BaseBall america®
ALMANAC 2005

PAGE
404
439

BASEBALL AMERICA INC.
Durham, N.C.

BaseBall america®
ALMANAC 2005

A Comprehensive Review of the 2004 Season, Featuring Statistics and Commentary

PUBLISHED BY
Baseball America Inc.

EDITOR
Allan Simpson

ASSISTANT EDITORS
J.J. Cooper, Aaron Fitt, Gary Martin

CONTRIBUTING EDITORS
Kevin Goldstein, Will Kimmey, Will Lingo

CONTRIBUTING WRITERS
Jim Callis, Chris Kline, John Manuel, Alan Matthews, John Perrotto

DESIGN & PRODUCTION
Phillip Daquila, Matthew Eddy, Linwood Webb

STATISTICAL CONSULTANTS
SportsTicker, Bristol, Conn.
The Sports Network, Hatboro, Pa.

BaseBall america

PRESIDENT/CEO Catherine Silver
VICE PRESIDENT/PUBLISHER Lee Folger
EDITOR IN CHIEF Allan Simpson
MANAGING EDITOR Will Lingo
DESIGN & PRODUCTION DIRECTOR Phillip Daquila

COVER PHOTOS Red Sox by Larry Goren; Jeff Francis by John Williamson;
Jered Weaver by Larry Goren; Matt Bush by Bill Mitchell

EDITOR'S NOTE
 • Major league statistics are based on final, unofficial 2004 averages.
 • The 2004 minor league statistics that appear in this publication were compiled by and provided to Baseball America courtesy of The Sports Network, official statistician for Minor League Baseball. The 2004 statistics for the Gulf Coast and Arizona Leagues, as well as all independent leagues, were provided by SportsTicker.
 • The organization statistics, which begin on page 55, include all players who participated in at least one game during the 2004 season. Pitchers' batting statistics are not included, nor are the pitching statistics of field players who pitched in less than two games. For players who played with more than one team in the same league, the player's cumulative statistics appear on the line immediately after the player's last-team statistics.
 • Innings pitched have been rounded off to the nearest full inning.

TABLE OF
CONTENTS

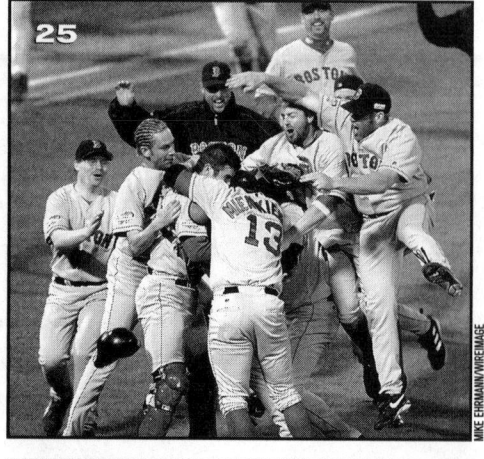

MIKE EHRMANN/WIREIMAGE

MAJOR
LEAGUES

2004 IN REVIEW

Ten years after devastation, baseball rebuilds popularity

Lots of full ballparks
More than 73 million fans came to major league games in 2004

BY JOHN PERROTTO

On Aug. 12, 1994, a 232-day strike began that wiped out the remainder of that year's regular season along with the playoffs and World Series, and delayed the start of the following season for nearly a month.

Many people said the strike would forever kill Major League Baseball's popularity. Attendance and television ratings did suffer when owners and players finally reached accord in 1995, but the game made progress each year as attention turned back to the field.

Along with great feats between the lines, owners and players also accomplished their greater feat by reaching a labor agreement without a work stoppage in 2002. So maybe it shouldn't have been a surprise that 10 years later, baseball was alive and well.

Barry Bonds hit his 700th home run. Ichiro Suzuki broke the single-season hits record, which had stood for 84 years. Greg Maddux won his 300th game. Ken Griffey Jr. hit his 500th homer and Gary Sheffield and Jim Thome belted their 400th. Randy Johnson pitched a perfect game at age 40. Eric Gagne ran his consecutive saves streak to an amazing 84 before finally having it broken.

The Boston Red Sox finally won another World Series. And more fans bought tickets to major league games than ever before.

The major leagues set a single-season attendance record with 73,022,969, surpassing the mark set in 2000. The Anaheim Angels, Boston Red Sox, Chicago Cubs, Houston Astros, New York Yankees, Philadelphia Phillies and San Diego Padres all set franchise attendance marks, and Minor League Baseball set an attendance record of its own.

"Setting the all-time attendance record is further evidence that this great sport has never been more popular," said commissioner Bud Selig, whose contract was extended three years in August, taking him through the 2009 season. "I think the sport has made an amazing amount of progress over the last 10 years and showed amazing durability. The heartbreak of 1994-95 was horrible and painful, but I'm really happy with what has happened since then. The focus is back on the field and it's never been more popular.

"In fact, you can make a case that 2004 was our greatest season ever."

It certainly was for Bonds, the San Francisco Giants left fielder who continued his pursuit of Henry Aaron's all-time home run record. Bonds moved into third on the homer chart with 703, passing his godfather Willie Mays, when he hit No. 661 off the Brewers' Ben Ford, a blast that landed in McCovey Cove beyond the right-field stands at SBC Park in San Francisco.

Bonds seemed overwhelmed by passing Mays, his boyhood idol. Bobby Bonds, Barry's father, was teammates with Mays from 1968-72 with the Giants.

FOLLOW THE CROWD

Major League Baseball set an overall attendance record in 2004, drawing more than 73 million fans to break a mark set in 2000. It's natural for total attendance to be higher because there are 30 big league teams now, but average attendance was also at its third-highest level ever. That record (for a full season) was set in 1993 and likely would have been bettered in 1994 before the strike hit. After several years in decline, average attendance went back over 30,000 again.

The attendance surge was reflected in the numbers of the individual clubs. Nine teams surpassed the three million mark in total attendance, and 11 more clubs drew more than two million. For individual club attendance, see Pages 33 and 45.

Year	American	National	Total	Average
1993	33,332,603	36,923,856	70,256,459	30,964
1994	24,202,197	25,807,819	50,010,016	31,612
1995	25,358,988	25,110,248	50,469,236	25,260
1996	29,718,093	30,379,288	60,097,381	26,889
1997	31,283,321	31,885,368	63,168,689	28,288
1998	31,947,900	38,424,321	70,372,221	29,285
1999	31,816,532	38,322,848	70,139,380	29,152
2000	32,897,543	39,737,552	72,635,095	30,099
2001	32,709,153	39,558,391	72,267,544	30,012
2002	30,910,469	36,948,707	67,859,176	28,168
2003	30,907,838	36,660,559	67,568,397	27,817
2004	32,801,668	40,221,301	73,022,969	30,401

Bonds walks away with more honors

Spectacular offensive seasons by Barry Bonds have become almost commonplace.

What made his 2004 performance as awesome as it was unfathomable, however, was that fans knew it could have been even better. Bonds' unique 2004 was a year that earned him Baseball America's Major League Player of the Year award for the third time in four years, but it was also a year in which he was the bull side-stepped by others.

PLAYER *of the* **YEAR**

Of all the numbers that Bonds put up in 2004—the .362 batting average, the 45 home runs in just 373 official at-bats, the all-time record 1.421 on-base plus slugging percentage—none of them elicits quite the reaction of his 232 walks, 34 more than the record he already owned and 62 more than any other major leaguer ever.

Because as much as his other numbers testify to his talent, the walks stand as proof of how opponents gave up before giving Bonds a fair fight.

Had Bonds walked as many times as fellow monster Albert Pujols of the Cardinals (84), say, and produced at the same rates as otherwise, he would have hit .362-63-141, probably the greatest single season in the history of the game. Those extra 18 home runs would have given him 721 for his career, well past Babe Ruth and on a 2005 collision course with Hank Aaron.

Still, Bonds surpassed 700 and seemed to be well on his way to passing Ruth and Aaron in 2005. He also passed his hero and godfather Willie Mays in April, hitting No. 660 into McCovey Cove with Mays on hand to give him a hug and congratulate him. Mays has always been a mentor to Bonds, particularly after Bonds' father Bobby died in August 2003.

Perhaps most impressive of all, Bonds and righthander Jason Schmidt carried a Giants team devoid of impact talent beyond them to the brink of the playoffs again. San Francisco was in the thick of the race to the last weekend, finishing two games out in the National League West and one game out of the wild card.

That's due in large part to the fact that Bonds is an unselfish player, in spite of his off-field churlishness. Given how teams give him nothing to hit, rather than reach

BILL NICHOLS

for what's best for him, he does what's best for the team. A full 120 of Bonds' walks were intentional, almost doubling his own record of 68, and many of the others were all but predetermined as well.

Bonds never begrudged this treatment, still viewing baseball as a team game. After the archrival Dodgers walked him intentionally in the ninth inning of a 3-2 September win, then five times the next day (three times intentionally), he commented, "The walks actually got them out of innings. You can't blame them for doing it."

Padres lefthander David Wells might have a promising approach. Having already been taken deep by Bonds in a September game, Wells came upon his own solution. He didn't want to walk him. But he also didn't want to mess around, trying to put the ball on the corner only to watch Bonds crush it anyway. Wells worked two strikes on Bonds before unveiling his secret weapon, the pitch no one expected him to throw.

It was a fastball right down the pipe. Bonds was so shocked he watched it sail across the plate for strike three. He walked away, undoubtedly amused, knowing that no would ever try that again.

They didn't. They wouldn't dare.

WALK IN HISTORY

Barry Bonds' walk totals in the last four seasons are all among the best in major league history, and in 2004 he was in a different galaxy altogether. Here are the top single-season walks totals in baseball:

1.	Barry Bonds	232	2004
2.	Barry Bonds	198	2002
3.	Barry Bonds	177	2001
4.	Babe Ruth	170	1923
5.	Mark McGwire	162	1998
	Ted Williams	162	1947
	Ted Williams	162	1949
8.	Ted Williams	156	1946
9.	Barry Bonds	151	1996
	Eddie Yost	151	1956
11.	Babe Ruth	150	1920
12.	Jeff Bagwell	149	1999
	Eddie Joost	149	1949
14.	Barry Bonds	148	2003
	Eddie Stanky	148	1945
	Jimmy Wynn	148	1969

PREVIOUS WINNERS

1998—Mark McGwire, 1b, Cardinals
1999—Pedro Martinez, rhp, Red Sox
2000—Alex Rodriguez, ss, Mariners
2001—Barry Bonds, of, Giants
2002—Alex Rodriguez, ss, Rangers
2003—Barry Bonds, of, Giants

"Willie Mays will always be my mentor," Barry Bonds said. "He will always be the one I look up to. He will always be the best baseball player of all time. That isn't ever going to change.

"Passing Willie just kind of bound us all together: Willie, my dad and myself. It kind of completed the circle of my family."

Bonds became only the third player in history to reach 700 homers, joining Aaron and Babe Ruth on Sept. 17 by connecting off San Diego's Jake Peavy in San Francisco. However, Bonds said his 700th homer wasn't as big a deal as No. 661.

"The good thing is I get to sleep now and stop having nightmares about this," he said, nonchalantly.

Bonds finished the season with 45 homers, 11 from Ruth's 714 and 52 from Aaron's 755. That left Aaron feeling it wouldn't be long before his name moved down a line in the record book.

"I think it's just a matter of time—maybe a year, two years," Aaron said. "I think he will break it. I'll be happy. Everybody will be after him then. They won't be involving me. Records are made to be broken."

That may be the case, but it seemed George Sisler's single-season hits record of 257 might last forever. It had stood since 1920 and hadn't been seriously challenged since before World War II, despite the major league schedule expanding from 154 games to 162 in 1961.

Suzuki, the Mariners' right fielder and leadoff hitter, finally became the man to pass Sisler as he finished 2004 with 262 hits. Suzuki broke the record with two days left in the season when he grounded a single up the middle off the Rangers' Ryan Drese at Safeco Field in Seattle.

"Through my career, I think this is the best moment," said Suzuki, who starred in Japan for nine seasons before joining Seattle in 2001. "I can't really put it into words."

Fireworks exploded after Suzuki's big hit reached the outfield, and his teammates mobbed him at first base. With the fans still cheering, Suzuki ran over to the first-base seats and shook hands with Sisler's 81-year-old daughter, Frances Sisler Drochelman, and other members of the Hall of Famer's family.

"My father would have been delighted," Drochelman said. "He would be so happy to know such a fine young man was doing so well."

Cubs righthander Greg Maddux has done well for a long time, as he extended his major league record by winning at least 15 games for a 17th consecutive season after returning to Chicago. That longevity added up to Maddux posting his 300th career victory on Aug. 7 by beating the Giants in San Francisco.

Maddux struggled in becoming the 22nd 300-game

MICHAEL WALBY

Ichiro Suzuki

TOP 10 MAJOR LEAGUE STORIES OF 2004

1 **Boston Red Sox are World Series champions.** Generations of Sox fans thought they would never read those words (and some of them were right), but a history-making playoff comeback against the Yankees provided the springboard to a dominant World Series sweep over the Cardinals.

2 **Baseball attendance returns to post-war, post-strike heights.** In addition to the growing popularity of amateur baseball from college on down, both the major leagues and minor leagues set attendance records in 2004.

3 **Healthy returns on Bonds.** People keep waiting for Barry Bonds to slow down, but the only thing that could slow him down in 2004 was a pitcher's willingness to walk him. Still, Bonds put up another amazing offensive season and put himself in position to become baseball's home run king in 2005.

4 **Expos finally find a city that wants them.** After ownership by Major League Baseball that lasted years longer than it should have, the Expos finally found out they would move to Washington, D.C., for 2005. Now all they have to do is find an owner, build a front office, rebuild the team and get a new ballpark.

5 **Steroid cloud won't go away.** In addition to receiving continued criticism for its steroid testing policy, Major League Baseball also couldn't bring an end to talk about performance-enhancing drugs as the federal investigation into BALCO dragged on.

6 **A-Rod adds to Red Sox-Yankees rivalry.** The pursuit of Alex Rodriguez began after the 2003 season, when the Rangers searched for payroll relief. The Red Sox looked like the only team in the running, but after they couldn't pull the deal off, the Yankees swooped in and grabbed him—to play third base.

7 **Ichiro keeps hitting and hitting and hitting.** Ichiro Suzuki didn't do much other than hit singles, but he hit lots and lots of them, piling up 262 hits to break a record set by George Sisler with the St. Louis Browns in 1920.

8 **Clemens' short retirement boosts Houston.** After Andy Pettitte signed with the Astros, he persuaded Roger Clemens to join him. Injuries sidetracked Pettitte, but Clemens was his usual self and helped Houston win the first playoff series in franchise history.

9 **Season of milestones.** In addition to the Braves winning their 13th straight division title, Eric Gagne converted 84 straight save opportunities, Ken Griffey Jr. reached 500 home runs and Greg Maddux got his 300th win.

10 **Diamondbacks start over.** Less than two years after winning the World Series, Arizona sank to the bottom of the baseball standings, costing Bob Brenly his job as manager and Jerry Colangelo his position as team president.

winner, a feat that could become more difficult as pitchers' workloads are watched more carefully with each passing year. He left in the sixth inning with a 6-3 lead, no outs and two runners on, and the bullpen closed out the win.

"Obviously to win 300 games, you've got to have a lot of help," Maddux said. "I've played on a lot of good teams, and a lot of times, you're only as good as the guys behind you. Today was a good example."

While Maddux was modest, his teammates appreciated his milestone and the work he put in to reach it.

"The most amazing thing about him is if you saw him going about his business, you'd think he was just another guy trying to stay in the big leagues," said Cubs relief pitcher Mike Remlinger, who was also a teammate of Maddux with the Braves. "He's there every day, doing all the little things you need to do to be successful. It makes you strive to have the same approach."

Griffey's approach has been altered by a multitude of injuries in recent seasons. In fact, the Reds center fielder had another injury-marred season in 2004 as a torn right hamstring sidelined him for the final seven weeks. However, Griffey did stay healthy long enough to become the 20th player to reach 500 homers when he connected off the Cardinals' Matt Morris on Father's Day at Busch Stadium.

At 34, Griffey was also the sixth-youngest to reach that

plateau. He was the fastest to 350, 400 and 450 before the injuries began to strike in 2001.

"Never in my wildest dreams did I think I'd ever accomplish this," Griffey said. "All the aches and pains I've had the past few years were gone for like two minutes. It was awesome."

After being congratulated by his teammates, Griffey went to a box next to the Reds' dugout and hugged his father Ken, who spent 19 seasons as a major league outfielder from 1973-91. The elder Griffey said Junior told him, simply, "Happy Father's Day."

Sheffield, the Yankees' right fielder, and Thome, the Phillies' first baseman, put themselves in position to join Griffey in the 500 Club by hitting their 400th homers. Thome reached the milestone June 14, homering off Cincinnati's Jose Acevedo at Citizens Bank Park in Philadelphia.

"It's an awesome thing," Thome said. "Looking back at all the work, all the time in the cage, it makes this very enjoyable."

Sheffield got to No. 400 on July 27 when he connected off the Blue Jays' Micheal Nakamura at SkyDome in Toronto.

"This means everything because I never thought I'd reach 400 home runs," Sheffield said. "I was just hoping to get 100. When I came in the league they told me I'd be a speed guy. I'm thrilled to death to get this milestone."

Johnson, the Diamondbacks' ace lefthander, has reached plenty of milestones in his great career. He added a perfect game to that list May 18 against the Braves at Turner Field, the first no-hitter in Arizona franchise history. It was the second no-hit game of Johnson's career, and at 40 he became the oldest pitcher in baseball history to throw a perfect game. His no-hitter came way back in 1990 against the Tigers, and it was the first no-hitter in Mariners history.

"That was far from perfect," Johnson recalled. "I was a very young pitcher who didn't have any idea where the ball was going. As a power pitcher, you don't want to think you're losing your stuff and I don't think I am. I feel my stuff is as good or better than when I won the no-hitter but I'd like to think I've gotten better as a pitcher."

Diamondbacks center fielder Steve Finley had a good view of Johnson's pitches and was amazed with their movement.

"Almost nothing went over the middle of the plate," Finley said. "He was hitting the corners all night, but the problem for the hitters was that most of those pitches came in there at 97, 98 and 99 miles an hour."

Gagne has continually overpowered hitters with a 97 mph fastball in recent seasons, but the Los Angeles Dodgers' closer saw his dominance come to a temporary end July 5 when the Diamondbacks scored two runs in the ninth to pin the first blown save on him since Aug. 26, 2002.

Entering with a 5-3 lead, Gagne was two outs away

LARRY GOREN

Game over
Eric Gagne converted 84 straight save opportunities

from keeping his 84-save streak alive, but Shea Hillenbrand singled and scored on pinch-hitter Luis Gonzalez' double to right, and Chad Tracy following by grounding a tying RBI single off first baseman Olmedo Saenz' glove.

"It will be interesting to see if any of us are alive when and if this kind of streak happens again," Dodgers manager Jim Tracy said.

"The streak was an unbelievable thing to be a part of and witness day and night," Dodgers first baseman/outfielder Shawn Green said. "You can never say never, but it feels untouchable like (Joe) DiMaggio, Cal Ripken Jr. or what Orel Hershiser did."

Sox Victory Caps Postseason To Remember

The Red Sox won more than just a World Series. They ended a lifetime of frustration for their fans.

The Red Sox swept the St. Louis Cardinals, who led the major leagues with 105 wins in the regular season, in four games. That marked Boston's first World Series victory since 1918, a span of 86 years.

Boston starting pitchers Curt Schilling, Pedro Martinez and Derek Lowe did not allow a run in a combined 20 innings over the last three games. Left fielder Manny Ramirez was named series MVP after going 7-for-17 (.412) with one homer and four RBIs.

"All of our fans have waited all their lives for this night. These guys did it for you, New England," Boston owner John Henry said after the Red Sox won 3-0 in Game Four.

New England was ready to celebrate when the team returned, as a crowd estimated at more than three million turned out for a celebration the weekend after the Red Sox won the title. The turnout was so great that the team's victory parade route was extended to the Charles River, where players rode amphibious vehicles to soak up all the good wishes.

The Red Sox advanced to the World Series with a stirring seven-game victory over the New York Yankees in

3,000-K CLUB

No.	Player	Strikeouts
1.	Nolan Ryan	5,714
2.	**Roger Clemens**	**4,317**
3.	**Randy Johnson**	**4,161**
4.	Steve Carlton	4,136
5.	Bert Blyleven	3,701
6.	Tom Seaver	3,640
7.	Don Sutton	3,574
8.	Gaylord Perry	3,534
9.	Walter Johnson	3,508
10.	Phil Niekro	3,342
11.	Ferguson Jenkins	3,192
12.	Bob Gibson	3,117

Active players in bold

the American League Championship Series. The Red Sox lost the first three games and were three outs from being swept when they rallied with four straight wins to become the first team in baseball history to overcome a 3-0 deficit in a postseason series.

The dramatic postseason led to more great television ratings, building on the success of 2003. World Series ratings on Fox were up 23 percent from 2003, with an average audience that made it the most-watched World Series since 1995 and the most popular ever on Fox.

The last night of the World Series marked the 12th evening during October that the baseball playoffs beat all other primetime competition, including "Monday Night Football." The World Series was the highest-rated sporting event on television since Super Bowl 38, and its ratings and share were 45 percent higher than the highest-rated NASCAR race in history.

The Boston-New York rivalry has long been spirited, and it gained an edge in recent years when Red Sox president Larry Lucchino began referring to the Yankees as the "Evil Empire." In Game Seven of the 2003 ALCS, the Red Sox blew a 5-2 lead in the eighth inning and lost 6-5 on Aaron Boone's homer off Tim Wakefield in the bottom of the 10th. "All empires fall sooner or later," Lucchino said.

Almost unnoticed next to the Red Sox-Yankees series filled with instant classics, the National League Championship Series also went the full seven games, with the Cardinals pulling it out with victories over the Houston Astros in the final two games.

St. Louis trailed 2-1 in the bottom of the sixth inning of Game Seven, but Albert Pujols hit a tying double off Roger Clemens and Scott Rolen followed with a game-winning two-run home run as the Cardinals rallied for a 5-2 victory. Pujols took MVP honors as he hit .500 with four homers and nine RBIs.

"It's every little boy's dream to go to the World Series," Pujols said. "I'm glad to have won the MVP but that trophy is going to stay right in this room because everybody here is an MVP."

Carlos Beltran was the postseason hero for the Astros, hitting four homers in the Division Series against the Braves and eight overall. That tied a record, but more importantly to the Astros it helped them win the franchise's first postseason series in eight tries.

Steroid Rumors Persist

While Barry Bonds continued to cement his standing as one of the greatest players in the history of the game, a large cloud hung over the Giants left fielder's head throughout the season.

In early March, citing information given to federal

No.	Player	Wins
1.	Cy Young	511
2.	Walter Johnson	417
3.	Grover Alexander	373
	Christy Mathewson	373
5.	Warren Spahn	363
6.	Pud Galvin	361
	Kid Nichols	361
8.	Tim Keefe	342
9.	Steve Carlton	329
10.	**Roger Clemens**	**328**
	John Clarkson	328
12.	Eddie Plank	326
13.	Nolan Ryan	324
	Don Sutton	324
15.	Phil Niekro	318
16.	Gaylord Perry	314
17.	Tom Seaver	311
18.	Old Hoss Radbourn	309
19.	Mickey Welch	307
20.	**Greg Maddux**	**305**
21.	Lefty Grove	300
	Early Wynn	300

300-WINS CLUB

Active players in bold

investigators, the San Francisco Chronicle reported that Bonds, along with Yankees sluggers Jason Giambi and Gary Sheffield, received performance-enhancing drugs—a human growth hormone called THG—from the Bay Area Laboratory Cooperative (BALCO), a nutritional supplements lab in Burlingame, Calif.

Human growth hormone works like a steroid, building muscle mass and helping athletes recover from training. Standard drug tests are unable to detect it.

The newspaper reported that the drugs were obtained through Greg Anderson, Bonds' personal trainer who had been charged with taking part in a steroid distribution ring that provided the substances to professional athletes. BALCO founder Victor Conte, lab vice president James Valente and track coach Remi Korchemny were also charged in the case. All four pleaded not guilty.

Bonds, Giambi and Sheffield were among major league players to testify following the 2003 season before a grand jury investigating the case. Other current or former major leaguers who testified included Bobby Estalella, Jeremy Giambi, Armando Rios and Benito Santiago.

Citing a source familiar with Anderson, the Chronicle added that the trainer obtained steroids and human growth hormones for Bonds dating to 2001. That was the season when he hit a record 73 homers.

Bonds and his attorney Michael Rains denied the allegations. "We continue to adamantly deny that Barry was provided, furnished or supplied any of those substances at any time by Greg Anderson," Rains said.

For his part, Bonds said he wasn't bothered by the whole controversy. "It doesn't faze me at all," he said. "There isn't anybody investigating me, as far as I know. I ain't being investigated."

Conte also denied supplying Bonds with performance-enhancing drugs.

"I would like the world to know that I have never given anabolic steroids or any other performance enhancing drugs to Barry Bonds," Conte said. "In fact, I have never even had a discussion about anabolic steroids with Barry Bonds. And that is the truth.

Gary Sheffield

LARRY GOREN

"I would also like to say that if anyone, and I mean anyone, says anything differently than what I am saying, they are not telling the truth."

Sheffield, though, told Sports Illustrated late in the regular season that he used a steroid cream he got from BALCO after Bonds introduced him to the lab's products. He said he did not realize it contained steroids.

Sheffield told the magazine he thought "the cream" was cortisone-based—he applied it to his surgically repaired knee—and that he so little suspected its true ingredients that he openly kept it in his locker. He said he was shocked and angry when it was reported that BALCO's "the cream" and "the clear" were designer steroids.

"I was mad. I want everybody to be on an even playing field," Sheffield said.

The two stars trained together and Sheffield even lived at Bonds' home for several weeks before the 2002 season. According to Sports Illustrated, Bonds also introduced Sheffield to Conte.

"(Bonds) said, 'I got guys here, they can get your urine

2004 MAJOR LEAGUE ALL-STARS

Vladimir Guerrero carried the Angels back to the playoffs

Johan Santana was dominant in the second half of the season

Selected by Baseball America

FIRST TEAM

Pos.	Player, Team	B-T	Ht.	Wt.	Age	AVG	AB	R	H	2B	3B	HR	RBI	SB
C	Ivan Rodriguez, Tigers	R-R	5-9	220	32	.334	527	72	176	32	2	19	86	7
1B	Albert Pujols, Cardinals	R-R	6-3	225	24	.331	592	133	196	51	2	46	123	5
2B	Mark Loretta, Padres	R-R	6-0	185	32	.335	620	108	208	47	2	16	76	5
3B	Adrian Beltre, Dodgers	R-R	5-11	220	25	.334	598	104	200	32	0	48	121	7
SS	Miguel Tejada, Orioles	R-R	5-9	200	28	.311	653	107	203	40	2	34	150	4
OF	Barry Bonds, Giants	L-L	6-2	240	40	.362	373	129	135	27	3	45	101	6
OF	Vladimir Guerrero, Angels	R-R	6-3	220	28	.337	612	124	206	39	2	39	126	15
OF	Gary Sheffield, Yankees	R-R	6-0	200	35	.290	573	117	166	30	1	36	121	5
DH	David Ortiz, Red Sox	L-L	6-4	230	28	.301	582	94	175	47	3	41	139	0

Pos.	Player, Team	B-T	Ht.	Wt.	Age	W	L	ERA	G	SV	IP	H	BB	SO
SP	Roger Clemens, Astros	R-R	6-4	235	41	18	4	2.98	33	0	214	169	79	218
	Randy Johnson, Diamondbacks	R-L	6-10	230	40	16	14	2.60	35	0	246	177	44	290
	Johan Santana, Twins	L-L	6-0	190	25	20	6	2.61	34	0	228	156	54	265
	Curt Schilling, Red Sox	R-R	6-5	235	37	21	6	3.26	32	0	227	206	35	203
RP	Mariano Rivera, Yankees	R-R	6-2	185	34	4	2	1.94	74	53	79	65	20	66

SECOND TEAM

Pos.	Player, Team	B-T	Ht.	Wt.	Age	AVG	AB	R	H	2B	3B	HR	RBI	SB
C	Jason Varitek, Red Sox	B-R	6-2	230	32	.296	463	67	137	30	1	18	73	10
1B	Todd Helton, Rockies	L-L	6-2	200	30	.347	547	115	190	49	2	32	96	3
2B	Alfonso Soriano, Rangers	R-R	6-1	180	26	.280	608	77	170	32	4	28	91	18
3B	Scott Rolen, Cardinals	R-R	6-4	240	29	.314	500	109	157	32	4	34	124	4
SS	Derek Jeter, Yankees	R-R	6-3	195	30	.292	643	111	188	44	1	23	78	23
OF	J.D. Drew, Braves	L-R	6-1	200	28	.305	518	118	158	28	8	31	93	12
OF	Jim Edmonds, Cardinals	L-L	6-1	210	34	.301	498	102	150	38	3	42	111	8
OF	Ichiro Suzuki, Mariners	L-R	5-9	170	30	.372	704	101	262	24	5	8	60	36
DH	Manny Ramirez, Red Sox	R-R	6-0	200	32	.308	568	108	175	44	0	43	130	2

Pos.	Player, Team	B-T	Ht.	Wt.	Age	W	L	ERA	G	SV	IP	H	BB	SO
SP	Roy Oswalt, Astros	R-R	6-0	175	26	20	10	3.49	36	0	237	233	62	206
	Carl Pavano, Marlins	R-R	6-5	235	28	18	8	3.00	31	0	222	212	49	139
	Jason Schmidt, Giants	R-R	6-5	205	31	18	7	3.20	32	0	225	165	77	251
	Carlos Zambrano, Cubs	B-R	6-5	240	23	16	8	2.75	31	0	210	174	81	188
RP	Brad Lidge, Astros	R-R	6-5	210	27	6	5	1.90	80	29	95	57	30	157

Ages as of July 1, 2004

Player of the Year: Barry Bonds, of, Giants. **Pitcher of the Year:** Johan Santana, lhp, Twins. **Rookie of the Year:** Khalil Greene, ss, Padres. **Manager of the Year:** Bobby Cox, Braves. **Executive of the Year:** Terry Ryan, Twins.

and blood and prescribe a vitamin specifically for your blood type and what your body needs,' " Sheffield said. "And that's what I did."

With little fanfare, MLB and its players agreed to ban the use of androstenedione, the supplement made famous by Mark McGwire in 1998 when he became the first player to hit 70 home runs in a season.

The Food and Drug Administration banned the sale of andro on April 12. MLB's decision took effect the same day and means players who test positive for andro face penalties, including suspensions after two positive tests. Andro is used by the body to make testosterone. Many players were caught by surprise by MLB's ban.

"I think it's a good move, but I thought it was already done," New York Mets infielder Todd Zeile said. "I thought they had done it the year after Mark McGwire in 1998."

Though MLB was drawing criticism from many corners about having a steroid policy that was not strict enough, commissioner Selig insisted the sport was making progress in that area.

"The illegal use of steroids and other performance-enhancing substances is detrimental to the integrity of the game and the long-term health of the athletes who use them," Selig said. "We in Major League Baseball are fully committed to eliminating those dangerous substances and reaching zero tolerance as soon as possible."

JOHN WILLIAMSON

Ken Caminiti

One player who admitted to using steroids during his career, Ken Caminiti, died on Oct. 10 of a heart attack in a New York hotel room at age 41. Caminiti's career included a National League MVP award with the Padres in 1996, but his life had been in turmoil since his 15-year career ended with the Braves in 2001.

Just five days before his death, Caminiti admitted in a Houston court that he violated his probation by testing positive for cocaine a month earlier, and was sentenced to 180 days in jail. However, Judge William Harmon gave Caminiti credit for the 189 days he already served in jail and a treatment facility after he was sentenced to three years probation for a cocaine arrest in March 2001. He had pleaded guilty in March 2002.

During the same period, Caminiti told Sports Illustrated that he used steroids during his MVP season, when he hit a career-high .326 with 40 home runs and 130 RBIs. He estimated half the players in the major leagues were also using them.

Expos Finally Find A Home—Maybe

The Montreal Expos' situation was a blight on Major League Baseball for three seasons.

The other 29 owners bought the Expos from Jeffrey Loria just before the start of spring training in 2002, with the idea they would own the club for only one season. However, one season turned into three and led to the atrophy of the organization as well as creating the impression of a large conflict of interest.

Finally, in the first week of the 2004 season, the saga moved toward an end when Selig announced the Expos would move to Washington, D.C., for the 2005 season. It would be the first franchise shift since the Washington

Senators moved to the Dallas-Fort Worth area prior to the 1972 season and became the Texas Rangers.

"After 30 years of waiting and waiting and waiting, and lots of hard work and more than a few prayers, there will be baseball in Washington in 2005," Washington Mayor Anthony Williams exclaimed in making the announcement.

The announcement came on the same day the Expos played their final home game at Olympic Stadium. A crowd of 31,395 watched the Florida Marlins roll to a 9-1 victory.

Some Expos fans weren't so happy with their team being uprooted. The game was delayed 10 minutes in the third inning after someone threw a golf ball that landed near second base and the players were pulled off the field.

"It's a day when the sun is setting in Montreal, but it's rising in Washington," Expos president Tony Tavares said.

At least, it wasn't as ugly a scene that played out one day short of 33 years earlier at RFK Stadium, when the Senators were forced to forfeit their last home game to the New York Yankees when souvenir-seeking fans overran the field.

Washington also lost a major league team following the 1960 season, when the original Senators moved to Minneapolis-St. Paul and became the Minnesota Twins. The expansion Senators then lasted only 11 years. Despite the poor track record, Selig said the time was right to return to the nation's capitol.

"There has been tremendous growth in the Washington, D.C., area over the last 33 years, and we in Major League Baseball believe that baseball will be welcomed there and will be a great success," Selig said.

The team planned to play for three seasons at RFK Stadium while a new ballpark is built, but many hurdles remained for the team to move and get the ballpark built. Local government was in the process of considering financing for the new ballpark, which would be built on the Anacostia waterfront in southeast Washington.

The cost of the project, which the city's chief financial officer estimated at $530 million, would be paid for through a gross receipts tax on large businesses, a tax on concessions and an annual rent payment by the team. It was still the subject of intense local debate, and the first city council hearing on the plan drew more than 250 speakers and lasted from 10 a.m. until 1 the next morning.

Tony Tavares

The most notable member of the opposition was former D.C. mayor Marion Barry. "I am opposed to this financing plan," Barry said at the hearing, noting that Abe Pollin, owner of the Washington Wizards basketball team, paid for much of the construction of MCI Center while Barry was mayor. "This is the biggest stickup by Major League Baseball since Jesse James was doing train robberies."

Las Vegas; Norfolk, Va.; Monterrey, Mexico; Portland, Ore.; and Northern Virginia also made bids for the Expos, but Washington was the easy choice because of its wealthy population base and a financial package that would build a new stadium primarily with taxpayers' money.

A crucial hurdle cleared in the process came when MLB

MAJOR LEAGUES

Twins reload with next young crop

Among teams that spend a lot of money, the Braves and Yankees have won acclaim in recent years for their ability to build consistent contenders.

And among the more budget-conscious organizations, the poster child has been the Athletics—particularly after "Moneyball" hit the national stage—for their knack for finding winning players at a lower price.

Then there are the Minnesota Twins. Marked for extinction a few years ago, the organization has continued to persevere. But the Twins have done much more than survive; they have thrived. With a payroll even smaller than that of the more ballyhooed A's, the Twins won their third straight American League Central title. After the Indians drew close at midseason, Minnesota cruised from there and ended up winning the division by nine games over the White Sox.

ORGANIZATION
of the **YEAR**

Once again they won with good young players, who for the most part have been developed in the organization. But even more interesting, the Twins have continued to win in spite of having to turn their roster over year after year because of budget constraints. So the young cast that helped carry the team to 92 wins in 2004 was not the same group that won 94 games in 2002.

In 2002, for instance, the Twins' catcher was A.J. Pierzynski. The leading hitter was first baseman was Doug Mientkiewicz. Lefthander Eric Milton won 15 games and Eddie Guardado and LaTroy Hawkins shared closer duties. By the time the 2004 postseason rolled around, they and others had moved on through trades or free agency. In part it was because of money, but Minnesota also has been able to let so many players go because of the supply of young talent that continues to come up from below.

Joe Nathan

In Mientkiewicz' case, for example, the Twins were comfortable letting him go because top prospect Justin Morneau was more than ready to step in at first base. Morneau stepped right into the cleanup spot for the Twins and hit 19 home runs in 74 games. Minnesota found its next closer in the Pierzynski trade with the Giants, and Joe Nathan saved 44 games. And Johan Santana, who split 2002 between Triple-A and the big leagues, emerged as the ace of the rotation with what may have been the best season for a starter in the big leagues in 2004.

In addition to the young players who have provided the next wave of

Next in line from Minnesota's crop of young talent
Justin Morneau stepped into the middle of the Twins lineup

talent in Minnesota, the Twins farm system is also as healthy as it has ever been. Through astute drafting and trading, the Twins have built an organization as talented as any in baseball.

It has been boosted by the emergence of such players as outfielder Jason Kubel, who had a season as strong as anyone in the minor leagues in 2004. And premium catching prospect Joe Mauer, Baseball America's Minor League Player of the Year in 2003, still hasn't made his full impact in Minnesota. His rookie season was short-circuited by injuries, so he'll be among the young players who will inevitably be called on in 2005.

Of course, it all comes back to a stable and cohesive front office that has a track record together unmatched in professional baseball—or professional sports, for that matter. General manager Terry Ryan joined the organization as scouting director in 1986 and has been in Minnesota ever since, rising to the GM position in 1994. Ryan was succeeded as scouting director by Mike Radcliff, who is not only the longest-tenured scouting director in baseball but also has been with the Twins since 1987. And yet they pale in comparison to the service of farm director Jim Rantz, who has been a member of the Twins organization since its inception in 1961. He has been a player, manager and executive in the organization and has been farm director since 1986.

It adds up to a winning combination for the Twins, proving the names on the field can change as long as the front office stays the same.

PREVIOUS WINNERS
1982—Oakland Athletics
1983—New York Mets
1984—New York Mets
1985—Milwaukee Brewers
1986—Milwaukee Brewers
1987—Milwaukee Brewers
1988—Montreal Expos
1989—Texas Rangers
1990—Montreal Expos
1991—Atlanta Braves
1992—Cleveland Indians
1993—Toronto Blue Jays
1994—Kansas City Royals
1995—New York Mets
1996—Atlanta Braves
1997—Detroit Tigers
1998—New York Yankees
1999—Oakland Athletics
2000—Chicago White Sox
2001—Houston Astros
2002—Minnesota Twins
2003—Florida Marlins

reached an agreement with Baltimore Orioles owner Peter Angelos, who had previously objected to having a team move just 40 miles from Oriole Park at Camden Yards. "Our aim was to protect and preserve the Orioles franchise and the economic benefits it has generated for Baltimore for the past 50 years," Angelos said. "Equally important was our efforts to protect Maryland's investment in Camden Yards."

Under the deal, an appraiser would establish a value for the Orioles franchise, and MLB would guarantee its value for an undisclosed period of time. The commissioner's office also would guarantee Baltimore's locally generated revenue for an undisclosed period of time and assist in the creation of a regional sports network.

Omar Minaya

The team's most immediate problem, however, was getting up and running for 2005. Team president Tony Tavares and a skeleton crew were working in Washington, while employees in Montreal were shutting down operations there and wondering when they might move. Tavares said a simple lack of manpower was the team's biggest problem.

"It's not having enough people to blitz this task," he said. "We have a very short time frame to get this thing up and running. Every time I hire a person, life gets less complicated. It's one more person with expertise that can do the job they need to do."

That included hiring a new general manager until former Cincinnati Reds GM Jim Bowden was appointed to the job Nov. 1. Omar Minaya, who ran the team's baseball operation after it moved to MLB ownership, left the organization to become the Mets GM and executive vice president of baseball operations.

Minaya, a native of the Dominican Republic who grew up just a few blocks away from Shea Stadium, became the first GM of Hispanic descent when he took over the Expos. The challenge of turning around his hometown team was too tempting to pass up. Jim Duquette, who succeeded Steve Phillips as GM in 2003, was demoted to senior vice president of baseball operations and will report to Minaya.

"We know as New Yorkers nobody wants to hear excuses. Get it done. That's it," Minaya said. "I have this dream of someday winning the World Series here in New York, a New York kid winning the World Series, and having a parade down Broadway. That's my dream."

MLB also was approaching the end of another perceived conflict of interest when Los Angeles investor Mark Attanasio signed a letter of intent to buy the Milwaukee Brewers for a reported $220 million.

The Brewers had been owned primarily by the Selig family since 1970, though Bud Selig put his shares in trust and turned over control of the franchise to his daughter, Wendy Selig-Prieb, when he became full-time commissioner.

Milwaukee had its 12th consecutive losing season in 2004, joining the Pittsburgh Pirates for the longest current streak of sub-.500 seasons. Attanasio was undeterred by the Brewers' failure.

"Now it's our job to start winning more games," Attanasio said. "Everything we do is going to be directed to winning more games."

Red Sox-Yankees Battle Starts With A-Rod

An inkling that the 2004 season would be an eventful one came early.

As the Yankees and Devil Rays gathered on the Gulf Coast of Florida on Valentine's Day to begin spring training early in preparation for their season-opening series in Japan, came news of a blockbuster trade.

The Yankees acquired American League MVP Alex Rodriguez and cash from the Rangers for all-star second baseman Alfonso Soriano and minor league infielder Joaquin Arias.

"This is a big, big one. It ranks with when we signed Reggie," said Yankees owner George Steinbrenner, referring to when he signed Hall of Famer Reggie Jackson as a free agent prior to the 1977 season.

Texas decided it wanted to trade Rodriguez in order to free up payroll and expedite its rebuilding process. Rodriguez signed a 10-year, $252 million contract—the largest in the history of professional sports—as a free agent following the 2000 season, which became baseball's last offseason of irrational exuberance. The salaries of many of the players signed that winter had become burdens to their clubs.

The Rangers had a deal in place in December to ship Rodriguez to the Red Sox for left fielder Manny Ramirez, who had signed an eight-year, $160 million contract just

400-HOME RUN CLUB

No. Player	Home Runs
1. Hank Aaron	755
2. Babe Ruth	714
3. Barry Bonds	**703**
4. Willie Mays	660
5. Frank Robinson	586
6. Mark McGwire	583
7. Sammy Sosa	**574**
8. Harmon Killebrew	573
9. Reggie Jackson	563
10. Mike Schmidt	548
11. Rafael Palmeiro	**541**
12. Mickey Mantle	536
13. Jimmie Foxx	534
14. Ted Williams	521
Willie McCovey	521
16. Eddie Mathews	512
Ernie Banks	512
18. Mel Ott	511
19. Eddie Murray	504
20. Ken Griffey Jr.	**501**
21. Lou Gehrig	493
Fred McGriff	**493**
23. Stan Musial	475
Willie Stargell	475
25. Dave Winfield	465
26. Jose Canseco	462
27. Carl Yastrzemski	452
28. Jeff Bagwell	**446**
29. Dave Kingman	442
30. Andre Dawson	438
31. Frank Thomas	**436**
32. Juan Gonzalez	**434**
33. Cal Ripken	431

Ken Griffey Jr.

34. Billy Williams	426
35. Jim Thome	**423**
36. Gary Sheffield	**415**
37. Darrell Evans	414
38. Duke Snider	407

Active players in bold

Waiting in the Wings

No. Player	Home Runs
39. Andres Galarraga	399
42. Manny Ramirez	390
49. Alex Rodriguez	381
53. Mike Piazza	378
60. Larry Walker	368

LARRY GOREN

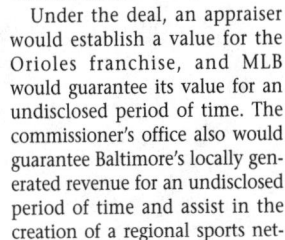

Greene's play gets him noticed

Khalil Greene has never sought the spotlight. With his often spectacular play at the plate and in the field, however, the spotlight has found him.

Even though his 2004 season was cut short by a broken right index finger on Sept. 13, Greene handled 458 chances in 134 games and was involved in 81 double plays, making 20 errors. And he displayed surprising power, hitting .273-15-65 while bouncing from the sixth and eighth spots in the batting order to leadoff. He set a club record for home runs and extra-base hits by a shortstop (50).

ROOKIE *of the* **YEAR**

For his spectacular season, Greene earned Baseball America's Rookie of the Year award, edging Pirates outfielder Jason Bay, who also happened to be his roommate for a short time in Triple-A when Bay was in the Padres organization.

"I really appreciate it," Greene said of the honor, "but I'm really not into awards and things. And I don't think Jason is, either."

Greene wasn't blowing smoke. He is a member of the Baha'i Faith, which espouses a Zen-like philosophy, and grew up in Key West, Fla. He is perhaps the most laid-back player in the big leagues and prefers to lead by example, not getting wrapped up in all the hype that followed him in 2004.

Greene, whose first name means friend of God, tended toward spectacular play on the season, but he rarely showed emotion on or off the field.

"He's a very quiet kid, keeps to himself," veteran Padres lefthander

All-around contributor
Khalil Greene excelled with bat and glove

David Wells says. "He doesn't join in a lot of stuff in the clubhouse, but he'll laugh along with the pranks.

"More importantly, he's as good a shortstop as I've had play behind me."

Greene made all the plays in 2004 in the big leagues, even though he didn't play shortstop in college until his junior year at Clemson, manning third base for the Tigers for two seasons.

"I really enjoy shortstop," Greene says. "You're so much more involved in the game. You have room to range at short and have more opportunity to make plays."

Still, going into the 2001 draft scouts said Greene didn't have the glove for short or the bat for third, so he wasn't drafted until the 14th round by the Cubs. So Greene returned for his senior season and proved himself both on the field and at the plate. He finished third in batting in NCAA Division I by batting .470-27-91 in 285 at-bats. The Padres took Greene, Baseball America's 2002 College Player of the Year, with the 13th pick overall after he led the Tigers to the College World Series.

He isn't the most toolsy shortstop around, but all he needed was a chance to prove himself. The Padres knew what he brought to the table with his makeup and drive. "I firmly believe good players will succeed if given the opportunity," Greene says. "Right out of the gate, San Diego told me I was their shortstop of the future, that I'd move up at my own pace. They showed faith in me. I feel fortunate to have moved up so quickly."

While he put up good minor league numbers, compiling a .290 average in 768 at-bats, he stumbled a bit in his major league debut. In 65 at-bats at the end of 2003, Greene hit just .215-2-6.

His coming-out party didn't start until he was given the opportunity to play everyday in San Diego in 2004. And while he subscribes to the theory that the game is the same, no matter where you might be in terms of development, being on center stage was eye-opening.

"I knew if I put the time and effort in, I'd be successful," Greene says. "But the big leagues are a definite step up: the media, the fans and the players. There is so much more involved here.

"I never put a number and said I need to hit X home runs, or want to make fewer than X errors. That limits you. My only goal was to get better. And I feel I've done that."

"Khalil changes the course of a game with his glove," Padres manager Bruce Bochy said. "I'm amazed at the plays he makes. And he doesn't just make plays, he turns them into double plays."

—JOHN MAFFEI

ALL-ROOKIE TEAM

Pos. Player, Club	PCT	AB	H	HR	RBI	SB
C John Buck, Royals	.235	238	56	12	30	1
1B Adam LaRoche, Braves	.278	324	90	13	45	0
2B Aaron Milles, Rockies	.293	522	153	6	47	12
3B David Wright, Mets	.293	263	77	14	40	6
SS Khalil Greene, Padres	.273	484	132	15	65	4
OF Jason Bay, Pirates	.282	411	116	26	82	4
OF Matt Holliday, Rockies	.290	400	116	14	57	3
OF Terrmel Sledge, Expos	.269	398	107	15	62	3
DH Bobby Crosby, Athletics	.239	545	130	22	64	7

	W-L	ERA	IP	H	BB	SO
P Zack Greinke, Royals	8-11	3.97	145	143	26	100
P Noah Lowry, Giants	6-0	3.82	92	91	28	72
P Bobby Madritsch, Mariners	6-3	3.27	88	74	33	60
P Akinori Otsuka, Padres	7-2	1.75	77	56	26	87
P Shingo Takatsu, White Sox	6-4	2.31	62	40	21	50

PREVIOUS WINNERS

1989—Gregg Olson, rhp, Orioles	
1990—Sandy Alomar, c, Indians	
1991—Jeff Bagwell, 1b, Astros	
1992—Pat Listach, ss, Brewers	
1993—Mike Piazza, c, Dodgers	
1994—Raul Mondesi, of, Dodgers	
1995—Hideo Nomo, rhp, Dodgers	
1996—Derek Jeter, ss, Yankees	
1997—Nomar Garciaparra, ss, Red Sox	
1998—Kerry Wood, rhp, Cubs	
1999—Carlos Beltran, of, Royals	
2000—Rafael Furcal, ss/2b, Braves	
2001—Albert Pujols, of/3b/1b, Cardinals	
2002—Eric Hinske, 3b, Blue Jays	
2003—Brandon Webb, rhp, Diamondbacks	

days before Rodriguez agreed to his big deal with Texas. The Red Sox would have then dealt Garciaparra to the White Sox for right fielder Magglio Ordonez. The Major League Baseball Players Association nixed the deal because it involved a restructured contract for Rodriguez that significantly reduced its value.

The Yankees had merely been observers, but they suddenly had a need for a third baseman in late January when Aaron Boone injured his knee in a pick-up basketball game, knocking him out for the entire 2004 season. Though Rodriguez had won Gold Gloves at shortstop, the Yankees began talking trade with the Rangers to get A-Rod for their hole at the hot corner.

The two sides quickly reached an agreement when the Rangers agreed to pay $67 million of the remaining $179 million on Rodriguez' contract and Rodriguez agreed to move to third base.

"Everyone dreams of being a Yankee and I still feel like someone's going to pinch me, wake me up and tell me this was just a dream and that the trade never happened," Rodriguez said at his introductory press conference at Yankee Stadium. "This is unbelievable."

Less than a month earlier, after failing to trade him, the Rangers named Rodriguez their captain. Rodriguez vowed then that his goal was to lead Texas to its first World Series title. Things changed quickly.

"This trade is about flexibility," Rangers general manager John Hart said. "We've traded the best player in the game, and we're getting tremendous financial flexibility to achieve a championship faster doing this deal than not making this deal."

Hart's words proved prophetic when Texas made a surprise run for the American League West title, before being eliminated in the final days. Rodriguez helped the Yankees to the AL East title, though the year ended bitterly with the playoff loss to the Red Sox. One of the enduring images of the 2004 Yankees-Red Sox series will be Rodriguez' attempt to knock the ball out of Bronson Arroyo's glove during Game Six.

The addition of Rodriguez also gave the Yankees a $188 million payroll on Opening Day. That was the largest in baseball history and drew howls from owners of other clubs.

John Hart

"The disparity in payrolls is not healthy for the sport," then Diamondbacks president Jerry Colangelo said. "But everyone runs their team the way they see fit, and they did it by the rules."

While the Red Sox didn't move Garciaparra during the offseason, they did send the two-time AL batting champion packing at the July 31 trade deadline as part of a four-team deal.

Boston dealt Garciaparra, minor league outfielder Matt Murton and cash to the Cubs and wound up getting shortstop Orlando Cabrera from the Expos and first baseman Doug Mientkiewicz from the Twins. The Expos got shortstop Alex Gonzalez, reliever Francis Beltran and infielder Brendan Harris from the Cubs, while Chicago minor league pitcher Justin Jones was shipped to the Twins.

"If it was in my control, I'd still be wearing a Red Sox uniform, because it's the place I know, I love," Garciaparra

Ended up in pinstripes
Pursuit of Alex Rodriguez was one of the offseason's big stories

said. "All of those fans, I'll always remember."

The Red Sox' objective was to strengthen their defense by adding two Gold Glove winners in Cabrera and Mientkiewicz. The plan worked as they went 42-18 after the trade to win the AL wild card. "I thought there was a flaw on the club that we couldn't allow to become a fatal flaw, that the defense on this team was not championship caliber," Boston GM Theo Epstein said.

There were plenty of other major trades in the 24 hours leading up to the deadline

The Marlins shipped righthander Brad Penny, first baseman Hee Seop Choi and minor league pitcher Bill Murphy to the Dodgers for catcher Paul Lo Duca, reliever Guillermo Mota and right fielder Juan Encarnacion. The Dodgers then sent Murphy and two other prospects, catcher Koyie Hill and outfielder Reggie Abercrombie, to the Diamondbacks for center fielder Steve Finley and catcher Brent Mayne. The Dodgers had fervently pursued Randy Johnson, but ultimately were unwilling to meet Arizona's trade demands.

The White Sox traded righthander Esteban Loaiza to the Yankees for righthander Jose Contreras and cash. The Mets, in an ill-advised attempt to try to boost themselves into the NL wild-card race, acquired righthander Kris Benson from the Pirates for third basemen Ty Wigginton and Jose Bautista and pitching prospect Matt Peterson, while also picking up righthander Victor Zambrano from the Devil Rays for 20-year-old lefthander Scott Kazmir, who pitched his way to the big leagues by the end of the season. Meanwhile, Zambrano missed the last six weeks of the season with elbow inflammation.

Clemens Hops Out Of His Rocking Chair

Before the Yankees acquired Rodriguez from the Rangers, the biggest move of the 2003-04 offseason came when the Astros lured 300-game winner and Houstonian Roger Clemens out of retirement with a one-year, $5 million contract.

Clemens had announced his retirement from the

Ryan earns respect of all his peers

Few people in baseball can compete with Terry Ryan when it comes to his ability to deflect credit.

Unfortunately for him, few people can compete when it comes to building a front office and a winning team on the field, either.

EXECUTIVE
of the **YEAR**

So while the Twins continue to bring in team honors, including their third straight American League Central title, with one of the smallest payrolls in baseball—$53.6 million in 2004, lowest of any playoff team and only the 19th-highest in all of baseball—it's time to recognize the man who has steadfastly led the Twins through their darkest seasons back to the levels of success they experienced in the early 1990s. That's why the Minnesota general manager is Baseball America's 2004 Executive of the Year.

Stability at the top
Twins general manager Terry Ryan

Ryan broke into professional baseball in 1972 as a 35th-round draft pick of the Twins out of high school in Wisconsin. He pitched in the organization for four seasons but had his career cut short by injuries, so he went to college and earned his degree at Wisconsin in 1979. He returned to baseball in 1980 as a scout with the Mets, and he remained with New York until

PREVIOUS WINNERS
1998—Doug Melvin, Rangers
1999—Jim Bowden, Reds
2000—Walt Jocketty, Cardinals
2001—Pat Gillick, Mariners
2002—Billy Beane, Athletics
2003—Brian Sabean, Giants

the Twins brought him back as scouting director in January 1986. He rose to vice president of player personnel after the 1991 season and became GM in September 1994.

Taking over leadership of a major league team during the sport's worst labor dispute perhaps prepared Ryan to guide the Twins through adversity, and they faced plenty of that in subsequent years. Ryan had to rebuild an organization torn down for budget reasons, and he did so slowly but surely through scouting and player development. He built a talented, loyal staff and watched the staff and players grow together.

Then came talk of contraction in the 2001-02 offseason, but Ryan remained steadfast in his leadership, never wavering as the leader of the Twins' ship in spite of many opportunities to work with bigger budgets for more prominent teams. In the process he not only built respect in his own organization, but also throughout the baseball industry.

So while other executives might get more ink, you'd be hard pressed to find another who has done more for his organization than Ryan.

Cox leads Braves to yet another title

Ever since the Braves won their first division title, doubters have lined up the next spring to find reasons to bet against them.

Never were they more prevalent than in 2004, when conventional wisdom said the Braves had finally lost enough of their winning pieces that they would cede a division title to the Marlins or Phillies, or even the Mets.

MANAGER
of the **YEAR**

The payroll, while by no means at the poverty line, dropped by about $16 million from 2003 to 2004, and players like Javy Lopez, Greg Maddux and Gary Sheffield moved on to bigger paydays. The departure of Maddux seemed to symbolize the end of the Braves' great pitching tradition, and the team would have to rely on new faces like J.D. Drew—who arrived with a great deal of talent but huge questions about his ability to stay

LARRY GOREN

Names change, results don't
Braves manager Bobby Cox

PREVIOUS WINNERS
1998—Larry Dierker, Astros
1999—Jimy Williams, Red Sox
2000—Dusty Baker, Giants
2001—Lou Piniella, Mariners
2002—Mike Scioscia, Angels
2003—Jack McKeon, Marlins

healthy—to keep its head above water. Then when the season actually got under way, the Braves were knocked back by early injuries to key players like Chipper Jones and Rafael Furcal.

At the end of the season, though, the Braves were in familiar territory: Back in the playoffs after winning their 13th straight division title. And most people agreed that in his 23rd year as a manager and 15th straight at the Braves' helm, Cox did his best job yet.

Cox has many positive qualities as a manager, but his best may be the way he always stands behind his players yet demands the best from them. "He gets those guys to subjugate their individual egos and blend them into one team ego," Braves general manager John Schuerholz said. "It's an ego of one."

And it's led to one successful year after another in Atlanta.

Yankees during the 2003 season. He then had an emotional farewell when he was removed during Game Four of the 2003 World Series against the Florida Marlins at Pro Player Stadium in Miami.

The situation started to change in December, though, when former Yankees rotation-mate Andy Pettitte decided to sign with his hometown Astros as a free agent. A month later, Clemens ended his retirement at 78 days to follow his friend's lead.

The 42-year-old future Hall of Famer went on to have another great season, as he went 18-4 with a 2.98 ERA in 33 starts to help the Astros win the National League wild-card spot.

As part of his contract, the Astros included a provision that didn't require Clemens to travel if he wasn't scheduled to pitch. He could even travel separately from the team to spend more time with his wife Debbie and their four sons: Koby, 17; Kory, 15; Kacy, 9; and Kody, 8.

"I've had a smile on my face every day, win or lose, to drive home in 15 minutes," Clemens said late in the season. "I haven't seen my yard this green in 20 years. I can't tell you what a pleasure it is, balancing this and getting to see my kids play ball."

Clemens also revitalized baseball in football-mad Houston with his performance.

"The town is abuzz and it's kind of snowballed," Astros catcher Brad Ausmus said. "People talk about the Astros all the time. People pay attention. It makes it fun to come to the field."

"He's energized everybody from the city to the club to the whole organization," Astros GM Gerry Hunsicker said. "He's just a special person and a special pitcher.

"There's no question the confidence level of the ballclub has been lifted by the signings of the offseason. We expect to win every night."

Clemens was one of 12 players age 40 or older to appear in a major league game in 2004, and many of them made significant contributions to their teams, including the aforementioned Randy Johnson.

Bonds won the NL batting title for the second time in three years with a .362 average, while also hitting his 700th career homer. He also broke his single-season records, set in 2002, with a .609 on-base percentage, 232 walks and 120 intentional walks.

Bonds' .812 slugging percentage led the major leagues for a fourth straight season. He also hit 45 homers to match Hank Aaron's NL record of eight 40-homer seasons. Furthermore, Bonds became the first major league player with 13 consecutive 30-homer seasons.

LARRY GOREN

Roger Clemens

Reds shortstop Barry Larkin made the NL all-star team and Braves first baseman Julio Franco became the oldest player to hit a grand slam at 45. Red Sox outfielder Ellis Burks, Mets reliever John Franco, Angels first baseman Andres Galarraga (who overcame a second bout with cancer), Mariners DH Edgar Martinez and lefthander Jamie Moyer and Orioles first baseman Rafael Palmeiro also had their moments.

However, 40-year-old first baseman Fred McGriff may have seen his career and bid for 500 home runs end July 27 when he was released by the Devil Rays. He batted just .181 with two home runs and seven RBIs in 27 games, leaving him with 493 career homers.

Longest Interim Service Ever

In 2003, Selig indicated he would retire when his term as commissioner ended. He changed his tune in 2004.

Selig received a three-year contract extension in August in a unanimous vote of the 29 owners. His contract now runs through the 2009 season. If Selig serves out the new term, he will have held the job for 17 years. That would be the second-longest tenure for a baseball leader behind Kenesaw Mountain Landis, who became the first commissioner in 1920 and held the job until he died in 1944.

Selig took over leadership of MLB in September 1992 when commissioner Fay Vincent resigned. At the time he was chairman of ownership's Executive Council and said he was serving on a temporary basis, but he led baseball until he was formally named commissioner in July 1998. Selig was given a five-year term in July 1998 and three years later owners extended it through 2006.

Bud Selig

"In September 1992, I told my wife when I got off the plane, she asked how long it would be, and I said, 'Two to four months,' " Selig said. "It's got to be the longest two to four months in history."

Though Selig talked of retirement in 2003, he was persuaded to change his mind by his fellow owners.

"I had a series of owners who asked me after that time not to close my mind and they were a little surprised that I had said that," Selig said. "Once they articulated that, I believe that my responsibility and my feeling for the sport is such that I want to do what they think is in the best interests of the sport.

"I finally felt it was the right thing to do."

Several owners said Selig will be able to serve as commissioner as long as he wants.

"If he had wanted six years, seven years, 10 years, I think he would have gotten it," Rockies vice chairman Jerry McMorris said.

Under Selig, Major League Baseball expanded the playoffs from four to eight teams in 1995, started interleague play in 1997, increased revenue sharing among its clubs, and got players to agree to a luxury tax on high-payroll clubs. Most significantly, in 2002 players and owners agreed to a labor contract without a work stoppage for the first time since the players established a legitimate union.

"This sport was a dinosaur. It didn't change, and then when you tried to change it, it obviously had a lot of critics," Selig said. "But the competition among other forms of entertainment and other sports will just intensify, and we have to be smart enough to always stay ahead of that curve."

Saying Their Goodbyes

Paul Molitor became the first player in history to play the majority of his games at DH and win election to the Hall of Fame. A few months later, the man considered baseball's greatest DH since the rule went into effect in 1973 retired.

The Mariners' Edgar Martinez hung it up after 18 sea-

sons, all in Seattle. He hit .312 with 309 homers and 1,261 RBIs. He played in seven All-Star Games and twice won the American League batting title. Martinez was a rarity among professional athletes as someone who stayed with the same organization for his entire career.

"It was important to stay in Seattle because not many players do that any more," Martinez said. "I always felt great in Seattle. I loved to play for Seattle. I always enjoyed it immensely to play in Seattle."

Martinez was one of a number of players who retired in 2004, including Ellis Burks, who decided to end his 18-year career after an injury-plagued season with the Red Sox. Burks spent nearly the entire season on the disabled list and had two knee operations. He finished his 18-year career with a .291 batting average, 352 homers and 1,206 RBIs.

"You can't play forever," Burks said. "As much as I'd like to, you tend to realize there's times when you have to let it go and leave it up to some of the younger guys."

Robin Ventura retired after the Dodgers lost to the Cardinals in the NL Division Series, finishing his 16-year career. Ventura left with 294 home runs, 1,182 RBIs and a .267 batting average while winning six Gold Gloves at third base. "I've realized that it's time to go, and that's it," Ventura said.

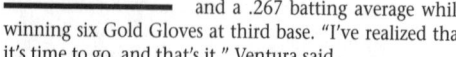

Edgar Martinez

MICHAEL WALBY

The Mets' Todd Zeile also retired after 16 seasons. Zeile played for 11 different teams, hitting .265 with 253 homers and 1,110 RBIs. Zeile broke in to the big leagues as a catcher but spent most of his career at third base and first base.

Blue Jays righthander Pat Hentgen and Padres lefthander Sterling Hitchcock didn't wait until the end of the season to retire.

Hentgen, the 1996 AL Cy Young Award winner, walked away July 24 after going 2-9 with a 6.95 ERA. He had a 131-112 lifetime record with a 4.32 ERA in 14 seasons.

"It's been a tough grind for me, mentally and physically," Hentgen said. "I always told myself I would retire from baseball if I felt like I couldn't do what I'm used to doing."

Hitchcock retired on Sept. 3 after being plagued by rib, groin and elbow injuries, limiting him to four starts. Hitchcock had a 74-76 career record with a 4.80 ERA during his 13-year career. "This is not the way you want to go out, obviously," he said. "There are very few who get to choose the way they want to go out."

Starting Over In Arizona

In 2001, the Diamondbacks won the World Series in just their fourth season of existence. Three years later, they lost a major league-worst 111 games and were in total upheaval.

The man who brought Major League Baseball to the desert in 1998, Jerry Colangelo, left the organization in the process and manager Bob Brenly, who guided the Diamondbacks to their title, was fired July 2.

Colangelo was forced out as chief executive by the four businessmen who became majority owners in 2002, with the promise of a $160 million cash infusion over a decade. In the same move, high-powered agent Jeff Moorad was appointed to replace Colangelo.

Colangelo helped land the expansion team for

JOHN WILLIAMSON

Beating up on his former teammate
Alfonso Soriano took the All-Star Game MVP

American League stars spoil Clemens' homecoming party

The 2004 All-Star Game was supposed to be Roger Clemens' show.

The game was played at Houston's Minute Maid Park, and Clemens was the starting pitcher for the National League in his first season with the Astros after coming out of a brief retirement.

However, Clemens wound up getting bashed in his homecoming bash as the Rangers' Alfonso Soriano and the Red Sox' Manny Ramirez homered during a six-run first inning to lead the American League to a 9-4 victory.

"I put our guys in a hole," Clemens said.

He certainly did, and the NL couldn't dig out. For the second year, the win meant home-field advantage in the World Series for the AL and Boston. (For the second year, it didn't matter as the Red Sox swept the Cardinals in October.)

The Red Sox' David Ortiz also homered for the AL and the Yankees' Derek Jeter got three hits. With the win, the AL closed its All-Star Game deficit to 40-33-2. Soriano was the game's MVP, after he finished 2-for-3 with three RBIs and one run.

"I felt a little sorry because he's been nice to me all of the time," Soriano said of Clemens, a teammate when both were with the Yankees in 2003. "But you know, I had to do my job in the game. I am sorry, but you know, I am happy right now."

The crowd of 41,886 had little to cheer for until the fourth, when the NL scored three runs off Cleveland's C.C. Sabathia. Jeff Kent knocked a two-out single, followed by a base hit by Astros teammate Carlos Beltran, who was selected for the game as an injury replacement after playing most of the first

half with the Royals. Edgar Renteria plated Kent with a ground-rule double down the left-field line, and two more runs scored on a double by Albert Pujols.

Much of the pregame buildup centered on the checkered past between Clemens and his starting batterymate, Mets catcher Mike Piazza. Clemens beaned Piazza in the 2000 regular season, then threw the barrel of a broken bat toward him in the World Series later that year.

Even prior to the first pitch, it was clear their feud was still simmering. Clemens and Piazza stood a few feet apart before the team picture was taken near the hill in center field at Minute Maid Park, but did not speak to each other.

Mike Piazza

STEVE MOORE

While winning pitcher Mark Mulder of the Athletics warmed up with Tigers catcher Ivan Rodriguez, Clemens started getting ready with a bullpen catcher. Piazza caught just a couple of pitches before leaving the bullpen for pregame introductions.

—JOHN PERROTTO

TOP VOTE-GETTERS

AMERICAN LEAGUE

CATCHER: 1. Ivan Rodriguez, Tigers, 2,537,586; 2. Jorge Posada, Yankees, 1,565,305; 3. Jason Varitek, Red Sox, 1,122,901.

FIRST BASE: 1. Jason Giambi, Yankees, 1,784,443; 2. Frank Thomas, White Sox, 978,623; 3. Carlos Delgado, Blue Jays, 717,341.

SECOND BASE: 1. Alfonso Soriano, Rangers, 3,466,447; 2. Pokey Reese, Red Sox, 1,082,772; 3. Bret Boone, Mariners, 990,776.

THIRD BASE: 1. Alex Rodriguez, Yankees, 2,915,901; 2. Hank Blalock, Rangers, 1,254,876; 3. Bill Mueller, Red Sox, 868,968.

SHORTSTOP: 1. Derek Jeter, Yankees, 2,052,880; 2. Nomar Garciaparra, Red Sox, 1,620,187; 3. Michael Young, Rangers, 1,248,498.

OUTFIELD: 1. Vladimir Guerrero, Angels, 3,024,870; 2. Manny Ramirez, Red Sox, 2,682,121; 3. Ichiro Suzuki, Mariners, 1,891,136; 4. Hideki Matsui, Yankees, 1,855,118; 5. Gary Sheffield, Yankees, 1,688,921; 6. Johnny Damon, Red Sox, 1,319,984; 7. Bernie Williams, Yankees, 1,017,844; 8. Torii Hunter, Twins, 847,586; 9. Magglio Ordoñez, White Sox, 666,066

NATIONAL LEAGUE

CATCHER: 1. Mike Piazza, Mets, 2,296,667; 2. Brad Ausmus, Astros, 1,518,827; 3. Mike Matheny, Cardinals, 1,014,882.

FIRST BASE: 1. Albert Pujols, Cardinals, 2,649,013; 2. Jeff Bagwell, Astros, 1,918,071; 3. Jim Thome, Phillies, 1,111,478.

SECOND BASE: 1. Jeff Kent, Astros, 2,898,381; 2. Tony Womack, Cardinals, 1,034,014; 3. Luis Castillo, Marlins, 767,994.

THIRD BASE: 1. Scott Rolen, Cardinals, 3,187,710; 2. Morgan Ensberg, Astros, 1,150,751; 3. Aramis Ramirez, Cubs, 1,068,706.

SHORTSTOP: 1. Edgar Renteria, Cardinals, 2,028,840; 2. Adam Everett, Astros, 1,814,814; 3. Kazuo Matsui, Mets, 1,160,731.

OUTFIELD: 1. Barry Bonds, Giants, 2,952,237; 2. Ken Griffey, Jr., Reds, 2,837,526; 3. Sammy Sosa, Cubs, 2,197,255; 4. Lance Berkman, Astros, 2,109,526; 5. Craig Biggio, Astros, 1,722,278; 6. Jim Edmonds, Cardinals, 1,468,061; 7. Carlos Beltran, Royals/Astros, 1,369,178; 8. Moises Alou, Cubs, 1,265,592; 9. Richard Hidalgo, Astros/Mets, 929,867.

ROSTERS

AMERICAN LEAGUE

PITCHERS: Francisco Cordero, Rangers; Tom Gordon, Yankees; x-Tim Hudson, Athletics; Ted Lilly, Blue Jays; Esteban Loaiza, White Sox; **Mark Mulder, Athletics**; Joe Nathan, Twins; Mariano Rivera, Yankees; Francisco Rodriguez, Angels; Kenny Rogers, Rangers; C.C. Sabathia, Indians; x-Curt Schilling, Red Sox; Javier Vazquez, Yankees; Jake Westbrook, Indians.

CATCHERS: Victor Martinez, Indians; **Ivan Rodriguez, Tigers**.

INFIELDERS: Ron Belliard, Indians; Hank Blalock, Rangers; **Jason Giambi, Yankees (1b)**; Carlos Guillen, Tigers; Ken Harvey, Royals; **Derek**

Jeter, Yankees (ss); David Ortiz, Red Sox; **Alex Rodriguez, Yankees (3b)**; **Alfonso Soriano, Rangers (2b)**; Miguel Tejada, Orioles; Michael Young, Rangers.

OUTFIELDERS: Carl Crawford, Devil Rays; **Vladimir Guerrero, Angels (rf)**; Matt Lawton, Indians; Hideki Matsui, Yankees; **Manny Ramirez, Red Sox (lf)**; Gary Sheffield, Yankees; **Ichiro Suzuki, Mariners (cf)**.

DESIGNATED HITTER: **Edgar Martinez, Mariners**; Carl Everett, White Sox.

NATIONAL LEAGUE

PITCHERS: Armando Benitez, Marlins; **Roger Clemens, Astros**; Eric Gagne, Dodgers; Tom Glavine, Mets; Danny Graves, Reds; Livan Hernandez, Expos; Randy Johnson, Diamondbacks; Danny Kolb, Brewers; Carl Pavano, Marlins; Jason Schmidt, Giants; Ben Sheets, Brewers; Carlos Zambrano, Cubs.

CATCHERS: Johnny Estrada, Braves; Paul Lo Duca, Dodgers; **Mike Piazza, Mets**.

INFIELDERS: x-Sean Casey, Reds; Todd Helton, Rockies; **Jeff Kent, Astros (2b)**; Barry Larkin, Reds; Mark Loretta, Padres; Mike Lowell, Marlins; **Albert Pujols, Cardinals (1b)**; **Edgar Renteria, Cardinals (ss)**; **Scott Rolen, Cardinals (3b)**; Jim Thome, Phillies; Jack Wilson, Pirates.

OUTFIELDERS: Bobby Abreu, Phillies; Moises Alou, Cubs; Carlos Beltran, Phillies; **Lance Berkman, Astros (cf)**; **Barry Bonds, Giants (lf)**; Miguel Cabrera, Marlins; x-Ken Griffey, Jr., Reds; **Sammy Sosa, Cubs (rf)**.

Starters in bold
x-Injured, did not play.

July 13 in Houston
American League 9, National League 4

AMERICAN	ab	r	h	bi	NATIONAL	ab	r	h	bi
Suzuki, cf	4	1	1	0	Renteria, ss	3	1	1	1
Vazquez, p	0	0	0	0	Wilson, ss	2	0	0	0
Belliard, 2b	1	0	0	0	Pujols, 1b	3	1	2	2
Rodriguez, I, c	4	1	2	1	Thome, 1b	2	0	0	0
Martinez, c	1	0	0	0	Bonds, lf	2	0	0	0
Guerrero, rf	4	1	1	0	Pavano, p	0	0	0	0
Lilly, p	0	0	0	0	Glavine, p	0	0	0	0
Tejada, ss	1	0	0	0	Abreu, ph	1	0	0	0
Ramirez, lf	2	1	1	2	Sheets, p	0	0	0	0
Ortiz, ph-1b	1	2	1	2	Lo Duca, c	0	0	0	0
Rodriguez, A, 3b	3	0	1	1	Rolen, 3b	1	0	1	0
Blalock, ph-3b	2	0	0	0	Lowell, ph-3b	2	0	0	0
Giambi, 1b	2	1	1	0	Sosa, rf	2	0	1	1
Crawford, ph-lf	2	0	0	0	Cabrera, rf	2	0	0	0
Matsui, ph-lf	1	0	0	0	Piazza, c	2	0	0	0
Jeter, ss	3	1	3	0	Estrada, c	2	0	0	0
Lawton, cf	2	0	1	0	Gagne, p	0	0	0	0
Soriano, 2b	3	1	2	3	Berkman, cf	2	0	0	0
Sheffield, rf	1	0	0	0	Alou, lf	2	0	1	0
Mulder, p	1	0	0	0	Kent, 2b	2	1	1	0
Harvey, ph	1	0	0	0	Loretta, ph-2b	2	0	1	0
Loaiza, p	0	0	0	0	Clemens, p	0	0	0	0
Sabathia, p	0	0	0	0	Kolb, p	0	0	0	0
Young, ph-ss	2	0	0	0	Larkin, ph	1	0	0	0
Nathan, p	0	0	0	0	Johnson, p	0	0	0	0
Gordon, p	0	0	0	0	Zambrano, p	0	0	0	0
Rodriguez, F, p	0	0	0	0	Beltran, ph-cf	2	1	1	0
Rivera, p	0	0	0	0	Helton, ph	1	0	0	0
Totals	**41**	**9**	**14**	**9**	**Totals**	**36**	**4**	**9**	**4**

American	600	102	000—9
National	100	300	000—4

LOB—National 6, American 8. **2B**—Suzuki, Pujols 2, Renteria. **3B**—Rodriguez, I., Rodriguez, A. **HR**—Ramirez, Soriano, Ortiz.

AMERICAN	ip	h	r	er	bb	so	NATIONAL	ip	h	r	er	bb	so
Mulder	2	2	1	1	0	1	Clemens	1	5	6	3	0	2
Loaiza	1	1	0	0	1	0	Kolb	1	1	0	0	0	0
Sabathia	1	4	3	3	0	0	Johnson	1	3	0	0	0	1
Vazquez	1	0	0	0	0	2	Zambrano	1	1	1	1	1	1
Lilly	1	2	0	0	0	1	Pavano	2	3	2	2	0	1
Nathan	1	0	0	0	0	2	Glavine	1	0	0	0	0	1
Gordon	⅓	0	0	0	0	0	Sheets	1	0	0	0	0	1
Rodriguez, F	⅔	0	0	0	0	0	Gagne	1	0	0	0	1	2
Rivera	1	0	0	0	0	0							

HBP—Rolen (by Mulder).

Umpires: HP—Ed Montague; **1B**—John Hirschbeck; **2B**—Doug Eddings; **3B**—Jim Reynolds; **LF**—Marvin Hudson; **RF**—Sam Holbrook. **T**—2:59. **A**—41,886.

Phoenix in 1998, but over the years he took the team into steep debt in his efforts to build a winner. It resulted in success on the field, when the Diamondbacks beat the Yankees in the World Series three years later. But it also led to millions of dollars in deferred payments and opened the way for partners from outside his personal circle to sign on and eventually bring his ouster.

"Anyone with any experience would say that it's always difficult to run any organization or any business by committee," Colangelo said. "Ultimately, someone needs to have the authority to make decisions. That is the best way, but it's not necessarily the way it is any more."

Brenly was fired after the Diamondbacks got off to a 29-50 start and saw attendance dwindle. Brenly compiled a 303-262 record in three-plus seasons.

"The blame does not solely fall on Bob's shoulders, as we have failed in many facets on the field and in the clubhouse," Colangelo said. "However, with disappointments come change and our ownership group and management feel that now is the time to relieve Bob of his duties."

Jerry Colangelo

Third-base coach Al Pedrique finished out the season as interim manager. The Diamondbacks then hired their Class A Lancaster manager and former big leaguer Wally Backman to manage the team, but his tenure lasted less than a week after issues about his background emerged, involving brushes with the law and financial problems. Arizona replaced Backman with Bob Melvin, the team's former bench coach before he managed the Mariners.

Brenly was one of five managers fired during the season along with the Astros' Jimy Williams (July 14), the Blue Jays' Carlos Tosca (Aug. 8), the New York Mets' Art Howe (Sept. 15) and the Phillies' Larry Bowa (Oct. 2).

The move in Houston worked wonders. The Astros were 44-44 under Williams in 2004 when the team finally jettisoned him the day after it hosted the All-Star Game at Minute Maid Park. Many observers felt the move should have been made much sooner and that it would be too late for the Astros to get back into the playoff race.

Former Brewers and Tigers manager Phil Garner took his place and rallied the Astros to a 48-26 record the rest of the way and the NL wild card. Houston then won its first playoff series in franchise history, overcoming the Braves in five games before losing to the Cardinals in the NL Championship Series.

"There was a cloud that hung over our team for so long," said GM Gerry Hunsicker, who surprisingly resigned

himself after the season. "We needed a dramatic change."

A year after leading the Blue Jays to a surprising 86-win season, Tosca was axed with his team's record just 47-64. Tosca took over June 3, 2002, and compiled a 189-191 record during his tenure.

"We were starting to mail it in a little bit," Toronto GM J.P. Ricciardi said. "The team was showing signs of not playing hard. It wasn't an easy decision. It never is when you have to tell someone who does what he loves that it's being taken away from him."

First-base coach John Gibbons replaced Tosca on an interim basis then got the job at season's end.

Howe finished the season in a strange position, still managing the club despite being fired several weeks earlier. The Mets asked Howe to stay on for the remainder of the season and he agreed.

"I saw strength and courage and conviction when I met Art Howe and I said, 'Let's go,' and hired him," Mets owner Fred Wilpon said. "I take full responsibility that the results weren't there."

The Mets were 71-91 in 2004 and 137-186 in Howe's two seasons despite having one of the highest payrolls in the major leagues.

The ax fell on Bowa with two days left in a season filled with speculation about his job security, much too late to save a year that Phillies fans had such high hopes for. The Phillies moved into Citizens Bank Park with hopes of winning the National League and ending the Braves' record string of 12 division titles. Instead, Philadelphia finished 86-76 and missed the playoffs for the 11th consecutive year. Bowa had a 337-308 record in four years, but his fiery personality eventually worked against him.

"There were times over the last four years where there were players who haven't been able to adjust to his style," Phillies GM Ed Wade said.

Larry Bowa

Melvin was fired in Seattle the day after the Mariners ended a 63-99 season, their worst in 12 years. "This was not easy to do and there is a point where you shed a tear," Mariners GM Bill Bavasi said. "It is awful but it crystalized in my mind that we needed to make a change."

Former Indians and Orioles manager Mike Hargrove replaced Melvin, who had a 156-168 record in two years on the job, his first as a big league manager.

The Dodgers changed general managers two days before spring training started, when Dan Evans was replaced by Athletics assistant GM Paul DePodesta. It was the first major move made by Boston developer Frank McCourt after he bought the Dodgers from News Corp. for $430 million in the offseason. At 31, DePodesta became the third-youngest person to be hired as a GM. Theo Epstein was 28 when the Red Sox hired him in 2002 and Randy Smith was hired as by the Padres at 29 in 1993. The Dodgers won the NL West in DePodesta's first year on the job.

"My mission is to be on a relentless quest for baseball knowledge," DePodesta said. "I know that will lead us in a positive direction. What I'm committed to is finding a way to

MANAGERIAL CHANGES

Six big league teams made managerial changes before, during or after the 2004 season, one more change than the year before. Here are the changes and the six new managers for 2005:

Team	Original Manager	In-Season Change	2005 Manager
Arizona	Bob Brenly	Al Pedrique	Bob Melvin
Houston	Jimy Williams	Phil Garner	Phil Garner
New York (NL)	Art Howe	—	Willie Randolph
Philadelphia	Larry Bowa	Gary Varsho	Charlie Manuel
Seattle	Bob Melvin	—	Mike Hargrove
Toronto	Carlos Tosca	John Gibbons	John Gibbons

win. I've been given a mandate by Frank and also the resources to be as aggressive as we possibly can."

Getting Their Place In The Hall

Dennis Eckersley and Paul Molitor comprised the Hall of Fame's Class of 2004 when they were inducted in Cooperstown on July 25.

In 24 seasons with the Indians (1975-77), Red Sox (1978-84, 1998), Cubs (1984-85), Athletics (1987-95) and Cardinals (1996-97), Eckersley appeared in 1,071 games, the most of any Hall of Fame pitcher. He began his career as a starter, then remade himself as perhaps the best closer in baseball history. He finished with a record of 197-171, with 390 saves and a 3.50 ERA.

Eckersley grew up in the Oakland area and his parents were always near when he was playing baseball. His father Wallace would leave work early to watch him play, coached Little League and even dragged the infield before and after games in his Ford Ranchero while his mother Bernice worked the snack bar.

They were there in Cooperstown, even though Wallace was confined to a wheelchair and was breathing with the help of an oxygen tank because of emphysema.

"My parents were there for me, and they're here for me now," Eckersley said. "My dad struggled to get here today, and both of us knew nothing could have stood in the way of us sharing this moment together."

Molitor collected 3,319 hits in his 21-year career with the Brewers (1978-92), Blue Jays (1993-95) and Twins (1996-98), batting .306 with 234 homers and 1,307 RBIs. Molitor also praised his parents, who are deceased.

"Somehow, in the midst of raising eight kids, my mother managed to see me play a lot of games," Molitor said. "But my mom always thought she was a jinx. She'd come to the games and watch them from her car or she'd hide behind a tree. It continued even to the major leagues. I'd leave her seats in the family section and I couldn't find her. She'd walk around looking for an empty seat."

Also inducted were longtime Oakland and San Francisco Giants voice Lon Simmons, who won the Ford Frick Award for contributions to baseball broadcasting. The New York

Times' Murray Chass gained entrance as the J.G. Taylor Spink Award recipient for contributions to baseball writing.

New Parks, Same Old Results

The Padres and Phillies moved into new homes, but both teams fell short of their hopes of making the playoffs. Both franchise set single-season attendance records as 3,016,752 watched the Padres at Petco Park in San Diego and 3,250,092 watched the Phillies at Citizens Bank Park.

The Padres christened Petco Park with a win, edging the Giants 4-3 on April 8. Sean Burroughs' two-out RBI single capped a two-run 10th as San Diego rallied for the win. The Padres' Brian Giles, a native of the San Diego area, singled for the first hit in park history.

Philadelphia suffered a 4-1 loss to the Reds in its first game at Citizens Bank Park on April 12. Reds pitcher Paul Wilson spoiled the party by allowing only one run in 7⅓ innings. Cincinnati's D'Angelo Jimenez had the park's first hit, a double, while the Phillies' Bobby Abreu hit the first home run.

Cooperstown bound
Hall of Fame inducted Paul Molitor and Dennis Eckersley in 2004

MAJOR LEAGUE DEBUTS, 2004

AMERICAN LEAGUE

Anaheim Angels

Dusty Bergman, lhp	June 9
Scott Dunn, rhp	Sept. 11
Matt Hensley, rhp	May 4
Casey Kotchman, 1b	May 9
Dallas McPherson, 3b	Sept. 10

Baltimore Orioles

Denny Bautista, rhp	May 25
Jose Bautista, 3b	April 4
Daniel Cabrera, rhp	May 13
John Maine, rhp	July 23
Val Majewski, of	Aug. 20
Darnell McDonald, of	April 30
Aaron Rakers, rhp	Sept. 8
Eddy Rodriguez, rhp	May 31

Boston Red Sox

Abe Alvarez, lhp	July 22
Jamie Brown, rhp	May 20
Lenny DiNardo, lhp	April 23
Andy Dominique, c	May 25
Anastacio Martinez, rhp	May 22
Phil Seibel, lhp	April 15
Kevin Youkilis, 3b	May 15

Chicago White Sox

Jeff Bajenaru, rhp	Sept. 4
Felix Diaz, rhp	May 13
Arnie Munoz, lhp	June 19
Shingo Takatsu, rhp	April 9
Wilson Valdez, ss	Sept. 7

Cleveland Indians

Cliff Bartosh, lhp	May 15
Fernando Cabrera, rhp	Aug. 20
Francisco Cruceta, rhp	Sept. 21
Kyle Denney, rhp	Sept. 14
Jeremy Guthrie, rhp	Aug. 28
Jake Robbins, rhp	Sept. 20
Grady Sizemore, of	July 21
Kazuhito Tadano, rhp	April 27

Detroit Tigers

Curtis Granderson, of	Sept. 13
Nook Logan, of	July 21
Roberto Novoa, rhp	July 29
Ryan Raburn, 2b	Sept. 12
Chris Shelton, c	April 15
Lino Urdaneta, rhp	Sept. 9

Kansas City Royals

Andres Blanco, ss	April 17
Shawn Camp, rhp	April 5
Byron Gettis, of	May 27
Ruben Gotay, 2b	Aug. 3
Zack Greinke, rhp	May 22
Justin Huisman, rhp	April 25
Donnie Murphy, 2b	Sept. 18
Paul Phillips, c	Sept. 9
Jimmy Serrano, rhp	Aug. 7
Rich Thompson, of	April 7
Mike Tonis, c	June 20
Jorge Vasquez, rhp	Aug. 13
Eduardo Villacis, rhp	May 1

Minnesota Twins

Jason Bartlett, ss	Aug. 3
Jesse Crain, rhp	Aug. 5
J.D. Durbin, rhp	Sept. 8
Matt Guerrier, rhp	June 17
Jason Kubel, of	Aug. 31
Joe Mauer, c	April 5
Terry Tiffee, 3b	Sept. 1

New York Yankees

Alex Graman, lhp	April 20
Brad Halsey, lhp	June 19
Sam Marsonek, rhp	July 11
Dioner Navarro, c	Sept. 7
Juan Padilla, rhp	July 16
Andy Phillips, 3b	Sept. 14
Scott Proctor, rhp	April 20

Oakland Athletics

Joe Blanton, rhp	Sept. 21
Ramon Castro, 3b	June 21
Jairo Garcia, rhp	Aug. 9

Justin Lehr, rhp	June 20
Mike Rose, c	Oct. 1
Nick Swisher, of	Sept. 3

Seattle Mariners

Scott Atchison, rhp	July 31
Cha Seung Baek, rhp	Aug. 8
Travis Blackley, lhp	July 1
Greg Dobbs, 3b	Sept. 8
Bucky Jacobsen, 1b	July 16
Justin Leone, 3b	July 2
Jose Lopez, ss	July 31
Mickey Lopez, 2b	Sept. 6
Bobby Madritsch, lhp	July 21
Clint Nageotte, rhp	June 1
Jeremy Reed, of	Sept. 8
Rene Rivera, c	Sept. 22
George Sherrill, lhp	July 16
Matt Thornton, lhp	June 27
Randy Williams, rhp	Sept. 11

Tampa Bay Devil Rays

Jorge Cantu, 2b	July 17
Bartolome Fortunato, rhp	June 29
Joey Gathright, of	June 25
Scott Kazmir, lhp	Aug. 23
Franklin Nunez, rhp	Aug. 14
B.J. Upton, ss	Aug. 2
John Webb, rhp	Aug. 2

Texas Rangers

Frank Francisco, rhp	May 14
Adrian Gonzalez, 1b	April 18
Travis Hughes, rhp	Sept. 26
Kameron Loe, rhp	Sept. 26
Sam Narron, lhp	July 30
Nick Regilio, rhp	July 9
Ryan Snare, lhp	Aug. 6
Chris Young, rhp	Aug. 24

Toronto Blue Jays

Russ Adams, ss	Sept. 3
David Bush, rhp	July 2
Gustavo Chacin, lhp	Sept. 20
Eric Crozier, 1b	Sept. 4
Jason Frasor, rhp	April 16
Gabe Gross, of	Aug. 7
Brandon League, rhp	Sept. 21
Adam Peterson, rhp	June 24
Simon Pond, of	April 7
Guillermo Quiroz, c	Sept. 4
Alexis Rios, of	May 27

NATIONAL LEAGUE

Arizona Diamondbacks

Greg Aquino, rhp	July 2
Brian Bruney, rhp	May 8
Lance Cormier, rhp	June 19
Casey Daigle, rhp	April 9
Doug DeVore, of	May 6
Jerry Gil, ss	Aug. 22
Mike Gosling, lhp	Sept. 9
Andy Green, 3b	June 12
Scott Hairston, 2b	May 7
Josh Kroeger, of	Sept. 2
Tim Olson, 3b	May 30
Chris Snyder, c	Aug. 21
Chad Tracy, 3b	April 21

Atlanta Braves

Jose Capellan, rhp	Sept. 12
Ramon Colon, rhp	Aug. 21
Nick Green, 2b	May 15
Adam LaRoche, 1b	April 7
Sam McConnell, lhp	June 25
Dan Meyer, rhp	Sept. 14
Charles Thomas, of	June 23

Chicago Cubs

Jason Dubois, of	May 19
Brendan Harris, 2b/3b	July 6
Jon Leicester, rhp	June 9
Michael Wuertz, rhp	April 5

Colorado Rockies

J.D. Closser, c	June 30
Scott Dohmann, rhp	May 15

Jeff Francis, lhp	Aug. 25
Choo Freeman, of	June 4
Chris Gissell, rhp	Aug. 22
Luis Gonzalez, 2b	April 6
Brad Hawpe, of	May 1
Matt Holliday, of	April 16
Jorge Piedra, of	Aug. 7
Allan Simpson, rhp	May 17

Florida Marlins

Chris Aguila, of	June 28
Franklyn Gracesqui, lhp	April 29
Logan Kensing, rhp	Sept. 10
Matt Treanor, c	June 2
Josh Willingham, c	July 6

Houston Astros

Jason Alfaro, ss	Sept. 9
John Buck, c	June 25
Chris Burke, 2b	July 4
Chad Qualls, rhp	July 22
Willy Taveras, of	Sept. 6

Los Angeles Dodgers

Yhency Brazoban, rhp	Aug. 5

Milwaukee Brewers

Mike Adams, rhp	May 18
Jeff Bennett, rhp	April 6
Jorge de la Rosa, lhp	Aug. 14
Matt Erickson, 2b/ss	July 9
Corey Hart, of	May 25
Ben Hendrickson, rhp	June 2
Dave Krynzel, of	Sept. 1
Pedro Liriano, rhp	Aug. 27
Chris Saenz, rhp	April 24

Montreal Expos

Chad Bentz, lhp	April 7
Ryan Church, of	Aug. 21
Shawn Hill, rhp	June 29
Joe Horgan, lhp	June 12
Maicer Izturis, ss	Aug. 27
Josh Labandeira, ss/2b	Sept. 17
Gary Majewski, rhp	Aug. 26
Val Pascucci, of	April 26
Terrmel Sledge, of	April 6

New York Mets

Heath Bell, rhp	Aug. 24
Craig Brazell, 1b	Aug. 17
Victor Diaz, of	Sept. 11
Joe Hietpas, c	Oct. 3
Jeff Keppinger, 2b	Aug. 20
Kazuo Matsui, ss	April 6
David Wright, 3b	July 21
Tyler Yates, rhp	April 9

Philadelphia Phillies

Gavin Floyd, rhp	Sept. 3
Ryan Howard, 1b	Sept. 1
Elizardo Ramirez, rhp	May 25

Pittsburgh Pirates

Frank Brooks, lhp	Aug. 27
Sean Burnett, lhp	May 30
Jose Castillo, 2b	April 7
Mike Johnston, lhp	April 7
Ian Snell, rhp	Aug. 20
John Van Benschoten, rhp	Aug. 18

St. Louis Cardinals

Carmen Cali, lhp	Sept. 8
Hector Luna, ss/2b	April 8
Yadier Molina, c	June 3

San Diego Padres

Justin Germano, rhp	May 22
Freddy Guzman, of	Aug. 17
Jon Knott, of	May 30
Marty McLeary, rhp	Aug. 22
Akinori Otsuka, rhp	April 6
Jason Szuminski, rhp	April 11
Steve Watkins, rhp	Aug. 21

San Francisco Giants

David Aardsma, rhp	April 6
Brian Dallimore, 2b/3b	April 29
Brad Hennessey, rhp	Aug. 7
Justin Knoedler, c	Oct. 3
Merkin Valdez, rhp	Aug. 1

BY JOHN PERROTTO

The 100th World Series, on the surface, appeared to be an event lacking drama.

The Boston Red Sox rolled to a four-game victory over the St. Louis Cardinals for the 18th sweep in World Series history. The Red Sox also became the fourth team to never trail in a World Series, joining the 1963 Dodgers, 1966 Orioles and 1989 Athletics.

"They ended up outplaying us in every category," Cardinals manager Tony La Russa said. "It ended up not being terrific competition."

No, it didn't. However, that doesn't mean this World Series wasn't without a great storyline and won't go down as very memorable for an entire region of the United States.

The Red Sox won their first World Series since 1918, a span that covered 86 often tortured years. That drought was the third-longest among teams who had won a championship, behind only the two Chicago teams—the Cubs (1908) and White Sox (1917).

The Red Sox had lost in Game Seven in each of their four previous World Series trips: 1946 and 1967 to St. Louis, 1975 to the Reds and 1986 to the Mets. That was all part of the supposed "Curse of The Bambino" that was placed on the Red Sox following the 1919 season when they sold the great Babe Ruth to the Yankees in order for Boston owner Harry Frazee to fund the Broadway play, "No, No Nanette."

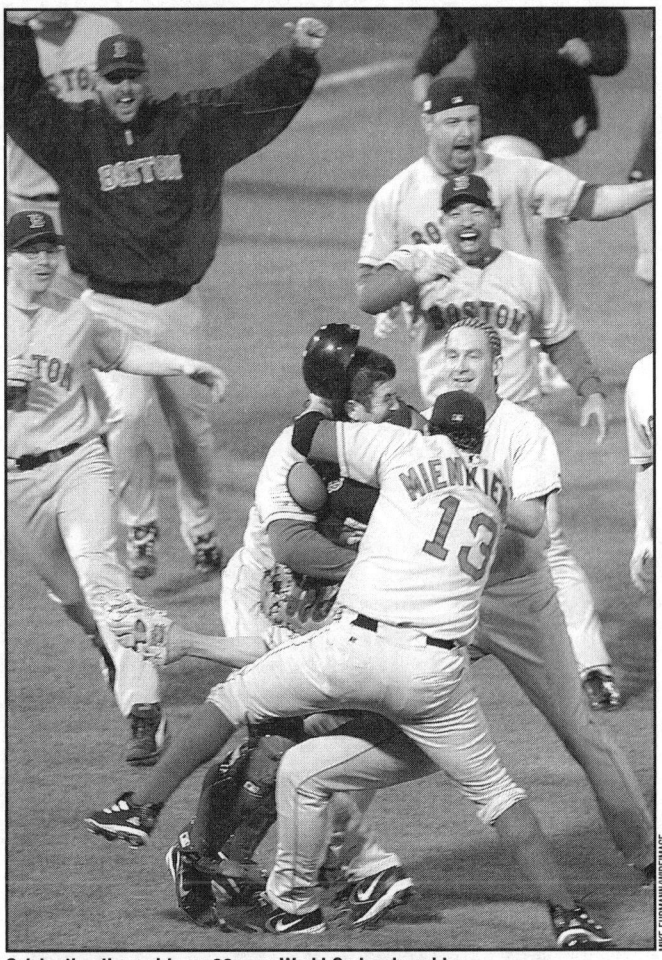

Celebrating the end to an 86-year World Series drought
Red Sox captured the 2004 series in four straight games, having never trailed

MIKE EHRMANN/WIREIMAGE

However, all the sins of the Red Sox' past seem to be lifted when they completed the sweep with a 3-0 win at Busch Stadium in Game Four. All was forgotten, including the sale of Ruth, Johnny Pesky holding the ball in 1946, Jim Lonborg running out of gas in 1967, Ed Armbrister colliding with Carlton Fisk in a non-interference call in 1975, Bucky Dent homering in 1978, Bill Buckner letting the ball go through his legs in 1986 and Aaron Boone going deep in 2003.

"I didn't believe in any curse," said Boston's Terry Francona, who became the seventh first-year manager to win a World Series after replacing Grady Little the previous winter.

"We can't reverse what went on a long time ago. I'm sure there are a lot of people in New England who are dancing in the streets right now. As far as the other stuff, this is this year's team. This team had nothing to do with any other team. We couldn't do anything about any other

year."

Yet, the 2004 Red Sox were able to do what so many other Boston teams couldn't through two world wars, the Great Depression, men on the moon and the rise and fall of the Soviet Union.

Celebration Consumes New England

Their triumph was cause for a raucous celebration in the clubhouse and Boston players and coaches milled about the floor of Busch Stadium more than an hour after the final out, while more than 1,000 fans who made the trip west from New England chanted "Thank you, Red Sox." Three days later, an estimated 3.2 million fans jammed the streets of Boston for one of the largest victory parades in professional sports history.

In the streets outside Boston's Fenway Park in the

WORLD SERIES YEAR-BY-YEAR

Year	Winner	Manager	Loser	Manager	Result	MVP
1903	Boston (AL)	Jimmy Collins	Pittsburgh (NL)	Fred Clarke	5-3	None Selected
1904	NO SERIES					
1905	New York (NL)	John McGraw	Philadelphia (AL)	Connie Mack	4-1	None Selected
1906	Chicago (AL)	Fielder Jones	Chicago (NL)	Frank Chance	4-2	None Selected
1907	Chicago (NL)	Frank Chance	Detroit (AL)	Hugh Jennings	4-0	None Selected
1908	Chicago (NL)	Frank Chance	Detroit (AL)	Hugh Jennings	4-1	None Selected
1909	Pittsburgh (NL)	Fred Clarke	Detroit (AL)	Hugh Jennings	4-3	None Selected
1910	Philadelphia (AL)	Connie Mack	Chicago (NL)	Frank Chance	4-1	None Selected
1911	Philadelphia (AL)	Connie Mack	New York (NL)	John McGraw	4-2	None Selected
1912	Boston (AL)	Jake Stahl	New York (NL)	John McGraw	4-3-1	None Selected
1913	Philadelphia (AL)	Connie Mack	New York (NL)	John McGraw	4-1	None Selected
1914	Boston (NL)	George Stallings	Philadelphia (AL)	Connie Mack	4-0	None Selected
1915	Boston (AL)	Bill Carrigan	Philadelphia (NL)	Pat Moran	4-1	None Selected
1916	Boston (AL)	Bill Carrigan	Brooklyn (NL)	Wilbert Robinson	4-1	None Selected
1917	Chicago (AL)	Pants Rowland	New York (NL)	John McGraw	4-2	None Selected
1918	Boston (AL)	Ed Barrow	Chicago (NL)	Fred Mitchell	4-2	None Selected
1919	Cincinnati (NL)	Pat Moran	Chicago (AL)	Kid Gleason	5-3	None Selected
1920	Cleveland (AL)	Tris Speaker	Brooklyn (NL)	Wilbert Robinson	5-2	None Selected
1921	New York (NL)	John McGraw	New York (AL)	Miller Huggins	5-3	None Selected
1922	New York (NL)	John McGraw	New York (AL)	Miller Huggins	4-0	None Selected
1923	New York (AL)	Miller Huggins	New York (NL)	John McGraw	4-2	None Selected
1924	Washington (AL)	Bucky Harris	New York (NL)	John McGraw	4-3	None Selected
1925	Pittsburgh (NL)	Bill McKechnie	Washington (AL)	Bucky Harris	4-3	None Selected
1926	St. Louis (NL)	Rogers Hornsby	New York (AL)	Miller Huggins	4-3	None Selected
1927	New York (AL)	Miller Huggins	Pittsburgh (NL)	Donie Bush	4-0	None Selected
1928	New York (AL)	Miller Huggins	St. Louis (NL)	Bill McKechnie	4-0	None Selected
1929	Philadelphia (AL)	Connie Mack	Chicago (NL)	Joe McCarthy	4-1	None Selected
1930	Philadelphia (AL)	Connie Mack	St. Louis (NL)	Gabby Street	4-2	None Selected
1931	St. Louis (NL)	Gabby Street	Philadelphia (AL)	Connie Mack	4-3	None Selected
1932	New York (AL)	Joe McCarthy	Chicago (NL)	Charlie Grimm	4-0	None Selected
1933	New York (NL)	Bill Terry	Washington (AL)	Joe Cronin	4-1	None Selected
1934	St. Louis (NL)	Frankie Frisch	Detroit (AL)	Mickey Cochrane	4-3	None Selected
1935	Detroit (AL)	Mickey Cochrane	Chicago (NL)	Charlie Grimm	4-2	None Selected
1936	New York (AL)	Joe McCarthy	New York (NL)	Bill Terry	4-2	None Selected
1937	New York (AL)	Joe McCarthy	New York (NL)	Bill Terry	4-1	None Selected
1938	New York (AL)	Joe McCarthy	Chicago (NL)	Gabby Hartnett	4-0	None Selected
1939	New York (AL)	Joe McCarthy	Cincinnati (NL)	Bill McKechnie	4-0	None Selected
1940	Cincinnati (NL)	Bill McKechnie	Detroit (AL)	Del Baker	4-3	None Selected
1941	New York (AL)	Joe McCarthy	Brooklyn (NL)	Leo Durocher	4-1	None Selected
1942	St. Louis (NL)	Billy Southworth	New York (AL)	Joe McCarthy	4-1	None Selected
1943	New York (AL)	Joe McCarthy	St. Louis (NL)	Billy Southworth	4-1	None Selected
1944	St. Louis (NL)	Billy Southworth	St. Louis (AL)	Luke Sewell	4-2	None Selected
1945	Detroit (AL)	Steve O'Neill	Chicago (NL)	Charlie Grimm	4-3	None Selected
1946	St. Louis (NL)	Eddie Dyer	Boston (AL)	Joe Cronin	4-3	None Selected
1947	New York (AL)	Bucky Harris	Brooklyn (NL)	Burt Shotton	4-3	None Selected
1948	Cleveland (AL)	Lou Boudreau	Boston (NL)	Billy Southworth	4-2	None Selected
1949	New York (AL)	Casey Stengel	Brooklyn (NL)	Burt Shotton	4-1	None Selected
1950	New York (AL)	Casey Stengel	Philadelphia (NL)	Eddie Sawyer	4-0	None Selected
1951	New York (AL)	Casey Stengel	New York (NL)	Leo Durocher	4-2	None Selected
1952	New York (AL)	Casey Stengel	Brooklyn (NL)	Chuck Dressen	4-3	None Selected
1953	New York (AL)	Casey Stengel	Brooklyn (NL)	Chuck Dressen	4-2	None Selected
1954	New York (NL)	Leo Durocher	Cleveland (AL)	Al Lopez	4-0	None Selected
1955	Brooklyn (NL)	Walter Alston	New York (AL)	Casey Stengel	4-3	Johnny Podres, p, Brooklyn
1956	New York (AL)	Casey Stengel	Brooklyn (NL)	Walter Alston	4-3	Don Larsen, p, New York
1957	Milwaukee (NL)	Fred Haney	New York (AL)	Casey Stengel	4-3	Lew Burdette, p, Milwaukee
1958	New York (AL)	Casey Stengel	Milwaukee (NL)	Fred Haney	4-3	Bob Turley, p, New York
1959	Los Angeles (NL)	Walter Alston	Chicago (AL)	Al Lopez	4-2	Larry Sherry, p, Los Angeles
1960	Pittsburgh (NL)	Danny Murtaugh	New York (AL)	Casey Stengel	4-3	Bobby Richardson, 2b, New York
1961	New York (AL)	Ralph Houk	Cincinnati (NL)	Fred Hutchinson	4-1	Whitey Ford, p, New York
1962	New York (AL)	Ralph Houk	San Francisco (NL)	Alvin Dark	4-3	Ralph Terry, p, New York
1963	Los Angeles (NL)	Walter Alston	New York (AL)	Ralph Houk	4-0	Sandy Koufax, p, Los Angeles
1964	St. Louis (NL)	Johnny Keene	New York (AL)	Yogi Berra	4-3	Bob Gibson, p, St. Louis
1965	Los Angeles (NL)	Walter Alston	Minnesota (AL)	Sam Mele	4-3	Sandy Koufax, p, Los Angeles
1966	Baltimore (AL)	Hank Bauer	Los Angeles (NL)	Walter Alston	4-0	Frank Robinson, of, Baltimore
1967	St. Louis (NL)	Red Schoendienst	Boston (AL)	Dick Williams	4-3	Bob Gibson, p, St. Louis
1968	Detroit (AL)	Mayo Smith	St. Louis (NL)	Red Schoendienst	4-3	Mickey Lolich, p, Detroit
1969	New York (NL)	Gil Hodges	Baltimore (AL)	Earl Weaver	4-1	Donn Clendenon, 1b, New York
1970	Baltimore (AL)	Earl Weaver	Cincinnati (NL)	Sparky Anderson	4-1	Brooks Robinson, 3b, Baltimore
1971	Pittsburgh (NL)	Danny Murtaugh	Baltimore (AL)	Earl Weaver	4-3	Roberto Clemente, of, Pittsburgh
1972	Oakland (AL)	Dick Williams	Cincinnati (NL)	Sparky Anderson	4-3	Gene Tenace, c, Oakland
1973	Oakland (AL)	Dick Williams	New York (NL)	Yogi Berra	4-3	Reggie Jackson, of, Oakland
1974	Oakland (AL)	Alvin Dark	Los Angeles (NL)	Walter Alston	4-1	Rollie Fingers, p, Oakland
1975	Cincinnati (NL)	Sparky Anderson	Boston (AL)	Darrell Johnson	4-3	Pete Rose, 3b, Cincinnati
1976	Cincinnati (NL)	Sparky Anderson	New York (AL)	Billy Martin	4-0	Johnny Bench, c, Cincinnati
1977	New York (AL)	Billy Martin	Los Angeles (NL)	Tom Lasorda	4-2	Reggie Jackson, of, New York
1978	New York (AL)	Bob Lemon	Los Angeles (NL)	Tom Lasorda	4-2	Bucky Dent, ss, New York
1979	Pittsburgh (NL)	Chuck Tanner	Baltimore (AL)	Earl Weaver	4-3	Willie Stargell, 1b, Pittsburgh
1980	Philadelphia (NL)	Dallas Green	Kansas City (AL)	Jim Frey	4-2	Mike Schmidt, 3b, Philadelphia
1981	Los Angeles (NL)	Tom Lasorda	New York (AL)	Bob Lemon	4-2	Cey/Guerrero/Yeager, L.A.
1982	St. Louis (NL)	Whitey Herzog	Milwaukee (AL)	Harvey Kuenn	4-3	Darrell Porter, c, St. Louis
1983	Baltimore (AL)	Joe Altobelli	Philadelphia (NL)	Paul Owens	4-1	Rick Dempsey, c, Baltimore
1984	Detroit (AL)	Sparky Anderson	San Diego (NL)	Dick Williams	4-1	Alan Trammell, ss, Detroit
1985	Kansas City (AL)	Dick Howser	St. Louis (NL)	Whitey Herzog	4-3	Bret Saberhagen, p, Kansas City
1986	New York (NL)	Dave Johnson	Boston (AL)	John McNamara	4-3	Ray Knight, 3b, New York
1987	Minnesota (AL)	Tom Kelly	St. Louis (NL)	Whitey Herzog	4-3	Frank Viola, p, Minnesota
1988	Los Angeles (NL)	Tom Lasorda	Oakland (AL)	Tony La Russa	4-1	Orel Hershiser, p, Los Angeles
1989	Oakland (AL)	Tony La Russa	San Francisco (NL)	Roger Craig	4-0	Dave Stewart, p, Oakland
1990	Cincinnati (NL)	Lou Piniella	Oakland (AL)	Tony La Russa	4-0	Jose Rijo, p, Cincinnati
1991	Minnesota (AL)	Tom Kelly	Atlanta (NL)	Bobby Cox	4-3	Jack Morris, p, Minnesota
1992	Toronto (AL)	Cito Gaston	Atlanta (NL)	Bobby Cox	4-2	Pat Borders, c, Toronto
1993	Toronto (AL)	Cito Gaston	Philadelphia (NL)	Jim Fregosi	4-2	Paul Molitor, dh, Toronto
1994	NO SERIES					
1995	Atlanta (NL)	Bobby Cox	Cleveland (AL)	Mike Hargrove	4-2	Tom Glavine, p, Atlanta
1996	New York (AL)	Joe Torre	Atlanta (NL)	Bobby Cox	4-2	John Wetteland, p, New York
1997	Florida (NL)	Jim Leyland	Cleveland (AL)	Mike Hargrove	4-3	Livan Hernandez, p, Florida
1998	New York (AL)	Joe Torre	San Diego (NL)	Bruce Bochy	4-0	Scott Brosius, 3b, New York
1999	New York (AL)	Joe Torre	Atlanta (NL)	Bobby Cox	4-0	Mariano Rivera, p, New York
2000	New York (AL)	Joe Torre	New York (NL)	Bobby Valentine	4-1	Derek Jeter, ss, New York
2001	Arizona (NL)	Bob Brenly	New York (AL)	Joe Torre	4-3	Johnson, p/Schilling, p, Arizona
2002	Anaheim (AL)	Mike Scioscia	San Francisco (NL)	Dusty Baker	4-3	Troy Glaus, 3b, Anaheim
2003	Florida (NL)	Jack McKeon	New York (AL)	Joe Torre	4-2	Josh Beckett, p, Florida
2004	Boston (AL)	Terry Francona	St. Louis (NL)	Tony La Russa	4-0	Manny Ramirez, of, Boston

moments after the Red Sox wrapped up their victory, a fan was seen kneeling on the sidewalk, crying and yelling "Thank you, God," over and over.

"All of our fans have waited all their lives for this night and it's finally here," Red Sox owner John Henry said. "These guys did it for you, New England."

"We know people who are 90 years old who have said: 'Just one championship before I die,' " Red Sox chairman Tom Werner said.

"I'm so happy," Boston pitcher Curt Schilling said. "I'm happy for the fans in Boston. I'm happy for Johnny Pesky, for Bill Buckner, for (Bob) Stanley and (Calvin) Schiraldi and all the great Red Sox players who can be remembered for being the great players that they were, instead of part of some curse that never really existed."

Surprisingly Dominant

The World Series figured to be a slugfest as it matched the highest-scoring team in each league. Instead, it was the Red Sox' starting pitching—after a wild Tim Wakefield gave up five runs in 3⅔ innings in Game One, which Boston won 11-9—that made the difference.

Schilling, Pedro Martinez and Derek Lowe did not allow an earned run in 20 innings over the final three games; Schilling worked six innings on a bad ankle and Martinez and Lowe pitched seven innings each. They combined to allow 10 hits and four walks while striking out 14.

Conversely, St. Louis' big bats were silenced.

Third baseman and cleanup hitter Scott Rolen was 0-for-15 and center fielder Jim Edmonds, the No. 5 hitter, went 1-for-15. No. 3 hitter and first baseman Albert Pujols had five hits but did not drive in a run.

The Cardinals batted just .190 in the series. Their 24 hits were the fewest in a World Series since the Orioles had 23 in 1969 and their 12 runs were the fewest in a Fall Classic since the Braves managed only nine in 1999.

"I don't think they pitched us tough, we just hit some balls good and they made some good plays," Pujols said. "That's the way it goes. What can you do? It's over."

Still, the Cardinals were left shaking their heads over being swept, particularly after leading the major leagues with 105 wins in the regular season. Only one other team had ever been swept after winning more games in the regular season—the 111-win 1954 Indians, who lost to the New York Giants.

"It's amazing to think we couldn't even get one lead in this series," Game One starting pitcher Woody Williams said. "We were talking about that on the bench: Let's get one lead and see what happens. But it

Heroic effort by Red Sox righthander
Curt Schilling won Game Two, despite a damaged ankle

JIM ROGASH/WIREIMAGE

never happened."

Momentum From Yankees Series

St. Louis ran into a Boston team that was red hot after an improbable comeback to beat the archrival Yankees in the American League Championship Series.

The Red Sox became the first team in major league history to rally from a 3-0 deficit in the postseason to win a seven-game series when they rallied against the Yankees.

The Yankees had beaten out the Red Sox for the AL East title in the regular season, after beating them in the 2003 ALCS on Boone's home run in the 10th inning of Game Seven. However, the Red Sox got their revenge in the postseason and became the third straight wild card winner to capture a World Series title after the Angels in 2002 and Marlins in 2003.

The Red Sox then took four in a row from the Cardinals to become the first team to ever win eight straight games in the same postseason. The 1976 Reds, 1995 Braves and 1998 Yankees had won seven in a row.

"We had a great season and beat two tough teams to get here," Cardinals chairman Bill DeWitt Jr. said. "Whoever you play in the World Series is going to be a great team and we caught a great team that was hot.

"They won their last eight games. When you get on a roll like that it's hard to stop."

Ramirez Singled Out For MVP

Boston left fielder Manny Ramirez was named the series Most Valuable Player as he batted .412 (7-for-17) with one homer and four RBIs. His seven hits led the Red Sox.

POST-SEASON ALL-STARS							
Selected by Baseball America							
Pos. Player, Team	AVG	AB	R	H	HR	RBI	SB
C Jason Varitek, Red Sox	.245	53	10	13	3	11	0
1B Albert Pujols, Cardinals	.414	58	15	24	6	14	0
2B Mark Bellhorn, Red Sox	.191	47	8	9	3	8	0
3B Alex Rodriguez, Yankees	.320	50	11	16	3	8	2
SS Orlando Cabrera, Red Sox	.288	59	9	17	0	11	1
OF Carlos Beltran, Astros	.435	46	21	20	8	14	6
OF Hideki Matsui, Yankees	.412	51	12	21	3	13	0
OF Manny Ramirez, Red Sox	.350	60	8	21	2	11	0
DH David Ortiz, Red Sox	.400	55	13	22	5	19	0

	W-L	ERA	SV	IP	H	BB	SO
P Keith Foulke, Red Sox	1-0	0.64	3	14	7	8	19
P Brad Lidge, Astros	1-0	0.75	3	12	5	3	20
P Derek Lowe, Red Sox	3-0	1.89	0	19	11	3	10
P Curt Schilling, Red Sox	3-1	3.52	0	23	9	5	13

Ramirez was nearly traded to the Rangers in the previous offseason for shortstop Alex Rodriguez. However, the Major League Baseball Players Association nixed the deal because they disagreed with how Rodriguez planned to restructure the rest of his record 10-year, $252-million contract with the Red Sox.

Rodriguez wound up being traded to the hated Yankees instead.

"I went through a lot of drama during the winter but I kept my mind positive and I told my wife before the season started, 'Hey, baby, this is going to be my year. This is the year,' " Ramirez said. "And we did it. We're the champs.'

"I left everything in God's hands. I said, well, if they want me to go back to Boston, I'm going to go back to Boston. If they want me to be in Texas, I'm going to prepare myself to have a great year. God sent me back to Boston for a reason."

Ramirez was nearly the goat in Game One at Fenway Park as he made two errors during St. Louis' two-run eighth that tied the game at 9-9. However, second baseman Mark Bellhorn hit a two-run homer off the right-field foul pole—the Pesky Pole—against losing pitcher Julian Tavarez in the bottom of the eighth to give Boston an 11-9 win.

Ramirez had three hits in the wild game while DH David Ortiz homered and drove in four runs and Bellhorn scored three times. Keith Foulke pitched 1⅔ scoreless innings for the win.

Cardinals right fielder Larry Walker had a home run among his four hits.

Boston's pitching took over from there as Schilling, playing with a sutured right ankle, gave up one unearned run in six innings, to get credit for the win in Boston's 6-2 triumph in Game Two.

Schilling tore a tendon in his ankle in Game One of Boston's American League Division Series victory over the Angels.

After being rocked for six runs in three innings in Game

Pivotal play of World Series
Cardinals' Jeff Suppan was thrown out at third base in Game Three

One of the ALCS by the Yankees, Red Sox team doctor Bill Morgan stitched the tendon together before Game Six and Schilling beat New York that night. Morgan performed the same procedure before Game Two against the Cardinals.

Pujols was the only St. Louis hitter who could figure out Schilling as he had three hits in a losing cause.

The series shifted to St. Louis for Game Three but home-field advantage wasn't enough to give the Cardinals any momentum.

Martinez pitched seven shutout innings as Boston took a commanding 3-0 lead with a 4-1 victory. Walker helped the Cardinals avoid being shut out when he homered in the ninth off Foulke.

The Cardinals did have two chances to grab the lead early against Martinez, but frittered away the opportunities with bad baserunning. Martinez escaped a first-inning jam when Ramirez threw Walker out at the plate after Walker tagged up on a shallow fly ball.

Then, in the third inning, St. Louis had Suppan on third base and Edgar Renteria on second with no outs. Walker hit a grounder to second baseman Mark Bellhorn, who threw to first, conceding the run. But Suppan froze between third and home, changed direction three times and was thrown out going back to the bag by Ortiz, who was playing first base for the first time in the postseason.

"I screwed up," Suppan said. "I really just screwed up—I don't know how to describe it or explain it."

After that, Martinez cruised, retiring the next 14 St. Louis hitters before exiting for a pinch-hitter in the eighth.

The Red Sox wrapped up the sweep the next night with a 3-0 victory as Lowe allowed three hits in seven innings and combined with Bronson Arroyo, Alan Embree and Foulke on a four-hit shutout.

Boston leadoff hitter Johnny Damon set the tone when he hit losing pitcher Jason Marquis' fourth pitch of the game for a home run. Trot Nixon added a two-run double in the third inning and finished with three two-base hits.

"Any time you don a Red Sox uniform, you have to talk about the history of this team and not having a World Series championship since 1918," Nixon said. "Sooner or later, that hex had to stop. Everybody thought it was a curse, but to us it was just a five-letter word."

Thankful he stayed with the Red Sox
World Series MVP Manny Ramirez hit .412-1-4

GAME ONE: October 23
Boston 11, St. Louis 9

St. Louis	ab	r	h	bi	bb	so	Boston	ab	r	h	bi	bb	so
Renteria, ss	4	1	2	1	1	1	Damon, cf	6	1	2	1	0	0
Walker, rf	5	1	4	2	0	0	Cabrera, ss	4	2	1	1	1	0
Pujols, 1b	3	0	0	0	1	1	Ramirez, lf	5	0	3	2	0	0
Rolen, 3b	5	0	0	0	0	0	Ortiz, dh	3	1	2	4	2	0
Edmonds, cf	4	2	1	0	1	2	Millar, 1b	5	1	0	0	0	0
Sanders, dh	3	1	0	0	2	2	Mientkiewicz, 1b	0	0	0	0	0	0
Womack, 2b	1	1	0	0	1	0	Nixon, rf	3	0	0	0	1	0
Anderson, 2b	2	0	1	0	0	0	Kapler, ph-rf	1	0	0	0	0	1
Matheny, c	2	0	1	2	0	1	Mueller, 3b	3	1	1	1	2	0
Marquis, pr	0	1	0	0	0	0	Mirabelli, c	3	1	1	0	0	1
Molina, c	1	0	0	0	0	0	Varitek, ph-c	2	1	0	0	0	1
Taguchi, lf	3	1	1	1	0	1	Bellhorn, 2b	3	3	2	2	2	0
Cedeno, ph-lf	2	1	1	0	0	1	Reese, 2b	0	0	0	0	0	0
Totals	35	9	11	6	6	9	Totals	38	11	13	11	8	3

St. Louis			011 302 020— 9
Boston			403 000 22x—11

E—Ramirez 2 (2), Arroyo (1), Millar (1), Renteria (1). DP—Boston.
LOB—St. Louis 9, Boston 12. 2B—Anderson (1), Damon, (1), Millar (1),
Renteria (1), Walker 2 (2). HR—Bellhorn (1), Ortiz (1), Walker (1). SH—
Womack. SF—Matheny 2.

St. Louis	ip	h	r	er	bb	so	Boston	ip	h	r	er	bb	so
Williams	2⅓	8	7	7	3	1	Wakefield	3⅔	5	5	5	5	2
Haren	3⅔	2	0	0	3	1	Arroyo	2⅓	4	4	2	0	4
Calero	⅓	1	2	2	2	0	Timlin	1⅓	1	1	1	0	0
King	⅓	1	0	0	0	1	Embree	0	1	1	0	0	0
Eldred	⅓	0	0	0	0	1	Foulke W	1⅔	2	0	0	1	3
Tavarez L	1	1	2	1	0	0							

Embree pitched to one hitter in eighth.

IBB—Pujols (by Foulke). HBP—Cabrera (by Williams), Pujols (by
Wakefield).
Umpires: HP—Ed Montague; 1B—Dale Scott; 2B—Brian Gorman; 3B—
Chuck Meriwether; LF—Gerry Davis; RF—Charlie Reliford.
T—4:00. A—35,035.

GAME TWO: October 24
Boston 6, St. Louis 2

St. Louis	ab	r	h	bi	bb	so	Boston	ab	r	h	bi	bb	so
Renteria, ss	3	1	0	0	1	0	Damon, cf	5	1	1	0	0	1
Walker, rf	4	0	0	0	0	2	Cabrera, ss	4	0	1	2	1	0
Pujols, 1b	4	1	3	0	0	0	Ramirez, lf	4	1	1	0	1	1
Rolen, 3b	3	0	0	1	0	0	Kapler, lf	0	0	0	0	0	0
Edmonds, cf	4	0	0	0	0	2	Ortiz, dh	3	1	0	0	1	1

Dominant in Game Three
Red Sox righthander Pedro Martinez struck out six

Delivered game-winning homer
Red Sox second baseman Mark Bellhorn led the way in Game One

St. Louis							Boston						
Sanders, lf	3	0	0	0	1	1	Varitek, c	3	0	1	2	0	0
Womack, 2b	4	0	1	0	0	1	Millar, 1b	1	1	0	0	2	1
Matheny, c	4	0	1	0	0	1	Mientkiewicz, pr-1b	0	0	0	0	0	0
Anderson, dh	2	0	0	0	0	1	Nixon, rf	4	1	1	0	0	1
Taguchi, dh	1	0	0	0	0	0	Mueller, 3b	3	1	2	0	1	0
							Bellhorn, 2b	3	0	1	2	0	0
							Reese, 2b	1	0	0	0	0	0
Totals	32	2	5	1	2	9	Totals	31	6	8	6	6	5

St. Louis			000 100 010—2
Boston			200 202 00x—6

E—Mueller 3 (3). DP—St. Louis 1, Boston 2. LOB—St. Louis 6, Boston
9. 2B—Bellhorn (1), Mueller (1), Pujols 2 (2). 3B—Varitek (1). SF—Rolen.
PB—Mirabelli.

St. Louis	ip	h	r	er	bb	so	Boston	ip	h	r	er	bb	so
Morris L	4⅓	4	4	4	4	3	Schilling W	6	4	1	0	1	4
Eldred	1⅓	4	2	2	0	1	Embree	1	0	0	0	0	3
King	⅓	0	0	0	1	0	Timlin	⅔	1	1	1	1	0
Marquis	1	0	0	0	2	0	Foulke	1⅓	0	0	0	0	2
Reyes	1	0	0	0	0	0							

HBP—Millar (by Morris), Varitek (by Eldred).
Umpires: HP—Dale Scott; 1B—Brian Gorman; 2B—Chuck Meriwether;
3B—Gerry Davis; LF—Charlie Reliford; RF—Ed Montague.
T—3:20. A—35,001.

GAME THREE: October 26
Boston 4, St. Louis 1

Boston	ab	r	h	bi	bb	so	St. Louis	ab	r	h	bi	bb	so
Damon, cf	5	1	1	0	0	0	Renteria, ss	4	0	1	0	0	1
Cabrera, ss	4	1	2	0	1	0	Walker, rf	3	1	1	1	1	0
Ramirez, lf	4	1	2	2	1	1	Pujols, 1b	4	0	1	0	0	1
Ortiz, 1b	4	0	1	0	0	0	Rolen, 3b	3	0	0	0	1	1
Mientkiewicz, 1b	0	0	0	0	0	0	Edmonds, cf	3	0	0	0	0	1
Varitek, c	4	0	0	1	1	1	Sanders, lf	3	0	0	0	0	2
Mueller, 3b	4	1	2	1	0	0	Womack, 2b	3	0	0	0	0	1
Nixon, rf	3	0	1	1	0	0	Matheny, c	2	0	0	0	0	1
Kapler, ph-rf	1	0	0	0	0	0	Cedeno, ph	1	0	0	0	0	0
Bellhorn, 2b	3	0	0	0	0	1	Tavarez, p	0	0	0	0	0	0
Reese, 2b	0	0	0	0	0	0	Suppan, p	1	0	1	0	0	0
Martinez, p	2	0	0	0	1	2	Reyes, p	0	0	0	0	0	0
Millar, ph	1	0	0	0	0	0	Anderson, ph	1	0	0	0	0	0
Timlin, p	0	0	0	0	0	0	Calero, p	0	0	0	0	0	0
Foulke, p	0	0	0	0	0	0	King, p	0	0	0	0	0	0
							Mabry, ph	1	0	0	0	0	0
							Molina, c	0	0	0	0	0	0
Totals	34	4	9	4	4	5	Totals	29	1	4	1	2	8

Boston			100 120 000—4
St. Louis			000 000 001—1

DP—Boston 2, St. Louis 2. LOB—Boston 8, St. Louis 3. 2B—Cabrera
(1), Damon (2), Meuller (2), Renteria (2). HR—Ramirez (1), Walker (2).

Boston	ip	h	r	er	bb	so		St. Louis	ip	h	r	er	bb	so
Martinez W	7	3	0	0	2	6		Suppan L	4⅔	8	4	4	1	4
Timlin	1	0	0	0	0	0		Reyes	⅓	0	0	0	0	0
Foulke	1	1	1	1	0	2		Calero	1	1	0	0	2	0
								King	2	0	0	0	1	0
								Tavarez	1	0	0	0	0	1

HBP—Bellhorn (by Suppan).
Umpires: HP—Brian Gorman; **1B**—Chuck Meriwether; **2B**—Gerry Davis; **3B**—Charlie Reliford; **LF**—Ed Montague; **RF**—Dale Scott.
T—2:58. **A**—52,015.

GAME FOUR: October 27
Boston 3, St. Louis 0

Boston	ab	r	h	bi	bb	so		St. Louis	ab	r	h	bi	bb	so
Damon, cf	5	1	2	1	0	0		Womack, 2b	3	0	1	0	0	0
Cabrera, ss	5	0	0	0	0	1		Luna, ph-2b	1	0	0	0	0	1
Ramirez, lf	4	0	1	0	1	1		Walker, rf	2	0	0	0	1	0
Ortiz, 1b	3	1	1	0	1	0		Pujols, 1b	4	0	1	0	0	1
Mientkiewicz, 1b	1	0	0	0	0	0		Rolen, 3b	4	0	0	0	0	0
Varitek, c	5	1	1	0	0	2		Edmonds, cf	4	0	0	0	0	1
Mueller, 3b	4	0	1	0	1	0		Renteria, ss	4	0	2	0	0	0
Nixon, rf	4	0	3	2	0	0		Mabry, lf	3	0	0	0	0	2
Kapler, pr-rf	0	0	0	0	0	0		Isringhausen, p	0	0	0	0	0	0
Bellhorn, 2b	1	0	0	0	3	1		Molina, c	2	0	0	0	0	1
Reese, pr-2b	0	0	0	0	0	0		Cedeno, ph	1	0	0	0	0	0
Lowe, p	2	0	0	0	0	1		Matheny, c	0	0	0	0	0	0
Millar, ph	1	0	0	0	0	1		Marquis, p	1	0	0	0	0	0
Arroyo, p	0	0	0	0	0	0		Anderson, ph	1	0	0	0	0	0
Embree, p	0	0	0	0	0	0		Haren, p	0	0	0	0	0	0
Foulke, p	0	0	0	0	0	0		Sanders, lf	0	0	0	0	1	0
Totals	35	3	9	3	6	7		**Totals**	30	0	4	0	2	6

Boston	102 000 000	—3
St. Louis	000 000 000	—0

LOB—Boston 12, St. Louis 6. **2B**—Nixon 3 (3), Ortiz (1), Renteria (3). **3B**—Damon (1). **HR**—Damon (1). **SB**—Sanders (1). **SH**—Lowe, Walker.

Boston	ip	h	r	er	bb	so		St. Louis	ip	h	r	er	bb	so
Lowe W	7	3	0	0	1	4		Marquis L	6	6	3	3	5	4
Arroyo	⅓	0	0	0	0	0		Haren	1	2	0	0	0	1
Embree	⅔	0	0	0	0	1		Isringhausen	2	1	0	0	1	2
Foulke S	1	0	0	0	1	0								

WP—Lowe. **IBB**—Bellhorn (by Marquis).
Umpires: HP—Chuck Meriwether; **1B**—Gerry Davis; **2B**—Charlie Reliford; **3B**—Ed Montague; **LF**—Dale Scott; **RF**—Brian Gorman.
T—3:14. **A**—52,037.

COMPOSITE BOX

BOSTON

Player, Pos.	AVG	G	AB	R	H	2B	3B	HR	RBI	BB	SO	SB
Bill Mueller, 3b	.429	4	14	3	6	2	0	0	2	4	0	0
Manny Ramirez, lf	.412	4	17	2	7	0	0	1	4	3	3	0
Trot Nixon, rf	.357	4	14	1	5	3	0	0	3	1	1	0
Doug Mirabelli, c	.333	1	3	1	1	0	0	0	0	0	1	0
David Ortiz, dh-1b	.308	4	13	3	4	1	0	1	4	4	1	0
Mark Bellhorn, 2b	.300	4	10	3	3	1	0	1	4	5	2	0
Johnny Damon, cf	.286	4	21	4	6	2	1	1	2	0	1	0
Orlando Cabrera, ss	.235	4	17	3	4	1	0	0	3	3	1	0
Jason Varitek, c	.154	4	13	2	2	0	1	0	2	1	4	0
Kevin Millar, 1b-ph	.125	4	8	2	1	0	0	0	2	2	2	0
Gabe Kapler, ph-rf	.000	4	2	0	0	0	0	0	0	0	1	0
Pedro Martinez, p	.000	1	2	0	0	0	0	0	0	0	1	0
Derek Lowe, p	.000	1	2	0	0	0	0	0	0	0	1	0
Doug Mientkiewicz, 1b	.000	4	1	0	0	0	0	0	0	0	0	0
Pokey Reese, 2b	.000	4	1	0	0	0	0	0	0	0	0	0
Totals	.283	4	138	24	39	11	2	4	24	24	20	0

Pitcher	W	L	ERA	G	GS	SV	IP	H	R	ER	BB	SO
Pedro Martinez	1	0	0.00	1	1	0	7	3	0	0	2	6
Derek Lowe	1	0	0.00	1	1	0	7	3	0	0	1	4
Curt Schilling	1	0	0.00	1	1	0	6	4	1	1	0	4
Alan Embree	0	0	1.80	3	0	0	2	1	1	0	0	4
Keith Foulke	1	0	1.80	4	0	1	5	4	1	1	1	8
Mike Timlin	0	0	6.00	3	0	0	3	2	2	2	1	0
Bronson Arroyo	0	0	6.75	2	0	0	3	4	2	2	1	4
Tim Wakefield	0	0	12.27	1	1	0	4	3	5	5	5	2
Totals	4	0	2.50	4	4	1	36	24	12	10	12	32

Won deciding Game Four
Derek Lowe pitched seven scoreless innings

LARRY GOREN

ST. LOUIS

Player, Pos.	AVG	G	AB	R	H	2B	3B	HR	RBI	BB	SO	SB
Jeff Suppan, p	1.000	1	1	0	1	0	0	0	0	0	0	0
Larry Walker, rf	.357	4	14	2	5	2	0	2	3	2	2	0
Albert Pujols, 1b	.333	4	15	1	5	2	0	0	0	1	3	0
Edgar Renteria, ss	.333	4	15	2	5	3	0	0	1	2	2	0
Mike Matheny, c	.250	4	8	0	2	0	0	0	2	0	3	0
Roger Cedeno, ph-lf	.250	3	4	1	1	0	0	0	0	0	1	0
So Taguchi, lf	.250	2	4	1	1	0	0	0	1	0	2	0
Tony Womack, 2b	.182	4	11	1	2	0	0	0	0	1	2	0
Marlon Anderson, ph-2b	.167	4	6	0	1	1	0	0	0	0	1	0
Jim Edmonds, cf	.067	4	15	2	1	0	0	0	0	1	6	0
Scott Rolen, 3b	.000	4	15	0	0	0	0	0	1	1	1	0
Reggie Sanders, dh-lf	.000	4	9	1	0	0	0	0	0	4	5	1
John Mabry, ph-lf	.000	2	4	0	0	0	0	0	0	0	0	0
Yadier Molina, c	.000	3	3	0	0	0	0	0	0	0	1	0
Jason Marquis, p-rp	.000	3	1	1	0	0	0	0	0	0	0	0
Hector Luna, ph	.000	1	1	0	0	0	0	0	0	0	1	0
Totals	.190	4	126	12	24	8	0	2	8	12	32	1

Pitcher	W	L	ERA	G	GS	SV	IP	H	R	ER	BB	SO
Dan Haren	0	0	0.00	2	0	0	5	4	0	0	3	2
Ray King	0	0	0.00	3	0	0	1	1	0	0	1	1
Jason Isringhausen	0	0	0.00	1	0	0	2	1	0	0	1	2
Al Reyes	0	0	0.00	1	0	0	1	0	0	0	0	0
Jason Marquis	0	1	3.86	2	1	0	7	6	3	3	7	4
Julian Tavarez	0	1	4.50	2	0	0	2	1	2	1	0	1
Jeff Suppan	0	1	7.71	1	1	0	5	8	4	4	1	4
Matt Morris	0	1	8.31	1	1	0	4	4	4	4	4	3
Cal Eldred	0	0	10.80	2	0	0	2	4	2	2	0	2
Kiko Calero	0	0	13.50	2	0	0	1	2	2	2	4	0
Woody Williams	0	0	27.00	1	1	0	2	8	7	7	3	1
Totals	0	4	6.09	4	4	0	34	39	24	23	24	20

SCORE BY INNING

Boston	805 322 220—24
St. Louis	011 402 031—12

E—Mueller 3, Ramirez 2, Arroyo, Bellhorn, Millar, Renteria. **DP**—Boston 5, St. Louis 3. **LOB**—Boston 41, St. Louis 24. **SB**—Sanders. **SH**—Womack, Walker. **SF**—Matheny 2, Rolen. **IBB**—Bellhorn (by Marquis), Pujols (by Foulke). **HBP**—Bellhorn (by Suppan), Cabrera (by Williams), Millar (by Morris), Pujols (by Wakefield), Varitek (by Eldred). **WP**—Lowe. **PB**—Mirabelli.

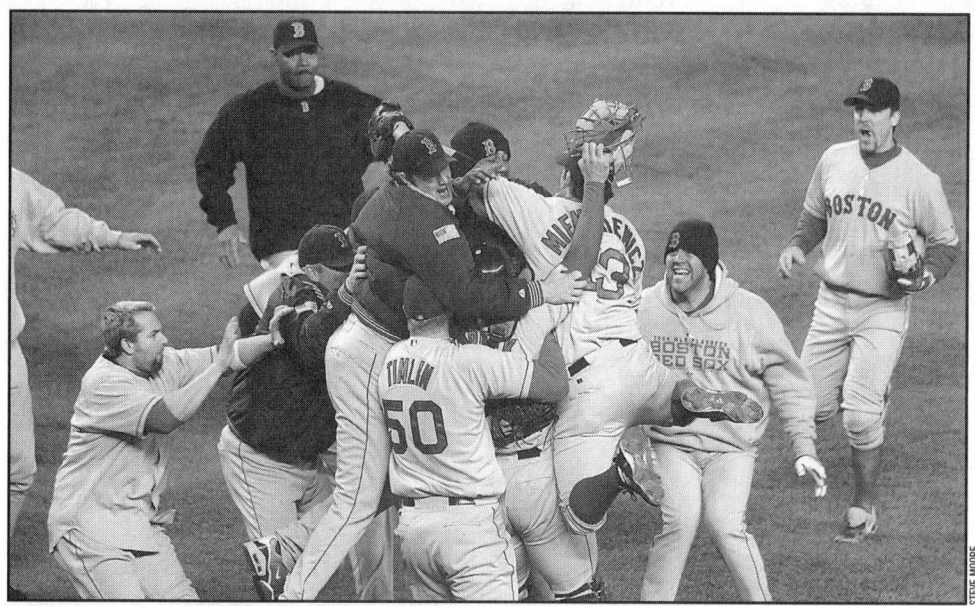

STEVE MOORE

Red Sox players celebrate their ALCS victory over the Yankees, the greatest comeback in baseball history
After being down 3-0, Boston rallied to beat New York four games to three

BY AARON FITT

It was, quite simply, the greatest comeback in baseball history. Maybe in sports history. But it was so much more than that.

It was Yankees-Red Sox in the American League Championship Series—again. It was baseball's fiercest rivals going head to head for the American League pennant again, only a year after their epic seven-game ALCS ended with Aaron Boone's 11th-inning home run—which is really when the buildup for the 2004 rematch began.

The feud escalated during the offseason, as owners traded barbs and the arms race continued. The Red Sox failed to land 2003 AL MVP Alex Rodriguez, so the Yankees dealt for him after Boone injured his knee, knocking him out for the year. Rodriguez moved from shortstop to third base in deference to Derek Jeter.

Boston added Curt Schilling and Keith Foulke; New York added Javier Vazquez, Kevin Brown and Gary Sheffield. By the time the teams met for the first time in spring training, the excitement was already high as fans camped out for tickets and vendors sold commemorative pins—for exhibition games.

LARRY GOREN

Curt Schilling

The Red Sox won six of the first seven regular-season meetings between the teams, including a three-game sweep at Yankee Stadium. Boston finished April 15-6 and led New York by 4½ games, but by July 24 the Red Sox found themselves 9½ games behind the Yankees with a 52-44 record. Along the way, they lost a classic 13-inning affair at Yankee Stadium on July 1, which saw Jeter crash into the stands after a foul ball, bloodying his face, while Boston shortstop Nomar Garciaparra sat alone on the bench, appearing uninterested.

But a few things happened to wake Boston up. First was another classic game against New York on July 24 at Fenway Park. The game featured a benches-clearing melee that started when Rodriguez and Sox catcher Jason Varitek came to blows, and in the bottom of the ninth Boston's Bill Mueller hit a walkoff home run against Yankee closer Mariano Rivera to complete the 11-10 Red Sox comeback.

The Sox were still scuffling when the July 31 trade deadline rolled around. Boston general manager Theo Epstein decided something needed to be done about his team's dismal defense, so he traded Garciaparra in a four-way deal that brought back Gold Glove infielders Orlando Cabrera and Doug Mientkiewicz. It took fans some time to get over the trade of the ever-popular Garciaparra, who ended up with the Cubs.

"I thought there was a flaw on the club that we couldn't allow to become a fatal flaw, that the defense on this team is not championship caliber," Epstein said. "In my mind, we were not going to win a World Series with our defense the way it was."

Shortly after that the Red Sox went on a remarkable run, winning 26 of their next 31 games, and cut their division deficit from 10½ to two games. New York never gave back the division lead, however. The two teams split their final six meetings in September, and the Yankees held on to win the division by three games.

NO-DIVISION FORMAT

	PENNANT	PCT	GA		PENNANT	PCT	GA		PENNANT	PCT	GA
1901	Chicago	.610	4	1924	Washington	.597	2	1947	New York	.630	12
1902	Philadelphia	.610	5	1925	Washington	.636	8½	1948	Cleveland	.626	1
1903	Boston	.659	14½	1926	New York	.591	3	1949	New York	.630	1
1904	Boston	.617	1½	1927	New York	.714	19	1950	New York	.636	3
1905	Philadelphia	.622	2	1928	New York	.656	2½	1951	New York	.636	5
1906	Chicago	.616	3	1929	Philadelphia	.693	18	1952	New York	.617	2
1907	Detroit	.613	1½	1930	Philadelphia	.662	8	1953	New York	.656	8½
1908	Detroit	.588	½	1931	Philadelphia	.704	13½	1954	Cleveland	.721	8
1909	Detroit	.645	3½	1932	New York	.695	13	1955	New York	.623	3
1910	Philadelphia	.680	14½	1933	Washington	.651	7	1956	New York	.630	9
1911	Philadelphia	.669	13½	1934	Detroit	.656	7	1957	New York	.636	8
1912	Boston	.691	14	1935	Detroit	.616	3	1958	New York	.597	10
1913	Philadelphia	.627	6½	1936	New York	.667	19½	1959	Chicago	.610	5
1914	Philadelphia	.651	8½	1937	New York	.662	13	1960	New York	.630	8
1915	Boston	.669	2½	1938	New York	.651	9½	1961	New York	.673	8
1916	Boston	.591	2	1939	New York	.702	17	1962	New York	.593	5
1917	Chicago	.649	9	1940	Detroit	.584	1	1963	New York	.646	10½
1918	Boston	.595	2½	1941	New York	.656	17	1964	New York	.611	1
1919	Chicago	.629	3½	1942	New York	.669	9	1965	Minnesota	.630	7
1920	Cleveland	.636	2	1943	New York	.636	13½	1966	Baltimore	.606	9
1921	New York	.641	4½	1944	St. Louis	.578	1	1967	Boston	.568	1
1922	New York	.610	1	1945	Detroit	.575	1½	1968	Detroit	.636	12
1923	New York	.645	16	1946	Boston	.675	12				

TWO-DIVISION FORMAT

	EAST	PCT	GA	WEST	PCT	GA	PENNANT		MVP
1969	Baltimore	.673	19	Minnesota	.599	9	Baltimore	3-0	Harmon Killebrew, 1b-3b, Minnesota
1970	Baltimore	.667	15	Minnesota	.605	9	Baltimore	3-0	Boog Powell, 1b, Baltimore
1971	Baltimore	.639	12	Oakland	.627	16	Baltimore	3-0	Vida Blue, lhp, Oakland
1972	Detroit	.551	½	Oakland	.600	5½	Oakland	3-2	Dick Allen, 1b, Chicago
1973	Baltimore	.599	8	Oakland	.580	6	Oakland	3-2	Reggie Jackson, of, Oakland
1974	Baltimore	.562	2	Oakland	.556	5	Oakland	3-1	Jeff Burroughs, of, Texas
1975	Boston	.594	4½	Oakland	.605	7	Boston	3-0	Fred Lynn, of, Boston
1976	New York	.610	10½	Kansas City	.556	2½	New York	3-2	Thurman Munson, c, New York
1977	New York	.617	2½	Kansas City	.630	8	New York	3-2	Rod Carew, 1b, Minnesota
1978	New York	.613	1	Kansas City	.568	5	New York	3-1	Jim Rice, of, Boston
1979	Baltimore	.642	8	California	.543	3	Baltimore	3-1	Don Baylor, dh, California
1980	New York	.636	3	Kansas City	.599	14	Kansas City	3-0	George Brett, 3b, Kansas City
1981	New York*	.607	2	Oakland**	.587	—	New York	3-0	Rollie Fingers, rhp, Milwaukee
	Milwaukee	.585	1½	Kansas City	.566	1			
1982	Milwaukee	.586	1	California	.574	3	Milwaukee	3-2	Robin Yount, ss, Milwaukee
1983	Baltimore	.605	6	Chicago	.611	20	Baltimore	3-1	Cal Ripken, ss, Baltimore
1984	Detroit	.642	15	Kansas City	.519	3	Detroit	3-0	Willie Hernandez, lhp, Detroit
1985	Toronto	.615	2	Kansas City	.562	1	Kansas City	4-3	Don Mattingly, 1b, New York
1986	Boston	.590	5½	California	.568	5	Boston	4-3	Roger Clemens, rhp, Boston
1987	Detroit	.605	2	Minnesota	.525	2	Minnesota	4-1	George Bell, of, Toronto
1988	Boston	.549	1	Oakland	.642	13	Oakland	4-0	Jose Canseco, of, Oakland
1989	Toronto	.549	2	Oakland	.611	7	Oakland	4-1	Robin Yount, of, Milwaukee
1990	Boston	.543	2	Oakland	.636	9	Oakland	4-0	Rickey Henderson, of, Oakland
1991	Toronto	.562	7	Minnesota	.586	8	Minnesota	4-1	Cal Ripken, ss, Baltimore
1992	Toronto	.593	4	Oakland	.593	6	Toronto	4-2	Dennis Eckersley, rhp, Oakland
1993	Toronto	.586	7	Chicago	.580	8	Toronto	4-2	Frank Thomas, 1b, Chicago

* Won first half; defeated Milwaukee 3-2 in best-of-5 playoff.   ** Won first half, defeated Kansas City 3-0 in best-of-5 playoff.

THREE-DIVISION FORMAT/WILD CARD

	EAST	PCT	GA	CENTRAL	PCT	GA	WEST	PCT	GA	WILD CARD	PCT
1994	New York	.619	6½	Chicago	.593	1	Texas	.456	1	None	
	PENNANT: None (season incomplete)						MVP: Frank Thomas, 1b, Chicago				
1995	Boston	.597	7	Cleveland	.694	30	Seattle	.545	1	New York (East)	.549
	PENNANT: Cleveland def. Seattle 4-2						MVP: Mo Vaughn, 1b, Boston				
1996	New York	.568	4	Cleveland	.615	14½	Texas	.556	4	Baltimore (East)	.543
	PENNANT: New York def. Baltimore 4-1						MVP: Juan Gonzalez, of, Texas				
1997	Baltimore	.605	2	Cleveland	.534	6	Seattle	.556	6	New York (East)	.593
	PENNANT: Cleveland def. Baltimore 4-2						MVP: Ken Griffey, of, Seattle				
1998	New York	.704	22	Cleveland	.549	9	Texas	.543	3	Boston (East)	.568
	PENNANT: New York def. Cleveland 4-2						MVP: Juan Gonzalez, of, Texas				
1999	New York	.605	4	Cleveland	.599	21½	Texas	.586	8	Boston (East)	.580
	PENNANT: New York def. Boston 4-1						MVP: Ivan Rodriguez, c, Texas				
2000	New York	.540	2½	Chicago	.586	5	Oakland	.565	½	Seattle (West)	.562
	PENNANT: New York def. Seattle 4-2						MVP: Jason Giambi, 1b, Oakland				
2001	New York	.594	13½	Cleveland	.562	6	Seattle	.716	14	Oakland (West)	.630
	PENNANT: New York def. Seattle 4-1						MVP: Ichiro Suzuki, of, Seattle				
2002	New York	.640	10½	Minnesota	.584	13½	Oakland	.636	4	Anaheim (West)	.611
	PENNANT: Anaheim def. Minnesota 4-1						MVP: Miguel Tejada, ss, Oakland				
2003	New York	.623	6	Minnesota	.556	4	Oakland	.593	3	Boston (East)	.586
	PENNANT: New York def. Boston 4-3						MVP: Alex Rodriguez, ss, Texas				
2004	New York	.623		Minnesota	.568	9	Anaheim	.568	1	Boston (East)	.605
	PENNANT: Boston def. New York 4-3										

Page	EAST	W	L	Pct.	GB	Manager	General Mangaer(s)	Attend.	Avg.	Last Penn.
187	New York Yankees	101	61	.623	—	Joe Torre	Brian Cashman	3,775,292	47,788	2003
86	*Boston Red Sox	98	64	.605	3	Terry Francona	Theo Epstein	2,837,304	35,028	1986
78	Baltimore Orioles	78	84	.481	23	Lee Mazzilli	Jim Beattie/Mike Flanagan	2,744,013	34,300	1993
254	Tampa Bay Devil Rays	70	91	.435	30½	Lou Piniella	Chuck LaMar	1,275,011	16,139	None
268	Toronto Blue Jays	67	94	.416	33½	C. Tosca/J. Gibbons	J.P. Ricciardi	1,900,041	23,457	1983
Page	CENTRAL	W	L	Pct.	GB	Manager	General Manager	Attend.	Avg.	Last Penn.
172	Minnesota Twins	92	70	.568	—	Ron Gardenhire	Terry Ryan	1,879,222	23,490	1991
94	Chicago White Sox	83	79	.512	9	Ozzie Guillen	Ken Williams	1,930,537	24,437	1959
115	Cleveland Indians	80	82	.494	12	Eric Wedge	Mark Shapiro	1,814,401	22,400	1997
130	Detroit Tigers	72	90	.444	20	Alan Trammell	Dave Dombrowski	1,917,004	23,962	1984
151	Kansas City Royals	58	104	.358	34	Tony Pena	Allard Baird	1,661,478	21,031	1985
Page	WEST	W	L	Pct.	GB	Manager	General Manager	Attend.	Avg.	Last Penn.
57	Anaheim Angels	92	70	.568	—	Mike Scioscia	Bill Stoneman	3,375,677	41,675	2002
203	Oakland Athletics	91	71	.562	1	Ken Macha	Billy Beane	2,201,516	27,179	1990
261	Texas Rangers	89	73	.549	3	Buck Showalter	John Hart	2,513,685	31,818	None
247	Seattle Mariners	63	99	.389	29	Bob Melvin	Bill Bavasi	2,940,731	36,305	None

*Won wild-card playoff berth

NOTE: Team's individual batting, pitching and fielding statistics can be found on page indicated in lefthand column

Sheffield played through pain to emerge as New York's offensive leader, making a run at the MVP award with a .290-36-121 season. Rodriguez didn't quite live up to expectations, but he still put up a strong .286-35-106 season. Offense wasn't the problem, though. Pitching was the main concern. Mainstays Roger Clemens and Andy Pettitte left for Houston before the season, and newcomers Vazquez and Brown had proven unreliable in big spots.

In the American League Division Series, Boston swept Anaheim in three games, though the clincher was no cinch. Boston led 6-0 at one point, but a seventh-inning Vladimir Guerrero grand slam tied the score, setting the stage for David Ortiz' home run in the 10th inning.

New York escaped a hard-fought series with Minnesota, which won the series-opener in the Bronx and blew late leads in the second and fourth games. With the Yankees up two games to one, a Ruben Sierra homer tied Game Four in the eighth inning, and Rodriguez scored the game-winner in the 11th, sending the Yankees home to take on Boston.

Keyed the Red Sox' improbable comeback
Boston DH David Ortiz

LARRY GOREN

Rematch, At Long Last

After all those months of buildup, many expected the ALCS showdown to be a letdown. Then the Yankees jumped out to an 8-0 lead against Schilling in Game One, and the letdown was on. Boston made the first game interesting, getting back to within 8-7 before falling 10-7, but after the game doctors said Schilling had a dislocated tendon in his ankle and likely would not pitch again in the postseason.

New York took Game Two against Pedro Martinez, 3-1, and blew out the Sox, 19-8, in Game Three at Fenway Park. The 19 runs were an ALCS record, and the end seemed near for Boston. In the history of baseball, no team had ever come back from a 3-0 deficit to win a postseason series. Of the 25 previous teams that had fallen behind 3-0, 20 were swept and just two had even forced six games.

"It's as big a hole as you can dig yourself, but obviously you're going to keep fighting them and try to dig your way out of it," said Red Sox righthander Bronson Arroyo, who started Game Three and got shelled. "What else are you going to do?"

In the fourth game, New York took a 4-3 lead into the ninth inning and sent Mariano Rivera, perhaps the best postseason closer of all time, to the mound against the bottom half of Boston's lineup. Rivera had never blown a save in ALCS play and had blown just three in 35 postseason chances in his career.

But Kevin Millar worked a walk, and pinch-runner Dave Roberts stole second base on a close play. Mueller, who had beaten Rivera in that season-turning win in late July, knocked a single to center field to tie the game. Each team's bullpen was depleted from the slugfest in Game Three, but they held each other scoreless until the 12th inning, when Ortiz hit a two-run homer against Paul Quantrill. Ortiz became the first player ever to hit two walkoff homers in the same postseason—and there were more heroics to come.

The Yankees had a chance to close it out again in Game Five. They led 4-2 entering Boston's half of the

MAJOR LEAGUES

Year	Batting Average	Home Runs	RBIs
1926	Heinie Manush, Detroit .377	Babe Ruth, New York 47	Babe Ruth, New York 145
1927	Harry Heilmann, Detroit .398	Babe Ruth, New York 60	Lou Gehrig, New York 175
1928	Goose Goslin, Washington .379	Babe Ruth, New York 54	Two tied at 142
1929	Lew Fonseca, Cleveland .369	Babe Ruth, New York 46	Al Simmons, Philadelphia 157
1930	Al Simmons, Philadelphia .381	Babe Ruth, New York 49	Lou Gehrig, New York 174
1931	Al Simmons, Philadelphia .390	Two tied at 46	Lou Gehrig, New York 184
1932	Dale Alexander, Detroit-Boston .367	Jimmie Foxx, Philadelphia 58	Jimmie Foxx, Philadelphia 169
1933	Jimmie Foxx, Philadelphia .356	Jimmie Foxx, Philadelphia 48	Jimmie Foxx, Philadelphia 163
1934	Lou Gehrig, New York .363	Lou Gehrig, New York 49	Lou Gehrig, New York 165
1935	Buddy Myer, Washington .349	Two tied at 36	Hank Greenberg, Detroit 170
1936	Luke Appling, Chicago .388	Lou Gehrig, New York 49	Hal Trosky, Cleveland 162
1937	Charlie Gehringer, Detroit .371	Joe DiMaggio, New York 46	Hank Greenberg, Detroit 183
1938	Jimmie Foxx, Boston .349	Hank Greenberg, Detroit 58	Jimmie Foxx, Boston 175
1939	Joe DiMaggio, New York .381	Jimmie Foxx, Boston 35	Ted Williams, Boston 145
1940	Joe DiMaggio, New York .352	Hank Greenberg, Detroit 41	Hank Greenberg, Detroit 150
1941	Ted Williams, Boston .406	Ted Williams, Boston 37	Joe DiMaggio, New York 125
1942	Ted Williams, Boston .356	Ted Williams, Boston 36	Ted Williams, Boston 137
1943	Luke Appling, Chicago .328	Rudy York, Detroit 34	Rudy York, Detroit 118
1944	Lou Boudreau, Cleveland .327	Nick Etten, New York 22	Vern Stephens, St. Louis 109
1945	Snuffy Stirnweiss, New York .309	Vern Stephens, St. Louis 24	Nick Etten, New York 111
1946	Mickey Vernon, Wash. .352	Hank Greenberg, Detroit 44	Hank Greenberg, Detroit 127
1947	Ted Williams, Boston .343	Ted Williams, Boston 32	Ted Williams, Boston 114
1948	Ted Williams, Boston .369	Joe DiMaggio, New York 39	Joe DiMaggio, New York 155
1949	George Kell, Detroit .343	Ted Williams, Boston 43	Two tied at 159
1950	Billy Goodman, Boston .354	Al Rosen, Cleveland 37	Two tied at 144
1951	Ferris Fain, Philadelphia .344	Gus Zernial, Chicago-Phil. 33	Gus Zernial, Chicago-Phil. 129
1952	Ferris Fain, Philadelphia .327	Larry Doby, Cleveland 32	Al Rosen, Cleveland 105
1953	Mickey Vernon, Washington .337	Al Rosen, Cleveland 43	Al Rosen, Cleveland 145
1954	Bobby Avila, Cleveland .341	Larry Doby, Cleveland 32	Larry Doby, Cleveland 126
1955	Al Kaline, Detroit .340	Mickey Mantle, New York 37	Two tied at 116
1956	Mickey Mantle, New York .353	Mickey Mantle, New York 52	Mickey Mantle, New York 130
1957	Ted Williams, Boston .388	Roy Sievers, Washington 42	Roy Sievers, Washington 114
1958	Ted Williams, Boston .328	Mickey Mantle, New York 42	Jackie Jensen, Boston 122
1959	Harvey Kuenn, Detroit .353	Two tied at 42	Jackie Jensen, Boston 112
1960	Pete Runnels, Boston .320	Mickey Mantle, New York 40	Roger Maris, New York 112
1961	Norm Cash, Detroit .361	Roger Maris, New York 61	Roger Maris, New York 142
1962	Pete Runnels, Boston .326	Harmon Killebrew, Minnesota 48	Harmon Killebrew, Minnesota 126
1963	Carl Yastrzemski, Boston .321	Harmon Killebrew, Minnesota 45	Dick Stuart, Boston 118
1964	Tony Oliva, Minnesota .323	Harmon Killebrew, Minnesota 49	Brooks Robinson, Baltimore 118
1965	Tony Oliva, Minnesota .321	Tony Conigliaro, Boston 32	Rocky Colavito, Cleveland 108
1966	Frank Robinson, Baltimore .316	Frank Robinson, Baltimore 49	Frank Robinson, Baltimore 122
1967	Carl Yastrzemski, Boston .326	Two tied at 44	Carl Yastrzemski, Boston 121
1968	Carl Yastrzemski, Boston .301	Frank Howard, Washington 44	Ken Harrelson, Boston 109
1969	Rod Carew, Minnesota .332	Harmon Killebrew, Minnesota 49	Harmon Killebrew, Minnesota 140
1970	Alex Johnson, California .329	Frank Howard, Washington 44	Frank Howard, Washington 126
1971	Tony Oliva, Minnesota .337	Bill Melton, Chicago 33	Harmon Killebrew, Minnesota 119
1972	Rod Carew, Minnesota .318	Dick Allen, Chicago 37	Dick Allen, Chicago 113
1973	Rod Carew, Minnesota .350	Reggie Jackson, Oakland 32	Reggie Jackson, Oakland 117
1974	Rod Carew, Minnesota .364	Dick Allen, Chicago 32	Jeff Burroughs, Texas 118
1975	Rod Carew, Minnesota .359	Two tied at 36	George Scott, Milwaukee 109
1976	George Brett, Kansas City .333	Graig Nettles, New York 32	Lee May, Baltimore 109
1977	Rod Carew, Minnesota .388	Jim Rice, Boston 39	Larry Hisle, Minnesota 119
1978	Rod Carew, Minnesota .333	Jim Rice, Boston 46	Jim Rice, Boston 139
1979	Fred Lynn, Boston .333	Gorman Thomas, Milwaukee 45	Don Baylor, California 139
1980	George Brett, Kansas City .390	Two tied at 41	Cecil Cooper, Milwaukee 122
1981	Carney Lansford, Boston .336	Four tied at 22	Eddie Murray, Baltimore 78
1982	Willie Wilson, Kansas City .332	Two tied at 39	Hal McRae, Kansas City 133
1983	Wade Boggs, Boston .361	Jim Rice, Boston 39	Two tied at 126
1984	Don Mattingly, New York .343	Tony Armas, Boston 43	Tony Armas, Boston 123
1985	Wade Boggs, Boston .368	Darrell Evans, Detroit 40	Don Mattingly, New York 145
1986	Wade Boggs, Boston .357	Jesse Barfield, Toronto 40	Joe Carter, Cleveland 121
1987	Wade Boggs, Boston .363	Mark McGwire, Oakland 49	George Bell, Toronto 134
1988	Wade Boggs, Boston .366	Jose Canseco, Oakland 42	Jose Canseco, Oakland 124
1989	Kirby Puckett, Minnesota .339	Fred McGriff, Toronto 36	Ruben Sierra, Texas 119
1990	George Brett, Kansas City .329	Cecil Fielder, Detroit 51	Cecil Fielder, Detroit 132
1991	Julio Franco, Texas .341	Two tied at 44	Cecil Fielder, Detroit 133
1992	Edgar Martinez, Seattle .343	Juan Gonzalez, Texas 43	Cecil Fielder, Detroit 124
1993	John Olerud, Toronto .363	Juan Gonzalez, Texas 46	Albert Belle, Cleveland 129
1994	Paul O'Neill, New York .359	Ken Griffey, Seattle 40	Kirby Puckett, Minnesota 112
1995	Edgar Martinez, Seattle .356	Albert Belle, Cleveland 50	Two tied at 126
1996	Alex Rodriguez, Seattle .358	Mark McGwire Oakland 52	Albert Belle, Cleveland 148
1997	Frank Thomas, Chicago .347	Ken Griffey, Seattle 56	Ken Griffey, Seattle 147
1998	Bernie Williams, New York .339	Ken Griffey, Seattle 56	Juan Gonzalez, Texas 157
1999	Nomar Garciaparra, Boston .357	Ken Griffey, Seattle 48	Manny Ramirez, Cleveland 165
2000	Nomar Garciaparra, Boston .372	Troy Glaus, Anaheim 47	Edgar Martinez, Seattle 145
2001	Ichiro Suzuki, Seattle .350	Alex Rodriguez, Texas 52	Bret Boone, Seattle 141
2002	Manny Ramirez, Boston .349	Alex Rodriguez, Texas 57	Alex Rodriguez, Texas 142
2003	Bill Mueller, Boston .326	Alex Rodriguez, Texas 47	Carlos Delgado, Toronto 145
2004	Ichiro Suzuki, Seattle .372	Manny Ramirez, Boston 43	Miguel Tejada, Baltimore 150

eighth inning, when Tom Gordon gave up a solo homer to Ortiz to make it 4-3. Three batters later, Varitek tied the game against Rivera with a sacrifice fly to center, once again scoring pinch-runner Roberts. After consecutive marathon games, both bullpens could have used a breather, but they didn't get one.

Somehow, the two best offenses in the AL were held in check until the 14th inning. For the Red Sox, Mike Timlin, Keith Foulke, Bronson Arroyo, Mike Myers, Alan Embree and Tim Wakefield combined for eighth shutout innings after New York scored four runs against starter Pedro Martinez.

The Yankee pen was just as strong until the 14th, when Ortiz came to the plate with two outs and Johnny Damon on second base. He fouled off eight two-strike pitches, then floated a single to center field to score the game-winning run—his major league record third game-ending hit of the postseason. The game lasted five hours, 49 minutes to become the longest game in postseason history in terms of time, and it came just 15 hours after the two teams played a five-hour, two-minute Game Four.

Even after two dramatic wins, though, the Red Sox still had to win two games at Yankee Stadium to complete the comeback, and they had no idea what to expect from Schilling. The Boston ace was scheduled to have ankle surgery after the season ended, but he ended up being able to take the mound for Game Six. Boston doctors developed a procedure using sutures to keep the tendon in place.

Schilling gutted out seven innings of one-run, four-hit ball. Blood seeped through his sock, and he spent much of his time in the dugout between innings with his head in his hands, praying. The offense did its part, and the Red Sox won 4-2 thanks to a Mark Bellhorn home run and another strong bullpen performance, especially Foulke.

Twice in the game, the umpires got together and (correctly) reversed calls in Boston's favor. Bellhorn's shot was originally called a double but later ruled a homer, and Rodriguez was called out after slapping the ball out of reliever Bronson Arroyo's glove, thwarting a Yankee rally.

BILL NICHOLS

Mark Bellhorn

That turned things ugly, as fans littered the field with baseballs and other debris, causing a delay and forcing police in riot gear to line the field.

Boston gave Derek Lowe the ball in Game Seven—on two days rest—against New York's Kevin Brown, who had gone just two innings in the third game of the series. Brown could not even get through two innings, and Lowe was outstanding in six innings of one-run, one-hit ball. Two home runs by Damon—including a grand slam—and one apiece by Bellhorn and series MVP Ortiz paced the Red Sox to a 10-3 blowout win, putting an exclamation point on an ALCS for the ages.

"Sweet revenge," Boston lefthander Alan Embree said. "We felt like we had unfinished business all year long with these guys. We played them tough. They thought they had us. We were the only ones that believed we could do it."

No longer was it certain that the Yankees would always

JOHN WILLIAMSON

Baseball's best pitcher over second half of 2004
Twins lefthander Johan Santana

get the better of the Red Sox. No longer was it impossible to come back from a 3-0 series deficit. The incontrovertible had been controverted, the impossible achieved.

Amazing Santana Carries Twins

While Minnesota's playoff run came to a disappointing conclusion against the Yankees, the Twins still had a lot to be happy about in 2004. Behind the remarkable season of lefthander Johan Santana, Minnesota cruised to its third consecutive AL Central title, topping the White Sox by nine games.

Santana went 20-6 and led the AL with a 2.61 ERA and 265 strikeouts. His second half was as good as any stretch by any pitcher: 13-0, 1.21 in 15 starts after the all-star break. He became the first pitcher since Martinez in 1999 to win AL pitcher of the month honors in three straight months (July, August and September). At times he was simply unhittable, thanks to a wicked changeup and outstanding fastball.

Minnesota's offense struggled at times but was bolstered when first baseman Justin Morneau was called up from Triple-A Rochester in July. Morneau was immediately inserted into the cleanup spot, and he responded by hitting .271-19-58 in just 280 at-bats. He wasn't the only young player to factor into Minnesota's 92-win season. Closer Joe Nathan, acquired from San Francisco prior to the 2004 season for catcher A.J. Pierzynski, converted 44 saves and posted a 1.62 ERA, becoming one of baseball's best relievers.

For a while, the Indians mounted a challenge to the Twins in the Central. Cleveland's resurgence was led by outstanding young players like catcher Victor Martinez (.283-23-108), DH Travis Hafner (.311-28-109), second baseman Ronnie Belliard (.282-12-70) and righthander Jake Westbrook (14-9, 3.38) and lefthander Cliff Lee (14-8, 5.43). The Indians eventually fell back to the pack, finishing 80-82, but they established themselves as potential contenders for 2005.

AL YEAR-BY-YEAR PITCHING LEADERS

SINCE 1926

Year	Wins	ERA	Strikeouts
1926	George Uhle, Cleveland ... 27	Lefty Grove, Philadelphia ... 2.51	Lefty Grove, Philadelphia ... 194
1927	Two tied at ... 22	Wilcy Moore, New York ... 2.28	Lefty Grove, Philadelphia ... 174
1928	Two tied at ... 24	Garland Braxton, Washington ... 2.52	Lefty Grove, Philadelphia ... 183
1929	George Earnshaw, Philadelphia ... 24	Lefty Grove, Philadelphia ... 2.82	Lefty Grove, Philadelphia ... 170
1930	Lefty Grove, Philadelphia ... 28	Lefty Grove, Philadelphia ... 2.54	Lefty Grove, Philadelphia ... 209
1931	Lefty Grove, Philadelphia ... 31	Lefty Grove, Philadelphia ... 2.05	Lefty Grove, Philadelphia ... 175
1932	General Crowder, Washington ... 26	Lefty Grove, Philadelphia ... 2.84	Red Ruffing, New York ... 190
1933	Two tied at ... 24	Monte Pearson, Cleveland ... 2.33	Lefty Gomez, New York ... 163
1934	Lefty Gomez, New York ... 26	Lefty Gomez, New York ... 2.33	Lefty Gomez, New York ... 158
1935	Wes Ferrell, Boston ... 25	Lefty Grove, Boston ... 2.70	Tommy Bridges, Detroit ... 163
1936	Tommy Bridges, Detroit ... 23	Lefty Grove, Boston ... 2.81	Tommy Bridges, Detroit ... 175
1937	Lefty Gomez, New York ... 21	Lefty Gomez, New York ... 2.33	Lefty Gomez, New York ... 194
1938	Red Ruffing, New York ... 21	Lefty Grove, Philadelphia ... 3.07	Bob Feller, Cleveland ... 240
1939	Bob Feller, Cleveland ... 24	Lefty Grove, Philadelphia ... 2.54	Bob Feller, Cleveland ... 246
1940	Bob Feller, Cleveland ... 27	Bob Feller, Cleveland ... 2.62	Bob Feller, Cleveland ... 261
1941	Bob Feller, Cleveland ... 25	Thornton Lee, Chicago ... 2.37	Bob Feller, Cleveland ... 260
1942	Tex Hughson, Boston ... 22	Ted Lyons, Chicago ... 2.10	Two tied at ... 113
1943	Two tied at ... 20	Spud Chandler, New York ... 1.64	Allie Reynolds, Cleveland ... 151
1944	Hal Newhouser, Detroit ... 29	Dizzy Trout, Detroit ... 2.12	Hal Newhouser, Detroit ... 187
1945	Hal Newhouser, Detroit ... 25	Hal Newhouser, Detroit ... 1.81	Hal Newhouser, Detroit ... 212
1946	Two tied at ... 26	Hal Newhouser, Detroit ... 1.94	Bob Feller, Cleveland ... 348
1947	Bob Feller, Cleveland ... 20	Spud Chandler, New York ... 2.46	Bob Feller, Cleveland ... 196
1948	Hal Newhouser, Detroit ... 21	Gene Bearden, Cleveland ... 2.43	Bob Feller, Cleveland ... 164
1949	Mel Parnell, Boston ... 25	Mel Parnell, Boston ... 2.78	Virgil Trucks, Detroit ... 153
1950	Bob Lemon, Cleveland ... 23	Early Wynn, Cleveland ... 3.20	Bob Lemon, Cleveland ... 170
1951	Bob Feller, Cleveland ... 22	Saul Rogovin, Detroit-Chicago ... 2.78	Vic Raschi, New York ... 164
1952	Bobby Shantz, Philadelphia ... 24	Allie Reynolds, New York ... 2.07	Allie Reynolds, New York ... 160
1953	Bob Porterfield, Washington ... 22	Eddie Lopat, New York ... 2.43	Billy Pierce, Chicago ... 186
1954	Two tied at ... 23	Mike Garcia, Cleveland ... 2.64	Bob Turley, Baltimore ... 185
1955	Three tied at ... 18	Billy Pierce, Chicago ... 1.97	Herb Score, Cleveland ... 245
1956	Frank Lary, Detroit ... 21	Whitey Ford, New York ... 2.47	Herb Score, Cleveland ... 263
1957	Two tied at ... 20	Bobby Shantz, New York ... 2.45	Early Wynn, Cleveland ... 184
1958	Bob Turley, New York ... 21	Whitey Ford, New York ... 2.01	Early Wynn, Chicago ... 179
1959	Early Wynn, Chicago ... 22	Hoyt Wilhelm, Baltimore ... 2.19	Jim Bunning, Detroit ... 201
1960	Two tied at ... 18	Frank Baumann, Chicago ... 2.68	Jim Bunning, Detroit ... 201
1961	Whitey Ford, New York ... 25	Dick Donovan, Washington ... 2.40	Camilo Pascual, Minnesota ... 221
1962	Ralph Terry, New York ... 23	Hank Aguirre, Detroit ... 2.21	Camilo Pascual, Minnesota ... 206
1963	Whitey Ford, New York ... 24	Gary Peters, Chicago ... 2.33	Camilo Pascual, Minnesota ... 202
1964	Two tied at ... 20	Dean Chance, Los Angeles ... 1.65	Al Downing, New York ... 217
1965	Mudcat Grant, Minnesota ... 21	Sam McDowell, Cleveland ... 2.18	Sam McDowell, Cleveland ... 325
1966	Jim Kaat, Minnesota ... 25	Gary Peters, Chicago ... 1.98	Sam McDowell, Cleveland ... 225
1967	Two tied at ... 22	Joel Horlen, Chicago ... 2.06	Jim Lonborg, Boston ... 246
1968	Denny McLain, Detroit ... 31	Luis Tiant, Cleveland ... 1.60	Sam McDowell, Cleveland ... 283
1969	Denny McLain, Detroit ... 24	Dick Bosman, Washington ... 2.19	Sam McDowell, Cleveland ... 279
1970	Three tied at ... 24	Diego Segui, Oakland ... 2.56	Sam McDowell, Cleveland ... 304
1971	Mickey Lolich, Detroit ... 25	Vida Blue, Oakland ... 1.82	Mickey Lolich, Detroit ... 308
1972	Two tied at ... 24	Luis Tiant, Boston ... 1.91	Nolan Ryan, California ... 329
1973	Wilbur Wood, Chicago ... 24	Jim Palmer, Baltimore ... 2.40	Nolan Ryan, California ... 383
1974	Two tied at ... 25	Catfish Hunter, Oakland ... 2.49	Nolan Ryan, California ... 367
1975	Two tied at ... 23	Jim Palmer, Baltimore ... 2.09	Frank Tanana, California ... 269
1976	Jim Palmer, Baltimore ... 22	Mark Fidrych, Detroit ... 2.34	Nolan Ryan, California ... 327
1977	Three tied at ... 20	Frank Tanana, California ... 2.54	Nolan Ryan, California ... 341
1978	Ron Guidry, New York ... 25	Ron Guidry, New York ... 1.74	Nolan Ryan, California ... 260
1979	Mike Flanagan, Baltimore ... 23	Ron Guidry, New York ... 2.78	Nolan Ryan, California ... 223
1980	Steve Stone, Baltimore ... 25	Rudy May, New York ... 2.47	Len Barker, Cleveland ... 187
1981	Steve McCatty, Oakland ... 14	Steve McCatty, Oakland ... 2.32	Len Barker, Cleveland ... 127
1982	LaMarr Hoyt, Chicago ... 19	Rick Sutcliffe, Cleveland ... 2.96	Floyd Bannister, Seattle ... 209
1983	LaMarr Hoyt, Chicago ... 21	Rick Honeycutt, Texas ... 2.42	Jack Morris, Detroit ... 232
1984	Mike Boddicker, Baltimore ... 20	Mike Boddicker, Baltimore ... 2.79	Mark Langston, Seattle ... 204
1985	Ron Guidry, New York ... 22	Dave Stieb, Toronto ... 2.48	Bert Blyleven, Cleve.-Minnesota ... 206
1986	Roger Clemens, Boston ... 24	Roger Clemens, Boston ... 2.48	Mark Langston, Seattle ... 245
1987	Two tied at ... 20	Jimmy Key, Toronto ... 2.76	Mark Langston, Seattle ... 262
1988	Frank Viola, Minnesota ... 24	Allan Anderson, Minnesota ... 2.45	Roger Clemens, Boston ... 291
1989	Bret Saberhagen, K.C. ... 23	Bret Saberhagen, Kansas City ... 2.16	Nolan Ryan, Texas ... 301
1990	Bob Welch, Oakland ... 27	Roger Clemens, Boston ... 1.93	Nolan Ryan, Texas ... 232
1991	Two tied at ... 20	Roger Clemens, Boston ... 2.62	Roger Clemens, Boston ... 241
1992	Two tied at ... 21	Roger Clemens, Boston ... 2.41	Randy Johnson, Seattle ... 241
1993	Jack McDowell, Chicago ... 22	Kevin Appier, Kansas City ... 2.56	Randy Johnson, Seattle ... 308
1994	Jimmy Key, New York ... 17	Steve Ontiveros, Oakland ... 2.65	Randy Johnson, Seattle ... 204
1995	Mike Mussina, Baltimore ... 19	Randy Johnson, Seattle ... 2.48	Randy Johnson, Seattle ... 294
1996	Andy Pettitte, New York ... 21	Juan Guzman, Toronto ... 2.93	Roger Clemens, Boston ... 257
1997	Roger Clemens, Toronto ... 21	Roger Clemens, Toronto ... 2.05	Roger Clemens, Toronto ... 292
1998	Three tied at ... 20	Roger Clemens, Toronto ... 2.65	Roger Clemens, Toronto ... 271
1999	Pedro Martinez, Boston ... 23	Pedro Martinez, Boston ... 2.07	Pedro Martinez, Boston ... 313
2000	Two tied at ... 20	Pedro Martinez, Boston ... 1.74	Pedro Martinez, Boston ... 284
2001	Mark Mulder, Oakland ... 21	Freddy Garcia, Seattle ... 3.05	Hideo Nomo, Boston ... 220
2002	Barry Zito, Oakland ... 23	Pedro Martinez, Boston ... 2.26	Pedro Martinez, Boston ... 239
2003	Roy Halladay, Toronto ... 22	Pedro Martinez, Boston ... 2.22	Esteban Loaiza, Chicago ... 207
2004	Curt Schilling, Boston ... 21	Johan Santana, Minnesota ... 2.61	Johan Santana, Minnesota ... 265

BILL NICHOLS

Lifted Angels to A.L. West crown
Anaheim outfielder Vladimir Guerrero

AL: BEST TOOLS

A Baseball America survey of American League managers, conducted at midseason 2004, ranked AL players with the best tools:

BEST HITTER
1. Manny Ramirez, Red Sox
2. Ivan Rodriguez, Tigers
3. Vladimir Guerrero, Angels

BEST POWER
1. Manny Ramirez, Red Sox
2. Alex Rodriguez, Yankees
3. David Ortiz, Red Sox

BEST BUNTER
1. Alex Sanchez, Tigers
2. Ichiro Suzuki, Mariners
3. Omar Vizquel, Indians

BEST STRIKE-ZONE JUDGMENT
1. Frank Thomas, White Sox
2. Manny Ramirez, Red Sox
3. Rafael Palmeiro, Orioles

BEST HIT-AND-RUN BATTER
1. David Eckstein, Angels
2. Derek Jeter, Yankees
3. Omar Vizquel, Indians

BEST BASERUNNER
1. Ichiro Suzuki, Mariners
2. Carl Crawford, Devil Rays
3. Derek Jeter, Yankees

FASTEST BASERUNNER
1. Carl Crawford, Devil Rays
2. Ichiro Suzuki, Mariners
3. Rocco Baldelli, Devil Rays

BEST PITCHER
1. Mark Mulder, Athletics
2. Curt Schilling, Red Sox
3. Tim Hudson, Athletics

BEST FASTBALL
1. Francisco Cordero, Rangers
2. Curt Schilling, Red Sox
3. Jorge Julio, Orioles

BEST CURVEBALL
1. Barry Zito, Athletics
2. Mike Mussina, Yankees
3. Tom Gordon, Yankees

BEST SLIDER
1. Francisco Rodriguez, Angels
2. Victor Zambrano, Devil Rays
3. Pedro Martinez, Red Sox

BEST CHANGEUP
1. Keith Foulke, Red Sox
2. Johan Santana, Twins
3. Pedro Martinez, Red Sox

BEST CONTROL
1. Curt Schilling, Red Sox
2. Brad Radke, Twins
3. Pedro Martinez, Red Sox

BEST PICKOFF MOVE
1. Brian Anderson, Royals
2. Kenny Rogers, Rangers
3. Terry Mulholland, Twins

BEST RELIEVER
1. Mariano Rivera, Yankees
2. Joe Nathan, Twins
3. Francisco Cordero, Rangers

BEST DEFENSIVE C
1. Ivan Rodriguez, Tigers
2. Benji Molina, Angels
3. Jason Varitek, Red Sox

BEST DEFENSIVE 1B
1. Doug Mientkiewicz, Twins
2. Rafael Palmeiro, Orioles
3. John Olerud, Mariners

BEST DEFENSIVE 2B
1. Bret Boone, Mariners
2. Adam Kennedy, Angels
3. Brian Roberts, Orioles

BEST DEFENSIVE 3B
1. Alex Rodriguez, Yankees
2. Eric Chavez, Athletics
3. Hank Blalock, Rangers

BEST DEFENSIVE SS
1. Derek Jeter, Yankees
2. Miguel Tejada, Athletics
3. Omar Vizquel, Indians

BEST INFIELD ARM
1. Alex Rodriguez, Yankees
2. Nomar Garciaparra, Red Sox
3. Miguel Tejada, Athletics

BEST DEFENSIVE OF
1. Ichiro Suzuki, Mariners
2. Torii Hunter, Twins
3. Rocco Baldelli, Devil Rays

BEST OUTFIELD ARM
1. Vladimir Guerrero, Angels
2. Ichiro Suzuki, Mariners
3. Jose Guillen, Angels

MOST EXCITING PLAYER
1. Vladimir Guerrero, Angels
2. Ichiro Suzuki, Mariners
3. Carl Crawford, Devil Rays

BEST MANAGER
1. Joe Torre, Yankees
2. Mike Scioscia, Angels
3. Lou Piniella, Devil Rays

Chicago, meanwhile, did what it always does when chasing the Twins: trade for Carl Everett. White Sox GM Ken Williams acquired the enigmatic center fielder at the trade deadline for the second straight year in 2004, this time from Montreal. But Everett wasn't the answer, because Chicago's fate was already sealed. Magglio Ordonez got hurt and Esteban Loaiza could not regain his form of 2003, when he was second in the American League Cy Young Award balloting. The Sox eventually shipped him to the Yankees for righthander Jose Contreras.

The Tigers made the biggest improvement in the majors in 2004: 29 games. Of course, Detroit lost an AL-record 119 games the previous year, but progress is progress. The signing of free-agent catcher Ivan Rodriguez (.334-19-86) made the biggest difference for the Tigers, but the emergence of shortstop Carlos Guillen (.318-20-97) and the maturation of their young pitching staff also played key roles.

Replacing Detroit in the AL Central basement was Kansas City, which followed up a surprising 83-win 2003 season with a disaster. The Royals lost a franchise-record 104 games, along the way trading Carlos Beltran to the Astros. Kansas City finished 34 games out of first place.

Down To The Wire Out West

Anaheim's path to the playoffs was not an easy one. Preseason expectations were high for the Angels, who had signed free agents Vladimir Guerrero, Bartolo Colon and Kelvim Escobar during the offseason. But injuries hit hard early in the year. Brendan Donnelly was hurt in spring training, Troy Glaus lost most of his season to shoulder surgery, Darin Erstad blew out his hamstring, Garret Anderson lost 42 games with arthritis symptoms, and Troy Percival battled elbow problems.

"Injuries are going to be part of any championship-caliber team," Angels manager Mike Scioscia said. "We are not going to hang our hat to say, 'Hey, we had some injuries,' and 'Hey, maybe we should have had a stronger lineup during the year.'

"We don't feel cheated at all."

Role players like Chone Figgins, Jeff DaVanon and Robb Quinlan plugged holes for the Angels and helped keep them close in the West. And Guerrero was as good as expected. He carried the team for stretches, putting up MVP-caliber numbers (.337-39-126). He played his best baseball in September, batting .371-10-23.

Anaheim spent much of the second half chasing Oakland, and the two teams were tied heading into a three-game series in the season's final weekend. The Angels won the first two to take the division, rallying for three runs in the eighth inning for a 5-4 win in the clincher. It was an Erstad two-run double that tied the score, followed by an Anderson single to give Anaheim its first division title in 18 years.

The Angels got help from Oakland, which was uncharacteristically bad in September. The A's had won the division three of the previous four years and made the play-

AMERICAN LEAGUE
DEPARTMENT LEADERS

INDIVIDUAL BATTING

GAMES
Miguel Tejada, Orioles 162
Hideki Matsui, Yankees 162
Ichiro Suzuki, Mariners 161
Michael Young, Rangers 160
Hank Blalock, Rangers 159
Brian Roberts, Orioles 159

AT-BATS
Ichiro Suzuki, Mariners 704
Michael Young, Rangers 690
Miguel Tejada, Orioles 653
Derek Jeter, Yankees 643
Brian Roberts, Orioles 641

RUNS
Vladimir Guerrero, Angels 124
Johnny Damon, Red Sox 123
Gary Sheffield, Yankees 117
Michael Young, Rangers 114
Alex Rodriguez, Yankees 112

HITS
Ichiro Suzuki, Mariners 262
Michael Young, Rangers 216
Vladimir Guerrero, Angels 206
Miguel Tejada, Orioles 203
Mark Kotsay, Athletics 190

TOTAL BASES
Vladimir Guerrero, Angels 366
David Ortiz, Red Sox 351
Miguel Tejada, Orioles 349
Manny Ramirez, Red Sox 348
Michael Young, Rangers 333

SINGLES
Ichiro Suzuki, Mariners 225
Michael Young, Rangers 152
Mark Kotsay, Athletics 135
Johnny Damon, Red Sox 131
Carl Crawford, Devil Rays 129
David Eckstein, Angels 129

DOUBLES
Brian Roberts, Orioles 50
Ronnie Belliard, Indians 48
David Ortiz, Red Sox 47
Manny Ramirez, Red Sox 44
Derek Jeter, Yankees 44

TRIPLES
Carl Crawford, Devil Rays 19
Chone Figgins, Angels 17

Carl Crawford: 19 triples, 59 steals

Miguel Tejada: 150 RBIs

Carlos Guillen, Tigers 10
Omar Infante, Tigers 9
Michael Young, Rangers 9

HOME RUNS
Manny Ramirez, Red Sox 43
David Ortiz, Red Sox 41
Paul Konerko, White Sox 41
Vladimir Guerrero, Angels 39
Mark Teixeira, Rangers 38

HOME RUN RATIO
(At-bats per home run)
Manny Ramirez, Red Sox 13.2
Paul Konerko, White Sox 13.7
David Ortiz, Red Sox 14.2
Carlos Delgado, Blue Jays 14.3
Mark Teixeira, Rangers 14.3

RUNS BATTED IN
Miguel Tejada, Orioles 150
David Ortiz, Red Sox 139
Manny Ramirez, Red Sox 130
Vladimir Guerrero, Angels 126
Gary Sheffield, Yankees 121

SACRIFICE BUNTS
Omar Vizquel, Indians 20
Derek Jeter, Yankees 16
Brian Roberts, Orioles 15
David Eckstein, Angels 14
Cristian Guzman, Twins 13

SACRIFICE FLIES
Miguel Tejada, Orioles 14
Carlos Delgado, Blue Jays 11
Rafael Palmeiro, Orioles 9
Eight tied at 8

HIT BY PITCHES
Travis Hafner, Indians 17
Kevin Millar, Red Sox 17
Jose Guillen, Angels 15
Miguel Cairo, Yankees 14
Derek Jeter, Yankees 14

WALKS
Eric Chavez, Athletics 95
Gary Sheffield, Yankees 92
Jorge Posada, Yankees 88
Mark Bellhorn, Red Sox 88
Hideki Matsui, Yankees 88

INTENTIONAL WALKS
Ichiro Suzuki, Mariners 19

Rafael Palmeiro, Orioles 15
Manny Ramirez, Red Sox 15
Vladimir Guerrero, Angels 14
Carlos Delgado, Blue Jays 12
Mark Teixeira, Rangers 12

STOLEN BASES
Carl Crawford, Devil Rays 59
Ichiro Suzuki, Mariners 36
Chone Figgins, Angels 34
Brian Roberts, Orioles 29
Alex Rodriguez, Yankees 28

CAUGHT STEALING
Carl Crawford, Devil Rays 15
Chone Figgins, Angels 13
Coco Crisp, Indians 13
Alex Sanchez, Tigers 13
Brian Roberts, Orioles 12

STRIKEOUTS
Mark Bellhorn, Red Sox 177
Hank Blalock, Rangers 149
Carlos Pena, Tigers 146
Bobby Crosby, Athletics 141
Casey Blake, Indians 139
Jose Valentin, White Sox 139

TOUGHEST TO STRIKE OUT
(At-bats per SO)
David Eckstein, Angels 11.6
Scott Hatteberg, Athletics 11.5
Ichiro Suzuki, Mariners 11.2
Omar Vizquel, Indians 9.1
Rafael Palmeiro, Orioles 9.0

GROUNDED INTO DOUBLE PLAYS
Jorge Posada, Yankees 24
Miguel Tejada, Orioles 24
Torii Hunter, Twins 23
Paul Konerko, White Sox 23
Eric Chavez, Athletics 21
Matt Lawton, Indians 21

HITTING STREAKS
Carlos Lee, White Sox 28
Robb Quinlan, Angels 21
Ichiro Suzuki, Mariners 21
Miguel Tejada, Orioles 19
David Eckstein, Angels 18

MULTIPLE-HIT GAMES
Ichiro Suzuki, Mariners 80
Michael Young, Rangers 70
Melvin Mora, Orioles 60
Vladimir Guerrero, Angels 59
Javy Lopez, Orioles 59

ON-BASE PERCENTAGE
Melvin Mora, Orioles .... .419
Ichiro Suzuki, Mariners .... .414
Travis Hafner, Indians .... .410
Jorge Posada, Yankees .... .400
Eric Chavez, Athletics .... .397

SLUGGING PERCENTAGE
Manny Ramirez, Red Sox .... .613
David Ortiz, Red Sox .... .603
Vladimir Guerrero, Angels .... .598
Travis Hafner, Indians .... .583
Melvin Mora, Orioles .... .562
Mark Teixeira, Rangers .... .560

PITCHING

WINS
Curt Schilling, Red Sox 21
Johan Santana, Twins 20
Bartolo Colon, Angels 18
Kenny Rogers, Rangers 18
Mark Mulder, Athletics 17

LOSSES

Darrell May, Royals	19
Ryan Franklin, Mariners	16
Mark Hendrickson, Devil Rays	15
Jason Johnson, Tigers	15
Sidney Ponson, Orioles	15

WINNING PERCENTAGE

Curt Schilling, Red Sox	.778
Johan Santana, Twins	.769
Mark Mulder, Athletics	.680
Kenny Rogers, Rangers	.667
Tim Hudson, Athletics	.667

GAMES

Paul Quantrill, Yankees	86
Tom Gordon, Yankees	80
Juan Rincon, Twins	77
B.J. Ryan, Orioles	76
Mike Timlin, Red Sox	76

GAMES STARTED

Mark Buehrle, White Sox	35
Kenny Rogers, Rangers	35
Bartolo Colon, Angels	34
Kyle Lohse, Twins	34
Brad Radke, Twins	34
Johan Santana, Twins	34
Barry Zito, Athletics	34

COMPLETE GAMES

Mark Mulder, Athletics	5
Sidney Ponson, Orioles	5
Jake Westbrook, Indians	5
Mark Buehrle, White Sox	4
Tim Hudson, Athletics	3
Darrell May, Royals	3
Curt Schilling, Red Sox	3

SHUTOUTS

Jeremy Bonderman, Tigers	2
Tim Hudson, Athletics	2
Sidney Ponson, Orioles	2
Twenty-seven tied at	1

GAMES FINISHED

Mariano Rivera, Yankees	69
Francisco Cordero, Rangers	63
Joe Nathan, Twins	63
Keith Foulke, Red Sox	61
Danys Baez, Devil Rays	59

SAVES

Mariano Rivera, Yankees	53
Francisco Cordero, Rangers	49
Joe Nathan, Twins	44
Troy Percival, Angels	33
Keith Foulke, Red Sox	32

INNINGS PITCHED

Mark Buehrle, White Sox	245
Johan Santana, Twins	228
Curt Schilling, Red Sox	227
Mark Mulder, Athletics	226
Brad Radke, Twins	220

HITS ALLOWED

Sidney Ponson, Orioles	265
Mark Buehrle, White Sox	257
Carlos Silva, Twins	255
Kenny Rogers, Rangers	248
Mike Maroth, Tigers	244

RUNS ALLOWED

Derek Lowe, Red Sox	138
Sidney Ponson, Orioles	136
Darrell May, Royals	130
Kyle Lohse, Twins	128
Jamie Moyer, Mariners	127

HOME RUNS ALLOWED

Jamie Moyer, Mariners	44
Bartolo Colon, Angels	38
Darrell May, Royals	38
Jon Garland, White Sox	34
Brian Anderson, Royals	33
Mark Buehrle, White Sox	33

WALKS

Miguel Batista, Blue Jays	96
Victor Zambrano, Devil Rays	96
Daniel Cabrera, Orioles	89
Ted Lilly, Blue Jays	89
Jose Contreras, Yankees/White Sox	84

FEWEST WALKS PER 9 INNINGS

Jon Lieber, Yankees	0.92
Brad Radke, Twins	1.07
Curt Schilling, Red Sox	1.39
Carlos Silva, Twins	1.55
Mark Buehrle, White Sox	1.87

HIT BATSMEN

Bronson Arroyo, Red Sox	20
Pedro Martinez, Red Sox	16
Tim Wakefield, Red Sox	16
Victor Zambrano, Devil Rays	16
Chan Ho Park, Rangers	13

STRIKEOUTS

Johan Santana, Twins	265
Pedro Martinez, Red Sox	227
Curt Schilling, Red Sox	203
Kelvim Escobar, Angels	191
Freddy Garcia, Mariners/White Sox	184

STRIKEOUTS PER 9 INNINGS

Johan Santana, Twins	10.46
Pedro Martinez, Red Sox	9.41
Kelvim Escobar, Angels	8.25
Jeremy Bonderman, Tigers	8.22
Cliff Lee, Indians	8.09

PICKOFFS

Mark Buehrle, White Sox	10
Mark Mulder, Athletics	9
Mark Redman, Athletics	9
Kenny Rogers, Rangers	6
Scott Schoeneweis, White Sox	6

WILD PITCHES

Jose Contreras, Yankees/ White Sox	17
Kevin Gregg, Angels	13
Miguel Batista, Blue Jays	12
Daniel Cabrera, Orioles	12
Javier Vazquez, Yankees	12

BALKS

Ted Lilly, Blue Jays	4
Jeremy Affeldt, Royals	3
Ryan Franklin, Mariners	3
Ramon Ortiz, Angels	3
Twelve tied at	2

OPPONENT BATTING AVERAGE

Johan Santana, Twins	.192
Ted Lilly, Blue Jays	.230
Pedro Martinez, Red Sox	.238
Curt Schilling, Red Sox	.239
Freddy Garcia, Mariners/White Sox	.242

FIELDING

PITCHER

PCT	Freddy Garcia, Mariners/White Sox	1.000
	Mike Maroth, Tigers	1.000

Mariano Rivera: 53 saves

Mark Buehrle: 245 innings

PO	Bronson Arroyo, Red Sox	24
	Jake Westbrook, Indians	24
A	Mark Buehrle, White Sox	51
	Mark Mulder, Athletics	51
E	John Parrish, Orioles	6
TC	Jake Westbrook, Indians	76
DP	Three tied at	5

CATCHER

PCT	Damian Miller, Athletics	.999
PO	Jason Varitek, Red Sox	880
A	Victor Martinez, Indians	61
E	Ivan Rodriguez, Tigers	11
TC	Victor Martinez, Indians	932
DP	Jorge Posada, Yankees	13
PB	Doug Mirabelli, Red Sox	15

FIRST BASE

PCT	John Olerud, Mariners/Yankees	.998
PO	Scott Hatteberg, Athletics	1281
A	Mark Teixeira, Rangers	98
E	Scott Hatteberg, Athletics	10
	Mark Teixeira, Rangers	10
TC	Scott Hatteberg, Athletics	1377
DP	Paul Konerko, White Sox	136

SECOND BASE

PCT	Marco Scutaro, Athletics	.995
PO	Alfonso Soriano, Rangers	308
A	Orlando Hudson, Blue Jays	450
E	Alfonso Soriano, Rangers	23
TC	Alfonso Soriano, Rangers	749
DP	Alfonso Soriano, Rangers	104

THIRD BASE

PCT	Eric Hinske, Blue Jays	.978
PO	Melvin Mora, Orioles	122
A	Hank Blalock, Rangers	279
E	Casey Blake, Indians	26
TC	Casey Blake, Indians	423
DP	Hank Blalock, Rangers	33

SHORTSTOP

PCT	David Eckstein, Angels	.988
PO	Derek Jeter, Yankees	273
A	Miguel Tejada, Orioles	526
E	Angel Berroa, Royals	28
TC	Miguel Tejada, Orioles	813
DP	Miguel Tejada, Orioles	118

OUTFIELD

PCT	Carlos Lee, White Sox	1.000
PO	Randy Winn, Mariners	416
A	Vladimir Guerrero, Angels	13
	Bobby Higginson, Tigers	13
E	Craig Monroe, Tigers	11
TC	Ichiro Suzuki, Mariners	387
DP	Four tied at	4

2004 AMERICAN LEAGUE STATISTICS

CLUB BATTING

	AVG	G	AB	R	H	2B	3B	HR	BB	SO	SB
Anaheim	.282	162	5675	836	1603	272	37	162	450	942	143
Boston	.282	162	5720	949	1613	373	25	222	659	1189	68
Baltimore	.281	162	5736	842	1614	319	18	169	528	949	101
Cleveland	.276	162	5676	858	1565	345	29	184	606	1009	94
Detroit	.272	162	5623	827	1531	284	54	201	518	1144	86
Seattle	.270	162	5722	698	1544	276	20	136	492	1058	110
Oakland	.270	162	5728	793	1545	336	15	189	608	1061	47
New York	.268	162	5527	897	1483	281	20	242	670	982	84
Chicago	.268	162	5534	865	1481	284	19	242	499	1030	78
Texas	.266	162	5615	860	1492	323	34	227	500	1099	69
Minnesota	.266	162	5623	780	1494	310	24	191	513	982	116
Toronto	.260	161	5531	719	1438	290	34	145	513	1083	58
Kansas City	.259	162	5538	720	1432	261	29	150	461	1057	67
Tampa Bay	.258	161	5483	714	1416	278	46	145	469	944	132

CLUB PITCHING

	ERA	G	CG	SV	IP	H	HR	R	ER	BB	SO
Minnesota	4.03	162	4	48	1476	1494	191	780	661	513	982
Oakland	4.17	162	10	35	1471	1545	189	793	682	608	1061
Boston	4.18	162	4	36	1451	1613	222	949	674	659	1189
Anaheim	4.28	162	2	50	1454	1603	162	836	692	450	942
Texas	4.53	162	5	52	1440	1492	227	860	724	500	1099
New York	4.69	162	1	59	1444	1483	242	897	752	670	982
Baltimore	4.70	162	8	27	1455	1614	169	842	760	528	949
Seattle	4.76	162	7	28	1459	1544	136	698	772	492	1058
Tampa Bay	4.81	161	3	35	1417	1416	145	714	757	469	944
Cleveland	4.81	162	8	32	1467	1565	184	858	784	606	1009
Toronto	4.91	161	6	37	1421	1438	145	719	775	513	1083
Chicago	4.91	162	8	34	1432	1481	242	865	782	499	1030
Detroit	4.93	162	7	35	1440	1531	201	827	788	518	1144
Kansas City	5.15	162	6	25	1420	1432	150	720	813	461	1057

CLUB FIELDING

	PCT	PO	A	E	DP		PCT	PO	A	E	DP
Oakland	.986	4414	1810	91	172	Seattle	.983	4378	1474	103	140
Anaheim	.985	4363	1512	90	126	Baltimore	.982	4366	1683	110	161
Toronto	.985	4263	1631	91	150	Boston	.981	4354	1650	118	129
Minnesota	.984	4428	1658	101	158	Texas	.981	4319	1606	117	152
Chicago	.984	4297	1669	100	167	Tampa Bay	.980	4251	1530	119	139
New York	.984	4331	1572	99	148	Kansas City	.978	4261	1636	131	169
Cleveland	.983	4400	1676	106	152	Detroit	.977	4319	1711	144	160

INDIVIDUAL BATTING LEADERS
(Minimum 502 Plate Appearances)

	AVG	G	AB	R	H	2B	3B	HR	RBI	BB	SO	SB
Suzuki, Ichiro, Seattle	.372	161	704	101	262	24	5	8	60	49	63	36
Mora, Melvin, Baltimore	.340	140	550	111	187	41	0	27	104	66	95	11
Guerrero, Vladimir, Anaheim	.337	156	612	124	206	39	2	39	126	52	74	15
Rodriguez, Ivan, Detroit	.334	135	527	72	176	32	2	19	86	41	91	7
Durazo, Erubiel, Oakland	.321	142	511	80	164	35	1	22	88	56	104	3
Guillen, Carlos, Detroit	.318	136	522	97	166	37	10	20	97	52	87	12
Lopez, Javy, Baltimore	.316	150	579	83	183	33	3	23	86	47	97	0
Kotsay, Mark, Oakland	.314	148	606	78	190	37	3	15	63	55	70	8
Young, Michael, Texas	.313	160	690	114	216	33	9	22	99	44	89	12
Hafner, Travis, Cleveland	.311	140	482	96	150	41	3	28	109	68	111	3

INDIVIDUAL PITCHING LEADERS
(Minimum 162 Innings)

	W	L	ERA	G	GS	CG	SV	IP	H	R	ER	BB	SO
Santana, Johan, Minnesota	20	6	2.61	34	34	1	0	228	156	70	66	54	265
Schilling, Curt, Boston	21	6	3.26	32	32	3	0	227	206	84	82	35	203
Westbrook, Jake, Cleveland	14	9	3.38	33	30	5	0	216	208	95	81	61	116
Radke, Brad, Minnesota	11	8	3.48	34	34	1	0	220	229	92	85	26	143
Hudson, Tim, Oakland	12	6	3.53	27	27	3	0	189	194	82	74	44	103
Lopez, Rodrigo, Baltimore	14	9	3.59	37	23	1	0	171	164	71	68	54	121
Garcia, Freddy, Seattle/Chicago	13	11	3.81	31	31	1	0	210	192	92	89	64	184
Buehrle, Mark, Chicago	16	10	3.89	35	35	4	0	245	257	119	106	51	165
Martinez, Pedro, Boston	16	9	3.90	33	33	1	0	217	193	99	94	61	227
Escobar, Kelvim, Anaheim	11	12	3.93	33	33	0	0	208	192	91	91	76	191

Ichiro Suzuki: .372 average

Michael Young: 216 hits

Melvin Mora: Hit .340-27-104

offs in all four of those seasons, but they went 13-18 in the final month of the 2004 season, including a 4-9 stretch to end the year.

"It's weird," Oakland third baseman Eric Chavez said. "It's very apparent to the rest of baseball what our problems are. If you ask me, we should have run away with this division this year."

Mark Mulder

Oakland's problems were indeed obvious: They didn't hit well and their trademark pitching was ineffective down the stretch. After losing shortstop Miguel Tejada to free agency before the season (to the Orioles), the A's knew it would be more difficult to score runs in 2004, but they figured their top three starters—

Tim Hudson, Mark Mulder and Barry Zito—gave them a good chance. It went according to plan early, as Mulder went 12-2, 3.21 in the first half to start the All-Star Game and Hudson went 7-3, 2.98 to join him in the game.

But Mulder went winless in his last seven starts, going 0-4, 7.27 amid speculation that he was trying to pitch through injury. Hudson missed more than a month with a strained stomach muscle and finished with 12 wins. Zito was inconsistent all year and finished 11-11.

Complicating matters in the West was the resurgence of the Rangers, who traded away Rodriguez for second baseman Alfonso Soriano and then went from 71 wins and a last-place finish in 2003 to 89 wins and a third-place finish in 2004. Texas spent 46 days in first place in 2004 and remained in contention until an 11-inning loss to Anaheim in the 158th game. They finished just three games behind the Angels.

The key was the Rangers' young infield of Soriano (.280-28-91), first baseman Mark Teixeira (.281-38-112), third baseman Hank Blalock (.276-32-110) and shortstop Michael Young (.313-22-99). Young, who moved to shortstop from second base after the trade, made the Rangers forget about Rodriguez with his energetic play, strong defense and surprising pop.

Hank Blalock

"We got better, and the biggest thing is we believe we are a good team now," Young said. "We believe we are a postseason club. I think that we proved that to people the way we played."

There was one other significant accomplishment out of the West, even though it came from a dismal Mariners team that lost 99 games. Seattle right fielder Ichiro Suzuki broke George Sisler's 84-year-old record for hits in a season. Suzuki's 262 hits broke the record of 257 set by Sisler of the St. Louis Browns in 1920. Suzuki hit .372 to lead the league, and he was able to break the record largely because his speed gave him the ability to run out infield hits and drag bunts. He set a new major league record with 233 singles in 2004. Because of his lack of extra-base hits, some players and media members questioned the significance of Suzuki's hit record, but baseball commissioner Bud Selig did not.

"I'm not sure this is getting the recognition it deserves," Selig said. "I think this is a stunning record."

AMERICAN LEAGUE
DIVISION SERIES
NEW YORK vs. MINNESOTA
COMPOSITE BOX

NEW YORK

Player, Pos.	AVG	G	AB	R	H	2B	3B	HR	RBI	BB	SO	SB
Alex Rodriguez, 3b	.421	4	19	3	8	3	0	1	3	2	1	2
Hideki Matsui, lf	.412	4	17	3	7	1	0	1	3	3	4	0
Derek Jeter, ss	.316	4	19	3	6	1	0	1	4	1	4	1
Bernie Williams, cf	.278	4	18	2	5	1	0	1	3	1	2	0
Kenny Lofton, cf	.250	1	4	0	1	0	0	0	1	0	1	0
Gary Sheffield, rf	.222	4	18	2	4	1	0	1	2	3	1	0
Jorge Posada, c	.222	4	18	2	4	0	0	0	0	6	6	0
John Olerud, 1b	.214	4	14	2	3	2	0	0	0	1	2	0
Miguel Cairo, 2b	.214	4	14	3	3	1	0	0	1	2	5	0
Ruben Sierra, dh	.167	3	12	1	2	0	0	1	3	2	3	1
Tony Clark, 1b	.000	1	1	0	0	0	0	0	0	0	1	0
Bubba Crosby, rf-pr	.000	2	0	0	0	0	0	0	0	0	0	0
Totals	**.279**	**4**	**154**	**21**	**43**	**10**	**0**	**6**	**20**	**15**	**30**	**4**

Pitcher	W	L	ERA	G	GS	SV	IP	H	R	ER	BB	SO
Paul Quantrill	1	0	0.00	2	0	0	2	2	0	0	0	1
Esteban Loaiza	0	0	0.00	1	0	0	2	4	0	0	0	0
Mariano Rivera	1	0	0.00	4	0	0	6	2	0	0	0	2
Kevin Brown	1	0	1.50	1	1	0	6	8	1	1	0	1
Mike Mussina	0	1	2.57	1	1	0	7	7	2	2	1	7
Jon Lieber	0	0	4.05	1	1	0	7	7	3	3	1	4
Tom Gordon	0	0	4.91	3	0	0	4	2	2	2	0	3
Tanyon Sturtze	0	0	6.75	2	0	0	3	4	2	2	3	4
Javier Vazquez	0	0	9.00	1	1	0	5	7	5	5	2	6
Felix Heredia	0	0	54.00	1	0	0	0	2	2	2	0	0
Totals	**3**	**1**	**3.73**	**4**	**4**	**0**	**41**	**43**	**17**	**17**	**7**	**28**

MINNESOTA

Player, Pos.	AVG	G	AB	R	H	2B	3B	HR	RBI	BB	SO	SB
Michael Cuddyer, 2b	.467	4	15	1	7	0	0	0	2	0	3	0
Torii Hunter, cf	.353	4	17	5	6	1	0	1	2	1	1	2
Cristian Guzman, ss	.333	4	15	2	5	0	0	0	0	2	3	1
Matthew LeCroy, ph	.333	3	3	0	1	0	0	0	0	1	1	0
Corey Koskie, 3b	.308	4	13	2	4	1	0	0	2	3	2	0
Jacque Jones, rf	.300	4	20	3	6	1	0	2	2	0	6	0
Lew Ford, dh-lf	.273	3	11	1	3	1	0	0	0	2	2	1
Henry Blanco, c	.250	4	8	1	2	0	0	1	2	0	2	0
Justin Morneau, 1b	.235	4	17	1	4	2	0	0	2	0	3	0
Shannon Stewart, lf-dh	.200	4	20	1	4	0	0	0	2	0	2	0
Jason Kubel, dh-ph	.143	2	7	0	1	1	0	0	0	0	0	0
Jose Offerman, ph	.000	3	3	0	0	0	0	0	1	0	0	0
Pat Borders, c	.000	2	2	0	0	0	0	0	0	0	1	0
Luis Rivas, 2b	.000	3	1	0	0	0	0	0	0	0	0	0
Totals	**.283**	**4**	**152**	**17**	**43**	**7**	**0**	**4**	**17**	**7**	**28**	**4**

Pitcher	W	L	ERA	G	GS	SV	IP	H	R	ER	BB	SO
Grant Balfour	0	0	0.00	2	0	0	3	0	0	0	0	2
Jesse Crain	0	0	0.00	1	0	0	1	0	0	0	0	0
Johan Santana	1	0	0.75	2	2	0	12	14	1	1	4	12
Terry Mulholland	0	0	3.00	1	0	0	3	3	1	1	0	0
Joe Nathan	0	1	3.60	3	0	1	5	2	2	2	5	6
Kyle Lohse	0	1	4.50	1	0	0	2	1	1	1	0	3
Brad Radke	0	0	7.11	1	1	0	6	8	5	5	3	0
J.C. Romero	0	0	9.00	2	0	0	1	0	1	1	1	1
Juan Rincon	0	0	10.80	3	0	0	3	4	4	4	2	5
Carlos Silva	0	1	10.80	1	1	0	5	10	6	6	0	1
Totals	**1**	**3**	**4.65**	**4**	**4**	**1**	**41**	**43**	**21**	**21**	**15**	**30**

SCORE BY INNINGS

Minnesota	321	131	023 001—17
New York	133	014	240 012—21

E—Blanco, Guzman, Jeter. **DP**—Minnesota 9, New York 4. **LOB**—Minnesota 28, New York 30. **CS**—Cuddyer 2, Ford, Jones, Rodriguez, Sheffield. **SF**—Blanco, Hunter, Koskie, Matsui, Stewart. **HBP**—Ford (by Heredia), Ford (by Vazquez), Koskie (by Heredia), Koskie (by Vazquez), Olerud (by Santana). **IBB**—Matsui (by Nathan), Sheffield (by Nathan). **WP**—Gordon, Lohse, Rincon. **PB**—Borders, Posada.

BOSTON vs. ANAHEIM
COMPOSITE BOX

CHAMPIONSHIP SERIES
BOSTON vs. NEW YORK
COMPOSITE BOX

BOSTON

Player, Pos.	AVG	G	AB	R	H	2B	3B	HR	RBI	BB	SO	SB
David Ortiz, dh	.545	3	11	4	6	2	0	1	4	5	2	0
Doug Mientkiewicz,1b-pr	.500	3	4	0	2	0	0	0	1	0	0	0
Johnny Damon, cf	.467	3	15	4	7	1	0	0	0	1	2	3
Manny Ramirez, lf	.385	3	13	3	5	2	0	1	7	1	4	0
Bill Mueller, 3b	.333	3	12	3	4	0	0	0	0	1	1	0
Kevin Millar, 1b	.300	3	10	2	3	0	0	1	4	1	1	0
Trot Nixon, rf	.250	2	8	0	2	0	0	0	2	2	1	0
Gabe Kapler, rf	.200	2	5	2	1	0	0	0	0	0	0	0
Jason Varitek, c	.167	3	12	3	2	0	0	1	2	2	5	0
Orlando Cabrera, ss	.154	3	13	1	2	1	0	0	3	2	2	0
Mark Bellhorn, 2b	.091	3	11	2	1	0	0	0	0	5	4	0
Kevin Youkilis, 3b	.000	1	2	0	0	0	0	0	0	0	1	0
Pokey Reese, 2b-pr	.000	3	0	1	0	0	0	0	0	0	0	0
Dave Roberts, pr	.000	0	0	0	0	0	0	0	0	0	0	0
Totals	.302	3	116	25	35	6	0	4	23	20	23	3

Pitcher	W	L	ERA	G	GS	SV	IP	H	R	ER	BB	SO
Alan Embree	0	0	0.00	2	0	0	1	0	0	0	1	0
Derek Lowe	1	0	0.00	1	0	0	1	1	0	0	1	0
Keith Foulke	0	0	0.00	2	0	1	3	2	0	0	1	5
Curt Schilling	1	0	2.70	1	1	0	7	9	3	2	2	4
Bronson Arroyo	0	0	3.00	1	1	0	6	3	2	2	2	7
Pedro Martinez	1	0	3.86	1	1	0	7	6	3	3	2	6
Mike Timlin	0	0	9.00	3	0	0	3	3	3	3	1	5
Mike Myers	0	0	27.00	2	0	0	0	0	1	1	1	1
Totals	3	0	3.54	3	3	1	28	24	12	11	11	28

ANAHEIM

Player, Pos.	AVG	G	AB	R	H	2B	3B	HR	RBI	BB	SO	SB
Darin Erstad, 1b	.500	3	10	2	5	1	0	1	2	3	1	0
Troy Glaus, dh	.364	3	11	3	4	2	0	2	3	2	4	0
David Eckstein, ss	.333	3	12	2	4	0	0	0	0	0	1	0
Jose Molina, c	.333	2	3	2	1	0	0	0	0	2	0	0
Jeff DaVanon, lf	.200	3	10	1	2	0	0	0	0	2	1	0
Vladimir Guerrero, rf	.167	3	12	1	2	0	0	1	6	2	4	0
Bengie Molina, c	.167	3	6	0	1	0	0	0	0	0	2	0
Garret Anderson, cf	.154	3	13	1	2	0	0	0	0	0	3	0
Chone Figgins, 3b-2b	.143	3	14	0	2	0	0	0	0	0	5	1
Dallas McPherson, 3b-ph	.111	3	9	0	1	0	0	0	1	0	4	0
Alfredo Amezaga, 2b	.000	2	2	0	0	0	0	0	0	0	2	0
Curtis Pride, ph	.000	2	2	0	0	0	0	0	0	0	1	0
Casey Kotchman, ph	.000	2	1	0	0	0	0	0	0	0	0	0
Adam Riggs, ph-lf	.000	2	1	0	0	0	0	0	0	0	0	0
Totals	.226	3	106	12	24	3	0	4	12	11	28	1

Pitcher	W	L	ERA	G	GS	SV	IP	H	R	ER	BB	SO
Kevin Gregg	0	0	0.00	1	0	0	2	3	0	0	1	0
Francisco Rodriguez	0	2	3.86	2	0	0	5	4	2	2	3	5
Bartolo Colon	0	0	4.50	1	1	0	6	7	3	3	3	3
Ramon Ortiz	0	0	4.50	1	0	0	2	1	1	1	1	0
Scot Shields	0	0	6.00	2	0	0	3	5	2	2	2	3
Kelvim Escobar	0	0	8.10	1	1	0	3	5	5	3	5	4
Jarrod Washburn	0	1	10.80	2	1	0	3	6	8	4	3	3
Brendan Donnelly	0	0	10.80	2	0	0	3	3	4	4	2	5
Totals	0	3	5.86	3	3	0	28	35	24	18	20	23

SCORE BY INNINGS
Boston	112	(10)12	114	2—25
Anaheim	010	220	700	0—12

E—Figgins 2, Eckstein, Schilling. DP—Anaheim 2, Boston 2. LOB—Anaheim 24, Boston 31. CS—DaVanon. SF—Ramirez 2. HBP—Erstad (by Martinez), Figgins (by Arroyo), Varitek (by Rodriguez). IBB—Guerrero (by Foulke), Nixon (by Shields), D. Ortiz (by Donnelly), D. Ortiz (by R. Ortiz), D. Ortiz (by Rodriguez), Varitek (by Donnelly), Varitek (by Escobar). WP—Rodriguez 2, Donnelly, Gregg.

BOSTON

Player, Pos.	AVG	G	AB	R	H	2B	3B	HR	RBI	BB	SO	SB
Doug Mientkiewicz, 1b-ph	.500	4	4	0	2	1	0	0	0	0	1	0
David Ortiz, dh	.387	7	31	6	12	0	1	3	11	4	7	0
Orlando Cabrera, ss	.379	7	29	5	11	2	0	0	5	3	5	1
Gabe Kapler, pr-rf	.333	2	3	0	1	0	0	0	0	0	0	0
Jason Varitek, c	.321	7	28	5	9	1	0	2	7	2	6	0
Manny Ramirez, lf	.300	7	30	3	9	1	0	0	5	4	0	0
Bill Mueller, 3b	.267	7	30	4	8	1	0	0	1	2	1	0
Kevin Millar, 1b	.250	7	24	4	6	3	0	0	2	5	4	0
Trot Nixon, rf	.207	7	29	4	6	1	0	1	3	0	5	0
Mark Bellhorn, 2b	.192	7	26	3	5	2	0	2	4	5	11	0
Johnny Damon, cf	.171	7	35	5	6	0	0	2	7	2	8	2
Pokey Reese, 2b-pr	.000	3	1	0	0	0	0	0	0	0	1	0
Doug Mirabelli, c	.000	1	1	0	0	0	0	0	0	0	0	0
Dave Roberts, pr	.000	2	0	2	0	0	0	0	0	0	0	1
Total	.277	7	271	41	75	12	1	10	40	28	53	4

Pitcher	W	L	ERA	G	GS	SV	IP	H	R	ER	BB	SO
Keith Foulke	0	0	0.00	5	0	1	6	1	0	0	6	8
Derek Lowe	1	0	3.18	2	2	0	11	7	4	4	1	6
Alan Embree	0	0	3.86	6	0	0	5	9	2	2	1	2
Ramiro Mendoza	0	0	4.50	2	0	0	2	2	1	1	0	1
Mike Timlin	0	0	4.76	5	0	0	6	10	3	3	5	2
Pedro Martinez	0	0	6.23	3	2	0	13	14	9	9	9	14
Curt Schilling	1	1	6.30	2	2	0	10	10	7	7	2	5
Mike Myers	0	0	7.71	3	0	0	2	5	2	2	1	4
Tim Wakefield	1	0	8.59	3	0	0	7	9	7	7	3	6
Curtis Leskanic	1	0	10.13	3	0	0	3	3	3	3	3	2
Bronson Arroyo	0	0	15.75	3	1	0	4	8	7	7	2	3
Total	4	3	5.87	7	7	1	69	78	45	45	33	51

NEW YORK

Player, Pos.	AVG	G	AB	R	H	2B	3B	HR	RBI	BB	SO	SB
Hideki Matsui, lf	.412	7	34	9	14	6	1	2	10	2	4	0
Ruben Sierra, dh	.333	5	21	1	7	1	1	0	2	3	4	0
Gary Sheffield, rf	.333	7	30	7	10	3	0	1	5	6	8	0
Bernie Williams, cf	.306	7	36	4	11	2	1	2	10	0	5	0
Kenny Lofton, dh	.300	3	10	1	3	0	0	1	2	2	3	1
Miguel Cairo, 2b	.280	7	25	4	7	3	0	0	0	2	4	1
Jorge Posada, c	.259	7	27	4	7	1	0	0	2	7	1	0
Alex Rodriguez, 3b	.258	7	31	8	8	2	0	2	5	4	6	0
Derek Jeter, ss	.200	7	30	5	6	1	0	0	5	6	2	1
John Olerud, 1b	.167	4	12	1	2	0	0	0	1	2	1	0
Tony Clark, 1b	.143	5	21	0	3	1	0	0	1	0	9	0
Bubba Crosby, pr-rf	.000	1	0	1	0	0	0	0	0	0	0	0
Totals	.282	7	277	45	78	20	3	9	44	33	51	3

Pitcher	W	L	ERA	G	GS	SV	IP	H	R	ER	BB	SO
Felix Heredia	0	0	0.00	3	0	0	1	1	0	0	0	1
Mariano Rivera	0	0	1.29	5	0	2	7	6	1	1	2	6
Esteban Loaiza	0	1	1.42	2	0	0	6	5	1	1	3	5
Tanyon Sturtze	0	0	2.70	4	0	0	3	2	1	1	2	2
Jon Lieber	1	1	3.14	2	2	0	14	12	5	5	1	5
Mike Mussina	1	0	4.26	2	2	0	13	10	6	6	2	15
Paul Quantrill	0	1	5.40	4	0	0	3	8	2	2	0	2
Orlando Hernandez	0	0	5.40	1	1	0	5	3	3	3	5	6
Tom Gordon	0	0	8.10	6	0	0	7	10	6	6	2	3
Javier Vazquez	1	0	9.95	2	0	0	6	9	7	7	6	5
Kevin Brown	0	1	21.60	2	2	0	3	9	9	8	4	2
Totals	3	4	5.17	7	7	2	70	75	41	40	28	53

SCORE BY INNINGS
Boston	482	630	762	002	01—41
New York	61(10)	529	732	000	00—45

E—Jeter 2, Clark, Loaiza, Ramirez. DP—Boston 4, New York 9. LOB—Boston 53, New York 69. CS—Damon, Ortiz. SF—Cabrera, Posada, Varitek. HBP—Cairo (by Foulke), Cairo (by Lowe), Cairo (by Martinez), Cairo (by Mendoza), Mueller (by Lieber), Posada (by Mendoza), Rodriguez 2 (by Martinez 2). IBB—Posada 2 (by Wakefield 2), Sheffield (by Embree). WP—Brown, Gordon, Lieber, Timlin. PB—Varitek 3, Posada.

BY AARON FITT

While much of America was fixated on the dramatic playoff series between Boston and New York, there was another series going on that lacked nothing for drama. Those who missed the 2004 National League Championship Series between the Cardinals and Astros missed something special.

Home-field advantage never seemed so important as it did in the 2004 NLCS. All seven games were won by the home team—and Game Seven was played in Busch Stadium, the Cardinals' reward for winning a league-high 105 games. Of course, Houston felt pretty confident with future Hall of Famer Roger Clemens on the mound in the decisive game, against Jeff Suppan.

"That makes me feel pretty good, because he's been in these situations a lot," Houston center fielder Carlos Beltran said. "He can deal with the pressure; he'll be fine."

He wasn't done yet
Roger Clemens helped the Astros get within a game of the World Series

He sure started out fine. The 42-year-old Clemens, who had come out of retirement during the offseason at the urging of good friend Andy Pettitte, limited the vaunted St. Louis offense to one run through the first five innings, and the Astros had a 2-1 lead. But the Cardinals finally broke through in the sixth, scoring three runs on an RBI double by Albert Pujols and a two-run homer by Scott Rolen. Just as important, center fielder Jim Edmonds denied Houston the chance to build a big lead early. He made a remarkable, sprawling catch on a Brad Ausmus drive in the second inning to save at least two runs. It was one of the great postseason catches in baseball history.

"If anyone thinks that play Jim Edmonds made didn't turn the game around a little bit, (they weren't) really paying attention," Astros first baseman Jeff Bagwell said. "There's two runs right there. They make the plays—that's why they're so good."

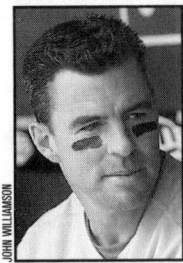

Jim Edmonds

Both teams made quite a few memorable plays in the series. After St. Louis took the opener, 10-7, thanks to a six-run sixth inning, Albert Pujols and Scott Rolen propelled the Cardinals to a 6-4 win in Game Two with back-to-back solo homers in the eighth inning, breaking a tie. St. Louis scored all its runs via the long ball—Rolen had two in the game—overpowering Beltran, who hit his sixth home run in seven postseason games in the first inning.

As the series shifted to Houston with the Cardinals up two games to none, many in the media pronounced the Astros dead, the series all but over. That couldn't have been farther from the truth. Houston had its two Cy Young contenders—Clemens and Roy Oswalt—scheduled to pitch the third and fourth games, and the Astros had only lost once in their last 20 games at Minute Maid Park, counting the Division Series.

Clemens did his part, throwing seven strong innings of four-hit, two-run ball in a 5-2 Houston win. Dominant closer Brad Lidge struck out five in two innings of work to pick up the save.

Then things really started getting interesting. Oswalt struggled somewhat in Game Four, allowing five earned runs in six innings, but Beltran saved the day. With the score tied at 5 in the seventh inning, Beltran blasted a Julian Tavarez pitch down by his ankles out of the park, and then Lidge picked up another two-inning save.

"Barry Bonds is the best hitter in baseball, but I don't think Barry would have hit that pitch," said Tavarez, who broke two bones in his non-throwing hand when he took out his frustration on a dugout phone after the Beltran homer. Had Houston gone on to win the series, Beltran would certainly have taken MVP honors. He ended up breaking an LCS record with 12 runs and tying an LCS record with four home runs. In just two playoff series, he tied records for single-postseason homers (8), RBIs (14), total bases (47) and extra-base hits (11), and he set a new record with 21 runs.

In Game Five, as much of the nation watched a five-hour, 49-minute marathon between Boston and New York, the Astros took care of business in a tidy 2 hours, 23 minutes. Those who opted to tune in to the NLCS were treated to brilliant pitching performances by Houston's Brandon Backe and St. Louis' Woody Williams. The 26-year-old Backe took a no-hitter through 5⅔ innings—the longest no-hit stretch to start an NLCS game ever—before Tony Womack singled in the sixth. That was the last hit of the game for the Cardinals, as Backe went eight innings and allowed no runs.

Yet Backe left the game with a no-decision, because

MAJOR LEAGUES

NO-DIVISION FORMAT

	PENNANT	PCT	GA
1901	Pittsburgh	.647	1½
1902	Pittsburgh	.741	27½
1903	Pittsburgh	.650	6½
1904	New York	.693	13
1905	New York	.686	9
1906	Chicago	.763	20
1907	Chicago	.704	17
1908	Chicago	.643	1
1909	Pittsburgh	.724	6½
1910	Chicago	.675	13
1911	New York	.647	7½
1912	New York	.682	10
1913	New York	.664	12½
1914	Boston	.614	10½
1915	Philadelphia	.592	7
1916	Brooklyn	.610	2½
1917	New York	.636	10
1918	Chicago	.651	10½
1919	Cincinnati	.686	9
1920	Brooklyn	.604	7
1921	New York	.614	4
1922	New York	.604	7
1923	New York	.621	4½

	PENNANT	PCT	GA
1924	New York	.608	1½
1925	Pittsburgh	.621	8½
1926	St. Louis	.578	2
1927	Pittsburgh	.610	1½
1928	St. Louis	.617	2
1929	Chicago	.645	10½
1930	St. Louis	.597	2
1931	St. Louis	.656	13
1932	Chicago	.584	4
1933	New York	.599	5
1934	St. Louis	.621	2
1935	Chicago	.649	4
1936	New York	.597	5
1937	New York	.625	3
1938	Chicago	.586	2
1939	Cincinnati	.630	4½
1940	Cincinnati	.654	12
1941	Brooklyn	.649	2½
1942	St. Louis	.688	2
1943	St. Louis	.682	18
1944	St. Louis	.682	14½
1945	Chicago	.636	3
1946	St. Louis	.628	2

	PENNANT	PCT	GA
1947	Brooklyn	.610	5
1948	Boston	.595	6½
1949	Brooklyn	.630	1
1950	Philadelphia	.591	2
1951	New York	.624	1
1952	Brooklyn	.627	4½
1953	Brooklyn	.682	13
1954	New York	.630	5
1955	Brooklyn	.641	13½
1956	Brooklyn	.604	1
1957	Milwaukee	.617	8
1958	Milwaukee	.597	8
1959	Los Angeles	.564	2
1960	Pittsburgh	.617	7
1961	Cincinnati	.604	4
1962	San Francisco	.624	1
1963	Los Angeles	.611	6
1964	St. Louis	.574	1
1965	Los Angeles	.599	2
1966	Los Angeles	.586	1½
1967	St. Louis	.627	10½
1968	St. Louis	.599	9

TWO-DIVISION FORMAT

	EAST	PCT	GA	WEST	PCT	GA	PENNANT		MVP
1969	New York	.617	8	Atlanta	.574	3	New York	3-0	Willie McCovey, 1b, San Francisco
1970	Pittsburgh	.549	5	Cincinnati	.630	14½	Cincinnati	3-0	Johnny Bench, c, Cincinnati
1971	Pittsburgh	.599	7	San Francisco	.556	1	Pittsburgh	3-1	Joe Torre, 3b, St. Louis
1972	Pittsburgh	.619	11	Cincinnati	.617	10½	Cincinnati	3-2	Johnny Bench, c, Cincinnati
1973	New York	.509	1½	Cincinnati	.611	3½	New York	3-2	Pete Rose, of, Cincinnati
1974	Pittsburgh	.543	1½	Los Angeles	.630	4	Los Angeles	3-1	Steve Garvey, 1b, Los Angeles
1975	Pittsburgh	.571	6½	Cincinnati	.667	20	Cincinnati	3-0	Joe Morgan, 2b, Cincinnati
1976	Philadelphia	.623	9	Cincinnati	.630	10	Cincinnati	3-0	Joe Morgan, 2b, Cincinnati
1977	Philadelphia	.623	5	Los Angeles	.605	10	Los Angeles	3-1	George Foster, of, Cincinnati
1978	Philadelphia	.556	1½	Los Angeles	.586	2½	Los Angeles	3-1	Dave Parker, of, Pittsburgh
1979	Pittsburgh	.605	2	Cincinnati	.559	1½	Pittsburgh	3-0	Hernandez, St. Louis; Stargell, Pittsburgh
1980	Philadelphia	.562	1	Houston	.571	1	Philadelphia	3-2	Mike Schmidt, 3b, Philadelphia
1981	Montreal*	.566	½	Los Angeles**	.632	½	Los Angeles	3-2	Mike Schmidt, 3b, Philadelphia
	Philadelphia	.618	1½	Houston	.623	1			
1982	St. Louis	.568	3	Atlanta	.549	1	St. Louis	3-0	Dale Murphy, of, Atlanta
1983	Philadelphia	.556	6	Los Angeles	.562	3	Philadelphia	3-1	Dale Murphy, of, Atlanta
1984	Chicago	.596	6½	San Diego	.568	12	San Diego	3-2	Ryne Sandberg, 2b, Chicago
1985	St. Louis	.623	3	Los Angeles	.586	5½	St. Louis	4-2	Willie McGee, of, St. Louis
1986	New York	.667	21½	Houston	.593	10	New York	4-2	Mike Schmidt, 3b, Philadelphia
1987	St. Louis	.586	3	San Francisco	.556	6	St. Louis	4-3	Andre Dawson, of, Chicago
1988	New York	.625	15	Los Angeles	.584	7	Los Angeles	4-3	Kirk Gibson, of, Los Angeles
1989	Chicago	.571	6	San Francisco	.568	3	San Francisco	4-1	Kevin Mitchell, of, San Francisco
1990	Pittsburgh	.586	4	Cincinnati	.562	5	Cincinnati	4-2	Barry Bonds, of, Pittsburgh
1991	Pittsburgh	.605	14	Atlanta	.580	1	Atlanta	4-3	Terry Pendleton, 3b, Atlanta
1992	Pittsburgh	.593	9	Atlanta	.605	8	Atlanta	4-3	Barry Bonds, of, Pittsburgh
1993	Philadelphia	.599	3	Atlanta	.642	1	Philadelphia	4-2	Barry Bonds, of, San Francisco

*Won second half; defeated Philadelphia 3-2 in best-of-5 playoff. **Won first half; defeated Houston 3-2 in best-of-5 playoff.

THREE-DIVISION FORMAT/WILD CARD

	EAST	PCT	GA	CENTRAL	PCT	GA	WEST	PCT	GA	WILD CARD	PCT
1994	Montreal	.649	6	Cincinnati	.593	½	Los Angeles	.509	3½	None	
	PENNANT: None (season incomplete)						MVP: Jeff Bagwell, 1b, Houston				
1995	Atlanta	.625	21	Cincinnati	.590	9	Los Angeles	.542	1	Colorado (West)	.535
	PENNANT: Atlanta def. Cincinnati, 4-2						MVP: Barry Larkin, ss, Cincinnati				
1996	Atlanta	.593	8	St. Louis	.543	6	San Diego	.562	1	Los Angeles (West)	.556
	PENNANT: Atlanta def. St. Louis 4-3						MVP: Ken Caminiti, 3b, Houston				
1997	Atlanta	.623	9	Houston	.519	5	San Francisco	.556	2	Florida (East)	.568
	PENNANT: Florida def. Atlanta 4-2						MVP: Larry Walker, of, Colorado				
1998	Atlanta	.654	18	Houston	.630	12½	San Diego	.605	9½	Chicago (Central)	.552
	PENNANT: San Diego def. Atlanta 4-2						MVP: Sammy Sosa, of, Chicago				
1999	Atlanta	.636	6½	Houston	.599	1½	Arizona	.617	14	New York (East)	.595
	PENNANT: Atlanta def. New York 4-2						MVP: Chipper Jones, 3b, Atlanta				
2000	Atlanta	.586	½	St. Louis	.586	10	San Francisco	.599	11	New York (East)	.580
	PENNANT: New York def. St. Louis 4-1						MVP: Jeff Kent, 2b, San Francisco				
2001	Atlanta	543	2	Houston	574	—	Arizona	.568	2	St. Louis (Central)	.574
	PENNANT: Arizona def. Atlanta 4-1						MVP: Barry Bonds, of, San Francisco				
2002	Atlanta	.631	19	St. Louis	.599	13	Arizona	.605	2½	San Francisco (West)	.590
	PENNANT: San Francisco def. St. Louis 4-1						MVP: Barry Bonds, of, San Francisco				
2003	Atlanta	.623	10	Chicago	.543	1	San Francisco	.621	15½	Florida (East)	.562
	PENNANT: Florida def. Chicago 4-3						MVP: Barry Bonds, of, San Francisco				
2004	Atlanta	.593	10	St. Louis	.648	13	Los Angeles	.574	2	Houston (Central)	.568
	PENNANT: St. Louis def. Houston 4-3										

Page	EAST	W	L	Pct.	GB	Manager(s)	General Mangaer	Attendance	Avg.	Last Penn.
71	Atlanta Braves	96	66	.593	—	Bobby Cox	John Schuerholz	2,322,565	29,399	1999
210	Philadelphia Phillies	86	76	.531	10	Larry Bowa/Gary Varsho	Ed Wade	3,206,532	40,589	1993
137	Florida Marlins	83	79	.512	13	Jack McKeon	Larry Beinfest	1,723,105	22,091	2003
195	New York Mets	71	91	.438	25	Art Howe	Jim Duquette	2,318,321	28,979	2000
179	Montreal Expos	67	95	.414	29	Frank Robinson	Omar Minaya	748,550	9,356	None

Page	CENTRAL	W	L	Pct.	GB	Manager(s)	General Manager	Attendance	Avg.	Last Penn.
224	St. Louis Cardinals	105	57	.648	—	Tony La Russa	Walt Jocketty	3,048,427	37,634	1987
144	*Houston Astros	92	70	.568	13	Jimy Williams/Phil Garner	Gerry Hunsicker	3,087,872	38,121	None
101	Chicago Cubs	89	73	.549	16	Dusty Baker	Jim Hendry	3,170,184	39,138	1945
108	Cincinnati Reds	76	86	.469	29	Dave Miley	Dan O'Brien	2,287,250	28,237	1990
217	Pittsburgh Pirates	72	89	.447	32½	Lloyd McClendon	Dave Littlefield	1,583,031	21,107	1979
165	Milwaukee Brewers	67	94	.416	37½	Ned Yost	Doug Melvin	2,062,382	25,461	None

Page	WEST	W	L	Pct.	GB	Manager(s)	General Manager	Attendance	Avg.	Last Penn.
158	Los Angeles Dodgers	93	69	.574	—	Jim Tracy	Paul DePodesta	3,488,283	43,065	1988
240	San Francisco Giants	91	71	.562	2	Felipe Alou	Brian Sabean	3,258,864	40,232	2002
232	San Diego Padres	87	75	.537	6	Bruce Bochy	Kevin Towers	3,040,046	37,531	1998
123	Colorado Rockies	68	94	.420	25	Clint Hurdle	Dan O'Dowd	2,338,069	29,595	None
64	Arizona Diamondbacks	51	111	.315	42	Bob Brenly/Al Pedrique	Joe Garagiola Jr.	2,519,560	31,105	2001

*Won wild-card playoff berth

NOTE: Teams' individual batting, pitching and fielding statistics can be found on page indicated in lefthand column

Williams was just as terrific. He also yielded just one hit and no runs in his seven innings of work, leaving the game in the hands of the bullpens. The unhittable Lidge shut down St. Louis in the top of the ninth, but Cardinals closer Jason Isringhausen ran into some trouble in the bottom of the inning, allowing a leadoff single to Beltran, who stole second. St. Louis decided to walk Lance Berkman to pitch to second baseman Jeff Kent. Big mistake. Kent crushed a first-pitch cutter to left field, giving the Astros a 3-0 win and bringing them one win away from their first World Series appearance.

"A no-doubter, walkoff, how-you-doin'," Houston third baseman Morgan Ensberg said. "This is what baseball's all about."

In a series chock full of drama, there was really only one fitting way to follow the walkoff home run in Game Five: with a walkoff home run in Game Six. Edmonds delivered just such an encore with the score tied at four in the 12th inning. His two-run blast against Dan Miceli marked the first time in NLCS history that consecutive games ended with walkoff homers.

It wouldn't even have been necessary if the Cardinals had held onto the lead that series MVP Albert Pujols staked them to with a two-run homer in the first and a double and run in the third. But Isringhausen blew his second straight save, giving up a game-tying RBI single to Bagwell. Lidge threw three more incredible scoreless innings, but he had to exit eventually, and the Cardinals capitalized.

"I was just trying to get a hit, actually," Edmonds said. "I wasn't trying to go deep."

Leading the attack
Albert Pujols was the heart of the Cardinals offense

LARRY GOREN

But he did, setting the stage for Game Seven. The ALCS had ended the previous night, so the deciding Houston-St. Louis game was played where it belonged to be: in prime time, on center stage.

It's In The Cards

Few preseason prognosticators even pegged the Cardinals to win their own division in 2004, let alone 105 games and the National League pennant. But that's just what St. Louis did, on the strength of the NL's highest-scoring offense and its most spectacular and consistent defense.

The Cardinals drew much of their success from the fearsome heart of their batting order. No. 3 hitter Pujols continued the greatest beginning to a major league career since Ted Williams and Joe DiMaggio. Pujols went .331-46-123 with 84 walks and just 52 strikeouts in 2004, becoming the third player ever to drive in 100 runs in his first four seasons and the only player of all time to hit at least 30 home runs in each of his first four years. If not for San Francisco's Bonds, Pujols likely would have been the favorite for league MVP honors. He certainly made the Cardinals glad they extended his contract for seven years, $100 million after his .359-43-124 campaign in 2003.

"It was a typical case of a guy that got a big contract and hasn't let up at all," Cardinals general manager Walt Jocketty said. "He's trying to find ways to get better."

Of course, it always helps to have Rolen and Edmonds hitting behind you. Cleanup hitter Rolen batted .314-34-124, despite hitting just three homers in just 35 September at-bats because of a strained calf. Rolen's terrif-

NL YEAR-BY-YEAR BATTING LEADERS
SINCE 1926

Year	Batting Average	Home Runs	RBIs
1926	Bubbles Hargrave, Cincinnati .353	Hack Wilson, Chicago 21	Jim Bottomley, St. Louis 120
1927	Paul Waner, Pittsburgh .380	Two tied at 30	Paul Waner, Pittsburgh 131
1928	Rogers Hornsby, St. Louis .370	Two tied at 31	Jim Bottomley, St. Louis 136
1929	Lefty O'Doul, Philadelphia .398	Chuck Klein, Philadelphia 43	Hack Wilson, Chicago 159
1930	Bill Terry, New York .401	Hack Wilson, Chicago 56	Hack Wilson, Chicago 190
1931	Chick Hafey, St. Louis .349	Chuck Klein, Philadelphia 31	Chuck Klein, Philadelphia 121
1932	Lefty O'Doul, Brooklyn .368	Two tied at 38	Frank Hurst, Philadelphia 143
1933	Chuck Klein, Philadelphia .368	Chuck Klein, Philadelphia 28	Chuck Klein, Philadelphia 120
1934	Paul Waner, Pittsburgh .362	Two tied at 35	Mel Ott, New York 135
1935	Arky Vaughan, Pittsburgh .385	Wally Berger, Boston 34	Wally Berger, Boston 130
1936	Paul Waner, Pittsburgh .373	Mel Ott, New York 33	Joe Medwick, St. Louis 138
1937	Joe Medwick, St. Louis .374	Two tied at 31	Joe Medwick, St. Louis 154
1938	Ernie Lombardi, Cincinnati .342	Mel Ott, New York 36	Joe Medwick, St. Louis 122
1939	Johnny Mize, St. Louis .349	Johnny Mize, St. Louis 28	Frank McCormick, Cincinnati 128
1940	Debs Garms, Pittsburgh .355	Johnny Mize, St. Louis 43	Johnny Mize, St. Louis 137
1941	Pete Reiser, Brooklyn .343	Dolf Camilli, Brooklyn 34	Dolf Camilli, Brooklyn 120
1942	Ernie Lombardi, Boston .330	Mel Ott, New York 30	Johnny Mize, New York 110
1943	Stan Musial, St. Louis .357	Bill Nicholson, Chicago 29	Bill Nicholson, Chicago 128
1944	Dixie Walker, Brooklyn .357	Bill Nicholson, Chicago 33	Bill Nicholson, Chicago 122
1945	Phil Cavarretta, Chicago .355	Tommy Holmes, Boston 28	Dixie Walker, Brooklyn 124
1946	Stan Musial, St. Louis .365	Ralph Kiner, Pittsburgh 23	Enos Slaughter, St. Louis 130
1947	Harry Walker, St.Louis-Phil. .363	Two tied at 51	Johnny Mize, New York 138
1948	Stan Musial, St. Louis .376	Two tied at 40	Stan Musial, St. Louis 131
1949	Jackie Robinson, Brooklyn .342	Ralph Kiner, Pittsburgh 54	Ralph Kiner, Pittsburgh 127
1950	Stan Musial, St. Louis .346	Ralph Kiner, Pittsburgh 47	Del Ennis, Philadelphia 126
1951	Stan Musial, St. Louis .355	Ralph Kiner, Pittsburgh 42	Monte Irvin, New York 121
1952	Stan Musial, St. Louis .336	Two tied at 37	Hank Sauer, Chicago 121
1953	Carl Furillo, Brooklyn .344	Eddie Mathews, Milwaukee 47	Roy Campanella, Brooklyn 142
1954	Willie Mays, New York .345	Ted Kluszewski, Cincinnati 49	Ted Kluszewski, Cincinnati 141
1955	Richie Ashburn, Philadelphia .338	Willie Mays, New York 51	Duke Snider, Brooklyn 136
1956	Hank Aaron, Milwaukee .328	Duke Snider, Brooklyn 43	Stan Musial, St. Louis 109
1957	Stan Musial, St. Louis .351	Hank Aaron, Milwaukee 44	Hank Aaron, Milwaukee 132
1958	Richie Ashburn, Philadelphia .350	Ernie Banks, Chicago 47	Ernie Banks, Chicago 129
1959	Hank Aaron, Milwaukee .355	Eddie Mathews, Milwaukee 46	Ernie Banks, Chicago 143
1960	Dick Groat, Pittsburgh .325	Ernie Banks, Chicago 41	Hank Aaron, Milwaukee 126
1961	Roberto Clemente, Pittsburgh .351	Orlando Cepeda, San Francisco 46	Orlando Cepeda, San Francisco 142
1962	Tommy Davis, Los Angeles .346	Willie Mays, San Francisco 49	Tommy Davis, Los Angeles 153
1963	Tommy Davis, Los Angeles .326	Two tied at 44	Hank Aaron, Milwaukee 130
1964	Roberto Clemente, Pittsburgh .339	Willie Mays, San Francisco 47	Ken Boyer, St. Louis 119
1965	Roberto Clemente, Pittsburgh .329	Willie Mays, San Francisco 52	Deron Johnson, Cincinnati 130
1966	Matty Alou, Pittsburgh .342	Hank Aaron, Atlanta 44	Hank Aaron, Atlanta 127
1967	Roberto Clemente, Pittsburgh .357	Hank Aaron, Atlanta 39	Orlando Cepeda, San Francisco 111
1968	Pete Rose, Cincinnati .335	Willie McCovey, San Francisco 36	Willie McCovey, San Francisco 105
1969	Pete Rose, Cincinnati .348	Willie McCovey, San Francisco 45	Willie McCovey, San Francisco 126
1970	Rico Carty, Atlanta .366	Johnny Bench, Cincinnati 45	Johnny Bench, Cincinnati 148
1971	Joe Torre, St. Louis .363	Willie Stargell, Pittsburgh 48	Joe Torre, St. Louis 137
1972	Billy Williams, Chicago .333	Johnny Bench, Cincinnati 40	Johnny Bench, Cincinnati 125
1973	Pete Rose, Cincinnati .338	Willie Stargell, Pittsburgh 44	Willie Stargell, Pittsburgh 119
1974	Ralph Garr, Atlanta .353	Mike Schmidt, Philadelphia 36	Johnny Bench, Cincinnati 129
1975	Bill Madlock, Chicago .354	Mike Schmidt, Philadelphia 38	Greg Luzinski, Philadelphia 120
1976	Bill Madlock, Chicago .339	Mike Schmidt, Philadelphia 38	George Foster, Cincinnati 121
1977	Dave Parker, Pittsburgh .338	George Foster, Cincinnati 52	George Foster, Cincinnati 149
1978	Dave Parker, Pittsburgh .334	George Foster, Cincinnati 40	George Foster, Cincinnati 120
1979	Keith Hernandez, St. Louis .344	Dave Kingman, Chicago 48	Dave Winfield, San Diego 118
1980	Bill Buckner, Chicago .324	Mike Schmidt, Philadelphia 48	Mike Schmidt, Philadelphia 121
1981	Bill Madlock, Pittsburgh .341	Mike Schmidt, Philadelphia 31	Mike Schmidt, Philadelphia 91
1982	Al Oliver, Montreal .331	Dave Kingman, New York 37	Two tied at 109
1983	Bill Madlock, Pittsburgh .323	Mike Schmidt, Philadelphia 40	Dale Murphy, Atlanta 121
1984	Tony Gwynn, San Diego .351	Two tied at 36	Two tied at 106
1985	Willie McGee, St. Louis .353	Dale Murphy, Atlanta 37	Dave Parker, Cincinnati 125
1986	Tim Raines, Montreal .334	Mike Schmidt, Philadelphia 37	Mike Schmidt, Philadelphia 119
1987	Tony Gwynn, San Diego .370	Andre Dawson, Chicago 49	Andre Dawson, Chicago 137
1988	Tony Gwynn, San Diego .313	Darryl Strawberry, New York 39	Will Clark, San Francisco 109
1989	Tony Gwynn, San Diego .336	Kevin Mitchell, San Francisco 47	Kevin Mitchell, San Francisco 125
1990	Willie McGee, St. Louis .335	Ryne Sandberg, Chicago 40	Matt Williams, San Francisco 122
1991	Terry Pendleton, Atlanta .319	Howard Johnson, New York 38	Howard Johnson, New York 117
1992	Gary Sheffield, San Diego .330	Fred McGriff, San Diego 35	Darren Daulton, Philadelphia 109
1993	Andres Galarraga, Colorado .370	Barry Bonds, San Francisco 46	Barry Bonds, San Francisco 123
1994	Tony Gwynn, San Diego .394	Matt Williams, San Francisco 43	Jeff Bagwell, Houston 116
1995	Tony Gwynn, San Diego .368	Dante Bichette, Colorado 40	Dante Bichette, Colorado 128
1996	Tony Gwynn, San Diego .353	Andres Galarraga, Colorado 47	Andres Galarraga, Colorado 150
1997	Tony Gwynn, San Diego .372	Larry Walker, Colorado 49	Andres Galarraga, Colorado 140
1998	Larry Walker, Colorado .363	Mark McGwire, St. Louis 70	Sammy Sosa, Chicago 158
1999	Larry Walker, Colorado .379	Mark McGwire, St. Louis 65	Mark McGwire, St. Louis 147
2000	Todd Helton, Colorado .372	Sammy Sosa, Chicago 50	Todd Helton, Colorado 147
2001	Larry Walker, Colorado .350	Barry Bonds, San Francisco 73	Sammy Sosa, Chicago 160
2002	Barry Bonds, San Francisco .370	Sammy Sosa, Chicago 49	Lance Berkman, Houston 128
2003	Albert Pujols, St. Louis .359	Jim Thome, Philadelphia 47	Preston Wilson, Colorado 141
2004	Barry Bonds, San Francisco .362	Adrian Beltre, Los Angeles 48	Vinny Castilla, Colorado 131

ic season at the plate, combined with his trademark Gold Glove defense at third base, made him a contender for the MVP award, too—at least until the final weeks.

Edmonds, another perennial Gold Glover, had the best offensive season of his excellent career, hitting .301-42-111 to tie his career high in homers and set a new career mark for RBIs. After an early-August trade, Edmonds was joined in the St. Louis outfield by five-time all-star and former NL MVP Larry Walker, making the Cardinals' offense even more dangerous. They ranked first in the NL in runs (855), batting average (.278) and on-base plus slugging percentage (.804) and ranked second in home runs (214, one behind league-leader Philadelphia).

And the Cardinals' pitching more than held its own. The staff ERA (3.75) was second best in the league, thanks to a good bullpen and consistent starters. Suppan, acquired before the season began, led the team with 16 wins, while the resurgent Chris Carpenter led the starting rotation with a 3.46 ERA to go along with 15 wins. Matt Morris, Jason Marquis and Williams each totaled double-digit wins, while Isringhausen (47 saves) anchored the deep pen.

All the ingredients added up to a jaunt to the NL Central title, which the Cardinals won by 13 games over another playoff team, wild-card entry Houston.

Astro-nomical Shakeup In The Central

After signing free-agent lefthander Pettitte in the off-season, Houston became a favorite to win the division. When Pettitte convinced Clemens to come back (under special conditions that would allow Clemens to travel with the team on his terms so he could spend as much time as possible with his Houston-based family), the Astros' chances looked even brighter.

But Pettitte was never fully healthy after injuring his left elbow while batting during his first game of the season. He made just 15 starts, going 6-4, 3.90, before shutting it down for the season and having surgery on a torn flexor tendon in the elbow. When Wade Miller injured his rotator cuff in June, the Astros were reeling, despite the terrific season by Clemens, who started the All-Star Game in Houston en route to an 18-4, 2.98 season.

The Astros were a disappointing 44-44 at the break, and manager Jimy Williams was fired and replaced by Phil Garner. His energy, combined with the June trade for Beltran from Kansas City, proved pivotal in Houston's turnaround. The Astros traded closer Octavio Dotel to get Beltran, allowing Lidge to slide into the closer's role, where he was nothing short of spectacular. Lidge set a major league record for most strikeouts in a season by a reliever with 157 in 95 innings.

GEORGE GOJKOVICH

Phil Garner

But the Astros' turnaround was not immediate; on August 15 they were four games under .500 and trailing five teams in the wild card race. Then they went on an amazing run, winning 36 of their final 46 games—including 18 in a row at home—to clinch a playoff berth on the final day of the season.

One of the teams Houston leapfrogged in that dash for the wild card was fellow NL Central contender Chicago. Like the Astros, the Cubs were a preseason favorite to contend for the World Series, boasting a deep pitching

BILL NICHOLS

Smashing the record books
Barry Bonds became just the third player to hit 700 home runs

staff and a potent offense. But righthander Mark Prior missed the first two months of the season with a sore Achillies tendon and elbow, and never got comfortable upon his return, going 6-4, 4.02 in 119 innings. Fellow ace Kerry Wood missed significant time with triceps tendonitis and finished 8-9, 3.72.

But Carlos Zambrano (16-8, 2.75) emerged as one of the NL's top pitchers, Matt Clement and free-agent signee Greg Maddux were steady, and seven Cubs had 15 or more home runs, led by Moises Alou's 39. Chicago only got stronger at the trading deadline, acquiring star Red Sox shortstop Nomar Garciaparra, who hit .297-4-20 in 165 at-bats for Chicago.

And there the Cubs were, 1½ games up in the wild-card race with nine games to play, six of them against the weakling Mets and Reds. But in the first of those nine games, New York rookie Victor Diaz hit a two-out, two-strike, three-run homer in the bottom of the ninth inning to send the send the game into extra innings, where the Cubs fell. They lost six of their next seven after that and were eliminated from postseason contention by the Braves in the second-to-last game of the year.

"I'm not used to my teams playing like this," Cubs manager Dusty Baker said. "Next year, it isn't going to be like this. It will be a better team. I expect it."

It might be better, depending on how the Cubs handle the situation with superstar Sammy Sosa, who left the meaningless final game of the year without dressing and then lashed out at Baker.

"I'm tired of being blamed by Dusty Baker for all the failures of this club," Sosa told the Chicago Sun-Times. "I'm always the guy they are going to blame. They blame me for not going to the World Series last year. They blame me for not going to the playoffs this year. I'm tired of it."

Dodgers Squeak By Giants

It's hard to believe, but Bonds might have actually had his best season in 2004—at the age of 40—but it still

NL YEAR-BY-YEAR PITCHING LEADERS
SINCE 1926

Year	Wins	ERA	Strikeouts
1926	Four tied at 20	Ray Kremer, Pittsburgh 2.61	Dazzy Vance, Brooklyn 140
1927	Charlie Root, Chicago 26	Ray Kremer, Pittsburgh 2.47	Dazzy Vance, Brooklyn 184
1928	Two tied at 25	Dazzy Vance, Brooklyn 2.09	Dazzy Vance, Brooklyn 200
1929	Pat Malone, Chicago 22	Bill Walker, New York 3.08	Pat Malone, Chicago 166
1930	Two tied at 20	Dazzy Vance, Brooklyn 2.61	Bill Hallahan, St. Louis 177
1931	Three tied at 19	Bill Walker, New York 2.26	Bill Hallahan, St. Louis 159
1932	Lon Warneke, Chicago 22	Lon Warneke, Chicago 2.37	Dizzy Dean, St. Louis 191
1933	Carl Hubbell, New York 23	Carl Hubbell, New York 1.66	Dizzy Dean, St. Louis 199
1934	Dizzy Dean, St. Louis 30	Carl Hubbell, New York 2.30	Dizzy Dean, St. Louis 195
1935	Dizzy Dean, St. Louis 28	Cy Blanton, Pittsburgh 2.59	Dizzy Dean, St. Louis 182
1936	Carl Hubbell, New York 26	Carl Hubbell, New York 2.31	Van Lingle Mungo, Brooklyn 238
1937	Carl Hubbell, New York 22	Jim Turner, Boston 2.38	Carl Hubbell, New York 159
1938	Bill Lee, Chicago 22	Bill Lee, Chicago 2.66	Clay Bryant, Chicago 135
1939	Bucky Walters, Cincinnati 27	Bucky Walters, Cincinnati 2.29	Two tied at 137
1940	Bucky Walters, Cincinnati 22	Bucky Walters, Cincinnati 2.48	Kirby Higbe, Philadelphia 137
1941	Two tied at 22	Elmer Riddle, Cincinnati 2.24	Johnny Vander Meer, Cincinnati 202
1942	Mort Cooper, St. Louis 22	Mort Cooper, St. Louis 1.77	Johnny Vander Meer, Cincinnati 186
1943	Three tied at 21	Howie Pollet, St. Louis 1.75	Johnny Vander Meer, Cincinnati 174
1944	Bucky Walters, Cincinnati 23	Ed Heusser, Cincinnati 2.38	Bill Voiselle, New York 161
1945	Red Barrett, Boston-St.Louis 23	Hank Borowy, Chicago 2.14	Preacher Roe, Pittsburgh 148
1946	Howie Pollet, St. Louis 21	Howie Pollet, St. Louis 2.10	John Schmitz, Chicago 135
1947	Ewell Blackwell, Cincinnati 22	Warren Spahn, Boston 2.33	Ewell Blackwell, Cincinnati 193
1948	Johnny Sain, Boston 24	Harry Brecheen, St. Louis 2.24	Harry Brecheen, St. Louis 149
1949	Warren Spahn, Boston 21	Dave Koslo, New York 2.50	Warren Spahn, Boston 151
1950	Warren Spahn, Boston 21	Jim Hearn, St.Louis-New York 2.49	Warren Spahn, Boston 191
1951	Two tied at 23	Chet Nichols, Boston 2.88	Two tied at 164
1952	Robin Roberts, Philadelphia 28	Hoyt Wilhelm, New York 2.43	Warren Spahn, Boston 183
1953	Two tied at 23	Warren Spahn, Milwaukee 2.10	Robin Roberts, Philadelphia 198
1954	Robin Roberts, Philadelphia 23	John Antonelli, New York 2.29	Robin Roberts, Philadelphia 185
1955	Robin Roberts, Philadelphia 23	Bob Friend, Pittsburgh 2.84	Sam Jones, Chicago 198
1956	Don Newcombe, Brooklyn 27	Lew Burdette, Milwaukee 2.71	Sam Jones, Chicago 176
1957	Warren Spahn, Milwaukee 21	Johnny Podres, Brooklyn 2.66	Jack Sanford, Philadelphia 188
1958	Two tied at 22	Stu Miller, San Francisco 2.47	Sam Jones, St. Louis 225
1959	Three tied at 21	Sam Jones, San Francisco 2.82	Don Drysdale, Los Angeles 242
1960	Two tied at 21	Mike McCormick, San Francisco 2.70	Don Drysdale, Los Angeles 246
1961	Two tied at 21	Warren Spahn, Milwaukee 3.01	Sandy Koufax, Los Angeles 269
1962	Don Drysdale, Los Angeles 25	Sandy Koufax, Los Angeles 2.54	Don Drysdale, Los Angeles 232
1963	Two tied at 25	Sandy Koufax, Los Angeles 1.88	Sandy Koufax, Los Angeles 306
1964	Larry Jackson, Chicago 24	Sandy Koufax, Los Angeles 1.74	Bob Veale, Pittsburgh 250
1965	Sandy Koufax, Los Angeles 26	Sandy Koufax, Los Angeles 2.04	Sandy Koufax, Los Angeles 382
1966	Sandy Koufax, Los Angeles 27	Sandy Koufax, Los Angeles 1.73	Sandy Koufax, Los Angeles 317
1967	Mike McCormick, S.F. 22	Phil Niekro, Atlanta 1.87	Jim Bunning, Philadelphia 253
1968	Juan Marichal, San Francisco 26	Bob Gibson, St. Louis 1.12	Bob Gibson, St. Louis 268
1969	Tom Seaver, New York 25	Juan Marichal, San Francisco 2.10	Ferguson Jenkins, Chicago 273
1970	Two tied at 23	Tom Seaver, New York 2.81	Tom Seaver, New York 283
1971	Ferguson Jenkins, Chicago 24	Tom Seaver, New York 1.76	Tom Seaver, New York 289
1972	Steve Carlton, Philadelphia 27	Steve Carlton, Philadelphia 1.98	Steve Carlton, Philadelphia 310
1973	Ron Bryant, San Francisco 24	Tom Seaver, New York 2.08	Tom Seaver, New York 251
1974	Two tied at 20	Buzz Capra, Atlanta 2.28	Steve Carlton, Philadelphia 240
1975	Tom Seaver, New York 23	Randy Jones, San Diego 2.24	Tom Seaver, New York 243
1976	Randy Jones, San Diego 22	John Denny, St. Louis 2.52	Tom Seaver, New York 235
1977	Steve Carlton, Philadelphia 23	John Candelaria, Pittsburgh 2.34	Phil Niekro, Atlanta 252
1978	Gaylord Perry, San Diego 21	Craig Swan, New York 2.43	J.R. Richard, Houston 303
1979	Two tied at 21	J.R. Richard, Houston 2.71	J.R. Richard, Houston 313
1980	Steve Carlton, Philadelphia 24	Don Sutton, Los Angeles 2.21	Steve Carlton, Philadelphia 286
1981	Tom Seaver, Cincinnati 14	Nolan Ryan, Houston 1.69	Fernando Valenzuela, L.A. 180
1982	Steve Carlton, Philadelphia 23	Steve Rogers, Montreal 2.40	Steve Carlton, Philadelphia 286
1983	John Denny, Philadelphia 19	Atlee Hammaker, San Francisco 2.25	Steve Carlton, Philadelphia 275
1984	Joaquin Andujar, St. Louis 20	Alejandro Pena, Los Angeles 2.48	Dwight Gooden, New York 276
1985	Dwight Gooden, New York 24	Dwight Gooden, New York 1.53	Dwight Gooden, New York 268
1986	Fernando Valenzuela, L.A. 21	Mike Scott, Houston 2.22	Mike Scott, Houston 306
1987	Rick Sutcliffe, Chicago 18	Nolan Ryan, Houston 2.76	Nolan Ryan, Houston 270
1988	Two tied at 23	Joe Magrane, St. Louis 2.18	Nolan Ryan, Houston 228
1989	Mike Scott, Houston 20	Scott Garrelts, San Francisco 2.28	Jose DeLeon, St. Louis 201
1990	Doug Drabek, Pittsburgh 22	Danny Darwin, Houston 2.21	David Cone, New York 233
1991	Two tied at 20	Dennis Martinez, Montreal 2.39	David Cone, New York 241
1992	Two tied at 20	Bill Swift, San Francisco 2.08	John Smoltz, Atlanta 215
1993	Two tied at 22	Greg Maddux, Atlanta 2.36	Jose Rijo, Cincinnati 227
1994	Two tied at 16	Greg Maddux, Atlanta 1.56	Andy Benes, San Diego 189
1995	Greg Maddux, Atlanta 19	Greg Maddux, Atlanta 1.63	Hideo Nomo, Los Angeles 236
1996	John Smoltz, Atlanta 24	Kevin Brown, Florida 1.89	John Smoltz, Atlanta 276
1997	Denny Neagle, Atlanta 20	Pedro Martinez, Montreal 1.90	Curt Schilling, Philadelphia 319
1998	Tom Glavine, Atlanta 20	Greg Maddux, Atlanta 2.22	Curt Schilling, Philadelphia 300
1999	Mike Hampton, Houston 22	Randy Johnson, Arizona 2.48	Randy Johnson, Arizona 364
2000	Tom Glavine, Atlanta 21	Kevin Brown, Los Angeles 2.58	Randy Johnson, Arizona 347
2001	Two tied at 22	Randy Johnson, Arizona 2.49	Randy Johnson, Arizona 372
2002	Randy Johnson, Arizona 24	Randy Johnson, Arizona 2.32	Randy Johnson, Arizona 334
2003	Russ Ortiz, Atlanta 21	Jason Schmidt, San Francisco 2.34	Kerry Wood, Chicago 266
2004	Roy Oswalt, Houston 20	Jake Peavy, San Diego 2.27	Randy Johnson, Arizona 290

wasn't enough to get San Francisco back to the playoffs. Bonds hit .362-45-101 despite only logging 373 official at-bats because he was walked an astounding 232 times, 120 of them intentional. He also hit his 660th career home run, tying him with his godfather Willie Mays for third place on the all-time list, and his 700th home run.

But the Giants just didn't have the depth to get back to the post-season. Marquis Grissom exploded with a .279-22-90 season, and Pedro Feliz broke out with a .276-22-84 campaign, but they still weren't exactly intimidating at the plate, and San Francisco had little else in the way of offense.

BILL NICHOLS

Jason Schmidt

Righthanded ace Jason Schmidt was an easy favorite for the NL Cy Young award—until he faltered down the stretch, going 2-2, 5.53 in September to finish 18-7, 3.20 overall. And San Francisco just didn't have any other frontline pitchers to pick him up.

Yet somehow, the Giants were in contention for the NL West title until a series against the Dodgers the final weekend of the season, and they were alive in the wild card race until the season's final day.

The fatal blow to the Giants was the Dodgers' biggest moment of the season. If the Giants held onto their three-run, ninth-inning lead over Los Angeles in the second-to-last game of the season, they could have tied for the division crown with a win the next day. But San Fransisco's lack of a dominant closer in lieu of the injured Robb Nen came back to haunt them at the worst possible moment. The Dodgers tied the game at three and still had the bases loaded for Steve Finley. He ended the game and captured the division title in the most dramatic way: with a walkoff grand slam.

"This is the perfect ending," Dodgers outfielder Shawn Green said. "The game sums up our team and our season. We are scrappy. We come from behind. Just when everything thinks we're out of it, we get the job done. It couldn't be more of a storybook finish."

LARRY GOREN

Steve Finley

It sure made rookie GM Paul DePodesta look good. He took a major risk at the trading deadline, with the Dodgers holding a 2½ game lead in the division over San Diego and 4½ over the Giants. But DePodesta was not convinced his team was built for October, so he traded clubhouse leader Paul Lo Duca, outfielder Juan Encarnacion and one of baseball's best setup men, righthander Guillermo Mota, to Florida for starter Brad Penny, first baseman Hee Seop Choi and minor leaguer Bill Murphy. And DePodesta wasn't done. Next he traded Murphy and two other top prospects to Arizona for Finley and catcher Brent Mayne. It was Finley's experience in big games that made him particularly appealing.

"Steve Finley adds yet another power bat to our lineup and a terrific defensive player," DePodesta said. "In addition, Steve provides a strong veteran presence as well as a significant postseason resume."

And the Dodgers could afford to lose Mota, partly because they still boasted the best closer in the game. Eric

Gagne entered 2004 having converted 63 consecutive save chances, and he extended that streak to 84 before blowing his first save in nearly two years. He finished the season 7-3, 2.19 with 45 saves in 47 chances. Though Penny was lost to injury before the playoffs, the Dodgers felt good about their chances in the Division Series against St. Louis with Gagne at the back of a pitching staff anchored by Odalis Perez (7-6, 3.25) and the rejuvenated Jose Lima (13-5, 4.07).

But the Cardinals took the first two games of the series at Busch Stadium, before Lima—signed to a minor league deal in spring training—twirled a five-hit, complete-game shutout in Game Three at Dodger Stadium. It gave L.A. hope, but Pujols erased that hope in Game Four with four RBIs, as the Cards ended the Dodgers' season, 6-2.

Braves Keep On Truckin'

It was supposed to be the year Atlanta finally missed the playoffs. The Braves won their 12th straight NL East title in 2003, but that was sure to be the swan song. After

MAJOR LEAGUES

NATIONAL LEAGUE
DEPARTMENT LEADERS

BATTING

GAMES
Juan Pierre, Marlins	162
Steve Finley, Diamondbacks/Dodgers	162
Derrek Lee, Cubs	161
Adam Dunn, Reds	161
Lance Berkman, Astros	160
Brad Wilkerson, Expos	160
Miguel Cabrera, Marlins	160

AT-BATS
Juan Pierre, Marlins	678
Cesar Izturis, Dodgers	670
Jimmy Rollins, Phillies	657
Jack Wilson, Pirates	652
Scott Podsednik, Brewers	640

RUNS
Albert Pujols, Cardinals	133
Barry Bonds, Giants	129
Jimmy Rollins, Phillies	119
Bobby Abreu, Phillies	118
J.D. Drew, Braves	118

HITS
Juan Pierre, Marlins	221
Mark Loretta, Padres	208
Jack Wilson, Pirates	201
Adrian Beltre, Dodgers	200
Albert Pujols, Cardinals	196

TOTAL BASES
Albert Pujols, Cardinals	389
Adrian Beltre, Dodgers	376
Todd Helton, Rockies	339
Moises Alou, Cubs	335
Adam Dunn, Reds	323

SINGLES
Juan Pierre, Marlins	184
Cesar Izturis, Dodgers	148
Jason Kendall, Pirates	148
Luis Castillo, Marlins	143
Mark Loretta, Padres	143

DOUBLES
Lyle Overbay, Brewers	53
Albert Pujols, Cardinals	51
Todd Helton, Rockies	49
Bobby Abreu, Phillies	47
Craig Biggio, Astros	47
Mark Loretta, Padres	47

TRIPLES
Juan Pierre, Marlins	12

Juan Pierre: 221 hits

Adrian Beltre: 48 home runs

Jimmy Rollins, Phillies	12
Jack Wilson, Pirates	12
Cesar Izturis, Dodgers	9
Four tied at	8

HOME RUNS
Adrian Beltre, Dodgers	48
Adam Dunn, Reds	46
Albert Pujols, Cardinals	46
Barry Bonds, Giants	45
Jim Edmonds, Cardinals	42
Jim Thome, Phillies	42

HOME RUN RATIO
(At-bats per home run)
Barry Bonds, Giants	8.3
Jim Edmonds, Cardinals	11.9
Jim Thome, Phillies	12.1
Adam Dunn, Reds	12.3
Adrian Beltre, Dodgers	12.5

RUNS BATTED IN
Vinny Castilla, Rockies	131
Scott Rolen, Cardinals	124
Albert Pujols, Cardinals	123
Adrian Beltre, Dodgers	121
Miguel Cabrera, Marlins	112

SACRIFICE BUNTS
Royce Clayton, Rockies	24
Adam Everett, Astros	22
Kris Benson, Pirates/Mets	15
Livan Hernandez, Expos	15
Juan Pierre, Marlins	15

SACRIFICE FLIES
Mark Loretta, Padres	16
Jeff Kent, Astros	11
Tony Batista, Expos	10
Edgar Renteria, Cardinals	10
Brian Giles, Padres	9
Albert Pujols, Cardinals	9

HIT BY PITCHES
Craig Wilson, Pirates	30
Jason LaRue, Reds	24
Jason Kendall, Pirates	19
Alex Cora, Dodgers	18
Craig Biggio, Astros	15
A.J. Pierzynski, Giants	15

WALKS
Barry Bonds, Giants	232
Bobby Abreu, Phillies	127
Lance Berkman, Astros	127
Todd Helton, Rockies	127
J.D. Drew, Braves	118

INTENTIONAL WALKS
Barry Bonds, Giants	120
Jim Thome, Phillies	26
Todd Helton, Rockies	19
Lance Berkman, Astros	14
Mike Piazza, Mets	14

STOLEN BASES
Scott Podsednik, Brewers	70
Juan Pierre, Marlins	45
Bobby Abreu, Phillies	40
Ryan Freel, Reds	37
Dave Roberts, Dodgers	33

CAUGHT STEALING
Juan Pierre, Marlins	24
Scott Podsednik, Brewers	13
Milton Bradley, Dodgers	11
Edgar Renteria, Cardinals	11
Ryan Freel, Reds	10

STRIKEOUTS
Adam Dunn, Reds	195
Craig Wilson, Pirates	169
Corey Patterson, Cubs	168
Geoff Jenkins, Brewers	152
Brad Wilkerson, Expos	152

TOUGHEST TO STRIKE OUT
(At-bats per SO)
Juan Pierre, Marlins	19.4
A.J. Pierzynski, Giants	17.4
Sean Casey, Reds	15.9
Jason Kendall, Pirates	14.0
Mark Loretta, Padres	13.8

GROUNDED INTO DOUBLE PLAYS
A.J. Pierzynski, Giants	27
Aramis Ramirez, Cubs	25
Andruw Jones, Braves	24
Jeff Kent, Astros	23
Vinny Castilla, Rockies	22
Marquis Grissom, Giants	22
Paul Lo Duca, Marlins	22

HITTING STREAKS
Jeff Kent, Astros	25
J.D. Drew, Braves	22
Danny Bautista, Diamondbacks	21
Jason Kendall, Pirates	20
Jose Vidro, Expos	19

MULTIPLE-HIT GAMES
Juan Pierre, Marlins	70
Mark Loretta, Padres	68
Adrian Beltre, Dodgers	63
Cesar Izturis, Dodgers	58
Sean Casey, Reds	57

ON-BASE PERCENTAGE
Barry Bonds, Giants	.609
Todd Helton, Rockies	.469
Lance Berkman, Astros	.450
J.D. Drew, Braves	.436
Bobby Abreu, Phillies	.428

SLUGGING PERCENTAGE
Barry Bonds, Giants	.812
Albert Pujols, Cardinals	.657
Jim Edmonds, Cardinals	.643
Adrian Beltre, Dodgers	.629
Todd Helton, Rockies	.620

PITCHING

WINS
Roy Oswalt, Astros	20
Roger Clemens, Astros	18
Carl Pavano, Marlins	18

Jason Schmidt, Giants 18
Four tied at 16

LOSSES
Brandon Webb, Diamondbacks 16
Casey Fossum, Diamondbacks 15
Livan Hernandez, Expos 15
Five tied at 14

WINNING PERCENTAGE
Roger Clemens, Astros .... .818
Chris Carpenter, Cardinals .... .750
Jose Lima, Dodgers .... .722
Jason Schmidt, Giants .... .720
Jake Peavy, Padres .... .714

GAMES
Jim Brower, Giants 89
Ray King, Cardinals 86
Rheal Cormier, Phillies 84
Chris Reitsma, Braves 84
Salomon Torres, Pirates 84

GAMES STARTED
Livan Hernandez, Expos 35
Randy Johnson, Diamondbacks 35
Roy Oswalt, Astros 35
Brandon Webb, Diamondbacks 35
Seven tied at 34

COMPLETE GAMES
Livan Hernandez, Expos 9
Cory Lidle, Reds/Phillies 5
Ben Sheets, Brewers 5
Randy Johnson, Diamondbacks 4
Jason Schmidt, Giants 4

SHUTOUTS
Cory Lidle, Reds/Phillies 3
Jason Schmidt, Giants 3
Six tied at 2

GAMES FINISHED
Jason Isringhausen, Cardinals 66
Jose Mesa, Pirates 65
John Smoltz, Braves 61
Shawn Chacon, Rockies 60
Braden Looper, Mets 60

SAVES
Armando Benitez, Marlins 47
Jason Isringhausen, Cardinals 47
Eric Gagne, Dodgers 45
John Smoltz, Braves 44
Jose Mesa, Pirates 43

INNINGS PITCHED
Livan Hernandez, Expos 255
Randy Johnson, Diamondbacks 246
Roy Oswalt, Astros 237
Ben Sheets, Brewers 237
Jason Schmidt, Giants 225

HITS ALLOWED
Jason Jennings, Rockies 241
Livan Hernandez, Expos 234
Roy Oswalt, Astros 233
Brian Lawrence, Padres 226
Kirk Rueter, Giants 225

RUNS ALLOWED
Shawn Estes, Rockies 133
Jason Jennings, Rockies 125
Cory Lidle, Reds/Phillies 123
Matt Morris, Cardinals 116
Adam Eaton, Padres 113
Brett Myers, Phillies 113

HOME RUNS ALLOWED
Eric Milton, Phillies 43
Greg Maddux, Cubs 35
Matt Morris, Cardinals 35
José Lima, Dodgers 33
Ismael Valdez, Padres/Marlins 33

WALKS
Brandon Webb, Diamondbacks 119
Russ Ortiz, Braves 112
Shawn Estes, Rockies 105
Jason Jennings, Rockies 101
Kazuhisa Ishii, Dodgers 98

FEWEST WALKS PER 9 INNINGS
David Wells, Padres 0.92
Ben Sheets, Brewers 1.22
Greg Maddux, Cubs 1.40
Randy Johnson, Diamondbacks 1.61
Jose Lima, Dodgers 1.80

HIT BATSMEN
Carlos Zambrano, Cubs 20
Jerome Williams, Giants 17
Jeff Weaver, Dodgers 14
Sun-Woo Kim, Expos 13
Matt Clement, Cubs 12

STRIKEOUTS
Randy Johnson, Diamondbacks 290
Ben Sheets, Brewers 264
Jason Schmidt, Giants 251
Oliver Perez, Pirates 239
Roger Clemens, Astros 218

STRIKEOUTS PER 9 INNINGS
Oliver Perez, Pirates 10.97
Randy Johnson, Diamondbacks 10.62
Jason Schmidt, Giants 10.04
Ben Sheets, Brewers 10.03
Matt Clement, Cubs 9.45

PICKOFFS
Chris Capuano, Brewers 6
Shawn Estes, Rockies 5
Jeff Fassero, Diamondbacks 5
Joe Kennedy, Rockies 5
Al Leiter, Mets 5
Dontrelle Willis, Marlins 5

WILD PITCHES
Brandon Webb, Diamondbacks 17
Matt Clement, Cubs 14
Woody Williams, Cardinals 12
Jim Brower, Giants 10
Brett Tomko, Giants 10

BALKS
Carl Pavano, Marlins 3
Shawn Estes, Rockies 2
Casey Fossum, Diamondbacks 2
Mike Hampton, Braves 2
Odalis Perez, Dodgers 2
Horacio Ramirez, Braves 2
Steve Trachsel, Mets 2
Carlos Zambrano, Cubs 2

OPPONENT BATTING AVERAGE
Randy Johnson, Diamondbacks .... .197
Jason Schmidt, Giants .... .202
Oliver Perez, Pirates .... .207
Roger Clemens, Astros .... .217
Al Leiter, Mets .... .218

FIELDING

PITCHER
PCT Steve Trachsel, Mets 1.000

Randy Johnson: 290 strikeouts

PO	Three tied at	21
A	Livan Hernandez, Expos	61
E	Brandon Webb, Diamondbacks	5
TC	Livan Hernandez, Expos	84
DP	Livan Hernandez, Expos	10

CATCHER
PCT	Mike Matheny, Cardinals	.999
PO	Michael Barrett, Cubs	1035
A	Jason Kendall, Pirates	78
E	Jason Kendall, Pirates	10
TC	Michael Barrett, Cubs	1088
DP	Brian Schneider, Expos	16
PB	Jason LaRue, Reds	15

FIRST BASE
PCT	Todd Helton, Rockies	.997
PO	Albert Pujols, Cardinals	1458
A	Todd Helton, Rockies	144
E	Shea Hillenbrand, Diamondbacks	13
	Phil Nevin, Padres	13
TC	Albert Pujols, Cardinals	1582
DP	Albert Pujols, Cardinals	136

SECOND BASE
PCT	Placido Polanco, Phillies	.995
PO	D'Angelo Jimenez, Reds	297
A	Mark Loretta, Padres	451
E	Ray Durham, Giants	16
TC	Mark Loretta, Padres	749
DP	Mark Loretta, Padres	101

THIRD BASE
PCT	Vinny Castilla, Rockies	.987
PO	Vinny Castilla, Rockies	124
A	Scott Rolen, Cardinals	325
E	Chad Tracy, Diamondbacks	25
TC	Adrian Beltre, Dodgers	452
DP	Tony Batista, Expos	35

SHORTSTOP
PCT	Royce Clayton, Rockies	.986
PO	Cesar Izturis, Dodgers	234
	Jack Wilson, Pirates	234
A	Jack Wilson, Pirates	492
E	Rafael Furcal, Braves	24
TC	Jack Wilson, Pirates	743
DP	Jack Wilson, Pirates	129

OUTFIELD
PCT	Corey Patterson, Cubs	.997
PO	Scott Podsednik, Brewers	392
A	Richard Hidalgo, Astros/Mets	14
	Juan Rivera, Expos	14
E	Craig Biggio, Astros	9
	Miguel Cabrera, Marlins	9
TC	Andruw Jones, Braves	402
DP	Endy Chavez, Expos	5
	Corey Patterson, Cubs	5

Roy Oswalt: 20 wins

2004 NATIONAL LEAGUE STATISTICS

CLUB BATTING

	AVG	G	AB	R	H	2B	3B	HR	BB	SO	SB
St. Louis	.278	162	5555	855	1544	319	24	214	548	1085	111
Colorado	.275	162	5577	833	1531	331	34	202	568	1181	44
San Diego	.273	162	5573	768	1521	304	32	139	566	910	52
San Francisco	.270	162	5546	850	1500	314	33	183	705	874	43
Atlanta	.270	162	5570	803	1503	304	37	178	587	1158	86
Chicago	.268	162	5628	789	1508	308	29	235	489	1080	66
Philadelphia	.267	162	5643	840	1505	303	23	215	645	1133	100
Houston	.267	162	5468	803	1458	294	36	187	590	999	89
Florida	.264	162	5486	718	1447	275	32	148	499	968	96
Los Angeles	.262	162	5542	761	1450	226	30	203	536	1092	102
Pittsburgh	.260	161	5483	680	1428	267	39	142	415	1066	63
Arizona	.253	162	5544	615	1401	295	38	135	441	1022	53
Cincinnati	.250	162	5518	750	1380	287	28	194	599	1335	77
New York	.249	162	5532	684	1376	289	20	185	512	1159	107
Montreal	.249	162	5474	635	1361	276	27	151	496	925	109
Milwaukee	.248	161	5483	634	1358	295	32	135	540	1312	138

CLUB PITCHING

	ERA	G	CG	SV	IP	H	HR	R	ER	BB	SO
Atlanta	3.74	162	4	48	1450	1503	178	803	603	587	1158
St. Louis	3.75	162	4	57	1454	1544	214	855	605	548	1085
Chicago	3.81	162	3	42	1465	1508	235	789	621	489	1080
Los Angeles	4.01	162	2	51	1453	1450	203	761	647	536	1092
San Diego	4.03	162	3	44	1441	1521	139	768	645	566	910
Houston	4.05	162	2	47	1443	1458	187	803	650	590	999
New York	4.09	162	2	31	1449	1376	185	684	658	512	1159
Florida	4.10	162	6	53	1439	1447	148	718	655	499	968
Milwaukee	4.24	161	6	42	1442	1358	135	634	679	540	1312
Pittsburgh	4.29	161	3	46	1428	1428	142	680	680	415	1066
San Francisco	4.29	162	8	46	1457	1500	183	850	695	705	874
Montreal	4.33	162	11	31	1447	1361	151	635	696	496	925
Philadelphia	4.45	162	4	43	1463	1505	215	840	724	645	1133
Arizona	4.98	162	5	33	1436	1401	135	615	794	441	1022
Cincinnati	5.19	162	5	47	1444	1380	194	750	832	599	1335
Colorado	5.54	162	3	36	1435	1531	202	833	883	568	1181

CLUB FIELDING

	PCT	PO	A	E	DP		PCT	PO	A	E	DP
Los Angeles	.988	4360	1666	73	145	Houston	.983	4329	1620	101	136
Philadelphia	.987	4388	1629	81	142	Pittsburgh	.983	4284	1693	103	189
Chicago	.986	4396	1579	86	126	San Diego	.982	4323	1601	108	146
Colorado	.986	4306	1824	89	161	Atlanta	.981	4350	1792	116	171
Florida	.986	4317	1604	86	153	Cincinnati	.981	4331	1641	113	123
St. Louis	.985	4361	1834	97	154	Milwaukee	.981	4326	1592	117	132
Montreal	.984	4341	1700	99	172	New York	.978	4347	1747	137	144
San Francisco	.984	4371	1739	101	153	Arizona	.977	4308	1717	139	144

INDIVIDUAL BATTING LEADERS
(Minimum 502 Plate Appearances)

	AVG	G	AB	R	H	2B	3B	HR	RBI	BB	SO	SB
Bonds, Barry, San Francisco	.362	147	373	129	135	27	3	45	101	232	41	6
Helton, Todd, Colorado	.347	154	547	115	190	49	2	32	96	127	72	3
Loretta, Mark, San Diego	.335	154	620	108	208	47	2	16	76	58	45	5
Beltre, Adrian, Los Angeles	.334	156	598	104	200	32	0	48	121	53	87	7
Pujols, Albert, St. Louis	.331	154	592	133	196	51	2	46	123	84	52	5
Pierre, Juan, Florida	.326	162	678	100	221	22	12	3	49	45	35	45
Casey, Sean, Cincinnati	.324	146	571	101	185	44	2	24	99	46	36	2
Kendall, Jason, Pittsburgh	.319	147	574	86	183	32	0	3	51	60	41	11
Ramirez, Aramis, Chicago	.318	145	547	99	174	32	1	36	103	49	62	0
Berkman, Lance, Houston	.316	160	544	104	172	40	3	30	106	127	101	9

INDIVIDUAL PITCHING LEADERS
(Minimum 162 Innings)

	W	L	ERA	G	GS	CG	SV	IP	H	R	ER	BB	SO
Peavy, Jake, San Diego	15	6	2.27	27	27	0	0	166	146	49	42	53	173
Johnson, Randy, Arizona	16	14	2.60	35	35	4	0	246	177	88	71	44	290
Sheets, Ben, Milwaukee	12	14	2.70	34	34	5	0	237	201	85	71	32	264
Zambrano, Carlos, Chicago	16	8	2.75	31	31	1	0	210	174	73	64	81	188
Clemens, Roger, Houston	18	4	2.98	33	33	0	0	214	169	76	71	79	218
Perez, Oliver, Pittsburgh	12	10	2.98	30	30	2	0	196	145	71	65	81	239
Pavano, Carl, Florida	18	8	3.00	31	31	2	0	222	212	80	74	49	139
Schmidt, Jason, San Francisco	18	7	3.20	32	32	4	0	225	165	84	80	77	251
Leiter, Al, New York	10	8	3.21	30	30	0	0	174	138	65	62	97	117
Perez, Odalis, Los Angeles	7	6	3.25	31	31	0	0	196	180	76	71	44	128

Todd Helton: .347 average

Jake Peavy: 2.27 ERA

Ben Sheets: 264 strikeouts

all, Gary Sheffield had bolted to the Yankees after the season, Greg Maddux had signed with the Cubs, and Javy Lopez had left for the Orioles. The once-vaunted Atlanta staff was now populated with less familiar names like John Thomson, Jaret Wright and Russ Ortiz.

But when the dust cleared on the 2004 season, there were the Braves atop the division for a 13th consecutive year, and it wasn't even close. Atlanta won the division by 10 games over the second-place Phillies and 13 games over the defending World Series champion Marlins. But for the third straight year, the Braves went down in the division series.

Of course, it was a credit to manager Bobby Cox and his staff that Atlanta even got there. They got as much as could possibly have been expected out of their pitching, including Wright (15-8, 3.28), Thomson (14-8, 3.72) and Ortiz (15-9, 4.13). Closer John Smoltz, the lone holdover from the beginning of Atlanta's run on division titles, was outstanding once again, posting a 2.76 ERA and 44 saves.

Offensively, former Cardinals outfielder J.D. Drew put together a career year, batting .305-31-118 in his first season after signing with the Braves. Chipper Jones started horridly, batting .214-12-34 before the all-star break, but he recovered to hit 30 home runs, playing better after moving from left field back to his old position at third base. Several young player made important strides in their development, such as second baseman Marcus Giles (.311-8-48), catcher Johnny Estrada (.314-9-76), first baseman Adam LaRoche (.278-13-45) and rookie outfielder Charles Thomas (.288-7-31).

Those players filled the void left by the departed free agents, allowing Atlanta to cruise past preseason East favorites Philadelphia and Florida. The Phillies never got into a groove and were plagued by injuries, most notably to closer Billy Wagner. First baseman Jim Thome performed up to his usual standards, hitting .274-42-105, and outfielder Bobby Abreu once again proved he is the best outfielder no one talks about, going .301-30-116 with 40 stolen bases in 45 attempts.

The Marlins, meanwhile, contended for the wild card for most of the year before fading fast in September. Juan Pierre was once again a bright spot, hitting .326 and stealing 45 bases, and phenom Miguel Cabrera teetered on the brink of superstardom, hitting .294-33-112 at age 21.

The Braves ran into the red-hot Astros in the division series. They split the first two games in Atlanta, and Houston took Game Three at Minute Maid Park. Atlanta finally put an end to Houston's 19-game home winning streak in Game Four, as LaRoche tied the score with a three-run homer in the sixth inning and Drew hit a go-ahead RBI single in the ninth. Game Five at Turner Field was much closer than the final score indicated, as the Braves trailed just 3-2 after five innings. But a pair of Beltran home runs helped seal Atlanta's fate, and the Astros rolled to a 12-3 win.

"We really felt like we were going to win this game," Smoltz said. "There was a lot of doubt and a lot of uncertainty about how we were going to win the few games that we did. This was such a great feeling, and now it's a very terrible feeling."

LARRY GOREN

J.D. Drew

ST. LOUIS vs. LOS ANGELES
COMPOSITE BOX

ST. LOUIS

Player, Pos.	AVG	G	AB	R	H	2B	3B	HR	RBI	BB	SO	SB
Jeff Suppan, p	.667	1	3	0	2	0	0	0	0	0	0	0
Roger Cedeno, ph	.500	2	2	0	1	0	0	0	0	0	0	0
Edgar Renteria, ss	.455	4	11	4	5	2	0	0	4	3	1	1
Albert Pujols, 1b	.333	4	15	4	5	0	0	2	5	3	0	0
Larry Walker, rf	.333	4	15	6	5	1	0	2	3	2	5	1
Mike Matheny, c	.286	4	14	1	4	0	0	1	5	0	2	0
Reggie Sanders, lf	.286	4	14	3	4	0	0	1	1	0	2	1
Jim Edmonds, cf	.267	4	15	1	4	0	0	1	2	1	9	0
Tony Womack, 2b	.158	4	19	2	3	0	1	0	1	0	2	1
Scott Rolen, 3b	.000	4	12	1	0	0	0	0	0	6	3	0
Marlon Anderson, ph	.000	3	3	0	0	0	0	0	0	0	1	0
Matt Morris, p	.000	1	2	0	0	0	0	0	0	0	0	0
Woody Williams, p	.000	1	2	0	0	0	0	0	0	1	0	0
Dan Haren, p	.000	1	1	0	0	0	0	0	0	0	0	0
John Mabry, ph	.000	1	1	0	0	0	0	0	0	0	1	0
Jason Marquis, p	.000	1	1	0	0	0	0	0	0	0	0	0
Totals	.254	4	130	22	33	3	1	7	21	15	26	4

Pitcher	W	L	ERA	G	GS	SV	IP	H	R	ER	BB	SO
Cal Eldred	0	0	0.00	2	0	0	1	1	0	0	2	0
Kiki Calero	0	0	0.00	1	0	0	1	0	0	0	0	2
Steve Kline	0	0	0.00	2	0	0	1	0	0	0	0	0
Ray King	0	0	0.00	3	0	0	2	0	0	0	0	1
Julian Tavarez	0	0	0.00	2	0	0	2	2	0	0	0	3
Dan Haren	1	0	0.00	1	0	0	2	1	0	0	1	3
Jeff Suppan	1	0	2.57	1	1	0	7	2	2	2	3	2
Woody Williams	1	0	3.00	1	1	0	6	8	2	2	1	2
Jason Isringhausen	0	0	4.50	2	0	0	2	1	1	1	2	2
Matt Morris	0	1	5.14	1	1	0	7	6	4	4	2	5
Jason Marquis	0	0	8.10	1	1	0	3	4	3	3	4	0
Totals	3	1	3.09	4	4	0	35	25	12	12	15	20

LOS ANGELES

Player, Pos.	AVG	G	AB	R	H	2B	3B	HR	RBI	BB	SO	SB
Tom Wilson, c	1.000	2	1	1	1	0	0	1	1	0	0	0
Brent Mayne, c	.333	4	6	1	2	0	0	0	0	2	0	0
Jayson Werth, lf	.286	4	14	3	4	1	0	2	3	3	4	0
Milton Bradley, rf	.273	4	11	1	3	1	0	1	1	5	2	2
Adrian Beltre, 3b	.267	4	15	1	4	0	0	0	1	0	3	0
Shawn Green, 1b	.250	4	16	3	4	0	0	3	3	0	3	0
Cesar Izturis, ss	.176	4	17	1	3	1	0	0	0	1	2	0
Alex Cora, 2b	.133	4	15	1	2	0	1	0	1	0	3	0
Steve Finley, cf	.125	4	16	0	2	1	0	0	2	1	0	0
Robin Ventura, ph	.000	3	3	0	0	0	0	0	0	0	1	0
David Ross, c	.000	2	3	0	0	0	0	0	0	0	1	0
Jason Grabowski, ph	.000	3	2	0	0	0	0	0	0	0	1	0
Jose Lima, p	.000	1	2	0	0	0	0	0	0	0	2	0
Odalis Perez, p	.000	2	2	0	0	0	0	0	0	0	0	0
Jeff Weaver, p	.000	1	2	0	0	0	0	0	0	0	1	0
Hee Seop Choi, ph	.000	1	1	0	0	0	0	0	0	0	0	0
Jose Hernandez, ph	.000	1	0	0	0	0	0	0	0	1	0	0
Totals	.198	4	126	12	25	4	1	7	12	15	20	2

Pitcher	W	L	ERA	G	GS	SV	IP	H	R	ER	BB	SO
Mike Venafro	0	0	0.00	2	0	0	1	0	0	0	0	1
Duaner Sanchez	0	0	0.00	2	0	0	2	1	0	0	1	3
Eric Gagne	0	0	0.00	2	0	0	3	1	0	0	1	3
Jose Lima	1	0	0.00	1	1	1	9	5	0	0	1	4
Yhency Brazoban	0	0	3.00	2	0	0	3	1	1	1	2	2
Elmer Dessens	0	0	6.75	1	0	0	1	1	1	1	0	1
Giovanni Carrara	0	0	9.00	3	0	0	2	4	2	2	1	1
Wilson Alvarez	0	1	10.80	2	0	0	3	4	4	4	0	4
Jeff Weaver	0	1	11.57	1	1	0	5	8	6	6	2	4
Odalis Perez	0	1	14.40	2	2	0	5	8	8	8	7	3
Totals	1	3	5.82	4	4	1	34	33	22	22	15	26

SCORE BY INNINGS

Los Angeles	203	312	001—12
St. Louis	146	430	400—22

E—Perez, Ross, Weaver. **DP**—Los Angeles 3, St. Louis 3. **LOB**—Los Angeles 27, St. Louis 25. **CS**—Edmonds, Renteria. **SF**—Beltre. **HBP**—Cora (by Morris), Renteria (by Brazoban), Sanders (by Weaver), Walker (by Weaver). **IBB**—Mayne (by Morris). **WP**—Carrara, Weaver. **PB**—Ross.

HOUSTON vs. ATLANTA
COMPOSITE BOX

HOUSTON

Player, Pos.	AVG	G	AB	R	H	2B	3B	HR	RBI	BB	SO	SB
Raul Chavez, c	.600	2	5	1	3	0	0	1	1	0	0	0
Jason Lane, rf-lf	.600	5	5	2	3	0	0	1	2	0	1	0
Carlos Beltran, cf	.455	5	22	9	10	2	0	4	9	1	4	2
Lance Berkman, rf	.409	5	22	5	9	1	0	1	3	3	6	0
Craig Biggio, lf	.400	5	20	5	8	2	0	1	4	2	4	1
Morgan Ensberg, 3b	.368	5	19	1	7	2	0	0	5	3	1	0
Brad Ausmus, c	.333	5	9	3	3	0	0	1	1	3	3	0
Jeff Bagwell, 1b	.318	5	22	5	7	2	0	2	5	3	3	0
Orlando Palmeiro, ph-lf	.250	5	4	0	1	0	0	0	0	0	0	0
Jeff Kent, 2b	.227	5	22	3	5	3	0	0	3	2	5	0
Jose Vizcaino, ss	.105	5	19	2	2	0	0	0	1	1	2	0
Mike Lamb, ph	.000	4	3	0	0	0	0	0	1	0	0	0
Roger Clemens, p	.000	2	3	0	0	0	0	0	0	1	1	0
Roy Oswalt, p	.000	2	3	0	0	0	0	0	0	0	1	0
Eric Bruntlett, ss	.000	2	1	0	0	0	0	0	0	1	0	0
Brandon Backe, p	.000	1	1	0	0	0	0	0	0	0	0	0
Totals	.322	5	180	36	58	12	0	11	36	21	30	3

Pitcher	W	L	ERA	G	GS	SV	IP	H	R	ER	BB	SO
Chad Harville	0	0	0.00	1	0	0	1	0	0	0	0	0
Dan Wheeler	0	0	0.00	1	0	0	1	0	0	0	0	0
Brad Lidge	0	0	2.08	3	0	1	4	4	1	1	1	6
Roy Oswalt	1	0	2.38	2	2	0	11	15	3	3	4	8
Roger Clemens	1	0	3.00	2	2	0	12	12	5	4	8	12
Brandon Backe	1	0	3.00	1	1	0	6	5	2	2	2	5
Mike Gallo	0	0	4.50	3	0	0	2	3	1	1	1	4
Dan Miceli	0	0	5.40	3	0	0	3	2	2	2	1	2
Chad Qualls	0	0	6.75	4	0	0	4	4	3	3	1	3
Russ Springer	0	1	18.00	2	0	0	2	3	4	4	1	5
Totals	3	2	3.86	5	5	1	47	48	21	20	19	45

ATLANTA

Player, Pos.	AVG	G	AB	R	H	2B	3B	HR	RBI	BB	SO	SB
John Smoltz, p	1.000	2	1	0	1	0	0	0	0	0	0	0
Andruw Jones, cf	.526	5	19	4	10	2	0	2	5	2	3	1
Mike Hampton, p	.500	2	2	0	1	0	0	0	0	0	1	0
Paul Byrd, p	.500	2	2	0	1	0	0	0	1	0	1	0
Rafael Furcal, ss	.381	5	21	5	8	0	1	2	4	3	3	3
Johnny Estrada, c	.353	5	17	3	6	0	0	2	4	3	3	0
Charles Thomas, lf	.250	5	16	1	4	0	0	0	0	2	5	1
Adam LaRoche, 1b	.235	5	17	1	4	1	0	1	4	2	5	0
Chipper Jones, 3b	.200	5	20	4	4	0	0	0	3	6	2	0
Eli Marrero, ph-lf	.200	3	5	0	1	0	0	0	0	0	2	0
J.D. Drew, rf	.200	5	20	1	4	0	0	0	1	4	7	1
DeWayne Wise, ph	.200	5	5	1	1	1	0	0	0	0	2	0
Marcus Giles, 2b	.125	5	24	1	3	0	0	0	1	0	6	1
Julio Franco, ph-1b	.000	3	4	0	0	0	0	0	0	0	1	0
Eddie Perez, c	.000	3	3	0	0	0	0	0	0	0	1	0
Jaret Wright, p	.000	2	3	0	0	0	0	0	0	0	2	0
Russ Ortiz, p	.000	1	1	0	0	0	0	0	0	0	1	0
Totals	.267	5	180	21	48	4	1	7	20	19	45	7

Pitcher	W	L	ERA	G	GS	SV	IP	H	R	ER	BB	SO
John Smoltz	1	0	0.00	2	0	0	5	4	0	0	2	4
John Thomson	0	0	0.00	1	1	0	4	1	0	0	1	0
Kevin Gryboski	0	0	2.08	5	0	0	4	3	1	1	1	3
Mike Hampton	0	0	2.45	2	1	0	7	4	2	2	4	6
Antonio Alfonseca	1	0	4.91	4	0	0	4	2	2	2	0	3
Paul Byrd	0	1	6.35	2	0	0	6	8	4	4	3	3
Jaret Wright	0	2	9.31	2	2	0	10	14	10	10	1	7
Juan Cruz	0	0	9.82	3	0	0	4	6	4	4	4	4
Russ Ortiz	0	0	15.00	1	1	0	3	7	5	5	1	1
Chris Reitsma	0	0	18.00	3	0	0	3	5	6	6	1	2
Tom Martin	0	0	54.00	2	0	0	0	4	2	2	1	0
Totals	2	3	7.04	5	5	0	46	58	36	36	21	30

SCORE BY INNING

Houston	178	054	731	00—36
Atlanta	120	234	241	02—21

E—Bagwell, Berkman, Chavez, Drew. DP—Atlanta 7, Houston 4. LOB—Atlanta 43, Houston 34. CS—Berkman, Drew, Ensberg. SF—Clemens, Estrada, Lamb, Vizcaino. HBP—Beltran (by Cruz), Furcal (by Springer), Thomas (by Backe). IBB—Thomas (by Backe), Vizcaino (by Byrd). WP—Clemens 3, Reitsma.

CHAMPIONSHIP SERIES
ST. LOUIS vs. HOUSTON
COMPOSITE BOX

ST. LOUIS

Player, Pos.	AVG	G	AB	R	H	2B	3B	HR	RBI	BB	SO	SB
Albert Pujols, 1b	.500	7	28	10	14	2	0	4	9	4	3	0
Jason Marquis, p	.500	1	2	0	1	0	0	0	0	0	0	0
Marlon Anderson, ph-2b	.333	5	3	1	1	0	0	0	0	1	0	0
Scott Rolen, 3b	.310	7	29	6	9	2	0	3	6	2	9	0
Jim Edmonds, cf	.292	7	24	2	7	2	0	2	7	2	6	0
Tony Womack, 2b	.269	7	26	5	7	1	0	0	1	1	3	2
Woody Williams, p	.250	2	4	1	1	1	0	0	0	0	0	0
Yadier Molina, c	.250	1	4	0	1	0	0	0	0	0	0	0
Larry Walker, rf	.241	7	29	6	7	1	1	2	5	3	8	0
Reggie Sanders, lf	.190	6	21	1	4	2	0	0	0	1	5	0
Edgar Renteria, ss	.167	7	24	1	4	0	0	0	2	2	5	0
Roger Cedeno, ph	.167	6	6	1	1	0	0	0	1	0	2	0
John Mabry, ph-lf	.167	4	6	0	1	0	0	0	1	0	3	0
Mike Matheny, c	.105	7	19	0	2	0	0	0	0	1	8	0
Hector Luna, ss	.000	2	4	0	0	0	0	0	0	0	2	0
So Taguchi, lf	.000	3	2	0	0	0	0	0	0	0	1	0
Jeff Suppan, p	.000	2	2	0	0	0	0	0	0	1	0	0
Matt Morris, p	.000	2	2	0	0	0	0	0	0	0	1	0
Totals	.255	7	235	34	60	12	1	11	33	17	56	2

Pitcher	W	L	ERA	G	GS	SV	IP	H	R	ER	BB	SO
Cal Eldred	0	0	0.00	1	0	0	0	0	0	0	1	0
Steve Kline	0	0	0.00	1	0	0	0	2	0	0	0	0
Woody Williams	1	0	2.77	2	2	0	13	5	4	4	3	9
Julian Tavarez	2	1	3.00	5	0	0	6	3	2	2	2	3
Jeff Suppan	1	1	3.00	2	2	0	12	8	5	4	4	9
Kiko Calero	0	0	3.86	5	0	0	7	8	3	3	1	7
Jason Isringhausen	0	1	4.70	6	0	3	8	4	4	4	4	3
Matt Morris	0	0	5.40	2	2	0	10	11	6	6	8	6
Jason Marquis	0	0	6.75	1	1	0	4	5	3	3	2	2
Ray King	0	0	10.80	4	0	0	2	4	2	2	0	1
Dan Haren	0	0	10.80	2	0	0	2	3	2	2	0	2
Totals	4	3	4.26	7	7	3	63	53	31	30	25	42

HOUSTON

Player, Pos.	AVG	G	AB	R	H	2B	3B	HR	RBI	BB	SO	SB
Carlos Beltran, cf	.417	7	24	12	10	1	0	4	5	8	4	4
Mike Lamb, ph-3b	.400	2	5	2	2	0	0	2	2	1	1	0
Orlando Palmeiro, ph-lf	.333	7	6	0	2	1	0	0	0	0	0	0
Lance Berkman, rf	.292	7	24	7	7	2	0	3	9	5	4	1
Jeff Bagwell, 1b	.259	7	27	1	7	2	0	0	3	4	5	1
Jose Vizcaino, ss-2b	.250	7	28	1	7	1	0	0	0	1	6	0
Raul Chavez, c	.250	2	4	0	1	0	0	0	1	0	1	0
Jeff Kent, 2b	.240	7	25	3	6	2	0	3	7	3	5	0
Craig Biggio, lf	.188	7	32	3	6	1	0	1	1	0	4	0
Morgan Ensberg, 3b	.136	7	22	2	3	0	0	1	2	1	3	0
Brad Ausmus, c	.105	7	19	0	2	0	0	0	0	2	8	0
Roger Clemens, p	.000	2	4	0	0	0	0	0	0	0	3	0
Pete Munro, p	.000	2	2	0	0	0	0	0	0	1	0	0
Adam Everett, ss-ph	.000	3	1	0	0	0	0	0	0	0	0	0
Roy Oswalt, p	.000	2	2	0	0	0	0	0	0	0	0	0
Jason Lane, lf-rf	.000	2	1	0	0	0	0	0	0	0	0	0
Brandon Backe, p-ph	.000	3	5	0	0	0	0	0	0	0	3	0
Eric Bruntlett, ph-ss	.000	4	2	0	0	0	0	0	0	0	0	0
Totals	.227	7	233	31	53	10	0	14	30	25	42	6

Pitcher	W	L	ERA	G	GS	SV	IP	H	R	ER	BB	SO
Brad Lidge	1	0	0.00	4	0	0	8	0	0	0	2	14
Dan Wheeler	1	0	0.00	4	0	0	7	4	0	0	0	9
Brandon Backe	0	0	2.84	2	2	0	13	6	4	4	4	10
Roger Clemens	1	1	4.15	2	2	0	13	10	6	6	2	9
Roy Oswalt	0	0	6.75	2	1	0	8	11	6	6	4	2
Pete Munro	0	0	9.00	2	2	0	7	14	7	7	1	5
Chad Qualls	0	1	11.25	4	0	0	4	8	5	5	2	4
Chad Harville	0	0	13.50	3	0	0	1	3	2	2	1	3
Dan Miceli	0	2	27.00	2	0	0	1	3	4	4	1	0
Totals	3	4	4.91	7	7	2	62	60	34	34	17	56

SCORE BY INNING

Houston	904	412	245	000—31
St. Louis	814	169	030	002—34

E—Edmonds, Munro, Vizcaino. DP—Houston 2, St. Louis 5. LOB—Houston 44, St. Louis 40. CS—Bagwell, Biggio, Ensberg, Vizcaino. SF—Berkman, Edmonds. HBP—Anderson (by Lidge), Edmonds (by Backe), Ensberg (by Isringhausen), Ensberg (by Williams), Kent (by Suppan), Kent (by Tavarez), Palmeiro (by Calero). IBB—Ausmus (by Morris), Beltran (by Isringhausen), Berkman (by Isringhausen), Berkman (by Tavarez), Matheny (by Qualls). WP—Morris 2, Clemens, Tavarez. PB—Chavez

ORGANIZATION
STATISTICS

BY BILL SHAIKIN

The Angels spent the money and won their division in 2004, but there was something vaguely unsatisfying about it all.

In 2002, as an underdog and a wild-card team, they  beat the bullies—the Yankees and Barry Bonds—and won the World Series. After owner Arte Moreno spent $145 million on four top free agents, the Angels sported a payroll exceeded only by the Yankees and Red Sox. The Angels were the big dogs now.

They won the American League West, their first division championship in 18 years, but by one game and only after erasing a three-game deficit with nine to play. Then they were swept from the playoffs by the Red Sox. That was it?

The Angels set the division title as a goal, and met it, to raucous applause. They obliterated their home attendance record, selling out 45 of 81 home games and drawing 3.4 million.

For all the perils of big spending, the free agents largely delivered. Vladimir Guerrero produced an MVP-caliber season, hitting .337-39-126 and ranking among the top four in the league in every Triple Crown category. He led the league and set a club record by scoring 124 runs. He drove in nine in one game, carried the Angels into the playoffs by hitting six home runs in the final seven games and hit a grand slam in the final playoff game. He became the first Angel outfielder voted into an All-Star Game starting lineup since Reggie Jackson in 1984.

Outfielder Jose Guillen hit .294-27-104, although the Angels kicked him off the team with one week left in the season for insubordination. Righthander Kelvim Escobar went 11-12, 3.93, with the best ERA and worst run support among Angel starters, and ranked fourth in the

Vladimir Guerrero

Dallas McPherson

PLAYERS of the YEAR

MAJOR LEAGUE: Vladimir Guerrero, of

In his first season as an Angel, Guerrero put up MVP-caliber numbers, going .337-39-126. He was at his best down the stretch, hitting .560-6-11 in the final six games of the season to carry the Angels past Oakland for the AL West crown.

MINOR LEAGUE: Dallas McPherson, 3b

Everywhere McPherson played in 2004, he hit. Overall, the heir apparent to Troy Glaus batted .317-40-126 in 135 games split between Double-A Arkansas and Triple-A Salt Lake. The 24-year-old did make 29 errors at the hot corner, however, and might eventually move to first base or the outfield.

league in strikeouts. Righthander Bartolo Colon started 5-8, 6.57 but finished 13-4, 3.65, and his 18 victories ranked third in the league behind Curt Schilling and Johan Santana.

But injuries exhausted the depth among position players, and the starting pitchers exhausted the bullpen. The Angels fielded their projected 2004 lineup for one game.

Outfielder Garret Anderson, the All-Star Game MVP in 2003, signed a $48-million contract extension and almost immediately thereafter missed seven weeks while doctors ran him through extensive tests, then diagnosed him with arthritis. Third baseman Troy Glaus, the World Series MVP in 2002, missed three months after shoulder surgery. DH Tim Salmon missed two months with shoulder and knee injuries that required eventual surgery. Second baseman Adam Kennedy tore up a knee in September and will miss much of the 2005 season for rehabilitation.

The minor league season was highlighted by the spectacular summer of third baseman Dallas McPherson, who hit .317-40-126 between Double-A Arkansas and Triple-A Salt Lake. After Kennedy's injury forced the Angels to move Chone Figgins to second base, the Angels employed McPherson at third base in September and in the playoffs. He hit three homers in 16 games but struck out 17 times in 40 at-bats.

First baseman Casey Kotchman also made his major league debut, sandwiching a .224-0-15 effort in Anaheim between overall .371-8-56 numbers at Arkansas and Salt Lake.

Tom Kotchman, Casey's father, managed short-season Provo to the Pioneer League championship, the first title for an Angels affiliate since Arkansas was awarded the Texas League crown in 2001.

ORGANIZATION LEADERS

BATTING

*AVG	Casey Kotchman, Salt Lake/Arkansas	.371
R	Dallas McPherson, Salt Lake/Arkansas	107
H	Erick Aybar, Rancho Cucamonga	189
TB	Dallas McPherson, Salt Lake/Arkansas	349
2B	Dallas McPherson, Salt Lake/Arkansas	36
3B	Dallas McPherson, Salt Lake/Arkansas	14
HR	Dallas McPherson, Salt Lake/Arkansas	40
RBI	Dallas McPherson, Salt Lake/Arkansas	126
BB	Mike Napoli, Rancho Cucamonga	88
SO	Dallas McPherson, Salt Lake/Arkansas	169
SB	Erick Aybar, Rancho Cucamonga	51
*OBP	Casey Kotchman, Salt Lake/Arkansas	.429
*SLG	Dallas McPherson, Salt Lake/Arkansas	.670

PITCHING

W	Jake Woods, Salt Lake/Arkansas	15
L	Steve Green, Salt Lake	17
#ERA	Micah Posey, Rancho Cucamonga/Cedar Rapids	2.91
G	Dustin Griffith, Salt Lake/Arkansas/Rancho Cuca.	56
	Von Stertzbach, Rancho Cucamonga/Cedar Rapids	56
CG	Chris Bootcheck, Salt Lake	3
	Willie Collazo, Arkansas	3
SV	Von Stertzbach, Rancho Cucamonga/Cedar Rapids	26
IP	Jake Woods, Salt Lake/Arkansas	173
BB	Steve Green, Salt Lake	85
SO	Steven Shell, Rancho Cucamonga	190

*Minimum 250 at-bats #Minimum 75 Innings

ANAHEIM ANGELS

Manager: Mike Scioscia.

2004 Record: 92-70, .568 (1st, AL West).

BATTING	AVG	G	AB	R	H	2B	3B	HR	RBI	BB	SO	SB	CS	OBP	SLG	B	T	HT	WT	DOB	1st Yr	Resides
Amezaga, Alfredo	.161	73	93	12	15	2	0	2	11	3	24	3	2	.212	.247	S	R	5-10	165	1-16-78	1999	Obregon, Mexico
Anderson, Garret	.301	112	442	57	133	20	1	14	75	29	75	2	1	.343	.446	L	L	6-3	225	6-30-72	1990	Tustin, Calif.
DaVanon, Jeff	.277	108	285	41	79	11	4	7	34	46	54	18	3	.372	.418	S	R	6-0	185	12-8-73	1995	Scottsdale, Ariz.
Eckstein, David	.276	142	566	92	156	24	1	2	35	42	49	16	5	.339	.332	R	R	5-7	165	1-20-75	1997	Sanford, Fla.
Erstad, Darin	.295	125	495	79	146	29	1	7	69	37	74	16	1	.346	.400	L	L	6-2	210	6-4-74	1995	Fargo, N.D.
Figgins, Chone	.296	148	577	83	171	22	17	5	60	49	94	34	13	.350	.419	S	R	5-8	155	1-22-78	1997	Seffner, Fla.
Galarraga, Andres	.300	7	10	1	3	0	0	1	2	0	3	0	0	.364	.600	R	R	6-3	265	6-18-61	1984	West Palm Beach, Fla.
Glaus, Troy	.251	58	207	47	52	11	1	18	42	31	52	2	3	.355	.575	R	R	6-5	240	8-3-76	1998	Corona, Calif.
Guerrero, Vladimir	.337	156	612	124	206	39	2	39	126	52	74	15	3	.391	.598	R	R	6-3	220	2-9-76	1994	Nizao Bani, D.R.
Guillen, Jose	.294	148	565	88	166	28	3	27	104	37	92	5	4	.352	.497	R	R	5-11	190	5-17-76	1994	San Cristobal, D.R.
Halter, Shane	.202	46	114	10	23	5	0	4	13	7	30	1	1	.248	.351	R	R	6-0	190	11-8-69	1991	Overland Park, Kan.
Kennedy, Adam	.278	144	468	70	130	20	5	10	48	41	92	15	5	.351	.406	L	R	6-1	185	1-10-76	1997	Yorba Linda, Calif.
Kotchman, Casey	.224	38	116	7	26	6	0	0	15	7	11	3	0	.289	.276	L	L	6-3	210	2-22-83	2001	Seminole, Fla.
McPherson, Dallas	.225	16	40	5	9	1	0	3	6	3	17	1	0	.279	.475	L	R	6-4	230	7-23-80	2001	Randleman, N.C.
Molina, Bengie	.276	97	337	36	93	13	0	10	54	18	35	0	1	.313	.404	R	R	5-11	220	7-20-74	1993	Yuma, Ariz.
Molina, Jose	.261	73	203	26	53	10	2	3	25	10	52	4	1	.296	.374	R	R	6-2	220	6-3-75	1993	Vega Alta, P.R.
Mondesi, Raul	.118	8	34	2	4	1	0	1	1	2	4	0	1	.189	.235	R	R	5-11	230	3-2-71	1990	San Cristobal, D.R.
Paul, Josh	.243	46	70	11	17	3	0	2	10	7	17	2	1	.308	.371	R	R	6-1	200	5-19-75	1996	Naperville, Ill.
Pride, Curtis	.250	35	40	5	10	3	0	0	3	0	11	1	0	.268	.325	L	R	6-0	210	12-17-68	1986	West Palm Beach, Fla.
Quinlan, Robb	.344	56	160	23	55	14	0	5	23	14	26	3	1	.401	.525	R	R	6-1	200	3-17-77	1999	Maplewood, Minn.
Riggs, Adam	.194	16	36	2	7	3	0	0	3	1	10	1	0	.216	.278	R	R	6-0	195	10-4-72	1994	The Woodlands, Texas
Salmon, Tim	.253	60	186	15	47	7	0	2	23	14	41	1	0	.306	.323	R	R	6-3	235	8-24-68	1989	Scottsdale, Ariz.

PITCHING	W	L	ERA	G	GS	CG	SV	IP	H	R	ER	BB	SO	AVG	B	T	HT	WT	DOB	1st Yr	Resides
Bergman, Dusty	0	0	13.50	1	0	0	0	2	4	3	3	1	1	.444	L	L	6-5	200	2-1-78	1999	Carson City, Nev.
Colon, Bartolo	18	12	5.01	34	34	0	0	208	215	122	116	71	158	.265	R	R	5-11	240	5-24-73	1994	Westlake, Ohio
Donnelly, Brendan	5	2	3.00	40	0	0	0	42	34	14	14	15	56	.224	R	R	6-3	240	7-4-71	1992	Hilton Head, S.C.
Dunn, Scott	0	0	9.00	3	0	0	0	3	7	3	3	1	2	.438	R	R	6-3	180	5-23-78	1999	San Antonio, Texas
Escobar, Kelvim	11	12	3.93	33	33	0	0	208	192	91	91	76	191	.244	R	R	6-1	210	4-11-76	1994	Caracas, Venez.
Gregg, Kevin	5	2	4.21	55	0	0	1	88	86	43	41	28	84	.255	R	R	6-6	220	6-20-78	1996	Corvallis, Ore.
Hensley, Matt	0	2	4.88	16	0	0	0	28	32	15	15	7	30	.294	R	R	6-2	220	8-18-78	2000	San Diego, Calif.
Lackey, John	14	13	4.67	33	32	1	0	198	215	108	103	60	144	.278	R	R	6-6	235	10-23-78	1999	Bothell, Wash.
Ortiz, Ramon	5	7	4.43	34	14	0	0	128	139	64	63	38	82	.280	R	R	6-0	175	3-23-73	1995	Cotui, D.R.
Percival, Troy	2	3	2.90	52	0	0	33	50	43	19	16	19	33	.230	R	R	6-3	235	8-9-69	1990	Riverside, Calif.
Rodriguez, Francisco	4	1	1.82	69	0	0	12	84	51	21	17	33	123	.172	R	R	6-0	180	1-7-82	1999	Caracas, Venez.
Sele, Aaron	9	4	5.05	28	24	0	0	132	163	84	74	51	51	.310	R	R	6-3	220	6-25-70	1991	Bellevue, Wash.
Shields, Scot	8	2	3.33	60	0	0	4	105	97	42	39	40	109	.238	R	R	6-1	170	7-22-75	1997	Livonia, Mich.
Turnbow, Derrick	0	0	0.00	4	0	0	0	6	2	0	0	7	3	.105	R	R	6-3	210	1-25-78	1997	Franklin, Tenn.
Washburn, Jarrod	11	8	4.64	25	25	1	0	149	159	81	77	40	86	.269	L	L	6-1	195	8-13-74	1995	Danbury, Wisc.
Weber, Ben	0	2	8.06	18	0	0	0	22	37	24	20	15	11	.363	R	R	6-4	205	11-17-69	1991	Beaumont, Texas

FIELDING

Catcher	PCT	G	PO	A	E	DP	PB
B. Molina	.995	89	597	56	3	5	6
J. Molina	.994	70	441	37	3	4	3
Paul	.993	37	134	9	1	2	2

First Base	PCT	G	PO	A	E	DP
Erstad	.996	124	986	66	4	83
Galarraga	1.000	1	9	1	0	2
Halter	1.000	4	10	1	0	2
Kotchman	.988	34	231	15	3	17
J.Molina	1.000	2	5	1	0	2
Riggs	1.000	1	1	1	0	0

Second Base	PCT	G	PO	A	E	DP
Amezaga	.960	16	7	17	1	2
Figgins	.986	20	27	42	1	8

Halter	1.000	6	4	7	0	2
Kennedy	.982	144	255	388	12	71
Riggs	1.000	1	0	1	0	0

Third Base	PCT	G	PO	A	E	DP
Amezaga	.923	26	3	9	1	3
Figgins	.944	92	57	129	11	9
Glaus	.950	19	11	27	2	2
Halter	.878	33	26	46	10	2
McPherson	1.000	14	9	22	0	1
Quinlan	.983	32	13	44	1	1

Shortstop	PCT	G	PO	A	E	DP
Amezaga	.990	32	38	58	1	5
Eckstein	.988	138	198	309	6	75
Figgins	.956	13	19	24	2	5

Halter	1.000	3	3	4	0	1

Outfield	PCT	G	PO	A	E	DP
Anderson	.991	94	211	4	2	1
Davanon	.993	81	142	2	1	2
Figgins	.990	57	100	1	1	0
Guerrero	.973	143	308	13	9	2
Guillen	.979	136	270	9	6	1
Mondesi	1.000	7	20	1	0	0
Paul	1.000	4	2	0	0	0
Pride	1.000	24	27	0	0	0
Quinlan	1.000	9	4	0	0	0
Riggs	1.000	8	11	1	0	0
Salmon	1.000	8	15	1	0	0

Director, Player Development: Tony Reagins.

Class	Farm Team	League	W	L	Pct.	Finish*	Manager	Affiliate Since
AAA	Salt Lake (Utah) Stingers	Pacific Coast	56	88	.389	16th (16)	Mike Brumley	2001
AA	Arkansas Travelers (Little Rock)	Texas	59	80	.424	7th (8)	Tyrone Boykin	2001
High A	Rancho Cucamonga (Calif.) Quakes	California	69	71	.493	**6th (10)**	Bobby Meacham	2001
Low A	Cedar Rapids (Iowa) Kernels	Midwest	75	64	.540	**t-4th (14)**	Bobby Magallanes	1993
Rookie	Provo (Utah) Angels	Pioneer	44	32	.579	**+1st (8)**	Tom Kotchman	2001
Rookie	Mesa (Ariz.) Angels	Arizona	12	43	.218	9th (9)	Brian Harper	2001

*Finish in overall standings (No. of teams in league)/playoff teams in **boldface**   +League champion

SALT LAKE STINGERS   Class AAA

PACIFIC COAST LEAGUE

BATTING	AVG	G	AB	R	H	2B	3B	HR	RBI	BB	SO	SB	CS	OBP	SLG	B	T	HT	WT	DOB	1st Yr	Resides
Amezaga, Alfredo	.259	32	135	15	35	5	2	2	14	13	18	7	0	.329	.370	S	R	5-10	165	1-16-78	1999	Obregon, Mexico
Boyer, Billy	.000	7	10	0	0	0	0	0	1	1	5	0	0	.083	.000	R	R	6-0	185	3-8-84	2003	Sumner, Wash.
Budde, Ryan	.235	5	17	0	4	0	0	0	1	1	7	0	0	.263	.235	R	R	5-11	200	8-15-79	2002	Midwest City, Okla.
DaVanon, Jeff	.625	3	8	4	5	0	0	1	1	2	0	1	1	.7001	.000	S	R	6-0	185	12-8-73	1995	Scottsdale, Ariz.
Del Chiaro, Brent	.000	3	6	1	0	0	0	0	2	0	0	0	0	.250	.000	R	R	6-3	217	6-26-79	2001	Oakley, Calif.
Erstad, Darin	.125	4	16	2	2	0	0	0	3	1	1	0	0	.176	.125	L	L	6-2	210	6-4-74	1995	Fargo, N.D.
Galarraga, Andres	.304	25	102	10	31	3	0	4	19	6	24	0	0	.342	.451	R	R	6-3	265	6-18-61	1984	West Palm Beach, Fla.
Gibson, Derrick	.292	48	168	17	49	11	1	6	26	12	36	1	1	.341	.476	R	R	6-2	240	2-5-75	1993	Winter Haven, Fla.
Gordon, Brian	.259	127	475	80	123	24	4	22	70	30	145	6	2	.305	.465	L	R	6-0	180	8-16-78	1997	Round Rock, Texas
Gorneault, Nick	.316	6	19	4	6	1	0	1	5	1	7	0	0	.381	.526	R	R	6-3	220	4-19-79	2001	Springfield, Mass.
Gregorio, Tom	.232	58	207	20	48	12	2	6	32	12	56	3	0	.280	.396	R	R	6-2	200	5-5-77	1999	Staten Island, N.Y.
Gutierrez, Victor	.234	22	77	14	18	5	0	1	6	6	12	2	0	.286	.338	R	R	5-9	170	12-23-77	1995	Santo Domingo, D.R.
Halter, Shane	.275	35	131	18	36	7	1	6	18	15	21	2	3	.349	.481	R	R	6-0	190	11-8-69	1991	Overland Park, Kan.
Johnson, Gary	.253	91	304	44	77	13	5	6	36	39	71	1	2	.346	.388	L	L	6-3	210	10-29-75	1999	Atherton, Calif.
Kotchman, Casey	.372	49	199	32	74	22	0	5	38	14	25	0	0	.423	.558	L	L	6-3	210	2-22-83	2001	Seminole, Fla.
McPherson, Dallas	.313	67	259	54	81	19	8	20	57	23	95	6	3	.370	.680	L	R	6-4	230	7-23-80	2001	Randleman, N.C.
Mondesi, Raul	.333	2	6	1	2	0	0	1	2	1	2	0	0	.429	.833	R	R	5-11	230	3-2-71	1990	San Cristobal, D.R.
Nieves, Wil	.297	108	421	60	125	22	8	10	53	12	64	3	6	.316	.458	R	R	6-0	190	9-25-77	1996	Santurce, P.R.
Pelaez, Alex	.317	92	353	43	112	18	2	9	60	20	48	1	1	.349	.456	R	R	5-9	190	4-6-76	1998	Chula Vista, Calif.
Pride, Curtis	.431	19	65	13	28	8	1	2	10	4	12	2	0	.465	.677	L	R	6-0	210	12-17-68	1986	West Palm Beach, Fla.
Quinlan, Robb	.296	27	108	15	32	9	1	2	17	14	14	1	1	.377	.454	R	R	6-1	200	3-17-77	1999	Maplewood, Minn.
Riggs, Adam	.331	112	450	104	149	33	8	29	90	30	80	8	3	.373	.633	R	R	6-0	195	10-4-72	1994	The Woodlands, Texas
Rodriguez, Javy	.263	20	80	9	21	3	1	1	7	6	13	1	4	.310	.363	R	R	5-11	170	1-16-79	2002	Miami, Fla.
Smith, Casey	.273	69	256	32	70	9	2	2	27	18	37	8	2	.322	.348	R	R	6-2	200	3-18-79	2001	Ashford, Ala.
Sorensen, Zach	.309	95	359	73	111	16	4	3	37	45	58	22	5	.380	.401	S	R	6-0	190	1-3-77	1998	St. George, Utah
Specht, Brian	.237	54	190	30	45	10	2	3	15	17	45	8	1	.306	.358	S	R	5-11	170	10-19-80	2000	Colorado Springs, Colo.
Thrower, Jake	.298	120	456	73	136	29	2	7	65	41	53	5	2	.356	.417	S	R	5-11	180	11-19-75	1997	Yuma, Ariz.
Wesson, Barry	.233	45	163	17	38	10	3	4	16	4	35	4	1	.297	.350	R	R	6-2	210	4-6-77	1995	Glen Allan, Miss.

PITCHING	W	L	ERA	G	GS	CG	SV	IP	H	R	ER	BB	SO	AVG	B	T	HT	WT	DOB	1st Yr	Resides
Andrade, Steve	0	1	4.61	12	0	0	3	14	15	7	7	8	17	.294	R	R	6-1	220	2-6-78	2001	Woodland, Calif.
Arnold, Mitchell	0	0	13.50	4	0	0	0	7	15	10	10	4	2	.455	R	R	6-9	230	1-31-82	2002	Saratoga, Wyo.
Astacio, Hector	0	0	2.70	1	0	0	0	3	2	1	1	2	2	.231	R	R	6-0	160	8-10-83	2001	Hato Mayor, D.R.
Bergman, Dusty	1	2	2.85	45	0	0	1	73	82	35	23	13	54	.280	L	L	6-5	200	2-1-78	1999	Carson City, Nev.
Bootcheck, Chris	11	9	5.12	28	28	3	0	163	202	109	93	60	105	.301	R	R	6-5	200	10-24-78	2001	Phoenix, Ariz.
Brunet, Mike	2	8	6.51	13	12	0	0	65	85	57	47	29	49	.318	R	R	6-2	160	3-5-77	1998	Land O'Lakes, Fla.
Cox, Jason	0	0	54.00	1	0	0	0	1	2	2	1	2	0	1.000	R	R	6-6	215	4-7-83	2003	Albuquerque, N.M.
Cyr, Eric	0	0	1.08	2	2	0	0	8	3	1	1	7	6	.107	L	L	6-4	200	2-11-79	1999	Ada, Okla.
Donnelly, Brendan	0	0	7.71	3	0	0	0	2	2	2	2	2	6	.250	R	R	6-3	240	7-4-71	1992	Hilton Head, S.C.
Dunn, Scott	10	4	3.21	46	6	0	1	90	72	36	32	56	84	.224	R	R	6-3	210	5-23-78	1999	San Antonio, Texas
Emanuel, Brandon	5	8	6.08	38	7	0	3	84	115	68	57	26	75	.320	R	R	6-3	210	4-9-76	1998	Tampa, Fla.
Esslinger, Cameron	1	0	7.43	8	0	0	0	13	19	11	11	8	8	.333	R	R	5-11	180	12-28-76	1999	Hewitt, N.J.
Green, Steve	5	17	7.66	29	29	1	0	136	186	131	116	85	93	.330	R	R	6-2	190	1-26-78	1998	Longueuil, Quebec
Griffith, Dustin	0	1	3.86	3	1	0	0	7	7	4	3	1	5	.241	R	R	6-4	190	9-16-80	2002	Littleton, Colo.
Hensley, Matt	1	3	2.93	30	0	0	5	43	29	16	14	12	49	.185	R	R	6-2	200	8-18-78	2000	San Diego, Calif.
James, Delvin	0	1	5.03	4	4	0	0	20	24	12	11	8	6	.316	R	R	6-4	240	1-3-78	1996	Nacogdoches, Texas
Jenks, Bobby	0	1	8.03	3	3	0	0	12	19	15	11	6	13	.358	R	R	6-3	240	3-14-81	2000	Bothell, Wash.
Jones, Greg	1	4	5.74	36	0	0	3	53	63	38	34	19	43	.297	R	R	6-2	195	11-15-76	1997	Seminole, Fla.
Lee, Corey	0	1	7.64	4	4	0	0	18	21	15	15	16	16	.300	L	L	6-2	185	12-26-74	1996	Raleigh, N.C.
Middlebrook, Jason	7	10	6.94	29	29	0	0	156	220	126	120	50	93	.336	R	R	6-3	215	6-26-75	1997	Grass Lake, Mich.
Mizuo, Yoshitaka	0	4	6.18	24	2	0	0	39	56	30	27	15	27	.327	L	L	5-11	180	5-2-68	2004	Tokyo, Japan
Peralta, Joel	4	2	4.98	39	0	0	1	56	64	33	31	18	68	.284	R	R	5-11	160	3-23-76	1997	Bonao, D.R.
Turnbow, Derrick	2	6	5.06	46	3	0	6	75	75	46	42	42	56	.275	R	R	6-3	210	1-25-78	1997	Franklin, Tenn.
Weber, Ben	0	2	8.64	15	0	0	1	17	27	25	16	9	18	.346	R	R	6-4	205	11-17-69	1991	Beaumont, Texas
Woods, Jake	6	4	6.07	15	14	1	0	83	108	67	56	42	60	.312	L	L	6-1	190	9-3-81	2001	Kingsburg, Calif.

FIELDING

Catcher	PCT	G	PO	A	E	DP	PB
Budde	1.000	4	27	1	0	0	0
Del Chiaro	1.000	3	12	2	0	1	0
Gregorio	.981	55	326	37	7	5	7
Nieves	.992	85	602	58	5	4	9

First Base	PCT	G	PO	A	E	DP
Erstad	.963	4	21	5	1	3

Galarraga	1.000	4	26	1	0	3
Halter	1.000	4	32	3	0	2
Kotchman	.992	42	340	26	3	42
Nieves	.990	23	187	9	2	23
Pelaez	.991	28	188	22	2	13
Quinlan	.996	23	200	25	1	19
Riggs	.972	11	96	10	3	10

Rodriguez	1.000	1	7	0	0	1
Smith	.976	8	76	4	2	8
Thrower	1.000	7	38	4	0	4

Second Base	PCT	G	PO	A	E	DP
Boyer	1.000	7	8	10	0	2
Gutierrez	1.000	4	5	8	0	4
Halter	1.000	6	10	8	0	2

	PCT	G	PO	A	E	DP
Pelaez	1.000	7	11	16	0	6
Riggs	.909	4	5	5	1	0
Rodriguez	.909	5	15	15	3	6
Smith	.987	14	28	46	1	10
Sorensen	.981	12	21	32	1	2
Specht	.973	53	96	155	7	34
Thrower	.972	41	69	103	5	21

Third Base	PCT	G	PO	A	E	DP
Gutierrez	.800	4	1	3	1	0
Halter	1.000	3	2	8	0	0
McPherson	.885	62	39	92	17	8
Pelaez	.962	36	20	56	3	4
Quinlan	.818	5	3	6	2	0
Riggs	1.000	8	4	18	0	3

	PCT	G	PO	A	E	DP
Rodriguez	.933	6	5	9	1	1
Smith	.913	11	9	12	2	0
Specht	.833	1	0	5	1	0
Thrower	.973	14	15	21	1	2

Shortstop	PCT	G	PO	A	E	DP
Amezaga	.961	32	53	118	7	23
Gutierrez	.929	15	22	43	5	10
Halter	.971	7	9	25	1	3
Rodriguez	.923	6	11	25	3	6
Smith	.961	26	46	77	5	17
Sorensen	.954	27	55	89	7	25
Thrower	.958	34	46	90	6	16

Outfield	PCT	G	PO	A	E	DP
DaVanon	1.000	3	7	0	0	0

	PCT	G	PO	A	E	DP
Gibson	.967	38	53	6	2	1
Gordon	.970	129	249	14	8	6
Gorneault	.909	6	10	0	1	0
Halter	.972	17	35	0	1	0
Johnson	.991	67	107	6	1	2
McPherson	1.000	1	1	1	0	0
Mondesi	.800	2	3	1	1	0
Pride	1.000	16	38	0	0	0
Quinlan	1.000	2	2	0	0	0
Riggs	.982	64	105	6	2	0
Rodriguez	1.000	2	3	0	0	0
Sorensen	.978	57	127	6	3	1
Thrower	.909	8	9	1	1	0
Wesson	1.000	46	102	1	0	0

ARKANSAS TRAVELERS — Class AA

TEXAS LEAGUE

BATTING	AVG	G	AB	R	H	2B	3B	HR	RBI	BB	SO	SB	CS	OBP	SLG	B	T	HT	WT	DOB	1st Yr	Resides
Aspito, Jason	.230	89	296	36	68	10	1	8	42	23	59	1	4	.303	.351	L	R	6-0	200	1-3-79	2000	Itasca, Ill.
Callaspo, Alberto	.284	136	550	76	156	29	2	6	48	47	25	15	14	.338	.376	S	R	5-11	173	4-19-83	2001	Maracay, Venez.
Del Chiaro, Brent	.228	38	114	14	26	3	0	4	14	7	52	1	0	.288	.360	R	R	6-3	217	6-26-79	2001	Oakley, Calif.
Duenas, Tommy	.000	3	8	0	0	0	0	0	0	0	5	0	0	.111	.000	R	R	5-11	200	7-16-84	2002	Miami, Fla.
Duncan, Carlos	.261	46	153	20	40	7	3	2	16	6	43	4	2	.298	.386	R	R	6-1	190	6-30-77	1995	San Pedro de Macoris, D.R.
Eylward, Mike	.260	115	392	36	102	15	0	6	58	35	77	3	1	.335	.344	R	R	6-2	210	11-28-79	2001	Clearwater, Fla.
Gibson, Derrick	.232	50	185	29	43	11	0	10	26	11	47	1	1	.294	.454	R	R	6-2	240	2-5-75	1993	Winter Haven, Fla.
Gomez, Rudy	.264	119	439	56	116	25	3	5	38	41	41	4	4	.333	.369	R	R	5-11	180	9-14-74	1996	Miami, Fla.
Gorneault, Nick	.281	130	495	91	139	28	4	21	81	45	128	7	5	.341	.481	R	R	6-3	220	4-19-79	2001	Springfield, Mass.
Guerrero, Christian	.276	54	192	18	53	13	4	3	23	12	42	4	2	.319	.432	R	R	6-5	200	7-12-80	1998	Bani, D.R.
2-team (56 S.A.)	.250	110	388	46	97	20	5	11	46	20	92	11	7	.287	.412							
Gutierrez, Victor	.279	58	190	15	53	13	2	2	16	12	24	4	2	.322	.400	R	R	5-9	170	12-23-77	1995	Santo Domingo, D.R.
Kotchman, Casey	.368	28	114	19	42	11	0	3	18	10	7	0	0	.438	.544	L	L	6-3	210	2-22-83	2001	Seminole, Fla.
Mathis, Jeff	.227	117	432	57	98	24	3	14	55	49	102	2	1	.310	.394	R	R	6-0	180	3-31-83	2001	Marianna, Fla.
McPherson, Dallas	.321	68	262	53	84	17	6	20	69	34	74	6	5	.404	.660	L	R	6-4	230	7-23-80	2001	Randleman, N.C.
Murphy, Tommy	.260	129	477	77	124	24	6	7	45	36	113	27	5	.310	.379	R	R	6-0	185	8-27-79	2000	Boynton Beach, Fla.
Rodriguez, Javy	.300	37	140	14	42	7	1	2	11	9	28	6	3	.340	.407	R	R	5-11	170	1-16-79	2002	Miami, Fla.
Smith, Casey	.282	44	170	25	48	9	3	0	19	10	24	3	3	.320	.371	R	R	6-2	200	3-18-79	2001	Ashford, Ala.
Sugden, Jason	.000	2	6	0	0	0	0	0	0	0	3	0	0	.143	.000	R	R	6-3	190	10-11-81	2002	Harrisburg, Pa.
Turner, Justin	.182	21	66	5	12	3	0	1	3	2	22	0	1	.214	.273	L	R	6-1	190	12-19-79	2001	Cape Coral, Fla.

PITCHING	W	L	ERA	G	GS	CG	SV	IP	H	R	ER	BB	SO	AVG	B	T	HT	WT	DOB	1st Yr	Resides
Andrade, Steve	2	2	2.44	35	0	0	9	48	37	16	13	12	59	.206	R	R	6-1	220	2-6-78	2001	Woodland, Calif.
Astacio, Hector	0	0	5.02	6	0	0	0	14	15	10	8	10	10	.263	R	R	6-0	160	8-10-83	2001	Hato Mayor, D.R.
Bilke, Austin	0	0	4.50	2	0	0	0	2	3	1	1	0		.300	R	R	6-2	220	8-13-79	2002	Beaver Dam, Wisc.
Bittner, Tim	8	6	4.46	22	22	0	0	119	113	65	59	57	82	.251	L	L	6-2	200	6-9-80	2001	Wilmington, Del.
Brunet, Mike	1	1	1.42	2	2	0	0	13	8	2	2	4	8	.178	R	R	6-2	160	3-5-77	1998	Land O`Lakes, Fla.
Collazo, Willie	6	10	4.56	32	20	3	0	148	156	88	75	38	100	.268	L	L	5-9	175	11-7-79	2001	Miami, Fla.
Cyr, Eric	4	3	3.17	11	8	0	0	54	48	23	19	15	44	.239	R	L	6-4	200	2-11-79	1999	Ada, Okla.
Del Chiaro, Brent	0	0	0.00	2	0	0	0	1	1	0	0	0		.333	R	R	6-3	217	6-26-79	2001	Oakley, Calif.
Emanuel, Brandon	0	0	4.50	1	1	0	0	4	5	2	2	1	5	.294	R	R	6-3	210	4-9-76	1998	Tampa, Fla.
Esslinger, Cameron	2	4	3.60	44	0	0	5	60	53	27	24	36	44	.242	R	R	5-11	180	12-28-76	1999	Hewitt, N.J.
Fischer, Rich	3	8	9.57	19	9	0	0	53	88	66	56	19	33	.371	R	R	6-3	170	10-21-80	2002	Riverside, Calif.
Gil, David	1	6	7.29	11	11	0	0	54	89	58	44	24	30	.379	R	R	6-4	215	12-26-74	2000	Miami, Fla.
Gomez, Rudy	0	0	18.00	1	0	0	0	1	2	3	2	1	0	.333	R	R	5-11	180	9-14-74	1996	Miami, Fla.
Grezlovski, Ben	2	2	6.60	11	0	0	0	15	14	17	11	13	5	.233	R	R	5-11	180	11-22-76	1999	Miami, Fla.
Griffith, Dustin	0	0	4.50	3	0	0	0	4	5	2	2	3	3	.294	R	R	6-4	190	9-16-80	2002	Littleton, Colo.
Lee, Corey	2	6	4.27	14	14	0	0	65	63	40	31	30	53	.252	L	L	6-2	185	12-26-74	1996	Raleigh, N.C.
Mizuo, Yoshitaka	1	1	6.48	9	2	0	0	17	23	13	12	4	9	.319	L	L	5-11	180	5-2-68	2004	Tokyo, Japan
Mozingo, Dan	0	5	5.85	11	4	0	0	32	43	24	21	12	14	.314	L	L	6-2	190	6-3-80	1999	Ashtabula, Ohio
O'Sullivan, Mark	5	5	7.46	45	4	0	1	80	117	74	66	46	53	.346	R	R	6-2	200	10-24-78	2001	Andover, Mass.
Roberts, Nick	2	3	5.54	12	11	0	0	67	78	42	41	12	33	.294	R	R	6-2	185	11-6-76	1999	Annabella, Utah
Rouwenhorst, Jon	4	7	4.06	52	0	0	11	69	67	39	31	32	65	.252	L	L	6-1	180	9-25-79	2001	Anaheim, Calif.
Santana, Ervin	2	1	3.30	8	8	0	0	44	41	19	16	18	48	.244	R	R	6-2	150	11-28-83	2001	San Cristobal, D.R.
Saunders, Joe	4	3	5.77	8	8	0	0	39	51	26	25	14	25	.333	L	L	6-2	200	6-16-81	2002	Springfield, Va.
Schneider, Scott	3	5	5.29	54	2	0	0	95	110	63	56	34	67	.285	R	R	6-4	210	5-4-78	2000	Virginia Beach, Va.
Smith, Cliff	0	0	9.00	18	0	0	0	22	37	26	22	10	15	.370	R	R	6-6	200	10-13-79	2001	Haverhill, Mass.
Woods, Jake	9	2	2.70	14	14	1	0	90	86	29	27	19	60	.253	L	L	6-1	190	9-3-81	2001	Kingsburg, Calif.

FIELDING

Catcher	PCT	G	PO	A	E	DP	PB
Del Chiaro	.988	35	233	20	3	1	5
Duenas	1.000	3	18	0	0	0	0
Mathis	.980	104	626	61	14	3	12

First Base	PCT	G	PO	A	E	DP
Eylward	.992	99	821	71	7	70
Gomez	.993	17	134	10	1	11
Kotchman	1.000	25	234	18	0	24

Second Base	PCT	G	PO	A	E	DP
Callaspo	1.000	3	5	10	0	2
Duncan	1.000	2	4	6	0	1
Gomez	.967	28	42	77	4	13
Gutierrez	.965	47	109	114	8	25

	PCT	G	PO	A	E	DP
Rodriguez	.931	16	23	44	5	12
Smith	.971	25	54	82	4	24
Turner	.990	21	40	55	1	8

Third Base	PCT	G	PO	A	E	DP
Aspito	.000	1	0	0	1	0
Eylward	.789	6	3	12	4	0
Gomez	.928	25	36	105	11	12
Gutierrez	1.000	4	1	13	0	2
McPherson	.929	57	42	114	12	8
Rodriguez	.840	9	2	19	4	1
Smith	.839	14	14	33	9	1

Shortstop	PCT	G	PO	A	E	DP
Callaspo	.956	122	200	363	26	65

	PCT	G	PO	A	E	DP
Gomez	1.000	4	4	11	0	3
Gutierrez	.882	6	12	18	4	5
Rodriguez	.882	3	4	11	2	2
Smith	.885	5	11	12	3	5

Outfield	PCT	G	PO	A	E	DP
Aspito	.970	79	126	4	4	0
Duncan	.986	37	63	7	1	0
Gibson	.778	5	6	1	2	0
Gorneault	.977	126	279	14	7	5
Guerrero	.945	53	82	4	5	1
Murphy	.979	120	311	10	7	2
Rodriguez	1.000	6	12	0	0	0
Sugden	1.000	2	3	0	0	0

CALIFORNIA LEAGUE

ORGANIZATION STATISTICS

BATTING	AVG	G	AB	R	H	2B	3B	HR	RBI	BB	SO	SB	CS	OBP	SLG	B	T	HT	WT	DOB	1st Yr	Resides
Abram, Matt	.148	21	54	4	8	4	0	0	3	2	17	0	0	.193	.222	R	R	6-0	180	6-13-80	2001	Scottsdale, Ariz.
Abruzzo, Jared	.252	94	329	33	83	18	0	11	46	36	90	0	0	.332	.407	S	R	6-3	210	11-15-81	2000	La Mesa, Calif.
Anderson, Garret	.444	3	9	1	4	0	0	1	1	1	1	0	0	.500	.778	L	L	6-3	225	6-30-72	1990	Tustin, Calif.
Aybar, Erick	.330	136	573	102	189	25	11	14	65	26	66	51	36	.370	.485	S	R	5-11	170	1-14-84	2002	Bani, D.R.
Budde, Ryan	.251	99	358	54	90	17	0	13	51	27	76	3	5	.313	.408	R	R	5-11	200	8-15-79	2002	Midwest City, Okla.
Cates, Zach	.162	16	37	7	6	2	0	0	1	7	13	1	0	.295	.216	L	R	6-3	210	9-21-79	2002	Tempe, Ariz.
Duncan, Carlos	.286	23	84	12	24	8	1	2	12	5	17	7	1	.319	.476	R	R	6-1	190	6-30-77	1995	San Pedro de Macoris, D.R.
Gates, David	.268	120	456	63	122	31	3	20	86	35	122	2	1	.329	.480	R	R	6-1	200	9-23-80	2001	Huntsville, Ala.
Glaus, Troy	.200	5	15	4	3	0	0	2	4	6	5	0	0	.429	.600	R	R	6-5	240	8-3-76	1998	Corona, Calif.
Halter, Shane	.211	5	19	4	4	1	0	0	1	2	4	2	0	.318	.263	R	R	6-0	190	11-8-69	1991	Overland Park, Kan.
Heath, Demetrius	.338	22	74	15	25	2	1	0	10	4	11	5	3	.372	.392	R	R	5-10	170	1-23-81	2001	Bethel, N.C.
Kimpton, Nick	.155	26	58	5	9	1	0	1	6	6	15	1	1	.231	.224	L	L	6-1	180	10-27-83	2001	Canberra, Australia
Melgarejo, Ransel	.282	74	238	49	67	13	4	3	35	32	52	20	6	.378	.408	R	R	6-0	180	8-28-81	2001	Miami, Fla.
Mondesi, Raul	.125	2	8	2	1	0	0	0	1	2	0	0	0	.222	.125	R	R	5-11	230	3-2-71	1990	San Cristobal, D.R.
Napoli, Michael	.282	132	482	94	136	29	4	29	118	88	166	9	5	.394	.539	R	R	6-0	200	10-31-81	2000	Cooper City, Fla.
Nunez, Felix	.167	15	24	4	4	0	0	0	2	5	5	0	1	.310	.167	R	R	6-1	170	10-9-82	2001	El Tigre, Venez.
Pavkovich, Adam	.227	107	375	59	85	33	2	10	44	36	70	4	5	.296	.405	R	R	6-2	185	11-23-81	2003	Venice, Fla.
Porter, Greg	.318	86	349	48	111	26	5	6	45	17	67	1	3	.357	.473	L	R	6-4	220	8-15-80	2001	Roanoke, Texas
Rodriguez, Javy	.262	14	42	4	11	2	0	4	4	6	5	5	3	.313	.310	R	R	5-11	170	1-16-79	2002	Miami, Fla.
Salmon, Tim	.348	7	23	5	8	1	1	2	6	4	6	0	0	.444	.739	R	R	6-3	235	8-24-68	1989	Scottsdale, Ariz.
Sugden, Jason	.238	78	214	33	51	8	7	1	27	12	71	2	2	.297	.355	S	R	6-3	190	10-11-81	2002	Harrisburg, Pa.
Turner, Justin	.194	19	67	9	13	2	0	2	5	6	23	1	0	.267	.313	L	R	6-1	190	12-19-79	2001	Cape Coral, Fla.
Weed, B.J.	.280	122	447	47	125	14	5	3	52	13	54	19	8	.300	.353	S	R	5-10	180	11-11-79	2003	Maybrook, N.Y.
Willits, Reggie	.285	135	526	99	150	17	5	5	52	73	112	45	15	.374	.365	S	R	5-11	185	5-30-81	2003	Noble, Okla.

PITCHING	W	L	ERA	G	GS	CG	SV	IP	H	R	ER	BB	SO	AVG	B	T	HT	WT	DOB	1st Yr	Resides
Astacio, Hector	1	1	5.54	16	1	0	0	26	24	20	16	7	20	.245	R	R	6-0	160	8-10-83	2001	Hato Mayor, D.R.
Austen, David	0	1	6.08	17	0	0	1	24	37	23	16	10	18	.359	R	R	6-1	185	5-21-81	2003	Coconut Creek, Fla.
Bilke, Austin	0	1	6.11	25	0	0	6	28	29	19	19	18	16	.269	R	R	6-2	220	8-13-79	2002	Beaver Dam, Wisc.
Carroll, James	4	3	4.10	47	0	0	1	68	76	45	31	33	33	.283	R	R	6-0	185	2-1-80	2003	Arlington, Texas
Davidson, Daniel	12	7	4.57	28	28	0	0	163	196	92	83	41	121	.301	L	L	6-4	225	1-9-81	2003	Lynn Haven, Fla.
Donnelly, Brendan	0	0	0.00	2	0	0	0	3	3	0	0	1	5	.250	R	R	6-3	240	7-4-71	1992	Hilton Head, S.C.
Dowdy, Justin	2	3	4.11	15	3	0	0	31	27	15	14	17	32	.233	L	L	6-1	160	8-13-83	2001	Chula Vista, Calif.
Griffith, Dustin	2	6	3.99	50	0	0	0	59	67	36	26	15	53	.277	R	R	6-4	190	9-16-80	2002	Littleton, Colo.
Jenks, Bobby	0	1	19.64	1	1	0	0	4	5	8	8	7	3	.357	R	R	6-3	240	3-14-81	2000	Bothell, Wash.
Lugo, Ozzie	3	0	4.50	18	0	0	0	22	22	12	11	15	17	.275	R	R	6-0	220	12-22-80	2002	Miami, Fla.
Peralta, Joel	0	0	9.00	1	0	0	0	2	5	2	2	1	1	.455	R	R	5-11	160	3-23-76	1997	Bonao, D.R.
Petke, Tim	0	0	3.38	3	0	0	0	5	6	2	2	3	1	.375	R	R	6-3	225	4-17-80	2003	Portland, Ore.
Posey, Micah	2	2	3.66	8	7	0	0	39	38	20	16	12	24	.257	L	L	6-5	220	10-18-82	2003	Tallahassee, Fla.
Saunders, Joe	9	7	3.41	19	19	0	0	106	106	49	40	23	76	.261	L	L	6-2	200	6-16-81	2002	Springfield, Va.
Shell, Steven	12	7	3.59	28	28	2	0	165	151	76	66	40	190	.242	R	R	6-5	190	3-10-83	2001	Cleburne, Texas
Smith, Cliff	0	1	8.68	7	0	0	0	9	12	10	9	4	6	.308	R	R	6-6	200	10-13-79	2001	Haverhill, Mass.
Stertzbach, Von	1	3	3.38	47	0	0	21	48	52	23	18	13	54	.271	R	R	6-2	190	5-15-81	2003	Plantation, Fla.
Thompson, Richard	3	2	3.94	41	5	0	4	78	76	36	34	33	71	.259	R	R	6-1	170	7-1-84	2002	Sydney, Australia
Toledo, Jean	7	10	4.85	25	25	2	0	128	148	84	69	55	70	.288	R	R	6-1	160	3-6-83	2001	Barcelona, Venez.
Touchstone, Nick	0	0	5.40	3	0	0	0	3	5	2	2	6	3	.333	L	L	6-5	220	11-19-81	2003	Niceville, Fla.
Washburn, Jarrod	0	0	2.25	1	1	0	0	4	4	1	1	3	5	.250	L	L	6-1	195	8-13-74	1995	Danbury, Wisc.
Wilhite, Matt	6	4	3.75	53	0	0	0	86	89	45	36	20	61	.272	R	R	6-1	185	7-3-81	2003	Franklin, Ky.
Wilson, Phil	3	9	6.59	38	16	0	0	109	132	96	80	58	75	.300	R	R	6-8	200	4-1-81	2000	Ramona, Calif.
Woody, Dominic	2	3	4.41	6	6	0	0	35	39	21	17	12	22	.289	R	R	6-3	210	8-17-78	1999	Richland, Wash.

FIELDING

Catcher	PCT	G	PO	A	E	DP	PB
Abruzzo	1.000	5	11	2	0	0	1
Budde	.980	66	477	61	11	0	7
Napoli	.986	72	484	84	8	4	7

First Base	PCT	G	PO	A	E	DP
Abram	1.000	19	102	4	0	7
Abruzzo	.976	53	429	20	11	40
Budde	.983	13	99	15	2	8
Cates	1.000	13	100	5	0	10
Halter	1.000	1	24	2	0	1
Kimpton	1.000	1	1	0	0	0
Napoli	.987	36	281	17	4	26
Porter	.983	13	114	4	2	11
Turner	.970	7	62	3	2	2

Second Base	PCT	G	PO	A	E	DP
Aybar	1.000	1	2	1	0	1
Heath	.962	19	24	52	3	9
Pavkovich	.970	35	59	102	5	18
Rodriguez	.938	12	10	20	2	3
Turner	.949	3	12	25	2	8
Weed	.965	82	125	209	12	39

Third Base	PCT	G	PO	A	E	DP
Halter	1.000	2	1	2	0	0
Napoli	1.000	2	0	2	0	0
Pavkovich	.921	72	64	123	16	16
Porter	.899	72	43	126	19	9
Weed	.800	2	2	2	1	0

Shortstop	PCT	G	PO	A	E	DP
Aybar	.954	132	266	391	32	80

	PCT	G	PO	A	E	DP
Halter	1.000	1	4	2	0	0
Pavkovich	.909	3	5	5	1	3
Rodriguez	.882	3	2	13	2	2
Weed	1.000	4	3	7	0	1

Outfield	PCT	G	PO	A	E	DP
Anderson	1.000	3	8	0	0	0
Duncan	.917	14	21	1	2	0
Gates	.962	81	126	2	5	1
Kimpton	.966	20	26	2	1	0
Melgarejo	1.000	75	141	8	0	0
Mondesi	1.000	1	1	0	0	0
Nunez	1.000	16	18	1	0	0
Sugden	.943	74	108	7	7	1
Weed	.963	53	75	2	3	0
Willits	.982	137	322	13	6	3

MIDWEST LEAGUE

BATTING	AVG	G	AB	R	H	2B	3B	HR	RBI	BB	SO	SB	CS	OBP	SLG	B	T	HT	WT	DOB	1st Yr	Resides
Abram, Matt	.192	23	78	6	15	3	0	3	15	3	28	0	0	.229	.346	R	R	6-0	180	6-13-80	2001	Scottsdale, Ariz.
Balkcom, Blake	.264	105	401	48	106	32	2	4	49	15	104	12	4	.303	.384	R	R	6-2	225	8-8-82	2003	Chipley, Fla.
Boyer, Billy	.228	28	101	9	23	4	0	1	8	8	38	1	3	.284	.297	S	R	6-0	185	3-8-84	2003	Sumner, Wash.
Brown, Matt	.233	122	437	67	102	20	4	23	82	33	126	6	6	.303	.455	R	R	6-0	200	8-8-82	2001	Hayden, Idaho
Casilla, Alexi	.310	9	29	6	9	2	1	0	1	5	4	1	1	.412	.448	S	R	5-9	160	6-20-84	2003	San Cristobal, D.R.
Collins, Michael	.218	33	110	10	24	6	0	1	12	13	21	0	3	.323	.300	R	R	6-3	210	7-18-84	2001	Canberra, Australia

BATTING	AVG	G	AB	R	H	2B	3B	HR	RBI	BB	SO	SB	CS	OBP	SLG	B	T	HT	WT	DOB	1st Yr	Resides
Cosby, Quan	.247	119	454	70	112	8	12	5	34	35	82	24	10	.303	.350	S	R	5-10	195	12-23-82	2001	Mart, Texas
Duenas, Tommy	.211	76	265	26	56	21	0	10	31	10	89	3	2	.247	.404	R	R	5-11	200	7-16-84	2002	Miami, Fla.
Guzman, Jose	.189	13	37	7	7	1	0	0	2	4	17	4	2	.268	.216	S	R	6-0	160	10-19-83	2001	Santo Domingo, D.R.
Kendrick, Howard	.367	75	313	66	115	24	6	10	49	12	41	15	6	.398	.578	R	R	5-10	180	7-12-83	2002	Callahan, Fla.
Kimpton, Nick	.290	37	131	20	38	5	1	0	12	12	25	10	4	.354	.344	L	L	6-1	180	10-27-83	2001	Canberra, Australia
Leahy, Ryan	.266	25	94	16	25	2	0	1	4	11	13	2	1	.355	.319	R	R	5-10	190	7-8-81	2004	Salem, Mass.
Lopez, Baltazar	.314	64	236	34	74	14	3	9	35	19	65	6	1	.368	.513	L	L	6-1	180	11-22-83	2003	Caborca, Mexico
Madrigal, Warner	.275	26	91	10	25	3	1	2	10	7	24	1	1	.330	.396	R	R	6-0	190	3-21-84	2001	San Pedro de Macoris, D.R.
Maher, Caleb	.201	38	144	15	29	5	2	4	13	12	45	1	3	.268	.347	R	R	6-2	200	3-22-83	2002	Ceres, Calif.
Martinez, Brett	.000	1	2	1	0	0	0	0	0	0	0	0	0	.333	.000	R	R	6-0	174	10-14-83	2003	Redlands, Calif.
Nunez, Felix	.269	20	78	14	21	2	1	2	9	9	12	5	1	.345	.397	R	R	6-1	170	10-9-82	2001	El Tigre, Venez.
Pali, Matt	.256	111	407	55	104	18	5	10	57	42	84	10	11	.343	.398	L	L	6-1	215	12-10-80	2003	Houston, Texas
Peel, Aaron	.216	62	208	25	45	6	1	9	24	17	66	4	4	.289	.385	R	R	6-1	190	2-8-83	2002	Seminole, Texas
Rodriguez, Sean	.250	57	196	35	49	8	4	4	17	18	54	14	4	.333	.393	R	R	6-0	180	4-26-85	2003	Miami, Fla.
Wilson, Bobby	.268	105	396	45	106	23	0	8	64	30	55	4	2	.320	.386	R	R	6-0	205	4-8-83	2003	Seminole, Fla.
Wood, Brandon	.251	125	478	65	120	30	5	11	64	46	117	21	5	.322	.404	R	R	6-3	185	3-2-85	2003	Scottsdale, Ariz.

PITCHING	W	L	ERA	G	GS	CG	SV	IP	H	R	ER	BB	SO	AVG	B	T	HT	WT	DOB	1st Yr	Resides
Austen, David	1	3	3.13	30	0	0	1	60	62	28	21	17	60	.256	R	R	6-1	185	5-21-81	2003	Coconut Creek, Fla.
Buckley, Allen	3	1	4.04	47	0	0	1	71	67	41	32	33	68	.245	R	R	6-6	230	9-18-79	2003	Brandon, Miss.
Dowdy, Justin	0	1	4.76	1	1	0	0	6	7	3	3	0	6	.333	L	L	6-1	160	8-13-83	2001	Chula Vista, Calif.
Hedden, Wayne	1	1	5.92	20	0	0	2	24	25	17	16	17	15	.275	R	R	6-2	200	10-27-82	2003	Tampa, Fla.
Hindman, Scott	1	1	6.75	27	0	0	0	35	28	27	26	40	39	.212	L	L	6-4	220	3-6-81	2002	Inverness, Ill.
Hunter, Chris	9	7	3.86	25	22	0	0	135	129	72	58	45	81	.251	R	R	6-4	205	12-12-80	2004	Lindon, Utah
Jepsen, Kevin	8	10	3.43	27	27	1	0	144	122	68	55	77	136	.228	R	R	6-3	200	7-26-84	2002	Sparks, Nev.
Morban, Carlos	2	0	5.67	28	0	0	1	40	42	27	25	22	36	.268	R	R	6-6	180	1-29-83	2001	Santo Domingo, D.R.
Moreno, Abel	10	8	3.41	25	25	0	0	143	141	69	54	31	120	.255	R	R	6-2	185	6-15-83	2001	Santo Domingo, D.R.
Posey, Micah	6	0	2.36	9	8	1	0	53	39	15	14	14	34	.211	L	L	6-5	220	10-18-82	2003	Tallahassee, Fla.
Pullin, Aaron	8	2	4.10	47	0	0	2	75	63	37	34	29	70	.226	R	R	6-3	200	2-17-81	2003	Midland, Texas
Ray, Ronnie	3	0	0.87	6	3	0	0	21	13	5	2	4	10	.191	R	R	6-3	190	5-11-84	2002	Pacific, Mo.
Rodriguez, Rafael	1	5	6.48	7	7	0	0	33	36	27	24	19	36	.267	R	R	6-1	170	9-24-84	2002	Santo Domingo, D.R.
Simard, Michel	7	5	3.51	19	18	0	0	92	101	41	36	27	91	.284	R	R	6-3	200	9-4-81	2003	Charlesburg, Quebec
Smith, Jesse	4	7	5.32	39	6	0	0	88	99	70	52	45	69	.280	R	R	6-2	210	7-11-80	2003	Lincoln, Neb.
Stertzbach, Von	0	0	0.00	9	0	0	5	14	7	0	0	1	18	.156	R	R	6-2	190	5-15-81	2003	Plantation, Fla.
Touchstone, Nick	7	7	4.22	24	22	0	0	117	101	75	55	68	97	.235	L	L	6-5	220	11-19-81	2003	Niceville, Fla.
Zimmermann, Bob	4	6	2.26	53	0	0	24	68	48	21	17	21	82	.202	R	R	6-5	225	11-17-81	2003	St. Louis, Mo.

FIELDING

Catcher	PCT	G	PO	A	E	DP	PB
Collins	.989	13	78	16	1	2	1
Duenas	.974	61	453	37	13	0	13
Wilson	.987	69	549	66	8	2	5

First Base	PCT	G	PO	A	E	DP
Abram	.991	16	102	7	1	9
Lopez	.975	61	512	33	14	52
Maher	.989	18	163	10	2	16
Pali	.997	41	334	26	1	36
Wilson	.978	8	77	11	2	6

Second Base	PCT	G	PO	A	E	DP
Abram	1.000	2	4	5	0	1
Boyer	.956	25	63	68	6	20
Brown	.957	5	8	14	1	3
Casilla	.949	9	17	20	2	4
Guzman	1.000	2	1	2	0	0
Kendrick	.976	64	135	197	8	38
Leahy	.955	11	25	38	3	7
Rodriguez	.960	26	45	76	5	19

Third Base	PCT	G	PO	A	E	DP
Abram	1.000	2	2	5	0	1
Brown	.913	112	86	217	29	19
Leahy	.750	5	0	6	2	0
Rodriguez	1.000	10	2	19	0	1
Wilson	.838	12	7	24	6	1

Shortstop	PCT	G	PO	A	E	DP
Boyer	.962	4	10	15	1	6
Brown	1.000	1	3	4	0	1
Leahy	1.000	4	4	14	0	2
Rodriguez	.960	6	9	15	1	3
Wood	.948	125	206	322	29	81

Outfield	PCT	G	PO	A	E	DP
Balkcom	.976	94	159	5	4	1
Cosby	.979	117	231	6	5	1
Guzman	.905	10	19	0	2	0
Kimpton	.950	35	54	3	3	0
Lopez	1.000	2	3	0	0	0
Madrigal	.976	26	39	2	1	0
Nunez	.971	21	34	0	1	0
Pali	1.000	61	77	1	0	0
Peel	.982	41	53	2	1	1
Rodriguez	.962	16	23	2	1	1

PROVO ANGELS — Rookie

PIONEER LEAGUE

BATTING	AVG	G	AB	R	H	2B	3B	HR	RBI	BB	SO	SB	CS	OBP	SLG	B	T	HT	WT	DOB	1st Yr	Resides
Boyer, Billy	.239	23	71	12	17	3	1	2	10	10	26	2	0	.357	.394	S	R	6-0	185	3-8-84	2003	Sumner, Wash.
Brewster, Jon	.000	2	1	1	0	0	0	0	0	0	0	0	0	.500	.000	R	R	6-0	190	10-8-81	2004	Sherman Oaks, Calif.
Casilla, Alexi	.333	4	12	4	4	1	1	0	1	4	0	1	0	.529	.583	S	R	5-9	160	6-20-84	2003	San Cristobal, D.R.
Duff, Tim	.298	43	151	31	45	11	0	2	24	28	37	1	0	.410	.411	R	R	6-2	205	4-23-82	1997	Coatesville, Pa.
Giannotti, Richard	.248	61	206	57	51	8	4	3	22	42	69	21	6	.393	.369	B	R	6-3	180	8-9-83	2004	Plantation, Fla.
Hughes, Michael	.186	41	118	18	22	9	0	0	15	16	27	2	2	.310	.263	R	R	6-3	225	9-8-81	2004	Hoffman Estates, Ill.
Johnson, Ben	.265	44	166	27	44	7	1	6	34	12	30	2	2	.344	.428	S	R	6-0	196	10-17-81	2004	Bellevue, Wash.
Leahy, Ryan	.305	25	95	19	29	1	0	0	8	8	8	2	1	.359	.316	R	R	5-10	190	7-8-81	2004	Salem, Mass.
Leblanc, Josh	.299	53	184	39	55	8	4	4	30	27	43	15	3	.395	.451	L	R	6-2	185	9-15-81	2004	Houston, Texas
Maher, Caleb	.316	50	177	36	56	12	1	6	36	25	59	3	1	.405	.497	R	R	6-2	200	3-22-83	2002	Ceres, Calif.
Martinez, Brett	.333	3	6	0	2	0	0	0	0	0	1	0	0	.333	.333	R	R	6-0	174	10-14-83	2003	Redlands, Calif.
Nunez, Felix	.211	5	19	1	4	0	0	0	1	0	4	2	0	.286	.211	R	R	6-1	170	10-9-82	2001	El Tigre, Venez.
Perdomo, Mike	.247	53	170	28	42	7	0	5	20	11	55	3	1	.301	.376	R	R	6-2	180	6-29-81	2002	Miami, Fla.
Remole, Clifton	.273	60	198	36	54	11	1	1	24	30	22	3	3	.374	.354	L	L	6-0	197	10-24-82	2004	Powder Springs, Ga.
Renz, Jordan	.279	63	226	34	63	18	1	8	45	27	84	1	1	.363	.473	S	R	6-2	200	7-21-83	2002	Broken Arrow, Okla.
Rodriguez, Sean	.338	64	225	64	76	14	4	10	55	51	62	9	3	.486	.569	R	R	6-0	180	4-26-85	2003	Miami, Fla.
Solorzano, Marlon	.000	3	3	0	0	0	0	0	0	0	0	0	0	.000	.000	R	R	5-10	200	5-22-82	2004	Miami, Fla.
Sutton, Nate	.328	54	180	46	59	6	3	1	34	37	40	7	2	.453	.411	L	R	6-0	195	9-1-82	1992	Santa Cruz, Calif.
Toussaint, Andrew	.289	55	194	39	56	12	2	12	52	34	68	6	4	.411	.557	R	R	6-2	175	10-24-82	2004	Los Angeles, Calif.
Walston, Chris	.265	45	162	22	43	10	0	5	35	9	41	1	0	.303	.420	R	R	6-6	230	10-1-84	2002	Lakeside, Calif.

GAMES BY POSITION: C—Duff 43, Johnson 34, Martinez 3. **1B**—Maher 7, Remole 34, Walston 41. **2B**—Boyer 9, Brewster 2, Casilla 3, Leahy 19, Leblanc 51. **3B**—Boyer 2, Casilla 1, Sutton 53, Toussaint 27. **SS**—Boyer 13, Leahy 7, Rodriguez 62. **OF**—Giannotti 59, Hughes 41, Johnson 9, Nunez 5, Perdomo 50, Remole 25, Renz 62, Rodriguez 3.

PITCHING

PITCHING	W	L	ERA	G	GS	CG	SV	IP	H	R	ER	BB	SO	AVG	B	T	HT	WT	DOB	1st Yr	Resides
Arnold, Mitchell	2	0	2.48	25	0	0	13	33	12	10	9	14	41	.112	R	R	6-9	230	1-31-82	2002	Saratoga, Wyo.
Carney, Frederic	1	1	5.10	19	0	0	1	30	33	19	17	10	25	.284	R	R	6-3	220	8-21-82	2004	Norwalk, Conn.
Corbett, Jason	0	0	2.70	3	0	0	0	3	3	1	1	5	2	.250	R	R	6-7	230	1-8-84	2003	Palm Harbor, Fla.
Cordova, Francisco	2	5	5.37	14	11	1	0	52	59	41	31	26	33	.285	R	R	6-4	225	8-26-83	2004	Colorado, Mexico
Cox, Jason	1	2	7.94	15	0	0	1	23	33	21	20	7	12	.363	R	R	6-6	215	4-7-83	2003	Albuquerque, N.M.
Cox, Michael	0	0	3.38	1	0	0	0	3	2	1	1	2	1	.200	L	L	5-11	205	11-3-78	2004	Pasadena, Texas
Cruz, Rafael	0	0	0.00	2	0	0	0	4	2	0	0	1	3	.133	R	R	6-2	170	8-20-85	2002	Veracruz, Mexico
Douglas, Jaime	0	1	8.84	18	0	0	0	18	22	18	18	20	12	.293	L	L	6-4	205	3-19-83	2004	Orlando, Fla.
Edwards, Bill	6	1	2.82	20	0	0	1	38	29	13	12	12	24	.210	R	R	6-3	185	3-26-81	2004	Germantown, Tenn.
Gelinas, Karl	4	3	5.44	14	7	0	0	43	69	31	26	9	28	.379	R	R	6-4	200	8-6-83	2003	Iberville, Quebec
Green, Nick	4	3	3.86	17	10	0	0	51	55	28	22	20	44	.272	R	R	6-4	180	8-20-84	2004	Tifton, Ga.
Hedden, Wayne	3	0	1.93	16	0	0	0	28	21	6	6	10	24	.206	R	R	6-2	200	10-27-82	2003	Tampa, Fla.
Layman, Billy	2	2	4.91	13	12	0	0	40	44	24	22	22	51	.277	R	R	6-3	195	11-25-82	2004	Tequesta, Fla.
Mutter, Casey	0	0	9.91	18	0	0	0	26	39	33	29	21	31	.331	R	R	6-4	220	2-23-82	2004	Rialto, Calif.
Pawelczyk, Kyle	2	3	8.47	17	5	0	0	34	47	38	32	24	35	.322	L	L	6-5	180	11-18-81	2002	Elkins, W.Va.
Ray, Ronnie	5	2	5.00	13	6	0	0	36	32	23	20	21	30	.235	R	R	6-3	190	5-11-84	2002	Pacific, Mo.
Requena, Ricardo	2	0	7.09	17	1	0	0	33	51	27	26	10	36	.349	R	R	6-0	160	5-27-84	2001	Maracay, Venez.
Rodriguez, Fernando	4	3	4.14	14	12	0	0	59	64	35	27	18	54	.282	R	R	6-3	210	6-18-84	2003	El Paso, Texas
Shearer, Kelly	0	0	7.94	2	1	0	0	6	7	5	5	7	9	.318	L	L	6-3	200	4-8-85	2003	Missouri City, Texas
Sweeney, Mike	0	0	24.00	4	0	0	0	3	8	9	8	4	1	.444	L	L	6-1	210	8-5-82	2004	Middleburg, Fla.
Waters, Chris	5	3	2.91	21	0	0	1	46	51	19	15	11	47	.287	R	R	6-0	170	8-17-80	2000	Wellington, Fla.
Whittington, Anthony	1	3	8.35	11	11	0	0	37	57	45	34	36	29	.373	L	L	6-5	220	10-9-84	2003	Buffalo, W.Va.

AZL ANGELS — Rookie

ARIZONA LEAGUE

BATTING	AVG	G	AB	R	H	2B	3B	HR	RBI	BB	SO	SB	CS	SLG	OBP	B	T	HT	WT	DOB	1st Yr	Resides
Arredondo, Jose	.191	28	68	6	13	2	0	0	3	1	13	1	2	.221	.203	R	R	6-0	170	3-30-84	2002	San Pedro de Macoris, D.R.
Casilla, Alexi	.258	45	163	29	42	1	4	0	10	15	10	24	8	.313	.332	S	R	5-9	160	7-20-84	2003	San Cristobal, D.R.
Cowles, Josh	.201	50	169	16	34	11	0	0	10	26	59	9	3	.266	.306	R	R	6-2	185	6-7-84	2003	Redlands, Calif.
Davies, Josh	.255	40	137	14	35	3	2	1	10	5	37	4	1	.328	.285	R	R	6-4	176	9-12-85	2004	Strathfield, Australia
Day, Devin	.274	22	73	12	20	1	0	0	6	6	22	4	1	.288	.354	R	R	6-1	185	9-3-80	2003	Gilbert, Ariz.
Doddo, Brandon	.250	22	76	5	19	4	0	0	10	3	15	2	0	.303	.278	L	R	5-10	195	8-8-83	2004	Cooper City, Fla.
Hernandez, David	.257	33	109	9	28	4	1	2	12	7	27	1	4	.367	.325	R	R	6-0	175	5-6-85	2004	Miami, Fla.
Kendrick, Howard	.250	3	12	1	3	1	0	0	0	1	0	2	0	.333	.308	R	R	5-10	180	7-12-83	2002	Callahan, Fla.
Maldonado, Martin	.217	25	60	5	13	1	0	0	4	3	13	2	1	.233	.277	R	R	6-1	180	8-16-86	2004	Miami, Fla.
Martinez, Brett	.235	40	162	13	38	8	1	0	21	11	26	3	2	.296	.286	R	R	6-0	174	10-14-83	2003	Redlands, Calif.
McDowell, D.T.	.310	21	58	8	18	3	2	1	7	6	12	3	5	.483	.379	R	R	6-0	190	8-16-85	2004	Atlanta, Ga.
Newton, Andy	.257	9	35	1	9	1	1	0	1	0	7	0	1	.343	.257	R	R	6-0	190	5-12-82	2004	Tucson, Ariz.
Pride, Curtis	.214	4	14	1	3	1	0	0	3	1	6	1	0	.286	.250	L	R	6-0	210	12-17-68	1986	West Palm Beach, Fla.
Reinhardt, Doug	.205	47	151	10	31	4	1	2	9	15	42	1	1	.285	.305	R	R	6-3	210	10-22-85	2004	Laguna Beach, Calif.
Rivera, Luis	.218	42	124	15	27	6	0	0	10	24	45	4	1	.266	.361	R	R	6-0	185	10-12-86	2004	Rio Piedras, P.R.
Rosario, Anderson	.277	45	173	24	48	5	3	2	16	9	51	8	5	.376	.315	R	R	6-0	170	3-25-83	2003	Santo Domingo, D.R.
Shankle, Brooks	.225	50	178	21	40	12	2	3	26	24	52	3	3	.365	.346	R	R	6-3	200	2-4-83	2004	Boerne, Texas
Smith, Stan	.182	37	137	8	25	2	4	0	8	4	37	4	5	.255	.210	R	R	6-4	215	10-21-83	2004	Decatur, Ga.
Wesson, Barry	.385	4	13	3	5	2	0	0	8	1	2	0	0	.538	.429	R	R	6-2	210	4-6-77	1995	Glen Allan, Miss.

GAMES BY POSITION: C—Hernandez 18, Maldonado 23, Martinez 28. **1B**—Cowles 1, Davies 2, Martinez 11, Reinhardt 4, Shankle 42. **2B**—Casilla 33, Davies 3, Day 14, Kendrick 1, Reinhardt 9. **3B**—Cowles 3, Davies 16, Doddo 9, Reinhardt 33, Shankle 6. **SS**—Arredondo 20, Casilla 11, Davies 26, Day 10, Reinhardt 1. **OF**—Cowles 43, Hernandez 8, McDowell 13, Newton 8, Pride 2, Rivera 33, Rosario 40, Smith 27, Wesson 4.

PITCHING	W	L	ERA	G	GS	CG	SV	IP	H	R	ER	BB	SO	AVG	B	T	HT	WT	DOB	1st Yr	Resides
Abreu, Francis	1	1	5.52	4	3	0	0	15	17	12	9	2	7	.293	R	R	6-2	180	6-2-83	2003	San Cristobal, D.R.
Aldridge, Ryan	0	3	6.25	13	5	0	1	40	41	30	28	28	43	.257	R	R	6-2	190	9-10-83	2004	Screven, Ga.
Arredondo, Jose	0	0	2.92	8	0	0	1	12	14	10	4	4	14	.000	R	R	6-0	170	3-30-84	2002	San Pedro de Macoris, D.R.
Corbett, Jason	2	3	3.72	17	0	0	0	19	13	15	8	13	22	.175	R	R	6-7	230	1-8-84	2003	Palm Harbor, Fla.
Cruz, Rafael	1	4	3.77	13	1	0	0	31	31	15	13	9	20	.269	R	R	6-2	170	8-20-85	2002	Veracruz, Mexico
Cyr, Eric	0	0	0.00	1	0	0	0	1	0	0	0	1	3	.000	R	L	6-4	200	2-11-79	1999	Ada, Okla.
Fuller, Justin	0	0	9.00	1	0	0	0	1	1	1	1	0	0	.250	L	L	6-1	190	6-20-80	2002	South Windsor, Conn.
Gamboa, Felix	0	0	6.16	9	2	0	0	19	20	14	13	17	23	.270	R	R	6-5	170	7-18-85	2002	Barcelona, Venez.
Guzman, Jose	0	1	4.50	3	0	0	0	4	5	2	2	0	0	.312	R	R	6-0	190	10-27-82	2000	Santo Domingo, D.R.
Hill, Andy	0	1	8.85	11	2	0	0	20	28	22	20	8	20	.333	R	R	6-4	195	10-31-84	2003	Okanogan, Wash.
James, Delvin	0	0	0.00	1	1	0	0	1	0	0	0	0	2	.000	R	R	6-4	240	1-3-78	1996	Nacogdoches, Texas
Jenks, Bobby	0	0	8.10	1	1	0	0	3	2	3	3	3	5	.181	R	R	6-3	240	3-14-81	2000	Bothell, Wash.
MacKenzie, Aaron	0	4	5.84	8	4	0	0	25	34	20	16	9	23	.323	R	R	6-4	207	4-14-81	2004	Perth, Australia
Moreno, Victor	0	2	4.71	14	1	0	2	29	31	17	15	7	23	.267	R	R	6-3	166	7-19-83	2003	Santo Domingo, D.R.
Morillo, Lennyn	1	5	7.41	13	6	0	0	38	42	37	31	31	30	.302	R	R	6-3	160	7-17-84	2003	Santo Domingo, D.R.
Pena, Henry	0	0	2.17	11	3	0	0	29	29	11	7	2	23	.263	R	R	6-1	170	5-23-85	2002	Santo Domingo, D.R.
Peralta, Joel	0	0	2.08	2	0	0	0	4	1	1	1	0	9	.076	R	R	5-11	160	3-23-76	1996	Bonao, D.R.
Rodriguez, Rafael	0	2	6.46	4	4	0	0	15	18	12	11	5	13	.295	R	R	6-1	170	9-24-84	2001	Santo Domingo, D.R.
Roque, Christopher	0	5	3.15	20	0	0	3	20	22	9	7	12	13	.285	R	R	6-3	180	10-13-82	2003	Miami, Fla.
Rowe, Joe	1	3	4.78	13	4	0	0	38	33	22	20	14	34	.246	L	R	6-9	215	3-29-84	2004	Millbrook, Ala.
Shearer, Kelly	2	3	2.82	13	9	0	0	51	42	22	16	23	36	.238	L	L	6-3	200	4-8-85	2003	Missouri City, Texas
Sweeney, Mike	0	0	15.12	10	0	0	0	8	18	16	14	8	13	.422	L	L	6-1	210	8-5-82	2004	Middleburg, Fla.
Valencia, Jose	2	4	5.23	14	1	0	0	21	28	14	12	3	25	.314	R	R	6-2	170	11-17-84	2001	El Tigre, Venez.
Weber, Ben	0	0	0.00	1	1	0	0	1	0	0	0	0	2	.000	R	R	6-4	200	11-17-69	1991	Beaumont, Texas
Whittington, Anthony	1	1	0.64	3	3	0	0	14	14	3	1	6	15	.269	R	L	6-5	225	10-9-84	2003	Buffalo, W.Va.
Wilson, Brendan	1	2	3.96	14	5	0	0	39	47	24	17	21	35	.297	R	R	6-1	170	10-7-85	2004	Aspendale, Australia

ARIZONA DIAMONDBACKS

BY JACK MAGRUDER

Talk about your extreme makeover.

Three years after setting a speed record by winning the World Series in its fourth season, Arizona took an unexpected U-turn in 2004. The Diamondbacks posted the worst record in the major leagues (51-111) in an injury-marred season that also included an exodus at the highest levels.

First to go in bottom-line-driven offseason moves were key components of the 2001 championship team, including righthander Curt Schilling, and infielders Craig Counsell and Junior Spivey. The latter two were packaged for cleanup hitter/iron man Richie Sexson, who played every inning of every game in 2003.

But Sexson suffered a shoulder injury on a checkswing in May that ultimately caused him to undergo surgery and miss the rest of the season. Soon to follow out the door was manager Bob Brenly, who was replaced by third-base coach Al Pedrique on July 2 as the Diamondbacks struggled to find offense without Sexson.

The most drastic blow came two months later when former managing general partner Jerry Colangelo was pushed out of the ownership group. Colangelo had lost much of his power in a re-organization by new money men Ken Kendrick, Dale Jensen, Mike Chipman and Jeff Royer, who pledged $160 million over 10 years when they bought into the franchise in 2002.

Colangelo, the man hand-picked by then-Milwaukee owner Bud Selig and White Sox managing partner Jerry Reinsdorf to spearhead the effort to bring baseball to Phoenix in the mid 1990s, was replaced by former power agent Jeff Moorad, although the change did not go into effect until after the regular season ended.

Sexson was hardly the only key on-field component the D'backs were forced to do without. With the season

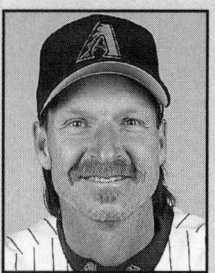 

Randy Johnson   Carlos Quentin

LARRY GOREN

PLAYERS of the YEAR

MAJOR LEAGUE: Randy Johnson, lhp

Johnson was the hot commodity around the trade deadline in July, but stayed with a bad Arizona club and still went 16-14, 2.60 with a National League-leading 290 strikeouts. He surpassed Steve Carlton with his 4,137th career strikeout, setting the all-time mark for lefthanders.

MINOR LEAGUE: Carlos Quentin, of

A member of "The Three Amigos," along with outfielder Conor Jackson and third baseman Jamie D'Antona, Quentin wreaked havoc at Class A Lancaster and followed up with a solid performance at Double-A El Paso. Overall, Quentin hit .331-21-89 in 452 at-bats, and was hit by pitches 43 times, a minor league record.

all but lost, Luis Gonzalez opted to forgo the final two months in order to undergo Tommy John surgery.

Closer Matt Mantei and top setup men Jose Valverde and Oscar Villarreal missed most of the season with arm injuries, and after the trading deadline deal of Steve Finley to Los Angeles, the D'backs were left to compete with the incomparable Randy Johnson and a cast of younger players being force-fed at the highest level.

Johnson again put up Cy Young-caliber numbers—16-14, 2.60 and a major league-leading 290 strikeouts—while leaving more milestones in his rear-view mirror. Johnson threw the 17th perfect game in major league history on May 18 in Atlanta, striking out 13, and recorded his 4,000th career strikeout on June 29.

Several top prospects continued to shine as they worked their way through the system. Outfielders Conor Jackson and Carlos Quentin, first-round picks in 2003, put up big numbers as teammates—first at low Class A Lancaster and then at Double-A El Paso.

Lancaster manager Wally Backman, in his first season in the organization, won praise for guiding the JetHawks to division titles in both halves of the high Class A California League. The Diamondbacks hired him as big league manager after the season, but he was dismissed after questions arose about his background and replaced by former Arizona bench coach Bob Melvin.

But the system took a hit when the pitcher formerly known as Adriano Rosario—considered a top prospect with a 96 mph fastball and quality slider—was found to be three years older than his stated 19. He gave his cousin's identity when signing for a $400,000 bonus in 2002.

ORGANIZATION LEADERS

BATTING

*AVG	Chris Carter, South Bend/Yakima	.339
R	Carlos Quentin, El Paso/Lancaster	103
H	Conor Jackson, El Paso/Lancaster	157
TB	Josh Kroeger, Tucson/El Paso	266
2B	Josh Kroeger, Tucson/El Paso	51
3B	Brian Barden, Tucson/El Paso	11
	Victor Hall, Tucson/El Paso	11
HR	Kyle Nichols, Tucson/El Paso	21
	Carlos Quentin, El Paso/Lancaster	21
RBI	Conor Jackson, El Paso/Lancaster	91
BB	Conor Jackson, El Paso/Lancaster	69
SO	Brian Barden, Tucson/El Paso	131
SB	Marland Williams, El Paso	49
*OBP	Carlos Quentin, El Paso/Lancaster	.435
*SLG	Chris Carter, South/Yakima	.590

PITCHING

W	Clint Goocher, El Paso/Lancaster	15
L	Matt Chico, El Paso/South Bend	12
	Clint Goocher, El Paso/Lancaster	12
#ERA	Lance Cormier, Tucson/El Paso	2.46
G	Carlton Wells, Lancaster	71
CG	Sergio Lizarraga, Tucson/El Paso	3
SV	Jason Bulger, El Paso/Lancaster	19
IP	Clint Goocher, El Paso/Lancaster	177
BB	Chris Kinsey, South Bend	70
SO	Matt Chico, El Paso/South Bend	148

* Minimum 250 at-bats #Minimum 75 innings

ORGANIZATION STATISTICS

ARIZONA DIAMONDBACKS

Managers: Bob Brenly, Al Pedrique.

2004 Record: 51-111 .315 (5th, NL West).

BATTING	AVG	G	AB	R	H	2B	3B	HR	RBI	BB	SO	SB	CS	OBP	SLG	B	T	HT	WT	DOB	1st Yr	Resides
Alomar, Roberto	.309	38	110	14	34	5	2	3	16	12	18	0	2	.382	.473	S	R	6-0	185	2-5-68	1985	Bradenton, Fla.
Baerga, Carlos	.235	79	85	6	20	2	0	2	11	6	12	0	0	.309	.329	S	R	5-11	215	11-4-68	1986	Bayamon, D.R.
Bautista, Danny	.286	141	539	64	154	27	1	11	65	35	66	6	2	.332	.401	R	R	5-11	225	5-24-72	1989	Santo Domingo, D.R.
Brito, Juan	.205	54	171	17	35	7	0	3	12	9	41	1	0	.246	.298	R	R	5-11	205	11-7-79	1997	Santiago Rodriguez, D.R.
Cintron, Alex	.262	154	564	56	148	31	7	4	49	31	59	3	3	.301	.363	S	R	6-2	200	12-17-78	1997	Yabucoa, P.R.
Colbrunn, Greg	.111	20	27	1	3	0	0	0	1	1	5	0	0	.143	.111	R	R	6-0	215	7-26-69	1988	Mount Pleasant, S.C.
Devore, Doug	.224	50	107	5	24	3	2	3	13	7	31	1	1	.272	.374	L	L	6-4	215	12-14-77	1999	Dublin, Ohio
Estalella, Bobby	.143	7	14	2	2	0	0	2	4	0	6	0	0	.143	.571	R	R	6-1	225	8-23-74	1993	Weston, Fla.
Finley, Steve	.275	104	404	61	111	16	1	23	48	40	52	8	4	.338	.490	L	L	6-2	195	3-12-65	1987	Del Mar, Calif.
Gil, Jerry	.174	29	86	3	15	2	1	0	8	0	33	2	0	.182	.221	R	R	6-3	183	10-14-82	2000	Santo Domingo, D.R.
Gonzalez, Luis	.259	105	379	69	98	28	5	17	48	68	58	2	2	.373	.493	L	R	6-2	200	9-3-67	1988	Scottsdale, Ariz.
Green, Andy	.202	46	109	13	22	2	1	1	4	5	17	1	1	.241	.266	R	R	5-9	180	7-7-77	2000	Lexington, Ky.
Hairston, Scott	.248	101	339	39	84	15	6	13	29	21	88	3	3	.293	.442	R	R	6-0	190	5-25-80	2001	Oro Valley, Ariz.
Hammock, Robby	.241	62	195	22	47	16	2	4	18	13	39	3	3	.287	.405	R	R	5-10	185	5-13-77	1998	Dacula, Ga.
Hill, Koyie	.250	13	36	3	9	1	0	1	6	2	6	1	0	.289	.361	S	R	6-0	190	3-9-79	2000	Lawton, Okla.
Hillenbrand, Shea	.310	148	562	68	174	36	3	15	80	24	49	2	0	.348	.464	R	R	6-1	210	7-27-75	1996	Mesa, Ariz.
Kata, Matt	.247	42	162	17	40	9	2	2	13	13	29	4	1	.301	.364	S	R	6-1	185	3-14-78	1999	Cleveland, Ohio
Kroeger, Josh	.167	22	54	5	9	3	0	0	2	1	21	0	1	.182	.222	L	L	6-2	200	8-31-82	2000	San Diego, Calif.
Mayne, Brent	.255	36	94	9	24	6	1	0	10	13	17	1	0	.343	.340	L	R	6-1	190	4-19-68	1989	Corona, Calif.
McCracken, Quinton	.288	55	156	20	45	11	1	2	13	13	23	2	4	.341	.410	S	R	5-7	190	8-16-70	1992	Scottsdale, Ariz.
Olson, Tim	.186	48	97	8	18	7	0	2	5	16	18	1	0	.301	.320	R	R	6-2	200	8-1-78	2000	Bismarck, N.D.
Sadler, Donnie	.130	18	23	1	3	2	0	0	1	7	0	0	0	.167	.217	R	R	5-6	175	6-17-75	1994	Waco, Texas
Sexson, Richie	.233	23	90	20	21	4	0	9	23	14	21	0	0	.337	.578	R	R	6-7	235	12-29-74	1993	Vancouver, Wash.
Snyder, Chris	.240	29	96	10	23	6	0	5	15	13	25	0	0	.327	.458	R	R	6-3	220	2-12-81	2002	Houston, Texas
Terrero, Luis	.245	62	229	21	56	14	0	4	14	20	78	10	2	.319	.358	R	R	6-2	206	5-18-80	1998	Barahona, D.R.
Tracy, Chad	.285	143	481	45	137	29	3	8	53	45	60	2	3	.343	.407	L	R	6-2	200	5-22-80	2001	Charlotte, N.C.
Zinter, Alan	.206	28	34	2	7	2	0	1	6	4	5	0	0	.353		S	R	6-2	195	5-19-68	1989	Oro Valley, Ariz.

PITCHING	W	L	ERA	G	GS	CG	SV	IP	H	R	ER	BB	SO	AVG	B	T	HT	WT	DOB	1st Yr	Resides
Aquino, Greg	0	2	3.06	34	0	0	16	35	24	15	12	17	26	.194	R	R	6-1	188	1-11-79	1996	Palenque, D.R.
Bruney, Brian	3	4	4.31	30	0	0	0	31	20	16	15	27	34	.189	R	R	6-3	225	2-17-82	2000	Warrenton, Ore.
Choate, Randy	2	4	4.62	74	0	0	0	51	52	26	26	28	49	.267	L	L	6-2	195	9-5-75	1997	Tampa, Fla.
Cormier, Lance	1	1	8.14	17	5	0	0	45	62	42	41	25	24	.333	R	R	6-1	190	8-19-80	2002	Lafayette, La.
Daigle, Casey	2	3	7.16	10	10	0	0	49	63	41	39	27	17	.320	R	R	6-5	217	4-4-81	2000	Vinton, La.
Dessens, Elmer	1	6	4.75	38	9	0	2	85	107	54	45	23	55	.301	R	R	5-10	200	1-13-71	1993	Hermosillo, Mexico
Durbin, Chad	1	1	8.68	7	0	0	0	9	9	10	9	11	10	.237	R	R	6-2	200	12-3-77	1996	Baton Rouge, La.
Fassero, Jeff	0	0	0.00	1	0	0	0	1	0	0	0	0	1	.000	L	L	6-1	200	1-5-63	1984	Paradise Valley, Ariz.
2-team (40 Colorado)	3	8	5.46	41	12	0	0	112	136	73	68	44	60	.304							
Fetters, Mike	0	1	8.68	23	0	0	1	19	23	22	18	14	14	.299	R	R	6-4	230	12-19-64	1986	Chandler, Ariz.
Fossum, Casey	4	15	6.65	27	27	0	0	142	171	111	105	63	117	.302	S	L	6-1	165	1-6-78	1999	Waco, Texas
Gonzalez, Edgar	0	9	9.32	10	10	0	0	46	72	49	48	18	31	.362	R	R	6-0	215	2-23-83	2002	San Nicolas, Mexico
Good, Andrew	1	2	5.31	17	2	0	0	41	43	25	24	13	26	.272	R	R	6-1	210	9-19-79	1998	Rochester Hills, Mich.
Gosling, Mike	1	1	4.62	6	4	0	0	25	26	13	13	13	14	.274	L	L	6-2	200	9-23-80	2002	Las Vegas, Nev.
Johnson, Randy	16	14	2.60	35	35	4	0	246	177	88	71	44	290	.197	R	L	6-10	231	9-10-63	1985	Scottsdale, Ariz.
Koplove, Mike	4	4	4.05	76	0	0	2	87	86	42	39	37	55	.269	R	R	5-10	180	8-30-76	1998	Philadelphia, Pa.
Mantei, Matt	0	3	11.81	12	0	0	4	11	17	15	14	6	13	.354	R	R	6-1	200	7-7-73	1991	Sawyer, Mich.
Nance, Shane	1	1	5.84	19	0	0	0	12	19	11	8	12	9	.352	L	L	5-8	191	9-7-77	2000	Houston, Texas
Randolph, Stephen	2	5	5.51	45	6	0	0	82	73	56	50	76	62	.235	L	L	6-3	200	5-1-74	1995	Austin, Texas
Reynolds, Shane	0	1	4.50	1	1	0	0	6	6	1	2	0	.500	R	R	6-3	215	3-26-68	1989	Houston, Texas
Service, Scott	1	1	7.08	21	0	0	0	20	24	17	16	10	17	.286	R	R	6-6	250	2-26-67	1986	Cincinnati, Ohio
Sparks, Steve	3	7	6.04	29	18	0	0	121	139	89	81	45	57	.287	R	R	6-0	195	7-2-65	1987	Sugar Land, Texas
Valverde, Jose	1	2	4.25	29	0	0	8	30	23	17	14	17	38	.213	R	R	6-4	254	7-24-79	1997	Santo Domingo, D.R.
Villafuerte, Brandon	0	3	4.05	20	0	0	0	20	25	9	9	14	13	.313	R	R	5-11	195	12-17-75	1995	Morgan Hill, Calif.
Villarreal, Oscar	0	2	7.00	17	0	0	0	18	25	14	14	7	17	.342	L	R	6-0	205	11-22-81	1999	Monterrey, Mexico
Webb, Brandon	7	16	3.59	35	35	1	0	208	194	111	83	119	164	.248	R	R	6-2	230	5-9-79	2000	Ashland, Ky.

FIELDING

Catcher	PCT	G	PO	A	E	DP	PB
Brito	.990	54	385	30	4	2	6
Estalella	1.000	6	19	2	0	0	0
Hammock	.997	46	313	21	1	8	5
Hill	.984	11	57	5	1	0	0
Mayne	.990	30	182	18	2	0	4
Snyder	1.000	29	213	19	0	2	3

First Base	PCT	G	PO	A	E	DP
Baerga	1.000	6	32	4	0	2
Colbrunn	1.000	2	7	1	0	0
Hillenbrand	.989	131	1127	72	13	105
Sexson	.996	23	199	27	1	19
Tracy	.970	11	29	3	1	2
Zinter	.978	8	41	3	1	1

Second Base	PCT	G	PO	A	E	DP
Alomar	.971	28	48	53	3	10
Cintron	.975	19	17	33	2	6

	PCT	G	PO	A	E	DP
Green	.969	14	16	15	1	4
Hairston	.972	85	174	207	11	47
Kata	.989	38	75	111	2	25
Sadler	1.000	2	2	1	0	1

Third Base	PCT	G	PO	A	E	DP
Cintron	1.000	1	1	0	0	0
Green	.918	18	12	33	4	1
Hammock	1.000	1	1	0	0	0
Hillenbrand	.921	17	6	29	3	3
Kata	1.000	3	4	4	0	0
Olson	.963	19	17	35	2	2
Sadler	1.000	2	1	0	0	0
Tracy	.935	135	104	258	25	28

Shortstop	PCT	G	PO	A	E	DP
Cintron	.972	133	141	382	15	61
Gil	.955	28	34	73	5	18
Kata	1.000	1	3	5	0	2

Olson	.920	17	18	29	4	8
Sadler	1.000	3	3	3	0	1

Outfield	PCT	G	PO	A	E	DP
Bautista	.986	137	271	8	4	1
Devore	1.000	31	53	2	0	1
Finley	.991	103	214	5	2	3
Gonzalez	.965	104	162	2	6	0
Green	9	10	1	0	0
Hairston	.000	3	0	0	0	0
Hammock	.955	12	20	1	1	0
Kroeger	1.000	19	38	0	0	0
McCracken	.979	37	45	2	1	0
Olson	1.000	4	7	0	0	0
Sadler	1.000	6	2	0	0	0
Terrero	.938	61	117	5	8	3
Tracy	1.000	1	2	0	0	0

FARM SYSTEM

Director, Player Development: Tommy Jones/**Assistant General Manager:** Bob Miller.

Class	Farm Team	League	W	L	Pct.	Finish*	Manager	Affiliate Since
AAA	Tucson (Ariz.) Sidewinders	Pacific Coast	74	70	.514	7th (16)	Chip Hale	1998
AA	#El Paso (Texas) Diablos	Texas	48	89	.350	8th (8)	Scott Coolbaugh	1999
High A	Lancaster (Calif.) JetHawks	California	86	54	.614	**2nd (10)**	Wally Backman	2001
Low A	South Bend (Ind.) Silver Hawks	Midwest	77	63	.550	**t-2nd (14)**	Tony Perezchica	1997
SS A	Yakima (Wash.) Bears	Northwest	35	41	.461	7th (8)	Bill Plummer	1999
Rookie	Missoula (Mont.) Osprey	Pioneer	27	46	.370	8th (8)	Jim Presley	1999

*Finish in overall standings (No. of teams in league)/playoff teams in **boldface**   #Affiliate will operate in Tennessee (Southern) in 2005

TUCSON SIDEWINDERS — Class AAA

PACIFIC COAST LEAGUE

BATTING	AVG	G	AB	R	H	2B	3B	HR	RBI	BB	SO	SB	CS	OBP	SLG	B	T	HT	WT	DOB	1st Yr	Resides
Alomar, Roberto	.400	2	5	2	2	0	0	0	0	1	2	0	0	.500	.400	S	R	6-0	185	2-5-68	1985	Bradenton, Fla.
Ansman, Craig	.251	104	342	59	86	19	1	19	58	36	117	1	1	.326	.480	R	R	6-3	222	3-10-78	2000	West Islip, N.Y.
Baerga, Carlos	.250	1	4	1	1	0	0	0	0	0	0	0	0	.250	.500	S	R	5-11	215	11-4-68	1986	Bayamon, D.R.
Barden, Brian	.283	89	332	50	94	30	5	8	50	18	83	3	1	.324	.476	R	R	5-11	200	4-2-81	2002	Corvallis, Ore.
Brito, Juan	.314	34	102	22	32	5	2	3	16	6	25	1	0	.358	.490	R	R	5-11	205	11-7-79	1997	Santiago Rodriguez, D.R.
Castillo, Wilkin	.150	6	20	2	3	1	0	0	2	3	3	0	0	.261	.200	S	R	6-0	170	6-1-84	2003	Bani, D.R.
Colbrunn, Greg	.300	3	10	1	3	1	0	1	5	0	2	0	0	.300	.700	R	R	6-0	215	7-26-69	1988	Mount Pleasant, S.C.
DeRenne, Keoni	.307	87	290	39	89	19	2	0	41	23	30	3	2	.353	.386	S	R	5-7	165	4-30-79	2000	Honolulu, Hawaii
Devore, Doug	.269	61	234	32	63	13	0	14	43	21	67	3	2	.328	.504	L	L	6-4	215	12-14-77	1999	Dublin, Ohio
Franklin, Micah	.294	29	68	10	20	5	0	4	12	8	21	4	0	.367	.544	S	R	6-0	220	4-25-72	1990	San Francisco, Calif.
Garrabrants, Steve	.400	6	20	7	8	1	1	1	4	2	2	0	0	.455	.700	R	R	5-10	170	11-18-81	2003	Phoenix, Ariz.
Gil, Jerry	.278	114	421	53	117	31	8	11	58	12	94	12	1	.299	.468	R	R	6-3	183	10-14-82	2000	Santo Domingo, D.R.
Green, Andy	.327	77	309	56	101	31	3	9	45	34	45	10	4	.394	.534	R	R	5-9	180	7-7-77	2000	Lexington, Ky.
Hairston, Scott	.313	28	115	29	36	8	3	5	20	11	21	0	3	.375	.565	R	R	6-0	190	5-25-80	2001	Oro Valley, Ariz.
Hall, Victor	.250	42	136	24	34	4	5	1	9	18	29	2	2	.338	.375	L	L	5-11	170	9-16-80	1998	Arleta, Calif.
Hammock, Robby	.286	8	21	1	6	1	0	0	4	2	1	2	0	.333	.333	R	R	5-10	185	5-13-77	1998	Dacula, Ga.
Kroeger, Josh	.332	59	208	30	69	23	0	10	41	15	47	2	1	.376	.587	L	L	6-2	200	8-31-82	2000	San Diego, Calif.
Magallanes, Ever	.263	16	38	7	10	1	0	0	3	4	5	2	0	.349	.289	L	L	5-10	160	11-6-65	1987	Downey, Calif.
Mayne, Brent	.091	5	11	1	1	0	0	0	1	4	0	0	0	.167	.091	L	R	6-1	190	4-19-68	1989	Corona Del Mar, Calif.
McCracken, Quinton	.328	15	58	7	19	5	1	1	8	3	5	2	2	.361	.500	S	R	5-9	190	8-16-70	1992	Scottsdale, Ariz.
Mercado, Orlando	.000	2	2	0	0	0	0	0	0	1	0	0	0	.000	.000	R	R	5-10	195	3-13-85	2003	Arecibo, P.R.
Myers, Corey	.289	57	180	25	52	12	1	7	25	22	43	0	1	.369	.483	R	R	6-2	220	6-5-80	1999	Henderson, Nev.
Neal, Steve	.279	119	373	52	104	22	3	15	58	45	109	2	2	.356	.475	L	L	6-2	258	2-14-77	1998	Pine Bluff, Ark.
Nichols, Kyle	.293	58	167	33	49	10	0	14	39	26	64	0	0	.390	.605	R	R	6-2	160	3-29-78	2001	Southport, Fla.
Olivares, Juan	.000	1	1	0	0	0	0	0	0	0	1	0	0	.000	.000	R	R	6-2	160	8-2-84	2002	San Pedro de Macoris, D.R.
Olson, Tim	.299	37	147	32	44	11	0	7	25	16	28	5	1	.373	.517	R	R	6-2	190	8-1-78	2000	Bismarck, N.D.
Ramirez, Julio	.272	125	441	67	120	26	9	7	64	22	118	21	11	.310	.420	R	R	5-11	159	8-10-77	1994	Santo Domingo, D.R.
Terrero, Luis	.313	58	217	36	68	9	6	9	35	17	48	15	3	.374	.535	R	R	6-2	206	5-18-80	1998	Barahona, D.R.
Tracy, Chad	.400	11	40	7	16	4	0	2	11	8	5	2	0	.490	.650	L	R	6-2	205	5-22-80	2001	Charlotte, N.C.
Varner, Noochie	.321	100	343	64	110	18	3	6	37	41	62	4	1	.396	.443	R	R	6-0	185	12-7-80	2000	Cynthiana, Ky.
Waldron, Jeff	.000	3	2	0	0	0	0	0	0	1	1	0	0	.333	.000	L	R	6-1	220	10-4-76	1999	Lynn, Mass.
Zinter, Alan	.335	54	179	28	60	12	2	7	39	24	33	0	0	.403	.542	S	R	6-2	195	5-19-68	1989	Oro Valley, Ariz.

PITCHING	W	L	ERA	G	GS	CG	SV	IP	H	R	ER	BB	SO	AVG	B	T	HT	WT	DOB	1st Yr	Resides
Abreu, Winston	1	0	5.68	28	0	0	3	44	44	28	28	25	41	.257	R	R	6-2	155	4-5-77	1994	Cotui, D.R.
2-team (14 Las Vegas)....	2	2	6.42	42	1	0	3	67	64	48	48	45	64	.248							
Aquino, Greg	1	3	6.37	21	2	0	1	30	33	25	21	18	19	.270	R	R	6-1	188	1-11-79	1996	Palenque, D.R.
Barber, Kevin	0	0	6.75	2	0	0	0	5	8	4	4	1	2	.348	R	R	6-3	205	12-12-78	2000	Belton, S.C.
Bruney, Brian	2	0	1.18	31	0	0	5	38	18	8	5	20	42	.141	R	R	6-3	225	2-17-82	2000	Warrenton, Ore.
Cannon, Jon	9	8	4.29	33	19	0	1	122	127	65	58	54	98	.271	R	L	6-3	200	1-1-75	1996	Los Altos, Calif.
Carque, Joe	0	0	27.00	1	0	0	0	1	4	3	2	0	0	.571	R	R	6-1	185	5-20-81	2003	Henderson, Nev.
Cervantes, Chris	1	0	12.15	5	0	0	0	7	10	9	9	3	2	.333	L	L	6-1	160	2-4-79	1998	Tucson, Ariz.
Choate, Randy	0	0	5.68	15	0	0	1	13	10	8	8	8	7	.222	L	L	6-2	195	9-5-75	1997	Tampa, Fla.
Cormier, Lance	3	3	2.68	8	8	2	0	50	50	17	15	17	37	.260	R	R	6-1	190	8-19-80	2002	Lafayette, La.
Daigle, Casey	4	6	6.88	18	15	0	0	101	154	85	77	24	51	.348	R	R	6-5	217	4-4-81	2000	Vinton, La.
Fetters, Mike	0	0	4.50	7	0	0	1	8	11	5	4	1	10	.314	R	R	6-4	230	12-19-64	1986	Chandler, Ariz.
Fossum, Casey	0	0	0.00	3	3	0	0	15	11	2	0	3	16	.196	S	L	6-1	155	1-6-78	1999	Waco, Texas
Freed, Mark	3	2	4.35	57	0	0	2	70	74	37	34	35	45	.273	L	L	6-4	225	8-10-78	2000	Pennsville, N.J.
Gonzalez, Edgar	5	5	4.88	15	15	1	0	94	99	52	51	25	66	.277	R	R	6-0	215	2-23-83	2002	San Nicolas, Mexico
Good, Andrew	2	3	3.04	5	3	0	0	24	25	12	8	4	17	.266	R	R	6-1	210	9-19-79	1998	Rochester Hills, Mich.
Gosling, Mike	9	5	5.82	24	21	0	0	128	160	101	83	53	67	.305	L	L	6-2	190	9-23-80	2002	Las Vegas, Nev.
Hansell, Greg	1	0	4.87	15	0	0	0	20	25	11	11	13	23	.309	R	R	6-5	220	3-12-74	1989	La Palma, Calif.
Henrie, Matt	1	4	6.70	8	7	0	0	44	63	34	33	10	17	.346	L	R	6-4	190	11-28-79	2002	Jupiter, Fla.
Lizarraga, Sergio	1	1	9.90	3	2	0	0	10	19	14	11	7	9	.413	R	R	6-4	190	7-23-81	2001	Mazatlan, Mexico
Lyon, Brandon	2	3	15.12	6	3	0	0	8	15	14	14	4	4	.375	R	R	6-1	180	8-10-79	2000	Salt Lake City, Utah
Medders, Brandon	0	0	4.26	11	0	0	0	13	15	7	6	4	17	.273	R	R	6-2	195	1-24-80	2001	Duncanville, Ala.
Nance, Shane	2	4	6.35	46	2	0	2	45	61	38	32	22	48	.314	L	L	5-8	191	9-7-77	2000	Houston, Texas
Parque, Jim	3	2	6.30	12	8	0	0	50	73	39	35	14	17	.348	L	L	5-11	170	2-8-76	1997	Puyallup, Wash.
Perrault, Josh	0	0	1.80	1	1	0	0	5	7	2	1	1	0	.350	R	R	6-3	205	6-11-82	2003	Mesa, Ariz.
Raggio, Brady	5	6	5.81	56	2	0	2	84	113	65	54	23	68	.319	R	R	6-4	210	9-17-72	1992	Danville, Calif.
Reynolds, Shane	2	1	5.27	5	5	1	0	27	30	16	16	3	28	.268	R	R	6-3	215	3-26-68	1989	Houston, Texas
Rocha, Angel	0	0	19.29	1	1	0	0	2	6	5	5	4	1	.500	L	L	6-3	205	11-15-84	2002	Santo Domingo, D.R.
Schultz, Mike	0	0	5.00	7	0	0	0	9	12	7	5	5	4	.333	R	R	6-7	210	11-28-79	2000	Reseda, Calif.
Service, Scott	5	0	3.24	24	0	0	9	25	28	9	9	6	28	.283	R	R	6-6	250	2-26-67	1986	Cincinnati, Ohio
Silva, Jose	2	3	7.07	9	8	0	0	42	59	33	33	18	31	.343	R	R	6-2	205	12-19-73	1992	Sarasota, Fla.

ORGANIZATION STATISTICS

Conor Jackson: Led the system in hits and RBIs

Carlos Quentin: Topped organization with a .435 on-base percentage

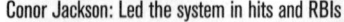

PITCHING

	W	L	ERA	G	GS	CG	SV	IP	H	R	ER	BB	SO	AVG	B	T	HT	WT	DOB	1st Yr	Resides
Stockman, Phil	3	2	5.75	12	12	0	0	56	60	39	36	36	35	.287	R	R	6-6	200	1-25-80	1998	Mt. Warren Park, Australia
Vaillancourt, Tim	0	1	4.15	1	1	0	0	4	5	2	2	0	7	.278	R	R	6-4	195	12-5-81	2003	Bear, Del.
Valverde, Jose	1	1	4.22	10	1	0	3	11	9	5	5	5	5	.225	R	R	6-4	254	7-24-79	1997	Santo Domingo, D.R.
Villafuerte, Brandon	2	2	2.64	23	0	0	4	31	27	10	9	10	23	.233	R	R	5-11	195	12-17-75	1995	Morgan Hill, Calif.
Villarreal, Oscar	0	2	14.34	6	5	0	0	11	20	17	17	4	12	.385	L	R	6-0	205	11-22-81	1999	Monterrey, Mexico
Ward, Jeremy	1	0	10.50	6	0	0	0	6	10	7	7	3	1	.370	R	R	6-2	235	2-24-78	1999	Rocky Mount, N.C.

FIELDING

Catcher	PCT	G	PO	A	E	DP	PB
Ansman	.990	93	547	45	6	7	6
Brito	.995	31	168	14	1	0	0
Hammock	.968	6	29	1	1	0	0
Mayne	1.000	5	14	3	0	0	1
Myers	.981	30	142	16	3	1	3
Zinter	1.000	2	16	1	0	0	1

First Base	PCT	G	PO	A	E	DP
Colbrunn	1.000	1	7	1	0	0
Franklin	1.000	1	11	1	0	0
Myers	.971	5	33	1	1	5
Neal	.998	105	816	78	2	75
Nichols	.995	26	180	11	1	19
Zinter	.986	28	196	20	3	15

Second Base	PCT	G	PO	A	E	DP
Alomar	1.000	2	9	2	0	0
Barden	.982	25	41	70	2	17
DeRenne	.988	64	117	200	4	47

Garrabrants	1.000	5	7	11	0	2
Green	.979	30	62	80	3	16
Hairston	.933	21	36	47	6	7
Magallanes	.960	8	8	16	1	0
Olson	1.000	2	2	3	0	0

Third Base	PCT	G	PO	A	E	DP
Barden	.970	67	37	127	5	17
Castillo	1.000	4	4	3	0	0
DeRenne	.938	8	1	14	1	0
Green	.922	34	23	71	8	3
Magallanes	.500	2	0	1	1	0
Myers	.918	22	10	35	4	5
Olson	.895	8	0	17	2	1
Tracy	.909	8	7	23	3	1
Zinter	.947	10	3	15	1	0

Shortstop	PCT	G	PO	A	E	DP
DeRenne	.950	13	13	25	2	3
Gil	.946	111	195	317	29	67

Green	1.000	8	10	17	0	2
Olson	.966	20	37	48	3	12

Outfield	PCT	G	PO	A	E	DP
Castillo	1.000	2	4	0	0	0
DeVore	.951	59	76	2	4	0
Franklin	1.000	8	14	3	0	0
Green	1.000	6	7	0	0	0
Hairston	1.000	5	11	0	0	0
Hall	.984	33	60	3	1	0
Kroeger	.964	62	132	3	5	0
McCracken	1.000	13	22	2	0	0
Neal	1.000	6	8	0	0	0
Olson	1.000	10	16	0	0	0
Ramirez	.978	118	261	10	6	2
Terrero	.978	57	127	5	3	0
Tracy	1.000	3	5	0	0	0
Varner	.994	90	151	5	1	2

EL PASO DIABLOS   Class AA

TEXAS LEAGUE

BATTING	AVG	G	AB	R	H	2B	3B	HR	RBI	BB	SO	SB	CS	OBP	SLG	B	T	HT	WT	DOB	1st Yr	Resides
Aguirre, Rodrigo	.429	2	7	3	3	1	0	0	1	0	0	1	0	.429	.571	L	R	5-9	165	8-1-83	2004	Hermosillo, Mexico
Barden, Brian	.303	48	195	33	59	10	6	3	28	10	48	1	2	.335	.462	R	R	5-11	200	4-2-81	2002	Corvallis, Ore.
Brooks, Doc	.283	16	46	7	13	5	1	0	8	3	13	0	0	.353	.435	R	R	5-10	190	1-21-80	2001	Phenix City, Ala.
Brown, Neb	.284	22	81	8	23	4	0	0	7	9	13	6	2	.356	.333	L	R	6-0	185	11-7-79	2002	Stillwater, Okla.
Cota, Jesus	.290	94	366	50	106	21	4	10	59	18	61	2	2	.324	.451	L	R	6-3	220	11-7-81	2001	Tucson, Ariz.
D'Antona, Jamie	.211	19	71	2	15	3	1	0	7	2	16	0	0	.230	.282	R	R	6-2	210	5-12-82	2003	Trumbull, Conn.
DeRenne, Keoni	.361	17	61	16	22	4	2	0	9	15	4	1	1	.487	.492	S	R	5-7	165	4-30-79	2000	Honolulu, Hawaii
DiRosa, Mike	.214	65	192	27	41	12	1	3	31	36	63	1	0	.336	.333	L	R	5-11	190	1-17-80	2001	Miami, Fla.
Garrabrants, Steve	.250	31	112	20	28	7	1	2	12	10	29	6	3	.323	.384	R	R	5-10	170	11-18-81	2003	Phoenix, Ariz.
Garthwaite, Jay	.189	42	122	9	23	5	2	2	13	5	37	2	0	.229	.311	R	R	6-2	210	11-26-80	2002	Kent, Wash.
Goss, Michael	.325	12	40	1	13	2	0	0	6	1	7	1	2	.341	.375	L	L	5-11	185	9-26-80	2002	Louisville, Miss.
Haley, Adam	.229	42	153	16	35	6	3	0	18	12	27	0	2	.298	.307	L	R	6-0	170	9-4-80	2002	Louisville, Ky.

BATTING

BATTING	AVG	G	AB	R	H	2B	3B	HR	RBI	BB	SO	SB	CS	OBP	SLG	B	T	HT	WT	DOB	1st Yr	Resides
Hall, Victor	.344	58	192	27	66	8	6	2	18	23	36	12	9	.412	.479	L	L	5-11	170	9-16-80	1998	Arleta, Calif.
Jackson, Conor	.301	60	226	33	68	13	2	6	37	24	36	3	3	.367	.456	R	R	6-3	205	5-7-82	2003	Woodland Hills, Calif.
Kroeger, Josh	.331	65	245	44	81	28	4	9	46	21	48	2	1	.393	.588	L	L	6-2	200	8-31-82	2000	San Diego, Calif.
Luellwitz, Sean	.198	26	86	12	17	4	0	3	7	9	19	0	0	.303	.349	R	R	6-5	220	11-16-79	2002	Brookfield, Wis.
Morgan, Matt	.164	19	55	8	9	5	0	0	7	12	13	0	0	.309	.255	R	R	6-2	170	8-10-81	2002	Orosi, Calif.
Nichols, Kyle	.292	49	144	23	42	9	0	7	35	21	43	0	2	.376	.500	R	R	6-2	225	3-29-78	2001	Southport, Fla.
Quentin, Carlos	.357	60	210	39	75	19	0	6	38	18	23	0	6	.443	.533	R	R	6-2	220	8-28-82	2004	Chula Vista, Calif.
Richar, Danny	.207	26	82	6	17	3	0	0	5	7	17	2	0	.286	.244	L	R	6-0	180	6-6-83	2002	La Romana, D.R.
Santana, Mayobanex	.222	16	27	2	6	1	0	0	2	1	6	0	1	.250	.259	R	R	6-3	185	8-23-81	1999	Santo Domingo, D.R.
Santos, Sergio	.282	89	347	53	98	19	5	11	52	24	89	3	2	.332	.461	R	R	6-3	190	7-4-83	2002	Hacienda Heights, Calif.
Snyder, Chris	.301	99	346	66	104	31	0	15	57	46	57	3	1	.389	.520	R	R	6-3	220	2-12-81	2002	Houston, Texas
Uggla, Dan	.258	83	295	29	76	12	2	4	30	15	55	10	7	.301	.353	R	R	5-11	195	3-11-80	2001	Columbia, Tenn.
Varner, Noochie	.330	32	115	15	38	4	1	1	10	10	23	2	1	.384	.409	R	R	6-0	185	12-7-80	2000	Cynthiana, Ky.
Waldron, Jeff	.320	15	50	4	16	4	0	1	6	6	9	0	1	.393	.460	L	R	6-1	220	10-4-76	1999	Lynn, Mass.
West, Todd	.251	66	215	24	54	10	1	0	24	18	37	12	3	.311	.307	R	R	5-11	160	3-2-79	2000	El Paso, Texas
Williams, Marland	.259	121	487	82	126	21	10	8	44	40	116	49	8	.317	.392	R	R	5-9	175	6-22-81	2002	Williston, Fla.

PITCHING

PITCHING	W	L	ERA	G	GS	CG	SV	IP	H	R	ER	BB	SO	AVG	B	T	HT	WT	DOB	1st Yr	Resides
Barber, Scott	1	3	5.44	38	1	0	1	81	98	51	49	24	47	.302	R	R	6-3	205	12-12-78	2000	Belton, S.C.
Biggs, Billy	0	1	1.35	14	0	0	0	20	15	5	3	6	16	.208	R	R	6-0	200	9-9-79	2002	Scott Depot, W.Va.
Bulger, Jason	0	3	3.91	24	0	0	8	25	25	12	11	19	26	.255	R	R	6-4	210	12-6-78	2001	Snellville, Ga.
Cervantes, Chris	1	1	8.53	21	3	0	1	44	64	47	42	25	28	.335	L	L	6-1	160	2-4-79	1998	Tucson, Ariz.
Chico, Matt	3	7	5.78	14	12	0	0	62	82	53	40	36	59	.315	L	L	5-11	190	6-10-83	2003	Fallbrook, Calif.
Cormier, Lance	2	3	3.29	10	8	0	0	63	66	19	16	17	58	.277	R	R	6-1	190	8-19-80	2002	Lafayette, La.
Doyle, Jared	0	1	3.97	11	0	0	0	11	10	6	5	10	9	.227	R	L	6-0	190	1-30-81	2002	Orlando, Fla.
Fossum, Casey	0	0	2.08	2	2	0	0	4	3	1	1	3	5	.188	S	L	6-1	165	1-6-78	1999	Waco, Texas
Goocher, Clint	6	10	5.23	17	13	0	0	86	103	61	50	27	41	.295	L	L	6-2	200	6-15-82	2003	Denton, Texas
Good, Andrew	0	0	0.93	4	4	0	0	10	7	2	1	3	9	.212	R	R	6-1	210	9-19-79	1998	Rochester Hills, Mich.
Henrie, Matt	9	4	5.28	17	15	1	0	102	128	68	60	20	60	.310	L	R	6-4	205	11-28-79	2002	Jupiter, Fla.
Juarez, William	3	7	5.00	13	13	0	0	76	80	47	42	22	68	.269	R	R	6-2	205	4-22-81	2000	Chinandega, Nicaragua
Leclair, Aric	4	2	4.38	30	0	0	0	39	41	20	19	20	33	.270	L	L	6-0	190	4-12-78	2000	Swanzey, N.H.
Lizarraga, Sergio	4	10	5.04	29	17	3	0	123	140	71	69	36	102	.289	R	R	6-4	190	7-23-81	2001	Mazatlan, Mexico
Murphy, Bill	3	3	6.68	6	6	0	0	31	41	28	23	17	24	.328	L	L	6-0	190	5-9-81	2002	Riverside, Calif.
Nippert, Dustin	2	5	3.64	14	14	0	0	72	77	45	29	40	73	.267	R	R	6-7	200	5-6-81	2002	Beallsville, Ohio
Perez, Beltran	2	6	4.41	37	8	0	3	104	102	56	51	46	77	.261	R	R	6-2	180	10-24-81	1999	San Fran. de Macoris, D.R.
Reynolds, Shane	0	1	5.79	2	2	0	0	5	7	3	3	2	3	.350	R	R	6-3	215	3-26-68	1989	Houston, Texas
Rosario, Adriano	3	3	5.44	7	7	0	0	43	47	27	26	5	36	.280	R	R	6-1	190	5-16-85	2002	San Fran. de Macoris, D.R.
Schultz, Matt	0	0	4.61	12	0	0	1	14	16	7	7	13	14	.308	R	R	6-7	210	11-28-79	2000	Reseda, Calif.
Sikaras, Pete	0	3	3.72	39	0	0	9	46	51	28	19	30	46	.280	R	R	6-2	200	5-5-79	2000	Niles, Ill.
Slaten, Doug	0	1	10.00	11	0	0	0	9	16	13	10	10	6	.390	L	L	6-5	190	2-4-80	2000	Venice, Calif.
Smith, Sam	2	5	7.55	18	6	0	0	48	76	45	40	26	39	.360	R	R	6-4	210	8-23-79	2002	Rio Rancho, N.M.
Stockman, Phil	1	3	2.67	6	6	1	0	27	17	13	8	20	21	.179	R	R	6-6	200	1-25-80	1998	Mt. Warren Park, Australia
Ward, Jeremy	0	2	7.94	7	0	0	0	6	10	8	5	1	4	.435	R	R	6-2	235	2-24-78	1999	Rocky Mount, N.C.
White, Bill	2	3	7.39	31	0	0	0	35	42	37	29	34	40	.302	L	L	6-3	215	11-20-78	2000	Alexander City, Ala.
Wilkinson, Matt	0	2	10.80	5	0	0	2	3	8	4	4	3	5	.444	L	R	6-3	195	10-25-77	2001	Chicago, Ill.

FIELDING

Catcher
Catcher	PCT	G	PO	A	E	DP	PB
DiRosa	.977	50	308	27	8	1	2
Morgan	1.000	5	29	2	0	0	1
Snyder	.988	83	580	54	8	3	8
Waldron	.983	8	53	6	1	0	0

First Base
First Base	PCT	G	PO	A	E	DP
Cota	.991	92	777	59	8	69
D'Antona	1.000	2	9	3	0	0
Luellwitz	.988	26	221	29	3	27
Morgan	1.000	3	19	2	0	4
Nichols	.980	14	92	6	2	7
Santana	1.000	8	22	1	0	1
Snyder	.984	8	58	2	1	4

Second Base
Second Base	PCT	G	PO	A	E	DP
Aguirre	1.000	2	6	7	0	2
Brown	1.000	18	33	61	0	13
Garrabrants	.947	29	54	90	8	12

	PCT	G	PO	A	E	DP
Richar	.965	24	44	67	4	15
Uggla	.940	18	24	55	5	11
West	.985	55	89	167	4	35

Third Base
Third Base	PCT	G	PO	A	E	DP
Barden	.933	48	21	77	7	6
Brown	.875	3	1	6	1	0
D'Antona	.917	18	6	38	4	4
Haley	.886	14	15	24	5	3
Jackson	1.000	6	0	5	0	0
Morgan	.857	8	4	14	3	4
Santana	1.000	4	2	6	0	0
Uggla	.933	45	27	84	8	4
West	1.000	4	3	1	0	0

Shortstop
Shortstop	PCT	G	PO	A	E	DP
DeRenne	.971	15	22	46	2	10
Haley	.955	29	45	83	6	22
Richar	1.000	2	5	5	0	3

		PCT	G	PO	A	E	DP
Santana	1.000	1	1	4	0	0
Santos	.935	87	138	223	25	47
West	1.000	9	13	23	0	7

Outfield
Outfield	PCT	G	PO	A	E	DP
Brooks	.889	12	8	0	1	0
Cota	1.000	3	3	0	0	0
Garthwaite	.966	38	55	1	2	0
Goss	.941	12	15	1	1	0
Hall	.945	47	85	1	5	0
Jackson	.966	47	83	1	3	0
Kroeger	.943	66	112	4	7	1
Luellwitz	.000	1	0	0	1	0
Quentin	.981	57	100	5	2	0
Santana	1.000	1	1	0	0	0
Uggla	.957	20	21	1	1	0
Varner	1.000	25	39	1	0	1
West	1.000	1	2	0	0	0
Williams	.957	116	240	7	11	0

LANCASTER JETHAWKS — High Class A

CALIFORNIA LEAGUE

BATTING	AVG	G	AB	R	H	2B	3B	HR	RBI	BB	SO	SB	CS	OBP	SLG	B	T	HT	WT	DOB	1st Yr	Resides
Abercrombie, Reggie	.342	29	120	24	41	10	2	3	19	2	24	8	1	.358	.533	R	R	6-3	220	7-15-80	2000	Columbus, Ga.
Avias, Phil	.315	109	384	64	121	22	8	13	68	29	54	5	4	.359	.516	R	R	5-11	175	12-17-82	2002	North Hills, Calif.
Ball, Jarred	.297	125	472	82	140	26	6	15	66	45	123	17	9	.359	.472	S	R	6-1	170	4-18-83	2001	Tomball, Texas
Biguenet, Michael	.140	24	57	8	8	1	1	3	3	26	1	1	.258	.246	R	R	5-11	185	11-20-81	2004	Mandeville, La.
Brooks, Doc	.332	90	301	67	100	20	2	15	47	30	82	7	7	.401	.561	R	R	5-10	190	1-21-80	2001	Phenix City, Ala.
Brown, Neb	.290	63	245	48	71	11	4	4	31	28	28	14	7	.367	.416	L	R	6-0	185	11-7-79	2002	Stillwater, Okla.
Cota, Jesus	.403	16	62	15	25	4	1	3	22	4	6	1	0	.435	.645	L	R	6-3	220	11-7-81	2001	Tucson, Ariz.
D'Antona, Jamie	.315	68	273	45	86	18	1	13	57	16	36	2	3	.353	.531	R	R	6-2	210	5-12-82	2003	Trumbull, Conn.
DeRenne, Keoni	.246	15	61	11	15	4	1	0	10	6	7	2	2	.309	.344	S	R	5-7	165	4-30-79	2000	Honolulu, Hawaii
Garrabrants, Steve	.270	60	215	33	58	6	1	3	30	22	49	11	3	.346	.349	R	R	5-10	170	11-18-81	2003	Phoenix, Ariz.
Garthwaite, Jay	.311	63	238	49	74	17	3	12	41	17	55	5	3	.357	.559	R	R	6-2	210	11-26-80	2002	Kent, Wash.
Haley, Adam	.314	57	159	23	50	4	1	0	14	10	33	5	8	.360	.352	L	R	6-0	170	9-4-80	2002	Louisville, Ky.

BATTING

BATTING	AVG	G	AB	R	H	2B	3B	HR	RBI	BB	SO	SB	CS	OBP	SLG	B	T	HT	WT	DOB	1st Yr	Resides
Hammock, Robby	.667	2	9	2	6	2	0	0	3	1	1	0	0	.700	.889	R	R	5-10	185	5-13-77	1998	Dacula, Ga.
Jackson, Conor	.345	67	258	64	89	19	2	11	54	45	36	4	3	.438	.562	R	R	6-3	205	5-7-82	2003	Austin, Texas
Luellwitz, Sean	.270	93	367	50	99	29	1	10	51	19	84	4	0	.309	.436	R	R	6-5	220	11-16-79	2002	Brookfield, Wis.
McStoots, Jason	.154	12	26	3	4	1	0	0	3	1	6	1	1	.185	.192	L	R	5-10	185	5-10-80	2003	West Brooklyn, Ill.
Morgan, Matt	.241	75	228	31	55	12	0	4	25	19	46	3	5	.300	.346	R	R	6-2	170	8-10-81	2002	Orosi, Calif.
Myers, Corey	.410	10	39	9	16	2	0	2	9	5	3	0	0	.477	.615	R	R	6-2	220	6-5-80	1999	Henderson, Nev.
Quentin, Carlos	.310	65	242	64	75	14	1	15	51	25	33	5	1	.428	.562	R	R	6-2	220	8-28-82	2004	Chula Vista, Calif.
Reynolds, Mark	.083	4	12	1	1	0	0	0	1	0	4	0	0	.083	.083	R	R	6-1	200	8-3-83	2004	Virginia Beach, Va.
Richar, Danny	.282	96	383	51	108	13	4	6	44	16	78	22	8	.312	.384	L	R	6-0	180	6-6-83	2002	La Romana, D.R.
Santana, Mayobanex	.219	20	64	10	14	1	0	1	9	5	12	1	1	.282	.281	R	R	6-3	185	8-23-81	1999	Santo Domingo, D.R.
Simon, Brandon	.182	35	77	11	14	2	0	0	6	3	22	4	2	.226	.208	L	L	6-0	175	9-9-80	2002	Fresno, Calif.
Tosca, Daniel	.252	84	250	26	63	14	0	7	37	37	61	3	4	.355	.392	L	R	6-0	180	11-1-80	1999	Seffner, Fla.
Uggla, Dan	.336	37	140	29	47	13	3	6	38	17	21	2	4	.419	.600	R	R	5-11	195	3-11-80	2001	Columbia, Tenn.
Zeringue, Jon	.335	56	230	36	77	14	3	10	41	14	53	9	5	.374	.552	R	R	6-2	205	8-29-83	2004	Thibodaux, La.

PITCHING

PITCHING	W	L	ERA	G	GS	CG	SV	IP	H	R	ER	BB	SO	AVG	B	T	HT	WT	DOB	1st Yr	Resides
Bass, Adam	10	8	5.03	28	27	1	0	147	180	90	82	49	117	.304	R	R	6-6	210	7-31-81	2003	Madison, Ala.
Belson, Greg	3	1	6.34	29	0	0	1	38	51	37	27	23	23	.321	R	R	5-10	170	8-16-78	2000	Staten Island, N.Y.
Bulger, Jason	0	1	1.52	21	0	0	11	24	14	4	4	10	31	.171	R	R	6-4	210	12-6-78	2002	Snellville, Ga.
Doyle, Jared	1	2	11.39	8	5	0	0	21	39	29	27	10	11	.402	R	L	6-0	190	1-30-81	2002	Orlando, Fla.
Glant, Dustin	3	3	6.14	13	2	0	3	22	28	17	15	13	12	.311	R	R	6-2	200	7-20-81	2003	Fort Wayne, Ind.
Gonzalez, Enrique	13	6	3.22	42	17	0	0	142	128	64	51	44	110	.242	R	R	5-10	195	7-14-82	2000	Bolivar, Venez.
Goocher, Clint	9	2	3.67	14	14	1	0	91	94	39	37	12	82	.266	L	L	6-2	200	6-15-82	2003	Denton, Texas
Holsten, Ryan	7	6	5.77	43	5	0	0	83	103	60	53	38	45	.313	R	R	6-4	210	5-5-79	2001	Wilmington, Del.
Liebeck, Jered	1	0	11.57	5	2	0	0	7	10	9	9	5	4	.323	R	R	6-1	200	1-27-81	2003	Phoenix, Ariz.
McMachen, Clifford	1	4	4.09	37	5	0	2	70	80	37	32	29	64	.279	L	L	6-1	205	1-14-81	2001	North Las Vegas, Nev.
Morgan, Matt	0	0	13.50	2	1	0	0	3	5	5	5	2	1	.333	R	R	6-2	170	8-10-81	2002	Orosi, Calif.
Schultz, Mike	1	1	3.00	13	0	0	2	18	19	13	6	13	18	.260	R	R	6-7	210	11-28-79	2000	Reseda, Calif.
Shappi, A.J.	1	0	3.00	2	1	0	0	6	6	2	2	1	8	.261	R	R	6-2	195	10-16-82	2004	Yorba Linda, Calif.
Silva, Jesus	11	7	4.38	28	27	0	0	152	168	89	74	56	126	.276	R	R	5-11	170	12-24-82	2000	Maracay, Venez.
Smith, Sam	5	5	5.40	18	12	0	1	68	86	46	41	24	53	.310	R	R	6-4	210	8-23-79	2002	Rio Rancho, N.M.
Watson, Mike	6	1	4.46	57	0	0	1	69	66	44	34	44	62	.256	R	R	6-1	180	9-28-80	2002	Altoona, Pa.
Wechsler, Justin	4	1	2.48	56	0	0	18	80	63	25	22	27	96	.221	R	R	6-2	240	4-6-80	2001	Pendleton, Ind.
Wells, Carlton	3	1	4.68	71	0	0	1	67	87	41	35	24	33	.318	L	L	6-2	210	3-25-80	2000	Tampa, Fla.
Whatley, Keith	2	4	7.19	12	10	0	0	51	70	51	41	27	47	.318	L	L	6-2	215	4-23-80	2002	Atlanta, Texas
White, Bill	1	1	1.96	14	0	0	1	18	16	8	4	7	23	.232	L	L	6-3	215	11-20-78	2000	Alexander City, Ala.
Zamora, Pete	3	3	6.15	13	13	0	0	67	91	50	46	22	37	.324	L	L	6-3	180	8-13-75	1997	Mission Viejo, Calif.

FIELDING

Catcher	PCT	G	PO	A	E	DP	PB
Avlas	.980	106	741	91	17	1	5
Hammock	1.000	1	5	1	0	0	0
Morgan	.992	20	114	18	1	0	4
Myers	1.000	3	16	1	0	0	2
Tosca	.978	22	128	8	3	2	0

First Base	PCT	G	PO	A	E	DP
Cota	.990	13	96	6	1	8
Garthwaite	.864	4	17	2	3	1
Luellwitz	.995	93	788	43	4	74
McStoots	1.000	1	5	0	0	0
Morgan	.985	11	62	5	1	6
Myers	.946	4	34	1	2	2
Santana	.988	19	149	15	2	16
Uggla	1.000	6	47	4	0	2

Second Base	PCT	G	PO	A	E	DP
Biguenet	.964	17	35	46	3	8
Brown	.970	62	148	172	10	35

	PCT	G	PO	A	E	DP
DeRenne	1.000	1	1	4	0	1
Garrabrants	.962	12	19	31	2	4
Haley	.962	5	13	12	1	3
McStoots	.960	6	9	15	1	2
Morgan	.974	34	59	93	4	22
Uggla	.979	19	29	64	2	9

Third Base	PCT	G	PO	A	E	DP
Biguenet	.875	5	1	6	1	0
D'Antona	.908	64	58	109	17	9
Garrabrants	.948	46	37	55	5	9
Garthwaite	.600	2	0	3	2	0
Haley	.905	19	10	28	4	0
Morgan	1.000	4	7	9	0	0
Myers	.833	1	4	1	1	0
Reynolds	.857	3	0	6	1	0
Santana	1.000	1	0	1	0	0
Uggla	.867	8	6	20	4	2

Shortstop	PCT	G	PO	A	E	DP
DeRenne	.971	14	25	41	2	9
Haley	.908	32	56	92	15	19
Morgan	.875	6	14	14	4	4
Reynolds	.750	1	1	2	1	0
Richar	.945	91	152	274	25	54
Uggla	.920	8	8	15	2	2

Outfield	PCT	G	PO	A	E	DP
Abercrombie	.985	29	63	3	1	1
Ball	.983	122	226	6	4	1
Brooks	.931	59	92	3	7	0
Cota	1.000	1	2	0	0	0
Garthwaite	.901	42	62	2	7	0
Jackson	.971	61	99	3	3	0
Morgan	.833	4	5	0	1	0
Quentin	.981	58	100	2	2	0
Simon	.956	33	43	0	2	0
Zeringue	1.000	45	76	7	0	1

SOUTH BEND SILVER HAWKS — Low Class A

MIDWEST LEAGUE

BATTING

BATTING	AVG	G	AB	R	H	2B	3B	HR	RBI	BB	SO	SB	CS	OBP	SLG	B	T	HT	WT	DOB	1st Yr	Resides
Aguirre, Rodrigo	.235	6	17	0	4	0	0	0	1	0	2	0	0	.235	.235	L	R	5-9	165	8-1-83	2004	Hermosillo, Mexico
Bonafacio, Emilio	.260	120	411	59	107	9	6	1	37	25	122	40	10	.306	.319	R	R	5-10	160	4-23-85	2002	Santo Domingo, D.R.
Carter, Chris	.385	6	26	3	10	3	0	2	7	0	2	0	0	.385	.731	L	L	6-0	220	9-16-82	2004	Concord, Calif.
Cook, Jeff	.289	120	405	55	117	23	6	3	59	23	64	10	8	.331	.398	L	R	5-10	190	10-4-80	2003	Hattiesburg, Miss.
Firlit, Dan	.083	4	12	2	1	0	0	0	0	2	5	1	0	.214	.083	R	R	6-1	190	11-22-78	2000	Orland Park, Ill.
Frazier, Alex	.313	125	464	73	145	36	3	20	80	27	92	21	5	.366	.532	R	R	6-4	215	12-21-80	2002	Dunnellon, Fla.
Garcia, Lino	.257	113	319	43	82	14	3	4	25	22	74	12	7	.319	.357	R	R	6-3	180	10-12-83	2001	San Fernando, Venez.
Gonzalez, Alberto	.241	102	328	41	79	15	6	2	27	16	46	9	7	.297	.341	R	R	5-11	160	4-18-83	2003	Maracaibo, Venez.
Gonzalez, Carlos	.262	12	42	3	11	4	0	1	6	1	10	2	0	.279	.429	L	L	6-1	178	10-17-85	2003	Maracaibo, Venez.
Goss, Michael	.287	81	282	40	81	8	3	0	26	18	52	7	7	.340	.337	L	L	5-11	185	9-26-80	2002	Louisville, Miss.
Kaplan, Jon	.263	103	377	62	99	23	5	9	39	32	57	25	8	.329	.422	R	R	6-9	180	1-11-80	2003	Chesterfield, Mo.
McCreery, Andrew	.140	18	50	6	7	0	0	1	4	5	10	1	3	.232	.200	R	R	6-3	215	11-15-81	2002	Solana Beach, Calif.
Milons, Jereme	.172	11	29	1	5	0	1	0	1	0	10	1	1	.200	.241	R	R	6-2	205	2-5-83	2002	Starkville, Miss.
Montero, Miguel	.263	115	403	47	106	22	2	11	59	36	74	8	2	.330	.409	L	R	5-11	195	7-9-83	2001	Caracas, Venez.
Mottram, John	.272	53	184	26	50	11	0	7	36	12	31	0	0	.330	.446	R	R	6-1	190	6-24-81	2003	North Andover, Mass.
Murillo, Augie	.263	101	357	46	94	16	1	4	38	23	48	10	5	.316	.347	R	R	6-3	195	5-5-82	2003	Tijuana, Mexico
Reynolds, Mark	.067	4	15	0	1	1	0	0	0	1	5	0	0	.125	.133	R	R	6-1	200	8-3-83	2004	Virginia Beach, Va.
Reynolds, Tila	.262	91	302	38	79	14	1	1	26	25	69	15	4	.319	.325	R	R	5-11	180	2-7-81	2003	Renton, Wash.
Rose, Brian	.238	75	240	31	57	14	0	11	40	19	54	1	1	.326	.433	R	R	6-2	230	9-17-80	2003	Miami, Fla.
Varela, Edgar	.261	127	471	54	123	25	1	8	61	25	59	2	4	.304	.369	L	R	6-1	200	8-9-80	2002	E. Rancho Dominguez, Calif.

PITCHING	W	L	ERA	G	GS	CG	SV	IP	H	R	ER	BB	SO	AVG	B	T	HT	WT	DOB	1st Yr	Resides
Biggs, Billy	4	1	1.23	31	0	0	18	44	25	10	6	10	42	.163	R	R	6-0	200	9-9-79	2002	Scott Depot, W.Va.
Chico, Matt	8	5	2.57	14	14	2	0	88	59	26	25	27	89	.188	L	L	5-11	190	6-10-83	2003	Fallbrook, Calif.
Coffin, Ryan	0	3	3.13	43	0	0	1	69	63	34	24	28	63	.245	R	R	6-5	210	8-5-81	2002	Tempe, Ariz.
Cremidan, Alexander	1	2	3.27	32	1	0	7	41	49	20	15	14	45	.288	L	R	6-3	210	1-15-81	2003	San Diego, Calif.
Glant, Dustin	5	5	4.06	29	12	1	8	89	103	45	40	27	44	.294	R	R	6-2	200	7-20-81	2003	Fort Wayne, Ind.
Juarez, William	3	1	1.55	7	7	0	0	46	38	10	8	7	47	.222	R	R	6-2	205	4-22-81	2003	Chinandega, Nicaragua
Kinsey, Chris	8	11	4.90	28	27	1	0	151	171	87	82	70	87	.294	R	R	6-3	230	10-18-82	2003	Elk Grove, Calif.
Leclair, Aric	0	1	1.23	11	0	0	2	15	9	2	2	3	19	.176	L	L	6-0	190	4-12-78	2000	Swanzey, N.H.
Liebeck, Jered	5	2	3.23	12	8	0	0	53	39	22	19	15	63	.202	R	R	6-1	200	1-27-81	2003	Phoenix, Ariz.
Mock, Garrett	3	2	3.00	8	8	1	0	54	49	21	18	12	37	.243	R	R	6-4	215	4-25-83	2004	Grand Prairie, Texas
Mosquea, Daniel	3	3	5.63	41	1	0	2	56	60	37	35	22	64	.280	L	L	6-1	170	2-3-80	2003	Del Norte, D.R.
Muegge, Danny	14	4	3.12	26	25	1	0	153	149	66	53	42	104	.253	L	R	6-5	180	3-6-81	2003	Brenham, Texas
Novosel, Walt	0	0	0.00	1	0	0	0	1	1	0	0	0	1	.200	L	L	6-3	215	6-16-81	2003	Pulaski, Pa.
Rocha, Angel	2	3	6.55	9	9	0	0	45	44	39	33	31	38	.250	L	L	6-3	180	11-15-84	2002	Santo Domingo, D.R.
Rosen, Mark	0	6	5.94	29	6	0	2	64	80	48	42	35	56	.317	L	L	5-11	200	6-30-84	2002	Randolph, Mass.
Sager, Brian	0	0	19.80	4	0	0	0	5	10	11	11	6	2	.417	R	R	6-5	230	10-30-79	2002	Branford, Conn.
Scarbery, Chad	12	9	3.81	30	22	2	0	149	155	71	63	52	107	.270	R	R	6-3	215	9-23-80	2003	Clovis, Calif.
Slaten, Doug	5	2	2.25	36	0	0	5	44	44	13	11	13	40	.260	L	L	6-5	190	2-4-80	2000	Venice, Calif.
Vicente, Ruben	4	3	4.94	45	0	0	2	62	73	37	34	18	44	.294	R	R	6-0	160	3-3-80	2000	La Romana, D.R.

FIELDING

Catcher	PCT	G	PO	A	E	DP	PB
Montero	.982	85	575	70	12	0	9
Mottram	1.000	5	30	1	0	0	1
Rose	.991	63	404	33	4	2	4

First Base	PCT	G	PO	A	E	DP
Frazier	1.000	2	5	0	0	0
McCreery	.967	10	83	4	3	6
Montero	1.000	16	130	1	0	7
Mottram	.978	28	205	22	5	16
Murillo	1.000	2	3	0	0	1
T. Reynolds	1.000	3	5	0	0	0
Varela	.988	95	766	61	10	78

Second Base	PCT	G	PO	A	E	DP
Aguirre	.889	3	5	3	1	1

Bonafacio	.958	115	217	303	23	68
A. Gonzalez	.976	19	37	44	2	9
T. Reynolds	.972	11	21	14	1	2

Third Base	PCT	G	PO	A	E	DP
Aguirre	.333	1	0	1	2	0
McCreery	1.000	3	1	4	0	1
Murillo	.931	96	60	170	17	15
M. Reynolds	1.000	4	2	8	0	1
T. Reynolds	.853	20	10	19	5	0
Varela	.934	33	20	65	6	5

Shortstop	PCT	G	PO	A	E	DP
Aguirre	1.000	2	2	2	0	1
Firlit	.833	4	7	8	3	1

A. Gonzalez	.962	83	141	237	15	54
Kaplan	.700	1	1	6	3	0
T. Reynolds	.955	63	90	189	13	30

Outfield	PCT	G	PO	A	E	DP
Cook	.972	120	202	8	6	1
Frazier	.929	60	75	4	6	0
Garcia	.979	113	224	4	5	0
A. Gonzalez	1.000	2	2	0	0	0
C. Gonzalez	1.000	12	23	0	0	0
Goss	.969	65	94	1	3	0
Kaplan	.989	119	174	11	2	3
Milons	.938	11	15	0	1	0

YAKIMA BEARS — Short-Season Class A

NORTHWEST LEAGUE

BATTING	AVG	G	AB	R	H	2B	3B	HR	RBI	BB	SO	SB	CS	OBP	SLG	B	T	HT	WT	DOB	1st Yr	Resides
Aguirre, Rodrigo	.256	40	125	20	32	2	0	3	16	10	19	1	0	.326	.344	L	R	5-9	165	8-1-83	2004	Hermosillo, Mexico
Buchanan, Todd	.244	55	156	23	38	8	1	2	17	26	29	0	0	.365	.346	L	L	6-2	200	9-16-80	2003	Roswell, Ga.
Buhagiar, Josh	.000	4	9	0	0	0	0	0	0	0	5	0	0	.000	.000	L	L	6-1	180	2-23-81	2004	La Habra Heights, Calif.
Burgess, Brandon	.203	51	177	20	36	7	0	6	27	14	62	0	0	.291	.345	R	R	6-3	225	2-24-83	2004	Sebastopol, Calif.
Carter, Chris	.335	70	257	47	86	15	1	15	63	46	35	2	3	.436	.576	L	R	6-0	220	9-16-82	2004	Concord, Calif.
Gonzalez, Carlos	.277	73	300	44	83	15	2	9	44	22	69	2	0	.330	.430	L	L	6-1	178	10-17-85	2003	Maracaibo, Venez.
Hendricks, Trey	.230	65	226	17	52	7	0	4	26	13	42	0	1	.278	.314	S	R	6-4	215	8-8-82	2004	Spring, Texas
Lange, B.J.	.213	47	108	13	23	2	0	1	7	9	14	2	3	.295	.259	R	R	5-11	195	2-3-84	2004	Riverdale, Ga.
Lockin, Billy	.200	17	60	5	12	2	0	0	7	2	11	1	1	.234	.233	R	R	5-8	155	11-27-82	2004	Simi Valley, Calif.
Melendez, Cris	.190	13	21	4	4	1	0	0	0	8	0	1	0	.227	.238	R	R	6-2	185	11-9-80	2003	Padillas, P.R.
Mena, Steve	.139	55	180	10	14	1	0	0	11	8	48	0	1	.221	.149	R	R	6-3	195	1-24-85	2004	Miami, Fla.
Mercado, Orlando	.266	69	252	35	67	16	3	3	40	32	24	1	1	.353	.389	R	R	5-10	195	3-13-85	2004	Arecibo, P.R.
Pohlman, Dan	.254	40	118	14	30	7	1	1	18	16	22	1	1	.336	.356	R	R	6-1	215	1-2-84	2004	North Barrington, Ill.
Polimar, Aldwin	.122	21	41	3	5	0	0	1	1	3	0	0	0	.250	.195	R	R	6-2	190	6-15-82	2001	Santo Domingo, D.R.
Reynolds, Mark	.274	64	234	58	64	19	1	12	41	25	66	5	1	.372	.517	R	R	6-1	200	8-3-83	2004	Virginia Beach, Va.
Schindewolf, Erik	.308	73	273	65	84	10	2	4	37	51	37	15	2	.421	.403	L	R	5-11	180	10-1-81	2004	Spring, Texas
Simon, Brandon	.329	47	152	25	50	5	2	1	13	6	32	11	3	.382	.408	L	L	6-0	175	9-9-80	2002	Fresno, Calif.

GAMES BY POSITION: C—Mercado 41, Pohlman 30, Polimar 15. **1B**—Buchanan 51, Carter 13, Hendricks 22, Polimar 2. **2B**—Aguirre 7, Lockin 1, Reynolds 1, Schindewolf 71. **3B**—Aguirre 32, Hendricks 29, Lockin 4, Mena 16, Reynolds 15. **SS**—Aguirre 3, Lockin 14, Mena 28, Reynolds 46. **OF**—Buchanan 1, Buhagiar 3, Burgess 49, Carter 32, Gonzalez 76, Hendricks 1, Lange 42, Melendez 12, Simon 47.

PITCHING	W	L	ERA	G	GS	CG	SV	IP	H	R	ER	BB	SO	AVG	B	T	HT	WT	DOB	1st Yr	Resides
Carque, Joe	0	6	5.40	24	4	0	0	55	79	53	33	15	34	.333	R	R	6-2	185	5-20-81	2003	Henderson, Nev.
Clark, Chad	0	2	7.50	5	0	0	0	12	10	10	10	11	7	.320	L	R	6-6	215	7-30-80	2003	Glendora, Calif.
Guerrero, Hipolito	1	0	3.98	16	0	0	0	20	19	9	9	3	21	.241	L	L	6-0	140	6-13-83	2001	Santo Domingo, D.R.
Jackson, Steven	1	0	4.56	9	2	0	0	24	24	12	12	6	18	.273	R	R	6-5	220	3-15-82	2004	Summerville, S.C.
Kemlo, Chris	5	2	5.12	31	0	0	0	39	45	25	22	19	48	.296	R	R	6-2	185	9-23-83	2002	Oshawa, Ontario
Kerbs, Reuben	5	2	5.50	23	1	0	0	36	38	24	22	18	20	.279	L	L	6-2	185	10-19-80	2003	Dodge City, Kan.
Kolberg, Koley	1	3	5.13	22	0	0	3	26	27	15	15	7	31	.281	R	R	6-1	176	11-26-82	2004	Coppell, Texas
Liebeck, Jered	4	2	4.53	11	10	0	0	60	65	37	30	19	52	.273	R	R	6-1	200	1-27-81	2003	Phoenix, Ariz.
Mock, Garrett	2	0	1.54	5	5	0	0	23	18	8	4	4	14	.212	R	R	6-4	215	4-25-83	2004	Grand Prairie, Texas
Novosel, Walt	0	0	6.48	7	0	0	0	8	13	10	6	6	11	.371	L	L	6-3	215	6-16-81	2003	Pulaski, Pa.
Ohlendorf, Ross	2	3	2.79	7	7	0	0	29	22	14	9	9	28	.200	R	R	6-4	235	8-8-82	2004	Austin, Texas
Perrault, Josh	2	4	4.07	14	13	0	0	66	79	42	30	22	37	.295	R	R	6-3	205	6-11-82	2004	Mesa, Ariz.
Pohlman, Dan	0	0	2.25	3	0	0	0	4	3	1	1	2	5	.188	R	R	6-1	215	1-1-82	2004	North Barrington, Ill.
Raab, Kellen	3	3	4.38	19	8	0	0	62	67	33	30	19	56	.275	L	L	6-6	225	2-16-82	2004	Bellevue, Neb.
Rocha, Angel	2	3	6.56	5	5	0	0	23	24	19	17	18	19	.258	L	L	6-3	180	11-15-84	2002	Santo Domingo, D.R.
Shappi, A.J.	4	1	1.75	12	11	0	0	67	64	17	13	6	65	.253	R	R	6-2	195	10-16-82	2004	Simi Valley, Calif.
Thompson, Chris	1	3	2.34	32	0	0	0	42	38	15	11	27	38	.244	R	R	6-3	195	1-8-82	2004	Oxford, Miss.
Van, Robbie	0	1	3.52	5	0	0	0	8	6	3	3	6	8	.200	L	L	6-2	210	11-3-81	2003	Las Vegas, Nev.
Vasquez, Esmerling	0	0	6.35	5	0	0	1	6	10	6	4	0	7	.357	R	R	6-1	150	11-7-83	2003	Tenares, D.R.
Whatley, Keith	1	6	7.13	8	8	0	0	35	45	38	28	15	24	.313	L	L	6-2	230	4-23-80	2002	Atlanta, Texas

PITCHING	W	L	ERA	G	GS	CG	SV	IP	H	R	ER	BB	SO	AVG	B	T	HT	WT	DOB	1st Yr	Resides
White, Mike	0	0	10.13	14	0	0	0	19	34	29	21	16	15	.382	L	L	6-2	215	9-12-82	2002	Clearwater, Fla.
Wilkinson, Matt	1	0	3.00	2	0	0	0	3	1	2	1	0	4	.125	L	R	6-3	195	10-25-77	2001	Chicago, Ill.

MISSOULA OSPREY — Rookie

PIONEER LEAGUE

BATTING	AVG	G	AB	R	H	2B	3B	HR	RBI	BB	SO	SB	CS	OBP	SLG	B	T	HT	WT	DOB	1st Yr	Resides
Brito, Javier	.310	67	232	36	72	17	1	8	44	16	37	0	1	.365	.496	R	R	6-3	210	3-25-83	2002	Puerto la Cruz, Venez.
Bruce, Derek	.271	60	225	29	61	8	2	2	25	12	32	4	7	.331	.351	R	R	6-2	190	8-3-82	2004	Lewiston, Idaho
Buhagiar, Josh	.260	31	96	17	25	7	2	2	11	9	21	4	1	.360	.438	L	L	6-1	180	2-23-81	2004	Sebastopol, Calif.
Castillo, Wilkin	.272	62	243	32	66	13	5	4	32	8	40	5	2	.308	.416	S	R	6-0	170	6-1-84	2003	Bani, D.R.
Centeno, Jaen	.296	56	196	34	58	12	2	4	34	33	48	3	5	.403	.439	R	R	6-3	180	1-1-84	2004	Santa Teresa, Venez.
Currei, Frank	.278	12	36	8	10	2	0	0	5	5	9	0	0	.349	.333	R	R	6-4	215	12-4-82	2004	Weymouth, Mass.
Del Campo, Manny	.258	16	31	4	8	2	0	1	4	4	6	0	0	.395	.419	R	R	5-10	200	5-11-83	2004	San Luis, Ariz.
Downing, Ramon	.290	27	100	18	29	7	1	3	22	9	28	4	2	.353	.470	S	R	5-10	187	9-1-83	2004	San Juan, P.R.
Gulick, Travis	.250	59	192	34	48	6	3	12	37	25	55	6	2	.339	.500	R	R	6-3	180	5-17-83	2004	East Lansing, Mich.
Matos, Miguel	.256	59	199	43	51	11	1	4	24	31	41	17	4	.373	.382	R	R	5-11	190	8-18-81	2003	Jimani, D.R.
Mercado, Richard	.283	58	187	26	53	10	2	4	29	33	31	2	1	.401	.422	R	R	6-0	220	4-29-74	2004	San Clemente, Calif.
Moreno, Juan	.333	4	3	0	1	0	0	0	1	1	0	0	0	.500	.667	L	R	5-9	180	8-16-81	2000	Santo Domingo, D.R.
Olivares, Juan	.239	57	184	19	44	10	2	2	16	0	41	2	2	.246	.348	R	R	6-2	160	8-2-84	2002	San Pedro de Macoris, D.R.
Rodriguez, Francisco	.263	34	99	8	26	6	1	1	11	5	24	1	1	.305	.374	S	R	6-0	160	4-23-84	2002	Santo Domingo, D.R.
Santiago, Jayson	.171	25	35	8	6	0	0	0	1	10	12	0	0	.356	.171	L	L	6-1	175	10-9-85	2003	Vega Alta, P.R.
Sosa, Ricardo	.309	51	178	30	55	10	2	4	26	18	42	6	0	.379	.455	R	R	6-1	200	5-24-84	2004	Miami Lakes, Fla.
Terrell, Josh	.222	14	36	3	8	1	0	0	9	2	5	1	0	.275	.250	R	R	6-5	225	9-3-83	2004	Princeton, Texas
Townsend, Marcus	.294	44	126	31	37	5	1	11	27	22	48	4	1	.414	.611	R	R	6-4	200	4-20-82	2004	Missouri City, Texas
Williams, Kevin	.192	34	78	19	15	3	0	0	3	9	29	10	4	.308	.231	S	L	6-1	175	10-30-81	2004	Columbus, Ga.

GAMES BY POSITION: C—Castillo 34, Curreri 10, Del Campo 12, Mercado 26. **1B**—Brito 66, Castillo 2, Rodriguez 2, Terrell 14. **2B**—Bruce 20, Castillo 6, Downing 22, Rodriguez 31. **3B**—Bruce 19, Castillo 17, Olivares 1, Sosa 41. **SS**—Bruce 26, Olivares 55. **OF**—Buhagiar 26, Centeno 48, Gulick 52, Matos 52, Santiago 11, Townsend 20, Williams 20.

PITCHING	W	L	ERA	G	GS	CG	SV	IP	H	R	ER	BB	SO	AVG	B	T	HT	WT	DOB	1st Yr	Resides
Bauer, Garrett	0	2	6.92	16	2	0	0	26	27	23	20	27	37	.267	R	L	6-1	175	9-4-81	2004	Kennesaw, Ga.
Clark, Chad	1	1	4.50	12	0	0	1	12	15	11	6	14	10	.306	L	R	6-6	215	7-30-80	2003	Glendora, Calif.
Davis, Vince	3	2	4.19	16	8	0	0	54	51	38	25	28	47	.254	R	L	6-6	245	8-22-82	2004	Chicago, Ill.
Dove, Shane	4	9	4.97	15	12	1	0	71	85	50	39	25	77	.302	L	L	6-1	170	7-22-84	2003	Tega Cay, S.C.
Duran, Emmanuel	2	1	5.13	23	1	0	2	33	49	21	19	16	38	.338	R	R	6-1	178	11-7-84	2003	Valverde Mao, D.R.
Elliott, Matt	3	1	3.12	12	0	0	6	17	16	6	6	14	22	.267	R	R	6-0	175	4-6-84	2004	Las Vegas, Nev.
Guerrero, Hipolito	0	0	9.82	7	0	0	0	11	22	16	12	7	7	.431	L	L	6-0	140	6-13-83	2001	Santo Domingo, D.R.
Howard, Adam	1	1	4.36	9	5	0	0	33	36	18	16	7	27	.277	R	R	6-4	210	8-16-83	2004	Chattanooga, Tenn.
Jackson, Steven	0	1	3.60	7	0	0	0	10	16	9	4	2	8	.327	R	R	6-5	220	3-15-82	2004	Summerville, S.C.
Julio, Donald	2	4	4.07	24	0	0	1	42	40	20	19	16	42	.250	R	R	6-1	160	8-12-83	2001	Panama City, Panama
Krantz, Ben	3	5	5.82	14	14	0	0	68	72	55	44	40	37	.269	R	R	6-2	195	7-28-80	2003	Toronto, Ontario
Nippert, Derik	0	3	15.43	3	3	0	0	12	30	21	20	3	6	.484	R	R	6-7	220	5-6-81	2003	Beallsville, Ohio
Novosel, Walt	0	0	5.87	6	0	0	0	8	3	5	5	5	13	.115	L	L	6-3	215	6-16-81	2003	Pulaski, Pa.
Sanchez, Ramon	1	1	9.13	18	1	0	0	24	33	34	24	18	18	.344	R	R	6-3	180	6-6-84	2003	Nigua, D.R.
Stein, Todd	2	2	6.38	17	0	0	1	24	31	23	17	9	28	.313	L	L	6-0	175	6-9-81	2004	St. Louis, Mo.
Vaillancourt, Tim	4	4	4.16	14	14	1	0	76	78	47	35	31	67	.268	R	R	6-4	195	12-5-81	2003	Bear, Del.
Valdez, Salvador	0	1	8.80	8	3	0	0	15	23	20	15	14	13	.329	R	R	6-3	210	5-8-83	2004	Culiacan, Mexico
Vasquez, Esmerling	3	2	3.52	19	0	0	5	31	22	15	12	21	33	.208	R	R	6-1	150	11-7-83	2003	Tenares, D.R.
Yamaguchi, Tetsuya	0	5	6.26	13	10	0	0	55	81	46	38	20	50	.351	L	L	6-0	165	11-11-83	2002	Yokohama, Japan
Yonezawa, Kosuke	0	0	11.42	8	0	0	0	9	8	13	11	9	9	.229	R	R	6-2	209	11-5-85	2004	Naka-gun, Japan

BY BILL BALLEW

In a season that many expected to be a rebuilding year in Atlanta, the Braves showed that until someone can prove otherwise, the situation remains business as usual in the National League East.

The Braves overcame countless injuries to add to their professional sports record by winning their 13th consecutive division title in 2004. The team achieved the feat with relatively ease, topping second-place Philadelphia by 10 games. Despite being three games below the .500 mark at the end of June, Atlanta put together back-to-back 20-win months to finish at 96-66, the second-best record in the NL and fourth-best overall.

The strong showing during the regular season seemed to ease the disappointment October brought once again. The Braves lost in five games to Houston in the Division Series, thereby leaving Atlanta with just one World Series crown to show for all the division titles since 1991.

"This team has surpassed anything I thought was possible," said closer John Smoltz, the lone player to experience all 13 seasons of excellence. "I didn't think there was any way we could compete for a division title this year. As far as the regular season is concerned, I enjoyed this year as much as any season we've had."

The lower expectations began when Time Warner required a payroll slashing of approximately $15 million. With the budget reduced to $82 million, such free agents as Gary Sheffield, Javy Lopez, Greg Maddux and Vinny Castilla wound up signing elsewhere.

But some new blood helped keep the Braves successful. Johnny Estrada stepped into the starting role at catcher and responded with an all-star season and a team-best .314 batting average. Rookie first baseman Adam LaRoche overcame a dislocated shoulder at midseason to provide some pop from the left side of the plate.

J.D. Drew | Jose Capellan

PLAYERS of the YEAR

MAJOR LEAGUE: J.D. Drew, of
Drew, a Georgia native, had a career year in his first season for the Braves. The former St. Louis outfielder hit .305-31-93 in 145 games. The key for the Florida State product was his ability to stay healthy, which he did in 2004.

MINOR LEAGUE: Jose Capellan, rhp
Capellan jumped from high Class A Myrtle Beach to the big leagues in 2004, blazing a fiery trail of strikeouts along the way. A true power pitcher that maintains his high 90s velocity deep into games, Capellan struck out 152 in 139 innings while going 14-4, 2.33.

General manager John Schuerholz also played a major role with his trade to acquire outfielders J.D. Drew and Eli Marrero from St. Louis and the free-agent signing of John Thomson. Drew had an MVP-caliber season by producing a career-best 31 homers and 93 RBIs while ranking fourth in the NL with 118 runs. Thomson pitched well by using both sides of the plate to win a career-best 14 games.

"When we look back on our season, I think most of the guys will be proud of the way they handled themselves," said Chipper Jones, who fell just four shy of recording his ninth straight 100-RBI season, thanks to a strong second half that coincided with his return to third base from left field.

Manager Bobby Cox did another masterful job while becoming only the ninth skipper in major league history to win 2,000 games.

The Braves also enjoyed success in the minors, posting an overall mark of 351-333 for a .512 winning percentage, equaling the organization's best since 1993. Triple-A Richmond had its first winning season in a decade by taking the International League's South Division before dropping the Governor's Cup to Buffalo in four games. Rookie-level Danville won the Appalachian League's East Division prior to falling in two games to Greeneville in the championship series.

Pitcher Jose Capellan used his 100-mph fastball to climb from Class A Myrtle Beach to the major leagues and emerge as the top pitching prospect the Braves have developed in several seasons. Outfielder Jeff Francoeur was tabbed the top prospect in the Carolina League, while third baseman Andy Marte garnered the same honor in the Southern League.

ORGANIZATION LEADERS

BATTING

*AVG	Napoleon Calzado, Richmond/Greenville	.353
R	Ryan Langerhans, Richmond	103
H	Napoleon Calzado, Richmond/Greenville	165
TB	Ryan Langerhans, Richmond	236
2B	Kelly Johnson, Greenville	35
	Brian McCann, Myrtle Beach	35
3B	Pete Orr, Richmond	10
HR	James Jurries, Richmond/Greenville	25
RBI	Scott Thorman, Greenville/Myrtle Beach	80
BB	Ryan Langerhans, Richmond	70
SO	Steve Doetsch, Rome	152
SB	Onil Joseph, Myrtle Beach	32
*OBP	Ryan Langerhans, Richmond	.397
*SLG	Mike Hessman, Richmond	.562

PITCHING

W	Jose Capellan, Richmond/Greenville/Myrtle Beach	14
L	Three tied at	10
#ERA	Chuck James, Rome	2.24
G	Matt Whiteside, Richmond	57
CG	Ten tied at	1
SV	Matt Whiteside, Richmond	38
IP	Blaine Boyer, Myrtle Beach	154
BB	Bryan Digby, Rome	71
SO	Kyle Davies, Richmond/Greenville/Myrtle Beach	173

*Minimum 250 at-bats #Minimum 75 Innings

ORGANIZATION STATISTICS

Manager: Bobby Cox.

2004 Record: 96-66, .593 (1st, NL East).

BATTING	AVG	G	AB	R	H	2B	3B	HR	RBI	BB	SO	SB	CS	OBP	SLG	B	T	HT	WT	DOB	1st Yr	Resides
Betemit, Wilson	.170	22	47	2	8	0	0	0	3	4	16	0	1	.231	.170	S	R	6-3	190	7-28-80	1997	Santo Domingo, D.R.
DeRosa, Mark	.239	118	309	33	74	16	0	3	31	23	53	1	3	.293	.320	R	R	6-1	205	2-26-75	1996	Atlanta, Ga.
Drew, J.D.	.305	145	518	118	158	28	8	31	93	118	116	12	3	.436	.569	L	R	6-1	200	11-20-75	1997	Hahira, Ga.
Estrada, Johnny	.314	134	462	56	145	36	0	9	76	39	66	0	0	.378	.450	S	R	5-11	209	6-27-76	1997	Salisbury, N.C.
Franco, Julio	.309	125	320	37	99	18	3	6	57	36	68	4	2	.378	.441	R	R	6-1	188	8-23-58	1984	San Pedro de Macoris, D.R.
Furcal, Rafael	.279	143	563	103	157	24	5	14	59	58	71	29	6	.344	.414	S	R	5-10	165	10-24-77	1997	Loma de Cabrera, D.R.
Garcia, Jesse	.252	50	115	14	29	4	1	1	10	1	16	1	2	.265	.330	R	R	5-10	170	9-24-73	1993	Robstown, Texas
Giles, Marcus	.311	102	379	61	118	22	2	8	48	36	70	17	4	.378	.443	R	R	5-8	180	5-18-78	1997	El Cajon, Calif.
Green, Nick	.273	95	264	40	72	15	3	3	26	12	63	1	2	.312	.386	R	R	6-0	180	9-10-78	1999	Duluth, Ga.
Hessman, Mike	.130	29	69	8	9	3	0	2	5	1	24	0	0	.155	.261	R	R	6-5	215	3-5-78	1996	Westminster, Calif.
Hollins, Damon	.364	7	22	3	8	2	0	0	5	0	4	0	0	.364	.455	R	L	5-11	180	6-12-74	1992	Fairfield, Calif.
Jones, Andruw	.261	154	570	85	149	34	4	29	91	71	147	6	6	.345	.488	R	R	6-1	210	4-23-77	1994	Willemstad, Curacao
Jones, Chipper	.248	137	472	69	117	20	1	30	96	84	96	2	0	.362	.485	S	R	6-4	220	4-24-72	1990	Alpharetta, Ga.
LaRoche, Adam	.278	110	324	45	90	27	1	13	45	27	78	0	0	.333	.488	L	L	6-3	180	11-6-79	2000	Fort Scott, Kan.
Marrero, Eli	.320	90	250	37	80	18	1	10	40	23	50	4	1	.374	.520	R	R	6-1	180	11-17-73	1993	Miami, Fla.
Perez, Eddie	.229	74	170	14	39	12	0	3	13	11	29	0	0	.286	.353	R	R	6-1	220	5-4-68	1987	Duluth, Ga.
Thomas, Charles	.288	83	236	35	68	8	4	7	31	21	45	3	1	.368	.445	L	L	6-0	190	12-26-78	2000	Asheville, N.C.
Wise, DeWayne	.228	77	162	24	37	9	4	6	17	9	28	6	1	.272	.444	L	L	6-1	175	2-24-78	1997	Chapin, S.C.

PITCHING	W	L	ERA	G	GS	CG	SV	IP	H	R	ER	BB	SO	AVG	B	T	HT	WT	DOB	1st Yr	Resides
Alfonseca, Antonio	6	4	2.57	79	0	0	0	74	71	24	21	28	45	.255	R	R	6-5	250	4-16-72	1991	La Romana, D.R.
Almanza, Armando	1	0	6.17	13	0	0	0	12	9	8	8	7	13	.200	L	L	6-3	240	10-26-72	1993	El Paso, Texas
Byrd, Paul	8	7	3.94	19	19	0	0	114	123	57	50	19	79	.270	R	R	6-1	185	12-3-70	1991	Louisville, Ky.
Capellan, Jose	0	1	11.25	3	2	0	0	8	14	10	10	5	4	.400	R	R	6-4	235	1-13-81	1999	Cotui, D.R.
Colon, Roman	2	1	3.32	18	0	0	0	19	18	9	7	8	15	.254	R	R	6-3	170	8-13-79	1996	Monte Cristi, D.R.
Cruz, Juan	6	2	2.75	50	0	0	0	72	59	24	22	30	70	.224	R	R	6-2	165	10-15-78	1998	Bonao, D.R.
Cunnane, Will	1	1	7.30	9	0	0	0	12	18	10	10	4	11	.346	R	R	6-1	200	4-24-74	1993	Rockland, N.Y.
Drew, Tim	0	0	4.50	11	0	0	0	16	21	11	8	5	7	.318	R	R	6-1	200	8-31-78	1997	Hahira, Ga.
Gryboski, Kevin	3	2	2.84	69	0	0	2	51	54	22	16	23	24	.280	R	R	6-5	235	11-15-73	1995	Plains, Pa.
Hampton, Mike	13	9	4.28	29	29	1	0	172	198	86	82	65	87	.290	R	L	5-10	180	9-9-72	1990	Evergreen, Colo.
Martin, Tom	0	1	3.71	29	0	0	0	17	17	7	7	5	12	.270	L	L	6-1	205	5-21-70	1989	Panama City, Fla.
2-team (47 Los Angeles)	0	2	3.97	76	0	0	1	45	49	20	20	19	30	.283							
McConnell, Sam	1	0	3.86	10	0	0	0	9	11	4	4	4	4	.289	L	L	6-5	230	12-31-75	1997	Fairfield, Ohio
Meyer, Dan	0	0	0.00	2	0	0	0	2	2	0	0	1	1	.286	R	L	6-3	190	7-3-81	2002	Mickleton, N.J.
Nitkowski, C.J.	1	0	4.50	22	0	0	0	20	22	11	10	10	16	.275	L	L	6-3	205	3-9-73	1994	Houston, Texas
Ortiz, Russ	15	9	4.13	34	34	2	0	205	197	98	94	112	143	.258	R	R	6-1	210	6-5-74	1995	Gilbert, Ariz.
Ramirez, Horacio	2	4	2.39	10	9	1	0	60	51	24	16	30	31	.226	L	L	6-1	170	11-24-79	1997	Inglewood, Calif.
Reitsma, Chris	6	4	4.07	84	0	0	2	80	89	38	36	20	60	.284	R	R	6-5	235	12-31-77	1996	Calgary, Alberta
Smith, Travis	2	3	6.20	16	4	0	0	41	48	28	28	12	26	.293	R	R	5-10	170	11-7-72	1995	Bend, Ore.
Smoltz, John	0	1	2.76	73	0	0	44	82	75	25	25	13	85	.245	R	R	6-3	220	5-15-67	1986	Duluth, Ga.
Thomson, John	14	8	3.72	33	33	0	0	198	210	93	82	52	133	.276	R	R	6-3	190	10-1-73	1993	Sulphur, La.
Wright, Jaret	15	8	3.28	32	32	0	0	186	168	79	68	70	159	.242	R	R	6-2	230	12-29-75	1994	Newport Beach, Calif.

FIELDING

Catcher	PCT	G	PO	A	E	DP	PB
Estrada	.989	133	776	44	9	8	8
Perez	.990	66	290	22	3	4	2

First Base	PCT	G	PO	A	E	DP
Franco	.997	84	627	48	2	68
Hessman	.962	16	96	4	4	6
LaRoche	.994	98	740	41	5	87
Perez	1.000	1	10	0	0	1

Second Base	PCT	G	PO	A	E	DP
DeRosa	1.000	5	3	11	0	4
Furcal	.000	1	0	0	0	0
Garcia	.946	11	16	19	2	5

Giles	.975	97	186	289	12	69
Green	.977	75	137	203	8	44

Third Base	PCT	G	PO	A	E	DP
Betemit	1.000	7	2	6	0	2
DeRosa	.939	72	27	126	10	7
Garcia	.750	3	0	3	1	0
Green	1.000	5	0	2	0	0
Hessman	.889	7	2	14	2	1
C. Jones	.975	96	58	177	6	13

Shortstop	PCT	G	PO	A	E	DP
Betemit	.933	11	12	30	3	5
DeRosa	.933	11	10	18	2	7

Furcal	.962	131	190	411	24	101
Garcia	.963	25	31	72	4	14

Outfield	PCT	G	PO	A	E	DP
DeRosa	.000	3	0	0	0	0
Drew	.990	142	296	12	3	0
Green	.000	1	0	0	0	0
Hessman	1.000	3	4	0	0	0
Hollins	1.000	6	8	1	0	0
A. Jones	.993	154	389	10	3	2
C. Jones	1.000	29	35	2	0	1
Marrero	.992	73	121	6	1	1
Thomas	.993	71	138	7	1	2
Wise	1.000	56	61	2	0	0

Director, Player Development: Dayton Moore.

Class	Farm Team	League	W	L	Pct.	Finish*	Manager	Affiliate Since
AAA	Richmond (Va.) Braves	International	79	62	.560	**2nd (14)**	Pat Kelly	1996
AA	#Greenville (S.C.) Braves	Southern	63	76	.453	9th (10)	Brian Snitker	1984
High A	Myrtle Beach (S.C.) Pelicans	Carolina	75	63	.543	3rd (8)	Randy Ingle	1999
Low A	Rome (Ga.) Braves	South Atlantic	70	70	.500	t-7th (16)	Rocket Wheeler	2003
Rookie	Danville (Va.) Braves	Appalachian	41	25	.621	**1st (10)**	Jim Saul	1993
Rookie	Kissimmee (Fla.) Braves	Gulf Coast	23	36	.390	10th (12)	Ralph Henriquez	1998

*Finish in overall standings (No. of teams in league)/playoff teams in **boldface**   #Franchise will operate in Pearl, Miss., in 2005

RICHMOND BRAVES — Class AAA

INTERNATIONAL LEAGUE

BATTING	AVG	G	AB	R	H	2B	3B	HR	RBI	BB	SO	SB	CS	OBP	SLG	B	T	HT	WT	DOB	1st Yr	Resides
Betemit, Wilson	.278	105	356	48	99	24	2	13	59	32	99	3	3	.336	.466	S	R	6-3	190	7-28-80	1997	Santo Domingo, D.R.
Boscan, J.C.	.311	21	61	4	19	2	0	0	6	9	14	0	1	.403	.344	R	R	6-2	160	12-26-79	1997	Maracaibo, Venez.
Branyan, Russell	.179	11	28	5	5	0	0	1	4	13	11	1	0	.452	.286	L	R	6-3	195	12-19-75	1994	Kathleen, Ga.
Calzado, Napoleon	.211	5	19	2	4	1	0	0	2	0	2	0	0	.211	.263	R	R	6-3	181	2-9-77	1997	Santo Domingo, D.R.
DePastino, Joe	.231	93	299	34	69	12	1	6	43	29	52	2	2	.304	.338	R	R	6-2	210	9-4-73	1992	Sarasota, Fla.
Evans, Lee	.239	58	180	25	43	8	0	7	20	21	57	0	1	.320	.400	S	R	6-1	185	7-20-77	1996	Northport, Ala.
Garcia, Jesse	.218	20	78	6	17	2	0	0	2	4	13	0	2	.265	.244	R	R	5-10	170	9-24-73	1993	Robstown, Texas
Green, Nick	.377	22	77	8	29	4	1	0	11	6	9	0	0	.443	.455	R	R	6-0	180	9-10-78	1999	Duluth, Ga.
Hessman, Mike	.287	78	265	48	76	14	1	19	54	28	65	4	0	.365	.562	R	R	6-5	215	3-5-78	1996	Westminster, Calif.
Hollins, Damon	.301	109	356	50	107	26	2	20	67	24	57	5	3	.341	.553	R	L	5-11	180	6-12-74	1992	Fairfield, Calif.
Jackson, Ryan	.224	16	58	7	13	3	0	2	4	1	15	2	0	.237	.379	L	L	6-2	200	11-15-71	1994	Sarasota, Fla.
Jurries, James	.267	102	318	46	85	16	0	18	56	32	96	0	1	.336	.487	R	R	6-0	190	4-13-79	2002	Lake Jackson, Texas
Langerhans, Ryan	.298	135	456	103	136	34	3	20	72	70	113	5	9	.397	.518	L	L	6-3	195	2-20-80	1998	Round Rock, Texas
LaRoche, Adam	.182	4	11	1	2	0	0	1	2	1	0	0	0	.250	.455	L	L	6-3	180	11-6-79	2000	Fort Scott, Kan.
Lopez, Luis	.332	69	232	37	77	18	0	9	51	30	27	0	0	.412	.526	R	R	6-0	200	10-5-73	1995	Brooklyn, N.Y.
Marrero, Eli	.208	6	24	1	5	2	0	0	3	1	3	0	0	.240	.292	R	R	6-1	180	11-17-73	1993	Miami, Fla.
McCarthy, Bill	.354	54	178	26	63	13	1	6	23	14	32	0	2	.407	.539	R	R	6-2	200	12-2-79	2001	Sewell, N.J.
Nilsson, Dave	.236	16	55	3	13	1	0	1	4	7	15	0	0	.323	.309	L	R	6-3	230	12-14-69	1987	Samford, Australia
Orr, Pete	.320	115	460	69	147	16	10	1	35	20	59	24	11	.349	.404	L	R	6-1	170	6-8-79	2000	Newmarket, Ontario
Terveen, Bryce	.195	15	41	3	8	0	1	1	7	5	7	0	0	.313	.317	L	R	6-1	200	3-1-78	1999	Modesto, Calif.
Thomas, Charles	.358	61	215	31	77	18	4	4	32	16	40	7	5	.416	.535	L	L	6-0	190	12-26-78	2000	Asheville, N.C.
Tyner, Jason	.288	64	243	40	70	12	1	1	16	15	22	18	6	.346	.358	L	L	6-1	160	4-23-77	1998	Beaumont, Texas
Velandia, Jorge	.215	129	390	39	84	21	1	6	25	41	67	1	1	.298	.321	R	R	5-9	180	1-12-75	1992	Roadhouse, Ill.
Velazquez, Juan	.146	13	41	4	6	0	0	0	1	4	9	1	0	.239	.146	S	R	5-11	150	8-22-78	1997	San Lorenzo, P.R.
Wise, DeWayne	.314	34	118	18	37	4	6	5	16	5	19	5	0	.341	.576	L	L	6-1	175	2-24-78	1997	Chapin, S.C.

PITCHING	W	L	ERA	G	GS	CG	SV	IP	H	R	ER	BB	SO	AVG	B	T	HT	WT	DOB	1st Yr	Resides
Aguilar, Ray	2	4	6.21	9	9	0	0	42	59	36	29	17	31	.324	S	L	5-11	200	1-18-80	2001	South El Monte, Calif.
Almanza, Armando	1	1	3.55	20	0	0	1	25	26	13	10	15	20	.255	L	L	6-3	240	10-26-72	1993	El Paso, Texas
Barry, Kevin	3	3	2.52	30	0	0	2	36	25	15	10	25	40	.210	R	R	6-2	210	8-18-78	2001	Princeton Junction, N.J.
Byrd, Paul	0	1	7.71	1	1	0	0	5	3	4	4	2	5	.167	R	R	6-1	185	12-3-70	1991	Louisville, Ky.
Capellan, Jose	4	2	2.51	7	7	0	0	43	33	13	12	15	37	.214	R	R	6-4	235	1-13-81	1999	Cotui, D.R.
Colon, Roman	4	1	3.65	51	0	0	0	74	72	33	30	22	64	.258	R	R	6-3	170	8-13-79	1996	Monte Cristi, D.R.
Cunnane, Will	1	7	5.23	35	2	0	2	43	52	27	25	22	42	.304	R	R	6-1	200	4-24-74	1993	Rockland, N.Y.
Curtis, Daniel	0	1	5.40	2	2	0	0	8	8	5	5	5	8	.267	R	R	6-3	215	11-3-79	1998	Chattanooga, Tenn.
Davies, Kyle	0	1	9.00	1	1	0	0	5	5	5	5	3	5	.263	R	R	6-2	190	9-9-83	2001	Dover, Fla.
Drew, Tim	4	5	3.31	19	13	0	1	82	92	35	30	24	44	.292	R	R	6-1	200	8-31-78	1997	Hahira, Ga.
Evert, Brett	2	1	7.03	7	5	0	0	24	26	19	19	15	20	.277	L	R	6-6	200	10-23-80	1998	Salem, Ore.
Fesh, Sean	1	5	3.74	40	1	0	0	53	50	27	22	28	41	.253	L	L	6-2	180	11-3-72	1991	Bethel, Conn.
Glynn, Ryan	1	1	5.60	11	0	0	0	18	26	11	11	14	19	.351	R	R	6-3	200	11-1-74	1995	Grand Prairie, Texas
Hernandez, Buddy	7	2	2.42	47	0	0	0	67	45	21	18	26	60	.190	R	R	5-9	170	3-3-79	2000	Birdsboro, Pa.
Hodges, Trey	5	2	4.82	10	10	0	0	52	51	29	28	18	41	.256	R	R	6-3	185	6-29-78	2000	Spring, Texas
McConnell, Sam	7	7	3.91	22	18	1	0	104	102	51	45	28	56	.254	L	L	6-5	230	12-31-75	1997	Fairfield, Ohio
Meyer, Dan	3	3	2.79	12	11	0	0	61	62	23	19	25	60	.264	R	L	6-3	190	7-3-81	2002	Mickleton, N.J.
Ramirez, Horacio	0	0	8.00	2	2	0	0	9	15	8	8	1	3	.385	L	L	6-1	170	11-24-79	1997	Inglewood, Calif.
Romano, Mike	13	5	3.42	40	16	0	0	124	130	51	47	51	99	.278	R	R	6-2	190	3-3-72	1993	Chalmette, La.
Smith, Chuck	9	4	3.72	29	24	1	0	143	125	62	59	47	129	.233	R	R	6-1	180	10-21-69	1991	Hillside, Ill.
Smith, Travis	10	2	2.59	20	19	1	0	108	98	31	31	26	93	.246	R	R	5-10	170	11-7-72	1995	Bend, Ore.
Whiteside, Matt	2	4	3.23	57	0	0	38	64	56	23	23	16	59	.235	R	R	6-0	200	8-8-67	1990	Arlington, Texas

FIELDING

Catcher	PCT	G	PO	A	E	DP	PB
Boscan	1.000	21	137	10	0	2	3
DePastino	.995	84	602	28	3	5	2
Evans	1.000	27	178	15	0	3	4
Nilsson	1.000	1	1	1	0	0	0
Terveen	1.000	14	95	9	0	1	7

First Base	PCT	G	PO	A	E	DP
DePastino	1.000	5	25	4	0	2
Evans	.977	17	114	12	3	11
Hessman	.988	31	156	8	2	24
Jackson	.962	11	95	7	4	11

	PCT	G	PO	A	E	DP
Jurries	.988	68	486	23	6	53
LaRoche	1.000	3	27	3	0	1
Lopez	.988	24	152	10	2	15
Nilsson	1.000	6	44	2	0	2

Second Base	PCT	G	PO	A	E	DP
Garcia	.942	20	37	44	5	16
Green	.967	20	34	55	3	14
Hessman	1.000	3	5	0	2	
Orr	.993	92	150	251	3	56
Velandia	.933	5	4	10	1	1
Velazquez	.972	8	20	15	1	6

Third Base	PCT	G	PO	A	E	DP
Betemit	.945	89	68	121	11	9
Calzado	1.000	2	2	3	0	0
Green	1.000	1	2	2	0	0
Hessman	.981	41	26	75	2	8
Jurries	.857	4	1	5	1	0
Lopez	.926	9	9	16	2	0
Orr	1.000	12	6	36	0	4

Shortstop	PCT	G	PO	A	E	DP
Betemit	.917	19	20	35	5	6
Garcia	1.000	1	1	1	0	0

Orr	1.000	2	1	11	0	3
Velandia	.959	126	161	325	21	80
Velazquez	1.000	5	7	8	0	2

Outfield	PCT	G	PO	A	E	DP
Branyan	1.000	10	12	0	0	0

Calzado	.875	3	7	0	1	0
Hessman	1.000	13	13	2	0	1
Hollins	.967	101	195	11	7	7
Jackson	1.000	1	1	1	0	0
Langerhans	.989	133	250	9	3	1

Marrero	1.000	6	13	1	0	0
McCarthy	.987	47	76	2	1	1
Orr	1.000	8	12	0	0	0
Thomas	.969	48	89	6	3	1
Tyner	1.000	57	101	6	0	1
Wise	.986	30	72	1	1	1

SOUTHERN LEAGUE

BATTING	AVG	G	AB	R	H	2B	3B	HR	RBI	BB	SO	SB	CS	OBP	SLG	B	T	HT	WT	DOB	1st Yr	Resides
Aldridge, Cory	.242	39	132	17	32	5	2	2	13	6	47	1	2	.275	.356	L	R	6-1	220	6-13-79	1997	Abilene, Texas
Boscan, J.C.	.221	53	163	15	36	10	0	1	15	25	40	1	1	.326	.301	R	R	6-2	160	12-26-79	1997	Maracaibo, Venez.
Butler, Brent	.246	70	195	22	48	9	0	4	23	19	34	0	1	.315	.354	R	R	6-0	180	2-11-78	1996	Laurinburg, N.C.
Calzado, Napoleon	.359	119	449	68	161	28	7	8	59	22	59	18	8	.395	.506	R	R	6-3	181	2-9-77	1997	Santo Domingo, D.R.
Evans, Lee	.208	21	72	7	15	3	0	4	14	6	26	1	0	.272	.417	S	R	6-1	185	7-20-77	1996	Northport, Ala.
Francoeur, Jeff	.197	18	76	8	15	2	0	3	9	0	14	1	0	.208	.342	R	R	6-4	165	1-8-84	2002	Lilburn, Ga.
Herr, Aaron	.272	94	283	37	77	20	2	7	32	28	88	7	3	.341	.431	R	R	5-11	180	3-7-81	2000	Lancaster, Pa.
Iorg, Isaac	.074	12	27	2	2	1	0	0	2	10	1	0	.167	.111	R	R	6-1	190	6-5-79	2001	Knoxville, Tenn.
Jansen, Ardley	.500	5	12	3	6	2	0	1	2	3	2	0	0	.563	.917	R	R	6-2	190	2-16-83	2000	Willemstad, Curacao
Johnson, Kelly	.282	135	479	70	135	35	3	16	50	49	102	9	9	.350	.468	L	R	6-1	180	2-22-82	2000	Tucson, Ariz.
Jurries, James	.306	18	72	15	22	4	0	7	14	5	15	1	2	.359	.653	R	R	6-0	190	4-13-79	2002	Lake Jackson, Texas
Marrero, Eli	.417	3	12	3	5	1	0	2	5	2	6	0	0	.500	1.000	R	R	6-1	180	11-17-73	1993	Miami, Fla.
Marte, Andy	.269	107	387	52	104	28	1	23	68	58	105	1	1	.364	.525	R	R	6-1	180	10-21-83	2001	Villa Tapia, D.R.
McCarthy, Bill	.300	67	233	30	70	12	2	9	42	26	67	1	2	.375	.485	R	R	6-2	200	12-2-79	2001	Sewell, N.J.
Melian, Jackson	.193	53	161	18	31	8	3	3	13	15	38	2	0	.271	.335	R	R	6-2	200	1-7-80	1997	Barcelona, Venez.
Pena, Brayan	.314	77	277	30	87	10	4	2	30	15	29	3	5	.349	.401	S	R	5-11	210	1-7-82	2001	San Jose, Costa Rica
Pena, Tony	.255	130	495	65	126	22	0	11	34	16	108	25	13	.280	.366	R	R	6-1	180	3-23-81	2000	Santiago, D.R.
Stern, Adam	.322	102	394	64	127	26	6	8	47	35	58	27	10	.378	.480	L	R	5-11	180	2-12-80	2001	London, Ontario
Thorman, Scott	.252	94	345	31	87	14	3	11	51	39	73	5	3	.326	.406	L	R	6-3	200	1-6-82	2000	Cambridge, Ontario
Velazquez, Juan	.222	76	167	20	37	8	0	1	14	19	43	2	2	.309	.287	S	R	5-11	150	8-22-78	1997	San Lorenzo, P.R.

PITCHING	W	L	ERA	G	GS	CG	SV	IP	H	R	ER	BB	SO	AVG	B	T	HT	WT	DOB	1st Yr	Resides
Aguilar, Ray	2	3	2.29	8	7	1	0	51	35	17	13	8	32	.192	S	L	5-11	200	1-18-80	2001	South El Monte, Calif.
Almanza, Armando	0	3	8.10	5	2	0	0	7	12	6	6	3	5	.429	L	L	6-3	240	10-26-72	1993	El Paso, Texas
Barry, Kevin	2	1	0.73	20	0	0	4	25	15	2	2	10	31	.172	R	R	6-2	210	8-18-78	2001	Princeton Junction, N.J.
Byrd, Paul	1	1	7.11	3	3	0	0	13	13	10	10	5	8	.271	R	R	6-1	185	12-3-70	1991	Louisville, Ky.
Capellan, Jose	5	1	2.50	9	9	0	0	50	15	14	19	53	.270	R	R	6-4	235	1-13-81	1999	Cotui, D.R.
Coenen, Matt	3	5	3.09	36	6	0	2	79	77	28	27	42	54	.263	L	L	6-6	230	3-13-80	2001	St. Michaels, Md.
Colon, Roman	1	0	0.00	3	0	0	0	3	1	1	0	0	5	.091	R	R	6-3	170	8-13-79	1996	Monte Cristi, D.R.
Curtis, Daniel	7	3	3.12	33	6	0	0	95	90	39	33	35	88	.254	R	R	6-3	215	11-3-79	1998	Chattanooga, Tenn.
Davies, Kyle	4	0	2.32	11	10	0	0	62	40	18	16	22	73	.183	R	R	6-2	190	9-9-83	2001	Dover, Fla.
Elder, Dave	0	1	3.00	8	0	0	0	9	8	3	3	4	6	.229	R	R	6-0	180	9-23-75	1997	Conyers, Ga.
Emiliano, Jamie	4	3	3.50	51	0	0	11	62	59	34	24	35	53	.250	R	R	5-10	210	8-2-74	1995	Andrews, Texas
Evert, Brett	4	3	4.07	22	9	0	0	73	65	35	33	28	72	.240	L	L	6-6	200	10-23-80	1999	Salem, Ore.
Fesh, Sean	0	1	2.45	1	0	0	0	4	4	3	1	2	0	.286	L	L	6-2	180	11-3-72	1991	Bethel, Conn.
Langen, Brian	1	0	4.91	15	0	0	2	18	14	11	10	15	18	.215	L	L	6-7	210	3-13-78	1998	Farmersville, Ill.
McBride, Macay	1	7	4.44	38	12	0	0	103	113	59	51	46	102	.279	L	L	5-11	180	10-24-82	2001	Sylvania, Ga.
Merricks, Matt	1	3	4.91	6	5	0	0	22	26	21	12	11	27	.292	L	L	5-11	180	8-6-82	2000	Oxnard, Calif.
Meyer, Dan	6	3	2.22	14	13	0	0	65	50	17	16	12	86	.209	L	L	6-3	190	7-3-81	2002	Mickleton, N.J.
Miner, Zach	6	10	5.22	27	22	1	0	129	132	87	75	55	111	.270	R	R	6-3	190	3-12-82	2001	Jupiter, Fla.
Moehler, Brian	3	9	4.17	20	20	0	0	108	113	58	50	27	57	.272	R	R	6-3	235	12-31-71	1993	Marietta, Ga.
Pineda, Isauro	5	7	4.60	32	10	1	5	76	77	51	39	38	79	.270	R	R	6-0	160	11-10-78	1997	Mazatlan, Mexico
Ramirez, Horacio	2	0	3.09	3	2	0	0	12	15	4	4	3	2	.349	L	L	6-1	170	11-24-79	1997	Inglewood, Calif.
Richardson, Jason	0	0	7.20	4	0	0	1	10	9	8	8	6	4	.237	R	R	6-2	200	6-11-80	1999	Lakeland, Fla.
Roberts, Ralph	0	1	4.50	8	0	0	0	14	17	7	7	5	12	.298	R	R	6-2	200	3-28-80	2001	Cherryville, N.C.
Smyth, Steve	1	1	5.64	7	4	0	0	22	25	20	14	19	15	.291	L	L	6-1	200	6-3-78	1999	Temecula, Calif.
Sturkie, Scott	1	3	4.33	19	0	0	4	27	25	16	13	11	13	.253	R	R	6-3	210	6-12-79	2001	West Columbia, S.C.
Zumwalt, Alec	3	7	5.09	46	0	0	1	76	84	52	43	38	67	.283	R	R	6-2	190	1-20-81	1999	Kernersville, N.C.

FIELDING

Catcher	PCT	G	PO	A	E	DP	PB
Boscan	.993	50	385	36	3	5	5
Evans	.989	20	156	17	2	3	0
B. Pena	.988	73	568	28	7	4	4
Velazquez	1.000	1	2	0	0	0	0

First Base	PCT	G	PO	A	E	DP
Boscan	.917	2	10	1	1	2
Butler	1.000	2	4	0	0	1
Calzado	.970	29	214	12	7	25
Iorg	1.000	3	18	1	0	1
Jurries	.993	17	137	5	1	13
Thorman	.994	94	796	42	5	86

Second Base	PCT	G	PO	A	E	DP
Butler	.968	40	79	103	6	33

Third Base	PCT	G	PO	A	E	DP
Butler	.875	6	4	10	2	1
Calzado	.962	24	18	57	3	8
Iorg	.833	4	0	10	2	3
Johnson	.900	3	2	7	1	0
Marte	.941	106	69	202	17	20
Velazquez	1.000	1	0	1	0	0

Shortstop	PCT	G	PO	A	E	DP
Butler	1.000	6	6	16	0	2
T. Pena	.954	128	167	371	26	82

Calzado	1.000	3	4	9	0	1
Herr	.955	74	128	168	14	45
Velazquez	.986	39	66	79	2	20

Outfield	PCT	G	PO	A	E	DP
Aldridge	.975	28	37	2	1	1
Calzado	.989	56	79	10	1	2
Francoeur	.978	20	41	3	1	1
Jansen	.750	5	3	0	1	0
Johnson	.956	132	203	16	10	2
Marrero	1.000	4	5	0	0	0
McCarthy	.970	62	93	3	3	2
Melian	.979	46	93	1	2	0
Stern	.990	96	198	10	2	2
Velazquez	1.000	1	1	0	0	

Velazquez	.966	10	7	21	1	4

CAROLINA LEAGUE

BATTING	AVG	G	AB	R	H	2B	3B	HR	RBI	BB	SO	SB	CS	OBP	SLG	B	T	HT	WT	DOB	1st Yr	Resides
Bernard, Miguel	.197	24	71	8	14	6	0	0	1	7	15	1	1	.288	.282	R	R	5-11	170	1-1-81	1998	San Pedro de Macoris, D.R.
Blanco, Gregor	.269	119	435	73	117	17	9	8	41	47	114	25	9	.342	.405	L	L	5-11	170	12-12-83	2001	Caracas, Venez.

BATTING	AVG	G	AB	R	H	2B	3B	HR	RBI	BB	SO	SB	CS	OBP	SLG	B	T	HT	WT	DOB	1st Yr	Resides
Downing, Juan	.192	9	26	3	5	0	0	0	4	6	0	0	0	.300	.192	S	R	5-10	180	12-29-78	2004	San Juan, P.R.
Duran, Carlos	.261	66	234	19	61	7	5	3	28	12	47	13	1	.295	.372	L	L	6-1	160	12-27-82	2000	Barquisimeto, Venez.
Francoeur, Jeff	.293	88	334	56	98	26	0	15	52	22	70	10	6	.346	.506	R	R	6-4	165	1-8-84	2002	Lilburn, Ga.
Giles, Marcus	.077	4	13	1	1	0	0	0	2	1	4	0	0	.133	.154	R	R	5-8	180	5-18-78	1997	El Cajon, Calif.
Hemingway, Jamie	.202	48	173	12	35	6	0	2	10	3	33	2	3	.223	.272	R	R	6-3	215	10-31-80	2003	Greensboro, N.C.
Hernandez, Luis	.272	117	401	49	109	23	4	6	45	16	70	8	6	.306	.394	S	R	5-10	140	6-26-84	2001	Quibor, Venez.
Iorg, Isaac	.274	80	281	33	77	13	1	3	25	19	43	5	5	.334	.359	R	R	6-1	190	6-5-79	2001	Knoxville, Tenn.
James, Willie	.189	45	111	10	21	1	0	0	11	14	28	8	6	.281	.198	S	R	5-8	160	4-30-81	2002	Moreno Valley, Calif.
Jansen, Ardley	.246	32	114	16	28	4	1	0	8	7	40	1	2	.295	.298	R	R	6-2	190	2-16-83	2000	Willemstad, Curacao
Joseph, Onil	.272	113	423	63	115	13	1	2	36	48	90	32	10	.354	.322	R	R	6-2	165	2-12-82	2000	San Pedro de Macoris, D.R.
McCann, Brian	.278	111	385	45	107	35	0	16	66	31	54	2	2	.337	.494	L	R	6-3	210	2-20-84	2002	Satellite Beach, Fla.
Ruelas, Alonzo	.274	57	157	22	43	6	1	2	16	19	39	3	2	.361	.363	R	R	6-1	190	4-2-81	2001	El Paso, Texas
Salas, Jose	.146	14	41	5	6	1	0	0	1	0	5	0	0	.143	.171	S	R	6-3	210	2-16-82	1999	Caracas, Venez.
Schuerholz, Jonathan	.207	122	376	34	78	12	5	1	33	49	77	14	9	.303	.274	R	R	5-11	188	6-25-80	2002	Atlanta, Ga.
Serrano, Ray	.259	33	116	19	30	8	0	5	23	3	18	0	2	.289	.457	R	R	5-9	180	1-19-81	1999	Ponce, P.R.
Thomas, Ben	.213	81	272	21	58	13	1	1	26	28	63	7	4	.288	.279	L	L	6-0	200	6-20-82	2003	Rapid City, S.D.
Thorman, Scott	.299	43	154	20	46	11	1	4	29	12	19	1	0	.358	.461	L	R	6-3	200	1-6-82	2000	Cambridge, Ontario
Timmons, Wesley	.277	113	383	48	106	24	2	3	45	55	32	10	5	.387	.373	R	R	6-0	190	7-12-79	2002	Jacksonville Beach, Fla.
Wise, DeWayne	.250	4	16	1	4	0	1	0	0	0	6	0	0	.250	.375	L	L	6-1	175	2-24-78	1997	Chapin, S.C.

PITCHING	W	L	ERA	G	GS	CG	SV	IP	H	R	ER	BB	SO	AVG	B	T	HT	WT	DOB	1st Yr	Resides
Acosta, Manny	4	0	4.24	11	0	0	0	23	20	12	11	11	21	.227	R	R	5-1	170	5-1-81	1998	Colon, Panama
Aguilar, Ray	2	0	2.25	4	0	0	0	20	15	5	5	1	12	.208	S	L	5-11	200	1-18-80	2001	South El Monte, Calif.
Basner, Ryan	3	4	3.22	38	0	0	8	59	73	23	21	9	63	.299	R	R	6-3	225	7-15-81	2003	West Chester, Pa.
Blakeney, Jacob	1	1	5.51	22	0	0	1	33	36	22	20	21	18	.281	R	R	6-1	200	7-26-80	2003	Mendenhall, Miss.
Boyer, Blaine	10	10	2.98	28	28	0	0	154	138	63	51	49	95	.241	R	R	6-3	215	7-11-81	2000	Marietta, Ga.
Bush, Paul	5	3	3.56	24	4	0	0	66	58	27	26	25	78	.244	R	R	6-1	190	10-5-79	2002	Titusville, Fla.
Capellan, Jose	5	1	1.94	8	8	1	0	46	27	11	10	11	62	.168	R	R	6-4	235	1-13-81	1999	Cotui, D.R.
Davies, Kyle	9	2	2.63	14	14	0	0	75	55	24	22	32	95	.204	R	R	6-2	190	9-9-83	2001	Dover, Fla.
Iorg, Isaac	0	0	0.00	1	0	0	0	0	0	0	0	0	1	.000	R	R	6-1	190	6-5-79	2001	Knoxville, Tenn.
Lerew, Anthony	8	9	3.75	27	27	0	0	144	145	75	60	46	125	.266	L	R	6-3	220	10-28-82	2001	Wellsville, Pa.
McClendon, Matt	2	1	3.26	11	0	0	0	19	17	8	7	9	23	.230	R	R	6-6	220	10-13-77	1999	Orlando, Fla.
Merricks, Matt	5	3	3.31	13	12	1	0	73	61	32	27	24	67	.228	L	L	5-11	180	8-6-82	2000	Oxnard, Calif.
Mueller, Mike	0	2	5.57	20	0	0	0	32	31	23	20	22	29	.258	R	R	6-5	220	8-22-80	2002	West Bend, Wisc.
Peralta, Efigenio	3	3	4.07	31	8	0	3	80	69	42	36	36	75	.234	R	R	6-2	192	1-31-82	2002	San Cristobal, D.R.
Richardson, Jason	0	4	4.45	14	1	0	2	28	29	17	14	20	22	.259	R	R	6-2	200	3-28-80	2001	Cherryville, N.C.
Roberts, Ralph	3	5	3.52	32	0	0	3	54	47	23	21	22	36	.228	R	R	6-3	210	6-12-79	2001	West Columbia, S.C.
Sturkie, Scott	2	1	3.86	12	1	0	0	28	30	14	12	8	23	.278	R	R	6-3	200	4-9-81	2003	Plantation, Fla.
Tucker, Glenn	3	1	1.64	48	0	0	21	66	55	13	12	26	56	.232	R	R	6-3	200	8-17-80	2000	Wellington, Fla.
Waters, Chris	0	1	12.27	4	1	0	0	7	14	10	10	4	4	.452	R	R	6-4	195	4-25-81	2003	Mercer Island, Wash.
White, Sean	6	6	3.60	18	10	0	0	70	62	34	28	24	41	.238	R	R	6-3	200	1-14-82	2003	Lorena, Texas
Wright, Matt	4	6	3.39	24	21	1	0	125	115	55	47	58	133	.249	R	R	6-4	225	3-13-82	2000	Lorena, Texas

FIELDING

Catcher	PCT	G	PO	A	E	DP	PB
Bernard	.975	21	140	17	4	4	7
McCann	.990	78	540	66	6	4	7
Ruelas	.989	34	241	17	3	1	2
Salas	.973	8	66	7	2	0	1
Serrano	.981	14	95	8	2	1	1

First Base	PCT	G	PO	A	E	DP
Iorg	.987	56	407	39	6	36
Ruelas	1.000	5	19	1	0	0
Salas	1.000	1	2	1	0	0
Thomas	.994	36	301	11	2	23
Thorman	.997	43	361	19	1	28
Timmons	.985	8	64	3	1	6

Second Base	PCT	G	PO	A	E	DP
Downing	1.000	2	4	4	0	0

	PCT	G	PO	A	E	DP
Giles	1.000	3	6	5	0	0
Iorg	1.000	3	1	6	0	0
James	.933	15	22	34	4	6
Schuerholz	.954	118	178	367	26	51
Timmons	1.000	3	1	2	0	1

Third Base	PCT	G	PO	A	E	DP
Downing	1.000	2	3	3	0	1
Iorg	.917	6	2	9	1	0
James	.923	9	3	9	1	1
Thomas	.921	34	13	45	5	2
Timmons	.962	96	68	136	8	14

Shortstop	PCT	G	PO	A	E	DP
Downing	.889	2	4	4	1	2
Hernandez	.977	116	195	305	12	56

	PCT	G	PO	A	E	DP
Iorg	1.000	4	1	9	0	0
James	.935	16	15	28	3	11
Schuerholz	1.000	1	3	2	0	1
Timmons	1.000	6	15	21	0	2

Outfield	PCT	G	PO	A	E	DP
Blanco	.961	115	216	3	9	0
Duran	.983	54	105	11	2	2
Francoeur	.975	82	150	8	4	1
Hemingway	.989	43	85	1	1	0
Jansen	.947	30	48	6	3	0
Joseph	.973	109	166	12	5	2
Timmons	1.000	1	2	0	0	0
Wise	1.000	3	6	0	0	0

ROME BRAVES — Low Class A

SOUTH ATLANTIC LEAGUE

BATTING	AVG	G	AB	R	H	2B	3B	HR	RBI	BB	SO	SB	CS	OBP	SLG	B	T	HT	WT	DOB	1st Yr	Resides
Barthel, Cole	.280	22	50	13	14	2	0	0	3	1	6	2	0	.333	.320	R	R	6-2	200	8-11-82	2001	Decatur, Ala.
Bernard, Miguel	.277	75	278	37	77	18	3	10	47	13	36	1	1	.326	.471	R	R	5-11	170	1-1-81	1998	San Pedro de Macoris, D.R.
Burrus, Josh	.272	126	503	82	137	30	3	11	46	33	123	30	10	.330	.410	R	R	5-11	180	8-20-83	2001	Marietta, Ga.
Campbell, Eric	.136	7	22	0	3	0	0	1	2	7	0	0	0	.240	.136	R	R	6-0	195	8-6-85	2004	Owensville, Ind.
Doetsch, Steve	.286	128	479	74	137	24	8	9	67	47	152	18	11	.355	.426	R	R	6-2	200	12-2-83	2003	St. Petersburg, Fla.
Downing, Juan	.233	8	30	4	7	1	0	0	3	2	4	0	1	.314	.267	S	R	5-10	180	12-29-78	2004	San Juan, P.R.
Esquivel, Matt	.285	114	411	69	117	32	3	16	64	35	140	14	4	.356	.494	R	R	6-2	220	12-17-82	2002	San Antonio, Texas
Giles, Marcus	.000	1	2	0	0	0	0	0	0	0	0	0	0	.500	.000	R	R	5-8	180	5-18-78	1997	El Cajon, Calif.
Guzman, Carlos	.252	103	329	44	83	26	3	13	52	38	111	6	3	.348	.468	R	R	6-3	180	7-5-83	2000	La Vega, D.R.
Hanson, Mike	.182	72	214	15	39	7	2	2	13	6	35	2	4	.209	.262	R	R	5-11	175	5-2-81	2003	Smyrna, Ga.
Hemingway, Jamie	.275	15	51	7	14	3	0	0	4	2	8	3	0	.302	.333	R	R	6-3	215	10-31-80	2003	Greensboro, N.C.
Hernandez, Diory	.271	90	306	40	83	20	1	3	38	26	67	7	4	.325	.373	R	R	6-0	170	4-8-84	2003	San Pedro de Macoris, D.R.
Jansen, Ardley	.254	66	228	37	58	8	0	8	24	25	67	8	4	.336	.395	R	R	6-2	190	2-16-83	2000	Willemstad, Curacao
Jones, Chipper	.000	1	2	0	0	0	0	0	0	0	0	0	0	.000	.000	S	R	6-4	220	4-24-72	1990	Alpharetta, Ga.
Prado, Martin	.315	107	429	68	135	25	6	3	38	30	47	14	10	.363	.422	R	R	6-1	170	10-27-83	2001	Maracay, Venez.
Pyzik, Steve	.303	50	122	15	37	9	1	0	19	7	13	0	0	.356	.393	R	R	5-11	175	5-18-81	2003	Mt. Airy, N.C.
Saltalamacchia, Jarrod	.272	91	323	42	88	19	2	10	51	34	83	1	0	.348	.437	S	R	6-4	195	5-2-85	2003	West Palm Beach, Fla.
Schade, Scott	.244	105	377	44	92	21	4	15	55	23	92	2	2	.296	.440	R	R	6-0	205	2-22-82	2003	Lewisburg, Ga.
Serrano, Ray	.258	17	62	5	16	5	1	1	7	1	7	0	0	.270	.419	R	R	5-9	180	1-19-81	1999	Ponce, P.R.

BATTING	AVG	G	AB	R	H	2B	3B	HR	RBI	BB	SO	SB	CS	OBP	SLG	B	T	HT	WT	DOB	1st Yr	Resides
Shehan, Jonathon	.250	2	4	0	1	0	0	0	1	1	0	0	0	.400	.250	R	R	5-9	200	5-13-82	2004	Strasburg, Pa.
Silva, Johan	.154	7	26	1	4	0	0	1	3	3	9	2	1	.241	.269	S	R	5-11	170	1-30-85	2002	Valencia, Venez.
Thomas, Ben	.236	27	89	8	21	5	0	1	9	4	22	1	0	.269	.326	L	L	6-0	200	6-20-82	2003	Rapid City, S.D.
White, Dean	.224	102	317	40	71	8	2	2	23	16	94	11	4	.264	.281	R	R	6-2	180	2-12-83	2001	Perth, Australia
Wise, DeWayne	.333	5	15	4	5	0	0	2	4	1	5	1	0	.412	.733	L	L	6-1	175	2-24-78	1997	Chapin, S.C.

PITCHING	W	L	ERA	G	GS	CG	SV	IP	H	R	ER	BB	SO	AVG	B	T	HT	WT	DOB	1st Yr	Resides
Anderson, Devin	0	2	7.00	5	0	0	0	9	12	10	7	5	9	.343	L	L	6-5	220	1-24-84	2003	Ocoee, Fla.
Ascanio, Jose	3	3	3.84	34	0	0	9	66	58	39	28	15	64	.235	R	R	6-0	150	5-2-85	2002	Maracay, Venez.
Bakker, Kyle	3	0	1.91	20	0	0	1	28	23	8	6	21	21	.228	L	L	6-9	255	10-21-81	2004	Omaha, Neb.
Blakeney, Jacob	0	2	2.35	17	0	0	5	23	16	8	6	5	18	.190	R	R	6-1	200	7-26-80	2003	Mendenhall, Miss.
Burrows, Angelo	1	2	4.73	8	0	0	0	13	7	7	7	11	7	.149	L	R	5-11	170	7-2-80	2000	Freeport, Bahamas
Digby, Bryan	8	10	5.75	27	27	1	0	144	189	112	92	71	107	.327	R	R	6-3	225	12-31-81	2000	Peachtree City, Ga.
Franzenburg, Luke	0	0	3.00	9	0	0	2	12	12	5	4	3	8	.255	L	L	5-11	190	5-27-81	2004	Keystone, Iowa
Garza, Rolando	1	1	6.75	10	0	0	0	21	21	18	16	12	13	.269	R	R	6-3	237	12-14-79	1997	Coachella, Calif.
James, Chuck	10	5	2.24	26	22	1	0	133	92	41	33	48	156	.195	L	L	6-0	170	11-9-81	2003	Mableton, Ga.
Letson, Wesley	2	0	3.24	11	0	0	1	17	19	6	6	8	12	.292	L	L	6-0	200	9-13-82	2004	Hartselle, Ala.
Long, Jeffery	2	2	8.53	13	0	0	0	25	37	27	24	13	19	.346	R	R	6-4	200	11-4-81	2004	Smyrna, Ga.
Lopez, Gonzalo	8	4	3.67	22	21	0	0	101	97	47	41	21	109	.249	R	R	6-2	175	10-6-83	2001	Managua, Nicaragua
Morton, Charles	7	9	4.86	27	18	0	2	117	140	76	63	67	102	.295	R	R	6-5	204	10-12-83	2002	Redding, Conn.
Mueller, Mike	0	3	5.64	15	1	0	0	30	39	21	19	14	32	.322	R	R	6-5	220	8-22-80	2002	West Bend, Wisc.
Nelson, Brad	0	2	5.40	20	0	0	3	27	38	25	16	13	18	.328	L	L	6-2	220	12-23-82	2001	Algona, Iowa
Nieves, Roberto	1	4	6.88	22	1	0	0	34	43	41	26	41	29	.314	R	R	6-2	195	11-23-82	2002	Vega Alta, P.R.
Reyes, Jo Jo	2	4	5.35	15	14	1	0	74	84	49	44	25	71	.288	L	L	6-2	200	11-20-84	2003	Riverside, Calif.
Rodriguez, Ricardo	5	3	3.26	31	0	0	12	50	42	21	18	16	61	.222	R	R	6-0	140	4-28-81	1999	Caracas, Venez.
Russell, Stephen	5	6	4.29	22	15	0	2	101	94	57	48	39	87	.248	R	R	6-5	185	12-20-83	2002	Las Vegas, Nev.
Smith, Danny	0	0	7.71	1	1	0	0	5	5	5	4	2	5	.263	L	L	6-5	225	9-9-83	2003	Fort Myers, Fla.
Stevens, Jacob	9	5	2.27	27	19	0	2	135	100	41	34	39	140	.204	L	L	6-3	210	3-15-85	2003	Cape Coral, Fla.
White, Sean	3	3	6.44	13	1	0	1	36	43	30	26	12	20	.301	R	R	6-4	195	4-25-81	2003	Mercer Island, Wash.

FIELDING

Catcher	PCT	G	PO	A	E	DP	PB
Bernard	.980	47	365	35	8	5	10
Pyzik	.992	43	217	19	2	4	1
Saltalamacchia	.982	50	415	31	8	3	13
Serrano	.975	13	112	5	3	0	0
Shehan	1.000	2	16	0	0	0	1

First Base	PCT	G	PO	A	E	DP
Guzman	.992	93	618	38	5	58
Pyzik	1.000	1	4	1	0	0
Schade	.997	53	354	24	1	30
Thomas	1.000	2	13	2	0	0

Second Base	PCT	G	PO	A	E	DP
Downing	1.000	2	4	5	0	2

	PCT	G	PO	A	E	DP
Hanson	.955	35	50	78	6	15
Hernandez	1.000	1	3	4	0	1
Prado	.978	101	175	222	9	52
White	.917	4	4	7	1	1

Third Base	PCT	G	PO	A	E	DP
Barthel	.786	12	7	15	6	0
Campbell	.938	7	2	13	1	0
Schade	.917	48	21	78	9	8
Thomas	.970	18	14	18	1	0
White	.882	62	26	109	18	10

Shortstop	PCT	G	PO	A	E	DP
Downing	.970	6	12	20	1	11
Hanson	.977	25	36	50	2	17

	PCT	G	PO	A	E	DP
Hernandez	.922	85	111	195	26	28
White	.940	28	42	68	7	14

Outfield	PCT	G	PO	A	E	DP
Burrus	.967	111	185	17	7	4
Doetsch	.981	112	255	5	5	2
Esquivel	.980	102	231	9	5	1
Guzman	1.000	6	6	0	0	0
Hanson	.875	6	5	2	1	0
Hemingway	.929	14	24	2	2	0
Jansen	.965	57	133	4	5	2
Jones	1.000	1	2	0	0	0
Silva	.933	7	14	0	1	0
White	1.000	3	6	0	0	0
Wise	1.000	1	1	0	0	0

DANVILLE BRAVES

Rookie

APPALACHIAN LEAGUE

BATTING	AVG	G	AB	R	H	2B	3B	HR	RBI	BB	SO	SB	CS	OBP	SLG	B	T	HT	WT	DOB	1st Yr	Resides
Armstrong, Cole	.316	49	174	30	55	9	0	6	46	29	17	0	0	.411	.471	L	R	6-3	210	8-24-83	2003	Surrey, B.C.
Arnold, Derrick	.185	49	135	18	25	4	0	3	14	16	43	2	1	.279	.281	B	R	5-9	160	2-4-86	2004	Pace, Fla.
Brown, Bo	.083	9	12	1	1	0	0	0	0	0	5	0	0	.214	.083	R	R	6-0	175	4-3-83	2004	Pensacola, Fla.
Cruz, Ramon	.125	12	24	0	3	1	0	0	1	0	10	0	0	.160	.167	R	R	6-1	180	10-22-83	2001	Santo Domingo, D.R.
Eichas, Keith	.305	59	220	31	67	16	1	2	29	7	39	2	0	.364	.414	R	R	6-2	200	6-29-83	2003	Georgetown, Texas
Harp, Troy	.200	3	5	1	1	0	0	0	0	0	2	0	0	.200	.200	R	R	6-0	190	11-5-81	2004	Louisville, Ky.
Holt, J.C.	.321	51	209	38	67	15	0	1	21	18	34	17	5	.377	.407	L	R	5-10	172	12-8-82	2004	Seiper, La.
Jones, Brandon	.297	57	209	35	62	6	5	3	33	23	33	4	2	.366	.416	L	R	6-1	190	12-10-83	2004	Wewahitchka, Fla.
Jurich, Mark	.281	57	203	39	57	10	1	16	47	28	33	0	1	.363	.556	L	L	5-11	180	4-19-82	2003	Louisville, Ky.
Loadenthal, Carl	.307	64	238	60	73	9	4	5	32	32	34	12	3	.390	.441	L	L	5-11	180	12-27-81	2003	Southampton, Pa.
Moreta, Carlos	.236	36	106	14	25	3	0	4	18	10	31	1	0	.311	.377	R	R	6-2	180	1-5-83	2000	Barahona, D.R.
Ponce, Angel	.302	22	43	6	13	0	0	4	2	13	1	2	.333	.302	R	R	5-11	187	7-8-82	2003	Veracruz, Mexico
Pope, Van	.270	60	233	39	63	18	2	5	39	11	44	5	1	.333	.429	R	R	6-0	180	2-26-84	2004	Jackson, Miss.
Romak, Jamie	.190	48	158	25	30	5	1	5	22	14	56	1	1	.287	.329	R	R	6-2	220	9-30-85	2003	London, Ontario
Rozema, Mike	.282	49	156	31	44	10	1	2	19	15	32	5	2	.353	.397	L	R	6-2	180	9-16-81	2004	Ridgewood, N.J.
Sammons, Clint	.288	40	132	19	38	7	2	0	17	18	26	5	1	.368	.371	R	R	6-0	195	5-15-82	2004	Stone Mountain, Ga.

GAMES BY POSITION: C—Armstrong 23, Cruz 11, Harp 3, Sammons 40. **1B**—Eichas 59, Moreta 14. **2B**—Arnold 3, Brown 2, Holt 51, Rozema 20. **3B**—Pope 47, Romak 20. **SS**—Arnold 43, Brown 4, Rozema 29. **OF**—Jones 57, Jurich 55, Loadenthal 64, Moreta 19, Ponce 17.

PITCHING	W	L	ERA	G	GS	CG	SV	IP	H	R	ER	BB	SO	AVG	B	T	HT	WT	DOB	1st Yr	Resides
Anderson, Devin	1	0	0.75	3	2	0	0	12	9	3	1	1	10	.188	L	L	6-5	220	1-24-84	2003	Ocoee, Fla.
Atilano, Luis	5	1	4.20	13	13	0	0	64	64	32	30	10	54	.255	R	R	6-3	180	5-10-85	2003	San Juan, P.R.
Bacot, Paul	3	1	4.70	13	13	0	0	61	60	40	32	14	38	.254	R	R	6-6	205	8-16-84	2003	Atlanta, Ga.
Bakker, Kyle	0	0	10.80	2	0	0	0	2	3	2	2	6	2	.333	L	L	6-9	255	10-21-81	2004	Omaha, Neb.
Collins, Danny	4	4	4.55	11	2	0	1	28	25	17	14	5	18	.243	L	L	6-3	175	4-12-83	2003	Fort Pierce, Fla.
Cuevas, Jairo	0	0	0.00	1	1	0	0	4	1	0	0	4	3	.077	R	R	6-3	210	1-24-84	2003	Santo Domingo, D.R.
Endl, Brady	2	3	2.89	16	0	0	1	28	24	10	9	7	33	.231	R	R	6-5	235	4-14-82	2004	Jefferson, Wisc.
Harrison, Matt	4	4	4.09	13	12	1	0	66	72	36	30	10	49	.275	L	L	6-5	205	8-16-85	2003	Stem, N.C.
Jimenez, Rodny	1	1	2.89	14	0	0	2	28	21	10	9	14	39	.208	R	R	6-2	170	3-16-82	2000	Santo Domingo, D.R.
Johnson, Bryan	2	1	3.32	12	0	0	2	19	20	9	7	8	14	.263	L	L	6-1	185	11-9-82	2004	Selah, Wash.
Letson, Wes	0	0	2.79	5	0	0	1	10	8	3	3	2	13	.211	L	L	6-0	200	9-13-82	2004	Hartselle, Ala.
Long, Jeffery	1	2	7.56	6	0	0	1	8	10	7	7	6	15	.294	R	R	6-4	200	11-4-81	2004	Smyrna, Ga.

PITCHING	W	L	ERA	G	GS	CG	SV	IP	H	R	ER	BB	SO	AVG	B	T	HT	WT	DOB	1st Yr	Resides
Nelson, Brad	3	2	4.85	20	0	0	5	26	28	18	14	4	23	.259	L	R	6-2	220	12-23-82	2001	Algona, Iowa
Paul, Jason	2	2	5.65	17	0	0	1	29	35	19	18	9	26	.310	R	R	6-2	180	10-10-85	2004	Henniker, N.H.
Payano, Nelson	2	0	4.13	9	3	0	0	24	14	13	11	13	34	.169	L	L	5-11	150	11-13-82	2001	Santo Domingo, D.R.
Santiago, Jose	1	2	5.01	6	4	0	0	23	25	16	13	11	23	.266	R	R	6-4	180	8-1-81	2001	Altagracia, D.R.
Smith, Danny	3	1	2.27	14	2	0	1	40	24	10	10	16	52	.173	L	L	6-5	225	9-9-83	2003	Fort Myers, Fla.
Stanley, Adam	0	0	0.00	1	0	0	0	1	0	0	0	2	0	.000	L	L	6-2	195	11-20-84	2003	Raleigh, N.C.
Villa, Kelvin	3	0	1.93	15	4	0	1	42	35	15	9	21	41	.229	L	L	5-10	160	12-14-85	2003	Tenares, D.R.
Vines, Chris	6	3	3.28	13	10	0	0	60	58	25	22	14	72	.248	R	R	6-5	205	2-26-85	2004	Birmingham, Ala.

GULF COAST LEAGUE

BATTING	AVG	G	AB	R	H	2B	3B	HR	RBI	BB	SO	SB	CS	SLG	OBP	B	T	HT	WT	DOB	1st Yr	Resides
Barksdale, James	.255	20	47	8	12	3	0	2	4	4	14	0	0	.447	.327	R	R	6-2	200	12-7-81	2004	Madison, Miss.
Bressoud, C.J.	.191	23	47	4	9	4	0	0	1	6	14	0	1	.277	.283	R	R	6-2	195	5-12-85	2003	Kennesaw, Ga.
Brezeale, Danny	.202	37	104	8	21	4	0	1	10	4	32	4	0	.269	.241	R	R	5-11	200	5-13-86	2004	Monck's Corner, S.C.
Brown, Bo	.152	22	46	4	7	0	0	0	1	2	18	0	0	.152	.216	R	R	6-0	175	4-3-83	2004	Cantonment, Fla.
Campbell, Eric	.251	56	211	30	53	7	0	7	29	15	47	3	1	.384	.306	R	R	6-0	195	8-6-85	2004	Owensville, Ind.
Guerra, Junior	.216	33	88	10	19	8	0	1	14	4	18	0	0	.341	.255	R	R	5-11	180	1-16-85	2002	Guayana, Venez.
Harp, Troy	.000	1	1	0	0	0	0	0	0	0	0	0	0	.000	.000	R	R	6-0	190	11-5-81	2004	Louisville, Ky.
Koko, Rubi	.125	42	104	13	13	2	1	2	5	9	62	8	4	.221	.195	R	R	6-3	185	3-25-86	2004	Willemstad, Curacao
Marte, Andy	.467	3	15	4	7	4	0	1	6	2	2	0	0	.933	.529	R	R	6-1	180	10-21-83	2001	Villa Tapia, D.R.
Ortega, Raul	.226	36	93	11	21	2	0	0	5	8	26	2	0	.247	.298	S	R	6-1	160	5-21-84	2001	Valencia, Venez.
Owings, Jon Mark	.226	44	124	14	28	1	3	3	7	13	38	5	1	.355	.304	R	R	6-4	192	4-4-85	2004	Gainesville, Ga.
Ramirez, Maximiliano ..	.275	57	204	20	56	16	1	8	35	19	50	1	0	.480	.339	R	R	5-11	170	10-11-84	2003	Barquisimeto, Venez.
Rodriguez, Manuel	.251	50	179	18	45	10	0	5	17	7	26	0	1	.391	.278	L	L	6-3	190	1-6-85	2002	Chitre, Panama
Rodriguez, Michael	.258	9	31	1	8	0	0	1	4	3	3	1	0	.355	.314	L	L	6-1	160	7-8-85	2002	Miranda, Venez.
Shehan, Jonathan	.200	18	35	6	7	0	0	0	1	6	7	0	0	.200	.333	R	R	5-9	200	5-13-82	2004	Strasburg, Pa.
Silva, Johan	.273	52	172	28	47	4	2	6	24	22	42	8	4	.424	.362	R	R	5-11	170	1-30-85	2001	Valencia, Venez.
Suero, Ovandy	.232	49	168	27	39	0	3	0	9	10	56	30	2	.268	.291	S	R	5-10	160	6-20-82	2002	Villa Gonzales, D.R.
Terrazas, Ivan	.282	37	117	14	33	7	1	4	20	4	18	2	1	.462	.311	S	R	5-11	190	11-18-82	2002	Mexico City, Mexico
Williams, Larry	.200	40	115	6	23	8	0	0	6	15	31	0	1	.270	.292	L	R	6-2	200	4-6-85	2004	Lawndale, Calif.

GAMES BY POSITION: C—Barksdale 12, Bressoud 23, Guerra 29, Harp 1, Shehan 17. **1B**—Brezeale 1, Ma. Rodriguez 44, Mi. Rodriguez 1, Williams 19. **2B**—Brezeale 10, Brown 8, Marte 1, Ortega 11, Suero 48. **3B**—Campbell 14, Marte 1, Ortega 5, Ramirez 42, Terrazas 1. **SS**—Brown 12. Campbell 36, Ortega 16. **OF**—Brezeale 25, Brown 1, Koko 38, Ortega 1, Owings 41, Mi. Rodriguez 5, Silva 51, Terrazas 33, Williams 9.

PITCHING	W	L	ERA	G	GS	CG	SV	IP	H	R	ER	BB	SO	AVG	B	T	HT	WT	DOB	1st Yr	Resides
Acosta, Manny	0	0	3.38	2	0	0	0	3	5	2	1	2	2	.454	R	R	6-4	170	5-1-81	1998	Colon, Panama
Aguilar, Ray	0	1	12.71	2	2	0	0	6	11	8	8	0	4	.392	S	L	5-11	200	1-18-80	2001	South El Monte, Calif.
Blackford, Todd	1	2	7.86	19	2	0	0	26	44	28	23	9	18	.369	L	R	6-3	200	6-10-85	2004	Bourbon, Ind.
Burrows, Angelo	1	3	3.75	14	0	0	3	24	22	11	10	7	23	.241	L	R	5-11	170	7-2-80	1999	Freeport, Bahamas
Collins, Danny	0	1	2.25	4	2	0	0	12	14	5	3	3	7	.291	L	L	6-3	175	4-12-83	2003	Fort Pierce, Fla.
Cross, Blake	3	3	2.96	17	0	0	4	27	23	12	9	16	28	.221	R	R	5-11	190	2-16-82	2004	Jamestown, N.C.
Cuevas, Jairo	2	3	3.09	9	7	0	1	35	29	13	12	7	39	.218	R	R	6-3	210	1-24-84	2003	Santo Domingo, D.R.
Demme, Asher	2	4	8.90	10	7	0	0	29	37	32	29	10	22	.305	R	R	6-3	200	11-1-84	2003	Reston, Va.
Franzenburg, Luke	0	0	4.50	3	0	0	0	6	9	4	3	1	2	.333	L	L	5-11	190	5-27-81	2004	Keystone, Iowa
Garza, Rolando	0	0	0.00	1	0	0	0	2	0	0	0	1	2	.000	R	R	6-4	210	12-14-79	1997	Coachella, Calif.
Hendricks, Donovan	2	0	5.01	15	0	0	0	32	41	24	18	7	23	.310	L	L	6-0	175	3-9-86	2003	South Victoria, Australia
Jackson, Drew	1	0	1.76	6	0	0	0	15	13	5	3	5	11	.224	L	L	6-0	200	10-12-83	2004	Farmington, N.M.
Katz, Jeff	0	1	5.11	5	2	0	0	12	15	11	7	9	13	.288	R	R	6-4	217	4-18-86	2004	Quinnipiac, Conn.
Parr, James	3	2	4.24	10	10	0	0	40	39	19	19	12	40	.251	R	R	6-1	185	2-27-86	2004	Albuquerque, N.M.
Payano, Nelson	1	1	0.52	5	1	0	0	17	10	3	1	8	15	.172	L	L	5-11	150	11-13-82	2000	Santo Domingo, D.R.
Peck, Mike	1	0	8.22	11	0	0	0	23	30	23	21	11	22	.303	R	R	6-5	200	8-6-83	2004	Irvine, Calif.
Richards, Glen	1	1	0.33	17	0	0	1	28	22	6	1	9	29	.220	R	L	5-11	170	10-27-84	2001	Mulgrave, Australia
Rivas, Carlos	3	2	3.52	12	8	0	1	46	40	23	18	24	44	.235	L	L	6-3	160	1-3-85	2002	Barquisimeto, Venez.
Rosario, Eduardo	0	1	0.00	7	2	0	0	12	12	8	0	10	14	.266	L	L	6-1	160	6-7-84	2001	Valencia, Venez.
Schreiber, Zach	0	0	3.60	3	1	0	0	5	5	2	2	3	5	.263	R	R	6-2	200	6-24-82	2004	Cedar Rapids, Iowa
Valenzuela, Sergio	1	2	3.00	5	3	0	0	21	15	9	7	3	16	.187	R	R	6-0	170	9-15-84	2001	Hermosillo, Mexico
Venters, Jonny	1	6	5.74	11	8	0	0	42	53	31	27	12	54	.296	L	L	6-3	175	3-20-85	2004	Altamonte Springs, Fla.
Wiggins, Trae	0	3	6.37	9	4	0	0	30	33	25	21	18	28	.270	L	L	6-3	195	10-15-82	2004	Stockbridge, Ga.

BALTIMORE ORIOLES

BY ROCH KUBATKO

It wasn't cause for breaking out champagne and covering the lockers in plastic, but the Orioles had reason to feel good about their 2004 season. Though they finished with a losing record for the seventh consecutive year, they no longer were a fourth-place team.

The Orioles went 78-84, their best record since 1999, and moved up to third place in the American League East after winning 21 of their last 33 games. They also moved manager Lee Mazzilli to tears after he met with his players for the last time.

"This has been the best year of my life," Mazzilli said. "I loved every minute of it."

Well, maybe not every minute.

Mazzilli's first season as manager brought intense speculation about his job status after the Orioles sunk to the bottom of the division at the all-star break. But they went 41-35 in the second half and continued to play hard until the end.

If not for a 3-14 start in June and a 12-game losing streak in August, Baltimore might have climbed above .500 and challenged for the wild card.

"I'm proud of what this team has done, but I don't think anybody is satisfied," Mazzilli said. "We have a mission that we're set on doing, and we're on that track. We've made a lot of progress, and we're looking to build on that."

Though Mazzilli kept his job, Ray Miller replaced Mark Wiley as pitching coach on June 26. The Orioles were last in team ERA before the switch, but they ranked second under Miller.

"Ray's been a definite plus for us," Mazzilli said.

Pitching wasn't a prime concern in the winter before the 2004 season, when the Orioles were throwing money at shortstop Miguel Tejada, catcher Javy Lopez and first

RICH ABEL

Miguel Tejada   Val Majewski

PLAYERS of the YEAR

MAJOR LEAGUE: Miguel Tejada, ss

Tejada's Orioles debut lived up to—and maybe even exceeded—expectations. The former AL MVP led the majors with 150 RBIs, to go along with a .311 average and 34 home runs. And as usual, he played all 162 games, much like another great Baltimore shortstop used to.

MINOR LEAGUE: Val Majewski, of

It was a season of distinctions for Majewski. He got a chance to play in the Futures Game and the Double-A All-Star Game, and he was called up to the parent club in mid-August after putting together a .307-15-80 campaign at Bowie.

baseman Rafael Palmeiro. They re-signed Sidney Ponson for $22.5 million over three years and made him the No. 1 starter, but mostly by default. The other four members of the rotation didn't have a full season in the majors. Ponson didn't have a full season of success in 2004, going 3-12 in the first half and 8-3 in the second.

Rodrigo Lopez led the staff with 14 wins, but he began the season in the bullpen. Daniel Cabrera started out at Double-A Bowie before an unexpected promotion led to a 12-8 record.

"I don't care if you have five 20-game winners," Mazzilli said. "You never have enough pitching."

Tejada was a bargain at $72 million over six years, driving in a franchise-record 150 runs and being named team MVP. Palmeiro rose to 10th on baseball's all-time home run list with 551, but he didn't heat up until September.

Third baseman Melvin Mora batted .340, the highest average in team history, and Brian Roberts hit a franchise-record 50 doubles. But center fielder Luis Matos and second baseman/outfielder Jerry Hairston had season-ending surgery, and right fielder Jay Gibbons and DH David Segui missed significant time with injuries.

All six coaches were invited back for 2005, but the Orioles didn't renew the contracts of farm director Doc Rodgers and scouting director Tony DeMacio. They also lost the negotiating rights to pitcher Wade Townsend, their No. 1 draft pick, who returned to Rice.

None of the club's six affiliates made the playoffs, finishing a combined 59 games below .500. Outfielder Val Majewski was named the organization's minor league Player of the Year after batting .307-15-80 at Double-A Bowie. The Orioles purchased his contract on Aug. 18.

ORGANIZATION LEADERS

BATTING

*AVG	Jose Leon, Ottawa	322
R	Walter Young, Bowie	88
H	Mike Fontenot, Ottawa	146
TB	Walter Young, Bowie	261
2B	Ed Rogers, Bowie	33
3B	Nate Spears, Delmarva	11
HR	Walter Young, Bowie	33
RBI	Walter Young, Bowie	98
BB	Jack Cust, Ottawa	65
SO	Walter Young, Bowie	145
SB	Jarod Rine, Delmarva	31
*OBP	Jose Leon, Ottawa	.382
*SLG	Jose Leon, Ottawa	.583

PITCHING

W	Hayden Penn, Bowie/Frederick/Delmarva	13
L	Fredy Deza, Frederick/Delmarva	14
#ERA	Zach Dixon, Frederick/Delmarva	2.53
G	Ryan Keefer, Frederick	63
	Nick McCurdy, Frederick	63
CG	Three tied at	2
SV	Jacobo Sequea, Bowie	27
IP	John Maine, Ottawa/Bowie	148
BB	Brian Forystek, Ottawa/Bowie	73
SO	John Maine, Ottawa/Bowie	139

* Minimum 250 at-bats #Minimum 75 innings

ORGANIZATION STATISTICS

Manager: Lee Mazzilli.

2004 Record: 78-84, .481 (3rd, AL East).

BATTING	AVG	G	AB	R	H	2B	3B	HR	RBI	BB	SO	SB	CS	OBP	SLG	B	T	HT	WT	DOB	1st Yr	Resides
Bigbie, Larry	.280	139	478	76	134	23	1	15	68	45	113	8	3	.341	.427	L	L	6-4	205	11-4-77	1999	Hobart, Ind.
Bautista, Jose	.273	16	11	3	3	0	0	0	1	3	0	0	0	.333	.273	R	R	6-0	190	10-19-80	2001	Santo Domingo, D.R.
Cust, Jack	.000	1	1	0	0	0	0	0	0	0	1	0	0	.000	.000	L	R	6-1	200	1-16-79	1997	Flemington, N.J.
Garcia, Karim	.212	23	66	9	14	0	0	3	11	4	15	0	0	.247	.348	L	L	6-0	210	10-29-75	1993	Ciudad Obregon, Mexico
Gibbons, Jay	.246	97	346	36	85	14	1	10	47	29	64	1	1	.303	.379	L	L	6-0	193	3-2-77	1998	Lakewood, Calif.
Gil, Geronimo	.281	12	32	1	9	2	0	0	4	3	5	0	0	.343	.344	R	R	6-2	227	8-7-75	1995	Oaxaca, Mexico
Hairston, Jerry	.303	86	287	43	87	19	1	2	24	29	29	13	8	.378	.397	R	R	5-10	185	5-29-76	1997	Pikesville, Md.
Huckaby, Ken	.167	8	12	1	2	1	0	0	0	0	0	0	0	.167	.250	R	R	6-0	210	1-27-71	1991	Philadelphia, Pa.
Leon, Jose	.182	31	66	4	12	2	0	2	8	2	19	0	0	.203	.303	R	R	6-0	210	12-8-76	1994	Cayey, P.R.
Lopez, Javy	.316	150	579	83	183	33	3	23	86	47	97	0	0	.370	.503	R	R	6-3	225	11-5-70	1988	Ponce, P.R.
Lopez, Luis	.182	56	88	7	16	5	0	1	8	3	20	0	0	.211	.273	S	R	5-11	185	9-4-70	1988	Cidra, P.R.
Machado, Robert	.151	37	73	5	11	3	0	1	3	4	18	0	0	.195	.233	R	R	6-1	220	6-3-73	1991	Caracas, Venez.
Majewski, Val	.154	9	13	3	2	1	0	0	1	0	1	0	0	.154	.231	L	L	6-2	200	6-19-81	2002	Freehold, N.J.
Matos, Luis	.224	89	330	36	74	18	0	6	28	19	60	12	4	.275	.333	R	R	6-0	180	10-30-78	1996	Bayamon, P.R.
McDonald, Darnell	.156	17	32	3	5	1	0	0	1	2	6	1	0	.206	.188	R	R	5-11	210	11-17-78	1998	Glendale, Colo.
Mora, Melvin	.340	140	550	111	187	41	0	27	104	66	95	11	6	.419	.562	R	R	5-11	200	2-2-72	1992	Bel Air, Md.
Mottola, Chad	.143	6	14	2	2	1	0	1	3	2	3	0	0	.250	.429	R	R	6-3	220	10-15-71	1992	Casselberry, Fla.
Newhan, David	.311	95	373	66	116	15	7	8	54	27	72	11	1	.362	.453	L	R	5-10	180	9-7-73	1995	Yorba Linda, Calif.
Osik, Keith	.080	11	25	0	2	0	0	0	0	0	7	0	0	.080	.080	R	R	6-0	200	10-22-68	1990	Shoreham, N.Y.
Palmeiro, Rafael	.258	154	550	68	142	29	0	23	88	86	61	2	1	.359	.436	L	L	6-0	215	11-24-64	1985	Colleyville, Texas
Raines Tim	.255	48	94	14	24	6	0	0	5	4	16	7	3	.293	.319	S	R	5-10	190	8-31-79	1998	Heathrow, Fla.
Roberts, Brian	.273	159	641	107	175	50	2	4	53	71	95	29	12	.344	.376	S	R	5-9	175	10-9-77	1999	Chapel Hill, N.C.
Segui, David	.339	18	59	8	20	3	0	1	7	5	13	0	1	.400	.441	S	L	6-1	215	7-19-66	1988	Kansas City, Kan.
Surhoff, B.J.	.309	100	343	49	106	12	1	8	50	30	46	2	0	.365	.420	L	R	6-1	215	8-4-64	1985	Cockeysville, Md.
Tejada, Miguel	.311	162	653	107	203	40	2	34	150	48	73	4	1	.360	.534	R	R	5-9	210	5-25-76	1994	Santo Domingo, D.R.

PITCHING	W	L	ERA	G	GS	CG	SV	IP	H	R	ER	BB	SO	AVG	B	T	HT	WT	DOB	1st Yr	Resides
Ainsworth, Kurt	0	1	9.68	7	7	0	0	31	39	34	33	20	20	.320	R	R	6-3	192	9-9-78	1999	Baton Rouge, La.
Bauer, Rick	2	1	4.70	23	2	0	0	54	49	31	28	20	37	.238	R	R	6-6	218	1-10-77	1997	Erie, Pa.
Bautista, Denny	0	0	36.00	2	0	0	0	2	6	8	8	2	1	.545	R	R	6-5	170	10-23-82	2000	Santo Domingo, D.R.
Bedard, Erik	6	10	4.59	27	26	0	0	137	149	83	70	71	121	.270	L	L	6-1	190	3-6-79	1999	Navan, Ontario
Borkowski, Dave	3	4	5.14	17	8	0	0	56	65	37	32	15	45	.289	R	R	6-1	220	2-7-77	1995	Monroe, Mich.
Cabrera, Daniel	12	8	5.00	28	27	1	1	148	145	85	82	89	76	.259	R	R	6-7	230	5-21-81	1999	San Pedro de Macoris, D.R.
Chen, Bruce	2	1	3.02	8	7	1	0	48	39	19	16	16	32	.220	L	L	6-2	210	6-19-77	1994	Panama City, Panama
Cubillan, Darwin	0	0	6.30	7	0	0	0	10	13	7	7	7	8	.302	R	R	6-2	177	11-15-72	1994	Tampa, Fla.
DeJean, Mike	0	5	6.13	37	0	0	0	40	49	29	27	28	36	.308	R	R	6-4	217	9-28-70	1992	Castle Rock, Colo.
DuBose, Eric	0	1	5.06	1	1	0	0	5	4	3	3	6	2	.263	L	L	6-3	233	5-15-76	1997	Houston, Texas
Grimsley, Jason	2	4	4.21	41	0	0	0	36	37	25	17	20	21	.261	R	R	6-3	205	8-7-67	1985	Lafayette, La.
2-team (32 Kansas City)	5	7	3.86	73	0	0	0	63	61	36	27	35	39	.251							
Groom, Buddy	4	1	4.78	60	0	0	0	53	67	30	28	16	32	.309	L	L	6-2	205	7-10-65	1987	Ovilla, Texas
Julio, Jorge	2	5	4.57	65	0	0	22	69	59	35	35	39	70	.228	R	R	6-1	223	3-3-79	1996	Caracas, Venez.
Lopez, Rodrigo	14	9	3.59	37	23	1	0	171	164	71	68	54	121	.252	R	R	6-1	190	12-14-75	1994	Mexico City, Mexico
Maine, John	0	1	9.82	1	1	0	0	4	7	4	4	3	1	.438	R	R	6-4	190	5-8-81	2002	Hartwood, Va.
Parrish, John	6	3	3.46	56	1	0	1	78	68	39	30	55	71	.238	L	L	5-11	190	11-26-77	1996	Owings Mills, Md.
Ponson, Sidney	11	15	5.30	33	33	5	0	216	265	136	127	69	115	.305	R	R	6-1	265	11-2-76	1994	Baltimore, Md.
Rakers, Aaron	0	0	4.15	3	0	0	0	4	5	2	2	1	3	.278	R	R	6-3	205	1-22-77	1999	Trenton, Ill.
Riley, Matt	3	4	5.63	14	13	0	0	64	60	43	40	44	60	.244	L	L	6-1	207	8-2-79	1998	Corona, Calif.
Rodriguez, Eddy	1	0	4.78	29	0	0	0	43	36	23	23	30	37	.231	R	R	6-1	195	8-8-81	1999	San Pedro de Macoris, D.R.
Ryan, B.J.	4	6	2.28	76	0	3	0	87	64	24	22	35	122	.200	L	L	6-6	250	12-28-75	1998	Bossier City, La.
Williams, Todd	2	0	2.87	29	0	0	0	31	26	10	10	9	13	.232	R	R	6-3	210	2-13-71	1991	Land O'Lakes, Fla.

FIELDING

Catcher	PCT	G	PO	A	E	DP	PB
Gil	1.000	11	64	4	0	1	0
Huckaby	1.000	8	25	2	0	0	1
J. Lopez	.994	132	848	49	5	11	10
Machado	.994	35	157	14	1	6	2
Osik	1.000	11	43	3	0	1	2

First Base	PCT	G	PO	A	E	DP
Garcia	1.000	1	10	1	0	0
Gibbons	.992	14	111	13	1	11
Leon	1.000	16	83	10	0	9
J. Lopez	.957	6	22	0	1	1
Newhan	1.000	2	10	1	0	2
Palmeiro	.993	130	1090	95	8	114
Segui	1.000	2	17	0	0	1
Surhoff	1.000	10	46	4	0	6

Second Base	PCT	G	PO	A	E	DP
Hairston	.983	12	22	37	1	9
L. Lopez	1.000	6	3	9	0	2
Roberts	.988	150	235	426	8	92

Third Base	PCT	G	PO	A	E	DP
J. Bautista	.000	4	0	0	0	0
Hairston	1.000	1	0	1	0	0
Leon	.900	6	1	8	1	1
L. Lopez	.840	11	6	15	4	2
Mora	.948	137	122	258	21	21
Newhan	.872	17	11	23	5	2

Shortstop	PCT	G	PO	A	E	DP
L. Lopez	.944	14	7	10	1	3
Mora	.000	1	0	0	0	0
Tejada	.970	162	263	526	24	118

Outfield	PCT	G	PO	A	E	DP
J. Bautista	1.000	6	4	1	0	0
Bigbie	.993	134	289	3	2	0
Garcia	1.000	19	33	0	0	0
Gibbons	.984	66	116	6	2	1
Hairston	.991	52	105	3	1	1
Majewski	1.000	4	11	0	0	0
Matos	.996	89	220	3	1	1
McDonald	1.000	13	21	0	0	0
Mottola	1.000	5	7	0	0	0
Newhan	1.000	42	73	3	0	0
Raines	1.000	38	61	2	0	0
Surhoff	.986	70	133	3	2	2

Brian Roberts: Stole a career-high 29 bases

Melvin Mora: Finished second in AL batting race at .340

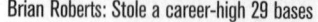

FARM SYSTEM

Director, Minor League Operations: Doc Rodgers.

Class	Farm Team	League	W	L	Pct.	Finish*	Manager	Affiliate Since
AAA	Ottawa (Ontario) Lynx	International	66	78	.458	t-11th (14)	Tim Leiper	2003
AA	Bowie (Md.) Baysox	Eastern	73	69	.514	5th (12)	Dave Trembley	1993
High A	Frederick (Md.) Keys	Carolina	52	87	.374	8th (8)	Tom Lawless	1989
Low A	Delmarva (Md.) Shorebirds	South Atlantic	69	69	.500	t-7th (16)	Bien Figueroa	1997
SS A	Aberdeen (Md.) IronBirds	New York-Penn	35	40	.467	8th (14)	Don Buford	2002
Rookie	Bluefield (W.Va.) Orioles	Appalachian	28	39	.418	8th (10)	Gary Kendall	1958

*Finish in overall standings (No. of teams in league)/playoff teams in **boldface**

OTTAWA LYNX
Class AAA

INTERNATIONAL LEAGUE

BATTING	AVG	G	AB	R	H	2B	3B	HR	RBI	BB	SO	SB	CS	OBP	SLG	B	T	HT	WT	DOB	1st Yr	Resides
Bellinger, Clay	.229	67	218	29	50	15	2	8	27	14	48	3	0	.281	.427	R	R	6-3	190	11-18-68	1989	Chandler, Ariz.
Cust, Jack	.235	102	344	55	81	15	1	17	55	65	127	4	0	.358	.433	L	R	6-1	200	1-16-79	1997	Flemington, N.J.
Done, Mike	1.000	1	1	0	1	1	0	0	0	0	0	0	0	01.000	2.000	S	R	5-11	190	7-27-79	2002	Aurora, Colo.
Fontenot, Mike	.279	136	524	73	146	30	10	8	49	48	111	14	7	.346	.420	L	R	5-8	160	6-9-80	2002	Slidell, La.
Garabito, Eddy	.298	124	450	52	134	27	5	6	37	40	48	19	12	.359	.420	S	R	5-8	186	12-2-76	1996	Manrreza, D.R.
Gil, Geronimo	.259	106	375	55	97	24	0	6	34	32	67	2	1	.327	.371	R	R	6-2	227	8-7-75	1995	Oaxaca, Mexico
Guzman, Edwards	.254	62	248	22	63	11	0	2	32	11	28	3	2	.286	.323	L	R	5-11	200	9-11-76	1996	Naranjito, P.R.
2-team (25 Durham)	.241	87	332	29	80	15	0	2	39	13	36	4	2	.270	.304							
Hammond, Joey	.236	90	271	27	64	7	1	1	30	22	42	3	2	.292	.320	R	R	6-1	189	10-27-77	1998	Frederick, Md.
Leon, Jose	.322	83	283	45	91	21	1	17	54	24	68	1	1	.382	.583	R	R	6-0	210	12-8-76	1994	Cayey, P.R.
Machado, Robert	.317	34	126	22	40	12	0	3	20	10	20	0	1	.368	.484	R	R	6-0	210	6-3-73	1991	Caracas, Venez.
Martinez, Octavio	.125	2	8	0	1	0	0	0	1	0	2	0	0	.125	.125	R	R	6-0	185	7-30-79	1999	Bakersfield, Calif.
McDonald, Darnell	.234	107	410	44	96	32	1	7	44	34	100	12	6	.294	.368	R	R	5-11	210	11-17-78	1998	Glendale, Colo.
McGee, Tom	.219	22	64	5	14	8	0	1	4	1	13	0	0	.242	.391	R	R	5-11	200	1-29-75	1997	Frederick, Md.
Mendez, Carlos	.256	80	305	29	78	17	1	4	37	10	30	2	0	.285	.357	R	R	6-0	228	6-18-74	1992	Caracas, Venez.
Mottola, Chad	.265	117	457	60	121	22	0	22	69	22	90	8	0	.308	.457	R	R	6-3	220	10-15-71	1992	Casselberry, Fla.
Raines Jr, Tim	.262	72	267	32	70	13	1	1	23	18	69	24	7	.314	.330	S	R	5-10	190	8-31-79	1998	Heathrow, Fla.
Rios, Armando	.341	13	44	9	15	4	0	1	6	10	11	2	0	.463	.500	L	L	5-9	190	9-13-71	1994	Pembroke Pines, Fla.
Swann, Pedro	.271	126	458	59	124	32	1	15	54	40	84	5	3	.339	.443	L	R	6-0	200	10-27-70	1991	Townsend, Del.
Walker, Matt	.375	3	8	1	3	0	0	0	1	0	3	1	0	.375	.375	R	R	6-2	200	12-3-77	2000	Gibsonia, Pa.

PITCHING	W	L	ERA	G	GS	CG	SV	IP	H	R	ER	BB	SO	AVG	B	T	HT	WT	DOB	1st Yr	Resides
Ainsworth, Kurt	0	0	9.00	1	1	0	0	4	7	4	4	1	6	.412	R	R	6-3	192	9-9-78	1999	Baton Rouge, La.
Bauer, Rick	3	5	4.00	11	11	0	0	63	69	28	28	19	42	.285	R	R	6-6	218	1-10-77	1997	Erie, Pa.
Bedard, Erik	0	1	7.20	2	2	0	0	5	8	4	4	3	3	.348	L	L	6-1	190	3-6-79	1999	Navan, Ontario

PITCHING	W	L	ERA	G	GS	CG	SV	IP	H	R	ER	BB	SO	AVG	B	T	HT	WT	DOB	1st Yr	Resides
Bergman, Sean	7	10	4.94	20	18	2	0	102	119	68	56	33	89	.285	R	R	6-4	220	4-11-70	1991	Joliet, Ill.
Borkowski, Dave	6	9	4.85	16	16	0	0	85	99	53	46	26	56	.294	R	R	6-1	220	2-7-77	1995	Monroe, Mich.
Byrdak, Tim	2	1	4.19	33	1	0	2	34	46	20	16	12	43	.322	L	L	5-11	180	10-31-73	1994	Oak Forest, Ill.
Chen, Bruce	4	3	3.22	22	17	1	0	95	85	41	34	30	108	.235	L	L	6-2	210	6-19-77	1994	Panama City, Panama
2-team (3 Syracuse)	4	4	3.76	25	20	1	0	105	102	53	44	35	116	.249							
Childs, Ryan	0	1	12.00	1	1	0	0	3	5	4	4	2	0	.417	L	R	6-3	210	6-16-81	2003	Gaithersburg, Md.
Cubillan, Darwin	3	4	4.59	51	0	0	24	51	52	26	26	17	53	.269	R	R	6-2	177	11-15-72	1994	Tampa, Fla.
DeWitt, Matt	2	4	7.71	25	5	0	1	54	70	47	46	20	25	.320	R	R	6-3	220	9-4-77	1995	Las Vegas, Nev.
DiFelice, Mark	9	4	3.54	36	4	0	1	89	74	42	35	27	70	.226	R	R	6-1	180	8-23-76	1998	Havertown, Pa.
Fiore, Tony	3	1	1.80	25	0	0	3	45	36	11	9	10	32	.222	R	R	6-4	220	10-12-71	1992	Tampa, Fla.
Forsythe, Brian	3	5	5.58	12	11	0	0	61	71	46	38	32	43	.302	L	L	6-1	182	10-30-78	2000	Palos Park, Ill.
Gannon, Joe	0	4	10.24	4	4	0	0	19	20	23	22	26	10	.282	L	R	6-1	190	3-15-75	2002	Buffalo, N.Y.
Hammond, Joey	0	0	9.00	2	2	0	0	2	3	2	2	0	0	.375	R	R	6-1	189	10-27-77	1998	Frederick, Md.
House, Craig	0	0	7.43	11	0	0	0	13	13	11	11	13	12	.241	R	R	6-2	220	7-8-77	1999	Nashville, Tenn.
Lorraine, Andrew	5	4	4.50	28	19	0	0	120	137	65	60	36	74	.287	L	L	6-3	200	8-11-72	1993	Scottsdale, Ariz.
Maine, John	5	7	3.91	22	22	0	0	120	123	59	52	52	105	.266	R	R	6-4	190	5-8-81	2002	Hartwood, Va.
Martinez, Javier	0	0	10.80	1	1	0	0	2	4	4	2	4	0	.500	R	R	6-2	230	2-5-77	1994	Toa Alta, P.R.
Ormond, Rodney	3	2	5.55	28	0	0	1	47	50	29	29	29	38	.275	R	R	6-4	210	6-17-77	1999	Princeton, N.C.
Paradis, Mike	0	0	15.32	9	0	0	0	12	22	22	21	18	8	.386	R	R	6-3	198	5-3-78	1999	Clemson, S.C.
Perez, Carlos	0	0	36.00	1	0	0	0	1	4	4	4	1	1	.667	L	L	6-1	185	5-20-82	2000	San Pedro de Macoris, D.R.
Rakers, Aaron	4	5	2.75	54	1	0	1	79	65	27	24	25	80	.229	R	R	6-3	205	1-22-77	1998	Trenton, Ill.
Riley, Matt	1	2	1.71	10	10	0	0	42	26	9	8	23	51	.181	L	L	6-1	207	8-2-79	1998	Corona, Calif.
Rodriguez, Eddy	1	0	5.12	28	0	0	3	32	34	19	18	18	31	.266	R	R	6-1	195	8-8-81	1999	San Pedro de Macoris, D.R.
Rodriguez, Joe	2	0	7.56	20	0	0	0	25	30	25	21	16	17	.288	L	L	6-1	200	12-18-74	1997	Cayey, P.R.
Spencer, Sean	0	1	5.79	9	0	0	0	19	21	12	12	11	14	.288	L	L	5-11	180	5-29-75	1997	Port Orchard, Wash.
Spradlin, Jerry	2	4	6.89	11	0	0	1	16	16	14	12	13	12	.276	S	R	6-7	240	6-14-67	1988	Anaheim, Calif.
Williams, Todd	1	1	3.05	14	0	0	2	21	19	7	7	3	11	.250	R	R	6-3	210	2-13-71	1991	Land O`Lakes, Fla.

FIELDING

Catcher	PCT	G	PO	A	E	DP	PB
Gil	.991	95	715	46	7	8	9
Guzman	1.000	2	8	0	0	0	0
Machado	.991	27	186	32	2	3	8
Martinez	1.000	2	14	1	0	0	1
McGee	.992	22	117	11	1	1	1
Mendez	1.000	5	22	0	0	0	0

First Base	PCT	G	PO	A	E	DP
Bellinger	.987	23	142	12	2	19
Gil	.957	4	21	1	1	1
Guzman	.986	26	192	15	3	21
Hammond	.995	28	165	22	1	24
Leon	1.000	1	2	0	0	0
Mendez	.996	62	488	42	2	48
Mottola	.977	18	123	6	3	12

Second Base	PCT	G	PO	A	E	DP
Bellinger	1.000	1	0	1	0	0
Done	1.000	1	1	1	0	0
Fontenot	.964	135	252	330	22	85
Garabito	1.000	4	10	10	0	6
Hammond	.947	6	6	12	1	6

Third Base	PCT	G	PO	A	E	DP
Bellinger	.930	17	9	31	3	2
Guzman	.976	29	28	54	2	6
Hammond	.945	30	23	63	5	5
Leon	.921	79	54	157	18	17

Shortstop	PCT	G	PO	A	E	DP
Bellinger	.975	18	33	44	2	16
Garabito	.957	117	174	295	21	67

Hammond	.980	13	19	30	1	6

Outfield	PCT	G	PO	A	E	DP
Bellinger	.750	3	3	0	1	0
Cust	.966	34	55	1	2	0
Garabito	1.000	1	1	0	0	0
Hammond	1.000	9	22	0	0	0
McDonald	.973	104	246	4	7	1
Mottola	.980	91	188	9	4	1
Raines	.982	70	160	3	3	1
Rios	1.000	13	21	0	0	0
Swann	.966	115	192	7	7	0
Walker	1.000	3	7	0	0	0

BOWIE BAYSOX — Class AA

EASTERN LEAGUE

BATTING	AVG	G	AB	R	H	2B	3B	HR	RBI	BB	SO	SB	CS	OBP	SLG	B	T	HT	WT	DOB	1st Yr	Resides
Burkhart, Lance	.230	47	148	23	34	6	0	11	31	18	39	0	0	.327	.493	R	R	5-9	220	12-16-74	1997	Florissant, Mo.
Calzado, Napoleon	.267	4	15	2	4	1	0	0	0	1	2	0	0	.313	.333	R	R	6-3	181	2-9-77	1997	Santo Domingo, D.R.
Cates, Gary	.255	111	400	52	102	18	1	4	40	21	51	12	6	.295	.335	R	R	5-7	163	7-3-81	1999	Brandon, Fla.
Clendenin, Morgan	.333	4	6	0	2	0	0	0	1	1	1	0	0	.429	.333	L	R	6-0	201	10-2-81	2003	Ripley, W.Va.
Cliffords, Woody	.216	32	97	7	21	1	0	1	7	13	20	2	0	.306	.258	L	R	6-2	193	12-2-80	2001	West Hills, Calif.
Done, Mike	.000	1	4	0	0	0	0	0	1	0	1	0	0	.000	.000	S	R	5-11	190	7-27-79	2002	Aurora, Colo.
Fahey, Brandon	.236	63	208	20	49	7	1	1	15	17	27	3	1	.293	.293	L	R	6-2	183	1-18-81	2002	Dallas, Texas
Florence, Branden	.286	11	35	3	10	1	0	1	4	1	3	0	0	.342	.400	R	R	6-0	200	4-3-78	2001	Boise, Idaho
Gibbons, Jay	.067	5	15	3	1	0	0	0	1	2	2	0	0	.167	.067	L	L	6-0	193	3-2-77	1998	Lakewood, Calif.
Gonzalez, Patrick	.000	1	0	0	0	0	0	0	0	0	0	0	0	.000	.000	R	R	5-10	170	11-21-79	2002	Ontario, Calif.
Guerrero, Francisco	.125	3	8	0	1	0	0	0	0	0	2	0	0	.125	.125	R	R	6-0	160	5-5-83	2001	San Pedro de Macoris, D.R.
Hairston, Jerry	.154	5	13	4	2	1	0	0	2	3	0	2	0	.313	.231	R	R	5-10	185	5-29-76	1997	Pikesville, Md.
Hammond, Joey	.214	5	14	2	3	1	0	0	0	6	3	1	0	.450	.286	R	R	6-1	189	10-27-77	1998	Frederick, Md.
Huggins, Michael	.237	76	249	22	59	16	0	4	30	33	53	2	4	.334	.349	L	R	6-3	212	8-29-80	2002	San Antonio, Texas
Kingsale, Eugene	.288	43	156	35	45	8	3	3	13	22	14	6	3	.381	.436	S	R	6-0	190	8-20-76	1994	Oranjestad, Aruba
Lofton, James	.267	29	101	13	27	4	0	2	13	7	12	0	1	.322	.366	S	R	5-10	210	3-6-74	1993	Los Angeles, Calif.
Majewski, Val	.307	112	433	71	133	24	5	15	80	33	68	14	4	.359	.490	L	L	6-2	200	6-19-81	2002	Freehold, N.J.
Martinez, Octavio	.254	21	59	8	15	4	0	0	2	1	7	0	0	.302	.322	R	R	6-0	185	7-30-79	1999	Bakersfield, Calif.
Morban, Jose	.209	67	244	35	51	9	2	9	23	21	74	9	3	.279	.373	B	R	6-1	170	12-2-79	1997	Santiago, D.R.
Mota, Tony	.268	83	291	39	78	18	3	2	37	25	54	6	2	.324	.371	R	R	6-1	170	10-31-77	1996	Miami, Fla.
Reed, Keith	.295	121	464	62	137	32	0	16	65	31	101	3	6	.345	.468	R	R	6-4	205	10-8-78	1999	Yarmouth Port, Mass.
Rogers, Ed	.284	124	482	71	137	33	1	4	37	37	78	20	7	.340	.382	R	R	6-1	183	8-29-78	1998	San Pedro de Macoris, D.R.
Rogers, Omar	.056	7	18	1	1	0	0	0	2	3	4	0	1	.190	.056	R	R	6-0	182	10-12-79	1999	San Pedro de Macoris, D.R.
Segui, David	.364	3	11	2	4	1	0	0	1	0	3	0	0	.417	.455	S	L	6-1	216	7-19-66	1988	Kansas City, Kan.
Walker, Matt	.302	13	43	4	13	3	0	1	7	1	14	1	0	.333	.442	R	R	6-2	210	12-3-77	2000	Gibsonia, Pa.
Whiteside, Eli	.253	90	297	41	75	18	0	18	60	25	65	2	2	.310	.495	R	R	6-2	213	10-22-79	2001	New Albany, Miss.
Wilken, Kris	.255	120	388	52	99	18	0	3	35	45	80	0	2	.330	.325	S	R	5-11	195	4-11-79	2000	Albuquerque, N.M.
Young, Walter	.272	133	486	88	132	28	1	33	98	47	145	2	3	.341	.537	L	R	6-5	298	2-18-80	1999	Purvis, Miss.

PITCHING	W	L	ERA	G	GS	CG	SV	IP	H	R	ER	BB	SO	AVG	B	T	HT	WT	DOB	1st Yr	Resides
Averette, Robert	5	1	3.02	10	9	0	0	51	54	20	17	14	27	.278	R	R	6-2	190	9-30-77	1997	Sylacauga, Ala.
Bauer, Rick	0	0	0.00	1	1	0	0	3	2	0	0	0	1	.200	R	R	6-6	218	1-10-77	1997	Erie, Pa.
Bautista, Denny	3	5	4.74	14	13	0	0	63	58	37	33	33	72	.243	R	R	6-5	170	10-23-82	2000	Santo Domingo, D.R.

PITCHING	W	L	ERA	G	GS	CG	SV	IP	H	R	ER	BB	SO	AVG	B	T	HT	WT	DOB	1st Yr	Resides
Bruback, Matt	5	5	4.32	14	13	0	0	75	80	41	36	36	83	.271	R	R	6-7	210	1-12-79	1998	Sarasota, Fla.
Cabrera, Daniel	0	1	2.63	5	5	0	0	27	11	10	8	12	35	.118	R	R	6-7	230	5-21-81	1999	San Pedro de Macoris, D.R.
Crouthers, Dave	9	9	5.03	27	27	0	0	140	134	81	78	68	138	.252	R	R	6-3	202	12-18-79	2001	Edwardsville, Ill.
Finch, Brian	2	6	8.69	11	10	0	0	48	73	46	46	16	32	.354	R	R	6-4	195	9-27-81	2003	Brazoria, Texas
Forystek, Brian	5	5	5.74	15	15	0	0	85	94	57	54	41	75	.284	L	L	6-1	182	10-30-78	2000	Palos Park, Ill.
Gannon, Joe	0	1	15.00	1	1	0	0	3	5	6	5	3	2	.385	L	R	6-1	190	3-15-75	2002	Buffalo, N.Y.
House, Craig	0	1	2.67	18	0	0	1	27	21	10	8	10	25	.214	R	R	6-2	220	7-8-77	1999	Nashville, Tenn.
Hundley, Jeff	1	3	2.90	35	4	0	0	62	55	23	20	17	52	.235	L	L	6-2	200	2-19-77	1998	Warren, Ohio
Jacquez, Tom	4	3	5.90	21	0	0	0	29	38	24	19	16	19	.319	L	L	6-2	190	12-29-75	1997	Stockton, Calif.
Maine, John	4	0	2.25	5	5	0	0	28	16	8	7	7	34	.160	R	R	6-4	190	5-8-81	2002	Hartwood, Va.
Martinez, Javier	2	0	6.75	11	0	0	0	13	12	11	10	18	18	.235	R	R	6-2	230	2-5-77	1994	Toa Alta, P.R.
Mitchell, Andy	3	2	2.95	54	0	0	0	98	77	35	32	35	78	.216	R	R	6-3	206	9-10-78	2001	Conyers, Ga.
Morris, Cory	3	6	5.98	12	12	0	0	59	60	39	39	39	59	.274	R	R	6-2	189	6-2-79	2001	Beckville, Texas
Ormond, Rodney	2	0	3.32	32	0	0	1	41	43	20	15	16	44	.276	R	R	6-4	210	6-17-77	1999	Princeton, N.C.
Paradis, Mike	0	0	18.00	2	0	0	0	5	5	4	4	5	1	.500	R	R	6-3	198	5-3-78	1999	Clemson, S.C.
Penn, Hayden	3	0	4.87	4	4	0	0	20	22	12	11	9	20	.282	R	R	6-3	185	10-13-84	2003	Santee, Calif.
Piersoll, Chris	2	8	3.99	16	10	0	0	56	64	28	25	20	39	.282	R	R	6-4	190	9-25-77	1997	Carlsbad, Calif.
Quevedo, Ruben	0	0	0.00	1	0	0	0	2	1	0	0	1	2	.167	R	R	6-1	255	1-5-79	1996	Valencia, Venez.
Rice, Scott	6	5	3.66	41	10	0	1	96	94	48	39	40	61	.259	L	L	6-6	217	9-21-81	1999	Simi Valley, Calif.
Rleal, Sendy	4	0	2.66	39	0	0	3	47	41	16	14	12	60	.232	R	R	6-1	165	6-21-80	2000	San Pedro de Macoris, D.R.
Rodriguez, Joe	0	2	5.14	12	2	0	0	21	31	19	12	4	19	.330	L	L	6-1	200	12-18-74	1997	Cayey, P.R.
Sequea, Jacobo	3	5	3.62	59	0	0	27	65	51	25	19	25	53	.213	R	R	6-1	194	8-31-81	1998	Anaco, Venez.
Spencer, Sean	2	0	2.63	9	0	0	1	14	12	4	4	1	16	.235	L	L	5-11	180	5-29-75	1997	Port Orchard, Wash.
Spradlin, Jerry	3	1	2.60	14	0	0	0	17	10	6	5	10	25	.156	S	R	6-7	240	6-14-67	1988	Anaheim, Calif.
Wilken, Kris	0	0	9.00	1	0	0	0	1	2	1	1	1	0	.500	S	R	5-11	195	4-11-79	2000	Albuquerque, N.M.
Wilson, Jeff	2	0	3.75	10	1	0	0	24	25	11	10	10	18	.242	L	L	6-2	199	5-30-76	1997	Greensboro, N.C.

FIELDING

Catcher	PCT	G	PO	A	E	DP	PB
Burkhart	.991	43	320	29	3	3	4
Clendenin	1.000	4	12	1	0	0	1
Martinez	.979	19	130	11	3	1	6
Whiteside	.986	86	660	48	10	3	14

First Base	PCT	G	PO	A	E	DP
Hammond	1.000	2	13	0	0	1
Huggins	.988	54	459	43	6	44
Wilken	.994	24	162	16	1	14
Young	.983	66	480	42	9	44

Second Base	PCT	G	PO	A	E	DP
Cates	.970	75	111	180	9	36
Done	1.000	1	1	3	0	0
Gonzalez	1.000	1	1	1	0	1

	PCT	G	PO	A	E	DP
Guerrero	1.000	2	4	3	0	0
Hairston	.929	5	5	8	1	3
Lofton	.963	20	23	56	3	4
Morban	1.000	1	4	6	0	2
Rogers	.980	51	67	127	4	24

Third Base	PCT	G	PO	A	E	DP
Hammond	1.000	2	4	1	0	0
Huggins	1.000	1	0	3	0	0
Rogers	.946	66	54	105	9	8
Rogers	.571	3	1	3	3	0
Wilken	.938	81	48	104	10	10

Shortstop	PCT	G	PO	A	E	DP
Fahey	.976	63	93	189	7	39
Hammond	1.000	1	3	2	0	1

	PCT	G	PO	A	E	DP
Morban	.965	65	108	143	9	31
Rogers	1.000	15	25	39	0	13

Outfield	PCT	G	PO	A	E	DP
Calzado	.750	5	3	0	1	0
Cates	1.000	34	56	2	0	0
Cliffords	.978	32	44	1	1	0
Florence	1.000	8	5	0	0	0
Gibbons	1.000	4	4	0	0	0
Kingsale	.989	42	86	1	1	0
Lofton	.889	4	7	1	1	0
Majewski	.978	118	211	7	5	2
Mota	.984	71	119	1	2	0
Reed	.961	122	211	10	9	4
Walker	1.000	12	20	1	0	0
Wilken	1.000	8	10	0	0	0

FREDERICK KEYS

CAROLINA LEAGUE

BATTING	AVG	G	AB	R	H	2B	3B	HR	RBI	BB	SO	SB	CS	OBP	SLG	B	T	HT	WT	DOB	1st Yr	Resides
Alvarez, Gera	.251	112	383	56	96	14	0	12	37	34	64	5	2	.324	.381	R	R	5-10	182	10-31-79	2002	Vista, Calif.
Arko, Tommy	.152	11	33	3	5	1	0	2	3	6	16	0	1	.300	.364	R	R	6-1	197	8-28-82	2000	Abilene, Texas
Bastida-Martinez, Evel	.098	15	51	4	5	0	1	2	4	7	0	0	0	.179	.176	L	R	6-0	190	2-28-79	2002	Hialeah, Fla.
Bigbie, Larry	.400	1	5	2	2	0	0	2	2	0	1	0	0	.400	1.600	L	L	6-4	205	11-4-77	1999	Hobart, Ind.
Bock, Brian	.196	18	51	4	10	1	0	1	1	5	4	0	0	.293	.275	R	R	6-1	210	8-24-81	2003	Bakersfield, Calif.
Carter, Chris	.271	98	343	39	93	16	1	11	45	41	115	6	4	.351	.420	R	R	6-1	195	2-13-79	2002	Conway, S.C.
Cliffords, Woody	.293	87	314	52	92	20	0	5	39	37	53	4	4	.373	.404	L	R	6-2	193	12-2-80	2001	West Hills, Calif.
Davies, Gregg	.200	12	25	3	5	0	0	0	3	2	8	0	0	.241	.200	L	L	6-1	190	1-8-80	2002	Olney, Md.
Diaz, Rafael	.381	6	21	2	8	1	0	0	2	0	3	1	0	.381	.429	R	R	6-0	185	6-13-81	2000	La Romana, D.R.
Done, Mike	.215	76	251	27	54	7	0	4	26	37	71	1	0	.324	.291	S	R	5-11	190	7-27-79	2002	Aurora, Colo.
Duncan, Jacob	.344	21	64	11	22	4	0	3	14	1	17	0	2	.354	.547	L	L	5-11	190	11-20-81	2003	Marshall, Texas
Fahey, Brandon	.271	62	181	20	49	7	0	3	19	22	20	3	3	.354	.359	L	R	6-2	183	1-18-81	2002	Dallas, Texas
Florence, Branden	.317	63	230	33	73	17	0	12	49	9	12	0	1	.347	.548	R	R	6-0	200	4-3-78	2001	Boise, Idaho
Gibbons, Jay	.182	3	11	2	2	1	0	0	1	2	2	0	0	.308	.545	L	L	6-0	193	3-2-77	1998	Lakewood, Calif.
Gredvig, Doug	.274	118	427	38	117	23	1	7	53	43	102	0	4	.337	.382	R	R	6-3	231	8-25-79	2000	Sacramento, Calif.
Harris, Cory	.224	34	116	13	26	10	1	2	12	14	16	6	3	.316	.379	R	R	5-10	180	12-7-79	1999	Davenport, Iowa
Houston, Matt	.235	30	85	9	20	2	1	1	9	6	20	0	0	.313	.318	R	R	5-11	195	2-1-82	2003	Oklahoma City, Okla.
Hubele, Ryan	.253	93	296	31	75	14	0	6	23	29	72	2	1	.321	.361	R	R	5-11	190	9-9-80	2002	Paradise Valley, Ariz.
Johnson, Tripper	.269	129	465	62	125	19	2	21	74	51	93	14	5	.343	.454	R	R	6-1	200	4-28-82	2000	Bellevue, Wash.
Keylor, Cory	.254	122	433	64	110	21	0	17	72	50	120	11	9	.332	.420	L	R	6-3	194	8-25-79	2001	Westerville, Ohio
Littleton, B.J.	.294	102	378	56	111	18	6	2	25	31	71	22	9	.357	.389	S	L	5-10	166	10-3-79	2000	Arlington, Texas
Martinez, Octavio	.250	8	32	4	8	0	0	0	2	1	4	1	0	.294	.250	R	R	6-0	185	7-30-79	1999	Bakersfield, Calif.
Morban, Jose	.235	56	200	34	47	9	0	3	13	19	65	17	5	.303	.325	B	R	6-1	170	12-2-79	1997	Santiago, D.R.
Morel, Elvis	.233	11	43	5	10	1	0	0	2	8	1	1	0	.267	.256	R	R	6-0	155	2-25-81	2001	Santo Domingo, D.R.
Mota, Tony	.214	3	14	3	3	2	0	0	0	3	1	0	0	.214	.357	S	R	6-1	170	10-31-77	1996	Miami, Fla.
Robinson, Levi	.183	26	71	6	13	3	0	1	6	4	14	1	0	.247	.268	R	R	6-0	180	3-28-80	2002	Anchorage, Alaska
Segui, David	.100	3	10	1	1	0	0	1	2	1	2	0	0	.167	.400	S	L	6-1	216	7-19-66	1988	Kansas City, Kan.
Walker, Matt	.224	15	58	6	13	6	0	0	6	4	17	0	0	.274	.328	R	R	6-2	200	12-3-77	2000	Gibsonia, Pa.
Wilken, Kris	.200	1	5	0	1	0	0	0	1	3	1	5	0	1	.250	.400	S	R	5-11	195	4-11-79	2000	Albuquerque, N.M.

PITCHING	W	L	ERA	G	GS	CG	SV	IP	H	R	ER	BB	SO	AVG	B	T	HT	WT	DOB	1st Yr	Resides
Alvarez, Gera	0	0	6.00	3	1	0	0	3	6	2	2	0	2	.429	R	R	5-10	182	10-31-79	2002	Vista, Calif.
Benitez, Fabricio	0	0	4.35	7	0	0	0	10	12	5	5	5	8	.286	R	R	6-3	170	5-10-78	1998	Santo Domingo, D.R.
Birkins, Kurt	5	2	4.50	27	6	0	2	68	70	36	34	22	55	.267	L	L	6-2	188	8-11-80	2001	Canoga Park, Calif.

PITCHING

	W	L	ERA	G	GS	CG	SV	IP	H	R	ER	BB	SO	AVG	B	T	HT	WT	DOB	1st Yr	Resides
Caughey, Trevor	0	1	6.17	4	2	0	0	12	15	8	8	3	5	.333	L	L	6-1	165	11-23-82	2002	San Luis Obispo, Calif.
Coppinger, Joe	0	5	5.31	13	6	0	0	41	44	25	24	19	29	.280	R	R	6-3	218	7-23-82	2001	El Paso, Texas
Deza, Fredy	1	3	5.61	5	5	0	0	26	33	22	16	2	20	.306	R	R	6-2	167	12-11-82	2000	La Romana, D.R.
Dixon, Zach	1	1	2.50	3	3	0	0	18	15	6	5	4	15	.234	L	L	6-2	195	11-29-80	2003	Houston, Texas
Done, Mike	0	0	0.00	2	0	0	0	2	1	0	0	0	1	.143	S	R	5-11	190	7-27-79	2002	Aurora, Colo.
Finch, Brian	1	4	7.96	9	9	0	0	37	59	35	33	15	22	.358	R	R	6-4	195	9-27-81	2003	Brazoria, Texas
Hannaman, Ryan	0	1	8.03	5	4	0	0	12	11	14	11	16	9	.239	L	L	6-3	190	8-28-81	2000	Mobile, Ala.
Henington, Justin	0	0	10.38	3	0	0	0	4	10	7	5	1	4	.435	R	R	6-4	210	2-24-82	2004	Leaksville, Miss.
Henry, Paul	2	5	7.42	35	9	0	0	87	115	82	72	38	88	.317	R	R	6-3	190	6-27-81	2002	Chattanooga, Tenn.
House, Craig	2	2	3.45	12	0	0	1	16	9	7	6	13	18	.167	R	R	6-2	220	7-8-77	1999	Nashville, Tenn.
Johnson, James	0	0	9.00	1	1	0	0	3	6	4	3	1	6	.429	R	R	6-5	213	6-27-83	2001	Endicott, N.Y.
Keefer, Ryan	4	4	3.09	63	0	0	4	87	89	32	30	26	73	.266	L	R	6-3	202	8-10-81	2000	Catawissa, Penn.
Levinski, Don	1	6	6.48	31	11	0	0	82	95	72	59	55	69	.284	R	R	6-4	200	10-20-82	2001	Weimar, Texas
Lewis, Rommie	1	7	5.61	47	4	0	0	87	92	67	54	41	52	.273	L	L	6-3	205	9-2-82	2001	Bellevue, Wash.
Loewen, Adam	0	2	6.75	2	2	1	0	8	7	6	6	9	3	.269	L	L	6-6	230	4-9-84	2003	Surrey, B.C.
Makowsky, Carl	0	2	10.32	8	0	0	0	11	20	13	13	12	10	.400	R	R	6-1	200	12-13-79	2002	Conroe, Texas
McCurdy, Nick	6	3	3.77	63	0	0	3	91	91	43	38	32	61	.266	R	R	6-3	185	1-24-80	2002	Thomasville, Ala.
Montani, Jerome	0	2	10.80	11	0	0	1	12	20	14	14	11	8	.364	R	R	5-11	174	11-22-80	2001	Liverpool, N.Y.
Morris, Cory	0	2	7.48	11	6	0	1	22	30	19	18	20	23	.330	R	R	6-2	189	6-2-79	2001	Beckville, Texas
Neal, Tony	2	6	4.33	50	0	0	18	62	48	30	30	25	64	.212	R	R	6-2	210	9-12-80	2003	Eight Mile, Ala.
Penn, Hayden	6	5	3.80	13	13	0	0	73	59	33	31	20	61	.222	R	R	6-3	185	10-13-84	2003	Santee, Calif.
Piersoll, Chris	2	4	4.56	19	5	0	1	51	51	27	26	21	48	.263	R	R	6-4	190	9-25-77	1997	Carlsbad, Calif.
Potter, Josh	0	0	0.00	1	0	0	0	2	1	0	0	1	0	.250	R	R	6-4	170	4-8-83	2002	Philipsburg, Pa.
Ray, Chris	6	3	3.80	14	14	1	0	73	82	31	31	20	74	.287	R	R	6-3	200	1-12-82	2003	Tampa, Fla.
Stahl, Richard	7	8	4.96	19	19	0	0	82	80	52	45	50	56	.259	R	L	6-7	222	4-11-81	2000	Covington, Ga.
Tiller, Jim	2	4	4.34	17	8	0	0	58	58	35	28	21	33	.264	R	R	6-5	194	4-13-83	2001	Elysian Fields, Texas
Wilson, Jeff	3	4	5.02	14	12	0	1	61	73	35	34	14	58	.298	L	L	6-2	199	5-30-76	1997	Greensboro, N.C.

FIELDING

Catcher	PCT	G	PO	A	E	DP	PB
Arko	.986	10	60	8	1	0	2
Bock	.980	18	125	20	3	1	1
Houston	.990	29	196	9	2	0	3
Hubele	.990	83	565	36	6	9	24
Martinez	.965	8	50	5	2	0	2

First Base	PCT	G	PO	A	E	DP
Davies	1.000	8	60	4	0	5
Diaz	1.000	2	12	0	0	2
Done	.992	26	216	18	2	16
Gredvig	.992	107	967	88	9	85
Hubele	1.000	1	8	0	0	1
Segui	1.000	1	12	1	0	1

Second Base	PCT	G	PO	A	E	DP
Alvarez	.979	78	124	254	8	54

	PCT	G	PO	A	E	DP	PB
Bastida-Martinez	.980	10	11	37	1	7	
Done	.971	37	50	85	4	12	
Morel	.953	10	15	26	2	4	
Robinson	.944	19	33	68	6	10	

Third Base	PCT	G	PO	A	E	DP
Alvarez	1.000	12	11	18	0	1
Bastida-Martinez	.800	3	0	4	1	1
Diaz	1.000	2	0	2	0	0
Johnson	.942	122	69	208	17	15
Robinson	1.000	2	2	2	0	0
Wilken	1.000	2	3	3	0	1

Shortstop	PCT	G	PO	A	E	DP
Alvarez	.953	28	42	80	6	15
Bastida-Martinez	1.000	2	4	5	0	1
Diaz	.800	1	3	1	1	0

	PCT	G	PO	A	E	DP
Fahey	.977	60	87	169	6	32
Morban	.940	55	74	160	15	31
Morel	1.000	2	1	6	0	0
Robinson	1.000	1	3	2	0	2

Outfield	PCT	G	PO	A	E	DP
Carter	.983	93	165	4	3	2
Cliffords	.983	77	112	7	2	3
Davies	1.000	2	2	0	0	0
Duncan	.917	17	22	0	2	0
Florence	1.000	5	5	0	0	0
Harris	.957	31	44	1	2	0
Keylor	.950	101	148	5	8	1
Littleton	.989	96	172	5	2	3
Walker	1.000	12	20	0	0	0
Wilken	1.000	2	5	0	0	0

DELMARVA SHOREBIRDS

Low Class A

SOUTH ATLANTIC LEAGUE

BATTING	AVG	G	AB	R	H	2B	3B	HR	RBI	BB	SO	SB	CS	OBP	SLG	B	T	HT	WT	DOB	1st Yr	Resides
Ascencion, Quincy	.209	38	129	15	27	5	1	1	14	7	22	3	1	.270	.287	R	R	6-0	215	11-1-82	2001	Willemstad, Curacao
Bass, Bryan	.239	122	389	53	93	23	3	9	54	54	125	16	3	.342	.383	S	R	6-1	180	4-12-82	2001	Seminole, Fla.
Bastida-Martinez, Evel	.194	23	67	6	13	3	0	1	7	9	14	3	1	.291	.284	L	R	6-0	190	2-28-79	2002	Hialeah, Fla.
Bock, Brian	.202	26	89	10	18	6	0	0	11	3	9	0	0	.229	.270	R	R	6-1	210	8-24-81	2003	Bakersfield, Calif.
Brown, Travis	.286	115	420	69	120	19	2	1	36	35	76	4	8	.353	.348	R	R	5-11	180	8-1-80	2003	Kankakee, Ill.
Carter, Chris	.306	10	36	8	11	2	0	0	4	7	10	1	0	.432	.361	R	R	6-1	195	2-13-79	2002	Conway, S.C.
Cates, Gary	.333	7	24	8	8	3	1	0	1	0	2	0	1	.360	.542	R	R	5-7	163	7-3-81	1999	Brandon, Fla.
Diaz, Rafael	.207	28	92	9	19	4	0	0	9	5	20	1	0	.250	.250	R	R	6-0	185	6-13-81	2000	La Romana, D.R.
Done, Mike	.212	9	33	3	7	0	0	1	2	2	13	1	0	.278	.303	S	R	5-11	190	7-27-79	2002	Aurora, Colo.
Fiorentino, Jeff	.296	49	179	40	53	12	2	10	36	20	50	2	2	.374	.570	L	R	6-1	185	4-14-83	2004	Hollywood, Fla.
Fransz, Jason	.317	28	101	19	32	6	0	6	25	11	25	1	0	.385	.554	S	R	6-3	210	2-5-81	2002	Corona, Calif.
Grimm, Eric	.221	55	163	20	36	10	1	0	20	25	46	1	2	.328	.294	S	R	6-0	185	4-30-81	2003	Parkersburg, W.Va.
Guerrero, Francisco	.167	5	6	1	1	0	0	0	1	0	0	0	0	.286	.167	R	R	6-0	160	5-5-83	2001	San Pedro de Macoris, D.R.
Gutierrez, Juan	.230	70	261	32	60	17	2	5	34	21	53	2	1	.298	.368	S	R	6-0	180	8-1-81	2003	Miami, Fla.
Harris, Cory	.311	55	206	37	64	18	0	9	41	19	30	6	3	.381	.529	R	R	5-10	180	12-7-79	1999	Davenport, Iowa
Houston, Matt	.265	51	151	19	40	6	2	13	18	33	21	1	1	.365	.450	R	R	5-11	195	2-1-82	2003	Oklahoma City, Okla.
Markakis, Nick	.299	96	355	57	106	23	3	11	64	42	66	12	3	.371	.470	L	L	6-1	175	11-17-83	2003	Woodstock, Ga.
McCurdy, Josh	.274	68	248	40	68	13	0	6	33	17	36	10	3	.328	.399	R	R	6-6	220	12-28-79	2003	Thornhill, Ontario
Morel, Elvis	.274	18	62	14	17	0	1	3	6	6	8	5	1	.333	.452	R	R	6-0	155	2-25-81	2001	Santo Domingo, D.R.
Rine, Jarod	.257	122	460	79	118	16	8	7	57	60	89	31	7	.345	.372	L	R	6-1	190	11-14-81	2003	Moundsville, W.Va.
Robinson, Levi	.040	7	25	1	1	0	0	0	1	1	8	2	0	.077	.040	R	R	6-0	180	3-28-80	2002	Anchorage, Alaska
Robinson-Pierce, Whitney	.083	20	48	5	4	0	0	0	3	11	22	1	0	.290	.083	R	R	6-3	210	3-4-82	2002	Fresno, Calif.
Russell, Mike	.239	75	230	31	55	15	0	12	47	25	84	2	1	.327	.461	R	R	6-0	193	8-14-81	2000	Bothell, Wash.
Scott, Lorenzo	.184	16	38	5	7	1	1	0	2	11	25	4	1	.392	.263	L	L	6-3	210	3-1-82	2003	St. Louis, Mo.
Spears, Nate	.275	97	371	50	102	12	11	5	38	47	63	7	6	.358	.407	L	R	5-11	180	5-3-85	2003	Port Charlotte, Fla.
Sultemeier, Eric	.128	12	39	3	5	1	0	0	4	1	9	0	0	.190	.154	R	R	6-2	180	6-28-82	2003	New Braunfels, Texas
Yount, Dustin	.257	99	339	40	87	26	2	8	59	59	80	1	1	.378	.416	L	R	6-1	200	10-27-82	2001	Scottsdale, Ariz.

PITCHING	W	L	ERA	G	GS	CG	SV	IP	H	R	ER	BB	SO	AVG	B	T	HT	WT	DOB	1st Yr	Resides
Acosta, Richal	1	2	4.94	17	0	0	3	27	29	16	15	7	26	.269	R	R	6-1	145	2-5-84	2001	San Rafael del Yuma, D.R.
Bass, Bryan	0	0	0.00	1	1	0	0	1	0	0	0	0	0	.000	S	R	6-1	180	4-12-82	2001	Seminole, Fla.
Britton, Chris	9	4	3.75	27	8	1	1	84	76	38	35	31	80	.244	R	R	6-4	228	12-16-82	2001	Plantation, Fla.

PITCHING

PITCHING	W	L	ERA	G	GS	CG	SV	IP	H	R	ER	BB	SO	AVG	B	T	HT	WT	DOB	1st Yr	Resides
Cahill, Casey	0	0	3.38	4	0	0	0	8	6	4	3	2	7	.194	R	R	6-3	180	3-15-82	2002	New Brunswick, N.J.
Caughey, Trevor	4	2	3.14	37	2	0	3	86	79	32	30	21	73	.248	L	L	6-1	165	11-23-82	2002	San Luis Obispo, Calif.
Chamberlin, Bryce	0	3	7.15	3	3	0	0	11	18	9	9	7	12	.367	R	R	6-2	195	12-22-82	2004	Okanogan, Wash.
Childs, Ryan	0	1	5.23	7	0	0	1	10	11	8	6	6	8	.250	L	R	6-3	210	6-16-81	2003	Gaithersburg, Md.
Cierlik, Jason	0	0	10.80	7	0	0	0	5	4	6	6	15	3	.211	L	L	6-0	205	2-21-81	2002	Brooklyn Park, Minn.
Coppinger, Joe	0	1	4.35	9	3	0	1	21	20	13	10	20	15	.263	R	R	6-3	218	7-23-82	2001	El Paso, Texas
Deza, Fredy	8	11	3.31	22	21	2	0	120	102	52	44	21	93	.226	R	R	6-2	167	12-11-82	2000	La Romana, D.R.
Dixon, Zach	9	4	2.54	24	21	0	0	121	97	52	34	65	105	.222	L	L	6-2	195	11-29-80	2003	Houston, Texas
Finch, Brian	2	2	1.44	5	5	0	0	25	23	11	4	2	14	.225	R	R	6-4	195	9-27-81	2003	Brazoria, Texas
Hart, Kevin	2	0	3.77	4	2	0	0	14	13	6	6	5	16	.245	R	R	6-4	220	12-29-82	2004	Dallas, Texas
Johnson, James	8	7	3.29	20	17	0	0	107	97	44	39	30	93	.243	R	R	6-5	213	6-27-83	2001	Endicott, N.Y.
Loewen, Adam	4	5	4.11	20	19	1	0	85	77	47	39	58	82	.249	L	L	6-6	230	4-9-84	2003	Surrey, B.C.
McCrory, Bob	0	1	7.59	8	0	0	0	11	13	16	9	15	11	.277	R	R	6-1	205	5-3-82	2004	Steens, Miss.
Montani, Jeff	1	4	4.79	35	0	0	1	62	68	37	33	22	53	.274	R	R	5-11	174	11-22-80	2001	Liverpool, N.Y.
Neal, Tony	1	0	2.57	7	0	0	2	14	8	5	4	10	20	.163	R	R	6-2	210	9-12-80	2003	Eight Mile, Ala.
Paradis, Mike	0	0	0.00	1	0	0	0	2	0	2	2	0	0	.000	R	R	6-3	198	5-3-78	1999	Clemson, S.C.
Patitucci, Mike	3	1	5.66	43	0	0	4	56	57	38	35	44	65	.259	L	L	6-0	195	11-6-80	2002	Uniontown, Pa.
Penn, Hayden	4	1	3.32	13	6	0	1	43	30	18	16	19	41	.195	R	R	6-3	185	10-13-84	2003	Santee, Calif.
Petrick, Russ	0	1	5.25	11	0	0	0	12	19	9	7	8	13	.345	L	L	6-6	185	2-12-83	2003	Monroe, Wash.
Potter, Josh	0	4	5.40	23	1	0	0	50	59	32	30	22	46	.292	R	R	6-4	170	4-8-83	2002	Philipsburg, Pa.
Ramirez, Luis	1	0	1.38	5	2	0	0	13	7	2	2	6	13	.159	R	R	6-4	180	6-9-82	2000	Barcelona, Venez.
Ray, Chris	2	3	3.42	10	9	0	0	50	43	21	19	17	46	.230	R	R	6-3	200	1-12-82	2003	Tampa, Fla.
Robinson, Dennis	3	0	0.50	3	3	0	0	18	11	2	1	4	7	.177	R	R	6-3	190	10-4-62	2004	Putnam Valley, N.Y.
Salas, Marino	2	4	2.15	40	0	0	13	50	51	15	12	17	46	.256	S	R	6-0	181	2-2-81	1998	Hato Mayor, D.R.
Spillers, Brandon	0	2	13.91	11	0	0	4	11	12	18	17	19	12	.293	R	R	6-3	210	3-12-82	2000	Roberta, Ga.
Tiller, Jim	5	6	5.72	16	13	1	1	74	89	59	47	14	47	.298	R	R	6-5	194	4-13-83	2001	Elysian Fields, Texas

FIELDING

Catcher

Catcher	PCT	G	PO	A	E	DP	PB
Bock	.967	24	178	24	7	1	2
Gutierrez	.996	30	223	18	1	2	10
Houston	.980	50	360	26	8	2	7
Robinson-Pierce	1.000	19	130	10	0	1	1
Russell	.980	27	183	11	4	1	6

First Base

First Base	PCT	G	PO	A	E	DP
Bastida-Martinez	1.000	1	5	0	0	0
Diaz	1.000	12	78	9	0	14
Gutierrez	.967	4	29	0	1	0
Russell	.983	33	218	12	4	20
Yount	.971	98	783	35	24	64

Second Base

Second Base	PCT	G	PO	A	E	DP
Bastida-Martinez	.988	18	44	41	1	11
Brown	1.000	11	16	27	0	3
Cates	.966	6	11	17	1	5
Done	1.000	5	6	13	0	2

	PCT	G	PO	A	E	DP
Grimm	.988	22	33	48	1	11
Guerrero	.875	4	3	11	2	2
Morel	1.000	1	1	5	0	1
Robinson	.955	4	5	16	1	4
Spears	.960	77	135	204	14	42

Third Base

Third Base	PCT	G	PO	A	E	DP
Bass	.901	109	56	181	26	16
Bastida-Martinez	1.000	1	0	2	0	0
Brown	.000	1	0	0	1	0
Diaz	.923	5	4	8	1	1
Diaz	.786	8	1	10	3	1
Grimm	.974	18	5	32	1	6
Russell	1.000	6	0	7	0	0

Shortstop

Shortstop	PCT	G	PO	A	E	DP
Bass	.941	3	5	11	1	1
Brown	.939	101	185	261	29	55
Diaz	1.000	3	3	6	0	1

	PCT	G	PO	A	E	DP
Grimm	.846	5	0	11	2	1
Morel	.905	15	16	41	6	8
Robinson	1.000	2	2	4	0	0
Spears	1.000	14	23	39	0	9

Outfield

Outfield	PCT	G	PO	A	E	DP
Ascencion	.974	33	37	1	1	0
Bass	1.000	2	6	1	0	0
Carter	1.000	7	14	0	0	0
Fiorentino	.949	48	88	6	5	0
Fransz	1.000	7	10	1	0	0
Harris	1.000	45	91	4	0	0
Markakis	.986	74	133	4	2	0
McCurdy	.985	60	123	5	2	1
Rine	.988	119	233	7	3	0
Scott	.962	13	24	1	1	0
Sultemeier	.947	12	18	0	1	0

ABERDEEN IRONBIRDS

Short-Season Class A

NEW YORK-PENN LEAGUE

BATTING	AVG	G	AB	R	H	2B	3B	HR	RBI	BB	SO	SB	CS	OBP	SLG	B	T	HT	WT	DOB	1st Yr	Resides
Ascencion, Quincy	.253	72	269	37	68	12	4	2	32	19	27	12	7	.307	.349	R	R	6-0	215	11-1-82	2001	Willemstad, Curacao
Bock, Brian	.393	12	28	3	11	5	0	0	7	0	4	0	0	.379	.571	R	R	6-1	210	8-24-81	2003	Bakersfield, Calif.
Boudon, Chad	.250	2	4	0	1	0	0	0	1	0	1	0	0	.400	.250	R	R	6-2	215	6-9-81	2003	Seattle, Wash.
Brannon, Evan	.180	29	50	3	9	2	0	0	2	4	9	0	0	.241	.220	R	R	5-11	165	3-26-82	2004	St. Petersburg, Fla.
Braun, Ron	.263	13	19	2	5	2	0	0	2	1	6	0	0	.300	.368	R	R	5-10	200	5-15-82	2004	Stony Brook, N.Y.
Burkhart, Lance	.667	2	6	2	4	1	1	1	2	1	0	0	0	.7141	.667	R	R	5-9	220	12-16-74	1997	Florissant, Mo.
Clendenin, Morgan	.191	46	131	11	25	6	1	5	22	1	35	1	1	.207	.366	L	R	6-0	201	10-2-81	2003	Ripley, W.Va.
Costello, Mike	.224	46	125	14	28	7	2	1	11	15	46	3	1	.317	.336	R	R	6-1	210	2-19-81	2003	Baltimore, Md.
Diaz, Rafael	.242	46	157	11	38	6	0	11	5	25	2	5	.265	.280	R	R	6-0	185	6-13-81	2000	La Romana, D.R.
Duncan, Jacob	.271	31	70	9	19	5	2	3	15	12	13	0	1	.369	.529	L	L	5-11	190	11-20-81	2003	Marshall, Texas
Fiorentino, Jeff	.348	14	46	9	16	7	1	2	12	9	4	3	1	.474	.674	L	R	6-0	185	4-14-83	2004	Hollywood, Fla.
Guerrero, Francisco	.000	1	1	0	0	0	0	0	0	0	0	0	0	.500	.000	R	R	6-0	160	5-5-83	2001	San Pedro de Macoris, D.R.
Hanan, Blake	.256	66	168	23	43	11	1	0	10	13	31	7	6	.321	.333	S	R	5-9	165	8-20-82	2004	Clifton Park, N.Y.
Kingsale, Eugene	.400	3	10	1	4	0	1	0	0	0	3	2	0	.400	.600	S	R	6-3	190	8-20-76	1994	Oranjestad, Aruba
Lofton, James	.308	4	13	1	4	0	0	0	2	3	2	0	0	.471	.308	S	R	5-10	210	3-6-74	1993	Los Angeles, Calif.
Marconi, Rob	.325	34	114	21	37	9	2	2	14	17	34	8	1	.406	.491	R	R	6-2	210	9-14-82	2004	La Grange, Ill.
Martinez, Octavio	.348	9	23	2	8	2	0	0	2	2	0	1	0	.423	.435	R	R	6-0	185	7-30-79	1999	Bakersfield, Calif.
Mendez, Carlos	.291	15	55	6	16	3	1	1	2	1	7	1	0	.304	.436	R	R	6-0	228	6-18-74	1992	Caracas, Venez.
Moffitt, Drew	.219	20	64	11	14	4	1	2	11	11	16	0	0	.325	.406	R	R	6-2	215	8-19-81	2004	McPherson, Kan.
Morel, Elvis	.229	11	48	7	11	1	0	0	6	3	5	6	1	.288	.250	R	R	6-0	155	2-25-81	2001	Santo Domingo, D.R.
Rivas, Arturo	.255	55	184	18	47	8	0	3	21	15	52	4	4	.310	.348	R	R	6-0	189	2-2-84	2001	San Francisco, Venez.
Robinson, Levi	.254	68	252	41	64	11	1	0	16	23	49	18	4	.338	.306	R	R	6-3	210	3-28-80	2002	Anchorage, Alaska
Robinson-Pierce, Whitney	.174	7	23	2	4	0	0	0	3	8	8	0	1	.240	.174	R	R	6-3	210	3-4-82	2003	Fresno, Calif.
Shafer, Corey	.195	44	149	11	29	4	0	2	15	5	33	0	0	.221	.262	L	L	6-2	215	12-17-82	2003	Choctaw, Okla.
Smith, C.J.	.242	61	207	28	50	14	3	3	19	24	50	3	0	.318	.382	R	R	6-3	210	2-22-82	2004	Tampa, Fla.
Smith, Chris	.368	9	19	5	7	0	1	2	3	4	5	0	0	.478	.789	L	L	5-11	217	12-10-79	2001	Wantagh, N.Y.
Sultemeier, Eric	.235	64	234	29	55	7	4	1	21	20	48	8	4	.301	.312	R	R	6-2	180	6-28-82	2003	New Braunfels, Texas
Wargo, Cody	.192	33	78	5	15	4	0	0	4	12	27	2	0	.297	.244	R	R	6-2	215	12-13-81	2004	Owins, Md.

GAMES BY POSITION: C—Bock 10, Braun 5, Burkhart 1, Clendenin 28, Fiorentino 1, Martinez 7, Mendez 4, Robinson-Pierce 7, Wargo 31. **1B**—Boudon 2, Costello 20, Diaz 2, Mendez 3, Smith 56. **2B**—Brannon 6, Lofton 2, Marconi 7, Morel 2, Robinson 64. **3B**—Costello 17, Diaz 39, Marconi 25. **SS**—Brannon 23, Hanan 65, Morel 9. **OF**—Ascencion 69, Duncan 4, Fiorentino 13, Kingsale 2, Morel 1, Rivas 52, Shafer 40, Sultemeier 60.

PITCHING	W	L	ERA	G	GS	CG	SV	IP	H	R	ER	BB	SO	AVG	B	T	HT	WT	DOB	1st Yr	Resides
Acosta, Richal	3	0	4.03	11	0	0	1	22	21	12	10	6	22	.241	R	R	6-1	145	2-5-84	2001	San Rafael del Yuma, D.R.
Ainsworth, Kurt	0	1	1.35	2	2	0	0	7	2	1	1	3	8	.095	R	R	6-3	192	9-9-78	1999	Baton Rouge, La.
Azze, Justin	0	1	5.82	20	0	0	1	34	38	22	22	13	29	.281	L	L	6-3	190	9-14-82	2003	Fountain Valley, Calif.
Baysinger, Trent	0	4	4.57	27	0	0	1	41	48	23	21	8	22	.296	L	L	6-1	185	9-1-81	2004	Moscow, Idaho
Boehm, Kyle	2	2	5.14	19	2	0	0	42	48	33	24	28	42	.271	R	R	6-1	190	4-20-83	2004	Rockford, Mich.
Brocato, Russ	3	5	6.64	15	12	0	0	60	76	51	44	26	36	.305	R	R	6-6	200	11-9-82	2003	New Freedom, Pa.
Cahill, Casey	2	0	2.45	21	0	0	1	37	35	13	10	11	29	.250	R	R	6-3	180	3-15-82	2002	New Brunswick, N.J.
Chamberlin, Bryce	1	6	6.03	13	6	0	0	37	33	30	25	19	42	.229	R	R	6-2	195	12-22-82	2004	Okanogan, Wash.
Childs, Ryan	3	3	3.71	21	6	0	1	51	57	29	21	17	30	.291	L	R	6-3	210	6-16-81	2003	Gaithersburg, Md.
Dumesnil, Bryan	1	0	4.32	4	0	0	0	8	11	4	4	5	5	.344	R	L	6-3	210	9-19-83	2002	Nanaimo, B.C.
Felix, Wilken	1	0	5.19	7	0	0	0	9	13	7	5	3	3	.371	R	R	6-1	170	3-16-83	2000	San Pedro de Macoris, D.R.
Haehnel, David	3	1	1.24	28	0	0	16	36	23	8	5	11	58	.178	L	L	6-4	185	7-21-82	2004	Wheeling, Ill.
Hart, Kevin	3	0	3.77	9	0	0	1	14	10	7	6	7	16	.192	R	R	6-4	220	12-29-82	2004	Dallas, Texas
Hoey, James	0	1	9.45	2	2	0	0	7	12	8	7	1	6	.387	R	R	6-6	200	12-30-82	2003	Hamilton, N.J.
McCrory, Bob	0	0	27.00	1	1	0	0	1	3	3	3	2	1	.600	R	R	6-1	205	5-3-82	2004	Steens, Miss.
Mendez, Wimer	1	1	3.06	4	4	0	0	18	18	10	6	8	11	.265	R	R	5-11	169	1-5-84	2001	Santo Domingo, D.R.
Paradis, Mike	0	0	0.00	2	0	0	0	3	0	0	0	3		.000	R	R	6-3	198	5-3-78	1999	Clemson, S.C.
Perez, Carlos	3	5	3.53	15	14	0	0	79	68	41	31	28	77	.234	L	L	6-1	185	5-20-82	2000	San Pedro de Macoris, D.R.
Petrick, Russ	2	4	5.52	20	6	0	0	46	57	35	28	24	44	.300	L	L	6-6	185	2-12-83	2003	Monroe, Wash.
Potter, Josh	1	0	8.31	3	0	0	0	4	6	4	4	1	1	.333	R	R	6-4	170	4-8-83	2002	Philipsburg, Pa.
Ramirez, Luis	1	2	4.76	11	11	0	0	51	46	27	27	12	75	.242	R	R	6-4	180	6-9-82	2000	Barcelona, Venez.
Robinson, Dennis	0	0	2.00	2	1	0	0	9	9	3	2	3	9	.281	R	R	6-3	190	10-4-82	2004	Putnam Valley, N.Y.
Schwabe, Ryan	0	0	1.06	3	3	0	0	17	14	2	2	6	18	.233	L	L	6-3	200	2-24-82	2004	Carroll, Iowa
Smith, Chris	1	0	3.38	4	4	0	0	13	13	9	5	5	13	.236	L	L	5-11	217	12-10-79	2001	Wantagh, N.Y.
Spencer, Sean	1	0	0.00	5	0	0	0	5	2	0	0	2	10	.118	L	L	5-11	180	5-29-75	1997	Port Orchard, Wash.
Spillers, Brandon	3	3	3.26	13	0	0	5	19	19	9	7	7	11	.284	R	R	6-3	210	3-12-82	2000	Roberta, Ga.
Stahl, Richard	0	0	0.00	1	1	0	0	3	1	0	0	0	1	.111	R	L	6-7	222	4-11-81	2000	Covington, Ga.

APPALACHIAN LEAGUE

BATTING	AVG	G	AB	R	H	2B	3B	HR	RBI	BB	SO	SB	CS	OBP	SLG	B	T	HT	WT	DOB	1st Yr	Resides
Avila, Angel	.263	47	167	19	44	4	1	5	20	8	62	9	4	.322	.389	R	R	6-1	170	6-26-84	2001	San Pedro de Macoris, D.R.
Braun, Ron	.172	8	29	2	5	0	0	1	5	1	8	0	0	.294	.172	R	R	6-2	215	5-15-82	2004	Stony Brook, N.Y.
Davis, Zach	.216	45	125	17	27	5	1	2	8	21	37	8	3	.329	.320	L	L	6-0	170	2-20-84	2002	Mabelvale, Ark.
Finan, Ryan	.333	36	123	27	41	12	0	5	21	18	16	0	1	.429	.553	R	R	6-5	220	1-5-82	2004	Beaumont, Texas
Guerrero, Francisco	.200	4	10	0	2	0	0	0	0	0	2	0	0	.200	.200	R	R	6-0	160	5-5-83	2001	San Pedro de Macoris, D.R.
Guerrero, Henry	.176	41	125	16	22	4	0	2	15	16	29	1	0	.273	.256	R	R	6-0	180	4-4-82	2000	Valencia, Venez.
Gutierrez, Juan	.349	36	126	19	44	8	0	8	29	17	14	0	1	.430	.603	S	R	6-0	190	8-1-81	2003	Miami, Fla.
Howell, Joey	.273	12	44	7	12	4	0	1	4	3	17	2	0	.319	.432	R	R	6-2	205	9-22-85	2004	West Palm Beach, Fla.
Kitch, Denver	.251	56	195	18	49	8	2	1	23	14	53	8	0	.316	.328	R	R	6-2	185	11-25-80	2004	Yukon, Okla.
Kotch, Kevin	.225	28	80	9	18	4	1	0	7	8	31	2	0	.303	.300	L	R	6-4	235	8-3-84	2004	Franklin Park, N.J.
Melendez, Alcides	.118	32	76	9	9	1	0	0	6	10	13	6	1	.225	.132	L	R	5-11	183	5-18-83	2001	Valencia, Venez.
Mendez, Carlos	.221	42	145	17	32	3	3	0	8	12	27	2	2	.283	.283	R	R	6-2	190	5-25-84	2002	Portuguesa, Venez.
Pacheco, Joel	.204	29	103	12	21	2	1	3	9	5	41	3	0	.248	.330	R	R	6-2	190	3-2-82	2003	Santo Domingo, D.R.
Puente, Dan	.140	15	50	4	7	3	0	0	7	9	21	0	0	.271	.200	R	R	6-2	205	12-3-81	2004	Oak Park, Ill.
Pulley, Matthew	.253	62	225	25	57	18	1	3	25	20	52	1	2	.312	.382	L	R	6-3	200	5-15-85	2003	Woodland, Calif.
Scott, Lorenzo	.237	62	219	36	52	6	1	3	16	27	75	12	2	.320	.315	L	L	6-3	210	3-1-82	2003	St. Louis, Mo.
Shafer, Corey	.312	20	77	11	24	4	1	3	12	7	17	0	1	.365	.506	L	L	6-2	215	12-17-82	2003	Choctaw, Okla.
Tucker, Jonathan	.250	16	56	7	14	3	0	0	1	3	12	1	1	.300	.304	R	R	5-7	170	7-2-83	2004	El Sobrante, Calif.
Wiggins, Brad	.264	49	163	26	43	9	2	6	22	17	59	7	4	.351	.454	L	L	6-0	185	7-9-83	2004	Fort Worth, Texas
Zapata, Jose	.220	29	91	8	20	4	0	0	13	3	28	2	1	.250	.264	R	R	6-4	184	4-4-84	2001	Quisqeya, D.R.

GAMES BY POSITION: C—Braun 8, Guerrero 41, Gutierrez 7, Kotch 13, Puente 6. 1B—Finan 34, Gutierrez 14, Pacheco 17, Pulley 4. 2B—F. Guerrero 1, Melendez 16, Mendez 41, Tucker 9, Zapata 8. 3B—F. Guerrero 1, Melendez 9, Pulley 53, Tucker 1, Zapata 7. SS—F. Guerrero 1, Kitch 56, Zapata 13. OF—Avila 44, Davis 44, Howell 10, Pacheco 6, Scott 60, Shafer 16, Wiggins 37.

PITCHING	W	L	ERA	G	GS	CG	SV	IP	H	R	ER	BB	SO	AVG	B	T	HT	WT	DOB	1st Yr	Resides
Bastardo, Alberto	1	1	1.86	3	2	0	1	10	9	3	2	4	10	.243	L	L	6-1	160	4-6-84	2002	Estado Aragua, Venez.
Bergesen, Brad	0	0	6.14	5	0	0	0	7	9	5	5	4	9	.290	R	R	6-2	215	8-25-85	2004	Pleasanton, Calif.
Brnardic, Ryan	3	1	3.67	17	1	0	1	42	39	19	17	17	35	.244	R	R	6-3	205	11-4-81	2003	Windsor, Ontario
Dumesnil, Bryan	1	1	4.15	14	0	0	1	26	29	15	12	11	28	.279	R	L	6-3	210	9-19-83	2002	Nanaimo, B.C.
Felix, Wilken	2	2	3.05	15	0	0	5	21	24	11	7	12	29	.296	R	R	6-1	170	3-16-83	2000	San Pedro de Macoris, D.R.
Furrow, Jason	1	2	4.74	13	13	0	0	57	75	40	30	15	31	.318	L	L	6-4	184	12-31-84	2003	Converse, Texas
Henington, Justin	0	3	3.73	16	0	0	1	31	30	22	13	13	39	.238	R	R	6-4	210	2-24-82	2004	Leaksville, Miss.
Hernandez, Moises	2	5	5.07	13	13	0	0	60	63	42	34	27	43	.278	R	R	5-11	171	3-18-84	2002	Valencia, Venez.
Lozado, Henry	0	2	5.61	15	0	0	0	26	28	24	16	13	27	.259	R	R	6-3	180	1-19-84	2003	Bayamon, P.R.
Lucas, Franklin	1	1	5.33	18	0	0	2	25	30	15	15	5	22	.300	R	R	6-2	155	1-1-84	2001	San Cristobal, D.R.
McCrory, Bob	4	3	1.92	11	11	0	0	52	42	21	11	32	51	.221	R	R	6-1	205	5-3-82	2004	Steens, Miss.
Mendez, Wimer	5	4	3.38	11	11	0	0	53	50	27	20	20	46	.251	R	R	5-11	169	1-5-84	2001	Santo Domingo, D.R.
Minor, Zach	2	4	4.80	16	0	0	0	30	34	18	16	19	32	.291	L	L	6-3	180	4-24-82	2004	Moline, Ill.
Pascual, Dionis	4	4	3.62	17	1	0	2	37	31	16	15	13	37	.217	R	R	6-0	194	9-6-83	2001	San Pedro de Macoris, D.R.
Pascual, Juan	1	2	3.93	15	3	0	0	37	37	20	16	8	38	.257	R	R	6-0	194	12-12-82	2000	San Pedro de Macoris, D.R.
Schindling, Andy	0	1	13.50	3	0	0	0	9	12	16	13	9	7	.333	R	R	6-2	165	8-15-86	2004	Bowie, Md.
Schwabe, Ryan	0	5	4.93	11	11	0	0	49	51	33	27	15	47	.263	L	L	6-3	200	2-24-82	2004	Carroll, Iowa
Soriano, Julio	0	1	6.10	3	1	0	0	10	6	7	7	10	17	.200	R	R	6-2	167	9-24-84	2002	San Pedro de Macoris, D.R.

BOSTON RED SOX

BY JOHN TOMASE

Keith Foulke fielded Edgar Renteria's comebacker with a flick of the glove and took four steps toward first base. In the millisecond before he underhanded to Doug Mientkiewicz, the very fabric of the Red Sox ruptured, disintegrated and reassembled itself into something glorious.

Goodbye, Babe Ruth. Goodbye, 1918. Goodbye, Bucky and Buckner and Boone. Hello, World Series champions. The Red Sox are cursed no more.

Closing the book on one of the most compelling and at times quixotic quests in sports history, the Red Sox swept the Cardinals to claim the club's first World Series title in 86 years. Making the story even better, they got there by becoming the first team in history to win a series after dropping the first three games, and they did it at the expense of their most hated rivals, the Yankees.

"Now 1918 is just another year the Red Sox won the World Series," general manager Theo Epstein said. "You still have all the history and angst, but you can point to the glorious year of 2004 and everything that went right for us."

Nothing went more right than the American League Championship Series. The Red Sox got blitzed 19-8 in Game Three and appeared headed for an early vacation. But David Ortiz won the next two games with walkoff hits in extra innings, starting pitcher Curt Schilling dramatically returned from an ankle injury to win Game Six, and the Sox exploded for four home runs in the 10-3 clincher.

From there, the World Series was anticlimactic. Manny Ramirez claimed MVP honors and the Red Sox never trailed while sweeping away the Cardinals.

It put the capper on a wild season that basically began on the morning of Oct. 17, 2003, when Aaron Boone's 11th-inning home run knocked the Red Sox from the 2003 ALCS.

First, they put Ramirez on unconditional waivers in an attempt to jettison his $20 million annual salary and found no takers. That nearly led to a trade with Texas for reigning MVP Alex Rodriguez, but the union squashed it on the grounds it decreased the value of his contract.

Manager Grady Little was replaced with former Phillies skipper Terry Francona, who subsequently proved instrumental in swaying Schilling to waive his no-trade clause from Arizona when the Red Sox swung a deal for the 2001 World Series MVP.

The season started promisingly. The Sox won six of seven against the Yankees in April to open a four-game division lead. But over the next three months, the Red Sox went 45-44 and fell 10 games behind New York.

On July 31, Epstein pulled off a stunner, trading franchise linchpin Nomar Garciaparra to the Cubs in a four-team trade that netted Orlando Cabrera and Doug Mientkiewicz.

After the Garciaparra trade, they took off. They went 25-4 over a 29-game stretch to salt away the wild card, then swept the Angels in the first round of the playoffs, setting up their ALCS and World Series heroics.

Stars for the Red Sox included Ramirez, who led the American League with 43 home runs, and Ortiz, who tied for second at 41 and drove in 139.

On the pitching side, Schilling led the majors with 21 victories and inspired the team in the postseason by winning two games with a bloody ankle after having surgery to stabilize a dislocated tendon.

In the minors, outfielder Brandon Moss came out of nowhere to hit a combined .353-15-111 between Class A Augusta and Sarasota.

Manny Ramirez | Brandon Moss

PLAYERS of the YEAR

MAJOR LEAGUE: Manny Ramirez, of

Ramirez was nearly traded for Alex Rodriguez prior to the 2004 season, but then he made Red Sox fans glad he was still around. Ramirez led the AL with 43 homers and ranked third with 130 RBIs, leading Boston to 98 wins and the wild card.

MINOR LEAGUE: Brandon Moss, of

There wasn't a lot left for Moss to prove at low Class A Augusta after he racked up 100 RBIs in early August, so the Red Sox promoted him to high A Sarasota. Moss continued his success there, hitting .422 in 23 games to post combined .353-15-111 numbers on the 2004 season.

ORGANIZATION LEADERS

BATTING

*AVG	Brandon Moss, Sarasota/Augusta	.353
R	Adam Hyzdu, Pawtucket	92
H	Brandon Moss, Sarasota/Augusta	182
TB	Earl Snyder, Pawtucket	300
2B	Earl Snyder, Pawtucket	43
3B	Sheldon Fulse, Portland	7
	Brandon Moss, Sarasota/Augusta	7
HR	Earl Snyder, Pawtucket	36
RBI	Brandon Moss, Sarasota/Augusta	111
BB	Adam Hyzdu, Pawtucket	84
SO	Jeremy Owens, Pawtucket	140
SB	Sheldon Fulse, Portland	29
*OBP	Adam Hyzdu, Pawtucket	.412
*SLG	Stefan Bailie, Portland/Sarasota	.576

PITCHING

W	Jarrett Gardner, Portland/Augusta	14
L	Kyle Jackson, Augusta	13
#ERA	Anibal Sanchez, Lowell	1.77
G	Matt Duff, Pawtucket	53
CG	Jamie Brown, Pawtucket	2
	Jon Papelbon, Sarasota	2
SV	Cla Meredith, Sarasota/Augusta	18
IP	Frank Castillo, Pawtucket	168
BB	Charlie Zink, Portland/Sarasota	81
SO	Jon Papelbon, Sarasota	153

*Minimum 250 at-bats #Minimum 75 Innings

BOSTON RED SOX

Manager: Terry Francona.

2004 Record: 98-64, .605 (2nd, AL East).

BATTING	AVG	G	AB	R	H	2B	3B	HR	RBI	BB	SO	SB	CS	OBP	SLG	B	T	HT	WT	DOB	1st Yr	Resides
Bellhorn, Mark	.264	138	523	93	138	37	3	17	82	88	177	6	1	.373	.444	S	R	6-1	205	8-23-74	1995	Oviedo, Fla.
Burks, Ellis	.182	11	33	6	6	0	0	1	1	3	8	2	0	.270	.273	R	R	6-2	200	9-11-64	1984	Englewood, Colo.
Cabrera, Orlando	.294	58	228	33	67	19	1	6	31	11	23	4	1	.320	.465	R	R	5-9	180	11-2-74	1994	Cartagena, Colombia
Crespo, Cesar	.165	52	79	6	13	2	1	0	2	0	20	2	0	.165	.215	S	R	5-10	180	5-23-79	1998	Miami Beach, Fla.
Damon, Johnny	.304	150	621	123	189	35	6	20	94	76	71	19	8	.380	.477	L	L	6-2	190	11-5-73	1992	Overland Park, Kan.
Daubach, Brian	.227	30	75	9	17	8	0	2	8	10	21	0	0	.326	.413	L	R	6-1	230	2-11-72	1990	Belleville, Ill.
Dominique, Andy	.182	7	11	0	2	0	0	1	0	3	0	0	.182	.182	R	R	6-0	220	10-30-75	1997	Granada Hills, Calif.
Garciaparra, Nomar	.321	38	156	24	50	7	3	5	21	8	16	2	0	.367	.500	R	R	6-0	190	7-23-73	1994	Boston, Mass.
Gutierrez, Ricky	.275	21	40	6	11	1	0	0	3	2	6	1	0	.310	.300	R	R	6-1	195	5-23-70	1988	Pembroke Pines, Fla.
Hyzdu, Adam	.300	17	10	3	3	2	0	1	2	1	2	0	0	.364	.800	R	R	6-2	220	12-6-71	1990	Mesa, Ariz.
Kapler, Gabe	.272	136	290	51	79	14	1	6	33	15	49	5	4	.311	.390	R	R	6-2	210	7-31-75	1995	Sherman Oaks, Calif.
Martinez, Sandy	.000	3	4	0	0	0	0	0	0	2	0	0	.000	.000	L	R	6-2	215	10-8-70	1991	Santo Domingo, D.R.
2-team (1 Cleveland)	.000	4	6	0	0	0	0	0	0	3	0	0	.000	.000							
McCarty, David	.258	91	151	24	39	8	1	4	17	14	40	1	0	.327	.404	R	L	6-5	215	11-23-69	1991	Piedmont, Calif.
Mientkiewicz, Doug	.215	49	107	13	23	6	1	1	10	10	18	0	1	.286	.318	L	R	6-2	205	6-19-74	1995	Estero, Fla.
2-team (78 Minn.)	.238	127	391	47	93	24	1	6	35	48	56	2	3	.326	.350							
Millar, Kevin	.297	150	508	74	151	36	0	18	74	57	91	1	1	.383	.474	R	R	6-0	210	9-24-71	1993	Encino, Calif.
Mirabelli, Doug	.281	59	160	27	45	12	0	9	32	19	46	0	0	.368	.525	R	R	6-1	220	10-18-70	1992	Orlando, Fla.
Mueller, Bill	.283	110	399	75	113	27	1	12	57	51	56	2	2	.365	.446	S	R	5-10	180	3-17-71	1993	Maryland Heights, Mo.
Nixon, Trot	.315	48	149	24	47	9	1	6	23	15	24	0	0	.377	.510	L	L	6-2	210	4-11-74	1994	Wilmington, N.C.
Ortiz, David	.301	150	582	94	175	47	3	41	139	75	133	0	0	.380	.603	L	L	6-4	230	11-18-75	1994	Haina, D.R.
Ramirez, Manny	.308	152	568	108	175	44	0	43	130	82	124	2	4	.397	.613	R	R	6-0	200	5-30-72	1991	Fort Lauderdale, Fla.
Reese, Pokey	.221	96	244	32	54	7	2	3	29	17	60	6	2	.271	.303	R	R	5-11	180	6-10-73	1991	Charlotte, N.C.
Roberts, Dave	.256	45	86	19	22	10	0	2	14	10	17	5	2	.330	.442	L	L	5-10	180	5-31-72	1994	Oceanside, Calif.
Snyder, Earl	.250	1	4	0	1	0	0	0	0	1	0	0	0	.250	.250	R	R	6-0	207	5-6-76	1998	New Britain, Conn.
Varitek, Jason	.296	137	463	67	137	30	1	18	73	62	126	10	3	.390	.482	S	R	6-2	230	4-11-72	1995	Suwanee, Ga.
Youkilis, Kevin	.260	72	208	38	54	11	0	7	35	33	45	0	1	.367	.413	R	R	6-1	220	3-15-79	2001	Cincinnati, Ohio

PITCHING	W	L	ERA	G	GS	CG	SV	IP	H	R	ER	BB	SO	AVG	B	T	HT	WT	DOB	1st Yr	Resides
Adams, Terry	2	0	6.00	19	0	0	0	27	35	19	18	6	21	.321	R	R	6-3	220	3-6-73	1991	Semmes, Ala.
2-team (42 Toronto)	6	4	4.76	61	0	0	3	70	84	39	37	28	56	.302							
Alvarez, Abe	0	1	9.00	1	1	0	0	5	8	5	5	5	2	.400	L	L	6-2	190	10-17-82	2003	Fontana, Calif.
Anderson, Jimmy	0	0	6.00	5	0	0	0	6	10	4	4	3	3	.400	L	L	6-1	210	1-22-76	1994	Chesapeake, Va.
Arroyo, Bronson	10	9	4.03	32	29	0	0	179	171	99	80	47	142	.249	R	R	6-2	210	2-24-77	1995	Brooksville, Fla.
Astacio, Pedro	0	0	10.38	5	1	0	0	9	13	10	10	5	6	.342	R	R	6-2	210	11-28-69	1989	Hato Mayor, D.R.
Brown, Jamie	0	0	5.87	4	0	0	0	8	15	7	5	4	6	.417	R	R	6-2	200	3-31-77	1997	Collinsville, Miss.
Castillo, Frank	0	0	0.00	2	0	0	0	1	1	0	0	1	0	.333	R	R	6-1	198	4-1-69	1987	Cave Creek, Ariz.
Dinardo, Lenny	0	0	4.23	22	0	0	0	28	34	17	13	12	21	.298	L	L	6-4	195	9-19-79	2001	High Springs, Fla.
Embree, Alan	2	2	4.13	71	0	0	0	52	49	28	24	11	37	.244	L	L	6-2	190	1-23-70	1990	Vancouver, Wash.
Foulke, Keith	5	3	2.17	72	0	0	32	83	63	22	20	15	79	.206	R	R	6-0	210	10-19-72	1994	Huffman, Texas
Jones, Bobby	0	1	5.40	3	0	0	0	3	3	2	2	8	3	.273	R	L	6-0	170	4-11-72	1992	East Rutherford, N.J.
Kim, Byung-Hyun	2	1	6.23	7	3	0	0	17	17	15	12	7	6	.258	R	R	5-9	180	1-21-79	1999	Gwangju, Korea
Leskanic, Curtis	3	2	3.58	32	0	0	2	28	24	11	11	16	22	.247	R	R	6-0	185	4-2-68	1990	Longwood, Fla.
2-team (19 Kansas City)	3	5	5.19	51	0	0	4	43	47	27	25	30	37	.280							
Lowe, Derek	14	12	5.42	33	33	0	0	183	224	138	110	71	105	.299	R	R	6-6	215	6-1-73	1991	Fort Myers, Fla.
Malaska, Mark	1	1	4.50	19	0	0	0	20	21	11	10	12	12	.266	L	L	6-3	191	1-17-78	2000	Youngstown, Ohio
Martinez, Anastacio	2	1	8.44	11	0	0	0	11	13	10	10	6	5	.289	R	R	6-2	180	11-3-78	1998	Santo Domingo, D.R.
Martinez, Pedro	16	9	3.90	33	33	1	0	217	193	99	94	61	227	.238	R	R	5-11	180	10-25-71	1990	Santo Domingo, D.R.
McCarty, David	0	0	2.45	3	0	0	0	4	2	1	1	1	4	.154	R	L	6-5	215	11-23-69	1991	Piedmont, Calif.
Mendoza, Ramiro	2	1	3.52	27	0	0	0	31	25	12	12	7	13	.225	R	R	6-2	190	6-15-72	1993	Los Santos, Panama
Myers, Mike	1	0	4.20	25	0	0	0	15	16	7	7	6	9	.267	L	L	6-3	220	6-26-69	1990	Highlands Ranch, Colo.
2-team (50 Seattle)	5	1	4.64	75	0	0	0	43	45	22	22	23	32	.274							
Nelson, Joe	0	0	16.88	3	0	0	0	3	4	5	5	3	5	.364	R	R	6-2	180	10-25-74	1996	Alameda, Calif.
Schilling, Curt	21	6	3.26	32	32	3	0	227	206	84	82	35	203	.239	R	R	6-5	235	11-14-66	1986	Paradise Valley, Ariz.
Seibel, Phil	0	0	0.00	2	0	0	0	4	0	0	0	5	1	.000	L	L	6-1	195	1-28-79	2001	Austin, Texas
Timlin, Mike	5	4	4.13	76	0	0	1	76	75	35	35	19	56	.257	R	R	6-4	210	3-10-66	1987	Oldsmar, Fla.
Wakefield, Tim	12	10	4.87	32	30	0	0	188	197	121	102	63	116	.264	R	R	6-2	210	8-2-66	1988	Melbourne, Fla.
Williamson, Scott	0	1	1.26	28	0	0	1	29	11	6	4	18	28	.115	R	R	6-0	180	2-17-76	1997	Friendswood, Texas

FIELDING

Catcher	PCT	G	PO	A	E	DP	PB
Dominique	1.000	1	1	0	0	0	0
S. Martinez	1.000	3	6	0	0	0	1
Mirabelli	.993	53	285	18	2	2	15
Varitek	.998	130	880	49	2	11	5

First Base	PCT	G	PO	A	E	DP
Daubach	.982	14	100	10	2	9
Dominique	.963	5	25	1	1	2
McCarty	.991	67	287	30	3	23
Mientkiewicz	.997	47	263	25	1	14
Millar	.989	69	466	58	6	45

Second Base	PCT	G	PO	A	E	DP
Ortiz	.986	34	253	21	4	23
Bellhorn	.980	124	189	349	11	61
Crespo	1.000	11	12	19	0	3
Gutierrez	1.000	14	15	24	0	6
Mientkiewicz	1.000	1	2	2	0	1
Mueller	.949	14	22	34	3	6
Reese	.991	30	49	63	1	15

Third Base	PCT	G	PO	A	E	DP
Bellhorn	.932	16	10	31	3	2

	PCT	G	PO	A	E	DP
Mueller	.943	96	71	162	14	15
Snyder	1.000	1	2	3	0	0
Youkilis	.968	65	47	106	5	7

Shortstop	PCT	G	PO	A	E	DP
Bellhorn	1.000	1	2	3	0	1
Cabrera	.966	57	78	147	8	23
Crespo	.943	27	20	30	3	8
Garciaparra	.957	37	52	81	6	17
Gutierrez	.941	6	7	9	1	3
Reese	.979	71	85	190	6	37

Outfield	PCT	G	PO	A	E	DP
Crespo	1.000	19	13	0	0	0
Damon	.986	148	349	4	5	2
Daubach	1.000	7	8	1	0	0
Hyzdu	1.000	14	6	0	0	0
Kapler	.978	127	170	6	4	0
McCarty	1.000	17	13	1	0	1
Millar	.976	74	121	1	3	0
Nixon	.985	40	63	1	1	0
Ramirez	.967	132	198	4	7	0
Roberts	.982	38	53	1	1	1

FARM SYSTEM

Director, Player Development: Ben Cherington.

Class	Farm Team	League	W	L	Pct.	Finish*	Manager	Affiliate Since
AAA	Pawtucket (R.I.) Red Sox	International	73	71	.507	t-5th (14)	Buddy Bailey	1973
AA	Portland (Maine) Sea Dogs	Eastern	69	73	.486	t-7th (12)	Ron Johnson	2003
High A	#Sarasota (Fla.) Red Sox	Florida State	76	61	.555	4th (12)	Todd Claus	1994
Low A	@Augusta (Ga.) GreenJackets	South Atlantic	66	73	.475	12th (16)	Chad Epperson	1999
SS A	Lowell (Mass.) Spinners	New York-Penn	32	44	.421	11th (14)	Luis Alicea	1996
Rookie	Fort Myers (Fla.) Red Sox	Gulf Coast	34	24	.586	**4th (12)**	Ralph Treuel	1993

*Finish in overall standings (No. of teams in league)/playoff teams in **boldface**
#Affiliate will operate in Wilmington (Carolina) in 2005   @Affiliate will operate in Capital City (South Atlantic) in 2005

PAWTUCKET RED SOX   Class AAA

INTERNATIONAL LEAGUE

BATTING	AVG	G	AB	R	H	2B	3B	HR	RBI	BB	SO	SB	CS	OBP	SLG	B	T	HT	WT	DOB	1st Yr	Resides
Alvarez, Jimmy	.218	31	101	8	22	6	0	3	13	8	20	3	2	.273	.366	S	R	5-10	160	10-4-79	1997	Santo Domingo, D.R.
Bailey, Jeff	.300	3	10	2	3	1	0	0	3	3	0	0	0	.462	.400	R	R	6-2	200	11-19-78	1997	Kelso, Wash.
Bellhorn, Mark	.167	2	6	1	1	1	0	0	0	2	0	0	0	.167	.333	S	R	6-1	205	8-23-74	1995	Oviedo, Fla.
Burks, Ellis	.000	1	2	1	0	0	0	0	0	0	0	0	0	.333	.000	R	R	6-2	200	9-11-64	1984	Englewood, Colo.
Casanova, Raul	.270	23	74	4	20	2	1	1	9	10	15	0	0	.353	.365	S	R	6-0	220	8-23-72	1990	Ponce, P.R.
Coquillette, Trace	.244	61	197	17	48	12	1	3	22	17	54	1	2	.324	.360	R	S	5-11	180	6-4-74	1993	Orangevale, Calif.
Crespo, Cesar	.271	55	221	30	60	13	3	4	19	21	53	10	2	.333	.412	S	R	5-10	190	5-23-79	1998	Miami Beach, Fla.
Curry, Mike	.262	50	164	29	43	5	0	0	16	24	43	12	4	.359	.293	L	R	5-10	190	2-15-77	1998	Jacksonville, Fla.
Daubach, Brian	.274	93	336	63	92	23	0	21	81	71	93	0	1	.403	.530	L	R	6-1	230	2-11-72	1990	Belleville, Ill.
Dominique, Andy	.267	111	419	54	112	28	0	15	69	55	87	0	2	.360	.442	R	R	6-1	220	10-30-75	1997	Granada Hills, Calif.
Febles, Carlos	.257	68	261	43	67	11	3	3	28	20	42	13	2	.319	.356	R	R	5-11	185	5-24-76	1994	La Romana, D.R.
Garciaparra, Nomar	.238	6	21	1	5	1	0	1	3	1	3	0	0	.273	.429	R	R	6-0	190	7-23-73	1994	Boston, Mass.
Hyzdu, Adam	.301	129	465	92	140	33	2	29	79	84	106	8	4	.413	.568	R	R	6-2	220	12-6-71	1990	Mesa, Ariz.
Kilburg, Joe	.000	4	4	0	0	0	0	0	0	1	3	0	0	.200	.000	L	R	5-11	180	12-20-75	1997	Bay Village, Ohio
Lombard, George	.276	55	192	38	53	8	3	3	23	20	33	16	3	.371	.396	L	R	6-0	215	9-14-75	1994	Atlanta, Ga.
McCarty, David	.286	3	7	2	2	0	0	0	1	4	2	0	0	.583	.286	R	L	6-5	215	11-23-69	1991	Piedmont, Calif.
Medrano, Jesus	.235	13	34	3	8	1	2	1	5	2	3	0	0	.289	.441	R	R	6-0	180	9-11-78	1997	La Puente, Calif.
Mueller, Bill	.308	4	13	1	4	2	0	0	2	2	0	0	0	.400	.462	S	R	5-10	180	3-17-71	1993	Maryland Heights, Mo.
Nixon, Trot	.333	6	21	2	7	1	0	0	2	3	0	0	0	.391	.381	L	L	6-2	210	4-11-74	1994	Wilmington, N.C.
Owens, Jeremy	.228	112	347	52	79	16	1	12	41	37	140	5	4	.303	.383	R	R	6-1	200	12-9-76	1998	Johnson City, Tenn.
Schrager, Tony	.266	122	436	63	116	29	0	15	49	47	88	2	2	.341	.436	R	R	6-1	170	6-14-77	1998	Omaha, Neb.
Sherrod, Justin	.267	104	341	55	91	20	5	17	51	25	108	6	2	.323	.504	R	R	6-2	205	1-11-78	2000	Boynton Beach, Fla.
Shoppach, Kelly	.233	113	399	62	93	25	0	22	64	46	138	0	0	.320	.461	R	R	5-11	210	4-29-80	2002	Fort Worth, Texas
Snyder, Earl	.273	136	538	85	147	43	1	36	104	35	128	1	1	.323	.558	R	R	6-0	207	5-6-76	1998	New Britain, Conn.
Stanley, Henri	.299	51	164	30	49	17	1	3	17	23	27	2	2	.383	.470	L	L	5-10	185	12-15-77	2000	Columbia, S.C.
Youkilis, Kevin	.262	36	145	21	38	12	0	3	17	27	27	2	0	.343	.407	R	R	6-1	220	3-15-79	2001	Cincinnati, Ohio

PITCHING	W	L	ERA	G	GS	CG	SV	IP	H	R	ER	BB	SO	AVG	B	T	HT	WT	DOB	1st Yr	Resides
Almonte, Edwin	5	6	5.63	51	0	0	7	72	89	49	45	22	37	.310	R	R	6-3	220	12-17-76	1998	New York, N.Y.
Anderson, Jimmy	0	0	5.40	1	0	0	0	2	1	1	1	1	1	.167	L	L	6-1	210	1-22-76	1994	Chesapeake, Va.
Astacio, Pedro	0	1	2.89	2	2	0	0	9	9	4	3	1	7	.250	R	R	6-2	210	11-28-69	1989	Hato Mayor, D.R.
Beech, Matt	1	1	8.44	4	4	0	0	16	26	18	15	9	9	.388	L	L	6-2	180	1-20-72	1995	Clearwater, Fla.
Brown, Jamie	4	6	4.82	23	20	2	0	127	128	76	68	17	92	.257	R	R	6-2	200	3-31-77	1997	Collinsville, Miss.
Cameron, Ryan	1	1	3.94	10	0	0	0	16	17	10	7	14	20	.262	R	R	6-1	175	9-13-77	1998	Williamstown, Mass.
Cassidy, Scott	5	3	3.46	28	12	0	1	81	72	34	31	38	72	.238	R	R	6-2	180	10-3-75	1998	Clay, N.Y.
Castillo, Frank	10	9	4.38	27	25	0	0	168	169	87	82	34	123	.260	R	R	6-1	198	4-1-69	1987	Cave Creek, Ariz.
Coquillette, Trace	0	0	9.00	2	1	0	0	2	5	2	2	1	1	.455	R	R	5-11	180	6-4-74	1993	Orangevale, Calif.
Dinardo, Lenny	0	0	0.00	1	1	0	0	3	3	0	0	4		.250	L	L	6-4	195	9-19-79	2001	High Springs, Fla.
Donaldson, Bo	0	0	0.00	1	1	0	0	2	1	0	0	1	3	.167	R	R	6-0	200	10-10-74	1997	Wesley Chapel, Fla.
Duff, Matt	7	4	3.93	53	0	0	7	73	72	32	32	36	68	.254	R	R	6-1	215	10-6-74	1997	Alligator, Miss.
Hamulack, Tim	7	4	6.98	35	0	0	2	30	44	26	23	19	25	.352	L	L	6-4	210	11-14-76	1996	Edgewood, Md.
Hebson, Bryan	1	0	5.73	7	0	0	0	11	13	7	7	4	9	.277	R	R	6-5	210	3-12-76	1998	Phenix City, Ala.
Johnson, James	0	2	4.13	16	0	0	0	24	28	12	11	13	17	.292	S	L	6-1	170	8-7-76	1998	San Diego, Calif.
Kester, Tim	12	10	4.09	27	23	1	0	163	181	84	74	19	74	.283	R	R	6-4	190	12-1-71	1993	Coral Springs, Fla.
Kim, Byung-Hyun	2	6	5.34	22	19	0	0	61	71	43	36	12	39	.289	R	R	5-9	180	1-21-79	1999	Gwangju, Korea
Leskanic, Curtis	0	0	0.00	1	0	0	0	1	0	0	0	0		.000	R	R	6-0	185	4-2-68	1990	Longwood, Fla.
Malaska, Mark	1	1	4.21	33	0	0	1	36	42	17	17	11	31	.292	L	L	6-3	191	1-17-78	2000	Youngstown, Ohio
Martinez, Anastacio	3	3	3.74	38	0	0	1	67	73	37	28	31	57	.277	R	R	6-2	190	11-3-78	1998	Santo Domingo, D.R.
Mendoza, Ramiro	0	1	4.15	6	0	0	0	9	13	5	4	0	3	.351	R	R	6-2	190	6-15-72	1993	Los Santos, Panama
Nelson, Joe	0	0	4.64	16	0	0	0	21	27	14	11	9	33	.307	R	R	6-2	180	10-25-74	1996	Alameda, Calif.
Puffer, Brandon	3	2	3.26	24	0	0	10	30	31	11	11	11	21	.263	R	R	6-3	190	10-5-75	1994	Round Rock, Texas
Seibel, Phil	1	2	3.02	8	7	0	0	45	42	16	15	12	31	.255	L	L	6-1	195	1-28-79	2001	Austin, Texas
Stephens, John	9	6	4.47	24	21	1	0	143	148	74	71	32	101	.268	R	R	6-1	212	11-15-79	1997	Berala, Australia
Stevens, Josh	1	0	5.00	5	4	0	0	27	45	16	15	4	11	.381	R	R	6-4	200	6-6-79	1998	Riverside, Calif.
Thomas, Brad	0	1	10.38	4	1	0	0	9	5	6	5	6	1	.353	L	L	6-4	220	10-12-77	1996	Sydney, Australia
Williamson, Scott	1	0	12.27	1	1	0	0	4	3	5	5	6	6	.231	R	R	6-0	180	2-17-76	1997	Friendswood, Texas
Yarnall, Ed	0	1	4.26	2	2	0	0	6	7	3	3	2	4	.259	L	L	6-3	235	12-4-75	1997	Baton Rouge, La.

FIELDING

Catcher	PCT	G	PO	A	E	DP	PB
Bailey	1.000	1	6	0	0	0	0
Casanova	.979	13	84	8	2	3	1
Dominique	.975	36	213	17	6	2	3
Shoppach	.988	101	621	61	8	7	3

First Base	PCT	G	PO	A	E	DP
Casanova	1.000	5	44	2	0	2
Coquillette	.991	16	101	7	1	5
Daubach	.992	78	609	41	5	55
Dominique	1.000	18	154	8	0	12
Kilburg	.900	1	9	0	1	0
McCarty	1.000	2	15	1	0	1
Snyder	.992	30	235	23	2	24
Youkilis	.929	2	13	0	1	3

Second Base	PCT	G	PO	A	E	DP
Alvarez	1.000	7	12	21	0	4

	PCT	G	PO	A	E	DP	PB
Bellhorn	1.000	2	2	7	0	0	
Coquillette	.989	21	38	53	1	13	
Crespo	.976	7	20	21	1	6	
Febles	.984	13	22	41	1	6	
Medrano	.918	13	20	25	4	2	
Schrager	.995	96	196	208	2	56	

Third Base	PCT	G	PO	A	E	DP
Daubach	1.000	1	1	3	0	0
Mueller	.857	4	2	4	1	0
Schrager	.976	21	14	26	1	1
Snyder	.958	94	60	189	11	16
Youkilis	.956	34	23	63	4	5

Shortstop	PCT	G	PO	A	E	DP
Alvarez	.956	24	34	52	4	15
Crespo	.963	49	80	126	8	31

	PCT	G	PO	A	E	DP
Febles	.944	58	91	144	14	28
Garciaparra	1.000	6	9	9	0	0
Schrager	.955	11	11	31	2	6
Snyder	.972	11	11	24	1	7

Outfield	PCT	G	PO	A	E	DP
Coquillette	1.000	9	15	0	0	0
Curry	.987	45	75	3	1	1
Daubach	1.000	4	6	0	0	0
Hyzdu	.976	120	239	5	6	1
Lombard	.991	53	112	1	1	0
Nixon	.750	4	3	0	1	0
Owens	.993	104	261	6	2	3
Sherrod	.984	95	173	7	3	0
Snyder	.917	8	11	0	1	0
Stanley	.984	39	62	1	1	1

PORTLAND SEA DOGS
Class AA

EASTERN LEAGUE

BATTING	AVG	G	AB	R	H	2B	3B	HR	RBI	BB	SO	SB	CS	OBP	SLG	B	T	HT	WT	DOB	1st Yr	Resides
Alvarez, Jimmy	.151	19	53	7	8	2	0	0	5	8	16	2	2	.262	.189	S	R	5-10	160	10-4-79	1997	Santo Domingo, D.R.
Bailey, Jeff	.294	91	299	57	88	23	3	13	58	46	80	2	0	.404	.522	R	R	6-2	200	11-19-78	1997	Kelso, Wash.
Bailie, Stefan	.309	37	139	23	43	15	0	8	28	10	34	0	0	.364	.590	R	R	6-0	210	5-16-80	2001	Mesa, Wash.
Campo, Mike	.233	54	172	32	40	12	1	6	20	25	39	6	2	.353	.419	L	R	5-10	185	11-14-76	2000	Absecon, N.J.
Chauncey, Clint	.194	29	98	11	19	6	0	1	8	7	35	0	0	.259	.286	R	R	6-1	180	1-1-81	2000	Jacksonville, Fla.
2-team (1 Akron)	.190	30	100	11	19	6	0	1	8	7	36	0	0	.255	.280							
Concepcion, Alberto	.214	4	14	0	3	1	0	0	1	0	1	0	0	.214	.286	R	R	6-1	220	4-18-81	2002	El Segundo, Calif.
Fulse, Sheldon	.245	102	355	58	87	15	7	9	39	50	104	29	11	.339	.403	S	R	6-3	170	11-10-81	1999	Bartow, Fla.
Hattig, John	.295	75	264	53	78	21	1	12	35	47	68	3	3	.411	.519	S	R	6-2	210	2-27-80	1999	Dededo, Guam
Headley, Justin	.233	17	60	9	14	3	1	0	2	10	10	0	0	.352	.317	L	L	6-2	200	4-27-76	1998	Memphis, Tenn.
Johnson, Eric	.221	40	122	9	27	9	2	2	16	14	38	3	2	.312	.377	R	R	6-1	210	8-14-77	1999	Shallotte, N.C.
Johnson, James	.500	4	14	3	7	1	0	1	4	0	2	1	1	.467	.786	S	L	6-1	170	8-7-76	1998	San Diego, Calif.
Kelly, Dustin	.267	4	15	1	4	1	0	0	3	0	4	0	0	.267	.333	R	R	6-2	200	2-4-70	1990	Mesa, Ariz.
Kilburg, Joe	.261	95	303	37	79	17	2	3	38	38	71	8	4	.351	.360	L	R	5-11	180	12-20-75	1997	Bay Village, Ohio
Lockwood, Mike	.280	74	296	46	83	21	2	9	39	34	46	2	4	.360	.456	L	L	6-0	190	12-27-76	1999	Powell, Ohio
Lombard, George	.381	16	63	11	24	3	3	2	11	7	8	7	0	.443	.619	L	R	6-0	215	9-14-75	1994	Atlanta, Ga.
Lopez-Cao, Mike	.255	21	55	9	14	3	0	3	11	13	16	0	0	.380	.473	L	L	5-9	180	8-14-75	1997	Miami, Fla.
Martinez, Edgar	.163	53	141	9	23	3	0	1	10	3	20	0	0	.207	.206	R	R	6-0	160	10-23-81	1999	Guigue, Venez.
McGowan, Sean	.262	69	275	31	72	13	0	3	32	20	46	0	2	.312	.342	R	R	6-6	240	5-15-77	1999	Burlington, Mass.
Medrano, Jesus	.251	57	227	27	57	11	4	3	19	12	48	12	6	.292	.374	R	R	6-1	210	9-11-78	1997	La Puente, Calif.
Nathans, John	.000	1	1	0	0	0	0	0	0	0	1	0	0	.000	.000	R	R	6-1	210	6-10-79	2001	Warwick, N.Y.
Nieves, Raul	.222	98	311	37	69	9	1	4	19	28	54	5	4	.291	.296	S	R	6-2	180	1-1-79	2000	Barranquitas, P.R.
O'Keefe, Mike	.248	133	472	50	117	21	4	19	68	63	99	2	4	.340	.430	L	L	5-10	200	6-28-78	1999	Hamden, Conn.
Perez, Kenny	.280	109	400	47	112	31	5	5	61	23	59	12	4	.323	.420	S	R	6-2	190	9-28-81	2000	Miami, Fla.
Ramirez, Hanley	.310	32	129	26	40	7	2	5	10	12	26	12	3	.360	.512	S	R	6-3	195	12-23-83	2001	Santo Domingo, D.R.
Roneberg, Brett	.278	124	474	67	132	30	3	17	77	59	74	9	3	.360	.462	L	L	6-2	210	2-5-79	1996	Cairns, Australia
Schneidmiller, Gary	.233	8	30	4	7	2	0	0	6	4	10	1	0	.306	.300	R	R	6-1	185	1-26-80	1998	Chino, Calif.

PITCHING	W	L	ERA	G	GS	CG	SV	IP	H	R	ER	BB	SO	AVG	B	T	HT	WT	DOB	1st Yr	Resides
Alvarez, Abe	10	9	3.59	26	26	0	0	135	132	65	54	32	108	.252	L	L	6-2	190	10-17-82	2003	Fontana, Calif.
Astacio, Pedro	0	0	0.00	1	1	0	0	4	3	0	0	1	4	.214	R	R	6-2	210	11-28-69	1989	Hato Mayor, D.R.
Brooks, Conor	0	0	4.50	1	0	0	0	2	1	1	1	0	1	.143	R	R	6-1	190	6-11-78	2000	Sarasota, Fla.
Cameron, Ryan	4	6	4.30	23	15	0	0	90	94	50	43	37	83	.268	R	R	6-1	175	9-13-77	1998	Williamstown, Mass.
Deschenes, Marc	1	1	2.45	27	0	0	11	33	29	9	9	12	34	.228	R	R	6-0	210	4-26-78	1999	Quebec City, Quebec
Dinardo, Lenny	1	0	9.53	3	0	0	0	6	8	6	6	1	4	.333	L	L	6-4	195	9-19-79	2001	High Springs, Fla.
Donaldson, Bo	4	3	5.05	30	2	0	0	73	72	45	41	24	72	.254	R	R	6-0	200	10-10-74	1997	Wesley Chapel, Fla.
Ehrlich, Drew	1	0	2.45	2	0	0	0	4	5	1	1	2	3	.333	L	R	6-5	235	2-1-82	2004	Merced, Calif.
Gabbard, Kason	3	6	5.77	14	14	0	0	53	61	42	34	26	35	.280	L	L	6-4	200	4-8-82	2001	Royal Palm Beach, Fla.
Gamble, Jerome	4	2	3.94	14	10	0	0	62	62	32	27	18	36	.262	R	R	6-2	200	4-5-80	1998	Alexander City, Ala.
Gardner, Jarrett	1	0	5.40	1	1	0	0	5	6	3	3	1	2	.286	R	R	6-1	175	3-26-81	2003	Moore, Okla.
Glaser, Eric	7	6	4.67	31	12	0	2	96	98	55	50	26	78	.259	R	R	6-6	230	1-23-78	1997	Fort Thomas, Ky.
Hamulack, Tim	2	0	3.52	7	0	0	0	15	16	6	6	7	16	.271	L	L	6-4	210	11-14-76	1996	Edgewood, Md.
Hebson, Bryan	1	0	4.26	12	0	0	2	25	19	14	12	11	20	.198	R	R	6-5	210	3-12-76	1998	Phenix City, Ala.
Howell, Jason	3	5	7.20	23	0	0	0	40	46	34	32	19	23	.289	L	L	6-2	195	5-25-79	2001	Millers Creek, N.C.
Johnson, James	0	2	7.65	21	0	0	0	38	49	35	32	15	38	.306	S	L	6-1	170	8-7-76	1998	San Diego, Calif.
Lambert, Jeremy	0	1	9.95	4	0	0	0	6	9	8	7	3	4	.333	R	R	6-1	220	1-10-79	1997	Taylorsville, Utah
Larson, Ryan	6	3	5.36	26	0	0	3	40	49	26	24	20	36	.306	R	R	5-10	190	5-13-79	2000	Rocklin, Calif.
Montalbano, Greg	0	2	3.00	6	5	0	0	18	21	11	6	8	11	.273	L	L	6-2	180	8-24-77	2000	Fort Myers, Fla.
Nelson, Joe	3	2	1.78	25	0	0	13	30	16	8	6	15	49	.152	R	R	6-2	180	10-25-74	1996	Alameda, Calif.
Nieves, Raul	0	0	13.50	1	0	0	0	1	2	1	1	1	0	.500	S	R	6-2	180	1-1-79	2000	Barranquitas, P.R.
Perez, Juan	5	1	4.14	46	0	0	6	78	72	46	36	37	79	.242	R	L	6-0	150	2-10-81	1999	Villa Rivas, D.R.
Rogers, Joe	0	2	5.17	5	2	0	0	16	20	14	9	11	14	.299	L	L	6-2	175	7-19-81	2001	Fullerton, Calif.
Seibel, Phil	0	1	7.50	3	1	0	0	6	8	5	5	2	6	.320	L	L	6-1	195	1-28-79	2001	Austin, Texas
Smith, Chris	5	2	3.75	14	14	0	0	74	77	34	31	15	85	.267	R	R	6-2	200	4-9-81	2002	Hesperia, Calif.
Stevens, Josh	6	9	5.24	20	20	1	0	125	148	80	73	20	107	.291	R	R	6-2	190	6-6-79	1998	Riverside, Calif.
Vaughan, Beau	0	0	12.27	1	1	0	0	4	5	5	5	4	4	.313	R	R	6-4	230	6-4-81	2003	Glendale, Ariz.
Weatherby, Charles	1	1	5.50	9	0	0	1	18	21	12	11	3	15	.280	R	R	6-0	200	12-23-78	2001	Beaufort, N.C.
Young, Colin	1	1	5.68	36	0	0	2	59	67	39	37	28	36	.293	L	L	6-0	185	8-1-77	1999	West Newbury, Mass.
Zink, Charlie	1	8	5.79	18	18	0	0	93	101	70	60	72	50	.282	R	R	6-1	190	8-26-79	2001	El Dorado Hills, Calif.

Catcher	PCT	G	PO	A	E	DP	PB
Bailey	.987	66	441	19	6	6	5
Chauncey	.992	29	219	26	2	3	3
Concepcion	.949	4	37	0	2	0	1
Lopez-Cao	.982	11	54	1	1	0	0
Martinez	.962	52	321	38	14	2	9

First Base	PCT	G	PO	A	E	DP
Bailey	.973	4	31	5	1	3
Bailie	.982	26	205	14	4	16
Kilburg	1.000	4	21	1	0	3
McGowan	.990	25	189	19	2	10
O`Keefe	.989	80	592	44	7	50
Roneberg	.987	12	65	10	1	6

Second Base	PCT	G	PO	A	E	DP
Alvarez	.981	12	20	32	1	7

	PCT	G	PO	A	E	DP
Kelly	1.000	3	6	5	0	1
Kilburg	.958	29	35	56	4	11
Lopez-Cao	.900	4	1	8	1	1
Medrano	.957	53	87	112	9	20
Nieves	.982	43	75	90	3	20
Perez	.935	14	25	33	4	5

Third Base	PCT	G	PO	A	E	DP
Alvarez	1.000	2	0	0	0	0
Hattig	.944	71	44	124	10	10
Kilburg	.919	36	18	61	7	5
Nieves	.901	31	29	44	8	3
Schneidmiller	1.000	8	7	21	0	3

Shortstop	PCT	G	PO	A	E	DP
Alvarez	1.000	2	2	6	0	1
Kelly	1.000	1	1	5	0	1

	PCT	G	PO	A	E	DP
Nieves	.979	25	35	60	2	14
Perez	.938	89	136	199	22	35
Ramirez	.978	32	52	82	3	12

Outfield	PCT	G	PO	A	E	DP
Bailey	1.000	22	27	2	0	0
Campo	.963	23	50	2	2	0
Fulse	.979	102	279	4	6	0
Headley	1.000	14	23	0	0	0
Johnson	1.000	39	83	2	0	1
Kilburg	.966	25	27	1	1	0
Lockwood	.993	80	138	6	1	2
Lombard	.968	15	30	0	1	0
Lopez-Cao	1.000	2	4	0	0	0
O`Keefe	.976	25	40	0	1	0
Roneberg	.981	111	202	6	4	1

SARASOTA RED SOX — High Class A

FLORIDA STATE LEAGUE

BATTING	AVG	G	AB	R	H	2B	3B	HR	RBI	BB	SO	SB	CS	OBP	SLG	B	T	HT	WT	DOB	1st Yr	Resides
Bailie, Stefan	.306	58	222	37	68	23	1	11	48	20	40	1	0	.383	.568	R	R	6-0	210	5-16-80	2001	Mesa, Wash.
Boran, Patrick	.221	41	145	10	32	6	1	1	15	7	35	3	2	.260	.297	S	R	6-2	200	8-8-80	2002	Pottsville, Pa.
Brown, Dusty	.229	38	118	11	27	3	0	1	8	15	28	2	0	.321	.280	R	R	6-0	195	6-19-82	2001	Prescott Valley, Ariz.
Buckley, Jim	.202	70	203	24	41	13	0	8	29	26	54	0	1	.291	.384	R	R	6-1	230	9-14-79	2002	Ocean City, N.J.
Concepcion, Alberto	.281	98	331	47	93	23	1	5	51	35	85	4	3	.364	.402	R	R	6-1	220	4-18-81	2002	El Segundo, Calif.
Cronkhite, Ian	.121	15	33	4	4	0	0	2	3	7	15	0	0	.293	.303	L	L	6-1	189	8-11-83	2002	Edmond, Okla.
Curtis, Lee	.162	11	37	4	6	1	0	0	3	3	6	0	0	.225	.189	R	R	5-11	185	7-21-81	2003	Greer, S.C.
Durbin, Chris	.279	125	470	75	131	32	6	7	44	39	79	8	10	.344	.417	R	R	6-0	180	9-8-81	2003	Wylie, Texas
Johnson, Eric	.125	19	56	5	7	1	0	1	5	6	15	2	0	.219	.196	R	R	6-1	210	8-14-77	1999	Shallotte, N.C.
LeVier, Brett	.304	19	69	6	21	5	0	0	4	2	8	0	1	.315	.377	R	R	6-3	195	4-26-83	2004	Whittier, Calif.
Moss, Brandon	.422	23	83	16	35	2	1	2	10	7	15	2	0	.462	.542	L	R	6-0	180	9-16-83	2002	Monroe, Ga.
Murphy, David	.261	73	272	35	71	11	0	4	38	25	46	3	5	.323	.346	L	L	6-4	192	10-18-81	2003	Spring, Texas
Murton, Matt	.301	102	376	60	113	16	4	11	55	42	61	5	4	.372	.452	R	R	6-1	215	10-3-81	2003	Kissimmee, Fla.
Nixon, Trot	.667	1	3	1	2	1	0	0	1	0	0	0	0	.667	1.000	L	L	6-2	210	4-11-74	1994	Wilmington, N.C.
Ontiveros, Jeff	.202	33	84	17	17	4	0	5	18	22	24	2	0	.367	.429	R	R	6-0	220	4-26-79	2002	Round Rock, Texas
Pedroia, Dustin	.336	30	107	23	36	8	3	2	14	13	4	0	2	.417	.523	R	R	5-8	180	8-17-83	2004	Woodland, Calif.
Penalo, Alex	.175	15	40	4	7	0	1	0	5	5	8	0	2	.271	.225	S	R	6-1	170	5-24-82	2002	Santo Domingo, D.R.
Ramirez, Hanley	.310	62	239	33	74	8	4	1	24	17	39	12	7	.364	.389	R	R	6-3	195	12-23-83	2001	Santo Domingo, D.R.
Ramos, Jason	.104	23	67	6	7	1	0	0	4	13	19	1	0	.250	.119	S	R	5-11	185	8-9-83	2003	Miami, Fla.
Schneidmiller, Gary	.189	37	90	11	17	4	0	2	11	15	19	0	0	.305	.300	R	R	6-1	185	1-26-80	1998	Chino, Calif.
Sitzman, Jay	.270	92	304	45	82	12	2	4	31	42	66	10	2	.361	.362	L	L	6-3	190	3-13-78	1999	Scottsdale, Ariz.
Spann, Chad	.252	61	214	26	54	9	0	4	22	9	53	6	2	.291	.350	R	R	6-1	190	10-25-83	2002	Buena Vista, Ga.
Stone, Greg	.174	35	121	8	21	3	2	0	5	8	20	1	1	.231	.231	L	R	5-11	170	2-19-81	2002	Claremore, Okla.
Suarez, Ignacio	.257	82	307	42	79	10	3	1	23	31	51	12	4	.331	.319	R	R	5-11	165	5-3-81	2003	Corona, N.Y.
Turner, Chris	.273	3	11	1	3	1	0	0	0	0	2	0	0	.273	.364	R	R	5-11	195	12-2-83	2003	El Dorado, Ark.
Turner, Justin	.129	9	31	2	4	0	0	0	1	8	8	0	0	.176	.129	R	R	6-1	190	12-19-79	2001	Cape Coral, Fla.
West, Jeremy	.293	124	461	60	135	28	4	18	68	37	83	0	3	.347	.488	R	R	6-0	200	11-8-81	2003	Las Vegas, Nev.

PITCHING	W	L	ERA	G	GS	CG	SV	IP	H	R	ER	BB	SO	AVG	B	T	HT	WT	DOB	1st Yr	Resides
Brooks, Conor	0	2	2.77	8	0	0	1	13	7	4	4	3	19	.163	L	R	6-1	190	6-11-78	2000	Sarasota, Fla.
Cedeno, Juan	7	6	4.64	25	22	1	0	120	145	70	62	40	78	.300	L	L	6-1	160	8-19-83	2001	Higuey, D.R.
Cochran, Thomas	0	0	16.50	4	0	0	0	6	12	11	11	3	1	.444	L	L	6-2	195	10-16-82	2003	Wilmington, Del.
Corporan, Willy	2	2	3.53	14	0	0	0	36	28	15	14	10	25	.219	R	R	6-4	185	9-2-81	2004	San Pedro de Macoris, D.R.
Delcarmen, Manuel	3	6	4.68	19	18	0	0	73	84	43	38	20	76	.291	R	R	6-2	190	2-16-82	2001	Hyde Park, Mass.
Dennison, Michael	1	1	6.94	18	0	0	5	23	27	18	18	12	24	.290	R	R	6-0	200	1-9-81	2003	Overland Park, Kan.
Gabbard, Kason	3	2	2.70	10	7	0	1	43	43	17	13	16	30	.253	L	L	6-4	200	4-8-82	2001	Royal Palm Beach, Fla.
Hebson, Bryan	0	0	0.00	1	1	0	0	2	1	0	0	0	2	.167	R	R	6-5	210	3-12-76	1998	Phenix City, Ala.
Howell, Jason	5	0	2.70	19	0	0	0	23	25	10	7	12	14	.272	L	L	6-2	195	5-25-79	2001	Millers Creek, N.C.
Kim, Byung-Hyun	0	0	0.00	1	1	0	0	2	0	0	0	0	2	.000	R	R	5-9	180	1-21-79	1999	Gwangju, Korea
Larson, Ryan	2	0	1.77	11	0	0	1	20	18	5	4	9	22	.250	R	R	5-10	190	5-13-79	2000	Rocklin, Calif.
Lester, Jon	7	6	4.28	21	20	0	0	90	82	46	43	37	97	.244	L	L	6-3	190	1-7-84	2002	Puyallup, Wash.
Marshall, Brian	1	1	3.49	27	0	0	1	39	35	15	15	15	39	.233	L	L	6-5	190	8-30-82	2003	Chesterfield, Va.
Mendoza, Luis	8	7	3.74	25	25	1	0	137	133	76	57	54	51	.254	L	R	6-3	180	10-31-83	2001	Mexico City, Mexico
Mendoza, Ramiro	0	1	4.50	2	2	0	0	4	6	2	2	0	3	.353	R	R	6-2	190	6-15-72	1993	Los Santos, Panama
Meredith, Cla	0	2	2.20	16	0	0	12	16	15	4	4	3	16	.254	R	R	6-1	185	6-4-83	2004	Richmond, Va.
Morla, Carlos	1	1	7.71	13	0	0	0	21	28	19	18	9	16	.308	R	R	6-0	177	4-15-82	2000	San Pedro de Macoris, D.R.
Ool, Kevin	0	0	4.70	3	0	0	0	8	7	4	4	3	8	.250	L	L	5-11	190	1-4-81	2003	Middletown, N.Y.
Pahucki, David	5	4	1.81	43	0	0	5	60	46	15	12	15	40	.211	R	R	6-2	210	10-17-82	2002	New Hampton, N.Y.
Papelbon, Jon	12	7	2.64	24	24	2	0	130	97	43	38	43	153	.206	R	R	6-4	230	11-23-80	2003	Jacksonville, Fla.
Rhodes, Shane	0	1	7.43	6	0	0	0	13	15	12	11	5	9	.273	L	L	6-2	200	1-19-80	2001	Monkton, Md.
Rodriguez, Eladio	0	0	3.38	5	1	0	0	8	10	5	3	4	5	.313	R	R	5-11	170	4-4-79	1998	Mao Valverde, D.R.
Rogers, Joe	8	5	3.72	36	2	0	1	82	76	45	34	47	48	.248	L	L	6-2	175	7-19-81	2001	Fullerton, Calif.
Shipman, Andrew	1	1	3.65	20	0	0	13	25	19	11	10	13	22	.221	R	R	6-3	185	10-18-81	2003	Bellevue, Wash.
Stone, Greg	0	0	0.00	1	0	0	0	2	0	0	0	3	1	.000	L	R	5-11	170	2-19-81	2002	Claremore, Okla.
Sturge, Justin	4	3	2.80	39	2	0	0	80	78	36	25	29	71	.249	R	L	6-4	200	5-4-81	2003	Syracuse, N.Y.
Thompson, Matt	0	0	21.21	3	0	0	0	5	10	11	11	6	5	.476	R	R	6-2	200	8-28-81	1999	Boise, Idaho
Vaquedano, Jose	5	1	3.95	14	8	0	0	68	65	34	30	21	60	.253	R	R	6-4	170	7-9-81	2002	San Antonio, Texas
Young, Colin	0	0	0.00	2	0	0	0	2	1	1	0	2	2	.091	L	L	6-0	185	8-1-77	1999	West Newbury, Mass.
Zink, Charlie	0	2	5.65	3	3	0	0	14	22	13	9	9	3	.379	R	R	6-1	190	8-26-79	2001	El Dorado Hills, Calif.

FIELDING

Catcher	PCT	G	PO	A	E	DP	PB
Brown	.982	32	200	22	4	3	15
Buckley	.993	68	411	27	3	4	24
Concepcion	.992	43	334	22	3	4	5
Ontiveros	1.000	6	29	3	0	1	1

First Base	PCT	G	PO	A	E	DP
Bailie	.981	28	240	15	5	17
Boran	.985	9	59	8	1	7
Concepcion	1.000	6	20	1	0	3
Ontiveros	.993	19	126	13	1	10
West	.989	86	680	60	8	58

Second Base	PCT	G	PO	A	E	DP
Boran	1.000	18	27	37	0	9
Curtis	.966	7	14	14	1	1
Penalo	.920	7	12	11	2	2
Ramos	.951	12	24	34	3	8
Schneidmiller	.900	13	23	31	6	5

	PCT	G	PO	A	E	DP/PB
Stone	.962	24	51	49	4	11
Suarez	.978	57	105	162	6	34
J. Turner	1.000	7	11	23	0	4

Third Base	PCT	G	PO	A	E	DP
Boran	.926	6	9	16	2	1
Concepcion	.938	45	26	65	6	7
Curtis	.900	3	3	6	1	1
LeVier	.970	18	15	50	2	6
Schneidmiller	.972	14	12	23	1	1
Spann	.894	54	45	81	15	9
Stone	1.000	5	7	14	0	1
J. Turner	.667	1	2	2	2	0

Shortstop	PCT	G	PO	A	E	DP
Boran	1.000	3	4	3	0	0
Pedroia	1.000	30	44	85	0	17
Penalo	.786	4	3	8	3	1
Ramirez	.939	61	78	169	16	30

	PCT	G	PO	A	E	DP
Ramos	.914	10	13	19	3	2
Stone	.923	6	5	19	2	4
Suarez	.950	26	39	74	6	15
J. Turner	.667	1	0	2	1	0

Outfield	PCT	G	PO	A	E	DP
Bailie	1.000	1	0	1	0	0
Boran	1.000	6	11	1	0	0
Cronkhite	.929	12	12	1	1	0
Curtis	1.000	2	3	0	0	0
Durbin	.985	128	243	21	4	5
Johnson	1.000	17	32	1	0	0
Moss	1.000	21	35	2	0	1
Murphy	.986	69	132	5	2	1
Murton	.990	103	188	13	2	4
Sitzman	.990	70	95	3	1	2
C. Turner	1.000	3	9	0	0	0

AUGUSTA GREENJACKETS — Low Class A

SOUTH ATLANTIC LEAGUE

BATTING	AVG	G	AB	R	H	2B	3B	HR	RBI	BB	SO	SB	CS	OBP	SLG	B	T	HT	WT	DOB	1st Yr	Resides
Arias, Claudio	.273	54	209	31	57	10	1	8	34	14	53	2	2	.322	.445	R	R	6-2	200	5-9-82	2002	Bani, D.R.
Bonvechio, Brett	.250	10	32	4	8	1	1	1	9	8	9	0	0	.381	.438	L	R	6-1	190	11-13-82	2001	Santa Clara, Calif.
Borowiak, Zach	.237	123	448	52	106	19	3	6	40	38	70	9	9	.307	.333	R	R	6-1	185	5-18-81	2003	Nashville, Ill.
Burgess, Tim	.233	58	206	30	48	8	0	3	31	33	52	3	2	.343	.316	L	L	6-2	205	11-3-81	2004	Temple, Ga.
Chauncey, Clint	.171	9	35	2	6	2	0	0	4	3	18	0	0	.231	.229	R	R	6-1	180	1-1-81	2000	Jacksonville, Fla.
Chavez, Dirimo	.250	100	376	60	94	9	2	1	23	50	53	4	5	.341	.293	R	R	6-0	170	8-10-83	2001	Cabudare, Venez.
Ciofrone, Peter	.286	67	248	40	71	16	3	1	33	35	39	3	5	.383	.387	L	R	5-11	190	9-28-83	2002	Nesconset, N.Y.
Cloninger, Erich	.222	6	18	1	4	1	0	0	5	1	6	0	0	.250	.278	R	R	5-11	190	11-6-80	2003	Lynchburg, Va.
Cronkhite, Ian	.216	82	264	31	57	9	2	1	26	26	56	6	5	.287	.277	L	L	6-1	189	8-13-82	2003	Edmond, Okla.
Curtis, Lee	.133	4	15	0	2	0	0	0	2	0	2	0	0	.188	.133	R	R	5-11	185	7-21-81	2003	Greer, S.C.
DeVries, Jon	.257	73	245	33	63	8	0	5	35	29	74	1	2	.371	.351	R	R	6-3	200	8-22-82	2001	Irvine, Calif.
Evans, Robert	.230	50	187	17	43	10	2	2	21	17	29	5	0	.295	.337	L	L	5-11	185	3-1-81	2003	Birmingham, Ala.
Guzman, Heriberto	.147	26	95	11	14	2	1	3	10	4	43	0	1	.214	.284	R	R	6-1	180	1-26-84	2001	Bajo de Haina, D.R.
Hall, Mickey	.246	118	403	67	99	24	5	13	63	58	134	13	4	.342	.427	L	L	6-1	195	5-20-85	2003	Marietta, Ga.
Jordan, Scooter	.240	57	200	30	48	4	1	0	14	34	41	7	9	.360	.270	L	R	5-8	160	12-15-80	2003	Rowlett, Texas
LeVier, Brett	.229	26	96	14	22	5	2	1	14	7	16	1	0	.283	.354	R	R	6-3	195	4-26-83	2004	Whittier, Calif.
McClain, Justin	.235	41	132	21	31	6	0	0	10	20	37	4	0	.354	.280	R	R	6-1	205	11-4-80	2003	Cartersville, Ga.
Moss, Brandon	.339	109	433	66	147	25	6	13	101	46	75	19	8	.402	.515	L	R	6-0	180	9-16-83	2002	Monroe, Ga.
Ontiveros, Jeff	.240	44	150	20	36	3	0	3	15	27	52	1	1	.393	.353	R	R	6-0	220	4-26-79	2001	Round Rock, Texas
Paniagua, Salvador	.233	32	116	13	27	5	0	2	17	5	39	0	0	.274	.328	R	R	6-1	190	5-21-83	2001	San Juan, D.R.
Pedroia, Dustin	.400	12	50	11	20	5	0	1	5	6	3	2	0	.474	.560	R	R	5-8	180	8-17-83	2004	Woodstock, Calif.
Schartz, Lance	.111	10	27	3	3	0	0	1	3	3	8	0	0	.250	.222	R	R	6-0	215	1-26-83	2003	Larned, Kan.
Stachowsky, Mitch	.192	23	78	10	15	0	0	2	7	6	40	1	0	.284	.269	R	R	6-3	230	10-2-84	2004	Pocatello, Idaho
Suarez, Ignacio	.270	38	141	28	38	6	2	1	15	21	29	7	1	.373	.362	R	R	5-11	165	5-3-81	2003	Corona, N.Y.
Vankirk, Robert	.000	3	6	0	0	0	0	0	1	0	2	0	0	.000	.000	R	R	5-10	200	2-11-81	2003	Sunshine Ranches, Fla.
White, Scott	.281	123	474	60	133	34	2	6	55	25	61	21	9	.333	.399	R	R	6-3	190	10-18-83	2003	Pembroke Pines, Fla.

PITCHING	W	L	ERA	G	GS	CG	SV	IP	H	R	ER	BB	SO	AVG	B	T	HT	WT	DOB	1st Yr	Resides
Beam, Randy	2	1	0.00	18	0	0	10	23	10	1	0	4	27	.127	L	L	6-3	205	5-21-82	2004	Bradenton, Fla.
Blackley, Adam	4	3	3.39	12	12	0	0	61	61	27	23	20	59	.257	L	L	6-1	190	2-22-85	2003	Melbourne, Australia
Borland, Curt	0	1	6.27	10	0	0	0	19	29	15	13	3	14	.358	R	R	6-2	210	10-13-79	2003	Broomfield, Colo.
Corporan, Willy	0	3	6.49	8	8	0	0	35	44	32	25	8	19	.308	R	R	6-4	185	9-2-81	2004	San Pedro de Macoris, D.R.
Delgado, Jesus	1	5	5.22	21	16	0	0	59	61	40	34	26	34	.275	R	R	6-0	170	4-19-84	2001	Maracay, Venez.
Dennison, Michael	5	3	5.12	29	0	0	2	46	64	31	26	9	51	.318	R	R	6-0	200	1-9-81	2003	Overland Park, Kan.
Farley, Chris	3	5	4.94	39	1	0	2	75	69	52	41	30	57	.244	R	R	6-2	180	2-24-83	2001	Orange, Mass.
Galvez, Gary	7	10	5.14	30	22	1	0	140	153	86	80	36	102	.279	R	R	6-3	210	3-24-84	2003	Santo Domingo, D.R.
Gardner, Jarrett	13	5	2.51	25	23	0	0	136	130	49	38	11	92	.251	R	R	6-1	175	3-26-81	2003	Moore, Okla.
Guanchez, Argimiro	4	4	4.95	35	0	0	3	44	55	36	24	23	33	.314	L	L	6-0	170	12-30-82	2003	Valencia, Venez.
Hertzler, Barry	4	4	8.50	25	1	0	1	36	56	37	34	13	21	.364	R	R	6-2	215	2-15-81	2003	East Providence, R.I.
Hilario, Elpidio	0	0	9.00	5	0	0	0	6	7	7	6	7	7	.259	R	R	6-2	276	12-14-83	2002	San Francisco de Macoris, D.R.
Jackson, Kyle	3	13	4.64	31	21	0	1	142	156	87	73	36	130	.277	R	R	6-3	180	4-9-83	2002	Litchfield, N.H.
Martinez, Edgar	1	0	0.90	10	0	0	0	8	8	1	1	4	5	.229	R	R	6-0	160	10-23-81	1999	Guigue, Venez.
Meredith, Cla	1	0	0.00	13	0	0	6	15	8	0	0	3	18	.154	R	R	6-1	185	6-4-83	2004	Richmond, Va.
Morla, Carlos	1	1	1.56	22	0	0	2	35	34	10	6	11	34	.266	R	R	6-1	140	5-5-84	2003	San Pedro de Macoris, D.R.
Ool, Kevin	3	2	4.76	27	0	0	1	45	56	28	24	11	36	.299	L	L	5-11	185	1-4-81	2003	Middletown, N.Y.
Penny, Davey	0	1	8.68	3	0	0	0	9	18	11	9	1	7	.375	R	R	6-3	210	9-9-81	2003	Benson, N.C.
Santos, Arty	2	3	5.79	16	6	0	0	42	57	34	27	12	26	.328	R	R	6-0	180	2-20-82	2003	Miami, Fla.
Simon, Billy	1	4	4.32	3	3	0	0	8	9	4	4	1	8	.273	R	R	6-6	220	11-11-82	2001	Wellington, Fla.
Tavarez, Milton	1	4	4.55	47	0	0	5	63	69	41	32	26	63	.268	R	R	6-2	190	3-29-82	2000	Higuey, D.R.
Vaquedano, Jose	4	2	1.88	11	11	0	0	67	59	22	14	12	66	.236	R	R	6-4	170	7-9-81	2002	San Antonio, Texas
Vaughan, Beau	7	3	3.30	14	13	0	0	71	58	30	26	27	73	.218	B	R	6-4	230	6-4-81	2003	Glendale, Ariz.
Willey, Cory	1	0	6.16	20	1	0	0	31	34	26	21	15	31	.281	R	L	6-3	185	4-22-81	2004	Cambridge, Md.
Wilson, Jonathan	0	0	12.27	1	1	0	0	4	8	5	5	0	1	.471	R	R	6-0	210	11-24-82	2003	Aurora, Colo.

FIELDING

Catcher	PCT	G	PO	A	E	DP	PB
Chauncey	.986	8	62	6	1	0	0
Cloninger	1.000	5	35	1	0	0	0
DeVries	.987	67	498	46	7	4	8
Ontiveros	1.000	2	8	1	0	0	0

	PCT	G	PO	A	E	DP	PB
Paniagua	.978	31	197	24	5	2	7
Schartz	1.000	10	65	1	0	1	1
Stachowsky	.993	23	144	4	1	0	7
Van Kirk	1.000	3	16	0	0	0	0

First Base	PCT	G	PO	A	E	DP
Bonvechio	1.000	4	44	1	0	4
Burgess	.989	53	425	19	5	43
Ciofrone	.972	14	99	7	3	12
DeVries	.875	1	7	0	1	0

Guzman	.975	4	39	0	1	1
McClain	.977	24	201	13	5	18
Ontiveros	.987	31	273	21	4	36
White	.993	14	134	1	1	10

Second Base	PCT	G	PO	A	E	DP
Borowiak	.988	46	93	152	3	36
Chavez	.956	50	99	118	10	29
Ciofrone	.953	27	58	65	6	18
Curtis	.833	3	2	3	1	1
Suarez	.968	17	39	53	3	10

Third Base	PCT	G	PO	A	E	DP
Chavez	.950	31	20	75	5	8
Guzman	.949	14	10	27	2	4
McClain	.667	2	0	2	1	0
White	.901	98	65	200	29	18

Shortstop	PCT	G	PO	A	E	DP
Borowiak	.920	74	100	232	29	45
Chavez	.977	9	13	30	1	6
LeVier	.947	25	38	88	7	14
Pedroia	1.000	12	11	34	0	7

Suarez	.933	21	32	66	7	15

Outfield	PCT	G	PO	A	E	DP
Arias	.964	44	74	7	3	0
Chavez	1.000	4	3	0	0	0
Cronkhite	.966	79	171	2	6	0
Evans	.966	41	81	5	3	0
Hall	.929	113	172	11	14	2
Jordan	.976	47	78	2	2	0
Moss	.963	104	201	8	8	2

LOWELL SPINNERS — Short-Season Class A

NEW YORK-PENN LEAGUE

BATTING	AVG	G	AB	R	H	2B	3B	HR	RBI	BB	SO	SB	CS	OBP	SLG	B	T	HT	WT	DOB	1st Yr	Resides
Ciaramella, Matt	.189	45	164	8	31	6	1	1	20	12	35	0	3	.242	.256	S	L	6-1	190	10-25-82	2004	Salt Lake City, Utah
Cloninger, Erich	.226	22	62	7	14	2	0	0	4	7	15	0	1	.300	.258	R	R	5-11	190	11-6-80	2003	Lynchburg, Va.
Curtis, Lee	.250	22	80	11	20	7	1	0	11	15	14	1	0	.371	.363	R	R	5-11	185	7-21-81	2003	Greer, S.C.
De la Cruz, Carlos	.274	64	237	29	65	6	3	1	16	21	55	15	10	.341	.338	S	L	6-0	160	7-2-84	2001	Santo Domingo, D.R.
Evans, Robert	.326	22	86	16	28	7	1	2	13	15	20	6	2	.431	.500	L	L	5-11	185	3-1-81	2003	Birmingham, Ala.
Guzman, Heriberto	.233	60	219	32	51	13	2	7	29	22	74	5	2	.319	.406	R	R	6-1	180	1-26-84	2001	Bajo de Haina, D.R.
Jeroloman, Chuck	.170	48	159	14	27	5	1	1	13	23	61	1	0	.285	.233	R	R	6-1	188	8-14-82	2004	Wellington, Fla.
Lara, Christian	.277	32	119	21	33	3	2	0	10	24	23	10	5	.404	.336	S	R	5-11	150	4-11-85	2003	Bolivar, Venez.
McCarty, David	.667	1	3	1	2	1	0	0	1	1	0	0	0	.750	1.000	R	L	6-5	215	11-23-69	1991	Piedmont, Calif.
Otness, John	.276	63	232	23	64	12	0	2	29	12	18	5	3	.327	.353	R	R	6-1	190	9-15-81	2004	Tacoma, Wash.
Paniagua, Salvador	.222	50	189	23	42	16	2	6	32	7	63	0	0	.260	.423	R	R	6-1	190	5-21-83	2001	San Juan, D.R.
Penalo, Alex	.139	11	36	3	5	2	0	0	2	0	11	1	0	.162	.194	S	R	6-1	170	5-2-84	2002	Santo Domingo, D.R.
Perry, Patrick	.176	33	102	9	18	2	0	0	9	10	22	0	1	.254	.196	L	R	6-0	200	10-3-82	2004	Niwot, Colo.
Pinckney, Andrew	.275	65	244	24	67	9	1	3	25	22	75	2	8	.339	.357	B	R	6-1	195	4-7-82	2004	Atlanta, Ga.
Ramos, Jason	.200	46	115	14	23	5	0	0	12	15	27	4	3	.303	.243	R	R	5-11	185	8-9-83	2003	Miami, Fla.
Schartz, Lance	.200	2	5	0	1	0	0	0	0	0	2	0	0	.200	.200	R	R	6-0	215	1-26-83	2004	Larned, Kan.
Sorensen, Logan	.273	11	44	7	12	5	1	0	14	2	4	2	0	.292	.432	L	L	5-11	187	8-12-81	2004	Riverton, Utah
Turner, Chris	.241	42	162	17	39	2	4	5	21	4	53	2	3	.265	.395	R	R	5-11	195	12-2-83	2003	El Dorado, Ark.
Vanderbosch, Matt	.276	60	225	52	62	8	6	3	21	35	44	28	1	.380	.404	L	R	5-8	190	4-12-82	2004	Hastings, Minn.
Williams, Dee	.203	47	118	15	24	3	2	0	6	20	40	8	9	.338	.263	S	R	5-10	180	8-8-83	2002	Greensboro, Ala.
Youkilis, Kevin	.750	2	4	1	3	1	0	0	2	0	0	0	0	.857	1.500	R	R	6-1	220	3-15-79	2001	Cincinnati, Ohio

GAMES BY POSITION: C—Cloninger 12, Paniagua 48, Perry 25. **1B**—Cloninger 3, Guzman 22, McCarty 1, Otness 20, Pinckney 7, Sorensen 11. **2B**—Curtis 16, Jeroloman 26, Penalo 11, Pinckney 10, Ramos 24, Williams 2. **3B**—Curtis 1, Guzman 34, Otness 26, Pinckney 18, Youkilis 2. **SS**—Jeroloman 23, Lara 32, Pinckney 5, Ramos 20. **OF**—Ciaramella 32, De la Cruz 51, Evans 23, Otness 6, Turner 41, Vanderbosch 52, Williams 41.

PITCHING	W	L	ERA	G	GS	CG	SV	IP	H	R	ER	BB	SO	AVG	B	T	HT	WT	DOB	1st Yr	Resides
Beam, Randy	1	2	1.62	9	0	0	2	17	10	3	3	3	19	.169	L	L	6-3	205	5-21-82	2004	Bradenton, Fla.
Blackley, Adam	0	1	7.71	1	1	0	0	5	8	6	4	0	4	.381	L	L	6-1	190	2-22-85	2003	Melbourne, Australia
Bono, Kyle	0	1	3.00	6	5	0	0	12	4	4	4	5	17	.108	R	R	6-3	200	6-29-83	2004	Lake Mary, Fla.
Cochran, Thomas	0	4	5.00	22	0	0	3	36	39	24	20	12	33	.269	L	L	6-2	195	10-16-82	2003	Wilmington, Del.
Dobies, Andrew	0	2	2.03	14	14	0	0	27	17	9	6	8	36	.181	L	L	6-1	180	4-20-83	2004	Wexford, Penn.
Eddy, Cooper	2	3	4.29	21	0	0	2	36	41	22	17	8	27	.291	R	R	6-1	205	4-14-82	2004	West Des Moines, Iowa
Ehrlich, Drew	1	3	3.09	14	0	0	0	32	27	14	11	10	26	.223	L	R	6-5	235	2-1-82	2004	Merced, Calif.
Garcia, Harvey	4	6	5.16	14	14	0	0	61	61	40	35	30	54	.260	R	R	6-2	170	3-16-84	2001	Guarenas, Venez.
Glanzmann, Jake	1	2	13.11	5	0	0	0	12	21	19	17	8	5	.404	L	L	6-4	215	12-10-82	2004	Springfield, Va.
Goodson, Matt	1	2	5.10	12	1	0	0	30	22	20	17	12	23	.200	R	R	6-3	205	9-26-82	2004	Galveston, Texas
Hertzler, Barry	4	3	2.67	15	9	0	0	81	70	25	24	23	73	.234	R	R	6-2	215	2-15-81	2003	East Providence, R.I.
Hottovy, Tommy	0	1	0.89	14	14	0	0	30	24	5	3	4	39	.214	L	L	6-1	195	7-9-81	2004	Parkville, Mo.
James, Mike	4	10	10.90	20	0	0	1	35	53	43	42	17	34	.353	R	R	6-1	205	6-2-81	2004	Roswell, Ga.
Ramos, Jason	0	0	0.00	1	0	0	0	0	0	0	0	0	0	.000	S	R	5-11	185	8-9-83	2003	Miami, Fla.
Rodriguez, Eladio	1	3	4.75	25	0	0	5	36	34	22	19	25	38	.246	R	R	5-11	170	4-4-79	1998	Mao Valverde, D.R.
Sanchez, Anibal	4	4	1.77	15	15	0	0	76	43	24	15	29	101	.157	R	R	6-0	180	2-27-84	2001	Maracay, Venez.
Sanders, David	2	2	6.35	17	0	0	0	28	42	20	20	10	17	.372	L	L	6-4	195	1-5-82	2003	Tulsa, Okla.
Schroyer, Ryan	4	2	4.44	14	2	0	0	49	46	29	24	23	57	.249	R	R	6-1	215	9-28-81	2004	Oracle, Ariz.
Shoemaker, Scott	2	0	2.48	17	0	0	3	33	32	15	9	8	52	.244	R	R	6-4	210	9-21-81	2004	San Diego, Calif.
Swindle, R.J.	5	1	1.94	12	1	0	0	51	42	18	11	4	56	.221	L	L	6-3	195	7-7-83	2004	Orlando, Fla.

GCL RED SOX — Rookie

GULF COAST LEAGUE

BATTING	AVG	G	AB	R	H	2B	3B	HR	RBI	BB	SO	SB	CS	SLG	OBP	B	T	HT	WT	DOB	1st Yr	Resides
Arias, Claudio	.417	7	24	6	10	3	0	1	3	2	4	0	0	.667	.481	R	R	6-2	200	5-9-82	2002	Bani, D.R.
Bawden, Thomas	.244	39	127	20	31	8	0	2	15	19	0	2	.354	.324	R	R	5-11	175	7-24-84	2003	Chesterfield, Mo.
Boran, Patrick	.150	7	20	5	3	2	0	1	3	6	4	0	0	.400	.357	R	R	6-2	200	8-8-80	2002	Pottsville, Pa.
Caple, Tom	.282	46	149	30	42	7	1	1	19	22	14	6	2	.362	.385	R	R	6-0	185	8-20-80	2004	San Diego, Calif.
Easley, Austin	.380	13	50	6	19	4	0	0	3	4	14	5	0	.460	.415	R	R	6-2	215	1-15-82	2004	Broken Arrow, Okla.
Fulse, Sheldon	.400	2	5	1	2	0	0	0	0	1	2	1	0	.400	.500	R	R	6-3	170	11-10-81	1999	Bartow, Fla.
Headley, Justin	.256	12	39	11	10	4	0	1	11	5	5	0	0	.436	.333	L	L	6-2	200	4-27-76	1998	Memphis, Tenn.
Jordan, Scooter	.301	24	83	16	25	1	0	0	4	18	16	5	6	.313	.437	L	R	5-8	160	12-15-80	2003	Rowlett, Texas
Justice, Jeff	.302	34	116	13	35	4	0	0	14	7	14	2	4	.336	.362	R	R	6-1	200	5-31-81	2004	Pendicktown, N.J.
Kelly, Dustin	.263	43	152	15	40	7	1	1	15	16	22	8	3	.342	.349	R	R	6-0	185	5-23-83	2004	Santa Maria, Calif.
Lara, Christian	.433	15	60	14	26	8	2	0	9	7	10	8	0	.633	.493	S	R	5-11	150	4-11-85	2002	Bolivar, Venez.
Leonard, Mike	.237	30	93	7	22	2	0	0	10	12	12	0	0	.258	.343	R	R	6-0	210	5-4-82	2004	Vernon, Conn.
LeVier, Bret	.333	7	24	3	8	2	0	0	2	4	3	2	0	.417	.467	R	R	6-1	195	4-26-83	2004	Whittier, Calif.
Medrano, Jesus	.300	3	10	0	3	0	0	0	2	2	2	0	0	.300	.417	R	R	6-0	180	9-11-78	1997	La Puente, Calif.
Mota, Willy	.295	35	129	19	38	9	3	2	18	6	41	6	1	.457	.328	R	R	6-1	160	10-25-85	2002	San Pedro de Macoris, D.R.
Murphy, David	.278	5	18	3	5	1	0	0	1	1	2	1	0	.333	.316	L	L	6-4	192	10-18-81	2003	Spring, Texas
Otness, John	.400	3	10	2	4	1	0	0	1	1	0	0	0	.500	.538	R	R	5-11	200	9-15-81	2004	Tacoma, Wash.

Penalo, Alex	.294	22	85	15	25	4	0	0	11	6	17	5	0	.341	.341	S	R	6-1	170	5-2-84	2002	Santo Domingo, D.R.
Pritz, Bryan	.267	29	90	15	24	5	0	1	10	6	10	4	1	.356	.313	R	R	5-10	180	5-5-82	2004	Willmette, Ill.
Purvis, Nate	.200	7	20	1	4	1	0	0	1	3	5	0	0	.250	.304	L	R	6-4	210	5-16-81	2004	Florence, Miss.
Ramirez, Hanley	.400	6	20	5	8	0	1	0	7	2	3	1	0	.500	.462	S	R	6-1	170	12-23-83	2000	Santo Domingo, D.R.
Soto, Luis	.261	36	134	22	35	9	2	5	16	5	22	4	1	.470	.289	S	R	6-1	180	12-7-85	2004	Bani, D.R.
Spann, Chad	.333	7	24	3	8	2	0	0	4	2	1	0	0	.417	.385	R	R	6-1	190	10-25-83	2002	Buena Vista, Ga.
Stachowsky, Mitch	.236	15	55	6	13	5	0	0	11	2	10	0	0	.327	.300	R	R	6-3	230	10-2-84	2004	Pocatello, Idaho
Stone, Greg	.250	2	8	1	2	0	0	0	0	0	1	0	0	.250	.250	L	R	5-11	170	2-19-81	2002	Claremore, Okla.
Suarez, Jose	.265	16	49	5	13	1	0	1	7	3	18	0	0	.347	.321	R	R	6-1	170	6-9-83	2002	Nueva Esparta, Venez.
Torres, Carlos	.257	42	148	26	38	7	0	8	31	19	38	1	2	.466	.368	R	R	6-4	190	4-3-84	2003	Carabobo, Venez.
Turner, Chris	.250	16	68	12	17	3	3	4	18	3	17	1	2	.559	.293	R	R	5-11	195	12-2-83	2003	El Dorado, Ark.
Underwood, Bret	.189	18	53	4	10	0	0	0	4	3	9	1	0	.189	.224	L	R	6-0	215	3-30-82	2004	Wilmington, Del.
Vankirk, Robert	.217	21	60	7	13	1	1	1	6	9	12	0	0	.317	.319	R	R	5-10	200	2-11-81	2003	Sunshine Ranches, Fla.

GAMES BY POSITION: C—Leonard 22, Stachowsky 14, Suarez 14, Vankirk 13. **1B**—Headley 9, Otness 2, Purvis 2, Torres 38, Underwood 12. **2B**—Bawden 37, Boran 2, Jordan 4, Kelly 16, Medrano 3, Penalo 1, Ramirez 1, Stone 1. **3B**—Bawden 5, Boran 4, Kelly 21, Lara 9, Leonard 6, LeVier 6, Penalo 9, Spann 5, Stone 1, Underwood 1. **SS**—Kelly 8, Lara 7, Penalo 14, Ramirez 5, Soto 30. **OF**—Arias 5, Caple 40, Easley 6, Fulse 2, Jordan 19, Justice 33, Leonard 1, Mota 33, Murphy 4, Otness 1, Penalo 1, Pritz 24, Soto 1, Turner 14.

PITCHING	W	L	ERA	G	GS	CG	SV	IP	H	R	ER	BB	SO	AVG	B	T	HT	WT	DOB	1st Yr	Resides
Albury, James	5	0	1.15	11	2	0	0	39	26	6	5	16	21	.195	L	R	6-3	170	1-4-86	2003	Brisbane, Australia
Astacio, Olivo	3	4	3.13	12	8	1	0	46	46	27	16	18	32	.255	R	R	6-5	200	7-28-84	2002	San Pedro de Macoris, D.R.
Astacio, Pedro	1	0	0.00	2	1	0	0	5	4	3	0	0	6	.210	R	R	6-2	210	11-28-69	1988	Hato Mayor, D.R.
Beech, Matt	0	0	0.00	3	3	0	0	5	5	0	0	1	3	.294	L	L	6-2	180	1-20-72	1994	Clearwater, Fla.
Blackley, Adam	1	0	3.00	2	0	0	0	9	7	4	3	1	11	.205	L	L	6-1	190	2-22-85	2003	Melbourne, Australia
Delgado, Jesus	0	0	10.80	1	0	0	0	2	4	2	2	0	2	.500	R	R	6-0	170	4-19-84	2001	Maracay, Venez.
Dinardo, Lenny	0	0	0.00	2	1	0	0	3	3	0	0	0	5	.272	L	L	6-4	195	9-19-79	2001	High Springs, Fla.
Frias, Junior	1	2	3.48	10	8	0	0	34	34	19	13	14	43	.263	R	R	6-3	200	8-26-84	2002	Santo Domingo, D.R.
Gamble, Jerome	0	0	0.00	2	2	0	0	4	2	0	0	4	4	.142	R	R	6-3	200	4-5-80	1998	Alexander City, Ala.
Glanzmann, Jake	0	0	10.29	5	0	0	0	7	12	9	8	5	3	.375	L	L	6-3	200	12-10-82	2004	Springfield, Va.
Guanchez, Argimiro	0	1	7.36	3	0	0	0	4	4	3	3	3	1	.285	L	L	6-0	170	12-30-82	1999	Valencia, Venez.
Hebson, Bryan	0	0	4.50	2	1	0	0	2	2	1	1	0	2	.210	R	R	6-1	190	12-31-81	2004	West Palm Beach, Fla.
Hoffar, Brad	2	1	5.28	10	0	0	0	15	16	12	9	8	10	.271	R	R	6-2	170	10-16-84	2002	La Sabana, Venez.
James, Jimmy	5	1	2.33	11	9	0	0	46	51	19	12	15	35	.271	R	R	6-2	170	10-16-84	2002	La Sabana, Venez.
Lester, Jon	0	0	0.00	1	1	0	0	1	0	0	0	2	1	.000	L	L	6-4	190	1-7-84	2002	Puyallup, Wash.
Martes, Jose	0	2	6.28	9	2	0	0	14	10	11	10	17	13	.222	L	L	6-4	160	12-23-85	2002	Azua, D.R.
Montalbano, Greg	0	2	4.85	5	4	0	0	13	17	8	7	2	10	.333	L	L	6-2	180	8-24-77	2000	Fort Myers, Fla.
Moser, Nolan	0	4	2.57	18	0	0	7	21	21	9	6	9	22	.259	R	R	6-0	185	4-14-81	2004	Capistrano Beach, Calif.
Newsom, Randy	2	2	2.81	18	0	0	4	32	32	13	10	9	25	.258	R	R	6-2	200	5-6-82	2004	Cincinnati, Ohio
Newton, Willie	0	1	2.61	5	0	0	0	10	10	7	3	6	5	.227	L	L	6-2	170	9-3-84	2004	Orem, Utah
Pena, Mario	4	3	3.94	12	6	0	0	48	54	27	21	6	34	.276	L	L	6-2	150	12-7-84	2003	Managua, Nicaragua
Peralta, Yader	3	0	2.10	16	0	0	3	34	29	10	8	10	38	.228	R	R	6-1	170	2-22-86	2004	Santo Domingo, D.R.
Rhodes, Shane	0	0	9.00	1	1	0	0	1	2	1	1	1	1	.400	L	L	6-2	200	1-19-80	2001	Monkton, Md.
Sanders, David	1	0	2.25	2	0	0		4	4	2	1	1	3	.133	L	L	6-4	195	1-5-82	2003	Tulsa, Okla.
Santos, Arty	0	0	1.29	3	0	0	0	7	6	1	1	0	6	.230	R	R	6-0	180	2-20-82	2003	Miami, Fla.
Seibel, Phil	0	0	2.25	3	3	0	0	4	2	1	1	1	6	.142	L	L	6-1	195	1-28-79	2000	Austin, Texas
Snapp, Mike	0	0	2.42	14	0	0	4	22	17	6	6	4	18	.204	R	R	6-0	205	9-25-81	2004	Joshua, Texas
Willey, Cory	1	0	4.50	2	0	0	0	2	0	1	1	1	1	.000	R	L	6-3	185	4-22-81	2004	Cambridge, Md.
Wilson, Jonathan	5	1	2.50	11	6	0	0	54	44	21	15	11	39	.231	R	R	6-0	210	11-24-82	2003	Aurora, Colo.

CHICAGO WHITE SOX

BY PHIL ROGERS

If home runs were all it took to win baseball games, the White Sox would have been one of the best teams in the majors in 2004. Instead, they are being reminded on an annual basis that there is a whole lot more to the sport.

The White Sox hit more than 200 home runs for the fifth year in a row, keeping pace with the Yankees. But they missed the American League playoffs for the fourth consecutive season, getting 83 wins from a team managed by newcomer Ozzie Guillen, the former shortstop who was expected to inspire a better effort than his predecessor, Jerry Manuel.

Guillen did have a good excuse for finishing nine games behind Minnesota. The Sox lost their Nos. 3 and No. 4 hitters, Magglio Ordonez and Frank Thomas, for a combined 198 games.

Ordonez had arthroscopic knee surgery on June 5 and played just 10 games after returning due to an ensuing case of bone marrow edema in that left knee. Thomas was lost for the season on June 6 with a stress fracture in his left ankle, which also was slow to heal. He had surgery in October.

After a 46-38 first half, the White Sox ran out of steam without Thomas and Ordonez, the latter of which opted for free agency after the season. Things would have been worse without a huge season from first baseman Paul Konerko, was finished second in the AL with 41 home runs. Konerko batted .277 and drove in a team-high 117 runs.

The White Sox also received double-figure home runs from Carlos Lee (31), Jose Valentin (30), Aaron Rowand (24), Juan Uribe (23), Joe Crede (21) and Thomas (18). Rowand was extremely productive, hitting .310.

But in the end, the Sox were third in the AL in runs scored and eighth in on-base percentage. Guillen, like Manuel before him, vowed to retool this one-dimension-

Paul Konerko   Brandon McCarthy

PLAYERS of the YEAR

MAJOR LEAGUE: Paul Konerko, 1b

A year after hitting a disappointing .234-18-65, Konerko re-emerged as a legitimate power threat in 2004. His 41 home runs were tied for second in the American League, and he led the White Sox with 117 RBIs.

MINOR LEAGUE: Brandon McCarthy, rhp

McCarthy rode a 12-game winning streak through three levels in 2004. He finished 17-5, 3.14 in 27 starts between low Class A Kannapolis, high A Winston-Salem and Double-A Birmingham. McCarthy also led the minors with 202 strikeouts in 172 innings.

al team into one based on more of a National League model—that is, pitching, defense and speed.

He felt many of the building blocks were in place in 2004—namely starting pitchers Mark Buehrle (an AL-high 245 innings pitched), Freddy Garcia, Jose Contreras and Jon Garland. Garcia and Contreras were acquired in midseason trades from the Mariners and the Yankees, respectively.

Closer Shingo Takatsu, the all-time saves leader in Japan, established himself at the back end of a contending staff. He started the year as a setup man but converted 19 of 20 save situations after replacing Billy Koch as the closer.

It was a challenging season for the player development staff, as highly-regarded pitchers Kris Honel and Ryan Wing were lost early in the year with injuries and switch-hitting outfielder Joe Borchard, in whom the organization invested a record $5.3 million signing bonus, batted just .174 with nine homers in 63 games after taking over for the injured Ordonez.

Double-A Birmingham and high Class A Winston-Salem returned to their league playoffs, with the Warthogs surging in the second half behind veteran manager Nick Leyva, who replaced Ken Dominguez after a slow start. Great Falls also advanced to the Pioneer League playoffs.

Righthander Brandon McCarthy, 21, went 17-5 with a 3.14 ERA and a minor league-high 202 strikeouts between Birmingham, Winston-Salem and low-A Kannapolis. Third baseman Josh Fields, a former quarterback at Oklahoma State, paid immediate dividends after being selected with the 18th pick overall in the June draft. He hit .285-7-39 in 66 games at Winston-Salem.

ORGANIZATION LEADERS

BATTING

*AVG	Boomer Berry, Great Falls	.307
R	Casey Rogowski, Winston-Salem	88
H	Bryant Nelson, Charlotte	161
TB	Bryant Nelson, Charlotte	272
2B	Brian Becker, Birmingham/Winston-Salem	38
3B	Ruddy Yan, Birmingham	10
HR	Darren Blakely, Birmingham/Winston-Salem	29
RBI	Brian Becker, Birmingham/Winston-Salem	93
BB	Casey Rogowski, Winston-Salem	91
SO	Chris Young, Kannapolis	146
SB	Ruddy Yan, Birmingham	35
*OBP	Casey Rogowski, Winston-Salem	.401
*SLG	Darren Blakely, Birmingham/Winston-Salem	.573

PITCHING

W	Brandon McCarthy, Birmingham/Win.-Salem/Kannapolis	17
L	Rafael Flores, Kannapolis	11
#ERA	Matt Smith, Birmingham	1.83
G	Matt Smith, Birmingham	70
CG	Brandon McCarthy, Birmingham/Win-Salem/Kannapolis	3
SV	Dwayne Pollok, Winston-Salem	38
IP	Brandon McCarthy, Birmingham/Win.-Salem/Kannapolis	172
BB	Brian Miller, Winston-Salem/Kannapolis	70
SO	Brandon McCarthy, Birmingham/Win.-Salem/Kannapolis	202

*Minimum 250 at-bats #Minimum 75 innings

CHICAGO WHITE SOX

Manager: Ozzie Guillen.

2004 Record: 83-79, .512 (2nd, AL Central).

BATTING	AVG	G	AB	R	H	2B	3B	HR	RBI	BB	SO	SB	CS	OBP	SLG	B	T	HT	WT	DOB	1st Yr	Resides
Alomar, Roberto	.180	18	61	4	11	1	0	1	8	2	13	0	0	.203	.246	S	R	6-0	185	2-5-68	1985	Bradenton, Fla.
Alomar, Sandy	.240	50	146	15	35	4	0	2	14	11	13	0	0	.298	.308	R	R	6-5	230	6-18-66	1984	Chicago, Ill.
Borchard, Joe	.174	63	201	26	35	4	1	9	20	19	57	1	0	.249	.338	S	R	6-5	220	11-25-78	2000	Camarillo, Calif.
Burke, Jamie	.333	57	120	22	40	9	0	0	15	10	13	0	0	.386	.408	R	R	6-0	190	9-24-71	1993	Roseburg, Ore.
Crede, Joe	.239	144	490	67	117	25	0	21	69	34	81	1	2	.299	.418	R	R	6-2	190	4-26-78	1996	Westphalia, Mo.
Davis, Ben	.231	54	160	21	37	9	0	6	16	9	40	1	1	.276	.400	S	R	6-4	225	3-10-77	1995	West Chester, Pa.
2-team (14 Seattle)	.207	68	193	22	40	9	0	6	18	12	49	1	1	.256	.347							
Dransfeldt, Kelly	.333	15	30	5	10	0	0	0	4	0	6	0	0	.333	.333	R	R	6-2	190	4-15-75	1996	Morris, Ill.
Everett, Carl	.266	43	154	21	41	7	1	5	21	8	26	1	0	.320	.422	S	R	6-0	215	6-3-71	1990	Brandon, Fla.
Gload, Ross	.321	110	234	28	75	16	0	7	44	20	37	0	3	.375	.479	L	L	6-0	180	4-5-76	1997	East Hampton, N.Y.
Harris, Willie	.262	129	409	68	107	15	2	2	27	51	79	19	7	.343	.323	L	R	5-9	175	6-22-78	1999	Cairo, Ga.
Konerko, Paul	.277	155	563	84	156	22	0	41	117	69	107	1	0	.359	.535	R	R	6-2	215	3-5-76	1994	Scottsdale, Ariz.
Lee, Carlos	.305	153	591	103	180	37	0	31	99	54	86	11	5	.366	.525	R	R	6-2	235	6-20-76	1994	Aguadulce, Panama
Olivo, Miguel	.270	46	141	21	38	7	2	7	26	10	29	5	4	.316	.496	R	R	6-0	220	7-15-78	1997	Ceres, Calif.
Ordonez, Magglio	.292	52	202	32	59	8	2	9	37	16	22	0	2	.351	.485	R	R	6-0	210	1-28-74	1992	Miami, Fla.
Perez, Timo	.246	103	293	38	72	12	0	5	40	15	29	3	1	.285	.338	L	L	5-9	165	4-8-75	1994	San Cristobal, D.R.
Rowand, Aaron	.310	140	487	94	151	38	2	24	69	30	91	17	5	.361	.544	R	R	6-1	210	8-29-77	1998	Las Vegas, Nev.
Thomas, Frank	.271	74	240	53	65	16	0	18	49	64	57	0	2	.434	.563	R	R	6-5	270	5-27-68	1989	Chicago, Ill.
Uribe, Juan	.283	134	502	82	142	31	6	23	74	32	96	9	11	.327	.506	R	R	5-11	175	7-22-79	1997	Palenque, D.R.
Valdez, Wilson	.233	19	43	8	10	1	0	1	4	2	5	1	2	.267	.326	R	R	5-11	160	5-20-78	1997	Nizao, D.R.
Valentin, Jose	.216	125	450	73	97	20	3	30	70	43	139	8	6	.287	.473	S	R	5-10	180	10-12-69	1987	Manati, P.R.

PITCHING	W	L	ERA	G	GS	CG	SV	IP	H	R	ER	BB	SO	AVG	B	T	HT	WT	DOB	1st Yr	Resides
Adkins, Jon	2	3	4.65	50	0	0	0	62	75	35	32	20	44	.305	L	R	6-0	200	8-30-77	1999	Wayne, W.Va.
Bajenaru, Jeff	0	1	10.80	9	0	0	0	8	15	10	10	6	8	.405	R	R	6-1	190	3-21-78	2000	Rancho Cucamonga, Calif.
Buehrle, Mark	16	10	3.89	35	35	4	0	245	257	119	106	51	165	.271	L	L	6-2	200	3-23-79	1999	St. Charles, Mo.
Contreras, Jose	5	4	5.30	13	13	0	0	75	73	48	44	42	68	.256	R	R	6-4	230	12-6-71	2003	Managua, Nicaragua
2-team (18 New York) ..	13	9	5.50	31	31	0	0	170	166	114	104	84	150	.253							
Cotts, Neal	4	4	5.65	56	1	0	0	65	61	45	41	30	58	.247	L	L	6-2	200	3-25-80	2001	Lebanon, Ill.
Darensbourg, Vic	0	0	0.00	2	0	0	0	1	1	0	0	1	0	.333	L	L	5-10	180	11-13-70	1992	Henderson, Nev.
Diaz, Felix	2	5	6.75	18	7	0	0	49	62	38	37	16	33	.310	R	R	6-1	180	7-27-80	1998	Las Mata de Farfan, D.R.
Garcia, Freddy	9	4	4.46	16	16	0	0	103	96	53	51	32	102	.247	R	R	6-4	240	6-10-76	1994	Baruta, Venez.
2-team (15 Seattle) ..	13	11	3.81	31	31	1	0	210	192	92	89	64	184	.242							
Garland, Jon	12	11	4.89	34	33	1	0	217	223	125	118	76	113	.269	R	R	6-6	200	9-27-79	1997	Granada Hills, Calif.
Grilli, Jason	2	3	7.40	8	8	1	0	45	52	38	37	20	26	.294	R	R	6-4	185	11-11-76	1998	Orlando, Fla.
Jackson, Mike	2	0	5.01	45	0	0	0	47	55	27	26	15	26	.294	R	R	6-0	220	12-22-64	1984	Spring, Texas
Koch, Billy	1	1	5.40	24	0	0	8	23	24	15	14	16	25	.255	R	R	6-3	210	12-14-74	1997	Clearwater, Fla.
Marte, Damaso	6	5	3.42	74	0	0	6	74	56	28	28	34	68	.217	L	L	6-2	200	2-14-75	1994	Santo Domingo, D.R.
Munoz, Arnie	0	1	10.05	11	1	0	0	14	20	16	16	12	11	.333	L	L	5-9	170	6-21-82	1999	Mao, D.R.
Politte, Cliff	0	0	4.38	54	0	0	1	51	52	26	25	22	48	.261	R	R	5-11	195	2-27-74	1996	St. Louis, Mo.
Rauch, Jon	1	1	6.23	2	2	0	0	9	16	6	6	4	4	.432	R	R	6-11	260	9-27-78	1999	Tucson, Ariz.
Schoeneweis, Scott	6	9	5.59	20	19	0	0	113	129	74	70	49	69	.291	L	L	6-0	190	10-2-73	1996	Fountain Hills, Ariz.
Stewart, Josh	0	1	15.26	3	2	0	0	8	16	13	13	3	5	.444	L	L	6-3	205	12-5-78	1999	Ledbetter, Ky.
Takatsu, Shingo	6	4	2.31	59	0	0	19	62	40	17	16	21	50	.182	R	R	5-10	160	11-25-68	2004	Tokyo, Japan
Wright, Dan	0	4	8.15	4	4	0	0	18	24	17	16	11	6	.320	R	R	6-5	240	12-14-77	1999	Batesville, Ark.
Wunsch, Kelly	0	0	0.00	3	0	0	0	2	2	0	0	1	1	.286	L	L	6-5	220	7-12-72	1993	Houston, Texas

FIELDING

Catcher	PCT	G	PO	A	E	DP	PB
S. Alomar	.990	49	278	15	3	2	4
Burke	.987	45	215	11	3	1	1
Davis	.991	53	329	17	3	1	5
Olivo	.984	46	237	10	4	5	4

First Base	PCT	G	PO	A	E	DP
Burke	1.000	2	4	2	0	1
Gload	1.000	42	219	12	0	15
Konerko	.995	139	1150	78	6	136
Thomas	1.000	4	31	3	0	2

Second Base	PCT	G	PO	A	E	DP
R. Alomar	.982	13	23	32	1	14

	PCT	G	PO	A	E	DP
Harris	.990	92	163	223	4	46
Uribe	.984	77	154	208	6	49
Valdez	1.000	5	9	4	0	3

Third Base	PCT	G	PO	A	E	DP
Burke	.000	2	0	0	0	0
Crede	.965	144	91	243	12	23
Dransfeldt	1.000	3	2	0	0	0
Uribe	.965	27	14	41	2	5

Shortstop	PCT	G	PO	A	E	DP
Dransfeldt	.947	8	4	14	1	1
Uribe	.983	38	54	115	3	31

	PCT	G	PO	A	E	DP
Valdez	.973	12	13	23	1	3
Valentin	.965	122	186	373	20	85

Outfield	PCT	G	PO	A	E	DP
Borchard	.972	56	101	4	3	0
Burke	1.000	2	2	0	0	0
Everett	1.000	1	1	0	0	0
Gload	.952	39	59	1	3	0
Harris	.983	30	57	1	1	0
Lee	1.000	148	282	11	0	2
Ordonez	.990	43	95	1	1	0
Perez	.986	80	135	8	2	4
Rowand	.975	137	304	10	8	1

Director, Player Development: David Wilder.

Class	Farm Team	League	W	L	Pct.	Finish*	Manager(s)	Affiliate Since
AAA	Charlotte (N.C.) Knights	International	68	74	.479	9th (14)	Nick Capra	1999
AA	Birmingham (Ala.) Barons	Southern	73	66	.525	t-2nd (10)	Razor Shines	1986
High A	Winston-Salem (N.C.) Warthogs	Carolina	74	66	.529	4th (8)	Ken Dominguez/Nick Leyva	1997
Low A	Kannapolis (N.C.) Intimidators	South Atlantic	69	70	.496	10th (16)	Chris Cron	2001
Rookie	Bristol (Va.) White Sox	Appalachian	27	38	.415	9th (10)	Jerry Hairston	1995
Rookie	Great Falls (Mont.) White Sox	Pioneer	42	33	.560	2nd (8)	John Orton	2003

*Finish in overall standings (No. of teams in league)/playoff teams in **boldface**

CHARLOTTE KNIGHTS — Class AAA

INTERNATIONAL LEAGUE

BATTING

	AVG	G	AB	R	H	2B	3B	HR	RBI	BB	SO	SB	CS	OBP	SLG	B	T	HT	WT	DOB	1st Yr	Resides
Aceves, Jon	.285	49	151	22	43	10	0	7	17	15	35	1	1	.363	.490	R	R	6-2	220	3-7-78	1997	Sonora, Mexico
Bell, Mike	.235	124	456	56	107	20	2	25	80	31	117	12	3	.300	.452	R	R	6-2	190	12-7-74	1993	Chandler, Ariz.
Bikowski, Scott	.197	21	66	8	13	1	0	1	4	9	18	0	1	.293	.258	L	L	6-0	190	2-12-77	1999	Suffield, Conn.
Borchard, Joe	.266	82	301	44	80	21	0	16	48	30	68	4	3	.333	.495	S	R	6-5	220	11-25-78	2000	Camarillo, Calif.
Burke, Jamie	.231	37	134	12	31	6	0	2	12	9	15	0	0	.286	.321	R	R	6-0	190	9-24-71	1993	Roseburg, Ore.
Burkhart, Morgan	.111	6	18	1	2	1	0	0	2	9	0	0	0	.200	.167	S	L	5-11	220	1-29-72	1995	St. Louis, Mo.
Cesar, Dionys	.300	28	80	5	24	4	0	1	9	6	13	3	1	.345	.388	S	R	5-10	150	8-27-76	1994	Santo Domingo, D.R.
2-team (18 Lou.)	.254	46	134	12	34	8	0	1	15	10	21	4	1	.308	.336							
Dransfeldt, Kelly	.249	88	305	34	76	18	1	5	30	15	63	5	2	.287	.364	R	R	6-2	190	4-15-75	1996	Morris, Ill.
Hankins, Ryan	.296	89	301	35	89	25	3	7	34	30	33	5	1	.366	.468	R	R	5-11	200	6-30-76	1998	Simi Valley, Calif.
McNeal, Aaron	.243	32	111	9	27	2	0	3	13	9	30	0	0	.311	.342	R	R	6-2	230	4-28-78	1996	Discovery Bay, Calif.
Moore, Michael	.083	9	24	1	2	0	0	0	2	10	0	0	0	.154	.125	R	R	6-4	225	3-7-71	1992	San Pedro, Calif.
Nelson, Bryant	.288	142	560	81	161	37	4	22	83	56	50	13	8	.350	.486	S	R	5-10	205	1-27-74	1994	Crossett, Ark.
Nicholson, Tommy	.000	1	3	0	0	0	0	0	0	0	1	0	0	.000	.000	L	R	5-9	160	8-23-79	2000	Anaheim, Calif.
Paz, Rich	.263	29	95	10	25	0	2	2	7	17	11	0	0	.381	.347	R	R	5-8	170	7-30-77	1994	Los Teques, Venez.
Reed, Jeremy	.275	73	276	44	76	14	1	8	37	36	34	12	1	.357	.420	L	L	6-0	185	6-15-81	2002	La Verne, Calif.
Reyes, Guillermo	.118	6	17	1	2	0	0	0	0	1	7	0	0	.167	.118	S	R	5-9	170	12-29-81	1999	Villa Vasquez, D.R.
Rivera, Mike	.100	11	40	3	4	0	1	0	2	3	12	0	0	.178	.150	R	R	6-0	210	9-8-76	1997	Bayamon, P.R.
Sadler, Donnie	.143	3	7	0	1	0	0	0	1	0	3	0	0	.250	.143	R	R	5-6	175	6-17-75	1994	Waco, Texas
Smith, Bobby	.272	134	508	84	138	37	2	28	89	40	117	12	4	.333	.518	R	R	6-3	210	4-10-74	1992	Oakland, Calif.
Stewart, Chris	.071	5	14	1	1	1	0	0	1	3	0	0	0	.188	.143	R	R	6-4	205	2-19-82	2002	Moreno Valley, Calif.
Taylor, Reggie	.290	58	210	34	61	14	0	11	30	21	45	11	4	.357	.514	L	R	6-1	180	1-12-77	1995	Newberry, S.C.
2-team (61 Lou.)	.274	119	401	62	110	23	1	20	54	34	91	21	7	.333	.462							
Torres, Andres	.295	87	322	49	95	11	4	8	26	35	74	23	7	.371	.429	S	R	5-10	195	1-26-78	1998	Aguada, P.R.
Valdez, Wilson	.302	70	281	37	85	7	2	2	15	12	41	13	5	.338	.363	R	R	5-11	160	5-20-78	1997	Nizao, D.R.
Valentin, Jose	.065	8	31	1	2	0	0	0	2	2	15	0	0	.121	.065	S	R	5-10	180	10-12-69	1987	Manati, P.R.
Valenzuela, Mario	.263	119	429	67	113	20	2	25	66	22	81	3	3	.307	.494	R	R	6-2	210	3-10-77	1996	Isla San Marcos, Mexico

PITCHING

	W	L	ERA	G	GS	CG	SV	IP	H	R	ER	BB	SO	AVG	B	T	HT	WT	DOB	1st Yr	Resides
Bajenaru, Jeff	1	2	1.80	16	0	0	10	20	12	6	4	3	16	.171	R	R	6-1	190	3-21-78	2000	Rancho Cucamonga, Calif.
Campos, Francisco	2	3	4.26	5	5	0	0	32	36	16	15	5	16	.293	R	R	6-0	175	8-12-72	1991	Guaymas, Mexico
Darensbourg, Vic	3	3	2.64	24	0	0	31	25	10	9	9	33	.229	L	L	5-10	180	11-13-70	1992	Henderson, Nev.
Diaz, Felix	10	2	2.97	19	17	0	0	115	95	41	38	24	96	.226	R	R	6-1	180	7-27-80	1998	Las Mata de Farfan, D.R.
Duncan, Courtney	1	0	2.03	18	0	0	1	31	20	11	7	14	22	.183	L	R	6-0	190	10-9-74	1996	Huntsville, Ala.
Grilli, Jason	9	9	4.83	25	25	2	0	153	163	95	82	58	101	.276	R	R	6-4	185	11-11-76	1998	Orlando, Fla.
Kohlmeier, Ryan	3	10	6.24	23	17	1	0	102	116	75	71	23	74	.282	R	R	6-2	225	6-25-77	1997	Cottonwood Falls, Kan.
Larson, Adam	0	2	7.36	6	1	0	0	15	18	12	12	5	6	.310	R	R	6-3	230	12-6-79	2002	Terre Haute, Ind.
Lopez, Orionny	1	0	6.00	2	1	0	0	6	7	4	4	3	7	.280	R	R	6-2	170	4-1-84	2002	West Palm Beach, Fla.
Majewski, Gary	3	3	3.19	35	0	0	14	42	30	16	15	16	41	.208	R	R	6-1	190	2-26-80	1999	Houston, Texas
McNichol, Brian	0	1	6.75	6	1	0	0	12	16	9	9	7	6	.340	L	L	6-5	220	5-20-74	1995	Woodbridge, Va.
Mieses, Jose	0	0	1.80	2	0	0	0	5	2	1	1	3	4	.133	R	R	6-1	175	10-14-77	1997	Santo Domingo, D.R.
Munoz, Arnie	2	6	5.68	13	13	0	0	70	81	48	44	29	60	.288	L	L	5-9	170	6-21-82	1998	Mao, D.R.
Pacheco, Enemencio	0	1	4.82	15	1	0	0	19	18	11	10	15	13	.257	R	R	6-1	170	8-31-78	1997	Santo Domingo, D.R.
Purvis, Rob	0	0	15.00	2	0	0	0	6	11	10	10	5	1	.423	R	R	6-2	200	8-11-77	1999	Tipton, Ind.
Rauch, Jon	6	3	3.11	14	13	0	0	72	57	27	25	25	61	.218	R	R	6-11	260	9-27-78	1999	Tucson, Ariz.
Rodriguez, Ryan	0	1	6.00	1	1	0	0	6	8	4	4	3	6	.348	L	L	6-4	215	7-10-84	2002	Keller, Texas
Sanders, Dave	2	2	6.06	40	0	0	2	52	61	35	35	24	45	.300	L	L	6-0	200	8-29-79	1999	Derby, Kan.
Santiago, Jose	9	9	4.34	57	1	0	7	87	89	51	42	35	47	.268	R	R	6-3	225	11-5-74	1994	Loiza, P.R.
Stewart, Josh	8	7	3.93	25	25	0	0	149	155	70	65	44	82	.275	L	L	6-3	205	12-5-78	1999	Ledbetter, Ky.
Ulacia, Dennis	1	0	1.42	1	1	0	0	6	6	1	1	0	4	.240	L	L	6-1	180	4-2-81	1999	Hialeah, Fla.
Winkelsas, Joe	0	0	6.30	5	0	0	0	10	15	7	7	3	5	.385	R	R	6-2	192	9-14-73	1996	Buffalo, N.Y.
Wright, Dan	0	2	28.69	2	2	0	0	5	17	19	17	6	3	.515	R	R	6-5	240	12-14-77	1999	Batesville, Ark.
Wunsch, Kelly	1	0	2.93	27	0	0	2	28	21	9	9	12	29	.216	L	L	6-5	220	7-12-72	1993	Houston, Texas
Wylie, Mitch	1	4	5.74	28	1	0	1	53	63	41	34	24	42	.306	R	R	6-3	190	1-14-77	1998	Princeton, Iowa
Yofu, Tetsu	5	4	4.62	21	17	1	0	113	107	64	58	33	111	.247	R	R	6-0	185	6-26-73	2003	Fujisaw City, Japan

FIELDING

Catcher	PCT	G	PO	A	E	DP	PB
Aceves	.997	41	284	20	1	5	6
Burke	.993	34	256	29	2	4	5
Hankins	1.000	65	392	43	0	7	9
Stewart	.897	5	25	1	3	0	0

First Base	PCT	G	PO	A	E	DP
Aceves	1.000	1	5	0	0	2

Bell	.994	81	621	38	4	70
Hankins	1.000	6	51	4	0	6
McNeal	1.000	10	90	7	0	11
Paz	.991	11	97	8	1	8
Rivera	.974	9	72	3	2	5
Smith	.995	24	188	17	1	19

Second Base	PCT	G	PO	A	E	DP
Nelson	.977	109	202	256	11	68
Nicholson	1.000	1	1	6	0	1
Paz	1.000	4	10	14	0	3
Smith	.960	29	57	86	6	23

Third Base	PCT	G	PO	A	E	DP
Bell	.921	35	19	63	7	7

	PCT	G	PO	A	E	DP
Cesar	1.000	5	2	4	0	1
Dransfeldt	.974	53	47	104	4	20
Hankins	.882	7	4	11	2	1
Nelson	.875	4	2	5	1	1
Paz	1.000	13	14	18	0	2
Reyes	.667	2	0	2	1	0
Smith	.922	31	16	55	6	7

Shortstop	PCT	G	PO	A	E	DP
Dransfeldt	.978	35	49	85	3	22
Reyes	1.000	4	4	7	0	2
Smith	.971	32	57	77	4	19
Valdez	.979	69	109	176	6	45
Valentin	.895	4	7	10	2	2

Outfield	PCT	G	PO	A	E	DP
Bikowski	1.000	8	20	0	0	0

	PCT	G	PO	A	E	DP
Borchard	.980	79	188	5	4	1
Cesar	1.000	18	31	0	0	0
Moore	1.000	7	9	2	0	0
Nelson	.938	12	15	0	1	0
Reed	.995	73	180	6	1	1
Smith	1.000	2	4	0	0	0
Taylor	.980	57	140	4	3	1
Torres	.975	88	224	6	6	3
Valenzuela	.990	97	183	15	2	5

BIRMINGHAM BARONS — Class AA

SOUTHERN LEAGUE

BATTING	AVG	G	AB	R	H	2B	3B	HR	RBI	BB	SO	SB	CS	OBP	SLG	B	T	HT	WT	DOB	1st Yr	Resides
Aceves, Jon	.225	13	40	10	9	0	0	3	7	12	9	2	0	.404	.450	R	R	6-2	220	3-7-78	1997	Sonora, Mexico
Anderson, Brian	.270	48	185	26	50	9	3	4	27	19	30	3	2	.346	.416	R	R	6-2	205	3-11-82	2003	Tucson, Ariz.
Becker, Brian	.237	25	93	14	22	8	0	4	17	8	21	0	0	.288	.452	R	R	6-7	230	5-26-75	1996	Tempe, Ariz.
Bikowski, Scott	.307	73	257	48	79	15	1	5	40	45	48	4	3	.411	.432	L	L	6-0	190	2-12-77	1999	Suffield, Conn.
Blakely, Darren	.214	27	84	16	18	5	4	4	15	12	32	3	0	.350	.512	B	R	6-1	190	3-14-77	1998	Pensacola, Fla.
Franklin, Micah	.122	25	82	5	10	1	0	1	4	10	25	4	1	.242	.171	S	R	6-0	220	4-25-72	1990	San Francisco, Calif.
Gonzalez, Andy	.170	36	112	19	19	3	0	3	8	10	17	1	0	.262	.277	R	R	6-2	180	12-15-81	2001	Rio Piedras, P.R.
Lopez, Pedro	.217	7	23	3	5	0	1	0	0	5	2	2	0	.379	.304	R	R	6-1	178	4-28-84	2001	Moca, D.R.
Maldonado, Carlos	.265	108	388	48	103	30	1	12	68	52	81	0	3	.353	.441	R	R	6-2	235	1-3-79	1996	Maracaibo, Venez.
Martel, Normand	.301	89	279	38	84	15	2	10	35	25	35	5	3	.356	.477	L	R	6-2	180	8-4-78	2001	Newport News, Va.
McNeal, Aaron	.260	93	350	39	91	16	0	15	53	27	105	2	4	.313	.434	R	R	6-2	230	4-28-78	1996	Discovery Bay, Calif.
Morse, Michael	.287	54	209	30	60	9	5	11	38	15	46	0	4	.336	.536	R	R	6-4	180	3-22-82	2000	Plantation, Fla.
Murphy, Nate	.278	90	335	49	93	11	4	13	45	22	104	10	3	.325	.451	L	L	6-0	215	4-15-75	1996	Tucson, Ariz.
Nicholson, Tommy	.278	38	115	11	32	14	0	0	13	12	32	2	0	.354	.400	R	R	5-9	160	8-23-79	2000	Anaheim, Calif.
Paz, Rich	.233	66	215	26	50	7	0	1	23	35	39	2	1	.357	.279	R	R	5-8	170	7-30-77	1994	Los Teques, Venez.
Reyes, Guillermo	.274	40	124	17	34	3	0	0	7	10	13	8	1	.328	.298	S	R	5-9	170	12-29-81	1999	Villa Vasquez, D.R.
Sasser, Rob	.242	122	418	58	101	24	3	10	55	51	80	11	6	.324	.385	R	R	6-3	210	3-9-75	1993	Oakland, Calif.
Shaffer, Josh	.177	28	79	9	14	4	0	0	3	10	23	1	1	.270	.228	L	R	6-1	180	6-26-80	1999	Yorba Linda, Calif.
Spidale, Mike	.306	126	484	87	148	27	7	4	47	61	72	26	15	.393	.434	R	R	6-2	190	3-12-82	2000	Broadview, Ill.
Stewart, Chris	.231	83	260	26	60	11	2	1	17	22	59	2	4	.299	.300	R	R	6-4	205	2-19-82	2002	Moreno Valley, Calif.
Yan, Ruddy	.267	128	494	56	132	12	10	1	48	31	82	35	19	.315	.338	S	R	6-0	170	1-13-82	1999	La Romana, D.R.

PITCHING	W	L	ERA	G	GS	CG	SV	IP	H	R	ER	BB	SO	AVG	B	T	HT	WT	DOB	1st Yr	Resides
Allen, Wyatt	0	4	4.93	33	2	0	0	49	52	30	27	19	55	.272	R	R	6-4	205	4-12-80	2001	Brentwood, Tenn.
Bajenaru, Jeff	2	0	1.34	32	0	0	12	34	19	9	5	11	51	.158	R	R	6-1	190	3-21-78	2000	Rancho Cucamonga, Calif.
Bullard, Jim	8	4	3.47	37	15	0	0	114	107	52	44	44	74	.245	L	L	6-7	230	12-29-79	2001	West Covina, Calif.
Duncan, Courtney	0	0	0.93	4	2	0	0	10	4	2	1	3	5	.125	L	R	6-0	190	10-9-74	1996	Huntsville, Ala.
Fields, Josh	3	4	2.55	52	0	0	4	74	54	22	21	21	72	.204	R	R	6-1	175	1-20-80	2001	Hungry Horse, Mont.
Honel, Kris	0	1	9.00	3	1	0	0	6	4	6	6	5	7	.200	R	R	6-5	205	11-7-82	2001	Bourbonnais, Ill.
Keller, Kris	0	3	8.25	15	0	0	0	24	35	26	22	7	14	.324	R	R	6-2	260	3-1-78	1996	Atlantic Beach, Fla.
LaMura, B.J.	4	4	3.69	24	2	0	2	39	31	19	16	21	39	.214	R	R	6-1	200	1-1-81	2002	Ronkonkoma, N.Y.
Lubisich, Nik	0	0	2.42	10	3	0	0	26	30	8	7	3	15	.294	L	L	6-2	195	4-19-79	2001	Portland, Ore.
McCarthy, Brandon	3	1	3.46	4	4	0	0	26	23	10	10	6	29	.235	R	R	6-7	180	7-7-83	2002	Colorado Springs, Colo.
McNichol, Brian	7	2	1.48	42	0	0	2	61	39	10	10	21	41	.185	L	L	6-5	220	5-20-74	1995	Woodbridge, Va.
Meaux, Ryan	7	9	4.04	29	21	0	0	140	163	68	63	46	103	.298	L	L	5-11	170	10-5-78	2001	Denver, Colo.
Munoz, Arnie	7	2	2.05	13	13	0	0	75	52	24	17	22	68	.195	L	L	5-9	170	6-21-82	1999	Mao, D.R.
Murray, Brad	0	4	9.50	11	0	0	1	18	31	20	19	9	7	.383	L	L	5-11	170	8-20-78	2000	La Belle, Fla.
Pacheco, Enemencio	0	0	3.55	5	2	0	0	13	10	6	5	5	3	.208	R	R	6-1	180	8-31-78	1997	Santo Domingo, D.R.
Phillips, Heath	12	10	4.02	27	26	0	0	154	179	78	69	36	107	.295	L	L	6-3	235	3-24-82	2001	Evansville, Ind.
Purvis, Rob	0	0	3.78	11	0	0	0	17	10	8	7	7	10	.175	R	R	6-2	200	8-11-77	1999	Tipton, Ind.
Smith, Matt	3	4	1.83	70	0	0	13	79	58	21	16	26	50	.212	R	R	6-5	240	8-14-78	1999	Godfrey, Ill.
Ulacia, Dennis	8	8	3.77	28	23	0	0	129	137	63	54	36	107	.269	L	L	6-1	180	4-2-81	1999	Hialeah, Fla.
Villacis, Eduardo	6	4	3.28	19	18	0	0	96	93	40	35	34	71	.257	R	R	6-2	180	8-29-79	1998	Miranda, Venez.
Yofu, Tetsu	3	2	2.63	7	7	0	0	41	39	13	12	9	41	.258	R	R	6-0	185	6-26-73	2003	Fujisawa City, Japan

FIELDING

Catcher	PCT	G	PO	A	E	DP	PB
Aceves	.983	8	53	6	1	0	1
Maldonado	1.000	61	391	34	0	5	3
Stewart	.985	76	555	41	9	4	14

First Base	PCT	G	PO	A	E	DP
Becker	1.000	22	208	10	0	13
Maldonado	.974	5	34	3	1	0
McNeal	.993	84	660	56	5	60
Murphy	1.000	1	11	0	0	3
Sasser	.990	31	269	22	3	18

Second Base	PCT	G	PO	A	E	DP
Nicholson	1.000	8	14	30	0	5
Reyes	.957	6	11	11	1	2

		1.000	2	0	1	0	0
Shaffer		1.000	2	0	1	0	0
Yan		.980	127	226	323	11	56

Third Base	PCT	G	PO	A	E	DP
Gonzalez	.833	1	2	3	1	1
Nicholson	.952	24	17	43	3	5
Paz	.943	52	35	98	8	12
Reyes	.833	5	2	8	2	0
Sasser	.889	55	29	83	14	12
Shaffer	.886	16	10	21	4	2

Shortstop	PCT	G	PO	A	E	DP
Gonzalez	.941	34	59	84	9	16
Lopez	.969	7	10	21	1	3
Morse	.944	54	59	125	11	21

	PCT	G	PO	A	E	DP
Nicholson	1.000	1	0	2	0	0
Paz	.975	17	30	48	2	6
Reyes	.958	27	29	62	4	9
Shaffer	1.000	10	12	17	0	3

Outfield	PCT	G	PO	A	E	DP
Anderson	.990	44	95	2	1	1
Bikowski	.987	66	141	7	2	2
Blakely	1.000	29	52	2	0	0
Franklin	.947	15	17	1	1	0
Martel	.971	66	128	5	4	0
Murphy	.984	84	175	4	3	2
Sasser	1.000	14	24	0	0	0
Spidale	.985	122	252	4	4	0
Yan	1.000	1	1	0	0	0

WINSTON-SALEM WARTHOGS — High Class A

CAROLINA LEAGUE

BATTING	AVG	G	AB	R	H	2B	3B	HR	RBI	BB	SO	SB	CS	OBP	SLG	B	T	HT	WT	DOB	1st Yr	Resides
Amador, Chris	.257	103	335	36	86	20	1	5	32	8	91	18	5	.282	.367	R	R	5-10	160	12-14-82	2000	Camuy, P.R.
Anderson, Brian	.319	69	254	43	81	22	4	8	46	29	44	10	1	.394	.531	R	R	6-2	205	3-11-82	2003	Tucson, Ariz.
Becker, Brian	.302	109	397	59	120	30	4	22	76	30	94	0	2	.349	.564	R	R	6-7	230	5-26-75	1996	Tempe, Ariz.

BATTING

	AVG	G	AB	R	H	2B	3B	HR	RBI	BB	SO	SB	CS	OBP	SLG	B	T	HT	WT	DOB	1st Yr	Resides
Blakely, Darren	.275	84	305	49	84	17	2	25	58	15	77	10	1	.322	.590	B	R	6-1	190	3-14-77	1998	Pensacola, Fla.
Brice, Thomas	.273	43	161	19	44	13	1	3	23	13	32	5	1	.333	.422	L	L	6-5	210	8-24-81	2002	Mile End, South Australia
Cameron, Troy	.175	13	40	2	7	3	1	0	3	2	10	0	0	.233	.300	S	R	5-11	180	8-31-78	1997	Plantation, Fla.
Fields, Josh	.285	66	256	36	73	12	4	7	39	18	74	0	0	.333	.445	R	R	6-2	210	12-14-82	2004	Stillwater, Okla.
Garcia, Cip	.188	11	16	4	3	0	0	0	0	3	5	0	0	.316	.188	R	R	6-0	200	10-23-78	1997	Albuquerque, N.M.
Gonzalez, Andy	.255	83	318	61	81	19	1	8	31	52	57	3	3	.369	.396	R	R	6-2	180	12-15-81	2001	Rio Piedras, P.R.
Lee, Carlos	.195	37	133	10	26	3	0	1	19	8	17	1	0	.243	.241	R	R	6-1	238	9-29-81	2000	Provincia, Panama
Lopez, Pedro	.292	112	432	62	126	13	0	4	35	23	35	12	9	.331	.350	R	R	6-1	178	4-28-84	2001	Moca, D.R.
Martel, Normand	.206	26	68	9	14	1	0	1	3	2	8	5	1	.239	.265	L	R	6-0	180	8-4-78	2001	Newport News, Va.
Molina, Gustavo	.286	25	77	10	22	6	0	3	14	5	16	0	0	.333	.481	R	R	6-2	180	2-24-82	2000	La Guaira, Venez.
Myers, Mike	.286	13	21	4	6	1	0	0	3	4	3	0	0	.423	.333	R	R	6-1	190	12-11-79	2002	St. Petersburg, Fla.
Nanita, Ricardo	.241	55	187	21	45	8	1	2	28	23	46	7	4	.327	.326	L	L	6-1	180	6-12-81	2003	Santo Domingo, D.R.
Nicholson, Tommy	.259	60	205	37	53	12	0	2	10	32	50	6	4	.361	.346	L	R	5-9	160	8-23-79	2000	Anaheim, Calif.
Perez, Melvin	.214	12	28	3	6	0	0	0	1	1	6	0	0	.241	.214	R	R	6-1	190	2-2-84	2002	San Cristobal, D.R.
Rogowski, Casey	.286	136	465	88	133	28	2	18	90	91	94	16	9	.401	.471	L	L	6-4	250	5-1-81	1999	Livonia, Mich.
Rosa, Wally	.225	84	271	23	61	11	0	1	17	25	52	3	3	.291	.277	R	R	6-1	185	11-28-81	2000	Miami, Fla.
Shaffer, Josh	.103	29	87	2	9	1	0	1	7	4	29	0	2	.143	.149	L	R	6-1	180	6-26-80	1999	Yorba Linda, Calif.
Sweeney, Ryan	.283	134	515	71	146	22	3	7	66	40	65	8	6	.342	.379	L	L	6-3	200	2-20-85	2003	Cedar Rapids, Iowa
Wade, Ryan	.235	6	17	0	4	1	0	0	0	1	4	0	0	.278	.294	R	R	6-5	220	10-31-75	1998	Moore, Okla.
Williams, Peanut	.213	22	61	8	13	2	0	2	7	4	12	0	0	.258	.344	R	R	6-3	210	10-3-77	1996	Nacogdoches, Texas

PITCHING

	W	L	ERA	G	GS	CG	SV	IP	H	R	ER	BB	SO	AVG	B	T	HT	WT	DOB	1st Yr	Resides
An, Byeong-Hak	2	5	5.89	31	9	0	1	70	84	61	46	31	35	.296	L	L	6-2	230	7-1-80	2001	Bu Chun City, Korea
Castro, Fabio	1	1	1.69	8	0	0	0	11	4	2	2	3	11	.114	L	L	5-8	150	1-20-85	2002	Monte Cristi, D.R.
Castro, Julio	3	3	5.54	37	0	0	0	52	40	34	32	18	61	.206	R	R	6-1	165	6-30-81	1998	San Pedro de Macoris, D.R.
Dizard, Fraser	0	0	0.00	1	0	0	0	2	0	0	0	0	2	.000	L	L	6-0	195	8-6-81	2003	Edmonds, Wash.
Espinal, Jose	8	2	3.48	42	2	0	1	75	69	34	29	23	71	.247	R	R	6-2	205	8-31-76	1994	Pedernales, D.R.
Hernandez, Fernando	0	0	0.00	2	0	0	0	2	1	0	0	1	1	.167	R	R	5-11	190	7-31-84	2003	Miami, Fla.
Hudson, Jeremy	0	3	8.36	13	3	0	0	38	48	41	35	25	13	.320	R	R	6-7	210	3-15-80	2002	Cullman, Ala.
Hummel, Rick	0	0	34.71	3	0	0	0	2	11	9	9	2	1	.647	R	R	6-2	190	9-12-80	2002	Wonder Lake, Ill.
LaMura, B.J.	4	5	5.58	12	11	2	0	61	77	45	38	29	47	.313	R	R	6-1	200	1-1-81	2002	Ronkonkoma, N.Y.
Larson, Adam	1	1	8.82	11	1	0	1	16	25	16	16	8	12	.352	R	R	6-3	230	12-6-79	2002	Terre Haute, Ind.
Little, Jeff	0	0	2.25	2	0	0	1	4	4	1	1	0	0	.250	R	R	6-3	200	4-30-80	2002	West Lafayette, Ind.
Lubisich, Nik	5	7	4.35	22	16	0	0	103	129	56	50	23	56	.311	L	L	6-2	195	4-19-79	2001	Portland, Ore.
Lumsden, Tyler	3	1	4.12	15	3	0	0	39	45	25	18	20	31	.283	L	L	6-4	205	5-9-83	2004	Roanoke, Va.
McCarthy, Brandon	6	0	2.08	8	8	0	0	52	31	12	12	3	60	.168	R	R	6-7	180	7-7-83	2002	Colorado Springs, Colo.
Mieses, Jose	3	5	5.40	21	5	0	0	45	51	30	27	29	33	.297	R	R	6-1	175	10-14-77	1997	Santo Domingo, D.R.
Miller, Brian	1	1	4.81	7	7	0	0	34	34	19	18	16	19	.270	R	R	6-3	200	10-18-82	2002	Charlotte, Mich.
Murray, Brad	3	4	3.82	48	0	0	2	64	68	32	27	13	30	.278	L	R	5-11	170	8-20-78	2000	La Belle, Fla.
Pollok, Dwayne	2	4	3.28	58	0	0	38	60	59	23	22	8	49	.260	R	R	6-4	200	11-12-80	2003	San Antonio, Texas
Purvis, Rob	4	5	4.89	34	6	0	0	77	93	45	42	45	29	.313	R	R	6-2	200	8-11-77	1999	Tipton, Ind.
Ray, Kenny	12	8	4.08	29	18	0	1	124	124	63	56	43	99	.267	R	R	6-2	200	12-27-74	1993	Phoenix, Ariz.
Reynoso, Paulino	3	2	3.95	25	19	0	1	84	79	42	37	41	70	.248	L	L	6-3	215	8-10-80	1999	Santiago, D.R.
Stumm, Jason	1	2	5.68	8	0	0	0	13	15	9	8	5	7	.300	R	R	6-2	210	4-13-81	1999	Centralia, Wash.
Tracey, Sean	9	8	2.73	27	27	0	0	148	109	60	45	69	130	.210	L	R	6-3	205	11-14-80	2002	Upland, Calif.
Wasserman, Ehren	1	0	2.70	10	0	0	1	10	11	4	3	5	5	.268	R	R	6-0	185	12-6-80	2003	Birmingham, Ala.
Whisler, Wes	2	1	3.38	5	5	0	0	27	17	10	10	7	13	.185	L	L	6-5	235	4-7-83	2004	Noblesville, Ind.
Winkelsas, Joe	0	0	6.75	1	0	0	0	1	4	1	1	0	1	.500	R	R	6-2	192	9-14-73	1996	Buffalo, N.Y.

FIELDING

Catcher	PCT	G	PO	A	E	DP	PB
Lee	.981	30	188	15	4	0	10
Molina	1.000	23	160	11	0	1	7
Rosa	.990	82	520	79	6	3	20
Wade	1.000	6	28	1	0	0	2

First Base	PCT	G	PO	A	E	DP
Becker	1.000	30	282	19	0	17
Brice	1.000	1	7	0	0	2
Cameron	1.000	1	5	0	0	0
Garcia	1.000	1	2	1	0	0
Molina	1.000	2	3	0	0	0
Rogowski	.989	114	951	84	11	91
Shaffer	1.000	1	1	1	0	1

Second Base	PCT	G	PO	A	E	DP
Amador	.952	95	158	254	21	60
Cameron	1.000	1	2	1	0	0

	PCT	G	PO	A	E	DP
Gonzalez	1.000	9	9	18	0	3
Lopez	1.000	5	5	10	0	2
Myers	1.000	6	17	13	0	3
Nicholson	.959	17	26	44	3	9
Shaffer	.964	15	22	31	2	6

Third Base	PCT	G	PO	A	E	DP
Cameron	.929	12	12	14	2	3
Fields	.931	58	33	116	11	4
Gonzalez	.908	39	33	66	10	3
Myers	1.000	1	2	2	0	0
Nicholson	.984	24	11	51	1	4
Perez	.955	12	11	10	1	2
Shaffer	.857	4	2	4	1	0

Shortstop	PCT	G	PO	A	E	DP
Gonzalez	.941	35	53	123	11	22
Lopez	.971	104	187	316	15	64

	PCT	G	PO	A	E	DP
Myers	1.000	4	2	0	0	0
Nicholson	1.000	3	6	10	0	2
Shaffer	1.000	1	0	2	0	1

Outfield	PCT	G	PO	A	E	DP
Amador	1.000	1	0	1	0	0
Anderson	.993	67	131	5	1	0
Blakely	.981	78	154	5	3	0
Brice	.986	43	67	4	1	0
Martel	.939	16	30	1	2	1
Myers	1.000	1	0	0	0	0
Nanita	.968	58	87	3	3	0
Nicholson	1.000	10	15	1	0	0
Rogowski	.962	14	25	0	1	0
Sweeney	.973	132	241	14	7	3
Williams	.939	21	29	2	2	0

KANNAPOLIS INTIMIDATORS — Low Class A

SOUTH ATLANTIC LEAGUE

BATTING

	AVG	G	AB	R	H	2B	3B	HR	RBI	BB	SO	SB	CS	OBP	SLG	B	T	HT	WT	DOB	1st Yr	Resides
Bounds, Brandon	.265	86	306	42	81	21	3	11	44	15	83	1	2	.299	.461	L	R	6-5	190	8-10-81	2001	Arlington, Texas
Brice, Thomas	.315	59	219	38	69	16	2	7	32	29	48	10	4	.397	.502	L	L	6-5	210	8-24-81	2002	Mile End, Australia
Castillo, Cesar	.143	11	28	3	4	0	0	0	2	3	5	2	0	.226	.143	R	R	5-10	180	6-26-79	2002	Yuma, Ariz.
Cook, David	.210	61	195	31	41	8	1	8	28	31	63	5	5	.336	.385	R	R	5-11	195	7-21-81	2003	Columbus, Ohio
Daigle, Leo	.292	119	445	56	130	29	2	18	90	45	82	5	2	.368	.488	R	R	6-3	220	9-18-79	1998	Spring Valley, Calif.
Gonzalez, Andy	.271	12	48	6	13	1	0	1	3	4	8	1	2	.333	.354	R	R	6-2	180	12-15-81	2001	Rio Piedras, P.R.
Gray, Antoin	.294	123	480	82	141	32	4	13	49	39	97	10	5	.356	.458	R	R	5-9	195	3-3-83	2003	Hattiesburg, Miss.
Haggerty, Cory	.251	82	251	42	63	15	0	4	23	39	67	8	5	.366	.359	L	R	6-0	180	8-25-81	2003	Manlius, N.Y.
Kelly, Chris	.105	6	19	0	2	0	0	0	2	6	0	0		.190	.105	R	R	6-1	195	2-23-82	2003	Las Vegas, Nev.
King, Clint	.218	34	119	11	26	11	0	2	7	12	28	0	0	.286	.361	L	R	5-11	205	8-6-82	2003	Pearl, Miss.
Lee, Carlos	.315	30	108	10	34	7	0	4	15	3	10	1	0	.339	.491	R	R	6-1	238	9-29-81	2000	Provincia, Panama

BATTING	AVG	G	AB	R	H	2B	3B	HR	RBI	BB	SO	SB	CS	OBP	SLG	B	T	HT	WT	DOB	1st Yr	Resides
Lisk, Charlie	.193	91	301	25	58	8	1	9	43	12	112	8	2	.234	.316	R	R	6-3	200	1-3-83	2001	Fort Mill, S.C.
Molina, Gustavo	.162	37	105	16	17	3	0	4	17	12	24	2	1	.273	.305	R	R	6-2	180	2-24-82	2000	La Guaira, Venez.
Morris, Seth	.193	82	244	25	47	13	1	7	25	11	80	3	1	.230	.340	R	R	6-2	200	8-25-80	2002	Hamilton, Ohio
Nanita, Ricardo	.316	61	225	32	71	12	2	1	31	26	32	5	4	.391	.400	L	L	6-1	180	6-12-81	2003	Santo Domingo, D.R.
Schnurstein, Micah	.278	132	493	53	137	33	0	6	59	27	104	15	4	.322	.381	R	R	6-1	200	7-18-84	2002	Henderson, Nev.
Valido, Robert	.251	123	458	66	115	25	0	4	44	36	59	28	13	.313	.332	R	R	6-2	180	5-16-85	2003	Miami, Fla.
Whisler, Wes	.289	11	38	2	11	2	0	1	5	1	7	0	0	.308	.421	L	L	6-5	235	4-7-83	2004	Noblesville, Ind.
Whitesides, Jake	.223	33	103	14	23	3	4	1	12	5	23	2	0	.259	.359	L	R	5-11	200	6-23-81	2000	Columbia, Mo.
Young, Chris	.261	136	467	83	122	31	5	24	56	67	146	31	9	.365	.503	R	R	6-2	170	9-5-83	2002	Houston, Texas

PITCHING	W	L	ERA	G	GS	CG	SV	IP	H	R	ER	BB	SO	AVG	B	T	HT	WT	DOB	1st Yr	Resides
An, Byeong Hak	0	2	3.60	2	2	0	0	10	8	7	4	10	3	.205	L	L	6-2	230	7-1-80	2001	Bu Chun City, Korea
Banks, Demetrius	0	0	9.00	5	0	0	0	5	5	6	5	5	11	.250	L	L	6-0	160	5-23-83	2002	Austell, Ga.
Bello, Juan	0	0	6.00	2	0	0	0	3	4	2	2	3	3	.308	R	R	6-2	170	5-24-84	2002	San Pedro de Macoris, D.R.
Castro, Fabio	4	0	3.00	37	0	0	3	51	44	20	17	23	44	.227	L	L	5-8	150	1-20-85	2002	Monte Cristi, D.R.
Deininger, Todd	1	1	5.80	26	1	0	0	36	35	26	23	35	25	.259	R	R	6-3	200	9-4-81	2002	Joliet, Ill.
Dizard, Fraser	0	1	2.83	27	1	0	1	48	38	19	15	33	39	.226	L	L	6-0	195	8-6-81	2003	Edmonds, Wash.
Flores, Rafael	8	11	3.75	23	22	0	0	127	139	71	53	33	65	.279	R	R	6-7	220	4-26-84	2003	El Paso, Texas
Gonzalez, Gio	1	2	3.76	8	8	0	0	41	39	20	17	20	34	.244	R	L	5-11	180	9-19-85	2004	Hialeah, Fla.
Haeger, Charles	1	3	2.01	5	5	0	0	31	31	17	7	12	21	.267	R	R	6-0	180	8-25-81	2003	Manilus, N.Y.
Haggerty, Cory	0	0	0.00	1	0	0	0	0	0	0	0	0	0	.000	R	R	6-0	170			
Haigwood, Daniel	10	4	4.87	22	22	0	0	116	102	68	63	59	101	.238	S	L	6-2	200	11-19-83	2002	Pleasant Plains, Ark.
Hernandez, Fernando	3	3	2.74	28	0	0	4	46	42	20	14	16	61	.251	R	R	5-11	190	7-31-84	2003	Miami, Fla.
Hudson, Jeremy	0	0	1.74	5	0	0	0	10	9	2	2	5	5	.281	R	R	6-7	210	3-15-80	2002	Cullman, Ala.
Hummel, Rick	0	0	36.00	2	0	0	0	1	4	4	4	0	0	.571	R	R	6-2	190	9-12-80	2002	Wonder Lake, Ill.
Hurd, John	0	0	3.60	13	0	0	0	20	19	9	8	12	17	.271	R	R	5-11	185	1-29-83	2003	Fruitvale, B.C.
Kane, Kyle	0	0	2.08	4	0	0	0	4	5	5	1	3	6	.278	L	R	6-3	210	2-4-76	1998	Reno, Nev.
Larson, Adam	3	1	4.20	18	0	0	2	30	35	17	14	8	23	.292	R	R	6-3	230	12-6-79	2002	Terre Haute, Ind.
Lopez, Orionny	2	3	2.75	33	0	0	1	56	48	21	17	18	51	.234	R	R	6-2	170	4-1-84	2002	West Palm Beach, Fla.
McCarthy, Brandon	8	5	3.64	15	15	3	0	94	80	41	38	21	113	.232	R	R	6-3	200	10-18-82	2002	Colorado Springs, Colo.
Miller, Brian	8	9	3.86	21	21	0	0	112	103	57	48	54	84	.246	R	R	6-1	190	10-25-81	2003	Boulder, Colo.
Moat, Mike	3	2	4.79	23	0	0	3	47	52	29	25	22	45	.287	R	R	6-2	200	8-13-80	2002	Tucson, Ariz.
Morris, Seth	0	0	7.71	3	0	0	0	2	5	2	2	2	1	.455	R	R	6-2	200	8-25-80	2002	Hamilton, Ohio
Novoa, Yunior	0	0	4.91	2	0	0	0	4	5	3	2	2	5	.333	L	L	6-3	170	9-11-84	2003	Santo Domingo, D.R.
Pena, Luis	0	4	6.29	10	2	0	0	24	27	22	17	6	25	.270	R	R	6-0	170	1-21-81	2001	La Vega, D.R.
Rodriguez, Ryan	10	9	4.04	26	26	0	0	147	150	83	66	59	100	.265	L	L	6-4	215	7-10-84	2002	Keller, Texas
Russell, Adam	0	2	9.00	2	2	0	0	10	18	11	10	7	3	.383	R	R	6-5	190	4-14-83	2004	North Olmsted, Ohio
Tisch, Tim	1	4	5.27	12	6	1	0	41	43	26	24	18	25	.277	L	L	6-5	190	4-11-80	2002	Santee, Calif.
Wasserman, Ehren	2	3	2.56	51	0	0	30	56	44	20	16	16	42	.221	S	R	6-0	185	12-6-80	2003	Birmingham, Ala.
Whisler, Wes	4	1	3.18	10	7	0	0	45	52	29	16	11	28	.281	L	L	6-5	235	4-7-83	2004	Noblesville, Ind.

FIELDING

Catcher	PCT	G	PO	A	E	DP	PB
Castillo	.970	10	61	3	2	1	1
Lee	.976	21	142	20	4	1	5
Lisk	.983	80	522	65	10	1	36
Molina	.993	36	262	41	2	3	5

First Base	PCT	G	PO	A	E	DP
Bounds	.990	27	193	15	2	6
Brice	1.000	1	7	0	0	0
Daigle	.995	110	850	67	5	45
Kelly	.964	6	50	3	2	5
Lee	1.000	1	6	1	0	1
Molina	1.000	1	1	0	0	0
Morris	1.000	1	1	0	0	0

Second Base	PCT	G	PO	A	E	DP
Gonzalez	1.000	2	5	4	0	1
Gray	.940	98	176	260	28	35
Haggerty	.966	35	61	79	5	5
Valido	1.000	9	11	26	0	3
Whitesides	1.000	1	1	2	0	0

Third Base	PCT	G	PO	A	E	DP
Daigle	1.000	2	1	4	0	0
Gonzalez	1.000	2	0	4	0	0
Gray	.909	11	6	24	3	0
Schnurstein	.923	127	94	195	24	8

Shortstop	PCT	G	PO	A	E	DP
Gonzalez	.949	9	15	22	2	4

Haggerty	.947	27	33	56	5	6
Schnurstein	1.000	1	1	0	0	1
Valido	.948	111	175	335	28	35

Outfield	PCT	G	PO	A	E	DP
Brice	.969	52	91	2	3	0
Cook	.971	50	96	6	3	0
Daigle	.667	4	2	0	1	0
Haggerty	.882	12	14	1	2	0
King	1.000	20	30	2	0	0
Morris	.962	76	136	14	6	1
Nanita	.961	63	116	7	5	1
Whitesides	.966	30	56	0	2	0
Young	.969	132	335	11	11	1

GREAT FALLS WHITE SOX — Rookie

PIONEER LEAGUE

BATTING	AVG	G	AB	R	H	2B	3B	HR	RBI	BB	SO	SB	CS	OBP	SLG	B	T	HT	WT	DOB	1st Yr	Resides
Alvarez, Fernando	.209	38	129	20	27	8	0	3	13	12	43	4	3	.277	.341	L	L	6-1	205	7-29-80	2004	Miami, Fla.
Berry, Boomer	.307	65	254	55	78	10	1	4	29	34	35	14	3	.399	.402	L	R	5-11	180	12-5-80	2004	Topeka, Kan.
Collaro, Tom	.287	66	268	48	77	7	6	18	67	13	82	4	3	.331	.560	R	R	6-4	210	4-4-83	2002	Sunrise, Fla.
Cook, Aaron	.301	34	113	26	34	3	1	8	22	20	26	2	2	.410	.558	R	R	5-11	195	7-21-81	2003	Columbus, Ohio
Cooper, Caleb	.274	21	73	17	20	10	0	1	7	5	19	2	0	.346	.452	R	R	6-0	215	12-25-82	2004	Hayward, Calif.
Deuchler, Matt	.244	43	160	16	39	11	1	3	27	21	36	3	2	.342	.381	R	R	5-11	205	4-6-81	2003	Ellicott City, Md.
Hansen, Josh	.290	40	145	26	42	11	2	5	17	22	39	2	1	.387	.497	R	R	6-2	215	12-15-80	2003	Wyoming, Minn.
Kelly, Chris	.315	65	270	45	85	14	1	11	51	15	75	1	1	.356	.496	R	R	6-1	195	2-23-82	2003	Las Vegas, Nev.
Lucy, Donny	.239	50	176	19	42	7	1	1	26	17	36	13	1	.312	.307	R	R	6-3	210	8-8-82	2004	Fallbrook, Calif.
Martin, Scott	.288	59	219	37	63	15	2	7	33	18	57	14	10	.363	.470	R	R	6-1	205	5-16-81	2003	Middletown, Del.
McCarthy, Ryan	.260	44	173	33	45	9	1	4	24	23	45	6	2	.363	.393	R	R	6-3	200	9-4-84	2004	Thousand Oaks, Calif.
McNeil, Derrick	.205	44	146	23	30	7	0	2	13	19	67	6	3	.302	.295	R	R	5-11	185	11-4-81	2004	Lutz, Fla.
Perez, Melvin	.200	18	55	7	11	1	0	0	2	8	14	2	1	.313	.218	R	R	6-1	170	2-2-84	2002	San Cristobal, D.R.
Ricks, Adam	.305	52	203	38	62	20	1	3	28	28	29	7	2	.411	.458	S	R	5-10	195	9-24-82	2004	San Ramon, Calif.
Rivera, Jhonny	.238	26	84	14	20	2	3	1	9	2	16	1	2	.253	.369	R	R	6-1	170	7-4-83	2000	Guarenas, Venez.
Roberts, Daron	.252	38	139	17	35	4	0	3	24	17	34	4	5	.298	.345	R	R	6-0	215	2-25-83	2004	Portland, Ore.

GAMES BY POSITION: C—Deuchler 32, Hansen 2, Lucy 44. **1B**—Alvarez 1, Collaro 10, Hansen 19, Kelly 55, Roberts 1. **2B**—Berry 65, McNeil 2, Ricks 13. **3B**—Cooper 16, Kelly 12, Perez 15, Ricks 37. **SS**—Berry 1, McCarthy 31, McNeil 41, Perez 3, Ricks 2. **OF**—Alvarez 27, Collaro 56, Cook 35, Martin 58, Rivera 25, Roberts 36.

PITCHING	W	L	ERA	G	GS	CG	SV	IP	H	R	ER	BB	SO	AVG	B	T	HT	WT	DOB	1st Yr	Resides
Bakker, Garry	4	2	4.50	13	12	0	0	64	64	38	32	24	50	.259	R	R	6-2	208	3-28-83	2004	Sloatsburg, N.Y.
Banks, Demetrius	1	0	2.00	21	0	0	3	36	19	12	8	22	48	.153	L	L	6-0	160	5-23-83	2002	Austell, Ga.
Doyle, Travis	1	2	3.60	11	4	0	1	25	25	13	10	15	27	.255	L	L	6-6	205	8-15-83	2004	Applegate, Mich.
Egbert, John	4	1	3.38	17	9	0	0	59	51	25	22	33	52	.243	L	R	6-3	205	5-12-83	2004	Rutherford, N.J.
Everly, Eric	3	4	4.35	18	8	0	0	52	66	33	25	19	54	.306	R	R	6-3	200	12-8-83	2004	Dallas, Texas
Hansen, Grant	1	2	5.64	6	5	0	0	22	23	17	14	19	16	.284	R	R	6-6	225	2-25-83	2004	Edmond, Okla.
Hurd, John	4	4	6.38	25	2	0	3	37	47	32	26	17	29	.309	R	R	5-11	185	1-29-83	2003	Fruitvale, B.C.
Johnson, J.D.	1	3	6.98	12	0	0	0	19	18	21	15	16	21	.243	R	R	6-5	190	12-10-82	2002	Moriarty, N.M.
Kane, Kyle	1	0	6.35	7	0	0	2	6	5	4	4	3	7	.227	L	R	6-3	210	2-4-76	1998	Reno, Nev.
Liotta, Ray	5	1	2.54	14	11	0	0	64	59	27	18	28	65	.248	L	L	6-3	220	4-3-83	2004	Kenner, La.
Little, Jeff	0	1	2.63	13	0	0	5	14	14	5	4	6	14	.259	R	R	6-3	200	4-30-80	2002	West Lafayette, Ind.
Logan, Boone	3	7	5.60	18	9	0	1	64	74	48	40	31	48	.287	R	L	6-5	200	8-13-84	2003	Helotes, Texas
Marshall, Jay	2	0	3.45	4	2	0	0	16	19	9	6	6	17	.302	L	L	6-5	185	2-25-83	2003	Manchester, Mo.
McGary, Gerron	0	1	2.08	21	0	0	0	30	23	9	7	29	38	.213	L	L	6-0	180	2-14-82	2002	Texarkana, Texas
Nachreiner, Matt	1	0	6.88	11	0	0	0	17	14	13	13	13	12	.237	L	R	6-2	190	11-17-84	2003	Cedar Park, Texas
Reed, Rylan	1	1	18.90	5	0	0	0	3	7	12	7	7	1	.389	R	R	6-7	260	11-18-81	2001	Round Rock, Texas
Russell, Adam	4	0	2.37	15	4	0	0	38	31	11	10	18	33	.223	R	R	6-8	250	4-14-83	2004	North Olmsted, Fla.
Suarez, Sony	5	2	5.37	18	9	0	2	64	66	46	38	41	62	.269	R	R	6-0	160	5-8-83	2000	Monte Cristi, D.R.
Thompson, Sean	0	1	5.40	8	0	0	0	8	13	6	5	5	7	.371	L	L	6-2	190	1-3-81	2003	Goletia, Calif.
Zaleski, Matt	1	1	3.35	24	0	0	3	40	53	18	15	6	34	.325	R	R	6-0	205	12-2-81	2004	North Aurora, Ill.

BRISTOL WHITE SOX — Rookie

APPALACHIAN LEAGUE

BATTING	AVG	G	AB	R	H	2B	3B	HR	RBI	BB	SO	SB	CS	OBP	SLG	B	T	HT	WT	DOB	1st Yr	Resides
Alcantara, Gilbert	.185	38	81	8	15	1	0	0	2	11	34	4	1	.298	.198	R	R	6-0	170	11-27-83	2002	Santo Domingo, D.R.
Allen, Brandon	.205	58	185	17	38	9	1	3	23	16	60	2	3	.280	.314	L	R	6-2	235	2-12-86	2004	Montgomery, Texas
Castillo, Cesar	.118	6	17	1	2	1	0	0	0	4	3	0	0	.286	.176	R	R	5-10	180	6-26-79	2002	Yuma, Ariz.
Castillo, Javier	.271	60	207	40	56	8	1	6	35	30	58	3	2	.372	.406	R	R	6-2	185	8-29-83	2002	Chitre, Panama
De los Santos, Jose	.314	54	204	29	64	10	1	0	35	5	21	1	2	.338	.373	R	R	5-11	160	8-10-84	2002	La Vega, D.R.
Foust, J.D.	.284	28	109	14	31	7	1	4	19	4	21	2	5	.319	.477	R	R	6-4	200	5-7-81	2003	Norwood, Ohio
Guest, Garret	.133	20	45	9	6	0	0	0	1	5	10	0	1	.235	.133	R	R	5-11	170	7-3-83	2004	Homer Glen, Ill.
Gulan, Mike	.250	10	32	4	8	2	0	2	10	4	10	0	0	.308	.500	R	R	6-1	200	12-18-70	1992	Steubenville, Ohio
Hernandez, Francisco	.326	53	181	32	59	13	1	5	30	13	32	0	0	.372	.492	S	R	5-9	160	2-4-86	2003	La Victoria, D.R.
Johnson, Brandon	.223	53	166	21	37	7	1	3	23	15	44	3	2	.291	.331	L	R	6-0	190	7-23-84	2004	Brunswick, Ga.
Lenderman, Matthew	.163	17	43	3	7	1	0	2	4	2	18	1	0	.217	.326	R	R	5-11	205	4-18-84	2003	Plano, Texas
Matthews, Dustin	.167	14	18	2	3	0	0	0	1	1	12	0	0	.250	.167	R	R	6-3	180	7-17-80	2004	Chicago, Ill.
Oxendine, Chad	.125	5	16	2	2	0	0	0	3	1	6	0	0	.176	.125	R	R	6-0	200	8-21-77	1995	San Antonio, Texas
Perez, Melvin	.130	7	23	3	3	0	0	0	1	1	10	0	0	.167	.130	R	R	6-1	170	2-2-84	2002	San Cristobal, D.R.
Rodriguez, Manuel	.221	38	140	16	31	6	3	5	13	5	44	1	1	.262	.414	R	R	6-2	180	5-24-83	2001	Chitre, Panama
Salgado, Eduardo	.250	2	4	0	1	0	0	0	1	1	2	0	0	.400	.250	R	R	6-2	210	8-7-79	2004	Miami, Fla.
Santana, Jeudy	.234	32	64	7	15	3	1	0	6	5	23	1	3	.310	.313	R	R	6-0	150	9-21-84	2002	Higuey, D.R.
Schmidt, J.J.	.243	47	140	17	34	12	0	2	19	11	29	2	3	.299	.371	R	R	6-3	210	8-15-85	2003	San Diego, Calif.
Shafer, Dustin	.195	49	159	19	31	6	0	2	9	5	33	2	0	.231	.270	R	R	6-3	185	3-31-85	2004	Ashland, Ky.
Swain, Michael	.277	40	112	19	31	5	0	3	17	10	22	1	0	.339	.402	L	R	6-0	190	4-3-84	2004	Evansville, Ind.
Tartaglia, Evan	.262	59	191	39	50	6	3	0	16	46	52	19	8	.416	.335	L	L	5-11	165	5-21-82	2004	Poughkeepsie, N.Y.
Torres, Andres	.364	6	22	8	8	0	0	1	2	3	4	5	0	.462	.500	S	R	5-10	175	1-26-78	1998	Aguadilla, P.R.

GAMES BY POSITION: C—C. Castillo 4, Hernandez 47, Lenderman 14, Oxendine 5, Salgado 2. **1B**—Allen 50, Gulan 4, Hernandez 1, Lenderman 2, Schmidt 18, Shafer 2. **2B**—De los Santos 11, Guest 9, Johnson 34, Santana 20, Swain 6. **3B**—De los Santos 18, Guest 6, Perez 2, Schmidt 22, Swain 26. **SS**—C. Castillo 2, J. Castillo 58, De los Santos 6, Matthews 3, Santana 2. **OF**—Alcantara 40, Allen 8, Foust 31, Guest 5, Johnson 4, Rodriguez 37, Shafer 47, Tartaglia 59, Torres 3.

PITCHING	W	L	ERA	G	GS	CG	SV	IP	H	R	ER	BB	SO	AVG	B	T	HT	WT	DOB	1st Yr	Resides
Bello, Juan	3	1	4.22	18	1	0	0	43	31	28	20	30	46	.203	R	R	6-2	170	5-24-84	2002	San Pedro de Macoris, D.R.
Casey, James	1	4	7.61	12	9	0	0	37	30	34	31	41	42	.222	R	R	6-4	215	9-22-84	2003	Azle, Texas
Davern, Mike	0	0	6.75	11	0	0	1	13	13	11	10	8	21	.241	R	R	6-4	210	11-22-81	2004	Brea, Calif.
Gonzalez, Gio	1	2	2.25	7	6	0	0	24	17	8	6	8	36	.198	R	L	5-11	180	9-19-85	2004	Hialeah, Fla.
Haeger, Charles	1	6	5.02	10	10	0	0	57	70	41	32	22	23	.308	R	R	6-1	200	9-19-83	2001	Plymouth, Mich.
Harrell, Lucas	3	5	5.59	13	9	0	0	48	53	39	30	32	33	.283	S	R	6-2	200	6-3-85	2004	Ozark, Kan.
Honel, Kris	0	0	108.00	1	1	0	0	0	1	4	4	3	0	.500	R	R	6-5	205	11-7-82	2001	Bourbonnais, Ill.
Lemon, Nick	2	2	7.88	15	0	0	0	24	15	27	21	31	25	.176	R	R	6-3	195	10-4-81	2004	Elk Grove, Calif.
Marshall, Jay	1	6	3.59	11	11	0	0	58	63	31	23	8	52	.274	L	L	6-5	185	2-25-83	2003	Manchester, Mo.
Murphey, Tim	1	3	4.63	15	3	0	0	35	25	20	18	19	38	.198	L	L	6-3	170	3-4-85	2004	Norwood, Ga.
Nachreiner, Matt	1	2	5.86	6	6	0	0	28	26	19	18	14	33	.250	L	R	6-2	190	11-17-84	2003	Cedar Park, Texas
Novoa, Yunior	3	2	3.58	13	8	0	0	50	39	27	20	22	49	.206	L	L	6-2	180	4-13-84	2003	Santo Domingo, D.R.
Pena, Luis	2	0	1.45	10	0	0	4	19	8	3	3	6	22	.131	R	R	6-0	170	1-21-81	2001	La Vega, D.R.
Perez, Carlos	3	0	2.17	13	0	0	2	29	28	9	7	10	21	.262	L	L	6-2	190	2-19-84	2002	Carabobo, Venez.
Polanco, Yestin	3	2	3.33	15	0	0	2	27	22	12	10	21	26	.224	L	L	5-10	190	11-29-84	2003	Santo Domingo, D.R.
Rodriguez, Francisco	0	0	5.59	6	0	0	0	10	16	8	6	5	9	.381	L	L	6-2	164	10-5-84	2003	Tenares, D.R.
Roelle, Justin	0	1	9.75	10	1	0	0	12	15	16	13	12	15	.306	L	L	6-4	180	5-28-81	2004	North Platte, Neb.
Torres, Carlos	2	2	5.00	19	0	0	1	36	41	29	20	11	28	.281	R	R	6-2	180	10-22-82	2004	Manhattan, Kan.
Veloz, Yonatan	0	0	7.11	13	0	0	1	13	22	15	10	8	13	.393	L	L	6-1	173	12-3-84	2002	Moca, D.R.

CHICAGO CUBS

BY JEFF VORVA

The Cubs can be excused for wondering "what if?" in 2004.

What if, on Sept. 25 at Shea Stadium, closer LaTroy Hawkins didn't give up that two-out, two-strike homer to Mets rookie Victor Diaz with a 3-0 lead?

Diaz's three-run homer tied the score and Craig Brazell hit an 11th-inning homer off Kent Mercker to give the New York Mets a 4-3 victory, sending the Cubs into a downward spiral. They lost eight of their final 10 games of the season to fall out of the wild-card race. Before that game, the Cubs had a 1½ game lead in the wild-card standings.

"The night before that game, everyone was talking about (Cubs manager Dusty Baker) and his magic," Cubs general manager Jim Hendry said. "But we lost it and had a bad week after that."

The Cubs, who were five outs away from the World Series in 2003, finished 89-73 in 2004, putting together back-to-back winning seasons for the first time since 1971-72. But it wasn't enough for some Cubs fans and media members, who had no trouble using the word "choke" during the closing week.

"It's a very strong word," Baker said. "It's disheartening that people feel like that. I would describe it that it just didn't end right. (The final) week was like a nightmare."

The Cubs were eliminated from the playoffs with one game left in the season. And when star right fielder Sammy Sosa said he was injured and then left the season finale 15 minutes into the game without permission, that ended the campaign on a more bitter note. Sosa was fined a day's pay—$87,400—by the club.

It was a season filled with Cubs players battling numerous injuries, umpires, media members and their

Aramis Ramirez   Brian Dopirak

PLAYERS of the YEAR

MAJOR LEAGUE: Aramis Ramirez, 3b

Ramirez had a career year in 2004, hitting .318-36-103 in 145 games. The last time the Dominican native had a season that good was in 2001 with the Pirates, though he lowered his strikeout totals to 62 and was the offensive anchor for the Cubs all season.

MINOR LEAGUE: Brian Dopirak, 1b

Dopirak fell three homers shy of Jeff Jones' 22-year-old Midwest League record of 42 at low Class A Lansing, but he should have a much brighter future as Jones never went deep in a 16-game big league career. In 2004, Dopirak hit .307-39-120 in 541 at-bats.

own announcers. But all would have been well if they just had shined the final week and gotten into the National League playoffs.

There were some highlights in the disappointing season.

Righthander Carlos Zambrano (16-8, 2.75) kept the Cubs in contention in a season that saw injuries to pitchers Mark Prior (6-4, 4.02) and Kerry Wood (8-9, 3.72). Veteran Greg Maddux also finished with 16 victories and provided the team with the most special moment of the season when he claimed his 300th career victory on Aug. 7.

The Cubs also found a long-term solution at third base when 26-year-old Aramis Ramirez (.318-36-103) shined, and they look solid at first with Derrek Lee (.278-32-98) inked for another two years. Trade deadline acquisition Nomar Garciaparra, formerly the longtime Red Sox shortstop, provided a late-season boost, hitting .297-4-20 in 165 at-bats. He became a free agent after the season, however.

The Cubs minor leaguers enjoyed a successful season, with Triple-A Iowa and short-season Boise making it to postseason play while Class A Daytona was named co-champion of the Florida State League.

Four Cubs farmhands—Lansing's Brian Dopirak and Kevin Collins, Daytona's Brandon Sing and Iowa's Jason Dubois—hit 30 or more home runs in 2004.

Sing, Dopirak and Double-A West Tenn's Richard Lewis were named MVPs of their respective leagues. Lewis, however, broke his leg in early September with Iowa.

The team's top pitching prospect heading into 2004, Angel Guzman, was coming off shoulder surgery and was 0-3, 5.60 in four starts at West Tenn after going 3-1, 4.20 in seven rehab appearances at Daytona.

ORGANIZATION LEADERS

BATTING

*AVG	Trenidad Hubbard, Iowa	.330
R	Trenidad Hubbard, Iowa	101
H	Brian Dopirak, Lansing	166
TB	Brian Dopirak, Lansing	321
2B	Brian Dopirak, Lansing	38
	Russ Johnson, Iowa	38
3B	Adam Greenberg, Iowa/West Tenn/Daytona	14
HR	Brian Dopirak, Lansing	39
RBI	Brian Dopirak, Lansing	120
BB	Brandon Sing, Daytona	84
SO	Dwaine Bacon, West Tenn	139
SB	Dwaine Bacon, West Tenn	60
	Chris Walker, Lansing	60
*OBP	Trenidad Hubbard, Iowa	.407
*SLG	Jason Dubois, Iowa	.629

PITCHING

W	Carlos Marmol, Lansing	14
L	Rocky Cherry, Daytona	10
	Andy Sisco, Daytona	10
#ERA	Clay Rapada, Lansing	2.33
G	Russ Rohlicek, West Tenn	60
CG	Jon Connolly, West Tenn/Daytona	3
SV	Jermaine Van Buren, Iowa/West Tenn/Lansing	22
IP	Ronald Bay, Lansing	168
BB	Renyel Pinto, Iowa/West Tenn	80
SO	Renyel Pinto, Iowa/West Tenn	188

*Minimum 250 at-bats #Minimum 75 innings

ORGANIZATION STATISTICS

MIKE JANES

CHICAGO CUBS

Manager: Dusty Baker.

2004 Record: 89-73, .549 (3rd, NL Central).

ORGANIZATION STATISTICS

BATTING	AVG	G	AB	R	H	2B	3B	HR	RBI	BB	SO	SB	CS	OBP	SLG	B	T	HT	WT	DOB	1st Yr	Resides
Alou, Moises	.293	155	601	106	176	36	3	39	106	68	80	3	0	.361	.557	R	R	6-3	220	8-3-66	1986	Santo Domingo, D.R.
Bako, Paul	.203	49	138	13	28	8	0	1	10	15	29	1	0	.288	.283	L	R	6-2	210	6-20-72	1993	Lafayette, La.
Barrett, Michael	.287	134	456	55	131	32	6	16	65	33	64	1	4	.337	.489	R	R	6-2	200	10-22-76	1995	Alpharetta, Ga.
Difelice, Mike	.000	4	3	0	0	0	0	0	0	0	1	0	0	.000	.000	R	R	6-2	205	5-28-69	1991	Safety Harbor, Fla.
Dubois, Jason	.217	20	23	2	5	0	1	1	5	1	7	0	0	.240	.435	R	R	6-4	200	3-26-79	2001	Virginia Beach, Va.
Garciaparra, Nomar	.297	43	165	28	49	14	0	4	20	16	14	2	1	.364	.455	R	R	6-0	190	7-23-73	1994	Boston, Mass.
Gonzalez, Alex	.217	37	129	15	28	10	0	3	8	4	26	1	1	.241	.364	R	R	6-0	200	4-8-73	1991	Coral Gables, Fla.
Goodwin, Tom	.200	77	105	11	21	8	0	0	3	8	22	5	0	.254	.276	L	R	6-0	195	7-27-68	1989	Grapevine, Texas
Grieve, Ben	.250	15	16	2	4	2	0	1	6	0	5	0	0	.316	.563	L	R	6-4	210	5-4-76	1994	Flower Mound, Texas
2-team (108 Mil.)	.260	123	250	30	65	17	0	8	35	39	70	0	0	.361	.424							
Grudzielanek, Mark	.307	81	257	32	79	12	1	6	23	15	32	1	1	.347	.432	R	R	6-1	190	6-30-70	1991	West Palm Beach, Fla.
Harris, Brendan	.222	3	9	0	2	1	0	0	1	1	1	0	0	.300	.333	R	R	6-1	190	8-26-80	2001	Queensbury, N.Y.
Hollandsworth, Todd	.318	57	148	28	47	6	2	8	22	17	26	1	1	.392	.547	L	L	6-2	225	4-20-73	1991	Castle Rock, Colo.
Jackson, Damian	.067	7	15	1	1	0	0	1	1	3	6	0	0	.222	.267	R	R	5-11	185	8-16-73	1992	Concord, Calif.
Kelton, David	.100	8	10	1	1	1	0	0	0	0	3	0	0	.100	.200	R	R	6-3	195	12-17-79	1998	La Grange, Ga.
Lee, Derrek	.278	161	605	90	168	39	1	32	98	68	128	12	5	.356	.504	R	R	6-5	245	9-6-75	1993	El Dorado Hills, Calif.
Macias, Jose	.268	98	194	23	52	6	3	3	22	5	38	4	1	.292	.376	S	R	5-8	190	1-25-72	1994	Panama City, Panama
Martinez, Ramon	.246	102	260	22	64	15	1	3	30	26	40	1	0	.313	.346	R	R	6-1	190	10-10-72	1993	Toa Alta, P.R.
Murray, Calvin	.200	11	5	2	1	0	0	0	1	1	0	0	0	.333	.200	R	R	5-11	180	7-30-71	1993	Spring, Texas
Ordonez, Rey	.164	23	61	2	10	3	0	1	5	2	14	0	0	.190	.262	R	R	5-9	160	1-11-71	1993	Parkland, Fla.
Patterson, Corey	.266	157	631	91	168	34	6	24	72	45	168	32	9	.320	.452	L	R	5-9	180	8-13-79	1999	Marietta, Ga.
Perez, Neifi	.371	23	62	12	23	5	0	2	6	3	10	1	0	.400	.548	S	R	6-0	175	6-2-73	1993	Santo Domingo, D.R.
2-team (103 S.F.)	.255	126	381	40	97	17	1	4	39	24	41	1	1	.296	.336							
Ramirez, Aramis	.318	145	547	99	174	32	1	36	103	49	62	0	2	.373	.578	R	R	6-1	215	6-25-78	1995	Santo Domingo, D.R.
Sosa, Sammy	.253	126	478	69	121	21	0	35	80	56	133	0	0	.332	.517	R	R	6-0	220	11-12-68	1986	Santo Domingo, D.R.
Walker, Todd	.274	129	372	60	102	19	4	15	50	43	52	0	3	.352	.468	L	R	6-0	185	5-25-73	1994	Castle Rock, Colo.

PITCHING	W	L	ERA	G	GS	CG	SV	IP	H	R	ER	BB	SO	AVG	B	T	HT	WT	DOB	1st Yr	Resides
Anderson, Jimmy	0	0	4.66	7	0	0	1	10	9	5	5	3	3	.243	L	L	6-1	210	1-22-76	1994	Chesapeake, Va.
Beltran, Francis	2	2	4.63	34	0	0	0	35	27	19	18	22	40	.214	R	R	6-6	230	11-29-79	1997	Santo Domingo, D.R.
Borowski, Joe	2	4	8.02	22	0	0	9	21	27	19	19	15	17	.303	R	R	6-2	225	5-4-71	1990	Bayonne, N.J.
Clement, Matt	9	13	3.68	30	30	0	0	181	155	79	74	77	190	.229	R	R	6-3	210	8-12-74	1994	Butler, Pa.
Dempster, Ryan	1	1	3.92	23	0	0	2	21	16	9	9	13	18	.208	R	R	6-3	215	5-3-77	1995	Denver, Colo.
Farnsworth, Kyle	4	5	4.73	72	0	0	0	67	67	39	35	33	78	.260	R	R	6-4	235	4-14-76	1995	Canton, Ga.
Hawkins, LaTroy	5	4	2.63	77	0	0	25	82	72	27	24	14	69	.233	R	R	6-5	215	12-21-72	1991	Frisco, Texas
Leicester, Jon	5	1	3.89	32	0	0	0	42	40	20	18	15	35	.256	R	R	6-3	230	2-7-79	2000	Huntington Beach, Calif.
Maddux, Greg	16	11	4.02	33	33	2	0	213	218	103	95	33	151	.269	R	R	6-0	185	4-14-66	1984	Las Vegas, Nev.
Mercker, Kent	3	1	2.55	71	0	0	0	53	39	15	15	27	51	.205	L	L	6-2	205	2-1-68	1986	Dublin, Ohio
Mitre, Sergio	2	4	6.62	12	9	0	0	52	71	38	38	20	37	.327	R	R	6-4	210	2-16-81	2001	San Ysidro, Calif.
Pratt, Andy	0	1	21.60	4	0	0	0	2	4	4	4	7	1	.000	L	L	6-0	185	8-27-79	1998	Chino Valley, Ariz.
Prior, Mark	6	4	4.02	21	21	0	0	119	112	53	53	48	139	.251	R	R	6-5	230	9-7-80	2002	Chicago, Ill.
Remlinger, Mike	1	2	3.44	48	0	0	2	37	33	16	14	16	35	.246	L	L	6-1	215	3-23-66	1987	Paradise Valley, Ariz.
Rusch, Glendon	6	2	3.47	32	16	0	2	130	127	54	50	33	90	.256	L	L	6-1	220	11-7-74	1993	Tujunga, Calif.
Wellemeyer, Todd	2	1	5.92	20	0	0	0	24	27	16	16	20	30	.287	R	R	6-3	205	8-30-78	2000	Louisville, Ky.
Wood, Kerry	8	9	3.72	22	22	0	0	140	127	62	58	51	144	.244	R	R	6-5	225	6-16-77	1995	Scottsdale, Ariz.
Wuertz, Michael	1	0	4.34	31	0	0	1	29	22	14	14	17	30	.218	R	R	6-3	200	12-15-78	1998	Burnsville, Minn.
Zambrano, Carlos	16	8	2.75	31	31	1	0	210	174	73	64	81	188	.225	S	R	6-5	255	6-1-81	1998	Puerto Cabello, Venez.

FIELDING

Catcher	PCT	G	PO	A	E	DP	PB
Bako	.989	47	332	30	4	2	1
Barrett	.994	130	1035	47	6	9	8
DiFelice	1.000	4	6	0	0	0	0

First Base	PCT	G	PO	A	E	DP
Dubois	1.000	1	2	0	0	0
Hollandsworth	.952	3	16	4	1	1
Lee	.996	161	1259	130	6	113
Walker	1.000	5	7	1	0	1

Second Base	PCT	G	PO	A	E	DP
Grudzielanek	.985	76	136	186	5	30
Jackson	.957	5	8	14	1	5
Macias	1.000	16	15	24	0	3

Third Base						
Martinez	1.000	6	3	6	0	0
Perez	1.000	2	4	4	0	3
Walker	.981	89	150	213	7	32

Third Base	PCT	G	PO	A	E	DP
Harris	.889	3	4	4	1	0
Macias	.957	18	10	12	1	1
Martinez	.917	24	12	21	3	4
Ramirez	.969	144	92	221	10	15

Shortstop	PCT	G	PO	A	E	DP
Garciaparra	.982	42	69	94	3	17
Gonzalez	.967	37	65	82	5	18
Martinez	.977	73	80	174	6	34
Ordonez	.959	22	31	39	3	9

Perez	.968	19	20	41	2	10

Outfield	PCT	G	PO	A	E	DP
Alou	.969	154	240	7	8	2
Dubois	1.000	5	5	0	0	0
Goodwin	1.000	28	30	0	0	0
Grieve	1.000	4	3	0	0	0
Hollandsworth	1.000	36	59	2	0	0
Kelton	1.000	3	2	0	0	0
Macias	1.000	28	30	2	0	0
Murray	1.000	8	7	0	0	0
Patterson	.997	157	324	8	1	5
Sosa	.984	124	238	5	4	2
Walker	1.000	1	1	0	0	0

Moises Alou: Led the Cubs with 39 home runs

Carlos Zambrano: Led an impressive Cubs staff with a 2.75 ERA

FARM SYSTEM

Director, Player Development: Oneri Fleita.

Class	Farm Team	League	W	L	Pct.	Finish*	Manager	Affiliate Since
AAA	Iowa Cubs (Des Moines)	Pacific Coast	79	64	.552	**4th (16)**	Mike Quade	1981
AA	West Tenn Diamond Jaxx (Jackson)	Southern	70	68	.507	5th (10)	Bobby Dickerson	1998
High A	Daytona (Fla.) Cubs	Florida State	70	56	.556	+5th (12)	Steve McFarland	1993
Low A	#Lansing (Mich.) Lugnuts	Midwest	77	63	.550	t-2nd (14)	Julio Garcia	1999
SS A	Boise (Idaho) Hawks	Northwest	42	34	.553	+t-1st (8)	Tom Beyers	2001
Rookie	Mesa (Ariz.) Cubs	Arizona	27	29	.482	6th (9)	Trey Forkerway	1997

*Finish in overall standings (No. of teams in league)/playoff teams in **boldface**   +League champion
#Affiliate will operate in Peoria (Midwest) in 2005

IOWA CUBS   Class AAA

PACIFIC COAST LEAGUE

BATTING	AVG	G	AB	R	H	2B	3B	HR	RBI	BB	SO	SB	CS	OBP	SLG	B	T	HT	WT	DOB	1st Yr	Resides
Arteaga, Josh	.267	15	45	8	12	2	0	1	6	5	6	0	0	.382	.378	R	R	5-9	170	3-14-80	2001	Homestead, Fla.
Cookson, Brent	.333	12	24	4	8	0	0	2	6	1	5	0	0	.346	.583	R	R	5-11	200	9-7-69	1991	Santa Paula, Calif.
Creighton, Matt	.394	31	66	16	26	6	2	4	18	5	9	1	0	.432	.727	R	R	6-0	190	2-22-79	2002	Weldon, Calif.
Dawkins, Gookie	.329	67	164	31	54	15	2	6	28	20	34	11	0	.402	.555	R	R	6-1	186	5-12-79	1997	Chappells, S.C.
2-team (48 Omaha)	.276	115	330	53	91	22	3	10	45	30	75	13	2	.336	.452							
Dubois, Jason	.314	109	385	75	121	26	1	31	99	41	97	2	0	.388	.629	R	R	6-4	200	3-26-79	2001	Virginia Beach, Va.
Gil, Benji	.257	35	113	14	29	7	1	1	13	7	24	0	0	.306	.363	R	R	6-2	210	10-6-72	1991	Grapevine, Texas
Gonzalez, Alex	.333	8	24	7	8	3	0	0	0	4	7	1	0	.429	.458	R	R	6-0	200	4-8-73	1991	Coral Gables, Fla.
Greenberg, Adam	.000	1	4	0	0	0	0	0	0	1	0	0	0	.200	.000	L	R	5-9	180	2-21-81	2002	Sparta, N.J.
Grudzielanek, Mark	.250	8	28	6	7	3	0	2	4	0	4	0	0	.250	.571	R	R	6-1	190	6-30-70	1991	West Palm Beach, Fla.
Gutierrez, Ricky	.368	21	68	5	25	5	0	0	10	6	10	0	1	.419	.441	R	R	6-1	190	5-23-70	1988	Pembroke Pines, Fla.
Harris, Brendan	.311	69	254	48	79	21	1	11	35	16	46	0	2	.353	.531	R	R	6-1	200	8-26-80	2001	Queensbury, N.Y.
Hocking, Denny	.288	39	104	20	30	12	0	3	22	11	20	0	2	.359	.490	S	R	5-10	180	4-2-70	1990	Tustin, Calif.
Hoffpauir, Micah	.333	1	3	0	1	1	0	0	1	1	0	0	0	.500	.667	L	L	6-3	180	3-1-80	2002	Jacksonville, Texas
Hubbard, Trenidad	.330	129	473	101	156	28	4	9	49	62	59	36	8	.407	.463	R	R	5-9	200	5-11-66	1986	Houston, Texas
Jackson, Damian	.278	28	97	18	27	6	5	3	13	11	20	3	1	.352	.536	R	R	5-11	185	8-16-73	1992	Concord, Calif.
Johnson, Russ	.296	129	415	71	123	38	2	14	78	70	63	7	3	.399	.499	R	R	5-10	180	2-22-73	1995	Denham Springs, La.
Kelton, David	.248	121	420	57	104	26	1	19	68	33	92	7	2	.305	.450	R	R	6-3	195	12-17-79	1998	La Grange, Ga.
Kopitzke, Casey	.215	81	251	19	54	10	0	1	17	12	38	1	1	.257	.267	R	R	6-2	205	5-31-78	1999	DePere, Wis.
Leon, Donny	.277	118	397	49	110	26	0	13	60	30	54	0	0	.336	.441	R	R	6-1	190	5-7-76	1995	Ponce, P.R.
Lewis, Richard	.246	32	118	14	29	8	1	3	11	4	21	4	0	.280	.407	R	R	6-1	190	6-29-80	2001	Marietta, Ga.
Lunar, Fernando	.252	78	254	30	64	8	0	5	23	10	46	0	0	.298	.343	R	R	6-1	230	5-25-77	1994	Alamogordo, N.M.
Martinez, Felix	.190	7	21	1	4	1	0	1	3	0	3	0	0	.190	.381	S	R	6-0	200	5-18-74	1993	Nagua, D.R.
Medlin, C.J.	.000	1	1	0	0	0	0	0	0	0	1	0	0	.000	.000	R	R	6-2	200	3-3-82	2002	Broken Arrow, Okla.

BATTING	AVG	G	AB	R	H	2B	3B	HR	RBI	BB	SO	SB	CS	OBP	SLG	B	T	HT	WT	DOB	1st Yr	Resides
Murray, Calvin	.311	130	457	84	142	24	7	7	54	43	65	25	4	.368	.440	R	R	5-11	180	7-30-71	1993	Spring, Texas
Ordonez, Rey	.292	6	24	3	7	2	0	0	3	1	1	0	0	.320	.375	R	R	5-9	160	1-11-71	1993	Parkland, Fla.
Perez, Neifi	.206	10	34	1	7	1	0	0	3	0	5	0	0	.206	.235	S	R	6-0	175	6-2-73	1993	Santo Domingo, D.R.
Selby, Bill	.275	119	407	60	112	31	5	17	77	30	59	2	4	.321	.501	L	R	5-10	195	6-11-70	1992	Southhaven, Miss.

PITCHING	W	L	ERA	G	GS	CG	SV	IP	H	R	ER	BB	SO	AVG	B	T	HT	WT	DOB	1st Yr	Resides
Anderson, Jimmy	6	5	4.28	16	15	0	0	95	108	54	45	35	42	.292	L	L	6-1	210	1-22-76	1994	Chesapeake, Va.
Beltran, Francis	0	0	2.84	6	0	0	4	6	5	2	2	1	6	.208	R	R	6-5	230	11-29-79	1997	Santo Domingo, D.R.
Bland, Nate	8	4	4.68	53	0	0	1	73	82	51	38	33	45	.293	L	L	6-5	190	12-27-74	1993	Birmingham, Ala.
Blasdell, Jared	0	1	10.80	1	0	0	0	2	1	2	2	5	2	.200	R	R	6-3	185	5-14-79	2001	Las Vegas, Nev.
Borowski, Joe	0	3	8.22	7	3	0	0	8	9	8	7	4	2	.290	R	R	6-2	225	5-4-71	1990	Bayonne, N.J.
Carrara, Giovanni	1	2	3.81	20	0	0	1	28	29	12	12	8	23	.279	R	R	6-2	235	3-4-68	1991	Edo Anzoategui, Venez.
Cash, David	1	0	1.59	3	3	0	0	17	12	4	3	4	14	.194	R	R	6-1	180	7-25-79	2001	Modesto, Calif.
Chiasson, Scott	1	0	3.15	15	0	0	0	20	16	7	7	7	20	.225	R	R	6-4	200	8-14-77	1998	Norwich, Conn.
Corey, Bryan	2	0	3.38	10	0	0	5	13	10	5	5	5	13	.208	R	R	6-0	170	10-21-73	1993	Phoenix, Ariz.
Dempster, Ryan	1	1	3.86	6	4	0	0	21	19	9	9	10	20	.244	R	R	6-3	215	5-3-77	1995	Denver, Colo.
Eckenstahler, Eric	2	0	3.60	8	0	0	0	10	11	4	4	12	11	.280	L	L	6-7	220	12-17-76	2000	Lake Villa, Ill.
Gerk, Jordan	0	1	4.50	1	1	0	0	4	7	2	2	1	2	.412	L	L	6-1	180	7-6-79	2000	Kelowna, B.C.
Glover, Gary	3	2	7.92	20	1	0	0	31	43	29	27	14	18	.328	R	R	6-5	205	12-3-76	1994	DeLand, Fla.
Izquierdo, Hansel	0	0	6.53	21	1	0	1	30	33	23	22	18	24	.275	R	R	6-1	200	1-2-77	1995	Miami, Fla.
Johnson, Russ	0	0	6.75	2	0	0	0	4	5	3	3	2	1	.313	R	R	5-10	180	2-22-73	1995	Denham Springs, La.
Koronka, John	12	9	4.34	29	23	2	0	153	164	86	74	65	116	.275	L	L	6-1	180	7-3-80	1998	Clermont, Fla.
Leicester, Jon	6	2	3.70	12	12	0	0	66	61	31	27	36	60	.244	R	R	6-3	200	2-7-79	2000	Huntington Beach, Calif.
Manning, David	0	4	4.34	7	3	0	0	19	14	11	9	9	11	.212	R	R	6-3	210	8-14-72	1992	West Palm Beach, Fla.
McGlinchy, Kevin	0	4	5.45	7	6	0	0	36	55	22	22	8	29	.357	R	R	6-5	220	6-28-77	1996	Orlando, Fla.
Meyer, Jake	1	1	3.86	4	3	0	0	19	13	9	8	4	11	.194	R	R	6-1	200	1-7-75	1997	San Diego, Calif.
Mitchell, Nathan	0	0	9.00	1	0	0	0	1	2	1	1	2	1	.400	R	R	6-0	190	5-2-80	2002	Houston, Texas
Mitre, Sergio	6	4	2.98	18	15	1	1	103	97	38	34	39	95	.255	R	R	6-4	210	2-16-81	2001	San Ysidro, Calif.
Nolasco, Ricky	2	3	9.30	9	9	0	0	41	68	42	42	16	28	.384	R	R	6-2	220	12-13-82	2001	Rialto, Calif.
O'Malley, Ryan	0	2	8.62	8	3	0	0	16	23	15	15	6	8	.365	R	L	6-1	200	4-9-80	2002	Springfield, Ill.
Ohman, Will	3	3	4.30	45	1	0	0	52	53	28	25	29	75	.265	L	L	6-2	200	8-13-77	1998	Mesa, Ariz.
Pinto, Renyel	0	0	7.71	2	2	0	0	9	9	9	8	8	9	.250	L	L	6-4	195	7-8-82	1999	Cupira, Venez.
Pratt, Andy	0	4	19.00	4	4	0	0	9	14	19	19	15	8	.400	L	L	6-0	185	8-27-79	1998	Chino Valley, Ariz.
Prior, Mark	1	0	3.38	1	1	0	0	5	3	2	2	1	10	.158	R	R	6-5	230	9-7-80	2002	Chicago, Ill.
Remlinger, Mike	0	0	16.20	2	0	0	0	2	3	3	3	0	1	.375	L	L	6-1	215	3-23-66	1987	Paradise Valley, Ariz.
Rusch, Glendon	2	0	1.89	4	0	0	0	19	18	6	4	1	16	.257	L	L	6-1	200	11-7-74	1993	Tujunga, Calif.
Ryu, Jae-Kuk	0	0	40.50	1	0	0	0	1	2	4	3	1	0	.500	R	R	6-3	210	5-30-83	2001	Seoul, Korea
Sedlacek, Shawn	10	7	4.32	22	22	1	0	131	151	70	63	42	95	.291	R	R	6-4	200	6-29-77	1998	Cedar Rapids, Iowa
Shibilo, Andy	0	0	6.23	9	0	0	0	13	17	11	9	9	9	.321	R	R	6-7	220	9-16-76	1998	Belleville, N.J.
Szuminski, Jason	3	2	4.94	41	2	0	8	51	57	40	28	35	31	.289	R	R	6-5	220	12-11-78	2000	San Antonio, Texas
Tolar, Kevin	4	0	3.45	51	0	0	0	57	55	30	22	40	77	.251	R	L	6-3	230	1-28-71	1989	Sarasota, Fla.
Van Buren, Jermaine	0	0	2.08	3	0	0	1	4	3	1	1	1	0	.188	R	R	6-1	200	7-2-80	1998	Hattiesburg, Miss.
Wellemeyer, Todd	1	1	3.91	14	4	0	0	23	24	11	10	12	23	.273	R	R	6-3	205	8-30-78	2000	Louisville, Ky.
Wood, Kerry	1	0	0.00	1	1	0	0	5	2	0	0	1	4	.111	R	R	6-5	225	6-16-77	1995	Scottsdale, Ariz.
Wuertz, Michael	1	1	2.42	37	0	0	19	45	30	13	12	15	59	.186	R	R	6-3	200	12-15-78	1998	Burnsville, Minn.

FIELDING

Catcher	PCT	G	PO	A	E	DP	PB
Kopitzke	.989	79	492	49	6	5	5
Lunar	.993	77	542	55	4	11	5

First Base	PCT	G	PO	A	E	DP
Creighton	1.000	14	106	9	0	10
Dubois	.978	25	165	10	4	20
Hoffpauir	.857	1	6	0	1	1
Johnson	.989	34	265	14	3	35
Kelton	1.000	1	10	0	0	0
Kopitzke	1.000	1	2	0	0	1
Leon	1.000	19	140	12	0	13
Selby	.988	73	547	39	7	64

Second Base	PCT	G	PO	A	E	DP
Dawkins	1.000	2	4	2	0	0
Gil	1.000	4	6	15	0	2
Grudzielanek	1.000	7	5	6	0	2
Gutierrez	1.000	4	10	12	0	5
Harris	.992	53	103	157	2	42
Hocking	1.000	5	10	13	0	4

	PCT	G	PO	A	E	DP
Jackson	1.000	1	3	1	0	0
Johnson	.986	50	96	109	3	33
Lewis	.986	31	62	82	2	20
Ordonez	1.000	1	2	0	0	0
Selby	.956	11	16	27	2	6

Third Base	PCT	G	PO	A	E	DP
Dawkins	1.000	3	2	3	0	0
Gil	.864	16	7	31	6	4
Gutierrez	1.000	1	0	1	0	0
Harris	1.000	7	0	6	0	0
Hocking	1.000	13	5	27	0	4
Johnson	.883	28	14	39	7	3
Leon	.932	92	59	148	15	22
Martinez	1.000	1	0	2	0	0
Selby	.833	5	4	1	1	0

Shortstop	PCT	G	PO	A	E	DP
Arteaga	.983	14	17	42	1	8
Dawkins	.948	49	74	125	11	37
Gil	1.000	13	17	48	0	11

	PCT	G	PO	A	E	DP
Gonzalez	1.000	8	10	12	0	4
Gutierrez	.962	15	15	36	2	11
Harris	.912	12	12	19	3	1
Hocking	.951	13	15	43	3	10
Jackson	.989	22	31	60	1	14
Martinez	.850	4	7	10	3	3
Ordonez	.969	6	8	23	1	4
Perez	1.000	10	11	23	0	3

Outfield	PCT	G	PO	A	E	DP
Cookson	1.000	6	12	0	0	0
Dubois	1.000	83	120	5	0	1
Greenberg	1.000	1	4	0	0	0
Hocking	1.000	2	5	1	0	0
Hubbard	.974	125	177	11	5	0
Jackson	1.000	3	4	1	0	1
Kelton	.983	105	169	5	3	1
Murray	.992	118	244	7	2	4
Selby	.949	26	35	2	2	0

WEST TENN DIAMOND JAXX

SOUTHERN LEAGUE

Class AA

BATTING	AVG	G	AB	R	H	2B	3B	HR	RBI	BB	SO	SB	CS	OBP	SLG	B	T	HT	WT	DOB	1st Yr	Resides
Arteaga, Josh	.219	82	224	20	49	18	1	3	27	14	59	1	1	.272	.348	R	R	5-9	170	3-14-80	2001	Homestead, Fla.
Bacon, Dwaine	.248	129	444	80	110	10	11	3	32	81	139	60	20	.373	.340	S	R	6-0	180	4-11-79	2001	Fort Washington, Md.
Cedeno, Ronny	.279	116	384	39	107	19	5	6	44	74	10	10	.328	.401	R	R	6-0	180	2-2-83	2000	Carabobo, Venez.
Craig, Matt	.275	112	375	63	103	20	4	20	63	49	101	3	2	.363	.509	S	R	6-3	200	4-16-81	2002	Dallas, Texas
Creighton, Matt	.250	76	232	29	58	18	2	3	25	8	45	2	0	.296	.384	R	R	6-0	190	2-22-79	2002	Weldon, Calif.
Dzurilla, Mike	.244	120	381	49	93	21	5	7	59	45	54	5	8	.330	.381	R	R	6-0	190	5-4-78	1999	Bayside, N.Y.
Greenberg, Adam	.274	33	113	22	31	7	2	3	10	14	30	3	0	.364	.451	L	L	5-9	180	2-21-81	2002	Sparta, N.J.
Hoffpauir, Micah	.306	94	340	58	104	20	6	11	75	27	61	1	4	.347	.497	L	L	6-3	180	3-1-80	2002	Jacksonville, Texas
Hood, Donny	.250	10	12	2	3	1	0	0	2	1	1	0	0	.357	.333	R	R	6-1	180	12-30-78	2002	Powder Springs, Ga.
Kweon, Yoon-Min	.167	5	6	1	1	0	1	0	0	0	1	0	0	.167	.500	R	R	6-2	210	1-22-79	2000	Inchon, Korea
Lewis, Richard	.329	99	380	68	125	27	10	10	69	37	94	7	6	.391	.532	R	R	6-1	190	6-29-80	2001	Marietta, Ga.

BATTING

BATTING	AVG	G	AB	R	H	2B	3B	HR	RBI	BB	SO	SB	CS	OBP	SLG	B	T	HT	WT	DOB	1st Yr	Resides
Mallory, Mike	.258	105	291	31	75	20	1	7	36	23	81	2	3	.326	.405	R	R	6-4	210	12-8-80	1999	Dinwiddie, Va.
O'Toole, Paul	.258	63	182	21	47	9	1	4	20	15	40	5	2	.318	.385	L	R	6-1	200	2-24-80	2002	South Bend, Ind.
Sosa, Sammy	.333	2	6	0	2	1	0	0	1	1	2	0	0	.429	.500	R	R	6-0	220	11-12-68	1986	Santo Domingo, D.R.
Soto, Geovany	.271	104	332	47	90	16	0	9	48	40	71	1	0	.355	.401	R	R	6-1	230	1-20-83	2001	San Juan, P.R.
Spearman, Jemel	.243	55	148	19	36	4	3	0	14	13	24	6	5	.315	.311	R	R	6-0	190	12-27-80	2002	Lawrenceville, Ga.
Weston, Aron	.287	123	425	62	122	20	9	4	46	31	90	10	9	.337	.405	L	L	6-3	190	11-5-80	1999	Solon, Ohio

PITCHING

PITCHING	W	L	ERA	G	GS	CG	SV	IP	H	R	ER	BB	SO	AVG	B	T	HT	WT	DOB	1st Yr	Resides
Arteaga, Josh	1	0	33.75	2	0	0	0	1	4	5	5	3	1	.571	R	R	5-9	170	3-14-80	2001	Homestead, Fla.
Blasdell, Jared	2	4	4.80	49	0	0	2	60	59	40	32	43	60	.253	R	R	6-3	185	5-14-79	2001	Las Vegas, Nev.
Blasko, Chad	5	4	5.67	13	13	0	0	67	77	45	42	24	65	.292	R	R	6-7	220	3-9-81	2003	Mishawaka, Ind.
Brownlie, Bobby	9	9	3.36	26	26	2	0	147	127	62	55	36	114	.236	R	R	6-0	215	10-5-80	2003	Edison, N.J.
Cabrera, Yunior	0	1	9.53	6	0	0	0	6	8	7	6	8	6	.308	L	L	6-0	170	10-25-79	1997	San Pedro de Macoris, D.R.
Castellanos, Hugo	1	0	3.52	22	0	0	1	23	21	9	9	16	14	.250	R	R	6-4	200	6-30-80	1998	Nuevo Laredo, Mexico
Chiasson, Scott	2	0	2.25	12	0	0	0	16	12	4	4	2	15	.214	R	R	6-3	200	8-14-77	1998	Norwich, Conn.
Christensen, Ben	0	1	4.91	9	1	0	0	11	11	7	6	7	12	.250	R	R	6-4	210	2-7-78	1999	Wichita, Kan.
Connolly, Jon	1	0	1.50	1	1	0	0	6	4	1	1	1	8	.190	R	L	6-0	200	8-24-83	2001	Oneonta, N.Y.
Cueto, Jose	0	0	21.21	4	0	0	0	5	11	11	11	3	7	.458	R	R	6-2	190	9-13-76	1996	San Pedro de Macoris, D.R.
Dzurilla, Mike	0	0	5.40	2	0	0	0	2	4	1	1	1	0	.571	R	R	6-0	190	5-4-78	1999	Bayside, N.Y.
Fahrner, Evan	2	4	3.39	58	0	0	7	77	70	35	29	34	85	.241	R	R	6-2	200	3-4-78	1999	Peoria, Ill.
Gerk, Jordan	5	1	4.46	24	2	0	1	42	43	24	21	15	28	.267	L	L	6-1	180	7-6-79	2000	Kelowna, B.C.
Guzman, Angel	0	3	5.60	4	4	0	0	18	20	11	11	4	13	.286	R	R	6-3	190	12-14-81	2000	Caracas, Venez.
Marshall, Sean	2	2	5.90	6	6	0	0	29	36	20	19	12	23	.310	L	L	6-5	185	8-30-82	2003	Chesterfield, Va.
Mitchell, Nathan	3	4	2.95	26	0	0	0	43	27	20	14	29	35	.175	R	R	6-2	220	12-13-82	2001	Rialto, Calif.
Nolasco, Ricky	6	4	3.70	19	19	0	0	107	104	50	44	37	115	.257	R	R	6-2	190	4-9-80	2002	Springfield, Ill.
O'Malley, Ryan	2	3	3.72	16	7	0	0	56	49	25	23	20	37	.240	R	L	6-1	200	4-8-80	2002	Mokena, Ill.
Pignatiello, Carmen	9	7	4.56	27	27	1	0	148	167	89	75	39	137	.286	L	L	6-0	190	9-12-82	2000	Mokena, Ill.
Pinto, Renyel	11	8	2.92	25	25	0	0	142	107	50	46	72	179	.213	L	L	6-4	195	7-8-82	1999	Cupira, Venez.
Pratt, Andy	0	5	9.28	6	5	0	0	21	24	27	22	21	26	.282	L	L	6-0	185	8-27-79	1998	Chino Valley, Ariz.
Ransom, Robert	0	0	4.91	1	1	0	0	4	3	2	2	1	4	.214	R	R	6-3	225	8-25-81	2004	Nashville, Tenn.
Rohlicek, Russ	5	5	2.09	60	0	0	2	69	44	19	16	42	67	.190	L	L	6-6	245	12-26-79	2001	Pleasant Hill, Calif.
Ryu, Jae-Kuk	1	0	2.95	14	0	0	0	18	22	8	6	10	19	.289	R	R	6-3	210	5-30-83	2001	Seoul, Korea
Sanchez, Felix	0	0	7.11	7	0	0	0	6	11	5	5	4	5	.379	R	L	6-3	180	8-3-81	1999	Puerto Plata, D.R.
Tavarez, Anderson	0	1	17.18	1	1	0	0	4	6	9	7	3	3	.400	R	R	6-1	170	2-14-82	2001	Santiago, D.R.
Van Buren, Jermaine	3	2	1.87	51	0	0	21	53	23	11	11	24	64	.134	R	R	6-1	220	7-2-80	1998	Hattiesburg, Miss.

FIELDING

Catcher	PCT	G	PO	A	E	DP	PB
Dzurilla	1.000	1	2	1	0	0	0
O'Toole	.988	45	310	31	4	3	3
Soto	.994	102	837	89	6	11	14

First Base	PCT	G	PO	A	E	DP
Craig	.973	10	66	5	2	6
Creighton	.975	35	245	23	7	23
Dzurilla	.984	19	113	9	2	9
Hoffpauir	.996	86	636	62	3	60
Hood	.500	1	1	0	1	0
O'Toole	1.000	1	9	0	0	0
Soto	1.000	1	3	0	0	0

Second Base	PCT	G	PO	A	E	DP
Arteaga	.936	15	23	21	3	4
Creighton	.889	8	13	11	3	2
Dzurilla	1.000	18	33	39	0	9
Lewis	.995	98	182	229	2	54
Spearman	.931	11	12	15	2	3

Third Base	PCT	G	PO	A	E	DP
Arteaga	.935	22	17	41	4	2
Craig	.933	90	51	172	16	11
Dzurilla	1.000	4	1	4	0	0
Hood	1.000	1	2	0	0	0
Spearman	.908	26	12	47	6	3

Shortstop	PCT	G	PO	A	E	DP
Arteaga	.989	26	38	53	1	15
Cedeno	.963	116	168	303	18	60
Spearman	1.000	2	2	4	0	1

Outfield	PCT	G	PO	A	E	DP
Bacon	.960	124	261	3	11	0
Creighton	1.000	2	2	0	0	0
Dzurilla	.984	58	59	4	1	0
Greenberg	.962	33	46	5	2	0
Hoffpauir	.917	11	8	3	1	0
Mallory	.978	91	131	3	3	0
O'Toole	1.000	13	11	1	0	0
Spearman	1.000	7	11	1	0	0
Weston	.962	126	167	11	7	2

DAYTONA CUBS — High Class A

FLORIDA STATE LEAGUE

BATTING	AVG	G	AB	R	H	2B	3B	HR	RBI	BB	SO	SB	CS	OBP	SLG	B	T	HT	WT	DOB	1st Yr	Resides
Butler, Keith	.255	103	369	48	94	14	2	4	47	23	54	24	10	.308	.336	R	R	5-10	180	8-11-80	2002	Marietta, Ga.
Coats, Buck	.292	113	418	64	122	23	4	8	56	32	91	28	9	.341	.423	L	R	6-3	190	6-9-82	2000	Hahira, Ga.
Greenberg, Adam	.291	91	323	52	94	10	12	3	28	42	65	16	8	.381	.424	L	R	5-9	180	2-21-81	2002	Sparta, N.J.
Gutierrez, Ricky	.077	4	13	1	1	0	0	0	3	1	3	0	0	.235	.077	R	R	6-1	190	5-23-70	1988	Pembroke Pines, Fla.
Hood, Donny	.237	23	76	6	18	7	0	2	9	6	12	0	1	.310	.408	R	R	6-1	180	12-30-78	2002	Powder Springs, Ga.
Jackson, Nic	.340	13	47	8	16	4	1	1	9	6	13	1	0	.418	.532	R	R	6-3	205	9-25-79	2000	Richmond, Va.
Johnson, J.J.	.279	109	390	42	109	16	5	6	62	28	79	9	2	.327	.392	R	R	6-2	210	11-3-81	2000	Appling, Ga.
Jones, Nick	.250	15	40	1	10	1	0	0	0	1	11	0	0	.268	.275	R	R	6-1	185	3-29-82	2003	Roanoke, Va.
Kweon, Yoon-Min	.174	11	23	2	4	1	0	0	1	1	5	1	0	.208	.217	R	R	6-2	210	1-22-79	2000	Inchon, Korea
Marquez, Uriak	.154	5	13	1	2	0	1	0	0	1	3	0	0	.214	.308	L	R	6-0	170	8-17-83	2001	Caracas, Venez.
McGehee, Casey	.261	119	449	56	117	30	0	10	66	33	69	2	1	.310	.394	R	R	6-1	195	10-12-82	2003	Aptos, Calif.
McKnight, Lukas	.242	45	120	10	29	5	1	1	12	11	23	1	2	.311	.325	L	R	6-0	200	2-19-80	2000	Libertyville, Ill.
Montanez, Luis	.215	21	79	8	17	4	2	1	7	7	16	2	3	.292	.354	R	R	6-2	180	12-15-81	2000	Miami, Fla.
Murton, Matt	.253	24	79	13	20	1	1	2	8	8	10	2	0	.326	.367	R	R	6-1	215	10-3-81	2003	Kissimmee, Fla.
2-team (102 Sarasota)	.292	126	455	73	133	17	5	13	63	50	71	7	4	.364	.437							
Ordonez, Rey	.125	3	8	0	1	1	0	0	1	0	1	0	0	.111	.250	R	R	5-9	160	1-11-71	1993	Parkland, Fla.
Pie, Felix	.299	105	412	79	123	17	9	8	47	38	113	31	16	.361	.442	L	L	6-2	170	2-8-85	2002	La Romana, D.R.
Reyes, Jose	.226	80	261	27	59	12	1	2	17	13	54	1	4	.276	.303	S	R	5-11	185	2-26-84	2000	Barahona, D.R.
Salas, Issmael	.225	63	209	31	47	12	1	5	23	16	32	3	0	.281	.364	R	R	5-9	190	7-25-82	2001	Tijuana, Mexico
Sing, Brandon	.270	122	408	86	110	27	0	32	94	84	101	1	3	.399	.571	R	R	6-5	210	3-13-81	1999	Joliet, Ill.
Spearman, Jemel	.289	12	45	12	13	0	0	0	5	7	4	1	.389	.289	R	R	6-0	190	12-27-80	2002	Lawrenceville, Ga.	
Theriot, Ryan	.273	103	330	47	90	14	3	1	34	48	43	13	11	.367	.342	S	R	5-11	170	12-7-79	2001	Baton Rouge, La.

PITCHING	W	L	ERA	G	GS	CG	SV	IP	H	R	ER	BB	SO	AVG	B	T	HT	WT	DOB	1st Yr	Resides
Atlee, Thomas	3	3	3.58	46	0	0	15	50	52	26	20	20	37	.263	R	R	5-10	190	9-6-79	2002	Houston, Texas
Baez, Federico	8	2	3.55	48	0	0	1	71	67	37	28	26	53	.253	R	R	6-2	190	8-4-81	2001	Dorado, P.R.
Blasdell, Jared	0	0	5.79	2	0	0	0	5	3	3	3	0	5	.176	R	R	6-3	185	5-14-79	2001	Las Vegas, Nev.

PITCHING

PITCHING	W	L	ERA	G	GS	CG	SV	IP	H	R	ER	BB	SO	AVG	B	T	HT	WT	DOB	1st Yr	Resides
Cherry, Rocky	5	10	5.20	27	22	1	0	125	139	79	72	46	104	.287	R	R	6-5	210	8-19-79	2003	Coppell, Texas
Connolly, Jon	9	5	2.40	21	21	3	0	131	123	47	35	24	101	.247	R	L	6-0	200	8-24-83	2001	Oneonta, N.Y.
2-team (4 Lakeland)	11	7	2.59	25	25	3	0	153	151	59	44	29	109	.256							
Gerk, Jordan	1	2	4.11	18	0	0	0	35	39	19	16	15	31	.279	L	L	6-1	180	7-6-79	2000	Kelowna, B.C.
Green, Craig	2	0	6.75	11	0	0	0	11	16	8	8	5	4	.348	R	R	6-3	210	11-8-81	2003	Bakersfield, Calif.
Guzman, Angel	3	1	4.20	7	7	0	0	30	27	15	14	0	40	.237	R	R	6-3	190	12-14-81	2000	Caracas, Venez.
Hill, Rich	7	6	4.03	28	19	0	0	109	88	64	49	72	136	.215	L	L	6-5	190	3-11-80	2002	Milton, Mass.
Jongejan, Ferenc	2	1	3.60	21	0	0	3	30	29	13	12	9	24	.276	L	L	6-2	170	10-20-78	2001	Utrecht, Netherlands
Kweon, Yoon-Min	0	0	0.00	1	0	0	0	1	0	0	0	1	0	1.000	R	R	6-2	210	1-22-79	2000	Inchon, Korea
Martin, Nick	2	2	3.99	26	0	0	3	38	39	17	17	13	34	.262	L	L	6-3	190	3-5-80	2001	Houston, Texas
Mitchell, Nathan	1	0	3.38	4	0	0	0	5	6	2	2	4	5	.286	R	R	6-0	190	5-2-80	2002	Houston, Texas
Mowday, Chris	3	1	1.98	39	0	0	3	55	38	22	12	31	58	.190	R	R	6-4	210	8-24-81	1998	Strathpine, Australia
O'Malley, Ryan	4	1	2.64	16	1	0	0	31	27	9	9	6	28	.245	R	L	6-1	200	4-9-80	2002	Springfield, Ill.
Overholt, Sean	1	1	7.63	10	0	0	1	31	35	30	26	12	27	.280	R	R	6-1	195	5-20-82	2003	Sandy, Utah
Ransom, Robert	1	0	1.57	5	2	0	1	23	18	5	4	5	13	.214	R	R	6-3	225	8-25-81	2004	Nashville, Tenn.
Shipman, Andrew	1	1	3.18	15	0	0	4	17	10	6	6	6	22	.164	R	R	6-3	185	10-18-81	2003	Bellevue, Neb.
2-team (20 Sarasota)	2	2	3.46	35	0	0	17	42	29	17	16	19	44	.197							
Sisco, Andy	4	10	4.21	26	25	0	0	126	118	64	59	65	134	.253	L	L	6-9	260	1-13-83	2001	Scottsdale, Ariz.
Tavarez, Anderson	7	5	4.32	19	13	0	1	77	84	41	37	19	41	.282	R	R	6-1	170	2-14-82	2001	Santiago, D.R.
Vasquez, Carlos	6	5	3.87	16	16	0	0	79	86	54	34	31	51	.272	L	L	6-2	215	12-6-82	2000	Sucre, Venez.
Wylie, Jason	0	0	12.60	3	0	0	0	5	11	7	7	2	6	.458	R	R	6-5	230	5-27-81	2002	West Jordan, Utah

FIELDING

Catcher	PCT	G	PO	A	E	DP	PB
Kweon	.833	3	5	0	1	0	0
McGehee	.986	28	190	14	3	2	6
McKnight	.968	30	173	8	6	0	1
Reyes	.993	80	586	77	5	5	4

First Base	PCT	G	PO	A	E	DP
Hood	1.000	12	73	6	0	3
Salas	.986	7	65	4	1	6
Sing	.985	111	923	57	15	85

Second Base	PCT	G	PO	A	E	DP
Coats	1.000	1	0	1	0	0
Gutierrez	1.000	1	1	0	0	0
Jones	.971	9	18	16	1	6
Marquez	.846	3	6	5	2	2

	PCT	G	PO	A	E	DP
Montanez	.942	20	25	56	5	7
Salas	.973	22	25	48	2	8
Spearman	.891	9	20	21	5	6
Theriot	.971	64	124	205	10	51

Third Base	PCT	G	PO	A	E	DP
Coats	.851	22	9	31	7	2
Hood	.818	6	5	13	4	0
Marquez	1.000	1	0	1	0	0
McGehee	.969	82	48	169	7	13
Salas	1.000	4	4	9	0	1
Salas	.941	20	15	33	3	5
Theriot	.750	1	1	2	1	1

Shortstop	PCT	G	PO	A	E	DP
Coats	.920	86	122	212	29	46

	PCT	G	PO	A	E	DP
Gutierrez	1.000	1	2	1	0	1
Johnson	1.000	1	0	5	0	1
Marquez	1.000	1	1	2	0	0
Ordonez	1.000	3	3	3	0	2
Salas	.875	1	2	5	1	0
Theriot	.957	38	58	96	7	21

Outfield	PCT	G	PO	A	E	DP
Butler	.990	77	100	3	1	1
Greenberg	1.000	95	178	4	0	1
Johnson	.944	91	155	13	10	2
McKnight	1.000	5	10	0	0	0
Murton	1.000	19	28	1	0	0
Pie	.979	104	223	10	5	0
Sing	1.000	3	2	0	0	0

LANSING LUGNUTS

Low Class A

MIDWEST LEAGUE

BATTING

BATTING	AVG	G	AB	R	H	2B	3B	HR	RBI	BB	SO	SB	CS	OBP	SLG	B	T	HT	WT	DOB	1st Yr	Resides
Boyer, Kyle	.205	13	44	2	9	1	0	1	3	3	20	2	1	.271	.295	R	R	6-1	195	11-23-81	2003	Temecula, Calif.
Chirinos, Robinson	.241	84	319	56	77	18	6	7	39	25	70	7	2	.313	.401	R	R	6-1	180	6-5-84	2001	Punto Fijo, Venez.
Collins, Kevin	.290	110	397	72	115	26	2	33	86	45	126	3	1	.369	.615	L	L	6-2	210	5-6-81	2000	Land O'Lakes, Fla.
Dopirak, Brian	.307	137	541	94	166	38	0	39	120	48	123	4	3	.363	.593	R	R	6-4	230	12-20-83	2002	Crystal Beach, Fla.
Fitzgerald, Ryan	.272	81	250	35	68	11	2	3	29	28	60	9	6	.345	.368	R	R	6-2	195	11-29-80	2003	West Des Moines, Iowa
Fox, Jake	.287	97	366	49	105	19	3	14	55	17	75	2	1	.331	.470	R	R	5-11	210	7-20-82	2003	Greenfield, Ind.
Francisco, Alfredo	.096	24	83	6	8	2	0	0	2	4	27	2	1	.148	.120	R	R	6-3	200	8-27-84	2002	San Pedro de Macoris, D.R.
Garcia, Alberto	.304	68	227	34	69	8	4	7	25	4	41	2	2	.321	.467	R	R	6-1	180	6-5-83	2002	Bonao, D.R.
Granato, Anthony	.269	32	108	18	29	4	1	1	15	25	3	1		.365	.352	B	R	6-0	205	3-18-81	2004	Burlingame, Calif.
Larsen, Drew	.243	99	342	55	83	24	2	11	51	25	101	8	2	.319	.421	R	R	6-0	190	3-9-83	2003	South Jordan, Utah
Marquez, Uriak	.243	43	140	15	34	6	0	1	14	4	20	1	1	.262	.307	L	R	6-0	170	8-17-83	2001	Caracas, Venez.
McQuade, Tony	.294	92	333	51	98	24	4	7	48	38	65	7	5	.363	.453	S	R	6-2	205	12-24-81	2003	Gainesville, Fla.
Medlin, C.J.	.279	14	43	8	12	3	0	1	12	6	11	0	0	.360	.419	R	R	6-2	200	3-3-82	2002	Broken Arrow, Okla.
Mejia, Carlos	.223	63	238	23	53	12	2	4	33	5	46	3	2	.246	.340	R	R	6-3	170	5-16-83	2003	San Pedro de Macoris, D.R.
Rick, Alan	.256	84	301	40	77	22	2	9	36	31	87	1	1	.336	.432	L	R	6-3	210	9-8-83	2002	Palatka, Fla.
Rojas, Carlos	.219	132	493	62	108	11	2	0	32	41	74	6	4	.283	.249	R	R	6-1	170	1-11-84	2001	Altagracia, Venez.
Salas, Issmael	.280	20	75	9	21	2	1	2	13	7	5	0	0	.349	.413	R	R	5-9	190	7-25-82	2001	Tijuana, Mexico
Tidball, Adam	.125	8	24	2	3	0	1	1	6	0	0			.192	.250	R	R	6-4	218	4-22-82	2003	Bethesda, Md.
Walker, Chris	.282	123	489	75	138	19	5	3	41	45	78	60	17	.346	.360	R	R	5-8	170	7-3-80	2002	Alpharetta, Ga.

PITCHING

PITCHING	W	L	ERA	G	GS	CG	SV	IP	H	R	ER	BB	SO	AVG	B	T	HT	WT	DOB	1st Yr	Resides
Bay, Ronald	11	9	3.10	28	28	0	0	168	166	71	58	30	139	.257	R	R	6-2	160	8-7-83	2003	Houston, Texas
Campusano, Ed	2	1	4.76	9	1	0	0	17	19	9	9	7	17	.271	L	L	6-4	185	7-14-82	2002	San Pedro de Macoris, D.R.
Dempster, Ryan	0	0	1.96	5	5	0	0	18	20	5	4	2	21	.270	R	R	6-3	215	5-3-77	1995	Denver, Colo.
Ferreras, Yorkin	2	2	4.10	13	7	0	1	42	42	20	19	6	29	.264	L	L	6-1	180	1-28-81	1998	Santo Domingo, D.R.
Fischer, Sam		1	6.08	18	0	0	0	24	20	17	16	33	28	.257	R	R	6-0	170	9-20-80	2002	Orland Park, Ill.
Gross, Kris	2	0	3.00	23	0	0	2	39	39	14	13	8	28	.257	R	R	6-2	190	12-28-80	2003	Lee`s Summit, Mo.
Jones, Justin	3	3	3.78	14	14	0	0	64	62	33	27	22	59	.254	L	L	6-4	195	9-25-84	2002	Virginia Beach, Va.
Kalita, Joe	1	3	2.67	18	0	0	1	34	30	11	10	8	23	.333	R	R	6-2	210	2-2-81	2003	Oak Park, Ill.
Marmol, Carlos	14	8	3.20	26	24	0	0	155	131	64	55	53	154	.234	R	R	6-2	190	10-14-82	2000	Bonao, D.R.
Marshall, Sean	2	0	1.11	7	7	1	0	49	29	7	6	4	51	.171	L	L	6-5	185	8-30-82	2003	Chesterfield, Va.
Mateo, Juan	4	1	3.27	53	1	0	9	74	66	28	27	19	60	.244	R	R	6-2	180	12-17-82	2002	Bani, D.R.
Mendez, Adalberto	5	7	4.62	56	0	0	20	64	63	37	33	28	55	.257	R	R	6-2	160	2-22-82	2003	Azua, D.R.
Nolen, Walt	0	0	3.00	3	1	0	0	6	4	2	2	4	3	.182	R	R	6-1	180	10-11-81	2004	Lake Charles, La.
O'Brien, Weston	0	1	1.33	16	0	0	1	20	11	3	3	6	23	.164	R	R	6-6	235	10-4-82	2001	Chino, Calif.
Pablos, Rene	0	1	6.10	8	0	0	0	10	14	7	7	9	4	.333	R	R	6-2	200	10-5-82	2003	Obregon, Mexico
Petrick, Billy	13	7	3.50	26	24	0	0	147	149	66	57	43	113	.267	S	R	6-6	240	4-29-84	2002	Morris, Ill.
Pratt, Andy	0	0	8.68	5	2	0	0	9	13	10	9	4	6	.325	L	L	6-0	185	8-27-79	1998	Chino Valley, Ariz.
Prior, Mark	0	0	1.23	2	2	0	0	7	2	1	1	1	13	.087	R	R	6-5	230	9-7-80	2002	Chicago, Ill.
Ransom, Robert	5	2	2.47	11	9	1	0	62	53	21	17	6	37	.233	R	R	6-3	225	8-25-81	2004	Nashville, Tenn.

PITCHING

	W	L	ERA	G	GS	CG	SV	IP	H	R	ER	BB	SO	AVG	B	T	HT	WT	DOB	1st Yr	Resides
Rapada, Clay	6	6	2.33	57	0	0	3	85	65	30	22	30	91	.212	R	L	6-5	180	3-9-81	2002	Chesapeake, Va.
Van Buren, Jermaine	0	1	1.80	3	0	0	0	5	6	1	1	5	7	.300	R	R	6-1	220	7-2-80	1998	Hattiesburg, Miss.
Wells, Randy	6	7	4.43	36	15	0	1	108	112	64	53	40	121	.267	R	R	6-4	200	8-28-82	2002	Lebanon, Ill.
Willett, Reid	0	3	5.21	26	0	0	0	38	44	25	22	18	27	.293	R	R	6-5	205	3-25-82	2003	Nashua, N.H.

FIELDING

Catcher	PCT	G	PO	A	E	DP	PB
Fox	.980	78	569	78	13	1	25
Medlin	.949	5	36	1	2	0	2
Rick	.992	58	465	38	4	3	13
Tidball	1.000	5	34	2	0	0	1

	PCT	G	PO	A	E	DP
Garcia	1.000	1	1	2	0	1
Granato	.978	23	56	76	3	18
Larsen	.905	6	10	9	2	2
Marquez	.944	21	41	44	5	11
Salas	1.000	10	23	37	0	12

Shortstop	PCT	G	PO	A	E	DP
Chirinos	1.000	1	1	5	0	0
Larsen	.947	5	10	8	1	4
Marquez	1.000	4	5	9	0	3
Rojas	.980	132	222	414	13	77

First Base	PCT	G	PO	A	E	DP
Collins	.989	12	90	3	1	8
Dopirak	.986	115	967	59	15	85
Garcia	1.000	13	54	5	0	8
Larsen	.986	12	67	5	1	8
Salas	1.000	1	3	0	0	1

Third Base	PCT	G	PO	A	E	DP
Francisco	.911	23	10	41	5	2
Garcia	.913	45	37	78	11	3
Granato	1.000	1	7	0	0	2
Larsen	.904	43	23	80	11	10
Marquez	.933	16	5	23	2	5
Salas	1.000	9	8	16	0	4

Outfield	PCT	G	PO	A	E	DP
Boyer	.952	13	20	0	1	0
Collins	1.000	78	92	5	0	1
Fitzgerald	.984	81	117	6	2	1
Garcia	.833	5	5	0	1	0
Marquez	1.000	1	1	0	0	0
McQuade	.982	91	162	4	3	0
Mejia	.981	63	98	7	2	0
Walker	.993	123	268	6	2	1

Second Base	PCT	G	PO	A	E	DP
Chirinos	.961	82	159	232	16	44

BOISE HAWKS — Short-Season Class A

NORTHWEST LEAGUE

BATTING

	AVG	G	AB	R	H	2B	3B	HR	RBI	BB	SO	SB	CS	OBP	SLG	B	T	HT	WT	DOB	1st Yr	Resides
Balcom, Jasha	.278	60	227	37	63	5	2	1	23	18	32	11	7	.331	.330	L	R	5-11	180	7-7-82	2003	Dublin, Ga.
Bernard, Oscar	.258	37	128	14	33	4	1	2	12	5	24	3	1	.284	.352	R	R	6-2	170	6-27-83	2001	San Pedro De Macoris, D.R.
Boyer, Kyle	.304	67	247	35	75	13	3	7	37	15	65	6	5	.344	.466	R	R	6-1	195	11-23-81	2003	Temecula, Calif.
Dawkins, Lance	.143	2	7	0	1	0	0	0	0	0	2	0	0	.143	.143	R	R	6-3	190	1-31-82	2003	Columbus, Miss.
Deeb, Bobby	.303	51	188	33	57	11	1	1	13	18	33	10	6	.405	.388	R	R	5-10	170	1-22-82	2004	West St. Paul, Minn.
Francisco, Alfredo	.187	61	209	19	39	10	0	4	27	10	50	2	0	.225	.292	R	R	6-3	200	8-27-84	2002	San Pedro de Macoris, D.R.
Granato, Anthony	.268	29	97	27	26	1	1	3	7	22	30	6	3	.418	.392	B	R	6-0	205	3-18-81	2004	Burlingame, Calif.
Gresky, David	.221	50	131	23	29	8	1	3	14	20	27	3	2	.342	.366	L	L	6-3	210	6-8-82	2003	North Royalton, Ohio
Griffin, Preston	.151	21	53	5	8	3	0	0	5	4	8	1	2	.286	.208	R	R	5-11	185	11-6-81	2004	Long Beach, Calif.
Harvey, Ryan	.268	58	231	42	62	8	0	14	43	20	77	2	2	.331	.485	R	R	6-5	220	8-30-84	2003	Palm Harbor, Fla.
Jones, Nick	.231	6	13	3	3	0	0	0	0	1	2	1	0	.333	.231	R	R	6-1	185	3-29-82	2003	Roanoke, Va.
Kweon, Yoon-Min	.000	4	10	3	0	0	0	0	2	3	1	0	0	.250	.000	R	R	6-2	210	1-22-79	2000	Inchon, Korea
Marquez, Uriak	.308	10	26	4	8	4	1	1	10	0	4	0	2	.296	.654	L	R	6-0	170	8-17-83	2001	Caracas, Venez.
Montanez, Luis	.293	72	266	47	78	15	7	8	48	35	54	5	4	.377	.492	R	R	6-2	175	12-15-81	2000	Miami, Fla.
Norwood, Ryan	.296	73	277	33	82	17	2	9	53	10	59	2	1	.327	.469	R	L	6-4	230	2-18-83	2004	Richmond, Va.
Perez, Leonel	.500	2	4	0	2	1	0	0	0	0	0	0	0	.600	.750	R	R	6-2	175	1-3-84	2002	Monte Plata, D.R.
Puello, Elvin	.000	2	5	0	0	0	0	0	0	0	3	0	0	.000	.000	R	R	6-2	175	12-18-84	2003	Romana, D.R.
Richie, Tony	.314	51	175	19	55	8	1	1	24	13	21	3	2	.373	.389	R	R	6-2	215	2-9-82	2003	Jacksonville, Fla.
Rios, Jose	.194	65	206	21	40	4	1	1	14	7	23	0	3	.230	.238	R	R	6-1	160	4-6-84	2003	Barranquitas, P.R.
Serrano, Julian	.286	5	7	2	2	0	0	0	0	1	3	0	0	.375	.286	R	R	5-8	200	4-8-84	2004	Santo Domingo, D.R.
Smith, Dustin	.128	14	39	1	5	0	0	0	1	0	9	2	0	.128	.128	R	R	5-11	185	5-27-81	2004	Leesville, La.
Tidball, Adam	.308	5	13	2	4	0	0	0	2	3	0	0	0	.400	.308	R	R	6-4	218	4-22-82	2003	Bethesda, Md.
Wick, Olin	.154	8	13	3	2	2	0	0	0	2	6	0	0	.267	.308	S	R	5-11	185	5-6-82	2004	Bellevue, Wash.

GAMES BY POSITION: C—Bernard 29, Perez 1, Richie 42, Tidball 5, Wick 7. **1B**—Norwood 73, Richie 4, Serrano 2. **2B**—Dawkins 2, Deeb 49, Granato 18, Griffin 4, Jones 4, Marquez 5, Smith 4. **3B**—Francisco 60, Granato 8, Griffin 4, Puello 1, Smith 8. **SS**—Granato 6, Griffin 14, Marquez 2, Rios 64. **OF**—Balcom 59, Bernard 1, Boyer 55, Gresky 34, Harvey 38, Montanez 58.

PITCHING

	W	L	ERA	G	GS	CG	SV	IP	H	R	ER	BB	SO	AVG	B	T	HT	WT	DOB	1st Yr	Resides
Blevins, Jerry	6	1	1.62	23	0	0	5	33	18	7	6	21	42	.158	L	L	6-6	185	9-6-83	2004	Swanton, Ohio
Brito, Luis	6	4	4.72	15	15	0	0	76	87	46	40	20	45	.281	R	R	6-3	180	10-19-83	2002	Monagas, Venez.
Campusano, Ed	0	5	5.29	14	5	0	0	34	37	29	20	15	24	.272	L	L	6-4	185	7-14-82	2002	San Pedro de Macoris, D.R.
Carter, Brian	0	1	8.59	5	0	0	1	7	12	8	7	3	5	.364	L	L	6-5	220	11-21-81	2003	Gig Harbor, Wash.
Downs, Darin	5	3	4.95	14	13	0	0	60	55	36	33	35	61	.248	R	L	6-1	176	12-26-84	2003	Boynton Beach, Fla.
Fenton, Will	1	0	2.93	20	0	0	4	31	28	13	10	13	35	.246	R	R	6-2	180	4-7-83	2004	Kingston, Wash.
Ferreras, Yorkin	3	2	2.55	5	5	0	0	25	21	8	7	3	23	.223	L	L	6-1	180	1-28-81	1998	Santo Domingo, D.R.
Fischer, Sam	0	0	0.66	7	0	0	1	14	10	1	1	2	19	.204	R	R	6-0	170	9-20-80	2002	Orland Park, Ill.
Green, Craig	0	1	6.61	9	0	0	0	16	24	15	12	3	8	.343	R	R	6-3	210	11-8-81	2003	Bakersfield, Calif.
Gross, Kris	4	1	3.21	19	0	0	5	28	26	15	10	15	27	.245	R	R	6-2	190	12-28-80	2003	Lee`s Summit, Mo.
Hagerty, Luke	0	2	12.00	4	3	0	0	9	15	13	12	9	5	.385	R	R	6-9	230	11-30-82	2004	North Plainfield, N.J.
Hunton, Jonathan	1	1	4.03	21	0	0	2	29	26	15	13	24	34	.250	R	R	6-2	210	2-2-81	2003	Oak Park, Ill.
Kalita, Ryan	1	0	6.00	5	0	0	0	6	8	4	4	1	5	.308	R	R	6-2	210	8-22-82	2004	Exeter, N.H.
Kosow, Jason	0	0	3.15	11	0	0	1	20	18	7	7	13	13	.247	R	R	6-3	200	8-22-82	2004	Exeter, N.H.
Krawiec, Aaron	0	1	4.22	3	2	0	0	11	16	6	5	0	8	.340	L	L	6-3	200	3-17-79	2000	Hamburg, N.Y.
Mathes, J.R.	3	0	3.50	12	8	0	0	54	50	25	21	10	51	.272	L	L	6-2	200	11-9-81	2004	Granger, Ind.
Mejia, Anderson	4	5	5.04	27	0	0	0	45	44	30	25	33	24	.265	R	R	6-2	200	7-15-82	1999	Hato Mayor, D.R.
Pablos, Rene	0	0	2.45	6	0	0	0	7	5	4	2	3	2	.208	R	R	6-2	200	11-20-84	2002	Obregon, Mexico
Rodriguez, Pedro	0	0	0.00	1	0	0	0	1	1	0	0	0	1	.200	R	R	6-7	200	11-20-84	2002	Anoco, Venez.
Ryu, Jae Kuk	0	2	2.57	5	0	0	0	7	7	3	2	5	7	.259	R	R	6-3	210	5-30-83	2001	Seoul, Korea
Schappert, Paul	2	2	6.08	9	0	0	1	13	15	10	9	8	13	.288	L	L	6-5	215	12-21-81	2004	Southlake, Texas
Shaver, Chris	0	0	3.54	13	10	0	0	41	40	20	16	19	24	.256	L	L	6-7	235	8-21-81	2004	Williamsburg, Va.
Urena, Jose	0	1	14.85	7	0	0	0	7	12	13	11	6	5	.400	R	R	6-3	160	6-8-81	1998	San Francisco de Macoris, D.R.
Weber, Matt	5	1	2.95	14	14	0	0	76	72	27	25	18	46	.254	R	R	6-3	200	5-5-85	2003	Roscoe, Ill.
Willett, Reid	1	0	6.65	14	1	0	0	23	23	18	17	11	20	.280	R	R	6-5	205	3-25-82	2003	Nashua, N.H.

ORGANIZATION STATISTICS

ARIZONA LEAGUE

BATTING	AVG	G	AB	R	H	2B	3B	HR	RBI	BB	SO	SB	CS	SLG	OBP	B	T	HT	WT	DOB	1st Yr	Resides
Andrews, Greg	.239	27	88	16	21	6	0	0	11	16	31	0	0	.307	.358	R	R		200	3-11-81	2004	Peoria, Ill.
Canzler, Russell	.248	32	105	12	26	2	3	1	13	9	35	0	1	.352	.310	R	R	6-2	190	4-11-86	2004	Conyngham, Pa.
Deeb, Bobby	.167	5	18	4	3	1	1	0	1	3	6	0	0	.333	.318	R	R	5-10	185	1-22-82	2004	West St. Paul, Minn.
Douillard, Jonathan	.275	11	40	2	11	2	0	0	11	2	9	0	1	.325	.310	L	R	6-0	190	1-24-82	2004	Acworth, Ga.
Green, Zane	.278	42	133	19	37	2	4	1	17	20	38	3	2	.376	.369	L	L	5-11	190	5-17-82	2004	Lake Park, Ga.
Griffin, Preston	.429	15	49	15	21	4	1	1	6	8	5	6	1	.612	.576	R	R	5-11	185	11-6-81	2004	Long Beach, Calif.
Harvey, Ryan	.400	2	10	1	4	3	0	0	5	0	4	0	0	.700	.400	R	R	6-5	220	8-30-84	2003	Palm Harbor, Fla.
Hoffpauir, Brad	.186	30	97	10	18	1	1	0	8	9	21	2	0	.216	.252	R	R	6-0	170	5-18-82	2004	Jacksonville, Texas
Joseph, Alfred	.268	44	142	17	38	2	2	0	20	11	37	5	7	.310	.333	R	R	5-11	185	7-25-86	2004	Corpus Christi, Texas
Martinez, Jose	.333	3	6	2	2	1	0	0	1	0	1	0	0	.500	.333	L	L	6-5	190	10-8-84	2001	Higuerote, Venez.
Mejia, Carlos	.283	26	106	15	30	5	2	1	17	2	25	1	1	.396	.310	R	R	6-3	170	5-16-83	2002	San Pedro de Macoris, D.R.
Miller, Gerald	.200	4	15	1	3	0	0	0	0	0	4	0	0	.200	.200	L	R	5-11	180	4-25-82	2004	Denver, Colo.
Morales, Saul	.197	34	142	25	28	1	0	0	8	5	33	6	5	.204	.228	R	R	5-10	175	1-26-82	2003	Carabobo, Venez.
Morgan, Ryan	.250	47	156	24	39	10	3	1	14	36	35	4	2	.372	.402	L	R	6-1	180	8-13-82	2004	Weymouth, Mass.
Perez, Leonel	.239	31	109	16	26	7	0	0	11	9	33	1	1	.303	.325	R	R	6-2	170	1-3-84	2002	Monte Plata, D.R.
Puello, Elvin	.302	53	189	26	57	7	3	1	37	12	38	1	4	.386	.380	R	R	6-2	175	12-18-84	2003	La Romana, D.R.
Quinones, Carlos	.315	53	216	28	68	12	1	0	28	19	33	9	7	.380	.373	S	R	6-2	170	3-12-83	2003	Mao Valverde, D.R.
Reed, Mark	.351	10	37	5	13	5	1	1	7	4	8	0	1	.622	.429	L	R	5-11	175	4-13-86	2004	La Verne, Calif.
Serrano, Julian	.186	13	43	3	8	3	0	0	1	0	8	1	0	.256	.222	R	R	6-2	210	12-1-81	2004	Santo Domingo, D.R.
Smith, Aaron	.259	33	116	21	30	7	4	1	12	18	25	1	0	.414	.371	R	R	6-1	185	4-9-82	2004	Everett, Wash.
Smith, Dustin	.067	4	15	2	1	1	0	0	1	1	3	1	1	.133	.222	R	R	5-11	185	5-27-81	2004	Leesville, La.
Speier, Cole	.000	12	24	0	0	0	0	0	0	1	9	0	0	.000	.040	R	R	5-11	180	3-18-84	2004	Paradise Valley, Ariz.
Tidball, Adam	.333	3	9	2	3	0	0	0	1	0	1	0	0	.333	.333	R	R	6-4	218	4-22-82	2003	Bethesda, Md.
Wick, Olin	.327	13	49	9	16	3	2	0	5	5	11	0	0	.469	.400	S	R	6-0	180	5-6-82	2004	Bellevue, Wash.

GAMES BY POSITION: C—Douillard 8, Perez 26, Reed 9, Speier 6, Tidball 2, Wick 12. **1B**—Douillard 1, Morgan 43, Perez 3, Puello 7, Serrano 2. **2B**—Andrews 25, Deeb 3, Griffin 1, Hoffpauir 28, Morales 5, A.Smith 1. **3B**—Canzler 18, Morgan 2, Puello 3, Serrano 6. **SS**—Andrews 5, Deeb 1, Griffin 13, Hoffpauir 2, Martinez 2, Puello 1, A. Smith 33, D. Smith 1. **OF**—Douillard 1, Green 32, Joseph 41, Mejia 3, Miller 3, Morales 28, Quinones 48.

PITCHING	W	L	ERA	G	GS	CG	SV	IP	H	R	ER	BB	SO	AVG	B	T	HT	WT	DOB	1st Yr	Resides
Atkins, Mitch	2	2	7.89	10	8	0	0	30	42	33	26	14	20	.333	R	R	6-3	215	10-1-85	2004	Browns Summit, N.C.
Caldwell, Daniel	1	1	3.29	14	2	0	2	38	37	15	14	11	49	.255	R	R	6-0	185	10-10-80	2004	Wake Forest, N.C.
Corbin, John	0	0	0.00	1	0	0	0	1	0	0	0	0	1	.000	L	L	6-3	205	6-11-82	2000	Hollywood, Fla.
Delie, Franky	1	3	7.00	5	0	0	0	9	10	10	7	6	8	.270	R	R	6-2	170	2-23-83	2001	La Romana, D.R.
Gallagher, Sean	1	2	3.12	10	9	0	0	35	38	19	12	11	44	.275	R	R	6-1	210	12-30-85	2004	Fort Lauderdale, Fla.
Hagerty, Luke	0	1	2.63	4	3	0	0	14	13	7	4	5	7	.260	R	L	6-7	230	4-1-81	2002	Defiance, Ohio
Haro, Jeremy	0	1	3.38	7	0	0	0	13	10	7	5	10	13	.192	R	R	5-10	160	10-18-79	2004	Palmdale, Calif.
Jones, Aaron	0	3	7.56	14	0	0	2	17	20	15	14	8	10	.307	R	R	6-0	195	9-9-81	2004	Torrance, Calif.
Jones, Brian	2	1	9.64	8	0	0	0	9	13	10	10	6	14	.333	R	R	6-1	185	11-12-81	2004	San Diego, Calif.
Koerber, Scott	1	2	5.14	15	0	0	0	28	35	19	16	18	23	.327	L	L	6-4	215	9-30-82	2004	Harper Woods, Mich.
Kosow, Jason	0	1	2.70	9	0	0	2	13	13	6	4	5	15	.250	R	R	6-3	200	8-22-82	2004	Exeter, N.H.
Krawiec, Aaron	0	1	2.57	4	3	0	0	14	16	8	4	2	6	.271	L	L	6-6	220	3-17-79	2000	Hamburg, N.Y.
Layden, Tim	1	1	2.62	12	9	0	0	45	42	19	13	26	28	.251	L	L	6-2	180	12-22-82	2004	Deer Park, N.Y.
Marsello, Jake	0	0	0.00	3	0	0	0	6	3	2	0	2	7	.142	R	R	6-2	210	12-17-82	2004	Lynn, Mass.
Mathes, J.R.	1	0	5.06	3	0	0	0	5	9	5	3	1	9	.360	L	L	6-3	205	11-9-81	2004	Granger, Ind.
Nolen, Walt	3	1	4.28	11	0	0	0	27	24	15	13	8	32	.242	R	R	6-1	180	10-11-81	2004	Lake Charles, La.
Ortiz, Jose	4	1	4.19	12	4	0	1	39	36	19	18	14	33	.244	R	R	6-2	160	11-17-83	2003	San Francisco de Macoris, D.R.
Pedrozo, Jose	0	0	0.00	1	1	0	0	1	0	0	0	0	0	.000	L	L	6-3	180	10-8-84	2002	Maracaibo, Venez.
Pratt, Andy	1	0	6.75	4	3	0	0	8	5	6	6	4	10	.166	L	L	6-0	180	8-27-79	1998	Chino Valley, Ariz.
Rodriguez, Pedro	0	2	13.24	10	1	0	1	17	29	32	25	9	20	.349	R	R	6-7	200	11-20-84	2001	Anoco, Venez.
Ryu, Jae-Kuk	0	0	4.50	2	0	0	0	4	4	2	2	0	5	.250	R	R	6-3	210	5-30-83	2001	Seoul, Korea
Santana, Andy	3	2	1.61	10	3	0	0	45	39	14	8	18	45	.243	L	L	6-3	160	8-17-83	2001	San Pedro de Macoris, D.R.
Schappert, Paul	2	0	2.84	7	0	0	1	13	12	4	4	3	13	.250	L	L	6-5	215	12-21-81	2004	Southlake, Texas
Shaver, Chris	0	1	10.13	2	0	0	0	3	6	8	3	3	6	.428	L	L	6-7	235	8-21-81	2004	Williamsburg, Va.
Thompson, Nick	2	1	2.40	11	0	0	1	15	14	5	4	7	18	.245	R	R	6-0	180	8-12-81	2004	Savannah, Tenn.
Wylie, Jason	0	0	8.10	3	0	0	0	3	4	4	3	2	1	.285	R	R	6-5	230	5-27-81	2002	West Jordan, Utah
Yepez, Jesus	1	2	3.66	12	8	0	0	47	44	27	19	24	44	.252	L	L	6-1	170	4-15-84	2002	Lara, Venez.

BY JOHN FAY

The Reds' 2004 season went like a lot of other recent ones: Things started out well, injuries took their toll and it all fell apart.

The club was 47-41 at the all-star break. But what happened three days before the break pretty much sealed the deal for the Reds.

Ken Griffey Jr. landed awkwardly while tracking down a fly ball in the right-center gap at Miller Park in Milwaukee.

Griffey partially tore his right hamstring on the play. He had 20 home runs and 60 RBIs at the time. He had just been named to the all-star team for the 12th time. The players hitting around him—Sean Casey and Adam Dunn—were enjoying the benefits of having Griffey's bat in the lineup.

The injury, at the time, was considered fairly minor. Griffey walked off the field without a limp.

He was back in the lineup in less than a month. He made his first start in right field as a Red on Aug. 3. The idea was that he would have to cover less ground in right than he would in center, so there would be less chance of aggravating the injury.

But in the first game, Griffey made a sliding stop to cut a ball off. He felt something pop. Again, the injury was not considered that serious and Griffey appeared twice as a pinch-hitter after suffering it.

But the hamstring didn't respond to treatment and when the club returned to Cincinnati, an MRI revealed a complete tear. Griffey had season-ending surgery two days later.

The season was in a major tailspin by then. The Reds started the second half 4-13 and finished at 76-86 for its fourth consecutive losing season. It is the longest such

 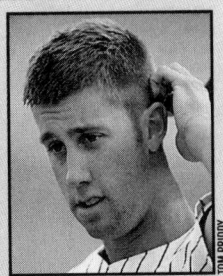

Adam Dunn   Richie Gardner

PLAYERS of the YEAR

MAJOR LEAGUE: Adam Dunn, of

Dunn fully reached his power potential in 2004, hitting 46 homers and driving in 102 runs to lead the Cincinnati offense. Though he set a major league single-season strikeout record with 195, he also drew 108 walks and scored 105 runs.

MINOR LEAGUE: Richie Gardner, rhp

Gardner was impressive in his first season as a pro, beginning at high Class A Potomac, where he was 8-3, 2.50. He was the starting pitcher for the Carolina League in the all-star game and was promoted to Double-A Chattanooga soon after, where he went 5-2, 2.56. Overall, he struck out 139 and walked just 26 in 156 innings.

streak for the organization since a stretch of 11 straight sub-.500 seasons from 1945-55.

Pitching, or lack thereof, played a major role in the Reds' demise. The club set records for ERA (5.19), runs allowed (907), home runs (236) and relief appearances (497).

But the team was in contention until the injuries caught up. In addition to Griffey, right fielder Austin Kearns lost 98 games to injuries and rehab. Paul Wilson, Aaron Harang, Casey, Jason LaRue, Mike Matthews and Danny Graves also spent time on the disabled list.

Dunn had one of the more interesting years statistically. He hit .266, raising his average 51 points from the year before. He also hit 46 home runs, scored 105 runs, drove in 102 and walked 108 times—thus becoming the first Red with 100 RBIs, 100 walks and 100 runs in a season since Joe Morgan in 1976, the second of Morgan's MVP years. But Dunn struck out a major league record 195 times.

Outfielder Wily Mo Pena also made huge strides, hitting .259-26-66 in 336 at-bats. Casey (.324-24-99) was probably the team MVP.

There doesn't appear to be a lot of help in the immediate future in the minors.

The best prospects played for Double-A Chattanooga, the only Reds' affiliate that finished above .500 in 2004. Third baseman Edwin Encarnacion (.281-17-82) will get a shot at the third base job—if the switch of Kearns to third fails.

Todd Coffey, a hard-throwing righthanded reliever, will get a chance in the bullpen. He struck out 64 and walked only six in stops at Chattanooga and Louisville.

ORGANIZATION LEADERS

BATTING

*AVG	Joey Votto, Potomac/Dayton	.301
R	Chris Denorfia, Chattanooga/Potomac	82
H	Joey Votto, Potomac/Dayton	143
TB	Joey Votto, Potomac/Dayton	237
2B	Edwin Encarnacion, Chattanooga	35
	Stephen Smitherman, Louisville	35
3B	Kenny Kelly, Louisville/Chattanooga	7
	Ray Olmedo, Louisville	7
HR	Tony Blanco, Chattanooga/Potomac	29
RBI	Joey Votto, Potomac/Dayton	93
BB	Joey Votto, Potomac/Dayton	90
SO	Walter Olmstead, Dayton	132
SB	William Bergolla, Chattanooga	36
*OBP	Joey Votto, Potomac/Dayton	.413
*SLG	Robert Mosby, Billings	.522

PITCHING

W	Richie Gardner, Chattanooga/Potomac	13
	Brian Rose, Louisville/Chattanooga	13
L	Alexander Farfan, Dayton/Billings	12
	Bubba Nelson, Louisville/Chattanooga	12
#ERA	Richie Gardner, Chattanooga/Potomac	2.53
G	Brian Shackelford, Louisville	59
CG	Seth Etherton, Louisville/Chattanooga	3
SV	Todd Coffey, Louisville/Chattanooga	24
IP	Matt Belisle, Louisville	163
BB	Jeffrey Bruksch, Potomac	63
SO	Calvin Medlock, Potomac/Dayton	157

*Minimum 250 at-bats #Minimum 75 Innings

ORGANIZATION STATISTICS

TOM PRIDDY

CINCINNATI REDS

Manager: Dave Miley.

2004 Record: 76-86, .469 (4th, NL Central).

BATTING	AVG	G	AB	R	H	2B	3B	HR	RBI	BB	SO	SB	CS	OBP	SLG	B	T	HT	WT	DOB	1st Yr	Resides
Bragg, Darren	.191	38	94	11	18	3	1	4	9	8	29	1	0	.255	.372	L	R	5-9	180	9-7-69	1991	Roswell, Ga.
2-team (9 San Diego)	.188	47	101	13	19	3	1	4	9	10	31	1	0	.261	.356							
Casey, Sean	.324	146	571	101	185	44	2	24	99	46	36	2	0	.381	.534	L	R	6-4	225	7-2-74	1995	Jupiter, Fla.
Castro, Juan	.244	111	299	36	73	21	2	5	26	14	51	1	0	.277	.378	R	R	5-11	195	6-20-72	1991	Glendale, Ariz.
Clark, Jermaine	.133	14	30	4	4	1	0	0	2	1	8	1	0	.212	.167	L	R	5-10	170	9-29-76	1997	Vacaville, Calif.
Cruz, Jacob	.224	96	147	22	33	8	0	3	28	16	43	0	0	.317	.340	L	L	6-0	210	1-28-73	1994	Gilbert, Ariz.
Dunn, Adam	.266	161	568	105	151	34	0	46	102	108	195	6	1	.388	.569	L	R	6-6	240	11-9-79	1998	Porter, Texas
Freel, Ryan	.277	143	505	74	140	21	8	3	28	67	88	37	10	.375	.368	R	R	5-10	178	3-8-76	1995	Jacksonville, Fla.
Griffey, Ken	.253	83	300	49	76	18	0	20	60	44	67	1	0	.351	.513	L	L	6-3	205	11-21-69	1987	Orlando, Fla.
Hummel, Tim	.218	56	110	10	24	4	0	1	7	8	17	1	0	.281	.282	R	R	6-2	190	11-18-78	2000	Montgomery, N.Y.
Jimenez, D`Angelo	.270	152	563	76	152	28	3	12	67	82	99	13	7	.364	.394	S	R	6-0	195	12-21-77	1995	Santo Domingo, D.R.
Kearns, Austin	.230	64	217	28	50	10	2	9	32	28	71	2	1	.321	.419	R	R	6-3	220	5-20-80	1998	Lexington, Ky.
Larkin, Barry	.289	111	346	55	100	15	3	8	44	34	39	2	0	.352	.419	R	R	6-0	185	4-28-64	1985	Orlando, Fla.
Larson, Brandon	.212	40	118	13	25	6	0	3	14	14	35	1	0	.304	.339	R	R	6-0	210	5-24-76	1997	San Antonio, Texas
LaRue, Jason	.251	114	390	46	98	24	2	14	55	26	108	0	2	.334	.431	R	R	5-11	200	3-19-74	1995	San Antonio, Texas
Lopez, Felipe	.242	79	264	35	64	18	2	7	31	25	81	1	1	.314	.405	S	R	6-1	185	5-12-80	1998	Altamonte Springs, Fla.
Machado, Anderson	.268	17	56	6	15	5	1	0	4	10	26	3	1	.379	.393	S	R	5-11	165	1-25-81	1998	Caracas, Venez.
Miller, Corky	.026	13	39	2	1	0	0	0	3	6	12	0	0	.204	.026	R	R	6-1	225	3-18-76	1998	Calimesa, Calif.
Olmedo, Ray	.000	8	1	0	0	0	0	0	0	1	0	0	0	.500	.000	S	R	5-11	155	5-31-81	1999	Maracay, Venez.
Pena, Wily Mo	.259	110	336	45	87	10	1	26	66	22	108	5	2	.316	.527	R	R	6-3	215	1-23-82	1999	Tampa, Fla.
Romano, Jason	.154	22	26	3	4	0	0	1	3	2	10	0	0	.214	.269	R	R	6-0	185	6-24-79	1997	Tampa, Fla.
Valentin, Javier	.233	82	202	18	47	10	1	6	20	17	36	0	0	.293	.381	S	R	5-10	190	9-19-75	1993	Manati, P.R.
Vander Wal, John	.118	42	51	2	6	2	0	2	4	4	20	0	0	.182	.275	L	L	6-1	210	4-29-66	1987	Grand Rapids, Mich.

PITCHING	W	L	ERA	G	GS	CG	SV	IP	H	R	ER	BB	SO	AVG	B	T	HT	WT	DOB	1st Yr	Resides
Acevedo, Jose	5	12	5.94	39	27	0	0	158	188	108	104	45	117	.292	R	R	6-0	185	12-18-77	1997	Santiago, D.R.
Bong, Jung Keun	1	1	4.70	3	3	0	0	15	13	8	10	11	20	.270	L	L	6-3	175	7-15-80	1998	Norcross, Ga.
Claussen, Brandon	2	8	6.14	14	14	0	0	66	80	50	45	35	45	.299	L	L	6-2	200	5-1-79	1999	Roswell, N.M.
Graves, Danny	1	6	3.95	68	0	0	41	68	77	39	30	13	40	.282	R	R	6-0	185	8-7-73	1994	Lake Mary, Fla.
Hancock, Josh	5	1	4.45	12	0	0	0	55	60	34	27	25	31	.273	R	R	6-3	215	4-11-78	1998	Tupelo, Miss.
2-team (4 Philadelphia)	5	2	5.09	16	11	0	0	64	73	43	36	28	36	.282							
Harang, Aaron	10	9	4.86	28	28	1	0	161	177	90	87	53	125	.280	R	R	6-7	240	5-9-78	1999	San Diego, Calif.
Haynes, Jimmy	0	3	9.60	5	4	0	0	15	26	17	16	7	8	.388	R	R	6-4	220	9-5-72	1991	La Grange, Ga.
Hudson, Luke	4	2	2.42	9	9	0	0	48	36	16	13	25	38	.208	R	R	6-3	195	5-2-77	1998	Fountain Valley, Calif.
Jones, Todd	8	2	3.79	51	0	0	1	57	49	25	24	25	37	.243	B	R	6-3	230	4-24-68	1989	Pell City, Ala.
Lidle, Cory	7	10	5.32	24	24	3	0	149	170	95	88	44	93	.288	R	R	5-11	190	3-22-72	1991	Las Vegas, Nev.
Matthews, Mike	2	1	6.30	35	0	0	0	30	31	22	21	16	15	.265	L	L	6-2	170	10-24-73	1992	Woodbridge, Va.
Myette, Aaron	0	0	8.31	5	0	0	0	4	3	4	4	8	6	.188	R	R	6-4	210	9-26-77	1997	Gig Harbor, Wash.
Norton, Phil	2	5	5.07	69	0	0	0	66	71	41	37	38	48	.284	R	L	6-0	215	2-1-76	1996	Texarkana, Texas
Padilla, Juan	1	0	10.67	12	0	0	0	14	23	17	17	8	12	.359	R	R	6-0	200	2-17-77	1998	Levittown, P.R.
Reith, Brian	2	2	7.27	22	0	0	0	26	30	21	21	19	24	.269	R	R	6-5	220	2-28-78	1996	Fort Wayne, Ind.
Riedling, John	5	3	5.10	70	0	0	0	78	90	54	44	40	46	.286	R	R	5-11	190	8-29-75	1994	Wellington, Fla.
Sanchez, Jesus	0	2	7.53	3	3	0	0	14	18	12	12	9	8	.305	L	L	5-10	165	10-11-74	1994	Nizao Bani, D.R.
Valentine, Joe	2	3	5.22	24	1	0	4	29	23	18	17	25	29	.211	R	R	6-2	210	12-24-79	1999	Pensacola, Fla.
Van Poppel, Todd	4	6	6.09	48	11	0	0	115	136	80	78	32	72	.298	R	R	6-5	230	12-9-71	1990	Southlake, Texas
Wagner, Ryan	3	2	4.70	49	0	0	0	52	59	31	27	27	37	.284	R	R	6-4	210	7-15-82	2003	Yoakum, Texas
White, Gabe	1	2	6.23	40	0	0	1	39	39	27	27	5	33	.257	L	L	6-2	205	11-20-71	1990	Sebring, Fla.
Wilson, Paul	11	6	4.36	29	29	1	0	184	192	93	89	63	117	.271	R	R	6-5	215	3-28-73	1994	Palm City, Fla.

FIELDING

Catcher	PCT	G	PO	A	E	DP	PB
LaRue	.989	111	648	59	8	8	15
Miller	.989	12	84	5	1	1	1
Valentin	.988	55	305	31	4	2	1

First Base	PCT	G	PO	A	E	DP
Casey	.994	145	1233	56	8	86
Castro	1.000	4	27	2	0	2
Cruz	1.000	6	10	1	0	2
Dunn	1.000	10	76	4	0	5
Hummel	1.000	13	43	8	0	6
Valentin	1.000	7	37	1	0	5
Vander Wal	1.000	4	8	0	0	0

Second Base	PCT	G	PO	A	E	DP
Castro	.977	12	15	28	1	6
Clark	1.000	2	4	3	0	1

Third Base	PCT	G	PO	A	E	DP
Castro	.958	78	38	75	5	7
Freel	.925	54	42	107	12	11
Hummel	.941	32	17	47	4	5
Larson	.937	35	24	50	5	4
Lopez	.936	24	24	49	5	1

Shortstop	PCT	G	PO	A	E	DP
Castro	.981	31	32	72	2	16
Hummel	.000	1	0	0	0	0
Jimenez	1.000	5	7	7	0	1
Larkin	.988	85	106	216	4	33

	PCT	G	PO	A	E	DP	PB
Freel	1.000	15	25	23	0	4	
Hummel	1.000	1	1	0	0	0	
Jimenez	.990	146	297	388	7	74	
Lopez	.667	2	1	1	1	1	

	PCT	G	PO	A	E	DP
Lopez	.957	51	65	137	9	25
Machado	.937	17	23	36	4	7
Olmedo	1.000	7	4	4	0	1

Outfield	PCT	G	PO	A	E	DP
Bragg	.984	26	61	2	1	0
Clark	1.000	8	10	1	0	0
Cruz	1.000	29	36	1	0	0
Dunn	.970	156	250	10	8	1
Freel	.985	89	185	8	3	3
Griffey	.994	77	173	4	1	1
Kearns	.975	60	118	1	3	0
LaRue	1.000	1	1	0	0	0
Pena	.969	91	212	6	7	0
Romano	1.000	11	9	1	0	0
Vander Wal	1.000	7	12	1	0	0

Ken Griffey: Became the 20th member of the 500-homer club

Sean Casey: Tied a career high with 99 RBIs

FARM SYSTEM

Director, Player Development: Tim Naehring.

Class	Farm Team	League	W	L	Pct.	Finish*	Manager	Affiliate Since
AAA	Louisville (Ky.) RiverBats	International	67	77	.465	10th (14)	Rick Burleson	2000
AA	Chattanooga (Tenn.) Lookouts	Southern	87	53	.621	**1st (10)**	Jayhawk Owens	1988
High A	#Potomac (Va.) Cannons	Carolina	67	72	.482	**5th (8)**	Edgar Caceres	2003
Low A	Dayton (Ohio) Dragons	Midwest	48	92	.343	14th (14)	Alonzo Powell	2000
Rookie	Billings (Mont.) Mustangs	Pioneer	37	37	.500	**5th (8)**	Donnie Scott	1974
Rookie	Sarasota (Fla.) Reds	Gulf Coast	20	37	.351	12th (12)	Freddie Benavides	1999

*Finish in overall standings (No. of teams in league)/playoff teams in **boldface**   #Affiliate will operate in Sarasota (Florida State) in 2005

LOUISVILLE BATS
Class AAA

INTERNATIONAL LEAGUE

BATTING	AVG	G	AB	R	H	2B	3B	HR	RBI	BB	SO	SB	CS	OBP	SLG	B	T	HT	WT	DOB	1st Yr	Resides
Alviso, Jerome	.192	15	26	3	5	0	0	0	5	4	3	0	0	.300	.192	S	R	6-1	160	9-4-75	1997	Livermore, Calif.
Bragg, Darren	.239	13	46	4	11	1	0	2	4	5	13	1	0	.314	.391	L	R	5-9	180	9-7-69	1991	Roswell, Ga.
2-team (70 Columbus)	.276	83	319	45	88	22	3	10	33	42	58	8	2	.359	.458							
Burnham, Gary	.261	69	222	30	58	15	0	5	30	19	33	2	3	.327	.396	L	L	5-11	200	10-13-74	1997	South Windsor, Conn.
Castro, Juan	.167	5	18	1	3	1	0	0	3	1	2	0	0	.200	.222	R	R	5-11	195	6-20-72	1991	Glendale, Ariz.
Cesar, Dionys	.185	18	54	7	10	4	0	0	6	4	8	1	0	.254	.259	S	R	5-10	150	8-27-76	1994	Santo Domingo, D.R.
Chamblee, Jim	.262	123	397	73	104	23	5	11	63	52	117	3	2	.364	.428	R	R	6-4	185	5-6-75	1995	Denton, Texas
Christensen, McKay	.294	5	17	1	5	1	0	0	3	1	4	1	0	.333	.353	L	L	5-11	180	8-14-75	1995	Alpine, Utah
Clark, Jermaine	.284	115	398	77	113	15	5	10	52	63	54	24	9	.386	.422	L	R	5-10	170	9-29-76	1997	Vacaville, Calif.
Cruz, Jacob	.315	17	54	12	17	4	0	3	7	10	10	0	0	.415	.556	L	L	6-0	210	1-28-73	1994	Gilbert, Ariz.
Hill, Jason	.143	3	7	0	1	0	0	0	0	0	1	0	0	.250	.143	R	R	6-3	210	3-17-77	1998	Danville, Calif.
Holbert, Aaron	.271	115	380	66	103	16	3	4	46	41	66	32	14	.350	.361	R	R	6-1	190	1-9-73	1990	Wesley Chapel, Fla.
Hummel, Tim	.289	42	152	18	44	13	0	2	20	12	27	2	0	.345	.414	R	R	6-2	190	11-18-78	2000	Montgomery, N.Y.
Kearns, Austin	.337	25	83	19	28	7	1	2	15	19	16	3	1	.471	.518	R	R	6-3	220	5-20-80	1998	Lexington, Ky.
Kelly, Kenny	.254	78	268	44	68	15	4	9	43	24	71	7	4	.320	.440	R	R	6-3	180	1-26-79	1997	Lutz, Fla.
Larson, Brandon	.282	32	117	14	33	5	0	9	25	5	39	0	0	.315	.556	R	R	6-0	210	5-24-76	1995	San Antonio, Texas
LaRue, Jason	.100	3	10	3	1	0	0	1	4	1	3	0	0	.214	.400	R	R	5-11	200	3-19-74	1995	San Antonio, Texas
Lomasney, Steve	.252	55	131	14	33	5	1	3	27	11	49	2	0	.310	.374	R	R	6-0	207	8-29-77	1995	Peabody, Mass.
Lopez, Felipe	.273	75	293	50	80	11	3	9	43	25	71	2	2	.329	.423	S	R	6-1	185	5-12-80	1998	Altamonte Springs, Fla.
Machado, Anderson	.229	31	109	14	25	5	2	0	12	10	26	3	2	.295	.312	S	R	5-11	165	1-25-81	1998	Caracas, Venez.
2-team (78 Scranton)	.228	109	404	65	92	17	7	6	38	60	99	14	8	.326	.349							
Miller, Corky	.220	74	227	31	50	14	0	6	37	25	44	0	0	.316	.361	R	R	6-1	185	3-18-76	1998	Calimesa, Calif.
Olmedo, Ray	.286	82	294	33	84	13	7	2	26	23	40	2	3	.342	.398	S	R	5-11	155	5-31-81	1999	Maracay, Venez.
Patchett, Gary	.000	4	2	1	0	0	0	0	0	0	0	0	0	.000	.000	R	R	6-2	180	9-25-78	2000	Gardena, Calif.

BATTING

BATTING	AVG	G	AB	R	H	2B	3B	HR	RBI	BB	SO	SB	CS	OBP	SLG	B	T	HT	WT	DOB	1st Yr	Resides
Romano, Jason	.337	40	163	22	55	12	4	2	16	3	24	3	1	.347	.497	R	R	6-0	185	6-24-79	1997	Tampa, Fla.
Sardinha, Dane	.262	89	324	32	85	17	1	9	40	10	94	0	1	.294	.404	R	R	6-0	215	4-8-79	2001	Gulfport, Miss.
Smitherman, Stephen	.272	129	452	55	123	35	1	10	52	42	107	5	5	.340	.420	R	R	6-4	235	9-1-78	2000	Hartshorne, Okla.
Stratton, Robert	.353	34	119	23	42	10	2	12	34	9	35	0	1	.392	.773	R	R	6-2	250	10-7-77	1996	Santa Barbara, Calif.
Taylor, Reggie	.257	61	191	28	49	9	1	9	24	13	46	10	3	.304	.455	L	R	6-1	180	1-12-77	1995	Newberry, S.C.
Vander Wal, John	.188	16	48	5	9	3	0	2	5	10	2	0	.264	.250	L	L	6-1	210	4-29-66	1987	Grand Rapids, Mich.

PITCHING

PITCHING	W	L	ERA	G	GS	CG	SV	IP	H	R	ER	BB	SO	AVG	B	T	HT	WT	DOB	1st Yr	Resides
Belisle, Matt	9	11	5.26	28	28	2	0	163	192	104	95	51	106	.301	S	R	6-3	190	6-6-80	1999	Austin, Texas
Bong, Jung Keun	8	8	5.82	19	19	0	0	94	118	66	61	31	65	.313	L	L	6-3	175	7-15-80	1998	Norcross, Ga.
Booker, Chris	0	1	4.50	7	0	0	0	12	10	6	6	10	9	.227	R	R	6-3	230	12-9-76	1995	Monroeville, Ala.
Cerros, Juan	2	5	3.15	30	6	0	1	71	63	33	25	38	47	.241	R	R	6-1	200	11-25-76	1996	Nuevo Leon, Mexico
Claussen, Brandon	8	6	4.66	18	18	0	0	100	98	56	52	47	111	.256	R	L	6-2	200	5-1-79	1999	Roswell, N.M.
Coffey, Todd	1	0	5.27	15	0	0	4	14	15	8	8	2	11	.273	R	R	6-5	230	9-9-80	1998	Forest City, N.C.
Etherton, Seth	5	6	3.47	19	19	3	0	112	107	45	43	32	110	.252	R	R	6-1	200	10-17-76	1998	Monarch Beach, Calif.
Harang, Aaron	0	1	12.00	1	1	0	0	3	9	8	4	3	3	.529	R	R	6-7	240	5-9-78	1999	San Diego, Calif.
Hartmann, Pete	0	0	13.50	3	0	0	0	2	5	4	3	1	4	.455	L	L	6-2	200	5-13-71	1993	Scottsdale, Ariz.
Hudson, Luke	2	1	2.84	3	3	0	0	19	15	8	6	5	17	.214	R	R	6-3	195	5-2-77	1998	Fountain Valley, Calif.
Mallette, Brian	1	0	2.27	40	0	0	5	44	35	12	11	12	36	.213	R	R	6-0	180	1-19-75	1997	Glenwood, Ga.
Matthews, Mike	1	0	1.53	15	0	0	1	18	12	3	3	5	16	.188	L	L	6-2	170	10-24-73	1992	Woodbridge, Va.
Moseley, Dustin	2	4	4.65	12	12	0	0	72	78	38	37	34	48	.286	R	R	6-4	190	12-26-81	2001	Texarkana, Texas
Moss, Damian	0	3	10.13	4	3	0	0	19	29	23	21	15	12	.363	R	L	6-0	180	11-24-76	1994	Dublin, Ga.
2-team (20 Durham)	5	12	6.60	24	20	0	0	108	138	91	79	80	79	.321							
Myette, Aaron	3	3	2.89	41	1	0	19	62	45	27	20	36	58	.193	R	R	6-4	210	9-26-77	1997	Gig Harbor, Wash.
Nelson, Joe	1	10	7.09	12	12	0	0	60	74	56	47	26	45	.312	R	R	6-2	200	8-26-81	2000	Fort Washington, Md.
Randall, Scott	1	4	4.98	27	1	0	0	43	48	29	24	19	30	.287	R	R	6-3	225	10-29-75	1995	Goleta, Calif.
Reith, Brian	2	3	3.72	26	1	0	0	36	51	17	15	13	32	.342	R	R	6-5	220	2-28-78	1996	Fort Wayne, Ind.
Rose, Brian	3	2	3.31	6	6	0	0	35	39	13	13	10	26	.283	R	R	6-3	210	2-13-76	1995	Dartmouth, Mass.
Sanchez, Jesus	3	2	3.00	22	5	0	1	60	49	22	20	28	51	.225	L	L	5-10	165	10-11-74	1994	Nizao Bani, D.R.
Shackelford, Brian	8	1	3.58	59	0	0	0	73	58	31	29	42	63	.220	L	L	6-1	190	8-30-76	1998	Norman, Okla.
Shearn, Tom	0	1	2.55	11	0	0	0	18	10	6	5	6	12	.167	R	R	6-4	200	8-28-77	1996	Columbus, Ohio
Valentine, Joe	5	5	5.01	30	0	0	0	65	63	41	36	32	61	.258	R	R	6-2	210	12-24-79	1999	Pensacola, Fla.
Wagner, Ryan	1	0	2.70	15	0	0	1	17	13	5	5	9	19	.210	R	R	6-4	210	7-15-82	2003	Yoakum, Texas
Watson, Mark	1	0	4.71	23	0	0	1	21	23	12	11	10	7	.274	R	L	6-3	240	1-23-74	1996	Atlanta, Ga.

FIELDING

Catcher	PCT	G	PO	A	E	DP	PB
Hill	1.000	1	5	0	0	0	
LaRue	.917	3	11	0	1	0	0
Lomasney	.987	23	142	9	2	0	2
Miller	.990	52	384	31	4	6	7
Sardinha	.987	72	508	33	7	4	2

First Base	PCT	G	PO	A	E	DP
Alviso	1.000	5	34	2	0	3
Burnham	.994	58	432	40	3	50
Chamblee	1.000	11	65	5	0	9
Cruz	1.000	4	29	3	0	3
Holbert	.984	37	229	22	4	29
Hummel	1.000	10	74	6	0	7
Lomasney	.990	16	81	14	1	11
Smitherman	.984	18	117	7	2	16
Vander Wal	1.000	8	52	1	0	6

Second Base	PCT	G	PO	A	E	DP
Alviso	1.000	1	3	3	0	0
Castro	1.000	1	1	1	0	0
Cesar	1.000	4	2	10	0	1

	PCT	G	PO	A	E	DP
Chamblee	.933	4	8	6	1	4
Clark	.991	31	53	58	1	21
Holbert	.989	46	80	102	2	35
Hummel	1.000	9	14	23	0	7
Lopez	.940	8	22	25	3	8
Olmedo	.974	59	126	174	8	48
Patchett	1.000	2	1	1	0	0

Third Base	PCT	G	PO	A	E	DP
Castro	1.000	1	0	4	0	0
Cesar	1.000	1	1	0	0	0
Chamblee	.923	90	62	178	20	31
Clark	.909	6	3	7	1	1
Holbert	1.000	2	2	5	0	1
Hummel	.927	20	6	32	3	1
Larson	.910	31	12	59	7	5
Lopez	1.000	1	0	1	0	0

Shortstop	PCT	G	PO	A	E	DP
Alviso	.800	6	2	6	2	3
Castro	.933	3	4	10	1	2
Cesar	.878	12	15	21	5	7

	PCT	G	PO	A	E	DP
Chamblee	1.000	1	2	0	0	0
Holbert	.979	11	15	32	1	6
Lopez	.959	67	79	154	10	41
Machado	.932	31	56	68	9	20
Olmedo	.947	24	33	56	5	16
Patchett	1.000	1	0	1	0	0

Outfield	PCT	G	PO	A	E	DP
Bragg	1.000	13	33	0	0	0
Chamblee	.962	15	23	2	1	0
Christensen	.889	4	8	0	1	0
Clark	1.000	78	141	1	0	0
Cruz	1.000	9	9	1	0	0
Darula	1.000	10	8	0	0	0
Holbert	1.000	10	14	2	0	0
Kearns	.949	22	55	1	3	0
Kelly	.973	79	172	8	5	1
Romano	.989	39	90	1	1	0
Smitherman	.966	110	162	10	6	1
Stratton	.912	14	30	1	3	0
Taylor	.973	56	101	6	3	1
Vander Wal	1.000	4	4	0	0	0

CHATTANOOGA LOOKOUTS — Class AA

SOUTHERN LEAGUE

BATTING	AVG	G	AB	R	H	2B	3B	HR	RBI	BB	SO	SB	CS	OBP	SLG	B	T	HT	WT	DOB	1st Yr	Resides
Anderson, Bryan	.279	35	61	7	17	7	1	0	9	10	16	0	0	.365	.426	R	R	6-2	170	7-10-78	2000	San Antonio, Texas
Bannon, Jeff	.252	134	473	68	119	31	2	13	73	43	111	5	2	.316	.408	R	R	6-4	185	8-21-79	2001	Camarillo, Calif.
Beattie, Andrew	.300	101	347	51	104	18	6	6	43	47	67	8	4	.381	.484	S	R	5-10	165	2-28-78	1998	Sarasota, Fla.
Bergolla, William	.283	116	466	79	132	26	1	4	38	40	63	36	6	.342	.369	R	R	6-0	175	2-4-83	2000	Valencia, Venez.
Blanco, Tony	.245	58	220	25	54	8	1	12	31	15	53	0	0	.300	.455	R	R	6-1	175	11-10-81	1999	Haina, D.R.
Cesar, Dionys	.297	49	165	27	49	8	1	6	35	23	35	4	1	.384	.467	S	R	5-10	150	8-27-76	1994	Santo Domingo, D.R.
Darula, Bobby	.366	48	153	38	56	8	0	6	27	16	16	8	2	.427	.536	L	R	5-10	185	10-29-74	1996	Greenwich, Conn.
Denorfia, Chris	.249	61	221	30	55	10	2	6	27	30	40	5	2	.340	.394	R	R	6-1	185	7-15-80	2002	Southington, Conn.
Durham, Chad	.255	73	216	32	55	10	2	2	16	26	52	16	5	.343	.356	R	R	5-8	170	6-23-78	1997	Charlotte, N.C.
Encarnacion, Edwin	.281	120	469	73	132	35	1	13	76	53	79	17	3	.352	.443	R	R	6-1	180	1-7-83	2000	La Romana, D.R.
Gutierrez, Jesse	.292	127	487	74	142	32	4	17	82	36	64	0	0	.352	.478	R	R	6-2	195	6-16-78	2001	McAllen, Texas
Hill, Jason	.297	78	232	30	69	10	0	3	30	20	32	1	0	.350	.405	R	R	6-3	210	3-17-77	1998	Danville, Calif.
Kelly, Kenny	.356	51	191	33	68	15	3	5	28	26	46	13	7	.441	.545	R	R	6-3	180	1-26-79	1997	Lutz, Fla.
Larson, Brandon	.286	2	7	1	2	1	0	1	1	0	4	0	0	.286	.857	R	R	6-0	210	5-24-76	1997	San Antonio, Texas
Moreta, Ramon	.231	91	234	31	54	8	2	19	22	46	9	7	.295	.432	R	R	5-11	160	9-5-75	1994	La Romana, D.R.
Peterson, Brian	.300	93	313	40	94	21	3	6	40	24	61	3	1	.361	.444	R	R	6-2	205	10-22-78	2000	Greencastle, Ind.
Senjem, Guye	.190	11	21	3	4	2	0	0	2	6	8	0	0	.370	.286	L	R	6-0	210	5-2-75	1997	Kenyon, Minn.
Wilson, Travis	.277	109	264	28	73	16	1	6	36	21	76	3	0	.338	.413	R	R	6-2	180	7-10-77	1997	Christchurch, New Zealand

PITCHING

PITCHING	W	L	ERA	G	GS	CG	SV	IP	H	R	ER	BB	SO	AVG	B	T	HT	WT	DOB	1st Yr	Resides
Baez, Benito	3	1	2.12	12	0	0	1	17	13	4	4	7	18	.210	L	L	6-0	160	5-6-77	1994	Bonao, D.R.
Beech, Matt	3	0	0.64	6	1	0	1	14	5	1	1	10	17	.114	L	L	6-2	180	1-20-72	1994	Clearwater, Fla.
Booker, Chris	2	0	1.38	28	0	0	5	39	26	6	6	25	57	.184	R	R	6-3	230	12-9-76	1995	Monroeville, Ala.
Caracioli, Lance	2	1	3.00	12	6	0	0	39	29	14	13	29	37	.215	L	L	6-4	200	12-14-77	1998	Walker, La.
Childress, Daylan	3	5	3.42	29	9	0	7	82	73	37	31	31	77	.241	R	R	6-1	200	7-31-78	2001	Floresville, Texas
Coffey, Todd	4	1	2.38	40	0	0	20	45	36	13	12	4	53	.216	R	R	6-5	230	9-9-80	1998	Forest City, N.C.
Crawford, Paxton	1	1	3.93	18	0	0	0	34	33	21	15	10	27	.252	R	R	6-3	210	8-4-77	1995	Morrilton, Ark.
DeHart, Casey	6	6	4.26	48	0	0	1	76	72	41	36	37	76	.249	L	L	6-1	180	11-1-77	1998	Burleson, Texas
Etherton, Seth	4	1	1.98	7	7	0	0	41	31	12	9	9	46	.207	R	R	6-1	200	10-17-76	1998	Monarch Beach, Calif.
Gardner, Richie	5	2	2.56	11	11	0	0	70	68	24	20	13	59	.248	R	R	6-3	185	2-1-82	2004	Santa Rosa, Calif.
Gil, David	0	1	6.00	17	0	0	0	24	32	17	16	10	18	.323	R	R	6-4	215	12-26-74	2000	Miami, Fla.
Hudson, Luke	7	7	3.32	16	16	0	0	87	71	35	32	25	91	.225	R	R	6-3	195	5-2-77	1998	Fountain Valley, Calif.
Kelly, Steve	12	7	2.96	28	28	0	0	161	156	69	53	48	116	.250	R	R	6-1	195	9-30-79	2001	Hamilton, Ohio
MacRae, Scott	2	0	3.00	5	4	0	0	21	25	9	7	6	12	.298	R	R	6-3	205	8-13-74	1995	Marietta, Ga.
Manning, Charlie	4	4	5.12	13	13	1	0	70	79	42	40	21	71	.287	L	L	6-2	180	3-31-79	2001	Winter Haven, Fla.
Meyer, Jake	1	1	3.15	4	0	0	0	20	21	8	7	3	16	.280	R	R	6-1	200	1-7-75	1997	San Diego, Calif.
Moseley, Dustin	3	2	2.66	8	8	0	0	47	33	16	14	10	40	.196	R	R	6-4	190	12-26-81	2001	Texarkana, Texas
Nelson, Bubba	1	2	4.08	10	9	0	0	53	61	32	24	12	35	.288	R	R	6-2	200	8-26-81	2000	Fort Washington, Md.
Ramirez, Elizardo	1	0	3.19	5	5	1	0	31	35	11	11	4	23	.282	R	R	6-0	145	1-28-83	2000	Santo Domingo, D.R.
Rose, Brian	10	3	3.30	20	18	0	0	106	106	44	39	17	85	.264	R	R	6-3	210	2-13-76	1995	Dartmouth, Mass.
Salmon, Brad	4	2	4.27	39	1	0	3	65	68	35	31	22	53	.271	L	R	6-4	220	1-3-80	1999	Cantonment, Fla.
Shearn, Tom	6	4	4.40	37	0	0	5	61	56	34	30	27	67	.243	R	R	6-4	200	8-27-77	1996	Columbus, Ohio
Thompson, Travis	3	1	1.83	18	0	0	3	34	27	10	7	9	34	.214	R	R	6-5	225	7-3-77	1999	Matthews, N.C.
Wilson, Travis	0	1	3.38	3	0	0	0	8	5	5	3	6		.185	R	R	6-2	180	7-10-77	1997	Christchurch, New Zealand

FIELDING

Catcher	PCT	G	PO	A	E	DP	PB
Hill	.989	58	425	39	5	6	5
Peterson	.986	87	714	69	11	8	10

First Base	PCT	G	PO	A	E	DP
Darula	1.000	1	7	0	0	3
Gutierrez	.994	124	984	87	7	84
Hill	1.000	2	3	0	0	1
Wilson	.985	18	121	10	2	15

Second Base	PCT	G	PO	A	E	DP
Anderson	.962	14	20	30	2	7
Bannon	.977	14	37	47	2	11
Beattie	.980	13	25	23	1	6
Bergolla	.965	92	183	208	14	51

Cesar	1.000	12	25	23	0	5

Third Base	PCT	G	PO	A	E	DP
Bannon	.870	9	8	12	3	2
Beattie	.923	5	4	8	1	1
Cesar	.813	6	3	10	3	
Encarnacion	.921	119	97	196	25	11
Wilson	.944	8	6	11	1	2

Shortstop	PCT	G	PO	A	E	DP
Bannon	.937	93	142	244	26	53
Beattie	.935	8	13	16	2	2
Bergolla	.944	23	28	57	5	15
Cesar	.944	19	26	59	5	9

Outfield	PCT	G	PO	A	E	DP
Anderson	1.000	1	2	0	0	0
Bannon	1.000	11	15	0	0	0
Beattie	.967	70	108	8	4	4
Blanco	.961	51	73	0	3	0
Darula	1.000	33	50	2	0	0
Denorfia	.987	60	151	5	2	3
Durham	1.000	62	106	7	0	1
Hill	1.000	2	5	0	0	0
Kelly	1.000	51	117	3	0	0
Moreta	.983	71	111	4	2	2
Senjem	1.000	6	9	0	0	0
Wilson	.948	40	54	1	3	0

POTOMAC CANNONS — High Class A

CAROLINA LEAGUE

BATTING	AVG	G	AB	R	H	2B	3B	HR	RBI	BB	SO	SB	CS	OBP	SLG	B	T	HT	WT	DOB	1st Yr	Resides
Blanco, Tony	.306	62	216	42	66	10	0	17	47	27	66	2	0	.403	.588	R	R	6-1	175	11-10-81	1999	Haina, D.R.
Cairns, Troy	.234	35	77	7	18	3	0	0	8	4	24	1	0	.298	.273	R	R	6-0	160	9-29-80	2002	Blue Springs, Mo.
Correll, Brad	.281	112	423	72	119	23	1	9	66	51	76	8	6	.367	.404	R	R	6-2	205	6-17-81	2002	Gastonia, N.C.
Denorfia, Chris	.312	75	269	52	84	18	4	11	51	48	66	10	6	.416	.532	R	R	6-1	185	7-15-80	2002	Southington, Conn.
Dickerson, Chris	.200	15	45	5	9	2	0	0	5	7	14	3	1	.321	.244	L	L	6-4	212	4-10-82	2003	Van Nuys, Calif.
Durham, Chad	.242	56	227	29	55	4	2	3	27	17	49	8	4	.298	.317	R	R	5-8	170	6-23-78	1997	Charlotte, N.C.
Hanigan, Ryan	.296	119	429	58	127	21	0	5	56	49	51	6	5	.369	.380	R	R	5-11	195	8-16-80	2002	Andover, Mass.
Howard, Kevin	.284	124	468	68	133	24	0	11	79	58	70	8	7	.364	.406	L	R	6-2	180	6-25-81	2003	Thousand Oaks, Calif.
Lewis, Domonique	.204	71	221	26	45	9	1	0	19	22	75	14	7	.278	.253	R	R	5-9	160	8-6-79	2001	Channelview, Texas
Logan, Matt	.274	50	186	27	51	9	1	4	26	17	32	2	3	.341	.398	L	R	6-0	200	7-22-79	1998	Brampton, Ontario
Motooka, Rafael	.150	10	20	1	3	0	0	1	2	1	5	0	0	.190	.300	R	R	6-2	180	9-25-78	2000	Gardena, Calif.
Patchett, Gary	.235	50	162	14	38	5	0	1	15	11	42	1	5	.295	.284	R	R	6-3	190	9-25-83	2001	Guatire, Venez.
Perez, Miguel	.232	18	69	7	16	2	0	0	5	1	12	1	0	.239	.261	R	R	6-3	190	11-4-78	2001	Smyrna, Ga.
Prince, Bryan	.211	76	251	30	53	8	0	6	31	33	45	0	0	.306	.315	R	R	6-2	180	6-7-80	2001	Manteca, Calif.
Ruiz, Junior	.284	102	349	78	99	20	2	2	38	65	41	24	9	.401	.370	L	R	5-10	195	6-2-80	2003	San Antonio, Texas
Schramek, Mark	.228	110	359	52	82	18	2	11	48	55	113	5	2	.348	.382	L	R	6-3	230	12-8-78	2000	San Antonio, Texas
Smith, Nestor	.217	15	60	7	13	0	0	3	4	14	0	1	.266	.217	S	R	5-11	180	1-21-78	1995	Maturin, Venez.
Tiburcio, Hector	.261	111	421	66	110	24	3	5	48	35	89	17	11	.317	.368	S	R	6-0	150	6-11-81	2000	San Cristobal, D.R.
Vavao, Jason	.262	89	279	37	73	24	2	12	35	32	100	6	2	.343	.455	R	R	6-3	200	5-5-81	2001	Carson, Calif.
Votto, Joey	.298	24	84	11	25	7	0	5	20	11	21	1	1	.385	.560	L	R	6-3	200	9-10-83	2002	Toronto, Ontario

PITCHING	W	L	ERA	G	GS	CG	SV	IP	H	R	ER	BB	SO	AVG	B	T	HT	WT	DOB	1st Yr	Resides
Aramboles, Ricardo	4	10	5.21	26	21	0	1	107	125	74	62	55	82	.295	R	R	6-4	220	12-4-81	1997	Santo Domingo, D.R.
Austin, Jeff	0	0	5.79	8	0	0	1	14	14	9	9	5	9	.264	R	R	6-0	180	10-19-76	1998	Kingwood, Texas
Barreto, Joel	10	7	4.70	43	6	0	6	92	85	51	48	37	102	.244	R	R	5-11	150	10-14-80	1998	La Guaira, Venez.
Boughner, Anthony	0	1	8.59	3	1	0	0	7	12	9	7	3	6	.353	L	L	6-3	212	11-1-78	2002	Beallsville, Ohio
Bruksch, Jeffrey	6	7	3.72	32	19	0	1	133	118	62	55	63	104	.238	R	R	6-4	205	4-29-80	2002	Los Angeles, Calif.
Cairns, Troy	0	0	4.50	1	0	0	0	2	2	1	1	0	0	.250	R	R	6-0	160	9-29-80	2002	Blue Springs, Mo.
Edens, Kyle	2	4	5.32	14	5	0	0	47	56	34	28	15	23	.295	R	R	5-10	190	1-25-80	2003	San Antonio, Texas
Frias, Juan	1	1	4.28	18	2	0	0	34	35	20	16	19		.271	L	L	5-11	170	8-7-79	1999	Santa Rosa, Calif.
Gardner, Richard	8	3	2.50	18	12	0	1	86	77	31	24	13	80	.229	R	R	6-3	185	2-1-82	2004	Barcelona, Venez.
Granado, Jan	4	4	5.40	18	8	0	1	65	85	43	39	17	39	.321	L	L	6-0	190	9-26-82	2000	Marietta, Ga.
MacRae, Scott	0	1	2.25	5	1	0	1	12	16	5	3	1	10	.308	R	R	6-3	205	8-13-74	1995	Marietta, Ga.
McWilliams, Matt	2	2	2.21	29	0	0	0	37	26	12	9	21	40	.191	L	L	6-3	210	4-27-79	2001	Lawrenceburg, Ky.
Medlock, Calvin	3	4	6.36	11	9	0	1	47	49	36	33	22	46	.265	R	R	5-10	175	11-8-82	2003	Houston, Texas
Mendoza, Chuy	4	5	3.54	35	0	0	2	53	56	27	21	30	35	.277	R	R	6-1	170	3-16-78	1997	Santo Domingo, D.R.
Paduch, Jim	3	2	5.21	26	13	0	0	95	108	61	55	26	79	.288	R	R	6-3	185	11-2-82	2003	Elmwood Park, Ill.
Pauly, Thomas	8	7	2.97	28	19	0	0	121	96	47	40	26	135	.215	R	R	6-1	195	7-28-81	2003	Atlantic Beach, Fla.

PITCHING

	W	L	ERA	G	GS	CG	SV	IP	H	R	ER	BB	SO	AVG	B	T	HT	WT	DOB	1st Yr	Resides
Salmon, Brad	1	0	0.54	5	1	0	0	17	12	1	1	3	16	.188	L	R	6-4	220	1-3-80	1999	Cantonment, Fla.
Schmidt, Jeremy	2	4	2.45	35	0	0	3	51	44	25	14	15	40	.226	R	R	6-2	190	11-15-79	2002	Sarasota, Fla.
Shafer, David	0	0	0.00	3	0	0	3	4	5	0	0	0	5	.294	R	R	6-3	185	3-7-82	2002	Flagstaff, Ariz.
Sugarman, Jeremy	0	1	4.26	9	1	0	0	19	28	13	9	6	3	.350	R	R	6-2	205	8-4-79	2003	Malibu, Calif.
Thurman, Corey	1	2	1.61	5	3	0	0	22	20	5	4		21	.230	R	R	6-1	210	11-5-78	1996	Wake Village, Texas
Valdez, Eddy	8	6	4.06	30	18	0	3	140	139	71	63	44	103	.266	R	R	6-1	190	2-8-80	2000	Nizao, D.R.
Vavao, Jason	0	1	18.00	1	0	0	0	1	1	2	2	2	0	.333	R	R	6-4	205	5-5-81	2001	Carson, Calif.

FIELDING

Catcher	PCT	G	PO	A	E	DP	PB
Hanigan	.986	65	466	43	7	7	3
Motooka	.976	10	39	1	1	0	1
Perez	.962	15	121	6	5	3	1
Prince	.981	55	370	38	8	3	3

First Base	PCT	G	PO	A	E	DP
Blanco	.973	35	268	24	8	24
Logan	.984	33	279	23	5	13
Prince	1.000	5	35	4	0	4
Ruiz	1.000	1	2	0	0	2
Vavao	.984	54	396	28	7	38
Votto	1.000	21	154	16	0	16

Second Base	PCT	G	PO	A	E	DP
Cairns	1.000	11	13	20	0	5

	PCT	G	PO	A	E	DP
Howard	.954	118	196	327	25	65
Lewis	.929	8	9	17	2	3
Patchett	1.000	11	18	29	0	6
Ruiz	.000	1	0	0	1	0

Third Base	PCT	G	PO	A	E	DP
Cairns	.920	12	4	19	2	0
Correll	.950	12	7	12	1	0
Lewis	.800	4	1	3	1	1
McWilliams	1.000	1	1	0	0	0
Patchett	.938	11	5	10	1	2
Schramek	.929	106	68	155	17	12

Shortstop	PCT	G	PO	A	E	DP
Cairns	.921	11	13	22	3	4

	PCT	G	PO	A	E	DP
Patchett	.936	29	44	73	8	14
Tiburcio	.933	108	175	281	33	58

Outfield	PCT	G	PO	A	E	DP
Blanco	.933	15	14	0	1	0
Correll	.942	99	154	8	10	2
Denorfia	.979	72	183	4	4	1
Dickerson	.931	13	26	1	2	1
Durham	1.000	56	114	4	0	1
Lewis	.933	55	93	4	7	0
Logan	1.000	3	3	1	0	0
Ruiz	.980	98	187	10	4	0
Smith	.895	13	17	0	2	0
Vavao	.920	15	23	0	2	0

DAYTON DRAGONS — Low Class A

MIDWEST LEAGUE

BATTING

	AVG	G	AB	R	H	2B	3B	HR	RBI	BB	SO	SB	CS	OBP	SLG	B	T	HT	WT	DOB	1st Yr	Resides
Beltre, Elvin	.205	34	122	13	25	3	3	3	15	10	50	3	5	.267	.352	R	R	6-3	200	1-19-81	1999	San Cristobal, D.R.
Bolivar, Luis	.234	123	495	65	116	25	5	11	52	36	105	31	10	.294	.372	S	R	6-1	150	2-15-81	1999	Aragua, Venez.
Cairns, Troy	.231	15	52	3	12	0	0	0	1	3	13	0	0	.273	.231	R	R	6-0	160	9-29-80	2002	Blue Springs, Mo.
Campos, Tiago	.196	31	102	4	20	3	1	1	10	3	34	1	0	.217	.275	R	R	6-2	170	3-18-81	2000	Sao Paulo, Brazil
Conley, Evan	.268	37	123	12	33	8	0	0	6	16	24	1	0	.366	.333	R	R	6-2	195	2-25-81	2003	Bradenton, Fla.
Dickerson, Chris	.303	84	314	50	95	15	3	4	34	51	92	27	14	.410	.408	L	L	6-4	212	4-10-82	2003	Van Nuys, Calif.
Fry, Ryan	.218	44	174	21	38	12	0	10	30	7	72	0	0	.253	.460	R	R	6-1	200	5-11-80	2001	Stockertown, Pa.
Gray, Matt	.151	24	86	4	13	2	2	0	4	7	34	0	0	.223	.221	L	L	6-2	205	4-18-84	2003	Overland Park, Kan.
Hernandez, Habelito	.211	96	374	31	79	17	2	3	29	6	70	4	1	.223	.291	R	R	6-0	180	1-11-81	2000	Bonao, D.R.
Himes, Ben	.212	90	312	37	66	18	5	10	45	29	121	5	6	.280	.397	L	R	6-5	210	3-9-81	2003	Austin, Texas
Hudson, Will	.197	81	254	43	50	7	2	3	25	46	63	14	7	.333	.276	S	R	6-2	190	1-26-81	2002	Fountain Valley, Calif.
Kroski, Chris	.308	16	52	7	16	3	0	4	11	2	13	0	2	.333	.596	L	R	6-1	228	5-15-82	2002	Clearwater, Fla.
Mejia, Jorge	.245	32	94	14	23	4	0	0	9	20		2	1	.324	.287	R	R	6-0	165	8-15-82	1999	Scottsdale, Ariz.
Moran, Javon	.383	25	94	11	36	2	0	0	7	10	15	11	3	.448	.404	R	R	5-11	175	9-30-82	2003	Valdosta, Ga.
Olmstead, Walter	.261	106	380	61	99	20	4	14	53	26	132	0	4	.331	.445	R	R	6-6	240	12-5-80	2002	San Antonio, Texas
Perez, Miguel	.237	74	249	22	59	7	0	1	22	16	62	2	2	.309	.277	R	R	6-3	190	9-25-83	2001	Guatire, Venez.
Piepkorn, Jeremiah	.168	28	101	10	17	3	1	1	9	5	30	0	0	.222	.248	R	R	6-4	200	2-18-81	2004	Sauk Rapids, Minn.
Purdom, John	.283	17	60	4	17	4	1	0	7	4	17	0	0	.328	.383	R	R	6-1	230	5-28-81	2004	Cincinnati, Ohio
Schmidt, Jarrod	.171	34	117	12	20	3	0	1		15	43	0	1	.287	.222	R	R	6-2	215	10-2-80	2002	Marietta, Ga.
Smith, Kyle	.182	76	269	25	49	15	1	9	27	24	129	2	2	.266	.304	R	R	6-2	200	5-17-81	2003	Houston, Texas
Strait, Cody	.209	56	220	15	46	10	2	0	13	13	81	3	3	.266	.273	R	R	6-1	185	5-28-83	2003	Sauer Lake, Texas
Urgelles, Jeff	.233	62	210	27	49	11	0	4	29		52	2	2	.335	.343	R	R	6-1	200	6-19-82	2003	Miami, Fla.
Votto, Joey	.302	111	391	60	118	26	2	14	73	79	110	9	2	.419	.486	L	R	6-3	200	9-10-83	2002	Toronto, Ontario

PITCHING

	W	L	ERA	G	GS	CG	SV	IP	H	R	ER	BB	SO	AVG	B	T	HT	WT	DOB	1st Yr	Resides
Bohorquez, Carlos	3	4	4.82	25	0	0	1	37	39	23	20	26	42	.275	R	R	5-11	165	10-6-81	1999	Maracaibo, Venez.
Boughner, Anthony	2	3	3.25	7	6	0	0	36	33	18	13	8	23	.234	L	L	6-3	212	11-1-78	2002	Beallsville, Ohio
Edens, Kyle	0	3	2.36	15	4	0	2	42	34	14	11	11	30	.222	R	R	5-10	190	1-25-80	2003	San Antonio, Texas
Ellison, Phillip	0	1	18.00	2	0	0	0	3	8	9	6	5	3	.533	R	R	6-6	250	12-28-81	2004	Douglasville, Ga.
Farfan, Alexander	0	7	5.65	22	3	0	0	51	48	38	32	33	40	.246	R	R	6-3	175	1-6-83	2000	Maracay, Venez.
Feliz, Ranier	0	2	10.19	6	3	0	0	18	25	20	20	9	13	.338	R	R	6-6	205	3-22-83	2001	Methuen, Mass.
Gemmell, Don	1	0	10.80	5	0	0	0	5	7	7	6	2	5	.304	R	R	6-1	215	7-15-79	2002	Manteca, Calif.
George, Brad	2	1	7.22	22	0	0	0	29	34	31	23	10	34	.279	R	R	6-5	210	5-31-82	2000	New Braunfels, Texas
George, Jon	1	7	5.56	18	12	0	1	66	81	54	41	15	43	.298	R	R	6-4	220	7-6-84	2002	Pennsauken, N.J.
Gillman, Justin	1	2	9.00	11	6	0	0	31	41	34	31	25	26	.318	R	R	6-2	175	6-27-83	2001	Panama City, Fla.
Granado, Jan	1	4	4.53	13	8	0	2	50	52	30	25	14	44	.265	L	L	6-0	190	9-26-82	2000	Barcelona, Venez.
Guevara, Carlos	3	4	2.86	44	0	0	9	57	47	22	18	24	90	.221	R	R	6-0	175	3-18-82	2003	Uvalde, Texas
Hawk, Derek	0	3	6.97	16	3	0	0	31	40	31	24	19	24	.310	R	R	6-6	200	11-13-82	2003	Ukiah, Calif.
Hudson, Will	0	0	2.25	3	0	0	0	4	3	1	1	1	5	.200	S	R	6-2	190	1-26-81	2002	Fountain Valley, Calif.
Keller, Frankie	0	5	8.31	11	9	0	0	39	54	36	36	23	27	.335	L	L	6-2	220	1-12-80	2002	Midland, Texas
Knoff, Justin	1	1	2.08	5	0	0	0	17	18	6	4	6	14	.257	R	R	6-4	195	6-22-81	2002	Burlington, N.J.
Mallett, Justin	4	5	4.02	18	13	0	0	78	93	42	35	28	65	.299	R	R	6-7	215	11-11-81	2003	East St. Louis, Ill.
Medlock, Calvin	8	3	2.57	22	15	0	0	95	74	33	27	21	111	.208	R	R	5-10	175	3-14-83	2003	Houston, Texas
Noriega, Luis	2	1	5.20	8	4	0	0	28	20	18	16	17	19	.200	R	R	6-3	140	7-5-82	1999	Sucre, Venez.
Pelland, Tyler	1	7	8.66	14	10	0	0	45	66	49	43	20	38	.340	R	L	6-0	200	10-9-83	2003	Bristol, Ver.
Rice, Trey	3	4	4.60	38	1	0	0	76	79	41	39	26	70	.264	L	L	6-3	215	6-5-83	2003	Angelton, Texas
Segovia, Omar	1	0	3.19	10	4	0	2	37	23	13	13	13	40	.176	L	L	6-2	210	5-28-83	2003	Cagua, Venez.
Shafer, David	5	3	2.92	31	7	0	5	77	60	32	25	16	84	.214	R	R	6-3	185	3-7-82	2002	Flagstaff, Ariz.
Thigpen, Josh	4	5	6.22	16	8	0	1	55	61	44	38	29	43	.284	R	R	6-4	210	6-27-82	2000	Killen, Ala.
Till, Brock	5	7	5.05	39	11	0	3	109	123	72	61	43	98	.285	R	R	5-10	195	7-1-80	2001	Lewistown, Ill.
Ursin, Dirt	0	6	5.87	21	8	0	2	69	77	51	45	44	42	.279	R	R	6-0	197	11-27-82	2003	Gramercy, La.
Wachman, Robbie	0	0	4.32	3	0	0	0	8	11	4	4	1	7	.324	R	R	6-4	205	10-16-80	2004	Valdsota, Ga.
Wilson, Joe	0	4	9.30	5	5	0	0	27	24	21		7	12	.310	L	L	6-3	195	8-2-82	2003	Fairfield, Conn.

ORGANIZATION STATISTICS

FIELDING

Catcher	PCT	G	PO	A	E	DP	PB
Conley	1.000	3	16	1	0	0	1
Kroski	.983	9	53	6	1	0	1
Perez	.975	73	565	69	16	3	10
Purdom	.981	7	48	4	1	0	3
Schmidt	.750	1	3	0	1	0	0
Urgelles	.968	54	423	37	15	1	10

First Base	PCT	G	PO	A	E	DP
Campos	1.000	2	2	1	0	0
Himes	1.000	4	10	0	0	0
Kroski	1.000	6	48	5	0	6
Mejia	1.000	1	3	0	0	1
Olmstead	.994	39	304	19	2	23
Purdom	.961	6	47	2	2	6
Votto	.986	90	662	45	10	53

Second Base	PCT	G	PO	A	E	DP
Bolivar	.952	36	66	73	7	14
Cairns	1.000	4	5	13	0	3
Conley	.967	9	11	18	1	2
Hernandez	.961	50	113	136	10	29
Hudson	1.000	14	31	27	0	7
Mejia	.961	31	46	76	5	20

Third Base	PCT	G	PO	A	E	DP
Cairns	.917	9	2	20	2	0
Conley	.891	20	10	31	5	4
Hernandez	.891	39	20	70	11	4
Hudson	.895	7	7	10	2	4
Olmstead	.868	56	38	93	20	11
Piepkorn	.919	15	13	21	3	0

Shortstop	PCT	G	PO	A	E	DP
Bolivar	.932	88	116	238	26	35
Hudson	.961	55	85	139	9	28

Outfield	PCT	G	PO	A	E	DP
Beltre	.962	34	73	3	3	0
Campos	1.000	25	35	0	0	0
Dickerson	.977	83	206	8	5	3
Fry	.963	34	48	4	2	0
Gray	.967	17	29	0	1	0
Himes	.964	79	129	4	5	1
Hudson	1.000	2	7	0	0	0
Moran	.961	24	48	1	2	1
Olmstead	1.000	5	5	0	0	0
Piepkorn	1.000	10	23	1	0	0
Schmidt	.958	21	43	3	2	0
Smith	.988	49	82	1	1	0
Strait	.976	54	110	13	3	2

BILLINGS MUSTANGS — Rookie

PIONEER LEAGUE

BATTING	AVG	G	AB	R	H	2B	3B	HR	RBI	BB	SO	SB	CS	OBP	SLG	B	T	HT	WT	DOB	1st Yr	Resides
Anderson, Drew	.254	54	197	40	50	10	4	2	29	39	42	14	4	.377	.376	S	R	5-9	170	2-2-83	2004	Brownsburg, Ind.
Belcher, Jordan	.182	3	11	1	2	0	0	0	1	1	0	0	0	.250	.182	R	R	6-2	185	2-17-84	2003	Grovetown, Ga.
Beltre, Elvin	.254	30	114	18	29	3	2	3	15	8	34	7	0	.309	.395	R	R	6-3	200	1-19-81	1999	San Cristobal, D.R.
Campos, Tiago	.341	14	44	7	15	3	2	0	6	6	11	1	2	.426	.500	R	R	6-2	170	3-18-81	2000	Sao Paulo, Brazil
Ellis, Jason	.250	19	48	6	12	5	0	1	5	8	14	2	0	.357	.417	R	R	5-11	190	9-22-79	2003	Batavia, Ohio
Esparragoza, Eyoxy	.306	12	49	9	15	5	0	1	9	4	12	3	0	.370	.469	R	R	6-0	185	9-9-84	2002	El Sombrero, Venez.
Gentry, Philip	.335	62	242	39	81	21	3	4	31	21	47	5	6	.393	.496	L	R	5-11	195	9-2-80	2003	Desoto, Texas
Gonzalez, Reynaldo	.000	2	5	0	0	0	0	0	0	1	1	0	0	.167	.000	R	R	6-0	185	8-16-84	2002	Carabobo, Venez.
Gutierrez, Tonys	.339	18	59	12	20	3	0	2	12	12	15	2	1	.480	.492	L	L	6-2	180	8-18-83	2001	Aragua, Venez.
Janish, Paul	.263	66	205	39	54	11	0	2	22	45	45	7	3	.406	.346	R	R	6-2	180	10-12-82	2004	Cypress, Texas
Kaats, Travis	.187	56	166	22	31	2	1	1	16	20	59	3	2	.303	.229	R	R	6-1	205	4-27-82	2004	Scottsdale, Ariz.
Key, Brad	.242	67	264	37	64	14	2	6	34	23	50	15	3	.322	.406	R	R	6-2	180	12-18-82	2004	Wilmington, N.C.
Lawhorn, Trevor	.240	56	217	28	52	11	2	7	34	23	50	15	3	.322	.406	R	R	6-0	195	12-18-81	2004	Littleton, Colo.
Levering, Matt	.091	4	11	0	1	0	0	0	1	6	7	0	0	.412	.091	R	R	6-0	195	12-18-81	2004	Littleton, Colo.
Mejia, Jorge	.350	14	40	6	14	4	0	0	1	8	10	1	1	.458	.450	R	R	6-1	165	8-15-82	1999	Scottsdale, Ariz.
Mosby, Robert	.263	69	255	51	67	5	2	19	52	42	87	1	0	.374	.522	R	R	6-3	240	4-9-82	2002	Belleville, Ill.
Phillips, Drew	.271	38	133	21	36	2	0	0	15	9	10	2	4	.324	.286	R	R	6-2	180	4-12-81	2004	Dewey, Okla.
Roberts, Brandon	.219	10	32	3	7	2	0	0	3	5	11	5	1	.375	.281	L	R	6-3	212	8-8-81	2004	Highland Village, Texas
Ronda, Willy Jo	.257	13	35	7	9	1	0	2	3	5	11	2	0	.366	.457	S	R	6-2	170	6-8-85	2003	San Juan, P.R.
Strait, Cody	.388	12	49	10	19	1	3	2	11	1	14	3	2	.444	.653	R	R	6-1	185	5-28-83	2004	Sauer Lake, Texas
Szymanski, B.J.	.259	22	81	13	21	4	2	3	17	9	26	2	1	.330	.469	S	R	6-5	215	10-1-82	2004	Wichita Falls, Texas
Tatum, Craig	.221	42	149	19	33	8	3	2	21	21	36	2	0	.322	.356	R	R	6-1	215	3-18-83	2004	Hattiesburg, Miss.
Ziemendorf, Chad	.296	31	81	12	24	5	0	0	11	16	23	3	2	.458	.358	R	R	5-10	175	4-3-85	2003	Los Altos, Calif.

GAMES BY POSITION: C—Ellis 10, Gonzalez 2, Tatum 42, Ziemendorf 29. 1B—Ellis 6, Gutierrez 16, Kaats 1, Mosby 51, Phillips 1, Roberts 6. 2B—Anderson 7, Lawhorn 55, Mejia 9, Ronda 4. 3B—Anderson 8, Key 67, Levering 2. SS—Anderson 3, Janish 66, Mejia 3, Phillips 1, Ronda 5. OF—Anderson 30, Belcher 3, Beltre 12, Campos 13, Esparragoza 12, Gentry 61, Kaats 50, Phillips 29, Strait 11, Szymanski 15.

PITCHING	W	L	ERA	G	GS	CG	SV	IP	H	R	ER	BB	SO	AVG	B	T	HT	WT	DOB	1st Yr	Resides
Cherry, Brad	0	0	2.25	3	0	0	1	4	1	1	1	2	6	.071	R	R	6-3	195	2-12-81	2003	Texarkana, Ark.
Dillard, Johnny	0	1	7.17	22	0	0	1	21	13	18	17	22	22	.188	R	R	6-1	160	1-14-81	2004	Iowa Park, Texas
Farfan, Alexander	1	5	6.30	16	8	0	1	50	53	38	35	29	34	.290	R	R	6-3	175	1-6-83	2000	Maracay, Venez.
Feliz, Ranier	3	5	6.28	18	11	0	0	57	75	44	40	31	44	.321	R	R	6-6	205	3-22-83	2001	Methuen, Mass.
Gillihan, Adam	1	0	0.00	3	0	0	0	4	6	1	0	4	3	.375	R	R	6-3	200	9-28-83	2004	Bentonville, Ark.
Goetz, Greg	1	5	7.16	17	8	0	0	44	51	42	35	39	35	.298	L	L	6-4	195	1-25-84	2004	Bellevue, Wash.
Griffin, David	1	0	6.48	10	0	0	0	17	24	13	12	8	17	.329	L	L	6-3	200	8-16-81	2004	Chowchilla, Calif.
Gruler, Chris	0	0	19.29	1	1	0	0	2	4	5	5	2	2	.364	R	R	6-3	200	9-11-83	2002	Fremont, Calif.
Hawk, Derek	0	2	4.26	17	7	0	1	57	52	30	27	18	64	.248	R	R	6-6	200	11-13-82	2003	Ukiah, Calif.
Jenson, Drew	2	0	2.00	19	0	0	0	18	14	4	4	11	16	.226	L	L	6-2	200	12-31-81	2004	Lakeside, Calif.
Johnson, T.J.	4	1	3.68	18	1	0	0	29	26	16	12	10	35	.239	L	L	6-3	210	11-29-80	2004	Byron, Mich.
Knoff, Justin	0	0	1.86	6	0	0	0	10	8	4	2	4	9	.222	R	R	6-4	195	6-22-81	2004	Tucson, Ariz.
Kupper, Dustin	0	0	9.82	4	0	0	0	4	6	7	4	4	2	.400	R	R	6-5	195	2-22-81	2001	Tucson, Ariz.
Lingenfelter, Adam	1	2	6.12	9	4	0	0	25	28	17	17	9	22	.283	R	R	6-5	220	11-21-79	2004	Gainesville, Fla.
Meque, Jacobo	1	1	4.56	18	7	0	0	49	45	32	25	36	46	.243	L	L	6-2	175	10-1-83	2002	Villa Altagracia, D.R.
Morenko, Brad	2	1	4.03	19	0	0	4	22	25	12	10	5	20	.291	R	R	6-4	215	8-5-81	2004	Marysville, Mich.
Noriega, Luis	3	3	6.20	18	2	0	0	41	34	31	28	38	37	.245	R	R	6-3	140	7-5-82	1999	Sucre, Venez.
O'Neal, Charles	0	0	0.00	2	0	0	0	2	1	0	0	1	3	.167	R	L	6-4	175	9-12-83	2004	Roberta, Ga.
Pelland, Tyler	9	3	3.44	15	15	0	0	73	67	36	28	39	81	.245	R	L	6-0	200	10-9-83	2003	Bristol, Ver.
Ramirez, Ramon	4	3	6.39	17	12	0	1	74	64	36	28	36	60	.243	R	R	6-0	170	9-16-82	2000	Cagua, Venez.
Sanders, Jared	4	1	2.00	23	0	0	5	27	20	6	6	6	22	.204	R	R	6-2	210	11-19-81	2004	Bend, Ore.
Stott, Zach	0	1	17.18	2	1	0	0	4	7	8	7	6	2	.438	R	R	6-5	210	7-6-83	2004	Logan, Utah
Vazquez, Camilo	1	0	0.00	2	0	0	0	3	1	0	0	3	6	.125	L	L	6-0	180	10-3-83	2003	Hialeah, Fla.

GCL REDS — Rookie

GULF COAST LEAGUE

BATTING	AVG	G	AB	R	H	2B	3B	HR	RBI	BB	SO	SB	CS	SLG	OBP	B	T	HT	WT	DOB	1st Yr	Resides
Belcher, Jordan	.228	38	123	18	28	3	2	1	13	23	22	7	1	.309	.347	R	R	6-2	185	2-17-84	2004	Grovetown, Ga.
Character, Johntavis	.100	10	20	0	2	1	0	0	1	3	10	0	0	.150	.250	R	R	6-4	215	1-16-85	2004	Decatur, Ga.
Cleveland, Clay	.192	10	26	4	5	0	0	0	2	4	4	1	0	.192	.323	R	R	6-4	250	9-21-80	2003	Daphne, Ala.
Esparragoza, Eyoxy	.000	7	20	1	0	0	0	0	0	0	10	0	0	.000	.048	R	R	6-0	185	9-9-84	2002	El Sombrero, Venez.
Franco, Ambiorix	.190	20	58	2	11	1	0	0	5	3	12	0	1	.207	.242	R	R	6-3	190	12-21-82	2003	Villa Mella, D.R.

BATTING	AVG	G	AB	R	H	2B	3B	HR	RBI	BB	SO	SB	CS	SLG	OBP	B	T	HT	WT	DOB	1st Yr	Resides
Gonzalez, Reynaldo	.135	32	96	7	13	4	0	2	8	6	34	1	2	.240	.192	R	R	6-0	185	8-16-84	2002	Valencia, Venez.
Gray, Matthew	.275	28	102	13	28	4	3	2	16	6	23	0	4	.431	.327	L	L	6-2	205	4-18-84	2003	Overland Park, Kan.
Gutierrez, Tonys	.275	12	40	2	11	3	2	1	7	8	5	0	0	.525	.380	L	L	6-2	180	8-18-83	2001	Aragua, Venez.
Hawkins, Pedro	.196	20	51	10	10	4	1	0	4	8	21	2	1	.314	.349	R	R	5-10	195	11-30-83	2004	Seattle, Wash.
Hernandez, Habelito	.462	3	13	2	6	2	0	0	2	0	2	1	0	.615	.462	R	R	6-0	180	1-11-81	2000	Bonao, D.R.
Holden, Josh	.348	26	89	15	31	1	3	0	4	8	25	10	6	.427	.420	L	L	6-2	220	12-10-80	2004	Powell, Ohio
Honey, Blake	.114	17	35	2	4	0	0	0	4	7	13	1	0	.114	.304	R	R	6-1	175	12-24-85	2004	Lewisville, Ark.
Infante, Ray	.157	26	70	8	11	3	0	0	4	7	12	5	1	.200	.268	R	R	5-10	160	10-1-84	2002	Maracaibo, Venez.
Kroski, Chris	.000	5	9	0	0	0	0	0	0	1	2	0	0	.000	.182	L	R	6-2	220	5-15-82	2002	Clearwater, Fla.
Langham, James	.156	28	77	14	12	4	1	1	7	8	34	6	1	.273	.316	R	R	6-0	205	9-3-82	2004	Gray, Ga.
Lewis, Kenny	.273	8	22	5	6	1	0	0	2	3	8	1	2	.318	.346	L	L	5-9	195	10-31-83	2003	Danville, Va.
Pena, Hannsel	.188	34	101	14	19	4	0	4	12	9	49	6	2	.347	.281	R	R	5-11	180	1-30-84	2003	LaGuna Salada, D.R.
Purdom, John	.259	20	54	6	14	1	0	1	5	6	9	0	0	.333	.339	R	R	6-1	230	5-28-81	2004	Cincinnati, Ohio
Reininger, J.D.	.221	27	86	12	19	6	2	1	10	13	25	2	0	.372	.343	R	R	6-2	182	12-3-82	2004	Spring Branch, Texas
Roa, Lonny	.154	20	65	5	10	1	0	1	5	5	28	1	0	.215	.247	R	R	6-3	215	11-28-85	2004	San Juan, P.R.
Roberts, Brandon	.220	39	123	11	27	4	0	1	8	19	30	3	1	.276	.338	L	R	6-4	215	8-8-81	2004	Highland Village, Texas
Ronda, Willy Jo	.198	26	96	10	19	3	1	1	7	6	30	0	1	.281	.240	S	R	6-2	175	6-8-85	2003	San Juan, P.R.
Salbaran, Orlando	.208	14	48	4	10	1	0	1	4	5	9	0	0	.292	.283	R	R	6-2	160	11-16-81	1998	Maracaibo, Venez.
Sanchez, Carlos	.208	44	144	11	30	8	1	1	13	15	35	5	2	.299	.294	R	R	6-1	180	9-19-84	2003	Culiacan, Mexico
Sandoval, Mayker	.255	46	161	22	41	10	5	5	30	15	50	17	4	.472	.332	R	R	5-11	170	2-9-84	2002	Barquisimeto, Venez.
Soto, Melvin	.233	13	30	0	7	0	0	0	2	2	5	0	0	.233	.281	S	R	6-0	150	10-31-84	2002	Bani, D.R.

GAMES BY POSITION: C—Gonzalez 32, Kroski 2, Purdom 10, Roa 19, Sulbaran 3. **1B**—Cleveland 5, Franco 5, Gutierrez 11, Kroski 1, Purdom 4, Reininger 1, Roberts 29, Sulbaran 7. **2B**—Hernandez 2, Infante 6, Ronda 10, Sandoval 43, Soto 2. **3B**—Franco 12, Reininger 20, Sanchez 27. **SS**—Honey 17, Infante 20, Ronda 16, Sanchez 2, Soto 10. **OF**—Belcher 38. Character 6, Esparragoza 6, Gray 27, Hawkins 19, Holden 23, Langham 26, Lewis 1, Pena 33, Purdom 2, Roberts 5.

PITCHING	W	L	ERA	G	GS	CG	SV	IP	H	R	ER	BB	SO	AVG	B	T	HT	WT	DOB	1st Yr	Resides
Adames, Geovanny	1	2	5.11	10	2	0	0	25	20	20	14	18	28	.224	R	R	6-2	185	1-15-83	2001	Santo Domingo, D.R.
Austin, Jeff	0	0	2.04	5	4	0	1	18	8	5	4	8	14	.133	R	R	6-0	180	10-19-76	1999	Kingwood, Texas
Bailey, Homer	0	1	4.38	6	3	0	0	12	14	7	6	3	9	.274	R	R	6-4	185	5-3-86	2004	LaGrange, Texas
Bong, Jung	0	0	12.00	2	2	0	0	3	3	5	4	2	3	.230	L	L	6-3	170	7-15-80	1997	Norcross, Ga.
Cherry, Brad	1	1	3.54	15	0	0	4	20	18	8	8	6	18	.230	R	R	6-2	200	2-11-84	2004	Texarkana, Ark.
DeLuna, David	1	5	6.61	12	4	0	0	33	45	33	24	17	22	.328	R	L	6-2	175	7-1-85	2004	Santo Domingo, D.R.
Ellison, Philip	1	2	2.63	12	0	0	0	14	14	11	4	14	6	.241	R	R	6-6	250	12-28-81	2004	Douglasville, Ga.
Geiersbach, Ken	0	1	0.77	12	0	0	0	12	11	3	1	6	14	.250	R	R	6-1	190	10-2-82	2004	Martinsville, Ind.
George, Brad	2	0	0.00	4	0	0	1	7	4	0	0	2	8	.166	R	R	6-5	210	5-31-82	2000	New Braunfels, Texas
Gonzalez, Rafael	1	6	4.20	12	8	0	0	41	38	25	19	18	32	.258	R	R	6-3	225	3-21-86	2004	Bronx, N.Y.
Gruler, Chris	2	1	1.75	7	5	0	0	26	20	7	5	13	10	.219	R	R	6-3	200	9-11-83	2002	Fremont, Calif.
Hendley, Blake	3	0	0.92	10	0	0	1	20	15	4	2	7	16	.205	R	R	6-3	195	9-1-81	2004	Edmond, Okla.
Herrera, Carlos	0	0	12.00	10	0	0	0	12	13	21	16	9	14	.265	R	R	6-0	210	8-17-81	2003	La Romana, D.R.
Jimenez, Santos	1	1	7.71	12	1	0	0	19	23	19	16	8	14	.306	R	R	6-1	181	9-2-83	2004	Catia La Mar, Venez.
Keller, Frankie	0	3	4.74	6	5	0	0	25	30	16	13	5	24	.294	L	L	6-2	220	1-12-80	2002	Midland, Texas
MacRae, Scott	0	1	1.50	2	0	0	0	6	4	1	1	2	1	.200	R	R	6-3	205	8-13-74	1995	Marietta, Ga.
O'Neal, Charles	4	4	2.58	13	7	0	0	45	41	20	13	19	29	.239	R	L	6-4	165	9-12-83	2004	Roberta, Ga.
Olivares, Francisco	0	0	1.38	8	0	0	0	13	14	6	2	8	13	.259	R	R	6-2	180	4-22-83	2001	Mexico City, Mexico
Sparks, Terrance	0	2	2.38	12	0	0	0	11	11	6	3	12	8	.244	L	L	6-0	170	2-19-83	2004	Huntington, Texas
Stott, Zach	2	2	2.82	12	8	0	0	51	54	20	16	10	34	.272	R	R	6-5	200	7-26-83	2004	Logan, Utah
Vazquez, Camilo	0	2	12.27	3	3	0	0	4	5	5	5	2	6	.312	L	L	6-0	180	10-3-83	2003	Hialeah, Fla.
Wachman, Robbie	1	2	5.12	13	5	0	1	46	46	29	26	18	49	.261	R	R	6-4	205	4-10-82	2004	Valdosta, Ga.
Young, Terrell	0	1	3.86	10	0	0	0	14	12	6	6	9	8	.240	R	R	6-3	175	8-7-85	2004	Granada, Miss.

BY JIM INGRAHAM

In a 2004 season devoted to rebuilding, the Indians rebuilt faster than they expected. But in the end, they learned, painfully, that they still had more work to do.

The Indians did finish with a record of 80-82, increas-ing their win total by 12 from the previous season. The Indians also had some important breakout seasons individually. And by the end of the season club officials felt confident that the team was ready to be a legitimate contender in the American League Central in 2005.

"Some things were much better than we thought, some weren't as good. But overall, I think we made great strides and took huge steps," general manager Mark Shapiro said. "And in the process, we won more games than a lot of people thought we'd win."

The high-water mark was reached on Aug. 14 when the Indians, thanks to a 20-9 spurt, had a record of 63-55 and were one game behind the division-leading Twins.

But then the bottom fell out. The Indians went 9-23 over their next 32 games, dropping out of the race. But that humbling tumble did not diminish what was otherwise an encouraging season.

Perhaps the biggest surprise came in mid-July, when the Indians had five players selected to the A.L. all-star team, and could have had seven. Travis Hafner, who was among the league leaders in RBIs, and pitcher Cliff Lee, who was 9-1, were not selected.

Those who were chosen were catcher Victor Martinez, second baseman Ron Belliard, outfielder Matt Lawton, and pitchers C.C. Sabathia and Jake Westbrook.

In his first full season at the major league level, Martinez emerged as one of the best young catchers in the majors, hitting .283-23-108, leading all major league catchers in home runs and RBIs.

Martinez teamed with Hafner, who hit .311-28-109, to

Victor Martinez | Jhonny Peralta

PLAYERS of the YEAR

MAJOR LEAGUE: Victor Martinez, c

Martinez emerged as one of the top catchers in the majors with a .283-23-108 campaign in 2004. Not bad for a guy with 191 career big league at-bats entering the season. Martinez and first baseman Travis Hafner make up the powerful nucleus of a talented young Cleveland team poised to make a run in the AL Central.

MINOR LEAGUE: Jhonny Peralta, ss

Peralta laid claim to the Indians' 2005 starting shortstop job, hitting .326-15-86 with 44 doubles and 109 runs to capture Triple-A International League MVP honors in 2004. The heir apparent to Omar Vizquel, Peralta led Buffalo to the IL title.

give the Indians a formidable middle of the lineup, triggering an offensive revival that saw the team go from at or near the bottom of the league in most offensive categories in 2003 to at or near the top in most categories in 2004.

The Indians seemed to be on some sort of streak, good or bad, virtually all year. They had 12 winning streaks of three or more games, including one six-gamer, one five-gamer, and five four-gamers. They also had 10 losing streaks of three or more games, including one nine-gamer, a seven-gamer, and two five-gamers.

Much of that streakiness was due to a chaotic bullpen, especially in the first half of the season, when the Indians blew many late leads, costing themselves a chance to remain in contention all season.

Through all the bullpen tribulations, however, the offense continued to produce. It was a balanced, one-through-nine attack.

And there's more help on the way. Four of the Indians' minor league affiliates won their league championships in 2004: Triple-A Buffalo, high Class A Kinston, Short season Mahoning Valley and the team's entry in the Dominican Summer League. That made the Indians the first team since the 1990 Dodgers to have four minor league teams win championships in the same season.

Leading the way was Buffalo, which produced the International League's MVP in shortstop Jhonny Peralta.

Reinforcements began to arrive at the big league level in September, chiefly in the form of outfielder Grady Sizemore, who flashed all the tools that excited scouts in the minor leagues, making him the favorite to be the club's starting center fielder in 2005.

ORGANIZATION LEADERS

BATTING

*AVG	Pat Osborn, Kinston	.342
R	Jhonny Peralta, Buffalo	109
H	Jhonny Peralta, Buffalo	181
TB	Jhonny Peralta, Buffalo	274
2B	Jhonny Peralta, Buffalo	44
3B	Mike Conroy, Lake County	10
HR	Ryan Goleski, Lake County	28
RBI	Ryan Goleski, Lake County	104
BB	Corey Smith, Buffalo/Akron	64
SO	John Van Every, Kinston	129
SB	Eider Torres, Kinston	48
*OBP	Pat Osborn, Kinston	.424
*SLG	Russ Branyan, Buffalo	.591

PITCHING

W	Brian Slocum, Kinston	15
L	Francisco Cruceta, Buffalo/Akron	13
#ERA	Chris Cooper, Akron/Kinston	1.66
G	Lee Gronkiewicz, Buffalo/Akron	53
CG	Four tied at	2
SV	Lee Gronkiewicz, Buffalo/Akron	20
	Todd Pennington, Kinston/Mahoning Valley	20
IP	Francisco Cruceta, Buffalo/Akron	172
BB	Francisco Cruceta, Buffalo/Akron	69
SO	Adam Miller, Kinston/Lake County	152

*Minimum 250 at-bats #Minimum 75 innings

CLEVELAND INDIANS

Manager: Eric Wedge.

2004 Record: 80-82, .494 (3rd, AL Central).

BATTING	AVG	G	AB	R	H	2B	3B	HR	RBI	BB	SO	SB	CS	OBP	SLG	B	T	HT	WT	DOB	1st Yr	Resides
Bard, Josh	.421	7	19	5	8	2	0	1	4	3	0	0	0	.478	.684	S	R	6-3	210	3-30-78	2000	Chandler, Ariz.
Belliard, Ronnie	.282	152	599	78	169	48	1	12	70	60	98	3	2	.348	.426	R	R	5-8	200	4-7-75	1994	Miami, Fla.
Blake, Casey	.271	152	587	93	159	36	3	28	88	68	139	5	8	.354	.486	R	R	6-2	210	8-23-73	1996	Indianola, Iowa
Broussard, Ben	.275	139	418	57	115	28	5	17	82	52	95	4	2	.370	.484	L	L	6-2	220	9-24-76	1999	Beaumont, Texas
Crisp, Coco	.297	139	491	78	146	24	2	15	71	36	69	20	13	.344	.446	S	R	6-0	180	11-1-79	1999	Desert Hot Springs, Calif.
Escobar, Alex	.211	46	152	20	32	8	2	1	12	23	42	1	1	.318	.309	R	R	6-1	190	9-6-78	1996	Valencia, Venez.
Gerut, Jody	.252	134	481	72	121	31	5	11	51	54	59	13	6	.334	.405	L	L	6-0	190	9-18-77	1999	Lombard, Ill.
Gonzalez, Raul	.091	7	11	0	1	0	0	0	0	4	0	0	0	.091	.091	R	R	5-9	190	12-27-73	1991	Carolina, P.R.
Hafner, Travis	.311	140	482	96	150	41	3	28	109	68	111	3	2	.410	.583	L	R	6-3	240	6-3-77	1997	Sykeston, N.D.
Laker, Tim	.214	44	117	12	25	2	0	3	17	7	28	0	0	.262	.308	R	R	6-3	225	11-27-69	1988	Simi Valley, Calif.
Lawton, Matt	.277	150	591	109	164	25	0	20	70	74	84	23	9	.366	.421	L	R	5-10	190	11-3-71	1992	Saucier, Miss.
Little, Mark	.200	11	20	0	4	0	0	0	2	0	7	0	0	.261	.200	R	R	6-0	190	7-11-72	1994	Edwardsville, Ill.
Ludwick, Ryan	.220	15	50	3	11	2	0	2	4	2	14	0	0	.278	.380	R	L	6-3	205	7-13-78	1999	Las Vegas, Nev.
Martinez, Sandy	.000	1	2	0	0	0	0	0	0	0	1	0	0	.000	.000	L	R	6-2	210	10-9-70	1990	Santo Domingo, D.R.
Martinez, Victor	.283	141	520	77	147	38	1	23	108	60	69	0	1	.359	.492	S	R	6-2	195	12-23-78	1997	Ciudad Bolivar, Venez.
McDonald, John	.204	66	93	17	19	5	1	2	7	4	11	0	0	.237	.344	R	R	5-11	175	9-24-74	1996	East Lyme, Conn.
Merloni, Lou	.289	71	190	25	55	12	1	4	28	14	41	1	2	.343	.426	R	R	5-10	200	4-6-71	1993	Framingham, Mass.
Peralta, Jhonny	.240	8	25	2	6	1	0	0	2	3	6	0	1	.321	.280	R	R	6-1	180	5-28-82	1999	Santiago, D.R.
Phelps, Josh	.303	24	76	13	23	6	0	5	10	4	20	0	0	.338	.579	R	R	6-3	220	5-12-78	1996	Rathdrum, Idaho
2-team (79 Toronto)	.251	103	371	51	93	19	2	17	61	22	93	0	0	.304	.450							
Phillips, Brandon	.182	6	22	1	4	2	0	1	2	5	0	2	0	.250	.273	R	R	5-11	190	6-28-81	1999	Stone Mountain, Ga.
Sizemore, Grady	.246	43	138	15	34	6	2	4	24	14	34	2	0	.333	.406	L	L	6-2	200	8-2-82	2000	Mill Creek, Wash.
Vizquel, Omar	.291	148	567	82	165	28	3	7	59	57	62	19	6	.353	.388	S	R	5-9	185	4-24-67	1984	Issaquah, Wash.
Young, Ernie	.500	3	4	0	2	0	0	0	1	2	0	0	0	.600	.500	R	R	6-1	230	7-8-69	1990	Gilbert, Ariz.

PITCHING	W	L	ERA	G	GS	CG	SV	IP	H	R	ER	BB	SO	AVG	B	T	HT	WT	DOB	1st Yr	Resides
Anderson, Jason	0	0	45.00	1	0	0	0	1	1	5	5	4	1	.250	L	R	6-0	170	6-9-79	2000	Danville, Ill.
Bartosh, Cliff	1	0	4.66	34	0	0	0	19	22	10	10	11	25	.275	L	L	6-2	175	9-5-79	1998	Duncanville, Texas
Betancourt, Rafael	5	6	3.92	68	0	0	4	67	71	32	29	18	76	.268	R	R	6-2	200	4-29-75	1994	Cumana, Venez.
Cabrera, Fernando	0	0	3.38	4	0	0	0	5	3	3	2	1	6	.167	R	R	6-4	170	11-16-81	2000	Toa Baja, P.R.
Cressend, Jack	0	1	6.32	11	0	0	0	16	22	11	11	10	8	.333	R	R	6-1	190	5-13-75	1996	Mandeville, La.
Cruceta, Francisco	0	1	9.39	2	2	0	0	8	10	9	8	4	9	.303	R	R	6-2	180	7-4-81	1999	La Vega, D.R.
D'Amico, Jeff	1	2	7.63	7	7	0	0	31	45	29	26	6	16	.333	R	R	6-7	250	12-27-75	1994	Palm Harbor, Fla.
Davis, Jason	2	7	5.51	26	19	0	0	114	148	81	70	51	72	.311	R	R	6-6	210	5-8-80	2000	Charleston, Tenn.
Dawley, Joe	0	0	5.40	2	2	0	0	8	7	5	5	7	8	.233	R	R	6-4	205	9-19-71	1993	Moreno Valley, Calif.
Denney, Kyle	1	2	9.56	4	4	0	0	16	32	17	17	8	13	.421	R	R	6-2	195	7-27-77	1999	Prague, Okla.
Durbin, Chad	5	6	6.66	17	8	1	0	51	63	40	38	24	38	.301	R	R	6-2	200	12-3-77	1996	Baton Rouge, La.
Elarton, Scott	3	5	4.53	21	21	1	0	117	107	62	59	42	80	.240	R	R	6-8	240	2-23-76	1994	Denver, Colo.
Guthrie, Jeremy	0	0	4.63	6	0	0	0	12	9	6	6	6	7	.214	R	R	6-1	200	4-8-79	2003	Las Vegas, Nev.
Howry, Bob	4	2	2.74	37	0	0	0	43	37	14	13	12	39	.228	L	R	6-5	220	8-4-73	1994	Glendale, Ariz.
Jimenez, Jose	1	7	8.42	31	0	0	8	36	45	37	34	14	21	.296	R	R	6-3	230	7-7-73	1994	Boca China, D.R.
Lee, Cliff	14	8	5.43	33	33	0	0	179	188	113	108	81	161	.268	L	L	6-3	190	8-30-78	2000	Benton, Ark.
Lee, David	0	0	10.38	4	0	0	0	4	8	7	5	4	4	.348	R	R	6-1	200	3-12-73	1996	Pittsburgh, Pa.
Miller, Matt	4	1	3.09	57	0	0	1	55	42	22	19	23	55	.216	R	R	6-3	215	11-23-71	1996	Greenville, Miss.
Pote, Lou	0	0	9.00	2	0	0	0	3	3	3	3	1	5	.250	R	R	6-3	208	8-21-71	1991	Phoenix, Ariz.
Riske, David	7	3	3.72	72	0	0	5	77	69	32	32	41	78	.240	R	R	6-2	195	10-23-76	1997	Kent, Wash.
Robbins, Jake	0	0	5.40	2	0	0	0	2	3	1	1	0	0	.375	R	R	6-5	190	5-23-76	1997	Charlotte, N.C.
Robertson, Jeriome	1	1	12.21	8	0	0	0	14	22	22	19	9	6	.349	L	L	6-1	200	3-30-77	1996	Exeter, Calif.
Sabathia, C.C.	11	10	4.12	30	30	1	0	188	176	90	86	72	139	.252	L	L	6-7	290	7-21-80	1998	Vallejo, Calif.
Stanford, Jason	0	1	0.82	2	2	0	0	11	12	1	1	5	5	.279	L	L	6-2	200	1-23-77	2000	Tucson, Ariz.
Stewart, Scott	0	2	7.24	23	0	0	0	14	23	14	11	6	18	.365	R	L	6-2	225	8-14-75	1994	Mt. Holly, N.C.
Tadano, Kazuhito	1	1	4.65	14	4	0	0	50	55	30	26	18	39	.272	R	R	6-0	180	4-25-80	2003	Tokyo, Japan
Westbrook, Jake	14	9	3.38	33	30	5	0	216	208	95	81	61	116	.255	R	R	6-3	215	9-29-77	1996	Danielsville, Ga.
White, Rick	5	5	5.29	59	0	0	1	78	88	52	46	29	44	.293	R	R	6-4	230	12-23-68	1990	Springfield, Ohio
Wickman, Bob	0	2	4.25	30	0	0	13	30	33	14	14	10	26	.282	R	R	6-1	240	2-6-69	1990	Wausaukee, Wisc.

FIELDING

Catcher	PCT	G	PO	A	E	DP	PB
Bard	1.000	7	47	4	0	1	0
Laker	.984	41	233	21	4	0	5
S. Martinez	1.000	1	7	1	0	0	1
V. Martinez	.994	132	865	61	6	11	9

First Base	PCT	G	PO	A	E	DP
Blake	1.000	8	12	0	0	2
Broussard	.994	133	991	77	6	108
Hafner	1.000	11	81	9	0	4
Merloni	.997	42	282	14	1	18
Phelps	.978	8	43	2	1	1

Second Base	PCT	G	PO	A	E	DP
Belliard	.981	151	278	427	14	89
McLemore	.975	47	113	123	6	37
Merloni	.967	7	12	17	1	4
Phillips	.973	6	17	19	1	4

Third Base	PCT	G	PO	A	E	DP
Blake	.939	152	121	276	26	24
McDonald	1.000	9	1	12	0	0
Merloni	.955	10	1	20	1	0
Peralta	1.000	2	1	2	0	0

Shortstop	PCT	G	PO	A	E	DP
McDonald	.947	30	25	65	5	16

		G	PO	A	E	DP
Peralta	.889	7	7	17	3	2
Vizquel	.982	147	200	396	11	91

Outfield	PCT	G	PO	A	E	DP
Crisp	.986	128	286	5	4	1
Gerut	.986	131	267	7	4	2
Gonzalez	1.000	4	7	0	0	0
Lawton	.986	142	266	9	4	3
Little	1.000	11	12	1	0	0
Ludwick	.970	15	32	0	1	0
Merloni	.750	4	2	1	1	0
Sizemore	.991	42	105	0	1	0

Travis Hafner: Breakthrough year, .311-28-109

Jake Westbrook: Staff leader with 216 innings pitched

FARM SYSTEM

Director, Player Development: John Farrell.

Class	Farm Team	League	W	L	Pct.	Finish*	Manager	Affiliate Since
AAA	Buffalo (N.Y.) Bisons	International	83	61	.576	+1st (14)	Marty Brown	1995
AA	Akron (Ohio) Aeros	Eastern	63	78	.447	11th (12)	Brad Komminsk	1997
High A	Kinston (N.C.) Indians	Carolina	88	50	.638	+1st (8)	Torey Lovullo	1987
Low A	Lake County (Ohio) Captains	South Atlantic	73	66	.525	5th (16)	Luis Rivera	2003
SS A	Mahoning Valley (Ohio) Indians	New York-Penn	42	34	.553	+4th (14)	Mike Sarbaugh	1999
Rookie	Burlington (N.C.) Indians	Appalachian	31	35	.470	7th (10)	Rouglas Odor	1986

*Finish in overall standings (No. of teams in league)/playoff teams in **boldface**   +League champion

BUFFALO BISONS   Class AAA

INTERNATIONAL LEAGUE

BATTING	AVG	G	AB	R	H	2B	3B	HR	RBI	BB	SO	SB	CS	OBP	SLG	B	T	HT	WT	DOB	1st Yr	Resides
Abernathy, Brent	.294	103	354	68	104	24	3	10	56	33	29	27	5	.357	.463	R	R	6-1	191	9-23-77	1997	Marietta, Ga.
Bard, Josh	.263	40	156	25	41	10	0	4	18	11	23	0	0	.310	.404	S	R	6-3	210	3-30-78	2000	Chandler, Ariz.
Branyan, Russell	.288	82	313	58	90	16	2	25	75	42	102	5	2	.374	.591	L	R	6-3	195	12-19-75	1994	Kathleen, Ga.
2-team (11 Richmond)	.279	93	341	63	95	16	2	26	79	55	113	6	2	.382	.566							
Clapinski, Chris	.312	107	369	65	115	24	4	11	63	46	62	18	6	.390	.488	S	R	6-0	170	8-20-71	1992	Cape Canaveral, Fla.
Cooper, Jason	.176	16	51	6	9	1	0	3	7	9	15	1	1	.300	.373	L	L	6-2	220	12-6-80	2002	Moses Lake, Wash.
Crozier, Eric	.297	84	296	55	88	21	0	20	53	36	67	5	1	.375	.571	L	L	6-4	200	8-11-78	2000	Columbus, Ohio
Dunwoody, Todd	.167	22	66	11	11	2	0	4	7	5	15	0	1	.236	.379	L	L	6-1	210	4-11-75	1993	West Lafayette, Ind.
Escobar, Alex	.286	16	63	10	18	5	0	4	10	4	15	0	1	.348	.556	R	R	6-1	190	9-6-78	1996	Valencia, Venez.
Garko, Ryan	.350	5	20	2	7	1	0	0	4	2	3	0	0	.391	.400	R	R	6-2	225	1-2-81	2003	Walnut, Calif.
Gonzalez, Raul	.310	56	232	36	72	13	1	9	40	13	19	5	5	.346	.491	R	R	5-9	190	12-27-73	1991	Carolina, P.R.
2-team (18 Norfolk)	.300	74	297	41	89	19	2	10	46	19	28	6	7	.343	.478							
Grindell, Nate	.359	23	64	12	23	5	0	2	9	8	16	0	0	.419	.531	R	R	6-1	180	4-9-77	1998	Carrollton, Texas
Gutierrez, Franklin	.148	7	27	4	4	1	0	1	3	1	11	0	0	.179	.296	R	R	6-2	175	2-21-83	2001	Caracas, Venez.
Little, Mark	.314	68	239	37	75	17	4	11	39	9	40	4	6	.349	.556	R	R	6-0	190	7-11-72	1994	Edwardsville, Ill.
Luderer, Brian	.250	2	8	2	2	1	0	0	2	0	1	0	0	.333	.375	R	R	5-11	190	8-19-78	1996	Tarzana, Calif.
Ludwick, Ryan	.271	44	166	25	45	15	0	8	30	16	52	0	0	.346	.506	R	L	6-3	205	7-13-78	1999	Las Vegas, Nev.
Martinez, Sandy	.274	62	197	29	54	8	1	17	47	12	44	2	0	.316	.584	L	R	6-2	215	10-8-70	1991	Santo Domingo, D.R.
Peralta, Jhonny	.326	138	556	109	181	44	2	15	86	54	126	8	4	.384	.493	R	R	6-1	180	5-28-82	1999	Santiago, D.R.
Phillips, Brandon	.303	135	521	83	158	34	4	8	50	44	56	14	11	.363	.430	R	R	5-11	190	6-28-81	1999	Stone Mountain, Ga.
Pratt, Scott	.333	1	3	1	1	0	0	0	0	1	0	0	0	.500	.333	L	R	5-10	185	2-4-77	1998	Gilbert, Ariz.
Sizemore, Grady	.287	101	418	73	120	23	8	8	51	42	72	15	10	.360	.438	L	L	6-2	200	8-2-82	2000	Mill Creek, Wash.
Smith, Corey	.111	5	18	0	2	1	0	0	1	1	6	0	0	.200	.167	R	R	6-1	200	4-15-82	2000	Piscataway, N.J.
Sorensen, Zach	.000	4	8	0	0	0	0	0	0	1	3	0	0	.111	.000	S	R	6-0	190	1-3-77	1998	St. George, Utah

ORGANIZATION STATISTICS

BATTING	AVG	G	AB	R	H	2B	3B	HR	RBI	BB	SO	SB	CS	OBP	SLG	B	T	HT	WT	DOB	1st Yr	Resides
Tyner, Jason	.345	38	139	25	48	4	1	0	16	18	15	5	0	.417	.388	L	L	6-1	160	4-23-77	1998	Beaumont, Texas
2-team (64 Richmond)	.309	102	382	65	118	16	2	1	32	33	37	23	6	.373	.369							
Wathan, Dusty	.303	75	238	41	72	15	1	1	24	17	30	3	0	.379	.387	R	R	6-4	215	8-22-73	1994	Peoria, Ariz.
Young, Ernie	.299	115	441	71	132	26	2	27	100	40	104	2	2	.368	.551	R	R	6-1	230	7-8-69	1990	Gilbert, Ariz.

PITCHING	W	L	ERA	G	GS	CG	SV	IP	H	R	ER	BB	SO	AVG	B	T	HT	WT	DOB	1st Yr	Resides
Alvarez, Oscar	0	0	0.00	1	0	0	0	3	4	0	0	2	0	.333	L	L	6-0	160	9-17-80	1999	Barcelona, Venez.
Anderson, Jason	2	1	2.76	9	0	0	1	16	15	5	5	2	11	.254	L	R	6-0	170	6-9-79	2000	Danville, Ill.
Bartosh, Cliff	0	3	2.80	28	0	0	3	35	26	11	11	8	46	.202	L	L	6-2	175	9-5-79	1998	Duncanville, Texas
Brown, Andrew	1	0	0.00	1	1	0	0	5	4	0	0	3	4	.222	R	R	6-6	230	2-17-81	1999	Deltona, Fla.
Cabrera, Fernando	4	3	3.79	45	0	0	5	76	57	37	32	43	93	.208	R	R	6-4	170	11-16-81	2000	Toa Baja, P.R.
Carmona, Fausto	1	0	6.00	1	1	0	0	6	6	4	4	3	2	.261	R	R	6-4	185	12-7-83	2001	Santo Domingo, D.R.
Cressend, Jack	10	1	5.13	24	4	0	1	53	73	30	30	10	41	.333	R	R	6-1	190	5-13-75	1996	Mandeville, La.
Cruceta, Francisco	6	5	3.25	14	14	1	0	83	78	35	30	36	62	.252	R	R	6-2	180	7-4-81	1999	La Vega, D.R.
D'Amico, Jeff	0	0	10.45	3	3	0	0	10	18	12	12	3	6	.391	R	R	6-7	250	12-27-75	1994	Palm Harbor, Fla.
Davis, Jason	3	2	3.00	9	9	0	0	54	53	26	18	18	39	.261	R	R	6-6	210	5-8-80	2000	Charleston, Tenn.
Davis, Kane	3	2	6.15	32	0	0	0	45	59	35	31	25	45	.319	R	R	6-3	190	6-25-75	1993	Reedy, W.Va.
Dawley, Joe	0	0	0.00	1	1	0	0	6	4	3	0	1	7	.190	R	R	6-4	205	9-19-71	1993	Moreno Valley, Calif.
Denney, Kyle	10	5	4.41	24	24	1	0	135	134	74	66	39	113	.251	R	R	6-2	195	7-27-77	1999	Prague, Okla.
Douglas, Shea	0	0	0.00	1	0	0	1	2	0	0	0	1	3	.000	L	L	6-1	190	2-3-81	2002	Vicksburg, Miss.
Durbin, Chad	3	3	3.46	9	9	0	0	52	55	22	20	16	40	.271	R	R	6-2	200	12-3-77	1996	Baton Rouge, La.
Elarton, Scott	1	1	3.15	3	3	1	0	20	19	7	7	5	10	.250	R	R	6-8	240	2-23-76	1994	Denver, Colo.
Ellis, Robert	3	4	6.83	10	10	0	0	55	65	42	42	16	35	.294	R	R	6-5	220	12-15-70	1991	Carthage, Texas
Evans, Kyle	0	1	7.36	1	1	0	0	4	4	5	3	5	1	.308	R	R	6-3	190	10-10-78	2000	Waco, Texas
Gronkiewicz, Lee	0	0	0.00	1	0	0	0	1	0	0	0	0	0	.000	R	R	5-11	180	8-21-78	2001	Lancaster, S.C.
Guthrie, Jeremy	1	2	7.91	4	4	0	0	19	23	19	17	18	10	.333	S	R	6-1	200	4-8-79	2003	Las Vegas, Nev.
Hackman, Luther	2	2	10.89	11	0	0	0	19	31	24	23	16	13	.360	R	R	6-4	195	10-10-74	1994	Columbus, Miss.
Hanson, Adam	1	0	5.79	1	0	0	0	5	6	3	3	0	0	.300	R	R	6-2	195	8-6-81	2003	Medford, N.J.
Howry, Bob	1	1	5.19	18	0	0	0	26	22	15	15	6	24	.222	L	R	6-5	220	8-4-73	1994	Glendale, Ariz.
Jimenez, Jose	0	0	0.00	2	0	0	0	3	3	0	0	1	3	.300	R	R	6-3	230	7-7-73	1994	Boca China, D.R.
Lee, David	2	4	4.88	51	0	0	9	66	63	37	36	35	55	.256	R	R	6-1	200	3-12-73	1996	Pittsburgh, Pa.
Martin, J.D.	0	0	10.80	1	1	0	0	5	9	6	6	2	2	.375	R	R	6-4	170	1-2-83	2001	Ridgecrest, Calif.
Miller, Matt	1	2	1.93	13	0	0	2	14	10	4	3	6	17	.196	R	R	6-3	215	11-23-71	1996	Greenville, Miss.
Porzio, Mike	0	0	6.00	1	1	0	0	3	7	6	2	2	2	.467	L	L	6-3	205	8-20-72	1993	Norwalk, Conn.
Ramsey, Keith	1	1	3.60	2	2	0	0	10	11	4	4	2	5	.275	L	L	6-1	170	3-4-80	2002	Los Angeles, Calif.
Rayborn, Kenny	8	2	3.64	23	22	0	0	124	122	57	50	40	65	.259	R	R	6-4	210	11-24-77	1997	Purvis, Miss.
Robbins, Jake	6	1	3.20	32	2	0	0	65	51	24	23	29	40	.214	R	R	6-5	190	5-23-76	1994	Charlotte, N.C.
Robertson, Jeriome	4	5	7.27	14	12	0	0	64	91	58	52	22	28	.331	L	L	6-1	200	3-30-77	1996	Exeter, Calif.
Sadler, Carl	0	1	12.46	3	0	0	0	4	5	6	6		4	.333	L	L	6-2	190	10-11-76	1996	Perry, Fla.
Stanford, Jason	0	0	0.00	1	1	0	0	3	2	0	0	3	4	.167	L	L	6-2	200	1-23-77	2000	Tucson, Ariz.
Stewart, Scott	3	1	4.22	27	0	0	6	32	37	15	15	9	21	.285	R	L	6-2	225	8-14-75	1994	Mt. Holly, N.C.
Tadano, Kazuhito	2	4	5.44	12	8	0	0	45	49	28	27	14	39	.275	R	R	6-0	180	4-25-80	2003	Tokyo, Japan
Tallet, Brian	0	0	4.15	5	0	0	0	9	7	4	4	3	7	.226	L	L	6-7	210	9-21-77	2000	Bethany, Okla.
Thomas, Evan	3	1	5.04	8	4	0	0	30	37	19	17	12	29	.294	R	R	5-10	170	6-14-74	1996	Pembroke Pines, Fla.
Wathan, Dusty	0	0	0.00	1	0	0	0	2	0	0	0	2	0	.000	R	R	6-4	215	8-22-73	1994	Peoria, Ariz.
White, Matt	2	2	5.97	13	4	0	0	32	45	25	21	19	24	.336	R	L	6-1	180	8-19-77	1998	Windsor, Mass.
Wickman, Bob	1	0	10.13	6	1	0	0	5	4	6	6	4	4	.211	R	R	6-1	240	2-6-69	1990	Wausaukee, Wis.
Young, Tim	0	1	17.28	5	0	0	0	8	17	16	16	7	9	.436	L	L	5-9	170	10-15-73	1996	Bristol, Fla.

FIELDING

Catcher	PCT	G	PO	A	E	DP	PB
Bard	.988	33	238	19	3	1	3
Garko	1.000	2	19	0	0	0	
Luderer	1.000	2	16	1	0	1	0
Martinez	.992	52	327	28	3	3	9
Wathan	.991	64	401	26	4	4	3

First Base	PCT	G	PO	A	E	DP
Branyan	.991	33	309	26	3	28
Clapinski	1.000	5	30	3	0	4
Crozier	.988	58	472	35	6	46
Garko	1.000	3	26	1	0	4
Grindell	1.000	3	22	1	0	1
Wathan	1.000	11	75	9	0	5
Young	.997	33	272	15	1	33

Second Base	PCT	G	PO	A	E	DP
Abernathy	.975	58	100	168	7	41
Clapinski	.960	19	32	40	3	13
Grindell	1.000	1	4	2	0	0
Phillips	.973	69	140	187	9	0
Pratt	1.000	1	2	0	1	0

Third Base	PCT	G	PO	A	E	DP
Abernathy	.921	35	28	54	7	7
Branyan	.964	29	21	59	3	4
Clapinski	.943	16	13	37	3	4
Grindell	1.000	4	2	10	0	0
Peralta	.923	59	38	130	14	12
Smith	.667	5	3	3	3	1

Shortstop	PCT	G	PO	A	E	DP
Clapinski	1.000	2	2	6	0	1
Peralta	.962	77	106	221	13	51
Phillips	.932	66	94	168	19	36

Outfield	PCT	G	PO	A	E	DP
Abernathy	1.000	4	6	0	0	0
Branyan	1.000	14	29	0	0	0
Clapinski	.984	63	112	11	2	2
Cooper	.968	14	30	0	1	0
Crozier	1.000	17	30	1	0	0
Dunwoody	1.000	12	17	0	0	0
Escobar	1.000	14	22	2	0	0
Gonzalez	.984	55	116	10	2	3
Grindell	.962	14	24	1	1	0
Little	.984	67	120	4	2	0
Ludwick	.980	29	49	1	1	0
Sizemore	.996	101	252	7	1	2
Sorensen	1.000	3	8	0	0	0
Tyner	1.000	38	71	1	0	0
Young	.944	6	16	1	1	1

AKRON AEROS — Class AA

EASTERN LEAGUE

BATTING	AVG	G	AB	R	H	2B	3B	HR	RBI	BB	SO	SB	CS	OBP	SLG	B	T	HT	WT	DOB	1st Yr	Resides
Aubrey, Michael	.261	38	134	13	35	7	0	5	22	15	18	0	0	.340	.425	L	L	6-0	195	4-15-82	2003	Shreveport, La.
Bard, Josh	.167	10	30	5	5	1	0	0	5	7	5	0	0	.324	.200	S	R	6-3	210	3-30-78	2000	Chandler, Ariz.
Camacaro, Armando	.167	18	60	5	10	2	0	1	6	5	13	0	0	.239	.250	R	R	5-11	170	4-6-79	1999	Guarenas, Venez.
Chauncey, Clint	.000	1	2	0	0	0	0	0	0	0	1	0	0	.000	.000	R	R	6-1	180	1-1-81	2000	Jacksonville, Fla.
Choy Foo, Rodney	.194	51	165	19	32	6	4	1	10	13	40	7	2	.261	.297	S	R	6-1	180	12-12-81	2001	Waimanalo, Hawaii
Cooper, Jason	.239	111	422	54	101	24	6	14	69	47	106	2	2	.321	.424	L	L	6-2	220	12-6-80	2002	Moses Lake, Wash.
Francisco, Ben	.254	133	497	72	126	29	3	15	71	50	86	21	5	.326	.414	R	R	6-1	180	10-23-81	2002	Anaheim, Calif.
Garko, Ryan	.331	43	172	29	57	15	0	6	38	14	28	1	0	.397	.523	R	R	6-2	225	1-2-81	2003	Walnut, Calif.
Grindell, Nate	.287	98	363	45	104	24	2	6	66	32	55	3	5	.341	.413	R	R	6-1	180	4-9-77	1998	Carrollton, Texas
Gutierrez, Franklin	.302	70	262	38	79	24	2	5	35	23	77	6	3	.372	.466	R	R	6-2	175	2-21-83	2001	Caracas, Venez.
Herrera, Javier	.133	5	15	1	2	0	0		1	1	3	0	0	.188	.133	R	R	6-1	195	1-8-81	2003	Miami, Fla.

BATTING	AVG	G	AB	R	H	2B	3B	HR	RBI	BB	SO	SB	CS	OBP	SLG	B	T	HT	WT	DOB	1st Yr	Resides
Inglett, Joe	.320	67	266	49	85	19	7	1	20	31	28	3	5	.393	.455	L	R	5-10	170	6-29-78	2000	Citrus Heights, Calif.
Kouzmanoff, Kevin	.208	7	24	3	5	1	1	1	6	2	5	0	0	.259	.458	R	R	6-1	200	7-25-81	2003	Evergreen, Colo.
Luderer, Brian	.207	43	140	13	29	7	0	0	13	12	15	0	2	.288	.257	R	R	5-11	190	8-19-78	1996	Tarzana, Calif.
Ludwick, Ryan	.269	8	26	4	7	2	0	1	5	1	5	0	0	.286	.462	R	L	6-3	205	7-13-78	1999	Las Vegas, Nev.
Lunetta, Anthony	.308	7	13	1	4	2	0	0	1	2	3	0	0	.400	.462	R	R	5-9	185	1-9-80	2003	Riverside, Calif.
Matulich, Mario	1.000	1	1	1	1	0	0	0	0	0	0	0	0	1.000	1.000	R	R	6-3	225	9-22-82	2004	Mineola, N.Y.
Minges, Tyler	.267	90	307	44	82	13	7	11	40	26	46	6	1	.330	.463	R	R	6-0	180	11-15-79	1998	Hamilton, Ohio
Orie, Kevin	1.000	1	2	1	2	0	0	0	0	0	0	0	0	1.000	1.000	R	R	6-4	220	9-1-72	1993	Pittsburgh, Pa.
Pinckney, Brandon	.311	68	244	32	76	9	1	2	33	14	30	4	3	.355	.381	R	R	5-10	165	4-12-82	2003	Elk Grove, Calif.
Pratt, Scott	.267	114	405	73	108	27	5	4	44	31	90	22	8	.329	.388	L	R	5-10	185	2-4-77	1998	Gilbert, Ariz.
Salazar, Oscar	.221	44	163	18	36	6	0	6	21	11	30	2	1	.269	.368	R	R	6-0	180	6-27-78	1995	Maracay, Venez.
Sherrill, J.J.	.156	20	64	6	10	2	0	1	4	5	25	3	0	.229	.234	S	R	5-7	170	8-11-80	1999	Seaside, Calif.
Smith, Corey	.249	128	454	79	113	14	3	19	66	63	106	3	2	.347	.419	R	R	6-1	200	4-15-82	2000	Piscataway, N.J.
Sorensen, Zach	.258	26	93	12	24	2	1	1	9	17	19	9	1	.366	.333	S	R	6-0	190	1-3-77	1998	St. George, Utah
Spilman, Ryan	.000	2	2	1	0	0	0	0	0	1	2	0	0	.333	.000	R	R	6-2	180	8-25-84	2004	Mount Vernon, Ind.
Valencia, Victor	.229	15	48	10	11	4	0	2	5	6	16	0	0	.333	.438	R	R	6-2	185	5-30-77	1994	Maracay, Venez.
Wallace, David	.213	47	141	19	30	4	0	6	19	25	58	0	0	.333	.369	R	R	6-4	230	10-17-79	2002	Brentwood, Tenn.
West, Todd	.125	4	8	1	1	1	0	0	1	2	1	1	0	.300	.250	R	R	5-11	160	3-2-79	2000	El Paso, Texas
Youngbauer, Scott	.233	61	219	41	51	12	4	6	28	28	41	5	2	.320	.406	S	R	6-1	179	1-14-79	2000	Powder Springs, Ga.
2-team (61 Reading)	.253	122	458	81	116	22	7	15	49	47	90	13	4	.324	.430							

PITCHING	W	L	ERA	G	GS	CG	SV	IP	H	R	ER	BB	SO	AVG	B	T	HT	WT	DOB	1st Yr	Resides
Alvarez, Oscar	7	2	3.36	23	5	0	1	67	62	26	25	24	50	.242	L	L	6-0	160	9-17-80	1999	Barcelona, Venez.
Bere, Jason	0	1	11.12	2	2	0	0	6	10	7	7	4	4	.417	R	R	6-3	225	5-26-71	1990	North Andover, Mass.
Betancourt, Rafael	0	0	0.00	1	0	0	0	1	0	0	0	1	2	.000	R	R	6-2	200	4-29-75	1994	Cumana, Venez.
Brannon, Nick	0	0	27.00	1	0	0	0	2	6	5	5	1	0	.600	L	L	6-5	190	4-23-78	2001	Sevierville, Tenn.
Brown, Andrew	3	6	4.66	17	17	0	0	77	66	44	40	36	67	.227	R	R	6-6	230	2-17-81	1999	Deltona, Fla.
Carmona, Fausto	4	8	4.76	15	15	0	0	87	114	52	46	21	63	.320	R	R	6-4	185	12-7-83	2001	Santo Domingo, D.R.
Cooper, Chris	5	1	1.72	27	0	0	2	37	37	11	7	10	28	.264	L	L	5-11	190	10-31-78	2001	Sewickley, Penn.
Cruceta, Francisco	4	8	5.28	15	15	1	0	89	89	58	52	33	45	.261	R	R	6-2	180	7-4-81	1999	La Vega, D.R.
Davis, Kane	0	0	3.00	1	0	0	0	3	2	1	1	0	3	.182	R	R	6-3	190	6-25-75	1993	Reedy, W.V.
Dawley, Joe	0	1	0.00	1	1	0	0	0	3	3	3	1	0	1.000	R	R	6-4	205	9-19-71	1993	Moreno Valley, Calif.
Denham, Dan	5	3	4.74	14	13	1	0	76	84	52	40	30	50	.280	R	R	6-2	190	12-24-82	2001	Stateline, Nev.
Dittler, Jake	5	12	5.02	21	20	1	0	108	119	73	60	40	85	.275	R	R	6-4	220	11-24-82	2001	Henderson, Nev.
Douglas, Shea	1	0	3.44	9	0	0	0	18	17	9	7	7	15	.239	L	L	6-1	190	2-3-81	2002	Vicksburg, Miss.
Evans, Kyle	1	3	7.71	8	7	0	0	33	39	36	28	16	24	.291	R	R	6-3	190	10-10-78	2000	Waco, Texas
Foley, Travis	1	4	6.99	7	7	0	0	28	35	22	22	17	23	.307	R	R	6-1	180	3-11-83	2001	Louisville, Ky.
Gomez, Mariano	0	1	5.31	7	3	0	0	20	27	14	12	8	15	.321	L	L	65	170	9-12-82	2000	San Pedro Sula, Honduras
Gronkiewicz, Lee	1	4	3.03	52	0	0	20	65	65	24	22	21	68	.259	R	R	5-11	180	8-21-78	2001	Lancaster, S.C.
Guthrie, Jeremy	8	8	4.21	23	21	1	0	130	145	76	61	42	94	.277	S	R	6-1	200	4-8-79	2003	Las Vegas, Nev.
Hanson, Adam	0	0	6.75	1	0	0	0	3	3	3	2	1	3	.273	R	R	6-2	195	8-6-81	2003	Medford, N.J.
Harris, Josh	2	0	0.00	2	0	0	0	3	3	0	0	0	2	.250	R	R	6-0	205	11-23-80	2004	Belton, Texas
Kleine, Victor	4	4	4.95	25	9	0	0	87	91	55	48	40	54	.270	L	L	6-4	180	9-12-79	2000	Florence, Ky.
Martinez, Dave	0	0	0.00	1	1	0	0	5	5	1	0	1	1	.250	L	L	6-1	210	6-7-80	1997	Ciudad Bolivar, Venez.
Mendoza, Marcos	0	0	27.00	1	0	0	0	2	3	5	5	3	1	.429	L	L	5-10	180	10-31-80	2001	El Cajon, Calif.
Pesco, Nick	1	0	0.00	1	1	0	0	5	3	0	0	1	10	.176	R	R	6-6	200	9-17-83	2003	Lodi, Calif.
Prahm, Ryan	0	0	2.22	15	0	0	1	24	19	9	6	20	22	.209	R	R	6-5	210	5-17-79	2001	Cedar Rapids, Iowa
Rayborn, Kenny	1	1	6.75	6	0	0	0	12	13	9	9	5	6	.283	R	R	6-4	210	11-22-74	1997	Purvis, Miss.
Robbins, Jake	2	1	3.28	12	0	0	1	25	16	10	9	7	21	.182	R	R	6-5	190	5-23-76	1994	Charlotte, N.C.
Sadler, Carl	1	1	2.93	23	0	0	3	43	36	17	14	15	41	.218	L	L	6-2	190	10-11-76	1996	Perry, Fla.
Sturkie, Scott	2	1	1.78	13	1	0	0	25	22	8	5	11	10	.237	R	R	6-3	210	6-12-79	2001	West Columbia, S.C.
Tallet, Brian	1	1	5.56	14	0	0	1	23	26	15	14	13	23	.292	L	L	6-7	210	9-21-77	2000	Bethany, Okla.
Van Dusen, Derrick	1	3	5.67	26	2	0	1	54	70	40	34	22	42	.308	L	L	6-3	180	6-6-81	2000	Fontana, Calif.
Vargas, Jose	3	3	3.51	33	0	0	2	56	46	22	22	27	64	.224	R	R	6-0	170	3-25-77	1998	Barahona, D.R.
Warden, Jim Ed	0	1	9.53	4	0	0	0	6	7	7	6	7	5	.350	R	R	6-7	195	5-7-79	2001	Murfreesboro, Tenn.
Wickman, Bob	0	0	0.00	1	1	0	0	1	0	0	0	2	1	.000	R	R	6-1	240	2-6-69	1990	Wausaukee, Wis.

FIELDING

Catcher	PCT	G	PO	A	E	DP	PB
Bard	1.000	4	20	3	0	0	0
Camacaro	.969	17	111	16	4	2	3
Garko	.993	24	138	12	1	1	1
Herrera	1.000	5	38	3	0	0	1
Luderer	.981	37	240	13	5	1	5
Spilman	1.000	2	4	1	0	0	0
Valencia	.974	15	103	8	3	1	1
Wallace	.979	45	314	19	7	2	6

First Base	PCT	G	PO	A	E	DP
Aubrey	.976	27	185	19	5	16
Garko	.979	16	129	12	3	18
Grindell	.987	66	554	52	8	42
Luderer	.982	6	49	7	1	4
Salazar	1.000	7	47	7	0	4
Youngbauer	.989	25	170	16	2	15

Second Base	PCT	G	PO	A	E	DP
Choy Foo	.974	43	63	122	5	20
Inglett	.954	51	97	129	11	26
Pratt	.938	20	24	51	5	5
Salazar	.926	11	19	31	4	7
West	1.000	1	1	3	0	1
Youngbauer	.969	18	36	57	3	15

Third Base	PCT	G	PO	A	E	DP
Choy Foo	1.000	1	1	0	0	0
Kouzmanoff	.813	7	5	8	3	0
Pratt	1.000	5	4	5	0	0
Salazar	1.000	2	3	3	0	0
Smith	.891	125	108	195	37	18
Youngbauer	1.000	3	2	3	0	0

Shortstop	PCT	G	PO	A	E	DP
Lunetta	1.000	4	5	13	0	3
Pinckney	.950	67	87	162	13	38
Pratt	.931	18	23	44	5	4
Salazar	.936	20	34	39	5	10
Sorensen	.981	25	41	63	2	21
West	1.000	2	4	5	0	1
Youngbauer	.976	12	16	24	1	4

Outfield	PCT	G	PO	A	E	DP
Cooper	.984	91	177	4	3	2
Francisco	.984	133	292	9	5	2
Grindell	1.000	13	13	0	0	0
Gutierrez	.969	52	121	5	4	0
Ludwick	1.000	5	6	0	0	0
Minges	.973	82	165	12	5	2
Pratt	1.000	35	88	1	0	1
Salazar	1.000	1	1	0	0	0
Sherrill	.953	20	40	1	2	0
Sorensen	1.000	2	3	0	0	0
Youngbauer	1.000	3	6	0	0	0

KINSTON INDIANS — High Class A

CAROLINA LEAGUE

BATTING	AVG	G	AB	R	H	2B	3B	HR	RBI	BB	SO	SB	CS	OBP	SLG	B	T	HT	WT	DOB	1st Yr	Resides
Aubrey, Michael	.339	60	218	34	74	14	1	10	60	27	26	3	1	.438	.550	L	L	6-0	195	4-15-82	2003	Shreveport, La.
Brock, Caleb	.254	41	134	19	34	13	0	3	19	8	27	2	0	.324	.418	R	R	5-11	200	3-30-80	2003	Lexington, Ky.

BATTING	AVG	G	AB	R	H	2B	3B	HR	RBI	BB	SO	SB	CS	OBP	SLG	B	T	HT	WT	DOB	1st Yr	Resides
Camacaro, Armando	.268	25	82	6	22	3	0	1	10	3	14	0	0	.310	.341	R	R	5-11	170	4-6-79	1999	Guarenas, Venez.
Cashman, Brandon	.250	1	4	1	1	0	0	0	1	1	3	0	0	.400	.250	R	R	5-10	205	10-31-79	2003	Eagan, Minn.
Choy Foo, Rodney	.215	54	191	24	41	10	1	1	20	17	40	8	2	.281	.293	S	R	6-1	180	12-12-81	2001	Waimanalo, Hawaii
Cotto, Luis	.211	12	38	9	8	2	0	0	2	3	7	0	0	.268	.263	R	R	5-10	180	7-9-81	2000	Rio Piedras, P.R.
Dyson, Trey	.179	12	39	5	7	2	0	1	5	7	7	0	0	.319	.308	L	L	6-4	220	3-11-80	2002	Blythewood, S.C.
Garko, Ryan	.328	65	238	44	78	17	1	16	58	26	34	4	1	.425	.609	R	R	6-2	225	1-2-81	2003	Walnut, Calif.
Herrera, Javier	.245	42	151	24	37	7	0	5	24	17	23	0	2	.339	.391	R	R	6-1	195	1-8-81	2003	Miami, Fla.
Larkin, Shaun	.260	118	435	67	113	25	0	12	62	37	67	3	3	.318	.400	L	R	5-9	170	9-7-79	2002	Cypress, Calif.
Lunetta, Anthony	.211	71	218	30	46	8	0	2	16	25	41	3	2	.309	.275	R	R	5-8	185	1-9-80	2003	Riverside, Calif.
Magness, Pat	.270	41	141	18	38	8	0	7	32	28	41	0	1	.401	.475	L	L	6-3	230	1-19-78	2000	Overland Park, Kan.
Malave, Dennis	.247	64	182	30	45	11	0	4	20	18	36	5	6	.322	.374	L	L	5-9	165	1-6-80	1997	Caracas, Venez.
McCullough, Clayton	.222	4	9	1	2	0	0	0	2	0	3	0	0	.222	.222	L	R	5-10	180	12-27-79	2002	Greenville, N.C.
Ochoa, Ivan	.237	66	257	41	61	9	3	1	26	21	56	11	4	.308	.307	R	R	5-10	140	12-16-82	2000	Guacara, Venez.
Osborn, Pat	.342	86	307	69	105	16	6	10	55	40	52	6	6	.424	.531	R	R	6-3	210	2-27-81	2002	Gainesville, Fla.
Panther, Nathan	.256	120	457	79	117	15	2	7	50	51	118	11	4	.345	.344	L	L	6-2	180	7-12-81	2002	Muscatine, Iowa
Parker, Brett	.174	12	23	3	4	2	0	0	1	1	5	0	0	.240	.261	R	R	6-0	190	8-27-80	2003	Mobile, Ala.
Santana, Mayobanex	.143	8	28	2	4	0	0	1	4	1	10	0	0	.172	.250	R	R	6-3	185	8-23-81	1999	Santo Domingo, D.R.
Sherrill, J.J.	.241	97	324	49	78	12	3	12	51	40	92	8	2	.337	.407	S	R	5-7	170	8-11-80	1999	Seaside, Calif.
Snyder, Brad	.355	29	110	20	39	7	1	6	21	13	28	4	2	.424	.600	L	L	6-2	180	5-25-82	2003	Bellevue, Ohio
Torres, Eider	.302	113	440	68	133	24	3	3	46	22	46	48	6	.337	.391	S	R	5-8	160	1-16-83	2000	Maracaibo, Venez.
Van Every, John	.276	113	392	67	108	22	2	21	71	52	129	11	3	.367	.503	L	L	6-1	190	11-27-79	2001	Brandon, Miss.
Wallace, David	.206	39	136	12	28	9	0	1	14	11	45	1	2	.268	.294	R	R	6-4	230	10-17-79	2002	Brentwood, Tenn.
West, Todd	.444	4	9	2	4	0	0	0	3	2	2	0	0	.545	.444	R	R	5-11	160	3-2-79	2000	El Paso, Texas

PITCHING	W	L	ERA	G	GS	CG	SV	IP	H	R	ER	BB	SO	AVG	B	T	HT	WT	DOB	1st Yr	Resides
Brannon, Nick	1	0	9.64	4	0	0	0	5	9	5	5	3	5	.409	L	L	6-5	190	4-23-78	2001	Sevierville, Tenn.
Carmona, Fausto	5	2	2.83	13	13	0	0	70	68	28	22	20	57	.249	R	R	6-4	185	12-7-83	2001	Santo Domingo, D.R.
Cooper, Chris	3	3	1.60	25	0	0	1	39	36	11	7	10	44	.242	L	L	5-11	190	10-31-78	2003	Sewickley, Pa.
Davis, Matt	3	2	3.13	41	0	0	4	83	85	35	29	26	61	.264	R	R	6-2	205	11-19-81	2003	Mason, Ohio
Denham, Dan	7	4	4.18	13	13	0	0	71	73	34	33	29	62	.274	R	R	6-1	190	12-24-82	2001	Stateline, Nev.
Douglas, Shea	3	0	0.56	16	1	0	1	32	18	4	2	10	32	.157	L	L	6-1	190	2-3-81	2002	Vicksburg, Miss.
Eisentrager, Dan	6	4	4.05	45	0	0	4	73	78	37	33	24	46	.272	R	R	6-3	170	12-30-80	2003	Elk Grove, Calif.
Foley, Travis	2	0	1.37	13	0	0	0	26	16	4	4	7	25	.167	R	R	6-3	190	3-11-83	2001	Louisville, Ky.
Lara, Juan	4	3	5.66	35	8	0	1	84	106	60	53	38	74	.307	R	L	6-2	190	1-26-81	1999	Bani, D.R.
Martin, J.D.	11	10	4.39	25	24	2	0	148	139	75	72	41	98	.255	R	R	6-4	170	1-2-83	2001	Ridgecrest, Calif.
Martinez, Dave	2	3	5.51	19	6	0	0	51	42	38	31	28	37	.227	L	L	6-1	210	6-7-80	1997	Ciudad Bolivar, Venez.
Mattison, Kieran	3	1	7.77	13	2	0	0	22	22	19	19	17	19	.268	L	R	6-0	200	6-21-80	2002	Greenville, N.C.
Miller, Adam	3	2	2.08	8	8	0	0	43	29	17	10	12	46	.192	R	R	6-4	175	11-26-84	2003	McKinney, Texas
Parker, Brett	0	0	0.00	1	1	0	0	1	1	1	0	1	0	.200	R	R	6-0	190	8-27-80	2003	Mobile, Ala.
Pennington, Todd	0	2	2.76	28	0	0	19	29	25	11	9	16	39	.229	R	R	6-2	214	4-6-80	2001	McClure, Ill.
Perez, Rafael	0	0	11.57	1	1	0	0	5	10	6	6	2	3	.435	L	L	6-3	170	5-15-82	2002	Santo Domingo, D.R.
Pesco, Nick	1	2	3.21	3	3	0	0	14	15	9	5	4	12	.273	R	R	6-6	200	9-17-83	2003	Lodi, Calif.
Prahm, Ryan	1	0	1.25	31	0	0	14	36	21	7	5	24	43	.165	R	R	6-5	210	5-17-79	2001	Cedar Rapids, Iowa
Ramsey, Keith	10	4	3.86	24	23	2	0	138	139	65	59	34	95	.270	L	L	6-1	170	3-4-80	2002	Los Angeles, Calif.
Rich, Dan	0	0	13.50	4	0	0	0	3	4	4	4	3	1	.333	L	L	6-2	230	8-31-79	2002	Rocky River, Ohio
Slocum, Brian	15	6	4.33	25	25	2	0	135	136	66	65	41	102	.265	R	R	6-4	190	3-27-81	2002	East Chester, N.Y.
Smith, Sean	0	1	8.00	2	2	0	0	9	14	10	8	4	8	.350	R	R	6-4	180	10-13-83	2002	Zephyr Cove, N.Y.
Stockman, Landon	2	1	1.23	16	0	0	1	22	16	3	3	7	20	.198	R	R	6-2	190	8-28-79	2001	Dickson, Tenn.
Van Dusen, Derrick	6	0	1.64	9	9	0	0	49	38	10	9	26	36	.218	L	L	6-3	180	6-6-81	2000	Fontana, Calif.

FIELDING

Catcher	PCT	G	PO	A	E	DP	PB
Brock	.989	16	81	7	1	0	0
Camacaro	.990	24	171	23	2	4	1
Cashman	1.000	1	6	1	0	0	0
Garko	.982	21	149	16	3	2	3
Herrera	.982	42	301	23	6	2	5
McCullough	1.000	3	15	1	0	0	0
Wallace	1.000	37	256	18	0	1	5

First Base	PCT	G	PO	A	E	DP
Aubrey	.991	50	405	23	4	39
Choy Foo	.986	24	193	15	3	16
Garko	1.000	26	224	17	0	17
Larkin	1.000	4	14	0	0	2
Magness	.994	35	290	18	2	16
Santana	1.000	2	14	2	0	2

Second Base	PCT	G	PO	A	E	DP
Choy Foo	1.000	12	29	34	0	5
Larkin	.960	14	18	30	2	9
Lunetta	.800	2	0	4	1	0
Parker	1.000	6	5	7	0	2
Torres	.981	112	170	307	9	57

Third Base	PCT	G	PO	A	E	DP
Choy Foo	.880	8	7	15	3	3
Cotto	1.000	1	0	1	0	0
Larkin	.968	69	50	101	5	5
Lunetta	.900	18	8	28	4	5
Osborn	.929	51	36	81	9	7

Shortstop	PCT	G	PO	A	E	DP
Choy Foo	1.000	2	6	4	0	1
Cotto	.900	11	15	21	4	3

	PCT	G	PO	A	E	DP
Larkin	.800	2	3	1	1	0
Lunetta	.960	43	58	108	7	19
Ochoa	.968	66	109	195	10	38
Osborn	.900	18	27	45	8	7
Parker	.929	6	6	7	1	0
West	.917	3	2	9	1	2

Outfield	PCT	G	PO	A	E	DP
Brock	1.000	2	1	0	0	0
Dyson	1.000	11	22	0	0	0
Malave	.961	55	94	4	4	0
Panther	.992	116	247	8	2	2
Santana	1.000	4	8	0	0	0
Sherrill	.981	96	205	7	4	1
Snyder	1.000	28	48	1	0	0
van Every	.955	116	205	5	10	2

LAKE COUNTY CAPTAINS   Low Class A

SOUTH ATLANTIC LEAGUE

BATTING	AVG	G	AB	R	H	2B	3B	HR	RBI	BB	SO	SB	CS	OBP	SLG	B	T	HT	WT	DOB	1st Yr	Resides
Brock, Caleb	.244	50	168	22	41	10	0	3	20	14	23	2	3	.330	.357	R	R	5-11	200	3-30-80	2003	Lexington, Ky.
Clem, Chris	.259	8	27	5	7	0	0	0	5	3	7	0	0	.344	.259	R	R	6-0	190	2-3-84	2003	Brisbane, Australia
Conroy, Mike	.268	111	400	51	107	17	10	5	52	27	78	12	6	.321	.398	L	L	6-3	190	10-3-82	2001	Fort Myers, Fla.
Cotto, Luis	.266	53	158	19	42	9	1	16	10	32	2	2	.324	.342	R	R	5-10	180	7-9-81	2000	Rio Piedras, P.R.
De la Cruz, Chris	.275	109	414	68	114	12	7	3	53	23	53	13	3	.317	.360	S	R	6-0	160	5-3-82	2001	Monte Plata, D.R.
Encarnacion, Teodoro	.213	17	61	7	13	0	1	1	3	1	15	0	1	.250	.295	R	R	6-2	190	3-26-83	2001	Santo Domingo, D.R.
Goleski, Ryan	.297	130	505	83	150	22	5	28	104	55	100	6	7	.372	.527	R	R	6-3	225	3-19-82	2003	Lake Orion, Mich.
Herrera, Javier	.263	46	160	28	42	9	2	5	22	17	32	0	0	.364	.438	R	R	6-1	195	1-8-81	2003	Miami, Fla.
Kouzmanoff, Kevin	.330	123	473	74	156	35	5	16	87	44	75	5	4	.394	.526	R	R	6-1	200	7-25-81	2003	Evergreen, Colo.
McCullough, Clayton	.205	28	83	9	17	1	0	1	7	12	22	1	1	.305	.253	L	R	5-10	180	12-27-79	2002	Greenville, N.C.
Mulhern, Ryan	.255	103	372	48	95	28	1	7	43	32	87	3	2	.319	.392	R	R	6-2	195	11-29-80	2003	Highlands Ranch, Colo.

BATTING	AVG	G	AB	R	H	2B	3B	HR	RBI	BB	SO	SB	CS	OBP	SLG	B	T	HT	WT	DOB	1st Yr	Resides
Noviskey, Josh	.290	22	69	14	20	1	1	1	11	8	22	0	0	.378	.377	S	R	6-4	215	3-15-83	2001	Newton, N.J.
Peavey, Bill	.242	65	223	30	54	8	0	11	35	28	49	0	0	.331	.426	L	L	6-4	250	1-16-79	2002	Brisbane, Calif.
Peterson, Derrick	.074	8	27	1	2	0	0	0	6	7	0	1	2	.242	.074	R	R	6-3	190	5-23-82	2004	Petersburg, Mich.
Pinckney, Brandon	.364	40	165	31	60	10	0	3	22	10	12	6	4	.401	.479	R	R	5-10	165	4-12-82	2003	Elk Grove, Calif.
Rojas, Ricardo	.251	104	394	72	99	14	3	5	39	24	94	27	14	.310	.340	R	R	6-0	160	2-2-83	2000	Puerto Plata, D.R.
Schilling, Micah	.250	115	396	58	99	16	4	5	43	52	105	3	4	.337	.348	L	R	5-11	180	12-27-82	2002	Zachary, La.
Snyder, Brad	.280	79	304	52	85	15	5	10	54	48	78	11	4	.382	.461	L	L	6-3	200	5-25-82	2003	Bellevue, Ohio
Valdes, Juan	.237	25	97	18	23	0	0	1	10	15	23	20	3	.345	.268	S	R	6-0	150	6-22-85	2003	Manati, P.R.
Whitney, Matt	.256	55	195	21	50	11	0	5	31	23	81	0	0	.347	.390	R	R	6-4	190	2-13-84	2002	Palm Beach Gardens, Fla.
Woodson, Mike	.286	3	7	0	2	1	0	0	1	2	0	0	0	.375	.429	R	R	5-11	180	12-11-84	2003	Salinas, P.R.

PITCHING	W	L	ERA	G	GS	CG	SV	IP	H	R	ER	BB	SO	AVG	B	T	HT	WT	DOB	1st Yr	Resides
Allen, Blake	5	4	4.86	23	0	0	0	54	57	33	29	21	49	.277	L	L	6-2	200	7-17-81	2002	Humboldt, Tenn.
Ashabraner, Bo	5	2	2.54	29	0	0	3	50	45	17	14	11	51	.236	R	R	6-7	230	2-19-81	2003	Yorba Linda, Calif.
Burton, T.J.	2	1	3.80	39	0	0	2	95	95	44	40	47	72	.260	R	R	6-3	170	7-30-83	2002	Ottawa, Ontario
Cevette, Dan	2	0	2.47	9	9	0	0	44	43	13	12	14	41	.254	L	L	6-3	180	10-19-83	2002	Elkland, Pa.
D'Amico, Jeff	0	0	0.00	2	1	0	0	2	1	0	0	1	0	.143	R	R	6-7	250	12-27-75	1994	Palm Harbor, Fla.
Hanson, Adam	3	6	4.55	35	0	0	0	63	74	33	32	32	62	.294	R	R	6-2	195	8-6-81	2003	Medford, N.J.
Hiraldo, Nelson	6	6	5.38	26	2	0	2	72	82	52	43	26	66	.279	R	R	6-0	195	9-17-83	2001	Puerto Plata, D.R.
Laffey, Aaron	3	7	6.45	19	15	0	1	74	79	58	53	44	69	.271	L	L	6-0	170	4-15-85	2003	Cumberland, Md.
Marceau, Pierre Luc	0	0	6.20	6	4	0	0	20	26	14	14	8	16	.302	L	L	6-2	190	4-11-81	2000	Fleurimont, Quebec
2-team (13 Savannah)	0	0	5.29	19	4	0	0	48	55	31	28	25	37	.286							
Martin, Kevin	1	3	6.75	9	0	0	0	11	17	12	8	6	8	.347	R	R	6-2	185	1-3-79	2001	Ridgecrest, Calif.
Martinez, Dave	0	0	9.00	1	0	0	0	2	4	2	2	1	2	.400	L	L	6-1	210	6-7-80	1997	Ciudad Bolivar, Venez.
Mattison, Kieran	1	2	2.70	13	0	0	2	30	26	10	9	16	22	.234	R	R	6-0	200	6-21-80	2002	Greenville, N.C.
Mercedes, Gerson	0	1	1.80	1	1	0	0	5	5	1	1	1	4	.250	R	R	6-1	192	7-8-81	2001	Santo Domingo, D.R.
Miller, Adam	7	4	3.36	19	19	1	0	91	79	39	34	28	106	.238	R	R	6-4	175	11-26-84	2003	McKinney, Texas
Mujica, Edward	7	7	4.65	26	19	1	2	124	130	77	64	32	89	.271	R	R	6-2	180	5-10-84	2002	Yagua, Venez.
Niesel, Chris	1	1	5.85	5	5	0	0	20	24	13	13	1	23	.286	R	R	5-11	195	11-18-82	2004	Plantation, Fla.
Perez, Rafael	7	6	4.85	23	22	0	0	115	121	75	62	47	99	.273	L	L	6-3	170	5-15-82	2002	Santo Domingo, D.R.
Pesco, Nick	6	7	3.91	21	21	0	0	106	96	49	46	30	97	.241	R	R	6-6	200	9-17-83	2003	Lodi, Calif.
Rich, Dan	0	0	10.13	3	0	0	0	5	8	6	6	0	6	.333	L	L	6-2	230	8-31-79	2002	Rocky River, Ohio
Roehl, Scott	1	5	5.14	29	3	0	2	70	87	52	40	15	68	.296	R	R	6-1	195	8-19-81	2003	Somers, Wis.
Santos, Reid	0	0	6.75	3	3	0	0	13	20	13	10	5	12	.357	L	L	6-1	170	8-24-82	2003	Kaneohe, Hawaii
Smith, Sean	7	2	3.99	13	13	0	0	61	50	24	23	28	48	.223	R	R	6-4	180	10-13-83	2002	Zephyr Cove, N.Y.
Southerland, Chip	3	2	4.03	20	0	0	5	22	20	10	10	6	26	.233	R	R	6-3	230	5-3-82	2003	Santa Ana, Calif.
Tallet, Brian	0	0	0.00	2	1	0	0	2	1	0	0	0	1	.143	L	L	6-7	210	9-21-77	2000	Bethany, Okla.
Warden, Jim Ed	5	1	3.00	41	1	0	13	54	43	22	18	27	63	.224	R	R	6-7	195	5-7-79	2001	Murfreesboro, Tenn.

FIELDING

Catcher	PCT	G	PO	A	E	DP	PB
Brock	.995	49	350	42	2	5	8
Herrera	.987	45	357	36	5	1	7
McCullough	.992	28	219	15	2	1	1
Noviskey	1.000	22	180	15	0	2	3
Woodson	.900	2	9	0	1	0	1

First Base	PCT	G	PO	A	E	DP
Cotto	1.000	1	1	0	0	0
Mulhern	.981	95	755	59	16	65
Peavey	.986	45	341	19	5	28

Second Base	PCT	G	PO	A	E	DP
Clem	1.000	3	3	10	0	0

Cotto	1.000	14	21	26	0	8
De La Cruz	.925	9	15	22	3	2
Pinckney	1.000	5	8	13	0	4
Schilling	.944	110	206	251	27	46

Third Base	PCT	G	PO	A	E	DP
Clem	1.000	1	0	3	0	0
Cotto	.929	14	7	19	2	3
Kouzmanoff	.950	115	83	185	14	14
Peterson	.958	8	6	17	1	3
Pinckney	.917	3	2	9	1	1

Shortstop	PCT	G	PO	A	E	DP
Clem	.913	4	6	15	2	2

Cotto	.933	20	25	58	6	12
De La Cruz	.950	94	141	254	21	50
Pinckney	.969	24	27	68	3	10

Outfield	PCT	G	PO	A	E	DP
Conroy	.970	96	156	7	5	0
Cotto	1.000	2	2	0	0	0
Encarnacion	1.000	13	18	3	0	0
Goleski	.974	117	211	11	6	3
Rojas	.996	96	216	10	1	3
Snyder	.975	71	152	4	4	2
Valdes	1.000	25	47	1	0	1

MAHONING VALLEY SCRAPPERS

Short-Season Class A

NEW YORK-PENN LEAGUE

BATTING	AVG	G	AB	R	H	2B	3B	HR	RBI	BB	SO	SB	CS	OBP	SLG	B	T	HT	WT	DOB	1st Yr	Resides
Butia, Mike	.315	62	232	32	73	17	1	5	44	24	54	0	1	.396	.461	L	R	6-2	215	11-29-82	2004	Pittsburgh, Penn.
Casillas, Omar	.185	24	65	10	12	0	0	0	2	11	10	0	0	.308	.185	R	R	6-1	170	9-17-83	2003	Cidra, P.R.
Clem, Chris	.217	42	138	20	30	4	0	1	16	12	36	2	1	.310	.268	R	R	6-0	190	2-3-84	2003	Brisbane, Australia
Cruz, Jose	.225	15	40	6	9	0	1	0	1	6	7	1	0	.326	.275	S	R	5-11	180	10-21-82	2002	Rio Piedras, P.R.
Encarnacion, Teodoro	.233	60	215	21	50	7	2	5	27	12	58	0	0	.270	.353	R	R	6-2	190	3-26-83	2001	Santo Domingo, D.R.
Finegan, Brian	.255	69	263	41	67	13	2	3	34	22	48	5	5	.320	.354	R	R	6-0	190	12-15-81	2004	Fresno, Calif.
Gimenez, Chris	.300	71	260	40	78	23	3	10	38	30	62	2	2	.419	.527	R	R	6-2	190	12-27-82	2004	Gilroy, Calif.
Matulich, Mario	.247	23	81	6	20	7	1	1	9	3	29	0	0	.282	.395	R	R	6-3	225	9-22-82	2004	Mineola, N.Y.
Merloni, Lou	.250	2	8	1	2	0	0	1	4	0	3	0	0	.250	.625	R	R	5-10	200	4-6-71	1993	Framingham, Mass.
Montgomery, Tim	.269	65	242	37	65	14	2	7	32	26	67	0	1	.342	.430	R	R	6-3	205	6-2-82	2004	Sammamish, Wash.
Pacheco, Fernando	.253	60	198	28	50	10	1	5	37	33	49	0	1	.363	.389	L	L	6-1	190	10-1-84	2002	San Ysidro, Calif.
Parker, Brett	.273	64	238	43	65	19	1	4	27	23	53	10	1	.347	.412	R	R	6-0	190	8-27-80	2003	Mobile, Ala.
Reyes, Argenis	.312	73	324	53	101	11	0	0	20	15	36	27	9	.349	.346	S	R	5-10	160	9-25-82	2001	Santiago, D.R.
Szabo, Marshall	.294	26	109	13	32	3	2	1	9	3	15	5	0	.310	.385	R	R	5-10	180	2-13-83	2004	Alpharetta, Ga.
Toregas, Wyatt	.294	59	214	38	63	18	1	7	48	11	26	1	2	.338	.486	R	R	5-11	200	2-22-82	2004	Ashburn, Va.

GAMES BY POSITION: C—Casillas 23, Encarnacion 1, Gimenez 3, Matulich 6, Toregas 53. **1B**—Gimenez 18, Matulich 5, Pacheco 57. **2B**—Clem 21, Parker 19, Reyes 17, Szabo 23. **3B**—Clem 20, Gimenez 28, Parker 33, Reyes 2. **SS**—Finegan 68, Parker 10. **OF**—Butia 47, Cruz 15, Encarnacion 55, Gimenez 22, Montgomery 58, Reyes 42.

PITCHING	W	L	ERA	G	GS	CG	SV	IP	H	R	ER	BB	SO	AVG	B	T	HT	WT	DOB	1st Yr	Resides
Cevette, Dan	3	0	1.25	7	6	0	0	36	24	5	5	6	39	.182	L	L	6-3	180	10-19-83	2002	Elkland, Penn.
Collins, Kyle	4	1	3.86	14	2	0	0	28	25	19	12	16	31	.231	R	R	6-1	165	8-17-81	2004	San Jose, Calif.
De los Santos, Richard	1	5	5.26	13	9	0	0	51	53	34	30	19	45	.268	R	R	6-1	170	6-1-84	2001	Elias Pina, D.R.
Foley, Travis	0	0	7.71	3	0	0	0	5	4	4	4	3	7	.222	R	R	6-1	180	3-11-83	2001	Louisville, Ky.
Gomez, Mariano	0	0	0.00	1	1	0	0	2	2	0	0	0	3	.250	L	L	6-5	170	9-12-82	2000	San Pedro Sula, Honduras
Harris, Mark	3	2	3.03	29	0	0	15	36	35	16	12	19	23	.254	R	R	6-3	205	2-17-81	2003	Loveland, Ohio

ORGANIZATION STATISTICS

PITCHING	W	L	ERA	G	GS	CG	SV	IP	H	R	ER	BB	SO	AVG	B	T	HT	WT	DOB	1st Yr	Resides
Haynes, Matt	4	4	4.87	18	2	0	0	41	33	26	22	26	49	.214	L	R	6-3	180	4-18-83	2002	Maroochydore, Australia
Hernandez, Michael	1	0	2.57	10	0	0	0	14	6	10	4	11	18	.115	L	L	6-4	190	4-8-81	2002	Fresno, Calif.
Hiraldo, Nelson	1	2	7.14	7	7	0	0	29	47	30	23	4	22	.367	R	R	6-0	195	9-17-83	2001	Puerto Plata, D.R.
Hoyman, Justin	0	0	2.08	5	5	0	0	13	9	3	3	4	8	.200	R	R	6-3	195	4-17-82	2004	Melbourne, Fla.
Jecmen, Mark	3	1	5.35	20	0	0	0	34	32	21	20	25	30	.262	R	R	6-8	235	2-16-83	2004	Diamond Bar, Calif.
Knippschild, Ryan	4	3	3.93	15	13	0	0	69	79	40	30	17	39	.286	L	L	6-1	195	9-24-82	2004	Lawrence, Kan.
Knox, Matt	3	4	2.25	23	0	0	3	40	33	15	10	12	61	.221	R	R	6-4	210	12-29-79	2001	Lebanon, Pa.
Laffey, Aaron	3	1	1.24	8	8	0	0	44	38	15	6	10	30	.229	L	L	6-0	170	4-15-85	2003	Cumberland, Md.
Lewis, Scott	0	1	5.40	2	2	0	0	3	2	2	2	1	9	.167	B	L	6-3	180	9-26-83	2004	Washington Courthouse, Ohio
Lincoln, Roger	3	3	3.51	24	0	0	0	41	37	19	16	15	39	.239	L	L	5-10	175	7-19-80	2003	Northford, Conn.
Lubrano, Paul	1	0	1.93	10	1	0	0	23	24	9	5	10	23	.258	L	L	6-1	170	12-19-81	2004	Winter Springs, Fla.
Niesel, Chris	2	0	2.30	5	4	0	0	27	13	8	7	4	20	.138	R	R	5-11	195	11-18-82	2004	Plantation, Fla.
Pekarek, Justin	0	1	6.23	7	2	0	0	17	23	14	12	7	15	.311	L	L	6-4	195	12-4-80	2004	Staplehurst, Neb.
Pennington, Todd	0	1	1.93	3	1	0	1	5	5	1	1	1	7	.294	R	R	6-2	214	4-6-80	2001	McClure, Ill.
Porzio, Mike	0	0	3.00	2	2	0	0	6	6	2	2	1	5	.286	L	L	6-3	205	8-20-72	1993	Norwalk, Conn.
Roehl, Scott	2	1	4.11	11	0	0	0	15	16	9	7	4	20	.258	R	R	6-1	195	8-19-81	2003	Somers, Wis.
Santana, Hector	1	2	9.55	20	0	0	1	27	33	33	29	25	15	.287	R	R	6-0	160	7-13-82	2000	San Pedro de Macoris, D.R.
Sipp, Tony	3	1	3.16	10	10	0	0	43	33	23	15	13	74	.202	L	L	6-0	185	7-12-83	2004	Moss Point, Miss.
Southerland, Chip	0	1	3.44	11	0	0	0	18	19	8	7	5	18	.268	R	R	6-3	230	5-3-82	2002	Santa Ana, Calif.
Tallet, Brian	0	0	0.00	2	1	0	0	3	3	3	0	0	2	.273	L	L	6-7	210	9-21-77	2000	Bethany, Okla.

BURLINGTON INDIANS — Rookie

APPALACHIAN LEAGUE

BATTING	AVG	G	AB	R	H	2B	3B	HR	RBI	BB	SO	SB	CS	OBP	SLG	B	T	HT	WT	DOB	1st Yr	Resides
Clark, Boodle	.242	46	153	25	37	11	1	5	32	23	35	1	1	.344	.425	R	R	6-0	195	12-28-83	2004	Bristol, Tenn.
Cumberbatch, Cirillo	.262	37	126	15	33	4	1	1	7	7	35	1	1	.304	.333	R	R	6-2	176	7-11-86	2004	Panama City, Panama
DeLeon, Evandy	.208	44	154	23	32	9	4	3	19	12	54	10	2	.262	.377	R	R	6-0	170	6-29-83	2003	Azua, D.R.
Denham, Jason	.144	38	104	13	15	0	1	0	4	21	40	5	5	.291	.163	L	L	6-0	170	5-1-86	2004	Antioch, Calif.
Garcia, Julio	.250	58	204	32	51	9	0	0	14	25	48	11	6	.341	.294	S	R	5-11	160	10-18-84	2002	Santo Domingo, D.R.
Hiser, P.J.	.322	49	177	28	57	9	4	10	35	14	53	7	5	.374	.588	R	R	6-0	195	8-18-81	2004	Hagerstown, Md.
Holmes, Justin	.233	30	103	10	24	4	1	0	6	5	18	5	2	.275	.294	R	R	5-11	185	11-28-81	2004	Athens, Ga.
Lofgren, Chuck	.231	6	13	2	3	0	0	0	0	4	2	0	0	.412	.231	L	L	6-3	190	1-29-86	2004	Burlingame, Calif.
Longworth, Chad	.292	50	178	19	52	12	0	0	22	12	45	7	5	.344	.360	R	R	6-3	190	6-11-83	2003	Wise, Va.
Ortega, Jose	.269	46	171	23	46	10	0	0	15	21	24	1	1	.352	.327	R	R	5-9	170	12-29-80	2004	Anaheim, Calif.
Ortiz, Rafael	.162	36	105	5	17	3	1	0	9	7	23	2	0	.226	.210	R	R	6-2	160	12-6-81	2002	Nizao de Bani, D.R.
Peterson, Derrick	.273	37	121	22	33	7	0	2	19	22	30	5	3	.386	.380	R	R	6-3	190	5-23-82	2004	Petersburg, Mich.
Roberts, Josh	.195	17	41	4	8	0	0	0	4	5	15	2	0	.286	.195	L	R	6-1	191	7-7-86	2004	Ipswich, Australia
Spilman, Ryan	.194	33	98	7	19	1	0	0	4	7	24	1	0	.257	.204	R	R	6-0	150	8-25-84	2004	Mount Vernon, Ind.
Valdes, Juan	.267	38	135	24	36	4	4	1	5	17	27	21	3	.357	.378	S	R	6-0	150	6-22-85	2003	Manati, P.R.
Vasquez, Domingo	.206	47	160	8	33	8	0	0	17	3	37	2	1	.224	.256	R	R	6-1	200	9-16-83	2001	Guarcara, Venez.
Woodson, Mike	.213	33	94	6	20	3	0	0	7	5	27	0	1	.257	.245	R	R	5-11	180	11-28-84	2003	Salinas, P.R.

GAMES BY POSITION: C—Holmes 1, Roberts 12, Spilman 33, Woodson 32. **1B**—Clark 20, Hiser 2, Ortega 4, Ortiz 4, Vasquez 41. **2B**—Clark 2, Garcia 56, Holmes 10, Ortega 1. **3B**—Clark 13, Holmes 3, Ortega 4, Ortiz 12, Peterson 37. **SS**—Garcia 1, Holmes 13, Ortega 37, Ortiz 18, Vasquez 1. **OF**—Cumberbatch 25, DeLeon 42, Denham 32, Hiser 41, Longworth 37, Valdes 34.

PITCHING	W	L	ERA	G	GS	CG	SV	IP	H	R	ER	BB	SO	AVG	B	T	HT	WT	DOB	1st Yr	Resides
Alwert, Garrett	4	4	6.06	14	9	0	0	52	74	36	35	7	51	.330	L	L	6-2	200	10-22-80	2004	Puyallup, Wash.
Amaya, Jose	2	2	4.82	12	3	0	0	47	48	26	25	20	40	.279	R	R	6-2	205	9-7-81	2004	San Jose, Calif.
Bunkleman, Cody	2	1	6.53	17	0	0	0	30	32	26	22	11	23	.283	R	R	6-3	200	1-1-00	2004	Chippewa Falls, Wis.
Collins, Kyle	3	0	2.12	4	3	0	0	17	12	4	4	3	17	.207	R	R	6-1	165	8-17-81	2004	San Jose, Calif.
Gabino, Armando	0	1	4.26	5	4	0	0	19	20	13	9	5	12	.260	R	R	6-3	200	8-31-83	2001	Santiago, D.R.
Guzman, Daniel	1	5	5.09	13	10	0	0	46	58	35	26	15	38	.307	R	R	6-1	180	2-5-82	2000	Caracas, Venez.
Harris, Josh	2	0	1.41	19	0	0	7	32	22	6	5	6	40	.193	R	R	6-0	205	11-23-80	2004	Belton, Texas
Kite, Josh	1	2	4.61	19	0	0	0	27	19	15	14	17	32	.198	L	L	6-2	190	3-2-82	2004	Greeneville, Tenn.
Lofgren, Chuck	0	0	6.04	9	9	0	0	22	25	16	15	13	23	.287	L	L	6-3	190	1-29-86	2004	Burlingame, Calif.
Lubrano, Paul	0	0	1.38	3	3	0	0	13	8	2	2	5	13	.182	L	L	6-1	170	12-19-81	2004	Winter Springs, Fla.
Mercedes, Gerson	5	5	5.03	13	13	0	0	59	57	33	33	16	62	.254	R	R	6-1	192	7-8-81	2001	Santo Domingo, D.R.
Rickert, Brandon	2	2	3.52	19	0	0	2	38	38	19	15	5	27	.259	R	R	6-3	205	1-23-83	2003	DeLand, Fla.
Roddy, Dustin	3	0	5.03	20	0	0	0	34	33	22	19	15	25	.252	R	R	6-2	195	11-10-82	2004	Searcy, Ark.
Santos, Reid	3	5	2.78	12	12	0	0	65	52	27	20	17	67	.220	L	L	6-1	170	8-24-82	2003	Kaneohe, Hawaii
Schau, Adrian	1	6	3.24	19	0	0	2	33	32	17	12	13	38	.258	R	R	6-2	200	1-8-82	2004	Novato, Calif.
Soto, Jesus	2	2	2.92	19	0	0	5	25	23	10	8	4	26	.240	L	L	5-11	170	8-26-80	2001	San Cristobal, D.R.

BY BARNEY HUTCHINSON

The Rockies played at full strength for only 25 games during the 2004 season.

No one could have predicted it before the season, but injuries to Larry Walker (strained left groin) and Preston Wilson (a balky left knee) limited manager Clint Hurdle to a scant 45-day period between June 22 and Aug. 5 where he had the lineup he envisioned in spring training.

After Walker missed the first 68 games of the season, he doubled in his debut June 22. With Walker and Wilson both in the starting lineup, the Rockies went 15-10.

A disastrous start forced the Rockies to experiment with a four-man rotation for a brief period, which wound up depleting their bullpen. After the starting rotation seemed to stabilize in the second half of the season, the bullpen ran out of gas.

The Rockies went through a 4-20 stretch that sunk their season from mid-May to mid-June. The return of Walker with Wilson to go with Todd Helton, Vinny Castilla and Jeromy Burnitz could not salvage the year.

So the Rockies went from a veteran team to a youth movement, trading away Walker to the eventual National League champion Cardinals on Aug. 6 and using a club-record 19 rookies during the season. In the process, they uncovered players such as outfielder Matt Holliday, second baseman Aaron Miles, shortstop Clint Barmes, utility player Luis Gonzalez and catcher J.D. Closser.

Unfortunately, the combination did not play well at Coors Field. The Rockies went 38-43 at home, their worst record in their 10-year history at Coors Field and only the second time they finished under .500 at the stadium. The 1999 team went 39-42.

Playing poorly at home led to a 68-94 finish, second-worst in club history. Only the inaugural expansion team's 65-97 record in 1993 was worse. It was the third time the Rockies finished with at least 90 losses.

Todd Helton   Jeff Francis

PLAYERS of the YEAR

MAJOR LEAGUE: Todd Helton, 1b

Despite the inflated numbers associated with playing home games at Denver's Coors Field, Helton does the same thing year in and year out: hit for both average and power. He put up huge numbers again in 2004, hitting .347-32-96 in 547 at-bats, and also walked 127 times.

MINOR LEAGUE: Jeff Francis, lhp

Francis was dominant from the start in 2004, earning Baseball America's Minor League Player of the Year award. He jumped from Double-A to Triple-A to the big leagues, winning 19 games in the process. The 23-year-old lefthander isn't overpowering but wins with exceptional command.

Hurdle and general manager Dan O'Dowd both agreed to two-year contract extensions prior to the start of the 2004 season, an indication ownership believes in patience and a payoff from the minor league system built by O'Dowd and scouting director Bill Schmidt.

Disappointments outweighed the highlights, however.

By midseason, fans grew restless with closer Shawn Chacon. He blew nine saves and finished 1-9, 7.11 despite a 35-save season. A final save-situation meltdown in Los Angeles on Sept. 28, in which he walked four consecutive batters trying to preserve a 4-0 lead, ended the experiment.

Helton had another standout season offensively to lead the highlights. Helton hit .347-32-96, finishing second in the league in average to the Giants' Barry Bonds. Burnitz finished eighth in home runs with 38. Fan favorite Vinny Castilla, returning to the club after a five-year absence, led the NL in RBIs with 131.

The Rockies got two decent starting pitching efforts from lefthanders Shawn Estes (15-8, 5.84) and Joe Kennedy (9-7, 3.66). Jason Jennings overcame a rough start to finish 11-12 in 33 starts, while Aaron Cook (6-4, 4.28) just began to find his way at the major league level when sidelined by blood clots in his lung in August.

The projected future gem on the mound, lefthander Jeff Francis, put together a sterling minor league season before his promotion to the major leagues.

Francis is the start of a wave of minor league jewels the Rockies are counting on for future improvement. Third baseman Ian Stewart, center fielder Jeff Salazar, relief pitcher Ryan Speier and first-round draft choice Chris Nelson are considered the organization's future.

ORGANIZATION LEADERS

BATTING

*AVG	Garrett Atkins, Colorado Springs	.366
R	Jeff Salazar, Tulsa/Visalia	118
H	Clint Barmes, Colorado Springs	175
TB	Ian Stewart, Asheville	300
2B	Garrett Atkins, Colorado Springs	43
3B	Jeff Salazar, Tulsa/Visalia	11
HR	Andy Tracy, Colorado Springs	33
RBI	Andy Tracy, Colorado Springs	120
BB	K.J. Hendricks, Visalia	85
SO	Shawn Garrett, Colorado Springs/Tulsa	132
SB	Christian Colonel, Asheville	35
*OBP	Garrett Atkins, Colorado Springs	.434
*SLG	Brad Hawpe, Colorado Springs	.652

PITCHING

W	Jeff Francis, Colorado Springs/Tulsa	16
L	Brian Tollberg, Colorado Springs	13
#ERA	Jeff Francis, Colorado Springs/Tulsa	2.21
G	Ryan Speier, Tulsa	61
CG	Alberto Arias, Asheville	4
SV	Ryan Speier, Tulsa	37
IP	Marc Kaiser, Asheville	181
BB	Justin Hampson, Tulsa	63
SO	Jeff Francis, Colorado Springs/Tulsa	196

*Minimum 250 at-bats #Minimum 75 Innings

COLORADO ROCKIES

Manager: Clint Hurdle.

2004 Record: 68-94, .420 (4th, NL West).

BATTING	AVG	G	AB	R	H	2B	3B	HR	RBI	BB	SO	SB	CS	OBP	SLG	B	T	HT	WT	DOB	1st Yr	Resides
Atkins, Garrett	.357	15	28	3	10	2	0	1	8	4	3	0	0	.424	.536	R	R	6-3	210	12-12-79	2000	Irvine, Calif.
Barmes, Clint	.282	20	71	14	20	3	1	2	10	3	10	0	1	.320	.437	R	R	6-0	175	3-6-79	2000	Vincennes, Ind.
Burnitz, Jeromy	.283	150	540	94	153	30	4	37	110	58	124	5	6	.356	.559	L	R	6-0	210	4-14-69	1990	Poway, Calif.
Castilla, Vinny	.271	148	583	93	158	43	3	35	131	51	113	0	0	.332	.535	R	R	6-1	200	7-4-67	1990	Littleton, Colo.
Clayton, Royce	.279	146	574	95	160	36	4	8	54	48	125	10	5	.338	.397	R	R	6-0	185	1-2-70	1988	Scottsdale, Ariz.
Closser, J.D.	.319	36	113	5	36	6	0	1	10	6	22	0	0	.364	.398	S	R	5-10	175	1-15-80	1998	Alexandria, Ind.
Freeman, Choo	.189	45	90	15	17	3	2	1	11	14	21	1	1	.298	.300	R	R	6-2	200	10-20-79	1998	Dallas, Texas
Gonzalez, Luis	.292	102	322	42	94	17	2	12	40	15	67	1	5	.328	.469	R	R	5-11	170	6-26-79	1997	El Tigre, Venez.
Greene, Todd	.282	75	195	23	55	14	0	10	35	13	38	0	0	.327	.508	R	R	5-10	210	5-8-71	1993	Alpharetta, Ga.
Hawpe, Brad	.248	42	105	12	26	3	2	3	9	11	34	1	1	.322	.400	L	L	6-3	200	6-22-79	2000	Fort Worth, Texas
Helton, Todd	.347	154	547	115	190	49	2	32	96	127	72	3	0	.469	.620	L	L	6-2	205	8-20-73	1995	Thornton, Colo.
Hocking, Denny	.202	55	94	7	19	2	0	0	4	7	20	0	1	.257	.223	S	R	5-10	180	4-2-70	1990	Tustin, Calif.
Holliday, Matt	.290	121	400	65	116	31	3	14	57	31	86	3	3	.349	.488	R	R	6-4	230	1-15-80	1998	Chico, Texas
Johnson, Charles	.236	109	305	42	72	20	0	13	47	49	91	2	1	.350	.430	R	R	6-3	250	7-20-71	1993	Plantation Acres, Fla.
Miles, Aaron	.293	134	522	75	153	15	3	6	47	29	53	12	7	.329	.368	S	R	5-8	170	12-15-76	1995	Antioch, Calif.
Pellow, Kit	.240	59	121	15	29	5	1	2	10	8	43	1	0	.308	.347	R	R	6-1	205	8-28-73	1996	Olathe, Kan.
Piedra, Jorge	.297	38	91	15	27	8	0	3	10	5	19	0	1	.340	.484	L	L	6-0	190	4-17-79	1998	Van Nuys, Calif.
Reyes, Rene	.148	28	61	5	9	2	0	0	1	5	17	0	0	.212	.180	S	R	5-11	215	2-21-78	1997	Margarita, Venez.
Sweeney, Mark	.266	122	177	25	47	12	2	9	40	32	51	1	0	.377	.508	L	L	6-1	215	10-26-69	1991	Scottsdale, Ariz.
Tracy, Andy	.188	15	16	1	3	1	0	0	1	1	8	0	0	.235	.250	L	R	6-3	220	12-11-73	1996	Columbus, Ohio
Walker, Larry	.324	38	108	22	35	9	3	6	20	25	23	2	0	.464	.630	L	R	6-3	235	12-1-66	1985	Maple Ridge, B.C.
Wilson, Preston	.248	58	202	24	50	11	0	6	29	17	49	2	1	.315	.391	R	R	6-2	215	7-19-74	1993	Miami, Fla.

PITCHING	W	L	ERA	G	GS	CG	SV	IP	H	R	ER	BB	SO	AVG	B	T	HT	WT	DOB	1st Yr	Resides
Bernero, Adam	1	1	5.57	16	2	0	0	32	36	20	20	17	21	.283	R	R	6-4	210	11-28-76	1999	Elk Grove, Calif.
Chacon, Shawn	1	9	7.11	66	0	0	35	63	71	52	50	52	52	.282	R	R	6-3	210	12-23-77	1996	Greeley, Colo.
Cook, Aaron	6	4	4.28	16	16	1	0	97	112	47	46	39	40	.294	R	R	6-3	170	2-8-79	1997	Hamilton, Ohio
Dohmann, Scott	0	3	4.11	41	0	0	0	46	41	22	21	19	49	.236	R	R	6-1	180	2-13-78	2000	Morgan City, La.
Driskill, Travis	0	0	6.48	5	0	0	0	8	13	6	6	3	6	.361	R	R	6-0	215	8-1-71	1993	Austin, Texas
Elarton, Scott	0	6	9.80	8	8	0	0	41	57	45	45	20	23	.328	R	R	6-8	240	2-23-76	1994	Denver, Colo.
Estes, Shawn	15	8	5.84	34	34	1	0	202	223	133	131	105	117	.291	R	L	6-2	200	2-18-73	1991	San Francisco, Calif.
Fassero, Jeff	3	8	5.51	40	12	0	0	111	136	73	68	44	59	.306	L	L	6-1	200	1-5-63	1984	Paradise Valley, Ariz.
Francis, Jeff	3	2	5.15	7	7	0	0	37	42	22	21	13	32	.286	L	L	6-5	200	1-8-81	2002	Sammamish, Wash.
Fuentes, Brian	2	4	5.64	47	0	0	0	45	46	30	28	19	48	.269	L	L	6-4	220	8-9-75	1996	Merced, Calif.
Gissell, Chris	0	1	14.54	5	1	0	0	9	20	14	14	3	11	.465	R	R	6-5	210	1-4-78	1996	Vancouver, Wash.
Harikkala, Tim	4	6	4.74	55	0	0	0	63	55	34	33	23	30	.235	R	R	6-2	180	7-15-71	1992	Lake Worth, Fla.
Jarvis, Kevin	0	0	27.00	2	0	0	0	2	6	6	6	4	0	.600	L	R	6-2	200	8-1-69	1991	Lexington, Ky.
Jennings, Jason	11	12	5.51	33	33	0	0	201	241	125	123	101	133	.299	L	R	6-2	245	7-17-78	1999	Rockwall, Texas
Kennedy, Joe	9	7	3.66	27	27	1	0	162	163	68	66	67	117	.265	R	L	6-4	230	5-24-79	1998	Indian Shores, Fla.
Kroon, Marc	0	0	6.00	6	0	0	0	7	4	4	10	3	.350	R	R	6-2	190	4-2-73	1991	Phoenix, Ariz.
Lopez, Javier	1	2	7.52	64	0	0	0	41	45	34	34	26	20	.287	L	L	6-4	200	7-11-77	1998	Fairfax, Va.
Nunez, Vladimir	3	3	7.01	22	0	0	0	26	26	22	20	14	22	.280	R	R	6-4	240	3-15-75	1996	Miami, Fla.
Reed, Steve	3	8	3.68	65	0	0	0	66	72	29	27	17	38	.281	R	R	6-2	210	3-11-65	1988	Golden, Colo.
Simpson, Allan	2	1	5.08	32	0	0	0	39	44	26	22	20	46	.289	R	R	6-4	180	8-26-77	1997	Las Vegas, Nev.
Stark, Denny	0	5	11.42	6	6	0	0	26	53	43	33	18	10	.427	R	R	6-2	210	10-27-74	1996	Edgerton, Ohio
Tsao, Chin-Hui	0	0	3.86	10	0	0	1	9	7	4	4	1	11	.200	R	R	6-2	175	6-2-81	2000	Hualien, Taiwan
Wendell, Turk	0	0	7.02	12	0	0	0	17	21	13	13	12	11	.328	L	R	6-2	200	5-19-67	1988	Castle Rock, Colo.
Wright, Jamey	2	3	4.12	14	14	0	0	79	82	39	36	45	41	.266	R	R	6-5	230	12-24-74	1993	Phoenix, Ariz.
Young, Jason	0	1	12.96	2	2	0	0	8	15	12	12	5	7	.385	R	R	6-5	215	9-28-79	2001	Bodega, Calif.

FIELDING

Catcher	PCT	G	PO	A	E	DP	PB
Closser	.986	32	195	17	3	4	6
Greene	.989	53	258	15	3	1	2
Johnson	.988	91	523	44	7	8	7
Pellow	1.000	4	11	0	0	0	0

First Base	PCT	G	PO	A	E	DP
Atkins	1.000	3	22	1	0	6
Helton	.997	153	1356	144	4	130
Pellow	.967	5	26	3	1	3
Sweeney	1.000	15	68	5	0	9

Second Base	PCT	G	PO	A	E	DP
Barmes	.979	9	19	27	1	5
Gonzalez	.994	40	84	96	1	27
Hocking	1.000	8	13	16	0	3

Miles	.984	128	273	353	10	70	

Third Base	PCT	G	PO	A	E	DP
Atkins	1.000	4	2	4	0	1
Castilla	.987	148	124	316	6	30
Gonzalez	.971	18	13	21	1	1
Hocking	1.000	2	1	0	0	0
Pellow	1.000	4	2	1	0	0
Tracy	1.000	1	0	1	0	0

Shortstop	PCT	G	PO	A	E	DP
Barmes	.981	9	17	36	1	7
Clayton	.986	144	213	417	9	88
Gonzalez	1.000	10	9	18	0	5
Hocking	.927	13	13	25	3	6

Outfield	PCT	G	PO	A	E	DP
Atkins	1.000	3	5	0	0	0
Burnitz	.974	143	255	10	7	1
Freeman	.986	41	69	1	1	0
Gonzalez	1.000	29	33	0	0	0
Hawpe	.982	34	54	1	1	1
Hocking	.975	30	39	0	1	0
Holliday	.963	115	177	4	7	1
Pellow	1.000	36	29	2	0	1
Piedra	1.000	34	49	1	0	1
Reyes	1.000	21	31	1	0	1
Sweeney	1.000	28	42	3	0	1
Walker	1.000	34	64	4	0	1
Wilson	.953	52	119	3	6	1

Director, Player Development: Bill Geivett.

Class	Farm Team	League	W	L	Pct.	Finish*	Manager	Affiliate Since
AAA	Colorado Springs (Colo.) Sky Sox	Pacific Coast	78	65	.545	6th (16)	Marv Foley	1993
AA	Tulsa (Okla.) Drillers	Texas	71	68	.511	**5th (8)**	Tom Runnells	2003
High A	#Visalia (Calif.) Oaks	California	56	84	.400	9th (10)	Stu Cole	2003
Low A	Asheville (N.C.) Tourists	South Atlantic	64	75	.460	13th (16)	Joe Mikulik	1994
SS A	Tri-City (Wash.) Dust Devils	Northwest	40	36	.526	5th (8)	Ron Gideon	2001
Rookie	Casper (Wyo.) Rockies	Pioneer	33	40	.452	7th (8)	P.J. Carey	2001

*Finish in overall standings (No. of teams in league)/playoff teams in **boldface**   #Affiliate will operate in Modesto (California) in 2005

COLORADO SPRINGS SKY SOX   Class AAA

PACIFIC COAST LEAGUE

BATTING	AVG	G	AB	R	H	2B	3B	HR	RBI	BB	SO	SB	CS	OBP	SLG	B	T	HT	WT	DOB	1st Yr	Resides
Almonte, Erick	.318	123	450	91	143	26	4	17	74	64	87	14	8	.402	.507	R	R	6-2	180	2-1-78	1996	Santo Domingo, D.R.
Atkins, Garrett	.366	122	445	88	163	43	3	15	94	57	45	0	0	.434	.578	R	R	6-3	210	12-12-79	2000	Irvine, Calif.
Barmes, Clint	.328	125	533	104	175	42	2	16	51	28	61	20	8	.376	.505	R	R	6-0	195	3-6-79	2000	Vincennes, Ind.
Bibee, Hal	.167	6	6	2	1	0	0	0	0	1	0	0	.167	.167	R	R	6-0	190	5-8-79	2002	Knoxville, Tenn.
Closser, J.D.	.299	83	298	53	89	19	1	7	54	41	47	0	2	.384	.440	S	R	5-10	175	1-15-80	1998	Alexandria, Ind.
Conway, Dan	.053	6	19	0	1	0	0	0	1	1	6	0	0	.143	.053	R	R	6-3	190	10-13-79	2000	Delmar, N.Y.
Donnels, Chris	.262	96	195	30	51	8	0	7	31	38	49	1	2	.386	.410	L	R	6-0	180	4-21-66	1987	Coto de Caza, Calif.
Freeman, Choo	.297	103	360	58	107	21	7	10	50	26	84	7	3	.350	.478	R	R	6-2	200	10-20-79	1998	Dallas, Texas
Garrett, Shawn	.371	30	116	25	43	12	0	3	23	9	28	5	2	.416	.552	S	R	6-3	210	11-2-78	1998	Kinmundy, Ill.
Greene, Todd	.333	4	12	2	4	1	0	1	4	1	3	0	0	.385	.667	R	R	5-10	210	5-8-71	1993	Alpharetta, Ga.
Hawpe, Brad	.322	92	345	62	111	19	1	31	86	36	91	3	2	.384	.652	L	L	6-3	200	6-22-79	2000	Fort Worth, Texas
Holliday, Matt	.364	6	22	8	8	5	0	2	4	5	6	2	0	.481	.864	R	R	6-4	230	1-15-80	1998	Chico, Texas
Matos, Pascual	.258	18	62	9	16	4	0	2	12	6	12	0	0	.333	.419	R	R	6-2	180	12-23-74	1992	Barahona, D.R.
Miles, Aaron	.333	12	54	8	18	3	0	0	8	2	4	2	2	.345	.389	S	R	5-8	170	12-15-76	1995	Antioch, Calif.
Morales, Willie	.261	22	46	6	12	3	0	1	8	2	13	0	0	.300	.391	R	R	5-9	200	9-7-72	1993	Tucson, Ariz.
Ortiz, Hector	.265	46	155	18	41	7	0	1	15	10	26	1	1	.315	.329	R	R	6-0	200	10-14-69	1988	Canovanas, P.R.
Pellow, Kit	.357	13	42	10	15	4	0	3	14	4	7	0	0	.417	.667	R	R	6-1	205	8-28-73	1996	Olathe, Kan.
Pena, Elvis	.271	96	269	39	73	16	3	2	30	35	45	4	2	.359	.375	S	R	5-11	160	8-15-74	1994	Santo Domingo, D.R.
Piedra, Jorge	.334	99	377	71	126	29	5	15	55	23	56	4	3	.372	.557	L	L	6-0	190	4-17-79	1998	Van Nuys, Calif.
Reyes, Rene	.307	87	313	44	96	23	1	6	47	18	60	10	5	.348	.444	S	R	5-11	215	2-21-78	1997	Margarita, Venez.
Sanders, Anthony	.316	24	79	11	25	5	0	4	12	8	26	3	0	.379	.532	R	R	6-2	200	3-2-74	1993	Tucson, Ariz.
Tracy, Andy	.315	126	464	98	146	42	3	33	120	58	115	4	2	.390	.631	L	R	6-3	220	12-11-73	1996	Columbus, Ohio

PITCHING	W	L	ERA	G	GS	CG	SV	IP	H	R	ER	BB	SO	AVG	B	T	HT	WT	DOB	1st Yr	Resides
Almonte, Hector	3	2	8.57	12	0	0	0	21	29	22	20	15	12	.333	R	R	6-2	190	10-17-75	1994	Santo Domingo, D.R.
2-team (29 Nashville)	4	3	8.02	41	2	0	0	64	79	60	57	43	48	.305							
Bernero, Adam	3	2	3.17	9	8	0	0	48	57	23	17	10	48	.294	R	R	6-4	210	11-28-76	1999	Elk Grove, Calif.
Billingsley, Brent	0	2	12.19	5	1	0	0	10	15	14	14	9	7	.357	L	L	6-2	200	4-19-75	1996	Chino Hills, Calif.
Bouknight, Kip	1	3	6.75	19	9	0	0	63	83	54	47	32	38	.325	R	R	6-0	190	11-16-78	2001	Gaston, S.C.
Bowles, Brian	2	0	3.91	13	0	0	0	23	28	14	10	12	17	.292	R	R	5-10	220	8-18-76	1995	Manhattan Beach, Calif.
Bumatay, Mike	2	4	6.28	37	0	0	0	53	60	38	37	44	45	.288	L	L	6-0	170	10-9-79	1998	Clovis, Calif.
Cook, Aaron	3	1	2.74	7	7	1	0	46	34	15	14	8	25	.206	R	R	6-3	170	2-8-79	1997	Hamilton, Ohio
Cosgrove, Mike	0	0	6.75	1	0	0	0	1	5	1	1	1	0	.625	R	R	6-1	195	2-14-76	1997	Downey, Calif.
Dohmann, Scott	1	0	1.64	18	0	0	2	22	22	5	4	7	31	.250	R	R	6-1	180	2-13-78	2000	Morgan City, La.
Driskill, Travis	5	5	5.40	28	13	0	2	112	141	70	67	24	81	.311	R	R	6-0	215	8-17-71	1993	Austin, Texas
Francis, Jeff	3	2	2.85	7	7	0	0	41	35	16	13	7	49	.230	L	L	6-5	200	1-8-81	2002	Sammamish, Wash.
Fuentes, Brian	0	0	0.00	5	5	0	0	5	1	0	0	3	6	.063	L	L	6-4	220	8-9-75	1996	Merced, Calif.
Gilfillan, Jason	6	3	5.37	50	0	0	1	69	67	49	41	45	65	.255	R	R	6-5	220	8-31-76	1997	Blacksburg, S.C.
Gissell, Chris	14	2	3.67	24	8	0	0	91	80	41	37	17	74	.233	R	R	6-5	210	1-4-78	1996	Vancouver, Wash.
Harikkala, Tim	0	0	4.50	4	0	0	3	4	5	2	2	2	5	.263	R	R	6-2	180	7-15-71	1992	Lake Worth, Fla.
Herrera, Alex	6	3	5.24	37	7	0	1	77	77	49	45	57	72	.261	L	L	5-11	190	11-5-76	1998	Maracaibo, Venez.
Jarvis, Kevin	0	4	5.79	6	6	1	0	37	44	34	24	10	25	.293	L	R	6-2	200	8-1-69	1991	Lexington, Ky.
Kennedy, Joe	1	1	7.11	3	2	0	0	13	17	11	10	2	12	.321	R	L	6-4	230	5-24-79	1998	Indian Shores, Fla.
Kroon, Marc	2	3	2.72	50	0	0	20	56	44	23	15	26	72	.232	R	R	6-2	190	4-2-73	1991	Phoenix, Ariz.
Lopez, Javier	0	1	4.00	8	0	0	0	9	10	4	4	2	9	.294	L	L	6-4	200	7-11-77	1998	Fairfax, Va.
Martinez, Luis	2	2	6.83	5	4	0	0	28	34	22	21	16	21	.298	L	L	6-6	200	1-20-80	1997	Boca Chica, D.R.
2-team (7 Memphis)	2	7	5.76	12	11	0	0	70	87	48	45	39	56	.310							
Nunez, Vladimir	2	5	5.68	23	8	0	3	63	76	44	40	22	60	.299	R	R	6-4	240	3-15-75	1996	Miami, Fla.
Simpson, Allan	2	1	2.80	27	0	0	4	35	30	14	11	10	43	.236	R	R	6-4	180	8-26-77	1997	Las Vegas, Nev.
Stark, Denny	8	2	3.50	14	13	0	0	80	73	36	31	26	51	.244	R	R	6-2	210	10-27-74	1996	Edgerton, Ohio
Tollberg, Brian	6	13	6.80	28	26	0	0	150	198	122	113	27	99	.318	R	R	6-3	195	9-16-72	1994	Bradenton, Fla.
Tsao, Chin-Hui	1	1	8.53	4	4	0	0	13	22	12	12	5	14	.379	R	R	6-2	175	6-2-81	2000	Hualien, Taiwan
Wendell, Turk	0	1	5.79	12	8	0	0	14	19	10	9	4	8	.328	L	R	6-2	200	5-19-67	1988	Castle Rock, Colo.
Young, Jason	5	2	4.73	7	7	0	0	40	54	26	21	12	20	.340	R	R	6-5	215	9-28-79	2001	Bodega, Calif.

FIELDING

Catcher	PCT	G	PO	A	E	DP	PB
Closser	.983	76	544	44	10	3	6
Conway	1.000	4	46	3	0	0	2
Donnels	1.000	1	3	1	0	0	1
Greene	1.000	3	14	2	0	0	0
Matos	.983	16	113	4	2	1	2
Morales	1.000	2	10	2	0	0	1
Ortiz	.997	42	275	22	1	0	2

First Base	PCT	G	PO	A	E	DP
Atkins	1.000	7	58	2	0	7
Donnels	1.000	36	280	10	0	31
Greene	1.000	1	1	0	0	1
Morales	1.000	5	41	1	0	3
Pellow	1.000	2	19	4	0	0
Tracy	.993	100	788	56	6	80
Pellow	.947	3	17	1	1	0	1

Second Base	PCT	G	PO	A	E	DP
Almonte	.976	72	131	200	8	43
Barmes	.963	5	10	16	1	4
Miles	.968	12	35	25	2	11
Pena	.989	61	120	150	3	34

Third Base	PCT	G	PO	A	E	DP
Almonte	.951	23	17	60	4	9
Atkins	.917	105	46	187	21	19

Pellow	.333	2	0	1	2	0
Tracy	.872	14	7	34	6	2

Shortstop	PCT	G	PO	A	E	DP
Almonte	.973	24	40	67	3	17
Barmes	.964	118	164	342	19	60
Pena	.933	2	5	9	1	4

Outfield	PCT	G	PO	A	E	DP
Donnels	1.000	7	8	1	0	0
Freeman	.983	102	223	7	4	2
Garrett	.978	30	44	1	1	0
Hawpe	.984	86	172	7	3	3
Holliday	1.000	6	9	0	0	0
Matos	1.000	2	2	0	0	0

Pellow	1.000	4	8	0	0	0
Pena	.933	14	13	1	1	1
Piedra	.978	93	168	7	4	0
Reyes	.957	74	128	7	6	0
Sanders	.969	25	31	0	1	0
Tracy	1.000	3	5	1	0	1

TULSA DRILLERS — Class AA

TEXAS LEAGUE

BATTING

BATTING	AVG	G	AB	R	H	2B	3B	HR	RBI	BB	SO	SB	CS	OBP	SLG	B	T	HT	WT	DOB	1st Yr	Resides
Baker, Jeff	.297	24	91	10	27	5	1	4	20	7	22	1	0	.343	.505	R	R	6-2	210	6-21-81	2003	Woodbridge, Va.
Barker, Sean	.229	22	83	9	19	3	0	2	12	7	24	2	0	.289	.337	R	R	6-3	220	5-26-80	2002	Bakersfield, Calif.
Bibee, Hal	.250	2	4	1	1	0	0	0	0	0	2	0	0	.250	.250	R	R	6-0	190	5-8-79	2002	Knoxville, Tenn.
Conway, Dan	.260	78	242	24	63	14	0	4	24	24	70	3	2	.344	.368	R	R	6-3	190	10-13-79	2000	Delmar, N.Y.
Garrett, Shawn	.307	103	374	73	115	16	3	12	51	41	104	14	10	.382	.463	S	R	6-3	210	11-2-78	1998	Kinmundy, Ill.
Harrison, Adonis	.226	106	318	39	72	14	1	5	28	38	58	9	6	.308	.324	L	R	5-9	160	9-28-76	1995	Pasadena, Calif.
Miller, Tony	.273	112	414	61	113	17	2	11	36	68	99	20	12	.385	.403	R	R	5-9	180	3-18-80	2001	Lorain, Ohio
Morales, Willie	.229	11	35	2	8	0	0	1	4	2	9	0	0	.270	.314	R	R	5-9	200	9-7-72	1993	Tucson, Ariz.
Nix, Jayson	.213	123	456	58	97	17	1	14	58	40	101	14	3	.292	.346	R	R	5-11	160	8-26-82	2001	Midland, Texas
Phillips, Dan	.233	10	30	2	7	2	0	0	2	0	9	0	0	.258	.300	R	R	6-3	188	8-23-78	1999	Northridge, Calif.
Piniella, Juan	.229	113	371	51	85	17	2	9	45	29	90	15	6	.289	.358	R	R	5-10	183	3-13-78	1996	Woodbridge, Va.
Rosamond, Mike	.246	60	179	23	44	10	1	5	30	12	53	3	4	.306	.397	R	R	6-5	230	4-18-78	1999	Madison, Miss.
Salazar, Jeff	.223	58	224	39	50	13	2	1	17	35	31	10	3	.331	.313	L	L	6-0	180	11-24-80	2002	Port Bolivar, Texas
Sandoval, Danny	.319	133	530	73	169	37	4	8	66	37	64	22	10	.365	.442	S	R	5-11	180	4-7-79	1997	Lara, Venez.
Senjem, Guye	.223	40	103	13	23	7	0	1	11	12	29	0	1	.305	.320	L	R	6-0	210	5-2-75	1997	Kenyon, Minn.
Shealy, Ryan	.318	132	469	88	149	32	3	29	99	61	123	1	1	.411	.584	R	R	6-5	240	8-29-79	2002	Fort Lauderdale, Fla.
Slavik, Corey	.228	113	364	32	83	16	5	3	47	21	79	4	2	.282	.324	L	R	6-0	190	3-24-80	2001	St. Petersburg, Fla.
Walker, Larry	.222	5	9	3	2	0	0	0	1	2	1	0	0	.462	.556	L	R	6-3	235	12-1-66	1985	Evergreen, Colo.
Wilson, Preston	.412	6	17	4	7	1	0	1	2	3	4	1	1	.524	.647	R	R	6-2	215	7-19-74	1993	Miami, Fla.
Winchester, Jeff	.222	79	243	19	54	13	1	5	29	11	52	0	2	.264	.346	R	R	6-0	211	1-21-80	1998	Metairie, La.

PITCHING

PITCHING	W	L	ERA	G	GS	CG	SV	IP	H	R	ER	BB	SO	AVG	B	T	HT	WT	DOB	1st Yr	Resides
Anderson, Travis	0	1	7.25	11	2	0	0	22	25	23	18	15	14	.272	R	R	6-4	240	3-18-78	1999	Bellevue, Wash.
Bausher, Tim	4	8	4.15	16	13	1	0	82	84	39	38	22	85	.264	R	R	6-4	200	4-23-79	2001	Bechtelsville, Pa.
Bernero, Adam	1	0	0.00	1	1	0	0	6	2	0	0	1	3	.105	R	R	6-4	210	11-28-76	1999	Elk Grove, Calif.
Bouknight, Kip	1	2	5.55	6	6	0	0	36	50	29	22	11	19	.340	R	R	6-0	190	11-16-78	2001	Gaston, S.C.
Bumatay, Mike	1	0	3.18	12	0	0	0	11	10	4	4	9	12	.250	L	L	6-0	170	10-9-79	1998	Clovis, Calif.
Cosgrove, Mike	1	4	4.71	21	0	0	1	29	37	18	15	7	15	.316	R	R	6-1	195	2-14-76	1997	Downey, Calif.
Esposito, Mike	10	6	3.33	24	24	1	0	143	138	57	53	35	90	.256	R	R	6-0	190	9-27-81	2003	Las Vegas, Nev.
Francis, Jeff	13	1	1.98	17	17	1	0	114	73	26	25	22	147	.180	L	L	6-5	200	1-8-81	2002	Sammamish, Wash.
Green, Sean	4	3	3.03	52	0	0	2	77	63	32	26	29	50	.223	R	R	6-3	230	4-20-79	2000	Louisville, Ky.
Hampson, Justin	10	9	3.49	27	27	1	0	170	176	82	66	63	104	.270	L	L	6-1	180	5-24-80	2000	Worden, Ill.
Kent, Steve	3	1	2.03	39	0	0	1	31	27	7	7	11	23	.248	L	L	5-11	170	10-3-78	1999	Killeen, Texas
McClellan, Zach	4	7	4.15	26	23	1	1	139	145	69	64	36	111	.269	R	R	6-5	210	11-25-78	2000	Toledo, Ohio
Narveson, Chris	0	3	3.15	4	4	0	0	20	16	14	7	13	14	.222	L	L	6-3	180	12-20-81	2000	Arden, N.C.
Parker, Zack	4	8	5.84	22	17	0	0	91	108	67	59	33	45	.296	R	L	6-2	205	8-19-81	2001	Austin, Texas
Ramirez, Emmanuel	3	5	3.58	48	0	0	6	65	46	29	26	42	68	.204	R	R	5-9	180	11-2-79	1999	Santo Domingo, D.R.
Serrano, Alex	3	4	3.38	14	0	0	0	24	22	9	9	4	27	.244	R	R	6-1	200	2-18-81	1998	Barcelona, Venez.
Simpson, Gerrit	5	4	4.42	39	3	0	0	73	75	50	36	27	51	.262	R	R	6-3	200	12-19-79	2001	Austin, Texas
Speier, Ryan	3	1	2.04	61	0	0	37	62	33	14	14	25	70	.153	R	R	6-7	200	7-24-79	2001	Springfield, Va.
Tsao, Chin-Hui	1	1	2.77	2	2	0	0	13	12	4	4	2	10	.261	R	R	6-2	175	6-2-81	2000	Hualien, Taiwan

FIELDING

Catcher	PCT	G	PO	A	E	DP	PB
Bibee	1.000	2	5	1	0	0	0
Conway	.982	71	437	47	9	5	4
Morales	.941	4	13	3	1	0	0
Slavik	1.000	2	2	0	0	0	0
Winchester	.985	73	504	35	8	2	11

First Base	PCT	G	PO	A	E	DP
Conway	1.000	1	1	0	0	1
Morales	1.000	1	7	1	0	0
Senjem	1.000	6	49	3	0	3
Shealy	.997	127	1141	68	4	120

Slavik	.986	8	65	7	1	6

Second Base	PCT	G	PO	A	E	DP
Harrison	.946	21	54	69	7	21
Nix	.971	119	253	392	19	85

Third Base	PCT	G	PO	A	E	DP
Baker	.924	20	10	51	5	6
Harrison	.918	30	18	60	7	8
Slavik	.945	93	64	177	14	17

Shortstop	PCT	G	PO	A	E	DP
Harrison	.970	7	10	22	1	5
Sandoval	.952	132	182	392	29	90

Outfield	PCT	G	PO	A	E	DP
Barker	1.000	21	39	3	0	1
Garrett	.984	79	122	5	2	1
Miller	.981	112	203	8	4	2
Phillips	1.000	7	14	0	0	0
Piniella	.994	99	167	5	1	1
Rosamond	.970	48	61	3	2	0
Salazar	.977	59	122	5	3	0
Senjem	1.000	3	3	0	0	0
Walker	1.000	5	5	0	0	0
Wilson	1.000	4	4	0	0	0

VISALIA OAKS — High Class A

CALIFORNIA LEAGUE

BATTING

BATTING	AVG	G	AB	R	H	2B	3B	HR	RBI	BB	SO	SB	CS	OBP	SLG	B	T	HT	WT	DOB	1st Yr	Resides
Baker, Jeff	.330	72	267	60	88	23	1	11	64	47	70	1	0	.439	.547	R	R	6-2	210	6-21-81	2003	Woodbridge, Va.
Balet, Pichi	.217	22	83	8	18	1	0	1	5	6	17	0	0	.309	.265	R	R	6-0	210	11-17-77	2001	West Palm Beach, Fla.
2-team (61 Inl. Empire)	.274	83	307	37	84	13	1	4	32	16	36	2	2	.337	.332							
Barker, Sean	.308	105	412	75	127	29	5	20	97	40	89	11	3	.373	.549	R	R	6-3	220	5-26-80	2002	Bakersfield, Calif.
Barre, Brian	.275	76	298	41	82	16	5	8	50	32	64	3	4	.343	.443	L	L	5-9	180	5-26-80	2002	Garden Grove, Calif.
Bernier, Doug	.273	102	348	56	95	13	1	3	24	45	93	5	4	.359	.342	R	R	5-11	170	6-24-80	2002	Santa Maria, Calif.
Colina, Alvin	.251	95	334	43	84	23	0	11	47	24	81	0	1	.312	.419	R	R	6-3	209	12-26-81	1999	Puerto Cabello, Venez.
Fallon, Chris	.254	115	398	68	101	22	1	16	81	67	89	0	1	.358	.435	L	R	6-2	180	3-9-79	2001	Bayonne, N.J.
Frome, Jason	.195	13	41	8	8	1	1	1	2	2	12	0	0	.233	.341	L	L	6-0	190	7-3-79	2001	Appleton, Wis.
Gonzalez, Bernie	.260	101	385	39	100	21	1	4	39	22	92	5	4	.303	.351	R	R	6-2	200	5-10-80	2002	Miami, Fla.

BATTING	AVG	G	AB	R	H	2B	3B	HR	RBI	BB	SO	SB	CS	OBP	SLG	B	T	HT	WT	DOB	1st Yr	Resides
Hendricks, K.J.	.286	126	475	100	136	20	5	3	54	85	74	34	9	.400	.368	S	R	5-7	160	2-20-81	2002	Killeen, Texas
Madera, Sandy	.303	28	99	10	30	9	0	1	20	9	16	1	2	.375	.424	R	R	6-2	210	8-11-80	1998	Santo Domingo, D.R.
Peck, Bryan	.240	105	408	48	98	24	0	6	52	40	77	1	2	.318	.343	R	R	5-11	190	8-9-77	2000	Athens, Texas
Phillips, Dan	.170	14	53	4	9	1	0	1	5	0	19	0	1	.185	.245	R	R	6-3	188	8-23-78	1999	Northridge, Calif.
Reinking, Kevin	.171	31	105	14	18	2	1	3	8	7	41	0	0	.248	.295	R	R	6-1	190	1-25-79	2001	Long Beach, N.Y.
Robledo, Nelson	.000	5	13	2	0	0	0	0	0	1	5	0	0	.071	.000	R	R	6-1	180	6-13-84	2002	Panama City, Panama
Salazar, Jeff	.347	75	314	79	109	18	9	13	44	38	33	17	2	.419	.586	L	L	6-0	180	11-24-80	2002	Port Bolivar, Texas
Sardinha, Duke	.033	11	30	1	1	1	0	0	1	4	12	0	1	.147	.067	R	R	6-0	200	11-4-80	2002	Kailua, Hawaii
Spilborghs, Ryan	.259	125	444	59	115	26	3	8	57	64	98	8	6	.357	.385	R	R	6-1	190	9-5-79	2002	Santa Barbara, Calif.
Street, Dan	.200	10	35	6	7	4	1	0	2	2	10	0	0	.263	.371	R	R	6-2	200	10-27-80	2002	Purcellville, Va.
Tena, Hector	.243	104	362	37	88	19	4	5	38	22	79	3	2	.305	.359	R	R	6-0	175	6-20-82	1999	San Cristobal, D.R.

PITCHING	W	L	ERA	G	GS	CG	SV	IP	H	R	ER	BB	SO	AVG	B	T	HT	WT	DOB	1st Yr	Resides
Arakawa, Yusuke	3	3	3.03	29	0	0	0	39	40	16	13	13	37	.270	R	R	6-0	160	3-26-78	2003	Saitama, Japan
Asahina, Jon	4	9	5.40	34	22	0	0	135	165	94	81	46	71	.302	S	R	5-11	185	12-31-80	2001	Fresno, Calif.
Beckstead, Jentry	3	6	4.18	40	0	0	9	56	65	33	26	16	55	.288	R	R	5-11	165	6-9-80	2001	Sandy, Utah
Cable, Taft	5	7	5.30	39	7	0	1	107	117	69	63	48	93	.275	R	R	6-2	220	7-25-80	2001	Browns Summit, N.C.
Cartier, Rich	6	10	6.52	32	19	0	0	106	129	91	77	54	55	.298	R	R	6-1	180	10-9-79	2002	Simi Valley, Calif.
Castleman, Steve	0	0	3.21	9	0	0	0	14	16	6	5	3	10	.286	R	R	6-4	195	11-6-79	2003	Biloxi, Miss.
Clarke, Darren	1	3	7.39	8	7	0	0	35	54	35	29	16	27	.335	R	R	6-8	230	3-18-81	2001	Tampa, Fla.
Cosgrove, Mike	3	2	1.96	33	0	0	16	37	30	10	8	12	31	.216	R	R	6-3	200	12-19-79	2002	Topsfield, Mass.
DiAngelo, Jason	0	0	3.86	4	0	0	0	7	7	3	3	0	6	.250	R	R	6-1	200	9-9-80	2003	McMurray, Penn.
Gallagher, Buddy	4	4	8.37	15	15	0	0	67	106	66	62	36	33	.358	L	L	5-11	175	1-3-79	2001	Billings, Mont.
Jimenez, Ubaldo	4	1	2.23	9	9	1	0	44	29	15	11	12	61	.186	R	R	6-2	165	1-22-84	2001	San Cristobal, D.R.
Johnson, Doug	4	11	8.29	35	14	0	0	97	133	94	89	46	60	.343	R	R	6-1	180	12-1-80	2002	Pelham, N.H.
Lynch, Brian	0	5	6.41	26	4	0	0	53	83	45	38	32	37	.362	R	R	6-2	195	9-21-80	2003	Connersville, Ind.
Mendoza, Marcos	0	0	3.47	31	0	0	0	36	35	19	14	18	33	.248	L	L	5-10	180	10-31-80	2001	El Cajon, Calif.
Morel, Eudy	2	2	4.46	29	0	0	1	36	33	18	18	15	37	.241	R	R	5-10	160	8-31-79	2000	Monte Cristi, D.R.
Pavlik, Isaac	1	1	8.61	23	0	0	0	23	35	26	22	12	19	.330	R	L	5-8	170	5-19-80	2002	Rutherford, N.J.
Perez, Elvis	2	3	4.92	13	9	0	0	53	59	36	29	18	40	.284	R	R	6-4	228	7-4-79	1996	Orlando, Fla.
Silva, Doug	0	0	6.75	2	0	0	0	4	6	3	3	1	4	.400	R	R	6-0	190	2-7-81	2003	Roseville, Calif.
Ulloa, Enmanuel	2	3	5.09	6	6	0	0	35	45	20	20	9	36	.319	R	R	6-2	185	11-26-78	1998	New York, N.Y.
Young, Chris	8	3	3.60	52	0	0	2	85	95	38	34	15	77	.287	R	R	6-4	205	4-19-81	2002	Stow, Ohio

FIELDING

Catcher	PCT	G	PO	A	E	DP	PB
Colina	.987	93	595	73	9	5	13
Madera	.977	19	117	10	3	1	4
Peck	.000	1	0	0	0	0	0
Reinking	.982	30	199	14	4	2	5
Robledo	1.000	5	28	1	0	0	1

First Base	PCT	G	PO	A	E	DP
Balet	.929	3	11	2	1	0
Fallon	.991	75	624	69	6	53
Madera	.983	7	58	1	1	5
Peck	.987	57	489	33	7	44

Second Base	PCT	G	PO	A	E	DP
Bernier	.953	8	20	21	2	4
Hendricks	.975	120	207	307	13	57
Sardinha	1.000	4	7	12	0	4
Tena	1.000	12	19	27	0	6

Third Base	PCT	G	PO	A	E	DP
Baker	.900	68	67	114	20	14
Balet	.900	20	18	36	6	4
Bernier	.944	38	20	65	5	1
Peck	.800	5	4	8	3	1
Sardinha	.833	6	7	8	3	2
Street	.833	9	7	8	3	0

	PCT	G	PO	A	E	DP
Tena	.500	1	0	1	1	0

Shortstop	PCT	G	PO	A	E	DP
Bernier	.975	58	84	186	7	29
Tena	.941	92	148	254	25	50

Outfield	PCT	G	PO	A	E	DP
Barker	.976	90	191	10	5	3
Barre	.963	58	97	6	4	2
Frome	1.000	8	12	0	0	0
Gonzalez	.938	85	123	14	9	3
Phillips	.964	12	25	2	1	1
Salazar	.995	72	187	9	1	2
Spilborghs	.981	102	246	11	5	2

ASHEVILLE TOURISTS

Low Class A

SOUTH ATLANTIC LEAGUE

BATTING	AVG	G	AB	R	H	2B	3B	HR	RBI	BB	SO	SB	CS	OBP	SLG	B	T	HT	WT	DOB	1st Yr	Resides
Barre, Brian	.232	30	112	23	26	3	1	6	16	18	24	4	1	.341	.438	L	L	5-9	180	5-26-80	2002	Garden Grove, Calif.
Bibee, Hal	.243	21	70	12	17	5	0	1	9	10	21	0	0	.346	.357	R	R	6-0	190	5-8-79	2002	Knoxville, Tenn.
Blood, Randy	.286	113	426	54	122	22	1	10	63	48	92	1	4	.359	.413	L	R	5-10	180	1-7-81	2003	Costa Mesa, Calif.
Colonel, Christian	.249	119	429	62	107	23	0	9	65	49	73	35	8	.343	.366	R	R	6-2	210	12-25-81	2003	Pocatello, Idaho
Czarniecki, Jordan	.315	105	381	72	120	25	3	16	58	48	69	30	6	.400	.522	R	R	6-1	175	10-4-80	2003	Anderson, Ind.
Ferrer, Simon	.232	61	198	22	46	9	0	11	33	18	56	5	3	.295	.444	R	R	5-10	175	6-24-80	2002	Santa Ynez, Calif.
Fuller, Casey	.215	33	135	19	29	4	0	6	12	5	40	1	2	.241	.378	L	L	6-6	215	2-9-79	2002	Marysville, Calif.
Gaetti, Joe	.257	111	370	62	95	24	1	16	55	55	107	16	6	.370	.457	R	R	5-11	205	10-16-81	2003	Raleigh, N.C.
George, Trey	.235	95	336	48	79	13	3	14	57	38	98	1	5	.321	.417	R	R	6-2	200	1-26-83	2002	Houston, Texas
Guance, Luis	.263	104	395	71	104	37	2	14	53	40	98	20	3	.335	.473	R	R	5-9	160	3-6-82	2000	Sabana Grande, D.R.
Herrera, Jonathan	.279	95	380	71	106	20	2	6	35	26	80	21	12	.335	.389	S	R	5-9	160	11-3-84	2002	Maracaibo, Zulia, Venez.
Iannetta, Chris	.314	36	121	23	38	5	1	5	17	27	29	0	1	.454	.496	R	R	5-11	195	4-8-83	2004	Providence, R.I.
Montague, Eddie	.259	83	309	50	80	15	0	10	44	27	60	9	2	.322	.405	L	R	6-0	195	3-23-80	2002	San Mateo, Calif.
Stewart, Ian	.319	131	505	92	161	31	9	30	101	66	112	19	9	.398	.594	L	R	6-3	205	4-5-85	2003	Garden Grove, Calif.
Street, Dan	.123	18	57	7	7	2	0	2	8	3	17	0	0	.194	.263	R	R	6-2	200	10-27-80	2002	Purcellville, Va.
Sweeney, James	.138	9	29	4	4	1	0	0	3	5	9	2	0	.306	.172	R	R	6-1	197	6-13-83	2001	Austin, Texas
Vasquez, Jose	.117	18	60	5	7	2	0	2	5	6	27	0	0	.197	.250	L	L	6-3	220	12-28-82	2000	Sarasota, Fla.
Wilson, Neil	.240	96	334	41	80	27	1	7	48	32	70	1	0	.312	.389	R	R	6-1	190	12-7-83	2002	Vero Beach, Fla.

PITCHING	W	L	ERA	G	GS	CG	SV	IP	H	R	ER	BB	SO	AVG	B	T	HT	WT	DOB	1st Yr	Resides
Arias, Alberto	8	9	5.00	26	24	4	1	135	153	86	75	36	83	.289	R	R	5-11	150	10-14-83	2001	Santo Domingo, D.R.
Burch, Jason	0	2	5.59	8	0	0	1	10	15	7	6	3	14	.349	R	R	6-5	215	10-15-82	2003	Papillion, Neb.
Castleman, Steve	1	1	6.85	18	0	0	0	24	29	18	18	2	19	.299	R	R	6-4	195	11-6-79	2003	Biloxi, Miss.
Corpas, Manuel	2	2	3.05	43	0	0	3	44	48	20	15	13	52	.277	R	R	6-3	170	12-3-82	2000	Panama City, Panama
DiAngelo, Jason	1	7	3.78	41	2	0	8	48	49	24	20	20	52	.261	R	R	6-1	200	9-9-80	2003	McMurray, Penn.
Gagne, J.P.	0	3	14.21	10	0	0	0	13	29	21	20	4	9	.453	R	R	6-1	195	10-27-80	2003	Bloomington, Minn.
Ion, Mark	4	2	4.65	34	0	0	8	41	41	26	21	21	32	.265	R	R	6-2	220	1-8-81	2003	Plantation, Fla.
Kaiser, Marc	11	11	4.33	27	27	3	0	181	197	106	87	37	105	.275	R	R	6-2	205	5-7-82	2003	Reno, Nev.
Lo, Ching-Lung	4	3	5.05	17	9	0	1	62	70	49	35	30	49	.288	R	R	6-6	190	8-20-85	2002	Tainan, Taiwan
Lynch, Brian	1	0	3.86	10	3	0	0	26	30	13	11	10	8	.291	R	R	6-2	195	9-21-80	2003	Connersville, Ind.

PITCHING	W	L	ERA	G	GS	CG	SV	IP	H	R	ER	BB	SO	AVG	B	T	HT	WT	DOB	1st Yr	Resides
Marsden, Aaron	11	8	4.58	27	24	1	0	165	176	95	84	43	107	.273	L	L	6-5	225	11-18-81	2003	Grand Forks, N.D.
Merrell, Darric	8	12	5.41	28	28	2	0	151	179	105	91	53	87	.294	R	R	6-4	210	1-22-82	2003	Temecula, Calif.
Morel, Eudy	1	0	1.88	11	0	0	0	14	12	3	3	1	18	.240	R	R	5-10	160	8-31-79	2000	Monte Cristi, D.R.
Robles, Larry	7	3	3.54	23	19	0	3	122	120	58	48	31	85	.261	R	R	6-2	200	10-29-80	2003	San Pedro, Calif.
Rosario, Melvin	1	1	6.89	14	0	0	0	16	16	13	12	5	11	.254	L	L	6-1	172	9-22-78	1998	Carolina, P.R.
Silva, Doug	2	2	4.98	29	0	0	0	43	45	25	24	12	35	.263	R	R	6-0	190	2-7-81	2003	Roseville, Calif.
Songster, Judd	0	0	2.25	2	0	0	0	4	1	1	1	1	5	.077	R	R	6-3	195	12-26-79	2001	North Platte, Neb.
Thomas, Steve	1	0	6.75	15	0	0	1	19	28	17	14	7	15	.333	R	R	6-2	185	8-19-69	1990	Huntsville, Ala.
Tsao, Chin-Hui	1	0	1.80	2	2	0	0	10	8	2	2	1	14	.211	R	R	6-2	175	6-2-81	2000	Hualien, Taiwan
Vazquez, Willie	0	2	5.59	10	0	0	0	19	19	13	12	12	15	.264	R	R	6-0	140	12-26-79	2000	Guayama, P.R.
Watchko, Jeff	1	6	6.23	35	0	0	1	48	56	38	33	22	49	.293	R	R	6-3	195	11-7-80	2003	Canton, Ga.

FIELDING

Catcher	PCT	G	PO	A	E	DP	PB
Bibee	1.000	20	127	9	0	0	6
Iannetta	.988	32	221	21	3	0	4
Sweeney	.971	7	29	5	1	0	0
Wilson	.994	81	505	36	3	1	16

Second Base	PCT	G	PO	A	E	DP
Blood	.956	84	162	254	19	56
Ferrer	.980	9	17	32	1	7
Guance	.979	49	104	131	5	33
Montague	.889	3	2	6	1	1

Shortstop	PCT	G	PO	A	E	DP
Ferrer	.933	12	22	34	4	8
Guance	.944	38	58	129	11	25
Herrera	.947	94	102	325	24	50

First Base	PCT	G	PO	A	E	DP
Colonel	.994	108	1065	34	7	87
Ferrer	.991	21	200	11	2	26
Montague	.973	5	35	1	1	3
Street	1.000	7	66	2	0	11

Third Base	PCT	G	PO	A	E	DP
Colonel	.867	5	3	10	2	1
Ferrer	.935	13	7	36	3	5
Guance	.889	9	3	21	3	1
Stewart	.941	116	89	308	25	27

Outfield	PCT	G	PO	A	E	DP
Barre	.957	29	44	1	2	0
Czarniecki	.992	105	231	5	2	1
Fuller	.967	19	26	3	1	0
Gaetti	.968	109	176	6	6	1
George	.970	86	120	8	4	0
Montague	.985	75	124	7	2	1
Street	1.000	4	1	0	0	0

NORTHWEST LEAGUE

BATTING	AVG	G	AB	R	H	2B	3B	HR	RBI	BB	SO	SB	CS	OBP	SLG	B	T	HT	WT	DOB	1st Yr	Resides
Almonte, Sandy	.261	6	23	4	6	1	1	0	0	1	1	1	1	.292	.391	S	R	5-11	150	11-16-82	2000	Puerto Plata, D.R.
Dean, Erik	.313	59	217	43	68	12	1	4	26	32	36	4	1	.410	.433	L	R	6-0	195	2-7-82	2002	Santa Clara, Calif.
Gentry, Garret	.421	15	57	11	24	5	1	3	14	6	6	1	1	.469	.702	L	R	5-10	210	6-27-81	1999	Victorville, Calif.
Ghutzman, Stephen	.283	41	145	29	41	9	1	2	20	21	30	0	2	.372	.400	S	R	6-0	210	12-2-80	2003	Spring, Texas
Guarno, Rick	.229	28	105	11	24	1	0	0	6	5	20	0	0	.311	.238	R	R	6-0	202	8-16-82	2003	Rochester, N.Y.
Hahn, Dustin	.250	4	16	3	4	0	0	0		3	4	0	0	.368	.250	R	R	6-1	195	10-21-82	2004	Elk Grove, Calif.
Koshansky, Joe	.234	66	239	41	56	18	0	12	43	31	84	1	0	.330	.460	L	L	6-4	225	5-26-82	2004	Fairfax, Va.
Macri, Matt	.333	52	195	33	65	17	4	7	43	23	52	4	5	.410	.569	R	R	6-2	200	5-29-82	2004	Clive, Iowa
Miller, Matt	.269	43	167	17	45	8	0	8	25	13	18	0	0	.337	.461	R	R	6-2	210	12-26-79	2003	La Grange, Texas
Nunez, Florentino	.257	48	187	22	48	9	0	4	25	16	37	0	2	.321	.369	S	R	6-0	165	3-23-84	2001	Villa Mella, D.R.
Restrepo, John	.256	11	43	8	11	2	0	0	4	7	3		1	.377	.302	L	L	6-1	185	7-27-82	2003	Santa Ana, Calif.
Robledo, Nelson	.212	45	165	13	35	5	1		16	12	38	0	0	.278	.297	R	R	6-1	180	6-13-84	2001	Panama City, Panama
Sakamoto, Mitsuru	.222	31	108	11	24	4	1	0	12	4	24	0	3	.261	.278	R	R	6-2	170	10-7-80	2003	Fukuoka, Japan
Sargent, Luke	.163	19	49	4	8	2	0	0	3	4	20	0	0	.226	.204	R	R	5-9	180	7-14-82	2004	Costa Mesa, Calif.
Smith, Seth	.259	9	27	6	7	1	1	2	5	1	3	0	0	.313	.593	L	L	6-3	215	9-30-82	2004	Terry, Miss.
Spivey, Brett	.200	38	130	9	26	4	0	0	13	24	23	3	5	.327	.231	L	L	5-9	185	6-4-81	2003	Charleston, S.C.
Strop, Pedro	.200	55	190	20	38	6	1	3	20	17	64	2	1	.286	.289	R	R	6-2	185	6-13-85	2002	San Cristobal, D.R.
Thigpen, Jud	.310	58	239	43	74	14	5	10	37	14	50	8	0	.363	.536	R	R	5-11	185	6-27-82	2004	Cleveland, Miss.
Valdez, Angel	.154	4	13	1	2	1	0	0	1	0	4	0	0	.154	.231	R	R	6-0	145	8-2-84	2001	La Romana, D.R.
Valdez, Jose	.219	43	169	22	37	4	2	2	11	21	30	3	3	.304	.302	L	R	6-1	185	9-6-83	2002	La Vega, D.R.
Van Kooten, Jason	.236	16	55	10	13	1	0	0	1	5	10	0	1	.364	.255	R	R	6-1	175	9-1-84	2004	Aurora, Colo.
Vasquez, Jose	.348	13	46	9	16	7	0	0	9	6	14	0	1	.407	.500	L	L	6-3	220	12-28-82	2000	Sarasota, Fla.

GAMES BY POSITION: C—Ghutzman 5, Guarno 23, Robledo 39, Sargent 13. **1B**—Gentry 1, Ghutzman 10, Koshansky 65, Robledo 3. **2B**—Almonte 4, Dean 47, Strop 18, J. Valdez 5, Van Kooten 3. **3B**—Dean 10, Hahn 4, Macri 49, Strop 9, J. Valdez 5. **SS**—Almonte 2, Strop 28, J. Valdez 33, Van Kooten 13. **OF**—Ghutzman 11, Miller 1, Miller 39, Nunez 40, Postlewait 1, Restrepo 11, Sakamoto 9, Smith 8, Spivey 43, Thigpen 54, A. Valdez 4.

PITCHING	W	L	ERA	G	GS	CG	SV	IP	H	R	ER	BB	SO	AVG	B	T	HT	WT	DOB	1st Yr	Resides
Beerer, Scott	0	0	3.38	6	0	0	0	5	6	2	2	2	5	.273	R	R	6-1	200	7-4-82	2003	Mission, Texas
Bright, Adam	3	4	4.93	23	0	0	0	38	38	25	21	22	36	.270	L	L	6-0	180	8-11-84	2003	Victoria, Australia
Buechner, Chris	3	1	2.45	19	0	0	3	26	16	8	7	6	31	.180	R	R	6-3	235	8-23-83	2004	Orange, Texas
Edsall, Stephen	2	0	3.55	12	0	0	0	25	19	10	10	10	23	.202	R	R	6-4	205	10-19-81	2004	North Hutchinson Island, Fla.
Gagne, J.P.	4	1	4.29	24	0	0	0	50	49	30	24	16	47	.244	R	R	6-1	205	10-27-80	2003	Bloomington, Minn.
Grube, Jarrett	4	3	4.24	17	9	0	0	57	62	38	27	13	55	.268	R	R	6-4	210	11-5-81	2004	Corunna, Ind.
Ion, Mark	2	0	1.93	4	0	0	1	9	6	2	2	2	9	.182	R	R	6-2	220	1-8-81	2003	Plantation, Fla.
Lira, Efren	1	1	5.19	20	0	0	0	35	36	24	20	20	26	.265	R	R	6-3	240	7-17-82	2004	Walnut, Calif.
Miller, Jim	1	1	0.97	34	0	0	17	37	21	6	4	11	65	.162	R	R	6-1	200	4-28-82	2004	North Fort Myers, Fla.
Morillo, Juan	3	2	2.98	14	14	0	0	66	56	34	22	41	73	.225	R	R	6-3	190	11-5-83	2001	San Pedro de Macoris, D.R.
Postlewait, Jake	3	5	5.70	14	12	0	0	54	65	41	34	31	35	.305	S	L	6-0	195	11-3-81	2004	Corvallis, Ore.
Prendergast, Matt	0	1	13.50	3	0	0	0	6	6	6	3	3		.294	R	R	6-4	210	3-26-82	2004	Herndon, Va.
Register, Steven	6	7	3.63	15	15	0	0	79	68	41	32	20	63	.229	R	R	6-1	170	5-16-83	2004	Columbus, Ga.
Rosario, Melvin	1	1	1.26	9	0	0	0	14	10	6	2	4	15	.185	L	L	6-1	172	9-22-78	1998	Carolina, P.R.
Santiago, Tomas	4	3	3.57	14	13	0	0	76	67	34	30	27	66	.232	R	R	6-4	210	10-30-81	2002	Cidra, P.R.
Songster, Judd	1	0	0.63	10	0	0	1	14	5	1	1	5	16	.106	R	R	6-3	195	12-26-79	2001	North Platte, Neb.
Tetuan, John	3	8	6.98	14	13	0	0	59	68	51	46	34	37	.291	R	R	6-0	200	9-16-80	2002	Topeka, Kan.
Thomas, Steven	2	0	1.33	11	0	0	0	14	8	3	2	8	18	.134	R	R	6-2	185	10-22-81	2004	Kingwood, Texas
Watchko, Jeff	0	0	6.23	8	0	0	0	13	12	10	9	8	10	.235	R	R	6-3	195	11-7-80	2003	Canton, Ga.
Webb, Nick	0	0	81.00	1	0	0	0	0	3	5	3	2	0	.750	L	L	6-3	205	7-8-79	2000	Houston, Texas

PIONEER LEAGUE

BATTING	AVG	G	AB	R	H	2B	3B	HR	RBI	BB	SO	SB	CS	OBP	SLG	B	T	HT	WT	DOB	1st Yr	Resides
Allen, Trevor	.212	33	113	14	24	4	1	1	11	14	30	2	1	.321	.292	R	R	6-2	215	12-26-79	2004	Haxtun, Colo.
Almonte, Sandy	.538	8	39	12	21	4	1	1	6	3	5	4	2	.571	.769	S	R	5-11	150	11-16-82	2000	Puerto Plata, D.R.
Baldwin, Bruce	.217	28	83	17	18	4	1	1	7	6	20	1	2	.309	.325	R	R	6-1	185	10-19-82	2004	Pembroke Pines, Fla.
Boggs, Steven	.221	41	149	23	33	3	0	0	23	21	36	14	6	.318	.242	S	R	5-11	180	2-29-84	2004	San Diego, Calif.
Davies, Mike	.332	61	232	44	77	16	1	9	55	25	70	1	3	.398	.526	L	L	6-3	190	3-29-81	2000	Beaverton, Ore.
Dragicevich, Jeff	.249	51	177	31	44	7	1	0	13	26	39	1	2	.354	.299	R	R	6-2	200	8-1-82	2004	Westlake Village, Calif.
Fox, Ryan	.242	48	153	43	37	7	2	12	36	44	66	7	3	.421	.549	R	R	6-3	220	10-13-80	2003	Rogers, Ark.
Hahn, Dustin	.308	63	240	56	74	18	1	8	43	51	55	10	2	.433	.492	R	R	6-1	195	10-21-82	2004	Elk Grove, Calif.
Hosgood, Rob	.281	27	96	18	27	4	2	2	15	13	36	1	2	.364	.427	L	L	6-2	210	12-5-81	2004	Clifton Park, N.Y.
Nelson, Chris	.347	38	147	36	51	6	3	4	20	20	42	6	5	.432	.510	R	R	5-11	175	9-3-85	2004	Decatur, Ga.
Nelson, Justin	.282	60	220	55	62	12	3	13	45	34	59	6	1	.379	.541	L	L	6-3	205	4-23-82	2004	San Diego, Calif.
Rodriguez, Ramon	.299	36	107	17	32	3	0	0	15	23	23	2	2	.425	.327	R	R	5-11	190	9-3-84	2002	Santiago City, D.R.
Sakamoto, Mitsuru	.227	7	22	1	5	0	0	0	3	1	6	1	0	.292	.227	L	R	6-2	170	10-7-80	2003	Fukuoka, Japan
Smith, Seth	.369	56	233	46	86	21	3	9	61	25	47	9	1	.427	.601	L	L	6-3	215	9-30-82	2004	Terry, Miss.
Van Kooten, Jason	.311	26	106	21	33	3	0	2	16	13	14	7	3	.390	.396	R	R	6-1	175	9-1-84	2004	Aurora, Colo.
Veracierto, Fernando	.304	39	148	17	45	7	0	0	21	8	25	0	3	.335	.351	R	R	5-11	170	8-18-82	2000	Miranda, Venez.
Wilson, Kyle	.262	51	187	21	49	6	0	4	34	15	31	1	1	.343	.358	R	R	6-1	215	8-23-82	2004	Santa Maria, Calif.
Young, Eric	.264	23	87	20	23	5	1	0	7	20	13	14	1	.407	.345	S	R	5-10	165	5-25-85	2004	Piscataway, N.J.

GAMES BY POSITION: C—Fox 36, Rodriquez 34, Wilson 9. **1B**—Davies 54, Wilson 23. **2B**—Almonte 4, Baldwin 12, Van Kooten 14, Veracierto 25, Young 23. **3B**—Hahn 33, Veracierto 9, Wilson 1, Wilson 19. **SS**—Dragicevich 46, C. Nelson 17, Van Kooten 10, Veracierto 5. **OF**—Allen 27, Baldwin 2, Boggs 39, Hahn 26, Hosgood 26, J. Nelson 58, Sakamoto 7, Smith 45.

PITCHING	W	L	ERA	G	GS	CG	SV	IP	H	R	ER	BB	SO	AVG	B	T	HT	WT	DOB	1st Yr	Resides
Buechner, Chris	1	1	3.95	13	0	0	4	14	11	6	6	1	14	.212	R	R	6-3	235	8-23-83	2004	Orange, Texas
Chivilli, Pedro	0	1	6.75	5	5	0	0	17	26	13	13	6	11	.371	R	R	6-0	170	2-21-83	2002	Santo Domingo, D.R.
Daley, Matt	2	1	4.75	21	0	0	0	30	31	19	16	5	30	.265	R	R	6-2	180	6-23-82	2004	Garden City, N.Y.
Deduno, Samuel	6	4	3.18	15	15	0	0	76	62	40	27	32	118	.216	R	R	6-1	150	7-2-83	2003	San Pedro de Macoris, D.R.
Delgado, George	2	1	5.67	25	0	0	7	33	44	22	21	19	35	.319	R	R	6-2	170	3-22-84	2002	Zulia, Venez.
Edsall, Stephen	1	4	12.19	5	5	0	0	21	43	30	28	6	10	.448	R	R	6-4	205	10-19-81	2004	North Hutchinson Island, Fla.
Lindsay, Shane	1	1	6.75	17	0	0	0	21	22	24	16	19	31	.256	R	R	6-1	205	1-25-85	2004	Bacchus Marsh, Australia
Manzueta, Radhames	1	3	8.42	7	1	0	0	26	36	29	24	12	25	.333	R	R	6-2	170	4-13-83	2002	San Cristobal, D.R.
Mattheus, Ryan	3	3	4.94	7	7	0	0	27	27	16	15	14	16	.257	R	R	6-3	220	11-10-83	2004	Elk Grove, Calif.
Merino, Josh	2	3	9.24	8	6	0	0	25	38	29	26	13	26	.342	R	R	6-6	205	7-31-82	2003	Vinton, Iowa
Metzger, Jay	2	5	9.84	14	4	0	0	32	58	42	35	14	31	.379	L	L	6-0	170	12-21-81	2004	Vernon, Conn.
Morales, Franklin	6	4	7.62	15	15	1	0	65	92	61	55	39	82	.336	L	L	6-0	170	1-24-86	2003	San Juan Morros, Venez.
Mosqueda, Juan	0	0	8.10	8	0	0	0	13	19	17	12	10	9	.345	R	R	5-10	160	2-25-82	2000	Estado Miranda, Venez.
Newman, Josh	1	2	3.48	27	0	0	1	34	30	17	13	8	46	.231	L	L	6-1	200	6-11-82	2004	Wheelersburg, Ohio
Patton, David	2	3	6.30	17	7	0	0	50	60	48	35	30	43	.296	R	R	6-3	175	5-18-84	2004	Enumclaw, Wash.
Sanchez, Rafael	0	1	7.71	22	0	0	1	35	53	36	30	20	28	.333	R	R	6-2	170	9-20-82	2002	San Juan, D.R.
Stanley, Pat	1	1	4.93	20	2	0	0	49	54	32	27	15	55	.274	R	R	6-7	200	1-4-83	2004	Ramsey, N.J.
Vargas, Buzz	0	1	5.54	21	0	0	1	26	37	16	16	7	30	.333	R	R	6-6	225	10-21-83	2004	Bay City, Texas
Veracierto, Fernando	0	0	45.00	1	0	0	0	1	2	5	5	3	0	.400	R	R	5-11	170	8-18-82	2000	Miranda, Venez.
White, Jeremey	2	1	8.24	20	0	0	0	32	46	36	29	16	25	.324	L	L	6-2	205	1-15-82	2004	Palmdale, Calif.

BY PAT CAPUTO

Nowhere to go but up.

It is a cliche commonly uttered by last-place teams, but in the Tigers' case it rang particularly true after they went 43-119 in 2003, narrowly avoiding the 1962 New York Mets' record of 120 losses in a single season.

Even given that, the Tigers took a significant leap forward in 2004. Not only did they stay on the fringe of contention in the American League Central until the second half of the season and win 72 games overall, but the organization seemed to rid itself of the dismal mindset that had mostly prevailed during an 11-year stretch that has not produced a winning season.

General manager Dave Dombrowski pulled off a couple key moves that paid off with a 29-game improvement and, more importantly, a speck of a light at the end of the tunnel.

Catcher Ivan Rodriguez, forgotten by most other teams on the open market despite his heroics with the World Series champion Marlins in 2003, signed a four-year contract with the Tigers as a free agent that contained more loopholes than the tax code. It represented a calculated risk by both the player and the organization, but it turned out well for both parties. Rodriguez, disproving the theory catchers hit a wall at age 32, had his typically strong season and provided much-needed leadership.

Dombrowski also hit the jackpot when he traded with Seattle for shortstop Carlos Guillen. Guillen posted by far the best statistics of his career, showed exceptional range in the field and, like Rodriguez, emerged as an excellent leader.

The Tigers also got an unexpected boost from two young players from their much-maligned player development system. Brandon Inge, replaced by Rodriguez at

Ivan Rodriguez

Curtis Granderson

PLAYERS of the YEAR

MAJOR LEAGUE: Ivan Rodriguez, c
Rodriguez proved a worthy free-agent signing, as he was a major reason for the Tigers' return to respectability in 2004. The perennial Gold Glove catcher hit .334-19-86, leading the Tigers to a 29-game improvement from their miserable 2003 season.

MINOR LEAGUE: Curtis Granderson, of
Granderson proved to be a hitting machine in his first season at Double-A Erie. He hit .301-21-94 with 80 walks in 2004, earning a September callup to Detroit. Granderson's tools are not outstanding, but he's a hard worker and a smart player.

catcher, had a breakout season as a hitter. He played in the outfield and at third base. He was particularly effective at third base, where he often played brilliant defense.

Omar Infante, a major disappointment in 2003, replaced the injured Fernando Vina early in the season and became the regular second baseman. He displayed surprising power and could develop quickly into an all-star-caliber player.

The Tigers' major problems stemmed from three areas. They lacked a legitimate No. 1 starter at the top of their rotation; their outfield was, for the most part, unproductive, and their lack of bullpen depth was alarming. They also made an inordinate number of errors and will have to improve defensively if they are to take another leap forward in 2005.

Two players who started out slowly but closed strong were outfielder Craig Monroe and first baseman Carlos Pena. The biggest disappointments among the position players were outfielder Bobby Higginson and infielder Eric Munson. Higginson will be entering the final season of a five-year, $36 million deal the Tigers are eagerly anticipating getting off the books. Munson, a first-round draft pick in 1999, simply has not produced on a consistent basis.

The best player coming up from the minor league system was lefthander Wil Ledezma, who pitched well enough after a strong season at Double-A Erie that he will likely have a spot in the starting rotation in 2005. Ledezma was joined at Erie by promising righthanders Kyle Sleeth (4-4, 6.30) and Preston Larrison (5-4, 3.05) to form one of the most intriguing rotations in the minors.

ORGANIZATION LEADERS

BATTING

*AVG	Tony Giarratano, Lakeland/West Michigan	.335
R	David Espinosa, Erie	89
	Curtis Granderson, Erie	89
H	Kelly Hunt, West Michigan	150
TB	Kelly Hunt, West Michigan	241
2B	Chris Maples, Lakeland	33
3B	Kody Kirkland, West Michigan	11
HR	Kurt Airoso, Erie	34
RBI	Kelly Hunt, West Michigan	102
BB	Kurt Airoso, Erie	82
SO	Garth McKinney, West Michigan	175
SB	Nook Logan, Toledo	38
*OBP	Curtis Granderson, Erie	.405
*SLG	Kurt Airoso, Erie	.548

PITCHING

W	Matt Vasquez, West Michigan	14
L	Pat Ahearne, Toledo	12
#ERA	Danile Zell, West Michigan	2.27
G	Jason Karnuth, Toledo/Erie	56
CG	Five tied at	3
SV	Franklyn German, Toledo	27
IP	Pat Ahearne, Toledo	179
BB	Jordan Tata, West Michigan	68
SO	Humberto Sanchez, Erie/Lakeland	130

*Minimum 250 at-bats #Minimum 75 innings

DETROIT TIGERS

Manager: Alan Trammell.

2004 Record: 72-90, .444 (4th, AL Central).

BATTING	AVG	G	AB	R	H	2B	3B	HR	RBI	BB	SO	SB	CS	OBP	SLG	B	T	HT	WT	DOB	1st Yr	Resides
Difelice, Mike	.136	13	22	3	3	0	1	0	2	3	3	0	0	.240	.227	R	R	6-2	205	5-28-69	1991	Safety Harbor, Fla.
Granderson, Curtis	.240	9	25	2	6	1	1	0	0	3	8	0	0	.321	.360	L	R	6-1	180	3-16-81	2002	Lynwood, Ill.
Guillen, Carlos	.318	136	522	97	166	37	10	20	97	52	87	12	5	.379	.542	S	R	6-1	200	9-30-75	1994	Maracay, Venez.
Higginson, Bobby	.246	131	448	63	110	24	2	12	64	70	84	5	2	.353	.388	L	R	5-11	190	8-18-70	1992	Bloomfield Hills, Mich.
Infante, Omar	.264	142	503	69	133	27	9	16	55	40	112	13	7	.317	.449	R	R	6-0	176	12-26-81	1999	Guanta, Venez.
Inge, Brandon	.287	131	408	43	117	15	7	13	64	32	72	5	4	.340	.453	R	R	5-11	195	5-19-77	1998	Ann Arbor, Mich.
Logan, Nook	.278	47	133	12	37	5	2	0	10	13	24	8	2	.340	.346	S	R	6-2	180	11-28-79	2000	Natchez, Miss.
Monroe, Craig	.293	128	447	65	131	27	3	18	72	29	79	3	4	.337	.488	R	R	6-1	210	2-27-77	1995	Texarkana, Texas
Munson, Eric	.212	109	321	36	68	14	2	19	49	29	90	1	1	.289	.445	L	R	6-3	220	10-3-77	1999	Chandler, Ariz.
Norton, Greg	.174	41	86	9	15	1	0	2	12	21	0	0		.276	.256	R	R	6-1	200	7-6-72	1993	Denver, Colo.
Pena, Carlos	.241	142	481	89	116	22	4	27	82	70	146	7	1	.338	.472	L	L	6-2	210	5-17-78	1998	Haverhill, Mass.
Raburn, Ryan	.138	12	29	4	4	1	0	0	1	2	15	1	0	.194	.172	R	R	6-0	180	4-17-81	2001	Plant City, Fla.
Rodriguez, Ivan	.334	135	527	72	176	32	2	19	86	41	91	7	4	.383	.510	R	R	5-9	220	11-30-71	1989	Miami, Fla.
Sanchez, Alex	.322	79	332	41	107	9	3	2	26	7	50	19	13	.335	.386	L	L	5-10	150	8-26-76	1996	Coral Gables, Fla.
Shelton, Chris	.196	27	46	6	9	1	0	1	3	9	14	0	0	.321	.283	R	R	6-0	220	6-26-80	2001	Salt Lake City, Utah
Smith, Jason	.239	61	155	20	37	7	4	5	19	8	37	1	2	.280	.432	L	R	6-3	190	7-24-77	1997	Coatopa, Ala.
Thames, Marcus	.255	61	165	24	42	12	0	10	33	16	42	0	1	.326	.509	R	R	6-2	205	3-6-77	1997	Louisville, Miss.
Torres, Andres	.000	3	0	1	0	0	0	0	0	0	1	0	0	.000	.000	S	R	5-10	175	1-26-78	1998	Aguada, P.R.
Vina, Fernando	.226	29	115	21	26	5	0	0	7	9	9	2	1	.308	.270	L	R	5-9	180	4-16-69	1991	Stateline, Nev.
White, Rondell	.270	121	448	76	121	21	2	19	67	39	77	1	2	.337	.453	R	R	6-1	220	2-23-72	1990	Gray, Ga.
Young, Dmitri	.272	104	389	72	106	23	2	18	60	33	71	0	1	.336	.481	S	R	6-2	240	10-11-73	1991	Parkland, Fla.

PITCHING	W	L	ERA	G	GS	CG	SV	IP	H	R	ER	BB	SO	AVG	B	T	HT	WT	DOB	1st Yr	Resides
Bonderman, Jeremy	11	13	4.89	33	32	2	0	184	168	101	100	73	168	.242	R	R	6-2	210	10-28-82	2002	Pasco, Wash.
Colyer, Steve	1	0	6.47	41	0	0	0	32	33	24	23	24	31	.270	L	L	6-4	205	2-22-79	1998	St. Peters, Mo.
Cornejo, Nate	1	3	8.42	5	5	0	0	26	42	25	24	11	12	.375	R	R	6-5	240	9-24-79	1998	Wellington, Kan.
Dingman, Craig	2	2	6.75	24	0	0	0	29	33	22	22	22	16	.295	R	R	6-4	210	3-12-74	1994	Wichita, Kan.
Ennis, John	0	0	8.44	12	0	0	1	16	20	16	15	5	13	.290	R	R	6-7	220	10-17-79	1998	Panorama, Calif.
German, Franklyn	1	0	7.36	16	0	0	0	15	17	15	12	11	8	.279	R	R	6-7	270	1-20-80	1997	San Cristobal, D.R.
Johnson, Jason	8	15	5.13	33	33	2	0	197	222	121	112	60	125	.284	R	R	6-6	217	10-27-73	1992	Tampa, Fla.
Knotts, Gary	7	6	5.25	36	19	0	2	135	142	83	79	58	81	.267	R	R	6-4	230	2-12-77	1996	Decatur, Ala.
Ledezma, Wilfredo	4	3	4.39	15	8	0	0	53	55	28	26	18	29	.272	L	L	6-3	150	1-21-81	1998	Maracay, Venez.
Levine, Al	3	4	4.58	65	0	0	0	71	83	37	36	24	32	.295	L	R	6-3	190	5-22-68	1991	Gilbert, Ariz.
Maroth, Mike	11	13	4.31	33	33	2	0	217	244	112	104	59	108	.288	L	L	6-0	190	8-17-77	1998	Orlando, Fla.
Novoa, Roberto	1	1	5.57	16	0	0	0	21	25	15	13	6	15	.309	R	R	6-5	220	8-15-79	2000	Santo Domingo, D.R.
Patterson, Danny	0	4	4.75	37	0	0	2	42	44	24	22	16	24	.282	R	R	6-0	190	2-17-71	1990	Colleyville, Texas
Robertson, Nate	12	10	4.90	34	32	1	1	197	210	116	107	66	155	.274	R	L	6-2	210	9-3-77	1999	Valley Center, Kan.
Urbina, Ugueth	4	6	4.50	54	0	0	21	54	38	28	27	32	56	.194	R	R	6-1	168	11-20-79	1997	Guarenas, Venez.
Urdaneta, Lino	0	0	0.00	1	0	0	0	0	5	6	6	1	1	01.000	R	R	6-1	200	2-15-74	1991	Ocumare Del Tuy, Venez.
Walker, Jamie	3	4	3.20	70	0	0	1	65	69	28	23	12	53	.263	L	L	6-2	190	7-1-71	1992	Overland Park, Kan.
Yan, Esteban	3	6	3.83	69	0	0	7	87	92	43	37	32	69	.274	R	R	6-4	250	6-22-75	1993	San Pedro de Marocos, D.R.

FIELDING

Catcher	PCT	G	PO	A	E	DP	PB
DiFelice	1.000	12	40	6	0	1	0
Inge	.988	39	209	30	3	1	4
Munson	.000	1	0	0	0	0	0
Rodriguez	.987	124	770	52	11	6	3
Shelton	1.000	6	10	0	0	0	3

First Base	PCT	G	PO	A	E	DP
Norton	1.000	7	36	2	0	6
Pena	.995	135	1142	77	6	128
Shelton	1.000	8	22	4	0	3
Young	1.000	25	203	17	0	15

Second Base	PCT	G	PO	A	E	DP
Infante	.976	105	204	281	12	73
Raburn	.969	11	9	22	1	5

	PCT	G	PO	A	E	DP
Smith	.987	34	68	87	2	21
Vina	.970	29	73	86	5	23

Third Base	PCT	G	PO	A	E	DP
Infante	1.000	10	2	8	0	2
Inge	.935	73	42	131	12	12
Munson	.934	94	51	177	16	17
Norton	.963	18	7	19	1	0
Smith	.833	5	5	5	2	2
Young	1.000	1	1	1	0	0

Shortstop	PCT	G	PO	A	E	DP
Guillen	.974	135	219	418	17	90
Infante	.960	23	28	67	4	11
Smith	.981	20	16	35	1	5

Outfield	PCT	G	PO	A	E	DP
Granderson	1.000	8	16	1	0	0
Higginson	.975	115	223	13	6	1
Infante	1.000	5	10	0	0	0
Inge	.980	26	43	5	1	1
Logan	.984	46	117	3	2	1
Monroe	.960	125	261	5	11	1
Norton	1.000	6	2	0	0	0
Sanchez	.952	78	177	2	9	1
Shelton	1.000	1	1	0	0	0
Thames	1.000	52	94	3	0	1
Torres	.000	1	0	0	0	0
White	.977	74	127	2	3	0
Young	1.000	2	2	0	0	0

Director, Minor League Operations: Rick Bennett.

Class	Farm Team	League	W	L	Pct.	Finish*	Manager	Affiliate Since
AAA	Toledo (Ohio) Mud Hens	International	65	78	.455	14th (14)	Larry Parrish	1987
AA	Erie (Pa.) Sea Wolves	Eastern	80	62	.563	**3rd (12)**	Rick Sweet	2001
High A	Lakeland (Fla.) Tigers	Florida State	51	81	.386	12th (12)	Gary Green	1967
Low A	West Michigan Whitecaps (Grand Rapids)	Midwest	69	70	.496	**+11th (14)**	Matt Walbeck	1997
SS A	Oneonta (N.Y.) Tigers	New York-Penn	33	41	.446	10th (14)	Mike Rojas	1999
Rookie	Lakeland (Fla.) Tigers	Gulf Coast	24	36	.400	9th (12)	Kevin Bradshaw	1995

*Finish in overall standings (No. of teams in league)/playoff teams in **boldface**

TOLEDO MUD HENS — Class AAA

INTERNATIONAL LEAGUE

BATTING	AVG	G	AB	R	H	2B	3B	HR	RBI	BB	SO	SB	CS	OBP	SLG	B	T	HT	WT	DOB	1st Yr	Resides
Alexander, Chad	.256	60	203	26	52	14	3	3	16	21	36	2	0	.327	.399	R	R	6-1	190	5-22-74	1995	Norfolk, Va.
Barkett, Andy	.283	114	413	59	117	29	1	19	66	38	80	6	4	.344	.496	L	L	6-1	205	9-5-74	1995	Raleigh, N.C.
Bautista, Rayner	.218	63	211	19	46	16	1	1	19	9	58	3	1	.267	.318	R	R	5-11	150	9-17-78	1996	Nizao, D.R.
Cleveland, Russ	.429	2	7	0	3	0	1	0	0	0	1	0	0	.429	.714	R	R	6-3	210	12-26-79	1998	Las Vegas, Nev.
Daigle, Leo	.000	1	1	0	0	0	0	0	0	0	1	0	0	.000	.000	R	R	6-3	220	9-18-79	1998	Spring Valley, Calif.
DiFelice, Mike	.270	64	237	20	64	14	0	5	36	14	37	1	0	.311	.392	R	R	6-2	205	5-28-69	1991	Safety Harbor, Fla.
Gil, Benji	.176	14	51	1	9	4	0	0	3	4	13	0	0	.236	.255	R	R	6-2	210	10-6-72	1991	Grapevine, Texas
Gomez, Rich	.261	75	249	37	65	9	3	5	25	17	56	19	4	.314	.382	R	R	5-11	190	7-19-76	1997	San Francisco de Macoris, D.R.
Harper, Brandon	.190	21	58	10	11	0	0	3	7	6	10	0	1	.294	.345	R	R	6-4	200	4-29-76	1997	Hobbs, N.M.
Klassen, Danny	.253	110	395	52	100	26	4	5	38	31	105	10	4	.315	.377	R	R	6-0	190	9-22-75	1993	Stuart, Fla.
Logan, Nook	.263	105	426	67	112	14	9	2	27	23	95	38	11	.303	.352	S	R	6-2	180	11-28-79	2000	Natchez, Miss.
Monroe, Craig	.320	6	25	4	8	4	0	2	6	0	6	0	0	.308	.720	R	R	6-1	210	2-27-77	1995	Texarkana, Texas
Morris, Warren	.287	102	397	55	114	29	3	8	51	29	71	5	4	.334	.436	L	R	5-11	190	1-11-74	1997	Alexandria, La.
Nicholson, Derek	.274	24	62	12	17	8	1	1	11	11	10	2	1	.373	.484	L	R	6-0	200	6-17-76	1998	Redondo Beach, Calif.
Norton, Greg	.207	53	184	26	38	6	1	4	16	24	48	1	1	.297	.315	R	R	6-1	200	7-6-72	1993	Denver, Colo.
Owens, Eric	.251	120	442	37	111	11	1	3	32	19	50	15	6	.283	.301	R	R	6-0	200	2-3-71	1992	Phoenix, Ariz.
Petrick, Ben	.000	3	10	0	0	0	0	0	0	1	7	0	0	.091	.000	R	R	6-0	200	4-7-77	1996	Hillsboro, Ore.
Rodriguez, Guillermo	.187	72	219	17	41	8	2	7	21	14	45	2	2	.244	.338	R	R	5-11	195	5-12-78	1996	Barquisimeto, Venez.
Rodriguez, Luis	.200	2	5	0	1	1	0	0	0	0	1	0	0	.200	.400	R	R	5-11	195	1-3-74	1994	Tampa, Fla.
Sanchez, Alex	.000	2	10	0	0	0	0	0	0	0	6	0	0	.000	.000	L	L	5-10	150	8-26-76	1996	Coral Gables, Fla.
Shelton, Chris	.339	18	62	5	21	2	0	0	7	10	13	0	0	.425	.371	R	R	6-0	220	6-26-80	2001	Salt Lake City, Utah
Smith, Jason	.270	33	122	18	33	8	2	3	13	6	26	5	1	.300	.443	L	R	6-3	190	7-24-77	1997	Coatopa, Ala.
Thames, Marcus	.329	64	234	57	77	21	1	24	59	33	40	4	1	.410	.735	R	R	6-2	205	3-6-77	1997	Louisville, Miss.
Toca, Jorge	.254	16	63	4	16	1	0	1	6	1	14	2	1	.262	.317	R	R	6-3	230	1-7-75	1999	Miami, Fla.
Ust, Brant	.254	111	406	47	103	17	2	10	41	15	97	3	3	.283	.379	R	R	6-1	210	7-17-78	1999	Redmond, Wash.
Vitiello, Joe	.328	86	323	52	106	19	0	16	70	27	61	2	2	.386	.536	R	R	6-3	220	4-11-70	1991	Stoneham, Mass.
Young, Dmitri	.500	2	10	1	5	1	1	1	5	4	1	0	0	.545	1.100	S	R	6-2	240	10-11-73	1991	Parkland, Fla.

PITCHING	W	L	ERA	G	GS	CG	SV	IP	H	R	ER	BB	SO	AVG	B	T	HT	WT	DOB	1st Yr	Resides
Ahearne, Pat	9	12	4.01	28	28	3	0	179	182	101	80	45	123	.261	R	R	6-3	215	12-10-69	1992	Atascadero, Calif.
Anderson, Matt	0	5	5.82	34	0	0	1	34	41	26	22	23	25	.291	R	R	6-4	200	8-17-76	1998	Louisville, Ky.
Baldwin, James	5	7	3.73	18	16	3	1	116	110	52	48	20	61	.255	R	R	6-3	230	7-15-71	1990	Southern Pines, N.C.
2-team (5 Norfolk)	8	9	3.56	23	21	3	1	147	144	63	58	25	85	.260							
Burnside, Adrian	4	7	6.13	26	14	0	0	76	87	61	52	40	62	.289	R	L	6-3	210	3-15-77	1996	Bradenton, Fla.
Colyer, Steve	2	1	4.21	25	0	0	0	26	26	13	12	23	25	.265	L	L	6-4	205	2-22-79	1998	St. Peters, Mo.
Cornejo, Nate	0	0	4.15	4	3	0	0	9	11	4	4	2	8	.314	R	R	6-5	240	9-24-79	1998	Wellington, Kan.
Cortes, David	1	0	3.95	14	0	0	0	14	12	6	6	6	10	.240	R	R	5-11	190	10-15-73	1994	El Centro, Calif.
Cuello, Felix	0	0	0.00	1	0	0	0	2	1	0	0	1	1	.167	R	R	6-3	180	9-17-79	2000	Santo Domingo, D.R.
Dingman, Craig	1	2	4.56	21	0	0	0	26	26	14	13	11	31	.260	R	R	6-4	210	3-12-74	1994	Wichita, Kan.
Eckenstahler, Eric	1	2	5.15	42	0	0	0	44	58	32	25	30	45	.317	L	L	6-7	220	12-17-76	2000	Lake Villa, Ill.
Ennis, John	9	5	3.58	38	13	0	10	103	100	49	41	36	77	.258	R	R	6-5	220	10-17-79	1998	Panorama, Calif.
German, Franklyn	3	5	4.59	49	0	0	27	49	46	25	25	25	60	.246	R	R	6-7	270	1-20-80	1997	San Cristobal, D.R.
Haynes, Jimmy	0	1	8.78	5	3	0	0	13	19	13	13	6	9	.328	R	R	6-4	220	9-5-72	1991	La Grange, Ga.
Karnuth, Jason	5	2	3.74	46	0	0	2	55	45	26	23	16	34	.221	R	R	6-2	190	5-15-76	1997	Memphis, Tenn.
Kirsten, Rick	3	4	5.86	14	6	0	0	51	63	36	33	23	27	.315	R	R	6-0	180	7-23-78	1999	Rolling Meadows, Ill.
Loux, Shane	7	11	5.29	22	22	1	0	133	154	86	78	34	86	.294	R	R	6-2	230	8-31-79	1997	Gilbert, Ariz.
Mears, Chris	1	1	3.83	30	1	0	0	40	37	21	17	20	29	.247	R	R	6-4	190	1-20-78	1996	Victoria, B.C.
Patterson, Danny	1	0	4.15	3	0	0	0	4	3	2	2	2	3	.188	R	R	6-0	190	2-17-71	1990	Colleyville, Texas
Prieto, Ariel	1	1	3.68	4	4	0	0	22	20	10	9	5	19	.247	R	R	6-3	240	10-22-69	1995	Miami, Fla.
Rodriguez, Guillermo	0	0	9.00	1	0	0	0	1	3	1	1	0	0	.500	R	R	5-11	195	5-12-78	1996	Barquisimeto, Venez.
Roney, Matt	2	1	3.86	5	5	0	0	30	30	13	13	10	18	.270	R	R	6-3	230	1-10-80	1998	Edmond, Okla.
Schmack, Brian	1	2	4.26	24	0	0	0	51	54	29	24	14	35	.266	R	R	6-2	205	12-7-73	1995	Barrington, Ill.
Urdaneta, Lino	0	2	9.69	9	1	0	0	13	22	14	14	3	4	.379	R	R	6-1	168	11-20-79	1997	Guarenas, Venez.
Van Hekken, Andy	9	7	4.96	28	27	0	0	152	179	97	84	59	101	.300	R	L	6-3	185	7-31-79	1998	Holland, Mich.

FIELDING

Catcher	PCT	G	PO	A	E	DP	PB
Cleveland	1.000	2	12	2	0	0	0
DiFelice	.990	58	348	41	4	2	6
Harper	.978	20	120	12	3	1	2
G. Rodriguez	.985	70	407	44	7	5	4
L. Rodriguez	1.000	2	13	3	0	0	0

	PCT	G	PO	A	E	DP
Gil	1.000	2	22	1	0	0
Nicholson	1.000	1	4	0	0	0
Norton	1.000	3	25	1	0	4
Shelton	.973	9	64	8	2	11
Ust	1.000	9	92	6	0	11
Vitiello	.993	29	263	29	2	25

	PCT	G	PO	A	E	DP
Gil	.944	7	13	21	2	6
Morris	.972	90	155	266	12	62
Ust	.970	23	36	61	3	13

Third Base	PCT	G	PO	A	E	DP
Bautista	1.000	8	1	13	0	3
Nicholson	.906	13	6	23	3	1
Norton	.975	51	34	121	4	16
G. Rodriguez	.333	1	0	1	2	0

First Base	PCT	G	PO	A	E	DP
Barkett	.986	98	884	65	13	85

Second Base	PCT	G	PO	A	E	DP
Bautista	.985	30	49	80	2	15

ORGANIZATION STATISTICS

Shortstop	PCT	G	PO	A	E	DP
Smith	.938	33	26	65	6	5
Ust	.917	43	21	101	11	10

Shortstop	PCT	G	PO	A	E	DP
Bautista	.975	22	30	49	2	9
Gil	.833	1	3	2	1	1
Klassen	.969	109	172	328	16	78
Ust	.957	16	27	40	3	9

Outfield	PCT	G	PO	A	E	DP
Alexander	.968	58	114	7	4	2
Barkett	1.000	9	9	1	0	0
Gomez	.957	31	45	0	2	0
Logan	.979	105	228	7	5	1
Monroe	1.000	5	9	1	0	0
Morris	1.000	9	17	0	0	0
Nicholson	1.000	4	7	0	0	0

	PCT	G	PO	A	E	DP
Owens	.987	121	214	13	3	2
Petrick	1.000	3	4	0	0	0
Sanchez	1.000	2	6	0	0	0
Thames	.979	63	94	1	2	0
Toca	1.000	8	12	1	0	0
Ust	1.000	21	41	2	0	0
Vitiello	1.000	6	8	0	0	0

ERIE SEAWOLVES — Class AA

EASTERN LEAGUE

BATTING	AVG	G	AB	R	H	2B	3B	HR	RBI	BB	SO	SB	CS	OBP	SLG	B	T	HT	WT	DOB	1st Yr	Resides
Airoso, Kurt	.260	122	427	78	111	15	3	34	94	82	127	7	0	.381	.548	R	R	6-2	190	2-12-75	1996	Tulare, Calif.
Bautista, Rayner	.238	36	126	16	30	7	1	3	10	12	27	2	2	.309	.381	R	R	5-11	150	9-17-78	1996	Nizao, D.R.
Cleveland, Russ	.185	18	54	7	10	3	1	2	7	6	19	0	0	.279	.389	R	R	6-3	210	12-26-79	1998	Las Vegas, Nev.
Espinosa, David	.264	134	511	89	135	23	5	19	52	80	134	20	7	.366	.440	S	R	6-2	190	12-16-81	2001	Miami, Fla.
Gomez, Rich	.240	21	75	12	18	5	0	2	10	9	18	9	1	.352	.387	R	R	5-11	180	7-19-76	1997	San Francisco de Macoris, D.R.
Granderson, Curtis	.301	123	462	89	139	19	8	21	94	80	95	14	8	.405	.513	L	R	6-1	180	3-16-81	2002	Lynwood, Ill.
Hannahan, Jack	.273	108	374	48	102	21	1	8	39	53	60	7	3	.365	.398	L	R	6-2	200	3-4-80	2001	St. Paul, Minn.
Harper, Brandon	.289	48	166	26	48	12	0	9	29	16	31	2	1	.372	.524	R	R	6-4	200	4-29-76	1997	Hobbs, N.M.
Hernandez, Anderson	.274	101	394	65	108	19	3	5	29	26	89	17	6	.326	.376	S	R	5-9	160	10-30-82	2001	Santo Domingo, D.R.
Jenkins, Neil	.216	61	232	15	50	13	1	6	29	7	78	0	0	.241	.388	R	R	6-5	200	7-17-80	1999	Jupiter, Fla.
Kelly, Donald	.228	28	101	17	23	6	2	0	9	15	13	3	1	.331	.327	L	L	6-4	190	2-15-80	2001	Pittsburgh, Pa.
Knoedler, Jason	.177	27	79	9	14	5	0	2	9	6	23	1	0	.241	.316	R	R	6-1	190	7-17-80	2001	Springfield, Ill.
Meyers, Chad	.313	34	134	26	42	10	1	8	17	16	18	11	3	.395	.582	R	R	5-11	190	8-8-75	1996	Omaha, Neb.
Nicholson, Derek	.271	61	221	31	60	13	1	10	37	23	47	1	0	.337	.475	L	R	6-0	200	6-17-76	1998	Redondo Beach, Calif.
Rabelo, Mike	.100	5	20	0	2	0	0	2	1	4	0	0	0	.182	.100	S	R	6-1	200	1-17-80	2001	New Port Richey, Fla.
Raburn, Ryan	.301	98	366	66	110	29	4	16	63	47	96	3	0	.390	.533	R	R	6-0	185	4-17-81	2001	Plant City, Fla.
St. Pierre, Maxim	.248	84	290	31	72	15	0	8	33	25	41	2	1	.315	.383	R	R	6-0	170	4-17-80	1997	Montreal, Quebec
Tejeda, Juan	.289	125	457	71	132	29	3	23	92	51	102	0	0	.362	.516	R	R	6-2	195	1-26-82	1999	Santiago, D.R.
Tousa, Scott	.220	95	259	38	57	10	3	4	27	35	56	3	4	.345	.328	L	R	5-11	180	8-3-79	2001	St. George, Utah

PITCHING	W	L	ERA	G	GS	CG	SV	IP	H	R	ER	BB	SO	AVG	B	T	HT	WT	DOB	1st Yr	Resides
Baugh, Kenny	8	8	3.72	24	24	1	0	143	154	70	59	41	107	.274	R	R	6-4	190	2-5-79	2001	Houston, Texas
Birtwell, John	0	0	3.52	6	0	0	0	8	6	3	3	2	7	.207	R	R	6-2	220	9-4-79	2001	Walpole, Mass.
Cordova, Jorge	2	1	5.10	22	3	0	0	42	55	28	24	19	32	.325	R	R	6-0	200	1-13-78	1996	La Asuncion, Venez.
Cuello, Felix	1	0	5.66	9	1	0	0	21	18	14	13	16	12	.234	R	R	6-3	180	9-17-79	2000	Santo Domingo, D.R.
Diaz, Pedro	1	1	4.42	4	3	0	0	18	21	13	9	6	14	.284	R	R	6-3	190	9-9-82	2002	Gurabo, P.R.
Hamman, Corey	0	0	6.75	2	1	0	0	7	10	6	5	3	3	.303	L	L	6-2	200	4-12-80	2002	Flanders, N.J.
Henkel, Rob	1	1	4.70	3	3	0	0	15	14	9	8	8	10	.246	R	L	6-2	210	8-3-78	2001	La Mesa, Calif.
Karnuth, Jason	0	0	6.97	10	0	0	6	10	14	8	8	6	9	.318	R	R	6-2	190	5-15-76	1997	Memphis, Tenn.
Kirsten, Rick	3	2	3.43	17	11	0	0	63	63	31	24	13	36	.253	R	R	6-4	200	7-23-78	1999	Rolling Meadows, Ill.
Larrison, Preston	5	4	3.05	20	20	0	0	118	122	54	40	36	59	.264	R	R	6-4	230	11-19-80	2001	Aurora, Ill.
Ledezma, Wilfredo	10	3	2.42	17	16	2	0	112	95	36	30	24	98	.228	L	L	6-3	150	1-21-81	1998	Maracay, Venez.
Lontayo, Alex	3	4	5.21	37	7	0	0	74	82	50	43	41	62	.284	L	L	6-2	200	11-20-78	2001	Cheswick, Penn.
McDowell, Kevin	1	0	1.69	7	0	0	0	11	7	2	2	13	7	.179	L	L	6-2	200	1-20-78	1996	Victoria, BC, Canada
Mears, Chris	4	1	3.54	13	0	0	0	20	21	10	8	5	12	.269	R	R	6-4	190	1-20-78	1998	Redondo Beach, Calif.
Nicholson, Derek	0	0	22.50	2	0	0	0	2	7	5	5	1	0	.538	L	R	6-0	200	6-17-76	1998	Redondo Beach, Calif.
Novoa, Roberto	7	0	2.96	41	0	0	4	79	63	32	26	18	59	.216	R	R	6-5	200	8-15-79	2000	Santo Domingo, D.R.
Palma, Rick	2	11	4.41	53	3	0	10	65	67	35	32	15	54	.269	L	L	6-1	160	9-26-79	1997	Maracay, Venez.
Rodney, Lee	4	1	3.13	24	0	0	1	37	40	17	13	8	19	.274	R	R	6-3	230	11-6-77	2000	Dacula, Ga.
Roney, Matt	9	9	4.93	22	22	3	0	133	163	79	73	33	89	.299	R	R	6-3	230	1-10-80	1998	Edmond, Okla.
Sanchez, Felix	2	2	7.24	14	0	0	0	14	18	11	11	6	12	.305	R	L	6-3	180	8-3-81	1999	Puerto Plata, D.R.
Sanchez, Humberto	1	0	2.13	2	2	0	0	13	10	5	3	6	15	.213	R	R	6-6	230	5-28-83	2002	Bronx, N.Y.
Schmack, Brian	4	4	4.40	26	0	0	5	31	25	16	15	7	15	.236	R	R	6-2	205	12-7-73	1995	Barrington, Ill.
Sleeth, Kyle	4	4	6.30	13	13	0	0	80	93	58	56	34	57	.297	R	R	6-5	205	12-20-81	2004	Westminster, Colo.
Tousa, Scott	0	0	0.00	1	0	0	0	1	0	0	0	3	0	.000	L	R	5-11	180	8-3-79	2001	St. George, Utah
Woodyard, Mark	6	4	3.52	43	9	0	5	102	102	53	40	37	55	.263	R	R	6-2	190	12-19-78	2000	Grand Bay, Ala.
Zumaya, Joel	2	2	6.30	4	4	0	0	20	19	20	14	10	29	.238	R	R	6-3	210	11-9-84	2002	Chula Vista, Calif.

FIELDING

Catcher	PCT	G	PO	A	E	DP	PB
Cleveland	.947	17	84	6	5	0	2
Harper	.981	41	290	19	6	6	2
Rabelo	1.000	5	32	4	0	0	0
St. Pierre	.996	84	487	54	2	1	7

First Base	PCT	G	PO	A	E	DP
Cleveland	1.000	1	1	0	0	0
Harper	1.000	1	1	0	0	0
Jenkins	.970	3	29	3	1	2
Nicholson	.989	21	170	12	2	18
Tejeda	.986	122	1091	75	16	93
Tousa	1.000	6	28	1	0	4

Second Base	PCT	G	PO	A	E	DP
Bautista	.985	15	18	49	1	6
Meyers	.000	1	0	0	1	0
Raburn	.950	95	189	306	26	63
Tousa	.988	36	66	96	2	28

Third Base	PCT	G	PO	A	E	DP
Bautista	.846	6	1	10	2	0
Hannahan	.951	102	65	228	15	27
Nicholson	.909	3	2	8	1	2
Tousa	.967	39	28	88	4	13

Shortstop	PCT	G	PO	A	E	DP
Bautista	.927	14	7	31	3	5
Hannahan	1.000	1	0	2	0	0

	PCT	G	PO	A	E	DP
Hernandez	.966	99	160	291	16	57
Kelly	.931	27	29	79	8	13
Tousa	.885	5	6	17	3	1

Outfield	PCT	G	PO	A	E	DP
Airoso	.968	21	27	3	1	1
Espinosa	.970	135	249	14	8	2
Gomez	1.000	21	34	1	0	0
Granderson	.991	123	303	10	3	2
Jenkins	.991	58	106	3	1	0
Knoedler	.979	23	43	3	1	0
Meyers	1.000	36	56	3	0	0
Nicholson	.964	23	27	0	1	0
Tousa	1.000	4	6	0	0	0

LAKELAND TIGERS — High Class A

FLORIDA STATE LEAGUE

BATTING	AVG	G	AB	R	H	2B	3B	HR	RBI	BB	SO	SB	CS	OBP	SLG	B	T	HT	WT	DOB	1st Yr	Resides
Amezquita, Octavio	.071	9	28	0	2	1	0	0	0	0	3	0	0	.071	.107	R	R	6-0	175	3-11-82	2004	Stockton, Calif.
Barnes, Justin	.400	2	5	1	2	0	0	0	0	1	2	0	0	.500	.400	R	R	6-3	210	10-13-80	2003	Gallion, Ala.

ORGANIZATION STATISTICS

BATTING

BATTING	AVG	G	AB	R	H	2B	3B	HR	RBI	BB	SO	SB	CS	OBP	SLG	B	T	HT	WT	DOB	1st Yr	Resides
Cleveland, Russ	.175	22	63	7	11	3	2	0	3	6	20	0	1	.243	.286	R	R	6-3	210	12-26-79	1998	Las Vegas, Nev.
Clevlen, Brent	.223	117	421	49	94	23	6	6	50	44	127	2	1	.300	.349	R	R	6-2	190	10-27-83	2002	Cedar Park, Texas
Cotto, Pedro	.214	61	182	17	39	4	1	0	17	11	21	0	1	.259	.247	L	L	5-11	170	5-26-82	2002	San Juan, P.R.
Doyle, Nathan	.143	7	14	4	2	2	0	0	2	0	5	0	0	.200	.286	R	R	6-1	195	1-30-81	2003	Wilmington, Del.
Giarratano, Tony	.376	53	202	30	76	11	0	5	25	16	38	14	8	.423	.505	S	R	6-0	180	11-29-82	2003	Marlboro, N.J.
Gil, Luis	.282	24	71	12	20	4	0	0	6	3	23	4	0	.307	.338	R	R	6-1	170	2-12-84	2002	Castillo, D.R.
Hernandez, Anderson	.289	26	97	14	28	3	3	0	9	6	19	5	0	.327	.381	S	R	5-9	160	10-30-82	2001	Santo Domingo, D.R.
Jenkins, Neil	.248	43	149	18	37	5	1	4	12	8	54	5	0	.300	.376	R	R	6-5	200	7-17-80	1999	Jupiter, Fla.
Maples, Chris	.269	122	431	66	116	33	1	17	74	37	88	7	11	.338	.469	R	R	5-10	180	10-31-79	2002	Hillsborough, N.C.
Mattle, David	.242	101	335	44	81	16	2	4	37	31	72	1	1	.310	.337	L	R	6-0	200	12-21-79	2001	Barberton, Ohio
Mejia, Gilberto	.266	96	354	50	94	13	5	7	31	35	76	16	10	.330	.390	S	R	5-9	160	9-1-82	2000	Bani, D.R.
Mendez, Victor	.241	120	402	53	97	20	9	12	58	42	100	8	7	.313	.425	R	R	5-11	180	6-28-80	1999	Las Matas de Farfan, D.R.
Moore, Scott	.223	118	391	52	87	13	4	14	56	49	125	2	4	.322	.384	L	R	6-2	180	11-17-83	2002	Long Beach, Calif.
Rabelo, Mike	.287	92	327	36	94	20	2	0	38	25	56	3	2	.349	.361	S	R	6-1	200	1-17-80	2001	New Port Richey, Fla.
Raburn, Ryan	.273	3	11	1	3	1	0	1	3	1	6	0	0	.333	.636	R	R	6-0	185	4-17-81	2001	Plant City, Fla.
Reynolds, Wilton	.171	26	82	8	14	3	2	1	10	7	27	0	0	.244	.293	R	R	6-4	190	3-5-80	2003	Sacramento, Calif.
Roa, Joel	.091	4	11	1	1	0	0	0	0	1	4	0	0	.167	.091	R	R	6-0	170	1-2-84	2001	Santo Domingo, D.R.
Roughton, Jody	.261	92	314	37	82	16	4	5	37	22	70	2	4	.316	.385	L	R	6-1	190	5-6-81	2002	Carthage, Mo.
Trezza, Alex	.217	28	69	7	15	3	2	0	12	10	22	0	1	.321	.319	L	R	6-3	210	9-1-80	2001	Middletown, N.Y.
Woods, Michael	.281	68	270	45	76	16	4	2	23	20	52	9	3	.333	.393	R	R	6-1	200	9-11-80	2001	Baton Rouge, La.

PITCHING

PITCHING	W	L	ERA	G	GS	CG	SV	IP	H	R	ER	BB	SO	AVG	B	T	HT	WT	DOB	1st Yr	Resides
Baldwin, Andy	1	5	6.17	17	6	0	0	47	69	36	32	19	36	.348	R	R	6-2	190	2-28-82	2003	Campbellsville, Ky.
Bechtel, Chuck	0	0	0.00	3	0	0	0	4	4	1	0	0	4	.250	R	R	6-4	215	11-12-79	2003	Royersford, Pa.
Bierd, Randor	1	5	7.00	7	7	0	0	36	38	29	28	21	30	.277	R	R	6-4	190	3-14-84	2003	Santo Domingo, D.R.
Birtwell, John	1	3	3.09	20	0	0	1	32	28	14	11	9	26	.237	R	R	6-2	220	9-4-79	2001	Walpole, Mass.
Connolly, Jon	2	2	3.68	4	4	0	0	22	28	12	9	5	8	.304	R	L	6-0	200	8-24-83	2001	Oneonta, N.Y.
Cordova, Jorge	0	2	4.91	8	0	0	0	11	9	7	6	5	13	.231	R	R	6-0	200	1-13-78	1996	La Asuncion, Venez.
Cuello, Felix	2	2	4.42	27	3	0	0	55	58	29	27	28	35	.279	R	R	6-3	180	9-17-79	2000	Santo Domingo, D.R.
Garcia, Felipe	0	3	4.12	10	0	0	0	20	22	12	9	15	16	.297	R	R	5-11	160	9-20-82	2001	San Pedro de Macoris, D.R.
Hamman, Corey	6	3	4.20	35	12	2	1	96	116	49	45	27	31	.300	L	L	6-2	200	4-12-80	2002	Flanders, N.J.
Harper, Landon	0	2	7.30	10	0	0	0	12	15	10	10	7	11	.283	R	R	6-1	210	2-1-82	2004	Hays, Kan.
Hensen, Brian	1	1	2.43	20	0	0	0	30	25	10	8	5	11	.229	L	L	6-4	170	6-12-82	2004	Clemson, S.C.
Howell, Mike	3	9	8.16	27	13	0	0	86	125	87	78	29	51	.333	R	R	6-4	200	11-9-79	2001	Binghamton, N.Y.
Johnson, Jeremy	3	6	4.87	14	14	0	0	68	79	39	37	26	42	.289	R	R	6-1	180	5-6-78	2000	Tamms, Ill.
Kobow, Mike	0	2	3.75	40	0	0	13	50	52	26	21	25	29	.269	R	R	6-4	190	4-9-79	2001	Hutchinson, Minn.
Lontayo, Alex	0	0	3.86	3	1	0	0	7	4	3	3	4	5	.182	L	L	6-1	190	12-1-75	1999	Chula Vista, Calif.
McDowell, Kevin	0	1	1.50	16	0	0	0	18	13	3	3	6	13	.210	L	L	6-2	190	11-20-78	2001	Cheswick, Pa.
Moates, Jason	0	4	2.55	17	0	0	0	25	24	10	7	9	20	.264	R	R	6-2	210	8-22-78	2001	Columbia, Tenn.
Myers, Damien	3	0	1.82	9	2	0	0	25	20	5	5	5	16	.220	L	L	6-0	180	11-3-80	2002	New York, N.Y.
Ostlund, Ian	1	0	2.25	14	0	0	1	24	15	6	6	3	24	.181	R	L	6-0	190	11-27-78	2001	Singers Glen, Va.
Parris, Matt	9	9	4.71	25	24	2	0	130	141	78	68	43	42	.279	R	R	6-4	200	10-4-82	2000	Ventura, Calif.
Pender, Matt	0	0	7.20	4	0	0	0	5	7	4	4	3	2	.350	R	R	6-5	210	6-11-81	2002	Kathleen, Ga.
Perez, Ezequiel	0	0	7.36	2	0	0	0	4	6	3	3	0	0	.375	R	R	6-1	185	9-10-81	2003	San Juan, P.R.
Rodney, Lee	2	1	0.67	19	0	0	7	27	19	3	2	5	22	.198	R	R	6-2	180	11-6-77	2000	Dacula, Ga.
Sanchez, Humberto	7	11	5.21	19	19	3	0	105	103	67	61	51	115	.258	R	R	6-6	230	5-28-83	2002	Bronx, N.Y.
Sleeth, Kyle	3	4	3.67	9	9	1	0	54	47	26	22	15	55	.230	R	R	6-5	205	12-20-81	2004	Westminster, Colo.
Trezza, Alex	0	0	11.57	3	0	0	0	2	7	3	3	1	1	.538	L	R	6-3	210	9-1-80	2001	Middletown, N.Y.
Urbina, Ugueth	0	0	0.00	2	0	0	0	2	3	0	0	0	1	.273	R	R	6-0	200	2-15-74	1991	Ocumare Del Tuy, Venez.
Urdaneta, Lino	0	2	11.57	2	2	0	0	2	5	3	3	0	0	.455	R	R	6-1	168	11-20-79	1997	Guarenas, Venez.
Zumaya, Joel	6	4	3.54	16	16	1	0	94	65	41	37	43	98	.198	R	R	6-3	210	11-9-84	2002	Chula Vista, Calif.

FIELDING

Catcher

Catcher	PCT	G	PO	A	E	DP	PB
Barnes	1.000	2	5	0	0	0	
Cleveland	.975	21	109	6	3	1	5
Maples	1.000	1	8	1	0	0	
Rabelo	.988	85	514	48	7	4	11
Roa	1.000	4	18	0	0	0	1
Trezza	.986	27	122	15	2	0	3

First Base

First Base	PCT	G	PO	A	E	DP
Bechtel	1.000	7	60	6	0	6
Jenkins	1.000	1	2	0	0	0
Maples	.995	46	366	38	2	29
Roughton	.993	82	673	58	5	72

Second Base

Second Base	PCT	G	PO	A	E	DP
Doyle	1.000	4	5	10	0	1

Gil	1.000	10	10	19	0	6
Maples	1.000	30	47	95	0	20
Mejia	.961	31	43	80	5	17
Raburn	.810	3	8	9	4	1
Woods	.965	66	112	187	11	44

Third Base

Third Base	PCT	G	PO	A	E	DP
Doyle	1.000	1	1	0	0	0
Maples	.945	16	13	39	3	6
Mejia	1.000	1	0	1	0	0
Moore	.903	115	84	177	28	14

Shortstop

Shortstop	PCT	G	PO	A	E	DP
Amezquita	.977	8	19	24	1	9
Doyle	1.000	1	0	1	0	0

Giarratano	.968	53	89	150	8	34
Gil	.983	14	18	40	1	11
Hernandez	.983	26	35	84	2	20
Mejia	.969	35	54	100	5	15

Outfield

Outfield	PCT	G	PO	A	E	DP
Clevlen	.934	116	200	14	15	3
Cotto	.988	43	80	2	1	0
Jenkins	.983	31	54	3	1	1
Mattle	.971	62	96	3	3	2
Mejia	1.000	19	37	3	0	0
Mendez	.993	120	290	14	2	2
Reynolds	.949	19	33	4	2	0

WEST MICHIGAN WHITECAPS — Low Class A

MIDWEST LEAGUE

BATTING	AVG	G	AB	R	H	2B	3B	HR	RBI	BB	SO	SB	CS	OBP	SLG	B	T	HT	WT	DOB	1st Yr	Resides
Blue, Vincent	.260	134	497	66	129	19	4	2	43	49	97	19	11	.328	.326	L	R	6-2	180	2-8-83	2001	Houston, Texas
Burgos, Richard	.205	27	88	8	18	3	0	3	8	5	19	0	0	.247	.341	R	R	6-0	190	4-18-82	2003	Glendora, Calif.
Doyle, Nathan	.225	41	120	16	27	6	3	1	12	7	53	2	0	.326	.350	R	R	6-1	195	1-30-81	2003	Wilmington, Del.
Flowers, Bo	.273	6	22	4	6	1	0	1	1	0	6	0	1	.360	.455	R	R	6-0	190	11-12-83	2002	Maywood, Ill.
Francia, Juan	.320	111	413	73	132	11	3	0	32	34	44	37	19	.384	.361	S	R	5-9	150	1-4-82	1999	San Antonio de los Altos, Venez.
Giarratano, Tony	.285	43	165	20	47	6	1	1	13	25	22	11	3	.383	.352	S	R	6-0	180	11-29-82	2003	Marlboro, N.J.
Graham, Andrew	.253	26	83	8	21	4	1	1	9	5	21	0	1	.303	.361	R	R	6-4	215	4-27-82	2003	Sydney, Australia
Hunt, Kelly	.275	136	546	71	150	28	0	21	102	22	107	2	3	.308	.441	R	R	6-5	240	4-15-81	2003	Bowling Green, Ohio
Kirkland, Kody	.236	129	496	50	117	30	11	10	61	15	149	6	8	.276	.401	R	R	6-4	200	6-9-83	2002	Pocatello, Idaho
Knoedler, Jason	.242	70	198	33	48	7	4	4	21	33	59	8	4	.346	.379	S	R	6-1	190	7-17-80	2001	Springfield, Ill.

BATTING

BATTING	AVG	G	AB	R	H	2B	3B	HR	RBI	BB	SO	SB	CS	OBP	SLG	B	T	HT	WT	DOB	1st Yr	Resides
Llamas, Juan	.200	1	5	1	1	0	0	0	2	0	0	0	0	.200	.200	R	R	6-1	160	6-24-80	1998	Cartagena, Columbia
McIntyre, Nick	.240	39	129	19	31	6	2	1	15	7	37	3	0	.277	.341	S	R	5-10	185	3-11-81	2003	Lafayette, Ind.
McKinney, Garth	.228	117	412	59	94	14	2	19	41	46	175	11	7	.313	.410	R	R	6-3	210	5-7-82	2002	Johnson City, Tenn.
Piantek, Kurt	.200	33	115	15	23	3	0	5	19	8	38	0	0	.254	.357	R	R	6-3	215	6-19-81	2003	Wallingford, Conn.
Reynolds, Wilton	.165	26	91	11	15	4	0	2	7	9	32	0	0	.248	.275	R	R	6-4	190	3-5-80	2002	Sacramento, Calif.
Rodland, Eric	.263	128	471	63	124	26	6	4	50	38	85	8	4	.331	.369	L	R	6-1	180	2-23-80	2003	Snohomish, Wash.
Sabino, Luis	.234	103	384	54	90	22	6	9	47	36	144	10	3	.302	.393	S	R	6-2	190	5-24-83	2003	Canovanas, P.R.
Sanchez, Danilo	.294	87	309	33	91	22	0	8	46	26	59	0	0	.355	.443	R	R	5-11	210	10-25-80	1998	Santo Domingo, D.R.
Trezza, Alex	.199	49	171	15	34	11	0	2	22	7	43	0	0	.235	.298	L	R	6-3	210	9-1-80	2001	Middletown, N.Y.

PITCHING

PITCHING	W	L	ERA	G	GS	CG	SV	IP	H	R	ER	BB	SO	AVG	B	T	HT	WT	DOB	1st Yr	Resides
Baldwin, Andy	8	4	2.76	14	14	0	0	88	73	29	27	21	61	.231	R	R	6-2	190	2-28-82	2003	Campbellsville, Ky.
De la Cruz, Eulogio	2	4	3.83	54	0	0	17	54	51	30	23	33	44	.244	R	R	5-11	177	3-12-84	2002	Santo Domingo, D.R.
Homer, Chris	0	3	4.57	39	0	0	12	45	48	28	23	21	50	.268	R	R	6-1	190	3-6-81	2003	Jamesville, N.Y.
Knoedler, Jason	0	0	9.00	1	0	0	0	1	2	1	1	1	0	.400	S	R	6-1	190	7-17-80	2001	Springfield, Ill.
Martinez, Cristhian	5	2	2.44	12	12	1	0	74	59	27	20	20	45	.220	R	R	5-11	180	3-18-79	2002	Las Vegas, Nev.
Myers, Damien	1	2	3.33	24	0	0	0	27	30	13	10	9	25	.273	L	L	6-0	180	11-3-80	2002	New York, N.Y.
Righter, Matt	0	0	0.00	5	0	0	0	6	3	0	0	2	1	.167	R	R	6-5	195	8-7-81	2004	Shippenville, Pa.
Rodriguez, Jermy	5	2	3.42	37	0	0	0	55	47	21	21	24	48	.233	R	R	5-10	160	1-10-80	2002	Esperanza, D.R.
Rogers, Brian	6	8	4.55	25	25	0	0	142	163	76	72	44	120	.287	R	R	6-4	190	7-17-82	2003	Marietta, Ga.
Ronz, Kenon	2	6	4.87	52	0	0	0	57	48	31	31	13	58	.223	L	L	5-11	185	4-30-81	2003	Scottsdale, Ariz.
Santo, Brian	3	4	2.77	45	0	0	1	62	65	27	19	25	58	.270	R	R	6-8	240	10-26-80	2003	Oberlin, Ohio
Steinborn, Chris	8	11	3.99	27	27	3	0	160	173	94	71	37	105	.277	L	L	6-4	210	3-23-82	2002	Akron, Ohio
Tata, Jordan	8	11	3.35	28	28	1	0	166	167	77	62	68	116	.266	R	R	6-6	220	9-20-81	2003	Dallas, Texas
Tomey, Anthony	2	3	2.72	41	0	0	4	50	35	15	15	37	61	.200	R	R	6-4	245	8-17-81	2003	Northville, Mich.
Vasquez, Matt	14	6	3.64	27	27	0	0	168	156	73	68	34	120	.245	R	R	6-3	205	6-7-82	2003	Santa Barbara, Calif.
Zell, Daniel	5	4	2.27	30	6	0	2	75	69	23	19	24	52	.254	L	L	6-5	210	11-27-81	2003	Cypress, Texas

FIELDING

Catcher	PCT	G	PO	A	E	DP	PB
Graham	.985	26	173	21	3	3	6
McIntyre	1.000	1	0	0	0	0	0
Sanchez	.988	74	493	74	7	2	8
Trezza	.979	48	293	38	7	5	4

First Base	PCT	G	PO	A	E	DP
Burgos	1.000	3	33	3	0	3
Doyle	1.000	2	6	3	0	0
Hunt	.992	131	1155	101	10	118
Kirkland	1.000	1	8	0	0	1
Piantek	.961	4	49	0	2	7

Second Base	PCT	G	PO	A	E	DP
Doyle	.971	10	13	21	1	5
Francia	.875	4	10	11	3	6
McIntyre	1.000	5	5	11	0	3
Rodland	.983	124	245	331	10	87

Third Base	PCT	G	PO	A	E	DP
Doyle	.889	2	0	8	1	1
Kirkland	.917	122	84	237	29	22
McIntyre	.833	19	15	20	7	7

Shortstop	PCT	G	PO	A	E	DP
Doyle	.909	6	6	14	2	3

	PCT	G	PO	A	E	DP
Francia	.942	92	171	280	28	68
Giarratano	.974	42	76	146	6	29
McIntyre	.909	5	5	15	2	3

Outfield	PCT	G	PO	A	E	DP
Blue	.981	128	260	1	5	0
Doyle	1.000	8	9	0	0	0
Flowers	1.000	6	14	0	0	0
Knoedler	.992	62	116	7	1	1
McIntyre	1.000	4	4	0	0	0
McKinney	.954	113	180	6	9	1
Reynolds	.833	4	5	0	1	0
Sabino	.970	99	186	8	6	4

ONEONTA TIGERS

Short-Season Class A

NEW YORK-PENN LEAGUE

BATTING	AVG	G	AB	R	H	2B	3B	HR	RBI	BB	SO	SB	CS	OBP	SLG	B	T	HT	WT	DOB	1st Yr	Resides
Amezquita, Octavio	.296	23	71	7	21	1	0	1	9	2	6	2	2	.333	.352	R	R	6-0	175	3-11-82	2004	Stockton, Calif.
Barnes, Justin	.205	32	73	9	15	0	0	4	10	1	25	2	1	.224	.370	R	R	6-3	210	10-13-84	2003	Gallion, Ala.
Castro, Francisco	.221	66	231	26	51	3	3	0	10	19	58	17	10	.280	.260	B	R	5-10	170	6-13-83	2001	Santo Domingo, D.R.
Colvin, Brooks	.260	64	235	28	61	7	0	1	15	21	53	10	6	.327	.302	R	R	5-10	175	12-11-81	2004	O'Fallon, Mo.
Dlugach, Brent	.213	47	183	17	39	7	2	1	12	8	59	5	4	.256	.290	R	R	6-4	200	3-3-83	2004	Germantown, Tenn.
Flowers, Bo	.280	66	246	38	69	7	6	4	26	19	65	16	9	.341	.407	R	R	6-0	190	11-12-83	2002	Maywood, Ill.
Frazier, Jeff	.304	20	79	15	24	5	1	1	13	9	11	2	1	.387	.430	R	R	6-4	215	12-21-80	2004	Toms River, N.J.
Graham, Andrew	.280	8	25	0	7	2	0	0	3	1	2	0	0	.308	.360	R	R	6-4	215	4-27-82	2003	Sydney, Australia
Justice, Justin	.216	69	259	30	56	14	7	3	25	12	108	2	2	.262	.359	L	L	6-0	175	2-19-85	2004	Leesburg, Fla.
Llamas, Juan	.303	74	284	38	86	20	4	7	55	16	27	11	7	.343	.475	R	R	6-1	160	6-24-80	1998	Cartagena, Columbia
McRae, Aaron	.185	22	54	4	10	4	0	0	6	2	20	0	0	.262	.259	L	R	6-2	205	4-11-80	2003	Surrey, B.C.
Mendez, Rafael	.220	70	246	18	54	17	1	2	29	18	88	10	6	.281	.321	R	R	6-0	200	4-24-84	2002	Caguas, P.R.
Parrish, Matt	.136	20	59	3	8	1	1	0	3	1	26	1	1	.164	.186	R	R	5-11	205	8-25-82	2004	Yorba Linda, Calif.
Roa, Joel	.196	18	46	3	9	3	0	1	2	2	23	0	0	.229	.326	R	R	6-0	170	1-2-84	2001	Santo Domingo, D.R.
Ryan, Dusty	.274	54	157	20	43	11	1	4	26	24	52	6	4	.369	.433	R	R	6-3	200	9-2-84	2004	Merced, Calif.
Sovie, Robbie	.095	10	21	3	2	0	0	0	1	1	1	0	0	.174	.095	R	R	6-1	180	11-24-83	2002	Macon, Ga.
Tulk, Robbie	.220	51	150	21	33	10	3	1	11	15	48	3	3	.299	.347	L	R	5-11	180	7-5-81	2004	Davis, Calif.
Williams, Matt	.197	39	71	11	14	3	0	1	4	9	26	7	4	.296	.282	B	R	6-2	173	11-18-83	2001	Los Angeles, Calif.

GAMES BY POSITION: C—Barnes 23, Graham 8, McRae 3, Roa 18, Ryan 44. **1B**—Llamas 4, McRae 1, Mendez 70. **2B**—Amezquita 8, Castro 64, Colvin 6, Williams 3. **3B**—Colvin 12, Llamas 63. **SS**—Amezquita 7, Colvin 22, Dlugach 47. **OF**—Flowers 65, Frazier 17, Justice 68, McRae 1, Parrish 21, Sovie 7, Tulk 36, Williams 24.

PITCHING	W	L	ERA	G	GS	CG	SV	IP	H	R	ER	BB	SO	AVG	B	T	HT	WT	DOB	1st Yr	Resides
Bumstead, Nate	3	1	2.03	11	9	0	0	58	47	21	13	15	75	.218	R	R	6-2	210	5-5-82	2004	Las Vegas, Nev.
Carmosino, Dominic	0	0	5.23	6	1	0	0	10	10	8	6	12	6	.250	L	L	6-2	230	7-28-82	2004	Cincinnati, Ohio
Clelland, Ed	5	0	1.90	26	0	0	3	43	42	14	9	13	38	.264	L	L	6-0	165	6-27-82	2004	Pasadena, Calif.
Contreras, Manuel	1	2	9.00	5	0	0	0	8	21	8	8	1	7	.500	R	R	6-0	170	3-20-81	2002	Villa Altagracia, D.R.
Figueroa, Juan	1	2	5.68	9	0	0	1	13	10	8	8	17	14	.208	R	R	6-0	190	10-18-81	2001	San Juan, P.R.
Jacobson, Tyler	1	0	3.25	19	0	0	1	28	22	11	10	7	17	.216	R	R	6-2	205	5-5-83	2004	Sumner, Wash.
Jurrjens, Jair	1	5	5.31	7	7	0	0	39	50	25	23	10	31	.313	R	R	6-1	160	1-29-86	2003	Curacao, Curacao
Kauten, Josh	2	5	3.92	12	12	1	0	64	61	41	28	16	43	.247	R	R	6-4	210	4-5-82	2004	Vinton, Iowa
Konecny, Dan	3	7	4.02	14	9	0	0	54	61	31	24	20	46	.284	R	R	6-4	210	9-5-81	2004	Ripon, Wis.
Kown, Andrew	1	2	2.85	9	9	0	0	41	40	19	13	13	37	.253	L	R	6-7	210	10-7-82	2004	Marietta, Ga.
Lewis, Lavon	1	5	4.90	12	12	0	0	61	61	37	33	27	39	.263	R	R	6-3	185	12-17-83	2003	Warrensburg, Mo.
Lyons, Tom	1	1	2.61	2	2	0	0	10	11	6	3	5	10	.268	R	R	6-2	200	3-22-83	2001	Downers Grove, Ill.
Mahoney, Collin	1	0	4.94	21	0	0	2	31	34	24	17	23	31	.297	R	R	6-4	245	12-26-82	2004	Patterson, N.Y.

PITCHING	W	L	ERA	G	GS	CG	SV	IP	H	R	ER	BB	SO	AVG	B	T	HT	WT	DOB	1st Yr	Resides
Martinez, Cristhian	1	0	2.08	2	2	0	0	13	9	3	3	1	12	.200	R	R	6-1	160	3-6-82	2003	San Cristobol, D.R.
Myers, Damien	5	1	2.16	20	0	0	3	42	33	16	10	18	48	.214	L	L	6-0	180	11-3-80	2002	New York, N.Y.
Pender, Matt	1	1	2.16	6	0	0	1	8	5	5	2	6	9	.179	R	R	6-5	210	6-11-81	2002	Kathleen, Ga.
Peralta, Tony	3	0	1.80	22	0	0	0	40	24	8	8	13	38	.173	L	L	6-2	187	9-13-83	2004	West Orange, N.J.
Perez, Ezequil	2	2	3.44	23	0	0	5	34	35	14	13	15	26	.265	R	R	6-1	185	9-10-81	2003	San Juan, P.R.
Rainwater, Josh	0	6	4.22	11	11	0	0	49	46	28	23	35	52	.253	R	R	6-2	220	4-9-85	2004	De Ridder, La.
Righter, Matt	0	1	4.43	14	0	0	0	22	23	15	11	10	13	.271	R	R	6-5	195	8-7-81	2004	Shippenville, Pa.

GULF COAST LEAGUE

ORGANIZATION STATISTICS

BATTING	AVG	G	AB	R	H	2B	3B	HR	RBI	BB	SO	SB	CS	SLG	OBP	B	T	HT	WT	DOB	1st Yr	Resides
Berry, Vince	.159	24	63	7	10	0	0	1	8	9	31	1	1	.206	.284	R	R	5-9	170	9-1-83	2004	Cincinnati, Ohio
Collet, Cody	.194	17	36	2	7	2	0	0	1	2	15	1	1	.250	.237	R	R	6-0	195	1-22-85	2003	Newbury Park, Calif.
De Leon, Santo	.273	38	139	14	38	8	3	1	15	5	30	1	0	.396	.308	R	R	6-2	175	11-1-83	2003	Azua, D.R.
Foster, Jordan	.213	19	61	4	13	4	0	1	9	5	12	2	0	.328	.273	R	R	6-1	205	10-19-81	2004	Arlington, Texas
Gil, Luis	.243	23	74	7	18	1	1	1	12	6	20	3	0	.324	.309	R	R	6-1	170	2-12-84	2002	Castillo, D.R.
Grullon, Leonardo	.217	48	175	18	38	7	3	3	20	3	33	9	2	.343	.253	R	R	6-3	210	5-8-82	2004	Tampa, Fla.
Kelly, Donald	.400	3	10	2	4	0	0	0	0	0	2	1	0	.400	.400	L	R	6-4	190	2-15-80	2001	Pittsburgh, Pa.
Kropf, Michael	.208	23	53	5	11	2	0	1	6	7	10	2	0	.302	.302	S	R	6-5	230	11-11-81	2004	Roswell, Ga.
Laster, Jeramy	.242	43	149	23	36	6	4	4	17	17	63	10	1	.416	.317	R	R	6-1	185	4-5-85	2003	Nashville, Tenn.
Lee, Josh	.228	38	114	14	26	2	0	3	10	18	39	1	1	.325	.338	L	R	6-4	220	9-13-82	2004	Abilene, Texas
Linares, Miguel	.236	44	148	16	35	2	1	0	10	13	36	4	1	.264	.302	R	R	6-2	180	12-16-83	2004	Santo Domingo, D.R.
McIntyre, Nick	.125	5	16	1	2	1	0	0	2	1	3	0	0	.188	.176	S	R	5-10	185	3-11-81	2003	Lafayette, Ind.
Middleton, Cory	.234	43	145	15	34	5	1	4	10	5	32	2	3	.366	.288	R	R	6-1	185	10-3-85	2004	Pensacola, Fla.
Miller, Cole	.269	40	130	14	35	4	1	5	16	5	37	3	2	.431	.292	R	R	5-11	200	10-20-84	2004	Yreka, Calif.
Parrish, Anthony	.264	25	87	16	23	5	0	2	14	15	23	4	2	.391	.393	R	R	5-11	205	8-25-82	2004	Yorba Linda, Calif.
Peeples, Jamaal	.205	30	44	4	9	0	0	0	3	4	24	4	1	.205	.286	L	R	6-1	210	8-28-86	2004	Philadelphia, Miss.
Roa, Joel	.167	3	6	1	1	1	0	0	2	0	2	0	0	.333	.167	R	R	6-0	170	1-2-84	2001	Santo Domingo, D.R.
Roberts, Lionel	.207	19	58	2	12	1	0	1	5	3	29	0	0	.276	.242	R	R	6-3	290	5-9-86	2004	New Orleans, La.
Saba, Anthony	.176	15	34	3	6	1	1	0	4	4	12	0	1	.265	.300	R	R	6-0	180	6-5-85	2002	San Cristobal, D.R.
Skelton, James	.140	23	43	3	6	1	0	0	2	7	11	0	0	.163	.260	L	R	5-11	165	10-28-85	2004	West Covina, Calif.
Soto, Maximo	.228	39	101	15	23	2	1	3	9	10	38	0	1	.356	.304	R	R	6-3	210	7-16-82	2002	San Pedro de Macoris, D.R.
Timm, Brandon	.232	41	125	21	29	3	1	0	12	17	36	7	1	.272	.329	R	R	6-2	200	12-4-84	2004	Broken Arrow, Okla.
Young, Stephen	.281	42	153	27	43	4	1	2	14	22	17	9	3	.359	.399	S	R	5-9	165	4-9-82	2004	North Hills, Calif.

GAMES BY POSITION: C—Collet 14, Kropf 18, Miller 31, Roa 3, Skelton 21. **1B**—Lee 36, Roberts 9, Soto 26. **2B**—Gil 4, Linares 15, McIntyre 4, Roberts 1, Young 41. **3B**—De Leon 36, Middleton 28. **SS**—Gil 19, Kelly 3, Linares 29, McIntyre 2, Middleton 13. **OF**—Berry 24, Foster 10, Grullon 46, Laster 41, Parrish 24, Peeples 23, Saba 9, Timm 29, Young 1.

PITCHING	W	L	ERA	G	GS	CG	SV	IP	H	R	ER	BB	SO	AVG	B	T	HT	WT	DOB	1st Yr	Resides
Bierd, Randor	1	3	2.78	11	1	0	0	32	23	11	10	5	39	.196	R	R	6-4	190	3-14-84	2003	Santo Domingo, D.R.
Caraballo, Jesse	0	3	4.18	16	1	0	0	32	27	16	15	18	24	.225	R	R	6-1	190	7-17-86	2003	San Cristobal, D.R.
Carmosino, Dominic	2	6	6.41	11	0	0	0	20	18	15	14	11	28	.236	L	L	6-4	220	7-28-82	2004	Cincinnati, Ohio
Cruz, Rhinel	0	1	4.78	16	0	0	0	32	37	20	17	19	26	.298	R	R	6-2	165	11-1-86	2004	Santo Domingo, D.R.
Fragaso, Jose	3	3	3.07	23	0	0	1	29	25	14	10	12	33	.227	R	R	6-0	170	11-12-84	2003	Santiago, D.R.
French, Luke	1	3	2.74	11	10	0	0	49	43	21	15	19	49	.233	L	L	6-4	220	9-13-85	2004	Littleton, Colo.
Garcia, Felipe	2	0	0.39	14	0	0	2	23	12	2	1	9	22	.162	R	R	5-11	160	9-20-82	2001	San Pedro de Macoris, D.R.
Harper, Landon	2	0	2.13	7	0	0	0	13	11	4	3	3	12	.239	R	R	6-1	210	2-21-82	2004	Hays, Kan.
Hensen, Brian	0	0	0.00	2	0	0	0	5	2	0	0	0	3	.117	L	L	6-4	170	8-12-82	2004	Clemson, S.C.
Jurrjens, Jair	4	2	2.27	6	6	2	0	40	25	16	10	10	39	.171	R	R	6-1	160	1-29-86	2003	Willemstad, Curacao
Pender, Matt	0	0	0.00	1	0	0	0	1	2	0	0	2	2	.400	R	R	6-5	210	6-11-81	2002	Kathleen, Ga.
Perdomo, Orlando	1	6	7.18	12	8	0	1	36	47	36	29	22	36	.307	R	R	6-0	160	5-3-84	2002	Ciudad Ojeda, Venez.
Pickford, Troy	0	0	0.00	3	3	0	0	6	2	0	0	0	9	.100	R	R	6-8	220	8-9-79	2002	Fresno, Calif.
Righter, Matt	0	0	3.86	2	0	0	0	2	3	1	1	0	3	.333	R	R	6-5	195	8-7-81	2004	Shippenville, Pa.
Santos, Adriano	3	4	4.96	12	10	0	0	49	61	36	27	21	41	.303	R	R	6-2	170	9-8-84	2004	Bani, D.R.
Sborz, Jay	1	4	4.48	12	12	0	0	60	52	32	30	44	62	.230	R	R	6-4	210	1-24-85	2003	Riverview, Fla.
Trahern, Dallas	1	2	0.59	7	6	0	0	31	22	8	2	7	24	.192	R	R	6-3	190	11-29-85	2004	Owasso, Okla.
Vasquez, Sendy	2	2	5.46	17	2	0	3	28	29	19	17	21	32	.266	S	R	6-1	160	8-10-82	2003	Hato Mayor Del Rey, D.R.
Wilkins, Philip	2	2	5.47	13	1	0	0	26	28	17	16	12	28	.269	R	R	6-2	200	8-29-82	2004	Winnsboro, S.C.

FLORIDA MARLINS

BY MIKE BERARDINO

The Marlins achieved something in 2004 that they had never done before: a second straight winning season.

However, unlike the only other two winning seasons in club history, they did not win a World Series. They

didn't even return to the playoffs, a great disappointment despite a significant retooling that cost them Ivan Rodriguez, Derrek Lee and Mark Redman in the offseason.

Injuries and inconsistency held back the Marlins, who nonetheless held at least a share of first place in the National League East for all but four days through the end of June. Eventually, the Atlanta Braves blew past them as holes in the Marlins' bullpen and limitations in the offense undercut manager Jack McKeon's first full season in the dugout.

Valued setup man Chad Fox was lost for the year on April 28 with an elbow injury, leaving closer import Armando Benitez to shoulder a heavier burden than expected. Benitez, pitching on a one-year contract, thrived nonetheless, nailing down a club-record 47 saves.

In an effort to replace Fox, the Marlins acquired former closer Billy Koch from the White Sox in mid-June. Control problems kept Koch from being effective in his new role and locale, however, and eventually forced the Marlins to make a blockbuster deal with the Dodgers on July 30.

In an effort to bolster their catching and setup spots, the Marlins sent righthander Brad Penny, first baseman Hee Seop Choi and Double-A lefthander Bill Murphy, their only Futures Game participant, to the Dodgers for catcher Paul Lo Duca, reliever Guillermo Mota and right fielder Juan Encarnacion.

The Marlins briefly caught fire after the trade, pulling within a game of the wild-card lead in early September.

Carl Pavano

Joe Dillon

PLAYERS of the YEAR

MAJOR LEAGUE: Carl Pavano, rhp

Pavano anchored a staff that was depleted during the 2004 season, due to injuries and trades, and blossomed in his role as a No. 1 starter, putting up Cy Young-caliber numbers. Pavano went 18-8, 3.00 in 222 innings, upping his value heading into free agency.

MINOR LEAGUE: Joe Dillon, 3b

Dillon did not play professional baseball in 2003, opting to return to Texas Tech, his alma mater, as an assistant coach. Signed in the offseason as a free agent, Dillon responded by hitting a combined .328-39-117 in 520 at-bats between Double-A Carolina and Triple-A Albuquerque.

However, multiple hurricanes hit the state and forced the Marlins to play three doubleheaders in an 11-day span, effectively wiping out their pitching staff.

Rookie righthander Logan Kensing was recalled from Class A Jupiter to make three key September starts. He went 0-3, 12.65, and the Marlins never recovered. They lost 14 of their last 21 games to finish in third place in the NL East.

Aside from Benitez, the biggest bright spot was the work of righthander Carl Pavano, who won a career-best 18 games and made the all-star team for the first time. Sent to the bullpen for the start of the playoffs in 2003, Pavano emerged as the workhorse ace of a ballyhooed staff.

The successful comeback of righthander A.J. Burnett from reconstructive elbow surgery was another high point. Burnett was activated in early June, a little more than 13 months after having the surgery, and soon was back to throwing in the high 90s with regularity.

He established a regular-season club mark with 14 strikeouts in an Aug. 29 game against Colorado. However, Burnett missed nearly three weeks after suffering elbow inflammation following a Sept. 12 start in Chicago.

World Series MVP Josh Beckett suffered through another year of starts and stops, spending three different stints on the disabled list, including two for blister-related problems.

In the minors, the reigning Organization of the Year didn't produce the way it had in 2003. The system went a combined 63 games under .500, although 39 of those came courtesy of the overmatched Greensboro Bats, who went 50-89 in the South Atlantic League.

Of the top five affiliates, only Double-A Carolina (73-66) had a winning record.

ORGANIZATION LEADERS

BATTING

*AVG	Larry Sutton, Albuquerque	.370
R	Joe Dillon, Albuquerque/Carolina	122
H	Joe Dillon, Albuquerque/Carolina	171
TB	Joe Dillon, Albuquerque/Carolina	348
2B	Joe Dillon, Albuquerque/Carolina	46
3B	Joe Dillon, Albuquerque/Carolina	7
HR	Joe Dillon, Albuquerque/Carolina	39
RBI	Joe Dillon, Albuquerque/Carolina	117
BB	Josh Willingham, Carolina	91
SO	Jai Miller, Greensboro	163
SB	Billy Hall, Albuquerque/Carolina	40
*OBP	Larry Sutton, Albuquerque	.472
*SLG	Larry Sutton, Albuquerque	.682

PITCHING

W	Nic Ungs, Carolina	11
	Ross Wolf, Jupiter	11
L	Jon Nickerson, Greensboro/Jamestown	13
#ERA	Ross Wolf, Jupiter	2.60
G	Randy Messenger, Carolina	58
CG	Yorman Bazardo, Jupiter	2
	Aaron Small, Albuquerque	2
SV	Randy Messenger, Carolina	21
IP	Peter Bauer, Albuquerque/Carolina	162
BB	Bill Murphy, Carolina	59
SO	Adam Bostick, Greensboro	163

*Minimum 250 at-bats #Minimum 75 innings

FLORIDA MARLINS

Manager: Jack McKeon.

2004 Record: 83-79, .512 (3rd, NL East).

BATTING	AVG	G	AB	R	H	2B	3B	HR	RBI	BB	SO	SB	CS	OBP	SLG	B	T	HT	WT	DOB	1st Yr	Resides
Aguila, Chris	.222	29	45	10	10	2	1	3	5	2	12	0	0	.255	.511	R	R	5-11	180	2-23-79	1997	Reno, Nev.
Cabrera, Miguel	.294	160	603	101	177	31	1	33	112	68	148	5	2	.366	.512	R	R	6-2	185	4-18-83	2000	Maracay, Venez.
Castillo, Luis	.291	150	564	91	164	12	7	2	47	75	68	21	4	.373	.348	S	R	5-11	190	9-12-75	1994	Santo Domingo, D.R.
Castro, Ramon	.135	32	96	9	13	3	0	3	8	11	30	0	0	.231	.260	R	R	6-3	235	3-1-76	1994	Vega Baja, P.R.
Choi Hee Seop	.270	95	281	48	76	16	1	15	40	52	78	1	0	.388	.495	L	L	6-5	240	3-16-79	1999	Kwang Ju, Korea
Conine, Jeff	.280	140	521	55	146	35	1	14	83	48	78	5	5	.340	.432	R	R	6-1	220	6-27-66	1988	Weston, Fla.
Cordero, Wil	.197	27	66	6	13	3	0	1	6	3	19	1	0	.239	.288	R	R	6-2	215	10-3-71	1988	Westlake, Ohio
Easley, Damion	.238	98	223	26	53	20	1	9	43	24	36	4	1	.331	.457	R	R	5-11	190	11-11-69	1989	Glendale, Ariz.
Encarnacion, Juan	.238	49	160	21	38	12	1	3	19	17	33	2	1	.320	.381	R	R	6-3	215	3-8-76	1994	Santo Domingo, D.R.
2-team (86 L.A.)	.236	135	484	63	114	30	2	16	62	38	86	5	4	.299	.405							
Gonzalez, Alex	.232	159	561	67	130	30	3	23	79	27	126	3	1	.269	.419	R	R	6-0	200	2-15-77	1994	Miami Lakes, Fla.
Harris, Lenny	.211	79	95	7	20	5	0	1	17	3	8	0	0	.232	.295	L	R	5-10	220	10-28-64	1984	Miami, Fla.
Lo Duca, Paul	.258	52	186	27	48	11	1	3	31	14	22	2	1	.314	.376	R	R	5-10	210	4-12-72	1993	San Antonio, Texas
2-team (91 L.A.)	.286	143	535	68	153	29	2	13	80	36	49	4	5	.338	.421							
Lowell, Mike	.293	158	598	87	175	44	1	27	85	64	77	5	1	.365	.505	R	R	6-3	215	2-24-74	1995	Miami, Fla.
Mordecai, Mike	.226	69	84	7	19	3	0	1	5	6	18	0	1	.278	.298	R	R	5-10	185	12-13-67	1989	Kennesaw, Ga.
Nunez, Abraham	.172	58	64	9	11	1	1	1	5	9	21	1	2	.274	.266	S	R	6-3	210	2-5-77	1997	Haina, D.R.
Pierre, Juan	.326	162	678	100	221	22	12	3	49	45	35	45	24	.373	.407	L	L	6-0	180	8-14-77	1998	Lone Tree, Colo.
Redmond, Mike	.256	81	246	19	63	15	0	2	25	14	28	1	0	.310	.341	R	R	5-11	210	5-5-71	1993	Veradale, Wash.
Sutton, Larry	.200	8	5	0	1	0	0	0	1	1	2	0	0	.333	.200	L	L	6-0	195	5-14-70	1992	Overland Park, Kan.
Treanor, Matt	.236	29	55	7	13	2	0	1	4	13	0	0	.311	.273	R	R	6-2	220	3-3-76	1994	Anaheim, Calif.
Willingham, Josh	.200	12	25	2	5	0	0	1	1	4	8	0	0	.310	.320	R	R	6-1	200	2-17-79	2000	Florence, Ala.

PITCHING	W	L	ERA	G	GS	CG	SV	IP	H	R	ER	BB	SO	AVG	B	T	HT	WT	DOB	1st Yr	Resides
Beckett, Josh	9	9	3.79	26	26	1	0	157	137	72	66	54	152	.235	R	R	6-5	220	5-15-80	2000	Spring, Texas
Benitez, Armando	2	2	1.29	64	0	0	47	70	36	11	10	21	62	.152	R	R	6-4	230	11-3-72	1991	San Pedro de Macoris, D.R.
Borland, Toby	1	1	5.40	18	0	0	0	18	18	11	11	11	12	.254	R	R	6-6	214	5-29-69	1988	Quitman, La.
Bump, Nate	2	4	5.01	50	2	0	0	74	84	46	41	32	44	.297	R	R	6-2	180	7-24-76	1998	Jupiter, Fla.
Burnett, A.J.	7	6	3.68	20	19	1	0	120	102	50	49	38	113	.231	R	R	6-4	230	1-3-77	1995	Miramar, Fla.
Fox, Chad	0	1	6.75	12	0	0	0	11	9	8	8	8	17	.225	R	R	6-3	190	9-3-70	1992	Houston, Texas
Gracesqui, Franklyn	0	1	11.25	7	0	0	1	4	6	5	5	3	1	.333	S	L	6-5	210	8-20-79	1998	New York, N.Y.
Howard, Ben	1	1	5.50	31	0	0	0	38	37	23	23	21	33	.261	R	R	6-0	220	1-15-79	1997	Jackson, Tenn.
Kensing, Logan	0	3	9.88	5	3	0	0	14	19	15	15	9	7	.345	R	R	6-1	185	7-3-82	2003	Boerne, Texas
Koch, Billy	1	2	3.51	23	0	0	0	26	21	10	10	20	25	.226	R	R	6-3	210	12-14-74	1997	Clearwater, Fla.
Manzanillo, Josias	3	3	6.12	26	0	0	1	32	38	24	22	15	27	.292	R	R	6-0	200	10-16-67	1984	Hyde Park, Mass.
Mota, Guillermo	1	4	4.81	26	0	0	3	34	24	18	18	10	33	.200	R	R	6-4	210	7-25-73	1993	San Pedro de Macoris, D.R.
2-team (52 L.A.)	9	8	3.07	78	0	0	4	97	75	33	33	37	85	.218							
Neu, Mike	0	0	4.50	1	0	0	0	4	5	2	2	2	2	.313	S	R	5-10	175	3-9-78	1999	Napa, Calif.
Oliver, Darren	2	3	6.44	18	8	0	0	59	75	44	42	17	33	.319	R	L	6-2	220	10-6-70	1988	Southlake, Texas
Pavano, Carl	18	8	3.00	31	31	2	0	222	212	80	74	49	139	.253	R	R	6-5	235	1-8-76	1994	Palm Beach Gardens, Fla.
Penny, Brad	8	8	3.15	21	21	0	0	131	124	50	46	39	105	.249	R	R	6-4	250	5-24-78	1996	Broken Arrow, Okla.
Perisho, Matt	5	3	4.40	66	0	0	0	47	45	23	23	26	42	.247	L	L	6-0	200	6-8-75	1993	Chandler, Ariz.
Phelps, Tommy	1	1	4.76	19	4	0	0	34	34	20	18	12	28	.268	L	L	6-3	190	3-4-74	1993	Tampa, Fla.
Seanez, Rudy	3	1	2.74	23	0	0	0	23	18	7	7	8	25	.212	R	R	5-11	200	10-20-68	1986	El Centro, Calif.
Small, Aaron	0	0	8.27	7	0	0	0	16	24	15	15	7	8	.343	R	R	6-5	220	11-23-71	1989	Loudon, Tenn.
Tejera, Michael	0	1	18.00	2	2	0	0	4	6	8	8	6	3	.375	L	L	5-9	192	10-18-76	1995	Miami, Fla.
Valdez, Ismael	9	4	4.50	11	11	0	0	56	61	30	28	18	30	.277	R	R	6-4	220	8-21-73	1991	Victoria, Mexico
2-team (23 San Diego)	14	9	5.19	34	31	1	0	170	202	105	98	49	67	.294							
Wayne, Justin	3	3	5.79	19	1	0	0	33	35	24	21	18	20	.282	R	R	6-3	205	4-16-79	2000	Jupiter, Fla.
Weathers, David	1	0	2.70	8	2	0	0	17	13	5	5	7	10	.232	R	R	6-3	230	9-25-69	1988	Loretto, Tenn.
3-team (32 N.Y./26 Hou.)	7	7	4.15	66	2	0	0	82	85	44	38	35	61	.274							
Willis, Dontrelle	10	11	4.02	32	32	2	0	197	210	99	88	61	139	.273	L	L	6-4	200	1-12-82	2000	Alameda, Calif.

FIELDING

Catcher	PCT	G	PO	A	E	DP	PB
Castro	.990	31	192	12	2	2	0
Lo Duca	.997	49	330	23	1	5	5
Mordecai	1.000	1	9	0	0	0	0
Redmond	.996	79	488	34	2	7	4
Treanor	.976	27	117	6	3	0	0
Willingham	.938	5	15	0	1	0	2

First Base	PCT	G	PO	A	E	DP
Choi	.990	89	720	41	8	59
Conine	.992	57	473	50	4	47
Cordero	.991	13	105	4	1	10
Easley	.984	18	119	8	2	16
Sutton	1.000	1	1	0	0	0

Second Base	PCT	G	PO	A	E	DP
Castillo	.991	148	275	406	6	97
Easley	.965	25	29	53	3	11
Mordecai	.800	4	2	2	1	0

Third Base	PCT	G	PO	A	E	DP
Easley	1.000	6	4	11	0	0
Lowell	.982	154	117	272	7	30
Harris	.000	3	0	0	0	0
Mordecai	.929	19	10	16	2	3

Shortstop	PCT	G	PO	A	E	DP
Easley	.968	15	6	24	1	3
Gonzalez	.976	158	225	425	16	99

	PCT	G	PO	A	E	DP
Mordecai	1.000	3	5	8	0	4
Outfield	**PCT**	**G**	**PO**	**A**	**E**	**DP**
Aguila	.909	20	19	1	2	0
Cabrera	.968	158	262	13	9	1
Conine	.994	83	174	5	1	2
Cordero	1.000	3	5	0	0	0
Easley	.909	5	10	0	1	0
Encarnacion	.980	48	96	2	2	0
Harris	1.000	14	12	0	0	0
Nunez	1.000	48	43	0	0	0
Pierre	.995	162	364	3	2	1
Willingham	1.000	3	6	0	0	0

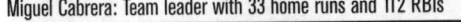

| Miguel Cabrera: Team leader with 33 home runs and 112 RBIs | Juan Pierre: Second in NL with 45 steals |

MORRIS FOSTOFF

MORRIS FOSTOFF

Miguel Cabrera: Team leader with 33 home runs and 112 RBIs

Juan Pierre: Second in NL with 45 steals

FARM SYSTEM

Director, Player Development: Marc DelPiano.

Class	Farm Team	League	W	L	Pct.	Finish*	Manager	Affiliate Since
AAA	Albuquerque (N.M.) Isotopes	Pacific Coast	67	77	.465	12th (16)	Tracy Woodson	2003
AA	Carolina (Zebulon, N.C.) Mudcats	Southern	73	66	.525	t-2nd (10)	Ron Hassey	2003
High A	Jupiter (Fla.) Hammerheads	Florida State	64	71	.474	8th (12)	Luis Dorante	2002
Low A	Greensboro (N.C.) Bats	South Atlantic	50	89	.360	15th (16)	Steve Phillips	2003
SS A	Jamestown (N.Y.) Jammers	New York-Penn	30	45	.400	12th (14)	Benny Castillo	2002
Rookie	Jupiter (Fla.) Marlins	Gulf Coast	31	29	.517	t-6th (12)	Tim Cossins	1992

*Finish in overall standings (No. of teams in league)/Playoffs teams in **boldface**

ALBUQUERQUE ISOTOPES — Class AAA

PACIFIC COAST LEAGUE

BATTING	AVG	G	AB	R	H	2B	3B	HR	RBI	BB	SO	SB	CS	OBP	SLG	B	T	HT	WT	DOB	1st Yr	Resides
Aguila, Chris	.312	97	330	61	103	23	2	11	56	37	82	8	3	.380	.494	R	R	5-11	180	2-23-79	1997	Reno, Nev.
Ashby, Chris	.239	73	213	24	51	11	0	5	25	20	31	2	1	.304	.362	R	R	6-3	190	12-15-74	1993	Boca Raton, Fla.
Banks, Brian	.231	67	216	31	50	12	2	6	30	27	46	0	0	.319	.389	S	R	6-3	220	9-28-70	1993	Mesa, Ariz.
Christenson, Ryan	.264	65	227	43	60	16	4	2	17	34	45	8	2	.364	.396	R	R	6-0	190	3-28-74	1995	Apple Valley, Calif.
Colangelo, Mike	.325	97	292	64	95	27	2	16	73	45	66	0	3	.422	.596	R	R	6-1	180	10-22-76	1998	Dumfries, Va.
Dillon, Joe	.325	108	403	96	131	33	7	30	86	46	85	12	3	.400	.665	R	R	6-2	200	8-25-75	1997	Rockin, Calif.
Hall, Billy	.209	18	43	7	9	1	1	0	3	0	10	0	1	.209	.279	S	R	5-9	180	6-17-69	1991	Wichita, Kan.
Hooper, Kevin	.277	39	155	21	43	3	2	0	17	14	24	6	5	.335	.323	R	R	5-10	160	12-7-76	1999	Lawrence, Kan.
Jorgensen, Ryan	.259	61	201	20	52	11	0	8	29	10	51	0	0	.292	.433	R	R	6-2	200	5-4-79	2000	Kingwood, Texas
Nannini, Mike	.143	24	35	1	5	0	0	0	2	0	14	0	0	.167	.143	R	R	5-11	190	8-9-80	1998	Las Vegas, Nev.
Niles, Drew	.259	111	278	39	72	9	2	4	29	41	73	3	3	.355	.349	S	R	6-1	185	3-17-77	1998	Irmo, S.C.
Osik, Keith	.179	19	56	5	10	3	1	1	5	5	7	0	0	.254	.321	R	R	6-0	200	10-22-68	1990	Shoreham, N.Y.
Padgett, Matthew	.267	131	435	65	116	28	4	24	93	36	123	1	5	.325	.515	L	L	6-2	215	7-22-77	1998	Lexington, S.C.
Ryan, Rob	.150	17	60	7	9	1	2	0	3	7	9	1	1	.239	.233	L	L	5-11	190	6-24-73	1996	Renton, Wash.
2-team (55 N.O.)	.227	72	198	19	45	7	2	3	15	18	30	2	1	.300	.328							
Sutton, Larry	.370	91	308	70	114	31	1	21	71	59	61	3	1	.472	.682	L	L	6-0	195	5-14-70	1992	Overland Park, Kan.
Treanor, Matt	.258	62	198	32	51	8	0	8	38	33	44	2	0	.385	.419	R	R	6-2	220	3-3-76	1994	Anaheim, Calif.
Valdez, Wilson	.319	66	285	36	91	11	3	2	25	16	35	19	12	.357	.400	R	R	5-11	160	5-20-78	1997	Nizao, D.R.
Wathan, Derek	.302	106	414	74	125	26	5	10	47	33	74	15	10	.354	.461	S	R	6-3	190	12-13-76	1998	Blue Springs, Mo.
Wilson, Josh	.279	56	240	32	67	12	2	5	23	19	51	6	1	.337	.408	R	R	6-1	160	3-26-81	1999	Pittsburgh, Penn.
Wood, Jason	.245	102	375	44	92	21	2	8	49	40	74	2	1	.322	.376	R	R	6-1	200	12-16-69	1991	Fresno, Calif.

PITCHING	W	L	ERA	G	GS	CG	SV	IP	H	R	ER	BB	SO	AVG	B	T	HT	WT	DOB	1st Yr	Resides
Alvarez, Juan	2	3	5.87	48	0	0	1	54	75	38	35	19	42	.333	L	L	6-0	170	8-9-73	1995	Miami, Fla.
Ashby, Chris	0	0	9.45	5	3	0	0	7	10	7	7	2	2	.333	R	R	6-3	190	12-15-74	1993	Boca Raton, Fla.

PITCHING	W	L	ERA	G	GS	CG	SV	IP	H	R	ER	BB	SO	AVG	B	T	HT	WT	DOB	1st Yr	Resides
Baker, Ryan	0	0	0.00	1	1	0	0	3	3	0	0	1	1	.273	R	R	6-0	200	3-20-78	2000	Linthicum, Md.
Bauer, Peter	1	0	1.29	1	1	0	0	7	6	1	1	3	4	.240	L	R	6-7	250	11-6-78	2000	Hagerstown, Md.
Blank, Matt	4	8	6.44	34	23	1	1	138	180	105	99	47	75	.323	L	L	6-2	190	4-5-76	1997	Arlington, Texas
Borland, Toby	4	2	2.29	34	0	0	11	39	24	10	10	12	38	.182	R	R	6-6	214	5-29-69	1988	Quitman, La.
Bump, Nate	0	0	1.38	3	2	0	0	13	7	2	2	1	12	.159	R	R	6-2	180	7-24-76	1998	Jupiter, Fla.
Burnett, A.J.	0	0	10.80	1	1	0	0	3	7	4	4	2	6	.412	R	R	6-4	230	1-3-77	1995	Miramar, Fla.
Flannery, Mike	4	3	8.49	29	0	0	2	35	48	33	33	18	25	.333	R	R	6-1	195	9-20-79	2000	Collings Lakes, N.J.
Florie, Bryce	1	1	2.45	11	0	0	0	15	12	4	4	5	9	.231	R	R	5-11	195	5-21-70	1988	Goose Creek, S.C.
Flury, Patrick	0	1	13.00	9	0	0	0	9	15	13	13	4	6	.375	R	R	6-2	210	3-14-73	1993	Sparks, Nev.
Gaal, Bryan	1	0	23.14	4	0	0	0	5	11	12	12	2	4	.423	R	R	6-4	205	12-17-76	1999	Syracuse, N.Y.
Gracesqui, Franklyn	1	0	3.27	19	0	0	1	22	10	9	8	19	16	.139	S	L	6-5	210	8-20-79	1998	New York, N.Y.
Hartmann, Pete	0	1	8.07	25	0	0	0	29	40	28	26	11	29	.323	L	L	6-2	200	5-13-71	1993	Scottsdale, Ariz.
Howard, Ben	3	0	3.67	23	0	0	1	34	29	16	14	22	28	.228	R	R	6-0	220	1-15-79	1997	Jackson, Tenn.
Mahomes, Pat	0	4	7.29	16	0	0	0	21	31	19	17	9	15	.341	R	R	6-4	220	8-9-70	1988	Lindale, Texas
Manzanillo, Josias	0	1	5.25	11	0	0	5	12	15	8	7	1	9	.300	R	R	6-0	200	10-16-67	1984	Hyde Park, Mass.
McNutt, Mike	2	1	5.08	12	4	0	0	28	35	21	16	5	19	.292	R	R	6-2	190	10-18-79	2000	Cincinnati, Ohio
Michalak, Chris	1	1	6.35	17	1	0	0	34	44	24	24	15	20	.324	L	L	6-2	195	1-4-71	1993	Keller, Texas
Nannini, Mike	9	10	5.29	29	25	1	0	151	156	99	89	42	111	.264	R	R	5-11	190	8-9-80	1998	Las Vegas, Nev.
Neu, Mike	1	2	6.34	35	0	0	6	38	47	33	27	24	28	.303	S	R	5-10	175	3-9-78	1999	Napa, Calif.
Olsen, Kevin	3	3	4.37	10	10	0	0	56	58	30	27	13	47	.270	R	R	6-2	195	7-26-76	1998	Norco, Calif.
Sanders, Scott	3	10	7.90	20	20	0	0	98	152	90	86	29	72	.354	R	R	6-4	220	3-25-69	1990	Poway, Calif.
Small, Aaron	9	9	5.06	27	24	2	0	155	199	95	87	29	109	.315	R	R	6-5	220	11-23-71	1989	Loudon, Tenn.
Sodowsky, Clint	9	7	5.40	48	0	0	2	68	76	45	41	32	39	.292	L	R	6-4	220	7-13-72	1991	Lamont, Okla.
Tejera, Michael	8	4	3.97	22	19	0	0	113	109	56	50	39	88	.253	L	L	5-9	192	10-18-76	1995	Miami, Fla.
Wayne, Justin	1	5	6.58	13	13	0	0	66	82	53	48	34	43	.307	R	R	6-3	205	4-16-79	2000	Jupiter, Fla.
Westmoreland, Clay	0	0	5.14	5	0	0	0	7	4	4	4	8	6	.167	R	R	5-10	185	6-6-82	2004	Mesa, Ariz.

FIELDING

Catcher	PCT	G	PO	A	E	DP	PB
Ashby	.991	16	96	9	1	1	1
Jorgensen	.989	56	336	31	4	4	3
Osik	1.000	18	109	12	0	3	2
Treanor	.991	61	399	30	4	2	6

First Base	PCT	G	PO	A	E	DP
Ashby	.996	32	236	18	1	27
Banks	.991	15	98	10	1	16
Dillon	1.000	2	18	0	0	0
Niles	1.000	4	38	5	0	2
Sutton	.990	70	630	48	7	60
Wathan	1.000	3	13	5	0	0
Wood	.997	36	272	17	1	35

Second Base	PCT	G	PO	A	E	DP
Dillon	.956	25	57	51	5	17

	PCT	G	PO	A	E	DP
Hooper	.984	38	66	115	3	22
Niles	.982	48	95	128	4	34
Wathan	.984	42	79	106	3	23
Wood	1.000	7	20	20	0	5

Third Base	PCT	G	PO	A	E	DP
Dillon	.943	65	27	122	9	12
Hall	.950	9	3	16	1	3
Niles	.895	18	2	15	2	0
Wathan	1.000	17	6	34	0	5
Wood	.940	55	34	108	9	11

Shortstop	PCT	G	PO	A	E	DP
Hooper	1.000	3	1	5	0	0
Niles	1.000	14	22	38	0	6
Valdez	.982	65	108	221	6	51

	PCT	G	PO	A	E	DP
Wathan	.978	10	13	32	1	7
Wilson	.972	56	97	178	8	36

Outfield	PCT	G	PO	A	E	DP
Aguila	.986	106	199	8	3	1
Ashby	.929	12	13	0	1	0
Banks	.983	43	58	0	1	0
Christenson	.979	62	138	2	3	0
Colangelo	.979	71	85	10	2	0
Dillon	.935	27	38	5	3	1
Hall	1.000	4	2	0	0	0
Padgett	.990	116	196	8	2	3
Ryan	1.000	16	36	0	0	0
Sutton	1.000	5	4	0	0	0
Wathan	.985	38	62	2	1	0

CAROLINA MUDCATS — Class AA

SOUTHERN LEAGUE

BATTING	AVG	G	AB	R	H	2B	3B	HR	RBI	BB	SO	SB	CS	OBP	SLG	B	T	HT	WT	DOB	1st Yr	Resides
Alfonzo, Eliezer	.000	4	4	0	0	0	0	0	0	0	4	0	0	.000	.000	R	R	6-0	200	2-7-79	1996	Lecherias, Venez.
Ambres, Chip	.241	137	452	81	109	28	3	20	62	76	117	26	9	.352	.449	R	R	6-1	190	12-19-79	1999	Beaumont, Texas
Anderson, Dennis	.231	91	221	15	51	10	1	2	29	27	44	1	1	.315	.312	S	R	6-0	200	2-1-78	1999	Tucson, Ariz.
Arnerich, Tony	.000	1	2	0	0	0	0	0	0	0	2	0	0	.000	.000	R	R	6-0	190	12-24-79	2001	Santa Rosa, Calif.
Brown, Greg	.000	3	4	0	0	0	0	0	1	1	0	0	0	.333	.000	R	R	5-11	195	5-4-80	2003	Pembroke Pines, Fla.
Demarco, Matt	.273	106	359	47	98	24	2	4	45	20	51	1	5	.319	.384	L	R	5-10	160	1-24-80	1999	Clayton, N.J.
Dillon, Joe	.342	33	117	26	40	13	0	9	31	14	29	3	2	.426	.684	R	R	6-2	200	8-25-75	1997	Rockin, Calif.
Frazier, Charles	.179	24	67	5	12	2	0	1	4	1	19	3	2	.214	.254	R	R	6-3	185	7-6-80	1999	Toms River, N.J.
Goelz, Jimmy	.188	56	154	14	29	5	0	1	10	9	34	1	1	.233	.240	R	R	5-10	170	2-13-76	1998	St. James, N.Y.
Hall, Billy	.300	95	350	53	105	18	4	4	30	42	46	40	15	.375	.409	S	R	5-9	180	6-17-69	1991	Wichita, Kan.
Inglin, Jeff	.289	80	263	46	76	17	0	6	35	39	30	1	2	.389	.422	R	R	5-11	180	10-8-75	1996	Petaluma, Calif.
Kavourias, Jim	.111	18	54	3	6	1	0	1	3	3	26	0	0	.155	.185	R	R	6-4	230	10-4-79	2000	Strongsville, Ohio
Magness, Pat	.211	69	180	22	38	12	1	5	28	28	54	0	0	.314	.372	L	L	6-3	230	1-19-78	2000	Overland Park, Kan.
Minor, Ryan	.250	48	176	23	44	14	1	8	33	12	51	1	1	.304	.477	R	R	6-7	240	1-5-74	1996	Edmond, Okla.
Niles, Drew	.000	2	6	0	0	0	0	0	0	0	1	0	0	.000	.000	S	R	6-1	185	3-17-77	1998	Irmo, S.C.
Reed, Eric	.306	55	222	32	68	9	6	3	14	14	55	24	5	.345	.441	L	L	5-11	170	12-2-80	2002	College Station, Texas
Rohleder, Andy	.257	66	183	18	47	16	1	2	26	13	49	1	1	.315	.388	R	R	6-0	190	2-27-80	2002	Ferdinand, Ind.
Rundgren, Rex	.268	44	142	12	38	6	2	0	13	6	36	2	0	.307	.338	R	R	6-1	170	11-22-80	2001	Sacramento, Calif.
Ryan, Rob	.217	30	92	10	20	7	1	2	10	16	14	1	1	.348	.380	L	L	5-11	190	6-24-73	1996	Renton, Wash.
Shanks, James	.435	13	23	3	10	1	0	1	7	6	6	1	1	.533	.609	R	R	6-0	180	1-26-79	1998	Appling, Ga.
Stokes, Jason	.272	106	394	66	107	26	0	23	78	42	121	5	0	.345	.513	R	R	6-4	225	1-23-82	2001	Coppell, Texas
Tucker, Michael	.191	55	131	12	25	5	0	2	15	15	44	0	2	.277	.275	R	R	6-3	205	11-7-79	2001	Lakeland, Fla.
Willingham, Josh	.281	112	338	81	95	24	0	24	76	91	87	6	3	.449	.565	R	R	6-1	200	2-17-79	2000	Florence, Ala.
Wilson, Josh	.315	81	311	63	98	21	1	10	41	42	50	8	6	.396	.486	R	R	6-1	160	3-26-81	1999	Pittsburgh, Pa.

PITCHING	W	L	ERA	G	GS	CG	SV	IP	H	R	ER	BB	SO	AVG	B	T	HT	WT	DOB	1st Yr	Resides
Baker, Ryan	5	3	3.34	40	1	0	0	65	65	27	24	31	46	.265	R	R	6-0	200	3-20-78	2000	Linthicum, Md.
Bauer, Peter	5	10	4.35	27	25	0	0	155	161	83	75	40	103	.274	L	R	6-7	250	11-6-78	2000	Hagerstown, Md.
Belizario, Ronald	3	5	5.55	15	15	0	0	73	75	52	45	43	58	.270	R	R	6-2	150	12-31-82	2000	Aragua, Venez.
Cave, Kevin	0	4	5.73	20	0	0	6	22	23	14	14	15	19	.271	R	R	6-2	220	5-25-80	2001	Levittown, Pa.
Flannery, Mike	4	2	5.29	25	0	0	2	32	40	21	19	13	23	.301	R	R	6-1	195	9-20-79	2000	Collings Lakes, N.J.
Flury, Patrick	3	4	2.56	42	0	0	1	60	42	19	17	38	68	.198	R	R	6-2	210	3-14-73	1993	Sparks, Nev.
Fuell, Jerrod	0	1	4.15	17	0	0	1	22	18	10	10	6	17	.222	R	R	6-4	210	10-3-80	2001	Tucson, Ariz.
Fulchino, Jeff	6	5	4.47	17	17	0	0	91	93	45	45	37	84	.266	R	R	6-4	235	11-28-79	2001	Hollis, N.H.

PITCHING

PITCHING	W	L	ERA	G	GS	CG	SV	IP	H	R	ER	BB	SO	AVG	B	T	HT	WT	DOB	1st Yr	Resides
Gaal, Bryan	2	4	4.99	24	0	0	2	31	39	21	17	11	23	.312	R	R	6-4	205	12-17-76	1999	Syracuse, N.Y.
Grzecka, Casey	0	0	0.00	1	0	0	1	1	0	0	1	0	.250	R	R	6-2	200	11-12-79	2002	Laguna Niguel, Calif.
Hartman, Pete	1	0	1.17	5	0	0	0	8	6	1	1	3	12	.222	L	L	6-2	200	5-13-71	1993	Scottsdale, Ariz.
Hutchinson, Trevor	10	7	4.23	24	24	0	0	123	133	70	58	38	86	.281	R	R	6-5	220	10-8-79	2003	Irving, Texas
Iehl, Jason	1	0	3.14	4	3	0	0	14	13	5	5	10	7	.250	R	R	6-2	200	4-23-84	2002	Woodridge, Ill.
Lugo, Ruddy	0	1	4.91	8	1	0	0	15	16	10	8	9	6	.271	R	R	5-10	205	5-22-80	1999	Brooklyn, N.Y.
McNutt, Mike	4	1	4.89	24	5	0	0	57	51	33	31	23	53	.236	R	R	6-2	190	10-18-79	2000	Cincinnati, Ohio
Messenger, Randy	6	3	2.58	58	0	0	21	66	67	21	20	29	71	.262	R	R	6-2	220	8-13-81	1999	Sparks, Nev.
Moser, Todd	0	0	6.75	20	0	0	0	27	29	20	20	15	17	.279	L	L	6-5	180	10-28-76	1999	Davie, Fla.
Murphy, Bill	6	4	4.08	20	20	0	0	104	80	48	47	59	113	.215	L	L	6-0	190	5-9-81	2002	Riverside, Calif.
Pearson, Jason	0	1	1.88	16	0	0	0	14	15	5	3	4	14	.250	L	L	6-2	200	12-29-75	1998	Freeport, Ill.
Rodriguez, Joe	0	0	3.18	7	0	0	0	6	6	2	2	5	4	.261	L	L	6-1	200	12-18-74	1997	Cayey, P.R.
Russ, James	0	0	0.00	1	0	0	0	1	0	0	0	1	1	.000	R	R	6-4	210	10-24-80	2003	Concord, N.C.
Sodowsky, Clint	1	2	10.80	8	0	0	0	10	18	12	12	6	8	.400	L	R	6-4	200	7-13-72	1991	Lamont, Okla.
Strelitz, Brian	5	1	6.33	30	0	0	0	48	66	35	34	16	24	.332	R	R	6-1	210	1-8-80	2001	Temple City, Calif.
Ungs, Nic	11	8	4.24	28	28	0	0	161	178	85	76	35	134	.276	R	R	6-2	220	9-3-79	2001	Dyersville, Iowa

FIELDING

Catcher	PCT	G	PO	A	E	DP	PB
Anderson	.993	60	373	35	3	3	6
Grzecka	.957	11	43	2	2	0	0
Willingham	.994	78	590	50	4	4	10
Tucker	1.000	14	17	21	0		6

First Base	PCT	G	PO	A	E	DP
Magness	.992	19	112	6	1	5
Stokes	.992	103	861	55	7	83
Tucker	1.000	7	44	5	0	1
Willingham	1.000	17	143	10	0	14

Second Base	PCT	G	PO	A	E	DP
Demarco	.974	75	136	168	8	44
Goelz	.993	36	53	89	1	12
Hall	.965	34	61	76	5	19
Niles	1.000	2	5	0	0	1

Third Base	PCT	G	PO	A	E	DP
Anderson	1.000	1	0	1	0	0
Demarco	.935	15	9	20	2	5
Dillon	.973	33	22	85	3	4
Hall	.931	37	25	56	6	4
Minor	.960	41	24	72	4	7
Tucker	.959	22	12	35	2	3

Shortstop	PCT	G	PO	A	E	DP
Demarco	1.000	14	15	37	0	10
Goelz	.946	9	10	25	2	6
Hall	.818	3	2	7	2	2
Rundgren	.969	43	66	124	6	29
Wilson	.949	80	96	201	16	33

Outfield	PCT	G	PO	A	E	DP
Ambres	.984	133	291	8	5	2
Frazier	1.000	21	30	1	0	0
Goelz	1.000	2	3	0	0	0
Hall	1.000	23	38	3	0	0
Inglin	.974	65	110	4	3	1
Kavourias	.969	16	30	1	1	0
Magness	.979	37	45	1	1	1
Minor	1.000	6	10	0	0	0
Reed	.982	53	105	4	2	0
Rohleder	.981	54	98	5	2	0
Ryan	1.000	29	57	0	0	0
Shanks	1.000	7	11	0	0	0
Willingham	.933	8	13	1	1	0

JUPITER HAMMERHEADS | High Class A

FLORIDA STATE LEAGUE

BATTING	AVG	G	AB	R	H	2B	3B	HR	RBI	BB	SO	SB	CS	OBP	SLG	B	T	HT	WT	DOB	1st Yr	Resides
Alfonzo, Eliezer	.281	105	399	51	112	12	2	18	70	22	105	6	4	.335	.456	R	R	6-0	200	2-7-79	1996	Lecherias, Venez.
Andino, Robert	.281	48	196	18	55	7	2	0	15	7	43	6	2	.304	.337	R	R	6-0	170	4-25-84	2002	Miami, Fla.
Aponte, Jose	.213	101	328	33	70	17	6	3	29	27	83	9	6	.276	.329	L	R	5-10	160	1-4-83	2001	Aragua, Venez.
Arlis, Patrick	.083	3	12	0	1	1	0	0	1	1	4	0	0	.154	.167	R	R	6-0	180	12-18-80	2002	Glendale Heights, Ill.
Arnerich, Tony	.175	35	97	12	17	6	1	2	12	12	20	0	0	.273	.320	R	R	6-2	190	12-24-79	2001	Santa Rosa, Calif.
Bass, Chris	.273	119	421	54	115	20	1	3	37	55	77	6	4	.366	.347	R	R	6-2	190	10-18-81	2000	Madison, Ind.
Bonner, Adam	.200	55	160	23	32	0	0	5	15	44	50	1	1	.376	.294	L	R	6-2	205	3-11-81	2000	Hueytown, Ala.
Brown, Greg	.148	14	27	2	4	1	0	0	1	3	11	0	0	.233	.185	R	R	5-11	195	5-4-80	2003	Pembroke Pines, Fla.
Cordero, Wil	.500	3	8	3	4	0	0	2	5	1	1	0	0	.556	1.250	R	R	6-2	215	10-3-71	1988	Westlake, Ohio
Demarco, Matt	.333	18	57	8	19	5	0	1	7	6	9	1	1	.424	.474	L	R	5-10	175	1-24-80	1999	Clayton, N.J.
Ezi, Travis	.223	81	242	45	54	10	4	2	19	28	76	19	7	.312	.322	S	L	6-0	175	9-5-81	2001	Baltimore, Md.
Figueroa, Juan	.313	5	16	1	5	0	0	0	1	2	3	0	1	.389	.313	R	R	6-3	240	6-24-75	1996	Santo Domingo, D.R.
Frazier, Charles	.234	92	303	53	71	9	1	6	21	50	81	36	14	.354	.330	R	R	6-4	200	7-6-80	1999	Toms River, N.J.
Fulton, Jonathan	.217	6	23	2	5	2	0	0	1	5		0	0	.250	.304	R	R	6-2	200	12-1-83	2003	Danville, Va.
Grzecka, Casey	.245	59	212	18	52	18	0	3	26	14	40	1	0	.293	.373	R	R	6-2	200	11-12-79	2002	Laguna Niguel, Calif.
Hermida, Jeremy	.297	91	340	53	101	17	1	10	50	42	73	10	3	.377	.441	L	R	6-4	200	1-30-84	2002	Marietta, Ga.
Kavourias, Jim	.153	30	111	10	17	3	1	2	9	10	41	1	0	.223	.252	R	R	6-2	170	9-19-82	2000	Chicago, Ill.
Krga, Mike	.000	2	4	0	0	0	0	0	0	1	2	0	0	.200	.000	R	R	6-1	190	8-4-80	2002	East Meadow, N.Y.
Merkle, Thomas	.213	44	150	9	32	6	0	0	11	12	25	0	1	.279	.253	R	R	6-1	198	4-21-82	2003	Carterville, Ga.
Mitchell, Lee	.216	119	426	48	92	14	6	12	58	34	135	1	2	.278	.362	R	R	6-2	205	5-28-80	2002	West Covina, Calif.
Ordorica, Eric	.257	56	171	18	44	10	0	2	21	14	38	3	0	.310	.351	R	R	5-9	170	12-15-84	2003	Tinley Park, Ill.
Restko, J.T.	.227	7	22	1	5	2	0	0	2	3	5	0	0	.320	.318	R	R	6-0	190	2-27-80	2002	Ferdinand, Ind.
Rohleder, Andy	.310	31	100	14	31	9	0	2	12	19	19	3	2	.431	.460	L	R	6-1	170	11-22-80	2001	Sacramento, Calif.
Rundgren, Rex	.279	73	283	27	79	11	1	0	26	13	60	3	1	.316	.325	R	R	6-0	180	1-26-79	1998	Appling, Ga.
Shanks, James	.333	35	132	20	44	7	2	5	20	5	25	4	2	.362	.530	R	R	6-1	210	1-8-80	2001	Temple City, Calif.
Strelitz, Brian	.000	1	0	0	0	0	0	0	0	0	0	0	0	.000	.000	R	R	6-1	210	11-7-79	2001	Lakeland, Fla.
Tucker, Michael	.220	55	177	20	39	14	1	3	27	19	44	1	1	.305	.362	R	R	6-3	205	5-10-82	2003	Vista, Calif.
Wyman, Spencer	.000	4	11	0	0	0	0	0	0	1	4	0	0	.000	.000	R	R	6-2	205	8-10-80	2003	Albuquerque, N.M.
Young, Dustin	.063	7	16	0	1	1	0	0	0	1	3	5	0	.250	.125	R	R	5-11	175			

PITCHING	W	L	ERA	G	GS	CG	SV	IP	H	R	ER	BB	SO	AVG	B	T	HT	WT	DOB	1st Yr	Resides
Akens, Phil	0	0	6.52	5	0	0	0	10	13	8	7	6	9	.342	R	R	6-6	200	8-9-82	2000	Bel Air, Md.
Arnerich, Tony	1	0	0.82	4	0	0	0	11	3	2	1	6	10	.083	R	R	6-0	190	12-24-79	2001	Santa Rosa, Calif.
Bazardo, Yorman	5	9	3.27	25	25	2	0	154	161	78	56	30	95	.266	R	R	6-2	170	7-11-84	2001	Maracay, Venez.
Belizario, Ronald	1	1	0.00	6	0	0	1	9	2	1	0	4	7	.074	R	R	6-2	150	12-31-82	2000	Aragua, Venez.
Burnett, A.J.	0	0	0.00	1	0	0	0	4	2	1	0	2	4	.143	R	R	6-4	230	1-3-77	1995	Miramar, Fla.
Byers, Waylon	0	0	5.68	5	0	0	0	6	8	4	4	4	6	.308	R	L	5-11	180	5-6-80	2002	Milo, Iowa
Campbell, Jarrett	2	1	4.03	21	0	0	0	38	37	20	17	10	17	.259	R	R	6-2	190	9-6-79	1999	Corpus Christi, Texas
Cave, Kevin	2	1	3.00	19	0	0	2	24	21	9	8	13	19	.228	R	R	6-2	220	5-25-80	2001	Levittown, Pa.
Demontel, Jimmy	0	0	5.27	14	0	0	10	14	17	9	8	5	13	.298	R	R	6-4	240	6-7-80	2002	Wichita Falls, Texas
Evans, Louis	1	1	2.25	10	0	0	0	16	8	5	4	16	15	.151	L	L	6-6	205	10-5-80	2001	San Jose, Calif.
Forster, Scott	0	1	9.28	11	0	0	0	11	12	11	11	9	6	.316	R	L	6-2	185	10-27-71	1994	Flourtown, Pa.
Fulchino, Jeff	2	2	2.72	8	0	0	0	43	39	17	13	16	48	.248	R	R	6-4	235	11-26-79	2001	Hollis, N.H.
Greusel, Evan	1	2	7.33	15	0	0	0	27	31	23	22	17	29	.284	R	R	6-3	210	8-22-79	2002	Norman, Okla.
Humen, David	0	0	0.00	1	0	0	0	1	0	0	0	1	1	.333	R	R	6-2	210	6-11-81	2003	Bedford, Texas

PITCHING

PITCHING	W	L	ERA	G	GS	CG	SV	IP	H	R	ER	BB	SO	AVG	B	T	HT	WT	DOB	1st Yr	Resides
Johnson, Josh	5	12	3.38	23	22	1	0	114	124	63	43	47	103	.278	L	R	6-7	220	1-31-84	2002	Tulsa, Okla.
Kensing, Logan	6	7	2.96	23	23	1	0	128	120	53	42	35	100	.251	R	R	6-1	185	7-3-82	2003	Boerne, Texas
Lerch, Zach	1	0	4.15	3	0	0	0	4	8	5	2	0	4	.400	L	R	6-4	188	11-23-82	2004	Cedar Rapids, Iowa
Lugo, Ruddy	1	7	5.26	31	0	0	11	39	42	31	23	15	33	.278	R	R	5-10	205	5-22-80	1999	Brooklyn, N.Y.
Olsen, Scott	7	6	2.97	25	25	1	0	136	127	57	45	54	158	.246	L	L	6-4	190	1-12-84	2002	Lake in the Hills, Ill.
Orloski, Joe	1	2	3.98	14	0	0	0	20	22	10	9	8	14	.275	R	R	6-3	180	5-17-79	1998	Las Vegas, Nev.
Overman, Matt	5	4	4.19	32	6	0	0	82	83	43	38	16	48	.267	R	R	6-0	185	9-10-80	2003	Casper, Wyo.
Phelps, Tommy	0	0	0.00	1	0	0	0	1	2	3	0	0	1	.333	L	L	6-3	190	3-4-74	1993	Tampa, Fla.
Reynolds, Eric	0	3	9.49	9	0	0	0	12	15	15	13	10	13	.319	L	L	6-3	210	4-20-80	2000	Guntown, Miss.
Russ, James	8	1	1.98	24	0	0	0	82	61	18	18	26	64	.208	R	R	6-4	210	10-24-80	2003	Concord, N.C.
Shanks, James	0	0	3.68	3	0	0	1	7	8	3	3	1	4	.276	R	R	6-0	180	1-26-79	1998	Appling, Ga.
Strelitz, Brian	2	0	4.18	15	0	0	0	24	27	13	11	5	12	.293	R	R	6-1	210	1-8-80	2001	Temple City, Calif.
Tejera, Michael	0	1	0.00	1	1	0	0	3	3	1	0	3	1	.231	L	L	5-9	192	10-18-76	1995	Miami, Fla.
Vandenhurk, Henricus	2	3	3.26	14	14	0	0	58	54	22	21	31	43	.250	R	R	6-5	190	5-22-85	2003	Eindhoven, Holland
Warpinski, Ryan	0	1	1.93	3	0	0	0	5	6	1	1	0	2	.300	R	R	6-3	210	6-30-81	2002	Maribel, Wis.
Wayne, Justin	0	0	0.00	2	1	0	0	3	3	0	0	0	2	.250	R	R	6-3	205	4-16-79	2000	Jupiter, Fla.
Wolf, Ross	11	7	2.60	43	0	0	5	90	87	33	26	28	58	.256	R	R	6-0	180	10-18-82	2002	Wheeler, Ill.

FIELDING

Catcher	PCT	G	PO	A	E	DP	PB
Alfonzo	.994	43	285	40	2	2	5
Arlis	.947	3	16	2	1	0	0
Arnerich	.984	33	227	26	4	1	8
Brown	.986	14	62	7	1	0	2
Grzecka	.984	52	343	36	6	1	11
Wyman	1.000	2	6	2	0	0	0

First Base	PCT	G	PO	A	E	DP
Alfonzo	.990	41	353	24	4	26
Bonner	.968	18	137	15	5	10
Cordero	1.000	1	7	0	0	0
Figueroa	.948	5	52	3	3	4
Merkle	.977	42	403	18	10	34
Restko	1.000	1	8	0	0	0
Tucker	.984	37	285	23	5	24
Wyman	1.000	1	8	0	0	0

Second Base	PCT	G	PO	A	E	DP
Bass	.973	95	170	266	12	48
Demarco	1.000	5	8	11	0	3
Mitchell	1.000	1	2	1	0	0
Ordorica	.968	35	57	93	5	19
Rundgren	1.000	2	3	5	0	3
Young	.917	2	8	3	1	1

Third Base	PCT	G	PO	A	E	DP
Alfonzo	.500	1	0	1	1	0
Bass	1.000	1	0	1	0	0
Demarco	.727	7	1	7	3	0
Fulton	1.000	1	2	1	0	0
Krga	1.000	1	1	2	0	0
Mitchell	.938	107	74	196	18	12
Ordorica	.941	7	4	12	1	2
Tucker	.975	19	11	28	1	2

Shortstop	PCT	G	PO	A	E	DP
Andino	.965	48	62	129	7	21
Demarco	1.000	1	1	0	0	0
Fulton	.867	5	6	20	4	3
Ordorica	.946	12	9	26	2	3
Rundgren	.953	71	96	248	17	45
Young	.909	3	1	9	1	1

Outfield	PCT	G	PO	A	E	DP
Aponte	.986	86	130	6	2	2
Bonner	1.000	38	63	4	0	0
Ezi	1.000	73	133	4	0	0
Frazier	.994	85	148	5	1	0
Hermida	.936	78	125	7	9	0
Kavourias	1.000	16	33	0	0	0
Rohleder	.956	27	41	2	2	1
Shanks	.988	35	79	2	1	2
Young	1.000	1	1	0	0	0

GREENSBORO BATS

Low Class A

SOUTH ATLANTIC LEAGUE

BATTING	AVG	G	AB	R	H	2B	3B	HR	RBI	BB	SO	SB	CS	OBP	SLG	B	T	HT	WT	DOB	1st Yr	Resides
Alen, Luis	.217	9	23	5	0	0	0	0	3	3	0	0		.345	.217	R	R	6-1	170	4-16-85	2002	Puerto Ordaz, Venez.
Andino, Robert	.281	76	295	27	83	10	1	8	46	18	83	9	2	.321	.403	R	R	6-0	170	4-25-84	2002	Miami, Fla.
Arlis, Patrick	.227	61	207	23	47	5	1	2	17	18	59	3	1	.292	.290	R	R	6-0	210	12-18-80	2002	Glendale Heights, Ill.
Arnerich, Tony	.333	16	54	8	18	7	0	3	6	3	6	0	0	.373	.630	R	R	6-0	190	12-24-79	2001	Santa Rosa, Calif.
Arroyo, Xavier	.232	91	293	43	68	11	2	5	29	31	91	27	11	.309	.334	S	R	6-1	170	8-9-84	2002	San Juan, P.R.
Bear, Ryan	.242	135	499	66	121	25	2	17	69	48	104	3	1	.317	.403	R	R	6-2	220	1-26-81	2003	Panama City, Fla.
Blake, Ryan	.285	91	295	44	84	20	0	17	52	33	91	0	0	.379	.525	R	R	6-2	180	2-7-83	2003	Kernersville, N.C.
Bonner, Adam	.233	27	90	13	21	6	0	3	11	11	29	0	0	.314	.400	L	R	6-5	200	3-11-81	2000	Hueytown, Ala.
Gendron, Steve	.187	52	187	20	35	2	0	0	13	18	45	4	0	.263	.198	R	R	6-3	195	11-25-81	2004	Tampa, Fla.
Mazzuca, Joe	.207	67	198	36	41	11	1	7	22	30	49	14	1	.350	.379	R	R	6-0	185	5-21-81	2003	Elmwood Park, Ill.
McMillan, Beau	.250	6	16	3	4	1	1	0	2	3	4	1	0	.400	.438	R	R	6-0	185	9-15-81	2004	West Palm Beach, Fla.
Miller, Jai	.205	113	390	51	80	15	3	12	49	32	163	11	4	.273	.351	R	R	6-4	195	1-17-85	2003	Selma, Ala.
Molina, Angel	.284	130	469	67	133	27	2	18	79	55	110	0	2	.370	.465	R	R	6-2	200	11-4-81	2000	Santa Isabel, P.R.
Ramistella, John	.170	31	94	12	16	4	2	3	9	7	39	2	2	.264	.351	R	R	6-2	220	8-29-81	2001	Monterey, Calif.
Randel, Kevin	.299	35	134	20	40	10	1	4	21	12	27	2	2	.369	.478	L	R	6-1	180	6-11-81	2002	Montclair, Calif.
Rohleder, Andy	.242	25	99	11	24	7	0	2	13	8	27	0	0	.303	.374	R	R	6-0	190	2-27-80	2002	Ferdinand, Ind.
Schade, Ryan	.226	72	199	33	45	5	0	1	17	16	50	6	2	.284	.266	R	R	5-9	170	11-21-78	2003	Lewisburg, Pa.
Seifrig, Cole	.196	121	443	56	87	20	3	4	30	13	128	6	1	.228	.282	R	R	6-3	190	9-10-84	2003	Santa Claus, Ind.
Shanks, James	.322	59	245	45	79	16	3	8	32	14	52	18	3	.369	.510	R	R	6-0	180	1-26-79	1998	Appling, Ga.
Sosa, Pablo	.261	72	272	25	71	10	5	2	28	10	47	4	3	.290	.357	R	R	6-1	180	8-11-82	2002	San Cristobal, D.R.
Wyman, Spencer	.155	19	58	7	9	0	1	6	8	22	1	0		.254	.207	L	R	6-0	205	5-10-82	2003	Vista, Calif.
Young, Dustin	.133	12	30	2	4	1	0	0	1	3	8	0	0	.212	.167	R	R	5-11	175	8-10-80	2003	Albuquerque, N.M.

PITCHING	W	L	ERA	G	GS	CG	SV	IP	H	R	ER	BB	SO	AVG	B	T	HT	WT	DOB	1st Yr	Resides
Akens, Phil	1	3	8.31	8	8	0	0	35	48	33	32	14	34	.322	R	R	6-6	200	8-9-82	2000	Bel Air, Md.
Benitez, Gabriel	3	3	6.41	11	10	0	0	39	48	34	28	22	32	.310	R	R	6-4	165	3-1-83	2000	Aragua, Venez.
Bonner, Adam	0	0	0.00	1	0	0	0	1	0	0	0	1		.000	L	R	6-5	200	3-11-81	2000	Hueytown, Ala.
Bostick, Adam	2	8	3.79	23	22	0	0	114	100	57	48	58	163	.235	L	L	6-1	220	3-17-83	2001	Greensburg, Penn.
Chick, Travis	6	4	4.04	28	11	0	0	91	79	51	41	27	112	.228	R	R	6-3	220	6-10-84	2002	Tyler, Texas
Cillo, Cody	1	3	5.82	14	0	0	0	22	27	17	14	11	23	.300	R	R	6-2	200	7-17-80	2003	Longmont, Colo.
Demontel, Jimmy	2	2	6.57	25	0	0	2	37	44	29	27	15	43	.289	R	R	6-4	240	6-7-80	2002	Wichita Falls, Texas
Glynn, Josh	0	1	4.50	5	0	0	0	10	13	7	5	4	2	.317	R	R	6-2	195	4-28-81	2003	Marysville, Calif.
Greusel, Evan	3	7	5.63	14	14	0	0	62	73	48	39	18	59	.292	R	R	6-3	210	8-22-79	2002	Norman, Okla.
Iehl, Jason	1	2	7.57	17	1	0	0	27	33	23	23	9	31	.289	R	R	6-2	180	4-23-84	2002	Woodridge, Ill.
Koehler, Kurt	0	1	7.20	2	2	0	0	5	7	6	4	2	3	.318	R	R	5-11	185	9-5-84	2004	Pinole, Calif.
Lovato, Nick	0	0	3.60	4	0	0	0	5	5	2	2	3	4	.263	L	L	6-4	215	12-20-80	2003	Anaheim, Calif.
Martinez, Carlos	2	3	3.04	40	0	0	9	47	41	20	16	11	34	.232	R	R	6-2	170	5-26-82	2001	Villa Vasquez, D.R.
Mazzuca, Joe	0	0	0.00	1	0	0	0	1	1	0	0	0	4	.333	R	R	6-0	185	5-21-81	2003	Elmwood Park, Ill.
McCormack, Zach	3	3	5.89	35	0	0	1	44	48	41	29	33	49	.265	L	L	6-3	210	11-8-80	2003	Fairfield, Calif.
Mildren, Paul	5	7	5.22	39	4	0	1	102	116	71	59	40	83	.289	R	L	6-1	160	5-3-84	2002	Melbourne, Australia
Nestor, Scott	2	0	6.35	23	0	0	0	40	46	33	28	25	34	.282	R	R	6-4	225	8-20-84	2003	Glendora, Calif.

PITCHING	W	L	ERA	G	GS	CG	SV	IP	H	R	ER	BB	SO	AVG	B	T	HT	WT	DOB	1st Yr	Resides
Nickerson, Jon	0	9	6.10	14	14	0	0	59	61	44	40	27	44	.264	L	R	6-5	180	12-4-84	2003	Millbrook, Ala.
Nowicki, Nathan	3	5	4.26	43	2	0	4	99	113	53	47	37	48	.289	R	R	6-4	190	4-25-82	2003	Littleton, Colo.
Pillsbury, Chris	0	2	7.30	10	5	0	0	25	36	26	20	12	24	.324	R	R	6-4	190	10-13-81	2003	Orange Park, Fla.
Prieto, Victor	0	8	13.16	10	9	0	0	27	32	44	39	33	19	.299	R	R	6-2	175	4-24-83	2000	Villa de Cura, Venez.
Resop, Chris	3	1	2.11	42	0	0	13	43	28	12	10	8	71	.181	R	R	6-3	200	11-4-82	2001	Naples, Fla.
Russ, James	0	3	7.80	4	4	0	0	15	15	13	13	10	16	.250	R	R	6-4	210	10-24-80	2003	Concord, N.C.
Saucedo, Matthew	2	5	5.45	23	0	0	1	35	30	26	21	21	25	.233	R	R	5-11	170	5-17-80	2003	Highland, Calif.
Schade, Ryan	0	1	13.50	4	1	0	0	3	8	5	5	3	3	.471	R	R	5-9	170	11-21-78	2003	Lewisburg, Penn.
Treanor, Bryan	1	0	0.00	2	0	0	0	2	2	0	0	2	3	.250	R	R	5-11	180	2-11-80	2002	San Luis Obispo, Calif.
Vargas, Jason	2	2	2.37	3	3	0	0	19	9	5	5	2	17	.143	L	L	6-0	215	2-2-83	2004	Apple Valley, Calif.
Warpinski, Ryan	5	4	4.21	13	12	0	0	58	61	34	27	23	46	.265	R	R	6-3	210	6-30-81	2002	Maribel, Wis.
Wood, Tim	2	3	4.22	24	8	0	1	70	73	47	33	22	70	.262	R	R	6-1	185	11-16-82	2003	Tucson, Ariz.
Yourkin, Matt	0	0	10.50	3	0	0	0	6	12	8	7	3	2	.400	R	L	6-3	225	7-4-81	2004	Napa, Calif.
Zarate, Maruro	1	4	8.45	10	10	0	0	44	69	46	41	12	29	.361	R	R	6-1	180	2-8-83	2001	Valencia, Venez.

FIELDING

Catcher	PCT	G	PO	A	E	DP	PB
Alen	.961	9	71	2	3	1	3
Arlis	.985	58	474	37	8	1	20
Arnerich	.992	15	114	12	1	0	4
Blake	.985	33	239	17	4	0	6
Molina	.991	15	109	7	1	0	4
Wyman	.988	18	148	12	2	0	8

First Base	PCT	G	PO	A	E	DP
Bear	.992	130	1021	56	9	67
Molina	.955	10	60	3	3	6

Second Base	PCT	G	PO	A	E	DP
Randel	.968	7	12	18	1	2
Schade	1.000	18	30	29	0	8

	PCT	G	PO	A	E	DP
Seifrig	.974	114	190	289	13	53
Young	.909	2	6	4	1	1

Third Base	PCT	G	PO	A	E	DP
Mazzuca	.822	34	18	65	18	4
McMillan	.824	6	0	14	3	2
Randel	.867	8	9	17	4	2
Schade	.926	28	17	46	5	5
Sosa	.922	67	46	119	14	7
Young	.875	3	2	5	1	0

Shortstop	PCT	G	PO	A	E	DP
Andino	.937	76	91	221	21	27
Gendron	.939	50	81	136	14	23
Randel	.900	2	1	8	1	0

	PCT	G	PO	A	E	DP
Schade	.971	9	12	22	1	3
Young	1.000	5	4	4	0	0

Outfield	PCT	G	PO	A	E	DP
Arroyo	.981	88	158	1	3	0
Bonner	.942	27	46	3	3	2
Mazzuca	.909	6	8	2	1	0
Miller	.960	112	233	7	10	1
Molina	.970	77	119	9	4	0
Ramistella	.927	28	36	2	3	0
Rohleder	.966	26	28	0	1	0
Schade	1.000	12	16	3	0	0
Shanks	.948	58	103	6	6	1

JAMESTOWN JAMMERS — Short-Season Class A

NEW YORK-PENN LEAGUE

BATTING	AVG	G	AB	R	H	2B	3B	HR	RBI	BB	SO	SB	CS	OBP	SLG	B	T	HT	WT	DOB	1st Yr	Resides
Alen, Luis	.250	44	120	11	30	9	0	0	12	10	11	1	0	.316	.325	R	R	6-1	170	4-16-85	2002	Puerto Ordaz, Venez.
Carroll, Brett	.251	60	211	27	53	16	1	6	28	15	57	1	0	.321	.422	R	R	6-0	190	10-3-82	2004	Knoxville, Tenn.
Cleveland, Brian	.259	63	255	33	66	14	2	2	20	11	54	4	1	.301	.353	R	R	6-4	205	1-7-82	2004	San Jose, Calif.
Davis, Brad	.289	43	152	23	44	12	1	0	14	10	20	3	3	.341	.382	R	R	6-2	185	12-29-82	2004	Mission Viejo, Calif.
Ewen, Nick	.245	51	163	18	40	7	1	3	13	19	51	5	4	.322	.356	L	R	6-4	210	3-8-83	2003	Roselle, Ill.
Fulton, Jonathan	.254	65	252	39	64	12	5	11	40	20	82	2	1	.312	.472	R	R	6-4	200	12-1-83	2003	Danville, Va.
Gaston, Jared	.273	53	176	24	48	2	3	2	17	17	53	3	2	.342	.352	R	R	6-3	195	11-25-81	2004	Tampa, Fla.
Gendron, Steve	.261	17	69	8	18	2	1	0	10	3	15	1	0	.292	.319	R	R	6-2	195	5-16-81	2004	Oklahoma City, Okla.
Ledbetter, Ted	.222	3	9	1	2	0	0	0	2	2	1	0		.364	.222	R	R	6-3	180	11-1-81	2003	San Pedro de Macoris, D.R.
Lindesey, Juan	.237	42	139	19	33	3	1	1	19	8	37	3	1	.282	.295	R	R	6-3	180	12-9-82	2004	Duluth, Ga.
McCann, Brad	.277	29	112	16	31	6	2	3	18	7	16	0	1	.328	.446	R	R	6-0	185	9-15-81	2004	West Palm Beach, Fla.
McMillan, Beau	.264	29	106	18	28	6	1	0	10	14	34	4	2	.347	.340	L	R	6-0	190	12-13-82	2004	Omaha, Neb.
Pietro, Joe	.282	66	238	36	67	1	4	0	20	30	65	13	9	.364	.319	L	R	6-0	190	12-15-84	2003	Tinley Park, Ill.
Restko, J.T.	.238	72	290	40	69	11	1	6	46	16	74	0	2	.285	.345	R	R	6-5	190	1-28-81	2004	Round Lake, Ill.
Sewell, Kevin	.294	58	201	27	59	13	6	6	33	9	39	1	2	.332	.507	L	R	5-11	208	1-28-81	2004	Vista, Calif.
Wyman, Spencer	.275	26	80	14	22	7	0	2	13	10	25	0	1	.356	.438	R	R	5-11	175	5-10-82	2003	Albuquerque, N.M.
Young, Dusty	.250	3	4	2	1	0	0	0	1	2	0	0		.400	.250					8-10-80		

GAMES BY POSITION: C—Alen 39, Davis 39, Wyman 9. **1B**—McCann 3, Restko 67, Wyman 6. **2B**—Carroll 10, Cleveland 24, Gendron 12, McMillan 28, Sewell 1, Young 1. **3B**—Carroll 33, Cleveland 18, McCann 24. **SS**—Cleveland 13, Fulton 61, Gendron 2, Young 1. **OF**—Carroll 12, Cleveland 6, Ewen 50, Gaston 42, Ledbetter 3, Lindesey 19, Pietro 65, Sewell 50.

PITCHING	W	L	ERA	G	GS	CG	SV	IP	H	R	ER	BB	SO	AVG	B	T	HT	WT	DOB	1st Yr	Resides
Alexander, Stuart	0	1	8.00	2	0	0	0	9	14	11	8	1	6	.341	R	R	6-4	225	10-25-84	2004	Windsor, Calif.
Barone, Daniel	3	6	5.08	19	2	0	0	51	60	31	29	11	45	.291	R	R	6-3	195	4-24-83	2001	Hollister, Calif.
Baxter, Allen	0	4	6.17	10	10	0	0	35	34	31	24	32	27	.262	R	R	6-4	215	7-6-83	2001	Sandston, Va.
Brandenburg, Adam	0	0	0.00	3	0	0	0	5	5	3	0	4	8	.217	L	L	6-5	225	8-17-81	2003	Snellville, Ga.
Gogal, Jeff	1	4	4.56	11	11	0	0	51	62	36	26	16	53	.294	R	L	6-2	195	6-10-82	2004	Kearny, N.J.
Hoff, Brian	0	3	3.50	19	0	0	0	36	40	23	14	11	26	.272	R	R	6-4	225	1-28-82	2004	Yorba Linda, Calif.
Hogan, Patrick	0	2	4.45	25	0	0	12	28	32	15	14	13	29	.288	R	R	6-4	235	4-10-81	2004	Columbia, S.C.
Humen, David	1	2	5.87	13	0	0	0	23	27	19	15	10	22	.293	R	R	6-1	215	10-17-82	2004	Pensacola, Fla.
James, Rhett	5	1	3.12	17	4	0	0	43	37	17	15	12	47	.228	R	R	6-1	205	4-20-81	2004	Hattiesburg, Miss.
Lacher, Jeffery	0	3	5.88	16	0	0	0	41	54	35	27	9	29	.302	R	R	6-1	205	5-26-81	2004	Cedar Rapids, Iowa
Lerch, Zach	5	4	4.76	13	13	0	0	64	72	46	34	16	56	.275	R	R	6-4	215	11-23-82	2004	Anaheim, Calif.
Lovato, Nick	0	0	6.75	2	0	0	0	5	8	4	4	4	3	.381	L	L	6-0	190	10-7-82	2003	Birmingham, Ala.
Lybarger, Craig	0	0	10.80	2	0	0	0	2	2	2	2	2	2	.333	L	L	6-0	188	10-7-82	2003	Birmingham, Ala.
Mobley, Chris	1	1	2.72	17	6	0	2	53	50	27	16	20	52	.248	R	R	5-11	171	8-16-83	2004	Kingsport, Tenn.
Molldrem, Craig	0	2	5.50	5	5	0	0	18	26	15	11	4	14	.338	R	R	6-6	205	9-17-81	2003	Boscobel, Wis.
Nickerson, Jon	2	4	5.09	9	8	0	0	41	45	26	23	31	29	.290	L	R	6-5	180	12-4-84	2003	Millbrook, Ala.
Prieto, Victor	0	0	189.00	1	0	0	0	0	3	8	7	4	0	.750	R	R	6-2	175	4-24-83	2000	Villa de Cura, Venez.
Tankersley, Taylor	1	1	3.38	6	6	0	0	27	21	14	10	8	32	.208	L	L	6-2	225	3-7-83	2004	Hammond, La.
Tillman, Derek	6	2	2.60	25	1	0	0	45	34	20	13	15	46	.206	R	R	6-2	180	7-12-80	2004	Long Beach, Calif.
Vargas, Jason	3	1	1.96	8	8	0	0	41	35	17	9	13	41	.224	L	L	6-0	215	2-2-83	2004	Apple Valley, Calif.
Yourkin, Matt	2	3	3.94	24	0	0	1	32	26	17	14	10	32	.217	R	L	6-3	225	7-4-81	2004	Napa, Calif.

GULF COAST LEAGUE

BATTING

BATTING	AVG	G	AB	R	H	2B	3B	HR	RBI	BB	SO	SB	CS	SLG	OBP	B	T	HT	WT	DOB	1st Yr	Resides
Adduci, James	.207	49	164	21	34	4	1	0	27	24	42	6	1	.244	.327	L	L	6-2	185	5-15-85	2003	Evergreen Park, Ill.
Brown, Greg	.143	5	14	2	2	0	0	0	3	3	6	0	0	.143	.316	R	R	5-11	195	5-4-80	2003	Pembroke Pines, Fla.
Burns, Greg	.243	42	136	28	33	5	4	0	7	26	48	7	7	.338	.372	L	L	6-2	185	11-7-86	2004	Pomona, Calif.
Campusano, Jose	.255	59	196	24	50	8	4	1	16	10	38	11	10	.352	.319	S	R	5-11	160	12-19-83	2003	Santo Domingo, D.R.
Ciprian, Jorge	.209	46	129	19	27	10	0	0	10	9	28	6	2	.287	.275	R	R	6-0	170	7-2-81	2003	La Romana, D.R.
De Vrieze, Jeffrey	.188	21	32	2	6	2	0	0	5	1	17	0	0	.250	.257	R	R	6-0	180	1-20-86	2003	Almere, Netherlands
Encarnacion, Seferino	.202	33	104	11	21	5	0	1	13	6	28	0	1	.279	.270	R	R	6-4	215	8-26-82	2003	Orange Park, Fla.
Ezi, Travis	.111	4	9	1	1	0	0	0	1	0	5	0	0	.111	.111	S	L	6-0	175	9-5-81	2000	Baltimore, Md.
Figueroa, Juan	.240	50	167	27	40	14	1	3	35	32	34	1	5	.389	.373	L	L	6-0	200	12-9-81	2004	Aguado, P.R.
Franco, Luis	.152	33	79	7	12	2	0	0	4	10	28	1	0	.177	.253	S	R	6-0	180	9-27-84	2003	Barquisimeto, Venez.
Kavourias, Jim	.200	4	10	3	2	0	0	1	3	5	3	0	0	.500	.438	R	R	6-4	230	10-4-79	2003	Strongsville, Ohio
McMillan, Beau	.304	20	69	13	21	4	2	0	4	4	18	3	0	.420	.342	R	R	5-11	185	9-15-81	2004	West Palm Beach, Fla.
Messner, Nathan	.310	44	155	23	48	7	0	2	29	13	36	2	4	.394	.357	R	R	6-3	210	11-21-85	2004	Muncy, Pa.
Randel, Kevin	.250	12	36	7	9	5	0	0	6	9	4	5	0	.389	.400	L	R	6-1	180	6-11-81	2002	Montclair, Calif.
Rodriguez, Jesus	.250	56	200	25	50	6	0	0	17	11	24	3	1	.280	.293	R	R	5-11	175	10-30-84	2002	Lara, Venez.
Rogers, Tanner	.278	37	108	22	30	8	2	0	18	12	32	6	0	.389	.400	R	R	6-0	180	1-11-85	2003	Littleton, Colo.
Smolarsky, Fred	.261	28	88	11	23	7	0	2	12	4	18	1	0	.409	.316	R	R	6-1	180	2-3-84	2003	Valencia, Venez.
Stokes, Jason	.250	3	8	1	2	1	0	1	1	1	3	0	0	.750	.333	R	R	6-4	225	1-23-82	2000	Coppell, Texas
Verley, Brandon	.048	10	21	1	1	0	0	0	3	2	6	1	1	.048	.167	L	L	6-2	202	6-25-85	2004	White Salmon, Wash.
Walton, Jamar	.238	42	143	17	34	3	1	1	13	13	32	6	3	.294	.296	L	R	6-4	195	1-5-86	2004	Emporia, Va.
Young, Dusty	.302	19	63	8	19	3	0	0	10	10	13	3	0	.349	.429	R	R	5-11	175	8-10-80	2003	Albuquerque, N.M.

GAMES BY POSITION: C—Brown 5, De Vrieze 19, Rogers 35, Smolarsky 17. **1B**—Adduci 1, Ciprian 1, Figueroa 39, Messner 22. **2B**—Franco 32, McMillan 15, Randel 9, Rodriguez 4, Young 16. **3B**—Campusano 1, McMillan 4, Messner 7, Randel 1, Rodriguez 52, Young 2. **SS**—Campusano 57, Franco 1, McMillan 2, Rodriguez 2, Young 5. **OF**—Adduci 42, Burns 41. Ciprian 42, Encarnacion 22, Ezi 4, Kavourias 1, Rodriguez 1, Verley 3, Walton 30.

PITCHING

PITCHING	W	L	ERA	G	GS	CG	SV	IP	H	R	ER	BB	SO	AVG	B	T	HT	WT	DOB	1st Yr	Resides
Alexander, Stuart	2	1	0.75	5	5	0	0	24	14	4	2	2	26	.162	R	R	6-5	210	10-25-84	2004	Windsor, Calif.
Belizario, Ronald	0	0	0.00	2	0	0	0	2	1	0	0	0	2	.166	R	R	6-2	150	12-31-82	1999	Aragua, Venez.
Berkenbosch, Kenny	1	0	1.64	7	0	0	0	11	13	5	2	2	6	.288	R	R	6-2	200	3-17-85	2002	Flevoland, Netherlands
Brandenburg, Adam	1	1	0.75	10	0	0	0	12	7	4	1	2	8	.159	L	L	6-5	225	8-17-81	2003	Snellville, Ga.
Brito, Joel	0	0	1.80	3	0	0	0	5	4	2	1	0	6	.200	R	R	6-1	175	3-23-84	2001	Santiago, D.R.
Camilo, Juan	3	1	2.76	11	10	0	0	46	42	21	14	20	45	.244	R	R	6-3	160	4-22-83	2003	San Francisco de Macoris, D.R.
Castor, Parrish	2	3	5.36	11	8	0	0	40	40	26	24	20	31	.259	L	L	6-2	180	9-18-83	2004	Keene, N.H.
Cillo, Cody	1	0	0.98	11	0	0	1	18	14	2	2	6	22	.229	R	R	6-2	200	7-17-80	2003	Longmont, Colo.
Davis, Lance	0	0	0.00	2	0	0	0	2	1	0	0	2	1	.142	R	R	6-2	190	1-18-83	2001	Lucedale, Miss.
Easton, Aaron	2	6	5.13	13	13	0	0	53	49	34	30	19	32	.253	L	R	6-10	240	9-8-81	2004	Waterford, Maine
Evans, Louis	2	0	1.13	6	0	0	0	8	5	3	1	2	9	.166	L	L	6-6	205	10-8-81	2001	Redding, Calif.
Gracesqui, Frank	0	1	0.00	2	2	0	0	3	1	1	0	4	4	.111	S	L	6-5	210	8-20-79	1998	New York, N.Y.
Griffin, Daniel	0	0	0.00	1	0	0	0	1	1	0	0	0	1	.250	R	R	6-3	190	2-21-78	1997	San Pedro de Macoris, D.R.
Humen, David	0	0	1.69	5	0	0	0	5	1	1	1	1	8	.062	R	R	6-2	210	6-11-81	2003	Bedford, Texas
Iehl, Jay	1	0	3.00	7	0	0	0	9	7	3	3	4	10	.225	R	R	6-2	180	4-23-84	2002	Woodridge, Ill.
Joseph, Jamaal	1	2	4.13	14	1	0	0	28	36	16	13	6	22	.307	R	R	6-4	220	8-8-81	2003	Richmond Hill, Calif.
Koehler, Kurt	0	0	4.50	1	1	0	0	2	4	1	1	0	4	.400	R	R	6-1	190	9-5-84	2004	Pinole, Calif.
Lovato, Nick	1	1	5.56	10	0	0	2	11	14	8	7	4	8	.325	L	L	6-4	215	12-20-80	2003	Anaheim, Calif.
Lybarger, Craig	1	1	3.50	13	0	0	0	18	21	11	7	5	13	.280	L	L	6-0	190	10-7-82	2003	Birmingham, Ala.
Marchbanks, David	2	1	4.20	14	9	0	0	41	37	24	19	19	24	.237	L	L	6-3	205	2-3-82	2003	Simpsonville, S.C.
Mattison, Justin	1	0	6.00	11	0	0	2	12	15	10	8	7	12	.288	L	L	6-0	190	6-24-81	2003	Dominguez Hills, Calif.
Olivo, Haydersman	0	0	2.63	11	0	0	0	14	7	5	4	19	17	.166	R	R	6-2	185	6-7-85	2004	Caracas, Venez.
Phelps, Tommy	0	0	0.00	1	1	0	0	1	0	0	0	0	1	.000	L	L	6-3	190	3-4-74	1993	Tampa, Fla.
Pie, Esequier	2	2	3.98	12	5	0	0	43	42	23	19	18	39	.257	R	R	6-2	165	3-6-84	2000	San Pedro de Macoris, D.R.
Prieto, Victor	0	3	4.40	5	4	0	0	14	6	8	7	16	8	.127	R	R	6-2	175	4-24-83	1999	Villa de Cura, Venez.
Santos, Jarrett	5	1	3.09	17	0	0	0	23	27	12	8	3	18	.287	R	R	6-4	215	8-18-81	2004	Tulare, Calif.
Sosa, Alexis	0	0	0.00	1	0	0	0	1	0	0	0	0	2	.000	S	L	6-0	175	6-25-83	2001	Santo Domingo, D.R.
Treanor, Bryan	0	1	3.52	7	1	0	0	8	8	3	3	5	7	.275	R	R	5-11	180	2-11-80	2002	San Luis Obispo, Calif.
Westmoreland, Clay	1	2	2.30	16	0	0	4	16	9	6	4	7	21	.160	R	R	5-10	185	6-6-82	2004	Mesa, Ariz.
Zarate, Mauro	2	2	2.36	17	0	0	3	42	35	18	11	7	28	.216	R	R	6-1	180	2-8-83	2001	Valencia, Venez.

TOM HALLIBURTON

Their 2004 accomplishments made sense but the Astros' wacky season plot became a mind-boggling trip.

When the Astros signed Houston-area pitchers Andy Pettitte and Roger Clemens in the off-season, it figured  the franchise planned to win a post-season series for the first time ever. And the Astros did, winning the National League Division Series against NL East champion Atlanta.

It's not surprising, either, that the Astros extended NL Central champion St. Louis to seven games in the NLCS before the Cardinals reached their 16th World Series. With returning veteran sluggers Lance Berkman, Jeff Kent, Jeff Bagwell and Craig Biggio to support Clemens, Pettitte and youngsters Roy Oswalt and Wade Miller, the Astros were supposed to be good.

They were not supposed to be 44-44 at the all-star break when the club fired manager Jimy Williams and hired Phil Garner as interim skipper for the rest of the season. Their June 24 acquisition of outfielder Carlos Beltran from Kansas City suggested they intended to compete for an improbable playoff berth.

They were not supposed to be 56-60 on the morning of Aug. 15—seven games off the NL wild card chase. That's when the Astros changed gears, going 36-10 in the final 46 regular-season games, to edge the Giants by one game for the club's eighth post-season appearance.

"It was a real roller-coaster ride," said Biggio, who hit a career-high 24 home runs and became a NL career record-holder for most home runs (41) by a leadoff batter.

Ironically, the arm which led Houston to the verge of its first World Series—Clemens—was tagged with the loss in Game 7 of the NLCS at St. Louis. Clemens became baseball's second all-time strikeout leader, trailing only

Roger Clemens | Chris Burke

PLAYERS of the YEAR

MAJOR LEAGUE: Roger Clemens, rhp

Everyone expected Clemens to provide a presence when he came out of retirement to play for his hometown Astros, but no one could have predicted another Cy Young-caliber season from the 41-year-old righthander. But that's exactly what happened as The Rocket went 18-4, 2.98 with 218 strikeouts in 214 innings.

MINOR LEAGUE: Chris Burke, 2b

Burke repeated a level at Double-A Round Rock in 2003, putting himself back on the prospect map. He followed it up with a strong showing at Triple-A New Orleans, setting career highs in most offensive categories and earning two stints in Houston. At New Orleans, Burke batted .315-16-52.

ORGANIZATION LEADERS

BATTING

*AVG	Ben Zobrist, Tri-City	.339
R	Josh Anderson, Salem/Lexington	114
H	Josh Anderson, Salem/Lexington	172
TB	Luke Scott, Round Rock/Salem	249
2B	Brooks Conrad, Round Rock	39
	Royce Huffman, New Orleans	39
3B	Edwin Maysonet, Lexington	10
HR	Mike Coolbaugh, New Orleans	30
	Phil Hiatt, New Orleans	30
RBI	Luke Scott, Round Rock/Salem	97
BB	Todd Self, Round Rock	89
SO	Charlton Jimerson, Round Rock	163
SB	Josh Anderson, Salem/Lexington	79
*OBP	Ben Zobrist, Tri-City	.438
*SLG	Mike Coolbaugh, New Orleans	.592

PITCHING

W	Ezequiel Astacio, Round Rock	13
L	Four tied at	11
#ERA	Mike Burns, Round Rock	1.67
G	Monte Mansfield, Salem	59
	Aaron Williams, Lexington	59
CG	Jared Fernandez, New Orleans	3
	D.J. Houlton, Round Rock	3
SV	Santiago Ramirez, Round Rock	32
IP	Jared Fernandez, New Orleans	196
BB	Derick Grigsby, Lexington	92
SO	Ezequiel Astacio, Round Rock	185

*Minimum 250 at-bats #Minimum 75 innings

Nolan Ryan.

The 42-year-old righthander led the major leagues with an .818 (18-4) winning percentage and remained baseball's leader in most wins by an active player—328.

A huge crowd favorite, Clemens helped the Astros set a new season home attendance record of 3,087,872 and earned the honor of the NL's starting pitcher in the All-Star Game. Clemens lifted Southeast Texas baseball interest to an all-time high.

Injuries to Pettitte and Miller caused Garner to patch together a starting rotation led by Oswalt's career-high 20 wins and closer Brad Lidge's 29 saves and 1.90 ERA. Oswalt became the only NL pitcher to win 20 games. He won 11 of his last 13 decisions, despite working through a painful left rib cage injury.

Beltran and Berkman paced Houston's offense in the postseason. Beltran hit .435 with a record-tying eight postseason home runs. Berkman batted .348 over 12 postseason games, adding four home runs.

While New Orleans finished its final season as a Houston farm club, Zephyrs infielder Chris Burke (.315-16-52) became the farm system's brightest star, earning a selection to the 2004 Futures Game.

Houston's Triple-A home moves to Round Rock in 2005, where the Express captured Texas League West Division titles in the first and second halves.

Tri-City advanced to the New York-Penn League championship in its second season and captured its first-ever playoff berth with a 50-25 regular season. Greeneville compiled a 41-26 record to win the Appalachian League championship under first-year skipper Tim Bogar.

HOUSTON ASTROS

Managers: Jimy Williams, Phil Garner.

2004 Record: 92-70, .568 (2nd, NL Central).

ORGANIZATION STATISTICS

BATTING	AVG	G	AB	R	H	2B	3B	HR	RBI	BB	SO	SB	CS	OBP	SLG	B	T	HT	WT	DOB	1st Yr	Resides
Alfaro, Jason	.182	7	11	1	2	0	0	0	0	0	5	0	0	.182	.182	R	R	5-10	185	11-29-77	1997	Fort Worth, Texas
Ausmus, Brad	.248	129	403	38	100	14	1	5	31	33	56	2	2	.306	.325	R	R	5-11	190	4-14-69	1988	San Diego, Calif.
Bagwell, Jeff	.266	156	572	104	152	29	2	27	89	96	131	6	4	.377	.465	R	R	6-0	210	5-27-68	1989	Houston, Texas
Beltran, Carlos	.258	90	333	70	86	17	7	23	53	55	57	28	0	.368	.559	S	R	6-1	190	4-24-77	1995	Manati, P.R.
Berkman, Lance	.316	160	544	104	172	40	3	30	106	127	101	9	7	.450	.566	S	L	6-1	220	2-10-76	1997	Houston, Texas
Biggio, Craig	.281	156	633	100	178	47	0	24	63	40	94	7	2	.337	.469	R	R	5-11	185	12-14-65	1987	Houston, Texas
Bruntlett, Eric	.250	45	52	14	13	2	0	4	8	7	13	4	0	.328	.519	R	R	6-0	200	3-29-78	2000	Lafayette, Ind.
Burke, Chris	.059	17	17	2	1	0	0	0	0	3	3	0	0	.200	.059	R	R	5-11	180	3-11-80	2001	Knoxville, Tenn.
Chavez, Raul	.210	64	162	9	34	8	0	0	23	10	38	0	1	.256	.259	R	R	5-11	215	3-18-73	1990	Valencia, Venez.
Ensberg, Morgan	.275	131	411	51	113	20	3	10	66	36	46	6	4	.330	.411	R	R	6-2	220	8-26-75	1998	Orlando, Fla.
Everett, Adam	.273	104	384	66	105	15	2	8	31	17	56	13	2	.317	.385	R	R	6-0	160	2-2-77	1998	Kennesaw, Ga.
Hidalgo, Richard	.256	58	199	21	51	15	2	4	30	17	53	1	2	.309	.412	R	R	6-3	220	6-28-75	1992	Guarenas, Venez.
Kent, Jeff	.289	145	540	96	156	34	8	27	107	49	96	7	3	.348	.531	R	R	6-1	190	3-7-68	1989	Foster City, Calif.
Lamb, Mike	.288	112	278	38	80	14	3	14	58	31	63	1	1	.356	.511	L	R	6-1	190	8-9-75	1997	Valinda, Calif.
Lane, Jason	.272	107	136	21	37	10	2	4	19	16	33	1	0	.348	.463	R	L	6-2	220	12-22-76	1999	Sebastopol, Calif.
Palmeiro, Orlando	.241	102	133	19	32	5	0	3	12	18	19	2	1	.344	.346	L	L	5-11	180	1-19-69	1991	Miami, Fla.
Taveras, Willy	.000	10	1	2	0	0	0	0	0	0	1	1	0	.000	.000	R	R	6-0	160	12-25-81	1999	Tenares, D.R.
Vizcaino, Jose	.274	138	358	34	98	21	3	3	33	20	39	1	1	.311	.374	S	R	6-1	190	3-26-68	1987	Poway, Calif.

PITCHING	W	L	ERA	G	GS	CG	SV	IP	H	R	ER	BB	SO	AVG	B	T	HT	WT	DOB	1st Yr	Resides
Backe, Brandon	5	3	4.30	33	9	0	0	67	75	33	32	27	54	.290	R	R	6-0	180	4-5-78	1998	Texas City, Texas
Bullinger, Kirk	1	0	6.16	27	0	0	1	31	36	22	21	10	11	.286	R	R	6-2	170	10-28-69	1992	Gretna, La.
Clemens, Roger	18	4	2.98	33	33	0	0	214	169	76	71	79	218	.217	R	R	6-4	235	8-4-62	1984	Houston, Texas
Dotel, Octavio	0	4	3.12	32	0	0	14	35	27	15	12	15	50	.213	R	R	6-0	200	11-25-73	1993	Santo Domingo, D.R.
Duckworth, Brandon	1	2	6.86	19	6	0	0	39	55	30	30	13	23	.337	R	R	6-2	195	1-23-76	1998	Kearns, Utah
Fernandez, Jared	0	0	54.00	2	1	0	0	1	6	6	6	5	0	.750	R	R	6-1	225	2-2-72	1994	Ogden, Utah
Gallo, Mike	2	0	4.74	69	0	0	0	49	55	27	26	20	34	.282	L	L	6-0	175	4-2-77	1999	Long Beach, Calif.
Griffiths, Jeremy	0	0	10.38	1	1	0	0	4	4	5	5	3	5	.235	R	R	6-6	240	3-22-78	1999	Avon Lakes, Ohio
Harville, Chad	3	2	4.75	56	0	0	0	53	54	35	28	26	46	.260	R	R	5-9	185	9-16-76	1997	Savannah, Tenn.
Hernandez, Carlos	1	3	6.43	9	9	0	0	42	50	31	30	23	26	.303	S	L	5-10	180	4-22-80	1997	Yagua, Venez.
Lidge, Brad	6	5	1.90	80	0	0	29	95	57	21	20	30	157	.174	R	R	6-5	210	12-23-76	1998	Englewood, Colo.
Miceli, Dan	6	6	3.59	74	0	0	2	78	74	34	31	27	83	.247	R	R	6-0	215	9-9-70	1990	Winter Springs, Fla.
Miller, Wade	7	7	3.35	15	15	0	0	89	76	35	33	44	74	.228	R	R	6-2	210	9-13-76	1996	Douglassville, Pa.
Munro, Pete	4	7	5.15	21	19	0	0	100	120	59	57	26	63	.302	R	R	6-3	210	6-14-75	1994	Little Neck, N.Y.
Oliver, Darren	1	0	3.86	9	2	0	0	14	12	6	6	4	13	.240	R	L	6-2	220	10-6-70	1988	Southlake, Texas
2-team (18 Florida)	3	3	5.94	27	10	0	0	73	87	50	48	21	46	.305							
Oswalt, Roy	20	10	3.49	36	35	2	0	237	233	100	92	62	206	.260	R	R	6-0	185	8-29-77	1997	Weir, Miss.
Pettitte, Andy	6	4	3.90	15	15	0	0	83	71	37	36	31	79	.226	L	L	6-5	225	6-15-72	1991	Deer Park, Texas
Qualls, Chad	4	0	3.55	25	0	0	1	33	34	13	13	8	24	.266	R	R	6-5	220	8-17-78	2001	Reno, Nev.
Redding, Tim	5	7	5.72	27	17	0	0	101	125	73	64	43	56	.309	R	R	6-0	200	2-12-78	1997	Churchville, N.Y.
Springer, Russ	0	1	2.63	16	0	0	0	14	15	4	4	6	9	.278	R	R	6-4	215	11-7-68	1989	Pollack, La.
Stone, Ricky	1	1	5.68	16	0	0	0	19	26	12	12	7	16	.317	R	R	6-1	195	2-28-75	1994	Hamilton, Ohio
Weathers, David	1	4	4.78	26	0	0	0	32	31	20	17	13	26	.261	R	R	6-3	230	9-25-69	1988	Loretto, Tenn.
Wheeler, Dan	3	1	4.29	46	1	0	0	65	76	33	31	20	55	.216	R	R	6-3	220	12-10-77	1997	Warwick, R.I.

FIELDING

Catcher	PCT	G	PO	A	E	DP	PB
Ausmus	.995	128	920	61	5	10	2
Chavez	.991	61	395	29	4	2	2
Tremie	.000	1	0	0	0	0	0

First Base	PCT	G	PO	A	E	DP
Bagwell	.995	152	1190	98	6	109
Berkman	1.000	4	5	1	0	2
Lamb	1.000	10	76	4	0	7
Lane	.933	3	13	1	1	3
Vizcaino	1.000	8	42	3	0	2

Second Base	PCT	G	PO	A	E	DP
Bruntlett	1.000	5	3	5	0	0

	PCT	G	PO	A	E	DP
Burke	1.000	7	7	15	0	3
Kent	.989	139	276	374	7	74
Lamb	.955	7	9	12	1	0
Vizcaino	1.000	37	45	51	0	17

Third Base	PCT	G	PO	A	E	DP
Ensberg	.949	118	80	164	13	23
Lamb	.919	57	41	106	13	9
Vizcaino	.840	21	10	11	4	0

Shortstop	PCT	G	PO	A	E	DP
Alfaro	1.000	3	2	3	0	1
Bruntlett	.938	33	17	28	3	9
Ensberg	.000	1	0	0	0	0

	PCT	G	PO	A	E	DP
Everett	.977	99	137	279	10	56
Vizcaino	.969	64	65	153	7	27

Outfield	PCT	G	PO	A	E	DP
Beltran	.977	89	201	8	5	2
Berkman	.992	160	243	11	2	1
Biggio	.966	149	250	4	9	0
Bruntlett	1.000	2	1	0	0	0
Hidalgo	.982	56	107	4	2	0
Lane	.984	76	60	2	1	0
Palmeiro	1.000	37	37	0	0	0
Taveras	1.000	7	1	0	0	0

148 • BASEBALL AMERICA 2005 ALMANAC

Assistant GM/Director, Player Development: Tim Purpura.

Class	Farm Team	League	W	L	Pct.	Finish*	Manager	Affiliate Since
AAA	#New Orleans (La.) Zephyrs	Pacific Coast	66	78	.458	13th (16)	Chris Maloney	1997
AA	@Round Rock (Texas) Express	Texas	86	54	.614	**1st (8)**	Jackie Moore	2000
High A	Salem (Va.) Avalanche	Carolina	65	74	.468	6th (8)	Russ Nixon	2003
Low A	Lexington (Ky.) Legends	South Atlantic	67	72	.482	11th (16)	Ivan DeJesus	2001
SS A	Tri-City ValleyCats (Troy, N.Y.)	New York-Penn	50	25	.667	**2nd (14)**	Gregg Langbehn	2001
Rookie	Greeneville (Tenn.) Astros	Appalachian	41	26	.612	**+2nd (10)**	Tim Bogar	1999

*Finish in overall standings (No. of teams in league)/Playoff teams in **boldface**   +League champion
#Affiliate will operate in Round Rock in 2005   @Affiliate will operate in Corpus Christi, Texas, in 2005

NEW ORLEANS ZEPHYRS   Class AAA

ORGANIZATION STATISTICS

PACIFIC COAST LEAGUE

BATTING	AVG	G	AB	R	H	2B	3B	HR	RBI	BB	SO	SB	CS	OBP	SLG	B	T	HT	WT	DOB	1st Yr	Resides
Alfaro, Jason	.325	126	465	62	151	32	0	13	67	26	58	3	6	.363	.477	R	R	5-10	185	11-29-77	1997	Fort Worth, Texas
Brown, Emil	.337	26	92	12	31	10	1	2	17	4	20	4	2	.386	.533	R	R	6-2	200	12-29-74	1994	Chicago, Ill.
2-team (19 Memphis)	.315	45	149	19	47	13	1	2	21	9	29	5	3	.372	.456							
Bruntlett, Eric	.250	86	332	50	83	12	4	6	37	35	72	14	4	.331	.364	R	R	6-0	200	3-29-78	2000	Lafayette, Ind.
Buck, John	.300	65	227	31	68	11	0	12	35	21	39	0	1	.368	.507	R	R	6-3	210	7-7-80	1998	Salt Lake City, Utah
Burke, Chris	.315	123	483	93	152	33	6	16	52	55	76	37	14	.396	.507	R	R	5-11	180	3-11-80	2001	Knoxville, Tenn.
Coolbaugh, Mike	.295	123	404	74	119	30	0	30	82	47	96	2	1	.368	.592	R	R	6-1	190	6-5-72	1990	San Antonio, Texas
Eckelman, Alex	.286	75	185	23	53	10	2	2	16	10	24	2	3	.325	.395	R	R	5-11	190	7-14-74	1997	St. Louis, Mo.
Fatheree, Danny	.250	23	36	4	9	1	0	1	2	4	9	0	1	.325	.361	R	R	5-11	230	8-25-78	1997	Grand Prairie, Texas
Hiatt, Phil	.235	140	485	80	114	15	4	30	77	64	140	5	1	.331	.468	R	R	6-4	205	5-1-69	1990	Pensacola, Fla.
Hill, Mike	.270	88	233	32	63	10	1	6	39	23	52	3	2	.335	.399	R	R	6-4	205	9-30-76	1999	Lawton, Okla.
Huffman, Royce	.309	144	531	81	164	39	3	10	60	71	94	8	2	.393	.450	R	R	6-0	205	1-11-77	1999	Missouri City, Texas
Logan, Kyle	.248	121	399	35	99	21	3	4	33	23	48	17	2	.301	.346	L	R	6-0	202	7-11-75	1997	Hattiesburg, Miss.
Norris, Dax	.233	29	90	7	21	3	0	2	9	4	13	1	0	.266	.333	R	R	5-10	190	1-14-73	1996	La Grange, Ga.
Ryan, Rob	.261	55	138	12	36	6	0	3	12	11	21	1	0	.327	.370	L	L	5-11	190	6-24-73	1996	Renton, Wash.
Stegall, Ryan	.200	4	5	0	1	0	0	0	4	2	2	0	0	.375	.400	R	R	6-1	190	11-13-79	2001	Liberty, Mo.
Thompson, Ryan	.247	70	235	24	58	11	1	8	39	9	46	1	0	.278	.404	R	R	6-3	210	11-4-67	1987	Indianapolis, Ind.
Tremie, Chris	.241	69	195	23	47	6	1	2	24	24	30	0	1	.332	.313	R	R	6-0	210	10-17-69	1992	New Waverly, Texas
Whiteman, Tommy	.276	25	98	11	27	6	0	0	9	8	21	2	2	.336	.337	R	R	6-3	180	7-14-79	2000	Edmond, Okla.

PITCHING	W	L	ERA	G	GS	CG	SV	IP	H	R	ER	BB	SO	AVG	B	T	HT	WT	DOB	1st Yr	Resides
Babula, Shaun	2	1	6.35	26	0	0	1	28	39	23	20	11	19	.320	S	L	6-1	183	5-21-77	1999	Burlington, N.J.
Backe, Brandon	6	5	2.80	19	9	0	0	64	57	26	20	26	74	.241	R	R	6-0	180	4-5-78	1998	Texas City, Texas
Barzilla, Philip	1	1	4.32	27	0	0	0	33	42	21	16	21	21	.307	L	L	6-0	180	1-25-79	2001	Sugar Land, Texas
Bost, Heath	4	1	4.41	44	0	0	3	49	41	25	24	21	40	.232	R	R	6-3	205	10-13-74	1995	Taylorsville, N.C.
Buchholz, Taylor	6	7	5.23	20	17	1	0	98	107	60	57	29	74	.273	R	R	6-4	220	10-13-81	2000	Springfield, Pa.
Bullinger, Kirk	3	1	3.00	28	0	0	14	30	24	10	10	9	14	.226	R	R	6-2	170	10-28-69	1992	Gretna, La.
Chouinard, Bobby	3	4	5.73	26	0	0	1	33	36	21	21	13	28	.290	R	R	6-1	180	5-1-72	1990	Forest Grove, Ore.
Duckworth, Brandon	5	5	5.53	14	13	0	0	70	81	44	43	28	63	.286	R	R	6-2	195	1-23-76	1998	Kearns, Utah
Eckelman, Alex	0	0	24.00	2	0	0	0	3	11	8	8	0	1	.524	R	R	5-11	190	7-14-74	1997	St. Louis, Mo.
Enochs, Chris	6	8	4.14	38	14	1	0	113	114	61	52	35	93	.260	R	R	6-3	225	10-11-75	1997	Newell, W.Va.
Fernandez, Jared	7	11	4.77	35	28	3	0	196	209	120	104	46	98	.272	R	R	6-4	220	10-12-71	1992	Tampa, Fla.
Fiore, Tony	2	2	4.63	23	1	0	2	35	42	20	18	11	24	.309	R	R	6-0	175	4-2-77	1999	Long Beach, Calif.
Gallo, Mike	0	0	0.00	3	0	0	1	4	0	0	0	2	4	.000	L	L	6-0	175	4-2-77	1999	Avon Lakes, Ohio
Griffiths, Jeremy	3	6	5.85	15	14	0	0	80	95	55	52	26	58	.300	R	R	6-2	200	3-22-78	1999	Avon Lakes, Ohio
Harris, Reggie	2	0	7.04	7	0	0	0	8	3	6	6	6	11	.125	R	R	6-2	210	8-12-68	1987	Waynesboro, Va.
Hernandez, Carlos	9	4	3.60	23	23	0	0	128	115	54	51	46	81	.247	S	L	5-10	180	4-22-80	1997	Yagua, Venez.
Powell, Greg	0	0	7.59	5	0	0	0	11	13	9	9	6	5	.325	R	R	6-4	200	8-26-78	2001	Holland, Pa.
Qualls, Chad	3	6	5.57	32	14	1	1	107	134	69	66	30	72	.312	R	R	6-5	220	8-17-78	2001	Reno, Nev.
Redding, Tim	1	3	6.04	5	5	0	0	28	30	21	19	12	26	.268	R	R	6-0	200	2-12-78	1998	Churchville, N.Y.
Saarloos, Kirk	2	0	15.43	2	2	0	0	7	17	15	12	1	6	.447	R	R	6-0	180	5-23-79	2001	Houston, Texas
Saladin, Miguel	1	6	4.04	49	0	0	6	65	51	30	29	30	42	.222	R	R	5-11	190	5-22-75	1996	San Pedro de Macoris, D.R.
Sessions, Doug	0	3	9.18	5	4	0	0	17	23	18	17	3	14	.329	R	R	6-1	205	9-28-76	1998	Orange Park, Fla.
Springer, Russ	1	2	3.48	26	0	0	6	31	31	13	12	14	33	.263	R	R	6-4	215	11-7-68	1989	Pollack, La.
Stone, Ricky	1	0	4.50	2	0	0	0	2	1	1	1	0	0	.250	R	R	6-1	190	2-28-75	1994	Hamilton, Ohio

FIELDING

Catcher	PCT	G	PO	A	E	DP	PB
Buck	.971	61	330	34	11	8	7
Eckelman	1.000	2	12	1	0	1	0
Fatheree	.970	8	32	0	1	0	0
Norris	.994	22	154	7	1	0	1
Tremie	.982	65	387	38	8	3	7

First Base	PCT	G	PO	A	E	DP
Coolbaugh	.967	5	27	2	1	4
Hiatt	.985	15	123	7	2	11
Huffman	.997	130	1174	78	4	102
Norris	1.000	2	5	0	0	1

Second Base	PCT	G	PO	A	E	DP
Alfaro	.938	8	8	22	2	3

	PCT	G	PO	A	E	DP	PB
Bruntlett	1.000	5	8	10	0	2	
Burke	.983	121	265	377	11	86	
Eckelman	.985	16	24	43	1	11	

Third Base	PCT	G	PO	A	E	DP
Alfaro	.983	43	38	80	2	7
Coolbaugh	.967	98	51	211	9	13
Eckelman	1.000	17	5	25	0	4
Huffman	1.000	1	0	1	0	0

Shortstop	PCT	G	PO	A	E	DP
Alfaro	.959	53	76	132	9	32
Bruntlett	.967	64	99	221	11	43
Coolbaugh	.952	6	7	13	1	3

	PCT	G	PO	A	E	DP
Stegall	1.000	3	1	2	0	1
Whiteman	.972	25	38	66	3	11

Outfield	PCT	G	PO	A	E	DP
Alfaro	.978	23	43	1	1	0
Brown	.981	26	51	1	1	0
Bruntlett	.978	20	42	2	1	0
Eckelman	1.000	11	10	1	0	0
Hiatt	.989	122	177	8	2	0
Hill	.978	62	85	3	2	1
Huffman	1.000	10	13	0	0	0
Logan	.962	114	216	9	9	3
Ryan	.974	42	73	3	2	0
Thompson	.938	54	89	2	6	2

ORGANIZATION STATISTICS

TEXAS LEAGUE

BATTING	AVG	G	AB	R	H	2B	3B	HR	RBI	BB	SO	SB	CS	OBP	SLG	B	T	HT	WT	DOB	1st Yr	Resides
Acevedo, Anthony	.160	10	25	2	4	1	0	0	3	4	6	0	1	.276	.200	L	L	6-5	195	5-5-78	2000	Bakersfield, Calif.
Coffie, Ivanon	.206	71	214	30	44	8	1	11	37	18	43	2	1	.280	.407	L	R	6-1	190	5-16-77	1996	Willemstad, Curacao
Conrad, Brooks	.290	129	480	84	139	39	6	13	83	63	105	8	7	.365	.477	S	R	5-11	190	1-16-80	2001	Spring Valley, Calif.
Gimenez, Hector	.245	97	331	38	81	16	3	6	46	18	64	2	0	.284	.366	S	R	5-10	180	9-28-82	2000	San Felipe, Venez.
Hill, Mike	.284	22	88	8	25	5	0	0	11	7	20	2	1	.340	.341	R	R	6-4	205	9-30-76	1999	Lawton, Okla.
Jimerson, Charlton	.238	131	488	78	116	22	5	18	53	31	163	39	6	.290	.414	R	R	6-3	210	9-22-79	2001	Hayward, Calif.
Matranga, David	.242	112	392	61	95	20	2	7	48	34	81	14	4	.327	.357	R	R	6-0	170	1-8-77	1998	Aliso Viejo, Calif.
Norris, Dax	.319	57	204	24	65	13	0	6	33	13	24	0	0	.357	.417	R	R	5-10	190	1-14-73	1996	La Grange, Ga.
Obradovich, Mark	.182	11	33	8	6	1	0	1	3	8	13	1	0	.341	.303	R	R	6-2	175	10-26-80	2001	Tuscaloosa, Ala.
Orie, Kevin	.329	22	76	12	25	7	0	4	20	7	12	1	0	.384	.579	R	R	6-4	220	9-1-72	1993	Pittsburgh, Pa.
Rodriguez, Mike	.267	105	397	59	106	23	5	4	53	39	55	16	10	.331	.380	L	L	5-10	180	10-15-80	2001	Cooper City, Fla.
Scott, Luke	.298	63	208	45	62	17	0	19	62	33	43	0	2	.401	.654	L	R	6-0	210	6-25-78	2002	Deleon Springs, Fla.
Self, Todd	.315	131	476	86	150	34	1	11	81	89	95	8	0	.420	.460	L	R	6-5	215	11-9-78	2000	Stonewall, La.
Taveras, Willy	.335	103	409	76	137	13	1	2	27	38	76	55	11	.402	.386	R	R	6-0	160	12-25-81	1999	Tenares, D.R.
Topolski, Jon	.230	80	226	42	52	17	0	9	33	40	64	4	4	.351	.425	L	R	5-10	180	1-29-80	2000	Houston, Texas
Whiteman, Tommy	.336	68	277	39	93	14	0	8	45	20	45	5	3	.381	.473	R	R	6-3	180	7-14-79	2000	Edmond, Okla.
Zamora, Junior	.267	95	318	47	85	21	3	6	44	29	53	3	0	.330	.409	R	R	6-1	190	5-3-76	1994	Church Hill, Tenn.

PITCHING	W	L	ERA	G	GS	CG	SV	IP	H	R	ER	BB	SO	AVG	B	T	HT	WT	DOB	1st Yr	Resides
Astacio, Ezequiel	13	10	3.89	28	28	1	0	176	155	89	76	56	185	.238	R	R	6-3	150	11-4-79	1998	Hato Mayor, D.R.
Babula, Shaun	0	1	7.04	4	0	0	0	8	9	7	6	0	5	.265	S	L	6-1	183	5-21-77	1999	Burlington, N.J.
Barzilla, Philip	1	3	2.54	17	1	0	0	39	33	13	11	17	31	.231	L	L	6-0	180	1-25-79	2001	Sugar Land, Texas
Burns, Mike	11	3	1.67	56	0	0	9	81	63	18	15	15	94	.215	R	R	6-1	190	7-14-78	2000	Diamond Bar, Calif.
Carlson, Jesse	5	0	5.04	41	0	0	1	55	57	33	31	21	51	.265	L	L	6-1	160	12-31-80	2002	Kensington, Conn.
Gothreaux, Jared	9	7	3.96	27	24	2	0	157	172	82	69	35	110	.279	R	R	6-0	200	1-27-80	2002	Lake Charles, La.
Harville, Chad	0	0	0.00	2	2	0	0	3	0	0	0	2	2	.000	R	R	5-9	185	9-16-76	1997	Savannah, Tenn.
Houlton, D.J.	12	5	2.94	28	28	3	0	159	141	59	52	47	159	.237	R	R	6-4	220	8-12-79	2001	Yorba Linda, Calif.
McClaskey, Tim	7	9	4.62	34	19	0	2	140	148	81	72	36	94	.268	R	R	5-10	170	1-11-76	1996	Melbourne, Fla.
McDaniel, Denny	4	3	3.36	48	0	0	2	75	66	30	28	24	69	.234	L	L	6-3	210	8-12-76	1996	Austin, Texas
Nieve, Fernando	2	0	1.56	3	3	0	0	17	12	4	3	8	17	.197	R	R	6-0	195	7-15-82	2000	San Felipe, Venez.
Pettitte, Andy	0	0	2.25	2	2	0	0	8	4	2	2	2	9	.143	L	L	6-5	225	6-15-72	1991	Deer Park, Texas
Poland, Trey	0	0	3.09	6	0	0	0	12	11	4	4	5	7	.256	L	L	6-1	190	4-3-75	1997	Shreveport, La.
Powell, Greg	2	5	8.26	26	8	0	0	69	110	65	63	33	28	.375	R	R	6-4	200	8-26-78	2001	Holland, Pa.
Ramirez, Santiago	6	4	2.63	55	0	0	32	59	71	24	23	38	83	.244	R	R	5-11	200	8-15-78	1997	Bonao, D.R.
Rodriguez, Wandy	11	6	4.48	26	25	1	0	143	159	77	71	57	115	.283	L	L	5-11	160	1-18-79	1999	Santiago Rodriguez, D.R.
Saladin, Miguel	1	0	0.00	3	0	0	1	5	3	1	0	2	6	.188	R	R	5-11	190	5-22-75	1996	San Pedro de Macoris, D.R.
Sampson, Chris	0	0	0.00	1	0	0	0	2	3	0	0	0	1	.375	R	R	6-0	170	5-23-78	1999	Lubbock, Texas

FIELDING

Catcher	PCT	G	PO	A	E	DP	PB
Gimenez	.989	91	693	52	8	2	10
Norris	.989	45	327	33	4	5	2
Obradovich	.974	11	71	4	2	0	5

First Base	PCT	G	PO	A	E	DP
Norris	.978	6	40	5	1	2
Orie	1.000	8	47	3	0	2
Self	.994	127	1056	73	7	101
Topolski	1.000	3	22	0	0	1

Second Base	PCT	G	PO	A	E	DP
Coffie	.913	14	25	38	6	7
Conrad	.979	124	246	354	13	74

	PCT	G	PO	A	E	DP
Matranga	1.000	1	1	2	0	0
Topolski	.800	2	3	1	1	0

Third Base	PCT	G	PO	A	E	DP
Coffie	.851	21	15	25	7	0
Gimenez	1.000	1	1	0	0	0
Matranga	.970	39	28	69	3	8
Norris	1.000	2	0	2	0	0
Topolski	.731	20	13	7	0	0
Zamora	.958	79	48	136	8	10

Shortstop	PCT	G	PO	A	E	DP
Coffie	.895	5	8	9	2	3
Matranga	.979	67	87	192	6	29

	PCT	G	PO	A	E	DP
Whiteman	.956	68	104	197	14	46
Zamora	.929	3	4	9	1	4

Outfield	PCT	G	PO	A	E	DP
Acevedo	1.000	3	5	0	0	0
Hill	.975	23	37	2	1	0
Jimerson	.978	128	251	12	6	2
Rodriguez	.975	101	154	3	4	0
Scott	.987	42	75	1	1	0
Self	1.000	7	10	0	0	0
Taveras	.974	103	207	14	6	3
Topolski	.956	40	43	0	2	0

CAROLINA LEAGUE

BATTING	AVG	G	AB	R	H	2B	3B	HR	RBI	BB	SO	SB	CS	OBP	SLG	B	T	HT	WT	DOB	1st Yr	Resides
Anderson, Josh	.268	66	280	45	75	13	6	2	21	13	53	31	4	.314	.379	L	L	6-2	195	8-10-82	2003	Eubank, Ky.
Fagan, John	.256	113	356	49	91	15	1	9	45	49	103	9	3	.358	.407	R	R	6-5	200	8-8-79	2001	San Jose, Calif.
Helquist, Jon	.219	115	370	49	81	19	3	3	29	28	79	8	1	.292	.311	R	R	6-0	170	8-17-80	1999	Jacksonville, Fla.
Kochen, Ryan	.254	96	338	40	86	16	2	5	33	19	52	5	1	.300	.358	R	R	6-2	195	6-13-79	2001	Batavia, Ill.
Likely, Cameron	.200	49	135	16	27	2	0	1	11	8	33	7	5	.255	.237	R	R	5-10	160	2-2-78	2001	Port St. Joe, Fla.
Mackor, Jeff	.235	65	221	20	52	6	0	1	20	11	46	1	1	.282	.276	R	R	6-1	215	6-17-80	2002	Salem, N.H.
Obradovich, Mark	.176	51	153	19	27	4	0	1	15	27	35	0	0	.301	.222	R	R	6-2	175	10-26-80	2001	Tuscaloosa, Ala.
Peavey, Pat	.275	131	476	47	131	25	0	7	62	33	54	3	1	.332	.372	R	R	6-1	195	5-5-80	2002	Brisbane, Calif.
Robinson, Wade	.262	128	507	69	133	24	3	3	61	35	101	15	7	.307	.339	L	R	6-2	165	1-12-81	2003	Bastrop, La.
Ruiz, Reinaldo	.333	24	78	8	26	4	0	0	9	6	14	1	0	.384	.385	R	R	6-4	200	2-4-80	1997	Falcon, Venez.
Saccomanno, Mark	.261	136	513	71	134	25	2	22	80	48	134	2	1	.330	.446	R	R	6-1	195	4-30-80	2003	Spring, Texas
Scott, Luke	.278	66	241	45	67	20	1	8	35	41	58	6	1	.369	.469	L	R	6-0	210	6-25-78	2002	Deleon Springs, Fla.
Seuss, Adam	.283	104	361	38	102	20	0	7	64	44	63	1	1	.370	.396	L	R	6-1	190	8-31-80	2002	La Quinta, Calif.
Skaug, Brian	.000	3	5	0	0	0	0	0	0	0	1	0	0	.000	.000	R	R	6-1	190	4-13-81	2003	Moses Lake, Wash.
Stegall, Ryan	.232	109	393	42	91	13	0	1	33	28	65	8	2	.293	.272	R	R	6-1	190	11-13-79	2001	Liberty, Mo.
Wright, Gavin	.270	54	163	20	44	7	1	1	12	8	32	1	2	.310	.344	R	R	6-2	175	5-6-79	1999	Lufkin, Texas

PITCHING	W	L	ERA	G	GS	CG	SV	IP	H	R	ER	BB	SO	AVG	B	T	HT	WT	DOB	1st Yr	Resides
France, Ryan	2	2	3.16	20	0	0	0	37	42	20	13	19	25	.294	S	R	6-2	196	3-25-80	2003	Austin, Texas
Freeman, Daniel	4	3	4.86	54	0	0	11	67	82	40	36	40	32	.313	R	R	6-2	215	8-3-82	2002	Jonesboro, La.
Heitzman, Aaron	0	4	7.06	29	2	0	0	51	76	50	40	35	25	.347	L	L	6-0	180	11-21-79	2002	New Ulm, Minn.
Hirsh, Jason	11	7	4.01	26	23	0	0	130	128	66	58	57	96	.262	R	R	6-8	250	2-20-82	2003	Las Vegas, Nev.
Kesten, Michael	0	1	3.77	2	2	1	0	14	13	6	6	6	8	.255	S	L	6-3	225	9-22-81	1999	Bellflower, Calif.

PITCHING	W	L	ERA	G	GS	CG	SV	IP	H	R	ER	BB	SO	AVG	B	T	HT	WT	DOB	1st Yr	Resides
Lipari, Tom	0	1	6.86	9	0	0	0	21	31	17	16	11	16	.356	L	L	6-5	180	4-23-79	2002	Omaha, Neb.
Mansfield, Monte	9	3	3.20	59	0	0	9	98	81	39	35	41	83	.226	R	R	6-4	215	3-22-81	2000	Hesperia, Calif.
McLemore, Mark	7	7	3.66	37	14	1	6	93	80	38	38	44	79	.228	L	L	6-2	220	10-9-80	2002	Granite Bay, Calif.
Merchant, Jamie	3	11	4.61	25	17	0	0	105	121	58	54	38	77	.290	R	R	6-4	260	3-19-81	2003	Colchester, Ver.
Nieve, Fernando	10	6	2.96	24	24	2	0	149	136	52	49	40	117	.242	R	R	6-0	195	7-15-82	2000	San Felipe, Venez.
Peguero, Jailen	5	6	3.87	51	1	0	8	86	93	51	37	32	79	.282	R	R	6-0	195	1-4-81	2000	Azua, D.R.
Pena, Francisco	1	2	5.86	11	10	0	0	35	39	26	23	26	31	.289	R	R	5-11	175	3-9-79	1997	Bonao, D.R.
Rodaway, Brian	5	8	4.87	34	19	0	2	131	158	77	71	30	67	.298	L	L	6-3	190	9-11-78	2001	Lincoln, Neb.
Sampson, Chris	7	11	3.80	27	27	2	0	152	170	72	64	26	101	.288	R	R	6-0	170	5-23-78	1999	Lubbock, Texas
Westhoff, Bill	1	2	5.84	20	0	0	0	37	44	26	24	23	14	.328	L	R	6-0	195	1-18-80	2002	Frisco, Texas

FIELDING

Catcher	PCT	G	PO	A	E	DP	PB
Mackor	.991	65	399	60	4	7	5
Obradovich	.997	51	327	51	1	6	7
Ruiz	.980	24	134	12	3	1	7

First Base	PCT	G	PO	A	E	DP
Fagan	.997	47	351	26	1	45
Peavey	.994	33	290	27	2	26
Saccomanno	.990	69	669	44	7	63

Second Base	PCT	G	PO	A	E	DP
Helquist	.972	113	223	370	17	76

Peavey	.982	32	56	104	3	22	
Skaug	1.000	3	2	10	0	2	
Stegall	1.000	2	0	1	0	0	

Third Base	PCT	G	PO	A	E	DP
Helquist	1.000	1	0	1	0	0
Peavey	.923	43	17	79	8	6
Saccomanno	.778	4	1	6	2	0
Stegall	.955	97	67	165	11	14

Shortstop	PCT	G	PO	A	E	DP
Robinson	.936	128	235	425	45	105

Stegall	.944	11	23	28	3	12

Outfield	PCT	G	PO	A	E	DP
Anderson	.977	66	160	7	4	3
Fagan	.969	66	123	4	4	1
Kochen	.986	96	137	4	2	0
Likely	.980	46	49	0	1	0
Scott	.992	66	116	6	1	1
Seuss	.990	58	96	4	1	0
Wright	1.000	51	76	4	0	2

LEXINGTON LEGENDS — Low Class A

SOUTH ATLANTIC LEAGUE

BATTING	AVG	G	AB	R	H	2B	3B	HR	RBI	BB	SO	SB	CS	OBP	SLG	B	T	HT	WT	DOB	1st Yr	Resides
Acevedo, Freddy	.217	109	341	50	74	17	2	10	43	37	97	16	4	.303	.367	R	R	6-2	200	9-23-81	1999	La Romana, D.R.
Alcantara, Ervin	.277	131	477	66	132	25	2	16	83	59	111	28	11	.355	.438	R	R	6-2	175	10-3-80	2002	San Pedro de Macoris, D.R.
Anderson, Josh	.326	73	298	69	97	12	3	4	31	33	47	48	9	.403	.426	L	L	6-2	195	8-10-82	2003	Eubank, Ky.
Davidson, Kevin	.216	48	148	20	32	4	0	1	17	26	18	7	3	.330	.264	R	R	5-9	185	7-21-80	2002	Port Richey, Fla.
Fernando, Osvaldo	.254	116	433	76	110	21	2	4	51	32	76	30	13	.320	.339	R	R	6-0	175	10-15-80	2001	San Pedro de Macoris, D.R.
Hearod, Beau	.257	118	428	68	110	22	0	25	68	51	135	1	2	.355	.484	R	R	5-10	205	4-3-81	2003	Jennings, La.
Hudgson, Maximiliano	.143	7	7	0	1	0	0	0	1	4	0	0	0	.333	.143	S	R	5-11	160	8-6-80	2000	Cali, Colombia
Humphries, Justin	.269	62	219	28	59	13	1	9	37	19	55	0	1	.327	.461	R	R	6-4	220	2-24-83	2001	Richmond, Texas
Koman, Brock	.276	82	294	35	81	22	1	3	43	19	44	0	0	.338	.388	R	R	6-0	205	10-11-80	2003	Pueblo West, Colo.
Maysonet, Edwin	.261	109	391	79	102	22	10	11	64	64	91	18	7	.372	.453	R	R	6-1	180	10-17-81	2003	Vega Baja, P.R.
Melendez, German	.227	77	238	34	54	12	0	1	19	29	61	11	2	.325	.290	R	R	6-0	180	9-13-80	1999	Mariara, Venez.
Prosser, Chad	.238	70	244	33	58	10	6	30	18	39	10	3	.301	.352	R	R	5-6	155	5-11-81	2003	Austell, Ga.
Riera, Zack	.272	26	81	11	22	6	0	1	7	10	16	2	0	.372	.383	S	R	5-9	185	4-16-79	2000	Tallahassee, Fla.
Robinson, Scott	.263	123	457	63	120	28	1	4	46	46	64	7	7	.333	.354	L	S	6-1	185	10-14-83	2003	Fairbanks, Alaska
Torres, Saul	.252	122	453	49	114	15	2	7	62	35	91	4	1	.321	.340	R	R	6-3	200	2-18-82	2000	Curarigua, Venez.
Tucker, Mamon	.211	41	123	26	4	1	0	12	12	24	0	2	.277	.260	R	R	6-3	180	10-18-79	1998	Austin, Texas

PITCHING	W	L	ERA	G	GS	CG	SV	IP	H	R	ER	BB	SO	AVG	B	T	HT	WT	DOB	1st Yr	Resides
Adler, Anthony	1	3	3.14	14	0	0	2	29	27	12	10	6	25	.257	R	R	6-4	195	6-6-80	2004	Dallas, Texas
Albers, Matt	8	3	3.31	22	21	0	0	111	95	51	41	57	140	.228	L	R	6-0	205	1-20-83	2002	Sugar Land, Texas
Beltre, Jonathan	4	5	3.08	46	0	0	0	79	63	29	27	53	79	.223	L	L	6-0	160	7-7-80	2000	Azua, D.R.
Collar, Mike	2	6	8.45	38	6	0	1	87	128	89	82	48	57	.344	R	R	6-3	210	10-16-81	2003	Scarborough, Maine
DeLeon, Joey	4	5	4.30	37	2	0	1	82	90	44	39	46	72	.282	R	R	5-11	190	10-21-82	2001	Nixon, Texas
Diaz, Raymar	1	3	4.43	24	1	0	2	43	31	21	21	26	37	.199	R	R	6-7	190	11-13-83	2003	Canovanas, P.R.
Douglass, Chance	9	10	5.33	29	24	0	0	137	156	99	81	73	106	.289	R	R	6-1	200	2-24-84	2002	Amarillo, Texas
France, Ryan	3	0	1.83	22	0	0	2	39	20	8	8	12	44	.150	S	R	6-2	196	3-25-80	2003	Austin, Texas
Grigsby, Derick	7	11	4.75	27	26	0	0	135	129	86	71	92	139	.254	R	R	6-0	190	6-30-82	2003	Marshall, Texas
Humphries, Justin	0	0	27.00	2	2	0	0	1	4	4	4	1	1	.500	R	R	6-4	220	2-24-83	2001	Richmond, Texas
Muecke, Josh	9	1	3.94	37	8	0	2	105	82	48	46	48	91	.214	L	L	6-3	195	1-9-82	2003	San Diego, Calif.
Ramsey, Robert	1	1	18.00	9	0	0	0	8	15	23	16	14	9	.405	R	R	6-2	185	9-26-81	2003	Austin, Texas
Shortell, Rory	1	3	7.06	7	7	0	0	29	26	23	23	13	21	.239	R	R	6-3	205	6-3-81	2003	Portland, Ore.
Stiehl, Robert	4	5	4.09	18	18	0	0	62	58	36	28	21	74	.246	R	R	6-2	230	12-9-80	2000	Torrance, Calif.
Talbot, Mitch	10	10	3.83	27	27	1	0	153	145	78	65	49	115	.247	R	R	6-2	175	10-17-83	2002	Cedar City, Utah
Wheatland, Matt	0	0	3.12	18	0	0	0	35	33	15	12	16	25	.252	R	R	6-5	210	10-18-81	2000	Poway, Calif.
Williams, Aaron	4	6	3.20	59	0	0	18	79	75	32	28	24	53	.253	R	R	6-1	180	10-7-80	2002	Oakfield, N.Y.

FIELDING

Catcher	PCT	G	PO	A	E	DP	PB
Davidson	.998	47	398	30	1	6	2
Humphries	1.000	3	16	0	0	0	2
Melendez	.982	75	560	51	11	4	13
Riera	.979	16	134	8	3	3	2

First Base	PCT	G	PO	A	E	DP
Humphries	.983	14	107	9	2	12
Koman	1.000	6	46	2	0	2
Melendez	1.000	2	10	0	0	1
Robinson	.985	120	950	75	16	90

Second Base	PCT	G	PO	A	E	DP
Fernando	1.000	3	8	3	0	1
Maysonet	.964	80	134	212	13	64
Prosser	.966	62	80	177	9	26

Third Base	PCT	G	PO	A	E	DP
Koman	.886	21	12	27	5	2
Prosser	.750	2	0	3	1	1
Torres	.955	118	86	212	14	18

Shortstop	PCT	G	PO	A	E	DP
Fernando	.950	112	171	304	25	68
Maysonet	.955	31	46	81	6	11

Outfield	PCT	G	PO	A	E	DP
Acevedo	.981	109	192	15	4	3
Alcantara	.973	136	245	10	7	3
Anderson	.968	73	150	2	5	0
Hearod	.969	82	126	1	4	0
Hudgson	.833	5	5	0	1	0
Tucker	.983	37	59	0	1	0

TRI-CITY VALLEYCATS — Short-Season Class A

NEW YORK-PENN LEAGUE

BATTING	AVG	G	AB	R	H	2B	3B	HR	RBI	BB	SO	SB	CS	OBP	SLG	B	T	HT	WT	DOB	1st Yr	Resides
Alvarez, Wilner	.206	23	63	6	13	0	0	0	5	5	14	6	2	.275	.206	R	R	6-0	175	7-14-82	2001	Caracas, Venez.
Ash, Jonny	.297	61	239	50	71	7	3	2	25	25	16	5	4	.388	.377	L	R	5-9	180	9-11-82	2004	Oakland, Calif.

BATTING	AVG	G	AB	R	H	2B	3B	HR	RBI	BB	SO	SB	CS	OBP	SLG	B	T	HT	WT	DOB	1st Yr	Resides
Averill, Brandon	.222	34	108	15	24	5	1	2	11	10	40	1	0	.294	.343	R	R	6-4	215	10-18-81	2004	Anaheim, Calif.
Babilonia, Edgar	.299	48	147	19	44	6	2	0	19	7	18	8	2	.340	.367	R	R	5-10	160	8-5-83	2000	Cartagena, Colombia
Barganier, Luke	.230	42	139	13	32	2	2	0	8	14	31	5	2	.299	.273	L	R	6-0	175	5-5-83	2004	Temple, Texas
Caraballo, Francisco	.275	57	207	27	57	12	1	7	33	16	51	4	2	.335	.444	R	R	6-1	185	10-21-83	2001	Anaco, Venez.
Clark, James	.256	38	125	21	32	5	0	5	19	14	35	2	0	.336	.416	R	R	6-3	200	8-10-82	2004	Richmond, Ky.
Cooper, James	.232	45	125	28	29	4	1	1	14	18	39	9	1	.333	.304	R	R	6-3	185	2-12-82	2004	Cullen, La.
Einertson, Mitch	.143	2	7	1	1	0	0	1	1	0	2	0	0	.143	.571	R	R	5-10	178	4-4-86	2004	Oceanside, Calif.
Garza, Mario	.238	66	239	38	57	11	1	15	65	36	61	3	1	.343	.481	L	R	6-0	202	5-26-81	2003	Melbourne, Fla.
Koch, Brady	.279	14	43	9	12	2	0	2	12	4	10	1	0	.353	.465	R	R	6-2	180	4-7-83	2004	Manhattan Beach, Calif.
Koenig, Lance	.270	20	63	9	17	3	0	1	4	5	17	0	1	.324	.365	R	R	6-3	170	12-10-80	2003	Brielle, N.J.
Pence, Hunter	.296	51	199	36	59	18	1	8	37	23	30	3	5	.369	.518	R	R	6-4	200	4-13-83	2004	Arlington, Texas
Santangelo, Lou	.201	47	164	28	33	5	2	6	20	21	58	2	1	.299	.366	R	R	6-1	200	3-16-83	2004	Holmdel, N.J.
Skaug, Brian	.364	5	11	2	4	1	0	0	1	0	2	1	0	.364	.455	R	R	6-1	190	4-13-81	2003	Moses Lake, Wash.
Sutton, Drew	.280	63	250	43	70	10	0	1	16	39	50	2	4	.379	.332	S	R	6-3	185	6-30-83	2004	Jackson, Tenn.
Vital, Kevin	.240	60	183	24	44	9	2	7	36	27	59	4	0	.344	.426	L	R	6-0	245	2-9-80	2003	Loreauville, La.
Walls, Michael	.292	12	24	6	7	2	0	1	5	2	4	1	0	.333	.500	R	R	6-1	190	8-9-81	2003	Hockessin, Del.
Zobrist, Ben	.339	68	257	50	87	14	3	4	45	43	31	15	4	.438	.463	S	R	6-3	200	5-26-81	2004	Eureka, Ill.

GAMES BY POSITION: C—Clark 7, Koch 9, Koenig 20, Santangelo 43. **1B**—Averill 1, Garza 49, Vital 34. **2B**—Ash 15, Babilonia 11, Sutton 54. **3B**—Ash 43, Averill 28, Babilonia 7, Skaug 4, Sutton 2. **SS**—Babilonia 8, Sutton 3, Zobrist 68. **OF**—Alvarez 21, Babilonia 22, Barganier 42, Caraballo 42, Cooper 42, Pence 51, Vital 25.

PITCHING	W	L	ERA	G	GS	CG	SV	IP	H	R	ER	BB	SO	AVG	B	T	HT	WT	DOB	1st Yr	Resides
Alvarado, Andy	4	3	3.58	11	10	1	0	50	47	23	20	24	41	.254	R	R	6-1	210	12-3-82	2004	Union City, Calif.
Brown, Casey	4	1	3.11	21	0	0	4	46	37	17	16	13	40	.213	R	R	6-0	210	2-13-82	2004	Tulsa, Okla.
DeWitt, Anthony	1	0	3.00	13	0	0	0	21	18	10	7	11	18	.225	R	R	6-0	225	5-30-82	2004	Hattiesburg, Miss.
Diaz, Raymar	7	5	3.19	15	15	0	0	79	70	36	28	31	70	.238	R	R	6-7	190	11-13-83	2003	Canovanas, P.R.
Edmiston, Bo	3	1	3.74	20	0	0	2	46	38	23	19	10	43	.221	R	R	6-5	220	8-1-81	2003	Greenville, Miss.
Englebrook, Evan	2	4	3.94	14	14	0	0	62	58	30	27	28	71	.251	R	R	6-8	225	4-28-82	2004	Mechanicsburg, Pa.
Escobar, Rodrigo	8	0	1.33	25	2	0	7	54	38	9	8	16	62	.196	R	R	5-11	165	2-11-83	2000	Cartagena, Colombia
Estrada, Paul	5	1	2.81	23	0	0	8	42	26	13	13	17	56	.177	R	R	6-1	215	9-10-82	2000	Ciudad Bolivar, Venez.
Martinez, Ronnie	11	2	1.96	15	15	1	0	92	62	21	20	20	81	.190	R	R	5-11	180	7-6-83	2002	Cotui, D.R.
McKeller, Ryan	4	4	4.86	14	14	0	0	74	74	44	40	39	64	.261	R	R	6-5	210	7-8-83	2003	Pflugerville, Texas
Murdy, Garrett	0	1	3.94	7	1	0	1	16	14	9	7	6	12	.230	R	R	6-4	215	3-15-83	2004	Laguna Hills, Calif.
Reineke, Chad	0	2	2.45	23	0	0	3	37	27	13	10	23	52	.206	R	R	6-6	210	4-9-82	2004	Defiance, Ohio
Romero, Levi	0	0	4.32	4	0	0	1	8	6	5	4	4	9	.200	R	R	6-1	170	4-12-84	2001	Anzoategui, Venez.
Shortell, Rory	0	0	1.86	3	3	0	0	10	8	2	2	3	10	.235	R	R	6-3	205	6-3-81	2003	Portland, Ore.
Soto, Enyelbert	0	0	4.50	1	0	0	0	2	2	1	1	0	3	.250	L	L	6-1	190	8-20-82	2000	Maracaibo, Venez.
Wigdahl, Jeff	1	1	3.51	19	1	0	0	33	20	15	13	19	35	.180	L	L	6-0	190	6-4-84	2004	San Antonio, Texas

GREENEVILLE ASTROS — Rookie

APPALACHIAN LEAGUE

BATTING	AVG	G	AB	R	H	2B	3B	HR	RBI	BB	SO	SB	CS	OBP	SLG	B	T	HT	WT	DOB	1st Yr	Resides
Acosta, Jose	.269	35	108	20	29	6	1	3	22	8	22	3	1	.341	.426	R	R	6-2	170	4-18-83	2001	Bonao, D.R.
Cavers, Eric	.200	18	45	5	9	2	0	0	3	4	18	2	1	.308	.244	R	R	6-1	205	11-9-82	2004	Otisfield, Maine
Corapci, Jason	.191	26	68	3	13	3	0	0	5	13	13	0	1	.233	.235	R	R	5-8	170	10-11-81	2003	Orange, Calif.
Einertson, Mitch	.308	63	227	53	70	15	0	24	67	32	70	4	4	.415	.692	R	R	5-10	178	4-4-86	2004	Oceanside, Calif.
Espinoza, Pedro	.265	33	83	10	22	3	0	0	14	5	12	4	2	.322	.301	R	R	6-2	162	5-6-85	2003	El Tocuyo, Venez.
Garcia, Antonio	.316	44	152	18	48	10	0	4	20	12	39	0	2	.369	.461	R	R	6-5	235	8-21-82	2004	Panama City, Panama
Hernandez, Jose	.264	39	106	20	28	3	1	2	12	16	32	11	2	.366	.368	R	R	6-0	160	8-22-84	2003	Villa De Cura, Venez.
Hudson, Maximiliano	.273	10	22	4	6	2	0	0	3	3	4	1	3	.407	.364	S	R	5-11	160	8-6-80	2000	Cali, Colombia
Kady, David	.133	15	15	2	2	1	0	0	0	2	5	0	0	.316	.200	L	R	6-0	205	7-29-80	2004	Highland Park, N.J.
Parraz, Jordan	.244	53	180	35	44	6	5	4	21	24	44	9	5	.349	.400	R	R	6-3	212	10-18-84	2004	Henderson, Nev.
Reed, Ryan	.227	48	172	34	39	7	0	2	20	24	40	9	5	.321	.302	L	L	6-4	200	12-19-83	2004	Lake Charles, La.
Sellers, Neil	.285	50	158	23	45	11	0	2	30	23	30	3	4	.387	.392	R	R	6-0	190	4-3-82	2004	Robards, Ky.
Sheldon, Ole	.217	53	166	23	36	4	1	3	19	14	23	8	0	.283	.307	R	R	6-3	210	11-25-82	2004	Roseburg, Ore.
Sutil, Waladimir	.298	53	188	31	56	9	0	0	29	17	24	24	8	.372	.346	R	R	5-10	140	10-31-84	2004	Caracas, Venez.
Torbert, Beau	.225	35	111	18	25	3	0	0	15	13	30	6	4	.320	.252	R	R	6-4	205	5-11-83	2004	Phenix City, Ala.
Towles, J.R.	.243	39	111	17	27	6	0	0	8	12	23	4	3	.370	.297	R	R	6-2	190	2-11-84	2004	Crosby, Texas
Triplett, Bryan	.279	44	147	31	41	11	1	1	18	26	32	9	5	.399	.388	R	R	6-0	185	4-16-82	2004	Leesville, S.C.
Uhle, Chris	.214	37	98	17	21	7	0	0	7	18	35	4	0	.345	.286	R	R	5-10	180	9-11-82	2004	Morton Grove, Ill.

GAMES BY POSITION: C—Acosta 27, Cavers 10, James 1, Kady 8, Towles 37. **1B**—Corapci 1, Garcia 27, Sheldon 48. **2B**—Corapci 10, Espinoza 18, Triplett 19, Uhle 29. **3B**—Corapci 13, Sellers 45, Triplett 14, Uhle 1. **SS**—Corapci 2, Espinoza 12, Sutil 53, Triplett 8, Uhle 2. **OF**—Corapci 2, Einertson 55, Hernandez 37, Hudgson 9, Parraz 38, Torbert 31.

PITCHING	W	L	ERA	G	GS	CG	SV	IP	H	R	ER	BB	SO	AVG	B	T	HT	WT	DOB	1st Yr	Resides
Adler, Anthony	1	0	1.59	10	0	0	4	17	8	3	3	3	10	.143	R	R	6-4	195	6-6-80	2004	Dallas, Texas
Arguello, Douglas	1	0	2.92	16	0	0	0	25	16	8	8	13	22	.184	L	L	6-1	175	11-24-84	2002	Managua, Nicaragua
Barthmaier, Jimmy	4	3	3.78	13	13	0	0	69	70	32	29	22	65	.258	R	R	6-4	210	1-6-84	2003	Roswell, Ga.
Chedister, Brad	0	0	10.20	11	0	0	0	15	15	20	17	20	11	.242	R	R	6-5	220	4-28-81	2004	Fort Walton Beach, Fla.
Davis, Cliff	0	1	3.60	5	5	0	0	25	29	13	10	8	19	.282	R	R	6-5	205	12-31-84	2003	Europa, Miss.
DeWitt, Anthony	2	1	0.47	7	0	0	0	19	13	3	1	3	15	.188	R	R	6-0	225	5-30-82	2004	Hattiesburg, Miss.
Gonzalez, Juan	0	1	7.71	3	0	0	0	5	3	4	4	6	5	.188	R	R	5-11	160	1-29-83	2001	La Isabela, D.R.
Gutierrez, Juan	8	2	3.70	13	13	0	0	66	74	31	27	30	59	.290	R	R	6-3	200	7-14-83	2001	Puerto la Cruz, Venez.
James, Brad	2	6	4.44	13	10	0	0	63	63	36	26	36	38	.238	R	R	6-2	205	6-19-84	2004	Prosper, Texas
Murdy, Garrett	2	3	6.43	8	3	1	1	21	31	19	15	6	20	.341	R	R	6-4	215	3-15-83	2004	Laguna Hills, Calif.
O'Donnell, Matthew	4	0	1.91	15	0	0	0	28	25	7	6	7	22	.248	L	R	6-1	190	8-19-81	2004	Marlborough, Mass.
Patton, Troy	2	2	1.93	4	4	0	0	28	23	8	6	5	32	.215	B	L	6-1	185	9-3-85	2004	Magnolia, Texas
Paulino, Felipe	1	3	7.59	10	10	0	0	32	30	30	27	24	37	.248	R	R	6-2	180	10-5-83	2002	Los Teques, Venez.
Romero, Levi	8	0	2.19	13	7	0	0	53	41	18	13	22	43	.215	R	R	6-1	170	4-12-84	2001	Anzoategui, Venez.
Solis, Marcos	1	1	8.07	16	0	0	0	35	37	28	26	12	20	.298	R	R	6-1	155	5-16-85	2002	Panama City, Panama
Soto, Enyelbert	1	1	1.03	24	0	0	13	35	30	10	4	2	47	.224	L	L	6-1	190	8-20-82	2000	Maracaibo, Venez.
Sotro, Chris	0	2	4.35	13	0	0	1	21	22	14	10	10	18	.256	R	R	6-0	195	12-8-80	2004	Upland, Calif.
Thompson, Ryan	4	0	2.25	15	0	0	0	36	33	11	9	4	33	.250	R	R	6-4	220	8-6-82	2004	Lakeland, Fla.

KANSAS CITY ROYALS

BY ALAN ESKEW

It has been 20 years since the Royals won the 1985 World Series.

That was also the last season the Royals made the American League playoffs, but entering the 2004 season there were expectations the team could return to the playoffs after winning 83 games in 2003.

Instead, the Royals finished last in the A.L. Central and lost a franchise-record 104 games, becoming only the second team in major league history to sandwich two 100-loss seasons around a winning season. The Royals were 62-100 in 2002.

The Royals thought they had beefed up their offense before the 2004 season with the signing of free agents Juan Gonzalez, a two-time A.L. MVP with 434 career home runs, and Benito Santiago, a five-time National League all-star catcher.

Gonzalez ended up playing 33 games and hitting five home runs before being sidelined with a bad back. Gonzalez proved a costly sign, $4.5 million for 2004, for a budget-conscious club. Santiago played in just 49 games before a fractured left hand ended his season on June 17.

They were not alone in spending ample time on the disabled list. The only Opening Day position player starter who avoided the disabled list was Carlos Beltran, who was traded to the Astros in a three-team deal for June 24 for prospects catcher John Buck, righthanded pitcher Mike Wood and third baseman Mark Teahen. The Royals lost 12 of 13 immediately after the Beltran trade.

The Beltran trade was yet another warning signal that the Royals continue to have problems keeping their star players once they become close to free agency. The Royals also traded away outfielders Johnny Damon and Jermaine Dye in recent years before they could file for free agency.

For the second straight year, team captain Mike Sweeney missed more than 50 games with recurring back

Zack Greinke   Billy Butler

PAUL JASIENSKI

PLAYERS of the YEAR

MAJOR LEAGUE: Zack Greinke, rhp

Greinke was one of the few bright spots on a hugely disappointing Royals team in 2004. Playing the entire season as a 20-year-old, Greinke went 8-11, 3.97 after his callup from Triple-A Omaha and showed an advanced feel for pitching.

MINOR LEAGUE: Billy Butler, 3b

Despite being one of the youngest players in the Rookie-level Pioneer League in 2004, the 18-year-old Butler made a run at the league's triple crown. Demonstrating remarkable plate discipline and potentially huge power, Butler led the league with a .373 average and 68 RBIs to go along with 10 homers.

injuries.

Royals' pitchers were also besieged by injuries. Young starting pitchers Runelvys Hernandez, Miguel Asencio and Kyle Snyder missed the entire season after surgeries, while veteran Kevin Appier made but two starts before a forearm and elbow injury finished his season in April.

The Royals went through a club-record 58 players in 2004, one shy of the major league record for a season. They sent 25 pitchers to the mound and for the first time in club history did not have a pitcher win 10 games.

The Royals went to a youth movement midway through the 2004 season, starting as many as seven rookies in games late in the season.

Righthander Zack Greinke, the sixth-overall pick in the 2002 draft, looks like a future staff ace. Greinke, who did not turn 21 until after the season, had a 3.97 ERA, which was lowest among all big league rookies with at least 100 innings pitched.

Rookie David DeJesus, who replaced Beltran in center, had two 15-game hitting streaks, including one to end the season. Buck showed power, hitting 12 home runs in 238 at-bats. Second baseman Ruben Gotay, who was named the Royals minor league player of the year, hit .270 in 44 games after being promoted from Double-A Wichita.

Billy Butler, the Royals' top pick in the 2004 draft, led the Pioneer League with a .373 average, .488 on-base percentage and 68 RBIs. Luis Cota, a draft-and-follow from 2003 who likely would have been a first-round pick in 2004 had he re-entered the draft, has a mid-90s mph fastball and went 2-1 with a 5.81 in 14 games with Idaho Falls.

ORGANIZATION LEADERS

BATTING

*AVG	Billy Butler, Idaho Falls	.373
R	Mel Stocker, Wichita/Wilmington	85
H	Mitch Maier, Wilmington/Burlington	141
TB	Jed Hansen, Omaha	234
2B	Mike Aviles, Wilmington	40
3B	Alexis Gomez, Omaha	8
HR	Calvin Pickering, Omaha	35
RBI	Brandon Berger, Omaha/Wichita	87
BB	Calvin Pickering, Omaha	70
SO	Chad Santos, Wichita	119
SB	Mel Stocker, Wichita/Wilmington	47
*OBP	Billy Butler, Idaho Falls	.486
*SLG	Calvin Pickering, Omaha	.712

PITCHING

W	Les Walrond, Omaha/Wichita	14
L	Greg Atencio, Burlington	14
#ERA	Trae McGill, Wilmington	2.08
G	J.J. Trujillo, Wichita	59
CG	Three tied at	2
SV	Ryan Braun, Wilmington	24
IP	Kris Wilson, Omaha	167
BB	Ambiorix Burgos, Burlington	75
SO	Ambiorix Burgos, Burlington	172

*Minimum 250 at-bats #Minimum 75 innings

KANSAS CITY ROYALS

Manager: Tony Pena. **2004 Record:** 58-104, .358 (5th, AL Central).

BATTING	AVG	G	AB	R	H	2B	3B	HR	RBI	BB	SO	SB	CS	OBP	SLG	B	T	HT	WT	DOB	1st Yr	Resides
Bautista, Jose	.200	13	25	1	5	1	0	0	1	1	12	0	0	.231	.240	R	R	6-0	190	10-19-80	2001	Santo Domingo, D.R.
Beltran, Carlos	.278	69	266	51	74	19	2	15	51	37	44	14	3	.367	.534	S	R	6-1	190	4-24-77	1995	Manati, P.R.
Berger, Brandon	.200	11	35	5	7	2	0	0	2	0	7	1	1	.200	.257	R	R	5-11	200	2-21-75	1996	Fort Mitchell, Ky.
Berroa, Angel	.262	134	512	72	134	27	6	8	43	23	87	14	8	.308	.385	R	R	6-0	175	1-27-78	1998	Santo Domingo, D.R.
Blanco, Andres	.317	19	60	9	19	2	2	0	5	5	6	1	2	.379	.417	S	R	5-10	155	4-11-84	2001	Moron, Venez.
Brown, Adrian	.273	5	11	0	3	0	0	0	0	0	2	0	0	.273	.273	S	R	6-0	200	2-7-74	1992	Summit, Miss.
Brown, Dee	.251	59	195	19	49	7	0	4	24	11	50	2	2	.293	.349	L	R	6-0	225	3-27-78	1996	Orlando, Fla.
Buck, John	.235	71	238	36	56	9	0	12	30	15	79	1	1	.280	.424	R	R	6-3	210	7-7-80	1998	Salt Lake City, Utah
Castillo, Alberto	.270	29	89	12	24	6	0	1	11	14	10	0	2	.365	.371	R	R	6-0	215	2-10-70	1987	Port St. Lucie, Fla.
DeJesus, David	.287	96	363	58	104	15	3	7	39	33	53	8	11	.360	.402	L	L	6-0	175	12-20-79	2002	Manalapan, N.J.
Gettis, Byron	.179	21	39	7	7	1	1	0	1	8	14	0	1	.327	.256	R	R	6-0	240	3-13-80	1998	East St. Louis, Ill.
Gomez, Alexis	.276	13	29	1	8	1	0	0	4	2	8	0	0	.323	.310	L	L	6-2	180	8-6-78	1997	Dajabon, D.R.
Gonzalez, Juan	.276	33	127	17	35	4	1	5	17	9	19	0	1	.326	.441	R	R	6-3	220	10-16-69	1986	Levittown, P.R.
Gotay, Ruben	.270	44	152	17	41	7	3	1	16	9	36	0	1	.315	.375	S	R	5-11	160	12-25-82	2001	Fajardo, P.R.
Graffanino, Tony	.263	75	278	37	73	11	0	3	26	27	38	10	2	.332	.335	R	R	6-1	190	6-6-72	1990	Marietta, Ga.
Guerrero, Wilton	.219	24	32	7	7	0	1	0	1	0	4	1	0	.219	.281	S	R	6-0	175	10-24-74	1993	Bratenahl, Ohio
Guiel, Aaron	.156	42	135	15	21	4	0	5	13	17	42	1	1	.263	.296	L	R	5-10	200	10-5-72	1993	Langley, B.C.
Harvey, Ken	.287	120	456	47	131	20	1	13	55	28	89	1	1	.338	.421	R	R	6-2	240	3-1-78	1999	Cerritos, Calif.
Jackson, Damian	.133	14	15	1	2	2	0	0	2	1	6	0	0	.188	.267	R	R	5-11	185	8-16-73	1992	Concord, Calif.
Lopez, Mendy	.105	18	38	4	4	0	0	1	4	4	9	0	0	.209	.184	R	R	6-2	200	10-15-73	1994	Santo Domingo, D.R.
Mateo, Ruben	.194	32	93	9	18	4	3	0	7	3	20	1	1	.235	.301	R	R	6-0	210	2-10-78	1995	San Cristobal, D.R.
Murphy, Donnie	.185	7	27	1	5	3	0	0	3	0	7	1	0	.185	.296	R	R	5-10	180	3-10-83	2002	Anaheim, Calif.
Nunez, Abraham	.226	59	221	31	50	9	0	5	29	25	48	0	1	.304	.335	L	R	6-3	210	2-5-77	1997	Haina, D.R.
Phillips, Paul	.200	4	5	2	1	0	0	0	1	0	1	0	0	.333	.200	R	R	5-11	185	4-15-77	1998	Bailey, Miss.
Pickering, Calvin	.246	35	122	21	30	8	1	7	26	18	42	0	0	.338	.500	L	L	6-5	260	9-29-76	1995	Temple Terrace, Fla.
Randa, Joe	.287	128	485	65	139	31	2	8	56	40	77	0	1	.343	.408	R	R	5-11	190	12-18-69	1991	Overland Park, Kan.
Relaford, Desi	.221	114	380	45	84	14	0	6	34	34	56	5	4	.296	.305	S	R	5-9	180	9-16-73	1991	Jacksonville, Fla.
Santiago, Benito	.274	49	175	18	48	10	0	6	23	8	32	1	2	.312	.434	R	R	6-1	200	3-9-65	1984	Pembroke Pines, Fla.
Stairs, Matt	.267	126	439	48	117	21	3	18	66	49	92	1	0	.345	.451	L	R	5-9	210	2-27-68	1989	Bangor, Maine
Stinnett, Kelly	.305	20	59	10	18	0	0	3	7	5	16	0	0	.379	.458	R	R	5-11	225	2-4-70	1990	Mesa, Ariz.
Sweeney, Mike	.287	106	411	56	118	23	0	22	79	33	44	3	2	.347	.504	R	R	6-3	225	7-22-73	1991	Overland Park, Kan.
Thompson, Rich	.000	6	1	1	0	0	0	0	0	0	1	0	0	.000	.000	L	R	6-3	180	4-23-79	2000	Montrose, Pa.
Tonis, Mike	.000	2	6	0	0	0	0	0	0	1	0	0	0	.143	.000	R	R	6-3	220	2-9-79	2000	Elk Grove, Calif.

PITCHING	W	L	ERA	G	GS	CG	SV	IP	H	R	ER	BB	SO	AVG	B	T	HT	WT	DOB	1st Yr	Resides
Affeldt, Jeremy	3	4	4.95	38	8	0	13	76	91	49	42	32	49	.302	L	L	6-4	215	6-6-79	1997	Medical Lake, Wash.
Anderson, Brian	6	12	5.64	35	26	2	0	166	217	123	104	53	70	.320	R	L	6-1	185	4-26-72	1993	Bratenahl, Ohio
Appier, Kevin	0	1	13.50	2	2	0	0	4	7	8	6	3	2	.368	R	R	6-2	215	12-6-67	1987	Paola, Kan.
Bautista, Denny	0	4	6.51	5	5	0	0	28	38	20	20	11	18	.333	R	R	6-5	170	10-23-82	2000	Santo Domingo, D.R.
2-team (2 Baltimore)	0	4	8.49	7	5	0	0	30	44	28	28	13	19	.352							
Bukvich, Ryan	0	0	3.68	9	0	0	1	7	4	3	3	7	7	.182	R	R	6-2	250	5-13-78	2000	Brandon, Miss.
Camp, Shawn	2	2	3.92	42	0	0	2	67	74	37	29	16	51	.285	R	R	6-1	200	11-18-75	1997	Fairfax, Va.
Carrasco, D.J.	2	2	4.84	30	0	0	0	35	41	22	19	15	22	.287	R	R	6-1	210	4-12-77	1998	Safford, Ariz.
Cerda, Jaime	1	4	3.15	53	0	0	2	46	41	21	16	30	33	.244	L	L	6-0	190	10-26-78	2000	Selma, Calif.
Field, Nate	2	3	4.26	43	0	0	3	44	40	25	21	19	30	.241	R	R	6-2	200	12-11-75	1998	Littleton, Colo.
George, Chris	1	2	7.23	10	7	0	0	42	60	39	34	25	15	.331	L	L	6-2	200	9-16-79	1998	Spring, Texas
Gobble, Jimmy	9	8	5.35	25	24	1	0	148	157	94	88	43	49	.270	L	L	6-3	190	7-19-81	1999	Bristol, Va.
Greinke, Zack	8	11	3.97	24	24	0	0	145	143	64	64	26	100	.256	R	R	6-2	200	10-21-83	2002	Apopka, Fla.
Grimsley, Jason	3	3	3.38	32	0	0	0	27	24	11	10	15	18	.238	R	R	6-3	200	8-7-67	1985	Lafayette, La.
Huisman, Justin	0	0	6.84	14	0	0	1	25	36	20	19	8	13	.336	R	R	6-1	195	4-16-79	2000	Thornton, Ill.
Kinney, Matt	0	3	7.16	11	0	0	0	16	27	14	13	7	21	.365	R	R	6-5	220	12-16-76	1995	Bangor, Maine
Leskanic, Curtis	0	3	8.04	19	0	0	2	16	23	16	14	14	15	.324	R	R	6-0	185	4-2-68	1990	Longwood, Fla.
MacDougal, Mike	1	1	5.56	13	0	0	1	11	16	8	7	9	14	.314	S	R	6-4	195	3-5-77	1999	Marco Island, Fla.
May, Darrell	9	19	5.61	31	31	3	0	186	234	130	116	55	120	.306	L	L	6-2	185	6-13-72	1992	Rogue River, Ore.
Reyes, Dennys	4	4	4.75	40	12	0	0	108	114	64	57	50	91	.273	R	L	6-3	245	4-19-77	1994	Higuera de Zaragoza, Mexico
Seanez, Rudy	0	1	3.91	16	0	0	0	23	21	10	10	11	21	.244	R	R	5-11	200	10-20-68	1986	El Centro, Calif.
Serrano, Jimmy	1	2	4.68	10	5	0	0	33	35	17	17	12	25	.288	R	R	5-10	170	5-9-76	1998	Grand Junction, Colo.
Sullivan, Scott	3	4	4.77	49	0	0	0	60	73	34	32	24	45	.308	R	R	6-3	210	3-13-71	1993	Livingston, Ala.
Vasquez, Jorge	0	0	8.10	2	0	0	0	3	4	4	3	1	4	.267	R	R	6-1	166	7-16-78	2000	Nagua, D.R.
Villacis, Eduardo	0	1	13.50	1	1	0	0	3	6	5	5	4	0	.375	R	R	6-2	180	8-29-79	1998	Miranda, Venez.
Wood, Mike	3	8	5.94	17	17	0	0	100	112	67	66	28	54	.286	R	R	6-3	210	4-26-80	2001	West Palm Beach, Fla.

FIELDING

Catcher	PCT	G	PO	A	E	DP	PB
Buck	.992	68	376	14	3	4	7
Castillo	.995	29	199	11	1	0	1
Phillips	1.000	4	11	1	0	0	0
Santiago	.996	49	228	18	1	3	6
Stinnett	.971	20	97	4	3	0	1
Tonis	1.000	2	13	1	0	0	2

First Base	PCT	G	PO	A	E	DP
Guerrero	1.000	2	3	0	0	1

	PCT	G	PO	A	E	DP
Harvey	.994	73	610	52	4	73
Lopez	.000	2	0	0	0	0
Pickering	1.000	8	60	3	0	6
Randa	1.000	3	20	2	0	4
Stairs	.986	30	208	11	3	25
Sweeney	.992	55	467	36	4	44

Second Base	PCT	G	PO	A	E	DP
Gotay	.983	42	78	97	3	29

	PCT	G	PO	A	E	DP
Graffanino	.988	75	185	219	5	67
Guerrero	.960	8	8	16	1	2
Jackson	.000	1	0	0	0	0
Lopez	.941	6	10	6	1	2
Murphy	1.000	7	12	17	0	8
Relaford	.982	36	69	94	3	22

Third Base	PCT	G	PO	A	E	DP
J. Bautista	.957	11	5	17	1	2

	PCT	G	PO	A	E	DP
Guerrero	.000	2	0	0	0	0
Lopez	.900	4	2	7	1	1
Randa	.967	119	85	241	11	22
Relaford	.927	42	24	78	8	5
Shortstop	PCT	G	PO	A	E	DP
Berroa	.955	133	207	389	28	94
Blanco	.959	19	30	64	4	17
Guerrero	1.000	3	1	2	0	0
Jackson	.000	1	0	0	0	0
Lopez	1.000	4	2	2	0	2

	PCT	G	PO	A	E	DP
Relaford	1.000	12	14	28	0	7
Outfield	PCT	G	PO	A	E	DP
J. Bautista	.000	1	0	0	0	0
Beltran	.985	69	197	4	3	1
Berger	1.000	11	25	1	0	1
A. Brown	1.000	5	9	0	0	0
D. Brown	.970	53	93	4	3	0
DeJesus	.984	94	246	3	4	0
Gettis	.930	21	38	2	3	1
Gonzalez	.948	29	52	3	3	1

	PCT	G	PO	A	E	DP
Guerrero	1.000	3	2	0	0	0
Guiel	.966	39	82	3	3	0
Harvey	1.000	4	4	0	0	0
Jackson	1.000	5	2	0	0	0
Lopez	.857	4	6	0	1	0
Mateo	1.000	30	52	4	0	1
Nunez	.993	57	135	3	1	0
Relaford	.981	32	51	2	1	0
Stairs	.986	71	131	5	2	2
Thompson	1.000	3	2	0	0	0

FARM SYSTEM

Director, Player Development: Shaun McGinn.

Class	Farm Team	League	W	L	Pct.	Finish*	Manager	Affiliate Since
AAA	Omaha (Neb.) Royals	Pacific Coast	71	73	.493	9th (16)	Mike Jirschele	1969
AA	Wichita (Kan.) Wranglers	Texas	73	66	.525	3rd (8)	Frank White	1995
High A	#Wilmington (Del.) Blue Rocks	Carolina	77	62	.554	**2nd (8)**	Billy Gardner	1993
Low A	Burlington (Iowa) Bees	Midwest	56	84	.400	13th (14)	Jim Gabella	2001
Rookie	Idaho Falls (Idaho) Chukars	Pioneer	42	35	.545	**3rd (8)**	Brian Rupp	2004
Rookie	Surprise (Ariz.) Royals	Arizona	29	27	.518	5th (9)	Lloyd Simmons	2003

*Finish in overall standings (No. of teams in league)/Playoff teams in **boldface**   #Affiliate will operate in High Desert (California) in 2005

OMAHA ROYALS   Class AAA

PACIFIC COAST LEAGUE

BATTING	AVG	G	AB	R	H	2B	3B	HR	RBI	BB	SO	SB	CS	OBP	SLG	B	T	HT	WT	DOB	1st Yr	Resides
Berger, Brandon	.233	39	146	25	34	9	0	14	37	19	22	1	1	.327	.582	R	R	5-11	200	2-21-75	1996	Fort Mitchell, Ky.
Brown, Adrian	.266	114	444	69	118	17	7	5	51	57	74	28	4	.347	.329	S	R	6-0	200	2-7-74	1992	Summit, Miss.
Brown, Dee	.125	10	40	2	5	0	0	2	5	0	12	0	0	.125	.275	L	R	6-0	225	3-27-78	1996	Orlando, Fla.
Casanova, Raul	.332	58	223	37	74	12	0	10	49	15	36	1	0	.379	.520	S	R	6-0	220	8-23-72	1990	Ponce, P.R.
Castillo, Alberto	.255	48	161	15	41	9	0	1	15	20	20	0	0	.348	.329	R	R	6-0	215	2-10-70	1987	Port St. Lucie, Fla.
Dawkins, Gookie	.223	48	166	22	37	7	1	4	17	10	41	2	2	.267	.349	R	R	6-1	186	5-12-79	1997	Chappells, S.C.
DeJesus, David	.315	50	197	38	62	14	4	6	16	21	30	7	6	.400	.518	L	L	6-0	175	12-20-79	2002	Manalapan, N.J.
Falu, Irving	.500	3	6	1	3	0	0	0	0	0	1	0	0	.500	.500	S	R	6-0	174	6-6-83	2003	Carolina, P.R.
Gettis, Byron	.257	51	179	23	46	7	0	4	19	33	61	4	1	.366	.363	R	R	6-0	240	3-13-80	1998	East St. Louis, Ill.
Gomez, Alexis	.251	109	383	45	96	17	8	7	34	19	96	8	6	.285	.392	L	L	6-2	180	8-6-78	1997	Dajabon, D.R.
Graffanino, Tony	.214	4	14	2	3	0	0	1	2	3	5	0	0	.353	.429	R	R	6-1	190	6-6-72	1990	Marietta, Ga.
Guerrero, Wilton	.326	72	282	30	92	14	4	3	40	8	33	12	8	.349	.436	S	R	6-0	175	10-24-74	1993	Bratenahl, Ohio
Guiel, Aaron	.310	30	116	29	36	6	0	10	30	21	33	0	2	.438	.621	L	R	5-10	200	10-5-72	1993	Langley, B.C.
Hansen, Jed	.272	125	463	82	126	19	4	27	82	66	118	7	4	.366	.505	R	R	6-1	190	8-19-72	1994	Olympia, Wash.
Hart, Corey	.262	21	65	8	17	3	0	1	2	3	15	0	0	.294	.354	S	R	6-0	190	9-5-75	1998	Oklahoma City, Okla.
Hooper, Kevin	.163	27	92	12	15	2	0	0	4	9	14	2	2	.245	.185	R	R	5-10	160	12-7-76	1999	Lawrence, Kan.
2-team (39 Alb.)	.235	66	247	33	58	5	2	0	21	23	38	8	7	.301	.271							
Jackson, Damian	.308	48	169	46	52	13	1	8	27	30	36	12	2	.425	.538	R	R	5-11	185	8-16-73	1992	Concord, Calif.
2-team (28 Iowa)	.297	76	266	64	79	19	6	11	40	41	56	15	3	.400	.538							
Lopez, Mendy	.293	31	123	20	36	6	1	13	26	9	31	1	2	.341	.675	R	R	6-2	200	10-15-73	1994	Santo Domingo, D.R.
Patterson, Jarrod	.264	104	356	60	94	16	0	11	51	59	68	0	0	.382	.402	L	R	6-1	190	9-7-73	1993	Clanton, Ala.
Phillips, Paul	.312	86	311	40	97	17	1	6	41	20	36	4	3	.358	.431	R	R	5-11	185	4-15-77	1998	Bailey, Miss.
Pickering, Calvin	.314	89	299	65	94	12	1	35	79	70	85	0	1	.451	.712	L	L	6-5	260	9-29-76	1995	Temple Terrace, Fla.
Relaford, Desi	.267	4	15	1	4	1	0	0	3	2	1	0	0	.353	.333	S	R	5-9	180	9-16-73	1991	Jacksonville, Fla.
Short, Rick	.282	89	316	30	89	16	0	7	48	15	39	1	1	.320	.399	R	R	6-0	200	12-6-72	1994	Peoria, Ill.
Teahen, Mark	.280	66	246	33	69	15	1	8	31	21	69	0	0	.344	.447	L	R	6-3	210	9-6-81	2002	Yucaipa, Calif.
2-team (20 Sac.)	.279	86	315	42	88	23	1	8	41	32	91	0	1	.353	.435							
Ullery, Dave	.188	11	32	2	6	0	0	0	0	3	11	0	0	.257	.188	L	R	6-3	220	12-16-74	1997	Brazil, Ind.

PITCHING	W	L	ERA	G	GS	CG	SV	IP	H	R	ER	BB	SO	AVG	B	T	HT	WT	DOB	1st Yr	Resides
Affeldt, Jeremy	0	0	0.00	4	0	0	3	4	2	0	0	0	5	.154	L	L	6-4	215	6-6-79	1997	Medical Lake, Wash.
Appier, Kevin	0	0	6.75	1	1	0	0	4	7	3	3	2	2	.438	R	R	6-2	215	12-6-67	1987	Paola, Kan.
Bukvich, Ryan	3	4	4.37	38	0	0	7	47	33	25	23	30	60	.193	R	R	6-2	250	5-13-78	2000	Brandon, Miss.
Camp, Shawn	1	1	5.32	15	0	0	1	22	26	14	13	6	21	.289	R	R	6-1	200	11-18-75	1997	Fairfax, Va.
Carrasco, D.J.	2	1	3.20	32	1	0	3	56	60	22	20	18	50	.278	R	R	6-1	210	4-12-77	1998	Safford, Ariz.
Cerda, Jaime	0	0	3.00	4	0	0	0	6	8	2	2	3	2	.348	L	L	6-0	190	10-26-78	2000	Selma, Calif.
Cumberland, Chris	0	0	11.57	4	0	0	0	5	7	6	6	7	3	.368	L	L	6-1	188	1-15-73	1993	Mandeville, La.
Dawley, Joe	1	2	3.19	9	3	0	0	31	26	14	11	8	29	.222	R	R	6-4	205	9-19-71	1993	Moreno Valley, Calif.
Dickson, Jason	4	5	6.93	13	12	0	0	61	95	53	47	13	26	.349	L	R	6-0	190	3-30-73	1994	Chandler, Ariz.
George, Chris	8	6	3.42	20	19	2	0	105	97	45	40	40	74	.251	L	L	6-2	200	9-16-79	1998	Spring, Texas
Gobble, Jimmy	3	1	4.58	4	4	0	0	20	25	20	10	7	15	.298	L	L	6-3	190	7-19-81	1999	Bristol, Va.
Greinke, Zack	1	1	2.51	6	6	0	0	29	25	8	8	4	23	.225	R	R	6-2	200	10-21-83	2002	Apopka, Fla.
Huisman, Justin	4	2	3.61	15	0	0	4	42	50	23	17	18	37	.286	R	R	6-1	195	4-16-79	2000	Thornton, Ill.
Linton, Doug	3	9	7.59	27	13	1	1	100	143	86	84	18	81	.332	R	R	6-1	190	9-2-65	1987	Overland Park, Kan.
MacDougal, Mike	0	1	5.65	14	0	0	2	14	12	9	9	11	8	.222	S	R	6-4	195	3-5-77	1999	Marco Island, Fla.
Nina, Elvin	0	1	6.75	6	0	0	0	5	8	4	4	3	5	.348	R	R	6-0	185	11-25-75	1997	Tempe, Ariz.
2-team (10 Las Vegas)	0	3	6.75	16	0	0	0	20	27	18	15	11	15	.318							
Randall, Scott	1	2	4.89	12	1	0	5	35	39	22	19	14	21	.285	R	R	6-3	225	10-29-75	1995	Goleta, Calif.
2-team (3 Edmonton)	1	2	5.31	15	1	0	5	41	50	27	24	16	28	.307							
Ryan, Jason	1	3	6.03	8	6	0	0	34	45	26	23	9	23	.310	S	R	6-3	185	1-23-76	1994	Charlotte, N.C.
2-team (14 Memphis)	2	10	6.91	22	19	0	0	100	143	88	77	39	57	.334							
Seanez, Rudy	2	1	1.57	24	0	0	3	34	19	8	6	12	41	.152	R	R	5-11	200	10-20-68	1986	El Centro, Calif.
Serrano, Jimmy	1	1	5.01	16	1	0	0	32	32	23	18	21	14	.256	R	R	5-10	170	5-9-76	1998	Grand Junction, Colo.

ORGANIZATION STATISTICS

PITCHING	W	L	ERA	G	GS	CG	SV	IP	H	R	ER	BB	SO	AVG	B	T	HT	WT	DOB	1st Yr	Resides
Ullery, Dave	0	0	3.38	2	0	0	0	3	4	1	1	1	1	.364	L	R	6-3	220	12-16-74	1997	Brazil, Ind.
Venafro, Mike	2	4	4.37	35	0	0	2	58	70	30	28	19	41	.308	L	L	5-10	180	8-2-73	1995	Fort Myers, Fla.
Voyles, Brad	3	2	3.27	10	8	0	0	41	40	19	15	21	43	.245	R	R	6-0	195	12-30-76	1998	Casco, Wis.
Walrond, Les	11	5	3.06	19	19	1	0	124	114	46	42	41	107	.243	L	L	6-0	210	11-7-76	1998	Brentwood, Tenn.
White, Matt	2	2	6.18	23	4	0	1	55	71	45	38	34	43	.313	R	L	6-1	180	8-19-77	1998	Windsor, Mass.
Wilson, Kris	10	13	5.65	28	28	0	0	167	201	116	105	28	97	.301	R	R	6-4	225	8-6-79	1997	Palm Harbor, Fla.
Wright, Jamey	8	6	4.21	18	18	1	0	105	111	58	49	35	70	.273	R	R	6-5	230	12-24-74	1993	Phoenix, Ariz.

FIELDING

Catcher	PCT	G	PO	A	E	DP	PB
Casanova	.988	26	151	8	2	0	0
Castillo	.985	41	300	20	5	2	7
Phillips	.995	77	522	44	3	2	8
Ullery	1.000	5	24	0	0	0	0

First Base	PCT	G	PO	A	E	DP
Casanova	.991	14	102	6	1	13
Castillo	1.000	1	6	0	0	0
Hansen	.996	29	242	16	1	21
Patterson	.994	55	452	30	3	35
Pickering	.975	55	441	26	12	47
Ullery	1.000	2	9	2	0	1

Second Base	PCT	G	PO	A	E	DP
Falu	.909	3	3	7	1	1
Graffanino	1.000	3	4	12	0	1
Guerrero	.959	55	83	130	9	31
Hansen	1.000	23	47	60	0	11
Hart	.969	16	26	37	2	12
Hooper	.978	25	51	81	3	21
Jackson	1.000	3	10	16	0	4
Lopez	1.000	5	7	15	0	3
Relaford	1.000	1	4	0	0	0
Short	.990	20	42	56	1	8

Third Base	PCT	G	PO	A	E	DP
Hansen	.818	5	1	8	2	0
Hart	1.000	5	2	9	0	0
Patterson	.929	11	6	20	2	2
Short	.950	58	42	129	9	10
Teahen	.932	66	41	136	13	9

Shortstop	PCT	G	PO	A	E	DP
Dawkins	.955	48	78	133	10	33
Guerrero	.909	3	4	6	1	0
Hansen	.907	23	27	80	11	15
Hooper	1.000	4	3	3	0	0
Jackson	.956	44	69	125	9	26
Lopez	.964	27	33	74	4	15
Relaford	1.000	1	3	3	0	1

Outfield	PCT	G	PO	A	E	DP
Berger	.983	31	56	3	1	0
Brown	.987	108	225	10	3	2
Brown	.875	6	7	0	1	0
DeJesus	.991	50	107	1	1	1
Gettis	.966	51	78	6	3	1
Gomez	.971	107	197	3	6	2
Guerrero	1.000	2	1	0	0	0
Guiel	.980	29	43	6	1	0
Hansen	.989	50	84	2	1	1
Phillips	1.000	1	1	0	0	0
Short	1.000	6	8	0	0	0

WICHITA WRANGLERS — Class AA

TEXAS LEAGUE

BATTING	AVG	G	AB	R	H	2B	3B	HR	RBI	BB	SO	SB	CS	OBP	SLG	B	T	HT	WT	DOB	1st Yr	Resides
Aldridge, Cory	.239	79	280	49	67	12	5	18	45	41	87	9	7	.343	.511	L	R	6-1	220	6-13-79	1997	Abilene, Texas
Arnerich, Tony	.000	2	6	0	0	0	0	0	0	0	4	0	0	.000	.000	R	R	6-0	190	12-24-79	2001	Santa Rosa, Calif.
Berger, Brandon	.281	70	267	42	75	18	2	12	50	34	40	3	2	.360	.498	R	R	5-11	200	2-21-75	1996	Fort Mitchell, Ky.
Berroa, Angel	.314	11	51	8	16	1	0	3	10	2	8	3	2	.340	.510	R	R	6-0	175	1-27-78	1998	Santo Domingo, D.R.
Blanco, Andres	.247	93	324	34	80	10	2	0	21	18	44	7	6	.299	.290	S	R	5-10	155	4-11-84	2001	Moron, Venez.
Brown, Dee	.303	61	241	42	73	19	2	12	50	24	38	1	4	.367	.548	L	R	6-0	225	3-27-78	1996	Orlando, Fla.
Fenster, Darren	.306	30	111	14	34	3	0	1	11	14	14	0	1	.389	.360	R	R	5-9	175	9-11-78	2000	Middletown, N.J.
Gemoll, Justin	.271	124	421	60	114	16	2	8	37	44	80	8	4	.353	.375	R	R	6-2	205	11-19-77	2000	San Jose, Calif.
Gettis, Byron	.362	17	58	6	21	4	1	2	11	8	12	0	1	.448	.569	R	R	6-0	240	3-13-80	1998	East St. Louis, Ill.
Gotay, Ruben	.289	106	405	71	117	22	6	9	68	51	60	9	10	.373	.440	S	R	5-11	160	12-25-82	2001	Fajardo, P.R.
Groves, Brett	.238	27	84	9	20	4	0	0	4	11	18	0	3	.333	.286	B	R	6-0	180	10-1-78	2002	Tampa, Fla.
Guiel, Aaron	.250	6	20	7	5	0	0	0	0	8	6	2	0	.516	.250	L	R	5-10	200	10-5-72	1993	Langley, B.C.
Hart, Corey	.229	75	240	37	55	13	0	1	29	42	52	0	6	.345	.296	S	R	6-0	190	9-5-75	1998	Oklahoma City, Okla.
Hopper, Norris	.278	98	363	48	101	5	3	0	40	33	44	17	7	.345	.309	R	R	5-9	200	3-24-79	1998	Passaic, N.J.
Jones, Jaime	.271	69	251	32	68	6	1	6	38	30	56	0	0	.357	.375	L	L	6-3	190	8-2-76	1995	Temecula, Calif.
Keppinger, Billy	1.000	1	1	1	1	0	0	0	0	0	0	0	0	1.000	1.000	L	R	6-0	180	12-15-78	2000	Auburn, Ga.
Ruan, Wilkin	.276	54	196	26	54	7	2	3	15	10	21	11	3	.313	.378	R	R	6-0	182	9-18-78	1997	Guaymate, D.R.
Santos, Chad	.261	130	471	59	123	27	3	21	68	46	119	3	1	.330	.465	L	L	5-11	220	4-28-81	1999	Kaneohe, Hawaii
Stocker, Mel	.150	14	40	7	6	1	0	0	1	4	5	3	1	.277	.175	S	R	5-10	160	8-15-80	2001	Tucson, Ariz.
Terrell, Jim	.260	28	96	14	25	3	0	2	12	10	13	1	0	.324	.354	L	R	6-1	170	9-8-77	1996	Blue Springs, Mo.
Tonis, Mike	.228	78	263	24	60	13	1	3	29	23	53	0	0	.289	.319	R	R	6-3	220	2-9-79	2000	Elk Grove, Calif.
Ullery, Dave	.228	18	57	8	13	0	0	2	8	7	17	0	0	.313	.333	L	R	6-3	220	12-16-74	1997	Brazil, Ind.
Walter, Scott	.248	104	387	53	96	22	1	13	55	26	65	5	2	.307	.411	R	R	6-1	200	12-28-78	2000	Manhattan Beach, Calif.

PITCHING	W	L	ERA	G	GS	CG	SV	IP	H	R	ER	BB	SO	AVG	B	T	HT	WT	DOB	1st Yr	Resides
Appier, Kevin	0	0	4.91	4	4	0	0	15	19	9	8	4	3	.306	R	R	6-2	215	12-6-67	1987	Paola, Kan.
Baerlocher, Ryan	5	2	5.26	19	5	0	1	53	59	35	31	20	47	.281	R	R	6-5	220	8-6-77	1999	Lewiston, Idaho
Bass, Brian	0	4	7.96	9	9	0	0	32	48	28	28	20	16	.353	R	R	6-0	190	1-6-82	2000	Montgomery, Ala.
Bautista, Denny	4	3	2.53	12	12	2	0	82	68	32	23	32	73	.227	R	R	6-5	170	10-23-82	2000	Santo Domingo, D.R.
Griffin, Colt	1	1	4.02	26	0	0	1	31	29	14	14	16	26	.246	R	R	6-4	200	9-29-82	2001	Marshall, Texas
Herndon, Junior	7	3	3.38	12	11	1	0	69	69	34	26	12	41	.261	R	R	6-1	190	9-11-78	1997	Craig, Colo.
Keppinger, Billy	3	3	6.08	48	2	0	2	74	95	54	50	17	50	.318	L	R	6-0	180	12-15-78	2000	Auburn, Ga.
Linton, Doug	1	0	1.69	1	1	0	0	5	8	2	1	0	4	.320	R	R	6-1	190	9-2-65	1987	Overland Park, Kan.
MacDougal, Mike	1	0	1.47	17	2	0	1	18	14	7	3	14	13	.209	S	R	6-4	195	3-5-77	1999	Marco Island, Fla.
Markray, Thad	1	5	3.86	8	8	0	0	42	37	20	18	10	40	.234	R	R	6-4	220	9-20-79	1997	Springhill, La.
Middleton, Kyle	8	8	4.74	28	27	0	0	161	177	97	85	55	88	.281	R	R	6-6	230	6-13-80	2000	Pensacola, Fla.
Natale, Mike	8	5	6.21	44	3	0	0	84	110	65	58	23	72	.315	R	R	6-0	195	9-2-79	2000	Whittier, Calif.
Serrano, Jimmy	3	1	1.96	11	11	1	0	64	42	18	14	18	74	.181	R	R	5-10	170	5-9-76	1998	Grand Junction, Colo.
Shiery, Shaun	2	0	4.67	5	3	0	0	17	21	11	9	14	4	.304	L	L	6-4	180	12-8-78	2001	Katy, Texas
Tamayo, Danny	12	7	3.98	25	25	0	0	142	166	66	63	36	123	.294	R	R	6-1	240	6-3-79	2001	Miami, Fla.
Thompson, Eric	0	2	5.48	7	5	0	0	21	24	13	13	13	21	.279	R	R	6-2	195	9-7-77	1998	Fairborn, Ohio
Trujillo, J.J.	7	10	3.17	59	2	0	8	97	95	42	34	22	79	.259	R	R	6-0	180	10-9-75	1999	Corpus Christi, Texas
Vasquez, Jorge	4	5	4.68	49	0	0	18	60	52	34	31	27	71	.227	R	R	6-1	166	7-16-78	2000	Nagua, D.R.
Villacis, Eduardo	2	0	2.67	8	3	0	0	30	22	11	9	6	21	.195	R	R	6-2	180	8-29-79	1998	Miranda, Venez.
Walrond, Les	3	3	4.38	8	6	0	0	39	30	19	19	17	34	.210	L	L	6-0	210	11-7-76	1998	Brentwood, Tenn.
Wilkerson, Wes	1	4	5.18	49	0	0	3	75	96	48	43	26	55	.310	R	R	6-3	200	9-11-76	2000	Nashville, Tenn.

FIELDING

Catcher	PCT	G	PO	A	E	DP	PB
Arnerich	1.000	1	6	0	0	0	0
Tonis	.993	62	401	35	3	3	6
Ullery	.990	12	96	4	1	1	2
Walter	,989	70	482	45	6	2	10

First Base	PCT	G	PO	A	E	DP
Gemoll	1.000	3	18	2	0	5
Hart	.962	3	25	0	1	2
Santos	.988	128	1145	76	15	107
Terrell	.931	4	25	2	2	2

ORGANIZATION STATISTICS

	PCT	G	PO	A	E	DP
Walter	.976	4	38	3	1	3

Second Base	PCT	G	PO	A	E	DP
Fenster	.993	28	50	83	1	14
Gotay	.971	105	190	316	15	57
Groves	1.000	3	8	10	0	5
Hart	1.000	2	1	6	0	2
Hopper	.875	4	4	3	1	2

Third Base	PCT	G	PO	A	E	DP
Fenster	.500	1	0	1	1	0
Gemoll	.949	117	78	204	15	17
Groves	1.000	5	5	11	0	0

	PCT	G	PO	A	E	DP
Hart	.926	11	4	21	2	1
Terrell	.935	10	8	21	2	3

Shortstop	PCT	G	PO	A	E	DP
Berroa	1.000	11	19	30	0	5
Blanco	.951	93	141	270	21	67
Groves	.909	3	4	6	1	3
Hart	.965	38	61	105	6	24
Terrell	1.000	5	6	10	0	2

Outfield	PCT	G	PO	A	E	DP
Aldridge	.977	76	122	3	3	0
Berger	.974	44	73	2	2	0

	PCT	G	PO	A	E	DP
Brown	.989	52	82	5	1	0
Gettis	.926	17	25	0	2	0
Groves	1.000	17	26	0	0	0
Guiel	.933	6	14	0	1	0
Hart	1.000	1	1	0	0	0
Hopper	1.000	79	186	9	0	3
Jones	.975	66	113	2	3	0
Ruan	.991	52	108	5	1	0
Stocker	1.000	14	19	1	0	0
Terrell	1.000	5	6	0	0	0
Walter	.778	7	6	1	2	0

WILMINGTON BLUE ROCKS — High Class A

CAROLINA LEAGUE

BATTING

	AVG	G	AB	R	H	2B	3B	HR	RBI	BB	SO	SB	CS	OBP	SLG	B	T	HT	WT	DOB	1st Yr	Resides
Alleva, J.D.	.211	66	218	19	46	11	1	1	24	17	30	0	1	.267	.284	L	R	5-11	190	11-2-78	2001	Durham, N.C.
Aviles, Mike	.300	126	463	66	139	40	4	6	68	39	57	2	5	.352	.443	R	R	5-11	193	3-13-81	2003	Middletown, N.Y.
Chapman, Travis	.234	27	94	12	22	4	0	5	16	7	24	0	0	.321	.436	R	R	6-2	210	6-5-78	2000	Dayton, Ohio
Clark, Daryl	.217	27	83	6	18	7	0	1	12	20	28	1	0	.383	.337	L	R	6-2	210	9-25-79	2000	Boalsburg, Pa.
Costa, Shane	.308	123	451	70	139	20	4	7	60	32	43	9	4	.364	.417	L	R	6-0	200	12-12-81	2003	Visalia, Calif.
Draper, Kevin	.189	64	180	17	34	7	0	2	8	15	31	5	2	.259	.261	R	R	6-2	190	8-11-80	2001	Whittier, Calif.
Espino, Damaso	.255	124	470	35	120	18	1	1	58	44	111	3	2	.319	.304	S	R	6-1	190	5-8-83	2000	Panama City, Panama
Fallon, Chris	.500	1	2	0	1	0	0	0	1	2	1	0	0	.750	.500	L	R	6-2	180	3-9-79	2001	Bayonne, N.J.
Fenster, Darren	.304	84	303	55	92	20	1	0	37	51	46	2	1	.411	.376	R	R	5-9	175	9-11-78	2000	Middletown, N.J.
Frend, Tim	.237	58	207	27	49	15	1	5	28	19	41	0	0	.312	.391	R	R	6-2	180	5-20-80	2002	Charlotte, N.C.
Groves, Brett	.069	15	29	5	2	0	0	0	2	9	6	0	1	.308	.069	B	R	6-0	180	10-1-78	2002	Tampa, Fla.
Jensen, David	.208	21	72	9	15	5	0	0	2	0	22	1	0	.219	.278	L	L	6-3	210	12-16-79	2002	Henderson, Nev.
Keim, Adam	.289	59	201	28	58	7	2	9	27	10	41	2	0	.325	.478	R	R	6-0	180	1-5-81	2002	Lebanon, Pa.
Maier, Mitch	.264	51	174	25	46	9	2	3	17	15	29	10	2	.326	.391	L	R	6-2	200	6-30-82	2003	Howell, Mich.
Murphy, Donnie	.254	129	485	67	123	32	4	10	73	52	96	1	1	.326	.398	R	R	5-10	180	3-10-83	2002	Anaheim, Calif.
Sevilla, Walter	.143	4	14	1	2	0	0	0	1	5	1	0		.200	.143	R	R	5-8	170	8-24-81	2003	Miami, Fla.
Solis, Eddie	.227	8	22	4	5	2	0	0	2	6	6	0	0	.393	.318	R	R	5-11	185	9-19-84	2003	San Diego, Calif.
Stephens, Bernard	.274	111	391	56	107	17	5	4	52	40	88	13	8	.345	.373	L	R	6-0	190	11-11-79	2002	North Augusta, S.C.
Stocker, Mel	.213	115	441	78	94	19	7	2	29	51	69	44	15	.311	.302	S	R	5-10	160	8-15-80	2001	Tucson, Ariz.
Tupman, Matt	.300	108	330	38	99	24	0	3	35	33	59	0	1	.361	.400	L	R	5-11	180	11-25-79	2002	Concord, N.H.

PITCHING

	W	L	ERA	G	GS	CG	SV	IP	H	R	ER	BB	SO	AVG	B	T	HT	WT	DOB	1st Yr	Resides
Ackerman, Eric	6	6	4.65	36	9	0	1	89	125	56	46	31	55	.333	L	L	6-0	190	10-19-79	2002	Denver, Colo.
Armitage, Barry	4	7	2.19	53	0	0	11	86	66	32	21	31	78	.214	R	R	6-4	250	5-11-79	2000	Durban, South Africa
Bayliss, Jonah	6	6	4.89	24	24	0	0	110	117	69	60	44	78	.277	R	R	6-2	200	8-13-80	2002	Williamstown, Mass.
Braun, Ryan	2	3	3.21	51	0	0	24	57	48	25	14	25	58	.227	R	R	6-2	205	7-29-80	2003	Mooresville, N.C.
Bray, Steve	5	0	3.45	10	0	0	0	16	15	6	6	2	16	.250	R	R	6-1	190	12-22-80	2003	Branford, Conn.
Chamberlain, Steve	7	2	3.82	47	0	0	1	61	56	26	26	22	41	.250	L	R	6-3	200	7-20-80	2002	Pullman, Wash.
Endicott, Drew	7	3	4.00	43	1	0	1	88	86	46	39	35	45	.265	R	R	6-3	180	3-30-81	2002	Carthage, Mo.
Gragg, John	0	1	2.60	4	2	0	0	17	19	6	5	5	9	.288	L	L	5-10	185	5-9-81	2003	Beaumont, Texas
Griffin, Colt	1	4	8.73	8	8	0	0	33	40	35	32	28	28	.313	R	R	6-4	200	9-29-82	2001	Marshall, Texas
Hoelscher, Nate	6	2	6.15	51	0	0	2	84	70	23	20	15	70	.227	L	L	6-2	190	11-11-79	2002	St. Joseph, Minn.
Hughes, Dusty	5	5	2.41	18	18	0	0	108	95	37	29	31	68	.235	L	L	5-9	195	6-29-83	2003	Horn Lake, Miss.
Kaanoi, Kahi	4	0	1.37	9	7	0	0	46	23	9	7	13	24	.150	L	R	6-0	205	8-19-82	2000	Kaneohe, Hawaii
Lowery, Devon	9	9	3.66	28	28	1	0	145	139	74	59	52	115	.253	L	R	6-1	190	3-24-83	2001	Belmont, N.C.
McGill, Trae	9	2	2.08	21	18	1	0	113	98	32	26	26	66	.237	R	R	6-0	190	8-7-77	2001	Mobile, Ala.
Shiery, Shaun	2	3	2.08	17	8	0	1	56	43	22	13	16	28	.212	L	L	6-4	180	12-8-78	2001	Katy, Texas
Stiles, Brad	2	2	4.55	21	0	0	0	28	30	15	14	15	13	.280	L	L	6-5	230	2-9-81	1999	Lamar, Colo.
Stodolka, Mike	3	2	4.33	14	14	0	0	62	66	35	30	18	33	.268	L	L	6-2	210	9-24-81	2000	Corona, Calif.
Tamayo, Danny	0	1	9.53	3	3	0	0	11	16	12	12	5	10	.320	R	R	6-1	240	6-3-79	2001	Miami, Fla.

FIELDING

Catcher	PCT	G	PO	A	E	DP	PB
Alleva	1.000	11	54	2	0	0	1
Draper	.962	38	207	19	9	2	7
Tupman	.990	102	606	55	7	6	10

First Base	PCT	G	PO	A	E	DP
Alleva	.985	51	426	25	7	41
Clark	.952	14	109	11	6	12
Espino	.985	38	362	20	6	32
Fallon	1.000	1	11	0	0	0
Jensen	.980	17	131	18	3	9
Keim	.979	27	214	21	5	25

Second Base	PCT	G	PO	A	E	DP
Fenster	.964	26	54	78	5	16
Keim	1.000	8	13	24	0	3
Murphy	.978	104	198	343	12	73
Sevilla	.967	4	15	14	1	8
Solis	1.000	2	1	5	0	1

Third Base	PCT	G	PO	A	E	DP
Chapman	.875	3	2	5	1	0
Espino	.902	66	40	107	16	8
Fenster	.937	26	15	44	4	5
Groves	1.000	3	0	1	0	0
Maier	.938	48	33	87	8	8
Solis	1.000	2	0	3	0	0

Shortstop	PCT	G	PO	A	E	DP
Aviles	.966	121	190	355	19	66
Fenster	1.000	3	2	4	0	1
Murphy	.914	15	20	54	7	15
Solis	1.000	4	7	8	0	3

Outfield	PCT	G	PO	A	E	DP
Costa	.973	112	169	10	5	2
Draper	.955	9	20	1	1	0
Fenster	1.000	8	13	0	0	0
Frend	.975	49	77	2	2	0
Groves	1.000	11	16	0	0	0
Keim	.963	19	25	1	1	0
Stephens	.974	110	214	12	6	1
Stocker	.981	113	261	4	5	0

BURLINGTON BEES — Low Class A

MIDWEST LEAGUE

BATTING

	AVG	G	AB	R	H	2B	3B	HR	RBI	BB	SO	SB	CS	OBP	SLG	B	T	HT	WT	DOB	1st Yr	Resides
Barry, Jeff	.226	110	336	51	76	4	3	2	33	33	69	16	6	.303	.274	R	R	6-0	190	8-1-81	2003	Essex Junction, Ver.
Donachie, Adam	.189	67	228	17	43	7	0	1	21	21	41	5	2	.261	.232	B	R	6-2	180	3-3-84	2002	Orlando, Fla.
Figuereo, Anibal	.174	34	92	10	16	8	0	1	8	7	30	0	0	.238	.293	R	R	6-2	210	1-21-82	2000	Barahona, D.R.
Foster, Brian	.294	7	17	3	5	1	0	0	4	6	1	0	0	.429	.353	R	R	6-2	200	8-21-81	1999	Burlington, N.C.
Gaffney, Mike	.207	88	271	31	56	7	1	2	31	14	56	6	3	.263	.262	R	R	6-1	195	11-11-81	2003	Westbury, N.Y.
Gonzalez, Luis	.261	52	180	26	47	11	0	2	20	8	43	3	0	.327	.356	R	R	6-1	205	11-8-82	2000	Guanta, Venez.

BATTING

	AVG	G	AB	R	H	2B	3B	HR	RBI	BB	SO	SB	CS	OBP	SLG	B	T	HT	WT	DOB	1st Yr	Resides
Graham, Bryan	.182	84	269	28	49	12	0	2	26	38	68	2	3	.282	.249	L	L	6-1	195	6-8-81	2003	Medford, N.J.
Groves, Brett	.242	28	91	13	22	2	0	0	8	24	21	3	2	.410	.264	B	R	6-0	180	10-1-78	2002	Tampa, Fla.
Hilt, Cole	.236	35	110	16	26	5	0	2	8	19	40	0	0	.368	.336	R	R	6-5	200	1-22-81	2004	Temecula, Calif.
Johnson, Josh	.167	4	12	1	2	0	0	0	1	1	3	0	0	.231	.167	B	R	5-11	170	1-11-86	2004	Tampa, Fla.
Kaaihue, Kila	.246	125	390	57	96	23	2	15	62	64	98	1	0	.360	.431	L	R	6-3	225	3-29-84	2002	Kailua, Hawaii
Keim, Adam	.149	19	67	1	10	3	0	1	5	3	12	0	1	.186	.239	R	R	6-0	180	1-5-81	2002	Lebanon, Penn.
Lubanski, Chris	.275	127	483	64	133	26	7	9	56	43	104	16	11	.336	.414	L	L	6-3	200	3-24-85	2003	Oldsmar, Fla.
Lucas, Ed	.202	24	89	12	18	5	1	0	10	5	21	2	2	.258	.281	R	R	6-4	205	5-21-81	2004	Deltona, Fla.
Maier, Mitch	.300	82	317	41	95	24	3	4	36	27	51	34	10	.354	.432	L	R	6-2	200	6-30-82	2003	Howell, Mich.
McDonald, Chamar	.111	9	18	2	2	1	0	1	3	2	13	0	0	.200	.333	R	R	6-4	200	6-18-83	2001	Madison, Miss.
McFall, Brian	.172	53	151	16	26	7	0	4	14	13	48	7	2	.270	.219	R	R	6-3	205	6-17-84	2003	Flagstaff, Ariz.
Moye, Alan	.234	13	47	9	11	1	0	0	3	10	16	1	2	.362	.255	R	R	6-2	200	10-8-82	2001	Longview, Texas
Powell, Brandon	.267	90	307	41	82	16	5	5	34	40	60	7	6	.359	.401	L	R	6-0	185	8-15-80	2003	Johnsonville, S.C.
Reinking, Kevin	.223	32	103	15	23	10	0	3	18	8	31	0	2	.302	.408	R	R	6-1	190	1-25-79	2001	Long Beach, N.Y.
Sanchez, Angel	.252	96	357	37	90	13	1	2	25	18	51	16	7	.303	.311	R	R	6-2	175	9-20-83	2001	Las Piedras, P.R.
Sevilla, Walter	.205	82	254	23	52	12	0	2	27	34	64	11	6	.305	.276	R	R	5-8	170	8-24-81	2003	Miami, Fla.
Springer, Kenard	.235	85	315	39	74	11	2	1	27	10	64	7	6	.274	.292	R	R	5-11	205	9-18-83	2002	Nettleton, Miss.

PITCHING

	W	L	ERA	G	GS	CG	SV	IP	H	R	ER	BB	SO	B	T	HT	WT	DOB	1st Yr	Resides
Atencio, Greg	7	14	5.60	28	28	0	0	149	157	109	93	68	118	.269	R	R	6-3	210	7-15-81	2002	Albuquerque, N.M.
Begnaud, Rusty	1	0	0.00	1	0	0	0	3	0	0	0	1	1	.000	R	R	6-1	190	12-19-80	2004	New Iberia, La.
Bray, Steve	3	3	3.29	24	0	0	6	63	58	30	23	13	73	.240	R	R	6-1	190	12-22-80	2003	Branford, Conn.
Brown, Ira	0	0	2.57	5	0	0	0	7	7	2	2	2	8	.259	R	R	6-4	210	8-3-82	2001	Conroe, Texas
Burgos, Ambiorix	7	11	4.38	27	26	0	0	134	109	70	65	75	172	.221	R	R	6-3	230	4-19-84	2001	Nagua, D.R.
Christensen, Danny	0	1	15.00	1	1	0	0	3	6	8	5	3	2	.353	L	L	6-1	205	8-10-83	2002	Vero Beach, Fla.
Coughlin, Chris	5	5	4.50	14	14	1	0	80	89	47	40	10	60	.283	R	R	6-0	190	9-30-80	2003	Southport, N.C.
Crist, Kyle	1	1	6.75	3	2	0	0	12	15	10	9	5	11	.306	R	R	6-3	180	6-27-83	2004	Granite Bay, Calif.
DeHoyos, Gabe	1	2	2.28	16	0	0	5	24	19	6	6	11	26	.229	R	R	6-0	220	4-14-80	2002	Artesia, N.M.
Dossett, Dusty	3	5	3.41	38	0	0	5	74	71	33	28	24	54	.250	R	R	6-2	175	4-11-80	2001	Athens, Texas
Encarnacion, Alexis	4	2	5.13	27	0	0	4	72	74	45	41	22	60	.261	R	R	6-0	170	9-26-82	2000	Santo Domingo, D.R.
Goodman, Chris	4	13	5.95	23	21	1	1	115	146	85	76	38	56	.310	R	R	6-0	180	8-30-81	2003	Marietta, Ga.
Gragg, John	3	10	4.40	26	19	2	1	129	119	71	63	51	105	.246	L	L	5-10	185	5-9-81	2003	Beaumont, Texas
Hughes, Dusty	4	2	1.56	8	8	0	0	52	39	12	9	15	36	.209	L	L	5-9	195	6-29-83	2003	Horn Lake, Miss.
Kaanoi, Kahi	2	1	2.83	23	4	0	3	54	45	21	17	15	42	.231	L	R	6-0	205	8-19-82	2000	Kaneohe, Hawaii
McClellan, Robbie	2	5	4.50	19	4	0	0	64	65	34	32	23	60	.261	R	R	6-1	170	1-31-81	2003	Liberal, Kan.
Metzger, Jon	0	1	6.94	6	0	0	0	12	14	11	9	6	13	.292	L	L	6-2	200	10-27-78	2000	Fairfax Station, Va.
Moore, Nate	2	1	4.15	19	0	0	3	35	30	16	16	12	32	.233	R	R	6-3	215	6-14-83	1999	Kinston, Ala.
Mullis, Jake	1	2	6.82	14	2	0	1	32	38	27	24	8	19	.288	R	R	6-2	215	1-22-81	2003	Arden, N.C.
Rosa, Carlos	0	5	4.67	8	8	0	0	35	41	24	18	17	23	.291	R	R	6-0	165	9-21-84	2002	San Francisco de Macoris, D.R.
Sherman, Justin	3	1	4.26	4	3	1	0	25	33	13	12	3	18	.317	R	R	6-4	195	12-6-80	2003	Las Vegas, Nev.
Stiles, Brad	2	1	2.57	13	0	0	2	28	27	12	8	9	27	.260	L	L	6-5	230	2-9-81	1999	Lamar, Colo.

FIELDING

Catcher	PCT	G	PO	A	E	DP	PB
Donachie	.986	66	513	42	8	2	9
Foster	1.000	2	3	0	0	0	1
Gonzalez	.995	48	359	27	2	2	9
Reinking	.989	28	170	9	2	0	4
Sanchez	1.000	1	5	0	0	0	1

First Base	PCT	G	PO	A	E	DP
Figuereo	.973	20	126	17	4	11
Gaffney	.900	2	9	0	1	1
Graham	.962	3	25	0	1	2
Hilt	1.000	1	6	0	0	1
Kaaihue	.989	119	952	60	11	86
McDonald	.980	8	45	4	1	6

Second Base	PCT	G	PO	A	E	DP
Gaffney	.933	3	6	8	1	1

	PCT	G	PO	A	E	DP
Groves	1.000	5	8	18	0	6
Johnson	1.000	1	2	5	0	1
Keim	.927	15	27	49	6	7
Powell	.964	78	126	222	13	46
Sanchez	.850	3	8	9	3	3
Sevilla	.957	40	65	90	7	19

Third Base	PCT	G	PO	A	E	DP
Gaffney	.974	35	27	49	2	4
Groves	1.000	12	11	16	0	1
Hilt	.906	13	8	21	3	4
Lucas	.971	18	11	23	1	4
Maier	.903	71	47	140	20	13

Shortstop	PCT	G	PO	A	E	DP
Gaffney	.957	22	28	60	4	8

	PCT	G	PO	A	E	DP
Groves	.909	2	5	5	1	2
Johnson	.833	2	2	3	1	1
Lucas	.933	5	4	10	1	2
Sanchez	.950	88	140	242	20	50
Sevilla	.966	33	35	77	4	17

Outfield	PCT	G	PO	A	E	DP
Barry	.951	107	188	7	10	0
Gaffney	1.000	10	21	1	0	0
Graham	.975	56	73	5	2	1
Groves	1.000	7	7	0	0	0
Lubanski	.980	125	242	4	5	0
McFall	.960	50	63	9	3	1
Moye	.957	14	20	2	1	1
Springer	.954	75	136	10	7	4

IDAHO FALLS CHUKARS — Rookie

PIONEER LEAGUE

BATTING

	AVG	G	AB	R	H	2B	3B	HR	RBI	BB	SO	SB	CS	OBP	SLG	B	T	HT	WT	DOB	1st Yr	Resides
Batista, Alexander	.296	69	291	59	86	21	2	3	37	20	57	12	5	.345	.412	R	R	6-0	180	8-11-83	2001	Puerto Plata, D.R.
Brown, Rusty	.321	45	137	26	44	13	0	8	34	26	36	0	2	.424	.591	R	R	6-3	220	8-19-81	2004	North Fort Myers, Fla.
Butler, Billy	.373	72	260	74	97	22	3	10	68	57	63	5	0	.486	.596	R	R	6-2	225	4-18-86	2004	Jacksonville, Fla.
Cerulo, Nick	.571	2	7	3	4	0	0	0	1	2	1	0	0	.667	.571	R	R	6-1	205	9-14-81	2004	Woodbridge, N.J.
Del Rosario, Felipe	.263	34	99	16	26	3	0	3	17	12	28	0	2	.342	.424	R	R	5-10	180	9-8-84	2002	La Romana, D.R.
Ferrara, Matt	.290	42	124	27	36	6	3	3	19	12	39	6	3	.364	.460	R	R	6-1	200	9-27-82	2002	Miramar, Fla.
Haney, Josh	.190	5	21	4	4	3	0	0	3	3	0	2	.346	.333	R	R	5-10	180	3-6-82	2004	Midland, Texas
Hayes, Brad	.284	53	208	43	59	15	0	1	34	23	51	5	6	.362	.370	R	R	6-0	180	3-25-82	2004	Paragould, Ark.
Infante, Jefferson	.261	28	92	16	24	5	1	2	16	7	23	1	0	.337	.402	R	R	5-11	205	10-5-82	2004	Bronx, N.Y.
Lisson, Mario	.289	70	256	60	74	10	2	8	49	44	82	15	6	.398	.438	R	R	6-2	195	5-31-84	2002	Caracas, Venez.
Lucas, Ed	.312	41	154	30	48	6	1	0	29	14	18	7	3	.379	.364	R	R	6-4	205	5-21-81	2004	Deltona, Fla.
McFall, Brian	.363	68	262	64	95	23	1	14	68	30	64	23	2	.438	.618	R	R	6-3	205	6-17-84	2003	Flagstaff, Ariz.
Norman, Derek	.190	18	63	6	12	3	0	4	8	10	0	1	.282	.238	R	R	6-0	190	2-21-82	2004	Knoxville, Tenn.
Salazar, Darwinson	.318	55	195	39	62	10	3	2	31	27	52	17	6	.408	.431	R	R	6-3	175	12-12-82	2000	Higuerote, Venez.
Solis, Eddie	.366	63	246	48	90	15	2	2	54	19	41	3	0	.418	.467	R	R	5-11	185	9-19-84	2003	San Diego, Calif.
Valentin, Geraldo	.351	65	259	55	91	21	6	4	44	19	28	7	5	.397	.525	R	R	6-0	175	9-8-82	2003	Rio Piedras, P.R.

GAMES BY POSITION: C—Del Rosario 32, Ferrara 10, Infante 25, Norman 18. **1B**—Brown 22, Del Rosario 2, Ferrara 5, Hayes 47, Lisson 9. **2B**—Ferrara 25, Haney 5, Solis 50. **3B**—Butler 49, Ferrara 2, Hayes 4, Lisson 21, Solis 3. **SS**—Ferrara 1, Lisson 34, Lucas 34, Solis 1, Valentin 12. **OF**—Batista 65, Brown 2, Cerulo 2, McFall 64, Salazar 51, Valentin 50.

PITCHING	W	L	ERA	G	GS	CG	SV	IP	H	R	ER	BB	SO	AVG	B	T	HT	WT	DOB	1st Yr	Resides
Beeson, Bobby	2	4	5.47	15	14	0	0	53	56	37	32	24	48	.277	L	L	6-3	225	11-25-82	2004	Magnolia, Ark.
Blackwell, Chad	1	1	3.27	21	0	0	7	33	32	15	12	16	46	.244	R	R	6-1	145	1-7-83	2004	Clewiston, Fla.
Buckner, Billy	2	2	3.93	8	5	0	0	34	44	18	15	8	37	.317	R	R	6-2	215	8-27-83	2004	Conyers, Ga.
Campbell, Matt	0	2	8.44	4	4	0	0	11	11	10	10	10	10	.275	L	L	6-2	170	12-27-82	2004	Gray Court, S.C.
Carlson, Zane	2	1	4.50	19	0	0	10	22	21	11	11	13	30	.244	R	R	6-2	180	8-11-80	2004	DeSoto, Texas
Cota, Luis	2	1	5.81	13	12	0	0	48	61	37	31	21	40	.311	R	R	6-1	180	7-23-85	2004	Tucson, Ariz.
Crist, Kyle	3	2	3.55	12	8	0	0	46	47	27	18	16	27	.257	R	R	6-3	180	6-27-83	2004	Granite Bay, Calif.
Green, Patrick	3	1	5.23	13	9	0	1	52	52	37	30	25	39	.257	L	R	6-3	187	8-20-84	2004	Alpharetta, Ga.
Hicklen, Patrick	2	2	5.00	6	1	0	0	18	27	14	10	1	19	.360	R	R	6-4	204	12-30-81	2004	Murfreesboro, Tenn.
Howell, J.P.	3	1	2.77	6	4	0	0	26	16	9	8	12	38	.176	L	L	6-0	180	4-25-83	2004	Sacramento, Calif.
McConiga, Jacob	0	2	9.27	12	3	0	0	33	57	42	34	22	29	.358	L	L	5-10	180	1-21-81	2003	Elverta, Calif.
Mullis, Jake	3	4	6.99	14	6	1	1	55	71	49	43	19	40	.317	R	R	6-2	215	1-22-81	2003	Arden, N.C.
Nendza, Brian	5	3	5.86	24	0	0	1	43	50	37	28	25	52	.289	L	L	6-6	200	12-9-80	2003	Palos Park, Ill.
Palmer, Lucas	3	2	7.86	17	1	0	2	45	65	48	39	20	33	.332	R	R	6-3	200	5-7-83	2002	Baker, Ore.
Rowe, Adam	2	3	4.73	23	0	0	4	27	30	17	14	11	24	.278	L	L	6-2	190	1-24-82	2004	Wooster, Ohio
Saxton, Chris	1	2	6.55	21	0	0	0	33	43	30	24	14	17	.319	R	R	6-0	180	12-2-81	2004	Lake Worth, Fla.
Sherman, Justin	8	1	5.54	10	9	0	0	50	68	34	31	19	28	.325	R	R	6-4	195	12-6-80	2003	Las Vegas, Nev.
Trammell, Travis	0	0	7.98	20	0	0	0	29	50	37	26	9	21	.385	R	R	6-5	240	8-19-81	2004	Lowell, Ark.

AZL ROYALS — Rookie

ARIZONA LEAGUE

BATTING	AVG	G	AB	R	H	2B	3B	HR	RBI	BB	SO	SB	CS	SLG	OBP	B	T	HT	WT	DOB	1st Yr	Resides
Adkison, Blake	.169	28	71	6	12	2	0	1	5	12	25	1	0	.239	.322	R	R	6-3	220	12-3-80	2004	Tyler, Texas
Caballero, Carlos	.265	36	117	17	31	6	1	0	11	5	25	5	4	.333	.326	R	R	6-0	170	12-5-83	2002	San Juan, P.R.
Chapman, Travis	.309	17	55	12	17	2	1	1	8	8	9	1	0	.436	.449	R	R	6-2	180	6-5-78	2000	Dayton, Ohio
Ellis, Jared	.229	53	188	37	43	11	5	4	28	23	81	9	4	.404	.348	R	R	6-2	215	3-27-82	2004	Chickisha, Okla.
Eusebio, Juan	.160	29	75	8	12	0	0	0	11	6	17	3	1	.160	.229	R	R	5-11	180	2-4-84	2001	Hato Mayor, D.R.
Falu, Irving	.274	54	223	33	61	8	3	1	15	26	19	23	10	.350	.362	S	R	6-0	174	6-6-83	2003	Carolina, P.R.
Figuereo, Anibal	.364	6	22	1	8	2	1	0	6	2	6	0	0	.545	.400	R	R	6-2	200	1-21-82	1999	Barahona, D.R.
Gonzalez, Juan	.346	9	26	6	9	5	0	0	5	6	8	0	0	.538	.455	R	R	6-3	220	10-16-69	1986	Levittown, P.R.
Grana, Robert	.234	39	124	16	29	8	1	0	15	22	37	2	1	.315	.349	R	R	6-3	200	8-4-83	2003	Las Vegas, Nev.
Guiel, Aaron	.471	4	17	3	8	1	0	2	5	0	2	0	0	.882	.500	L	R	5-10	200	10-5-72	1993	Langley, B.C.
Johnson, Josh	.213	53	178	44	38	5	6	0	22	55	38	23	13	.309	.413	S	R	5-11	170	1-11-86	2004	Tampa, Fla.
McConnell, Chris	.339	37	124	22	42	5	0	3	11	17	19	8	4	.452	.420	R	R	5-11	170	12-18-85	2004	Franklinville, N.J.
Moye, Alan	.275	12	40	8	11	2	2	1	12	8	14	3	1	.500	.388	R	R	6-2	200	10-8-82	2001	Longview, Texas
Norman, Derek	.222	3	9	1	2	0	0	0	3	3	0	0	0	.222	.417	R	R	6-0	190	2-21-82	2004	Knoxville, Tenn.
Pena, Jose	.241	18	58	5	14	3	0	3	7	2	25	0	0	.448	.274	R	R	6-0	190	10-24-84	2002	Monte Cristi, D.R.
Qualls, Darrell	.235	34	98	9	23	4	3	0	12	10	33	0	4	.337	.301	R	R	6-3	205	7-17-83	2004	Middleburg, Fla.
Santana, Ethien	.236	52	191	26	45	5	0	0	17	20	35	23	9	.262	.323	L	L	5-11	153	1-25-84	2004	San Juan, P.R.
Thomas, Jonathan	.077	9	13	1	1	0	0	0	1	2	2	0	0	.077	.200	L	R	5-11	175	10-23-81	2004	Newark, N.J.
Vega, Miguel	.275	56	229	36	63	15	5	10	44	16	74	6	1	.515	.328	R	R	6-3	205	7-31-85	2003	Arroyo, P.R.

GAMES BY POSITION: C—Grana 39, Norman 2, Pena 16, Thomas 4. **1B**—Adkison 16, Figuereo 3, Vega 44. **2B**—Falu 44, Johnson 12. **3B**—Chapman 13, Falu 3, Figuereo 2, Qualls 31, Vega 18. **SS**—Johnson 30, McConnell 29. **OF**—Caballero 35, Ellis 50, Eusebio 27, Gonzalez 3, Guiel 3, Moye 9, Santana 52.

PITCHING	W	L	ERA	G	GS	CG	SV	IP	H	R	ER	BB	SO	AVG	B	T	HT	WT	DOB	1st Yr	Resides
Bass, Brian	0	1	2.55	5	5	0	0	18	17	6	5	3	23	.246	R	R	6-0	190	1-6-82	2000	Montgomery, Ala.
Begnaud, Rusty	4	3	3.74	14	10	0	1	65	71	36	27	10	75	.276	R	R	6-1	195	12-19-80	2004	New Iberia, La.
Clow, Josh	1	1	4.57	12	0	0	1	22	20	14	11	17	19	.238	R	R	6-2	235	1-13-83	2004	Knoxville, Tenn.
Coffey, Andrew	1	0	1.71	13	0	0	0	26	16	7	5	11	26	.170	L	L	5-11	195	11-2-85	2004	Cottonwood, Ariz.
Cordier, Erik	2	4	5.19	11	11	0	0	35	38	27	20	21	22	.279	R	R	6-3	190	2-25-86	2004	Sturgeon Bay, Wis.
Damico, Yovany	1	0	0.28	20	0	0	6	32	19	3	1	10	24	.169	R	R	6-1	170	8-18-84	2003	Mariara, Venez.
Eckley, Jacob	2	1	3.68	8	0	0	0	15	18	8	6	6	14	.305	L	L	6-4	210	6-27-83	2004	Omaha, Neb.
Garcia, Eliszer	2	7	3.94	19	0	0	3	32	31	16	14	6	24	.250	L	L	6-1	150	6-7-84	2002	Edo Bolivar, Venez.
Goins, Mitch	2	0	4.36	13	9	0	0	54	60	38	26	17	44	.280	R	R	6-3	235	1-18-83	2004	Bloomfield, N.M.
McCleland, Bruce	3	2	3.15	11	4	0	0	34	37	17	12	8	22	.274	R	R	6-5	210	12-16-84	2002	Capetown, South Africa
Morales, Angelo	6	4	3.96	14	10	0	0	61	76	34	27	9	45	.296	R	R	6-1	170	5-2-86	2004	Chiriqui, Panama
Nelson, Justin	0	0	2.84	6	1	0	1	13	10	4	4	5	6	.212	L	L	6-4	200	12-15-82	2001	Kersey, Colo.
Rosa, Carlos	0	0	4.91	4	4	0	0	11	14	6	6	9	8	.325	R	R	6-2	170	9-21-84	2002	San Francisco de Macoris, D.R.
Rosario, Julio	3	2	2.48	15	0	0	0	36	37	13	10	13	23	.264	R	R	6-0	160	11-17-83	2002	La Romana, D.R.
Sokoll, John	0	0	9.39	16	2	0	0	15	22	21	16	16	14	.333	L	L	6-6	210	11-9-84	2004	Solon, Iowa
Tennyson, Adam	2	2	3.96	15	0	0	0	25	22	11	11	21	22	.236	R	R	6-0	165	10-15-83	2004	Tuscaloosa, Ala.

BY JILL PAINTER

The Dodgers had a champagne celebration for the first time in eight years as they returned to the playoffs in 2004. The celebration, however, didn't last long.

They won the National League West with 93 victories but lost to the Cardinals in the division series, posting just one win.

Throughout the season, there was one constant: change.

There was a new owner in Frank McCourt, new general manager in Paul DePodesta and a slew of deadline trades. There also was a new player, of sorts, in Adrian Beltre.

The Dodgers third baseman, in his sixth full year in the major leagues, had a breakthrough year to say the least, finally fulfilling the promise the Dodgers saw in him as a teenager. He hit 48 home runs—one shy of Shawn Green's franchise record—and batted .334 with 121 RBIs in a contract year.

Beltre, 25, provided a much-needed boost in the lineup and was moved to the cleanup spot with Green batting fifth. Green batted .266-28-86 after a slow start.

The Dodgers' starting rotation was anything but solidified, as it was in 2003, but it received an unexpected yet inspirational performance by Jose Lima. He was signed to a minor league contract in spring training and ended up tied for a team-best with 13 wins. And he was the only pitcher to win a postseason game, shutting out the Cardinals in a complete-game, 4-0 victory in Game 3 of the best-of-five series. It was the Dodgers' first postseason win since 1988, when they won the World Series.

And in typical Hollywood fashion, there was always drama in Los Angeles. The Dodgers had 53 comeback wins, the most impressive engineered by Steve Finley, who was acquired before the July 31 trade deadline from Arizona for minor leaguers. Despite a 3-0 San Francisco

Adrian Beltre   Joel Guzman

ROBERT GURGANUS

PLAYERS of the YEAR

MAJOR LEAGUE: Adrian Beltre, 3b

Beltre always showed flashes of brilliance early in his career with the Dodgers, but it all came together for the 25-year-old—in MVP-caliber fashion in 2004. Beltre hit .334-48-121 in 598 at-bats, and led the Dodgers to the National League West title.

MINOR LEAGUE: Joel Guzman, ss

Guzman moved from high Class A Vero Beach to Double-A Jacksonville in 2004, and the 6-foot-6 Dominican shortstop more than held his own. Guzman hit .307-14-51 in 329 at-bats prior to the promotion and .280-9-35 in 182 at-bats after the promotion.

lead in the bottom of the ninth, Finley hit a grand slam to clinch the NL West title for Los Angeles.

DePodesta traded five major league players before the deadline in an effort to get a starting pitcher for the playoffs.

He made an unpopular trade as he sent catcher Paul Lo Duca, a fan favorite, righthanded reliever Guillermo Mota and outfielder Juan Encarnacion to the Marlins in a deal for righthander Brad Penny and first baseman Hee-Seop Choi. DePodesta made the trade to get a No. 1 starter but Penny didn't throw a pitch in the playoffs as he injured a nerve in his arm Aug. 8, in just his second start with the Dodgers. He ran off the mound but tried to make a comeback in September that resulted in re-injury.

The Dodgers traded with Cleveland for the volatile Milton Bradley the day before the season started and it was a roller-coaster ride. Bradley was ejected from four games, the final time resulting in a suspension for the last five games of the regular season. He slammed a beer bottle—which was thrown at him by a fan—into the stands and stormed off field.

The Dodgers' top two prospects were hampered by injuries in 2004. A strained right forearm limited righthander Edwin Jackson and lefthander Greg Miller missed the entire season after Tommy John surgery.

But other prospects had major breakout seasons. Righthander Chad Billingsley, the team's top draft pick in 2003, emerged as one of the top pitching prospects in baseball after going 4-0, 2.98 at high Class A Vero Beach and then 7-4, 2.35 at Double-A Jacksonville. He struck out a combined 158 batters in 134 innings between the two levels.

ORGANIZATION LEADERS

BATTING

*AVG	John Barnes, Las Vegas	.348
R	Shane Victorino, Las Vegas/Jacksonville	98
H	Luis Garcia, Las Vegas	156
TB	Luis Garcia, Las Vegas	290
2B	Jason Repko, Las Vegas/Jacksonville	37
3B	Joel Guzman, Jacksonville/Vero Beach	11
HR	Luis Garcia, Las Vegas	32
RBI	Luis Garcia, Las Vegas	95
BB	Russell Martin, Vero Beach	72
SO	Delwyn Young, Vero Beach	134
SB	Alex Requena, Vero Beach	50
*OBP	Jose Flores, Las Vegas	.407
*SLG	Chin-Feng Chen, Las Vegas	.584

PITCHING

W	Chad Billingsley, Jacksonville/Vero Beach	11
	Jonathan Broxton, Vero Beach	11
L	Mark Johnson, Las Vegas	12
#ERA	Marcos Carvajal, Jacksonville/Columbus	1.80
G	Troy Brohawn, Las Vegas	72
CG	Julio Pimentel, Columbus	2
SV	Jose Diaz, Vero Beach/Columbus	20
IP	Heath Totten, Las Vegas	160
BB	Glenn Bott, Las Vegas	75
	Joel Hanrahan, Las Vegas	75
SO	Chad Billingsley, Jacksonville/Vero Beach	158

*Minimum 250 at-bats   #Minimum 75 innings

LOS ANGELES DODGERS

Manager: Jim Tracy.

2004 Record: 93-69, .574 (1st, NL West).

BATTING	AVG	G	AB	R	H	2B	3B	HR	RBI	BB	SO	SB	CS	OBP	SLG	B	T	HT	WT	DOB	1st Yr	Resides
Beltre, Adrian	.334	156	598	104	200	32	0	48	121	53	87	7	2	.388	.629	R	R	5-11	220	4-7-79	1995	Santo Domingo, D.R.
Bradley, Milton	.267	141	516	72	138	24	0	19	67	71	123	15	11	.362	.424	S	R	6-0	205	4-15-78	1996	Long Beach, Calif.
Chen, Chin-Feng	.000	8	8	1	0	0	0	0	0	2	3	0	0	.200	.000	R	R	6-1	189	10-28-77	1999	Tainan City, Taiwan
Choi, Hee Seop	.161	31	62	5	10	5	0	6	11	18	0	0	.289	.242	L	L	6-5	240	3-16-79	1999	Vancouver, Wash.
2-team (95 Florida)	.251	126	343	53	86	21	1	15	46	63	96	1	0	.370	.449							
Cora, Alex	.264	138	405	47	107	9	4	10	47	47	41	3	4	.364	.380	L	R	6-0	200	10-18-75	1996	Caguas, P.R.
Encarnacion, Juan	.235	86	324	42	76	18	1	13	43	21	53	3	3	.289	.417	R	R	6-3	215	3-8-76	1993	Santo Domingo, D.R.
Finley, Steve	.263	58	224	31	59	12	0	13	46	21	30	1	3	.324	.491	L	L	6-2	194	3-12-65	1987	Del Mar, Calif.
2-team (104 Arizona)	.271	162	628	92	170	28	1	36	94	61	82	9	7	.333	.490							
Flores, Jose	.250	9	4	0	1	0	0	0	0	1	2	0	0	.400	.250	R	R	5-11	180	6-28-73	1994	Corpus Christi, Texas
Grabowski, Jason	.220	113	173	18	38	7	0	7	20	19	50	0	0	.297	.382	L	R	6-3	200	5-24-76	1997	Clinton, Conn.
Green, Shawn	.266	157	590	92	157	28	1	28	86	71	114	5	2	.352	.459	L	L	6-4	200	11-10-72	1992	Newport Beach, Calif.
Hernandez, Jose	.289	95	211	32	61	12	1	13	29	26	61	3	1	.370	.540	R	R	6-1	190	7-14-69	1987	Dorado, P.R.
Izturis, Cesar	.288	159	670	90	193	32	9	4	62	43	70	25	9	.330	.381	S	R	5-9	175	2-10-80	1997	Barquisimeto, Venez.
Lo Duca, Paul	.301	91	349	41	105	18	1	10	49	22	27	2	4	.351	.444	R	R	5-10	185	4-12-72	1993	San Antonio, Texas
Mayne, Brent	.188	47	96	5	18	0	0	0	5	14	24	0	0	.286	.188	L	R	6-1	190	4-19-68	1989	Corona Del Mar, Calif.
2-team (36 Arizona)	.221	83	190	14	42	6	1	0	15	27	41	1	0	.314	.263							
Perez, Antonio	.231	13	13	5	3	1	0	0	0	0	5	1	0	.286	.308	R	R	5-11	170	1-26-80	1998	Bani, D.R.
Roberts, Dave	.253	68	233	45	59	4	7	2	21	28	31	33	1	.340	.356	L	L	5-10	180	5-31-72	1994	Oceanside, Calif.
Ross, David	.170	70	165	13	28	3	1	5	15	15	62	0	0	.253	.291	R	R	6-2	215	3-19-77	1998	Tallahassee, Fla.
Saenz, Olmedo	.279	77	111	17	31	1	0	8	22	12	33	0	0	.352	.505	R	R	5-11	220	10-8-70	1991	Chitre Herrera, Panama
Thurston, Joe	.176	17	17	1	3	1	1	0	1	0	5	0	0	.167	.353	L	R	5-11	175	9-29-79	1999	Vallejo, Calif.
Ventura, Robin	.243	102	152	19	37	3	0	5	28	22	31	0	0	.337	.362	L	R	6-1	200	7-14-67	1989	Greenwich, Conn.
Werth, Jayson	.262	89	290	56	76	11	3	16	47	30	85	4	1	.338	.486	R	R	6-5	210	5-20-79	1997	Chatham, Ill.
Wilson, Tom	.125	9	8	1	1	0	0	0	0	3	0	0	0	.125	.125	R	R	6-3	220	12-19-70	1991	Lake Havasu City, Ariz.
2-team (14 New York)	.167	13	12	1	2	0	0	0	1	5	0	0	.231	.167							

PITCHING	W	L	ERA	G	GS	CG	SV	IP	H	R	ER	BB	SO	AVG	B	T	HT	WT	DOB	1st Yr	Resides
Alvarez, Wilson	7	6	4.03	40	15	0	1	121	109	56	54	31	102	.244	L	L	6-1	255	3-24-70	1987	Bradenton, Fla.
Brazoban, Yhency	6	2	2.48	31	0	0	0	33	25	9	9	15	27	.219	R	R	6-1	170	6-11-80	1998	Santo Domingo, D.R.
Carrara, Giovanni	5	2	2.18	42	0	0	2	54	46	15	13	20	48	.228	R	R	6-2	235	3-4-68	1991	Anzoategui, Venez.
Dessens, Elmer	1	0	3.20	12	1	0	0	20	16	7	7	8	18	.216	R	R	5-10	198	1-13-72	1994	Hermosillo, Mexico
2-team (38 Arizona)	2	6	4.46	50	10	0	2	105	123	61	52	31	73	.287							
Dreifort, Darren	1	4	4.44	60	0	0	1	51	43	25	25	36	63	.232	R	R	6-2	210	5-3-72	1994	Wichita, Kan.
Falkenborg, Brian	1	0	7.53	6	0	0	0	14	19	14	12	9	11	.322	R	R	6-6	195	1-18-78	1996	Redmond, Wash.
Gagne, Eric	7	3	2.19	70	0	0	45	82	53	24	20	22	114	.181	R	R	6-2	235	1-7-76	1996	Montreal, Quebec
Ishii, Kazuhisa	13	8	4.71	31	31	2	0	172	155	97	90	98	99	.246	L	L	6-0	200	9-9-73	2002	Tokyo, Japan
Jackson, Edwin	2	1	7.30	8	5	0	0	25	31	20	20	11	16	.307	R	R	6-3	190	9-9-83	2001	Columbus, Ga.
Kida, Masao	0	0	0.00	3	0	0	0	5	4	0	0	1	5	.235	R	R	6-3	210	9-12-68	1999	Tokyo, Japan
Lima, Jose	13	5	4.07	36	24	0	0	170	178	81	77	34	93	.271	R	R	6-2	205	9-30-72	1990	Houston, Texas
Martin, Tom	0	1	4.13	47	0	0	1	28	32	13	13	14	18	.291	L	L	6-1	200	5-21-70	1989	Panama City, Fla.
Mota, Guillermo	8	4	2.14	52	0	0	1	63	51	15	15	27	52	.228	R	R	6-4	210	7-25-73	1991	San Pedro de Macoris, D.R.
Myers, Rodney	0	0	0.00	1	0	0	0	2	1	0	0	0	1	.167	R	R	6-1	200	6-26-69	1990	Chandler, Ariz.
Nomo, Hideo	4	11	8.25	18	18	0	0	84	105	77	77	42	54	.312	R	R	6-2	235	8-31-68	1995	Tokyo, Japan
Penny, Brad	1	2	3.09	3	3	0	0	12	6	5	4	6	4	.154	R	R	6-4	250	5-24-78	1996	Broken Arrow, Okla.
2-team (21 Florida)	9	10	3.15	24	24	0	0	143	130	55	50	45	111	.243							
Perez, Odalis	7	6	3.25	31	31	0	0	196	180	76	71	44	128	.250	L	L	6-0	220	6-11-77	1995	Las Matas de Farfan, D.R.
Sanchez, Duaner	3	1	3.38	67	0	0	0	80	81	34	30	27	44	.266	R	R	6-0	189	10-14-79	1997	Cotui, D.R.
Stewart, Scott	1	0	5.84	11	0	0	0	12	20	8	8	6	8	.392	R	L	6-2	225	8-14-75	1994	Mt. Holly, N.C.
Venafro, Mike	0	0	4.00	17	0	0	0	9	11	5	4	3	6	.306	L	L	5-10	180	8-2-73	1995	Fort Myers, Fla.
Weaver, Jeff	13	13	4.01	34	34	0	0	220	219	103	98	67	153	.260	R	R	6-5	200	8-22-76	1998	Simi Valley, Calif.

FIELDING

Catcher	PCT	G	PO	A	E	DP	PB
Lo Duca	.995	81	513	42	3	4	7
Mayne	1.000	47	224	12	0	2	2
Ross	.992	67	355	21	3	0	6
Wilson	1.000	7	11	0	0	0	

First Base	PCT	G	PO	A	E	DP
Choi	.994	23	161	10	1	19
Grabowski	1.000	3	2	1	0	0
Green	.995	111	879	53	5	82
Hernandez	1.000	8	15	2	0	3
Lo Duca	1.000	3	11	1	0	1
Saenz	.986	25	125	12	2	16
Ventura	1.000	40	214	14	0	15

Second Base	PCT	G	PO	A	E	DP
Cora	.987	138	261	343	8	91
Flores	.000	1	0	0	0	0
Hernandez	.980	50	80	113	4	21
Perez	.750	2	2	1	1	1
Thurston	1.000	4	2	3	0	1

Third Base	PCT	G	PO	A	E	DP
Beltre	.978	155	120	322	10	32
Flores	1.000	1	0	1	0	0
Hernandez	1.000	12	4	8	0	1
Saenz	1.000	2	0	2	0	0
Ventura	1.000	11	13	11	0	6

Shortstop	PCT	G	PO	A	E	DP
Beltre	1.000	1	0	1	0	0

Hernandez	.971	13	8	26	1	5
Izturis	.985	159	234	430	10	96
Perez	1.000	1	1	2	0	1

Outfield	PCT	G	PO	A	E	DP
Bradley	.977	138	332	8	8	1
Chen	1.000	3	8	0	0	0
Encarnacion	.976	85	161	3	4	0
Finley	.993	55	145	0	1	0
Grabowski	.977	31	42	0	1	0
Green	.976	52	81	2	2	1
Hernandez	1.000	9	6	0	0	0
Lo Duca	1.000	9	13	0	0	0
Roberts	.976	62	118	2	3	1
Werth	.974	79	146	6	4	2

FARM SYSTEM

Field Coordinator, Minor League Operations: Terry Collins.

Class	Farm Team	League	W	L	Pct.	Finish*	Manager	Affiliate Since
AAA	Las Vegas (Nev.) 51s	Pacific Coast	67	76	.469	11th (16)	Terry Kennedy	2001
AA	Jacksonville (Fla.) Suns	Southern	66	71	.482	7th (10)	Dino Ebel	2002
High A	Vero Beach (Fla.) Dodgers	Florida State	77	57	.575	**1st (12)**	Scott Little	1980
Low A	Columbus (Ga.) Catfish	South Atlantic	69	69	.500	t-7th (16)	Dann Bilardello	2002
Rookie	Ogden (Utah) Raptors	Pioneer	35	40	.467	6th (8)	Travis Barbary	2003
Rookie	Vero Beach (Fla.) Dodgers	Gulf Coast	31	29	.517	t-6th (12)	Luis Salazar	2001

*Finish in overall standings (No. of teams in league)/Playoff teams in **boldface**

LAS VEGAS 51s — Class AAA

PACIFIC COAST LEAGUE

BATTING

	AVG	G	AB	R	H	2B	3B	HR	RBI	BB	SO	SB	CS	OBP	SLG	B	T	HT	WT	DOB	1st Yr	Resides
Barnes, John	.348	65	250	39	87	17	0	9	43	13	21	2	2	.379	.524	R	R	6-2	210	4-24-76	1996	Mesa, Ariz.
Bell, Rick	.302	125	460	68	139	36	1	12	54	23	75	7	3	.336	.463	R	R	6-2	180	4-5-79	1997	Scottsdale, Ariz.
Chen, Chin-Feng	.289	81	308	59	89	19	6	20	65	35	78	6	2	.359	.584	R	R	6-1	189	10-28-77	1999	Tainan City, Taiwan
Flores, Jose	.313	99	319	64	100	20	1	7	51	49	30	6	2	.407	.448	R	R	5-11	180	6-28-73	1994	Corpus Christi, Texas
Garcia, Luis	.314	129	497	76	156	32	3	32	95	32	104	1	1	.354	.584	R	R	6-4	190	11-5-78	1996	Guadalajara, Mexico
Garcia, Sergio	.161	16	31	5	5	1	0	1	1	4	7	1	1	.257	.290	R	R	5-9	175	3-29-80	2002	Paramount, Calif.
Giambi, Jeremy	.130	11	23	3	3	0	0	1	1	3	8	0	0	.231	.261	L	L	5-11	216	9-30-74	1996	Las Vegas, Nev.
Hill, Koyie	.286	91	350	57	100	26	0	13	54	28	69	0	1	.339	.471	S	R	6-0	190	3-9-79	2000	Lawton, Okla.
Holt, Daylan	.265	39	98	11	26	2	0	4	13	7	19	2	1	.308	.408	R	R	6-1	200	10-4-78	2000	Mesquite, Texas
Kellner, Ryan	.187	65	187	20	35	7	0	6	23	10	56	0	0	.235	.321	R	R	6-2	205	12-9-77	1998	Morganton, N.C.
Langill, Eric	.192	14	26	0	5	1	0	0	2	0	6	0	0	.192	.231	R	R	5-9	190	4-4-79	2000	Kirkland, Quebec
Michaelis, Derek	.200	4	15	2	3	1	0	0	2	0	6	0	0	.294	.267	L	L	6-7	240	12-2-78	2000	Waco, Texas
Myrow, Brian	.359	50	153	29	55	15	2	6	29	21	47	2	3	.444	.601	L	R	5-11	190	9-4-76	1999	Fort Worth, Texas
Perez, Antonio	.296	125	476	92	141	24	6	22	88	61	87	23	12	.379	.511	R	R	5-11	170	1-26-80	1998	Bani, D.R.
Repko, Jason	.311	75	302	55	94	26	4	7	41	18	57	13	5	.355	.493	R	R	5-11	175	12-27-80	1999	West Richland, Wash.
Riggs, Eric	.231	52	130	14	30	6	0	3	14	20	21	1	2	.331	.346	S	R	6-2	190	8-19-76	1998	Miami, Fla.
Ross, Cody	.273	60	238	44	65	17	2	14	49	18	43	2	0	.328	.538	R	L	5-11	180	12-23-80	1999	Carlsbad, N.M.
Stanley, Henri	.284	26	88	13	25	8	1	3	12	4	25	2	1	.319	.500	L	L	5-10	185	12-15-77	2000	Columbia, S.C.
2-team (28 Portland)	.265	54	189	24	50	14	2	5	24	17	36	3	1	.325	.439							
Theodorou, Nick	.282	89	294	47	83	14	3	4	32	36	36	9	7	.368	.391	S	R	5-11	182	6-7-75	1998	Rialto, Calif.
Thurston, Joe	.284	101	317	38	90	17	3	4	23	20	46	7	2	.356	.394	L	R	5-11	175	9-29-79	1999	Vallejo, Calif.
Victorino, Shane	.235	55	200	28	47	9	1	3	20	11	37	7	2	.278	.335	S	R	5-9	160	11-30-80	1999	Wailuku, Hawaii
Werth, Jayson	.412	14	51	13	21	2	1	5	20	8	10	2	0	.500	.784	R	R	6-5	210	5-20-79	1997	Chatham, Ill.
Wilson, Tom	.421	9	38	10	16	2	0	4	9	4	10	0	0	.476	.789	R	R	6-3	220	12-19-70	1991	Lake Havasu City, Ariz.
2-team (14 Sacramento)	.325	23	80	16	26	4	0	5	14	19	23	0	0	.455	.563							

PITCHING

	W	L	ERA	G	GS	CG	SV	IP	H	R	ER	BB	SO	AVG	B	T	HT	WT	DOB	1st Yr	Resides
Abreu, Winston	1	2	7.83	14	1	0	0	23	20	20	20	20	23	.230	R	R	6-2	155	4-5-77	1994	Cotui, D.R.
Brazoban, Yhency	2	0	2.19	10	0	0	1	12	14	3	3	1	17	.286	R	R	6-1	170	6-11-80	1998	Santo Domingo, D.R.
Brohawn, Troy	7	5	5.42	72	1	0	5	91	122	58	55	26	74	.316	L	L	6-0	190	1-14-73	1994	Woolford, Md.
Carrara, Giovanni	0	1	2.51	11	0	0	2	14	11	4	4	8	15	.208	R	R	6-2	235	3-4-68	1991	Anzoategui, Venez.
2-team (20 Iowa)	1	3	3.37	31	0	0	3	43	40	16	16	16	38	.255							
Eckert, Harold	4	3	6.35	31	9	0	0	84	103	66	59	42	81	.308	R	R	6-3	220	7-18-77	2001	Edison, N.J.
Falkenborg, Brian	4	6	6.17	18	15	0	1	89	104	66	61	25	87	.286	R	R	6-6	195	1-18-78	1996	Redmond, Wash.
Farmer, Tom	7	7	4.59	47	7	0	3	82	105	54	42	34	70	.306	R	R	6-3	185	7-27-79	2001	Miami, Fla.
Hanrahan, Joel	7	7	5.05	25	22	0	0	119	128	78	67	75	97	.276	R	R	6-3	215	10-6-81	2000	Norwalk, Iowa
Jackson, Edwin	6	4	5.86	19	19	0	0	91	90	65	59	55	70	.265	R	R	6-3	190	9-9-83	2001	Columbus, Ga.
Jarvis, Matt	0	0	10.80	2	0	0	0	2	7	2	2	0	1	.583	R	R	6-4	180	2-22-72	1991	Albuquerque, N.M.
Johnson, Mark	6	12	5.39	37	21	0	2	140	171	91	84	42	89	.304	R	R	6-3	220	5-2-75	1997	Leesburg, Fla.
Ketchner, Ryan	0	0	1.29	1	1	0	0	7	5	1	1	0	4	.200	L	L	6-1	190	4-19-82	2000	Lantana, Fla.
Kida, Masao	3	1	5.97	9	5	0	0	38	40	25	25	16	32	.274	R	R	6-3	210	9-12-68	1999	Tokyo, Japan
Knott, Eric	0	2	5.00	12	0	0	0	18	18	13	10	6	9	.265	L	L	6-1	180	9-23-74	1997	Sebring, Fla.
Mathews, T.J.	1	0	4.50	13	0	0	5	18	17	9	9	4	12	.258	R	R	6-1	220	1-19-70	1992	Las Vegas, Nev.
Montero, Agustin	1	4	7.69	42	0	0	3	46	55	47	39	26	38	.289	R	R	6-3	212	8-26-77	1995	San Pedro de Macoris, D.R.
Myers, Rodney	4	1	4.74	24	0	0	0	38	42	22	20	11	25	.278	R	R	6-1	190	6-26-69	1990	Chandler, Ariz.
Nickle, Doug	2	2	4.73	19	1	0	2	32	35	19	17	21	19	.287	R	R	6-4	210	10-2-74	1997	Sonoma, Calif.
Nina, Elvin	0	2	6.75	10	0	0	0	15	19	14	11	8	10	.306	R	R	6-0	185	11-25-79	1997	Tempe, Ariz.
Nomo, Hideo	1	1	5.71	4	4	0	0	17	22	11	11	8	25	.324	R	R	6-2	235	8-31-68	1995	Tokyo, Japan
Osoria, Franquelis	0	0	6.48	4	0	0	0	8	13	6	6	1	3	.351	R	R	6-0	165	9-12-81	2000	Santiago, D.R.
Ruhl, Nathan	0	0	7.56	6	0	0	0	8	8	7	7	9	5	.276	R	R	6-4	230	7-16-76	1996	Lee's Summit, Mo.
Shuey, Paul	0	1	18.00	3	0	0	0	3	9	6	6	2	2	.529	R	R	6-2	235	9-16-70	1992	Wake Forest, N.C.
Smith, Roy	3	6	3.23	30	3	0	0	48	70	38	33	27	40	.350	R	R	6-6	230	5-18-76	1994	Pinellas Park, Fla.
Stewart, Scott	0	0	2.45	4	0	0	0	4	3	1	1	1	7	.231	R	L	6-2	225	8-14-75	1994	Mt. Holly, N.C.
Sturtze, Tanyon	0	0	0.52	6	6	0	0	36	26	11	10	12	32	.203	R	R	6-5	200	10-12-70	1990	St. Petersburg, Fla.
Totten, Heath	8	11	5.46	28	27	1	0	160	213	107	97	29	93	.321	R	R	6-3	210	9-30-78	2000	Lumberton, Texas
Venafro, Mike	0	1	7.11	5	0	0	1	6	8	5	5	2	4	.320	L	L	5-10	180	8-2-73	1995	Fort Myers, Fla.
2-team (35 Omaha)	2	5	6.44	40	0	0	3	64	78	35	33	21	45	.310							
White, Rick	0	0	0.00	6	0	0	2	12	4	0	0	1	14	.105	R	R	6-4	230	12-23-68	1990	Springfield, Ohio

FIELDING

Catcher	PCT	G	PO	A	E	DP	PB
Hill	.994	81	562	56	4	4	10
Kellner	.977	56	355	28	9	3	10
Langill	1.000	8	39	1	0	0	0
Wilson	.986	9	65	6	1	1	4

First Base	PCT	G	PO	A	E	DP
Bell	.981	34	231	23	5	24
Chen	1.000	2	16	0	0	5
Garcia	.987	95	785	72	11	78
Hill	.909	2	10	0	1	1
Myrow	.988	25	219	18	3	17

Second Base	PCT	G	PO	A	E	DP
Bell	1.000	2	4	3	0	0
Flores	1.000	5	3	17	0	1

	PCT	G	PO	A	E	DP
Garcia	1.000	4	9	13	0	7
Perez	.978	48	84	140	5	32
Riggs	1.000	1	1	1	0	1
Theodorou	1.000	11	19	27	0	6
Thurston	.977	85	171	249	10	47

Third Base	PCT	G	PO	A	E	DP
Bell	.941	89	53	169	14	10
Flores	.953	32	16	45	3	2
Garcia	.909	4	1	9	1	1
Hill	1.000	1	1	2	0	0
Riggs	.955	28	15	48	3	4

	PCT	G	PO	A	E	DP
Theodorou	.789	7	4	11	4	1

Shortstop	PCT	G	PO	A	E	DP
Flores	.955	56	82	150	11	36
Garcia	1.000	1	1	2	0	0
Perez	.952	79	97	201	15	46
Riggs	.957	7	9	13	1	6
Theodorou	.962	16	24	27	2	7

Outfield	PCT	G	PO	A	E	DP
Barnes	.991	55	98	7	1	1
Chen	.967	76	112	5	4	0
Garcia	1.000	4	5	1	0	0

	PCT	G	PO	A	E	DP
Garcia	1.000	2	2	0	0	0
Giambi	1.000	6	8	0	0	0
Holt	1.000	28	37	5	0	1
Michaelis	1.000	4	6	0	0	0
Myrow	1.000	16	22	0	0	0
Repko	.988	69	162	4	2	0
Riggs	1.000	5	7	1	0	0
Ross	.972	61	99	4	3	0
Stanley	.975	22	39	0	1	0
Theodorou	.989	53	88	3	1	0
Victorino	.984	50	118	9	2	1
Werth	1.000	13	14	0	0	0

JACKSONVILLE SUNS — Class AA

SOUTHERN LEAGUE

BATTING	AVG	G	AB	R	H	2B	3B	HR	RBI	BB	SO	SB	CS	OBP	SLG	B	T	HT	WT	DOB	1st Yr	Resides
Abercrombie, Reggie	.173	41	168	17	29	6	4	4	20	4	66	3	3	.193	.327	R	R	6-3	220	7-15-80	2000	Columbus, Ga.
Alvarez, Nick	.249	80	217	30	54	11	0	7	29	17	32	5	3	.315	.396	R	R	6-3	205	2-8-77	2000	Miami, Fla.
Aybar, Willy	.276	126	482	56	133	27	0	15	77	50	77	8	10	.346	.425	S	R	6-0	185	3-9-83	2000	Bani, D.R.
Bellorin, Edwin	.281	86	285	27	80	15	1	1	30	18	51	1	0	.331	.351	R	R	5-11	180	2-21-82	1999	Edo Bolivar, Venez.
Castro, Nelson	.243	118	399	48	97	15	3	11	45	29	99	17	7	.303	.378	R	R	5-10	200	6-4-76	1994	Monte Cristi, D.R.
Dowdy, Brett	.273	36	66	9	18	1	1	0	5	8	20	0	0	.347	.318	R	R	6-0	189	2-22-82	2003	Bradenton, Fla.
Garcia, Sergio	.254	83	169	24	43	3	0	4	18	23	40	4	2	.352	.343	R	R	5-9	175	3-29-80	2002	Paramount, Calif.
Guzman, Joel	.280	46	182	25	51	11	3	9	35	13	44	1	2	.325	.522	R	R	6-4	198	11-24-84	2002	San Pedro de Macoris, D.R.
Holt, Daylan	.213	75	178	22	38	8	1	10	22	15	49	2	0	.281	.438	R	R	6-1	200	10-4-78	2000	Mesquite, Texas
Hoorelbeke, Jesse	.193	29	83	10	16	7	0	4	15	14	31	0	1	.323	.422	R	R	6-3	225	10-13-77	2002	Hansen, Idaho
King, Brennan	.277	131	480	61	133	29	1	13	47	30	109	1	6	.332	.423	R	R	6-3	205	1-20-81	1999	Murfreesboro, Tenn.
Langill, Eric	.133	6	15	1	2	1	0	0	0	4	6	0	0	.333	.200	R	R	5-9	190	4-4-79	2000	Kirkland, Quebec
Loney, James	.238	104	395	39	94	19	2	4	35	42	75	6	5	.314	.327	L	L	6-3	220	5-7-84	2002	Missouri City, Texas
McGee, Tom	.212	11	33	2	7	0	0	1	3	3	8	0	1	.278	.303	R	R	5-11	200	1-29-75	1997	Frederick, Md.
Michaelis, Derek	.264	110	330	47	87	26	1	10	41	38	104	5	5	.345	.439	L	L	6-7	240	12-2-78	2000	Waco, Texas
Repko, Jason	.291	46	189	26	55	11	2	6	19	13	43	10	5	.341	.466	R	R	5-11	175	12-27-80	1999	West Richland, Wash.
Riggs, Eric	.323	18	62	10	20	1	0	1	5	11	14	0	1	.425	.387	S	R	6-2	190	8-19-76	1998	Miami, Fla.
Ruan, Wilkin	.208	55	178	19	37	5	0	1	8	10	26	9	3	.250	.253	R	R	6-0	182	9-18-78	1997	Guaymate, D.R.
Schifano, Tony	.176	6	17	2	3	1	0	0	1	2	5	2	0	.333	.235	R	R	6-1	190	11-11-74	1997	Anaheim Hills, Calif.
Socarras, Tony	.205	49	151	10	31	9	0	2	10	12	53	1	1	.277	.305	L	R	6-0	205	11-8-79	2000	Miami, Fla.
Victorino, Shane	.327	75	294	70	96	13	7	16	43	20	65	9	7	.373	.582	S	R	5-9	160	11-30-80	1999	Wailuku, Hawaii

PITCHING	W	L	ERA	G	GS	CG	SV	IP	H	R	ER	BB	SO	AVG	B	T	HT	WT	DOB	1st Yr	Resides
Abreu, Winston	1	1	5.59	3	2	0	0	10	10	7	6	7	12	.278	R	R	6-2	155	4-5-77	1994	Cotui, D.R.
Billingsley, Chad	4	0	2.98	8	8	0	0	42	32	16	14	22	47	.213	R	R	6-2	215	7-29-84	2003	Defiance, Ohio
Bott, Glenn	4	11	4.37	28	27	1	0	146	143	81	71	75	120	.255	L	L	6-0	170	9-17-81	2001	Houston, Texas
Brazoban, Yhency	4	4	2.65	37	0	0	13	51	38	18	15	22	61	.210	R	R	6-1	170	6-11-80	1998	Santo Domingo, D.R.
Brown, Andrew	1	3	4.02	8	8	0	0	40	36	23	18	14	58	.232	R	R	6-6	230	2-17-81	1999	Deltona, Fla.
Carvajal, Marcos	0	0	0.00	1	0	0	0	3	2	0	0	2	2	.182	R	R	6-4	175	4-19-84	2001	Ciudad Bolivar, Venez.
Eckert, Harold	2	0	2.65	3	3	0	0	17	14	6	5	5	22	.226	R	R	6-3	220	7-18-77	2001	Edison, N.J.
Gonzalez, Luis	1	3	4.73	45	1	0	0	65	73	41	34	47	66	.293	L	L	6-0	190	2-27-83	2001	Carolina, P.R.
Hamilton, Jamaal	0	0	4.50	1	0	0	0	2	3	1	1	1	1	.333	L	L	6-2	200	9-13-83	2002	Lubbock, Texas
Hull, Eric	4	3	4.18	21	8	0	0	60	70	29	28	26	39	.289	R	R	5-11	185	12-3-79	2001	Selah, Wash.
Ketchner, Ryan	8	7	3.02	21	21	1	0	119	118	43	40	36	98	.264	L	L	6-1	190	4-19-82	2000	Lantana, Fla.
Leek, Randy	2	3	4.32	9	9	0	0	50	52	26	24	5	22	.277	L	L	5-11	175	4-18-77	1999	Levittown, N.Y.
Montero, Agustin	2	0	2.40	21	0	0	4	30	20	10	8	16	36	.190	R	R	6-3	212	8-26-77	1995	San Pedro de Macoris, D.R.
Nall, T.J.	8	9	4.14	32	20	1	1	143	146	74	66	36	123	.264	R	R	6-1	195	11-4-80	1999	Schaumburg, Ill.
Nina, Elvin	5	2	2.50	33	0	0	2	58	46	21	16	26	64	.230	R	R	6-0	185	11-25-75	1997	Tempe, Ariz.
Osoria, Franquelis	8	5	3.56	51	0	0	5	81	71	36	32	18	73	.237	R	R	6-0	165	9-12-81	2000	Santiago, D.R.
Reina, Dimas	1	4	7.39	9	7	0	0	35	55	36	29	14	31	.355	R	R	6-0	170	2-23-82	1999	Caracas, Venez.
Rojas, Jose	1	0	4.65	28	0	0	0	50	44	28	26	37	46	.234	R	R	5-10	165	3-20-82	1999	San Pedro de Macoris, D.R.
Ruhl, Nathan	1	0	4.11	9	0	0	0	15	13	7	7	5	14	.232	R	R	6-4	230	7-16-76	1996	Lee`s Summit, Mo.
Schmoll, Steve	0	2	1.83	11	0	0	2	20	14	7	4	7	18	.206	R	R	6-2	200	2-4-80	2003	Rockville, Md.
Steffek, Brian	4	7	4.87	36	1	0	3	57	69	38	31	27	49	.308	R	R	6-2	205	3-2-78	2000	Stafford, Texas
Thompson, Derek	5	7	3.72	22	22	0	0	119	132	53	49	51	100	.288	L	L	6-2	190	1-8-81	2000	Land O'Lakes, Fla.

FIELDING

Catcher	PCT	G	PO	A	E	DP	PB
Alvarez	1.000	1	2	0	0	0	0
Bellorin	.990	83	653	58	7	8	4
Langill	1.000	5	29	1	0	0	0
McGee	1.000	10	65	5	0	1	0
Socarras	.991	47	389	29	4	2	6

First Base	PCT	G	PO	A	E	DP
Alvarez	.972	12	63	6	2	6
Hoorelbeke	.986	17	134	12	2	9
Loney	.987	102	778	86	11	86
Michaelis	.978	13	85	6	2	10

Second Base	PCT	G	PO	A	E	DP
Aybar	.975	125	267	319	15	86
Dowdy	1.000	1	0	2	0	0

	PCT	G	PO	A	E	DP
Garcia	1.000	18	28	39	0	11
Schifano	1.000	1	1	2	0	0

Third Base	PCT	G	PO	A	E	DP
Castro	1.000	5	0	12	0	2
Dowdy	.500	3	1	0	1	0
Garcia	1.000	10	4	9	0	2
King	.949	128	82	197	15	22
Riggs	.500	2	1	0	1	0

Shortstop	PCT	G	PO	A	E	DP
Castro	.968	82	123	211	11	45
Garcia	.913	6	11	10	2	4
Guzman	.949	44	55	111	9	24
Riggs	.913	6	8	13	2	1
Schifano	.958	4	6	17	1	3

Outfield	PCT	G	PO	A	E	DP
Abercrombie	.958	43	90	2	4	1
Alvarez	.931	42	50	4	4	0
Castro	1.000	25	39	3	0	0
Dowdy	1.000	17	17	1	0	0
Garcia	.911	31	38	3	4	0
Holt	1.000	51	59	6	0	2
Hoorelbeke	.800	3	4	0	1	0
Michaelis	.955	77	102	3	5	1
Repko	.966	48	81	4	3	2
Riggs	.957	10	21	1	1	0
Ruan	.973	45	104	5	3	0
Victorino	.989	74	179	9	2	2

VERO BEACH DODGERS — High Class A

FLORIDA STATE LEAGUE

BATTING	AVG	G	AB	R	H	2B	3B	HR	RBI	BB	SO	SB	CS	OBP	SLG	B	T	HT	WT	DOB	1st Yr	Resides
Abercrombie, Reggie	.271	34	133	18	36	4	5	5	12	6	33	16	5	.305	.489	R	R	6-3	220	7-15-80	2000	Columbus, Ga.

BATTING	AVG	G	AB	R	H	2B	3B	HR	RBI	BB	SO	SB	CS	OBP	SLG	B	T	HT	WT	DOB	1st Yr	Resides
Abreu, Tony	.419	11	43	8	18	3	1	0	3	1	8	4	1	.435	.535	R	R	5-11	160	11-13-84	2003	Puerto Plata, D.R.
Bagley, David	.212	10	33	5	7	1	0	0	2	4	8	0	0	.289	.242	R	R	6-2	200	12-26-80	2002	Poway, Calif.
Dowdy, Brett	.209	42	115	13	24	2	0	1	7	14	20	4	1	.300	.252	R	R	6-0	189	2-22-82	2003	Bradenton, Fla.
Dyson, Trey	.273	74	253	36	69	14	1	6	36	30	41	4	2	.357	.407	L	L	6-4	220	3-11-80	2002	Blythewood, S.C.
Ellis, A.J.	.219	40	114	15	25	4	0	2	22	24	20	1	0	.357	.307	R	R	6-3	240	4-9-81	2003	Lexington, Ky.
Garcia, Sergio	.000	1	5	0	0	0	0	0	0	0	1	0	0	.000	.000	R	R	5-9	175	3-29-80	2002	Paramount, Calif.
Gillitzer, Scott	.230	93	331	50	76	11	3	7	35	19	53	2	2	.276	.344	R	R	6-1	185	6-11-79	2001	Prairie du Chien, Wis.
Goelz, Bryan	.261	103	295	32	77	9	2	2	33	35	55	10	8	.346	.325	L	L	6-1	180	4-10-80	2002	St. James, N.Y.
Guzman, Joel	.307	87	329	52	101	22	8	14	51	21	78	8	5	.347	.550	R	R	6-4	198	11-24-84	2002	San Pedro de Macoris, D.R.
Hoorelbeke, Jesse	.217	65	207	32	45	6	0	13	39	23	74	3	1	.305	.435	R	R	6-3	225	10-13-77	2002	Hansen, Idaho
Hu, Chin-Lung	.307	20	75	12	23	4	1	0	10	5	6	3	1	.350	.387	R	R	5-9	150	2-2-84	2003	Tainan City, Taiwan
Kemp, Matt	.351	11	37	5	13	5	0	1	9	4	12	2	1	.405	.568	R	R	6-4	210	9-23-84	2003	Midwest City, Okla.
LaRoche, Andy	.233	62	219	26	51	13	0	10	35	17	42	2	3	.290	.429	R	R	6-1	200	9-13-83	2003	Fort Scott, Kan.
Marcos, Emilio	.125	19	48	3	6	1	0	0	3	7	14	2	2	.271	.146	R	R	6-2	160	3-21-81	2003	Villa Altagracia, D.R.
Martin, Russell	.250	122	416	74	104	24	1	15	64	72	54	9	5	.366	.421	R	R	5-11	202	2-15-83	2002	Chelsea, Quebec
McGee, Tom	.083	4	12	1	1	0	0	0	1	1	6	0	0	.143	.083	R	R	5-11	200	1-29-75	1997	Frederick, Md.
Milons, Jereme	.205	11	39	5	8	1	0	0	2	3	9	4	0	.256	.231	R	R	6-2	205	2-5-83	2002	Starkville, Miss.
Mitchell, Russell	.249	46	169	12	42	8	1	0	17	4	32	1	1	.278	.308	R	R	6-1	182	2-15-85	2003	Cartersville, Ga.
Requena, Alex	.245	111	413	64	101	7	5	2	23	44	103	50	15	.318	.300	S	R	5-11	150	8-13-80	1999	Maracay, Venez.
Roberts, Dave	.000	2	8	0	0	0	0	0	0	0	0	0	0	.000	.000	L	L	5-10	180	5-31-72	1994	Oceanside, Calif.
Rohan, Jimmy	.321	7	28	3	9	1	0	1	3	1	4	1	0	.345	.464	R	R	6-1	190	5-13-84	2002	Valencia, Calif.
Sprout, Brian	.285	89	305	49	87	15	2	12	45	37	56	5	5	.385	.466	R	R	6-0	205	6-28-80	2002	Lake City, Minn.
Testa, Chris	.215	37	135	14	29	6	3	1	6	10	38	2	2	.291	.326	L	L	6-2	180	5-23-81	1999	Palmdale, Calif.
Van Buizen, Rodney	.162	47	154	12	25	2	0	0	15	10	33	4	2	.237	.175	R	R	6-0	190	9-25-80	1999	Sydney, Australia
Young, Delwyn	.281	129	470	76	132	36	3	22	85	57	134	11	4	.364	.511	S	R	5-10	180	6-30-82	2002	Santa Barbara, Calif.

PITCHING	W	L	ERA	G	GS	CG	SV	IP	H	R	ER	BB	SO	AVG	B	T	HT	WT	DOB	1st Yr	Resides
Bailey, Chad	0	0	3.60	3	0	0	0	5	4	2	2	1	2	.235	L	L	6-4	190	6-24-83	2003	Ewa Beach, Hawaii
Baisley, Brad	0	3	4.79	9	6	0	0	36	47	30	19	15	26	.311	R	R	6-8	240	8-24-79	1998	Tampa, Fla.
Bartlett, Richard	4	3	2.23	40	0	0	7	69	57	23	17	29	57	.224	R	R	6-3	216	10-6-81	2000	Kennewick, Wash.
Billingsley, Chad	7	4	2.35	18	18	0	0	92	68	32	24	49	111	.202	R	R	6-2	215	7-29-84	2003	Defiance, Ohio
Broxton, Jonathan	11	6	3.23	23	23	1	0	128	110	49	46	43	144	.231	R	R	6-4	240	6-16-84	2002	Waynesboro, Ga.
Dannemiller, Beau	2	4	2.93	36	0	0	7	74	47	25	24	32	71	.183	R	R	6-0	210	12-26-79	2001	Munroe Falls, Ohio
De la Cruz, Julian	0	0	27.00	1	0	0	0	1	3	3	3	0	0	.500	R	R	5-11	170	7-23-84	2002	La Victoria, D.R.
Diaz, Jose	0	1	1.64	9	0	0	6	11	7	3	2	5	15	.179	R	R	6-4	230	2-27-84	2001	La Romana, D.R.
Figueroa, Jonathan	0	1	7.00	23	1	0	1	27	35	22	21	17	22	.318	L	L	6-5	205	9-15-83	2002	Acarigua, Venez.
Gonzalez, Alfredo	1	0	3.86	8	0	0	0	14	15	10	6	6	14	.288	S	R	5-11	185	9-17-79	1998	Nagua, D.R.
Hamilton, Jamaal	4	1	4.02	25	0	0	0	31	36	14	14	10	20	.286	L	L	6-3	220	9-13-83	2002	Lubbock, Texas
Hoorelbeke, Casey	6	4	4.01	18	14	0	0	76	81	40	34	31	56	.270	R	R	6-8	245	4-4-80	2002	Coeur d'Alene, Idaho
Hosford, Clint	5	2	4.71	22	8	1	1	71	63	41	37	24	53	.232	R	R	6-2	185	8-8-80	1999	Vancouver, B.C.
Hull, Eric	3	1	4.18	9	0	0	0	52	48	25	24	8	49	.254	R	R	5-11	185	12-3-79	2001	Selah, Wash.
Megrew, Mike	7	6	3.41	22	22	0	0	106	84	45	40	43	125	.214	L	L	6-6	210	1-29-84	2002	Hope Valley, R.I.
Merricks, Matt	2	2	3.12	6	5	0	0	26	30	9	9	10	16	.294	L	L	5-11	180	8-6-82	2000	Oxnard, Calif.
Ojeda, Alvis	0	0	2.25	4	1	0	0	12	8	3	3	2	8	.190	R	R	6-0	170	9-23-83	2001	Maracaibo, Venez.
Plummer, Jarod	4	4	3.86	11	11	0	0	63	65	29	27	14	49	.264	R	R	6-5	200	1-27-84	2002	Garland, Texas
Reina, Dimas	5	4	3.23	16	9	1	1	64	57	28	23	21	55	.239	R	R	6-0	170	2-23-82	1999	Caracas, Venez.
Rodriguez, Mike	7	3	4.98	28	7	0	1	69	71	39	38	26	49	.270	R	R	6-1	180	8-31-82	2002	Roseville, Calif.
Schmoll, Steve	3	3	1.80	37	0	0	10	65	57	18	13	18	58	.237	R	R	6-2	200	2-4-80	2003	Rockville, Md.
Simmons, Justin	0	0	0.77	5	0	0	0	12	7	1	1	5	6	.175	L	L	6-3	215	10-5-81	2004	DeSoto, Texas
Steffek, Brian	3	2	1.66	13	0	0	3	22	25	9	4	8	24	.294	R	R	6-2	205	3-2-78	2000	Stafford, Texas
Stults, Eric	2	1	2.70	7	0	0	1	10	11	4	3	4	6	.282	L	L	6-3	215	12-9-79	2002	Mishawaka, Ind.
Tequida, Mauricio	0	2	5.25	5	0	0	0	12	15	9	7	4	4	.319	R	R	6-1	180	2-5-82	2003	Obregon, Mexico
Testa, Chris	0	0	2.25	3	0	0	0	4	2	1	1	3	5	.125	L	L	6-2	180	5-23-81	1999	Palmdale, Calif.
Warriax, Brandon	1	0	3.46	8	0	0	0	13	14	8	5	7	12	.259	R	R	6-0	160	6-23-79	1997	Maxton, N.C.
Wayne, Brett	0	0	9.00	5	0	0	0	10	12	13	10	8	12	.293	R	R	6-0	175	4-28-80	2002	Simi Valley, Calif.

FIELDING

Catcher	PCT	G	PO	A	E	DP	PB
Ellis	.993	35	245	26	2	2	4
Martin	.990	101	845	91	9	6	13

First Base	PCT	G	PO	A	E	DP
Dowdy	1.000	2	15	0	0	2
Dyson	.994	38	306	31	2	15
Ellis	1.000	1	6	1	0	0
Gillitzer	.995	27	166	24	1	9
Hoorelbeke	.979	39	305	22	7	21
Requena	1.000	1	6	0	0	0
Rohan	1.000	5	50	3	0	6
Sprout	.969	15	116	9	4	5
Testa	.989	10	80	7	1	5
Van Buizen	.955	6	40	2	2	5

Second Base	PCT	G	PO	A	E	DP
Dowdy	1.000	8	11	14	0	3
Gillitzer	.957	11	17	28	2	7
Mitchell	.923	3	3	9	1	0

Young	PCT	G	PO	A	E	DP
Young	.951	115	166	276	23	39

Third Base	PCT	G	PO	A	E	DP
Dowdy	1.000	4	1	5	0	0
Garcia	1.000	1	0	2	0	0
Gillitzer	.929	23	14	38	4	0
Laroche	.901	54	26	83	12	4
Mitchell	.928	38	29	48	6	4
Rohan	.500	1	0	1	1	0
Sprout	.941	12	2	14	1	0
Van Buizen	.909	5	2	8	1	4

Shortstop	PCT	G	PO	A	E	DP
Abreu	.930	11	22	18	3	1
Bartlett	.750	1	2	1	1	0
Dowdy	.833	3	3	2	1	0
Gillitzer	.943	10	11	22	2	3
Guzman	.972	87	138	237	11	33
Hu	.950	19	21	55	4	14

Outfield	PCT	G	PO	A	E	DP
Abercrombie	.985	33	61	3	1	0
Dowdy	1.000	21	25	0	0	0
Dyson	1.000	7	9	0	0	0
Gillitzer	1.000	22	36	4	0	1
Goelz	.974	102	181	7	5	1
Hoorelbeke	1.000	1	1	0	0	0
Kemp	.957	11	21	1	1	0
Marcos	.946	19	34	1	2	0
Milons	1.000	11	27	0	0	0
Requena	.961	113	213	10	9	2
Roberts	1.000	2	4	0	0	0
Sprout	.987	49	74	3	1	0
Testa	.857	20	30	0	5	0
Van Buizen	1.000	31	41	2	0	0

COLUMBUS CATFISH — Low Class A

SOUTH ATLANTIC LEAGUE

BATTING	AVG	G	AB	R	H	2B	3B	HR	RBI	BB	SO	SB	CS	OBP	SLG	B	T	HT	WT	DOB	1st Yr	Resides
Abreu, Tony	.302	104	358	50	108	21	8	8	54	8	59	16	12	.327	.472	R	R	5-11	160	11-13-84	2003	Puerto Plata, D.R.
Bagley, David	.273	41	139	16	38	7	2	2	25	16	31	2	0	.374	.396	R	R	6-2	200	12-26-80	2002	Poway, Calif.

BATTING

BATTING	AVG	G	AB	R	H	2B	3B	HR	RBI	BB	SO	SB	CS	OBP	SLG	B	T	HT	WT	DOB	1st Yr	Resides
Carter, Brandon	.154	4	13	2	2	1	0	0	0	3	4	0	0	.313	.231	L	R	5-8	165	11-12-82	2004	Palm Beach Gardens, Fla.
Castillo, Albenis	.192	7	26	4	5	0	0	0	0	3	6	1	1	.300	.192	R	R	6-4	178	12-24-83	2001	Cocle, Panama
Castillo, Luis	.203	41	133	13	27	7	0	2	19	9	33	0	2	.257	.301	R	R	6-3	175	1-18-84	2002	Estado Guarico, Venez.
De Aza, Alejandro	.255	102	341	63	87	17	2	4	45	38	55	24	10	.346	.352	L	L	6-0	174	4-11-84	2001	La Romana, D.R.
Hu, Chin-Lung	.298	84	332	58	99	6	6	25	20	10	7	7	.342	.422	R	R	5-9	150	2-2-84	2003	Tainan City, Taiwan
Jimenez, Luis	.288	110	392	62	113	24	1	20	75	51	104	6	2	.372	.508	L	L	6-4	205	5-7-82	1999	Bobure, Venez.
Kemp, Matt	.288	112	423	67	122	22	8	17	66	24	100	8	7	.330	.499	R	R	6-4	210	9-23-84	2003	Midwest City, Okla.
Laroche, Andy	.283	65	244	52	69	20	0	13	42	29	30	12	5	.375	.525	R	R	6-1	200	9-13-83	2003	Fort Scott, Kan.
Laurin, Dominique	.233	65	189	29	44	15	1	4	28	27	59	3	3	.342	.386	R	R	6-0	185	10-7-82	2003	North Vancouver, B.C.
Marcos, Emilio	.250	21	72	9	18	3	1	0	11	2	14	4	1	.289	.319	R	R	6-2	160	3-21-81	2003	Villa Altagracia, D.R.
Milons, Jereme	.273	103	436	70	119	14	6	10	53	30	99	25	8	.321	.401	R	R	6-2	205	2-5-83	2002	Starkville, Miss.
Mitchell, Russell	.201	63	209	24	42	12	1	0	14	10	49	2	4	.257	.268	R	R	6-1	182	2-15-85	2003	Cartersville, Ga.
Nixon, Mike	.261	90	333	49	87	20	2	5	50	26	68	6	8	.323	.378	R	R	6-3	210	8-17-83	2002	Phoenix, Ariz.
Paul, Matt	.174	9	23	4	4	0	1	0	2	7	7	2	1	.367	.261	R	R	5-10	190	10-10-85	2004	Slidell, La.
Paul, Xavier	.265	126	460	69	122	26	6	9	72	54	124	10	6	.342	.407	L	R	6-0	200	2-25-85	2003	Slidell, La.
Price, Jared	.240	53	171	26	41	12	0	6	22	14	52	3	1	.302	.415	R	R	6-1	190	3-18-82	2000	Rupert, Idaho
Rohan, Jimmy	.281	89	281	43	79	11	2	1	30	18	37	5	3	.338	.345	R	R	6-1	190	5-13-81	2002	Valencia, Calif.
Sapp, Steven	.063	6	16	0	1	0	0	0	1	1	3	0	0	.118	.063	R	R	6-3	190	11-17-85	2003	Los Angeles, Calif.

PITCHING

PITCHING	W	L	ERA	G	GS	CG	SV	IP	H	R	ER	BB	SO	AVG	B	T	HT	WT	DOB	1st Yr	Resides
Alvarez, Carlos	1	0	6.65	15	0	0	0	22	31	18	16	8	32	.341	L	L	5-9	160	3-31-85	2002	Maracaibo, Venez.
Bailey, Chad	2	3	2.17	26	2	0	2	62	63	28	15	21	46	.273	L	L	6-4	190	6-24-83	2003	Ewa Beach, Hawaii
Carvajal, Marcos	4	2	1.88	36	0	0	1	72	50	19	15	35	72	.199	R	R	6-4	175	4-19-84	2001	Ciudad Bolivar, Venez.
Castillo, Albenis	1	1	5.21	9	0	0	1	19	26	17	11	13	21	.306	R	R	6-4	178	12-24-83	2001	Cocle, Panama
De los Santos, Omar	1	2	9.00	12	0	0	0	18	24	23	18	19	21	.312	R	R	6-0	162	8-13-81	1999	San Pedro de Macoris, D.R.
Diaz, Jose	1	4	2.12	28	0	0	14	34	21	13	8	12	59	.175	R	R	6-4	230	2-27-84	2001	La Romana, D.R.
Figueroa, Jonathan	3	7	6.90	14	13	0	0	60	67	48	46	25	70	.284	L	L	6-5	205	9-15-83	2002	Acariuga, Venez.
Hamilton, Jamaal	1	0	0.36	14	0	0	2	25	15	2	1	7	27	.176	L	L	6-3	220	9-13-83	2002	Lubbock, Texas
Hammes, Zach	5	8	4.55	24	23	0	0	113	147	79	57	54	73	.318	R	R	6-6	225	5-15-84	2002	Iowa City, Iowa
Hoorelbeek, Casey	0	1	2.57	3	3	0	0	14	13	7	4	2	8	.245	R	R	6-8	245	4-4-80	2002	Coeur d'Alene, Idaho
Kuo, Hong-Chih	1	0	4.50	3	0	0	0	6	8	3	3	4	10	.348	L	L	6-0	200	7-23-81	2000	Tainan City, Taiwan
Looney, Marshal	0	2	6.55	3	3	0	0	11	12	9	8	9	16	.279	L	L	6-4	251	3-23-84	2002	Lapine, Ore.
Lopez, Arturo	5	4	4.76	29	7	0	0	87	88	51	46	30	83	.263	L	L	5-10	165	2-22-83	2001	Culiacan, Mexico
Ojeda, Alvis	8	2	3.59	30	3	0	2	85	74	47	34	29	86	.231	R	R	6-0	170	9-23-83	2001	Maracaibo, Venez.
Pimentel, Julio	10	8	3.48	23	23	2	0	111	106	56	43	47	102	.254	R	R	6-1	190	12-14-85	2003	La Romana, D.R.
Plaisance, Kenny	2	0	7.88	3	0	0	0	8	11	7	7	2	6	.333	R	R	6-2	200	4-15-80	2004	Lockport, La.
Plummer, Jarod	2	1	2.45	4	4	0	0	22	13	8	6	5	23	.167	R	R	6-5	200	1-27-84	2002	Garland, Texas
Rodriguez, Mike	1	0	1.26	5	0	0	0	14	4	2	2	6	18	.089	R	R	6-1	180	8-31-82	2002	Roseville, Calif.
Rodriguez, Ozzie	3	3	5.01	20	2	0	2	41	40	24	23	26	43	.263	R	R	5-10	168	6-10-84	2003	Hatillo Palma, D.R.
Sobkow, Phil	2	2	7.36	7	6	0	0	22	21	20	18	17	18	.239	R	R	6-5	210	6-11-83	2003	Calder, Sask.
Stults, Eric	1	2	2.49	12	0	0	3	22	18	8	6	6	16	.225	L	L	6-3	215	12-9-79	2002	Mishawaka, Ind.
Testa, Chris	1	2	6.48	20	0	0	0	42	38	37	30	44	53	.233	L	L	6-2	180	5-23-81	1999	Palmdale, Calif.
Tiffany, Chuck	5	2	3.70	22	22	1	0	100	76	42	41	40	141	.208	L	L	6-1	195	1-25-85	2003	Covina, Calif.
Wayne, Brett	2	4	2.66	27	0	0	5	68	45	28	20	31	71	.187	R	R	6-0	175	4-28-80	2002	Simi Valley, Calif.
Weeden, Brandon	7	9	5.39	27	27	0	0	122	119	86	73	73	106	.258	R	R	6-4	190	10-14-83	2002	Oklahoma City, Okla.

FIELDING

Catcher	PCT	G	PO	A	E	DP	PB
Nixon	.992	88	805	66	7	5	18
Price	.993	52	413	37	3	1	10

First Base	PCT	G	PO	A	E	DP
A. Castillo	1.000	6	40	2	0	2
L. Castillo	.964	21	127	8	5	13
De Aza	1.000	1	2	0	0	0
Jimenez	.989	84	654	43	8	73
Nixon	1.000	1	3	0	0	1
Rohan	.990	36	276	17	3	28

Second Base	PCT	G	PO	A	E	DP
Abreu	.950	96	164	231	21	62
Carter	1.000	3	9	3	0	3

	PCT	G	PO	A	E	DP
Laurin	.977	21	36	49	2	11
Mitchell	1.000	10	21	15	0	4
M. Paul	.923	9	8	16	2	2
Rohan	.923	10	12	12	2	3

Third Base	PCT	G	PO	A	E	DP
A. Castillo	.939	15	3	28	2	0
LaRoche	.942	62	45	101	9	12
Laurin	.833	8	5	10	3	1
Mitchell	.945	53	31	106	8	8
Rohan	.778	3	1	6	2	1

Shortstop	PCT	G	PO	A	E	DP
Abreu	.857	2	1	5	1	0
Carter	.667	1	0	2	1	0

	PCT	G	PO	A	E	DP
Hu	.963	84	117	251	14	49
Laurin	.945	31	35	68	6	21
Rohan	.926	30	41	72	9	16

Outfield	PCT	G	PO	A	E	DP
De Aza	.940	75	123	3	8	0
Kemp	.965	105	184	10	7	2
Marcos	.964	21	52	2	2	1
Milons	.976	102	199	5	5	0
X. Paul	.934	119	118	9	9	2
Rohan	1.000	3	2	0	0	0
Sapp	.875	6	13	1	2	0

OGDEN RAPTORS — Rookie

PIONEER LEAGUE

BATTING	AVG	G	AB	R	H	2B	3B	HR	RBI	BB	SO	SB	CS	OBP	SLG	B	T	HT	WT	DOB	1st Yr	Resides
Arias, Hector	.252	29	107	13	27	6	1	2	14	7	27	1	1	.296	.383	R	R	6-3	200	9-5-84	2003	Bani, D.R.
Batz, Daniel	.335	55	206	29	69	10	3	3	28	19	21	4	0	.409	.456	R	R	6-1	195	3-19-82	2004	Mohnton, Pa.
Bruce, Cole	.233	25	73	15	17	4	0	2	6	6	17	1	1	.288	.370	R	R	6-3	200	1-20-82	2004	Clute, Texas
Carter, Brandon	.386	25	83	20	32	7	1	0	14	15	16	9	3	.475	.494	L	R	5-8	165	11-12-82	2004	Palm Beach Gardens, Fla.
Castillo, Luis	.343	35	137	36	47	9	0	7	28	13	33	0	0	.408	.562	R	R	6-3	175	1-18-84	2002	Estado Guarico, Venez.
Denker, Travis	.311	57	225	44	70	17	1	12	43	24	52	5	3	.372	.556	R	R	5-9	170	8-5-85	2003	Brea, Calif.
DeWitt, Blake	.284	70	299	61	85	19	3	12	47	28	78	1	1	.350	.488	L	R	5-11	175	8-20-85	2004	Sikeston, Mo.
Dunlap, Cory	.351	71	245	57	86	18	1	7	53	68	40	0	0	.492	.518	L	L	6-1	230	4-13-84	2004	Alameda, Calif.
Lynch, Mike	.234	27	94	9	22	2	0	0	7	21	0	0	.287	.255	R	R	6-3	220	10-31-82	2002	Oak Forest, Ill.
Marcos, Emilio	.364	23	107	25	39	7	3	3	15	1	19	10	2	.398	.570	R	R	6-2	160	3-21-81	2003	Villa Altagracia, D.R.
May, Lucas	.286	34	147	25	42	5	2	5	30	8	37	4	3	.329	.449	R	R	6-0	190	10-24-84	2003	Chesterfield, Mo.
Nicholson, David	.263	41	137	24	36	5	2	0	12	27	31	4	1	.396	.328	R	R	6-0	175	8-22-82	2004	Anaheim, Calif.
Piazza, Tom	.100	5	10	1	1	0	0	0	2	2	2	0	0	.231	.100	L	R	6-0	200	10-9-81	2003	Boynton Beach, Fla.
Pujols, Kengshill	.221	37	131	13	29	6	1	1	13	5	38	3	1	.275	.305	R	R	6-0	180	3-3-85	2003	Bani, D.R.
Richmond, B.J.	.267	49	187	31	50	9	0	1	22	12	33	4	1	.314	.332	L	L	6-3	190	2-3-84	2004	Belmont, N.C.
Ruggiano, Justin	.329	46	155	26	51	12	0	7	36	23	38	6	1	.428	.542	R	R	6-2	205	4-12-82	2004	College Station, Texas

BATTING	AVG	G	AB	R	H	2B	3B	HR	RBI	BB	SO	SB	CS	OBP	SLG	B	T	HT	WT	DOB	1st Yr	Resides
Russ, Ryan	.327	31	107	26	35	8	4	1	15	19	25	6	2	.446	.505	S	R	6-2	193	3-7-81	2004	Comfort, Texas
Westervelt, Chris	.341	49	176	41	60	12	0	10	37	27	46	1	0	.438	.580	R	R	5-11	210	11-20-81	2004	Batesville, Ark.

GAMES BY POSITION: C—Lynch 14, Pujols 37, Westervelt 27. **1B**—Bruce 2, L. Castillo 20, Dunlap 50, Lynch 6. **2B**—Bruce 3, Carter 15, Denker 47, Nicholson 11. **3B**—Bruce 1, Denker 10, DeWitt 65. **SS**—Bruce 13, Carter 5, May 34, Nicholson 27. **OF**—Arias 28, Batz 53, Lynch 6, Marcos 23, Piazza 3, Richmond 47, Ruggiano 46, Russ 29.

PITCHING	W	L	ERA	G	GS	CG	SV	IP	H	R	ER	BB	SO	AVG	B	T	HT	WT	DOB	1st Yr	Resides
Akin, Brian	1	1	6.04	21	0	0	0	48	65	36	32	22	63	.320	R	R	6-3	195	10-13-81	2004	Louisville, Ky.
Alexander, Mark	4	1	2.65	25	0	0	9	34	30	10	10	8	37	.236	R	R	5-11	200	12-6-80	2004	Independence, Mo.
Alvarez, Carlos	3	0	3.26	20	0	0	0	30	29	13	11	5	38	.248	L	L	5-9	160	3-31-85	2002	Maracaibo, Venez.
Alvarez, Gabriel	1	1	4.30	16	0	0	3	29	32	18	14	12	36	.271	R	R	5-11	178	9-10-84	2002	Guadalupe, Mexico
Castillo, Albenis	2	2	5.01	12	1	0	0	32	27	20	18	19	30	.233	R	R	6-4	178	12-24-83	2001	Cocle, Panama
Elbert, Scott	2	3	5.26	12	12	0	0	50	47	33	29	30	45	.253	L	L	6-2	190	5-13-85	2004	Seneca, Mo.
Garcia, Javier	2	3	9.20	16	7	0	0	46	64	51	47	26	39	.320	R	R	6-5	175	1-5-84	2001	Aragua, Venez.
Johnson, Blake	3	3	6.47	13	12	0	0	57	73	46	41	19	57	.317	R	R	6-5	195	6-14-85	2004	Baton Rouge, La.
Klusman, Aaron	2	1	5.71	21	0	0	5	35	48	26	22	13	25	.329	R	R	6-4	215	9-9-80	2004	Phoenix, Ariz.
Obispo, Jose	1	2	13.86	5	4	0	0	12	13	21	19	20	10	.277	R	R	6-1	160	11-5-84	2002	Santo Domingo, D.R.
Orenduff, Justin	3	4	4.74	13	10	0	0	44	46	26	23	25	57	.272	R	R	6-4	205	5-27-83	2004	Chesapeake, Va.
Parker, David	5	2	4.94	19	0	0	2	51	52	31	28	41	44	.263	R	R	6-4	185	8-18-83	2002	Winnipeg, Manitoba
Pfeiffer, David	1	4	6.20	8	8	0	0	41	50	34	28	22	33	.301	L	L	6-3	185	8-17-85	2004	Port St. Lucie, Fla.
Pratt, Jordan	2	6	9.50	12	12	0	0	48	74	60	51	36	46	.356	R	R	6-3	195	5-17-85	2003	Monmouth, Ore.
Shuey, Paul	0	0	3.38	2	2	0	0	3	2	2	1	4	4	.222	R	R	6-2	235	9-16-70	1992	Wake Forest, N.C.
Sobkow, Phil	0	2	5.84	6	5	0	0	25	28	22	16	19	32	.289	R	R	6-5	210	6-17-81	2003	Calder, Sask.
Wade, Cory	1	5	5.14	8	0	0	0	14	24	9	8	4	19	.369	R	R	6-2	180	5-28-83	2004	Indianapolis, Ind.
Wright, Wesley	3	3	6.29	17	2	0	0	44	56	43	31	23	66	.299	R	L	5-10	160	1-28-85	2003	Grady, Ala.
Zuleta, Howar	0	1	12.46	3	0	0	0	4	5	6	6	4	8	.294	R	R	6-0	180	1-8-86	2003	Maracaibo, Venez.

GULF COAST LEAGUE

BATTING	AVG	G	AB	R	H	2B	3B	HR	RBI	BB	SO	SB	CS	SLG	OBP	B	T	HT	WT	DOB	1st Yr	Resides
Bagley, David	.500	2	4	1	2	0	0	0	0	4	2	1	0	.500	.750	R	R	6-2	200	12-26-80	2002	Poway, Calif.
Barnes, John	.364	6	22	3	8	2	0	0	6	0	1	0	0	.455	.364	R	R	6-2	210	4-24-76	1996	Mesa, Ariz.
Crist, Justin	.311	33	74	10	23	4	0	0	4	4	9	3	1	.365	.354	R	R	5-10	175	8-6-82	2004	Tucson, Ariz.
Giambi, Jeremy	.267	6	15	2	4	1	0	1	3	5	4	0	0	.533	.476	L	L	5-11	210	9-30-74	1996	Las Vegas, Nev.
Gil, Rotsen	.304	29	79	11	24	4	5	1	10	3	15	0	0	.519	.337	S	R	5-10	195	3-2-84	2001	Anzoategui, Venez.
Harper, Tony	.264	29	110	9	29	10	1	1	10	2	18	2	2	.400	.293	L	R	6-0	200	10-15-84	2004	South Milwaukee, Wis.
Hoffmann, Jamie	.310	60	229	40	71	8	7	4	36	24	38	14	5	.459	.374	L	R	6-4	220	8-8-84	2004	New Ulm, Minn.
Jackson, Derry	.208	47	106	17	22	2	1	0	12	12	43	5	6	.245	.303	R	R	6-1	190	6-13-84	2004	Portland, Ore.
Ludwig, Mike	.094	22	32	1	3	0	0	0	1	7	0	0	0	.094	.147	R	R	6-2	214	4-30-81	2003	Blaine, Minn.
McDonald, James	.224	46	125	15	28	2	1	0	10	12	44	3	2	.256	.291	L	R	6-5	195	10-19-84	2003	Long Beach, Calif.
Medero-Stullz, Carlos	.195	31	77	5	15	0	0	1	9	5	15	0	0	.234	.261	R	R	5-8	190	5-30-86	2004	Hialeah, Fla.
Mora, Jesus	.277	43	141	16	39	10	0	3	15	4	32	2	3	.411	.306	R	R	6-3	200	12-25-83	2002	Santo Domingo, D.R.
Ndungidi, Sambu	.135	17	52	5	7	3	1	0	4	4	15	0	0	.231	.196	S	R	6-3	200	5-9-85	2002	Pierre Fonds, Quebec
Paul, Matthew	.156	26	64	11	10	3	0	0	3	15	18	6	1	.203	.325	R	R	5-10	190	9-3-82	2004	Slidell, La.
Pena, Carlos	.217	39	115	15	25	4	4	4	21	6	38	3	2	.426	.268	R	R	6-2	190	12-28-83	2001	La Romana, D.R.
Peterson, James	.295	47	176	19	52	14	2	6	32	13	38	2	1	.500	.344	L	L	6-0	210	10-14-83	2003	Winterset, Iowa
Purkey, Bryan	.182	8	11	2	2	0	0	0	2	2	4	1	0	.182	.308	R	R	6-0	200	8-28-81	2003	Port St. Lucie, Fla.
Raglani, Anthony	.300	6	20	2	6	1	0	0	1	2	4	2	0	.350	.364	L	L	6-2	215	4-6-83	2004	Indiana, Pa.
Rivera, Juan	.243	52	185	28	45	6	0	0	14	13	30	5	0	.276	.296	S	R	6-0	180	3-17-87	2003	San Pedro de Macoris, D.R.
Sapp, Steven	.255	31	94	15	24	3	0	0	6	6	16	5	1	.287	.327	R	R	6-3	190	11-17-85	2003	Los Angeles, Calif.
Soto, Jesus	.292	48	171	33	50	11	2	4	18	10	18	5	3	.450	.342	S	R	5-11	180	9-7-86	2003	Valencia, Venez.
Steidl, Sam	.129	11	31	6	4	0	0	0	3	7	3	0	1	.129	.300	L	L	5-10	185	5-9-81	2004	Alexandria, Minn.
Sutherland, David	.301	50	153	22	46	2	3	0	14	9	15	4	0	.353	.357	L	L	6-6	175	5-2-85	2003	Ferny Grove, Australia

GAMES BY POSITION: C—Gil 29, Harper 18, Jackson 1, Medero-Stullz 31, Purkey 5. **1B**—Giambi 3, Ludwig 8, Peterson 20, Sutherland 43. **2B**—Crist 20, Paul 17, Rivera 1, Soto 38. **3B**—Crist 4, Hoffman 58, Ludwig 8. **SS**—Crist 7, Paul 2, Rivera 51, Soto 12. **OF**—Barnes 6, Giambi 3, Jackson 44, Ludwig 1, McDonald 41, Mora 39, Ndungidi 10, Pena 38, Raglani 4, Sapp 29, Steidl 9.

PITCHING	W	L	ERA	G	GS	CG	SV	IP	H	R	ER	BB	SO	AVG	B	T	HT	WT	DOB	1st Yr	Resides
Bassham, Johnnie	0	0	3.95	10	0	0	0	14	13	10	6	12	19	.245	L	L	6-1	195	8-20-82	2004	Benbroo, Texas
De la Cruz, Julian	4	6	5.58	18	4	0	4	50	60	39	31	22	47	.292	R	R	5-11	170	7-23-84	2002	La Victoria, D.R.
Garrison, Kale	2	2	6.48	18	0	0	1	25	26	19	18	17	24	.257	L	L	6-1	175	3-1-82	2003	Gilbert, Ariz.
Gearhart, Kalen	3	0	1.89	18	0	0	0	33	30	7	7	7	22	.234	R	R	6-2	180	8-12-85	2004	Lewistown, Pa.
Gonzalez, Alfredo	1	2	5.25	5	3	0	0	12	16	10	7	7	8	.326	S	R	5-11	165	9-17-79	1997	Nagua, D.R.
Guerra, Javy	4	1	3.38	11	9	0	0	40	31	18	15	19	36	.213	R	R	6-1	185	10-31-85	2004	Denton, Texas
Hayes, Alvin	3	1	3.58	16	8	0	0	50	29	26	20	35	51	.169	R	R	6-6	195	8-19-83	2003	Century, Fla.
Hochgesang, Nathan	1	1	1.54	7	2	0	0	23	16	7	4	7	21	.186	R	R	6-4	220	12-18-81	2004	Fullerton, Calif.
Kida, Masao	0	0	0.00	2	2	0	0	4	2	0	0	0	0	.142	R	R	6-3	210	9-12-68	1998	Tokyo, Japan
Looney, Marshall	0	1	2.55	7	7	0	0	18	15	8	5	9	19	.227	L	L	6-4	251	3-23-84	2002	Lapine, Ore.
Lorenzo, Pedro	0	1	5.79	4	4	0	0	14	9	9	9	8	12	.272	R	R	6-4	180	2-4-86	2003	Nizao, D.R.
Norrito, Giuseppe	0	0	0.00	4	0	0	1	4	1	0	0	0	4	.071	R	R	5-10	180	8-4-82	2004	Pembroke Pines, Fla.
Obispo, Jose	1	0	1.00	4	1	0	0	14	9	2	0	4	9	.191	R	R	6-1	160	11-5-84	2002	Santo Domingo, D.R.
Pfeiffer, David	2	0	0.40	5	3	0	0	22	17	2	1	2	20	.202	L	L	6-3	185	8-17-85	2004	Port St. Lucie, Fla.
Plaisance, Kenny	4	3	3.63	18	1	0	0	40	40	19	16	13	20	.277	R	R	6-5	200	9-22-83	2004	Lockport, La.
Ramirez, Miguel	1	5	5.44	15	8	0	1	48	58	33	29	15	39	.310	R	R	5-11	178	7-15-83	2003	Vicente Noble, D.R.
Rodriguez, Osvaldo	0	0	4.41	5	3	0	0	16	17	10	8	8	15	.265	R	R	5-10	168	6-10-84	2002	Hatillo Palma, D.R.
Simmons, Justin	1	0	0.92	7	1	0	0	20	10	2	2	8	17	.151	L	L	6-3	225	10-5-81	2004	DeSoto, Texas
Wade, Cory	2	1	3.03	11	2	0	1	33	28	12	11	1	26	.227	R	R	6-2	180	5-28-83	2004	Indianapolis, Ind.
White, Cody	1	1	2.53	5	0	0	0	11	11	4	3	6	10	.297	L	L	6-3	185	2-27-85	2003	Pleasant Grove, Texas
Zuleta, Howar	1	3	2.14	23	2	0	7	42	30	12	10	19	51	.189	R	R	6-0	180	1-8-86	2003	Maracaibo, Venez.

MILWAUKEE BREWERS

BY TOM HAUDRICOURT

In 2004, the Brewers made the kind of history that no club wants in the record book.

After a surprising first half in which they forged a 45-41 record, the Brewers suffered the worst second-half col-

lapse in major league history by a team that made it to the All-Star Game break with a winning mark. They went 22-53, a .293 winning percentage that wiped the '75 Brewers off the books as the biggest second-half tumblers.

In the process, the Brewers posted their 12th consecutive losing season, tying Pittsburgh for the longest active skid, and finished last in the National League Central for the third year in a row. For a rebuilding program in its second year under general manager Doug Melvin and manager Ned Yost, it was a discouraging turn of events.

Ever the optimist, Yost tried to put a positive spin on the massive second-half collapse.

"We knew it was going to be a process," he said. "I think we've taken some positive steps that don't show up in the won-lost record. I think they'll show up next year. I look at the total picture."

Even with that broader perspective, all parties involved agreed the offense was a disaster in 2004. Scoring runs became a daily chore as the Brewers finished last or next-to-last in nearly every important offensive category, including batting average, runs, total bases, slugging percentage, times shutout and total strikeouts.

The poster boy for the Brewers' Jekyll-and-Hyde season was first baseman Lyle Overbay, who batted .344-10-62 before the break and .245-6-25 afterward. Overbay had to collect a hit in his final at-bat to salvage a .300 batting average.

The dreadful offense sabotaged a much-improved pitching staff, especially the work of the top two starters, Ben Sheets and Doug Davis. Sheets compiled a 2.70 ERA

Ben Sheets   Prince Fielder

PLAYERS of the YEAR

MAJOR LEAGUE: Ben Sheets, rhp
Despite going 12-14 overall, Sheets came into his own in 2004, striking out 264 in 237 innings and carrying a 2.70 ERA on one of the weakest teams in the National League. His overhand curveball and mid-90s fastball are his two best pitches, and he finished third in the N.L. in ERA and second in strikeouts.

MINOR LEAGUE: Prince Fielder, 1b
The Brewers lost shortstop J.J. Hardy for the season due to a shoulder injury and second base prospect Rickie Weeks' struggled in Double-A. But Fielder solidified his spot as a future star in Milwaukee, holding his own in the Double-A Southern League at age 20, hitting .272-23-78 in 497 at-bats.

and set a franchise record with 264 strikeouts but was saddled with a 12-14 record, thanks to a total of 19 runs in his defeats.

Davis' 3.39 ERA and 166 strikeouts were more indicative of the way he pitched than his 12-12 record.

Despite the collapse, four club records were set. Beyond Podsednik's stolen base total and Sheets' strikeouts, Overbay led the majors with 53 doubles and all-star closer Dan Kolb recorded 39 saves while getting precious few opportunities down the stretch.

Making the year even more sobering was an injury-plagued season in the Brewers' heralded farm system. Shortstop J.J. Hardy missed most of the year due to shoulder surgery and righthander Mike Jones pitched only six times before having shoulder surgery that will sideline him for all of 2005.

There were other physical setbacks as well as growing pains associated with pushing young players such as Rickie Weeks and Prince Fielder to higher levels in the system. Weeks and Fielder skipped high Class A ball and went to Double-A Huntsville, where they struggled for extended periods but were ranked among the Southern League's top prospects.

One shining breakthrough was righthander Ben Hendrickson, the pitcher of the year and ERA leader in the International League (11-3, 2.02). Hendrickson then found the majors much tougher, going 1-8, 6.22 in 10 outings with the Brewers.

Also, second baseman Hernan Iribarren emerged from the Dominican Summer League to bat .439 and earn MVP honors in the Arizona Rookie League.

ORGANIZATION LEADERS

BATTING
*AVG	Steve Sollmann, Helena	.364
R	Callix Crabbe, High Desert	89
H	Travis Hinton, High Desert	163
TB	Travis Hinton, High Desert	273
2B	Travis Hinton, High Desert	36
3B	Callix Crabbe, High Desert	11
HR	Prince Fielder, Huntsville	23
RBI	Vinny Rottino, Beloit	124
BB	Prince Fielder, Huntsville	65
SO	Brad Nelson, Huntsville	146
SB	Terry Trofholz, Beloit	48
*OBP	Steve Sollmann, Helena	.487
*SLG	Grant Richardson, Beloit/Helena	.523

PITCHING
W	Ben Hendrickson, Indianapolis	11
L	Khalid Ballouli, High Desert	14
#ERA	Ben Hendrickson, Indianapolis	2.02
G	Brian Adams, Huntsville	52
	Roberto Giron, Indianapolis/Huntsville	52
CG	Ben Hendrickson, Indianapolis	2
SV	John Novinsky, Indianapolis/Huntsville	17
IP	Ryan Costello, Huntsville/High Desert	141
BB	Dennis Sarfate, Huntsville	78
SO	Jeff Housman, Indianapolis/Huntsville	134

*Minimum 250 at-bats #Minimum 75 innings

MILWAUKEE
BREWERS

Manager: Ned Yost.   **2004 Record:** 67-94, .416 (6th, NL Central).

BATTING	AVG	G	AB	R	H	2B	3B	HR	RBI	BB	SO	SB	CS	OBP	SLG	B	T	HT	WT	DOB	1st Yr	Resides
Bennett, Gary	.224	75	219	18	49	14	0	3	20	22	32	1	0	.297	.329	R	R	6-0	210	4-17-72	1990	Waukegan, Ill.
Branyan, Russell	.234	51	158	21	37	11	1	11	27	20	68	1	0	.324	.525	L	R	6-3	195	12-19-75	1994	Kathleen, Ga.
Clark, Brady	.280	138	353	41	99	18	1	7	46	53	48	15	8	.385	.397	R	R	6-2	190	4-18-73	1997	Beaverton, Ore.
Counsell, Craig	.241	140	473	59	114	19	5	2	23	59	88	17	4	.328	.315	L	R	6-0	185	8-21-70	1992	Mequon, Wis.
Durrington, Trent	.232	53	82	13	19	2	3	2	4	4	23	4	0	.267	.402	R	R	5-10	188	8-27-75	1994	Broadbeach Waters, Australia
Erickson, Matt	.167	4	6	0	1	0	0	0	0	1	0	0	0	.167	.167	L	R	5-11	190	7-30-75	1997	Appleton, Wis.
Ginter, Keith	.262	113	386	47	101	23	2	19	60	37	100	8	1	.333	.479	R	R	5-10	195	5-5-76	1998	Fullerton, Calif.
Grieve, Ben	.261	108	234	28	61	15	0	7	29	39	65	0	0	.364	.415	L	R	6-4	210	5-4-76	1994	Flower Mund, Texas
Hall, Bill	.238	126	390	43	93	20	3	9	53	20	119	12	6	.276	.374	R	R	6-0	170	12-28-79	1998	Nettleton, Miss.
Hart, Corey	.000	1	1	0	0	0	0	0	0	0	1	0	0	.000	.000	R	R	6-6	200	3-24-82	2000	Bowling Green, Ky.
Helms, Wes	.263	92	274	24	72	13	1	4	28	24	60	0	1	.333	.361	R	R	6-4	230	5-12-76	1994	Atlanta, Ga.
Jenkins, Geoff	.264	157	617	88	163	36	6	27	93	46	152	3	1	.325	.473	L	R	6-1	213	7-21-74	1995	Scottsdale, Ariz.
Johnson, Mark	.091	7	11	1	1	0	0	0	2	3	2	0	0	.267	.091	L	R	6-0	200	9-12-75	1994	Warner Robins, Ga.
Kieschnick, Brooks	.270	77	63	2	17	3	0	1	7	5	16	0	0	.324	.365	L	R	6-4	220	6-6-72	1993	Caldwell, Texas
Krynzel, Dave	.220	16	41	6	9	1	0	0	3	3	15	0	0	.319	.244	L	L	6-1	180	11-7-81	2000	Henderson, Nev.
Liefer, Jeff	.214	16	28	2	6	2	0	1	5	2	8	0	0	.258	.393	L	R	6-3	210	8-17-74	1996	Costa Mesa, Calif.
Magruder, Chris	.236	56	89	11	21	6	1	2	10	8	21	0	1	.310	.393	S	R	5-11	200	4-26-77	1998	Mesa, Ariz.
Moeller, Chad	.208	101	317	25	66	13	1	5	27	21	74	0	1	.265	.303	R	R	6-3	215	2-18-75	1996	Scottsdale, Ariz.
Overbay, Lyle	.301	159	579	83	174	53	1	16	87	81	128	2	1	.385	.478	L	L	6-2	225	1-28-77	1999	Centralia, Wash.
Podsednik, Scott	.244	154	640	85	156	27	7	12	39	58	105	70	13	.313	.364	L	L	6-0	170	3-18-76	1994	West, Texas
Spivey, Junior	.272	59	228	33	62	13	0	7	28	25	48	5	3	.359	.421	R	R	6-0	200	1-28-75	1996	Phoenix, Ariz.

PITCHING	W	L	ERA	G	GS	CG	SV	IP	H	R	ER	BB	SO	AVG	B	T	HT	WT	DOB	1st Yr	Resides
Adams, Mike	2	3	3.40	46	0	0	0	53	50	21	20	14	39	.248	R	R	6-2	190	4-8-70	1991	Kirkland, Wash.
Bennett, Jeff	1	5	4.79	60	0	0	0	71	78	43	38	26	45	.278	R	R	6-3	200	6-10-80	1998	Brush Creek, Tenn.
Burba, Dave	3	1	4.08	45	0	0	2	71	63	36	32	24	47	.237	R	R	6-4	240	7-6-66	1987	Gilbert, Ariz.
Capuano, Chris	6	8	4.99	17	17	0	0	88	91	55	49	37	80	.269	L	L	6-2	220	8-19-78	2000	West Springfield, Mass.
Davis, Doug	12	12	3.39	34	34	0	0	207	192	84	78	79	166	.247	R	L	6-4	190	9-21-75	1996	Cedar Hill, Texas
De la Rosa, Jorge	0	3	6.35	5	5	0	0	23	29	20	16	14	5	.309	L	L	6-1	190	4-5-81	1998	San Nicolas, Mexico
Ford, Ben	1	1	6.38	19	0	0	0	24	25	17	17	10	13	.269	R	R	6-7	230	8-15-75	1994	Cedar Rapids, Iowa
Glover, Gary	2	1	3.50	4	3	0	0	18	18	9	7	8	8	.265	R	R	6-5	205	12-3-76	1994	DeLand, Fla.
Hendrickson, Ben	1	8	6.22	10	9	0	0	46	58	33	32	20	29	.310	R	R	6-4	190	2-4-81	2000	Eden Prairie, Minn.
Hernandez, Adrian	0	2	8.44	6	1	0	0	16	20	18	15	14	14	.294	R	R	6-1	180	3-25-75	2000	Tampa, Fla.
Kieschnick, Brooks	1	1	3.77	32	0	0	0	43	44	19	18	13	28	.262	L	R	6-4	220	6-6-72	1993	Caldwell, Texas
Kolb, Danny	0	4	2.98	64	0	0	39	57	50	22	19	15	21	.234	R	R	6-4	210	3-29-75	1995	Walnut, Ill.
Liriano, Pedro	0	0	4.02	11	0	0	0	16	15	10	7	3	10	.238	R	R	6-2	170	10-23-80	1999	Cotui, D.R.
Obermueller, Wes	6	8	5.80	25	20	1	0	118	138	80	76	42	59	.291	R	R	6-2	190	12-22-76	1999	North Liberty, Iowa
Phelps, Travis	0	1	10.50	4	0	0	0	6	8	7	7	3	3	.286	R	R	6-2	160	7-25-77	1997	Rocky Comfort, Mo.
Saenz, Chris	1	0	0.00	1	1	0	0	6	2	0	0	3	7	.100	R	R	6-3	200	8-14-81	2001	Tucson, Ariz.
Santos, Victor	11	12	4.97	31	28	0	0	154	169	95	85	57	115	.278	R	R	6-3	190	10-2-76	1995	San Pedro de Macoris, D.R.
Sheets, Ben	12	14	2.70	34	34	5	0	237	201	85	71	32	264	.226	R	R	6-1	220	7-18-78	1999	St. Amant, La.
Vizcaino, Luis	4	4	3.75	73	0	0	1	72	61	35	30	24	63	.228	R	R	5-11	180	8-6-74	1995	Bani, D.R.
Wise, Matt	1	2	4.44	30	3	0	0	53	51	27	26	15	30	.252	R	R	6-4	195	11-18-75	1997	Yorba Linda, Calif.

FIELDING

Catcher	PCT	G	PO	A	E	DP	PB
Bennett	.993	75	379	31	3	3	3
Johnson	.952	5	18	2	1	0	0
Moeller	.999	100	718	46	1	4	4

First Base	PCT	G	PO	A	E	DP
Branyan	1.000	2	7	0	0	1
Helms	.973	10	68	3	2	7
Overbay	.992	158	1311	113	11	110

Second Base	PCT	G	PO	A	E	DP
Durrington	1.000	6	12	12	0	1
Erickson	1.000	1	1	3	0	1
Ginter	.973	54	91	127	6	19

	PCT	G	PO	A	E	DP
Hall	.959	50	95	113	9	29
Spivey	.963	58	111	177	11	41
Third Base						
Branyan	.962	44	35	91	5	7
Counsell	.000	1	0	0	0	0
Durrington	.789	11	3	12	4	0
Ginter	.973	47	28	80	3	10
Helms	.904	66	45	105	16	10
Hall	.933	11	6	22	2	4
Shortstop	PCT	G	PO	A	E	DP
Counsell	.983	129	165	357	9	70
Erickson	1.000	1	0	4	0	0

	PCT	G	PO	A	E	DP
Hall	.956	37	59	116	8	23
Spivey	1.000	1	1	1	0	0
Outfield	PCT	G	PO	A	E	DP
Clark	.984	133	248	5	4	3
Ginter	1.000	2	5	0	0	0
Grieve	.964	65	106	0	4	0
Jenkins	.996	156	261	10	1	3
Krynzel	.968	10	29	1	1	1
Liefer	1.000	3	4	0	0	0
Magruder	1.000	24	32	1	0	0
Podsednik	.990	153	392	5	4	2

Director, Player Development: Reid Nichols.

Class	Farm Team	League	W	L	Pct.	Finish*	Manager	Affiliate Since
AAA	#Indianapolis (Ind.) Indians	International	66	78	.458	t-11th (14)	Cecil Cooper	2000
AA	Huntsville (Ala.) Stars	Southern	65	75	.464	8th (10)	Frank Kremblas	1999
High A	@High Desert (Calif.) Mavericks	California	49	91	.350	10th (10)	Mel Queen	2001
Low A	&Beloit (Wis.) Snappers	Midwest	72	68	.514	t-7th (14)	Don Money	1982
Rookie	Helena (Mont.) Brewers	Pioneer	40	37	.519	4th (8)	Johnny Narron	2003
Rookie	Phoenix (Ariz.) Brewers	Arizona	24	32	.429	8th (9)	Mike Guerrero	2001

*Finish in overall standings (No. of teams in league)/Playoff teams in **boldface**   @Affiliate will operate in Brevard County (Florida State) in 2005
#Affiliate will operate in Nashville (Pacific Coast) in 2005   &Affiliate will operate in Charleston, W.Va. (South Atlantic) in 2005

INDIANAPOLIS INDIANS   Class AAA

INTERNATIONAL LEAGUE

BATTING	AVG	G	AB	R	H	2B	3B	HR	RBI	BB	SO	SB	CS	OBP	SLG	B	T	HT	WT	DOB	1st Yr	Resides
Bergeron, Peter	.274	82	318	46	87	10	8	3	22	20	40	12	7	.318	.384	L	R	6-0	190	11-9-77	1996	St. Petersburg, Fla.
Coste, Chris	.296	78	260	34	77	21	1	2	26	21	37	2	3	.358	.408	R	R	6-1	200	2-4-73	1995	Fargo, N.D.
Delgado, Alex	.218	65	206	9	45	10	0	0	28	5	21	1	1	.243	.267	R	R	6-0	160	1-11-71	1988	Palmarejo, Venez.
Durrington, Trent	.222	51	162	19	36	1	0	1	9	16	34	17	5	.298	.247	R	R	5-10	188	8-27-75	1994	Broadbeach Waters, Australia
Erickson, Matt	.270	122	400	57	108	27	1	2	34	45	69	12	10	.359	.358	L	R	5-11	190	7-30-75	1997	Appleton, Wis.
Figueroa, Luis	.272	116	383	44	104	14	0	5	47	24	24	5	6	.314	.347	S	R	5-9	145	2-16-74	1997	Vega Alta, P.R.
Gemoll, Brandon	.278	80	248	30	69	19	1	3	34	14	65	3	2	.319	.399	L	L	6-2	210	9-15-80	2001	San Jose, Calif.
Ginter, Keith	.214	4	14	3	3	2	0	1	3	1	4	0	0	.267	.571	R	R	5-10	195	5-5-76	1998	Fullerton, Calif.
Hardy, J.J.	.277	26	101	17	28	10	0	4	20	9	8	0	0	.330	.495	R	R	6-2	180	8-19-82	2001	Tucson, Ariz.
Hart, Corey	.282	121	440	68	124	29	8	15	67	42	92	17	7	.344	.486	R	R	6-6	200	3-24-82	2000	Bowling Green, Ky.
Helms, Wes	.316	6	19	4	6	1	0	0	1	3	4	0	0	.409	.368	R	R	6-4	230	5-12-76	1994	Atlanta, Ga.
Johnson, Mark	.256	88	281	39	72	18	0	5	38	43	44	3	2	.355	.374	L	R	6-0	200	9-12-75	1994	Warner Robins, Ga.
Knox, Ryan	.264	43	174	24	46	12	0	1	14	15	33	10	10	.323	.351	R	R	6-1	190	6-28-77	1999	Peoria, Ill.
Krynzel, Dave	.271	69	258	36	70	10	4	6	26	20	63	10	8	.327	.411	L	L	6-1	180	11-7-81	2000	Henderson, Nev.
Liefer, Jeff	.281	107	370	60	104	25	1	20	83	47	63	1	0	.364	.516	L	R	6-3	210	8-17-74	1996	Costa Mesa, Calif.
Magruder, Chris	.272	79	305	37	83	17	4	6	39	21	55	7	4	.337	.413	S	R	5-11	200	4-26-77	1998	Mesa, Ariz.
Nunnally, Jon	.217	79	240	35	52	9	1	9	34	39	55	4	4	.324	.375	L	R	5-10	205	11-9-71	1992	Keeling, Va.
Scarborough, Steve	.246	112	342	39	84	27	4	4	37	43	73	2	0	.342	.383	R	R	6-0	160	3-10-78	1999	College Station, Texas
Sheldon, Scott	.230	41	113	12	26	8	0	5	10	10	26	0	1	.288	.434	R	R	6-3	215	11-20-68	1991	Pearland, Texas

PITCHING	W	L	ERA	G	GS	CG	SV	IP	H	R	ER	BB	SO	AVG	B	T	HT	WT	DOB	1st Yr	Resides
Adams, Mike	2	0	2.61	10	2	0	0	31	23	10	9	4	37	.209	R	R	6-5	190	7-29-78	2001	Sinton, Texas
Bowles, Brian	1	1	6.17	10	0	0	1	12	13	8	8	8	15	.289	R	R	6-5	220	8-18-76	1995	Manhattan Beach, Calif.
Capuano, Chris	0	1	8.31	2	2	0	0	9	10	9	8	5	9	.294	L	L	6-2	220	8-19-78	2000	West Springfield, Mass.
Childers, Jason	0	1	1.26	24	0	0	15	29	20	4	4	9	27	.198	R	R	6-0	160	1-13-75	1997	Douglas, Ga.
Childers, Matt	5	5	4.87	35	10	0	2	98	100	55	53	27	65	.263	R	R	6-5	190	12-3-78	1997	Augusta, Ga.
De La Rosa, Jorge	5	6	4.52	20	20	0	0	86	80	45	43	36	86	.249	L	L	6-1	190	4-5-81	1998	San Nicolas, Mexico
Erdos, Todd	2	8	8.36	42	0	0	0	56	69	57	52	33	39	.304	R	R	6-1	200	11-21-73	1992	Meadville, Pa.
2-team (4 Rochester)	2	8	7.93	46	0	0	0	59	70	57	52	34	42	.297							
Farnsworth, Jeff	2	6	8.18	11	8	0	0	47	64	46	43	19	26	.314	R	R	6-2	195	10-6-75	1996	Pensacola, Fla.
Ford, Ben	2	2	4.85	32	1	0	9	43	53	25	23	21	36	.317	R	R	6-7	230	8-15-75	1994	Cedar Rapids, Iowa
Giron, Roberto	5	0	1.86	21	0	0	3	29	25	11	6	7	18	.234	R	R	6-2	170	3-24-76	1994	Villa Mella, D.R.
Glover, Gary	3	3	3.98	8	6	0	0	41	47	19	18	11	18	.307	R	R	6-5	205	12-3-76	1994	DeLand, Fla.
2-team (5 Rochester)	3	4	5.24	13	10	0	0	57	74	34	33	16	26	.332							
Hendrickson, Ben	11	3	2.02	21	21	2	0	125	114	32	28	26	93	.246	R	R	6-4	190	2-4-81	2000	Eden Prairie, Minn.
Hernandez, Adrian	0	8	5.72	20	15	0	0	94	111	61	60	39	83	.301	R	R	6-1	180	3-25-75	2000	Tampa, Fla.
Housman, Jeff	1	1	7.71	5	3	0	0	19	31	16	16	13	13	.383	L	L	6-3	180	8-4-81	2002	Visalia, Calif.
Kieschnick, Brooks	0	0	0.00	2	2	0	0	2	1	0	0	0	1	.143	L	R	6-4	220	6-6-72	1993	Caldwell, Texas
Liriano, Pedro	3	10	5.20	29	21	1	1	126	149	81	73	50	97	.300	R	R	6-2	170	10-23-80	1999	Cotui, D.R.
Michalak, Chris	2	6	5.18	37	0	0	1	49	65	37	28	18	29	.327	L	L	6-2	195	1-4-71	1993	Keller, Texas
Novinsky, John	0	0	0.00	1	0	0	0	1	0	0	0	0	0	.500	R	R	6-3	190	4-25-79	2001	Hauppauge, N.Y.
Obermueller, Wes	0	3	5.19	4	4	1	0	26	30	16	15	7	17	.294	R	R	6-2	190	12-22-76	1999	North Liberty, Iowa
Parker, Mark	0	1	7.36	1	0	0	0	4	7	3	3	1	3	.438	R	R	6-3	210	12-13-78	1999	Hartsfield, Ga.
Phelps, Travis	8	5	4.37	28	14	0	0	107	114	58	52	25	84	.273	R	R	6-2	160	7-25-77	1997	Rocky Comfort, Mo.
Reichert, Dan	7	4	3.74	49	0	0	1	87	89	44	36	38	73	.271	R	R	6-3	170	7-12-76	1997	Turlock, Calif.
Rivard, Reggie	1	0	9.00	1	0	0	0	2	2	2	2	1	0	.250	L	R	6-2	190	3-13-78	2000	Bonnyville, Alberta
Santos, Victor	0	0	3.48	3	3	0	0	10	12	4	4	4	11	.308	R	R	6-3	190	10-2-76	1995	San Pedro de Macoris, D.R.
Scarborough, Steve	0	0	0.00	3	2	0	0	2	2	0	0	0	1	.286	R	R	6-0	160	3-10-78	1999	College Station, Texas
Stewart, Paul	0	2	10.80	6	1	0	0	12	20	16	14	6	8	.377	R	R	6-5	220	10-21-78	1996	Raleigh, N.C.
Weibl, Clint	4	3	3.78	24	9	0	0	81	83	43	34	26	61	.263	R	R	6-3	180	3-17-75	1996	Dawson, Ga.
Wise, Matt	1	0	1.80	7	1	0	0	20	12	4	4	4	20	.176	R	R	6-4	195	11-18-75	1997	Yorba Linda, Calif.
Woolard, Glenn	0	0	0.00	1	1	0	0	6	3	0	0	1	4	.150	R	R	6-1	200	4-18-81	2002	Lititz, Pa.

FIELDING

Catcher	PCT	G	PO	A	E	DP	PB
Coste	.985	27	180	15	3	2	0
Delgado	.988	61	382	35	5	5	5
Johnson	.992	70	433	35	4	3	2

First Base	PCT	G	PO	A	E	DP
Coste	1.000	13	89	7	0	8
Durrington	1.000	1	7	0	0	0
Gemoll	.997	52	351	31	1	41

	PCT	G	PO	A	E	DP
Hart	.857	2	11	1	2	0
Johnson	1.000	9	51	2	0	6
Liefer	.994	79	649	64	4	73
Sheldon	1.000	7	51	3	0	5

Second Base	PCT	G	PO	A	E	DP
Coste	1.000	5	6	10	0	2
Durrington	.963	32	67	62	5	15
Erickson	.990	69	115	186	3	45

	PCT	G	PO	A	E	DP
Figueroa	.984	31	62	62	2	16
Ginter	1.000	2	3	3	0	1
Scarborough	.937	23	48	56	7	17

Third Base	PCT	G	PO	A	E	DP
Coste	.924	34	18	55	6	5
Durrington	.792	9	5	14	5	3
Erickson	.978	41	17	72	2	6
Figueroa	.988	31	25	59	1	8

	PCT	G	PO	A	E	DP
Ginter	1.000	1	1	1	0	0
Helms	.857	5	3	9	2	2
Liefer	1.000	8	8	14	0	1
Scarborough	.925	20	5	44	4	5
Sheldon	.914	13	7	25	3	6

Shortstop	PCT	G	PO	A	E	DP
Erickson	.976	11	13	28	1	5

	PCT	G	PO	A	E	DP
Figueroa	.991	52	92	132	2	31
Hardy	.953	25	29	72	5	16
Scarborough	.955	65	86	190	13	40

Outfield	PCT	G	PO	A	E	DP
Bergeron	.983	83	157	13	3	0
Durrington	1.000	6	17	1	0	0
Figueroa	1.000	2	1	1	0	0

Gemoll	1.000	11	10	1	0	0
Hart	.961	92	163	10	7	4
Knox	.981	41	102	1	2	0
Krynzel	.993	63	141	6	1	1
Liefer	1.000	14	34	0	0	0
Magruder	1.000	74	119	5	0	1
Nunnally	.973	58	103	6	3	3

HUNTSVILLE STARS — Class AA

SOUTHERN LEAGUE

BATTING

	AVG	G	AB	R	H	2B	3B	HR	RBI	BB	SO	SB	CS	OBP	SLG	B	T	HT	WT	DOB	1st Yr	Resides
Alvarado, Joel	.146	69	205	15	30	9	0	1	13	32	49	2	2	.265	.205	R	R	6-2	190	6-30-80	2001	Cayey, P.R.
Barnwell, Chris	.246	138	484	43	119	24	4	6	51	36	76	11	14	.310	.349	R	R	5-10	180	3-1-79	2001	Jacksonville, Fla.
Belcher, Jason	.289	47	128	17	37	10	0	3	17	10	21	2	2	.357	.434	L	R	6-1	190	1-13-82	2000	Walnut Ridge, Ark.
Chavez, Ozzie	.211	84	266	18	56	9	1	2	17	21	57	1	4	.269	.274	S	R	6-2	190	7-13-83	2000	Villa Mella, D.R.
Corredor, Nestor	.100	6	20	0	2	0	0	0	0	0	7	0	0	.100	.100	R	R	6-1	180	5-25-84	2002	Portuguesa, Venez.
Cruz, Enrique	.188	35	101	14	19	3	1	2	5	14	37	2	1	.284	.297	R	R	6-1	180	11-21-81	1999	Santo Domingo, D.R.
Delgado, Alex	.111	5	18	2	2	0	0	1	3	0	1	0	0	.111	.278	R	R	6-0	160	1-11-71	1988	Palmarejo, Venez.
Fielder, Prince	.272	136	497	70	135	29	1	23	78	65	93	11	7	.366	.473	L	R	6-0	260	5-9-84	2002	Melbourne, Fla.
Gann, Jamie	.256	59	195	21	50	7	2	6	28	13	54	6	4	.305	.405	R	R	6-1	190	5-1-75	1996	Oklahoma City, Okla.
Gemoll, Brandon	.205	30	78	7	16	3	0	3	9	3	22	0	0	.235	.359	L	L	6-2	210	9-15-80	2001	San Jose, Calif.
Gwynn, Anthony	.243	138	534	74	130	20	5	2	37	53	95	35	16	.318	.311	L	R	6-0	185	10-4-82	2003	Poway, Calif.
Johnson, Kade	.259	69	224	26	58	9	1	5	28	21	41	6	2	.325	.375	R	R	6-1	205	9-28-78	2000	Baytown, Texas
Knox, Ryan	.287	66	181	25	52	10	0	4	19	19	35	10	7	.353	.409	R	R	6-1	190	6-28-77	1999	Peoria, Ill.
Nelson, Brad	.254	137	500	61	127	31	1	19	77	47	146	11	10	.321	.434	R	R	6-3	220	1-5-82	2003	Cary, N.C.
Raburn, Johnny	.248	115	314	38	78	12	3	1	23	37	53	16	8	.326	.315	S	R	6-1	160	2-16-79	2000	Plant City, Fla.
Van Iderstine, Ben	.288	17	52	1	15	2	0	1	3	0	12	0	1	.288	.385	L	L	6-2	200	1-20-78	2001	Regina, Sask.
Weeks, Rickie	.259	133	479	67	124	35	6	8	42	55	107	11	12	.366	.407	R	R	6-0	195	9-13-82	2003	Altamonte Springs, Fla.

PITCHING

	W	L	ERA	G	GS	CG	SV	IP	H	R	ER	BB	SO	AVG	B	T	HT	WT	DOB	1st Yr	Resides
Adams, Brian	3	2	4.25	32	0	0	3	85	92	47	40	26	67	.283	L	L	6-3	190	10-2-77	2000	Bishopville, S.C.
Bausher, Tim	1	6	3.67	11	9	0	0	49	53	28	20	19	54	.272	R	R	6-4	200	4-23-79	2001	Bechtelsville, Pa.
Costello, Ryan	8	8	3.89	24	23	1	0	125	124	66	54	49	105	.259	R	L	6-6	210	7-13-79	2001	Marlton, N.J.
Eveland, Dana	0	2	2.28	4	4	0	0	24	23	9	6	4	14	.253	L	L	6-1	220	10-29-83	2003	Palmdale, Calif.
Ford, Matt	2	6	3.94	21	18	0	0	91	89	50	40	49	47	.262	S	L	6-1	170	4-8-81	1999	Tamarac, Fla.
Giron, Roberto	2	2	1.86	31	0	0	8	39	22	10	8	10	50	.163	R	R	6-2	170	3-24-76	1994	Villa Mella, D.R.
Harper, Jesse	0	0	3.18	1	1	0	0	6	6	2	2	0	4	.250	R	R	6-4	210	11-11-80	2001	Clute, Texas
Housman, Jeff	5	8	3.13	23	20	0	1	112	108	55	39	38	121	.247	L	L	6-3	180	8-4-81	2002	Visalia, Calif.
Jones, Mike	1	4	4.18	6	6	0	0	24	22	14	11	13	16	.247	R	R	6-4	200	4-23-83	2001	Phoenix, Ariz.
Miller, Ryan	1	1	2.19	6	0	0	0	12	9	3	3	4	20	.200	R	R	6-1	200	2-12-78	2000	Newburgh, Ind.
Novinsky, John	7	1	2.93	45	0	0	17	61	53	23	20	15	60	.230	R	R	6-3	190	4-25-79	2001	Hauppauge, N.Y.
Parra, Manny	0	1	4.50	3	3	0	0	6	6	3	3	0	10	.240	L	L	6-3	200	10-30-82	2002	Citrus Heights, Calif.
Pratt, Andy	1	0	1.80	1	1	0	0	5	5	1	1	0	6	.250	L	L	6-0	185	8-27-79	1998	Chino Valley, Ariz.
2-team (6 West Tenn)	1	5	7.86	7	6	0	0	26	29	28	23	21	32	.276							
Raburn, Johnny	1	0	0.00	3	1	0	0	4	3	0	0	1	2	.214	S	R	6-1	160	2-16-79	2000	Plant City, Fla.
Rijo, Fernando	3	5	3.52	39	0	0	2	61	52	29	24	23	57	.326	R	R	5-11	173	11-15-77	1995	La Romana, D.R.
Rivard, Reggie	3	1	6.55	22	1	0	0	34	50	31	25	9	21	.342	L	R	6-2	190	3-13-78	2000	Bonnyville, Alberta
Rivera, Saul	2	1	1.62	26	0	0	1	33	30	11	6	16	25	.252	R	R	5-11	150	12-7-77	1998	San Juan, P.R.
Saenz, Chris	5	5	4.15	14	14	0	0	85	76	41	39	18	84	.238	R	R	6-3	200	8-14-81	2001	Tucson, Ariz.
Sarfate, Dennis	7	12	3.98	28	25	0	0	129	128	71	57	78	113	.266	R	R	6-4	210	4-9-81	2001	Chandler, Ariz.
Shelley, Jason	2	4	4.09	15	2	0	0	33	33	18	15	17	29	.250	R	R	6-2	190	3-19-77	1999	Plainfield, Ill.
Stewart, Paul	5	3	2.98	41	2	0	2	94	93	36	31	16	74	.262	R	R	6-5	220	10-21-78	1996	Raleigh, N.C.
Woolard, Glenn	6	2	2.73	23	11	0	1	82	61	29	25	35	67	.209	R	R	6-1	200	4-18-81	2002	Lititz, Pa.
Zamora, Peter	0	1	6.14	10	0	0	0	15	18	13	10	7	4	.316	L	L	6-3	180	8-13-75	1997	Mission Viejo, Calif.

FIELDING

Catcher	PCT	G	PO	A	E	DP	PB
Alvarado	.992	66	467	59	4	6	12
Corredor	.980	6	44	5	1	1	2
Delgado	.977	5	38	4	1	0	0
Johnson	.987	63	503	42	7	4	6
Raburn	1.000	3	14	0	0	0	0

First Base	PCT	G	PO	A	E	DP
Alvarado	1.000	2	9	0	0	0
Fielder	.987	133	1079	56	15	96
Gemoll	1.000	1	9	0	0	1
Nelson	.900	1	9	0	1	0
Raburn	1.000	6	41	1	0	1

Second Base	PCT	G	PO	A	E	DP
Raburn	.950	12	23	34	3	4
Weeks	.969	131	238	293	17	69

Third Base	PCT	G	PO	A	E	DP
Alvarado	1.000	1	2	0	0	0
Barnwell	.943	138	127	271	24	26
Raburn	1.000	3	1	7	0	0

Shortstop	PCT	G	PO	A	E	DP
Chavez	.944	77	104	200	18	39
Cruz	.921	32	28	89	10	15
Knox	.857	1	1	5	1	2

Raburn	.934	39	41	115	11	16

Outfield	PCT	G	PO	A	E	DP
Barnwell	1.000	1	0	1	0	0
Belcher	1.000	25	37	1	0	0
Fielder	1.000	2	1	0	0	0
Gann	.970	52	93	4	3	2
Gemoll	1.000	15	22	0	0	0
Gwynn	.974	135	324	10	9	0
Knox	.984	45	58	4	1	0
Nelson	.982	136	199	17	4	2
Raburn	.978	28	41	3	1	1
Van Iderstine	1.000	7	13	0	0	0

HIGH DESERT MAVERICKS — High Class A

CALIFORNIA LEAGUE

BATTING

	AVG	G	AB	R	H	2B	3B	HR	RBI	BB	SO	SB	CS	OBP	SLG	B	T	HT	WT	DOB	1st Yr	Resides
Bibbs, Kennard	.280	120	496	75	139	16	10	2	36	40	64	40	18	.334	.365	L	L	5-9	160	3-5-80	2002	Houston, Texas
Boyd, Dan	.293	69	266	47	78	21	2	11	51	29	57	3	2	.394	.511	R	R	5-11	190	9-28-78	2001	Dade City, Fla.
Candelaria, Ben	.095	5	21	2	2	0	0	0	0	3	0	1		.095	.095	L	R	5-11	160	1-29-75	1992	Hatillo, P.R.
Candelaria, Scott	.246	58	224	22	55	7	1	3	23	8	42	0	1	.277	.326	R	R	6-2	190	11-2-78	2000	Albuquerque, N.M.
Chavez, Ozzie	.323	39	130	19	42	4	1	1	23	7	26	2	5	.364	.392	S	R	6-2	190	7-13-83	2000	Villa Mella, D.R.
Crabbe, Callix	.291	132	540	89	157	26	11	7	62	59	64	37	11	.366	.419	S	R	5-8	190	2-14-83	2002	Lithonia, Ga.
Cruz, Enrique	.283	97	360	53	102	19	0	17	65	36	82	12	7	.347	.478	R	R	6-1	180	11-21-81	1999	Santo Domingo, D.R.
Eure, Jeff	.240	92	366	45	88	23	4	10	51	26	102	6	8	.297	.407	R	R	6-1	200	8-17-80	2001	Pillow, Penn.

BATTING	AVG	G	AB	R	H	2B	3B	HR	RBI	BB	SO	SB	CS	OBP	SLG	B	T	HT	WT	DOB	1st Yr	Resides
Farnsworth, Troy	.259	78	263	40	68	14	1	12	46	27	66	2	2	.341	.456	R	R	6-2	210	2-4-76	1998	West Valley City, Utah
Frost, Jeremy	.268	89	325	39	87	19	2	9	38	18	71	8	1	.307	.422	R	R	6-3	210	11-19-79	2002	Oviedo, Fla.
Hamilton, Mark	.300	21	80	12	24	3	0	3	15	6	14	1	0	.356	.450	L	L	6-3	200	4-23-78	2000	Hurst, Texas
Henderson, Eric	.148	9	27	5	4	1	0	1	2	2	11	0	0	.207	.296	L	L	6-4	210	9-5-79	2000	Litchfield Park, Ariz.
Hinton, Travis	.304	136	536	80	163	36	4	22	88	48	99	3	1	.364	.509	L	L	6-1	210	11-21-80	2001	Chandler, Ariz.
Mendez, Mario	.277	92	336	53	93	14	6	15	50	22	95	9	7	.328	.488	R	R	6-0	170	8-21-81	1999	Azua, D.R.
Morris, Chris	.286	39	126	24	36	7	0	0	16	22	31	25	9	.393	.341	S	R	5-8	180	7-1-79	2000	Andrews, S.C.
Rasmussen, Pete	.177	35	96	11	17	4	2	1	10	8	30	0	1	.257	.292	R	R	5-9	185	8-20-80	2003	McHenry, Ill.
Serfass, Jake	.120	9	25	4	3	1	0	0	4	1	6	0	0	.154	.160	L	L	6-2	215	12-15-81	2004	Fairless Hills, Pa.
Van Iderstine, Ben	.372	46	191	23	71	15	1	2	17	8	19	1	1	.402	.492	L	L	6-2	200	1-20-78	2001	Regina, Sask.
Vanden Berg, John	.281	72	256	34	72	16	2	6	32	29	65	1	0	.358	.430	R	R	6-2	210	2-5-80	2002	Cedarburg, Wis.
Villanueva, Froilan	.265	70	272	43	72	17	1	13	39	11	94	3	0	.305	.478	R	R	6-2	150	10-5-78	1998	Santo Domingo, D.R.

PITCHING	W	L	ERA	G	GS	CG	SV	IP	H	R	ER	BB	SO	AVG	B	T	HT	WT	DOB	1st Yr	Resides
Alliston, Josh	0	0	0.00	1	0	0	0	0	0	0	0	0	0	.000	R	R	6-5	230	2-29-80	2002	Long Beach, Calif.
Ballouli, Khalid	6	14	5.95	27	25	0	0	138	182	106	91	34	128	.318	R	R	6-2	190	3-20-80	2002	Austin, Texas
Bradley, David	7	11	4.76	31	23	0	1	138	151	93	73	54	129	.275	R	R	6-1	170	8-28-77	1999	Parkersburg, W.Va.
Breslow, Craig	1	3	7.19	23	0	0	0	41	54	39	33	24	41	.318	L	L	6-1	180	8-8-80	2002	Trumbull, Conn.
Bruso, Greg	1	7	5.48	12	12	0	0	66	82	50	40	12	50	.301	L	R	6-3	190	5-5-80	2002	South Lake Tahoe, Calif.
Capuano, Chris	0	1	27.00	1	1	0	0	2	6	6	6	3	2	.600	L	L	6-2	220	8-19-78	2000	West Springfield, Mass.
Costello, Ryan	1	3	9.92	6	2	0	0	16	19	19	18	9	15	.284	R	L	6-6	210	7-13-79	2001	Marlton, N.J.
Hall, Bo	5	9	6.55	27	24	0	0	133	169	102	97	42	127	.310	R	R	6-0	180	5-5-80	2002	Ormond Beach, Fla.
Hamilton, Mark	2	2	5.45	12	2	0	0	33	42	25	20	13	26	.323	L	L	6-3	200	4-23-78	2000	Hurst, Texas
Harper, Jesse	3	3	4.01	9	9	0	0	49	46	26	22	15	51	.247	R	R	6-4	210	11-11-80	2001	Clute, Texas
Henderson, Eric	4	5	6.98	25	9	0	1	88	116	87	68	48	58	.320	L	L	6-4	210	9-5-79	2000	Litchfield Park, Ariz.
Kolb, Dan	3	3	5.42	37	0	0	3	83	91	60	50	44	75	.277	R	R	6-1	190	6-5-80	2001	Palmetto, Fla.
Kusiewicz, Mike	0	1	4.14	26	0	0	1	37	46	19	17	16	44	.305	R	L	6-2	185	11-1-76	1995	Nepean, Ontario
Martin, Forest	1	4	5.25	10	9	0	0	48	53	35	28	18	40	.280	R	R	6-2	190	8-21-81	1998	Azua, D.R.
Mendez, Manny	0	0	7.71	3	0	0	0	2	3	2	2	3	2	.300	R	R	6-0	180	1-30-81	2003	Huntington Beach, Calif.
Needham, Joel	0	0	3.00	2	0	0	0	3	4	3	1	1	4	.333	R	R	6-3	173	7-15-80	1999	Riverside, Calif.
Neugebauer, Nick	0	0	18.00	1	1	0	0	1	2	2	2	0	0	.400	R	R	6-3	200	4-3-79	2001	Rialto, Calif.
Nolasco, David	3	6	7.40	44	1	0	1	83	110	79	68	50	56	.318	R	R	6-2	200	10-30-82	2002	Citrus Heights, Calif.
Parra, Manny	5	2	3.48	13	12	1	0	67	76	41	26	19	64	.284	L	L	6-3	200	3-13-78	2000	Bonnyville, Alberta
Rivard, Reggie	1	3	2.33	17	0	0	3	19	17	10	5	8	12	.243	L	R	6-2	190	3-13-78	2000	Bonnyville, Alberta
Rivera, Homero	1	1	6.84	20	0	0	4	25	35	25	19	14	25	.318	R	L	5-10	160	8-13-77	1995	Nizao, D.R.
Slack, Nick	2	6	4.98	45	0	0	9	60	70	40	33	19	71	.288	R	R	6-1	215	1-5-83	2003	Deltona, Fla.
Stetter, Mitchel	1	4	8.15	8	7	0	0	39	54	39	35	14	29	.323	L	L	6-4	195	1-16-81	2003	Huntingburg, Ind.
Teeter, Travis	1	1	7.71	4	0	0	0	16	29	15	14	1	23	.327	R	R	6-1	210	7-13-80	2002	Cohoes, N.Y.
Vanden Berg, John	0	0	13.50	1	0	0	0	1	2	1	1	0	1	.500	R	R	6-2	210	2-5-80	2002	Cedarburg, Wis.
Woolard, Glenn	1	2	4.69	12	2	0	0	48	58	31	25	21	46	.299	R	R	6-1	190	4-18-81	2002	Lititz, Pa.

FIELDING

Catcher	PCT	G	PO	A	E	DP	PB
Frost	.967	13	103	14	4	0	4
Vanden Berg	.975	69	503	53	14	4	12
Villanueva	.983	64	496	66	10	4	17

First Base	PCT	G	PO	A	E	DP
Farnsworth	1.000	5	25	2	0	1
Frost	.969	7	60	3	2	4
Hamilton	1.000	1	6	1	0	0
Hinton	.984	130	1090	73	19	86

Second Base	PCT	G	PO	A	E	DP
B. Candelaria	.800	1	3	1	1	1
S. Candelaria	.944	6	4	13	1	3

	PCT	G	PO	A	E	DP
Crabbe	.966	132	241	356	21	62
Eure	.909	5	4	6	1	0

Third Base	PCT	G	PO	A	E	DP
Eure	.913	83	58	173	22	10
Farnsworth	.892	38	29	70	12	2
Frost	.778	5	2	5	2	0
Villanueva	1.000	1	1	3	0	0

Shortstop	PCT	G	PO	A	E	DP
S. Candelaria	.905	4	7	12	2	2
Chavez	.951	39	68	127	10	29
Cruz	.960	97	168	241	17	43

	PCT	G	PO	A	E	DP
Eure	1.000	3	7	7	0	2

Outfield	PCT	G	PO	A	E	DP
Bibbs	.983	120	278	11	5	3
Boyd	.962	68	92	9	4	1
B. Candelaria	.909	5	10	0	1	0
S. Candelaria	1.000	30	41	2	0	2
Frost	.954	45	61	1	3	0
Hamilton	.913	11	21	0	2	0
Mendez	.910	88	144	7	15	0
Morris	.938	8	15	0	1	0
Rasmussen	.810	14	15	2	4	0
Serfass	1.000	9	10	0	0	0
Van Iderstine	.987	45	74	1	1	0

BELOIT SNAPPERS — Low Class A

MIDWEST LEAGUE

BATTING	AVG	G	AB	R	H	2B	3B	HR	RBI	BB	SO	SB	CS	OBP	SLG	B	T	HT	WT	DOB	1st Yr	Resides
Acosta, Gilberto	.167	43	132	14	22	3	0	0	9	11	24	1	1	.234	.189	S	R	6-1	150	10-5-82	2000	Valencia, Venez.
Anderson, Drew	.307	123	456	64	140	22	5	5	59	45	95	13	4	.372	.410	L	R	6-2	195	6-9-81	2003	Kearney, Neb.
Campana, Wandel	.301	35	123	15	37	10	0	0	10	4	17	1	2	.343	.382	R	R	6-0	175	6-6-78	1998	Santo Domingo, D.R.
Corporan, Carlos	.228	63	197	20	45	7	2	1	16	7	65	1	3	.261	.299	S	R	6-3	212	1-7-84	2003	Catano, P.R.
Deevers, Robby	.238	73	235	27	56	17	2	8	28	10	77	6	5	.279	.430	R	R	5-10	190	6-23-80	2003	Elgin, Okla.
Heether, Adam	.252	128	476	65	120	35	4	17	72	37	93	2	1	.313	.450	R	R	6-0	200	1-14-82	2003	Ripon, Calif.
Iribarren, Hernan	.373	15	67	12	25	6	1	0	10	5	16	1	0	.411	.657	L	R	6-1	160	6-29-84	2002	Barquisimeto, Venez.
Lewis, Will	.328	38	137	28	45	11	0	5	21	16	22	4	3	.401	.518	R	R	5-10	180	8-18-81	2003	Texarkana, Ark.
Marks, Tim	.193	35	114	12	22	2	0	0	6	9	13	0	0	.258	.211	R	R	6-3	230	6-1-81	2003	Kankakee, Ill.
Moss, Steve	.235	102	362	41	85	17	4	8	34	35	90	6	4	.318	.370	R	R	6-2	180	1-12-84	2002	Sherman Oaks, Calif.
Murray, Joshua	.160	50	188	21	30	5	0	4	15	9	50	1	2	.209	.250	R	R	6-2	184	2-12-82	2002	Lutz, Fla.
Palmisano, Lou	.293	113	409	59	120	22	3	7	65	43	93	3	2	.371	.413	R	R	6-1	185	9-16-82	2003	Fort Lauderdale, Fla.
Ramirez, Manuel	.236	86	296	36	70	21	1	5	35	16	54	1	0	.274	.365	R	R	6-0	165	9-7-82	2001	Acarigua, Venez.
Richardson, Grant	.223	28	94	17	21	3	0	6	17	10	25	1	0	.315	.447	R	R	6-1	210	2-26-83	2004	Richland, Wash.
Rodriguez, Guilder	.265	95	351	64	93	6	0	0	27	45	50	14	6	.352	.282	S	R	6-1	160	7-24-83	2001	Barquisimeto, Venez.
Rottino, Vinny	.304	139	529	78	161	29	9	17	124	40	71	5	1	.352	.482	R	R	6-0	195	4-7-80	2003	Racine, Wis.
Septimo, Agustin	.133	6	15	4	2	0	0	1	3	2	2	0	0	.235	.333	S	R	6-1	160	5-27-84	2003	Santo Domingo, D.R.
Trofholz, Terry	.300	119	460	86	138	14	5	2	42	33	96	48	10	.343	.365	R	R	6-2	190	9-11-80	2003	Plano, Texas

PITCHING	W	L	ERA	G	GS	CG	SV	IP	H	R	ER	BB	SO	AVG	B	T	HT	WT	DOB	1st Yr	Resides
Barnes, Justin	1	3	8.27	4	3	0	0	16	22	15	15	5	12	.333	R	R	6-3	205	8-21-83	2003	Port St. Lucie, Fla.
Beresford, Simon	4	4	4.50	38	5	0	1	92	84	50	46	50	87	.246	R	R	6-6	215	1-2-83	2003	Glen Waverley, Australia
Capuano, Chris	0	0	3.38	1	1	0	0	3	3	1	1	1	4	.300	L	L	6-2	220	8-19-78	2000	West Springfield, Mass.

PITCHING

PITCHING	W	L	ERA	G	GS	CG	SV	IP	H	R	ER	BB	SO	AVG	B	T	HT	WT	DOB	1st Yr	Resides
Dillard, Timo	2	5	3.94	43	1	0	10	78	88	46	34	22	61	.283	S	R	6-4	200	7-19-83	2003	Saltillo, Miss.
Durost, Ken	7	7	3.63	24	18	0	0	104	82	47	42	55	116	.216	R	R	6-4	190	10-10-81	2003	Palmdale, Calif.
Eveland, Dana	9	6	2.84	22	16	1	2	117	108	48	37	24	119	.242	L	L	6-2	219	10-29-83	2003	Palmdale, Calif.
Gallardo, Yovani	0	1	12.27	2	2	0	0	7	12	10	10	4	8	.375	R	R	6-3	160	9-19-85	2004	Fort Worth, Texas
Grybash, Daniel	4	2	4.98	40	0	0	2	72	75	46	40	52	55	.268	R	R	6-1	205	12-26-80	2003	Palatine, Ill.
Hawk, Tommy	0	2	15.88	2	1	0	0	6	9	10	10	7	2	.360	R	R	6-3	210	2-7-85	2003	Lompoc, Calif.
Kloosterman, Greg	2	8	7.57	19	14	0	0	63	77	60	53	42	57	.302	L	L	6-3	205	6-21-82	2003	Bristol, Ind.
McKenna, Daniel	1	0	8.00	11	0	0	0	18	18	16	16	13	13	.254	R	R	6-5	210	1-30-81	2003	Marlton, N.J.
Montalbo, Brian	6	6	4.74	24	19	0	1	108	107	64	57	57	65	.257	S	R	6-4	210	11-22-81	2003	Anchorage, Alaska
Moreira, Greg	8	8	4.29	27	20	1	1	130	128	73	62	44	86	.255	R	R	6-5	210	5-29-83	2001	Apopka, Fla.
Pena, Luis	9	3	3.92	21	16	0	0	99	101	50	43	35	76	.262	R	R	6-5	160	1-10-83	2000	La Victoria, Venez.
Rauch, Brian	0	1	4.50	1	0	0	0	2	3	2	1	1	4	.333	R	R	6-2	220	11-30-80	2003	Rockledge, Fla.
Rival, Kevin	1	1	2.81	13	0	0	2	26	17	9	8	10	28	.185	R	R	6-2	210	12-22-78	2003	New Britain, Conn.
Stanczyk, Ben	3	0	2.25	3	0	0	1	4	5	1	1	0	1	.333	R	R	6-2	210	9-26-82	2004	Waukesha, Wis.
Stetter, Mitchel	4	0	1.70	24	3	0	6	53	31	12	10	12	57	.171	L	L	6-4	195	1-16-81	2003	Huntingburg, Ind.
Taubenheim, Ty	5	3	3.59	47	0	0	12	90	78	40	36	17	106	.234	R	R	6-5	200	11-17-82	2003	Lynden, Wash.
Villanueva, Carlos	8	8	3.77	25	21	1	1	115	102	67	48	30	113	.230	S	R	6-2	190	11-28-83	2002	Santo Domingo, D.R.

FIELDING

Catcher	PCT	G	PO	A	E	DP	PB
Corporan	.980	29	217	26	5	1	4
Marks	.981	27	180	24	4	1	2
Palmisano	.994	85	621	53	4	5	10
Ramirez	1.000	2	4	2	0	0	1
Rottino	.973	5	33	3	1	0	1

	PCT	G	PO	A	E	DP
Campana	1.000	2	3	3	0	0
Iribarren	.944	14	25	43	4	10
Lewis	.961	35	60	88	6	23
Rodriguez	.978	78	148	212	8	37
Rottino	.963	5	8	18	1	4
Septimo	.909	2	5	5	1	0

	PCT	G	PO	A	E	DP
Campana	.919	30	31	82	10	15
Murray	.968	54	74	139	7	33
Rodriguez	.985	16	26	39	1	9
Rottino	1.000	1	0	1	0	0
Septimo	.800	4	0	8	2	1

First Base	PCT	G	PO	A	E	DP
Corporan	.985	35	245	11	4	21
Deevers	1.000	1	1	0	0	0
Ramirez	.987	78	619	47	9	47
Richardson	.974	27	176	10	5	18
Rottino	.977	12	79	5	2	5

Third Base	PCT	G	PO	A	E	DP
Campana	1.000	3	1	3	0	1
Heether	.944	127	75	211	17	11
Ramirez	.667	2	1	1	1	0
Rottino	.895	14	10	24	4	4

Outfield	PCT	G	PO	A	E	DP
Acosta	1.000	1	2	0	0	0
Anderson	.995	120	208	5	1	1
Deevers	.960	71	113	8	5	1
Moss	.966	95	220	4	8	1
Rottino	1.000	34	53	2	0	0
Trofholz	.990	113	199	5	2	0

Second Base	PCT	G	PO	A	E	DP
Acosta	.964	5	8	19	1	4

Shortstop	PCT	G	PO	A	E	DP
Acosta	.952	37	54	103	8	12

HELENA BREWERS
Rookie

PIONEER LEAGUE

BATTING	AVG	G	AB	R	H	2B	3B	HR	RBI	BB	SO	SB	CS	OBP	SLG	B	T	HT	WT	DOB	1st Yr	Resides
Acosta, Gilberto	.221	33	95	12	21	7	1	0	5	8	22	9	1	.282	.316	S	R	6-1	150	10-5-82	2000	Valencia, Venez.
Bates, Dallas	.286	35	119	21	34	5	0	2	10	12	38	3	3	.358	.378	L	L	5-8	170	7-20-84	2002	Chandler, Ariz.
Blevins, Clay	.243	30	103	11	25	6	0	0	12	14	14	1	1	.339	.301	L	R	6-0	180	5-1-83	2004	Dale, Okla.
Brady, Josh	.363	29	113	24	41	9	4	5	24	13	24	5	3	.433	.646	R	R	6-0	170	10-24-80	2004	Lubbock, Texas
Corredor, Nestor	.056	5	18	1	1	0	0	0	2	2	5	0	0	.143	.056	R	R	5-10	230	5-25-84	2002	Portuguesa, Venez.
De la Cruz, Carlos	.343	34	108	20	37	5	0	2	15	14	21	1	2	.411	.444	R	R	6-3	175	3-1-82	2004	La Artagracia, D.R.
Escobar, Alcides	.281	67	231	38	65	8	0	2	24	20	44	20	9	.345	.342	R	R	6-1	155	12-16-88	2003	Vargas, Venez.
Fermaint, Charlie	.229	58	218	30	50	14	2	5	39	19	83	8	2	.300	.381	R	R	5-10	170	10-11-85	2003	Vega Alta, P.R.
Festa, Tony	.305	67	226	51	69	19	0	7	53	56	39	6	1	.463	.482	L	R	6-3	210	12-1-80	2004	Danville, Calif.
Lozada, Charlie	.224	43	134	18	30	4	1	0	13	7	24	2	5	.264	.269	R	R	5-11	190	6-28-83	2003	Caracas, Venez.
Mannon, Adam	.255	72	259	41	66	22	2	8	52	41	70	10	3	.371	.448	L	L	6-3	200	12-12-83	2003	Queen Creek, Ariz.
Rasheed, Hasan	.299	49	174	45	52	7	2	4	23	37	50	13	8	.422	.431	L	L	5-8	175	1-26-84	2004	Nashville, Tenn.
Richardson, Grant	.367	44	166	35	61	16	1	5	42	32	20	2	4	.481	.566	R	R	6-1	210	2-26-83	2004	Richland, Wash.
Segura, Alberto	.278	41	144	22	40	10	0	1	24	17	25	1	0	.350	.368	R	R	5-11	180	11-9-83	2001	Los Llanos, D.R.
Septimo, Agustin	.317	37	101	15	32	2	0	1	11	4	32	12	3	.367	.366	S	R	6-1	160	5-27-84	2003	Santo Domingo, D.R.
Serfass, Jake	.192	31	99	13	19	6	0	1	8	20	32	0	2	.333	.283	L	R	6-2	215	12-15-81	2002	Fairless Hills, Pa.
Sollmann, Steve	.364	72	272	59	99	12	2	1	40	52	30	23	8	.487	.434	R	R	5-11	190	4-1-82	2004	Cincinnati, Ohio

GAMES BY POSITION: C—Blevins 30, Corredor 5, Lozada 9, Segura 38. **1B**—Acosta 1, Brady 23, De la Cruz 1, Lozada 17, Richardson 39. **2B**—Acosta 1, Septimo 8, Sollmann 72. **3B**—Acosta 2, Brady 2, De la Cruz 4, Festa 65, Septimo 9. **SS**—Acosta 15, Escobar 66, Septimo 3. **OF**—Bates 22, Brady 4, De la Cruz 1, Fermaint 58, Mannon 2, Rasheed 49, Serfass 30.

PITCHING	W	L	ERA	G	GS	CG	SV	IP	H	R	ER	BB	SO	AVG	B	T	HT	WT	DOB	1st Yr	Resides
Baker, Josh	1	1	3.66	15	8	0	2	52	37	22	21	20	44	.203	R	R	6-5	220	3-28-83	2004	Houston, Texas
Barnes, Justin	3	2	3.98	11	5	0	1	41	39	22	18	9	55	.242	R	R	6-3	205	8-21-83	2003	Port St. Lucie, Fla.
Bates, Dallas	0	1	0.00	2	0	0	0	2	1	5	0	3	1	.143	L	L	5-8	170	7-20-84	2002	Chandler, Ariz.
Berger, Garrett	0	0	37.80	1	0	0	0	2	3	7	7	5	1	.375	R	R	6-3	240	5-11-83	2003	Carmel, Ind.
De la Cruz, Carlos	1	0	5.40	4	0	0	0	5	4	3	3	4	4	.235	R	R	6-3	175	3-1-82	2004	La Artagracia, D.R.
DeCarlo, Derek	5	3	6.18	15	2	0	0	44	45	33	30	15	35	.260	R	R	6-4	175	3-24-83	2004	Miami, Fla.
Garcia, Miguel	0	1	18.90	0	0	0	0	3	10	11	7	2	3	.526	R	R	6-2	160	6-29-85	2002	Barinas, Venez.
Garner, Jeff	1	2	6.95	12	1	0	0	22	29	20	17	9	19	.322	R	R	6-2	195	4-23-80	2004	Freeland, Mich.
Hawk, Tommy	4	0	6.40	13	5	0	0	32	56	26	23	8	23	.384	R	R	6-3	210	2-7-85	2003	Lompoc, Calif.
Hinton, Robert	4	4	5.15	15	5	0	1	51	55	31	29	17	50	.275	R	R	6-2	190	8-13-84	2004	Sarasota, Fla.
Hundt, Brandon	1	1	4.41	10	0	0	2	16	20	11	8	2	16	.299	R	R	6-1	190	12-1-81	2004	Chula Vista, Calif.
Johnson, David	1	0	2.25	4	0	0	1	8	6	2	2	1	5	.207	R	R	6-5	210	8-25-82	2004	Manhattan Beach, Calif.
Marion, Ryan	1	1	8.15	20	3	0	2	35	39	43	32	33	25	.273	R	R	6-1	200	9-23-84	2003	Kernersville, N.C.
Martinez, Alvaro	3	7	6.02	17	13	0	1	58	64	41	39	16	49	.283	R	R	6-7	197	6-29-85	2001	Caracas, Venez.
McKenna, Daniel	0	1	7.92	12	0	0	0	25	33	27	22	17	17	.308	R	R	6-5	210	1-30-81	2003	Marlton, N.J.
Murray, Brandon	0	2	11.32	18	0	0	0	21	33	29	26	23	23	.367	R	L	6-1	200	8-21-81	2004	Norwich, Conn.
Needham, Joel	2	2	6.43	8	0	0	3	14	18	11	10	8	11	.316	R	R	6-0	180	1-30-81	2003	Huntington Beach, Calif.
Stanczyk, Ben	0	1	4.63	7	5	0	0	23	23	12	12	6	24	.247	R	R	6-2	210	9-26-82	2004	Waukesha, Wis.
Theodorakos, Jared	0	0	6.11	9	0	0	0	28	32	21	19	15	19	.276	L	L	6-3	240	3-15-81	2004	St. Louis, Mo.
Wahpepah, Josh	2	4	4.40	15	7	0	2	47	58	28	23	17	35	.307	R	R	6-5	195	7-17-84	2004	Shawnee, Okla.
Walker, Edwin	4	2	5.57	15	9	0	0	52	61	39	32	21	47	.303	R	L	6-3	190	10-26-83	2002	San Antonio, Texas
Wilson, David	1	1	6.00	3	3	0	0	15	8	1	0	5	13	.163	L	L	6-3	195	5-22-82	2004	Mesa, Ariz.

PITCHING	W	L	ERA	G	GS	CG	SV	IP	H	R	ER	BB	SO	AVG	B	T	HT	WT	DOB	1st Yr	Resides
Wooley, Robert	3	3	3.52	17	5	0	2	64	69	31	25	18	48	.278	R	R	6-1	190	12-7-84	2003	Kokomo, Ind.

ARIZONA LEAGUE

BATTING	AVG	G	AB	R	H	2B	3B	HR	RBI	BB	SO	SB	CS	SLG	OBP	B	T	HT	WT	DOB	1st Yr	Resides
Angulo, Oscar	.277	26	83	10	23	2	1	1	11	2	13	6	4	.361	.307	R	R	5-11	165	2-1-84	2004	Barquisimeto, Venez.
Arias, Francis	.174	14	23	7	4	1	0	0	1	4	8	2	0	.217	.345	R	R	6-0	170	6-11-84	2004	Santo Domingo, D.R.
Ayala, Angel	.255	31	106	10	27	9	0	0	13	9	31	2	3	.340	.310	L	R	6-2	208	7-24-86	2004	Vega Baja, P.R.
Blanc, Jhonathan	.263	37	114	8	30	3	0	4	14	5	35	5	5	.395	.300	R	R	6-3	180	3-22-85	2004	Santo Domingo, D.R.
Chapman, Stephen	.229	49	192	33	44	7	7	4	18	17	50	4	3	.401	.290	L	L	6-0	180	10-12-85	2004	Marianna, Fla.
Corredor, Nestor	.276	28	76	3	21	7	1	1	7	3	11	0	1	.434	.304	R	R	5-10	230	5-25-84	2002	Portuguesa, Venez.
De la Cruz, Fredy	.270	48	178	22	48	15	3	0	23	13	44	4	2	.388	.325	R	R	6-2	180	10-17-85	2004	Galvan, D.R.
De la Rosa, Anderson	.197	24	61	5	12	3	1	0	3	2	21	3	1	.279	.222	R	R	6-0	166	8-1-84	2004	Barquisimeto, Venez.
Gallardo, Carlos	.291	41	134	18	39	7	1	0	14	12	19	1	1	.358	.377	R	R	6-0	200	3-31-83	2004	Mission, Texas
Iribarren, Hernan	.439	46	189	40	83	6	9	4	36	19	23	15	7	.630	.490	L	R	6-1	160	6-29-84	2002	Barquisimeto, Venez.
Krynzel, Dave	.500	5	16	8	8	1	1	0	0	3	2	2	0	.688	.600	L	L	6-1	180	11-7-81	2000	Henderson, Nev.
Leclercq, Lenny	.253	45	162	24	41	6	1	1	8	19	61	9	4	.321	.341	R	R	6-2	180	9-7-85	2003	West Terre Haute, Ind.
Lopez, Yonnata	.333	4	9	0	3	1	0	0	1	0	3	0	0	.444	.333	L	R	6-2	170	3-2-85	2003	Valencia, Venez.
Opdyke, Bryan	.175	40	114	16	20	3	1	0	9	25	39	5	5	.219	.345	L	R	6-2	190	8-7-84	2003	Tucson, Ariz.
Parejo, Freddy	.275	55	222	31	61	15	3	3	40	12	25	12	7	.410	.320	R	R	6-2	170	10-16-84	2003	La Guaira, Venez.
Rivera, Joel	.176	27	68	12	12	1	2	0	4	15	26	2	2	.250	.337	R	R	6-1	169	10-19-85	2004	Hoboken, N.J.
Salome, Angel	.235	20	81	7	19	7	0	0	8	4	14	2	0	.321	.271	R	R	5-7	190	6-8-86	2004	Wadsworth Terrace, N.Y.
Tua, Franklin	.192	15	26	2	5	0	0	0	3	1	8	1	0	.192	.222	R	R	6-2	170	11-6-84	2004	Cobudare, Venez.
Vicioso, Osvaldo	.189	30	95	14	18	4	2	0	6	10	35	4	3	.274	.267	S	R	6-2	171	11-12-86	2003	Santo Domingo, D.R.

GAMES BY POSITION: C—Corredor 28, Lopez 2, Opdyke 26, Salome 12, Tua 2. **1B**—Arias 1, Ayala 18. Chapman 1, Gallardo 39, Opdyke 3, Tua 9. **2B**—Angulo 2, Arias 3, Iribarren 46, Tua 1, Vicioso 8. **3B**—Angulo 2, De La Cruz 46, Parejo 1, Vicioso 8. **SS**—Leclercq 45, Vicioso 14. **OF**—Blanc 33. Chapman 48, De La Cruz 1, Delarosa 21, Krynzel 4, Opdyke 1, Parejo 54, Rivera 26, Salome 1.

PITCHING	W	L	ERA	G	GS	CG	SV	IP	H	R	ER	BB	SO	AVG	B	T	HT	WT	DOB	1st Yr	Resides
Angulo, Oscar	0	0	0.00	2	0	0	0	3	4	0	0	4	3	.000	R	R	5-11	165	2-1-84	2004	Barquisimeto, Venez.
Arias, Victor	2	0	2.53	8	2	0	0	21	13	13	6	15	15	.178	R	R	6-4	180	1-1-84	2004	San Cristobal, D.R.
Bernal, Luis	0	1	5.89	10	2	0	0	18	20	14	12	8	12	.277	R	R	6-1	195	1-24-83	2004	Bisbee, Ariz.
Breshears, Richard	1	2	4.55	12	1	0	1	30	28	17	15	10	28	.259	R	R	6-4	190	8-12-83	2004	Midwest City, Okla.
Bruso, Greg	1	0	1.13	2	1	0	0	8	3	1	1	1	6	.115	R	R	6-3	190	5-5-80	2002	South Lake Tahoe, Calif.
Diggins, Ben	0	0	0.00	4	4	0	0	6	6	2	0	5	4	.272	R	R	6-7	230	6-13-79	2000	Tucson, Ariz.
Fermin, Jorge	0	1	6.11	13	1	0	0	28	35	30	19	18	15	.284	R	R	6-3	175	9-23-85	2004	Santiago, D.R.
Gallardo, Yovani	0	0	0.47	6	6	0	0	19	14	3	1	4	23	.202	R	R	6-2	190	2-27-86	2004	Fort Worth, Texas
Garcia, Miguel	4	2	3.38	8	2	0	0	27	23	12	10	10	20	.232	R	R	6-2	160	6-29-85	2001	Barinas, Venez.
Garner, Jeff	2	2	1.80	8	0	0	0	15	13	4	3	3	9	.240	R	R	6-2	200	4-23-80	2004	Freeland, Mich.
Hawk, Tommy	0	1	5.40	2	0	0	0	5	6	4	3	0	2	.333	R	R	6-3	210	2-7-85	2003	Lompoc, Calif.
Johnson, David	0	1	10.03	5	3	0	0	12	24	15	13	4	8	.444	R	R	6-5	210	8-25-82	2004	Manhattan Beach, Calif.
Labasta, William	2	0	10.33	13	1	0	0	27	42	35	31	15	18	.368	R	R	6-3	175	9-7-85	2004	Santo Domingo, D.R.
Laureano, Wilfrido	0	1	3.34	14	2	0	1	35	33	23	13	17	26	.242	L	L	6-6	170	3-4-84	2001	El Seybo, D.R.
Lluveres, Rafael	2	4	2.80	12	8	0	0	45	35	20	14	26	39	.214	L	L	6-4	150	9-21-84	2002	Haina, D.R.
Malave, Ronny	2	2	4.24	15	0	0	4	23	26	14	11	10	16	.288	R	R	6-1	181	1-1-86	2003	Aragua, Venez.
Montes, Oscar	2	5	5.27	13	7	0	0	43	39	28	25	26	50	.250	R	R	6-3	220	2-10-85	2003	Pembroke Pines, Fla.
Morrison, Tyler	2	2	3.41	15	0	0	3	34	35	18	13	16	27	.271	R	R	6-0	200	5-1-85	2003	Glendora, Calif.
Mosquea, Dany	4	0	4.34	13	3	0	0	37	41	23	18	28	31	.294	R	R	6-2	180	4-8-85	2002	Villa Mella, D.R.
Needham, Joel	1	1	1.17	5	0	0	1	8	8	2	1	4	4	.258	R	R	6-3	220	8-16-81	2004	Huntington Beach, Calif.
Parillo, Brandon	1	2	1.52	9	7	0	0	24	12	8	4	9	25	.139	L	L	5-10	185	9-22-85	2004	Huntington Beach, Calif.
Rogers, Mark	0	3	4.73	9	6	0	0	27	30	21	14	14	35	.294	R	R	6-2	205	1-30-86	2004	Orr's Island, Maine

ORGANIZATION STATISTICS

BY JOHN MILLEA

The Twins have routinely been a team of change. Thanks to a limited payroll and a regular stable of youngsters who have earned a shot at the big leagues, Minnesota general manager Terry Ryan has never shied away from shaking up the roster.

The results are proof positive that Ryan knows what he is doing. The Twins won the American League Central title for the third consecutive year in 2004, then lost to the Yankees in the first round of the playoffs for the second year in a row.

If there is a theme to this franchise, it is this: good enough to win, not good enough to go all the way. The 2004 season left the Twins with regrets about their power hitting and about the bottom end of their rotation, and concerns about what their roster will look like in 2005.

The single biggest highlight of 2004 was the performance of lefthander Johan Santana, who went on a second-half surge for the second consecutive year. In 2003 Santana joined the rotation in July and went 11-2, 2.86 after that to finish at 12-3, 3.07. In 2004, his first full year as a starter, the 25-year-old Venezuelan began slowly after offseason elbow surgery. But after the all-star break, Santana was the best pitcher in the game. He went 13-0, 1.21 in 15 starts after the break and was the A.L. pitcher of the month in July, August and September. He finished with a 20-6 record and led the league in ERA (2.61) and strikeouts (265).

The groundwork for the 2004 Twins was laid in offseason moves. The trade of all-star catcher A.J. Pierzynski to San Francisco brought in Joe Nathan, who was brilliant in his first season as a closer. He was named an all-star, converting 44 of 47 save opportunities. During one par-

Johan Santana

Jason Kubel

PLAYERS of the YEAR

MAJOR LEAGUE: Johan Santana, lhp

Santana had one of the better second halves in baseball history. The lefthander went 13-0, 1.21 in 15 starts after the all-star break to lead the Twins to their third straight AL Central title. On the season, Santana led the American League in ERA (2.61) and strikeouts (265) and placed second in wins (20).

MINOR LEAGUE: Jason Kubel, of

Kubel demonstrated outstanding strike zone judgment and hitting ability in 2004. He was leading the Double-A Eastern League with a .377 batting average when he was called up to Triple-A Rochester, where he hit .343-15-71. Kubel earned a September callup and playing time in the postseason.

ticularly strong run, he did not give up a run in 28 straight outings.

Another big move came at the July 31 trading deadline, when first baseman Doug Mientkiewicz and his .246 batting average were shipped to Boston. That opened the door for another minor league star, Justin Morneau. The third-round pick from the 1999 draft had proven everything he could down on the farm, and he did not disappoint after getting the call to the big club. Morneau took over at first base, where he wasn't as talented defensively as Mientkiewicz, but he hit .271-19-58 in 280 at-bats.

Morneau's emergence helped relieve some of the concern about power hitting, but problems remained. Behind Santana and Brad Radke (11-8, 3.48), who both had 34 starts, the rest of the rotation had more downs than ups. While Santana and Radke combined for a 31-14 record, Carlos Silva, Kyle Lohse and Terry Mullholland posted a combined 28-30 total mark.

In the minor leagues, success along individual lines continued but none of the Twins six farm clubs made the playoffs. Triple-A Rochester finished 73-71 and was the only club to finish above .500.

The biggest minor league star was outfielder Jason Kubel, who led the Eastern League (at the time of his promotion to Triple-A) and International League in hitting before earning a September callup. Righthander Scott Baker marked himself as a possible big leaguer in 2005, getting all-star notice in both the Florida State and Eastern leagues before ending the season in Triple-A.

ORGANIZATION LEADERS

BATTING
*AVG	Jason Kubel, Rochester/New Britain	.352
R	Jason Kubel, Rochester/New Britain	96
H	Jason Kubel, Rochester/New Britain	172
TB	Garrett Jones, New Britain/Fort Myers	291
2B	Kevin West, Rochester/New Britain	43
3B	Doug Deeds, Fort Myers	12
	Scott Whitrock, Quad Cities	12
HR	Garrett Jones, New Britain/Fort Myers	31
RBI	Kevin West, Rochester/New Britain	109
BB	Brock Peterson, Quad Cities	56
	J.R. Taylor, Quad Cities	56
SO	Scott Whitrock, Quad Cities	155
SB	Josh Rabe, Rochester	26
*OBP	Jason Bartlett, Rochester	.415
*SLG	Justin Morneau, Rochester	.615

PITCHING
W	Dave Gassner, Rochester	16
L	Henry Bonilla, Rochester/New Britain	12
	Jeff Randazzo, Fort Myers	12
#ERA	Travis Bowyer, New Britain/Fort Myers	1.29
G	Bobby Korecky, New Britain	55
CG	Scott Baker, Rochester/New Britain/Fort Myers	2
	Matt Yeatman, Fort Myers	2
SV	Bobby Korecky, New Britain	31
IP	Dave Gassner, Rochester	174
BB	Adam Harben, Quad Cities	68
SO	Francisco Liriano, New Britain/Fort Myers	174

*Minimum 250 at-bats #Minimum 75 innings

ORGANIZATION STATISTICS

MINNESOTA TWINS

Manager: Ron Gardenhire.

2004 Record: 92-70, .568 (1st, AL Central).

ORGANIZATION STATISTICS

BATTING	AVG	G	AB	R	H	2B	3B	HR	RBI	BB	SO	SB	CS	OBP	SLG	B	T	HT	WT	DOB	1st Yr	Resides
Bartlett, Jason	.083	8	12	2	1	0	0	0	1	1	1	2	0	.154	.083	R	R	6-0	170	10-30-79	2001	Norman, Okla.
Blanco, Henry	.206	114	315	36	65	19	1	10	37	21	56	0	3	.260	.368	R	R	5-11	225	8-29-71	1990	Guarenas, Venez.
Borders, Pat	.286	19	42	3	12	4	0	0	5	0	10	2	0	.302	.381	R	R	6-2	200	5-14-63	1984	Lake Wales, Fla.
2-team (19 Seattle)	.232	38	95	9	22	6	0	1	10	1	22	3	1	.247	.326							
Bowen, Rob	.111	17	27	1	3	0	0	1	2	4	10	0	0	.226	.222	S	R	6-3	220	2-24-81	1999	Fort Myers, Fla.
Cuddyer, Michael	.263	115	339	49	89	22	1	12	45	37	74	5	5	.339	.440	R	R	6-2	220	3-27-79	1998	Fort Myers, Fla.
Ford, Lew	.299	154	569	89	170	31	4	15	72	67	75	20	2	.381	.446	R	R	6-0	190	8-12-76	1999	Lufkin, Texas
Guzman, Cristian	.274	145	576	84	158	31	4	8	46	30	64	10	5	.309	.384	S	R	6-0	205	3-21-78	1995	Santo Domingo, D.R.
Hunter, Torii	.271	138	520	79	141	37	0	23	81	40	101	21	7	.330	.475	R	R	6-2	210	7-18-75	1993	The Colony, Texas
Jones, Jacque	.254	151	555	69	141	22	1	24	80	40	117	13	10	.315	.427	L	L	5-10	200	4-25-75	1996	San Diego, Calif.
Koskie, Corey	.251	118	422	68	106	24	2	25	71	49	103	9	3	.342	.495	L	R	6-3	220	6-28-73	1994	Fort Myers, Fla.
Kubel, Jason	.300	23	60	10	18	2	0	2	7	6	9	1	1	.358	.433	L	R	5-11	190	5-25-82	2000	Palmdale, Calif.
LeCroy, Matthew	.269	88	264	25	71	14	0	9	39	16	60	0	0	.321	.424	R	R	6-2	230	12-13-75	1998	Belton, S.C.
Mauer, Joe	.308	35	107	18	33	8	1	6	17	11	14	1	0	.369	.570	L	R	6-4	220	4-19-83	2001	Fort Myers, Fla.
Mientkiewicz, Doug	.246	78	284	34	70	18	0	5	25	38	38	2	2	.340	.363	L	R	6-2	200	6-19-74	1995	Estero, Fla.
Morneau, Justin	.271	74	280	39	76	17	0	19	58	28	54	0	0	.340	.536	L	R	6-4	220	5-15-81	1999	Fort Myers, Fla.
Offerman, Jose	.256	77	172	22	44	14	2	2	22	29	31	1	1	.363	.395	S	R	6-0	195	11-11-68	1988	Toluca Lake, Calif.
Ojeda, Augie	.339	30	59	16	20	1	0	2	7	10	3	1	1	.429	.458	S	R	5-8	170	12-20-74	1997	South Gate, Calif.
Prieto, Alex	.250	16	32	4	8	1	0	1	4	3	9	0	1	.306	.375	R	R	5-11	200	6-19-76	1993	Wichita, Kan.
Punto, Nick	.253	38	91	17	23	0	0	2	12	12	19	6	0	.340	.319	R	R	5-9	176	11-8-77	1998	Mission Viejo, Calif.
Restovich, Michael	.255	29	47	9	12	3	0	2	6	4	10	0	0	.314	.447	R	R	6-4	240	1-3-79	1998	Fort Myers, Fla.
Rivas, Luis	.256	109	336	44	86	19	5	10	34	13	53	15	1	.283	.432	R	R	5-11	185	8-30-79	1996	La Guaira, Venez.
Ryan, Michael	.239	36	71	9	17	2	1	0	7	4	16	1	1	.280	.296	L	R	6-0	180	7-6-77	1996	Indiana, Pa.
Stewart, Shannon	.304	92	378	46	115	17	2	11	47	47	44	6	3	.380	.447	R	R	5-11	210	2-25-74	1992	Miami, Fla.
Tiffee, Terry	.273	17	44	7	12	4	0	2	8	3	3	0	0	.333	.500	R	R	6-3	210	4-21-79	2000	North Little Rock, Ark.

PITCHING	W	L	ERA	G	GS	CG	SV	IP	H	R	ER	BB	SO	AVG	B	T	HT	WT	DOB	1st Yr	Resides
Balfour, Grant	4	1	4.35	36	0	0	0	39	35	19	19	21	42	.238	R	R	6-2	190	12-30-77	1997	Sydney, Australia
Beimel, Joe	0	0	43.20	3	0	0	0	2	8	8	8	2	2	.615	L	L	6-3	220	4-19-77	1998	Cranberry Township, Pa.
Crain, Jesse	3	0	2.00	22	0	0	0	27	17	6	6	12	14	.179	R	R	6-0	190	7-5-81	2002	Austin, Texas
Durbin, J.D.	0	1	7.36	4	1	0	0	7	12	6	6	6	6	.387	R	R	6-0	190	2-24-82	2000	Scottsdale, Ariz.
Fultz, Aaron	3	3	5.04	55	0	0	1	50	51	28	28	23	37	.267	L	L	6-0	200	9-4-73	1992	Fayette, Ala.
Greisinger, Seth	2	5	6.18	12	9	0	0	51	68	40	35	15	36	.319	R	R	6-3	180	7-29-75	1997	Falls Church, Va.
Guerrier, Matt	0	1	5.68	9	2	0	0	19	22	13	12	6	11	.293	R	R	6-3	220	8-2-78	1999	Birmingham, Ala.
Lohse, Kyle	9	13	5.34	35	34	1	0	194	240	128	115	76	111	.305	R	R	6-2	200	10-4-78	1997	Fort Myers, Fla.
Mulholland, Terry	5	9	5.18	39	15	0	0	123	163	76	71	33	60	.327	R	L	6-3	220	3-9-63	1984	Scottsdale, Ariz.
Nathan, Joe	1	2	1.62	73	0	0	44	72	48	14	13	23	89	.187	R	R	6-4	205	11-22-74	1995	Chandler, Ariz.
Pulido, Carlos	0	0	8.74	6	0	0	0	11	16	13	11	4	9	.333	L	L	6-0	180	8-5-71	1989	Caracas, Venez.
Radke, Brad	11	8	3.48	34	34	1	0	220	229	92	85	26	143	.267	R	R	6-2	185	10-27-72	1991	Largo, Fla.
Rincon, Juan	11	6	2.63	77	0	0	2	82	52	27	24	32	106	.181	R	R	5-11	200	1-23-79	1997	Maracaibo, Venez.
Roa, Joe	2	3	4.50	48	0	0	0	70	84	38	35	24	47	.297	R	R	6-2	200	10-11-71	1989	Royal Oak, Mich.
Romero, J.C.	7	4	3.51	74	0	0	1	74	61	32	29	38	69	.224	S	L	5-11	200	6-4-76	1997	San Juan, P.R.
Santana, Johan	20	6	2.61	34	34	1	0	228	156	70	66	54	265	.192	L	L	6-0	205	3-13-79	1996	Tovar, Venez.
Silva, Carlos	14	8	4.21	33	33	1	0	203	255	100	95	35	76	.310	R	R	6-4	240	4-23-79	1996	Bolivar, Venez.
Thomas, Brad	0	0	16.88	3	0	0	0	3	7	5	5	1	0	.500	L	L	6-4	220	10-12-77	1996	Sydney, Australia

FIELDING

Catcher	PCT	G	PO	A	E	DP	PB
Blanco	.991	114	685	45	7	7	5
Borders	.968	19	82	9	3	3	0
Bowen	.985	15	65	1	1	1	0
LeCroy	.967	26	114	4	4	0	1
Mauer	.991	32	212	10	2	0	0

First Base	PCT	G	PO	A	E	DP
Cuddyer	1.000	10	34	2	0	3
LeCroy	.994	23	172	3	1	17
Mientkiewicz	.994	77	661	37	4	61
Morneau	.995	61	523	41	3	54
Offerman	.983	7	52	6	1	11
Tiffee	1.000	1	2	0	0	0

Second Base	PCT	G	PO	A	E	DP
Bartlett	1.000	1	0	1	0	0
Cuddyer	.982	48	54	113	3	17
Offerman	.750	3	3	3	2	1
Ojeda	.969	20	19	43	2	8
Prieto	1.000	8	10	21	0	6
Punto	.982	19	20	34	1	10
Rivas	.994	109	176	317	3	75

Third Base	PCT	G	PO	A	E	DP
Cuddyer	.923	43	33	51	7	6
Koskie	.963	115	79	207	11	14
Ojeda	1.000	4	1	6	0	1
Prieto	1.000	5	1	3	0	0
Punto	.000	2	0	0	0	0
Tiffee	.966	12	11	17	1	0

Shortstop	PCT	G	PO	A	E	DP
Bartlett	.889	5	5	11	2	3

	PCT	G	PO	A	E	DP
Guzman	.983	145	234	440	12	103
Ojeda	1.000	7	8	14	0	4
Prieto	1.000	3	4	4	0	2
Punto	1.000	11	16	33	0	9

Outfield	PCT	G	PO	A	E	DP
Cuddyer	1.000	15	16	0	0	0
Ford	.986	126	268	7	4	0
Hunter	.988	126	311	5	4	0
Kubel	1.000	10	14	1	0	1
Jones	.994	142	318	5	2	1
Punto	1.000	2	2	1	0	0
Restovich	1.000	19	20	0	0	0
Ryan	.947	15	18	0	1	0
Stewart	.972	71	103	2	3	0

Director, Minor Leagues: Jim Rantz.

Class	Farm Team	League	W	L	Pct.	Finish*	Manager	Affiliate Since
AAA	Rochester (N.Y.) Red Wings	International	73	71	.507	t-5th (14)	Phil Roof	2003
AA	New Britain (Conn.) Rock Cats	Eastern	70	70	.500	6th (12)	Stan Cliburn	1995
High A	Fort Myers (Fla.) Miracle	Florida State	61	74	.452	9th (12)	Jose Marzan	1993
Low A	#Swing of the Quad Cities (Davenport, Iowa)	Midwest	68	68	.500	10th (14)	Kevin Boles	1999
Rookie	Elizabethton (Tenn.) Twins	Appalachian	38	29	.567	4th (10)	Ray Smith	1974
Rookie	Fort Myers (Fla.) Twins	Gulf Coast	31	26	.544	5th (12)	Riccardo Ingram	1989

*Finish in overall standings (No. of teams in league)/Playoff teams in **boldface**   #Affiliate will operate in Beloit (Midwest) in 2005

ROCHESTER RED WINGS   Class AAA

INTERNATIONAL LEAGUE

BATTING	AVG	G	AB	R	H	2B	3B	HR	RBI	BB	SO	SB	CS	OBP	SLG	B	T	HT	WT	DOB	1st Yr	Resides
Bartlett, Jason	.331	67	269	54	89	15	7	3	29	33	37	7	3	.415	.472	R	R	6-0	170	10-30-79	2001	Norman, Okla.
Corporan, Elvis	.467	5	15	4	7	0	0	1	1	1	4	0	0	.500	.667	S	R	6-3	200	6-9-80	1999	Catano, P.R.
Diaz, Juan	.270	39	137	23	37	5	0	11	24	14	43	0	0	.346	.547	R	R	6-2	260	2-19-74	1996	Santo Domingo, D.R.
Dunwoody, Todd	.305	85	308	42	94	25	3	9	50	11	60	8	2	.335	.494	L	L	6-1	210	4-11-75	1993	West Lafayette, Ind.
2-team (22 Buffalo)	.281	107	374	53	105	27	3	13	57	16	75	8	3	.317	.473							
Ford, Lew	.200	1	5	0	1	0	0	0	0	0	1	0	0	.200	.200	R	R	6-0	190	8-12-76	1999	Lufkin, Texas
Heintz, Chris	.279	86	294	33	82	14	0	8	45	16	40	0	2	.318	.408	R	R	6-1	200	8-6-74	1996	Clearwater, Fla.
Kubel, Jason	.343	90	350	71	120	28	0	16	71	34	40	16	3	.398	.560	L	R	5-11	190	5-25-82	2000	Palmdale, Calif.
Marsters, Brandon	.209	60	187	24	39	14	0	3	18	12	51	1	1	.267	.332	R	R	5-11	210	3-14-75	1996	Fort Myers, Fla.
Mauer, Joe	.316	5	19	1	6	3	0	0	2	1	4	0	0	.333	.474	L	R	6-4	220	4-19-83	2001	Fort Myers, Fla.
Maza, Luis	.258	8	31	6	8	2	1	0	1	1	3	1	0	.324	.387	R	R	5-9	180	6-22-80	1998	Cumana, Venez.
Morneau, Justin	.306	72	288	51	88	23	0	22	63	32	47	1	1	.377	.615	L	R	6-4	230	5-15-81	1999	Fort Myers, Fla.
Ojeda, Augie	.242	90	331	49	80	19	0	2	21	39	33	7	5	.331	.317	S	R	5-8	170	12-20-74	1997	South Gate, Calif.
Owens, Ryan	.218	42	101	13	22	5	2	1	14	22	33	1	1	.362	.337	R	R	6-2	200	3-18-78	1999	Anaheim Hills, Calif.
Prieto, Alex	.249	84	289	39	72	13	0	6	22	29	52	2	3	.316	.356	R	R	5-11	200	6-19-76	1993	Wichita, Kan.
Rabe, Josh	.263	122	429	54	113	27	0	7	45	40	76	26	5	.333	.375	R	R	6-2	210	10-15-78	2000	Mendon, Ill.
Restovich, Michael	.247	106	425	65	105	20	3	20	63	25	104	4	3	.291	.449	R	R	6-4	240	1-3-79	1998	Fort Myers, Fla.
Rivas, Luis	.214	3	14	2	3	0	0	0	1	0	2	1	0	.267	.214	R	R	5-11	185	8-30-79	1996	La Guaira, Venez.
Rodriguez, Luis	.286	127	486	73	139	33	1	5	52	53	49	3	3	.353	.389	S	R	5-9	180	6-27-80	1997	Cojedes, Venez.
Ryan, Michael	.211	50	175	29	37	7	1	6	16	16	38	3	4	.281	.366	L	R	6-0	180	7-6-77	1996	Indiana, Pa.
Scanlon, Matt	.192	29	73	4	14	0	0	1	6	12	12	1	1	.314	.233	L	R	5-11	180	6-19-78	1999	Richfield, Minn.
Simmons, Brian	.224	82	299	33	67	12	0	9	37	17	64	3	2	.270	.355	S	R	6-2	190	9-4-73	1995	McMurray, Pa.
Stewart, Shannon	.333	3	9	3	3	1	0	0	1	2	0	0	0	.400	.444	R	R	5-11	210	2-25-74	1992	Miami, Fla.
Tiffee, Terry	.307	82	316	42	97	26	3	12	68	21	26	0	0	.357	.522	S	R	6-3	210	4-21-79	2000	North Little Rock, Ark.
Torres, Gabby	.226	10	31	1	7	4	0	0	3	0	6	0	0	.250	.355	R	R	5-10	200	3-22-78	1996	Acarigua, Venez.
West, Kevin	.278	20	79	10	22	8	0	4	22	4	19	0	0	.306	.532	R	R	6-2	200	1-1-80	1999	Redwood Valley, Calif.

PITCHING	W	L	ERA	G	GS	CG	SV	IP	H	R	ER	BB	SO	AVG	B	T	HT	WT	DOB	1st Yr	Resides
Baker, Scott	1	3	4.97	9	9	0	0	54	65	31	30	15	36	.295	R	R	6-4	190	9-19-81	2003	Shreveport, La.
Beimel, Joe	2	4	6.97	49	1	0	2	62	83	54	48	24	44	.322	L	L	6-3	220	4-19-77	1998	Cranberry Township, Pa.
Bonilla, Henry	1	2	3.24	3	2	0	0	17	16	8	6	2	11	.254	R	R	6-0	190	8-16-78	2000	Reno, Nev.
Bonser, Boof	1	0	1.29	1	1	0	0	7	5	1	1	1	7	.192	R	R	6-4	230	10-14-81	2000	Pinellas Park, Fla.
Crain, Jesse	3	2	2.49	41	0	0	19	51	38	20	14	17	64	.208	R	R	6-1	200	7-5-81	2002	Austin, Texas
Durbin, J.D.	3	2	4.54	7	7	0	0	36	49	27	18	16	38	.329	R	R	6-0	190	2-24-82	2000	Scottsdale, Ariz.
Erdos, Todd	0	0	0.00	4	0	0	0	3	1	0	0	1	3	.111	R	R	6-1	200	11-21-73	1992	Meadville, Pa.
Eyre, Willie	6	7	3.64	36	21	1	4	136	131	60	55	53	91	.255	R	R	6-2	200	7-21-78	1999	Taylorsville, Utah
Fultz, Aaron	0	0	0.00	7	0	0	0	8	6	1	0	5	5	.194	L	L	6-0	200	9-4-73	1992	Fayette, Ala.
Gassner, Dave	16	8	3.41	28	28	0	0	174	175	72	66	30	93	.262	R	L	6-2	190	12-14-78	2000	Hortonville, Wis.
Glover, Gary	0	1	8.44	5	4	0	0	16	27	15	15	5	8	.386	R	R	6-5	205	12-3-76	1994	Deland, Fla.
Greisinger, Seth	5	5	4.96	13	13	0	0	74	94	44	41	19	44	.319	R	R	6-3	190	7-29-75	1997	Falls Church, Va.
Guerrier, Matt	5	10	3.19	24	23	0	0	144	135	65	51	25	97	.248	R	R	6-3	180	8-2-78	1999	Birmingham, Ala.
Helling, Rick	1	0	0.00	1	1	0	0	7	4	0	0	1	2	.167	R	R	6-3	241	12-15-70	1992	Southlake, Texas
Hodge, James	3	6	3.41	49	1	0	4	74	78	34	28	9	63	.279	R	R	5-11	180	10-28-76	1998	Bryan, Texas
Johnson, Adam	5	4	6.07	38	6	0	1	83	100	59	56	30	86	.300	R	R	6-2	210	7-12-79	2000	Fort Myers, Fla.
Kemp, Beau	6	3	3.54	36	0	0	4	48	46	23	19	19	35	.266	R	R	6-0	190	10-31-80	2000	Tulsa, Okla.
Marsters, Brandon	0	0	0.00	1	0	0	0	1	1	0	0	0	0	.500	R	R	5-11	210	3-14-75	1996	Fort Myers, Fla.
Mills, Ryan	1	0	6.10	15	0	0	1	21	25	14	14	13	16	.313	R	L	6-5	190	7-21-77	1998	Scottsdale, Ariz.
Moreno, Victor	1	0	6.35	6	0	0	0	11	12	10	8	6	12	.273	R	R	6-0	180	6-10-79	1998	Puerto Cabello, Venez.
Munro, Pete	6	3	3.88	10	10	0	0	51	51	30	22	11	34	.258	R	R	6-3	210	6-14-75	1994	Little Neck, N.Y.
Palki, Jeromy	2	0	4.44	42	1	0	3	73	74	40	36	37	74	.257	R	R	6-0	200	4-14-76	1995	Oakland, Ore.
Pulido, Carlos	1	3	11.72	5	5	0	0	18	29	24	23	7	12	.367	L	L	6-0	180	8-5-71	1989	Caracas, Venez.
Romero, J.C.	0	0	2.25	3	3	0	0	8	4	2	2	5	11	.143	S	L	5-11	200	6-4-76	1997	San Juan, P.R.
Schoening, Brent	4	8	4.56	44	8	0	1	95	103	51	48	37	80	.278	R	R	6-1	180	4-7-78	1999	Houston, Texas

FIELDING

Catcher	PCT	G	PO	A	E	DP	PB
Corporan	1.000	1	1	0	0	0	0
Heintz	.993	85	543	34	4	0	10
Marsters	.998	59	389	30	1	4	1
Mauer	1.000	2	8	1	0	0	0
Torres	1.000	9	61	6	0	1	1

First Base	PCT	G	PO	A	E	DP
Diaz	1.000	1	6	0	0	0

	PCT	G	PO	A	E	DP
Dunwoody	.979	47	339	37	8	35
Morneau	.994	68	565	63	4	60
Owens	.965	10	74	8	3	5
Prieto	.993	15	139	13	1	20
Tiffee	.982	8	51	4	1	5

Second Base	PCT	G	PO	A	E	DP
Bartlett	1.000	1	1	8	0	1
Maza	.972	8	19	16	1	5

	PCT	G	PO	A	E	DP
Ojeda	1.000	9	18	26	0	5
Owens	1.000	3	2	2	0	0
Prieto	.982	11	29	27	1	8
Rivas	1.000	3	5	13	0	2
Rodriguez	.979	112	222	279	11	77

Third Base	PCT	G	PO	A	E	DP
Heintz	.750	2	2	1	1	0
Ojeda	.950	10	5	14	1	1

	PCT	G	PO	A	E	DP
Owens	.867	16	11	28	6	2
Prieto	.920	45	23	69	8	9
Rodriguez	1.000	8	3	12	0	2
Scanlon	.714	6	1	4	2	1
Tiffee	.930	67	53	119	13	12
Shortstop	**PCT**	**G**	**PO**	**A**	**E**	**DP**
Bartlett	.944	65	107	216	19	42

	PCT	G	PO	A	E	DP
Ojeda	.978	64	93	180	6	45
Prieto	.985	16	29	37	1	12
Rodriguez	1.000	2	3	8	0	1
Outfield	**PCT**	**G**	**PO**	**A**	**E**	**DP**
Dunwoody	1.000	30	60	2	0	1
Ford	1.000	1	5	0	0	0
Kubel	.990	86	190	10	2	3

	PCT	G	PO	A	E	DP
Owens	1.000	1	3	0	0	0
Rabe	.989	104	173	4	2	0
Restovich	.975	98	189	6	5	3
Ryan	.987	38	77	1	1	0
Scanlon	1.000	8	9	0	0	0
Simmons	.995	80	195	7	1	0
West	1.000	2	4	0	0	0

NEW BRITAIN ROCK CATS — Class AA

EASTERN LEAGUE

BATTING	AVG	G	AB	R	H	2B	3B	HR	RBI	BB	SO	SB	CS	OBP	SLG	B	T	HT	WT	DOB	1st Yr	Resides
Bowen, Rob	.197	77	249	28	49	10	0	9	24	31	76	3	0	.292	.345	S	R	6-3	220	2-24-81	1999	Fort Myers, Fla.
Corporan, Elvis	.176	6	17	0	3	0	0	0	2	2	8	0	0	.250	.176	S	R	6-3	200	6-9-80	1999	Catano, P.R.
Davidson, Seth	.235	94	272	50	64	16	7	0	8	12	32	7	4	.280	.346	R	R	6-0	180	2-26-79	2001	San Diego, Calif.
Garbe, B.J.	.201	114	374	42	75	20	0	3	35	39	69	12	8	.283	.278	R	R	6-2	190	2-3-81	1999	Moses Lake, Wash.
Jones, Garrett	.311	122	450	68	140	33	2	30	92	28	98	11	4	.356	.593	L	L	6-4	220	6-21-81	1999	Tinley Park, Ill.
Kennedy, Bryan	.251	67	203	17	51	4	0	6	24	15	30	2	0	.308	.360	L	R	6-2	210	10-4-78	2001	Riverside, Calif.
Kubel, Jason	.377	37	138	25	52	14	4	6	29	19	19	0	2	.453	.667	L	R	5-11	190	5-25-82	2000	Palmdale, Calif.
Kuhaulua, Kaulana	.136	7	22	1	3	1	0	0	0	0	8	0	0	.136	.182	R	R	6-0	160	1-30-80	2001	Waianae, Hawaii
Mauer, Jake	.258	101	283	29	73	11	2	0	31	24	25	3	0	.325	.311	R	R	6-2	180	12-20-78	2001	St. Paul, Minn.
Maza, Luis	.311	126	492	64	153	26	8	12	66	28	70	5	6	.365	.470	R	R	5-9	180	6-22-80	1998	Cumana, Venez.
Munoz, Billy	.246	36	138	25	34	5	0	8	27	10	40	0	0	.293	.457	L	L	6-2	220	6-30-75	1998	Mesa, Ariz.
Owens, Ryan	.204	63	206	24	42	12	0	8	31	23	43	4	0	.282	.379	R	R	6-2	200	3-18-78	1999	Anaheim Hills, Calif.
Scanlon, Matt	.230	74	248	29	57	7	2	5	33	22	65	0	1	.297	.335	L	R	5-11	180	6-19-78	1999	Richfield, Minn.
Tomlin, James	.216	139	490	58	106	18	1	1	34	23	75	13	9	.253	.263	R	R	6-1	170	8-12-82	2000	Los Angeles, Calif.
Torres, Gabby	.266	54	173	14	46	12	0	3	18	9	22	0	0	.328	.387	R	R	5-10	200	3-22-78	1996	Acarigua, Venez.
Watkins, Tommy	.267	116	397	64	106	21	1	8	47	45	77	20	9	.346	.385	R	R	5-8	200	6-18-80	1998	Fort Myers, Fla.
West, Kevin	.293	119	434	68	127	35	1	25	87	41	98	2	3	.359	.551	R	R	6-2	210	1-1-80	1999	Redwood Valley, Calif.

PITCHING	W	L	ERA	G	GS	CG	SV	IP	H	R	ER	BB	SO	AVG	B	T	HT	WT	DOB	1st Yr	Resides
Abbott, Jim	3	6	5.06	21	17	0	0	94	101	54	53	31	38	.277	R	R	6-3	190	10-12-79	2000	Caledonia, Mich.
Baker, Scott	5	3	2.43	10	10	0	0	70	44	23	19	13	72	.173	R	R	6-4	190	9-19-81	2003	Shreveport, La.
Bonilla, Henry	11	10	4.54	25	22	1	0	143	180	75	72	36	67	.319	R	R	6-0	190	8-16-78	2000	Reno, Nev.
Bonser, Boof	12	9	4.37	27	27	0	0	154	160	89	75	56	146	.266	R	R	6-4	230	10-14-81	2000	Pinellas Park, Fla.
Bowyer, Travis	6	3	1.76	31	0	0	3	61	42	17	12	38	65	.196	R	R	6-3	220	8-3-81	1999	Big Island, Va.
Cameron, Kevin	1	3	1.94	26	0	0	3	46	47	20	10	21	47	.260	R	R	6-1	180	12-15-79	2001	Joliet, Ill.
Corona, Ronnie	0	1	10.13	3	3	0	0	11	20	13	12	5	7	.400	R	R	6-0	180	1-27-79	2000	Apple Valley, Calif.
Durbin, J.D.	4	1	2.52	13	13	0	0	64	62	21	18	22	53	.251	R	R	6-0	190	2-24-82	2000	Scottsdale, Ariz.
Gutierrez, Jannio	0	1	6.61	10	0	0	0	16	16	12	12	12	18	.267	R	R	5-10	200	5-3-82	2001	Maracaibo, Venez.
Helling, Rick	1	2	4.94	5	5	0	0	31	30	18	17	11	21	.252	R	R	6-3	241	12-15-70	1992	Southlake, Texas
Kemp, Beau	3	3	2.73	18	0	0	3	30	27	10	9	12	24	.260	R	R	6-0	190	10-31-80	2000	Tulsa, Okla.
Korecky, Bobby	3	4	3.36	55	0	0	31	67	52	29	25	20	57	.212	R	R	5-11	180	9-16-79	2002	Saline, Mich.
Liriano, Francisco	3	2	3.18	7	7	0	0	40	45	14	14	17	49	.276	L	L	6-2	185	10-26-83	2001	San Cristobal, D.R.
Lohse, Erik	1	1	5.04	7	4	0	0	25	29	18	14	11	13	.293	R	R	6-0	200	6-5-80	2001	Glenn, Calif.
Miller, Colby	3	7	5.83	14	14	0	0	79	87	55	51	31	38	.286	R	R	6-2	190	3-19-82	2000	Weatherford, Okla.
Miller, Jason	0	2	4.28	33	1	0	2	40	33	19	19	21	42	.219	L	L	6-1	200	7-20-82	2000	Sarasota, Fla.
Moreno, Victor	7	2	2.27	33	5	0	2	75	56	20	19	42	86	.207	R	R	6-10	200	6-10-79	1998	Puerto Cabello, Venez.
Neshek, Pat	2	1	3.82	26	0	0	2	35	34	15	15	18	38	.252	S	R	6-2	200	9-4-80	2002	Brooklyn Park, Minn.
Pridie, Jon	3	6	5.44	36	7	0	1	93	100	57	56	40	81	.283	R	R	6-3	220	12-7-79	1998	Prescott, Ariz.
Richardson, Jason	1	2	5.79	11	5	0	0	28	33	21	18	19	19	.303	R	R	6-2	200	6-11-80	1999	Lakeland, Fla.
Wolfe, Brian	1	1	8.18	7	0	0	0	11	16	10	10	3	6	.348	R	R	6-2	200	11-29-80	1999	Fullerton, Calif.

FIELDING

Catcher	PCT	G	PO	A	E	DP	PB
Bowen	.985	66	484	32	8	3	7
Corporan	1.000	4	20	5	0	0	1
Kennedy	.990	51	289	22	3	3	8
Torres	1.000	31	222	12	0	3	4

First Base	PCT	G	PO	A	E	DP
Jones	.983	121	875	127	17	90
Mauer	1.000	1	1	1	0	0
Munoz	1.000	19	152	26	0	16

Second Base	PCT	G	PO	A	E	DP
Davidson	.989	23	31	56	1	9

	PCT	G	PO	A	E	DP
Maza	.989	124	214	330	6	67

Third Base	PCT	G	PO	A	E	DP
Mauer	.943	91	61	105	10	15
Maza	1.000	1	1	3	0	0
Owens	.951	34	26	52	4	4
Scanlon	1.000	4	7	5	0	0
Watkins	.956	20	12	31	2	0

Shortstop	PCT	G	PO	A	E	DP
Davidson	.969	51	92	129	7	35
Kuhaulua	1.000	7	9	12	0	4

	PCT	G	PO	A	E	DP
Mauer	.920	7	7	16	2	5
Scanlon	1.000	1	1	4	0	0
Watkins	.957	79	118	196	14	46

Outfield	PCT	G	PO	A	E	DP
Garbe	.981	120	256	7	5	1
Kubel	.961	36	70	4	3	0
Owens	.927	25	38	0	3	0
Scanlon	.947	43	68	4	4	0
Tomlin	.991	138	312	11	3	2
Watkins	.933	15	25	3	2	1
West	1.000	71	103	9	0	1

FORT MYERS MIRACLE — High Class A

FLORIDA STATE LEAGUE

BATTING	AVG	G	AB	R	H	2B	3B	HR	RBI	BB	SO	SB	CS	OBP	SLG	B	T	HT	WT	DOB	1st Yr	Resides
Burgos, Omar	.208	31	101	8	21	7	0	0	6	8	30	1	2	.292	.277	R	R	6-2	210	11-11-82		Maturin, Venez.
Corporan, Elvis	.209	41	148	17	31	9	0	1	17	15	26	0	0	.282	.291	S	R	6-3	200	6-9-80	1999	Catano, P.R.
Deeds, Doug	.294	123	436	71	128	28	12	5	57	43	86	11	3	.363	.447	L	L	6-2	180	6-2-81	2002	Columbus, Ohio
Geiger, Kyle	.197	29	76	3	15	1	0	0	7	7	14	0	0	.259	.211	R	R	6-3	230	5-8-82	2003	Greenwood, Ind.
Gomon, Dusty	.200	2	5	1	1	0	0	0	4	0	0			.200	.200	R	R	6-4	220	9-3-82	2001	Jacksonville, Fla.
Guzman, Garrett	.269	78	275	35	74	10	5	4	31	22	42	3	2	.321	.385	L	L	5-10	170	2-7-83	2001	Henderson, Nev.
Jones, Garrett	.242	19	66	6	16	5	0	1	6	4	19	2	0	.286	.364	L	L	6-4	220	6-21-81	1999	Tinley Park, Ill.
Kennedy, Bryan	.167	2	6	0	1	0	0	0	0	0	3	0	0	.167	.167	L	R	6-2	210	10-4-78	2001	Riverside, Calif.
Kuhaulua, Kaulana	.235	98	340	42	80	15	2	5	43	16	85	12	6	.279	.335	R	R	6-0	160	1-30-80	2001	Waianae, Hawaii
Matienzo, Danny	.305	123	455	51	139	27	1	5	65	43	88	1	0	.366	.402	R	R	5-11	190	9-3-80	2002	Miami, Fla.
Mauer, Joe	.667	2	6	0	4	0	0	0	2	2	2	0	0	.750	.667	L	R	6-4	220	4-19-83	2001	Fort Myers, Fla.
Merchan, Jesus	.287	79	247	23	71	10	2	0	21	14	18	5	1	.336	.344	R	R	5-11	180	3-26-81	2000	Maracay Venez.

BATTING

BATTING	AVG	G	AB	R	H	2B	3B	HR	RBI	BB	SO	SB	CS	OBP	SLG	B	T	HT	WT	DOB	1st Yr	Resides
Molina, Felix	.240	103	321	49	77	22	4	3	39	37	63	7	5	.321	.361	S	R	5-8	170	5-5-83	2001	Mayaguez, P.R.
Morales, Jose	.287	91	331	30	95	13	4	4	46	29	77	0	1	.340	.387	S	R	5-11	180	2-20-83	2001	San Juan, P.R.
Oeltjen, Trent	.278	90	324	45	90	8	5	2	28	18	61	25	8	.337	.352	L	L	6-1	180	2-28-83	2001	Sydney, Australia
Pattee, Ben	.230	48	148	16	34	3	1	0	17	18	21	0	1	.317	.264	R	R	6-0	185	9-24-81	2003	Ukiah, Calif.
Perodin, Ron	.265	100	328	43	87	2	2	0	20	20	47	24	7	.315	.284	L	L	5-9	170	10-13-80	2002	Los Angeles, Calif.
Romero, Alex	.292	104	380	59	111	21	2	6	42	54	47	6	4	.387	.405	S	R	6-0	170	9-9-83	2001	Maracaibo, Venez.
Sandoval, Michael	.179	49	156	16	28	7	1	6	21	19	30	0	1	.284	.353	R	R	5-10	200	7-8-81	1998	Puerto Cabello, Venez.
Tamburrino, Brett	.270	77	248	28	67	8	1	0	18	28	48	13	6	.349	.310	S	R	5-11	190	11-10-81	1999	Sunbury, Australia
Tintor, Eli	.176	7	17	1	3	0	0	0	1	2	3	1	0	.333	.176	R	R	6-2	195	12-24-84	2003	Hibbing, Minn.

PITCHING	W	L	ERA	G	GS	CG	SV	IP	H	R	ER	BB	SO	AVG	B	T	HT	WT	DOB	1st Yr	Resides
Baker, Scott	4	2	2.40	7	7	0	0	45	40	13	12	6	37	.233	R	R	6-4	190	9-19-81	2003	Shreveport, La.
Barrett, Ricky	5	1	3.52	17	4	0	0	38	29	20	15	25	41	.216	L	L	5-11	180	3-9-81	2002	West Sacramento, Calif.
Blackburn, Nick	3	6	6.27	9	7	0	0	37	51	30	26	7	21	.327	R	R	6-4	210	2-24-82	2002	Norman, Okla.
Bowyer, Travis	3	0	0.30	17	0	0	2	30	18	6	1	17	32	.182	R	R	6-3	220	8-3-81	1999	Big Island, Va.
Cameron, Kevin	2	3	3.13	22	0	0	1	32	23	13	11	13	22	.197	R	R	6-1	180	12-15-79	2003	Joliet, Ill.
Contreras, J.C.	0	0	6.00	3	0	0	0	3	7	3	2	0	1	.583	L	L	6-0	150	4-24-82	1999	Caracas, Venez.
Fisher, Pete	0	1	4.50	2	0	0	0	2	2	1	1	0	1	.250	R	R	6-3	220	7-7-77	1998	Stoneham, Mass.
Gray, Josh	2	10	5.77	33	12	0	0	87	103	64	56	40	56	.293	L	L	6-4	195	11-20-80	2003	Orange, Texas
Gutierrez, Jannio	3	2	2.18	25	0	0	3	41	38	15	10	19	48	.233	R	R	5-10	200	5-3-82	2001	Maracaibo, Venez.
Hill, Josh	0	1	2.70	3	0	0	0	7	5	2	2	9	5	.238	R	R	6-3	210	3-27-83	2001	Warilla, Australia
Hines, Matthew	0	0	11.25	3	0	0	0	4	7	5	5	3	2	.412	R	R	6-7	220	5-13-81	2002	Coal City, Ill.
Liriano, Francisco	6	7	4.00	21	21	0	0	117	118	56	52	43	125	.263	L	L	6-2	185	10-26-83	2001	San Cristobal, D.R.
Lohse, Erik	3	4	3.52	33	0	0	0	54	50	30	21	15	46	.249	R	R	6-0	200	6-5-80	2001	Glenn, Calif.
Miller, Jason	1	0	1.53	19	0	0	1	29	16	5	5	11	40	.158	L	L	6-1	200	7-20-82	2000	Sarasota, Fla.
Moseley, Marcus	3	1	5.70	28	7	0	2	66	71	55	42	44	38	.275	R	R	6-3	230	8-12-80	1998	Hohenwald, Tenn.
Neshek, Pat	0	1	2.95	16	0	0	10	18	16	7	6	2	19	.222	S	R	6-2	200	9-4-80	2002	Brooklyn Park, Minn.
Olson, Justin	7	7	2.88	45	6	0	8	78	60	34	25	46	85	.221	R	R	6-3	215	4-5-80	2003	Oak Park, Ill.
Randazzo, Jeff	5	12	4.93	27	26	0	0	133	153	96	73	61	79	.285	R	L	6-7	200	8-12-81	2000	Broomall, Pa.
Speigner, Levale	4	3	1.75	22	1	0	2	46	46	15	9	14	49	.251	R	R	5-11	170	9-24-80	2003	Thomasville, Ga.
Tejada, Manny	5	4	3.52	22	14	0	0	95	91	44	37	25	63	.251	R	R	6-3	210	4-16-82	1999	Center Point, Iowa
Thomas, John	2	5	3.55	34	7	1	0	66	69	34	26	25	69	.268	L	L	6-2	190	7-24-81	2001	Orcutt, Calif.
Yeatman, Matt	3	7	4.30	23	23	2	0	111	106	72	53	48	88	.254	R	R	6-4	200	8-2-82	2001	Tomball, Texas

FIELDING

Catcher	PCT	G	PO	A	E	DP	PB
Corporan	.989	31	165	12	2	0	11
Geiger	.970	27	149	12	5	1	6
Kennedy	1.000	2	16	0	0	0	1
Matienzo	1.000	2	7	1	0	0	0
Mauer	1.000	1	7	0	0	0	0
Morales	.976	81	587	59	16	6	10
Tintor	1.000	6	47	3	0	0	2

First Base	PCT	G	PO	A	E	DP
Corporan	1.000	5	34	0	0	4
Gomon	1.000	1	6	1	0	0
Jones	.995	19	161	20	1	16
Matienzo	.987	102	756	64	11	73
Sandoval	1.000	1	3	0	0	0

	1.000	16	96	11	0	9
Tamburrino	1.000	16	96	11	0	9

Second Base	PCT	G	PO	A	E	DP
Kuhaulua	.920	12	17	29	4	6
Merchan	.977	39	70	97	4	23
Molina	.962	74	132	172	12	47
Pattee	.974	10	16	22	1	2
Tamburrino	.943	12	21	29	3	5

Third Base	PCT	G	PO	A	E	DP
Burgos	.935	30	19	53	5	5
Corporan	.900	8	3	15	2	1
Merchan	1.000	2	0	2	0	0
Pattee	.908	35	19	60	8	8
Sandoval	.923	37	20	52	6	3
Tamburrino	.928	30	9	55	5	0

Shortstop	PCT	G	PO	A	E	DP
Kuhaulua	.953	82	106	236	17	56
Merchan	.959	30	57	82	6	20
Molina	.898	26	32	65	11	12

Outfield	PCT	G	PO	A	E	DP
Deeds	.982	93	153	9	3	2
Guzman	.980	54	87	12	2	3
Oeltjen	.994	83	163	1	1	1
Pattee	.750	1	3	0	1	0
Perodin	.977	90	163	4	4	0
Romero	.989	83	183	4	2	2
Sandoval	1.000	2	2	0	0	0
Tamburrino	1.000	18	26	1	0	0

SWING OF THE QUAD CITIES

Low Class A

MIDWEST LEAGUE

BATTING	AVG	G	AB	R	H	2B	3B	HR	RBI	BB	SO	SB	CS	OBP	SLG	B	T	HT	WT	DOB	1st Yr	Resides
Arneson, Justin	.250	63	216	32	54	10	5	3	19	21	64	9	4	.332	.384	R	R	5-11	170	12-27-81	2002	Fergus Falls, Minn.
Burgos, Omar	.206	94	330	32	68	11	2	1	26	33	76	5	4	.288	.261	R	R	6-2	210	11-11-82	2000	Maturin, Venez.
Garcia, Alex	.245	90	322	36	79	6	3	1	27	14	60	11	7	.294	.292	S	R	6-0	150	1-16-82	2002	Nizao, D.R.
Geiger, Kyle	.291	53	189	22	55	8	2	2	25	15	43	0	0	.349	.386	R	R	6-3	230	5-8-82	2003	Greenwood, Ind.
Gomon, Dusty	.182	79	291	29	53	15	0	6	29	11	74	0	1	.224	.296	R	R	6-4	210	9-3-82	2001	Jacksonville, Fla.
Johnson, Josh	.144	48	146	10	21	5	0	0	11	6	30	0	1	.191	.178	R	R	5-11	205	11-3-82	2001	Ridgway, Pa.
Moses, Matt	.223	29	112	16	25	7	0	3	14	12	25	0	0	.304	.366	L	R	6-1	210	2-20-85	2003	Richmond, Va.
Pattee, Ben	.259	36	143	9	37	7	0	2	15	5	20	2	1	.280	.350	R	R	6-0	185	9-24-81	2003	Ukiah, Calif.
Peterson, Brock	.256	124	454	66	116	21	0	7	65	56	104	5	4	.344	.348	R	R	6-3	215	11-20-83	2003	Chehalis, Wash.
Phillips, Kyle	.228	97	347	49	79	10	0	11	44	38	69	1	0	.304	.369	L	R	6-2	205	4-3-84	2002	El Cajon, Calif.
Punto, Nick	.438	4	16	4	7	1	0	1	6	2	2	1	0	.500	.688	S	R	5-9	176	11-8-77	1998	Mission Viejo, Calif.
Rutgers, Paul	.202	77	248	26	50	7	2	0	16	36	66	7	1	.310	.246	R	R	5-10	190	1-17-84	2002	Melbourne, Australia
Span, Denard	.267	64	240	29	64	4	3	0	14	34	49	15	8	.363	.308	L	L	6-1	180	2-27-84	2003	Tampa, Fla.
Spataro, Ryan	.241	83	261	41	63	9	3	0	21	30	59	13	7	.323	.299	L	R	5-10	180	9-1-82	2001	Barrie, Ontario
Taylor, J.R.	.265	108	411	58	109	29	4	4	57	56	65	21	5	.357	.384	S	R	5-7	165	11-6-82	2001	San Leandro, Calif.
Tyler, John	.333	2	6	1	2	0	0	0	2	0	1	1	0	.500	.333	R	R	6-5	240	8-20-82	2001	Downingtown, Pa.
Whitrock, Scott	.254	124	449	59	114	19	12	13	61	38	155	17	9	.321	.437	R	R	6-0	205	12-18-80	2001	Wisconsin Rapids, Wis.
Zamojc, Mark	.239	96	335	45	80	15	7	1	46	25	75	10	3	.295	.334	L	R	6-2	195	12-21-81	2004	Burlington, Ontario

PITCHING	W	L	ERA	G	GS	CG	SV	IP	H	R	ER	BB	SO	AVG	B	T	HT	WT	DOB	1st Yr	Resides
Barrett, Ricky	2	1	2.77	13	12	0	0	62	48	25	19	30	59	.211	L	L	5-11	180	3-9-81	2002	West Sacramento, Calif.
Blackburn, Nick	6	4	2.77	20	13	1	1	84	69	37	26	23	66	.220	R	R	6-4	210	2-24-82	2002	Norman, Okla.
Brandon, Eric	3	9	3.67	45	0	0	7	61	70	27	25	21	55	.283	R	R	6-1	220	2-18-81	2003	Nashville, Tenn.
Crawford, Tristan	3	3	2.79	21	0	0	2	48	37	16	15	9	43	.216	R	R	6-2	200	7-22-82	2000	Browns Plains, Australia
Culpepper, Kevin	2	4	5.53	35	0	0	4	55	64	40	34	22	44	.294	L	L	6-5	190	6-28-82	2003	Toccoa, Ga.
DePaula, Julio	12	7	3.05	49	0	0	9	91	81	37	31	39	88	.238	R	R	6-0	178	12-31-82	2000	Santo Domingo, D.R.
Garcia, Angel	2	1	4.50	7	2	0	0	16	13	8	8	5	16	.220	R	R	6-7	220	10-28-83	2001	Dorado, P.R.
Harben, Adam	9	7	3.09	26	26	0	0	143	114	60	49	68	171	.218	R	R	6-5	205	8-19-83	2002	Maumelle, Ark.
Hines, Matthew	0	0	6.00	7	0	0	0	9	12	6	6	8	5	.316	R	R	6-7	220	5-13-81	2002	Coal City, Ill.

PITCHING

PITCHING	W	L	ERA	G	GS	CG	SV	IP	H	R	ER	BB	SO	AVG	B	T	HT	WT	DOB	1st Yr	Resides
Jones, Justin	0	2	5.31	7	4	0	0	20	20	17	12	14	17	.256	L	L	6-4	195	9-25-84	2002	Virginia Beach, Va.
2-team (14 Lansing)	3	5	4.15	21	18	0	0	85	82	50	39	36	76	.255							
Mauer, Billy	0	3	4.19	23	2	0	0	34	34	22	16	18	21	.254	R	R	6-4	200	5-6-80	2003	St. Paul, Minn.
Meek, Evan	0	0	11.12	3	3	0	0	6	7	7	7	15	3	.350	R	R	6-0	207	5-12-83	2003	Bothell, Wash.
Perkins, Glen	2	1	1.30	9	9	0	0	48	33	9	7	12	49	.192	L	L	6-0	190	3-2-83	2004	Lakeland, Minn.
Prunty, T.J.	0	0	5.93	10	2	0	0	14	14	9	9	7	9	.264	R	R	6-3	210	7-5-81	2002	Inver Grove Heights, Minn.
Sawatski, Jay	0	1	1.37	15	0	0	0	26	14	6	4	10	29	.156	R	L	6-2	195	5-7-82	2004	Little Rock, Ark.
Schutt, Chris	7	9	4.03	29	24	0	0	143	133	75	64	62	104	.245	R	R	6-1	215	2-8-82	2003	Park Ridge, Ill.
Simonitsch, Errol	6	2	2.56	20	20	0	0	109	100	41	31	36	107	.244	L	L	6-4	225	8-24-82	2003	Glendale, Calif.
Speigner, Levale	2	2	2.84	22	0	0	0	32	27	14	10	15	29	.225	R	R	5-11	170	9-24-80	2003	Thomasville, Ga.
Tautor, Peter	2	6	5.43	42	0	0	1	56	64	44	34	28	54	.301	R	R	6-5	240	6-26-81	2003	Wantina South, Australia
Tyler, Scott	7	4	2.60	22	19	0	0	104	73	33	30	64	132	.201	R	R	6-2	190	8-20-82	2001	Downingtown, Pa.
Uhl, Jon	3	2	5.52	17	0	0	1	29	34	21	18	17	22	.288	R	R	6-2	190	10-6-80	2003	Tampa, Fla.

FIELDING

Catcher

Catcher	PCT	G	PO	A	E	DP	PB
Geiger	.993	43	362	35	3	1	6
Johnson	.990	44	284	28	3	3	5
Phillips	.989	59	471	51	6	2	6

First Base

First Base	PCT	G	PO	A	E	DP
Gomon	.983	50	390	23	7	28
Johnson	1.000	1	2	1	0	1
Peterson	.994	74	579	45	4	44
Phillips	1.000	1	5	0	0	1
Zamojc	.985	15	124	5	2	12

Second Base

Second Base	PCT	G	PO	A	E	DP
Garcia	.948	53	79	142	12	29
Pattee	.965	17	30	53	3	11
Punto	1.000	1	2	3	0	1
Rutgers	.956	60	104	157	12	20
Taylor	.938	6	12	18	2	5

Third Base

Third Base	PCT	G	PO	A	E	DP
Burgos	.892	93	55	151	25	12
Moses	.824	13	12	16	6	1
Pattee	.960	14	12	12	1	1
Peterson	.778	7	2	5	2	0
Punto	1.000	1	0	1	0	0
Rutgers	.750	8	2	7	3	0
Taylor	.500	1	0	1	1	0

Shortstop

Shortstop	PCT	G	PO	A	E	DP
Garcia	.908	31	37	82	12	16
Pattee	1.000	1	2	8	0	2
Punto	1.000	2	6	4	0	1
Taylor	.935	101	151	269	29	55
Tyler	1.000	2	5	6	0	2

Outfield

Outfield	PCT	G	PO	A	E	DP
Arneson	.955	60	101	4	5	1
Johnson	1.000	2	2	0	0	0
Pattee	1.000	3	7	1	0	0
Peterson	.833	3	5	0	1	0
Rutgers	.944	8	16	1	1	0
Span	.992	64	123	2	1	1
Spataro	.948	81	141	6	8	2
Whitrock	.961	124	254	17	11	4
Zamojc	.956	73	127	4	6	0

ELIZABETHTON TWINS

Rookie

APPALACHIAN LEAGUE

BATTING

BATTING	AVG	G	AB	R	H	2B	3B	HR	RBI	BB	SO	SB	CS	OBP	SLG	B	T	HT	WT	DOB	1st Yr	Resides
Anderson, Heath	.095	15	42	2	4	0	0	0	1	6	21	0	0	.204	.095	R	R	6-4	190	4-29-84	2003	Panama City, Fla.
Burns, Deacon	.314	63	255	49	80	20	4	12	49	18	53	9	2	.368	.565	L	L	5-8	185	10-28-82	2004	Brownwood, Texas
Burt, Landon	.287	43	164	25	47	10	1	1	15	20	17	8	2	.362	.366	L	L	5-10	180	8-16-82	2004	Bermuda Dunes, Calif.
Hughes, Luke	.284	44	141	20	40	8	1	3	19	9	30	1	3	.338	.418	R	R	5-11	191	8-2-84	2003	Morley, Australia
Lahey, Tim	.202	26	84	7	17	2	0	3	11	13	38	0	0	.317	.333	R	R	6-4	235	2-7-82	2004	Worcester, Mass.
Lopez, Javier	.244	46	160	17	39	10	1	4	15	6	49	4	2	.276	.394	R	R	6-2	190	10-19-83	2002	Juana Diaz, P.R.
Ortiz, Patrick	.268	19	56	9	15	2	0	2	10	15	3	2		.379	.304	S	R	5-11	165	7-30-85	2003	Maunabo, P.R.
Patterson, Terrence	.224	43	170	27	38	4	3	7	16	4	37	7	2	.250	.406	R	R	5-8	170	6-12-84	2002	Bartow, Fla.
Pickrel, Jeremy	.266	49	177	28	47	10	2	4	27	27	61	5	4	.357	.412	L	R	6-4	225	4-3-83	2004	Henderson, Ill.
Plouffe, Trevor	.283	60	237	29	67	7	2	4	28	19	34	3	1	.340	.380	R	R	6-1	175	6-15-86	2004	Northridge, Calif.
Sanchez, Javi	.271	43	144	19	39	8	2	2	17	16	20	0	0	.364	.396	R	R	6-2	205	11-8-81	2004	Miami, Fla.
Tolbert, Matt	.308	33	104	23	32	7	2	3	18	12	13	3	2	.376	.500	B	R	6-0	180	5-4-82	2004	Woodville, Miss.
Winfree, David	.286	59	217	31	62	8	0	8	37	18	51	1	1	.349	.433	R	R	6-3	215	8-5-85	2003	Virginia Beach, Va.
Woodard, Johnny	.309	57	194	37	60	8	4	8	35	24	56	5	2	.386	.515	L	R	6-4	208	9-15-84	2003	Fairfield, Calif.
Yaconetti, Jay	.224	34	107	17	24	7	0	4	19	5	41	1	0	.265	.402	R	R	6-2	210	2-17-82	2004	Gilbert, Ariz.

GAMES BY POSITION: C—Anderson 10, Lahey 22, Lankford 6, Sanchez 38. **1B**—Winfree 13, Woodard 56. **2B**—Hughes 40, Tolbert 28. **3B**—Hughes 1, Winfree 42, Yaconetti 28. **SS**—Ortiz 18, Plouffe 52. **OF**—Burns 40, Burt 42, Lopez 43, Patterson 39, Pickrel 46.

PITCHING

PITCHING	W	L	ERA	G	GS	CG	SV	IP	H	R	ER	BB	SO	AVG	B	T	HT	WT	DOB	1st Yr	Resides
Aselton, Kyle	1	4	4.54	15	4	0	1	38	30	21	19	19	38	.224	R	L	6-5	215	2-28-83	2004	Corvallis, Calif.
Bowlin, Jason	1	3	3.25	23	0	0	3	28	26	13	10	8	27	.243	R	R	6-0	185	8-4-82	2003	Fairfield, Ohio
Culpepper, Kevin	0	3	5.29	9	0	0	0	17	18	12	10	7	20	.261	L	L	6-5	190	6-28-82	2003	Toccoa, Ga.
Duguay, Steven	4	4	3.36	12	11	0	0	56	55	28	21	11	70	.256	R	R	6-1	200	10-29-82	2003	Fleetwood, N.C.
Fox, Matthew	2	1	5.40	8	5	0	0	27	27	18	16	8	32	.257	R	R	6-3	192	12-4-82	2004	Parkland, Fla.
Lankford, Kris	0	0	12.60	5	0	0	0	5	7	7	7	2	6	.304	S	R	6-3	195	7-15-82	2003	Altus, Okla.
Marini, Chris	4	2	2.91	11	8	0	0	53	55	24	17	8	52	.263	L	L	6-1	190	2-11-83	2003	Glendale, Ariz.
Martinez, Javier	1	0	5.34	12	2	0	0	29	23	18	17	22	25	.225	L	L	5-11	160	6-13-84	2002	Maracaibo, Venez.
Martinez, J.P.	3	2	3.86	20	1	0	1	40	39	25	17	16	47	.248	R	R	6-2	205	6-8-82	2004	Metairie, La.
Mata, Frank	2	2	3.73	26	1	0	13	31	22	15	13	6	39	.193	R	R	6-2	205	3-11-84	2002	Anzoategui, Venez.
Medina, Dennis	2	1	4.42	13	4	0	0	39	50	21	19	10	38	.309	R	R	6-3	190	1-17-83	2001	Cabimas, Venez.
Meek, Evan	1	2	8.44	11	0	0	0	21	18	26	20	23	21	.231	R	R	6-0	207	5-12-83	2003	Bothell, Wash.
Mousser, Jeff	2	0	4.63	18	0	0	1	23	25	12	12	11	24	.278	R	R	6-2	215	9-10-81	2004	Tempe, Ariz.
Perkins, Glen	1	0	2.25	3	3	0	0	12	8	3	3	4	22	.195	L	L	6-0	190	3-2-83	2004	Lakeland, Minn.
Sawatski, Jay	1	0	2.35	4	0	0	0	8	6	3	2	2	9	.207	R	L	6-2	195	5-7-82	2004	Little Rock, Ark.
Shinske, David	7	3	4.19	11	11	0	0	54	59	31	25	17	28	.282	R	R	6-3	206	10-2-85	2003	Eindhoven, Netherlands
Smit, Alexander	1	1	2.54	6	5	0	0	28	25	9	8	10	43	.243	L	L	6-3	206	10-27-85	2004	Knoxville, Tenn.
Waldrop, Kyle	2	0	3.24	4	4	0	0	25	10	9	3		25	.221	R	R	6-5	205	10-27-85	2004	Knoxville, Tenn.
Williams, John	3	1	5.40	14	5	0	0	38	46	27	23	14	50	.288	R	L	6-2	200	12-19-81	2004	Murfreesboro, Tenn.

GCL TWINS

Rookie

GULF COAST LEAGUE

BATTING

BATTING	AVG	G	AB	R	H	2B	3B	HR	RBI	BB	SO	SB	CS	SLG	OBP	B	T	HT	WT	DOB	1st Yr	Resides
Abellera, Joe	.174	15	46	6	8	0	0	0	4	3	11	1	0	.174	.250	R	R	6-4	200	8-2-85	2004	Minnetonka, Minn.
Arratia, Jilmer	.320	49	175	16	56	9	2	2	29	10	25	12	1	.429	.365	R	R	5-11	170	6-28-84	2002	Maiquetia, Venez.
Bartlett, Jason	.357	5	14	1	5	1	0	0	1	0	3	0	0	.429	.400	R	R	6-0	170	10-30-79	2001	Norman, Okla.
Blancarte, Dante	.234	36	111	10	26	3	0	0	15	23	17	1	0	.261	.370	L	L	6-0	220	5-12-82	2004	South Berwick, Maine

ORGANIZATION STATISTICS

BATTING	AVG	G	AB	R	H	2B	3B	HR	RBI	BB	SO	SB	CS	SLG	OBP	B	T	HT	WT	DOB	1st Yr	Resides
Brown, Chris	.259	38	139	19	36	5	1	2	19	8	28	1	1	.353	.297	R	R	6-2	215	12-28-82	2004	Largo, Fla.
Contreras, J.C.	.000	3	3	0	0	0	0	0	0	0	1	0	0	.000	.000	L	L	6-0	150	4-24-82	1998	Caracas, Venez.
Dangler, Andy	.276	19	58	3	16	5	1	0	7	9	13	1	0	.397	.382	R	R	6-4	230	2-1-81	2004	Chambersburg, Pa.
Feiner, Korey	.170	22	53	7	9	3	0	0	4	8	7	2	0	.226	.318	R	R	5-10	210	9-25-81	2004	Sun Prairie, Minn.
Fletcher, Simon	.207	22	58	11	12	1	0	1	3	7	24	6	0	.276	.324	R	R	6-1	210	6-16-85	2003	Sydney, Australia
Jones, Larry	.171	30	82	10	14	0	0	1	6	6	31	4	1	.207	.244	R	R	6-1	210	9-19-84	2003	Stockton, Ala.
Kalin, Travis	.244	27	86	10	21	5	0	1	11	8	18	1	0	.337	.309	R	R	6-3	180	7-30-84	2003	Lake Mary, Fla.
Lysaught, Michael	.186	28	70	5	13	2	1	0	7	11	18	1	2	.243	.293	R	R	5-11	170	9-30-85	2003	Sydney, Australia
McIlvaine, Tim	.231	14	26	4	6	0	0	0	6	7	0	0	0	.231	.375	R	R	6-3	200	4-21-81	2004	Eastchester, N.Y.
Moses, Matt	.250	1	4	0	1	0	0	0	1	0	0	0	0	.250	.250	L	R	6-0	210	2-20-85	2003	Richmond, Va.
Najac, Greg	.258	38	120	31	31	5	2	0	13	10	20	1	0	.333	.318	L	R	6-0	210	4-28-85	2003	Nanuet, N.Y.
Ortiz, Yancarlos	.263	29	95	11	25	3	0	0	7	12	14	6	2	.295	.352	S	R	5-9	140	9-15-84	2003	San Cristobal, D.R.
Ovalle, Edward	.279	45	172	26	48	12	3	2	27	7	36	5	8	.419	.312	R	R	5-11	170	6-15-85	2002	Santo Domingo, D.R.
Portes, Juan	.327	44	168	24	55	8	1	8	31	12	28	4	2	.530	.380	R	R	5-11	170	11-26-85	2004	Malden, Mass.
Robinson, Mark	.215	41	135	11	29	3	1	1	14	5	24	4	3	.274	.259	R	R	6-1	180	4-7-86	2004	Glendora, Calif.
Spann, Denard	.375	5	16	1	6	2	0	0	1	3	3	0	1	.500	.474	S	R	6-0	200	10-9-82	2004	Tampa, Fla.
Tintor, Eli	.228	25	79	14	18	4	0	1	8	3	9	2	1	.316	.274	S	R	6-2	195	12-24-84	2003	Hibbing, Minn.
Valdez, Odannys	.252	46	143	37	36	8	0	0	10	20	25	12	2	.308	.393	S	R	5-10	150	5-9-85	2003	Santo Domingo, D.R.

GAMES BY POSITION: C—Brown 1, Dangler 2, Feiner 22, Hernandez 10, Najac 14, Tintor 22. **1B**—Abellera 1, Blancarte 30, Brown 28, Kalin 1, Tintor 1. **2B**—Arratia 8, Kalin 1, Lysaught 11, Portes 1, Valdez 44. **3B**—Abellera 14, Arratia 10, Kalin 17, Lysaught 3, Portes 17. **SS**—Bartlett 5, Kalin 11, Lysaught 13, Ortiz 27, Portes 13. **OF**—Arratia 34, Fletcher 19, Jones 30, Lysaught 19, Najac 19, Ortiz 1, Ovalle 42, Robinson 40, Tintor 2, Spann 5.

PITCHING	W	L	ERA	G	GS	CG	SV	IP	H	R	ER	BB	SO	AVG	B	T	HT	WT	DOB	1st Yr	Resides
Brown, Jeremy	0	2	11.00	4	1	0	0	9	18	11	11	4	1	.418	R	R	6-3	210	1-3-79	2001	London, Ky.
Bryant, Patrick	2	2	4.26	12	4	0	1	32	31	23	15	13	21	.248	R	R	6-4	190	10-26-85	2004	Gulf Breeze, Fla.
Contreras, J.C.	0	0	0.00	2	0	0	1	4	2	1	0	0	5	.000	L	L	6-0	150	4-24-82	1998	Caracas, Venez.
Fisher, Pete	1	0	4.50	3	0	0	0	4	1	2	2	1	6	.076	R	R	6-3	220	7-7-77	1998	Stoneham, Mass.
Garcia, Angel	0	0	0.00	6	1	0	0	8	6	2	0	3	9	.181	R	R	6-7	210	10-28-83	2001	Dorado, P.R.
Gault, Joe	3	2	5.18	13	3	0	1	33	48	25	19	11	21	.331	R	R	6-5	190	12-24-85	2003	Canyon Country, Calif.
Hebert, Robbie	1	0	1.98	11	1	0	2	14	13	4	3	4	13	.236	R	R	6-3	210	12-12-81	2004	Thibodaux, La.
Hill, Shaggy	0	1	0.90	6	2	0	0	10	9	1	1	6	9	.250	R	R	6-3	210	3-27-83	2001	Warilla, Australia
Lynch, John	1	0	1.64	5	0	0	0	11	8	2	2	1	12	.200	L	L	6-1	190	5-23-81	2002	Rogers, Minn.
Merricks, Alex	0	0	12.21	14	0	0	0	14	14	20	19	26	19	.264	L		5-11	180	12-23-83	2002	Oxnard, Calif.
Mijares, Jose	4	0	2.43	19	0	0	5	30	22	9	8	15	25	.207	L	L	6-0	180	10-29-84	2002	Canacas Distaito, Venez.
Morlan, Eduardo	1	2	2.84	11	2	0	1	25	25	14	8	10	28	.245	R	R	6-2	210	3-1-86	2004	Miami, Fla.
Pineda, Valentin	1	0	4.35	10	0	0	1	10	8	6	5	3	8	.210	R	R	6-4	180	6-4-85	2002	Villa Altagracia, D.R.
Rainville, Jay	3	2	1.83	8	7	0	0	34	39	19	7	3	38	.272	R	R	6-3	230	10-16-85	2004	Pawtucket, R.I4
Rogers, Mike	3	3	4.02	11	7	0	1	47	46	27	21	23	53	.251	L	L	5-10	175	6-11-85	2004	Del City, Okla.
Schoenbachler, Jeff	2	3	3.92	12	7	0	1	39	43	30	17	16	45	.268	L	L	6-1	185	9-13-85	2004	Reno, Nev.
Sosa, Oswaldo	1	2	2.20	8	5	0	0	29	27	13	7	4	30	.238	R	R	6-2	180	9-19-85	2002	Tovar, Venez.
Swarzak, Anthony	5	3	2.63	11	9	0	1	48	46	20	14	6	42	.251	R	R	6-3	195	9-10-85	2004	Fort Lauderdale, Fla.
Thwaites, Luke	0	0	7.27	10	1	0	0	17	31	18	14	5	16	.369	R	R	6-5	200	5-18-85	2003	Queensland, Australia
Vais, Danny	0	2	2.86	16	0	0	0	22	25	14	7	5	15	.280	R	R	6-1	210	11-21-84	2004	Arvada, Colo.
Waldrop, Kyle	3	2	1.42	7	7	0	0	38	32	9	6	4	30	.228	R	R	6-4	190	10-27-85	2004	Knoxville, Tenn.

MONTREAL EXPOS

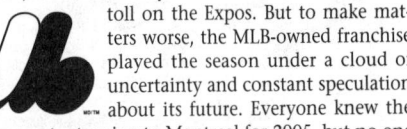

BY AARON FITT

The 2004 season could not have been much more trying for the Montreal Expos.

Splitting their home games between Montreal and San Juan, P.R., for the second year in a row took enough of a toll on the Expos. But to make matters worse, the MLB-owned franchise played the season under a cloud of uncertainty and constant speculation about its future. Everyone knew the team was not returning to Montreal for 2005, but no one was quite sure where the franchise would end up.

It turns out the answer was Washington, D.C., despite the concerns of Orioles owner Peter Angelos that a team based in the nation's capital would severely curtail Baltimore's revenues.

The Expos saw their revenues stunted by dismal attendance figures in 2004, not to anyone's surprise. The franchise's lame-duck status kept some fans away, and others were undoubtedly repelled by the last-place product that Montreal fielded.

The Expos finished 67-95, 29 games out of first place in the National League East. They traded former all-star shortstop Orlando Cabrera to Boston in a July 31 trade deadline deal, months after the offseason trade of ace Javier Vasquez to the Yankees and free agent right fielder Vladimir Guerrero's signing with the Angels.

What remained were young players learning the ropes and a few veterans playing through a difficult situation. Rookie Terrmel Sledge was one of the most pleasant surprises for the Expos in 2004, hitting .269-15-62 in 398 at-bats. Brad Wilkerson and Tony Batista each hit 32 home runs, although neither player hit above .255. Wilkerson did become the first Expo to hit 30 homers, score 100 runs and draw 100 walks in a season. Jose Vidro, who signed a contract extension during the season, put together a solid .294-14-60 campaign before having season-ending knee

Brad Wilkerson   Ryan Church

PLAYERS of the YEAR

MAJOR LEAGUE: Brad Wilkerson, 1b-of
Wilkerson may have been a bargain-priced player at $375,000, but he put up big power numbers in 2004, in the Expos' final season in Montreal. The 27-year-old hit 39 doubles and 32 home runs in mostly a leadoff role, while walking 106 times and scoring 112 runs. He hit hit .255 and drove in 67 runs.

MINOR LEAGUE: Ryan Church, of
Church came with shortstop Maicer Izturis in an offseason trade with the Indians for lefty reliever Scott Stewart. He immediately blossomed, hitting .343-17-78 in 347 at-bats at Triple-A Edmonton before being called up to the big leagues in mid-August.

surgery in August, and Juan Rivera hit .307-12-49.

Veteran righthander Livan Hernandez was one of the few bright spots on the Expos pitching staff. Hernandez was a workhorse, going 11-15, 3.60 with nine complete games and 255 innings. Zach Day (5-10, 3.93) and Tomo Ohka (3-7, 3.40) also pitched well in limited starts. At the back of the staff, Chad Cordero emerged as a solid closer, notching 14 saves and a 2.94 ERA with 83 strikeouts in 83 innings.

Expos manager Frank Robinson said the entire rotation is up for grabs in 2005.

"I don't think anyone after Livan has proven themselves to the point where they have a job, except maybe Ohka," Robinson said. "Then again, with some of these arms, it makes you look forward to next year—but we still need help."

Lefthander Scott Downs posted a 5.14 ERA in 63 major league innings, but he was much better at Triple-A Edmonton. Downs went 10-6, 3.52 for the Trappers and threw a no-hitter against Las Vegas on July 11, on his way to Pacific Coast League pitcher of the year honors. Downs was the first Edmonton lefty to reach the double-digit win plateau since 1992.

The end of 2004 saw a few more changes in the organization, other than the obvious move to Washington. General manager Omar Minaya, who did everything he could for the Expos despite an extremely limited budget, left to become GM of the Mets. And there were some affiliation changes: the Expos replaced their now-defunct Edmonton affiliate with New Orleans, and their Brevard County affiliate was replaced with Potomac (Carolina).

ORGANIZATION LEADERS

BATTING

*AVG	Ryan Church, Edmonton	.346
R	Alejandro Machado, Harrisburg/Brevard County	88
H	Alejandro Machado, Harrisburg/Brevard County	163
TB	Kory Casto, Savannah	229
2B	Kory Casto, Savannah	35
3B	Shawn Norris, Harrisburg/Brevard County	10
HR	Val Pascucci, Edmonton	25
RBI	Val Pascucci, Edmonton	92
BB	Shawn Norris, Harrisburg/Brevard County	84
SO	Shawn Norris, Harrisburg/Brevard County	117
SB	Alejandro Machado, Harrisburg/Brevard County	30
	Jerry Owens, Savannah	30
*OBP	Ryan Church, Edmonton	.430
*SLG	Ryan Church, Edmonton	.622

PITCHING

W	Mike Hinckley, Harrisburg/Brevard County	11
L	Luke Lockwood, Harrisburg	17
#ERA	Danny Rueckel, Edmonton/Harrisburg	2.11
G	Three tied at	49
CG	Wilton Chavez, Edmonton	3
SV	Gus Hlebovy, Vermont	16
IP	Wilton Chavez, Edmonton	164
BB	Devin Perrin, Savannah	62
SO	Mike Hinckley, Harrisburg/Brevard County	131

*Minimum 250 at-bats #Minimum 75 innings

MONTREAL EXPOS

Manager: Frank Robinson.　　　　**2004 Record:** 67-95, .414 (5th, NL East).

BATTING	AVG	G	AB	R	H	2B	3B	HR	RBI	BB	SO	SB	CS	OBP	SLG	B	T	HT	WT	DOB	1st Yr	Resides
Batista, Tony	.241	157	606	76	146	30	2	32	110	26	78	14	6	.272	.455	R	R	6-0	208	12-9-73	1992	Mao Valverde, D.R.
Bergeron, Peter	.214	11	42	2	9	0	0	0	1	2	16	0	1	.250	.214	L	R	6-0	190	11-9-77	1996	St. Petersburg, Fla.
Cabrera, Orlando	.246	103	390	41	96	19	2	4	31	28	31	12	3	.298	.336	R	R	5-9	180	11-2-74	1994	Cartagena, Colombia
Calloway, Ron	.167	46	84	4	14	2	0	1	10	5	22	2	0	.211	.226	L	L	6-1	210	9-4-76	1997	Los Banos, Calif.
Carroll, Jamey	.289	102	218	36	63	14	2	0	16	32	21	5	1	.378	.372	R	R	5-9	175	2-18-74	1996	Evansville, Ind.
Cepicky, Matt	.217	32	60	4	13	4	0	1	3	1	18	1	0	.230	.333	L	R	6-2	225	11-10-77	1999	Sun City Center, Fla.
Chavez, Endy	.277	132	502	65	139	20	6	5	34	30	40	32	7	.318	.371	L	L	5-9	170	2-7-78	1996	Valencia, Venez.
Church, Ryan	.175	30	63	6	11	1	0	1	6	7	16	0	0	.257	.238	L	L	6-1	190	10-14-78	2000	Lompoc, Calif.
Diaz, Einar	.223	55	139	9	31	6	1	1	11	11	10	2	0	.293	.302	R	R	5-10	195	12-28-72	1992	Chesnee, S.C.
Everett, Carl	.252	39	127	8	32	10	0	2	14	8	19	0	0	.319	.378	S	R	6-0	215	6-3-71	1990	Brandon, Fla.
Fox, Andy	.093	34	43	2	4	0	0	1	1	0	16	0	0	.093	.163	L	R	6-4	200	1-12-71	1989	Fair Oaks, Calif.
Gonzalez, Alex	.241	35	133	19	32	7	0	4	16	8	32	1	1	.289	.383	R	R	6-0	200	4-8-73	1991	Coral Gables, Fla.
Harris, Brendan	.160	20	50	4	8	2	0	1	2	2	11	0	0	.208	.260	R	R	6-1	200	8-26-80	2001	Queensbury, N.Y.
2-team (3 Chicago)	.169	23	59	4	10	3	0	1	3	3	12	0	0	.222	.271							
Izturis, Maicer	.206	32	107	10	22	5	2	1	4	10	20	4	0	.286	.318	S	R	5-8	150	9-12-80	1998	Barquisimeto, Venez.
Johnson, Nick	.251	73	251	35	63	16	0	7	33	40	58	6	3	.359	.398	L	L	6-3	195	9-19-78	1996	Sacramento, Calif.
Labandeira, Josh	.000	7	14	0	0	0	0	0	0	0	4	0	0	.000	.000	R	R	5-7	180	2-25-79	2001	Porterville, Calif.
Lopez, Luis	.154	11	26	0	4	0	0	0	0	0	9	0	0	.185	.154	R	R	6-0	205	10-5-73	1995	Brooklyn, N.Y.
Mateo, Henry	.273	40	44	3	12	2	0	0	1	9	2	3	.289	.318	S	R	5-11	180	10-14-76	1995	Santo Domingo, D.R.
Pascucci, Val	.177	32	62	6	11	1	0	2	6	10	22	1	0	.297	.290	R	R	6-6	235	11-17-78	1999	Cerritos, Calif.
Rivera, Juan	.307	134	391	48	120	24	1	12	49	34	45	6	2	.364	.465	R	R	6-2	170	7-3-78	1996	Guarenas, Venez.
Schneider, Brian	.257	135	436	40	112	20	3	12	49	42	63	0	1	.325	.399	L	R	6-0	200	11-26-76	1995	West Palm Beach, Fla.
Sledge, Terrmel	.269	133	398	45	107	20	6	15	62	40	66	3	3	.336	.462	L	L	6-0	180	3-18-77	1999	Granada Hills, Calif.
Vidro, Jose	.294	110	412	51	121	24	0	14	60	49	43	3	1	.367	.454	S	R	5-11	195	8-27-74	1992	Sabana Grande, P.R.
Wilkerson, Brad	.255	160	572	112	146	39	2	32	67	106	152	13	6	.374	.498	L	L	6-0	205	6-1-77	1999	Owensboro, Ky.

PITCHING	W	L	ERA	G	GS	CG	SV	IP	H	R	ER	BB	SO	AVG	B	T	HT	WT	DOB	1st Yr	Resides
Armas, Tony	2	4	4.88	16	16	0	0	72	66	41	39	45	54	.247	R	R	6-3	225	4-29-78	1995	Puerto Piritu, Venez.
Ayala, Luis	6	12	2.69	81	0	0	2	90	92	30	27	15	63	.268	R	R	6-2	170	1-12-78	1997	Los Mochis, Mexico
Beltran, Francis	0	0	7.53	11	0	0	1	14	20	12	12	5	8	.333	R	R	6-5	230	11-29-79	1997	Santo Domingo, D.R.
2-team (34 Chicago)	2	2	5.47	45	0	0	1	49	47	31	30	27	48	.253							
Beltran, Rigo	0	0	13.50	2	0	0	0	1	1	1	1	0	0	.333	L	L	5-11	215	11-13-69	1991	Delray Beach, Fla.
Bentz, Chad	0	3	5.86	36	0	0	0	28	23	19	18	23	18	.228	R	L	6-2	215	5-5-80	2001	Juneau, Alaska
Biddle, Rocky	4	8	6.92	47	9	0	11	78	98	69	60	31	51	.307	R	R	6-3	230	5-21-76	1997	San Dimas, Calif.
Corcoran, Roy	0	0	6.75	5	0	0	0	5	7	4	4	5	4	.304	R	R	5-10	170	5-11-80	2001	Slaughter, La.
Cordero, Chad	7	3	2.94	69	0	0	14	83	68	28	27	43	83	.221	R	R	6-0	190	3-18-82	2003	Chino, Calif.
Day, Zach	5	10	3.93	19	19	1	0	117	117	53	51	45	61	.265	R	R	6-4	210	6-15-78	1996	Cincinnati, Ohio
Downs, Scott	3	6	5.14	12	12	1	0	63	79	47	36	23	38	.310	L	L	6-2	190	3-17-76	1997	Lexington, Ky.
Eischen, Joey	0	1	3.93	21	0	0	0	18	16	10	8	8	17	.232	L	L	6-0	215	5-25-70	1989	Rotonda West, Fla.
Fikac, Jeremy	1	2	5.40	19	0	0	0	25	26	16	15	13	22	.274	R	R	6-2	185	4-8-75	1998	Shiner, Texas
Hernandez, Livan	11	15	3.60	35	35	9	0	255	234	105	102	83	186	.248	R	R	6-2	240	2-20-75	1996	Miami Beach, Fla.
Hill, Shawn	1	2	16.00	3	3	0	0	9	17	16	16	7	10	.415	R	R	6-2	185	4-28-81	2000	Georgetown, Ontario
Horgan, Joe	4	1	3.15	47	0	0	2	40	35	18	14	22	30	.230	L	L	6-1	200	6-7-77	1996	Rancho Cordova, Calif.
Kim, Sun-Woo	4	6	4.58	43	17	0	0	136	145	80	69	55	87	.275	R	R	6-1	185	9-4-77	1998	Seoul, Korea
Majewski, Gary	0	1	3.86	16	0	0	1	21	28	15	9	5	12	.326	R	R	6-2	200	2-26-80	1999	Houston, Texas
Ohka, Tomo	3	7	3.40	15	15	0	0	85	98	40	32	20	38	.288	R	R	6-1	180	3-18-76	1999	Kyoto, Japan
Patterson, John	4	7	5.03	19	19	0	0	98	100	58	55	46	99	.260	R	R	6-5	210	1-30-78	1997	Scottsdale, Ariz.
Rauch, Jon	3	0	1.54	9	2	0	0	23	14	4	4	7	18	.175	R	R	6-11	260	9-27-78	1999	Tucson, Ariz.
Tucker, T.J.	4	2	3.72	54	1	0	0	68	73	28	28	17	44	.275	R	R	6-3	266	8-20-78	1997	New Port Richey, Fla.
Vargas, Claudio	5	5	5.25	45	14	0	0	118	120	75	69	64	89	.266	R	R	6-3	225	6-19-78	1996	Santiago, D.R.

FIELDING

Catcher	PCT	G	PO	A	E	DP	PB
Diaz	.990	44	264	19	3	6	3
Schneider	.998	133	814	59	2	16	4

First Base	PCT	G	PO	A	E	DP
Fox	1.000	1	2	0	0	0
Johnson	.994	73	618	43	4	69
Lopez	1.000	8	53	2	0	5
Pascucci	.933	5	14	0	1	1
Sledge	1.000	10	63	6	0	3
Wilkerson	.995	86	694	67	4	68

Second Base	PCT	G	PO	A	E	DP
Carroll	.995	51	84	97	1	32
Fox	1.000	3	0	5	0	0
Harris	.972	11	15	20	1	3
Izturis	.977	10	18	25	1	6

Labandeira	.000	2	0	0	0	0	
Mateo	.879	9	12	17	4	3	
Vidro	.987	105	176	270	6	71	

Third Base	PCT	G	PO	A	E	DP
Batista	.954	155	82	308	19	35
Carroll	.944	13	8	26	2	1
Diaz	.000	1	0	0	0	0
Fox	1.000	3	1	6	0	0
Harris	.833	4	2	3	1	0

Shortstop	PCT	G	PO	A	E	DP
Cabrera	.984	101	147	290	7	69
Carroll	1.000	10	11	16	0	4
Fox	1.000	5	0	5	0	0
Gonzalez	.960	33	57	88	6	24
Izturis	.937	23	33	71	7	15

Labandeira	.833	3	2	3	1	0

Outfield	PCT	G	PO	A	E	DP
Bergeron	.913	11	21	0	2	0
Calloway	1.000	20	27	0	0	0
Carroll	1.000	2	2	0	0	0
Cepicky	1.000	11	24	0	0	0
Chavez	.984	127	301	9	5	5
Church	1.000	18	35	3	0	0
Everett	.955	33	61	2	3	0
Mateo	1.000	1	1	0	0	0
Pascucci	1.000	17	29	0	0	0
Rivera	.986	121	192	14	3	3
Sledge	.987	114	216	5	3	1
Wilkerson	.982	80	159	8	3	3

Tony Batista: Led Expos with 110 RBIs

Livan Hernandez: League leader with 255 innings pitched

FARM SYSTEM

Director, Player Development: Adam Wogan.

Class	Farm Team	League	W	L	Pct.	Finish*	Manager	Affiliate Since
AAA	#Edmonton (Alberta) Trappers	Pacific Coast	69	74	.483	10th (16)	Dave Huppert	2003
AA	Harrisburg (Pa.) Senators	Eastern	52	90	.366	12th (12)	Dave Machemer	1991
High A	@Brevard County (Fla.) Manatees	Florida State	53	72	.424	10th (12)	Tim Raines	2002
Low A	Savannah (Ga.) Sand Gnats	South Atlantic	58	80	.420	14th (16)	Bob Henley	2003
SS A	Vermont Expos (Burlington)	New York-Penn	34	38	.472	7th (14)	Jose Alguacil	1994
Rookie	Melbourne (Fla.) Expos	Gulf Coast	22	38	.367	11th (12)	Arturo DeFreites	1998

*Finish in overall standings (No. of teams in league)/Playoff teams in **boldface**
#Affiliate will operate in New Orleans (Pacific Coast) in 2005   @Affiliate will operate in Potomac (Carolina) in 2005

EDMONTON TRAPPERS   Class AAA

PACIFIC COAST LEAGUE

BATTING	AVG	G	AB	R	H	2B	3B	HR	RBI	BB	SO	SB	CS	OBP	SLG	B	T	HT	WT	DOB	1st Yr	Resides
Bergeron, Peter	.512	11	41	8	21	4	1	1	5	3	1	2	0	.545	.732	L	R	6-0	190	11-9-77	1996	St. Petersburg, Fla.
Brown, Jason	.143	6	21	0	3	2	0	0	2	0	6	0	0	.143	.238	R	R	6-2	200	5-22-74	1997	Rolling Hills Estates, Calif.
Calloway, Ron	.283	59	223	36	63	17	1	5	46	34	39	13	5	.385	.435	L	L	6-1	210	9-4-76	1997	Los Banos, Calif.
Carroll, Wes	.207	12	29	2	6	1	0	0	1	3	7	1	0	.281	.241	R	R	5-11	180	1-5-79	2001	Evansville, Ind.
Cepicky, Matt	.269	82	312	51	84	15	3	15	67	18	75	2	1	.305	.481	L	R	6-2	225	11-10-77	1999	Sun City Center, Fla.
Chavez, Endy	.344	14	61	9	21	3	2	0	7	7	7	5	2	.406	.459	L	L	5-9	170	2-7-78	1996	Valencia, Venez.
Church, Ryan	.346	98	347	74	120	29	8	17	79	51	62	0	1	.430	.622	R	R	6-1	190	10-14-78	2000	Lompoc, Calif.
2-team (69 Iowa)	.297	104	384	68	114	27	1	17	59	26	61	0	2	.341	.505							
Harris, Brian	.300	100	297	47	89	13	2	3	33	40	50	1	3	.391	.387	S	R	5-10	170	4-28-75	1997	Carmel, Ind.
Hodges, Scott	.212	38	118	12	25	6	0	1	18	11	29	1	0	.279	.288	L	R	6-0	190	12-26-78	1997	Lexington, Ky.
Hoover, Paul	.289	69	194	27	56	14	1	1	20	20	46	4	0	.361	.387	R	R	6-1	210	4-14-76	1997	Steubenville, Ohio
Izturis, Maicer	.338	99	376	65	127	19	2	3	36	57	30	14	12	.428	.423	S	R	5-8	150	9-12-80	1998	Barquisimeto, Venez.
Johnson, Nick	.222	3	9	2	2	1	0	0	0	4	3	0	0	.462	.333	L	L	6-3	195	9-19-78	1996	Sacramento, Calif.
Knorr, Randy	.269	83	286	32	77	16	0	2	37	37	63	0	0	.352	.346	R	R	6-2	215	11-12-68	1986	Tampa, Fla.
Lopez, Luis	.206	23	68	9	14	1	0	1	9	9	11	0	0	.295	.265	R	R	6-0	200	10-5-73	1984	Brooklyn, N.Y.
Mateo, Henry	.303	30	119	23	36	8	3	0	9	8	16	10	1	.354	.420	S	R	5-11	180	10-14-76	1995	Santo Domingo, D.R.
Matos, Julius	.287	49	167	16	48	13	1	2	22	11	21	2	2	.335	.413	R	R	5-11	170	12-17-74	1994	Racine, Wis.
Medrano, Anthony	.309	117	418	60	129	25	2	2	42	41	48	3	4	.373	.392	R	R	5-10	170	12-8-74	1993	Long Beach, Calif.
Ortiz, Luis	.196	22	51	2	10	1	1	0	4	6	5	0	0	.293	.255	R	R	6-0	180	5-25-70	1991	North Richland, Texas
2-team (75 Memphis)	.234	97	214	19	50	6	1	4	25	18	26	0	0	.294	.327							
Pascucci, Val	.298	109	393	83	117	32	1	25	92	78	96	9	2	.422	.575	R	R	6-6	235	11-17-78	1999	Cerritos, Calif.
Short, Rick	.342	40	152	13	52	13	0	2	19	10	7	1	1	.384	.467	R	R	6-0	200	12-6-72	1994	Peoria, Ill.
2-team (89 Omaha)	.301	129	468	43	141	29	0	9	67	25	46	2	2	.341	.421							
Toca, Jorge	.302	55	159	19	48	12	0	4	21	4	31	0	2	.319	.453	R	R	6-3	230	1-7-75	1999	Miami, Fla.
Ware, Jeremy	.250	26	64	5	16	2	0	0	5	5	6	0	0	.310	.281	R	R	6-0	200	10-23-75	1995	Guelph, Ontario
Watson, Brandon	.293	139	526	74	154	17	3	2	41	31	68	22	10	.332	.348	L	R	6-1	170	9-30-81	1999	Inglewood, Calif.
Wilson, John	.256	37	117	10	30	7	0	3	11	10	11	2	0	.318	.393	R	R	6-1	210	9-29-78	2000	Newbury Park, Calif.

PITCHING	W	L	ERA	G	GS	CG	SV	IP	H	R	ER	BB	SO	AVG	B	T	HT	WT	DOB	1st Yr	Resides
Armas, Tony	0	0	1.80	2	2	0	0	10	11	4	2	1	8	.268	R	R	6-3	225	4-29-78	1995	Puerto Piritu, Venez.
Beltran, Francis	0	0	1.50	6	0	0	3	6	4	1	1	2	8	.190	R	R	6-5	230	11-29-79	1997	Santo Domingo, D.R.
2-team (6 Iowa)	0	0	2.19	12	0	0	7	12	9	3	3	3	14	.200							
Beltran, Rigo	3	2	3.64	25	8	0	3	64	65	27	26	17	52	.267	L	L	5-11	215	11-13-69	1991	Delray Beach, Fla.
Bentz, Chad	0	0	3.60	5	0	0	0	5	5	2	2	3	2	.278	R	L	6-2	215	5-5-80	2001	Juneau, Alaska
Borbon, Pedro	0	0	7.00	8	0	0	0	9	14	7	7	3	10	.359	L	L	6-1	230	11-15-67	1988	Houston, Texas
Chavez, Wilton	5	12	4.61	28	27	3	0	164	177	104	84	43	114	.272	R	R	6-2	160	6-13-78	1998	Monte Cristi, D.R.
Chiavacci, Ron	4	6	5.17	25	8	0	0	78	72	48	45	52	72	.247	R	R	6-2	220	9-5-77	1998	Scranton, Pa.
Childers, Jason	0	3	4.50	14	0	0	5	14	15	8	7	9	13	.278	R	R	6-0	160	1-13-75	1997	Douglas, Ga.
Coco, Pasqual	1	0	12.27	4	0	0	0	4	4	5	5	4	2	.286	R	R	6-1	180	9-8-77	1995	Santo Domingo, D.R.
Corcoran, Roy	6	1	3.05	30	0	0	5	44	39	16	15	24	35	.245	R	R	5-10	170	5-11-80	2001	Slaughter, La.
Downs, Scott	10	6	3.52	22	22	2	0	135	143	57	53	26	67	.274	L	L	6-2	190	3-17-76	1997	Lexington, Ky.
Ferrari, Anthony	3	2	5.43	39	0	0	0	65	80	41	39	30	31	.310	L	L	5-9	165	6-22-78	2000	Greenbrae, Calif.
Fikac, Jeremy	5	5	5.88	28	0	0	1	41	45	30	27	21	34	.274	R	R	6-2	185	4-8-75	1998	Shiner, Texas
Horgan, Joe	1	0	3.18	13	0	0	0	17	15	6	6	4	11	.234	L	L	6-1	200	6-7-77	1996	Rancho Cordova, Calif.
2-team (10 Memphis)	1	1	4.39	23	0	0	0	27	29	13	13	7	19	.279							
Johnson, Mike	6	6	5.93	30	14	1	0	102	128	70	67	29	77	.305	L	R	6-2	180	10-3-75	1993	Jupiter, Fla.
Karp, Josh	4	10	5.95	24	24	0	0	127	147	91	84	51	102	.295	R	R	6-5	210	9-21-79	2002	Bothell, Wash.
Mahomes, Pat	4	4	4.88	20	0	0	6	24	25	14	13	14	19	.275	R	R	6-4	220	8-9-70	1988	Lindale, Texas
Majewski, Gary	1	2	3.86	15	0	0	1	16	18	8	7	8	17	.295	R	R	6-2	200	2-26-80	1999	Houston, Texas
Parker, Christian	1	3	8.07	8	7	0	0	29	46	26	26	13	17	.362	R	R	6-1	200	7-3-75	1996	Albuquerque, N.M.
Randall, Scott	0	0	7.94	3	0	0	0	6	11	5	5	2	7	.423	R	R	6-3	225	10-29-75	1995	Goleta, Calif.
Rauch, Jon	1	1	4.50	3	3	0	0	18	17	9	9	2	13	.246	R	R	6-11	260	9-27-78	1999	Tucson, Ariz.
Robertson, Jeriome	1	3	5.73	7	7	0	0	33	44	21	21	10	22	.331	L	L	6-3	180	3-30-77	1996	Exeter, Calif.
Rodriguez, Wilfredo	0	1	30.60	3	1	0	0	5	19	18	17	7	2	.655	L	L	6-3	180	3-20-79	1996	San Felix, Venez.
Rueckel, Danny	1	0	2.89	7	0	0	1	9	14	3	3	7	10	.359	R	R	6-0	170	9-25-79	2002	Dunwoody, Ga.
Schroder, Chris	2	1	4.39	17	1	0	0	27	24	13	13	15	32	.242	R	R	6-3	210	8-20-78	2001	Okarche, Okla.
Sessions, Doug	1	1	4.07	7	3	0	0	24	31	13	11	6	11	.323	R	R	6-1	205	9-28-76	1998	Orange Park, Fla.
2-team (15 New Orleans)	1	4	6.15	12	7	0	0	41	54	31	28	9	25	.325							
Song, Seung	3	1	4.26	13	13	0	0	63	70	35	30	29	59	.278	R	R	6-1	190	6-29-80	1999	Pusan, Korea
Stanifer, Rob	4	4	4.27	37	0	0	1	59	65	29	28	18	46	.279	R	R	6-2	220	3-10-72	1994	Largo, Fla.
Stevenson, Jason	0	0	3.60	3	0	0	0	5	7	2	2	1	3	.350	L	L	6-1	175	8-8-81	2001	Redding, Calif.
Tucker, T.J.	2	0	4.86	3	3	0	0	17	26	15	9	5	5	.342	R	R	6-3	266	8-20-78	1997	New Port Richey, Fla.

FIELDING

Catcher	PCT	G	PO	A	E	DP	PB
Brown	1.000	5	24	5	0	0	0
Hoover	.990	33	190	17	2	1	5
Knorr	.992	75	460	24	4	6	4
Wilson	.996	33	234	24	1	3	2

First Base	PCT	G	PO	A	E	DP
Cepicky	1.000	1	1	0	0	1
Hoover	1.000	4	24	2	0	6
Johnson	1.000	3	24	2	0	3
Lopez	1.000	16	134	11	0	18
Matos	1.000	1	8	1	0	1
Ortiz	.983	10	53	5	1	6
Pascucci	.990	75	622	55	7	70
Short	.991	13	108	4	1	8
Toca	.987	28	204	28	3	17

Second Base	PCT	G	PO	A	E	DP
Brian Harris	.983	62	111	171	5	45
Izturis	.978	9	14	31	1	11
Mateo	.937	27	51	67	8	13
Medrano	.991	48	76	133	2	27
Short	1.000	10	21	24	0	7

Third Base	PCT	G	PO	A	E	DP
Carroll	.833	9	5	10	3	1
Brendan Harris	.943	34	21	62	5	4
Brian Harris	.872	22	7	27	5	2
Hodges	.898	59	25	38	6	4
Hoover	.842	19	8	24	6	2
Matos	.900	28	23	40	7	9
Medrano	1.000	9	5	14	0	1
Pascucci	1.000	3	0	4	0	0
Short	1.000	10	10	14	0	1

Shortstop	PCT	G	PO	A	E	DP
Izturis	.968	89	117	217	11	47
Matos	1.000	4	7	7	0	6
Medrano	.976	56	93	151	6	46

Outfield	PCT	G	PO	A	E	DP
Bergeron	1.000	11	16	2	0	0
Calloway	.982	58	105	7	2	1
Cepicky	.975	75	154	4	4	0
Chavez	1.000	14	27	2	0	0
Church	.990	95	184	6	2	3
Matos	1.000	13	21	2	0	0
Pascucci	.964	30	50	4	2	3
Toca	1.000	3	2	0	0	0
Ware	.972	22	35	0	1	0
Watson	.981	130	310	6	6	2

HARRISBURG SENATORS — Class AA

EASTERN LEAGUE

BATTING	AVG	G	AB	R	H	2B	3B	HR	RBI	BB	SO	SB	CS	OBP	SLG	B	T	HT	WT	DOB	1st Yr	Resides
Ambrosini, Dominick	.234	47	158	11	37	4	1	2	19	11	31	2	1	.284	.310	L	L	5-10	185	2-21-81	1999	Ronkonkoma, N.Y.
Belcher, Jason	.279	70	244	23	68	18	0	2	33	17	35	2	2	.327	.377	L	R	6-1	190	1-13-82	2000	Walnut Ridge, Ark.
Broadway, Larry	.271	130	473	69	128	20	0	22	71	68	102	2	3	.362	.452	L	L	6-4	230	12-17-80	2002	Scotts Hill, Tenn.
Brown, Jason	.283	45	120	16	34	11	0	5	18	5	32	0	0	.315	.500	R	R	6-2	200	5-22-74	1997	Rolling Hills Estates, Calif.
Camilo, Juan	.262	117	363	54	95	20	3	11	52	43	98	12	6	.341	.424	R	R	6-0	200	6-24-76	1996	Santo Domingo, D.R.
Carroll, Wes	.237	23	59	2	14	2	0	0	3	5	5	2	1	.297	.271	R	R	5-11	180	1-5-79	2001	Evansville, Ind.
Dorta, Melvin	.262	71	225	20	59	11	2	0	22	15	23	12	4	.311	.329	R	R	5-11	160	1-15-82	1999	Guscara, Venez.
Labandeira, Josh	.271	133	510	71	138	21	4	9	32	52	90	9	5	.356	.380	R	R	5-7	180	2-25-79	2001	Porterville, Calif.
Lane, Rich	.293	127	484	66	142	29	2	7	57	43	90	4	4	.352	.405	L	L	6-3	195	1-4-80	1999	Tustin, Calif.
Liriano, Pedro	.189	33	122	10	23	5	0	0	10	4	28	8	4	.213	.230	R	R	5-11	160	2-20-77	1999	Pimentel, D.R.
Machado, Alejandro	.280	93	346	54	97	5	4	4	26	41	39	19	9	.365	.353	S	R	6-0	160	4-26-82	1999	Caracas, Venez.
Manriquez, Salomon	.148	11	27	2	4	1	0	1	2	0	4	0	0	.148	.296	R	R	6-1	190	9-15-82	2000	Guacara, Venez.
McKinley, Josh	.240	83	296	39	71	16	4	9	42	50	72	10	5	.349	.412	S	R	6-1	205	9-14-79	1998	Windermere, Fla.
McMillan, Drew	.214	54	173	13	37	8	0	2	17	12	45	0	0	.275	.295	R	R	6-3	200	10-25-80	1999	Yorba Linda, Calif.
Norris, Shawn	.315	37	124	16	39	10	2	3	33	25	37	1	1	.429	.500	L	R	6-2	170	8-1-80	2001	Draper, Utah
Raymundo, G.J.	.301	35	103	13	31	7	0	2	13	7	14	0	0	.354	.427	R	R	5-11	189	3-3-77	1999	Clovis, Calif.
Rombley, Danny	.174	40	121	16	21	3	0	0	5	10	42	8	1	.246	.198	R	R	6-1	185	11-26-79	1999	Amersfoort, Netherlands
Rooi, Vince	.148	36	108	8	16	2	0	1	7	8	33	1	1	.214	.194	R	R	6-1	195	12-13-81	1999	Amsterdam, Netherlands
Storey, Eric	.135	19	52	4	7	0	0	1	3	5	18	0	0	.211	.192	R	R	6-1	170	10-12-77	2000	Indianapolis, Ind.
Taylor, Seth	.157	14	51	5	8	3	1	1	11	1	21	0	1	.200	.314	R	R	6-1	180	8-23-77	1999	Louisville, Miss.
Ware, Jeremy	.222	53	189	23	42	10	0	2	14	14	37	2	3	.280	.307	R	R	6-0	200	10-23-75	1995	Guelph, Ontario
Wilson, John	.206	44	131	8	27	6	2	2	13	13	27	5	1	.276	.328	R	R	6-1	190	9-29-78	2000	Newbury Park, Calif.

PITCHING	W	L	ERA	G	GS	CG	SV	IP	H	R	ER	BB	SO	AVG	B	T	HT	WT	DOB	1st Yr	Resides
Bentz, Chad	0	1	8.59	5	1	0	1	7	5	7	7	8	2	.200	R	L	6-2	215	5-5-80	2001	Juneau, Alaska
Bergmann, Jason	0	2	9.00	2	0	0	0	4	7	5	4	2	3	.412	R	R	6-4	190	9-25-81	2002	Manalapan, N.J.

PITCHING	W	L	ERA	G	GS	CG	SV	IP	H	R	ER	BB	SO	AVG	B	T	HT	WT	DOB	1st Yr	Resides
Bridges, Donnie	3	5	5.07	18	13	0	0	76	65	52	43	45	56	.230	R	R	6-4	220	12-10-78	1997	Purvis, Miss.
Casadiego, Gerardo	1	2	8.38	10	0	0	0	19	26	22	18	10	10	.325	R	R	6-0	180	12-19-80	1998	Barquisimeto, Venez.
Crumpton, Chuck	0	0	6.59	6	0	0	0	14	25	11	10	3	5	.397	R	R	6-4	210	12-30-76	1999	Mesquite, Texas
Douglass, Ryan	2	4	6.23	36	0	0	0	65	93	56	45	23	53	.335	R	R	6-3	210	12-3-78	1997	Pittsburgh, Pa.
Echols, Justin	3	8	6.94	21	11	1	0	73	88	57	56	42	60	.307	R	R	6-3	180	10-6-80	1999	Roby, Mo.
Ferrari, Anthony	0	0	1.80	3	0	0	2	5	5	1	1	0	4	.278	L	L	5-9	165	6-22-78	2000	Greenbrae, Calif.
Hill, Shawn	5	7	3.39	17	17	2	0	88	90	39	33	20	53	.272	R	R	6-2	185	4-28-81	2000	Georgetown, Ontario
Hinckley, Mike	5	2	2.87	16	16	0	0	94	83	34	30	23	80	.242	R	L	6-3	170	10-5-82	2001	Moore, Okla.
Lockwood, Luke	3	17	4.95	33	19	0	1	136	168	83	75	30	86	.305	L	L	6-3	170	7-21-81	1999	Victorville, Calif.
Marrero, Darwin	0	0	10.80	2	2	0	0	8	13	10	10	2	7	.351	R	R	6-1	190	2-9-81	1998	Valencia, Venez.
Mata, Gustavo	0	0	9.00	1	0	0	0	3	6	3	3	1	2	.400	R	R	6-1	190	5-20-83	2001	Carupano, Venez.
Maust, David	3	8	6.43	44	7	0	0	85	107	65	61	37	44	.305	L	L	6-2	200	11-6-78	2001	Morgantown, W.Va.
Patterson, John	0	0	0.00	1	1	0	0	4	0	0	0	2	9	.000	R	R	6-5	210	1-30-78	1997	Scottsdale, Ariz.
Puello, Ignacio	0	0	6.75	10	0	0	0	15	17	12	11	10	16	.283	R	R	6-1	170	10-16-80	1998	San Pedro de Macoris, D.R.
Rasner, Darrell	1	1	1.21	5	5	0	0	30	21	4	4	9	15	.214	R	R	6-3	210	1-13-81	2002	Carson City, Nev.
Rijo, Fernando	0	0	4.32	4	0	0	0	8	9	4	4	6	7	.281	R	R	5-11	173	11-15-77	1995	La Romana, D.R.
Rivera, Saul	0	2	7.84	18	0	0	3	21	27	22	18	12	15	.321	R	R	5-11	150	12-7-77	1998	San Juan, P.R.
Rodriguez, Wilfredo	0	1	5.40	4	0	0	0	8	11	5	5	8	3	.314	L	L	6-3	180	3-20-79	1996	San Felix, Venez.
Rueckel, Danny	6	5	2.01	41	0	0	8	76	70	28	17	16	55	.247	R	R	6-0	170	9-25-79	2002	Dunwoody, Ga.
Rundles, Rich	2	6	3.43	19	19	0	0	97	103	48	37	32	60	.275	L	L	6-5	180	6-3-81	1999	Livingston, Ala.
Schroder, Chris	2	2	2.42	32	0	0	11	48	39	13	13	17	51	.223	R	R	6-3	200	8-20-78	2001	Okarche, Okla.
Searles, Jon	3	3	5.05	30	0	0	0	46	45	32	26	25	27	.265	R	R	6-3	200	1-18-81	1999	Huntington, N.Y.
Sessions, Doug	3	1	6.48	5	4	0	0	25	34	18	18	5	18	.330	R	R	6-1	205	9-28-76	1998	Orange Park, Fla.
Skrmetta, Matt	0	1	5.40	5	0	0	1	7	5	4	4	6	2	.208	R	R	6-5	230	11-6-72	1993	Satellite Beach, Fla.
Stevenson, Jason	8	10	4.06	24	22	0	1	135	132	66	61	46	75	.261	L	L	6-1	175	8-8-81	2001	Redding, Calif.
Thurman, Corey	1	2	9.31	5	5	0	0	19	31	22	20	6	15	.360	R	R	6-1	210	11-5-78	1996	Wake Village, Texas

FIELDING

Catcher	PCT	G	PO	A	E	DP	PB
Belcher	.955	19	97	8	5	0	2
Brown	.965	28	127	9	5	1	2
Manriquez	1.000	6	22	3	0	0	1
McKinley	.984	10	57	4	1	1	1
McMillan	.991	52	299	33	3	1	3
Storey	1.000	3	13	4	0	0	0
Wilson	.976	41	259	25	7	4	2

First Base	PCT	G	PO	A	E	DP
Broadway	.993	121	1069	93	8	111
Lane	.978	24	163	17	4	20

Second Base	PCT	G	PO	A	E	DP
Carroll	.929	8	12	14	2	3
Dorta	.970	28	45	86	4	23
Liriano	.980	30	52	96	3	24

Machado	.992	80	154	226	3	57
Raymundo	1.000	1	2	0	0	
Taylor	1.000	2	3	6	0	

Third Base	PCT	G	PO	A	E	DP
Belcher	.714	3	0	5	2	0
Dorta	.947	33	20	52	4	4
McKinley	.333	2	0	1	2	0
Norris	.972	37	33	73	3	9
Raymundo	.935	20	16	27	3	3
Rooi	.938	34	23	68	6	3
Storey	1.000	5	1	5	0	0
Taylor	.914	12	12	20	3	0
Wilson	1.000	1	0	2	0	0

Shortstop	PCT	G	PO	A	E	DP
Dorta	.857	4	6	6	2	4

Labandeira	.952	128	226	394	31	83
Machado	.982	13	17	39	1	10

Outfield	PCT	G	PO	A	E	DP
Ambrosini	.987	44	72	3	1	0
Belcher	.952	33	59	1	3	0
Bridges	1.000	12	12	1	0	0
Brown	1.000	1	1	0	0	0
Camilo	.959	106	178	8	8	1
Carroll	1.000	13	17	1	0	0
Dorta	1.000	4	8	1	0	0
Lane	.974	99	178	9	5	1
McKinley	.948	62	124	3	7	1
Raymundo	1.000	4	6	0	0	0
Rombley	.976	39	75	5	2	0
Storey	1.000	2	1	0	0	0
Ware	.990	47	100	1	1	0

BREVARD COUNTY MANATEES · High Class A

FLORIDA STATE LEAGUE

BATTING	AVG	G	AB	R	H	2B	3B	HR	RBI	BB	SO	SB	CS	OBP	SLG	B	T	HT	WT	DOB	1st Yr	Resides
Ambrosini, Anthony	.154	4	13	0	2	0	0	0	1	1	2	0	0	.214	.154	R	R	5-9	185	9-22-78	2001	Ronkonkoma, N.Y.
Ambrosini, Dominick	.193	57	202	11	39	7	1	2	23	16	54	2	5	.256	.267	L	L	5-10	185	2-21-81	1999	Ronkonkoma, N.Y.
Apodaca, Luis	.277	15	47	5	13	2	0	0	2	3	8	0	0	.333	.319	R	R	5-11	170	8-15-82	1998	Caracas, Venez.
Batista, Rafael	.000	2	5	0	0	0	0	0	0	0	3	0	0	.000	.000	S	R	5-8	150	2-20-82	2003	Santo Domingo, D.R.
Bergeron, Peter	.176	4	17	3	3	0	1	0	0	0	2	3	0	.176	.294	L	R	6-0	190	11-9-77	1996	St. Petersburg, Fla.
Bynum, Seth	.235	20	51	7	12	3	1	1	3	4	20	0	0	.291	.392	R	R	6-1	185	12-19-80	2004	Louisville, Ky.
Camilo, Juan	.250	1	4	1	1	0	0	0	0	0	2	0	0	.250	.250	L	R	6-0	200	6-24-76	1996	Santo Domingo, D.R.
Carroll, Wes	.244	78	307	32	75	11	2	1	28	27	46	0	3	.308	.303	R	R	5-11	180	1-5-79	2001	Evansville, Ind.
Chavez, Ender	.380	20	71	12	27	3	1	0	8	11	12	4	5	.463	.451	L	L	6-0	185	5-9-81	1999	Valencia, Venez.
Chop, Chad	.218	122	444	47	97	16	0	9	46	48	66	3	6	.296	.315	L	L	6-4	210	3-21-80	2002	Santa Ana, Calif.
Clanton, Ja'Mar	.067	7	15	0	1	0	0	0	1	0	3	0	0	.067	.067	R	R	6-0	170	7-14-81	2002	Bellwood, Ill.
Contreras, Jose	.429	4	14	3	6	0	0	0	2	1	0	0	0	.467	.429	R	R	6-0	170	4-26-85	2002	Miranda, Venez.
Diaz, Frank	.242	114	413	46	100	17	8	8	57	31	76	16	6	.303	.380	R	R	6-2	180	10-6-83	2001	Valencia, Venez.
Ditter, Brad	.200	3	5	1	1	0	0	0	0	0	2	0	0	.200	.200	L	R	6-0	180	7-22-80	2003	Redmond, Wash.
Ellerson, Brian	.257	37	113	14	29	3	0	8	15	23	0	4	8	.288	.283	R	R	6-1	190	9-28-79	2002	Bayonne, N.J.
Emmerick, Josh	.234	46	124	11	29	7	1	2	13	29	35	1	0	.379	.355	R	R	6-4	190	2-22-81	2000	Oceanside, Calif.
Everett, Carl	.400	5	15	2	6	1	0	0	3	2	3	0	0	.444	.467	S	R	6-0	215	6-3-71	1990	Brandon, Fla.
Hodges, Scott	.222	2	9	2	2	0	0	0	2	1	2	0	0	.300	.222	L	R	6-0	190	12-26-78	1997	Lexington, Ky.
Johnson, Nick	.190	6	21	3	4	0	0	1	5	4	6	0	0	.320	.333	L	L	6-3	195	9-19-78	1996	Sacramento, Calif.
Machado, Alejandro	.355	46	186	34	66	10	2	1	19	22	27	11	6	.424	.446	S	R	6-0	160	4-26-82	1999	Caracas, Venez.
Manriquez, Salomon	.250	16	52	5	13	5	0	1	2	1	14	0	0	.264	.404	R	R	6-0	190	9-15-82	2000	Guacara, Venez.
Margalski, Ben	.231	34	108	14	25	2	1	3	18	11	28	0	0	.306	.352	L	R	6-2	210	9-2-79	2001	High Ridge, Mo.
McMillan, Drew	.250	18	64	14	16	4	0	3	12	8	15	1	0	.347	.453	R	R	6-3	200	10-25-80	1999	Yorba Linda, Calif.
Montz, Luke	.500	1	2	0	1	1	0	0	0	2	1	0	0	.7501.000		R	R	6-2	205	7-7-83	2003	Lafayette, La.
Norris, Shawn	.273	98	352	48	96	15	8	2	48	60	80	5	2	.379	.378	L	R	6-2	170	8-1-80	2001	Draper, Utah
Rodriguez, Robert	.143	3	7	2	1	0	0	1	2	0	0	0	0	.143	.571	R	R	5-10	180	12-17-80	2002	Miami, Fla.
Rombley, Danny	.234	61	205	22	48	6	2	0	12	24	51	4	4	.319	.283	R	R	6-1	185	11-26-79	1999	Amersfoort, Netherlands
Rooi, Vince	.200	65	210	20	42	4	0	6	19	24	50	3	0	.297	.305	R	R	6-1	195	12-13-81	1999	Amsterdam, Netherlands
Thissen, Greg	.225	82	267	28	60	17	1	7	32	26	70	7	1	.298	.375	R	R	6-4	185	6-1-81	2001	Davenport, Iowa
Tuttle, Jason	.272	92	279	41	76	6	1	0	14	30	25	13	8	.348	.301	L	L	5-9	170	11-27-79	2002	Winston-Salem, N.C.
Vroman, Doug	.063	5	16	0	1	0	0	0	0	1	4	1	0	.118	.063	R	R	6-2	200	2-9-81	2003	Westport, Conn.
Williams, Clyde	.238	106	357	39	85	14	7	12	40	25	87	4	1	.288	.417	L	L	6-2	190	7-7-79	1998	Sanford, Fla.

BATTING	AVG	G	AB	R	H	2B	3B	HR	RBI	BB	SO	SB	CS	OBP	SLG	B	T	HT	WT	DOB	1st Yr	Resides
Wong, Ivanosky	.667	1	3	0	2	0	0	0	1	0	0	0		.750	.667	R	R	5-11	170	11-26-83	2001	Bolivar, Venez.
Yepez, Marcos	.226	16	53	7	12	2	1	0	3	5	16	1	2	.305	.302	S	R	5-10	160	12-29-81	1999	Caracas, Venez.

PITCHING	W	L	ERA	G	GS	CG	SV	IP	H	R	ER	BB	SO	AVG	B	T	HT	WT	DOB	1st Yr	Resides
Armas, Tony	0	1	6.75	3	3	0	0	9	5	7	7	7	7	.179	R	R	6-3	225	4-29-78	1995	Puerto Piritu, Venez.
Barlow, Chris	4	9	4.27	27	17	0	4	112	109	56	53	24	48	.255	R	R	6-6	210	11-11-80	2002	Cazenovia, N.Y.
Bergmann, Jason	3	2	1.14	24	0	0	8	32	20	7	4	18	28	.189	R	R	6-4	190	9-25-81	2002	Manalapan, N.J.
Bray, Bill	0	2	4.91	6	0	0	1	7	9	5	4	1	6	.290	L	L	6-3	215	6-5-83	2004	Virginia Beach, Va.
Campbell, Brett	1	0	3.86	4	0	0	0	7	6	3	3	4	2	.250	R	R	6-0	170	10-17-81	2004	Douglasville, Ga.
Davis, Stockton	1	7	4.97	28	0	0	2	51	57	36	28	33	33	.285	L	R	6-3	210	9-8-79	2002	Owasso, Okla.
Douglass, Ryan	1	1	1.04	7	0	0	4	9	5	1	1	2	5	.179	R	R	6-3	210	12-3-78	1997	Pittsburgh, Pa.
Echols, Justin	0	5	5.88	7	4	0	0	34	40	27	22	10	29	.284	R	R	6-3	180	10-6-80	1999	Roby, Mo.
Eischen, Joey	0	0	0.00	4	4	0	0	6	5	4	0	1	7	.217	L	L	6-0	215	5-25-70	1989	Rotonda West, Fla.
Everts, Clint	2	2	2.25	4	4	0	0	20	16	5	5	10	19	.222	R	R	6-2	170	8-10-84	2003	Cypress, Texas
Felfoldi, Jon	0	1	3.72	2	2	0	0	10	10	6	4	4	1	.270	L	L	6-1	180	7-6-81	2002	San Diego, Calif.
Girdley, Josh	0	3	5.24	9	5	0	0	34	37	24	20	15	19	.272	L	L	6-3	185	8-29-80	1999	Jasper, Texas
Goodman, Chris	0	2	7.11	16	1	0	1	32	42	27	25	9	24	.326	S	R	6-1	180	11-9-81	2003	Benson, Ariz.
Hinckley, Mike	6	2	2.61	10	10	0	0	62	47	23	18	18	51	.206	R	L	6-3	170	10-5-82	2001	Moore, Okla.
Lira, Oscar	0	0	0.00	2	0	0	0	4	1	0	0	3	3	.091	R	R	6-3	180	7-17-82	2001	Caracas, Venez.
Marceau, Pierre Luc	1	1	4.28	18	0	0	0	27	18	17	13	33	21	.212	L	L	6-2	190	4-11-81	2000	Fleurimont, Quebec
Marrero, Darwin	1	0	1.04	3	1	0	0	9	5	1	1	2	4	.172	R	R	6-1	190	2-9-81	1998	Valencia, Venez.
Martinez, Samuel	1	5	5.29	14	0	0	1	17	22	14	10	8	14	.310	R	R	6-2	160	3-22-79	2000	Santo Domingo, D.R.
Mata, Gustavo	1	0	2.12	3	3	0	0	17	11	6	4	9	13	.186	R	R	6-1	190	5-20-83	2001	Carupano, Venez.
Morales, Alex	2	6	4.55	32	4	0	3	63	60	36	32	41	55	.256	R	R	5-11	170	4-8-82	2003	Mt. Prospect, Ill.
Norderum, Jason	0	2	6.83	35	2	0	0	58	58	52	44	53	63	.271	L	L	6-3	220	11-21-81	2000	Redding, Calif.
O'Connor, Michael	8	8	4.11	26	14	0	0	103	98	51	47	42	104	.253	L	L	6-3	170	8-17-80	2002	Ellicott City, Md.
Patterson, John	0	0	0.00	2	2	0	0	8	3	0	0	1	7	.111	R	R	6-5	210	1-30-78	1997	Scottsdale, Ariz.
Price, Brett	6	4	3.53	23	19	0	0	99	88	47	39	53	100	.236	L	L	5-10	165	12-7-79	2001	Leesville, S.C.
Quintero, Mayque	3	2	2.75	21	1	0	0	36	29	12	11	15	32	.230	R	R	6-2	220	4-19-78	2002	Miami, Fla.
Rasner, Darrell	6	5	3.17	22	21	0	0	119	133	55	42	31	88	.284	R	R	6-3	210	1-13-81	2002	Carson City, Nev.
Rodriguez, Wilfredo	2	3	7.71	9	5	0	0	30	34	28	26	23	26	.281	L	L	6-3	180	3-20-79	1996	San Felix, Venez.
Rundles, Rich	0	1	6.00	1	1	0	0	3	4	2	2	2	0	.333	L	L	6-5	180	6-3-81	1999	Livingston, Ala.
Santillan, Manny	0	1	6.00	7	0	0	0	12	12	9	8	10	10	.250	R	R	6-0	215	8-20-79	1997	La Romana, D.R.
Searles, Jon	4	0	1.59	19	0	0	4	28	12	6	5	9	23	.129	R	R	6-3	220	1-18-81	1999	Huntington, N.Y.
Skrmetta, Matt	1	0	0.00	3	0	0	0	2	0	0	0	2	5	.000	S	R	6-3	220	11-6-72	1993	Satellite Beach, Fla.
Smith, Dan	0	0	2.25	3	0	0	0	4	5	1	1	1	2	.357	R	R	6-3	225	9-15-75	1993	Carl Junction, Kan.
Song, Seung	0	0	6.75	3	2	0	0	12	14	11	9	3	10	.280	R	R	6-1	190	6-29-80	1999	Pusan, Korea
Yost, Wendell	0	0	0.00	1	0	0	0	1	1	0	0	1	2	.250	R	R	6-3	185	6-23-81	2004	Lynchburg, Va.

FIELDING

Catcher	PCT	G	PO	A	E	DP	PB
A. Ambrosini	1.000	4	21	4	0	0	3
Apodaca	.973	14	97	10	3	0	3
Emmerick	.984	44	277	25	5	3	9
Manriquez	.976	14	70	13	2	2	4
Margalski	.996	30	239	29	1	2	5
McMillan	.993	18	127	18	1	1	3
Montz	1.000	1	8	1	0	0	0
Rodriguez	.944	2	17	0	1	0	0
Wong	1.000	1	12	1	0	0	0

First Base	PCT	G	PO	A	E	DP
Chop	.993	35	284	21	2	29
Ellerson	1.000	7	47	1	0	4
Johnson	1.000	6	48	6	0	2
Williams	.987	84	710	54	10	78

Second Base	PCT	G	PO	A	E	DP
Carroll	.972	26	53	85	4	15

	PCT	G	PO	A	E	DP
Clanton	1.000	3	2	10	0	1
Machado	.967	5	17	12	1	7
Norris	.959	21	46	70	5	12
Thissen	.980	70	137	212	7	52
Yepez	.917	4	5	17	2	2

Third Base	PCT	G	PO	A	E	DP
Carroll	.895	14	11	23	4	4
Clanton	1.000	2	1	2	0	0
Ellerson	.850	11	6	11	3	1
Hodges	.833	2	1	4	1	0
Norris	.940	43	42	84	8	10
Rooi	.914	58	38	101	13	11
Yepez	1.000	4	1	4	0	0

Shortstop	PCT	G	PO	A	E	DP
Bynum	.931	19	12	42	4	10
Carroll	.947	30	46	97	8	28
Clanton	1.000	3	5	4	0	1

	PCT	G	PO	A	E	DP
Contreras	.875	4	12	9	3	2
Machado	.960	38	63	107	7	16
Norris	.977	30	55	74	3	19
Yepez	.905	3	6	13	2	3

Outfield	PCT	G	PO	A	E	DP
D. Ambrosini	.947	48	69	3	4	1
Batista	1.000	1	1	0	0	0
Bergeron	1.000	4	7	0	0	0
Chavez	.963	15	25	1	1	0
Chop	.986	53	70	1	1	0
Diaz	.972	114	225	16	7	2
Ellerson	1.000	1	1	0	0	0
Everett	1.000	3	3	0	0	0
Rombley	.960	60	114	6	5	2
Thissen	1.000	12	12	2	0	1
Tuttle	.985	86	129	4	2	0
Vroman	1.000	1	2	0	0	0

SAVANNAH SAND GNATS — Low Class A

SOUTH ATLANTIC LEAGUE

BATTING	AVG	G	AB	R	H	2B	3B	HR	RBI	BB	SO	SB	CS	OBP	SLG	B	T	HT	WT	DOB	1st Yr	Resides
Apodaca, Luis	.206	61	204	19	42	7	0	5	18	12	43	1	1	.280	.314	R	R	5-11	170	8-15-82	1999	Caracas, Venez.
Baez, Edgardo	.173	50	191	16	33	10	0	5	29	19	56	1	0	.259	.304	R	R	6-2	190	7-12-85	2003	Dorado, P.R.
Bernadina, Rogearvin	.238	129	450	67	107	24	7	7	66	60	113	24	2	.338	.369	L	L	6-0	170	6-12-84	2002	Den Haag, Netherlands
Bynum, Seth	.250	24	72	11	18	2	0	1	3	9	24	0	0	.333	.319	R	R	6-1	185	12-19-80	2004	Louisville, Ky.
Casto, Kory	.286	124	483	67	138	35	4	16	88	31	70	1	2	.337	.474	L	R	6-1	180	12-8-81	2003	Aurora, Ore.
Castro, Ofilio	.189	10	37	2	7	2	0	0	1	0	12	0	0	.184	.243	R	R	6-0	160	8-18-83	2001	Managua, Nicaragua
Clanton, Ja`Mar	.200	15	30	3	6	0	1	0	2	1	10	0	0	.226	.267	R	R	6-0	170	7-14-81	2002	Bellwood, Ill.
Conlisk, Jason	.215	111	349	38	75	20	2	5	37	41	87	7	2	.298	.327	S	R	5-10	180	7-8-81	2002	Ridgewood, N.Y.
Emmerick, Josh	.188	24	69	7	13	1	0	1	5	10	19	0	1	.305	.246	R	R	6-4	190	2-22-81	2000	Oceanside, Calif.
Fitzpatrick, Reggie	.245	90	323	45	79	13	6	3	27	29	74	13	11	.310	.350	L	L	5-11	180	2-28-83	2001	Atlanta, Ga.
Ivany, Devin	.170	32	106	7	18	4	0	0	4	8	21	2	0	.239	.208	R	R	6-2	185	7-27-82	2004	Fort Lauderdale, Fla.
Jimenez, Franklyn	.214	72	229	26	49	6	0	5	27	7	43	5	0	.239	.306	R	R	6-2	180	2-23-82	2002	Bayamon, P.R.
Mancebo, Melvin	.429	2	7	3	3	0	0	1	2	0	1	0	0	.375	.857	R	R	6-1	190	9-8-83	2004	San Cristobal, D.R.
Manriquez, Salomon	.265	32	117	11	31	7	0	3	18	8	33	0	1	.315	.402	R	R	6-2	170	9-15-82	2000	Guacara, Venez.
Nunez, Eduardo	.000	2	1	2	0	0	0	0	0	4	1	1	0	.800	.000	R	R	6-2	170	9-21-85	2003	San Sebastian, P.R.
Owens, Jerry	.292	108	418	69	122	17	2	1	37	46	59	30	13	.365	.349	L	L	6-3	195	2-16-81	2003	Newhall, Calif.
Rodriguez, Alfredo	.143	2	7	2	1	0	0	0	0	1	3	0	0	.250	.143	R	R	5-11	180	11-1-77	1995	Zalaya, Santiago, D.R.
Rodriguez, Rob	.250	22	56	7	14	5	0	0	7	8	26	0	0	.338	.339	R	R	5-10	180	12-17-80	2002	Miami, Fla.
San Pedro, Erick	.200	14	40	3	8	2	0	1	4	9	17	0	0	.347	.325	R	R	6-1	210	10-5-83	2004	Hialeah, Fla.
Sucre, Antonio	.240	103	363	44	87	11	3	8	46	35	114	3	5	.327	.353	R	R	6-2	180	8-13-83	2001	Puerto la Cruz, Venez.
Tuttle, Jason	.333	4	12	1	4	0	0	0	0	0	0	0	0	.333	.333	L	L	5-9	170	11-27-79	2002	Winston-Salem, N.C.

BATTING	AVG	G	AB	R	H	2B	3B	HR	RBI	BB	SO	SB	CS	OBP	SLG	B	T	HT	WT	DOB	1st Yr	Resides
Webb, Trey	.241	78	274	39	66	10	0	4	30	28	48	7	4	.313	.321	R	R	6-1	170	2-11-82	2003	Mansfield, Texas
Whitesell, Josh	.250	113	380	56	95	29	0	16	54	58	91	0	1	.352	.453	L	L	6-3	220	4-14-82	2003	Redlands, Calif.
Yepez, Marcos	.238	77	265	35	63	14	2	2	24	30	85	12	2	.329	.328	S	R	5-10	160	12-29-81	1999	Caracas, Venez.

PITCHING	W	L	ERA	G	GS	CG	SV	IP	H	R	ER	BB	SO	AVG	B	T	HT	WT	DOB	1st Yr	Resides
Bergmann, Jason	3	7	4.85	13	13	0	0	65	67	43	35	34	58	.265	R	R	6-4	190	9-25-81	2002	Manalapan, N.J.
Everts, Clint	7	3	2.49	17	17	1	0	90	67	29	25	21	103	.206	R	R	6-2	170	8-10-84	2003	Cypress, Texas
Felfoldi, Jon	2	3	3.51	5	5	0	0	26	28	17	10	17	20	.292	L	L	6-1	180	7-6-81	2002	San Diego, Calif.
Galarraga, Armando	5	5	4.65	23	19	1	0	110	104	64	57	31	94	.247	R	R	6-4	170	1-15-82	1999	Caracas, Venez.
Gomez, Warmar	4	7	3.80	43	0	0	4	66	83	37	28	25	37	.304	R	R	6-2	210	5-8-83	2001	Rio Grande, P.R.
Goodman, Chris	0	0	2.45	8	1	0	2	18	16	5	5	2	20	.232	S	R	6-1	180	11-9-81	2003	Benson, Ariz.
Jimenez, Franklyn	0	0	0.00	2	0	0	0	1	0	0	0	0	1	.000	R	R	6-2	180	2-23-82	2002	Bayamon, P.R.
Long, Nick	5	9	4.89	28	17	0	0	105	102	76	57	61	81	.254	R	R	6-3	180	11-24-82	2001	Columbus, Ga.
Marceau, Pierre Luc	0	0	4.61	13	0	0	0	27	29	17	14	17	21	.274	L	L	6-2	190	4-11-81	2000	Fleurimont, Quebec
Marrero, Darwin	1	1	4.91	2	2	1	0	11	10	6	6	3	8	.238	R	R	6-1	190	2-9-81	1998	Valencia, Venez.
Martinez, Samuel	2	2	4.58	11	5	0	0	39	38	27	20	16	32	.255	R	R	6-2	160	3-22-79	2000	Santo Domingo, D.R.
Mitchell, Thomas	1	0	9.00	11	0	0	1	23	29	24	23	16	10	.302	R	R	6-2	180	11-20-80	2000	Bladenboro, N.C.
Nyquist, Brett	4	12	5.67	22	20	0	0	106	139	84	67	27	79	.309	L	L	6-7	200	5-7-81	2003	Duluth, Minn.
Pearson, Anthony	1	4	3.81	33	3	0	1	85	61	40	36	49	106	.203	R	R	6-3	190	8-14-81	2002	Baton Rouge, La.
Perrin, Brian	5	6	4.50	36	15	0	0	122	112	64	61	62	108	.252	R	R	6-2	225	5-14-81	2003	Glendale, Ariz.
Plexico, Gerald	8	5	2.63	49	0	0	6	82	59	27	24	25	101	.194	L	L	6-4	210	2-24-80	2003	Chapin, S.C.
Reid, Brett	5	4	1.98	46	0	0	15	64	51	17	14	20	84	.221	R	R	6-0	175	10-19-79	2003	Liberty, Mo.
Sandoval, Francisco	1	0	13.97	7	0	0	0	10	16	16	15	4	4	.381	R	R	6-1	170	3-11-84	2001	Valencia, Venez.
Thompson, Daryl	4	9	5.08	25	21	0	0	103	117	66	58	30	79	.290	R	R	6-1	170	11-2-85	2003	Mechanicsville, Md.
Thorne, David	0	3	5.30	15	0	0	0	19	20	13	11	12	16	.274	R	R	6-3	180	9-18-81	2002	Sydney, Australia

FIELDING

Catcher	PCT	G	PO	A	E	DP	PB
Apodaca	.986	59	421	61	7	2	7
Emmerick	1.000	24	179	15	0	0	3
Ivany	.995	23	174	17	1	0	0
Manriquez	.967	15	104	15	4	2	3
A. Rodriguez	1.000	1	12	0	0	0	0
R. Rodriguez	1.000	22	136	13	0	2	6
San Pedro	.983	6	53	5	1	0	1

First Base	PCT	G	PO	A	E	DP
Bynum	1.000	1	1	0	0	0
Jimenez	.990	30	188	9	2	10
Manriquez	.988	13	82	3	1	5
Whitesell	.984	104	810	56	14	70
Yepez	1.000	3	7	1	0	3

Second Base	PCT	G	PO	A	E	DP
Bynum	1.000	5	6	6	0	0

Clanton	.953	8	16	25	2	6
Conlisk	.977	82	171	203	9	43
Jimenez	.970	21	45	53	3	17
Nunez	1.000	1	1	0	0	0
Yepez	.944	26	35	49	5	9

Third Base	PCT	G	PO	A	E	DP
Casto	.870	112	59	176	35	10
Castro	.970	10	5	27	1	1
Jimenez	.750	2	1	2	1	0
Manriquez	.833	2	1	4	1	1
Yepez	.902	14	4	33	4	2

Shortstop	PCT	G	PO	A	E	DP
Bynum	.906	14	14	34	5	3
Clanton	.625	2	1	4	3	1
Conlisk	.935	23	45	71	8	18

Webb	.936	73	118	202	22	34
Yepez	.959	29	48	94	6	16

Outfield	PCT	G	PO	A	E	DP
Baez	.971	41	64	3	2	0
Bernadina	.960	113	223	15	10	3
Clanton	1.000	1	0	0	0	0
Fitzpatrick	.972	82	135	5	4	1
Jimenez	.967	17	27	2	1	0
Mancebo	.000	1	0	0	1	0
Owens	.969	70	91	2	3	0
A. Rodriguez	.667	1	2	0	1	0
Sucre	.936	94	151	10	11	0
Tuttle	1.000	4	3	0	0	0
Yepez	1.000	3	7	0	0	0

VERMONT EXPOS — Short-Season Class A

NEW YORK-PENN LEAGUE

BATTING	AVG	G	AB	R	H	2B	3B	HR	RBI	BB	SO	SB	CS	OBP	SLG	B	T	HT	WT	DOB	1st Yr	Resides
Baez, Edgardo	.248	46	165	18	41	6	1	7	27	20	34	2	1	.332	.424	R	R	6-2	190	7-12-85	2003	Dorado, P.R.
Castro, Ofilio	.263	68	240	38	63	14	1	3	32	39	47	7	6	.365	.354	R	R	6-0	170	8-18-83	2001	Managua, Nicaragua
Clanton, Ja'Mar	.235	17	51	5	12	1	1	0	3	4	16	2	4	.291	.294	R	R	6-1	190	5-23-84	2002	Rocky Mount, N.C.
Cobb, Maurice	.114	16	35	5	4	2	0	0	2	4	13	5	1	.262	.171	R	R	6-1	190	4-26-85	2002	Miranda, Venez.
Contreras, Jose	.241	53	170	27	41	3	0	0	11	18	43	12	6	.312	.259	R	R	6-0	170	4-26-85	2002	Miranda, Venez.
Conway, Brandon	.188	36	112	10	21	2	2	0	5	9	38	1	3	.248	.241	L	R	6-3	190	11-9-83	2004	Shenandoah Jctn., W.Va.
Desmond, Ian	.250	4	12	2	3	0	0	1	1	0	2	0	1	.308	.500	R	R	6-2	185	9-20-85	2004	Sarasota, Fla.
Ditter, Brad	.302	52	192	24	58	6	2	3	27	17	27	9	3	.360	.401	L	R	6-0	180	7-22-80	2003	Redmond, Wash.
Ivany, Devin	.136	11	44	4	6	0	0	0	1	1	5	1	0	.156	.136	R	R	6-2	185	7-27-82	2004	Fort Lauderdale, Fla.
Legrande, Duron	.144	37	139	11	20	1	0	0	8	9	46	10	2	.212	.151	L	L	6-2	185	6-6-81	2004	Greensboro, N.C.
Louisa, Lorvin	.184	15	49	6	9	1	0	1	4	3	27	0	3	.245	.265	R	R	6-4	200	2-7-83	2000	Willemstad, Curacao
Lowrance, Marvin	.286	53	185	23	53	6	1	3	20	28	35	1	1	.392	.378	L	L	6-0	215	7-16-84	2004	Whittier, Calif.
Manriquez, Salomon	.290	10	31	2	9	3	0	1	5	2	3	0	0	.333	.484	R	R	6-1	190	9-15-82	2000	Guacara, Venez.
Montz, Luke	.251	62	203	31	51	11	0	10	34	33	41	2	1	.363	.453	R	R	6-2	205	7-7-83	2003	Lafayette, La.
Mortimer, Steve	.238	65	214	31	51	13	0	7	29	29	64	8	2	.354	.397	L	L	6-3	215	6-10-81	2004	Issaquah, Wash.
Poppert, John	.219	31	114	14	25	6	0	2	9	7	26	0	0	.268	.325	R	R	6-0	185	4-14-82	2004	Raleigh, N.C.
Sandora, Robert	.182	13	22	2	4	0	0	0	2	9	7	0	0	.419	.182	L	R	6-0	200	8-5-81	2003	West Babylon, N.Y.
Travis, David	.168	30	95	8	16	6	0	2	12	7	44	0	1	.233	.295	L	L	6-4	210	12-15-80	2004	Springfield, Ill.
Vroman, Douglas	.236	71	229	42	54	16	0	8	30	41	55	10	6	.352	.410	R	R	6-2	200	2-9-81	2003	Westport, Conn.

GAMES BY POSITION: C—Ivany 9, Jenkins 1, Manriquez 7, Montz 28, Poppert 28, Sandora 3. **1B**—Manriquez 1, Montz 25, Mortimer 44, Travis 5. **2B**—Clanton 12, Contreras 17, Ditter 47. **3B**—Castro 51, Clanton 2, Conway 17, Travis 10. **SS**—Castro 16, Contreras 39, Conway 19, Desmond 4. **OF**—Baez 43, Cobb 11, Legrande 28, Lowrance 48, Mortimer 20, Sandora 9, Vroman 68.

PITCHING	W	L	ERA	G	GS	CG	SV	IP	H	R	ER	BB	SO	AVG	B	T	HT	WT	DOB	1st Yr	Resides
Bunn, Greg	3	0	3.00	9	5	0	0	24	16	8	8	11	27	.186	R	R	6-1	210	2-3-83	2004	Wake Forest, N.C.
Campbell, Brett	0	1	4.09	11	0	0	0	22	24	14	10	10	25	.273	R	R	6-0	170	10-17-81	2004	Douglasville, Ga.
Cerezo, Hector	1	0	3.68	9	0	0	1	15	11	8	6	3	21	.208	L	L	6-2	180	2-28-82	2000	Miranda, Venez.
Cook, Steven	2	7	5.33	12	10	0	0	54	69	37	32	9	40	.297	R	R	6-4	205	11-26-81	2004	Bryson City, N.C.
Cox, Ben	2	0	2.97	22	0	0	3	33	31	18	11	20	38	.250	R	R	6-2	220	9-20-81	2004	Baytown, Texas
Diaz, Eddie	1	3	7.45	17	0	0	0	29	34	25	24	14	39	.291	R	R	6-0	170	1-25-83	2001	Orlando, Fla.
Felfoldi, Jon	2	3	2.72	9	9	0	0	50	41	20	15	15	46	.225	L	L	6-1	180	7-6-81	2002	San Diego, Calif.
Garza, Rudy	0	0	0.00	2	0	0	0	3	2	0	0	2	3	.182	R	R	6-2	190	4-10-84	2004	Sherman, Texas
Goodman, Chris	1	3	5.14	8	1	0	4	42	54	25	24	13	27	.316	S	R	6-1	180	11-9-81	2003	Benson, Ariz.
Henderson, Jim	2	6	2.59	14	13	0	0	76	61	34	22	27	39	.225	L	R	6-4	190	10-21-82	2003	Calgary, Alberta
Hlebovy, Gus	3	0	4.13	30	0	0	16	33	37	17	15	18	48	.282	R	R	5-11	170	7-6-82	2003	Campbell, Ohio

PITCHING	W	L	ERA	G	GS	CG	SV	IP	H	R	ER	BB	SO	AVG	B	T	HT	WT	DOB	1st Yr	Resides
Jenkins, Ricky	2	3	5.33	6	5	0	0	25	27	20	15	15	13	.273	R	R	6-3	200	6-12-82	2003	North Charleston, S.C.
Morales, Ricardo	1	0	3.00	1	1	0	0	6	3	2	2	1	5	.143	L	L	6-1	170	12-9-83	2001	La Romana, D.R.
Ochoa, Nehomar	0	3	4.70	5	5	0	0	15	20	10	8	11	7	.313	R	R	6-3	170	9-18-82	2000	Tacarigua, Venez.
Sandora, Robert	0	0	2.25	1	1	0	0	4	6	2	1	2	3	.286	L	R	6-0	200	8-5-81	2003	West Babylon, N.Y.
Sandoval, Francisco	5	2	5.87	21	0	0	1	46	68	39	30	23	32	.362	R	R	6-1	170	3-11-84	2001	Valencia, Venez.
Sosa, Gabriel	2	1	5.06	4	4	1	0	16	16	10	9	6	11	.262	L	L	5-9	170	9-27-85	2003	Vega Baja, P.R.
Thorne, David	0	0	33.75	2	0	0	0	1	4	5	5	3	1	.571	R	R	6-3	180	9-18-81	2002	Sydney, Australia
Trahan, David	3	2	2.59	20	1	0	0	49	41	20	14	28	47	.230	R	R	6-3	185	2-27-81	2004	Santa Fe, Texas
Wideman, Aaron	3	1	1.81	10	10	0	0	45	26	9	9	13	38	.167	R	L	5-11	190	6-8-85	2003	Mississauga, Ontario
Wilson, Thomas	1	1	3.86	7	0	0	0	12	11	5	5	1	9	.239	R	L	6-2	195	5-21-82	2004	Smithfield, N.C.
Wright, Isaiah	1	1	10.20	11	0	0	0	15	19	22	17	20	10	.311	R	R	6-1	170	7-21-83	2002	Dover, Del.

GCL EXPOS — Rookie

GULF COAST LEAGUE

BATTING	AVG	G	AB	R	H	2B	3B	HR	RBI	BB	SO	SB	CS	SLG	OBP	B	T	HT	WT	DOB	1st Yr	Resides
Ambrosini, Anthony	.222	5	18	1	4	2	0	0	1	0	0	0	0	.333	.222	R	R	5-9	180	9-22-78	2001	Ronkonkoma, N.Y.
Batista, Rafael	.225	54	160	26	36	4	0	1	11	29	31	7	8	.269	.362	S	R	5-8	150	2-20-82	2003	Santo Domingo, D.R.
Cobb, Maurice	.230	18	61	7	14	4	2	1	8	3	21	1	0	.410	.273	R	R	6-1	170	5-23-84	2002	Rocky Mount, N.C.
Cordova, Luis	.269	44	160	15	43	9	3	2	28	10	30	2	2	.400	.320	S	R	6-1	170	6-4-83	2000	Bolivar, Venez.
Davis, Leonard	.182	42	143	18	26	6	1	3	14	19	58	2	3	.301	.295	L	R	5-10	195	12-24-83	2004	Dos Palos, Calif.
Desmond, Ian	.227	55	216	28	49	11	0	1	27	10	40	13	3	.292	.272	R	R	6-2	185	9-20-85	2004	Sarasota, Fla.
Diaz, Ramon	.215	39	130	10	28	6	1	0	6	12	32	1	0	.277	.301	R	R	6-2	210	1-13-81	2004	Bronx, N.Y.
Emmerick, Josh	.125	5	8	0	1	0	0	0	0	1	1	0	0	.125	.222	R	R	6-4	190	2-22-81	2000	Oceanside, Calif.
Hamisevicz, Victor	.206	52	160	21	33	5	0	0	9	31	35	2	0	.238	.343	L	L	6-4	205	12-4-84	2003	Dunn Loring, Va.
Louisa, Lorvin	.308	11	39	4	12	3	0	0	7	3	14	0	1	.385	.372	R	R	6-4	200	2-7-83	1999	Willemstad, Curacao
Mancebo, Melvin	.291	33	103	16	30	6	1	4	14	9	36	4	0	.485	.354	R	R	6-1	190	9-8-83	2004	San Cristobal, D.R.
Mateo, Henry	.286	5	14	7	4	2	0	0	2	6	2	4	0	.429	.545	S	R	5-11	180	10-14-76	1995	Santo Domingo, D.R.
Nunez, Eduardo	.223	41	139	19	31	4	2	2	8	21	39	6	4	.324	.333	R	R	6-0	170	9-21-85	2003	San Sebastian, P.R.
Ovalles, Jose	.213	41	108	9	23	2	0	4	15	28	9	5	.231	.323	R	R	5-10	170	7-7-84	2003	Santo Domingo, D.R.
Rojas, Luis	.240	37	125	15	30	6	1	2	19	14	26	3	4	.352	.315	R	R	6-0	190	9-18-81	1999	Santo Domingo, D.R.
San Pedro, Erick	.083	4	12	1	1	0	0	0	4	2	4	0	0	.083	.214	R	R	6-0	205	10-5-83	2004	Miami, Fla.
Sandora, Robert	.095	7	21	0	2	0	0	0	2	1	5	0	0	.095	.167	L	R	6-0	200	8-5-81	2003	West Babylon, N.Y.
Simmons, Lyndsey	.167	23	54	7	9	3	0	0	4	11	8	0	0	.222	.308	L	R	6-0	200	10-15-81	2004	Smithtown, N.Y.
Soto, Abel	.182	7	22	2	4	0	0	0	1	2	8	0	0	.182	.250	R	R	6-2	180	2-1-85	2003	Bani, D.R.
Suarez, Gabriel	.210	41	124	8	26	0	0	1	9	7	32	5	2	.234	.259	R	R	6-0	170	12-14-84	2004	Scottsdale, Ariz.
Wong, Ivanosky	.211	13	38	2	8	0	0	0	3	6	7	0	0	.211	.340	R	R	5-11	170	11-26-83	2001	Bolivar, Venez.

GAMES BY POSITION: C—Ambrosini 4, Batista 1, Emmerick 4, Mancebo 17, San Pedro 4, Simmons 21, Soto 7, Wong 13. **1B**—Hamisevicz 52, Rojas 11. **2B**—Batista 1, Mateo 5, Nunez 37, Ovalles 20. **3B**—Davis 39, Ovalles 19, Rojas 7. **SS**—Desmond 51, Suarez 9. **OF**—Batista 53. Cobb 18. Cordoba 10, Davis 3, Diaz 39, Emmerick 1, Mancebo 15, Rojas 14, Sandora 7, Simmons 3, Suarez 28.

PITCHING	W	L	ERA	G	GS	CG	SV	IP	H	R	ER	BB	SO	AVG	B	T	HT	WT	DOB	1st Yr	Resides
Balester, Colin	1	2	2.19	5	4	0	0	25	20	8	6	5	21	.215	R	R	6-5	190	6-6-86	2004	Huntington Beach, Calif.
Campbell, Brett	0	1	3.86	5	0	0	1	7	6	3	3	6	11	.222	R	R	6-0	170	10-17-81	2004	Douglasville, Ga.
Cook, Steven	0	0	2.08	1	0	0	0	4	6	3	1	1	4	.300	R	R	6-4	205	11-26-81	2004	Bryson City, N.C.
Eischen, Joey	0	0	0.00	1	1	0	0	1	0	0	0	0	2	.000	L	L	6-0	210	5-25-70	1989	Rotonda West, Fla.
Engles, Terrence	0	4	9.75	10	6	0	2	24	31	28	26	12	17	.313	R	R	6-4	190	11-12-85	2004	Staten Island, N.Y.
Garza, Rudy	0	5	4.75	12	2	0	1	30	37	19	16	15	28	.300	R	R	6-2	190	4-10-84	2004	Sherman, Texas
Harrison, Ryan	1	2	4.29	13	3	0	2	36	35	18	17	13	22	.253	R	R	6-0	175	7-12-86	2004	Woodbine, Md.
Jackson, Aaron	1	3	4.02	13	2	0	0	31	23	16	14	16	24	.205	S	R	6-0	175	3-28-86	2004	St. Augustine, Fla.
Jenkins, Ricky	0	0	0.00	3	1	0	0	3	1	1	0	1	7	.083	R	R	6-3	200	6-12-82	2003	North Charleston, S.C.
Johnson, Anthony	0	2	8.00	9	3	0	0	18	29	21	16	8	16	.362	R	R	6-1	180	5-23-83	2004	Yazoo City, Miss.
Lehman, James	0	1	4.40	11	2	0	0	31	34	19	15	6	14	.274	R	R	6-2	185	3-14-85	2003	Brampton, Ontario
Lira, Oscar	1	3	5.08	11	4	0	1	34	38	26	19	11	24	.281	R	R	6-3	180	7-17-82	2001	Caracas, Venez.
Lugo, Ruddy	2	1	1.67	12	2	0	2	43	43	20	8	12	34	.260	R	R	6-1	185	11-10-86	2004	Hoboken, N.J.
Marrero, Darwin	0	0	33.75	1	1	0	0	1	5	5	5	0	1	.500	R	R	6-1	190	2-9-81	1997	Valencia, Venez.
Mata, Gustavo	0	2	6.00	2	2	0	0	6	9	4	4	0	7	.333	R	R	6-1	190	5-20-83	2001	Carupano, Venez.
Morales, Ricardo	1	7	4.55	12	8	0	0	57	59	37	29	12	55	.262	L	L	6-1	170	12-9-83	2001	La Romana, D.R.
Perks, Matt	0	7	7.09	11	2	0	0	27	36	24	21	15	18	.321	R	R	6-7	200	8-20-85	2004	Hamilton Square, N.J.
Roznovsky, Brandon	2	2	4.19	13	0	0	4	19	23	13	9	9	19	.291	R	R	6-2	195	9-24-81	2004	Brenham, Texas
Skrmetta, Matt	1	0	1.59	4	2	0	0	6	2	1	1	2	8	.100	S	R	6-3	220	11-6-72	1993	Satellite Beach, Fla.
Song, Seung	1	0	5.79	2	2	0	0	9	10	6	6	4	3	.270	R	R	6-1	190	6-29-80	1999	Pusan, Korea
Sosa, Gabriel	5	2	2.29	11	9	0	0	51	36	16	13	23	63	.196	L	L	5-9	170	9-27-85	2003	Vega Baja, P.R.
Yost, Wendell	6	1	3.79	11	4	0	0	36	35	16	15	5	23	.251	R	L	6-3	185	6-23-81	2004	Lynchburg, Va.

NEW YORK YANKEES

BY GEORGE KING

The hours felt as long as days. The days? They seemed like months? The months? Each one a year.

That's how the Yankees' winter of 2004-05 went. There have been other Yankee offseasons where it took a while

to get over disappointment. Heck, it was only three years earlier that the Diamondbacks won Game Seven of the World Series on Luis Gonzalez' broken-bat single off Mariano Rivera in the ninth inning. The next year the Angels ushered the Yankees out of the postseason in the first round.

However, never in their storied history did the Yankees have to deal with the angst and grief that came with losing to the Red Sox in the American League Championship Series in 2004. Not only were they eliminated by their blood rivals, they were the first team in baseball history to flush a 3-0 lead. And they were three outs away with Rivera on the mound in Game Four. Against the Red Sox!

Nothing in their glorious past prepared them for the gut-wrenching winter. It would have been hard enough just to lose to the Red Sox. But dropping four straight was tough to swallow. And right behind that bitter pill was the Red Sox taking four in a row from the Cardinals in the World Series.

For five days nothing stirred in the Yankees universe. George Steinbrenner was quiet. Joe Torre, Brian Cashman and the players said they weren't going out of their way to watch the World Series. Then The Boss called his Inner Circle to Tampa for three days of meetings to map out what could be done to ensure the Yankees return to the World Series, something they haven't won since 2000 when they copped their third straight title by beating the Mets.

"Congratulations to the Boston Red Sox, to their ownership and to the people of Boston. The Red Sox deserve

Gary Sheffield   Robinson Cano

PLAYERS of the YEAR

MAJOR LEAGUE: Gary Sheffield, of

Sheffield garnered MVP consideration in 2004 by playing through injury and carrying a high-paid yet often underachieving Yankees batting order. He hit .290-36-121 in his first season in the Bronx, overshadowing the New York debut of third baseman Alex Rodriguez.

MINOR LEAGUE: Robinson Cano, 2b

Cano put himself in the mix for the Yankees starting second base job with a solid 2004 campaign. He hit .283-13-77 in 508 at-bats between Double-A Trenton and Triple-A Columbus, and he increased his walk total from 16 in 2003 to 42 in 2004.

all the credit for what they have accomplished," The Boss said. "But make no mistake about it. We are hard at work and will be back with a strong team for our loyal New York Yankee fans."

Nothing the Yankees accomplished in 2004 looked good after the Colossal Collapse. Their seventh straight AL East title was nothing. Beating the Twins in the A.L. Division Series meant very little. Gary Sheffield's MVP-type season was reduced to a footnote. Alex Rodriguez' Yankee debut didn't matter. When a 3-0 lead against the Red Sox vanished the Yankee universe crashed.

The three-day summit in Tampa concentrated on upgrading Joe Torre's pitching staff. Torre professed his faith that Vazquez can bounce back from a 14-10 first year in pinstripes to be an ace. After going the entire season without a lefty being a big part of the rotation, the Yankees went into the winter looking for one.

Beyond the pitching picture, what Jason Giambi's future is remains a huge question. With four more years and $80 million left on his contract, the Yankees entered the offseason not knowing what they had in the 33-year-old lefthanded first baseman/DH.

Due to a benign tumor, Giambi was limited to 80 games in which he batted .208-12-40.

Throughout the season, the Yankees' beleaguered minor league system took a beating. Seattle told the Yankees they didn't have enough to get Freddy Garcia. Kansas City said the same thing about Carlos Beltran. And Randy Johnson stayed in Arizona because the Diamondbacks didn't like Dioner Navarro or Robinson Cano, New York's two best upper-tier prospect.

"We have to get better," said minor league head Mark Newman.

ORGANIZATION STATISTICS

ORGANIZATION LEADERS

BATTING

*AVG	Andy Phillips, Columbus/Trenton	.319
R	Kevin Reese, Columbus/Trenton	98
H	Kevin Reese, Columbus/Trenton	168
TB	Andy Phillips, Columbus/Trenton	274
	Kevin Reese, Columbus/Trenton	274
2B	Kevin Reese, Columbus/Trenton	50
3B	Robinson Cano, Columbus/Trenton	10
	John Rodriguez, Columbus	10
HR	Mitch Jones, Trenton	39
RBI	Andy Phillips, Columbus/Trenton	100
BB	Eric Duncan, Tampa/Battle Creek	69
SO	Mitch Jones, Trenton	152
SB	Kevin Thompson, Trenton/Tampa	38
*OBP	Craig Wilson, Trenton	.435
*SLG	Andy Phillips, Columbus/Trenton	.576

PITCHING

W	Jon Skaggs, Tampa	13
L	Javier Ortiz, Columbus/Trenton	12
#ERA	Colter Bean, Columbus	2.29
G	Paul Thorp, Battle Creek	55
CG	Three tied at	3
SV	Edwardo Sierra, Tampa	28
IP	Sean Henn, Trenton	163
BB	Abel Gomez, Battle Creek	73
SO	Abel Gomez, Battle Creek	149

*Minimum 250 at-bats #Minimum 75 innings

NEW YORK YANKEES

Manager: Joe Torre.　　　　　　　　　　**2004 Record:** 101-61, .623 (1st, AL East).

BATTING	AVG	G	AB	R	H	2B	3B	HR	RBI	BB	SO	SB	CS	OBP	SLG	B	T	HT	WT	DOB	1st Yr	Resides
Bush, Homer	.000	9	7	2	0	0	0	0	0	0	2	1	0	.125	.000	R	R	5-10	175	11-12-72	1991	Keller, Texas
Cairo, Miguel	.292	122	360	48	105	17	5	6	42	18	49	11	3	.344	.417	R	R	6-1	210	5-4-74	1992	Bakersfield, Calif.
Clark, Tony	.221	106	253	37	56	12	0	16	49	26	92	0	0	.297	.458	S	R	6-7	245	6-15-72	1990	Glendale, Ariz.
Crosby, Bubba	.151	55	53	8	8	2	0	2	7	2	13	2	0	.196	.302	L	L	5-11	185	8-11-76	1998	Bellaire, Texas
Escalona, Felix	.000	5	8	1	0	0	0	0	0	0	2	0	0	.111	.000	R	R	6-0	190	3-12-79	1996	Puerto Cabello, Venez.
Flaherty, John	.252	47	127	11	32	9	0	6	16	5	25	0	2	.286	.465	R	R	6-1	200	10-21-67	1988	Lutz, Fla.
Giambi, Jason	.208	80	264	33	55	9	0	12	40	47	62	0	1	.342	.379	L	R	6-3	235	1-8-71	1992	Covina, Calif.
Jeter, Derek	.292	154	643	111	188	44	1	23	78	46	99	23	4	.352	.471	R	R	6-3	195	6-26-74	1992	Tampa, Fla.
Lee, Travis	.105	7	19	1	2	1	0	0	2	1	3	0	0	.150	.158	L	R	6-3	205	5-26-75	1997	Henderson, Nev.
Lofton, Kenny	.275	83	276	51	76	10	7	3	18	31	27	7	3	.346	.395	L	L	6-0	190	5-31-67	1988	Tucson, Ariz.
Matsui, Hideki	.298	162	584	109	174	34	2	31	108	88	103	3	0	.390	.522	L	R	6-2	210	6-12-74	2003	Tokyo, Japan
Navarro, Dioner	.429	5	7	2	3	0	0	0	1	0	0	0	0	.429	.429	S	R	5-10	190	2-9-84	2001	Caracas, Venez.
Olerud, John	.280	49	164	16	46	7	0	4	26	21	20	0	0	.367	.396	L	L	6-5	220	8-5-68	1989	Fall City, Wash.
2-team (78 Seattle)	.259	127	425	45	110	20	1	9	48	61	61	0	0	.359	.374							
Phillips, Andy	.250	5	8	1	2	0	0	1	2	0	1	0	0	.250	.625	R	R	6-0	205	4-6-77	1999	Demopolis, Ala.
Posada, Jorge	.272	137	449	72	122	31	0	21	81	88	92	1	3	.400	.481	S	R	6-2	205	8-17-71	1991	Tampa, Fla.
Rodriguez, Alex	.286	155	601	112	172	24	2	36	106	80	131	28	4	.375	.512	R	R	6-3	210	7-27-75	1994	Dallas, Texas
Sheffield, Gary	.290	154	573	117	166	30	1	36	121	92	83	5	6	.393	.534	R	R	6-0	190	11-18-68	1986	St. Petersburg, Fla.
Sierra, Ruben	.244	107	307	40	75	12	1	17	65	25	55	1	0	.296	.456	S	R	6-1	210	10-6-65	1984	Miami, Fla.
Williams, Bernie	.262	148	561	105	147	29	1	22	70	85	96	1	5	.360	.435	S	R	6-2	205	9-13-68	1986	Armonk, N.Y.
Wilson, Enrique	.213	93	240	19	51	9	0	6	31	15	20	1	2	.254	.325	S	R	5-11	195	7-27-73	1992	Santo Domingo, D.R.

PITCHING	W	L	ERA	G	GS	CG	SV	IP	H	R	ER	BB	SO	AVG	B	T	HT	WT	DOB	1st Yr	Resides
Brown, Kevin	10	6	4.09	22	22	0	0	132	132	65	60	35	83	.262	R	R	6-4	200	3-14-65	1986	Macon, Ga.
De Paula, Jorge	0	1	5.00	3	1	0	0	9	9	6	5	4	2	.281	R	R	6-1	160	11-10-78	1997	Santo Domingo, D.R.
Gordon, Tom	9	4	2.21	80	0	0	4	90	56	23	22	23	96	.180	R	R	5-10	190	11-18-67	1986	Avon Park, Fla.
Graman, Alex	0	0	19.80	3	2	0	0	5	14	11	11	2	4	.500	L	L	6-4	200	11-17-77	1999	Huntingburg, Ind.
Halsey, Brad	1	3	6.47	8	7	0	0	32	41	26	23	14	25	.306	L	L	6-1	180	2-14-81	2002	Austin, Texas
Heredia, Felix	1	1	6.28	47	0	0	0	39	44	28	27	20	25	.278	L	L	6-0	180	6-8-75	1993	Miami, Fla.
Hernandez, Orlando	8	2	3.30	15	15	0	0	85	73	31	31	36	84	.230	R	R	6-2	220	10-11-69	1998	Miami, Fla.
Karsay, Steve	0	0	2.70	7	0	0	0	7	5	3	2	2	4	.217	R	R	6-3	215	3-24-72	1990	Scottsdale, Ariz.
Lieber, Jon	14	8	4.33	27	27	0	0	177	216	95	85	18	102	.301	R	R	6-3	230	4-2-70	1992	Mobile, Ala.
Loaiza, Esteban	10	7	5.70	31	27	2	0	183	217	124	116	71	117	.296	R	R	6-3	210	12-31-71	1991	Southlake, Texas
Marsonek, Sam	0	0	0.00	1	0	0	0	2	2	0	0	0	0	.333	R	R	6-6	225	7-10-78	1997	Tampa, Fla.
Mussina, Mike	12	9	4.59	27	27	1	0	165	178	91	84	40	132	.276	L	R	6-2	185	12-8-68	1990	Montoursville, Pa.
Nitkowski, C.J.	1	1	7.62	19	0	0	0	13	18	11	11	6	10	.327	L	L	6-3	205	3-9-73	1994	Houston, Texas
Osborne, Donovan	2	0	7.13	9	2	0	0	18	25	16	14	5	10	.347	L	L	6-2	195	6-21-69	1990	Carson City, Nev.
Padilla, Juan	0	0	3.97	6	0	0	0	11	16	5	5	4	5	.348	R	R	6-0	200	2-17-77	1998	Levittown, P.R.
Prinz, Bret	1	0	5.08	26	0	0	0	28	28	17	16	14	22	.259	R	R	6-2	215	6-15-77	1998	Peoria, Ariz.
Proctor, Scott	2	1	5.40	26	0	0	0	25	29	18	15	14	21	.284	R	R	6-1	198	1-2-77	1998	Jensen Beach, Fla.
Quantrill, Paul	7	3	4.72	86	0	0	1	95	124	54	50	20	37	.316	L	R	6-1	200	11-3-68	1989	Tarpon Springs, Fla.
Rivera, Mariano	4	2	1.94	74	0	0	53	79	65	17	17	20	66	.225	R	R	6-2	185	11-29-69	1990	La Chorrera, Panama
Sturtze, Tanyon	6	2	5.47	28	3	0	1	77	75	49	47	33	56	.254	R	R	6-5	200	10-12-70	1990	St. Petersburg, Fla.
Vazquez, Javier	14	10	4.91	32	32	0	0	198	195	114	108	60	150	.255	R	R	6-2	200	7-25-76	1994	Ponce, P.R.

FIELDING

Catcher	PCT	G	PO	A	E	DP	PB
Flaherty	.989	46	255	19	3	3	4
Navarro	1.000	4	9	0	0	0	0
Posada	.990	134	835	53	9	13	9

First Base	PCT	G	PO	A	E	DP
Cairo	1.000	1	2	0	0	0
Clark	.994	99	603	49	4	64
Giambi	.990	47	372	14	4	30
Lee	1.000	6	44	4	0	2
Olerud	.997	47	367	25	1	34

Second Base	PCT	G	PO	A	E	DP
Bush	1.000	4	7	4	0	3

Third Base	PCT	G	PO	A	E	DP
Cairo	.987	113	195	275	6	59
Wilson	.977	80	124	179	7	23

Third Base	PCT	G	PO	A	E	DP
Cairo	.895	8	4	13	2	0
Escalona	.000	1	0	0	0	0
Phillips	1.000	4	2	5	0	0
Rodriguez	.965	155	100	262	13	25
Sheffield	.000	2	0	0	1	0

Shortstop	PCT	G	PO	A	E	DP
Cairo	1.000	3	0	5	0	1
Escalona	1.000	4	3	7	0	1
Jeter	.981	154	273	392	13	96

	PCT	G	PO	A	E	DP
Rodriguez	1.000	2	1	1	0	1
Wilson	.972	16	10	25	1	6

Outfield	PCT	G	PO	A	E	DP
Crosby	.973	45	36	0	1	0
Lofton	.989	74	180	4	2	4
Matsui	.978	160	307	8	7	2
Sheffield	.983	136	271	11	5	3
Sierra	.977	29	41	1	1	0
Williams	.995	97	214	2	1	1

STEVE MOORE

Derek Jeter: Paced Yankees with 188 hits and 44 doubles

STEVE MOORE

Mariano Rivera: Set new career-high with 53 saves

FARM SYSTEM

Vice President, Player Personnel: Mark Newman

Class	Farm Team	League	W	L	Pct.	Finish*	Manager(s)	Affiliate Since
AAA	Columbus (Ohio) Clippers	International	80	64	.556	**3rd (14)**	Bucky Dent	1979
AA	Trenton (N.J.) Thunder	Eastern	64	78	.451	10th (12)	Stump Merrill	2003
High A	Tampa (Fla.) Yankees	Florida State	75	58	.564	**+3rd (12)**	Bill Masse	1994
Low A	#Battle Creek (Mich.) Yankees	Midwest	71	68	.511	9th (14)	Mitch Seoane/Bill Mosiello	2003
SS A	Staten Island (N.Y.) Yankees	New York-Penn	28	44	.389	13th (14)	Tommy John	1999
Rookie	Tampa (Fla.) Yankees	Gulf Coast	36	23	.610	**+1st (12)**	Oscar Acosta	1980

*Finish in overall standings (No. of teams in league)/Playoff teams in **boldface**   +League champion
#Affiliate will operate in Charleston, S.C. (South Atlantic) in 2005

COLUMBUS CLIPPERS
Class AAA

INTERNATIONAL LEAGUE

BATTING	AVG	G	AB	R	H	2B	3B	HR	RBI	BB	SO	SB	CS	OBP	SLG	B	T	HT	WT	DOB	1st Yr	Resides
Betts, Todd	.270	44	159	23	43	8	0	4	16	13	31	0	0	.330	.396	L	R	6-0	185	6-24-73	1993	Scarborough, Ontario
Bragg, Darren	.282	70	273	41	77	21	3	8	29	37	45	7	2	.367	.469	L	R	5-9	180	9-7-69	1991	Roswell, Ga.
Bush, Homer	.275	63	233	35	64	15	0	2	18	11	41	2	3	.312	.365	R	R	5-10	175	11-12-72	1991	Keller, Texas
Cano, Robinson	.259	61	216	22	56	9	2	6	30	18	27	0	1	.316	.403	L	R	6-0	170	10-22-82	2001	San Pedro de Macoris, D.R.
Cosme, Caonabo	.250	63	232	30	58	10	1	3	33	21	56	4	1	.315	.341	R	R	6-2	160	3-18-79	1996	La Vega, D.R.
Crosby, Bubba	.276	33	116	18	32	5	2	1	15	14	26	3	3	.365	.379	L	L	5-11	185	8-11-76	1998	Bellaire, Texas
Deardorff, Jeff	.269	122	432	66	116	13	3	18	76	50	113	10	6	.345	.438	R	R	6-3	220	8-14-78	1997	Clermont, Fla.
Escalona, Felix	.309	130	447	79	138	32	1	7	59	31	56	2	4	.373	.432	R	R	6-0	190	3-12-79	1996	Puerto Cabello, Venez.
Fasano, Sal	.233	76	236	21	55	15	1	10	33	10	46	0	0	.278	.432	R	R	6-2	254	8-10-71	1993	Overland Park, Kan.
Fuentes, Omar	.111	5	9	0	1	0	0	0	0	0	1	0	0	.200	.111	R	R	6-1	175	4-6-80	1997	Maracay, Venez.
Hooper, Kevin	.195	28	87	6	17	1	0	0	4	5	11	3	1	.239	.207	R	R	5-10	160	12-7-76	1999	Lawrence, Kan.
Kelly, Mike	.253	84	297	49	75	13	0	15	50	33	66	10	2	.336	.448	R	R	6-4	190	6-2-70	1991	Los Alamitos, Calif.
McDonald, Donzell	.196	28	92	14	18	5	3	3	10	9	22	4	0	.272	.413	S	R	5-11	180	2-20-75	1995	Glendale, Colo.
Melian, Jackson	.300	11	30	1	9	4	2	0	4	4	7	0	0	.400	.567	R	R	6-2	200	1-7-80	1997	Barcelona, Venez.
Myrow, Brian	.268	47	164	28	44	12	3	3	15	23	37	3	4	.365	.433	L	R	5-11	190	9-4-76	1999	Fort Worth, Texas
Navarro, Dioner	.250	40	136	18	34	8	2	1	16	14	17	1	0	.316	.360	S	R	5-10	190	2-9-84	2001	Caracas, Venez.
Parrish, Dave	.268	32	97	12	26	7	1	0	12	7	23	0	0	.317	.361	R	R	6-3	220	6-13-79	2000	Yorba Linda, Calif.
Phillips, Andy	.316	115	434	82	137	19	6	25	84	51	61	2	1	.386	.560	R	R	6-0	205	4-6-77	1999	Demopolis, Ala.
Reese, Kevin	.323	53	217	41	70	13	3	8	28	12	34	4	4	.370	.521	L	L	5-11	195	3-11-78	2000	San Diego, Calif.
Rodriguez, John	.300	112	377	78	113	29	10	16	69	48	82	9	3	.388	.557	L	L	6-0	185	1-20-78	1997	New York, N.Y.
Spencer, Shane	.250	15	48	6	12	3	0	0	4	7	14	1	0	.368	.313	R	R	6-0	220	2-20-72	1990	Tampa, Fla.
Torrealba, Steve	.462	4	13	3	6	1	0	2	4	0	3	0	0	.4621	.000	R	R	6-0	195	2-24-78	1995	Barquisimeto, Venez.
Vento, Michael	.273	122	451	64	123	28	1	15	73	34	78	2	3	.331	.439	R	R	6-0	195	5-25-78	1998	Corrales, N.M.

PITCHING	W	L	ERA	G	GS	CG	SV	IP	H	R	ER	BB	SO	AVG	B	T	HT	WT	DOB	1st Yr	Resides
Adkins, Tim	0	0	4.50	1	0	0	0	2	2	1	1	1	1	.250	L	L	6-0	190	5-12-74	1992	Huntington, W.Va.
Anderson, Jason	1	3	4.63	36	0	0	1	45	48	24	23	12	38	.264	L	R	6-0	170	6-9-79	2000	Danville, Ill.
2-team (9 Buffalo)	3	4	4.13	45	0	0	2	61	63	29	28	14	49	.261							
Beal, Andy	4	6	5.24	29	16	1	0	115	146	76	67	38	51	.313	L	L	6-2	185	10-31-78	2000	Paducah, Ky.

PITCHING

PITCHING	W	L	ERA	G	GS	CG	SV	IP	H	R	ER	BB	SO	AVG	B	T	HT	WT	DOB	1st Yr	Resides
Bean, Colter	9	3	2.29	53	0	0	1	83	61	24	21	23	109	.205	R	R	6-6	255	1-16-77	2000	Anniston, Ala.
Brown, Kevin	0	0	4.50	1	1	0	0	4	5	2	2	1	3	.313	R	R	6-4	200	3-14-65	1986	Macon, Ga.
Carlyle, Buddy	8	5	4.15	19	18	0	0	104	111	51	48	25	94	.272	L	R	6-3	170	12-21-77	1996	Bellevue, Neb.
Contreras, Jose	2	0	3.29	2	2	0	0	14	11	5	5	5	19	.216	R	R	6-4	230	12-6-71	2003	Managua, Nicaragua
Davis, Lance	4	2	5.48	8	7	0	0	46	54	28	28	8	20	.302	R	L	6-0	170	9-1-76	1995	Polk City, Fla.
Graman, Alex	11	6	3.37	24	22	1	0	131	115	56	49	53	129	.235	L	L	6-4	200	11-17-77	1999	Huntingburg, Ind.
Halsey, Brad	11	4	2.63	24	23	3	0	144	128	46	42	37	109	.237	L	L	6-1	180	2-14-81	2002	Austin, Texas
Heredia, Felix	0	0	0.00	3	0	0	0	4	2	0	0	1	5	.154	L	L	6-0	180	6-8-75	1993	Miami, Fla.
Hernandez, Orlando	2	1	5.60	3	3	0	0	18	17	11	11	3	16	.243	R	R	6-2	220	10-11-69	1998	Miami, Fla.
Izquierdo, Hansel	1	1	2.33	11	0	0	0	19	20	7	5	7	12	.260	R	R	6-1	200	1-2-77	1995	Miami, Fla.
Karsay, Steve	0	0	5.56	11	0	0	0	11	12	10	7	6	8	.255	R	R	6-3	215	3-24-72	1990	Scottsdale, Ariz.
Mann, Jim	3	1	5.97	25	1	0	0	38	48	30	25	15	25	.314	R	R	6-3	220	11-17-74	1994	Holbrook, Mass.
Manning, Charlie	1	1	3.65	11	0	0	0	12	10	6	5	6	11	.233	L	L	6-2	180	3-31-79	2001	Winter Haven, Fla.
Marsonek, Sam	1	5	3.15	35	0	0	17	40	36	20	14	12	28	.240	R	R	6-6	225	7-10-78	1997	Tampa, Fla.
Mussina, Mike	0	0	0.00	1	1	0	0	3	2	0	0	0	5	.182	L	R	6-2	185	12-8-68	1990	Montoursville, Pa.
Nitkowski, C.J.	0	0	1.42	16	0	0	0	13	8	3	2	3	11	.182	L	L	6-3	205	3-9-73	1994	Houston, Texas
Ortiz, Javier	1	5	7.50	9	9	0	0	42	66	38	35	19	33	.357	R	R	6-0	155	11-28-79	1997	Cartagena, Colombia
Padilla, Juan	2	1	2.03	44	0	0	2	58	49	20	13	6	52	.232	R	R	6-0	200	2-17-77	1998	Levittown, P.R.
Prinz, Bret	3	1	3.52	29	0	0	11	31	27	12	12	9	33	.241	R	R	6-2	215	6-15-77	1998	Peoria, Ariz.
Proctor, Scott	2	3	2.86	35	0	0	4	44	37	15	14	18	42	.233	R	R	6-1	198	1-2-77	1998	Jensen Beach, Fla.
Ramirez, Ramon	0	3	8.50	4	4	0	0	18	25	19	17	8	17	.329	R	R	5-11	170	8-31-81	1997	Santiago, D.R.
Reyes, Carlos	2	1	5.88	5	5	0	0	26	43	17	17	10	12	.381	S	R	6-1	190	4-4-69	1991	Tampa, Fla.
Rodriguez, Nerio	5	8	8.10	11	10	0	0	47	63	48	42	15	47	.328	R	R	6-2	205	3-4-71	1991	San Pedro de Macoris, D.R.
Schmitt, Eric	5	5	6.05	20	16	1	0	86	103	66	58	17	69	.293	R	R	6-4	210	7-23-78	2000	Fairfax, Va.
Thurman, Mike	0	0	15.43	2	0	0	0	2	5	4	4	2	2	.500	R	R	6-5	220	7-22-73	1994	West Palm Beach, Fla.
Wang, Chien-Ming	5	1	2.01	6	5	2	0	40	31	9	9	8	35	.215	R	R	6-3	200	3-31-80	2000	Tampa, Fla.

FIELDING

Catcher	PCT	G	PO	A	E	DP	PB
Fasano	.993	76	524	49	4	2	7
Fuentes	.939	5	31	0	2	0	0
Navarro	.994	39	287	28	2	7	1
Parrish	.990	32	201	7	2	1	4
Torrealba	1.000	4	25	1	0	0	1

First Base	PCT	G	PO	A	E	DP
Betts	1.000	14	121	6	0	12
Deardorff	.984	9	56	6	1	4
Myrow	.980	40	312	23	7	31
Phillips	.991	86	689	67	7	68

Second Base	PCT	G	PO	A	E	DP
Bush	1.000	17	44	43	0	0

	PCT	G	PO	A	E	DP
Cano	.985	61	118	140	4	35
Cosme	.978	45	96	126	5	27
Hooper	.991	18	37	69	1	20
Phillips	.868	7	9	24	5	6

Third Base	PCT	G	PO	A	E	DP
Bush	.944	37	18	67	5	6
Deardorff	.900	94	54	135	21	16
Escalona	.920	9	2	21	2	3
Phillips	.941	7	4	12	1	2

Shortstop	PCT	G	PO	A	E	DP
Bush	1.000	4	7	9	0	1
Cosme	.978	18	28	63	2	14

	PCT	G	PO	A	E	DP
Escalona	.960	120	144	354	21	67
Hooper	.960	9	8	16	1	1

Outfield	PCT	G	PO	A	E	DP
Bragg	.991	69	102	3	1	0
Crosby	1.000	27	57	1	0	0
Kelly	1.000	47	87	3	0	1
McDonald	.982	29	55	1	1	1
Melian	1.000	8	18	1	0	1
Reese	.980	51	92	4	2	0
Rodriguez	.969	102	217	4	7	1
Spencer	1.000	10	13	0	0	0
Vento	.982	109	210	7	4	2

TRENTON THUNDER — Class AA

EASTERN LEAGUE

BATTING	AVG	G	AB	R	H	2B	3B	HR	RBI	BB	SO	SB	CS	OBP	SLG	B	T	HT	WT	DOB	1st Yr	Resides
Brown, Andy	.000	1	1	0	0	0	0	0	0	0	0	0	0	.000	.000	L	L	6-6	190	4-14-80	1998	Richmond, Ind.
Cannizaro, Andy	.314	85	328	44	103	18	0	3	44	36	31	7	9	.385	.396	R	R	5-10	170	12-19-78	2001	Mandeville, La.
Cano, Robinson	.301	74	292	43	88	20	8	5	44	24	40	2	4	.356	.497	L	R	6-0	170	10-22-82	2001	San Pedro de Macoris, D.R.
Cosme, Caonabo	.308	14	52	7	16	4	1	1	5	2	13	3	0	.357	.481	R	R	6-2	160	3-18-79	1996	La Vega, D.R.
Fuentes, Omar	.251	68	211	23	53	11	0	5	31	25	30	0	1	.329	.374	R	R	6-1	175	4-6-80	1997	Maracay, Venez.
Griffin, Nate	.000	1	3	0	0	0	0	0	0	0	0	0	0	.000	.000	L	R	6-1	215	10-13-74	1995	Hazel Crest, Ill.
Grove, Jason	.293	120	376	47	110	24	2	11	68	32	91	2	2	.358	.455	L	L	6-2	200	8-15-78	2001	Walla Walla, Wash.
Jones, Mitch	.246	137	496	92	122	25	4	39	97	64	152	8	1	.334	.548	R	R	6-2	215	10-15-77	2000	Orem, Utah
Lofton, Kenny	.214	4	14	0	3	1	0	0	2	1	3	0	0	.267	.286	L	L	6-0	190	5-31-67	1988	Tucson, Ariz.
Madera, Sandy	.250	12	28	2	7	3	0	1	1	0	5	0	0	.250	.464	R	R	6-2	210	8-11-80	1998	Santo Domingo, D.R.
Melian, Jackson	.264	41	121	19	32	6	3	3	15	13	31	1	1	.343	.438	R	R	6-2	200	1-7-80	1997	Barcelona, Venez.
Navarro, Dioner	.271	70	255	32	69	14	1	3	29	33	44	1	0	.354	.369	S	R	5-10	190	2-9-84	2001	Caracas, Venez.
Olivares, Teuris	.201	72	179	25	36	7	1	6	27	19	29	1	1	.277	.352	R	R	6-0	165	12-15-78	1996	San Pedro de Macoris, D.R.
Parrish, David	.231	38	117	8	27	2	0	1	14	9	23	1	1	.281	.274	R	R	6-3	220	6-13-79	2000	Yorba Linda, Calif.
Phillips, Andy	.357	10	42	8	15	2	1	4	16	3	1	3	0	.383	.738	R	R	6-0	205	4-6-77	1999	Demopolis, Ala.
Reese, Kevin	.298	78	329	57	98	37	4	6	40	23	48	13	5	.348	.489	L	L	5-11	195	3-11-78	2000	San Diego, Calif.
Rifkin, Aaron	.252	127	468	62	118	27	1	23	82	49	118	4	1	.321	.462	L	L	6-3	220	3-12-79	2001	Upland, Calif.
Sardinha, Bronson	.267	72	266	37	71	11	1	6	29	37	65	4	1	.356	.383	L	L	6-1	195	4-6-83	2001	Kahuku, Hawaii
Stotts, J.T.	.233	54	172	23	40	6	0	3	15	17	23	3	3	.311	.320	R	R	5-11	185	1-21-80	2001	Valencia, Calif.
Tejeda, Ferdin	.174	30	86	8	15	1	0	0	3	6	19	3	0	.228	.186	S	R	5-11	170	9-15-82	2001	Santo Domingo, D.R.
Thompson, Kevin	.281	69	270	43	76	17	0	9	17	30	40	29	10	.362	.444	R	R	5-10	185	9-18-79	2000	Fort Worth, Texas
Weber, Jake	.262	111	363	52	95	18	3	6	38	29	47	4	5	.320	.377	L	R	5-11	180	4-22-76	1998	Wappinger Falls, N.Y.
Wilson, Craig	.306	80	268	49	82	12	0	3	27	56	35	3	3	.435	.384	R	R	6-0	180	9-3-70	1993	Phoenix, Ariz.
Winrow, Tommy	.218	15	55	3	12	0	1	1	4	2	14	1	1	.246	.309	L	L	6-2	185	7-12-80	1999	Fort Myers, Fla.

PITCHING	W	L	ERA	G	GS	CG	SV	IP	H	R	ER	BB	SO	AVG	B	T	HT	WT	DOB	1st Yr	Resides
Adkins, Tim	1	4	4.47	52	1	0	1	56	64	37	28	27	44	.290	L	L	6-0	190	5-12-74	1992	Huntington, W.Va.
Blackwell, Brad	0	0	18.00	1	0	0	0	3	3	2	2	0	2	.500	R	R	6-2	215	5-8-82	2003	Bixby, Okla.
Blankenship, John	1	1	9.00	13	0	0	1	15	19	15	15	10	10	.297	L	L	5-10	180	11-6-78	2000	Logan, Ala.
Brown, Kevin	0	1	13.50	1	1	0	0	2	7	5	3	0	1	.500	R	R	6-4	200	3-14-65	1986	Macon, Ga.
Carlyle, Buddy	4	0	0.72	8	5	0	0	37	23	4	3	4	48	.174	L	R	6-3	170	12-21-77	1996	Bellevue, Neb.
Currier, Rik	4	6	6.06	34	8	0	0	82	91	65	55	51	74	.281	R	R	5-10	185	5-26-78	2001	Aliso Viejo, Calif.
DeSalvo, Matt	2	2	6.59	5	5	0	0	27	27	20	20	10	24	.260	R	R	6-0	170	9-11-80	2003	New Castle, Pa.
Elder, Dave	2	2	3.06	17	0	0	1	18	13	8	6	15	24	.206	R	R	6-0	180	9-23-75	1997	Conyers, Ga.
Goetz, Geoff	0	0	5.19	9	0	0	0	9	11	5	5	3	6	.306	L	L	6-0	185	4-3-79	1997	Lutz, Fla.
Henn, Sean	6	8	4.41	27	27	0	0	163	173	94	80	63	118	.273	R	L	6-5	200	4-23-81	2001	Fort Worth, Texas

PITCHING	W	L	ERA	G	GS	CG	SV	IP	H	R	ER	BB	SO	AVG	B	T	HT	WT	DOB	1st Yr	Resides
Heredia, Felix	0	1	5.40	3	1	0	0	5	7	6	3	0	8	.350	L	L	6-0	180	6-8-75	1993	Miami, Fla.
Isaacson, Charlie	1	1	3.18	10	0	0	1	17	21	10	6	4	12	.304	R	R	6-2	190	5-5-80	2002	Overland Park, Kan.
Izquierdo, Hansel	1	1	3.29	11	0	0	3	14	17	5	5	5	11	.315	R	R	6-1	200	1-2-77	1995	Miami, Fla.
Julianel, Ben	1	2	5.68	6	0	0	0	6	6	4	4	3	5	.250	S	L	6-2	180	9-4-79	2001	Belmont, Calif.
Karsay, Steve	1	0	7.50	4	0	0	0	6	6	5	5	4	7	.273	R	R	6-3	215	3-24-72	1990	Scottsdale, Ariz.
Kaye, Justin	1	0	5.14	3	0	0	0	7	11	4	4	4	7	.379	R	R	6-4	190	6-9-76	1995	Fort Lauderdale, Fla.
Kennard, Jeff	0	1	10.13	7	0	0	0	8	14	9	9	9	7	.368	R	R	6-2	195	7-26-81	2001	Centerville, Ohio
King, Jeremy	0	0	6.75	2	0	0	0	3	3	2	2	2	2	.300	R	R	6-2	210	11-12-81	2000	Nocatee, Fla.
Manning, Charlie	2	1	4.07	15	1	0	0	24	31	11	11	6	19	.310	L	L	6-2	180	3-31-79	2001	Winter Haven, Fla.
Moore, Ben	0	0	0.00	1	0	0	0	1	0	0	0	0	1	.000	R	R	6-1	170	6-10-81	2003	St. Croix Falls, Wis.
Orloski, Joe	1	2	9.00	6	0	0	0	8	12	9	8	5	7	.333	R	R	6-3	180	5-17-79	1998	Las Vegas, Nev.
Ortiz, Javier	6	7	4.10	19	18	1	0	105	110	54	48	33	77	.269	R	R	6-0	155	11-28-79	1997	Cartagena, Colombia
Padilla, Juan	0	0	9.00	3	0	0	0	4	4	4	4	3	4	.267	R	R	6-0	200	2-17-77	1998	Levittown, P.R.
Pope, Justin	3	4	4.06	18	10	2	0	75	78	37	34	18	53	.266	S	R	6-1	180	11-8-79	2001	Lake Worth, Fla.
Ramirez, Ramon	4	6	4.66	18	18	1	0	114	115	60	59	32	128	.260	R	R	5-11	170	8-31-81	1997	Santiago, D.R.
Reyes, Carlos	1	6	5.68	15	12	1	0	78	106	52	49	15	60	.323	S	R	6-1	190	4-4-69	1991	Tampa, Fla.
Shepard, David	4	7	3.54	51	0	0	20	69	57	30	27	28	52	.226	R	R	6-1	195	2-6-74	1996	Sarasota, Fla.
Smith, Matt	4	4	4.96	14	11	0	0	62	67	34	34	31	56	.286	L	L	6-5	225	6-15-79	2000	Henderson, Nev.
Villegas, Francisco	1	4	5.94	20	6	0	2	50	64	36	33	15	67	.309	R	R	5-10	180	3-23-78	2001	San Luis, Ariz.
Wang, Chien-Ming	6	5	4.05	18	18	0	0	109	112	53	49	26	90	.266	R	R	6-3	200	3-31-80	2000	Tampa, Fla.
Ward, Jeremy	3	3	4.85	41	0	0	3	43	47	28	23	12	33	.281	R	R	6-2	235	2-24-78	1999	Rocky Mount, N.C.
Wiggins, Scott	1	1	5.14	16	0	0	1	14	11	8	8	11	15	.229	L	L	6-3	200	3-24-76	1997	Newport, Ky.
Zamora, Peter	0	0	36.00	1	0	0	0	1	3	4	4	1	1	.500	L	L	6-3	180	8-13-75	1997	Mission Viejo, Calif.

FIELDING

Catcher	PCT	G	PO	A	E	DP	PB
Fuentes	.990	63	452	34	5	2	9
Griffin	1.000	1	6	0	0	0	0
Madera	.923	6	19	5	2	1	0
Navarro	.984	54	394	37	7	5	13
Parrish	.984	32	225	18	4	5	5

First Base	PCT	G	PO	A	E	DP
Fuentes	1.000	3	27	0	0	3
Jones	1.000	21	141	10	0	18
Phillips	1.000	5	34	6	0	3
Rifkin	.987	118	956	60	13	79
Wilson	1.000	7	33	0	0	2

Second Base	PCT	G	PO	A	E	DP
Cano	.967	70	126	201	11	44

Cosme	.978	12	21	24	1	5
Olivares	.991	35	30	84	1	17
Wilson	.994	44	73	102	1	25

Third Base	PCT	G	PO	A	E	DP
Cano	.909	4	3	7	1	0
Cosme	1.000	1	1	0	0	
Olivares	.929	7	6	7	1	1
Phillips	.933	6	5	9	1	1
Sardinha	.831	57	30	68	20	7
Stotts	.925	45	18	68	7	3
Wilson	.986	34	18	54	1	5

Shortstop	PCT	G	PO	A	E	DP
Cannizaro	.962	84	116	240	14	55

Cosme	1.000	1	1	3	0	1
Olivares	.972	27	37	68	3	9
Stotts	.963	9	10	16	1	4
Tejeda	.974	30	42	72	3	18

Outfield	PCT	G	PO	A	E	DP
Grove	.969	108	181	6	6	1
Jones	.973	127	202	13	6	2
Lofton	1.000	4	6	0	0	0
Melian	1.000	15	15	0	0	0
Reese	.988	81	165	6	2	2
Thompson	.992	67	115	4	1	0
Weber	1.000	57	88	5	0	2
Winrow	1.000	15	34	2	0	2

TAMPA YANKEES
High Class A

FLORIDA STATE LEAGUE

BATTING	AVG	G	AB	R	H	2B	3B	HR	RBI	BB	SO	SB	CS	OBP	SLG	B	T	HT	WT	DOB	1st Yr	Resides
Brown, Andy	.162	27	74	4	12	2	0	3	9	5	26	0	1	.215	.311	L	L	6-6	190	4-14-80	1998	Richmond, Ind.
Cabrera, Melky	.288	85	333	48	96	20	3	8	51	23	59	3	1	.341	.438	S	L	5-11	170	8-11-84	2002	Santo Domingo, D.R.
Carson, Matt	.171	37	129	16	22	7	0	3	17	6	33	2	1	.213	.295	R	R	6-2	200	7-1-81	2002	Yucaipa, Calif.
Cruz, Jose Enrique	.115	9	26	7	3	0	0	1	4	7	11	1	0	.303	.231	R	R	5-10	185	7-13-81	2003	Houston, Texas
Drobiak, Jayson	.229	81	288	41	66	13	4	11	43	25	71	5	1	.293	.417	L	R	6-2	190	3-3-79	1999	Jewett City, Conn.
Duncan, Eric	.254	52	177	24	45	20	2	4	26	31	47	0	2	.364	.458	L	R	6-3	195	12-7-84	2003	Florham Park, N.J.
Duncan, Shelley	.248	123	424	65	105	27	1	19	78	54	119	6	3	.336	.450	R	R	6-5	215	9-29-79	2001	Tucson, Ariz.
Giambi, Jason	.167	2	6	0	1	0	0	0	1	1	0	0	0	.286	.167	L	R	6-3	235	1-8-71	1992	Covina, Calif.
Guillen, Rodolfo	.264	79	307	40	81	16	2	1	42	22	59	1	0	.313	.339	R	R	6-3	185	11-23-83	2001	Santo Domingo, D.R.
Holman, Mario	.286	4	7	1	2	1	0	0	3	0	3	0	0	.286	.429	S	R	6-0	160	5-21-84	2003	Managua, Nicaragua
Koutnik, Jared	.291	104	381	57	111	19	2	10	62	30	72	1	2	.348	.430	R	R	6-3	190	11-9-79	2002	Milwaukee, Wis.
Lee, Travis	.250	3	12	2	3	1	0	0	3	1	4	0	0	.308	.333	L	R	6-3	225	5-26-75	1997	Henderson, Nev.
Lopez, Gabe	.256	106	403	56	103	23	4	3	46	42	48	5	0	.327	.355	R	R	5-8	170	3-11-80	2002	Pico Rivera, Calif.
Madera, Sandy	.333	3	6	2	2	2	0	0	3	0	0	0	0	.375	.667	R	R	6-2	210	8-11-80	1998	Santo Domingo, D.R.
Mejia, Manuel	.287	42	115	14	33	9	1	0	19	10	31	0	0	.366	.383	R	R	6-2	190	11-5-78	1997	Santo Domingo, D.R.
Mendez, Deivi	.310	20	71	13	22	7	1	1	8	4	8	0	0	.355	.479	R	R	6-1	160	6-24-83	2000	Santo Domingo, D.R.
Santos, Omir	.286	37	119	18	34	6	1	2	13	6	17	1	0	.341	.403	R	R	6-1	200	4-29-81	2001	Toa Baja, P.R.
Sardinha, Bronson	.315	63	248	37	78	12	2	2	33	29	39	9	2	.389	.403	L	R	6-1	195	4-6-83	2001	Kahuku, Hawaii
Spencer, Shane	.444	3	9	0	4	0	0	0	2	1	1	0	0	.500	.444	R	R	6-0	210	2-20-72	1990	Tampa, Fla.
Sprowl, Jon-Mark	.256	66	219	30	56	10	1	1	29	41	24	0	3	.381	.324	L	R	6-1	225	8-1-80	1999	Panama City, Fla.
Stotts, J.T.	.233	36	116	14	27	4	1	0	11	9	23	0	0	.289	.284	R	R	5-11	185	1-21-80	2001	Valencia, Calif.
Tejeda, Ferdin	.236	50	174	21	41	7	0	0	15	13	32	3	0	.293	.276	S	R	5-11	170	9-15-82	2001	Santo Domingo, D.R.
Thompson, Kevin	.356	11	45	12	16	4	0	2	6	4	7	9	2	.420	.578	R	R	5-10	185	9-18-79	2000	Fort Worth, Texas
Van Meetren, Jason	.179	8	28	0	5	1	0	0	1	9	0	1	.233	.214	R	R	6-3	200	10-4-79	2001	Henderson, Nev.
Vechionacci, Marcos	.250	1	4	1	1	0	0	0	0	2	1	0	0	.250	.250	S	R	6-2	170	8-7-86	2003	Valencia, Venez.
Verbryke, Eric	.250	101	340	57	85	19	3	5	34	36	69	11	2	.337	.368	L	L	6-2	220	8-6-81	2002	Santa Maria, Calif.
Winrow, Tommy	.330	93	339	56	112	20	2	4	41	26	55	1	5	.379	.437	L	L	6-2	185	7-12-80	1999	Fort Myers, Fla.

PITCHING	W	L	ERA	G	GS	CG	SV	IP	H	R	ER	BB	SO	AVG	B	T	HT	WT	DOB	1st Yr	Resides
Abreu, Eric	2	0	1.06	3	3	1	0	17	7	2	2	6	15	.127	R	R	6-0	170	6-2-83	2003	Santo Domingo, D.R.
Artiles, Carlos	3	3	4.22	13	0	0	0	21	17	10	10	13	13	.218	L	L	5-11	165	1-21-81	1998	Santo Domingo, D.R.
Blankenship, Jon	0	2	7.94	11	1	0	0	17	23	16	15	12	6	.319	L	L	5-10	180	11-6-78	2000	Logan, Ala.
Borrell, Danny	0	1	6.23	4	2	0	0	9	8	7	6	4	8	.242	L	L	6-3	200	1-24-79	2000	Sanford, N.C.
Brumit, Matthew	1	0	5.29	10	0	0	1	17	25	11	10	6	7	.338	R	R	6-4	220	10-28-79	2002	Akron, Ohio
DeLeon, Juan	3	3	2.93	33	1	0	0	61	54	26	20	25	73	.225	R	R	5-11	160	6-24-81	2001	Santo Domingo, D.R.
DeSalvo, Matt	6	3	1.43	13	13	0	0	75	48	20	12	30	80	.176	R	R	5-10	170	9-11-80	2003	New Castle, Pa.
Esquivia, Manuel	0	0	15.88	5	0	0	0	6	7	10	10	10	2	.304	R	R	6-0	165	5-30-80	1997	Cartagena, Colombia
Goetz, Geoff	1	0	0.98	14	0	0	2	18	13	5	2	16	6	.213	L	L	6-0	185	4-3-79	1997	Lutz, Fla.

PITCHING

PITCHING	W	L	ERA	G	GS	CG	SV	IP	H	R	ER	BB	SO	AVG	B	T	HT	WT	DOB	1st Yr	Resides
Heredia, Felix	0	0	1.80	2	2	0	0	5	4	1	1	3	3	.222	L	L	6-0	180	6-8-75	1993	Miami, Fla.
Hernandez, Orlando	1	0	1.50	3	3	0	0	12	3	4	2	7	11	.079	R	R	6-2	220	10-11-69	1998	Miami, Fla.
Isaacson, Charlie	4	4	3.63	23	11	1	0	87	75	37	35	38	78	.240	R	R	6-2	190	5-5-80	2002	Overland Park, Kan.
Julianel, Ben	5	5	2.49	44	0	0	10	61	53	23	17	24	72	.235	S	L	6-2	180	9-4-79	2001	Belmont, Calif.
Karstens, Jeffrey	6	9	4.02	24	24	1	0	139	151	70	62	31	116	.276	R	R	6-3	175	9-24-82	2003	San Diego, Calif.
Kennard, Jeff	1	1	5.56	13	0	0	0	23	23	16	14	10	21	.256	R	R	6-2	195	7-26-81	2001	Centerville, Ohio
King, Jeremy	7	3	3.65	28	4	0	0	62	53	29	25	28	60	.226	R	R	6-2	210	11-12-81	2000	Nocatee, Fla.
Lieber, Jon	1	0	0.00	1	1	0	0	7	2	0	0	0	4	.083	R	R	6-2	230	4-2-70	1992	Mobile, Ala.
Marsonek, Sam	0	0	0.00	3	0	0	0	4	3	0	0	0	3	.214	R	R	6-6	225	7-10-78	1997	Tampa, Fla.
Moore, Ben	2	0	2.14	12	0	0	0	21	18	7	5	8	13	.234	R	R	6-1	170	6-10-81	2003	St. Croix Falls, Wis.
Pope, Justin	4	4	3.80	13	9	1	0	66	66	32	28	7	44	.262	S	R	6-0	180	11-8-79	2001	Lake Worth, Fla.
Sevilla, Wilton	0	0	4.50	1	0	0	0	2	2	1	1	1	2	.286	R	R	5-7	170	7-19-83	2004	Leon, Nicaragua
Sierra, Edwardo	2	3	3.33	45	0	0	28	49	44	22	18	45	57	.246	R	R	6-3	185	4-15-82	1999	San Cristobal, D.R.
Skaggs, Jon	13	9	3.87	27	27	2	0	163	142	84	70	70	116	.235	R	R	6-5	225	3-27-78	2001	Houston, Texas
Valdez, Jose	7	7	4.27	23	20	0	0	112	116	69	53	38	76	.265	R	R	6-4	185	1-23-83	2001	Santo Domingo, D.R.
Villegas, Francisco	0	0	3.09	15	0	0	2	23	18	8	8	18	24	.231	R	R	5-10	180	3-23-78	2001	San Luis, Ariz.
White, Steven	6	2	2.56	12	12	1	0	60	51	26	17	19	44	.226	R	R	6-5	205	6-15-81	2004	League City, Texas

FIELDING

Catcher	PCT	G	PO	A	E	DP	PB
Madera	1.000	2	11	0	0	0	0
Mejia	.987	37	202	30	3	0	8
Santos	.993	37	277	24	2	0	1
Sprowl	.994	64	459	40	3	1	13

First Base	PCT	G	PO	A	E	DP
Brown	1.000	2	7	1	0	1
Carson	1.000	1	4	0	0	0
Drobiak	.988	51	452	35	6	48
S. Duncan	.986	82	651	55	10	58
Giambi	1.000	2	10	1	0	1
Lee	1.000	3	19	1	0	2
Verbryke	1.000	1	2	0	0	0

Second Base	PCT	G	PO	A	E	DP
Cruz	.969	7	10	21	1	3
Holman	.900	3	3	6	1	0

	PCT	G	PO	A	E	DP
Koutnik	.985	15	23	41	1	8
Lopez	.978	100	177	302	11	55
Stotts	.982	10	23	32	1	11

Third Base	PCT	G	PO	A	E	DP
Drobiak	1.000	3	1	1	0	0
E. Duncan	.939	48	25	68	6	4
Koutnik	.911	17	13	28	4	4
Lopez	1.000	1	0	3	0	1
Sardinha	.865	61	35	112	23	7
Stotts	1.000	4	2	11	0	1
Vechionacci	1.000	1	1	3	0	1

Shortstop	PCT	G	PO	A	E	DP
Cruz	1.000	1	1	3	0	0
Koutnik	.912	46	47	118	16	25
Lopez	.500	1	1	0	1	0
Mendez	.903	20	33	60	10	8

	PCT	G	PO	A	E	DP
Stotts	.936	17	33	55	6	16
Tejeda	.979	49	84	146	5	32

Outfield	PCT	G	PO	A	E	DP
Brown	1.000	18	48	1	0	0
Cabrera	.983	82	167	5	3	1
Carson	1.000	35	62	3	0	2
E. Duncan	1.000	1	1	0	0	0
S. Duncan	1.000	6	8	0	0	0
Guillen	.981	75	149	6	3	1
Koutnik	1.000	8	16	1	0	0
Lofton	1.000	1	1	0	0	0
Spencer	1.000	2	4	0	0	0
Van Meetren	1.000	5	8	0	0	0
Verbryke	.975	98	147	7	4	0
Winrow	.969	80	118	6	4	0

BATTLE CREEK YANKEES — Low Class A

MIDWEST LEAGUE

BATTING	AVG	G	AB	R	H	2B	3B	HR	RBI	BB	SO	SB	CS	OBP	SLG	B	T	HT	WT	DOB	1st Yr	Resides
Andrus, Erold	.291	137	553	83	161	34	1	12	74	38	86	14	5	.338	.421	S	L	6-2	170	8-16-84	2001	Maracay, Venez.
Cabrera, Edwin	.167	8	18	1	3	1	0	0	3	1	7	1	0	.211	.222	S	R	6-0	170	8-14-83	2001	Santo Domingo, D.R.
Cabrera, Melky	.333	42	171	35	57	16	3	0	16	15	23	7	2	.383	.462	S	L	5-11	170	8-11-84	2002	Santo Domingo, D.R.
Carson, Matt	.304	95	381	59	116	23	2	12	58	22	78	21	7	.355	.470	R	R	6-2	200	7-1-81	2002	Yucaipa, Calif.
Cruz, Jose Enrique	.231	83	264	40	61	9	1	8	26	30	68	13	5	.329	.364	R	R	5-10	185	7-13-81	2003	Houston, Texas
Duncan, Eric	.260	78	288	52	75	23	2	12	57	38	84	7	1	.351	.479	L	R	6-3	195	12-7-84	2003	Florham Park, N.J.
Gonzalez, Edwar	.214	14	28	4	6	2	1	0	4	1	10	0	2	.267	.357	R	R	5-10	200	1-1-83	2002	Miami, Fla.
Harris, Estee	.214	57	192	17	41	8	2	3	20	21	82	5	1	.305	.323	L	R	5-11	170	1-8-85	2003	Central Islip, N.Y.
Kartler, Bryce	.252	92	329	51	83	13	2	11	43	36	81	12	6	.335	.404	L	L	6-2	215	6-9-80	2003	Phoenix, Ariz.
Made, Hector	.289	128	515	68	149	30	1	5	52	33	76	12	10	.336	.381	R	R	6-1	155	12-18-84	2002	Santo Domingo, D.R.
Robles, Luis	.196	33	92	8	18	8	0	1	11	4	12	0	0	.227	.315	R	R	6-4	180	3-2-82	2003	Rialto, Calif.
Rodriguez, Rafael	.295	70	220	29	65	14	1	5	30	6	57	4	2	.314	.436	R	R	5-11	160	1-11-84	2001	San Pedro de Macoris, D.R.
Rojas, Tommy	.272	79	250	31	68	15	0	6	50	21	68	1	2	.345	.404	R	R	6-1	185	3-31-82	2001	Henderson, Nev.
Santos, Omir	.240	56	171	21	41	7	0	2	16	7	27	4	0	.277	.316	R	R	6-1	200	4-29-81	2001	Toa Baja, P.R.
Treadway, Jared	.189	19	37	3	7	0	2	1	3	1	19	0	1	.205	.378	R	R	6-0	180	12-21-79	2002	Bay Village, Ohio
Urick, John	.283	118	396	61	112	29	0	15	65	52	85	1	4	.369	.470	L	L	6-2	210	2-22-82	2003	Blue Springs, Mo.
Van Meetren, Jason	.286	58	196	36	56	8	0	2	30	25	46	1	6	.367	.357	R	R	6-3	200	10-4-79	2001	Henderson, Nev.
Vasquez, Willie	.243	108	362	50	88	22	1	8	44	46	96	2	6	.332	.376	S	R	6-0	150	12-26-83	2000	Piritu, Venez.
Villanova, Robert	.091	7	11	1	1	0	0	0	1	2	2	0	0	.231	.091	L	R	6-2	200	7-8-82	2004	Mahopac, N.Y.
Walsh, Nick	.318	54	195	33	62	7	0	0	22	37	22	7	5	.435	.354	L	R	5-8	180	5-6-80	2004	Alamo, Calif.

PITCHING	W	L	ERA	G	GS	CG	SV	IP	H	R	ER	BB	SO	AVG	B	T	HT	WT	DOB	1st Yr	Resides
Baisley, Brad	0	2	9.88	7	2	0	0	14	21	18	15	4	5	.350	R	R	6-9	200	8-24-79	1998	Tampa, Fla.
Barkley, Richard	0	0	4.91	4	0	0	0	7	9	4	4	3	5	.290	R	R	6-1	180	8-6-81	2003	Sumter, S.C.
Beam, T.J.	2	5	4.35	11	7	0	0	41	34	20	20	17	54	.224	R	R	6-7	215	8-8-80	2003	Scottsdale, Ariz.
Blackwell, Brad	1	0	18.69	6	0	0	0	4	8	9	9	9	3	.400	R	R	6-2	215	5-8-82	2003	Bixby, Okla.
Brumit, Matthew	4	2	3.95	40	0	0	1	57	57	28	25	16	82	.252	R	R	6-4	220	10-28-79	2002	Akron, Ohio
Castle, Heath	1	1	5.63	42	0	0	1	54	67	42	34	16	36	.307	L	L	6-0	200	1-6-82	2003	Lomansville, Ky.
Clippard, Tyler	10	10	3.44	26	25	1	0	149	153	71	57	32	145	.261	R	R	6-4	170	2-14-85	2003	Trinity, Fla.
Esquivia, Manuel	0	0	10.80	2	0	0	0	5	5	6	6	8	3	.250	R	R	6-0	165	5-30-80	1997	Cartagena, Colombia
Gardner, Mike	1	2	3.40	43	0	0	0	56	54	23	21	16	44	.251	R	R	6-0	190	5-23-81	2002	Louisville, Ky.
Gomez, Abel	9	10	3.66	29	25	0	0	143	115	73	58	73	149	.222	L	L	6-0	170	11-24-84	2002	Santo Domingo, D.R.
Harmsen, Brandon	10	3	3.53	35	16	0	1	130	166	68	51	32	80	.308	R	R	6-3	200	12-13-81	2002	Jenison, Mich.
Jones, Jason	3	1	2.87	6	6	0	0	31	38	11	10	3	19	.300	R	R	6-5	225	11-20-82	2004	Pasadena, Md.
Kemlo, Chris	0	1	5.06	5	0	0	0	11	17	6	6	4	9	.347	R	R	6-5	200	9-23-83	2002	Oshawa, Ontario
Martinez, Mike	1	1	6.00	4	0	0	1	6	9	4	4	3	5	.346	R	R	6-0	190	4-12-81	2004	Anaheim, Calif.
Moore, Ben	7	3	3.88	27	6	0	1	70	66	33	30	18	60	.253	R	R	6-1	170	6-10-81	2003	St. Croix Falls, Wis.
Quezada, Elvys	2	6	4.11	15	15	1	0	72	59	43	33	23	75	.211	R	R	6-1	210	12-15-81	2003	New York, N.Y.
Sevilla, Wilton	0	1	0.00	2	0	0	0	2	4	5	0	1	2	.400	R	R	5-7	170	7-19-83	2002	Leon, Nicaragua
Smith, Josh	5	2	5.42	34	10	0	0	90	106	61	54	42	71	.293	R	R	6-4	225	11-15-81	2003	McGregor, Texas
Stephens, Amad	1	2	3.42	13	0	0	0	24	25	14	9	8	21	.269	R	R	6-0	215	6-1-79	2001	San Diego, Calif.
Thorp, Paul	2	4	3.08	55	0	0	26	64	61	25	22	14	65	.246	R	R	6-0	200	9-23-80	2002	Carrollton, Texas

PITCHING	W	L	ERA	G	GS	CG	SV	IP	H	R	ER	BB	SO	AVG	B	T	HT	WT	DOB	1st Yr	Resides
Vanderplow, Randy	1	1	3.72	14	0	0	0	19	12	8	8	3	24	.182	R	R	6-3	210	7-21-80	2004	Tustin Ranch, Calif.
Wheeler, Adam	0	0	4.26	5	0	0	1	6	8	3	3	2	8	.286	R	R	6-6	180	4-26-83	2001	Smyrna, Ga.
White, Steven	5	2	2.65	9	9	2	0	58	36	19	17	26	56	.183	R	R	6-5	205	6-15-81	2004	League City, Texas
Wiseman, Steven	1	1	6.10	8	0	0	0	10	16	7	7	6	14	.340	R	R	5-11	170	4-23-80	2002	Winchester, Tenn.
Wright, Chase	5	8	5.44	18	18	0	0	86	100	60	52	57	51	.288	L	L	6-2	190	2-8-83	2001	Iowa Park, Texas

FIELDING

Catcher	PCT	G	PO	A	E	DP	PB
Robles	1.000	25	147	10	0	0	0
Rojas	.990	77	524	51	6	1	9
Santos	.991	55	416	43	4	1	7

First Base	PCT	G	PO	A	E	DP
Gonzalez	1.000	5	21	1	0	0
Kartler	1.000	1	7	2	0	0
Robles	.978	7	43	1	1	3
Urick	.984	104	746	50	13	72
Vasquez	.992	38	244	15	2	15

Second Base	PCT	G	PO	A	E	DP
Cruz	.967	75	148	173	11	37
Rodriguez	.951	41	61	95	8	18

	PCT	G	PO	A	E	DP
Vasquez	1.000	15	18	40	0	4
Walsh	.969	14	29	34	2	8

Third Base	PCT	G	PO	A	E	DP
Cruz	1.000	1	0	1	0	0
Duncan	.901	75	58	124	20	9
Rodriguez	.840	19	18	24	8	2
Van Meetren	.667	1	2	0	1	0
Vasquez	.928	39	28	62	7	10
Walsh	.960	11	8	16	1	3

Shortstop	PCT	G	PO	A	E	DP
Made	.944	128	203	333	32	58
Vasquez	.958	14	15	31	2	9

Outfield	PCT	G	PO	A	E	DP
Andrus	.984	138	298	4	5	1
E. Cabrera	1.000	1	1	0	0	0
M. Cabrera	.991	41	103	3	1	2
Carson	.964	96	197	15	8	3
Gonzalez	1.000	5	1	0	0	0
Harris	.955	42	63	1	3	0
Kartler	.945	32	52	0	3	0
Treadway	1.000	14	13	0	0	0
Van Meetren	.941	39	78	2	5	0
Vasquez	1.000	9	9	0	0	0
Villanova	1.000	5	3	0	0	0
Walsh	1.000	16	26	0	0	0

NEW YORK-PENN LEAGUE

BATTING	AVG	G	AB	R	H	2B	3B	HR	RBI	BB	SO	SB	CS	OBP	SLG	B	T	HT	WT	DOB	1st Yr	Resides
Allen, Rod	.234	35	94	12	22	5	0	2	10	8	18	5	1	.324	.351	R	R	6-2	210	9-21-82	2004	Phoenix, Ariz.
Battle, Tim	.246	53	199	28	49	8	2	1	20	14	74	13	6	.302	.322	R	R	6-2	185	9-10-85	2003	Riverdale, Ga.
Cabrera, Edwin	.182	6	22	2	4	0	0	1	5	3	6	0	0	.308	.318	R	R	6-0	176	9-14-83	2001	Santo Domingo, D.R.
Caradonna, Troy	.234	36	111	9	26	5	1	0	9	10	11	0	1	.298	.297	S	R	6-3	219	4-13-81	2003	Tampa, Fla.
Christian, Justin	.274	50	208	29	57	9	2	7	33	19	39	15	4	.336	.438	R	R	6-1	188	4-3-80	2004	San Mateo, Calif.
DeVoir, Jordan	.205	27	83	9	17	2	0	0	5	2	26	1	1	.230	.229	R	R	6-3	210	8-13-82	2004	Kennewick, Wash.
Ehlers, Cody	.191	45	157	11	30	7	1	1	18	12	25	0	0	.253	.268	L	L	5-11	184	4-16-82	2004	Stillwater, Okla.
Gonzalez, Edwar	.223	33	130	18	29	6	1	3	14	7	27	1	0	.279	.354	R	R	5-10	200	1-1-83	2002	Miami, Fla.
Haag, Ryan	.299	22	67	8	20	2	1	0	6	4	15	2	5	.338	.358	L	R	5-10	180	11-20-81	2004	Santa Clarita, Calif.
Harris, Estee	.243	52	173	32	42	10	2	6	26	18	65	9	3	.327	.428	L	R	5-11	170	1-8-85	2003	Central Islip, N.Y.
Jones, Ben	.280	41	150	16	42	6	0	6	26	12	47	0	0	.337	.440	R	R	6-3	195	7-3-81	2004	Monroe, La.
Mendez, Deivi	.277	25	94	7	26	5	0	0	6	3	12	1	1	.296	.330	R	R	6-1	160	6-24-83	2000	Santo Domingo, D.R.
Nelson, Kevin	.258	27	89	9	23	6	1	1	7	9	19	0	0	.347	.382	R	R	6-1	180	4-8-81	2003	Arlington Heights, Ill.
Pilittere, Pat	.215	34	121	9	26	6	0	0	11	3	18	1	1	.252	.264	R	R	6-0	215	11-23-81	2004	Walnut, Calif.
Plumley, Grant	.252	62	258	30	65	11	2	0	19	13	45	2	1	.297	.310	R	R	6-0	185	12-21-81	2004	Lake Forest, Calif.
Rich, Scott	.243	42	136	19	33	7	0	2	14	12	38	2	1	.300	.338	R	L	6-3	210	8-18-82	2004	Hamilton Square, N.J.
Rodriguez, Rafael	.279	12	43	6	12	0	3	0	3	1	11	1	0	.295	.419	R	R	5-11	160	1-11-84	2001	San Pedro de Macoris, D.R.
Tierce, Evan	.184	11	38	4	7	1	1	1	5	4	9	0	0	.256	.342	L	L	6-0	190	7-19-82	2004	Keller, Texas
Vechionacci, Marcos	.292	19	72	13	21	5	0	0	8	11	13	0	0	.393	.361	S	R	6-2	170	8-7-86	2003	Valencia, Venez.
Villanova, Robert	.219	29	96	12	21	1	1	1	9	7	22	0	0	.279	.281	L	R	6-2	200	7-8-82	2004	Mahopac, N.Y.
Zamora, Hector	.289	55	187	30	54	10	1	3	20	35	47	0	1	.412	.401	L	R	6-1	210	10-19-82	2002	Culver City, Calif.

GAMES BY POSITION: C—Caradonna 22, Nelson 25, Pilittere 31. **1B**—Ehlers 38, Gonzalez 1, Jones 35, Pilittere 3. **2B**—Christian 29, DeVoir 3, Haag 17, Mendez 6, Plumley 4, Rodriguez 11, Vechionacci 7. **3B**—Christian 1, DeVoir 16, Haag 5, Mendez 7, Plumley 1, Vechionacci 12, Zamora 40. **SS**—DeVoir 2, Mendez 12, Plumley 57, Vechionacci 3. **OF**—Allen 32, Battle 51, Christian 3, DeVoir 5, Ehlers 2, Gonzalez 28, Harris 51, Rich 31, Tierce 11, Villanova 28.

PITCHING	W	L	ERA	G	GS	CG	SV	IP	H	R	ER	BB	SO	AVG	B	T	HT	WT	DOB	1st Yr	Resides
Abreu, Eric	3	0	1.63	7	2	0	1	28	24	5	5	6	47	.229	R	R	6-0	170	6-2-83	2003	Santo Domingo, P.R.
Barkley, Richard	1	1	1.35	4	0	0	0	7	6	1	1	4	2	.286	R	R	6-1	180	8-6-81	2003	Sumter, S.C.
Beam, T.J.	2	4	2.57	12	12	1	0	67	61	28	19	14	69	.242	R	R	6-7	215	8-28-80	2003	Scottsdale, Ariz.
Blackwell, Brad	1	1	2.31	21	0	0	1	35	27	9	9	21	25	.213	R	R	6-2	215	5-8-82	2003	Bixby, Okla.
Brown, Kevin	0	1	3.00	1	1	0	0	6	6	4	2	1	6	.240	R	R	6-4	200	3-14-65	1986	Macon, Ga.
Coke, Phil	0	0	6.75	3	1	0	0	8	9	6	6	3	7	.281	L	L	6-0	200	7-19-82	2003	Stockton, Calif.
Cuen, David	2	2	6.51	20	0	0	0	37	44	27	27	21	35	.297	L	L	6-4	190	8-4-83	2001	Somerton, Ariz.
De la Rosa, Dane	0	0	0.00	1	0	0	0	2	1	2	0	2	1	.167	R	R	6-6	220	2-1-83	2003	Wildomar, Calif.
Edwards, Drew	1	5	5.92	15	7	0	0	49	57	35	32	15	39	.289	R	R	6-5	215	11-22-81	2004	Queens, N.Y.
Hoover, Jesse	2	1	1.78	16	9	0	1	56	28	14	11	26	90	.151	R	R	6-3	210	1-8-82	2004	Fort Wayne, Ind.
Jones, Jason	2	3	2.44	8	8	1	0	48	42	15	13	3	27	.239	R	R	6-5	225	11-20-82	2004	Pasadena, Md.
Karsay, Steve	0	0	0.00	3	0	0	0	3	1	0	0	1	1	.100	R	R	6-3	215	3-24-72	1990	Scottsdale, Ariz.
King, Ben	0	0	13.50	2	0	0	0	2	5	3	3	0	0	.556	L	L	6-2	185	12-10-80	2004	Grapevine, Texas
Knox, Mike	3	6	5.43	15	10	0	0	61	84	41	37	29	44	.326	R	R	6-4	190	9-19-83	2003	Plano, Texas
Kramer, Jason	1	3	4.54	12	2	0	0	38	54	31	19	14	24	.331	L	L	6-6	185	7-21-83	2004	New Windsor, N.Y.
Marquez, Jeff	2	4	2.96	11	11	0	0	52	51	26	17	20	37	.254	R	R	6-2	175	10-18-84	2004	Vacaville, Calif.
Martinez, Mike	0	0	1.62	17	0	0	8	17	12	3	3	1	14	.188	R	R	6-0	190	4-12-81	2004	Anaheim, Calif.
Parker, Shaun	3	2	3.79	19	0	0	0	55	59	31	23	18	32	.281	L	L	6-3	200	7-30-81	2004	Westampton, N.J.
Perez, Alex	2	0	0.00	2	0	0	0	8	7	0	0	1	5	.233	L	L	6-4	230	3-24-82	2004	Perth Amboy, N.J.
Santana, Miguel	1	3	10.13	6	3	0	0	16	21	19	18	8	13	.313	R	R	6-0	180	5-19-82	2001	Santo Domingo, D.R.
Scheinbaum, Ben	1	4	3.04	15	0	0	0	24	23	12	8	18	20	.274	L	L	6-6	225	11-2-81	2004	Henderson, Nev.
Sevilla, Wilton	0	0	12.00	2	0	0	0	3	5	5	4	1	2	.357	R	R	5-7	170	7-19-83	2002	Leon, Nicaragua
Soto, Edgar	1	2	2.91	4	4	0	0	22	20	9	7	7	9	.250	L	L	5-11	175	12-28-84	2002	Maracaibo, Venez.
Stephens, Amad	0	0	0.00	1	0	0	0	3	0	0	0	0	1	.000	R	R	6-1	215	6-1-79	2003	San Diego, Calif.
Stevens, Jason	1	0	5.40	1	1	0	0	5	10	4	3	0	1	.435	R	R	6-2	210	1-1-83	2003	Cape Coral, Fla.
Villalona, Bryan	0	0	0.00	1	0	0	0	1	2	1	0	0	0	.400	R	R	6-2	170	9-15-82	2002	San Pedro de Macoris, D.R.
Wagner, Mike	0	0	13.50	1	0	0	0	1	3	2	2	2	1	.429	L	L	6-4	225	3-28-85	2004	Fort Pierce, Fla.
Wright, Chase	0	1	9.00	1	1	0	0	3	5	5	3	3	3	.333	L	L	6-2	190	2-8-83	2001	Iowa Park, Texas

GULF COAST LEAGUE

BATTING	AVG	G	AB	R	H	2B	3B	HR	RBI	BB	SO	SB	CS	SLG	OBP	B	T	HT	WT	DOB	1st Yr	Resides
Almario-Cabrera, Yosvany	.346	41	133	23	46	9	4	2	17	16	24	7	2	.519	.413	R	R	5-11	190	6-21-80	2004	Miami, Fla.
Amador, Anderson	.211	46	161	26	34	5	1	6	17	8	60	2	2	.366	.254	R	R	6-2	180	11-4-84	2002	Azua, D.R.
Battle, Tim	.320	12	50	11	16	3	3	1	4	4	15	5	2	.560	.364	R	R	6-2	185	9-10-85	2003	Riverdale, Ga.
Christian, Justin	.571	3	7	1	4	3	0	0	4	4	0	0	0	01.000	.727	R	R	6-1	188	4-3-80	2004	San Mateo, Calif.
Corona, Reegie	.261	36	92	12	24	5	0	0	4	5	13	8	2	.315	.299	S	R	6-0	160	11-7-86	2003	San Antonio, Venez.
Dominguez, Raul	.274	45	113	15	31	2	0	1	12	14	20	1	0	.319	.362	L	L	6-1	180	7-25-81	2001	Panama City, Panama
Duenas, Yobal	.182	4	11	2	2	0	0	0	1	1	0	0	0	.182	.250	R	R	6-3	220	5-4-72	2004	Havana, Cuba
Gonzalez, Hector	.290	34	93	15	27	4	0	0	12	11	18	2	2	.333	.377	S	R	6-2	180	2-23-85	2003	Estado Miranda, Venez.
Griffin, Nathan	.247	31	73	7	18	3	0	0	9	3	15	0	0	.288	.295	R	R	6-0	195	12-7-81	2004	Dallas, Texas
Guillen, Rudy	.429	4	14	1	6	0	0	0	1	0	0	0	0	.429	.429	R	R	6-3	185	11-23-83	2000	Santo Domingo, D.R.
Guy, Jason	.000	1	2	0	0	0	0	0	0	0	1	0	0	.000	.000	L	L	5-10	170	4-30-82	2001	Fort Myers, Fla.
Haag, Ryan	.250	9	20	3	5	1	0	0	1	5	6	2	0	.300	.423	L	R	5-9	180	11-20-81	2004	Santa Clarita, Calif.
Harris, Estee	.067	4	15	1	1	0	0	1	2	0	6	0	0	.267	.067	L	R	5-11	170	1-8-85	2003	Central Islip, N.Y.
Holmann, Mario	.258	20	66	12	17	1	1	1	7	13	17	10	4	.348	.370	S	R	6-0	160	5-21-84	2003	Managua, Nicaragua
Levy, Carlos	.229	20	48	4	11	0	0	2	8	1	25	2	0	.354	.260	L	L	6-4	180	2-5-84	2000	Panama City, Panama
Mendez, Deivi	.161	8	31	3	5	2	0	0	3	1	4	0	1	.226	.188	R	R	6-1	160	6-24-83	1999	Santo Domingo, D.R.
Perez, Jose	.202	36	99	8	20	2	0	0	12	16	28	12	3	.222	.316	L	L	6-1	185	9-15-85	2003	Oceanside, Calif.
Phillips, Nate	.242	47	157	15	38	5	0	0	14	15	47	1	6	.274	.320	S	R	6-2	190	1-24-86	2004	Arlington, Texas
Plaza, William	.341	20	41	3	14	2	0	0	6	8	6	0	1	.390	.460	R	R	6-0	185	10-6-82	2004	San Jose, Costa Rica
Poterson, Jon	.202	56	198	24	40	7	1	7	30	22	60	1	0	.354	.280	S	R	6-1	215	2-10-86	2004	Chandler, Ariz.
Rojas, Irwil	.253	30	91	7	23	4	1	0	13	4	7	1	0	.319	.303	L	R	6-1	175	8-11-84	2002	Carabobo, Venez.
Romero, Luis	.188	36	101	14	19	1	0	1	8	12	21	0	0	.228	.308	S	R	6-1	195	9-8-83	2001	Maturin, Venez.
Tierce, Evan	.361	40	147	26	53	11	1	1	14	14	16	13	4	.469	.420	L	L	5-10	190	7-19-82	2004	Keller, Texas
Vechionacci, Marcos	.336	36	131	24	44	9	1	4	22	12	19	5	3	.511	.392	S	R	6-2	170	8-7-86	2002	Valencia, Venez.
Walsh, Nick	.000	1	3	0	0	0	0	0	0	0	1	0	0	.000	.250	L	R	5-8	180	5-6-80	2004	Alamo, Calif.

GAMES BY POSITION: C—Dominguez 1, Griffin 30, Plaza 14, Rojas 27, Romero 6. **1B**—Almario-Cabrera 1, Dominguez 42, Romero 28. **2B**—Almario-Cabrera 4, Christian 2, Corona 29, Duenas 3, Gonzalez 2, Haag 8, Holmann 19, Phillips 1, Walsh 1. **3B**—Almario-Cabrera 13, Corona 1, Gonzalez 2, Phillips 6, Vechionacci 24. **SS**—Almario-Cabrera 1, Amador 1, Christian 1, Corona 1, Gonzalez 6, Mendez 8, Phillips 40, Vechionacci 8. **OF**—Almario-Cabrera 14, Amador 43, Battle 12, Dominguez 1, Guillen 2, Guy 1, Harris 3, Levy 8, Perez 1, Perez 32, Phillips 1, Poterson 40, Tierce 33.

PITCHING	W	L	ERA	G	GS	CG	SV	IP	H	R	ER	BB	SO	AVG	B	T	HT	WT	DOB	1st Yr	Resides
Antigua, Erick	1	0	1.46	6	0	0	2	12	6	2	2	2	14	.142	R	R	6-1	170	8-9-83	2002	Santo Domingo, D.R.
Berg, Justin	3	2	5.87	15	1	0	1	31	40	22	20	15	29	.317	R	R	6-3	195	6-7-84	2004	Antigo, Wis.
Borrell, Danny	0	0	1.38	4	4	0	0	13	8	2	2	2	18	.177	L	L	6-3	200	1-24-79	2000	Sanford, N.C.
Coke, Phil	0	1	3.97	7	1	0	0	11	18	7	5	3	13	.360	L	L	6-1	210	7-19-82	2003	Stockton, Calif.
De la Rosa, Dane	2	0	2.88	14	1	0	1	34	25	13	11	12	32	.190	R	R	6-6	220	2-1-83	2003	Wildomar, Calif.
De Leon, Juan	1	0	1.80	1	1	0	0	5	3	1	1	2	2	.176	R	R	5-11	160	6-24-81	2001	Santo Domingo, D.R.
Garcia, Christian	3	4	2.84	13	6	0	0	38	26	13	12	17	47	.188	R	R	6-4	175	8-24-85	2004	Miami, Fla.
Hughes, Philip	0	0	0.00	3	3	0	0	5	4	0	0	0	8	.222	R	R	6-5	220	6-24-86	2004	Santa Ana, Calif.
Kennard, Jeff	0	0	4.50	2	0	0	0	2	4	2	1	0	3	.444	R	R	6-2	195	7-26-81	2001	Centerville, Ohio
Lara, Toni	3	1	3.51	15	10	0	0	49	40	23	19	18	47	.224	L	L	6-0	155	1-31-84	2002	Santo Domingo, D.R.
Marquez, Jeff	2	0	0.63	4	2	0	0	14	10	1	1	4	18	.188	R	R	6-2	175	8-10-84	2004	Vacaville, Calif.
Marsonek, Sam	0	0	3.00	2	1	0	1	3	2	1	1	0	3	.181	R	R	6-6	225	7-10-78	1997	Tampa, Fla.
Moscat, Marvin	2	3	2.70	16	2	0	5	37	24	11	11	9	47	.180	R	R	6-0	170	5-15-82	2002	Bani, D.R.
Nelson, Maximo	6	3	2.63	12	9	0	0	55	48	16	16	12	54	.235	R	R	6-5	160	4-21-82	2001	Santo Domingo, D.R.
Omana, Edgar	1	1	2.70	13	0	0	2	13	11	5	4	5	21	.215	L	L	6-3	175	9-12-83	2001	Maracaibo, Venez.
Perez, Alex	2	1	2.82	12	0	0	1	22	24	7	7	3	29	.269	L	L	6-4	230	3-24-82	2004	Perth Amboy, N.J.
Sevilla, Wilton	1	0	0.00	4	0	0	1	6	2	0	0	0	6	.100	R	R	6-0	160	7-19-83	2002	Leon, Nicaragua
Stephens, Jay	5	3	2.61	13	8	0	1	48	55	23	14	10	48	.279	R	R	6-4	190	10-16-84	2003	Tallmadge, Ohio
Stuart, Cory	0	0	4.50	2	0	0	1	2	2	1	1	1	4	.250	R	R	6-2	185	3-15-82	2003	Surrey, B.C.
Tadeo, Jose	1	1	3.00	16	0	0	3	18	11	7	6	8	22	.169	S	R	6-2	180	4-3-82	2004	Bellflower, Calif.
Villalona, Guillermo	2	2	4.30	6	5	0	0	23	26	13	11	2	17	.279	R	R	6-2	170	9-15-82	2002	Santo Domingo, D.R.
Wagner, Mike	0	1	2.29	15	5	0	1	35	30	11	9	10	31	.217	L	L	6-4	225	3-28-85	2004	Fort Pierce, Fla.
Watts, Joey	1	0	1.84	8	0	0	0	15	9	3	3	4	16	.169	L	L	5-11	170	2-22-82	2004	Brandon, Fla.

NEW YORK METS

BY MARTY NOBLE

Shortly after the 1981 season, Mets general manager Frank Cashen said the most accurate way to measure the status of an organization is not by games won and lost but by jobs lost. Cashen had just dismissed Joe Torre as manager when he said, "The number of jobs lost will tell you, because it incorporates everything—wins, losses, performance, expectations, disappointment, stability and the future."

Twenty-three years later, with Cashen long absent from the firing line, the Mets were all about jobs lost in 2004. As the World Series began, they were awash in rolling heads, vacancies and anxious employees.

New York's wretched 2004 season prompted more dismissals than George Steinbrenner or Donald Trump could execute on an angry day. Another manager, Art Howe, was discarded before season's end, though he stayed on through Game 162 (and loss 91). Most of his staff was purged as well, even the bullpen coach and the trainer. And the dismissal of Don Baylor meant the job of batting coach had been vacated for the second time in less than six months.

General manager Jim Duquette wasn't fired, but the late-September appointment of Omar Minaya as GM subordinated Duquette—and made him the senior vice president of baseball operations—before he had served a year of his three-year contract. And Triple-A manager John Stearns was reassigned as well.

If the Mets weren't starting over again, they were close to it. Since their appearance in the 2000 World Series, they have had three managers (including Howe's successor), three general managers, four batting coaches and four pitching coaches.

And relatively little success.

Other than the summer emergence of 21-year-old third

David Wright

David Wright

PLAYERS of the YEAR

MAJOR LEAGUE: David Wright, 3b

The Mets called up Wright from Triple-A Norfolk in July, and the 21-year-old third baseman had an immediate impact at the big league level, hitting .293-14-40 in 263 at-bats. He is New York's cornerstone of the future as the rebuilding effort gets underway.

MINOR LEAGUE: David Wright, 3b

Wright also led the way for the Mets at the minor league level in 2004, despite playing little more than half a season between Double-A Binghamton and Norfolk. At the two levels, Wright hit a combined .341-18-57 in 337 at-bats.

baseman David Wright, an early-July sweep of the Yankees, a brief flirtation with first place two weeks later and Todd Zeile's fun September, the most positive aspect of 2004 for the Mets was Montreal denying them a third straight last-place finish. They took steps back in almost every other area.

Their offseason efforts to reinforce their defense blew up. Japanese import Kaz Matsui proved he wasn't a major league shortstop. Jose Reyes missed significant time because of injury. Shifting Mike Piazza to first base proved to be a mistake. And free agent center fielder Mike Cameron didn't perform up to the defensive standards he previously had established. Among National League teams, only the Diamondbacks committed more errors than the Mets, not a good thing for a pitching staff with the second-lowest strikeouts-per-nine-innings ratio (6.07) in the league.

Most of all, the Mets didn't hit. Only four National League teams scored fewer runs. The extended absence of Reyes and Piazza, Piazza's quiet second half, the failure of the other catchers to produce, the nagging injuries to Cliff Floyd, and Matsui's offensive performance—which wasn't as bad as his defensive failure—conspired to put most of the Mets' final offensive totals near the bottom of the league.

With Reyes and Wright having reached the big leagues in successive summers, with Kazmir and one-time catching prospect Justin Huber traded, the Mets' minor league system likely won't provide much immediate help. Righthanded pitcher Yusmeiro Petit is coming quickly, but September probably is his earliest possible ETA. Outfielder Lastings Milledge, the team's first-round draft pick in 2003, is a 2006—if then—callup.

ORGANIZATION LEADERS

BATTING

*AVG	Ian Bladergroen, Capital City	.342
R	Blake Whealy, Capital City	100
H	Victor Diaz, Norfolk	154
TB	Victor Diaz, Norfolk	259
2B	Prentice Redman, Norfolk/Binghamton	46
3B	Angel Pagan, Norfolk/Binghamton	11
HR	Jamar Hill, Capital City	26
RBI	Victor Diaz, Norfolk	94
BB	Blake Whealy, Capital City	66
SO	Corey Ragsdale, Norfolk/St. Lucie	156
SB	Wayne Lydon, Binghamton	65
*OBP	David Wright, Norfolk/Binghamton	.441
*SLG	David Wright, Norfolk/Binghamton	.605

PITCHING

W	Blake McGinley, Norfolk/Binghamton	12
	Yusmeiro Petit, Binghamton/St. Lucie/Capital City	12
L	Three tied at	10
#ERA	Greg Ramirez, Capital City	2.06
G	P.J. Bevis, Norfolk/Binghamton	49
CG	Bryan Edwards, Binghamton/St. Lucie	2
SV	Heath Bell, Norfolk/Binghamton	16
	Jose Parra, Norfolk/Binghamton	16
IP	Brian Bannister, Binghamton/St. Lucie	155
BB	Jose Diaz, Binghamton	70
SO	Yusmeiro Petit, Binghamton/St. Lucie/Capital City	200

*Minimum 250 at-bats #Minimum 75 innings

NEW YORK METS

Manager: Art Howe.　　　　　　**2004 Record:** 71-91, .438 (4th, NL East).

BATTING	AVG	G	AB	R	H	2B	3B	HR	RBI	BB	SO	SB	CS	OBP	SLG	B	T	HT	WT	DOB	1st Yr	Resides
Brazell, Craig	.265	24	34	3	9	2	0	1	3	1	7	0	0	.286	.412	L	R	6-3	210	5-10-80	1998	Montgomery, Ala.
Buchanan, Brian	.000	2	3	0	0	0	0	0	0	1	1	0	0	.250	.000	R	R	6-4	230	7-21-73	1994	Fort Myers, Fla.
2-team (38 S.D.)	.190	40	63	7	12	2	0	2	6	7	20	0	0	.278	.317							
Cameron, Mike	.231	140	493	76	114	30	1	30	76	57	143	22	6	.319	.479	R	R	6-2	200	1-8-73	1991	McDonough, Ga.
Delgado, Wilson	.292	42	130	11	38	4	1	2	13	15	29	1	0	.366	.385	S	R	5-11	165	7-15-72	1994	San Cristobal, D.R.
Diaz, Victor	.294	15	51	8	15	3	0	3	8	1	15	0	0	.321	.529	R	R	6-0	200	12-10-81	2001	Chicago, Ill.
Duncan, Jeff	.067	13	15	2	1	0	0	0	1	1	5	3	0	.125	.067	L	L	6-2	188	12-9-78	2000	Frankfort, Ill.
Floyd, Cliff	.260	113	396	55	103	26	0	18	63	47	103	11	4	.352	.462	L	R	6-4	230	12-5-72	1991	Plantation, Fla.
Garcia, Danny	.232	58	138	23	32	7	1	3	17	22	34	3	0	.371	.362	R	R	6-1	175	4-12-80	2001	Anaheim, Calif.
Garcia, Karim	.234	62	192	24	45	7	2	7	22	10	35	3	0	.272	.401	L	L	6-0	210	10-29-75	1993	Ciudad Obregon, Mexico
Gutierrez, Ricky	.175	24	63	2	11	2	0	0	5	6	8	0	0	.257	.206	R	R	6-1	195	5-23-70	1988	Pembroke Pines, Fla.
Hidalgo, Richard	.228	86	324	46	74	11	1	21	52	27	76	3	2	.296	.463	R	R	6-3	220	7-2-75	1992	Guarenas, Venez.
2-team (58 Houston)	.239	144	523	67	125	26	3	25	82	44	129	4	4	.301	.444							
Hietpas, Joe	.000	1	0	0	0	0	0	0	0	0	0	0	0	.000	.000	R	R	6-3	220	5-1-79	2001	Appleton, Wis.
Keppinger, Jeff	.284	33	116	9	33	2	0	3	9	6	7	2	1	.317	.379	R	R	6-0	180	4-21-80	2002	Auburn, Ga.
Matsui, Kazuo	.272	114	460	65	125	32	2	7	44	40	97	14	3	.331	.396	S	R	5-10	185	10-23-75	2004	Tokyo, Japan
McEwing, Joe	.254	75	138	17	35	3	1	1	16	9	32	4	1	.297	.312	R	R	5-11	165	10-19-72	1992	Yardley, Pa.
Phillips, Jason	.218	128	362	34	79	18	0	7	34	35	42	0	1	.298	.326	R	R	6-1	210	9-27-76	1997	El Cajon, Calif.
Piazza, Mike	.266	129	455	47	121	21	0	20	54	68	78	0	0	.362	.444	R	R	6-3	215	9-4-68	1989	Boynton Beach, Fla.
Reyes, Jose	.255	53	220	33	56	16	2	2	14	5	31	19	2	.271	.373	S	R	6-0	175	6-11-83	2000	Santiago, D.R.
Snead, Esix	.000	1	0	0	0	0	0	0	0	0	0	0	0	.000	.000	S	R	5-10	170	6-7-76	1998	Williston, Fla.
Spencer, Shane	.281	74	185	21	52	10	1	4	26	13	37	6	0	.332	.411	R	R	6-0	200	2-20-72	1990	Tampa, Fla.
Valent, Eric	.267	130	270	39	72	15	2	13	34	28	61	0	1	.337	.481	L	L	5-11	195	4-4-77	1998	Anaheim, Calif.
Wigginton, Ty	.285	86	312	46	89	23	2	12	42	23	48	6	1	.334	.487	R	R	6-0	210	10-11-77	1998	Chula Vista, Calif.
Williams, Gerald	.233	57	129	17	30	8	1	4	11	8	26	2	1	.277	.419	R	R	6-2	185	8-10-66	1987	Tampa, Fla.
Wilson, Tom	.250	4	0	1	0	0	0	0	1	2	0	0	0	.400	.250	R	R	6-3	220	12-19-70	1991	Lake Havasu City, Ariz.
Wilson, Vance	.274	79	157	18	43	10	1	4	21	11	24	1	0	.335	.427	R	R	5-11	190	3-17-73	1994	Springdale, Ark.
Wright, David	.293	69	263	41	77	17	1	14	40	14	40	6	0	.332	.525	R	R	6-0	200	12-20-82	2001	Chesapeake, Va.
Zeile, Todd	.233	137	348	30	81	16	0	9	35	44	83	0	0	.319	.356	R	R	6-1	200	9-9-65	1986	Thousand Oaks, Calif.

PITCHING	W	L	ERA	G	GS	CG	SV	IP	H	R	ER	BB	SO	AVG	B	T	HT	WT	DOB	1st Yr	Resides
Baldwin, James	0	2	15.00	2	2	0	0	6	13	10	10	5	1	.448	R	R	6-3	230	7-15-71	1990	Southern Pines, N.C.
Bell, Heath	0	2	3.33	17	0	0	0	24	22	9	9	6	27	.253	R	R	6-3	230	9-29-77	1998	Tustin, Calif.
Benson, Kris	4	4	4.50	11	11	1	0	68	65	37	34	17	51	.244	R	R	6-4	195	11-7-74	1997	Wexford, Pa.
2-team (20 Pittsburgh)	12	12	4.31	31	31	1	0	200	202	106	96	61	134	.263							
Bottalico, Ricky	3	2	3.38	60	0	0	0	69	54	30	26	34	61	.215	L	R	6-1	215	8-26-69	1991	Rocky Hill, Conn.
Darensbourg, Vic	0	1	7.94	5	0	0	0	6	10	5	5	2	1	.435	L	L	5-10	180	11-13-70	1992	Henderson, Nev.
DeJean, Mike	0	0	1.69	17	0	0	0	21	21	5	4	5	24	.263	R	R	6-4	217	9-28-70	1992	Castle Rock, Colo.
Erickson, Scott	0	1	7.88	2	2	0	0	8	15	9	7	4	3	.395	R	R	6-4	230	2-2-68	1989	Stateline, Nev.
Feliciano, Pedro	1	1	5.40	22	0	0	0	18	14	12	11	12	14	.209	L	L	5-10	185	8-25-76	1995	Dorado, P.R.
Fortunato, Bartolome	1	1	3.86	15	0	0	1	19	14	8	8	13	20	.203	R	R	6-4	210	8-24-74	1997	Santo Domingo, D.R.
Franco, John	2	7	5.28	52	0	0	0	46	46	28	27	24	36	.258	L	L	5-10	185	9-17-60	1984	Staten Island, N.Y.
Ginter, Matt	1	3	4.54	15	14	0	0	69	82	41	35	20	38	.289	R	R	5-11	220	12-24-77	1999	Winchester, Ky.
Glavine, Tom	11	14	3.60	33	33	1	0	212	204	94	85	70	109	.252	L	L	6-0	185	3-25-66	1984	Alpharetta, Ga.
Heilman, Aaron	1	3	5.46	5	4	0	0	28	27	17	17	13	22	.257	R	R	6-5	220	11-12-78	2001	Logansport, Ind.
Leiter, Al	10	8	3.21	30	30	0	0	174	138	65	62	97	117	.218	L	L	6-3	220	10-23-65	1984	Weston, Fla.
Looper, Braden	2	5	2.70	71	0	0	29	83	86	28	25	16	60	.266	R	R	6-3	220	10-28-74	1997	Pembroke Pines, Fla.
Moreno, Orber	3	1	3.38	33	0	0	1	35	29	17	13	11	29	.221	R	R	6-0	200	4-27-77	1994	Los Altos, Venez.
Parra, Jose	1	0	3.21	13	0	0	0	14	14	6	5	6	14	.255	R	R	5-11	160	11-28-72	1990	Santiago, D.R.
Roberts, Grant	0	0	17.36	4	0	0	0	5	9	9	9	6	1	.429	R	R	6-3	205	9-13-77	1995	El Cajon, Calif.
Seo, Jae	5	10	4.90	24	21	0	0	118	133	67	64	50	54	.299	R	R	6-1	215	5-24-77	1998	La Canada, Calif.
Stanton, Mike	2	6	3.16	83	0	0	0	77	70	32	27	33	58	.237	L	L	6-1	215	7-2-67	1987	Houston, Texas
Trachsel, Steve	12	13	4.00	33	33	0	0	203	203	104	90	83	117	.262	R	R	6-4	205	10-31-70	1991	Mesa, Ariz.
Weathers, Dave	5	3	4.28	32	0	0	0	34	41	19	16	15	25	.304	R	R	6-3	230	9-25-69	1988	Loretto, Tenn.
Wheeler, Dan	3	1	4.80	32	1	0	0	51	65	29	27	17	46	.307	R	R	6-3	220	12-10-77	1997	Warwick, R.I.
Yates, Tyler	2	4	6.36	21	7	0	0	47	61	36	33	25	35	.311	R	R	6-4	220	8-7-77	1998	Koloa, Hawaii
Zambrano, Victor	2	0	3.86	3	3	0	0	14	12	9	6	6	14	.222	R	R	6-0	200	8-6-75	1994	Valencia, Venez.

FIELDING

Catcher	PCT	G	PO	A	E	DP	PB
Hietpas	1.000	1	2	0	0	0	0
Phillips	.998	87	486	37	1	4	3
Piazza	.982	50	260	15	5	1	5
T. Wilson	1.000	3	11	0	0	0	0
V. Wilson	.993	69	257	23	2	2	4
Zeile	1.000	2	12	0	0	0	0

First Base	PCT	G	PO	A	E	DP
Brazell	.974	7	34	4	11	1
Buchanan	1.000	1	8	1	0	1
Phillips	1.000	38	259	16	0	20
Piazza	.985	68	498	35	8	44
Spencer	1.000	1	13	0	0	0

Valent	.996	27	202	21	1	21
Zeile	.995	67	386	23	2	35

Second Base	PCT	G	PO	A	E	DP
D. Garcia	.969	44	97	91	6	19
Keppinger	.987	32	61	86	2	20
Matsui	.923	3	4	8	1	3
McEwing	.981	34	50	55	2	10
Reyes	.980	43	75	117	4	26

Third Base	PCT	G	PO	A	E	DP
McEwing	.000	1	0	0	0	0
Wigginton	.924	66	29	116	12	8
Wright	.942	69	39	140	11	10

Zeile	.933	46	38	73	8	7

Shortstop	PCT	G	PO	A	E	DP
Delgado	.957	39	49	128	8	28
Matsui	.956	110	174	323	23	65
McEwing	.982	13	19	36	1	5
Reyes	.957	10	18	26	2	5

Outfield	PCT	G	PO	A	E	DP
Buchanan	1.000	18	12	0	0	0
Cameron	.978	135	354	6	8	2
Diaz	.935	14	29	0	2	0
Duncan	1.000	4	7	0	0	0
Floyd	.988	106	164	5	2	1

Tom Glavine: Posted a 3.60 ERA with help of a terrific first half

Al Leiter: His 3.21 ERA was ninth-best in the National League

FARM SYSTEM

Director, Minor League Operations: Kevin Morgan.

Class	Farm Team	League	W	L	Pct.	Finish*	Manager	Affiliate Since
AAA	Norfolk (Va.) Tides	International	72	72	.500	7th (14)	John Stearns	1969
AA	Binghamton (N.Y.) Mets	Eastern	76	66	.535	**4th (12)**	Ken Oberkfell	1992
High A	St. Lucie (Fla.) Mets	Florida State	64	65	.496	7th (12)	Tim Teufel	1988
Low A	#Capital City Bombers (Columbia, S.C.)	South Atlantic	89	47	.654	**1st (16)**	Jack Lind	1983
SS A	Brooklyn (N.Y.) Cyclones	New York-Penn	43	31	.581	**3rd (14)**	Tony Tijerina	2001
Rookie	Kingsport (Tenn.) Mets	Appalachian	32	36	.471	6th (10)	Mookie Wilson	1980
Rookie	St. Lucie (Fla.) Mets	Gulf Coast	36	24	.600	**t-2nd (12)**	Brett Butler	2004

*Finish in overall standings (No. of teams in league)/Playoff teams in **boldface**   #Affiliate will operate in Hagerstown (South Atlantic) in 2005

NORFOLK TIDES   Class AAA

INTERNATIONAL LEAGUE

BATTING	AVG	G	AB	R	H	2B	3B	HR	RBI	BB	SO	SB	CS	OBP	SLG	B	T	HT	WT	DOB	1st Yr	Resides
Bacani, David	.264	44	144	20	38	9	3	2	14	17	34	4	2	.350	.410	R	R	5-7	170	7-30-79	2001	Long Beach, Calif.
Basak, Chris	.223	58	193	25	43	11	4	6	19	10	58	5	3	.260	.415	R	R	6-2	190	12-6-78	2000	Joliet, Ill.
Brazell, Craig	.265	121	475	66	126	22	2	23	67	21	99	1	2	.300	.465	L	R	6-3	210	5-10-80	1998	Montgomery, Ala.
Caligiuri, Jay	.000	4	9	0	0	0	0	0	0	0	2	0	0	.000	.000	R	R	6-0	195	3-29-80	2001	Camarillo, Calif.
Cardona, Javier	.111	26	63	2	7	1	0	1	4	5	14	0	0	.186	.175	R	R	6-1	210	9-15-75	1994	Dorado, P.R.
Collins, Mike	.162	35	74	1	12	3	0	0	5	3	16	0	2	.188	.203	R	R	5-9	166	1-29-77	1998	Phoenix, Ariz.
Delgado, Wilson	.261	108	352	40	92	18	5	3	23	27	73	1	6	.317	.366	S	R	5-11	165	7-15-72	1994	San Cristobal, D.R.
Detienne, David	.174	11	23	2	4	0	0	0	1	1	4	0	0	.200	.174	R	R	6-3	190	8-16-79	1998	Dartmouth, N.S.
Diaz, Victor	.292	141	528	81	154	31	1	24	94	31	133	6	8	.332	.491	R	R	6-0	200	12-10-81	2001	Chicago, Ill.
Duncan, Jeff	.257	55	202	26	52	12	1	2	14	23	52	11	5	.332	.356	L	L	6-2	188	12-9-78	2000	Frankfort, Ill.
Garcia, Danny	.260	63	242	28	63	14	1	2	19	15	35	9	5	.322	.351	R	R	6-1	175	4-12-80	2001	Anaheim, Calif.
Glavine, Mike	.216	87	204	14	44	9	0	8	23	23	45	0	1	.305	.377	L	L	6-3	210	1-24-73	1995	Billerica, Mass.
Gonzalez, Raul	.262	18	65	5	17	6	1	1	6	6	9	1	2	.333	.431	R	R	5-9	190	12-27-73	1991	Carolina, P.R.
Huber, Justin	.313	5	16	3	5	2	0	0	3	3	3	0	0	.421	.438	R	R	6-5	190	7-1-82	2001	Emerald, Australia
Jacobs, Mike	.177	27	96	8	17	3	0	2	6	9	30	0	0	.245	.271	L	R	6-2	200	10-30-80	1999	San Diego, Calif.
Keppinger, Jeff	.316	6	19	1	6	1	0	0	2	4	2	0	0	.458	.368	R	R	6-0	180	4-21-80	2002	Auburn, Ga.
Levis, Jesse	.370	10	27	3	10	2	0	0	3	1	0	0	0	.393	.444	L	R	5-9	200	4-14-68	1989	Elkins Park, Pa.
Nye, Rodney	.277	130	423	44	117	27	0	5	50	33	81	0	4	.330	.376	R	R	6-4	215	12-2-76	1995	Cameron, Okla.
Pachot, John	.262	85	290	26	76	10	0	6	32	12	41	0	1	.293	.359	R	R	6-2	210	11-11-74	1993	Ponce, P.R.
Pagan, Angel	.289	12	45	13	13	3	3	0	1	4	8	4	1	.347	.489	S	R	6-1	180	7-2-81	2000	Rio Piedras, P.R.

BATTING

	AVG	G	AB	R	H	2B	3B	HR	RBI	BB	SO	SB	CS	OBP	SLG	B	T	HT	WT	DOB	1st Yr	Resides
Ragsdale, Corey	.250	6	20	1	5	1	0	0	1	1	4	1	0	.286	.300	R	R	6-4	185	11-10-82	2001	Jonesboro, Ark.
Redman, Prentice	.254	62	213	29	54	17	2	4	30	17	57	9	3	.308	.408	R	R	6-2	191	8-26-79	1999	Duncanville, Ala.
Slack, Jon	.200	6	15	3	3	0	0	0	0	0	4	0	0	.250	.200	L	L	6-0	177	12-9-81	2002	Henderson, Nev.
Snead, Esix	.268	79	269	42	72	10	2	0	21	35	53	40	10	.352	.320	S	R	5-10	170	6-7-76	1998	Williston, Fla.
Socarras, Tony	.273	13	22	3	6	1	0	1	3	1	10	0	1	.292	.455	L	R	6-0	205	11-8-78	2000	Miami, Fla.
Timmons, Ozzie	.274	30	106	13	29	6	0	4	18	12	18	0	0	.347	.443	R	R	6-2	220	9-18-70	1991	Tampa, Fla.
Velazquez, Gil	.091	17	33	4	3	1	0	0	0	5	12	1	0	.211	.121	R	R	6-3	180	10-17-79	1998	Paramount, Calif.
Williams, Gerald	.305	63	246	37	75	10	3	7	28	9	35	6	9	.335	.455	R	R	6-2	185	8-10-66	1987	Tampa, Fla.
Wilson, Tom	.322	34	115	26	37	10	0	7	22	25	24	0	1	.443	.591	R	R	6-2	220	12-19-70	1991	Lake Havasu City, Ariz.
Wilson, Vance	.500	1	4	1	2	0	0	1	1	0	0	0	0	.500	1.250	R	R	5-11	190	3-17-73	1994	Springdale, Ark.
Wright, David	.298	31	114	18	34	8	0	8	17	16	19	2	4	.388	.579	R	R	6-0	200	12-20-82	2001	Chesapeake, Va.

PITCHING

	W	L	ERA	G	GS	CG	SV	IP	H	R	ER	BB	SO	AVG	B	T	HT	WT	DOB	1st Yr	Resides
Acosta, Domingo	0	0	0.00	1	0	0	0	2	2	0	0	0	0	.286	R	R	6-3	185	10-5-80	2001	New York, N.Y.
Bacani, David	0	0	0.00	2	2	0	0	4	1	0	0	1	1	.071	R	R	5-7	170	7-30-79	2001	Long Beach, Calif.
Baldwin, James	3	2	2.90	5	5	0	0	31	34	11	10	5	24	.281	R	R	6-3	230	7-15-71	1990	Southern Pines, N.C.
Bell, Heath	3	1	3.23	45	0	0	16	56	42	21	20	24	69	.210	R	R	6-3	230	9-29-77	1998	Tustin, Calif.
Bevis, P.J.	1	2	5.06	22	0	0	2	27	28	24	15	23	16	.272	R	R	6-3	175	7-28-80	1998	Capalaba, Australia
Bottalico, Ricky	0	0	0.00	5	0	0	0	7	7	1	0	4	8	.233	L	R	6-1	215	8-26-69	1991	Rocky Hill, Conn.
Byard, David	0	0	6.00	2	0	0	0	3	5	2	2	2	0	.385	R	R	6-2	240	6-1-78	2000	Mt. Vernon, Ohio
Cole, Joey	1	0	0.00	1	0	0	0	1	0	0	0	1	2	.000	L	R	6-8	225	9-15-77	1999	Nacogdoches, Texas
Darensbourg, Vic	1	1	3.18	18	0	0	0	23	13	9	8	12	21	.169	L	L	5-10	180	11-13-70	1992	Henderson, Nev.
2-team (24 Charlotte)	4	4	2.87	42	0	0	0	53	38	19	17	21	54	.204							
Erickson, Scott	3	3	4.50	8	8	0	0	52	56	30	26	12	30	.279	R	R	6-4	230	2-2-68	1989	Stateline, Nev.
Feliciano, Pedro	4	3	5.30	32	0	0	2	36	35	25	21	15	25	.259	L	L	5-10	185	8-25-76	1995	Dorado, P.R.
Fortunato, Bartolome	0	0	3.38	6	0	0	0	5	4	2	2	3	5	.211	R	R	6-1	180	8-24-74	1997	Santo Domingo, D.R.
2-team (34 Durham)	4	3	2.52	40	0	0	9	50	32	16	14	24	59	.186							
Ginter, Matt	1	5	2.95	11	11	0	0	64	55	26	21	8	49	.228	R	R	6-1	220	12-24-77	1999	Winchester, Ky.
Griffiths, Jeremy	5	2	3.47	13	13	0	0	70	63	30	27	29	31	.254	R	R	6-6	240	3-22-78	1999	Avon Lakes, Ohio
Heilman, Aaron	7	10	4.33	26	26	1	0	152	156	88	73	66	123	.264	R	R	6-5	220	11-12-78	2001	Logansport, Ind.
Joseph, Jake	1	1	4.08	15	1	0	0	29	37	15	13	7	15	.308	R	R	6-1	220	1-24-78	1999	Citrus Heights, Calif.
Keisler, Randy	6	7	3.81	22	21	1	0	130	145	72	55	45	110	.282	L	L	6-3	190	2-24-76	1998	Richards, Texas
Keppel, Bob	3	7	4.71	17	16	1	0	94	111	51	49	22	42	.304	R	R	6-5	205	6-11-82	2000	Chesterfield, Mo.
McGinley, Blake	3	3	4.05	13	0	0	2	27	30	15	12	7	28	.280	R	L	6-1	175	8-2-78	2001	Bakersfield, Calif.
Meyers, Mike	1	1	5.54	16	4	0	0	39	44	26	24	17	20	.297	R	R	6-2	210	10-18-77	1997	Molina, Ill.
Musser, Neal	2	4	6.25	7	7	0	0	36	39	30	25	17	24	.283	L	L	6-1	215	8-25-80	1999	Otterbein, Ind.
Olson, Ryan	0	0	0.00	1	0	0	0	1	0	0	0	0	2	.000	S	L	6-5	193	1-16-80	2001	Oakhurst, Calif.
Parra, Jose	2	1	1.63	24	0	0	16	28	19	6	5	10	35	.192	R	R	5-11	160	11-28-72	1990	Santiago, D.R.
Pineda, Luis	0	0	2.00	5	0	0	0	9	5	4	2	5	13	.152	R	R	6-1	170	10-17-74	1995	San Cristobal, D.R.
Ring, Royce	3	1	3.63	29	0	0	2	35	37	15	14	12	22	.274	L	L	6-0	220	12-21-80	2002	La Mesa, Calif.
Roach, Jason	2	5	3.47	39	8	1	0	91	90	44	35	30	80	.256	R	R	6-4	206	4-20-76	1997	Kinston, N.C.
Rodriguez, Jose	1	0	4.91	2	0	0	0	4	4	2	2	1	1	.333	R	R	6-1	170	1-15-82	1999	Aragua, Venez.
Seo, Jae	0	2	2.82	4	4	0	0	22	22	7	7	8	20	.272	R	R	6-1	215	5-24-77	1998	La Canada, Calif.
Strange, Pat	10	9	5.25	29	19	1	1	135	152	85	79	53	88	.283	R	R	6-5	243	8-23-80	1998	Springfield, Mass.
Wheeler, Dan	1	0	2.45	5	0	0	0	7	8	2	2	2	10	.276	R	R	6-3	220	12-10-77	1997	Warwick, R.I.
Yates, Tyler	6	2	3.18	30	1	0	4	40	28	18	14	22	43	.194	R	R	6-4	220	8-7-77	1998	Koloa, Hawaii

FIELDING

Catcher	PCT	G	PO	A	E	DP	PB
Cardona	.980	19	132	16	3	5	3
Huber	1.000	5	28	0	0	1	1
Jacobs	.992	16	118	3	1	1	1
Levis	.946	8	32	3	2	0	1
Pachot	.998	75	487	37	1	3	6
Socarras	1.000	10	42	1	0	0	1
T. Wilson	.980	19	143	3	3	0	2
V. Wilson	1.000	1	10	1	0	0	0

First Base	PCT	G	PO	A	E	DP
Brazell	.989	95	742	64	9	89
Caligiuri	1.000	2	16	2	0	3
Detienne	1.000	1	5	0	0	1
Garcia	1.000	2	13	1	0	1
Glavine	.989	53	343	27	4	35
Jacobs	1.000	1	7	1	0	0
Nye	.929	3	11	2	1	0
T. Wilson	.917	4	20	2	2	4

Second Base	PCT	G	PO	A	E	DP
Bacani	.980	34	62	82	3	23
Basak	.976	27	54	68	3	23
Collins	1.000	24	48	51	0	16
Delgado	1.000	3	8	13	0	3
Detienne	1.000	4	0	6	0	1
Garcia	.955	48	72	97	8	26
Keppinger	1.000	4	7	13	0	3
Nye	.963	13	21	31	2	5
Velazquez	.939	9	14	17	2	1

Third Base	PCT	G	PO	A	E	DP
Basak	1.000	6	1	13	0	2
Cardona	.000	1	0	0	1	0
Detienne	.875	4	5	2	1	0
Garcia	1.000	3	0	4	0	0
Nye	.936	104	75	204	19	24
Velazquez	1.000	4	0	3	0	0
T. Wilson	.750	3	1	5	2	1
Wright	.933	31	27	71	7	5

Shortstop	PCT	G	PO	A	E	DP
Bacani	.857	2	3	9	2	1
Basak	.963	26	31	73	4	21
Collins	1.000	2	0	1	0	0
Delgado	.977	104	149	285	10	62
Garcia	.857	15	19	29	8	7
Ragsdale	.933	6	15	13	2	4
Velazquez	1.000	3	1	3	0	1

Outfield	PCT	G	PO	A	E	DP
Brazell	1.000	18	12	1	0	0
Diaz	.969	132	267	12	9	4
Duncan	.982	55	110	2	2	0
Garcia	1.000	10	8	0	0	0
Gonzalez	1.000	16	24	1	0	0
Pagan	1.000	12	23	1	0	1
Redman	.974	66	108	6	3	0
Slack	1.000	3	8	0	0	0
Snead	.970	73	194	3	6	1
Timmons	1.000	24	28	1	0	0
Williams	.993	55	131	5	1	0

BINGHAMTON METS
Class AA

EASTERN LEAGUE

BATTING

	AVG	G	AB	R	H	2B	3B	HR	RBI	BB	SO	SB	CS	OBP	SLG	B	T	HT	WT	DOB	1st Yr	Resides
Acuna, Ron	.300	129	500	61	150	27	4	1	57	26	99	22	12	.333	.376	R	R	6-0	215	2-1-81	1996	Valencia, Venez.
Anderson, Jimmy	.182	3	11	1	2	1	0	0	2	0	4	0	0	.167	.273	R	R	6-2	200	8-3-81	2002	Riverside, Calif.
Bacani, David	.329	58	158	21	52	9	3	4	29	19	29	8	6	.414	.500	R	R	5-7	170	7-30-79	2001	Long Beach, Calif.
Baldiris, Aarom	.235	21	81	8	19	3	1	0	8	6	13	0	0	.284	.296	R	R	6-2	195	1-5-83	2000	St. Lucia Miranda, Venez.
Basak, Chris	.256	80	273	42	70	21	5	8	41	38	67	10	5	.351	.458	R	R	6-2	190	12-6-78	2000	Joliet, Ill.
Cardona, Javier	.257	21	70	6	18	5	0	1	15	2	7	0	0	.286	.371	R	R	6-1	210	9-15-75	1994	Dorado, P.R.
Clements, Zac	.185	9	27	5	5	0	0	1	1	2	12	0	0	.267	.296	R	R	6-0	215	1-17-80	2002	Memphis, Tenn.
Detienne, David	.232	61	168	24	39	7	2	0	14	17	62	5	3	.325	.298	R	R	5-9	190	8-16-79	1998	Dartmouth, N.S.
Duncan, Jeff	.256	38	133	19	34	6	1	0	9	21	38	10	2	.367	.316	L	L	6-2	188	12-9-78	2000	Frankfort, Ill.
Garcia, Karim	.083	3	12	1	1	1	0	0	3	1	2	0	0	.143	.167	L	L	6-0	210	10-29-75	1993	Ciudad Obregon, Mexico

BATTING

BATTING	AVG	G	AB	R	H	2B	3B	HR	RBI	BB	SO	SB	CS	OBP	SLG	B	T	HT	WT	DOB	1st Yr	Resides
Gonzalez, Jimmy	.268	20	56	7	15	3	0	0	4	5	13	0	0	.359	.321	R	R	6-3	230	3-8-73	1991	Hartford, Conn.
Harper, Brett	.247	45	174	24	43	12	0	7	26	14	60	0	0	.309	.437	L	R	6-4	180	7-31-81	2001	Scottsdale, Ariz.
Hietpas, Joe	.230	43	139	13	32	10	0	3	19	19	41	0	2	.335	.367	R	R	6-3	220	5-1-79	2001	Appleton, Wis.
Huber, Justin	.271	70	236	44	64	16	1	11	33	46	57	2	2	.414	.487	R	R	6-5	190	7-1-82	2001	Emerald, Australia
Jiannetti, Joe	.353	5	17	1	6	1	0	1	3	0	3	0	0	.353	.588	R	R	6-0	187	9-25-81	2001	St. Petersburg, Fla.
Keppinger, Jeff	.362	14	47	14	17	3	1	0	5	6	2	2	1	.426	.468	R	R	6-0	180	4-21-80	2002	Auburn, Ga.
2-team (81 Altoona)	.340	95	362	58	123	20	3	1	38	33	17	12	6	.392	.420							
Lambin, Chase	.244	121	410	64	100	22	4	10	65	48	103	4	2	.331	.390	S	R	6-1	180	7-7-79	2002	Houston, Texas
Lydon, Wayne	.270	123	507	78	137	18	6	5	43	49	119	65	20	.339	.359	R	R	6-2	190	4-17-81	1999	Jessup, Pa.
Malek, Bobby	.222	14	54	7	12	2	0	1	1	2	13	0	0	.263	.315	L	R	6-3	205	7-6-81	2002	Canton, Mich.
Pagan, Angel	.288	112	448	71	129	25	8	4	63	42	96	29	5	.346	.406	S	R	6-1	180	7-2-81	2000	Rio Piedras, P.R.
Pressley, Josh	.300	101	340	44	102	30	0	3	62	46	64	0	0	.383	.415	L	R	6-6	220	4-2-80	1998	Fort Lauderdale, Fla.
Redman, Prentice	.286	63	245	46	70	29	1	13	49	28	68	9	4	.367	.571	R	R	6-2	191	8-26-79	1999	Duncanville, Ala.
Reyes, Jose	.111	4	18	2	2	0	0	0	3	2	4	3	1	.190	.111	S	R	6-0	175	6-11-83	2000	Santiago, D.R.
Velazquez, Gil	.239	104	356	42	85	16	3	5	38	30	94	3	2	.300	.343	R	R	6-3	180	10-17-79	1998	Paramount, Calif.
Wilson, Vance	.333	1	3	2	1	0	0	1	1	0	0	0	0	.500	1.333	R	R	5-11	190	3-17-73	1994	Springdale, Ark.
Wright, David	.363	60	223	44	81	27	0	10	40	39	41	20	6	.467	.619	R	R	6-0	200	12-20-82	2001	Chesapeake, Va.

PITCHING

PITCHING	W	L	ERA	G	GS	CG	SV	IP	H	R	ER	BB	SO	AVG	B	T	HT	WT	DOB	1st Yr	Resides
Bannister, Brian	3	3	4.06	8	8	0	0	44	45	23	20	17	28	.276	R	R	6-1	205	2-28-81	2003	Paradise Valley, Ariz.
Bell, Heath	0	0	0.00	1	0	0	0	2	2	0	0	0	0	.250	R	R	6-3	230	9-29-77	1998	Tustin, Calif.
Bevis, P.J.	1	2	3.06	27	0	0	12	32	26	12	11	8	32	.217	R	R	6-3	175	7-28-80	1998	Capalaba, Australia
Byard, David	0	0	0.00	3	0	0	0	6	5	1	0	0	5	.217	R	R	6-2	240	6-1-78	2000	Mt. Vernon, Ohio
Caracioli, Lance	1	4	5.72	28	0	0	1	46	55	33	29	28	41	.299	L	L	6-4	200	12-14-77	1998	Walker, La.
Chenard, Ken	9	6	4.45	27	17	0	3	123	101	66	61	48	122	.221	R	R	6-3	195	8-30-78	1999	Victorville, Calif.
Cole, Joey	0	0	7.04	7	0	0	0	8	9	6	6	13	4	.259	L	R	6-8	225	9-15-77	1999	Nacogdoches, Texas
Diaz, Jose	4	7	5.18	21	19	1	0	83	59	53	48	70	90	.203	R	R	6-0	175	4-13-80	1997	San Pedro de Macoris, D.R.
Edwards, Brian	1	0	3.00	2	1	0	0	9	6	3	3	6	2	.207	R	R	6-3	190	5-28-81	2003	Littleton, Colo.
Hill, Jeremy	2	3	2.08	24	0	0	10	30	20	10	7	19	34	.183	R	R	5-11	200	8-8-77	1996	Dallas, Texas
Joseph, Jake	6	0	3.32	25	0	0	1	43	32	18	16	14	28	.208	R	R	6-1	180	1-24-78	1999	Citrus Heights, Calif.
Kazmir, Scott	2	1	1.73	4	4	0	0	26	16	6	5	9	29	.188	L	L	6-0	170	1-24-84	2002	Houston, Texas
Lavigne, Tim	4	5	5.70	40	4	0	2	84	94	62	53	39	44	.283	R	R	5-10	210	7-4-78	2000	Virginia Beach, Va.
Mangrum, Micah	1	0	4.88	14	0	0	0	31	33	17	17	4	22	.266	R	R	6-2	170	9-11-77	2000	Sandy, Utah
McGinley, Blake	9	2	3.73	32	0	0	1	70	60	31	29	14	82	.226	R	L	6-1	175	8-2-78	2001	Bakersfield, Calif.
Meyers, Mike	0	3	6.10	5	4	0	1	21	23	16	14	10	11	.274	R	R	6-2	210	10-18-77	1997	Molina, Ill.
Musser, Neal	3	6	3.41	19	19	0	0	108	103	52	41	40	70	.254	L	L	6-1	215	8-25-80	1999	Otterbein, Ind.
Ough, Wayne	2	5	6.99	15	15	0	0	67	81	55	52	34	46	.297	R	R	6-2	210	11-27-78	2000	Manly, Australia
Parra, Jose	0	0	0.00	1	0	0	0	1	0	0	0	0	2	.000	R	R	5-11	170	11-28-72	1989	Santiago, D.R.
Peterson, Matt	6	4	3.27	19	18	0	0	105	97	44	38	45	90	.253	R	R	6-5	210	2-11-82	2001	Alexandria, La.
Petit, Yusmeiro	1	1	4.50	2	2	0	0	12	10	6	6	5	16	.222	R	R	6-0	180	11-22-84	2002	Maracaibo, Venez.
Ring, Royce	2	2	3.77	19	0	0	1	29	25	13	12	11	23	.234	L	L	6-0	220	12-21-80	2002	La Mesa, Calif.
Roman, Orlando	2	2	4.35	8	5	0	0	31	26	16	15	15	31	.224	R	R	6-1	210	11-28-78	1999	Vega Baja, P.R.
Scobie, Jason	5	5	2.82	26	24	0	1	147	137	57	46	49	95	.247	R	R	6-1	195	9-1-78	2001	Austin, Texas
Sedlacek, Shawn	0	1	11.20	8	1	0	0	14	24	18	17	2	11	.387	R	R	6-4	200	6-29-77	1998	Cedar Rapids, Iowa
Strayhorn, Kole	5	4	5.22	39	0	0	8	50	49	34	29	27	43	.254	R	R	6-0	185	10-1-82	2001	Shawnee, Okla.

FIELDING

Catcher	PCT	G	PO	A	E	DP	PB
Anderson	1.000	3	20	1	0	0	0
Cardona	.987	20	138	11	2	1	3
Clements	1.000	1	8	1	0	0	0
Gonzalez	.982	15	104	8	2	1	1
Hietpas	.982	43	298	23	6	4	4
Huber	.992	66	461	37	4	3	10
Wilson	1.000	1	5	1	0	0	0

First Base	PCT	G	PO	A	E	DP
Cardona	1.000	1	2	0	0	0
Detienne	.996	31	202	22	1	16
Garcia	.955	3	20	1	1	1
Gonzalez	1.000	1	2	0	0	0
Harper	.985	41	354	28	6	36
Huber	.971	5	33	0	1	4

Second Base	PCT	G	PO	A	E	DP
Pressley	.988	75	583	57	8	51
Bacani	.979	32	53	90	3	15
Basak	1.000	4	7	5	0	3
Detienne	1.000	2	2	9	0	1
Keppinger	1.000	11	19	25	0	5
Lambin	.946	96	166	258	24	55
Reyes	1.000	4	8	12	0	4

Third Base	PCT	G	PO	A	E	DP
Bacani	1.000	1	0	1	0	0
Baldiris	.946	21	17	36	3	2
Basak	.957	45	26	85	5	7
Detienne	.961	18	14	35	2	1
Keppinger	.889	2	1	7	1	0
Wright	.943	59	40	92	8	5

Shortstop	PCT	G	PO	A	E	DP
Basak	.965	33	42	95	5	23
Detienne	.952	8	7	13	1	4
Velazquez	.974	104	180	301	13	60

Outfield	PCT	G	PO	A	E	DP
Acuna	.957	99	149	7	7	1
Clements	.875	7	0	1	0	0
Detienne	1.000	3	4	0	0	0
Duncan	.972	39	69	1	2	0
Jiannetti	1.000	2	2	0	0	0
Lydon	.952	119	213	7	11	0
Malek	1.000	16	24	2	0	1
Pagan	.991	103	215	11	2	2
Pressley	1.000	1	4	0	0	0
Redman	.973	56	107	1	3	0

ST. LUCIE METS — High Class A

FLORIDA STATE LEAGUE

BATTING	AVG	G	AB	R	H	2B	3B	HR	RBI	BB	SO	SB	CS	OBP	SLG	B	T	HT	WT	DOB	1st Yr	Resides
Anderson, Jimmy	.250	2	4	1	1	0	0	0	0	1	0	0	0	.250	.250	R	R	6-2	200	8-3-81	2002	Riverside, Calif.
Bacon, Matt	.200	5	10	2	2	0	0	1	1	6	0	0	2	.273	.200	L	R	6-2	203	2-18-81	2004	Pensacola, Fla.
Baldiris, Aarom	.305	107	406	57	124	15	5	4	45	46	64	6	6	.384	.397	R	R	6-2	195	1-5-83	2000	Miranda, Venez.
Batista, Wilson	.165	29	97	5	16	0	0	0	5	8	20	5	1	.231	.165	S	R	6-0	170	2-7-81	2001	Vietnan los Mina, D.R.
Brinkley, Dante	.250	5	16	4	4	1	0	1	1	4	4	1	1	.400	.500	R	R	5-10	183	8-21-81	2003	Fairview Heights, Ill.
Caligiuri, Jay	.238	104	365	52	87	15	1	18	69	54	83	1	1	.339	.433	R	R	6-0	195	3-29-80	2001	Camarillo, Calif.
Clements, Zac	.313	52	150	16	47	11	2	3	14	11	40	6	9	.373	.473	R	R	6-0	215	1-17-80	2002	Memphis, Tenn.
Floyd, Cliff	.500	1	4	2	2	0	0	0	1	0	2	0	0	.500	.500	L	R	6-4	230	12-5-72	1991	Plantation, Fla.
Garcia, Miguel	.280	9	25	1	7	0	0	0	2	1	7	0	1	.333	.280	L	L	6-1	180	4-8-82	2000	Santo Domingo, D.R.
Garcia, Travis	.000	2	4	0	0	0	0	0	0	0	2	0	0	.000	.000	R	R	6-2	205	4-3-82	2003	Bronx, N.Y.
Harper, Brett	.350	60	220	32	77	18	1	9	55	35	53	1	1	.440	.564	L	R	6-4	180	7-31-81	2001	Scottsdale, Ariz.
Hietpas, Joe	.251	55	191	23	48	15	1	2	27	18	51	1	1	.329	.372	R	R	6-3	220	5-1-79	2001	Appleton, Wis.
Huber, Justin	.283	15	53	13	15	2	0	2	10	5	8	2	0	.356	.434	R	R	6-5	190	7-1-82	2001	Emerald, Australia
Jiannetti, Joe	.255	81	271	31	69	12	2	5	28	18	38	11	8	.306	.369	R	R	6-0	187	9-25-81	2001	St. Petersburg, Fla.
Lawson, Forrest	.205	28	78	10	16	3	2	1	6	11	20	0	2	.319	.333	R	R	6-2	185	11-9-80	1999	Federal Way, Wash.

BATTING

BATTING	AVG	G	AB	R	H	2B	3B	HR	RBI	BB	SO	SB	CS	OBP	SLG	B	T	HT	WT	DOB	1st Yr	Resides
Malek, Bobby	.266	111	425	63	113	23	6	13	58	32	82	15	6	.321	.440	L	R	6-3	205	7-6-81	2002	Canton, Mich.
McIntyre, Robert	.208	88	274	33	57	10	0	3	21	12	70	5	7	.253	.277	R	R	5-10	175	12-8-80	1999	Tampa, Fla.
Milledge, Lastings	.235	22	81	6	19	6	2	2	8	9	21	3	2	.319	.432	R	R	6-1	185	4-5-85	2003	Palmetto, Fla.
Parker, Rashad	.294	12	34	3	10	3	0	0	2	3	9	1	0	.368	.382	R	R	5-11	177	9-1-79	2003	Westchester, Calif.
Piazza, Mike	.500	2	6	0	3	1	0	0	2	1	0	0	0	.500	.667	R	R	6-3	215	9-4-68	1989	Boynton Beach, Fla.
Piazza, Tony	.000	1	1	0	0	0	0	0	0	0	1	0	0	.000	.000	R	R	6-2	215	6-22-80	2003	Cody, Wyo.
Ragsdale, Corey	.221	124	421	65	93	19	5	7	38	42	152	24	14	.305	.340	R	R	6-4	185	11-10-82	2001	Jonesboro, Ark.
Reaver, David	.290	21	62	9	18	2	0	0	7	5	15	3	1	.362	.323	R	R	6-0	192	5-16-81	2003	Union Bridge, Md.
Reyes, Jose	.261	6	23	3	6	2	0	0	1	0	3	2	0	.261	.348	S	R	6-0	175	6-11-83	2000	Santiago, D.R.
Rodriguez, Andres	.238	55	160	15	38	5	1	3	16	8	50	1	2	.275	.338	R	R	6-4	220	2-14-79	1998	San Cristobal, D.R.
Rodriguez, Edgar	.273	10	22	2	6	1	1	0	4	1	8	0	1	.360	.409	R	R	6-0	185	11-29-79	1997	San Pedro de Macoris, D.R.
Seuss, Adam	.143	2	7	1	1	0	0	0	0	0	2	0	0	.250	.143	L	R	6-0	185	8-31-80	2002	La Quinta, Calif.
Slack, Jon	.258	108	445	66	115	18	3	6	30	41	75	30	5	.327	.353	L	L	6-0	177	12-9-81	2002	Henderson, Nev.
Turay, Alhaji	.256	86	308	35	79	12	0	16	44	22	81	11	6	.313	.451	R	R	6-1	207	9-22-82	2001	Auburn, Wash.
Wigginton, Ty	.375	2	8	1	3	0	0	0	1	0	0	1	0	.375	.375	R	R	6-0	200	10-11-77	1998	Chula Vista, Calif.
Wilson, Andrew	.429	5	14	2	6	2	0	0	2	6	2	2	0	.500	.857	R	R	6-2	210	11-20-80	2003	Vero Beach, Fla.
Wilson, Brandon	.140	29	93	4	13	8	0	0	6	4	38	1	1	.175	.226	R	R	6-4	181	9-1-82	2000	Baton Rouge, La.

PITCHING

PITCHING	W	L	ERA	G	GS	CG	SV	IP	H	R	ER	BB	SO	AVG	B	T	HT	WT	DOB	1st Yr	Resides
Acosta, Domingo	0	0	1.42	4	0	0	0	6	5	2	1	1	8	.208	R	R	6-3	185	10-5-80	2001	New York, N.Y.
Bannister, Brian	5	7	4.24	20	20	0	0	110	111	63	52	27	106	.263	R	R	6-1	205	2-28-81	2003	Paradise Valley, Ariz.
Byard, David	5	5	4.55	37	0	0	4	57	62	35	29	28	26	.279	R	R	6-2	240	6-1-78	2000	Mt. Vernon, Ohio
Cole, Joey	1	3	4.85	24	0	0	9	26	24	16	14	20	20	.253	L	R	6-8	225	9-15-77	1999	Nacogdoches, Texas
Cordova, Vincent	1	2	3.13	4	3	1	0	23	22	8	8	4	19	.253	R	R	6-3	210	4-16-82	2003	Whittier, Calif.
Cox, Michael	2	1	3.23	21	3	0	0	31	16	13	11	35	33	.154	L	L	5-11	205	11-3-78	2000	Pasadena, Texas
Deaton, Kevin	6	3	2.99	19	19	0	0	96	94	38	32	23	73	.258	R	R	6-5	235	8-7-81	2000	Merritt Island, Fla.
Edwards, Brian	5	6	3.30	38	6	2	4	90	88	36	33	19	35	.267	R	R	6-3	190	5-28-81	2003	Littleton, Colo.
Erickson, Scott	1	0	0.00	2	2	0	0	7	6	0	0	5		.222	R	R	6-4	220	2-2-68	1989	Stateline, Nev.
Hawk, Shane	2	0	3.55	8	0	0	2	13	9	6	5	5	10	.205	L	L	6-6	188	9-10-81	2003	Cibolo, Texas
Kazmir, Scott	1	2	3.42	11	11	0	0	50	49	20	19	22	51	.257	L	L	6-0	170	1-24-84	2002	Houston, Texas
Keisler, Randy	1	0	0.00	1	0	0	0	4	3	0	0	1		.231	L	L	6-3	190	2-24-76	1998	Richards, Texas
Keppel, Bob	1	0	0.90	2	2	0	0	10	7	2	1	2	6	.200	R	L	6-5	205	6-11-82	2000	Chesterfield, Mo.
Lindstrom, Matt	5	5	3.73	14	14	1	0	80	83	44	33	20	50	.272	R	R	6-4	205	2-11-80	2002	Rexburg, Idaho
Mangrum, Micah	1	0	0.73	4	1	0	0	12	7	2	1	3	5	.171	R	R	6-2	170	9-11-77	2000	Sandy, Utah
McNab, Tim	4	4	4.65	38	0	0	1	72	91	40	37	22	53	.307	R	R	6-0	170	6-4-80	2002	Hollywood, Fla.
Meyers, Mike	1	1	5.71	4	3	0	0	17	20	11	11	3	14	.308	R	R	6-2	210	10-18-77	1997	Molina, Ill.
Moreno, Orber	0	0	27.00	1	0	0	0	1	4	3	3	0	2	.571	R	R	6-3	200	4-27-77	1994	Los Altos, Venez.
Nunez, Jose	0	0	8.10	2	0	0	0	3	4	3	3	2	1	.308	L	L	6-2	175	3-14-79	1996	Monte Cristi, D.R.
Ochoa, Javier	1	0	0.00	3	0	0	0	7	7	3	0	1	6	.259	R	R	6-2	200	1-8-79	1996	Maracay, Venez.
Olson, Ryan	1	1	4.38	41	0	0	1	49	39	27	24	37	46	.218	S	L	6-5	193	1-16-80	2001	Oakhurst, Calif.
Ough, Wayne	1	3	8.82	4	4	0	0	16	22	20	16	11	13	.319	R	R	6-2	210	11-27-78	2000	Manly, Australia
Paulk, Robert	8	6	3.70	31	10	0	3	92	111	45	38	23	60	.302	R		5-11	170	3-14-81	2002	Madison, Fla.
Petit, Yusmeiro	2	3	1.22	9	9	1	0	44	27	9	6	14	62	.175	R	R	6-0	180	11-22-84	2002	Maracaibo, Venez.
Pinango, Miguel	2	2	2.75	4	3	0	0	20	18	6	6	1	16	.247	R	R	6-1	160	1-20-83	2000	St. Teresa, Venez.
Pineda, Luis	1	0	2.84	5	0	0	1	6	5	2	2	1	10	.217	R	R	6-1	170	10-17-74	1995	San Cristobal, D.R.
Portobanco, Luz	1	3	3.77	34	2	0	0	76	75	43	32	32	58	.258	R	R	6-2	190	9-15-79	2000	Miami, Fla.
Rodriguez, Jose	1	0	0.00	4	0	0	1	8	2	1	0	2	5	.077	R	R	6-0	170	1-15-82	1999	Aragua, Venez.
Roman, Orlando	4	5	3.71	20	16	1	2	102	82	44	42	33	99	.220	R	R	6-1	210	11-28-78	1999	Vega Baja, P.R.
Strickland, Scott	0	1	9.45	6	1	0	0	7	11	8	7	2	5	.344	R	R	5-11	180	4-26-76	1997	Spring, Texas

FIELDING

Catcher	PCT	G	PO	A	E	DP	PB
Anderson	1.000	2	9	0	0	0	0
Bacon	.952	3	19	1	0	2	
Clements	.969	50	283	34	10	5	12
Hietpas	.983	55	349	48	7	1	6
Huber	1.000	4	31	4	0	0	0
T. Piazza	1.000	1	3	0	0	0	0
B. Wilson	.977	29	188	23	5	2	5

First Base	PCT	G	PO	A	E	DP
Caligiuri	.992	71	598	46	5	71
Harper	.988	39	387	15	5	39
M. Piazza	1.000	1	6	0	0	0
A. Rodriguez	.995	27	187	14	1	17

Second Base	PCT	G	PO	A	E	DP
Batista	.941	27	56	71	8	17
McIntyre	.977	81	153	237	9	59

	PCT	G	PO	A	E	DP
Reaver	.944	15	30	37	4	9
Reyes	.917	6	8	14	2	3
A. Rodriguez	1.000	2	6	5	0	1
E. Rodriguez	.926	7	9	16	2	4

Third Base	PCT	G	PO	A	E	DP
Baldiris	.935	104	69	219	20	17
Caligiuri	.925	14	4	33	3	2
T. Garcia	1.000	2	0	4	0	1
Jiannetti	.765	9	4	9	4	0
Reaver	.500	1	1	0	1	0
A. Rodriguez	1.000	1	1	0	0	0
Wigginton	1.000	2	2	1	0	0
A. Wilson	1.000	2	0	6	0	0

Shortstop	PCT	G	PO	A	E	DP
Batista	.889	2	2	6	1	0
McIntyre	1.000	2	0	3	0	0
Ragsdale	.941	124	237	387	39	96
Reaver	1.000	4	6	12	0	2

Outfield	PCT	G	PO	A	E	DP
Brinkley	1.000	5	12	2	0	0
Clements	1.000	1	1	1	0	0
Floyd	1.000	1	1	0	0	0
M. Garcia	1.000	5	5	0	0	0
Jiannetti	.971	61	96	3	3	1
Lawson	.925	27	36	1	3	0
Malek	.972	106	163	10	5	2
Milledge	.920	22	43	4	0	0
Parker	.952	12	20	0	1	0
A. Rodriguez	1.000	1	1	0	0	0
Seuss	1.000	2	3	1	0	0
Slack	.991	107	221	9	2	1
Turay	.916	63	83	4	8	0
A. Wilson	1.000	2	4	0	0	0

CAPITAL CITY BOMBERS — Low Class A

SOUTH ATLANTIC LEAGUE

BATTING	AVG	G	AB	R	H	2B	3B	HR	RBI	BB	SO	SB	CS	OBP	SLG	B	T	HT	WT	DOB	1st Yr	Resides
Anderson, Jimmy	.245	37	106	13	26	8	0	2	12	6	30	0	0	.302	.377	R	R	6-2	200	8-3-81	2002	Riverside, Calif.
Batista, Wilson	.260	84	319	70	83	15	1	3	35	49	57	35	8	.363	.342	S	R	6-0	170	2-7-81	2001	Vietnam los Mina, D.R.
Bennett, Stacy	.067	6	15	1	1	0	0	0	0	2	5	0	0	.176	.067	L	R	6-3	196	4-2-82	2003	Watkinsville, Ga.
Bergeron, Jean	.278	23	72	18	20	5	0	5	17	18	23	0	1	.429	.556	R	R	6-3	220	12-19-81	2004	Chesterfield, N.H.
Bladergroen, Ian	.342	72	269	39	92	23	3	13	74	25	55	1	1	.397	.595	L	L	6-5	210	2-23-83	2003	Albuquerque, N.M.
Bowman, Shawn	.255	116	396	65	101	17	1	18	66	39	121	5	4	.336	.439	R	R	6-2	190	12-9-84	2003	Coquitlam, B.C.
Brinkley, Dante	.228	32	101	20	23	7	2	2	14	9	41	2	2	.295	.396	R	R	5-10	180	8-21-81	2003	Fairview Heights, Ill.
Davidson, Tyler	.233	57	206	33	48	12	2	5	32	22	49	5	1	.315	.383	R	R	6-5	240	9-23-80	2003	Edmonds, Wash.
Garcia, Yunir	.270	78	222	39	60	9	0	10	34	38	72	2	1	.386	.446	R	R	6-1	200	8-3-82	1999	San Pablo, Venez.
Harvey, Ryan	.325	115	425	89	138	32	5	11	72	35	48	12	5	.395	.501	R	R	6-0	190	12-17-79	2003	Riverside, Calif.

ORGANIZATION STATISTICS

BATTING

BATTING	AVG	G	AB	R	H	2B	3B	HR	RBI	BB	SO	SB	CS	OBP	SLG	B	T	HT	WT	DOB	1st Yr	Resides
Hill, Jamar	.271	121	458	83	124	21	1	26	89	37	110	20	11	.334	.491	R	R	6-4	200	9-20-82	2002	Juneau, Alaska
Linares, Jesus	.294	81	204	43	60	10	0	6	33	29	59	1	2	.393	.431	S	R	6-0	190	6-7-82	1999	El Tocuyo, Venez.
Milledge, Lastings	.340	65	262	66	89	22	1	13	58	17	53	23	6	.399	.580	R	R	6-1	185	4-5-85	2003	Palmetto, Fla.
Parker, Rashad	.225	70	240	40	54	12	1	2	17	15	54	9	2	.293	.308	R	R	5-11	177	9-1-79	2003	Westchester, Calif.
Piazza, Tony	.143	7	21	4	3	1	0	0	0	3	11	0	0	.250	.190	R	R	6-2	215	6-22-80	2003	Cody, Wyo.
Pietsch, Seth	.229	10	35	8	8	0	1	1	9	2	12	1	0	.293	.371	R	R	5-9	197	9-16-81	2003	Grants Pass, Ore.
Reaver, David	.154	37	123	15	19	2	0	0	6	10	26	1	0	.228	.171	R	R	6-0	192	5-16-81	2003	Union Bridge, Md.
Reynoso, Danilo	.245	15	49	3	12	2	0	0	4	3	17	1	1	.283	.286	R	R	5-11	205	4-5-82	1998	San Cristobal, D.R.
Stewart, Caleb	.314	25	86	20	27	6	0	5	15	13	11	0	1	.396	.558	R	R	6-2	230	6-11-82	2001	Rush, Ky.
Watts, Derran	.228	27	92	12	21	4	3	1	8	11	29	5	1	.330	.370	R	R	6-3	185	6-28-80	2001	Brampton, Ontario
Whealy, Blake	.283	124	428	100	121	32	5	23	82	66	126	10	5	.387	.542	R	R	6-1	180	5-27-80	2002	River Forest, Ill.
Wilson, Andrew	.286	104	370	63	106	32	0	19	70	43	80	2	0	.364	.527	R	R	6-2	210	11-20-80	2003	Vero Beach, Fla.
Wilson, Brandon	.209	20	67	9	14	2	0	1	2	2	22	0	0	.254	.284	R	R	6-4	181	9-1-82	2000	Baton Rouge, La.

PITCHING

PITCHING	W	L	ERA	G	GS	CG	SV	IP	H	R	ER	BB	SO	AVG	B	T	HT	WT	DOB	1st Yr	Resides
Acosta, Domingo	1	2	3.86	29	0	0	6	42	43	23	18	26	35	.257	R	R	6-3	185	10-5-80	2001	New York, N.Y.
Brewer, Jeff	0	0	16.20	1	0	0	0	2	5	3	3	1		.556	R	R	6-3	190	10-5-80	2003	Fredericton, N.B.
Cordova, Vincent	8	7	4.25	24	19	0	0	121	138	73	57	14	100	.285	R	R	6-3	210	4-16-82	2003	Whittier, Calif.
Danly, Ryan	3	3	4.33	11	9	1	0	44	59	31	21	18	38	.321	L	L	6-8	195	6-23-81	2001	Cedar Rapids, Iowa
Foli, Daniel	1	0	2.97	17	0	0	2	30	19	13	10	11	32	.184	R	R	6-1	180	3-30-81	2001	Kodak, Tenn.
Garcia, Anderson	9	2	4.50	35	5	0	2	84	92	57	42	47	75	.275	R	R	6-2	170	3-23-81	2001	Santo Domingo, D.R.
Gomez, Jose	3	1	3.18	11	0	0	0	17	8	7	6	12	23	.140	R	R	6-3	240	12-16-80	1998	Brooksville, Fla.
Hawk, Shane	1	1	2.20	25	0	0	8	33	25	9	8	9	44	.208	L	L	6-6	188	9-10-81	2003	Cibolo, Texas
King, Bryan	8	0	4.02	40	0	0	2	69	64	39	31	23	69	.242	R	R	6-1	185	5-20-81	2002	Englewood, Colo.
Lindstrom, Matt	3	2	3.21	12	11	0	0	56	47	26	20	10	64	.223	R	R	6-4	205	2-11-80	2002	Rexburg, Idaho
MacLane, Evan	5	2	2.39	14	10	0	0	68	57	21	18	10	66	.225	L	L	6-2	185	11-4-82	2003	Quincy, Calif.
Maldonado, Ivan	4	4	7.38	14	8	0	0	46	65	40	38	15	35	.333	R	R	6-3	210	6-7-80	2002	Cayey, P.R.
Mangrum, Micah	1	0	2.25	7	0	0	1	12	13	5	3	4	12	.277	R	R	6-2	170	9-11-77	2000	Sandy, Utah
Miramontes, Mateo	0	3	12.24	11	6	0	1	25	46	43	34	23	23	.371	R	R	6-4	200	12-24-81	2003	Pleasanton, Calif.
Muniz, Carlos	4	0	4.29	16	0	0	7	21	11	10	10	8	19	.159	R	R	6-1	180	3-12-81	2003	Wilmington, Calif.
Ochoa, Javier	2	1	5.18	24	0	0	1	40	38	26	23	22	38	.242	R	R	6-2	200	1-8-79	1996	Maracay, Venez.
Osberg, Tanner	11	7	5.89	28	26	0	0	141	169	103	92	54	79	.307	L	R	6-3	185	9-10-82	2000	Red Deer, Alberta
Perez, Marcelo	0	0	0.00	3	0	0	0	5	1	0	0		6	.059	R	R	6-1	160	7-4-82	2000	Loma de Cabrera, D.R.
Petit, Yusmeiro	9	2	2.39	15	15	0	0	83	47	29	22	22	122	.159	R	R	6-0	180	11-22-84	2002	Maracaibo, Venez.
Ramirez, Greg	7	0	2.06	38	8	0	10	96	81	39	22	28	105	.226	R	R	6-4	205	9-12-80	2003	Oxnard, Calif.
Rodriguez, Jose	0	1	2.08	6	0	0	0	9	6	2	2	5	8	.200	R	R	6-0	170	1-15-82	1999	Carora, Venez.
Rondon, Celso	3	3	4.71	22	0	0	1	36	32	19	19	14	41	.242	R	R	6-0	215	4-7-84	2001	Cumana Sucre, Venez.
Walker, Brian	5	5	3.45	22	13	0	0	78	78	41	30	34	69	.263	L	L	6-3	210	2-20-80	2001	Miami, Fla.
Worthington, Tim	1	1	6.04	7	6	0	0	28	27	21	19	16	33	.245	R	R	6-2	200	7-29-80	2003	Redwood City, Calif.

FIELDING

Catcher	PCT	G	PO	A	E	DP	PB
Anderson	.974	37	248	17	7	1	5
Bennett	1.000	6	44	3	0	0	1
Garcia	.987	71	564	35	8	0	4
Piazza	1.000	3	26	3	0	0	2
Reynoso	.967	15	105	13	4	1	5
B. Wilson	1.000	19	167	11	0	1	4

First Base	PCT	G	PO	A	E	DP
Bergeron	.993	17	136	9	1	14
Bladergroen	.992	44	325	34	3	28
Davidson	.997	35	284	7	1	22
Garcia	1.000	1	4	0	0	0
Linares	.973	5	34	2	1	3
A. Wilson	.994	41	308	16	2	36

	PCT	G	PO	A	E	DP
B. Wilson	1.000	1	2	0	0	0

Second Base	PCT	G	PO	A	E	DP
Linares	.971	30	37	63	3	11
Reaver	1.000	4	3	5	0	0
Whealy	.946	104	203	254	26	55
A. Wilson	.919	14	29	28	5	6

Third Base	PCT	G	PO	A	E	DP
Bowman	.927	113	63	244	24	25
Linares	.829	22	6	23	6	1
A. Wilson	.943	15	6	27	2	0

Shortstop	PCT	G	PO	A	E	DP
Batista	.922	84	115	226	29	40
Linares	.952	31	42	76	6	13

	PCT	G	PO	A	E	DP
Reaver	.923	31	44	87	11	16

Outfield	PCT	G	PO	A	E	DP
Brinkley	1.000	32	54	6	0	2
Harvey	.954	100	141	3	7	0
Hill	.961	112	191	7	8	1
Linares	1.000	1	1	0	0	0
Milledge	.920	62	97	6	9	1
Parker	.966	65	110	3	4	0
Pietsch	.947	8	18	0	1	0
Stewart	1.000	19	31	3	0	1
Watts	.982	27	54	2	1	0
A. Wilson	.867	11	13	0	2	0

BROOKLYN CYCLONES — Short-Season Class A

NEW YORK-PENN LEAGUE

BATTING	AVG	G	AB	R	H	2B	3B	HR	RBI	BB	SO	SB	CS	OBP	SLG	B	T	HT	WT	DOB	1st Yr	Resides
Bennett, Stacy	.106	17	47	4	5	1	0	0	2	4	16	0	1	.222	.128	L	R	6-3	196	4-2-82	2003	Watkinsville, Ga.
Bergeron, Jabe	.111	3	9	0	1	1	0	0	1	1	4	0	0	.273	.222	R	R	6-3	230	12-19-81	2004	Chesterfield, N.H.
Brinkley, Dante	.316	62	234	47	74	9	1	6	30	25	59	14	1	.396	.440	R	R	5-10	180	8-21-81	2003	Fairview Heights, Ill.
Brown, Kyle	.167	5	6	1	1	0	0	0	0	1	2	1	1	.167	.167	R	R	6-0	187	10-4-81	2004	Schenectady, N.Y.
Burt, Jim	.280	48	168	20	47	11	2	4	23	14	28	6	2	.368	.440	R	L	5-11	230	4-23-81	2004	Saddle River, N.J.
Coles, Corey	.278	64	237	40	66	6	5	2	20	17	31	10	5	.338	.371	L	L	6-1	170	1-30-82	2003	Lafayette, La.
Concepcion, Ambiorix	.305	66	259	38	79	14	3	8	46	13	54	28	11	.338	.475	R	R	6-2	180	10-15-83	2001	Santo Domingo, D.R.
Coultas, Ryan	.252	44	155	16	39	5	1	1	10	5	31	2	0	.287	.316	R	R	6-3	185	4-24-82	2004	Ventura, Calif.
Davidson, Tyler	.305	65	243	36	74	15	4	6	45	22	64	3	1	.376	.473	R	R	6-5	240	9-23-80	2003	Edmonds, Wash.
Fisher, Matt	.246	34	126	17	31	7	2	3	11	10	13	2	0	.299	.405	R	R	5-9	180	9-3-81	2004	Chatsworth, Calif.
Flores, Jesus	.333	3	6	1	2	0	0	1	3	0	1	0	0	.333	.833	R	R	6-1	180	10-26-84	2002	Carupano, Venez.
Garcia, Travis	.143	11	35	0	5	2	0	0	2	2	6	0	0	.189	.200	R	R	6-2	205	4-18-82	2003	Bronx, N.Y.
Garcia, Yunir	.189	12	37	2	7	0	0	1	3	3	13	1	0	.286	.270	R	R	6-1	200	8-3-82	1999	San Pablo, Venez.
Hathaway, Aaron	.206	40	131	17	27	5	0	0	12	8	25	1	0	.250	.244	R	R	6-0	190	12-2-82	2004	Vancouver, Wash.
Housel, David	.000	1	3	0	0	0	0	0	0	1	1	0	0	.250	.000	S	R	6-1	160	9-6-81	2001	DeBary, Fla.
Psomas, Grant	.233	65	223	23	52	13	2	3	29	25	48	4	1	.310	.350	R	R	6-3	195	9-2-82	2004	Carnegie, Pa.
Reynoso, Danilo	.190	14	42	3	8	0	0	1	3	1	17	0	0	.209	.262	R	R	5-11	205	4-5-82	1998	San Cristobal, D.R.
Rios, Kevin	.177	55	158	17	28	4	1	1	12	10	40	2	3	.239	.234	R	R	6-2	180	7-21-81	2003	Santa Ana, Calif.
Stewart, Caleb	.210	26	81	8	17	5	2	0	12	5	25	3	2	.253	.321	R	R	6-2	230	6-11-82	2004	Rush, Ky.
Triplett, Russ	.000	2	4	0	0	0	0	0	0	0	0	0	0	.000	.000	R	R	5-11	180	1-18-81	2004	West Columbia, S.C.
Watts, Derran	.267	53	187	32	50	7	3	2	13	21	47	17	3	.344	.369	R	R	6-3	185	6-28-80	2001	Brampton, Ontario
Wendt, Justin	.125	3	8	1	1	0	0	0	2	1	1	0	0	.222	.250	L	R	6-3	230	12-24-81	2000	Waterloo, Ontario
Zech, Bryan	.143	21	63	6	9	1	0	0	5	8	16	0	0	.236	.159	R	R	5-10	175	5-27-81	2004	Wellington, Fla.

GAMES BY POSITION: C—Bennett 16, Flores 3, Y. Garcia 12, Hathaway 40, Reynoso 14. **1B**—Bergeron 2, Burt 27, Davidson 44, Wendt 3. **2B**—Fisher 34, Housel 1, Rios 21, Triplett 1, Zech 21. **3B**—Bennett 1, T. Garcia 11, Psomas 61, Rios 6. **SS**—Coultas 43, Psomas 4, Rios 29, Triplett 1. **OF**—Brinkley 55, Brown 2, Coles 61, Concepcion 59, Davidson 1, Stewart 16, Watts 42.

PITCHING	W	L	ERA	G	GS	CG	SV	IP	H	R	ER	BB	SO	AVG	B	T	HT	WT	DOB	1st Yr	Resides
Alfonzo, Edgar	3	2	3.21	20	1	0	0	42	50	21	15	12	33	.294	L	L	5-10	160	12-14-84	2002	Estado Miranda, Venez.
Almenar, Aristedes	0	1	1.46	7	0	0	0	12	11	2	2	3	14	.256	R	R	6-0	170	12-27-83	2001	Valencia, Venez.
Bergeron, Jabe	0	0	1.59	1	1	0	0	6	4	1	1	2	6	.286	R	R	6-3	230	12-19-81	2004	Chesterfield, N.H.
Camacho, Eddy	3	2	1.10	20	0	0	1	41	23	6	5	11	39	.168	L	L	6-1	185	9-17-82	2004	Sylmar, Calif.
Danly, Ryan	1	0	0.00	1	0	0	0	4	2	0	0	1	3	.143	L	L	6-8	195	6-21-81	2001	Cedar Rapids, Iowa
Devaney, Michael	5	0	1.95	14	14	0	0	69	58	19	15	29	56	.240	R	R	6-4	220	7-31-82	2004	Camas, Wash.
Eager, Blake	0	0	0.00	2	0	0	0	3	0	0	0	0	4	.000	R	R	6-5	190	5-19-82	2004	Tucson, Ariz.
Foli, Daniel	0	1	3.38	3	0	0	0	5	4	2	2	5	6	.211	R	R	6-1	180	3-30-81	2001	Kodak, Tenn.
Freitas, Julio	1	0	5.19	10	0	0	0	17	18	11	10	7	11	.273	R	R	6-0	197	5-30-82	2000	Anzoategui, Venez.
Hernandez, Gaby	1	0	0.00	1	0	0	0	3	2	0	0	0	6	.200	R	R	6-3	215	5-2-86	2004	Homestead, Fla.
Hyde, Scott	4	4	4.03	10	10	0	0	51	44	24	23	18	46	.230	R	R	6-5	215	3-24-83	2004	Grants Pass, Ore.
Landing, Jeffrey	0	3	9.95	8	3	0	0	19	30	25	21	9	15	.361	R	R	6-3	190	7-31-83	2004	Jamestown, N.C.
MacLane, Evan	5	3	3.16	13	13	0	0	74	70	35	26	6	70	.244	L	L	6-2	185	11-4-82	2003	Quincy, Calif.
Maldonado, Ivan	1	0	4.22	2	2	0	0	11	13	5	5	3	5	.283	R	R	6-3	210	6-7-80	2002	Cayey, P.R.
Meyers, Ryan	0	0	3.00	1	0	0	0	3	4	1	1	0	3	.333	L	R	6-5	195	7-17-85	2003	Springville, Ariz.
Muniz, Carlos	3	2	3.07	12	0	0	3	15	14	8	5	3	20	.246	R	R	6-1	180	3-12-81	2003	Wilmington, Calif.
Perez, Marcelo	1	3	6.53	17	0	0	2	30	41	26	22	16	21	.325	R	R	6-1	160	7-4-82	2000	Loma de Cabrera, D.R.
Quaglieri, Will	1	1	3.86	11	5	0	0	35	35	17	15	7	26	.255	R	R	6-4	210	3-14-81	2004	Reno, Nev.
Regas, Kris	0	0	4.15	3	0	0	0	4	6	4	2	0	6	.333	S	L	6-4	210	11-15-79	2002	Bourbonnais, Ill.
Rengel, Orlando	0	0	3.00	1	0	0	0	3	1	1	1	0	4	.100	R	R	6-1	170	5-11-83	2001	Piritu Anzoategui, Venez.
Rodriguez, Jose	2	2	3.57	9	0	0	0	18	15	9	7	5	16	.242	R	R	6-0	170	1-15-82	1999	Carora, Venez.
Rondon, Celso	3	2	1.51	26	0	0	12	36	17	6	6	15	47	.139	R	R	6-0	215	4-7-84	2001	Cumana Sucre, Venez.
Smith, Chuck	0	0	1.93	7	0	0	1	9	7	3	2	3	11	.212	R	R	6-3	205	12-13-81	2004	Florence, Ala.
Swindell, Mike	4	1	2.69	12	11	0	0	64	47	24	19	22	62	.212	R	R	6-1	190	9-26-81	2004	Wildomar, Calif.
Torres, David	0	0	1.69	4	0	0	0	5	4	4	1	2	3	.211	R	R	6-1	205	3-23-81	2003	Orlando, Fla.
Williams, Joe	5	4	2.28	15	15	0	0	75	62	26	19	26	64	.225	L	L	6-2	220	4-8-81	2004	Orland Park, Ill.
Worthington, Tim	0	0	6.00	2	0	0	0	3	5	3	2	4	3	.357	R	R	6-2	200	7-29-80	2003	Redwood City, Calif.

KINGSPORT METS

Rookie

APPALACHIAN LEAGUE

BATTING	AVG	G	AB	R	H	2B	3B	HR	RBI	BB	SO	SB	CS	OBP	SLG	B	T	HT	WT	DOB	1st Yr	Resides
Arroyo, Rafael	.258	42	124	24	32	5	1	6	26	30	35	1	3	.425	.460	R	R	5-9	170	10-26-82	2004	Panorama City, Calif.
Bergeron, Jabe	.291	28	103	15	30	2	1	5	16	4	25	1	0	.318	.476	R	R	6-3	230	12-19-81	2004	Chesterfield, N.H.
Cabral, Marcos	.267	34	116	20	31	8	0	2	10	15	25	3	3	.356	.388	R	R	6-0	180	4-4-84	2003	Miami, Fla.
Camacho, Johan	.183	31	109	9	20	3	0	2	8	9	35	0	0	.256	.266	S	R	6-3	245	8-13-83	2000	Barquisimeto, Lara, Venez.
Cerda, Felix	.167	44	156	16	26	3	0	1	10	15	49	0	1	.238	.205	L	L	6-0	170	9-15-83	2001	Vietnan Los Mina, D.R.
Gamero, Jesus	.323	44	161	31	52	7	4	3	32	13	28	3	1	.395	.472	R	R	5-11	170	1-24-84	2001	Higuerote, Venez.
Garcia, Travis	.310	46	171	25	53	9	1	9	36	16	37	1	3	.373	.532	R	R	6-2	205	4-18-82	2003	Bronx, N.Y.
Gomez, Carlos	.287	38	150	24	43	10	4	1	20	5	29	8	1	.333	.427	R	R	6-4	190	12-4-81	2003	Santiago, D.R.
Gonzalez, Humberto	.074	9	27	5	2	0	0	2	6	6	10	1	5	.257	.074	R	R	5-9	160	3-5-81	2003	Des Moines, Wash.
Lawrence, Horace	.362	27	105	11	38	6	1	5	24	12	17	6	3	.429	.581	L	L	6-4	215	1-6-81	2003	Richmond, Calif.
Petersen, Josh	.253	53	186	27	47	9	2	3	29	21	49	1	2	.341	.371	R	R	6-4	215	1-2-84	2004	Palm Beach Gardens, Fla.
Piazza, Tommy	.194	18	62	8	12	2	1	2	8	4	19	1	0	.254	.355	R	R	6-0	200	10-9-81	2003	Boynton Beach, Fla.
Pietsch, Seth	.291	56	206	44	60	6	5	11	45	22	37	9	2	.371	.529	R	R	5-9	197	9-16-81	2003	Grants Pass, Ore.
Purkey, Bryan	.000	3	3	1	0	0	0	0	0	2	3	0	0	.400	.000	R	R	6-0	200	8-28-81	2003	Port St. Lucie, Fla.
Santana, Luis	.109	16	46	7	5	0	0	1	2	9	14	1	0	.255	.174	R	R	5-11	180	2-26-85	2003	Dajabon, D.R.
Sgueglia, Thomas	.118	6	17	1	2	0	0	0	2	3	7	0	0	.238	.118	R	R	6-2	205	1-13-84	2004	Bronx, N.Y.
Triplett, Russ	.288	52	198	32	57	13	1	1	13	20	31	2	4	.363	.379	R	R	5-11	180	1-18-81	2004	West Columbia, S.C.
Wyrick, Josh	.287	60	254	41	73	9	4	4	24	16	53	13	7	.338	.402	L	L	6-3	190	3-11-82	2004	Bakersfield, Calif.
Zech, Bryan	.233	25	90	16	21	6	0	0	2	10	3	27	3	1	.281	.367	R	R	5-10	175	5-27-81	2004	Wellington, Fla.

GAMES BY POSITION: C—Arroyo 41, Piazza 14, Santana 16. **1B**—Bergeron 16, Camacho 13, Cerda 28, Petersen 14. **2B**—Cabral 20, Gonzalez 8, Swindell 1, Triplett 17, Zech 23. **3B**—Camacho 17, Garcia 23, Petersen 27, Sgueglia 5. **SS**—Cabral 13, Garcia 23, Triplett 34. **OF**—Cerda 5, Gamero 36, Gomez 37, Lawrence 24, Petersen 9, Pietsch 45, Wyrick 58.

PITCHING	W	L	ERA	G	GS	CG	SV	IP	H	R	ER	BB	SO	AVG	B	T	HT	WT	DOB	1st Yr	Resides
Almenar, Aristedes	1	2	2.20	9	9	0	0	41	40	16	10	13	34	.255	R	R	6-0	170	12-27-83	2001	Valencia, Venez.
Brewer, Jeff	5	3	3.81	17	2	0	4	52	54	24	22	17	53	.269	R	R	6-3	190	10-5-80	2002	Fredericton, N.B.
Freites, Julio	0	0	4.26	6	0	0	1	13	12	7	6	3	11	.261	R	R	6-0	197	5-30-82	2000	Clarines Anzoategui, Venez.
Fry, Troy	5	2	4.06	14	8	0	0	58	68	29	26	7	49	.288	R	R	6-5	220	6-23-81	2003	Wind Gap, Penn.
Gomez, Jose	0	2	4.86	8	2	0	2	17	14	11	9	7	25	.226	R	R	6-3	240	12-16-80	1998	Santo Domingo, D.R.
Gonzalez, Humberto	0	0	6.35	2	0	0	0	6	10	6	4	1	5	.370	R	R	5-9	160	3-5-81	2003	Des Moines, Wash.
Gonzalez, Marino	1	2	11.40	6	1	0	0	15	30	20	19	5	13	.423	R	R	6-4	190	11-4-82	2001	Puerto Plata, D.R.
Landing, Jeff	0	4	9.64	6	6	0	0	23	34	27	25	11	24	.327	R	R	6-3	190	7-31-83	2004	Jamestown, N.C.
Mannix, Kevin	1	1	4.11	10	0	0	0	15	11	9	7	13	16	.196	R	R	6-2	207	12-20-80	2004	Syosset, N.Y.
Marte, German	1	0	5.19	9	6	0	0	26	30	19	15	9	32	.280	R	R	6-1	180	4-29-80	2003	San Cristobal, D.R.
Meyers, Ryan	0	0	7.50	2	1	0	0	6	7	5	5	3	3	.292	L	R	6-5	195	7-17-85	2003	Springville, Ariz.
Miramontes, Mateo	0	0	7.50	4	0	0	0	12	17	13	10	11	12	.340	R	R	6-4	200	12-24-81	2003	Pleasanton, Calif.
Myers, Rodney	0	2	23.14	2	1	0	0	2	5	7	6	4	3	.417	R	R	6-1	200	6-26-69	1990	Chandler, Ariz.
Quaglieri, Will	1	1	4.50	1	1	0	0	4	6	4	2	0	5	.316	R	R	6-4	210	3-14-81	2004	Reno, Nev.
Rengel, Orlando	5	4	3.26	14	13	1	0	69	52	27	25	18	63	.204	R	R	5-11	170	5-11-83	2001	Anzoategui, Venez.
Sides, Andy	3	1	2.95	6	0	0	0	21	21	7	7	5	15	.247	L	R	6-7	215	8-5-84	2003	DeSoto, Mo.
Smith, Chuck	1	1	4.15	4	0	0	0	13	14	8	6	2	11	.292	R	R	6-3	205	12-13-81	2004	Florence, Ala.
Smith, David	2	3	6.39	17	0	0	1	31	39	23	22	16	20	.307	L	L	6-2	185	3-12-82	2003	Asheboro, N.C.
Swindell, Mike	0	0	1.35	2	0	0	0	7	3	1	1	2	7	.136	R	R	6-1	190	9-26-81	2004	Wildomar, Calif.
Torres, David	2	0	2.52	15	0	0	2	36	29	11	10	6	43	.222	R	R	6-1	205	3-23-81	2003	Orlando, Fla.
Weintraub, Jason	3	4	3.88	11	9	0	0	46	50	30	20	12	45	.270	R	R	6-4	170	8-13-82	2001	Tampa, Fla.
Weitzman, Billy	1	4	5.36	16	4	0	2	50	57	34	30	21	34	.271	R	R	6-3	195	11-29-83	2003	Oceanside, N.Y.
Worthington, Tim	1	0	1.74	6	3	0	0	21	17	7	4	4	21	.221	R	R	6-2	200	7-29-80	2003	Redwood City, Calif.

ORGANIZATION STATISTICS

GULF COAST LEAGUE

BATTING	AVG	G	AB	R	H	2B	3B	HR	RBI	BB	SO	SB	CS	SLG	OBP	B	T	HT	WT	DOB	1st Yr	Resides
Austin, Parris	.211	35	95	13	20	4	0	0	8	6	28	2	1	.253	.265	R	R	6-2	185	12-13-85	2004	Douglasville, Ga.
Bacon, Matt	.207	16	29	3	6	2	0	0	3	3	8	0	0	.276	.343	L	R	6-2	203	2-18-81	2004	Pensacola, Fla.
Carp, Mike	.267	57	191	30	51	12	0	4	26	22	51	2	1	.393	.358	L	R	6-2	205	6-30-86	2004	Lakewood, Fla.
Dulaney, Todd	.295	38	105	15	31	2	1	0	14	10	10	5	5	.333	.357	R	R	5-10	170	12-20-83	2003	Maywood, Ill.
Evans, Nick	.258	50	182	36	47	10	3	7	27	14	51	3	2	.462	.311	R	R	6-2	180	1-30-86	2004	Phoenix, Ariz.
Fisher, Matt	.271	16	59	12	16	4	1	0	8	2	11	2	2	.373	.313	R	R	5-9	180	9-3-81	2004	Chatsworth, Calif.
Flores, Jesus	.319	45	141	16	45	12	3	4	25	8	26	1	1	.532	.368	R	R	6-1	180	10-26-84	2002	Carupano Sucre, Venez.
Gaerlan, Armand	.259	55	185	34	48	7	4	1	15	42	35	6	4	.357	.396	R	R	5-10	180	8-22-82	2004	Fremont, Calif.
Garcia, Miguel	.164	34	73	7	12	1	0	0	2	8	17	1	1	.178	.274	L	L	6-1	180	4-8-82	1999	Santo Domingo, D.R.
Gomez, Carlos	.268	19	71	10	19	7	0	0	11	2	9	9	1	.366	.303	R	R	6-2	170	12-4-85	2002	Santiago, D.R.
Harper, Brett	.400	2	5	1	2	0	0	1	4	1	1	0	01.000	.500	L	R	6-4	180	7-31-81	2001	Scottsdale, Ariz.
Henry, Sean	.282	56	202	35	57	9	5	4	30	22	43	10	6	.436	.364	R	R	5-10	154	8-18-85	2004	Suisun City, Calif.
Lawrence, Horace	.339	22	62	8	21	3	1	1	16	4	8	5	1	.468	.391	L	L	6-00	177	1-6-81	2003	Richmond, Calif.
Maldonado, Brahiam	.185	47	151	21	28	3	1	1	12	15	49	8	2	.238	.272	R	R	6-0	185	9-18-85	2004	Loiza, P.R.
Oliveros, Ricky	.272	38	92	8	25	4	0	1	10	6	15	2	2	.348	.337	R	R	6-2	170	9-23-83	2001	Piritu, Venez.
Piazza, Tommy	.385	6	13	2	5	1	0	0	3	2	6	0	1	.462	.467	L	R	6-0	200	10-9-81	2003	Boynton Beach, Fla.
Santana, Luis	.148	12	27	1	4	0	0	0	2	1	7	0	0	.148	.207	R	R	5-11	180	2-26-85	2003	Dajabon, D.R.
Sgueglia, Thomas	.286	18	35	7	10	2	0	0	1	11	8	1	1	.343	.468	R	R	6-2	200	1-13-84	2004	Bronx, N.Y.
Suggs, Bryant	.234	37	77	12	18	0	1	0	6	11	11	4	7	.260	.352	L	L	5-9	160	10-17-83	2004	Tampa, Fla.
Timmons, Jeff	.259	19	27	3	7	0	0	0	3	6	8	0	2	.259	.429	R	R	6-1	195	10-2-82	1993	Hollywood, Fla.
Wells, Cory	.291	44	148	23	43	12	1	3	21	11	39	9	3	.446	.352	R	R	6-0	185	11-18-84	2003	Plant City, Fla.

GAMES BY POSITION: C—Bacon 12, Flores 43, Oliveros 1, Piazza 3, Santana 1, Timmons 17. **1B**—Carp 41, Dulaney 1, Harper 2, Oliveros 34, Timmons 1. **2B**—Austin 1, Dulaney 32, Fisher 15, Gaerlan 19, Henry 1, Santana 1, Sgueglia 4. **3B**—Carp 11, Dulaney 1, Evans 21, Gaerlan 24, Henry 3, Oliveros 1, Sgueglia 8. **SS**—Gaerlan 13, Garcia 1, Henry 50, Sgueglia 2. **OF**—Austin 31, Bacon 1. Carp 1, Dulaney 1, Garcia 33, Gomez 10, Lawrence 19, Maldonado 45, Oliveros 1, Suggs 29, Wells 42.

PITCHING	W	L	ERA	G	GS	CG	SV	IP	H	R	ER	BB	SO	AVG	B	T	HT	WT	DOB	1st Yr	Resides
Camacho, Edward	0	0	0.00	3	0	0	1	5	9	0	0	0	9	.000	L	L	6-1	180	9-17-82	2004	Sylmar, Calif.
Castillo, Jonathan	2	2	5.67	13	6	0	1	40	51	30	25	12	24	.300	R	R	5-11	195	12-27-83	2004	New York, N.Y.
Cole, Joey	0	0	4.50	2	1	0	0	2	3	1	1	0	3	.375	L	R	6-8	225	9-15-77	1999	Nacogdoches, Texas
Cox, Michael	0	0	5.40	11	1	0	0	20	16	12	12	21	28	.228	L	L	5-11	205	11-3-78	2000	Pasadena, Texas
Deaton, Kevin	0	0	3.00	2	2	0	0	3	3	1	1	0	5	.250	R	R	6-5	235	8-7-81	2000	Merritt Island, Fla.
Eager, Blake	4	3	3.93	13	7	0	0	53	57	25	23	17	43	.275	R	R	6-3	205	5-19-82	2004	Tucson, Ariz.
Elliot, Adam	0	0	0.00	1	1	0	0	1	0	0	0	0	0	.000	S	R	6-1	200	3-27-84	2002	Concord, Calif.
Garay, Kelvin	0	0	7.11	10	0	0	2	19	22	19	15	11	16	.318	L	L	6-5	230	1-18-85	2002	Trujillo Alto, P.R.
Gonzalez, Marino	2	2	7.50	7	1	0	0	12	14	10	10	5	16	.280	R	R	6-4	190	11-4-82	1999	Puerto Plata, D.R.
Hakey, Patrick	3	0	3.80	14	0	0	0	24	19	13	10	13	17	.218	L	R	6-7	210	1-21-82	2004	Fairfax, Va.
Heil, Ryan	0	0	6.61	10	0	0	0	16	17	14	12	17	7	.293	R	R	6-4	215	11-7-81	2004	San Diego, Calif.
Hernandez, Gaby	3	3	1.09	10	9	2	0	50	25	10	6	12	58	.150	R	R	6-3	215	5-21-86	2004	Homestead, Fla.
Hope, Travis	3	3	3.54	17	0	0	4	28	32	16	11	8	23	.273	R	R	6-3	210	1-29-81	2004	Marion, Ill.
Maldonado, Ivan	0	0	13.50	1	0	0	0	1	3	2	2	0	3	.428	R	R	6-3	210	6-7-80	2002	Cayey, P.R.
Marte, German	1	0	2.40	4	2	0	0	15	15	5	4	4	15	.254	R	R	6-1	180	4-29-85	2002	San Cristobal, D.R.
Mateo, Waner	2	0	4.14	13	6	0	0	41	39	29	19	21	34	.246	R	R	6-5	175	2-5-85	2003	San Cristobal, D.R.
Miramontes, Mateo	1	0	3.14	9	5	0	0	29	26	14	10	12	21	.234	R	R	6-4	200	12-24-81	2003	Pleasanton, Calif.
Moreno, Orber	0	1	40.50	1	1	0	0	1	4	3	3	1	1	.666	R	R	6-3	200	4-27-77	1994	Los Altos, Venez.
Nunez, Jose	2	0	0.00	6	1	0	1	10	6	0	0	0	12	.157	L	L	6-2	175	3-14-79	1996	Monte Cristi, D.R.
Pereyra, Reynaldo	3	1	4.50	18	0	0	0	26	28	17	13	13	28	.269	R	R	6-1	180	1-7-83	2003	Villa Mella, D.R.
Pineda, Luis	0	1	3.86	5	1	0	0	9	6	4	4	5	8	.206	R	R	6-1	170	10-17-74	1995	San Cristobal, D.R.
Rodriguez, Julio	0	0	0.00	3	0	0	0	4	2	0	0	0	4	.142	R	R	6-3	185	1-14-87	2004	
Sanchez, Jose	4	5	4.42	12	11	0	0	55	55	31	27	9	46	.253	R	R	6-0	170	5-12-84	2002	Maracaibo Venez.
Serfass, Joe	2	1	2.79	12	0	0	2	19	19	7	6	4	20	.260	R	R	6-3	215	5-6-81	2004	Newington, Conn.
Sides, Andy	0	2	2.45	5	3	0	0	11	9	4	3	4	9	.236	L	R	6-7	195	8-5-84	2003	DeSoto, Texas
Smith, Chuck	4	0	1.06	6	1	0	2	17	8	2	2	3	20	.137	R	R	6-3	205	12-13-81	2004	Florence, Ala.
Strickland, Scott	0	0	0.00	2	1	0	0	2	0	0	0	0	2	.000	R	R	5-11	180	4-26-76	1997	Spring, Texas

BY CASEY TEFERTILLER

The A's rebuilt and re-tooled for 2004. General manager Billy Beane had watched his team falter in the first round of the playoffs for four consecutive seasons, and 2004 would be a different concoction.

Beane brought in veterans who had achieved in clutch situations. Notably, he traded for Mark Kotsay, a former College World Series hero whose six-year major-league career had been spent with losing teams. Kotsay would assume the role of center fielder and leadoff man, critical jobs for the A's. Beane also added catcher Damian Miller and lefthander Mark Redman, both owners of World Series rings. He brought in Arthur Rhodes to take over as closer.

This talent was added to a base that included superior starting pitching behind Oakland's 'Big Three' of Tim Hudson, Mark Mulder and Barry Zito, plus upcoming starter Rich Harden. It would be arguably the most imposing rotation in baseball, backed by a firm defensive team that could score enough runs to win close games.

There were bumps along the way. Rhodes struggled in a closer role and Beane was forced to trade for Octavio Dotel from Houston to firm up the bullpen on June 24. The A's took off, assuming first place from in the American League West on Aug. 5 and seeming to control the division. By Sept. 4, the A's owned a four-game lead, and a fifth consecutive trip to the playoffs seemed inevitable. Then, it all fell apart.

Oakland lost five straight and 16 of its final 27 games as the Angels climbed forward to take over the division lead, finally knocking out the A's in Game 161 during a head-to-head, final weekend confrontation in Oakland.

In the end, it was the chill of that September fade that would haunt the A's.

The most vaunted members of the team—the starting

Mark Kotsay   Nick Swisher

PLAYERS of the YEAR

MAJOR LEAGUE: Mark Kotsay, of

A former first-round pick of the Marlins, Kotsay was acquired from the Padres prior to the 2004 season and enjoyed the best season of his seven-year major league career. He hit .315, played outstanding in center field and proved to be an effective leadoff hitter.

MINOR LEAGUE: Nick Swisher, of

Oakland's first-round pick in the 2002 draft had a breakout year in 2004. He hit .269-29-92 in 443 at-bats for Triple-A Sacramento, just a year after hitting .230 at Double-A. He also led the minor leagues with 103 walks. Swisher was called up to the parent club for the A's failed playoff push.

pitchers—had failed to deliver when it came to the crunch. Mulder's situation proved the most daunting. After beginning the year 17-4 and starting the All-Star Game, he simply lost his touch. In his final seven starts, Mulder went 0-4, 7.27.

"If I'd just won two of those starts, we'd be going to the playoffs," he said after a 10-0 loss to the Angels in the final series. Mulder swore there was no physical problem, leaving the A's to ponder what might have been.

Hudson missed six weeks with a rib injury and finished 12-6, 3.53. Zito started poorly, then rebounded in the second half to finish 11-11, 4.48. Harden was perhaps the team's top pitcher in the second half and finished 11-7, 3.99. The biggest breakdown came in the bullpen, which was charged with 28 blown saves.

While the big league A's were playing the tease, Oakland's organization put together a strong minor league season. Five of the six affiliates reached the playoffs and all six finished over .500 with a combined record of 400-295. Sacramento won the Pacific Coast League championship and Modesto took the title in the California League. Kane County reached the finals in the Midwest League, as did Vancouver in the Northwest League. Oakland farmhands won MVP awards in the PCL (first baseman Dan Johnson), the Cal League (outfielder Brian Stavisky) and the Northwest League (outfielder Javier Herrera).

Many of Oakland's minor leaguers had breakout years, none more dramatic than the 19-year-old Herrera, who hit .331-12-47, along with a .555 slugging percentage. Herrera has five workable tools, with a right-field arm and center-field speed.

ORGANIZATION LEADERS

BATTING

*AVG	Brian Stavisky, Modesto	.343
R	Nelson Cruz, Sacramento/Midland/Modesto	109
	Nick Swisher, Sacramento	109
H	Brian Stavisky, Modesto	176
TB	Nelson Cruz, Sacramento/Midland/Modesto	301
2B	Jason Perry, Midland/Modesto	44
3B	Freddie Bynum, Sacramento/Midland	7
HR	Dan Johnson, Sacramento	29
	Nick Swisher, Sacramento	29
RBI	Dan Johnson, Sacramento	111
BB	Nick Swisher, Sacramento	103
SO	Nelson Cruz, Sacramento/Midland/Modesto	149
SB	Freddie Bynum, Sacramento/Midland	39
*OBP	Brian Snyder, Kane County	.421
*SLG	Jason Perry, Midland/Modesto	.613

PITCHING

W	Steven Bondurant, Midland/Kane County	16
L	Brad Weis, Midland	12
#ERA	Mike McGirr, Kane County/Vancouver	2.37
G	Daniel Fyvie, Kane County	59
CG	Steven Bondurant, Midland/Kane County	2
	Drew Dickinson, Midland	2
SV	Jeff Coleman, Midland/Modesto	23
IP	Joe Blanton, Sacramento	176
BB	Brad Weis, Midland	69
SO	Brad Knox, Kane County	174

*Minimum 250 at-bats   #Minimum 75 innings

OAKLAND ATHLETICS

Manager: Ken Macha.

BATTING	AVG	G	AB	R	H	2B	3B	HR	RBI	BB	SO	SB	CS	OBP	SLG	B	T	HT	WT	DOB	1st Yr	Resides
Byrnes, Eric	.283	143	569	91	161	39	3	20	73	46	111	17	1	.347	.467	R	R	6-2	210	2-16-76	1998	Woodside, Calif.
Castro, Ramon	.133	9	15	2	2	1	0	0	3	1	3	0	0	.188	.200	S	R	6-0	190	10-23-79	1997	Valencia, Venez.
Chavez, Eric	.276	125	475	87	131	20	0	29	77	95	99	6	3	.397	.501	L	R	6-1	200	12-7-77	1997	Walnut Creek, Calif.
Crosby, Bobby	.239	151	545	70	130	34	1	22	64	58	141	7	3	.319	.426	R	R	6-3	195	1-12-80	2001	Cypress, Calif.
Durazo, Erubiel	.321	142	511	80	164	35	1	22	88	56	104	3	2	.396	.523	L	L	6-3	240	1-23-75	1997	Hermosillo, Mexico
Dye, Jermaine	.265	137	532	87	141	29	4	23	80	49	128	4	2	.329	.464	R	R	6-5	220	1-28-74	1993	Phoenix, Ariz.
German, Esteban	.250	31	60	9	15	1	1	0	7	4	13	0	1	.297	.300	R	R	5-9	165	1-26-78	1997	Santo Domingo, D.R.
Hatteberg, Scott	.284	152	550	87	156	30	0	15	82	72	48	0	0	.367	.420	L	R	6-1	210	12-14-69	1991	Salem, Ore.
Karros, Eric	.194	40	103	8	20	6	0	2	11	7	16	1	0	.243	.311	R	R	6-4	220	11-4-67	1988	Los Angeles, Calif.
Kielty, Bobby	.214	83	238	29	51	14	1	7	31	35	47	1	0	.321	.370	S	R	6-1	220	8-5-76	1999	Fort Myers, Fla.
Kotsay, Mark	.314	148	606	78	190	37	3	15	63	55	70	8	5	.370	.459	L	L	6-0	200	12-2-75	1996	Pembroke Pines, Fla.
McLemore, Mark	.248	77	250	29	62	14	0	2	21	41	33	0	2	.355	.328	S	R	5-11	200	10-4-64	1984	Southlake, Texas
McMillon, Billy	.185	52	92	10	17	4	0	3	11	8	22	0	1	.255	.326	L	L	5-11	195	11-17-71	1993	Columbia, S.C.
Melhuse, Adam	.257	69	214	23	55	11	0	11	31	16	47	0	1	.309	.463	S	R	6-2	200	3-27-72	1993	San Luis Obispo, Calif.
Menechino, Frank	.091	13	33	0	3	0	0	0	1	1	8	0	0	.143	.091	R	R	5-8	190	1-7-71	1993	Staten Island, N.Y.
Miller, Damian	.272	110	397	39	108	25	0	9	58	39	87	0	1	.339	.403	R	R	6-3	220	10-13-69	1990	La Crosse, Wis.
Rose, Mike	.000	2	2	1	0	0	0	0	0	0	2	0	0	.000	.000	S	R	6-1	185	8-25-76	1995	Elk Grove, Calif.
Scutaro, Marco	.273	137	455	50	124	32	1	7	43	16	58	0	0	.297	.393	R	R	5-10	170	10-30-75	1995	San Felipe, Venez.
Swisher, Nick	.250	20	60	11	15	4	0	2	8	8	11	0	0	.352	.417	S	L	6-0	190	11-25-80	2002	Parkersburg, W.Va.

PITCHING	W	L	ERA	G	GS	CG	SV	IP	H	R	ER	BB	SO	AVG	B	T	HT	WT	DOB	1st Yr	Resides
Blanton, Joe	0	0	5.63	3	0	0	0	8	6	5	5	2	6	.000	R	R	6-3	225	12-11-80	2002	Bowling Green, Ky.
Bradford, Chad	5	7	4.42	68	0	0	1	59	51	32	29	24	34	.000	R	R	6-5	205	9-14-74	1996	Raymond, Miss.
Dotel, Octavio	6	2	4.09	45	0	0	22	51	41	23	23	18	72	.000	R	R	6-0	200	11-25-73	1993	Santo Domingo, D.R.
Duchscherer, Justin	7	6	3.27	53	0	0	0	96	85	37	35	32	59	.000	R	R	6-3	190	11-19-77	1996	Colleyville, Texas
Garcia, Jairo	0	0	12.71	4	0	0	0	6	5	8	8	9	5	.000	R	R	6-0	165	3-7-83	2000	Juan Baron, D.R.
Hammond, Chris	4	1	2.68	41	0	0	1	54	56	21	16	13	34	.000	L	L	6-1	210	1-21-66	1988	Wedowee, Ala.
Harden, Rich	11	7	3.99	31	31	0	0	190	171	90	84	81	167	.000	R	R	6-1	180	11-30-81	2001	Victoria, B.C.
Harville, Chad	0	0	3.38	3	0	0	0	3	2	1	1	1	0	.000	R	R	5-9	185	9-16-76	1997	Savannah, Tenn.
Hudson, Tim	12	6	3.53	27	27	3	0	189	194	82	74	44	103	.000	R	R	6-1	165	7-14-75	1997	Apollo Beach, Fla.
Lehr, Justin	1	1	5.23	27	0	0	0	33	35	19	19	14	16	.000	R	R	6-1	200	8-3-77	1999	West Covina, Calif.
Mecir, Jim	0	5	3.59	65	0	0	2	48	45	21	19	19	49	.000	S	R	6-1	230	5-16-70	1991	Kildeer, Ill.
Mulder, Mark	17	8	4.43	33	33	5	0	226	223	119	111	83	140	.000	L	L	6-6	210	8-5-77	1999	Scottsdale, Ariz.
Redman, Mark	11	12	4.71	32	32	2	0	191	218	110	100	68	102	.000	L	L	6-5	245	1-5-74	1995	Catoosa, Okla.
Rhodes, Arthur	3	3	5.12	37	0	0	9	39	46	23	22	21	34	.000	L	L	6-2	210	10-24-69	1988	Baltimore, Md.
Rincon, Ricardo	1	1	3.68	67	0	0	0	44	45	22	18	22	40	.000	L	L	5-10	190	4-13-70	1994	Veracruz, Mexico
Saarloos, Kirk	2	1	4.44	6	5	0	0	24	27	13	12	12	10	.000	R	R	6-0	180	5-23-79	2001	Houston, Texas
Zito, Barry	11	11	4.48	34	34	0	0	213	216	116	106	81	163	.000	L	L	6-4	215	5-13-78	1999	Van Nuys, Calif.

FIELDING

Catcher	PCT	G	PO	A	E	DP	PB
Melhuse	.995	64	358	18	2	1	5
Miller	.999	109	701	49	1	4	9
Rose	1.000	2	1	0	0	0	0

First Base	PCT	G	PO	A	E	DP
Durazo	.882	4	14	1	2	2
Hatteberg	.993	148	1281	86	10	135
Karros	.989	22	165	17	2	15
McMillon	1.000	3	4	1	0	1
Melhuse	1.000	1	2	1	0	0
Swisher	1.000	3	19	0	0	3

Second Base	PCT	G	PO	A	E	DP
German	1.000	10	9	21	0	6

McLemore	.975	47	113	123	6	37
Menechino	.978	12	16	29	1	2
Scutaro	.995	123	232	311	3	78

Third Base	PCT	G	PO	A	E	DP
Castro	1.000	6	1	4	0	0
Chavez	.968	125	113	276	13	31
German	.935	15	8	21	2	3
McLemore	.984	27	17	46	1	2
Melhuse	.750	3	1	2	1	1
Scutaro	.000	1	0	0	0	0

Shortstop	PCT	G	PO	A	E	DP
Castro	1.000	1	0	2	0	0
Crosby	.975	151	241	505	19	107

Scutaro	.971	16	25	42	2	9

Outfield	PCT	G	PO	A	E	DP
Byrnes	.989	141	264	11	3	2
Chavez	1.000	1	2	0	0	0
Dye	.992	134	258	3	2	2
Kielty	.990	67	97	1	1	0
Kotsay	.984	145	347	11	6	4
McLemore	.000	1	0	0	0	0
McMillon	1.000	21	23	0	0	0
Swisher	.889	16	24	0	3	0

Mark Mulder: Won 15 games for the fourth consecutive season

Rich Harden: Led the Oakland staff with 167 strikeouts

FARM SYSTEM

Director, Player Development: Keith Lieppman.

Class	Farm Team	League	W	L	Pct.	Finish*	Manager	Affiliate Since
AAA	Sacramento (Calif.) RiverCats	Pacific Coast	79	65	.549	**+5th (16)**	Tony DeFrancesco	2000
AA	Midland (Texas) RockHounds	Texas	72	68	.514	4th (8)	Webster Garrison	1999
High A	#Modesto (Calif.) A's	California	90	50	.643	**+1st (10)**	Von Hayes	1975
Low A	Kane County Cougars (Geneva, Ill.)	Midwest	83	56	.597	**1st (14)**	Dave Joppie	2003
SS A	Vancouver (B.C.) Canadians	Northwest	42	34	.553	**t-1st (8)**	Dennis Rogers	2000
Rookie	Phoenix (Ariz.) Athletics	Arizona	34	22	.607	**2nd (9)**	Ruben Escalera	1988

*Finish in overall standings (No. of teams in league)/Playoff teams in **boldface**   #Affiliate will operate in Stockton (California) in 2005

SACRAMENTO RIVERCATS | Class AAA

PACIFIC COAST LEAGUE

BATTING	AVG	G	AB	R	H	2B	3B	HR	RBI	BB	SO	SB	CS	OBP	SLG	B	T	HT	WT	DOB	1st Yr	Resides
Baker, John	.347	14	49	11	17	3	0	0	10	6	23	0	0	.429	.408	L	R	6-1	215	1-20-81	2002	Walnut Creek, Calif.
Bynum, Freddie	.287	66	258	42	74	11	3	2	26	19	61	21	4	.343	.376	L	R	6-1	180	2-15-80	2000	Stantonsburg, N.C.
Castro, Ramon	.228	40	123	15	28	8	2	1	16	15	20	2	2	.317	.350	S	R	6-0	190	10-23-79	1997	Valencia, Venez.
Chavez, Eric	.308	3	13	2	4	1	0	0	0	1	2	0	0	.357	.385	L	R	6-1	200	12-7-77	1997	Walnut Creek, Calif.
Craig, Beau	.000	3	4	0	0	0	0	0	0	0	0	0	0	.000	.000	S	R	5-10	190	2-12-79	2000	Santee, Calif.
Cruz, Nelson	.231	4	13	4	3	1	0	1	2	1	7	0	0	.286	.538	R	R	6-3	175	7-1-81	1998	Monte Cristi, D.R.
Edwards, Mike	.287	140	551	91	158	41	0	13	81	76	100	11	2	.384	.432	R	R	6-1	190	11-24-76	1995	Mechanicsburg, Pa.
German, Esteban	.329	55	231	33	76	8	4	2	29	19	28	18	2	.380	.424	R	R	5-9	165	1-26-78	1997	Santo Domingo, D.R.
Gomez, Francis	.133	7	15	0	2	0	0	0	1	2	7	0	1	.235	.133	R	R	6-1	165	9-2-81	1999	La Romana, D.R.
Jackson, Steve	.333	5	9	2	3	0	0	0	1	1	3	0	0	.400	.333	R	R	6-5	235	12-13-77	2000	Yakima, Wash.
Johnson, Dan	.299	142	535	95	160	29	5	29	111	89	93	0	1	.403	.535	L	R	6-2	220	8-10-79	2001	Coon Rapids, Minn.
Kiger, Mark	.231	6	13	2	3	0	0	0	2	3	3	0	2	.375	.231	R	R	5-11	180	5-30-80	2002	San Diego, Calif.
Koonce, Graham	.241	120	439	73	106	25	0	22	77	77	129	0	0	.362	.449	L	L	6-4	225	5-15-75	1994	Julian, Calif.
Lockwood, Mike	.221	38	86	13	19	4	0	1	10	15	11	1	0	.350	.302	L	L	6-0	190	12-27-76	1998	Powell, Ohio
McLemore, Mark	.526	6	19	2	10	1	0	0	5	5	2	0	0	.625	.579	S	R	5-11	200	10-4-64	1984	Southlake, Texas
McMillon, Billy	.438	10	32	7	14	4	0	3	10	7	3	0	0	.550	.844	L	L	5-11	195	11-17-71	1993	Columbia, S.C.
Menechino, Frank	.267	4	15	2	4	0	0	0	1	1	0	0	0	.353	.267	R	R	5-8	190	1-7-71	1993	Staten Island, N.Y.
Morrissey, Adam	.291	109	392	61	114	26	1	9	56	40	89	1	1	.358	.431	R	R	5-11	185	6-8-81	1999	Ourimbah, Australia
Rivera, Mike	.224	49	170	12	38	7	2	5	20	10	34	1	1	.262	.376	R	R	6-0	210	9-8-76	1997	Bayamon, P.R.
Rose, Mike	.281	107	349	56	98	20	2	6	49	76	80	0	0	.407	.401	S	R	6-1	185	8-25-76	1995	Elk Grove, Calif.
Rouse, Mike	.276	99	323	53	89	11	2	10	40	50	68	0	4	.379	.415	L	R	5-11	190	4-25-80	2001	San Jose, Calif.
Stanley, Steve	.227	74	220	42	50	4	2	3	24	33	30	9	2	.324	.305	L	L	5-8	160	12-23-79	2002	Columbus, Ohio
Swisher, Nick	.269	125	443	109	119	28	2	29	92	103	109	3	3	.406	.537	S	L	6-0	190	11-25-80	2002	Parkersburg, W.Va.
Teahen, Mark	.275	20	69	9	19	8	0	0	10	11	22	0	1	.383	.391	L	R	6-3	210	9-6-81	2002	Yucaipa, Calif.
Watson, Matt	.305	125	476	79	145	37	3	19	96	54	75	3	4	.377	.515	L	R	5-11	210	9-5-78	1999	Lancaster, Pa.
Weber, Jon	.341	19	44	9	15	4	0	2	12	3	9	0	0	.383	.568	L	L	5-11	180	1-20-78	1999	Lakewood, Calif.
Wilson, Tom	.238	14	42	6	10	2	0	1	5	15	13	0	0	.439	.357	R	R	6-3	220	12-19-70	1991	Lake Havasu City, Ariz.

PITCHING

PITCHING	W	L	ERA	G	GS	CG	SV	IP	H	R	ER	BB	SO	AVG	B	T	HT	WT	DOB	1st Yr	Resides
Blanton, Joe	11	8	4.19	28	26	1	0	176	199	101	82	34	143	.284	R	R	6-3	225	12-11-80	2002	Bowling Green, Ky.
Bradford, Chad	0	0	0.00	2	0	0	0	2	1	0	0	0	3	.143	R	R	6-5	205	9-14-74	1996	Raymond, Miss.
Cammack, Eric	3	2	5.61	47	1	0	2	67	75	51	42	31	64	.277	R	R	6-1	180	8-14-75	1997	Port Neches, Texas
Flores, Ron	4	3	3.74	55	0	0	1	53	59	26	22	18	55	.274	L	L	5-11	190	8-9-79	2000	Pico Rivera, Calif.
Garcia, Jairo	1	2	3.95	11	0	0	1	14	10	6	6	9	21	.208	R	R	6-0	165	3-7-83	2000	Juan Baron, D.R.
Gomes, Wayne	3	2	3.87	52	0	0	2	79	100	42	34	27	54	.306	R	R	6-2	220	1-15-73	1993	Cherry Hill, N.J.
Gwyn, Marcus	0	1	6.35	12	0	0	0	17	20	16	12	8	19	.294	R	R	6-3	230	11-4-77	2000	The Woodlands, Texas
Hammond, Chris	0	0	0.00	3	3	0	0	4	6	0	0	0	5	.353	L	L	6-1	210	1-21-66	1986	Wedowee, Ala.
Harden, Rich	0	0	5.40	1	1	0	0	5	6	3	3	3	6	.300	L	R	6-1	180	11-30-81	2001	Victoria, B.C.
Hudson, Tim	0	0	6.00	1	1	0	0	3	2	2	2	2	3	.167	R	R	6-1	165	7-14-75	1997	Apollo Beach, Fla.
Kohn, Shawn	1	1	4.85	24	1	0	1	43	56	26	23	7	37	.306	R	R	6-2	200	1-28-80	2002	Snohomish, Wash.
Lehr, Justin	4	2	2.65	32	0	0	13	37	37	14	11	10	40	.250	R	R	6-1	200	8-3-77	1999	West Covina, Calif.
Mabeus, Chris	7	2	3.00	38	0	0	4	51	45	18	17	12	61	.236	R	R	6-3	210	2-11-79	2001	Soldotna, Alaska
O`Brien, Matt	0	1	7.71	4	0	0	0	7	13	8	6	4	3	.394	L	L	6-0	180	2-22-77	2000	Seattle, Wash.
Pettyjohn, Adam	3	1	6.32	10	9	1	0	53	55	38	37	14	44	.268	R	L	6-3	190	6-11-77	1998	Exeter, Calif.
2-team (21 Fresno)	6	7	5.78	31	23	1	0	132	158	96	85	39	87	.302							
Pote, Lou	1	2	3.38	19	0	0	2	27	23	10	10	12	20	.242	R	R	6-3	208	8-21-71	1991	Phoenix, Ariz.
Ramos, Mario	4	7	6.08	29	16	0	0	95	119	73	64	35	90	.304	L	L	5-11	180	10-19-77	2000	Pflugerville, Texas
Reames, Britt	3	5	4.67	34	3	0	8	52	55	27	27	28	57	.270	R	R	5-10	200	8-19-73	1995	Seneca, S.C.
Rheinecker, John	11	9	4.44	28	27	0	0	172	194	102	85	51	129	.283	L	L	6-2	210	5-29-79	2001	Waterloo, Ill.
Rhodes, Arthur	0	0	0.00	2	0	0	0	2	0	0	0	1	3	.000	L	L	6-2	210	10-24-69	1988	Baltimore, Md.
Saarloos, Kirk	2	0	3.54	5	5	0	0	20	19	8	8	9	17	.250	R	R	6-0	180	5-23-79	2001	Houston, Texas
2-team (2 New Orleans)	2	2	6.59	7	7	0	0	27	36	23	20	10	23	.316							
Street, Huston	0	0	0.00	1	0	0	0	1	2	0	0	0	2	.250	R	R	6-0	190	8-2-83	2004	Austin, Texas
Wood, Mike	11	3	2.80	15	15	1	0	90	83	42	28	24	66	.241	R	R	6-3	210	4-26-80	2001	West Palm Beach, Fla.
Woodard, Steve	8	6	4.85	18	18	0	0	108	133	64	58	16	59	.300	L	R	6-4	210	5-15-75	1994	Hartselle, Ala.
Ziegler, Mike	2	8	6.46	18	16	0	0	92	118	69	66	26	70	.307	R	R	6-3	220	7-25-79	2000	Glen Burnie, Md.

FIELDING

Catcher	PCT	G	PO	A	E	DP	PB
Baker	1.000	12	101	7	0	0	1
Jackson	1.000	3	4	0	0	0	0
Rivera	.980	45	325	22	7	1	3
Rose	.988	86	611	33	8	0	3
Wilson	1.000	5	29	2	0	0	1

First Base	PCT	G	PO	A	E	DP
Jackson	1.000	1	10	1	0	0
Johnson	.990	98	835	59	9	59
Koonce	.993	49	414	34	3	31
Rivera	1.000	1	2	0	0	0
Swisher	1.000	1	1	0	0	0
Wilson	1.000	2	5	0	0	1

Second Base	PCT	G	PO	A	E	DP
Bynum	.966	11	11	17	1	3
Castro	.889	3	3	5	1	2

	PCT	G	PO	A	E	DP	PB
German	.977	40	56	112	4	23	
Gomez	1.000	5	5	13	0	4	
Kiger	1.000	6	6	8	0	2	
McLemore	.933	3	7	7	1	3	
Menechino	1.000	2	4	6	0	1	
Morrissey	.977	79	98	202	7	27	
Rouse	.953	12	18	23	2	3	

Third Base	PCT	G	PO	A	E	DP
Bynum	.840	12	4	17	4	1
Castro	1.000	3	1	2	0	0
Edwards	.907	88	40	164	21	11
Morrissey	.957	27	17	50	3	2
Teahen	.983	20	18	39	1	3
Wilson	.833	3	2	3	1	0

Shortstop	PCT	G	PO	A	E	DP
Bynum	.960	19	23	49	3	5

	PCT	G	PO	A	E	DP
Castro	.956	33	42	89	6	17
German	.914	13	17	36	5	5
Gomez	1.000	1	2	1	0	0
Morrissey	1.000	1	0	2	0	0
Rouse	.967	85	107	249	12	42

Outfield	PCT	G	PO	A	E	DP
Bynum	1.000	31	58	1	0	0
Cruz	1.000	4	12	0	0	0
Edwards	.967	55	88	1	3	0
Johnson	.900	15	27	0	3	0
Lockwood	1.000	34	52	1	0	0
McMillon	1.000	5	6	0	0	0
Stanley	.973	66	140	2	4	0
Swisher	.977	121	287	6	7	0
Watson	.955	125	223	10	11	0
Weber	1.000	16	19	0	0	0

MIDLAND ROCKHOUNDS — Class AA

TEXAS LEAGUE

BATTING	AVG	G	AB	R	H	2B	3B	HR	RBI	BB	SO	SB	CS	OBP	SLG	B	T	HT	WT	DOB	1st Yr	Resides
Acosta, Jesse	.167	8	12	4	2	0	0	0	2	0	2	0	0	.154	.167	R	R	5-9	185	11-19-80	2003	Kerman, Calif.
Allegra, Matt	.382	18	68	10	26	8	1	1	13	4	19	1	1	.425	.574	R	R	6-3	195	8-10-81	2000	Lake Mary, Fla.
Baker, John	.280	117	439	67	123	32	5	15	78	37	94	0	2	.355	.478	L	R	6-1	215	1-20-81	2002	Walnut Creek, Calif.
Brown, Jeremy	.256	122	446	59	114	27	0	6	49	71	80	2	1	.361	.357	R	R	6-1	210	1-3-79	2001	London, Ky.
Bynum, Freddie	.268	65	265	38	71	13	4	1	22	24	56	18	7	.332	.358	L	R	6-1	180	2-15-80	2000	Stantonsburg, N.C.
Castro, Ramon	.247	28	93	16	23	2	3	0	12	12	18	3	2	.348	.333	S	R	6-0	190	10-23-79	1997	Valencia, Venez.
Colamarino, Brant	.272	78	309	40	84	22	2	8	50	27	60	0	0	.331	.434	L	L	5-11	205	12-4-80	2002	Pittsburgh, Pa.
Cruz, Nelson	.313	67	262	51	82	14	2	14	46	26	69	8	3	.377	.542	R	R	6-3	175	7-1-81	1998	Monte Cristi, D.R.
Gomez, Francis	.236	103	347	48	82	13	3	4	39	27	84	10	4	.297	.326	R	R	6-1	165	9-2-81	1999	La Romana, D.R.
Howe, Matt	.129	9	31	0	4	1	0	0	1	4	5	0	0	.229	.161	R	R	6-1	200	9-16-76	1998	Houston, Texas
Jackson, Steve	.243	73	247	28	60	12	0	11	39	18	62	0	2	.302	.425	R	R	6-5	235	12-13-77	2000	Yakima, Wash.
Kiger, Mark	.263	126	487	78	128	24	3	5	47	78	96	12	6	.369	.355	R	R	5-11	180	5-30-80	2002	San Diego, Calif.
McCurdy, John	.249	100	349	40	87	20	1	6	43	17	100	4	4	.284	.364	R	R	6-2	195	4-17-81	2002	Crofton, Md.
Menechino, Frank	.308	4	13	1	4	0	0	0	2	1	0	0	0	.400	.308	R	R	5-8	190	1-7-71	1993	Staten Island, N.Y.
Myers, Casey	.206	10	34	3	7	0	0	2	1	9	0	0	0	.250	.206	R	R	5-11	210	10-23-79	2001	Phoenix, Ariz.
Perry, Jason	.198	28	81	11	16	5	1	1	11	4	23	3	1	.275	.321	L	R	5-9	190	10-24-81	2003	El Paso, Texas
Quintanilla, Omar	.351	23	94	20	33	10	0	2	20	10	9	2	0	.419	.521	L	R	5-9	190	1-12-78	2000	Phoenix, Ariz.
Sellier, Brian	.279	130	491	75	137	30	6	4	62	67	86	13	4	.366	.389	L	R	6-0	200	1-12-78	2000	Phoenix, Ariz.
Stanley, Steve	.419	36	148	32	62	7	3	0	21	20	20	6	5	.480	.507	L	L	5-8	160	12-23-79	2002	Columbus, Ohio
Teahen, Mark	.335	53	197	31	66	15	4	6	36	29	44	0	0	.419	.543	L	R	6-3	210	9-6-81	2002	Yucaipa, Calif.
Weber, Jon	.280	111	421	64	118	24	5	15	68	46	103	10	5	.354	.468	L	L	5-11	180	1-20-78	1999	Lakewood, Calif.

PITCHING	W	L	ERA	G	GS	CG	SV	IP	H	R	ER	BB	SO	AVG	B	T	HT	WT	DOB	1st Yr	Resides
Bazzell, Shane	15	3	3.03	34	14	0	2	119	105	52	40	36	86	.239	L	R	6-2	180	3-2-79	1998	Columbus, Miss.
Bondurant, Steven	2	3	6.39	7	7	0	0	38	43	29	27	14	29	.289	L	L	6-0	185	3-3-80	2003	Matthews, N.C.
Coleman, Jeff	0	0	15.63	5	0	0	0	6	16	13	11	2	5	.444	R	R	5-11	190	10-6-80	2001	San Dimas, Calif.
Crowell, Kyle	2	0	4.54	40	0	0	0	67	70	40	34	29	70	.294	R	R	6-0	190	6-16-79	2000	Webster, Texas
Dickinson, Drew	8	11	4.90	27	26	2	0	147	198	90	80	46	75	.327	L	L	6-2	170	12-13-79	2002	Freeport, Ill.
Fischer, Steve	0	1	13.50	6	0	0	0	7	12	12	11	6	6	.375	R	R	6-0	200	6-20-78	2000	Benicia, Calif.
Fritz, Ben	7	4	5.63	20	20	1	0	104	118	69	65	50	77	.289	R	R	6-4	225	3-29-81	2002	Clovis, Calif.
Garcia, Jairo	2	0	1.50	13	0	0	2	18	10	3	3	15	32	.161	R	R	6-0	165	3-7-83	2000	Juan Baron, D.R.

PITCHING

PITCHING	W	L	ERA	G	GS	CG	SV	IP	H	R	ER	BB	SO	AVG	B	T	HT	WT	DOB	1st Yr	Resides
Gwyn, Marcus	3	4	2.94	44	0	0	13	67	59	25	22	19	72	.238	R	R	6-3	230	11-4-77	2000	The Woodlands, Texas
Komine, Shane	4	5	4.77	17	17	0	0	94	103	56	50	28	65	.278	R	R	5-9	175	10-18-80	2002	Honolulu, Hawaii
Mabeus, Chris	4	0	1.99	20	0	0	11	23	23	5	5	2	27	.261	R	R	6-3	210	2-11-79	2001	Soldotna, Alaska
Mattioni, Nick	1	3	2.93	19	0	0	3	31	24	12	10	17	15	.220	R	R	6-2	205	3-14-79	2000	Deerfield Beach, Fla.
Obenchain, Stephen	2	2	5.11	17	2	0	1	37	42	22	21	11	32	.294	R	R	6-5	210	7-29-81	2002	Henderson, Ky.
Oquist, Mike	2	5	6.11	27	7	0	0	63	76	47	43	24	34	.298	R	R	6-2	190	5-30-68	1989	Swink, Colo.
Sansom, Trevor	0	2	2.70	16	2	0	0	33	27	12	10	15	29	.239	R	R	6-4	190	5-6-76	1999	Winfield, W.Va.
Smyth, Steve	5	4	4.70	20	9	0	1	59	56	36	31	38	45	.249	L	L	6-1	200	6-3-78	1999	Temecula, Calif.
Snow, Bert	1	3	2.59	20	0	0	0	31	25	13	9	6	21	.227	R	R	6-1	200	3-23-77	1998	Brooksville, Fla.
Sonnier, Shawn	3	3	2.95	45	0	0	0	76	70	29	25	22	69	.252	R	R	6-5	220	7-5-76	1998	Carencro, La.
Street, Huston	1	0	1.35	10	0	0	3	13	10	2	2	3	14	.217	R	R	6-0	190	8-2-83	2004	Austin, Texas
Weis, Brad	7	12	5.78	28	28	0	0	146	173	106	94	69	70	.302	L	L	5-11	180	11-29-77	1999	Winter Park, Fla.
Ziegler, Mike	3	3	3.42	8	8	0	0	53	42	22	20	11	35	.222	R	R	6-3	220	7-25-79	2000	Glen Burnie, Md.

FIELDING

Catcher	PCT	G	PO	A	E	DP	PB
Baker	.983	50	315	24	6	1	7
Brown	.991	87	570	66	6	4	11
Jackson	.969	5	29	2	1	0	1
Myers	1.000	1	2	0	0	0	0

First Base	PCT	G	PO	A	E	DP
Baker	1.000	17	123	13	0	12
Colamarino	.993	70	640	33	5	71
Gomez	1.000	2	2	1	0	0
Howe	.963	6	50	2	2	2
Jackson	.988	48	364	37	5	37
Myers	1.000	7	71	2	0	5

Second Base	PCT	G	PO	A	E	DP
Acosta	1.000	5	8	10	0	1

	PCT	G	PO	A	E	DP
Bynum	1.000	4	5	6	0	3
Castro	.970	6	12	20	1	8
Colamarino	1.000	1	0	1	0	0
Gomez	.962	10	26	25	2	8
Kiger	.979	97	225	293	11	65
McCurdy	.913	23	41	54	9	8
Menechino	.750	2	1	2	1	0

Third Base	PCT	G	PO	A	E	DP
Castro	.943	16	4	46	3	5
Gomez	.960	54	45	99	6	14
Jackson	1.000	6	4	10	0	0
Kiger	.923	2	4	8	1	0
McCurdy	.909	17	10	30	4	1
Teahen	.968	53	38	113	5	12

Shortstop	PCT	G	PO	A	E	DP
Castro	.938	4	6	9	1	1
Gomez	.935	36	64	95	11	23
Kiger	.953	26	30	71	5	8
McCurdy	.955	54	90	142	11	35
Quintanilla	.969	23	29	97	4	22

Outfield	PCT	G	PO	A	E	DP
Allegra	1.000	17	21	3	0	0
Bynum	.985	62	128	3	2	1
Cruz	.972	67	128	9	4	2
Kiger	1.000	3	5	1	0	0
Perry	1.000	17	26	1	0	0
Sellier	.978	117	221	6	5	0
Stanley	.986	36	69	2	1	1
Weber	.967	110	218	16	8	3

MODESTO ATHLETICS — High Class A

CALIFORNIA LEAGUE

BATTING	AVG	G	AB	R	H	2B	3B	HR	RBI	BB	SO	SB	CS	OBP	SLG	B	T	HT	WT	DOB	1st Yr	Resides
Colamarino, Brant	.355	50	183	41	65	8	2	11	41	28	23	1	0	.450	.601	L	L	5-11	205	12-4-80	2002	Pittsburgh, Pa.
Cornejo, Eddie	.272	67	235	37	64	14	1	0	33	33	34	2	4	.371	.340	L	R	5-10	175	11-19-81	2003	Mira Loma, Calif.
Craig, Beau	.200	7	20	2	4	0	0	1	2	6	0	0	0	.304	.200	S	R	5-10	170	2-12-79	2000	Santee, Calif.
Cruz, Nelson	.345	66	261	54	90	27	1	11	52	24	73	8	4	.407	.582	R	R	6-3	175	7-1-81	1998	Monte Cristi, D.R.
Ethier, Andre	.313	99	419	72	131	23	5	7	53	45	64	2	5	.383	.442	L	R	6-3	195	4-10-82	2003	Phoenix, Ariz.
Garcia, Isaac	.300	117	426	65	128	41	3	9	73	13	85	1	3	.322	.474	R	R	6-1	165	11-6-78	1998	Las Matas., D.R.
McBeth, Marcus	.234	99	329	41	77	18	4	5	41	14	86	4	4	.288	.359	R	R	6-1	185	8-23-80	2002	Enoree, S.C.
McCurdy, John	.196	13	51	3	10	3	0	0	5	1	15	0	0	.226	.255	R	R	6-2	195	4-17-81	2002	Crofton, Md.
Morris, Jed	.267	91	303	39	81	20	3	1	37	43	48	1	3	.376	.363	L	R	5-11	185	3-4-80	2002	Ripon, Calif.
Myers, Casey	.318	63	214	32	68	10	1	4	27	30	23	0	0	.406	.430	R	R	5-11	210	10-29-79	2001	Phoenix, Ariz.
Perry, Jason	.338	83	325	81	110	39	1	24	80	34	87	4	4	.431	.686	L	R	6-0	200	8-18-80	2002	Jonesboro, Ga.
Quintanilla, Omar	.315	108	451	75	142	32	5	11	72	37	54	1	3	.370	.481	L	R	5-9	190	10-24-81	2003	El Paso, Texas
Rogers, Nick	.111	5	9	1	1	0	0	0	2	5	0	0	0	.333	.111	R	R	6-1	210	12-12-79	2002	Ponte Vedra Beach, Fla.
Santana, Mayobanex	.309	41	139	20	43	9	0	1	18	4	24	0	2	.331	.396	R	R	6-3	185	8-23-81	1999	Santo Domingo, D.R.
2-team (20 Lancaster)	.281	61	203	30	57	10	0	2	27	9	36	1	3	.315	.360							
Schneidmiller, Gary	.205	27	78	13	16	2	1	1	9	15	18	2	0	.354	.295	R	R	6-1	185	1-26-80	1998	Chino, Calif.
Stavisky, Brian	.343	130	513	108	176	39	5	19	83	54	89	6	4	.413	.550	L	R	6-3	230	7-6-80	2002	Port Allegheny, Pa.
Suomi, John	.297	134	545	84	162	35	4	12	100	41	72	3	1	.347	.442	L	R	5-11	180	10-5-80	2000	Toronto, Ontario
Sutton, Don	.175	12	40	7	7	3	0	0	9	5	10	0	0	.271	.250	R	R	6-1	220	11-21-83	2003	North Las Vegas, Nev.
Turner, Lloyd	.292	125	535	81	156	31	4	2	51	36	70	27	7	.348	.376	R	R	6-1	180	4-11-80	2002	Hephzibah, Ga.

PITCHING	W	L	ERA	G	GS	CG	SV	IP	H	R	ER	BB	SO	AVG	B	T	HT	WT	DOB	1st Yr	Resides
Avendano, Elvis	7	4	2.95	45	1	0	2	73	63	34	24	20	46	.229	R	R	6-5	195	2-8-83	2000	El Guayabo, Venez.
Brannon, Nick	0	0	3.45	15	0	0	0	16	10	6	6	12	17	.185	L	L	6-5	190	4-23-78	2001	Sevierville, Tenn.
Burton, Jared	3	2	4.78	10	3	0	0	32	34	19	17	20	25	.276	R	R	6-5	220	6-2-81	2002	Westminster, S.C.
Bystrowski, Bobby	0	0	8.16	12	0	0	0	14	19	13	13	8	11	.339	R	R	6-1	165	9-27-76	1997	Fair Oaks, Calif.
Cabaniel, Tomas	3	1	6.00	12	11	0	0	48	52	37	32	26	28	.287	R	R	6-1	165	2-10-83	2000	Caracas, Venez.
Coleman, Jeff	4	3	2.49	45	0	0	23	61	41	18	17	22	58	.192	R	R	5-11	190	10-6-80	2001	San Dimas, Calif.
Cornejo, Eddie	0	0	9.00	1	0	0	0	1	1	1	1	0	0	.200	L	R	5-10	175	11-19-81	2003	Mira Loma, Calif.
Fischer, Steve	1	2	6.44	21	0	0	0	36	50	30	26	29	22	.338	R	R	6-0	200	6-20-78	2000	Benicia, Calif.
Kohn, Shawn	3	0	2.30	23	0	0	4	43	32	12	11	4	68	.200	R	R	6-2	200	1-28-80	2002	Snohomish, Wash.
Landeros, Leonard	1	2	3.29	42	0	0	7	63	56	29	23	31	63	.236	L	L	6-3	170	12-12-80	2001	Hanford, Calif.
Lynch, Matt	13	3	3.93	27	27	0	0	151	165	75	66	38	111	.272	L	L	6-4	190	1-14-81	2003	Fort Pierce, Fla.
McCall, Derell	6	5	5.16	15	14	0	0	75	76	51	43	38	60	.256	R	R	6-3	205	9-22-81	2000	Cantonment, Fla.
Moak, Curtis	2	1	3.86	19	0	0	0	23	27	14	10	14	22	.284	L	L	6-0	185	11-19-78	2001	Hamilton, Ohio
Muessig, Jeff	2	1	3.38	9	7	0	0	32	30	12	12	9	26	.261	R	R	6-2	185	2-27-82	2001	Mt. Sinai, N.Y.
Obenchain, Stephen	3	3	4.76	23	5	0	1	64	74	43	34	29	53	.291	R	R	6-5	210	7-29-81	2002	Henderson, Ky.
Perez, Keith	6	2	4.90	21	10	0	0	68	82	42	37	28	44	.297	R	R	6-2	200	1-18-80	2003	Holly, Mich.
Robertson, Luke	0	0	5.25	4	1	0	0	12	11	7	7	5	6	.234	R	R	6-4	220	6-30-79	2002	Valley Center, Kan.
Sansom, Trevor	2	1	1.80	7	0	0	3	10	8	2	2	3	12	.222	R	R	6-4	190	5-6-76	1999	Winfield, W.Va.
Sauer, Michael	11	2	4.51	24	19	0	0	116	118	67	58	33	89	.262	R	R	6-2	190	6-30-80	1999	Gloucester, N.J.
Shank, Chris	6	5	3.99	49	0	0	3	86	84	47	38	30	81	.254	R	R	6-2	185	1-31-81	2002	Westminster, Mass.
Sullivan, Brad	8	11	4.65	27	27	0	0	147	180	89	76	48	99	.303	R	R	6-0	195	9-12-81	2003	Nederland, Texas
Ziegler, Brad	9	2	3.90	16	15	0	0	92	95	51	40	22	77	.261	R	R	6-4	190	10-10-79	2003	Springfield, Mo.

FIELDING

Catcher	PCT	G	PO	A	E	DP	PB
Craig	1.000	5	31	1	0	0	1
Morris	.984	35	228	16	4	1	6
Myers	.960	20	134	11	6	1	2
Suomi	.986	92	642	50	10	8	25
Sutton	1.000	1	8	1	0	0	1

First Base	PCT	G	PO	A	E	DP
Colamarino	.984	50	403	31	7	37
Myers	.974	18	143	8	4	25
Perry	1.000	2	14	1	0	4
Santana	.991	41	305	19	3	16
Stavisky	.979	34	261	24	6	16
Sutton	.980	6	48	2	1	5

Second Base	PCT	G	PO	A	E	DP
Cornejo	.978	34	52	84	3	12
Garcia	.939	15	25	21	3	8
Turner	.961	103	207	286	20	65

Third Base	PCT	G	PO	A	E	DP
Cornejo	.871	13	9	18	4	3
Garcia	.928	77	53	102	12	11
McCurdy	.935	12	10	19	2	1
Morris	1.000	2	1	1	0	0
Schneidmiller	.935	25	18	40	4	2
Suomi	.860	20	7	30	6	2
Turner	.929	9	8	18	2	2

Shortstop	PCT	G	PO	A	E	DP
Cornejo	.953	14	23	38	3	5
Garcia	.941	25	36	60	6	8
Quintanilla	.941	104	152	298	28	68
Turner	.600	1	0	3	2	0

Outfield	PCT	G	PO	A	E	DP
Cruz	.982	73	158	4	3	1
Ethier	.963	103	207	2	8	2
McBeth	.974	98	210	11	6	3
Perry	.964	73	128	5	5	3
Rogers	1.000	5	6	0	0	0
Stavisky	.975	93	150	7	4	1
Turner	1.000	23	33	1	0	0

KANE COUNTY COUGARS — Low Class A

MIDWEST LEAGUE

BATTING

BATTING	AVG	G	AB	R	H	2B	3B	HR	RBI	BB	SO	SB	CS	OBP	SLG	B	T	HT	WT	DOB	1st Yr	Resides
Acosta, Jesse	.122	22	41	8	5	1	0	0	7	11	10	0	1	.308	.146	R	R	5-9	185	11-19-80	2003	Kerman, Calif.
Appert, Luke	.274	128	464	88	127	28	3	13	60	80	63	3	1	.388	.431	L	R	6-0	185	7-14-80	2003	Cottage Grove, Minn.
Brown, Trevor	.287	73	195	29	56	11	4	2	29	37	54	0	3	.412	.415	R	R	5-9	185	8-14-80	2001	Eugene, Ore.
Castillo, David	.246	111	402	66	99	28	1	9	59	65	77	0	0	.359	.388	R	R	6-0	185	9-15-81	2003	Corpus Christi, Texas
Gibbons, Danny	.087	12	23	1	2	1	0	0	1	3	4	0	0	.222	.130	L	R	6-3	205	10-21-80	2002	Toronto, Ontario
Harriman, David	.242	54	186	20	45	7	0	4	23	20	45	1	1	.319	.344	R	R	6-0	200	10-15-80	2002	Surrey, B.C.
Ingram, Brian	.229	126	472	80	108	23	5	4	44	84	97	6	4	.347	.324	L	R	5-10	175	3-29-81	2003	Rural Hall, N.C.
Kim, Eddie	.254	113	405	42	103	21	2	10	71	45	86	0	1	.328	.390	L	R	6-3	260	4-16-81	2003	Fairfax, Va.
Majewski, Dustin	.274	127	464	75	127	23	2	12	62	48	105	20	6	.339	.409	L	L	5-11	190	8-16-81	2003	Brenham, Texas
Perez, Luis	.271	89	314	44	85	16	1	4	41	27	46	12	5	.341	.366	R	R	6-0	160	8-17-83	2002	Los Teques, Venez.
Putnam, Danny	.220	50	164	30	36	5	2	7	28	30	42	0	0	.348	.402	L	L	5-10	200	9-17-82	2004	Escondido, Calif.
Rogers, Nick	.240	94	283	52	68	15	4	3	33	44	81	14	5	.344	.353	R	R	6-1	210	12-12-79	2002	Ponte Vedra Beach, Fla.
Snyder, Brian	.311	101	366	54	114	18	3	13	61	67	82	3	2	.421	.484	R	R	6-0	195	3-17-82	2003	Wellington, Fla.
Spanos, Vasili	.311	97	331	58	103	26	1	12	80	54	76	11	5	.419	.505	R	R	6-1	225	2-25-81	2003	River Forest, Ill.
Tritle, Chris	.192	102	234	37	45	8	2	6	29	20	96	10	2	.262	.321	R	R	6-3	195	6-22-82	2000	Center Point, Iowa
Wayment, Kory	.235	98	328	46	77	20	2	9	48	29	89	4	3	.301	.390	R	R	6-1	165	2-18-81	2001	Ogden, Utah

PITCHING

PITCHING	W	L	ERA	G	GS	CG	SV	IP	H	R	ER	BB	SO	AVG	B	T	HT	WT	DOB	1st Yr	Resides
Bondurant, Steven	14	5	2.08	21	21	2	0	126	92	39	29	27	132	.200	L	L	6-0	185	3-3-80	2003	Matthews, N.C.
Braden, Dallas	2	1	4.70	5	5	0	0	23	22	13	12	6	33	.242	L	L	6-1	185	8-13-83	2004	Lubbock, Texas
Corchado, Jose	5	5	3.12	33	6	0	3	61	45	26	21	26	73	.204	R	R	6-0	195	4-5-84	2002	Isabela, P.R.
Crowder, Justin	2	1	4.73	34	0	0	1	32	32	20	17	7	37	.252	L	L	6-0	195	9-24-79	2002	Lewisville, Texas
Dunwell, Chris	11	8	4.41	28	28	0	0	157	179	90	77	36	145	.279	R	R	6-1	200	1-29-80	2002	El Cajon, Calif.
Friedberg, Drew	1	0	8.44	8	0	0	0	5	9	5	5	7	8	.360	L	L	6-2	200	3-3-79	2001	Middleton, Wis.
Fyvie, Daniel	4	1	3.69	59	0	0	5	78	70	36	32	22	72	.239	R	R	6-0	165	8-12-82	2002	Flint, Mich.
Garcia, Jairo	1	0	0.30	25	0	0	16	30	16	2	1	6	49	.154	R	R	6-0	165	3-7-83	2000	Juan Baron, D.R.
Knox, Brad	14	5	2.59	26	25	0	0	156	141	53	45	24	174	.235	R	R	6-3	210	5-27-82	2002	Houston, Texas
Leon, Brigmer	4	4	2.90	46	1	0	0	81	82	41	26	20	56	.263	R	R	6-3	165	4-7-81	1998	Cumana, Venez.
McAuliff, Jarod	0	1	4.15	3	0	0	0	4	5	2	2	1	4	.333	R	R	6-0	180	7-24-82	2004	Stillwater, Okla.
McGirr, Mike	1	3	4.37	16	3	0	0	35	41	24	17	15	38	.283	R	R	6-0	180	3-9-80	2003	Lexington, Mass.
Peterson, Trent	8	5	3.42	21	20	1	0	121	107	49	46	25	109	.242	R	L	6-1	180	11-16-81	2003	Tallahassee, Fla.
Pickens, J.R.	6	2	3.44	54	0	0	5	81	81	36	31	26	75	.258	L	R	6-1	210	6-22-80	2002	Liberty, Texas
Rodriguez, Manuel	2	3	6.35	40	3	0	1	72	89	52	51	26	43	.307	R	R	6-2	165	5-2-81	1999	Estrin, Monagas, Venez.
Sanchez, Adiel	0	1	16.20	8	0	0	0	7	16	13	12	9	4	.457	L	L	6-1	210	8-27-82	2002	Santo Domingo, D.R.
Street, Huston	0	1	1.69	9	0	0	4	11	9	2	2	5	14	.225	R	R	6-0	190	8-2-83	2004	Austin, Texas
Trout, Jared	7	10	5.88	28	27	1	0	132	153	100	86	42	101	.288	R	R	6-0	175	1-15-82	2003	Gilbertsville, Penn.
Windsor, Jason	1	0	2.77	9	0	0	3	13	11	4	4	5	13	.216	R	R	6-2	220	7-7-82	2004	Saratoga, Calif.

FIELDING

Catcher	PCT	G	PO	A	E	DP	PB
Brown	.979	25	129	11	3	0	5
Castillo	.993	87	683	76	5	2	6
Harriman	.997	40	330	25	1	0	8

First Base	PCT	G	PO	A	E	DP
Brown	.981	34	238	20	5	20
Kim	.991	86	703	63	7	56
Majewski	1.000	1	2	0	0	0
Spanos	.978	28	222	5	5	21

Second Base	PCT	G	PO	A	E	DP
Acosta	.833	2	5	0	1	0
Appert	.951	122	200	288	25	47
Ingram	.935	21	35	65	7	12

Third Base	PCT	G	PO	A	E	DP
Acosta	1.000	5	2	5	0	0
Snyder	.893	82	40	119	19	8
Spanos	.924	39	31	66	8	2
Wayment	.873	22	15	40	8	2

Shortstop	PCT	G	PO	A	E	DP
Acosta	.880	9	6	16	3	3
Ingram	.965	105	142	303	16	49
Snyder	1.000	4	5	11	0	1
Wayment	.945	32	52	86	8	21

Outfield	PCT	G	PO	A	E	DP
Gibbons	1.000	11	8	0	0	0
Majewski	.992	126	252	4	2	1
Perez	.966	83	110	5	4	1
Putnam	.988	45	83	2	1	0
Rogers	.968	81	121	1	4	0
Tritle	.984	98	122	3	2	2
Wayment	.954	39	55	7	3	0

VANCOUVER CANADIANS — Short-Season

NORTHWEST LEAGUE

BATTING	AVG	G	AB	R	H	2B	3B	HR	RBI	BB	SO	SB	CS	OBP	SLG	B	T	HT	WT	DOB	1st Yr	Resides
Beauregard, Josh	.207	18	58	12	12	2	1	1	4	8	12	3	3	.313	.328	L	R	6-0	190	3-7-81	2003	Swanzey, N.H.
Blasi, Nick	.299	71	271	57	81	14	2	0	26	38	66	3	2	.390	.365	R	R	5-11	195	9-23-81	2004	Wichita, Kan.
Bubalo, Ty	.182	17	44	4	8	1	0	0	4	3	12	0	0	.234	.205	R	R	6-3	215	8-8-83	2002	Beaverton, Ore.
Everidge, Tom	.274	74	292	42	80	13	1	6	52	23	72	0	0	.332	.387	R	R	6-1	215	4-20-83	2004	Glen Allen, Calif.
Harriman, David	.310	9	29	3	9	0	1	0	2	2	6	0	0	.375	.379	R	R	6-0	200	10-15-80	2002	Surrey, B.C.
Herrera, Javier	.331	65	263	50	87	15	4	12	47	24	59	23	1	.392	.555	R	R	5-11	200	4-9-85	2002	Caracas, Venez.
Leslie, Myron	.245	73	273	41	67	12	2	1	29	41	34	1	1	.339	.315	S	R	6-3	190	5-2-82	2004	Valrico, Fla.
Long, Wesley	.286	3	14	3	4	1	1	0	2	0	1	0	0	.286	.500	R	R	5-11	195	6-12-82	2004	Auburn, Ala.

ORGANIZATION STATISTICS

BATTING	AVG	G	AB	R	H	2B	3B	HR	RBI	BB	SO	SB	CS	OBP	SLG	B	T	HT	WT	DOB	1st Yr	Resides
Melillo, Kevin	.340	22	94	22	32	11	2	2	21	11	16	2	1	.422	.564	L	R	6-0	190	5-14-82	2004	Longwood, Fla.
Ogando, Alexi	.150	7	20	3	3	0	0	1	6	4	9	1	0	.320	.300	R	R	6-4	160	10-5-83	2002	San Pedro de Macoris, D.R.
Petit, Gregorio	.256	68	254	34	65	9	2	4	35	20	67	3	3	.315	.354	R	R	5-10	186	12-10-84	2002	Santa Teresa, Venez.
Powell, Landon	.244	38	135	24	33	6	1	3	19	26	22	0	0	.368	.370	S	R	6-3	235	3-19-82	2004	New Hill, N.C.
Putnam, Danny	.289	11	38	10	11	2	0	2	3	14	8	1	0	.481	.500	L	L	5-10	200	9-17-82	2004	Escondido, Calif.
Ramirez, Juan	.071	16	42	6	3	0	0	1	5	8	0	1	5	.188	.071	R	R	6-0	208	9-16-83	2001	Monte Plata, D.R.
Robnett, Richie	.299	43	164	26	49	14	1	4	36	28	43	1	2	.395	.470	L	L	5-10	195	9-17-83	2004	Visalia, Calif.
Ruiz, Ryan	.243	56	202	30	49	13	1	2	34	33	55	4	2	.357	.347	R	R	5-8	180	10-18-81	2004	Las Vegas, Nev.
Sutton, Don	.163	14	49	6	8	1	0	1	6	5	15	0	0	.255	.245	R	R	6-1	220	11-21-83	2003	North Las Vegas, Nev.
Suzuki, Kurt	.297	46	175	27	52	10	3	3	31	18	26	0	1	.394	.440	R	R	5-11	200	10-4-83	2004	Wailuku, Hawaii
Tietje, Chalon	.262	41	130	21	34	7	3	1	17	12	28	0	0	.336	.385	R	R	6-1	195	6-11-82	2004	San Luis Obispo, Calif.
Winslow, Ben	.159	24	63	6	10	2	0	0	4	7	20	5	0	.250	.190	R	R	6-2	200	10-16-79	2003	Prescott, Ariz.

GAMES BY POSITION: C—Bubalo 9, Harriman 8, Powell 20, Ramirez 14, Sutton 4, Suzuki 27. **1B**—Everidge 71, Melillo 2, Winslow 6. **2B**—Long 2, Melillo 21, Ruiz 47, Winslow 9. **3B**—Leslie 71, Winslow 4. **SS**—Petit 68, Ruiz 5, Winslow 4. **OF**—Beauregard 11, Blasi 72, Herrera 66, Ogando 7, Putnam 11, Robnett 46, Tietje 31.

PITCHING	W	L	ERA	G	GS	CG	SV	IP	H	R	ER	BB	SO	AVG	B	T	HT	WT	DOB	1st Yr	Resides
Acevedo, Danielin	2	1	3.20	5	2	0	0	20	22	11	7	6	7	.275	R	R	6-3	170	4-2-83	2002	Puerto Plata, D.R.
Barnett, Danny	0	3	6.59	9	0	0	0	14	19	12	10	9	13	.317	R	R	6-1	190	1-22-83	2004	Kearns, Utah
Basch, Zachary	1	3	5.40	18	0	0	0	23	25	17	14	14	22	.287	R	R	6-3	190	6-22-81	2003	Sylvania, Ohio
Braden, Dallas	2	0	2.33	8	0	0	2	19	15	7	5	3	30	.214	L	L	6-1	185	8-13-83	2004	Lubbock, Texas
Cabaniel, Tomas	6	3	4.59	15	15	0	0	82	88	48	42	24	74	.268	R	R	6-1	165	2-10-83	2000	Caracas, Venez.
Carter, Steven	0	0	22.50	3	0	0	0	2	6	5	5	0	0	.500	R	R	6-3	220	6-9-80	2004	Windsor, Ontario
Drucker, Scott	2	1	3.00	14	0	0	6	21	20	8	7	6	18	.244	R	R	6-1	192	5-30-82	2004	Miami, Fla.
Espinal, Leonardo	0	2	6.75	2	2	0	0	9	11	8	7	2	6	.297	R	R	6-3	200	2-6-84	2003	San Pedro de Macoris, D.R.
Ford, Ryan	4	0	3.66	15	11	0	2	71	76	36	29	15	49	.274	L	L	6-3	195	7-10-82	2004	Rochester, Mich.
Howay, Chris	3	1	5.65	20	0	0	2	29	35	19	18	13	32	.315	R	R	6-3	210	8-17-79	2001	New Westminster, B.C.
Martinez, Shawn	1	4	4.50	17	2	0	2	40	42	22	20	20	36	.276	R	R	6-3	235	3-7-82	2004	Colorado Springs, Colo.
McGirr, Mike	5	0	0.66	7	7	0	0	41	23	5	3	7	31	.162	R	R	6-0	180	3-9-81	2003	Lexington, Mass.
Robertson, Connor	0	0	3.60	3	0	0	0	5	4	2	2	2	5	.235	R	R	6-3	205	6-30-79	2004	Tuscaloosa, Ala.
Rogers, Michael	1	2	4.87	12	8	0	0	41	48	22	22	15	26	.291	R	R	6-1	195	10-24-82	2004	Hamilton, N.J.
Sanchez, Adiel	2	3	5.23	22	0	0	1	31	37	19	18	15	19	.296	L	L	6-1	210	8-27-82	2002	Santo Domingo, D.R.
Santana, Braulio	4	3	4.58	12	10	0	0	55	56	33	28	14	23	.259	R	R	5-9	210	4-3-85	2003	San Pedro de Macoris, D.R.
Schilsky, Stephen	0	3	8.31	8	0	0	1	13	19	13	12	10	4	.380	R	R	6-2	215	1-3-81	2002	Springfield, Ill.
Sharpe, Steven	6	3	4.48	16	14	0	0	72	59	40	36	30	53	.224	R	R	6-1	210	7-20-81	2004	Stillwell, Kan.
Tharpe, Derek	0	2	4.80	12	1	0	3	30	34	18	16	7	30	.288	L	L	5-11	188	10-30-81	2004	Knoxville, Tenn.
Tichota, Clay	3	0	4.71	16	4	0	1	42	47	27	22	12	36	.283	R	R	6-4	210	11-26-81	2004	Littleton, Colo.
Windsor, Jason	0	0	0.00	4	0	0	1	5	4	0	0	0	5	.222	R	R	6-2	220	7-7-82	2004	Saratoga, Calif.
Winslow, Ben	0	0	4.50	2	0	0	0	2	2	1	1	2	2	.250	R	R	6-2	200	10-16-79	2003	Prescott, Ariz.

ARIZONA LEAGUE

BATTING	AVG	G	AB	R	H	2B	3B	HR	RBI	BB	SO	SB	CS	SLG	OBP	B	T	HT	WT	DOB	1st Yr	Resides
Arias, Roberto	.153	29	59	9	9	1	2	0	5	7	18	1	1	.237	.239	R	R	6-1	170	1-2-83	2002	San Jose de Ocoa, D.R.
Beauregard, Josh	.279	28	104	27	29	6	1	1	10	20	22	11	6	.385	.400	L	L	6-0	195	3-7-81	2003	Deltona, Fla.
Best, Tyler	.205	30	88	15	18	2	0	1	11	26	32	3	1	.261	.418	L	R	6-0	208	4-24-81	2004	Tacoma, Wash.
Boyd, Chad	.207	35	116	19	24	4	1	1	13	16	21	3	2	.284	.311	L	L	5-10	180	4-21-85	2004	West Hills, Calif.
Carela, Carlos	.222	30	81	10	18	2	0	0	11	10	30	10	4	.247	.315	R	R	6-2	160	9-24-83	2004	San Pedro de Macoris, D.R.
Feliz, Nelson	.300	10	40	3	12	3	0	0	10	3	10	1	1	.375	.341	R	R	6-1	195	5-9-84	2001	San Cristobal, D.R.
Long, Wesley	.345	54	206	45	71	17	1	4	35	31	26	16	7	.495	.434	R	R	6-0	190	6-12-82	2004	Auburn, Ala.
Martinez, Frank	.207	47	174	25	36	7	5	3	21	13	51	5	5	.356	.271	R	R	6-1	160	7-19-85	2003	Santo Domingo, D.R.
Ogando, Alexi	.267	47	180	26	48	13	1	6	24	14	57	3	1	.450	.340	R	R	6-4	160	10-5-83	2002	San Pedro de Macoris, D.R.
Padron, Raul	.306	40	147	23	45	14	4	1	35	16	25	6	3	.476	.380	R	R	6-0	190	9-17-84	2003	San Antonio, Venez.
Perez, Wilber	.289	49	194	49	56	11	8	1	20	28	40	20	7	.443	.382	S	R	6-2	183	3-31-85	2001	Santo Domingo, D.R.
Piper-Jordan, Andre	.237	45	156	29	37	8	2	1	11	10	41	14	5	.333	.306	R	R	6-0	195	12-5-83	2004	Federal Way, Wash.
Pratt, Haas	.180	35	122	9	22	8	0	1	15	15	27	2	3	.270	.268	R	R	6-3	225	9-17-81	2004	Arvada, Colo.
Sutton, Donald	.241	25	87	11	21	7	1	4	21	9	27	0	1	.483	.330	R	R	6-1	220	11-21-83	2003	North Las Vegas, Nev.
Valdez, Alexander	.272	31	103	14	28	1	2	0	14	11	14	5	3	.320	.342	R	R	6-1	160	3-2-86	2003	Santo Domingo, D.R.

GAMES BY POSITION: C—Arias 17, Best 21, Feliz 5, Padron 13, Sutton 6. **1B**—Best 4, Feliz 3, Padron 16, Pratt 24, Sutton 13. **2B**—Martinez 2, Perez 43, Valdez 11. **3B**—Carela 3, Long 45, Valdez 9. **SS**—Carela 7, Long 4, Martinez 44, Valdez 1. **OF**—Arias 1, Beauregard 25, Boyd 30, Carela 13, Ogando 46, Perez 5, Piper-Jordan 44, Pratt 4, Valdez 6.

PITCHING	W	L	ERA	G	GS	CG	SV	IP	H	R	ER	BB	SO	AVG	B	T	HT	WT	DOB	1st Yr	Resides
Acevedo, Danielin	3	2	2.17	10	9	0	0	54	63	26	13	11	42	.293	R	R	6-3	170	4-2-83	2002	Puerto Plata, D.R.
Burton, Jared	1	0	4.15	5	5	0	0	22	21	12	10	4	15	.247	R	R	6-5	220	4-26-81	2002	Westminster, S.C.
Fairbanks, Scott	2	0	2.11	14	0	0	1	21	13	5	5	22	29	.175	R	R	6-3	200	4-26-81	2004	Bremerton, Wash.
Gray, Jeffrey	3	0	1.89	14	2	0	0	38	30	14	8	3	32	.211	R	R	6-3	205	11-19-81	2004	Chesterfield, Mo.
Heuser, James	3	2	3.11	15	0	0	0	38	33	22	13	16	28	.237	L	L	6-5	200	3-30-84	2003	Peru, Ill.
Mitchell, Michael	1	0	1.35	7	0	0	1	13	14	4	2	1	7	.274	R	R	6-2	185	10-27-81	2004	St. Peters, Mo.
Mola, Heydin	2	2	6.34	13	3	0	0	38	49	33	27	17	26	.312	R	R	6-2	160	3-25-84	2002	San Cristobal, D.R.
Muessig, Jeff	0	0	3.09	6	4	0	0	23	20	11	8	7	22	.238	R	R	6-2	185	2-27-82	2001	Mt. Sinai, N.Y.
Newby, Joey	2	3	4.04	14	11	0	0	56	68	35	25	10	46	.307	R	R	6-2	205	3-8-82	2004	Soldotna, Alaska
Piekarz, Joe	4	2	1.66	17	4	0	0	38	32	11	7	12	40	.225	R	L	6-2	175	1-1-82	2004	Streamwood, Ill.
Robertson, Connor	2	2	0.92	25	0	0	13	29	17	8	3	8	46	.157	R	R	6-3	215	6-30-79	2004	Tuscaloosa, Ala.
Robertson, Luke	0	1	0.71	4	3	0	0	13	9	2	1	3	17	.204	R	R	6-4	220	6-30-79	2001	Valley Center, Kan.
Rodriguez, William	2	0	4.91	5	0	0	0	7	7	7	4	7	6	.241	L	L	6-0	175	5-8-84	2001	Santiago, D.R.
Semerano, Robert	5	1	4.08	21	0	0	0	29	30	16	13	7	24	.272	R	R	6-1	185	7-18-81	2004	Port Jervis, N.Y.
Torres, Luis	3	5	5.06	15	8	0	0	53	67	35	30	23	35	.313	R	R	6-1	175	10-23-84	2002	Valencia, Venez.
Webb, Ryan	1	1	4.87	8	7	0	0	20	18	11	11	1	23	.227	R	R	6-6	190	2-5-86	2004	Palm Harbor, Fla.

PHILADELPHIA PHILLIES

BY JIM SALISBURY

The Phillies have played 122 seasons. Never had one been as eagerly anticipated as 2004.

The team had its second straight strong offseason, adding all-star closer Billy Wagner and lefthanded starter Eric Milton to a sturdy nucleus that included starter Kevin Millwood and sluggers Jim Thome and Bobby Abreu. With a club record $93 million payroll and four starting pitchers who'd been all-stars in their careers, the Phillies soared into stunning new Citizens Bank Park as the hands-down favorite to win the National League East.

Marred by injury and underachievement, the season was a bust. Sure, the Phils had just their fourth winning season in 18 years, but the franchise had passed the point where a winning season was good enough. The Phils finished second in the National League East, 10 games behind perennial champ Atlanta.

Arguably the most disappointing Phillies season since the collapse of 1964 ended with manager Larry Bowa out of a job and angry fans calling for general manager Ed Wade's head.

Wade survived and set out to find a manager "that can take us to the World Series."

The Phillies were 338-309 in four seasons under Bowa, but his tenure was marked by annual bouts of clubhouse tension and poor relations with players.

The Phils were in first place by a game in the NL East at the all-star break, but they faltered in the second half, going 25-31 in July and August as Atlanta pulled away. The Phils dropped from wild-card contention with a franchise-worst 1-9 homestand in August. They went 19-8 in September, but that couldn't save Bowa's job or the team's playoff hopes.

Injuries played a role in the team's wheel-spinning first half, and its second-half decline. Starting pitchers

Jim Thome   Ryan Howard

PLAYERS of the YEAR

MAJOR LEAGUE: Jim Thome, 1b

Thome carried the Phillies for a second straight season, belting 42 homers and driving in more than 100 runs for the sixth consecutive year. He was especially dangerous against righthanded pitchers, hitting .296 against them with an on-base plus slugging average of 1.089.

MINOR LEAGUE: Ryan Howard, 1b

Howard, 24, put up huge power numbers in 2004, leading the minor leagues with 46 home runs. He spent most of the season at Double-A Reading, where his 37 home runs snapped Greg Luzinski's 35-year-old franchise record. In all, Howard drove in 131 runs.

Millwood, Vicente Padilla and Randy Wolf all spent significant time on the disabled list, as did Wagner and valuable rookie reliever Ryan Madson. Phillies starters ended up 12th in the NL with just 71 quality starts, 26 fewer than the Braves.

Offensively, the Phils were third in the league in runs (840), second in homers (215), second in on-base percentage (.345) and fourth in slugging (.443). But they hit just .257 with runners in scoring position and stranded 1,236 runners, second most in the league.

In his second year in Philadelphia, Thome hit 42 homers, but he battled a hand injury all season. Abreu hit .301 with 30 homers and stole 40 bases while making his first All-Star Game appearance.

Shortstop Jimmy Rollins was one of the team's bright spots, hitting .289 with career-highs in walks (57) and RBIs (73). Rollins lowered his strikeouts from 113 to 73 and solidified the long troublesome leadoff spot. He played brilliant defense, making just nine errors as the Phils posted their highest fielding percentage (.987) in club history.

Citizens Bank Park was a big attraction, helping the club draw a franchise record 3.25 million fans. The Phils played in front of 44 sellout crowds, but if they don't make the playoffs soon, that number will surely go down.

In the minors, the Phils had mixed success. Righthander Gavin Floyd had a strong season in Double-A and won his major league debut in September. First baseman Ryan Howard led the minor leagues with 46 homers between Double-A and Triple-A, and 2003 draftee Michael Bourn emerged as a leadoff man/centerfielder of the future with a strong season at low Class A Lakewood.

ORGANIZATION LEADERS

BATTING

*AVG	Lou Collier, Scranton	.326
R	Ryan Howard, Scranton/Reading	94
H	John Castellano, Scranton/Reading/Clearwater	152
TB	Ryan Howard, Scranton/Reading	309
2B	Jake Blalock, Lakewood	40
3B	Mark Budzinski, Scranton	15
HR	Ryan Howard, Scranton/Reading	46
RBI	Ryan Howard, Scranton/Reading	131
BB	Michael Bourn, Lakewood	85
SO	Ryan Howard, Scranton/Reading	166
SB	Michael Bourn, Lakewood	58
*OBP	Michael Bourn, Lakewood	.431
*SLG	Ryan Howard, Scranton/Reading	.637

PITCHING

W	Dan Giese, Scranton	12
	C.J. Woodrow, Clearwater/Lakewood	12
L	Kyle Kendrick, Lakewood/Batavia	16
#ERA	Cory Schultz, Clearwater/Lakewood	2.24
G	Spike Lundberg, Scranton/Reading	56
CG	Alfredo Simon, Clearwater	4
SV	Jim Crowell, Scranton	16
IP	Erick Arteaga, Clearwater	159
BB	Nick Bourgeois, Clearwater	68
SO	Robinson Tejeda, Reading	133

*Minimum 250 at-bats #Minimum 75 innings

PHILADELPHIA PHILLIES

Managers: Larry Bowa/Gary Varsho.

2004 Record: 86-76, .531 (2nd, NL East).

BATTING	AVG	G	AB	R	H	2B	3B	HR	RBI	BB	SO	SB	CS	OBP	SLG	B	T	HT	WT	DOB	1st Yr	Resides
Abreu, Bobby	.301	159	574	118	173	47	1	30	105	127	116	40	5	.428	.544	L	R	6-0	200	3-11-74	1991	Aragua, Venez.
Bell, David	.291	143	533	67	155	33	1	18	77	57	75	1	1	.363	.458	R	R	5-10	195	9-14-72	1990	Seattle, Wash.
Burrell, Pat	.257	127	448	66	115	17	0	24	84	78	130	2	0	.365	.455	R	R	6-4	220	10-10-76	1998	Clearwater, Fla.
Byrd, Marlon	.228	106	346	48	79	13	2	5	33	22	68	2	2	.287	.321	R	R	6-0	225	8-30-77	1999	San Diego, Calif.
Collier, Lou	.278	32	36	7	10	1	0	1	4	5	10	1	0	.381	.389	R	R	5-10	190	8-21-73	1993	Chicago, Ill.
Glanville, Doug	.210	87	162	21	34	1	1	2	14	8	21	8	0	.244	.265	R	R	6-2	170	8-25-70	1991	Philadelphia, Pa.
Hinch, A.J.	.182	4	11	1	2	1	0	0	0	0	4	0	0	.182	.273	R	R	6-1	200	5-15-74	1997	Scottsdale, Ariz.
Howard, Ryan	.282	19	39	5	11	5	0	2	5	2	13	0	0	.333	.564	L	L	6-4	230	11-19-79	2001	Wildwood, Mo.
Ledee, Ricky	.285	73	123	19	35	7	0	7	26	22	27	2	0	.393	.512	L	L	6-1	200	11-22-73	1990	Salinas, P.R.
Lieberthal, Mike	.271	131	476	58	129	31	1	17	61	37	69	1	1	.335	.447	R	R	6-0	195	1-18-72	1990	Westlake Village, Calif.
Michaels, Jason	.274	115	299	44	82	12	0	10	40	42	80	2	2	.364	.415	R	R	6-0	205	5-4-76	1998	Tampa, Fla.
Perez, Tomas	.216	86	176	22	38	13	2	6	21	9	44	0	0	.257	.415	S	R	5-11	185	12-29-73	1993	Barquisimeto, Venez.
Polanco, Placido	.298	126	503	74	150	21	0	17	55	27	39	7	4	.344	.441	R	R	5-10	185	10-10-75	1994	Miami, Fla.
Pratt, Todd	.258	45	128	16	33	5	0	3	16	18	38	0	0	.351	.367	R	R	6-3	235	2-9-67	1985	Deerfield, Fla.
Rollins, Jimmy	.289	154	657	119	190	43	12	14	73	57	73	30	9	.348	.455	S	R	5-8	165	11-27-78	1996	Alameda, Calif.
Thome, Jim	.274	143	508	97	139	28	1	42	105	104	144	0	2	.396	.581	L	R	6-4	240	8-27-70	1989	Aurora, Ohio
Utley, Chase	.266	94	267	36	71	11	2	13	57	15	40	4	1	.308	.468	L	R	6-1	170	12-17-78	2000	Las Vegas, Nev.
Wooten, Shawn	.170	33	53	2	9	3	0	0	2	2	9	0	0	.228	.226	R	R	5-10	220	7-24-72	1993	Covina, Calif.

PITCHING	W	L	ERA	G	GS	CG	SV	IP	H	R	ER	BB	SO	AVG	B	T	HT	WT	DOB	1st Yr	Resides
Abbott, Paul	1	6	6.24	10	10	0	0	49	57	37	34	31	21	.000	R	R	6-3	205	9-15-67	1985	Fullerton, Calif.
Cormier, Rheal	4	5	3.56	84	0	0	0	81	70	32	32	26	46	.000	L	L	5-10	195	4-23-67	1989	Voorhees, N.J.
Crowell, Jim	0	0	3.00	4	0	0	0	3	6	2	1	0	1	.000	R	L	6-4	230	5-14-74	1995	Valparaiso, Ind.
Floyd, Gavin	2	0	3.49	6	4	0	0	28	25	11	11	16	24	.000	R	R	6-4	210	1-27-83	2002	Severna Park, Md.
Geary, Geoff	1	0	5.44	33	0	0	0	45	52	29	27	16	30	.000	R	R	6-0	165	8-26-76	1998	El Cajon, Calif.
Hancock, Josh	0	1	9.00	4	2	0	0	9	13	9	9	3	5	.333	R	R	6-3	210	4-11-78	1998	Tupelo, Miss.
Hernandez, Roberto	3	5	4.76	63	0	0	0	57	66	39	30	29	44	.000	R	R	6-4	250	11-11-64	1986	Largo, Fla.
Jones, Todd	3	3	4.97	27	0	0	1	25	35	14	14	8	22	.330	S	R	6-3	230	4-24-68	1989	Pell City, Ala.
2-team (51 Cincinnati)	11	5	4.15	78	0	0	2	82	84	39	38	33	59	.000							
Lidle, Cory	5	2	3.90	10	10	2	0	62	54	28	27	17	33	.236	R	R	5-11	190	3-22-72	1991	Las Vegas, Nev.
2-team (24 Cincinnati)	12	12	4.90	34	34	5	0	211	224	123	115	61	126	.000							
Madson, Ryan	9	3	2.34	52	1	0	1	77	68	23	20	19	55	.000	L	R	6-6	180	8-28-80	1998	Moreno Valley, Calif.
Millwood, Kevin	9	6	4.85	25	25	0	0	141	155	81	76	51	125	.000	R	R	6-4	220	12-24-74	1993	Duluth, Ga.
Milton, Eric	14	6	4.75	34	34	0	0	201	196	110	106	75	161	.000	L	L	6-3	225	8-4-75	1997	Fort Myers, Fla.
Myers, Brett	11	11	5.52	32	31	1	0	176	196	113	108	62	116	.000	R	R	6-4	215	8-17-80	1993	Jacksonville, Fla.
Padilla, Vicente	7	7	4.53	20	20	0	0	115	119	63	58	36	82	.000	R	R	6-2	215	11-27-77	1999	Chinandega, Nicaragua
Powell, Brian	1	2	5.03	17	2	0	0	39	39	23	22	16	24	.000	R	R	6-2	200	10-10-73	1995	Bainbridge, Ga.
Ramirez, Elizardo	0	0	4.80	7	0	0	0	15	17	8	8	5	9	.000	R	R	6-0	145	1-28-83	2000	Santo Domingo, D.R.
Rodriguez, Felix	2	3	3.00	23	0	0	1	21	18	7	7	10	28	.231	R	R	6-1	190	9-9-72	1991	Monte Cristi, D.R.
2-team (53 S.F.)	5	8	3.29	76	0	0	1	66	61	25	24	29	59	.000							
Telemaco, Amaury	0	2	4.31	42	0	0	0	54	51	27	26	19	32	.000	R	R	6-3	220	1-19-74	1992	La Romana, D.R.
Wagner, Billy	4	0	2.42	45	0	0	21	48	31	16	13	6	59	.000	L	L	5-11	195	7-25-71	1993	Charlottesville, Va.
Wolf, Randy	5	8	4.28	23	23	1	0	137	145	73	65	36	89	.000	L	L	6-0	200	8-22-76	1997	West Hills, Calif.
Worrell, Tim	5	6	3.68	77	0	0	19	78	75	36	32	21	64	.000	R	R	6-4	230	7-5-67	1990	Glendale, Ariz.

FIELDING

Catcher	PCT	G	PO	A	E	DP	PB
Hinch	1.000	4	14	5	0	0	0
Lieberthal	.993	129	859	43	6	7	6
Pratt	1.000	43	259	8	0	2	1

First Base	PCT	G	PO	A	E	DP
Howard	1.000	8	59	6	0	9
Perez	.964	10	49	5	2	4
Thome	.994	134	1091	84	7	103
Utley	1.000	13	94	11	0	6
Wooten	1.000	11	70	3	0	6

Second Base	PCT	G	PO	A	E	DP
Perez	1.000	17	26	32	0	7

	PCT	G	PO	A	E	DP
Polanco	.995	109	264	304	3	76
Utley	.982	50	100	123	4	29

Third Base	PCT	G	PO	A	E	DP
Bell	.943	142	89	308	24	22
Collier	1.000	1	0	1	0	1
Perez	.944	22	12	22	2	1
Polanco	1.000	13	15	26	0	4
Wooten	1.000	4	2	4	0	0

Shortstop	PCT	G	PO	A	E	DP
Perez	.952	10	14	26	2	5
Rollins	.986	154	214	399	9	88

Outfield	PCT	G	PO	A	E	DP
Abreu	.982	158	311	13	6	4
Burrell	.983	122	217	9	4	1
Byrd	.990	92	195	4	2	1
Collier	1.000	8	3	0	0	0
Glanville	1.000	68	112	0	0	0
Ledee	1.000	22	47	3	0	1
Michaels	.983	78	166	5	3	2

Director, Minor Leagues: Steve Noworyta.

Class	Farm Team	League	W	L	Pct.	Finish*	Manager	Affiliate Since
AAA	Scranton/W-B (Pa.) Red Barons	International	69	73	.486	8th (14)	Marc Bombard	1989
AA	Reading (Pa.) Phillies	Eastern	64	77	.454	9th (12)	Greg Legg	1967
High A	Clearwater (Fla.) Phillies	Florida State	55	82	.401	11th (12)	Mike Schmidt	1985
Low A	Lakewood (N.J.) Blue Claws	South Atlantic	70	66	.515	6th (16)	P.J. Forbes	2001
SS A	Batavia (N.Y.) Muckdogs	New York-Penn	28	46	.378	14th (14)	Luis Melendez	1988
Rookie	Clearwater (Fla.) Phillies	Gulf Coast	36	24	.600	t-2nd (12)	Roly deArmas	1999

*Finish in overall standings (No. of teams in league)/Playoff teams in **boldface**

SCRANTON/WILKES-BARRE RED BARONS — Class AAA

INTERNATIONAL LEAGUE

ORGANIZATION STATISTICS

BATTING

	AVG	G	AB	R	H	2B	3B	HR	RBI	BB	SO	SB	CS	OBP	SLG	B	T	HT	WT	DOB	1st Yr	Resides
Barker, Kevin	.194	12	36	3	7	1	0	2	4	3	8	0	0	.256	.389	L	L	6-3	200	7-26-75	1996	Mendota, Va.
Budzinski, Mark	.283	135	508	79	144	29	15	5	52	48	103	16	2	.345	.429	L	L	6-2	180	8-26-73	1995	Richmond, Va.
Byrd, Marlon	.263	37	152	13	40	11	1	2	17	10	18	2	3	.323	.388	R	R	6-0	225	8-30-77	1999	San Diego, Calif.
Castellano, John	.385	4	13	1	5	1	0	0	1	2	0	0	0	.467	.462	R	R	5-11	180	9-8-77	1998	Boynton Beach, Fla.
Collier, Lou	.326	101	387	62	126	26	3	14	66	34	82	14	3	.383	.517	R	R	5-10	190	8-21-73	1993	Chicago, Ill.
Hannahan, Buzz	.281	81	217	32	61	10	3	0	20	19	49	5	5	.357	.355	R	R	6-2	180	6-29-76	1998	St. Paul, Minn.
Hernandez, Michel	.255	77	231	34	59	9	0	6	31	25	24	0	1	.328	.372	R	R	6-0	210	8-12-78	1998	Caracas, Venez.
Hinch, A.J.	.234	77	265	21	62	9	1	2	32	24	48	0	0	.313	.298	R	R	6-1	200	5-15-74	1997	Scottsdale, Ariz.
Hitchcox, Brian	.235	47	136	22	32	10	1	1	5	18	16	3	0	.346	.346	L	R	5-11	175	7-21-78	1999	Clearwater, Fla.
Howard, Ryan	.270	29	111	21	30	10	0	9	29	14	37	0	0	.362	.604	L	L	6-4	230	11-19-79	2001	Wildwood, Mo.
Jacobson, Russ	.286	2	7	0	2	1	0	0	1	1	3	0	0	.375	.429	R	R	6-3	210	10-14-77	2000	Scottsdale, Ariz.
Keene, Kurt	.250	6	8	2	2	0	0	0	2	1	2	1	0	.300	.250	R	R	6-0	190	8-22-77	2000	Chattanooga, Tenn.
Machado, Anderson	.227	78	295	51	67	12	5	6	26	50	73	11	6	.337	.363	S	R	5-11	165	1-25-81	1998	Caracas, Venez.
Ozuna, Pablo	.307	126	472	77	145	27	3	6	76	22	43	31	12	.343	.415	R	R	5-10	185	8-25-75	1996	Boca Chica, D.R.
Padilla, Jorge	.253	117	364	51	92	12	0	7	45	48	75	11	7	.348	.343	R	R	6-2	200	8-11-79	1998	Carolina, P.R.
Polanco, Placido	.000	1	3	1	0	0	0	0	0	1	0	0	0	.250	.000	R	R	5-10	185	10-10-75	1994	Miami, Fla.
Roberge, J.P.	.256	70	238	17	61	12	1	1	16	18	42	1	1	.307	.328	R	R	6-0	180	9-12-72	1994	Arcadia, Calif.
Rushford, Jim	.275	134	517	71	142	30	4	10	75	45	54	1	2	.333	.406	L	L	6-1	190	3-24-74	1996	San Diego, Calif.
Smith, Mark	.281	116	398	54	112	29	1	11	62	42	69	3	1	.359	.442	R	R	6-3	220	5-7-70	1991	Flower Mound, Texas
Utley, Chase	.285	33	123	23	35	8	1	6	25	18	29	4	2	.368	.512	L	R	6-1	170	12-17-78	2000	Las Vegas, Nev.
Wooten, Shawn	.293	61	225	28	66	22	0	4	34	24	29	0	1	.370	.444	R	R	5-10	220	7-24-72	1993	Covina, Calif.

PITCHING

	W	L	ERA	G	GS	CG	SV	IP	H	R	ER	BB	SO	AVG	B	T	HT	WT	DOB	1st Yr	Resides
Abbott, Paul	1	2	6.15	5	5	1	0	26	26	18	18	17	19	.265	R	R	6-3	205	9-15-67	1985	Fullerton, Calif.
Bowers, Shane	1	3	5.37	15	9	1	0	52	65	36	31	19	36	.304	R	R	6-4	215	7-8-71	1993	Covina, Calif.
Coggin, David	2	3	4.73	16	8	0	0	53	50	30	28	18	39	.248	R	R	6-4	215	10-30-76	1995	Upland, Calif.
Condrey, Clay	9	9	5.46	27	27	2	0	155	206	106	94	34	70	.321	R	R	6-3	195	11-19-75	1998	Navasota, Texas
Crowell, Jim	7	3	2.40	46	0	0	16	64	61	22	17	14	44	.250	R	L	6-4	230	5-14-74	1995	Valparaiso, Ind.
Ellis, Robert	5	8	4.23	16	16	1	0	111	111	54	52	18	55	.256	R	R	6-5	220	12-15-70	1991	Carthage, Texas
2-team (10 Buffalo)	8	12	5.10	26	26	1	0	166	176	96	94	34	90	.269							
Floyd, Gavin	1	3	4.99	5	5	0	0	31	39	20	17	9	18	.312	R	R	6-4	210	1-27-83	2002	Severna Park, Md.
Geary, Geoff	1	2	2.31	21	0	0	10	23	20	7	6	13	23	.235	R	R	6-0	165	8-26-76	1998	El Cajon, Calif.
Giese, Dan	12	5	2.81	54	0	0	3	83	63	27	26	18	54	.211	R	R	6-3	215	5-19-77	1999	San Clemente, Calif.
Hancock, Josh	8	7	4.01	18	18	1	0	108	107	52	48	21	65	.263	R	R	6-3	215	4-11-78	1998	Tupelo, Miss.
Hernandez, Yoel	0	0	6.46	14	2	0	0	31	38	26	22	7	18	.311	R	R	6-2	170	4-15-80	1999	Ciudad Bolivar, Venez.
Hutchinson, Ryan	1	0	2.84	4	0	0	0	6	8	2	2	0	2	.308	R	R	6-0	200	8-9-78	2001	Vincennes, Ind.
Jimenez, Jason	0	2	5.33	14	0	0	0	27	32	23	16	14	20	.296	R	L	6-2	200	1-10-76	1997	Elk Grove, Calif.
Junge, Eric	4	9	9.91	9	5	0	0	26	42	29	29	16	17	.375	R	R	6-5	215	1-5-77	1999	New York, N.Y.
Kubes, Greg	5	4	3.84	49	0	0	0	75	95	44	32	26	46	.310	R	L	6-6	200	11-10-76	1998	East Bernard, Texas
Lee, Seung	2	3	4.57	35	6	0	1	81	89	45	41	24	67	.284	R	R	6-4	220	6-2-79	2001	Pusan, Korea
Lundberg, Spike	6	3	3.26	44	0	0	3	66	69	35	24	14	57	.270	S	R	6-1	185	5-4-77	1997	San Diego, Calif.
Padilla, Vicente	0	0	13.50	2	2	0	0	5	6	7	7	5	6	.286	R	R	6-2	215	11-27-77	1999	Chinandega, Nicaragua
Perez, Franklin	0	5	6.00	9	6	0	0	39	49	32	26	5	23	.304	R	R	6-2	228	6-10-78	1998	Bani, D.R.
Powell, Brian	3	1	1.62	8	8	2	0	44	27	11	8	6	29	.168	R	R	6-2	200	10-10-73	1995	Bainbridge, Ga.
Sanches, Brian	0	0	7.50	4	0	0	0	6	6	5	5	3	4	.333	R	R	6-0	190	8-8-78	1999	Nederland, Texas
Smith, Bud	0	1	6.00	1	1	0	0	3	3	4	2	2	0	.231	L	L	6-0	170	10-23-79	1998	Lakewood, Calif.
Telemaco, Amaury	0	0	0.00	1	1	0	0	1	0	0	0	0	2	.000	R	R	6-3	220	1-19-74	1992	La Romana, D.R.
Yarnall, Ed	5	5	3.97	24	23	0	0	118	103	54	52	56	93	.238	L	L	6-3	235	12-4-75	1997	Baton Rouge, La.

FIELDING

Catcher	PCT	G	PO	A	E	DP	PB
Hernandez	.984	72	388	37	7	4	5
Hinch	.992	75	435	34	4	3	3
Jacobson	1.000	2	19	1	0	0	1

First Base	PCT	G	PO	A	E	DP
Barker	1.000	6	32	3	0	6
Collier	1.000	2	10	0	0	1
Howard	.977	29	232	21	6	22
Roberge	.986	35	268	15	4	19
Rushford	.993	73	654	44	5	63
Wooten	1.000	2	12	1	0	0

Second Base	PCT	G	PO	A	E	DP
Hannahan	.966	27	54	60	4	22
Hitchcox	.973	9	15	21	1	3

	PCT	G	PO	A	E	DP
Keene	.957	4	11	11	1	3
Ozuna	.975	58	132	145	7	32
Polanco	1.000	1	1	1	0	0
Roberge	.989	19	38	51	1	10
Utley	.970	33	70	93	5	20

Third Base	PCT	G	PO	A	E	DP
Collier	.888	45	25	70	12	3
Hannahan	.982	19	13	41	1	1
Hitchcox	.880	27	8	58	9	4
Roberge	1.000	11	6	12	0	3
Wooten	.935	50	29	86	8	6

Shortstop	PCT	G	PO	A	E	DP
Hannahan	.938	11	12	18	2	6
Hitchcox	.900	1	3	6	1	1

	PCT	G	PO	A	E	DP
Machado	.943	78	111	220	20	43
Ozuna	.968	56	84	160	8	32

Outfield	PCT	G	PO	A	E	DP
Barker	1.000	3	5	0	0	0
Budzinski	.987	136	287	7	4	0
Byrd	.980	37	97	2	2	0
Castellano	1.000	2	4	0	0	0
Collier	.978	51	83	6	2	2
Hannahan	.983	18	55	2	1	1
Ozuna	1.000	3	9	0	0	0
Padilla	.977	116	288	9	7	4
Rushford	.979	56	93	2	2	0
Smith	.983	29	55	3	1	0

EASTERN LEAGUE

BATTING	AVG	G	AB	R	H	2B	3B	HR	RBI	BB	SO	SB	CS	OBP	SLG	B	T	HT	WT	DOB	1st Yr	Resides
Barker, Kevin	.286	111	405	69	116	38	3	18	58	53	95	2	1	.367	.528	L	L	6-3	200	7-26-75	1996	Mendota, Va.
Burrell, Pat	.200	4	15	2	3	0	0	2	4	3	7	0	0	.333	.600	R	R	6-4	220	10-10-76	1998	Clearwater, Fla.
Castellano, John	.340	103	368	50	125	25	1	18	68	32	55	0	3	.395	.560	R	R	5-11	180	9-8-77	1998	Boynton Beach, Fla.
Cosbey, Chris	.243	56	148	16	36	6	3	0	16	9	28	6	4	.292	.324	L	L	5-9	160	11-14-74	1998	Arcadia, Calif.
Deschaine, Jim	.282	79	277	36	78	16	1	9	38	35	38	3	1	.368	.444	R	R	6-0	200	9-18-77	1999	Bristol, Conn.
Fleming, Ryan	.260	110	388	56	101	14	7	7	38	48	47	17	4	.343	.387	L	L	5-11	180	2-11-76	1998	Ashville, Ohio
Gibbs, Kevin	.300	3	10	3	3	0	0	1	0	6	0	0	0	.300	.600	S	R	6-2	180	4-3-74	1995	Davidsonville, Md.
Gonzalez, Danny	.262	134	461	62	121	23	2	4	41	52	95	2	4	.349	.347	S	R	6-0	180	11-20-81	2001	Trujillo Alto, P.R.
Hitchcox, Brian	.257	45	140	27	36	4	1	7	18	22	25	-4	1	.377	.450	R	R	5-11	175	7-21-78	1999	Clearwater, Fla.
Howard, Ryan	.297	102	374	73	111	18	1	37	102	46	129	1	2	.386	.647	L	L	6-4	230	11-19-79	2001	Wildwood, Mo.
Jacobson, Russ	.178	54	174	12	31	8	0	2	17	11	37	0	0	.236	.259	R	R	6-3	210	10-14-77	2000	Scottsdale, Ariz.
Keene, Kurt	.281	111	391	56	110	12	4	12	41	21	54	6	4	.321	.425	R	R	6-0	190	8-22-77	2000	Chattanooga, Tenn.
Leon, Carlos	.128	26	78	7	10	2	1	0	6	6	12	4	2	.198	.179	S	R	5-10	160	8-31-79	1997	Cabimas, Venez.
Norman, Zach	.000	1	5	0	0	0	0	0	0	0	2	0	0	.000	.000	R	R	6-0	210	1-20-82	2003	Odessa, Mo.
Perez, Josue	.213	23	80	9	17	0	0	0	4	8	13	5	1	.289	.213	S	R	6-0	180	8-12-77	1998	Santo Domingo, D.R.
Phelps, Jeff	.259	87	282	39	73	17	0	6	30	29	70	3	4	.333	.383	R	R	6-0	190	11-20-78	2001	Yuma, Ariz.
Polanco, Placido	.667	1	3	0	2	0	0	0	0	0	0	0	0	.667	.667	R	R	5-10	185	10-10-75	1994	Miami, Fla.
Quintana, Miguel	.221	50	163	15	36	6	1	3	14	9	35	3	6	.270	.325	L	R	6-1	190	6-29-79	2001	Miami, Fla.
Richardson, Juan	.282	18	71	10	20	7	1	5	13	1	16	0	1	.297	.507	R	R	6-1	175	1-27-79	1999	Bani, D.R.
Ruiz, Carlos	.284	101	349	45	99	15	2	17	50	22	37	8	4	.338	.484	R	R	5-10	180	1-22-79	1999	Chiriqui, Panama
Walsh, Sean	.230	46	126	9	29	8	0	1	11	14	26	2	1	.322	.317	R	R	6-4	220	11-15-79	2001	Aiken, S.C.
Youngbauer, Scott	.272	61	239	40	65	10	3	9	21	19	49	8	2	.328	.452	S	R	6-1	179	1-14-79	2000	Powder Springs, Ga.

PITCHING	W	L	ERA	G	GS	CG	SV	IP	H	R	ER	BB	SO	AVG	B	T	HT	WT	DOB	1st Yr	Resides
Bowers, Shane	1	0	1.20	4	4	0	0	15	12	2	2	4	14	.218	R	R	6-4	215	7-8-71	1993	Covina, Calif.
Brito, Eude	8	6	4.42	43	7	1	4	98	95	56	48	41	84	.255	L	L	5-11	160	8-19-78	1999	Sabana de la Mar, D.R.
Bucktrot, Keith	4	7	4.87	20	20	0	0	105	140	65	57	39	60	.321	R	R	6-2	180	11-27-80	2000	Claremore, Okla.
Candelario, Eddie	0	3	7.36	16	4	0	0	37	45	33	30	23	21	.302	R	R	6-0	176	1-5-80	1998	La Carmelita, D.R.
Chantres, Carlos	1	3	6.91	6	5	0	0	29	35	23	22	19	25	.307	R	R	6-3	165	4-1-76	1994	Miami, Fla.
Culp, Brandon	2	1	4.38	4	4	0	0	25	23	12	12	8	28	.245	R	R	6-6	250	8-27-77	2000	Jemison, Ala.
Dawson, Layne	3	2	6.85	9	8	0	0	45	55	39	34	16	31	.299	R	R	6-2	180	9-13-79	2001	Somerville, Tenn.
Dougherty, Kevin	1	4	6.85	11	7	0	0	45	60	39	34	28	26	.341	L	L	6-5	200	3-4-78	1997	Voorhees, N.J.
Floyd, Gavin	6	6	2.57	20	20	2	0	119	93	39	34	46	94	.212	R	R	6-4	210	1-27-83	2002	Severna Park, Md.
Franco, Martire	4	4	3.30	48	0	0	15	85	73	31	31	20	63	.234	R	R	6-0	170	2-25-78	1998	Bani, D.R.
Gardner, Hayden	2	1	3.09	7	0	0	1	12	13	4	4	3	6	.295	R	R	6-2	200	10-7-80	2001	Stafford, Va.
Gwaltney, Lee	2	2	7.17	4	4	0	0	21	24	17	17	11	17	.293	R	R	6-5	210	5-6-80	2002	Willow Park, Texas
Hernandez, Yoel	1	2	2.01	20	0	0	6	31	24	12	7	15	33	.211	R	R	6-0	170	4-15-80	1999	Ciudad Bolivar, Venez.
Hiles, Cary	1	1	4.58	13	0	0	0	20	20	12	10	8	17	.260	R	R	5-10	170	11-29-75	1998	Memphis, Tenn.
Hutchinson, Ryan	1	1	3.18	12	1	0	0	23	25	9	8	6	15	.272	R	R	6-0	200	8-9-78	2001	Vincennes, Ind.
Jimenez, Jason	3	2	5.68	17	0	0	3	25	36	18	16	10	20	.353	R	L	6-2	200	1-10-76	1997	Elk Grove, Calif.
Lee, Seung	0	0	10.80	3	0	0	0	7	13	8	8	1	2	.433	R	R	6-4	220	6-2-79	2001	Pusan, Korea
Lundberg, Spike	1	1	2.84	12	0	0	2	13	15	7	4	6	10	.283	S	R	6-1	185	5-4-77	1997	San Diego, Calif.
Madson, Ryan	0	0	4.50	2	1	0	0	2	3	2	1	2	1	.375	R	R	6-6	180	8-28-80	1998	Moreno Valley, Calif.
Parcus, Kyle	0	1	6.75	5	0	0	0	5	8	4	4	4	2	.333	L	L	6-3	200	10-7-81	2003	Rosebud, Texas
Perez, Franklin	6	4	4.15	15	15	0	0	80	82	40	37	17	55	.271	R	R	6-2	228	6-10-78	1998	Bani, D.R.
Ramirez, Elizardo	2	5	6.68	8	8	1	0	34	51	34	25	14	20	.345	R	R	6-0	145	1-28-83	2000	Santo Domingo, D.R.
Sanches, Brian	4	2	2.71	41	0	0	3	70	55	22	21	25	60	.217	R	R	6-0	170	8-8-78	1999	Nederland, Texas
Spiegel, Mike	0	3	11.37	6	5	0	0	19	32	25	24	15	10	.386	L	L	6-5	200	11-24-75	1996	Carmichael, Calif.
Squires, Matt	0	1	3.62	26	0	0	1	32	35	17	13	15	26	.276	L	L	5-10	200	1-24-79	2001	Lewiston, Idaho
Tejeda, Robinson	8	14	5.15	27	26	0	0	150	148	93	86	59	133	.253	R	R	6-3	180	3-24-82	1999	Bani, D.R.
Villegas, Felix	3	1	3.35	31	0	0	0	48	35	19	18	28	37	.206	R	R	6-2	200	8-8-78	2000	San Juan, P.R.
Wagner, Billy	0	0	0.00	1	1	0	0	1	1	0	0	0	2	.250	L	L	5-11	195	7-25-71	1993	Charlottesville, Va.
Wolf, Randy	0	0	2.25	1	1	0	0	4	5	1	1	0	4	.333	L	L	6-0	200	8-22-76	1997	West Hills, Calif.

FIELDING

Catcher	PCT	G	PO	A	E	DP	PB
Castellano	.989	15	82	4	1	1	2
Jacobson	.980	47	282	18	6	3	3
Ruiz	.988	86	596	53	8	8	10

First Base	PCT	G	PO	A	E	DP
Barker	.991	19	102	14	1	9
Hitchcox	1.000	1	3	1	0	1
Howard	.992	97	786	53	7	75
Jacobson	.958	4	22	1	1	1
Keene	1.000	26	173	20	0	15
Walsh	1.000	2	9	0	0	1

Second Base	PCT	G	PO	A	E	DP
Hitchcox	.970	44	70	125	6	24

	PCT	G	PO	A	E	DP
Keene	.932	25	53	57	8	13
Leon	1.000	8	16	23	0	5
Phelps	.973	10	11	25	1	2
Polanco	1.000	1	1	2	0	0
Youngbauer	.967	59	126	168	10	41

Third Base	PCT	G	PO	A	E	DP
Keene	.981	27	19	33	1	5
Leon	1.000	10	5	10	0	1
Phelps	.949	51	51	134	10	15
Richardson	.853	15	12	17	5	2
Walsh	.947	30	21	50	4	3

Shortstop	PCT	G	PO	A	E	DP
Gonzalez	.945	133	199	297	29	71

	PCT	G	PO	A	E	DP
Keene	1.000	7	8	8	0	3
Leon	.975	10	21	18	1	3

Outfield	PCT	G	PO	A	E	DP
Barker	.994	79	166	7	1	2
Burrell	.923	4	12	0	1	0
Castellano	.988	46	82	3	1	1
Cosbey	.963	50	73	6	3	0
Deschaine	.991	67	97	8	1	1
Fleming	.981	106	252	6	5	4
Gibbs	1.000	3	6	0	0	0
Keene	.960	30	42	6	2	1
Perez	.976	23	39	2	1	1
Quintana	.989	51	89	1	1	0
Walsh	1.000	9	7	0	0	0

FLORIDA STATE LEAGUE

BATTING	AVG	G	AB	R	H	2B	3B	HR	RBI	BB	SO	SB	CS	OBP	SLG	B	T	HT	WT	DOB	1st Yr	Resides
Aquilino, Anthony	.260	17	50	3	13	2	1	0	1	2	13	1	1	.302	.340	R	R	5-8	180	6-23-82	1997	Pine Hill, N.J.
Barthelemy, Ryan	.297	132	475	62	141	27	4	14	77	51	93	4	6	.370	.459	L	R	6-3	220	5-19-80	2002	Miami, Fla.
Burford, Kevin	.182	32	99	14	18	5	0	1	8	16	32	1	1	.299	.263	L	L	6-1	215	11-7-77	1997	Westminster, Calif.
Castellano, John	.242	27	91	21	22	4	1	3	17	11	10	0	0	.337	.407	R	R	5-11	180	9-8-77	1998	Boynton Beach, Fla.

BATTING	AVG	G	AB	R	H	2B	3B	HR	RBI	BB	SO	SB	CS	OBP	SLG	B	T	HT	WT	DOB	1st Yr	Resides
Correll, Brad	.190	28	84	14	16	5	0	1	7	13	10	1	1	.307	.286	R	R	6-2	205	6-17-81	2002	Gastonia, N.C.
Cosbey, Chris	.216	55	167	26	36	4	2	1	19	24	26	8	2	.321	.281	L	L	5-9	160	11-14-74	1998	Arcadia, Calif.
Cruz, Edgar	.179	11	28	2	5	0	0	0	2	1	7	0	0	.207	.179	R	R	6-3	190	8-12-78	1997	Juncos, P.R.
Floyd, Mike	.261	107	349	61	91	19	5	10	39	40	98	7	6	.343	.430	R	R	6-2	180	1-15-80	2002	Severna Park, Md.
Gibbs, Kevin	.286	4	14	3	4	1	0	0	1	1	2	0	0	.333	.357	S	R	6-2	180	4-3-74	1995	Davidsonville, Md.
Gradoville, Tim	.246	63	187	18	46	10	1	4	26	12	53	0	4	.298	.374	R	R	6-3	195	1-30-80	2002	Aurora, Colo.
Guevara, Orlando	.000	2	2	0	0	0	0	0	0	0	0	0	0	.000	.000	S	R	6-1	170	9-13-83	2001	Guacara, Venez.
Hansen, Bryan	.300	3	10	1	3	1	0	0	1	1	2	0	0	.364	.400	L	L	6-2	175	5-8-83	2001	Coram, N.Y.
Harman, Brad	.000	1	0	1	0	0	0	0	0	1	0	0	0	1.000	.000	R	R	6-1	175	11-11-85	2004	Ferntree Gully, Australia
Italiano, Nick	.182	27	66	7	12	3	1	1	7	5	13	1	0	.250	.303	R	R	5-9	185	5-31-81	2003	Marlton, N.J.
Jones, Terry	.204	44	147	14	30	7	0	4	21	18	30	3	0	.300	.333	R	R	6-2	190	3-20-83	2001	Upland, Calif.
Klemm, Chris	.194	10	31	4	6	0	0	1	1	8	0	0	2	.242	.194	L	L	6-2	185	4-25-81	2003	Whittier, Calif.
Leon, Carlos	.287	48	150	27	43	8	2	1	14	15	16	7	2	.365	.387	S	R	5-10	160	8-31-79	1997	Cabimas, Venez.
Machado, Anderson	.227	7	22	0	5	0	0	0	1	4	2	0	0	.346	.227	S	R	5-11	165	1-25-81	1998	Caracas, Venez.
Pratt, Trent	.195	93	308	24	60	7	1	4	26	26	77	0	2	.265	.263	R	R	6-2	210	8-25-79	2002	Wichita, Kan.
Quintana, Miguel	.272	69	235	29	64	10	2	9	32	17	50	3	3	.320	.447	L	R	6-1	190	6-29-79	2001	Miami, Fla.
Richardson, Juan	.220	42	159	9	35	7	0	4	12	5	44	0	2	.248	.340	R	R	6-1	175	1-27-79	1999	Bani, D.R.
Roberson, Chris	.307	83	313	52	96	13	6	9	38	27	71	16	12	.371	.473	R	R	6-2	190	8-23-79	2001	San Pablo, Calif.
Roper, Zack	.121	19	58	4	7	0	1	0	0	4	14	0	0	.177	.155	R	R	6-2	200	9-26-77	2000	Pompano Beach, Fla.
2-team (4 Palm Beach)	.138	23	65	5	9	1	1	0	0	4	16	0	0	.188	.185							
Santana, Ralph	.286	87	315	43	90	13	1	0	15	24	44	11	14	.337	.333	L	R	6-1	170	9-30-80	2001	Orlando, Fla.
Santora, Jack	.236	105	322	27	76	16	2	2	28	44	51	7	9	.332	.317	S	R	5-9	160	10-6-76	1999	Monterey, Calif.
Tempesta, Nick	.230	98	317	26	73	17	0	0	22	16	57	1	3	.287	.284	R	R	5-10	180	11-20-78	2001	Brockton, Mass.
Vukovich, Vince	.167	63	186	17	31	12	1	0	21	23	36	0	2	.259	.242	L	R	6-1	200	5-6-80	2001	Voorhees, N.J.
Walsh, Sean	.196	59	184	19	36	7	0	3	25	20	39	4	3	.308	.283	R	R	6-4	220	11-15-79	2001	Aiken, S.C.

PITCHING	W	L	ERA	G	GS	CG	SV	IP	H	R	ER	BB	SO	AVG	B	T	HT	WT	DOB	1st Yr	Resides
Bourgeois, Nick	5	11	4.94	26	21	0	0	120	122	79	66	68	97	.264	L	L	6-4	210	10-26-80	2002	Lake Charles, La.
Butto, Francisco	5	11	4.85	36	14	0	2	111	112	71	60	47	94	.260	R	R	6-1	200	5-11-80	1999	Maturin, Venez.
Carlsen, Clary	0	1	5.06	3	0	0	0	5	8	7	3	2	3	.333	R	R	6-2	205	5-17-82	2004	Poulsbo, Wash.
Cerrato, Justin	1	0	2.45	2	0	0	0	4	4	1	1	1	4	.286	R	R	6-2	205	6-14-82	2003	Clearwater, Fla.
Culp, Brandon	1	3	2.64	26	3	0	0	61	54	23	18	28	45	.247	R	R	6-6	250	8-27-77	2000	Jemison, Ala.
Davis, Allen	1	0	0.00	3	1	1	0	11	8	0	0	1	10	.200	L	L	6-4	190	10-1-75	1998	Ovilla, Texas
Dawson, Layne	1	4	3.43	10	6	0	0	39	32	18	15	11	23	.219	R	R	6-2	180	9-13-79	2001	Somerville, Tenn.
Gardner, Hayden	2	4	4.97	26	0	0	6	38	37	26	21	18	28	.252	R	R	6-2	200	10-7-80	2000	Stafford, Va.
Gwaltney, Lee	3	9	3.71	19	19	1	0	112	115	50	46	35	79	.273	R	R	6-5	210	5-6-80	2002	Willow Park, Texas
Hamels, Cole	1	0	1.13	4	4	0	0	16	10	2	2	4	24	.182	L	L	6-3	175	12-27-83	2003	San Diego, Calif.
Hiles, Cary	2	2	4.67	16	0	0	0	27	31	17	14	11	26	.284	R	R	5-10	170	11-29-75	1998	Memphis, Tenn.
Hutchinson, Ryan	1	3	2.12	29	1	0	7	47	50	18	11	14	24	.279	R	R	6-2	200	8-9-78	2001	Vincennes, Ind.
Junge, Eric	0	1	6.43	5	5	0	0	14	15	12	10	5	14	.288	R	R	6-5	215	1-5-77	1999	New York, N.Y.
Mayfield, Brandon	2	2	3.80	48	0	0	1	73	97	45	31	37	35	.323	R	R	6-2	200	10-17-78	2000	Birmingham, Ala.
Mihalick, Mike	0	1	10.80	3	1	0	0	5	11	6	6	1	5	.423	R	R	6-3	210	3-22-82	2004	Nazareth, Pa.
Paddock, Josh	1	2	7.08	14	0	0	0	20	33	21	16	6	16	.344	R	R	6-2	200	10-15-80	2002	Covington, Ind.
Padilla, Vicente	0	1	9.00	1	1	0	0	2	3	2	2	1	1	.333	R	R	6-2	215	11-27-77	1999	Chinandega, Nicaragua
Ramirez, Elizardo	5	1	2.44	9	9	1	0	59	55	17	16	8	33	.249	R	R	6-0	145	1-28-83	2000	Santo Domingo, D.R.
Read, Robby	0	2	6.23	9	0	0	0	17	21	14	12	14	12	.304	R	R	6-1	190	7-12-81	2002	Tallahassee, Fla.
Reyes, Maximo	0	0	1.93	6	0	0	1	9	4	2	2	2	7	.129	R	R	5-9	170	9-24-81	2001	Clearwater, Fla.
Richardson, Beau	6	2	3.78	51	1	0	1	50	55	28	21	20	38	.281	L	L	6-2	200	9-23-79	2002	San Francisco, Calif.
Schultz, Cory	0	1	0.43	11	1	1	4	21	16	1	1	2	18	.222	R	R	6-1	205	9-26-80	2003	Dubuque, Iowa
Simon, Alfredo	7	9	3.27	22	21	3	0	135	121	58	49	38	107	.242	R	R	6-4	215	5-8-81	2000	Santiago, D.R.
Smith, Bud	0	1	3.95	5	5	0	0	14	13	6	6	5	12	.255	L	L	6-0	170	10-23-79	1998	Lakewood, Calif.
Sweeney, Matt	6	9	4.47	21	17	0	0	113	118	62	56	33	62	.274	R	R	6-2	185	2-25-83	2001	Yardville, N.J.
Wood, Brandon	0	0	3.38	3	1	0	0	5	2	2	2	2	3	.118	R	R	6-0	200	2-20-79	1999	Nacogdoches, Texas
Woodrow, C.J.	3	1	4.17	6	5	1	0	37	48	19	17	4	17	.308	R	R	6-3	200	8-21-81	2003	Plymouth, Minn.

FIELDING

Catcher	PCT	G	PO	A	E	DP	PB
Castellano	1.000	3	12	0	0	0	0
Cruz	1.000	7	31	4	0	1	0
Gradoville	.968	49	266	39	10	2	7
Guevara	1.000	2	5	2	0	0	0
Pratt	.987	84	545	53	8	7	12
Tempesta	.800	5	4	0	1	0	0

First Base	PCT	G	PO	A	E	DP
Barthelemy	.989	118	953	81	11	85
Burford	1.000	5	25	2	0	2
Castellano	1.000	7	57	4	0	8
Gradoville	1.000	1	2	0	0	1
Hansen	1.000	3	27	3	0	6
Roper	1.000	11	73	5	0	1
Walsh	1.000	1	5	0	0	1

Second Base	PCT	G	PO	A	E	DP
Aquilino	.977	13	18	24	1	6
Italiano	1.000	20	36	47	0	9
Leon	.984	25	43	79	2	18
Santana	.970	51	86	141	7	29
Santora	.988	41	58	101	2	11
Tempesta	1.000	8	5	19	0	3

Third Base	PCT	G	PO	A	E	DP
Aquilino	1.000	1	1	2	0	1
Barthelemy	.957	11	9	13	1	0
Castellano	.700	3	1	6	3	0
Jones	.891	41	23	59	10	5
Leon	1.000	4	2	7	0	2
Richardson	1.000	4	2	6	0	1
Santana	.840	7	6	15	4	0
Tempesta	.917	32	24	53	7	8
Walsh	.915	50	23	95	11	9

Shortstop	PCT	G	PO	A	E	DP
Aquilino	1.000	2	3	5	0	2
Leon	.988	20	32	52	1	7
Machado	.852	7	11	12	4	1
Santora	.945	67	102	173	16	39
Tempesta	.953	56	89	136	11	29
Walsh	1.000		0	1	0	0

Outfield	PCT	G	PO	A	E	DP
Barthelemy	.875	6	7	0	1	0
Burford	.900	5	9	0	1	0
Correll	1.000	29	43	3	0	0
Cosbey	.957	51	85	4	4	2
Floyd	.982	104	211	10	4	3
Gibbs	1.000	3	2	0	0	0
Gradoville	.900	5	8	1	1	0
Klemm	.938	7	15	0	1	0
Quintana	.986	74	130	6	2	1
Roberson	.957	81	195	6	9	2
Roper	1.000	7	10	0	0	0
Santana	1.000	23	46	7	0	0
Vukovich	1.000	50	71	5	0	0
Walsh	1.000	6	5	3	0	1

LAKEWOOD BLUECLAWS — Low Class A

SOUTH ATLANTIC LEAGUE

BATTING	AVG	G	AB	R	H	2B	3B	HR	RBI	BB	SO	SB	CS	OBP	SLG	B	T	HT	WT	DOB	1st Yr	Resides
Blalock, Jake	.271	131	517	81	140	40	2	16	90	61	126	4	3	.350	.449	R	R	6-4	215	8-6-83	2002	San Diego, Calif.
Bourn, Michael	.315	109	413	92	130	20	14	5	53	85	88	58	6	.431	.467	L	R	5-11	180	12-27-82	2003	Humble, Texas
Bramasco, Omar	.237	102	355	54	84	19	3	8	38	45	95	3	4	.332	.375	R	R	6-0	180	10-28-81	2002	Huntington Park, Calif.

BATTING	AVG	G	AB	R	H	2B	3B	HR	RBI	BB	SO	SB	CS	OBP	SLG	B	T	HT	WT	DOB	1st Yr	Resides
Cortez, Jose	.291	66	213	31	62	15	1	8	34	33	40	1	2	.390	.484	S	R	6-1	210	12-15-80	2003	Chino, Calif.
Gradoville, Tim	.145	24	62	9	9	2	1	1	9	10	24	4	1	.308	.258	R	R	6-3	195	1-30-80	2002	Aurora, Colo.
Hansen, Bryan	.273	127	462	77	126	28	5	9	59	74	65	1	3	.374	.413	L	L	6-2	175	5-8-83	2001	Coram, N.Y.
Isaacson, Greg	.125	3	8	0	1	0	0	0	2	1	0	0	0	.364	.125	L	R	6-1	205	2-18-82	2004	Aberdeen, Wash.
Italiano, Nick	.261	34	115	21	30	7	1	0	10	15	16	3	2	.353	.339	L	R	5-9	185	5-31-81	2003	Marlton, N.J.
Jarvis, Kyle	.174	12	46	5	8	3	0	0	7	6	11	1	0	.259	.239	L	L	6-5	225	9-5-80	2003	Renton, Wash.
Klemm, Chris	.304	63	204	22	62	13	2	2	33	22	51	3	2	.376	.417	L	L	6-2	185	4-25-81	2003	Whittier, Calif.
Lombardi, Mike	.200	3	10	0	2	2	0	0	1	1	2	0	0	.273	.400	R	R	6-1	190	12-14-81	2004	Brookhaven Hamlet, N.Y.
Lopez, Mauber	.100	6	20	3	2	1	0	0	2	6	2	0	0	.308	.150	R	R	5-10	170	6-30-81	2001	Carabobo, Venez.
Mader, Josh	.216	41	134	15	29	5	0	0	18	11	30	3	1	.285	.254	R	R	6-0	180	8-23-83	2004	Albuquerque, N.M.
Moni, Timi	.224	18	58	7	13	3	0	1	6	9	23	4	1	.343	.328	R	R	6-1	200	6-11-82	2002	Irvington, N.J.
Moran, Javon	.285	101	421	73	120	18	9	2	38	24	78	41	17	.340	.385	R	R	5-11	175	9-30-82	2003	Valdosta, Ga.
Moss, Tim	.256	78	273	31	70	15	1	2	28	24	75	10	8	.342	.341	R	R	5-10	175	1-26-82	2003	Lancaster, Texas
Norman, Zach	.333	12	48	10	16	3	0	5	14	2	15	2	0	.377	.708	R	R	6-0	210	1-20-82	2003	Odessa, Mo.
Rodriguez, Carlos	.268	112	440	56	118	27	2	6	57	26	68	20	10	.315	.380	S	R	6-0	170	10-4-83	2001	Santo Domingo, D.R.
Ruiz, Randy	.286	111	420	85	120	31	2	17	91	43	141	1	1	.366	.490	R	R	6-3	220	10-19-77	1999	Bronx, N.Y.
Tugwell, Marc	.286	56	203	27	58	19	0	5	33	13	30	2	3	.333	.453	R	R	6-0	190	4-16-81	2003	Springfield, Va.
Winegarden, Erik	.216	57	185	19	40	14	0	2	23	31	44	2	0	.350	.324	R	R	6-1	200	12-5-79	2002	Eden Prairie, Minn.

PITCHING	W	L	ERA	G	GS	CG	SV	IP	H	R	ER	BB	SO	AVG	B	T	HT	WT	DOB	1st Yr	Resides
Arteaga, Erick	10	9	4.81	27	26	1	0	159	207	94	85	21	87	.323	R	R	6-7	170	4-2-81	2000	Yaracuy, Venez.
Barrack, Jacob	0	0	5.51	9	0	0	0	16	17	11	10	5	14	.270	R	R	5-11	165	5-19-82	2004	Vista, Calif.
Cabrera, Nate	6	4	2.82	24	23	2	0	131	111	50	41	40	113	.230	R	R	6-5	235	1-25-83	2003	Arvada, Colo.
Cline, Zac	5	1	2.98	8	8	0	0	42	38	15	14	8	34	.238	L	L	6-3	215	7-17-83	2004	Union City, Pa.
Doble, Clemente	2	2	4.56	8	2	0	0	24	21	14	12	18	15	.256	R	R	6-2	170	1-23-82	2002	Villa Mella, D.R.
Evangelista, Nick	0	0	1.80	2	0	0	0	5	2	1	1	2	4	.125	R	R	6-4	215	3-17-82	2004	Shoemakersville, Pa.
Hodges, Daniel	2	3	2.96	31	0	0	7	46	54	16	15	10	31	.289	L	L	6-0	180	3-6-81	2003	Tallahassee, Fla.
Honsa, Chris	0	0	6.12	12	1	0	2	25	29	17	17	9	23	.276	R	R	6-3	185	8-13-83	2003	Chandler, Ariz.
Kendrick, Kyle	3	8	6.08	15	15	0	0	67	85	56	45	33	36	.313	R	R	6-3	190	8-26-84	2003	Mount Vernon, Wash.
Libey, Justin	0	0	6.52	5	0	0	0	10	13	8	7	3	4	.302	R	R	6-5	215	1-14-81	2003	Angola, Ind.
Mathieson, Scott	8	9	4.32	25	25	1	0	131	130	73	63	50	112	.254	R	R	6-3	190	2-27-84	2002	Aldergrove, B.C.
Menocal, Victor	1	4	6.33	30	0	0	2	54	66	47	38	22	28	.307	R	R	6-4	215	8-7-79	2002	Wilmington, N.C.
Overton, Brad	2	1	7.01	14	0	0	1	26	30	21	20	20	23	.291	R	R	6-2	190	4-27-81	2003	Winston-Salem, N.C.
Paddock, Josh	2	2	5.26	15	0	0	1	26	35	17	15	7	18	.315	R	R	6-2	200	10-15-80	2002	Covington, Ind.
Parcus, Kyle	4	4	3.32	41	0	0	4	76	68	34	28	17	78	.238	L	L	6-3	200	10-7-81	2003	Rosebud, Texas
Reyes, Maximo	9	3	2.31	42	0	0	10	62	50	24	16	12	67	.216	R	R	5-9	170	9-24-81	2001	Clearwater, Fla.
Schultz, Cory	3	1	2.88	29	0	0	1	59	59	22	19	15	41	.260	R	R	6-1	205	9-26-80	2003	Dubuque, Iowa
Shepard, Kevin	0	2	8.83	5	5	0	0	17	24	21	17	12	11	.323	L	L	6-0	185	6-13-83	2004	Andover, Mass.
Sweeney, Matt	0	2	7.83	5	5	0	0	23	27	22	20	12	11	.300	R	R	6-2	185	2-25-83	2001	Yardville, N.J.
Wilson, Aaron	0	4	5.85	16	0	0	0	32	38	28	21	22	22	.297	R	R	6-3	190	8-9-81	2004	San Diego, Calif.
Wilson, Joe	4	5	3.03	19	19	0	0	86	63	36	29	42	85	.205	L	L	6-3	195	8-2-82	2003	Fairfield, Conn.
Woodrow, C.J.	9	3	3.61	22	8	0	0	72	64	38	29	8	51	.229	R	R	6-3	200	8-21-81	2003	Plymouth, Minn.

FIELDING

Catcher	PCT	G	PO	A	E	DP	PB
Cortez	.983	63	379	38	7	8	10
Gradoville	.993	23	132	20	1	0	2
Lombardi	.966	3	27	1	1	0	0
Lopez	1.000	4	26	4	0	0	2
Norman	.968	4	28	4	1	2	0
Winegarden	.984	50	341	17	6	2	10

First Base	PCT	G	PO	A	E	DP
Hansen	.990	117	938	78	10	101
Jarvis	1.000	3	28	2	0	1
Ruiz	.970	18	155	8	5	15

Second Base	PCT	G	PO	A	E	DP
Bramasco	1.000	9	25	32	0	10
Isaacson	1.000	1	1	3	0	0
Italiano	.978	32	60	73	3	22
Mader	.957	10	22	23	2	8
Moss	.968	77	171	195	12	41
Tugwell	1.000	11	17	24	0	6

Third Base	PCT	G	PO	A	E	DP
Bramasco	.936	66	60	161	15	22
Isaacson	.750	2	1	2	1	0
Italiano	1.000	2	1	2	0	1
Mader	.925	27	24	50	6	6
Tugwell	.868	42	26	86	17	10

Shortstop	PCT	G	PO	A	E	DP
Bramasco	.954	26	41	84	6	14
Mader	.875	2	2	5	1	0
Rodriguez	.911	112	159	279	43	65

Outfield	PCT	G	PO	A	E	DP
Blalock	.982	126	213	9	4	3
Bourn	.979	108	228	10	5	2
Bramasco	1.000	1	5	1	0	0
Klemm	.947	62	103	4	6	0
Mader	1.000	1	2	1	0	0
Moni	.968	16	29	1	1	0
Moran	.980	101	237	2	5	1
Ruiz	1.000	8	17	1	0	1

BATAVIA MUCKDOGS — Short-Season Class A

NEW YORK-PENN LEAGUE

BATTING	AVG	G	AB	R	H	2B	3B	HR	RBI	BB	SO	SB	CS	OBP	SLG	B	T	HT	WT	DOB	1st Yr	Resides
Brant, Derek	.171	25	76	8	13	3	0	0	1	9	17	1	1	.284	.211	R	R	6-4	205	1-29-82	2004	St. Michael, Minn.
Buffone, Anthony	.202	38	129	8	26	3	1	0	8	10	12	2	4	.259	.240	B	R	6-0	185	8-9-82	2004	Manalapan, N.J.
Crosland, Jason	.183	55	208	28	38	9	1	6	22	9	90	2	0	.246	.322	R	R	6-2	215	8-30-82	2003	Lamar, Colo.
Dirnberger, Joe	.189	38	132	15	25	3	1	1	11	12	40	0	3	.267	.250	R	R	6-1	198	4-6-82	2004	Arvada, Colo.
Frith, Ryan	.243	66	255	36	62	11	2	11	41	19	86	13	3	.304	.431	R	R	6-2	185	8-17-82	2004	Baton Rouge, La.
Galloway, Carl	.210	42	157	14	33	7	1	5	15	7	49	2	2	.248	.363	R	R	6-0	215	5-8-83	2004	Carlsbad, Calif.
Gamble, Sean	.304	64	247	36	75	15	6	1	19	31	49	7	7	.383	.425	L	L	6-0	195	6-23-83	2004	Montgomery, Ala.
Hardy, John	.272	51	191	21	52	7	4	1	13	24	45	5	3	.356	.366	R	R	6-1	180	9-28-82	2004	Boise, Idaho
Isaacson, Greg	.203	58	207	17	42	13	3	2	23	16	62	3	4	.288	.324	L	R	6-1	205	2-18-82	2004	Aberdeen, Wash.
Jaramillo, Jason	.232	31	112	11	26	5	0	1	14	12	27	0	1	.307	.304	B	R	6-0	200	10-9-82	2004	Franksville, Wis.
Jarvis, Kyle	.233	9	30	4	7	1	0	1	6	8	4	0	0	.400	.367	L	L	6-5	225	9-5-80	2003	Renton, Wash.
Karlsen, Grant	.214	19	70	5	15	0	0	0	7	3	21	0	1	.263	.214	R	R	6-2	185	2-21-85	2003	Wheelers Hill, Australia
Mader, Josh	.268	12	41	7	11	0	0	1	4	5	10	5	0	.354	.341	R	R	6-0	180	8-23-83	2004	Albuquerque, N.M.
Moni, Timi	.211	21	76	12	16	1	1	2	8	6	25	5	2	.302	.329	R	R	6-1	200	6-11-82	2002	Irvington, N.J.
Norman, Zach	.242	25	95	13	23	4	2	1	8	7	23	1	4	.318	.358	R	R	6-0	210	1-20-82	2003	Odessa, Mo.
Orr, Sam	.227	57	220	15	50	8	2	5	21	12	64	4	1	.270	.350	L	R	6-2	190	6-1-83	2004	La Mirada, Calif.
Shimer, Nick	.244	64	238	30	58	8	2	3	32	38	61	6	3	.362	.361	R	R	6-2	190	10-14-81	2003	Fairfax, Va.

GAMES BY POSITION: C—Brant 24, Jaramillo 18, Karlsen 19, Norman 14. 1B—Buffone 10, Galloway 35, Jarvis 9, Norman 9, Shimer 11. 2B—Buffone 20, Hardy 9, Isaacson 42, Mader 5. 3B—Buffone 7, Dirnberger 32, Isaacson 9, Orr 27. SS—Hardy 42, Mader 7, Orr 27. OF—Crosland 34, Frith 63, Gamble 61, Moni 20, Shimer 45.

PITCHING	W	L	ERA	G	GS	CG	SV	IP	H	R	ER	BB	SO	AVG	B	T	HT	WT	DOB	1st Yr	Resides
Allen, Kyle	2	3	3.46	14	1	0	2	39	38	16	15	14	36	.255	R	L	6-0	190	7-27-83	2004	Murrieta, Calif.
Baldwin, Andy	4	6	5.17	15	15	0	0	71	96	50	41	14	54	.323	R	R	6-5	215	10-20-82	2004	Florence, Ore.
Barrack, Jacob	1	1	2.00	12	1	0	2	27	17	8	6	6	33	.179	R	R	5-11	165	5-19-82	2004	Vista, Calif.
Bisenius, Joe	0	1	1.43	11	11	0	0	50	39	12	8	14	38	.211	R	R	6-5	210	9-18-82	2004	Sioux City, Iowa
Cline, Zac	2	0	2.53	8	0	0	0	21	21	8	6	4	21	.250	L	L	6-3	215	7-17-83	2004	Union City, Pa.
Correa, Jose	3	2	5.35	22	0	0	2	37	38	28	22	15	34	.266	R	R	6-3	182	9-20-81	2004	Vineland, N.J.
Griffith, Derek	1	7	4.24	14	14	0	0	64	73	54	30	28	44	.287	L	L	6-6	205	10-28-82	2004	Arab, Ala.
Happ, J.A.	1	2	2.02	11	11	0	0	36	22	8	8	18	37	.180	L	L	6-5	202	10-19-82	2004	Peru, Ill.
Honsa, Chris	1	0	0.00	6	0	0	2	12	4	0	0	11	11	.103	R	R	6-3	185	8-13-83	2003	Chandler, Ariz.
Johnson, Nathan	2	6	4.78	18	4	0	0	53	54	38	28	11	49	.256	R	R	6-1	210	1-13-82	2004	Oskaloosa, Iowa
Kendrick, Kyle	2	8	5.48	13	12	0	0	71	94	52	43	18	53	.326	R	R	6-3	190	8-26-84	2003	Mount Vernon, Wash.
Martinez, Jason	0	2	5.80	19	3	0	0	40	56	33	26	20	27	.326	L	L	5-11	170	12-29-81	2004	Grand Junction, Calif.
Mihalik, Mike	1	0	3.60	4	0	0	1	10	6	4	4	3	9	.167	R	R	6-3	210	3-22-82	2004	Nazareth, Pa.
Overton, Brad	0	1	3.09	7	0	0	1	12	14	5	4	2	6	.304	R	R	6-2	190	4-27-81	2003	Winston-Salem, N.C.
Rose, Kevin	5	3	3.63	22	0	0	1	45	54	24	18	24	45	.290	R	R	6-2	180	1-25-82	2004	San Jose, Calif.
Santander, Nelson	3	1	5.63	17	0	0	2	24	30	16	15	9	11	.297	R	R	6-2	180	11-2-82	2001	Caracas, Venez.
Shepard, Kevin	0	1	1.29	2	2	0	0	7	9	6	1	2	4	.290	L	L	6-0	185	6-13-83	2004	Andover, Mass.
Tompkins, Jake	0	2	7.94	12	0	0	0	28	31	28	25	21	27	.277	R	R	6-0	190	3-10-80	2003	Cedar Hill, Texas
Wilson, Aaron	0	0	0.00	3	0	0	1	6	4	2	0	4	4	.167	R	R	6-3	190	8-9-81	2004	San Diego, Calif.

GCL PHILLIES — Rookie

GULF COAST LEAGUE

BATTING	AVG	G	AB	R	H	2B	3B	HR	RBI	BB	SO	SB	CS	SLG	OBP	B	T	HT	WT	DOB	1st Yr	Resides
Aquilino, Anthony	.263	22	76	14	20	4	0	2	11	9	15	2	1	.395	.364	R	R	5-8	180	6-23-82	2004	Pine Hill, N.J.
Baez, Welinson	.234	51	171	24	40	7	2	4	18	21	62	3	0	.368	.320	R	R	6-3	190	7-7-84	2003	Bani, D.R.
Cespedes, Cesar	.248	34	105	13	26	4	0	4	13	10	35	4	1	.400	.316	S	R	6-0	160	6-8-82	2002	Azua, D.R.
Cresswell, Charles	.245	16	49	4	12	1	0	0	9	4	23	0	0	.265	.309	L	R	6-3	205	7-5-85	2004	Perryton, Texas
Cuevas, Phillip	.259	27	27	3	7	0	0	0	2	0	5	0	0	.259	.259	R	R	5-11	160	6-25-85	2003	Sabana Grande de Palanque, D.R.
Deschaine, Jim	.231	3	13	2	3	1	0	1	3	0	1	0	0	.538	.231	R	R	6-0	200	9-18-77	1999	Bristol, Conn.
Galloway, Carl	.222	9	36	2	8	4	0	1	4	0	8	0	0	.417	.216	R	R	6-0	215	8-5-83	2004	Carlsbad, Calif.
Golson, Greg	.295	47	183	34	54	8	5	1	22	10	54	12	2	.410	.345	R	R	6-0	190	9-17-85	2004	Austin, Texas
Goodson, Robby	.186	30	97	12	18	1	0	4	14	15	24	2	0	.320	.292	L	R	6-3	240	4-21-82	2004	Vicksburg, Miss.
Graham, Mitch	.283	47	159	28	45	4	3	1	13	14	45	6	2	.365	.358	R	R	6-1	170	2-17-86	2004	Perth, Australia
Guevara, Orlando	.097	14	31	0	3	1	0	0	0	2	11	0	0	.129	.176	S	R	6-1	170	9-13-83	2001	Guacara, Venez.
Harman, Brad	.230	51	183	23	42	10	0	2	19	11	41	2	1	.317	.281	R	R	6-1	175	11-19-85	2004	Ferntree Gully, Australia
Jaramillo, Jason	.667	1	3	1	2	0	0	0	1	0	0	0	0	.667	.667	S	R	6-0	200	10-9-82	2004	Franksville, Wis.
Jones, Terry	.500	1	2	1	1	0	0	1	1	0	0	0	0	02.00	1.00	R	R	6-2	190	3-20-83	2001	Upland, Calif.
Leon, Carlos	.429	2	7	1	3	0	0	0	0	0	1	0	0	.429	.429	S	R	5-10	160	8-31-79	1997	Cabimas, Venez.
Lombardi, Michael	.279	26	68	12	19	6	0	1	16	9	18	0	2	.412	.364	R	R	6-1	190	12-14-81	2004	Brookhaven Hamlet, N.Y.
Macfarlane, Andrew	.229	46	166	20	38	10	2	1	19	13	36	6	0	.331	.301	R	L	5-11	190	8-18-83	2004	Fruitland, Idaho
Marson, Louis	.257	38	113	18	29	3	0	4	8	13	18	4	0	.389	.333	R	R	6-1	195	6-26-86	2004	Scottsdale, Ariz.
Mateo, Ruben	.133	5	15	2	2	0	0	0	1	4	4	0	0	.133	.188	S	R	6-1	190	8-19-84	2004	Bani, D.R.
Plumsky, R.T.	.295	35	112	20	33	6	0	6	25	17	28	5	0	.509	.394	R	R	6-0	200	1-19-84	2004	Newark, Del.
Shaw, Buck	.258	46	159	24	41	8	1	8	30	17	25	5	0	.472	.328	L	R	6-4	210	11-18-83	2004	Wagoner, Okla.
Szabo, Jordan	.200	29	90	5	18	1	0	0	7	8	14	2	1	.211	.273	R	R	6-3	195	8-24-83	2004	Oceanside, Calif.
Tugwell, Marc	.200	6	20	3	4	0	0	1	3	1	3	1	0	.350	.333	R	R	6-0	190	4-16-81	2003	Springfield, Va.
Williams, Julian	.292	12	24	1	7	0	1	0	1	2	5	1	1	.375	.333	R	R	5-11	175	7-27-83	2004	Upland, Calif.

GAMES BY POSITION: C—Creswell 11, Guevara 13, Jaramillo 1, Lombardi 22, Marson 29. **1B**—Galloway 6, Goodson 24, Harman 1, Shaw 33. **2B**—Aquilino 21, Cuevas 9, Graham 30, Leon 2, Tugwell 2. **3B**—Baez 50, Guevara 1, Harman 8, Jones 1, Shaw 1, Tugwell 2. **SS**—Baez 1, Graham 18, Harman 42. **OF**—Cespedes 30, Golson 40, Goodson 1, Macfarlane 43, Mateo 5, Plumsky 33, Shaw 28, Williams 8.

PITCHING	W	L	ERA	G	GS	CG	SV	IP	H	R	ER	BB	SO	AVG	B	T	HT	WT	DOB	1st Yr	Resides
Barb, Andrew	2	2	2.57	15	4	0	0	35	29	12	10	7	56	.211	R	R	6-3	190	10-6-84	2004	Kirkland, Wash.
Carlsen, Clary	3	0	2.86	15	0	0	1	22	18	7	7	4	24	.211	R	R	6-1	200	5-17-82	2004	Poulsbo, Wash.
Carrasco, Carlos	5	4	3.56	11	8	0	0	48	53	23	19	15	34	.276	R	R	6-3	178	3-21-87	2004	Barquisimeto, Venez.
Cerrato, Justin	0	0	0.00	2	1	0	0	3	2	0	0	0	2	.181	R	R	6-2	205	6-14-82	2003	Clearwater, Fla.
Coggin, Dave	0	0	0.00	1	0	0	0	2	0	0	0	0	3	.000	R	R	6-4	200	10-30-76	1995	Upland, Calif.
De la Cruz, Maximino	4	3	2.11	12	11	0	0	60	64	25	14	13	54	.274	R	R	6-1	160	5-29-85	2002	Santo Domingo, D.R.
DeChristofaro, Vinnie	0	0	0.00	1	0	0	0	1	0	0	0	0	1	.000	L	L	6-2	160	4-2-82	2001	Richmond Hill, Ga.
Doble, Clemente	1	0	2.45	14	0	0	5	22	18	7	6	6	15	.214	R	R	6-2	170	1-23-82	2001	Villa Mella, D.R.
Duiett, Cory	1	1	4.87	13	0	0	2	20	26	13	11	7	19	.285	R	R	6-0	212	8-16-82	2004	Hoover, Ala.
Encarnacion, Luis	0	0	6.00	5	0	0	0	6	12	11	4	5	4	.400	R	R	6-2	170	11-30-82	2002	Los Alcarrizos, D.R.
Evangelista, Nick	2	0	2.67	15	2	0	3	27	29	11	8	5	20	.278	R	R	6-4	215	3-17-82	2004	Shoemakerville, Pa.
Gazo, Lenin	3	4	4.95	11	10	0	0	44	48	32	24	16	24	.271	R	R	6-1	145	7-25-84	2004	Rivas, Nicaragua
Junge, Eric	0	1	7.36	2	2	0	0	4	6	4	3	4	4	.352	R	R	6-5	210	1-5-77	1999	New York, N.Y.
Linder, Matt	1	1	4.43	15	0	0	0	22	23	14	11	7	21	.255	R	R	6-5	195	9-15-84	2003	Thunder Bay, Ontario
Mendoza, Robert	2	2	2.51	15	0	0	1	29	28	12	8	10	28	.254	R	R	6-0	170	2-19-84	2001	Quibor Lara, Venez.
Mihalik, Mike	0	0	1.20	10	0	0	4	15	10	10	2	3	15	.181	R	R	6-3	210	3-22-82	2004	Nazareth, Pa.
Mitchinson, Scott	7	0	1.75	10	10	0	0	62	40	12	12	1	60	.181	R	R	6-3	185	12-28-84	2004	Leeming, Australia
Pichardo, Kelvin	5	5	2.79	12	11	0	0	58	41	21	18	15	62	.201	R	R	6-0	160	10-13-85	2003	Santiago, D.R.
Rosario, Jose	0	0	14.29	6	0	0	0	6	9	9	9	8	9	.375	L	L	6-1	170	10-27-82	2004	Santiago, D.R.
Tompkins, Jake	0	1	9.00	2	0	0	0	4	5	5	4	2	5	.277	R	R	6-0	190	3-10-80	2003	Cedar Hill, Texas
Wedel, Jeremy	0	0	0.00	1	1	0	0	1	0	0	0	1	1	.000	R	R	6-0	190	11-27-76	1998	Wasco, Calif.

BY JOHN PERROTTO

The Pirates began the 2004 season with seven rookies on the roster and finished with 13.

Youth was finally served in the Pirates' 12th consecutive losing season after years of trying to get by with a patchwork roster of veterans while a barren farm system was being rebuilt.

With youth comes inexperience, however, and inconsistency. The Pirates finished 72-89 and in fifth place in the six-team National League Central.

The Pirates had stretches in which they won 10 in a row, 10 of 14, nine of 11 and nine of 12. They also had stretches in which they lost nine in a row, 14 of 15, nine of 11, 14 of 18 and 21 of 25.

When it was over, the Pirates had fewer wins than the previous season for the first time in manager Lloyd McClendon's four-year tenure. The Pirates improved from 62 to 72 wins between 2001 and 2002, then increased their victory total to 75 in 2003 before dropping back to 72.

That left general manager Dave Littlefield knowing the Pirates were still not close to contending for a playoff berth.

"It's not satisfying," Littlefield said. "From our standpoint, nobody is in this thing to finish under .500. This is part of the process to get better and become a championship club. We've got a lot of work to do to become what we want to become."

McClendon, though, believes the Pirates are on track to becoming a good team. Though his team finished 17 games under .500, he felt 2004 was a season of progress.

"You're disappointed with the record, obviously," McClendon said. "I'm extremely happy with the effort and progress all these young players have made. As we move forward, it's only going to get better."

What gives the Pirates hope is that they had plenty of

Jason Bay   Zach Duke

BILL MITCHELL

PLAYERS of the YEAR

MAJOR LEAGUE: Jason Bay, of

One of the National League's leading candidates for Rookie of the Year honors, Bay exploded on the scene in 2004, hitting .282-26-82 in 411 at-bats. The 26-year-old outfielder from Trail, British Columbia, was a solid clutch hitter for the Pirates, though he struck out 129 times.

MINOR LEAGUE: Zach Duke, lhp

Duke had 17 consecutive outings in which he allowed two earned runs or less in 2004, and wound up leading the minors with a 1.46 ERA. The lefthander was named the pitcher of the year in the high A Carolina League, going 10-5, 1.39 for Lynchburg. At Double-A Altoona, Duke went 5-1, 1.58.

young players take positive steps forward.

Lefthander Oliver Perez emerged as a potentially dominating starting pitcher despite not turning 23 until late in the season. He was 12-10, 2.98, and his 239 strikeouts were the third-highest total in club history.

Left fielder Jason Bay stamped himself as a serious contender for the N.L. Rookie of the Year as he hit .282-26-82 in just 411 at bats. The 26 homers were a club rookie record and only San Francisco's Barry Bonds had more RBIs in fewer at-bats in 2004.

The Pirates acquired both Perez and Bay from San Diego in a trade for outfielder Brian Giles late in the 2003 season.

Shortstop Jack Wilson took a step toward stardom in his fourth season as he batted .308-11-59. Wilson carried a .246 lifetime batting average into the season but had 201 hits, the first 200-hit season by a Pirate since Dave Parker had 215 in 1977.

The Pirates did not quite match their success of recent years at the minor league level after having the best overall winning percentage in 2002 and sending all six farm clubs to the playoffs in 2003.

However, Pirates affiliates did combine to go 354-339, a third straight winning season after having sub-.500 marks in 32 of the previous 33 years. Low Class A Hickory won the South Atlantic League championship and Double-A Altoona lost in the Eastern League finals.

Lefthander Zach Duke and first baseman Brad Eldred had two of the best seasons in the entire minor leagues while splitting time between high Class A Lynchburg and Altoona. Duke was 15-6, 1.46 in 26 starts while Eldred hit .301-38-137 in 130 games.

ORGANIZATION LEADERS

BATTING

*AVG	Jeff Keppinger, Altoona	.337
R	Chris Truby, Nashville	96
H	Nate McLouth, Altoona	166
TB	Brad Eldred, Altoona/Lynchburg	292
2B	Chris Truby, Nashville	41
3B	Rich Thompson, Nashville	13
HR	Brad Eldred, Altoona/Lynchburg	38
RBI	Brad Eldred, Altoona/Lynchburg	137
BB	Adam Boeve, Hickory	61
SO	Brad Eldred, Altoona/Lynchburg	148
SB	Rajai Davis, Lynchburg	57
*OBP	Jon Benick, Hickory	.396
*SLG	Brad Eldred, Altoona/Lynchburg	.606

PITCHING

W	Zach Duke, Altoona/Lynchburg	15
L	John Van Benschoten, Nashville	11
#ERA	Zach Duke, Altoona/Lynchburg	1.46
G	Jeff Miller, Altoona	52
CG	Nelson Figueroa, Nashville	4
SV	Chris Hernandez, Hickory	24
IP	Nelson Figueroa, Nashville	152
BB	Josh Sharpless, Hickory	55
SO	Tom Gorzelanny, Lynchburg/Hickory	167

*Minimum 250 at-bats #Minimum 75 innings

PITTSBURGH
PIRATES

Manager: Lloyd McClendon.

BATTING	AVG	G	AB	R	H	2B	3B	HR	RBI	BB	SO	SB	CS	OBP	SLG	B	T	HT	WT	DOB	1st Yr	Resides
Alvarez, Tony	.211	24	38	5	8	2	0	1	8	4	7	0	0	.289	.342	R	R	6-1	200	5-10-79	1996	Los Teques, Venez.
Bautista, Jose	.200	23	40	1	8	2	0	0	2	18	0	0	.238	.250	R	R	6-0	190	10-19-80	2001	Santo Domingo, D.R.
Bay, Jason	.282	120	411	61	116	24	4	26	82	41	129	4	6	.358	.550	R	R	6-2	200	9-20-78	2000	Trail, B.C.
Castillo, Jose	.256	129	383	44	98	15	2	8	39	23	92	3	2	.298	.368	R	R	6-1	200	3-19-81	1998	Las Mercedes, Venez.
Cota, Humberto	.227	36	66	10	15	1	1	5	8	3	20	0	0	.271	.500	R	R	6-0	210	2-7-79	1997	San Luis, Mexico
Davis, J.J.	.143	25	35	4	5	1	0	0	3	4	10	2	0	.225	.171	R	R	6-5	240	10-25-78	1997	Charlotte, N.C.
Hill, Bobby	.266	126	233	28	62	7	2	2	27	20	39	0	3	.353	.339	S	R	5-9	180	4-3-78	2000	San Jose, Calif.
House, J.R.	.111	5	9	1	1	0	0	0	0	0	2	0	0	.111	.222	R	R	6-0	215	11-11-79	1999	Ormond Beach, Fla.
Kendall, Jason	.319	147	574	86	183	32	0	3	51	60	41	11	8	.399	.390	R	R	6-0	195	6-26-74	1992	Manhattan Beach, Calif.
Mackowiak, Rob	.246	155	491	65	121	22	6	17	75	50	114	13	4	.319	.420	L	R	5-10	195	6-20-76	1996	Sarasota, Fla.
Mateo, Ruben	.242	19	33	4	8	0	0	3	7	5	6	0	0	.359	.515	R	R	6-0	210	2-10-78	1995	San Cristobal, D.R.
Mondesi, Raul	.283	26	99	8	28	8	0	2	14	11	27	0	2	.355	.424	R	R	5-11	230	3-2-71	1990	San Cristobal, D.R.
Nunez, Abraham	.236	112	182	17	43	9	0	2	13	10	36	1	3	.275	.319	S	R	5-11	190	3-16-76	1994	Santo Domingo, D.R.
Redman, Tike	.280	155	546	65	153	19	4	8	51	23	52	18	6	.310	.374	L	L	5-11	170	3-10-77	1996	Duncanville, Ala.
Rivera, Carlos	.200	7	15	1	3	0	0	1	1	3	0	0	.250	.200	L	L	6-1	245	6-10-78	1996	Rio Grande, P.R.
Sanchez, Freddy	.158	9	19	2	3	0	0	2	0	3	0	0	.158	.158	R	R	5-11	185	12-21-77	2000	Burbank, Calif.
Simon, Randall	.194	61	175	14	34	6	0	3	14	15	17	0	0	.264	.280	L	L	6-0	240	5-26-75	1993	Willemstad, Curacao
Stynes, Chris	.216	74	162	16	35	10	0	1	16	9	23	0	0	.266	.296	R	R	5-9	205	1-19-73	1991	Deerfield Beach, Fla.
Ward, Daryle	.249	79	293	39	73	17	2	15	57	22	45	0	0	.305	.474	L	L	6-1	245	6-27-75	1994	Riverside, Calif.
Wigginton, Ty	.220	58	182	17	40	7	0	5	24	22	34	1	0	.306	.341	R	R	6-0	200	10-11-77	1998	Chula Vista, Calif.
2-team (86 New York)	.261	144	494	63	129	30	2	17	66	45	82	7	1	.324	.433							
Wilson, Craig	.264	155	561	97	148	35	5	29	82	50	169	2	2	.354	.499	R	R	6-2	220	11-30-76	1995	Huntington Beach, Calif.
Wilson, Jack	.308	157	652	82	201	41	12	11	59	26	71	8	4	.335	.459	R	R	6-0	190	12-29-77	1998	Thousand Oaks, Calif.

PITCHING	W	L	ERA	G	GS	CG	SV	IP	H	R	ER	BB	SO	AVG	B	T	HT	WT	DOB	1st Yr	Resides
Benson, Kris	4	4	4.50	11	11	1	0	68	65	37	34	17	51	.244	R	R	6-4	180	11-7-74	1997	Wexford, Pa.
Boehringer, Brian	1	1	4.62	21	0	0	0	25	27	14	13	17	20	.293	S	R	6-2	190	1-8-70	1991	Fenton, Mo.
Boyd, Jason	1	0	5.54	12	0	0	0	13	13	9	8	8	12	.260	R	R	6-3	180	2-23-73	1994	Edwardsville, Ill.
Brooks, Frank	0	1	4.67	11	1	0	0	17	13	10	9	9	18	.203	L	L	6-1	190	9-6-78	1999	Brooklyn, N.Y.
Burnett, Sean	5	5	5.02	13	13	1	0	72	86	41	40	28	30	.301	L	L	5-11	190	9-17-82	2000	Wellington, Fla.
Corey, Mark	1	2	4.54	31	0	0	0	36	39	20	18	19	28	.275	R	R	6-3	225	11-16-74	1995	Austin, Pa.
Figueroa, Nelson	0	3	5.72	10	3	0	0	28	32	18	18	11	10	.302	R	R	5-11	190	4-18-74	1995	Brooklyn, N.Y.
Fogg, Josh	11	10	4.64	32	32	0	0	178	193	98	92	66	82	.283	R	R	6-0	202	12-13-76	1998	Riverview, Fla.
Gonzalez, Mike	3	1	1.25	47	0	0	1	43	32	7	6	6	55	.201	R	L	6-2	205	5-23-78	1997	Pasadena, Texas
Grabow, John	2	5	5.11	68	0	0	1	62	81	39	35	28	64	.323	L	L	6-2	210	11-4-78	1997	San Gabriel, Calif.
Johnston, Mike	0	3	4.37	24	0	0	0	23	29	16	11	15	18	.315	L	L	6-3	200	3-30-79	1998	Colwyn, Pa.
Meadows, Brian	2	4	3.58	68	0	0	1	78	76	40	31	19	46	.259	R	R	6-4	230	11-21-75	1994	Troy, Ala.
Mesa, Jose	5	2	3.25	70	0	0	43	69	78	26	25	20	37	.291	R	R	6-3	230	5-22-66	1984	West Lake, Ohio
Perez, Oliver	12	10	2.98	30	30	2	0	196	145	71	65	81	239	.207	L	L	6-2	190	8-15-81	1999	Culiacan, Mexico
Roberts, Willis	0	0	5.25	9	0	0	0	12	12	7	7	9	7	.279	R	R	6-3	240	6-19-75	1993	San Cristobal, D.R.
Snell, Ian	0	1	7.50	3	1	0	0	12	14	10	10	9	9	.298	R	R	5-11	160	10-30-81	2000	Dover, Del.
Torres, Salomon	7	7	2.64	84	0	0	0	92	87	33	27	22	62	.256	R	R	5-11	210	3-11-72	1991	San Pedro de Macoris, D.R.
Van Benschoten, John	1	3	6.91	6	5	0	0	29	33	27	22	19	18	.300	R	R	6-4	215	4-14-80	2001	Milford, Ohio
Vogelsong, Ryan	6	13	6.50	31	26	0	0	133	148	97	96	67	92	.285	R	R	6-3	215	7-22-77	1998	Carlisle, Pa.
Wells, Kip	5	7	4.55	24	24	0	0	138	145	71	70	66	116	.270	R	R	6-3	200	4-21-77	1999	Houston, Texas
Williams, Dave	2	3	4.42	10	6	0	0	39	31	21	19	13	33	.217	L	L	6-2	210	3-12-79	1998	Tampa, Fla.

FIELDING

Catcher	PCT	G	PO	A	E	DP	PB
Cota	.991	24	101	4	1	1	0
House	1.000	3	17	0	0	0	0
Kendall	.991	146	998	78	10	13	2
Wilson	1.000	4	11	0	0	0	0

First Base	PCT	G	PO	A	E	DP
Mackowiak	.000	1	0	0	0	0
Rivera	1.000	7	35	2	0	6
Simon	.992	46	347	25	3	37
Ward	.991	71	548	34	5	73
Wilson	.994	65	460	34	3	53

Second Base	PCT	G	PO	A	E	DP
Castillo	.980	123	230	301	11	81

	PCT	G	PO	A	E	DP	PB
Hill	.994	40	70	89	1	22	
Nunez	.985	32	60	70	2	24	
Sanchez	1.000	3	3	4	0	1	

Third Base	PCT	G	PO	A	E	DP
Hill	.971	25	10	24	1	2
Mackowiak	.962	55	37	90	5	15
Nunez	.833	6	0	5	1	0
Sanchez	.000	1	0	0	0	0
Stynes	.992	71	28	89	1	9
Wigginton	.955	56	34	92	6	8

Shortstop	PCT	G	PO	A	E	DP
Castillo	.000	2	0	0	0	0
Nunez	1.000	13	10	15	0	4
Sanchez	.800	4	1	3	1	0
Wilson	.977	156	234	492	17	129

Outfield	PCT	G	PO	A	E	DP
Alvarez	1.000	16	17	0	0	0
Bautista	.864	12	19	0	3	0
Bay	.991	119	211	3	2	0
Davis	.895	17	16	1	2	0
Mackowiak	.974	118	138	9	4	3
Mateo	.933	10	13	1	1	1
Mondesi	.939	26	44	2	3	0
Redman	.986	147	338	3	5	1
Ward	1.000	12	10	0	0	0
Wilson	.977	100	167	2	4	0

ORGANIZATION STATISTICS

FARM SYSTEM

Director, Player Development: Brian Graham.

Class	Farm Team	League	W	L	Pct.	Finish*	Manager(s)	Affiliate Since
AAA	#Nashville (Tenn.) Sounds	Pacific Coast	63	79	.444	14th (16)	Trent Jewett	1998
AA	Altoona (Pa.) Curve	Eastern	85	56	.603	**1st (12)**	Tony Beasley	1999
High A	Lynchburg (Va.) Hillcats	Carolina	57	81	.413	7th (8)	Jay Loviglio/Tom Prince	1995
Low A	Hickory (N.C.) Crawdads	South Atlantic	85	55	.607	**+2nd (16)**	Dave Clark	1999
SS A	Williamsport (Pa.) Crosscutters	New York-Penn	34	40	.459	9th (14)	Jeff Branson	1999
Rookie	Bradenton (Fla.) Pirates	Gulf Coast	30	28	.517	6th (12)	Woody Huyke	1967

*Finish in overall standings (No. of teams in league)/Playoff teams in **boldface**   #Affiliate will operate in Indianapolis (International) in 2005

NASHVILLE SOUNDS
Class AAA

PACIFIC COAST LEAGUE

BATTING	AVG	G	AB	R	H	2B	3B	HR	RBI	BB	SO	SB	CS	OBP	SLG	B	T	HT	WT	DOB	1st Yr	Resides
Abad, Andy	.292	99	301	45	88	15	1	12	49	40	52	4	1	.382	.468	L	L	6-1	180	9-25-72	1993	Jupiter, Fla.
Allen, Luke	.258	122	414	53	107	18	2	17	43	33	94	3	6	.312	.435	L	R	6-2	220	8-4-78	1997	Covington, Ga.
Alvarez, Tony	.290	99	335	59	97	12	1	14	48	35	63	19	12	.365	.457	R	R	6-1	200	5-10-79	1996	Los Teques, Venez.
Bay, Jason	.400	4	10	3	4	2	0	1	3	3	5	0	0	.538	.900	R	R	6-2	200	9-20-78	2000	Trail, B.C.
Cota, Humberto	.259	8	27	4	7	0	0	1	2	3	7	0	0	.333	.370	R	R	6-0	210	2-7-79	1997	San Luis, Mexico
Davis, J.J.	.250	27	84	11	21	6	1	8	17	3	28	3	0	.270	.631	R	R	6-5	240	10-25-78	1997	Charlotte, N.C.
de la Rosa, Tomas	.283	63	173	22	49	6	2	7	29	16	34	3	0	.339	.462	R	R	5-10	185	12-28-78	1996	Santo Domingo, D.R.
Figueroa, Luis	.297	102	316	39	94	13	1	6	43	25	37	2	2	.355	.402	R	R	6-0	170	3-2-77	1995	Carolina, P.R.
House, J.R.	.288	92	309	38	89	21	1	15	49	23	72	1	1	.344	.508	R	R	6-0	215	11-11-79	1999	Ormond Beach, Fla.
Mateo, Ruben	.316	35	114	21	36	12	0	11	25	12	33	2	2	.391	.711	R	R	6-0	210	2-10-78	1995	San Cristobal, D.R.
McDonald, Keith	.255	92	274	29	70	16	0	6	30	34	58	1	2	.342	.380	R	R	6-2	230	2-8-73	1994	Anaheim Hills, Calif.
Moriarty, Mike	.216	97	259	32	56	15	4	6	22	33	71	7	3	.318	.375	R	R	6-0	180	3-8-74	1995	Mount Laurel, N.J.
Olszta, Eddie	.118	16	17	2	2	0	0	0	4	4	8	0	1	.286	.118	R	R	5-10	180	3-8-79	2001	New Lenox, Ill.
Rivera, Carlos	.292	93	312	46	91	19	0	17	50	24	54	6	7	.348	.516	L	L	6-1	245	6-10-78	1996	Rio Grande, P.R.
Sanchez, Freddy	.264	44	125	10	33	7	1	1	11	11	17	4	1	.326	.360	R	R	5-11	185	12-21-77	2000	Burbank, Calif.
Sheldon, Scott	.221	34	113	8	25	7	0	2	13	12	33	0	0	.241	.336	R	R	6-3	215	11-20-68	1991	Pearland, Texas
Shumpert, Terry	.256	69	211	41	54	15	1	11	36	23	38	3	1	.342	.493	R	R	6-0	200	8-16-66	1987	Lone Tree, Colo.
Simon, Randall	.266	17	64	5	17	4	0	1	6	2	8	1	0	.294	.375	L	L	6-0	240	5-26-75	1993	Willemstad, Curacao
Skrehot, Shaun	.293	39	116	18	34	7	0	5	15	10	21	5	2	.364	.483	R	R	5-10	180	12-5-75	1998	Spring, Texas
Snusz, Chris	.267	9	15	2	4	1	0	0	1	1	1	0	0	.313	.333	R	R	6-0	210	11-8-72	1995	West Seneca, N.Y.
Thompson, Rich	.287	112	411	73	118	7	13	5	36	26	62	41	15	.348	.404	L	R	6-3	180	4-23-79	2000	Montrose, Pa.
Truby, Chris	.300	130	466	96	140	41	2	25	83	47	96	11	2	.367	.558	R	R	6-2	215	12-9-73	1993	Noblesville, Ind.
Ward, Daryle	.281	28	96	14	27	7	0	7	17	5	16	0	0	.317	.573	L	L	6-1	245	6-27-75	1994	Riverside, Calif.

PITCHING	W	L	ERA	G	GS	CG	SV	IP	H	R	ER	BB	SO	AVG	B	T	HT	WT	DOB	1st Yr	Resides
Acevedo, Juan	0	4	9.00	18	0	0	1	23	38	23	23	10	18	.365	R	R	6-2	245	5-5-70	1992	Algonquin, II
Almonte, Hector	1	1	7.74	29	2	0	0	43	50	38	37	28	36	.291	R	R	6-2	190	10-17-75	1994	Santo Domingo, D.R.
Boyd, Jason	1	1	3.86	11	0	0	0	16	23	7	7	3	11	.333	R	R	6-3	180	2-23-73	1994	Edwardsville, Ill.
Brooks, Frank	6	3	4.10	42	8	0	2	83	81	42	38	22	55	.255	L	L	6-1	190	9-6-78	1999	Brooklyn, N.Y.
Burnett, Sean	1	5	5.36	10	10	0	0	47	58	29	28	17	25	.310	L	L	5-11	190	9-17-82	2000	Wellington, Fla.
Corey, Mark	1	4	4.42	34	0	0	16	39	40	21	19	15	39	.265	R	R	6-3	225	11-16-74	1995	Austin, Penn.
Crudale, Mike	0	1	9.00	5	0	0	0	7	8	7	7	4	5	.286	R	R	6-0	200	1-3-77	1999	Danville, Calif.
2-team (4 Fresno)	0	1	12.15	9	0	0	0	13	21	20	18	5	8	.356							
Figueroa, Nelson	12	8	4.19	25	23	4	0	152	168	79	71	36	129	.279	R	R	6-1	170	5-18-74	1995	Brooklyn, N.Y.
Fussell, Chris	2	5	4.97	51	1	0	2	67	73	39	37	32	50	.281	R	R	6-2	200	5-19-76	1994	Oregon, Ohio
Gonzalez, Mike	2	0	0.90	14	0	0	2	20	12	2	2	7	35	.185	R	L	6-2	205	5-23-78	1997	Pasadena, Texas
Hackman, Luther	1	5	5.36	37	0	0	1	44	42	29	26	15	45	.253	R	R	6-4	195	10-10-74	1994	Columbus, Miss.
Izquierdo, Hansel	1	1	4.26	5	4	0	0	19	24	10	9	4	20	.308	R	R	6-1	200	1-2-77	1995	Miami, Fla.
2-team (15 Iowa)	1	1	5.66	26	5	0	1	49	57	33	31	22	44	.288							
Jarvis, Kevin	2	5	4.11	11	11	1	0	66	93	31	30	12	46	.338	L	R	6-2	200	8-1-69	1991	Lexington, Ky.
2-team (6 Colo. Springs)	2	9	4.72	17	17	2	0	103	137	65	54	22	71	.322							
Johnston, Mike	0	0	8.40	19	0	0	0	15	19	14	14	13	6	.306	L	L	6-3	200	3-30-79	1998	Colwyn, Pa.
Mahomes, Pat	2	4	5.77	24	2	0	2	34	36	23	22	14	31	.273	R	R	6-4	220	8-9-70	1988	Lindale, Texas
3-team (20 Edm./16 Alb.)	6	12	5.90	60	2	0	8	79	92	56	52	37	65	.293							
Mann, Jim	1	3	11.47	20	0	0	0	24	40	32	31	9	25	.370	R	R	6-3	200	11-17-74	1994	Holbrook, Mass.
Martin, Greg	0	1	7.50	5	1	0	0	12	15	10	10	7	7	.319	L	L	6-1	190	4-10-80	2002	Scranton, Pa.
Mottl, Ryan	2	0	3.86	2	2	0	0	12	12	6	5	2	9	.255	S	R	6-3	200	12-9-77	2000	Florissant, Mo.
Reid, Justin	5	3	3.96	32	16	0	2	123	112	56	54	35	121	.246	R	R	6-5	210	6-30-77	1999	Folsom, Calif.
Roberts, Willis	6	3	5.87	35	0	0	5	38	45	26	25	13	32	.298	R	R	6-3	240	6-19-75	1993	San Cristobal, D.R.
Stein, Blake	0	1	10.24	8	0	0	0	10	14	11	11	9	7	.350	R	R	6-7	240	8-3-73	1994	Folsom, La.
Stewart, Cory	7	6	5.13	18	18	0	0	93	112	59	53	47	53	.302	L	L	6-4	180	11-14-79	1999	Boerne, Texas
Van Benschoten, John	4	11	4.72	23	23	0	0	132	135	75	69	49	101	.261	R	R	6-4	215	4-14-80	2001	Milford, Ohio
Williams, Dave	6	2	3.47	21	21	0	0	117	113	52	45	33	103	.252	L	L	6-2	210	3-12-79	1998	Tampa, Fla.

FIELDING

Catcher	PCT	G	PO	A	E	DP	PB
Cota	1.000	7	43	7	0	1	0
House	.993	63	428	29	3	1	6
McDonald	.997	80	546	33	2	8	4
Olszta	1.000	3	4	0	0	0	0
Snusz	1.000	6	16	0	0	0	1

	PCT	G	PO	A	E	DP	PB
House	.992	19	120	1	1	8	
Rivera	.992	76	574	30	5	56	
Sheldon	1.000	9	39	9	0	5	
Simon	1.000	11	76	6	0	9	
Truby	.976	22	148	14	4	8	
Ward	1.000	22	164	14	0	15	

	PCT	G	PO	A	E	DP	PB
Moriarty	1.000	49	71	100	0	27	
Sanchez	.989	25	40	49	1	11	
Sheldon	.941	7	7	9	1	3	
Shumpert	.981	45	82	128	4	26	
Skrehot	1.000	1	1	2	0	1	
Truby	.993	38	64	78	1	18	

First Base	PCT	G	PO	A	E	DP
Abad	.983	9	54	5	1	8

Second Base	PCT	G	PO	A	E	DP
de la Rosa	.978	15	14	30	1	6

Third Base	PCT	G	PO	A	E	DP
Allen	.882	8	3	12	2	0

	PCT	G	PO	A	E	DP
Figueroa	.948	80	43	123	9	10
Sheldon	.909	5	2	8	1	0
Truby	.961	79	54	142	8	18

Shortstop	PCT	G	PO	A	E	DP
de la Rosa	.922	46	52	101	13	10
Moriarty	.990	53	63	135	2	29
Sanchez	.968	9	10	20	1	6
Sheldon	.750	2	1	2	1	1

Outfield	PCT	G	PO	A	E	DP
Abad	.992	78	125	2	1	0
Allen	.974	120	216	7	6	2
Alvarez	.980	102	138	6	3	0
Bay	1.000	3	3	0	0	0

	PCT	G	PO	A	E	DP
Shumpert	1.000	7	8	19	0	3
Skrehot	.955	38	51	99	7	24
Truby	.966	6	12	16	1	5

	PCT	G	PO	A	E	DP
Davis	1.000	21	31	1	0	1
House	1.000	5	5	1	0	0
Mateo	.981	32	50	1	1	1
Olszta	1.000	4	4	0	0	0
Rivera	.947	14	18	0	1	0
Sheldon	1.000	15	20	0	0	0
Shumpert	.000	3	0	0	1	0
Thompson	.974	109	253	5	7	0
Ward	1.000	2	1	0	0	0

ALTOONA CURVE Class AA

EASTERN LEAGUE

BATTING

BATTING	AVG	G	AB	R	H	2B	3B	HR	RBI	BB	SO	SB	CS	OBP	SLG	B	T	HT	WT	DOB	1st Yr	Resides
Bonifay, Josh	.277	96	343	52	95	16	0	19	76	40	96	5	1	.360	.490	R	R	6-0	187	7-30-78	1999	Bradenton, Fla.
Chaves, Brandon	.231	40	104	16	24	2	3	1	15	19	19	2	0	.354	.337	S	R	6-3	180	8-5-79	2000	Hilo, Hawaii
Cockrell, Mike	.154	8	13	0	2	0	0	0	1	0	4	0	0	.143	.154	R	R	5-10	160	7-25-81	2001	Wilmington, Calif.
Cortes, Jorge	.288	38	139	17	40	8	1	6	19	13	24	0	1	.344	.489	L	L	6-0	180	10-17-80	1998	Barranquilla, Colombia
De la Rosa, Tomas	.333	8	18	3	6	1	0	1	4	1	2	1	1	.368	.556	R	R	5-10	185	1-28-78	1996	Santo Domingo, D.R.
DeCaster, Yurendell	.274	96	328	53	90	18	1	14	40	22	78	4	2	.328	.463	R	R	6-1	200	9-26-79	1997	Willemstad, Curacao
Doumit, Ryan	.262	67	221	31	58	20	0	10	34	21	49	0	1	.343	.489	S	R	6-0	190	4-3-81	1999	Moses Lake, Wash.
Duffy, Chris	.309	113	453	84	140	23	6	8	41	33	77	32	8	.378	.439	L	L	5-10	175	4-20-80	2001	Glendale, Ariz.
Eldred, Brad	.279	39	147	24	41	9	0	17	60	6	51	0	0	.329	.687	R	R	6-5	274	7-12-80	2002	Coconut Creek, Fla.
Evans, Tom	.308	33	120	25	37	9	1	4	22	18	20	4	1	.404	.500	R	R	6-1	200	7-9-74	1992	Issaquah, Wash.
Keppinger, Jeff	.337	81	315	44	106	17	2	1	33	27	15	10	5	.387	.413	R	R	6-0	180	4-21-80	2002	Auburn, Ga.
McLouth, Nate	.322	133	515	93	166	40	4	8	73	48	62	31	7	.384	.462	L	R	5-11	170	10-28-81	2001	Whitehall, Mich.
Mendez, Donaldo	.132	23	76	7	10	5	0	0	3	6	22	0	1	.241	.197	R	R	6-2	180	6-7-78	1996	Barquisimeto, Venez.
Moriarty, Mike	.303	20	66	17	20	9	0	0	6	11	13	1	0	.432	.439	R	R	6-0	190	3-8-74	1995	Mount Laurel, N.J.
Navarrete, Ray	.238	49	130	15	31	5	1	2	17	8	20	0	0	.304	.338	R	R	6-0	190	5-20-78	2000	Colts Neck, N.J.
Nicholson, Kevin	.215	78	261	28	56	13	2	4	36	23	37	2	0	.277	.326	S	R	5-10	190	3-29-76	1997	Surrey, B.C.
Paulino, Ronny	.285	98	365	54	104	23	2	15	58	32	61	3	2	.345	.482	R	R	6-3	210	4-21-81	1998	Santo Domingo, D.R.
Pena, Rudy	.500	1	4	0	2	0	0	0	0	1	0	0	0	.500	.500	R	R	6-0	219	3-7-79	1996	Monte Cristi, D.R.
Sadler, Ray	.266	119	428	60	114	24	1	20	72	23	89	16	6	.306	.467	R	R	6-1	200	9-19-80	2000	Waco, Texas
Sheldon, Scott	.183	18	60	5	11	2	0	1	9	6	14	1	0	.257	.267	R	R	6-3	215	11-20-68	1991	Pearland, Texas
Skrehot, Shaun	.263	67	243	33	64	12	1	1	16	15	24	5	2	.322	.333	R	R	5-10	180	12-5-75	1998	Spring, Texas
Snusz, Chris	.183	36	120	11	22	4	1	0	6	9	29	0	0	.246	.233	R	R	6-0	210	11-8-72	1995	West Seneca, N.Y.
Thomas, Gary	.228	29	92	13	21	8	2	2	8	9	14	0	0	.304	.424	R	R	5-7	175	9-6-79	1997	Houma, La.

PITCHING

PITCHING	W	L	ERA	G	GS	CG	SV	IP	H	R	ER	BB	SO	AVG	B	T	HT	WT	DOB	1st Yr	Resides
Agamennone, Brandon	3	1	4.54	19	0	0	0	34	35	18	17	11	36	.257	R	R	6-2	190	11-6-75	1998	Crofton, Md.
Alcala, Jason	1	0	0.00	1	0	0	0	3	2	0	0	3	.167	R	R	6-2	210	9-18-80	1998	Cumana, Venez.
Bimeal, Matt	1	0	12.27	3	0	0	0	4	7	5	5	0	5	.438	R	R	6-3	225	8-17-80	2000	Davidsville, Pa.
Borner, Brady	5	6	5.55	38	9	0	1	97	116	75	60	30	60	.293	L	L	5-10	192	4-12-79	2001	Chaska, Minn.
Bradley, Bobby	5	4	3.11	19	19	0	0	101	85	42	35	41	78	.229	R	R	6-1	180	12-15-80	1999	Wellington, Fla.
Bullington, Bryan	12	7	4.10	26	26	0	0	145	160	77	66	47	100	.283	R	R	6-5	220	9-30-80	2003	Indianapolis, Ind.
Candelario, Eddie	0	1	4.84	21	0	0	2	35	31	21	19	17	34	.233	R	R	6-0	176	1-5-80	1998	La Carmelita, D.R.
2-team (16 Reading)	0	4	6.12	37	0	4	2	72	76	54	49	40	55	.270							
Connolly, Mike	8	6	4.39	20	20	0	0	111	118	58	54	39	102	.270	L	L	6-0	180	6-2-82	2000	Oneonta, N.Y.
Crudale, Mike	1	0	5.67	23	0	0	2	33	35	23	21	22	24	.271	R	R	6-0	200	1-3-77	1999	Danville, Calif.
Duke, Zach	5	1	1.58	9	9	0	0	51	41	11	9	10	36	.227	L	L	6-2	207	4-19-83	2002	Waco, Texas
Harts, Jeremy	0	2	5.28	9	0	0	1	15	12	12	9	13	10	.222	S	L	6-1	219	6-6-80	1998	Decatur, Ga.
Jacobsen, Landon	5	2	4.99	15	14	0	0	70	83	46	39	23	47	.291	R	R	6-3	215	5-4-79	2000	Canova, S.D.
Lorraine, Andrew	0	0	0.00	6	0	0	0	7	4	0	0	1	7	.167	L	L	6-3	200	8-11-72	1993	Scottsdale, Ariz.
Lundquist, Dave	3	2	5.75	15	0	0	0	20	21	13	13	8	15	.273	R	R	6-2	200	6-4-73	1993	Hickory, N.C.
McDade, Neal	8	1	3.36	32	7	0	1	86	70	35	32	26	53	.227	R	R	6-2	205	6-16-76	1996	Orange Park, Fla.
Miller, Jeff	5	4	2.91	52	0	0	18	68	48	25	22	28	79	.198	R	R	6-4	220	2-1-80	2001	Springfield, N.J.
O'Brien, Patrick	1	0	0.00	2	0	0	0	4	1	0	0	3	1	.071	R	R	6-4	200	11-20-80	2000	Bath, Ohio
Peterson, Matt	3	2	6.25	7	7	0	0	36	36	25	25	22	29	.269	R	R	6-5	210	2-11-82	2001	Alexandria, La.
2-team (19 Binghamton)	9	6	4.03	26	25	0	0	141	133	69	63	67	119	.257							
Reid, Justin	0	1	9.00	1	1	0	0	3	6	4	3	1	3	.400	R	R	6-5	210	6-30-77	1999	Folsom, Calif.
Serrano, Elio	3	5	5.73	44	0	0	14	55	73	44	35	15	37	.323	R	R	6-3	210	12-4-78	1996	Valencia, Venez.
Shaffar, Ben	0	1	7.40	8	2	0	0	21	28	20	17	10	23	.318	S	R	6-3	190	9-28-77	1999	Leitchfield, Ky.
Snell, Ian	11	7	3.16	26	26	3	0	151	147	54	53	40	142	.259	R	R	5-11	160	10-30-81	2000	Dover, Del.
Stein, Blake	5	2	3.52	36	0	0	7	61	51	27	24	25	62	.222	R	R	6-7	240	8-3-73	1994	Folsom, La.

FIELDING

Catcher	PCT	G	PO	A	E	DP	PB
Doumit	.983	25	159	14	3	2	3
Paulino	.986	80	585	52	9	2	9
Pena	1.000	1	10	2	0	0	0
Snusz	.984	36	228	23	4	3	1

First Base	PCT	G	PO	A	E	DP
Bonifay	.993	73	546	50	4	47
DeCaster	.980	6	44	5	1	4
Eldred	.994	38	331	17	2	34
Navarrete	.993	20	145	6	1	10
Paulino	.985	8	60	6	1	6

Second Base	PCT	G	PO	A	E	DP
Keppinger	.982	60	142	193	6	31
Mendez	.953	16	31	51	4	10
Moriarty	.986	15	25	48	1	12

	PCT	G	PO	A	E	DP
Navarrete	.952	17	22	38	3	7
Nicholson	.957	12	12	32	2	8
Sheldon	.975	7	16	23	1	4
Skrehot	1.000	4	11	13	0	4

Third Base	PCT	G	PO	A	E	DP
Cockrell	.500	3	0	1	1	0
DeCaster	.919	85	69	123	17	16
Evans	.951	30	23	55	4	7
Navarrete	1.000	4	0	3	0	0
Nicholson	.891	25	11	30	5	4
Sheldon	1.000	3	3	3	0	1

Shortstop	PCT	G	PO	A	E	DP
Chaves	.952	40	53	85	7	18
Cockrell	.917	6	5	6	1	0

	PCT	G	PO	A	E	DP
De la Rosa	.692	7	4	5	4	0
Mendez	.905	5	8	11	2	5
Moriarty	1.000	5	8	16	0	3
Nicholson	.923	30	31	53	7	11
Skrehot	.980	62	79	163	5	38

Outfield	PCT	G	PO	A	E	DP
Bonifay	1.000	11	19	1	0	0
Cortes	.988	37	78	1	1	0
DeCaster	1.000	8	4	0	0	0
Duffy	.993	113	289	8	2	2
McLouth	.969	130	250	3	8	0
Sadler	.979	117	216	12	5	1
Sheldon	1.000	5	6	1	0	0
Thomas	1.000	25	52	1	0	0

CAROLINA LEAGUE

BATTING	AVG	G	AB	R	H	2B	3B	HR	RBI	BB	SO	SB	CS	OBP	SLG	B	T	HT	WT	DOB	1st Yr	Resides
Asprilla, Avelino	.283	121	452	50	128	22	3	9	53	21	81	6	4	.318	.405	R	R	5-11	170	1-1-81	1999	Panama City, Panama
Buttler, Vic	.241	101	365	36	88	19	5	5	37	23	61	8	3	.286	.362	L	L	6-0	170	8-12-80	2000	Hawthorne, Calif.
Chapman, Travis	.167	14	54	3	9	1	0	0	3	2	13	0	0	.196	.185	R	R	6-1	190	9-6-80	2001	Ft. Walton Beach, Fla.
Cortes, Jorge	.292	70	260	32	76	20	1	5	36	37	48	1	2	.385	.435	L	L	6-0	180	10-17-80	1998	Barranquilla, Colombia
Davis, Rajai	.314	127	509	91	160	27	7	5	38	59	60	57	15	.388	.424	S	R	5-11	188	10-19-80	2001	New London, Conn.
Eldred, Brad	.310	91	335	54	104	22	1	21	77	35	97	5	2	.397	.570	R	R	6-5	274	7-12-80	2002	Coconut Creek, Fla.
Hernandez, Jose	.200	64	215	16	43	5	0	0	11	14	35	0	2	.251	.223	R	R	6-0	165	11-3-80	1998	Valencia, Venez.
Herrera, Christian	.198	24	86	15	17	7	0	0	5	8	21	1	0	.268	.279	R	R	5-11	169	4-9-82	2000	Aguascalientes, Mexico
Lee, Taber	.248	93	315	38	78	11	2	3	37	48	71	11	9	.355	.324	S	R	6-1	180	10-18-80	2002	Olympia, Wash.
Lytle, Chaz	.277	99	354	37	98	14	2	0	24	18	54	22	8	.319	.328	L	L	6-0	190	10-27-80	2002	Lake Mary, Fla.
Macia, Wanell	.125	3	8	0	1	1	0	0	0	1	3	0	0	.222	.250	L	L	5-11	183	7-20-82	2001	La Romana, D.R.
Meath, Matt	.286	61	175	27	50	11	4	2	24	28	58	8	6	.386	.429	S	R	6-0	170	10-6-79	2001	Boca Raton, Fla.
Mercedes, Victor	.275	128	484	55	133	24	7	8	62	33	101	29	15	.324	.403	R	R	5-11	175	4-15-79	2000	Santo Domingo, D.R.
Navarrete, Ray	.300	62	247	29	74	11	1	8	46	9	37	0	1	.327	.449	R	R	6-0	190	5-20-78	2000	Colts Neck, N.J.
Newman, Ryan	.182	56	159	13	29	2	0	1	10	10	45	1	2	.229	.214	R	R	5-11	160	2-25-79	2002	Scottsdale, Ariz.
Nino, Denny	.200	25	70	5	14	2	1	0	2	3	14	0	0	.243	.257	R	R	6-1	200	6-4-83	2001	Caracas, Venez.
Olszta, Eddie	.125	7	16	0	2	1	0	0	2	3	11	1	0	.238	.188	R	R	5-10	180	3-8-79	2001	New Lenox, Ill.
Pena, Rudy	.171	40	123	5	21	2	0	2	9	2	23	0	1	.197	.236	R	R	6-0	219	3-7-79	1996	Monte Cristi, D.R.
Powell, Pedro	.344	8	32	9	11	2	0	0	2	2	4	8	2	.382	.406	R	R	5-7	150	5-20-84	2003	Hawkinsville, Ga.
Ravelo, Manny	.261	17	46	6	12	2	0	0	4	9	13	4	6	.393	.304	R	R	5-10	160	8-8-79	1998	Santo Domingo, D.R.
Rosamond, Mike	.216	37	134	16	29	10	0	1	13	7	37	2	1	.254	.313	R	R	6-5	230	4-18-78	1999	Madison, Miss.
Smith, Sean	.261	6	23	1	6	1	0	0	0	1	6	1	1	.292	.304	R	R	6-0	192	8-24-82	2000	Joliet, Ill.
Voshell, Chase	.201	58	164	16	33	8	0	2	16	18	46	2	0	.285	.287	R	R	6-2	185	3-29-77	2001	Milford, Ohio

PITCHING	W	L	ERA	G	GS	CG	SV	IP	H	R	ER	BB	SO	AVG	B	T	HT	WT	DOB	1st Yr	Resides
Albaladejo, Jonathan	8	8	4.33	24	24	1	0	131	150	72	63	25	92	.286	R	R	6-5	249	10-30-82	2001	Vega Alta, P.R.
Alcala, Jason	1	3	2.57	23	0	0	5	42	33	13	12	10	37	.214	R	R	6-2	210	9-18-80	1998	Cumana, Venez.
Alvarez, Basilio	0	0	5.40	2	2	0	0	10	12	6	6	5	6	.293	R	R	6-3	160	1-2-84	2001	San Pedro de Macoris, D.R.
Bimeal, Matt	0	0	3.38	4	0	0	0	8	8	3	3	1	7	.258	R	R	6-3	225	8-17-80	2000	Davidsville, Pa.
Candelario, Eddie	1	2	4.64	4	4	0	0	21	17	11	11	7	21	.215	R	R	6-0	176	1-5-80	1998	La Carmelita, D.R.
Davila, Marcus	5	9	4.39	51	0	0	8	84	89	49	41	27	43	.271	R	R	6-1	190	8-14-81	2002	Key West, Fla.
Duke, Zach	10	5	1.39	17	17	1	0	97	73	24	15	20	106	.207	L	L	6-2	207	4-19-83	2002	Waco, Texas
Gorzelanny, Tom	3	5	4.85	10	10	0	0	56	54	31	30	19	61	.255	L	L	6-2	202	7-12-82	2003	Orland Park, Ill.
Gravelle, Nick	5	10	3.62	26	25	1	0	152	157	70	61	45	109	.274	L	L	6-4	190	2-14-80	2002	Kelso, Wash.
Guerrero, Julio	4	8	5.63	33	12	1	1	96	125	64	60	19	59	.316	R	R	6-4	180	1-4-81	1999	San Pedro de Macoris, D.R.
Hart, Alex	0	1	3.63	3	0	0	0	15	16	12	6	8	7	.271	R	R	6-6	210	1-10-80	2002	Indian Harbor Beach, Fla.
Harts, Jeremy	0	0	8.68	10	0	0	0	9	11	9	9	14	7	.297	S	L	6-1	219	6-6-80	1998	Decatur, Ga.
Higgins, Josh	1	5	2.77	37	0	0	12	49	44	20	15	11	33	.235	R	R	6-5	180	6-19-79	2000	Santee, Calif.
Johnson, Russell	0	1	10.32	3	3	0	0	11	18	14	13	3	11	.360	L	R	6-2	200	1-6-85	2003	Alexander City, Ala.
Lord, Justin	2	2	2.96	14	2	0	0	24	24	11	8	11	19	.250	R	R	6-4	210	11-15-79	2001	Marianna, Fla.
Maholm, Paul	1	3	1.84	8	8	0	0	44	39	11	9	15	28	.236	L	L	6-2	215	6-25-82	2003	Holly Springs, Miss.
Martin, Greg	2	1	3.00	25	0	0	0	45	32	18	15	30	25	.203	L	L	6-1	190	4-10-80	2002	Scranton, Pa.
Michael, Mark	0	3	3.41	7	4	0	0	29	24	15	11	12	20	.216	R	R	6-3	185	1-20-81	2003	Lexington, Ky.
Mottl, Ryan	2	5	6.15	12	11	0	0	53	68	43	36	21	38	.309	S	R	6-3	200	12-9-77	2000	Florissant, Mo.
Newman, Ryan	0	0	0.00	1	0	0	0	1	0	0	0	0	0	.500	R	R	5-11	160	2-25-79	2002	Scottsdale, Ariz.
O'Brien, Patrick	4	4	4.47	25	13	0	0	93	100	47	46	26	58	.279	R	R	6-4	200	11-20-80	2000	Bath, Ohio
Owens, Henry	3	4	4.28	39	0	0	4	55	46	26	26	26	49	.236	R	R	6-3	230	4-23-79	2001	Miami, Fla.
Sharber, Jason	1	0	5.06	5	0	0	1	11	7	7	6	5	6	.175	R	R	6-3	220	2-24-82	2001	Murfreesboro, Tenn.
Youman, Shane	4	2	3.16	47	0	0	2	74	67	28	26	35	62	.242	L	L	6-4	217	10-11-79	2002	New Iberia, La.

FIELDING

Catcher	PCT	G	PO	A	E	DP	PB
Chapman	1.000	14	87	16	0	0	3
Hernandez	.986	63	387	42	6	3	11
Nino	.981	25	143	12	3	1	7
Olszta	1.000	7	54	6	0	1	2
Pena	.993	40	245	22	2	0	11

First Base	PCT	G	PO	A	E	DP
Eldred	.988	89	795	57	10	64
Navarrete	.989	45	409	26	5	33
Voshell	1.000	7	42	4	0	3

Second Base	PCT	G	PO	A	E	DP
Asprilla	1.000	2	3	5	0	2

	PCT	G	PO	A	E	DP
Herrera	1.000	4	3	9	0	1
Mercedes	.970	127	262	380	20	92
Newman	1.000	11	14	25	0	0

Third Base	PCT	G	PO	A	E	DP
Asprilla	.953	119	79	246	16	21
Navarrete	.889	7	4	12	2	1
Newman	.923	13	6	30	3	4
Voshell	1.000	10	3	11	0	0

Shortstop	PCT	G	PO	A	E	DP
Herrera	.958	19	25	43	3	7
Lee	.953	93	167	280	22	51
Newman	.925	30	41	58	8	12

Outfield	PCT	G	PO	A	E	DP
Buttler	.976	96	157	7	4	2
Cortes	.911	56	104	4	10	1
Davis	.968	119	232	8	8	1
Lytle	.987	82	148	0	2	0
Macia	.600	3	3	0	2	0
Meath	.969	29	31	0	1	0
Powell	.944	7	16	1	1	0
Rosamond	.979	25	44	2	1	0
Smith	1.000	6	8	0	0	0
Voshell	.750	5	3	0	1	0

SOUTH ATLANTIC LEAGUE

BATTING	AVG	G	AB	R	H	2B	3B	HR	RBI	BB	SO	SB	CS	OBP	SLG	B	T	HT	WT	DOB	1st Yr	Resides
Benick, Jon	.328	130	488	76	160	29	2	32	104	53	95	2	2	.396	.592	S	R	6-1	210	9-26-79	2001	Glen Lyon, Pa.
Bocchino, Anthony	.252	69	218	34	55	9	2	4	31	25	38	2	0	.336	.367	L	L	5-10	180	5-15-80	2002	Brooklyn, N.Y.
Boeve, Adam	.290	130	459	93	133	25	2	28	93	61	112	10	2	.385	.536	R	R	6-1	205	6-20-80	2003	Doon, Iowa
Chapman, Travis	.238	31	105	14	25	4	1	5	15	9	25	1	0	.296	.438	R	R	6-1	190	9-6-80	2001	Fort Walton Beach, Fla.
Cockrell, Mike	.281	84	317	62	89	18	0	10	54	30	44	2	2	.341	.432	R	R	5-10	160	7-25-81	2001	Wilmington, Calif.
Collum, Mike	.245	59	184	26	45	10	1	5	25	16	42	0	0	.324	.391	R	R	6-3	180	7-16-81	2001	Wellington, Fla.
Guzman, Javier	.306	124	470	75	144	20	12	2	63	20	78	31	14	.334	.413	R	R	5-11	160	5-4-84	2002	Santo Domingo, D.R.
Harris, James	.255	85	282	38	72	8	2	1	31	14	20	7	4	.304	.309	R	R	6-0	165	5-25-81	2003	Longwood, Fla.
Kingsbury, Bobby	.247	100	372	66	92	24	3	19	64	36	71	12	2	.317	.481	L	L	6-1	180	8-30-80	2002	Lyndhurst, Ohio
McCuistion, Mike	.255	86	286	41	73	24	2	4	23	36	55	2	0	.343	.395	L	R	6-2	210	5-14-82	2001	Yucaipa, Calif.

BATTING	AVG	G	AB	R	H	2B	3B	HR	RBI	BB	SO	SB	CS	OBP	SLG	B	T	HT	WT	DOB	1st Yr	Resides
Meath, Matt	.171	10	35	5	6	0	1	2	6	8	11	3	1	.326	.400	S	R	6-0	170	10-6-79	2001	Boca Raton, Fla.
Morgan, Nyjer	.255	134	514	83	131	16	7	4	41	53	120	55	16	.357	.337	L	L	6-0	180	7-2-80	2003	Willits, Calif.
Olszta, Eddie	.167	6	6	1	1	0	0	0	1	2	3	0	0	.375	.167	R	R	5-10	180	3-8-79	2001	New Lenox, Ill.
Rea, Brad	.293	109	410	60	120	31	1	8	60	38	73	4	1	.353	.432	R	R	6-4	220	7-29-79	2002	Gibsonia, Pa.
Reyes, Milver	.227	26	88	7	20	1	0	2	10	1	16	0	1	.239	.307	R	R	5-11	187	9-3-82	2000	San Felipe, Venez.
Smith, Sean	.274	34	95	20	26	10	5	0	9	8	15	8	1	.355	.484	R	R	6-0	192	8-24-82	2000	Joliet, Ill.
Stansberry, Craig	.286	106	391	57	112	14	5	9	67	52	88	20	8	.377	.417	R	R	6-0	185	3-8-82	2003	Plano, Texas

PITCHING	W	L	ERA	G	GS	CG	SV	IP	H	R	ER	BB	SO	AVG	B	T	HT	WT	DOB	1st Yr	Resides
Alcala, Jason	2	0	4.97	7	0	0	0	13	18	9	7	4	4	.340	R	R	6-2	210	9-18-80	1998	Cumana, Venez.
Capps, Matt	2	3	10.07	12	8	0	0	42	82	55	47	16	27	.402	R	R	6-3	236	9-3-83	2002	Douglasville, Ga.
Demaria, Chris	8	3	2.94	40	0	0	10	80	62	29	26	20	102	.209	R	R	6-3	210	9-28-80	2002	Torrance, Calif.
Gorzelanny, Tom	2	2	2.23	16	15	1	0	93	63	30	23	34	106	.193	L	L	6-2	202	7-12-82	2003	Orland Park, Ill.
Harts, Jeremy	0	1	4.95	16	0	0	0	20	12	16	11	23	19	.174	S	L	6-1	219	6-6-80	1998	Decatur, Ga.
Hernandez, Chris	1	2	1.93	44	0	0	24	51	48	14	11	19	68	.246	R	R	6-0	200	10-3-80	2003	Redlands, Calif.
Holliday, Brian	7	8	4.61	23	23	0	0	113	106	60	58	54	80	.249	L	L	6-2	180	6-1-84	2002	Moon Township, Pa.
Johnson, Blair	1	4	7.83	9	8	0	0	44	59	40	38	14	22	.326	R	R	6-4	210	3-25-84	2002	Topeka, Kan.
Lissir, Alexander	5	1	5.09	37	1	0	0	69	89	47	39	27	32	.314	R	R	6-0	190	12-29-82	2000	Tucacas, Venez.
Lord, Justin	0	1	12.00	2	2	0	0	6	9	8	8	3	3	.375	R	R	6-4	210	11-15-79	2001	Marianna, Fla.
Lundquist, Dave	4	0	0.93	10	0	0	0	19	12	2	2	5	21	.185	R	R	6-2	200	6-4-73	1993	Hickory, N.C.
Maholm, Paul	0	2	9.49	3	3	0	0	12	17	14	13	10	12	.354	L	L	6-2	215	6-25-82	2003	Holly Springs, Miss.
Nunez, Leo	10	4	3.13	27	20	3	1	144	121	53	50	46	140	.229	R	R	6-1	150	8-14-83	2001	Bonao, D.R.
Shafer, Kurt	2	1	4.46	25	5	0	1	67	69	39	33	22	52	.273	R	R	6-4	190	12-4-81	2000	Land O'Lakes, Fla.
Sharpless, Josh	6	2	3.03	44	0	0	5	74	42	28	25	55	109	.167	R	R	6-5	225	1-26-81	2003	Freedom, Pa.
Shortslef, Josh	11	5	4.34	30	18	0	0	124	134	65	60	38	92	.276	L	L	6-4	220	2-1-82	2000	Hannibal, N.Y.
Starling, Wardell	11	8	4.11	26	26	1	0	140	133	84	64	51	114	.249	R	R	6-3	203	3-14-83	2003	Missouri City, Texas
Torrealba, Yoann	8	8	4.80	28	11	0	2	109	125	66	58	30	61	.293	R	R	5-11	170	7-24-82	2000	Veroe, Yaracuy, Venez.

FIELDING

Catcher	PCT	G	PO	A	E	DP	PB
Chapman	.985	28	173	19	3	2	6
McCuistion	.989	82	667	49	8	2	18
Olszta	1.000	3	14	0	0	0	2
Reyes	.981	26	197	13	4	1	5

First Base	PCT	G	PO	A	E	DP
Benick	.992	111	914	69	8	83
Collum	1.000	4	16	0	0	1
Rea	.992	29	229	6	2	24

Second Base	PCT	G	PO	A	E	DP
Cockrell	.980	11	20	29	1	5

	PCT	G	PO	A	E	DP
Collum	.955	4	6	15	1	7
Harris	.983	25	45	72	2	11
Stansberry	.983	102	208	310	9	63

Third Base	PCT	G	PO	A	E	DP
Cockrell	.969	73	37	152	6	6
Collum	.916	38	24	74	9	8
Harris	.974	31	19	55	2	2

Shortstop	PCT	G	PO	A	E	DP
Collum	1.000	5	5	15	0	3
Guzman	.933	123	163	378	39	78
Harris	.943	12	19	31	3	6

Outfield	PCT	G	PO	A	E	DP
Bocchino	.972	42	62	8	2	1
Boeve	.973	120	175	3	5	1
Collum	.000	1	0	0	1	0
Harris	.958	14	21	2	1	1
Kingsbury	.974	96	179	8	5	0
Meath	.833	11	9	1	2	0
Morgan	.970	132	291	5	9	0
Smith	.975	32	38	1	1	0

WILLIAMSPORT CROSSCUTTERS

Short-Season Class A

NEW YORK-PENN LEAGUE

BATTING	AVG	G	AB	R	H	2B	3B	HR	RBI	BB	SO	SB	CS	OBP	SLG	B	T	HT	WT	DOB	1st Yr	Resides
Bixler, Brian	.276	59	228	40	63	7	4	0	21	15	51	14	5	.321	.342	R	R	6-1	188	10-22-82	2004	Sandusky, Ohio
Brown, Tim	.238	67	231	36	55	14	1	5	30	30	56	1	1	.343	.372	L	L	6-3	220	2-21-83	2001	Eugene, Ore.
Carlin, Mike	.274	41	117	19	32	7	1	6	22	15	22	4	1	.353	.504	R	R	6-0	200	7-6-81	2003	Pittsburgh, Pa.
Chance, Andy	.143	7	21	1	3	1	0	0	1	4	3	2	0	.308	.190	R	R	6-2	210	9-12-80	2003	Brews Bridge, La.
Elliott, Justin	.250	5	16	3	4	0	0	0	1	0	2	0	0	.250	.250	R	R	5-11	185	4-27-82	2002	Lakeland, Fla.
Grandstrand, Brett	.268	49	168	22	45	7	2	3	21	18	28	5	4	.335	.387	R	R	6-0	175	11-13-82	2004	New Castle, Wash.
Herrera, Christian	.282	25	78	8	22	3	1	0	3	7	20	5	3	.356	.346	R	R	5-11	169	4-9-82	2000	Aguascalientes, Mexico
Hicks, Joe	.159	20	63	4	10	3	1	0	4	2	22	0	0	.197	.238	R	R	5-11	188	4-22-84	2002	Houston, Texas
Hofius, Mike	.274	42	135	15	37	6	1	5	29	18	35	0	0	.365	.444	L	L	6-2	210	5-3-82	2004	Lakewood, Calif.
Holmes, Brett	.234	42	141	13	33	4	2	2	12	5	40	10	3	.259	.333	R	R	6-1	180	3-13-81	2003	Springfield, Mo.
Johnson, A.J.	.251	66	239	32	60	12	1	2	18	24	73	8	2	.326	.335	R	R	6-0	185	9-26-83	2004	Franklin, Tenn.
Lerud, Steve	.241	8	29	2	7	0	0	0	2	4	6	0	1	.353	.241	L	R	6-1	205	10-13-84	2004	Reno, Nev.
Lomack, Jermel	.283	44	152	27	43	4	0	0	8	18	27	29	4	.375	.309	S	R	5-8	157	5-13-83	2004	Gardena, Calif.
Macia, Wanell	.292	52	185	26	54	12	4	3	26	5	25	2	1	.311	.449	L	L	5-11	183	7-20-82	2001	La Romana, D.R.
Nino, Denny	.100	4	10	2	1	0	0	0	1	1	4	1	0	.182	.100	R	R	6-1	200	6-4-83	2001	Caracas, Venez.
Reddinger, Brandon	.140	30	86	4	12	1	0	0	7	7	24	0	0	.237	.151	R	R	6-2	210	8-16-82	2004	Pasco, Wash.
Reyes, Milver	.171	34	105	12	18	2	0	1	11	6	19	1	2	.230	.219	R	R	5-11	187	9-3-82	2000	San Felipe, Venez.
Santiago, John	.317	31	104	11	33	8	0	1	17	7	15	1	1	.368	.423	R	R	6-1	165	12-26-84	2003	Trujillo Alto, P.R.
Smith, John	.277	26	65	7	18	1	0	0	4	11	8	1	3	.385	.292	L	R	5-10	185	1-18-82	2004	Hawkinsville, Ga.
Smith, Sean	.235	47	170	27	40	10	2	4	24	12	41	18	1	.289	.388	R	R	6-0	192	8-24-82	2000	Joliet, Ill.
Solano, Euvi	.266	30	79	5	21	2	1	0	7	8	14	6	2	.333	.316	R	R	6-0	178	4-28-82	2000	San Cristobal, D.R.
Walker, Neil	.313	8	32	2	10	3	0	0	7	2	1	1	2	.343	.406	S	R	6-3	205	9-10-85	2004	Gibsonia, Pa.

GAMES BY POSITION: C—Elliott 5, Lerud 4, Nino 4, Reddinger 29, Reyes 34, Walker 4. **1B**—Brown 41, Carlin 16, Hofius 22. **2B**—Grandstrand 23, Herrera 6, Lomack 26, Smith 1, Solano 24. **3B**—Grandstrand 26, Herrera 3, Santiago 31, Smith 22, Solano 3. **SS**—Bixler 59, Grandstrand 5, Herrera 16. **OF**—Hicks 18, Holmes 39, Johnson 65, Lomack 14, Macia 46, Smith 48.

PITCHING	W	L	ERA	G	GS	CG	SV	IP	H	R	ER	BB	SO	AVG	B	T	HT	WT	DOB	1st Yr	Resides
Bimeal, Matt	0	1	7.79	15	0	0	3	17	23	16	15	7	18	.311	R	R	6-3	225	8-17-80	2000	Davidsville, Pa.
Bishop, Matt	1	4	4.74	21	0	0	0	25	34	16	13	4	22	.321	R	R	6-2	215	6-5-82	2004	Raleigh, N.C.
Bloom, Kyle	4	3	2.60	12	12	0	0	45	34	19	13	13	46	.210	L	L	6-4	185	2-21-83	2004	Bettendorf, Iowa
Capps, Matt	3	5	4.85	11	11	0	0	65	84	43	35	4	33	.315	R	R	6-3	236	9-3-83	2002	Douglasville, Ga.
Craig, Dustin	1	6	2.94	28	0	0	11	34	32	14	11	12	31	.244	R	R	6-4	235	4-9-82	2004	San Antonio, Texas
Drage, Derek	4	1	2.01	17	0	0	1	22	14	6	5	4	26	.173	L	R	6-3	195	12-10-81	2004	Green Bay, Wis.
Guillory, Matt	5	6	3.36	14	13	0	0	75	67	33	28	13	52	.239	R	R	6-4	190	3-13-83	2004	Lake Charles, La.
Hankins, Derek	6	4	3.14	14	14	0	0	83	74	33	29	14	57	.239	R	R	6-4	190	7-1-83	2004	Altamont, Ill.
Herce, Steve	2	2	3.46	18	0	0	0	42	40	19	16	11	25	.250	R	R	6-3	230	3-23-81	2004	Houston, Texas
Hummel, John	0	0	4.40	14	0	0	0	14	21	7	7	5	13	.344	L	L	6-5	227	4-18-84	2002	Hoffman Estates, Ill.

PITCHING	W	L	ERA	G	GS	CG	SV	IP	H	R	ER	BB	SO	AVG	B	T	HT	WT	DOB	1st Yr	Resides
Johnson, Blair	6	1	2.44	14	14	2	0	89	62	34	24	12	40	.193	R	R	6-4	210	3-25-84	2002	Topeka, Kan.
Kiley, Jason	0	2	11.81	4	0	0	0	5	12	9	7	2	5	.444	R	R	6-4	220	10-15-82	2001	St. Charles, Ill.
Michael, Mark	0	1	2.49	14	0	0	0	22	17	7	6	10	24	.224	R	R	6-3	185	1-20-81	2003	Lexington, Ky.
Munoz, Luis	2	4	4.57	15	8	0	0	61	80	40	31	14	36	.319	R	R	6-2	176	1-10-82	2001	San Pedro de Macoris, D.R.
Ortega, Joel	0	0	6.75	3	0	0	0	3	2	2	2	1	2	.200	R	R	6-1	196	2-4-84	2001	Aguadulce, Panama
Quarles, Jason	4	3	3.47	23	0	0	0	23	30	15	9	18	30	.294	R	R	6-1	190	4-20-83	2004	Indianapolis, Ind.
Ramos, Vic	0	0	0.96	3	0	0	0	9	6	3	1	2	8	.182	L	R	6-3	200	10-4-81	2000	Cayey, P.R.
Salas, Joe	0	0	6.52	13	0	0	1	10	5	7	7	8	6	.167	L	L	5-10	200	11-24-81	2004	Albuquerque, N.M.

GCL PIRATES — Rookie

GULF COAST LEAGUE

BATTING	AVG	G	AB	R	H	2B	3B	HR	RBI	BB	SO	SB	CS	SLG	OBP	B	T	HT	WT	DOB	1st Yr	Resides
Covington, Chris	.067	18	45	4	3	0	0	0	2	6	19	5	0	.067	.189	R	R	5-11	190	12-12-85	2004	Lawrenceville, Ga.
Diggs, Terry	.167	6	12	1	2	0	1	0	1	1	1	1	0	.333	.286	L	R	5-10	175	8-31-80	2004	Courtland, Ala.
Lerud, Steve	.246	48	175	22	43	12	1	5	20	17	38	0	1	.411	.297	L	R	6-1	200	10-13-84	2004	Reno, Nev.
Loyola, Maiko	.256	38	121	17	31	9	1	1	13	13	17	4	0	.372	.341	R	R	5-11	150	7-19-85	2002	San Cristobal, D.R.
Made, Kelington	.212	28	85	11	18	9	0	2	10	10	16	0	1	.388	.302	R	R	5-11	180	6-25-83	2001	San Cristobal, D.R.
Mendez, Donaldo	.263	11	38	4	10	1	0	2	7	1	8	1	1	.447	.300	R	R	6-1	155	6-7-78	1996	Barquisimeto, Venez.
Munos, David	.302	28	96	11	29	6	2	0	11	5	20	5	0	.406	.337	S	R	6-1	160	8-28-84	2002	Caracas, Venez.
Peabody, John	.220	21	59	5	13	1	1	0	6	9	25	2	0	.271	.351	R	R	6-4	215	8-24-85	2003	San Diego, Calif.
Peralta, Alexander	.343	32	108	22	37	4	1	0	11	8	12	3	1	.398	.405	R	R	5-11	170	12-27-84	2002	Loma de Cabrera, D.R.
Picart, Gregory	.256	25	86	12	22	3	0	0	6	7	16	0	3	.291	.333	S	R	5-11	175	9-25-85	2004	Guayama, P.R.
Poni, Francis	.258	32	97	13	25	10	0	3	17	6	22	0	0	.454	.318	R	R	6-0	200	8-1-83	2003	Carson, Calif.
Powell, Pedro	.243	46	177	33	43	2	3	0	4	13	42	22	3	.288	.302	R	R	5-7	150	5-20-84	2003	Hawkinsville, Ga.
Prasch, Eddie	.220	32	118	11	26	6	2	0	21	12	27	1	1	.305	.301	L	R	6-1	180	1-25-86	2004	Alpharetta, Ga.
Santiago, John	.253	20	75	6	19	3	0	2	11	5	9	1	0	.373	.317	R	R	6-1	170	12-26-84	2003	Trujillo Alto, P.R.
Schwartzbauer, Daniel	.366	35	123	23	45	9	0	1	24	13	14	5	3	.463	.424	R	R	5-11	175	11-2-81	2004	Glenshaw, Pa.
Stevens, Anthony	.221	26	77	10	17	2	1	1	11	3	26	0	2	.312	.250	R	R	6-0	180	8-27-84	2003	Knoxville, Tenn.
Walker, Neil	.271	52	192	28	52	12	3	4	20	10	33	3	1	.427	.313	S	R	6-3	205	9-10-85	2004	Gibsonia, Pa.
Westfield, Antonio	.171	15	41	5	7	1	0	1	2	7	13	2	0	.268	.292	R	R	6-1	205	10-10-84	2004	Cleveland, Tenn.
Wulf, Kent	.221	43	154	17	34	8	3	1	14	11	38	5	2	.331	.275	R	R	5-11	175	4-26-85	2003	Leona Valley, Calif.

GAMES BY POSITION: C—Lerud 25, Made 9, Poni 8, Walker 22. **1B**—Made 18, Peabody 20, Poni 23. **2B**—Peralta 31, Picart 16, Prasch 1, Schwartzbauer 12. **3B**—Diggs 1, Picart 2, Prasch 31, Santiago 20, Schwartzbauer 7. **SS**—Mendez 11, Munos 25, Picart 8, Schwartzbauer 17. **OF**—Covington 17, Diggs 4, Loyola 38, Powell 45, Stevens 25, Westfield 14, Wulf 42.

PITCHING	W	L	ERA	G	GS	CG	SV	IP	H	R	ER	BB	SO	AVG	B	T	HT	WT	DOB	1st Yr	Resides
Alvarez, Basilio	3	3	2.55	11	5	0	0	49	42	22	14	9	41	.224	R	R	6-3	160	1-2-84	2004	San Pedro de Macoris, D.R.
Arias, Keily	1	0	2.00	9	0	0	0	18	20	11	4	5	8	.273	L	L	6-0	160	7-23-85	2002	Esperanza, D.R.
Bauserman, Joseph	2	2	2.79	9	8	0	0	39	26	13	12	10	35	.187	R	R	6-2	220	10-4-85	2004	Tallahassee, Fla.
Bradley, Bobby	0	0	1.80	2	2	0	0	5	6	1	1	1	6	.300	R	R	6-1	180	12-15-80	1999	Wellington, Fla.
Cramer, Terry	0	0	0.00	1	0	0	0	2	2	0	0	0	3	.285	R	R	6-5	250	6-8-83	2004	Tampa, Fla.
Cuffman, Jacob	0	1	4.86	6	5	0	0	17	16	12	9	20	15	.253	R	R	6-4	185	3-3-85	2003	Butler, Pa.
Davidson, David	1	0	3.44	7	1	0	0	18	16	11	7	14	24	.235	L	L	6-1	180	4-23-84	2002	Thorold, Ontario
Garavito, Jean	2	3	2.04	13	0	0	2	18	10	5	4	7	16	.172	R	R	5-11	160	1-11-85	2002	San Felipe, Venez.
Gordon, Alex	2	2	2.68	10	0	0	1	37	34	14	11	11	22	.248	L	L	6-4	233	3-3-80	1998	Seattle, Wash.
Herbort, Ryan	0	3	19.64	5	4	0	0	7	13	17	16	11	6	.351	R	R	6-4	200	3-13-86	2004	Dalton, Ga.
Johnson, Russell	1	2	4.53	13	9	0	0	46	42	24	23	15	50	.253	L	R	6-2	200	1-6-85	2003	Alexander City, Ala.
Maholm, Paul	0	0	2.25	1	0	0	0	4	5	1	1	1	2	.294	L	L	6-2	215	6-25-82	2003	Holly Springs, Miss.
Miller, Kevin	0	0	3.00	3	0	0	0	3	3	1	1	3	3	.250	R	R	6-3	220	3-17-82	2004	Rochester, Pa.
Ortega, Joel	2	1	2.19	12	0	0	3	25	21	8	6	6	23	.225	R	R	6-1	150	2-4-84	2000	Aguadulce, Panama
Pearson, Kyle	0	0	18.00	1	1	0	0	3	7	6	6	2	1	.500	R	R	6-1	180	10-8-84	2003	Panama City, Fla.
Ramos, Kendy	1	0	1.04	5	0	0	0	9	11	4	1	2	7	.297	R	R	6-0	160	3-22-84	2002	Monte Cristi, D.R.
Ramos, Victor	1	2	1.93	11	0	0	1	23	14	7	5	7	16	.168	L	R	6-3	200	10-4-81	2000	Cayey, P.R.
Ridener, Eric	2	0	1.53	9	4	0	1	35	16	7	6	17	33	.134	R	R	6-5	230	9-11-85	2004	Coral Springs, Fla.
Salas, Joe	2	0	2.45	10	0	0	4	11	7	3	3	3	12	.179	L	L	5-10	200	11-24-81	2004	Albuquerque, N.M.
Stewart, Cory	0	1	8.44	2	2	0	0	5	8	5	5	2	4	.347	L	L	6-4	180	11-14-79	1999	Boerne, Texas
Suero, Nicolas	3	6	4.41	12	6	0	0	51	53	30	25	6	21	.266	R	R	6-2	170	12-10-84	2002	Santo Domingo, D.R.
Valdez, Luis	7	2	2.79	11	11	2	0	61	58	22	19	10	41	.248	R	R	6-2	150	5-7-84	2001	Sabana Grande, D.R.

ORGANIZATION STATISTICS

ST. LOUIS CARDINALS

BY DAVID WILHELM

The Cardinals' offense, overpowering for most of the 2004 season, was missing in action during the World Series.

The team that led the National League in victories (105), runs (855) and average (.278) scored just 12 runs and batted .190 (24-for-126) in being swept by the Boston Red Sox.

The Cardinals' starting rotation, which included four pitchers with at least 15 wins, was 0-3, 9.35.

"We weren't supposed to be here at the beginning, and we ended up opening a lot of eyes," said outfielder Reggie Sanders, desperately searching for a positive. "But for us, it's disappointing because we got swept four games. Nobody thought in a million years that would ever happen. The bats weren't there, and this is the outcome of it."

The lack of offense was shocking.

First baseman Albert Pujols, who batted .331-46-123 in the regular season, had no RBIs in the Series despite batting .333 (5-for-15). Third baseman Scott Rolen (.314-34-124), center fielder Jim Edmonds (.301-42-111) and Sanders (.260-22-67) combined to hit a microscopic .026 (1-for-39) with no homers, one RBI and 12 strikeouts.

Rolen was 0-for-15 with one RBI, Edmonds was 1-for-15 with six strikeouts and Sanders was 0-for-9 with five strikeouts.

"We had a great year," Pujols said. "It didn't end up where we wanted, but that's OK. We got there and we have a great group of guys. I'm pretty sure we're going to be with this great group of guys again next year, and hopefully we get another shot at it."

The Cardinals rode the hitting of their star players and surprisingly effective pitching to run away with the Central Division championship.

St. Louis already was in control in the division race

Albert Pujols

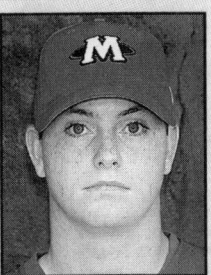

Brad Thompson

PLAYERS of the YEAR

MAJOR LEAGUE: Albert Pujols, 1b

Scott Rolen, Jim Edmonds and Pujols all had great years for the Cardinals in 2004, but Pujols led the big three in average (.331), slugging (.657), doubles (51) and home runs (46). Pujols also led the National League with 133 runs and 389 total bases.

MINOR LEAGUE: Brad Thompson, rhp

Thompson had possibly the most impressive streak in the minor leagues in 2004, with a consecutive scoreless inning string that reached 49 for Double-A Tennessee. He then went down with shoulder problems, but finished strong, going 9-2, 2.89 overall in 87 innings between Tennessee and Triple-A Memphis.

Aug. 6 when it traded three minor leaguers to Colorado for right fielder Larry Walker. Walker's arrival allowed the Cardinals to shift Sanders to left, a position that was being shared by John Mabry, Ray Lankford, So Taguchi, Roger Cedeño and Marlon Anderson.

The revamped rotation added righthanders Jason Marquis and Jeff Suppan, and neither disappointed. Marquis, acquired from Atlanta along with lefthanded reliever Ray King, was 15-7, 3.71 in 201 innings. Suppan, signed as a free agent, was 16-9, 4.16 in 188 innings and won the deciding games in playoff series against Los Angeles and Houston.

Veteran Woody Williams overcame a slow start to finish 11-8, 4.18 in 190 innings, and righthander Chris Carpenter—injured all of 2003—emerged as the staff ace by going 15-5, 3.46 with 152 strikeouts in 182 innings before being shut down late in the season and in the playoffs because of nerve irritation in his right biceps.

The bullpen was solid, led by closer Jason Isringhausen (47 saves), King (5-2, 2.61), newcomer Julian Tavarez (7-4, 2.38), Steve Kline (2-2, 1.79), Cal Eldred (4-2, 3.76) and Kiko Calero (3-1, 2.78).

Manager Tony La Russa, who fought back tears after the Game 4 loss to the Red Sox, wasted no time in announcing he planned to return in 2005 for his 10th season. In nine seasons under La Russa, the Cardinals are 794-663 with five playoff appearances.

Five of the Cardinals' six minor league teams finished above .500. Two of them have been relocated for 2005. Double-A Tennessee will move to Springfield, Mo., and low Class A Peoria will shift to Davenport, Iowa.

ORGANIZATION LEADERS

BATTING

*AVG	Brendan Ryan, Peoria	322
R	Anthony Monegan, Peoria	97
H	Skip Schumaker, Tennessee	163
TB	Kevin Witt, Memphis	286
2B	John Gall, Memphis	34
3B	Anthony Monegan, Peoria	9
HR	Kevin Witt, Memphis	36
RBI	Kevin Witt, Memphis	107
BB	Daric Barton, Peoria	69
SO	Terry Evans, Palm Beach/Peoria	121
SB	Papo Bolivar, Tennessee	51
*OBP	Daric Barton, Peoria	.445
*SLG	Kevin Witt, Memphis	.600

PITCHING

W	Stuart Pomeranz, Peoria	12
L	Luis Martinez, Memphis/Tennessee	12
	Kyle McClellan, Peoria	12
#ERA	Anthony Rawson, Memphis/Palm Beach	2.08
G	Josh Kinney, Tennessee/Palm Beach	57
CG	Tyler Adamczyk, Palm Beach	3
	Jordan Pals, Palm Beach/Peoria	3
SV	Al Reyes, Memphis	23
IP	Buddy Blair, Tennessee/Palm Beach	171
BB	Alan Benes, Memphis	79
SO	Dan Haren, Memphis	150

*Minimum 250 at-bats #Minimum 75 innings

ST. LOUIS CARDINALS

Manager: Tony La Russa.

2004 Record: 105-57, .648 (1st, NL Central).

BATTING	AVG	G	AB	R	H	2B	3B	HR	RBI	BB	SO	SB	CS	OBP	SLG	B	T	HT	WT	DOB	1st Yr	Resides
Anderson, Marlon	.237	113	253	31	60	12	0	8	28	12	38	6	2	.269	.379	L	R	5-11	200	1-6-74	1995	Vorhees, N.J.
Cedeno, Roger	.265	95	200	22	53	9	2	3	23	19	41	5	1	.329	.375	S	R	6-1	205	8-16-74	1992	Valencia, Venez.
Edmonds, Jim	.301	153	498	102	150	38	3	42	111	101	150	8	3	.418	.643	L	L	6-1	212	6-27-70	1988	Orange, Calif.
Hart, Bo	.154	11	13	0	2	0	0	0	2	1	3	0	0	.214	.154	R	R	5-11	175	9-27-76	1999	Laselva Beach, Calif.
Lankford, Ray	.255	92	200	36	51	14	1	6	22	29	55	2	2	.349	.425	L	L	5-11	200	6-5-67	1987	St. Louis, Mo.
Luna, Hector	.249	83	173	25	43	7	2	3	22	13	37	6	3	.304	.364	R	R	6-1	170	2-1-80	1999	Monte Cristi, D.R.
Mabry, John	.296	87	240	32	71	11	0	13	40	26	63	0	1	.363	.504	L	R	6-4	210	10-17-70	1991	St. Louis, Mo.
Matheny, Mike	.247	122	385	28	95	22	1	5	50	23	83	0	2	.292	.348	R	R	6-3	220	9-22-70	1991	St. Charles, Mo.
McKay, Cody	.230	35	74	7	17	2	0	0	6	2	14	0	0	.269	.257	L	R	6-0	210	1-11-74	1996	Scottsdale, Ariz.
Molina, Yadier	.267	51	135	12	36	6	0	2	15	13	20	0	1	.329	.356	R	R	5-11	225	7-13-82	2001	Vega Alta, P.R.
Porter, Colin	.314	23	35	3	11	1	0	1	2	0	13	0	0	.314	.429	L	L	6-2	210	11-23-75	1998	Tucson, Ariz.
Pujols, Albert	.331	154	592	133	196	51	2	46	123	84	52	5	5	.415	.657	R	R	6-3	225	1-16-80	2000	St. Louis, Mo.
Renteria, Edgar	.287	149	586	84	168	37	0	10	72	39	78	17	11	.327	.401	R	R	6-1	200	8-7-75	1992	Pembroke Pines, Fla.
Rolen, Scott	.314	142	500	109	157	32	4	34	124	72	92	4	3	.409	.598	R	R	6-4	240	4-4-75	1993	Holmes Beach, Fla.
Sanders, Reggie	.260	135	446	64	116	27	3	22	67	33	118	21	5	.315	.482	R	R	6-1	205	12-1-67	1988	Phoenix, Ariz.
Taguchi, So	.291	109	179	26	52	10	2	3	25	12	23	6	3	.337	.419	R	R	5-10	165	7-2-69	2002	Nishinomiya, Japan
Walker, Larry	.280	44	150	29	42	7	1	11	27	24	44	0	4	.393	.560	L	R	6-3	235	12-1-66	1985	Evergreen, Colo.
2-team (38 Colo.)	.298	82	258	51	77	16	4	17	47	49	57	6	0	.424	.589							
Womack, Tony	.307	145	553	91	170	22	3	5	38	36	60	26	5	.349	.385	L	R	5-9	170	9-25-69	1991	Greensboro, N.C.

PITCHING	W	L	ERA	G	GS	CG	SV	IP	H	R	ER	BB	SO	AVG	B	T	HT	WT	DOB	1st Yr	Resides
Ankiel, Rick	1	0	5.40	5	0	0	0	10	10	6	6	1	9	.256	L	L	6-1	215	7-19-79	1998	Fort Pierce, Fla.
Calero, Kiko	3	1	2.78	41	0	0	2	45	27	14	14	10	47	.176	R	R	6-1	185	1-9-75	1996	Rio Piedras, P.R.
Cali, Carmen	0	0	8.59	10	0	0	0	7	13	7	7	6	8	.394	L	L	5-10	185	11-4-78	2000	Naples, Fla.
Carpenter, Chris	15	5	3.46	28	28	1	0	182	169	75	70	38	152	.245	R	R	6-6	215	4-27-75	1994	Bedford, N.H.
Eldred, Cal	4	2	3.76	52	0	0	1	67	71	31	28	17	54	.276	R	R	6-4	240	11-24-67	1989	Chandler, Ariz.
Flores, Randy	1	0	1.93	9	1	0	0	14	13	3	3	3	7	.265	L	L	6-0	180	7-31-75	1997	Pico Rivera, Calif.
Haren, Danny	3	3	4.50	14	5	0	0	46	45	23	23	17	32	.265	R	R	6-5	220	9-17-80	2001	West Covina, Calif.
Isringhausen, Jason	4	2	2.87	74	0	0	47	75	55	27	24	23	71	.199	R	R	6-3	230	9-7-72	1992	Tarpon Springs, Fla.
King, Ray	5	2	2.61	86	0	0	0	62	43	19	18	24	40	.197	L	L	6-1	240	1-15-74	1995	Franklin, Wis.
Kline, Steve	2	2	1.79	67	0	0	3	50	37	12	10	17	35	.209	S	L	6-1	215	8-22-72	1993	Winfield, Pa.
Lincoln, Mike	3	2	5.19	13	0	0	0	17	10	12	10	6	14	.164	R	R	6-2	215	4-10-75	1996	Citrus Heights, Calif.
Marquis, Jason	15	7	3.71	32	32	0	0	201	215	90	83	70	138	.275	L	R	6-1	210	8-21-78	1996	Staten Island, N.Y.
Morris, Matt	15	10	4.72	32	32	3	0	202	205	116	106	56	131	.266	R	R	6-5	220	8-9-74	1995	Jupiter, Fla.
Pearce, Josh	0	0	3.86	3	0	0	0	2	3	1	1	0	0	.375	R	R	6-3	220	8-20-77	1999	Yakima, Wash.
Reyes, Al	0	0	0.75	12	2	0	0	12	3	1	1	2	11	.081	R	R	6-1	209	4-10-71	1989	Santo Domingo, D.R.
Simontacchi, Jason	0	0	5.28	13	0	0	0	15	17	10	9	7	3	.304	R	R	6-2	190	11-13-73	1996	Santa Clara, Calif.
Suppan, Jeff	16	9	4.16	31	31	0	0	188	192	98	87	65	110	.265	R	R	6-2	220	1-2-75	1993	Los Angeles, Calif.
Tavarez, Julian	7	4	2.38	77	0	0	4	64	57	21	17	19	48	.238	L	R	6-2	195	5-22-73	1992	Broadview, Ohio
Williams, Woody	11	8	4.18	31	31	0	0	190	193	93	88	58	131	.262	R	R	6-0	200	8-19-66	1988	Fresno, Texas

FIELDING

Catcher	PCT	G	PO	A	E	DP	PB
Matheny	.999	122	742	58	1	10	2
McKay	1.000	18	75	12	0	1	3
Molina	.993	51	256	16	2	1	4

First Base	PCT	G	PO	A	E	DP
Anderson	1.000	2	3	0	0	0
Edmonds	1.000	1	9	1	0	0
Mabry	.981	14	90	16	2	6
Matheny	1.000	1	1	0	0	0
McKay	1.000	1	2	0	0	0
Pujols	.994	150	1458	114	10	136

Second Base	PCT	G	PO	A	E	DP
Anderson	.969	37	55	70	4	20

	PCT	G	PO	A	E	DP
Hart	1.000	4	6	9	0	4
Luna	1.000	19	24	33	0	6
Womack	.976	133	225	391	15	81

Third Base	PCT	G	PO	A	E	DP
Luna	.920	16	4	19	2	3
Mabry	.925	20	10	27	3	3
McKay	.750	7	1	2	1	0
Rolen	.977	141	93	325	10	23

Shortstop	PCT	G	PO	A	E	DP
Hart	.000	1	0	0	0	0
Luna	.947	24	33	57	5	12
Renteria	.983	149	222	419	11	92

Outfield	PCT	G	PO	A	E	DP
Anderson	.939	36	44	2	3	1
Cedeno	1.000	54	47	2	0	0
Edmonds	.988	146	314	11	4	2
Lankford	.956	70	85	1	4	0
Luna	1.000	10	9	0	0	0
Mabry	.986	57	69	0	1	0
Porter	1.000	14	12	0	0	0
Sanders	.981	119	198	6	4	1
Simontacchi	.000	1	0	0	0	0
Taguchi	.980	103	99	1	2	0
Walker	.983	41	58	1	1	0

Jim Edmonds: Tied career-high with 42 home runs

Scott Rolen: Led potent Cardinals offense with 124 RBIs

FARM SYSTEM

Director, Player Development: Bruce Manno.

Class	Farm Team	League	W	L	Pct.	Finish*	Manager	Affiliate Since
AAA	Memphis (Tenn.) Redbirds	Pacific Coast	73	71	.507	8th (16)	Danny Sheaffer	1998
AA	#Tennessee Smokies (Kodak)	Southern	69	71	.493	6th (10)	Mark DeJohn	2003
High A	Palm Beach (Fla.) Cardinals	Florida State	73	61	.545	6th (12)	Tom Nieto	2003
Low A	@Peoria (Ill.) Chiefs	Midwest	75	64	.540	**t-4th (14)**	Joe Cunningham	1995
SS A	New Jersey Cardinals (Augusta)	New York-Penn	41	34	.547	5th (14)	Tommy Shields	1994
Rookie	Johnson City (Tenn.) Cardinals	Appalachian	33	35	.485	5th (10)	Tom Kidwell	1974

*Finish in overall standings (No. of teams in league)/Playoff teams in **boldface**
#Franchise will operate in Springfield, Mo. (Texas) in 2005   @Affiliation will operate in Quad Cities (Midwest) in 2005

MEMPHIS REDBIRDS   Class AAA

PACIFIC COAST LEAGUE

BATTING	AVG	G	AB	R	H	2B	3B	HR	RBI	BB	SO	SB	CS	OBP	SLG	B	T	HT	WT	DOB	1st Yr	Resides
Alviso, Jerome	.212	66	137	8	29	4	0	0	17	11	27	2	2	.270	.241	S	R	6-1	160	9-4-75	1997	Livermore, Calif.
Bowers, Jason	.254	120	389	49	99	20	3	7	38	23	73	9	1	.309	.375	R	R	5-11	170	1-27-78	1998	Uniontown, Pa.
Brown, Emil	.281	19	57	7	16	3	0	0	4	5	9	1	1	.349	.333	R	R	6-2	200	12-29-74	1994	Chicago, Ill.
Burnham, Gary	.292	35	89	15	26	5	0	3	13	7	13	1	1	.351	.449	L	L	5-11	200	10-13-74	1997	South Windsor, Conn.
Cedeno, Roger	.217	7	23	3	5	0	0	0	1	2	6	0	0	.280	.217	S	R	6-1	205	8-16-74	1992	Valencia, Venez.
Colina, Javier	.189	17	37	5	7	0	0	1	6	1	4	0	0	.205	.270	R	R	6-1	190	2-15-79	1997	Cocorote, Venez.
Cresse, Brad	.246	22	69	8	17	4	0	2	7	4	16	0	0	.288	.391	R	R	6-2	230	7-31-78	2000	Long Beach, Calif.
Gall, John	.292	135	506	77	148	34	0	22	84	48	68	1	1	.350	.490	R	R	6-0	195	4-2-78	2000	Portola Valley, Calif.
Hart, Bo	.297	146	445	81	132	25	7	8	45	25	66	8	7	.349	.438	R	R	5-11	175	9-27-76	1999	Laselva Beach, Calif.
Haynes, Dee	.335	58	182	29	61	5	0	14	33	7	25	1	0	.359	.593	R	R	6-0	205	2-22-78	2000	Columbus, Miss.
Hunter, Brian	.204	17	54	5	11	0	0	0	6	5	9	1	2	.271	.204	R	R	6-3	180	3-25-71	1989	Vancouver, Wash.
Lankford, Ray	.212	9	33	5	7	0	0	3	5	3	10	0	0	.297	.485	L	L	5-11	200	6-5-67	1987	St. Louis, Mo.
Mabry, John	.338	39	136	27	46	7	0	12	35	17	29	0	0	.406	.654	L	R	6-4	210	10-17-70	1991	St. Louis, Mo.
Mahoney, Mike	.300	79	270	32	81	16	1	5	32	22	37	1	4	.357	.422	R	R	6-1	205	12-5-72	1995	Des Moines, Iowa
McKay, Cody	.278	27	90	9	25	4	1	3	15	4	15	0	0	.323	.444	L	R	6-0	210	1-11-74	1996	Scottsdale, Ariz.
Molina, Yadier	.302	37	129	19	39	6	0	1	14	17	14	0	0	.387	.372	R	R	5-11	225	7-13-82	2001	Vega Alta, P.R.
Motte, Jason	.200	3	5	0	1	0	0	0	0	0	4	0	0	.200	.200	R	R	6-0	195	6-22-82	2003	Johnson City, Tenn.
Ortiz, Luis	.245	75	163	17	40	5	0	4	21	12	21	0	0	.294	.350	R	R	6-0	180	5-25-70	1991	North Richland, Texas
Porter, Colin	.261	101	330	46	86	20	2	10	34	25	75	13	5	.316	.424	L	L	6-2	210	11-23-75	1998	Tucson, Ariz.
Prieto, Chris	.284	130	451	73	128	17	6	3	41	51	56	28	8	.366	.368	L	L	5-11	180	8-24-72	1993	Fontana, Calif.
Quinn, Mark	.218	24	87	10	19	3	0	3	11	9	15	0	0	.299	.356	R	R	6-1	195	5-21-74	1995	West Covina, Calif.
Rios, Armando	.320	9	25	4	8	1	0	1	6	2	5	2	0	.370	.480	L	L	5-9	190	9-13-71	1994	Pembroke Pines, Fla.
Seabol, Scott	.304	138	514	92	156	26	1	31	78	37	93	6	3	.356	.539	R	R	6-4	200	5-17-75	1996	McKeesport, Pa.
Taguchi, So	.327	17	55	5	18	4	0	1	7	1	10	6	0	.362	.455	R	R	5-10	165	7-2-69	2002	Nishinomiya, Japan
Witt, Kevin	.306	131	477	81	146	30	1	36	107	28	112	2	0	.353	.600	L	R	6-4	220	1-5-76	1994	Bellaire, Texas

PITCHING	W	L	ERA	G	GS	CG	SV	IP	H	R	ER	BB	SO	AVG	B	T	HT	WT	DOB	1st Yr	Resides
Ankiel, Rick	1	0	0.00	1	1	0	0	6	1	1	0	0	5	.053	L	L	6-1	215	7-19-79	1998	Fort Pierce, Fla.
Benes, Alan	8	10	5.60	28	27	0	0	161	193	102	100	79	94	.304	R	R	6-5	240	1-21-72	1993	St. Louis, Mo.
Calero, Kiko	0	0	2.49	12	3	0	1	25	20	8	7	11	33	.222	R	R	6-1	185	1-9-75	1996	Rio Piedras, P.R.
Cali, Carmen	1	1	2.70	17	0	0	3	20	17	6	6	4	20	.227	L	L	5-10	185	11-4-78	2000	Naples, Fla.
Creek, Doug	2	1	4.71	33	0	0	0	29	28	16	15	11	39	.264	L	L	6-0	225	3-1-69	1991	Palm Harbor, Fla.
Cummings, Jeremy	0	1	4.50	1	1	0	0	6	9	7	3	1	5	.321	R	R	6-1	185	11-7-76	1999	Hurricane, W.Va.
Flores, Randy	5	7	3.82	36	15	1	2	123	115	60	52	46	99	.251	L	L	6-0	180	7-31-75	1997	Pico Rivera, Calif.
Haren, Danny	11	4	4.15	21	21	0	0	128	137	60	59	33	150	.276	R	R	6-5	220	9-17-80	2001	West Covina, Calif.
Horgan, Joe	0	1	6.52	10	0	0	0	10	14	7	7	3	8	.350	L	L	6-1	200	6-7-77	1996	Rancho Cordova, Calif.
Journell, Jimmy	0	0	0.00	4	0	0	1	3	4	0	0	1	5	.333	R	R	6-4	205	12-29-77	2000	Springfield, Ohio
Martinez, Luis	0	5	5.06	7	7	0	0	43	53	26	24	23	35	.317	L	L	6-6	200	1-20-80	1997	Boca Chica, D.R.
Nussbeck, Mark	2	1	3.50	3	3	1	0	18	21	7	7	4	14	.288	L	R	6-4	200	5-25-74	1996	Kansas City, Mo.
Paronto, Chad	5	3	2.13	47	0	0	4	55	46	20	13	25	38	.227	R	R	6-5	255	7-28-75	1996	Pittsfield, Mass.
Parrott, Rhett	2	2	5.29	7	7	1	0	34	44	21	20	15	15	.338	R	R	6-2	190	11-12-79	2001	Dalton, Ga.
Patterson, Danny	0	0	6.75	9	0	0	0	7	8	5	5	7	7	.296	R	R	6-0	190	2-17-71	1990	Colleyville, Texas
Pearce, Josh	3	2	3.26	26	0	0	1	30	35	12	11	6	31	.297	R	R	6-3	220	8-20-77	1999	Yakima, Wash.
Pearson, Jason	1	4	4.55	26	0	0	0	30	29	17	15	12	26	.252	L	L	6-0	205	12-29-75	1998	Freeport, Ill.
Rawson, Anthony	1	0	0.00	3	0	0	0	3	0	0	0	1	1	.000	L	L	5-11	180	7-31-80	2001	Kosciusko, Miss.
Reyes, Al	2	2	2.95	37	0	0	23	40	32	13	13	14	47	.219	R	R	6-1	209	4-10-71	1989	Santo Domingo, D.R.
Rodriguez, Nerio	5	3	5.67	16	13	0	0	73	80	50	46	30	46	.284	R	R	6-1	200	3-4-71	1991	San Pedro de Macoris, D.R.
Rust, Evan	3	1	5.74	28	5	0	0	47	57	35	30	21	36	.297	R	R	6-1	210	5-4-78	2000	Ben Lomond, Calif.
Ryan, Jason	1	7	7.36	14	13	0	0	66	98	62	54	30	34	.346	S	R	6-3	185	1-23-76	1994	Charlotte, N.C.
Simontacchi, Jason	7	4	4.33	33	8	0	2	81	101	44	39	12	55	.308	R	R	6-2	190	11-13-73	1996	Santa Clara, Calif.
Stemle, Steve	6	3	3.49	54	0	0	3	77	87	30	30	14	43	.292	R	R	6-4	200	5-20-77	1998	New Albany, Ind.
Stocks, Nick	1	0	6.84	15	1	0	1	26	28	20	20	17	23	.283	R	R	6-2	185	8-27-78	2000	Tampa, Fla.
Thompson, Brad	1	0	5.52	3	3	0	0	15	20	10	9	3	10	.323	R	R	6-1	190	1-31-82	2003	Las Vegas, Nev.
Wainwright, Adam	4	4	5.37	12	12	0	0	64	68	47	38	28	64	.267	R	R	6-8	205	8-30-81	2000	St. Simons Island, Ga.
Woodard, Steve	1	3	10.02	4	4	0	0	21	37	27	23	5	13	.374	L	R	6-4	210	5-15-75	1994	Hartselle, Ala.
2-team (18 Sac.)	9	9	5.68	22	22	0	0	128	170	91	81	21	72	.313							
Young, Tim	0	2	9.00	8	0	0	0	12	16	12	12	4	12	.308	L	L	5-9	170	10-15-73	1996	Bristol, Fla.

FIELDING

Catcher	PCT	G	PO	A	E	DP	PB
Cresse	.984	17	109	15	2	2	1
Mahoney	.986	76	530	46	8	3	5
McKay	.991	19	111	5	1	1	2
Molina	1.000	36	266	35	0	3	9
Motte	1.000	2	12	2	0	0	1

First Base	PCT	G	PO	A	E	DP
Burnham	.984	20	120	7	2	17
Gall	.991	17	104	7	1	6
Mabry	.994	23	159	14	1	22
Ortiz	1.000	29	195	16	0	15
Seabol	1.000	2	2	0	0	1
Witt	.994	85	623	43	4	73

Second Base	PCT	G	PO	A	E	DP
Alviso	.985	19	31	33	1	10
Bowers	.875	1	2	5	1	0

	PCT	G	PO	A	E	DP	PB
Colina	1.000	3	5	7	0	3	
Hart	.978	97	183	260	10	67	
Seabol	.983	44	71	104	3	25	

Third Base	PCT	G	PO	A	E	DP
Alviso	1.000	7	0	4	0	0
Bowers	1.000	1	1	1	0	0
Colina	1.000	10	5	10	0	0
Mabry	.941	5	5	11	1	2
McKay	.938	7	4	11	1	1
Seabol	.955	98	63	149	10	18
Witt	.893	43	18	49	8	7

Shortstop	PCT	G	PO	A	E	DP
Alviso	.989	25	34	55	1	14
Bowers	.976	113	170	322	12	79
Colina	.933	5	8	6	1	2
Hart	.963	21	28	49	3	15

Outfield	PCT	G	PO	A	E	DP
Alviso	1.000	2	3	0	0	0
Bowers	1.000	1	1	0	0	0
Brown	1.000	17	30	0	0	0
Burnham	1.000	5	2	1	0	0
Cedeno	1.000	7	10	0	0	0
Gall	.975	119	150	4	4	1
Haynes	.986	46	69	4	1	1
Hunter	1.000	16	29	0	0	0
Lankford	1.000	3	5	0	0	0
Mabry	1.000	19	24	3	0	0
Porter	.995	96	200	6	1	2
Prieto	.985	126	248	10	4	3
Quinn	.969	22	30	1	1	0
Rios	1.000	3	5	0	0	0
Taguchi	1.000	16	30	0	0	0

TENNESSEE SMOKIES   Class AA

SOUTHERN LEAGUE

BATTING	AVG	G	AB	R	H	2B	3B	HR	RBI	BB	SO	SB	CS	OBP	SLG	B	T	HT	WT	DOB	1st Yr	Resides
Bolivar, Papo	.295	126	451	71	133	25	2	15	60	55	86	51	17	.353	.459	R	R	5-10	168	10-18-78	1996	Catia La Mar, Venez.
Boyd, Shaun	.190	54	158	16	30	5	1	0	12	13	40	9	5	.256	.234	R	R	5-10	175	8-15-81	2000	Las Vegas, Nev.
Colina, Javier	.265	85	313	52	83	14	4	9	48	17	49	5	3	.302	.422	R	R	6-1	190	2-15-79	1997	Cocorote, Venez.
Cresse, Brad	.293	49	164	25	48	12	0	9	27	20	41	0	0	.372	.530	R	R	6-2	230	7-31-78	2000	Long Beach, Calif.
Duncan, Chris	.289	120	387	57	112	23	0	16	65	64	94	8	4	.393	.473	L	R	6-5	210	5-5-81	1999	Tucson, Ariz.
Ehrnsberger, Chad	.217	47	129	14	28	7	1	6	17	18	29	0	1	.320	.426	R	R	5-10	210	11-29-77	2002	Ottawa, Ohio
Eickhorst, Chris	.262	15	42	7	11	3	0	1	8	8	15	0	0	.380	.405	R	R	6-3	200	12-29-79	2002	New Brunswick, N.J.
Erickson, Corey	.181	100	293	38	53	17	1	13	45	31	82	4	0	.266	.379	R	R	5-11	205	1-10-77	1995	Springfield, Ill.
Espy, Nate	.274	114	277	45	76	15	4	11	38	39	50	5	2	.375	.477	L	R	6-3	210	4-24-78	1998	Pensacola, Fla.
Estrada, Kevin	.000	2	4	0	0	0	0	0	0	1	0	0	0	.000	.000	S	R	6-2	185	10-1-80	2003	El Segundo, Calif.
Gorecki, Reid	.320	7	25	1	8	3	0	0	1	2	3	1	0	.370	.440	R	R	6-1	180	12-22-80	2002	East Rockaway, N.Y.
Hamilton, Jon	.241	114	316	37	76	15	1	6	32	28	73	16	5	.301	.351	L	L	6-1	200	10-23-77	1997	San Ramon, Calif.
Haynes, Dee	.243	31	103	8	25	2	0	3	14	8	18	0	0	.328	.350	R	R	6-0	205	2-22-78	2000	Columbus, Miss.
Jaramillo, Milko	.223	69	184	22	41	3	0	5	29	20	37	1	1	.298	.321	R	R	5-11	165	1-21-80	1997	Caracas, Venez.
Johnson, Gabe	.267	127	450	64	120	27	0	18	66	43	118	7	1	.334	.447	R	R	6-1	195	9-21-79	1998	Delray Beach, Fla.
McCoy, Mike	.000	3	6	0	0	0	0	0	0	0	3	0	0	.000	.000	R	R	5-9	175	4-2-81	2002	El Cajon, Calif.
Moylan, Dan	.288	104	316	39	91	16	0	2	38	48	54	1	1	.389	.358	L	R	6-0	190	4-24-79	2000	Keene, N.H.
Nelson, John	.301	63	206	41	62	16	3	8	29	31	56	6	2	.396	.524	R	R	6-1	190	3-3-79	2001	Denton, Texas
Schumaker, Skip	.316	138	516	78	163	29	6	4	43	60	61	19	14	.389	.419	L	R	5-10	175	2-3-80	2001	Laguna Niguel, Calif.

PITCHING	W	L	ERA	G	GS	CG	SV	IP	H	R	ER	BB	SO	AVG	B	T	HT	WT	DOB	1st Yr	Resides
Ankiel, Rick	1	0	0.00	1	1	0	0	5	3	1	0	2	7	.100	L	L	6-1	215	7-19-79	1998	Fort Pierce, Fla.
Axelson, Josh	6	5	4.80	34	14	0	0	105	97	58	56	39	76	.251	R	R	6-1	201	12-4-78	2000	Brooklyn, Mich.
Bauer, Greg	1	0	0.00	10	0	0	0	13	8	2	0	5	11	.178	R	R	6-1	190	11-30-77	2000	Tulsa, Okla.
Blair, Buddy	0	1	6.75	3	3	0	0	9	14	7	7	5	5	.341	L	L	6-1	206	7-2-81	2003	Tulsa, Okla.
Cali, Carmen	1	2	2.91	38	0	0	14	46	43	19	15	19	47	.246	L	L	5-10	185	11-4-78	2000	Naples, Fla.
Cavazos, Andy	2	5	6.14	46	0	0	1	51	67	40	35	32	41	.325	R	R	6-3	185	1-5-81	1999	Clute, Texas
Ciprian, Wilson	1	2	5.85	14	0	0	0	17	17	13	11	6	9	.356	R	R	5-11	160	11-14-82	2000	Villa Mella, D.R.
Cook, Jeremy	8	3	4.19	29	16	0	0	116	118	70	54	21	67	.264	R	R	6-6	235	3-2-78	2000	Yuba City, Calif.

PITCHING

PITCHING	W	L	ERA	G	GS	CG	SV	IP	H	R	ER	BB	SO	AVG	B	T	HT	WT	DOB	1st Yr	Resides
Cummings, Jeremy	5	1	3.44	17	17	2	0	92	84	41	35	30	69	.243	R	R	6-2	215	11-7-76	1999	Hurricane, W.Va.
Johnson, Tyler	2	2	4.79	53	0	0	4	56	48	32	30	37	77	.230	S	L	6-2	180	6-7-81	2001	Newbury Park, Calif.
Kingrey, Jarrod	1	0	9.00	3	0	0	0	3	6	4	3	1	2	.429	R	R	6-1	214	8-23-76	1998	Forston, Ga.
Kinney, Josh	3	8	5.50	50	0	0	4	56	67	40	34	34	48	.307	R	R	6-1	195	3-31-79	2001	Port Allegany, Pa.
Leek, Randy	1	7	4.42	14	13	1	0	75	86	41	37	25	34	.296	L	L	5-11	175	4-18-77	1999	Levittown, N.Y.
2-team (9 Jacksonville)	.. 3	10	4.38	23	22	1	0	125	138	67	61	30	56	.288							
Martinez, Luis	7	7	4.10	16	16	0	0	94	96	51	43	36	77	.269	L	L	6-6	200	1-20-80	1997	Boca Chica, D.R.
Moser, Todd	2	5	5.36	10	9	1	0	49	63	31	29	18	29	.320	L	L	6-5	180	10-28-76	1999	Davie, Fla.
2-team (20 Carolina)	.. 2	5	5.85	30	9	1	0	75	92	51	49	33	46	.306							
Narveson, Chris	5	10	4.16	23	23	0	0	128	114	64	59	51	121	.240	L	L	6-3	180	12-20-81	2000	Arden, N.C.
Parker, Matt	2	2	5.05	25	1	0	0	36	40	22	20	24	36	.288	R	R	6-3	210	12-13-78	1999	Hartsfield, Ga.
Reyes, Anthony	6	2	3.03	12	12	0	0	74	62	27	25	13	102	.225	R	R	6-2	215	10-16-81	2004	Whittier, Calif.
Rust, Evan	3	1	2.59	22	0	0	6	24	18	9	7	12	22	.198	R	R	6-1	210	5-4-78	2000	Ben Lomond, Calif.
Stocks, Nick	4	3	3.66	31	0	0	2	39	29	17	16	20	43	.204	R	R	6-2	185	8-27-78	2000	Tampa, Fla.
Thompson, Brad	8	2	2.36	13	12	2	0	72	56	19	19	11	57	.212	R	R	6-1	190	1-31-82	2003	Las Vegas, Nev.
Wodnicki, Mike	0	2	10.67	12	2	0	0	27	45	33	32	6	9	.378	R	R	6-3	210	1-17-80	2001	Southington, Conn.
2-team (5 Mobile)	.. 0	3	10.29	17	3	0	0	35	58	42	40	10	14	.377							

FIELDING

Catcher

Catcher	PCT	G	PO	A	E	DP	PB
Cresse	.991	45	301	27	3	3	4
Eickhorst	1.000	12	70	5	0	1	2
Johnson	.982	18	94	13	2	0	2
Moylan	.988	78	547	40	7	6	5

	PCT	G	PO	A	E	DP	PB
Ehrnsberger	.977	35	80	87	4	29	
Erickson	.980	39	58	88	3	16	
Jaramillo	.967	6	11	18	1	2	
McCoy	1.000	2	0	3	0	2	

	PCT	G	PO	A	E	DP	PB
Estrada	1.000	1	0	2	0	1	
Jaramillo	.963	59	64	168	9	36	
Nelson	.967	60	63	170	8	28	

First Base

First Base	PCT	G	PO	A	E	DP
Duncan	.990	87	687	35	7	70
Erickson	1.000	3	2	0	0	0
Espy	.989	68	513	25	6	39
Hamilton	1.000	3	17	2	0	0
Moylan	1.000	2	3	0	0	0

Third Base

Third Base	PCT	G	PO	A	E	DP
Colina	.970	10	10	22	1	2
Erickson	.953	24	12	49	3	7
Johnson	.937	113	63	204	18	17
Schumaker	.857	6	4	8	2	0

Outfield

Outfield	PCT	G	PO	A	E	DP
Bolivar	.976	133	194	6	5	1
Boyd	.981	48	51	1	1	0
Duncan	.971	31	32	2	1	0
Ehrnsberger	1.000	8	6	0	0	0
Gorecki	1.000	7	16	0	0	0
Hamilton	.992	96	123	7	1	1
Haynes	.952	26	38	2	2	0
Moylan	1.000	15	18	2	0	0
Schumaker	.982	132	272	7	5	3

Second Base

Second Base	PCT	G	PO	A	E	DP
Colina	.967	75	152	167	11	40

Shortstop

Shortstop	PCT	G	PO	A	E	DP
Colina	1.000	2	2	1	0	0
Erickson	.980	38	38	106	3	18

PALM BEACH CARDINALS — High Class A

FLORIDA STATE LEAGUE

BATTING	AVG	G	AB	R	H	2B	3B	HR	RBI	BB	SO	SB	CS	OBP	SLG	B	T	HT	WT	DOB	1st Yr	Resides
Blasi, Blake	.266	72	158	23	42	7	2	1	22	23	32	4	4	.361	.354	S	R	5-8	160	5-23-79	2000	Wichita, Kan.
Boyd, Shaun	.344	39	157	23	54	12	1	4	26	11	22	7	6	.390	.510	R	R	5-10	175	8-15-81	2000	Las Vegas, Nev.
Catalanotte, Greg	.248	124	403	54	100	30	4	4	50	51	112	3	2	.343	.372	S	R	6-3	210	6-18-77	1999	Glendale, Ariz.
Clark, Daryl	.221	31	95	13	21	5	0	3	21	16	30	1	0	.336	.368	L	R	6-2	210	9-25-79	2000	Boalsburg, Pa.
Davis, John-Paul	.237	38	118	14	28	4	0	0	12	17	28	0	0	.355	.271	R	R	6-4	220	12-20-78	2001	Russellville, Ark.
Dryer, Matt	.250	1	4	0	1	0	0	0	1	0	1	0	0	.250	.250	R	R	6-2	190	11-12-79	2002	Rochester, N.Y.
Ehrnsberger, Chad	.245	71	208	33	51	15	2	4	32	35	41	5	3	.359	.394	R	R	5-10	210	11-29-77	2002	Ottawa, Ohio
Eickhorst, Chris	.120	10	25	2	3	1	0	0	1	2	9	0	0	.185	.160	R	R	6-3	200	12-29-79	2002	New Brunswick, N.J.
Estrada, Kevin	.263	91	312	39	82	19	5	3	47	29	36	20	6	.326	.385	S	R	6-2	185	10-1-80	2001	El Segundo, Calif.
Evans, Terry	.224	19	58	7	13	4	0	2	7	4	16	1	0	.281	.397	R	R	6-3	180	1-19-82	2002	Dublin, Ga.
Frome, Jason	.214	37	98	10	21	3	1	4	12	17	35	2	1	.330	.388	L	L	6-0	190	7-3-79	2001	Appleton, Wis.
Gorecki, Reid	.277	118	440	74	122	23	3	8	47	46	80	23	9	.343	.398	R	R	6-1	180	12-22-80	2002	East Rockaway, N.Y.
Hanson, Travis	.259	57	224	26	58	11	0	2	35	19	38	2	3	.321	.335	L	R	6-2	195	1-24-81	2002	Port Orchard, Wash.
Hunter, Brian	.182	3	11	1	2	0	0	0	0	1	1	1	0	.250	.182	R	R	6-3	180	3-25-71	1989	Vancouver, Wash.
Jaramillo, Milko	.283	15	53	7	15	1	0	1	11	2	7	1	2	.321	.358	R	R	5-11	165	1-21-80	1997	Caracas, Venez.
Laya, Rayner	.251	101	387	64	97	9	3	0	30	39	34	41	19	.319	.289	R	R	5-10	150	8-22-70	1998	La Sabana, Venez.
Lemanczyk, Matt	.232	89	302	38	70	7	2	1	25	25	55	33	11	.301	.278	R	R	6-2	195	10-5-80	2002	Rockville Centre, N.Y.
Marcelli, Brandon	.143	10	14	0	2	0	0	0	1	3	9	0	0	.333	.143	R	R	6-2	205	1-2-81	2004	Fresno, Calif.
McCoy, Mike	.299	62	177	34	53	12	1	2	23	31	32	7	4	.416	.412	R	R	5-9	175	4-2-81	2002	El Cajon, Calif.
Motte, Jason	.174	108	287	22	50	5	0	1	24	6	94	1	2	.193	.202	R	R	6-0	195	6-22-82	2003	Johnson City, Tenn.
Palmer, Cody	.000	1	1	0	0	0	0	0	0	0	0	0	0	.000	.000	R	R	6-0	200	8-25-81	2003	Mitchell, S.D.
Parker, Tyler	.273	9	33	5	9	2	0	0	3	0	12	0	0	.294	.333	R	R	6-3	210	5-13-81	2002	Marietta, Ga.
Pena, Omar	.286	2	7	2	2	1	0	0	0	1	1	0	0	.375	.429	R	R	5-11	175	3-2-82	2003	Haverhill, Mass.
Rodriguez, Marcos	.350	12	20	4	7	0	0	0	4	6	8	0	0	.481	.350	L	L	6-0	180	4-7-83	2001	Lara, Venez.
Roper, Zack	.286	4	7	1	2	1	0	0	0	0	2	0	0	.286	.429	R	R	6-2	200	9-26-77	2000	Pompano Beach, Fla.
Rosenthal, Ben	.257	52	105	11	27	4	0	3	17	13	23	1	2	.336	.381	L	R	6-0	210	7-25-79	2003	San Diego, Calif.
Santor, John	.210	41	124	16	26	6	1	4	21	9	43	0	1	.266	.371	R	R	6-1	215	11-16-81	2000	Palmdale, Calif.
Schutzenhofer, Andy	.292	121	373	65	109	15	2	3	56	51	36	3	2	.386	.367	L	L	6-0	200	1-24-81	2003	Swansea, Ill.
Tucker, Mamon	.264	42	140	15	37	5	2	1	17	7	31	3	2	.305	.350	R	R	6-3	180	10-18-79	1998	Austin, Texas

PITCHING	W	L	ERA	G	GS	CG	SV	IP	H	R	ER	BB	SO	AVG	B	T	HT	WT	DOB	1st Yr	Resides
Adamczyk, Tyler	5	10	5.00	26	25	3	0	137	143	85	76	71	81	.276	R	R	6-6	190	11-9-82	2002	Westlake, Calif.
Ankiel, Rick	0	1	2.08	3	3	0	0	9	5	4	2	0	11	.167	L	L	6-1	215	7-19-79	1998	Fort Pierce, Fla.
Batista, Roberto	4	5	4.55	53	0	0	1	59	68	38	30	22	35	.290	R	R	6-1	165	3-10-82	1999	Guaymate, D.R.
Blair, Buddy	11	10	4.40	26	26	1	0	162	178	85	79	38	101	.284	L	L	6-1	206	7-2-81	2003	Tulsa, Okla.
Brey, Josh	0	1	12.27	1	1	0	0	4	5	5	5	0	4	.313	R	L	6-0	185	8-26-79	2001	Allentown, Penn.
Caple, Chance	1	0	1.69	3	3	0	0	16	12	3	3	7	10	.214	R	R	6-6	240	8-9-78	1999	Southlake, Texas
Ciprian, Wilson	4	2	2.61	38	0	0	11	48	47	17	14	10	31	.255	R	R	5-11	160	11-14-82	2002	Villa Mella, D.R.
Cook, B.R.	0	0	7.50	3	2	0	0	6	9	6	5	4	3	.321	R	R	6-4	200	3-2-78	1999	Salem, Ore.
Cotton, Nate	0	0	0.00	1	0	0	0	1	0	0	0	1	0	1.000	L	R	6-2	195	7-19-79	2000	Southside, Ala.
Garza, Jonathan	6	1	2.53	27	0	0	10	32	28	9	9	14	19	.235	R	R	6-1	190	7-13-82	2003	Frederick, Okla.
Hawksworth, Blake	1	0	5.91	2	2	0	0	11	10	7	7	3	11	.250	R	R	6-3	195	3-1-83	2002	Sammamish, Wash.
Kinney, Josh	0	1	4.32	7	0	0	0	8	8	6	4	6	12	.258	R	R	6-1	195	3-31-79	2001	Port Allegany, Pa.
Lundgren, Wayne	0	1	4.26	8	0	0	0	13	8	7	6	1	5	.178	R	R	6-7	180	4-21-82	2002	Baulkham Hills, Australia
Mondesir, James	1	2	3.67	17	8	0	0	61	61	32	25	24	37	.256	S	R	6-4	210	6-10-79	2002	Jamaica, N.Y.

PITCHING

PITCHING	W	L	ERA	G	GS	CG	SV	IP	H	R	ER	BB	SO	AVG	B	T	HT	WT	DOB	1st Yr	Resides
Pals, Jordan	5	1	2.69	11	11	1	0	60	60	22	18	19	43	.263	R	R	6-8	205	10-18-80	2003	Effingham, Ill.
Petty, Chad	3	2	5.25	23	3	0	0	60	62	39	35	16	38	.267	L	L	6-4	220	2-17-82	2000	West Farmington, Ohio
Rawson, Anthony	0	2	2.16	53	0	0	5	75	55	23	18	23	44	.200	L	L	5-11	180	7-31-80	2001	Kosciusko, Miss.
Reyes, Anthony	2	0	4.40	6	6	0	0	31	32	17	15	7	36	.276	R	R	6-2	215	10-16-81	2004	Whittier, Calif.
Russ, Chris	0	0	0.00	7	0	0	5	8	4	0	0	2	2	.143	R	R	5-11	175	3-27-79	2001	Comfort, Texas
Scalamandre, Rich	3	2	4.08	40	0	0	0	46	41	22	21	26	48	.244	R	R	5-11	195	8-20-80	2002	Brooklyn, N.Y.
Smith, Jared	5	4	3.06	14	12	0	0	65	57	26	22	39	40	.251	L	R	6-2	200	12-1-78	2001	Birmingham, Ala.
Stemle, Steve	2	0	0.00	2	0	0	0	3	1	0	0	0	0	.111	R	R	6-4	200	5-20-77	1998	New Albany, Ind.
Teekel, Josh	9	6	3.93	26	25	0	0	142	134	67	62	57	96	.258	R	R	6-5	200	9-18-80	1999	Greenwell Springs, La.
Wallace, Shane	7	6	3.14	54	0	0	1	63	38	27	22	40	37	.172	L	L	6-2	225	12-29-80	1999	Carrollton, Texas
Wodnicki, Mike	2	2	3.81	6	5	0	0	28	27	14	12	2	17	.243	R	R	6-3	210	1-17-80	2001	Southington, Conn.

FIELDING

Catcher	PCT	G	PO	A	E	DP	PB
Eickhorst	1.000	10	42	5	0	0	1
Marcelli	1.000	10	31	4	0	0	1
Motte	.987	108	509	92	8	9	13
Palmer	1.000	1	1	0	0	0	0
Rosenthal	.980	48	176	16	4	0	8

First Base	PCT	G	PO	A	E	DP
Davis	.987	17	148	5	2	16
Ehrnsberger	1.000	4	5	0	0	0
Parker	1.000	3	38	1	0	2
Santor	.996	24	213	11	1	19
Schutzenhofer	.991	108	967	62	9	96

Second Base	PCT	G	PO	A	E	DP
Blasi	.946	34	53	87	8	18
Ehrnsberger	1.000	12	20	26	0	6

Hanson	.981	49	93	166	5	30
McCoy	.967	55	96	169	9	29
Pena	1.000	1	3	3	0	1

Third Base	PCT	G	PO	A	E	DP
Blasi	.750	8	3	6	3	1
Dryer	1.000	1	0	2	0	1
Ehrnsberger	.961	49	29	117	6	10
Estrada	.934	75	46	168	15	13
McCoy	.960	6	4	20	1	1
Roper	1.000	2	0	1	0	0

Shortstop	PCT	G	PO	A	E	DP
Blasi	.800	4	0	8	2	0
Estrada	.989	15	32	60	1	17
Jaramillo	.952	15	30	49	4	10
Laya	.954	101	173	344	25	73

McCoy	.833	1	1	4	1	1
Pena	1.000	1	0	2	0	0

Outfield	PCT	G	PO	A	E	DP
Boyd	1.000	42	78	1	0	0
Catalanotte	.974	109	144	6	4	0
Clark	.500	2	1	0	1	0
Evans	.938	18	30	0	2	0
Frome	.966	29	55	1	2	1
Gorecki	.965	115	234	12	9	2
Hunter	1.000	2	3	0	0	0
Lemanczyk	.993	84	132	4	1	0
Parker	.000	1	0	0	1	0
Rodriguez	1.000	11	5	0	0	0
Schutzenhofer	1.000	3	4	1	0	0
Tucker	.913	21	20	1	2	0

MIDWEST LEAGUE

BATTING	AVG	G	AB	R	H	2B	3B	HR	RBI	BB	SO	SB	CS	OBP	SLG	B	T	HT	WT	DOB	1st Yr	Resides
Barton, Daric	.313	90	313	63	98	23	0	13	77	69	44	4	4	.445	.511	L	R	6-0	205	8-16-85	2003	Huntington Beach, Calif.
Boyer, Kyle	.255	16	47	10	12	0	1	0	2	6	5	1	2	.352	.298	R	R	6-0	185	3-5-80	2002	Ogden, Utah
Davis, John-Paul	.296	68	240	45	71	14	0	10	38	31	57	0	0	.387	.479	R	R	6-4	220	12-20-78	2001	Russellville, Ark.
Dobson, Sean	.286	4	7	3	2	0	0	0	0	1	3	0	0	.444	.286	R	L	5-9	180	7-24-82	2004	Eastpointe, Mich.
Dryer, Matt	.294	72	235	38	69	18	0	7	51	44	59	0	1	.401	.460	R	R	6-2	190	11-12-79	2002	Rochester, N.Y.
Evans, Terry	.222	101	365	48	81	21	1	13	59	35	105	8	3	.301	.392	R	R	6-3	200	1-19-82	2002	Dublin, Ga.
Frisella, Sal	.263	51	156	25	41	4	2	5	26	18	43	4	1	.352	.410	R	R	6-1	215	4-10-81	2003	Sunset Hills, Mo.
Haerther, Cody	.316	86	326	48	103	20	2	5	45	32	59	7	3	.383	.436	L	R	6-0	190	7-14-83	2003	Chatsworth, Calif.
Hayes, Calvin	.304	41	158	28	48	2	0	2	12	16	25	6	3	.368	.354	R	R	5-9	190	3-21-84	2003	Salisbury, N.C.
Hileman, Jutt	.261	12	23	2	6	1	0	0	0	2	7	0	0	.320	.304	R	R	6-1	180	7-13-81	2000	Palmyra, Pa.
Hoffpauir, Jarrett	.271	67	247	35	67	21	1	5	31	32	23	3	6	.369	.425	R	R	5-9	175	6-18-83	2004	Vidalia, La.
Jaramillo, Milko	.274	22	62	7	17	3	1	0	8	10	1	1	1	.357	.355	R	R	5-11	165	1-21-80	1997	Caracas, Venez.
Marcelli, Brandon	.273	29	88	10	24	6	0	3	12	4	26	0	1	.304	.443	R	R	6-2	205	1-2-81	2004	Fresno, Calif.
Mather, Joe	.253	65	241	34	61	18	2	7	31	24	70	3	3	.333	.432	R	R	6-4	190	7-23-82	2001	Phoenix, Ariz.
McCoy, Mike	.208	50	178	25	37	7	3	2	16	21	33	8	1	.296	.315	R	R	5-9	175	4-2-82	2002	El Cajon, Calif.
Monegan, Anthony	.297	124	509	97	151	31	9	3	53	54	94	19	9	.367	.411	L	R	6-0	170	5-11-79	2000	Flossmoor, Ill.
Pagnozzi, Matt	.209	73	215	29	45	10	1	0	14	15	54	4	1	.277	.265	R	R	6-2	205	11-10-82	2003	Mesa, Ariz.
Palmer, Cody	.308	13	26	7	8	2	0	1	6	2	5	4	7	0	0	.387	.538	R	R	6-0	200	8-25-81	2003	Mitchell, S.D.
Parker, Tyler	.265	85	291	39	77	11	2	10	48	23	87	9	7	.326	.419	R	R	6-3	210	5-13-81	2002	Marietta, Ga.
Patrick, Chris	.308	7	26	7	8	2	0	1	6	2	2	0	0	.387	.500	R	R	5-9	180	2-20-82	2004	Fresno, Calif.
Pena, Omar	.276	83	246	38	68	9	1	3	19	16	48	3	5	.323	.358	R	R	5-11	175	3-2-82	2003	Haverhill, Mass.
Rodriguez, Marcos	.178	13	45	5	8	2	0	0	5	5	9	0	0	.260	.222	L	L	6-0	180	4-7-83	2001	Lara, Venez.
Rosenthal, Ben	.300	3	10	2	3	0	0	0	0	2	2	0	0	.417	.300	L	R	6-0	210	7-25-79	2003	San Diego, Calif.
Ryan, Brendan	.322	105	426	72	137	21	4	2	59	24	42	30	7	.356	.404	R	R	6-2	195	3-26-82	2003	Los Angeles, Calif.
Santor, John	.264	68	250	39	66	17	0	13	53	21	69	7	4	.330	.488	R	R	6-1	215	11-16-81	2000	Palmdale, Calif.
Sherman, Steve	.290	7	31	6	9	0	0	3	12	2	5	0	0	.333	.581	L	L	6-2	200	8-20-81	2004	Plano, Texas

PITCHING	W	L	ERA	G	GS	CG	SV	IP	H	R	ER	BB	SO	AVG	B	T	HT	WT	DOB	1st Yr	Resides
Acosta, Adam	0	0	13.50	5	1	0	0	7	13	13	11	4	9	.382	R	R	6-0	190	10-21-81	2004	Miami, Fla.
Aguero, Miguel	2	2	7.94	7	5	0	0	28	45	26	25	7	16	.357	R	R	6-0	185	5-19-82	2001	Lara, Venez.
Brey, Josh	3	2	3.34	34	4	0	0	62	66	27	23	23	47	.281	R	L	6-0	185	8-26-79	2001	Allentown, Pa.
Brown, Justin	0	0	0.00	4	0	0	0	3	1	0	0	5	2	.091	R	R	5-11	190	10-6-80	2004	Greenbrian, Tenn.
Burch, Jason	5	5	3.61	44	0	0	21	52	42	22	21	26	60	.219	R	R	6-5	215	10-15-82	2003	Papillion, Neb.
Correa, Cristobal	3	6	3.86	19	16	1	0	91	92	46	39	36	59	.267	R	R	6-1	175	12-5-79	1998	Guarico, Venez.
Davis, John-Paul	0	0	0.00	2	0	0	0	3	0	0	0	4	0	.000	R	R	6-4	220	12-20-78	2001	Russellville, Ark.
DeJaynes, Brandon	5	3	4.29	49	1	0	2	71	38	39	34	57	106	.156	R	R	6-2	190	9-10-80	2003	Quincy, Ill.
Dove, Dennis	0	1	7.04	2	2	0	0	8	7	7	6	7	3	.259	R	R	6-4	205	8-31-81	2003	Ocilla, Ga.
Drown, Eric	4	5	5.03	24	15	0	0	79	62	48	44	58	83	.218	R	R	6-2	200	2-21-80	2003	Ipswich, Mass.
Garza, Justin	5	1	1.51	29	0	0	2	36	28	13	6	11	28	.211	R	R	6-1	190	7-13-82	2003	Frederick, Okla.
Jordan, Brantley	3	3	3.17	50	0	0	2	54	47	23	19	21	54	.236	L	L	6-0	190	4-24-81	2003	Austin, Texas
Lambert, Chris	1	1	2.58	9	9	0	0	38	31	15	11	24	46	.218	R	R	6-1	205	8-31-79	2004	Manchester, N.H.
Lundgren, Wayne	2	2	3.94	33	1	0	0	46	44	25	20	11	43	.243	R	R	6-3	190	4-21-82	2000	Baulkham Hills, Australia
McClellan, Kyle	4	12	5.34	24	24	1	0	128	143	85	76	34	84	.283	R	R	6-2	185	6-12-84	2002	Florissant, Mo.
Michael, Mark	6	6	3.36	20	20	1	0	121	117	59	45	39	95	.260	R	R	6-4	215	8-20-82	2003	Gibbstown, N.J.
Mondesir, James	3	1	6.18	12	4	1	0	28	30	20	19	6	22	.275	S	R	6-4	210	6-10-79	2002	Jamaica, N.Y.
Pals, Jordan	5	3	2.84	12	12	2	0	73	66	30	23	15	36	.240	R	R	6-8	205	10-18-80	2003	Effingham, Ill.
Parisi, Michael	1	1	3.28	6	6	0	0	36	30	16	13	15	36	.229	R	R	6-3	215	4-18-83	2004	Lake Grove, N.Y.
Paz, Jackson	6	0	5.32	26	0	0	0	24	28	18	14	13	16	.289	R	L	6-1	160	7-10-82	2000	Maracaibo, Venez.
Petty, Chad	0	1	21.00	2	2	0	0	3	7	8	7	6	3	.467	L	L	6-4	220	2-17-82	2000	West Farmington, Ohio

PITCHING	W	L	ERA	G	GS	CG	SV	IP	H	R	ER	BB	SO	AVG	B	T	HT	WT	DOB	1st Yr	Resides
Pomeranz, Stuart	12	4	3.55	17	17	0	0	101	95	59	40	25	88	.244	R	R	6-7	220	12-17-84	2003	Collierville, Tenn.
Roper, Derek	1	1	5.79	6	0	0	0	14	18	10	9	2	16	.305	R	R	6-6	205	12-31-80	2003	Elk City, Okla.
Scalamandre, Rich	0	0	0.00	5	0	0	1	9	3	0	0	0	11	.107	R	R	5-11	195	8-20-80	2002	Brooklyn, N.Y.
Schweitzer, Scott	1	0	2.25	16	0	0	0	16	10	4	4	11	18	.167	L	L	6-3	235	5-4-80	2002	Alexandria, Ky.
Soteropoulos, Peter	1	0	3.52	20	0	0	0	31	24	16	12	6	32	.209	L	L	6-1	210	8-5-81	2003	Peabody, Mass.
Torres, Jaime	1	0	5.60	8	0	0	0	18	27	14	11	7	10	.351	R	R	5-11	195	1-12-82	2004	Riverside, Calif.
Weatherby, Charles	1	1	2.45	9	0	0	1	15	16	7	4	1	11	.281	R	R	6-0	200	12-23-78	2001	Beaufort, N.C.
Worrell, Mark	0	2	4.30	12	0	0	6	15	9	10	7	6	20	.176	R	R	6-1	190	3-18-82	2004	Boynton Beach, Fla.

FIELDING

Catcher	PCT	G	PO	A	E	DP	PB
Barton	.975	52	381	48	11	4	11
Marcelli	.989	21	155	19	2	0	0
Pagnozzi	.994	73	467	57	3	2	18
Palmer	1.000	11	43	2	0	0	1
Rosenthal	1.000	3	17	2	0	0	1
Jaramillo	1.000	8	10	16	0		1
McCoy	.974	13	32	42	2		7
Pena	.947	26	50	75	7		15

First Base	PCT	G	PO	A	E	DP
Davis	.988	65	543	41	7	51
Dryer	.950	5	17	2	1	2
Evans	1.000	4	11	2	0	2
Mather	.983	8	57	0	1	4
Santor	.990	68	629	40	7	56

Second Base	PCT	G	PO	A	E	DP
Boyer	.962	10	19	32	2	6
Hayes	.913	22	52	43	9	16
Hoffpauir	.962	67	120	183	12	49

Third Base	PCT	G	PO	A	E	DP
Davis	1.000	1	1	0	0	0
Dryer	.918	59	38	129	15	7
Hileman	.667	2	1	3	2	0
Jaramillo	1.000	2	0	1	0	0
Mather	.930	22	17	36	4	3
McCoy	.929	37	24	80	8	12
Patrick	.778	5	6	14	4	2
Pena	.949	32	13	43	3	7

Shortstop	PCT	G	PO	A	E	DP
Jaramillo	.952	12	22	37	3	7
McCoy	1.000	2	2	6	0	0
Patrick	1.000	1	2	3	0	0
Pena	.937	22	28	61	6	11
Ryan	.938	104	139	330	31	63

Outfield	PCT	G	PO	A	E	DP
Dobson	1.000	4	3	0	0	0
Evans	.981	92	148	5	3	0
Frisella	.958	21	21	2	1	0
Haerther	.963	58	72	5	3	2
Hayes	1.000	1	1	0	0	0
Hileman	1.000	8	11	0	0	0
Mather	.968	39	57	4	2	0
McCoy	1.000	1	1	0	0	0
Monegan	.979	121	229	7	5	0
Parker	.965	75	100	9	4	1
Rodriguez	1.000	13	19	0	0	0
Sherman	1.000	7	14	0	0	0

NEW JERSEY CARDINALS — Short-Season Class A

NEW YORK-PENN LEAGUE

BATTING	AVG	G	AB	R	H	2B	3B	HR	RBI	BB	SO	SB	CS	OBP	SLG	B	T	HT	WT	DOB	1st Yr	Resides
Boyer, Kyle	.167	14	48	2	8	0	0	1	4	1	10	1	1	.196	.229	R	R	6-0	185	3-5-80	2002	Ogden, Utah
Cantu, Tim	.203	29	64	13	13	2	0	1	8	5	23	1	1	.297	.281	R	R	6-1	190	2-2-83	2004	Castaic, Calif.
Davie, Andrew	.154	10	26	1	4	0	0	1	2	0	10	0	0	.154	.269	L	R	6-6	240	1-5-83	2001	Little Rock, Ark.
Delgado, Jose	.158	6	19	1	3	1	0	0	3	2	10	0	1	.227	.211	S	R	5-9	180	9-10-83	2004	San Juan, P.R.
Dobson, Sean	.269	62	227	35	61	8	1	0	18	24	27	11	5	.352	.313	R	L	5-9	180	7-24-82	2004	Eastpointe, Mich.
Ferris, Mike	.199	41	146	18	29	5	0	3	14	19	44	2	1	.295	.295	L	L	6-2	225	12-31-82	2004	Cincinnati, Ohio
Granadillo, Tony	.235	14	51	6	12	3	0	0	2	11		0	0	.264	.294	S	R	5-10	185	8-10-84	2002	Carabobo, Venez.
Grimm, Casey	.250	57	188	21	47	7	0	4	27	26	44	1	0	.336	.351	L	R	6-1	205	2-9-81	2003	Morristown, N.J.
Herbert, Sam	.245	18	53	6	13	1	0	1	6	4	11	4	3	.305	.321	R	R	5-10	185	10-21-81	2004	Davis, Calif.
Hoffpauir, Jarrett	.361	9	36	8	13	3	0	3	6	3	2	1	0	.410	.694	R	R	5-9	175	6-18-83	2004	Vidalia, La.
House, Kevin	.208	11	24	5	5	1	1	0	0	9	2	0		.240	.333	R	R	5-11	195	7-27-82	2003	Memphis, Tenn.
Mather, Joe	.125	3	8	0	1	0	0	0	0	2	2	0	0	.125	.125	R	R	6-4	190	7-23-82	2003	Phoenix, Ariz.
Mullinax, Jacob	.290	56	224	32	65	9	4	3	36	11	52	5	1	.336	.406	R	R	6-2	195	6-13-82	2004	Hesperia, Calif.
Palmer, Cody	.189	32	90	10	17	7	0	3	11	8	33	0	0	.270	.367	R	R	5-9	180	8-25-81	2003	Vancouver, Wash.
Patrick, Chris	.325	57	206	30	67	13	2	1	22	11	27	1	5	.367	.422	R	R	5-9	180	2-20-82	2004	Fresno, Calif.
Rodriguez, Marcos	.215	20	65	6	14	4	1	0	6	9	15	1	0	.320	.308	L	L	6-0	180	4-7-83	2001	Lara, Venez.
Shepherd, Matt	.232	71	254	27	59	8	0	0	23	23	44	17	7	.295	.264	R	R	6-2	200	5-5-83	2004	Hattiesburg, Miss.
Sherman, Steve	.263	62	217	22	57	8	3	3	27	24	41	3	0	.339	.369	L	L	6-2	200	8-20-81	2004	Plano, Texas
Swackhamer, Wes	.222	55	212	17	47	13	0	2	23	16	56	4	0	.274	.311	L	L	6-2	190	1-21-83	2004	Basking Ridge, N.J.
Taillon, Cory	.207	20	58	9	12	1	0	0	4	9	12	1	0	.313	.224	R	R	5-10	195	5-18-82	2004	Thousand Oaks, Calif.
Thomas, Tee	.333	2	6	1	2	1	0	0	0	0	3	0	0	.333	.500	R	R	5-11	187	6-13-81	2003	Starkville, Miss.
Toops, Brady	.206	33	97	11	20	3	2	0	9	8	26	2	1	.271	.278	L	R	6-2	220	7-31-81	2004	New London, Minn.
Webber, Levi	.244	58	180	26	44	10	1	6	21	19	48	2	2	.313	.411	R	R	6-2	220	6-30-82	2004	Portland, Maine
Williams, Simon	.353	6	17	3	6	0	0	0	3	4	5	0	1	.476	.353	S	R	6-1	190	10-14-82	2003	Mesa, Ariz.
Wootan, Tanner	.250	1	4	1	1	1	0	0	0	0	1	0	0	.250	.500	L	R	6-2	180	11-9-84	2003	Ellerbee, N.C.
Yarbrough, Brandon	.143	5	14	1	2	0	0	0	0	0	3	0	0	.200	.143	L	R	6-2	210	11-8-80	2004	Ellerbee, N.C.

GAMES BY POSITION: C—Palmer 31, Taillon 20, Toops 32, Yarbrough 2. **1B**—Davie 6, Ferris 39, Grimm 1, Rodriguez 1, Webber 35. **2B**—Cantu 17, Delgado 6, Hoffpauir 8, Mullinax 1, Patrick 46, Thomas 1. **3B**—Cantu 3, Granadillo 14, Mather 2, Mullinax 55, Patrick 1, Wootan 1. **SS**—Cantu 2, Patrick 4, Shepherd 70. **OF**—Boyer 14, Dobson 65, Herbert 18, House 10, Rodriguez 18, Sherman 58, Swackhamer 56, Webber 3, Williams 6.

PITCHING	W	L	ERA	G	GS	CG	SV	IP	H	R	ER	BB	SO	AVG	B	T	HT	WT	DOB	1st Yr	Resides
Acosta, Adam	1	1	2.50	8	1	0	0	18	20	7	5	4	14	.290	R	R	6-0	190	10-21-81	2004	Miami, Fla.
Aguero, Miguel	5	5	2.97	15	14	1	0	91	92	33	30	22	82	.267	R	R	6-2	185	5-19-82	2001	Lara, Venez.
Baird, Jack	0	1	1.50	4	0	0	0	6	5	1	1	2	3	.250	L	R	6-2	195	4-28-81	2004	Washington Depot, Conn.
Baysinger, Daniel	1	0	2.00	7	0	0	0	9	8	2	2	5	2	.286	R	R	6-2	195	1-27-82	2004	Scottsdale, Ariz.
Bova, Chris	1	4	3.76	19	6	0	1	53	49	29	22	16	32	.241	R	R	6-4	230	2-7-82	2004	Athens, Ohio
Brown, Justin	0	1	3.24	2	1	0	0	8	11	9	3	2	6	.314	R	R	5-11	190	10-6-80	2004	Greenbrier, Tenn.
Della Rocco, Chris	2	3	4.00	19	9	0	1	63	62	35	28	17	33	.254	R	R	6-1	195	1-17-82	2004	Wilmington, Del.
Dickerson, Bo	0	0	1.80	1	1	0	0	5	3	2	1	1	4	.176	R	R	6-0	190	11-12-83	2002	Maywood, Ill.
Dove, Dennis	0	5	8.18	6	6	0	0	22	31	20	20	13	24	.333	R	R	6-4	205	8-31-81	2003	Ocilla, Ga.
Doyne, Cory	2	0	2.33	30	0	0	12	39	19	10	10	12	48	.143	R	R	6-4	210	8-13-81	2000	Lutz, Fla.
Grant, Jessen	0	0	0.00	3	0	0	0	5	4	0	0	0	1	.211	R	R	6-4	235	10-4-81	2004	Greensboro, N.C.
Gross, Michael	3	1	0.98	13	0	0	3	18	14	3	2	7	12	.222	R	R	6-5	220	9-14-82	2004	Bloomington, Ill.
Haberer, Eric	0	2	3.27	8	3	0	0	19	14	7	5	9	12	.219	L	L	6-5	220	9-14-82	2004	Bloomington, Ill.
John, Jason	1	2	9.38	9	5	0	0	24	30	25	25	10	21	.294	R	R	6-5	230	11-3-81	2003	Corpus Christi, Texas
Parisi, Michael	4	2	4.42	7	7	0	0	37	40	18	18	6	26	.280	R	R	6-3	205	4-18-83	2004	Lake Grove, N.Y.
Paz, Jackson	1	0	1.50	16	0	0	1	18	9	4	3	5	16	.153	R	L	6-1	160	7-10-82	2000	Maracaibo, Venez.
Robertson, Quinton	3	2	3.41	6	6	1	0	32	29	12	12	6	20	.240	R	R	6-5	215	12-18-81	2001	Alpharetta, Ga.
Roper, Derek	6	0	3.38	13	5	0	1	48	54	21	18	11	51	.281	R	R	6-6	205	12-31-80	2003	Elk City, Okla.
Schweitzer, Scott	1	0	4.26	9	0	0	0	6	7	3	3	3	10	.280	L	L	6-3	235	5-4-80	2002	Alexandria, Ky.
Sillman, Michael	0	0	1.25	17	0	0	0	22	12	3	3	10	29	.169	R	R	6-1	190	12-3-81	2004	Omaha, Neb.

PITCHING	W	L	ERA	G	GS	CG	SV	IP	H	R	ER	BB	SO	AVG	B	T	HT	WT	DOB	1st Yr	Resides
Smith, Donnie	3	3	3.88	11	11	1	0	46	52	23	20	5	41	.283	R	R	6-2	195	1-14-83	2004	Portsmouth, Va.
Torres, Jaime	2	1	1.65	13	0	0	0	27	22	6	5	9	21	.224	R	R	5-11	195	1-12-82	2004	Riverside, Calif.
Tubb, Austin	4	1	2.84	23	0	0	0	32	33	14	10	12	28	.273	R	R	6-3	210	3-7-82	2004	Hoover, Ala.
Zick, Jeremy	1	1	4.55	18	0	0	1	28	30	14	14	12	28	.273	R	R	6-1	210	8-25-82	2004	Ontario, Calif.

JOHNSON CITY CARDINALS — Rookie

APPALACHIAN LEAGUE

BATTING	AVG	G	AB	R	H	2B	3B	HR	RBI	BB	SO	SB	CS	OBP	SLG	B	T	HT	WT	DOB	1st Yr	Resides
Becher, Billy	.286	58	168	30	48	7	1	11	41	29	50	2	1	.383	.536	L	R	6-4	230	3-8-82	2004	Chandler, Ariz.
Broome, Mark	.215	25	79	14	17	2	0	2	5	8	15	3	0	.292	.316	R	R	5-11	170	6-22-82	2004	Clinton, Miss.
Burton, Adam	.205	30	83	5	17	3	0	0	5	10	21	2	0	.289	.241	R	R	6-0	195	11-16-81	2004	Steele, Mo.
Chacin, Steward	.131	30	61	4	8	1	0	1	6	3	16	0	1	.169	.197	R	R	6-0	180	12-31-85	2003	Bolivar, Venez.
Delgado, Jose	.278	63	216	47	60	9	5	3	28	53	65	17	4	.431	.407	S	R	5-9	180	9-10-83	2004	San Juan, P.R.
Diaz, Sandy	.225	36	129	17	29	8	0	3	17	8	35	0	1	.301	.357	R	R	6-0	185	1-1-84	2001	Azua, D.R.
Gabriel, Chad	.269	57	197	38	53	14	1	5	37	12	40	5	1	.327	.426	R	R	6-1	190	5-19-84	2004	Norwalk, Calif.
Granadillo, Tony	.315	50	168	40	53	10	1	10	30	22	37	3	1	.413	.565	S	R	5-10	165	8-10-84	2002	Carabobo, Venez.
Herbert, Sam	.308	33	117	17	36	4	2	0	16	14	16	15	2	.382	.376	R	R	5-10	185	10-21-81	2004	Davis, Calif.
Jesson, Das	.231	53	182	30	42	11	0	9	34	28	53	6	3	.344	.440	S	R	6-2	180	11-16-84	2004	Pacific Palisades, Calif.
Lucena, Juan	.332	56	205	35	68	8	1	4	30	11	16	7	3	.365	.439	R	R	5-10	155	1-20-84	2002	Lara, Venez.
Miller, Mike	.209	42	115	19	24	5	0	5	18	11	34	1	2	.287	.383	R	R	6-2	195	4-21-83	2004	Newhall, Calif.
Nelson, Daniel	.258	42	124	20	32	9	2	0	11	13	31	7	1	.336	.363	S	R	5-11	180	2-12-84	2004	Los Angeles, Calif.
Schwarze, Brian	.069	23	29	3	2	0	0	0	0	3	10	1	0	.206	.069	R	R	6-1	180	3-11-81	2004	Chesterfield, Mo.
Sivira, Yonathan	.292	44	137	19	40	10	3	2	18	3	21	2	3	.329	.453	R	R	6-1	165	1-25-84	2002	Barquisimeto, Venez.
Williams, Simon	.272	46	136	19	37	3	2	3	13	14	30	1	2	.344	.390	R	L	6-2	180	6-30-82	2004	Portland, Maine
Yarbrough, Brandon	.326	48	175	37	57	10	1	6	33	25	55	3	1	.411	.497	L	R	6-2	180	11-9-84	2003	Ellerbee, N.C.

GAMES BY POSITION: C—Burton 26, Diaz 18, Yarbrough 34. **1B**—Becher 56, Jesson 26. **2B**—Chacin 16, Delgado 61, Nelson 2. **3B**—Broome 18, Chacin 12, Granadillo 46, Jesson 6. **SS**—Chacin 2, Lucena 45, Nelson 31. **OF**—Chacin 1, Gabriel 47, Herbert 36, Jesson 21, Miller 42, Schwarze 15, Sivira 47, Williams 46.

PITCHING	W	L	ERA	G	GS	CG	SV	IP	H	R	ER	BB	SO	AVG	B	T	HT	WT	DOB	1st Yr	Resides
Acosta, Adam	0	0	4.91	10	2	0	0	18	16	11	10	8	21	.229	R	R	6-0	190	10-21-81	2004	Miami, Fla.
Andersen, Phillip	5	1	4.01	13	13	0	0	61	55	30	27	26	52	.248	R	R	6-2	175	10-28-83	2004	Chandler, Ariz.
Brown, Justin	2	4	6.66	8	8	0	0	26	28	20	19	19	19	.283	R	R	5-11	190	10-6-80	2004	Greenbrian, Tenn.
Capellan, Domingo	2	3	6.16	25	0	0	1	31	27	24	21	14	30	.241	R	R	5-10	180	12-12-82	2000	Cotui, D.R.
Dickerson, Bo	0	1	6.00	3	2	0	0	6	4	6	4	5	6	.182	R	R	6-0	190	11-12-83	2002	Maywood, Ill.
Gomez, Luis	0	1	4.60	12	0	0	0	16	16	9	8	3	17	.276	R	R	6-0	170	11-5-82	2001	Sincerin, Colombia
Grant, Jessen	0	1	5.79	14	0	0	0	14	12	10	9	11	14	.226	R	R	6-4	210	6-25-82	2004	Cupertino, Calif.
Gross, Tim	1	1	5.68	16	0	0	3	19	26	17	12	4	13	.317	R	R	6-4	235	10-4-81	2004	Marietta, Ga.
Haberer, Eric	2	2	4.69	9	9	0	0	40	47	30	21	13	37	.283	L	L	6-5	220	11-9-84	2004	Bloomington, Ill.
John, Jason	1	2	4.38	9	0	0	0	12	11	8	6	7	17	.229	R	R	6-5	230	11-3-81	2003	Corpus Christi, Texas
Lemon, Tim	1	4	7.21	13	8	0	0	49	66	46	39	22	29	.330	R	R	6-1	180	9-23-80	1998	La Mirada, Calif.
Markham, Josh	0	0	11.57	2	0	0	0	2	5	4	3	3	0	.385	L	L	6-2	185	11-19-84	2003	Decatur, Ala.
Noonan, Chris	3	4	3.72	16	2	0	0	36	42	21	15	14	26	.292	L	L	6-2	190	3-5-81	2004	Atlantic Highlands, N.J.
Parish, Brian	1	2	6.75	20	0	0	0	19	17	21	14	20	17	.250	R	R	5-11	185	1-20-82	2004	Mahopac, N.Y.
Pleeter, Gregg	4	0	4.40	18	0	0	0	43	29	24	21	19	43	.188	R	R	6-5	195	1-29-82	2004	Chestnut Ridge, N.Y.
Powell, John	2	2	7.52	14	6	0	0	32	36	31	27	28	26	.281	R	R	6-5	205	7-30-84	2004	Tillar, Ark.
Robertson, Quinton	2	0	4.11	7	6	0	0	35	36	18	16	7	27	.257	R	R	6-5	215	12-18-81	2004	Alpharetta, Ga.
Scherer, Matt	2	5	4.03	13	12	0	0	60	62	36	27	16	43	.258	R	R	6-5	230	1-20-83	2004	Wappingers Falls, N.Y.
Siak, Joey	1	1	3.45	20	0	0	0	29	32	14	11	6	29	.269	L	L	6-1	200	8-3-82	2004	Hendersonville, N.C.
Sillman, Michael	1	1	2.00	6	0	0	1	9	5	2	2	2	13	.161	R	R	6-1	190	12-3-81	2004	Omaha, Neb.
Spring, Dan	2	0	0.00	3	0	0	0	4	3	0	0	2	3	.231	R	R	6-1	190	12-15-80	2004	Washington, D.C.
Treadway, Zack	0	0	6.75	5	0	0	0	4	5	3	3	5	4	.313	R	R	6-1	215	6-2-82	2004	Oxford, Ohio
Worrell, Mark	1	0	1.16	18	0	0	7	23	12	3	3	7	37	.156	R	R	6-1	200	3-18-82	2004	Boynton Beach, Fla.

SAN DIEGO PADRES

BY JOHN MAFFEI

The 2003 season was a 64-98 disaster for San Diego.

To coincide with moving into a new downtown ballpark in 2004, Padres general manager Kevin Towers added outfielders Jay Payton and Terrence Long, catcher Ramon Hernandez, lefthander David Wells and righthander Akinori Otsuka to make the team competitive.

It worked.

The club didn't make the postseason, but it finished 87-75, was in the battle for the wild-card spot until the last three days of the season and drew 3 million fans to Petco Park.

"When your plan is to make the playoffs and you don't, you can't consider a season a success," Towers said. "Still, we made great strides."

Towers had hoped for normal seasons from first baseman Phil Nevin, left fielder Ryan Klesko and right fielder Brian Giles.

Nevin, who missed three weeks after knee surgery, hit .289-26-105 and carried the offense of a team that was just 42-39 at home. Klesko, bothered by a sore shoulder most of the season, batted .291-9-66, well below expectations from a power standpoint. Giles hit .284-23-94—not bad, but less than hoped for.

The left side of the infield was composed of homegrown products—third baseman Sean Burroughs and rookie shortstop Khalil Greene. Greene was spectacular in the field and hit better than expected—.273-15-65—despite missing the last month of the season with a broken finger. He was Baseball America's 2004 Rookie of the Year. Burroughs, who missed the final two weeks of the season after knee surgery, hit .298-2-47 while hitting in the leadoff spot most of the year.

Second baseman Mark Loretta had his second straight sensational season, hitting .335-16-76 with 208 hits and 47 doubles. And he teamed with Greene to form an

Jake Peavy   Brad Baker

PLAYERS of the YEAR

MAJOR LEAGUE: Jake Peavy, rhp

Peavy led the Padres resurgence towards contention in the National League West by going 15-6, 2.27 in 166 innings. He started strong, but finished even stronger, going 4-0, 2.03 in August and allowed one earned run on six hits in 14 innings in the last week of September to win the N.L. ERA title.

MINOR LEAGUE: Brad Baker, rhp

Baker, a supplemental first-round pick of the Red Sox in 1999, moved permanently to the bullpen in 2004 and flourished in the role. He was dominant at Double-A Mobile, going 2-1, 1.57 with 30 saves in 55 appearances. He made eight more outings at Triple-A Portland and saved four more games while going 1-0, 0.93.

excellent double-play combination.

Hernandez, who missed a month after knee surgery, hit .276-18-63 and caught nearly every game down the stretch as the team battled for a postseason spot.

Two of the best young arms in the starting rotation—Brian Lawrence and Jake Peavy—were drafted by the Padres and developed through the farm system. Peavy (15-6, 2.27 ERA) won the NL ERA title and proved to be a front-of-the-rotation starter at 23.

In the bullpen, closer Trevor Hoffman regained his form after missing most of the 2003 season following shoulder surgery. He had 41 saves, the sixth time in his career he saved 40 or more games in a season.

Three San Diego farm teams—Triple-A Portland, Double-A Mobile and low Class A Fort Wayne—made it to the playoffs. Mobile was declared co-champion of the Southern League after the championship series with the Tennessee Smokies was canceled because of Hurricane Ivan.

Portland (84-60) posted the best regular-season record in Triple-A. Often, Triple-A teams are a collection of retreads and six-year free agents. Not so with the Beavers.

"I'm very happy with the way things went this season," farm director Tye Waller said. "Things are starting to come together. We have prospects at every level now.

"As an organization, we had a nice year, a real nice year. With all the injuries and movement on the big club, we really had to rely on the farm system to supply talent. I think we came through, helped the big club, and still were able develop our players and win games."

ORGANIZATION LEADERS

BATTING

*AVG	Xavier Nady, Portland	.333
R	Paul McAnulty, Lake Elsinore	98
H	Fernando Valenzuela, Fort Wayne	148
TB	Paul McAnulty, Lake Elsinore	258
2B	Paul McAnulty, Lake Elsinore	36
3B	Brian Wahlbrink, Fort Wayne	8
HR	Greg Sain, Mobile	28
RBI	Josh Barfield, Mobile	90
BB	Paul McAnulty, Lake Elsinore	88
SO	Kervin Jacobo, Lake Elsinore	171
SB	Freddy Guzman, Portland/Mobile	65
*OBP	George Kottaras, Fort Wayne	.415
*SLG	Xavier Nady, Portland	.632

PITCHING

W	Four tied at	11
L	Three tied at	12
#ERA	Roger Deago, Portland/Mobile/Lake Elsinore	2.01
G	Brad Baker, Portland/Mobile	63
CG	Three tied at	2
SV	Brad Baker, Portland/Mobile	34
IP	Brian Whitaker, Mobile/Lake Elsinore	169
BB	David Pauley, Lake Elsinore	60
SO	Sean Thompson, Fort Wayne	157

*Minimum 250 at-bats #Minimum 75 innings

SAN DIEGO PADRES

Manager: Bruce Bochy.

2004 Record: 87-75, .537 (3rd, NL West).

BATTING	AVG	G	AB	R	H	2B	3B	HR	RBI	BB	SO	SB	CS	OBP	SLG	B	T	HT	WT	DOB	1st Yr	Resides
Aurilia, Rich	.254	51	138	22	35	8	2	2	16	15	28	0	0	.331	.384	R	R	6-1	185	9-2-71	1992	Phoenix, Ariz.
Bragg, Darren	.143	9	7	2	1	0	0	0	2	2	0	0	0	.333	.143	L	R	5-9	180	8-7-69	1991	Roswell, Ga.
Buchanan, Brian	.200	38	60	7	12	2	0	2	6	6	19	0	0	.279	.333	R	R	6-4	230	7-21-73	1994	Fort Myers, Fla.
Burroughs, Sean	.298	130	523	76	156	23	3	2	47	31	52	5	4	.348	.365	L	R	6-2	200	9-12-80	1999	Long Beach, Calif.
Cirillo, Jeff	.213	33	75	12	16	3	0	1	7	5	14	0	0	.259	.293	R	R	6-1	200	9-23-69	1991	Redmond, Wash.
Fick, Robert	.167	13	12	2	2	0	0	0	2	4	0	0	0	.333	.167	L	R	6-1	205	3-15-74	1996	Manhattan Beach, Calif.
Giles, Brian	.284	159	609	97	173	33	7	23	94	89	80	10	3	.374	.475	L	L	5-10	205	1-20-71	1989	San Diego, Calif.
Gonzalez, Alex	.174	11	23	2	4	1	1	0	3	2	6	0	0	.240	.304	R	R	6-0	200	4-8-73	1991	Coral Gables, Fla.
3-team (37 Chi./Mon. 35)	.225	83	285	36	64	18	1	7	27	14	64	2	2	.263	.368							
Greene, Khalil	.273	139	484	67	132	31	4	15	65	53	94	4	2	.349	.446	R	R	5-11	210	10-21-79	2002	Key West, Fla.
Guzman, Freddy	.211	20	76	8	16	3	0	0	5	3	13	5	2	.250	.250	S	R	5-10	165	1-20-81	2000	Santo Domingo, D.R.
Hansen, Dave	.143	29	28	1	4	0	0	0	3	5	0	0	0	.226	.143	L	R	6-0	195	11-24-68	1986	San Juan Capistrano, Calif.
Hernandez, Ramon	.276	111	384	45	106	23	0	18	63	35	45	1	0	.341	.477	R	R	6-0	210	5-20-76	1994	Aragua, Venez.
Klesko, Ryan	.291	127	402	58	117	32	2	9	66	73	67	3	2	.399	.448	L	L	6-3	220	6-12-71	1989	Couington, Ga.
Knott, Jon	.214	9	14	1	3	2	0	0	1	1	5	0	0	.267	.357	R	R	6-3	220	8-4-78	2002	Nokomis, Fla.
Long, Terrence	.295	136	288	31	85	19	4	3	28	19	51	3	2	.335	.420	L	L	6-1	200	2-29-76	1994	Montgomery, Ala.
Loretta, Mark	.335	154	620	108	208	47	2	16	76	58	45	5	3	.393	.495	R	R	6-0	185	8-14-71	1993	Scottsdale, Ariz.
Nady, Xavier	.247	34	77	7	19	4	0	3	9	5	13	0	0	.301	.416	R	R	6-2	205	11-14-78	2000	Salinas, Calif.
Nevin, Phil	.289	147	547	78	158	31	1	26	105	66	121	0	0	.368	.492	R	R	6-2	230	1-19-71	1993	San Diego, Calif.
Ojeda, Miguel	.256	62	156	23	40	3	0	8	26	15	34	0	0	.322	.429	R	R	6-2	190	1-29-75	1993	Sonora, Mexico
Payton, Jay	.260	143	458	57	119	17	4	8	55	43	56	2	0	.326	.367	R	R	5-10	185	11-22-72	1994	Zanesville, Ohio
Quintero, Humberto	.250	23	72	7	18	3	0	2	10	5	16	0	2	.295	.375	R	R	6-1	190	8-2-79	2007	Maracaibo, Venez.
Robinson, Kerry	.293	80	92	20	27	4	0	0	5	5	8	11	4	.330	.337	L	L	6-0	175	10-3-73	1995	Chesterfield, Mo.
Vazquez, Ramon	.235	52	115	12	27	3	2	1	13	11	24	1	1	.297	.322	L	R	5-11	170	8-21-76	1995	Cayey, P.R.

PITCHING	W	L	ERA	G	GS	CG	SV	IP	H	R	ER	BB	SO	AVG	B	T	HT	WT	DOB	1st Yr	Resides
Ashby, Andy	0	0	0.00	2	0	0	0	2	1	0	0	0	2	.143	R	R	6-1	202	7-11-67	1986	Pittston, Pa.
Beck, Rod	0	2	6.38	26	0	0	0	24	27	18	17	9	15	.278	R	R	6-1	230	8-3-68	1986	Scottsdale, Ariz.
Bynum, Mike	0	1	54.00	2	0	0	0	1	4	4	3	0	1	.500	L	L	6-4	200	3-20-78	1999	Middleburg, Fla.
Eaton, Adam	11	14	4.61	33	33	0	0	199	204	113	102	52	153	.266	R	R	6-2	190	11-23-77	1997	Snohomish, Wash.
Germano, Justin	1	2	8.86	7	5	0	0	21	31	24	21	14	16	.341	R	R	6-2	190	8-6-82	2000	Claremont, Calif.
Hitchcock, Sterling	0	3	6.33	4	4	0	0	21	22	15	15	8	14	.265	L	L	6-0	205	4-29-71	1989	Tampa, Fla.
Hoffman, Trevor	3	3	2.30	55	0	0	41	55	42	14	14	8	53	.211	R	R	6-0	215	10-13-67	1989	Del Mar, Calif.
Lawrence, Brian	15	14	4.12	34	34	2	0	203	226	101	93	55	121	.287	R	R	6-0	195	5-14-76	1998	Linden, Texas
Linebrink, Scott	7	3	2.14	73	0	0	0	84	61	22	20	26	83	.209	R	R	6-2	200	8-4-76	1997	Taylor, Texas
McLeary, Marty	0	0	14.73	3	0	0	0	4	6	6	6	2	4	.438	R	R	6-5	220	10-26-74	1997	Mansfield, Ohio
Neal, Blaine	1	1	4.07	40	0	0	0	42	49	19	19	11	36	.295	L	R	6-5	240	4-6-78	1996	Haddon Heights, N.J.
Oropesa, Eddie	2	1	12.00	6	0	0	0	9	12	12	12	13	6	.188	L	L	6-0	205	11-23-71	1993	Miami, Fla.
Osuna, Antonio	2	1	2.45	31	0	0	0	37	32	11	10	11	36	.232	R	R	5-11	205	4-12-73	1991	Juan Jose Rios, Mexico
Otsuka, Akinori	7	2	1.75	73	0	0	2	77	56	16	15	26	87	.199	R	R	5-11	200	1-13-72	2004	Chiba, Japan
Peavy, Jake	15	6	2.27	27	27	0	0	166	146	49	42	53	173	.236	R	R	6-1	180	5-31-81	1999	Semmes, Ala.
Puffer, Brandon	0	1	5.50	14	0	0	0	18	24	13	11	11	12	.320	R	R	6-3	190	10-5-75	1994	Round Rock, Texas
Stone, Ricky	1	6	6.89	27	0	0	0	33	40	27	25	9	22	.301	R	R	6-1	190	2-28-75	1994	Hamilton, Ohio
2-team (16 Houston)	2	6	6.45	43	0	0	0	52	66	39	37	16	38	.307							
Sweeney, Brian	1	0	5.65	7	2	0	0	14	20	9	9	2	10	.328	R	R	6-2	185	6-13-74	1996	Yonkers, N.Y.
Szuminski, Jason	0	0	7.20	7	0	0	0	10	12	9	8	11	5	.286	R	R	6-5	225	12-11-78	2000	San Antonio, Texas
Tankersley, Dennis	0	5	5.14	9	6	0	0	35	35	25	20	17	29	.254	R	R	6-2	185	2-24-79	1999	St. Charles, Mo.
Valdes, Ismael	9	6	5.53	23	20	1	0	114	141	75	70	31	37	.303	R	R	6-4	220	8-21-73	1991	Victoria, Mexico
Watkins, Steve	0	0	6.28	11	0	0	0	14	17	10	10	4	7	.293	R	R	6-4	190	7-19-78	1998	Lubbock, Texas
Wells, David	12	8	3.73	31	31	0	0	196	203	85	81	20	101	.266	L	L	6-4	235	5-20-63	1984	Clearwater, Fla.
Witasick, Jay	0	1	3.21	44	0	0	1	62	57	28	22	26	57	.244	R	R	6-4	235	8-28-72	1993	Bel Air, Md.

FIELDING

Catcher	PCT	G	PO	A	E	DP	PB
Hernandez	.992	108	753	35	6	7	7
Nevin	1.000	1	4	0	0	0	0
Ojeda	.996	50	240	18	1	2	2
Quintero	1.000	21	130	10	0	0	0

First Base	PCT	G	PO	A	E	DP
Aurilia	1.000	1	7	0	0	0
Buchanan	1.000	3	9	0	0	1
Cirillo	1.000	10	61	1	0	3
Fick	1.000	1	9	0	0	1
Hansen	1.000	7	15	1	0	2
Klesko	.987	18	138	16	2	19
Nevin	.989	144	1131	92	13	108
Vazquez	1.000	3	8	0	0	0

Second Base	PCT	G	PO	A	E	DP
Aurilia	.938	7	6	9	1	3
Cirillo	.867	4	4	9	2	2
Loretta	.987	154	288	451	10	101
Vazquez	1.000	10	13	17	0	4

Third Base	PCT	G	PO	A	E	DP
Aurilia	.919	29	16	41	5	3
Burroughs	.957	125	100	209	14	25
Cirillo	1.000	11	8	10	0	1
Hansen	1.000	2	0	1	0	0
Vazquez	1.000	9	8	6	0	2

Shortstop	PCT	G	PO	A	E	DP
Aurilia	.962	6	8	17	1	2
Greene	.965	136	177	381	20	81

	PCT	G	PO	A	E	DP
Gonzalez	1.000	11	10	18	0	4
Vazquez	.983	22	22	35	1	5

Outfield	PCT	G	PO	A	E	DP
Buchanan	1.000	18	12	0	0	0
Cirillo	.000	1	0	0	0	0
Giles	.979	159	322	8	7	3
Guzman	.960	17	46	2	2	0
Klesko	.986	104	135	2	2	0
Knott	1.000	5	4	0	0	0
Long	.986	87	140	2	2	0
Nady	.923	22	23	1	2	0
Payton	.989	137	342	11	4	2
Robinson	1.000	49	48	1	0	0

Phil Nevin: Team leader in homers (26) and RBIs (105)

Jake Peavy: Led majors with 2.27 ERA

LARRY GOREN

BILL MITCHELL

FARM SYSTEM

Director, Player Development: Tye Waller.

Class	Farm Team	League	W	L	Pct.	Finish*	Manager	Affiliate Since
AAA	Portland (Ore.) Beavers	Pacific Coast	84	60	.583	**1st (16)**	Craig Colbert	2001
AA	Mobile (Ala.) BayBears	Southern	73	67	.521	**+4th (10)**	Gary Jones	1997
High A	Lake Elsinore (Calif.) Storm	California	68	72	.486	7th (10)	Rick Renteria	2001
Low A	Fort Wayne (Ind.) Wizards	Midwest	72	68	.514	**t-7th (14)**	Randy Ready	1999
SS A	Eugene (Ore.) Emeralds	Northwest	26	50	.342	8th (8)	Roy Howell	2001
Rookie	Peoria (Ariz.) Padres	Arizona	26	30	.464	7th (9)	Carlos Lezcano	2004

*Finish in overall standings (No. of teams in league)/Playoff teams in **boldface**   +League Champion

PORTLAND BEAVERS

Class AAA

PACIFIC COAST LEAGUE

BATTING	AVG	G	AB	R	H	2B	3B	HR	RBI	BB	SO	SB	CS	OBP	SLG	B	T	HT	WT	DOB	1st Yr	Resides
Bozied, Taggert	.315	57	213	41	67	17	1	16	58	18	29	0	0	.374	.629	R	R	6-3	210	7-24-79	2001	Sioux Falls, S.D.
Buchanan, Brian	.357	12	42	9	15	8	0	2	12	9	7	0	0	.481	.690	R	R	6-4	230	7-21-73	1994	Fort Myers, Fla.
Castro, Bernie	.263	90	308	38	81	8	1	0	20	22	30	17	9	.310	.295	S	R	5-10	165	7-14-79	1998	Santo Domingo, D.R.
Cirillo, Jeff	.348	7	23	3	8	3	0	0	2	5	1	1	0	.464	.478	R	R	6-1	200	9-23-69	1991	Redmond, Wash.
Fernandez, Alex	.260	113	377	45	98	21	1	7	52	16	53	9	3	.288	.377	L	L	6-1	200	5-15-81	1998	Cotui, D.R.
Fick, Robert	.380	12	50	8	19	4	0	2	6	2	11	1	0	.404	.580	L	R	6-1	205	3-15-74	1996	Manhattan Beach, Calif.
Furmaniak, J.J.	.292	120	425	71	124	24	4	17	73	33	86	8	5	.346	.487	R	R	6-0	190	7-31-79	2000	Bolingbrook, Ill.
Gautreau, Jake	.274	48	168	24	46	9	1	9	35	14	37	1	0	.333	.500	L	R	6-0	185	11-14-79	2001	South Padre Island, Texas
Gerber, Joseph	.258	49	124	16	32	9	1	1	9	18	30	0	0	.350	.371	L	L	6-1	210	8-27-78	2000	Portland, Ore.
Germano, Justin	.000	10	16	0	0	0	0	0	0	0	10	0	0	.059	.000	R	R	6-2	190	8-6-82	2000	Claremont, Calif.
Guzman, Freddy	.292	66	264	48	77	12	4	1	19	30	46	48	5	.365	.379	S	R	5-10	165	1-20-81	2000	Santo Domingo, D.R.
Haad, Yamid	.302	80	295	47	89	21	0	9	35	16	41	3	0	.338	.464	R	R	6-2	210	9-2-77	1995	Cartagena, Colombia
Hernandez, Ramon	.316	7	19	2	6	1	0	0	6	2	3	0	0	.381	.368	R	R	6-0	210	5-20-76	1994	Aragua, Venez.
Killian, Billy	.143	3	7	0	1	0	0	0	0	1	0	0	0	.250	.143	L	R	6-1	190	6-12-86	2004	Stanwood, Mich.
Kingsale, Eugene	.205	20	44	9	9	3	0	2	6	7	7	2	0	.327	.409	S	R	6-3	190	8-20-76	1994	Oranjestad, Aruba
Knott, Jon	.290	113	435	79	126	22	3	26	85	58	110	5	3	.376	.533	R	R	6-3	220	8-4-78	2002	Nokomis, Fla.
Lopez, Mauber	.000	1	1	0	0	0	0	0	0	0	0	0	0	.000	.000	R	R	5-10	170	6-30-81	2001	Carabobo, Venez.
Nady, Xavier	.333	74	291	52	97	19	1	22	70	22	42	3	0	.394	.632	R	R	6-2	210	11-14-78	2000	Salinas, Calif.
Nieves, Jose	.271	80	288	35	78	19	1	4	31	17	30	5	3	.311	.385	R	R	6-0	180	6-16-75	1992	Carabobo, Venez.
Ojeda, Miguel	.263	5	19	4	5	0	0	2	3	2	3	0	0	.333	.579	R	R	6-2	190	1-29-75	1996	Sonora, Mexico
Petrick, Ben	.225	24	80	14	18	6	1	2	11	11	18	0	0	.323	.400	R	R	6-0	200	4-7-77	1996	Hillsboro, Ore.
Quintero, Humberto	.317	68	259	36	82	25	0	5	30	8	18	0	0	.348	.471	R	R	6-1	190	8-2-79	1997	Maracaibo, Venez.
Richardson, Mike	.250	1	4	1	1	0	0	1	1	1	2	0	0	.400	1.000	R	R	5-10	210	7-11-79	2002	Inverness, Calif.
Risinger, Ben	.242	79	227	28	55	11	0	4	25	16	40	0	0	.310	.344	R	R	6-1	170	11-25-77	1998	Perth, Australia
Robinson, Kerry	.306	42	170	31	52	6	3	2	20	19	15	25	1	.383	.412	L	L	6-0	175	10-3-73	1995	Chesterfield, Mo.
Scales, Bobby	.235	73	213	26	50	13	2	1	24	27	56	3	1	.335	.329	S	R	6-0	170	10-4-77	1999	Roswell, Ga.
Sears, Todd	.000	1	3	0	0	0	0	0	0	0	1	0	0	.000	.000	L	R	6-5	215	10-23-75	1997	Ankeny, Iowa
Stanley, Henri	.248	28	101	11	25	6	1	2	12	13	11	1	0	.330	.386	L	L	5-10	185	12-15-77	2000	Columbia, S.C.

BATTING	AVG	G	AB	R	H	2B	3B	HR	RBI	BB	SO	SB	CS	OBP	SLG	B	T	HT	WT	DOB	1st Yr	Resides
Vazquez, Ramon	.299	53	184	36	55	21	1	8	34	33	28	2	0	.402	.554	L	R	5-11	170	8-21-76	1995	Cayey, P.R.
Washington, Rico	.192	47	104	10	20	6	0	1	13	13	15	0	0	.292	.279	L	R	5-9	190	5-30-78	1997	Gray, Ga.

PITCHING	W	L	ERA	G	GS	CG	SV	IP	H	R	ER	BB	SO	AVG	B	T	HT	WT	DOB	1st Yr	Resides
Baker, Brad	1	0	0.93	8	0	0	4	10	5	2	1	4	17	.143	R	R	6-2	180	11-6-80	1999	Leyden, Mass.
Bruback, Matt	1	8	5.84	14	12	0	0	69	85	49	45	30	49	.304	R	R	6-7	210	1-12-79	1998	Sarasota, Fla.
Bumstead, Mike	4	0	2.57	18	5	0	0	49	44	14	14	18	38	.242	R	R	6-3	210	7-8-77	2001	Big Bear Lake, Calif.
Bynum, Mike	6	6	3.19	62	0	0	6	79	72	33	28	44	75	.243	L	L	6-4	200	3-20-78	1999	Middleburg, Fla.
Byrdak, Tim	3	0	5.45	20	2	0	0	38	48	28	23	17	25	.312	L	L	5-11	180	10-31-73	1994	Oak Forest, III.
Deago, Roger	0	0	4.66	5	0	0	0	10	13	6	5	5	6	.333	R	L	5-10	180	6-21-77	2003	Chitre, Panama
Fernandez, Alfredo	0	0	3.86	1	1	0	0	5	4	2	2	2	3	.235	R	R	6-4	205	9-15-84	2002	Maracaibo, Venez.
Germano, Justin	9	5	3.38	20	20	2	0	123	113	48	46	25	98	.241	R	R	6-2	190	8-6-82	2000	Claremont, Calif.
Hamilton, Joey	0	2	5.36	11	10	0	0	47	61	36	28	15	23	.308	R	R	6-4	240	9-9-70	1992	Norcross, Ga.
Hampton, Matt	2	2	4.88	37	1	0	0	59	59	35	32	17	51	.261	R	L	6-4	200	6-20-77	2001	Wenatchee, Wash.
Hitchcock, Sterling	1	1	6.35	3	3	0	0	11	17	9	8	1	6	.327	L	L	6-0	205	4-29-71	1989	Tampa, Fla.
Huerta, Edgar	1	0	1.17	6	0	0	0	8	4	1	1	6	4	.182	L	L	5-11	145	2-9-80	1999	Culiacan, Mexico
McLeary, Marty	5	4	2.99	44	7	0	13	84	65	30	28	42	81	.215	R	R	6-5	220	10-26-74	1997	Mansfield, Ohio
Miadich, Bart	3	4	3.57	31	0	0	12	35	28	16	14	25	34	.217	R	R	6-4	205	2-3-76	1998	Lake Oswego, Ore.
Neal, Blaine	4	2	1.86	27	0	0	1	39	32	10	8	12	38	.225	R	R	6-5	240	4-6-78	1996	Haddon Heights, N.J.
Oropesa, Eddie	3	3	2.31	37	0	0	1	47	30	15	12	19	55	.185	L	L	6-0	205	11-23-71	1993	Miami, Fla.
Osborne, Donovan	2	2	8.56	7	2	0	0	14	26	14	13	5	12	.426	L	L	6-2	195	6-21-69	1990	Carson City, Nev.
Oxspring, Chris	6	4	3.99	17	17	0	0	86	82	45	38	44	81	.247	R	R	6-1	180	5-13-77	2000	Labrador, Australia
Pote, Lou	1	0	7.20	4	0	0	1	5	5	4	4	3	6	.250	R	R	6-3	208	8-21-71	1991	Phoenix, Ariz.
2-team (19 Sacramento)	2	2	3.98	23	0	0	3	32	28	14	14	15	26	.243							
Puffer, Brandon	1	1	3.34	22	0	0	2	32	32	15	12	10	19	.254	R	R	6-3	190	10-5-75	1994	Round Rock, Texas
Risinger, Ben	0	0	9.00	1	0	0	0	1	2	1	1	1	1	.400	R	R	6-1	170	11-25-77	1998	Perth, Australia
Rojas, Chris	1	2	12.71	6	2	0	0	11	19	22	16	9	5	.365	R	R	6-2	180	3-30-77	1998	Glendale, N.Y.
Stauffer, Tim	6	3	3.54	14	14	0	0	81	83	46	32	26	50	.261	R	R	6-2	205	6-2-82	2004	Saratoga Springs, N.Y.
Steik, Ricky	1	0	37.80	2	0	0	0	2	7	7	7	3	1	.636	R	R	6-0	180	1-1-00	2004	Buena Park, Calif.
Stone, Ricky	0	0	3.38	3	0	0	0	5	9	5	2	2	2	.409	R	R	6-1	190	2-28-75	1994	Hamilton, Ohio
2-team (2 New Orleans)	1	0	3.68	5	0	0	0	7	11	6	3	2	2	.367							
Sweeney, Brian	11	4	3.83	24	23	0	0	139	130	65	59	42	110	.242	R	R	6-2	185	6-13-74	1996	Yonkers, N.Y.
Tankersley, Dennis	7	4	3.15	19	19	0	0	120	114	52	42	37	86	.253	R	R	6-2	185	2-24-79	1999	St. Charles, Mo.
Watkins, Steve	5	3	3.07	22	6	0	0	56	53	20	19	19	58	.248	R	R	6-4	190	7-19-78	1998	Lubbock, Texas
Webb, Alan	0	0	3.86	8	0	0	0	12	12	5	5	8	8	.273	L	L	5-10	160	9-26-79	1997	Las Vegas, Nev.

FIELDING

Catcher	PCT	G	PO	A	E	DP	PB
Fick	1.000	1	1	0	0	0	0
Haad	.987	69	491	30	7	4	7
Hernandez	.938	7	24	6	2	0	0
Ojeda	.974	5	36	1	1	0	0
Quintero	.989	67	489	50	6	5	4
Richardson	1.000	1	6	1	0	0	0
Risinger	.975	8	38	1	1	0	0

First Base	PCT	G	PO	A	E	DP
Bozied	.994	57	435	45	3	35
Buchanan	.983	11	104	9	2	9
Cirillo	1.000	1	10	0	0	0
Fick	.990	12	87	10	1	8
Gerber	.989	27	162	14	2	15
Haad	.990	10	97	3	1	10
Knott	1.000	1	4	2	0	0
Nady	.990	13	90	7	1	9
Nieves	.956	5	40	3	2	5

	PCT	G	PO	A	E	DP
Petrick	.992	14	117	5	1	6
Risinger	.987	12	72	6	1	11
Sears	.875	1	6	1	1	1
Second Base	**PCT**	**G**	**PO**	**A**	**E**	**DP**
Castro	.978	64	115	147	6	30
Cirillo	1.000	1	2	1	0	0
Nieves	.979	16	21	25	1	9
Risinger	.971	17	29	38	2	5
Scales	.965	15	21	34	2	8
Vazquez	.995	46	69	117	1	19
Third Base	**PCT**	**G**	**PO**	**A**	**E**	**DP**
Cirillo	.917	3	2	9	1	0
Gautreau	.948	45	28	63	5	6
Nieves	.956	42	37	72	5	3
Risinger	.977	32	28	58	2	8
Scales	1.000	6	6	9	0	0
Vazquez	1.000	4	1	7	0	2
Washington	.894	29	12	64	9	9

Shortstop	PCT	G	PO	A	E	DP
Furmaniak	.954	117	183	357	26	67
Nieves	.957	19	26	41	3	4
Risinger	.893	11	8	17	3	2
Vazquez	.950	4	4	15	1	1
Outfield	**PCT**	**G**	**PO**	**A**	**E**	**DP**
Castro	1.000	3	11	0	0	0
Fernandez	.959	102	156	8	7	4
Gerber	1.000	16	11	1	0	0
Guzman	.983	66	166	3	3	2
Kingsale	.939	15	30	1	2	0
Knott	.989	107	171	3	2	0
Nady	.974	63	111	3	3	0
Petrick	1.000	10	13	0	0	0
Robinson	.986	40	66	2	1	0
Scales	.893	18	24	1	3	0
Stanley	.971	30	66	0	2	0

MOBILE BAYBEARS Class AA

SOUTHERN LEAGUE

BATTING	AVG	G	AB	R	H	2B	3B	HR	RBI	BB	SO	SB	CS	OBP	SLG	B	T	HT	WT	DOB	1st Yr	Resides
Agramonte, Marcos	.100	4	10	2	1	0	0	0	0	0	2	1	0	.100	.100	S	R	5-10	175	9-29-76	1998	Athens, Ga.
Barfield, Josh	.248	138	521	79	129	28	3	18	90	48	119	4	2	.313	.417	R	R	6-0	185	12-17-82	2001	Spring, Texas
Carter, Josh	.225	33	89	6	20	3	0	1	6	3	16	1	3	.258	.292	R	R	6-2	210	11-5-80	2001	Fallbrook, Calif.
Clements, Jason	.270	99	230	33	62	7	1	3	21	25	62	5	1	.352	.348	R	R	5-11	170	3-1-78	1999	Arlington, Texas
Donovan, Todd	.299	52	201	38	60	7	3	2	19	24	44	20	9	.386	.393	R	R	6-1	175	8-12-78	1999	East Lyme, Conn.
Furmaniak, J.J.	.196	14	51	10	10	4	0	1	8	7	15	1	0	.305	.333	R	R	6-0	190	7-31-79	2000	Bolingbrook, Ill.
Gautreau, Jake	.259	66	212	27	55	13	0	10	30	31	52	1	1	.351	.462	L	R	6-0	185	11-14-79	2001	South Padre Island, Texas
Gerber, Joseph	.219	61	155	17	34	5	0	7	26	9	56	0	1	.259	.387	L	L	6-1	210	8-27-78	2000	Portland, Ore.
Guzman, Freddy	.283	35	138	21	39	5	2	1	7	16	28	17	5	.359	.370	S	R	5-10	165	1-20-81	2000	Santo Domingo, D.R.
Johnson, Ben	.251	136	475	80	119	28	6	23	85	55	136	5	6	.335	.480	R	R	6-1	200	1-18-81	1999	Memphis, Tenn.
Jones, Kennard	.234	82	304	35	71	14	2	0	9	25	76	6	4	.302	.293	L	L	5-11	180	9-8-81	2002	Beltsville, Md.
Lima, Joseph	1.000	1	1	0	1	0	0	0	0	0	0	0	0	1.000	1.000	R	R	6-1	190	7-16-79	2002	San Diego, Calif.
Merrill, Ronnie	.252	92	326	41	82	21	3	6	32	31	59	5	4	.321	.390	S	R	5-11	180	11-13-78	2000	Seffner, Fla.
Morales, Steve	.224	56	156	14	35	6	0	5	17	9	30	0	0	.266	.359	R	R	5-10	190	5-4-78	1996	Mayaguez, P.R.
Morton, Colt	.333	3	3	1	1	0	0	1	1	1	0	0	0	.500	1.333	R	R	6-6	227	4-10-82	2003	Wellington, Fla.
Nettles, Marcus	.248	55	137	18	34	3	1	0	9	8	42	7	3	.304	.285	L	L	5-11	185	5-15-80	2001	Chicago, Ill.
Richardson, Mike	.222	22	45	10	10	0	1	2	3	7	11	0	0	.364	.400	R	R	5-10	210	7-11-79	2002	Inverness, Calif.
Roman, Jesse	.169	68	172	16	29	5	0	5	14	16	38	0	1	.238	.285	L	L	6-0	190	4-21-79	2001	Woodhaven, N.Y.
Sain, Greg	.235	133	456	64	107	22	0	28	74	66	140	1	0	.338	.467	R	R	6-2	220	12-26-79	2001	Torrance, Calif.
Scales, Bobby	.265	20	68	13	18	1	1	3	13	15	2	0	.405	.353	S	R	6-0	170	10-4-77	1999	Roswell, Ga.
Trzesniak, Nick	.211	108	346	26	73	18	2	7	42	28	91	2	3	.284	.335	R	R	6-0	210	11-19-80	1999	Tinley Park, Ill.
Washington, Rico	.291	68	244	36	71	12	1	9	45	33	42	0	2	.376	.459	L	R	5-9	190	5-30-78	1997	Gray, Ga.

PITCHING	W	L	ERA	G	GS	CG	SV	IP	H	R	ER	BB	SO	AVG	B	T	HT	WT	DOB	1st Yr	Resides
Baker, Brad	2	1	1.57	55	0	0	30	57	37	11	10	24	68	.179	R	R	6-2	180	11-6-80	1999	Leyden, Mass.
Bumstead, Mike	0	1	5.13	19	0	0	0	26	28	15	15	18	22	.298	R	R	6-3	210	7-8-77	2001	Big Bear Lake, Calif.
Cassel, Jack	4	2	3.74	57	0	0	1	75	77	35	31	27	52	.277	R	R	6-2	190	8-8-80	2000	Northridge, Calif.
Conden, Greg	0	1	15.00	1	1	0	0	3	6	5	5	2	1	.462	R	R	6-3	220	7-24-80	2003	California, Md.
Deago, Roger	3	2	1.69	22	8	0	0	69	52	17	13	26	50	.215	R	L	5-10	180	6-21-77	2003	Chitre, Panama
Germano, Justin	2	1	2.51	5	5	0	0	32	31	11	9	7	20	.258	R	R	6-2	190	8-6-82	2000	Claremont, Calif.
Gregg, Grant	0	0	0.00	1	0	0	0	2	3	0	0	0	1	.273	L	L	6-3	230	6-4-80	2003	Abilene, Texas
Hamilton, Clayton	1	0	1.80	1	1	0	0	5	5	2	1	2	6	.263	R	R	6-5	200	6-15-82	2004	Beaver Falls, Pa.
Hampton, Matt	3	0	3.00	13	0	0	1	12	10	4	4	3	8	.222	R	L	6-4	220	6-20-77	2001	Wenatchee, Wash.
Hensley, Clay	11	10	4.30	27	27	2	0	159	167	84	76	48	125	.276	R	R	5-11	190	8-31-79	2002	Pearland, Texas
Huerta, Edgar	0	2	9.00	6	0	0	0	7	12	9	7	6	7	.387	L	L	5-11	145	2-9-80	1999	Culiacan, Mexico
Jones, Geoff	0	0	3.00	6	0	0	0	9	6	3	3	5	13	.182	L	L	6-6	230	4-15-78	1999	Dolores, Colo.
McAdoo, Duncan	2	3	5.50	6	6	0	0	34	39	24	21	9	22	.277	R	R	6-1	200	4-15-78	2000	Houston, Texas
Miniel, Rene	1	2	4.64	30	0	0	0	43	39	26	22	22	38	.245	R	R	6-2	170	4-26-79	1998	Santo Domingo, D.R.
Peavy, Jake	0	1	5.79	1	1	0	0	5	7	4	3	2	4	.318	R	R	6-1	180	5-31-81	1999	Semmes, Ala.
Ribas, Gabe	2	7	8.35	13	12	0	0	51	78	49	47	25	18	.368	R	R	6-4	220	2-3-80	2002	Brunswick, Maine
Rivera, Homero	0	1	10.97	8	0	0	0	11	19	13	13	7	5	.404	R	L	5-10	160	8-13-77	1995	Nizao, D.R.
Rojas, Chris	7	5	3.31	19	19	0	0	103	88	46	38	46	77	.230	R	R	6-2	180	3-30-77	1998	Glendale, N.Y.
Sevier, Nate	0	0	1.47	11	0	0	0	18	10	4	3	7	13	.167	R	R	6-0	220	9-14-79	2002	Salinas, Calif.
Spiehs, R.D.	5	6	2.88	59	0	0	3	66	56	24	21	19	60	.238	R	R	6-3	210	10-18-79	2002	Grand Island, Neb.
Stauffer, Tim	3	2	2.63	8	8	1	0	51	56	17	15	13	33	.286	R	R	6-2	205	6-2-82	2004	Saratoga Springs, N.Y.
Thayer, Dale	1	1	3.68	8	0	0	0	7	8	3	3	1	7	.267	R	R	6-0	190	12-17-80	2003	Huntington Beach, Calif.
Thompson, Mike	10	2	3.41	35	18	0	0	121	129	50	46	31	69	.285	R	R	6-4	200	11-6-80	1999	Lamar, Colo.
Watkins, Steve	4	3	3.64	10	10	0	0	59	50	28	24	15	57	.231	R	R	6-4	190	7-26-78	1998	Lubbock, Texas
Webb, Alan	4	4	4.40	42	0	0	0	47	35	23	23	19	48	.212	L	L	5-10	160	9-26-79	1997	Las Vegas, Nev.
Whitaker, Brian	8	9	3.73	23	23	1	0	138	128	68	57	36	82	.249	R	R	6-4	200	11-5-79	2002	Salisbury, N.C.
Wodnicki, Mike	0	0	9.00	5	1	0	0	8	13	9	8	4	5	.371	R	R	6-3	210	1-17-80	2001	Southington, Conn.

FIELDING

Catcher	PCT	G	PO	A	E	DP	PB
Morales	.986	44	257	29	4	0	4
Morton	1.000	1	10	0	0	0	1
Richardson	1.000	2	9	1	0	0	1
Sain	.950	3	18	1	1	1	2
Trzesniak	.990	101	645	84	7	4	6

First Base	PCT	G	PO	A	E	DP
Gerber	.991	12	95	10	1	13
Roman	.988	18	159	7	2	16
Sain	.992	113	993	64	8	97
Washington	1.000	1	2	0	0	0

Second Base	PCT	G	PO	A	E	DP
Barfield	.981	136	293	396	13	95

	PCT	G	PO	A	E	DP
Clements	1.000	3	4	9	0	0
Scales	1.000	1	2	5	0	1

Third Base	PCT	G	PO	A	E	DP
Clements	.950	9	5	14	1	0
Gautreau	.940	63	40	116	10	8
Sain	1.000	7	3	14	0	0
Washington	.960	65	48	143	8	19

Shortstop	PCT	G	PO	A	E	DP
Agramonte	1.000	2	2	6	0	3
Clements	.945	38	56	98	9	24
Furmaniak	.970	14	23	42	2	8
Merrill	.961	89	125	274	16	59

Outfield	PCT	G	PO	A	E	DP
Carter	1.000	21	20	2	0	1
Clements	1.000	18	17	0	0	0
Donovan	.983	54	111	2	2	0
Gerber	.949	20	35	2	2	1
Guzman	.989	34	81	5	1	0
Johnson	.963	144	226	10	9	1
Jones	.980	81	187	7	4	1
Nettles	.964	37	52	2	2	0
Richardson	1.000	13	28	2	0	0
Roman	.969	24	30	1	1	0
Scales	.893	19	24	1	3	0
Trzesniak	1.000	1	2	0	0	0

LAKE ELSINORE STORM
High Class A

CALIFORNIA LEAGUE

BATTING	AVG	G	AB	R	H	2B	3B	HR	RBI	BB	SO	SB	CS	OBP	SLG	B	T	HT	WT	DOB	1st Yr	Resides
Adams, Skip	.156	9	32	2	5	0	1	1	5	1	11	0	0	.182	.313	R	R	6-0	200	10-18-79	2003	Albuquerque, N.M.
Aguilar, Trino	.000	3	3	1	0	0	0	0	1	0	0	0	0	.400	.000	R	R	5-10	170	8-27-83	2001	Guarico, Venez.
Baker, Casey	.283	80	297	45	84	13	3	3	36	16	54	15	8	.322	.377	R	R	5-9	160	8-7-80	1999	Wysox, Pa.
Baker, Steve	.254	72	283	35	72	14	3	4	34	21	72	10	3	.312	.367	R	R	6-3	200	4-20-80	2002	Rome, N.Y.
Buchanan, Brian	.300	4	10	1	3	2	0	0	1	3	0	0	0	.417	.500	R	R	6-4	230	7-21-73	1994	Fort Myers, Fla.
Burgamy, Brian	.268	38	123	16	33	5	0	1	18	11	22	1	4	.328	.333	S	R	5-10	180	12-20-80	2002	Aylmer, Quebec
Carlin, Luke	.262	37	107	12	28	7	0	1	12	10	19	0	1	.319	.355	S	R	5-11	180	12-20-80	2002	Aylmer, Quebec
Carter, Josh	.305	89	331	38	101	23	2	1	41	17	41	4	4	.345	.396	R	R	6-2	210	11-5-80	2001	Fallbrook, Calif.
Cruz, Luis	.277	124	512	75	142	35	3	8	72	24	56	3	7	.310	.404	R	R	6-0	180	2-10-84	2001	Sonora, Mexico
Jacobo, Kervin	.241	123	457	53	110	21	4	11	55	34	171	12	7	.299	.376	S	R	6-2	190	9-26-82	2000	Haina, D.R.
Johnson, Michael	.254	90	331	55	84	23	2	15	64	52	106	0	0	.353	.471	L	R	6-3	215	6-25-80	2003	Georgetown, S.C.
Jones, Kennard	.291	50	206	23	60	8	5	0	18	25	40	13	11	.369	.379	L	L	5-11	180	9-8-81	2002	Beltsville, Md.
Lauderdale, Matt	.333	2	6	1	2	0	1	0	3	0	0	0	0	.333	.833	R	R	5-10	200	4-14-81	2003	Roswell, Ga.
Lima, Joseph	.219	61	192	17	42	13	1	1	20	11	51	3	2	.267	.313	R	R	6-1	190	7-16-79	2002	San Diego, Calif.
McAnulty, Paul	.297	133	495	98	147	36	3	23	87	88	106	3	1	.404	.521	L	R	5-10	220	2-24-81	2002	Oxnard, Calif.
Merrill, Ronnie	.425	9	40	7	17	2	2	2	7	4	6	1	2	.477	.725	R	R	6-2	210	9-12-80	2002	Long Beach, Calif.
Miller, Chris	.278	12	36	5	10	1	0	3	6	4	9	0	1	.395	.556	L	L	5-11	185	5-15-80	2001	Chicago, Ill.
Nettles, Marcus	.271	52	203	32	55	1	4	0	7	16	44	15	4	.327	.315	L	L	5-11	180	3-18-81	1999	Yauco, P.R.
Pagan, Andres	.240	103	354	38	85	16	2	6	44	34	92	0	2	.311	.347	R	R	6-4	180	3-18-81	1999	Yauco, P.R.
Ramos, Peeter	.270	63	256	39	69	13	1	0	15	19	34	12	2	.324	.328	R	R	5-11	150	3-18-82	2001	Inverness, Calif.
Richardson, Mike	.257	78	280	47	72	12	1	11	47	44	70	1	3	.363	.425	R	R	6-0	190	4-21-79	2001	Woodhaven, N.Y.
Roman, Jesse	.263	51	194	22	51	9	0	6	27	15	43	0	0	.316	.402	L	L	6-0	190	4-21-79	2001	Woodhaven, N.Y.
Serrano, Eddie	.353	7	17	3	6	0	0	0	4	2	0	0	0	.476	.353	R	R	6-0	170	10-26-81	2000	David, Panama
Smyres, Justin	.239	16	46	11	11	3	2	1	9	8	10	0	0	.375	.457	R	R	6-0	175	5-8-81	2003	Paso Robles, Calif.
Tejeda, Ferdin	.257	14	35	6	9	0	0	0	4	8	1	2	2	.395	.257	S	R	5-11	170	9-15-82	2001	Santo Domingo, D.R.
Watson, Rob	.000	3	11	1	0	0	0	0	2	0	1	0	0	.000	.000	R	R	5-10	180	12-31-79	2002	Riverside, Calif.

PITCHING	W	L	ERA	G	GS	CG	SV	IP	H	R	ER	BB	SO	AVG	B	T	HT	WT	DOB	1st Yr	Resides
Beavers, Kevin	2	6	5.28	33	8	0	0	75	82	53	44	33	44	.278	L	L	6-5	190	10-24-79	2002	Irvine, Calif.
Bechtel, Chuck	0	2	3.77	9	0	0	1	14	15	9	6	5	9	.254	R	R	6-4	215	11-12-79	2003	Royersford, Pa.
Bonine, Eddie	5	10	5.45	21	21	0	0	112	121	82	68	39	96	.271	R	R	6-5	220	6-6-81	2003	Glendale, Ariz.
Bumstead, Mike	1	0	1.23	9	0	0	0	15	10	2	2	5	13	.192	R	R	6-3	210	7-8-77	2001	Big Bear Lake, Calif.
Coonrod, Aaron	3	2	3.51	22	1	0	0	33	27	17	13	19	37	.221	R	R	6-4	200	5-17-80	2002	Fremont, Ohio
Craker, Justin	2	1	9.88	9	0	0	0	14	14	16	15	18	9	.280	R	R	6-0	215	9-11-78	2001	Superior, Wis.
Deago, Roger	0	0	0.00	1	0	0	0	2	1	0	0	0	3	.200	R	L	5-10	180	6-21-77	2003	Chitre, Panama

ORGANIZATION STATISTICS

PITCHING

PITCHING	W	L	ERA	G	GS	CG	SV	IP	H	R	ER	BB	SO	AVG	B	T	HT	WT	DOB	1st Yr	Resides
Girardeau, Clark	3	2	4.53	12	9	0	0	54	57	32	27	18	38	.264	R	R	6-5	210	4-12-82	2003	Mobile, Ala.
Gregg, Grant	1	3	5.15	37	0	0	0	44	44	31	25	26	41	.254	L	L	6-3	230	6-4-80	2003	Abilene, Texas
Guthrie, Sazi	1	0	0.84	5	0	0	0	11	10	1	1	5	11	.256	R	R	6-4	205	12-14-79	2004	Santa Cruz, Calif.
Hayhurst, Dirk	1	2	5.56	5	5	0	0	23	25	18	14	16	18	.269	L	R	6-3	200	3-24-81	2003	Canton, Ohio
Hitchcock, Sterling	1	0	1.00	2	2	0	0	9	8	1	1	0	13	.250	L	L	6-0	205	4-29-71	1989	Tampa, Fla.
Huber, Jon	8	6	3.70	20	20	0	0	107	107	53	44	44	100	.260	R	R	6-2	190	7-1-81	2000	North Fort Myers, Fla.
Jones, Geoff	1	1	3.00	11	0	0	0	18	10	10	6	6	11	.159	L	L	6-6	230	8-10-79	1999	Dolores, Colo.
Mateo, Natanael	6	3	2.79	39	0	0	2	52	46	20	16	11	59	.248	R	R	6-1	160	12-24-80	1999	Dominican Republic
Miniel, Rene	0	1	7.33	16	0	0	1	27	39	23	22	14	29	.342	R	R	6-2	170	4-26-79	1998	Santo Domingo, D.R.
Osuna, Antonio	0	0	2.45	7	2	0	0	7	2	2	2	2	12	.083	R	R	5-11	205	4-12-73	1991	Juan Jose Rios, Mexico
Pauley, David	7	12	4.17	27	26	0	0	153	155	89	71	60	128	.262	R	R	6-2	170	6-17-83	2001	Longmont, Colo.
Ribas, Gabe	4	5	4.35	13	13	0	0	70	85	47	34	21	41	.298	R	R	6-4	220	2-3-80	2002	Brunswick, Maine
Sevier, Nate	0	0	3.10	38	1	0	1	52	54	24	18	12	46	.262	R	R	6-0	220	9-14-79	2002	Salinas, Calif.
Shanks, E.J.	0	0	0.00	1	0	0	0	1	0	0	0	0	0	.000	R	R	6-5	230	4-8-82	2004	Las Vegas, Nev.
Stauffer, Tim	2	0	1.78	6	6	0	0	35	28	10	7	9	30	.215	R	R	6-2	205	6-2-82	2003	Saratoga Springs, N.Y.
Thayer, Dale	2	1	1.63	50	0	0	23	55	36	12	10	11	54	.181	R	R	6-0	190	12-17-80	2003	Huntington Beach, Calif.
Tierney, Chris	2	5	6.96	8	8	0	0	43	56	38	33	19	18	.324	L	L	6-6	200	9-1-83	2001	Lockport, Ill.
Tucker, Rusty	0	0	7.71	8	0	0	0	7	9	8	6	5	6	.300	R	L	6-1	190	7-15-80	2001	Gloucester, Mass.
Villatoro, Wilmer	6	2	2.84	47	0	0	0	67	50	29	21	35	67	.218	R	R	6-0	150	6-27-83	2000	San Salvador, El Salvador
Webb, Alan	2	1	3.86	11	0	0	0	12	10	6	5	4	9	.227	L	L	5-10	160	9-25-79	1997	Las Vegas, Nev.
Wells, Jared	4	6	4.52	13	12	0	0	72	81	44	36	30	38	.289	R	R	6-4	200	10-31-81	2003	Brazoria, Texas
Whitaker, Brian	1	2	1.99	5	5	1	0	32	28	11	7	7	25	.235	R	R	6-4	200	11-5-79	2002	Salisbury, N.C.
Wiedmeyer, Jason	0	0	9.90	4	0	0	0	10	18	11	11	3	1	.391	L	L	6-3	200	10-15-78	2001	West Bend, Wis.
Wodnicki, Mike	3	1	6.04	17	1	0	7	22	36	17	15	3		.356	R	R	6-3	210	1-17-80	2001	Southington, Conn.

FIELDING

Catcher

Catcher	PCT	G	PO	A	E	DP	PB
Carlin	.985	36	237	32	4	3	5
Lauderdale	1.000	2	5	1	0	0	0
Miller	1.000	2	13	0	0	0	0
Pagan	.974	99	703	82	21	6	12
Richardson	.987	10	68	8	1	0	3

First Base

First Base	PCT	G	PO	A	E	DP
Buchanan	1.000	2	11	0	0	0
Johnson	.986	69	612	30	9	47
Lima	1.000	3	8	0	0	1
McAnulty	.992	26	246	13	2	20
Pagan	.917	2	11	0	1	1
Roman	.986	45	393	24	6	33

Second Base

Second Base	PCT	G	PO	A	E	DP
Adams	1.000	1	1	3	0	1
Aguilar	1.000	2	3	3	0	2
C. Baker	.962	12	21	30	2	9
Burgamy	.875	5	6	8	2	1
Lima	.964	41	73	116	7	18
Merrill	.929	5	10	16	2	2
Ramos	.944	63	107	195	18	29
Serrano	.870	6	14	3	2	
Smyres	.985	12	26	41	1	10
Tejeda	1.000	2	3	5	0	0
Watson	1.000	3	7	12	0	3

Third Base

Third Base	PCT	G	PO	A	E	DP
Burgamy	.925	13	14	23	3	5
Cruz	.880	6	16	3	3	
Jacobo	.901	115	69	203	30	6
Lima	.947	10	10	8	1	0
Smyres	.778	3	2	5	2	0

Shortstop

Shortstop	PCT	G	PO	A	E	DP
Adams	.907	8	17	32	5	4
C. Baker	1.000	2	2	1	0	1
Cruz	.936	116	194	376	39	70
Jacobo	.893	5	7	18	3	2
Lima	.667	1	1	3	2	2
Merrill	.857	3	4	8	2	2
Ramos	.714	1	3	2	2	1
Tejeda	.889	9	10	22	4	2

Outfield

Outfield	PCT	G	PO	A	E	DP
C. Baker	.978	67	127	4	3	0
S. Baker	.993	72	143	6	1	1
Buchanan	1.000	1	1	0	0	0
Burgamy	1.000	17	18	0	0	0
Carter	.977	74	120	8	3	2
Jones	.939	50	90	2	6	0
Lima	1.000	1	1	0	0	0
McAnulty	.949	68	101	10	6	0
Nettles	.959	52	93	1	4	0
Richardson	.984	39	60	3	1	0
Roman	.875	7	6	1	1	0

FORT WAYNE WIZARDS — Low Class A

MIDWEST LEAGUE

BATTING

BATTING	AVG	G	AB	R	H	2B	3B	HR	RBI	BB	SO	SB	CS	OBP	SLG	B	T	HT	WT	DOB	1st Yr	Resides
Adams, Skip	.177	63	203	28	36	6	0	7	25	16	82	3	1	.249	.310	R	R	6-0	200	10-18-79	2003	Albuquerque, N.M.
Baker, Casey	.248	29	117	13	29	7	0	0	9	5	29	1	4	.279	.308	R	R	5-9	160	8-7-80	1999	Wysox, Pa.
Bochy, Greg	.188	34	117	6	22	2	0	2	15	15	35	0	0	.276	.256	R	R	6-2	200	8-26-79	2002	Poway, Calif.
Bonvechio, Brett	.237	82	304	36	72	19	1	9	45	27	76	0	0	.309	.395	L	R	6-1	190	11-13-82	2001	Santa Clara, Calif.
Burgamy, Brian	.233	16	60	10	14	7	0	0	4	7	13	3	0	.309	.350	S	R	5-10	190	6-27-81	2002	Lawton, Okla.
Carlin, Luke	.212	27	99	10	21	6	3	0	12	11	23	1	0	.288	.333	S	R	5-11	180	12-20-80	2002	Aylmer, Quebec
Ciofrone, Peter	.261	42	157	20	41	3	2	1	15	16	28	0	0	.348	.325	L	R	5-11	190	9-28-82	2002	Nesconset, N.Y.
Ciriaco, Juan	.244	99	348	29	85	12	2	2	35	16	80	5	8	.280	.307	R	R	6-0	160	8-15-83	2003	Santo Domingo, D.R.
Figueroa, Baudilio	.115	8	26	3	3	0	0	0	1	3	6	0	0	.148	.231	S	R	6-0	160	6-28-83	2002	Puerto Plata, D.R.
Garay, Ernesto	.232	22	69	12	16	1	1	0	2	8	16	0	1	.312	.275	L	L	6-1	160	2-17-82	2001	Managua, Nicaragua
Hogan, Billy	.164	16	61	7	10	2	0	0	6	7	20	0	0	.246	.197	R	R	6-3	210	5-20-83	2003	Dallas, Texas
Johnson, Ryan	.089	12	45	2	4	1	0	0	2	2	10	0	0	.128	.111	L	L	6-2	205	1-11-81	2003	Laguna Hills, Calif.
Kazmar, Sean	.217	5	23	5	5	1	0	0	2	1	6	0	0	.308	.348	R	R	5-10	170	8-5-84	2004	Las Vegas, Nev.
Kolkhorst, Chris	.340	12	47	15	16	4	1	1	4	5	7	1	1	.429	.532	L	R	6-2	215	3-7-82	2004	Houston, Texas
Kottaras, George	.310	78	271	40	84	18	1	7	46	51	41	0	0	.415	.461	L	L	6-0	190	5-16-83	2003	Markham, Ontario
Lauderdale, Matt	.226	39	146	17	33	10	1	4	18	14	44	1	0	.307	.390	R	R	5-10	200	4-14-81	2003	Roswell, Ga.
Macias, Drew	.266	129	478	60	127	18	5	8	55	49	68	16	14	.340	.374	L	L	6-3	175	3-7-83	2003	Rancho Cucamonga, Calif.
McRoberts, Mark	.168	30	101	8	17	8	0	1	12	16	46	0	0	.282	.277	R	R	6-3	190	1-15-82	2000	El Cajon, Calif.
Miller, Chris	.202	24	89	8	18	2	0	3	14	2	16	0	0	.226	.326	R	R	6-2	210	9-12-80	2002	Long Beach, Calif.
Mora, Ruben	.284	23	81	12	23	2	0	1	5	10	19	1	1	.363	.346	S	R	6-0	170	10-1-82	2000	Colon, Panama
Morton, Colt	.150	36	127	10	19	5	1	4	11	16	45	0	0	.260	.299	R	R	6-6	227	4-10-82	2003	Wellington, Fla.
Pickens, Jordan	.240	106	392	68	94	23	0	17	58	42	112	1	0	.338	.429	R	R	6-2	190	6-10-81	2001	Atascadero, Calif.
Ramos, Peeter	.296	61	253	43	75	10	4	3	31	17	35	20	6	.343	.403	R	R	5-11	150	3-18-82	2001	Caracas, Venez.
Smith, Rashad	.056	5	18	2	1	0	0	0	1	5	1	0		.105	.056	L	R	6-4	200	1-20-80	2002	Bolivar, Tenn.
Smyres, Justin	.214	22	84	6	18	6	1	0	9	3	14	0	0	.250	.310	R	R	6-0	175	5-8-81	2003	Paso Robles, Calif.
Thayer, Matt	.667	1	3	0	2	0	0	0	2	1	0	1	0	.750	.667	R	R	6-1	200	2-21-82	2004	Woodland Hills, Calif.
Valenzuela, Fernando	.294	135	503	68	148	23	2	11	81	56	63	1	0	.373	.414	L	L	5-10	210	9-30-82	2003	Los Angeles, Calif.
Wahlbrink, Brian	.258	126	519	81	134	19	8	8	47	35	142	24	9	.312	.372	R	R	6-3	200	3-19-80	2003	Anaheim, Calif.

PITCHING

PITCHING	W	L	ERA	G	GS	CG	SV	IP	H	R	ER	BB	SO	AVG	B	T	HT	WT	DOB	1st Yr	Resides
Abraham, Paul	1	2	2.79	37	0	0	1	48	53	28	15	15	49	.279	R	R	6-1	200	1-10-80	2001	Centreville, Va.
Bechtel, Chuck	1	4	6.94	35	0	0	0	67	63	49	36	40	54	.318	R	R	6-4	215	11-12-79	2003	Royersford, Pa.
Bonine, Eddie	2	1	1.98	5	5	0	0	27	25	11	6	3	31	.236	R	R	6-5	220	6-6-81	2003	Glendale, Ariz.

PITCHING	W	L	ERA	G	GS	CG	SV	IP	H	R	ER	BB	SO	AVG	B	T	HT	WT	DOB	1st Yr	Resides
Chick, Travis	5	0	2.13	7	7	0	0	42	32	12	10	9	55	.206	R	R	6-3	220	6-10-84	2002	Tyler, Texas
Conden, Greg	4	7	4.30	23	12	0	1	82	70	49	39	33	85	.230	R	R	6-3	220	7-24-80	2003	California, Md.
Coonrod, Aaron	1	4	4.54	29	0	0	5	36	37	28	18	30	33	.266	R	R	6-4	210	5-17-80	2002	Fremont, Ohio
De la O, Danny	1	0	6.43	2	1	0	0	7	10	5	5	2	4	.333	L	L	6-0	185	8-25-83	2003	Marina del Ray, Calif.
Ekstrom, Michael	0	2	8.16	3	3	0	0	14	21	15	13	3	10	.344	R	R	6-2	215	8-30-83	2004	Gresham, Ore.
Garcia, Geivy	0	1	4.76	4	0	0	0	6	7	3	3	0	4	.304	R	R	6-1	174	7-8-82	2001	LaGuna Salada, D.R.
Girardeau, Clark	4	4	5.02	13	13	0	0	72	64	50	40	29	73	.233	R	R	6-5	210	4-12-82	2003	Mobile, Ala.
Gregg, Grant	1	2	5.09	12	0	0	0	18	22	13	10	5	16	.306	L	L	6-3	230	6-4-80	2003	Abilene, Texas
Guthrie, Sazi	2	4	4.23	35	3	0	1	77	84	48	36	32	57	.278	R	R	6-4	205	12-14-79	2004	Santa Cruz, Calif.
Hayhurst, Dirk	9	4	2.66	26	17	0	0	118	114	41	35	19	106	.252	L	R	6-3	200	3-24-81	2003	Canton, Ohio
Klatt, Ryan	4	0	2.79	25	0	0	3	29	19	10	9	6	35	.184	R	R	6-0	185	3-21-81	1999	Sale Creek, Tenn.
Mead, David	1	5	6.40	18	11	0	0	58	61	49	41	34	54	.280	R	R	6-5	180	6-24-82	2003	Spencer, N.C.
Moore, Daniel	1	3	7.41	4	4	0	0	17	27	14	14	10	14	.380	L	L	6-5	225	6-24-82	2003	Spencer, N.C.
Pence, Howie	4	3	2.83	44	0	0	2	48	45	24	15	24	49	.243	R	R	6-5	210	10-17-79	2003	Arlington, Texas
Perez, Henry	3	1	3.70	21	0	0	0	24	21	14	10	8	23	.231	R	R	6-3	210	10-27-82	2000	Santo Domingo, D.R.
Robinson, Ronnie	0	0	3.77	10	0	0	0	14	20	13	6	5	13	.328	R	R	6-3	195	4-22-81	2003	Atlanta, Ga.
Rosales, Leo	6	1	1.40	53	1	0	26	58	38	11	9	15	66	.183	R	R	6-1	185	5-28-81	2003	Los Angeles, Calif.
Steidlmayer, Luke	1	0	2.61	3	2	0	0	10	6	5	3	1	14	.158	R	R	6-5	190	8-13-80	2002	Colusa, Calif.
Sterry, Vern	2	0	2.40	5	5	0	0	30	27	9	8	5	26	.237	R	R	6-2	210	2-7-82	2004	Rowland Heights, Calif.
Thompson, Sean	9	6	3.10	27	27	0	0	148	125	60	51	57	157	.234	L	L	5-11	160	10-13-82	2002	La Junta, Colo.
Tierney, Chris	3	4	3.38	15	15	0	0	83	91	40	31	31	51	.285	L	L	6-6	200	9-1-83	2001	Lockport, Ill.
Upwood, Jake	1	2	6.00	19	0	0	0	21	24	20	14	12	17	.286	L	L	5-11	175	9-19-80	2003	Central Square, N.Y.
Varner, Matt	2	2	1.61	19	0	0	1	22	18	6	4	7	16	.231	R	R	5-11	200	1-16-82	2004	Brazoria, Texas
Wells, Jared	4	6	4.09	14	14	1	0	81	91	42	37	19	72	.278	R	R	6-4	200	10-31-81	2003	Brazoria, Texas

FIELDING

Catcher	PCT	G	PO	A	E	DP	PB
Carlin	.988	27	223	23	3	1	4
Kottaras	.991	50	399	27	4	2	5
Lauderdale	.975	21	176	18	5	0	3
Miller	.987	8	72	5	1	1	4
Morton	.986	36	331	29	5	1	2

First Base	PCT	G	PO	A	E	DP
Adams	1.000	2	7	0	0	0
Miller	1.000	1	4	0	0	1
Pickens	1.000	5	39	1	0	4
Valenzuela	.990	135	1065	78	12	98

Second Base	PCT	G	PO	A	E	DP
Adams	.947	4	8	10	1	3
Baker	.980	9	20	29	1	10
Burgamy	.942	16	25	40	4	7

	PCT	G	PO	A	E	DP
Ciofrone	.930	37	66	93	12	26
Ramos	.968	61	111	162	9	34
Smyres	.986	15	29	40	1	8

Third Base	PCT	G	PO	A	E	DP
Adams	.792	21	14	28	11	6
Baker	.000	2	0	0	1	0
Bochy	.910	34	19	52	7	2
Bonvechio	.955	82	54	159	10	8
Smyres	.929	4	4	9	1	1

Shortstop	PCT	G	PO	A	E	DP
Adams	.928	31	52	90	11	16
Ciriaco	.893	98	151	224	45	48
Figueroa	.867	5	6	7	2	1
Kazmar	.862	5	9	16	4	4
Smyres	.941	3	6	10	1	1

Outfield	PCT	G	PO	A	E	DP
Baker	.958	17	21	2	1	0
Garay	.880	22	22	0	3	0
Hogan	1.000	4	7	0	0	0
Johnson	.833	8	10	0	2	0
Kolkhorst	1.000	12	19	2	0	0
Macias	.970	129	250	8	8	1
McRoberts	.971	15	32	1	1	0
Mora	.973	21	33	3	1	0
Perez	1.000	1	4	0	0	0
Pickens	.969	72	122	3	4	0
Smith	1.000	2	5	0	0	0
Wahlbrink	.985	125	249	8	4	2

EUGENE EMERALDS — Short-Season Class A

NORTHWEST LEAGUE

BATTING	AVG	G	AB	R	H	2B	3B	HR	RBI	BB	SO	SB	CS	OBP	SLG	B	T	HT	WT	DOB	1st Yr	Resides
Aguilar, Trino	.278	48	151	15	42	11	0	3	17	8	28	3	0	.333	.411	R	R	5-10	170	7-27-83	2001	Guarico, Venez.
Burnham, Brett	.253	45	154	20	39	9	1	1	23	19	33	0	3	.346	.344	R	R	5-10	195	1-1-81	2003	South Windsor, Conn.
Bush, Matt	.222	8	27	1	6	2	0	0	3	2	9	0	0	.276	.296	R	R	5-10	170	2-8-86	2004	San Diego, Calif.
Dale, Lachlan	.247	74	283	45	70	18	1	15	49	16	87	1	0	.295	.477	R	R	6-2	195	6-22-83	2002	Kalamunda, Australia
Diaz, Orlando	.234	50	167	20	39	7	1	3	17	13	35	1	3	.305	.341	R	R	6-2	200	2-14-82	2004	Downers Grove, Iowa
Embrey, Rielly	.100	10	30	3	3	1	0	0	3	8	7	2	0	.289	.133	L	R	6-2	200	8-31-81	2004	Poway, Calif.
Figueroa, Baudilio	.185	16	54	3	10	1	0	0	5	3	15	1	1	.224	.204	S	R	6-2	195	6-28-83	2002	Puerto Plata, D.R.
Fryer, Brian	.170	14	47	4	8	2	0	0	2	2	11	3	1	.220	.213	R	R	6-1	185	8-16-82	2004	Las Vegas, Nev.
Garay, Ernesto	.310	25	100	16	31	3	0	1	8	5	12	3	1	.343	.370	L	L	6-1	160	2-17-82	2001	Managua, Nicaragua
Hogan, Billy	.236	58	199	22	47	13	1	3	22	18	66	3	0	.308	.357	R	R	6-3	210	5-20-83	2003	Dallas, Texas
Johnson, Craig	.273	27	77	13	21	8	0	0	4	7	28	0	3	.349	.377	L	L	6-1	185	4-11-82	2004	Sacramento, Calif.
Kazmar, Sean	.253	65	273	49	69	13	3	6	27	9	55	6	0	.279	.388	R	R	5-10	170	8-5-84	2004	Las Vegas, Nev.
Kolkhorst, Chris	.352	30	91	22	32	5	1	0	7	22	17	6	1	.496	.429	S	R	5-9	180	3-7-82	2002	Houston, Texas
Lobaton, Jose	.219	44	151	13	33	12	0	7	23	17	35	0	0	.298	.437	S	R	5-10	170	6-30-81	2001	Carabobo, Venez.
Lopez, Mauber	.200	5	10	1	2	0	0	0	0	3	5	0	0	.200	.200	R	R	6-3	190	1-15-82	2000	El Cajon, Calif.
McRoberts, Mark	.186	22	70	17	13	1	0	4	10	11	31	0	0	.305	.371	R	R	6-3	190	1-15-82	2000	El Cajon, Calif.
Mora, Ruben	.278	30	97	12	27	4	2	0	9	7	22	1	2	.333	.361	S	R	6-0	170	11-2-81	2002	Colon, Panama
Morton, Colt	.239	66	243	43	58	13	0	17	45	33	75	2	0	.340	.502	R	R	6-6	227	4-10-82	2003	Wellington, Fla.
Ramirez, Yordany	.200	4	15	1	3	0	0	1	3	1	5	0	0	.250	.400	R	R	6-1	160	7-31-84	2002	Boca Chica, D.R.
Rivera, Jodam	.125	3	8	1	1	0	0	0	0	1	2	0	0	.222	.125	S	R	5-10	180	2-4-86	2004	Hatillo, P.R.
Thayer, Matt	.284	46	183	29	52	10	0	3	25	17	39	8	4	.354	.388	L	R	5-10	175	2-21-82	2004	Woodland Hills, Calif.
Vincent, Tom	.234	56	175	24	41	11	2	4	18	14	60	7	2	.295	.389	L	R	6-3	215	3-3-82	2003	McKellar, Australia

GAMES BY POSITION: C—Lobaton 27, Lopez 5, Morton 49. **1B**—Dale 39, Diaz 27, Embrey 10, Vincent 4. **2B**—Aguilar 22, Burnham 33, Figueroa 4, Fryer 13, Kazmar 9, Rivera 2. **3B**—Aguilar 19, Dale 34, Diaz 33, Figueroa 3. **SS**—Aguilar 5, Bush 8, Figueroa 9, Kazmar 56. **OF**—Garay 21, Hogan 55, Johnson 22, Kolkhorst 26, McRoberts 17, Mora 23, Ramirez 2, Thayer 44, Vincent 31.

PITCHING	W	L	ERA	G	GS	CG	SV	IP	H	R	ER	BB	SO	AVG	B	T	HT	WT	DOB	1st Yr	Resides
Burks, Brian	2	2	2.25	26	0	0	4	32	33	16	8	9	21	.260	R	R	5-9	180	5-29-81	2004	Alpharetta, Ga.
Burnham, Brett	0	0	3.00	2	0	0	0	3	1	1	1	0	2	.100	R	R	5-10	195	1-1-81	2003	South Windsor, Conn.
Cespedes, Jose	1	0	2.48	24	0	0	0	36	29	14	10	12	25	.215	R	R	6-3	180	9-22-83	2004	Azua, D.R.
Colbert, Henry	0	2	8.80	21	0	0	0	31	44	36	30	24	35	.326	R	R	6-3	180	12-10-81	2003	Yakima, Wash.
Darby, James	1	3	8.53	25	0	0	0	25	24	32	24	35	10	.245	R	R	6-3	185	1-5-84	2002	Camden, Australia
De la O, Danny	3	6	7.02	18	10	0	0	67	78	56	52	29	55	.292	L	L	6-0	185	8-25-83	2003	Marina del Ray, Calif.
Delabar, Steve	1	1	2.65	3	3	0	0	17	13	7	5	3	11	.206	R	R	6-5	200	7-17-83	2004	Elizabethtown, Ky.
Ekstrom, Michael	3	1	3.69	12	7	0	0	39	38	18	16	10	42	.248	R	R	6-2	215	8-30-83	2004	Gresham, Ore.
Ellis, Jonathan	1	2	4.65	5	1	0	0	10	7	5	5	2	9	.206	R	R	6-0	190	10-3-81	2004	Thomasville, S.C.

PITCHING	W	L	ERA	G	GS	CG	SV	IP	H	R	ER	BB	SO	AVG	B	T	HT	WT	DOB	1st Yr	Resides
Fernandez, Alfredo	2	5	5.60	13	13	0	0	63	66	41	39	23	45	.276	R	R	6-4	205	9-15-84	2002	Maracaibo, Venez.
Gallegos, Gary	1	6	6.60	25	4	0	0	45	46	36	33	23	53	.271	L	L	6-4	210	3-29-82	2004	Riverside, Calif.
Hamilton, Clayton	1	1	5.86	8	5	0	0	28	22	21	18	13	31	.210	R	R	6-5	200	6-15-82	2004	Beaver Falls, Pa.
Kintzler, Brandon	0	0	0.00	3	0	0	3	3	0	0	0	4	.250	R	R	6-1	180	8-1-84	2004	Las Vegas, Nev.
Kroft, Adam	1	0	1.80	1	1	0	0	5	4	1	1	4	3	.222	R	R	6-5	230	12-30-81	2004	Ballston Lake, N.Y.
O'Hagan, David	1	0	2.57	8	0	0	1	7	4	3	2	5	12	.148	R	R	6-1	200	6-5-82	2004	Minnetonka, Minn.
Ponce, William	1	9	5.97	14	12	0	0	66	75	54	44	33	39	.277	R	R	6-1	190	9-9-84	2002	San Salvador, El Salvador
Rayborn, Chris	1	0	7.71	1	1	0	0	2	7	9	2	3	3	.438	R	R	6-3	210	8-19-83	2004	Purvis, Miss.
Robinson, Ronnie	0	0	4.66	9	0	0	0	10	8	6	5	5	8	.222	R	R	6-3	195	4-22-81	2003	Atlanta, Ga.
Santo, Joel	2	2	5.35	7	7	0	0	34	40	25	20	23	22	.294	R	R	6-3	180	6-4-84	2002	San Cristobal, D.R.
Shanks, E.J.	0	0	2.45	2	0	0	0	4	2	1	1	2	4	.167	R	R	6-5	230	4-8-82	2004	Las Vegas, Nev.
Steik, Ricky	1	1	3.26	16	0	0	2	19	21	8	7	9	18	.292	R	R	6-0	180	1-1-00	2004	Buena Park, Calif.
Sterry, Vern	2	3	3.96	9	9	0	0	50	43	24	22	11	52	.226	R	R	6-2	210	2-7-82	2004	Rowland Heights, Calif.
Upwood, Jake	1	2	3.71	17	0	0	0	17	15	7	7	7	12	.231	L	L	5-11	175	9-19-80	2003	Central Square, N.Y.
Varner, Matt	1	2	4.30	9	1	0	0	15	14	8	7	9	11	.246	R	R	5-11	200	1-16-82	2004	Brazoria, Texas
Vose, Jake	0	1	4.75	24	2	0	1	36	39	27	19	11	30	.267	L	L	5-10	185	2-13-82	2004	Las Vegas, Nev.

AZL PADRES   Rookie

ARIZONA LEAGUE

BATTING	AVG	G	AB	R	H	2B	3B	HR	RBI	BB	SO	SB	CS	SLG	OBP	B	T	HT	WT	DOB	1st Yr	Resides
Bush, Matt	.181	21	72	12	13	2	1	0	10	11	17	4	1	.236	.302	R	R	5-10	170	2-8-86	2004	San Diego, Calif.
Cruceta, Julio	.318	43	176	22	56	7	5	0	20	5	23	9	5	.415	.354	R	R	6-1	170	5-13-83	2001	La Vega, D.R.
Etheridge, Chad	.235	7	17	3	4	1	0	1	2	3	7	0	0	.471	.350	S	R	6-0	205	1-3-83	2003	Old Hickory, Tenn.
Figueroa, Baudilio	.308	15	52	9	16	4	0	2	6	6	10	1	0	.500	.373	R	R	6-2	160	6-28-83	2002	Puerto Plata, D.R.
Johnson, Craig	.288	34	125	18	36	8	0	0	19	11	30	1	0	.352	.386	L	L	6-1	185	4-11-82	2004	Sacramento, Calif.
Johnson, Michael	.345	8	29	4	10	5	0	0	3	4	12	1	0	.517	.424	L	R	6-3	215	6-25-80	2003	Georgetown, S.C.
Johnston, Trey	.262	37	126	16	33	5	0	1	16	7	34	0	0	.325	.312	R	R	5-11	190	7-4-85	2003	Bradenton, Fla.
Jones, Daryl	.295	36	149	19	44	11	0	1	25	7	38	1	1	.389	.327	R	R	6-3	200	9-1-86	2004	Gardena, Calif.
Killian, Billy	.230	40	135	17	31	7	2	0	13	11	21	3	1	.311	.293	L	R	6-1	190	6-12-86	2004	Stanwood, Mich.
Kolkhorst, Chris	.280	7	25	5	7	1	1	0	3	8	3	2	1	.400	.486	L	R	5-9	180	3-7-82	2004	Houston, Texas
Lopez, Luis	.222	13	36	3	8	1	0	0	2	8	1	0		.250	.263	R	R	6-2	180	1-8-84	2000	Santiago, Panama
Medley, Brian	.177	23	79	8	14	3	0	0	5	7	32	1	0	.215	.270	R	R	6-0	188	2-25-82	2004	Halifax, Va.
Ramirez, Yordany	.264	39	159	23	42	7	5	1	21	4	26	16	1	.390	.300	R	R	6-1	160	7-31-84	2002	Boca Chica, D.R.
Rivera, Jodam	.276	48	185	24	51	5	2	0	19	17	28	5	6	.324	.346	S	R	5-10	180	2-4-86	2004	Hatillo, P.R.
Sanchez, Luany	.202	34	109	12	22	3	0	1	8	6	15	1	0	.257	.267	R	R	6-1	180	6-18-85	2003	Jima Abajo, D.R.
Smyres, Justin	.273	3	11	1	3	1	0	0	1	0	2	0	1	.364	.273	R	R	6-0	175	5-8-81	2003	Paso Robles, Calif.
Vazquez, Kelvin	.272	49	180	30	49	12	4	1	18	22	38	6	4	.400	.362	S	R	6-1	170	9-30-83	2004	Gurabo, P.R.
White, Peter	.315	38	127	20	40	8	1	1	19	18	21	2	2	.402	.403	R	R	6-3	190	1-19-83	2004	Reno, Nev.
Whitney, Nate	.269	53	186	30	50	8	4	2	29	22	35	6	1	.387	.361	R	R	6-1	185	5-17-82	2004	Bloomington, Ill.

GAMES BY POSITION: C—Johnston 1, Killian 23, Lopez 11, Sanchez 32. **1B**—Etheridge 1, M. Johnson 7, Jones 24, Lopez 2, White 28. **2B**—Rivera 21, Smyres 3, Vazquez 39. **3B**—Cruceta 8, Figueroa 2, Johnston 36, Vazquez 10, White 6. **SS**—Bush 21, Figueroa 12, Rivera 28. **OF**—Cruceta 31, C. Johnson 31, Kolkhorst 7, Medley 39, Ramirez 2, Whitney 51.

PITCHING	W	L	ERA	G	GS	CG	SV	IP	H	R	ER	BB	SO	AVG	B	T	HT	WT	DOB	1st Yr	Resides
Baca, Daniel	4	2	1.93	23	0	0	0	28	26	9	6	11	23	.242	R	R	5-10	170	10-17-85	2003	Guadalupe, Mexico
Colbert, Henry	1	0	0.00	3	0	0	0	3	2	0	0	1	6	.166	R	R	6-3	180	12-10-81	2003	Yakima, Wash.
De Montigny, Mat	1	0	3.60	16	0	0	0	25	24	11	10	11	25	.250	R	R	6-1	170	9-22-84	2003	Trois Rivieres, Quebec
Delabar, Steven	3	4	4.37	14	6	0	0	45	51	32	22	21	39	.303	R	R	6-5	200	7-17-83	2004	Elizabethtown, Ky.
Geraldo, Jose	0	0	0.00	2	0	0	0	2	1	0	0	0	1	.125	R	R	6-3	180	9-22-83	2001	Azua, D.R.
Hamilton, Clayton	0	0	2.08	3	0	0	0	4	2	1	1	1	3	.125	R	R	6-5	200	6-15-82	2004	Beaver Falls, Pa.
Jenkins, B.J.	0	0	3.75	18	0	0	1	24	15	12	10	7	34	.174	R	R	6-2	195	8-4-81	2004	Hendersonville, Tenn.
Jimenez Angulo, Fabian	2	6	6.95	12	9	0	0	45	60	40	35	28	28	.329	L	L	6-3	170	8-27-86	2003	Cartagena, Colombia
Jimenez, Juan	1	0	0.89	1	1	0	0	20	12	4	2	2	14	.169	R	R	6-2	180	5-18-86	2003	Santiago, D.R.
Jones, Geoff	0	0	5.14	7	0	0	0	7	11	5	4	2	9	.333	L	L	6-6	230	8-10-79	1999	Dolores, Colo.
Kintzler, Brandon	3	2	2.38	21	0	0	6	34	36	12	9	9	38	.276	R	R	6-1	180	8-1-84	2004	Las Vegas, Nev.
Kroft, Adam	3	0	4.14	13	0	0	0	46	41	22	21	14	25	.251	R	R	6-5	230	12-30-81	2004	Ballston Lakes, N.Y.
Krosschell, Ben	1	3	2.42	14	11	0	0	48	48	21	13	19	40	.262	R	R	6-1	165	10-2-85	2004	Highland Ranch, Colo.
Moore, Daniel	0	0	5.19	3	3	0	0	9	11	6	5	2	5	.323	R	L	6-5	225	6-24-82	2003	Spencer, N.C.
Nourie, John	0	0	4.50	2	0	0	0	2	2	1	1	1	1	.250	L	L	6-3	205	6-11-82	2004	Munster, Ind.
Rayborn, Chris	3	3	5.19	13	9	0	0	50	56	35	29	11	27	.275	R	R	6-3	210	8-19-83	2004	Purvis, Miss.
Santo, Joel	0	3	4.60	5	5	0	0	16	20	13	8	9	9	.322	R	R	6-3	180	6-4-84	2002	San Cristobal, D.R.
Shanks, E.J.	2	1	1.63	19	0	0	2	28	19	9	5	5	19	.197	R	R	6-5	230	4-8-82	2004	Las Vegas, Nev.
Steidlmayer, Luke	0	0	3.60	3	3	0	0	10	9	4	4	1	11	.236	R	R	6-5	190	8-13-80	2002	Colusa, Calif.
Steik, Ricky	0	3	3.07	14	0	0	5	15	13	8	5	5	9	.232	L	R	6-3	210	1-24-84	2004	Buena Park, Calif.
Stutes, Kyle	2	2	3.52	20	0	0	0	31	34	18	12	5	37	.278	L	L	5-10	185	1-22-82	2004	Port Neches, Texas
Tucker, Rusty	0	1	4.22	10	1	0	1	11	9	6	5	4	8	.219	R	L	6-1	190	7-15-80	2001	Gloucester, Mass.

ORGANIZATION STATISTICS

BY ANDY BAGGARLY

The Giants were one of baseball's hottest and most resilient teams down the stretch in 2004, but problems in the bullpen and in the field were exposed in the final weekend, sabotaging their playoff hopes.

Despite a roster full of holes, the Giants won 18 of 28 games after Sept. 1, but they were eliminated from the National League West race in the next-to-last game of the season—a heartbreaking 7-3 loss at Dodger Stadium—then were eliminated from the wild card the following day.

Their deficiencies caught up with them in spectacular fashion in an Oct. 2 loss at Dodger Stadium, when they entered the ninth inning with a 3-0 lead. The Dodgers rallied for seven runs, clinching the division on Steve Finley's walk-off grand slam.

Dustin Hermanson, who had thrown 100 innings as a starting pitcher before he was converted to the bullpen in August, was throwing for a fifth straight day. Jim Brower, who tied the club record with 89 appearances, was unavailable after pitching in eight straight games (over nine days). And shortstop Cody Ransom, who entered as a defensive replacement to start the ninth, committed a fielding error that fueled the Dodgers' rally.

It was no surprise that general manager Brian Sabean said he would target pitching and defense over the winter as he sought to re-tool an aging, veteran club.

"It's obvious we have to improve our defense and our team speed," Sabean said.

The Giants faced many challenges, yet they appeared to overcome one of the biggest: the 232 walks to Barry Bonds, including 120 intentional passes. Both marks broke Bonds' own single-season records. His .609 on-base percentage set another record.

Bonds, who turned 40 on July 24, hit .362 to become

Barry Bonds   Matt Cain

BILL MITCHELL

PLAYERS of the YEAR

MAJOR LEAGUE: Barry Bonds, of

Even at age 40, Bonds' skills at the plate only seem to get better. He put together another monster season in 2004, leading the National League in walks (232), batting average (.362), on-base percentage (.609) and slugging percentage (.812) by wide margins. He also drilled 45 home runs and drove in 101.

MINOR LEAGUE: Matt Cain, rhp

Cain opened his second full season of professional baseball by going 7-1, 1.86 at Class A San Jose. He moved to Double-A Norwich for the final two months and went 6-4, 3.35. In 158 innings, the 19-year-old righthander walked 57 while striking out 161. His fastball and breaking ball already rate as major league average pitches.

the oldest player to win a batting title. He also hit 45 home runs, drove in 101 runs and tied his career high with 129 runs scored. Along the way, he passed his godfather, Willie Mays, on the all-time home run list and became the third member of the 700-homer club. Bonds will enter 2005 just 11 away from tying Babe Ruth on the all-time list and 52 away from tying Hank Aaron's all-time record.

Pitching appears to be a future strength. Jerome Williams and Jesse Foppert are expected to be healthy in 2005. Noah Lowry was 6-0 and pitched brilliantly as a rookie. Brad Hennessey also showed he could stand the heat.

Top prospects Matt Cain and Merkin Valdez remained in the system after Sabean held off dealing them at the trade deadline.

The Giants expect another Cy Young-caliber season from Jason Schmidt, and Brett Tomko could be emerging as a solid No. 2 starter after going 5-1, 1.43 over his last eight starts.

But the bullpen was a hodgepodge all season. In the trade that brought catcher A.J. Pierzynksi to San Francisco, the Giants gave up righthander Joe Nathan, who blossomed into one of the American League's best closers. The Giants also failed to re-sign Tim Worrell, who filled in ably for Robb Nen in 2003.

The Giants minor league system had a lackluster year. Only high Class A San Jose made the playoffs, posting an aggregate record of 74-66. Yet contributions from Lowry and Hennessey showed once again that the Giants know how to develop young pitching.

ORGANIZATION LEADERS

BATTING

*AVG	Brian Horwitz, Salem-Keizer	.347
R	Todd Linden, Fresno	93
H	Jason Ellison, Fresno	159
TB	Mike Cervenak, Fresno/Norwich	266
2B	Nate Schierholtz, San Jose/Hagerstown	40
3B	Doug Clark, Norwich	13
HR	Mike Cervenak, Fresno/Norwich	26
RBI	Mike Cervenak, Fresno/Norwich	98
BB	Fred Lewis, Fresno/San Jose	89
SO	Todd Linden, Fresno	149
SB	Fred Lewis, Fresno/San Jose	34
*OBP	Fred Lewis, Fresno/San Jose	.424
*SLG	Mike Cervenak, Fresno/Norwich	.586

PITCHING

W	Matt Cain, Norwich/San Jose	13
L	Josh Habel, Norwich	10
	Brian Stirm, San Jose	10
#ERA	Joe Bateman, Norwich/Hagerstown	2.30
G	Jeremy Accardo, Norwich/San Jose	57
	Lee Gardner, Fresno	57
CG	Pat Misch, Norwich	4
SV	Jeremy Accardo, Norwich/San Jose	28
IP	Ryan Jensen, Fresno	170
BB	Ryan Jensen, Fresno	81
SO	Matt Cain, Norwich/San Jose	161

*Minimum 250 at-bats #Minimum 75 innings

SAN FRANCISCO GIANTS

Manager: Felipe Alou.

2004 Record: 91-71, .562 (2nd, NL West).

BATTING	AVG	G	AB	R	H	2B	3B	HR	RBI	BB	SO	SB	CS	OBP	SLG	B	T	HT	WT	DOB	1st Yr	Resides
Alfonzo, Edgardo	.289	139	519	66	150	26	1	11	77	46	40	1	1	.350	.407	R	R	5-11	187	11-8-73	1991	Little Neck, N.Y.
Bonds, Barry	.362	147	373	129	135	27	3	45	101	232	41	6	1	.609	.812	L	L	6-2	230	7-24-64	1985	San Carlos, Calif.
Cruz, Deivi	.292	127	397	46	116	30	2	7	55	17	32	1	3	.322	.431	R	R	6-0	207	11-6-72	1993	Nizao, D.R.
Dallimore, Brian	.279	20	43	8	12	2	0	1	7	4	7	0	1	.347	.395	R	R	6-1	180	11-15-73	1996	Las Vegas, Nev.
Durham, Ray	.282	120	471	95	133	28	8	17	65	57	60	10	4	.364	.484	S	R	5-8	180	11-30-71	1990	Charlotte, N.C.
Ellison, Jason	.500	13	4	4	2	0	0	1	3	0	1	2	0	.500	1.250	R	R	5-10	180	4-4-78	2000	Lewiston, Idaho
Feliz, Pedro	.276	144	503	72	139	33	3	22	84	23	85	5	2	.305	.485	R	R	6-1	205	4-27-75	1994	Azua, D.R.
Grissom, Marquis	.279	145	562	78	157	26	2	22	90	37	83	3	1	.323	.450	R	R	5-11	190	4-17-67	1988	Fairburn, Ga.
Hammonds, Jeffrey	.211	40	95	14	20	5	0	3	6	15	22	1	0	.336	.358	R	R	6-0	205	3-5-71	1993	Cincinnati, Ohio
Knoedler, Justin	.000	1	1	0	0	0	0	0	0	0	0	0	0	.000	.000	R	R	6-2	210	7-17-80	2001	Springfield, Ill.
Ledee, Ricky	.113	31	53	6	6	2	0	0	4	5	20	1	0	.200	.151	L	L	6-1	200	11-22-73	1990	Salinas, P.R.
2-team (73 Phil.)	.233	104	176	25	41	9	0	7	30	27	47	3	0	.337	.403							
Linden, Todd	.156	16	32	6	5	1	0	0	1	5	7	0	0	.289	.188	S	R	6-3	210	6-30-80	2002	Bremerton, Wash.
Minor, Damon	.241	24	58	8	14	2	0	0	6	12	18	0	0	.405	.276	L	L	6-7	230	1-5-74	1996	Edmond, Okla.
Mohr, Dustan	.274	117	263	52	72	20	1	7	28	46	64	0	3	.394	.437	R	R	6-1	210	6-19-76	1997	Hattiesburg, Miss.
Perez, Neifi	.232	103	319	28	74	12	1	2	33	21	35	0	1	.276	.295	B	R	6-0	175	6-2-73	1993	Santo Domingo, D.R.
Pierzynski, A.J.	.272	131	471	45	128	28	2	11	77	19	27	0	1	.319	.410	L	R	6-3	220	12-30-76	1994	Fort Myers, Fla.
Ransom, Cody	.250	78	68	13	17	6	0	1	11	6	20	2	2	.320	.382	R	R	6-2	190	2-17-76	1998	Chandler, Ariz.
Snow, J.T.	.327	107	346	62	113	32	1	12	60	58	61	4	0	.429	.529	L	L	6-2	210	2-26-68	1989	San Mateo, Calif.
Torcato, Tony	.556	13	9	1	5	0	0	2	1	0	0	0	0	.583	.556	L	R	6-1	195	10-25-79	1998	Woodland, Calif.
Torrealba, Yorvit	.227	64	172	19	39	7	3	6	23	17	31	2	0	.302	.407	R	R	5-11	190	7-19-78	1995	Guarenas, Venez.
Tucker, Michael	.256	140	464	77	119	21	6	13	62	70	106	5	2	.352	.412	L	R	6-2	195	6-25-71	1993	Lehigh Acres, Fla.

PITCHING	W	L	ERA	G	GS	CG	SV	IP	H	R	ER	BB	SO	AVG	B	T	HT	WT	DOB	1st Yr	Resides
Aardsma, David	1	0	6.75	11	0	0	0	11	20	8	8	10	5	.417	R	R	6-5	200	12-27-81	2003	The Woodland, Texas
Brower, Jim	7	7	3.29	89	0	0	1	93	90	42	34	36	63	.259	R	R	6-3	210	12-29-72	1994	Sarasota, Fla.
Burba, Dave	1	0	5.68	6	0	0	0	6	7	4	4	2	3	.280	R	R	6-4	240	7-7-66	1987	Gilbert, Ariz.
2-team (45 Milwaukee)	4	1	4.21	51	0	0	2	77	70	40	36	26	50	.241							
Christiansen, Jason	4	3	4.50	60	0	0	3	36	34	20	18	26	22	.250	R	L	6-5	240	9-21-69	1991	Mesa, Ariz.
Cooper, Brian	0	2	8.78	5	2	0	0	13	15	13	13	5	7	.288	R	R	6-1	185	8-19-74	1995	Upland, Calif.
Correia, Kevin	0	1	8.05	12	1	0	0	19	25	20	17	10	14	.333	R	R	6-3	200	8-24-80	2002	San Diego, Calif.
Estrella, Leo	0	0	27.00	2	0	0	0	1	8	4	4	1	0	.727	R	R	6-1	185	2-20-75	1994	Port St. Lucie, Fla.
Eyre, Scott	2	2	4.10	83	0	0	1	53	43	26	24	27	49	.219	L	L	6-1	210	5-30-72	1992	Bradenton, Fla.
Foppert, Jesse	0	0	0.00	1	0	0	0	1	1	0	0	0	2	.250	R	R	6-6	210	7-10-80	2001	San Rafael, Calif.
Franklin, Wayne	2	1	6.39	43	2	0	0	51	55	37	36	22	40	.281	L	L	6-2	211	3-9-74	1996	Rising Sun, Md.
Hennessey, Brad	2	2	4.98	7	7	0	0	34	42	24	19	15	25	.294	R	R	6-2	185	2-7-80	2001	Toledo, Ohio
Herges, Matt	4	5	5.23	70	0	0	23	65	64	44	38	21	39	.338	L	R	6-0	200	4-1-70	1992	Champaign, Ill.
Hermanson, Dustin	6	9	4.53	47	18	0	17	131	132	71	66	46	102	.262	R	R	6-2	200	12-21-72	1994	Phoenix, Ariz.
Lowry, Noah	6	0	3.82	16	14	2	0	92	91	41	39	28	72	.259	R	L	6-2	190	10-10-80	2001	Ojai, Nev.
Rodriguez, Felix	3	5	3.43	53	0	0	0	45	43	18	17	19	31	.250	R	R	6-1	190	9-9-72	1990	Monte Cristi, D.R.
Rueter, Kirk	9	12	4.73	33	33	0	0	190	225	108	100	66	56	.296	L	L	6-2	210	12-1-70	1991	Nashville, Ill.
Schmidt, Jason	18	7	3.20	32	32	4	0	225	165	84	80	77	251	.202	R	R	6-5	205	1-29-73	1991	Longview, Wash.
Tomko, Brett	11	7	4.04	32	31	2	0	194	196	98	87	64	108	.260	R	R	6-4	215	4-7-73	1995	San Diego, Calif.
Valdez, Merkin	0	0	27.00	2	0	0	0	2	4	5	5	3	2	.444	R	R	6-3	170	11-5-81	2000	San Cristobal, D.R.
Walker, Kevin	0	0	16.20	5	0	0	0	2	3	3	3	2	1	.429	L	L	6-4	190	9-20-76	1995	Glen Rose, Texas
Walker, Tyler	5	1	4.24	52	0	0	1	64	69	31	30	24	48	.288	R	R	6-3	230	5-15-76	1997	Ross, Calif.
Williams, Jerome	10	7	4.24	22	22	0	0	129	123	69	61	44	80	.254	R	R	6-3	180	12-4-81	1999	Waipahu, Hawaii

FIELDING

Catcher	PCT	G	PO	A	E	DP	PB
Knoedler	1.000	1	2	0	0	0	0
Pierzynski	.999	118	697	56	1	6	9
Torrealba	.995	59	349	18	2	4	2

First Base	PCT	G	PO	A	E	DP
Feliz	.991	70	527	42	5	59
Minor	1.000	17	131	9	0	12
Snow	.995	100	801	55	4	69

Second Base	PCT	G	PO	A	E	DP
Alfonzo	.882	5	5	10	2	2
Cruz	.000	2	0	0	0	0
Dallimore	.963	9	8	18	1	3
Durham	.972	118	242	315	16	74

	PCT	G	PO	A	E	DP
Perez	.995	39	80	115	1	23
Ransom	.980	16	28	21	1	5

Third Base	PCT	G	PO	A	E	DP
Alfonzo	.965	129	88	246	12	20
Cruz	.000	1	0	0	0	0
Dallimore	.923	6	4	8	1	0
Feliz	.975	51	32	85	3	7
Perez	1.000	1	0	1	0	0
Ransom	.000	1	0	0	1	0

Shortstop	PCT	G	PO	A	E	DP
Cruz	.980	104	127	266	8	59
Feliz	.929	20	17	48	5	9
Perez	.978	57	67	158	5	29

	PCT	G	PO	A	E	DP
Ransom	.948	45	20	35	3	11

Outfield	PCT	G	PO	A	E	DP
Bonds	.983	133	214	11	4	0
Ellison	1.000	4	5	0	0	0
Feliz	1.000	4	1	0	0	0
Grissom	.994	142	341	3	2	2
Hammonds	1.000	28	49	3	0	0
Ledee	.960	15	24	0	1	0
Linden	1.000	11	9	0	0	0
Mohr	.981	95	153	6	3	2
Ransom	.000	1	0	0	0	0
Tucker	.978	124	262	2	6	2

Vice President, Player Personnel: Dick Tidrow.

Class	Farm Team	League	W	L	Pct.	Finish*	Manager	Affiliate Since
AAA	Fresno (Calif.) Grizzlies	Pacific Coast	62	82	.431	15th (16)	Fred Stanley	1998
AA	Norwich (Conn.) Navigators	Eastern	69	73	.486	t-7th (12)	Shane Turner	2003
High A	San Jose (Calif.) Giants	California	74	66	.529	**4th (10)**	Lenn Sakata	1988
Low A	#Hagerstown (Md.) Suns	South Atlantic	49	88	.358	16th (16)	Mike Ramsey	2001
SS A	Salem-Keizer (Ore.) Volcanoes	Northwest	37	39	.487	6th (8)	Joe Strain	1997
Rookie	Scottsdale (Ariz.) Giants	Arizona	36	19	.655	**+1st (9)**	Bert Hunter	2000

*Finish in overall standings (No. of teams in league)/Playoff teams in **boldface**   +League champion
#Affiliate will operate in Augusta (South Atlantic) in 2005

FRESNO GRIZZLIES — Class AAA

PACIFIC COAST LEAGUE

BATTING	AVG	G	AB	R	H	2B	3B	HR	RBI	BB	SO	SB	CS	OBP	SLG	B	T	HT	WT	DOB	1st Yr Resides
Athas, Jamie	.258	124	419	58	108	16	4	4	45	38	91	13	11	.326	.344	L	R	6-2	190	10-14-79	2001 Winston-Salem, N.C.
Cervenak, Michael	.250	10	44	7	11	1	0	5	10	0	7	0	0	.267	.614	R	R	5-11	180	8-17-76	1999 New Boston, Mich.
Cruz, Deivi	.310	12	42	5	13	3	0	1	6	3	2	0	0	.348	.452	R	R	6-0	207	11-6-72	1993 Nizao, D.R.
Dallimore, Brian	.324	111	432	72	140	21	4	8	67	40	53	9	2	.396	.447	R	R	6-1	180	11-15-73	1996 Las Vegas, Nev.
Doster, Dave	.311	120	424	50	132	36	0	9	66	26	42	2	5	.353	.460	R	R	5-10	180	10-8-70	1993 Fort Wayne, Ind.
Durham, Ray	.571	5	14	4	8	0	1	1	5	2	2	0	1	.647	.929	S	R	5-8	180	11-30-71	1990 Charlotte, N.C.
Ellison, Jason	.315	125	505	90	159	32	7	9	40	40	66	27	12	.368	.459	R	R	5-10	180	4-4-78	2000 Lewiston, Idaho
Haynes, Nathan	.250	1	4	1	1	0	0	0	0	0	1	1	0	.250	.750	L	L	5-9	180	9-7-79	1997 Vallejo, Calif.
Kuzmic, Craig	.237	78	228	33	54	7	1	8	30	35	61	0	2	.348	.382	S	R	6-0	185	5-2-77	1998 Fountain Valley, Calif.
Lewis, Fred	.304	6	23	3	7	1	0	1	2	5	5	1	1	.429	.478	L	R	6-2	190	12-9-80	2002 Wiggins, Miss.
Linden, Todd	.260	130	489	93	127	28	2	23	75	63	149	8	6	.349	.466	S	R	6-3	210	6-30-80	2002 Bremerton, Wash.
Lunsford, Trey	.252	118	404	39	102	21	2	5	41	35	83	3	2	.320	.351	R	R	6-1	195	5-25-79	2000 South Haven, Miss.
Minor, Damon	.302	97	338	48	102	23	3	17	56	50	78	0	0	.399	.538	L	L	6-7	230	1-5-74	1996 Edmond, Okla.
Munhall, Brian	.500	2	4	1	2	0	0	0	1	0	0	0	0	.600	.500	R	R	6-1	190	6-17-80	2002 Spokane, Wash.
Niekro, Lance	.298	67	242	42	72	21	4	12	47	14	32	1	1	.337	.566	R	R	6-3	210	1-29-79	2000 Lakeland, Fla.
Ransom, Cody	.309	36	136	29	42	6	2	10	21	19	30	8	0	.397	.603	R	R	6-2	190	2-17-76	1998 Chandler, Ariz.
Santos, Deivis	.269	75	208	22	56	9	1	4	31	9	37	0	0	.298	.380	L	L	6-1	175	3-9-74	1997 Santo Domingo, D.R.
Shabala, Adam	.313	119	402	63	126	17	5	9	48	32	81	21	3	.364	.448	L	R	6-1	190	2-6-78	2000 Streator, Ill.
Snow, J.T.	.286	2	7	1	2	0	0	1	2	0	1	0	0	.286	.714	L	L	6-2	210	2-26-68	1989 San Mateo, Calif.
Stratton, Robert	.183	33	109	6	20	3	0	3	12	2	54	1	0	.204	.294	R	R	6-2	250	10-7-77	1996 Santa Barbara, Calif.
Strong, Zach	.100	9	10	1	1	1	0	0	1	4	0	0	0	.182	.200	S	R	6-3	200	6-3-81	2003 Olympia, Wash.
Swanson, Brent	.000	2	2	0	0	0	0	0	0	0	2	0	0	.000	.000	L	R	5-11	190	9-11-80	2004 Richmond, B.C.
Torcato, Tony	.289	119	395	39	114	22	0	3	57	11	35	4	1	.314	.367	L	R	6-1	195	10-25-79	1998 Woodland, Calif.

PITCHING	W	L	ERA	G	GS	CG	SV	IP	H	R	ER	BB	SO	AVG	B	T	HT	WT	DOB	1st Yr Resides
Aardsma, David	6	4	3.09	44	0	0	11	55	46	21	19	30	53	.223	R	R	6-5	200	12-27-81	2003 The Woodlands, Texas
Anderson, Luke	0	1	9.00	4	0	0	0	3	4	4	3	5	2	.308	R	R	6-5	210	4-29-78	2000 Las Vegas, Nev.
Begg, Chris	2	5	6.97	9	9	0	0	41	55	32	32	18	17	.324	R	R	6-4	195	9-12-79	2001 Sutherland, Sask.
Cooper, Brian	0	2	2.08	4	4	0	0	22	19	9	5	6	15	.226	R	R	6-1	185	8-19-74	1995 Upland, Calif.
Correia, Kevin	3	7	4.53	29	16	0	0	105	118	61	53	35	70	.284	R	R	6-3	200	8-24-80	2002 San Diego, Calif.
Crudale, Mike	0	0	15.63	4	0	0	0	6	13	13	11	1	3	.419	R	R	6-0	200	1-3-77	1999 Danville, Calif.
Estrella, Leo	0	8	7.65	38	5	0	0	78	125	71	66	33	34	.368	R	R	6-1	185	2-20-75	1994 Port St. Lucie, Fla.
Eyre, Scott	0	0	0.00	3	0	0	0	3	3	0	0	2	1	.250	L	L	6-1	210	5-30-72	1992 Bradenton, Fla.
Foppert, Jesse	0	2	3.68	4	4	0	0	15	14	11	6	9	13	.241	R	R	6-6	210	7-10-80	2001 San Rafael, Calif.
Franklin, Wayne	0	2	3.86	3	3	0	0	9	6	4	4	4	5	.182	L	L	6-2	211	3-9-74	1996 Rising Sun, Md.
Garcia, James	0	1	5.19	8	7	0	0	35	35	20	20	16	34	.263	R	R	6-2	210	2-3-80	2002 Torrance, Calif.
Gardner, Lee	7	3	4.46	57	0	0	1	71	79	40	35	22	42	.290	R	R	6-0	215	1-16-75	1998 Hartland, Mich.
Hennessey, Brad	4	1	2.02	5	5	0	0	36	26	8	8	15	16	.202	R	R	6-2	185	2-7-80	2001 Toledo, Ohio
Jacome, Jason	0	2	3.49	35	2	0	0	67	81	29	26	17	43	.300	L	L	6-1	160	11-24-70	1991 Tucson, Ariz.
Jensen, Ryan	10	7	5.36	30	26	0	0	170	178	105	101	81	127	.273	R	R	6-0	205	9-17-75	1996 West Valley, Utah
Lowry, Noah	5	4	4.13	17	17	1	0	89	98	53	41	28	73	.278	R	L	6-1	190	10-10-80	2001 Ojai, Nev.
Mazone, Brian	1	1	4.63	2	2	0	0	12	17	6	6	3	6	.340	L	L	6-4	200	7-26-76	1998 Cardiff, Calif.
Munter, Scott	1	1	3.45	13	0	0	1	16	20	8	6	4	5	.303	R	R	6-6	235	3-7-80	2001 Wichita, Kan.
Pavon, Julio	1	1	5.52	5	2	0	0	15	19	9	9	8	11	.317	R	R	6-2	190	6-14-76	2000 Granada, Nicaragua
Pettyjohn, Adam	3	6	5.42	21	14	0	0	80	103	58	48	25	43	.324	R	L	6-3	190	6-11-77	1998 Exeter, Calif.
Pickford, Kevin	0	0	6.23	1	1	0	0	4	7	3	3	5	2	.389	L	L	6-4	200	3-12-75	1993 Fresno, Calif.
Taschner, Jack	4	7	9.28	18	9	0	0	53	71	59	55	32	44	.311	L	L	6-1	190	4-21-78	1998 Racine, Wis.
Tomko, Brett	0	0	5.40	1	1	0	0	5	4	3	3	2	4	.211	R	R	6-4	215	4-7-73	1995 San Diego, Calif.
Urban, Jeff	5	4	4.21	46	0	0	1	66	69	35	31	23	56	.272	R	L	6-8	215	1-25-77	1998 Alexandria, Ind.
Valdez, Merkin	0	0	7.20	1	1	0	0	5	6	4	4	4	5	.333	R	R	6-3	225	11-5-81	2000 San Cristobal, D.R.
Veres, Dave	0	4	5.97	29	0	0	12	29	34	22	19	9	22	.286	R	R	6-2	220	10-19-66	1986 Castle Rock, Colo.
Walker, Kevin	1	3	4.26	48	1	0	1	70	79	33	33	35	63	.298	L	L	6-4	190	9-20-76	1995 Glen Rose, Texas
Walker, Tyler	1	1	1.72	9	1	0	6	16	16	5	3	2	15	.250	R	R	6-3	230	5-15-76	1997 Ross, Calif.
Zerbe, Chad	6	6	4.29	33	14	0	0	107	131	63	51	35	51	.307	L	L	6-0	190	4-27-72	1991 Highland, Calif.

FIELDING

Catcher	PCT	G	PO	A	E	DP	PB
Kuzmic	.991	38	215	11	2	0	3
Lunsford	.991	116	697	47	7	4	14
Munhall	1.000	1	2	0	0	0	0

First Base	PCT	G	PO	A	E	DP
Doster	1.000	1	2	0	0	0
Minor	.994	62	509	33	3	50

	PCT	G	PO	A	E	DP	PB
Niekro	.991	34	310	20	3	31	
Santos	.993	37	266	25	2	31	
Snow	1.000	2	14	0	1		
Torcato	.994	23	160	8	1	22	

Second Base	PCT	G	PO	A	E	DP
Athas	.955	12	16	26	2	5
Cruz	1.000	6	8	12	0	3

	PCT	G	PO	A	E	
Dallimore	.982	49	98	126	4	29
Doster	.979	67	113	166	6	38
Durham	.944	5	11	23	2	6
Kuzmic	1.000	2	1	1	0	0
Ransom	.984	28	48	72	2	20

Third Base	PCT	G	PO	A	E	DP
Cervenak	.967	10	8	21	1	2

ORGANIZATION STATISTICS

Dallimore	.941	35	25	71	6	7
Doster	.968	60	44	107	5	7
Kuzmic	.924	35	23	50	6	3
Niekro	.950	24	20	37	3	7
Ransom	.857	2	1	5	1	0
Strong	1.000	3	1	1	0	0

Shortstop	PCT	G	PO	A	E	DP
Athas	.952	112	151	343	25	74
Cruz	.955	7	7	14	1	2
Dallimore	.960	32	43	78	5	14
Ransom	.967	7	4	25	1	5

Outfield	PCT	G	PO	A	E	DP
Dallimore	1.000	2	2	0	0	0

Ellison	.983	119	343	14	6	2
Haynes	.667	1	2	0	1	0
Lewis	.923	6	12	0	1	0
Linden	.976	132	262	19	7	1
Santos	1.000	15	14	2	0	0
Shabala	.985	104	181	16	3	1
Stratton	1.000	23	45	2	0	1
Torcato	.991	65	109	4	1	0

NORWICH NAVIGATORS — Class AA

EASTERN LEAGUE

BATTING

	AVG	G	AB	R	H	2B	3B	HR	RBI	BB	SO	SB	CS	OBP	SLG	B	T	HT	WT	DOB	1st Yr	Resides
Benavidez, Julian	.272	65	217	27	59	13	1	7	37	23	67	0	0	.348	.438	R	R	6-2	215	4-14-82	2001	Oakland, Calif.
Carter, Bryan	.224	117	389	42	87	24	4	4	32	29	104	10	4	.287	.337	L	L	6-0	194	2-25-78	2000	Frostproof, Fla.
Cervenak, Mike	.337	110	410	77	138	36	1	21	88	52	53	6	1	.414	.583	R	R	5-11	180	8-17-76	1999	New Boston, Mich.
Chavez, Angel	.198	89	308	22	61	8	2	0	21	24	53	6	4	.261	.237	R	R	6-1	180	7-22-81	1999	David Chiriqui, Panama
Clark, Doug	.292	140	537	82	157	23	13	10	71	44	103	33	8	.348	.439	L	R	6-2	205	3-5-76	1998	Springfield, Mass.
Cordido, Julio	.239	25	92	13	22	4	1	2	9	5	13	4	0	.283	.370	R	R	6-1	213	7-30-80	1997	Caracas, Venez.
Curry, Chris	.255	87	298	32	76	18	1	8	40	16	81	0	0	.304	.403	R	R	6-1	190	11-17-77	1999	Conway, Ark.
Garrido, Tomas	.154	6	13	0	2	0	0	0	0	0	4	0	0	.154	.154	R	R	6-2	155	8-27-81	1999	Valencia, Venez.
Knoedler, Justin	.274	115	409	64	112	28	3	9	47	32	98	5	3	.335	.423	R	R	6-2	210	7-17-80	2001	Springfield, Ill.
Knowlton, Jay	.400	13	30	4	12	3	0	0	2	5	6	0	0	.500	.500	R	R	6-1	195	12-8-79	2003	Milwaukie, Ore.
McMains, Derin	.271	110	436	58	118	23	1	5	55	29	40	12	2	.314	.362	S	R	6-0	180	11-9-79	2001	Little Rock, Ark.
Ortmeier, Dan	.252	106	377	55	95	23	6	10	48	47	110	18	2	.353	.424	S	L	6-4	220	5-11-81	2002	Highland Village, Texas
Pecci, Jay	.242	63	190	22	46	5	0	1	19	19	26	7	4	.339	.284	S	R	5-11	180	9-26-76	1998	Novato, Calif.
Santos, Deivis	.314	28	102	8	32	5	1	1	13	6	12	0	0	.352	.412	L	L	6-1	175	3-9-74	1997	Santo Domingo, D.R.
Valderrama, Carlos	.289	93	381	59	110	24	3	7	37	31	82	20	1	.345	.423	R	R	5-11	175	11-30-77	1995	Bachaquero, Venez.
Vericker, Brad	.192	17	52	6	10	3	0	0	2	10	20	0	0	.317	.250	L	L	6-2	210	5-8-81	2003	Marana, Ariz.
Von Schell, Tyler	.263	64	247	25	65	16	1	5	39	23	60	0	1	.328	.397	R	R	6-3	215	7-7-79	2001	Goleta, Calif.
Wald, Jacob	.210	52	162	19	34	8	1	2	13	17	49	0	3	.297	.309	R	R	6-2	180	2-8-81	2002	Alexandria, Va.
Walter, Randy	.111	13	45	1	5	0	0	0	2	2	15	0	0	.149	.111	R	R	6-2	210	4-14-81	2002	Ballantine, Mont.

PITCHING

	W	L	ERA	G	GS	CG	SV	IP	H	R	ER	BB	SO	AVG	B	T	HT	WT	DOB	1st Yr	Resides
Accardo, Jeremy	2	1	5.40	7	0	0	1	8	9	5	5	2	5	.290	R	R	6-2	180	12-8-81	2004	Mesa, Ariz.
Anderson, Luke	7	2	4.11	35	0	0	2	50	53	24	23	15	52	.265	R	R	6-5	210	4-29-78	2000	Las Vegas, Nev.
Bateman, Joe	1	3	2.78	12	1	0	0	23	20	7	7	8	17	.233	R	R	6-2	170	5-6-80	2002	Pittsfield, Mass.
Begg, Chris	9	1	2.30	16	14	0	0	94	87	27	24	11	61	.246	R	R	6-4	195	9-12-79	2001	Sutherland, Sask.
Cain, Matt	6	4	3.35	15	15	0	0	86	73	44	32	40	72	.227	R	R	6-3	180	10-1-84	2002	Collierville, Tenn.
Clark, Jeff	2	0	4.50	4	4	0	0	18	24	9	9	4	17	.316	R	R	6-6	240	5-6-80	2000	Ledyard, Conn.
Habel, Josh	4	10	4.36	27	25	1	0	136	130	76	66	50	123	.253	L	L	6-1	190	9-10-80	2002	Durango, Iowa
Hennessey, Brad	5	5	3.56	18	18	0	0	101	106	42	40	34	55	.272	R	R	6-2	185	2-7-80	2001	Toledo, Ohio
Markert, Jackson	0	1	5.61	15	0	0	0	26	36	18	16	15	9	.346	R	R	6-6	215	2-9-79	2000	Tulsa, Okla.
Mazone, Brian	1	1	2.08	7	1	0	2	17	13	8	4	2	19	.200	L	L	6-4	200	7-26-76	1998	Cardiff, Calif.
Misch, Pat	7	6	3.00	26	26	4	0	159	138	61	53	35	123	.235	R	L	6-2	170	8-18-81	2003	Northbrook, Ill.
Montes, Alberto	6	5	3.56	53	0	0	16	66	68	28	26	16	36	.274	R	R	6-2	210	12-11-79	2001	El Paso, Texas
Munter, Scott	2	4	2.35	42	0	0	3	65	63	19	17	22	30	.265	R	R	6-6	235	3-7-80	2001	Wichita, Kan.
Palmer, Matt	4	7	3.06	42	5	0	0	79	66	35	27	51	81	.231	R	R	6-2	200	3-21-79	2002	Caruthersville, Mo.
Pavon, Julio	2	3	4.70	17	5	0	0	44	43	26	23	10	20	.253	R	R	6-2	165	6-14-76	2000	Granada, Nicaragua
Sadler, Billy	0	3	3.86	17	0	0	0	30	22	16	13	18	24	.208	R	R	6-0	190	9-21-81	2003	Pensacola, Fla.
Taschner, Jack	3	1	2.48	14	10	0	0	58	47	17	16	16	55	.218	L	L	6-3	190	4-21-78	1999	Racine, Wis.
Treadway, Brion	1	4	6.03	7	7	0	0	37	44	25	25	17	29	.293	R	R	6-4	205	4-1-79	2000	Oxford, Ohio
Valdez, Merkin	1	4	4.32	10	7	0	1	42	35	21	20	15	31	.224	R	R	6-3	170	11-5-81	2000	San Cristobal, D.R.
Walk, Mitch	6	8	5.09	47	4	0	2	88	94	56	50	46	53	.276	L	L	6-2	185	4-7-78	2000	Mattoon, Ill.

FIELDING

Catcher	PCT	G	PO	A	E	DP	PB
Curry	.982	54	250	18	5	1	6
Knoedler	.991	102	681	64	7	2	15

First Base	PCT	G	PO	A	E	DP
Benavidez	.985	54	418	39	7	45
Cervenak	.975	14	108	8	3	13
Cordido	1.000	1	12	0	0	1
Curry	1.000	3	19	1	0	0
Santos	.987	18	145	8	2	14
Vericker	.968	3	26	4	1	3
Von Schell	.992	54	470	26	4	34

Second Base	PCT	G	PO	A	E	DP
Cervenak	1.000	1	3	4	0	1
Garrido	1.000	4	6	10	0	2

Knowlton	1.000	5	7	12	0	0
McMains	.992	103	218	310	4	64
Pecci	.957	27	46	65	5	11
Wald	.960	8	11	13	1	3

Third Base	PCT	G	PO	A	E	DP
Benavidez	.943	12	13	20	2	2
Cervenak	.970	95	67	162	7	14
Cordido	.902	18	9	28	4	1
Curry	1.000	1	0	1	0	1
Knowlton	1.000	1	2	1	0	0
Pecci	.963	20	14	38	2	5

Shortstop	PCT	G	PO	A	E	DP
Chavez	.962	88	141	240	15	58
Cordido	1.000	5	7	14	0	2

Knowlton	.947	4	4	14	1	1
McMains	1.000	1	0	2	0	0
Pecci	.909	6	8	12	2	3
Wald	.940	44	60	113	11	22

Outfield	PCT	G	PO	A	E	DP
Carter	.973	90	174	4	5	1
Clark	.989	134	269	10	3	0
Cordido	1.000	1	1	0	0	0
Knoedler	1.000	1	1	0	0	0
Ortmeier	.990	98	192	4	2	1
Santos	1.000	7	11	1	0	0
Valderrama	.995	88	180	2	1	1
Walter	.947	13	34	2	2	0

SAN JOSE GIANTS — High Class A

CALIFORNIA LEAGUE

BATTING

	AVG	G	AB	R	H	2B	3B	HR	RBI	BB	SO	SB	CS	OBP	SLG	B	T	HT	WT	DOB	1st Yr	Resides
Abreu, Yohany	.227	11	22	5	5	2	1	0	4	2	6	2	0	.292	.409	S	R	6-0	160	4-3-84	2002	San Cristobal, D.R.
Anderson, Keith	.241	47	158	21	38	7	0	3	27	23	31	0	1	.332	.342	R	R	6-1	205	1-6-79	2001	Escondido, Calif.
Benavidez, Julian	.161	46	149	14	24	7	0	6	24	20	37	0	1	.264	.329	R	R	6-2	215	4-14-82	2001	Oakland, Calif.
Bone, Kyle	.333	1	3	0	1	0	0	0	0	0	0	0	0	.333	.333	R	R	6-1	195	6-30-80	2004	Cooper City, Fla.
Buscher, Brian	.292	88	343	50	100	14	7	4	56	33	61	5	4	.359	.408	L	R	6-0	201	4-18-81	2003	Jacksonville, Fla.
Chavez, Angel	.389	12	54	12	21	5	0	1	16	4	7	2	2	.433	.537	R	R	6-1	180	7-22-81	1999	David Chiriqui, Panama
Ciesluk, Chris	.000	2	3	1	0	0	0	0	0	2	0	0	0	.250	.000	R	R	6-2	215	2-6-83	2001	Taunton, Mass.

ORGANIZATION STATISTICS

BATTING

BATTING	AVG	G	AB	R	H	2B	3B	HR	RBI	BB	SO	SB	CS	OBP	SLG	B	T	HT	WT	DOB	1st Yr	Resides
Cordido, Julio	.281	112	452	67	127	27	6	8	65	28	63	18	12	.333	.420	R	R	6-1	213	7-30-80	1997	Caracas, Venez.
Durham, Ray	.333	1	3	0	1	0	0	0	0	0	0	0	0	.333	.333	S	R	5-8	180	11-30-71	1990	Charlotte, N.C.
Holm, Steve	.259	61	201	27	52	12	0	9	29	33	52	1	2	.374	.453	R	R	6-0	208	10-21-79	2001	Tulsa, Okla.
Hornostaj, Aaron	.221	84	281	35	62	10	1	0	29	35	49	20	6	.301	.263	L	R	6-1	180	5-19-83	2002	Waterloo, Ontario
Ishikawa, Travis	.232	16	56	10	13	7	0	1	10	10	16	0	0	.353	.411	L	L	6-3	190	9-24-83	2002	Federal Way, Wash.
Jennings, Todd	.186	45	177	20	33	6	0	1	12	10	36	5	4	.246	.237	R	R	6-0	190	12-10-81	2003	Orangevale, Calif.
LaBarbera, A.J.	.302	99	378	60	114	18	3	4	47	41	51	16	5	.382	.397	R	R	5-10	190	3-17-80	2003	Whittier, Calif.
Lewis, Fred	.301	115	439	88	132	20	11	8	57	84	109	33	14	.424	.451	L	R	6-2	190	12-9-80	2002	Wiggins, Miss.
Martinez-Esteve, Eddy	.420	17	69	11	29	7	2	0	14	4	9	0	1	.446	.580	R	R	6-2	215	7-14-83	2004	Miami, Fla.
Munhall, Brian	.182	6	22	5	4	1	0	1	3	2	12	0	0	.250	.364	R	R	6-0	190	6-17-80	2002	Spokane, Wash.
Niekro, Lance	.311	15	61	13	19	7	1	1	14	2	5	0	0	.328	.508	R	R	6-3	210	1-29-79	2000	Lakeland, Fla.
Schierholtz, Nate	.295	62	258	39	76	18	9	3	31	15	41	3	1	.338	.469	L	R	6-2	215	2-15-84	2003	Danville, Calif.
Sobieraj, Aaron	.253	20	75	10	19	3	3	1	5	6	13	1	1	.325	.413	R	R	6-2	170	6-3-81	2002	Clearwater, Fla.
Sosa, Carlos	.253	97	344	50	87	16	6	10	46	36	101	7	1	.329	.422	R	R	6-1	195	10-20-81	2001	Santo Domingo, D.R.
Strong, Zach	.246	38	122	12	30	9	0	0	15	7	33	0	1	.293	.320	R	R	6-3	200	6-3-81	2003	Olympia, Wash.
Timpner, Clay	.280	6	25	4	7	2	0	0	2	1	2	1	0	.296	.360	L	L	6-2	197	5-13-83	2004	Alva, Fla.
Trumble, Dan	.240	95	334	56	80	16	2	17	48	48	119	12	8	.347	.452	R	R	6-2	220	9-29-79	2000	Nampa, Idaho
Vericker, Brad	.277	99	358	54	99	29	3	14	76	60	83	0	2	.375	.492	L	L	6-2	210	5-8-81	2003	Marana, Ariz.
Wald, Jacob	.197	44	147	18	29	5	1	1	13	10	33	4	1	.274	.265	R	R	6-2	180	2-8-81	2002	Alexandria, Va.
Walter, Randy	.263	89	300	43	79	14	5	6	34	24	79	10	3	.328	.403	R	R	6-2	215	4-14-81	2002	Ballantine, Mont.

PITCHING

PITCHING	W	L	ERA	G	GS	CG	SV	IP	H	R	ER	BB	SO	AVG	B	T	HT	WT	DOB	1st Yr	Resides
Accardo, Jeremy	1	2	4.25	50	0	0	27	55	57	28	26	15	43	.268	R	R	6-3	170	12-8-81	2004	Mesa, Ariz.
Broshuis, Garrett	4	3	5.19	14	8	0	0	52	60	32	30	16	47	.287	R	R	6-1	185	12-18-81	2004	Advance, Mo.
Burres, Brian	12	1	2.84	36	15	0	0	124	115	49	39	30	114	.249	L	L	6-1	171	4-8-81	2001	Clackamas, Ore.
Cain, Matt	7	1	1.86	13	13	0	0	73	58	25	15	17	89	.216	R	R	6-3	180	10-1-84	2002	Collierville, Tenn.
Cram, Josh	2	0	5.07	42	0	0	0	60	70	36	34	24	31	.298	R	R	6-2	195	8-22-80	2001	Edmonds, Wash.
Espineli, Geno	0	0	0.00	1	0	0	1	1	0	0	0	0	1	.000	L	L	6-4	200	9-8-82	2004	Katy, Texas
Foppert, Jesse	0	0	1.93	4	4	0	0	9	4	2	2	4	11	.133	R	R	6-6	210	7-10-80	2001	San Rafael, Calif.
Garcia, James	5	5	2.94	43	1	0	2	70	57	26	23	24	84	.222	R	R	6-2	210	2-3-80	2002	Torrance, Calif.
Markert, Jackson	3	3	4.10	25	0	0	0	26	31	13	12	12	23	.298	R	R	6-6	215	2-9-79	2000	Tulsa, Okla.
McNiven, Brooks	6	8	4.35	31	21	0	0	134	162	74	65	32	73	.295	R	R	6-5	175	6-19-81	2003	Vernon, B.C.
Pannone, Anthony	4	6	4.20	56	0	0	1	94	97	48	44	35	75	.265	R	R	6-3	220	7-7-81	2001	Olympia, Wash.
Pavon, Julio	1	5	4.50	15	8	0	0	60	66	33	30	9	41	.282	R	R	6-2	165	6-14-76	2000	Granada, Nicaragua
Pendley, Nathan	0	0	1.80	7	0	0	0	5	8	2	1	3	2	.381	L	L	6-4	220	9-5-81	2004	Albany, Ore.
Petersen, Jeffrey	5	8	4.82	27	13	0	0	84	93	60	45	32	45	.279	R	R	6-0	190	9-21-81	2003	Pensacola, Fla.
Sadler, Billy	2	2	2.38	30	3	0	0	57	29	17	15	40	66	.154	R	R	6-0	205	1-29-73	1991	Longview, Wash.
Schmidt, Jason	1	0	0.00	1	1	0	0	5	2	0	0	1	7	.118	R	R	6-5	205	1-29-73	1991	Longview, Wash.
Simon, Alfredo	1	2	5.68	6	6	0	0	32	44	24	20	12	21	.328	R	R	6-4	215	5-8-81	2000	Santiago, D.R.
Stirm, Brian	4	10	4.87	31	18	0	0	109	121	71	59	41	86	.282	R	R	6-8	216	3-13-82	2002	Saratoga, Calif.
Treadway, Brion	7	5	3.95	20	20	0	0	112	98	53	49	42	97	.240	R	R	6-4	205	4-1-79	2000	Oxford, Ohio
Valdez, Merkin	3	1	2.52	7	7	0	0	36	30	12	10	5	44	.219	R	R	6-3	170	11-5-81	2000	San Cristobal, D.R.
Waddell, Jason	6	4	4.08	47	2	0	0	71	76	39	32	24	60	.275	R	L	6-2	211	6-11-81	2001	Riverside, Calif.

FIELDING

Catcher	PCT	G	PO	A	E	DP	PB
Anderson	.980	44	365	35	8	5	5
Holm	.995	50	338	41	2	2	7
Jennings	.984	44	346	29	6	3	9
Munhall	.968	4	27	3	1	0	1

First Base	PCT	G	PO	A	E	DP
Benavidez	.985	31	251	15	4	15
Cordido	1.000	1	8	2	0	0
Holm	1.000	2	6	0	0	1
Ishikawa	1.000	16	153	8	0	15
Niekro	.993	15	139	4	1	14
Sosa	1.000	2	6	1	0	0
Strong	.981	8	46	5	1	4
Vericker	.994	76	651	46	4	56

Second Base	PCT	G	PO	A	E	DP
Durham	1.000	1	1	2	0	0

	PCT	G	PO	A	E	DP
Holm	.750	1	2	1	1	1
Hornostaj	.955	25	34	73	5	10
LaBarbera	.981	98	198	305	10	61
Sobieraj	.928	18	25	52	6	6

Third Base	PCT	G	PO	A	E	DP
Abreu	1.000	1	0	1	0	1
Benavidez	.500	1	2	0	2	0
Buscher	.926	17	11	39	4	5
Ciesluk	1.000	1	1	5	0	0
Cordido	.950	76	55	136	10	12
Holm	1.000	5	3	7	0	0
Hornostaj	.938	5	9	6	1	1
Schierholtz	.895	38	19	58	9	4
Strong	1.000	1	1	0	0	0

Shortstop	PCT	G	PO	A	E	DP
Abreu	.750	2	4	2	2	1

	PCT	G	PO	A	E	DP
Chavez	.937	12	22	37	4	10
Cordido	.949	34	48	120	9	19
Hornostaj	.919	52	73	143	19	30
Wald	.941	43	52	122	11	15

Outfield	PCT	G	PO	A	E	DP
Abreu	.818	7	8	1	2	0
Cordido	1.000	3	4	0	0	0
Lewis	.971	113	259	7	8	2
Martinez-Esteve	1.000	17	21	1	0	0
Schierholtz	.861	17	29	2	5	2
Sosa	.966	98	157	14	6	1
Strong	.938	19	27	3	2	0
Timpner	1.000	6	15	0	0	0
Trumble	.957	83	127	6	6	2
Walter	.972	86	166	6	5	2

HAGERSTOWN SUNS — Low Class A

SOUTH ATLANTIC LEAGUE

BATTING	AVG	G	AB	R	H	2B	3B	HR	RBI	BB	SO	SB	CS	OBP	SLG	B	T	HT	WT	DOB	1st Yr	Resides
Abreu, Johany	.223	35	121	16	27	4	1	1	4	1	27	6	1	.242	.298	S	R	6-0	160	4-3-84	2002	San Cristobal, D.R.
Anderson, Keith	.347	15	49	8	17	4	0	2	7	6	9	1	1	.411	.551	R	R	6-0	205	1-6-79	2003	Escondido, Calif.
Armitage, Jonathan	.239	124	447	50	107	23	4	12	63	52	111	9	3	.318	.389	S	R	6-5	210	10-29-80	2004	Athens, Ga.
Barrows, Derek	.213	62	211	18	45	6	0	3	16	11	40	4	5	.257	.284	R	R	6-1	187	11-20-80	2003	Sarasota, Fla.
Bone, Kyle	.204	15	49	4	10	1	2	0	11	7	14	0	1	.298	.306	R	R	6-1	195	6-30-80	2004	Cooper City, Fla.
Buller, Dayton	.202	35	114	11	23	8	1	2	9	13	35	1	1	.295	.342	R	R	6-0	190	6-22-81	2002	Oakhurst, Calif.
Columbus, Jason	.287	104	401	56	115	27	2	14	61	29	103	3	0	.353	.469	R	R	6-6	230	9-27-79	2003	St. Lucie, Fla.
Coutlangus, Jon	.194	71	227	29	44	5	0	2	19	31	52	12	4	.293	.242	L	L	6-1	180	10-21-80	2003	St. Lucie, Fla.
Dobson, Patrick	.247	101	381	49	94	21	2	7	31	39	92	10	5	.328	.367	R	R	6-3	210	12-8-80	2003	Santa Barbara, Calif.
Garrido, Tomas	.192	10	26	2	5	2	0	0	1	0	3	0	0	.192	.269	R	R	6-2	155	8-27-81	1999	Valencia, Venez.
Hornostaj, Aaron	.268	14	56	8	15	0	0	5	2	14	5	1	.300	.304	L	R	6-1	180	5-19-83	2002	Waterloo, Ontario
Hutting, Timothy	.248	125	427	62	106	18	2	2	42	47	38	5	5	.334	.314	R	R	6-0	190	10-29-81	2003	Newhall, Calif.
Ishikawa, Travis	.257	98	358	59	92	19	2	15	54	45	110	10	5	.357	.447	L	L	6-3	190	9-24-83	2002	Federal Way, Wash.
Knowlton, Jay	.244	58	217	34	53	12	1	1	20	23	50	1	4	.337	.323	R	R	6-1	195	12-8-79	2003	Milwaukie, Ore.
LaBarbera, A.J.	.235	11	34	5	8	1	0	0	4	7	5	0	0	.381	.265	R	R	5-10	190	3-17-80	2003	Whittier, Calif.
Martinez-Esteve, Eddy	.217	13	46	4	10	1	1	1	11	8	11	1	1	.339	.348	R	R	6-2	215	7-14-83	2004	Miami, Fla.

BATTING	AVG	G	AB	R	H	2B	3B	HR	RBI	BB	SO	SB	CS	OBP	SLG	B	T	HT	WT	DOB	1st Yr	Resides
Munhall, Brian	.275	62	200	24	55	6	2	4	22	18	42	3	1	.348	.385	R	R	6-0	190	6-17-80	2002	Spokane, Wash.
Schierholtz, Nate	.298	59	235	41	70	22	0	15	54	19	52	1	0	.356	.583	L	R	6-2	215	2-15-84	2003	Danville, Calif.
Schmidt, Jesse	.256	119	437	55	112	19	3	7	56	66	87	11	7	.359	.362	S	R	6-1	200	10-27-81	2003	Carlsbad, Calif.
Strong, Zach	.241	16	58	7	14	3	0	3	7	7	11	0	0	.323	.448	S	R	6-3	200	6-3-81	2003	Olympia, Wash.
Swanson, Brent	.229	21	70	7	16	2	0	1	7	6	17	0	0	.299	.300	L	R	5-11	190	9-11-80	2004	Richmond, B.C.
Wagner, Mike	.256	119	422	64	108	24	2	13	49	42	116	5	3	.350	.415	R	R	6-3	210	9-13-81	2003	Woodinville, Wash.

PITCHING	W	L	ERA	G	GS	CG	SV	IP	H	R	ER	BB	SO	AVG	B	T	HT	WT	DOB	1st Yr	Resides
Acosta, Kelyn	4	3	4.41	10	10	0	0	51	61	31	25	23	37	.296	R	R	6-1	170	4-24-85	2002	Azua, D.R.
Alvarez, Tim	4	9	3.69	51	0	0	22	61	50	29	25	28	41	.226	L	L	6-4	235	1-5-81	2003	Central Point, Ore.
Anez, Omar	2	7	4.81	14	14	0	0	79	81	50	42	25	56	.261	R	R	6-2	240	2-1-81	1998	Gustiro Miranda, Venez.
Bateman, Joe	7	5	2.14	36	0	0	1	71	48	19	17	20	80	.190	R	R	6-1	200	5-6-80	2002	Pittsfield, Mass.
Callahan, Ryan	0	4	4.56	7	5	0	0	24	28	16	12	10	17	.286	L	L	6-0	160	11-19-80	2004	Janesville, Wis.
English, Jesse	0	1	7.48	17	4	0	0	43	40	37	36	40	46	.245	L	L	6-3	220	9-13-84	2002	Vista, Calif.
Floyd, Jesse	4	8	4.60	32	18	0	2	121	130	74	62	42	125	.270	R	R	6-5	185	1-2-81	2003	Nederland, Texas
George, Chris	2	1	7.86	20	2	0	0	45	63	40	39	13	38	.330	R	R	6-1	180	10-13-80	2003	Santa Cruz, Calif.
Martin, Sean	4	3	3.65	44	0	0	2	94	93	50	38	23	83	.254	R	R	6-1	190	3-27-80	2003	Tucson, Ariz.
Millikan, Bryan	2	3	4.22	10	0	0	0	43	45	21	20	17	27	.280	R	R	6-5	190	8-13-83	2003	Olympia, Wash.
Musgrave, Mike	2	5	5.79	36	12	0	0	84	94	65	54	47	56	.286	R	R	6-2	185	4-10-84	2003	Ocala, Fla.
NeSmith, Travis	1	9	5.67	34	9	0	0	86	101	62	54	52	73	.301	L	L	6-3	225	4-26-82	2003	Miami, Fla.
Portorreal, Daniel	0	2	7.27	8	1	0	0	17	24	18	14	15	10	.343	R	R	6-2	160	1-29-82	2002	Santo Domingo, D.R.
Sadowski, Ryan	3	9	6.92	26	16	0	0	91	106	84	70	45	90	.294	R	R	6-4	185	10-4-82	2003	Davie, Fla.
Serrato, Juan	8	8	4.57	26	21	1	0	104	105	73	53	65	91	.258	R	R	6-2	200	11-4-81	2002	Riverside, Calif.
Sobieraj, Aaron	0	0	4.57	11	0	0	0	22	17	11	11	15	16	.221	R	R	6-2	170	6-3-81	2002	Clearwater, Fla.
Thurmond, Ben	4	6	2.54	19	14	1	1	92	87	39	26	28	73	.256	R	R	6-0	190	10-2-81	2003	Tempe, Ariz.
Wilson, Brian	2	5	5.34	23	3	0	3	57	63	37	34	22	41	.283	R	R	6-1	205	3-16-82	2004	Londonderry, N.H.

FIELDING

Catcher	PCT	G	PO	A	E	DP	PB
Anderson	1.000	15	111	19	0	1	3
Bone	.983	15	100	14	2	1	1
Buller	.983	34	262	29	5	2	6
Munhall	.981	62	433	41	9	4	7
Swanson	.985	19	120	8	2	1	5

First Base	PCT	G	PO	A	E	DP
Columbus	.986	33	255	23	4	25
Ishikawa	.994	94	773	55	5	54
Knowlton	1.000	1	11	0	0	0
Strong	.988	9	79	3	1	9

Second Base	PCT	G	PO	A	E	DP
Barrows	.937	16	38	51	6	9
Dobson	.961	95	179	240	17	39

	PCT	G	PO	A	E	DP
Garrido	1.000	3	7	9	0	2
Hornostaj	.964	5	11	16	1	5
Knowlton	.923	11	19	17	3	4
LaBarbera	.979	9	20	26	1	9

Third Base	PCT	G	PO	A	E	DP
Abreu	.909	12	8	22	3	2
Barrows	.896	41	29	66	11	7
Garrido	1.000	1	0	2	0	0
Hornostaj	.920	8	7	16	2	5
Knowlton	.882	23	16	44	8	4
Schierholtz	.914	55	34	105	13	7
Strong	.875	2	2	5	1	2

Shortstop	PCT	G	PO	A	E	DP
Abreu	1.000	4	6	10	0	1

	PCT	G	PO	A	E	DP
Barrows	.769	3	4	6	3	0
Garrido	.938	5	8	7	1	1
Hornostaj	1.000	1	0	1	0	0
Hutting	.943	123	144	334	29	47
Knowlton	.857	6	8	16	4	5
LaBarbera	1.000	1	0	3	0	0

Outfield	PCT	G	PO	A	E	DP
Abreu	1.000	14	30	1	0	0
Armitage	.964	117	201	14	8	3
Coutlangus	.975	67	143	12	4	2
Martinez-Esteve	1.000	9	16	1	0	0
Schmidt	.970	98	186	6	6	2
Strong	1.000	4	10	0	0	0
Wagner	.940	110	185	2	12	1

SALEM-KEIZER VOLCANOES

Short-Season Class A

NORTHWEST LEAGUE

BATTING	AVG	G	AB	R	H	2B	3B	HR	RBI	BB	SO	SB	CS	OBP	SLG	B	T	HT	WT	DOB	1st Yr	Resides
Acha, John	.165	38	109	12	18	3	1	2	12	8	31	2	1	.238	.266	R	R	6-0	200	6-3-81	2004	Turlock, Calif.
Babineaux, Charlie	.246	55	199	30	49	8	1	8	33	8	50	1	0	.286	.417	R	R	6-2	215	5-16-81	2004	New Iberia, La.
Bone, Kyle	.154	15	39	3	6	0	0	0	2	3	13	0	0	.214	.154	R	R	6-1	195	6-30-80	2004	Cooper City, Fla.
Bowker, John	.323	31	127	23	41	9	2	4	16	8	25	1	0	.390	.520	L	L	6-2	190	7-8-83	2004	Sacramento, Calif.
Conte, Nick	.215	44	135	12	29	2	0	0	10	14	23	1	1	.290	.230	R	R	5-10	175	1-18-82	2003	San Carlos, Calif.
Felix, Maximo	.210	21	62	9	13	3	1	1	7	2	19	0	0	.254	.339	R	R	6-0	190	11-9-82	2001	Santo Domingo, D.R.
Frandsen, Kevin	.296	25	98	22	29	5	0	3	14	9	9	0	1	.369	.439	R	R	6-0	175	5-24-82	2004	San Jose, Calif.
Groth, Brad	.050	13	40	1	2	1	0	0	0	7	10	1	1	.208	.075	R	R	6-2	197	5-13-83	2004	Lake Villa, Ill.
Haines, Kyle	.261	32	119	15	31	5	0	0	11	12	18	1	1	.328	.303	L	R	6-1	170	7-28-82	2004	Louisville, Ky.
Horwitz, Brian	.347	71	268	41	93	24	1	2	44	21	34	3	3	.407	.466	R	R	6-1	180	11-7-82	2004	Encino, Calif.
Jennings, Todd	.329	17	70	7	23	3	0	3	11	3	12	0	1	.356	.500	R	R	6-0	190	12-10-81	2003	Orangevale, Calif.
Klink, Simon	.258	62	260	41	67	12	0	11	44	27	78	3	1	.347	.431	S	R	6-1	212	12-21-81	2004	Auburn, Ind.
Martinez-Esteve, Eddy	.286	10	35	5	10	4	0	0	2	6	7	0	0	.405	.400	L	R	6-2	215	7-14-83	2004	Miami, Fla.
Mooney, Mike	.100	3	10	0	1	1	0	0	3	0	2	0	0	.100	.200	R	R	6-1	205	6-8-83	2003	Hillsborough, Calif.
Palumbo, Jeff	.288	65	260	44	75	10	1	0	25	34	29	6	0	.371	.335	S	R	5-10	180	3-6-82	2004	Bowie, Md.
Paulino, Adalberto	.176	14	34	3	6	2	0	2	7	1	6	0	0	.222	.412	R	R	5-11	179	9-6-82	2000	Nizao, D.R.
Strain, Ryan	.198	40	126	19	25	5	1	1	12	24	18	2	0	.333	.278	S	R	5-9	183	10-15-80	2003	Englewood, Colo.
Thompson, Will	.293	62	225	43	66	12	0	1	27	37	34	0	0	.400	.360	L	L	6-2	200	11-20-82	2004	Missoula, Mont.
Timpner, Clay	.293	68	294	37	86	7	2	5	28	20	35	16	5	.339	.381	L	L	6-2	197	5-13-83	2004	Alva, Fla.
Yens, Jose	.282	41	142	18	40	6	2	3	24	2	31	4	2	.302	.415	R	R	6-1	190	10-16-82	2003	Santo Domingo, D.R.

GAMES BY POSITION: C—Bone 15, Conte 44, Felix 17, Jennings 9. **1B**—Acha 12, Babineaux 7, Felix 1, Thompson 60. **2B**—Acha 1, Frandsen 19, Palumbo 26, Strain 32. **3B**—Acha 11, Klink 66. **SS**—Deltran 1, Frandsen 4, Groth 5, Haines 31, Palumbo 37. **OF**—Acha 5, Babineaux 33, Bowker 31, Horwitz 65, Martinez-Esteve 9, Mooney 3, Paulino 7, Timpner 68, Yens 20.

PITCHING	W	L	ERA	G	GS	CG	SV	IP	H	R	ER	BB	SO	AVG	B	T	HT	WT	DOB	1st Yr	Resides
Broshuis, Garrett	3	0	1.37	5	2	0	0	20	15	4	3	4	23	.203	R	R	6-3	170	12-18-81	2004	Advance, Mo.
Espineli, Geno	1	3	5.10	22	0	0	3	30	29	18	17	8	37	.254	L	L	6-4	200	9-8-82	2004	Katy, Texas
Gardner, Adam	2	0	2.54	19	0	0	0	50	38	19	14	30	59	.207	L	L	6-0	185	2-14-82	2004	Fairfax Station, Va.
Hedrick, Justin	1	2	3.27	11	4	0	0	33	22	14	12	17	44	.182	R	R	6-3	225	6-8-82	2004	Omaha, Neb.
Jenson, Kevin	0	1	10.45	6	0	0	0	10	14	13	12	9	11	.304	R	R	6-4	215	4-7-84	2004	Yuba City, Calif.
Kunes, Michael	1	1	4.09	21	0	0	4	33	34	19	15	14	30	.262	L	L	6-1	205	9-16-81	2003	Chatsworth, Calif.
Mackay, Douglas	3	4	6.18	16	9	0	0	51	67	39	35	23	39	.312	R	R	6-1	197	3-29-83	2004	Riverton, Utah
Minor, Matt	0	0	4.96	15	0	0	4	16	9	9	7	16	.273	R	R	6-0	190	9-20-82	2004	Las Vegas, Nev.
Moreno, Anthony	5	1	3.44	21	0	0	1	50	41	22	19	11	47	.227	R	R	5-11	198	5-4-83	2002	Mesa, Ariz.
Odom, John	2	4	5.01	20	5	0	0	59	82	39	33	19	55	.335	R	R	6-2	185	1-6-82	2004	Atlanta, Ga.

PITCHING	W	L	ERA	G	GS	CG	SV	IP	H	R	ER	BB	SO	AVG	B	T	HT	WT	DOB	1st Yr	Resides
Pendley, Nathan	2	0	2.45	15	0	0	2	18	14	6	5	8	20	.219	L	L	6-4	220	9-5-81	2004	Albany, Ore.
Raguse, Matt	0	3	7.16	14	6	0	0	28	39	26	22	16	33	.342	R	R	6-2	195	9-28-82	2004	Oxford, Ohio
Reina, Jesus	2	6	5.40	15	13	0	0	57	68	42	34	20	55	.296	L	L	6-0	140	4-20-84	2002	Maracay, Venez.
Sack, Darren	2	5	6.23	16	16	0	0	69	81	55	48	27	55	.287	R	R	6-4	190	7-19-82	2004	Anaheim, Calif.
Sanchez, Jonathan	2	1	4.84	6	6	0	0	22	16	13	12	19	34	.198	L	L	6-2	165	11-19-82	2004	Sabana Grande, P.R.
Smith, Chase	5	4	2.23	20	0	0	0	32	18	14	8	17	32	.162	L	R	6-0	200	11-19-82	2004	Hinton, Okla.
Sobieraj, Aaron	2	1	2.49	8	0	0	0	22	18	6	6	8	15	.237	R	R	6-2	170	6-3-81	2002	Clearwater, Fla.
Whitaker, Craig	4	2	3.44	15	15	0	0	71	58	33	27	43	77	.221	R	R	6-4	188	11-19-84	2003	Lufkin, Texas
Wohlgemuth, Trevor	0	1	6.14	7	0	0	0	7	8	7	5	6	4	.267	R	R	6-3	230	10-10-81	2004	Springfield, Ill.

AZL GIANTS — Rookie

ARIZONA LEAGUE

BATTING	AVG	G	AB	R	H	2B	3B	HR	RBI	BB	SO	SB	CS	SLG	OBP	B	T	HT	WT	DOB	1st Yr	Resides
Abreu, Johany	.281	11	32	3	9	1	0	0	0	3	3	3	0	.313	.361	S	R	6-0	160	4-3-84	2002	San Cristobal, D.R.
Bowker, John	.512	10	43	14	22	7	1	2	11	7	11	1	0	.860	.580	L	L	6-2	190	7-8-83	2004	Sacramento, Calif.
Buller, Dayton	.364	7	22	7	8	0	1	1	5	5	4	3	0	.591	.517	R	R	6-0	190	6-22-81	2002	Oakhurst, Calif.
Chavez, Angel	.375	4	16	2	6	0	0	1	5	1	3	2	0	.563	.389	R	R	6-1	180	7-22-81	1999	David Chiriqui, Panama
Ciesluk, Chris	.214	9	14	2	3	2	0	0	2	1	4	0	0	.357	.267	R	R	6-2	215	2-6-83	2001	Taunton, Mass.
Cividanes, Manny	.165	35	115	8	19	3	3	0	7	9	34	1	1	.243	.224	L	L	6-1	175	10-31-84	2004	San Juan, P.R.
DeSouza, Daniel	.255	54	216	50	55	7	5	0	25	37	50	13	6	.333	.364	L	L	6-1	175	11-27-84	2004	Queens, N.Y.
Disla, Lisandro	.351	48	168	27	59	7	1	0	25	18	29	4	5	.405	.424	R	R	6-0	170	4-6-84	2001	Mao, D.R.
Dixon, Dorian	.317	27	82	10	26	7	0	0	12	13	8	1	0	.402	.411	L	R	5-10	180	12-11-82	2004	San Diego, Calif.
Haines, Kyle	.339	19	59	12	20	8	0	0	12	4	3	3	3	.475	.394	L	R	6-1	170	7-28-82	2004	Louisville, Ill.
Jennings, Todd	.385	8	26	7	10	3	1	0	6	1	5	2	0	.577	.429	R	R	6-0	190	12-10-81	2003	Orangevale, Calif.
King, Lisandro	.163	21	49	4	8	0	0	0	6	5	17	1	0	.163	.232	R	R	6-1	170	5-27-86	2003	La Romana, D.R.
Kurtz, Jared	.237	17	59	9	14	7	0	0	6	9	19	2	0	.356	.338	R	R	6-0	215	11-12-81	2004	Fort Wayne, Ind.
Luster, Jeremiah	.271	19	70	11	19	3	0	0	7	5	17	3	2	.314	.314	R	R	5-10	175	8-31-86	2004	Oceanside, Calif.
Martinez-Esteve, Eddy	.357	4	14	2	5	2	0	0	4	0	2	2	0	.500	.375	R	R	6-2	215	7-14-83	2004	Miami, Fla.
Mooney, Mike	.312	55	215	43	67	11	7	6	57	25	45	7	6	.512	.394	R	R	6-1	205	6-8-83	2003	Hillsborough, Calif.
Morillo, Roberto	.252	36	103	17	26	3	2	2	18	11	29	3	1	.379	.330	S	R	6-0	155	7-24-84	2001	Maracaibo, Venez.
Richards, Judson	.271	56	218	35	59	11	3	5	37	22	60	10	0	.417	.339	L	L	6-2	205	12-25-80	2004	Carmel Valley, Calif.
Sanchez, Ivan	.176	13	34	5	6	1	0	1	4	3	14	0	0	.294	.237	R	R	6-3	190	3-17-83	2002	San Jose de Ocoa, D.R.
Sanders, Marcus	.292	55	209	54	61	12	4	3	21	35	45	28	4	.431	.415	R	R	6-0	180	8-25-85	2004	Sarasota, Fla.
Sandoval, Pablo	.266	46	177	21	47	9	5	0	26	5	17	4	1	.373	.287	S	R	5-11	180	8-11-86	2003	Carabobo, Venez.

GAMES BY POSITION: C—Buller 7, Dixon 4, Jennings 4, Kurtz 15, Sandoval 33. 1B—Ciesluk 3, Richards 56. 2B—Disla 3, Haines 1, King 3, Morillo 2, Sanders 54. 3B—Chavez 2. Ciesluk 4, Disla 45, King 8, Morillo 6. SS—Abreu 8. Chavez 2, Haines 12, King 9, Luster 14, Morillo 15. OF—Abreu 2, Bowker 10. Cividanes 34, Desouza 52, Martinez-Esteve 4, Mooney 54, Morillo 9, Sanchez 12.

PITCHING	W	L	ERA	G	GS	CG	SV	IP	H	R	ER	BB	SO	AVG	B	T	HT	WT	DOB	1st Yr	Resides
Callahan, Ryan	2	0	4.12	8	2	0	0	20	13	10	9	8	14	.180	L	L	6-0	160	11-19-80	2004	Janesville, Wis.
Cepeda, Benny	2	4	4.61	11	7	0	0	41	45	24	21	17	43	.284	R	R	6-2	175	5-2-83	2004	Rio Piedras, P.R.
Farach, Juan	2	1	4.22	9	4	0	0	32	33	25	15	13	30	.261	L	L	5-11	150	7-7-85	2002	Masaya, Nicaragua
Foppert, Jesse	0	0	9.00	1	1	0	0	1	3	1	1	0	2	.500	R	R	6-6	210	7-10-80	2001	San Rafael, Calif.
Gornati, T.J.	4	2	4.01	12	8	0	0	43	47	22	19	10	46	.281	R	R	6-1	205	3-16-81	2004	Pittsburgh, Pa.
Hedrick, Justin	0	0	10.13	2	0	0	0	3	6	3	3	1	4	.461	R	R	6-3	225	6-8-82	2004	Omaha, Neb.
Jenson, Kevin	1	1	1.59	12	0	0	0	11	9	3	2	2	12	.243	R	R	6-4	215	4-7-81	2004	Yuba City, Calif.
Ludwig, Kellen	3	2	2.28	11	7	0	1	47	43	17	12	11	55	.251	R	R	6-5	225	11-19-82	2003	Leesburg, Ga.
Lundwall, Todd	0	0	5.00	8	0	0	0	9	4	6	5	12	9	.133	R	R	6-2	205	12-24-80	2003	Los Angeles, Calif.
Matos, Osiris	2	0	2.44	11	8	0	1	48	43	23	13	20	47	.229	R	R	6-1	180	11-6-84	2002	Santo Domingo, D.R.
Mercado, Arnoldo	2	0	4.30	18	0	0	1	15	16	18	7	18	16	.262	R	R	6-1	160	12-28-81	2001	Sinaloa, Mexico
Millikan, Bryan	1	0	9.00	3	0	0	0	4	5	4	4	4	3	.312	R	R	6-5	190	8-13-83	2003	Olympia, Wash.
Minor, Matt	0	0	0.00	9	0	0	5	10	3	1	0	1	8	.096	R	R	6-0	180	9-20-82	2004	Las Vegas, Nev.
Portorreal, Daniel	0	0	4.35	7	3	0	0	21	22	13	10	10	18	.268	R	R	6-2	160	1-29-82	2002	Santo Domingo, D.R.
Putman, Rickey	1	0	1.59	8	0	0	1	17	5	4	3	10	22	.087	R	R	6-3	220	10-1-82	2004	Conroe, Texas
Salankey, Caleb	2	1	3.35	11	5	0	1	40	49	24	15	12	41	.296	R	R	6-1	180	5-10-82	2004	Arvada, Colo.
Sanchez, Jon	5	0	2.77	9	3	0	1	26	22	9	8	9	27	.229	L	L	6-2	165	11-19-82	2004	Sabana Grande, P.R.
Sanchez, Jose	1	1	3.26	17	0	0	5	19	18	7	7	5	30	.232	R	R	6-1	180	11-19-82	2002	Santo Domingo, D.R.
Solis, Hairo	3	2	3.25	22	0	0	2	28	22	13	10	9	42	.209	R	R	6-1	170	3-3-84	2001	Las Matas de Farfan, D.R.
Ventura, Robert	3	3	4.42	11	7	0	0	37	46	21	18	11	34	.296	R	R	6-2	160	11-26-81	2002	Santiago, D.R.
Yntema, Orlando	0	1	7.50	2	1	0	0	6	6	7	5	2	6	.240	R	R	6-3	180	2-21-86	2003	Cabarete, D.R.
Zbacnik, Billy	3	1	3.60	17	0	0	0	20	19	9	8	13	25	.260	L	L	6-5	235	4-20-81	2003	San Diego, Calif.

ORGANIZATION STATISTICS

SEATTLE MARINERS

BY COREY BROCK

There was nothing subtle about the Seattle Mariners' fall from grace in 2004.

The Mariners, who won 93 games in 2003, faltered early and by May were essentially out of contention in the American League West Division.

How far did Seattle fall? Just three seasons removed from winning 116 games, the Mariners nearly lost 100 games (63-99) in 2004.

So how did it happen? How did a team on the verge of making the playoffs one season completely drop off the postseason radar screen the next?

A number of factors—poor hitting, an aging team, a weakened bullpen, and others—conspired to send Seattle tumbling toward the club's worst record since the 103-loss season of 1983.

"A combination of things led to the year we had," said Mariners manager Bob Melvin, who was fired a day after the season ended. "But the middle-of-the-order guys we counted on to knock in runs all had off years. Guys are going to have off years, but you don't see that many having off years at the same time."

Second baseman Bret Boone, who drove in 141 runs during that magical 2001 season, was bothered by a nagging back injury all season and hit just .251-24-83.

"It's a humbling game," Boone said. "In '01, we'd make a bad play and still get a break. This year, we'd make a good play and get a bad call. I can't explain why. But it seemed like it happened (to all of us) at once."

Veterans John Olerud and Rich Aurilia—two players who had a history of driving in runs—never recovered from slow starts and were released by midseason. Olerud, who had 22 RBIs to show for the first four months of the season, later resurfaced with the Yankees.

By season's end, a handful of other players who were on the Opening Day roster were gone, too: Ben Davis, Quinton McCracken, Dave Hansen, Kevin Jarvis, Mike

Ichiro Suzuki

Felix Hernandez

BILL MITCHELL

PLAYERS of the YEAR

MAJOR LEAGUE: Ichiro Suzuki, of

Suzuki racked up 262 hits in 2004, breaking George Sisler's major league record of 257. He did so by hitting a record 225 singles for a last-place Mariners team, but still broke one of baseball's most hallowed marks. Suzuki's second-half push was remarkable—he hit .429 after the all-star break.

MINOR LEAGUE: Felix Hernandez, rhp

As an 18-year-old in 2004, Hernandez did nothing to diminish his "phenom" status. He went 9-3, 2.74 at Class A Inland Empire before a June promotion to Double-A San Antonio, where he was 5-1, 3.30. Hernandez, who often hit 97 mph with his fastball, also had 172 strikeouts in 149 innings overall.

Myers and Freddy Garcia, who was traded to the White Sox. Scott Spiezio, another free agent signee, struggled, hitting just .215 and was essentially benched in the second half of the season.

At the heart of Seattle's problems was an anemic offense that ranked last in the American League in runs scored, home runs and slugging percentage. DH Edgar Martinez hit .263 with 12 home runs and announced, in August, that the 2004 season would be his last with the Mariners.

There might as well have been a revolving door on the Mariners clubhouse in 2004. A total of 15 players made their major league debuts with Seattle. Some of those rookies—outfielder Jeremy Reed, first baseman Bucky Jacobsen and pitcher Bobby Madritsch—showed enough promise to warrant consideration for the opening day roster in 2005 with good showings.

By season's end, the Mariners' roster more resembled that of the Triple-A Tacoma Rainiers' Opening Day roster.

For all their woes in 2004, the Mariners did managed to make a little history—some good history, at that.

Right fielder Ichiro Suzuki had a career year with 262 hits to lead the American League in batting average while setting a major league record for hits in a season. But Ichiro provided about the only highlights in a season gone bad.

The organization's minor league highlight was undoubtedly the performance of 18-year-old phenom Felix Hernandez, who secured his place as the top pitching prospect in the minor leagues. The 6-foot-3, 170-pound righthander went 9-3, 2.74 at high Class A Inland Empire and then 5-1, 3.30 at Double-A San Antonio.

ORGANIZATION LEADERS

BATTING

*AVG	Carlos Arroyo, Inland Empire	.323
R	Gary Harris, Inland Empire	92
H	Shin-Soo Choo, San Antonio	163
TB	A.J. Zapp, Tacoma	266
2B	Jesus Guzman, Inland Empire	35
3B	Gary Harris, Inland Empire	18
HR	A.J. Zapp, Tacoma	29
RBI	A.J. Zapp, Tacoma	101
BB	Dustin Delucchi, San Antonio	71
SO	A.J. Zapp, Tacoma	184
SB	Shin-Soo Choo, San Antonio	40
*OBP	Bucky Jacobsen, Tacoma	.422
*SLG	Bucky Jacobsen, Tacoma	.661

PITCHING

W	Felix Hernandez, San Antonio/Inland Empire	14
L	Nibaldo Acosta, Wisconsin	14
#ERA	Cesar Jimenez, Inland Empire	2.32
G	Tim Rall, San Antonio	56
CG	Travis Blackley, Tacoma	2
SV	Rick Guttormson, San Antonio	25
IP	Bobby Livingston, Inland Empire	187
BB	Gustavo Martinez, Tacoma/San Antonio	82
SO	Thomas Oldham, Inland Empire/Wisconsin	188

*Minimum 250 at-bats #Minimum 75 innings

ORGANIZATION STATISTICS

SEATTLE MARINERS

Manager: Bob Melvin.

2004 Record: 63-99, .389 (4th, AL West).

BATTING	AVG	G	AB	R	H	2B	3B	HR	RBI	BB	SO	SB	CS	OBP	SLG	B	T	HT	WT	DOB	1st Yr Resides
Aurilia, Rich	.241	73	261	27	63	13	0	4	28	22	43	1	0	.304	.337	R	R	6-1	185	9-2-71	1992 Phoenix, Ariz.
Bloomquist, Willie	.245	93	188	27	46	10	0	2	18	10	48	13	2	.283	.330	R	R	5-11	185	2-21-83	1999 Port Orchard, Wash.
Bocachica, Hiram	.244	50	90	9	22	5	0	3	6	12	27	5	4	.337	.400	R	R	5-11	180	3-4-76	1994 Toa Alta, P.R.
Boone, Bret	.251	148	593	74	149	30	0	24	83	56	135	10	5	.317	.423	R	R	5-10	190	4-6-69	1990 Orlando, Fla.
Borders, Pat	..189	19	53	6	10	2	0	1	5	1	12	1	1	.204	.283	R	R	6-2	200	5-14-63	1982 Lake Wales, Fla.
Cabrera, Jolbert	.270	113	359	38	97	19	2	6	47	16	70	10	3	.312	.384	R	R	6-1	195	12-8-72	1991 Cartagena, Colombia
Davis, Ben	.091	14	33	1	3	0	0	0	2	3	9	0	0	.162	.091	S	R	6-4	220	3-10-77	1995 West Chester, Pa.
Dobbs, Greg	.226	18	53	4	12	1	0	1	9	1	14	0	0	.250	.302	L	R	6-1	200	7-2-78	2001 Moreno Valley, Calif.
Hansen, Dave	.282	57	78	14	22	5	0	2	12	18	16	0	0	.412	.423	L	R	6-0	195	11-24-68	1986 San Juan Capistrano, Calif.
Ibanez, Raul	.304	123	481	67	146	31	1	16	62	36	72	1	2	.353	.472	L	R	6-2	220	6-2-72	1992 Miami, Fla.
Jacobsen, Bucky	.275	42	160	17	44	9	0	9	28	14	47	0	0	.335	.500	R	R	6-4	220	8-30-75	1997 Hermiston, Ore.
Leone, Justin	.216	31	102	15	22	5	0	6	13	9	32	1	0	.298	.441	R	R	6-1	190	3-9-77	1999 Las Vegas, Nev.
Lopez, Jose	.232	57	207	28	48	13	0	5	22	8	31	0	1	.263	.367	R	R	6-2	170	11-24-83	2001 Barcelona, Venez.
Lopez, Mickey	.250	6	4	1	1	0	0	0	0	1	0	0	0	.500	.250	S	R	5-9	170	11-17-73	1995 Miami, Fla.
Martinez, Edgar	.263	141	486	45	128	23	0	12	63	58	107	1	1	.342	.385	R	R	5-11	205	1-2-63	1984 Kirkland, Wash.
McCracken, Quinton	.150	19	20	6	3	0	0	0	2	4	1	1	2	.227	.150	S	R	5-7	190	8-16-70	1992 Scottsdale, Ariz.
Olerud, John	.245	78	261	29	64	13	1	5	22	40	41	0	0	.354	.360	L	L	6-5	220	8-5-68	1989 Fall City, Wash.
Olivo, Miguel	.200	50	160	25	32	8	2	6	14	10	55	2	2	.260	.388	R	R	6-0	215	7-15-78	1997 Ceres, Calif.
2-team (46 Chicago)	.233	96	301	46	70	15	4	13	40	20	84	7	6	.286	.439						
Reed, Jeremy	.397	18	58	11	23	4	0	0	5	7	4	3	1	.470	.466	L	L	6-0	185	6-15-81	2002 La Verne, Calif.
Rivera, Rene	.000	2	3	0	0	0	0	0	0	0	1	0	0	.000	.000	R	R	5-10	190	7-31-83	2001 Bayamon, P.R.
Santiago, Ramon	.179	19	39	8	7	1	0	0	2	3	3	0	0	.256	.205	S	R	5-11	160	8-31-79	1999 Las Matas de Farfan, D.R.
Spiezio, Scott	.215	112	367	38	79	12	3	10	41	36	60	4	1	.288	.346	S	R	6-2	220	9-21-72	1993 Morris, Ill.
Suzuki, Ichiro	.372	161	704	101	262	24	5	8	60	49	63	36	11	.414	.455	L	R	5-9	170	10-22-73	2001 Kobe, Japan
Wilson, Dan	.251	103	319	23	80	13	0	2	33	26	57	0	1	.305	.310	R	R	6-3	215	3-25-69	1990 Seattle, Wash.
Winn, Randy	.286	157	626	84	179	34	6	14	81	53	98	21	7	.346	.427	S	R	6-2	195	6-9-74	1995 Danville, Calif.

PITCHING	W	L	ERA	G	GS	CG	SV	IP	H	R	ER	BB	SO	AVG	B	T	HT	WT	DOB	1st Yr Resides
Atchison, Scott	2	3	3.52	25	0	0	0	31	29	12	12	14	36	.250	R	R	6-2	180	3-29-76	1999 Fort Worth, Texas
Baek, Cha-Seung	2	4	5.52	7	5	0	0	31	35	23	19	11	20	.278	R	R	6-4	190	5-29-80	1999 Olympia, Wash.
Blackley, Travis	1	3	10.04	6	6	0	0	26	35	31	29	22	16	.321	L	L	6-3	190	11-4-82	2001 Chelienham, Australia
Franklin, Ryan	4	16	4.90	32	32	2	0	200	224	116	109	61	104	.285	R	R	6-3	180	3-5-73	1993 Spiro, Okla.
Garcia, Freddy	4	7	3.20	15	15	1	0	107	96	39	38	32	82	.236	R	R	6-4	240	6-10-76	1994 Baruta, Venez.
Guardado, Eddie	2	2	2.78	41	0	0	18	45	31	14	14	14	45	.194	R	L	6-0	205	10-2-70	1991 Stockton, Calif.
Hasegawa, Shigetoshi	4	6	5.16	68	0	0	0	68	67	42	39	31	46	.260	R	R	5-11	180	8-1-68	1997 Newport Beach, Calif.
Jarvis, Kevin	1	0	8.31	8	0	0	0	13	20	12	12	5	7	.345	L	R	6-2	200	8-1-69	1991 Lexington, Ky.
Kida, Masao	0	0	8.38	7	0	0	0	10	15	9	9	5	5	.366	R	R	6-3	210	9-12-68	1999 Tokyo, Japan
Madritsch, Bobby	6	3	3.27	15	11	1	0	88	74	33	32	33	60	.232	L	L	6-2	190	2-28-76	1998 Burbank, Ill.
Mateo, Julio	1	2	4.68	45	0	0	1	58	56	30	30	16	43	.251	R	R	6-0	175	8-2-77	1996 Bani, D.R.
Meche, Gil	7	7	5.01	23	23	1	0	128	139	73	71	47	99	.273	R	R	6-3	200	9-8-78	1996 Scott, La.
Moyer, Jamie	7	13	5.21	34	33	1	0	202	217	127	117	63	125	.272	L	L	6-0	180	11-18-62	1984 Seattle, Wash.
Myers, Mike	4	1	4.88	50	0	0	0	29	15	15	17	23	.279	L	L	6-3	220	6-26-69	1990 Highlands Ranch, Colo.
Nageotte, Clint	1	6	7.36	12	5	0	0	37	48	31	30	27	24	.324	R	R	6-3	200	10-25-80	2000 New Port Richey, Fla.
Pineiro, Joel	6	11	4.67	21	21	1	0	141	144	77	73	43	111	.265	R	R	6-1	200	9-25-78	1997 Rio Piedras, P.R.
Putz, J.J.	0	3	4.71	54	0	0	9	63	66	35	33	24	47	.274	R	R	6-5	220	2-22-77	1999 Trenton, Mich.
Sherrill, George	2	1	3.80	21	0	0	0	24	24	12	10	9	16	.258	L	L	6-0	210	4-19-77	1999 Memphis, Tenn.
Soriano, Rafael	0	3	13.50	6	0	0	0	3	9	6	5	3	3	.450	R	R	1-70	12-19-79	1997 San Jose, D.R.
Taylor, Aaron	0	0	9.82	5	0	0	0	4	5	4	4	3	4	.313	R	R	6-8	240	8-20-77	1996 Hahira, Ga.
Thornton, Matt	1	2	4.13	19	1	0	0	33	30	15	15	25	30	.250	L	L	6-6	220	9-15-76	1998 Allendale, Mich.
Villone, Ron	8	6	4.08	56	10	0	0	117	102	64	53	64	86	.232	L	L	6-3	245	1-16-70	1993 River Vale, N.J.
Williams, Randy	0	0	5.79	6	0	0	0	5	3	3	3	6	.188	L	L	6-3	190	9-18-75	1998 Houston, Texas

FIELDING

Catcher	PCT	G	PO	A	E	DP	PB
Borders	.992	19	121	9	1	1	1
Davis	1.000	14	71	5	0	3	1
Olivo	.997	49	273	19	1	2	9
Rivera	1.000	2	4	0	0	0	0
Wilson	.997	103	611	37	2	6	0

First Base	PCT	G	PO	A	E	DP
Bloomquist	.975	19	70	8	2	11
Cabrera	1.000	23	151	7	0	18
Hansen	1.000	7	25	4	0	1
Ibanez	.983	10	57	2	1	2
Jacobsen	.984	21	169	12	3	12
Olerud	.998	77	548	52	1	58
Spiezio	.986	42	251	24	4	22

Second Base	PCT	G	PO	A	E	DP
Bloomquist	.000	1	0	0	0	0

	PCT	G	PO	A	E	DP
Boone	.978	148	280	350	14	90
Cabrera	.987	18	37	40	1	12
M. Lopez	1.000	3	1	4	0	0

Third Base	PCT	G	PO	A	E	DP
Bloomquist	.923	31	24	36	5	6
Cabrera	.970	36	33	63	3	7
Dobbs	.929	14	5	21	2	3
Hansen	1.000	6	6	6	0	0
Leone	.901	28	25	48	8	2
J. Lopez	.000	1	0	0	0	0
Martinez	.000	1	0	0	0	0
Spiezio	.964	66	56	131	7	15

Shortstop	PCT	G	PO	A	E	DP
Aurilia	.990	73	113	186	3	39
Bloomquist	.955	20	27	36	3	11

	PCT	G	PO	A	E	DP
Cabrera	.960	14	11	13	1	2
Leone	.800	2	3	1	1	0
J. Lopez	.956	57	90	126	10	24
Santiago	.946	16	22	31	3	8

Outfield	PCT	G	PO	A	E	DP
Bloomquist	1.000	9	14	0	0	0
Bocachica	1.000	44	68	0	0	0
Cabrera	.980	23	46	2	1	0
Ibanez	.984	112	229	10	4	3
McCracken	1.000	8	11	1	0	0
Reed	.981	16	51	0	1	0
Suzuki	.992	158	372	12	3	2
Winn	.991	154	416	5	4	1

FARM SYSTEM

Director, Player Development: Frank Mattox.

Class	Farm Team	League	W	L	Pct.	Finish*	Manager	Affiliate Since
AAA	Tacoma (Wash.) Rainiers	Pacific Coast	79	63	.556	3rd (16)	Dan Rohn	1995
AA	San Antonio (Texas) Missions	Texas	66	72	.478	6th (8)	Dave Brundage	2001
High A	Inland Empire (Calif.) 66ers	California	77	63	.550	**3rd (10)**	Daren Brown	2001
Low A	Wisconsin Timber Rattlers (Appleton)	Midwest	57	82	.410	12th (14)	Steve Roadcap	1993
SS A	Everett (Wash.) AquaSox	Northwest	41	35	.539	t-3rd (8)	Pedro Grifol	1995
Rookie	Peoria (Ariz.) Mariners	Arizona	31	25	.554	4th (9)	Scott Steinmann	2001

*Finish in overall standings (No. of teams in league)/Playoff teams in **boldface**

TACOMA RAINIERS   Class AAA

PACIFIC COAST LEAGUE

BATTING	AVG	G	AB	R	H	2B	3B	HR	RBI	BB	SO	SB	CS	OBP	SLG	B	T	HT	WT	DOB	1st Yr	Resides
Bloomquist, Willie	.417	3	12	2	5	0	0	1	3	0	2	1	0	.417	.667	R	R	5-11	185	2-21-83	1999	Port Orchard, Wash.
Bocachica, Hiram	.287	40	136	22	39	5	1	10	25	17	36	12	3	.393	.559	R	R	5-11	180	3-4-76	1994	Toa Alta, P.R.
Borders, Pat	.255	36	137	16	35	5	1	5	13	3	28	0	1	.287	.416	R	R	6-2	200	5-14-63	1984	Lake Wales, Fla.
Christianson, Ryan	.258	44	151	19	39	6	1	6	24	15	35	0	0	.325	.430	R	R	6-2	210	4-21-81	1999	Riverside, Calif.
Collins, Mike	.182	25	77	5	14	1	0	0	4	7	21	0	2	.256	.195	R	R	5-9	166	1-29-77	1998	Phoenix, Ariz.
Davis, Ben	.248	39	141	18	35	9	0	4	15	15	29	1	0	.321	.397	S	R	6-4	225	3-10-77	1995	West Chester, Pa.
Dobbs, Greg	.271	67	255	28	69	9	2	8	31	5	36	4	3	.286	.416	L	R	6-1	200	7-2-78	2001	Moreno Valley, Calif.
Ellison, Josh	.227	8	22	1	5	1	0	0	1	10	0	0	0	.261	.273	L	R	5-10	200	7-24-83	2001	West Palm Beach, Fla.
Faison, Vince	.267	10	30	7	8	2	1	2	3	2	12	0	0	.313	.600	L	R	6-0	180	1-22-81	1999	Lyons, Ga.
Gerez, Francisco	.000	2	7	0	0	0	0	0	0	0	0	0	0	.000	.000	R	R	5-11	170	3-5-80	2001	Mao, D.R.
Gonzalez, Wiki	.308	13	52	9	16	5	0	5	14	2	3	0	0	.333	.692	R	R	5-11	205	5-17-74	1994	Palo Negro, Venez.
Guzman, Elpidio	.259	125	455	58	118	19	2	5	36	14	89	24	12	.280	.343	L	L	6-0	160	2-24-77	1996	Santo Domingo, D.R.
Horner, Jim	.190	39	126	9	24	5	0	4	15	6	22	0	1	.231	.325	R	R	6-0	210	11-11-73	1996	Twin Falls, Idaho
Ibanez, Raul	.235	4	17	2	4	1	0	0	1	0	6	0	0	.235	.294	L	R	6-2	200	6-2-72	1992	Miami, Fla.
Jacobs, Greg	.320	63	197	40	63	13	0	9	30	21	38	1	1	.388	.523	L	L	5-10	180	10-9-76	1998	Anaheim Hills, Calif.
Jacobsen, Bucky	.312	81	292	59	91	22	1	26	86	50	88	1	1	.422	.661	R	R	6-4	220	8-30-75	1997	Hermiston, Ore.
Leone, Justin	.269	68	253	56	68	10	5	21	51	26	82	5	6	.344	.597	R	R	6-2	170	3-9-77	1999	Las Vegas, Nev.
Lopez, Jose	.295	74	275	40	81	19	0	13	39	16	30	6	2	.342	.505	R	R	6-2	170	11-24-83	2001	Barcelona, Venez.
Lopez, Mickey	.286	109	391	70	112	20	5	10	41	45	59	13	10	.369	.440	S	R	5-9	170	11-17-73	1995	Miami, Fla.
Maduro, Jorge	.172	9	29	4	5	1	1	0	2	1	9	0	0	.200	.276	R	R	6-0	190	3-11-81	1999	Miami, Fla.
Moon, Brian	.232	16	56	5	13	3	0	2	9	0	11	0	0	.246	.393	S	R	6-0	190	7-15-77	1997	Mansfield, Ga.
Nesbit, Michael	.176	7	17	0	3	1	0	0	1	0	4	0	0	.176	.235	R	R	6-1	190	12-16-81	2004	Northridge, Calif.
Reed, Jeremy	.305	61	233	40	71	10	5	3	36	23	22	14	2	.366	.455	L	L	6-0	185	6-15-81	2002	La Verne, Calif.
Rivera, Rene	.400	4	15	3	6	1	0	1	1	0	3	0	0	.400	.667	R	R	5-10	190	7-31-83	2001	Bayamon, P.R.
Sandel, George	.122	16	41	3	5	1	0	0	4	4	13	0	1	.196	.146	R	L	5-10	175	12-4-80	2003	Palm Beach, Fla.
Santiago, Ramon	.193	71	243	35	47	7	2	1	24	24	31	9	6	.288	.251	S	R	5-11	180	8-31-79	1999	Las Matas de Farfan, D.R.
Strong, Jamal	.324	64	238	46	77	11	2	3	24	38	29	19	6	.421	.424	R	R	5-10	180	8-5-78	2000	Altadena, Calif.
Ugueto, Luis	.271	101	361	53	98	19	0	5	38	30	98	25	7	.341	.440	S	R	5-11	170	2-15-79	1996	Maracay, Venez.
Zapp, A.J.	.291	136	509	78	148	27	2	29	101	56	184	1	0	.365	.523	L	R	6-3	190	4-24-78	1996	Greenwood, Ind.
Zuniga, Tony	.280	9	25	3	7	0	1	0	3	3	8	0	1	.379	.360	R	R	6-0	200	12-13-75	1996	Anaheim, Calif.

PITCHING	W	L	ERA	G	GS	CG	SV	IP	H	R	ER	BB	SO	AVG	B	T	HT	WT	DOB	1st Yr	Resides
Anderson, Craig	4	8	5.65	24	0	0	2	92	115	63	58	42	65	.308	L	L	6-3	185	10-30-80	1999	Ourimbah, Australia
Atchison, Scott	5	3	4.15	40	1	0	7	69	71	35	32	26	76	.266	R	R	6-2	180	3-29-76	1999	Fort Worth, Texas
Baek, Cha-Seung	5	4	4.21	14	14	0	0	73	85	41	34	24	56	.290	R	R	6-4	190	5-29-80	2001	Olympia, Wash.
Blackley, Travis	8	6	3.83	19	18	2	0	110	100	49	47	47	80	.249	L	L	6-3	190	11-4-82	2001	Cheltenham, Australia
Christman, Tim	2	0	4.58	30	0	0	2	39	44	24	20	15	45	.286	L	L	6-0	200	3-31-75	1996	Oneonta, N.Y.
Evert, Brett	0	2	6.48	2	2	0	0	8	6	8	6	10	7	.188	L	R	6-6	200	10-23-80	1999	Salem, Ore.
Fulmer, T.A.	0	0	0.00	3	0	0	2	6	2	0	0	3	4	.105	R	R	6-3	200	1-14-80	2002	Charleston, S.C.
Harris, Jeff	5	3	4.34	26	8	1	1	75	60	37	36	26	53	.218	R	R	6-1	200	7-4-74	1995	San Pablo, Calif.
Heaverlo, Jeff	1	0	4.76	5	0	0	0	6	5	3	3	2	7	.217	R	R	6-1	215	1-13-78	1999	Moses Lake, Wash.
Hoerman, Jared	5	1	4.91	39	1	0	1	62	68	38	34	40	34	.274	R	R	6-4	210	4-25-77	1999	Ardmore, Okla.
Kelly, John	1	2	5.23	7	2	0	0	21	25	12	12	8	27	.301	R	R	6-0	205	12-13-72	1994	Melbourne, Fla.
Key, Chris	0	0	0.00	2	0	0	1	2	1	0	0	1	0	.167	R	L	6-3	210	10-30-77	2000	Reno, Nev.
Looper, Aaron	1	0	4.26	8	0	0	0	13	15	6	6	3	13	.313	R	R	6-2	180	9-7-76	1998	Ada, Okla.
Madritsch, Bobby	5	2	3.75	12	12	0	0	62	61	33	26	26	53	.251	L	L	6-2	190	2-28-76	1998	Burbank, Ill.
Martinez, Gustavo	6	7	4.89	18	17	0	1	99	118	61	54	55	70	.303	R	R	6-0	170	11-9-75	1998	Santo Domingo, D.R.
Maynard, Scott	2	11	11.91	3	2	0	0	11	20	19	15	8	3	.385	R	R	6-2	210	8-28-77	1995	Laguna Niguel, Calif.
Meche, Gil	3	1	3.05	10	10	0	0	57	55	37	32	27	45	.249	R	R	6-3	200	9-8-78	1996	Scott, La.
Nageotte, Clint	6	6	4.46	14	14	0	0	81	78	42	40	35	63	.256	R	R	6-3	200	10-25-80	2000	New Port Richey, Fla.
Nottingham, Shawn	0	0	13.50	3	0	0	0	2	4	3	3	3	2	.444	L	L	6-1	190	11-24-83	2002	Massillon, Ohio
Pulsipher, Bill	1	1	2.92	2	2	0	0	12	13	5	4	4	5	.277	S	L	6-3	228	10-9-73	1992	Port St. Lucie, Fla.
Putz, J.J.	0	0	4.32	7	0	0	3	8	10	5	4	3	13	.278	R	R	6-5	220	2-22-77	1999	Trenton, Mich.
Rose, Brad	0	0	0.00	1	0	0	0	0	0	0	0	2	0	.000	R	R	6-4	180	7-24-83	2003	Knoxville, Tenn.
Runion, Tony	1	0	5.93	12	0	0	5	14	14	9	9	9	16	.259	R	R	6-3	229	12-6-71	1993	Florence, Ky.
Sherrill, George	4	2	2.32	36	0	0	13	50	42	13	13	9	62	.223	L	L	6-0	210	4-19-77	1999	Memphis, Tenn.
Shibilo, Andy	1	1	8.74	16	0	0	0	23	35	23	22	20	21	.357	R	R	6-7	220	9-16-76	1998	Belleville, N.J.
2-team (9 Iowa)	1	1	7.82	25	0	0	0	36	52	34	31	29	30	.344							
Simas, Bill	1	1	3.86	9	0	0	0	12	10	5	5	2	8	.227	L	R	6-3	230	11-28-71	1992	Fresno, Calif.
Soriano, Rafael	0	0	2.45	3	0	0	0	4	2	1	1	2	5	.154	R	R	6-1	170	12-19-79	1997	San Jose, D.R.
Thornton, Matt	7	5	5.42	16	15	1	0	83	86	58	50	50	63	.273	L	L	6-6	220	9-15-76	1998	Allendale, Mich.
Ward, Bryan	1	1	4.10	7	7	0	0	42	46	25	19	12	34	.275	L	L	6-2	200	1-25-72	1993	Mt. Holly, N.J.
Wear, Greg	1	1	7.56	7	1	0	0	17	18	15	14	12	9	.269	R	R	6-5	220	7-7-79	2002	Orland Park, Ill.
Williams, Randy	7	2	3.63	50	0	0	8	79	68	37	32	46	64	.230	L	L	6-3	190	9-18-75	1998	Houston, Texas

ORGANIZATION STATISTICS

FIELDING

Catcher	PCT	G	PO	A	E	DP	PB
Borders	.996	36	248	21	1	3	1
Davis	.997	38	299	13	1	3	4
Gonzalez	.991	12	105	5	1	1	1
Horner	.996	33	213	11	1	2	3
Maduro	1.000	9	52	2	0	0	1
Moon	1.000	16	81	17	0	1	1
Rivera	1.000	4	36	1	0	0	0

First Base	PCT	G	PO	A	E	DP
Bocachica	.938	2	15	0	1	1
Jacobsen	.976	5	39	1	1	2
Ugueto	1.000	1	3	1	0	0
Zapp	.992	135	1047	101	9	112
Zuniga	1.000	1	7	1	0	0

Second Base	PCT	G	PO	A	E	DP
Collins	1.000	3	8	11	0	4
J. Lopez	1.000	9	21	16	0	3
M. Lopez	.974	100	212	304	14	62

	PCT	G	PO	A	E	DP
Sandel	.923	13	12	24	3	3
Santiago	1.000	10	19	25	0	8
Ugueto	.932	15	20	35	4	8

Third Base	PCT	G	PO	A	E	DP
Dobbs	.931	64	54	121	13	14
Leone	.900	45	42	75	13	3
J. Lopez	.920	22	11	35	4	2
M. Lopez	1.000	2	0	1	0	0
Ugueto	.895	8	5	12	2	2
Zuniga	.909	6	3	7	1	1

Shortstop	PCT	G	PO	A	E	DP
Bloomquist	1.000	2	1	2	0	0
Collins	.968	22	41	51	3	17
Leone	.961	12	16	33	2	9
J. Lopez	.926	42	78	121	16	31
M. Lopez	1.000	4	4	10	0	1
Santiago	.978	61	91	177	6	27

	PCT	G	PO	A	E	DP
Ugueto	.917	6	3	8	1	0

Outfield	PCT	G	PO	A	E	DP
Bloomquist	1.000	1	1	0	0	0
Bocachica	.957	38	66	1	3	1
Ellison	.923	9	12	0	1	0
Faison	1.000	8	11	3	0	2
Gerez	.500	2	1	0	1	0
Guzman	.970	125	212	13	7	5
Horner	1.000	4	6	0	0	0
Ibanez	1.000	2	2	0	0	0
Jacobs	.980	57	96	4	2	2
Leone	1.000	13	16	0	0	0
M. Lopez	1.000	1	2	0	0	0
Nesbit	1.000	6	14	0	0	0
Reed	.982	61	159	6	3	2
Sandel	1.000	2	2	1	0	0
Strong	.985	62	127	3	2	1
Ugueto	.948	73	105	5	6	0

SAN ANTONIO MISSIONS

TEXAS LEAGUE

BATTING	AVG	G	AB	R	H	2B	3B	HR	RBI	BB	SO	SB	CS	OBP	SLG	B	T	HT	WT	DOB	1st Yr	Resides
Arroyo, Jack	.000	4	4	1	0	0	0	0	0	2	0	0	0	.333	.000	R	R	6-1	175	9-7-80	2004	Prundale, Calif.
Balfe, Ryan	.213	36	141	10	30	3	0	0	12	7	42	1	0	.252	.234	S	R	6-1	180	11-11-75	1994	Cornwall, N.Y.
Bastida-Martinez, Evel	.216	12	37	3	8	1	0	0	1	1	8	1	0	.243	.250	L	R	6-0	190	2-28-79	2002	Hialeah, Fla.
Bohn, T.J.	.264	62	220	24	58	9	4	7	29	22	46	6	1	.336	.436	R	R	6-5	200	1-17-80	2002	Otsego, Minn.
Brown, Hunter	.286	124	441	69	126	19	4	13	52	56	80	20	8	.379	.435	R	R	6-2	200	10-24-79	2002	Houston, Texas
Bubela, Jaime	.223	46	166	13	37	3	0	2	15	8	42	2	2	.267	.277	L	R	6-1	200	6-6-78	2000	Houston, Texas
Choo, Shin-Soo	.315	132	517	89	163	17	7	15	84	56	97	40	8	.382	.462	L	L	5-11	170	7-13-82	2001	Pusan, Korea
Christianson, Ryan	.280	34	132	15	37	9	0	1	13	10	25	2	1	.329	.371	R	R	6-2	210	4-21-81	1999	Riverside, Calif.
Delucchi, Dustin	.272	127	486	82	132	23	2	4	32	71	75	23	15	.375	.352	L	L	6-0	180	12-23-77	2000	Burlingame, Calif.
Dobbs, Greg	.325	51	203	25	66	14	4	5	34	11	23	5	4	.373	.507	L	R	6-1	200	7-2-78	2001	Moreno Valley, Calif.
Ellison, Josh	.500	1	4	0	2	0	0	0	1	0	1	0	0	.500	.500	L	R	5-10	200	7-24-83	2001	West Palm Beach, Fla.
Faison, Vince	.288	17	59	8	17	6	0	3	11	8	13	0	2	.382	.542	L	R	6-0	180	1-22-81	1999	Lyons, Ga.
Gandolfo, Rob	.223	98	323	28	72	6	1	0	20	17	42	6	3	.270	.248	R	R	5-9	170	8-24-77	1999	Dumont, N.J.
Garbe, B.J.	.375	3	8	0	3	0	0	0	0	1	0	1	0	.444	.375	R	R	6-2	190	2-3-81	1999	Moses Lake, Wash.
Gerez, Francisco	.000	1	1	0	0	0	0	0	0	0	1	0	0	.000	.000	R	R	5-11	170	3-5-80	2001	Mao, D.R.
Guerrero, Christian	.224	56	196	28	44	7	1	8	23	8	50	7	5	.256	.393	R	R	6-5	200	7-12-80	1998	Bani, D.R.
Horner, Jim	.284	18	67	8	19	9	0	5	4	4	10	2	1	.347	.418	R	R	6-0	210	11-11-73	1996	Twin Falls, Idaho
Jacobs, Greg	.310	42	155	27	48	13	1	5	31	16	20	1	3	.370	.503	L	L	5-10	180	10-9-76	1998	Anaheim Hills, Calif.
Lindsey, John	.282	123	457	68	129	31	2	19	72	48	98	1	7	.365	.484	R	R	6-2	230	1-30-77	1995	Hattiesburg, Miss.
Menchaca, Eddie	.212	125	419	43	89	19	2	0	33	18	83	7	3	.252	.267	R	R	6-0	190	2-7-81	2001	Phoenix, Ariz.
Moon, Brian	.168	37	119	5	20	4	1	0	10	6	22	0	1	.215	.218	S	R	6-0	190	7-15-77	1997	Mansfield, Ga.
Morse, Michael	.274	41	157	18	43	10	1	6	33	9	27	0	2	.326	.465	R	R	6-4	180	3-22-82	2000	Plantation, Fla.
Oliveros, Luis	.229	80	279	24	64	19	0	4	22	13	42	0	4	.280	.341	R	R	6-1	180	6-18-83	2000	Guarenas, Venez.
Rodrigues, Rich	.235	7	17	1	4	0	0	0	2	2	1	0	0	.350	.235	R	R	6-2	215	9-11-75	2000	San Ramon, Calif.
Sandel, George	.000	3	5	0	0	0	0	0	0	1	2	0	0	.167	.000	R	L	5-10	175	12-4-80	2003	Palm Beach, Fla.
Slee, Gregory	.000	1	4	0	0	0	0	0	0	0	2	0	0	.000	.000	L	R	6-1	200	10-18-81	2004	Liberty Center, Ohio

PITCHING	W	L	ERA	G	GS	CG	SV	IP	H	R	ER	BB	SO	AVG	B	T	HT	WT	DOB	1st Yr	Resides
Baek, Cha-Seung	0	0	0.00	1	1	0	0	5	2	0	0	0	5	.125	R	R	6-4	190	5-29-80	1999	Olympia, Wash.
Bott, Glenn	0	0	3.86	1	1	0	0	5	4	2	2	2	4	.222	L	L	6-0	170	9-17-81	2001	Houston, Texas
Buglovsky, Chris	6	8	3.64	24	21	1	0	121	121	68	49	45	81	.268	L	R	6-2	165	11-22-79	2000	Iselin, N.J.
Cate, Troy	2	5	6.35	12	12	0	0	57	74	44	40	20	35	.316	L	L	6-1	200	10-21-81	2002	Temecula, Calif.
Christensen, Ben	0	0	9.35	5	0	0	0	9	13	9	9	10	5	.371	R	R	6-4	210	2-7-78	1999	Wichita, Kan.
Cortez, Renee	2	5	4.44	36	0	0	3	53	61	29	26	24	46	.300	R	R	6-4	170	12-9-82	2000	Valencia, Venez.
Devey, Phil	2	6	4.76	13	13	0	0	70	75	42	37	25	71	.265	L	L	6-0	170	5-31-77	1999	Lachute, Quebec
Done, Juan	10	10	5.34	27	27	0	0	153	165	99	91	70	86	.282	R	R	6-2	220	10-2-80	2001	Miami, Fla.
Dorman, Rich	8	4	3.48	20	20	1	0	109	93	44	42	64	137	.231	R	R	6-2	210	9-30-80	2000	Medford, Ore.
Flores, Ruben	0	0	5.40	1	0	0	0	2	0	1	1	3	2	.000	R	R	6-4	165	5-19-84	2003	El Paso, Texas
Fruto, Emiliano	3	3	5.66	43	1	0	1	68	77	47	43	37	56	.291	R	R	6-3	170	6-6-84	2001	Bolivar, Colombia
Fulmer, T.A.	0	2	5.58	9	4	0	0	31	33	21	19	12	31	.273	R	R	6-3	200	1-14-80	2002	Charleston, S.C.
Gil, David	1	1	6.35	5	0	0	0	6	9	4	4	0	7	.375	R	R	6-4	215	12-26-74	2000	Miami, Fla.
Guttormson, Rick	5	4	3.27	54	0	0	25	66	68	28	24	24	56	.267	R	R	6-2	180	1-11-77	1997	Anacortes, Wash.
Hernandez, Felix	5	1	3.30	10	10	1	0	57	47	23	21	21	58	.204	R	R	6-3	170	4-8-86	2003	Valencia, Venez.
Hoerman, Jared	0	1	3.00	11	0	0	0	8	12	13	4	4	10	.277	R	R	6-4	210	4-25-77	1999	Ardmore, Okla.
Key, Chris	5	4	4.68	36	12	0	1	102	119	66	53	27	63	.291	R	L	6-3	210	10-30-77	2000	Reno, Nev.
Levrault, Allen	1	0	8.00	11	0	0	0	9	14	9	8	6	8	.318	R	R	6-3	240	8-15-77	1996	Westport, Mass.
Martinez, Gustavo	2	3	3.75	10	8	0	0	50	42	23	21	27	39	.233	R	R	6-0	170	11-9-75	1998	Santo Domingo, D.R.
Nunez, Jose	1	0	6.19	10	0	0	0	16	21	13	11	12	11	.318	L	L	6-2	175	3-14-79	1996	Monte Cristi, D.R.
Perez, Elvis	1	6	7.56	10	7	0	0	33	47	31	28	18	35	.338	R	R	6-4	228	7-4-79	1996	Orlando, Fla.
Rall, Tim	3	5	4.57	56	0	0	1	65	62	34	33	35	78	.256	R	R	6-0	200	9-30-79	2003	Lynbrook, N.Y.
Rose, Brad	0	0	4.50	1	0	0	0	2	2	1	1	4	2	.333	R	R	6-4	180	7-24-83	2003	Knoxville, Tenn.
Soriano, Rafael	1	0	1.13	2	1	0	0	8	4	1	1	0	10	.154	R	R	6-1	170	12-19-79	1997	San Jose, D.R.
Taylor, Aaron	3	1	2.89	30	0	0	0	37	27	13	12	14	37	.200	R	R	6-8	240	8-20-77	1996	Hahira, Ga.
Thomas, Jared	5	3	3.62	33	0	0	1	60	57	24	24	38	64	.258	L	L	6-3	220	7-28-80	2002	Grand Blanc, Mich.

FIELDING

Catcher	PCT	G	PO	A	E	DP	PB
Christianson	.982	18	156	9	3	0	2
Horner	1.000	17	134	4	0	2	4

	PCT	G	PO	A	E	DP	PB
Moon	.991	30	204	25	2	3	2
Oliveros	.988	70	537	56	7	6	11
Rodrigues	1.000	5	35	1	0	0	0

First Base	PCT	G	PO	A	E	DP
Balfe	.970	16	119	11	4	15
Brown	.981	21	134	19	3	12

	PCT	G	PO	A	E	DP
Christianson	.976	4	38	2	1	10
Lindsey	.991	98	801	73	8	78
Menchaca	1.000	5	35	3	0	6

Second Base	PCT	G	PO	A	E	DP
Arroyo	.833	2	2	3	1	0
Bastida-Martinez	.949	12	24	13	2	2
Brown	.991	29	47	68	1	22
Gandolfo	.977	78	119	184	7	51
Menchaca	.983	24	52	67	2	20
Sandel	.833	1	3	2	1	0

Third Base	PCT	G	PO	A	E	DP
Brown	.957	79	66	154	10	18
Dobbs	.918	51	34	78	10	8
Gandolfo	.737	10	2	12	5	0
Oliveros	.667	1	2	0	1	0

Shortstop	PCT	G	PO	A	E	DP
Gandolfo	1.000	5	11	12	0	3
Menchaca	.974	96	150	264	11	72
Morse	.951	40	64	110	9	22

Outfield	PCT	G	PO	A	E	DP
Bohn	.993	58	137	5	1	0
Bubela	.949	21	36	1	2	0
Choo	.970	126	206	18	7	6
Delucchi	.992	119	240	7	2	0
Faison	1.000	12	20	1	0	1
Gandolfo	1.000	5	5	0	0	0
Garbe	1.000	2	1	0	0	0
Guerrero	.946	54	65	5	4	1
Jacobs	1.000	31	46	2	0	0

INLAND EMPIRE 66ERS

CALIFORNIA LEAGUE

BATTING	AVG	G	AB	R	H	2B	3B	HR	RBI	BB	SO	SB	CS	OBP	SLG	B	T	HT	WT	DOB	1st Yr	Resides
Arroyo, Carlos	.323	114	434	62	140	22	3	6	52	27	53	14	5	.358	.429	L	L	5-11	170	5-30-81	2000	Cartagena, Colombia
Balentien, Wladimir	.289	10	38	5	11	1	0	2	5	4	10	1	0	.357	.474	R	R	6-2	160	7-2-84	2001	Willemstad, Aruba
Balet, Frederico	.295	61	224	29	66	12	1	0	27	10	19	2	2	.348	.357	R	R	6-0	210	11-11-77	2001	West Palm Beach, Fla.
Bohn, T.J.	.283	71	240	46	68	9	3	7	37	44	61	6	4	.412	.433	R	R	6-5	200	1-17-80	2002	Otsego, Minn.
Castro, Ismael	.303	16	66	11	20	7	0	2	10	4	3	0	1	.343	.500	S	R	5-9	160	8-14-83	2000	Cartagena, Colombia
Cho, Hyung	.298	24	84	11	25	7	0	1	14	2	5	1	0	.322	.417	R	R	5-9	190	8-20-82	2004	Toronto, Ontario
Ellison, Josh	.390	31	118	17	46	7	0	0	13	10	23	3	2	.438	.449	L	R	5-10	200	7-24-83	2001	West Palm Beach, Fla.
Faison, Vince	.320	7	25	5	8	2	0	1	5	2	4	2	0	.370	.520	L	R	6-0	180	1-22-81	1999	Lyons, Ga.
Garciaparra, Michael	.226	70	234	48	53	12	3	1	26	31	44	5	4	.333	.316	R	R	6-1	160	4-2-83	2002	Harbor Heights, Calif.
Gonzalez, Juan	.291	129	519	79	151	22	7	2	59	51	95	26	17	.353	.372	S	R	6-0	160	2-23-82	1999	Valencia, Venez.
Guzman, Jesus	.310	114	442	80	137	35	3	6	71	57	105	10	9	.393	.443	R	R	6-1	160	6-14-84	2001	Sucre, Venez.
Harris, Matt	.231	101	347	49	80	9	1	9	47	32	93	6	2	.304	.401	R	R	6-4	210	1-3-80	2002	Greeley, Colo.
Harris, Gary	.279	134	562	92	157	20	18	8	78	29	107	34	12	.318	.422	L	R	5-10	180	9-9-79	2003	Resaca, Ga.
Lentz, Brian	.246	44	122	15	30	4	2	2	16	12	36	0	1	.311	.361	R	R	6-1	215	1-23-80	2003	Manchester, Mass.
Monzon, Erick	.339	31	115	24	39	6	1	7	18	5	28	4	1	.381	.591	R	R	6-0	190	11-30-81	2004	Carolina, P.R.
Nelson, Jon	.303	123	499	83	151	30	5	19	95	25	154	26	11	.348	.497	R	R	6-5	210	1-16-80	2002	Orem, Utah
Pullins, Taylor	.133	5	15	2	2	1	0	0	1	4	3	0	0	.316	.200	R	R	5-11	170	3-15-79	2004	Orem, Utah
Rivera, Rene	.235	107	379	41	89	22	1	6	53	28	70	0	1	.300	.346	R	R	5-10	190	7-31-83	2001	Bayamon, P.R.
Rogelstad, Matt	.248	106	375	43	93	8	6	2	41	30	57	5	3	.315	.317	L	R	6-3	185	9-13-82	2003	Hammond, La.
Slee, Gregory	.154	5	13	2	2	0	0	0	0	2	3	0	0	.267	.154	L	R	6-1	200	10-18-81	2004	Liberty Center, Ohio
Spiezio, Scott	.000	2	5	0	0	0	0	0	0	1	0	0	0	.000	.000	S	R	6-2	220	9-21-72	1993	Morris, Ill.

PITCHING	W	L	ERA	G	GS	CG	SV	IP	H	R	ER	BB	SO	AVG	B	T	HT	WT	DOB	1st Yr	Resides
Castillo, Ruben	1	0	0.00	5	0	0	0	7	4	1	0	1	4	.174	R	R	6-2	155	8-16-78	1996	San Pedro de Macoris, D.R.
Cate, Troy	3	0	2.61	7	3	0	0	21	21	8	6	6	24	.263	L	L	6-1	200	10-21-81	2002	Temecula, Calif.
Cicciello, Michael	0	0	9.00	1	0	0	0	2	4	2	2	0	1	.500	L	L	6-0	200	4-20-82	2004	Hartsdale, N.Y.
Dorman, Rich	3	2	2.68	7	7	0	0	37	35	13	11	12	36	.248	R	R	6-2	210	9-30-78	2000	Medford, Ore.
Fulmer, T.A.	6	7	5.16	17	17	1	0	96	109	61	55	21	86	.282	R	R	6-3	200	1-14-80	2002	Charleston, S.C.
Hernandez, Felix	9	3	2.74	16	15	0	0	92	85	31	28	26	114	.245	R	R	6-2	190	4-8-86	2003	Valencia, Venez.
Huber, Jon	4	1	6.12	7	5	0	0	32	42	24	22	14	38	.304	R	R	6-2	190	7-1-81	2000	North Fort Myers, Fla.
2-team (20 Lake Elsinore)	12	7	4.26	27	25	0	0	139	149	77	66	58	138	.271							
Jimenez, Cesar	6	7	2.32	43	2	0	6	85	80	28	22	18	80	.250	L	L	5-11	200	11-24-84	2002	Cumana Sucre, Venez.
Johnson, Rett	0	2	7.97	7	7	0	0	20	32	20	18	14	14	.368	L	R	6-2	210	7-6-79	2000	Aynor, S.C.
Livingston, Bobby	12	6	3.57	28	27	1	0	187	187	90	74	30	141	.261	L	L	6-3	190	9-3-82	2002	Lubbock, Texas
Martinez, Miguel	2	1	5.62	30	0	0	5	42	38	26	26	17	54	.238	R	R	6-2	190	10-22-82	2002	Carolina, D.R.
Martinez, Roman	0	0	0.00	1	0	0	0	1	1	0	0	1	1	.250	R	R	6-2	200	12-23-84	2003	Monte Cristi, D.R.
Oldham, Thomas	4	3	3.21	7	6	0	0	42	47	22	15	6	56	.280	L	L	6-2	210	5-18-82	2003	Fremont, Neb.
Pizarro, Melvin	4	4	3.86	41	0	0	8	70	64	39	30	24	58	.235	L	L	6-1	180	3-16-78	1995	Carolina, P.R.
Rowland-Smith, Ryan	5	3	3.70	29	12	0	3	100	107	50	41	30	119	.276	L	L	6-3	200	1-26-83	2001	Newcastle, Australia
Sandoval, Juan	11	11	4.12	27	27	1	0	168	184	91	77	43	119	.279	R	R	6-1	170	1-13-81	2001	Santo Domingo, D.R.
Soriano, Rafael	0	0	2.25	2	2	0	0	8	7	3	2	1	9	.241	R	R	6-1	170	12-19-79	1997	San Jose, D.R.
Soto, Darwin	4	4	3.19	42	0	0	10	68	61	34	24	24	54	.232	R	R	6-2	180	11-15-82	1999	Bani, D.R.
Steele, Mike	0	0	5.17	20	1	0	1	31	37	19	18	16	24	.296	R	R	6-2	200	8-22-78	2000	Midland, Mich.
Taylor, Aaron	0	1	13.50	1	1	0	0	1	2	3	2	1	2	.400	R	R	6-8	240	8-20-77	1996	Hahira, Ga.
Viane, David	2	3	3.38	20	0	0	0	27	26	15	10	12	12	.257	R	R	6-1	210	7-15-79	2002	Farmington Hills, Mich.
Watson, Tanner	2	4	5.06	25	5	0	4	69	75	43	39	22	57	.288	R	R	6-3	190	6-14-82	2001	Arnprior, Ontario
Wear, Greg	1	2	9.60	17	3	0	1	30	55	42	32	12	25	.379	R	R	6-5	220	7-7-79	2002	Orland Park, Ill.

FIELDING

Catcher	PCT	G	PO	A	E	DP	PB
Hagen	1.000	4	7	2	0	0	1
Lentz	.988	39	224	28	3	3	7
Rivera	.993	106	880	110	7	6	17
Slee	.968	4	29	1	1	0	0

First Base	PCT	G	PO	A	E	DP
Balet	.969	18	148	10	5	15
Hagen	.986	97	789	76	12	47
Lentz	1.000	1	1	0	0	0
Nelson	.975	8	39	0	1	3
Rogelstad	.980	23	180	12	4	17

Second Base	PCT	G	PO	A	E	DP
Castro	1.000	12	20	33	0	1

	PCT	G	PO	A	E	DP
Cho	.939	24	36	41	5	10
Garciaparra	.944	27	53	65	7	11
Gonzalez	.974	42	75	115	5	24
Monzon	.000	1	0	0	1	0
Pullins	.852	5	8	15	4	5
Rogelstad	.963	35	70	84	6	19

Third Base	PCT	G	PO	A	E	DP
Castro	1.000	4	5	11	0	0
Gonzalez	.966	8	3	25	1	2
Guzman	.894	111	59	185	29	10
Hagen	.667	2	2	0	1	0
Monzon	1.000	1	2	1	0	0
Rogelstad	.949	19	8	29	2	1
Spiezio	1.000	1	0	1	0	0

Shortstop	PCT	G	PO	A	E	DP
Garciaparra	.947	39	56	123	10	22
Gonzalez	.944	77	119	215	20	35
Guzman	1.000	4	7	10	0	2
Monzon	.956	19	27	59	4	15
Rogelstad	1.000	4	5	7	0	1

Outfield	PCT	G	PO	A	E	DP
Arroyo	.979	88	133	8	3	2
Balentien	.958	10	23	0	1	0
Bohn	.986	72	137	8	2	4
Ellison	.979	22	44	2	1	0
Faison	1.000	6	14	0	0	0
Harris	.979	131	265	9	6	1
Nelson	.950	99	145	8	8	2

WISCONSIN TIMBER RATTLERS

MIDWEST LEAGUE

BATTING	AVG	G	AB	R	H	2B	3B	HR	RBI	BB	SO	SB	CS	OBP	SLG	B	T	HT	WT	DOB	1st Yr	Resides
Balentien, Wladimir	.277	76	260	39	72	12	3	15	46	12	77	10	2	.315	.519	R	R	6-2	160	7-2-84	2001	Willemstad, Curacao

BATTING	AVG	G	AB	R	H	2B	3B	HR	RBI	BB	SO	SB	CS	OBP	SLG	B	T	HT	WT	DOB	1st Yr	Resides
Bastida-Martinez, Evel	.258	51	190	28	49	4	0	2	23	24	35	11	4	.352	.311	L	R	6-0	190	2-28-79	2002	Hialeah, Fla.
Blakeley, Eric	.287	86	261	43	75	19	2	5	24	32	52	8	6	.373	.433	R	R	6-2	180	9-8-79	2002	Greenville, Ohio
Bradford, Sam	.143	17	49	4	7	2	0	1	4	2	15	1	0	.176	.245	S	R	6-1	185	10-15-81	2003	Smyrna, Ga.
Cho, Hyung	.298	18	57	4	17	2	0	0	10	5	11	0	1	.365	.333	R	R	5-9	190	8-20-82	2004	Toronto, Ontario
Collins, Chris	.236	108	382	43	90	19	0	4	57	47	72	3	2	.320	.317	R	R	5-11	195	8-14-81	2001	Phoenix, Ariz.
Colton, Chris	.232	127	457	63	106	18	11	12	63	40	99	15	9	.302	.398	R	R	6-1	195	9-21-82	2002	Newnan, Ga.
Cox, Michael	.228	116	390	49	89	21	2	11	51	47	100	2	6	.314	.377	R	R	6-0	188	11-11-80	2003	Sarasota, Fla.
Dutton, Jeremy	.208	93	288	27	60	13	1	2	19	38	62	3	3	.307	.281	L	R	5-11	195	11-15-80	2003	Durham, N.C.
Ellison, Chris	.209	25	91	22	19	3	1	0	6	14	23	3	1	.327	.264	L	R	5-10	200	7-24-83	2001	West Palm Beach, Fla.
Gerez, Francisco	.320	9	25	2	8	2	0	0	5	2	5	3	0	.370	.400	R	R	5-11	170	3-5-80	2001	Mao, D.R.
Hrynio, Michael	.000	1	0	0	0	0	0	0	0	0	0	0	0	.000	.000	R	R	6-2	190	11-18-82	2001	Mine Hill, N.J.
Jones, Adam	.267	130	510	76	136	23	7	11	72	33	124	8	4	.314	.404	R	R	6-2	180	8-1-85	2003	San Diego, Calif.
LaHair, Bryan	.279	67	262	30	73	24	0	5	29	16	66	0	6	.323	.427	L	R	6-5	215	11-5-82	2003	Worcester, Mass.
Metheny, Brenton	.196	30	92	8	18	5	2	2	13	11	29	2	1	.279	.359	L	R	6-0	205	10-3-80	2003	Old Fields, W.Va.
Navarro, Oswaldo	.211	40	109	13	23	4	0	0	7	11	19	4	1	.295	.248	S	R	6-0	150	10-2-84	2002	Maracay, Venez.
Nesbit, Michael	.278	69	237	34	66	11	1	2	17	20	46	8	5	.336	.359	R	R	6-1	190	12-16-81	2004	Northridge, Calif.
Orlandos, Nick	.291	65	261	24	76	9	1	1	23	23	34	10	4	.354	.345	R	R	6-0	185	7-8-80	2002	Mission Viejo, Calif.
Ruchti, Justin	.222	79	230	15	51	15	0	1	22	20	51	1	3	.283	.300	R	R	6-2	200	12-11-80	2003	Houston, Texas
Sandel, George	.273	23	55	7	15	1	0	0	3	12	14	0	0	.403	.291	R	L	5-10	175	12-4-80	2003	Palm Beach, Fla.
Womack, Josh	.260	118	470	76	122	21	9	5	39	34	126	24	7	.314	.374	L	L	6-1	190	1-5-84	2002	San Diego, Calif.

PITCHING	W	L	ERA	G	GS	CG	SV	IP	H	R	ER	BB	SO	AVG	B	T	HT	WT	DOB	1st Yr	Resides
Abrams, Casey	1	3	12.74	37	1	0	0	30	57	48	42	24	27	.410	L	L	6-4	200	7-17-81	2003	Lebanon, Ohio
Acosta, Nibaldo	7	14	4.40	27	26	1	0	162	170	101	79	42	95	.266	R	R	6-1	180	3-6-83	2001	Maracaibo, Venez.
Bilke, Austin	0	2	3.29	17	1	0	3	27	31	12	10	10	20	.295	R	R	6-2	220	8-13-79	2002	Beaver Dam, Wis.
Castillo, Ruben	0	1	9.75	11	0	0	1	12	15	13	13	5	9	.294	R	R	6-2	155	8-16-78	1996	San Pedro de Macoris, D.R.
Chang, Kenly	0	2	5.40	40	2	0	1	63	70	43	38	20	48	.275	R	R	6-1	170	8-25-82	2001	Bluefields, Nicaragua
Ciccotelli, Michael	1	0	6.30	12	0	0	0	10	10	12	7	4	8	.238	L	L	6-0	200	4-20-82	2004	Hartsdale, N.Y.
Feierabend, Ryan	9	7	3.63	26	26	1	0	161	158	78	65	44	106	.259	L	L	6-3	190	8-22-85	2003	Grafton, Ohio
Fillinger, Chad	1	2	8.44	11	0	0	0	16	25	16	15	5	15	.342	R	R	6-4	210	10-26-82	2004	Petaluma, Calif.
Heaston, Bryan	3	1	6.69	26	0	0	0	35	33	26	26	24	32	.250	R	R	6-3	210	6-9-80	2002	Farmington, N.M.
Hrynio, Michael	4	4	3.75	54	0	0	9	62	47	26	26	33	82	.211	R	R	6-2	190	11-18-82	2001	Mine Hill, N.J.
Mackintosh, Jason	6	8	4.04	33	20	1	0	149	137	86	67	44	139	.245	R	L	6-0	205	7-2-80	2004	South Weber, Utah
Moorhead, Brandon	9	10	3.27	25	25	0	0	146	142	66	53	50	163	.250	R	R	6-1	205	6-28-81	2003	Bowersville, Ga.
O'Flaherty, Eric	3	3	6.12	12	10	0	0	57	83	43	39	23	38	.342	L	L	6-2	195	2-5-85	2003	Walla Walla, Wash.
Oldham, Thomas	6	6	2.93	19	19	1	0	117	108	47	38	30	132	.243	L	L	6-2	210	5-18-82	2003	Fremont, Neb.
Ovalles, Juan	5	4	6.39	25	1	0	0	38	41	29	27	21	45	.281	R	R	6-1	160	5-15-82	1999	Caracas, Venez.
Perry, Brandon	0	3	5.51	11	0	0	0	16	17	15	10	14	6	.262	L	L	6-1	180	9-27-84	2002	Graham, N.C.
Rose, Brad	0	1	13.50	15	0	0	0	14	26	27	21	12	11	.382	R	R	6-4	180	7-24-83	2003	Knoxville, Tenn.
Stitt, Brian	2	10	4.63	45	7	0	16	91	101	51	47	28	90	.278	R	R	6-0	185	8-26-82	2002	Wellington, Fla.
Tindell, Matt	0	1	7.88	6	1	0	0	8	9	8	7	8	8	.281	R	R	5-11	180	4-22-80	1999	Avon Park, Fla.

FIELDING

Catcher	PCT	G	PO	A	E	DP	PB
Collins	.991	71	509	51	5	2	13
Ruchti	.995	77	567	57	3	5	10

First Base	PCT	G	PO	A	E	DP
Blakeley	.818	3	8	1	2	0
Collins	1.000	10	77	4	0	5
Cox	.990	11	97	5	1	5
Dutton	.993	69	546	41	4	44
LaHair	.988	46	310	30	4	22
Metheny	1.000	14	130	10	0	15

Second Base	PCT	G	PO	A	E	DP
Bastida-Martinez	.813	4	3	10	3	0
Blakeley	.978	21	37	53	2	11
Cho	.900	8	9	9	2	1
Cox	.964	47	74	114	7	17

	PCT	G	PO	A	E	DP
Gerez	1.000	1	3	0	0	0
Navarro	.969	27	53	70	4	22
Orlandos	.936	26	50	67	8	10
Sandel	.974	18	28	46	2	9

Third Base	PCT	G	PO	A	E	DP
Bastida-Martinez	.892	25	8	50	7	3
Blakeley	.943	49	25	91	7	10
Cho	1.000	3	0	4	0	0
Collins	.905	18	4	34	4	2
Cox	.883	52	35	108	19	7
Jones	1.000	2	0	2	0	0
Metheny	.667	2	1	1	1	0

Shortstop	PCT	G	PO	A	E	DP
Blakeley	.900	10	12	15	3	5
Cox	.700	3	4	3	3	0

	PCT	G	PO	A	E	DP
Gerez	.786	7	8	14	6	3
Jones	.943	120	214	318	32	57
Navarro	1.000	8	9	21	0	3
Sandel	.938	3	5	10	1	3

Outfield	PCT	G	PO	A	E	DP
Balentien	.969	73	122	4	4	1
Blakeley	1.000	6	9	0	0	0
Bradford	1.000	12	13	0	0	0
Colton	.987	127	224	7	3	2
Ellison	.973	24	35	1	1	1
LaHair	.965	30	51	4	2	0
Metheny	1.000	2	2	0	0	0
Nesbit	.977	68	119	7	3	0
Womack	.989	113	178	10	2	5

EVERETT AQUASOX

NORTHWEST LEAGUE

BATTING	AVG	G	AB	R	H	2B	3B	HR	RBI	BB	SO	SB	CS	OBP	SLG	B	T	HT	WT	DOB	1st Yr	Resides
Cabrera, Asdrubal	.272	63	239	44	65	16	3	5	41	21	43	7	5	.330	.427	S	R	6-0	170	11-13-85	2004	Puerto la Cruz, Venez.
Chen, Yung-Chi	.300	49	200	37	60	13	1	3	34	16	36	25	3	.353	.420	R	R	5-11	172	7-13-83	2004	Kaohsiung City, Taiwan
Craig, Casey	.265	59	200	46	53	10	3	5	30	45	59	18	6	.398	.420	L	R	6-1	185	1-12-85	2003	La Mesa, Calif.
Cruz, Elvis	.208	32	106	12	22	7	0	3	19	8	35	1	1	.259	.358	R	R	6-3	180	11-23-83	2002	Santo Domingo, D.R.
Ellison, Josh	.400	5	20	4	8	2	0	0	2	2	3	0	0	.435	.500	L	R	5-10	200	7-24-83	2001	West Palm Beach, Fla.
Falcon, Omar	.222	46	158	32	35	7	1	5	24	19	54	1	3	.335	.373	R	R	6-0	190	9-1-82	2000	Miami, Fla.
Green, Brandon	.272	72	283	37	77	15	4	7	55	26	55	9	6	.333	.428	B	R	6-2	195	8-12-81	2004	Adair, Okla.
Heid, Trevor	.215	44	130	17	28	9	1	0	14	11	32	8	1	.297	.300	R	R	6-3	210	4-30-82	2004	St. George, Utah
Hubbard, Marshall	.275	55	189	20	52	14	1	2	24	22	52	3	3	.361	.392	L	R	6-2	215	4-16-82	2004	Ashland, Va.
Johnson, Brent	.300	66	233	51	70	13	0	1	31	33	27	12	4	.400	.369	R	R	6-2	185	5-21-82	2004	Las Vegas, Nev.
Johnson, Rob	.234	20	77	17	18	3	1	1	7	4	10	6	2	.286	.338	R	R	6-1	200	7-22-83	2004	Butte, Mont.
LaHair, Bryan	.440	7	25	5	11	6	0	1	7	1	3	0	0	.464	.800	L	R	6-5	215	11-5-82	2003	Worcester, Mass.
Navarro, Oswaldo	.273	68	267	38	73	27	1	1	30	21	59	17	4	.331	.393	S	R	6-0	150	10-2-84	2002	Maracay, Venez.
Olivo, Miguel	.000	2	6	0	0	0	0	0	0	0	2	0	0	.000	.000	R	R	6-0	215	7-15-78	1997	Ceres, Calif.
Ozoria, Pedro	1.000	1	2	1	2	1	0	0	2	0	0	0	0	1.000	1.500	R	R	6-3	170	2-22-84	2002	San Pedro De Macoris, D.R.
Santin, Daniel	.111	3	9	0	1	0	0	0	0	0	4	0	0	.111	.111	L	R	6-3	205	11-7-84	2004	Miami, Fla.
Schweiger, Brian	.264	32	72	18	19	5	0	3	13	20	24	1	4	.443	.458	R	R	6-0	195	8-21-82	2003	Rialto, Calif.
Soto, Luis	.259	9	27	4	7	1	0	0	3	1	5	2	0	.310	.296	R	R	5-9	190	7-30-83	2003	Peravia, D.R.
Tuiasosopo, Matt	.255	30	106	20	27	6	1	3	17	11	38	4	3	.350	.415	R	R	6-2	210	5-10-86	2004	Woodinville, Wash.
Wilson, Michael	.259	66	239	45	62	15	0	9	51	25	61	10	5	.357	.435	S	R	6-2	215	6-29-83	2002	Tulsa, Okla.

GAMES BY POSITION: C—Falcon 45, Johnson 6, Olivo 2, Santin 2, Schweiger 28. **1B**—Green 52, Hubbard 18, LaHair 7, Schweiger 1, Soto 7. **2B**—Cabrera 17, Chen 22, Green 6, Navarro 39. **3B**—Cabrera 5, Chen 27, Green 17, Johnson 31, Navarro 2, Ozoria 1. **SS**—Cabrera 42, Chen 3, Navarro 29, Tuiasosopo 5. **OF**—Craig 55, Cruz 28, Ellison 1, Heid 43, Hubbard 24, Johnson 37, Johnson 1, Wilson 65.

PITCHING	W	L	ERA	G	GS	CG	SV	IP	H	R	ER	BB	SO	AVG	B	T	HT	WT	DOB	1st Yr	Resides
Bello, Cibney	4	1	3.93	22	0	0	1	34	24	16	15	15	34	.214	L	R	6-5	180	9-10-82	2000	Vargas, Venez.
Bergdall, Kendall	3	3	6.55	15	10	0	0	55	68	49	40	40	41	.302	R	L	6-3	190	11-26-82	2002	Lahoma, Okla.
Blanco, Ivan	0	1	11.05	4	4	0	0	15	21	19	18	12	20	.339	R	R	6-1	190	9-24-83	2001	Guatire, Venez.
Cullen, Phil	1	2	2.97	15	1	0	0	30	22	13	10	17	20	.204	R	R	6-9	210	12-2-79	2001	Chelan, Wash.
Falconer, Kenny	0	0	14.21	8	0	0	0	6	11	12	10	5	4	.379	L	R	6-6	203	9-27-82	2003	Lethbridge, Alberta
Fillinger, Chad	1	0	5.94	11	0	0	1	17	22	11	11	5	25	.314	R	R	6-4	210	10-26-82	2004	Petaluma, Calif.
Flores, Ruben	2	4	5.20	11	11	0	0	54	50	36	31	24	40	.249	R	R	6-4	165	5-19-84	2003	El Paso, Texas
Forbes, Terry	1	2	4.50	9	0	0	0	20	29	16	10	7	11	.354	L	R	6-3	200	6-27-84	2002	Dartmouth, N.S.
Hall, Vance	3	0	5.71	18	0	0	1	35	42	28	22	17	25	.298	L	L	6-2	210	11-24-83	2003	Pittsburgh, Pa.
Jensen, Aaron	7	4	5.29	16	16	0	0	80	90	53	47	36	56	.280	R	R	6-2	180	6-11-84	2003	Springville, Utah
Lockwood, Jon	0	0	4.50	2	0	0	0	2	1	1	1	4	0	.143	R	R	6-2	210	12-12-81	2004	Toronto, Ontario
Lowe, Mark	1	2	4.93	18	3	0	7	38	42	22	21	14	38	.280	R	R	6-4	180	6-7-83	2004	Missouri City, Texas
Martinez, Roman	0	2	2.45	5	0	0	0	7	9	4	2	2	5	.321	R	R	6-3	160	8-9-84	2001	Puerto Plata, D.R.
Nottingham, Shawn	9	3	3.15	15	14	0	0	89	74	34	31	29	87	.223	L	L	6-1	190	1-22-85	2003	Massillon, Ohio
Perry, Brandon	1	0	6.99	17	0	0	1	28	40	28	22	17	26	.336	L	L	6-1	180	9-27-84	2002	Graham, N.C.
Rivera, Mumba	4	7	3.51	18	5	0	0	59	44	28	23	25	48	.202	R	R	6-5	205	12-10-80	2004	St. Croix, V.I.
Rose, Brad	0	0	3.38	4	0	0	0	5	6	2	2	4	3	.316	R	R	6-4	180	7-24-83	2003	Knoxville, Tenn.
Snyder, Jason	2	2	2.23	8	8	0	0	44	32	14	11	16	39	.205	R	R	6-5	205	4-6-83	2004	St. George, Utah
Trolia, Aaron	2	3	4.83	20	4	0	6	41	40	23	22	17	33	.258	R	R	6-2	210	5-10-81	2004	University Place, Wash.
Woerman, Joe	0	1	6.57	9	0	0	0	12	13	14	9	8	12	.260	R	R	6-3	200	12-12-82	2003	Coronado, Calif.

AZL MARINERS — Rookie

ARIZONA LEAGUE

BATTING	AVG	G	AB	R	H	2B	3B	HR	RBI	BB	SO	SB	CS	SLG	OBP	B	T	HT	WT	DOB	1st Yr	Resides
Arroyo, Jack	.310	23	84	23	26	7	0	1	11	12	14	5	0	.429	.414	R	R	6-1	175	9-7-80	2004	Prundale, Calif.
Balfe, Ryan	.400	1	5	2	2	1	1	0	3	0	2	0	0	1.000	.400	S	R	6-1	180	11-11-75	1994	Cornwall, N.Y.
Brock, Jermaine	.242	35	120	16	29	5	2	0	10	6	33	5	2	.317	.281	L	L	6-2	175	1-29-87	2004	Grand Rapids, Mich.
Bubela, Jaime	.343	16	67	12	23	3	1	2	12	4	9	2	1	.507	.375	L	R	6-1	200	6-6-78	2000	Houston, Texas
Cruz, Reynaldo	.261	24	92	14	24	6	2	1	13	9	31	2	1	.402	.324	R	R	6-3	180	1-7-83	2003	Haina, D.R.
Dominguez, Jeff	.222	45	162	18	36	2	1	0	15	12	39	10	0	.247	.288	S	R	6-2	153	7-31-86	2004	Carolina, P.R.
Emmons, John	.305	34	131	20	40	5	3	0	13	6	26	12	2	.389	.350	R	R	6-1	205	10-10-81	2004	San Antonio, Texas
Faison, Vince	1.000	1	2	2	2	0	0	0	0	0	0	0	0	1.000	1.000	L	R	6-0	180	1-22-81	1999	Lyons, Ga.
Flaig, Jeff	.252	32	107	16	27	5	1	0	12	10	19	4	2	.318	.347	R	R	6-2	170	3-3-85	2003	Placentia, Calif.
Garciaparra, Michael	.273	3	11	4	3	0	1	0	4	2	5	0	0	.455	.429	R	R	6-1	160	4-2-83	2001	Harbor Heights, Calif.
Gerez, Francisco	.383	23	94	19	36	4	1	1	11	9	18	10	2	.479	.448	R	R	6-1	160	5-3-80	2001	Mao, D.R.
Hall, David	.277	35	137	25	38	13	0	0	20	7	39	8	2	.372	.331	R	R	6-1	195	10-9-83	2004	Vista, Calif.
Hubbard, Marshall	.500	1	4	0	2	0	0	0	1	0	1	0	0	.500	.500	R	R	6-3	215	4-16-82	2004	Ashland, Va.
Jacobitz, Joe	.278	30	97	14	27	2	2	0	9	14	18	0	1	.340	.383	S	R	6-3	215	1-12-82	2004	San Francisco, Calif.
Johnson, Rob	.222	8	27	4	6	1	0	0	1	3	7	1	1	.259	.323	R	R	6-1	200	7-22-83	2004	Butte, Mont.
Lampe, Rayon	.221	29	95	10	21	2	0	1	10	5	32	2	3	.274	.302	R	R	6-2	180	11-20-86	2003	San Nicolas, Aruba
Lopez, Jose	.167	4	12	3	2	1	0	0	1	2	1	1	0	.250	.267	R	R	6-2	170	11-24-83	2001	Barcelona, Venez.
Monzon, Erick	.417	3	12	3	5	0	0	0	3	0	4	0	0	.417	.417	R	R	6-0	190	11-30-81	2004	Liberty Center, Ohio
Ozoria, Pedro	.254	38	138	24	35	6	0	3	21	16	38	6	1	.362	.340	R	R	6-3	180	2-22-84	2002	San Pedro de Macoris, D.R.
Quintero, Cesar	.250	7	28	3	7	3	0	0	8	2	5	1	1	.357	.281	R	R	6-1	200	11-16-82	2001	Monagrillo, Panama
Santin, Daniel	.325	41	160	31	52	13	2	4	28	10	21	2	1	.506	.384	L	L	6-3	205	11-7-84	2004	Miami, Fla.
Slee, Greg	.172	8	29	1	5	0	0	0	3	5	7	1	1	.172	.294	L	R	6-2	180	10-18-81	2004	Liberty Center, Ohio
Snelling, Chris	.313	10	32	8	10	4	1	0	9	7	3	1	0	.500	.476	L	L	5-10	160	12-3-81	1999	Gorokan, Australia
Soto, Luis	.331	37	148	35	49	12	3	2	27	13	22	2	4	.493	.392	R	R	6-0	190	7-30-83	2001	Peravia, D.R.
Tuiasosopo, Matt	.412	20	68	18	28	5	2	4	12	13	14	1	2	.721	.528	R	R	6-2	210	5-10-86	2004	Woodinville, Wash.
Wu, Chao	.293	21	75	9	22	5	0	1	12	4	10	3	0	.400	.337	L	R	6-3	180	5-25-84	2003	Kaohsiung City, Taiwan

GAMES BY POSITION: C—Quintero 5, Santin 34, Slee 8, Wu 9. **1B**—Flaig 8, Lampe 4, Quintero 2, Santin 1, Soto 31, Wu 12. **2B**—Arroyo 17, Dominguez 10, Garciaparra 2, Gerez 10, Lampe 18, Lopez 1, Monzon 1, Ozoria 3. **3B**—Arroyo 6, Gerez 7, Lampe 7, Lopez 2, Ozoria 36, Soto 3. **SS**—Arroyo 1, Dominguez 37, Garciaparra 1, Gerez 2, Lopez 2, Monzon 2, Tuiasosopo 15. **OF**—Brock 32, Bubela 11. Cruz 23, Emmons 34, Faison 1, Gerez 4, Hall 34, Hubbard 1, Jacobitz 26, Snelling 8, Soto 2.

PITCHING	W	L	ERA	G	GS	CG	SV	IP	H	R	ER	BB	SO	AVG	B	T	HT	WT	DOB	1st Yr	Resides
Arias, Oliver	6	2	5.59	12	11	0	0	56	63	41	35	26	60	.282	R	R	6-5	210	8-17-81	2003	Santo Domingo, D.R.
Baek, Cha-Seung	0	0	1.29	2	2	0	0	7	3	2	1	1	5	.120	R	R	6-4	190	5-29-80	1999	Olympia, Wash.
Brandt, Adam	2	1	3.38	13	0	0	4	21	16	14	8	8	26	.200	R	L	6-2	230	5-18-82	2004	Blacklick, Ohio
Carter, Eric	2	4	4.26	13	8	0	1	44	49	31	21	25	35	.289	R	R	6-2	210	10-31-83	2004	Dover, Del.
Ciccotelli, Michael	0	0	13.03	8	0	0	1	10	21	14	14	2	13	.437	R	L	6-0	200	4-20-82	2004	White Plains, N.Y.
Clement, Donald	4	4	4.45	15	0	0	0	28	38	25	14	7	17	.299	R	R	6-3	225	9-12-81	2004	Grand Junction, Colo.
Dorn, Tim	0	0	5.50	13	0	0	0	18	15	13	11	20	24	.220	R	R	6-8	245	12-30-82	2003	Monrovia, Calif.
Fagan, Paul	4	3	5.07	12	11	0	1	60	68	38	34	29	57	.282	L	L	6-5	195	4-13-85	2003	Jacksonville, Fla.
Forbes, Terry	1	1	0.00	8	0	0	0	12	7	4	0	4	6	.162	L	R	6-3	200	6-27-84	2002	Dartmouth, N.S.
Grasley, Stephen	4	0	3.18	16	0	0	0	28	32	14	10	1	37	.273	R	R	6-0	190	8-5-81	2004	Shoreview, Minn.
James, Craig	1	1	0.68	10	0	0	4	13	10	1	1	5	13	.217	R	R	6-1	170	3-10-83	2001	Miami, Fla.
Lamont, Tyrone	1	1	3.31	13	0	0	0	33	25	19	12	13	27	.208	R	R	6-4	210	4-3-85	2003	Durban, South Africa
Leaist, Ryan	0	0	2.35	10	0	0	1	15	8	5	4	10	18	.150	L	R	6-3	200	5-22-82	2003	Hamilton, Ontario
Lockwood, Jon	3	4	6.97	10	9	0	0	41	43	34	32	30	33	.277	R	R	6-2	210	12-12-81	2004	Toronto, Ontario
Martinez, Roman	2	1	5.82	10	1	0	0	22	27	20	14	10	21	.300	R	R	6-3	160	8-9-84	2001	Puerto Plata, D.R.
Santiago, Julio	2	0	1.80	3	1	0	0	10	5	3	2	1	12	.151	L	L	6-0	150	12-8-85	2002	San Estanislao, Colombia
Snyder, Jason	1	0	2.88	6	5	0	0	25	20	8	8	7	29	.229	R	R	6-2	205	4-6-83	2003	St. George, Utah
Steele, Mike	0	0	9.00	2	0	0	1	3	6	3	3	0	7	.400	R	R	6-3	190	8-22-78	2000	Midland, Mich.
Sundstrom, Matt	1	0	0.00	3	0	0	0	3	2	1	0	4	3	.142	R	R	6-3	160	6-7-84	2002	Sydney, Australia
Tindell, Jason	1	1	1.80	4	0	0	2	5	1	1	1	3	7	.062	R	R	5-11	180	4-22-80	1999	Avon Park, Fla.
Tucker, Cardoza	0	0	18.00	2	0	0	0	3	8	6	6	3	4	.533	R	R	6-2	180	11-11-84	2003	Fresno, Calif.
Wear, Greg	0	0	2.57	2	2	0	0	7	3	3	2	0	6	.111	R	R	6-5	220	7-7-79	2002	Orland Park, Ill.
Woerman, Joe	1	3	5.33	6	6	0	0	27	27	19	16	16	27	.267	R	R	6-3	200	12-12-82	2003	Coronado, Calif.

BY MARC TOPKINN

The Devil Rays had their most successful season in history in 2004, finishing out of last place in the American League East for the first time and winning a team-record 70 games. But they still have a long way to go.

The Rays were the talk of the baseball world after running off a 12-game mid-June winning streak and tearing through one-quarter of their schedule at a 30-10 pace. But they dropped off significantly in a disappointing second half—including a 12-game losing streak—and had to win two of three the final weekend to log the 70th win.

"It's a small step, but a step in the right direction," manager Lou Piniella said.

As usual with the Rays, most of the talk is about the future. With the continued improvement of their young major leaguers, the development of blue-chip prospects such as B.J. Upton and Delmon Young, the acquisition of a future star such as Scott Kazmir, and the drafting of (though not yet signing of) potential ace Jeff Niemann, the Rays remained convinced things are going to get better. They planned to raise their major league low $23-million payroll into somewhere in the low- to mid-$30-million range in 2005.

They went into the offseason hoping to add several veterans who can pitch at the front of their rotation and add power to the middle of their order.

"There's no question now in anybody's mind with Lou, his staff, the young players that have become stars in this league, with more young players on the way, that if we pick up the right veteran players over the next several years, the job will get done," general manager Chuck LaMar said.

The most significant development for the Rays in 2004 was the continued progress from their first wave of homegrown position players.

Carl Crawford | Delmon Young

PLAYERS of the YEAR

MAJOR LEAGUE: Carl Crawford, of

For the second straight year, Crawford led the American League in stolen bases by double digits in 2004. His 59 steals were 23 more than second-place Ichiro Suzuki of Seattle had. Crawford also led the majors with 19 triples and improved upon his 2003 season in every major offensive category.

MINOR LEAGUE: Delmon Young, of

Young, the top pick in the 2003 draft, proved he was one of the top prospects in baseball with a terrific 2004 season at low Class A Charleston. He led the South Atlantic League with 116 RBIs and 165 hits, and he ranked in the top five in batting (.322), runs (95), total bases (276) and slugging percentage (.538).

Aubrey Huff, coming off a breakout season that established him as one of the best young hitters in the game, fell just short of matching his 2003 numbers despite being pitched much more carefully and getting fewer opportunities. He also showed he could play third base on an everyday basis if needed, giving the Rays another option.

Center fielder Rocco Baldelli had to deal with several nagging injuries during his sophomore season but ended up making progress, hitting more homers while striking out less and playing better defense.

Leftfielder Carl Crawford was the team's big success story, making his first All-Star Game and threatening .300 while leading the majors in triples and winning a second straight AL stolen base title.

"Those are three legitimate impact players at the major league level," LaMar said. "They've proved they can play for any team in baseball."

Equally encouraging for the Rays were the early results by their next group of young players, with infielders Upton and Jorge Cantu both making impressive debuts. Plus, Young had a tremendous season at Class A Charleston and could be in the big leagues by the end of the 2005 season.

The pitching staff was not as promising, but the Rays did benefit from a solid bullpen, led by free agent acquisition Danys Baez, who finished with 30 saves.

At the minor league level, the Durham Bulls fell short of a third straight Triple-A International League championship, but it wasn't the fault of manager Bill Evers, who did a tremendous job with a roster that underwent constant change.

ORGANIZATION LEADERS

BATTING

*AVG	Matt Diaz, Durham	.332
R	Jason Pridie, Charleston	103
H	Matt Diaz, Durham	167
TB	Matt Diaz, Durham	287
2B	Matt Diaz, Durham	47
3B	Jason Pridie, Charleston	11
HR	Midre Cummings, Durham	27
RBI	Delmon Young, Charleston	116
BB	Midre Cummings, Durham	86
SO	Jared Sandberg, Durham	138
SB	Joey Gathright, Durham/Montgomery	43
	Elliot Johnson, Charleston	43
*OBP	B.J. Upton, Durham/Montgomery	.410
*SLG	Jorge Cantu, Durham	.576

PITCHING

W	Chris Seddon, Montgomery/Bakersfield	14
L	Mark Comolli, Bakersfield	15
#ERA	Jason Hammel, Bakersfield/Charleston	2.66
G	Joe Yarbrough, Bakersfield	60
CG	Jim Magrane, Durham/Montgomery	3
SV	Scott Vandermeer, Charleston	22
IP	Jason Hammel, Bakersfield/Charleston	166
BB	Mark Comolli, Bakersfield	131
SO	Jason Hammel, Bakersfield/Charleston	153

*Minimum 250 at-bats #Minimum 75 innings

TAMPA BAY
DEVIL RAYS

Manager: Lou Piniella.

2004 Record: 70-91, .435 (4th, AL East).

BATTING	AVG	G	AB	R	H	2B	3B	HR	RBI	BB	SO	SB	CS	OBP	SLG	B	T	HT	WT	DOB	1st Yr	Resides
Baldelli, Rocco	.280	136	518	79	145	27	3	16	74	30	88	17	4	.326	.436	R	R	6-4	190	9-25-81	2000	Cumberland, R.I.
Bautista, Jose	.167	12	12	1	2	0	0	1	3	7	0	1	0	.333	.167	R	R	6-0	190	10-19-80	2001	Santo Domingo, D.R.
3-team (16 Balt./13 K.C.)	.208	41	48	5	10	1	0	0	2	5	22	0	1	.283	.229							
Blum, Geoff	.215	112	339	38	73	21	0	8	35	24	58	2	3	.266	.348	S	R	6-3	200	4-26-73	1994	Los Angeles, Calif.
Cantu, Jorge	.301	50	173	25	52	20	1	2	17	9	44	0	0	.341	.462	R	R	6-1	184	1-30-82	1999	Mission, Mexico
Crawford, Carl	.296	152	626	104	185	26	19	11	55	35	81	59	15	.331	.450	L	L	6-2	210	8-5-81	1999	Houston, Texas
Cruz, Jose	.242	153	545	76	132	25	8	21	78	76	117	11	6	.333	.433	S	R	6-0	210	4-19-74	1995	Coral Gables, Fla.
Cummings, Midre	.278	22	54	10	15	4	0	2	7	5	12	1	0	.361	.463	L	R	6-0	190	10-14-71	1990	Tarpon Springs, Fla.
Diaz, Matt	.190	10	21	3	4	1	1	3	1	6	0	0	0	.292	.476	R	R	6-1	206	3-3-78	1999	Winter Haven, Fla.
Fick, Robert	.201	76	214	12	43	5	2	6	26	20	32	0	0	.273	.327	L	R	6-1	205	3-15-74	1996	Manhattan Beach, Calif.
Fordyce, Brook	.205	54	151	14	31	6	0	2	9	9	34	0	0	.259	.285	R	R	6-0	194	5-7-70	1989	Stuart, Fla.
Gathright, Joey	.250	19	52	11	13	0	0	0	1	2	14	6	1	.316	.250	L	R	5-10	175	4-22-82	2002	La Place, La.
Gipson, Charles	.500	5	4	1	2	0	0	0	0	0	1	1	0	.500	.500	R	R	6-0	190	12-16-72	1992	Orange, Calif.
Gomes, Jonny	.071	5	14	0	1	0	0	1	1	6	0	0	0	.133	.071	R	R	6-1	200	11-22-80	2001	Petaluma, Calif.
Hall, Toby	.255	119	404	35	103	21	0	8	60	24	41	0	2	.300	.366	R	R	6-3	240	10-21-75	1997	Tampa, Fla.
Huff, Aubrey	.297	157	600	92	178	27	2	29	104	56	74	5	1	.360	.493	L	R	6-4	230	12-20-76	1998	Gulfport, Fla.
Lugo, Julio	.275	157	581	83	160	41	4	7	75	54	106	21	5	.338	.396	R	R	6-1	180	11-16-75	1995	Brooklyn, N.Y.
Martinez, Tino	.262	138	458	63	120	20	1	23	76	66	72	3	1	.361	.461	L	R	6-2	230	12-7-67	1989	Tampa, Fla.
McGriff, Fred	.181	27	72	7	13	4	0	2	7	9	19	0	0	.272	.306	L	L	6-3	225	10-31-63	1984	Tampa, Fla.
Perez, Eduardo	.211	13	38	2	8	2	0	1	7	4	9	0	0	.286	.342	R	R	6-4	240	9-11-69	1991	Santurce, P.R.
Rolls, Damian	.162	53	117	12	19	5	0	0	9	10	36	2	1	.231	.205	R	R	6-2	210	9-15-77	1996	Tampa, Fla.
Romano, Jason	.125	4	8	0	1	0	0	0	1	0	2	0	0	.125	.125	R	R	6-0	185	6-24-79	1997	Tampa, Fla.
Sanchez, Rey	.246	91	285	23	70	14	3	2	26	12	28	0	1	.281	.337	R	R	5-9	170	10-5-67	1986	Trujillo Alto, P.R.
Simon, Randall	.118	8	17	2	2	0	0	0	3	2	0	0	0	.286	.118	L	L	6-0	240	5-26-75	1993	Willemstad, Curacao
Upton, B.J.	.258	45	159	19	41	8	2	4	12	15	46	4	1	.324	.409	R	R	6-3	180	8-21-84	2003	Chesapeake, Va.

PITCHING	W	L	ERA	G	GS	CG	SV	IP	H	R	ER	BB	SO	AVG	B	T	HT	WT	DOB	1st Yr	Resides
Abbott, Paul	2	5	6.70	10	9	0	0	47	49	39	35	27	25	.000	R	R	6-3	205	9-15-67	1985	Fullerton, Calif.
Baez, Danys	4	4	3.57	62	0	0	30	68	60	31	27	29	52	.000	R	R	6-3	215	9-10-77	2000	Miami, Fla.
Bell, Rob	8	8	4.46	24	19	1	0	123	121	71	61	41	57	.000	R	R	6-5	225	1-17-77	1995	Tampa, Florida
Brazelton, Dewon	6	8	4.77	22	21	0	0	121	121	71	64	53	64	.000	R	R	6-4	215	6-16-80	2002	Tullahoma, Tenn.
Carter, Lance	3	3	3.47	56	0	0	0	80	77	32	31	23	36	.000	R	R	6-1	190	12-18-74	1994	Bradenton, Fla.
Colome, Jesus	2	2	3.27	33	0	0	3	41	28	16	15	18	40	.000	R	R	6-4	205	12-23-77	1997	San Pedro de Macoris, D.R.
Fortunato, Bartolome	0	0	3.68	3	0	0	0	7	10	3	3	2	5	.000	R	R	6-1	180	8-24-74	1997	Santo Domingo, D.R.
Gaudin, Chad	1	2	4.85	26	4	0	0	43	59	27	23	16	30	.000	R	R	5-11	165	3-24-83	2002	Harahan, La.
Gonzalez, Dicky	0	0	6.14	4	0	0	0	7	9	5	5	2	7	.000	R	R	5-11	170	12-21-78	1996	Bayamon, P.R.
Gonzalez, Jeremi	5	6	6.97	11	8	0	0	50	72	42	39	20	22	.000	R	R	6-0	220	1-8-75	1992	Maracaibo, Venez.
Halama, John	7	6	4.70	34	14	0	0	119	134	68	62	27	59	.000	L	L	6-5	215	2-22-72	1994	Brooklyn, N.Y.
Harper, Travis	6	2	3.89	52	0	0	0	79	69	37	34	23	59	.000	L	R	6-4	190	5-21-76	1998	Riverton, W.Va.
Hendrickson, Mark	10	15	4.81	32	30	2	0	183	211	113	98	46	87	.000	L	L	6-9	230	6-23-74	1998	Mt. Vernon, Wash.
Kazmir, Scott	2	3	5.67	8	7	0	0	33	33	22	21	21	41	.000	L	L	6-0	170	1-24-84	2002	Houston, Texas
Miller, Trever	1	1	3.12	60	0	0	1	49	48	21	17	15	43	.000	R	L	6-3	200	5-29-73	1991	Mt. Washington, Ky.
Moss, Damian	0	1	16.88	5	2	0	0	8	13	15	15	5	6	.000	R	L	6-0	180	11-24-76	1994	Dublin, Ga.
Nunez, Franklin	0	3	5.91	8	0	0	0	11	11	8	7	7	14	.000	R	R	6-0	175	1-18-77	1995	Rincon, D.R.
Ritchie, Todd	0	2	9.00	4	2	0	0	8	12	9	8	6	4	.000	R	R	6-3	210	11-7-71	1990	Kerens, Texas
Seay, Bobby	0	0	2.38	21	0	0	0	23	21	6	6	5	17	.000	L	L	6-2	235	6-20-78	1997	West Gulfport, Miss.
Sosa, Jorge	4	7	5.53	43	8	0	1	99	100	67	61	54	94	.000	S	R	6-2	170	4-28-77	1995	San Jose, D.R.
Standridge, Jason	0	0	9.00	3	1	0	0	10	14	10	10	4	7	.000	R	R	6-4	230	11-9-78	1997	Pinson, Ala.
Waechter, Doug	5	7	6.01	14	14	0	0	70	68	54	47	33	36	.000	R	R	6-4	210	1-28-81	1999	St. Petersburg, Fla.
Webb, John	0	0	7.00	4	0	0	0	9	12	7	7	7	9	.000	R	R	6-3	220	5-23-79	1999	Pensacola, Fla.
Zambrano, Victor	9	7	4.43	23	22	0	0	128	107	68	63	96	109	.000	R	R	6-0	200	8-6-75	1994	Valencia, Venez.

FIELDING

Catcher	PCT	G	PO	A	E	DP	PB
Hall	.992	119	686	38	6	4	7
Fick	1.000	3	3	1	0	0	0
Fordyce	.990	51	274	11	3	3	1

First Base	PCT	G	PO	A	E	DP
Blum	1.000	2	13	0	0	2
Fick	.976	10	79	2	2	8
Huff	.997	38	262	27	1	24
Martinez	.997	114	876	67	3	85
McGriff	1.000	6	53	3	0	5
Perez	1.000	5	43	2	0	6
Rolls	.000	1	0	0	0	0
Simon	.000	1	0	0	0	0

Second Base	PCT	G	PO	A	E	DP
Blum	.994	52	76	104	1	22
Cantu	.964	33	48	85	5	19
Lugo	.970	8	16	16	1	3

Rolls	1.000	2	2	2	0	0
Romano	.500	1	1	0	1	0
Sanchez	.987	87	157	234	5	55

Third Base	PCT	G	PO	A	E	DP
Bautista	1.000	2	0	2	0	0
Blum	.934	59	35	78	8	8
Cantu	.921	11	9	26	3	1
Huff	.943	87	69	129	12	12
Perez	.000	1	0	0	0	0
Rolls	.953	19	16	25	2	3
Upton	.917	13	10	12	2	0

Shortstop	PCT	G	PO	A	E	DP
Blum	1.000	1	1	0	0	0
Cantu	1.000	1	2	2	0	0
Gipson	1.000	2	0	2	0	1
Lugo	.963	143	236	422	25	91
Sanchez	1.000	4	5	15	0	1

Upton	.901	16	23	41	7	8

Outfield	PCT	G	PO	A	E	DP
Baldelli	.978	124	342	11	8	2
Bautista	1.000	8	4	0	0	0
Blum	.929	7	12	1	1	1
Crawford	.994	145	350	5	2	1
Cruz	.970	152	315	10	10	0
Cummings	1.000	2	3	0	0	0
Diaz	1.000	4	11	0	0	0
Fick	.976	21	40	0	1	0
Gipson	1.000	2	3	0	0	0
Gathright	1.000	16	30	0	0	0
Huff	1.000	9	17	0	0	0
Perez	1.000	3	5	0	0	0
Rolls	1.000	24	35	1	0	0
Romano	1.000	1	2	1	0	0
Upton	1.000	1	0	0	0	0

Director, Player Personnel: Cam Bonifay.

Class	Farm Team	League	W	L	Pct.	Finish*	Manager	Affiliate Since
AAA	Durham (N.C.) Bulls	International	77	67	.535	**4th (14)**	Bill Evers	1998
AA	Montgomery (Ala.) Biscuits	Southern	57	83	.407	10th (10)	Charlie Montoyo	1999
High A	#Bakersfield (Calif.) Blaze	California	59	81	.421	8th (10)	Mako Oliveras	2001
Low A	@Charleston (S.C.) RiverDogs	South Atlantic	76	63	.547	**4th (16)**	Steve Livesey	1997
SS A	Hudson Valley (N.Y.) Renegades	New York-Penn	39	33	.542	6th (14)	Dave Howard	1996
Rookie	Princeton (W.Va.) Devil Rays	Appalachian	23	44	.343	10th (10)	Jamie Nelson	1997

*Finish in overall standings (No. of teams in league)/Playoff teams in **boldface**
#Affiliation will operate in Visalia (California) in 2005   @Affiliation will operate in Battle Creek (Midwest) in 2005

DURHAM BULLS   Class AAA

INTERNATIONAL LEAGUE

BATTING	AVG	G	AB	R	H	2B	3B	HR	RBI	BB	SO	SB	CS	OBP	SLG	B	T	HT	WT	DOB	1st Yr	Resides
Badeaux, Brooks	.326	58	193	26	63	8	2	1	18	16	23	1	2	.377	.404	S	R	5-10	170	10-20-76	1998	Scott, La.
Cancel, Robinson	.263	18	57	6	15	7	0	1	4	1	10	0	1	.288	.439	R	R	6-0	190	5-4-76	1994	Lajas, P.R.
Cantu, Jorge	.302	95	368	57	111	33	1	22	80	16	64	3	0	.335	.576	R	R	6-1	184	1-30-82	1999	Mission, Mexico
Cummings, Midre	.285	119	414	83	118	26	3	27	89	86	107	13	2	.408	.558	L	R	6-0	190	10-14-71	1990	Tarpon Springs, Fla.
Diaz, Matt	.332	134	503	81	167	47	5	21	93	26	96	15	4	.377	.571	R	R	6-0	206	3-3-78	1999	Winter Haven, Fla.
French, Anton	.227	31	110	19	25	2	1	4	12	14	27	15	1	.315	.373	L	R	5-11	170	7-25-75	1993	St. Louis, Mo.
Gathright, Joey	.326	60	236	34	77	9	1	0	8	19	46	33	13	.384	.373	L	R	5-10	175	4-22-82	2002	La Place, La.
Gipson, Charles	.296	96	297	50	88	14	3	2	35	57	8	8	.381	.384	R	R	6-0	190	12-16-72	1992	Orange, Calif.
Gomes, Jonny	.257	114	389	73	100	27	1	26	78	51	136	8	5	.368	.532	R	R	6-1	200	11-22-80	2001	Petaluma, Calif.
Guzman, Edwards	.202	25	84	7	17	4	0	0	7	2	8	1	0	.221	.250	L	R	5-11	200	9-11-76	1996	Naranjito, P.R.
Hoover, Paul	.296	16	54	9	16	1	0	1	8	4	15	0	0	.350	.370	R	R	6-1	210	4-14-76	1997	Steubenville, Ohio
LaForest, Pete	.222	84	275	37	61	19	0	7	31	35	64	1	1	.309	.367	L	R	6-2	210	1-27-78	1995	Montebello, Quebec
Massiatte, Dan	.146	32	89	6	13	4	1	0	5	10	30	0	0	.235	.213	R	R	5-11	180	7-25-78	2000	Houston, Texas
Maxwell, Jason	.264	100	363	41	96	13	1	13	55	20	55	0	1	.303	.413	R	R	6-0	185	3-26-72	1993	Franklin, Tenn.
McGriff, Fred	.238	7	21	4	5	0	0	1	4	5	6	0	0	.385	.381	L	L	6-3	225	10-31-63	1984	Tampa, Fla.
Ordaz, Luis	.255	103	361	39	92	27	6	3	34	11	51	1	4	.278	.388	R	R	5-9	182	8-12-75	1993	Maracaibo, Venez.
Osik, Keith	.244	26	82	6	20	0	0	1	8	6	10	0	0	.300	.280	R	R	6-0	190	10-22-68	1990	Shoreham, N.Y.
Rolls, Damian	.278	23	97	23	27	7	0	3	14	7	17	2	1	.346	.443	R	R	6-2	210	9-15-77	1996	Tampa, Fla.
Sandberg, Jared	.230	126	435	61	100	26	1	19	67	29	138	1	2	.281	.425	R	R	6-3	226	3-2-78	1996	Seattle, Wash.
Trammell, Bubba	.366	10	41	6	15	4	0	4	14	5	2	0	0	.435	.756	R	R	6-2	220	11-6-71	1994	Clearwater, Fla.
Upton, B.J.	.311	69	264	65	82	17	1	12	36	42	72	17	5	.411	.519	R	R	6-3	180	8-21-84	2003	Chesapeake, Va.

PITCHING	W	L	ERA	G	GS	CG	SV	IP	H	R	ER	BB	SO	AVG	B	T	HT	WT	DOB	1st Yr	Resides
Bell, Rob	5	0	1.69	7	7	0	0	37	28	7	7	8	35	.209	R	R	6-5	225	1-17-77	1995	Tampa, Fla.
Brazelton, Dewon	4	4	4.71	10	10	0	0	50	61	35	26	15	38	.299	R	R	6-4	215	6-16-80	2002	Tullahoma, Tenn.
Carnes, Matt	4	2	3.02	28	1	0	2	54	58	23	18	22	43	.278	R	R	6-3	210	8-18-75	1997	Miami, Okla.
Cloude, Ken	1	2	11.25	4	2	0	0	12	19	17	15	9	5	.373	R	R	6-1	200	1-9-75	1994	Baltimore, Md.
Colome, Jesus	2	1	3.52	18	0	0	2	31	27	12	12	16	17	.243	R	R	6-4	205	12-23-77	1997	San Pedro de Macoris, D.R.
Corcoran, Tim	3	3	3.91	33	0	0	0	51	46	22	22	33	40	.253	R	R	6-1	180	4-15-78	1997	Slaughter, La.
Fortunato, Bartolome	4	3	2.42	34	0	0	9	45	28	14	12	21	54	.183	R	R	6-3	190	10-7-79	1999	Dyer, Ind.
Frendling, Neal	0	0	3.00	1	0	0	0	3	5	1	1	2	2	.417	R	R	6-3	190	10-7-79	1999	Dyer, Ind.
Gaudin, Chad	1	3	4.72	17	7	0	2	48	48	26	25	17	52	.264	R	R	5-11	165	3-24-83	2002	Harahan, La.
Glen, Willie	0	1	12.27	4	0	0	0	4	5	5	5	2	4	.333	R	R	6-1	185	10-30-77	2001	Plainfield, Ind.
Gonzalez, Dicky	1	2	4.80	6	6	0	0	30	28	16	16	7	30	.252	R	R	5-11	170	12-21-78	1996	Bayamon, P.R.
Gonzalez, Jeremi	4	2	3.90	19	8	0	1	58	50	27	25	19	44	.233	R	R	6-0	220	1-8-75	1992	Maracaibo, Venez.
Harper, Travis	1	0	3.52	2	1	0	0	8	10	3	3	0	5	.294	L	R	6-4	190	5-21-76	1998	Riverton, W.Va.
Holtz, Mike	1	2	3.80	17	0	0	0	24	17	10	10	8	27	.200	L	L	5-9	185	10-10-72	1994	Hollidaysburg, Pa.
Magrane, Jim	8	5	3.93	25	21	2	0	133	160	67	58	42	65	.298	R	R	6-6	230	7-23-78	2000	Ottumwa, Iowa
McClung, Seth	2	1	3.29	11	0	0	0	14	10	5	5	7	12	.208	R	R	6-6	230	2-7-81	1999	Lewisburg, W.Va.
Minix, Travis	3	0	4.75	21	0	0	1	36	39	27	19	10	28	.264	R	R	6-1	180	8-8-77	1999	Hamlet, Ind.
Moss, Damian	5	9	5.87	20	17	0	0	109	108	68	58	65	67	.311	R	L	6-0	180	11-24-76	1994	Dublin, Ga.
Nunez, Franklin	4	2	2.81	40	0	0	9	51	36	21	16	34	70	.193	R	R	6-0	175	1-18-77	1995	Rincon, D.R.
Orvella, Chad	0	0	5.40	2	0	0	0	2	1	1	1	1	2	.143	R	R	5-11	190	10-1-80	2003	Sammamish, Wash.
Parker, Josh	0	1	3.00	12	0	0	0	12	15	4	4	7	7	.341	R	R	6-5	220	1-12-81	2001	Louisville, Ky.
Parker, Matt	0	0	5.79	1	1	0	0	5	8	3	3	1	7	.364	R	R	6-3	210	12-13-78	1999	Hartsfield, Ga.
2-team (1 Indianapolis)	0	1	6.48	2	1	0	0	8	15	6	6	2	10	.395							
Reyes, Al	2	1	2.45	20	0	0	10	22	22	6	6	5	22	.265	R	R	6-1	210	4-10-70	1989	Santo Domingo, D.R.
Ritchie, Todd	4	6	6.29	16	16	0	0	89	112	71	62	23	41	.303	R	R	6-3	210	11-7-71	1990	Kerens, Texas
Seay, Bobby	2	1	1.72	29	0	0	1	37	26	9	7	9	35	.191	L	L	6-2	235	6-20-78	1997	West Gulfport, Miss.
Sosa, Jorge	1	2	2.77	3	3	0	0	13	11	5	4	0	23	.224	S	R	6-2	170	4-28-77	1995	San Jose, D.R.
Standridge, Jason	8	4	3.85	20	20	2	0	119	120	56	51	44	76	.265	R	R	6-4	230	11-9-78	1997	Pinson, Ala.
Veras, Jose	6	5	5.34	30	10	0	0	84	101	55	50	33	63	.304	R	R	6-5	237	10-20-80	1998	Santo Domingo, D.R.
Waechter, Doug	0	2	6.75	8	8	0	0	29	33	22	22	17	22	.277	R	R	6-4	210	1-28-81	1999	St. Petersburg, Fla.
Webb, John	1	3	3.27	8	0	0	0	33	31	19	12	14	22	.246	R	R	6-3	220	5-23-79	1999	Pensacola, Fla.

FIELDING

Catcher	PCT	G	PO	A	E	DP	PB
Cancel	1.000	15	75	8	0	2	5
Guzman	1.000	1	2	0	0	0	1
Hoover	1.000	6	31	4	0	3	3
LaForest	.985	75	479	39	8	6	10
Massiatte	.992	30	233	22	2	3	2
Osik	1.000	25	166	8	0	0	1

First Base	PCT	G	PO	A	E	DP
Cancel	1.000	1	1	0	0	0
Cummings	1.000	1	1	0	0	0
Guzman	1.000	14	99	9	0	6
Hoover	1.000	4	42	3	0	4
LaForest	1.000	1	9	0	0	1
Maxwell	.993	63	535	32	4	59
McGriff	.909	1	10	0	1	2
Sandberg	.990	58	447	32	5	63
Trammell	.986	7	69	3	1	7

Second Base	PCT	G	PO	A	E	DP
Badeaux	.994	46	68	110	1	32
Cantu	.978	44	88	131	5	33
Gipson	.980	11	20	28	1	8

Maxwell	.971	11	10	23	1	4
Ordaz	.972	36	64	111	5	28
Rolls	1.000	3	5	11	0	1

Third Base	PCT	G	PO	A	E	DP
Badeaux	1.000	3	3	1	0	0
Cantu	.923	12	4	20	2	0
Gipson	.946	16	2	33	2	5
Guzman	.889	5	1	7	1	2
Hoover	.882	5	5	10	2	0
Maxwell	.960	17	10	38	2	7
Ordaz	.944	25	14	37	3	9

Rolls	1.000	4	4	7	0	2
Sandberg	.935	65	54	134	13	14

Shortstop	PCT	G	PO	A	E	DP
Cantu	.952	37	61	99	8	18
Gipson	.667	1	0	2	1	1
Maxwell	1.000	1	1	1	0	0
Ordaz	.968	41	58	121	6	28
Upton	.916	66	100	173	25	49

Outfield	PCT	G	PO	A	E	DP
Badeaux	1.000	7	10	0	0	0

Cummings	.982	29	54	2	1	0
Diaz	.974	132	250	15	7	6
French	.981	29	50	3	1	0
Gathright	.968	60	114	6	4	1
Gipson	.972	68	128	12	4	3
Gomes	.962	97	170	6	7	1
Guzman	1.000	3	1	0	0	0
Hoover	1.000	1	2	0	0	0
Rolls	1.000	16	33	0	0	0
Sandberg	1.000	2	4	0	0	0

MONTGOMERY BISCUITS — Class AA

SOUTHERN LEAGUE

BATTING	AVG	G	AB	R	H	2B	3B	HR	RBI	BB	SO	SB	CS	OBP	SLG	B	T	HT	WT	DOB	1st Yr	Resides
Bowser, Matt	.113	16	53	5	6	4	0	0	6	5	13	0	0	.190	.189	L	L	6-3	205	3-8-79	2000	Palm Harbor, Fla.
Brewer, Jace	.252	110	404	44	102	18	3	10	49	19	78	1	3	.290	.386	R	R	6-0	170	6-6-79	2000	Norman, Okla.
Cancel, Robinson	.214	51	159	15	34	10	1	4	24	15	27	0	2	.287	.365	R	R	6-0	190	5-4-76	1994	Lajas, P.R.
Clark, Aaron	.198	114	298	36	59	12	4	11	27	20	113	3	1	.260	.376	L	L	6-1	190	2-17-79	2001	Ennis, Texas
Cortez, Fernando	.287	94	359	51	103	20	5	3	30	32	60	8	7	.345	.396	L	R	6-1	170	8-10-81	2001	San Diego, Calif.
DeMent, Dan	.256	98	336	45	86	25	7	8	34	30	82	1	2	.318	.443	R	R	5-10	170	6-17-78	2000	Birmingham, Ala.
Espada, Joe	.265	27	98	8	26	1	1	0	5	7	14	2	3	.333	.296	R	R	5-10	170	8-30-75	1996	Carolina, P.R.
Feliciano, Jesus	.204	28	93	10	19	2	0	1	4	4	16	0	1	.242	.258	L	L	5-11	150	8-3-79	1998	Bayamon, P.R.
Franco, Iker	.209	63	187	17	39	6	0	3	14	15	32	1	0	.271	.289	R	R	6-1	210	5-5-81	1998	Ensenada, Mexico
Gathright, Joey	.341	32	126	23	43	5	1	0	8	11	30	10	6	.399	.397	L	R	5-10	175	4-22-82	2002	La Place, La.
German, Amado	.217	104	359	34	78	15	4	30	48	93	4	5	.310	.315	B	R	6-2	204	3-30-78	1998	San Pedro de Macoris, D.R.
Gomes, Joey	.270	25	89	12	24	7	0	2	8	6	17	0	0	.313	.416	R	R	6-2	210	11-2-79	2002	Petaluma, Calif.
Harrison, Vince	.266	57	184	21	49	6	2	5	27	24	34	5	3	.372	.402	R	R	5-11	200	11-27-79	2001	Springdale, Ohio
Isenia, Chairon	.303	57	195	22	59	13	1	2	24	10	34	0	0	.357	.410	R	R	5-11	210	1-23-79	1996	Willemstad, Curacao
Martin, Brian	.258	115	368	40	95	25	2	9	38	38	102	5	3	.332	.410	R	R	6-2	220	4-14-80	1998	El Centro, Calif.
Massiatte, Dan	.246	20	57	6	14	4	0	2	6	6	15	1	0	.338	.421	R	R	5-11	180	7-25-78	2000	Houston, Texas
Moore, Frank	.268	48	183	19	49	7	3	2	19	12	40	0	0	.322	.372	L	R	6-2	200	7-2-78	1998	Douglas, Ga.
Perez, Nestor	.321	42	131	18	42	8	1	0	11	2	10	1	0	.331	.397	R	R	5-10	170	11-24-76	1998	Tenerife Canary Islands
Reece, Eric	.236	58	216	22	51	11	1	4	26	11	49	1	0	.285	.352	L	R	6-3	210	6-16-78	2001	El Dorado Hills, Calif.
Riggans, Shawn	.222	10	36	3	8	1	0	2	7	2	14	0	0	.282	.417	R	R	6-2	190	7-25-80	2001	Fort Lauderdale, Fla.
Salas, Juan	.246	78	284	26	70	13	3	3	29	9	68	2	1	.277	.345	R	R	6-2	190	11-7-78	1999	Santo Domingo, D.R.
Upton, B.J.	.327	29	104	21	34	7	1	2	15	14	28	3	0	.407	.471	R	R	6-3	180	8-21-84	2003	Chesapeake, Va.
Velazquez, Jose	.260	65	223	25	58	5	2	3	32	31	32	1	0	.353	.341	L	L	6-2	200	8-24-75	1994	Guayama, P.R.

PITCHING	W	L	ERA	G	GS	CG	SV	IP	H	R	ER	BB	SO	AVG	B	T	HT	WT	DOB	1st Yr	Resides
Autrey, Scott	3	5	8.08	9	9	0	0	42	57	41	38	14	27	.341	R	R	6-2	210	1-26-81	2002	Arlington, Texas
Benedetti, John	2	0	2.52	28	0	0	0	39	35	17	11	13	29	.233	R	R	6-0	180	6-27-78	2000	Palatine, Ill.
Coose, Austin	5	4	3.18	43	0	0	2	57	51	22	20	23	60	.245	R	R	6-2	230	1-27-79	2001	Kokomo, Ind.
Corcoran, Tim	0	1	2.76	6	2	0	0	16	14	5	5	3	12	.246	R	R	6-2	205	4-15-78	1997	Slaughter, La.
Cromer, Jason	9	11	4.15	27	26	2	0	147	180	79	68	46	86	.308	R	L	6-4	220	12-11-80	1999	Des Moines, Iowa
Diaz, Jose	1	3	5.40	7	6	0	0	30	26	19	18	27	37	.243	R	R	6-4	230	2-27-84	2001	La Romana, D.R.
Flinn, Chris	0	1	6.41	21	0	0	1	39	46	32	28	11	38	.288	R	R	6-2	180	8-18-80	2001	Levittown, N.Y.
Frendling, Neal	1	1	7.15	6	1	0	0	11	18	10	9	2	7	.346	R	R	6-3	190	10-7-79	1999	Dyer, Ind.
Glen, Willie	4	4	4.48	29	8	0	0	78	81	41	39	33	81	.272	R	R	6-1	185	10-30-77	2001	Plainfield, Ind.
Henderson, Brian	1	0	2.91	20	0	0	2	22	26	14	7	7	15	.295	L	L	5-11	195	5-19-82	2003	Sugar Land, Texas
Hines, Carlos	4	2	4.41	43	1	0	5	80	82	43	39	22	64	.266	R	R	6-3	190	9-26-80	1999	Selma, N.C.
Kazmir, Scott	1	2	1.44	4	4	0	0	25	14	7	4	11	24	.171	L	L	6-0	170	1-24-84	2002	Houston, Texas
Magrane, Jim	1	2	6.35	3	3	1	0	17	17	14	12	7	9	.283	R	R	6-2	204	7-23-78	2000	Ottumwa, Iowa
Matthews, Jarod	3	7	3.67	24	15	1	0	101	85	49	41	25	84	.228	R	R	6-2	190	11-10-82	2002	Olympia, Wash.
McClung, Seth	1	1	4.73	3	3	0	0	13	10	7	7	4	8	.217	R	R	6-6	230	2-7-81	1999	Lewisburg, W.Va.
Minix, Travis	0	0	1.76	12	0	0	1	15	12	3	3	3	18	.214	R	R	6-1	190	8-8-77	1999	Hamlet, Ind.
Nunez, Franklin	0	1	0.84	6	0	0	0	11	4	3	1	3	19	.114	R	R	6-0	175	1-18-77	1995	Rincon, D.R.
Orvella, Chad	0	0	0.00	6	0	0	4	7	0	0	0	0	15	.000	R	R	5-11	180	10-24-80	2003	Sammamish, Wash.
Osting, Jimmy	0	3	9.90	4	4	0	0	10	14	11	11	8	9	.341	L	L	6-5	190	4-7-77	1995	Louisville, Ky.
Parker, Josh	0	2	3.94	42	0	0	19	48	44	23	21	12	54	.240	R	R	6-5	220	1-12-81	2001	Louisville, Ky.
Parker, Matt	1	6	5.01	12	6	0	0	41	42	26	23	20	22	.269	R	R	6-3	190	12-13-78	1999	Hartsfield, Ga.
2-team (25 Tennessee)	3	8	5.03	37	7	0	0	77	82	48	43	44	58	.278							
Prochaska, Mike	4	10	5.48	16	16	1	0	92	112	60	56	28	68	.302	L	L	6-1	200	5-23-80	2002	Raleigh, N.C.
Pruett, Jason	0	1	6.14	8	0	0	0	7	13	5	5	1	9	.406	L	L	6-3	180	11-21-79	1999	Princeton, Texas
Ritchie, Todd	1	0	2.45	2	2	0	0	11	8	4	3	3	4	.216	R	R	6-3	210	11-7-71	1990	Kerens, Texas
Seddon, Chris	9	10	4.39	21	21	1	0	119	129	67	58	44	102	.281	L	L	6-3	170	10-13-83	2001	Canyon Country, Calif.
Shields, Jamie	0	3	7.85	4	4	0	0	18	24	16	16	8	14	.329	R	R	6-3	190	12-20-81	2001	Valencia, Calif.
Standridge, Jason	1	0	3.60	2	2	0	0	10	13	4	4	4	8	.361	R	R	6-4	230	11-9-78	1997	Pinson, Ala.
Veras, Jose	1	0	6.30	3	3	0	0	10	10	7	7	7	6	.256	R	R	6-5	237	10-20-80	1998	Santo Domingo, D.R.
Waligora, T.P.	2	1	6.29	13	0	0	0	24	25	17	17	13	19	.266	R	R	6-8	250	8-7-76	1997	Richmond, Va.
Walton, Samuel	0	1	6.32	10	1	0	0	16	15	11	11	14	13	.263	L	L	6-4	200	12-1-78	1997	Dallas, Texas
Webb, John	2	1	4.10	9	3	0	0	26	26	12	12	8	12	.263	R	R	6-3	220	5-23-79	1999	Pensacola, Fla.

FIELDING

Catcher	PCT	G	PO	A	E	DP	PB
Cancel	.992	33	212	28	2	1	4
Franco	.986	60	387	51	6	3	8
Isenia	.977	30	196	14	5	0	8
Massiatte	.979	20	126	14	3	1	0
Reece	1.000	8	51	1	0	0	0
Riggans	1.000	6	34	6	0	0	0

First Base	PCT	G	PO	A	E	DP
Bowser	.946	6	39	2	0	3

Brewer	.800	1	4	0	1	0
Cancel	1.000	6	33	1	0	4
Clark	.990	19	96	6	1	9
Moore	.978	32	216	9	5	15
Reece	.990	40	274	13	3	22
Velazquez	.993	54	409	22	3	33

Second Base	PCT	G	PO	A	E	DP
Cortez	.976	94	196	219	10	38

DeMent	.968	19	24	37	2	6
Espada	.984	25	61	59	2	12
Moore	1.000	2	3	2	0	0
Perez	1.000	5	6	11	0	5

Third Base	PCT	G	PO	A	E	DP
Brewer	1.000	1	1	4	0	0
DeMent	.727	10	1	7	3	0
Harrison	.936	57	32	114	10	10

Salas	.938	78	54	111	11	11

Shortstop	PCT	G	PO	A	E	DP
Brewer	.969	82	99	211	10	37
Espada	1.000	2	1	2	0	0
Moore	.000	1	0	0	2	0
Perez	.991	36	32	80	1	7

Upton	.900	23	29	61	10	16

Outfield	PCT	G	PO	A	E	DP
Brewer	1.000	29	39	6	0	1
Cancel	1.000	3	3	0	0	0
Clark	.978	93	134	1	3	0
DeMent	.969	40	58	5	2	0

Feliciano	1.000	28	66	2	0	1
Gathright	.985	22	63	2	1	0
German	.989	105	266	6	3	1
Gomes	1.000	6	17	1	0	0
Martin	.974	124	218	11	6	1
Moore	1.000	20	36	3	0	0

BAKERSFIELD BLAZE — High Class A

CALIFORNIA LEAGUE

BATTING	AVG	G	AB	R	H	2B	3B	HR	RBI	BB	SO	SB	CS	OBP	SLG	B	T	HT	WT	DOB	1st Yr	Resides
Aracena, Sandy	.284	47	162	12	46	12	2	2	26	12	34	2	1	.337	.420	R	R	6-0	180	3-3-81	1998	La Vega, D.R.
Bouman, Robbie	.188	9	32	4	6	2	0	0	5	1	10	2	1	.257	.250	R	R	6-4	190	8-30-82	2004	Sterling, Va.
Centeno, Irwin	.186	21	70	10	13	3	0	1	5	8	17	4	3	.269	.271	R	R	6-2	170	6-1-81	1998	Maracay, Venez.
Cordell, Brent	.276	105	341	47	94	22	1	13	68	40	73	4	1	.368	.460	S	R	6-3	210	5-22-80	2001	Reno, Nev.
Cuevas, Aneudi	.182	5	11	1	2	0	0	1	2	4	6	1	1	.400	.455	R	R	6-1	160	10-6-81	1999	Nizao, D.R.
DePaula, Luis	.293	94	372	60	109	18	3	3	39	28	79	30	12	.348	.382	R	R	5-11	160	12-11-82	2000	Santo Domingo, D.R.
Dufner, Kris	.198	79	268	24	53	4	3	0	23	22	73	5	0	.263	.235	S	R	6-2	185	2-15-80	2003	Philadelphia, Pa.
Dukes, Elijah	.332	58	211	44	70	16	2	8	34	26	50	16	7	.416	.540	S	R	6-2	240	6-26-84	2003	Tampa, Fla.
Feliciano, Jesus	.303	68	251	41	76	13	3	0	23	18	20	9	4	.348	.378	L	L	5-11	150	6-6-79	1998	Bayamon, P.R.
Gomes, Joey	.300	72	277	41	83	17	1	7	45	18	44	7	1	.359	.444	R	R	6-2	210	11-2-79	2002	Petaluma, Calif.
Harrison, Vince	.281	69	256	46	72	17	1	11	42	45	49	8	5	.399	.484	R	R	5-11	200	11-27-79	2001	Springdale, Ohio
Jones, Mitch	.227	18	53	11	12	4	0	1	4	2	13	2	1	.267	.358	R	R	6-2	185	8-21-80	2003	Birmingham, Ala.
Lincoln, Justin	.263	51	167	21	44	13	0	5	16	20	62	2	2	.352	.431	R	R	6-3	205	4-4-79	1999	Sarasota, Fla.
Maniscalco, Matthew	.253	124	463	56	117	23	1	0	47	52	66	22	10	.329	.307	R	R	5-10	180	2-18-81	2003	Oxford, Ala.
Martinez, Gabriel	.323	116	436	54	141	39	3	4	47	30	90	4	8	.371	.454	L	R	6-2	160	5-17-83	2002	Sabana Grande, P.R.
Mateo, Luis	.300	120	476	59	143	28	2	19	69	10	131	13	3	.320	.487	R	R	6-2	190	8-9-81	1999	San Pedro de Macoris, D.R.
Merritt, Graig	.184	51	152	10	28	4	0	0	7	6	33	1	3	.228	.211	R	R	6-1	190	7-2-78	2001	Pitt Meadows, B.C.
Ramos, Carlos	.272	30	114	24	31	4	0	0	7	11	10	7	5	.339	.307	L	L	5-8	175	2-23-80	2004	Miami, Fla.
Reece, Eric	.263	54	213	31	56	9	2	7	35	13	49	3	0	.303	.423	L	R	6-3	210	6-16-78	2001	El Dorado Hills, Calif.
Rico, Matt	.228	97	338	44	77	10	3	7	33	23	94	6	4	.286	.337	R	R	6-2	190	10-8-81	2001	Visalia, Calif.
Riggans, Shawn	.346	34	127	20	44	11	0	5	22	15	23	0	1	.417	.551	R	R	6-2	190	7-25-80	2001	Fort Lauderdale, Fla.
Riley, Ryan	.188	5	16	2	3	0	0	0	2	4	1	0	.350	.188	R	R	5-10	180	11-10-78	1998	Seattle, Wash.
St. Clair, Jason	.000	6	15	1	0	0	0	0	0	0	7	0	1	.118	.000	R	R	5-10	170	9-27-82	2001	Phoenix, Ariz.

PITCHING	W	L	ERA	G	GS	CG	SV	IP	H	R	ER	BB	SO	AVG	B	T	HT	WT	DOB	1st Yr	Resides
Allen, Brian	1	1	4.30	11	0	0	0	23	27	15	11	7	18	.290	R	R	6-3	180	9-15-79	2002	Cairo, Ga.
Autrey, Scott	3	7	3.81	15	15	0	0	80	91	44	34	20	67	.294	R	R	6-2	210	1-26-81	2002	Arlington, Texas
Comolli, Mark	4	15	7.74	29	23	0	0	116	136	118	100	131	83	.299	R	R	6-0	190	3-11-79	2001	Millville, Del.
Cromer, Nathan	2	3	6.16	37	1	0	0	69	112	57	47	26	43	.375	L	L	6-4	200	12-11-80	1999	Des Moines, Iowa
DeBarr, Nick	1	4	4.91	26	10	0	1	66	59	41	36	55	45	.245	R	R	6-4	220	8-24-83	2002	Pleasanton, Calif.
Feliciano, Jesus	0	0	1.69	5	1	0	0	5	1	1	1	3	2	.067	L	L	5-11	150	6-6-79	1998	Bayamon, P.R.
Flinn, Chris	3	0	1.21	24	0	0	8	30	19	5	4	15	35	.183	R	R	6-2	180	8-18-80	2001	Levittown, N.Y.
Girdner, Jason	0	1	5.71	18	0	0	0	41	59	31	26	25	22	.353	R	R	6-1	200	12-17-80	2004	Welling, Okla.
Gor, Nick	0	0	11.91	9	0	0	0	11	18	15	15	8	2	.367	R	R	6-7	230	10-10-81	2004	Yorba Linda, Calif.
Hammel, Jason	6	2	1.89	11	11	0	0	71	52	18	15	20	65	.207	R	R	6-6	200	9-2-82	2002	Port Orchard, Wash.
Henderson, Brian	1	5	3.54	29	0	0	4	41	50	18	16	11	44	.311	L	L	5-11	195	5-19-82	2003	Sugar Land, Texas
Little, Joe	2	5	4.55	11	11	0	0	55	54	31	28	30	51	.255	L	L	6-1	170	3-10-82	2003	Arvada, Colo.
Lockwood, Brian	4	11	6.86	28	20	0	0	127	160	108	97	49	107	.313	R	R	6-2	170	2-20-81	2001	Torrance, Calif.
McCally, Ryan	4	3	3.35	25	0	0	2	43	43	16	16	14	32	.264	R	R	6-1	195	2-27-81	2003	Phoenix, Ariz.
Navaroli, Michael	0	5	5.77	32	0	0	2	39	51	28	25	25	25	.325	R	R	6-3	220	11-17-80	2002	North Palm Beach, Fla.
Orvella, Chad	0	1	3.06	15	0	0	4	18	13	7	6	4	24	.273	R	R	5-11	190	10-1-80	2003	Sammamish, Wash.
Prochaska, Mike	6	2	1.70	11	11	0	0	64	67	15	12	16	56	.273	L	L	6-1	200	5-23-80	2002	Raleigh, N.C.
Ridgway, Jeff	2	3	2.31	15	1	0	1	35	32	17	9	19	27	.248	R	L	6-3	180	8-17-80	2000	Port Angeles, Wash.
Seddon, Chris	5	0	0.65	7	7	0	0	41	30	4	3	8	41	.201	L	L	6-3	170	10-13-83	2001	Canyon Country, Calif.
Shields, Jamie	8	5	4.23	20	20	1	0	117	120	61	55	33	92	.270	R	R	6-3	190	12-20-81	2001	Valencia, Calif.
Walton, Samuel	2	5	3.93	23	10	0	2	73	62	45	32	38	82	.230	L	L	6-4	200	12-1-78	1997	Dallas, Texas
Yarbrough, Joe	5	3	5.14	60	0	0	8	68	72	40	39	39	48	.276	L	L	6-3	210	4-16-80	2002	Bessemer, Ala.

FIELDING

Catcher	PCT	G	PO	A	E	DP	PB
Aracena	.961	29	216	30	10	4	9
Cordell	.979	50	294	39	7	5	24
Merritt	.985	50	300	36	5	3	10
Reece	1.000	2	9	1	0	0	1
Riggans	.996	29	220	17	1	1	5

First Base	PCT	G	PO	A	E	DP
Aracena	1.000	2	8	4	0	1
Cordell	.986	39	306	38	5	23
Dufner	1.000	2	3	0	0	1
Jones	.833	2	9	1	2	1
Lincoln	.875	2	7	0	1	1
Martinez	.984	68	559	45	10	66
Reece	.977	36	323	15	8	43

Second Base	PCT	G	PO	A	E	DP
Bouman	1.000	7	13	13	0	3

	PCT	G	PO	A	E	DP	PB
DePaula	.985	87	171	234	6	66	
Dufner	.974	46	91	130	6	39	
Harrison	1.000	1	1	6	0	1	
Lincoln	1.000	1	1	0	0	0	
Martinez	1.000	2	5	8	0	0	
Riley	.900	2	4	5	1	0	
St. Clair	.875	4	8	6	2	1	

Third Base	PCT	G	PO	A	E	DP
Dufner	.968	20	16	45	2	2
Harrison	.938	67	51	115	11	11
Lincoln	.935	39	14	58	5	4
Martinez	.943	20	15	35	3	2
Merritt	1.000	1	0	1	0	0

Shortstop	PCT	G	PO	A	E	DP
Bouman	1.000	2	2	8	0	1
Cuevas	.870	4	10	10	3	1

	PCT	G	PO	A	E	DP
DePaula	.941	9	14	18	2	5
Dufner	1.000	5	6	10	0	1
Maniscalco	.963	124	209	387	23	95
Riley	1.000	2	4	5	0	2

Outfield	PCT	G	PO	A	E	DP
Aracena	1.000	1	1	0	0	0
Centeno	.900	20	26	1	3	0
Dukes	.984	55	118	5	2	0
Feliciano	.983	54	110	6	2	1
Gomes	1.000	40	59	2	0	0
Jones	.909	15	19	1	2	0
Jones	.750	1	3	0	1	0
Lincoln	1.000	2	2	0	0	0
Martinez	.897	29	34	1	4	0
Mateo	.930	111	168	18	14	6
Ramos	.965	33	54	1	2	0
Rico	.987	96	135	14	2	1

CHARLESTON RIVERDOGS — Low Class A

SOUTH ATLANTIC LEAGUE

BATTING	AVG	G	AB	R	H	2B	3B	HR	RBI	BB	SO	SB	CS	OBP	SLG	B	T	HT	WT	DOB	1st Yr	Resides
Aracena, Sandy	.173	31	98	5	17	3	0	0	3	6	27	0	0	.236	.204	R	R	6-0	180	3-3-81	1998	La Vega, D.R.

BATTING	AVG	G	AB	R	H	2B	3B	HR	RBI	BB	SO	SB	CS	OBP	SLG	B	T	HT	WT	DOB	1st Yr	Resides
Arhart, Josh	.262	71	244	36	64	8	0	5	33	31	28	1	4	.360	.357	R	R	6-1	220	9-13-79	2002	Garden Grove, Calif.
Bankston, Wes	.289	127	470	82	136	30	3	23	101	73	104	9	0	.390	.513	R	R	6-4	200	11-23-83	2002	Plano, Texas
Brignac, Reid	.500	3	14	3	7	1	0	0	5	1	2	0	0	.533	.571	L	R	6-1	185	1-16-86	2004	St. Amant, La.
Cuevas, Aneudi	.214	46	154	21	33	8	1	3	21	13	60	4	2	.278	.338	R	R	6-1	160	10-6-81	1999	Nizao, D.R.
Dion, Nate	.220	79	245	27	54	9	1	2	23	20	82	14	6	.293	.290	R	R	6-3	170	11-13-81	2000	Torrance, Okla.
Dukes, Elijah	.288	43	163	26	47	12	2	2	15	18	47	14	1	.368	.423	S	R	6-2	220	6-26-84	2003	Tampa, Fla.
Johnson, Elliot	.262	126	503	92	132	22	7	6	41	54	91	43	15	.339	.370	S	R	6-0	160	3-9-84	2002	Thatcher, Ariz.
Jones, Mitch	.211	21	57	7	12	0	0	5	7	14	1	0	.303	.211	R	R	6-2	185	8-21-80	2003	Birmingham, Ala.
Leandro, Francisco	.340	31	106	29	36	9	1	2	18	19	11	7	1	.440	.500	L	L	5-10	180	7-19-80	2004	Warrensburg, Mo.
Nichols, Tommy	.214	82	285	35	61	10	0	12	41	24	97	0	0	.282	.375	R	R	6-1	180	8-27-83	2001	Fairfield, Calif.
Pridie, Jason	.276	128	515	103	142	27	11	17	86	37	114	17	6	.327	.470	L	R	6-1	180	10-9-83	2002	Prescott, Ariz.
Schleicher, Mark	.235	104	375	35	88	15	4	4	43	17	100	4	6	.284	.328	R	R	6-1	180	1-1-82	2003	Matthews, N.C.
Schlichting, Travis	.260	94	331	50	86	19	1	2	34	36	71	6	4	.341	.341	R	R	6-3	180	10-19-84	2003	Round Rock, Texas
Simmons, Colt	.290	101	341	49	99	16	0	3	33	41	49	1	3	.383	.364	R	R	6-0	190	12-4-83	2002	Las Vegas, Nev.
Speigner, Brent	.200	29	50	2	10	0	0	0	4	6	18	0	1	.298	.200	R	R	6-1	200	4-3-81	2003	Vestavia Hills, Ala.
St. Clair, Jason	.243	53	185	26	45	8	2	3	28	12	43	8	3	.295	.357	R	R	5-10	170	9-27-82	2001	Phoenix, Ariz.
Touchstone, Josh	.242	23	62	14	15	2	1	0	4	12	0	1	.338	.306	R	R	5-11	185	2-10-81	2004	Semmes, Ala.
Young, Delmon	.322	131	513	95	165	26	5	25	116	53	120	21	6	.388	.538	R	R	6-3	205	9-14-85	2004	Camarillo, Calif.

PITCHING	W	L	ERA	G	GS	CG	SV	IP	H	R	ER	BB	SO	AVG	B	T	HT	WT	DOB	1st Yr	Resides
Allen, Brian	4	2	2.36	26	0	0	0	50	38	20	13	5	40	.209	R	R	6-3	180	9-15-79	2002	Cairo, Ga.
Basilio, Manuel	1	0	6.27	10	0	0	0	19	19	13	13	15	11	.268	R	R	6-3	190	10-20-79	1998	San Pedro De Macoris, D.R.
Bulger, Brian	10	8	3.58	37	17	0	1	123	103	58	49	50	120	.224	R	R	6-4	200	12-2-80	2002	Snellville, Ga.
Carpenter, Calvin	1	0	7.36	10	0	0	0	15	19	13	12	15	14	.317	R	R	6-3	190	9-23-82	2001	Natchitoches, La.
Cramer, Bob	6	4	3.32	35	0	0	4	62	52	27	23	12	48	.224	L	L	6-1	190	10-28-79	2003	Anaheim, Calif.
Dobyns, Jon	0	0	7.71	5	1	0	0	12	11	10	10	6	3	.250	R	R	6-2	210	9-8-81	2004	Phoenix, Ariz.
Flanagan, Jeremy	4	1	3.86	18	5	0	0	44	43	23	19	12	38	.249	R	R	6-3	190	4-14-81	2000	Richmond, Calif.
Gangi, Aaron	2	9	8.19	31	11	0	1	86	134	84	78	31	46	.363	L	L	6-3	190	12-7-81	2003	Ashland, Ohio
Gonzalez, Jino	9	5	4.56	24	23	0	0	120	128	74	61	53	98	.279	L	L	6-2	210	9-5-82	2003	Las Vegas, Nev.
Hammel, Jason	4	7	3.23	18	18	0	0	95	94	54	34	27	88	.253	R	R	6-6	200	9-2-82	2002	Port Orchard, Wash.
Houser, James	3	1	2.20	7	7	0	0	33	27	9	8	13	27	.225	L	L	6-4	185	12-15-84	2003	Sarasota, Fla.
King, Tim	0	3	23.14	3	2	0	0	7	14	20	18	11	4	.412	L	L	6-3	200	8-22-83	2001	Deer Park, Texas
Kranawetter, Josh	6	2	1.79	12	11	1	0	65	54	21	13	21	69	.227	R	R	5-10	185	5-21-80	2002	Jacob, Ill.
Little, Joe	1	3	6.49	10	9	0	0	43	54	36	31	17	44	.305	L	L	6-1	170	3-10-82	2003	Arvada, Colo.
McCally, Ryan	2	3	5.35	15	2	0	0	39	60	25	23	7	25	.368	R	R	6-1	195	2-27-81	2003	Phoenix, Ariz.
McClung, Seth	0	0	0.00	3	3	0	0	9	5	0	0	4	10	.152	R	R	6-6	230	2-7-81	1999	Lewisburg, W.Va.
Olson, Jordan	0	0	6.39	16	0	0	0	25	21	20	18	19	19	.219	L	L	6-3	190	2-19-81	2003	La Crescenta, Calif.
Orvella, Chad	1	0	1.33	22	0	0	4	47	28	9	7	5	76	.168	R	R	5-11	190	10-1-80	2003	Sammamish, Wash.
Peguero, Tony	10	6	3.32	23	23	1	0	133	135	61	49	22	87	.263	R	R	6-3	170	2-17-81	1999	San Pedro de Macoris, D.R.
Perez, Tony	4	3	2.17	45	0	0	1	75	77	38	18	22	51	.266	S	L	5-9	165	6-12-81	2003	Chula Vista, Calif.
Ritchie, Todd	1	1	4.09	2	2	0	0	11	13	6	5	3	13	.295	R	R	6-3	210	11-7-71	1990	Kerens, Texas
Sonnanstine, Andy	2	0	0.59	8	5	0	0	31	18	5	2	7	42	.167	L	R	6-3	185	3-18-83	2004	Wadsworth, Ill.
Speigner, Brent	0	0	5.40	2	0	0	0	2	1	1	1	1	0	.250	R	R	6-1	200	4-3-81	2003	Vestavia Hills, Ala.
Vandermeer, Scott	5	5	2.98	52	0	0	22	63	51	27	21	29	67	.215	R	R	6-4	180	2-16-81	1999	New Orleans, La.
Walker, Aaron	0	0	0.00	1	0	0	0	5	2	0	0	2	3	.118	L	L	6-3	195	2-4-82	2004	East Palestine, Ohio
Weimer, Andrew	0	0	12.00	6	0	0	0	9	18	12	12	5	10	.409	R	R	6-2	180	3-20-81	2003	New Hartford, N.Y.

FIELDING

Catcher	PCT	G	PO	A	E	DP	PB
Aracena	.978	29	199	20	5	5	8
Arhart	.992	63	475	46	4	5	4
Simmons	.997	47	293	27	1	1	15
Speigner	.990	24	93	7	1	0	1

First Base	PCT	G	PO	A	E	DP
Bankston	.994	95	745	57	5	66
Nichols	.985	50	433	29	7	36
Simmons	1.000	1	1	0	0	0

Second Base	PCT	G	PO	A	E	DP
Johnson	.972	125	249	342	17	76
Schleicher	.800	2	0	4	1	1

	PCT	G	PO	A	E	DP
St. Clair	.935	5	12	17	2	6
Touchstone	.979	15	21	26	1	5

Third Base	PCT	G	PO	A	E	DP
Schleicher	.932	33	20	62	6	4
Schlichting	.897	93	50	185	27	13
St. Clair	.938	14	5	25	2	1
Touchstone	.889	3	2	6	1	1

Shortstop	PCT	G	PO	A	E	DP
Brignac	.933	3	4	10	1	1
Cuevas	.944	45	75	145	13	38
Schleicher	.917	70	105	181	26	28
Schlichting	1.000	1	1	5	0	1

	PCT	G	PO	A	E	DP
St. Clair	.876	19	30	55	12	12
Touchstone	.929	6	6	7	1	1

Outfield	PCT	G	PO	A	E	DP
Bankston	1.000	10	7	0	0	0
Dion	.946	74	100	5	6	1
Dukes	.988	41	73	6	1	2
Jones	1.000	18	26	2	0	0
Leandro	.985	32	62	2	1	0
Pridie	.985	122	248	14	4	4
Schleicher	1.000	1	4	0	0	0
Simmons	1.000	8	8	0	0	0
St Clair	1.000	13	11	0	0	0
Young	.979	114	220	14	5	3

HUDSON VALLEY RENEGADES

Short-Season Class A

NEW YORK-PENN LEAGUE

BATTING	AVG	G	AB	R	H	2B	3B	HR	RBI	BB	SO	SB	CS	OBP	SLG	B	T	HT	WT	DOB	1st Yr	Resides
Asanovich, Josh	.292	58	219	32	64	16	2	3	33	19	31	9	1	.361	.425	R	R	6-2	185	1-31-83	2004	Gold Canyon, Ariz.
Baty, Ryan	.276	23	87	7	24	2	0	2	15	6	18	1	0	.323	.368	R	R	6-4	210	12-21-80	2004	Wichita, Kan.
Bolen, Josh	.143	2	7	2	1	0	0	0	1	1	0	0	0	.250	.143	R	R	6-3	225	5-5-80	2003	Pekin, Ill.
Bouman, Robbie	.111	5	18	3	2	0	0	0	1	1	4	0	0	.158	.111	R	R	6-4	190	8-30-82	2004	Sterling, Va.
Breen, Patrick	.222	56	180	19	40	7	2	5	20	14	48	3	1	.286	.367	L	L	6-3	210	6-23-82	2004	Santa Ana, Calif.
Cooper, Chad	.272	45	151	25	41	6	2	0	19	8	15	4	1	.329	.338	R	R	6-1	185	1-31-81	2003	Picture Rocks, Pa.
Cottrell, Patrick	.275	66	244	37	67	18	3	4	35	13	43	7	0	.314	.422	R	R	5-11	160	3-16-82	2004	Chatom, Ala.
Cumberland, Shaun	.329	50	164	25	54	7	4	1	11	11	23	9	1	.375	.439	L	R	6-2	185	8-1-84	2003	Pace, Fla.
Frias, Fernando	.214	38	103	12	22	2	4	3	14	3	31	1	0	.234	.398	R	R	6-1	160	9-27-81	2000	San Pedro de Macoris, D.R.
Jaso, John	.302	57	199	34	60	17	2	2	35	22	32	1	0	.378	.437	L	R	6-2	205	9-19-83	2003	McKinleyville, Calif.
Leandro, Francisco	.266	40	143	20	38	8	1	1	18	18	26	3	2	.359	.357	L	L	5-10	180	7-19-80	2004	Warrensburg, Mo.
Nowak, Chris	.279	62	219	26	61	18	3	1	32	16	35	1	2	.347	.402	R	R	6-6	225	2-21-83	2004	Spartanburg, S.C.
Paredes, Salvador	.194	51	160	20	31	7	0	1	18	4	50	1	1	.214	.256	R	R	6-1	170	6-16-84	2001	Santo Domingo, D.R.
Perez, Fernando	.233	69	266	46	62	8	5	2	20	30	70	24	4	.315	.323	R	R	6-1	185	4-28-83	2004	Princeton Junction, N.J.
Ritchie, Jake	.125	3	8	1	1	0	0	0	1	1	5	0	0	.300	.125	R	R	6-2	202	10-15-80	2004	Thibodaux, La.
Spring, Matt	.220	50	168	20	37	4	2	8	23	17	62	0	1	.298	.411	R	R	6-2	215	11-7-84	2004	Peoria, Ariz.

BATTING	AVG	G	AB	R	H	2B	3B	HR	RBI	BB	SO	SB	CS	OBP	SLG	B	T	HT	WT	DOB	1st Yr	Resides
Woodruff, Bud	.129	21	70	3	9	4	0	0	5	5	31	0	0	.184	.186	R	R	6-4	200	9-23-82	2002	Tuscaloosa, Ala.

GAMES BY POSITION: C—Jaso 25, Spring 35, Woodruff 16. **1B**—Baty 20, Jaso 14, Nowak 41. **2B**—Asanovich 38, Cooper 33, Cottrell 6. **3B**—Cottrell 55, Nowak 18, Paredes 1. **SS**—Asanovich 23, Bouman 5, Paredes 49. **OF**—Bolen 2, Breen 39, Cumberland 49, Frias 34, Leandro 40, Perez 69, Ritchie 3.

PITCHING	W	L	ERA	G	GS	CG	SV	IP	H	R	ER	BB	SO	AVG	B	T	HT	WT	DOB	1st Yr	Resides
Barratt, Jonathan	2	3	2.74	10	10	1	0	43	38	21	13	11	50	.230	R	L	5-9	165	3-19-85	2004	Springfield, Mo.
Barriger, Marcus	2	2	4.54	14	0	0	1	36	43	24	18	8	26	.299	R	R	6-1	215	8-5-82	2004	Swansea, Ill.
Bigda, Drew	0	0	0.00	2	0	0	0	2	1	0	0	2	.143	R	L	6-0	210	5-16-83	2004	Stamford, Conn.
Bitter, Ryan	3	1	0.95	21	0	0	5	28	17	6	3	3	37	.167	R	R	6-1	195	9-30-81	2004	Pacific Grove, Calif.
Cobb, Matthew	4	6	3.45	13	10	0	0	60	59	29	23	15	58	.254	L	L	6-3	180	6-30-83	2003	Prattville, Ala.
Delacruz, Eduardo	3	6	4.09	14	14	0	0	66	52	34	30	29	61	.213	R	R	6-3	170	10-6-81	2001	Pueblo Nuevo, D.R.
De la Cruz, Jose	2	0	1.02	18	0	0	8	44	30	8	5	13	46	.184	R	R	6-6	206	9-23-83	2003	Haina, D.R.
Dobyns, Jon	0	0	9.00	1	0	0	0	1	1	1	1	1	2	.200	R	R	6-2	210	9-8-81	2004	Phoenix, Ariz.
King, Tim	5	3	4.08	11	11	0	0	57	50	31	26	18	43	.236	L	L	6-3	200	8-22-83	2001	Deer Park, Texas
Lavergne, Jarrad	3	1	1.64	12	8	1	0	60	48	19	11	8	46	.220	L	L	6-2	200	2-18-83	2002	New Iberia, La.
Mann, Brandon	5	5	3.38	14	14	0	0	72	67	33	27	18	68	.245	L	L	6-2	160	5-16-84	2002	Des Moines, Wash.
Price, John	0	0	4.86	12	0	0	1	17	20	11	9	8	8	.282	L	L	6-2	220	7-10-81	2004	LaPlace, La.
Smith, Cole	0	0	4.50	3	0	0	0	4	2	2	2	6	2	.143	R	R	6-4	170	10-30-83	2002	Rockwall, Texas
Sonnanstine, Andy	3	1	1.00	9	2	0	1	27	18	4	3	3	24	.178	L	R	6-3	185	3-18-83	2004	Wadsworth, Ill.
Volquez, Angel	2	0	3.21	12	0	0	0	14	18	8	5	9	7	.340	R	R	6-3	210	7-3-80	1999	Santo Domingo, D.R.
Wagner, Nick	1	0	3.34	18	0	0	2	35	34	15	13	10	24	.262	R	R	6-2	215	6-16-83	2004	Springfield, Ill.
Walker, Aaron	4	2	2.70	14	3	0	2	30	21	12	9	9	36	.200	L	L	6-3	195	2-4-82	2004	East Palestine, Ohio
Weimer, Andrew	0	1	3.04	17	0	0	0	24	25	14	8	10	14	.272	R	R	6-2	180	3-20-81	2003	New Hartford, N.Y.

PRINCETON DEVIL RAYS — Rookie

APPALACHIAN LEAGUE

BATTING	AVG	G	AB	R	H	2B	3B	HR	RBI	BB	SO	SB	CS	OBP	SLG	B	T	HT	WT	DOB	1st Yr	Resides
Bouman, Robbie	.274	35	117	12	32	4	2	0	12	9	32	3	2	.331	.342	R	R	6-4	190	8-30-82	2004	Sterling, Va.
Brignac, Reid	.361	59	97	16	35	4	2	1	25	9	10	2	1	.413	.474	L	R	6-3	185	1-16-86	2004	St. Amant, La.
Crooks, Alex	.151	34	93	12	14	5	0	1	8	14	24	0	0	.262	.237	L	L	6-2	235	6-28-84	2004	Baldwin, Calif.
Cunningham, Chris	.259	55	174	31	45	8	2	4	36	23	45	1	5	.365	.397	R	R	6-1	200	8-24-82	2004	Homewood, Ill.
Delarosa, Jaria	.295	46	146	26	43	4	4	22	5	43	3	3	.346	.459	R	R	6-3	170	9-8-85	2004	La Victoria, D.R.
Hall, J.T.	.186	41	118	20	22	3	1	3	16	15	46	1	2	.302	.305	L	R	6-3	225	5-19-84	2004	Port Gibson, Miss.
Irvin, Blair	.208	39	101	15	21	1	0	0	5	7	24	14	3	.259	.218	L	R	6-2	170	5-16-83	2002	Patterson, La.
Lagreid, Thomas	.235	27	85	15	20	4	0	3	16	12	18	1	1	.340	.388	R	R	6-1	185	10-24-83	2004	Edmonds, Wash.
Lopez, Christian	.281	29	96	18	27	6	0	3	13	6	24	3	1	.333	.438	R	R	6-2	185	10-14-84	2004	Miami Lakes, Fla.
Markel, Craig	.245	37	106	12	26	2	0	1	12	16	14	0	0	.347	.292	R	R	5-10	214	6-17-80	2004	Carson, Calif.
Ramos, Carlos	.370	21	81	18	30	2	3	3	13	4	6	5	2	.409	.556	L	L	5-8	175	2-23-80	2004	Miami, Fla.
Ritchie, Jake	.287	47	167	31	48	13	0	6	28	21	50	4	1	.380	.473	R	R	6-2	202	10-15-80	2004	Thibodaux, La.
Roberson, Craig	.133	6	15	1	2	0	0	0	1	0	8	0	0	.133	.133	R	R	5-10	165	10-21-81	2004	West Monroe, La.
Rousseve, Brandon	.208	50	183	26	38	5	3	0	12	18	57	13	3	.306	.268	R	R	6-1	175	8-4-84	2004	New Orleans, La.
Royster, Ryan	.273	52	176	25	48	10	2	5	26	5	47	3	3	.297	.438	R	R	6-2	210	7-25-86	2004	Eugene, Ore.
Schultz, Blake	.291	42	141	20	41	3	1	2	14	16	27	5	0	.365	.369	R	R	6-3	200	9-26-81	2004	Urbandale, Ill.
Shelley, Shane	.158	6	19	3	3	0	0	1	0	1	1	1	3	.238	.158	S	R	5-11	170	4-17-84	2003	Belle Chasse, La.
Touchstone, Josh	.289	43	173	21	50	8	3	20	11	32	9	4	.333	.387	R	R	5-11	185	2-10-81	2004	Semmes, Ala.
Wiens, Logan	.174	42	144	13	25	6	0	1	13	7	44	1	0	.209	.236	R	R	6-6	210	1-13-86	2004	Merced, Calif.

GAMES BY POSITION: C—Lagreid 25, Lopez 28, Lopez 1, Markel 16. **1B**—Bouman 1, Crooks 30, Hall 5, Lopez 1, Markel 3, Wiens 40. **2B**—Bouman 1, Rousseve 42, Touchstone 27. **3B**—Bouman 22, Delarosa 13, Markel 1, Ritchie 21, Touchstone 15. **SS**—Bouman 12, Brignac 24, Delarosa 30, Rousseve 8. **OF**—Cunningham 47, Hall 18, Irvin 29, Ramos 21, Ritchie 19, Roberson 5, Royster 49, Schultz 34, Shelley 6.

PITCHING	W	L	ERA	G	GS	CG	SV	IP	H	R	ER	BB	SO	AVG	B	T	HT	WT	DOB	1st Yr	Resides
Bigda, Drew	1	1	3.43	18	0	0	0	21	18	10	8	15	21	.247	R	L	6-0	210	5-16-83	2004	Stamford, Conn.
Brehm, Derek	0	0	11.81	6	0	0	0	5	8	9	7	10	4	.348	L	L	6-1	190	10-31-80	2004	San Antonio, Texas
Brock, Ken	0	4	10.13	14	2	0	0	24	46	32	27	14	19	.407	L	L	6-1	220	1-3-83	2004	The Dalles, Ore.
Carpenter, Calvin	1	0	1.98	5	1	0	0	14	8	4	3	9	20	.170	R	R	6-2	190	9-23-82	2001	Natchitoches, La.
Davis, Wade	3	5	5.93	13	13	0	0	58	71	46	38	19	38	.302	R	R	6-5	220	9-7-85	2004	Lake Wales, Fla.
Dobyns, Jon	2	3	3.91	12	0	0	0	23	28	15	10	11	20	.289	R	R	6-2	210	9-8-81	2004	Phoenix, Ariz.
Evers, Billy	1	2	7.53	21	0	0	0	35	44	37	29	31	24	.303	R	R	6-2	195	8-31-82	2004	New Port Richey, Fla.
Geddes, Michael	0	1	4.15	9	0	0	0	13	8	6	6	9	14	.195	R	R	6-4	218	10-21-83	2003	Hudsonville, Mich.
Gil, Roberto	0	1	9.45	10	0	0	0	13	17	16	14	8	17	.288	R	R	6-1	160	5-20-84	2004	San Pedro de Macoris, D.R.
Gor, Nick	1	2	4.09	20	1	0	6	22	24	18	10	10	21	.286	R	R	6-7	230	10-10-81	2004	Yorba Linda, Calif.
Kelly, Chris	1	0	5.40	4	0	0	0	8	13	7	5	3	7	.342	R	R	6-3	200	7-14-82	2004	Sarasota, Fla.
Larson, Matt	1	2	4.12	6	3	0	1	20	22	12	9	9	22	.272	R	R	6-4	195	4-9-81	2004	Costa Mesa, Calif.
Lavergne, Jarrad	0	1	6.75	1	0	0	0	1	4	5	1	1	2	.444	L	L	6-2	200	2-18-83	2002	New Iberia, La.
Limas, Alejandro	0	9	6.83	13	12	0	0	54	63	54	41	35	53	.296	L	L	6-1	185	8-31-85	2004	Bonao, D.R.
Lopez, Romelio	1	1	2.96	5	5	0	0	24	27	11	8	13	29	.273	S	R	6-7	230	10-10-83	2003	Ciudad Piar Campo, Venez.
McGee, Jacob	5	1	3.97	12	12	0	0	57	49	30	25	25	53	.231	L	L	6-2	185	8-6-86	2004	Reno, Nev.
Muro, Joseph	1	3	10.25	10	6	0	0	26	36	34	30	34	21	.346	R	R	6-0	165	2-16-84	2004	Chino, Calif.
Redfern, Chad	1	3	7.56	10	8	0	0	33	44	34	28	18	21	.319	R	R	6-3	190	12-27-80	2003	Sylmar, Calif.
Rodriguez, Claudio	0	0	4.62	15	3	0	0	39	48	33	20	25	30	.298	R	R	6-5	220	6-29-83	2003	Bonao, D.R.
Rodriguez, Joan	0	1	5.79	5	0	0	0	9	10	8	6	6	7	.286	R	R	6-2	180	10-3-85	2003	San Francisco de Macoris, D.R.
Salas, Juan	1	0	4.82	8	0	0	0	9	10	7	5	6	6	.278	R	R	6-2	190	11-7-78	1999	Santo Domingo, D.R.
Smith, Cole	1	1	2.96	11	1	0	0	27	17	14	9	16	30	.173	R	R	6-4	170	10-30-83	2002	Rockwall, Texas
Sues, Jarret	1	2	6.29	24	0	0	2	34	50	29	24	17	33	.345	L	R	6-3	210	2-16-81	2004	Red Bank, N.J.

BY GERRY FRALEY

How is this for irony?

The Rangers subtracted the best player in the American League shortly before the start of the 2004 season and became a better team.

The Rangers, on a streak of four consecutive last-place finishes in the AL West, stunned their rivals all season. Texas led the division by 4½ games after a win at Oakland on July 23. The Rangers remained in contention until the final 10 days before a thin starting rotation caught up to them.

The Rangers finished third in a demanding division but had 89 wins, the club's most since 1999. The outlook went from gloomy to hopeful in just one season.

"I'm hoping this is a story to be continued," manager Buck Showalter said. "We'd like for it to be a chapter. The question is what chapter in the book is it?

"This is a cruel game. Just when you think you've got it all figured out, this game can grab you and say 'Wait a second.' We know we have more work to do."

The turnaround started with the trade of reigning AL Most Valuable Player Alex Rodriguez to the Yankees.

The deal changed the direction of the Rangers. They stopped kidding themselves into believing one more veteran would produce a winner and went all-out with young players, and those players blossomed without the heavy presence of Rodriguez.

Michael Young switched from second to shortstop and became an all-star as Rodriguez's replacement. Third baseman Hank Blalock also made the All-Star Game and with Young formed the best left side of an infield in the league. They played high-quality defense and also combined for 54 homers and 209 RBIs.

Blalock and Young were among five Rangers all-stars. First baseman Mark Teixeira will crack that level soon. He overcame a slow start caused by injuries to hit 38 homers

Michael Young | Ian Kinsler

BILL MITCHELL

PLAYERS of the YEAR

MAJOR LEAGUE: Michael Young, ss

All the Rangers asked Young to do in 2004 was replace the reigning American League MVP. Who would have thought Young would be up to the challenge? He nearly led the resurgent Rangers to the playoffs, batting .313-22-99 and collecting 211 hits while playing solid defense in his first season as a shortstop after moving from second base.

MINOR LEAGUE: Ian Kinsler, ss

Kinsler opened the 2004 season by hitting .402 in 224 at-bats at low Class A Clinton, so the Rangers decided to give him a real test. They moved him up two rungs to Double-A Frisco, where Kinsler proceeded to hit .300-9-46 to establish himself as one of the top prospects in the organization.

with 112 RBIs.

Add in all-star closer Francisco Cordero, emerging righthanded starter Ryan Drese and outfielders Kevin Mench and Laynce Nix, and the Rangers have a core of sub-30-years-old talent that should keep the club on the upswing.

The bullpen was the key to the Rangers' success.

Headed by closer Cordero, who had 49 saves in 54 chances, the bullpen ranked among the AL's best. Texas relievers led the league in wins (34) and ERA (3.46) while handling a heavy workload.

The rotation was a season-long headache. The Rangers used a club-record 17 starters in what was a rotation with no middle class. Ageless lefthander Kenny Rogers and Drese were the upper class. The Rangers were 43-25 in their starts and 46-48 in all other starts.

All six minor league affiliates posted winning records in 2004. The overall record of 381-314 was the third-best among all organizations. The top four affiliates reached the playoffs, and Double-A Frisco won the Texas League championship.

Righthander Kameron Loe and shortstop Ian Kinsler both had strong seasons while playing at two levels.

The strike-throwing Loe, who appeared with Frisco and Oklahoma leading up to a September callup, was the organization's Nolan Ryan award winner as pitcher of the year. Loe was 12-9, 3.17 overall.

Kinsler started the season at low Class A Clinton and leapfrogged to Frisco. He became a prospect after hitting a combined .345 with 51 doubles and 73 extra-base hits overall in 501 at-bats.

ORGANIZATION LEADERS

BATTING

*AVG	Chad Allen, Oklahoma	.358
R	Ian Kinsler, Frisco/Clinton	103
H	Ian Kinsler, Frisco/Clinton	174
TB	Ian Kinsler, Frisco/Clinton	289
2B	Ian Kinsler, Frisco/Clinton	51
3B	Joaquin Arias, Stockton	8
	Rick Asadoorian, Frisco	8
HR	Jason Botts, Frisco	24
RBI	Ian Kinsler, Frisco/Clinton	99
BB	Jason Botts, Frisco	77
SO	Nate Gold, Stockton	140
	Santiago Perez, Oklahoma/Frisco	140
SB	Cameron Coughlan, Stockton	35
*OBP	Ian Kinsler, Frisco/Clinton	.429
*SLG	Ian Kinsler, Frisco/Clinton	.573

PITCHING

W	Sam Narron, Oklahoma/Frisco	14
L	Three tied at	10
#ERA	Jason Andrew, Oklahoma/Frisco/Stockton	2.59
G	Brad Clontz, Oklahoma	59
CG	John Wasdin, Oklahoma	2
SV	Brad Clontz, Oklahoma	18
IP	Kameron Loe, Oklahoma/Frisco	166
BB	Kelvin Jimenez, Frisco	67
SO	John Hudgins, Oklahoma/Frisco/Stockton	145

*Minimum 250 at-bats #Minimum 75 innings

TEXAS RANGERS

Manager: Buck Showalter.

2004 Record: 89-73, .549 (3rd, AL West).

BATTING	AVG	G	AB	R	H	2B	3B	HR	RBI	BB	SO	SB	CS	OBP	SLG	B	T	HT	WT	DOB	1st Yr	Resides
Alexander, Manny	.238	21	21	3	5	2	0	0	3	1	7	0	0	.273	.333	R	R	5-10	180	3-20-71	1988	San Pedro de Macoris, D.R.
Allen, Chad	.241	20	58	4	14	4	1	0	6	2	13	0	1	.262	.345	R	R	6-1	200	2-6-75	1996	Dallas, Texas
Ardoin, Danny	.125	6	8	1	1	0	0	0	1	3	2	0	0	.364	.125	R	R	6-0	220	7-8-74	1995	Ville Platte, La.
Barajas, Rod	.249	108	358	50	89	26	1	15	58	13	63	0	1	.276	.453	R	R	6-2	220	9-5-75	1996	Scottsdale, Ariz.
Blalock, Hank	.276	159	624	107	172	38	3	32	110	75	149	2	2	.355	.500	L	R	6-1	200	11-21-80	1999	Carlsbad, Calif.
Conti, Jason	.182	22	55	6	10	3	0	0	4	5	19	0	2	.250	.236	L	R	5-11	180	1-27-75	1996	Phoenix, Ariz.
Dellucci, David	.242	107	331	59	80	13	1	17	61	47	88	9	4	.342	.441	L	L	5-11	189	10-31-73	1995	Baton Rouge, La.
Fox, Andy	.083	12	12	2	1	0	0	0	1	3	0	0	0	.154	.083	L	R	6-4	200	1-12-71	1989	Fair Oaks, Calif.
Fullmer, Brad	.233	76	258	41	60	19	1	11	33	27	30	1	2	.310	.442	L	R	6-0	220	1-17-75	1994	Henderson, Nev.
Gonzalez, Adrian	.238	16	42	7	10	3	0	1	7	2	6	0	0	.273	.381	L	L	6-2	190	5-8-82	2000	Bonita, Calif.
Huckaby, Ken	.132	16	38	3	5	2	0	0	5	1	12	0	0	.233	.184	R	R	6-1	200	1-27-71	1991	Philadelphia, Pa.
Jordan, Brian	.222	61	212	27	47	13	1	5	23	16	35	2	2	.275	.363	R	R	6-1	205	3-29-67	1988	Alpharetta, Ga.
Laird, Gerald	.224	49	147	20	33	6	0	1	16	12	35	0	1	.287	.286	R	R	6-2	220	11-13-79	1999	Garden Grove, Calif.
Matthews, Gary	.275	87	280	37	77	11	1	11	36	33	64	5	1	.350	.461	S	R	6-3	225	8-25-74	1994	Baltimore, Md.
Mench, Kevin	.279	125	438	69	122	30	3	26	71	33	63	0	0	.335	.539	R	R	6-0	225	1-7-78	1999	Newark, Del.
Nivar, Ramon	.222	7	18	3	4	0	0	0	4	0	7	1	1	.211	.222	R	R	5-10	170	2-22-80	1998	San Cristobal, D.R.
Nix, Laynce	.248	115	371	58	92	20	4	14	46	23	113	1	1	.293	.437	L	L	6-0	200	10-30-80	2000	Midland, Texas
Perry, Herbert	.224	49	134	13	30	2	1	5	17	14	19	0	0	.307	.366	R	R	6-2	230	9-15-69	1991	Mayo, Fla.
Soriano, Alfonso	.280	145	608	77	170	32	4	28	91	33	121	18	5	.324	.484	R	R	6-1	180	1-7-78	1999	San Pedro de Macoris, D.R.
Teixeira, Mark	.281	145	545	101	153	34	2	38	112	68	117	4	1	.370	.560	S	R	6-3	220	4-11-80	2002	Arlington, Texas
Young, Eric	.288	104	344	55	99	25	2	1	27	43	28	14	9	.377	.381	R	R	5-8	185	5-18-67	1989	Atlanta, Ga.
Young, Michael	.313	160	690	114	216	33	9	22	99	44	89	12	3	.353	.483	R	R	6-1	190	10-19-76	1997	Los Angeles, Calif.

PITCHING	W	L	ERA	G	GS	CG	SV	IP	H	R	ER	BB	SO	AVG	B	T	HT	WT	DOB	1st Yr	Resides
Almanzar, Carlos	7	3	3.72	67	0	0	0	73	66	32	30	19	44	.244	R	R	6-2	200	11-6-73	1994	Santo Domingo, D.R.
Bacsik, Mike	1	1	4.60	3	3	0	0	16	16	8	8	1	6	.267	L	L	6-3	190	11-11-77	1996	Duncanville, Texas
Benoit, Joaquin	3	5	5.68	28	15	0	0	103	113	67	65	31	95	.279	R	R	6-3	220	7-26-77	1996	Santiago, D.R.
Bierbrodt, Nick	1	1	5.82	4	4	0	0	17	14	11	11	9	10	.246	L	L	6-5	215	5-16-78	1996	Tierra Verde, Fla.
Brocail, Doug	4	1	4.13	43	0	0	1	52	54	29	24	20	43	.269	L	R	6-2	200	5-16-67	1986	Missouri City, Texas
Callaway, Mickey	0	1	7.94	4	3	0	0	11	18	10	10	7	9	.367	R	R	6-2	200	5-13-75	1996	Memphis, Tenn.
Cordero, Francisco	3	4	2.13	67	0	0	49	72	60	19	17	32	79	.226	R	R	6-2	235	5-11-75	1994	Santo Domingo, D.R.
Dickey, R.A.	6	7	5.61	25	15	0	1	104	136	77	65	33	57	.311	R	R	6-3	205	10-29-74	1997	Nashville, Tenn.
Dominguez, Juan	1	2	3.91	4	4	0	0	23	25	11	10	5	14	.281	R	R	6-2	180	5-18-80	2000	Valverde Mao, D.R.
Drese, Ryan	14	10	4.20	34	33	2	0	208	233	104	97	58	98	.285	R	R	6-3	220	4-5-76	1998	Oakland, Calif.
Erickson, Scott	1	3	6.16	4	4	0	0	19	23	13	13	16	6	.307	R	R	6-4	230	2-2-68	1989	Stateline, Nev.
Francisco, Frank	5	1	3.33	45	0	0	0	51	36	19	19	28	60	.198	R	R	6-2	180	9-11-79	1998	Santo Domingo, D.R.
Garcia, Rosman	0	0	5.40	4	0	0	0	7	9	5	4	5	5	.310	R	R	6-2	160	1-3-79	1996	San Joaquin, Venez.
Hughes, Travis	0	0	13.50	2	0	0	0	1	4	2	2	2	4	.500	R	R	6-5	224	5-25-78	1998	Beaver City, Neb.
Lewis, Colby	1	1	4.11	3	3	0	0	15	13	7	7	13	11	.228	R	R	6-4	230	8-2-79	1999	Bakersfield, Calif.
Loe, Kameron	0	0	5.40	2	1	0	0	7	6	5	4	6	3	.273	R	R	6-7	231	9-10-81	2002	Chatsworth, Calif.
Mahay, Ron	3	0	2.55	60	0	0	0	67	60	23	19	29	54	.235	L	L	6-2	185	6-28-71	1991	Manalapan, N.J.
Narron, Sam	0	0	13.50	1	1	0	0	3	5	4	4	4	1	.385	L	L	6-5	213	7-12-81	2002	Goldsboro, N.C.
Nelson, Jeff	0	1	5.32	29	0	0	1	24	17	16	14	19	22	.207	R	R	6-8	225	11-17-66	1984	Issaquah, Wash.
Park, Chan Ho	4	7	5.46	16	16	0	0	96	105	63	58	33	63	.281	R	R	6-2	210	7-30-73	1994	Arlington, Texas
Powell, Jay	1	1	3.38	23	0	0	0	24	24	11	9	11	17	.267	R	R	6-4	220	1-9-72	1993	Madison, Miss.
Ramirez, Erasmo	0	3	4.29	34	0	0	0	36	34	19	17	7	21	.252	L	L	6-0	190	4-29-76	1998	Santa Ana, Calif.
Regilio, Nick	0	4	6.05	6	4	0	0	19	20	16	13	15	12	.278	R	R	6-2	205	9-4-78	1999	Deltona, Fla.
Rodriguez, Ricardo	3	1	2.03	5	4	1	0	27	28	10	6	12	15	.262	R	R	6-3	190	5-21-78	1997	Guayubin, D.R.
Rogers, Kenny	18	9	4.76	35	35	2	0	212	248	117	112	66	126	.292	L	L	6-1	210	11-10-64	1984	Southlake, Texas
Shouse, Brian	2	0	2.23	53	0	0	0	44	36	12	11	18	34	.224	L	L	5-11	190	9-26-68	1990	Peoria, Ill.
Snare, Ryan	0	0	10.80	1	0	0	0	3	5	5	4	2	0	.333	L	L	6-0	190	2-8-79	2001	Palm Harbor, Fla.
Tejera, Michael	0	0	10.13	6	0	0	0	5	9	6	6	3	7	.360	L	L	5-9	192	10-18-76	1995	Miami, Fla.
Wasdin, John	2	4	6.78	15	10	0	0	65	83	52	49	23	36	.305	R	R	6-2	190	8-5-72	1993	Jacksonville, Fla.
Young, Chris	3	2	4.71	7	7	0	0	36	36	21	19	10	27	.250	R	R	6-10	260	5-25-79	2001	Dallas, Texas

FIELDING

Catcher	PCT	G	PO	A	E	DP	PB
Ardoin	.958	6	21	2	1	0	1
Barajas	.990	105	656	23	7	2	7
Huckaby	.978	16	81	7	2	1	2
Laird	.983	49	275	19	5	6	6

First Base	PCT	G	PO	A	E	DP
Barajas	1.000	2	3	1	0	0
Fullmer	1.000	4	15	0	0	5
Gonzalez	.990	11	94	6	1	13
Perry	1.000	15	104	3	0	12
Teixeira	.992	142	1210	98	10	114

Second Base	PCT	G	PO	A	E	DP
Alexander	.917	11	2	9	1	0

	PCT	G	PO	A	E	DP
Fox	1.000	3	3	9	0	2
Soriano	.969	142	308	418	23	104
E. Young	.938	20	39	51	6	11

Third Base	PCT	G	PO	A	E	DP
Alexander	.800	3	2	2	1	0
Blalock	.957	159	103	279	17	33
Fox	.000	2	0	0	0	0
Perry	.867	6	7	6	2	0
E. Young	1.000	1	0	1	0	0

Shortstop Base	PCT	G	PO	A	E	DP
Alexander	.944	7	6	11	1	1
E. Young	.857	8	2	4	1	1
M. Young	.972	158	225	423	19	98

Outfield	PCT	G	PO	A	E	DP
Allen	1.000	13	14	0	0	0
Conti	1.000	21	45	0	0	0
Dellucci	.989	94	177	0	2	0
Fox	1.000	2	2	0	0	0
Jordan	.990	44	94	1	1	0
Matthews	.990	85	195	8	2	1
Mench	.995	109	213	6	1	3
Nivar	1.000	6	12	1	0	0
Nix	.996	114	225	4	1	1
Teixeira	1.000	7	8	0	0	0
E. Young	.976	53	77	4	2	0

ORGANIZATION STATISTICS

Director, Minor League Operations: John Lombardo.

Class	Farm Team	League	W	L	Pct.	Finish*	Manager	Affiliate Since
AAA	Oklahoma RedHawks (Oklahoma City)	Pacific Coast	81	63	.563	**2nd (16)**	Bobby Jones	1983
AA	Frisco (Texas) RoughRiders	Texas	81	59	.579	**+2nd (8)**	Tim Ireland	2003
High A	#Stockton (Calif.) Ports	California	72	68	.514	**5th (10)**	Arnie Beyeler	2003
Low A	Clinton (Iowa) LumberKings	Midwest	74	64	.536	**6th (14)**	Carlos Subero	2003
SS A	Spokane (Wash.) Indians	Northwest	41	35	.539	**t-3rd (8)**	Darryl Kennedy	2003
Rookie	Surprise (Ariz.) Rangers	Arizona	32	24	.571	3rd (9)	Pedro Lopez	2003

*Finish in overall standings (No. of teams in league)/Playoff teams in **boldface**   #Affiliation will operate in Bakersfield (California) in 2005

OKLAHOMA REDHAWKS ,Class AAA
PACIFIC COAST LEAGUE

BATTING	AVG	G	AB	R	H	2B	3B	HR	RBI	BB	SO	SB	CS	OBP	SLG	B	T	HT	WT	DOB	1st Yr Resides
Alexander, Manny	.288	93	361	65	104	29	4	10	49	27	45	8	4	.338	.474	R	R	5-10	180	3-20-71	1988 San Pedro de Macoris, D.R.
Allen, Chad	.358	93	386	75	138	28	3	7	70	31	72	18	2	.407	.500	R	R	6-1	200	2-6-75	1996 Dallas, Texas
Ardoin, Danny	.308	68	237	50	73	12	0	10	44	41	66	1	1	.422	.485	R	R	6-0	220	7-8-74	1995 Ville Platte, La.
Asadoorian, Rick	.190	15	42	7	8	1	1	0	4	4	13	1	0	.306	.262	R	R	6-1	202	8-23-80	2000 Whitinsville, Mass.
Beinbrink, Andrew	.313	16	48	8	15	5	0	0	1	4	10	2	0	.370	.417	R	R	6-3	200	9-24-76	1999 San Diego, Calif.
Conti, Jason	.328	104	421	63	138	26	5	8	61	33	84	5	1	.381	.470	L	R	5-11	180	1-27-75	1996 Phoenix, Ariz.
Esposito, Brian	.000	1	4	0	0	0	0	0	1	0	1	0	0	.000	.000	R	R	6-1	190	2-24-79	2000 Willington, Conn.
Fox, Andy	.296	34	125	22	37	10	0	1	12	14	25	1	2	.385	.400	L	R	6-4	200	1-12-71	1989 Fair Oaks, Calif.
Gonzalez, Adrian	.304	123	457	61	139	28	3	12	88	39	73	1	1	.364	.457	L	L	6-2	190	5-8-82	2000 Bonita, Calif.
Hatcher, Justin	.333	2	6	0	2	0	0	0	0	0	3	0	0	.333	.333	R	R	5-10	200	5-12-80	2003 Fort Worth, Texas
Huckaby, Ken	.276	35	127	18	35	8	1	2	20	9	18	0	0	.317	.402	R	R	6-1	210	1-27-71	1991 Philadelphia, Pa.
Jones, Jason	.263	81	300	45	79	15	1	13	45	40	68	2	1	.350	.450	S	R	6-3	210	10-17-76	1999 Marietta, Ga.
Jordan, Brian	.385	7	26	3	10	2	0	0	8	3	3	1	0	.467	.462	R	R	6-1	205	3-29-67	1988 Alpharetta, Ga.
Laird, Gerald	.182	6	22	2	4	2	0	0	2	2	8	1	0	.250	.273	R	R	6-2	220	11-13-79	1999 Garden Grove, Calif.
Matthews, Gary	.324	38	145	33	47	9	4	9	36	23	29	4	1	.409	.628	S	R	6-3	225	8-25-74	1994 Baltimore, Md.
McDougall, Marshall	.282	94	354	48	100	24	0	19	69	35	80	2	1	.349	.511	R	R	6-1	200	12-19-78	2000 Tampa, Fla.
Newhan, David	.328	61	262	57	86	21	6	9	38	26	55	10	0	.387	.557	L	R	5-10	180	9-7-73	1995 Yorba Linda, Calif.
Nivar, Ramon	.264	113	462	62	122	21	0	10	52	14	43	15	15	.290	.374	R	R	5-10	170	2-22-80	1998 San Cristobal, D.R.
Perez, Santiago	.266	89	316	66	84	15	3	9	40	51	110	14	9	.375	.418	S	R	6-2	160	12-30-75	1994 Santo Domingo, D.R.
Pickler, Jeff	.311	86	354	64	110	22	5	1	51	34	49	15	3	.369	.410	R	R	5-10	180	1-6-76	1998 Santa Ana, Calif.
Smith, Jeff	.200	13	35	3	7	2	0	0	3	4	4	0	0	.300	.257	L	R	6-3	210	6-17-74	1996 Naples, Fla.
Waldron, Jeff	.228	34	101	9	23	3	1	0	8	12	35	0	0	.325	.277	L	R	6-2	160	10-4-76	1999 Lynn, Mass.
2-team (3 Tucson)	.223	37	103	9	23	3	1	0	8	13	36	0	0	.325	.272						
Zoccolillo, Peter	.293	128	484	83	142	37	1	23	96	65	94	4	2	.375	.517	L	R	6-2	200	2-6-77	1999 White Plains, N.Y.

PITCHING	W	L	ERA	G	GS	CG	SV	IP	H	R	ER	BB	SO	AVG	B	T	HT	WT	DOB	1st Yr Resides
Andrew, Jason	0	0	2.25	1	1	0	0	4	4	1	1	1	4	.250	R	R	6-1	160	1-29-80	2002 Tacoma, Wash.
Bacsik, Mike	8	6	4.55	34	9	0	0	95	106	58	48	23	50	.286	L	L	6-3	190	11-11-77	1996 Duncanville, Texas
Bierbrodt, Nick	1	3	7.30	5	5	0	0	25	26	21	20	22	26	.274	L	L	6-5	215	5-16-78	1996 Tierra Verde, Fla.
Brocail, Doug	2	0	4.19	12	0	0	0	19	20	9	9	2	19	.263	R	R	6-5	230	5-16-67	1986 Missouri City, Texas
Burke, Erick	0	1	5.29	24	0	0	0	32	37	23	19	22	28	.289	L	L	6-4	230	8-14-77	1999 Houston, Texas
Clontz, Brad	2	6	4.47	59	0	0	18	56	57	35	28	19	51	.268	R	R	6-1	195	4-25-71	1992 Alpharetta, Ga.
Dominguez, Juan	5	1	3.13	9	9	1	0	55	41	20	19	19	41	.205	R	R	6-2	180	5-18-80	2000 Valverde Mao, D.R.
Drese, Ryan	1	0	1.80	1	1	0	0	5	6	1	1	0	0	.300	R	R	6-3	220	4-5-76	1998 Oakland, Calif.
Erickson, Scott	0	1	9.82	2	2	0	0	11	17	13	12	9	11	.370	R	R	6-4	230	2-2-68	1989 Stateline, Nev.
Garcia, Rosman	4	6	4.65	41	0	0	2	72	87	41	37	36	49	.307	R	R	6-2	160	1-3-79	1996 San Joaquin, Venez.
Helling, Rick	1	4	9.00	6	6	0	0	31	59	35	31	11	20	.421	R	R	6-3	241	12-15-70	1992 Southlake, Texas
Hudgins, John	0	1	7.50	3	2	0	0	12	19	10	10	5	8	.365	R	R	6-2	195	8-31-81	2003 Mission Viejo, Calif.
Hughes, Travis	1	2	5.26	13	0	0	0	26	21	15	15	9	24	.221	R	R	6-5	224	5-25-78	1998 Beaver City, Neb.
Loe, Kameron	5	2	3.27	8	8	0	0	52	52	20	19	13	42	.265	R	R	6-7	231	9-10-81	2002 Chatsworth, Calif.
Miadich, Bart	1	0	4.60	21	0	0	2	29	24	15	15	22	35	.231	R	R	6-4	205	2-3-76	1998 Lake Oswego, Ore.
2-team (31 Portland)	4	4	4.04	52	0	0	14	65	52	31	29	47	69	.223						
Narron, Sam	8	2	4.43	17	16	1	0	102	123	55	50	24	31	.308	L	L	6-5	213	7-12-81	2002 Goldsboro, N.C.
Nelson, Jeff	0	1	16.20	2	2	0	0	2	3	3	3	0	3	.375	R	R	6-8	225	11-17-66	1984 Issaquah, Wash.
Park, Chan Ho	0	2	3.72	4	4	0	0	19	21	8	8	3	19	.273	R	R	6-2	200	7-30-73	1994 Arlington, Texas
Ramirez, Erasmo	1	0	6.16	14	0	0	0	19	23	15	13	4	9	.299	L	L	6-0	190	4-29-76	1998 Santa Ana, Calif.
Regilio, Nick	6	5	4.71	17	17	0	0	92	98	49	48	46	72	.282	R	R	6-2	205	9-4-78	1999 Deltona, Fla.
Rodriguez, Ricardo	2	2	5.11	6	6	1	0	37	42	23	21	12	18	.296	R	R	6-3	190	5-21-78	1997 Guayubin, D.R.
Shouse, Brian	0	0	6.14	9	0	0	0	7	12	5	5	4	3	.375	L	L	5-11	190	9-26-68	1990 Peoria, Ill.
Snare, Ryan	11	6	4.72	26	24	0	0	137	171	88	72	49	79	.306	L	L	6-0	190	2-8-79	2001 Palm Harbor, Fla.
Stamler, Keith	7	3	3.13	48	1	0	3	83	78	39	29	26	40	.250	R	R	5-11	190	10-20-79	2000 Stockholm, N.J.
Sylvester, Billy	1	4	6.05	19	5	0	0	42	49	28	28	22	53	.293	R	R	6-5	210	10-1-76	1997 Florence, S.C.
Thompson, Erik	0	0	9.00	1	1	0	0	5	10	5	5	0	2	.435	R	R	5-9	197	6-23-82	2002 Pensacola, Fla.
Vance, Cory	2	2	5.94	8	6	0	0	33	37	24	22	10	15	.274	L	L	6-1	195	6-20-79	2000 Vandalia, Ohio
Wasdin, John	7	1	3.46	18	14	2	0	104	94	43	40	19	81	.242	R	R	6-2	190	8-5-72	1993 Jacksonville, Fla.
Williams, Todd	2	2	3.03	27	0	0	9	30	37	15	10	7	11	.308	R	R	6-3	210	2-13-71	1991 Land O'Lakes, Fla.
Young, Chris	3	0	1.48	5	5	1	0	30	20	7	5	9	34	.189	R	R	6-10	260	5-25-79	2001 Dallas, Texas

FIELDING

Catcher	PCT	G	PO	A	E	DP	PB
Ardoin	.976	68	403	48	11	7	10
Esposito	1.000	1	6	0	0	0	0
Hatcher	1.000	2	10	0	0	0	0
Huckaby	.989	29	171	16	2	0	1
Laird	.955	4	21	0	1	0	1
Smith	1.000	13	86	5	0	0	1
Waldron	.995	34	207	10	1	3	0

First Base	PCT	G	PO	A	E	DP
Allen	1.000	1	9	1	0	2
Fox	.977	4	42	0	1	3
Gonzalez	.995	123	1112	99	6	141

	PCT	G	PO	A	E	DP
Huckaby	.983	6	58	1	1	8
Jones	1.000	4	27	1	0	4
Newhan	.986	7	69	3	1	9
Zoccolillo	1.000	2	16	0	0	2

Second Base	PCT	G	PO	A	E	DP
Newhan	.966	36	85	113	7	33
Nivar	.987	43	85	142	3	36
Perez	.960	6	14	10	1	6
Pickler	.985	63	138	195	5	57

Third Base	PCT	G	PO	A	E	DP
Beinbrink	.963	10	5	21	1	3

	PCT	G	PO	A	E	DP
Fox	.914	17	10	22	3	0
McDougall	.941	77	49	191	15	30
Newhan	.929	8	5	21	2	1
Perez	.882	31	17	73	12	7
Pickler	1.000	5	2	7	0	1

Shortstop	PCT	G	PO	A	E	DP
Alexander	.965	93	169	334	18	81
Fox	.882	3	3	12	2	1
McDougall	.961	16	26	47	3	12
Perez	.945	33	66	105	10	26

Outfield	PCT	G	PO	A	E	DP
Allen	.992	80	122	3	1	0
Asadoorian	1.000	15	25	1	0	0
Conti	.979	99	210	22	5	9
Fox	1.000	4	4	0	0	0
Jones	.978	52	85	3	2	0
Jordan	1.000	4	7	0	0	0
Matthews	.971	38	66	1	2	0
Nivar	.988	67	156	5	2	1
Perez	1.000	14	24	1	0	1
Zoccolillo	.985	72	128	3	2	1

FRISCO ROUGHRIDERS — Class AA

TEXAS LEAGUE

BATTING

	AVG	G	AB	R	H	2B	3B	HR	RBI	BB	SO	SB	CS	OBP	SLG	B	T	HT	WT	DOB	1st Yr	Resides
Asadoorian, Rick	.288	81	229	28	66	14	7	3	27	13	60	9	0	.328	.450	R	R	6-1	202	8-23-80	2000	Whitinsville, Mass.
Beinbrink, Andrew	.257	60	175	23	45	9	0	3	25	27	39	5	5	.351	.360	R	R	6-3	200	9-24-76	1999	San Diego, Calif.
Botts, Jason	.293	133	481	85	141	25	3	24	92	77	126	7	4	.399	.507	S	R	6-5	253	7-26-80	2000	Paso Robles, Calif.
Bourgeois, Jason	.255	138	530	73	135	19	7	2	58	44	81	30	10	.313	.328	R	R	5-9	185	1-4-82	2000	Houston, Texas
Boyd, Patrick	.188	69	223	28	42	7	3	7	28	20	76	5	2	.282	.341	S	R	6-3	212	9-7-78	2002	Palm Harbor, Fla.
Clark, Daryl	.222	21	54	2	12	3	0	0	4	8	16	0	1	.317	.278	L	R	6-2	210	9-25-79	2000	Boalsburg, Pa.
Curry, Mike	.271	54	199	38	54	7	0	3	17	20	44	20	6	.341	.352	L	R	5-10	190	2-15-77	1998	Jacksonville, Fla.
Eldridge, Rashad	.284	108	348	64	99	16	5	2	31	50	94	14	5	.381	.376	S	R	5-11	211	10-16-81	2000	Macon, Ga.
Esposito, Brian	.207	31	92	11	19	4	0	1	11	4	27	0	1	.232	.283	R	R	6-1	190	2-24-79	2000	Willington, Conn.
Gonzalez, Edgar	.289	106	394	58	114	25	4	8	55	36	83	6	2	.355	.434	R	R	5-11	183	6-14-78	2000	Chula Vista, Calif.
Jordan, Brian	.158	6	19	1	3	1	0	0	0	0	6	0	0	.158	.211	R	R	6-1	205	3-29-67	1988	Alpharetta, Ga.
Kinsler, Ian	.300	71	277	51	83	21	1	9	46	32	47	7	4	.400	.480	R	R	6-0	175	6-22-82	2003	Tucson, Ariz.
McDougall, Marshall	.315	18	73	17	23	7	0	2	14	8	12	0	0	.383	.493	R	R	6-1	200	12-19-78	2000	Tampa, Fla.
McKinley, Josh	.212	45	137	18	29	4	1	5	18	20	44	0	3	.321	.365	S	R	6-1	205	9-14-79	1998	Windermere, Fla.
Meadows, Tydus	.285	99	344	55	98	20	2	18	69	47	72	3	1	.380	.512	R	R	6-0	235	9-5-77	1998	Evans, Ga.
Mench, Kevin	.313	4	16	3	5	0	0	1	1	1	0	0	0	.353	.500	R	R	6-0	225	1-7-78	1999	Newark, Del.
Meyer, Drew	.241	59	232	35	56	6	2	2	13	22	43	4	2	.309	.310	L	R	5-9	202	8-29-81	2002	Charleston, S.C.
Mosquera, Julio	.310	31	116	23	36	4	0	8	36	9	17	0	0	.375	.552	R	R	6-0	190	1-29-72	1993	Clearwater, Fla.
Nix, Laynce	.269	7	26	2	7	1	0	0	2	1	10	0	1	.296	.308	L	L	6-0	200	10-30-80	2000	Midland, Texas
Perez, Santiago	.387	28	111	28	43	11	4	5	19	11	30	4	3	.452	.694	S	R	6-2	160	12-30-75	1994	Santo Domingo, D.R.
Perry, Herbert	.414	8	29	4	12	3	0	4	3	7	0	0	0	.455	.517	R	R	6-2	200	9-15-69	1991	Mayo, Fla.
Raymundo, G.J.	.288	19	52	5	15	0	2	1	15	5	11	0	1	.373	.423	R	R	5-11	189	3-3-77	1999	Clovis, Calif.
Senreiso, Juan	.348	11	46	7	16	1	1	2	5	2	7	0	1	.375	.543	R	R	6-0	203	8-4-81	2000	Guaymate, D.R.
Smith, Dustin	.081	16	37	2	3	0	0	0	2	2	11	0	0	.128	.081	R	R	6-1	215	5-8-81	2001	Girard, Kan.
Smith, Jeff	.330	69	221	23	73	15	0	3	28	20	32	0	0	.389	.439	L	R	6-3	210	6-17-74	1996	Naples, Fla.
Smith, Will	.283	87	315	48	89	19	3	8	57	21	46	6	5	.328	.438	R	R	5-11	180	5-7-77	2000	Prattville, Ala.
Teixeira, Mark	.000	1	3	0	0	0	0	0	0	0	1	0	0	.250	.000	S	R	6-3	220	4-11-80	2002	Arlington, Texas
Waldron, Jeff	.317	12	41	4	13	1	0	0	4	2	8	0	0	.378	.341	L	R	6-1	200	10-4-76	1999	Lynn, Mass.
2-team (15 El Paso)	.319	27	91	8	29	5	0	1	10	8	17	0	1	.386	.407							

PITCHING

	W	L	ERA	G	GS	CG	SV	IP	H	R	ER	BB	SO	AVG	B	T	HT	WT	DOB	1st Yr	Resides
Andrew, Jason	3	0	3.31	24	2	0	1	49	46	22	18	21	36	.251	R	R	6-1	160	1-29-80	2002	Tacoma, Wash.
Beasley, Ray	3	0	3.00	42	0	0	8	51	43	22	17	17	43	.225	R	L	5-11	160	10-26-76	1996	Lake City, Fla.
Benoit, Joaquin	0	0	0.00	1	1	0	0	2	0	0	0	0	6	.000	R	R	6-3	220	7-26-77	1996	Santiago, D.R.
Bierbrodt, Nick	1	2	4.68	5	5	0	0	25	29	14	13	11	21	.293	L	L	6-5	215	5-16-78	1996	Tierra Verde, Fla.
Brocail, Doug	0	0	2.08	1	1	0	0	4	2	1	1	0	6	.143	L	R	6-5	230	5-16-67	1986	Missouri City, Texas
Burke, Erick	4	2	1.77	25	0	0	0	41	32	11	8	20	35	.216	L	L	6-4	230	8-14-77	1999	Houston, Texas
Callaway, Mickey	2	0	0.00	2	2	0	0	12	3	0	0	4	9	.086	R	R	6-2	200	5-13-75	1996	Memphis, Tenn.
Dickey, RA	1	1	1.98	4	4	0	0	14	16	5	3	1	9	.286	R	R	6-3	205	10-29-74	1997	Nashville, Tenn.
Dittfurth, Ryan	0	0	12.60	3	0	0	0	5	8	7	7	6	4	.364	R	R	6-1	199	10-18-79	1998	McKinney, Texas
Dominguez, Juan	0	0	1.08	3	2	0	0	8	4	1	1	1	11	.143	R	R	6-2	180	5-18-80	2000	Valverde Mao, D.R.
Francisco, Frank	1	3	2.55	15	0	0	0	6	18	7	6	5	10	.119	R	R	6-2	180	9-11-79	1998	Santo Domingo, D.R.
Gardner, Hayden	1	0	9.00	9	0	0	0	13	14	14	13	12	8	.292	R	R	6-2	200	10-7-80	2000	Stafford, Va.
Hogan, Gary	0	0	0.00	2	0	0	0	4	1	0	0	3	3	.077	R	R	6-4	200	6-20-81	2002	North Little Rock, Ark.
Hudgins, John	5	3	3.13	12	12	0	0	69	57	29	24	18	64	.226	R	R	6-2	195	8-31-81	2003	Mission Viejo, Calif.
Hughes, Travis	3	6	3.73	40	0	0	7	63	63	34	26	33	66	.255	R	R	6-5	224	5-25-78	1998	Beaver City, Neb.
Jimenez, Kelvin	3	5	4.53	26	21	0	0	129	135	76	65	67	101	.267	R	R	6-0	178	10-27-80	2000	Santo Domingo, D.R.
Keller, Kris	1	0	7.79	14	0	0	1	17	25	15	15	4	13	.338	R	R	6-2	260	3-1-78	1996	Atlantic Beach, Fla.
Kozlowski, Ben	3	2	4.89	8	7	0	1	39	38	25	21	20	23	.270	L	L	6-6	220	8-16-80	1999	Seminole, Fla.
Loe, Kameron	7	7	3.10	19	19	0	0	113	122	42	39	29	97	.280	R	R	6-7	231	9-10-81	2002	Chatsworth, Calif.
Marcano, Luis	2	2	5.46	18	0	0	0	30	33	19	18	17	14	.284	R	R	6-0	170	1-12-81	1998	Cumana, Venez.
Masset, Nick	1	0	1.80	2	1	0	0	10	8	2	2	4	8	.242	R	R	6-4	190	5-17-82	2001	Largo, Fla.
Moreno, Edwin	5	6	6.04	18	13	0	0	70	90	51	47	18	37	.315	R	R	6-1	200	5-25-78	1998	El Mojan, Venez.
Narron, Sam	6	0	2.36	13	8	0	0	53	56	23	14	10	27	.264	L	L	6-5	213	7-12-81	2002	Goldsboro, N.C.
Nelson, Jeff	0	0	2.45	3	3	0	0	4	2	1	1	1	3	.154	R	R	6-8	225	11-17-66	1984	Issaquah, Wash.
Park, Chan Ho	0	2	8.74	2	2	0	0	11	16	11	11	5	5	.315	R	R	6-2	200	7-30-73	1994	Arlington, Texas
Rowe, Steven	8	2	3.59	54	0	0	3	83	63	38	33	34	72	.207	R	R	6-3	216	7-17-80	2002	Lubbock, Texas
Rupe, Josh	2	2	4.38	7	6	0	0	37	41	23	18	16	16	.277	R	R	6-2	198	8-18-82	2002	Chesapeake, Va.
Stamler, Keith	0	0	0.00	4	0	0	0	9	4	0	0	2	7	.138	R	R	5-11	190	10-20-79	2002	Stockholm, N.J.
Sylvester, Billy	4	1	2.34	30	0	0	12	42	21	14	11	22	62	.144	R	R	6-5	210	10-1-76	1997	Florence, S.C.
Thompson, Erik	6	6	2.98	15	15	1	0	91	78	35	30	14	65	.229	R	R	5-9	197	6-23-82	2002	Pensacola, Fla.
Thompson, Justin	3	2	2.61	23	0	0	0	38	35	19	11	11	26	.250	L	L	6-4	210	3-8-73	1991	Spring, Texas
Young, Chris	6	5	4.48	18	18	0	0	88	94	44	44	31	75	.269	R	R	6-10	260	5-25-79	2001	Dallas, Texas

FIELDING

Catcher	PCT	G	PO	A	E	DP	PB
Esposito	.986	30	197	20	3	2	6
McKinley	.970	21	89	8	3	0	3
Mosquera	.988	24	149	21	2	3	2
D. Smith	.989	16	84	4	1	0	2
J. Smith	.992	64	481	38	4	4	4
Waldron	1.000	6	43	3	0	0	0

First Base	PCT	G	PO	A	E	DP
Beinbrink	.984	17	117	10	2	5
Botts	.984	127	1105	46	19	94
Perry	1.000	1	7	0	0	2
J. Smith	1.000	1	1	0	0	1
Teixeira	1.000	1	9	0	0	0

Second Base	PCT	G	PO	A	E	DP
Bourgeois	.975	135	211	386	15	70
Gonzalez	1.000	8	9	15	0	4
Meyer	1.000	1	2	4	0	0
Raymundo	1.000	3	4	5	0	0

Third Base	PCT	G	PO	A	E	DP
Beinbrink	.914	27	15	38	5	4
Gonzalez	.936	87	63	155	15	8

	PCT	G	PO	A	E	DP
McDougall	.941	6	5	11	1	2
McKinley	.900	8	3	6	1	0
Meyer	1.000	1	1	5	0	0
Perez	.940	18	11	36	3	1
Raymundo	.968	13	6	24	1	1

Shortstop	PCT	G	PO	A	E	DP
Bourgeois	.833	3	2	3	1	1
Kinsler	.938	71	110	192	20	38
McDougall	1.000	10	11	29	0	8
Meyer	.926	55	62	113	14	24
Perez	.862	7	8	17	4	4

Outfield	PCT	G	PO	A	E	DP
Asadoorian	.984	81	174	6	3	1
Boyd	.992	81	118	2	1	0

	PCT	G	PO	A	E	DP
Clark	.889	12	8	0	1	0
Curry	.986	55	138	1	2	0
Eldridge	.980	97	146	2	3	0
Gonzalez	1.000	5	2	0	0	0
Jordan	1.000	4	4	0	0	0
McKinley	.941	10	16	0	1	0
Meadows	1.000	47	77	6	0	1
Mench	1.000	2	3	0	0	0
Meyer	1.000	3	2	1	0	0
Nix	1.000	7	12	0	0	0
Perez	1.000	3	7	0	0	0
Senreiso	1.000	9	18	1	0	0
W. Smith	.979	86	137	4	3	0

STOCKTON PORTS — High Class A

CALIFORNIA LEAGUE

BATTING

	AVG	G	AB	R	H	2B	3B	HR	RBI	BB	SO	SB	CS	OBP	SLG	B	T	HT	WT	DOB	1st Yr	Resides
Arias, Joaquin	.300	123	500	77	150	20	8	4	62	31	53	30	14	.344	.396	R	R	6-0	155	9-21-84	2002	Santo Domingo, D.R.
Boyd, Patrick	.213	48	183	31	39	9	1	3	30	18	56	6	1	.301	.322	S	R	6-3	212	9-7-78	2002	Palm Harbor, Fla.
Cleveland, Jeremy	.277	129	487	72	135	32	5	8	70	53	110	11	2	.354	.413	R	R	6-1	187	9-10-81	2003	Fairfax Station, Va.
Coughlan, Cameron	.253	127	455	71	115	9	5	1	38	69	107	35	10	.361	.301	S	R	5-11	181	8-12-81	2002	Malibu, Calif.
Esposito, Brian	.256	22	78	10	20	2	1	5	13	6	17	1	0	.310	.500	R	R	6-1	190	2-24-79	2000	Willington, Conn.
Fox, Adam	.240	131	483	64	116	24	4	15	77	60	106	4	3	.329	.400	R	R	5-9	195	11-23-81	2003	St. Mary`s, Pa.
Gold, Nate	.242	135	500	85	121	32	2	20	94	65	140	5	0	.337	.434	R	R	6-3	221	6-12-80	2002	Centerville, Utah
Hamblen, Chris	.244	13	41	1	10	3	0	0	5	3	13	0	0	.311	.317	S	R	6-1	190	2-17-80	2002	Ft. Thomas, Ky.
Hoffpauir, Joshua	.264	47	178	18	47	10	0	0	24	14	13	8	3	.318	.320	L	R	5-10	175	9-21-77	2000	Vidalia, La.
Jaile, Chris	.234	54	171	26	40	8	1	3	21	29	39	1	1	.353	.345	R	R	6-3	208	2-20-81	1999	Miami, Fla.
Margalski, Ben	.192	38	125	19	24	5	3	2	15	18	50	0	2	.294	.328	L	R	6-2	210	9-2-79	2001	High Ridge, Mo.
Ringe, Craig	.231	104	338	54	78	21	3	3	41	51	99	5	2	.341	.337	R	R	5-9	196	3-16-80	2002	Warrensburg, Mo.
Sandoval, Abigail	.222	20	72	6	16	3	1	0	11	6	14	0	2	.305	.292	R	R	5-11	160	1-23-82	2001	Bolivar, Venez.
Senreiso, Juan	.296	56	233	36	69	12	2	6	32	15	47	12	5	.344	.442	R	R	6-0	203	8-4-81	2000	Guaymate, D.R.
Shelley, Randall	.170	13	47	4	8	5	0	1	6	4	8	0	0	.231	.340	R	R	6-4	200	1-12-80	2001	Trabuco Canyon, Calif.
Sinisi, Vince	.310	63	248	39	77	13	3	7	40	33	45	7	3	.383	.472	L	L	6-0	203	11-7-81	2003	The Woodlands, Texas
Smith, Dustin	.330	62	209	29	69	15	1	6	21	18	31	1	2	.407	.498	R	R	6-1	215	5-8-81	2001	Girard, Kan.
Swope, Tobin	.333	3	9	2	3	0	0	0	1	1	2	0	0	.455	.333	R	R	5-10	197	1-15-81	2003	Dallas, Texas
Taylor, Seth	.231	7	26	1	6	2	0	0	3	0	9	0	0	.259	.308	R	R	6-1	180	8-23-77	1999	Louisville, Miss.
Webster, Anthony	.287	99	380	66	109	20	7	8	44	39	69	20	4	.363	.439	L	R	6-0	204	4-10-83	2001	Parsons, Tenn.

PITCHING

	W	L	ERA	G	GS	CG	SV	IP	H	R	ER	BB	SO	AVG	B	T	HT	WT	DOB	1st Yr	Resides
Akens, Phil	4	0	3.79	18	1	0	0	38	42	21	16	16	37	.282	R	R	6-6	200	8-9-82	2000	Bel Air, Md.
Andrew, Jason	5	2	1.59	8	5	0	0	34	25	10	6	7	20	.200	R	R	6-1	160	1-29-80	2002	Tacoma, Wash.
Beltre, Omar	4	5	2.45	46	0	0	6	59	60	32	16	24	47	.262	R	R	6-1	218	8-24-81	2000	Santo Domingo, D.R.
Bengochea, Kiki	1	5	7.55	19	5	0	0	48	63	45	40	19	39	.320	R	R	6-2	190	12-4-80	2002	Miami, Fla.
Danks, John	1	4	5.24	13	13	0	0	55	62	38	32	26	48	.290	L	L	6-1	190	4-15-85	2003	Round Rock, Texas
De los Santos, Francisco	1	0	0.00	3	0	0	0	6	2	0	0	8	4	.100	R	R	6-1	170	2-19-81	1998	Las Matas de Farfan, D.R.
Dittfurth, Ryan	0	1	24.55	6	1	0	0	7	13	21	20	15	9	.382	R	R	6-1	199	10-18-79	1998	McKinney, Texas
Garcia, Jose	4	7	7.00	22	12	0	0	72	104	64	56	26	51	.339	R	R	6-1	160	6-2-81	2000	Barcelona, Venez.
Gardner, Hayden	1	0	4.50	7	0	0	0	10	13	9	5	7	6	.310	R	R	6-2	200	10-7-80	2000	Stafford, Va.
Hill, Seth	0	0	4.80	19	0	0	1	30	29	17	16	8	14	.250	L	L	6-4	230	5-6-81	2003	Sandwich, Ill.
Hogan, Gary	1	3	4.41	27	2	0	1	67	66	37	33	28	37	.261	R	R	6-4	200	6-20-81	2000	North Little Rock, Ark.
Holubec, Ken	3	2	3.76	29	0	0	1	38	33	20	16	7	47	.224	L	L	6-0	220	9-1-78	2000	Houma, La.
Hudgins, John	3	1	2.35	15	11	0	2	65	49	19	17	18	73	.201	R	R	6-2	195	8-31-81	2003	Mission Viejo, Calif.
Jaile, Chris	0	0	0.00	1	0	0	0	1	0	0	0	1	2	.000	R	R	6-3	208	2-20-81	1999	Miami, Fla.
Keiter, Ben	3	6	6.80	12	8	0	0	45	52	37	34	26	38	.301	R	R	6-3	215	4-23-80	2001	Arvada, Colo.
Kirsten, Joel	0	0	7.36	5	3	0	0	15	23	16	12	4	10	.338	L	L	6-1	180	5-9-82	2003	Reseda, Calif.
Kozlowski, Ben	4	2	3.83	10	8	0	0	47	40	23	20	19	32	.234	L	L	6-6	220	8-16-80	1999	Seminole, Fla.
Littleton, Wes	8	10	4.15	30	23	0	0	141	139	76	65	56	72	.263	R	R	6-1	198	9-2-82	2003	Oceanside, Calif.
Lorenzo, Matt	1	3	4.60	9	8	0	1	43	42	27	22	11	39	.253	L	R	6-3	200	6-21-82	2003	Hartville, Ohio
Marcano, Luis	3	0	3.73	34	0	0	5	41	41	19	17	17	26	.266	R	R	6-0	170	1-12-81	1998	Cumana, Venez.
Masset, Nick	6	5	3.51	16	11	0	0	77	71	38	30	19	43	.241	R	R	6-4	190	5-17-82	2001	Largo, Fla.
Mazurek, David	8	2	3.07	54	0	0	8	70	58	25	24	27	59	.221	R	R	6-4	225	7-20-83	2003	Indian Head Park, Ill.
Perez, Roberto	0	0	7.20	2	1	0	0	5	3	4	4	6	3	.167	R	R	6-2	175	9-27-83	2002	Sabana Pulenque, D.R.
Rupe, Josh	2	0	0.98	4	3	0	0	18	12	4	2	4	14	.182	R	R	6-2	198	8-18-82	2002	Chesapeake, Va.
Russ, Chris	1	3	4.29	28	0	0	3	36	40	21	17	21	29	.253	L	L	6-3	188	9-26-79	2000	Laurel, Md.
Smith, Cody	4	6	3.91	32	17	1	2	124	161	61	54	31	60	.319	R	R	6-2	209	4-20-82	2003	Santa Maria, Calif.
Volquez, Edison	4	1	2.95	8	8	0	0	40	31	16	13	14	34	.214	R	R	6-0	190	7-3-83	2002	La Segunua, D.R.

FIELDING

Catcher	PCT	G	PO	A	E	DP	PB
Esposito	.992	19	103	20	1	0	4
Hamblen	.931	11	62	5	5	3	0
Jaile	.981	46	279	30	6	4	16
Margalski	.985	28	173	20	3	1	7
Smith	.985	48	307	31	5	0	7

First Base	PCT	G	PO	A	E	DP
Cleveland	1.000	1	4	1	0	1
Gold	.990	135	1222	102	13	109
Margalski	1.000	3	24	6	0	4
Sandoval	1.000	1	6	2	0	1
Shelley	1.000	1	8	0	0	2

Second Base	PCT	G	PO	A	E	DP
Coughlan	.949	16	40	35	4	8
Fox	1.000	15	24	46	0	7
Hoffpauir	.948	33	71	94	9	21
Ringe	.963	60	112	204	12	48
Sandoval	.979	19	36	58	2	7
Taylor	1.000	4	3	7	0	2
Ringe	.951	25	36	81	6	12
Swope	1.000	2	3	1	0	1
Taylor	1.000	2	3	13	0	4

Third Base	PCT	G	PO	A	E	DP
Fox	.929	113	69	220	22	15
Ringe	.894	17	12	30	5	2
Shelley	.933	12	13	29	3	0

Shortstop	PCT	G	PO	A	E	DP
Arias	.928	114	163	349	40	73

Outfield	PCT	G	PO	A	E	DP
Boyd	.968	44	89	2	3	1
Cleveland	.963	119	223	11	9	1
Coughlan	.984	68	116	8	2	1
Hoffpauir	1.000	5	6	0	0	0
Margalski	.000	1	0	0	1	0
Senreiso	.929	49	127	4	10	1
Sinisi	.981	56	101	5	2	0
Smith	1.000	2	2	0	0	0
Webster	.946	83	156	2	9	0

MIDWEST LEAGUE

BATTING

BATTING	AVG	G	AB	R	H	2B	3B	HR	RBI	BB	SO	SB	CS	OBP	SLG	B	T	HT	WT	DOB	1st Yr	Resides
Altman, Kevin	.000	1	4	1	0	0	0	0	0	1	2	0	0	.200	.000	R	R	6-2	170	12-24-84	2003	Riverside, Calif.
Benjamin, Casey	.192	57	151	20	29	6	1	0	11	27	45	1	3	.317	.245	R	R	6-2	190	8-1-80	2003	Cookeville, Tenn.
Bourassa, Adam	.290	57	217	37	63	6	1	0	21	33	27	14	4	.386	.327	L	L	5-8	165	3-31-81	2003	Apple Valley, Minn.
Bubela, Dane	.251	108	383	53	96	22	5	4	40	48	130	6	2	.343	.366	L	R	5-10	190	5-31-80	2003	Houston, Texas
Cashman, Brandon	.215	50	181	24	39	3	3	4	22	16	60	7	5	.289	.331	R	R	5-10	205	10-31-79	2003	Eagan, Minn.
Clark, Cody	.229	55	179	28	41	6	1	2	19	24	52	1	0	.332	.307	R	R	6-2	170	9-14-81	2003	Fayetteville, Ark.
Fransz, Jason	.278	42	162	16	45	12	0	5	25	11	42	3	2	.341	.444	R	R	6-3	210	2-5-81	2002	Corona, Calif.
Frostad, Emerson	.216	114	370	45	80	17	2	6	42	44	97	2	3	.308	.322	L	R	6-1	210	1-13-83	2004	Calgary, Alberta
Furtado, Micah	.303	84	300	56	91	17	3	4	35	46	69	17	12	.416	.420	L	R	5-7	170	6-9-82	2003	Kapaa, Hawaii
Grayson, Larry	.253	102	340	56	86	28	2	9	39	27	87	6	2	.313	.426	R	R	5-10	180	7-28-82	2002	Orlando, Fla.
Hatcher, Justin	.289	69	190	29	55	12	1	3	29	27	46	2	5	.388	.411	R	R	5-10	200	5-12-80	2003	Fort Worth, Texas
Jacobsen, Brock	.115	21	52	13	6	1	1	0	3	5	23	2	0	.207	.173	S	R	6-2	195	12-31-79	2003	Santa Clara, Utah
Kinsler, Ian	.401	60	227	52	91	30	1	11	53	26	37	16	6	.465	.687	R	R	6-0	175	6-22-82	2003	Tucson, Ariz.
Kreuzer, Josh	.265	105	362	46	96	34	3	10	65	53	87	2	0	.370	.459	R	R	6-6	240	9-28-82	2002	San Jose, Calif.
Pena, Antonio	.136	7	22	1	3	0	0	1	6	3	1	0	.333	.136	R	R	6-3	230	9-12-80	2002	Monti Cristi, D.R.
Richardson, Kevin	.221	102	349	50	77	19	0	13	55	33	124	1	1	.307	.387	R	R	6-3	230	9-12-80	2002	Bellingham, Wash.
Sandoval, Abigail	.231	99	351	46	81	16	2	3	33	34	87	8	6	.299	.313	R	R	5-11	160	1-23-82	2001	Bolivar, Venez.
Senreiso, Juan	.315	33	127	20	40	10	2	2	23	16	31	12	6	.390	.472	R	R	6-0	203	8-4-81	2000	Guaymate, D.R.
Swope, Tobin	.169	26	77	10	13	5	0	0	5	12	18	3	0	.298	.234	R	R	5-10	197	1-15-81	2003	Dallas, Texas
Wishy, Andrew	.256	124	422	58	108	22	0	14	70	63	114	13	6	.357	.408	L	R	6-3	210	9-27-82	2003	Kansas City, Mo.

PITCHING

PITCHING	W	L	ERA	G	GS	CG	SV	IP	H	R	ER	BB	SO	AVG	B	T	HT	WT	DOB	1st Yr	Resides
Adames, Emilio	0	1	6.75	1	1	0	0	4	6	3	3	1	3	.333	R	R	6-2	185	5-2-84	2003	San Pedro de Macoris, D.R.
Altman, Kevin	0	0	0.00	2	0	0	0	3	3	0	0	1	0	.231	R	R	6-2	170	12-24-84	2003	Riverside, Calif.
Bannister, John	0	0	1.80	1	1	0	0	5	5	1	1	1	5	.278	R	R	6-3	180	1-20-84	2003	Tucson, Ariz.
Benjamin, Casey	0	0	2.70	3	0	0	0	3	4	1	1	0	5	.286	R	R	6-2	190	8-1-80	2003	Cookeville, Tenn.
Bowman, Bobby	0	0	27.00	1	0	0	0	1	5	3	3	1	0	.625	R	R	6-6	220	8-16-80	2003	Pell City, Ala.
Cashman, Brandon	1	0	1.00	2	1	0	0	9	2	1	1	2	15	.067	R	R	5-10	205	10-31-79	2003	Eagan, Minn.
Chavez, Jesse	6	10	4.68	27	22	0	0	123	149	75	64	35	96	.303	R	R	6-2	153	8-21-83	2003	Riverside, Calif.
Cordeiro, Chris	5	4	3.14	29	0	0	6	57	59	24	20	12	33	.274	R	R	6-3	175	4-3-82	2003	Thousand Oaks, Calif.
Cunningham, Tim	0	5	7.00	26	6	0	0	45	44	43	35	49	27	.254	L	L	6-2	185	10-19-80	2003	Rocklin, Calif.
Danks, John	3	2	2.17	14	8	0	0	50	38	17	12	14	64	.202	L	L	6-1	190	4-15-85	2003	Round Rock, Texas
Diamond, Thomas	1	0	2.05	7	7	0	0	31	18	8	7	8	42	.167	R	R	6-3	230	4-6-83	2004	Kenner, La.
Farnum, Matt	8	8	4.45	28	23	0	2	131	142	70	65	42	101	.280	R	R	6-2	195	6-1-81	2003	Littleton, Colo.
Frydendall, Craig	6	3	4.74	37	0	0	0	63	66	36	33	25	51	.275	L	L	6-4	190	5-25-82	2002	Elkhart, Kan.
Garcia, Jose	2	2	2.89	9	9	0	0	47	37	19	15	13	40	.214	R	R	6-3	220	4-29-78	1996	Las Vegas, Nev.
Herrera, Cesar	8	3	3.65	44	3	0	6	86	89	40	35	26	63	.269	R	R	6-0	170	6-5-81	1999	La Romana, D.R.
Hogan, Gary	1	1	0.97	14	1	0	3	37	36	12	4	7	27	.259	R	R	6-4	200	2-14-82	2002	North Little Rock, Ark.
Ingram, Jesse	0	0	0.00	1	0	0	1	2	0	0	0	0	4	.000	R	R	6-1	200	4-27-82	2004	Lafayette, La.
Kirsten, Joel	7	1	2.35	38	3	0	5	77	66	23	20	23	65	.237	L	L	6-1	180	5-9-81	2002	Reseda, Calif.
Lorenzo, Matt	3	7	4.06	17	13	0	0	71	65	35	32	22	90	.239	L	R	6-3	200	6-21-82	2003	Hartville, Ohio
Mattoon, Brian	11	6	2.87	32	20	1	1	132	137	58	42	17	88	.272	L	L	6-3	210	9-15-80	2003	Liverpool, N.Y.
Sarmiento, Williams	1	3	4.55	8	5	0	0	30	31	16	15	7	24	.272	R	R	6-2	190	10-15-83	2002	Estado Carabobo, Venez.
Seely, Nick	0	0	0.00	6	0	0	0	7	8	0	0	3	8	.258	L	R	6-0	200	2-4-81	2004	Eureka, Calif.
Smiley, Gerald	0	0	3.18	6	0	0	2	11	7	4	4	2	12	.179	R	R	6-0	200	10-1-82	2001	Seattle, Wash.
Volquez, Edison	4	4	4.05	22	16	0	3	91	83	49	41	30	77	.241	R	R	6-0	190	7-3-83	2002	La Segunua, D.R.
Watts, Joldy	8	4	4.77	40	0	0	2	83	88	50	44	28	75	.269	R	R	6-2	190	6-12-82	2002	St. Anthony, Idaho

FIELDING

Catcher	PCT	G	PO	A	E	DP	PB
Benjamin	1.000	1	3	0	0	0	0
Clark	.995	49	350	41	2	1	6
Hatcher	.997	46	292	28	1	1	4
Richardson	.993	57	360	38	3	1	6

First Base	PCT	G	PO	A	E	DP
Benjamin	.981	12	46	7	1	5
Clark	1.000	3	17	1	0	2
Fransz	.968	7	57	4	2	3
Jacobsen	.984	16	118	5	2	12
Kreuzer	.984	81	708	29	12	53
Richardson	.984	35	276	23	5	27
Sandoval	1.000	4	5	1	0	4

Second Base	PCT	G	PO	A	E	DP
Benjamin	.966	9	8	20	1	3

	PCT	G	PO	A	E	DP
Furtado	.955	82	140	262	19	60
Garcia	1.000	3	2	2	0	0
Sandoval	.984	28	47	75	2	13
Swope	.962	21	19	57	3	5

Third Base	PCT	G	PO	A	E	DP
Benjamin	.818	18	11	16	6	1
Frostad	.915	113	71	177	23	17
Jacobsen	1.000	1	1	0	0	0
Sandoval	.938	12	6	24	2	1
Swope	1.000	5	5	10	0	1

Shortstop	PCT	G	PO	A	E	DP
Benjamin	.973	18	26	47	2	11
Frostad	1.000	1	1	0	0	0
Kinsler	.952	60	80	178	13	34

	PCT	G	PO	A	E	DP
Pena	1.000	7	15	21	0	5
Sandoval	.948	59	98	173	15	38

Outfield	PCT	G	PO	A	E	DP
Altman	1.000	1	2	0	0	0
Benjamin	1.000	6	1	0	0	0
Bourassa	.986	57	130	6	2	1
Bubela	.965	99	157	10	6	2
Cashman	.966	46	110	2	4	0
Cordeiro	1.000	8	13	0	0	0
Fransz	1.000	5	9	1	0	0
Grayson	.970	103	154	8	5	3
Hatcher	1.000	4	5	1	0	0
Jacobsen	1.000	4	5	0	0	0
Senreiso	.946	33	52	1	3	0
Wishy	.960	83	93	2	4	0

NORTHWEST LEAGUE

BATTING

BATTING	AVG	G	AB	R	H	2B	3B	HR	RBI	BB	SO	SB	CS	OBP	SLG	B	T	HT	WT	DOB	1st Yr	Resides
Alexander, Chris	.253	41	146	9	37	4	0	1	17	12	36	0	0	.317	.301	R	R	6-4	223	9-17-80	2003	Albuquerque, N.M.
Baez, Lizahio	.262	22	84	8	22	2	0	4	10	8	18	0	0	.323	.429	S	R	6-2	190	11-2-83	2001	San Cristobal, D.R.
Baldwin, Ryan	.189	19	53	6	10	0	0	1	6	4	15	0	0	.259	.245	R	R	5-9	180	11-23-80	2003	Tulsa, Okla.
Boggs, Brandon	.235	45	149	27	35	11	0	3	19	29	43	6	2	.373	.369	B	R	5-11	190	1-9-83	2004	Marietta, Ga.
Cashman, Brandon	.278	21	79	20	22	5	3	7	18	11	23	4	0	.400	.684	R	R	5-10	205	10-31-79	2003	Eagan, Minn.
Fasano, Jim	.266	69	274	30	73	21	0	8	45	24	65	0	1	.327	.431	L	R	6-5	240	7-20-83	2004	Horsham, Pa.
Guerra, Alex	.000	6	16	1	0	0	0	0	2	3	8	0	0	.158	.000	S	R	6-0	170	11-22-83	2000	Maturin Monagas, Venez.
Harrison, Ben	.271	55	214	41	58	11	0	11	33	22	64	2	0	.358	.477	R	R	6-4	203	9-18-81	2004	Key West, Fla.
Hulett, Tug	.279	70	247	54	69	17	0	0	23	66	67	19	7	.444	.348	L	R	5-10	185	2-28-83	2004	Shreveport, La.

BATTING	AVG	G	AB	R	H	2B	3B	HR	RBI	BB	SO	SB	CS	OBP	SLG	B	T	HT	WT	DOB	1st Yr	Resides
Jacobsen, Brock	.226	10	31	4	7	3	0	0	1	1	16	1	0	.250	.323	S	R	6-2	210	12-31-79	2001	Santa Clara, Utah
Lenoir, Bobby	.224	63	223	38	50	9	2	1	26	22	59	10	3	.307	.296	R	R	6-1	185	7-12-82	2004	Wilmington, Del.
Mahar, Kevin	.316	38	152	26	48	9	1	6	22	12	38	5	0	.379	.493	R	R	6-5	215	6-8-81	2004	Midland, Mich.
Mask, Michael	.252	47	159	26	40	9	1	3	22	27	38	2	4	.354	.377	L	L	5-9	180	6-24-81	2004	Sarasota, Fla.
Metcalf, Travis	.266	72	290	48	77	21	1	15	62	37	74	1	2	.348	.500	R	R	6-3	200	8-17-82	2004	Lawrence, Kan.
Nickeas, Mike	.288	61	233	42	67	18	0	10	55	33	53	2	0	.384	.494	R	R	6-0	205	2-13-83	2004	Westlake Village, Calif.
Sanchez, Angel	.200	3	10	2	2	0	0		1	1	3	0	0	.385	.400	R	R	5-11	190	1-14-85	2004	West Covina, Calif.
Susdorf, Billy	.211	58	199	31	42	7	0	4	22	37	48	9	2	.344	.307	R	R	6-1	215	5-7-83	2004	Newhall, Calif.
Swope, Tobin	.158	26	76	14	12	4	0	1	5	14	20	4	0	.304	.250	R	R	5-10	197	1-15-81	2003	Dallas, Texas

GAMES BY POSITION: C—Baez 5, Baldwin 18, Nickeas 54, Sanchez 3. **1B**—Alexander 16, Fasano 60. **2B**—Guerra 5, Hulett 66, Lenoir 8, Swope 3. **3B**—Guerra 1, Hulett 4, Metcalf 71, Swope 2. **SS**—Hulett 1, Lenoir 57, Swope 21. **OF**—Boggs 41, Cashman 19, Harrison 43, Jacobsen 7, Mahar 31, Mask 39, Susdorf 54.

PITCHING	W	L	ERA	G	GS	CG	SV	IP	H	R	ER	BB	SO	AVG	B	T	HT	WT	DOB	1st Yr	Resides
Altman, Kevin	1	4	6.42	18	9	0	0	48	68	50	34	19	29	.349	R	R	6-2	170	12-24-84	2003	Riverside, Calif.
Bannister, John	2	2	3.51	16	7	0	0	59	49	29	23	28	67	.223	R	R	6-3	180	1-20-84	2003	Tucson, Ariz.
Brannon, Clint	3	2	0.59	15	10	0	1	61	35	9	4	14	58	.164	S	L	5-11	205	12-24-82	2004	Bradford, Ark.
Burcie, Jarrad	3	0	1.74	23	0	0	8	31	23	7	6	5	40	.198	R	R	6-1	215	5-17-82	2004	Haltom, Texas
Cockroft, JD	1	6	4.01	16	5	0	0	43	49	29	19	15	27	.278	L	L	6-2	205	7-11-82	2004	Coral Gables, Fla.
Diamond, Thomas	0	2	2.35	5	3	0	1	15	13	5	4	5	26	.228	R	R	6-3	230	4-6-83	2004	Kenner, La.
Espinal, Willy	1	0	4.30	22	0	0	1	44	47	26	21	16	29	.273	R	R	6-0	178	12-9-82	2004	Villa Mella, D.R.
Figuereo, Victor	0	1	7.88	5	0	0	0	8	10	9	7	7	8	.303	R	R	5-10	186	12-24-84	2000	Las Matas de Farfan, D.R.
Herrera, Marcos	6	1	2.12	23	0	0	0	47	37	13	11	11	33	.214	R	R	6-5	197	2-24-82	2000	Santo Domingo, D.R.
Hurley, Eric	0	2	5.40	8	6	0	0	28	31	18	17	6	21	.279	R	R	6-4	195	9-17-85	2004	Jacksonville, Fla.
Ingram, Jesse	4	1	1.42	22	0	0	4	32	19	7	5	16	45	.167	R	R	6-1	200	4-27-82	2004	Lafayette, Calif.
Jerome, Clayton	3	3	6.85	19	4	0	0	47	74	48	36	15	32	.352	R	R	6-2	190	2-15-82	2004	Mesquite, Texas
Lensch, Justin	3	5	5.01	19	9	0	1	59	72	41	33	24	30	.299	L	L	6-2	190	2-10-82	2004	Phoenix, Ariz.
Lujan, John	1	0	2.20	4	3	0	0	16	17	4	4	9	17	.270	R	R	6-1	200	5-10-84	2004	Waco, Texas
Phillips, Shawn	6	1	3.93	18	10	0	0	71	69	33	31	8	53	.252	R	R	6-2	195	12-19-82	2004	Laurel, Del.
Roberts, Mark	4	5	3.54	12	7	0	0	48	42	22	19	14	54	.237	R	R	5-11	190	6-24-82	2004	Sperry, Okla.
Rupe, Josh	2	0	1.50	4	3	0	0	18	14	3	3	3	19	.209	R	R	6-2	198	8-18-82	2002	Chesapeake, Va.
Walker, Andy	1	0	5.93	7	0	0	1	14	14	9	9	6	11	.264	R	R	6-1	176	4-23-83	2004	Sparks, Okla.

AZL RANGERS   Rookie

ARIZONA LEAGUE

BATTING	AVG	G	AB	R	H	2B	3B	HR	RBI	BB	SO	SB	CS	SLG	OBP	B	T	HT	WT	DOB	1st Yr	Resides
Alvino, Hargeny	.056	6	18	2	1	0	0	0	2	5	10	0	0	.056	.261	R	R	6-2	190	8-21-81	2002	Nizao, D.R.
Backman, Wally	.172	28	93	8	16	2	2	0	10	13	38	1	3	.237	.284	L	R	6-2	200	1-7-86	2004	Prineville, Ore.
Charles, Larry	.161	8	31	2	5	0	0	1	9	6	12	0	1	.258	.297	R	R	6-1	190	12-29-83	2001	La Romana, D.R.
Gac, Ian	.235	40	153	19	36	8	1	5	31	13	59	2	0	.399	.292	R	R	6-3	210	8-10-85	2003	Seattle, Wash.
Gomez, Mauro	.246	34	126	12	31	9	2	1	16	10	33	0	2	.373	.301	R	R	6-2	190	9-7-84	2003	Bani, D.R.
Guzman, Juan	.091	3	11	0	1	0	0	0	1	1	8	2	0	.091	.167	S	R	6-3	190	5-17-84	2003	Caracas, Venez.
Herren, K.C.	.297	46	185	32	55	13	2	0	21	24	54	7	6	.389	.381	L	R	6-0	210	8-21-85	2004	Auburn, Wash.
Higashi, Jon	.350	13	40	7	14	3	2	1	9	3	8	0	0	.600	.422	R	R	5-11	200	7-20-82	2004	Canoga Park, Calif.
Hurba, Craig	.263	32	99	18	26	5	6	1	16	12	21	1	0	.465	.345	R	R	6-1	205	8-25-81	2004	Maryland, N.Y.
Mahar, Kevin	.280	27	100	20	28	5	1	5	18	9	28	7	1	.500	.348	R	R	6-5	215	6-8-81	2004	Midland, Mich.
Maldonado, Juan	.222	38	144	17	32	5	2	0	18	11	39	6	1	.285	.277	R	R	6-4	160	12-4-80	2001	Bajo de Haina, D.R.
Martinez, Eduardo	.206	23	63	13	13	1	1	1	5	8	23	3	3	.302	.297	R	R	6-1	160	12-9-82	2001	San Cristobal, D.R.
Meyer, Drew	.387	15	62	15	24	2	0	0	5	3	8	4	1	.419	.415	L	R	5-10	180	8-29-81	2002	Charleston, S.C.
Pena, Antonio	.268	37	142	22	38	7	3	1	13	15	26	5	3	.380	.358	R	R	5-11	160	9-16-84	2001	Monte Cristi, D.R.
Rodriguez, Luis	.252	35	127	26	32	5	1	3	15	22	26	3	1	.378	.371	R	R	5-11	175	7-12-83	2004	Arroyo, P.R.
Sanchez, Angel	.258	35	120	21	31	8	0	5	16	21	41	2	1	.450	.371	R	R	5-11	190	1-14-85	2003	West Covina, Calif.
Thon, Freddy	.291	51	203	31	59	12	1	4	36	13	23	9	3	.419	.339	L	L	6-2	215	4-9-84	2004	Guaynabo, P.R.
Torres, Jose	.220	44	132	25	29	5	1	1	7	33	45	9	2	.295	.408	R	R	5-10	197	11-20-83	2004	Corona, Calif.
Valdez, Riquelbi	.267	5	15	4	4	0	0	1	2	5		0	1	.467	.421	R	R	5-11	165	7-10-82	2001	San Cristobal, D.R.
Washington, Johnny	.219	12	32	7	7	1	0	0		8	13	2	1	.250	.375	R	R	5-11	165	5-6-84	2003	Compton, Calif.

GAMES BY POSITION: C—Higashi 11, Hurba 19, Sanchez 32. **1B**—Gac 18, Martinez 1, Thon 38. **2B**—Backman 6, Martinez 5, Meyer 2, Pena 29, Valdez 5, Washington 12. **3B**—Backman 16, Gomez 33, Martinez 6, Meyer 1. **SS**—Backman 6, Martinez 6, Meyer 7, Pena 7, Rodriguez 33, Washington 1. **OF**—Charles 8, Guzman 3, Herren 46, Hurba 1, Mahar 27, Maldonado 37, Martinez 3, Meyer 3, Torres 44.

PITCHING	W	L	ERA	G	GS	CG	SV	IP	H	R	ER	BB	SO	AVG	B	T	HT	WT	DOB	1st Yr	Resides
Adames, Emilio	4	0	5.24	16	3	0	0	46	58	36	27	9	31	.303	R	R	6-2	185	6-2-84	2003	San Pedro de Macoris, D.R.
Bowman, Bobby	0	0	5.19	8	0	0	0	9	7	8	5	4	10	.205	R	R	6-6	220	8-16-80	2003	Pell City, Ala.
Casanova, Nicholas	0	2	17.47	4	2	0	0	6	17	12	11	6	3	.548	R	R	6-2	190	8-19-85	2004	Corona, Calif.
De los Santos, Francisco	1	1	5.87	14	0	0	1	23	23	20	15	17	19	.244	R	R	6-1	170	2-19-81	2002	San Juan Maguana, D.R.
Diaz, Gener	3	1	5.40	11	0	0	0	10	9	9	6	6	8	.250	R	R	6-3	185	3-13-85	2003	Peravia, D.R.
Feldman, Scott	0	0	0.00	4	3	0	0	7	2	0	0	1	5	.090	L	R	6-5	210	2-7-83	2003	Burlington, Calif.
Fernando, Pedro	1	3	4.67	14	6	0	1	44	46	29	23	19	32	.270	R	R	6-3	170	11-23-81	2002	San Pedro de Macoris, D.R.
Foster, Ben	2	2	5.19	15	6	0	0	43	48	29	25	13	44	.277	L	L	5-11	195	4-2-82	2004	Farmington, Minn.
Hurley, Eric	0	1	2.35	8	2	0	0	15	20	8	4	4	15	.317	R	R	6-4	195	9-17-85	2004	Jacksonville, Fla.
Irvin, Tony	1	1	2.16	12	0	0	1	17	10	4	4	6	11	.185	R	R	6-5	230	12-13-82	2004	Tampa, Fla.
Jaimes, Jose	5	1	4.10	15	3	0	0	26	24	16	12	17	26	.240	R	R	6-2	180	6-28-84	2001	Los Teques, Venez.
Lujan, John	1	1	1.71	10	3	0	0	32	23	11	6	11	26	.200	R	R	6-1	200	5-10-84	2004	Waco, Texas
Melendez, Marlon	3	5	5.24	13	5	0	0	34	50	22	20	10	32	.349	R	R	6-4	233	10-15-84	2004	Fajardo, P.R.
Padgett, Michael	2	1	2.59	12	4	0	0	31	29	9	9	6	25	.245	R	R	6-4	210	5-6-82	2004	Reno, Nev.
Park, Chan Ho	1	1	1.71	4	0	0	0	21	15	6	4	6	20	.197	R	R	6-2	190	6-30-73	1994	Arlington, Texas
Perez, Roberto	4	3	3.61	14	6	0	0	57	50	24	23	17	48	.234	R	R	6-3	170	9-27-83	2001	Santiago, D.R.
Ramirez, Ivan	0	5	5.50	16	0	0	2	18	21	15	11	7	13	.291	L	L	5-9	167	7-2-82	2004	Santa Barbara, Calif.
Scheffel, Dustin	0	0	3.00	6	0	0	0	6	7	4	2	3	13	.280	R	R	6-5	200	5-6-81	2002	Cameron Park, Calif.
Schlact, Michael	1	1	3.52	10	5	0	0	31	28	18	12	9	22	.264	R	R	6-7	205	12-9-85	2004	Marietta, Ga.
Seely, Nick	3	2	3.50	15	0	0	4	18	20	8	7	4	16	.273	L	R	6-0	200	2-4-81	2004	Eureka, Calif.

BY LARRY MILLSON

The Blue Jays finally shook that third-place rut in 2004. The problem is they moved in the wrong direction.

Toronto finished last in the American League East with a 67-94 record, their highest loss total since 1980 when they were 67-95. They had finished third behind the Yankees and Red Sox from 1998 to 2003.

The Jays were 27-53 (.338) on the road, the worst winning percentage away from home since 1979 when they were 21-60 (.259). They never had a winning record on a road trip in 2004, and finished .500 on just two (3-3 each time).

The disappointing season cost manager Carlos Tosca his job. Tosca, who led the team to an 86-76 record in 2003, was fired after a loss to the Yankees in New York on Aug. 8 and replaced on an interim basis by first base coach John Gibbons. Gibbons dropped the interim tag the day after the season, after the Blue Jays went 20-30 under him. He was signed to a one-year deal.

The Blue Jays hitting took a big drop in 2004, as they finished 12th in the league in runs scored with 719. They were second in 2003 with 894. Toronto also ranked 11th in club ERA at 4.91 after being ninth at 4.69 ERA in 2003.

Injuries also were a factor, as 2003 Cy Young Award winner Roy Halladay, first baseman Carlos Delgado, center fielder Vernon Wells, outfielder Frank Catalanotto, catcher Greg Myers, relievers Justin Speier, Kerry Ligtenberg, Valerio De los Santos and Bob File, starter-reliever Justin Miller, second baseman Orlando Hudson, shortstop Chris Woodward and catcher Kevin Cash all spent time on the DL, many for a significant period.

Despite missing five weeks with a rib-cage injury, Delgado hit 32 home runs and drove in 99 in the final year of a four-year, $68 million contract. It was his eighth consecutive season with 30 or more homers and he just missed his seventh season in a row with 100 or more

RICH ABEL

Carlos Delgado | Gustavo Chacin

PLAYERS of the YEAR

MAJOR LEAGUE: Carlos Delgado, 1b

Delgado got off to a very slow start in 2004, but after a second-half surge his numbers looked much like they do every year—good. Delgado hit .305-22-63 after the All-Star break to reach 30 homers on the year for the seventh consecutive season.

MINOR LEAGUE: Gustavo Chacin, lhp

In his fourth straight season at Double-A, Chacin finally broke out, going 16-2, 2.92 in 25 starts at New Hampshire before promotions to Triple-A Syracuse and then the majors. The key to Chacin's success was the development of his cutter to complement his fastball and his changeup.

RBIs.

But even before the injuries hit, the team was playing poorly early in the season. Among the club's priorities in 2005 will be to play better in April. Toronto has had three poor Aprils in a row: 8-16 in 2002, 10-18 in 2003 and 7-15 in 2004.

"Spring training was a major concern last year and that's one of the things we addressed with the coaching staff," general manager J.P. Ricciardi said. "We need to play our kids a little longer. We're going to be more aggressive in spring training and play the last seven to 10 games like it's the start of the season."

On the positive side was the emergence of right fielder Alexis Rios, who was called up from Triple-A Syracuse on May 26. After a tentative start, Rios became a solid regular in the field and at the plate, with the promise of future power. He had 11 assists from the outfield.

Starting pitcher Dave Bush was called up from Syracuse for a July 2 start and he stayed in the rotation for the rest of the season. Shortstop Russ Adams made the most of his September callup and should be the starting shortstop in 2005. Lefthander Gustavo Chacin went 19-2 in the minor leagues and won his major league debut at Yankee Stadium.

In its first season as a Blue Jays affiliate after relocating from New Haven, Double-A New Hampshire won the Eastern League title. Chacin was the league's pitcher of the year and Mike Basso was manager of the year.

High Class A Dunedin lost in the Florida State League playoffs, but Omar Malave was the league's manager of the year. Righthander Ismael Ramirez was named the league's most valuable pitcher.

ORGANIZATION LEADERS

BATTING

*AVG	Anton French, Syracuse/New Hampshire	.319
R	Clint Johnston, Charleston	87
H	Dominic Rich, New Hampshire	143
TB	Ron Davenport, Dunedin	219
2B	Ron Davenport, Dunedin	40
3B	Justin Singleton, New Hampshire	11
HR	Glenn Williams, Syracuse	23
RBI	Ron Davenport, Dunedin	92
BB	Ryan Roberts, Dunedin/Charleston	91
SO	Justin Singleton, New Hampshire	152
SB	Tyrell Godwin, New Hampshire	42
*OBP	Howie Clark, Syracuse	.407
*SLG	Raul Tablado, Dunedin	.585

PITCHING

W	Gustavo Chacin, Syracuse/New Hampshire	18
L	Chris Baker, Syracuse/New Hampshire	12
#ERA	Mike MacDonald, Charleston/Auburn	1.71
G	Jordan DeJong, New Hampshire	57
CG	David Bush, Syracuse	2
SV	Bubbie Buzachero, Dunedin	24
IP	Ismael Ramirez, Dunedin	165
BB	Josue Matos, Syracuse	56
SO	Shaun Marcum, Dunedin/Charleston	155

*Minimum 250 at-bats #Minimum 75 innings

TORONTO BLUE JAYS

Managers: Carlos Tosca/John Gibbons.

2004 Record: 67-94, .416 (5th, AL Central).

BATTING

BATTING	AVG	G	AB	R	H	2B	3B	HR	RBI	BB	SO	SB	CS	OBP	SLG	B	T	HT	WT	DOB	1st Yr	Resides
Adams, Russ	.306	22	72	10	22	2	1	4	10	5	5	1	0	.359	.528	L	R	6-1	180	8-30-80	2002	Laurinburg, N.C.
Berg, Dave	.253	58	154	13	39	4	0	3	23	4	27	0	1	.278	.338	R	R	5-11	195	9-3-70	1993	Pembroke Pines, Fla.
Cash, Kevin	.193	60	181	18	35	9	0	4	21	10	59	0	0	.249	.309	R	R	6-0	190	12-6-77	2000	Lutz, Fla.
Catalanotto, Frank	.293	75	249	27	73	19	1	1	26	17	33	1	0	.344	.390	L	R	5-11	195	4-27-74	1992	Southlake, Texas
Clark, Howie	.217	40	115	17	25	6	0	3	12	13	15	0	0	.292	.348	L	R	5-11	185	2-13-74	1992	Lake Charles, La.
Crozier, Eric	.152	14	33	5	5	2	0	2	4	6	19	0	0	.282	.394	L	L	6-4	200	8-11-78	2000	Columbus, Ohio
Delgado, Carlos	.269	128	458	74	123	26	0	32	99	69	115	0	1	.373	.535	L	R	6-3	230	6-25-72	1989	Aguadilla, P.R.
Estalella, Bobby	.231	5	13	1	3	0	0	0	3	0	5	0	0	.412	.231	R	R	6-1	225	8-23-74	1993	Weston, Fla.
Gomez, Chris	.282	109	341	41	96	11	1	3	37	28	41	3	2	.337	.346	R	R	6-1	185	6-16-71	1992	Carlsbad, Calif.
Gross, Gabe	.209	44	129	18	27	4	0	3	16	19	31	2	2	.311	.310	L	R	6-3	210	10-21-79	2001	Dothan, Ala.
Hermansen, Chad	.000	4	7	0	0	0	0	0	0	0	3	0	0	.000	.000	R	R	6-2	190	9-10-77	1995	Las Vegas, Nev.
Hinske, Eric	.246	155	570	66	140	23	5	15	69	54	109	12	8	.312	.375	L	R	6-2	220	8-5-77	1998	Menasha, Wis.
Hudson, Orlando	.270	135	489	73	132	32	7	12	58	51	98	7	3	.341	.438	S	R	6-0	180	12-12-77	1998	Darlington, S.C.
Johnson, Reed	.270	141	537	68	145	25	2	10	61	28	98	6	3	.320	.380	R	R	5-10	180	12-8-76	1999	Temecula, Calif.
Menechino, Frank	.301	72	236	40	71	13	4	9	25	36	44	0	2	.400	.504	R	R	5-8	190	1-7-71	1993	Staten Island, N.Y.
2-team (13 Oakland)	.275	85	269	40	74	13	4	9	26	37	52	0	2	.371	.454							
Myers, Greg	.222	8	18	0	4	2	0	0	1	2	4	0	0	.300	.333	L	R	6-2	220	4-14-66	1984	Riverside, Calif.
Phelps, Josh	.237	79	295	38	70	13	2	12	51	18	73	0	0	.296	.417	R	R	6-3	220	5-12-78	1996	Rathdrum, Idaho
Pond, Simon	.163	16	49	4	8	2	0	1	6	5	12	0	0	.250	.265	L	R	6-1	205	10-27-76	1994	North Vancouver, B.C.
Quiroz, Guillermo	.212	17	52	2	11	2	0	0	6	2	8	1	0	.263	.250	R	R	6-1	210	11-29-81	1999	Maracaibo, Venez.
Rios, Alex	.286	111	426	55	122	24	7	1	28	31	84	15	3	.338	.383	R	R	6-5	195	2-18-81	1999	Guaynabo, P.R.
Wells, Vernon	.272	134	536	82	146	34	2	23	67	51	83	9	2	.337	.472	R	R	6-1	220	12-8-78	1997	Arlington, Texas
Woodward, Chris	.235	69	213	21	50	13	4	1	24	14	46	1	2	.283	.347	R	R	6-0	180	6-27-76	1995	Chino, Calif.
Zaun, Gregg	.269	107	338	46	91	24	0	6	36	47	61	0	2	.367	.393	S	R	5-10	190	4-14-71	1990	Houston, Texas

PITCHING

PITCHING	W	L	ERA	G	GS	CG	SV	IP	H	R	ER	BB	SO	AVG	B	T	HT	WT	DOB	1st Yr	Resides
Batista, Miguel	10	13	4.80	38	31	2	5	199	206	115	106	96	104	.273	R	R	6-1	195	2-19-71	1988	Weston, Fla.
Bush, Dave	5	4	3.69	16	16	1	0	98	95	47	40	25	64	.255	R	R	6-2	210	11-9-79	2002	Devon, Pa.
Chacin, Gustavo	1	1	2.57	2	2	0	0	14	8	4	4	3	6	.167	L	L	5-11	190	12-4-80	1998	Maracaibo, Venez.
Chulk, Vinnie	1	3	4.66	47	0	0	2	56	59	30	29	27	44	.271	R	R	6-2	195	12-19-78	2000	Miami, Fla.
De los Santos, Valerio	0	0	6.17	17	0	0	0	12	11	8	8	10	10	.250	L	L	6-2	218	10-6-72	1993	Santo Domingo, D.R.
Douglass, Sean	2	6	6.28	14	3	0	0	39	37	27	27	28	36	.252	R	R	6-6	218	4-28-79	1997	Lancaster, Calif.
File, Bob	1	0	4.81	24	0	0	0	34	45	19	18	12	15	.331	R	R	6-4	215	1-28-77	1998	Morrisville, Pa.
Frasor, Jason	4	6	4.08	63	0	0	17	68	64	31	31	36	54	.251	R	R	5-10	170	8-9-77	1999	Oak Forest, Ill.
Frederick, Kevin	0	2	6.59	22	0	0	0	29	32	21	21	16	22	.283	R	R	6-1	210	11-4-76	1998	Prairie View, Ill.
Glynn, Ryan	1	0	4.05	6	2	0	0	20	19	9	9	8	14	.250	R	R	6-3	200	11-1-74	1995	Grand Prairie, Texas
Halladay, Roy	8	8	4.20	21	21	1	0	133	140	66	62	39	95	.272	R	R	6-6	230	5-14-77	1995	Palm Harbor, Fla.
Hentgen, Pat	2	9	6.95	18	16	0	0	80	90	67	62	42	33	.283	R	R	6-2	195	11-13-68	1986	Tarpon Springs, Fla.
Kershner, Jason	0	1	6.04	24	2	0	0	22	30	16	15	8	15	.316	L	L	6-2	185	12-19-76	1995	Scottsdale, Ariz.
League, Brandon	1	0	0.00	3	0	0	0	5	3	0	0	1	2	.176	R	R	6-2	180	3-16-83	2001	Honolulu, Hawaii
Ligtenberg, Kerry	1	6	6.38	57	0	0	3	55	73	40	39	25	49	.313	R	R	6-2	220	5-11-71	1994	Inner Grove Heights, Minn.
Lilly, Ted	12	10	4.06	32	32	2	0	197	171	92	89	89	168	.230	L	L	6-1	190	1-4-76	1996	Oakhurst, Calif.
Lopez, Aquilino	1	1	6.00	18	0	0	0	21	21	15	14	13	13	.266	R	R	6-3	160	4-21-75	1997	Villa Altagracia, D.R.
Maurer, Dave	0	0	54.00	3	0	0	0	1	6	8	8	5	1	.600	L	L	6-2	205	2-23-75	1997	Burnsville, Minn.
Miller, Justin	3	4	6.06	19	15	0	0	82	101	58	55	42	47	.316	R	R	6-2	220	8-27-77	1997	Torrance, Calif.
Nakamura, Micheal	0	3	7.36	19	0	0	0	26	27	23	21	7	24	.262	R	R	5-10	170	9-6-76	1998	Ferntree Gully, Australia
Peterson, Adam	0	0	16.88	3	0	0	0	3	7	5	5	3	2	.467	R	R	6-3	220	5-18-79	2002	Abrams, Wis.
Speier, Justin	3	8	3.91	62	0	0	7	69	61	32	30	25	52	.239	R	R	6-4	205	11-6-73	1995	Paradise Valley, Ariz.
Towers, Josh	9	9	5.11	21	21	0	0	116	148	70	66	26	51	.310	R	R	6-1	190	2-26-77	1996	Owings Mills, Md.

FIELDING

Catcher	PCT	G	PO	A	E	DP	PB
Cash	.994	60	316	36	2	5	5
Estalella	1.000	3	20	1	0	0	0
Myers	1.000	4	27	2	0	1	0
Quiroz	.976	15	76	6	2	3	3
Zaun	.987	97	547	46	8	5	3

First Base	PCT	G	PO	A	E	DP
Berg	.959	7	44	3	2	8
Clark	1.000	11	106	6	0	8
Crozier	.972	5	33	2	1	2
Delgado	.996	120	1041	88	5	98
Gomez	.983	19	106	12	2	9
Phelps	.981	12	101	2	2	7

Second Base	PCT	G	PO	A	E	DP
Berg	1.000	4	5	9	0	1
Clark	.000	1	0	0	0	0
Gomez	1.000	3	6	2	0	2
Hudson	.984	133	275	450	12	90
Menechino	1.000	30	54	72	0	13

Third Base	PCT	G	PO	A	E	DP
Berg	.600	3	0	3	2	0
Clark	.000	1	0	0	0	0
Gomez	1.000	5	2	8	0	1
Hinske	.978	153	107	242	8	23
Menechino	1.000	7	4	14	0	2

Shortstop	PCT	G	PO	A	E	DP
Adams	.936	21	26	47	5	9

	PCT	G	PO	A	E	DP
Gomez	.969	77	108	206	10	46
Menechino	.981	14	26	26	1	9
Woodward	.981	64	87	171	5	42

Outfield	PCT	G	PO	A	E	DP
Berg	.974	31	37	1	1	0
Catalanotto	.971	41	67	1	2	1
Clark	.972	19	33	2	1	0
Gross	1.000	38	73	5	0	1
Hermansen	1.000	4	4	0	0	0
Johnson	.989	137	266	9	3	1
Pond	1.000	9	18	0	0	0
Rios	.991	111	218	11	2	4
Wells	.997	131	327	5	1	0

Director, Player Development: Dick Scott

Class	Farm Team	League	W	L	Pct.	Finish*	Manager	Affiliate Since
AAA	Syracuse (N.Y.) SkyChiefs	International	66	78	.458	t-11th (14)	Marty Pevey	1978
AA	New Hampshire Fisher Cats (Manchester)	Eastern	84	57	.596	+2nd (12)	Mike Basso	2003
High A	Dunedin (Fla.) Blue Jays	Florida State	76	57	.571	2nd (12)	Omar Malave	1987
Low A	#Charleston (W.Va.) Alley Cats	South Atlantic	84	56	.600	3rd (16)	Ken Joyce	2001
SS A	Auburn (N.Y.) Doubledays	New York-Penn	50	24	.676	1st (14)	Dennis Holmberg	2001
Rookie	Pulaski (Va.) Blue Jays	Appalachian	40	27	.597	3rd (10)	Gary Cathcart	2003

*Finish in overall standings (No. of teams in league)/Playoff teams in **boldface**   +League champion   #Affiliation will operate at Lansing (Midwest) in 2005

SYRACUSE SKYCHIEFS
Class AAA

INTERNATIONAL LEAGUE

BATTING

	AVG	G	AB	R	H	2B	3B	HR	RBI	BB	SO	SB	CS	OBP	SLG	B	T	HT	WT	DOB	1st Yr	Resides
Adams, Russ	.288	122	483	58	139	37	3	5	54	45	62	6	2	.351	.408	L	R	6-1	180	8-30-80	2002	Laurinburg, N.C.
Benard, Marvin	.211	33	123	15	26	5	2	4	18	9	21	0	1	.281	.382	L	L	5-9	190	1-20-70	1992	Richland, Wash.
Chiaffredo, Paul	.219	34	114	12	25	3	0	4	14	8	31	0	1	.270	.351	R	R	6-2	215	5-30-76	1997	Campbell, Calif.
Clapp, Stubby	.287	29	87	13	25	8	2	0	6	15	18	0	2	.410	.425	L	R	5-8	170	2-24-73	1996	Windsor, Ontario
Clark, Howie	.313	72	256	43	80	14	2	6	32	40	18	1	0	.407	.453	L	R	5-11	180	2-13-74	1992	Lake Charles, La.
Crozier, Eric	.277	25	94	12	26	8	0	1	16	16	27	3	2	.393	.394	L	L	6-4	200	8-11-78	2000	Columbus, Ohio
2-team (84 Buffalo)	.292	109	390	67	114	29	0	21	69	52	94	8	3	.380	.528							
Delgado, Carlos	.556	2	9	2	5	2	0	1	4	0	0	0	0	.556	1.111	L	R	6-3	230	6-25-72	1989	Aguadilla, P.R.
Estalella, Bobby	.250	6	24	3	6	0	0	2	3	1	6	0	0	.280	.500	R	R	6-1	225	8-23-74	1993	Weston, Fla.
Fagan, Shawn	.237	95	329	45	78	12	1	8	45	42	72	0	2	.328	.353	R	R	5-11	200	3-2-78	2000	Levittown, N.Y.
French, Anton	.349	36	149	37	52	10	2	7	23	12	33	13	6	.393	.584	L	R	5-11	170	7-25-75	1993	St. Louis, Mo.
2-team (31 Durham)	.297	67	259	56	77	12	3	11	35	26	60	28	7	.359	.494							
Gross, Gabe	.294	103	377	52	111	29	2	9	54	53	81	4	5	.381	.454	L	R	6-3	210	10-21-79	2001	Dothan, Ala.
Guiel, Jeff	.197	68	228	28	45	13	1	6	26	19	63	1	0	.264	.342	L	R	5-11	190	1-12-74	1997	Langley, B.C.
Hall, Noah	.233	58	176	28	41	3	3	2	15	25	38	4	4	.354	.318	R	R	5-11	200	7-9-77	1996	Aptos, Calif.
Hassey, Brad	.130	16	23	3	3	0	0	0	1	4	5	0	1	.259	.130	R	R	5-10	170	11-28-79	2002	Tucson, Ariz.
Hermansen, Chad	.240	42	146	18	35	9	1	6	18	16	52	0	0	.307	.438	R	R	6-2	190	9-10-77	1995	Las Vegas, Nev.
Matos, Julius	.293	73	297	49	87	18	1	7	42	15	20	1	1	.323	.431	R	R	5-11	170	12-12-74	1994	Racine, Wis.
Pond, Simon	.278	78	302	36	84	24	1	7	36	19	72	1	0	.325	.434	L	R	6-1	205	10-27-76	1994	North Vancouver, B.C.
Quiroz, Guillermo	.227	76	255	32	58	19	1	8	32	28	54	0	0	.309	.404	R	R	6-1	210	11-29-81	1999	Maracaibo, Venez.
Rios, Alex	.259	46	185	14	48	10	1	3	23	9	30	2	1	.292	.373	R	R	6-5	195	2-18-81	1999	Guaynabo, P.R.
Sanders, Anthony	.276	65	228	27	63	19	1	5	30	13	56	1	2	.320	.434	R	R	6-2	200	3-2-74	1993	Tucson, Ariz.
Sequea, Jorge	.269	97	335	53	90	16	3	4	31	35	63	10	6	.347	.370	R	R	5-10	160	10-1-80	1998	Anaco, Venez.
Solano, Danny	.200	9	25	3	5	1	0	0	3	4	6	0	0	.333	.240	R	R	5-9	150	12-3-75	1997	Santo Domingo, D.R.
Whittaker, Tim	.257	47	144	9	37	10	0	1	14	3	28	1	1	.272	.347	R	R	6-0	220	1-4-79	2001	Conway, S.C.
Williams, Glenn	.264	116	428	65	113	23	4	23	79	34	79	2	4	.324	.498	S	R	6-2	190	7-18-77	1994	Wattle Grove, Australia
Zaun, Gregg	.304	7	23	4	7	1	0	0	2	2	5	1	0	.346	.348	S	R	5-10	190	4-14-71	1990	Houston, Texas

PITCHING

	W	L	ERA	G	GS	CG	SV	IP	H	R	ER	BB	SO	AVG	B	T	HT	WT	DOB	1st Yr	Resides
Arnold, Jason	1	3	3.65	7	7	0	0	37	40	19	15	12	15	.276	R	R	6-3	210	5-2-79	2001	Palm Bay, Fla.
Baker, Chris	0	11	6.75	18	14	1	0	77	103	70	58	22	61	.322	R	R	6-1	200	8-24-77	1999	Valencia, Calif.
Bouknight, Kip	0	1	3.60	1	1	0	0	5	6	3	2	1	5	.300	R	R	6-0	190	11-16-78	2001	Gaston, S.C.
Bush, Dave	6	6	4.06	16	16	2	0	100	108	52	45	20	88	.276	R	R	6-2	210	11-9-79	2002	Devon, Pa.
Chacin, Gustavo	2	0	2.31	2	2	0	0	12	16	4	3	3	14	.327	L	L	5-11	190	12-4-80	1998	Maracaibo, Venez.
Chen, Bruce	0	1	8.71	3	3	0	0	10	17	12	10	5	8	.354	L	L	6-2	195	6-19-77	1994	Panama City, Panama
Chulk, Vinnie	4	2	2.83	18	0	0	3	29	27	13	9	11	26	.252	R	R	6-2	195	12-19-78	2000	Miami, Fla.
Douglass, Sean	5	6	4.75	18	18	1	0	89	92	53	47	37	74	.272	R	R	6-6	218	4-28-79	1997	Lancaster, Calif.
File, Bob	3	3	2.57	24	0	0	7	35	31	11	10	7	11	.237	R	R	6-4	215	1-28-77	1998	Morrisville, Penn.
Frasor, Jason	0	0	2.25	3	0	0	0	4	1	1	1	5	6	.077	R	R	5-10	170	8-9-77	1999	Oak Forest, Ill.
Frederick, Kevin	3	2	0.99	20	0	0	5	27	18	6	3	9	26	.180	L	R	6-1	210	11-4-76	1998	Prairie View, Ill.
Glynn, Ryan	7	2	3.40	16	16	1	0	93	82	38	35	34	75	.236	R	R	6-3	200	11-1-74	1995	Grand Prairie, Texas
2-team (11 Richmond)	8	3	3.75	27	16	1	0	110	108	49	46	48	94	.257							
Haines, Talley	4	2	3.87	44	0	0	3	79	80	37	34	15	53	.261	R	R	6-5	205	11-16-76	1998	Jackson, Mo.
Kershner, Jason	3	2	5.20	28	0	0	4	36	45	23	21	10	31	.313	L	L	6-2	185	12-19-76	1995	Scottsdale, Ariz.
Lopez, Aquilino	1	6	7.17	32	0	0	5	43	58	36	34	11	32	.326	R	R	6-3	160	4-21-75	1997	Villa Altagracia, D.R.
Lukasiewicz, Mark	4	2	7.68	32	0	0	4	36	38	33	31	11	33	.268	L	L	6-5	240	3-8-73	1994	Clay, N.Y.
Matos, Josue	7	6	5.04	29	23	0	0	141	144	89	79	56	112	.266	R	R	6-0	190	3-15-78	1997	Cabo Rojo, P.R.
Maurer, Dave	0	0	3.56	43	4	0	2	66	58	27	26	26	64	.242	R	L	6-2	205	2-23-75	1997	Burnsville, Minn.
Miller, Justin	1	1	2.16	3	3	0	0	17	16	6	4	4	21	.242	R	R	6-2	220	8-27-77	1997	Torrance, Calif.
Nakamura, Micheal	3	2	3.11	31	1	0	4	55	42	20	19	17	76	.213	R	R	5-10	170	9-6-76	1998	Ferntree Gully, Australia
Peterson, Adam	2	2	12.86	19	0	0	0	21	38	30	30	16	19	.404	R	R	6-3	220	5-18-79	2002	Abrams, Wis.
Reimers, Cameron	2	7	5.05	12	12	0	0	66	82	43	37	20	28	.305	R	R	6-5	200	9-15-78	1999	Missoula, Mont.
Sanchez, Jesus	1	4	6.84	7	4	0	0	25	28	21	19	13	20	.283	L	L	5-10	165	10-11-74	1994	Nizao Bani, D.R.
2-team (22 Louisville)	4	6	4.13	29	9	0	1	85	77	43	39	41	71	.243							
Smith, Mike	4	6	5.28	35	15	0	1	109	123	80	64	53	72	.280	R	R	5-11	190	9-19-77	2000	Westwood, Mass.
Towers, Josh	3	1	2.50	6	5	0	0	36	33	11	10	7	25	.246	R	R	6-1	190	2-26-77	1996	Owings Mills, Md.

FIELDING

Catcher	PCT	G	PO	A	E	DP	PB
Chiaffredo	.992	33	225	20	2	1	6
Estalella	1.000	5	37	5	0	0	0
Quiroz	.994	71	492	26	3	7	10
Whittaker	.983	35	218	19	4	3	2
Zaun	1.000	5	42	1	0	0	0

First Base	PCT	G	PO	A	E	DP
Clark	.966	6	52	5	2	5
Crozier	.983	24	213	15	4	24
Delgado	1.000	2	18	2	0	1
Fagan	.989	81	697	51	8	61
Guiel	.947	3	17	1	1	0

	PCT	G	PO	A	E	DP
Hassey	1.000	1	2	0	0	1
Matos	.993	17	127	11	1	17
Pond	1.000	7	57	3	0	5
Whittaker	.909	2	9	1	1	1
Williams	.984	8	56	4	1	9

Second Base	PCT	G	PO	A	E	DP
Clapp	.928	12	28	36	5	9
Clark	.988	18	28	56	1	12
Hassey	.929	4	7	6	1	1
Matos	1.000	6	11	18	0	8
Sequea	.969	87	152	220	12	57
Solano	1.000	6	8	13	0	1
Williams	.976	16	25	56	2	8

Third Base	PCT	G	PO	A	E	DP
Clapp	1.000	2	0	1	0	0
Clark	.900	7	3	15	2	1
Matos	.967	21	12	47	2	0

Nakamura	1.000	1	0	3	0	0
Pond	.913	22	10	32	4	3
Solano	1.000	3	2	4	0	0
Williams	.965	91	69	206	10	22

Shortstop	PCT	G	PO	A	E	DP
Adams	.939	121	179	325	33	82
Hassey	1.000	5	4	7	0	2
Matos	.935	23	32	68	7	11
Sequea	1.000	1	1	2	0	0

Outfield	PCT	G	PO	A	E	DP
Benard	.981	33	52	1	1	0

Clapp	1.000	16	36	2	0	0
Clark	.937	39	69	5	5	3
Fagan	1.000	4	5	0	0	0
French	.987	36	72	2	1	0
Gross	.957	34	64	3	3	0
Guiel	.992	61	114	3	1	2
Hall	.980	57	93	3	2	1
Hermansen	1.000	16	28	1	0	0
Matos	.905	9	18	1	2	0
Pond	.964	39	51	2	2	0
Rios	.964	46	101	6	4	0
Sanders	.977	61	126	4	3	1

NEW HAMPSHIRE FISHER CATS

Class AA

EASTERN LEAGUE

BATTING	AVG	G	AB	R	H	2B	3B	HR	RBI	BB	SO	SB	CS	OBP	SLG	B	T	HT	WT	DOB	1st Yr	Resides
Chiaffredo, Paul	.254	64	228	32	58	12	0	9	29	10	54	1	0	.293	.425	R	R	6-2	215	5-30-76	1997	Campbell, Calif.
Clapp, Stubby	.226	19	53	10	12	7	0	1	9	14	14	0	0	.349	.415	L	R	5-8	170	2-24-73	1996	Windsor, Ontario
Cosby, Robert	.529	5	17	2	9	1	0	1	6	0	1	0	0	.529	.765	S	R	6-2	200	4-2-81	1999	Rio Piedras, P.R.
French, Anton	.282	33	124	29	35	5	5	3	16	23	16	1	1	.362	.476	L	R	5-11	170	7-25-75	1993	St. Louis, Mo.
Godwin, Tyrell	.253	133	521	85	132	21	7	6	40	52	110	42	12	.326	.355	L	R	6-0	200	7-10-79	2001	Council, N.C.
Griffin, John-Ford	.248	129	467	66	116	28	1	22	81	56	128	1	1	.330	.454	L	L	6-2	215	11-19-79	2001	Sarasota, Fla.
Hassey, Brad	.154	23	65	6	10	1	0	2	6	3	14	0	0	.203	.262	R	R	5-10	170	11-28-79	2002	Tucson, Ariz.
Hattig, John	.296	40	142	24	42	7	0	10	30	12	41	0	1	.352	.556	S	R	6-2	210	2-27-80	1999	Dededo, Guam
2-team (75 Portland)	.296	115	406	77	120	28	1	22	65	59	109	3	4	.391	.532							
Hill, Aaron	.280	135	479	78	134	26	2	11	80	63	61	3	2	.369	.411	R	R	6-0	200	3-21-82	2003	Visalia, Calif.
Jova, Maikel	.277	122	462	46	128	28	2	10	63	12	90	1	1	.296	.411	R	R	6-0	190	3-5-81	2000	San Jose, Costa Rica
Kratz, Erik	.333	3	9	1	3	1	0	0	0	2	2	0	0	.500	.444	R	R	6-4	246	6-15-80	2002	Harrisonburg, Va.
Logan, Matt	.221	54	181	22	40	11	0	1	21	22	39	1	1	.307	.298	L	R	6-3	210	7-22-79	1998	Brampton, Ontario
Rich, Dominic	.279	136	513	79	143	30	3	8	71	53	72	3	2	.353	.396	L	R	5-10	190	8-22-79	2000	Herndon, Pa.
Singleton, Justin	.236	129	441	54	104	19	11	16	50	33	152	7	4	.291	.438	L	R	6-1	190	4-10-79	2001	Sparks, Md.
Snyder, Michael	.207	79	261	32	54	9	3	8	36	28	79	2	2	.282	.356	L	R	6-5	230	2-11-81	1999	Chino Hills, Calif.
Solano, Danny	.234	103	359	51	84	19	2	1	26	56	73	2	2	.343	.306	R	R	5-9	150	12-3-75	1997	Santo Domingo, D.R.
Umbria, Jose	.256	58	211	17	54	4	0	1	20	10	45	0	0	.290	.289	R	R	6-2	210	1-20-78	1996	Barquisimeto, Venez.
Valencia, Victor	.179	31	95	11	17	1	0	4	14	9	31	0	0	.255	.316	R	R	6-2	185	5-30-77	1994	Maracay, Venez.
2-team (15 Akron)	.196	46	143	21	28	5	0	6	19	15	47	0	0	.282	.357							
Waugh, Jason	.273	3	11	0	3	0	0	0	1	1	2	0	0	.333	.273	R	R	6-1	190	3-12-80	2002	Bakersfield, Calif.
Whittaker, Tim	.500	1	2	0	1	0	0	0	0	1	0	0	0	.667	.500	R	R	6-0	220	1-4-79	2001	Conway, S.C.

PITCHING	W	L	ERA	G	GS	CG	SV	IP	H	R	ER	BB	SO	AVG	B	T	HT	WT	DOB	1st Yr	Resides
Arnold, Jason	0	1	3.15	4	4	0	0	20	17	7	7	5	14	.230	R	R	6-3	210	5-2-79	2001	Palm Bay, Fla.
Baker, Chris	5	1	3.09	11	11	0	0	70	56	26	24	13	61	.221	R	R	6-1	200	8-24-77	1999	Valencia, Calif.
Banks, Josh	6	6	5.03	18	17	1	0	91	89	54	51	28	76	.251	R	R	6-3	195	7-18-82	2003	Arnold, Md.
Bouknight, Kip	0	0	3.86	3	1	0	1	9	10	5	4	4	4	.270	R	R	6-0	190	11-16-78	2001	Gaston, S.C.
Chacin, Gustavo	16	2	2.92	25	25	0	0	142	113	53	46	49	109	.215	L	L	5-11	190	12-4-80	1998	Maracaibo, Venez.
DeJong, Jordan	6	2	2.86	57	0	0	14	69	69	24	22	30	57	.263	R	R	6-2	170	4-12-79	2002	Yorba Linda, Calif.
Frederick, Kevin	2	0	1.27	18	0	0	1	21	15	7	3	5	26	.190	R	R	6-1	210	11-4-76	1998	Prairie View, Ill.
Houston, Ryan	7	4	4.33	34	8	0	0	98	93	50	47	50	102	.254	R	R	6-4	190	9-22-79	1999	Pensacola, Fla.
Jackson, Tim	3	10	4.80	53	0	0	3	69	63	42	37	30	66	.263	R	R	5-11	210	7-12-78	2001	Lyons, Ill.
League, Brandon	6	4	3.38	41	10	0	2	104	92	44	39	41	90	.240	R	R	6-2	180	3-16-83	2001	Honolulu, Hawaii
Lee, Derek	1	3	3.38	12	9	1	0	56	59	22	21	14	19	.285	L	L	6-4	180	8-20-74	1997	Ft. Worth, Texas
McGowan, Dustin	2	0	4.06	6	6	0	0	31	24	14	14	15	29	.207	R	R	6-3	220	3-24-82	2000	Ludowici, Ga.
Ogiltree, John	2	4	2.69	45	0	0	3	60	48	22	18	32	36	.217	R	R	6-6	220	6-3-78	2001	Mississauga, Ontario
Ozias, Todd	8	4	3.43	18	17	0	0	89	86	43	34	29	74	.250	R	R	6-1	190	8-19-76	1998	Coral Springs, Fla.
Peterson, Adam	2	2	2.54	27	0	0	15	28	20	8	8	10	38	.198	R	R	6-3	215	5-18-79	2002	Abrams, Wis.
Reimers, Cameron	7	4	2.78	15	15	0	0	94	87	33	29	20	42	.249	R	R	6-5	200	9-15-78	1999	Missoula, Mont.
Rosario, Francisco	2	4	4.31	12	12	0	0	48	48	25	23	16	45	.268	R	R	6-0	195	9-28-80	1999	San Rafael de Yuma, D.R.
Templet, Jordy	0	0	1.80	2	0	0	0	5	4	1	1	2	3	.211	R	R	6-0	165	8-19-81	2003	Gonzales, La.
Thompson, Travis	4	3	5.61	22	0	0	1	34	38	25	21	21	27	.286	R	R	5-5	225	7-3-77	1999	Matthews, N.C.
Torres, Andy	2	0	3.05	9	0	0	1	21	20	7	7	8	18	.256	R	R	5-9	160	4-12-78	2002	Bell Gardens, Calif.
Vermilyea, James	3	2	2.47	21	6	1	5	58	43	20	16	12	39	.204	R	R	6-4	195	2-10-82	2003	Tucson, Ariz.

FIELDING

Catcher	PCT	G	PO	A	E	DP	PB
Chiaffredo	.990	60	447	33	5	5	4
Kratz	1.000	3	24	2	0	0	1
Umbria	.992	54	385	26	3	1	5
Valencia	.977	26	160	10	4	2	3
Whittaker	1.000	1	12	0	0	0	0

First Base	PCT	G	PO	A	E	DP
Chiaffredo	1.000	1	10	0	0	1
Griffin	.978	16	127	8	3	15
Logan	.991	51	417	21	4	42
Snyder	.994	75	636	57	4	60
Umbria	1.000	3	24	1	0	2

Second Base	PCT	G	PO	A	E	DP
Clapp	.967	5	11	18	1	5
Hassey	1.000	13	18	41	0	8
Rich	.971	124	236	365	18	69
Solano	1.000	4	15	13	0	3

Third Base	PCT	G	PO	A	E	DP
Clapp	1.000	5	1	13	0	1
Cosby	1.000	5	2	9	0	0
Hassey	.857	7	1	11	3	0
Hattig	.990	35	28	68	1	4
Singleton	1.000	1	1	1	0	0
Solano	.975	90	57	213	7	23

Shortstop	PCT	G	PO	A	E	DP
Hill	.959	134	236	375	26	82
Solano	.968	7	11	19	1	5

Outfield	PCT	G	PO	A	E	DP
Clapp	1.000	1	2	0	0	0
French	.970	31	61	4	2	0
Godwin	.973	132	208	11	6	2
Griffin	1.000	29	36	2	0	1
Hassey	1.000	3	2	0	0	0
Jova	.956	108	186	8	9	1
Singleton	.977	129	248	6	6	2
Waugh	1.000	3	4	0	0	0

DUNEDIN BLUE JAYS

High Class A

FLORIDA STATE LEAGUE

BATTING	AVG	G	AB	R	H	2B	3B	HR	RBI	BB	SO	SB	CS	OBP	SLG	B	T	HT	WT	DOB	1st Yr	Resides
Chiaravalloti, Vito	.267	122	446	63	119	33	1	14	71	69	110	0	1	.378	.439	R	R	6-3	220	10-26-80	2003	Middletown, N.J.

BATTING

BATTING	AVG	G	AB	R	H	2B	3B	HR	RBI	BB	SO	SB	CS	OBP	SLG	B	T	HT	WT	DOB	1st Yr	Resides
Cota, Carlo	.294	116	463	81	136	37	1	11	63	45	101	2	1	.356	.449	R	R	5-10	180	9-18-80	2002	Calexico, Calif.
Davenport, Ron	.278	113	442	63	123	40	4	16	92	47	68	0	1	.345	.495	L	R	6-2	190	10-16-81	2000	Raleigh, N.C.
Delgado, Carlos	.250	2	8	1	2	0	1	2	0	0	0	0	0	.250	.625	L	R	6-3	230	6-25-72	1989	Aguadilla, P.R.
Dragicevich, Scott	.227	84	277	32	63	14	0	3	28	42	81	1	0	.329	.310	R	R	6-3	200	2-28-80	2002	Westlake, Calif.
Hassey, Brad	.280	22	82	10	23	4	1	0	8	7	15	1	1	.337	.354	R	R	5-10	170	11-28-79	2002	Tucson, Ariz.
Kratz, Erik	.286	14	49	6	14	4	0	1	6	2	16	0	0	.327	.429	R	R	6-4	246	6-15-80	2002	Harrisonburg, Va.
Mayorson, Manny	.217	90	300	33	65	8	0	0	26	25	23	2	2	.277	.243	R	R	5-10	160	3-10-83	2000	La Romana, D.R.
Medina, Rodney	.259	57	197	30	51	8	4	3	12	16	20	2	5	.321	.386	S	R	6-1	180	10-17-81	1999	Maracaibo, Venez.
Negron, Miguel	.269	99	372	46	100	16	5	9	48	38	81	3	1	.341	.411	L	L	6-2	170	8-22-82	2000	Caguas, P.R.
Raymundo, G.J.	.326	26	89	16	29	5	0	0	11	9	16	0	0	.388	.382	R	R	6-1	190	3-3-77	1999	Clovis, Calif.
Roberts, Ryan	.239	59	205	29	49	1	1	7	25	36	51	0	3	.350	.356	R	R	5-11	190	9-19-80	2003	North Richland Hills, Texas
Schneider, John	.206	58	170	26	35	8	0	6	28	41	69	0	0	.373	.359	R	R	6-3	220	2-14-80	2002	Lawrenceville, N.J.
Tablado, Raul	.303	84	323	62	98	28	0	21	76	24	91	0	0	.354	.585	R	R	6-2	170	3-3-82	2000	Miami, Fla.
Tingler, Jayce	.251	118	447	77	112	15	2	1	36	74	25	3	5	.373	.300	L	L	5-8	155	11-28-80	2003	Smithville, Mo.
Waugh, Jason	.249	86	317	42	79	16	0	1	33	22	59	2	2	.302	.309	R	R	6-1	190	3-12-80	2002	Bakersfield, Calif.
Whittaker, Tim	.161	17	56	4	9	3	0	0	3	9	19	0	0	.288	.214	R	R	6-0	170	1-4-79	2001	Conway, S.C.
Woodward, Chris	.313	6	16	2	5	2	0	1	3	1	2	0	0	.333	.625	R	R	6-0	180	6-27-76	1995	Chino, Calif.
Yepez, Jose	.192	62	213	26	41	11	0	4	22	16	36	0	0	.262	.300	R	R	6-0	170	11-3-80	1998	Lara, Venez.

PITCHING

PITCHING	W	L	ERA	G	GS	CG	SV	IP	H	R	ER	BB	SO	AVG	B	T	HT	WT	DOB	1st Yr	Resides
Arnold, Jason	1	1	4.35	3	3	0	0	10	13	5	5	2	11	.302	R	R	6-3	210	5-2-79	2001	Palm Bay, Fla.
Banks, Josh	7	1	1.80	11	11	0	0	60	49	17	12	8	60	.220	R	R	6-3	195	7-18-82	2003	Arnold, Md.
Buzachero, Bubbie	2	2	2.55	51	0	0	24	60	53	19	17	20	59	.233	R	R	5-11	180	6-13-81	2002	Livingston, Tenn.
Dragicevich, Scott	0	0	0.00	1	0	0	0	1	1	0	0	0	1	.200	R	R	6-3	200	6-28-80	2002	Westlake, Calif.
Flores, Neomar	6	10	5.72	27	23	0	0	118	151	83	75	36	79	.310	R	R	6-2	180	3-12-82	1999	Guarenas, Venez.
Harper, Jesse	3	0	1.00	4	3	0	0	18	14	2	2	4	18	.212	R	R	6-4	210	11-11-80	2001	Clute, Texas
Isenberg, Kurt	2	4	5.61	14	14	0	0	61	73	46	38	20	40	.299	R	L	6-0	190	1-15-82	2003	Virginia Beach, Va.
James, Justin	3	6	5.40	11	11	0	0	50	60	32	30	19	41	.299	R	R	6-3	212	9-13-81	2003	Yukon, Okla.
Kratz, Erik	0	0	0.00	1	0	0	0	1	0	0	0	1	0	.000	R	R	6-4	246	6-15-80	2002	Harrisonburg, Va.
Marcum, Shaun	3	2	3.12	12	12	0	0	69	74	30	24	4	72	.272	R	R	6-0	175	12-14-81	2003	Excelsior Springs, Mo.
Maureau, Justin	0	1	7.50	6	0	0	0	6	6	5	5	7	5	.261	R	L	6-1	170	12-17-80	2002	Highlands Ranch, Colo.
Mumma, Brad	0	1	14.73	2	1	0	0	4	9	7	6	3	3	.474	L	L	6-4	230	4-1-81	2003	La Porte, Ind.
Nunley, Derrek	3	3	7.68	26	0	0	2	34	41	31	29	31	27	.301	R	R	6-1	180	9-13-80	1999	Jacksonville, Fla.
Ozuna, Tommi	4	4	4.48	43	1	0	0	64	65	34	32	32	36	.263	L	L	6-2	180	5-17-81	1998	Santo Domingo, D.R.
Perkins, Vince	1	4	3.95	13	9	0	0	55	53	28	24	24	47	.250	L	R	6-5	220	9-27-81	2001	Victoria, B.C.
Pleiness, Chad	4	3	4.40	36	4	0	0	78	82	45	38	33	46	.274	R	R	6-6	230	3-5-80	2002	Scottville, Mich.
Ramirez, Ismael	15	6	2.72	28	27	0	0	165	151	57	50	25	131	.242	R	R	6-0	210	3-6-81	2003	Amory, Miss.
Reed, Brian	2	1	3.16	24	0	0	4	31	38	11	11	8	31	.290	R	R	6-2	160	6-18-80	1998	San Pedro de Macoris, D.R.
Romero, Felix	0	0	1.88	9	0	0	2	14	11	3	3	2	20	.196	R	R	6-0	195	9-28-80	1999	San Rafael de Yuma, D.R.
Rosario, Francisco	1	1	4.67	6	6	0	0	17	16	12	9	11	16	.229	R	R	6-0	175	9-28-80	1995	Paradise Valley, Ariz.
Speier, Justin	0	0	4.50	2	0	0	0	2	3	1	1	0	2	.333	R	R	6-4	205	11-6-73	1995	Paradise Valley, Ariz.
Templet, Jordy	0	0	13.50	3	0	0	0	3	3	4	4	3	3	.273	R	R	6-4	165	8-19-81	2003	Gonzales, La.
Thorpe, Tracy	3	2	3.64	39	0	0	1	59	39	25	24	30	53	.192	R	R	6-4	250	12-15-80	2000	Melbourne, Fla.
Torres, Andy	9	3	2.52	42	0	0	0	79	64	28	22	16	71	.230	R	R	5-9	160	4-12-78	2002	Bell Gardens, Calif.
Valdez, Santo	2	1	6.53	23	0	0	2	41	52	35	30	10	31	.299	R	R	6-1	170	3-30-82	1999	Bani, D.R.
Vermilyea, Jamie	5	1	3.09	18	6	0	0	55	54	21	19	13	37	.261	R	R	6-4	195	2-10-82	2003	Tucson, Ariz.
Waugh, Jason	0	0	0.00	1	0	0	0	1	1	0	0	1	0	.250	R	R	6-1	190	3-12-80	2002	Bakersfield, Calif.

FIELDING

Catcher	PCT	G	PO	A	E	DP	PB
Kratz	.991	13	94	11	1	0	1
Schneider	.993	56	397	34	3	3	4
Whittaker	1.000	6	46	5	0	0	2
Yepez	.987	62	427	45	6	3	5

First Base	PCT	G	PO	A	E	DP
Chiaravalloti	.984	77	620	60	11	60
Davenport	.984	19	170	14	3	14
Delgado	1.000	2	14	2	0	0
Dragicevich	1.000	28	223	14	0	19
Kratz	1.000	2	9	0	0	1
Whittaker	.989	10	81	6	1	4

Second Base	PCT	G	PO	A	E	DP
Cota	.959	66	113	194	13	35
Hassey	.971	7	11	22	1	3
Mayorson	1.000	3	4	10	0	0
Roberts	.958	59	119	158	12	36

Third Base	PCT	G	PO	A	E	DP
Cota	.942	50	34	96	8	5
Dragicevich	.938	43	23	67	6	2
Hassey	.846	7	0	11	2	0
Raymundo	.909	16	10	20	3	2
Tablado	.882	21	11	34	6	2

Shortstop	PCT	G	PO	A	E	DP
Dragicevich	1.000	6	9	16	0	4
Hassey	1.000	9	24	0	7	
Mayorson	.963	86	148	239	15	48
Raymundo	.833	3	5	10	3	1
Tablado	.906	32	51	84	14	25
Woodward	1.000	6	8	9	0	3

Outfield	PCT	G	PO	A	E	DP
Davenport	.966	72	135	7	5	2
Medina	.977	45	83	2	2	0
Negron	.981	94	208	4	4	1
Tingler	.990	116	187	15	2	0
Waugh	.965	78	133	3	5	0

CHARLESTON ALLEY CATS — Low Class A

SOUTH ATLANTIC LEAGUE

BATTING	AVG	G	AB	R	H	2B	3B	HR	RBI	BB	SO	SB	CS	OBP	SLG	B	T	HT	WT	DOB	1st Yr	Resides
Acey, Jermy	.295	53	200	26	59	4	2	5	22	21	46	5	3	.376	.410	S	R	5-11	185	5-24-81	2003	Elk Grove, Calif.
Arnold, Eric	.280	105	378	40	106	22	0	5	61	29	114	1	3	.329	.378	R	R	6-1	190	8-9-80	2002	La Porte, Texas
Davis, Morrin	.152	54	138	19	21	2	3	1	14	15	61	2	1	.248	.232	R	R	6-2	190	12-11-82	2000	Tampa, Fla.
Diaz, Robinson	.287	106	407	62	117	20	2	2	42	27	31	10	4	.342	.361	R	R	5-10	180	9-19-83	2001	Monte Plata, D.R.
Galloway, Mike	.246	109	366	45	90	16	4	7	44	30	129	2	4	.315	.369	R	R	6-2	210	5-9-81	2002	St. Thomas, Ontario
Johnston, Clint	.263	133	467	87	123	36	3	13	79	83	127	1	0	.372	.437	L	L	6-2	210	7-2-77	1998	Nashville, Tenn.
Macaluso, Mike	.167	5	12	2	2	0	0	0	1	2	1	0	0	.231	.167	R	R	5-11	165	4-9-81	2004	Tampa, Fla.
Medina, Rodney	.330	28	103	14	34	5	1	1	17	4	10	3	1	.352	.427	S	R	6-1	180	10-17-81	1999	Maracaibo, Venez.
Patrick, Brian	.249	83	253	35	63	10	2	1	35	36	44	3	1	.348	.316	S	R	5-10	185	11-29-80	2003	Fort Lauderdale, Fla.
Peralta, Juan	.228	118	438	57	100	15	1	2	43	39	78	8	5	.291	.281	S	R	6-0	170	6-24-83	2000	Santiago Rodriguez, D.R.
Reiman, Joey	.292	116	408	68	119	28	2	7	51	50	82	3	6	.386	.422	R	R	6-1	200	12-20-80	2003	Phoenix, Ariz.
Rivera, Willie	.208	99	336	40	70	9	0	3	28	24	92	5	3	.272	.262	L	R	6-0	150	12-28-81	2000	Caguas, P.R.
Roberts, Ryan	.284	64	225	38	64	9	0	13	39	55	50	0	0	.441	.498	R	R	5-11	190	9-19-80	2003	North Richland Hills, Texas
Smith, David	.278	121	436	74	121	27	2	12	63	53	119	5	0	.366	.431	R	R	6-1	190	1-12-81	2002	Charleston, W.Va.
Snavely, Christian	.254	111	331	50	84	22	1	3	48	59	53	115	6	2	.364	.459	L	R	6-3	200	5-7-82	2003	Defiance, Ohio

BATTING

BATTING	AVG	G	AB	R	H	2B	3B	HR	RBI	BB	SO	SB	CS	OBP	SLG	B	T	HT	WT	DOB	1st Yr	Resides
Wolfe, Joey	.219	57	146	16	32	5	2	3	16	16	40	1	2	.326	.342	L	R	5-9	205	10-10-80	2003	Saratoga, Calif.

PITCHING

PITCHING	W	L	ERA	G	GS	CG	SV	IP	H	R	ER	BB	SO	AVG	B	T	HT	WT	DOB	1st Yr	Resides
Canizal, Joaquin	8	2	4.16	42	0	0	1	80	82	41	37	29	75	.263	R	R	6-4	200	1-5-81	2003	Trujillo Alto, P.R.
Core, Daniel	10	8	3.32	28	28	1	0	157	137	70	58	53	132	.238	R	R	6-1	195	7-17-81	2003	Pembroke Pines, Fla.
Dalton, Matt	4	3	1.69	23	0	0	2	32	22	10	6	15	27	.191	R	R	6-4	200	9-21-79	2003	Monroeville, Pa.
Esaray, Brad	4	1	5.11	42	0	0	2	56	69	44	32	45	39	.312	L	L	6-3	170	9-20-78	2001	Concord, N.C.
Harper, Jeremy	1	2	4.08	13	4	0	1	35	37	22	16	20	33	.270	R	R	6-2	190	10-31-80	2003	Seneca Rocks, W.Va.
Isenberg, Kurt	3	4	3.88	11	10	0	0	51	48	25	22	15	34	.242	R	L	6-0	190	1-15-82	2003	Virginia Beach, Va.
James, Justin	5	4	3.00	14	14	0	0	78	67	31	26	24	83	.233	R	R	6-3	212	9-13-81	2003	Yukon, Okla.
MacDonald, Mike	3	0	1.93	7	6	0	0	33	29	14	7	9	23	.230	R	R	6-1	200	10-29-81	2004	Camden, Maine
Marcum, Shaun	7	4	3.19	13	13	1	0	79	64	32	28	16	83	.218	R	R	6-0	175	12-14-81	2003	Excelsior Springs, Mo.
Mastny, Thomas	10	3	2.17	27	27	0	0	149	123	44	36	41	143	.224	R	R	6-6	220	2-4-81	2003	Zionsville, Ind.
Mora, Ramon	5	4	6.00	14	12	0	0	63	76	50	42	18	49	.295	R	R	6-2	210	3-18-81	1998	Maturin, Venez.
Mumma, Brad	2	3	3.83	20	7	0	8	49	53	30	21	15	47	.272	L	L	6-4	230	4-1-81	2003	La Porte, Ind.
Nunley, Derrek	1	1	6.75	8	0	0	0	12	13	10	9	9	6	.289	R	R	6-1	180	9-13-80	1999	Jacksonville, Fla.
Patrick, Brian	0	0	0.00	2	1	0	0	2	2	0	0	0	0	.000	S	R	5-10	185	11-29-80	2003	Fort Lauderdale, Fla.
Reed, Brian	1	0	0.35	25	0	0	10	26	17	2	1	5	28	.181	R	R	6-1	210	3-6-81	2003	Amory, Miss.
Rico, Erik	3	1	1.75	8	4	0	0	26	22	7	5	8	14	.229	L	L	6-2	190	1-21-80	2002	Miami, Fla.
Romero, Davis	4	4	2.53	32	14	0	1	103	78	36	29	30	108	.210	L	L	5-10	140	3-30-83	2000	Aguadulce, Panama
Romero, Felix	9	4	2.96	42	0	0	3	73	62	27	24	20	102	.228	R	R	6-2	160	6-18-80	1998	San Pedro de Macoris, D.R.
Sandoval, Marcos	2	1	6.14	24	0	0	0	29	19	25	20	29	26	.184	R	R	6-1	180	12-29-80	1998	Carabobo, Venez.
Sopko, Mark	1	2	6.00	40	0	0	9	51	64	35	34	18	30	.308	R	R	5-11	190	12-16-81	2003	Joliet, Ill.
Templet, Jordy	0	2	4.09	16	0	0	2	22	25	10	10	10	18	.294	R	R	6-0	165	8-19-81	2003	Gonzales, La.
Tressler, Aaron	0	0	9.00	2	0	0	0	4	7	5	4	2	4	.368	R	R	6-1	188	3-28-82	2004	Pennsylvania Furnace, Pa.
Wesley, John	0	3	10.80	6	1	0	0	12	19	15	14	7	12	.373	R	R	6-6	230	10-14-80	2002	Westbury, N.Y.

FIELDING

Catcher	PCT	G	PO	A	E	DP	PB
Diaz	.985	77	603	63	10	5	9
Reiman	1.000	32	257	19	0	1	3
Wolfe	1.000	30	197	14	0	2	4

First Base	PCT	G	PO	A	E	DP
Johnston	.994	111	914	62	6	68
Reiman	1.000	23	172	15	0	17

Second Base	PCT	G	PO	A	E	DP
Acey	.935	43	69	105	12	17
Patrick	.912	7	15	16	3	3

Third Base	PCT	G	PO	A	E	DP
Peralta	1.000	2	2	1	0	0
Rivera	.990	27	46	57	1	10
Roberts	.972	61	149	166	9	26
Arnold	.928	95	58	162	17	11
Macaluso	1.000	4	5	2	0	0
Patrick	1.000	1	0	3	0	0
Rivera	.947	36	21	69	5	4

Shortstop	PCT	G	PO	A	E	DP
Macaluso	1.000	1	0	2	0	0

	PCT	G	PO	A	E	DP
Peralta	.940	106	156	296	29	49
Rivera	.964	30	37	95	5	15

Outfield	PCT	G	PO	A	E	DP
Davis	.925	44	58	4	5	1
Galloway	.973	94	139	4	4	0
Medina	.980	23	45	3	1	0
Patrick	.949	59	89	4	5	1
Smith	.985	110	191	7	3	4
Snavely	.978	98	129	6	3	0

AUBURN DOUBLEDAYS — Short-Season Class A

NEW YORK-PENN LEAGUE

BATTING

BATTING	AVG	G	AB	R	H	2B	3B	HR	RBI	BB	SO	SB	CS	OBP	SLG	B	T	HT	WT	DOB	1st Yr	Resides
Acey, Jermy	.400	3	10	4	4	1	0	0	3	2	0	0	0	.538	.500	S	R	5-11	185	5-24-81	2003	Elk Grove, Calif.
Armstrong, Jason	.260	45	123	24	32	9	0	1	12	13	20	6	0	.338	.358	R	R	6-0	175	11-13-81	2004	Menlo Park, Calif.
Cannon, Chip	.271	62	210	33	57	15	1	10	41	22	55	0	0	.338	.495	L	R	6-5	215	11-30-81	2004	Charleston, S.C.
Corrente, David	.257	35	113	15	29	4	1	1	12	12	28	0	0	.349	.336	R	R	6-2	200	10-13-83	2001	Chatham, Ontario
Esposito, Vinny	.251	60	199	30	50	18	1	3	38	29	66	1	1	.363	.397	L	R	6-0	195	8-22-80	2003	Middletown, N.J.
Gerlits, Gooby	.267	7	15	0	4	1	0	0	2	1	2	0	0	.313	.333	R	R	6-0	220	11-17-82	2004	Coral Springs, Fla.
Hall, Brian	.294	57	211	38	62	14	1	10	39	24	49	3	3	.367	.512	R	R	6-0	190	2-1-82	2004	Carlsbad, N.M.
Hicks, David	.270	16	37	3	10	0	1	2	4	8	0	1	1	.333	.351	L	R	6-5	215	11-22-81	2004	Raleigh, N.C.
Klosterman, Ryan	.275	66	269	50	74	13	4	5	32	22	55	16	2	.346	.409	R	R	5-11	175	5-28-82	2004	Clermont, Fla.
Kratz, Erik	.308	10	39	5	12	6	0	0	10	1	8	0	0	.317	.462	R	R	6-4	246	6-15-80	2002	Harrisonburg, Va.
Lind, Adam	.308	70	266	43	82	23	0	5	50	24	36	1	0	.367	.474	L	L	6-2	190	7-17-83	2004	Anderson, Ind.
Macaluso, Mike	.263	5	19	3	5	1	1	0	2	2	3	0	1	.364	.421	R	R	5-11	165	4-9-81	2004	Tampa, Fla.
Mangioni, Jarad	.262	43	122	19	32	7	1	3	12	14	34	2	1	.348	.410	R	R	6-3	185	2-8-84	2002	Sydney, Australia
Mathews, Aaron	.265	70	283	52	75	10	6	0	26	33	47	6	6	.349	.343	R	R	5-9	200	5-10-82	2004	John Day, Ore.
Metropoulos, Joey	.257	49	152	28	39	16	0	6	30	18	48	0	0	.362	.480	R	R	6-1	230	10-7-83	2004	Jamul, Calif.
Nielsen, Eric	.264	68	231	38	61	15	2	7	35	35	45	0	4	.383	.437	R	R	6-0	205	11-14-81	2004	Las Vegas, Nev.
Powers, Greg	.200	15	30	3	6	1	1	0	4	5	10	0	0	.314	.300	L	R	5-11	180	5-14-81	2004	Scottsdale, Ariz.
Thigpen, Curtis	.301	45	166	34	50	11	2	7	29	23	32	1	1	.388	.518	R	R	6-1	200	8-28-79	2002	Forney, Texas
Velez, Eugenio	.263	10	19	5	5	0	0	0	1	2	5	0	0	.391	.263	S	R	6-1	160	5-16-82	2002	San Pedro de Macoris, D.R.

GAMES BY POSITION: C—Corrente 32, Gerlits 6, Kratz 9, Thigpen 32. **1B**—Cannon 43, Hicks 11, Mangioni 1, Metropoulos 30. **2B**—Acey 3, Armstrong 13, Hall 55, Macaluso 1, Powers 9, Velez 1. **3B**—Armstrong 25, Esposito 57, Macaluso 1, Powers 2, Velez 2. **SS**—Armstrong 7, Klosterman 65, Macaluso 3, Powers 1, Velez 1. **OF**—Lind 61, Mangioni 36, Mathews 69, Metropoulos 3, Nielsen 69.

PITCHING

PITCHING	W	L	ERA	G	GS	CG	SV	IP	H	R	ER	BB	SO	AVG	B	T	HT	WT	DOB	1st Yr	Resides
Bell, Kristian	4	0	5.85	19	0	0	1	32	30	22	21	22	32	.243	R	R	6-1	185	1-11-84	2004	Houston, Texas
Cannon, Eddie	0	0	0.00	2	0	0	0	3	2	3	0	0	4	.167	R	R	6-0	170	11-13-81	2004	Seaburg, Fla.
Cheng, Chi-Hung	0	0	4.50	1	0	0	0	2	1	1	1	0	3	.143	L	L	6-1	193	6-20-80	2004	Kaohsiung City, Taiwan
Dalton, Matt	2	0	3.97	6	0	0	0	11	14	5	5	7	5	.311	R	R	6-4	200	9-21-79	2003	Monroeville, Pa.
Day, Dewon	0	3	1.44	28	0	0	9	25	25	8	4	10	29	.238	R	R	6-4	210	9-30-80	2003	Jackson, Miss.
Dicken, Randy	4	8	4.86	8	3	0	1	17	21	10	9	13	20	.296	R	R	6-1	190	8-19-82	2004	Martinsburg, Pa.
Grant, Brian	0	1	3.86	1	1	0	0	5	6	4	2	1	5	.286	R	R	6-4	190	8-16-84	2002	Goldsboro, N.C.
Harper, Jeremy	1	0	3.21	3	3	0	0	14	13	6	5	4	7	.232	R	R	6-2	190	10-31-80	2003	Seneca Rocks, W.Va.
Hill, Danny	0	0	1.59	8	0	0	3	11	9	3	2	3	6	.220	R	R	6-0	200	11-5-81	2004	Weimar, Texas
Jackson, Zach	0	0	5.40	4	0	0	0	15	20	9	9	6	11	.308	L	L	6-0	180	4-20-86	2004	Cranberry Township, Pa.
Janssen, Casey	3	1	3.60	10	10	0	0	50	46	21	20	10	43	.241	R	R	6-4	210	9-17-81	2004	Huntington Beach, Calif.
Leonard, Chris	4	4	4.40	20	10	0	2	61	67	40	30	22	63	.277	L	L	6-1	190	10-9-80	2004	Columbus, Ohio
MacDonald, Mike	4	1	1.55	8	8	0	0	46	30	8	8	6	30	.185	R	R	6-1	200	10-29-81	2004	Camden, Maine
Maureau, Justin	0	0	1.93	4	0	0	0	5	3	1	1	4	5	.176	R	L	6-1	170	12-17-80	2004	Highlands Ranch, Colo.
McKenzie, Casey	5	4	3.78	15	15	0	0	69	76	32	29	20	62	.278	R	R	6-3	206	7-26-82	2004	Tampa, Fla.

PITCHING	W	L	ERA	G	GS	CG	SV	IP	H	R	ER	BB	SO	AVG	B	T	HT	WT	DOB	1st Yr	Resides
McLaughlin, Joey	4	1	2.45	23	0	0	0	44	29	18	12	21	51	.188	R	R	6-0	178	2-11-82	2004	Sapulpa, Okla.
Mumma, Brad	0	0	0.00	1	1	0	0	6	2	1	0	2	2	.111	L	L	6-4	230	4-1-81	2003	La Porte, Ind.
Neylan, Chris	1	1	7.94	17	0	0	0	28	38	29	25	20	22	.311	R	L	6-6	200	9-27-82	2001	Tampa, Fla.
Perez, Juan	6	1	2.76	12	11	1	0	59	61	22	18	10	40	.265	R	R	6-4	170	12-27-81	2002	San Pedro de Macoris, D.R.
Purcey, David	1	0	1.50	3	2	0	0	12	6	2	2	1	13	.150	L	L	6-5	240	4-22-82	2004	Dallas, Texas
Rico, Erik	5	1	1.27	15	0	0	2	28	24	6	4	4	22	.226	L	L	6-2	190	1-21-80	2002	Miami, Fla.
Rodriguez, Jayson	5	3	3.19	21	0	0	2	37	29	16	13	15	30	.220	R	R	6-0	175	5-1-83	2003	Tampa, Fla.
Roy, Scott	1	0	2.70	15	0	0	4	20	14	9	6	4	17	.203	R	R	6-1	220	8-15-82	2004	Manchester, Conn.
Tate, Derek	4	1	2.20	5	2	0	0	16	17	5	4	6	24	.270	R	L	5-11	185	12-19-81	2004	Kennewick, Wash.
Timm, Jordan	0	0	1.42	2	2	0	0	6	6	1	1	1	8	.261	L	L	6-6	230	1-15-81	2004	Pine River, Wis.
Wesley, John	0	1	4.26	4	2	0	0	13	13	7	6	4	9	.271	R	R	6-6	230	10-14-80	2002	Westbury, N.Y.
Yates, Kyle	0	1	6.75	9	0	0	0	9	9	7	7	5	11	.265	R	R	6-4	220	8-7-77	1998	Koloa, Hawaii

PULASKI BLUE JAYS   Rookie

APPALACHIAN LEAGUE

BATTING	AVG	G	AB	R	H	2B	3B	HR	RBI	BB	SO	SB	CS	OBP	SLG	B	T	HT	WT	DOB	1st Yr	Resides
Anderson, Charlie	.311	52	151	37	47	14	0	6	20	29	39	0	0	.429	.523	L	R	6-3	210	10-2-81	2004	Dearborn, Mich.
Ashford, Jon	.255	49	137	24	35	8	2	6	30	19	61	2	2	.348	.474	L	R	6-3	195	8-20-83	2002	Conington, Tenn.
Badger, Graig	.240	34	75	22	18	2	0	0	10	24	20	2	1	.422	.267	R	R	5-9	175	2-11-81	2004	New Brunswick, N.J.
Bormaster, Brian	.252	45	143	21	36	7	0	5	22	22	28	0	1	.363	.406	R	R	5-10	190	10-19-81	2004	Houston, Texas
Chappell, Jon	.293	21	58	12	17	7	0	3	16	8	20	0	1	.391	.569	R	R	6-2	210	4-10-80	2004	Walkerville, Australia
Chourio, Junior	.258	35	97	16	25	5	0	3	15	1	23	1	2	.277	.402	R	R	6-3	170	3-23-83	2001	Maracaibo, Venez.
Garibaldi, Anthony	.287	47	143	36	41	5	2	5	24	17	48	0	2	.398	.455	R	R	6-2	190	12-19-80	2004	Hammond, La.
Gerlits, Gooby	.129	11	31	4	4	1	0	1	6	1	13	0	0	.152	.258	R	R	6-0	220	11-17-82	2004	Coral Springs, Fla.
Hetherington, Luke	.255	60	196	40	50	10	2	8	40	28	64	5	2	.376	.449	R	R	6-1	190	4-13-83	2001	Covington, Wash.
Hicks, David	.306	36	134	33	41	9	1	2	25	20	27	2	0	.409	.433	L	R	6-5	215	11-22-81	2004	Raleigh, N.C.
Land, Tim	.209	14	43	8	9	1	0	2	11	6	12	0	0	.314	.372	R	R	6-2	225	11-16-81	2004	Pensacola, Fla.
Lex, Joshua	.287	26	87	15	25	10	0	2	19	14	19	1	0	.411	.471	R	R	6-0	215	10-7-81	2004	Sacramento, Calif.
Macaluso, Mike	.219	36	128	19	28	4	0	0	10	19	17	2	0	.327	.250	R	R	5-11	165	4-9-81	2004	Tampa, Fla.
Powers, Greg	.230	24	61	13	14	3	0	0	6	11	12	0	1	.373	.279	L	R	5-11	180	5-14-81	2004	Scottsdale, Ariz.
Rodriguez, Yuber	.309	63	249	49	77	15	6	7	53	28	71	9	3	.396	.502	R	R	6-1	192	11-17-83	2001	Maracay, Venez.
Salas, Jose	.211	9	19	1	4	1	0	0	2	0	6	0	0	.250	.263	S	R	6-0	194	8-26-81	2002	Caracas, Venez.
Sena, Emmanuel	.241	53	162	24	39	2	3	1	15	29	53	1	4	.367	.309	S	R	6-1	150	10-15-84	2001	Santo Domingo, D.R.
Thomas, Nick	.280	55	193	34	54	12	0	8	43	42	50	0	0	.411	.466	R	R	6-3	220	2-2-83	2003	Elk Grove, Calif.
Velez, Eugenio	.292	44	168	27	49	14	4	1	26	12	32	1	4	.339	.440	S	R	6-1	160	5-16-82	2002	San Pedro de Macoris, D.R.

GAMES BY POSITION: C—Bormaster 42, Chappell 2, Gerlits 9, Land 14, Lex 10. **1B**—Anderson 23, Bormaster 1, Chappell 4, Garibaldi 1, Gerlits 2, Hicks 34, Lex 3, Salas 3, Thomas 3. **2B**—Badger 26, Macaluso 18, Powers 4, Salas 1, Sena 28. **3B**—Garibaldi 47, Lex 9, Powers 18, Salas 1, Sena 4, Velez 6. **SS**—Garibaldi 1, Macaluso 19, Salas 1, Sena 20, Velez 35. **OF**—Anderson 18, Ashford 44, Chourio 35, Hetherington 59, Rodriguez 63, Thomas 15.

PITCHING	W	L	ERA	G	GS	CG	SV	IP	H	R	ER	BB	SO	AVG	B	T	HT	WT	DOB	1st Yr	Resides
Bell, Bryon	0	0	27.00	1	0	0	0	1	3	3	3	0	2	.500	L	L	6-6	245	2-1-83	2004	New Hamburg, Ontario
Berroa, Yesson	3	3	6.60	10	9	0	0	36	51	28	24	12	32	.338	R	R	6-4	200	7-20-83	2001	San Pedro de Macoris, D.R.
Cannon, Eddie	3	0	2.95	19	0	0	0	40	36	16	13	11	40	.250	R	R	6-0	170	11-13-81	2004	Seaburg, Fla.
Charron, Joey	0	1	3.18	8	0	0	0	11	7	4	4	6	9	.167	L	L	5-9	158	4-5-82	2004	Tallahassee, Fla.
Cheng, Chi-Hung	1	3	2.82	14	14	0	0	61	47	27	19	35	74	.214	L	L	6-1	193	6-20-80	2004	Kaohsiung City, Taiwan
Gale, Bryan	1	3	6.28	12	0	0	0	14	13	11	10	8	19	.241	R	R	6-4	185	4-27-81	2004	Decatur, Mich.
Grant, Brian	3	1	2.94	10	9	0	0	49	54	23	16	12	29	.280	R	R	6-4	190	8-16-84	2002	Goldsboro, N.C.
Hahn, Cory	0	0	5.40	3	0	0	0	3	5	2	2	0	3	.333	R	R	6-0	235	10-25-81	2004	Louisville, Ky.
Harang, Daryl	3	1	4.71	15	0	0	0	21	16	11	11	7	23	.213	R	R	6-2	225	11-19-82	2004	San Diego, Calif.
Harrison, Ben	0	0	0.00	4	0	0	0	3	4	0	0	4	9	.267	L	L	6-1	175	4-14-84	2003	Colleyville, Texas
Martin, Adrian	3	2	3.54	18	7	0	0	56	65	28	22	12	51	.288	R	R	6-2	170	9-2-84	2003	Stuart, Fla.
Perez, Juan	1	0	1.50	1	1	0	0	6	5	1	1	0	1	.227	R	R	6-4	188	12-27-81	2002	Santo Domingo, D.R.
Pidutti, James	2	2	5.79	14	0	0	0	19	19	15	12	13	17	.253	R	R	6-2	205	11-22-81	2003	Coniston, Ontario
Rider, Michael	2	2	7.03	17	0	0	2	24	27	22	19	16	27	.297	R	R	6-3	187	11-21-83	2003	Fairfield, Calif.
Rodriguez, Edward	2	2	5.00	19	2	0	0	36	42	24	20	13	36	.292	R	R	6-3	170	10-6-84	2003	Santo Domingo, D.R.
Roy, Scott	1	0	2.08	8	0	0	2	13	13	5	3	3	13	.260	R	R	6-1	220	8-15-82	2004	Manchester, Conn.
Sanchez, Raymon	1	4	4.28	18	2	0	0	34	39	20	16	17	32	.279	L	L	6-0	170	1-7-84	2002	Santo Domingo, D.R.
Savickas, Russell	1	5	5.79	10	9	0	0	37	39	26	24	15	23	.273	R	R	6-4	170	7-30-83	2002	Johnston, R.I.
Tate, Derek	2	0	1.10	11	3	0	0	33	22	6	4	4	41	.186	R	L	5-11	185	12-19-81	2004	Kennewick, Wash.
Timm, Jordan	3	1	2.67	11	11	0	1	61	59	22	18	12	53	.253	L	L	6-6	230	1-15-81	2004	Pine River, Wis.
Tressler, Aaron	3	2	1.53	21	0	0	5	29	14	6	5	11	40	.137	R	R	6-1	188	3-28-82	2004	Pennsylvania Furnace, Pa.

MINOR
LEAGUES

After more than 50 years, minors break all-time attendence record

BY WILL LINGO

It would be nearly impossible to list all the ways minor league baseball now is different from minor league baseball after World War II. From the way teams obtain players to the way they sell tickets, just about everything has changed.

In most ways, today's version of minor league baseball is superior to its predecessor. The modern game had never been able to match one thing, however: attendance numbers. Back in 1949, 448 teams in 59 minor leagues drew nearly 40 million fans, a record that stood ever since. The minors drew close in 2003 but got knocked back by bad weather, drawing a shade over 39 million for the season.

The record finally fell in 2004, however, as teams in the affiliated minors drew 39,887,755 fans, an all-time record.

Promoted to Triple-A
Huge crowds in places like Round Rock spurred the minors' attendance boom

"Congratulations to our clubs, leagues and of course the fans who have made this possible," Minor League Baseball president Mike Moore said. "This is a proud accomplishment for our industry."

Unfortunately, no one found out about the accomplishment until every minor league team had closed its gates for the season. Minor League Baseball said right after the season that unofficial estimates put attendance at 39.5 million for the season.

The old record of 39,782,717 fans stood since 1949, and it represented the peak of the post-war boom. The new record came from 176 teams playing in 15 leagues.

The minor leagues have been approaching the attendance record for several years, with four of the five highest attendance totals in the 103 years of the National Association (which is now known as Minor League Baseball) coming in the last four years.

It also turned out that the old record was not as high as had been reported for years. Steve Densa, Minor League Baseball's assistant director of media relations, discovered the 1949 attendance numbers included league all-star games, which are not supposed to count toward regular season attendance. With those games taken out, the new figure is 39,640,443.

The journey from one peak to the next was long and arduous. To find this out, though, you don't have to go to history books. You can just call John Moss, the president of the South Atlantic League. He started the Western Carolina League in 1948 at the height of the post-war boom, and though he left for a few years to run the Rock Hill, S.C., club in the Tri-State League, he has been president of the league nearly ever since.

The Western Carolina League started with eight teams, all in western North Carolina. It endured through the bad times, though sometimes just barely. In 1976, arguably the absolute bottom of the minor league parabola, the league was down to four teams and played an interlocking schedule with the Carolina League, which also had just four teams.

Even then, though, Moss said he didn't fear the end of minor league baseball. "I've always been an eternal optimist," he said. "I've had the opportunity to be in the game through a lot of evolution. And right now I think we're at the peak of where we have ever been."

The Western Carolinas League became the South Atlantic League in 1980. It has grown to a current roster of 16 teams, stretching from Savannah, Ga., to suburban Cleveland. Where its four teams drew 134,217 fans in 1976, the 16 teams drew more than 3 million fans in 2004.

What is the league doing better? Better ballparks, better amenities for fans, better facilities for players, better people in the front offices, better promotion and marketing. You name it. "All the things we're doing are just a little better than they've been done before, to the best of my knowledge," Moss said.

It took the minors awhile to become adept at it, but now the sales, marketing and promotion efforts of many minor league teams are on par with any professional sports franchise. The last push came from new ballpark standards that prompted cities across America to pour millions into ballpark construction and renovation. Since 1988, new ballparks have been built for 104 affiliated teams. Construction reached a peak from 1993-97, when 46 new facilities sprung up.

New ballparks and new markets have provided the fuel to drive minor league attendance ever higher, but the real driving force has been people who have dedicated their lives to minor

A YEAR FOR THE AGES

Minor League Baseball set an all-time attendance record in 2004, drawing almost 250,000 more fans than the old record, set in 1949. The five largest attendance figures in history:

Year	No. of Teams	Attendance
2004	176	39,887,755
1949	448	*39,640,443
2003	176	39,069,707
2002	176	38,639,142
2001	176	38,808,339

*Revised in 2004 from the originally stated record of 39,782,717

league baseball.

"The secret is simple," Moore said. "Owners and operators who were willing to work hard 12 months a year and make the fans their main objective turned the game into a real part of the American fabric."

And in 2004, all the hard work paid off and brought minor league baseball full circle.

Onward And Upward

One of the major reasons minor league baseball has grown so much over the last 25 years has been its willingness to move teams to new, bigger markets.

The 2004 season brought just a few new cities, but those that did come in were immediately successful. The most notable move came in the Southern League, where the Montgomery Biscuits started play. The Biscuits drew 322,946 fans, ninth-best in Double-A and more than double the 150,051 who came out for the team's last season in Orlando.

Paul Payne was 15 when pro baseball returned to Chattanooga in 1976. Now a businessman in Montgomery and father of three, he was there for Opening Night. "We're looking for something our family can build memories around," he said. "There are a lot of us transplants here that don't pull for Alabama or Auburn. So this will be our team."

That's what Tom Dickson and his wife/business partner Sherrie Myers were counting on when they purchased the franchise and moved it into the new 7,000-seat, $26 mil-

lion Riverwalk Stadium on the banks of the Alabama River.

Even the club's logo—a google-eyed cartoon biscuit with a pat of butter for a tongue—gained acceptance. Most of the complaints were drowned out by the sound of cash registers, as Biscuits apparel became a bestseller.

"It was met with skepticism and, frankly, anger," Payne said. "But you know what? When you're looking at minor league baseball, you just want to be noticed. You want to stand out from the hundreds of other teams out there.

"Biscuits certainly does stand out."

Another new Double-A franchise found itself embroiled in an even bigger nickname controversy. When the Eastern League franchise that was moving from New Haven, Conn., to Manchester, N.H., announced its name would be the New Hampshire Primaries, the outcry was so great that the team changed the name to the New Hampshire Fisher Cats. The Fisher Cats also had a successful first season, drawing 215,961 fans, but they expect things to really take off when they open their new ballpark in 2005.

The final franchise move for 2004 came in the Appalachian League, where the Astros affiliate moved from Martinsville, Va., to Greeneville, Tenn., and shared a new ballpark with Tusculum College. The Astros drew 51,183 fans, tops in the Appy League and more than double what the team drew in its last season in Martinsville.

Things weren't as happy in another Greenville—this one in South Carolina. For five years the Greenville Braves said they needed a new stadium, and just before Opening Day the threatened move became reality. The Southern League franchise will move to Pearl, Miss., a suburb of Jackson, for the 2005 season. Although the city of Greenville put together a last-minute stadium deal, the offer was trumped by Pearl's offer of a $25 million stadium paid for with private money. (Greenville was likely to get another franchise soon, however, in the Southern or South Atlantic League.)

That announcement came just before the 2004 season, but a more surprising announcement came as the season ended, when John Q. Hammons' proclamations proved true. Hammons said he would bring a Double-A team to Springfield, Mo., to play in the $32 million ballpark he

ORGANIZATION STANDINGS

Cumulative farm club records for the 30 major league organizations, with winning percentages going back five years. Every organization has six affiliates, except the Mets, who have seven:

	2004 W	L	Pct.	2003 Pct.	2002 Pct.	2001 Pct.	2000 Pct.	1999 Pct.
Oakland	400	295	.576	.532	.509	.480	.551	.573
Toronto	400	299	.572	.531	.480	.460	.529	.534
Texas	381	313	.549	.547	.498	.478	.530	.541
New York-NL	412	341	.547	.503	.496	.524	.509	.516
Cleveland	380	324	.540	.576	.577	.543	.517	.500
Chicago-NL	365	314	.538	.474	.529	.512	.513	.480
Houston	375	329	.533	.500	.535	.598	.526	.499
St. Louis	364	336	.520	.451	.509	.423	.472	.442
New York-AL	354	335	.514	.501	.530	.543	.517	.558
Atlanta	351	332	.514	.497	.512	.489	.493	.496
Pittsburgh	354	339	.511	.581	.571	.467	.491	.487
Seattle	351	340	.508	.527	.471	.560	.577	.483
Chicago-AL	353	347	.504	.494	.466	.495	.483	.520
Boston	350	346	.503	.496	.454	.468	.522	.526
Los Angeles	345	342	.502	.485	.563	.538	.527	.457
Minnesota	341	338	.502	.503	.540	.541	.537	.496
San Diego	349	347	.501	.476	.513	.470	.485	.505
Kansas City	348	347	.501	.527	.521	.469	.457	.545
Arizona	347	363	.489	.513	.454	.477	.466	.483
Colorado	342	368	.482	.508	.473	.478	.502	.472
Tampa Bay	331	371	.472	.497	.445	.474	.478	.508
San Francisco	327	367	.471	.454	.463	.528	.444	.502
Cincinnati	326	368	.470	.480	.528	.567	.486	.521
Detroit	322	368	.467	.481	.509	.508	.478	.480
Philadelphia	322	368	.467	.462	.525	.504	.568	.523
Baltimore	323	382	.458	.486	.434	.445	.481	.453
Florida	315	377	.455	.502	.491	.539	.496	.477
Anaheim	315	378	.455	.510	.472	.499	.426	.486
Milwaukee	316	381	.453	.469	.462	.496	.495	.442
Montreal	288	392	.424	.437	.477	.435	.453	.493

MINOR LEAGUES

Francis takes smooth path to success

His rise was so sustained and carried Jeff Francis to such sublime heights, it's easy to forget his struggles the first two months of the 2003 season.

He finished 12-9, 3.47 the year at high Class A Visalia. A deeper look at his statistics there suggest dominance rather than hard times

 and a complete turnaround for Francis, a 6-foot-5 lefthander taken in the first round of the 2002 draft by the Rockies.

Francis had far more strikeouts (153) than walks (45) at Visalia, fewer hits (135) than innings (161), and on July 6 he threw a no-hitter. In short, Francis' first full professional season was a springboard to the 2004 brilliance that made him Baseball America's Minor League Player of the Year.

Francis went 16-4, 2.21 in 24 combined starts at Double-A Tulsa and Triple-A Colorado Springs. He totaled 155 innings and averaged 11.4 strikeouts per nine innings, which by itself would be impressive. But consider this: Francis' strikeouts—196, which led the minor leagues at the time of his promotion to Colorado—far exceeded the number of hits (108) and walks (29) he allowed.

The only thing Francis didn't do in 2004 was pitch in the Olympics. The Rockies announced in early August that Francis would not travel to Athens to pitch for his native Canada. Instead, the Rockies' schedule allowed Francis to make two starts at altitude in Colorado Springs and join the Rockies at the outset of a four-city road trip in late August.

For his part, Francis said he understood and agreed with the Rockies' decision. "I have zero regrets," Francis says. "Where I am now—I wouldn't trade it for anything. If I'd gone to the Olympics, (the Rockies) told me they would have shut me down after it."

But two months into the 2003 season, there's no way anyone would have expected Francis' destination in August 2004 to be the big leagues. After 11 starts at Visalia, Francis was 2-7, 6.88 and

Dream season
Jeff Francis was nearly unhittable in 2004

had surrendered 66 hits in 52 innings with 20 walks and 45 strikeouts.

In his next start, Francis pitched six scoreless innings, allowing three hits and two walks with 11 strikeouts. That outing on June 5 was the beginning of a stunning turnaround when Francis went 10-2, 1.83 in his final 16 starts. Take those starts with his performance in 2004, and he went 26-5, 2.40 over 40 starts with 54 walks, 304 strikeouts and 177 hits in 263 innings.

Marteese Robinson, professional scouting director for the Cardinals, saw three of Francis' starts with Tulsa and noticed opposing hitters rarely took good swings against him. Like Greg Maddux, Robinson said, Francis has the ability to paint the corners with his fastball.

"His delivery and mechanics are almost flawless," he says. "The fastball looks like the curveball, looks like the changeup and vice-versa. From the second he lifts the leg, he's coming at you. It's a chess game to him; every pitch has a purpose."

Fastball command and fastball extension are two of Francis' primary assets and will help him cope with Coors Field. It won't hurt that Francis, 23, is poised on the mound—he was a physics major at the University of British Columbia, after all—as well as perceptive, intelligent and adaptable.

Francis throws an average fastball in the 89-91 mph range, a curveball and a changeup. His miniscule walk totals are clear evidence of his superb fastball command. But coupled with that is the delivery extension that gives Francis an edge.

After going 0-2, 13.50 in his first two starts in the majors and giving up 13 hits, including five homers, in 9⅓ innings—Francis made strides when he "just kind of tried to slow things down" in his third start. He held the Padres to five hits in 5⅓ scoreless innings and came away with his first big league win and finished the season with a 3-2, 5.15 record in Colorado.

"I don't know if it's a relief," Francis said. "I want to go out there and keep pitching the way I can. It's not like I've done anything yet. It's just one game. It's a matter of putting a lot of those type of games together."

PREVIOUS **WINNERS**

1981—Mike Marshall, 1b, Albuquerque (Dodgers)	
1982—Ron Kittle, of, Edmonton (White Sox)	
1983—Dwight Gooden, rhp, Lynchburg (Mets)	
1984—Mike Bielecki, rhp, Hawaii (Pirates)	
1985—Jose Canseco, of, Huntsville/Tacoma (Athletics)	
1986—Gregg Jefferies, ss, Columbia/Lynchburg/Jackson (Mets)	
1987—Gregg Jefferies, ss, Jackson/Tidewater (Mets)	
1988—Tom Gordon, rhp, Appleton/Memphis/Omaha (Royals)	
1989—Sandy Alomar, c, Las Vegas (Padres)	
1990—Frank Thomas, 1b, Birmingham (White Sox)	
1991—Derek Bell, of, Syracuse (Blue Jays)	
1992—Tim Salmon, of, Edmonton (Angels)	
1993—Manny Ramirez, of, Canton/Charlotte (Indians)	
1994—Derek Jeter, ss, Tampa/Albany/Columbus (Yankees)	
1995—Andruw Jones, of, Macon (Braves)	
1996—Andruw Jones, of, Durham/Greenville/Richmond (Braves)	
1997—Paul Konerko, 1b, Albuquerque (Dodgers)	
1998—Eric Chavez, 3b, Huntsville/Edmonton (Athletics)	
1999—Rick Ankiel, lhp, Arkansas/Memphis (Cardinals)	
2000—Jon Rauch, rhp, Winston-Salem/Birmingham (White Sox)	
2001—Josh Beckett, rhp, Brevard County/Portland (Marlins)	
2002—Rocco Baldelli, of, Bakersfield/Orlando/Durham (Devil Rays)	
2003—Joe Mauer, c, Fort Myers/New Britain (Twins)	

built for Southwest Missouri State University. Then the Cardinals announced they were purchasing the Texas League's El Paso Diablos and moving them to Springfield for the 2005 season. The Springfield team will play at 8,000-seat Hammons Field. SMS played there in 2004, but it was built with Double-A baseball in mind.

Hammons, an 84-year-old hotelier who owns more than 50 hotels across the United States, paid for the bulk of the ballpark project. Because some of his hotels include interests in casinos, he is not permitted to own a minor league team, so the Cardinals stepped in. The El Paso Times reported the sales price was $9.8 million.

The Texas League will now stretch into Missouri, and that won't be the only change for the league in 2005. In a move that had been announced in 2003, the league's Round Rock franchise—arguably the most successful Double-A franchise ever—will move to Corpus Christi for 2005.

The move became necessary because Round Rock is moving up to Triple-A. The Pacific Coast League's Edmonton franchise played its last season in 2004 and will move to Round Rock for 2005. The team will keep the same name as the previous franchise, the Round Rock Express.

Cal League Gets Shuffled

Several of the pending franchise moves created accompanying affiliation changes, but otherwise it was the five new affiliations in the California League that highlighted an otherwise ho-hum session of trading partners after the 2004 season ended.

The biggest news came in Modesto, where the Athletics ended a 30-year affiliation to move to Stockton, which offered a new ballpark and a slightly better location. Modesto signed a two-year affiliation with the Rockies. The Rockies wanted to stay in the California League but were hoping to upgrade from Visalia, and Modesto was the best affiliate remaining.

The Brewers left the league to move their Class A affiliate east, so the Royals decided to move west to High Desert, which is closer to their spring training complex in Surprise, Ariz.

The Devil Rays remained in the Cal League but will move from Bakersfield to Visalia. The Oaks are still making improvements to Recreation Park to bring it up to Organized Baseball standards, and the club said a new clubhouse will be ready for the 2005 season. With that move, the only club left in the Cal League was Bakersfield, which announced an affiliation agreement with the Rangers. The Rangers were forced out of Stockton when the Athletics moved in.

The Devil Rays wanted to move their high Class A affiliate back to the East Coast, but they were squeezed out by other teams. One that took an open slot was the Brewers, who announced a two-year affiliation with Brevard County in the Florida State League. The Brewers' move from High Desert seems odd at first glance because their spring training base is in Arizona. But the team has made an

JetHawks lost players but just kept winning

The chain reaction should have decimated the Lancaster JetHawks. After all, adversity was widespread in the Diamondbacks organization in 2004.

The tumultuous season was peppered with injuries and trades that ravaged Arizona's big league roster.

Naturally, replacements came from the upper levels of the farm system, and that created a trickledown effect that meant the high Class A JetHawks lost many of their players as the season went on. The team that cruised to a first-half division title in the California League South was ravaged at the midway point of the season. Lancaster lost six players, including Carlos Quentin (.310-15-51 in the first half), Conor Jackson (.345-11-54) and Jamie D'Antona (.315-13-57)—the heart of a lineup that scored 263 runs in 36 games.

Despite all that, Lancaster managed to follow its 43-27 first half with a 43-27 second half, good enough for another division title. The JetHawks lost to Modesto in the decisive fifth game of an exciting championship series, but their perseverance in posting one of the best records in the minors with an ever-changing roster made them Baseball America's Minor League Team of the Year. "I've never been with a club that experienced this much turnover in a year before," manager Wally Backman said. "It was a big challenge for us as a staff to set the bar as high from the beginning of the year."

Lancaster won in the face of major turnover by turning new parts into equally effective every-

day players. Backman also relied on a few key players who spent the entire season at Lancaster. Outfielder Jarred Ball and catcher Phil Avlas, who both drove in more than 65 runs, were the most important position players, while Enrique Gonzalez and Justin Wechsler stabilized the pitching staff all year.

The team reflected Backman's influence as well, and he did a good job of putting players in the right roles. Backman's bunch also fed off his outgoing and animated style—illustrated by his six ejections and two suspensions, not to mention his frequent trash can-throwing, table-tossing tirades.

It's a unique combination of attributes, but it helped Backman created a group with uncommon camaraderie. After games, players would get together and cook out, watch "SportsCenter" or play pool. It wasn't uncommon for Backman and the coaches to spend time with their players off the field.

"The coaches don't separate themselves from us; they come out and hang out with us and keep us in line," Ball said. "I think that's probably the main factor with us winning, the way we play as a team. I'll remember this year as the most fun I've had. Usually at the end of the year you're ready to go home, but this year I've had so much fun, I'd rather stay here and keep playing."

PREVIOUS WINNERS

1993—Harrisburg/Eastern (Expos)
1994—Wilmington/Carolina (Royals)
1995—Norfolk/International (Mets)
1996—Edmonton/Pacific Coast (Athletics)
1997—West Michigan/Midwest (Tigers)
1998—Mobile/Southern (Padres)
1999—Trenton/Eastern (Red Sox)
2000—Round Rock/Texas (Astros)
2001—Lake Elsinore/California (Padres)
2002—Akron Aeros/Eastern (Indians)
2003—Sacramento/Pacific Coast (Athletics)

MINOR LEAGUES

effort to move its affiliates closer together on the East Coast, also switching its low Class A team from Beloit to Charleston, W.Va.

The Reds also moved into the FSL, signing an affiliation with Sarasota. Sarasota had been home of the Red Sox' high Class A team, but Boston moved north to Wilmington. The moves makes perfect sense for the Reds, who have held spring training in Sarasota since 1998.

The Reds' move also worked out well for the Carolina League's Potomac Cannons, who signed a two-year affiliation agreement with the Expos. The Cannons, based in the northern Virginia suburb of Woodbridge, announced the agreement just before Major League Baseball said it would move the Expos to Washington, D.C.

The Expos also established a new Triple-A affiliation in New Orleans. The Expos replace the Astros, who had been in New Orleans since 1997 but decided to switch over to the new Round Rock PCL franchise.

In other notable affiliation moves:

■ The Red Sox announced an agreement with Wilmington (Carolina), leaving Sarasota and the Florida State League. The move put four of the Sox' six minor league teams in the Northeast.

■ The Mets' move to low Class A Hagerstown ended a 22-year relationship with Capital City. The move was driven by the Bombers' shaky stadium situation. With a ballpark initiative in Columbia, S.C., apparently dead, Bombers ownership said the franchise was looking to move if it finds the right opportunity.

■ Quad Cities, where John O'Donnell Stadium went through a massive renovation for the 2004 season, booted the Twins and signed an affiliation deal with the Cardinals. The Cardinals left Peoria, and the Cubs stepped in there from Lansing.

For a complete rundown of affiliation moves, see the accompanying chart.

No Longer Accepting Visa

Construction and landscaping workers in the Sun Belt. Ski resort workers in Colorado. Dishwashers and housekeepers from Cape Cod to Lake Tahoe. Australian lifeguards on Long Island.

And baseball players?

All these groups were affected by the sudden end of visas for temporary foreign workers just before the 2004 season started. Known as H-2B visas, they dried up after U.S. Citizenship and Immigration Services handed out 66,000 by mid-March, leaving baseball and a variety of other industries scrambling to adjust.

"The visa situation is really unfortunate," Blue Jays scouting director Jon Lalonde said. "We had to discount Canadian players in the draft this year because they wouldn't be able to play in our system at all this summer.

"The larger impact, however, has been with our Latin players. There were six players we were hoping to bring in from our Dominican Summer League team this year, but we weren't able to due to the visa restriction."

Major league players weren't affected because they come under a visa classification for people in specialty occupations. Minor league players, however, are lumped in with non-agricultural, seasonal workers of every stripe.

The current system has been in place since the early 1990s, but immigration officials had never observed the limit before. Because of post-Sept. 11 security concerns and a sudden surge in applications, though, the government held to the 66,000 cap.

The final couple of moves in the 2004 affiliation dance wrapped up just at the deadline, with five California League clubs changing affiliations and the Expos placing their high Class A franchise near their new major league home in Washington, D.C.

TRIPLE-A Minor League Team	Old Affiliate	New Affiliate
Indianapolis (International)	Brewers	Pirates
Nashville (Pacific Coast)	Pirates	Brewers
New Orleans (Pacific Coast)	Astros	Expos
*Round Rock (Pacific Coast)	Expos	Astros
DOUBLE-A		
†Corpus Christi (Texas)	Astros	Astros
#Springfield (Texas)	Diamondbacks	Cardinals
Tennessee (Southern)	Cardinals	Diamondbacks
HIGH CLASS A		
Bakersfield (California)	Devil Rays	Rangers
Brevard County (Florida State)	Expos	Brewers
High Desert (California)	Brewers	Royals
Modesto (California)	Athletics	Rockies
Potomac (Carolina)	Reds	Expos
Sarasota (Florida State)	Red Sox	Reds
Stockton (California)	Rangers	Athletics
Wilmington (Carolina)	Royals	Red Sox
Visalia (California)	Rockies	Devil Rays
LOW CLASS A		
Augusta (South Atlantic)	Red Sox	Giants
Battle Creek (Midwest)	Yankees	Devil Rays
Beloit (Midwest)	Brewers	Twins
Capital City (South Atlantic)	Mets	Red Sox
Charleston, S.C. (South Atlantic)	Devil Rays	Yankees
Charleston, W.Va. (South Atlantic)	Blue Jays	Brewers
Hagerstown (South Atlantic)	Giants	Mets
Lansing (Midwest)	Cubs	Blue Jays
Peoria (Midwest)	Cardinals	Cubs
Quad Cities (Midwest)	Twins	Cardinals

*Franchise operated in Edmonton in 2004.
†Franchise operated in Round Rock in 2004.
#Franchise operated in El Paso in 2004.

Baseball felt the pinch. First, Latin American players who are ready to come to the United States weren't been able to get in, resulting in older players having to stay and play in the Latin American-based Rookie leagues, and a shortage of talent for domestic leagues as well, especially at the short-season levels.

The struggle for affiliated teams to fill out minor league rosters had a trickle-down effect on independent leagues, which saw more of their players signed by affiliated clubs and lost one of their usual sources of talent: released players.

The draft was also affected by the visa limit, forcing teams to change the way they assessed foreign players who were eligible for the draft. For example, teams drafted 37 Canadians in 2004, which is a bit below normal. Few of the 37 signed and played during the season.

But the visa difficulties seem certain to get worse in 2005 unless something changes. Baseball officials were lobbying to either increase the limit or change minor leaguers to a different visa classification.

Leagues Take Over Two Teams

In contrast with the rosy overall picture in the minor leagues, two franchises were taken over by their respective leagues in 2004 (and remained in that situation after the season ended) after they became awash in red ink.

A grand plan in Portland, Ore., involving tens of millions of dollars went sour, and the Pacific Coast League had to assume control when no one else would. The Beavers have been a financial sinkhole since returning to the PCL in 2001, and questions remained about who

MINOR LEAGUES

Selected by Baseball America

Chris Burke

Carlos Quentin

Jose Capellan

Yusmeiro Petit

FIRST TEAM

Pos.	Player, Team (League)	AVG	AB	R	H	2B	3B	HR	RBI	BB	SO	SB
C	Brian McCann, Myrtle Beach (Carolina)	.278	385	45	107	35	0	16	66	31	54	2
1B	Ryan Howard, Reading (EL)/Scranton/Wilkes-Barre (IL)	.291	485	94	141	28	1	46	131	60	166	1
2B	Chris Burke, New Orleans (Pacific Coast)	.315	483	93	152	33	6	16	52	55	76	37
3B	Ian Stewart, Asheville (South Atlantic)	.319	505	92	161	31	9	30	101	66	112	19
SS	B.J. Upton, Montgomery (SL)/Durham (IL)	.315	368	86	116	24	2	14	51	66	100	20
OF	Jason Kubel, New Britain (EL)/Rochester (IL)	.352	488	96	172	42	4	22	100	52	59	16
OF	Carlos Quentin, Lancaster (CAL)/El Paso (TL)	.332	452	103	150	33	1	21	89	43	56	5
OF	Delmon Young, Charleston, S.C. (South Atlantic)	.322	513	95	165	26	5	25	116	53	120	21
DH	Dallas McPherson, Arkansas (TL)/Salt Lake (PCL)	.317	521	107	165	36	14	40	126	60	169	12

Pos.	Player, Team (League)	W	L	ERA	G	GS	CG	SV	IP	H	BB	SO
SP	Jose Capellan, Myrtle Beach (CL)/Greenville (SL)/Rich. (IL)	14	4	2.32	24	23	1	0	140	113	45	152
SP	Jeff Francis, Tulsa (TL)/Colorado Springs (PCL)	16	3	2.85	24	24	1	0	155	108	29	196
SP	Brandon McCarthy, Kannapolis (SAL)/W-S (CL)/Birm. (SL)	17	6	3.14	27	27	3	0	172	134	30	202
SP	Yusmeiro Petit, Cap. City (SAL)/St. Lucie (FSL)/Bing. (EL)	12	6	2.20	26	26	1	0	139	84	41	200
RP	Brad Baker, Mobile (SL)/Portland (PCL)	3	1	1.48	63	0	0	34	67	42	28	85

SECOND TEAM

Pos.	Player, Team (League)	AVG	AB	R	H	2B	3B	HR	RBI	BB	SO	SB
C	Ryan Garko, Kinston (CL)/Akron (EL)/Buffalo (IL)	.330	430	75	142	33	1	22	100	42	65	5
1B	Brad Eldred, Lynchburg (CL)/Altoona (EL)	.302	473	77	143	31	1	37	135	41	144	5
2B	Delwyn Young, Vero Beach (Florida State)	.281	470	76	132	36	3	22	85	57	134	11
3B	David Wright, Binghamton (EL)/Norfolk (IL)	.341	337	62	115	35	0	18	57	55	60	22
SS	Ian Kinsler, Clinton (MWL)/Frisco (TL)	.345	504	103	174	51	2	20	99	58	84	23
OF	Conor Jackson, Lancaster (CAL)/El Paso (TL)	.324	484	97	157	32	4	17	91	69	72	7
OF	Brandon Moss, Augusta (SAL)/Sarasota (FSL)	.353	516	82	182	27	7	15	111	53	90	21
OF	Nick Swisher, Sacramento (Pacific Coast)	.269	443	109	119	28	2	29	92	103	109	3
DH	Brian Dopirak, Lansing (Midwest)	.307	541	94	166	38	0	39	120	48	123	4

Pos.	Player, Team (League)	W	L	ERA	G	GS	CG	SV	IP	H	BB	SO
SP	Gustavo Chacin, New Hampshire (EL)/Syracuse (IL)	18	2	2.88	27	27	0	0	153	129	52	123
SP	Kyle Davies, Myr. Beach (CL)/Greenville (SL)/Richmond (IL)	13	3	2.72	26	26	0	0	142	100	54	173
SP	Zach Duke, Lynchburg (CL)/Altoona (EL)	15	6	1.46	26	26	1	0	148	114	30	142
SP	Felix Hernandez, Inland Empire (CAL)/San Antonio (TL)	14	4	2.95	26	25	1	0	149	132	47	172
RP	Jairo Garcia, Kane Co. (MWL)/Midland (TL)/Sacramento (PCL)	4	2	1.46	49	0	0	19	62	36	30	102

would pick up the pieces and accept millions in losses, and whether the team has a long-term future in Portland.

The situation was so unsettled that it wasn't clear the franchise would be ready to open its gates until just before the season. The team's primary creditor, the Teachers Insurance and Annuity Association-College Retirement Equities Fund, and team owner Portland Family Entertainment agreed to an arrangement that allowed the PCL to take over the club. The league had to step in after the city of Portland said it would not allow the team to play at PGE Park unless the team's shaky financial picture was clarified.

The franchise was said to have potential buyers, but by the end of the season it remained under league control.

The takeover of the Bakersfield Blaze was more surpris-ing. Bakersfield is a charter member of the California League and has had a professional baseball team almost continuously since 1941, but years of declining atten-dance and the lack of a new ballpark on the horizon finally led to the league stepping in.

The root of the problem dates back to 2001, when a ballpark project fell apart. The Blaze has been one of the worst draws in the Cal League and averaged 999 fans a game in 2004, 163rd out of 176 minor league teams.

Even when the ballpark project was being discussed, league and city officials wanted the Patton family to sell the team. Lowell Patton bought the franchise in 1985 for $200,000 and longtime Blaze general manager Jack Patton, Lowell Patton's son, said the team was nearly sold again in the 2003-04 offseason. The deal fell through in

December, and when that happened the team had to scramble to get ready for the 2004 season. Three Cal League owners put up the money to buy the franchise and turn over operation to the league, while the league searches for new, permanent ownership.

Minor League Baseball president Mike Moore said he's not particularly concerned about having two teams under league control. "In both instances, the franchises were poorly operated, necessitating the takeovers," Moore said. "Properly operated, I would expect both to be successful franchises."

Careers On The Ropes

The careers of two of the most talented prospects in baseball were placed in jeopardy because of substance abuse. Devil Rays outfielder Josh Hamilton and Marlins righthander Jeff Allison, both of whom were first-round picks and former Baseball America High School Player of the Year award winners, missed all of the 2004 season, with their returns uncertain.

Hamilton's problems kept him off the field for all of the last two seasons, but the depth and severity of his

ALL-STAR FUTURES GAME

The 2004 All-Star Futures Game in Houston brought together some of the hardest-throwing pitchers in the minor leagues. Count David Wright among the most impressed onlookers.

A .351-16-52 first half earned the Mets third-base prospect a trip to Houston, where he faced Felix Hernandez (Mariners), Jose Capellan (Braves) and Merkin Valdez (Giants). All three touched 97 mph, with Capellan reaching 98. Wright went 1-for-3, striking out on a Hernandez curveball, singling against Capellan and grounding out versus Valdez.

"Those guys speak for themselves," said Wright, who went on to New York in the second half and fared better against big league pitching. "Those three might be the best three pitchers I've faced in my career. It's good to put the faces with the names. You read about them, and it's good meeting them. I just hope I don't have to see them too often in the future."

David Wright

Wright wasn't alone in seeing a steady diet of quality pitching. Many of the minor leagues' best arms were on hand for the Futures Game, and they overmatched the hitters even more than the final score would indicate: 4-3 in favor of the United States.

"The pitching was definitely dominating," Dodgers catcher Koyie Hill said. "That's as many swings and misses and soft-hit balls as you'll see from these hitters."

Dallas McPherson (Angels) was also one of the two best third-base prospects and he left Houston with two strikeouts in two at-bats, whiffing on a curveball from Jeff Francis (Rockies) and a 98 mph fastball from Capellan. And he had a blast.

"I had never heard of Capellan before this game," McPherson said. "It looked like he was 89-90 in warmups, then he's 96 with his first pitch, and I'm like, 'Whoa, where'd that come from?' That's what you get in a game like this."

All three offensive rallies—two-run outbursts by the United States in the third and fifth, and a three-run last gasp by the World in the seventh and final inning— were aided by catchable fly balls that outfielders couldn't make plays on. If not for the shaky defense, the Futures Game might have seen its first scoreless tie.

The United States moved its lead to 4-0 in the fifth on Blue Jays shortstop Aaron Hill's double, who was the last player added to the Futures Game rosters. Fellow Blue Jays shortstop Russ Adams originally was

slated to attend before a sore rib cage forced him to bow out. Hill ended up with the MVP award, joining a distinguished class that also includes Alfonso Soriano, Sean Burroughs and Jose Reyes.

UNITED STATES ROSTER

Pitchers: Joe Blanton (Athletics), Bryan Bullington (Pirates), Matt Cain (Giants), John Danks (Rangers), Clint Everts (Expos), Gavin Floyd (Phillies), Bill Murphy (Marlins), Kyle Sleeth (Tigers), Tim Stauffer (Padres), Brad Thompson (Cardinals).
Catchers: Koyie Hill (Dodgers), Jeff Mathis (Angels).
Infielders: Michael Aubrey (Indians), Chris Burke (Astros), Prince Fielder (Brewers), Aaron Hill (Blue Jays), Dallas McPherson (Angels), B.J. Upton (Devil Rays), Rickie Weeks (Brewers), David Wright (Mets).
Outfielders: Jason Kubel (Twins), Conor Jackson (Diamondbacks), Val Majewski (Orioles), Jeremy Reed (Mariners), Delmon Young (Devil Rays).

WORLD ROSTER

Pitchers: Jose Capellan (Braves), Fausto Carmona (Indians), Jeff Francis (Rockies), Jairo Garcia (Athletics), Felix Hernandez (Mariners), Wil Ledezma (Tigers), Arnie Munoz (White Sox), Juan Perez (Red Sox), Yusmeiro Petit (Mets), Merkin Valdez (Giants).
Catchers: Dioner Navarro (Yankees), Robinzon Diaz (Blue Jays).
Infielders: Jesus Cota (Diamondbacks), Justin Morneau (Twins), Robinson Cano (Yankees), Ruben Gotay (Royals), Edwin Encarnacion (Reds), Andy Marte (Braves), Andres Blanco (Royals), Joel Guzman (Dodgers).
Outfielders: Tony Blanco (Reds), Shin-Soo Choo (Mariners), Jorge Cortes (Pirates), Felix Pie (Cubs), Willy Taveras (Astros).

FUTURES GAME
Minute Maid Park, Houston
July 11, 2004

United States 4, World 3

WORLD	ab	r	h	rbi	USA	ab	r	h	rbi
Taveras, cf	2	0	0	0	Burke, 2b	2	1	1	0
Pie, cf	1	0	1	1	Weeks, 2b	1	0	0	0
Gotay, 2b	1	0	0	0	Upton, ss	2	0	0	0
Cano, 2b	2	0	0	1	Hill, ss	1	0	1	2
Morneau, 1b	4	0	0	0	McPherson dh	2	0	0	0
Encarnacion, 3b	2	0	2	0	Aubrey, dh	1	0	0	0
Marte, 3b	2	0	0	0	Fielder, 1b	3	0	1	0
Choo, rf	3	0	0	0	Wright, 3b	3	0	1	0
Blanco, dh	2	0	0	0	Hill, c	2	0	0	0
Cota, dh	1	0	0	0	Mathis, c	1	0	0	0
Cortes, lf	2	1	0	0	Reed, cf	1	0	0	0
Navarro, c	2	0	0	0	Jackson, lf	1	1	1	0
Diaz, c	1	1	1	0	Kubel, lf-rf	2	2	1	0
Guzman, ss	2	0	1	0	Young, rf	1	0	0	0
Blanco, ss	0	1	0	0	Majewski, cf	1	0	0	0
Totals	27	3	5	2	Totals	24	4	6	2
World					000	000		3—3	
USA					002	020		x—4	

E—Marte, Choo, Wright. **2B**—Diaz, Hill, Jackson.

WORLD	ip	h	r	er	bb	so	USA	ip	h	r	er	bb	so
Francis	1	0	0	0	0	2	Blanton	1	1	0	0	1	1
Hernandez	1	1	0	0	0	1	Stauffer	1	0	0	0	0	2
Ledezma, L	1	2	2	0	0	1	Danks, W	1	2	0	0	0	1
Capellan	1	1	0	0	0	2	Everts	1	0	0	0	0	1
Munoz	⅓	1	2	0	0	0	Murphy	1	0	0	0	1	2
Petit	⅔	1	0	0	0	1	Bullington	1	0	0	0	0	1
Valdez	⅔	0	0	0	0	0	Cain	0	1	3	3	2	0
Garcia	⅓	0	0	0	0	1	Floyd	⅔	1	0	0	0	1
							Sleeth, Sv	⅓	0	0	0	0	0

WP—Murphy, Floyd. **T**—2:08.

CLASSIFICATION ALL-STARS

Selected by Baseball America

Pos.	Player, Team (League)	AVG	AB	R	H	2B	3B	HR	RBI	BB	SO	SB
C	Koyie Hill, Las Vegas (Pacific Coast)	.286	350	57	100	26	0	13	54	28	69	0
1B	Justin Morneau, Rochester (International)	.306	288	51	88	23	0	22	63	32	47	1
2B	Chris Burke, New Orleans (Pacific Coast)	.315	483	93	152	33	6	16	52	55	76	37
3B	Dallas McPherson, Salt Lake (Pacific Coast)	.313	259	54	81	19	8	20	57	23	95	6
SS	Jhonny Peralta, Buffalo (International)	.326	556	109	181	44	2	15	86	54	126	8
OF	Matt Diaz, Durham (International)	.331	499	81	165	47	5	21	92	26	94	15
OF	Jason Kubel, Rochester (International)	.343	350	51	120	28	0	16	71	34	40	16
OF	Nick Swisher, Sacramento (Pacific Coast)	.269	443	109	119	28	2	29	92	103	109	3
DH	Calvin Pickering, Omaha (Pacific Coast)	.314	299	65	94	12	1	35	79	70	85	0

Pos.	Player, Team (League)	W	L	ERA	G	GS	CG	SV	IP	H	BB	SO
SP	Felix Diaz, Charlotte (International)	10	2	2.97	19	17	0	0	115	95	24	96
SP	Dave Gassner, Rochester (International)	16	8	3.41	28	28	0	0	174	175	30	93
SP	Brad Halsey, Columbus (International)	11	4	2.63	24	23	3	0	144	128	37	109
SP	Ben Hendrickson, Indianapolis (International)	11	3	2.02	21	21	2	0	125	114	26	93
RP	Al Reyes, Durham (IL)/Memphis (Pacific Coast)	4	3	2.71	58	0	0	33	63	54	20	69

Player of the Year: Jason Kubel, of, Rochester (International). **Manager of the Year:** Marty Brown, Buffalo (International). **Team of the Year:** Richmond (International).

PLAYER of the YEAR
Jason Kubel, of
Rochester

Pos.	Player, Team (League)	AVG	AB	R	H	2B	3B	HR	RBI	BB	SO	SB
C	Josh Willingham, Carolina (Southern)	.281	338	81	95	24	0	24	76	91	87	6
1B	Ryan Howard, Reading (Eastern)	.297	374	73	111	18	1	37	102	46	129	1
2B	Richard Lewis, West Tenn (Southern)	.329	380	68	125	27	10	10	59	37	94	7
3B	David Wright, Binghamton (Eastern)	.363	223	44	81	27	0	10	40	39	41	20
SS	Aaron Hill, New Hampshire (Eastern)	.280	479	78	134	26	2	11	80	63	61	3
OF	Shin-Soo Choo, San Antonio (Texas)	.315	517	89	163	17	7	15	84	56	97	40
OF	Curtis Granderson, Erie (Eastern)	.301	462	89	139	19	8	21	94	80	95	14
OF	Nate McLouth, Altoona (Eastern)	.322	515	93	166	40	4	8	73	48	62	31
DH	Ryan Shealy, Tulsa (Texas)	.318	469	88	149	32	3	29	99	61	123	1

Pos.	Player, Team (League)	W	L	ERA	G	GS	CG	SV	IP	H	BB	SO
SP	Gustavo Chacin, New Hampshire (Eastern)	16	2	2.92	25	25	0	0	142	113	49	109
SP	Jeff Francis, Tulsa (Texas)	13	1	1.98	17	17	1	0	114	73	22	147
SP	D.J. Houlton, Round Rock (Texas)	12	5	2.94	28	28	3	0	159	141	47	159
SP	Renyel Pinto, West Tenn (Southern)	11	8	2.92	25	25	0	0	142	107	72	179
RP	Brad Baker, Mobile (Southern)	2	1	1.57	55	0	0	30	57	37	24	68

Player of the Year: Jeff Francis, lhp, Tulsa (Texas). **Manager of the Year:** Tony Beasley, Altoona (Eastern). **Team of the Year:** New Hampshire (Eastern).

PLAYER of the YEAR
Jeff Francis, lhp
Tulsa

Pos.	Player, Team (League)	AVG	AB	R	H	2B	3B	HR	RBI	BB	SO	SB
C	Brian McCann, Myrtle Beach (Carolina)	.278	385	45	107	35	0	16	66	31	54	2
1B	Brad Eldred, Lynchburg (Carolina)	.308	331	53	102	22	1	20	75	35	96	5
2B	Delwyn Young, Vero Beach (Florida State)	.281	470	76	132	36	3	22	85	57	134	11
3B	Jeff Baker, Visalia (California)	.330	267	60	88	23	1	11	64	47	70	1
SS	Erick Aybar, Rancho Cucamonga (California)	.330	573	102	189	25	11	14	65	26	66	51
OF	Jeff Francoeur, Myrtle Beach (Carolina)	.293	334	56	98	26	0	15	52	22	70	10
OF	Conor Jackson, Lancaster (California)	.345	258	64	89	19	2	11	54	45	36	4
OF	Brian Stavisky, Modesto (California)	.343	513	108	176	39	5	19	83	54	89	6
DH	Michael Napoli, Rancho Cucamonga (California)	.282	482	94	136	29	4	29	118	88	166	9

Pos.	Player, Team (League)	W	L	ERA	G	GS	CG	SV	IP	H	BB	SO
SP	Matt Cain, San Jose (California)	7	1	1.86	13	13	0	0	73	58	17	89
SP	Zach Duke, Lynchburg (Carolina)	10	5	1.39	17	17	1	0	97	73	20	106
SP	Felix Hernandez, Inland Empire (California)	9	3	2.74	16	15	0	0	92	85	26	114
SP	Steven Shell, Rancho Cucamonga (California)	12	7	3.59	28	28	2	0	165	151	40	190
RP	Dwayne Pollok, Winston-Salem (Carolina)	2	4	3.28	58	0	0	38	60	59	8	49

Player of the Year: Erick Aybar, ss, Rancho Cucamonga (California). **Manager of the Year:** Torey Lovullo, Kinston (Carolina). **Team of the Year:** Lancaster (California).

PLAYER of the YEAR
Erick Aybar, ss
Rancho Cucamonga

---

problems emerged in 2004 and made it more a question of if he will ever play again rather than when.

Hamilton was suspended for the season as a result of multiple violations of Major League Baseball's drug program. Hamilton, 22, had already served a 30-day suspension for failing at least two drug tests. Based on the rules of the program, the additional discipline indicated he failed at least two more and used a "prohibited substance" deemed by MLB more severe than marijuana. He later revealed in a magazine article that he had abused cocaine since spring training 2002.

Hamilton signed with the Devil Rays for a $3.96 million bonus as the top pick in the 1999 draft. After a

promising start, he has been a huge bust, missing considerable time with injuries and all of the last two years with what were first described as personal problems.

Hamilton is the first player to be suspended by MLB for a full season for drug-related violations since Darryl Strawberry in February 2000. Hamilton joins a list that includes Dwight Gooden (November 1994), Pascual Perez (March 1992), Eddie Milner (March 1988) and Steve Howe (December 1983).

Yet with all of Hamilton's problems, Allison's situation might be worse. Allison, the Marlins' 2003 first-round pick, left spring training after testing positive for marijuana and had received treatment for an addiction to

LOW CLASS A — Midwest League, South Atlantic League

Pos.	Player, Team (League)	AVG	AB	R	H	2B	3B	HR	RBI	BB	SO	SB
C	Daric Barton, Peoria (Midwest)	.313	313	63	98	23	0	13	77	69	44	4
1B	Brian Dopirak, Lansing (Midwest)	.307	541	94	166	38	0	39	120	48	123	4
2B	Howie Kendrick, Cedar Rapids (Midwest)	.367	313	66	115	24	6	10	49	12	41	15
3B	Ian Stewart, Asheville (South Atlantic)	.319	505	92	161	31	9	30	101	66	112	19
SS	Ian Kinsler, Clinton (Midwest)	.401	227	52	91	30	1	11	53	26	37	16
OF	Michael Bourn, Lakewood (South Atlantic)	.315	410	91	129	19	14	5	53	84	88	58
OF	Brandon Moss, Augusta (South Atlantic)	.339	433	66	147	25	6	13	101	46	75	19
OF	Delmon Young, Charleston, S.C. (South Atlantic)	.322	513	95	165	26	5	25	116	53	120	21
DH	Vinny Rottino, Beloit (Midwest)	.304	529	78	161	25	9	17	124	40	71	5

Pos.	Player, Team (League)	W	L	ERA	G	GS	CG	SV	IP	H	BB	SO
SP	Chuck James, Rome (South Atlantic)	10	5	2.24	26	22	1	0	133	92	48	156
SP	Brad Knox, Kane County (Midwest)	14	5	2.59	26	25	0	0	156	141	24	174
SP	Tom Mastny, Charleston, W.Va. (South Atlantic)	10	3	2.17	27	27	0	0	149	123	41	143
SP	Yusmeiro Petit, Capital City (South Atlantic)	9	2	2.39	15	15	0	0	83	47	22	122
RP	Jairo Garcia, Kane County (Midwest)	1	0	0.30	25	0	0	16	30	16	6	49

Player of the Year: Delmon Young, of, Charleston, S.C. (South Atlantic). **Manager of the Year:** Dave Joppie, Kane County (Midwest). **Team of the Year:** Capital City (South Atlantic)

PLAYER of the **YEAR**
Delmon Young, of
Charleston, S.C.

SHORT-SEASON A — New York-Penn League, Northwest League

Pos.	Player, Team (League)	AVG	AB	R	H	2B	3B	HR	RBI	BB	SO	SB
C	Mike Nickeas, Spokane (Northwest)	.288	233	42	67	18	0	10	55	33	53	2
1B	Ryan Norwood, Boise (Northwest)	.296	277	33	82	17	2	9	53	10	59	2
2B	Brian Hall, Auburn (New York-Penn)	.294	211	38	62	14	1	10	39	24	49	3
3B	Matt Macri, Tri-City (Northwest)	.333	195	33	65	17	4	7	43	23	52	4
SS	Ben Zobrist, Tri-City (New York-Penn)	.339	257	50	87	14	3	4	45	43	31	15
OF	Ambiorix Concepcion, Brooklyn (New York-Penn)	.305	259	38	79	14	3	8	46	13	54	28
OF	Javier Herrera, Vancouver (Northwest)	.331	263	50	87	15	4	12	47	24	59	23
OF	Luis Montanez, Boise (Northwest)	.293	266	47	78	15	7	8	48	35	54	5
DH	Chris Carter, Yakima (Northwest)	.335	257	47	86	15	1	15	63	46	35	2

Pos.	Player, Team (League)	W	L	ERA	G	GS	CG	SV	IP	H	BB	SO
SP	Ronnie Martinez, Tri-City (New York-Penn)	11	2	1.96	15	15	1	0	92	62	20	81
SP	Shawn Nottingham, Everett (Northwest)	9	3	3.15	15	14	0	0	89	74	29	87
SP	Anibal Sanchez, Lowell (New York-Penn)	3	4	1.77	15	15	0	0	76	43	29	101
SP	A.J. Shappi, Yakima (Northwest)	4	1	1.75	12	11	0	0	67	64	8	65
RP	Jim Miller, Tri-City (Northwest)	1	1	0.97	34	0	0	17	37	21	11	65

Player of the Year: Javier Herrera, of, Vancouver (Northwest). **Manager of the Year:** Tom Beyers, Boise (Northwest). **Team of the Year:** Tri-City (New York-Penn).

PLAYER of the **YEAR**
Javier Herrera, of
Vancouver

ROOKIE — Appalachian League, Arizona League, Gulf Coast League, Pioneer League

Pos.	Player, Team (League)	AVG	AB	R	H	2B	3B	HR	RBI	BB	SO	SB
C	Francisco Hernandez, Bristol (Appalachian)	.326	181	32	59	13	1	5	30	13	32	0
1B	Cory Dunlap, Ogden (Pioneer)	.351	245	57	86	18	1	7	53	68	40	0
2B	Hernan Iribarren, Brewers (Arizona)	.439	189	40	83	6	9	4	36	19	23	15
3B	Billy Butler, Idaho Falls (Pioneer)	.373	260	74	97	22	3	10	68	57	63	5
SS	Sean Rodriguez, Provo (Pioneer)	.338	225	64	76	14	4	10	55	51	62	9
OF	Deacon Burns, Elizabethton (Appalachian)	.314	255	49	80	20	4	12	49	18	53	9
OF	Mitch Einertson, Greeneville (Appalachian)	.308	227	53	70	15	0	24	67	32	70	4
OF	Seth Smith, Casper (Pioneer)	.369	233	46	86	21	3	9	61	25	47	9
DH	Brian McFall, Idaho Falls (Pioneer)	.363	262	64	95	23	1	14	68	30	64	23

Pos.	Player, Team (League)	W	L	ERA	G	GS	CG	SV	IP	H	BB	SO
SP	Samuel Deduno, Casper (Pioneer)	6	4	3.18	15	15	0	0	76	62	32	118
SP	Ray Liotta, Great Falls (Pioneer)	5	1	2.54	14	11	0	0	64	59	28	65
SP	Scott Mitchinson, Phillies (Gulf Coast)	7	0	1.75	10	10	0	0	62	40	1	60
SP	Tyler Pelland, Billings (Pioneer)	9	3	3.44	18	12	0	0	73	67	39	81
RP	Enyelbert Soto, Greeneville (Appalachian)	1	1	1.03	24	0	0	13	35	30	2	47

Player of the Year: Mitch Einertson, of, Greeneville (Appalachian). **Manager of the Year:** Tim Bogar, Greeneville (Appalachian). **Team of the Year:** Greeneville (Appalachian).

PLAYER of the **YEAR**
Mitch Einertson, of
Greeneville

MINOR LEAGUES

OxyContin, a prescription painkiller.

Then he was admitted to a Lynn, Mass., hospital because of what one newspaper reported was a heroin overdose. The Salem News quoted Rob Nash, one of Allison's former coaches, as saying, "It's worse than any of us thought. The kid's got a sickness. He's hit rock bottom. The kid needs some support right now. You can draw your own conclusions."

Allison was placed on the restricted list, and the Marlins had no idea when he might return.

When A Streak Is Not A Streak

He received a standing ovation for setting a record for the longest scoreless inning streak in minor league history, but Cardinals pitching prospect Brad Thompson had to settle for holding a Southern League record.

When Thompson picked up the first out of the fifth inning in a game against West Tenn, extending his scoreless-innings streak to 56⅓, the Tennessee Smokies announced that he had broken a minor league record. The game was stopped, the crowd gave Thompson a standing ovation, and the game ball was pulled out for safekeeping.

There were a few problems, however. First, his streak stretched back to the 2003 season, so it involved different seasons and different leagues. According to most historians, that disqualifies it as a single streak.

More significantly, Thompson was still short of tying

Brown pulls different parts into team

MANAGER *of the* **YEAR**

Triple-A teams are always an interesting mix of young players and veterans, but the mix manager Marty Brown received at Buffalo in 2004 was especially jumbled.

The Bisons used 42 pitchers, and while that's not unheard of in Triple-A, Brown also had to deal with losing pitching coach Terry Clark, who was fired in early June. Clark was replaced by veteran Ken Rowe, whom Brown credited with turning the staff around.

As the pitching staff sorted itself out, the offense became red-hot. At one point in July, every hitter in the lineup was hitting over .300.

The club then lost first basemen Russell Branyan and Eric Crozier in trades, and outfielder Grady Sizemore to the big leagues, but Brown kept the team focused.

"Being a Triple-A manager is one of the most difficult jobs in baseball because of all the gaps you have to keep constantly filling in," Indians general manager Mark Shapiro said. "But Marty is the leader of that club. He believes in and pulls for his players. And as a leader, it's his job to rally them through it. And he's certainly done that this year."

Brown rallied the Bisons enough to win an International League-best 83 games in the regular season as well as the Governor's Cup playoffs. His ability to win and get the most out of his talent made him a clear choice as Baseball America's 2004 Minor League Manager of the Year.

Brown's players love playing for him because of his calm demeanor and the way he approaches each player in an individual manner.

"At this level, it's a little different because you have guys constantly coming down from

Players' manager
Marty Brown

the big leagues or coming up from Double-A," said Brown, 41. "The big league guys don't think they should be back here and the Double-A guys doubt themselves a little bit. It's tough for both sides to handle the fact that they're Triple-A players. It's really easy for them to get down."

The Reds drafted Brown out of Georgia in the 12th round in 1985. He played most of his career in the Cincinnati organization, making it to the big leagues for two brief stints with them and one with the Orioles in 1990. He started his managerial career in the Pirates organization in 1997, reaching Triple-A before the Indians brought him to Buffalo for the 2003 season.

"We were very fortunate to get him in here," farm director John Farrell said. "He's young, detailed and very energetic. And he knows how to deal with a mixed bag of motives and personalities."

But don't expect Brown to toot his own horn. "I always liked playing for guys who were about their players," he said. "The ones who truly cared about them and weren't into themselves. It made me want to play harder for them. So for me, it's all about those guys, not me."

the longest documented streak. His streak eventually reached 57⅔ innings, but it left him 1⅓ innings short of Irving "Kaiser" Wilhelm's 59 scoreless innings for Birmingham in 1907.

As Thompson neared the record, Memphis Redbirds general manager Dave Chase looked back through microfilm of the Memphis Commercial Appeal from the 1907 season. He found that Wilhelm's scoreless streak, thought to be 56 innings, was actually three innings longer.

Chase sent his information to Minor League Baseball. Minor League Baseball media-relations director Jim Ferguson called, e-mailed and faxed the information to the Smokies an hour before the game against West Tenn. The Smokies either did not receive the information, or did not relay it to the field before Thompson's appearance.

Thompson did have 49 scoreless innings to start the season, which was a Southern League record. At the end of the streak, his numbers were an unfathomable 7-0, 0.18. He earned a promotion to Triple-A, but injuries bothered him the rest of the season and he ended up

pitching just 87 innings overall, with a mark of 9-2, 2.90.

End Of Season Blown Away

Hurricanes caused havoc for teams on the East Coast at the end of the season, and not surprisingly the bulk of the problems were in Florida.

Hurricanes Charley and Frances brought an early end to the regular season in the Florida State League, then Hurricane Ivan led to abbreviated playoffs in the FSL and Southern League, with co-champions declared in each league.

Charley hit first, coming ashore within 45 miles of ballparks in Sarasota and Fort Myers, but both came through the storm relatively unscathed. Daytona's Jackie Robinson Stadium was not as fortunate.

Winds from the hurricane ripped up several of the team's advertising billboards in the outfield, destroyed a batting cage, blew away the batting eye in center field and knocked a light tower down onto the field.

After Charley hit central Florida, Frances came through a couple of weeks later and caused even more widespread

damage, knocking out power for millions across the state. Frances ended the FSL regular season early, and it kept the offices of Minor League Baseball in St. Petersburg shut down for five days around the Labor Day weekend.

With many places in Florida facing mandatory evacuations as the last weekend of the summer approached, the league decided to cancel games in advance, allowing players and coaches time to get out of town.

Jupiter's Roger Dean Stadium and St. Lucie's Tradition Field sustained the worst damage from Frances, whose winds also destroyed scoreboards at Vero Beach's Holman Stadium and Brevard County's Space Coast Stadium.

Hurricane Ivan was the biggest and most powerful yet, and it moved into the Gulf of Mexico and made landfall near Mobile, Ala., cancelling two league championships. Mobile was scheduled to play Tennessee in the Southern League, but the two were declared co-champions, as were Daytona and Tampa in the FSL.

Around The Minors

■ One of the Diamondbacks' top pitching prospects spent most of 2004 in the Dominican Republic after it turned out he had been using a false identity. Major League Baseball was investigating whether the pitcher known as Adriano Rosario is actually Ramon Antonio Pena Paulino, or Tony Pena, and is more than three years older than his listed age. Rosario/Pena's signing came under scrutiny after an ESPN expose. Ivan Noboa—a buscone, or independent developer of talent—took $100,000 from Arizona as part of a June 2002 deal but did not tell the pitcher of that payment when he took another $100,000 from his $400,000 signing bonus. Also, the Dodgers made a higher offer than the Diamondbacks that may not have been communicated to the player.

■ Before it started, concert promoter Don Sullivan was ready to declare the Bob Dylan-Willie Nelson tour a success. In a summer when many concert tours failed to meet expectations, Sullivan hit on a successful plan to play in 22 minor league ballparks. The Dylan-Nelson tour is not the first time minor league ballparks have been used for concerts, but it was the first tour in memory based solely in minor league parks.

■ Saying it was "a good way to complete my baseball life," Hall of Famer Mike Schmidt ended his minor league managerial career after just one season. He hadn't held a full-time position in baseball since retiring from the Phillies in 1989 and had no managerial experience, but because of his place in the franchise's pantheon he got the job at high Class A Clearwater. "People might think this is the wrong thing to say, but it's been tough for me to take this job financially. I've given up a lot of appearance income. I need to be out earning. I make more in two hours at a card show than I did in this job."

■ In an industry where wacky promotions are as much a part of the game as hot dogs and double plays, Brevard County Manatees (Florida State) intern John Van Vleet may have come up with promotion of the year. Van Vleet, 22, lived in a tent on the berm beyond the left-field fence at Brevard County's Space Coast Stadium by night, working in the ballpark during the day. He planned to stay for 152 days, but he had to end his stay at 147 because of the aforementioned hurricanes. Van Vleet has the resume for the job, as he once lived out of the back of his Jeep for two months in Jackson Hole, Wyo., while working for a fly fishing store.

TRIPLE-A ALL-STAR GAME

At the site of the longest game in professional baseball history, it was fitting that the 17th annual Triple-A All-Star Game became the first to go into extra innings. But it was strange that a member of the Yankees organization wound up being the hero at McCoy Stadium, home of the Pawtucket Red Sox and deep in the heart of Red Sox Nation. Couple all that with a pro-Sox crowd chanting "Bucky! Bucky!" in the late innings, and it was truly a surreal setting.

Columbus' Andy Phillips hit a two-out, walk-off home run in the bottom of the 10th inning to give the International League a 4-3 victory over the Pacific Coast League before a crowd of 11,192. Phillips' homer not only ended the game in dramatic fashion but also prevented the game from ending in a tie for the first time in its history. League officials previously decided the game would not go past 10 innings, no matter what the score.

Phillips, who drilled a 1-0 slider from Tacoma righthander Scott Atchison over the left-center wall for the game-winner, was the game's MVP, an honor that seemed destined for ex-Red Sox outfielder Midre Cummings. The 32-year-old veteran, who played for Durham in 2004, robbed Salt Lake City's Erick Almonte of extra bases with a tremendous catch at the wall in the top of the eighth inning, then belted a go-ahead homer in the bottom of the frame that gave the IL a 3-2 lead. The PCL scratched out a run in the ninth to set the stage for Phillips.

While Phillips played the hero's role, the feel-good story was Bucky Jacobsen, Tacoma's strapping first baseman. Jacobsen put on a show in the home run derby before the game and quickly became a fan favorite. However, he didn't play in the actual game, and for good reason: The 28-year-old minor league veteran received word that he was getting his first-ever promotion to the big leagues.

Triple-A All-Star Game
July 14 at Pawtucket
International League 4, Pacific Coast League 3

PCL	ab	r	h	bi	IL	ab	r	h	bi
Hubbard, cf	1	1	0	0	Cummings, cf	4	1	1	1
Theodorou, cf	2	0	0	0	Peralta, ss	2	0	0	0
Barmes, ss	3	0	0	0	Cantu, ss	2	0	0	0
Almonte, ss	2	0	0	0	Morneau, 1b	2	1	1	0
Dillon, 3b	3	0	0	0	Gil, c	1	0	0	0
Dallimore, 3b/2b	2	0	1	0	Sardinha, c	1	0	0	0
Sutton, 1b	3	1	1	0	Vitiello, dh	2	1	1	2
Neal, 1b	2	0	0	0	Hart, dh	1	0	0	0
Pickering, dh	4	1	2	1	Young, rf	2	0	0	0
Gall, lf	2	0	1	1	Rushford, rf	2	0	1	0
Riggs, lf	1	0	0	0	Snyder, 3b	2	0	0	0
Church, rf	2	0	0	0	Williams, 3b	2	0	0	0
Zoccolillo, rf	2	0	1	0	Collier, lf	4	0	0	0
Morrissey, 2b	1	0	0	0	Dominique, c	2	0	0	0
Huffman, 3b	1	0	0	0	Brazell, 1b	2	0	0	0
Ansman, c	2	0	1	0	Nelson, 2b	2	0	0	0
Nieves, c	2	0	0	0	Phillips, 2b	2	1	1	1
Totals	35	3	7	2	Totals	35	4	5	4

Pacific Coast League	2 0 0	0 0 0	0 0 1	0— 3
International League	0 0 0	2 0 0	0 1 0	1— 4

E—Sutton. DP—IL 2. LOB—PCL 7, IL 3. HR—Cummings, Phillips, Vitiello. SB—Hubbard.

PCL	ip	h	r	er	bb	so	IL	ip	h	r	er	bb	so
Haren	2	0	0	0	0	0	Hendrickson	2	3	2	2	3	1
Williams	2	2	2	2	0	2	Diaz	2	0	0	0	0	1
Wright	1	0	0	0	0	1	Gassner	1	1	0	0	0	0
Tolar	1	0	0	0	0	1	Graman	1	0	0	0	0	0
McCleary	⅔	1	0	0	1	1	Kester	1	0	0	0	1	1
Flores	1⅓	1	1	1	0	2	Giese	⅔	0	0	0	0	0
Atchison L	1⅔	1	1	1	0	0	Crowell	⅓	1	0	0	0	0
							Crain	⅓	2	1	0	1	1
							Whiteside W	1⅔	0	0	0	0	3

Two outs when winning run scored.
WP—McCleary. PB—Sardinha.
Time—2:50. A—11,192.

M I N O R L E A G U E
DEPARTMENT LEADERS
Full-season teams only

Zach Duke: 1.46 ERA

SACRIFICE BUNTS
Abigail Sandoval, Clinton/Stockton 22
Wilson Valdez, Albuquerque/Charlotte 21
Juan Francia, West Michigan 20
James Tomlin, New Britain 19
Three tied at 18

SLUGGING PERCENTAGE
Calvin Pickering, Omaha .... .712
Dallas McPherson, Arkansas/Salt Lake .... .670
Joe Dillon, Carolina/Albuquerque .... .669
Brad Hawpe, Colorado Springs .... .652
Ryan Howard, Reading/Scranton .... .637

ON-BASE PERCENTAGE
Calvin Pickering, Omaha .... .451
Josh Willingham, Carolina .... .449
Darric Barton, Peoria .... .445
David Wright, Binghamton/Norfolk .... .441
Carlos Quentin, Lancaster/El Paso .... .435

BATTING AVERAGE
By Position
(Minimum 378 Plate Appearances)

Catchers
Phil Avlas, Lancaster .... .315
Darric Barton, Peoria .... .313
Chris Snyder, El Paso .... .301
John Suomi, Modesto .... .297
Will Nieves, Salt Lake .... .297

First Basemen
Jon Benick, Hickory .... .328
Gabriel Martinez, Bakersfield .... .323
Ryan Shealy, Tulsa .... .318
Andy Phillips, Tampa/Trenton/Col. (IL) .... .316
Todd Self, Round Rock .... .315

Second Basemen
Jeff Keppinger, Altoona/Bing./Norfolk .... .339
Brian Dallimore, Fresno .... .324
Pete Orr, Richmond .... .320
Erick Almonte, Colorado Springs .... .318
Chris Burke, New Orleans .... .315

Third Basemen
Garrett Atkins, Colorado Springs .... .366
David Wright, Binghamton/Norfolk .... .341
Joe Dillon, Carolina/Albuquerque .... .329
Mike Cervenak, Norwich/Fresno .... .328
Kevin Kouzmanoff, Lake County/Akron .... .324

Shortstop
Ian Kinsler, Clinton/Frisco .... .345
Maicer Izturis, Edmonton .... .338
Tony Giarratano, West Mich./Lakeland .... .335
Brandon Pinckney, Lake County/Akron .... .333
Erick Aybar, Rancho Cucamonga .... .330

Outfielders
Chad Allen, Oklahoma .... .358
Napoleon Calzado, Bowie/Green./Rich. .... .356
Brandon Moss, Augusta/Sarasota .... .353
Jason Kubel, New Britain/Rochester .... .352

Ryan Church, Edmonton .... .346

EARNED RUN AVERAGE
(Minimum 112 Innings)
Zach Duke, Lynchburg/Altoona 1.46
Ben Hendrickson, Indianapolis 2.02
Trae McGill, Wilmington 2.08
Dusty Hughes, Burl. (MWL)/Wilm. 2.13
Thomas Mastny, Charleston, W.Va. 2.17
Yusmeiro Petit, Cap. City/St. Lucie/Bing. 2.20
Jeff Francis, Tulsa/Colorado Springs 2.21
Chuck James, Rome 2.24
Jake Stevens, Rome 2.27
Jose Capellan, Myrtle Beach/Green./Rich. 2.32

WORST ERA
Mark Comolli, Bakersfield 7.74
Steve Green, Salt Lake 7.66
Jason Middlebrook, Salt Lake 6.94
Brian Lockwood, Bakersfield 6.86
Brian Tollberg, Colorado Springs 6.80

WINS
Gustavo Chacin, New Hampshire/Syracuse 18
Brandon McCarthy, Kann./W-S/Birm. 17
Steven Bondurant, Kane County/Midland 16
Jeff Francis, Tulsa/Colorado Springs 16
Dave Gassner, Rochester 16

LOSSES
Steve Green, Salt Lake 17
Luke Lockwood, Harrisburg 17
Kyle Kendrick, Batavia/Lakewood 16
Mark Comolli, Bakersfield 15
Six tied at 14

GAMES
Troy Brohawn, Las Vegas 72
Carlton Wells, Lancaster 71
Matt Smith, Birmingham 70
Brad Baker, Mobile/Portland (PCL) 63
Ryan Keefer, Frederick 63
Nick McCurdy, Frederick 63
Agustin Montero, Vero/Jack./Las Vegas 63

COMPLETE GAMES
Alberto Arias, Asheville 4
Nelson Figueroa, Nashville 4
Pat Misch, Norwich 4
Alfredo Simon, Clearwater/San Jose 4
Twenty-three tied at 3

SAVES
Dwayne Pollok, Winston-Salem 38
Matt Whiteside, Richmond 38
Ryan Speier, Tulsa 37
Brad Baker, Mobile/Portland (PCL) 34
Al Reyes, Durham/Memphis 33

SHUTOUTS
Pat Misch, Norwich 3
Alfredo Simon, Clearwater/San Jose 3
Scott Baker, Fort Myers/N. Britain/Rochester 2
Yorman Bazardo, Jupiter 2
Travis Blackley, Tacoma 2

INNINGS
Jared Fernandez, New Orleans 196
Bobby Livingston, Inland Empire 187
Marc Kaiser, Asheville 181
Pat Ahearne, Toledo 179
Clint Goocher, Lancaster/El Paso 177

WALKS
Mark Comolli, Bakersfield 131
Derick Grigsby, Lexington 92
Steve Green, Salt Lake 85
Gustavo Martinez, San Antonio/Tacoma 82
Ryan Jensen, Fresno 81
Charlie Zink, Sarasota/Portland (EL) 81

STRIKEOUTS
Brandon McCarthy, Kann./W-S/Birm. 202
Yusmeiro Petit, Cap. City/St. Lucie/Bing. .. 200
Jeff Francis, Tulsa/Colorado Springs 196
Steven Shell, Rancho Cucamonga 190
Thomas Oldham, Wisc./Inland Empire 188

Renyel Pinto, West Tenn/Iowa 188

HITS
Jason Middlebrook, Salt Lake 220
Heath Totten, Las Vegas 213
Ben Crockett, Visalia 210
Jared Fernandez, New Orleans 209
Erick Arteaga, Lakewood 207

STRIKEOUTS PER NINE INNINGS
(Starters)
Yusmeiro Petit, Cap. City/St. Lucie/Bing. 12.92
Adam Bostick, Greensboro 12.87
Ambiorix Burgos, Burlington (MWL) 11.58
Jeff Francis, Tulsa/Colorado Springs 11.41
Travis Chick, Fort Wayne/Greensboro 11.24

STRIKEOUTS PER NINE INNINGS
(Relievers)
Jairo Garcia, Kane Co./Mid./Sacramento 14.89
Chad Orvella, Char./Bake./Mont./Dur. 14.23
Carlos Guevara, Dayton 14.29
Brandon DeJaynes, Peoria 13.37
Jose Diaz, Columbus (SAL)/Vero Beach 13.32

BATTING AVERAGE AGAINST
(Starters)
Yusmeiro Petit, Cap. City/St. Lucie/Bing . .170
Jeff Francis, Tulsa/Colorado Springs ...... .194
Chuck James, Rome .... .195
Kyle Davies, M. Beach/Green./Richmond .197
Jake Stevens, Rome .... .204

BATTING AVERAGE AGAINST
(Relievers)
Ryan Speier, Tulsa .... .153
Jermaine Van Buren, Lan./W.T./Iowa ...... .154
Brandon DeJaynes, Peoria .... .156
Chad Orvella, Char./Bake./Mont./Dur. .... .162
Josh Sharpless, Hickory .... .167

MOST STRIKEOUTS, ONE GAME
Julio Pimentel, Columbus (IL) 16
Brandon McCarthy, Winston-Salem 16
Thomas Oldham, Wisconsin 15
Luis Ramirez, Aberdeen 15
Scott Olsen, Jupiter 15
Anthony Reyes, Tennessee 15

BALKS
Jacobo Meque, Billings 7
Abel Moreno, Cedar Rapids 7
Wandy Rodriguez, Round Rock 6
Colin Young, Sarasota/Portland (EL) 6
Six tied at 5

MOST ERRORS
Juan Ciriaco, Fort Wayne 45
Wade Robinson, Salem 45
Carlos Rodriguez, Lakewood 43
Bronson Sardinha, Tampa/Trenton 43
Luis Cruz, Lake Elsinore 42

Jairo Garcia: strikeout leader

MINOR LEAGUE BEST TOOLS

	International/AAA	Pacific Coast/AAA	Eastern/AA	Southern/AA	Texas/AA	California/A	Carolina/A	Florida State/A	Midwest/A	South Atlantic/A
Best Batting Prospect	Jhonny Peralta, Buffalo	Ryan Church, Edmonton	David Wright, Binghamton	Rickie Weeks, Huntsville	Dallas McPherson, Arkansas	Conor Jackson, Lancaster	Michael Aubrey, Kinston	Felix Pie, Daytona	Ian Kinsler, Clinton	Ian Stewart, Asheville
Best Power Prospect	Justin Morneau, Rochester	Jason Dubois, Iowa	Ryan Howard, Reading	Jason Stokes, Carolina	Dallas McPherson, Arkansas	Carlos Quentin, Lancaster	Tony Blanco, Potomac	Brandon Sing, Daytona	Brian Dopirak, Lansing	Ian Stewart, Asheville
Best Strike-Zone Discipline	Grady Sizemore, Buffalo	Nick Swisher, Sacramento	David Wright, Binghamton	Prince Fielder, Huntsville	Todd Self, Round Rock	Jeff Salazar, Visalia	Michael Aubrey, Kinston	Jayce Tingler, Dunedin	Brian Snyder, Kane County	Josh Anderson, Lexington
Best Baserunner	David Krynzel, Indianapolis	Freddy Guzman, Portland	Wayne Lydon, Binghamton	Shane Victorino, Jacksonville	Willy Taveras, Round Rock	Jeff Salazar, Visalia	Josh Anderson, Salem	Alex Requena, Vero Beach	Mitch Maier, Burlington	Josh Anderson, Lexington
Fastest Baserunner	Joey Gathright, Durham	Freddy Guzman, Portland	Wayne Lydon, Binghamton	Ruddy Yan, Birmingham	Marland Williams, El Paso	Chris Morris, High Desert	Rajai Davis, Lynchburg	Felix Pie, Daytona	Chris Walker, Lansing	Josh Anderson, Lexington
Best Pitching Prospect	Ben Hendrickson, Indianapolis	Edwin Jackson, Las Vegas	Gavin Floyd, Reading	Jose Capellan, Greenville	Jeff Francis, Tulsa	Felix Hernandez, Inland Empire	Zach Duke, Lynchburg	Chad Billingsley, Vero Beach	Matt Chico, South Bend	Adam Miller, Lake County
Best Fastball	Jesse Crain, Rochester	Edwin Jackson, Las Vegas	Brandon League, New Hampshire	Jose Capellan, Greenville	Jeff Francis, Tulsa	Felix Hernandez, Inland Empire	Jose Capellan, Myrtle Beach	Edwardo Sierra, Tampa	Kevin Jepsen, Cedar Rapids	Jose Diaz, Columbus
Best Breaking Pitch	Ben Hendrickson, Indianapolis	Taylor Buchholz, New Orleans	Gavin Floyd, Reading	Arnie Munoz, Birmingham	Steven Andrade, Arkansas	Felix Hernandez, Inland Empire	Zach Duke, Lynchburg	Rich Hill, Daytona	Jason Burch, Peoria	Clint Everts, Savannah
Best Control	Dave Gassner, Rochester	Mike Wood, Sacramento	Wil Ledezma, Erie	Brad Thompson, Tennessee	Jeff Francis, Tulsa	Clint Goocher, Lancaster	Richie Gardner, Potomac	Chad Billingsley, Vero Beach	Brad Knox, Kane County	Yusmeiro Petit, Capital City
Best Reliever	Jesse Crain, Rochester	George Sherrill, Tacoma	Brandon League, New Hampshire	Brad Baker, Mobile	Ryan Speier, Tulsa	Jason Bulger, Lancaster	Dwayne Pollok, Winston-Salem	Edwardo Sierra, Tampa	Jairo Garcia, Kane County	Jose Diaz, Columbus
Best Defensive Catcher	Guillermo Quiroz, Syracuse	Yadier Molina, Memphis	Dioner Navarro, Trenton	Brian Peterson, Chattanooga	Jeff Mathis, Arkansas	Rene Rivera, Inland Empire	Brian McCann, Myrtle Beach	Jason Motte, Palm Beach	Miguel Montero, South Bend	Robinzon Diaz, Charleston, W.Va.
Best Defensive First Baseman	Justin Morneau, Rochester	Casey Kotchman, Salt Lake	Larry Broadway, Harrisburg	James Loney, Jacksonville	Chad Santos, Wichita	Brant Colamarino, Modesto	Michael Aubrey, Kinston	Andy Schutzenhofer, Palm Beach	Fernando Valenzuela, Fort Wayne	Christian Colonel, Asheville
Best Defensive Second Baseman	Brandon Phillips, Buffalo	Chris Burke, New Orleans	Robinson Cano, Trenton	Richard Lewis, West Tenn	Ruben Gotay, Wichita	Callix Crabbe, High Desert	Victor Mercedes, Lynchburg	Gabe Lopez, Tampa	Peeter Ramos, Fort Wayne	Etanislao Abreu, Columbus
Best Defensive Third Baseman	Glenn Williams, Syracuse	Mark Teahen, Sacramento/Omaha	David Wright, Binghamton	Andy Marte, Greenville	Mark Teahen, Midland	Jeff Baker, Visalia	Avelino Asprilla, Lynchburg	Aarom Baldiris, St. Lucie	Matt Brown, Cedar Rapids	Shawn Bowman, Capital City
Best Defensive Shortstop	J.J. Hardy, Indianapolis	Maicer Izturis, Edmonton	Josh Labandeira, Harrisburg	Josh Wilson, Carolina	Andres Blanco, Wichita	Erick Aybar, Rancho Cucamonga	Ivan Ochoa, Kinston	Hanley Ramirez, Sarasota	Carlos Rojas, Lansing	Chin-Lung Hu, Columbus
Best Infield Arm	B.J. Upton, Durham	Jerry Gil, Tucson	Josh Labandeira, Harrisburg	Andy Marte, Greenville	Sergio Santos, El Paso	Luis Cruz, Lake Elsinore	Mark Schramek, Potomac	Hanley Ramirez, Sarasota	Adam Jones, Wisconsin	Shawn Bowman, Capital City
Best Defensive Outfielder	Grady Sizemore, Buffalo	Jason Ellison, Fresno	Chris Duffy, Altoona	Anthony Gwynn, Huntsville	Willy Taveras, Round Rock	Jeff Salazar, Visalia	Gregor Blanco, Myrtle Beach	Chris Roberson, Clearwater	Dustin Majewski, Kane County	Josh Anderson, Lexington
Best Outfield Arm	Alex Escobar, Buffalo	Julio Ramirez, Tucson	Franklin Gutierrez, Akron	Skip Schumaker, Tennessee	Shin-Soo Choo, San Antonio	Luis Mateo, Bakersfield	Jeff Francoeur, Myrtle Beach	Felix Pie, Daytona	Scott Whitrock, Quad Cities	Lastings Milledge, Capital City
Most Exciting Player	B.J. Upton, Durham	Jose Lopez, Tacoma	David Wright, Binghamton	Rickie Weeks, Huntsville	Willy Taveras, Round Rock	Erick Aybar, Rancho Cucamonga	Jeff Francoeur, Myrtle Beach	Felix Pie, Daytona	Ian Kinsler, Clinton	Ian Stewart, Asheville
Best Manager Prospect	Marty Brown, Buffalo	Dan Rohn, Tacoma	Ken Oberkfell, Binghamton	Frank Kremblas, Huntsville	Tim Ireland, Frisco	Wally Backman, Lancaster	Torey Lovullo, Kinston	Tom Nieto, Palm Beach	Kevin Boles, Quad Cities	Rocket Wheeler, Rome

Selected at midseason 2004, by Baseball America in consultation with minor league managers

FREITAS AWARDS

Baseball America's annual Bob Freitas Awards are presented to franchises that show sustained excellence in the business of minor league baseball.

They were first presented in 1989, shortly after the death of Freitas, a longtime minor league operator, promoter and ambassador. Franchises must be in operation for at least five seasons before they're eligible, the only thing that kept three of 2004's winners from claiming a Freitas Award sooner.

■ **Sacramento** was regarded as one of the top markets without a team in Organized Baseball for years, until Art Savage brought the River Cats into the Pacific Coast  League in 2000. Now it's regarded as one of the top markets in minor league baseball.

The River Cats have been a hot ticket in Sacramento from the time they moved into privately financed Raley Field. Sacramento and Memphis have battled for the overall minor league attendance crown each year, with the River Cats winning in 2004 for overall attendance (751,156) and finishing just behind Memphis in average attendance (10,433). The front office has won numerous awards for its business practices and community work.

The River Cats have also enjoyed unparalleled success on the field—winning four division titles and back-t0-back PCL championship s in 2003 and '04.

■ Sacramento and Memphis will soon have another standout PCL franchise to compete with, on the field and in the stands. The **Round Rock** Express proved too good for  Double-A, earning a promotion to Triple-A for 2005. In the five seasons the franchise spent in the Texas League, however, the Express may have been the most successful Double-A franchise in minor league history.

Austin, Texas, also was regarded as a market that should have an affiliated team before the Express moved into Dell Diamond for the 2000 season in suburban Round Rock. Many new minor league franchises have found success in the suburbs of larger cities, and the Express is perhaps the best example.

With Nolan Ryan as one of the club's principal owners, the Express quickly became the Texas League's flagship franchise. Round Rock set Double-A attendance records in each of its five seasons, drawing 689,286 in 2004. That trailed only Sacramento and Memphis among all minor league teams, and the Express will add seats for 2005. The Texas League franchise will move to Corpus Christi.

■ Speaking of attendance records, the **Dayton** Dragons have set many of their own since debuting, like Sacramento and Round Rock, in the 2000 season. The  Dragons play in the Midwest League, but both their ballpark and their attendance go beyond what traditionally would be expected at the Class A level.

Like the Express, the Dragons set a new attendance record for their classification in each of their first five seasons. They drew 593,663 fans in 2004 to Fifth Third Field, a state-of-the-art stadium that is a part of a $30 million complex in the heart of downtown Dayton.

■ In contrast to the three other megafranchises that were honored in 2004, the **Burlington** Indians have more modest goals in the Appalachian League. But they have been no less successful in achieving them.

The Indians joined the league in 1986 and have been among its attendance leaders ever since. Miles Wolff has been team president since day one, and the Indians have also been the team's major league affiliate throughout that time, sending a steady stream of future big leaguers through Burlington.

The franchise has been just as successful in producing front-office members who have moved onward and upward in the baseball industry. The steady stream of new talent in the front office has lead to continual improvements at Burlington Athletic Stadium and a consistent level of success for the franchise over the last 20 years.

PREVIOUS WINNERS

Triple-A
1989—Columbus (International)	
1990—Pawtucket (International)	
1991—Buffalo (American Association)	
1992—Iowa (American Association)	
1993—Richmond (International)	
1994—Norfolk (International)	
1995—Albuquerque (Pacific Coast)	
1996—Indianapolis (American Association)	
1997—Rochester (International)	
1998—Salt Lake (Pacific Coast)	
1999—Louisville (International)	
2000—Edmonton (Pacific Coast)	
2001—Buffalo (International)	
2002—Memphis (Pacific Coast)	
2003—Pawtucket (International)	

Double-A
1989—El Paso (Texas)
1990—Arkansas (Texas)
1991—Reading (Eastern)
1992—Tulsa (Texas)
1993—Harrisburg (Eastern)
1994—San Antonio (Texas)
1995—Midland (Texas)
1996—Carolina (Southern)
1997—Bowie (Eastern)
1998—Trenton (Eastern)
1999—Portland (Eastern)
2000—Reading (Eastern)
2001—Mobile (Southern)
2002—Chattanooga (Southern)
2003—New Britain (Eastern)

Class A
1989—Durham (Carolina)
1990—San Jose (California)
1991—Asheville (South Atlantic)
1992—Springfield (Midwest)
1993—South Bend (Midwest)
1994—Kinston (Carolina)
1995—Kane County (Midwest)
1996—Wisconsin (Midwest)
1997—Rancho Cucamonga (California)
1998—West Michigan (Midwest)
1999—Wilmington (Carolina)
2000—Charleston, S.C. (South Atlantic)
2001—Delmarva (South Atlantic)
2002—Fort Myers (Florida State)
2003—Modesto (California)

Short-Season
1989—Eugene (Northwest)
1990—Salt Lake City (Pioneer)
1991—Spokane (Northwest)
1992—Boise (Northwest)
1993—Billings (Pioneer)
1994—Everett (Northwest)
1995—Great Falls (Pioneer)
1996—Bluefield (Appalachian)
1997—Oneonta (New York-Penn)
1998—Hudson Valley (New York-Penn)
1999—Portland (Northwest)
2000—Lowell (New York-Penn)
2001—Salem-Keizer (Northwest)
2002—Ogden (Pioneer)
2003—Spokane (Northwest)

BUFFALO BISONS

Buffalo was greater than the sum of its parts
Despite using 42 different pitchers and two pitching coaches, the Bisons posted an IL-best 83-61 record and won the Governor's Cup

BY CHRIS KLINE

As the Cleveland Indians continued to reap the dividends of player development at the major league level, the Tribe's affiliates stayed strong—winning four titles in the minor leagues in 2004.

Perhaps none was more impressive than what happened in Buffalo, as Baseball America Manager of the Year Marty Brown balanced a club that used 42 different arms and fired its pitching coach in early June to win the Governor's Cup for the first time since 1998.

The Bisons' quest for the IL title appeared to be in jeopardy during the first round of the playoffs after they fell into an 0-2 deficit to Durham, but the team rallied to win the final three games at home.

They then faced a hot Richmond club, but due to the threat of hurricanes hitting the Virginia area, all games of the championship series were played at Buffalo's Dunn Tire Park, giving the Bisons a distinct home-field advantage. They went on to win the series, 3-1.

"We were very fortunate to get him in here," farm director John Farrell said of Brown. "He's young, detailed and very energetic. And he knows how to deal with a mixed bag of motives and personalities. On top of that, he deals well with molding a team each year that requires a combination of needs and requests from the major league club. He's the right fit for us in so many ways."

RICH ABEL

Jhonny Peralta

The mix he received in 2004 was especially jumbled, particularly the pitching staff. Pitching coach Terry Clark was replaced by veteran Ken Rowe, whom Brown credited with turning the staff around.

"He's been around a long time and knows the game," Brown said. "A lot of the younger pitchers get here and are looking for a pat on the back. He'll give them that, but he makes them earn everything. But you can't put the blame or the praise on any one guy. When things are going well or when they're not going well, it's the whole thing that's not working—not just an individual."

As the pitching staff sorted itself out, the offense suddenly became red-hot. At one point in July, every hitter in the Bisons lineup was hitting over .300. The club then lost first basemen Russell Branyan and Eric Crozier in trades and outfielder Grady Sizemore to the big leagues for a brief stint, but Brown kept the team focused.

"I sent Russell to Milwaukee for basically nothing because it was the right thing to do," Cleveland general manager Mark Shapiro said. "He had a chance to play in the big leagues every day. I sent Crozier to the Blue Jays because it made sense to us."

Brown still had IL batting champion Jhonny Peralta and second baseman Brandon Phillips, who combined to be the true catalysts on the club down the stretch.

Peralta batted .326-15-86 in 556 at-bats and figures into the middle of the diamond for the big league club in 2005. Phillips hit .303-8-50 in 521 at-bats, but more importantly regained his focus after a season-long slump in 2003.

"Being a Triple-A manager is one of the most difficult jobs in baseball because of all the gaps you have to keep constantly filling in," Shapiro said. "But Marty is the leader of that club. He believes in and pulls for his players. And as a leader, it's his job to rally them through it. And he's certainly done that this year."

Road Warriors

No team played more games away from home in 2004 than Richmond, whose 51-year-old field was constantly criticized for its lack of proper drainage. The Braves went almost a month between games at The Diamond, having to move games to Harbor Park in Norfolk when the field was deemed unplayable due to rain . . . four days earlier.

The city proposed $18-20 million to renovate the stadi-

um, but the team was forced to not only play regular season home games on the road, but had to face Buffalo in the Governor's Cup with all five games scheduled in New York.

"It was tough playing so many games in different places and not getting back home," Braves reliever Buddy Hernandez said. "But it was probably tougher on the fans in Richmond than anybody else. Basically for the last month of the season, we were a road team and they couldn't share in a lot of the things we accomplished this year."

BILL MITCHELL

Jason Kubel

The Durham Bulls went into the 2004 season looking for their third straight IL title, and after taking the first two games at home against Buffalo, another appearance in the Governor's Cup Final appeared to be inevitable.

But then Buffalo suddenly woke up to win the next three, ending the Bulls championship run at back-to-back titles.

Prospect-Laden Wings

No IL team boasted more talent in 2004 than the Rochester Red Wings—even though they faltered and finished just two games over .500 at 73-71.

The Wings received standout performances from shortstop Jason Bartlett, first baseman Justin Morneau, third baseman Terry Tiffee, righthanded reliever Jesse Crain and starters J.D. Durbin, Dave Gassner and Scott Baker. But none had quite the impact of outfielder Jason Kubel, the league batting champion.

Kubel blew up most radar screens in 2004, hitting .343-16-71 in 350 at-bats after getting called up from Double-A New Britain. The 22-year-old was in the mix for the Twins' 2005 outfield before suffering a knee injury.

Perhaps the most impressive thing about Kubel was his consistency at recognizing pitches. He struck out 59 times and drew 53 walks in 127 games.

"I like his approach at the plate—he doesn't try to do too much in any situation," an AL scout said. "He doesn't strike out a lot for a power guy, and will take the walk or

the pitch the other way when it's there."

The Affiliation Shuffle

There wasn't as much affiliation movement in the IL as there was in the Pacific Coast League by season's end, but the IL said goodbye to the Milwaukee Brewers, who left Indianapolis for Nashville of the PCL.

Replacing the Brewers in Indy are the Pirates, who had been in Music City since 1997.

"We are very happy to agree to terms on a two-year working agreement with Indianapolis," Pirates GM Dave Littlefield said. "The Indianapolis organization and facilities are among the best and the Pirates look forward to working with the team and the city for years to come."

MINOR LEAGUES

STANDINGS

Page	NORTH	W	L	Pct.	GB	Manager	Attendance	Avg.	Last Penn.
119	Buffalo Bisons (Indians)	83	61	.576	—	Marty Brown	574,088	8,320	2004
88	Pawtucket Red Sox (Red Sox)	73	71	.507	10	Buddy Bailey	657,067	9,387	1984
176	Rochester Red Wings (Twins)	73	71	.507	10	Phil Roof	437,088	6,427	1997
215	Scranton/W-B Red Barons (Phillies)	69	73	.486	13	Marc Bombard	402,676	6,010	None
80	Ottawa Lynx (Orioles)	66	78	.458	17	Tim Leiper	159,619	2,347	1995
273	Syracuse SkyChiefs (Blue Jays)	66	78	.458	17	Marty Pevey	364,848	5,209	1976

Page	SOUTH	W	L	Pct.	GB	Manager	Attendance	Avg.	Last Penn.
73	Richmond Braves (Braves)	79	62	.560	—	Pat Kelly	368,436	6,699	1994
259	Durham Bulls (Devil Rays)	77	67	.535	3½	Bill Evers	490,615	7,110	2003
199	Norfolk Tides (Mets)	72	72	.500	8½	John Stearns	485,260	7,032	1985
96	Charlotte Knights (White Sox)	68	74	.479	11½	Nick Capra	265,271	4,080	1999

Page	WEST	W	L	Pct.	GB	Manager	Attendance	Avg.	Last Penn.
191	Columbus Clippers (Yankees)	80	64	.556	—	Bucky Dent	489,177	7,526	1996
111	Louisville RiverBats (Reds)	67	77	.465	13	Rick Burleson	648,092	9,392	2001
169	Indianapolis Indians (Brewers)	66	78	.458	14	Cecil Cooper	576,067	8,113	2000
134	Toledo Mud Hens (Tigers)	65	78	.455	14½	Larry Parrish	544,778	7,672	1967

GOVERNORS' CUP PLAYOFFS—Semifinals: Buffalo defeated Durham 3-2 and Richmond defeated Columbus 3-2 in best-of-5 series. **Finals:** Buffalo defeated Richmond 3-1 in best-of-5 series.

NOTE: Team's individual batting and pitching statistics can be found on page indicated in lefthand column.

CLUB BATTING

	AVG	G	AB	R	H	2B	3B	HR	BB	SO	SB
Buffalo	.297	144	4963	848	1472	311	33	188	465	926	114
Richmond	.280	141	4644	660	1301	252	34	141	432	928	78
Durham	.276	144	4733	733	1308	295	27	168	440	1034	119
Columbus	.276	144	4800	737	1325	271	44	147	452	898	67
Rochester	.273	144	4960	726	1352	304	21	146	434	846	85
Scranton/Wilkes-Barre	.272	142	4769	666	1298	271	39	92	473	835	103
Louisville	.267	144	4758	694	1269	258	42	122	448	1060	110
Syracuse	.266	144	4844	661	1290	294	31	119	467	940	52
Charlotte	.265	142	4740	639	1258	252	22	173	405	905	117
Ottawa	.265	144	4863	619	1289	291	24	119	401	962	103
Pawtucket	.264	144	4927	763	1303	310	23	192	577	1222	81
Toledo	.263	143	4825	626	1270	262	36	123	354	986	120
Norfolk	.261	144	4739	590	1239	253	28	117	373	1010	102
Indianapolis	.261	144	4732	620	1233	271	33	92	444	852	106

CLUB PITCHING

	ERA	G	CG	SV	IP	H	HR	R	ER	BB	SO
Richmond	3.70	141	3	45	1190	1164	94	543	489	445	976
Norfolk	4.03	144	5	43	1257	1272	118	661	563	463	957
Columbus	4.20	144	8	36	1247	1294	130	654	582	375	1041
Durham	4.24	144	4	37	1219	1264	134	657	574	491	958
Rochester	4.24	144	2	39	1271	1352	144	685	599	388	966
Louisville	4.38	144	5	33	1233	1260	123	674	600	517	1010
Scranton/Wilkes-Barre	4.39	142	8	33	1236	1318	152	689	603	359	807
Pawtucket	4.48	144	4	29	1260	1372	179	697	627	365	901
Charlotte	4.56	142	4	37	1241	1252	176	697	629	429	933
Indianapolis	4.58	144	4	33	1251	1350	128	706	636	439	974
Toledo	4.64	143	7	41	1242	1329	122	731	640	456	891
Ottawa	4.65	144	3	39	1260	1328	146	726	651	520	1034
Syracuse	4.66	144	5	38	1247	1326	163	738	646	424	995
Buffalo	4.71	144	3	32	1255	1326	130	724	657	494	961

CLUB FIELDING

	PCT	PO	A	E		PCT	PO	A	E
Richmond	.981	3597	1342	97	Columbus	.977	3740	1430	123
Charlotte	.981	3724	1343	100	Ottawa	.975	3781	1403	134
Indianapolis	.980	3753	1506	110	Scranton/W-B	.975	3707	1413	133
Rochester	.978	3814	1467	117	Syracuse	.974	3742	1454	140
Buffalo	.978	3766	1423	118	Norfolk	.974	3772	1450	141
Pawtucket	.977	3780	1403	120	Louisville	.973	3699	1429	144
Toledo	.977	3726	1618	126	Durham	.973	3658	1438	144

INDIVIDUAL BATTING LEADERS
(Minimum 389 Plate Appearances)

	AVG	G	AB	R	H	2B	3B	HR	RBI	BB	SO	SB
Kubel, Jason, Rochester	.343	90	350	71	120	28	0	16	71	34	40	16
Diaz, Matt, Durham	.332	134	503	81	167	47	5	21	93	26	96	15
Collier, Lou, Scranton	.326	101	384	62	126	26	3	14	66	34	82	14
Peralta, Jhonny, Buffalo	.326	138	556	109	181	44	2	15	86	54	126	8
Orr, Pete, Richmond	.320	115	460	69	147	16	10	1	35	20	59	24
Phillips, Andy, Columbus	.316	115	434	82	137	19	6	25	84	51	61	2
Clapinski, Chris, Buffalo	.312	107	369	65	115	24	4	11	63	46	62	18
Tyner, Jason, Rich./Buffalo	.309	102	382	65	118	16	2	1	32	33	37	23
Escalona, Felix, Columbus	.309	130	447	79	138	32	1	7	59	31	56	2
Ozuna, Pablo, Scranton	.307	126	472	77	145	27	3	6	76	22	43	31

INDIVIDUAL PITCHING LEADERS
(Minimum 115 Innings)

	W	L	ERA	G	GS	CG	SV	IP	H	R	ER	BB	SO
Hendrickson, Ben, Indianapolis	11	3	2.02	21	21	2	0	125	114	32	28	26	93
Halsey, Brad, Columbus	11	4	2.63	24	23	3	0	144	128	46	42	37	109
Diaz, Felix, Charlotte	10	2	2.97	19	17	0	0	115	95	41	38	24	96
Guerrier, Matt, Rochester	5	10	3.19	24	23	0	0	144	135	65	51	25	97
Graman, Alex, Columbus	11	6	3.37	24	22	1	0	131	115	56	49	53	129
Gassner, Dave, Rochester	16	8	3.41	28	28	0	0	174	175	72	66	30	93
Romano, Mike, Richmond	13	5	3.42	40	16	0	0	124	130	51	47	51	99
Baldwin, James, Norfolk/Toledo	8	9	3.53	23	21	3	1	147	144	63	58	25	85
Rayborn, Kenny, Buffalo	8	2	3.64	23	22	0	0	124	122	57	50	40	65
Eyre, Willie, Rochester	6	7	3.64	36	21	1	4	136	131	60	55	53	91

ALL-STAR TEAM

C—Kelly Shoppach, Pawtucket. **1B**—Justin Morneau, Rochester. **2B**—Pete Orr, Richmond. **3B**—Earl Snyder, Pawtucket. **SS**—Jhonny Peralta, Buffalo. **OF**—Matt Diaz, Durham; Adam Hyzdu, Pawtucket; Jason Kubel, Rochester. **DH**—Ernie Young, Buffalo. **UT**—Jorge Cantu, Durham. **SP**—Ben Hendrickson, Indianapolis. **RP**—Matt Whiteside, Richmond.

Most Valuable Player: Jhonny Peralta, Buffalo. **Most Valuable Pitcher:** Ben Hendrickson, Indianapolis. **Rookie of the Year:** Jason Kubel, Rochester. **Manager of the Year:** Marty Brown, Buffalo.

DEPARTMENT LEADERS

BATTING

G	Bryant Nelson, Charlotte	142
AB	Bryant Nelson, Charlotte	560
R	Jhonny Peralta, Buffalo	109
H	Jhonny Peralta, Buffalo	181
TB	Earl Snyder, Pawtucket	300
XBH	Earl Snyder, Pawtucket	80
2B	Matt Diaz, Durham	47
3B	Mark Budzinski, Scranton/W-B	15
HR	Earl Snyder, Pawtucket	36
RBI	Earl Snyder, Pawtucket	104
SH	Luis Rodriguez, Rochester	18
SF	Victor Diaz, Norfolk	9
	Jhonny Peralta, Buffalo	9
BB	Midre Cummings, Durham	86
IBB	Midre Cummings, Durham	13
HBP	Jonny Gomes, Durham	22
SO	Jeremy Owens, Pawtucket	140
SB	Esix Snead, Norfolk	40
CS	Aaron Holbert, Louisville	14
GIDP	Felix Escalona, Columbus	24
OBP	Adam Hyzdu, Pawtucket	.412
SLG	Jorge Cantu, Durham	.576

PITCHING

G	Brian Shackelford, Louisville	59
GS	Three tied at	28
CG	Four tied at	3
ShO	Brad Halsey, Columbus	2
	Ben Hendrickson, Indianapolis	2
GF	Matt Whiteside, Richmond	51
SV	Matt Whiteside, Richmond	38
W	Dave Gassner, Rochester	16
L	Three tied at	12
IP	Pat Ahearne, Toledo	179
H	Clay Condrey, Scranton/W-B	206
R	Clay Condrey, Scranton/W-B	106
ER	Matt Belisle, Louisville	95
HR	Frank Castillo, Pawtucket	28
HB	Kenny Rayborn, Buffalo	12
	Mike Smith, Syracuse	12
BB	Damian Moss, Durham/Louisville	80
SO	Alex Graman, Columbus	129
	Chuck Smith, Richmond	129
WP	Josue Matos, Syracuse	13
BK	Three tied at	4

FIELDING

C	PCT	John Pachot, Norfolk	.998
	PO	Geronimo Gil, Ottawa	715
	A	Kelly Shoppach, Pawtucket	61
	E	Pete LaForest, Durham	8
		Kelly Shoppach, Pawtucket	8
	DP	Geronimo Gil, Ottawa	8
	PB	Three tied at	10
1B	PCT	Andy Barkett, Toledo	.986
	PO	Andy Barkett, Toledo	884
	A	Andy Phillips, Columbus	67
	E	Andy Barkett, Toledo	13
	DP	Craig Brazell, Norfolk	89
2B	PCT	Tony Schrager, Pawtucket	.995
	PO	Mike Fontenot, Ottawa	252
	A	Mike Fontenot, Ottawa	330
	E	Mike Fontenot, Ottawa	22
	DP	Mike Fontenot, Ottawa	85
3B	PCT	Rodney Nye, Norfolk	.936
	PO	Rodney Nye, Norfolk	75
	A	Glenn Williams, Syracuse	206
	E	Jeff Deardorff, Columbus	21
	DP	Jim Chamblee, Louisville	31
SS	PCT	Wilson Delgado, Norfolk	.977
	PO	Russ Adams, Syracuse	179
	A	Felix Escalona, Columbus	354
	E	Russ Adams, Syracuse	33
	DP	Russ Adams, Syracuse	82
OF	PCT	Grady Sizemore, Buffalo	.996
	PO	Jorge Padilla, Scranton/W-B	.288
	A	Matt Diaz, Durham	15
		Mario Valenzuela, Charlotte	15
	E	Victor Diaz, Norfolk	9
	DP	Damon Hollins, Richmond	7

PACIFIC COAST LEAGUE
TRIPLE-A

BY AARON FITT

The Sacramento River Cats became the first team since Edmonton in 1996-97 to win back-to-back Pacific Coast League titles. Sacramento's three-game sweep of the Iowa Cubs in the 2004 championship series gave the River Cats 12 wins in their last 13 postseason games. It was the fifth time in the last nine years an Oakland affiliate won the PCL title.

"This was a lot of hard work and preparation," Sacramento manager Tony DeFrancesco said. "But it's a good feeling."

The River Cats, who rallied for three runs in the bottom of the ninth for a dramatic 5-4 win in Game Two against Iowa, rode an early Jon Weber three-run homer to a 4-3 win in the deciding third game. They reached the finals by taking three of four from Portland, the only team with an ERA below 4.00 in the bopper-friendly PCL. Iowa had advanced with a five-game series win against Oklahoma. Then the Cubs ran into a Sacramento team that had come together just in the nick of time: the River Cats lost eight of their final 12 regular-season contests, then fell in their first postseason game against Portland before winning six straight.

"They just played better than us," Cubs second baseman Russ Johnson told the Des Moines Register. "They pitched better, they hit better, they fielded better . . . they just played better. The right team won."

Sacramento first baseman Dan Johnson, who won regular season MVP honors with a .299-29-111 campaign, added to his trophy case with the postseason MVP award, batting .458-2-6 in seven games. Afterward, Johnson and righthanders Joe Blanton (11-8, 4.19) and Justin Lehr (13 saves, 2.65 ERA) were called up to aid Oakland's playoff run.

The prospect-laden River Cats were also paced for much of the season by outfielders Matt Watson (.305-19-96) and Nick Swisher (.269-29-92), before Swisher was

Call it a clean sweep
Dan Johnson won the regular-season and postseason MVP awards

called up to the parent club. But pitching was Sacramento's backbone. The River Cats staff posted a 4.55 ERA, second-best in the league, while leading the PCL with 1,071 strikeouts and walking a league-low 381.

Mediocre Year For Prospects

Across the league, however, pitching was disappointing in 2004. The best arm in the league belonged to Las Vegas

STANDINGS

Page	CENTRAL	W	L	Pct.	GB	Manager	Attendance	Avg.	Last Penn.
103	Iowa Cubs (Cubs)	79	64	.552	—	Mike Quade	540,055	7,298	None
127	Colorado Springs Sky Sox (Rockies)	78	65	.545	1	Marv Foley	236,022	3,576	1995
155	Omaha Royals (Royals)	71	73	.493	8½	Mike Jirschele	318,537	4,616	None
141	Albuquerque Isotopes (Marlins)	67	77	.465	12½	Tracy Woodson	575,607	8,222	None
Page	**EAST**	**W**	**L**	**Pct.**	**GB**	**Manager**	**Attendance**	**Avg.**	**Last Penn.**
266	Oklahoma RedHawks (Rangers)	81	63	.563	—	Bobby Jones	474,206	6,678	None
229	Memphis Redbirds (Cardinals)	73	71	.507	8	Danny Sheaffer	730,565	10,436	2000
149	New Orleans Zephyrs (Astros)	66	78	.458	15	Chris Maloney	324,324	4,769	2001
222	Nashville Sounds (Pirates)	63	79	.444	17	Trent Jewett	405,536	6,052	None
Page	**NORTH**	**W**	**L**	**Pct.**	**GB**	**Manager**	**Attendance**	**Avg.**	**Last Penn.**
237	Portland Beavers (Padres)	84	60	.583	—	Craig Colbert	312,678	4,403	1994
252	Tacoma Rainiers (Mariners)	79	63	.556	4	Dan Rohn	310,680	4,854	2001
183	Edmonton Trappers (Expos)	69	74	.483	14½	Dave Huppert	252,557	4,209	2002
58	Salt Lake Stingers (Angels)	56	88	.389	28	Mike Brumley	448,153	6,494	1979
Page	**SOUTH**	**W**	**L**	**Pct.**	**GB**	**Manager**	**Attendance**	**Avg.**	**Last Penn.**
208	Sacramento River Cats (Athletics)	79	65	.549	—	Tony DeFrancesco	751,156	10,432	2004
65	Tucson Sidewinders (Diamondbacks)	74	70	.514	5	Chip Hale	285,378	4,019	1993
162	Las Vegas 51's (Dodgers)	67	76	.469	11½	Terry Kennedy	306,628	4,318	1988
245	Fresno Grizzlies (Giants)	62	82	.431	17	Fred Stanley	531,040	7,375	None

PLAYOFFS—Semifinals: Sacramento defeated Portland 3-1 and Iowa defeated Oklahoma 3-2 in best-of-5 series. **Finals:** Sacramento defeated Iowa 3-0 in best-of-5 series.

NOTE: Team's individual batting and pitching statistics can be found on page indicated in lefthand column.

righthander Edwin Jackson, who pitched at 93-97 mph with his fastball and showed a nasty slider—when healthy. But Jackson suffered a strained forearm early in 2004 and never seemed 100 percent. He finished 6-4, 5.86 with 55 walks in 91 innings.

Baseball America's Minor League Player of the Year, lefthander Jeff Francis, also had a brief stint in the PCL with the Colorado Springs Sky Sox. Francis, who dominated the Double-A Texas League before arriving at Colorado Springs, went 3-2, 2.85 in 41 innings before getting called up to the Rockies.

The PCL's pitcher of the year was Edmonton lefthander Scott Downs, who went 10-6, 3.52 and threw the league's only no-hitter of the season July 11 against Las Vegas.

MIKE JAMES

Edwin Jackson

Downs was promoted to the parent Expos, but not before becoming the first Edmonton lefty to reach the double-digit win plateau since 1992.

The two best prospects in the league were Salt Lake infielders Casey Kotchman and Dallas McPherson.

Kotchman, a first baseman, filled in for the Angels' major league club early in the season, but he was sent down to Salt Lake on June 14, eight days before McPherson was promoted from Double-A Arkansas to the PCL. They wasted no time tearing up PCL pitching, as Kotchman notched three multi-hit games in his first four starts, and McPherson homered 10 times in his first 20 contests.

Kotchman's .372 batting average and McPherson's .680 slugging percentage would have led the league if they had enough plate appearances to qualify. But even those two top prospects could not salvage the Stingers' season; they finished 28 games back in the North Division due largely to their league-worst 5.70 ERA.

Terrero's Troubles

Another highly regarded prospect, Tucson's Luis Terrero, couldn't escape controversy in 2004. First, Terrero was suspended six weeks for throwing a baseball at a heckling fan following an on-field incident at Tucson.

Terrero had a pitch thrown over his head, and he attempted to charge the mound but was instead punched by the opposing catcher. After being ejected, Terrero picked up a ball from his dugout and threw it at a heckler, missing but hitting the fan next to him in the chest.

Terrero took an anger management course during his six-week suspension. In his first game back, he went 2-for-4 with a home run. After rounding the bases following the homer, Terrero stopped, got down on his knees and kissed home plate before getting up and pointing to the sky as he trotted to the dugout. Tucson manager Chip Hale pulled Terrero out of the game.

"It's not my way of playing the game. It's not the Diamondbacks' way of playing the game to ever show up an opponent," Hale said. "I don't know in his heart if he thought he was showing up the opponent, but he's got to learn that you just can't do those things."

Banner Year

Terrero's exploits notwithstanding, it was a successful season for the PCL. Sacramento led the minor leagues in

LEAGUE CHAMPIONS

Last 30 Years

Year	Regular Season*	Pct.	Playoff
1974	Spokane (Rangers)	.549	Spokane (Rangers)
1975	Hawaii (Padres)	.611	Hawaii (Padres)
1976	Salt Lake City (Angels)	.625	Hawaii (Padres)
1977	Phoenix (Giants)	.579	Phoenix (Giants)
1978	Tacoma (Yankees)	.584	Tacoma (Yankees)#
			Albuquerque (Dodgers)#
1979	Albuquerque (Dodgers)	.581	Salt Lake City (Angels)
1980	Tucson (Astros)	.595	Albuquerque (Dodgers)
1981	Albuquerque (Dodgers)	.712	Albuquerque (Dodgers)
1982	Albuquerque (Dodgers)	.594	Albuquerque (Dodgers)
1983	Albuquerque (Dodgers)	.594	Portland (Phillies)
1984	Hawaii (Pirates)	.621	Edmonton (Angels)
1985	Hawaii (Pirates)	.587	Vancouver (Brewers)
1986	Vancouver (Brewers)	.616	Las Vegas (Padres)
1987	Calgary (Mariners)	.596	Albuquerque (Dodgers)
1988	Albuquerque (Dodgers)	.605	Las Vegas (Padres)
1989	Albuquerque (Dodgers)	.563	Vancouver (White Sox)
1990	Albuquerque (Dodgers)	.641	Albuquerque (Dodgers)
1991	Albuquerque (Dodgers)	.580	Tucson (Astros)
1992	Colo. Springs (Indians)	.596	Colo. Springs (Indians)
1993	Portland (Twins)	.608	Tucson (Astros)
1994	Albuquerque (Dodgers)	.597	Albuquerque (Dodgers)
1995	Tucson (Astros)	.608	Colo. Springs (Rockies)
1996	Edmonton (Athletics)	.592	Edmonton (Athletics)
1997	Phoenix (Giants)	.615	Edmonton (Athletics)
1998	Iowa (Cubs)	.590	New Orleans (Astros)
1999	Vancouver (Athletics)	.592	Vancouver (Athletics)
2000	Salt Lake (Twins)	.629	Memphis (Cardinals)
2001	New Orleans (Astros)	.590	New Orleans (Astros)#
	Tacoma (Mariners)	.590	Tacoma (Mariners)#
2002	Las Vegas (Dodgers)	.590	Edmonton (Twins)
2003	Sacramento (Athletics)	.639	Sacramento (Athletics)
2004	Portland (Padres)	.583	Sacramento (Athletics)

*Best overall record   #Co-champions

attendance for the fifth consecutive year, drawing 751,156 fans, and Memphis was second in the minors for the fifth straight year, with 730,565.

The two franchises have dominated attendance figures since opening new Raley Field (in Sacramento) and AutoZone Park (in Memphis) in 2000. Overall, however, league attendance was slightly down from 2003's record mark of 6,998,344. PCL clubs drew 6,803,068 fans in 2004, the first time in five seasons the league had failed to set a new attendance record.

The PCL could cruise to a new record in 2005, however, thanks to the addition of Round Rock. The Express, which was third in the minors in attendance in 2004, moves from the Double-A Texas League into the PCL, replacing the now-defunct Edmonton Trappers, who began play in 1981 but were sold late in the 2003 season, making 2004 a lameduck campaign.

Coincidentally, the Montreal Expos, Edmonton's parent club in 2003 and 2004, also became a team of the past following the 2004 season after it was announced the franchise would relocate to Washington, D.C.

The franchise replaced its Edmonton affiliate with New Orleans, which was formerly an Astros affiliate. The Astros, in turn, moved to Round Rock, which had been their Double-A Texas League affiliate for four seasons.

The only other change in the PCL for 2005 is Nashville, which switched affiliations with Indianapolis of the International League. Nashville became a Brewers affiliate while Indianapolis teamed up with the Pirates.

BILL MITCHELL

Luis Terrero

2004 PACIFIC COAST LEAGUE STATISTICS

CLUB BATTING

	AVG	G	AB	R	H	2B	3B	HR	BB	SO	SB
Colorado Springs	.307	143	4880	859	1496	340	31	178	488	929	80
Oklahoma	.296	144	5075	844	1503	320	38	143	513	988	105
Edmonton	.290	143	4872	715	1414	282	31	97	513	818	92
Tucson	.290	144	5016	792	1453	330	55	162	447	1175	97
Salt Lake	.289	144	5040	785	1458	289	54	152	402	984	92
Las Vegas	.289	143	5036	806	1454	307	35	184	433	963	93
Fresno	.281	144	5056	717	1422	272	38	133	439	993	99
Iowa	.280	143	4845	760	1359	315	32	157	434	857	100
Albuquerque	.280	144	4938	791	1382	296	42	162	541	1067	90
Memphis	.279	144	4942	723	1381	247	22	174	373	869	82
Sacramento	.279	144	4933	830	1378	283	28	158	732	1021	70
Omaha	.278	144	4844	737	1346	232	33	185	533	987	90
Portland	.277	144	4938	738	1370	300	26	147	442	845	134
New Orleans	.274	144	4820	665	1321	264	26	147	450	937	100
Tacoma	.272	142	4793	731	1306	232	40	179	432	1038	136
Nashville	.272	142	4775	684	1301	257	30	180	421	995	117

CLUB PITCHING

	ERA	G	CG	SV	IP	H	HR	R	ER	BB	SO
Portland	3.86	144	2	40	1275	1254	119	635	547	491	1042
Sacramento	4.55	144	3	35	1271	1430	142	746	643	381	1071
Iowa	4.56	143	4	41	1243	1328	150	717	629	543	1024
Oklahoma	4.57	144	6	34	1267	1394	153	724	643	448	878
Tacoma	4.61	142	4	46	1233	1277	131	707	631	585	1014
Omaha	4.65	144	5	34	1240	1370	171	728	641	425	969
Memphis	4.74	144	3	41	1254	1403	183	728	661	461	1009
New Orleans	4.85	144	6	35	1242	1319	139	732	669	426	901
Edmonton	4.89	143	6	26	1221	1381	154	728	664	456	899
Nashville	4.91	142	5	33	1236	1364	148	722	674	437	1011
Fresno	4.92	144	1	27	1281	1476	159	789	701	504	881
Colorado Springs	5.05	143	2	36	1218	1365	165	775	684	455	1010
Tucson	5.37	144	4	34	1253	1495	169	835	748	483	898
Las Vegas	5.45	143	1	27	1263	1483	183	849	764	512	999
Albuquerque	5.66	144	4	30	1262	1489	209	862	794	448	905
Salt Lake	5.70	144	5	24	1239	1516	163	900	784	538	955

CLUB FIELDING

	PCT	PO	A	E		PCT	PO	A	E
Albuquerque	.982	3787	1587	98	Colo. Springs	.977	3655	1415	121
Memphis	.982	3762	1478	96	Las Vegas	.977	3788	1526	127
Nashville	.981	3709	1415	101	Oklahoma	.976	3800	1672	135
New Orleans	.979	3725	1563	114	Omaha	.975	3721	1488	133
Edmonton	.978	3663	1422	112	Portland	.975	3826	1456	136
Iowa	.978	3728	1508	119	Tacoma	.974	3699	1414	137
Fresno	.978	3844	1541	123	Salt Lake	.974	3716	1485	140
Tucson	.977	3760	1529	126	Sacramento	.974	3812	1459	143

INDIVIDUAL BATTING LEADERS
(Minimum 389 Plate Appearances)

	AVG	G	AB	R	H	2B	3B	HR	RBI	BB	SO	SB
Atkins, Garrett, Colo. Springs	.366	122	445	88	163	43	3	15	94	57	45	0
Allen, Chad, Oklahoma	.358	93	386	75	138	28	3	7	70	31	72	18
Church, Ryan, Edmonton	.346	98	347	74	120	29	8	17	79	51	62	0
Izturis, Maicer, Edmonton	.338	99	376	65	127	19	2	3	36	57	30	14
Piedra, Jorge, Colo. Springs	.334	99	377	71	126	29	5	15	55	23	56	4
Riggs, Adam, Salt Lake	.331	112	450	104	149	33	8	29	90	30	80	8
Hubbard, Trenidad, Iowa	.330	129	473	101	156	28	4	9	49	62	59	36
Barmes, Clint, Colo. Springs	.328	125	533	104	175	42	2	16	51	28	61	20
Conti, Jason, Oklahoma	.328	104	421	63	138	26	5	8	61	33	84	5
Dillon, Joe, Albuquerque	.325	108	403	96	131	33	7	30	86	46	85	12

INDIVIDUAL PITCHING LEADERS
(Minimum 115 Innings)

	W	L	ERA	G	GS	CG	SV	IP	H	R	ER	BB	SO
Walrond, Les, Omaha	11	5	3.06	19	19	1	0	124	114	46	42	41	107
Tankersley, Dennis, Portland	7	4	3.15	19	19	0	0	120	114	52	42	37	86
Germano, Justin, Portland	9	5	3.38	20	20	2	0	123	113	48	46	25	98
Williams, Dave, Nashville	6	2	3.47	21	21	0	0	117	113	52	45	33	103
Downs, Scott, Edmonton	10	6	3.52	22	22	2	0	135	143	57	53	26	67
Hernandez, Carlos, New Orl.	9	4	3.60	23	23	0	0	128	115	54	51	46	81
Flores, Randy, Memphis	5	7	3.82	36	15	1	2	123	115	60	52	46	99
Sweeney, Brian, Portland	11	4	3.83	24	23	0	0	139	130	65	59	42	110
Reid, Justin, Nashville	5	3	3.96	32	16	0	2	123	112	56	54	35	121
Haren, Dan, Memphis	11	4	4.15	21	21	0	0	128	137	60	59	33	150

ALL-STAR TEAM

C—Mike Rose, Sacramento. **1B**—Dan Johnson, Sacramento. **2B**—Chris Burke, New Orleans. **3B**—Garrett Atkins, Colorado Springs. **SS**—Clint Barmes, Colorado Springs. **OF**—Chad Allen, Oklahoma; Ryan Church, Edmonton; Adam Riggs, Salt Lake. **DH**—Calvin Pickering, Omaha. **RHP**—Brian Sweeney, Portland. **LHP**—Scott Downs, Edmonton. **RP**—Al Reyes, Memphis.

Most Valuable Player: Dan Johnson, Sacramento. **Pitcher of the Year:** Scott Downs, Edmonton. **Rookie of the Year:** Chris Burke, New Orleans. **Manager of the Year:** Dan Rohn, Sacramento.

BATTING
G	Royce Huffman, New Orleans	144
AB	Mike Edwards, Sacramento	551
R	Nick Swisher, Sacramento	109
H	Clint Barmes, Colorado Springs	175
TB	Andy Tracy, Colorado Springs	293
XBH	Andy Tracy, Colorado Springs	78
2B	Garrett Atkins, Colorado Springs	43
3B	Rich Thompson, Nashville	13
HR	Kevin Witt, Memphis	36
RBI	Andy Tracy, Colorado Springs	120
SH	Elvis Pena, Colorado Springs	13
SF	Peter Zoccolillo, New Orleans	11
BB	Nick Swisher, Sacramento	103
IBB	Ryan Church, Edmonton	8
	A.J. Zapp, Tacoma	8
HBP	Joey Thurston, Las Vegas	17
SO	A.J. Zapp, Tacoma	184
SB	Freddy Guzman, Portland	48
CS	Ramon Nivar, Oklahoma	15
	Rich Thompson, Nashville	15
GIDP	Garrett Atkins, Colorado Springs	24
SLG	Joe Dillon, Albuquerque	.665

PITCHING
G	Troy Brohawn, Las Vegas	72
GS	Steve Green, Salt Lake	29
	Jason Middlebrook, Salt Lake	29
CG	Nelson Figueroa, Nashville	4
ShO	Four tied at	2
GF	Brad Clontz, Oklahoma	48
SV	Al Reyes, Memphis	23
W	Chris Gissell, Colorado Springs	14
L	Steve Green, Salt Lake	17
IP	Jared Fernandez, New Orleans	196
H	Jason Middlebrook, Salt Lake	220
R	Steve Green, Salt Lake	131
ER	Jason Middlebrook, Salt Lake	120
HR	Kris Wilson, Omaha	39
HB	John Rheinecker, Sacramento	15
BB	Steve Green, Salt Lake	85
SO	Dan Haren, Memphis	150
WP	Ryan Jensen, Fresno	14
BK	John Koronka, Iowa	5

FIELDING
C	PCT	Keith McDonald, Nashville	.997
	PO	Trey Lunsford, Fresno	697
	A	Wil Nieves, Salt Lake	58
	E	Danny Ardoin, Oklahoma	11
		John Buck, New Orleans	11
	DP	Fernando Lunar, Iowa	11
	PB	Trey Lunsford, Fresno	14
1B	PCT	Steve Neal, Tucson	.998
	PO	Royce Huffman, New Orleans	1174
	A	A.J. Zapp, Tacoma	101
	E	Calvin Pickering, Omaha	12
	DP	Adrian Gonzalez, Oklahoma	141
2B	PCT	Chris Burke, New Orleans	.983
	PO	Chris Burke, New Orleans	265
	A	Chris Burke, New Orleans	377
	E	Mickey Lopez, Tacoma	14
	DP	Chris Burke, New Orleans	86
3B	PCT	Mike Coolbaugh, New Orleans	.967
	PO	Scott Seabol, Memphis	63
	A	Mike Coolbaugh, New Orleans	211
	E	Garrett Atkins, Colorado Springs	21
		Mike Edwards, Sacramento	21
	DP	Marshall McDougall, Oklahoma	30
SS	PCT	Jason Bowers, Memphis	.976
	PO	Jerry Gil, Tucson	195
	A	J.J. Furmaniak, Portland	357
	E	Jerry Gil, Tucson	29
	DP	Manny Alexander, Oklahoma	81
OF	PCT	Colin Porter, Memphis	.995
	PO	Jason Ellison, Fresno	343
	A	Jason Conti, Oklahoma	22
	E	Matt Watson, Sacramento	11
	DP	Jason Conti, Oklahoma	9

EASTERN LEAGUE

DOUBLE-A

BY ALAN MATTHEWS

It wasn't easy for the New Hampshire Fisher Cats to discover their identity. But once they settled into their new home in Manchester, N.H., the Fisher Cats won the 2004 Eastern League title, sweeping the Altoona Curve in the best-of-5 championship series.

RICH ABEL

Brandon League

First named the Primaries, the franchise—which relocated from New Haven, Conn., prior to the 2004 season—changed its nickname to Fisher Cats when the area's fans expressed discontent with the Primaries moniker. Fisher Cats are weasel-like rodents indigenous to New Hampshire, and the team's complexion was congruous, as New Hampshire weaseled its way back from a late-season deficit in the standings to edge Binghamton for the Northern Division pennant before cruising to the EL crown.

The Fisher Cats took seven consecutive games from Binghamton in mid-August and won the division with an 84-57 record behind the league's stingiest pitching staff. Righthander Brandon League earned the EL postseason Most Valuable Player award after going 2-0 with a save in four appearances during the playoffs. The 21-year old righthander, a native of Hawaii, recorded 10 strikeouts and had a 1.50 ERA in 12 innings of work during New Hampshire's first-round win over Binghamton and ensuing sweep of the Curve.

Following one-run victories in the first two games at Altoona, the Fisher Cats became the first Blue Jays affiliate in 12 years to win its league title, with a 2-0 shutout at home in Game Three.

Francisco Rosario, who made a strong return in 2004 from Tommy John surgery, tossed six scoreless innings, scattering three hits before Jamie Vermilyea and League slammed the door. New Hampshire third baseman John Hattig, who was traded to Toronto from the Red Sox and moved from Portland of the EL to the Fisher Cats in July, deposited a two-run homer into the Altoona bullpen in the bottom of the third inning for the game's lone offensive highlight.

It was an especially rewarding finish for 13 members of the Fisher Cats who played in the EL championship series in 2003 as members of the New Haven Ravens, losing to Akron.

The bulk of the Blue Jays' deep crop of minor league pitching prospects contributed to the Fisher Cats' impressive staff. Lefty Gustavo Chacin went 16-2, 2.86 in the regular season with New Hampshire and finished the year with 20 wins between Double-A, Triple-A and the majors.

Infielder Jeff Keppinger won the EL batting title with a .341-1-38 campaign. He opened the season with Altoona but, like Hattig, was traded in July only to relocate to another EL club. He didn't miss a beat in two months at Binghamton and became the second player—and first since 1923, the league's inaugural year—to win the EL batting title while playing for multiple teams. Earl Babbington batted .383 between Elmira and York in 1923.

Reading first baseman Ryan Howard hammered 37 of his minor-league leading 46 home runs in the EL prior to a promotion to Triple-A and eventually the majors. His 37 homers also set a Reading club record. However, Howard finished two homers behind Trenton's Mitch Jones for the league title. Reading also graduated Gavin Floyd, who captured the league's ERA crown, to the big leagues.

A record number of fans were on hand to witness the compelling play. A total of 3,914,027 fans attended EL games in 2004, eclipsing the previous attendance record of 3,868,732, which was set in 1999.

"I am very excited about breaking the all-time single-season attendance record that we set in 1999," EL president Joseph McEacharn said. "It proves that the Eastern League continues to thrill the fans throughout the Northeast with great baseball action and that our teams are putting forth a fantastic product both on and off the field."

Akron drew a league-best total of 478,611 fans, the sixth time in the past eight seasons the Aeros led the league in total attendance. By drawing 402,280 fans, Trenton became the first team below the Triple-A level to draw more than 400,000 fans in 10 consecutive seasons.

STANDINGS

Page	NORTH	W	L	Pct.	GB	Manager	Attendance	Avg.	Last Penn.
274	New Hampshire Fisher Cats (Blue Jays)	84	57	.596	—	Mike Basso	215,961	3,175	2004
200	Binghamton Mets (Mets)	76	66	.535	8½	Ken Oberkfell	216,493	3,280	1994
177	New Britain Rock Cats (Twins)	70	70	.500	13½	Stan Cliburn	311,671	4,722	2001
246	Norwich Navigators (Giants)	69	73	.486	15½	Shane Turner	168,559	2,553	2002
89	Portland Sea Dogs (Red Sox)	69	73	.486	15½	Ron Johnson	434,684	6,209	None
192	Trenton Thunder (Yankees)	64	78	.451	20½	Stump Merrill	402,280	6,095	None

Page	SOUTH	W	L	Pct.	GB	Manager	Attendance	Avg.	Last Penn.
223	Altoona Curve (Pirates)	85	56	.603	—	Tony Beasley	394,062	5,970	None
135	Erie Seawolves (Tigers)	80	62	.563	5½	Rick Sweet	245,117	3,605	None
81	Bowie Baysox (Orioles)	73	69	.514	12½	Dave Trembley	312,354	4,805	None
216	Reading Phillies (Phillies)	64	77	.454	21	Greg Legg	478,257	7,138	2001
120	Akron Aeros (Indians)	63	78	.447	22	Brad Komminsk	478,611	7,038	2003
184	Harrisburg Senators (Expos)	52	90	.366	33½	Dave Machemer	255,978	3,820	1999

PLAYOFFS—Semifinals: New Hampshire defeated Binghamton 3-1 and Altoona defeated Erie 3-0 in best-of-5 series. **Finals:** New Hampshire defeated Altoona 3-0 in best-of-5 series.

NOTE: Team's individual batting and pitching statistics can be found on page indicated in lefthand column.

CLUB BATTING

	AVG	G	AB	R	H	2B	3B	HR	BB	SO	SB
Altoona	.273	141	4695	697	1280	270	28	135	400	871	117
Binghamton	.272	142	4787	696	1300	296	40	89	516	1135	193
Trenton	.269	142	4793	684	1288	266	31	141	510	904	93
Reading	.266	141	4654	644	1240	226	30	158	447	923	74
Erie	.266	142	4749	734	1263	254	37	180	590	1079	102
Bowie	.264	142	4685	660	1235	252	17	128	414	922	87
Norwich	.262	142	4776	622	1250	264	39	93	418	1026	122
Portland	.261	142	4782	664	1247	280	41	126	531	1010	116
Akron	.259	141	4742	689	1226	257	46	114	484	952	98
New Britain	.258	140	4586	626	1181	245	28	124	371	855	82
New Hampshire	.254	141	4641	645	1179	230	36	114	449	1032	79
Harrisburg	.250	142	4695	565	1176	219	27	88	468	974	99

CLUB PITCHING

	ERA	G	CG	SV	IP	H	HR	R	ER	BB	SO
New Hampshire	3.49	141	3	46	1224	1096	114	534	474	438	975
Norwich	3.63	142	5	35	1228	1171	98	564	496	427	912
New Britain	4.08	140	3	47	1214	1214	110	610	550	479	987
Erie	4.10	142	6	32	1239	1289	139	665	564	411	872
Altoona	4.19	141	3	46	1215	1212	140	636	565	435	984
Bowie	4.23	142	0	34	1216	1188	128	642	571	519	1108
Binghamton	4.26	142	1	41	1223	1136	112	654	579	532	998
Akron	4.54	141	4	32	1223	1288	118	719	617	490	942
Reading	4.56	141	4	35	1200	1256	147	683	608	483	917
Trenton	4.72	142	5	33	1233	1336	99	721	647	450	1072
Harrisburg	4.73	142	3	28	1219	1328	149	725	640	446	839
Portland	4.77	142	1	40	1250	1317	134	757	662	478	1053

CLUB FIELDING

	PCT	PO	A	E		PCT	PO	A	E
Norwich	.979	3685	1433	108	Binghamton	.974	3710	1461	137
New Britain	.979	3642	1376	109	Bowie	.974	3648	1336	133
New Hampshire	.977	3671	1500	122	Harrisburg	.973	3683	1543	143
Trenton	.976	3700	1420	124	Erie	.973	3718	1555	146
Reading	.976	3601	1317	120	Portland	.973	3750	1297	141
Altoona	.975	3668	1316	126	Akron	.967	3669	1351	173

INDIVIDUAL BATTING LEADERS
(Minimum 383 Plate Appearances)

	AVG	G	AB	R	H	2B	3B	HR	RBI	BB	SO	SB
Keppinger, Jeff, Bing./Norfolk	.340	95	362	58	123	20	3	1	38	33	17	12
Castellano, John, Reading	.340	103	368	50	125	25	1	18	68	32	55	0
Cervenak, Michael, Norwich	.337	110	410	77	138	36	1	21	88	52	53	6
McLouth, Nate, Altoona	.322	133	515	93	166	40	4	8	73	48	62	31
Jones, Garrett, New Britain	.311	122	450	68	140	33	2	30	92	28	98	11
Maza, Luis, New Britain	.311	126	492	84	153	26	8	12	66	28	70	5
Duffy, Chris, Altoona	.309	113	453	84	140	23	6	8	41	33	77	32
Majewski, Val, Bowie	.307	112	433	71	133	24	5	15	80	33	68	14
Granderson, Curtis, Erie	.301	123	462	89	139	19	8	21	94	80	95	14
Raburn, Ryan, Erie	.301	98	366	66	110	29	4	16	63	47	96	3

INDIVIDUAL PITCHING LEADERS
(Minimum 114 Innings)

	W	L	ERA	G	GS	CG	SV	IP	H	R	ER	BB	SO
Floyd, Gavin, Reading	6	6	2.57	20	20	2	0	119	93	39	34	46	94
Scobie, Jason, Binghamton	5	5	2.82	26	24	0	1	147	137	57	46	49	95
Chacin, Gustavo, New Hampshire	16	2	2.92	25	25	0	0	142	113	53	46	49	109
Misch, Patrick, Norwich	7	6	3.00	26	26	4	0	159	138	61	53	35	123
Larrison, Preston, Erie	5	4	3.05	20	20	0	0	118	122	54	40	36	59
Snell, Ian, Altoona	11	7	3.16	26	26	3	0	151	147	54	53	49	142
Alvarez, Abe, Portland	10	9	3.59	26	26	0	0	135	132	65	54	32	108
Baugh, Kenny, Erie	8	8	3.72	24	24	1	0	143	154	70	59	41	107
Peterson, Matt, Norfolk/Bing.	9	6	3.99	26	25	0	0	141	133	69	63	67	119
Stevenson, Jason, Harrisburg	8	10	4.06	24	22	0	1	135	132	66	61	46	75

ALL-STAR TEAM

C—Ronny Paulino, Altoona. **1B**—Ryan Howard, Reading. **2B**—Jeff Keppinger, Altoona/Binghamton. **3B**—Mike Cervenak, Norwich. **SS**—Aaron Hill, New Hampshire. **OF**—Curtis Granderson, Erie; Val Majewski, Bowie; Kevin West, New Britain. **DH**—Mitch Jones, Trenton. **UT**—John Castellano, Reading. **RHP**—Ian Snell, Altoona. **LHP**—Gustavo Chacin, New Hampshire. **RP**—Bobby Korecky, New Britain.

Most Valuable Player: Ryan Howard, Reading. **Pitcher of the Year:** Gustavo Chacin, New Hampshire. **Rookie of the Year:** Ryan Howard, Reading. **Manager of the Year:** Mike Basso, New Hampshire.

DEPARTMENT LEADERS

BATTING
G	Doug Clark, Norwich	140
AB	Doug Clark, Norwich	537
R	Nate McLouth, Altoona	93
H	Nate McLouth, Altoona	166
TB	Mitch Jones, Trenton	272
XBH	Mitch Jones, Trenton	68
2B	Nate McLouth, Altoona	40
3B	Doug Clark, Norwich	13
HR	Mitch Jones, Trenton	39
RBI	Ryan Howard, Reading	102
SH	James Tomlin, New Britain	19
SF	Aaron Hill, New Hampshire	11
BB	Kurt Airoso, Erie	82
IBB	Three tied at	6
HBP	Chris Duffy, Altoona	17
	Scott Tousa, Erie	17
SO	Mitch Jones, Trenton	152
	Justin Singleton, New Hampshire	152
SB	Wayne Lydon, Binghamton	65
CS	Wayne Lydon, Binghamton	20
GIDP	Rich Lane, Harrisburg	25
OBP	Mike Cervenak, Norwich	.414
SLG	Ryan Howard, Reading	.647

PITCHING
G	Jacobo Sequea, Bowie	59
GS	Three tied at	27
CG	Pat Misch, Norwich	4
ShO	Pat Misch, Norwich	3
GF	Jacobo Sequea, Bowie	53
SV	Bobby Korecky, New Britain	31
W	Gustavo Chacin, New Hampshire	16
L	Luke Lockwood, Harrisburg	17
IP	Sean Henn, Trenton	163
H	Henry Bonilla, New Britain	180
R	Sean Henn, Trenton	94
ER	Robinson Tejeda, Reading	86
HR	Robinson Tejeda, Reading	29
HB	Jeremy Guthrie, Akron	16
BB	Charlie Zink, Portland	72
SO	Boof Bonser, New Britain	146
WP	Ken Chenard, Binghamton	15
BK	Colin Young, Portland	6

FIELDING
C	PCT	Maxim St. Pierre, Erie	.996
	PO	Justin Knoedler, Norwich	681
	A	Justin Knoedler, Norwich	64
	E	Edgar Martinez, Portland	14
	DP	Carlos Ruiz, Reading	8
	PB	Justin Knoedler, Norwich	15
1B	PCT	Larry Broadway, Harrisburg	.993
	PO	Larry Broadway, Harrisburg	1069
	A	Garrett Jones, New Britain	127
	E	Garrett Jones, New Britain	17
	DP	Larry Broadway, Harrisburg	111
2B	PCT	Derin McMains, Norwich	.992
	PO	Dominic Rich, New Hampshire	236
	A	Dominic Rich, New Hampshire	365
	E	Ryan Raburn, Erie	26
	DP	Dominic Rich, New Hampshire	69
3B	PCT	Mike Cervenak, Norwich	.970
	PO	Corey Smith, Akron	108
	A	Jack Hannahan, Erie	228
	E	Corey Smith, Akron	37
	DP	Jack Hannahan, Erie	27
SS	PCT	Gil Velazquez, Binghamton	.974
	PO	Aaron Hill, New Hampshire	236
	A	Josh Labandeira, Harrisburg	394
	E	Josh Labandeira, Harrisburg	31
	DP	Josh Labandeira, Harrisburg	83
OF	PCT	Chris Duffy, Altoona	.993
	PO	James Tomlin, New Britain	312
	A	David Espinosa, Erie	14
	E	Wayne Lydon, Binghamton	11
	DP	Ryan Fleming, Reading	4
		Keith Reed, Bowie	4

BY WILL LINGO

The Southern League tried to avoid it, but for the second time in four years the league couldn't settle its championship on the field and had to declare co-champions.

The league canceled its championship series in 2001 in the wake of Sept. 11, as did most minor leagues. In 2004, the problem was Hurricane Ivan, one of three hurricanes that plagued minor leagues in the Southeast at the end of the season.

The Mobile BayBears and Tennessee Smokies both won their semifinal series three games to one—clinching on Sept. 11, oddly enough—but the hurricane bore down in the Gulf of Mexico and the league decided it wasn't worth waiting it out.

Anthony Reyes

"If I was a player in Tennessee and my family was in Mobile, baseball would be the last thing on my mind," league president Don Mincher said. "For that reason, I knew it was the right decision to cancel this year's championship series. This is the toughest decision I've had to make in my presidency, but I know this is the safest possible option, and that is what is important at a time like this."

Ivan did eventually make landfall in Mobile on Sept. 15, the day the first finals game in Mobile had been scheduled.

At one point when officials were trying to decide what to do about the hurricane, they considered a one-game playoff for the title. "That was fine with me," Tennessee manager Mark DeJohn said, "because I would have had Reyes starting."

Righthander Anthony Reyes was the league's best starter in the second half of the season, going 6-2, 2.91 after getting promoted from high Class A in July. Mobile had the league's pitcher of the year, however, in closer Brad Baker.

Baker, a supplemental first-round pick of the Red Sox in 1999, looked like a washout but turned his career around after moving to the bullpen late in 2003. His fastball/changeup combination proved devastating, netting him 30 saves and 68 strikeouts in 57 innings.

Baker led Mobile to its second Southern League title, and its first since 1998. The BayBears joined the league in 1997 and have been a Padres affiliate through their entire

run. The Smokies got their first title since 1978, when the franchise was known as the Knoxville Sox, but lost the Cardinals after 2004, just the second season of their affiliation.

The Cardinals bought the Texas League's El Paso franchise and moved it to Springfield, Mo., so St. Louis will send its Double-A players there starting in 2005. That left the Diamondbacks without a Double-A affiliate, so they'll move to Tennessee in 2005, the only affiliation change that will affect the league.

The league will see at least one move, however, with the Greenville Braves moving to Pearl, Miss., and becoming the Mississippi Braves. The Braves had been in Greenville since 1984. It's unlikely the South Carolina city will be without minor league baseball for long, and rumors early in the offseason indicated West Tenn could move there for 2005. The team would get a new ballpark for 2006.

Richard Lewis

If 2004 was the last season for the Diamond Jaxx, at least fans there got to see two standout performances. Second baseman Richard Lewis was the league's MVP after ranking among the offensive leaders in several categories and batting .329-10-59 overall. He played in Greenville in 2003 and was traded from the Braves organization to the Cubs just before the start of the 2004 season in a deal involving Juan Cruz.

STANDINGS: SPLIT SEASON

FIRST HALF

EAST	W	L	PCT	GB
Tennessee	39	31	.557	—
Chattanooga	38	32	.543	1
Carolina	37	33	.529	2
Jacksonville	35	34	.507	3½
Greenville	26	43	.377	12½

WEST	W	L	PCT	GB
Mobile	40	30	.571	—
West Tenn	37	32	.536	2½
Birmingham	35	34	.507	4½
Huntsville	32	38	.457	8
Montgomery	29	41	.414	11

SECOND HALF

EAST	W	L	PCT	GB
Chattanooga	49	21	.700	—
Greenville	37	33	.529	12
Carolina	36	33	.522	12½
Jacksonville	31	37	.456	17
Tennessee	30	40	.429	19

WEST	W	L	PCT	GB
Birmingham	38	32	.543	—
West Tenn	33	36	.478	4½
Huntsville	33	37	.471	5
Mobile	33	37	.471	5
Montgomery	28	42	.400	10

PLAYOFFS—Semifinals: Tennessee defeated Chattanooga 3-1 and Mobile defeated Birmingham 3-1 in best-of-five series. **Finals:** Cancelled—Mobile and Tennessee were named co-champions.

STANDINGS: OVERALL

Page		W	L	Pct.	GB	Manager	Attendance	Avg.	Last Penn.
112	Chattanooga Lookouts (Reds)	87	53	.621	—	Jayhawk Owens	244,961	3,656	1988
97	Birmingham Barons (White Sox)	73	66	.525	13½	Razor Shines	280,879	4,255	2002
142	Carolina Mudcats (Marlins)	73	66	.525	13½	Ron Hassey	245,810	3,724	2003
238	Mobile BayBears (Padres)	73	67	.521	14	Gary Jones	193,885	2,893	2004
104	West Tenn Diamond Jaxx (Cubs)	70	68	.507	16	Bobby Dickerson	159,308	2,528	2000
230	Tennessee Smokies (Cardinals)	69	71	.493	18	Mark DeJohn	253,756	3,787	2004
163	Jacksonville Suns (Dodgers)	66	71	.482	19½	Dino Ebel	420,495	6,276	2001
170	Huntsville Stars (Brewers)	65	75	.464	22	Frank Kremblas	180,506	2,734	2001
74	Greenville Braves (Braves)	63	76	.453	23½	Brian Snitker	143,443	2,206	1997
260	Montgomery Biscuits (Devil Rays)	57	83	.407	30	Charlie Montoyo	322,946	4,820	1999

NOTE: Team's individual batting and pitching statistics can be found on page indicated in lefthand column.

2004 SOUTHERN LEAGUE STATISTICS

CLUB BATTING

	AVG	G	AB	R	H	2B	3B	HR	BB	SO	SB
Chattanooga	.276	140	4775	688	1318	285	32	110	473	963	128
Greenville	.270	139	4694	593	1268	254	33	125	409	1045	106
West Tenn	.265	138	4446	619	1177	232	61	90	433	1047	116
Birmingham	.262	139	4628	635	1214	224	43	105	494	956	123
Tennessee	.261	140	4593	634	1200	237	23	129	525	1015	134
Carolina	.257	139	4545	646	1170	270	23	131	537	1080	126
Montgomery	.253	140	4542	523	1148	225	42	80	371	1001	49
Jacksonville	.250	137	4582	567	1145	222	26	119	388	1088	84
Huntsville	.241	140	4497	510	1085	219	25	88	438	998	128
Mobile	.241	140	4529	601	1091	212	25	132	461	1140	78

CLUB PITCHING

	ERA	G	CG	SV	IP	H	HR	R	ER	BB	SO
Chattanooga	3.33	140	2	46	1248	1161	111	540	461	395	1131
Birmingham	3.43	139	0	34	1224	1170	80	535	466	391	969
Huntsville	3.57	140	1	35	1209	1156	107	590	479	447	1050
Mobile	3.82	140	4	35	1220	1192	109	584	518	424	911
Greenville	3.88	139	3	30	1216	1172	94	623	524	502	1073
Jacksonville	3.88	137	3	30	1215	1201	108	601	524	499	1102
West Tenn	3.99	138	3	27	1180	1094	118	597	523	511	1142
Tennessee	4.27	140	6	31	1198	1198	125	635	569	447	989
Carolina	4.34	139	0	33	1209	1235	129	639	583	488	991
Montgomery	4.53	140	6	34	1187	1237	128	672	597	425	975

CLUB FIELDING

	PCT	PO	A	E		PCT	PO	A	E
Carolina	.978	3626	1349	112	Jacksonville	.976	3644	1388	123
Mobile	.978	3661	1533	119	Birmingham	.975	3672	1415	129
Montgomery	.978	3562	1276	111	Greenville	.973	3648	1411	138
West Tenn	.978	3539	1331	112	Chattanooga	.971	3743	1342	150
Tennessee	.977	3594	1452	117	Huntsville	.970	3626	1390	154

INDIVIDUAL BATTING LEADERS
(Minimum 378 Plate Appearances)

	AVG	G	AB	R	H	2B	3B	HR	RBI	BB	SO	SB
Calzado, Napoleon, Greenville	.359	119	449	68	161	28	7	8	59	22	59	18
Lewis, Richard, West Tenn	.329	99	380	68	125	27	10	10	59	37	94	7
Stern, Adam, Greenville	.322	102	394	64	127	26	6	8	47	35	58	27
Schumaker, Skip, Tennessee	.316	138	516	78	163	29	6	4	43	60	61	19
Hoffpauir, Micah, West Tenn	.306	94	340	58	104	20	6	11	75	27	61	1
Spidale, Mike, Birmingham	.306	126	484	87	148	27	7	7	47	61	72	26
Hall, Billy, Carolina	.300	95	350	53	105	18	4	4	30	42	46	40
Beattie, Andrew, Chattanooga	.300	101	347	51	104	18	6	6	43	47	67	8
Bolivar, Papo, Tennessee	.295	126	451	71	133	25	2	15	60	55	86	51
Gutierrez, Jesse, Chattanooga	.292	127	487	74	142	32	4	17	82	36	64	0

INDIVIDUAL PITCHING LEADERS
(Minimum 112 Innings)

	W	L	ERA	G	GS	CG	SV	IP	H	R	ER	BB	SO
Pinto, Renyel, West Tenn	11	8	2.92	25	25	0	0	142	107	50	46	72	179
Kelly, Steve, Chattanooga	12	7	2.96	28	28	0	0	161	156	69	53	48	116
Ketchner, Ryan, Jacksonville	8	7	3.02	21	21	1	0	119	118	43	40	36	98
Housman, Jeff, Huntsville	5	8	3.13	23	20	0	1	112	108	55	39	38	121
Brownlie, Bobby, West Tenn	9	9	3.36	26	26	2	0	147	127	62	55	36	114
Thompson, Mike, Mobile	10	2	3.41	35	18	0	0	121	129	50	46	31	69
Bullard, Jim, Birmingham	8	4	3.47	37	15	0	14	107	52	44	44	74	
Thompson, Derek, Jacksonville	5	7	3.72	22	22	0	0	119	132	53	49	51	100
Whitaker, Brian, Mobile	8	9	3.73	23	23	1	0	138	128	68	57	36	82
Ulacia, Dennis, Birmingham	8	8	3.77	28	23	0	0	129	137	63	54	36	107

ALL-STAR TEAM

C—Josh Willingham, Carolina. **1B**—Jesse Gutierrez, Chattanooga. **2B**—Richard Lewis, West Tenn. **3B**—Edwin Encarnacion, Chattanooga. **SS**—Josh Wilson, Carolina. **OF**—Napoleon Calzado, Greenville; Brad Nelson, Huntsville; Skip Schumaker, Tennessee; Adam Stern, Greenville. **DH**—Greg Sain, Mobile. **UT**—William Bergola, Chattanooga. **RHP**—Brian Rose, Chattanooga. **LHP**—Renyel Pinto, West Tenn. **RP**—Brad Baker, Mobile.

Most Valuable Player: Richard Lewis, West Tenn. **Most Outstanding Pitcher:** Brad Baker, Mobile. **Manager of the Year:** Jayhawk Owens, Chattanooga.

DEPARTMENT LEADERS

BATTING
G	Four tied at	138
AB	Anthony Gwynn, Huntsville	534
R	Mike Spidale, Birmingham	87
H	Skip Schumaker, Tennessee	163
TB	Prince Fielder, Huntsville	235
XBH	Ben Johnson, Mobile	57
2B	Three tied at	35
3B	Dwaine Bacon, West Tenn	11
HR	Greg Sain, Mobile	28
RBI	Josh Barfield, Mobile	90
SH	Ruddy Yan, Birmingham	17
SF	Micah Hoffpauir, West Tenn	12
BB	Josh Willingham, Carolina	91
IBB	Chris Duncan, Tennessee	8
	Josh Willingham, Carolina	8
HBP	Rickie Weeks, Huntsville	28
SO	Brad Nelson, Huntsville	146
SB	Dwaine Bacon, West Tenn	60
CS	Dwaine Bacon, West Tenn	20
GIDP	William Bergola, Chattanooga	23
OBP	Josh Willingham, Carolina	.449
SLG	Josh Willingham, Carolina	.565

PITCHING
G	Matt Smith, Birmingham	70
GS	Steve Kelly, Chattanooga	28
	Nic Ungs, Carolina	28
CG	Five tied at	2
ShO	Brad Thompson, Tennessee	2
GF	Brad Baker, Mobile	49
SV	Brad Baker, Mobile	30
W	Steve Kelly, Chattanooga	12
	Heath Phillips, Birmingham	12
L	Dennis Sarfate, Huntsville	12
IP	Steve Kelly, Chattanooga	161
	Nic Ungs, Carolina	161
H	Jason Cromer, Montgomery	180
R	Carmen Pignatiello, West Tenn	89
ER	Clay Hensley, Mobile	76
	Nic Ungs, Carolina	76
HR	Nic Ungs, Carolina	24
HB	Trevor Hutchinson, Carolina	11
	Brian Rose, Chattanooga	11
BB	Dennis Sarfate, Huntsville	78
SO	Renyel Pinto, West Tenn	179
WP	Steve Kelly, Chattanooga	13
BK	Ryan Meaux, Birmingham	4

FIELDING
C	PCT	Josh Willingham, Carolina	.994
	PO	Geovany Soto, West Tenn	837
	A	Geovany Soto, West Tenn	89
	E	Brian Peterson, Chattanooga	11
	DP	Geovany Soto, West Tenn	11
	PB	Geovany Soto, West Tenn	14
		Chris Stewart, Birmingham	14
1B	PCT	Scott Thorman, Greenville	.994
	PO	Prince Fielder, Huntsville	1079
	A	Jesse Gutierrez, Chattanooga	87
	E	Prince Fielder, Huntsville	15
	DP	Greg Sain, Mobile	97
2B	PCT	Richard Lewis, West Tenn	.995
	PO	Josh Barfield, Mobile	293
	A	Josh Barfield, Mobile	396
	E	Rickie Weeks, Huntsville	17
	DP	Josh Barfield, Mobile	95
3B	PCT	Brennan King, Jacksonville	.949
	PO	Chris Barnwell, Huntsville	127
	A	Chris Barnwell, Huntsville	271
	E	Edwin Encarnacion, Chattanooga	25
	DP	Chris Barnwell, Huntsville	26
SS	PCT	Ronny Cedeno, West Tenn	.963
	PO	Ronny Cedeno, West Tenn	168
	A	Tony Pena, Greenville	371
	E	Jeff Bannon, Chattanooga	26
		Tony Pena, Greenville	26
	DP	Tony Pena, Greenville	82
OF	PCT	Jon Hamilton, Tennessee	.992
	PO	Anthony Gwynn, Huntsville	324
	A	Brad Nelson, Huntsville	17
	E	Dwaine Bacon, West Tenn	11
	DP	Andrew Beattie, Chattanooga	4

MINOR LEAGUES

BY JOHN MANUEL

Round Rock thought it had the right script for a perfect farewell to the Texas League.

The Express franchise, owned in part by Hall of Fame pitcher Nolan Ryan and operated by his son Reid, set another league attendance record, making it five in five seasons. The team won both halves of play in the West Division, earning a bye through the first round of the league playoffs.

But in its last series as a Double-A franchise—the Express move up to Triple-A in 2005, remaining an Astros affiliate—Round Rock got shell-shocked. The Frisco RoughRiders, in just their second season, swept Tulsa in a semifinal series before taking four of five from the Express for their first TL championship.

TOM PRIDDY

Willy Taveras

Frisco had won the season series between the two clubs, claiming 11 of the 16 regular-season games, before its easy win in the championship series. Frisco hit .306 in the playoffs while the pitching staff shackled the Drillers and Express, holding them to a .227 average.

"You have got to have the pitching," Frisco manager Tim Ireland said. "You need above-average starting pitching and average relief pitching, but that can change on any given night."

The RoughRiders' rotation was in constant flux and injuries decimated Texas' big league rotation. Thirty-three pitchers came and went for Ireland and pitching coach Steve Luebber, with righthander Kelvin Jimenez one of the few who was along the whole way. Jimenez saved his best for last, striking out 12 in seven shutout innings in Game Two of the championship series, leading Frisco to a 1-0 victory.

Round Rock had been the league's most prolific offensive team in the regular season with 744 runs, led by league batting champion Willy Taveras. The speedy outfielder, a Rule 5 draft pick from Cleveland the previous December (the Astros subsequently sent 15-game winner Jeriome Robertson to the Indians so they could send Taveras to the minor leagues without returning him to Cleveland), paid dividends with a .335 average, 55 stolen bases and 76 runs scored in just 103 games.

Unlike Frisco, Round Rock also had a steady rotation fronted by league strikeout leader Ezequiel Astacio (185

strikeouts, 13-10, 3.89). D.J. Houlton ranked second in the league in ERA during a 12-5, 2.94 season, and the Express had the league's top bullpen with the tandem of righthanders Mike Burns (11-3, 1.67, nine saves) and Santiago Ramirez (6-4, 2.63, 32 saves).

The top pitchers in the league, however, weren't in the playoffs. Tulsa lefthander Jeff Francis, who completely dominated the Texas League, was in the big leagues by the time the Drillers were being swept by Frisco. Francis led the league in the triple crown categories at the time he was promoted to Triple-A. He went 13-1, 1.98 with 147 strikeouts in 114 innings and was selected Baseball America's Minor League Player of the Year.

Arkansas began the year with one of the league's most talented rosters, featuring top Angels prospects such as shortstop Alberto Callaspo, outfielder Nick Gorneault, first baseman Casey Kotchman, catcher Jeff Mathis, third baseman Dallas McPherson, righthander Ervin Santana and lefthander Jake Woods. But poor team chemistry and the promotions of Kotchman and McPherson sent the team into a tailspin. The Travelers finished with a league-worst 59-89 record.

Round Rock's Double-A team moves to a new ballpark in Corpus Christi in 2005, remaining an Astros affiliate as the Ryans hope to duplicate their success in Round Rock. The club nearly reached 10,000 fans per game in 2004, drawing 689,286 in 70 opening dates, more than 1,800 more fans per game than Frisco (9,846 vs. 8,019).

A more unexpected change in the league for 2005 involves Springfield, Mo., as the St. Louis Cardinals bought the El Paso Diablos franchise for $9.8 million in order to move it to Springfield. After former Diablos officials made an unsuccessful effort to bring a Triple-A club in, El Paso's Cohen Stadium instead will house a team from the independent Central League in 2005.

STANDINGS: SPLIT SEASON

FIRST HALF					SECOND HALF				
EAST	W	L	PCT	GB	**EAST**	W	L	PCT	GB
Tulsa	38	31	.551	—	Frisco	45	25	.643	—
Wichita	37	32	.536	1	Wichita	36	34	.514	9
Frisco	36	34	.514	2½	Tulsa	33	37	.471	12
Arkansas	33	36	.478	5	Arkansas	26	44	.371	19
WEST	W	L	PCT	GB	**WEST**	W	L	PCT	GB
Round Rock	45	25	.643	—	Round Rock	41	29	.586	—
Midland	35	35	.500	10	San Antonio	36	32	.529	4
San Antonio	30	40	.429	15	Midland	37	33	.529	4
El Paso	24	45	.348	20½	El Paso	24	44	.353	16

PLAYOFFS—Semifinals: Frisco defeated Tulsa 3-0 in best-of-5 series; Round Rock received first-round bye. **Finals:** Frisco defeated Round Rock 4-1 in best-of-7 series.

STANDINGS: OVERALL

Page		W	L	Pct.	GB	Manager	Attendance	Avg.	Last Penn.
150	Round Rock Express (Astros)	86	54	.614	—	Jackie Moore	689,286	9,846	2000
267	Frisco RoughRiders (Rangers)	81	59	.579	5	Tim Ireland	553,312	8,019	2004
156	Wichita Wranglers (Royals)	73	66	.525	12½	Frank White	161,638	2,487	1999
209	Midland RockHounds (Athletics)	72	68	.514	14	Webster Garrison	256,110	3,822	1975
128	Tulsa Drillers (Rockies)	71	68	.511	14½	Tom Runnells	320,733	4,787	1998
253	San Antonio Missions (Mariners)	66	72	.478	19	Dave Brundage	278,080	3,972	2003
59	Arkansas Travelers (Angels)	59	80	.424	26½	Tyrone Boykin	178,655	2,928	2001
66	El Paso Diablos (Diamondbacks)	48	89	.350	36½	Scott Coolbaugh	229,315	3,422	1994

NOTE: Team's individual batting and pitching statistics can be found on page indicated in lefthand column.

MINOR LEAGUES

2004 TEXAS LEAGUE STATISTICS

CLUB BATTING

	AVG	G	AB	R	H	2B	3B	HR	BB	SO	SB
Frisco	.276	140	4820	736	1331	243	45	117	505	1050	120
El Paso	.276	137	4676	668	1291	273	52	94	419	980	119
Midland	.275	140	4834	716	1329	279	43	99	524	1040	92
Round Rock	.273	140	4750	744	1299	276	27	125	491	1002	160
Arkansas	.266	139	4681	641	1246	249	38	114	389	916	88
Wichita	.264	139	4639	652	1226	206	31	116	486	857	82
San Antonio	.262	138	4614	589	1211	222	30	92	395	851	125
Tulsa	.259	139	4622	628	1199	234	26	116	455	1052	121

CLUB PITCHING

	ERA	G	CG	SV	IP	H	HR	R	ER	BB	SO
Tulsa	3.67	139	5	42	1209	1142	117	573	493	407	958
Frisco	3.74	140	1	39	1243	1186	119	608	516	462	1004
Round Rock	3.86	140	7	47	1228	1217	100	589	526	398	1066
Wichita	4.30	139	4	34	1218	1287	109	661	582	404	960
Midland	4.47	140	3	36	1235	1310	102	695	613	463	908
San Antonio	4.53	138	3	40	1208	1254	109	684	608	547	1037
Arkansas	4.96	139	4	26	1209	1353	118	777	666	465	865
El Paso	5.04	137	5	25	1194	1383	99	787	669	518	950

CLUB FIELDING

	PCT	PO	A	E		PCT	PO	A	E
Wichita	.976	3654	1449	128	San Antonio	.974	3624	1413	136
Tulsa	.975	3627	1535	132	Frisco	.973	3728	1385	144
Round Rock	.975	3683	1412	133	El Paso	.969	3581	1498	165
Midland	.974	3705	1557	140	Arkansas	.968	3628	1505	170

INDIVIDUAL BATTING LEADERS
(Minimum 378 Plate Appearances)

	AVG	G	AB	R	H	2B	3B	HR	RBI	BB	SO	SB
Taveras, Willy, Round Rock	.335	103	409	76	137	13	1	2	27	38	76	55
Sandoval, Danny, Tulsa	.319	133	530	73	169	37	4	8	66	37	64	22
Shealy, Ryan, Tulsa	.318	132	469	88	149	32	3	29	99	62	97	3
Choo, Shin-Soo, San Antonio	.315	132	517	89	163	17	7	15	84	56	97	40
Self, Todd, Round Rock	.315	131	476	86	150	34	1	11	81	89	95	8
Garrett, Shawn, Tulsa	.307	103	374	73	115	16	3	12	51	41	104	14
Snyder, Chris, El Paso	.301	99	346	66	104	31	0	15	57	46	57	3
Botts, Jason, Frisco	.293	133	481	85	141	25	3	24	92	77	126	7
Cota, Jesus, El Paso	.290	94	366	50	106	21	4	10	59	18	61	2
Conrad, Brooks, Round Rock	.290	129	480	84	139	39	6	13	83	63	105	8

INDIVIDUAL PITCHING LEADERS
(Minimum 112 Innings)

	W	L	ERA	G	GS	CG	SV	IP	H	R	ER	BB	SO
Francis, Jeff, Tulsa	13	1	1.98	17	17	1	0	114	73	26	25	22	147
Houlton, D.J., Round Rock	12	5	2.94	28	28	3	0	159	141	59	52	47	159
Bazzell, Shane, Midland	15	3	3.03	34	14	0	2	119	105	52	40	36	86
Loe, Kameron, Frisco	7	7	3.10	19	19	0	0	113	122	42	39	29	97
Esposito, Mike, Tulsa	10	6	3.33	24	24	1	0	143	138	57	53	35	90
Hampson, Justin, Tulsa	10	9	3.49	27	27	1	0	170	176	82	66	63	104
Buglovsky, Chris, San Antonio	6	8	3.64	24	21	1	0	121	121	68	49	45	81
Astacio, Ezequiel, Round Rock	13	10	3.89	28	28	1	0	176	155	89	76	56	185
Gothreaux, Jared, Round Rock	9	7	3.96	27	24	2	0	157	172	82	69	35	110
Tamayo, Danny, Wichita	12	7	3.98	25	25	0	0	142	166	66	63	36	123

ALL-STAR TEAM

C—Chris Snyder, El Paso. **1B**—Ryan Shealy, Tulsa. **2B**—Ruben Gotay, Wichita. **3B**—Dallas McPherson, Arkansas. **SS**—Danny Sandoval, Tulsa. **OF**—Shin-Soo Choo, San Antonio; Nick Gorneault, Arkansas; Willy Taveras, Round Rock. **DH**—Jason Botts, Round Rock. **UT**—Brooks Conrad, Round Rock. **P**—Ezequiel Astacio, Round Rock; Shane Bazzell, Midland; Jeff Francis, Tulsa; D.J. Houlton, Round Rock; Kameron Loe, Frisco; Santiago Ramirez, Round Rock; Ryan Speier, Tulsa.

Player of the Year: Ryan Shealy, Tulsa. **Pitcher of the Year:** Jeff Francis, Tulsa. **Manager of the Year:** Jackie Moore, Round Rock.

DEPARTMENT LEADERS

BATTING
G	Jason Bourgeois, Frisco	138
AB	Alberto Callaspo, Arkansas	550
R	Nick Gorneault, Arkansas	91
H	Danny Sandoval, Tulsa	169
TB	Ryan Shealy, Tulsa	274
XBH	Ryan Shealy, Tulsa	64
2B	Brooks Conrad, Round Rock	39
3B	Marland Williams, El Paso	10
HR	Ryan Shealy, Tulsa	29
RBI	Ryan Shealy, Tulsa	99
SH	Juan Piniella, Tulsa	15
SF	Brooks Conrad, Round Rock	12
BB	Todd Self, Round Rock	89
IBB	Shawn Garrett, Tulsa	11
HBP	John Baker, Midland	17
	Dave Matranga, Round Rock	17
SO	Charlton Jimerson, Round Rock	163
SB	Willy Taveras, Round Rock	55
CS	Dustin Delucchi, San Antonio	15
GIDP	Jesus Cota, El Paso	23
OBP	Todd Self, Round Rock	.420
SLG	Ryan Shealy, Tulsa	.584

PITCHING
G	Ryan Speier, Tulsa	61
GS	Three tied at	28
CG	Three tied at	3
ShO	Willie Collazo, Arkansas	2
GF	Ryan Speier, Tulsa	58
SV	Ryan Speier, Tulsa	37
W	Shane Bazzell, Midland	15
L	Brad Weis, Midland	12
IP	Ezequiel Astacio, Round Rock	176
H	Drew Dickinson, Midland	198
R	Brad Weis, Midland	106
ER	Brad Weis, Midland	94
HR	Justin Hampson, Tulsa	22
HB	Brad Weis, Midland	15
BB	Juan Done, San Antonio	70
SO	Ezequiel Astacio, Round Rock	185
WP	Three tied at	12
BK	Wandy Rodriguez, Round Rock	6

FIELDING
C	PCT	Jeremy Brown, Midland	.991
	PO	Hector Gimenez, Round Rock	693
	A	Jeremy Brown, Midland	66
	E	Jeff Mathis, Arkansas	14
	DP	Luis Oliveros, San Antonio	6
	PB	Jeff Mathis, Arkansas	12
1B	PCT	Ryan Shealy, Tulsa	.997
	PO	Chad Santos, Wichita	1145
	A	Chad Santos, Wichita	76
	E	Jason Botts, Frisco	19
	DP	Ryan Shealy, Tulsa	120
2B	PCT	Mark Kiger, Midland	.979
	PO	Jayson Nix, Tulsa	253
	A	Jayson Nix, Tulsa	392
	E	Jayson Nix, Tulsa	19
	DP	Jayson Nix, Tulsa	85
3B	PCT	Justin Gemoll, Wichita	.949
	PO	Justin Gemoll, Wichita	78
	A	Justin Gemoll, Wichita	204
	E	Justin Gemoll, Wichita	15
		Edgar Gonzalez, Frisco	15
	DP	Hunter Brown, San Antonio	18
SS	PCT	Eddie Menchaca, San Antonio	.974
	PO	Alberto Callaspo, Arkansas	200
	A	Danny Sandoval, Tulsa	392
	E	Danny Sandoval, Tulsa	29
	DP	Danny Sandoval, Tulsa	85
OF	PCT	Juan Piniella, Tulsa	.994
	PO	Tommy Murphy, Arkansas	311
	A	Shin-Soo Choo, San Antonio	18
	E	Marland Williams, El Paso	11
	DP	Shin-Soo Choo, San Antonio	6

BY KEVIN GOLDSTEIN

The Modesto Athletics finished their 30-year affiliation with Oakland in grand style in 2004, with a league MVP (outfielder Brian Stavisky), manager of the year (Von Hayes), a league-best 90-50 record, and most importantly, their first California League title in 20 years.

A championship matchup between the A's, who won both halves of the Northern Division, and the Lancaster JetHawks, who did the same in the Southern Division, seemed almost inevitable. While the JetHawks cruised into the finals by taking three of four from the defending champion Inland Empire 66ers in the Southern Division finals, the A's needed a dramatic Game Five victory over the San Jose Giants to advance to the finals.

Trailing 6-5 in the bottom of the ninth with two outs, Jason Perry's RBI single to left field scored Lloyd Turner with the tying run. Shortstop Omar Quintanilla followed two batters later with the game-winning single off Jeremy Accardo to propel Modesto into the finals.

The best-of-five final allowed for more dramatics. After dropping two of the first three games to the JetHawks, the A's forced a decisive Game Five with a 12-8 victory behind Perry's five-hit, two home run effort.

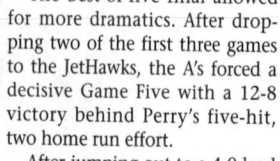

Jon Zeringue

After jumping out to a 4-0 lead in the finale, the A's held off a ninth-inning Lancaster rally to win 4-3, with catcher Phil Avlas flying out to Stavisky to end the game.

Stavisky, who hit .343 to lead the league during the regular season, went 20-for-40 in the post-season, while Perry, who hit 24 regular season home runs in 84 games, earned postseason MVP honors by batting .378-3-10 in 10 games. Lancaster was led by outfielder Jon Zeringue, who hit .335-10-41 in 56 regular-season games after being selected by the Diamondbacks in the second round of the June draft. He continued to impress in the postseason, batting .447 with 12 RBIs in nine games.

Talent-wise, it was a tale of two halves in the Cal League, as four of the top five prospects were showcasing their talent in Double-A by the end of June.

The first half was dominated by young righthanded pitching sensations, notably Inland Empire's Felix Hernandez and San Jose's Matt Cain, both of whom moved to Double-A and continued to pitch well despite still being teenagers. "Those two are both so special," one American League scout said. "They are so young and they obviously have amazing arms, but they both really know how to pitch, which is phenomenal."

The biggest offensive impact of the first half was made by Lancaster's "Three Amigos"—outfielders Conor Jackson and Carlos Quentin, and third baseman Jamie D'Antona. Arizona's first three picks in the 2003 draft combined to hit .323-39-162 in 70 games before being promoted as a group to Double-A El Paso.

The league's top position player according to scouts and managers was Rancho Cucamonga shortstop Eric Aybar, who led the league in hits (189) and stolen bases (51) while often playing spectacular defense.

The postseason affiliation shuffle affected no league more than the Cal League, as half of the league's 10 squads will have new parent teams in 2005. Four of the five changes involved existing Cal League participants.

Oakland will move its representative to Stockton for 2005, with Stockton's former parent club, the Rangers, taking over in Bakersfield. The Rockies move in at Modesto, leaving Bakersfield's former parent, the Devil Rays, with the Rockies' former squad, the Visalia Oaks, the least attended team in the circuit in 2004.

The only new organization entering the Cal League in 2005 will be the Royals, who will take over in High Desert after the previous tenants, the Brewers, reached an agreement with Brevard County (Florida State).

STANDINGS: SPLIT SEASON

FIRST HALF

NORTH	W	L	PCT	GB
Modesto	44	26	.629	—
San Jose	37	33	.529	7
Visalia	34	36	.486	10
Stockton	32	38	.457	12
Bakersfield	29	41	.414	15

SOUTH	W	L	PCT	GB
Lancaster	43	27	.629	—
Inland Empire	39	31	.557	4
Lake Elsinore	34	36	.486	9
Rancho Cucamonga	33	37	.471	10
High Desert	25	45	.357	18

SECOND HALF

NORTH	W	L	PCT	GB
Modesto	46	24	.657	—
Stockton	40	30	.571	6
San Jose	37	33	.529	9
Bakersfield	30	40	.429	16
Visalia	22	48	.314	24

SOUTH	W	L	PCT	GB
Lancaster	43	27	.614	—
Inland Empire	38	32	.543	5
Rancho Cucamonga	36	34	.514	7
Lake Elsinore	34	36	.486	9
High Desert	24	46	.343	19

PLAYOFFS—Quarterfinals: San Jose defeated Stockton 2-1 and Inland Empire defeated Rancho Cucamonga 2-0 in best-of-3 series. **Semifinals:** Modesto defeated San Jose 3-2 and Lancaster defeated Inland Empire 3-1 in best-of-5 series. **Finals:** Modesto defeated Lancaster 3-2 in best-of-5 series.

STANDINGS: OVERALL

Page		W	L	Pct.	GB	Manager	Attendance	Avg.	Last Penn.
210	Modesto A's (Athletics)	90	50	.643	—	Von Hayes	145,019	2,101	2004
67	Lancaster JetHawks (Diamondbacks)	86	54	.614	4	Wally Backman	129,442	1,876	None
254	Inland Empire 66ers (Mariners)	77	63	.550	13	Steve Roadcap	201,633	2,880	2003
246	San Jose Giants (Giants)	74	66	.529	16	Lenn Sakata	151,414	2,194	2001
268	Stockton Ports (Rangers)	72	68	.514	18	Arnie Beyeler	98,035	1,441	2002
60	Rancho Cucamonga Quakes (Angels)	69	71	.493	21	Bobby Meacham	286,198	4,148	1994
239	Lake Elsinore Storm (Padres)	68	72	.486	22	Rick Renteria	236,746	3,482	2001
261	Bakersfield Blaze (Devil Rays)	59	81	.421	31	Mako Oliveras	69,922	1,059	1989
128	Visalia Oaks (Rockies)	56	84	.400	34	Stu Cole	66,254	960	1978
170	High Desert Mavericks (Brewers)	49	91	.350	41	Mel Queen	122,265	1,747	1997

NOTE: Teams' individual batting and pitching statistics can be found on page indicated in lefthand column.

CLUB BATTING

	AVG	G	AB	R	H	2B	3B	HR	BB	SO	SB
Modesto	.302	140	5076	856	1531	354	40	118	461	886	62
Lancaster	.296	140	4914	856	1457	279	45	154	419	984	136
Inland Empire	.282	140	4856	744	1368	257	54	81	409	974	145
High Desert	.278	140	4936	720	1373	263	48	135	407	985	150
Bakersfield	.274	140	4821	663	1320	269	27	94	406	1037	149
Rancho Cucamonga	.273	140	4861	757	1329	254	49	125	448	1071	178
Visalia	.268	140	4904	758	1314	273	38	115	557	1071	87
Lake Elsinore	.267	140	4861	684	1298	257	39	99	468	1076	94
San Jose	.265	140	4835	725	1281	262	61	99	538	1051	140
Stockton	.263	140	4763	711	1252	245	47	92	533	1028	146

CLUB PITCHING

	ERA	G	CG	SV	IP	H	HR	R	ER	BB	SO
San Jose	3.92	140	0	31	1270	1279	107	646	553	419	1062
Inland Empire	4.03	140	3	38	1236	1303	100	665	554	351	1128
Lake Elsinore	4.19	140	1	35	1247	1264	89	716	580	480	1014
Modesto	4.22	140	0	43	1265	1308	98	699	593	469	1018
Stockton	4.29	140	1	30	1232	1274	90	700	587	465	893
Rancho Cucamonga	4.45	140	4	33	1245	1349	126	737	616	447	977
Bakersfield	4.56	140	1	32	1237	1332	96	735	627	594	1012
Lancaster	4.67	140	2	41	1246	1404	120	760	647	480	997
Visalia	5.43	140	3	29	1244	1493	138	861	751	459	943
High Desert	5.77	140	1	23	1237	1517	148	955	793	482	1119

CLUB FIELDING

	PCT	PO	A	E		PCT	PO	A	E
Visalia	.970	3733	1459	160	Rancho Cuca.	.966	3736	1521	183
Bakersfield	.969	3710	1537	167	Stockton	.966	3697	1557	186
Inland Empire	.969	3709	1481	167	Lancaster	.966	3737	1507	186
San Jose	.968	3809	1495	176	High Desert	.962	3710	1455	206
Modesto	.967	3794	1375	178	Lake Elsinore	.959	3741	1552	225

INDIVIDUAL BATTING LEADERS
(Minimum 378 Plate Appearances)

	AVG	G	AB	R	H	2B	3B	HR	RBI	BB	SO	SB
Stavisky, Brian, Modesto	.343	130	513	108	176	39	5	19	83	54	89	6
Perry, Jason, Modesto	.338	83	325	81	110	39	1	24	80	34	87	4
Aybar, Erick, Rancho Cucamonga	.330	136	573	102	189	25	11	14	65	26	66	51
Martinez, Gabriel, Bakersfield	.323	116	436	54	141	39	3	4	47	30	90	4
Arroyo, Carlos, Inland Empire	.323	114	434	62	140	22	3	6	52	27	53	14
Avlas, Phil, Lancaster	.315	109	384	64	121	22	8	13	68	29	54	5
Quintanilla, Omar, Modesto	.315	108	451	75	142	32	5	11	72	37	54	1
Ethier, Andre, Modesto	.313	99	419	72	131	23	5	7	53	45	64	2
Guzman, Jesus, Inland Empire	.310	114	442	80	137	35	3	6	71	57	105	10
Barker, Sean, Visalia	.308	105	412	75	127	29	5	20	97	40	89	11

INDIVIDUAL PITCHING LEADERS
(Minimum 112 Innings)

	W	L	ERA	G	GS	CG	SV	IP	H	R	ER	BB	SO
Burres, Brian, San Jose	12	1	2.84	36	15	0	0	124	115	49	39	30	114
Gonzalez, Enrique, Lancaster	13	6	3.22	42	17	0	0	142	128	64	51	44	110
Livingston, Bobby, Inland Empire	12	6	3.57	28	27	1	0	187	187	90	74	30	141
Shell, Steven, Rancho Cucamonga	12	7	3.59	28	28	2	0	165	151	76	66	40	190
Smith, Cody, Stockton	4	6	3.91	32	17	1	2	124	161	61	54	31	60
Lynch, Matt, Modesto	13	3	3.93	27	27	0	0	151	165	75	66	38	111
Sandoval, Juan, Inland Empire	11	11	4.12	27	27	1	0	168	184	91	77	43	119
Littleton, Wes, Stockton	8	10	4.15	30	23	0	0	141	139	76	65	56	72
Pauley, David, Lake Elsinore	7	12	4.17	27	26	0	0	153	155	89	71	60	128
Shields, Jamie, Bakersfield	8	5	4.23	20	20	1	0	117	120	61	55	33	92

ALL-STAR TEAM

C—Phil Avlas, Lancaster. **1B**—Travis Hinton, High Desert. **2B**—Callix Crabbe, High Desert. **3B**—Jeff Baker, Visalia. **SS**—Erick Aybar, Rancho Cucamonga. **OF**—Paul McAnulty, Lake Elsinore; Jeff Salazar, Visalia; Brian Stavisky, Modesto. **DH**—John Suomi, Modesto. **UT**—Mike Napoli, Rancho Cucamonga. **P**—Brian Burres, San Jose; Enrique Gonzalez, Lancaster; Bobby Livingston, Inland Empire; Steven Shell, Rancho Cucamonga.

Most Valuable Player: Brian Stavisky, Modesto. **Rookie of the Year:** Erick Aybar, Rancho Cucamonga. **Manager of the Year:** Von Hayes, Modesto.

DEPARTMENT LEADERS

BATTING
G	Erick Aybar, Rancho Cucamonga	136
	Travis Hinton, High Desert	136
AB	Erick Aybar, Rancho Cucamonga	573
R	Brian Stavisky, Modesto	108
H	Erick Aybar, Rancho Cucamonga	189
TB	Brian Stavisky, Modesto	282
XBH	Jason Perry, Modesto	64
2B	Issac Garcia, Modesto	41
3B	Gary Harris, Inland Empire	18
HR	Mike Napoli, Rancho Cucamonga	29
RBI	Mike Napoli, Rancho Cucamonga	118
SH	Luis DePaula, Bakersfield	14
SF	Adam Fox, Stockton	12
BB	Paul McAnulty, Lake Elsinore	88
	Mike Napoli, Rancho Cucamonga	88
IBB	Mike Napoli, Rancho Cucamonga	5
HBP	Carlos Quentin, Lancaster	27
SO	Kervin Jacobo, Lake Elsinore	171
SB	Erick Aybar, Rancho Cucamonga	51
CS	Erick Aybar, Rancho Cucamonga	36
GIDP	Rene Rivera, Inland Empire	21
OBP	Jason Perry, Modesto	.431
SLG	Jason Perry, Modesto	.686

PITCHING
G	Carlton Wells, Lancaster	71
GS	Three tied at	28
CG	Three tied at	2
ShO	Five tied at	1
GF	Jeremy Accardo, San Jose	44
SV	Jeremy Accardo, San Jose	27
W	Enrique Gonzalez, Lancaster	13
	Matt Lynch, Modesto	13
L	Mark Comolli, Bakersfield	15
IP	Bobby Livingston, Inland Empire	187
H	Ben Crockett, Visalia	210
R	Ben Crockett, Visalia	123
ER	Ben Crockett, Visalia	107
HR	Khalid Ballouli, High Desert	23
HB	Mark Comolli, Bakersfield	25
BB	Mark Comolli, Bakersfield	131
SO	Steven Shell, Rancho Cucamonga	190
WP	Mark Comolli, Bakersfield	25
BK	Darwin Soto, Inland Empire	4

FIELDING
C	PCT	Rene Rivera, Inland Empire	.993
	PO	Rene Rivera, Inland Empire	880
	A	Rene Rivera, Inland Empire	110
	E	Andres Pagan, Lake Elsinore	21
	DP	John Suomi, Modesto	8
	PB	John Suomi, Modesto	25
1B	PCT	Sean Luellwitz, Lancaster	.995
	PO	Nate Gold, Stockton	1222
	A	Nate Gold, Stockton	102
	E	Travis Hinton, High Desert	19
	DP	Nate Gold, Stockton	109
2B	PCT	A.J. LaBarbera, San Jose	.981
	PO	Callix Crabbe, High Desert	241
	A	Callix Crabbe, High Desert	356
	E	Callix Crabbe, High Desert	21
	DP	Luis DePaula, Bakersfield	66
3B	PCT	Adam Fox, Stockton	.929
	PO	Adam Fox, Stockton	69
		Kervin Jacobo, Lake Elsinore	69
	A	Adam Fox, Stockton	220
	E	Kervin Jacobo, Lake Elsinore	30
	DP	Adam Pavkovich, Rancho Cuca.	16
SS	PCT	Matthew Maniscalco, Bakersfield	.963
	PO	Erick Aybar, Rancho Cucamonga	266
	A	Erick Aybar, Rancho Cucamonga	391
	E	Joaquin Arias, Stockton	40
	DP	Matthew Maniscalco, Bakersfield	95
OF	PCT	Matt Rico, Bakersfield	.987
	PO	Reggie Willits, Rancho Cuca.	322
	A	Luis Mateo, Bakersfield	18
	E	Mario Mendez, High Desert	15
	DP	Luis Mateo, Bakersfield	6

MINOR LEAGUES

BY CHRIS KLINE

The Kinston Indians finally got over the hump in 2004. After appearing in the Carolina League playoffs each of the previous four seasons, the K-Tribe took home its first league title since 1995.

Nothing about it was easy, however, as the Indians faced elimination in five of eight playoff games.

First, they fell behind 1-0 to Winston-Salem in the best-of-3 Southern Division finals before winning the next two games to advance to the championship round.

Then, after dropping the first two games of the best-of-5 Mills Cup series at home to Wilmington, the Indians made the eight-hour trip north to Delaware with their backs against the wall.

But righthanders Adam Miller and J.D. Martin quickly changed all that and the Indians instead returned home champions.

Kinston won Game Three, 3-1, and then Miller dominated the Blue Rocks—hitting 100 mph on the radar gun twice—in a 4-0 K-Tribe win. Finally, it was Martin's turn and the 21-year-old did not disappoint, carrying a perfect game into the eighth inning of another 3-1 Kinston win to lock up the title.

Adam Miller

"We never got down on ourselves and never stopped believing we could accomplish what we started," Kinston manager Torey Lovullo said. "We started the season feeling like we had unfinished business and nothing was going to stop that. We just took it day-to-day and tried not to get caught up in the fact that we could be going home. We didn't want to go home without finishing what we started.

"We just got strong outings from our staff when we needed it most. Adam Miller saved his best performance for last and J.D. was nearly perfect. The rest of the team rallied around those performances and it carried us through."

Martin might have been nearly perfect in the postseason finale, but the K-Tribe tasted perfection on the final day of the regular season in Myrtle Beach, where lefthander Keith Ramsey tossed the first nine-inning perfect game against the Pelicans. Ramsey needed just 97 pitches to complete the first perfect game in the Carolina League since Peninsula's Marty Bystrom on Aug. 12, 1978.

While Kinston was the rage all season long—running away with the first half with the likes of first baseman

Michael Aubrey and catcher Ryan Garko—the season's top awards went to two Lynchburg players. Lefthander Zach Duke was named pitcher of the year and first baseman Brad Eldred won the league's most valuable player award—on a team that won just 22 more games after Duke and Eldred were promoted to Double-A in the second half.

Duke went 10-5, 1.39 in 97 innings for the Hillcats and wound up leading all the minors in ERA with a 1.46 mark between Lynchburg and Double-A Altoona. While most scouts considered Duke's stuff to be average across the board, the 21-year-old lefty featured a fastball in the low-to-mid 90's, outstanding curveball and changeup.

But it was Duke's quiet confidence and command that pushed him above all other hurlers in the league.

"I think the most impressive thing to me is the consistency," Hillcats pitching coach Scott Lovekamp said. "He made 17 starts with two earned runs or less. It was a quality start every time out and was something I'd never seen before, particularly from a 21-year-old."

Eldred put up huge power numbers, hitting .310-21-77 in 335 at-bats. The 24-year-old first baseman has light-tower power, and his pop is intriguing in a Pirates organization that lacks a true power hitter.

In other league developments in 2004, perennial Mills Cup contender Wilmington will have to adjust to a different organization. The Royals opted to end their 12-year affiliation with the Blue Rocks, moving to High Desert of the California League to be closer to the club's spring training complex in Surprise, Ariz. The Red Sox quickly moved in as the team's parent franchise.

Potomac also shuffled affiliations, ending its two-year deal with the Reds. The franchise is now an affiliate of the relocated Montreal Expos, now located across the Potomac River in Washington, D.C.

STANDINGS: SPLIT SEASON

FIRST HALF

NORTH	W	L	PCT	GB
Potomac	37	32	.536	—
Lynchburg	35	35	.500	2½
Wilmington	33	36	.478	4
Frederick	20	49	.290	17

SOUTH	W	L	PCT	GB
Kinston	45	24	.652	—
Myrtle Beach	40	28	.588	4½
Salem	38	32	.543	7½
Winston-Salem	29	41	.414	16½

SECOND HALF

NORTH	W	L	PCT	GB
Wilmington	44	26	.629	—
Frederick	32	38	.457	12
Potomac	30	40	.429	14
Lynchburg	22	46	.324	21

SOUTH	W	L	PCT	GB
Winston-Salem	45	25	.643	—
Kinston	43	26	.623	1½
Myrtle Beach	35	35	.500	10
Salem	27	43	.391	17½

PLAYOFFS—Semifinals: Wilmington defeated Potomac 2-1 and Kinston defeated Winston-Salem 2-1 in best-of-3 series. **Finals:** Kinston defeated Wilmington 3-2 in best-of-5 series.

STANDINGS: OVERALL

Page		W	L	Pct.	GB	Manager(s)	Attendance	Avg.	Last Penn.
121	Kinston Indians (Indians)	88	50	.638	—	Torey Lovullo	103,015	1,493	2004
157	Wilmington Blue Rocks (Royals)	77	62	.554	11½	Billy Gardner	320,788	4,860	1999
74	Myrtle Beach Pelicans (Braves)	75	63	.543	13	Randy Ingle	209,095	3,030	2000
97	Winston-Salem Warthogs (White Sox)	74	66	.529	15	Ken Dominguez/Nick Leyva	134,144	2,063	2003
113	Potomac Cannons (Reds)	67	72	.482	21½	Edgar Caceres	170,278	2,541	1989
150	Salem Avalanche (Astros)	65	74	.468	23½	Russ Nixon	224,991	3,515	2001
224	Lynchburg Hillcats (Pirates)	57	81	.413	31	Jay Loviglio/Tom Prince	148,067	2,313	2002
82	Frederick Keys (Orioles)	52	87	.374	36½	Tom Lawless	266,257	4,226	1990

NOTE: Team's individual batting and pitching statistics can be found on page indicated in lefthand column.

CLUB BATTING

	AVG	G	AB	R	H	2B	3B	HR	BB	SO	SB
Kinston	.269	138	4563	724	1227	236	23	124	471	952	128
Winston-Salem	.267	140	4649	657	1243	245	24	120	433	921	104
Potomac	.264	139	4619	690	1220	222	18	103	548	1007	117
Lynchburg	.263	138	4626	554	1216	225	34	72	391	939	167
Wilmington	.262	139	4630	618	1211	257	32	59	463	833	94
Frederick	.260	139	4606	591	1198	218	12	119	458	1005	96
Myrtle Beach	.257	138	4516	558	1159	227	32	71	397	873	142
Salem	.254	139	4590	577	1167	223	19	71	398	923	98

CLUB PITCHING

	ERA	G	CG	SV	IP	H	HR	R	ER	BB	SO
Wilmington	3.40	139	2	41	1211	1152	77	560	458	414	835
Myrtle Beach	3.44	138	3	38	1203	1097	65	533	460	456	1051
Kinston	3.71	138	6	45	1189	1140	91	559	490	427	965
Lynchburg	3.93	138	4	33	1208	1215	98	604	528	395	904
Potomac	4.03	139	0	27	1207	1209	105	639	541	415	987
Salem	4.20	139	6	36	1208	1294	78	638	564	468	850
Winston-Salem	4.32	140	2	47	1215	1232	94	674	584	467	886
Frederick	5.10	139	2	32	1202	1302	131	762	681	517	975

CLUB FIELDING

	PCT	PO	A	E		PCT	PO	A	E
Kinston	.976	3565	1375	120	Myrtle Beach	.973	3609	1375	139
Frederick	.976	3606	1533	125	Wilmington	.970	3633	1530	158
Winston-Salem	.975	3646	1540	133	Lynchburg	.970	3624	1505	157
Salem	.975	3623	1629	137	Potomac	.964	3621	1366	186

INDIVIDUAL BATTING LEADERS
(Minimum 378 Plate Appearances)

	AVG	G	AB	R	H	2B	3B	HR	RBI	BB	SO	SB
Davis, Rajai, Lynchburg	.314	127	509	91	160	27	7	5	38	59	60	57
Eldred, Brad, Lynchburg	.310	91	335	54	104	22	1	21	77	35	97	5
Costa, Shane, Wilmington	.308	123	451	70	139	20	4	7	60	32	43	9
Torres, Eider, Kinston	.302	113	440	68	133	24	3	3	46	22	46	48
Becker, Brian, Winston-Salem	.302	109	397	59	120	30	4	22	76	30	94	0
Aviles, Mike, Wilmington	.300	126	463	66	139	40	4	6	68	39	57	2
Hanigan, Ryan, Potomac	.296	119	429	58	127	21	0	5	56	49	51	6
Littleton, B.J., Frederick	.294	102	378	56	111	18	6	2	25	31	71	22
Lopez, Pedro, Winston-Salem	.292	112	432	62	126	13	0	4	35	23	35	12
Rogowski, Casey, Win.-Salem	.286	136	465	88	133	28	2	18	90	91	94	16

INDIVIDUAL PITCHING LEADERS
(Minimum 112 Innings)

	W	L	ERA	G	GS	CG	SV	IP	H	R	ER	BB	SO
McGill, Trae, Wilmington	9	2	2.08	21	18	1	0	113	98	32	26	26	66
Tracey, Sean, Winston-Salem	9	8	2.73	27	27	0	0	148	109	60	45	69	130
Nieve, Fernando, Salem	10	6	2.96	24	24	2	0	149	136	52	49	40	117
Pauly, Thomas, Potomac	8	7	2.97	28	19	0	0	121	96	47	40	26	135
Boyer, Blaine, Myrtle Beach	10	10	2.98	28	28	0	0	154	138	63	51	49	95
Wright, Matt, Myrtle Beach	4	6	3.39	24	21	1	0	125	115	55	47	58	133
Gravelle, Nick, Lynchburg	5	10	3.62	26	25	1	0	152	157	70	61	45	109
Lowery, Devon, Wilmington	9	9	3.66	28	28	1	0	145	139	74	59	52	115
Bruksch, Jeffrey, Potomac	6	7	3.72	32	19	0	1	133	118	62	55	63	104
Lerew, Anthony, Myrtle Beach	8	9	3.75	27	27	0	0	144	145	75	60	46	125

ALL-STAR TEAM

C—Brian McCann, Myrtle Beach. **1B**—Brad Eldred, Lynchburg. **2B**—Kevin Howard, Potomac. **3B**—Tripper Johnson, Frederick. **SS**—Mike Aviles, Wilmington. **UT IF**—Eider Torres, Kinston. **OF**—Shane Costa, Wilmington; Rajai Davis, Lynchburg; Jeff Francoeur, Myrtle Beach. **UT OF**—Ryan Sweeney, Winston-Salem. **DH**—Ryan Garko, Kinston. **SP**—Zach Duke, Lynchburg. **RP**—Dwayne Pollok, Winston-Salem.

Most Valuable Player: Brad Eldred, Lynchburg. **Pitcher of the Year:** Zach Duke, Lynchburg. **Manager of the Year:** Torey Lovullo, Kinston.

BATTING

G	Casey Rogowski, Winston-Salem	136
	Mark Saccomanno, Salem	136
AB	Ryan Sweeney, Winston-Salem	515
R	Rajai Davis, Lynchburg	91
H	Rajai Davis, Lynchburg	160
TB	Mark Saccomanno, Salem	229
XBH	Brian Becker, Winston-Salem	56
2B	Mike Aviles, Wilmington	40
3B	Gregor Blanco, Myrtle Beach	9
HR	Darren Blakely, Winston-Salem	25
RBI	Casey Rogowski, Winston-Salem	90
SH	Wade Robinson, Salem	17
	Jon Schuerholz, Myrtle Beach	17
SF	Ryan Hanigan, Potomac	9
	Shaun Larkin, Kinston	9
BB	Casey Rogowski, Winston-Salem	91
IBB	Casey Rogowski, Winston-Salem	11
HBP	Three tied at	15
SO	Mark Saccomanno, Salem	134
SB	Rajai Davis, Lynchburg	57
CS	Three tied at	15
GIDP	Donnie Murphy, Wilmington	22
OBP	Junior Ruiz, Potomac	.401
SLG	Brad Eldred, Lynchburg	.570

PITCHING

G	Ryan Keefer, Frederick	63
	Nick McCurdy, Frederick	63
GS	Blaine Boyer, Myrtle Beach	28
	Devon Lowery, Wilmington	28
CG	Six tied at	2
ShO	Three tied at	2
GF	Dwayne Pollok, Winston-Salem	53
SV	Dwayne Pollok, Winston-Salem	38
W	Brian Slocum, Kinston	15
L	Jamie Merchant, Salem	11
	Chris Sampson, Salem	11
IP	Blaine Boyer, Myrtle Beach	154
H	Chris Sampson, Salem	170
R	Paul Henry, Frederick	82
ER	Paul Henry, Frederick	72
	J.D. Martin, Kinston	72
HR	Keith Ramsey, Kinston	19
HB	Sean Tracey, Winston-Salem	23
BB	Sean Tracey, Winston-Salem	69
SO	Thomas Pauly, Potomac	135
WP	Richard Stahl, Frederick	14
BK	Nine tied at	2

FIELDING

C	PCT	Brian McCann, Myrtle Beach	.990
	PO	Matt Tupman, Wilmington	606
	A	Wally Rosa, Winston-Salem	79
	E	John Draper, Wilmington	9
	DP	Ryan Hubele, Frederick	9
	PB	Ryan Hubele, Frederick	24
1B	PCT	Doug Gredvig, Frederick	.992
	PO	Doug Gredvig, Frederick	967
	A	Doug Gredvig, Frederick	88
	E	Casey Rogowski, Win.-Salem	11
	DP	Casey Rogowski, Win.-Salem	91
2B	PCT	Eider Torres, Kinston	.981
	PO	Victor Mercedes, Lynchburg	262
	A	Victor Mercedes, Lynchburg	380
	E	Jon Schuerholz, Myrtle Beach	26
	DP	Victor Mercedes, Lynchburg	92
3B	PCT	Wes Timmons, Myrtle Beach	.962
	PO	Avelino Asprilla, Lynchburg	79
	A	Avelino Asprilla, Lynchburg	246
	E	Tripper Johnson, Frederick	17
		Mark Schramek, Potomac	17
	DP	Avelino Asprilla, Lynchburg	21
SS	PCT	Luis Hernandez, Myrtle Beach	.977
	PO	Wade Robinson, Salem	235
	A	Wade Robinson, Salem	425
	E	Wade Robinson, Salem	45
	DP	Wade Robinson, Salem	105
OF	PCT	Nathan Panther, Kinston	.992
	PO	Mel Stocker, Wilmington	261
	A	Ryan Sweeney, Winston-Salem	14
	E	Three tied at	10
	DP	Four tied at	3

MINOR LEAGUES

BY J.J. COOPER AND SEAN KERNAN

When the first hurricane arrived, the Florida State League weathered the storm in fine fashion.

Games were rained out, and Daytona's stadium lost a light pole, forcing the team to move some games. But all in all, the league survived Hurricane Charley with few problems.

Little did the league know that it would be only the first of a triple-whammy in 2004.

When Hurricane Frances arrived three weeks later, it washed out the final five days of the regular season, and forced the Vero Beach-Daytona semifinal series to be played in Clearwater, since neither team's stadium was ready after the storm.

That was bad enough, but with a third storm, Hurricane Ivan, bearing down on the state, FSL president Chuck Murphy decided that he had to cancel the championship series, as the Daytona Cubs and Tampa Yankees were declared co-champions.

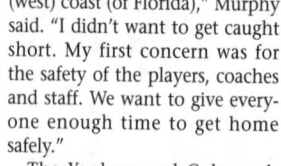

RODGER WOOD

Brandon Sing

"(Ivan) could come up the (west) coast (of Florida)," Murphy said. "I didn't want to get caught short. My first concern was for the safety of the players, coaches and staff. We want to give everyone enough time to get home safely."

The Yankees and Cubs each swept their best-of-three division series. The championship series was scheduled in Tampa for Games One and Two. The series was to shift to Clearwater's Bright House Networks Field—Daytona's "home" field because Jackie Robinson Ballpark was unplayable due to Hurricane Frances—for the last three games of the five-game set.

Murphy consulted with other league officials and player development representatives of the Cubs and Yankees before announcing the decision.

"We got two division winners," Murphy said. "We were able to get our division winners, so we'll take that. There really isn't anything else we can do. We thought about making it a best-of-three series, but then if you get a weather problem on Sunday what do you do?"

"I told our guys that we're pretty fortunate," Daytona manager Steve McFarland said. "What we've been through have been inconveniences. We had to move around a bit. We just had to take care of ourselves. Most of us don't have families here to take care of and most of us don't have personal property.

"You just watch the news and see people who have lost their homes, or are standing in line to get ice because they have no power, and you have to ask yourself—is baseball really that important?"

The soggy ending to the season meant that most teams played 10-15 games less than the scheduled 142. The shortened season kept Daytona first baseman Brandon Sing from likely breaking the league record for home runs. Because of the weather, the Cubs played only 124 games and Sing finished with 32 home runs, one short of the record.

Sing appeared to be on pace to break the record for most of the season—he had 25 home runs at the end of June—but a second-half slump, combined with the poor weather, kept him one short of the league record held by Miami's Jim Fuller in 1971.

In what turned out to be the Cubs' final regular-season game, Sing had a would-be home run blown foul by the wind. Sing did end up with the league MVP award, as he led the league in home runs, RBIs (94), runs (86) and on-base percentage (.399). He became the first FSL player to hit more than 30 home runs since Dunedin's Carlos Delgado in 1992.

STANDINGS: SPLIT SEASON

FIRST HALF

EAST	W	L	PCT	GB
Daytona	40	29	.580	—
St. Lucie	37	31	.544	2½
Palm Beach	37	32	.536	3
Vero Beach	36	34	.514	4½
Brevard County	31	36	.463	8
Jupiter	30	38	.441	9½

WEST	W	L	PCT	GB
Dunedin	41	29	.586	—
Sarasota	39	31	.557	2
Tampa	37	31	.544	3
Fort Myers	31	37	.456	9
Lakeland	29	39	.426	11
Clearwater	25	46	.352	16½

SECOND HALF

EAST	W	L	PCT	GB
Vero Beach	41	23	.641	—
Palm Beach	36	29	.554	5½
Daytona	30	27	.526	7½
Jupiter	34	33	.507	8½
St. Lucie	27	34	.443	12½
Brevard County	22	36	.379	16

WEST	W	L	PCT	GB
Tampa	38	27	.585	—
Dunedin	35	28	.556	2
Sarasota	37	30	.552	2
Clearwater	30	36	.455	8½
Fort Myers	30	37	.448	9
Lakeland	22	42	.344	15½

PLAYOFFS—Semifinals: Daytona defeated Vero Beach 2-0 and Tampa defeated Dunedin 2-0 in best-of-3 series. **Finals:** Cancelled— Daytona and Tampa declared co-champions.

STANDINGS: OVERALL

Page		W	L	Pct.	GB	Manager	Attendance	Avg.	Last Penn.
163	Vero Beach Dodgers (Dodgers)	77	57	.575	—	Scott Little	66,945	1,062	1990
274	Dunedin Blue Jays (Blue Jays)	76	57	.571	½	Omar Malave	36,844	594	None
193	Tampa Yankees (Yankees)	75	58	.564	1½	Bill Masse	71,648	1,214	2004
90	Sarasota Red Sox (Red Sox)	76	61	.555	2½	Todd Claus	40,715	667	1963
105	Daytona Cubs (Cubs)	70	56	.556	3	Steve McFarland	110,223	2,004	2004
231	Palm Beach Cardinals (Cardinals)	73	61	.545	4	Tom Nieto	92,806	1,406	None
201	St. Lucie Mets (Mets)	64	65	.496	10½	Tim Teufel	85,991	1,343	1998
143	Jupiter Hammerheads (Marlins)	64	71	.474	13½	Luis Dorante	95,903	1,522	1991
177	Fort Myers Miracle (Twins)	61	74	.452	16½	Jose Marzan	96,150	1,576	1985
185	Brevard County Manatees (Expos)	53	72	.424	19½	Tim Raines	98,430	1,822	2001
216	Clearwater Phillies (Phillies)	55	82	.401	23½	Mike Schmidt	135,082	2,078	1993
135	Lakeland Tigers (Tigers)	51	81	.386	25	Gary Green	32,301	557	1992

NOTE: Team's individual batting and pitching statistics can be found on page indicated in lefthand column.

2004 FLORIDA STATE LEAGUE STATISTICS

CLUB BATTING

	AVG	G	AB	R	H	2B	3B	HR	BB	SO	SB
Daytona	.267	126	4112	594	1096	199	43	86	404	805	139
Fort Myers	.266	135	4414	544	1173	196	42	42	399	814	111
Tampa	.265	133	4402	636	1166	250	30	80	427	870	58
Sarasota	.264	136	4494	613	1187	225	33	90	448	883	74
Dunedin	.258	133	4472	649	1153	253	19	99	523	883	16
St. Lucie	.256	129	4278	557	1095	202	32	97	394	1009	130
Palm Beach	.254	134	4341	603	1104	202	29	51	464	869	159
Lakeland	.254	132	4258	558	1082	215	48	78	378	1013	78
Vero Beach	.253	134	4389	618	1109	199	33	116	450	914	148
Jupiter	.248	135	4444	543	1101	202	29	81	448	1084	111
Brevard County	.245	125	4051	472	991	156	38	60	423	833	80
Clearwater	.242	136	4369	528	1059	198	31	71	422	898	75

CLUB PITCHING

	ERA	G	CG	SV	IP	H	HR	R	ER	BB	SO
Jupiter	3.41	135	5	30	1178	1148	51	559	446	417	920
Vero Beach	3.51	134	3	38	1173	1079	79	535	457	446	1075
Tampa	3.51	133	7	43	1136	1026	69	536	443	469	954
St. Lucie	3.69	129	6	28	1137	1104	62	550	466	393	898
Sarasota	3.81	136	4	40	1169	1136	76	585	495	444	942
Palm Beach	3.84	134	5	33	1159	1106	80	566	495	431	767
Clearwater	3.88	136	9	22	1168	1196	111	607	504	419	840
Fort Myers	3.89	135	3	29	1142	1122	78	624	494	475	969
Daytona	3.90	126	5	31	1084	1055	93	568	470	411	955
Dunedin	3.96	133	0	35	1158	1176	91	582	510	363	940
Brevard County	4.08	125	0	28	1077	1016	73	579	488	498	861
Lakeland	4.53	132	9	23	1098	1152	88	624	553	414	754

CLUB FIELDING

	PCT	PO	A	E		PCT	PO	A	E
Lakeland	.975	3295	1333	118	Jupiter	.970	3534	1433	151
Sarasota	.972	3507	1372	139	Dunedin	.970	3473	1385	148
Tampa	.971	3408	1381	141	Vero Beach	.970	3519	1289	148
Palm Beach	.971	3476	1651	151	Fort Myers	.968	3427	1361	156
Clearwater	.971	3503	1426	147	Daytona	.968	3253	1280	150
Brevard County	.971	3232	1328	138	St. Lucie	.965	3411	1448	174

INDIVIDUAL BATTING LEADERS
(Minimum 378 Plate Appearances)

	AVG	G	AB	R	H	2B	3B	HR	RBI	BB	SO	SB
Matienzo, Danny, Fort Myers	.305	123	455	51	139	27	1	5	65	43	88	1
Baldiris, Aarom, St. Lucie	.305	107	406	57	124	15	5	4	45	46	64	6
Murton, Matt, Sarasota	.301	102	376	60	113	16	4	11	55	42	61	5
Pie, Felix, Daytona	.299	105	412	79	123	17	9	8	47	38	113	31
Hermida, Jeremy, Jupiter	.297	91	340	53	101	17	1	10	50	42	73	10
Barthelemy, Ryan, Clearwater	.297	132	475	62	141	27	4	14	77	51	93	4
Cota, Carlo, Dunedin	.294	116	463	81	136	37	1	11	63	45	101	2
Deeds, Doug, Fort Myers	.294	123	436	71	128	28	12	5	57	43	86	11
West, Jeremy, Sarasota	.293	124	461	60	135	28	4	18	68	37	83	0
Schutzenhofer, Andy, Palm Beach	.292	121	373	65	109	15	2	3	56	51	36	3

INDIVIDUAL PITCHING LEADERS
(Minimum 112 Innings)

	W	L	ERA	G	GS	CG	SV	IP	H	R	ER	BB	SO
Connolly, Jon, Lake./Daytona	7	9	3.53	22	21	4	0	135	121	58	49	38	107
Papelbon, Jon, Sarasota	12	7	2.64	24	24	2	0	130	97	43	38	43	153
Ramirez, Ismael, Dunedin	15	6	2.72	28	27	0	0	165	151	57	50	25	131
Kensing, Logan, Jupiter	6	7	2.96	23	23	1	0	128	120	53	42	35	100
Olsen, Scott, Jupiter	7	6	2.97	25	25	1	0	136	127	57	45	54	158
Rasner, Darrell, Brevard County	6	5	3.17	22	21	0	0	119	133	55	42	31	88
Broxton, Jonathan, Vero Beach	11	6	3.23	23	23	1	0	128	110	49	46	43	144
Bazardo, Yorman, Jupiter	5	9	3.27	25	25	2	0	154	161	78	56	30	95
Simon, Alfredo, Clearwater	7	9	3.27	22	21	4	0	135	121	58	49	38	107
Johnson, Josh, Jupiter	5	12	3.38	23	22	1	0	114	124	63	43	47	103

ALL-STAR TEAM

C—Eliezer Alfonzo, Jupiter; Russell Martin, Vero Beach. **1B**—Brandon Sing, Daytona. **2B**—Delwyn Young, Vero Beach. **3B**—Aarom Baldiris, St. Lucie. **SS**—Joel Guzman, Vero Beach. **UT IF**—Carlo Cota, Dunedin. **OF**—Ron Davenport, Dunedin; Matt Murton, Sarasota; Felix Pie, Daytona. **UT OF**—Chris Roberson, Clearwater. **DH**—Jeremy West, Sarasota. **SP**—Jonathan Broxton, Vero Beach; Jon Connolly, Lakeland/Daytona; Jon Papelbon, Sarasota; Ismael Ramirez, Dunedin. **RP**—Bubbie Buzachero, Dunedin; Edwardo Sierra, Tampa.

Most Valuable Player: Brandon Sing, Daytona. **Most Valuable Pitcher:** Ismael Ramirez, Dunedin. **Manager of the Year:** Omar Malave, Dunedin.

DEPARTMENT **LEADERS**

BATTING

G	Ryan Barthelemy, Clearwater	132
AB	Ryan Barthelemy, Clearwater	475
R	Brandon Sing, Daytona	86
H	Ryan Barthelemy, Clearwater	141
TB	Delwyn Young, Vero Beach	240
XBH	Delwyn Young, Vero Beach	61
2B	Ron Davenport, Dunedin	40
3B	Doug Deeds, Fort Myers	12
	Adam Greenberg, Daytona	12
HR	Brandon Sing, Daytona	32
RBI	Brandon Sing, Daytona	94
SH	Jason Motte, Palm Beach	13
SF	Jay Caligiuri, St. Lucie	9
	Shelley Duncan, Tampa	9
BB	Brandon Sing, Daytona	84
IBB	Brandon Sing, Daytona	9
HBP	Jayce Tingler, Dunedin	16
SO	Corey Ragsdale, St. Lucie	152
SB	Alex Requena, Vero Beach	50
CS	Rayner Laya, Palm Beach	19
GIDP	Jeremy West, Sarasota	22
OBP	Brandon Sing, Daytona	.399
SLG	Brandon Sing, Daytona	.571

PITCHING

G	Shane Wallace, Palm Beach	54
GS	Ismael Ramirez, Dunedin	27
	Jon Skaggs, Tampa	27
CG	Alfredo Simon, Clearwater	4
ShO	Alfredo Simon, Clearwater	3
GF	Bubbie Buzachero, Dunedin	45
SV	Edwardo Sierra, Tampa	28
W	Ismael Ramirez, Dunedin	15
L	Josh Johnson, Jupiter	12
	Jeff Randazzo, Fort Myers	12
IP	Ismael Ramirez, Dunedin	165
H	Buddy Blair, Palm Beach	178
R	Jeff Randazzo, Fort Myers	96
ER	Buddy Blair, Palm Beach	79
HR	Michael Howell, Lakeland	20
HB	Rich Hill, Daytona	19
BB	Rich Hill, Daytona	72
SO	Scott Olsen, Jupiter	158
WP	Tyler Adamczyk, Palm Beach	26
BK	Rich Hill, Daytona	5

FIELDING

C	PCT	Jose Reyes, Daytona	.993
	PO	Russell Martin, Vero Beach	845
	A	Jason Motte, Palm Beach	92
	E	Jose Morales, Fort Myers	16
	DP	Jason Motte, Palm Beach	9
	PB	Jim Buckley, Sarasota	24
1B	PCT	Andy Schutzenhofer, P.B.	.991
	PO	Andy Schutzenhofer, P.B.	.967
	A	Ryan Barthelemy, Clearwater	81
	E	Brandon Sing, Daytona	15
	DP	Andy Schutzenhofer, P.B.	96
2B	PCT	Gabe Lopez, Tampa	.978
	PO	Gabe Lopez, Tampa	177
	A	Gabe Lopez, Tampa	302
	E	Delwyn Young, Vero Beach	23
	DP	Robert McIntyre, St. Lucie	59
3B	PCT	Lee Mitchell, Jupiter	.937
	PO	Scott Moore, Lakeland	84
	A	Aarom Baldiris, St. Lucie	219
	E	Scott Moore, Lakeland	28
	DP	Aarom Baldiris, St. Lucie	17
SS	PCT	Rayner Laya, Palm Beach	.954
	PO	Corey Ragsdale, St. Lucie	237
	A	Corey Ragsdale, St. Lucie	387
	E	Corey Ragsdale, St. Lucie	39
	DP	Corey Ragsdale, St. Lucie	96
OF	PCT	Adam Greenberg, Daytona	1.000
	PO	Victor Mendez, Lakeland	290
	A	Chris Durbin, Sarasota	21
	E	Brent Clevlen, Lakeland	15
	DP	Chris Durbin, Sarasota	5

BY AARON FITT

The Kane County Cougars, who finished with a league-best record of 83-56, were upset in the 2004 Midwest League championship series. The West Michigan Whitecaps topped the Cougars three games to two to capture their third league crown since 1996.

Kane County forced a decisive game with a 7-5 win in Game Four in a 16-inning, 5:35 affair that was won on catcher David Castillo's two-run home run. In Game Five, Danny Zell got the win for West Michigan with six solid innings in a 4-2 victory, as three errors by Cougars third baseman Vasili Spanos led to three unearned runs.

It was an unlikely conclusion to the 2004 season. The Whitecaps finished the first half 29-40, 12½ games out of first place in the East Division. As late as July 19, they were 37-51 on the year, and though they won their division's second half with a 40-30 record, they still entered the postseason one game under .500 for 2004. And Kane County, which won both halves in the West Division, took all eight regular-season games against West Michigan. Certainly, the Whitecaps were major underdogs, despite their second-half surge. But they never lost confidence.

MICHAEL WALBY

Brian Dopirak

"Before the season started we thought we could have a good year," Zell told the Grand Rapids Press. "We lost a lot of close games early, but it started clicking for us. Things just happened for us."

Despite winning the league title, West Michigan placed no players on the MWL's postseason all-star team and no players on Baseball America's manager's survey of the top-20 MWL prospects.

Kane County was paced by lefthander Steven Bondurant and righthander Brad Knox, both of whom went 14-5. They ranked 1-2 in the league in ERA (2.08 and 2.59, respectively) and struck out a combined 277.

The MWL's best prospect was obvious: league MVP Brian Dopirak. The 6-foot-4, 230-pound Lansing first baseman fell just three homers short of Jeff Jones' 22-year-old MWL record of 42. He had a 27-game hitting streak, the third longest in the minors in 2004. Overall, the 20-year-old hit .307-39-120.

The Midwest League was one of the first to begin the affiliation shuffle after the 2004 season. The Chicago Cubs, previously with Lansing, and Peoria, previously with the St. Louis Cardinals, got things started with an agreement, leaving the Cardinals looking for a MWL home. That was bad news for the Minnesota Twins. They had hoped to return to Quad Cities, where John O'Donnell Stadium just went through a massive renovation for the 2004 season.

But after getting only one year to enjoy the new facility, the Twins were booted out when the Swing decided to sign an affiliation deal with the Cardinals. The Twins then latched on to Beloit, which was vacated by the Brewers after a 22-year partnership. Milwaukee bolted for the South Atlantic League's Charleston Alley Cats.

Charleston's former parent club, the Blue Jays, signed a two-year agreement with Lansing. The Yankees left Battle Creek for the Sally League, opening the door for the Devil Rays to sign with Battle Creek.

STANDINGS: SPLIT SEASON

FIRST HALF

EAST	W	L	PCT	GB
South Bend	42	28	.600	—
Lansing	38	32	.543	4
Battle Creek	33	36	.478	8½
Fort Wayne	33	37	.471	9
West Michigan	29	40	.420	12½
Dayton	27	43	.386	15

WEST	W	L	PCT	GB
Kane County	43	26	.623	—
Cedar Rapids	42	27	.609	1
Peoria	38	31	.551	5
Beloit	38	32	.543	5½
Clinton	35	33	.515	7½
Quad Cities	33	33	.500	8½
Wisconsin	31	38	.449	12
Burlington	22	48	.314	21½

SECOND HALF

EAST	W	L	PCT	GB
West Michigan	40	30	.571	—
Fort Wayne	39	31	.557	1
Lansing	39	31	.557	1
Battle Creek	38	32	.543	2
South Bend	35	35	.500	5
Dayton	21	49	.300	19

WEST	W	L	PCT	GB
Kane County	40	30	.571	—
Clinton	39	31	.557	1
Peoria	37	33	.529	3
Quad Cities	35	35	.500	5
Beloit	34	36	.486	6
Burlington	34	36	.486	6
Cedar Rapids	33	37	.471	7
Wisconsin	26	44	.371	14

PLAYOFFS—Quarterfinals: Clinton defeated Cedar Rapids 2-0, South Bend defeated Fort Wayne 2-0, Kane County defeated Peoria 2-1 and West Michigan defeated Lansing 2-1 in best-of-3 series. **Semifinals:** Kane County defeated Clinton 2-0 and West Michigan defeated South Bend 2-0 in best-of-3 series. **Finals:** West Michigan defeated Kane County 3-2 in best-of-5 series.

STANDINGS: OVERALL

Page		W	L	Pct.	GB	Manager(s)	Attendance	Avg.	Last Penn.
211	Kane County Cougars (Athletics)	83	56	.597	—	Dave Joppie	522,042	7,677	2001
106	Lansing Lugnuts (Cubs)	77	63	.550	6½	Julio Garcia	392,256	5,768	2003
68	South Bend Silver Hawks (D'backs)	77	63	.550	6½	Tony Perezchica	212,531	3,220	1993
60	Cedar Rapids Kernels (Angels)	75	64	.540	8	Bobby Magallanes	177,929	2,578	1994
232	Peoria Chiefs (Cardinals)	75	64	.540	8	Joe Cunningham	211,598	3,158	2002
269	Clinton LumberKings (Rangers)	74	64	.536	8½	Carlos Subero	91,804	1,434	1991
171	Beloit Snappers (Brewers)	72	68	.514	9½	Don Money	96,677	1,487	1995
240	Fort Wayne Wizards (Padres)	72	68	.514	9½	Randy Ready	278,351	4,034	None
194	Battle Creek Yankees (Yankees)	71	68	.511	10	Mitch Seoane/Bill Mosiello	95,845	1,431	2000
178	Swing of the Quad Cities (Twins)	68	68	.500	13½	Kevin Boles	173,364	2,938	1990
136	West Michigan Whitecaps (Tigers)	69	70	.496	14	Matt Walbeck	390,033	5,571	2004
255	Wisconsin Timber Rattlers (Mariners)	57	82	.410	26	Steve Roadcap	206,487	3,081	1984
157	Burlington Bees (Royals)	56	84	.400	27½	Jim Gabella	62,976	953	1999
114	Dayton Dragons (Reds)	48	92	.343	35½	Alonzo Powell	593,663	8,361	None

NOTE: Team's individual batting and pitching statistics can be found on page indicated in lefthand column.

MINOR LEAGUES

2004 MIDWEST LEAGUE STATISTICS

CLUB BATTING

	AVG	G	AB	R	H	2B	3B	HR	BB	SO	SB
Peoria	.277	139	4761	759	1317	261	30	109	511	988	117
Battle Creek	.272	139	4669	683	1270	269	19	103	436	1029	112
South Bend	.266	140	4734	630	1258	238	38	85	312	887	162
Beloit	.265	140	4641	663	1232	226	40	87	367	953	108
Lansing	.264	140	4813	706	1273	250	36	144	392	1060	120
Cedar Rapids	.257	139	4686	650	1205	237	48	117	361	1110	144
Kane County	.257	139	4672	730	1200	251	29	110	664	1053	84
Clinton	.256	138	4508	671	1156	268	28	91	559	1191	123
West Michigan	.254	139	4715	619	1198	223	43	94	372	1190	117
Wisconsin	.251	140	4676	607	1172	228	40	79	443	1060	116
Fort Wayne	.246	139	4743	619	1167	217	33	90	447	1082	80
Quad Cities	.238	136	4516	564	1076	190	43	55	434	1036	118
Dayton	.236	140	4645	551	1096	218	34	93	446	1382	117
Burlington	.234	140	4504	553	1054	209	25	55	446	1010	138

CLUB PITCHING

	ERA	G	CG	SV	IP	H	HR	R	ER	BB	SO
Lansing	3.39	140	2	38	1249	1156	77	546	471	387	1109
Quad Cities	3.44	136	1	39	1192	1061	66	554	455	523	1123
West Michigan	3.52	139	5	36	1232	1189	68	565	482	413	964
Clinton	3.73	138	1	31	1199	1188	92	586	497	369	1011
Fort Wayne	3.77	140	1	40	1238	1216	95	669	518	454	1185
Kane County	3.79	139	4	38	1225	1200	83	606	516	335	1180
South Bend	3.82	140	8	47	1228	1221	90	599	521	432	992
Cedar Rapids	3.87	139	2	36	1220	1132	74	644	525	510	1069
Peoria	4.06	140	6	36	1213	1147	92	670	547	478	1058
Battle Creek	4.13	138	4	32	1209	1246	83	661	555	436	1086
Beloit	4.26	140	3	39	1204	1150	131	669	570	481	1069
Burlington	4.47	140	5	31	1201	1202	113	686	596	431	1016
Wisconsin	4.67	140	4	30	1215	1280	118	747	630	441	1074
Dayton	5.03	139	0	28	1218	1285	130	800	681	499	1095

CLUB FIELDING

	PCT	PO	A	E		PCT	PO	A	E
Lansing	.975	3746	1469	133	Battle Creek	.968	3628	1272	164
Beloit	.971	3612	1380	148	Cedar Rapids	.967	3661	1466	176
West Michigan	.970	3695	1537	160	Peoria	.967	3640	1512	177
Clinton	.970	3596	1464	156	Wisconsin	.966	3645	1440	177
South Bend	.969	3685	1444	163	Quad Cities	.964	3575	1308	180
Kane County	.969	3674	1406	162	Dayton	.962	3655	1312	195
Burlington	.969	3602	1390	161	Fort Wayne	.962	3713	1359	202

INDIVIDUAL BATTING LEADERS
(Minimum 378 Plate Appearances)

	AVG	G	AB	R	H	2B	3B	HR	RBI	BB	SO	SB
Ryan, Brendan, Peoria	.322	105	426	72	137	21	4	2	59	24	42	30
Francia, Juan, West Michigan	.320	111	413	73	132	11	3	0	32	34	44	37
Barton, Daric, Peoria	.313	90	313	63	98	23	0	13	77	69	44	4
Frazier, Alex, South Bend	.313	125	464	73	145	36	3	20	80	27	92	21
Snyder, Brian, Kane County	.311	101	366	54	114	18	3	13	61	67	82	3
Spanos, Vasili, Kane County	.311	97	331	58	103	26	1	12	80	54	76	11
Anderson, Drew, Beloit	.307	123	456	64	140	22	5	5	59	45	95	13
Dopirak, Brian, Lansing	.307	137	541	94	166	38	0	39	120	48	123	4
Carson, Matt, Battle Creek	.304	95	381	59	116	23	2	12	58	22	78	21
Rottino, Vinny, Beloit	.304	139	529	78	161	25	9	17	124	40	71	5

INDIVIDUAL PITCHING LEADERS
(Minimum 112 Innings)

	W	L	ERA	G	GS	CG	SV	IP	H	R	ER	BB	SO
Bondurant, Steven, Kane County	14	5	2.08	21	21	2	0	126	92	39	29	27	132
Knox, Brad, Kane County	14	5	2.59	26	25	0	0	156	141	53	45	24	174
Hayhurst, Dirk, Fort Wayne	9	4	2.66	26	17	0	0	118	114	41	35	19	106
Eveland, Dana, Beloit	9	6	2.84	22	16	1	2	117	108	48	37	24	119
Mattoon, Brian, Clinton	11	6	2.87	32	20	1	1	132	137	58	42	17	88
Oldham, Thomas, Wisconsin	6	6	2.93	19	19	1	0	117	108	47	38	30	132
Harben, Adam, Quad Cities	9	7	3.09	26	26	0	0	143	114	60	49	68	171
Bay, Ronald, Lansing	11	9	3.10	28	28	0	0	168	166	71	58	30	139
Thompson, Sean, Fort Wayne	9	6	3.10	27	27	0	0	148	125	60	51	57	157
Muegge, Danny, South Bend	14	4	3.12	26	25	1	0	153	149	66	53	42	104

ALL-STAR TEAM

C—Daric Barton, Peoria. **1B**—Brian Dopirak, Lansing. **2B**—Howie Kendrick, Cedar Rapids. **3B**—Eric Duncan, Battle Creek. **SS**—Ian Kinsler, Clinton. **OF**—Kevin Collins, Lansing; Chris Dickerson, Dayton; Alex Frazier, South Bend. **DH**—Vinny Rottino, Beloit. **RHP**—Brad Knox, Kane County. **LHP**—Steven Bondurant, Kane County. **RHRP**—Bob Zimmermann, Cedar Rapids. **LHRP**—Clay Rapada, Lansing.

Most Valuable Player: Brian Dopirak, Lansing. **Prospect of the Year:** Brian Dopirak, Lansing. **Manager of the Year:** Dave Joppie, Kane County.

DEPARTMENT LEADERS

BATTING
G	Vinny Rottino, Beloit	139
AB	Erold Andrus, Battle Creek	553
R	Anthony Monegan, Peoria	97
H	Brian Dopirak, Lansing	166
TB	Brian Dopirak, Lansing	321
XBH	Brian Dopirak, Lansing	77
2B	Brian Dopirak, Lansing	38
3B	Quan Cosby, Cedar Rapids	12
	Scott Whitrock, Quad Cities	12
HR	Brian Dopirak, Lansing	39
RBI	Vinny Rottino, Beloit	124
SH	Abigail Sandoval, Clinton	21
SF	Vinny Rottino, Beloit	10
BB	Brian Hagen, Kane County	84
IBB	Daric Barton, Peoria	10
HBP	Jordan Pickens, Fort Wayne	19
SO	Garth McKinney, West Michigan	175
SB	Chris Walker, Lansing	60
CS	Juan Francia, West Michigan	19
GIDP	Fernando Valenzuela, Fort Wayne	22
OBP	Daric Barton, Peoria	.445
SLG	Kevin Collins, Lansing	.615

PITCHING
G	Dan Fyvie, Kane County	59
GS	Four tied at	28
CG	Chris Steinborn, West Michigan	3
ShO	Ten tied at	1
GF	Bob Zimmermann, Cedar Rapids	50
SV	Leo Rosales, Fort Wayne	26
	Paul Thorp, Battle Creek	26
W	Five tied at	14
L	Nibaldo Acosta, Wisconsin	14
	Greg Atencio, Burlington	14
IP	Ronald Bay, Lansing	168
	Matt Vasquez, West Michigan	168
H	Chris Dunwell, Kane County	179
R	Greg Atencio, Burlington	109
ER	Greg Atencio, Burlington	93
HR	Carlos Villanueva, Beloit	20
HB	Nibaldo Acosta, Wisconsin	19
	Mark Michael, Peoria	19
BB	Kevin Jepsen, Cedar Rapids	77
SO	Brad Knox, Kane County	174
WP	Mark Michael, Peoria	23
BK	Abel Moreno, Cedar Rapids	7

FIELDING
C	PCT	Justin Ruchti, Wisconsin	.995
	PO	David Castillo, Kane County	683
	A	Jacob Fox, Lansing	78
	E	Miguel Perez, Dayton	16
	DP	Three tied at	5
	PB	Jacob Fox, Lansing	25
1B	PCT	Kelly Hunt, West Michigan	.992
	PO	Kelly Hunt, West Michigan	1155
	A	Kelly Hunt, West Michigan	101
	E	Brian Dopirak, Lansing	15
	DP	Kelly Hunt, West Michigan	118
2B	PCT	Eric Rodland, West Michigan	.983
	PO	Eric Rodland, West Michigan	245
	A	Eric Rodland, West Michigan	331
	E	Luke Appert, Kane County	25
	DP	Eric Rodland, West Michigan	87
3B	PCT	Adam Heether, Beloit	.944
	PO	Matt Brown, Cedar Rapids	86
	A	Kody Kirkland, West Michigan	237
	E	Matt Brown, Cedar Rapids	29
		Kody Kirkland, West Michigan	29
	DP	Kody Kirkland, West Michigan	22
SS	PCT	Carlos Rojas, Lansing	.980
	PO	Carlos Rojas, Lansing	222
	A	Carlos Rojas, Lansing	414
	E	Juan Ciriaco, Fort Wayne	45
	DP	Brandon Wood, Cedar Rapids	81
OF	PCT	Drew Anderson, Beloit	.995
	PO	Erold Andrus, Battle Creek	298
	A	Scott Whitrock, Quad Cities	17
	E	Scott Whitrock, Quad Cities	11
	DP	Josh Womack, Wisconsin	5

MINOR LEAGUES

SOUTH ATLANTIC LEAGUE

LOW CLASS A

BY JOHN MANUEL

Charleston South had the prospects. Charleston West had the veterans. Capital City had the league's best overall record and got a late-season fortification from the parent New York Mets.

But the unheralded Hickory Crawdads posted an undefeated record in postseason play and for the second time in three seasons, the 'Dads won the South Atlantic League championship. They beat Charleston (W.Va.) in the semifinals before sweeping Capital City in the finals.

Power fueled Hickory's perfect postseason. The Crawdads hit 12 home runs in five playoff games, including eight against the Bombers in the championship series, a three-game sweep. Hickory finished the sweep at home at L.P. Frans Stadium with three homers in a 9-2 victory, besting the Bombers in a matchup of the league's best two offenses.

BILL MITCHELL

Delmon Young

"I wish I could pinpoint something, other than to say that these kids wanted it," manager Dave Clark told the Hickory Daily Record. "They smelled it going into the last month of the season."

A pair of 24-year-olds, first baseman Jon Benick (.328-32-104) and outfielder Adam Boeve (.290-28-93), paced the Crawdads offense all season. The switch-hitting Benick, who finished the 2003 season with the Padres' Double-A affiliate, led the league in home runs.

Capital City had the league's most talented roster throughout the season. The Bombers beat Charleston (S.C.) in the semifinals, holding the River Dogs to one run in two games despite the best efforts of outfielder Delmon Young. The first overall pick in the 2003 draft started slowly in the SAL but had a torrid second half, hitting .368-16-67 after June 22. Young, who led the league in hits (165) and RBIs (116), was named the league's No. 1 prospect.

"He's ahead of the game for an 18-year-old," RiverDogs manager Steve Livesey said of Young, who turned 19 just after the RiverDogs were eliminated from the playoffs. "The main adjustment he made as the season went along was in better pitch selection. As the year went on, he didn't wear down; he just got stronger."

Young was nearly matched on the prospect front by Capital City outfielder Lastings Milledge and Asheville third baseman Ian Stewart, who led the league in slugging percentage (.594) while hitting 30 homers.

"The league was just outstanding," Augusta manager Chad Epperson said.

Epperson's Red Sox were one of five organizations that changed affiliates in the SAL when the season was over. The Sox relocated to Capital City, which spent the offseason trying to get a new ballpark plan in place during lengthy negotiations with the city and the University of South Carolina. The Gamecocks had tentative plans to build a park on their own, excluding the Bombers, leaving the franchise in limbo.

STANDINGS: SPLIT SEASON

FIRST HALF

NORTH	W	L	PCT	GB
Charleston, W.Va.	41	29	.586	—
Hickory	39	31	.557	2
Lexington	37	32	.536	3½
Lake County	36	34	.514	5
Delmarva	35	34	.507	5½
Kannapolis	34	35	.493	6½
Lakewood	31	36	.463	8½
Hagerstown	28	39	.418	11½

SOUTH	W	L	PCT	GB
Capital City	44	26	.629	—
Charleston, S.C.	40	29	.580	3½
Rome	40	30	.571	4
Columbus	38	32	.543	6
Asheville	31	39	.443	13
Augusta	31	39	.443	13
Savannah	31	40	.429	14
Greensboro	20	50	.286	24

SECOND HALF

NORTH	W	L	PCT	GB
Hickory	46	24	.657	—
Charleston, W.Va.	43	27	.614	3
Lakewood	39	30	.565	6½
Lake County	37	32	.536	8½
Kannapolis	35	35	.500	11
Delmarva	34	35	.493	11½
Lexington	30	40	.429	16
Hagerstown	21	49	.300	25

SOUTH	W	L	PCT	GB
Capital City	45	21	.682	—
Charleston, S.C.	36	34	.514	11
Augusta	35	34	.507	11½
Asheville	33	36	.478	13½
Columbus	31	37	.456	15
Greensboro	30	39	.435	16½
Rome	30	40	.429	17
Savannah	28	40	.412	18

PLAYOFFS—Semifinals: Hickory defeated Charleston, W.Va., 2-0 and Capital City defeated Charleston, S.C., 2-0 in best-of-3 series. **Finals:** Hickory defeated Capital City 3-0 in best-of-5 series.

STANDINGS: OVERALL

Page		W	L	Pct.	GB	Manager	Attendance	Avg.	Last Penn.
202	Capital City Bombers (Mets)	89	47	.654	—	Jack Lind	100,798	1,550	1998
224	Hickory Crawdads (Pirates)	85	55	.607	4	Dave Clark	178,439	2,549	2004
275	Charleston, W.Va., Alley Cats (Blue Jays)	84	56	.600	7	Ken Joyce	125,979	1,852	1990
261	Charleston, S.C., RiverDogs (Devil Rays)	76	63	.547	14½	Steve Livesey	255,793	3,654	None
122	Lake County Captains (Indians)	73	66	.525	17½	Luis Rivera	406,096	6,152	None
217	Lakewood BlueClaws (Phillies)	70	66	.515	19	P.J. Forbes	440,521	6,574	None
75	Rome Braves (Braves)	70	70	.500	21	Rocket Wheeler	246,674	3,737	2003
164	Columbus Catfish (Dodgers)	69	69	.500	21	Dann Bilardello	51,352	828	None
83	Delmarva Shorebirds (Orioles)	69	69	.500	21	Bien Figueroa	230,536	3,659	2000
98	Kannapolis Intimidators (White Sox)	69	70	.496	21½	Chris Cron	105,214	1,618	None
151	Lexington Legends (Astros)	67	72	.482	23½	Ivan DeJesus	401,191	5,899	2001
91	Augusta GreenJackets (Red Sox)	66	73	.475	24½	Chad Epperson	160,378	2,430	1999
129	Asheville Tourists (Rockies)	64	75	.460	26½	Joe Mikulik	140,634	2,232	1984
186	Savannah Sand Gnats (Expos)	58	80	.420	32	Bob Henley	113,359	1,828	1996
144	Greensboro Bats (Marlins)	50	89	.360	40½	Steve Phillips	200,477	3,084	1982
247	Hagerstown Suns (Giants)	49	88	.358	40½	Mike Ramsey	128,508	2,007	None

NOTE: Team's individual batting and pitching statistics can be found on page indicated in lefthand column.

2004 SOUTH ATLANTIC LEAGUE STATISTICS

CLUB BATTING

	AVG	G	AB	R	H	2B	3B	HR	BB	SO	SB
Hickory	.276	140	4720	758	1304	243	46	135	462	906	159
Capital City	.274	136	4566	853	1250	274	26	166	494	1111	135
Lake County	.272	139	4698	711	1278	219	44	111	453	997	111
Lakewood	.269	137	4607	718	1240	285	43	89	543	1025	163
Columbus	.267	138	4591	710	1227	247	45	107	390	984	146
Charleston, S.C.	.265	139	4712	733	1250	225	39	109	472	1090	150
Rome	.265	140	4671	650	1239	263	39	107	352	1128	123
Asheville	.264	139	4647	738	1228	268	24	165	521	1082	177
Charleston, W.Va.	.259	140	4644	673	1205	230	26	89	536	1140	54
Kannapolis	.259	139	4667	637	1209	271	25	125	420	1085	138
Lexington	.257	140	4634	690	1192	233	25	102	491	975	182
Delmarva	.257	138	4561	668	1172	243	39	97	517	1018	118
Augusta	.254	139	4684	655	1192	217	33	74	516	1041	109
Hagerstown	.250	137	4586	607	1146	230	25	105	479	1036	88
Greensboro	.243	139	4591	611	1115	213	27	117	394	1234	112
Savannah	.241	138	4483	569	1079	219	27	84	454	1050	107

CLUB PITCHING

	ERA	G	CG	SV	IP	H	HR	R	ER	BB	SO
Charleston, W.Va.	3.54	140	2	39	1223	1135	76	585	481	438	1116
Kannapolis	3.91	139	4	44	1218	1186	87	657	529	513	980
Delmarva	3.93	138	5	35	1197	1130	98	620	522	509	1054
Charleston, S.C.	3.96	139	2	33	1222	1219	94	666	538	414	1053
Columbus	4.14	138	3	34	1201	1134	123	683	553	566	1222
Capital City	4.16	136	1	41	1186	1171	103	680	548	426	1137
Hickory	4.23	140	5	43	1220	1201	114	659	573	471	1067
Lakewood	4.25	137	4	28	1190	1231	94	665	562	388	908
Rome	4.26	140	3	40	1201	1212	100	694	568	502	1109
Augusta	4.32	139	1	33	1221	1313	117	712	586	349	1014
Savannah	4.34	138	3	29	1173	1148	110	672	566	472	1062
Lake County	4.35	139	2	32	1207	1234	129	669	583	446	1104
Lexington	4.47	140	1	28	1213	1177	123	698	602	599	1088
Asheville	4.76	139	10	27	1194	1321	158	740	632	364	864
Hagerstown	4.80	137	2	31	1185	1236	110	756	632	530	1000
Greensboro	5.33	139	0	29	1186	1278	146	835	703	507	1124

CLUB FIELDING

	PCT	PO	A	E		PCT	PO	A	E
Hickory	.974	3661	1487	138	Delmarva	.967	3590	1369	170
Charleston, W.Va.	.973	3669	1428	143	Hagerstown	.966	3554	1386	176
Lexington	.971	3638	1373	149	Charleston, S.C.	.965	3667	1459	184
Lake County	.971	3621	1334	150	Lakewood	.965	3569	1379	178
Asheville	.971	3582	1599	157	Greensboro	.965	3559	1291	177
Kannapolis	.969	3655	1472	166	Augusta	.964	3662	1490	191
Columbus	.968	3604	1321	165	Capital City	.964	3558	1358	183
Rome	.967	3602	1247	165	Savannah	.963	3519	1362	190

INDIVIDUAL BATTING LEADERS
(Minimum 378 Plate Appearances)

	AVG	G	AB	R	H	2B	3B	HR	RBI	BB	SO	SB
Moss, Brandon, Augusta	.339	109	433	66	147	25	6	13	101	46	75	19
Kouzmanoff, Kevin, Lake County	.330	123	473	74	156	35	5	16	87	44	75	5
Benick, Jon, Hickory	.328	130	488	76	160	29	2	32	104	53	93	2
Harvey, Ryan, Capital City	.325	115	425	89	138	32	5	11	72	35	48	12
Young, Delmon, Charleston, S.C.	.322	131	513	95	165	26	5	25	116	53	120	21
Stewart, Ian, Asheville	.319	131	505	92	161	31	9	30	101	66	112	19
Czarniecki, Jordan, Asheville	.315	105	381	72	120	25	3	16	58	48	69	30
Bourn, Michael, Lakewood	.315	109	413	92	130	20	14	5	53	85	88	58
Prado, Martin, Rome	.315	107	429	68	135	25	6	3	38	30	47	14
Guzman, Javier, Hickory	.306	124	470	75	144	20	12	2	63	20	78	31

INDIVIDUAL PITCHING LEADERS
(Minimum 112 Innings)

	W	L	ERA	G	GS	CG	SV	IP	H	R	ER	BB	SO
Mastny, Thomas, Charleston, W.Va.	10	3	2.17	27	27	0	0	149	123	44	36	41	143
James, Chuck, Rome	10	5	2.24	26	22	1	0	133	92	41	33	48	156
Stevens, Jacob, Rome	9	5	2.27	27	19	0	2	135	100	41	34	39	140
Gardner, Jarrett, Augusta	13	5	2.51	25	23	0	0	136	130	49	38	11	92
Dixon, Zach, Delmarva	9	4	2.54	24	21	0	0	121	97	52	34	65	105
Cabrera, Nate, Lakewood	6	4	2.82	24	23	2	0	131	111	50	41	40	113
Nunez, Leo, Hickory	10	4	3.13	27	20	3	1	144	121	53	50	46	140
Deza, Fredy, Delmarva	8	11	3.31	22	21	2	0	120	102	52	44	21	93
Peguero, Tony, Charleston, S.C.	10	6	3.32	23	23	1	0	133	135	61	49	22	87
Core, Daniel, Charleston, W.Va.	10	8	3.32	28	28	1	0	157	137	70	58	53	132

ALL-STAR TEAM

C—Robinson Diaz, Charleston, W.Va.; Colt Simmons, Charleston, S.C. **1B**—Jon Benick, Hickory. **2B**—Martin Prado, Rome. **3B**—Ian Stewart, Asheville. **SS**—Chin-Lung Hu, Columbus. **UT IF**—Kevin Kouzmanoff, Lake County. **OF**—Josh Anderson, Lexington; Brandon Moss, Augusta; Delmon Young, Charleston, S.C. **UT OF**—Ryan Goleski, Lake County. **DH**—Ryan Harvey, Capital City. **RHP**—Thomas Mastny, Charleston, W.Va. **LHP**—Chuck James, Rome.

Most Valuable Player: Brandon Moss, Augusta. **Most Valuable Pitcher:** Chuck James, Rome. **Outstanding Prospect:** Delmon Young, Charleston, S.C. **Manager of the Year:** Jack Lind, Capital City.

DEPARTMENT LEADERS

BATTING
G	Chris Young, Kannapolis	136
AB	Jake Blalock, Lakewood	517
R	Jason Pridie, Charleston, S.C.	103
H	Delmon Young, Charleston, S.C.	165
TB	Ian Stewart, Asheville	300
XBH	Ian Stewart, Asheville	70
2B	Jake Blalock, Lakewood	40
3B	Michael Bourn, Lakewood	14
HR	Jon Benick, Hickory	32
RBI	Delmon Young, Charleston, S.C.	116
SH	Edwin Maysonet, Lexington	14
SF	Ryan Goleski, Lake County	10
BB	Michael Bourn, Lakewood	85
IBB	Wes Bankston, Charleston, S.C.	8
HBP	Nyjer Morgan, Hickory	32
SO	Jai Miller, Greensboro	163
SB	Michael Bourn, Lakewood	58
CS	Javon Moran, Lakewood	17
GIDP	Robinson Diaz, Charleston, W.Va.	24
OBP	Michael Bourn, Lakewood	.431
SLG	Ian Stewart, Asheville	.594

PITCHING
G	Aaron Williams, Lexington	59
GS	Danny Core, Charleston, W.Va.	28
	Darric Merrell, Asheville	28
CG	Alberto Arias, Asheville	4
ShO	Nate Cabrera, Lakewood	2
GF	Aaron Williams, Lexington	53
SV	Ehren Wasserman, Kannapolis	30
W	Jarrett Gardner, Augusta	13
L	Kyle Jackson, Augusta	13
IP	Marc Kaiser, Asheville	181
H	Erick Arteaga, Lakewood	207
R	Bryan Digby, Rome	112
ER	Bryan Digby, Rome	92
	Tanner Osberg, Capital City	92
HR	Aaron Marsden, Asheville	30
HB	Marc Kaiser, Asheville	25
BB	Derick Grigsby, Lexington	92
SO	Adam Bostick, Greensboro	163
WP	Bryan Digby, Rome	19
BK	Adam Loewen, Delmarva	4
	Edward Mujica, Lake County	4

FIELDING
C	PCT	Neil Wilson, Asheville	.994
	PO	Mike Nixon, Columbus	805
	A	Mike Nixon, Columbus	66
	E	German Melendez, Lexington	11
	DP	Chico Cortez, Lakewood	8
	PB	Charlie Lisk, Kannapolis	36
1B	PCT	Leo Daigle, Kannapolis	.995
	PO	Christian Colonel, Asheville	1065
	A	Bryan Hansen, Lakewood	78
	E	Dustin Yount, Delmarva	24
	DP	Bryan Hansen, Lakewood	101
2B	PCT	Craig Stansberry, Hickory	.983
	PO	Elliot Johnson, Charleston, S.C.	249
	A	Elliot Johnson, Charleston, S.C.	342
	E	Antoin Gray, Kannapolis	28
	DP	Elliot Johnson, Charleston, S.C.	76
3B	PCT	Saul Torres, Lexington	.955
	PO	Micah Schnurstein, Kannapolis	94
	A	Ian Stewart, Asheville	308
	E	Kory Casto, Savannah	35
	DP	Ian Stewart, Asheville	27
SS	PCT	Osvaldo Fernando, Lexington	.950
	PO	Travis Brown, Delmarva	185
	A	Javier Guzman, Hickory	378
	E	Carlos Rodriguez, Lakewood	43
	DP	Javier Guzman, Hickory	78
OF	PCT	Ricardo Rojas, Lake County	.996
	PO	Chris Young, Kannapolis	335
	A	Josh Burrus, Rome	17
	E	Mickey Hall, Augusta	14
	DP	Three tied at	4

BY AARON FITT

It was a double dose of despair for the Auburn Doubledays in 2004.

For the second consecutive year, the Blue Jays affiliate posted the best regular-season record in the New York-Penn League, and for the second straight year Auburn was swept in the first round of the playoffs by the wild-card entry. In 2003, Williamsport bounced the Doubledays and went on to win the league title; in 2004, Mahoning Valley knocked out Auburn before sweeping Tri-City in the championship series.

RICH ABEL

Ben Zobrist

It was a remarkable turnaround for the Scrappers, who were five games below .500 and 15½ games behind the first-place Doubledays in the Pinckney Division with four weeks left in the regular season. Auburn was having its way with Mahoning Valley, taking nine of 13 regular-season meetings between the clubs.

"It seems like Auburn just kills everybody in this league," first-year Mahoning Valley manager Mike Sarbaugh said late in the season.

But the Scrappers made a late playoff run, winning 11 of their final 14 games to squeak past New Jersey in the wild-card race. Leading the way offensively for the Scrappers were outfielder Argenis Reyes, who led the league in hits and runs, and third baseman Chris Gimenez, the league leader in doubles. Lefthanders Tony Sipp and Aaron Laffey anchored the pitching staff.

The Scrappers came from behind to take the first game of the best-of-three playoff series against Auburn. In the second game, Sipp allowed just two unearned runs and struck out six Doubledays in five innings, leading Mahoning Valley to a 7-3 win and the upset.

But it didn't get any easier in the championship series, where the Scrappers ran into a Tri-City team that featured righthander Ronnie Martinez—the league MVP—and shortstop Ben Zobrist, who led the NY-P with a .339 batting average.

"Zobrist will play in the major leagues," ValleyCats manager Greg Langbehn said. "First and foremost, he's a classy individual. His hitting ability is excellent, and his knowledge of the strike zone is without question the best that I've seen in the league."

Ironically, it was a Zobrist strikeout that essentially sealed Mahoning Valley's championship. After the Scrappers took a back-and-forth series opener on a walkoff RBI single by Brett Parker, they sent Justin Hoyman to the mound to try for the sweep. They got it, but not before Hoyman struck out Zobrist with the bases loaded in the fifth inning to protect the 4-2 win. It was Mahoning Valley's seventh straight victory.

Zobrist was probably the league's best player, but its best prospect was Brooklyn's Ambiorix Concepcion. A 20-year-old Dominican outfielder, Concepcion reminded several league managers of Vladimir Guerrero. He flashed five-tool potential while putting together a .305-8-46 season.

After Concepcion, the top talent was all pitching. Jamestown lefthanders Taylor Tankersley and Jason Vargas, the Marlins' top two draft picks in 2004, were dominant. Even more dominant were a couple of hard-throwing righthanders: Lowell's Anibal Sanchez (the league leader with a 1.77 ERA and 101 strikeouts in 76 innings) and Staten Island's Jesse Hoover (90 strikeouts in 56 innings). And of course, Martinez's stellar 11-2, 1.96 record carried him to the MVP award.

Overall, managers had mixed opinions about the level of talent in the NY-P in 2004.

"I think the New York-Penn League is becoming a very college-oriented league," Auburn manager Dennis Holmberg said. "I think a lot of organizations are steering more toward commonplace college kids who have traveled and packed suitcases, been away from home, who can handle this better than a high school kid."

STANDINGS

Page	McNAMARA	W	L	Pct.	GB	Manager	Attendance	Avg.	Last Penn.
203	Brooklyn Cyclones (Mets)	43	31	.581	—	Tony Tijerina	294,261	7,953	2001
233	New Jersey Cardinals (Cardinals)	41	34	.547	2½	Tommy Shields	115,324	3,203	1994
262	Hudson Valley Renegades (Devil Rays)	39	33	.542	3	Dave Howard	155,606	4,445	1999
84	Aberdeen Ironbirds (Orioles)	35	40	.467	8½	Don Buford	228,925	6,187	1983
225	Williamsport Crosscutters (Pirates)	34	40	.459	9	Jeff Branson	75,785	2,165	2003
195	Staten Island Yankees (Yankees)	28	44	.389	14	Tommy John	156,895	5,061	2002
Page	PINCKNEY	W	L	Pct.	GB	Manager	Attendance	Avg.	Last Penn.
276	Auburn Doubledays (Blue Jays)	50	24	.676	—	Dennis Holmberg	63,679	1,930	1998
123	Mahoning Valley Scrappers (Indians)	42	34	.553	9	Mike Sarbaugh	160,832	4,232	2004
145	Jamestown Jammers (Marlins)	30	45	.400	20½	Benny Castillo	57,523	1,692	1991
218	Batavia Muckdogs (Phillies)	28	46	.378	22	Luis Melendez	37,086	1,002	1963
Page	STEDLER	W	L	Pct.	GB	Manager	Attendance	Avg.	Last Penn.
151	Tri-City ValleyCats (Astros)	50	25	.667	—	Gregg Langbehn	110,497	3,069	1997
187	Vermont Expos (Expos)	34	38	.472	14½	Jose Alguacil	93,796	2,842	1996
137	Oneonta Tigers (Tigers)	33	41	.446	16½	Mike Rojas	42,100	1,275	1998
92	Lowell Spinners (Red Sox)	32	44	.421	18½	Luis Alicea	185,000	5,000	None

PLAYOFFS—Semifinals: Mahoning Valley defeated Auburn 2-0 and Tri-City defeated Brooklyn 2-1 in best-of-3 series. **Finals:** Mahoning Valley defeated Tri-City 2-0 in best-of-3 series.

NOTE: Teams' individual batting and pitching statistics can be found on page indicated in lefthand column.

2004 NEW YORK-PENN LEAGUE STATISTICS

CLUB BATTING

	AVG	G	AB	R	H	2B	3B	HR	BB	SO	SB
Auburn	.274	74	2514	427	689	165	21	61	288	553	36
Mahoning Valley	.273	76	2627	389	717	146	17	50	231	553	53
Tri-City	.267	75	2593	425	693	116	19	63	309	568	72
Jamestown	.262	75	2577	356	675	121	29	42	202	637	42
Hudson Valley	.255	72	2406	332	614	124	30	33	189	525	66
Williamsport	.253	74	2454	318	621	107	21	32	219	536	109
Brooklyn	.253	74	2462	329	622	107	26	39	196	542	94
Staten Island	.248	72	2528	313	626	112	19	35	207	587	53
Aberdeen	.247	75	2528	307	625	131	25	28	217	537	80
New Jersey	.245	75	2534	312	622	109	15	32	229	570	61
Lowell	.242	76	2605	327	631	115	28	31	269	658	91
Oneonta	.242	74	2490	291	602	115	29	31	185	708	98
Vermont	.235	72	2306	303	541	97	8	48	280	577	69
Batavia	.230	74	2484	280	572	98	25	44	206	681	54

CLUB PITCHING

	ERA	G	CG	SV	IP	H	HR	R	ER	BB	SO
Hudson Valley	2.99	72	2	20	620	544	27	272	206	179	554
Brooklyn	3.12	74	0	19	653	583	41	282	226	207	594
Tri-City	3.15	75	2	26	672	545	45	271	235	264	667
Auburn	3.40	74	1	24	645	611	26	296	244	221	574
New Jersey	3.46	75	3	22	676	650	36	302	260	201	564
Oneonta	3.57	74	1	16	667	649	32	342	265	277	592
Williamsport	3.62	74	2	16	644	637	47	323	259	154	474
Staten Island	3.75	72	2	11	653	667	35	338	272	239	555
Mahoning Valley	3.84	76	0	20	671	637	46	371	286	258	652
Lowell	3.95	76	0	16	686	636	48	362	301	239	711
Vermont	4.13	72	2	21	615	621	31	350	282	265	529
Batavia	4.13	74	0	14	653	700	42	392	300	227	543
Aberdeen	4.28	75	0	27	674	683	52	391	320	259	622
Jamestown	4.35	75	0	16	652	687	61	417	315	237	601

CLUB FIELDING

	PCT	PO	A	E		PCT	PO	A	E
New Jersey	.969	2028	852	91	Hudson Valley	.965	1859	747	94
Williamsport	.968	1931	873	92	Aberdeen	.962	2018	785	111
Brooklyn	.968	1958	831	93	Batavia	.961	1959	778	112
Staten Island	.967	1959	804	93	Oneonta	.960	2002	780	115
Tri-City	.967	2016	802	95	Vermont	.958	1844	688	111
Auburn	.967	1936	810	95	Lowell	.957	2057	732	125
Mahoning Valley	.966	2012	796	98	Jamestown	.955	1956	714	126

INDIVIDUAL BATTING LEADERS
(Minimum 205 Plate Appearances)

	AVG	G	AB	R	H	2B	3B	HR	RBI	BB	SO	SB
Zobrist, Ben, Tri-City	.339	68	257	50	87	14	3	4	45	43	31	15
Patrick, Chris, New Jersey	.325	57	206	30	67	13	2	1	22	11	27	1
Brinkley, Dante, Brooklyn	.316	62	234	47	74	9	1	6	30	25	59	14
Butia, Mike, Mahoning Valley	.315	62	232	32	73	17	1	5	44	24	54	0
Reyes, Argenis, Mahoning Valley	.312	73	324	53	101	11	0	0	20	15	36	27
Lind, Adam, Auburn	.308	70	266	43	82	23	0	7	50	24	36	1
Concepcion, Ambiorix, Bklyn.	.305	66	259	38	79	14	3	8	46	13	54	28
Davidson, Tyler, Brooklyn	.305	65	243	36	74	15	4	6	45	22	64	3
Gamble, Sean, Batavia	.304	64	247	36	75	15	6	1	19	31	49	7
Llamas, Juan, Oneonta	.303	74	284	38	86	20	4	7	55	16	27	11

INDIVIDUAL PITCHING LEADERS
(Minimum 61 Innings)

	W	L	ERA	G	GS	CG	SV	IP	H	R	ER	BB	SO
Sanchez, Anibal, Lowell	4	4	1.77	15	15	0	0	76	43	24	15	29	101
Devaney, Mike, Brooklyn	5	0	1.95	14	14	0	0	69	58	19	15	29	56
Martinez, Ronnie, Tri-City	11	2	1.96	15	15	1	0	92	62	21	20	20	81
Williams, Joe, Brooklyn	5	4	2.28	15	15	0	0	75	62	26	19	26	64
Johnson, Blair, Williamsport	6	1	2.44	14	14	2	0	89	62	34	24	12	40
Beam, T.J., Staten Island	2	4	2.57	12	12	1	0	67	61	28	19	14	69
Henderson, Jim, Vermont	2	6	2.59	14	13	0	0	76	61	34	22	27	39
Hertzler, Barry, Lowell	4	3	2.67	15	9	0	0	81	70	25	24	23	73
Swindell, Mike, Brooklyn	4	1	2.69	12	11	0	0	64	47	24	19	22	62
Aguero, Miguel, New Jersey	5	5	2.97	15	14	1	0	91	92	33	30	22	82

ALL-STAR TEAM

C—John Jaso, Hudson Valley; Curtis Thigpen, Auburn. **1B**—Mario Garza, Tri-City. **2B**—Chris Patrick, New Jersey. **3B**—Juan Llamas, Oneonta. **SS**—Ben Zobrist, Tri-City. **UT IF**—Chris Gimenez, Mahoning Valley. **OF**—Dante Brinkley, Brooklyn; Ambiorix Concepcion, Brooklyn; Adam Lind, Auburn; Argenis Reyes, Mahoning Valley. **DH**—Mike Butia, Mahoning Valley. **RHP**—Ronnie Martinez, Tri-City; Anibal Sanchez, Lowell. **LHP**—David Haehnel, Aberdeen; Joe Williams, Brooklyn.

Most Valuable Player: Ronnie Martinez, Tri-City. **Most Outstanding Prospect:** Ambiorix Concepcion, Brooklyn. **Manager of the Year:** Tom Shields, New Jersey.

DEPARTMENT LEADERS

BATTING

G	Juan Llamas, Oneonta	74
AB	Argenis Reyes, Mahoning Valley	324
R	Argenis Reyes, Mahoning Valley	53
H	Argenis Reyes, Mahoning Valley	101
TB	Chris Gimenez, Mahoning Valley	137
XBH	Chris Gimenez, Mahoning Valley	36
2B	Chris Gimenez, Mahoning Valley	23
	Adam Lind, Auburn	23
3B	Justin Justice, Oneonta	7
HR	Mario Garza, Tri-City	15
RBI	Mario Garza, Tri-City	65
SH	Grant Plumley, Staten Island	9
	Levi Robinson, Aberdeen	9
SF	Tim Brown, Williamsport	8
BB	Ben Zobrist, Tri-City	43
IBB	Eric Nielsen, Auburn	5
HBP	Chris Gimenez, Mahoning Valley	24
SO	Justin Justice, Oneonta	108
SB	Jermel Lomack, Williamsport	29
CS	Ambiorix Concepcion, Brooklyn	11
GIDP	Brian Cleveland, Jamestown	11
	Teodoro Encarnacion, M.V.	11
OBP	Ben Zobrist, Tri-City	.438
SLG	Chris Gimenez, Mahoning Valley	.527

PITCHING

G	Cory Doyne, New Jersey	30
	Gus Hlebovy, Vermont	30
GS	Six tied at	15
CG	Blair Johnson, Williamsport	2
ShO	Three tied at	1
GF	David Haehnel, Aberdeen	25
	Gus Hlebovy, Vermont	25
SV	David Haehnel, Aberdeen	16
	Gus Hlebovy, Vermont	16
W	Ronnie Martinez, Tri-City	11
L	Kyle Kendrick, Batavia	8
IP	Ronnie Martinez, Tri-City	92
H	Andy Baldwin, Batavia	96
R	Derek Griffith, Batavia	54
ER	Russ Brocato, Aberdeen	44
HR	Four tied at	9
HB	Mark Jecmen, Mahoning Valley	10
BB	Ryan McKeller, Tri-City	39
SO	Anibal Sanchez, Lowell	101
WP	Tim King, Hudson Valley	12
BK	Jayson Rodriguez, Auburn	3
	Tony Sipp, Mahoning Valley	3

FIELDING

C	PCT	Lou Santangelo, Tri-City	.995
	PO	Wyatt Toregas, M.V.	469
	A	Aaron Hathaway, Brooklyn	59
	E	Salvador Paniagua, Lowell	12
	DP	Aaron Hathaway, Brooklyn	3
	PB	Salvador Paniagua, Lowell	13
1B	PCT	C.J. Smith, Aberdeen	.991
	PO	Rafael Mendez, Oneonta	579
	A	Rafael Mendez, Oneonta	49
	E	J.T. Restko, Jamestown	14
	DP	Rafael Mendez, Oneonta	49
2B	PCT	Drew Sutton, Tri-City	.979
	PO	Francisco Castro, Oneonta	136
	A	Francisco Castro, Oneonta	198
	E	Francisco Castro, Oneonta	17
	DP	Drew Sutton, Tri-City	33
3B	PCT	Jacob Mullinax, New Jersey	.957
	PO	Ofilio Castro, Vermont	45
	A	Patrick Cottrell, Hudson Valley	130
	E	Brett Carroll, Jamestown	18
	DP	Jacob Mullinax, New Jersey	9
		Grant Psomas, Brooklyn	9
SS	PCT	Ben Zobrist, Tri-City	.959
	PO	Ben Zobrist, Tri-City	131
	A	Matt Shepherd, New Jersey	236
	E	Jonathan Fulton, Jamestown	23
	DP	Matt Shepherd, New Jersey	50
OF	PCT	Steve Sherman, New Jersey	1.000
	PO	Doug Vroman, Vermont	148
	A	Eric Sultemeier, Aberdeen	10
	E	Bo Flowers, Oneonta	10
	DP	Three tied at	3

MINOR LEAGUES

BY WILL KIMMEY

The short-season Northwest League played more like the National Football League than the NWL in 2004 as parity was prevalent. Five of the eight teams registered between 42 and 40 wins and the divisional races came down to the season's final weekend.

"I've never seen two divisions in a league be so close to each other the entire season," Tri-City manager Ron Gideon said. "It's been tight all year, nobody ran off with it."

Spokane, which led the league in attendance for the fifth straight year, and Everett took early leads in the Eastern and Western divisions, but the overall equity in the league allowed Boise and Vancouver to overtake them. Both won 42 games to take their divisions by one game.

That parity ended in the playoffs as Boise swept three games from Vancouver, notching wins of 7-4, 9-7 and 5-3 thanks to a stunning offensive barrage from outfielder Ryan Harvey.

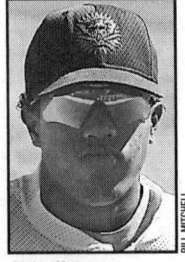

Javier Herrera

Harvey, 19, hit 14 regular-season home runs and then cranked at least one in each postseason game. He finished the series with four homers, a triple, six RBIs and five runs.

"He's got plus power," Vancouver manager Dennis Rogers said. "He hit two home runs off us that first night that went about 900 feet combined."

Boise's lefty-righty bullpen duo of Jerry Blevins and Will Fenton didn't yield a run while striking out 12 batters in seven combined postseason innings, with Blevins notching saves in each game.

Vancouver looked like it would be the story of the year. The Athletics affiliate began the season a bit short on talent after Oakland spent five of its first nine picks on players who competed in the College World Series through the end of June. The Canadians still sat at 23-26 one week into August.

"We were under .500 for a while even after the college guys filtered in," Rogers said. "It takes a while to adapt. We picked it up as we moved along because our guys stayed mentally tough. I think we really surprised some people the way we finished."

The arrivals of outfielder Richie Robnett, catchers Kurt Suzuki and Landon Powell and second baseman Kevin Melillo boosted an offense that had mostly relied on the shoulders of Javier Herrera. Herrera, a 19-year-old Venezuelan, missed most of the 2003 campaign in the Rookie-level Arizona League after crashing into an outfield fence and suffering a neck injury. He made a full recovery and won league MVP honors while ranking third in batting and second in steals. He also showed off five tools.

"For a young kid, how he handled himself, you thought he ought to be in advanced A-ball," Gideon said.

Everett held a four-game lead over Vancouver before the Canadians' potent lineup led them on a 19-8 stretch run to finish one-game better than the AquaSox. In contrast to a more college-heavy Canadians team, the AquaSox operated with few players over 20 years of age—which ultimately might have been the difference between them and the Canadians in the pennant race. "They were peaking late when our young guys were slowing down," Everett manager Pedro Grifol said.

Grifol's club featured an outstanding defensive infield based around Asdrubal Cabrera, Osvaldo Navarro and Yung Chen while lefthander Shawn Nottingham did the heavy lifting on the mound. Nottingham led the league in wins, strikeouts and innings thanks to an excellent changeup and pinpoint command overall.

Spokane righthander Clint Brannon proved even more dominant than Nottingham, however. He produced a record-setting 0.59 ERA while allowing just 35 hits in 61 innings. He needed to pitch 3⅓ innings on the season's final day to qualify for the record, so he worked on three days' rest.

Outside of Brannon's success, the league featured just one other ERA qualifier with a mark less than 3.00, Yakima's A.J. Shappi. In 2003, not a member of the 10-player ERA leader board had any number greater than 2 in front of his figure.

"I'll be honest, with the pitching in this league, you really had to see some guys on certain days for them to really jump out at you," Rogers said. "There were only a few guys who really had plus stuff."

Righthanders Garrett Mock of Yakima and Thomas Diamond of Spokane fit the bill but like several top 2004 draft picks, neither spent much time in the NWL.

"Mock and Diamond pitched one or two outings and moved up," Gideon said. "Some of the other organizations didn't let their top picks stay down."

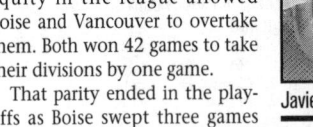

STANDINGS

Page	EAST	W	L	Pct.	GB	Manager	Attendance	Avg.	Last Penn.
107	Boise Hawks (Cubs)	42	34	.553	—	Tom Beyers	107,936	2,917	2004
269	Spokane Indians (Rangers)	41	35	.539	1	Darryl Kennedy	169,075	4,569	2003
130	Tri-City Dust Devils (Rockies)	40	36	.526	2	Ron Gideon	54,087	1,423	None
69	Yakima Bears (Diamondbacks)	35	41	.461	7	Bill Plummer	51,544	1,393	2000
Page	WEST	W	L	Pct.	GB	Manager	Attendance	Avg.	Last Penn.
211	Vancouver Canadians (Athletics)	42	34	.553	—	Dennis Rogers	140,037	3,685	None
255	Everett AquaSox (Mariners)	41	35	.539	1	Pedro Grifol	104,010	2,811	1985
248	Salem-Keizer Volcanoes (Giants)	37	39	.487	5	Joe Strain	118,929	3,129	2001
241	Eugene Emeralds (Padres)	26	50	.342	16	Roy Howell	117,547	3,176	1980

PLAYOFFS—Boise defeated Vancouver 3-0 in best-of-5 series for league championship.

NOTE: Teams' individual batting and pitching statistics can be found on page indicated in lefthand column.

MINOR LEAGUES

BILL MITCHELL

CLUB BATTING

	AVG	G	AB	R	H	2B	3B	HR	BB	SO	SB
Salem-Keizer	.268	76	2652	385	710	122	12	46	246	484	41
Vancouver	.267	76	2610	427	697	133	25	43	322	579	47
Everett	.267	76	2588	448	690	170	17	49	286	602	124
Boise	.262	76	2572	373	674	114	21	55	204	536	57
Yakima	.261	76	2610	403	680	117	13	62	283	541	41
Tri-City	.260	76	2592	370	673	131	21	58	266	576	30
Spokane	.255	76	2635	427	671	153	7	75	365	688	65
Eugene	.248	76	2605	354	647	144	12	68	233	675	47

CLUB PITCHING

	ERA	G	CG	SV	IP	H	HR	R	ER	BB	SO
Spokane	3.73	76	0	17	689	683	64	362	286	221	599
Tri-City	4.01	76	0	23	684	621	43	378	305	283	631
Boise	4.20	76	0	20	675	671	51	374	315	290	548
Vancouver	4.37	76	0	21	668	692	39	373	324	226	521
Yakima	4.46	76	0	13	668	739	50	423	331	260	562
Salem-Keizer	4.46	76	0	14	678	680	55	398	336	306	686
Everett	4.79	76	0	18	672	680	82	423	358	314	567
Eugene	5.13	76	0	11	663	676	72	456	378	305	567

CLUB FIELDING

	PCT	PO	A	E		PCT	PO	A	E
Vancouver	.971	2003	756	82	Everett	.966	2017	793	98
Salem-Keizer	.968	2035	747	92	Tri-City	.965	2052	780	104
Boise	.968	2026	847	96	Yakima	.962	2005	798	111
Spokane	.967	2068	797	98	Eugene	.958	1988	764	121

INDIVIDUAL BATTING LEADERS
(Minimum 205 Plate Appearances)

	AVG	G	AB	R	H	2B	3B	HR	RBI	BB	SO	SB
Horwitz, Brian, Salem-Keizer	.347	71	268	41	93	24	1	2	44	21	34	3
Carter, Chris, Yakima	.335	70	257	47	86	15	1	15	63	46	35	2
Macri, Matt, Tri-City	.333	52	195	33	65	17	4	7	43	23	52	4
Herrera, Javier, Vancouver	.331	65	263	50	87	15	4	12	47	24	59	23
Dean, Erik, Tri-City	.313	59	217	43	68	12	1	4	26	32	36	4
Thigpen, Jud, Tri-City	.310	58	239	43	74	14	5	10	37	14	50	8
Schindewolf, Erik, Yakima	.308	73	273	65	84	10	2	4	37	51	37	15
Boyer, Kyle, Boise	.304	67	247	35	75	13	3	7	37	15	65	6
Deeb, Bobby, Boise	.303	51	188	33	57	11	1	1	13	18	33	10
Johnson, Brent, Everett	.300	66	233	51	70	13	0	1	31	33	27	12

INDIVIDUAL PITCHING LEADERS
(Minimum 61 Innings)

	W	L	ERA	G	GS	CG	SV	IP	H	R	ER	BB	SO
Brannon, Clint, Spokane	3	2	0.59	15	10	0	1	61	35	9	4	14	58
Shappi, A.J., Yakima	4	1	1.75	12	11	0	0	67	64	17	13	8	65
Weber, Matt, Boise	5	1	2.95	14	14	0	0	76	72	27	25	18	46
Morillo, Juan, Tri-City	3	2	2.98	14	14	0	0	66	56	34	22	41	73
Nottingham, Shawn, Everett	9	3	3.15	15	14	0	0	89	74	34	31	29	87
Whitaker, Craig, Salem-Keizer	4	2	3.44	15	15	0	0	71	58	33	27	43	77
Santiago, Tomas, Tri-City	4	3	3.57	14	13	0	0	76	67	34	30	27	66
Register, Steven, Tri-City	6	7	3.63	15	15	0	0	79	68	41	32	20	63
Ford, Ryan, Vancouver	4	0	3.66	15	11	0	2	71	76	36	29	15	49
Phillips, Shawn, Spokane	6	1	3.93	18	10	0	0	71	69	33	31	8	53

ALL-STAR TEAM

C—Mike Nickeas, Spokane. **1B**—Lachlan Dale, Eugene. **2B**—Erik Dean, Tri-City. **3B**—Matt Macri, Tri-City. **SS**—Asdrubal Cabrera, Everett. **OF**—Javier Herrera, Vancouver; Brian Horwitz, Salem-Keizer; Luis Montanez, Boise. **DH**—Chris Carter, Yakima. **RHP**—A.J. Shappi, Yakima. **LHP**—Shawn Nottingham, Everett. **RHRP**—Jim Miller, Tri-City. **LHRP**—Jerry Blevins, Boise.

Most Valuable Player: Javier Herrera, Vancouver. **Manager of the Year:** Tom Beyers, Boise.

DEPARTMENT LEADERS

BATTING

G	Lachlan Dale, Eugene	74
	Tom Everidge, Vancouver	74
AB	Carlos Gonzalez, Yakima	300
R	Erik Schindewolf, Yakima	65
H	Brian Horwitz, Salem-Keizer	93
TB	Chris Carter, Yakima	148
XBH	Travis Metcalf, Spokane	37
2B	Oswaldo Navarro, Everett	27
3B	Luis Montanez, Boise	7
HR	Colt Morton, Eugene	17
RBI	Chris Carter, Yakima	63
SH	Jasha Balcom, Boise	12
SF	Travis Metcalf, Spokane	6
BB	Tug Hulett, Spokane	68
IBB	Joe Koshansky, Tri-City	3
	Mark Reynolds, Yakima	3
HBP	Bobby Deeb, Boise	14
SO	Lachlan Dale, Eugene	87
SB	Yung-Chi Chen, Everett	25
CS	Jasha Balcom, Boise	7
	Tug Hulett, Spokane	7
GIDP	Simon Klink, Salem-Keizer	13
OBP	Tug Hulett, Spokane	.444
SLG	Chris Carter, Yakima	.576

PITCHING

G	Jim Miller, Tri-City	34
GS	Aaron Jenson, Everett	16
	Darren Sack, Salem-Keizer	16
CG	None	
ShO	None	
GF	Jim Miller, Tri-City	32
SV	Jim Miller, Tri-City	17
W	Shawn Nottingham, Everett	9
L	William Ponce, Eugene	9
IP	Shawn Nottingham, Everett	89
H	Aaron Jenson, Everett	90
R	Danny De la O, Eugene	56
ER	Danny De la O, Eugene	52
HR	Darren Sack, Salem-Keizer	15
HB	Kevin Altman, Spokane	12
BB	Craig Whitaker, Salem-Keizer	43
SO	Shawn Nottingham, Everett	87
WP	Craig Whitaker, Salem-Keizer	14
BK	Kendall Bergdall, Everett	3

FIELDING

C	PCT	Tony Richie, Boise	.997
	PO	Mike Nickeas, Spokane	419
	A	Orlando Mercado, Yakima	38
	E	Nelson Robledo, Tri-City	9
	DP	Oscar Bernard, Boise	3
		Orlando Mercado, Yakima	3
	PB	Omar Falcon, Everett	18
1B	PCT	Todd Buchanan, Yakima	.992
	PO	Ryan Norwood, Boise	628
	A	Tom Everidge, Vancouver	57
	E	Ryan Norwood, Boise	10
		Will Thompson, Salem-Keizer	10
	DP	Ryan Norwood, Boise	63
2B	PCT	Tug Hulett, Spokane	.975
	PO	Tug Hulett, Spokane	121
	A	Tug Hulett, Spokane	186
	E	Bobby Deeb, Boise	13
	DP	Tug Hulett, Spokane	43
3B	PCT	Travis Metcalf, Spokane	.959
	PO	Myron Leslie, Vancouver	65
	A	Travis Metcalf, Spokane	155
	E	Lachlan Dale, Eugene	20
	DP	Travis Metcalf, Spokane	18
SS	PCT	Jose Rios, Boise	.958
	PO	Gregorio Petit, Vancouver	115
	A	Gregorio Petit, Vancouver	189
	E	Sean Kazmar, Eugene	23
	DP	Gregorio Petit, Vancouver	34
		Jose Rios, Boise	34
OF	PCT	Nick Blasi, Vancouver	1.000
	PO	Carlos Gonzalez, Yakima	163
	A	Carlos Gonzalez, Yakima	14
	E	Brandon Burgess, Yakima	8
	DP	Carlos Gonzalez, Yakima	3
		Michael Wilson, Everett	3

MINOR LEAGUES

BY WILL KIMMEY

The Rookie-level Appalachian League serves as the lowest stateside destination for seven major league organizations. Because a stricter visa application process limited the number of available Latin teenagers, a demographic that normally populates a large percentage of the league, more than the normal complement of players in their 20s traveled the Appy trails in 2004.

Managers agreed the older composition of the league raised its level of play and made the standout performances of the younger players that much more impressive.

"With the age rule that was lifted for this year, it was a college-aged league," Bluefield manager Gary Kendall said. "Definitely, we saw some kids that should have been playing in short-season A somewhere."

Mitch Einertson

No one caused more gasps than Greeneville outfielder Mitch Einertson. The Astros selected the 5-foot-10, 180-pounder from a California high school in the fifth round of the 2004 draft, and the 18-year-old tied Joy Gritts' 1960 league record by crushing 24 home runs. He added a league-best 67 RBIs and .692 slugging percentage while hitting .308.

"Coming out of high school and hitting over 20 home runs is almost impossible to do," Burlington manager Rouglas Odor said. "Manny Ramirez, when he was here (in 1991), he hit 19 home runs and had 63 RBIs."

Einertson went homerless in his last five games and failed to break the record, but he hit two in three playoff games before cranking another in his first game after a promotion to the short-season New York-Penn League. Ole Sheldon hit a 10th-inning home run to clinch Greeneville's 2-1 win in the decisive third game of the championship series, with an Einertson homer providing the Astros' other run.

"The story of the year has been Einertson—he ran away with it," Johnson City manager Tom Kidwell said.

The other story was the Tennessee town of Greeneville hosting a championship club during its first year as an Appy affiliate since the Burley Cubs played there in 1942.

The Astros moved their farm team from Martinsville, Va., to Greeneville, where it shares Pioneer Park with Tusculum College. Greeneville drew a league-best 51,183 fans, more than 15,000 better than Burlington, which ranked second.

A collection of already-solid arms benefited from Pioneer Park's major league dimensions, and the Greeneville staff ranked second in the league with a 3.78 team ERA. It rang up 516 strikeouts and allowed 549 hits in 576 innings. Standouts included righthanders Juan Gutierrez (8-2, 3.70) and Jimmy Barthmaier (4-3, 3.78) and lefty Troy Patton (2-2, 1.93), the team's three starters during the playoffs. Closer Enyelbert Soto, a lefty with pinpoint control and an aggressive approach, kept leads for those starters and tied for the league lead with 13 saves while posting a 1.03 ERA.

"My God, Greeneville had some pitchers that just dominated," Princeton manager Jamie Nelson said. "I don't care who you are and where you're pitching, their hits to innings pitched (ratio) are just incredible."

The Astros won the Western Division by three games over Elizabethton, another club stacked with talent. Outfielder/DH Deacon Burns led the Twins' offense. A lefthanded-hitting Kirby Puckett clone, Burns topped the league in hits and doubles while ranking among the top five in home runs, runs, RBIs, slugging percentage and extra-base hits. He also struck out 53 times.

"When Mr. Doubleday invented the rules, he gave you three strikes," Elizabethton manager Ray Smith said, "and Deacon uses all of his."

While Burns was a late-round find in the 2004 draft, all of the team's top picks also contributed at some point. Trevor Plouffe played shortstop behind fellow first-rounders Kyle Waldrop, Glen Perkins and Matt Fox on the mound.

"Minnesota's going to have prospects because they draft a lot of young guys and don't miss much," Kendall said.

Pulaski's roster sat near the other end of the spectrum, packed with plenty of college products. That experience allowed the Blue Jays to lead the league in team ERA at 3.78, thanks to 23-year-old league leader Jordan Timm (3-1, 2.67) and 19-year-old Chi-Hung Cheng (4-1, 2.82). A patient approach at the plate allowed Pulaski to top the league with 330 walks.

STANDINGS

Page	EAST	W	L	Pct.	GB	Manager	Attendance	Avg.	Last Penn.
76	Danville Braves (Braves)	41	25	.621	—	Jim Saul	32,194	1,073	None
277	Pulaski Blue Jays (Blue Jays)	40	27	.597	1½	Gary Cathcart	25,659	754	None
124	Burlington Indians (Indians)	31	35	.470	10	Rouglas Odor	34,219	1,140	1993
85	Bluefield Orioles (Orioles)	28	39	.418	13½	Gary Kendall	24,910	830	2001
263	Princeton Devil Rays (Devil Rays)	23	44	.343	18½	Jamie Nelson	25,374	792	1994
Page	WEST	W	L	Pct.	GB	Manager	Attendance	Avg.	Last Penn.
152	Greeneville Astros (Astros)	41	26	.612	—	Tim Bogar	51,183	1,599	2004
179	Elizabethton Twins (Twins)	38	29	.567	3	Ray Smith	27,017	900	2003
234	Johnson City Cardinals (Cardinals)	33	35	.485	8½	Tom Kidwell	19,940	623	1976
204	Kingsport Mets (Mets)	32	36	.471	9½	Mookie Wilson	30,765	992	1995
100	Bristol White Sox (White Sox)	27	38	.415	13	Jerry Hairston	21,120	704	2002

PLAYOFFS—Greeneville defeated Danville 2-1 in best-of-3 series for league championship.

NOTE: Teams' individual batting and pitching statistics can be found on page indicated in lefthand column.

MINOR LEAGUES

CLUB BATTING

	AVG	G	AB	R	H	2B	3B	HR	BB	SO	SB
Danville	.276	66	2257	386	624	113	17	52	223	452	55
Elizabethton	.270	67	2261	340	611	111	21	63	208	542	50
Pulaski	.269	67	2275	435	613	130	20	60	330	615	26
Johnson City	.268	68	2321	394	623	114	19	64	266	566	82
Kingsport	.265	68	2287	357	605	99	25	58	225	534	52
Greeneville	.260	67	2157	364	561	109	9	45	256	496	101
Princeton	.255	67	2236	336	571	88	20	40	198	562	69
Bristol	.246	65	2164	311	533	97	13	38	199	550	47
Bluefield	.244	67	2229	289	543	102	14	42	223	614	64
Burlington	.241	66	2137	266	516	94	17	22	210	537	81

CLUB PITCHING

	ERA	G	CG	SV	IP	H	HR	R	ER	BB	SO
Pulaski	3.77	67	0	10	587	580	42	300	246	211	574
Greeneville	3.78	67	1	19	576	549	34	296	242	222	516
Danville	3.83	66	1	16	578	542	36	290	246	177	560
Elizabethton	4.22	67	0	19	571	560	55	323	268	201	614
Burlington	4.25	66	0	16	562	555	45	307	265	172	535
Bluefield	4.27	67	0	13	582	599	56	354	276	247	554
Kingsport	4.48	68	1	12	585	620	44	360	291	199	544
Bristol	4.83	65	0	11	562	535	44	381	302	311	532
Johnson City	4.88	68	0	12	590	594	63	393	320	262	524
Princeton	5.72	67	0	9	573	666	65	474	364	345	515

CLUB FIELDING

	PCT	PO	A	E		PCT	PO	A	E
Danville	.968	1734	642	78	Elizabethton	.961	1713	642	95
Burlington	.967	1685	679	81	Bluefield	.958	1747	714	107
Johnson City	.966	1770	683	86	Kingsport	.957	1754	715	112
Greeneville	.963	1728	704	94	Bristol	.956	1687	675	109
Pulaski	.962	1762	725	98	Princeton	.943	1719	684	146

INDIVIDUAL BATTING LEADERS
(Minimum 184 Plate Appearances)

	AVG	G	AB	R	H	2B	3B	HR	RBI	BB	SO	SB
Lucena, Juan, Johnson City	.332	56	205	35	68	8	1	4	30	11	16	7
Hernandez, Francisco, Bristol	.326	53	181	32	59	13	1	5	30	13	32	0
Yarbrough, Brandon, Johnson City	.326	48	175	37	57	10	1	6	33	25	55	3
Gamero, Jesus, Kingsport	.323	44	161	31	52	7	4	3	32	13	28	3
Hiser, P.J., Burlington	.322	49	177	28	57	9	4	10	35	14	53	7
Holt, J.C., Danville	.321	51	209	38	67	15	0	1	21	18	34	17
Armstrong, Cole, Danville	.316	49	174	30	55	9	0	6	46	29	17	0
Granadillo, Tony, Johnson City	.315	50	168	40	53	10	1	10	30	22	37	3
Burns, Deacon, Elizabethton	.314	63	255	49	80	20	4	12	49	18	53	9
De los Santos, Jose, Bristol	.314	54	204	29	64	10	1	0	35	5	21	1

INDIVIDUAL PITCHING LEADERS
(Minimum 54 Innings)

	W	L	ERA	G	GS	CG	SV	IP	H	R	ER	BB	SO
Timm, Jordan, Pulaski	3	1	2.67	11	11	0	1	61	59	22	18	12	53
Santos, Reid, Burlington	3	5	2.78	12	12	0	0	65	52	27	20	17	67
Cheng, Chi-Hung, Pulaski	4	1	2.82	14	14	0	0	61	47	27	19	35	74
Rengel, Orlando, Kingsport	5	4	3.26	14	13	1	0	69	52	27	25	18	63
Vines, Chris, Danville	6	3	3.28	13	10	0	0	60	58	25	22	14	72
Duguay, Steven, Elizabethton	4	4	3.36	12	11	0	0	56	55	28	21	11	70
Martin, Adrian, Pulaski	3	2	3.54	18	7	0	0	56	65	28	22	12	51
Marshall, Jay, Bristol	1	6	3.59	11	11	0	0	58	63	31	23	8	52
Gutierrez, Juan, Greeneville	8	2	3.70	13	13	0	0	66	74	31	27	30	59
Barthmaier, Jimmy, Greeneville	4	3	3.78	13	13	0	0	69	70	32	29	22	65

ALL-STAR TEAM

C—Cole Armstrong, Danville. **1B**—Ryan Finan, Bluefield. **2B**—J.C. Holt, Danville. **3B**—Tony Granadillo, Johnson City. **SS**—Juan Lucena, Johnson City. **UT IF**—Jose de los Santos, Bristol. **OF**—Deacon Burns, Elizabethton; Yuber Rodriguez, Pulaski; Mitch Einertson, Greeneville. **UT OF**—Carl Loadenthal, Danville. **DH**—Seth Pietsch, Kingsport. **RHP**—Bob McCrory, Bluefield. **LHP**—Reid Santos, Burlington. **RP**—Enyelbert Soto, Greeneville.

Player of the Year: Mitch Einertson, Greeneville. **Pitchers of the Year:** Reid Santos, Burlington; Steven Duguay, Elizabethton. **Manager of the Year:** Tim Bogar, Greeneville.

BATTING

G	Carl Loadenthal, Danville	64
AB	Deacon Burns, Elizabethton	255
R	Carl Loadenthal, Danville	60
H	Deacon Burns, Elizabethton	80
TB	Mitch Einertson, Greeneville	157
XBH	Mitch Einertson, Greeneville	39
2B	Deacon Burns, Elizabethton	20
3B	Yuber Rodriguez, Pulaski	6
HR	Mitch Einertson, Greeneville	24
RBI	Mitch Einertson, Greeneville	67
SH	Wladimir Sutil, Greeneville	7
SF	Three tied at	5
BB	Jose Delgado, Johnson City	53
IBB	Seth Pietsch, Kingsport	4
	Yuber Rodriguez, Pulaski	4
HBP	Keith Eichas, Danville	14
SO	Lorenzo Scott, Bluefield	75
SB	Wladimir Sutil, Greeneville	24
CS	Wladimir Sutil, Greeneville	8
	Evan Tartaglia, Bristol	8
GIDP	Juan Lucena, Johnson City	11
OBP	Jose Delgado, Johnson City	.431
SLG	Mitch Einertson, Greeneville	.692

PITCHING

G	Frank Mata, Elizabethton	26
GS	Chi-Hung Cheng, Pulaski	14
CG	Three tied at	1
ShO	None	
GF	Frank Mata, Elizabethton	23
	Enyelbert Soto, Greeneville	23
SV	Frank Mata, Elizabethton	13
	Enyelbert Soto, Greeneville	13
W	Juan Gutierrez, Greeneville	8
	Levi Romero, Greeneville	8
L	Alejandro Limas, Princeton	9
IP	Jimmy Barthmaier, Greeneville	69
	Orlando Rengel, Kingsport	69
H	Jason Furrow, Bluefield	75
R	Alejandro Limas, Princeton	54
ER	Alejandro Limas, Princeton	41
HR	Gerson Mercedes, Burlington	9
HB	Billy Weitzman, Kingsport	15
BB	James Casey, Bristol	41
SO	Chi-Hung Cheng, Pulaski	74
WP	Nick Lemon, Bristol	13
BK	Three tied at	3

FIELDING

C	PCT	Henry Guerrero, Bluefield	.997
	PO	Francisco Hernandez, Bristol	347
	A	Francisco Hernandez, Bristol	55
	E	Francisco Hernandez, Bristol	13
	DP	Francisco Hernandez, Bristol	4
	PB	Henry Guerrero, Bluefield	14
1B	PCT	Ole Sheldon, Greeneville	.995
	PO	Johnny Woodard, Elizabethton	483
	A	Keith Eichas, Danville	37
	E	Johnny Woodard, Elizabethton	13
	DP	Ole Sheldon, Greeneville	40
		Johnny Woodard, Elizabethton	40
2B	PCT	J.C. Holt, Danville	.977
	PO	Jose Delgado, Johnson City	114
	A	Jose Delgado, Johnson City	157
	E	Jose Delgado, Johnson City	13
	DP	Jose Delgado, Johnson City	29
3B	PCT	Patrick Sellers, Greeneville	.935
	PO	Tony Granadillo, Johnson City	35
	A	Van Pope, Danville	102
	E	David Winfree, Elizabethton	15
	DP	Anthony Garibaldi, Pulaski	7
SS	PCT	Juan Lucena, Johnson City	.965
	PO	Javier Castillo, Bristol	90
		Wladimir Sutil, Greeneville	90
	A	Denver Kitch, Bluefield	174
	E	Javier Castillo, Bristol	20
	DP	Denver Kitch, Bluefield	40
OF	PCT	Chad Gabriel, Johnson City	1.000
	PO	Carl Loadenthal, Danville	127
	A	J.D. Foust, Bristol	7
	E	Angel Avila, Bluefield	7
		Ryan Reed, Greeneville	7
	DP	Three tied at	2

MINOR LEAGUES

BY ALAN MATTHEWS

After falling short three years in a row, the Provo Angels finally prevailed in the Pioneer League playoffs in 2004.

The Angels, who had lost in the league finals despite strong regular-season efforts in 2001, 2002 and 2003, came from behind to beat the Billings Mustangs 4-2 in the second game of the best-of-3 championship series. The title was the first for the franchise since 1991, when it was located in Salt Lake City.

With no outs and a runner aboard in the bottom of the eighth inning, Angels outfielder J.R. Renz drove a 1-0 pitch from Billings pitcher Brad Morenko over the left-field fence to snap a 2-2 tie. Righthander Mitchell Arnold struck out the side in the top of the ninth to close out the Mustangs.

"I've never won anything in my life," Renz said. "We had to win this one tonight. They're too tough to beat twice."

Renz almost never got his chance to win the game.

"It's ironic," Provo manager Tom Kotchman told the Deseret Morning News. "Renz bunted (late in the season) to win a ballgame and I told him I'm giving him one pitch to hit and then he might bunt. He got the pitch to hit. And hit it out."

Arnold struck out the side to secure the crown as the 2,062 fans in attendance erupted.

"It feels good to win obviously," Kotchman said. "We've had teams with better records since we've been here, but this was the team that won."

Billings, the defending champ, defeated the Angels in the championship series in 2001 and 2003. League MVP Sean Rodriguez was an integral member of the 2003 team that tied the league record for most regular season wins with 54. He rejoined Provo in 2004 after a slow start at Class A Cedar Rapids and batted .341-10-55 while playing a sound shortstop. Angels 2004 draft picks Josh Leblanc and Andrew Toussaint, who were college teammates at Southern, were also key cogs in Provo's lineup, which pounded out 44 runs in five post-season games.

Provo qualified for the playoffs by winning minor league baseball's tightest race. Seven of the league's eight teams had a shot at a division title entering the final

BILL MITCHELL

Sean Rodriguez

week of the first half. The Angels defeated Helena the final day of the half to clinch a tie-breaker victory over Idaho Falls based on head-to-head records in the Southern Division. Helena finished a half-game behind Billings in the Northern Division.

Idaho Falls lost in the first round of the playoffs to Provo, but the Chukars boasted the league's deepest talent pool. Third baseman Billy Butler won the batting title with a .373-10-68 rookie season. Butler, a Royals first-round pick, was flanked in the Chukars batting order by Eddie Solis, Brian McFall and Geraldo Valentin. The foursome finished in the top seven among league batting leaders and Idaho Falls paced the league with a .319 team average.

The Chukars pitching staff was loaded with intriguing arms also produced from the Royals 2004 draft class. South Carolina products Billy Buckner, Chad Blackwell and Matt Campbell provided the staff with a stabilizing force of players who had recently played in the College World Series. Luis Cota, a hard-throwing righthander who was a draft-and-follow selection in 2003, made his pro debut with the Chukars and ranked among the league's top 10 prospects.

Pitching was the strong suit of Great Falls. The White Sox entered the postseason riding a six-game winning streak and the second-half Northern Division crown before being swept by Billings. Great Falls posted the lowest team ERA in the PL at 4.24, in part because of the efforts of lefty Ray Liotta, the league's top pitching prospect. Liotta went 5-1, 2.54 with 65 strikeouts in 63 innings as the league's only hurler to post an ERA below 3.00.

Casper righthander Sam Deduno was dominant on the mound, as well. He racked up a league-best 118 strikeouts on his way to a 6-4, 3.18 record.

STANDINGS: SPLIT SEASON

FIRST HALF

NORTH	W	L	PCT	GB
Billings	21	16	.568	—
Helena	22	17	.564	—
Great Falls	17	20	.459	4
Missoula	15	23	.395	6½

SOUTH	W	L	PCT	GB
Provo	20	18	.526	—
Ogden	19	18	.514	½
Idaho Falls	20	19	.513	½
Casper	17	20	.459	2½

SECOND HALF

NORTH	W	L	PCT	GB
Great Falls	25	13	.658	—
Helena	18	20	.474	7
Billings	16	21	.432	8½
Missoula	12	23	.343	11½

SOUTH	W	L	PCT	GB
Provo	24	14	.632	—
Idaho Falls	22	16	.579	2
Casper	16	20	.444	7
Ogden	16	22	.421	8

PLAYOFFS—Semifinals: Billings defeated Great Falls 2-0 and Provo defeated Idaho Falls 2-1 in best-of-3 series. **Finals:** Provo defeated Billings 2-0 in best-of-3 series.

STANDINGS: OVERALL

Page		W	L	Pct.	GB	Manager	Attendance	Avg.	Last Penn.
61	Provo Angels (Angels)	44	32	.579	—	Tom Kotchman	43,920	1,292	2004
99	Great Falls White Sox (White Sox)	42	33	.560	1½	John Orton	109,779	2,888	2002
158	Idaho Falls Chukars (Royals)	42	35	.545	2½	Brian Rupp	61,237	1,655	2000
172	Helena Brewers (Brewers)	40	37	.519	4½	Johnny Narron	37,568	1,015	1984
115	Billings Mustangs (Reds)	37	37	.500	6	Donnie Scott	106,837	2,967	2001
165	Ogden Raptors (Dodgers)	35	40	.467	8½	Travis Barbary	133,886	3,719	None
131	Casper Rockies (Rockies)	33	40	.452	9½	P.J. Carey	42,938	1,192	None
70	Missoula Osprey (Diamondbacks)	27	46	.370	15½	Jim Presley	64,942	1,855	1999

NOTE: Team's individual batting and pitching statistics can be found on page indicated in lefthand column.

2004 PIONEER LEAGUE STATISTICS

CLUB BATTING

	AVG	G	AB	R	H	2B	3B	HR	BB	SO	SB
Idaho Falls	.319	76	2674	570	852	180	24	60	323	596	101
Ogden	.303	75	2631	496	798	156	22	73	311	577	56
Casper	.292	73	2539	492	741	130	20	66	362	617	87
Helena	.288	76	2580	456	742	152	15	44	368	573	116
Provo	.282	76	2564	514	722	138	23	65	371	676	81
Great Falls	.272	75	2607	441	710	139	20	74	259	656	85
Missoula	.272	73	2476	399	673	131	25	62	252	550	69
Billings	.264	74	2487	400	656	120	26	57	338	638	79

CLUB PITCHING

	ERA	G	CG	SV	IP	H	HR	R	ER	BB	SO
Great Falls	4.24	75	0	20	678	691	43	399	319	358	635
Billings	4.84	74	0	14	638	625	52	401	343	363	588
Provo	5.31	76	1	17	646	740	54	447	381	316	572
Helena	5.53	76	0	20	659	743	81	476	405	293	567
Missoula	5.54	73	2	16	629	738	70	491	387	328	589
Idaho Falls	5.75	76	1	26	657	801	72	509	420	285	578
Ogden	6.05	75	0	19	647	765	61	507	435	352	689
Casper	6.43	73	1	14	628	791	68	538	449	289	665

CLUB FIELDING

	PCT	PO	A	E		PCT	PO	A	E
Billings	.971	1914	806	80	Great Falls	.958	2033	826	124
Helena	.965	1977	793	100	Provo	.958	1939	835	121
Ogden	.959	1941	763	115	Casper	.952	1885	705	131
Idaho Falls	.959	1972	848	121	Missoula	.945	1887	689	149

INDIVIDUAL BATTING LEADERS

(Minimum 205 Plate Appearances)

	AVG	G	AB	R	H	2B	3B	HR	RBI	BB	SO	SB
Butler, Billy, Idaho Falls	.373	72	260	74	97	22	3	10	68	57	63	5
Smith, Seth, Casper	.369	56	233	46	86	21	3	9	61	25	47	9
Richardson, Grant, Helena	.367	44	166	35	61	16	1	5	42	32	20	2
Solis, Eddie, Idaho Falls	.366	63	246	48	90	15	2	2	54	19	41	3
Sollmann, Steve, Helena	.364	72	272	59	99	12	2	1	40	52	30	23
McFall, Brian, Idaho Falls	.363	68	262	64	95	23	1	14	68	30	64	23
Valentin, Geraldo, Idaho Falls	.351	65	259	55	91	21	6	4	44	19	28	7
Dunlap, Cory, Ogden	.351	71	245	57	86	18	1	7	53	68	40	0
Westervelt, Chris, Ogden	.341	49	176	41	60	12	0	10	37	27	46	1
Rodriguez, Sean, Provo	.338	64	225	64	76	14	4	10	55	51	62	9

INDIVIDUAL PITCHING LEADERS

(Minimum 61 Innings)

	W	L	ERA	G	GS	CG	SV	IP	H	R	ER	BB	SO
Liotta, Ray, Great Falls	5	1	2.54	14	11	0	0	64	59	27	18	28	65
Deduno, Samuel, Casper	6	4	3.18	15	15	0	0	76	62	40	27	32	118
Ramirez, Ramon, Billings	3	6	3.39	17	12	0	1	74	64	36	28	36	60
Pelland, Tyler, Billings	9	3	3.44	18	12	0	0	73	67	36	28	39	81
Wooley, Robert, Helena	3	3	3.52	17	5	0	2	64	69	31	25	18	48
Vaillancourt, Tim, Missoula	4	4	4.16	14	14	1	0	76	78	47	35	31	67
Bakker, Garry, Great Falls	4	2	4.50	13	12	0	0	64	64	38	32	24	50
Dove, Shane, Missoula	4	9	4.97	15	12	1	0	71	85	50	39	25	77
Suarez, Sony, Great Falls	5	2	5.37	18	9	0	2	64	66	46	38	41	62
Logan, Boone, Great Falls	3	7	5.60	18	9	0	1	64	74	48	40	31	48

ALL-STAR TEAM

C—Craig Tatum, Billings. **1B**—Cory Dunlap, Ogden. **2B**—Eddie Solis, Idaho Falls. **3B**—Billy Butler, Idaho Falls. **SS**—Sean Rodriguez, Provo. **OF**—Jaen Centeno, Missoula; Brian McFall, Idaho Falls; Seth Smith, Casper. **DH**—Andrew Toussaint, Provo. **RHP**—Samuel Deduno, Casper. **LHP**—Tyler Pelland, Billings. **RP**—Mitchell Arnold, Provo.

Most Valuable Player: Sean Rodriguez, Provo. **Pitcher of the Year:** Samuel Deduno, Casper. **Manager:** Tom Kotchman, Provo.

BATTING

G	Three tied at	72
AB	Blake DeWitt, Ogden	299
R	Billy Butler, Idaho Falls	74
H	Steve Sollmann, Helena	99
TB	Brian McFall, Idaho Falls	162
XBH	Brian McFall, Idaho Falls	38
2B	Brian McFall, Idaho Falls	23
3B	Tom Collaro, Great Falls	6
	Geraldo Valentin, Great Falls	6
HR	Robert Mosby, Billings	19
RBI	Billy Butler, Idaho Falls	68
	Brian McFall, Idaho Falls	68
SH	Phillip Gentry, Billings	9
SF	Brad Hayes, Idaho Falls	6
	Robert Mosby, Billings	6
BB	Cory Dunlap, Ogden	68
IBB	Tony Festa, Helena	4
HBP	Sean Rodriguez, Provo	15
SO	Robert Mosby, Billings	87
SB	Brian McFall, Idaho Falls	23
	Steve Sollmann, Helena	23
CS	Scott Martin, Great Falls	10
GIDP	Alex Batista, Idaho Falls	15
OBP	Cory Dunlap, Ogden	.492
SLG	Brian McFall, Idaho Falls	.618

PITCHING

G	Josh Newman, Casper	27
GS	Samuel Deduno, Casper	15
	Franklin Morales, Casper	15
CG	Five tied at	1
ShO	Franklin Morales, Casper	1
GF	Mark Alexander, Ogden	24
SV	Mitchell Arnold, Provo	13
W	Tyler Pelland, Billings	9
L	Shane Dove, Missoula	9
IP	Samuel Deduno, Casper	76
H	Franklin Morales, Casper	92
R	Franklin Morales, Casper	61
ER	Franklin Morales, Casper	55
HR	Ben Krantz, Missoula	11
HB	Jake Mullis, Idaho Falls	13
BB	David Parker, Ogden	41
	Sony Suarez, Great Falls	41
SO	Samuel Deduno, Casper	118
WP	Jacobo Meque, Billings	15
	Tyler Pelland, Billings	15
BK	Jacobo Meque, Billings	7

FIELDING

C	PCT	Donny Lucy, Great Falls	.988
	PO	Donny Lucy, Great Falls	357
	A	Tim Duff, Provo	63
	E	Wilkin Castillo, Missoula	11
	DP	Kengshill Pujols, Ogden	3
		Alberto Segura, Helena	3
	PB	Ryan Fox, Casper	29
1B	PCT	Chris Kelly, Great Falls	.994
	PO	Javier Brito, Missoula	452
		Chris Kelly, Great Falls	452
	A	Javier Brito, Missoula	30
	E	Mike Davies, Casper	9
	DP	Robert Mosby, Billings	51
2B	PCT	Trevor Lawhorn, Billings	.978
	PO	Boomer Berry, Great Falls	152
	A	Steve Sollmann, Helena	178
	E	Josh Leblanc, Provo	22
	DP	Trevor Lawhorn, Billings	41
		Steve Sollmann, Helena	41
3B	PCT	Tony Festa, Helena	.963
	PO	Blake DeWitt, Ogden	45
	A	Tony Festa, Helena	145
	E	Blake DeWitt, Ogden	20
	DP	Billy Butler, Idaho Falls	11
		Brad Key, Billings	11
SS	PCT	Paul Janish, Billings	.975
	PO	Sean Rodriguez, Provo	123
	A	Alcides Escobar, Helena	224
	E	Sean Rodriguez, Provo	27
	DP	Sean Rodriguez, Provo	52
OF	PCT	Phillip Gentry, Billings	1.000
	PO	Miguel Matos, Missoula	115
	A	Brian McFall, Idaho Falls	19
	E	Alex Batista, Idaho Falls	9
	DP	Five at	2

BY ALLAN SIMPSON

The crackdown on temporary visas to foreign players in 2004 affected every league at the entry level of professional baseball, but none was impacted to a greater degree than the Rookie-level Arizona League.

A league normally top-heavy in teenage talent of foreign origin, the AZL was allowed to relax its rules as they

Matt Tuiasosopo

pertain to age and prior experience, and the Giants and Athletics, with pitching staffs composed almost entirely of players ranging from 20 to 24, not unexpectedly dominated the league.

The Giants won the first half of the league's split-season schedule and the A's the second half, before the Giants beat the A's 3-2 in a one-game championship final. Righthanders Osiris Matos, 20, and Kellen Ludwig, 21, the team's two top starters during the regular season, combined to hold the A's to five hits, with Ludwig coming on in the top of the 7th inning to stop a two-run uprising. He blanked the A's the rest of the way to earn just his second save of the season. It was the first Arizona League title for the Giants.

Outfielder Mike Mooney, 21, was the only Giants player named to the league's all-star team. A second-year player, he led the league with 57 RBIs while finishing tied for second with six home runs.

Meanwhile, a high school shortstop from the 2004 draft earned the distinction of being the league's No. 1 prospect, though it wasn't the Padres Matt Bush, the first overall pick in the draft.

Bush's career got off on the wrong foot when he got in a bar fight on the eve of the Arizona League season, was charged with three misdemeanors and was suspended for several weeks by the Padres. Things didn't get a lot better when he was reinstated. His debut drew mixed reviews from managers, who expected to see a five-tool talent and didn't. He was overmatched at the plate, hitting .181-0-10 in 72 at-bats, and he battled a hamstring problem.

Mariners shortstop Matt Tuiasosopo, who signed a record $2.29 million bonus as a third-round pick, upstaged Bush and was named the league's best prospect. He made a statement in his first professional at-bat, homering off the Giants, and went on to hit

.412-4-12 in 68 at-bats before being promoted to short-season Everett.

"He overmatched this league," A's manager Ruben Escalera said. "He's got the whole package—all five tools."

The league's most dominant player was Brewers second baseman Hernan Iribarren, who ran away with the batting title and was named the league's Most Valuable Player. The lefthanded-hitting Iribarren finished 88 points ahead of his nearest competitor in the batting race. His .438 average was the second-highest in league history, topped only by the .451 mark compiled by the Padres' Tim McWilliam in 1988, the league's inaugural season. He also led the league in hits (83), on-base percentage (.490) and slugging percentage (.630).

"He was the most polished player in the league, by far, and should have been in a higher league from the start," Mariners manager Scott Steinmann said. "He's a solid little second baseman and really understands every part of the game."

While Bush didn't distinguish himself in his pro debut, neither did Brewers righthander Mark Rogers, the first high school pitcher drafted in 2004. Rogers didn't win a game, going 0-3, 4.73. But his stuff was the talk of the league and he was unhittable when he was on his game.

"He didn't have a great season, but we're satisfied with his progress," Brewers manager Mike Guerrero said. "You need to go slowly with him. He doesn't know what he's capable of yet. But he's a smart, coachable kid who applies what you teach him."

A's righthander Connor Robertson, 23, was typical of the older players that infiltrated the Arizona League in 2004. Robertson led the league with 13 saves—more than double his closest pursuer—while posting a 0.92 ERA. He also walked only eight while striking out 46 in 29 innings.

STANDINGS: SPLIT SEASON

FIRST HALF	W	L	PCT	GB	SECOND HALF	W	L	PCT	GB
Giants	18	9	.667	—	Athletics	20	8	.714	—
Royals	16	12	.571	2½	Giants	18	10	.643	2
Rangers	16	12	.571	2½	Rangers	16	12	.571	4
Mariners	16	12	.571	2½	Mariners	15	13	.536	5
Brewers	15	13	.536	3½	Cubs	15	13	.536	5
Athletics	14	14	.500	4½	Royals	13	15	.464	7
Padres	13	15	.464	5½	Padres	13	15	.464	7
Cubs	12	16	.429	6½	Brewers	9	19	.321	11
Angels	5	22	.185	13	Angels	7	21	.250	13

PLAYOFFS—Giants defeated Athletics in one-game playoff.

STANDINGS: OVERALL

Page		Complex Site	W	L	Pct.	GB	Manager	Last Penn.
249	Giants	Scottsdale	36	19	.655	—	Bert Hunter	2004
212	Athletics	Phoenix	34	22	.607	2½	Ruben Escalera	2001
270	Rangers	Surprise	32	24	.571	4½	Pedro Lopez	None
256	Mariners	Peoria	31	25	.554	5½	Scott Steinmann	2000
159	Royals	Surprise	29	27	.518	7½	Lloyd Simmons	2003
108	Cubs	Mesa	27	29	.482	9½	Trey Forkerway	2002
242	Padres	Peoria	26	30	.464	10½	Carlos Lezcano	None
173	Brewers	Phoenix	24	32	.429	12½	Mike Guerrero	1990
62	Angels	Mesa	12	43	.218	24	Brian Harper	None

NOTE: Team's individual batting and pitching statistics can be found on page indicated in lefthand column.

2004 ARIZONA LEAGUE STATISTICS

CLUB BATTING

	AVG	G	AB	R	H	2B	3B	HR	BB	SO	SB
Mariners	.288	56	1937	334	557	105	23	20	171	417	80
Giants	.283	56	1941	343	549	104	33	21	219	419	93
Padres	.267	56	1978	278	529	99	24	11	171	400	59
Brewers	.266	56	1949	270	518	98	33	18	175	468	79
Cubs	.263	56	1914	275	503	85	28	8	190	453	41
Athletics	.255	56	1857	314	474	104	28	24	230	441	100
Rangers	.254	56	1896	301	482	91	25	30	232	520	63
Royals	.252	56	1858	290	469	84	28	26	243	469	107
Angels	.236	56	1912	201	451	72	21	11	162	476	76

CLUB PITCHING

	ERA	G	CG	SHO	SV	IP	H	R	ER	BB	SO
Athletics	3.31	56	0	2	15	494	493	254	182	154	439
Giants	3.52	56	0	4	18	498	479	265	195	198	532
Royals	3.64	56	0	2	12	496	509	261	201	182	414
Padres	3.70	56	0	2	15	503	502	269	207	171	427
Rangers	4.10	56	0	4	11	495	511	288	226	173	414
Brewers	4.12	56	0	2	10	495	490	307	227	247	416
Cubs	4.27	56	0	2	10	499	519	311	237	215	482
Mariners	4.54	56	0	1	15	493	497	319	249	225	487
Angels	4.85	56	0	0	7	498.	532	332	269	226	453

CLUB FIELDING

	PCT	PO	A	E	DP		PCT	PO	A	E	DP
Royals	.958	1489	647	93	56	Padres	.953	1510	607	105	51
Cubs	.956	1497	599	96	45	Mariners	.952	1479	562	102	39
Rangers	.956	1485	637	98	50	Brewers	.949	1486	602	112	49
Giants	.955	1494	565	96	39	Angels	.948	1495	544	112	51
Athletics	.954	1483	616	101	45						

INDIVIDUAL BATTING LEADERS
(Minimum 151 Plate Appearances)

	AVG	G	AB	R	H	2B	3B	HR	RBI	BB	SO	SB
Iribarren, Hernan, Brewers	.439	46	189	40	83	6	9	4	36	19	23	15
Disla, Lisandro, Giants	.351	48	168	27	59	7	1	0	25	18	29	4
Long, Wesley, Athletics	.345	54	206	45	71	17	1	4	35	31	36	9
Soto, Luis, Mariners	.331	37	148	35	49	12	3	2	27	13	22	2
Santin, Daniel, Mariners	.325	41	160	31	52	13	2	4	28	10	21	2
Cruceta, Julio, Padres	.318	43	176	22	56	7	5	0	20	5	23	9
Quinones, Carlos, Cubs	.315	53	216	28	68	12	1	0	28	19	33	9
Mooney, Mike, Giants	.312	55	215	43	67	11	7	6	57	25	45	7
Padron, Raul, Athletics	.306	40	147	23	45	14	4	1	35	16	25	6
Puello, Elvin, Cubs	.302	53	189	26	57	7	3	1	37	12	38	1

INDIVIDUAL PITCHING LEADERS
(Minimum 45 Innings)

	W	L	ERA	G	GS	CG	SV	IP	H	R	ER	BB	SO
Acevedo, Danielin, Athletics	3	2	2.17	10	9	0	0	54	63	26	13	11	42
Ludwig, Kellen, Giants	3	2	2.28	11	7	0	1	47	43	17	12	11	55
Krosschell, Ben, Padres	1	3	2.42	14	11	0	0	48	48	21	13	19	40
Matos, Osiris, Giants	2	0	2.44	11	8	0	1	48	43	23	13	20	47
Lluveres, Rafael, Brewers	2	4	2.80	12	8	0	0	45	35	20	14	26	39
Shearer, Kelly, Angels	2	3	2.82	13	9	0	0	51	42	22	16	23	36
Perez, Roberto, Rangers	4	3	3.61	14	6	0	0	57	50	24	23	17	48
Yepez, Jesus, Cubs	1	2	3.66	12	8	0	0	47	44	27	19	24	44
Begnaud, Rusty, Royals	4	3	3.74	14	10	0	1	65	71	36	27	10	75
Morales, Angelo, Royals	6	4	3.96	14	10	0	0	61	76	34	27	9	45

ALL-STAR TEAM

C—Daniel Santin, Mariners. **1B**—Miguel Vega, Royals. **2B**—Hernan Iribarren, Brewers. **3B**—Wesley Long, Athletics. **SS**—Wilber Perez, Athletics. **OF**—Mike Mooney, Giants; Carlos Quinones, Cubs; K.C. Herren, Rangers. **DH**—Elvin Puello, Cubs. **RHP**—Rusty Begnaud, Royals. **LHP**—Andy Santana, Cubs. **RHRP**—Connor Robertson, Athletics. **LHRP**—Rafael Lluberes, Brewers.

Most Valuable Player: Hernan Iribarren, Brewers. **Manager of the Year:** Bert Hunter, Giants.

BATTING

G	Miguel Vega, Royals	56
	Judson Richards, Giants	56
AB	Miguel Vega, Royals	229
R	Marcus Sanders, Giants	54
H	Hernan Iribarren, Brewers	83
TB	Hernan Iribarren, Brewers	119
XBH	Miguel Vega, Royals	30
2B	Wesley Long, Athletics	17
3B	Hernan Iribarren, Brewers	9
HR	Miguel Vega, Royals	10
RBI	Mike Mooney, Giants	57
SH	Daniel Desouza, Giants	6
SF	Mike Mooney, Giants	6
BB	Josh Johnson, Royals	55
IBB	Several tied at	2
HBP	Jarred Ellis, Royals	13
	Elvin Puello, Cubs	13
SO	Jared Ellis, Royals	81
SB	Marcus Sanders, Giants	28
CS	Josh Johnson, Royals	13
GIDP	Elvin Puello, Cubs	10
OBP	Hernan Iribarren, Brewers	.490
SLG	Hernan Iribarren, Brewers	.630

PITCHING

G	Connor Robertson, Athletics	25
GS	Five tied at	11
CG	None	
ShO	None	
GF	Connor Robertson, Athletics	22
SV	Connor Robertson, Athletics	13
W	Oliver Arias, Mariners	6
	Angelo Morales, Royals	6
L	Eliszer Garcia, Royals	7
IP	Rusty Begnaud, Royals	65
H	Angelo Morales, Royals	76
R	Oliver Arias, Mariners	41
ER	Oliver Arias, Mariners	35
	Fabian Jimenez Angulo, Padres	35
HR	William Labasta, Brewers	7
HB	Chris Rayborn, Padres	9
	Joe Woerman, Mariners	9
BB	Lennyn Morillo, Angels	31
SO	Rusty Begnaud, Royals	75
WP	Tim Dorn, Mariners	11
BK	Several tied at	3

FIELDING

C	AVG	Nestor Corredor, Brewers	.989
	PO	Pablo Sandoval, Giants	300
	A	Pablo Sandoval, Giants	41
	E	Robert Grana, Royals	10
	DP	Angel Sanchez, Angels	4
	PB	Leonel Perez, Cubs	15
1B	AVG	Freddy Thon, Rangers	.989
	PO	Judson Richards, Giants	455
	A	Judson Richards, Giants	36
	E	Judson Richards, Giants	13
	DP	Freddy Thon, Rangers	35
2B	AVG	Irving Falu, Royals	.977
	PO	Hernan Iribarren, Brewers	113
	A	Hernan Iribarren, Brewers	142
	E	Marcus Sanders, Giants	14
	DP	Hernan Iribarren, Brewers	31
3B	AVG	Lisandro Disla, Giants	.933
	PO	Wesley Long, Athletics	139
	A	Freddy de la Cruz, Brewers	79
	E	Trey Johnston, Padres	13
		Wesley Long, Athletics	13
	DP	Freddy de la Cruz, Brewers	8
		Trey Johnston, Padres	8
SS	AVG	Frank Martinez, Athletics	.919
	PO	Frank Martinez, Athletics	63
	A	Frank Martinez, Athletics	133
	E	Lenny Leclercq, Brewers	28
	DP	Frank Martinez, Athletics	22
OF	AVG	Nate Whitney, Padres	.977
	PO	Freddy Parejo, Brewers	95
	A	Freddy Parejo, Brewers	9
	E	K.C. Herren, Rangers	8
	DP	Freddy Parejo, Brewers	3

BY ALLAN SIMPSON

Evan Tierce was barely on the radar for most of the 2004 Gulf Coast League season, but he certainly made his presence felt in the final days of the campaign.

Not only did the Yankees center fielder win the batting title on the last day of the season, but he was the offensive star for the Yankees as they won the league playoffs, beating the Red Sox in two straight games.

Tierce, a 17th-round draft pick out of Texas State, started the 2004 season at short-season Staten Island but was sent down after hitting only .184 in 38 at-bats. Though he was hitting .359 in the GCL entering the final game of the season, he didn't have enough plate appearances to officially qualify for the batting title. But by going 2-for-5 in the season finale, he pushed himself over the limit, finishing at .361.

Tierce then went 4-for-9 with three RBIs as the Northern Division champion Yankees swept the Red Sox in the league's best-of-3 final. Righthander Christian Garcia allowed one run and one hit in six innings in an

Kyle Waldrop
ROBERT GURGANUS

8-1 win in Game One, while Maximo Nelson allowed one run in five innings in an 11-2 win in game Two. It was the Yankees' first league title since 2001.

The Red Sox, winners of the Southern Division, defeated the Eastern Division champion Mets in a sudden-death semifinal, 9-2. The Red Sox jumped on league ERA leader Gaby Hernandez for seven runs in 2⅓ innings—one more earned run than he gave up in nine regular season starts.

For the second time in three years, the league's No. 1 prospect was a 6-foot-1, 170-pound, 18-year-old Red Sox shortstop from the Dominican Republic.

Hanley Ramirez was the rage of the league in 2002, when he hit .341-6-26 and flashed five-tool ability. Now 20 and on the fast track to Boston, Ramirez started the 2004 season at high Class A Sarasota and finished it at

Double-A Portland. He hit .310 at both stops.

The latest Red Sox phenom is Luis Soto, signed to a $500,000 bonus by the Red Sox in November, 2003. He hit only .261—80 points less than Ramirez in his U.S. debut—and committed 14 errors in 30 games. But he was no less a prospect than Ramirez in the eyes of GCL managers.

"He's the best in the league," said Reds manager Freddie Benavides, a former big league shortstop. "He can do it all, both ways. His tools are comparable to Ramirez, but he may be a better prospect because he has a much better attitude."

Had they pitched more, 2004 first-round picks Homer Bailey (Reds) and Philip Hughes (Yankees) might have wrested the No. 1 spot from Soto, but neither worked the required 20 innings to qualify for the list. Bailey, whose fastball touched 97 mph, was placed on a strict pitch count by the Reds after pitching nearly 100 innings in the spring at La Grange (Texas) High. He made six starts in the GCL but toiled only 12 innings. Hughes, who topped out at 95, was limited to three innings because of a tender arm.

Other first-rounders to debut in the league were Pirates catcher Neil Walker, Phillies center fielder Greg Golson and Twins righthander Kyle Waldrop.

The 6-foot-5 Waldrop, who went 22-0 in his final two years at Knoxville's Farragut High, was as advanced as any prep pitcher drafted. With three pitches he threw for strikes almost at will, he walked only four in 38 innings before being promoted to the more challenging Appalachian League, where he walked three in 25 innings.

"He's very advanced for 18," Twins manager Riccardo Ingram said. "He can pound the strike zone with three pitches. His fastball is 88-89 mph, but with a tall, slender body, you know there's more (velocity) in there."

No pitcher put together more impressive control numbers, however, than Phillies righthander Scott Mitchinson, an Australian who walked only one in 62 innings while striking out 60. He also tied for the league lead with seven wins while his 1.75 ERA ranked second.

STANDINGS

Page	EAST	Complex Site	W	L	Pct.	GB	Manager	Last Penn.
205	Mets	St. Lucie	36	24	.600	—	Brett Butler	None
146	Marlins	Jupiter	31	29	.517	5	Tim Cossins	None
166	Dodgers	Vero Beach	31	29	.517	5	Luis Salazar	1990
188	Expos	Melbourne	22	38	.367	14	Arturo DeFreites	1991
Page	**SOUTH**	**Complex Site**	**W**	**L**	**Pct.**	**GB**	**Manager**	**Last Penn.**
92	Red Sox	Fort Myers	34	24	.586	—	Ralph Treuel	None
179	Twins	Fort Myers	31	26	.544	2 ½	Riccardo Ingram	None
226	Pirates	Bradenton	30	28	.517	4	Woody Huyke	None
115	Reds	Sarasota	20	37	.351	13 ½	Freddie Benavides	None
Page	**NORTH**	**Complex Site**	**W**	**L**	**Pct.**	**GB**	**Manager**	**Last Penn.**
196	Yankees	Tampa	36	23	.610	—	Oscar Acosta	2004
219	Phillies	Clearwater	36	24	.600	½	Roly deArmas	2002
138	Tigers	Lakeland	24	36	.400	12 ½	Kevin Bradshaw	None
77	Braves	Kissimmee	23	36	.390	13	Ralph Henriquez	2003

PLAYOFFS—Semifinal: Red Sox defeated Mets in one-game playoff; Yankees received first-round bye. **Finals:** Yankees defeated Red Sox 2-0 in best-of-3 series.

NOTE: Teams' individual batting and pitching statistics can be found on page indicated in lefthand column.

2004 GULF COAST LEAGUE STATISTICS

CLUB BATTING

	AVG	G	AB	R	H	2B	3B	HR	BB	SO	SB
Red Sox	.277	58	1923	298	533	101	14	29	191	347	63
Yankees	.263	59	1897	257	498	79	13	27	190	428	72
Mets	.261	60	1970	297	515	95	21	27	207	441	70
Dodgers	.258	60	2086	288	539	90	27	25	163	427	63
Twins	.254	57	1853	245	471	79	12	19	171	362	64
Pirates	.253	58	1879	255	476	98	19	23	151	396	60
Phillies	.249	60	1909	267	475	79	14	42	177	476	55
Marlins	.241	60	1931	273	465	94	15	12	205	463	62
Braves	.236	59	1901	226	448	80	11	41	153	504	64
Tigers	.234	60	1964	234	459	62	18	32	178	555	64
Expos	.223	60	1856	216	414	73	11	17	212	458	60
Reds	.213	57	1759	198	374	69	21	23	190	509	70

CLUB PITCHING

	ERA	G	CG	SHO	SV	IP	H	R	ER	BB	SO
Yankees	2.87	59	0	10	20	492	428	184	157	139	529
Red Sox	2.99	58	1	3	18	490	462	222	163	161	403
Phillies	3.12	60	0	5	16	490	461	228	170	129	461
Pirates	3.31	58	2	2	12	486	430	224	179	162	384
Marlins	3.36	60	0	6	12	513	461	251	192	200	435
Dodgers	3.41	60	0	3	15	534	475	250	202	219	470
Twins	3.50	57	0	3	15	478	494	270	186	163	446
Tigers	3.79	60	2	3	7	515	469	268	217	233	512
Mets	3.84	60	2	5	13	513	479	269	219	192	463
Reds	3.98	57	0	4	8	476	468	280	211	217	381
Expos	4.39	60	0	3	13	499	518	304	244	176	421
Braves	4.42	59	0	3	10	494	522	304	243	197	461

CLUB FIELDING

	PCT	PO	A	E	DP		PCT	PO	A	E	DP
Tigers	.968	1546	548	70	45	Mets	.960	1539	567	87	27
Yankees	.967	1475	537	69	38	Phillies	.960	1469	546	84	55
Pirates	.966	1459	613	72	43	Marlins	.957	1539	602	96	51
Dodgers	.964	1601	633	83	34	Expos	.956	1498	571	95	23
Red Sox	.963	1471	641	81	45	Reds	.953	1428	580	100	58
Braves	.962	1483	543	80	40	Twins	.952	1434	565	101	39

INDIVIDUAL BATTING LEADERS
(Minimum 159 Plate Appearances)

	AVG	G	AB	R	H	2B	3B	HR	RBI	BB	SO	SB
Tierce, Evan, Yankees	.361	40	147	26	53	11	1	1	14	14	16	13
Portes, Juan, Twins	.327	44	168	24	55	8	1	8	30	12	28	4
Arratia, Jilmer, Twins	.320	49	175	16	56	9	2	2	29	10	25	12
Hoffmann, Jamie, Dodgers	.310	60	229	40	71	8	7	4	36	24	38	14
Messner, Nate, Marlins	.310	44	155	23	48	7	0	2	29	13	36	2
Sutherland, David, Dodgers	.301	50	153	22	46	2	3	0	14	9	15	4
Peterson, James, Dodgers	.295	47	176	19	52	14	2	6	32	13	38	2
Golson, Greg, Phillies	.295	47	183	34	54	8	5	1	22	10	54	12
Soto, Jesus, Dodgers	.292	48	171	33	50	11	2	4	18	10	18	5
Wells, Cory, Mets	.291	44	148	23	43	12	1	3	21	11	39	9

INDIVIDUAL PITCHING LEADERS
(Minimum 47 Innings)

	W	L	ERA	G	GS	CG	SV	IP	H	R	ER	BB	SO
Hernandez, Gaby, Mets	3	3	1.09	10	9	2	0	50	25	10	6	12	58
Mitchinson, Scott, Phillies	7	0	1.75	10	10	0	0	62	40	12	12	1	60
De la Cruz, Maximino, Phillies	4	3	2.11	12	11	0	0	60	64	25	14	13	54
Sosa, Gabriel, Expos	5	2	2.29	11	9	0	0	51	36	16	13	23	63
Wilson, Jonathan, Red Sox	5	1	2.50	11	6	0	0	54	44	21	15	11	39
Alvarez, Basilio, Pirates	3	3	2.55	11	5	0	0	49	42	22	14	9	41
Stephens, Jay, Yankees	5	3	2.61	13	8	0	1	48	55	23	14	10	48
Swarzak, Anthony, Twins	5	3	2.63	11	9	0	1	48	46	20	14	6	42
Nelson, Maximo, Yankees	6	3	2.63	12	9	0	0	55	48	16	16	12	54
French, Luke, Tigers	1	3	2.74	11	10	0	0	49	43	21	15	19	49

ALL-STAR TEAM

C—Jesus Flores, Mets. **1B**—Carlos Torres, Red Sox. **2B**—Jesus Soto, Dodgers. **3B**—Jamie Hoffmann, Dodgers. **SS**—Sean Henry, Mets. **OF**—Yosvani Almario-Cabrera, Yankees; Jilmer Arratia, Twins; Evan Tierce, Yankees. **SP**—Scott Mitchinson, Phillies. **RP**—Howar Zuleta, Dodgers.

Manager of the Year: Oscar Acosta, Yankees.

BATTING

G	Jamie Hoffmann, Dodgers	60
AB	Jamie Hoffmann, Dodgers	229
R	Jamie Hoffmann, Dodgers	40
H	Jamie Hoffmann, Dodgers	71
TB	Jamie Hoffmann, Dodgers	105
XBH	Maximiliano Ramirez, Braves	25
2B	Maximiliano Ramirez, Braves	16
3B	Jamie Hoffmann, Dodgers	7
HR	Four tied at	8
RBI	Jamie Hoffmann, Dodgers	36
SH	Todd Dulaney, Mets	5
SF	Edward Ovalle, Twins	6
BB	Armand Gaerlan, Mets	42
IBB	Jamie Hoffman, Dodgers	4
HBP	Odannys Valdez, Twins	14
SO	Jeramy Laster, Tigers	63
SB	Ovandy Suero, Braves	30
CS	Jose Campusano, Marlins	10
GIDP	Manuel Rodriguez, Braves	8
OBP	Evan Tierce, Yankees	.420
SLG	Juan Portes, Twins	.530

PITCHING

G	Jose Fragoso, Tigers	23
	Howar Zuleta, Dodgers	23
GS	Aaron Easton, Marlins	13
CG	Gaby Hernandez, Mets	2
	Jair Jurrjens, Tigers	2
ShO	Three tied at	1
GF	Blake Cross, Braves	16
	Howar Zuleta, Dodgers	16
SV	Nolan Moser, Red Sox	7
	Howar Zuleta, Dodgers	7
W	Scott Mitchinson, Phillies	7
	Luis Valdez, Pirates	7
L	Ricardo Morales, Expos	7
IP	Scott Mitchinson, Phillies	62
H	Maximo Delacruz, Phillies	64
R	Julian de la Cruz, Dodgers	39
ER	Julian de la Cruz, Dodgers	31
HR	Jay Sborz, Tigers	9
HB	Geovanny Adames, Reds	9
	Robbie Wachman, Reds	9
BB	Jay Sborz, Tigers	44
SO	Gabriel Sosa, Expos	63
WP	Orlando Perdomo, Tigers	16
BK	Mario Pena, Red Sox	4

FIELDING

C	AVG	Nathan Griffin, Yankees	1.000
	PO	Jesus Flores, Mets	289
	A	Reynaldo Gonzalez, Reds	36
	E	Tanner Rogers, Marlins	10
	DP	Reynaldo Gonzalez, Reds	5
	PB	Rotsen Gil, Reds	11
1B	AVG	David Sutherland, Dodgers	.997
	PO	Victor Hamisevicz, Expos	409
	A	Juan Figueroa, Marlins	30
	E	Brandon Roberts, Reds	7
	DP	Juan Figueroa, Marlins	30
2B	AVG	Stephen Young, Tigers	.983
	PO	Ovandy Suero, Braves	102
	A	Mayker Sandoval, Reds	109
	E	Mayker Sandoval, Reds	10
		Ovandy Suero, Braves	10
	DP	Ovandy Suero, Braves	29
3B	AVG	Jesus Rodriguez, Marlins	.955
	PO	Jamie Hoffmann, Dodgers	59
	A	Jamie Hoffmann, Dodgers	111
	E	Carlos Sanchez, Reds	14
	DP	Welinson Baez, Phillies	9
		Maximiliano Ramirez, Braves	9
SS	AVG	Brad Harman, Phillies	.928
	PO	Jose Campusano, Marlins	110
	A	Jose Campusano, Marlins	143
	E	Jose Campusano, Marlins	28
	DP	Jose Campusano, Marlins	28
OF	AVG	Kent Wulf, Pirates	1.000
	PO	Rafael Batista, Expos	94
	A	Rafael Batista, Expos	10
	E	Rafael Batista, Expos	8
	DP	Andrew Macfarlane, Phillies	4

DOMINICAN SUMMER LEAGUE

The Cleveland Indians didn't make the headway they hoped for at the major league level in 2004, finishing two games below .500. But their farm system had a banner '04 season with four teams winning league championships.

That included the more competitive of Cleveland's two entries in the sprawling 32-team Dominican Summer League. Indians I went 53-16 during the regular season to win the Santo Domingo East/American title by a handy nine-game margin, then won five of seven playoff games to win their second title in three years.

The Indians were stretched to the limit by Yankees I in the best-of-five final before prevailing 6-5 in 14 innings in the deciding game. Shortstop and series MVP Argenis Tavarez stroked a one-out double to center to drive home Luis Camacaro with the winning run. Tavarez had two homers, six RBIs and three stolen bases in the five-game series.

Cleveland (.768) and Kansas City (.778) received first-round byes in the playoffs because they posted the best overall records among six division champions. The Royals, however, lost 2-1 in the semifinals to Yankees I, who also beat the Mariners 2-1 in the quarterfinals.

Switch-hitting outfielder Jose Constanza, 20, led Indians I to the division title by topping the DSL with a .444 average, 72 runs, 115 hits and 19 triples. His average, hits and triples were all league records.

"He plays the game like he's been playing it forever," Indians Director of Latin American Operations Ross Atkins said. "He can drag bunt, push it out there or he'll square to bunt, pull the infield in and then rope a line drive over the third baseman's head. He has ridiculous bat control and it seemed like he got two hits every single day."

The league's most dominant pitcher was 25-year-old Cubs lefthander Raul Valdez, who went 7-2, 0.51 and overmatched younger players with a league record 152 strikeouts in 88 innings. In one seven-inning outing, he struck out 20.

Valdez normally would have pitched in the United States in 2004, but he was a victim of the temporary embargo on H-2B work visas imposed by the U.S. government and had to spend the season in the Dominican. Major League Baseball relaxed age and service time restrictions for the DSL and other short-season leagues to cope with the problem.

While the DSL has grown exponentially from its humble beginnings of four teams in 1985 to a record 35 teams in 2003, it actually experienced a decline in 2004 as three teams—the Brewers, Cardinals and Devil Rays—did not field teams. In addition to the Indians, the Athletics, Braves, Dodgers and Yankees all fielded two teams.

—ALLAN SIMPSON

ALL-STAR TEAM: C—Jonathan Jaspe, Blue Jays. **1B**—Angel Reyes, Tigers. **2B**—Jorge Patino, Tigers. **3B**—Manuel Rafael, Red Sox. **SS**—Garivaldis Perez, Royals. **OF**—Jose Constanza, Indians !; Jose Duarte, Royals; Jairo Hernandez, Mariners. **DH**—Joan Silva, Angels. **RHP**—Raul Valdez, Cubs. **LHP**—Johan Pino, Twins. **RP**—Samuel Gervacio, Astros.

Most Valuable Player: Jose Constanza, Indians 1. **Most Valuable Pitcher:** Johan Pino, Twins. **Manager of the Year:** Julio Bruno, Royals.

STANDINGS

SANTO DOMINGO EAST/American	W	L	PCT	GB
Indians I	53	16	.768	—
Tigers	44	25	.638	9
Indians II	36	31	.537	16
Twins	36	33	.522	17
Red Sox	33	35	.485	19½
SANTO DOMINGO EAST/National	**W**	**L**	**PCT**	**GB**
Giants	36	32	.529	—
Diamondbacks	33	36	.478	3½
Rockies	33	37	.471	4
Cubs	27	42	.391	9½
Reds	24	46	.343	13
Dodgers I	22	44	.333	13
SANTO DOMINGO NORTH	**W**	**L**	**PCT**	**GB**
Mariners	50	21	.704	—
Dodgers II	47	23	.671	2½
Athletics I	34	36	.486	15½
Phillies	31	39	.443	18½
Expos	30	38	.441	18½
Athletics II	18	53	.254	32
SANTO DOMINGO WEST	**W**	**L**	**PCT**	**GB**
Yankees I	50	21	.704	—
Padres	40	31	.563	10
Mets	34	37	.479	16
Yankees II	18	53	.254	32
SAN PEDRO de MACORIS	**W**	**L**	**PCT**	**GB**
Blue Jays	51	19	.729	—
Angels	45	26	.634	6½
Orioles	33	38	.465	18½
Astros	31	39	.443	20
Pirates	26	44	.371	25
Rangers	26	46	.361	26
CIBAO	**W**	**L**	**PCT**	**GB**
Royals	49	14	.778	—
White Sox	36	26	.581	12½
Marlins	29	36	.446	21
Braves II	27	36	.429	22
Braves I	17	46	.270	32

PLAYOFFS: Quarterfinals—Yankees I defeated Mariners 2-1 and Blue Jays defeated Giants 2-0 in best-of-3 series. **Semifinals**—Indians defeated Blue Jays 2-0 and Yankees I defeated Royals 2-1 in best-of-3 series. **Finals**—Indians defeated Yankees I 3-2 in best-of-5 series.

INDIVIDUAL BATTING LEADERS
(Minimum 150 At-Bats)

	AVG	AB	R	H	2B	3B	HR	RBI	SB
Constanza, Jose, Indians I	.444	259	72	115	12	19	1	40	37
Perez, Garivaldis, Royals	.366	227	55	83	13	4	2	26	19
Perez, Alwin, Royals	.353	190	39	67	8	3	0	35	8
Ciriaco, Pedro, Diamondbacks	.349	252	52	88	11	4	1	18	29
Perez, Eduardo, Dodgers II	.348	178	30	62	13	0	3	23	7
Acosta, Cristian, White Sox	.347	199	33	69	13	0	5	35	9
Infante, Larry, Angels	.344	218	45	75	12	5	0	24	24
Gonzalez, Jesus, Blue Jays	.339	230	38	78	14	5	7	44	0
Hernandez, Jairo, Mariners	.332	214	42	71	12	3	6	42	22
Sanchez, Salvador, White Sox	.330	209	35	69	13	2	4	37	4
Patino, Jorge, Tigers	.327	251	53	82	9	3	0	14	20
Gonzalez, Adolfo, Dodgers II	.325	206	28	67	10	1	1	36	5
Batista, Norberto, Marlins	.325	194	39	63	10	0	1	29	27
Moreno, Pedro, White Sox	.324	179	30	58	16	0	4	32	10
Duarte, Jose, Royals	.317	218	52	69	12	3	2	39	10
Rafael, Manuel, Red Sox	.315	257	50	81	20	5	1	45	9
Rivadeneira, Deivis, Braves II	.315	216	36	68	11	3	3	28	19
Silva, Johan, Angels	.314	204	37	64	16	3	2	40	9
Mercedes, Mario, Cubs	.311	177	20	55	4	1	2	18	0
Santana, Richard, Red Sox	.308	263	48	81	6	5	2	30	49
Veloz, Vladimir, Marlins	.308	172	32	53	14	1	3	30	6
Quinones, Carlos, Cubs	.304	224	37	68	11	2	0	26	6
Alvarado, Ramon, Athletics I	.303	195	29	59	12	3	1	27	7
Aguilar, Heliezer, Blue Jays	.303	218	47	66	14	1	3	22	9
Morel, Alvis, Royals	.301	219	52	66	6	1	2	23	16
Rodriguez, Orlando, Tigers	.300	230	41	69	16	2	0	29	9
Peralta, Felix, Royals	.299	204	38	61	10	3	0	35	7
Volquez, Bienvenido, Indians I	.298	228	43	68	11	6	2	30	7
Santos, Jose, Braves II	.297	222	38	66	6	4	0	29	25
Lachapelle, Alex, White Sox	.297	175	34	52	12	0	9	30	6

Player, Team	AVG	AB	R	H	2B	3B	HR	RBI	SB
De la Cruz, Angel, Rangers	.295	193	32	57	9	5	6	29	4
Sojo, Richard, Twins	.294	201	26	59	12	2	5	20	14
Corro, Abdiel, Expos	.294	211	24	62	12	1	3	28	2
Manzanillo, Gerson, Yankees I	.294	218	40	64	4	2	0	20	38
Palmares, Gregory, Cubs	.292	154	19	45	5	2	1	12	2
Garth, Ronald, Mariners	.290	207	37	60	11	0	2	21	18
Guzman, Francisco, Expos	.289	239	36	69	13	0	5	29	14
Matos, Willie, Royals	.289	166	31	48	15	2	6	36	0
Silverio, Rigoberto, Marlins	.288	191	33	55	6	2	0	16	10
Feliz, Moises, Rockies	.288	212	28	61	9	1	4	25	0
Arnal, Cristo, Indians II	.287	171	36	49	6	1	2	23	12
Perez, Hector, Giants	.286	217	27	62	8	3	6	25	12
Reyes, Angel, Tigers	.286	231	40	66	12	2	3	36	2
Morales, Saul, Cubs	.286	234	50	67	10	1	1	19	23
Amaro, Noel, Orioles	.284	155	27	44	9	5	0	22	11
Bautista, Pedruin, Tigers	.284	208	42	59	16	3	4	26	6
Pena, Virgilio, Indians II	.283	223	38	63	11	5	1	23	10
Sosa, Roberto, Red Sox	.282	177	33	50	15	1	6	35	1
Castro, Jonathan, Expos	.282	202	37	57	10	3	0	16	23
Gonzalez, Carlos, Phillies	.282	220	29	62	8	3	3	38	13
Cruz, Carlos, Padres	.280	175	23	49	9	3	1	24	13
Pimentel, Manelik, Mariners	.279	219	40	61	10	1	3	28	10
Herrera, Elian, Dodgers II	.278	187	39	52	5	2	0	18	22
Martinez, Abner, Phillies	.278	169	17	47	6	1	3	20	9
Martinez, Jose, Mets	.277	188	24	52	8	1	3	30	5
Camarena, Jose, Braves I	.277	177	22	49	13	2	2	26	4
Septimo, Leison, Diamondbacks	.276	221	29	61	9	3	2	25	8
Tavarez, Argenis, Indians I	.276	225	46	62	8	4	2	33	24
Obispo, Mario, Expos	.276	174	29	48	7	0	1	15	7
Herrera, Ronny, Rangers	.276	170	29	47	11	2	0	23	2
Escobar, Neison, Braves II	.276	163	23	45	17	1	1	18	13
Garcia, Santos, White Sox	.276	210	36	58	10	2	4	27	16
Caldera, Jose, Angels	.275	171	39	47	5	1	0	27	16
Carmona, Eliazar, Braves II	.274	168	28	46	6	1	0	15	17
Mesa, Maikol, Reds	.273	194	16	53	7	4	1	30	4
Montero, Lucas, Indians I	.272	180	35	49	6	5	4	26	10
Borg, Hector, Giants	.271	207	35	56	6	1	0	22	10
Guerrero, Santiago, Padres	.271	155	26	42	11	1	1	23	12
Dollis, Rafelito, Orioles	.271	181	28	49	6	2	2	22	1
Mejia, Jose, Mariners	.270	196	24	53	11	1	2	23	8
Baez, Juan, Astros	.270	226	36	61	13	3	1	23	8
Jaspe, Jonathan, Blue Jays	.270	233	43	63	20	2	4	41	3
Agustin, Juan, Marlins	.270	211	32	57	4	2	1	14	19
Hernandez, Eddy, Mariners	.269	197	18	53	10	1	2	31	6
Rodriguez, Concepcion, Braves I	.269	193	32	52	11	2	3	24	11
Hernandez, Ramon, Indians II	.268	164	27	44	2	1	0	11	18
Bermudez, Nestor, Blue Jays	.268	190	29	51	9	0	0	26	1
Cordero, Octavio, Blue Jays	.268	179	36	48	4	1	0	14	31
Nunez, Jose, Dodgers II	.267	232	38	62	13	1	6	28	3
Peralta, Johnny, Marlins	.267	176	18	47	9	4	1	26	13
Arnedo, Rolando, Expos	.266	158	20	42	10	0	1	15	4
Bonilla, Leury, Mariners	.266	229	38	61	7	2	2	29	27
Manzanillo, Jose, Twins	.265	155	19	41	16	0	1	18	0
Santana, Eddy, Orioles	.265	185	26	49	12	1	0	16	6
Florentino, Jhon, Astros	.265	238	41	63	14	3	6	36	9
DeJesus, Cristobal, White Sox	.265	155	32	41	3	2	2	13	16
Gonzalez, J.R., Reds	.264	182	21	48	9	4	1	23	4
Casso, Jorge, Braves I	.264	182	23	48	2	4	1	21	9
Almonte, Rafael, Cubs	.263	190	21	50	5	2	2	17	12
Garcia, Carlos, Phillies	.263	251	54	66	8	1	0	20	40
Medina, Erick, Braves II	.263	190	30	50	9	1	3	24	12
Ruiz, Donato, Mariners	.262	168	20	44	8	2	1	27	8
Bueno, Manuel, Astros	.262	248	31	65	7	2	1	17	22
Ramirez, Yorman, Indians II	.261	234	24	61	7	1	0	28	13
De los Santos, Deiby, Dodgers II	.261	222	36	58	17	4	2	31	20
Ortiz, Norberto, Angels	.261	199	30	52	11	0	2	19	8
Jimenez, Gustavo, Tigers	.261	203	23	53	12	1	4	35	0
Mayora, Daniel, Rockies	.261	261	35	68	14	6	1	35	24
Insunza, Miguel, Indians I	.260	204	32	53	13	0	3	33	4
Contreras, Rayner, Padres	.260	154	15	40	8	1	2	22	5
Ferrer, Manuel, Diamondbacks	.259	224	32	58	8	3	1	19	10
Rivas, Eduardo, Dodgers I	.259	166	31	43	7	4	2	18	20
Luque, William, Twins	.259	232	40	60	3	4	0	17	18
Gonzalez, Jarol, Padres	.259	189	27	49	8	1	0	22	5
#Santa, Moises, Red Sox	.257	202	24	52	7	1	**9**	36	6
#Moreno, Junior, Red Sox	.232	143	17	56	**21**	1	5	41	2
#Fermin, Angel, Yankees I	.211	166	22	35	7	0	**9**	26	1

INDIVIDUAL PITCHING LEADERS
(Minimum 50 Innings)

Player, Team	W	L	ERA	G	SV	IP	H	BB	SO
Valdez, Raul, Cubs	7	2	**0.51**	16	0	88	38	8	**152**
Pino, Joan, Twins	10	1	0.53	13	0	86	49	5	81
Paredes, Jesus, Yankees I	4	2	0.54	22	5	50	23	11	56
Vargas, Albert, Indians I	8	0	0.94	12	0	58	31	2	39
Lugo, Jose, Athletics I	5	1	1.05	13	0	68	45	25	61
Rosario, Francisco, Indians I	7	1	1.07	18	0	76	50	10	50
Soriano, Julio, Orioles	4	0	1.09	21	9	50	34	24	68
Valdez, Luis, Indians I	7	2	1.19	14	0	76	48	10	78
Gonzalez, Jose, Mets	8	0	1.21	13	0	74	53	17	68
Pinto, Julio, Indians I	8	2	1.24	15	1	87	50	12	95
Alvarez, Mario, Dodgers II	4	3	1.24	13	0	65	42	12	48
Morales, Jorge, Yankees I	5	2	1.29	11	1	63	38	5	47
Espinoza, Gustavo, Angels	6	2	1.36	14	0	92	46	16	105
Fernandez, Eddy, Mariners	5	1	1.37	12	0	72	47	17	65
Perez, Jackson, Padres	5	4	1.37	13	0	72	59	13	48
Perez, Heriberto, Braves II	3	2	1.37	14	0	59	53	14	61
Trifolio, Nelson, Royals	5	0	1.41	12	2	51	35	9	32
Mendez, Jesus, Yankees I	3	2	1.42	13	3	51	33	16	58
Chirinos, Carlos, Yankees II	3	3	1.42	12	0	51	37	8	23
Frieri, Ernesto, Padres	4	0	1.43	21	1	50	30	24	59
Garcia, Jose, Marlins	5	3	1.46	13	0	68	42	9	83
Soto, Sterling, Mariners	7	0	1.48	20	4	61	42	19	51
Gracia, Mario, Dodgers II	6	0	1.52	12	0	65	49	17	51
Joaquin, Waldis, Giants	6	1	1.61	14	0	61	51	28	44
Mercedes, Michel, Mariners	5	2	1.72	14	1	63	45	12	43
Martis, Shairon, Giants	4	3	1.79	14	0	70	55	17	63
Trias, Orlando, Blue Jays	9	3	1.80	14	0	95	70	16	79
Quevedo, Deiban, Athletics II	0	2	1.81	12	0	50	42	18	25
Arias, Marlon, Dodgers II	4	1	1.84	13	0	64	52	13	67
Trejo, Miguel, Tigers	3	3	1.85	15	1	68	47	11	59
Moscoso, Guillermo, Tigers	6	3	1.90	15	2	90	58	16	102
Brown, Luis, Mariners	6	3	1.93	13	1	61	57	26	49
Luces, Victor, Athletics I	6	3	1.94	13	0	56	36	39	44
Gervacio, Samuel, Astros	1	4	1.95	28	12	51	30	27	80
Polanco, Julio, Mets	5	2	1.99	17	0	68	38	27	91
Capellan, Jose, Red Sox	4	3	2.07	19	3	65	45	24	78
Perez, Oneli, White Sox	7	5	2.08	20	5	65	53	17	52
Riera, Jorge, Indians II	4	2	2.09	14	0	82	80	6	66
Polanco, Celson, Astros	4	2	2.09	13	1	73	55	11	56
Bruno, Antonio, Rockies	7	4	2.09	18	4	78	56	12	36
Mateo, Francisco, Blue Jays	11	3	2.11	15	0	98	59	26	122
Tejeda, Cristian, Rockies	4	2	2.11	16	0	60	38	17	56
Cordero, Angel, Padres	4	3	2.12	13	0	59	40	25	62
Mendoza, Nelson, Dodgers II	3	3	2.15	13	0	53	50	15	50
Cruz, Williander, Indians I	3	1	2.18	13	0	54	45	24	48
Reyes, Jorge, Mets	4	4	2.18	21	4	62	48	23	46
Morillo, Rafelin, Phillies	5	5	2.19	20	1	70	68	13	46
Gutierrez, Leonardo, Rockies	2	2	2.20	11	0	57	48	1	36
Martinez, Edwin, Mets	5	5	2.29	23	4	51	35	21	49
?Naval, Fernando, Orioles	5	4	2.29	13	0	75	50	36	83
Liz Gomez, Radamez, Orioles	7	3	2.29	13	0	75	45	23	99
Acosta, Jorge, Braves II	4	1	2.29	15	0	59	49	21	52
Arias, Henry, Royals	5	2	2.33	13	0	54	53	19	36
Montan, Miguel, Yankees II	1	5	2.36	12	0	53	39	9	47
Heredia, Felix, Indians II	5	1	2.39	19	0	68	56	18	69
Dolsi, Freddy, Tigers	6	7	2.39	14	0	83	60	31	97
Pena, Riqui, Rocies	3	4	2.42	13	0	74	47	22	44
Frias, Juseph, Mets	2	4	2.44	15	0	77	51	27	79
Patino, Geomar, Giants	6	3	2.45	13	0	70	55	13	46
Ortega, Anthony, Angels	2	6	2.45	13	0	81	64	13	61
Zerpa, Carlos, Indians II	6	2	2.47	13	0	66	52	20	48
Garcia, Ramon, Tigers	9	3	2.49	14	0	83	74	14	96
Quintana, Eduardo, Dodgers I	2	3	2.52	14	0	61	41	22	56
Alcantara, Omar, Padres	4	2	2.52	18	0	54	40	9	45
Payano, Leonardo, Expos	3	6	2.54	16	1	60	53	20	66
Perez, Wilfrido, Orioles	5	1	2.54	11	0	60	42	29	99
Rosario, Frank, White Sox	4	0	2.56	14	1	53	37	13	65
Lebron, Willy, Rangers	4	4	2.57	19	2	56	54	18	58
Cueto, Johnny, Reds	3	6	2.58	18	0	77	66	26	69
Florentino, Bladimir, Phillies	4	3	2.59	11	0	56	39	26	58
Toribio, Wilson, Rangers	3	4	2.60	20	1	55	46	11	37
Mateo, Marcos, Reds	4	2	2.61	15	0	69	62	17	57
Colon, Carlos, Mariners	7	4	2.61	14	0	62	44	32	72
Oliveros, Rayner, Royals	8	1	2.62	11	1	55	56	3	48
Montero, Joaniel, Indians II	1	5	2.68	11	0	57	49	14	27
Cabrera, Leonidas, Diamondbacks	3	6	2.73	13	0	56	36	30	45
De la Rosa, Alexis, Indians I	3	2	2.73	15	1	59	39	24	38
#Estevez, Joel, Rockies	4	2	3.34	**25**	**15**	30	32	10	35

VENEZUELAN SUMMER LEAGUE

Venezuela has been troubled by economic and security concerns, leading to civil unrest, since the established Venezuelan Winter League was forced to cancel part of its 2002-03 season in the wake of a general strike that crippled the country.

The eight-year-old Venezuelan Summer League con-

tinued to suffer its own fallout in 2004, when the league lost support from four more major league organizations and was forced to scrap its two-division format. With only two teams left in the Barquisimeto Division, the surviving clubs merged with teams in the Valencia Division to form one nine-team league.

The most significant organization to pull out of Venezuela in 2004 was the Cleveland Indians, whose San Felipe affiliate won the 2003 league championship and went 175-58 (a .751 clip) from 2001-03. The Blue Jays, Brewers and Twins also withdrew from the league, while the Red Sox joined the circuit. That left the number of big league teams supplying talent at 10—down from 18 in 2002, when the league fielded 12 teams.

Tronconero 2, a Mets affiliate, won the league title, rallying to beat Venoco 1 (Astros) 2-1 in the best-of-three championship series. The two teams tied for first in the regular season at 37-25.

After Tronconero 2 lost the opener 4-0 on a four-hitter by Victor Garate, series MVP Luis Martinez pitched eight shutout innings in Game Two as Tronconero 2 won 7-2. Tronconero 2 then won the finale 5-3, scoring all five runs in the first four innings.

Tronconero 2 gained a share of the regular-season title on the strength of outstanding pitching, led by league ERA leader Rafael Cova (6-0, 1.33). Outfielder Yonel Pacheco also led the league with 29 stolen bases while sharing the home run lead at nine.

Aguirre second baseman Luis Valbuena was named the league's most valuable player. He led the league in average (.365), hits (81), doubles (25) and triples (6).

—ALLAN SIMPSON

	AVG	AB	R	H	2B	3B	HR	RBI	SB
Fernandez, Jair, Aguirre	.301	136	15	41	10	0	1	22	0
Lasso, Jony, Cagua	.301	153	23	46	13	1	3	35	0
Rojo, Billy, Cagua	.301	173	34	52	9	4	1	18	6
Quintero, Cesar, Venoco 1	.301	146	29	44	7	1	4	21	8
Meza, Javier, Venoco 1	.300	210	30	63	7	1	0	23	7
Segovia, Luis, Ciudad Alianza	.297	236	53	70	17	1	1	17	21
Cambero, Alberto, Tronconero 1	.295	166	29	49	8	3	0	18	15
Serrano, Terry, Aguirre	.294	136	21	40	6	2	1	13	3
Thiel, Emile, Venoco 2	.293	188	29	55	4	4	1	17	4
Albornoz, Henry, Universidad	.292	212	32	62	21	2	3	36	9
Delgado, Ronny, Cagua	.286	182	26	52	11	1	5	**50**	1
Aguilar, Jose, Cagua	.285	144	33	41	13	2	0	16	5
Roman, Willman, San Joaquin	.281	199	21	56	9	0	2	27	0
Brown, Steve, Venoco 1	.281	192	38	54	18	1	2	30	12
Orfila, Pablo, Aguirre	.280	132	16	37	4	3	1	17	0
Calderon, Adolfo, Xiudad Alianza	.279	136	18	38	8	1	0	12	6
Hernandez, Quincy, Universidad	.279	201	45	56	17	4	5	26	15
Gonzalez, Esteban, Venoco 1	.279	122	16	34	2	0	0	9	8
Ramirez, Ronald, Venoco 1	.277	206	37	57	14	1	1	29	16
Bastardo, Jose, Cagua	.273	128	25	35	2	0	0	8	8
Paris, Juan, Venoco 1	.272	180	28	49	9	2	3	25	3
Lopez, Jose, Venoco 1	.271	133	26	36	4	3	3	24	3
Contreras, Efrain, Cagua	.271	155	20	42	4	0	1	17	3
Rodriguez, Yamber, Venoco 1	.270	185	34	50	11	2	1	18	18
Morales, Jaime, Tronconero 1	.269	167	25	45	12	2	0	20	6
Valero, Deywils, Tronconero 1	.268	179	24	48	7	3	1	22	8
Linares, Emilio, Ciudad Alianza	.267	236	36	63	10	2	5	42	8
Benitez, Deybis, Aguirre	.264	208	21	55	8	2	0	21	4
Castanon, Carlos, San Joaquin	.264	193	25	51	11	0	0	19	7
Sanchez, Julio, Venoco 2	.264	125	12	33	10	0	1	13	1
Moreno, Wilfredo, Venoco 2	.263	190	28	50	16	1	3	30	3
Hernandez, Xavier, Cagua	.262	195	24	51	7	1	2	25	0
Munoz, Joe, San Joaquin	.258	151	22	39	6	1	0	15	8
Bruzual, Edgar, Tronconero 2	.254	130	19	33	4	0	0	12	7
Ontivero, Emilio, Universidad	.254	169	21	43	6	0	2	14	7
Cedron, John, San Joaquin	.253	203	39	51	8	1	0	24	20
Hernandez, Fidel, Tronconero 1	.251	187	22	47	7	4	0	11	16
Garcia, Cristian, Tronconero 2	.251	203	43	51	7	**6**	0	22	7
Rodriguez, Junior, San Joaquin	.250	168	23	42	5	1	0	15	5
Vasquez, Robert, Venoco 2	.250	148	24	37	6	5	1	18	15

STANDINGS

	W	L	PCT	GB
Venoco I (Astros)	37	25	.594	—
Tronconero II (Mets)	37	25	.594	—
Universidad (Marlins/Padres)	34	29	.539	3½
Aguirre (Mariners)	32	28	.532	4
Tronconero I (Phillies)	29	31	.484	7
Ciudad Alianza (Red Sox)	29	33	.469	8
Cagua (Reds)	28	32	.468	8
San Joaquin (Pirates)	28	35	.445	9½
Venoco II (Orioles)	22	38	.373	14

PLAYOFFS: Tronconero II defeated Venoco I 2-1 in best-of-3 series.

ALL-STAR TEAM: C—Cesar Cordido, Tronconero II. **1B**—Douglas Morales, Tronconero I. **2B**—Luis Valbuena, Aguirre. **3B**—Gary Roche, Universidad (Marlins). **SS**—Christian Garcia, Tronconero II. **OF**—Steve Brown, Venoco I; Jose Graterol, Mariners; Yonel Pacheco, Tronconero II. **DH**—Jesus Garcia, Ciudad Alianza; Carlos Pistes, Cagua. **RHP**—Rafael Cova, Tronconero II. **LHP**—Alberto Bastardo, Venoco II. **RP**—Jose Rojas, Cagua.
Most Valuable Player: Luis Valbuena, Aguirre. **Most Outstanding Pitcher:** Alberto Bastardo, Venoco II; Rafael Cova, Tronconero II.

INDIVIDUAL BATTING LEADERS
(Minimum 115 At-Bats)

	AVG	AB	R	H	2B	3B	HR	RBI	SB
Valbuena, Luis, Aguirre	**.365**	222	45	**81**	**25**	**6**	2	35	11
Piste, Carlos, Cagua	.356	146	37	52	11	3	3	29	0
Morales, Douglas, Tronconero 1	.332	184	28	61	14	1	2	31	6
Garcia, Jesus, Ciudad Alianza	.329	216	40	71	12	1	**9**	41	2
Pacheco, Jonel, Tronconero 2	.321	224	41	72	18	2	**9**	44	**29**
Ramos, Renan, Ciudad Alianza	.316	187	36	59	11	3	1	23	6
Prieto, Michael, San Joaquin	.315	197	30	62	6	2	2	23	8
Graterol, Jose, Aguirre	.312	202	43	63	18	4	7	39	18
Lopez, Marcos, Tronconero 1	.311	161	30	50	5	1	0	20	10
Roche, Gary, Universidad	.307	202	38	62	15	0	5	32	2
Ochoa, Blake, Universidad	.302	126	9	38	8	0	0	21	2

INDIVIDUAL PITCHING LEADERS
(Minimum 40 Innings)

	W	L	ERA	G	SV	IP	H	BB	SO
Sanchez, Romulo, San Joaquin	4	2	1.03	21	6	44	33	7	49
Mendez, Julio, Tronconero 2	5	2	1.18	18	3	46	41	19	26
Cova, Rafael, Tronconero 2	6	0	**1.33**	11	0	54	37	32	50
Correa, Felix, Aguirre	2	1	1.79	12	0	40	29	18	34
Castro, Julio, San Joaquin	6	2	1.82	14	0	54	43	11	50
#Rojas, Jose, Cagua	4	2	1.86	28	**9**	39	36	19	23
Beltran, Hugo, Tronconero 2	2	1	1.96	12	2	41	39	15	31
Perdomo, Javier, Tronconero 2	**7**	2	1.98	12	0	64	54	13	44
Quijada, Fernando, Tronconero 1	2	4	2.11	12	1	47	40	17	45
Machi, Jean, Tronconero 1	2	2	2.18	9	0	41	29	10	39
#Contreras, Carlos, Universidad	3	2	2.27	27	**9**	40	33	18	46
Bastardo, Alberto, Venoco 2	3	4	2.27	14	0	79	67	13	**74**
Guaramato, Edgar, Aguirre	6	3	2.28	15	0	51	34	21	45
Escalona, Jose, Aguirre	3	2	2.30	11	0	43	27	23	42
Camacho, Gustavo, Venoco 2	6	2	2.30	13	0	70	69	15	30
Marrero, Alvaro, Venoco 2	3	1	2.31	12	0	58	52	22	42
Saenz, Jose, Tronconero 1	3	4	2.33	12	0	54	62	9	31
Mejias, Jose, Tronconero 1	5	2	2.40	12	0	64	55	15	51
Mayora, Cesar, Venoco 1	5	3	2.53	14	0	68	52	19	54
Sokolovich, Miguel, Ciudad Alianza	1	3	2.70	18	1	50	40	12	31
Vega, Marwin, Aguirre	3	4	2.83	11	0	48	36	23	43
Noel, Wilton, Venoco 1	3	3	2.86	13	0	66	57	24	41
Ortiz, Jose, Ciudad Alianza	4	3	3.02	15	0	57	41	18	67
Martinez, Yofri, San Joaquin	3	4	3.09	16	1	64	57	28	53
Bermudez, Jose, Tronconero 1	4	4	3.20	10	0	51	44	15	44
Rivero, Raul, Venoco 2	2	3	3.20	15	0	45	47	14	28
Martinez, Luis, Tronconero 2	2	3	3.20	12	0	65	51	14	49
Lugo, Victor, San Joaquin	1	4	3.21	16	0	53	51	23	38
Moncada, Jorge, Venoco 1	6	0	3.39	19	2	58	56	22	52
Monarrez, Israel, Cagua	2	2	3.45	17	0	44	35	31	44
Linares, Remo, Ciudad Alianza	3	3	3.47	13	0	60	50	26	50
Molina, Randy, Tronconero 2	4	1	3.52	14	2	54	42	20	48
Farias, Carlos, Universidad	**7**	3	3.54	15	0	84	65	40	58
Flores, Cesar, Universidad	3	4	3.61	12	1	67	68	11	51
Gaetano, Diomny, Aguirre	3	4	3.64	18	3	47	59	12	39
Rodriguez, Jorge, Ciudad Alianza	5	5	3.72	17	1	56	49	25	38
Izquierdo, Giovany, Cagua	1	1	3.80	16	0	47	46	25	28

Statistics in **boldface** indicate league leader
#League leader but non-qualifier

PROSPECTS

PROSPECT
POSITION RANKINGS

BY JOHN MANUEL

Baseball America ranked the game's top major league prospects, by position, following the 2004 season. Only players who have not exceeded the major league rookie eligibility standards of 130 at-bats for position players and 50 innings for pitchers were eligible.

Ages are as of Oct. 1, 2004. The highest level each player reached in 2004 is also noted.

RIGHTHANDED STARTERS

When the Dwight Gooden comparisons were thrown around prior to the 2004 season, Felix Hernandez seemed too good to be true. When he more than held his own as an 18-year-old in the Double-A Texas League, he proved to be for real. One of his few rivals was Matt Cain, who nearly matched him strikeout for strikeout in the California League and stayed healthy for a full season. Chad Billingsley's thick, strong body helped him thrive in a year that ended in Double-A. Adam Miller and Jose Capellan both hit 100 mph in the Carolina League in 2004 and have more going for them than just fastballs. Yusmeiro Petit and Brendan McCarthy were the only minor leaguers to record 200 or more strikeouts.

Rank, Player, Team	Age	Highest Level
1. Felix Hernandez, Mariners	18	Double-A
2. Matt Cain, Giants	20	Double-A
3. Chad Billingsley, Dodgers	20	Double-A
4. Adam Miller, Indians	19	High A
5. Jose Capellan, Braves	23	Majors
6. Gavin Floyd, Phillies	21	Majors
7. Edwin Jackson, Dodgers	21	Majors
8. Yusmeiro Petit, Mets	19	Double-A
9. Brendan McCarthy, White Sox	21	Double-A
10. Anthony Reyes, Cardinals	23	Double-A
11. Kyle Davies, Braves	21	Triple-A
12. Scott Baker, Twins	23	Triple-A
13. Denny Bautista, Royals	24	Majors
14. Thomas Diamond, Rangers	21	Low A
15. Merkin Valdez, Giants	22	Majors
16. Ben Hendrickson, Brewers	23	Majors
17. J.D. Durbin, Twins	22	Majors
18. Joe Blanton, Athletics	23	Majors
19. Richie Gardner, Reds	22	Double-A
20. Homer Bailey, Reds	18	Rookie
21. Mark Rogers, Brewers	18	Rookie
22. Justin Verlander, Tigers	21	Did not play
23. Adam Harben, Twins	21	Low A
24. Hayden Penn, Orioles	19	Double-A
25. Jonathan Broxton, Dodgers	20	High A

LEFTHANDED STARTERS

An elite trio of lefties saw plenty of tumult in 2004. The Mets traded Scott Kazmir to the Devil Rays and he became that pitching-poor organization's most important prospect. Cole Hamels (Phillies) and Greg Miller (Dodgers) missed most or all of the season with arm injuries, neither of which required surgery. However, both missed a full year of development time. The Rockies hope Minor League Player of the Year Jeff Francis can take the next step as a productive starter in Coors Field.

Rank, Player, Team	Age	Highest Level
1. Scott Kazmir, Devil Rays	20	Majors
2. Jeff Francis, Rockies	23	Majors
3. Mike Hinckley, Expos	21	Double-A
4. Scott Olsen, Marlins	20	High A
5. Greg Miller, Dodgers	19	Double-A
6. Cole Hamels, Phillies	20	High A
7. Dan Meyer, Braves	23	Triple-A
8. Zach Duke, Pirates	21	Double-A
9. John Danks, Rangers	19	High A
10. Chuck Tiffany, Dodgers	18	Low A

Injuries hampered his 2004 major league debut
Twins prospect Joe Mauer

11. Jeremy Sowers, Indians	21	Did not play
12. Adam Loewen, Orioles	20	High A
13. Jacob Stevens, Braves	19	Low A
14. Renyel Pinto, Cubs	22	Triple-A
15. Francisco Liriano, Twins	20	Double-A

RELIEVERS

The 2003 draft graduated three college closers to the major leagues in short order, and Oakland hopes Huston Street can do the same thing from the Class of 2004. Street reached Triple-A in his first season and has the pedigree on and off the field to close, though his stuff profiles better as a setup man. His biggest obstacle might be fellow Athletics farmhand Jairo Garcia, a former starter who stayed healthy and vaulted from the Midwest League to the majors in one season. Hawaii native Brandon League is the hardest thrower in the group but has never put up dominant strikeout numbers in the minors.

Rank, Player, Team	Age	Highest Level
1. Huston Street, Athletics	21	Triple-A
2. Jairo Garcia, Athletics	21	Majors
3. Jesse Crain, Twins	23	Majors
4. Brandon League, Blue Jays	21	Majors
5. Chad Orvella, Devil Rays	24	Triple-A
6. Chris Resop, Marlins	21	Low A
7. David Aardsma, Giants	22	Majors
8. Bill Bray, Expos	21	High A
9. Ryan Speier, Rockies	25	Double-A
10. Brad Baker, Padres	23	Triple-A

CATCHERS

This position isn't supposed to have a repeat winner. Then again, Joe Mauer isn't your typical prospect. Baseball America's 2003 Minor League Player of the Year was having a fine big league debut (he hit a career-high six homers in just 107 at-bats) before a recurring knee injury sidelined him for the rest of the season. The Twins even worked him out at third base, and the injury has raised questions whether or not Mauer will catch again. Jeff Mathis had a poor second half in 2004 but his all-

around tools make him the best of the rest of an uninspiring group. Daric Barton is a premier bat but may not stay at catcher. Guillermo Quiroz and Kelly Shoppach struggled offensively in Triple-A, but both have shown they can handle the position defensively and have shown above-average power.

Rank, Player, Team	Age	Highest Level
1. Joe Mauer, Twins	21	Majors
2. Jeff Mathis, Angels	21	Double-A
3. Daric Barton, Cardinals	19	Low A
4. Brian McCann, Braves	20	High A
5. Guillermo Quiroz, Blue Jays	22	Majors
6. Kelly Shoppach, Red Sox	24	Triple-A
7. Jarrod Saltalamacchia, Braves	19	Low A
8. Russell Martin, Dodgers	21	High A
9. Chris Snyder, Diamondbacks	23	Majors
10. Neil Walker, Pirates	19	Short-season

FIRST BASEMEN

A position for premium hitters has an eclectic mix of talent. Casey Kotchman isn't an elite power hitter—yet—but has batting champion and Gold Glove potential, and might have been the best hitter in the minor leagues in 2004. Prince Fielder handled the jump to Double-A and now has to handle his father Cecil's gambling scandal, but his power is undeniable. James Loney has yet to produce over a full season due to injury, but scouts rave about his swing, athletic ability and defense. Ryan Howard led the minors with 46 homers to further establish himself as a prospect.

Rank, Player, Team	Age	Highest Level
1. Casey Kotchman, Angels	21	Majors
2. Prince Fielder, Brewers	20	Double-A
3. James Loney, Dodgers	20	Double-A
4. Michael Aubrey, Indians	22	Double-A
5. Brian Dopirak, Cubs	20	Low A
6. Ryan Howard, Phillies	24	Majors
7. Dan Johnson, Athletics	25	Triple-A
8. Adrian Gonzalez, Rangers	22	Majors
9. Jason Stokes, Marlins	22	Double-A
10. Jason Botts, Rangers	24	Double-A

SECOND BASEMEN

Not traditionally a prospect haven, second base has fewer prospects now than it has had in some time. While Rickie Weeks and Josh Barfield have big tools, neither had overly productive 2004 seasons, though scouts still love Weeks' tools. Chris Burke's productive season at Triple-A has him set up to take over for Jeff Kent with the Astros in 2005. If the Yankees want to have a low-cost player, Robinson Cano could give them that option soon as well, bringing a power lefthanded bat to the Bronx. Howie Kendrick's offensive package draws comparisons to Ray Durham.

Rank, Player, Team	Age	Highest Level
1. Rickie Weeks, Brewers	22	Majors
2. Josh Barfield, Padres	21	Double-A
3. Chris Burke, Astros	24	Majors
4. Robinson Cano, Yankees	21	Triple-A
5. Howie Kendrick, Angels	21	Low A

THIRD BASEMEN

Few players that scouts saw in 2004 elicited more praise than Ian Stewart, who led the South Atlantic League in slugging percentage and showed better-than-expected defensive ability at the hot corner. Andy Marte had a fine season interrupted by an ankle injury, and either he or 40-homer Dallas McPherson—who finished the year on the Angels' playoff roster—easily could rank first on this list as well. Eric Duncan has significant offensive potential, but scouts aren't sold on his ability to stay at third defensively. Jeff Baker (repeated wrist problems) and Matt Moses (back) have significant offensive upside as well, but have had trouble staying healthy.

Rank, Player, Team	Age	Highest Level
1. Ian Stewart, Rockies	19	Low A
2. Andy Marte, Braves	20	Double-A
3. Dallas McPherson, Angels	24	Majors
4. Eric Duncan, Yankees	19	High A
5. Andy LaRoche, Dodgers	21	High A

6. Edwin Encarnacion, Reds	21	Double-A
7. Jeff Baker, Rockies	23	Double-A
8. Blake DeWitt, Dodgers	19	Rookie
9. Matt Moses, Twins	19	Low A
10. Mark Teahen, Royals	23	Triple-A

SHORTSTOPS

Devil Rays shortstop B.J. Upton was the No. 1 prospect in the minors for most of the 2004 season before an August promotion to Tampa Bay. His departure left the top spot open for players with a similar profile: more advanced offensively than defensively. As Upton learned quickly, defense is more of a priority in the major leagues, and it will be for these players to stay at baseball's glamour position. Joel Guzman made enormous progress offensively in 2004 and probably will hit enough for an eventual move to third base or a corner outfield spot. Hanley Ramirez has a better chance to stay at short. No organization has depth at the position like the Angels, and no shortstop had a bigger 2004 season than the Rangers' Ian Kinsler, who smacked 50 doubles and reached Double-A in his first full season.

Rank, Player, Team	Age	Highest Level
1. Joel Guzman, Dodgers	19	Double-A
2. Hanley Ramirez, Red Sox	20	Double-A
3. J.J. Hardy, Brewers	22	Triple-A
4. Chris Nelson, Rockies	19	Rookie
5. Erick Aybar, Angels	20	High A
6. Tony Giarratano, Tigers	21	High A
7. Sergio Santos, Diamondbacks	21	Double-A
8. Joaquin Arias, Rangers	20	High A
9. Jason Bartlett, Twins	24	Majors
10. Alberto Callaspo, Angels	21	Double-A
11. Ian Kinsler, Rangers	22	Double-A
12. Russ Adams, Blue Jays	24	Majors
13. Brandon Wood, Angels	19	Low A
14. Aaron Hill, Blue Jays	22	Double-A
15. Luis Soto, Red Sox	18	Rookie

OUTFIELDERS

Delmon Young and Lastings Milledge, teammates for USA Baseball's junior national team in 2002, brought exciting tools to their organizations and were scintillating in their first professional seasons. Jeff Francoeur translated his immense talent into major production and looks like Atlanta's Next Great Prospect. Jason Kubel hit his way onto the Twins' postseason roster, but his prospect stock took a hit when he tore up his left knee in the Arizona Fall League. Jeremy Hermida could follow Kubel's lead as a smooth hitter whose power blossoms after he leaves the spacious parks of the Florida State League. Leadoff hitters abound in the outfield, with Felix Pie, Fred Lewis, Michael Bourn and Joey Gathright all candidates to front big league lineups for years in the near future.

Rank, Player, Team	Age	Highest Level
1. Delmon Young, Devil Rays	19	Low A
2. Lastings Milledge, Mets	19	High A
3. Jeff Francoeur, Braves	20	Double-A
4. Grady Sizemore, Indians	22	Majors
5. Jeremy Hermida, Marlins	20	High A
6. Jason Kubel, Twins	22	Majors
7. Nick Swisher, Athletics	23	Majors
8. Carlos Quentin, Diamondbacks	22	Double-A
9. Franklin Gutierrez, Indians	21	Triple-A
10. Felix Pie, Cubs	19	High A
11. Brian Anderson, White Sox	22	Double-A
12. Ryan Sweeney, White Sox	19	High A
13. Jeremy Reed, Mariners	23	Majors
14. Shin-Soo Choo, Mariners	22	Double-A
15. Conor Jackson, Diamondbacks	22	Double-A
16. Curtis Granderson, Tigers	23	Majors
17. Fred Lewis, Giants	23	Triple-A
18. Javi Herrera, Athletics	19	Short-season
19. Elijah Dukes, Devil Rays	20	High A
20. Ryan Harvey, Cubs	20	Short-season
21. Mitch Einertson, Astros	18	Short-season
22. Michael Bourn, Phillies	21	Low A
23. Joey Gathright, Devil Rays	22	Majors
24. Brad Nelson, Brewers	22	Double-A
25. Greg Golson, Phillies	19	Rookie

As with most of the prospect lists that appear in Baseball America, the Minor League Top 20 Prospects lists are compiled with long-term major league potential in mind. While we like to see players do well now, what we're really looking for are future major league stars.

These lists do bring a slightly different perspective than Baseball America's traditional organizational Top 10 Prospects lists. Those lists have more of a scouting angle, while our league lists are based on conversations with league managers. Managers and scouts can often view players differently. Both look at a player's tools, but managers give more weight to what a player does on the field, while scouts look at what a player might eventually do. We think both perspectives are useful.

For a player to qualify for a league prospect list, he must have spent at least one-third of the season in a league to qualify. Position players must have one plate appearance per league game. In other words, for a league that plays 140 games, a player is eligible if he has at least 140 plate appearances.

Pitchers must pitch ⅓ inning per league game. Relievers must make at least 20 appearances in a full-season league or 10 appearances in a short-season league (* indicates since traded).

TRIPLE-A

INTERNATIONAL LEAGUE
1. B.J. Upton, ss, Durham (Devil Rays)
2. Justin Morneau, 1b, Rochester (Twins)
3. Grady Sizemore, of, Buffalo (Indians)
4. Jason Kubel, of, Rochester (Twins)
5. *Jeremy Reed, of, Charlotte (White Sox)
6. Alexis Rios, of, Syracuse (Blue Jays)
7. Ben Hendrickson, rhp, Indianapolis (Brewers)
8. Dan Meyer, lhp, Richmond (Braves)
9. Guillermo Quiroz, c, Syracuse (Blue Jays)
10. Jason Bartlett, ss, Rochester (Twins)
11. Joey Gathright, of, Durham (Devil Rays)
12. Jesse Crain, rhp, Rochester (Twins)
13. Jorge Cantu, 3b, Durham (Bulls)
14. Robinson Cano, 2b, Columbus (Yankees)
15. John Maine, rhp, Ottawa (Orioles)
16. Russ Adams, ss, Syracuse (Blue Jays)
17. David Krynzel, of, Indianapolis (Brewers)
18. Kelly Shoppach, c, Pawtucket (Red Sox)
19. Francisco Cruceta, rhp, Buffalo (Indians)
20. David Bush, rhp, Syracuse (Blue Jays)

PACIFIC COAST LEAGUE
1. Casey Kotchman, 1b, Salt Lake (Angels)
2. Dallas McPherson, 3b, Salt Lake (Angels)
3. Edwin Jackson, rhp, Las Vegas (Dodgers)
4. Nick Swisher, of, Sacramento (Athletics)
5. Jose Lopez, inf, Tacoma (Mariners)
6. Jeremy Reed, of, Tacoma (Mariners)
7. Chris Burke, 2b, New Orleans (Astros)
8. Joe Blanton, rhp, Sacramento (Athletics)
9. Juan Dominguez, rhp, Oklahoma (Rangers)
10. Yadier Molina, c, Memphis (Cardinals)
11. Clint Nageotte, rhp, Tacoma (Mariners)
12. Ryan Church, of, Edmonton (Expos)
13. Dan Johnson, 1b, Sacramento (Athletics)
14. Freddy Guzman, of, Portland (Padres)
15. Clint Barmes, ss, Colorado Springs (Rockies)
16. Luis Terrero, of, Tucson (Diamondbacks)
17. Garrett Atkins, 3b, Colorado Springs (Rockies)
18. Bobby Madritsch, lhp, Tacoma (Mariners)
19. Brendan Harris, inf, Edmonton (Expos)
20. Noah Lowry, lhp, Fresno (Giants)

DOUBLE-A

EASTERN LEAGUE
1. David Wright, 3b, Binghamton (Mets)
2. Jason Kubel, of, New Britain (Twins)
3. Matt Cain, rhp, Norwich (Giants)
4. Mike Hinckley, lhp, Harrisburg (Expos)
5. Gavin Floyd, rhp, Reading (Phillies)
6. Zach Duke, lhp, Altoona (Pirates)
7. Curtis Granderson, of, Erie (Tigers)
8. Ryan Howard, 1b, Reading (Phillies)
9. J.D. Durbin, rhp, New Britain (Twins)
10. Franklin Gutierrez, of, Akron (Indians)

Dominating phenom
The Mariners' Felix Hernandez

ANDREW WOOLLEY

11. Val Majewski, of, Bowie (Orioles)
12. Michael Aubrey, 1b, Akron (Indians)
13. Larry Broadway, 1b, Harrisburg (Expos)
14. Aaron Hill, ss, New Hampshire (Blue Jays)
15. Brandon League, rhp, New Hampshire (Blue Jays)
16. Robinson Cano, 2b, Trenton (Yankees)
17. Scott Baker, rhp, New Britain (Twins)
18. *Denny Bautista, rhp, Bowie (Orioles)
19. Ian Snell, rhp, Altoona (Pirates)
20. Francisco Rosario, rhp, New Hampshire (Blue Jays)

SOUTHERN LEAGUE
1. Andy Marte, 3b, Greenville (Braves)
2. Joel Guzman, ss, Jacksonville (Dodgers)
3. Rickie Weeks, 2b, Huntsville (Brewers)
4. Prince Fielder, 1b, Huntsville (Brewers)
5. Jose Capellan, rhp, Greenville (Braves)
6. Edwin Encarnacion, 3b, Chattanooga (Reds)
7. Anthony Reyes, rhp, Tennessee (Cardinals)
8. Kyle Davies, rhp, Greenville (Braves)
9. James Loney, 1b, Jacksonville (Dodgers)
10. Josh Barfield, 2b, Mobile (Padres)
11. Brian Anderson, of, Birmingham (White Sox)
12. Josh Willingham, c/1b, Carolina (Marlins)
13. Renyel Pinto, lhp, West Tenn (Cubs)
14. Freddy Guzman, of, Mobile (Padres)
15. Dan Meyer, lhp, Greenville (Braves)
16. *Michael Morse, ss, Birmingham (White Sox)
17. William Bergolla, 2b/ss, Chattanooga (Reds)

18. Arnie Munoz, lhp, Birmingham (White Sox)
19. Brad Thompson, rhp, Tennessee (Cardinals)
20. Brad Nelson, of/1b, Huntsville (Brewers)

TEXAS LEAGUE
1. Felix Hernandez, rhp, San Antonio (Mariners)
2. Dallas McPherson, 3b, Arkansas (Angels)
3. Jeff Francis, lhp, Tulsa (Rockies)
4. Shin-Soo Choo, of, San Antonio (Mariners)
5. Denny Bautista, rhp, Wichita (Royals)
6. Sergio Santos, ss, El Paso (Diamondbacks)
7. Carlos Quentin, of, El Paso (Diamondbacks)
8. Ezequiel Astacio, rhp, Round Rock (Astros)
9. Ian Kinsler, ss, Frisco (Rangers)
10. Alberto Callaspo, ss/2b, Arkansas (Angels)
11. Conor Jackson, of, El Paso (Diamondbacks)
12. Chris Snyder, c, El Paso (Diamondbacks)
13. Jeff Mathis, c, Arkansas (Angels)
14. Willy Taveras, of, Round Rock (Astros)
15. Jason Botts, 1b, Frisco (Rangers)
16. *Mark Teahen, 3b, Midland (Athletics)
17. Ryan Shealy, 1b, Tulsa (Rockies)
18. D.J. Houlton, rhp, Round Rock (Astros)
19. John Hudgins, rhp, Frisco (Rangers)
20. Dustin Nippert, rhp, El Paso (Diamondbacks)

HIGH CLASS A

CALIFORNIA LEAGUE
1. Felix Hernandez, rhp, Inland Empire (Mariners)
2. Matt Cain, rhp, San Jose (Giants)
3. Erick Aybar, ss, Rancho Cucamonga (Angels)
4. Carlos Quentin, of, Lancaster (Diamondbacks)
5. Conor Jackson, of, Lancaster (Diamondbacks)
6. Elijah Dukes, of, Bakersfield (Devil Rays)
7. Fred Lewis, of, San Jose (Giants)
8. Manny Parra, lhp, High Desert (Brewers)
9. Jon Zeringue, of, Lancaster (Diamondbacks)
10. Jeff Salazar, of, Visalia (Rockies)
11. John Danks, lhp, Stockton (Rangers)
12. Steven Shell, rhp, Rancho Cucamonga (Angels)
13. Jeff Baker, 3b, Visalia (Rockies)
14. Nate Schierholtz, 3b, San Jose (Giants)
15. Joaquin Arias, ss, Stockton (Rangers)
16. Jaime D'Antona, 3b, Lancaster (Diamondbacks)
17. Jason Hammel, rhp, Bakersfield (Devil Rays)
18. John Hudgins, rhp, Stockton (Rangers)
19. Omar Quintanilla, ss, Modesto (Athletics)
20. Enrique Gonzalez, rhp, Lancaster (Diamondbacks)

CAROLINA LEAGUE
1. Jeff Francoeur, of, Myrtle Beach (Braves)
2. Michael Aubrey, 1b, Kinston (Indians)
3. Brian Anderson, of, Winston-Salem (White Sox)
4. Zach Duke, lhp, Lynchburg (Pirates)
5. Kyle Davies, rhp, Myrtle Beach (Braves)

6. Brandon McCarthy, rhp, Winston-Salem (White Sox)
7. Ryan Sweeney, of, Winston-Salem (White Sox)
8. Brian McCann, c, Myrtle Beach (Braves)
9. Richie Gardner, rhp, Potomac (Reds)
10. Fernando Nieve, rhp, Salem (Astros)
11. Tom Gorzelanny, lhp, Lynchburg (Pirates)
12. Josh Fields, 3b, Winston-Salem (White Sox)
13. Ryan Garko, 1b/c, Kinston (Indians)
14. Brad Eldred, 1b, Lynchburg (Pirates)
15. Anthony Lerew, rhp, Myrtle Beach (Braves)
16. Chris Ray, rhp, Frederick (Orioles)
17. Sean Tracey, rhp, Winston-Salem (White Sox)
18. Rajai Davis, of, Lynchburg (Pirates)
19. Hayden Penn, rhp, Frederick (Orioles)
20. Mitch Maier, 3b, Wilmington (Royals)

FLORIDA STATE LEAGUE

1. Joel Guzman, ss, Vero Beach (Dodgers)
2. Chad Billingsley, rhp, Vero Beach (Dodgers)
3. Hanley Ramirez, ss, Sarasota (Red Sox)
4. *Scott Kazmir, lhp, St. Lucie (Mets)
5. Scott Olsen, lhp, Jupiter (Marlins)
6. Felix Pie, of, Daytona (Cubs)
7. Mike Hinckley, lhp, Brevard County (Expos)
8. Jeremy Hermida, of, Jupiter (Marlins)
9. Tony Giarratano, ss, Lakeland (Tigers)
10. Eric Duncan, 3b, Tampa (Yankees)
11. Francisco Liriano, lhp, Fort Myers (Twins)
12. Jonathan Broxton, rhp, Vero Beach (Dodgers)
13. Yusmeiro Petit, rhp, St. Lucie (Mets)
14. Jon Papelbon, rhp, Sarasota (Red Sox)
15. Jon Lester, lhp, Sarasota (Red Sox)
16. Andy LaRoche, 3b, Vero Beach (Dodgers)
17. Ismael Ramirez, rhp, Dunedin (Blue Jays)
18. Delwyn Young, 2b, Vero Beach (Dodgers)
19. Josh Banks, rhp, Dunedin (Blue Jays)
20. Kyle Sleeth, rhp, Lakeland (Tigers)

MIDWEST LEAGUE

1. Brian Dopirak, 1b, Lansing (Cubs)
2. Daric Barton, c, Peoria (Cardinals)
3. Eric Duncan, 3b, Battle Creek (Yankees)
4. John Danks, lhp, Clinton (Rangers)
5. Brandon Wood, ss, Cedar Rapids (Angels)
6. Jairo Garcia, rhp, Kane County (Athletics)
7. Joey Votto, 1b, Dayton (Reds)
8. Ian Kinsler, ss, Clinton (Rangers)
9. Sean Marshall, lhp, Lansing (Cubs)
10. Adam Harben, rhp, Quad Cities (Twins)
11. Wladimir Balentien, of, Wisconsin (Mariners)
12. Howie Kendrick, 2b, Cedar Rapids (Angels)
13. Adam Jones, ss, Wisconsin (Mariners)
14. Glen Perkins, lhp, Quad Cities (Twins)
15. Melky Cabrera, of, Battle Creek (Yankees)
16. Kevin Jepsen, rhp, Cedar Rapids (Angels)
17. Ambiorix Burgos, rhp, Burlington (Royals)
18. Billy Petrick, rhp, Lansing (Cubs)
19. Baltazar Lopez, 1b, Cedar Rapids (Angels)
20. Dana Eveland, lhp, Beloit (Brewers)

SOUTH ATLANTIC LEAGUE

1. Delmon Young, of, Charleston, S.C. (Devil Rays)
2. Ian Stewart, 3b, Asheville (Rockies)
3. Lastings Milledge, of, Capital City (Mets)
4. Adam Miller, rhp, Lake County (Indians)
5. Yusmeiro Petit, rhp, Capital City (Mets)
6. Chuck Tiffany, lhp, Columbus (Dodgers)
7. Jarrod Saltalamacchia, c, Rome (Braves)
8. Brandon McCarthy, rhp, Kannapolis (White Sox)
9. Andy LaRoche, 3b, Columbus (Dodgers)
10. Clint Everts, rhp, Savannah (Expos)
11. Michael Bourn, of, Lakewood (Phillies)
12. Jacob Stevens, lhp, Rome (Braves)
13. Tom Gorzelanny, lhp, Hickory (Pirates)
14. Josh Anderson, of, Lexington (Astros)
15. Chris Young, of, Kannapolis (White Sox)
16. Nate Schierholtz, 3b, Hagerstown (Giants)
17. Scott Mathieson, rhp, Lakewood (Phillies)
18. Matt Albers, rhp, Lexington (Astros)

A reason for Dodger Pride
Vero Beach shortstop Joel Guzman

19. Chin-Lung Hu, ss, Columbus (Dodgers)
20. Brandon Moss, of, Augusta (Red Sox)

NEW YORK-PENN LEAGUE

1. Ambiorix Concepcion, of, Brooklyn (Mets)
2. Anibal Sanchez, rhp, Lowell (Red Sox)
3. Jason Vargas, lhp, Jamestown (Marlins)
4. Taylor Tankersley, lhp, Jamestown (Marlins)
5. Ben Zobrist, ss, Tri-City (Astros)
6. Jesse Hoover, rhp, Staten Island (Yankees)
7. David Haehnel, lhp, Aberdeen (Orioles)
8. Tony Sipp, lhp, Mahoning Valley (Indians)
9. Christian Lara, ss, Lowell (Red Sox)
10. Jeff Marquez, rhp, Staten Island (Yankees)
11. Curtis Thigpen, c, Auburn (Blue Jays)
12. Mike Butia, of, Mahoning Valley (Indians)
13. Hunter Pence, of, Tri-City (Astros)
14. Tommy Hottovy, lhp, Lowell (Red Sox)
15. Jon Fulton, ss, Jamestown (Marlins)
16. Argenis Reyes, of, Mahoning Valley (Indians)
17. Blair Johnson, rhp, Williamsport (Pirates)
18. J.A. Happ, lhp, Batavia (Phillies)
19. Jake Mullinax, 3b, New Jersey (Cardinals)
20. Jon Barratt, lhp, Hudson Valley (Devil Rays)

NORTHWEST LEAGUE

1. Javier Herrera, of, Vancouver (Athletics)
2. Ryan Harvey, of, Boise (Cubs)
3. Carlos Gonzalez, of, Yakima (Diamondbacks)
4. Craig Whitaker, rhp, Salem-Keizer (Giants)
5. Matt Tuiasosopo, ss, Everett (Mariners)
6. Juan Morillo, rhp, Tri-City (Rockies)
7. Richie Robnett, of, Vancouver (Athletics)
8. Asdrubal Cabrera, ss, Everett (Mariners)
9. Matt Macri, 3b, Tri-City (Rockies)
10. Chris Carter, of/dh, Yakima (Diamondbacks)
11. Jim Miller, rhp, Tri-City (Rockies)
12. Kurt Suzuki, c, Vancouver (Athletics)
13. Eric Hurley, rhp, Spokane (Rangers)
14. Shawn Nottingham, lhp, Everett (Mariners)
15. A.J. Shappi, rhp, Yakima (Diamondbacks)
16. Landon Powell, c, Vancouver (Athletics)
17. Ross Ohlendorf, rhp, Yakima (Diamondbacks)
18. Orlando Mercado Jr., c, Yakima (Diamondbacks)
19. Mike Nickeas, c, Spokane (Rangers)
20. Tomas Santiago, rhp, Tri-City (Rockies)

APPALACHIAN LEAGUE

1. Mitch Einertson, of, Greeneville (Astros)
2. Francisco Hernandez, c, Bristol (White Sox)
3. Kyle Waldrop, rhp, Elizabethton (Twins)
4. Reid Brignac, ss, Princeton (Devil Rays)

5. Gio Gonzalez, lhp, Bristol (White Sox)
6. Trevor Plouffe, ss, Elizabethton (Twins)
7. Yuber Rodriguez, of, Pulaski (Blue Jays)
8. Brandon Yarbrough, c, Johnson City (Cardinals)
9. Alexander Smit, lhp, Elizabethton (Twins)
10. Troy Patton, lhp, Greeneville (Astros)
11. Matt Fox, rhp, Elizabethton (Twins)
12. Juan Gutierrez, rhp, Greeneville (Astros)
13. Jordan Parraz, of, Greeneville (Astros)
14. Van Pope, 3b, Danville (Braves)
15. Frank Mata, rhp Elizabethton (Twins)
16. J.C. Holt, 2b, Danville (Braves)
17. Javier Castillo, ss, Bristol (White Sox)
18. Juan Valdes, of, Burlington (Indians)
19. Jose Delgado, 2b, Johnson City (Cardinals)
20. Deacon Burns, of, Elizabethton (Twins)

PIONEER LEAGUE

1. Chris Nelson, ss, Casper (Rockies)
2. Blake DeWitt, 3b, Ogden (Dodgers)
3. Sean Rodriguez, ss, Provo (Angels)
4. Billy Butler, 3b, Idaho Falls (Royals)
5. Ray Liotta, lhp, Great Falls (White Sox)
6. Scott Elbert, lhp, Ogden (Dodgers)
7. Cory Dunlap, 1b, Ogden (Dodgers)
8. Sam Deduno, rhp, Casper (Rockies)
9. Luis Cota, rhp, Idaho Falls (Royals)
10. Seth Smith, of, Casper (Rockies)
11. Josh Wahpepah, rhp, Helena (Brewers)
12. B.J. Szymanski, of, Billings (Reds)
13. Billy Buckner, rhp, Idaho Falls (Royals)
14. Brian McFall, 1b, Idaho Falls (Royals)
15. Mitchell Arnold, rhp, Provo (Angels)
16. Andrew Toussaint, 3b/dh, Provo (Angels)
17. Blake Johnson, rhp, Ogden (Dodgers)
18. J.P. Howell, lhp, Idaho Falls (Royals)
19. Franklin Morales, lhp, Casper (Rockies)
20. Craig Tatum, c, Billings (Reds)

ARIZONA LEAGUE

1. Matt Tuiasosopo, ss, Mariners
2. Hernan Iribarren, 2b, Brewers
3. Mark Rogers, rhp, Brewers
4. Miguel Vega, 1b/3b, Royals
5. Matt Bush, ss, Padres
6. Daryl Jones, 1b, Padres
7. K.C. Herren, of, Rangers
8. Daniel Santin, c, Mariners
9. Elvin Puello, 3b/ss, Cubs
10. Marcus Sanders, 2b, Giants
11. Josh Johnson, ss, Royals
12. Erik Cordier, rhp, Royals
13. Yovani Gallardo, rhp, Brewers
14. Pablo Sandoval, c, Giants
15. Freddy Parejo, of, Brewers
16. Irving Falu, 2b, Royals
17. Andy Santana, lhp, Cubs
18. Alexi Ogando, of, Athletics
19. Alexi Casilla, 2b/ss, Angels
20. Connor Robertson, rhp, Athletics

GULF COAST LEAGUE

1. Luis Soto, ss, Red Sox
2. Gaby Hernandez, rhp, Mets
3. Greg Golson, of, Phillies
4. Kyle Waldrop, rhp, Twins
5. Neil Walker, c, Pirates
6. Christian Garcia, rhp, Yankees
7. Marcos Vechionacci, 3b, Yankees
8. Jay Rainville, rhp, Twins
9. Christian Lara, ss, Red Sox
10. Greg Burns, of, Marlins
11. Jose Campusano, ss, Marlins
12. Juan Portes, 3b, Twins
13. Jamie Hoffmann, 3b, Dodgers
14. Carlos Carrasco, rhp, Phillies
15. Anthony Swarzak, rhp, Twins
16. Jesus Flores, c, Mets
17. Johan Silva, of, Braves
18. Carlos Gomez, of, Mets
19. Willy Mota, of, Red Sox
20. Scott Mitchinson, rhp, Phillies

INDEPENDENT
LEAGUES

Indy players in demand in 2004 as record number sold to major clubs

BY J.J. COOPER

Five years ago, Schaumburg's Ben Van Iderstine would have had a legitimate shot to hit .400 in the Northern League. Chillicothe two-way star Mark Hamilton also could have vied for both the Frontier League's batting and ERA titles.

In 2004, however, both ended up as footnotes in their leagues' respective seasons. Neither was complaining. Nowadays, a couple of months of gaudy stats in an independent league is a good way to find yourself playing in Organized Baseball. It happened for Van Iderstine and Hamilton, who became teammates in 2004 with the high Class A High Desert Mavericks in the Brewers farm system.

In all, such player acquisitions happened a record 112 times during the 2004 season, as four of the five independent leagues set records for players sold. The Atlantic League led the way with 40 players sold to affiliated clubs.

The path from the independent leagues to affiliated baseball has gotten smoother and more frequent over the past few years, but the leagues had seen nothing like 2004. Because of U.S. government visa restrictions that limited the number of foreign players that could play in the states, affiliated teams had few other places to turn if they lost a player to injury.

"They've finally recognized that our guys can play," said Miles Wolff, commissioner of both the Northeast League and Central League. "Some teams had a superior attitude. Now, (Northeast League president) Dan Moushon takes calls from teams asking, 'Who are the best pitchers? We need one.' In the last year or two, the attitude of the major league clubs has turned around."

While all the player movement has been seen as a sign of acceptance, the downside for independent leagues was that while they were sending more players to affiliated ball, they had the same problems that the affiliated

Atlantic League celebration
Ex-big leaguers steer Ducks to 2004 title

teams were having in finding replacements.

"The talent pool is decreased because of the visa situation," said Northern League director of baseball operations Mike Marshall. "We're probably looking at 10 to 20 percent of the players with (visas in past years) aren't available this year."

So when a veteran pitcher was sold by an Atlantic League club in 2004, there wasn't the normal reservoir of talent waiting to replace him. It was a problem that teams around the indy leagues had to face all season.

"We've had more players taken because there seem to be less players out there," said Wolff, who also owns the Northeast League's Quebec City club. "Veteran hitters and veteran pitchers aren't out there. There are not enough players for our team, so there are even less for the traveling teams."

Both the Atlantic (Pennsylvania Road Warriors) and Northeast (Aces) leagues fielded road-only teams in 2004 that ostensibly served as reserve squads for the other teams in the league.

The Road Warriors have always been the weak sister of the Atlantic League, finishing last each of the past five years. But their 23-103 record in 2004 topped their previous worst mark by 7½ games. The Aces, a new traveling team in the Northeast League, had more success but still finished with a 28-64 record, worst in the league.

Moving Men

The arrival of a second traveling team in 2004 was proof that while indy ball is more stable than it has been at any point during the past decade, it still battles with finding stable markets for some of its teams.

The Aces were formed when the Allentown Ambassadors informed the

2004 INDEPENDENT LEAGUE ALL-STARS

Selected by Baseball America

Pos. Player, Team (League)	AVG	AB	R	H	2B	3B	HR	RBI	SB
C Kelley Gulledge, Fargo-Moorhead (Northern)	.320	347	64	111	31	2	8	55	2
1B Doug Jennings, Long Island (Atlantic)	.359	340	87	122	31	2	17	84	2
2B Anthony Angel, Edinburg (Central)	.308	347	68	107	20	4	6	66	8
SS Victor Rodriguez, Somerset (Atlantic)	.371	483	82	179	32	0	25	111	4
3B Wilton Veras, New Jersey (Northeast)	.369	320	46	118	29	1	5	59	1
OF Richard Austin, Rockford (Frontier)	.359	290	71	104	20	1	15	77	22
OF Kimera Bartee, Long Island (Atlantic)	.319	445	103	142	22	9	27	88	30
OF Adam Olow, St. Paul (Northern)	.376	340	76	128	29	4	7	70	16
DH Eddie Pearson, Kansas City (Northern)	.330	351	70	116	15	0	30	94	4

	W	L	ERA	G	SV	IP	H	BB	SO
SP Kevin Henthrorne, Atlantic City (Atlantic)	12	3	2.69	23	0	150	139	19	100
SP Brian Mazone, Joliet (Northern)	9	2	1.73	14	0	104	77	15	95
SP Hank Woodman, Schaumburg (Northern)	6	6	1.95	19	0	120	95	34	141
RP Chris Chavez, St. Paul (Northern)	2	0	2.20	43	29	45	29	11	63
RP Alex Santos, Quebec (Northeast)	2	1	1.06	31	22	34	19	5	49

PLAYER OF THE YEAR: Victor Rodriguez, ss, Somerset (Atlantic).

Northeast League that they were declaring bankruptcy and folding less than a month before the season began. The Road Warriors live on, in part, because the Atlantic League continues to search for a city and ownership to place its eighth franchise.

At the same time, the Central League scaled back from 10 franchises to eight when the Rio Grande Valley WhiteWings and the Alexandria Aces both folded before the 2004 season. And the Frontier League ran into financial and legal troubles with its Florence franchise, eventually forcing the league to take over the team, with hopes of selling it to new ownership before the 2005 season.

But while there were still potholes throughout the indy leagues, the surviving five leagues show plenty of signs of long-term stability. The five leagues formed a new association of independent leagues that hopes to work together on major issues. Among other things, the leagues have teamed up to hold their own joint offseason meetings. And the Northern League announced that Edmonton and Calgary, two former Triple-A cities, will join the league for the 2005 season.

While one upstart league (Arizona-Mexico) folded during the 2003 season, and another (Southeastern) folded after the season, no new leagues attempted to play in 2004. That should change in 2005, as the Golden Baseball League hopes to field eight teams in California and Arizona.

Growing Attendance

According to reported attendance figures, the five independent leagues saw only a marginal attendance increase in 2004. All together, the five leagues drew 6,560,539 fans, up from 6,376,618 in 2003. That growth came despite the Central League's decision to field eight teams, down from 10 in 2003.

The Northern League led the way with 2,001,268 fans—an average of 4,285 per game. The Atlantic (1,793,238) and Frontier (1,294,711) leagues both easily topped the 1 million fan mark, and the Northeast League saw an increase of nearly 100,000 fans, drawing 759,004. With 712,318 fans, the Central was the only league to see a decrease, largely because it cut back two teams. All five leagues topped 2,000 in average attendance.

The Northern League's Winnipeg franchise led the way, averaging 7,027 fans per game. Long Island (Atlantic) and St. Paul (Northern) topped 6,000 fans per game.

ATLANTIC LEAGUE

Every time Long Island manager Don McCormack shook hands and wished good luck to one of his departing pitchers in 2004, he wondered if he was watching

Rodriguez adds power

Even as he destroyed the Atlantic League record book in 2004, Victor Rodriguez was not fully appreciated by his own Somerset fans.

While the stats may have shown night after night of 2-for-4, 2 RBIs and a run scored, fans saw a runner who sometimes pulled up on a grounder before he reached first base.

PLAYER
of the **YEAR**

What they didn't know was that Rodriguez had an abdominal strain that made it painful to run. Given the choice between sitting his top hitter or telling him to push it, Somerset manager Sparky Lyle told Rodriguez to jog when needed and ignore the booing.

So as he put together one of the best seasons in Atlantic League history, Rodriguez occasionally heard boo-birds at home. It got to the point that Lyle asked the reporter who covered the Patriots to explain Rodriguez' condition in the newspaper. The booing slowed, but never fully subsided.

"I didn't want him out of the lineup," Lyle said. "I told him, 'I don't want you to get upset about this.' There are times when he

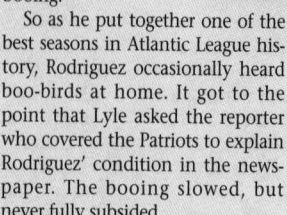
Victor Rodriguez

wouldn't run the whole way when he knew he was out. That looked bad, but it was of no concern to me, because I knew he was going out there hurt."

There was a good reason to keep Rodriguez in the No. 3 hole. The 28-year-old was on his way to breaking the league record for batting (.371) as well as hits (179) and RBIs (111). He also was second-best in the league in home runs (25). His record-breaking year was good enough to make Rodriguez Baseball America's Independent League Player of the Year for 2004.

Rodriguez, a second-round pick of the Florida Marlins out of a Puerto Rico high school in 1994, had spent the previous 10 years in affiliated ball, most of it as a shortstop in Double-A. He had a .277 career average, but just 26 career home runs.

"When we signed him, we knew he had the potential to hit, but we had no idea he'd hit for the power," Somerset director of player procurement Adam Gladstone said. "He got into a groove where every ball he hit took off. He never got into a slump."

—J.J. COOPER

the Ducks' chance at an Atlantic League title disappear.

During the first half of the season, the Ducks had one of the league's best offenses and one of the best pitching staffs as well, led by former big leaguers Bill Pulsipher, Bill Simas, Lance Davis and Matt Beech.

But all four were signed by big league clubs to Triple-A contracts during the season, and McCormack figured it would be impossible to fill those holes.

He didn't count on the Ducks' 2004 Reunion Tour. When they signed with affiliated clubs, all four said they could end up back in Long Island if they were released.

"You kind of hope they come back, but it doesn't often happen," McCormack said.

With just a week and a half left in the season, Pulsipher came back. The other three followed close behind. Pulsipher quickly developed a motto: "We're getting the band back together." He even made t-shirts proclaiming the fact.

With their clubhouse full again, the Ducks rode into the playoffs on a high. "When those guys come back, it gives you a breath of fresh air," McCormack said.

The Ducks lost their playoff opener but blew through their next five games to claim their first league title,

sweeping Camden in the championship series after rallying to beat Atlantic City in the semifinals.

"Having those guys back was tremendous," said playoff MVP Justin Davies, who hit .333 with six runs during the playoffs. "Having those guys back, we felt real confident going into the playoffs. It was back like it was during the first month of the season."

The winning pitcher in the final game? Pulsipher, who won two playoff games. The closer who pitched the final two innings? Simas, who didn't allow a run while picking up three saves in the playoffs.

While the return of the four pitchers lifted the Ducks to the title, it was the Long Island offense that got the team into the playoffs. First baseman Doug Jennings led the league in on-base (.505) and slugging percentage (.612) and was second in the

Bill Pulsipher

league in batting (.359), and outfielder Kimera Bartee completed a remarkable transformation. Bartee was a speedy center fielder who stole 218 bases in 883 minor league games, but slugged only .380. With the Ducks, Bartee continued to run, stealing 30 bases, but he also finished second in the league with 27 home runs, slugged .591 and drove in 88 runs while scoring a league-leading 103.

"As he was coming through organizations, he was told to be a speed guy," McCormack said. "Now he's told to look for pitches he can hit hard and a long way. Over the course of a couple of years, he has done that pretty well. This year, he would get in hitting counts and look for pitches up in the zone and hit them a long ways. He really concentrated."

While Bartee and Jennings had big seasons, Somerset shortstop/first baseman Victor Rodriguez rewrote parts of the league's record book, with a .372-25-112 season that set records for batting average, RBIs and hits (179). He was named the league's MVP.

STANDINGS

FIRST HALF

NORTH

NORTH	W	L	PCT	GB
Long Island Ducks	39	23	.629	--
Bridgeport Bluefish	38	24	.613	1
Nashua Pride	29	34	.460	10½
Pennsylvania Road Warriors	10	53	.159	29½

SOUTH	W	L	PCT	GB
Atlantic City Surf	38	24	.613	--
Camden Riversharks	36	26	.581	2
Somerset Patriots	33	29	.532	5
Newark Bears	26	36	.419	12

SECOND HALF

NORTH	W	L	PCT	GB
Nashua Pride	36	27	.571	--
Bridgeport Bluefish	34	29	.540	2
Long Island Ducks	25	38	.397	11
Pennsylvania Road Warriors	13	50	.206	23

SOUTH	W	L	PCT	GB
Camden Riversharks	39	23	.629	--
Newark Bears	36	27	.571	3½
Somerset Patriots	35	28	.556	4½
Atlantic City Surf	33	29	.532	6

PLAYOFFS: Semifinals—Long Island defeated Atlantic City 2-1 and Camden defeated Nashua 2-0 in best-of-5 series. **Finals**—Long Island defeated Camden 3-0 in best-of-5 series.

MANAGERS: Atlantic City—Jeff Ball. **Bridgeport**—Jose Lind. **Camden**—Wayne Krenchicki. **Long Island**—Don McCormack. **Nashua**—

Butch Hobson. **Newark**—Bill Madlock. **Pennsylvania**—Bert Pena. **Somerset**—Sparky Lyle.

ATTENDANCE: Long Island 440,540; Somerset 376,315; Camden 293,018; Bridgeport 242,608; Newark 189,468; Atlantic City 133,521; Nashua 117,768.

ALL-STAR TEAM: C—Chris Widger, Camden. **1B**—Doug Jennings, Long Island. **2B**—Emiliano Escandon, Somerset. **3B**—Jeff Nettles, Somerset. **SS**—Victor Rodriguez, Somerset. **OF**—Kimera Bartee, Long Island; Quincy Foster, Camden; Keith Maxwell, Newark; Ozzie Timmons, Atlantic City. **DH**—Jose Amado, Bridgeport. **UT**—Dario Delgado, Atlantic City. **LHP**—Bill Pulsipher, Long Island. **RHP**—Kevin Henthorne, Bridgeport. **RP**—Bill Simas, Long Island.

Most Valuable Player: Victor Rodriguez, Somerset. **Most Valuable Pitcher:** Kevin Henthorne, Bridgeport. **Manager of the Year:** Jeff Ball, Atlantic City.

INDIVIDUAL BATTING LEADERS
(Minimum 340 Plate Appearances)

	AVG	AB	R	H	2B	3B	HR	RBI	SB
Rodriguez, Victor, Somerset	.371	483	82	179	32	0	25	111	3
Jennings, Doug, Long Island	.359	340	87	122	31	2	17	84	2
Amado, Jose, Bridgeport	.339	437	69	148	33	1	13	93	9
Foster, Quincy, Camden	.330	455	82	150	13	10	2	54	51
Lennon, Pat, Long Island	.323	439	85	142	36	2	14	88	7
Bartee, Kimera, Long Island	.319	445	103	142	22	9	27	88	30
Nettles, Jeff, Somerset	.319	455	87	145	23	3	22	93	1
Delgado, Dario, Atlantic City	.313	447	83	140	26	1	24	83	10
Luuloa, Keith, Bridgeport	.313	396	60	124	29	0	6	51	0
Jones, Chris, Newark	.313	297	56	93	18	3	15	69	2

INDIVIDUAL PITCHING LEADERS
(Minimum 101 Innings)

	W	L	ERA	G	SV	IP	H	BB	SO
Henthorne, Kevin, Bridgeport	12	3	2.69	23	0	150	139	19	100
Mikkelsen, Lincoln, Camden	12	4	3.01	25	0	159	160	40	96
Cain, Tim, Bridgeport	12	4	3.12	24	0	153	132	37	91
Pulsipher, Bill, Long Island	9	5	3.67	18	0	115	121	34	85
Davis, Lance, Long Island	8	6	3.67	18	0	105	106	24	70
Cornett, Brad, Bridgeport	8	4	3.81	21	0	120	119	27	84
Gannon, Joe, Newark	7	4	3.90	20	0	108	87	62	58
Smith, Clint, Newark	6	9	3.97	27	1	116	123	24	59
Simon, Ben, Camden	6	9	4.05	20	0	127	126	33	81
Zwirchitz, Andy, Atlantic City	9	8	4.14	24	1	128	135	70	109

* Signed with affiliated minor league club during 2004 season

ATLANTIC CITY

BATTING	AVG	AB	R	H	2B	3B	HR	RBI	SB
Adolfo, Carlos, of	.278	54	12	15	1	0	6	17	1
*Alexander, Chad, of	.318	85	11	27	7	0	1	15	0
*Benard, Marvin, of	.361	36	5	13	2	1	0	6	1
Benjamin, Al, of	.287	188	26	54	14	0	7	34	3
3-team (15 Camden, 27 Nashua)	.301	345	52	104	20	2	12	50	5
Candelaria, Ben, dh	.360	125	23	45	14	2	5	23	1
2-team (29 Bridgeport)	.303	234	36	71	20	3	7	33	1
Delgado, Dario, 3b-1b	.313	447	83	140	26	1	24	83	10
Encarnacion, Henry, ss	.000	5	0	0	0	0	0	0	0
3-team (7 Camden, 28 Penn)	.164	110	8	18	4	2	0	3	2
Gambill, Chad, of	.283	46	7	13	3	0	1	5	0
Garland, Tim, of	.086	35	4	3	0	0	0	2	0
*Gutierrez, Vic, ss	.333	30	4	10	0	1	0	5	2
*Heath, Demetrius, 2b-of	.286	266	59	76	9	5	1	16	48
Housel, David, 2b-ss	.215	191	23	41	11	1	0	13	2
Johnson, Gary, of	.293	440	69	129	25	5	8	51	11
Lara, Eddie, 2b-3b	.250	48	3	12	1	0	0	6	0
3-team (18 Newark, 38 Bridgeport)	.284	250	32	71	13	2	8	46	7
Law, Jason, of	.226	124	11	28	4	2	0	14	0
Marval, Raul, ss-3b	.278	464	91	129	29	1	16	71	4
Matullo, Joe, c	.132	76	8	10	2	0	0	6	1
McDonald, Kevin, c	.188	133	19	25	7	0	1	11	1
Miller, Orlando, ss	.252	107	15	27	5	0	5	21	1
*Minor, Ryan, 3b-1b	.326	236	39	77	11	0	16	45	0
Quintana, Wil, of	.228	224	34	51	12	0	17	39	2
3-team (35 Newark, 2 Long Island)	.239	343	48	82	17	1	21	57	7
Rosario, Mel, c	.266	320	44	85	24	5	10	48	5
*Timmons, Ozzie, of	.373	287	57	107	22	2	21	73	2
Velazquez, Jose, 1b	.331	236	49	78	13	1	5	36	2

PITCHING	W	L	ERA	G	SV	IP	H	BB	SO
Barnett, Marty	2	3	6.75	9	0	44	62	19	28
*Brooks, Conor	1	2	4.06	30	16	31	25	11	33
Brownson, Mark	2	4	5.37	14	1	62	71	20	42
Castillo, Alberto	4	2	4.47	14	0	54	63	24	33
Chavez, Anthony	7	4	3.14	14	0	94	90	33	51
Corbin, Archie	6	2	2.70	15	0	50	31	24	60
Corrado, Rob	5	7	4.76	33	1	90	113	31	75
Darley, Ned	1	2	2.21	26	5	36	36	21	23
Davis, Ray	3	0	3.41	10	0	58	42	24	44

	W	L	ERA	G	SV	IP	H	BB	SO
Dickinson, Rodney	4	5	3.54	41	1	40	40	17	43
*Farnsworth, Jeff	2	0	2.96	4	0	27	26	3	19
Forbes, Derek	0	1	7.15	6	0	11	14	7	8
Goldwater, Kyle	5	4	4.87	28	0	136	160	30	70
High, Andy	2	1	3.44	4	0	18	16	3	20
McCarthy, Greg	1	0	7.20	12	1	10	14	11	8
Montane, Ivan	1	1	2.21	8	0	20	15	11	19
2-team (6 Somerset)	1	1	6.04	14	0	28	31	20	26
Newman, Alan	0	2	7.04	2	0	7	16	4	7
Odom, Lance	1	0	8.38	6	0	9	12	4	7
Persails, Mark	1	0	1.29	3	0	14	9	10	7
Ponce Deleon, Damon	12	5	3.92	49	2	87	94	32	71
Sanchez, Amaury	1	0	3.86	4	0	4	5	2	1
*Villegas, Felix	0	0	3.38	4	0	5	5	3	6
Wade, Terrell	1	1	5.46	7	0	31	36	22	25
2-team (6 Pennsylvania)	3	2	5.30	13	0	54	61	31	34
Young, Ray	0	0	7.50	3	0	6	7	7	3
Zwirchitz, Andy	9	8	4.14	24	1	128	135	70	109

BRIDGEPORT

BATTING	AVG	AB	R	H	2B	3B	HR	RBI	SB
Alley, Charles, c	.237	93	13	22	6	1	1	11	0
Amado, Jose, dh-1b	.339	437	69	148	33	1	13	93	9
Avila, Rolo, of	.262	416	68	109	18	0	2	39	15
Boston, D.J., 1b	.254	209	32	53	12	1	5	24	8
Candelaria, Ben, of	.239	109	13	26	6	1	2	10	0
Escobar, Gustavo, ss-2b	.277	405	65	112	11	11	1	53	31
Espada, Angel, 2b	.313	112	19	35	5	0	1	8	7
*Gann, Jamie, of	.369	149	34	55	13	4	8	42	5
Kuilan, Hector, c	.271	295	33	80	19	0	4	29	0
Lara, Eddie, 3b-2b	.306	144	21	44	9	2	4	27	5
Luuloa, Keith, 3b	.313	396	60	124	29	0	6	51	0
Marrero, Oreste, 1b-of	.209	234	37	49	8	0	4	29	1
Ortiz, Asbel, 2b	.250	220	23	55	8	3	4	26	1
Ortiz, Nick, ss	.229	323	40	74	12	2	6	32	7
Otanez, Willis, of	.293	184	21	54	10	0	7	37	0
Pennyfeather, William, of	.266	361	64	96	15	3	8	67	2
Rocha, Juan, of	.286	42	4	12	2	0	1	9	0
Sanchez, Tino, of-c	.290	252	33	73	16	1	7	29	3

PITCHING	W	L	ERA	G	SV	IP	H	BB	SO
Agosto, Stevenson	3	8	5.74	34	2	102	98	66	84
Arroyo, Luis	5	3	4.35	12	0	41	50	15	33
2-team (14 Pennsylvania)	10	10	4.68	26	0	127	150	57	86
Arthurs, Shane	5	6	4.86	49	2	70	78	38	36
Batson, Byron	2	2	5.09	5	0	17	20	4	10
Bell, Richard	3	1	3.00	17	2	24	31	6	16
Cain, Tim	12	3	3.12	24	0	152	132	37	91
Cornett, Brad	8	4	3.81	21	0	120	119	27	84
Henthorne, Kevin	12	3	2.69	23	0	150	139	19	100
Hill, Terrance	2	1	5.03	49	1	68	63	35	58
Langen, Brian	4	3	2.39	14	0	67	70	16	49
*Mathews, T.J.	1	3	4.25	17	5	36	43	5	40
Ramos, Eddy	1	1	1.38	23	13	26	20	9	33
2-team (26 Newark)	4	3	4.12	49	14	91	85	34	91
Rojas, Mel	0	0	2.08	17	9	17	14	2	14
Rosengren, Phil	2	3	4.66	23	0	58	67	27	34
Rosenkranz, Terry	0	3	11.52	11	0	25	45	16	19
Schurman, Ryan	5	3	3.73	23	1	41	38	14	34
2-team (12 Camden)	8	8	5.26	35	1	99	106	34	67
Warren, Brian	1	0	1.86	21	3	19	24	1	26
Wedel, Jeremy	1	0	5.87	8	0	7	11	5	4
Williams, Blake	5	6	3.86	23	0	95	103	28	70
2-team (4 Somerset)	6	9	4.68	27	0	117	131	37	83

CAMDEN

BATTING	AVG	AB	R	H	2B	3B	HR	RBI	SB
Anderson, Travis, c	.294	218	39	64	9	1	2	24	1
Barrett, Rich, of	.265	102	28	27	3	0	0	5	25
Benjamin, Al, of	.261	46	7	12	3	2	1	5	0
Briggs, Stoney, of	.259	379	49	98	26	4	11	65	11
Cameron, Troy, 3b-2b	.286	402	72	115	23	3	16	55	2
Dewey, Jason, c	.250	76	9	19	7	1	0	7	0
Encarnacion, Henry, 2b	.214	14	2	3	1	1	0	0	0
Foster, Quincy, of	.330	455	82	150	13	0	2	54	51
Hage, Tom, dh-1b	.290	272	36	79	13	0	8	41	0
Jones, Ryan, 1b	.297	411	67	122	26	2	15	85	1
Jordan, Kevin, 2b	.248	266	34	66	14	2	2	34	3
Maness, Dwight, of	.274	424	78	116	19	3	11	69	28
Mejia, Max, of	.077	13	1	1	0	0	0	1	0
Rivero, Eddie, of	.222	90	10	20	6	0	3	9	0
Rodriguez, Tony, ss	.286	409	52	117	16	1	5	52	15
Strauss, Brad, 3b-1b	.273	400	51	109	15	9	5	46	5
Wakeland, Chris, of	.143	28	2	4	1	0	0	2	0
2-team (68 Somerset)	.266	263	32	70	12	4	9	45	2

	AVG	AB	R	H	2B	3B	HR	RBI	SB
Widger, Chris, c	.267	202	37	54	12	1	16	43	5
Wilson, Kevin, 2b-ss	.174	69	9	12	1	0	0	2	1

PITCHING	W	L	ERA	G	SV	IP	H	BB	SO
Bullinger, Jim	3	0	3.55	6	0	33	31	9	20
Cedeno, Blas	1	2	3.89	22	2	34	39	18	19
*Davis, Kane	2	0	0.00	5	3	4	2	2	7
*Dougherty, Kevin	4	2	3.55	7	0	38	29	12	36
Forster, Scott	0	0	8.10	12	0	13	18	11	14
Foster, Cliff	3	4	5.71	24	2	34	36	25	24
Janzen, Marty	1	0	2.35	9	0	15	15	7	11
2-team (4 Nashua)	1	2	5.17	13	0	31	44	14	17
Laxton, Brett	8	8	4.34	23	0	145	163	48	84
Laxton, Josh	0	0	9.00	2	0	2	3	2	2
Markey, Barry	4	2	5.71	31	0	58	76	23	22
Mikkelsen, Lincoln	12	4	3.01	25	0	158	160	40	96
*Nussbeck, Mark	7	1	3.45	15	0	70	68	14	47
Rizzo, Nick	0	0	3.86	2	0	7	8	0	2
Rizzo, Todd	4	5	1.79	59	9	80	60	29	57
Schurman, Ryan	3	5	6.33	12	0	58	68	20	33
Simon, Ben	6	9	4.05	20	0	126	126	33	81
*Spradlin, Jerry	2	0	0.40	19	8	22	15	4	18
Steward, Jaime	4	6	4.19	29	1	77	69	49	68
Strong, Joe	3	0	2.20	29	15	28	19	11	31
*Thomas, Evan	8	1	3.62	13	0	87	76	25	66
*Ward, Bryan	1	0	3.46	2	0	13	17	2	16

LONG ISLAND

BATTING	AVG	AB	R	H	2B	3B	HR	RBI	SB
Baez, Kevin, ss-3b	.256	344	36	88	16	1	4	40	0
Bartee, Kimera, of	.319	445	103	142	22	9	27	88	30
Caruso, Mike, ss	.299	134	17	40	4	1	0	12	1
Davies, Justin, of	.266	369	63	98	12	2	2	36	18
Garrick, Matt, c	.240	204	18	49	9	0	4	26	0
Jennings, Doug, 1b	.359	340	87	122	31	2	17	84	2
Johnson, Jason, of	.278	360	78	100	14	6	11	58	36
Lennon, Pat, dh-1b	.323	439	85	142	36	2	14	88	7
Liniak, Cole, 3b-2b	.269	360	62	97	23	1	8	47	5
Magee, Wendell, of	.294	446	61	131	29	2	13	86	7
McCormack, Taylor, 3b-1b	.230	283	25	65	13	2	2	23	0
McNamara, Rusty, 2b-3b	.281	64	19	18	6	0	1	6	0
Owen, Ryan, c	.256	82	16	21	5	2	0	4	0
Quintana, Wil, of	.500	2	4	2	0	0	0	3	0
Rodriguez, L, c	.290	221	28	64	13	3	7	39	3
Salvo, Andrew, 2b-ss	.299	321	40	96	12	2	2	33	1

PITCHING	W	L	ERA	G	SV	IP	H	BB	SO
*Beech, Matt	3	1	2.28	7	0	43	26	18	53
Borbon, Pedro	0	0	7.71	1	0	4	8	4	1
Brewington, Jamie	1	2	8.37	27	2	23	39	13	20
Chavez, Carlos	1	0	4.37	18	0	22	26	7	13
Cotton, Joe	5	1	1.91	40	2	42	33	13	33
Davenport, Joe	1	3	9.53	7	0	17	28	10	7
*Davis, Lance	8	6	3.67	18	0	105	106	24	70
DeSilva, John	4	6	4.02	17	0	87	95	14	43
*Dewitt, Matt	1	0	2.35	14	2	15	13	2	17
Heredia, Julian	0	4	5.88	4	0	26	29	10	21
2-team (23 Pennsylvania)	3	18	5.55	27	0	168	189	53	139
Kolb, Brandon	0	0	15.43	3	0	2	5	3	0
2-team (38 Nashua)	2	3	4.35	41	0	60	72	23	34
Kozlowski, Kris	5	5	5.71	33	0	108	137	31	52
Lamber, Justin	5	1	4.18	44	0	75	88	22	60
Mattes, Troy	2	1	5.12	3	0	19	19	7	8
Navarro, Jason	5	3	3.61	12	0	72	74	25	59
2-team (13 Nashua)	8	8	4.95	25	0	129	155	54	106
*Pulsipher, Bill	9	5	3.67	18	0	115	121	34	85
Rekar, Bryan	2	4	5.87	11	0	53	70	15	36
Sheredy, Kevin	1	3	7.39	13	0	28	38	23	19
Shibilo, Andy	3	3	4.60	14	1	58	63	23	24
*Simas, Bill	2	4	1.95	44	17	50	37	14	53
Stoops, Jim	1	2	4.97	20	0	25	29	17	19
*Ulloa, Enmanuel	1	4	4.13	21	1	61	62	12	54
2-team (2 Pennsylvania)	2	4	3.73	23	1	70	64	15	62
*Weibl, Clint	2	1	3.55	4	0	25	21	10	12
Zimmerman, Jordan	3	2	2.28	50	2	47	48	16	36

NASHUA

BATTING	AVG	AB	R	H	2B	3B	HR	RBI	SB
Benjamin, Al, of	.342	111	19	38	3	0	4	11	2
Bichette, Dante, 1b-dh	.312	199	39	62	12	1	18	54	9
Burns, Kevan, of	.276	254	38	70	19	1	4	29	4
Cordova, Ricardo, ss-2b	.287	387	64	111	13	4	4	41	12
Figga, Mike, c	.233	30	4	7	1	0	1	5	1
Fonville, Chad, 2b	.182	33	6	6	1	0	0	1	0
Garcia, Omar, dh-of	.278	54	9	15	1	0	1	10	0

	AVG	AB	R	H	2B	3B	HR	RBI	SB
Hastings, Jeff, of	.036	28	4	1	1	0	0	1	0
Haverbusch, Kevin, 1b-of	.312	269	52	84	14	1	19	65	9
Hine, Dennis, 2b	.217	23	3	5	0	0	0	2	0
Howell, Pat, of-2b	.223	121	13	27	4	0	2	8	2
King, Brad, c	.190	100	12	19	3	0	5	15	0
2-team (48 Somerset)	.205	259	32	53	11	0	11	33	1
*Lofton, James, 2b-ss	.272	173	34	47	7	0	3	18	6
*Lopez-Cao, Mike, c-2b	.296	213	35	63	16	1	4	32	0
*Matos, Pascual, c	.254	173	24	44	11	1	8	30	4
Murray, Glenn, dh	.265	393	72	104	15	0	21	72	3
Petersen, Chris, ss	.271	166	17	45	8	0	1	13	2
*Pride, Curtis, of	.446	65	12	29	9	0	1	12	4
Robinson, Bo, 3b-1b	.272	448	63	122	26	0	7	62	3
Rodarte, Raul, of	.310	210	48	65	18	1	4	22	3
Rodriguez, Carlos, of	.307	417	59	128	19	2	13	76	20
Rodriguez, Henry, of	.301	163	34	49	11	0	13	36	0
Sanchez, Marcos, c	.292	24	3	7	2	0	1	1	1
Shanks, Eric, 3b-2b	.254	130	24	33	7	0	1	12	2
Tovar, Edgar, 2b-3b	.236	182	17	43	7	0	1	22	1
2-team (52 Pennsylvania)	.283	389	47	110	15	0	5	45	4

PITCHING	W	L	ERA	G	SV	IP	H	BB	SO
Andujar, Luis	1	0	3.86	42	2	56	59	12	51
Bichette, Dante	0	1	12.00	3	1	6	11	4	5
*Chantres, Carlos	4	0	2.88	4	0	25	19	11	21
Chrysler, Clint	5	2	4.97	46	0	70	94	32	42
*Deschenes, Marc	3	0	1.73	23	9	26	18	6	25
Guy, Brad	11	11	4.89	26	0	165	214	43	104
Hammons, Matt	5	6	5.74	13	0	62	84	18	49
Hardwick, Bubba	1	5	6.06	40	0	87	116	38	65
Harriger, Denny	4	3	3.31	9	0	65	63	22	37
Janzen, Marty	0	2	7.88	4	0	16	29	7	6
Juden, Jeff	0	2	10.64	7	0	11	21	6	5
Klemm, Tom	0	0	27.00	3	0	1	5	3	0
Kolb, Brandon	2	3	3.90	38	0	57	67	20	34
Looney, Brian	5	3	3.92	11	0	66	71	23	41
Navarro, Jason	3	5	6.67	13	0	56	81	29	47
Pearson, Terry	3	0	1.65	25	3	32	35	19	30
Pena, Juan	1	4	5.73	6	0	33	39	14	22
Pena, Juan	0	0	5.12	10	0	19	30	12	13
Smith, Cliff	1	0	3.38	17	0	24	22	13	23
Sparks, Jeff	5	4	2.70	45	10	53	42	22	69
Stevens, Dave	1	0	6.75	3	0	4	5	4	6
Teut, Nate	10	9	5.24	26	0	144	181	47	88
Williamson, Willie	0	0	27.00	3	0	1	0	10	0
Yennaco, Jay	0	1	25.14	11	0	9	23	11	5

NEWARK

BATTING	AVG	AB	R	H	2B	3B	HR	RBI	SB
Clyburn, Danny, of	.334	299	47	100	17	1	16	56	0
Coleman, Michael, of-1b	.269	379	65	102	21	0	27	76	3
DeLeon, Sandy, c	.256	133	16	34	3	1	0	12	3
Dewey, Jason, c	.254	193	23	49	14	1	5	34	0
2-team (24 Camden)	.253	269	32	68	21	2	5	41	0
Henderson, Rickey, dh-of	.281	303	70	85	16	2	9	31	37
Joffrion, Jack, 2b-ss	.269	361	59	97	25	4	10	41	3
Jones, Chris, of-1b	.313	297	56	93	18	3	15	69	2
LaFlair, Jay, c-3b	.203	79	9	16	4	0	0	3	3
Lara, Eddie, 2b	.259	58	8	15	3	0	4	13	2
Larkin, Stephen, of	.184	76	7	14	3	1	0	5	2
Maestrales, Pete, 3b-2b	.263	270	51	71	18	4	6	29	11
Martinez, Hipolito, of-1b	.283	92	15	26	1	2	2	10	1
Maxwell, Keith, 1b-of	.292	408	79	119	18	1	30	84	1
*Mosquera, Julio, c	.296	54	5	16	2	0	1	8	0
Olmeda, Jose, 3b-2b	.287	254	36	73	14	3	13	52	3
Perez, Jerson, ss	.294	428	77	126	24	8	10	68	7
Piercy, Mike, of	.268	190	31	51	4	1	1	9	19
Quintana, Wil, of	.243	111	12	27	3	1	4	15	5
Randolph, Andre, 2b	.149	47	3	7	1	0	0	3	3
Santora, Jack, 2b	.348	23	8	8	2	0	0	3	2
Torres, Jason, c	.161	31	2	5	0	0	2	7	0
VanRossum, Chris, of	.276	261	40	72	20	4	4	33	12

PITCHING	W	L	ERA	G	SV	IP	H	BB	SO
Anderson, Jason	0	0	17.36	4	0	4	7	8	3
Banks, Willie	1	3	9.64	5	0	14	21	9	4
*Bauer, Greg	4	6	4.95	15	0	76	96	35	48
Billingsley, Brent	5	1	3.83	9	0	51	50	23	40
Crampton, Steve	6	3	2.15	46	2	75	43	20	68
Crumpton, Chuck	7	4	4.38	12	0	63	74	17	26
Daneker, Pat	4	8	6.49	21	0	95	126	35	46
Dunn, Gerald	0	1	4.09	4	0	11	13	7	5
Foster, Cliff	3	1	4.96	16	0	32	35	28	21
2-team (24 Camden)	6	5	5.35	40	2	67	71	53	45
Gannon, Joe	7	4	3.90	20	0	108	87	62	58
Gaskill, Derek	0	0	0.00	4	0	5	3	2	7

	W	L	ERA	G	SV	IP	H	BB	SO
*Harris, Reggie	0	1	4.06	27	15	31	30	5	30
Langen, Brian	0	1	1.80	1	0	5	5	2	3
2-team (14 Bridgeport)	4	4	2.35	15	0	72	75	18	52
Linares, Ramon	1	0	10.43	11	0	14	23	11	12
Lopez, Jose	2	1	1.93	6	1	18	16	6	10
Maestrales, Pete	0	0	0.00	3	0	2	2	1	0
Montoya, Eric	0	0	2.25	3	0	8	10	2	3
Oakes, Gerry	0	0	15.26	6	0	7	12	19	7
Parks, Tommy	2	3	7.71	20	0	65	104	31	43
Ramos, Eddy	3	2	5.21	26	1	65	65	25	58
Reynoso, Edison	0	2	8.05	6	0	19	31	12	16
Richards, Dave	3	0	3.55	42	0	45	51	23	36
Ruhl, Nathan	0	2	10.03	7	0	11	14	5	5
Smith, Clint	6	9	3.97	27	1	115	123	24	59
Smith, Mike	3	2	5.48	5	0	23	26	12	17
Taylor, Tom	2	4	5.49	8	0	39	45	11	23
Viera, Rolando	1	1	4.41	4	0	16	23	6	13
Wade, Travis	3	4	2.45	42	4	69	66	12	50

PENNSYLVANIA

BATTING	AVG	AB	R	H	2B	3B	HR	RBI	SB
Agar, Cory, of	.242	66	6	16	5	1	0	7	1
Ayala, Abraham, c	.286	262	19	75	12	0	4	28	4
Bassett, Mike, of	.227	110	12	25	2	1	2	13	1
Bernazard, Oscar, 2b-ss	.162	272	19	44	6	1	0	18	6
Cafiero, Rob, 1b	.242	339	26	82	10	0	10	47	0
Camacho, Juan, dh	.189	53	3	10	1	0	2	7	0
Capodieci, Adam, c	.000	7	1	0	0	0	0	0	0
Chamizo, Ramiro, 3b-2b	.320	206	22	66	9	1	3	27	1
Cruz, Orlando, of	.181	166	11	30	8	0	2	12	2
Encarnacion, Henry, ss	.165	91	6	15	3	1	0	3	2
Falu, Melvin, ss-2b	.266	383	49	102	12	3	5	46	8
Goodwin, Curtis, of	.077	13	0	1	0	0	0	0	1
Iglasias, Isbel, of	.255	200	25	51	7	2	0	9	8
LeBron, Juan, of	.241	166	20	40	10	0	4	18	0
2-team (23 Somerset)	.236	254	26	60	13	1	4	22	1
Lynam, Guy, c-of	.282	220	17	62	13	0	2	20	5
Owen, Ryan, c	.241	79	8	19	3	1	1	6	0
2-team (25 Long Island)	.248	161	24	40	8	3	1	10	0
Reyes, Ivan, ss	.171	111	11	19	2	0	0	4	1
Santana, Gamalier, of	.221	303	33	67	18	1	5	18	27
Schmidt, Greg, of-3b	.266	64	3	17	3	0	0	6	0
Soto, Jose, of	.209	110	14	23	4	0	3	12	6
Stovall, DaRond, of	.259	263	47	68	17	4	6	27	6
Terebetski, Greg, ss	.077	39	3	3	0	0	0	1	0
Tindell, Matt, of	.120	25	4	3	0	0	0	1	0
Torres, Jason, c	.114	44	2	5	0	0	0	2	0
2-team (12 Newark)	.133	75	4	10	0	0	2	9	0
Tovar, Edgar, 2b-3b	.324	207	30	67	8	0	4	23	3
Williams, Brady, 1b-3b	.243	440	57	107	17	3	15	49	2

PITCHING	W	L	ERA	G	SV	IP	H	BB	SO
Arroyo, Luis	5	7	4.83	14	0	85	100	42	53
Benetiz, Edisbel	1	2	3.98	13	0	43	36	24	36
Collins, Pat	1	5	6.21	8	0	42	48	27	28
De Aza, Fernando	1	7	4.54	52	0	73	85	43	48
*Diaz, Pedro	1	3	3.56	24	1	43	35	16	34
Fernandez, Carlos	1	6	5.77	29	1	43	42	44	31
Figueroa, Juan	0	4	6.93	11	0	24	27	17	21
Guerrero, Jose	0	2	14.36	8	0	15	36	9	5
Heredia, Julian	3	14	5.49	23	0	142	160	43	118
Lee, Garrett	0	6	7.36	11	0	58	92	11	33
Linares, Ramon	0	5	2.54	39	5	46	36	36	45
2-team (11 Newark)	1	5	4.45	50	5	60	59	47	57
Matta, Felix	0	0	10.50	6	0	6	12	8	1
Miranda, Angel	0	0	7.27	7	0	8	14	1	6
Mozingo, Dan	2	3	4.55	18	0	55	51	34	40
2-team (5 Somerset)	4	4	5.82	23	0	77	85	46	49
Neitz, Josh	0	0	6.94	4	0	11	13	10	7
Ortiz, Julio	0	2	11.84	19	0	19	33	22	12
Peguero, Darwin	0	1	7.94	4	0	5	5	5	3
Polanco, Dionicio	1	0	10.32	14	0	11	19	11	7
Ramirez, Joslin	0	2	8.49	10	2	11	20	5	5
Rodriguez, Felix	2	18	7.83	27	0	123	164	89	76
Ruffin, Johnny	0	0	13.50	4	0	3	6	5	7
Saenz, Jason	2	7	7.46	16	0	70	93	43	46
Sanchez, Amaury	0	4	5.45	14	0	34	51	24	24
2-team (4 Atlantic City)	1	4	5.26	18	0	39	56	26	25
Stoops, Jim	1	2	5.79	4	0	18	22	6	9
2-team (20 Long Island)	2	4	5.32	24	0	44	51	23	28
Ulloa, Enmanuel	1	0	1.00	2	0	9	2	3	8
Wade, Terrell	2	1	5.09	6	0	23	25	9	9
Williamson, Willie	0	1	25.50	5	0	6	11	21	6
2-team (3 Nashua)	0	1	25.83	8	0	7	11	31	6

INDEPENDENT LEAGUES

SOMERSET

BATTING	AVG	AB	R	H	2B	3B	HR	RBI	SB
Cancel, Robinson, 3b	.250	20	2	5	1	0	0	3	0
Clemente, Edgard, of	.331	284	39	94	20	0	11	46	2
Diaz, Jorge, ss-3b	.302	63	14	19	2	2	0	3	1
Eickhorst, Chris, c	.257	74	16	19	5	0	0	2	0
Escandon, Emiliano, 2b	.308	373	77	115	24	6	5	57	6
Gsell, Tony, of	.244	197	22	48	11	1	5	23	2
Hutchins, Norm, of	.262	378	73	99	14	4	9	37	17
King, Brad, c	.214	159	20	34	8	0	6	18	1
LeBron, Juan, of	.227	88	6	20	3	1	0	4	1
Lemonis, Chris, 1b	.317	284	37	90	23	5	4	48	2
Lopez, Luis, 1b	.154	52	5	8	0	0	2	3	0
Nettles, Jeff, 3b	.319	455	87	145	23	3	22	93	1
Ottavinia, Paul, 1b	.333	159	26	53	14	1	4	25	4
Perez, Jhonny, ss-2b	.261	399	80	104	16	0	10	51	21
Radmanovich, Ryan, of	.244	328	48	80	25	1	11	41	1
Rodriguez, Victor, ss-1b	.371	483	82	179	32	0	25	111	3
Santana, Manny, c-1b	.245	245	26	60	20	1	5	36	0
Stovall, DaRond, of	.268	41	5	11	0	2	1	4	1
2-team (68 Pennsylvania)	.260	304	52	79	17	6	7	31	7
Todd, Jeremy, of	.200	35	5	7	2	0	2	7	0
Wakeland, Chris, of	.281	235	30	66	11	4	9	43	2

PITCHING	W	L	ERA	G	SV	IP	H	BB	SO
Aldred, Scott	3	3	3.00	20	3	57	57	22	50
*Beasley, Ray	0	0	5.23	6	0	10	12	8	6
*Carnes, Matt	3	0	1.82	5	0	34	35	9	33
Daneker, Pat	1	1	2.92	6	0	24	31	4	7
2-team (21 Newark)	5	9	5.76	27	0	120	157	39	53
Darnell, Paul	3	5	5.58	46	1	71	77	39	68
Davis, Jason	5	6	4.15	41	1	89	75	52	65
*Dickson, Jason	2	2	3.55	5	0	33	37	3	20
*Elder, Dave	4	0	1.34	21	5	33	17	16	37
Grunwald, Erik	3	5	6.67	14	0	58	76	32	31
Heams, Shane	6	2	4.90	40	0	68	72	46	61
Jensen, Justin	3	6	7.63	13	0	59	93	28	51
Kelley, Rich	8	3	5.34	14	0	87	98	25	48
Lukasiewicz, Mark	2	1	1.40	14	0	19	15	6	17
Malko, Bryan	5	10	6.11	23	0	119	160	56	74
Marquez, Rob	1	0	2.67	25	9	30	23	9	31
Modica, Greg	2	0	0.75	2	0	12	6	1	15
Montane, Ivan	0	0	15.75	6	0	8	16	9	7
Mozingo, Dan	2	1	9.00	5	0	22	34	12	9
Ricketts, Chad	2	2	2.25	38	0	48	39	20	55
Schwager, Matt	2	0	2.23	29	6	40	28	10	45
Shelley, Jason	0	2	15.30	4	0	10	13	20	8
Smith, Cam	7	4	4.32	16	0	91	102	34	101
Spiegel, Mike	3	2	5.03	8	0	39	45	21	20
Stechschulte, Gene	0	0	0.00	3	0	2	3	1	1
Williams, Blake	1	3	8.31	4	0	21	28	9	13
Winkelsas, Joe	0	0	7.36	7	0	11	18	4	4

CENTRAL LEAGUE

For most independent league managers, the season is filled with roster juggling. Between releasing players who didn't work out, filling in for injuries and replacing players who have signed with affiliated clubs, roster management is a full-time job.

Unless you're Edinburg manager Chad Tredaway. The Central League champion Roadrunners didn't have to overhaul their roster during the 2004 season—they hardly had to tweak it.

The Roadrunners signed Mexican Leaguer Pat O'Sullivan around the all-star break, released righthander Daniel Henderson and sold closer Jeremy Flanagan to the Devil Rays in late June. And that was it. With those exceptions, the team that sprayed champagne and beer in early September was the same team that arrived at spring training.

"That's what I'm most proud of. We made one release this year," Tredaway said. "That's so rare in professional sports. The team we started with in spring training is the one we won with, which I'm really proud of."

The Roadrunners dominated the playoffs like they had the regular season. They swept Amarillo in the first round and swept Shreveport in the finals. Edinburg

outscored its opponents 40-11 in the six games.

Edinburg led the league in ERA, paced by four starters who finished in double digits in wins. Rookie Julio Ruiz, 22, moved into the rotation at midseason and went 8-3, 2.24 to lead the league in ERA.

Edinburg had plenty of pitching in 2003, when it won both halves of the regular season but lost in the first round of the playoffs. Instead of viewing the loss as a fluke, Tredaway saw it as a reason to tweak.

"I think we had to make some improvements. We did have a great season, but I felt we were short a starter and short a bat. We knew we had to improve our clubhouse too," Tredaway said. "We took a chance on some guys."

Josh Kranawetter

In 2004, the offense was able to keep up with the pitching. The Roadrunners led the league in runs, paced by outfielders Ryan Webb (.338-8-41) and Ryan Lehr (.322-6-72), and O'Sullivan, who smashed 14 home runs in just 47 games.

Edinburg may have won the title, but the Pensacola Pelicans also earned plenty of respect with their Central League debut. The Pelicans had played in the now-defunct Southeastern League for the previous two seasons, but moved over to the Central League for the 2004 season.

With a roster that included several Southeastern League veterans, the Pelicans won the East Division's second-half title and finished with the league's second best record. The Pelicans' began the season with great pitching, including righthander Josh Kranawetter, who may have been the indy leagues find of the year.

Kranawetter was 4-3, 1.77 with Pensacola, and was equally impressive for the Devil Rays' low Class A Charleston (S.C.) club after Tampa Bay purchased his contract in late June. But when Kranawetter and lefthander Phil Devey signed with affiliated clubs, the team's hitting picked up the slack, led by outfielder Rafael Alvarez, who led the league in batting average (.353), slugging percentage (.642) and on-base percentage (.468).

STANDINGS

FIRST HALF				
EAST	**W**	**L**	**PCT**	**GB**
Shreveport Sports	27	20	.574	—
Fort Worth Cats	24	22	.522	2½
Pensacola Pelicans	24	23	.511	3
Jackson Senators	19	28	.404	8
WEST	**W**	**L**	**PCT**	**GB**
Edinburg Roadrunners	33	14	.702	—
Coastal Bend Aviators	24	24	.500	9½
San Angelo Colts	23	23	.500	9½
Amarillo Dillas	13	33	.283	19½
SECOND HALF				
EAST	**W**	**L**	**PCT**	**GB**
Pensacola Pelicans	31	17	.646	—
Fort Worth Cats	26	21	.553	4½
Shreveport Sports	23	25	.479	8
Jackson Senators	21	27	.438	10
WEST	**W**	**L**	**PCT**	**GB**
Edinburg Roadrunners	35	13	.729	—
Amarillo Dillas	23	25	.479	12
Coastal Bend Aviators	19	29	.396	16
San Angelo Colts	13	34	.277	21½

PLAYOFFS: Semifinals—Edinburg defeated Amarillo 3-0 and Shreveport defeated Pensacola 3-2 in best-of-5 series. **Finals**—Edinburg defeated Shreveport 3-0 in best-of-5 series.

MANAGERS: Amarillo—Murray Wilson. **Coastal Bend**—Glenn Wilson. **Edinburg**—Chad Tredaway. **Fort Worth**—Wayne Terwilliger. **Jackson**—Dan Shwam. **Pensacola**—Bernie Carbo. **San Angelo**—Toby Rumsfield/Eric Moore/John Harris. **Shreveport**—Terry Bevington/John Barlowe.

ATTENDANCE: Fort Worth 151,374; Edinburg 145,370; Coastal Bend 103,049; San Angelo 82,758; Jackson 71,349; Amarillo 58,627; Shreveport 55,207; Pensacola 44,584.

ALL-STAR TEAM: C—Trey Salinas, Coastal Bend. **1B**—Dan Meier, Amarillo. **2B**—Anthony Angel, Edinburg. **3B**—Ryan Lehr, Edinburg. **SS**—Joe Espada, Pensacola. **OF**—Rafael Alvarez, Pensacola; Juan Rocha, San Angelo/Shreveport; Ryan Webb, Edinburg. **DH**—Larry Bethea, Pensacola. **LHP**—Pedro Flores, Edinburg. **RHP**—Thad Markray, Shreveport.

Player of the Year: Rafael Alvarez, Pensacola. **Rookie Player of the Year:** Tim Hartshorn, Fort Worth. **Rookie Pitcher of the Year:** Julio Ruiz, Edinburg. **Manager of the Year:** Chad Tredaway, Edinburg.

INDIVIDUAL BATTING LEADERS
(Minimum 259 Plate Appearances)

	AVG	AB	R	H	2B	3B	HR	RBI	SB
Alvarez, Rafael, Pensacola	.353	218	60	77	21	3	12	52	20
Meier, Dan, Amarillo	.340	344	76	117	24	6	8	63	0
Webb, Ryan, Edinburg	.338	358	80	121	26	4	8	41	30
Espada, Joe, Pensacola	.336	271	53	91	4	2	4	47	18
McMann, Dallas, Amarillo	.328	265	35	87	15	3	3	33	1
Salinas, Trey, Coastal Bend	.323	251	39	81	15	1	7	37	12
Lehr, Ryan, Edinburg	.322	369	54	119	22	5	6	74	2
Todd, Jeremy, Amarillo	.322	264	50	85	15	5	11	66	0
Shannon, Josey, Pensacola	.316	244	27	77	19	1	6	50	8
Mendoza, Carlos, Pensacola	.314	328	55	103	21	3	6	44	11

INDIVIDUAL PITCHING LEADERS
(Minimum 77 Innings)

	W	L	ERA	G	SV	IP	H	BB	SO
Ruiz, Julio, Edinburg	9	3	2.24	25	0	92	64	39	79
Aragon, Angel, Fort Worth	8	3	2.34	13	0	92	76	18	78
Flores, Pedro, Edinburg	10	5	2.49	18	0	116	95	80	98
Montoya, Eric, Edinburg	10	2	2.59	19	0	122	103	45	85
Batson, Byron, Pensacola	8	3	3.01	30	2	108	104	23	71
Smith, Mike, Co.Bend/Fort Worth	11	6	3.02	23	1	155	163	32	135
Markray, Thad, Shreveport	8	2	3.05	12	0	83	75	26	87
Lopez, Jose, Coastal Bend	9	6	3.09	24	2	137	135	45	108
Creek, Ryan, Jackson	8	2	3.19	19	0	124	96	49	111
Davis, Allen, Fort Worth	10	7	3.38	20	0	130	129	29	126

* Signed with affiliated club

AMARILLO

BATTING	AVG	AB	R	H	2B	3B	HR	RBI	SB
Ayala, Odannys, of	.308	338	61	104	21	11	5	40	14
Craig, Beau, dh-of	.294	17	2	5	2	0	1	1	0
Craig, Benny, of	.271	310	47	84	17	2	20	65	0
Ellenbecker, Bix, c	.136	22	3	3	0	1	0	1	0
Figueroa, Carlos, 3b-2b	.331	160	26	53	12	2	2	17	7
Gonzales, Benino, c	.130	23	3	3	1	0	0	0	0
Huson, Tim, 3b-of	.167	36	2	6	1	0	0	1	0
January, Javerro, of	.197	61	7	12	1	1	0	6	2
2-team (5 Jackson)	.203	79	11	16	2	1	1	9	3
Lebron, Francisco, dh-1b	.280	125	20	35	4	0	3	24	0
Llanos, Alex, 2b-ss	.299	137	28	41	7	5	1	15	7
Mann, Matt, of-c	.293	225	37	66	13	0	5	21	10
2-team (35 Coastal Bend)	.277	354	54	98	21	0	7	37	13
Martin, Scott, of	.229	35	4	8	0	0	0	5	0
Maxwell, Mark, of	.083	12	0	1	0	0	0	0	1
McMann, Dallas, c-of	.328	265	35	87	15	3	3	33	1
Meier, Dan, 1b	.340	344	76	117	24	6	8	63	0
Oropeza, Asdrubal, ss	.262	191	35	50	12	1	7	29	12
2-team (18 Jackson)	.276	261	46	72	17	1	10	39	14
Otis, Trent, 2b-ss	.234	321	32	75	10	3	4	36	12
*Ramistella, John, of	.209	43	5	9	0	0	0	4	3
Tinius, Ben, 3b	.190	205	20	39	5	4	2	26	2
Todd, Jeremy, of-c	.322	264	50	85	15	5	11	66	0

PITCHING	W	L	ERA	G	SV	IP	H	BB	SO
Bernard, Jason	0	1	7.01	10	0	52	60	28	28
Blaylock, Don	0	0	13.89	9	0	11	19	9	6
Carter, Ramsey	2	0	7.59	6	0	10	13	10	8
Castillo, Marcus	5	5	2.69	11	0	80	84	20	49
2-team (13 Pensacola)	7	8	3.26	24	0	112	130	30	69
Collazo, Rafael	0	0	15.43	5	0	9	21	6	6
Ferguson, Keith	2	5	5.35	12	0	65	78	35	36
Flading, Cameron	2	1	8.51	10	1	37	57	19	45
Guzman, Jonathan	0	0	20.25	1	0	1	3	2	1
Lehr, George	0	2	11.08	13	0	13	24	8	16
Martin, Larry	1	1	15.88	7	0	5	10	7	6
Morgan, Shawn	5	5	5.66	37	8	41	53	22	24
Percosky, Mark	0	1	16.88	2	0	5	12	3	2
Rhodes, Kendall	0	2	8.39	10	0	24	27	19	15

Rosa, Cristy	5	5	4.55	11	0	59	71	8	35
Shaw, Elliott	2	6	7.58	16	0	65	65	59	42
Shuck, Danny	0	4	7.62	8	0	26	44	15	11
Singleton, Steven	0	3	11.68	26	0	37	63	34	34
Stark, Holden	0	1	9.31	8	0	9	12	11	5
*Stockman, Landon	1	2	4.21	18	2	25	23	11	29
Stockstill, Jason	10	9	3.90	20	0	136	121	61	104
Tevey, John	4	5	7.18	22	0	57	77	30	39

COASTAL BEND

BATTING	AVG	AB	R	H	2B	3B	HR	RBI	SB
Adolfo, Carlos, of	.290	221	44	64	18	2	7	32	14
Battersby, Eric, 1b-of	.303	267	34	81	10	4	10	52	4
Bell, David, c	.162	74	14	12	2	0	0	3	3
Castillo, Carlos, ss	.173	110	6	19	0	2	0	6	1
Coleman, Alph, of	.176	17	0	3	0	0	0	1	1
Colon, Cristobal, 3b	.281	196	16	55	11	1	3	22	2
2-team (33 San Angelo)	.271	321	31	87	19	2	4	41	2
Correa, Dalphie, ss	.159	69	4	11	1	0	0	2	7
Cortez, J.R., 3b-ss	.166	151	17	25	2	0	0	11	8
Ferrell, Lou, ss-2b	.216	148	14	32	4	1	0	13	4
Guerrero, Mike, dh-of	.272	276	47	75	27	2	7	38	7
Kasparek, Andrew, c	.310	29	2	9	1	1	0	5	0
Khalil, Rashid, of	.128	39	3	5	1	0	0	3	1
Knight, Marcus, of	.216	208	30	45	5	2	1	20	17
Lebron, Francisco, 1b	.241	108	6	26	4	0	1	14	1
2-team (33 Amarillo)	.262	233	26	61	8	0	4	38	1
Loeb, Bryan, c-3b	.178	129	12	23	7	2	1	10	4
Maldonado, Edwin, 2b	.248	323	32	80	22	2	3	37	16
Mann, Matt, of	.248	129	17	32	8	0	2	16	3
Peery, Noah, of	.240	25	5	6	1	0	1	1	1
*Ramistella, John, of	.296	115	27	34	5	2	7	26	12
2-team (14 Amarillo)	.272	158	32	43	5	2	7	30	15
Reeves, Kerry, 2b-ss	.091	11	0	1	0	0	0	0	0
Riggins, Auntwan, 3b-ss	.186	59	12	11	1	0	0	1	3
Salinas, Trey, c-1b	.323	251	39	81	15	1	7	37	12
Strickland, Greg, of	.233	103	26	24	3	1	0	6	20
2-team (54 Fort Worth)	.240	312	52	75	9	6	2	30	42
Van Allen, Larry, of	.194	31	2	6	1	0	0	0	2

PITCHING	W	L	ERA	G	SV	IP	H	BB	SO
Carter, Ramsey	0	0	11.25	3	0	4	6	4	1
2-team (6 Amarillo)	2	0	8.59	9	0	14	19	14	9
Chapa, Rey	0	1	11.25	6	0	4	11	4	3
Davidson, Andy	1	1	9.22	10	0	13	21	6	7
Dikdan, Brian	2	4	4.32	15	0	33	39	19	10
Elias, Rob	4	2	2.79	21	2	42	37	14	30
Garcia, Mike	0	3	11.42	4	0	8	14	4	5
Guzman, Jonathan	0	1	9.39	8	0	15	24	7	7
2-team (1 Amarillo)	0	1	10.26	9	0	16	27	9	8
Henderson, Sam	3	2	3.92	16	1	43	39	22	27
2-team (8 Edinburg)	6	3	4.78	24	1	79	81	42	49
Hinojosa, Hector	0	3	13.00	4	0	9	11	11	8
Huerta, Jorge	2	0	3.48	20	1	41	41	11	23
2-team (1 Pensacola)	2	0	4.60	21	1	45	52	12	26
Lira, James	1	1	0.00	3	0	4	3	2	3
Lopez, Jose	9	6	3.09	24	2	137	135	45	108
Makowsky, Bubba	0	1	4.58	29	0	53	48	27	22
Marquetti, Agustin	2	2	2.82	16	2	22	19	14	21
Martanovic, Eric	0	0	9.72	5	0	8	12	7	3
2-team (1 Pensacola)	0	0	8.10	6	0	10	12	8	5
Martinez, Marcus	0	0	3.00	4	0	6	6	5	6
Morgan, Lavelle	5	9	4.71	27	2	114	119	47	108
Persails, Mark	1	3	7.84	6	0	20	28	11	16
3-team (6 Jackson, 6 San Angelo)	5	8	5.66	18	0	90	109	40	64
Rafferty, Ryan	0	0	6.43	12	0	14	14	10	16
Ramon, Tim	1	1	11.37	4	0	6	13	4	4
Rohr, Matthew	1	3	3.97	4	0	22	21	9	9
Sanchez, Gilbert	0	0	9.00	2	0	1	1	4	2
Seibert, Kevin	2	3	4.76	39	3	58	73	28	51
Smith, Mike	9	5	2.83	19	1	127	126	26	115
Stout, Josh	1	4	4.66	5	0	9	18	5	9
Tower, Scott	0	3	18.69	3	0	4	8	10	4

EDINBURG

BATTING	AVG	AB	R	H	2B	3B	HR	RBI	SB
Alonzo, Aldo, 2b	.167	12	1	2	0	0	0	1	0
Angel, Anthony, 2b	.308	347	68	107	20	4	6	66	8
Argento, Shaun, 1b-c	.284	257	33	73	10	0	2	43	1
Fitzpatrick, Eddie, c	.226	283	33	64	7	0	2	31	1
Garanzuay, Hector, ss	.290	193	26	56	7	0	2	24	1
Gonzalez, Eric, of-3b	.305	311	63	95	29	0	10	53	11
Lehr, Ryan, 3b-1b	.322	369	54	119	22	5	6	74	2
Mendoza, Aaron, c-1b	.263	114	17	30	7	2	2	21	0
Moore, Vince, of	.269	327	60	88	18	2	3	48	18

BATTING	AVG	AB	R	H	2B	3B	HR	RBI	SB
O'Sullivan, Patrick, dh-1b	.333	192	34	64	10	1	14	43	4
Sisk, Aaron, ss-3b	.252	309	44	78	14	2	11	43	19
Webb, Ryan, of	.338	358	80	121	26	4	8	41	30
Zieour, Neesan, of	.297	327	52	97	18	4	2	34	9

PITCHING	W	L	ERA	G	SV	IP	H	BB	SO
*Flanagan, Jeremy	0	0	0.90	10	7	10	6	8	9
Flores, Pedro	10	5	2.49	18	0	115	95	80	98
Garza, Roel	2	1	3.80	27	0	42	44	20	32
Goodmann, Joe	5	3	1.17	37	7	46	33	15	55
Harris, Ryan	11	2	4.13	19	0	117	115	51	91
Henderson, Dan	3	1	5.86	8	0	35	42	20	22
Montoya, Eric	10	2	2.59	19	0	121	103	45	85
Ramirez, Luis	2	1	2.94	25	2	33	28	13	28
Ruiz, Julio	9	3	2.24	25	0	92	64	39	79
Valentin, Dan	10	5	3.82	20	0	129	122	58	119
Vasquez, Tim	4	1	2.60	36	1	52	50	25	50
Wilkerson, Steven	2	3	3.69	42	14	61	61	23	71

FORT WORTH

BATTING	AVG	AB	R	H	2B	3B	HR	RBI	SB
Adolfo, Carlos, of	.292	113	31	33	5	1	7	19	12
2-team (60 Coastal Bend)	.290	334	75	97	23	3	14	51	26
Albertson, Eli, of	.264	193	32	51	13	1	5	30	1
Allen, John, dh-of	.319	144	24	46	16	1	6	31	2
Barrett, Fred, 2b	.100	10	0	1	0	0	0	0	1
Essian, Jim, of	.235	311	70	73	21	3	10	39	39
Gomez, Ricky, ss-2b	.207	242	36	50	6	1	1	29	7
Green, Terence, 3b-1b	.273	362	53	99	23	1	8	55	28
Hannon, Pat, dh-of	.276	58	8	16	4	0	1	8	1
Hartshorn, Jr-2b, of	.300	250	60	75	15	4	12	38	9
Marshall, Jon, c	.063	48	3	3	0	0	0	3	0
Mejias, Erick, 2b	.159	69	6	11	2	1	1	5	2
Merriman, Terrell, of	.281	114	21	32	7	1	0	16	8
Pelfrey, Dennis, 2b-c	.206	170	24	35	4	0	3	21	4
Radwan, Jason, c	.246	293	40	72	12	1	13	62	3
Smith, Bryon, 1b-3b	.257	343	54	88	13	1	7	47	11
Smith, Jeremy, of	.235	98	14	23	4	1	4	17	0
Strickland, Greg, of	.244	209	46	51	6	5	2	24	22
Yarbrough, Shawn, ss-2b	.182	22	5	4	2	0	0	1	2

PITCHING	W	L	ERA	G	SV	IP	H	BB	SO
Anderson, Scott	0	0	6.75	2	0	2	1	4	3
Aragon, Angel	8	3	2.34	13	0	92	76	18	78
Cabrera, Walin	0	0	2.16	8	0	8	8	5	2
Carroll, James	0	2	10.80	5	0	6	11	2	8
*Davis, Allen	10	7	3.38	20	0	130	129	29	126
Fuqua, David	2	2	4.50	38	1	50	58	16	32
Harrington, Matt	1	2	2.77	7	0	26	20	7	22
Hughes, Andy	0	0	7.20	8	0	10	16	3	5
Montarbo, Adam	0	0	18.00	2	0	2	5	2	0
Plancich, Nick	0	0	0.00	2	0	2	4	1	1
Reinike, Chris	0	3	2.95	16	3	18	15	8	15
Rodriguez, Luis	0	1	5.19	10	0	17	21	8	9
2-team (2 Pensacola)	0	1	6.20	12	0	20	26	9	11
Sears, Kevin	1	0	5.87	6	0	7	9	2	6
Smith, Mike	2	1	3.86	4	0	28	37	6	20
2-team (19 Coastal Bend)	11	6	3.02	23	1	155	163	32	135
Stevens, Dave	2	6	4.33	33	11	72	74	19	66
Stokley, Billy	0	1	3.67	22	1	27	29	14	19
Stout, Logan	0	2	4.60	12	2	15	17	5	21
Weems, Ryan	5	2	4.22	12	0	53	57	20	49
Whalen, John	1	1	6.26	21	0	23	22	21	15
Williams, Shad	9	6	4.69	24	2	113	133	25	68
*Wood, Brandon	10	4	3.43	27	1	105	97	31	91

JACKSON

BATTING	AVG	AB	R	H	2B	3B	HR	RBI	SB
Bost, Tom, of	.286	98	29	28	3	1	7	21	6
Boston, Tyson, of	.252	155	28	39	10	0	4	23	4
Corbeil, Azarias, c-of	.248	101	17	25	10	0	1	14	0
Doezie, Ty, 2b-of	.155	110	15	17	2	0	1	6	0
Garland, Tim, of	.259	108	21	28	2	1	1	10	11
*Hoffpauir, Josh, 2b-ss	.269	201	36	54	13	3	0	20	11
January, Javerro, of-1b	.222	18	4	4	1	0	1	3	1
Langaigne, Selwyn, of	.305	302	57	92	22	2	8	51	28
Llanos, Alex, ss-2b	.285	235	34	67	14	3	4	28	19
2-team (35 Amarillo)	.290	372	62	108	21	8	5	43	26
McCall, Gerard, c	.228	263	25	60	15	0	3	29	2
Mejias, Erick, 2b-3b	.255	208	30	53	9	2	3	27	12
2-team (21 Fort Worth)	.231	277	36	64	11	3	4	32	14
Newsom, Steve, of	.298	171	29	51	6	1	4	25	5
Oropeza, Asdrubal, ss	.314	70	11	22	5	0	3	10	2
Paciorek, Mack, ss	.242	33	5	8	2	0	0	5	0
Peters, Samone, dh-1b	.234	124	11	29	7	1	6	27	0

BATTING	AVG	AB	R	H	2B	3B	HR	RBI	SB
Quero, Pedro, dh	.282	71	9	20	3	0	1	6	0
Rosario, Victor, of	.182	22	4	4	0	0	0	0	2
Sanchez, Matthew, 3b	.295	95	15	28	6	0	0	8	2
Shelley, Randall, 3b	.233	150	20	35	14	1	3	17	3
Sorensen, Nick, of	.254	197	25	50	13	2	2	21	8
2-team (10 Pensacola)	.230	226	27	52	13	2	2	21	9
Tranum, Josh, 1b	.269	323	51	87	22	1	15	74	1
Vasquez, Chris, of	.261	92	9	24	5	0	2	13	1
Wilson, Kasey, c	.190	42	3	8	1	0	0	2	1
2-team (61 San Angelo)	.248	250	28	62	11	0	5	29	2
York, Andrew, c	.209	43	5	9	1	0	0	0	0

PITCHING	W	L	ERA	G	SV	IP	H	BB	SO
Camp, Rusty	8	6	4.44	16	0	99	108	37	77
Casey, Reid	5	3	2.29	40	1	59	49	16	46
Cox, Adam	0	2	6.17	3	0	11	13	7	2
Creek, Ryan	8	2	3.19	19	0	124	96	49	111
Devenney, Nick	0	1	7.43	5	0	13	12	12	9
Garretson, Andrew	0	0	2.84	4	0	6	9	2	6
Guzman, Alexis	3	4	6.30	20	0	30	44	10	18
Ihlenburg, Marc	1	1	7.89	5	0	21	39	3	10
Jenkins, Cortney	0	3	12.71	4	0	5	12	1	5
Jones, Fontella	1	1	0.82	27	10	33	19	20	36
Kuiper, David	0	1	4.13	16	0	28	28	10	13
Kuklis, Kevin	2	5	4.61	21	5	70	73	16	35
Newman, Alan	0	1	9.88	9	0	13	18	9	11
Persails, Mark	3	3	4.50	6	0	32	38	12	15
Pezely, Frank	0	0	16.20	5	0	3	7	2	4
Runyon, Bob	0	2	4.26	3	0	6	9	4	4
Shack, Jermaine	0	2	8.28	12	0	25	27	21	22
Snyder, Ryan	4	11	4.25	20	0	127	139	19	63
Vandegriff, Nick	5	7	4.13	19	0	120	144	37	64

PENSACOLA

BATTING	AVG	AB	R	H	2B	3B	HR	RBI	SB
Alvarez, Osmel, c	.111	9	0	1	0	0	0	0	0
Alvarez, Rafael, of	.353	218	60	77	21	3	12	52	20
Bethea, Larry, 1b	.308	286	50	88	22	0	15	74	4
Branch, George, dh-of	.279	272	50	76	17	0	17	46	1
Cleveland, Clay, 1b	.242	66	8	16	4	0	2	8	3
DeMarco, Tony, 1b-3b	.111	36	0	4	0	0	0	1	0
Dodson, Bo, of	.000	2	1	0	0	0	0	0	0
Donaldson, Erik, of	.160	25	2	4	1	0	1	2	0
*Espada, Joe, ss	.336	271	53	91	4	2	4	47	18
Joyce, Tom, of	.232	99	11	23	5	1	3	13	3
Kelly, Heath, 3b	.240	242	42	58	14	1	7	31	6
Langs, Ronte, of	.200	10	1	2	1	0	0	2	0
Mendoza, Carlos, 2b	.314	328	55	103	21	3	6	44	11
Nunnari, Talmadge, dh	.278	18	5	5	2	0	0	4	0
Rodriguez, Mike, c-3b	.289	308	45	89	10	0	6	46	5
Salas, Jose, c	.316	155	33	49	8	1	4	25	3
Salas, Jose, ss	.218	87	14	19	2	1	3	7	8
Shannon, Josey, of	.316	244	27	77	19	1	6	50	8
Silva, Michael, c	.100	20	1	2	1	0	0	1	0
Smallwood, Erik, dh-1b	.220	50	5	11	3	0	1	8	0
Sorensen, Nick, of	.069	29	2	2	0	0	0	0	1
Vick, Hunter, ss-2b	.229	35	8	8	2	0	0	5	0
Wilke, Josh, dh	.043	23	2	1	0	0	0	1	1
Wilson, Andy, of	.314	341	73	107	13	2	5	35	13

PITCHING	W	L	ERA	G	SV	IP	H	BB	SO
Batson, Byron	8	3	3.01	30	2	107	104	23	71
Casadiego, Gerardo	6	2	3.29	43	8	54	52	26	58
Castillo, Marcus	2	3	6.40	13	0	32	46	10	20
*Devey, Phil	3	1	1.46	6	0	37	33	12	35
Dobson, Richard	5	5	4.09	44	4	72	75	26	62
Garner, Isiah	0	0	0.00	1	0	2	1	0	
Gregg, James	3	1	4.24	20	4	23	22	16	16
Griffin, Charles	2	1	2.85	27	1	41	23	21	38
Guzman, Alexis	1	0	5.40	5	0	11	13	1	8
3-team (20 Jackson, 12 San Angelo)	6	5	4.73	37	2	59	71	13	40
Hernandez, Santos	3	4	4.82	21	0	65	54	56	59
Huerta, Jorge	0	0	17.18	1	0	3	11	1	3
Kars, Jonathan	0	0	0.00	1	0	1	0	1	0
*Kranawetter, Josh	4	3	1.77	12	1	56	37	21	69
Martanovic, Eric	0	0	0.00	1	0	1	0	1	2
Martinez, Caleb	0	1	7.71	3	0	9	16	7	6
McCall, Derell	1	2	5.48	4	0	23	24	7	12
Mitchell, Kelvin	1	0	2.14	19	1	21	19	7	23
Norris, Jeff	6	1	3.59	15	0	67	61	27	46
Ramirez, Victor	0	0	6.75	5	0	5	5	6	2
Ring, Josh	0	0	27.00	4	0	2	9	3	4
Robinson, Jeff	2	0	5.56	4	0	11	13	3	11
Rodriguez, Luis	0	0	12.00	2	0	3	5	1	2
Semprun, Chris	0	0	0.00	1	0	0	1	1	0
Sigley, Jayson	3	3	5.80	9	0	40	39	18	34

	W	L	ERA	G	SV	IP	H	BB	SO
Sparks, Jeff	0	0	6.55	3	0	11	12	10	13
Stephens, Trey	6	8	4.52	21	0	99	99	40	103
*Tindell, Matt	0	0	0.00	9	0	9	2	12	10

SAN ANGELO

BATTING	AVG	AB	R	H	2B	3B	HR	RBI	SB
Aguilar, Bert, dh-1b	.258	252	28	65	14	0	8	35	1
Bischofberger, Sean, 1b-3b	.284	211	29	60	14	0	7	32	1
Boston, Tyson, of	.207	87	7	18	7	0	0	7	2
2-team (45 Jackson)	.236	242	35	57	17	0	4	30	6
Colon, Cristobal, 3b	.256	125	15	32	8	1	1	19	0
Deck, Ronnie, c	.079	38	1	3	0	0	1	2	0
Diaz, Jorge, 2b-ss	.287	352	68	101	19	3	1	25	50
Gerald, Eddie, of	.268	198	30	53	12	1	6	24	4
Gilbert, Joe, of-ss	.221	213	21	47	14	1	1	26	2
Hanson, Andrew, of	.095	21	3	2	0	0	0	0	0
James, Tony, of-3b	.284	335	51	95	13	1	11	40	19
Kent, Brian, c	.246	69	6	17	3	1	0	7	0
Laskowski, Lee, of	.234	47	6	11	2	0	1	6	0
Luna, Jaime, ss	.059	51	5	3	0	0	0	5	1
Magdaleno, Ricky, ss	.224	196	27	44	9	0	4	24	3
Matthews, Bobby, of	.029	35	2	1	0	0	0	0	0
Mercer, Joe, 3b	.316	38	7	12	2	0	0	10	0
Rocha, Juan, of	.310	281	48	87	12	0	15	63	1
Rumfield, Toby, 1b	.202	94	8	19	3	0	1	8	0
Sanchez, Matthew, 3b-of	.266	207	24	55	9	1	0	20	4
2-team (29 Jackson)	.275	302	39	83	15	1	0	28	6
Velez, Lanze, of	.000	3	0	0	0	0	0	0	0
Wilson, Kasey, c	.260	208	25	54	10	0	5	27	1
York, Andrew, c	.241	54	6	13	3	0	0	4	2
2-team (18 Jackson)	.227	97	11	22	4	0	0	4	2

PITCHING	W	L	ERA	G	SV	IP	H	BB	SO
Ahearne, Paul	1	0	6.17	7	0	11	13	4	10
Dobson, Dwayne	0	5	5.30	14	0	18	18	16	15
Flanagan, Chris	5	4	5.48	15	0	70	69	39	61
Greco, Sam	0	1	4.10	16	0	37	43	20	21
Gutierrez, Jon	1	2	5.84	8	0	24	25	12	22
Guzman, Alexis	2	1	1.56	12	2	17	14	2	14
Henry, Mike	8	6	4.40	19	0	118	119	49	87
Johnson, Chad	6	10	5.25	37	3	82	105	38	61
Jones, Quentin	0	0	5.40	13	5	15	11	6	21
Kennedy, Jodie	0	5	6.41	8	0	39	48	25	43
Mahan, Dallas	3	1	5.24	13	0	22	26	13	19
Persails, Mark	1	2	5.45	6	0	38	43	17	33
Runyon, Bob	0	1	8.71	16	0	20	28	10	13
2-team (3 Jackson)	0	3	7.67	19	0	27	37	16	17
Salazar, Luis	5	8	5.03	21	0	98	119	18	58
Sena, Jason	0	5	5.19	26	1	76	93	31	54
Therneau, Dave	3	5	2.96	11	0	73	68	14	70
Von Haefen, Jason	1	2	4.89	21	9	35	36	14	41
Watzek, Kurt	0	0	11.45	9	0	11	21	7	16

SHREVEPORT

BATTING	AVG	AB	R	H	2B	3B	HR	RBI	SB
Alvarez, Jorge, of-2b	.312	362	60	113	27	0	6	64	5
Anderson, Keto, of	.289	363	45	105	7	7	1	28	13
Bragg, Michael, of-c	.200	20	2	4	1	0	0	3	0
Dusan, Joe, 1b-of	.296	301	47	89	17	2	3	50	2
Gilliam, Bobby, of	.323	31	8	10	1	1	0	4	4
Gonzalez, Jose, ss-2b	.181	227	19	41	4	1	2	21	5
Hall, Chris, 3b	.260	173	29	45	7	1	3	28	0
Henderson, Derek, dh-1b	.273	348	52	95	18	0	7	67	6
Hicks, Michael, 2b	.258	151	22	39	12	0	2	18	1
Loeb, Bryan, c	.353	34	4	12	3	2	1	5	0
2-team (41 Coastal Bend)	.215	163	16	35	10	4	2	15	4
Mack, Tony, of	.248	117	14	29	2	0	0	13	2
Patterson, Derek, 3b-2b	.300	320	54	96	22	2	9	47	12
2-team (78 San Angelo)	.311	331	59	103	12	0	20	72	1
Schifano, Tony, ss-3b	.294	197	24	58	9	1	0	16	9
Spearman, Vernon, of	.240	254	50	61	8	6	0	19	14
Thompson, Adam, c	.143	28	3	4	2	0	1	3	0
Webster, Kevin, c	.237	198	22	47	9	0	3	26	1

PITCHING	W	L	ERA	G	SV	IP	H	BB	SO
Black, Keith	7	7	3.46	19	0	117	126	40	55
*Brown, Ira	4	1	2.00	6	0	36	24	20	40
Camp, Rusty	1	1	4.20	2	0	15	9	6	13
2-team (16 Jackson)	9	7	4.41	18	0	114	117	43	90
Council, Gabe	1	2	7.82	16	0	25	32	19	12
Cowling, Ross	0	2	27.00	2	0	2	8	0	1
Doiron, Ian	4	5	3.34	13	0	67	55	21	40
Frost, Pat	0	2	9.88	4	0	13	19	15	14
Gold, Joshua	9	7	4.15	19	0	119	123	33	60

	W	L	ERA	G	SV	IP	H	BB	SO
Kantz, Joe	1	4	3.70	42	3	48	38	25	57
Knox, Jerry	1	2	3.74	11	0	33	40	13	14
Kuiper, David	2	0	5.79	13	0	18	27	4	7
2-team (16 Jackson)	2	1	4.79	29	0	47	55	14	20
Makowsky, Carl	5	3	2.60	36	14	55	49	14	37
*Markray, Thad	8	2	3.05	12	0	82	75	26	87
Morrow, David	0	0	6.75	16	0	20	15	27	15
Perry, Trevor	0	0	6.23	2	1	4	5	3	3
*Poland, Trey	2	0	0.37	18	1	24	15	6	29
Ramirez, Victor	0	0	4.91	2	0	3	2	6	2
2-team (5 Pensacola)	0	0	6.00	7	0	9	7	12	4
Slanina, Jason	5	5	4.91	19	0	99	112	40	39
Smith, Aaron	0	0	4.91	4	0	7	6	6	7
Yates, Chad	0	2	4.43	4	0	20	17	16	10

FRONTIER LEAGUE

Rockford manager Bob Koopman says pitching and defense win championships, so it's no surprise his RiverHawks pitching staff is always among the Frontier League leaders.

The pitching was there again in 2004, but the addition of offense made the difference as Rockford won its first league title. The RiverHawks led the league in ERA (3.47) and were second in the league in runs scored (578).

Richard Austin

"When I came back for this season, I absolutely thought it would be a failure if we didn't win. We had too much talent not to win. I felt like we were the favorites," RiverHawks pitcher Scott Sobkowiak said.

Outfielder Richard Austin was the league MVP after hitting .359-15-77 with a league-leading .489 on-base percentage. First baseman Aaron McEachran hit .332-11-62, and the RiverHawks hit .289 as a team.

The RiverHawks averaged seven runs a game in the playoffs, including a 14-run outburst in the final game of a three-game sweep of Evansville in the championship series. Sobkowiak, a former Atlanta Braves prospect, set the tone for the series with eight strong innings in Game One, retiring 18 in a row at one point in a 7-4 win.

Olmo Rosario was the playoff MVP. Rosario lost his starting shortstop job at the midseason mark, but when he was pressed into duty as a DH for the playoffs, he responded by hitting .429.

It was Rockford's first professional title since 1950, when the Rockford Peaches won the All-American Girls Professional Baseball League.

On the other end of the spectrum, Windy City seemed to be in position to challenge Rockford for the title early in the season. But rarely has a season that started so well ended so poorly.

The Windy City Thunderbolts had the best record in the Frontier League three weeks into the season, after an 11-game winning streak pushed the team to a 20-8 record. Over the next two months the team slowly drifted back to .500, and with three weeks to go the Thunderbolts were 37-37, needing another winning streak to get back into the playoff race.

No one would have imagined the team had won its last game. Hurt by player sales, trades and a general slump, the T-Bolts collapsed, losing their final 20 games of the season to finish 37-57 overall. Manager Steve Maddock was fired during the losing streak, but new manager Joe Charboneau was unable to reverse the slide.

"We went on a road trip after an 11-game winning streak," general manager Lydia Bergeron said. "We lost some games, and we just never seemed to rebound after the road trip.

"Sometimes it works and sometimes it doesn't. Nothing seemed to work. Their hearts were in it, but it seemed we couldn't come back as we had during the winning streak. We didn't seem to have it toward the end."

Rockford's Austin was named the league's MVP, but until he was signed by the Brewers in late July, Mark Hamilton was the league's best value, as he managed to give Chillicothe two players for the price of one. Hamilton served as the ace of the Chillicothe staff, going 4-5, 2.25 to finish second in the league in ERA while leading the league in complete games. On the four days between his starts, he wandered out to the outfield, where he hit .323-3-31 with 11 steals, good enough to rank him in the top 10 in batting when his contract was sold.

"He's the kid who's been our best player both ways. Whether he's on the mound or in the outfield, he's the best player we've had," Paints manager Jamie Keefe said.

The league welcomed one new team to the league in 2004—the Springfield/Ozark Ducks arrived in a swap with the Central League, which received the Kenosha Mammoths in return and moved them to Pensacola, Fla. The league also opened a new stadium in Florence, but that team ran into serious financial troubles during the season, forcing the league to take over the team, with the hope of finding new ownership in the offseason.

STANDINGS

EAST	W	L	PCT	GB
Washington Wild Things	62	34	.646	—
Evansville Otters	54	42	.563	8
Kalamazoo Kings	51	45	.531	11
Chillicothe Paints	48	48	.500	14
Richmond Roosters	43	53	.448	19
Florence Freedom	31	65	.323	31

WEST	W	L	PCT	GB
Rockford Riverhawks	59	37	.615	—
Gateway Grizzlies	56	38	.596	2
River City Rascals	51	43	.543	7
Springfield-Ozark Ducks	52	44	.542	7
Windy City Thunderbolts	37	57	.394	21
Mid-Missouri Mavericks	28	66	.298	30

PLAYOFFS: Semifinals—Rockford defeated Gateway 3-2 and Evansville defeated Washington 3-0 in best-of-5 series. **Finals**—Rockford defeated Evansville 3-0 in best-of-5 series.

MANAGERS: Chillicothe—Jamie Keefe. **Evansville**—Greg Jelks. **Florence**—Tom Browning/Pete Rose Jr./Mike Easler. **Gateway**—Danny Cox. **Kalamazoo**—Fran Riordan. **Mid-Missouri**—Jack Clark/Jim Gentile. **Richmond**—Chris Mongiardo. **River City**—Randy Martz. **Rockford**—Bob Koopmann. **Springfield-Ozark**—Greg Tagert. **Washington**—John Massarelli. **Windy City**—Steve Maddock/Joe Charboneau.

ATTENDANCE: Gateway 217,500; River City 185,333; Washington 154,963; Kalamazoo 135,654; Evansville 121,733; Rockford 103,140; Chillicothe 82,183; Florence 68,250; Windy City 67,397; Springfield-Ozark 67,028; Richmond 46,019; Mid-Missouri 45,511.

ALL-STAR TEAM: C—Tony Cosentino, Chillicothe. **1B**—Phil Warren, Gateway. **2B**—Brian Stoecklein, Washington. **3B**—Greg Stevens, Gateway. **SS**—Adrian Gascon, Chillicothe. **OF**—Richard Austin, Rockford; Jack Headley, Washington; Fehlandt Lentini, Kalamazoo. **DH**—Trevor Hall, Richmond. **SP**—Grant Williams, Evansville. **RP**—Chad Sosebee, Richmond.

Most Valuable Player: Richard Austin, Rockford. **Most Valuable Pitcher:** Chad Sosebee, Richmond. **Rookie of the Year:** Kevin White, Richmond. **Manager of the Year:** John Massarelli, Washington.

INDIVIDUAL BATTING LEADERS
(Minimum 259 Plate Appearances)

	AVG	AB	R	H	2B	3B	HR	RBI	SB
Austin, Richard, Rockford	.359	290	71	104	20	1	15	77	22
McEachran, Aaron, Rockford	.332	331	67	110	23	1	11	62	1
Williams, Peanut, Windy City	.332	247	54	82	21	1	11	43	17
Brisson, Dustin, Chillicothe	.330	348	48	115	27	1	14	65	5
Headley, Jack, Washington	.325	311	58	101	15	4	3	38	18

Dreher, Doug, Chillicothe	.324	370	52	120	28	0	2	51	6
White, Kevin, Richmond	.322	289	57	93	8	5	11	37	4
Reese, Mike, Richmond	.319	348	60	111	14	4	4	42	32
Warren, Phil, Gateway	.314	357	71	112	20	0	23	66	0
Conner, Michael, River City	.313	233	57	73	18	1	11	52	21

INDIVIDUAL PITCHING LEADERS
(Minimum 77 Innings)

	W	L	ERA	G	SV	IP	H	BB	SO
Sosebee, Chad, Richmond	12	4	2.02	52	7	89	62	37	81
Hamilton, Mark, Chillicothe	4	5	2.25	11	0	88	71	30	95
Lewis, Jeremy, Evansville	9	4	2.47	20	0	135	132	29	120
Tomsu, Josh, Rockford	10	3	2.64	18	0	119	106	39	79
James, Frank, Rockford	7	3	2.65	16	0	78	65	30	47
Dooley, Joe, Gateway	10	3	2.75	19	0	128	116	47	102
Brook, Steven, River City	10	2	2.95	22	1	107	89	22	92
Williams, Grant, Evansville	10	2	2.97	19	0	130	95	47	119
Kesten, Michael, Chillicothe	7	8	3.02	19	0	128	104	47	141
Beshears, Joshua, Kalamazoo	11	3	3.03	19	0	113	100	37	113

* Signed with affiliated club

CHILLICOTHE

BATTING	AVG	AB	R	H	2B	3B	HR	RBI	SB
Blacken, Beau, of-3b	.271	321	49	87	21	0	17	58	1
Brightwell, Corey, of	.500	4	1	2	1	0	0	0	1
Brisson, Dustin, 1b	.330	348	48	115	27	1	14	65	5
Cosentino, Tony, c	.294	357	47	105	22	0	4	51	2
Dailey, D.J., 2b	.105	19	2	2	0	0	0	0	0
2-team (9 Gateway)	.116	43	4	5	0	0	0	1	0
Davenport, Juston, of	.211	114	14	24	5	1	1	11	1
Dreher, Doug, 2b	.324	370	52	120	28	0	2	51	6
Drummond, Charlie, c	.211	19	4	4	2	0	1	5	0
Edick, Denver, of-3b	.111	9	2	1	0	1	0	1	0
Gascon, Adrian, ss	.309	375	51	116	23	0	2	66	6
Goerdt, Eric, of	.227	97	8	22	5	0	1	11	0
Grutka, Marc, 2b	.250	4	1	1	0	0	0	0	0
2-team (2 Evansville)	.222	9	1	2	0	0	0	1	0
*Hamilton, Mark, of	.323	189	33	61	18	1	3	31	11
Heath, Darren, of	.286	49	9	14	1	0	0	3	5
Honce, Joe, ss	.000	5	0	0	0	0	0	0	0
L'Italien, Peter, dh	.143	7	1	1	0	0	1	1	0
Madrid, Mike, dh	.500	10	0	5	0	0	0	3	0
Navratil, Mike, of	.158	38	6	6	1	0	0	2	3
Pickens, Scott, c	.240	167	27	40	3	0	2	13	6
Pohle, Richard, dh-of	.387	62	13	24	4	0	1	9	0
Rodriguez, Jose, 3b	.258	190	29	49	14	1	1	29	4
Shorts, Adam, 3b-2b	.263	76	11	20	1	0	0	3	0
Spry, Michael, of	.281	203	33	57	7	8	1	19	1
Steppe, Nicholas, of	.203	64	7	13	6	0	0	3	0
Tuttle, Chris, of	.270	178	40	48	5	2	0	12	11
2-team (5 Richmond)	.265	196	42	52	6	2	0	13	12
Zimniewicz, Kurt, 3b	.167	24	4	4	0	0	1	0	0

PITCHING	W	L	ERA	G	SV	IP	H	BB	SO
Blanton, Matt	3	1	2.79	5	0	29	30	7	15
2-team (11 Springfield-Ozark)	8	4	4.91	16	0	84	97	39	56
Callahan, James	0	1	19.80	3	0	5	12	4	2
Cunningham, Perry	7	4	3.98	20	1	101	114	26	74
Durkee, Jeremy	1	4	6.21	27	1	37	42	18	44
Frary, Levi	0	0	0.00	1	0	1	1	0	0
Gits, Mike	6	3	3.11	47	2	81	92	19	49
Gordon, Dave	1	2	4.98	21	0	43	52	18	36
Hamilton, Mark	4	5	2.25	11	0	88	71	30	95
Hunter, Jeff	4	4	4.20	10	0	55	54	27	42
*Kesten, Michael	7	8	3.02	19	0	128	104	47	141
Lemieux, David	0	0	13.50	4	0	4	8	3	5
Martinez, John	5	4	4.57	13	0	86	110	20	73
Rahrer, Josh	7	4	4.62	16	0	89	103	31	59
Robinson, Justin	1	2	3.18	17	1	22	17	11	23
Royce, Ramon	2	5	4.82	33	17	46	52	15	44
Searle, Chris	0	1	11.37	6	0	6	12	7	6
2-team (2 Mid-Missouri)	0	1	16.88	8	0	8	19	9	9
Sonnier, Zachary	0	0	5.06	5	0	5	8	0	6
2-team (2 Windy City)	0	0	5.19	7	0	8	12	0	9
Williams, Jason	0	0	0.00	4	0	7	6	2	5

EVANSVILLE

BATTING	AVG	AB	R	H	2B	3B	HR	RBI	SB
Baywal, Tim, dh	.000	3	0	0	0	0	0	0	0
Brackley, Carlos, of	.336	220	40	74	8	0	9	42	6
Davie, Andrew, 1b	.243	136	20	33	5	1	3	26	0
Escobar, Luis, c	.167	18	2	3	0	0	0	1	0
Flanders, Brad, c	.259	27	1	7	1	0	0	4	1
Flynn, Sean, c	.228	250	28	57	19	2	8	37	1
Garza, O.J., of	.250	292	43	73	5	2	3	34	11

BATTING	AVG	AB	R	H	2B	3B	HR	RBI	SB
Ginther, Andy, c	.267	15	2	4	1	0	0	1	0
2-team (17 Spring./Ozark)	.290	62	8	18	3	0	1	6	2
Grutka, Marc, 2b	.200	5	0	1	0	0	0	1	0
*Hilt, Cole, 3b	.352	159	32	56	17	0	7	38	1
Julo, Chris, 2b-3b	.194	31	3	6	1	0	1	6	0
Lefler, Scott, 2b-3b	.167	6	1	1	0	0	0	0	0
Lipinski, Jim, dh	.244	41	4	10	3	0	0	6	0
Martin, Steve, of	.267	322	55	86	11	4	7	40	20
McClain, Terrence, of	.262	279	39	73	15	4	5	40	4
McCutchan, Brett, 1b	.196	97	16	19	3	0	4	12	0
McKenna, Brian, ss	.318	107	16	34	4	0	3	16	1
Mischo, Dave, 3b	.213	47	6	10	1	0	1	6	1
Radwan, Jason, c	.263	19	2	5	2	1	0	0	0
Ramirez, Johnathan, 2b-ss	.156	77	9	12	4	0	0	7	0
Scott, Frank, 2b	.232	211	48	49	5	1	1	18	13
2-team (4 Mid-Missouri)	.231	221	49	51	5	1	1	18	13
Stuckey, Denver, ss-3b	.290	372	68	108	17	2	3	43	8
Trujillo, David, dh	.297	300	41	89	18	3	6	53	1
Ward, Scott, of-3b	.293	123	19	36	3	2	3	12	8

PITCHING	W	L	ERA	G	SV	IP	H	BB	SO
Ampi, A.J.	5	3	1.48	28	1	30	27	12	24
Barber, Scott	3	4	5.24	11	0	56	75	17	38
Campbell, Dayle	0	0	5.12	14	2	19	18	9	13
Cassidy, Kevin	0	1	7.71	2	0	2	2	1	2
Faigin, Jason	3	3	5.20	26	2	36	41	23	28
Garcia, Justin	5	5	4.20	13	0	60	53	42	57
Heiberger, Heath	3	6	5.61	13	0	61	64	30	53
Jackson, J.J.	0	0	6.00	5	0	9	13	6	5
Langdon, Donny	0	1	5.14	5	0	7	3	11	12
Lewis, Jeremy	9	4	2.47	20	0	134	132	29	120
Miller, Kevin	0	0	3.00	5	0	3	3	3	2
Mischo, Dave	0	0	2.25	4	0	4	3	0	3
Palinkas, Steve	0	0	27.00	1	0	1	3	0	0
Parker, John	0	0	12.15	4	0	6	11	5	0
Read, Robby	3	2	4.23	7	0	38	32	22	29
Renes, Alex	0	0	11.00	7	0	9	13	7	6
Saunders, Tim	0	0	1.20	5	0	15	10	0	11
Simmering, Bryan	1	2	6.35	22	3	45	63	20	29
Simpson, Andre	7	6	4.88	24	2	103	111	44	87
*Stephens, Amad	4	0	1.44	19	14	25	17	7	37
Watzek, Kurt	1	3	8.34	6	0	22	37	11	17
White, Scott	0	0	13.50	3	0	3	8	2	5
Williams, Grant	10	2	2.97	19	0	130	95	47	119

FLORENCE

BATTING	AVG	AB	R	H	2B	3B	HR	RBI	SB
Athas, Mike, ss	.271	48	7	13	2	0	0	4	3
Burwell, Wilson, 3b	.252	115	10	29	4	0	2	13	0
Creighton, Tom, 2b	.280	200	41	56	5	2	11	37	17
Derhak, Alex, c	.261	203	18	53	5	0	0	18	2
Dworken, Mikaella, c	.238	21	2	5	2	0	0	4	0
Fenwick, Ron, 2b	.296	54	6	16	1	0	0	6	0
Ford, Jake, dh-1b	.283	138	21	39	6	2	4	31	2
*Foust, J.D., of	.302	192	29	58	9	1	4	27	15
Geswein, Kyle, 1b	.262	107	13	28	5	0	4	14	0
Hembree, Jon,P	.400	5	0	2	0	0	0	0	0
Hildebrant, Flip, of	.179	140	11	25	4	0	2	8	1
Ison, Jeremy, 3b-ss	.246	228	22	56	13	0	6	26	1
Jakubauskas, Chris, dh	.172	29	4	5	1	0	1	2	0
Levengood, Kyle, 1b-3b	.269	305	24	82	11	0	5	42	3
Pfister, Billy, ss	.200	15	3	3	0	0	1	3	0
Pickerell, Steve, c	.175	80	9	14	3	0	4	14	0
Rahschulte, Justin	.226	217	40	49	10	2	7	27	3
Schmidt, Zach, ss-2b	.223	188	23	42	6	1	5	17	2
Singer, Matt, of	.264	329	53	87	17	3	5	29	10
Stegbauer, Keith, 2b	.203	59	7	12	2	0	0	4	2
Steppe, Nicholas, of	.313	83	12	26	7	1	3	7	2
2-team (24 Chillicothe)	.265	147	19	39	13	1	3	10	2
Stone, Jon, c	.094	64	7	6	0	0	1	5	1
Thomas, Tee, of	.243	169	24	41	6	1	0	10	19
Turner, Tim, of	.270	37	4	10	0	0	0	3	5
Williamson, Chris, 1b-of	.215	65	8	14	1	0	4	9	0
Wilson, Kevin, ss	.250	48	4	12	2	0	0	2	0
Winkler, Shane, of	.200	20	2	4	0	0	0	2	0

PITCHING	W	L	ERA	G	SV	IP	H	BB	SO
Balzer, Ian	0	0	9.00	5	0	9	13	4	9
Bays, Leonard	4	8	6.22	39	5	76	83	47	85
Chafey, Hal	1	4	4.71	7	0	36	31	25	24
Chown, Eric	0	1	5.63	9	0	16	18	8	13
Davidson, Tom	3	3	3.27	24	0	55	51	32	39
Fischer, Eric	3	5	4.39	12	0	65	77	34	40
Flowers, Tyler	3	3	3.97	34	3	45	42	22	40
Gatch, Jeff	0	0	0.00	1	0	1	1	0	0
Graves, Bobby	0	6	8.06	13	0	41	47	47	27

PITCHING	W	L	ERA	G	SV	IP	H	BB	SO
Hansen, Chris	0	0	6.75	3	0	4	6	10	1
Hartzell, Ryan	2	0	3.86	16	2	18	17	9	19
2-team (18 Washington)	3	3	3.97	34	3	45	42	22	40
Hembree, Jon	1	1	7.71	24	0	18	16	18	9
Ihlenburg, Marc	2	3	4.74	10	0	38	52	11	19
Jakubauskas, Chris	0	2	7.50	7	0	24	34	9	18
Lantz, Doug	2	5	3.22	7	0	36	37	16	18
2-team (6 Washington)	4	5	4.09	13	0	55	58	18	27
Marksbury, Mike	1	1	7.58	24	0	29	32	20	32
Mendible, Frank	0	0	8.50	13	0	18	25	17	16
Meyer, Todd	0	1	6.06	14	0	16	16	11	13
Miller, Jason	0	1	7.20	3	0	5	9	4	4
Morrison, James	1	9	5.90	14	0	71	96	20	35
Palazzolo, Steve	1	3	7.54	9	0	37	46	25	14
Parr, Drew	0	2	10.38	3	0	8	18	5	4
Peters, Jamie	0	1	12.27	2	0	3	9	4	2
Posey, Joel	6	2	3.18	11	0	68	64	30	70
*Rival, Kevin	2	2	0.55	25	9	32	26	9	43
Rowland, Nick	1	1	12.32	15	1	19	38	7	13
Sibbersen, Justin	0	1	19.64	3	0	7	19	3	7
Steppe, Nicholas	0	0	6.75	3	0	2	3	3	3
Turner, Tim	0	1	3.79	13	0	19	19	12	16
Wiedeman, Matt	1	0	2.08	4	0	8	9	2	2
Williams, Jason	0	2	6.20	11	0	20	23	11	13
2-team (4 Chillicothe)	0	2	4.55	15	0	27	29	13	18

GATEWAY

BATTING	AVG	AB	R	H	2B	3B	HR	RBI	SB
Andrews, Greg, 2b	.111	18	3	2	1	0	0	1	0
Astrauskas, Wayne, c	.266	169	22	45	6	1	5	26	0
Bauder, Brad, of	.288	288	44	83	26	3	9	36	14
Bergheger, Jeremiah, 2b-3b	.231	52	13	12	1	0	1	5	4
Blaesing, Jamie, c	.000	1	0	0	0	0	0	0	0
Bollig, Jake, of	.217	23	5	5	0	0	2	6	0
Breyman, Mike, of	.324	145	33	47	12	1	6	29	0
Coyne, Tony, 2b	.306	170	29	52	5	1	7	29	1
Dailey, D.J., ss	.125	24	2	3	0	0	0	1	0
Gilbert, Gary, ss-2b	.251	191	28	48	8	1	4	21	1
Gilvin, Casey, of	.125	8	0	1	0	0	0	0	0
Hoffman, Eric, ss	.222	27	5	6	0	0	0	4	1
Lonon, T.J., of	.182	11	0	2	0	0	0	0	1
Monette, Daylon, of	.245	208	30	51	13	1	4	28	4
Oetting, Todd, dh	.294	327	52	96	21	1	12	53	5
Patrick, Sean, c	.238	42	6	10	0	0	0	3	0
Reiter, Jimmy, of	.268	351	55	94	17	2	8	40	20
Smarsh, Shawn, of-2b	.372	129	19	48	8	0	2	24	14
Stevens, Greg, 3b	.273	344	65	94	20	0	20	64	8
Sullivan, Ryan, 3b-2b	.254	224	25	57	15	0	7	33	0
Vargas, Oscar, ss	.265	117	18	31	6	0	3	16	3
Warren, Phil, 1b	.314	357	71	112	20	0	23	66	0

PITCHING	W	L	ERA	G	SV	IP	H	BB	SO
Buck, Pete	0	5	7.75	13	0	38	69	15	30
DeSalme, Gene	1	0	4.67	20	1	17	15	18	20
Dooley, Joe	10	3	2.75	19	0	127	116	47	102
Drewes, Brad	7	3	4.40	18	0	71	69	28	76
Forgione, Brian	0	1	23.14	1	0	2	5	3	1
Garrett, Brad	0	0	54.00	1	0	1	2	0	0
Golden, Mike	2	2	2.75	30	16	39	26	17	66
Hamilton, Ryan	4	1	0.81	23	3	33	21	15	42
Hendrix, Phillip	0	1	5.40	7	0	10	11	5	9
Kellbach, Brandon	0	2	6.46	4	0	15	17	7	9
Klahs, Dave	1	1	4.00	11	3	18	19	6	13
Lee, Kevin	9	5	5.10	19	0	100	111	46	87
Mault, Jeff	0	0	5.40	1	0	1	3	2	0
Mueller, Mark	1	0	10.80	4	0	11	19	6	9
Newland, Robert	1	4	4.86	20	1	37	43	26	38
Patterson, Scott	11	2	4.30	20	0	129	127	31	120
Rowe, Ted	2	0	1.76	15	1	30	27	9	28
Smith, Brandon	8	5	4.14	20	0	104	95	35	95
Smith, Dan	2	6	6.11	13	2	17	14	9	25
Sullivan, Ryan	0	0	9.00	2	0	3	2	4	1
Zaleski, Kyle	0	1	4.20	9	0	15	15	5	14

KALAMAZOO

BATTING	AVG	AB	R	H	2B	3B	HR	RBI	SB
Archer, Eric, 2b	.273	22	2	6	1	0	0	1	1
Archer, Phil, c	.223	148	16	33	5	0	6	22	1
Blaze, Darryl, of	.298	356	74	106	12	5	2	25	27
Daly, Rich, 1b	.143	35	2	5	2	0	0	2	0
DeGroote, Casey, 1b-3b	.284	285	52	81	18	0	11	54	1
Espinosa, Luis, dh	.255	110	14	28	7	0	3	9	0
Fenwick, Ron, 3b-2b	.127	63	7	8	1	0	0	4	0
2-team (20 Florence)	.205	117	13	24	2	0	0	10	0
Flamont, Sam, of	.255	55	8	14	2	0	2	8	2

BATTING	AVG	AB	R	H	2B	3B	HR	RBI	SB
Gomez, Arnie, 1b	.240	75	6	18	3	0	0	10	0
2-team (4 Richmond)	.233	90	7	21	3	0	0	10	0
Haven, Tory, dh	.233	60	8	14	1	0	4	8	1
Lentini, Fehlandt, of	.310	342	57	106	16	9	7	60	28
Malone, Billy, dh	.192	52	4	10	3	0	0	7	0
*McClain, Justin, 1b	.345	113	24	39	11	0	6	19	6
Pirman, Pete, of	.289	294	46	85	16	2	11	51	13
Riordan, Chris, ss	.000	3	0	0	0	0	0	0	0
Rogers, Brandon, c	.233	249	32	58	8	0	6	37	0
San Miguel, Javy, of	.333	12	0	4	0	0	0	0	1
Sepulveda, Carlos, of	.275	233	37	64	16	3	6	51	7
Shallenberger, Joe, ss	.185	65	6	12	1	0	3	11	0
Startari, Jason, 2b-ss	.224	313	40	70	16	1	2	26	9
Uranga, Darren, ss	.251	295	52	74	16	2	2	38	11

PITCHING	W	L	ERA	G	SV	IP	H	BB	SO
Auten, Brandon	0	0	6.23	4	0	4	6	3	3
Beever, James	0	1	12.79	5	1	6	9	6	5
Beshears, Joshua	11	3	3.03	19	0	113	100	37	113
Beuning, Brian	3	2	4.32	33	0	50	45	31	52
Brooks, Jake	1	2	2.06	34	15	39	25	14	52
Fuller, Justin	0	0	4.09	7	1	11	9	4	16
*Garner, Jeff	0	1	0.00	8	1	10	7	2	7
Huizinga, Jon	2	0	3.86	4	0	21	18	9	18
Jamison, Ryan	7	4	5.57	22	0	82	84	38	65
Keeling, Justin	3	6	4.06	44	1	51	57	26	42
Keeton, Glen	0	1	2.81	8	1	16	12	15	11
Lawson, Scott	1	3	7.40	12	1	20	29	6	13
Leishman, Mike	0	1	5.54	19	0	26	20	24	28
McWatters, David	5	8	4.50	20	0	126	134	41	95
Musialowski, Jonathan	1	1	5.49	11	0	19	20	10	8
Naplin, Lee	7	3	3.08	19	1	96	91	39	80
O'Neil, Pat	0	1	7.94	3	0	5	9	2	5
Padilla, Matt	0	0	1.80	4	0	10	8	6	7
Rohr, Charles	0	1	4.50	7	0	8	7	7	5
Streich, Isaac	0	0	12.00	5	0	3	4	4	1
Wiltshire, Greg	7	5	3.23	30	1	92	88	43	80
Yurek, Ryan	0	0	7.36	3	0	3	4	3	2
Ziroli, Mike	1	2	7.79	6	0	17	22	12	11
2-team (23 Windy City)	3	4	5.79	29	0	46	62	25	37

MID-MISSOURI

BATTING	AVG	AB	R	H	2B	3B	HR	RBI	SB
Acuff, Tarron, of	.077	13	1	1	0	0	0	0	0
Blase, Blake, 1b-of	.250	324	53	81	18	0	17	58	3
Bok, Matt, of	.100	10	1	1	0	0	0	2	0
Boruff, Gabe, of	.167	12	2	2	0	0	0	0	0
Burkhart, Damon, 3b	.186	43	14	8	0	1	1	4	1
Cashman, Thomas, 1b	.214	14	0	3	0	0	0	1	0
Darjean, Eric, of	.243	181	26	44	5	3	2	19	15
2-team (34 Windy City)	.251	283	43	71	11	7	2	26	30
Dennis, Jace, 2b	.250	4	0	1	0	0	0	0	0
Fewell, Wes, of	.105	38	0	4	2	0	0	2	0
Giorgis, David, of	.400	5	2	2	0	0	0	1	0
Goirigolzarri, Raymond, of	.179	56	9	10	2	0	2	6	2
Hillman, Dusty, 2b	.299	331	56	99	16	2	6	47	10
Lara, Rafael, ss-2b	.250	216	34	54	10	1	0	22	17
2-team (13 Richmond)	.258	264	41	68	12	1	2	31	19
Laskowski, Lee, of	.250	12	0	3	0	0	0	0	0
Lucas, Scott, 1b	.250	4	2	1	1	0	0	0	0
Matthews, Bobby, c	.273	11	3	3	0	0	0	3	0
McMahon, Justin, of	.250	28	3	7	1	0	1	3	0
Metheny, Brent, 3b-ss	.280	232	38	65	13	2	6	41	10
Nichols, Jace, of	.220	91	19	20	5	1	2	11	2
Oakes, Matt, c	.311	193	23	60	15	0	2	28	0
Oehler, John, c	.205	78	7	16	1	0	0	8	1
Peoples, Derrick, of	.218	55	10	12	3	0	0	2	5
Peters, Samone, 1b	.308	26	2	8	0	0	0	3	0
Quaney, Gator, of	.167	66	6	11	3	0	0	7	0
2-team (10 Windy City)	.175	80	8	14	4	1	0	7	0
Ramigawachi, Matt, 3b	.222	9	1	2	1	0	0	1	0
Rapacioli, Mike, 1b	.227	22	2	5	3	0	1	2	0
Richt, Tim, 3b	.500	4	0	2	1	0	0	1	0
Samples, Mike, 2b-ss	.083	12	0	1	0	0	0	0	0
Saunders, Nick, dh	.309	149	18	46	10	2	5	31	1
Scott, Frank, 2b	.200	10	1	2	0	0	0	0	0
Scott, Worth, of	.067	15	0	1	0	0	0	0	0
Sterbens, Chad, 3b-ss	.271	240	34	65	10	1	1	24	9
Story-Harden, Thomari, 1b	.249	173	29	43	3	1	11	38	4
Stricker, George, of	.186	97	6	18	1	1	2	15	3
Taylor, Lucas, of	.571	7	4	4	1	0	0	2	0
Teahen, Matt, 3b	.077	13	2	1	1	0	0	1	0
Thomas, Charles, of	.248	129	26	32	4	4	4	14	7
Turberville, Erik, ss	.280	25	1	7	2	0	0	1	1
Varon, Peter, ph	.000	1	0	0	0	0	0	0	0
Veloz, Gabe, 3b	.500	6	1	3	1	0	0	0	0
Weiss, Bryan, 1b-3b	.243	37	3	9	1	0	1	4	1
2-team (13 River City)	.220	50	4	11	2	0	1	7	1
Wittmus, Tony, of	.111	9	0	1	0	0	0	0	0
Wright, Jon, of	.264	110	16	29	6	4	2	16	3
2-team (27 Windy City)	.254	197	27	50	8	4	6	30	5
Wuerch, Jason, c	.192	26	2	5	1	0	0	1	0

PITCHING	W	L	ERA	G	SV	IP	H	BB	SO
Almand, Michael	0	2	16.43	3	0	7	19	5	2
Buck, Ben	0	2	10.80	6	0	5	9	5	3
Cauble, Greg	0	0	0.00	1	0	2	3	1	1
Craker, Justin	3	3	2.03	41	11	53	39	31	60
Cremeans, Keith	0	4	6.55	6	0	34	48	12	29
Dorsey, Brian	0	1	13.50	1	0	1	4	2	2
Elkins, Jason	0	0	6.59	8	0	13	14	11	14
Glascock, John-Paul	2	4	6.75	25	0	56	73	41	35
Hall, Courtney	0	2	9.00	2	0	6	11	3	6
Harvey, Reed	0	0	3.60	3	0	5	4	3	4
Heinrichs, Darren	0	1	4.26	8	0	31	28	16	25
3-team (6 Windy City, 3 Richmond)	0	2	4.87	17	0	44	43	22	40
Jackson, Jimmy	1	2	4.83	20	0	31	35	19	20
Jakubov, Ryan	0	2	36.00	3	0	4	14	9	3
Kennedy, Dajuan	0	0	13.50	2	0	2	4	1	1
Kline, Ty	2	3	6.14	14	0	44	65	14	28
2-team (7 Windy City)	5	4	5.59	21	0	77	111	24	59
Kozol, Anthony	0	4	10.07	13	0	22	37	6	18
Lemieux, David	6	2	3.93	22	0	34	30	18	34
2-team (4 Chillicothe)	6	2	5.08	26	0	39	38	21	39
Mahan, Dallas	0	1	27.00	3	0	1	6	0	0
Marko, Ed	0	0	18.00	2	0	2	4	4	0
Moellering, Dan	0	0	7.50	4	0	6	10	1	5
Mueller, Mark	1	1	2.70	9	0	13	10	5	11
2-team (4 Gateway)	1	2	6.48	13	0	25	29	11	20
Nevels, Kyle	0	1	11.39	10	0	21	33	16	16
Parish, Graham	0	1	11.25	2	0	4	6	2	0
Picco, John	1	7	8.40	15	0	65	74	52	62
Reyes, Luis	0	0	9.82	7	0	7	13	6	5
Roelle, Shane	0	2	8.56	4	0	13	23	9	14
Russell, Greg	1	4	10.80	15	0	23	25	25	25
Santillan, Manny	0	2	54.00	2	0	2	10	4	1
Searle, Chris	0	0	37.80	2	0	1	7	2	3
Shuck, Danny	5	2	3.96	11	0	61	71	19	38
Soja, Steve	4	4	4.58	16	0	88	97	27	71
2-team (1 River City)	4	4	4.98	17	0	90	102	29	72
Starcher, Greg	0	0	6.75	3	0	2	4	2	2
Tyson, Leo	0	0	12.00	2	0	3	5	3	1
Wiedmeyer, Jason	2	9	5.50	18	0	111	133	35	89
Wyatt, Blake	0	0	5.52	12	0	14	20	4	13

RICHMOND

BATTING	AVG	AB	R	H	2B	3B	HR	RBI	SB
Archer, Eric, 3b-ss	.220	127	20	28	6	0	2	18	2
3-team (7 Kalamazoo, 5 Rockford)	.240	154	25	37	8	0	3	22	3
Barclay, Mike, of	.069	29	5	2	1	0	0	0	1
Borque, Blair, c	.200	45	6	9	1	0	2	4	0
Brown, Kevin, 1b	.311	305	67	95	18	0	23	68	12
Cisneros, Josh, c	.167	6	2	1	0	0	0	0	0
Croley, Mike, 2b	.143	21	1	3	0	0	0	1	0
Donley, Ryan, of-3b	.240	50	4	12	3	0	0	6	1
Goedson, Todd, c	.000	1	0	0	0	0	0	0	0
Gomez, Arnie, of	.200	15	1	3	0	0	0	0	0
Hall, Trevor, dh-1b	.330	282	46	93	16	1	14	63	0
2-team (7 Windy City)	.310	306	48	95	16	1	15	66	0
Hancock, Justin, ss-of	.236	140	15	33	4	1	1	16	3
Hargrove, Taylor, 2b	.235	17	2	4	0	0	0	1	1
Hollingsworth, Josh, 3b-ss	.259	316	49	82	11	0	14	48	10
Lara, Rafael, 2b-ss	.292	48	7	14	2	0	2	9	2
Miller, Drew, of	.291	330	54	96	27	2	3	37	3
Newman, Cory, of	.000	6	0	0	0	0	0	0	0
2-team (8 Rockford)	.185	27	2	5	1	0	0	0	0
Patterson, Adam, dh	.218	55	5	12	1	0	0	4	0
Reese, Mike, of	.319	348	60	111	14	4	4	42	32
Romprey, Ed, ss	.160	50	6	8	3	0	0	4	0
Samples, Mike, 2b	.250	4	1	1	1	0	0	0	0
3-team (4 Mid-Missouri, 3 Windy City)	.130	23	2	3	1	0	0	0	2
Sandoval, Jose, 3b-ss	.213	61	13	13	4	1	1	8	3
Sanguinetti, Tony, c	.228	162	18	37	10	0	4	22	0
Scott, Dave, c	.000	7	0	0	0	0	0	0	0
Silva, Michael, c	.276	156	21	43	5	1	1	21	1
Turberville, Erik, 3b-2b	.238	63	6	15	3	1	0	4	0
2-team (9 Mid-Missouri)	.250	88	7	22	5	1	0	5	1
Tuttle, Chris, of	.222	18	2	4	1	0	0	1	1
White, Kevin, of	.322	289	57	93	8	5	11	37	4
White, Rick, of	.333	9	0	3	1	0	0	2	0

	AVG	AB	R	H	2B	3B	HR	RBI	SB
Woods, Blake, 2b	.288	222	48	64	17	0	11	38	9
2-team (9 Windy City)	.275	255	50	70	19	0	11	41	9

PITCHING	W	L	ERA	G	SV	IP	H	BB	SO
Anderson, Andy	0	0	27.00	2	0	1	4	2	1
*Barkley, Richard	4	3	2.97	10	0	60	44	16	64
Berger, Garrett	0	0	3.86	2	0	2	3	4	0
Butler, Jordan	0	0	0.00	2	0	1	2	1	1
Byrum, Pete	0	0	7.71	2	0	9	10	2	5
*Caldwell, David	0	0	12.27	4	0	3	3	2	2
Campos, David	1	5	5.30	32	0	93	112	48	67
Cartwright, Jim	0	0	12.46	5	0	8	14	7	6
Casoli, Tony	3	3	4.53	10	0	57	59	15	30
2-team (13 Springfield/Ozark)	.3	5	4.87	23	1	81	90	23	46
Corley, Klent	1	0	8.44	2	0	5	8	4	3
Donlin, Sean	1	0	7.71	3	0	7	8	11	8
Elkins, Jason	0	0	27.00	2	0	2	7	0	2
2-team (8 Mid-Missouri)	0	0	9.19	10	0	15	21	11	16
Gann, Jake	1	1	4.50	13	0	18	26	11	15
Gerbasi, Greg	0	1	15.43	1	0	2	7	2	0
Gonzales, Jamie	0	3	7.58	8	0	19	29	13	12
Graves, Bobby	0	2	17.18	2	0	3	6	7	3
2-team (13 Florence)	0	8	8.80	15	0	45	53	54	30
Heagen, Doug	0	0	13.50	1	0	3	7	0	3
2-team (2 Washington)	0	2	10.13	3	0	13	21	2	11
Heinrichs, Darren	0	1	10.38	3	0	4	9	4	6
Horvat, Jason	1	6	6.89	7	0	15	17	8	20
Joyce, Michael	0	1	7.36	1	0	3	3	2	1
Kupper, Dustin	1	2	1.83	13	3	19	16	6	13
*Mead, Dan	0	0	14.73	5	0	3	5	11	4
Miller, Jeff	0	0	7.20	2	0	5	8	3	3
Moenter, Curtis	2	4	7.25	13	0	49	60	34	35
Moore, Bo	1	6	6.75	15	0	56	71	24	39
Moran, Shane	0	0	13.50	2	0	1	2	2	2
Mott, Tyler	1	3	4.98	7	0	21	26	9	12
Murphy, Mike	0	0	5.40	4	0	6	8	3	3
Neitz, Josh	0	5	5.67	9	0	27	33	5	23
Pettibone, John	0	0	17.18	4	0	3	6	5	4
Pilkington, Jason	3	1	2.26	5	0	27	23	14	25
2-team (16 Rockford)	7	4	2.81	21	1	67	56	36	64
Quaempts, Justin	0	1	6.00	1	0	3	4	2	1
Rodriguez, Ricardo	0	1	1.46	11	0	12	8	3	9
Schweitzer, Matt	6	5	3.40	29	5	79	73	20	70
Shelnutt, Chad	0	0	6.75	2	0	1	2	2	1
Sosebee, Chad	12	4	2.02	52	7	89	62	37	81
Spigner, Chris	0	2	18.78	2	0	7	21	5	6
Strickland, Keith	0	0	0.00	2	0	1	2	0	1
Strohm, Steve	1	0	4.30	6	0	14	14	9	13
West, Ryan	4	2	5.30	48	2	73	75	17	52

RIVER CITY

BATTING	AVG	AB	R	H	2B	3B	HR	RBI	SB
Aqueron, Rene, of	.279	61	9	17	2	1	2	6	1
Bischofberger, Sean, 3b	.203	64	10	13	3	0	1	7	1
Calderon, Tony, ss	.283	46	9	13	2	0	0	4	2
Carver, Dane, c	.143	7	0	1	0	0	0	0	0
*Christian, Justin, ss	.450	120	31	54	11	2	5	22	26
Conner, Michael, of	.313	233	57	73	18	1	11	52	21
Dennis, Jace, 2b-ss	.167	6	3	1	0	0	0	0	1
2-team (3 Mid-Missouri)	.200	10	3	2	0	0	0	0	1
Dorame, Ricky, of	.182	66	8	12	3	0	1	5	1
Errante, Eric, 2b	.000	9	0	0	0	0	0	0	0
Honeycutt, Blake, 2b	.200	5	1	1	0	0	0	0	0
Howell, Ryan, 3b	.200	10	1	2	1	0	0	0	1
Jackson, Brody, of	.309	333	66	103	20	3	12	54	51
Kalczynski, Joe, c	.171	35	6	6	1	0	0	1	3
Klosterman, Chris, ss-3b	.303	343	45	104	27	2	7	52	7
Lewis, Brian, ph	1.000	1	0	1	1	0	0	0	0
Madrid, Mike, 1b	.293	324	55	95	19	0	19	83	5
2-team (3 Chillicothe)	.299	334	55	100	19	0	19	86	5
Moreno, Jhonny, 3b	.246	61	7	15	2	0	0	4	0
Munoz, Dan, 3b	.077	13	3	1	0	0	0	0	1
Negron, Jason, of	.205	39	5	8	1	0	0	5	0
Nowak, David, of	.286	28	5	8	2	0	0	5	3
Olsen, Kela, dh-of	.289	301	56	87	17	1	13	54	4
Ornelas, Rafael, 3b-2b	.278	162	24	45	5	2	0	18	6
*Riera, Zack, c	.316	209	43	66	18	3	13	46	8
Ury, Josh, of	.282	348	58	98	21	2	15	54	13
Vittitoe, Cooper, 2b	.279	269	64	75	10	1	6	37	26
Weiss, Bryan, 2b	.154	13	1	2	1	0	0	3	0
Williams, Jonny, c	.248	121	25	30	4	0	7	31	4

PITCHING	W	L	ERA	G	SV	IP	H	BB	SO
Brook, Steven	10	2	2.95	22	1	106	89	22	92
*Charron, Joey	0	1	6.23	4	0	4	5	3	2
Forbes, Derek	0	1	45.00	2	0	1	6	1	3

	W	L	ERA	G	SV	IP	H	BB	SO
*Gale, Bryan	4	2	3.62	7	0	32	24	10	28
Guntorius, Dave	3	1	3.57	29	2	40	32	12	36
Hendrix, Phillip	4	0	3.09	13	0	43	46	12	37
2-team (7 Gateway)	5	0	3.52	20	0	53	57	17	46
Johnson, Kelly	4	2	4.08	29	6	39	39	23	46
Krines, Dan	3	10	4.47	21	0	86	104	22	52
Laratta, E.J.	4	6	6.06	18	0	81	111	31	59
Larrick, Greg	0	0	13.50	4	0	5	9	6	3
Ledbetter, Aaron	6	4	3.94	13	0	75	81	19	72
McCool, Ricky	0	0	10.80	3	0	3	5	2	3
McReynolds, Steve	0	0	0.00	2	0	7	4	2	2
Miller, Joe	0	0	4.50	2	0	2	2	3	2
Modica, Greg	11	3	3.20	19	0	129	109	22	91
Newland, Robert	0	1	8.53	4	0	12	18	7	7
2-team (20 Gateway)	1	5	5.80	24	1	49	61	33	45
Niedbalski, Nick	0	2	6.59	12	0	28	34	8	18
Olsen, Kela	0	0	5.40	2	0	1	3	2	1
Schilsky, Steve	0	2	6.38	9	1	24	32	18	23
Soja, Steve	0	0	22.50	1	0	2	5	2	1
Thatcher, Joe	2	3	2.98	29	5	42	38	15	55
Tower, Scott	0	0	10.13	4	0	5	11	3	5
Weber, Kris	0	1	5.19	8	1	17	18	5	17
Wood, Bobby	0	2	5.92	5	0	24	25	12	27

ROCKFORD

BATTING	AVG	AB	R	H	2B	3B	HR	RBI	SB
Archer, Eric, 3b	.600	5	3	3	1	0	1	3	0
*Austin, Richard, of	.359	290	71	104	20	1	15	77	22
Baron, Brian, dh	.412	17	2	7	0	0	0	1	0
Bernstine, David, c	.249	181	22	45	8	2	3	26	1
Ciarrachi, Kevin, c	.259	193	22	50	16	0	0	25	1
Crowder, Chris, 2b	.400	5	1	2	1	0	0	1	0
DiBlasi, Chris, 1b	.182	66	10	12	4	0	0	5	1
Elkouri, Shaff, dh-2b	.305	236	43	72	12	1	6	35	8
Fjelland, Ben, 3b-2b	.287	348	53	100	27	1	5	56	5
Floyd, Dan, of	.307	137	20	42	13	0	0	18	3
Landry, Mike, c	.136	22	2	3	0	0	0	3	0
Larson, Ryan, 3b	.290	248	33	72	10	0	4	37	0
McEachran, Aaron, 1b	.332	331	67	110	23	1	11	62	1
Newman, Cory, of	.238	21	2	5	1	0	0	0	0
Rosario, Olmo, ss	.258	225	39	58	6	4	4	27	7
San Miguel, Javy, dh-of	.667	3	1	2	0	0	0	0	0
2-team (4 Kalamazoo)	.400	15	1	6	0	0	0	0	1
Santana, Ricardo, of	.284	359	68	102	23	3	5	65	27
Schutt, Doug, of	.286	311	63	89	11	4	3	32	39
Vaughn, Kiley, ss-2b	.256	328	54	84	15	2	1	42	10

PITCHING	W	L	ERA	G	SV	IP	H	BB	SO
Barbosa, Joe	1	2	3.72	20	1	58	59	19	59
Christensen, Mica	0	2	6.92	4	0	13	22	8	6
Crowley, Kevin	1	0	4.37	15	1	22	24	14	12
*Dowdy, Justin	4	1	2.39	10	2	52	35	18	53
Dulkowski, Marc	2	3	4.61	29	1	56	62	38	41
Ellison, Derrick	3	2	3.81	28	1	26	16	15	34
Glosser, Jason	0	0	8.31	3	0	4	7	0	5
James, Frank	7	3	2.65	16	0	78	65	30	47
Latimer, Josh	3	3	2.47	35	15	43	32	17	41
Mack, Bobby	0	0	2.41	13	0	18	12	11	10
Merle, Jesen	3	2	3.61	42	1	42	47	19	43
Miller, Danny	0	0	6.35	3	0	5	7	5	2
Olson, Justin	8	0	4.11	27	0	72	66	33	82
Palmer, Adam	1	4	3.72	11	0	48	54	15	17
Pilkington, Jason	4	3	3.18	16	1	39	33	22	39
Saldana, Jaime	4	2	2.59	9	0	38	26	24	47
Sobkowiak, Scott	8	7	4.20	15	0	96	100	45	89
Tomsu, Josh	10	3	2.64	18	0	119	106	39	79

SPRINGFIELD-OZARK

BATTING	AVG	AB	R	H	2B	3B	HR	RBI	SB
Balster, Scott, of	.222	18	3	4	0	0	0	1	2
Booth, Steve, c	.198	116	17	23	2	0	4	21	1
Fischer, David, dh-of	.296	223	36	66	12	1	4	30	4
Ginther, Andy, c	.298	47	6	14	2	0	1	5	2
Haake, Steve, of	.290	321	57	93	21	3	10	53	16
Harper, Eddie, of	.294	218	34	64	9	1	0	13	12
Kindle, Jud, c	.121	33	4	4	1	0	0	2	0
Kirby, Brian, of-1b	.256	308	46	79	13	2	16	55	6
Landon, Josh, 2b	.268	209	38	56	11	0	4	27	4
Leathers, Todd, 1b	.275	335	64	92	21	0	10	69	4
Munoz, David, ss	.232	311	35	72	12	1	4	33	7
Oligo, Kaliko, of	.228	193	28	44	3	1	0	18	8
Pelfrey, Dennis, of	.193	83	11	16	4	0	1	9	9
Pittullo, Clay, of	.125	16	2	2	0	0	0	1	1
Spencer, John, c	.265	117	16	31	4	0	2	16	0
Taylor, Alex, 2b-of	.257	148	25	38	7	1	3	17	9

BATTING	AVG	AB	R	H	2B	3B	HR	RBI	SB
Townsend, Tanner, 3b	.252	349	49	88	20	3	12	61	15
Uegawachi, Bryce, 2b-ss	.250	124	19	31	3	0	1	8	2
Wettlaufer, Josh, of	.333	21	8	7	1	0	1	3	2

PITCHING	W	L	ERA	G	SV	IP	H	BB	SO
Bennett, Jamie	10	5	3.70	19	0	121	113	33	110
Blanton, Matt	5	3	6.02	11	0	55	67	32	41
Casoli, Tony	0	2	5.70	13	1	23	31	8	16
Chenard, Ryan	2	0	6.17	32	1	46	46	22	34
Cooney, Jim	0	3	5.70	36	0	30	31	17	28
Dunkle, Peter	0	0	9.18	8	0	16	27	11	21
Fisher, Cody	7	8	3.79	19	0	123	141	34	82
Gonzalez, John	2	0	0.86	11	0	21	16	7	16
Miralles, Rodrigo	6	3	3.17	16	0	59	54	22	60
Rodriguez, Ricardo	0	2	1.13	22	1	24	19	10	20
2-team (11 Richmond)	0	3	1.24	33	1	36	27	13	29
Schaefer, Mike	4	9	4.85	19	0	102	105	56	67
Stephens, Brett	3	1	4.38	5	0	24	29	11	20
2-team (13 Windy City)	7	8	4.95	18	0	107	122	29	106
Stone, Nathan	2	1	2.23	33	8	44	44	11	49
Taylor, Scott	1	1	2.52	29	1	35	29	9	32
*Vanderplow, Randy	4	2	2.01	20	9	22	16	4	33
Villarreal, Luis	6	3	3.95	14	0	79	85	38	65

WASHINGTON

BATTING	AVG	AB	R	H	2B	3B	HR	RBI	SB
Arbinger, Mike, of	.299	355	71	106	27	2	6	51	6
Barden, Andy, c	.262	84	15	22	5	0	0	12	1
Barry, Gil, 3b-ss	.462	13	3	6	2	0	0	2	2
2-team (82 Windy City)	.272	290	45	79	12	1	2	23	17
Biernbaum, L.J., of	.278	334	64	93	16	1	13	58	6
Bok, Matt, dh-c	.240	96	11	23	7	1	4	21	1
2-team (3 Mid-Missouri)	.226	106	12	24	7	1	4	23	1
Buchenauer, Joel, 3b	.203	133	23	27	3	2	0	7	1
Cahill, Jon, ss	.274	317	38	87	11	0	6	49	1
Coakley, Jay, dh	.274	230	38	63	10	0	10	48	0
Cornell, Brandon, of	.229	118	26	27	1	5	0	7	10
Ellis, Ryan, 2b	.500	4	1	2	0	0	0	0	0
Gaub, Josh, c	.154	13	2	2	0	0	0	2	0
Greenwell, Bill, 1b	.293	334	53	98	15	1	13	72	1
Headley, Jack, of	.325	311	58	101	15	4	3	38	18
Kinyon, Chad, 3b	.292	195	26	57	13	1	4	33	1
McGarvey, Randy, c	.223	184	28	41	7	0	1	31	3
Nulton, Kevin, 3b	.176	74	14	13	1	1	0	8	5
Rynders, Wes, of	.129	31	3	4	1	0	0	6	1
Sandoval, Jjalil, 2b	.174	23	3	4	1	0	0	2	0
Stoecklein, Brian, 2b	.295	322	65	95	21	5	10	43	9

PITCHING	W	L	ERA	G	SV	IP	H	BB	SO
Augsburger, Kyle	4	0	4.53	28	2	51	62	16	40
Borsa, B.J.	7	1	2.12	35	19	46	30	14	50
Coughenour, Jory	0	2	4.57	5	0	21	23	9	22
Davis, Brendon	3	2	2.76	32	4	58	49	28	54
Dorn, Grant	4	5	4.52	17	0	79	89	27	74
Ewin, Ryan	9	2	5.38	17	0	80	81	30	53
Fischer, Eric	3	2	4.09	6	0	33	32	16	9
2-team (12 Mid-Missouri)	6	7	4.29	18	0	98	109	50	49
Hartzell, Ryan	1	3	4.05	18	1	26	25	13	21
Heagen, Doug	0	2	9.00	2	0	10	14	2	8
Holt, Eric	5	3	4.11	23	0	87	109	24	43
Lantz, Doug	2	0	5.79	6	0	18	21	2	9
McDonnell, Matt	7	5	4.46	19	0	105	112	35	70
Palmer, Adam	4	1	2.79	6	0	29	22	13	15
2-team (11 Rockford)	5	5	3.38	17	0	77	76	28	32
Popp, Jim	5	1	1.40	30	6	58	35	12	53
Powell, Matt	8	5	4.46	19	1	105	120	21	63
Sikorski, Mike	0	0	18.00	1	0	1	2	2	1

WINDY CITY

BATTING	AVG	AB	R	H	2B	3B	HR	RBI	SB
Baker, Brian, of	.303	274	56	83	16	4	18	62	19
Barry, Gil, ss-3b	.264	277	42	73	10	1	2	21	15
Bolton, Patrick, 3b	.273	11	0	3	0	0	0	1	0
Bragg, Michael, c	.226	53	7	12	4	0	0	1	1
Coleman, Alph, of	.214	56	10	12	4	0	1	8	4
Cunningham, Mike, of	.244	45	9	11	2	1	0	5	4
Daly, Rich, 1b	.253	99	13	25	6	0	1	15	0
Darjean, Eric, 3b-of	.265	102	17	27	6	4	0	7	15
Flamont, Sam, 2b-dh	.326	144	26	47	9	1	5	31	5
2-team (15 Kalamazoo)	.307	199	34	61	11	1	7	39	7
Fuller, Casey, of	.219	151	19	33	1	0	4	22	2
George, Kyle, ss-2b	.184	76	6	14	4	0	1	4	1
Guglielmelli, Brad, c	.271	214	27	58	17	1	5	22	2
Hall, Trevor, 1b	.083	24	2	2	0	0	1	3	0
Haven, Tory, dh	.212	52	5	11	2	0	2	16	0
2-team (19 Kalamazoo)	.223	112	13	25	3	0	6	24	1

BATTING	AVG	AB	R	H	2B	3B	HR	RBI	SB
Houston, Bobby Joe, 1b	.000	3	1	0	0	0	0	0	0
Johnson, Nick, of	.276	286	46	79	14	1	7	45	12
Kalczynski, Joe, c	.211	19	4	4	0	0	0	3	0
2-team (10 River City)	.185	54	10	10	1	0	0	4	3
Keefner, Eric, 3b	.125	16	4	2	1	0	0	0	1
Keesee, David, 2b-3b	.226	62	7	14	5	0	1	9	0
Kuecher, Matt, c	.000	8	0	0	0	0	0	0	0
Lawson, Forrest, of	.216	37	5	8	3	0	1	3	1
McCoy, Jerome, of-ss	.267	303	51	81	7	0	0	26	37
Murch, Jeremy, dh-of	.238	84	11	20	7	0	2	10	1
Quaney, Gator, c	.214	14	2	3	1	1	0	0	0
Rhomberg, Joe, 2b	.140	43	3	6	2	0	0	5	0
Samples, Mike, 2b	.143	7	1	1	0	0	0	0	1
Saunders, Nick, 3b-dh	.245	94	7	23	4	0	1	15	0
2-team (40 Mid-Missouri)	.284	243	25	69	14	2	6	46	1
Street, Dan, 1b-3b	.292	72	9	21	5	0	0	4	2
Sullivan, Kevin, c	.222	18	5	4	1	0	2	5	0
Walker, Keronn, c	.143	49	2	7	0	0	1	4	0
Wiens, Ranger, 3b	.111	27	1	3	0	0	0	0	3
*Williams, Peanut, 1b-of	.332	247	54	82	21	1	11	43	17
Woods, Blake, 3b	.182	33	2	6	2	0	0	3	0
Wright, Jon, dh-of	.241	87	11	21	2	0	4	14	2

PITCHING	W	L	ERA	G	SV	IP	H	BB	SO
Bell, Kory	1	0	3.97	7	0	11	13	8	8
Bogs, Brian	3	1	2.45	21	0	22	15	6	24
Bolton, Aaron	3	6	6.13	19	0	94	94	64	84
Buitron, Andy	3	1	7.06	19	0	29	38	9	23
Campbell, Andrew	0	1	9.00	5	0	11	17	5	9
Daly, Brian	0	0	0.00	2	0	2	3	1	0
Darby, Paul	0	5	8.35	5	0	18	28	6	12
Donlin, Sean	3	3	9.00	13	0	18	19	15	19
2-team (3 Richmond)	1	3	8.64	16	0	25	27	26	27
Edmundson, Marcus	0	0	6.75	3	0	2	0	5	3
Heinrichs, Darren	0	0	4.32	6	0	8	6	2	9
*Hines, Matt	2	1	4.43	19	13	20	20	8	21
Kline, Ty	3	1	4.86	7	0	33	46	10	31
Kozol, Anthony	1	0	5.87	13	0	15	22	9	19
2-team (13 Mid-Missouri)	1	4	8.36	26	0	37	59	15	37
Leishman, Mike	0	0	18.00	1	0	2	2	1	3
2-team (19 Kalamazoo)	0	1	6.43	20	0	28	22	25	31
Litchfield, B.J.	2	5	3.72	40	4	55	60	18	55
Matta, Felix	3	3	5.24	10	0	46	50	27	21
Regas, Kris	2	5	6.16	8	0	38	47	13	35
Reilly, Chris	4	6	4.37	16	0	92	88	38	79
Shelton, Brad	0	0	6.00	3	0	6	6	4	5
Sonnier, Zachary	0	0	5.40	2	0	3	4	0	3
St. Amant, John	0	1	11.05	3	0	7	11	7	10
Stephens, Brett	4	7	5.12	13	0	82	93	18	86
Tacker, Trevor	3	3	6.32	15	0	57	66	41	26
Villarreal, Luis	0	2	3.38	3	0	18	22	4	17
2-team (14 Springfield/Ozark)	6	5	3.84	17	0	98	107	42	82
Ziroli, Mike	2	2	4.60	23	0	29	40	13	26
Ziroli, Steve	1	4	5.33	26	0	50	58	20	54

NORTHERN LEAGUE

George Tsamis has won three championships in the past six seasons, and he says like children, every title is special. But he admits the 2004 Northern League title may be his favorite because of its improbable ending.

Adam Olow

Trailing Schaumburg by three runs with two outs in the ninth inning of the decisive Game Five of the league's championship series, Tsamis' St. Paul Saints rallied to score seven runs, winning the Northern League title, 10-6, on Marc Mirizzi's walk-off grand slam.

"This is the most incredible thing I've seen on a baseball diamond. It will be tough to ever top this," said Tsamis, the second-year manager of the Saints. "It's the closet thing to Joe Carter (hitting a home run to win the World Series) that you'll ever see."

Twice the Saints were down to their final strike, but two doubles, three singles and a walk set up Mirizzi, who

wouldn't have been in the game if not for a late-season thumb injury to first baseman Billy Munoz. The Saints had acquired Mirizzi at the trade deadline as insurance because starting shortstop Chas Terni had a sore hamstring.

"When I came over, you could just tell about this team," Mirizzi said. "When you walked into the locker room, the confidence was there."

Terni remained healthy for the playoffs, but when Munoz got hurt, Mirizzi got back on the field as a first baseman. He wasn't great in the playoffs, batting .235 in nine games, but with one swing he ensured he'll be remembered in St. Paul. In front of a home crowd, Mirizzi cranked a fastball down the left-field line. The only question was whether it would stay fair.

"I knew it had the distance. Yeah, I was giving it a little Carlton Fisk to make sure it stayed true," Mirizzi said. "I still don't remember touching any of the bases. Coming into home plate and getting swarmed like that, it's a natural high."

When it landed inside the foul pole, it set off a Saints celebration that kept going for a couple of hours. It was St. Paul's fourth title, but its first since 1996, and the most exciting finish in the Northern League's 12-year history.

"It was storybook," Mirizzi said.

It was a relatively storybook season for the league as a whole, as a number of records fell.

St. Paul's Adam Olow's .376 average broke Terry Lee's Northern League season batting record, which had stood since 1995. Schaumburg's Geoff McCallum set a record for hits with 138, Schaumburg's Mario Delgado set a record with 104 RBIs and Kansas City's Rick Prieto set records with 97 runs and 78 walks. Saints closer Chris Chavez set a career record for saves, while Lincoln third baseman Josh Patton broke the league's career marks for hits and games played.

The league announced expansion for 2005, as Edmonton and Calgary were scheduled to join the league, giving the league a link to Canada and potential further future westward expansion. The two Alberta cities most recently fielded teams in the Triple-A Pacific Coast League.

STANDINGS

FIRST HALF

NORTH	W	L	PCT	GB
Fargo-Moorhead RedHawks	32	16	.667	—
St. Paul Saints	30	17	.638	1½
Winnipeg Goldeyes	26	21	.553	5½
Sioux City Explorers	18	30	.375	14
Sioux Falls Canaries	16	32	.333	16

SOUTH	W	L	PCT	GB
Schaumburg Flyers	31	17	.646	—
Lincoln Saltdogs	29	19	.604	2
Joliet Jackhammers	24	24	.500	7
Kansas City T-Bones	20	28	.417	11
Gary Southshore Railcats	13	35	.271	18

SECOND HALF

NORTH	W	L	PCT	GB
St. Paul Saints	31	17	.646	—
Winnipeg Goldeyes	30	18	.625	1
Fargo-Moorhead Red Hawks	23	25	.479	8
Sioux City Explorers	21	27	.438	10
Sioux Falls Canaries	17	31	.354	14

SOUTH	W	L	PCT	GB
Kansas City T-Bones	28	20	.583	—
Schaumburg Flyers	27	21	.563	1
Joliet Jackhammers	25	23	.521	3
Lincoln Saltdogs	20	28	.417	8
Gary Southshore Railcats	18	30	.375	10

PLAYOFFS: Semifinals—St. Paul defeated Fargo-Moorhead 3-1 and Schaumburg defeated Kansas City 3-2 in best-of-5 series. **Finals**—St. Paul defeated Schaumburg 3-2 in best-of-5 series.

MANAGERS: Fargo-Moorhead—Doug Simunic. Gary—Garry Templeton. Joliet—Jeff Isom. Kansas City—Al Gallagher. Lincoln—Tim Johnson. St. Paul—George Tsamis. Schaumburg—Andy McCauley. Sioux City—Jay Kirkpatrick. Sioux Falls—Doc Edwards. Winnipeg—Hal Lanier.

ATTENDANCE: Winnipeg 323,241; St. Paul 280,375; Kansas City 238,745; Schaumburg 200,060; Joliet 198,250; Fargo-Moorhead 179,665; Gary 147,801; Sioux City 120,681; Sioux Falls 108,096.

ALL-STAR TEAM: C—Kelley Gulledge, Fargo-Moorhead. 1B—Mario Delgado, Schaumburg. 2B—Justin Hall, St. Paul. 3B—Pat Scalabrini, Winnipeg. SS—Geoff McCallum, Schaumburg. OF—Josh Loggins, Joliet; Adam Olow, St. Paul; Rick Prieto, Kansas City. DH—Eddie Pearson, Kansas City. RHP—Hank Woodman, Schaumburg. LHP—Brian Mazone, Joliet.

Player of the Year: Mario Delgado, Schaumburg. Pitcher of the Year: Rich Hyde, Joliet. Rookie Player of the Year: Casey Baker, Sioux City. Rookie Pitcher of the Year: Mike Peschel, Fargo-Moorhead. Manager of the Year: Andy McCauley, Schaumburg.

INDIVIDUAL BATTING LEADERS
(Minimum 259 Plate Appearances)

	AVG	AB	R	H	2B	3B	HR	RBI	SB
Olow, Adam, St. Paul	.376	340	76	128	29	4	7	70	16
Brown, Ray, Kansas City	.362	362	69	131	36	1	19	85	4
McCallum, Geoff, Schaumburg	.358	385	86	138	21	3	3	48	16
Brown, Tonayne, St. Paul	.344	349	53	120	17	1	8	62	10
Baker, Casey, Sioux City	.337	309	45	104	12	0	2	36	2
Gretz, Nick, St. Paul	.332	271	47	90	20	1	9	70	1
Pearson, Eddie, Kansas City	.330	351	70	116	15	0	30	94	4
Weekly, Chris, Schaumburg	.330	327	73	108	20	2	16	68	8
Longmire, Marcel, Sioux City	.327	364	62	119	29	0	11	72	20
Berrios, Harry, Winnipeg	.327	401	49	131	19	0	9	71	1

INDIVIDUAL PITCHING LEADERS
(Minimum 77 Innings)

	W	L	ERA	G	SV	IP	H	BB	SO
Mazone, Brian, Joliet	9	2	1.73	14	0	104	77	15	95
Woodman, Hank, Schaumburg	6	6	1.95	19	0	120	95	34	141
Peschel, Mike, Fargo-Moorhead	7	2	2.86	17	1	110	96	36	66
Krysa, Jonathan, Kansas City	9	7	3.10	25	0	165	159	55	139
Teeter, Travis, Lincoln	4	2	3.16	26	0	80	69	20	52
Hyde, Rich, Joliet	12	5	3.17	21	0	139	141	26	92
George, Todd, Fargo-Moorhead	9	4	3.31	18	0	109	111	32	67
Purcell, Brad, Winnipeg	10	5	3.33	19	0	127	110	41	119
Bicknell, Greg, Kansas City	13	3	3.56	20	0	134	147	22	106
Nagasaka, Nideki, Lincoln	8	7	3.58	20	0	116	117	49	94

* Signed with affiliated club

FARGO-MOORHEAD

BATTING	AVG	AB	R	H	2B	3B	HR	RBI	SB
Dormanen, Derek, 3b	.270	74	12	20	1	0	0	7	0
Fitzgerald, Jason, 1b-of	.269	386	67	104	23	3	7	59	40
Foley, Steve, of	.291	254	35	74	7	1	4	37	6
Gulledge, Kelley, c	.320	347	64	111	31	2	8	55	2
Hebrink, Ryan, 3b	.205	78	11	16	1	1	0	8	1
2-team (1 Schaumburg)	.195	82	11	16	1	1	0	8	1
Jeffcoat, Bryon, ss	.255	381	82	97	22	2	12	55	6
Kinchen, Jason, 1b	.233	73	7	17	2	0	3	10	0
2-team (34 Joliet)	.241	195	27	47	7	0	15	39	0
Kofler, Eric, dh	.288	320	51	92	14	0	18	80	0
Mathis, Joe, of	.284	416	80	118	24	7	6	38	24
Mazer, Brad, of-3b	.238	294	39	70	15	2	5	44	1
Nunez, Hector, of	.000	4	0	0	0	0	0	0	0
Paul, Corey, of	.250	36	6	9	2	0	1	7	2
Salazar, Ruben, 3b	.314	159	25	50	10	0	3	29	1
Smith, Demond, of	.227	154	28	35	3	3	3	23	10
Ward, Brian, 2b	.265	351	54	93	20	3	7	49	3

PITCHING	W	L	ERA	G	SV	IP	H	BB	SO
Bermudez, Manny	3	2	3.86	21	4	25	27	7	16
Bess, Steve	0	0	1.69	6	2	5	4	0	9
*Brannon, Nick	3	0	2.31	19	0	23	18	15	23
Clark, Ray	7	3	4.14	13	0	78	68	29	59
Dormanen, Derek	1	2	6.48	11	0	33	44	9	25
Franklin, Brent	2	1	5.75	33	2	36	35	15	34
2-team (4 Joliet)	2	2	5.05	37	2	41	37	19	40
Fuller, Justin	0	0	4.50	3	0	4	3	3	4
George, Todd	9	4	3.31	18	0	108	111	32	67
Gilbert, Rich	0	1	27.00	2	0	1	0	5	0
Grunwald, Erik	0	1	9.00	1	0	6	10	6	4
2-team (8 Kansas City)	1	3	7.58	9	0	29	41	15	21
Hooker, Jon	1	1	1.77	10	1	20	11	8	18
Houdek, Brian	0	2	3.04	17	1	26	25	15	12
2-team (12 Gary)	2	9	5.31	29	1	79	91	43	43
Jones, Sean	0	0	6.75	10	0	10	15	9	7
King, Ben	1	1	3.00	5	0	9	8	4	4
*Mattioni, Nick	3	3	1.64	24	8	33	17	7	32
Peschel, Mike	7	2	2.86	17	1	110	96	36	66

PITCHING	W	L	ERA	G	SV	IP	H	BB	SO
*Roberts, Nick	4	1	6.08	6	0	37	48	8	20
Saunders, Tim	1	0	8.71	11	1	20	28	10	10
Scheving, J.J.	3	7	5.79	18	0	102	114	52	48
Sergent, Joe	1	2	3.55	6	0	38	36	14	27
Spivey, Melvin	4	3	2.70	29	5	40	38	15	19
2-team (5 Sioux City)	4	7	4.43	34	5	61	68	24	31
Sprague, Kevin	0	1	6.43	4	0	21	22	16	15
Stavros, Tony	0	0	0.00	1	0	2	2	0	2
Whitney, Jake	5	4	4.48	10	0	66	79	10	46
3-team (4 St. Paul, 3 Lincoln)	7	8	5.24	17	0	101	143	15	70

GARY

BATTING	AVG	AB	R	H	2B	3B	HR	RBI	SB
Ayala, Elliott, of	.211	19	0	4	1	0	0	1	0
Beamon, Trey, dh	.209	67	9	14	1	0	1	3	0
Beshears, Scott, ss-3b	.063	16	0	1	0	0	0	0	0
3-team (39 Sioux City, 10 SF)	.225	178	19	40	7	1	1	16	0
Brown, Billy, of	.224	67	10	15	2	0	2	6	1
Brown, Michael, of	.230	122	18	28	3	1	4	15	3
Camacho, Juan, 3b	.263	186	27	49	10	1	8	30	1
Clinton, Ricky, c	.153	111	8	17	3	0	2	7	0
DeYoung, Peter, 1b-3b	.257	269	30	69	7	1	2	34	10
Dierks, Scott, of-3b	.219	32	1	7	3	0	0	0	0
2-team (3 Sioux City)	.171	41	3	7	3	0	0	0	1
Howe, Matt, 3b	.263	137	18	36	6	0	3	18	1
Iapoce, Anthony, of	.271	240	41	65	10	1	1	20	14
Kinsolving, Darin, 1b-of	.257	109	16	28	6	1	4	26	0
2-team (62 Sioux Falls)	.258	329	39	85	20	2	13	60	0
Knight, Dustin, dh-1b	.059	17	1	1	1	0	0	2	0
Lee, Curt, 2b	.264	360	43	95	14	1	3	47	0
Martinez, Hipolito, of	.287	265	41	76	14	2	9	36	0
Medlin, C.J., c	.208	48	6	10	3	0	0	6	0
3-team (11 Kansas City, 12 Schaum.)	.198	121	11	24	5	0	2	15	0
O'Neal, Brandon, ss	.263	99	14	26	6	2	5	24	1
Rios, Brian, dh	.300	10	1	3	1	0	1	1	0
2-team (19 Sioux City)	.364	77	9	28	4	0	2	12	2
*Rodrigues, Rich, c	.284	232	31	66	16	0	4	26	0
Roper, Zach, of	.286	7	0	2	0	0	0	0	0
Samuels, Scott, of	.299	77	14	23	3	0	3	10	8
2-team (58 St. Paul)	.274	292	50	80	15	0	9	47	16
Schell, Barry, of	.083	36	3	3	1	0	0	3	0
Shorts, Adam, ss	.125	24	3	3	1	0	0	2	0
Stoner, Mike, dh-1b	.281	153	20	43	11	0	3	17	0
Syska, Tom, 2b-3b	.290	31	9	9	1	2	0	3	0
3-team (1 Joliet, 1 Schaum.)	.263	38	10	10	1	2	0	3	0
Tolentino, Juan, of	.237	211	27	50	8	2	5	19	11
Welsh, Eric, 1b	.136	44	5	6	3	0	0	5	0
White, Kenny, ss	.222	185	23	41	10	0	1	16	1
*Woody, Dominic, c	.200	55	4	11	3	1	1	9	0

PITCHING	W	L	ERA	G	SV	IP	H	BB	SO
Andel, Chris	2	5	6.46	34	9	39	39	26	29
Bell, Kory	0	1	8.00	14	0	27	43	14	18
Coleman, Billy	0	4	8.10	6	0	30	48	11	28
Davidson, Tom	0	1	8.68	7	0	9	15	8	9
De Loera, Abel	1	0	4.91	21	0	22	19	18	16
Gilbert, Rich	0	1	7.88	6	0	8	11	3	6
2-team (2 Fargo-Moorhead)	0	2	9.35	8	0	8	11	8	6
Houdek, Brian	2	7	6.45	12	0	53	66	28	31
Illius, John	0	0	5.40	4	0	6	11	5	6
Kerber, Travis	2	8	4.92	27	2	78	85	23	49
Klemm, Tom	0	0	21.00	3	0	3	9	6	2
Lopez, Derek	1	1	4.76	15	1	22	21	8	21
2-team (14 Sioux Falls)	3	6	4.18	29	2	56	61	17	48
MacLane, Tommy	3	4	4.02	13	0	80	95	24	46
Miller, Benji	1	2	7.30	9	0	12	13	5	7
O'Donnell, Tony	4	11	5.98	20	0	111	144	38	68
Oldenburg, Quintin	0	1	2.91	5	0	21	19	4	14
Rohr, Matthew	2	2	5.67	5	0	27	30	12	19
Shafer, Adam	1	0	4.70	6	0	7	8	4	7
Shartzer, Bryan	4	2	5.94	33	0	50	58	17	25
Skyles, Matt	0	0	6.28	10	0	14	19	10	10
Sloan, Brandon	0	3	9.95	3	0	12	25	9	6
3-team (11 Sioux City, 4 SF)	0	7	10.35	18	3	35	64	21	23
Soria, Dan	6	6	4.68	18	0	105	123	38	51
Urvalek, Mike	0	2	7.43	7	0	23	32	18	19
White, Eric	0	1	4.61	11	0	13	19	6	12
*Woody, Dominic	2	3	3.16	18	0	51	45	20	40

JOLIET

BATTING	AVG	AB	R	H	2B	3B	HR	RBI	SB
Allensworth, Jermaine, of	.321	333	71	107	26	4	4	27	10
Cunningham, Mike, of	.240	25	2	6	0	0	0	1	2
Davis, Glenn, of-1b	.219	32	2	7	1	0	1	1	1
Delgado, Gabby, 2b	.289	301	44	87	12	4	4	39	12

BATTING	AVG	AB	R	H	2B	3B	HR	RBI	SB
Firlit, Dan, ss	.206	326	35	67	11	1	3	25	5
Fritz, Ben, c	.145	62	6	9	2	0	1	3	0
Goldbach, Jeff, c	.233	283	43	66	16	0	11	43	2
Gordon, David, 1b-3b	.178	118	19	21	3	1	5	11	1
Hymon, James, 2b	.042	24	2	1	0	0	1	0	0
Kinchen, Jason, dh	.246	122	20	30	5	0	12	29	0
Lackaff, John, 3b	.272	342	39	93	16	2	2	37	12
Loggins, Josh, of-1b	.305	380	58	116	17	4	20	76	14
Malone, Billy, 2b	.000	1	0	0	0	0	0	0	0
McCay, Matt, of	.277	292	35	81	13	0	3	32	6
Morton, Rickie, 1b	.318	85	10	27	3	1	5	14	0
Paul, Corey, of	.298	309	56	92	19	0	10	45	10
2-team (11 Fargo-Moorhead)	.293	345	62	101	21	0	11	52	12
Roberson, Kevin, of	.171	35	5	6	2	0	0	2	0
Smith, Bubba, dh-1b	.282	163	22	46	14	0	7	41	2
Syska, Tom, 2b	.000	3	0	0	0	0	0	0	0
Welsh, Eric, 1b	.200	15	1	3	1	0	0	0	0
2-team (12 Gary)	.153	59	6	9	4	0	0	5	0
Woods, Blake, 3b	.118	17	2	2	0	0	0	0	0

PITCHING	W	L	ERA	G	SV	IP	H	BB	SO
Ally, Ben	4	4	4.86	16	0	74	90	14	43
Donlin, Sean	0	0	5.51	8	1	16	13	11	15
Franklin, Brent	0	1	0.00	4	0	5	2	4	6
Garvin, Robert	1	4	3.40	43	21	42	51	9	42
Hecker, Steven	6	9	5.03	20	0	116	117	51	86
Hinderks, Jeremy	1	0	4.58	13	1	17	19	6	7
2-team (4 Winnipeg)	2	4	4.87	21	1	57	67	24	34
Hooker, Jon	4	2	5.40	22	0	28	29	17	22
2-team (10 Fargo-Moorhead)	5	3	3.88	32	1	48	40	25	40
Hyde, Rich	12	5	3.17	21	0	139	141	26	92
Jones, Sean	0	0	0.00	1	0	1	1	0	0
2-team (10 Fargo-Moorhead)	0	0	8.44	11	0	10	16	10	7
Kennedy, Jodie	3	2	6.75	7	0	29	39	17	11
Kent, Nathan	2	5	5.43	11	0	61	66	16	44
*Mazone, Brian	9	2	1.73	14	0	104	77	15	95
Medina, Julio	0	0	3.86	3	0	7	9	1	3
Miller, Matt	2	1	4.78	22	0	26	29	15	15
Ott, Mike	1	1	6.93	12	0	24	36	8	13
2-team (7 Schaumburg)	1	3	6.43	19	0	49	70	22	33
Petrusek, Matt	3	2	5.02	19	0	66	80	16	53
Runser, Greg	1	1	4.91	21	0	33	46	13	19
Spigner, Chris	0	3	9.82	6	0	18	33	10	7
Villarreal, Luis	0	1	4.58	4	0	19	21	12	14
Young, Doug	0	4	8.15	13	0	17	27	7	15

KANSAS CITY

BATTING	AVG	AB	R	H	2B	3B	HR	RBI	SB
Brown, Michael, 2b-of	.322	183	27	59	15	0	7	35	9
2-team (35 Gary)	.285	305	45	87	18	1	11	50	12
Brown, Ray, 1b	.362	362	69	131	36	1	19	85	4
Ceriani, Matt, c	.247	263	34	65	11	0	6	30	1
Fujimoto, Hiroshi, c-3b	.217	120	9	26	5	1	0	6	0
Hass, Mike, of-3b	.211	114	14	24	3	0	1	7	0
Hill, Chad, 2b-ss	.273	308	43	84	18	2	7	37	2
Holst, Micah, of	.100	10	0	1	0	0	0	0	1
Jones, Jack, ss	.191	267	23	51	6	6	6	29	8
LePine, Chris, of	.290	238	46	69	7	1	4	17	9
Medlin, C.J., c	.171	35	2	6	0	0	1	4	0
Nowlin, Cody, of	.282	344	37	97	22	3	8	51	2
Pearson, Eddie, dh	.330	351	70	116	15	0	30	94	4
Prieto, Rick, of-2b	.314	353	97	111	24	10	5	42	17
Shindle, Chad, 3b	.213	150	10	32	6	0	5	17	0
Thompson, Phil, of-3b	.232	233	32	54	15	1	4	25	9

PITCHING	W	L	ERA	G	SV	IP	H	BB	SO
Balbuena, Caleb	1	1	4.67	6	0	17	21	9	13
Bicknell, Greg	13	3	3.56	20	0	134	147	22	106
Clark, Wade	0	0	21.60	2	0	3	10	3	2
Forbes, Derek	2	1	3.21	20	3	28	23	14	24
Grunwald, Erik	1	2	7.23	8	0	23	31	9	17
Hader, Ryan	0	1	6.61	11	1	16	12	17	20
Horner, Eric	0	0	13.50	1	0	2	5	1	2
Howerton, John	2	3	2.95	40	3	64	68	15	34
Johnson, David	0	4	4.13	27	10	28	18	17	38
Krysa, Jonathan	9	7	3.10	25	0	165	159	55	139
Marcus, Clint	0	1	7.27	12	0	17	25	4	10
McCasland, Ralph	0	2	12.19	3	0	10	27	9	5
McClellan, Matt	8	6	3.90	30	0	99	92	19	95
McDonald, Jon	9	8	3.94	23	0	141	159	37	87
Muhammad, Damon	0	0	27.00	3	0	3	10	6	2
Oksen, Andrew	0	0	15.00	7	0	9	15	13	4
Read, Robby	0	0	31.50	1	0	2	4	6	1
Sigley, Jayson	0	2	11.17	2	0	9	17	3	7
Sprague, Kevin	0	1	5.09	9	0	17	15	8	9
3-team (4 Fargo-Moorhead, 8 SC)	1	3	5.60	21	0	70	86	39	46

	W	L	ERA	G	SV	IP	H	BB	SO
Sutton, Zach	0	0	13.50	1	0	2	8	1	0
Thompson, Phil	1	3	5.46	8	0	28	32	11	15
Viane, David	2	3	5.06	18	1	26	39	11	23

LINCOLN

BATTING	AVG	AB	R	H	2B	3B	HR	RBI	SB
Bonilla, Clemente, 2b	.231	121	10	28	3	1	1	15	5
3-team (17 SF, 12 St. Paul)	.245	220	24	54	10	1	2	27	7
Bouras, Brad, dh	.277	159	20	44	8	0	3	19	0
Cantalamessa, Jordan, ph	.000	1	0	0	0	0	0	0	0
Church, Ian, of	.253	95	13	24	3	1	2	13	1
Doskocil, Darren, 2b-of	.252	314	38	79	14	1	5	31	10
Foreman, JuJu, of	.276	351	63	97	9	3	1	34	27
Guidebeck, Wil, c	.150	20	4	3	0	0	0	3	0
Machado, Albenis, ss	.288	337	44	97	17	0	1	33	10
Moreno, Jorge, of	.285	393	66	112	27	1	7	44	25
Patton, Josh, 3b	.320	378	65	121	28	3	15	56	7
Peterson, Charles, dh-1b	.305	351	45	107	19	0	14	67	2
Rengifo, Daling, c	.000	1	0	0	0	0	0	0	0
Rose, Pete, 1b	.197	142	8	28	2	0	5	18	0
Santore, Todd, c	.143	63	1	9	0	0	0	4	0
Sullivan, Kevin, c	.268	213	32	57	8	2	5	32	5
Warner, Bryan, of-1b	.304	401	62	122	25	0	14	64	10
Wiseman, Jeb, c	.161	62	6	10	2	0	1	3	0
2-team (30 Sioux Falls)	.175	126	10	22	5	1	1	8	0

PITCHING	W	L	ERA	G	SV	IP	H	BB	SO
Beever, James	1	0	7.61	13	1	23	34	9	21
Carbajal, Alex	1	4	4.09	15	0	70	67	28	48
*Embry, Byron	3	3	1.46	42	10	55	37	13	90
Ford, Tom	3	1	6.52	7	0	38	48	18	15
Haverly, Matt	0	0	10.13	3	0	5	11	4	4
2-team (3 Winnipeg)	0	0	8.59	6	0	7	13	4	6
Huguet, George	2	1	1.17	11	0	15	10	8	8
Lesko, Adam	4	1	1.88	15	1	24	17	10	24
Nagasaka, Nideki	8	7	3.58	20	0	115	117	49	94
Parker, Brandon	0	0	7.71	3	0	2	3	4	5
3-team (3 St. Paul, 16 Sioux Falls)	1	2	3.27	22	3	22	18	22	30
Springston, Adam	5	4	3.87	14	0	74	65	32	69
*Teeter, Travis	4	2	3.16	26	0	79	69	20	52
Tremblay, Max	1	2	2.94	40	1	33	23	14	30
Truty, Darren	5	7	4.88	17	0	101	115	25	67
Trytten, Ryan	3	5	5.40	39	0	63	62	31	57
Weidert, Chris	1	0	3.00	25	12	27	20	4	26
Whitney, Jake	2	1	3.18	3	0	17	28	2	14
Zipser, Mike	6	9	4.84	20	0	119	120	38	68

ST. PAUL SAINTS

BATTING	AVG	AB	R	H	2B	3B	HR	RBI	SB
Bonilla, Clemente, 2b-ss	.270	37	4	10	4	0	1	6	0
Brown, Tonayne, of	.344	349	53	120	17	1	8	62	10
Cox, Kris, of	.302	43	8	13	4	0	0	6	1
2-team (4 Winnipeg)	.280	50	9	14	4	0	0	6	1
Dennison, Dan, of	.161	31	5	5	1	0	0	2	1
Dorsey, Ryan, 3b	.222	153	18	34	6	2	4	10	0
Dworken, Mikaella, c	.232	95	11	22	4	0	1	17	0
Gretz, Nick, dh-1b	.332	271	47	90	20	1	9	70	1
*Hall, Justin, 2b	.326	350	77	114	22	4	5	36	5
Howe, Matt, 3b	.289	38	5	11	3	0	2	6	0
Kohno, Kazuhiro, dh	.220	91	11	20	5	0	2	9	0
Lucca, Lou, 3b	.276	105	16	29	8	1	5	24	1
Marks, Tim, c	.189	53	6	10	0	0	2	5	0
Merritt, Tim, 1b	.301	83	14	25	7	1	2	14	4
Mirizzi, Marc, ss-1b	.245	49	6	12	4	0	0	5	1
2-team (77 Sioux Falls)	.298	352	51	105	21	1	7	59	6
Munoz, Billy, 1b	.188	16	2	3	0	0	1	3	0
Olow, Adam, of	.376	340	76	128	29	4	7	70	16
Renick, Josh, 1b-3b	.283	353	71	100	12	4	3	24	26
Samuels, Scott, of	.265	215	36	57	12	0	6	37	8
Senjem, Guye, of-1b	.254	126	22	32	9	0	4	21	2
Terni, Chas, ss	.282	308	42	87	18	0	5	39	1
Wallis, Jacob, c	.251	167	18	42	7	0	4	29	1
2-team (32 Sioux City)	.247	291	36	72	17	1	9	43	1
Wiseman, Jeb, c	.188	64	4	12	3	1	0	5	0

PITCHING	W	L	ERA	G	SV	IP	H	BB	SO
Aucoin, Eddie	6	1	4.34	34	0	56	77	10	42
Chavez, Chris	2	0	2.20	43	29	45	29	11	63
*Christman, Tim	1	0	3.86	4	1	16	16	2	20
Corona, Ronnie	1	0	3.00	1	0	6	3	2	6
Eason, Clay	1	1	4.43	4	0	20	25	6	11
Foster, Kevin	3	4	5.66	8	0	41	51	27	23
Gaal, Bryan	5	5	4.64	12	0	77	81	33	65
*Holubec, Ken	2	0	2.08	6	0	30	22	7	22
Lucy, Pat	0	0	11.57	8	0	16	26	16	7

	W	L	ERA	G	SV	IP	H	BB	SO
Martinez, Cesar	3	1	3.04	4	0	23	28	10	15
Meyer, Mike	8	7	4.35	19	0	122	140	38	83
Parker, Brandon	0	0	0.00	3	0	3	1	3	3
Perez, Julio	9	3	2.76	41	4	58	56	19	55
Rupert, Chris	0	0	7.62	17	0	13	20	10	13
Shafer, Adam	0	1	3.07	8	1	14	11	6	14
3-team (13 Sioux City, 6 Gary)	3	7	4.68	27	1	73	68	33	61
*Smith, Roy	1	1	2.35	2	0	15	13	4	15
Tisch, Tim	10	2	4.01	17	0	94	90	44	54
Truty, Darren	2	0	4.80	3	0	15	22	5	15
2-team (17 Lincoln)	7	7	4.87	20	0	116	137	30	82
Verdugo, Jason	5	5	4.05	17	0	109	105	24	77
Walters, Cory	1	0	9.95	4	0	6	13	1	1
Wells, Mark	1	0	8.28	18	0	29	48	18	14
Whitney, Jake	0	3	10.00	4	0	18	36	3	10

SCHAUMBURG

BATTING	AVG	AB	R	H	2B	3B	HR	RBI	SB
*Campana, Wandel, 2b	.306	121	18	37	7	1	2	24	4
Cole, Eric, of	.266	376	54	100	16	3	12	54	15
Collins, Jesse, of	.188	48	2	9	1	1	0	5	0
Delgado, Mario, 1b	.318	393	58	125	31	1	23	104	0
Doakes, Schuyler, of	.246	65	13	16	0	1	0	4	7
Gord, Nelson, of	.259	158	26	41	11	1	2	23	0
Hebrink, Ryan, of	.000	4	0	0	0	0	0	0	0
Hendrickson, Justin, of-1b	.278	317	54	88	18	2	18	60	1
Krause, Brent, of	.254	71	10	18	3	1	2	8	0
Malone, Billy, 2b	.200	85	13	17	2	0	3	9	0
2-team (1 Joliet)	.198	86	13	17	2	0	3	9	0
McCallum, Geoff, ss	.358	385	86	138	21	3	3	48	16
Medlin, C.J., c	.211	38	3	8	2	0	1	5	0
Merritt, Tim, 2b-1b	.313	115	20	36	7	1	0	14	2
2-team (25 St. Paul)	.308	198	34	61	14	2	2	28	6
Neal, Joe, c	.000	14	2	0	0	0	0	1	0
Pierce, Kirk, c	.247	263	41	65	15	1	7	42	0
Romprey, Ed, 2b-of	.255	55	7	14	0	0	1	6	2
Ruiz, Ryan, of	.233	43	7	10	2	0	0	6	2
2-team (80 Sioux City)	.310	371	70	115	22	2	5	43	35
Staton, T.J., dh	.269	275	52	74	12	0	11	38	13
Syska, Tom, of	.250	4	1	1	0	0	0	0	0
*Van Iderstine, Ben, of	.400	145	36	58	7	3	5	21	5
Weekly, Chris, 3b	.330	327	73	108	20	2	16	68	8

PITCHING	W	L	ERA	G	SV	IP	H	BB	SO
Bailie, Matt	9	5	5.03	23	0	102	104	34	83
Bennett, Derek	1	3	5.20	11	0	55	56	21	41
*Boughner, Anthony	7	1	2.09	10	0	73	71	7	53
Christensen, Mica	0	0	6.52	9	0	9	6	7	8
Cierlik, Jason	0	2	3.58	27	0	32	28	25	27
DeHart, Rick	2	2	5.76	5	0	29	27	6	25
*DeHoyos, Gabe	3	2	2.51	22	9	32	31	8	44
Fauske, Josh	3	1	3.09	18	0	23	28	9	16
Gray, Brett	2	2	6.61	8	0	32	42	10	23
Haynes, Brad	0	0	18.00	1	0	1	0	3	0
Hummel, Rick	3	0	2.79	18	5	19	19	7	16
Johnson, Ryan	1	2	8.27	8	0	16	28	5	12
Keppen, Dusty	0	0	8.64	14	2	16	22	7	15
Marcotte, Trevor	0	0	1.50	3	0	6	5	6	5
Ott, Mike	0	2	5.92	7	0	24	34	14	20
Prempas, Lyle	3	2	4.93	25	1	49	45	29	48
Salvevold, Greg	6	3	5.58	14	0	79	101	30	39
Silva, Cheech	1	2	6.00	9	0	21	25	21	21
Spencer, Johnny	0	0	5.40	1	0	1	3	1	1
Starck, Tom	0	2	12.79	3	0	6	11	8	4
Therneau, Dave	0	1	7.71	2	0	9	16	8	12
Thrasher, Jesse	0	0	9.00	4	0	5	3	10	1
Weber, Brett	7	1	2.54	37	3	46	34	19	46
Woodman, Hank	6	6	1.95	19	0	120	95	34	141
*Ziegler, Brad	3	0	1.50	4	0	24	12	1	26

SIOUX CITY

BATTING	AVG	AB	R	H	2B	3B	HR	RBI	SB
Baker, Casey, of	.337	309	45	104	12	0	2	36	2
Beshears, Scott, 3b	.246	126	15	31	6	1	1	16	0
Brock, Todd, ss	.303	343	66	104	24	5	7	50	20
Brown, Bobby, of	.283	357	43	101	21	2	7	70	6
Carroll, Justin, 3b	.211	109	14	23	4	1	1	14	0
Church, Ian, of	.229	109	14	25	8	0	2	17	4
2-team (33 Lincoln)	.240	204	27	49	11	1	4	30	5
Dierks, Scott, 3b	.000	9	2	0	0	0	0	0	1
Dworken, Mikaella, c	.221	145	13	32	2	0	1	14	0
2-team (26 St. Paul)	.225	240	24	54	6	0	2	31	0
Gamboa, Javier, dh	.250	4	1	1	0	0	0	0	0
Howe, Matt, 3b	.305	151	20	46	11	1	4	27	0
3-team (10 St. Paul, 36 Gary)	.285	326	43	93	20	1	9	51	1

	AVG	AB	R	H	2B	3B	HR	RBI	SB
Krause, Brent, of	.258	93	12	24	4	1	2	9	0
2-team (19 Schaumburg)	.273	22	2	6	1	0	0	1	0
Leavitt, Adam, 2b-3b	.237	76	11	18	2	1	0	6	3
Lemonis, Chris, 3b	.333	3	0	1	0	0	0	0	0
Longmire, Marcel, c-1b	.327	364	62	119	29	0	11	72	20
Paul, Jeremy, c	.000	1	0	0	0	0	0	0	0
Pinkerton, Danny, c	.190	84	12	16	4	0	1	8	0
Riggan, Zack, c	.091	11	0	1	0	0	0	0	0
Rios, Brian, dh-1b	.373	67	8	25	3	0	1	11	2
Ruiz, Ryan, of	.320	328	63	105	20	2	5	37	33
Sullivan, Jason, 2b-ss	.262	343	42	90	15	0	0	27	3
Wilson, Desi, 1b	.319	379	75	121	18	2	5	55	19

PITCHING	W	L	ERA	G	SV	IP	H	BB	SO
Charron, Joey	0	0	3.00	5	0	6	4	2	3
Evans, Tony	4	5	4.01	20	0	98	89	31	96
Flanagan, Chris	1	4	7.79	11	0	34	51	19	18
Ford, Tom	1	2	4.70	12	0	38	49	20	22
2-team (7 Lincoln)	4	3	5.61	19	0	77	97	38	37
Gagner, Jay	0	0	10.80	7	0	6	14	2	8
Giannetti, Chad	0	0	7.04	4	0	7	11	4	3
Glick, David	9	6	4.24	19	0	116	126	20	90
Kramer, Sean	1	4	5.12	40	9	51	52	30	66
Laroche, Jeff	0	1	9.95	5	0	6	13	4	4
Mabry, Barry	0	0	2.33	9	0	19	14	6	9
Mahan, Dallas	2	0	3.23	21	1	30	28	5	26
Marcotte, Trevor	3	1	4.74	6	0	24	18	17	20
2-team (3 Schaumburg)	3	1	4.11	9	0	30	23	23	25
Merrigan, Josh	1	3	8.31	9	0	30	41	18	11
2-team (7 Sioux Falls)	2	5	7.43	16	0	66	91	29	25
Miller, Nathan	0	0	5.19	6	0	8	12	4	4
Orga, Kevin	0	0	9.82	5	0	11	15	3	5
Scholten, J.D.	5	2	7.91	18	0	38	50	22	23
Shafer, Adam	2	6	5.15	13	0	50	49	23	40
Silva, Cheech	0	0	6.75	3	0	4	3	4	3
2-team (9 Schaumburg)	1	2	6.12	12	0	25	28	25	24
Sloan, Brandon	0	3	10.13	11	2	13	25	9	4
Spivey, Melvin	0	4	7.71	5	0	21	30	9	12
Sprague, Kevin	1	1	5.34	8	0	32	49	15	22
St. Amant, John	0	0	11.12	5	0	5	9	4	2
Swiatkiewicz, Chris	7	9	4.78	21	0	124	146	39	76
Wiebe, Jonathan	2	6	2.79	35	2	51	55	35	22

SIOUX FALLS

BATTING	AVG	AB	R	H	2B	3B	HR	RBI	SB
Allan, Josh, dh	.220	59	11	13	5	0	2	8	0
Beshears, Scott, 2b-of	.222	36	4	8	1	0	0	0	0
Bonilla, Clemente, 2b	.258	62	10	16	3	0	0	6	2
Brightwell, Corey, of	.100	10	1	1	0	0	0	0	0
Brown, Billy, of	.219	178	26	39	7	1	9	37	6
2-team (16 Gary)	.220	245	36	54	9	1	11	43	7
Carroll, Justin, c-3b	.271	70	9	19	4	0	3	10	0
2-team (41 Sioux City)	.235	179	23	42	8	1	4	24	0
Davis, Glenn, 1b-of	.278	284	42	79	11	0	17	55	1
2-team (10 Joliet)	.272	316	44	86	12	0	18	56	2
Fulton, Josh, ss	.260	50	7	13	1	0	0	4	0
Gaspar, Warren, of	.269	327	63	88	15	2	2	24	24
Hanson, Andrew, 1b-of	.133	15	4	2	0	0	0	4	0
Hernandez, Miguel, 3b	.276	76	6	21	5	0	0	5	0
Jacobson, Kerry, of	.118	17	3	2	0	0	0	1	0
Kinsolving, Darin, of-1b	.259	220	23	57	14	1	9	34	0
Mirizzi, Mark, ss	.307	303	45	93	17	1	7	54	5
Navratil, Mike, of	.257	35	2	9	1	0	0	4	0
Pagan, Carlos, c	.304	181	24	55	14	0	12	33	0
Pagan, Felix, 3b	.281	274	46	77	14	0	13	46	3
Parker, Clark, 2b	.211	279	38	59	10	0	2	22	12
Pena, Bert, 3b	.250	16	1	4	0	0	0	3	0
Rhomberg, Joe, of-1b	.250	140	21	35	12	2	1	13	1
Thomas, Juan, dh-2b	.304	191	35	58	5	1	14	31	3
Tolentino, Juan, of	.226	106	10	24	3	2	2	10	3
2-team (57 Gary)	.233	317	37	74	11	4	7	29	14
*Walker, Matt, of	.313	99	16	31	9	0	2	12	4
Wallis, Jacob, c	.242	124	18	30	10	1	5	14	0
Wright, Ron, dh	.303	109	16	33	6	0	3	19	0

PITCHING	W	L	ERA	G	SV	IP	H	BB	SO
Blake, Peter	0	0	2.45	3	0	3	4	2	5
Bright, Nathan	0	5	4.96	21	1	61	72	26	31
Dorn, Grant	1	2	2.92	9	1	12	13	3	12
Ellis, Rob	2	5	6.56	21	0	35	44	17	21
Faust, Wes	4	9	4.66	20	0	119	125	40	70
Foss, Brad	1	7	4.92	29	5	56	76	26	43
*Hoegh, Owen	0	0	4.26	19	0	25	31	15	18
Koziara, Matt	0	1	5.14	2	0	7	9	2	7
Lopez, Derek	2	5	3.78	14	1	33	40	9	27
Lyons, Mike	8	6	4.05	26	1	126	132	19	107

PITCHING (cont.)	W	L	ERA	G	SV	IP	H	BB	SO
Mendez, David	0	3	8.79	6	0	28	39	18	16
Merrigan, Josh	1	2	6.69	7	0	36	50	11	14
Mincks, Lincoln	1	4	6.17	35	0	54	78	23	31
Parker, Brandon	1	2	3.31	16	3	16	14	15	22
Robles, Jose	0	0	5.68	8	0	12	16	6	13
Santos, Alex	1	4	9.53	5	0	22	46	5	14
Sloan, Brandon	0	1	11.17	4	1	9	14	3	13
Sonnier, Zachary	0	0	12.15	3	0	6	15	2	1
Tribe, Phillip	0	1	12.91	3	0	7	15	4	6
Walters, Cory	9	5	3.71	22	0	131	118	21	92
2-team (4 St. Paul)	10	5	4.00	26	0	137	131	22	93
White, Eric	2	1	4.26	18	1	31	46	10	19

WINNIPEG

BATTING	AVG	AB	R	H	2B	3B	HR	RBI	SB
Barbier, Blair, 2b	.249	354	54	88	21	0	11	37	10
Berrios, Harry, dh-of	.327	401	49	131	19	0	9	71	1
Brinkley, Darryl, dh-of	.316	237	38	75	19	0	7	36	21
Chamberlain, Wes, 1b-of	.190	121	16	23	3	1	4	17	3
Clary, Casey, c	.222	36	6	8	0	0	1	7	0
Cox, Kris, of	.143	7	1	1	0	0	0	0	0
Forbes, Michael, of	.292	96	24	28	8	1	3	10	1
Garcia, Amaury, of	.298	188	35	56	7	2	3	16	17
Larned, Drew, c	.240	171	26	41	7	1	4	23	0
Morrison, Greg, 1b	.300	310	41	93	20	1	11	47	2
Nishiyama, Michitaka, of	.333	3	1	1	0	0	0	0	0
Poulin, Max, ss	.269	372	54	100	14	5	1	38	15
Scalabrini, Pat, 3b	.322	395	82	127	34	2	20	66	16
Soto, T.J., of	.269	320	47	86	21	7	10	62	26
Stewart, Andy, c	.291	127	19	37	7	0	2	18	0
Zoffinger, Billy, of	.254	197	29	50	11	2	1	28	5

PITCHING	W	L	ERA	G	SV	IP	H	BB	SO
Anderson, Scott	1	0	6.75	6	1	8	6	6	5
Blankenship, Jon	0	0	5.95	4	0	19	32	7	9
Bogs, Brian	0	0	0.00	4	0	1	2	0	0
Brooks, Jake	0	1	17.18	4	0	3	9	0	7
Bystrowski, Bobby	1	0	15.43	4	0	4	8	5	6
Cauble, Greg	0	0	6.00	1	0	3	2	2	4
Glick, David	1	1	3.22	3	0	22	18	7	17
2-team (19 Sioux City)	10	7	4.08	22	0	139	144	27	107
Graves, Don	2	3	5.28	9	0	46	63	12	21
Gross, Rafael	1	1	3.86	3	0	7	8	4	5
Haverly, Matt	0	0	4.50	3	0	2	2	0	2
Hinderks, Jeremy	1	4	4.99	8	0	39	48	18	27
Holbrook, Shayn	12	5	3.72	36	3	72	70	31	56
Keppen, Dusty	0	1	4.35	21	1	20	21	7	17
2-team (14 Schaumburg)	1	1	6.27	35	3	37	43	14	32
Luque, Roger	9	4	3.74	21	0	149	157	47	97
Magee, Jayson	0	0	12.00	4	0	3	4	1	0
Major, Marc	0	0	2.31	9	0	11	10	9	13
Marcus, Clint	1	0	4.32	19	0	8	11	1	4
2-team (12 Kansas City)	1	1	6.31	31	0	25	36	5	14
Montero, Oscar	2	2	2.32	43	22	42	34	27	69
Murray, Steve	8	6	4.53	21	0	105	123	26	55
Ovalles, Juan	1	1	5.40	15	0	28	25	14	18
Paull, K.P.	0	0	0.00	1	0	3	0	0	1
Purcell, Brad	10	5	3.33	19	0	127	110	41	119
Purvis, Ace	0	0	108.00	1	0	1	3	1	0
Rodriguez, Wil	0	0	6.75	1	0	4	3	5	3
Rohr, Charles	0	0	4.26	5	0	6	9	5	3
Rosengren, Phil	0	0	54.00	1	0	1	5	1	0
Smith, Donnie	2	0	4.30	17	0	14	18	7	9
Stanton, Travis	5	5	4.72	21	0	87	79	30	85

NORTHEAST LEAGUE

When Joel Bennett lost Game Two of the 2004 Northeast League championship series, he said goodbye to his teammates because he had to get back to his day job, teaching at a high school in Elmira, N.Y.

Bennett's New Jersey teammates headed north to Lynn, Mass., to try to come back from a 2-0 deficit against North Shore in the best-of-five series. He planned to follow the rest of the series from afar, until a pair of extra-inning wins forced a change in plans.

Fabricio Benitez, the Jackals closer, went 4⅔ innings in New Jersey's come-from-behind 7-4 win in 13 innings in Game Three. He wasn't available for Game Four, so projected Game Five starter Aaron Myers had to pitch the final two innings in a 4-2, 11-inning win.

"After we won Game Four, I called him and told him, 'Joel, I need you bad. Is there any way you can get off work?' " Jackals manager Joe Calfapietra said.

Bennett had just taken a couple of days off to attend the funeral of a family member, but he called his principal and asked if he could use his last personal day. His principal told him to go and win a championship.

So the next morning Bennett hopped in his car with

his wife and daughter and drove the seven hours to Lynn. He arrived at 3 p.m., took an hour-long nap and got to the ballpark in time for his normal warm-up.

Bennett had been a tough-luck loser in Game Two, allowing just two runs and striking out 15 in a complete-game effort. He didn't have the same stuff in Game Five, but he went

Wilton Veras

seven innings, allowing three runs on five hits before leaving with a 5-3 lead. Myers followed up to pitch two scoreless innings for the save and the Jackals' fourth Northeast League title.

Although the Jackals recovered from a 2-0 deficit, it was the team's second-most-impressive comeback of the season. New Jersey won five games in a span of three days to edge New Haven for the Southern Division first-half title. The furious finish capped off a 12-2 run to the title, as the Jackals won must-win game after must-win game down the stretch.

"It was some ride," Calfapietra said. "It happened so fast. We had to win, so we didn't realize what was happening. I didn't realize we won four in less than 24 hours until someone wrote an article about it."

The league had to scramble just before the start of the season, when the Allentown Ambassadors declared bankruptcy and announced that they would not play. That left the league to quickly form a traveling team (using uniforms from the defunct Central League's Alexandria Aces).

The Aces finished with the league's worst record, but they did close relatively strong, as they finished second in the South Division in the second half.

STANDINGS

FIRST HALF

NORTH	W	L	PCT	GB
North Shore Spirit	32	14	.696	—
Brockton Rox	27	19	.587	5
Bangor Lumberjacks	25	21	.543	7
Quebec Les Capitales	24	22	.522	8

SOUTH	W	L	PCT	GB
New Jersey Jackals	26	21	.553	—
New Haven County Cutters	25	22	.532	1
Elmira Pioneers	17	29	.370	8½
Aces	9	37	.196	16½

SECOND HALF

NORTH	W	L	PCT	GB
Quebec Les Capitales	34	12	.739	—
Bangor Lumberjacks	31	15	.674	3
North Shore Spirit	25	21	.543	9
Brockton Rox	18	28	.391	16

SOUTH	W	L	PCT	GB
New Jersey Jackals	28	18	.609	—
Aces	19	27	.413	9
Elmira Pioneers	15	31	.326	13
New Haven County Cutters	14	32	.304	14

PLAYOFFS: Semifinals—New Jersey defeated Bangor 3-1 and North Shore defeated Quebec 3-2 in best-of-5 series. **Finals**—New Jersey defeated North Shore 3-2 in best-of-5 series.

MANAGERS: Aces—Bob Flori. **Bangor**—Kash Beauchamp. **Brockton**—Ed Nottle. **Elmira**—Greg Keagle. **New Haven**—Jarvis Brown. **New Jersey**—Joe Calfapietra. **North Shore**—John Kennedy. **Quebec**—Daren Bush.

ATTENDANCE: Brockton 203,094; Quebec 156,899; North Shore 115,118; New Jersey 106,110; Bangor 62,987; New Haven County 56,982; Elmira 55,710.

ALL-STAR TEAM: C—Brian Jones, Brockton. **1B**—Vic Davilla, North Shore. **2B**—Mike Torres, Brockton. **SS**—Chris Rowan, New Jersey. **3B**—Wilton Veras, New Jersey. **OF**—Wady Almonte, New Jersey; Derry Hammond, Bangor; Benoit Emond, Quebec. **DH**—Eddie Lantigua, Quebec. **LHP**—Brian Buchanan, Brockton. **RHP**—Keith Dunn, Quebec.

Player of the Year: Wilton Veras, New Jersey. **Rookie Player of the Year:** Kris Zacuto, Brockton. **Rookie Pitcher of the Year:** Paul Jacinto, Quebec.

INDIVIDUAL BATTING LEADERS
(Minimum 248 Plate Appearances)

	AVG	AB	R	H	2B	3B	HR	RBI	SB
Veras, Wilton, New Jersey	.369	320	46	118	29	1	5	59	1
Matos, Francisco, Brockton	.359	234	33	84	20	1	3	24	7
Nerei, Yuji, Elmira	.351	231	44	81	20	1	6	44	0
Davilla, Vic, North Shore	.330	351	67	116	14	0	14	56	0
Fischer, Rob, North Shore	.328	244	48	80	16	2	9	38	7
Emond, Ben, Quebec	.327	342	65	112	22	1	2	39	12
Almonte, Wady, New Jersey	.327	321	49	105	29	2	9	64	5
Ross, Don, Bangor	.327	205	48	67	16	2	14	30	11
Corbeil, Al, Aces	.320	266	38	85	16	0	5	30	0
Lebron, Hector, New Haven	.319	342	43	109	18	1	4	44	2

INDIVIDUAL PITCHING LEADERS
(Minimum 74 Innings)

	W	L	ERA	G	SV	IP	H	BB	SO
Long, Jerry, Bangor	7	4	1.97	16	0	101	71	41	91
Morse, Bryan, North Shore	10	4	2.50	18	0	137	132	27	84
Kelly, John, North Shore	8	3	2.60	13	0	83	72	30	110
Sugarman, Jeremy, North Shore	10	0	2.88	11	0	75	77	17	44
Dunn, Keith, Quebec	10	2	3.06	18	0	121	130	26	88
Buchanan, Brian, Brockton	11	5	3.26	19	0	119	109	45	98
Pena, Alex, Aces	4	9	3.34	19	1	97	84	28	86
Keinath, Tim, New Haven	5	7	3.56	29	0	78	76	22	56
Myers, Aaron, New Jersey	7	5	3.64	20	0	116	109	26	113
Miller, Josh, New Jersey	8	3	3.76	21	0	110	119	28	76

* Signed with affiliated club

ACES

BATTING	AVG	AB	R	H	2B	3B	HR	RBI	SB
Beck, Ben, of	.250	52	4	13	4	0	0	2	0
Capodieci, Adam, c	.000	3	0	0	0	0	0	0	0
Corbeil, Al, of-c	.320	266	38	85	16	0	5	30	0
Correa, Dalphie, ss	.250	164	14	41	3	2	0	14	2
Davis, Mike, 2b	.275	244	32	67	19	2	4	31	3
Doakes, Schuyler, of	.231	104	11	24	5	0	0	2	10
Gambill, Chad, of	.316	196	35	62	13	1	6	35	1
Garcia, Eustaquio, ss	.201	134	9	27	2	0	0	11	1
Gerald, Eddie, of	.252	147	24	37	11	0	5	26	3
Hileman, Jutt, of	.198	116	7	23	3	0	1	8	0
Larkin, Stephen, 1b	.239	117	13	28	5	1	0	11	1
Neufeld, Andy, 2b	.147	75	11	11	3	0	0	7	0
Perez, Koby, dh-c	.222	36	1	8	3	0	0	4	0
Quezada, Dalmiro, 3b-2b	.179	145	14	26	6	0	0	5	0
Schmidt, Greg, 1b-of	.227	154	13	35	11	2	4	25	2
Schmidt, J.P., 3b	.251	251	30	63	11	1	5	26	2
Silvera, Andres, 3b	.000	15	1	0	0	0	0	0	0
Smith, Coby, of	.206	306	46	63	8	1	5	28	20
Torres, Jessie, c	.243	115	15	28	1	0	1	12	0
Valera, Yohanny, c	.274	296	35	81	18	1	4	39	0

PITCHING	W	L	ERA	G	SV	IP	H	BB	SO
Andrews, Clayton	1	2	5.57	4	0	21	23	6	16
Bernard, Jason	0	0	12.27	4	0	7	12	3	4
Bowe, Brandon	0	2	12.46	7	0	8	18	4	6
2-team (3 Bangor)	0	4	13.11	10	0	11	23	5	7
Busenitz, Jeff	0	1	4.45	21	0	30	30	11	15
Cerbone, Marc	6	5	4.67	16	0	86	97	26	57
Devenney, Nick	1	1	4.50	23	0	40	41	28	35
Emmerthal, Steve	0	3	4.59	21	0	51	58	23	41
Figueroa, Carlos	3	0	3.79	19	0	19	22	4	15
2-team (18 New Jersey)	7	3	4.34	37	0	45	46	19	38
Francis, Buzzy	0	4	9.60	22	0	30	40	24	17
Gonzalez, Mario	2	2	3.93	7	0	34	32	21	28
2-team (3 North Shore)	2	2	3.92	10	0	39	36	26	31
Kirkland, Aaron	1	1	1.86	17	1	19	23	2	13
Kuklis, Kevin	1	2	2.64	7	0	30	37	8	24
Lambo, Luke	0	3	5.03	12	0	19	23	13	14
Maness, Nick	0	1	5.68	6	0	6	11	4	5
Marcotte, Trevor	5	6	8.19	8	0	29	44	13	11
2-team (3 New Jersey)	0	6	9.00	11	0	39	60	21	18

	W	L	ERA	G	SV	IP	H	BB	SO
Mendoza, Geronimo	0	7	6.48	11	0	41	51	21	32
Miranda, Angel	3	4	4.76	20	10	39	42	23	15
Neitz, Josh	3	2	5.29	18	0	49	54	15	32
Newill, Max	3	6	7.44	17	0	65	86	30	61
Pena, Alex	4	9	3.34	19	1	97	84	28	86
Rivera, Raul	0	2	4.91	6	0	7	9	6	2
Saldana, Jaime	0	2	8.10	3	0	10	14	3	9
Sanchez, Amaury	0	0	7.20	4	0	5	10	1	3
Strickland, Keith	0	0	19.80	4	0	5	12	1	3

BANGOR

BATTING	AVG	AB	R	H	2B	3B	HR	RBI	SB
Baker, Brian, of	.146	41	6	6	1	1	2	6	2
Baywal, Tim, 3b	.308	13	2	4	2	0	0	1	1
Bello, Rolando, 2b-3b	.278	237	30	66	11	2	1	27	15
2-team (19 Elmira)	.274	285	34	78	13	2	1	30	15
Brooks, Jeff, dh-3b	.133	15	1	2	0	0	0	0	0
Burke, Mark, 1b	.286	322	55	92	18	0	17	53	6
Carminucci, Chris, 3b	.000	1	0	0	0	0	0	0	0
Davis, Mike, 3b-2b	.189	37	4	7	1	0	0	2	0
2-team (73 Aces)	.263	281	36	74	20	2	4	33	3
Dominguez, Carlos, 2b	.000	7	1	0	0	0	0	0	1
2-team (12 New Haven)	.167	24	5	4	0	0	0	1	2
Garcia, Jose, of	.304	336	59	102	21	3	6	38	21
Grasso, Mike, 2b	.211	76	7	16	1	1	0	3	3
Hammond, Derry, of	.287	282	53	81	20	1	23	66	3
Hargreaves, Brad, c	.233	322	45	75	12	1	1	40	9
Kane, Ryan, 3b	.083	36	5	3	1	0	0	0	0
2-team (60 New Haven)	.199	261	31	52	13	0	4	19	0
King, Willie, of-3b	.462	26	5	12	3	0	1	7	1
Kohno, Kazuhiro, of	.271	166	22	45	4	0	7	33	9
Martinez, Dave, of	.083	36	4	3	0	0	0	3	0
Misawa, Hide, c	.000	4	0	0	0	0	0	0	0
Powell, Paul, 3b-ss	.264	280	27	74	18	0	3	43	8
Ross, Don, dh-1b	.327	205	48	67	16	2	14	30	11
Sienko, Ryan, c	.189	37	5	7	2	0	1	7	0
Tranum, Josh, dh-1b	.255	55	7	14	3	0	1	11	1
Uchino, Shin, ss	.256	297	42	76	19	1	3	22	10
*Whitesides, Jake, of	.307	189	31	58	15	4	6	30	15

PITCHING	W	L	ERA	G	SV	IP	H	BB	SO
Andrews, Clayton	7	3	4.06	15	0	84	94	22	63
2-team (4 Aces)	8	5	4.36	19	0	105	117	28	79
Boker, John	4	0	0.00	30	2	33	13	16	28
Bowe, Brandon	0	2	15.00	3	0	3	5	1	1
Cabrera, Yunior	0	0	18.00	2	0	1	1	1	0
Calmus, Lance	5	3	3.68	23	10	71	73	14	48
Duffy, John	0	0	0.00	1	0	2	0	0	0
Fox, Ben	1	2	3.90	13	1	30	26	13	20
Gangemi, Joe	0	0	10.80	5	0	3	6	3	1
Huguet, J.C.	6	3	2.00	32	1	72	52	31	51
Kohl, Doug	0	0	12.00	3	0	6	9	1	5
Long, Jerry	7	4	1.97	16	0	100	71	41	91
Magee, Jayson	0	0	18.00	2	0	2	5	3	4
Mangieri, John	1	0	2.25	4	1	4	4	2	3
McKeller, Laine	3	1	5.55	17	0	35	42	14	28
Miller, Ernie	0	0	10.47	7	0	16	28	14	9
Odom, Lance	0	0	0.00	2	0	3	6	3	3
Parker, John	0	0	4.35	11	0	10	11	5	9
*Pavlik, Isaac	1	3	3.73	24	4	50	43	25	56
Pincavitch, Kevin	0	0	18.00	1	0	1	3	1	0
Rohlfing, Jon	1	3	3.70	20	2	24	23	9	33
Scheuing, Matt	11	5	3.99	19	0	108	116	26	58
Thomas, Adam	9	5	3.82	18	0	113	108	37	81
Thomas, Eric	0	0	8.10	2	0	3	4	4	1
Uhl, Jon	0	0	4.70	9	0	23	22	15	20

BROCKTON

BATTING	AVG	AB	R	H	2B	3B	HR	RBI	SB
Arroyo, Abner, of	.308	169	33	52	16	3	10	25	1
Beck, Ben, of	.313	16	3	5	0	0	0	1	1
2-team (15 Aces)	.265	68	7	18	4	0	0	3	1
Bustos, Saul, ss	.277	368	48	102	11	2	9	51	4
Daubert, Jake, 3b	.294	337	66	99	14	2	14	52	2
Doakes, Schuyler, of	.154	39	6	6	2	0	0	2	5
2-team (29 Aces)	.210	143	17	30	7	0	0	4	15
Fera, Aaron, of	.259	135	16	35	3	0	2	14	0
Henriquez, Hector, 2b	.246	138	7	34	2	0	1	9	2
Jones, Brian, c-1b	.248	318	46	79	15	0	12	55	2
Joyce, Tom, of	.250	28	6	7	1	0	0	2	1
Knight, Marcus, of	.273	22	5	6	4	0	0	2	0
Lewis, Craig, 1b	.265	102	17	27	4	1	5	19	0
Matos, Francisco, dh	.359	234	33	84	20	1	3	24	7
Medina, Junior, of	.222	9	2	2	0	0	0	0	0
Newsom, Steve, of	.313	48	6	15	2	0	0	10	1
Sandoval, Michael, of	.229	153	21	35	0	0	5	25	1

BATTING	AVG	AB	R	H	2B	3B	HR	RBI	SB
Smith, Nestor, of	.316	155	26	49	10	2	5	17	3
Stewart, Chad, of	.283	276	35	78	10	2	0	23	11
Torres, Mike, 2b	.277	300	46	83	19	4	10	51	8
Wildman, Dwight, of	.250	12	1	3	1	0	0	0	0
Winn, Brett, of	.152	33	3	5	2	0	0	2	0
Zacuto, Kris, 1b-c	.277	260	45	72	12	0	11	35	1

PITCHING	W	L	ERA	G	SV	IP	H	BB	SO
Andersen, Derek	6	10	4.84	19	0	119	138	24	85
*Averette, Robert	3	1	1.88	6	0	43	40	4	31
Baez, Miguel	0	1	6.97	5	0	10	16	4	9
Bennett, Matt	1	3	5.77	34	2	48	68	11	29
*Buchanan, Brian	11	5	3.26	19	0	118	109	45	98
Dunn, Gerald	0	2	10.32	8	0	11	21	2	4
Encarnacion, Orlando	0	0	5.14	3	0	7	10	5	0
Evans, Tony	0	0	0.00	2	0	2	1	3	1
Henry, Mike	3	0	1.93	4	0	28	18	9	17
Keelin, Chris	0	0	19.29	1	0	2	2	7	3
Knox, Jerry	0	0	1.93	4	0	4	5	1	1
Koch, Jon	1	3	5.47	15	0	51	66	19	20
Lynn, Kevin	3	1	5.02	28	1	80	112	22	54
MacLane, Tommy	2	0	2.31	7	0	11	9	11	9
Martin, Scott	5	8	6.43	19	0	92	132	23	41
Mendoza, Geronimo	2	5	7.75	8	0	33	48	12	23
2-team (11 Aces)	2	12	7.05	19	0	75	99	33	55
Parker, Aaron	0	0	4.00	5	0	9	11	3	1
Polanco, Dionicio	0	0	3.18	3	0	5	6	4	7
*Runion, Tony	1	2	2.67	28	15	27	23	6	30
Stevens, Dave	0	3	1.29	7	2	7	7	1	5
Stutz, Tony	5	3	3.56	47	3	55	54	23	53
Williams, Shad	2	0	4.91	3	0	22	21	7	11

ELMIRA

BATTING	AVG	AB	R	H	2B	3B	HR	RBI	SB
Abreu, Dennis, 3b	.306	183	34	56	12	5	3	18	12
Bello, Rolando, 3b	.250	48	4	12	2	0	0	3	0
Bryan, Jason, of	.221	290	35	64	22	1	7	36	17
Checksfield, Steven, of-1b	.275	309	44	85	23	2	11	44	4
2-team (6 New Jersey)	.271	325	49	88	24	2	11	44	6
Clary, Casey, c	.000	2	1	0	0	0	0	0	0
Cucurullo, Matt, of	.254	67	5	17	1	0	0	7	1
Davidson, Cleatus, ss	.259	351	42	91	25	1	5	42	12
Deck, Ronnie, of	.185	130	9	24	2	0	0	11	1
Dodson, Jeremy, of	.271	306	36	83	17	1	10	46	5
Edwards, Dytarious, 2b	.262	366	46	96	13	3	2	23	35
Elder, Rick, 1b	.284	81	15	23	5	0	5	11	1
2-team (21 New Jersey)	.246	142	21	35	9	0	6	17	1
Funaro, Jeff, 3b-c	.266	64	9	17	1	0	1	7	0
Funaro, Joe, c	.375	8	0	3	0	0	0	4	0
Grasso, Mike, 3b	.100	10	1	1	0	0	0	0	0
2-team (23 Bangor)	.198	86	8	17	1	1	0	3	3
Johnstone, Ben, dh	.091	11	1	1	0	0	0	0	2
Keating, Matt, 1b	.000	2	1	0	0	0	0	0	0
Kenning, Ryan, of	.059	17	2	1	0	0	1	1	0
Memmert, Gabe, 1b	.157	51	4	8	1	0	0	2	0
Morita, Jobu, of-3b	.271	203	22	55	12	1	3	21	4
Nerei, Yuji, dh-of	.351	231	44	81	20	1	6	44	0
Piantek, Kurt, 1b	.306	72	14	22	6	1	2	9	0
Smith, Ryan, c	.268	190	16	51	9	0	2	15	0
Watari, Shinya, dh	.143	21	3	3	1	0	0	1	0
Zimniewicz, Kurt, 2b	.000	10	0	0	0	0	0	1	0

PITCHING	W	L	ERA	G	SV	IP	H	BB	SO
Borland, Curt	2	8	6.10	29	0	69	88	32	42
Burch, Matt	2	6	6.23	23	4	73	87	33	55
Cook, Bradley	0	1	5.40	6	0	6	11	5	3
Cosentino, Ryan	0	1	5.68	12	0	12	5	23	15
Elfeldt, Matt	3	3	5.24	35	4	44	46	24	47
Ford, Brian	5	2	1.93	29	0	37	27	14	19
Henderson, Kenneth	0	2	8.44	5	0	21	30	20	14
Kamimura, Soichi	0	0	3.38	2	0	2	2	3	1
LaSalle, Julio	4	7	3.90	20	1	120	120	50	69
Morrison, Robbie	3	4	3.61	17	4	67	68	23	48
Solveson, Saul	3	7	2.54	20	0	63	64	23	38
Soto, Reyes	0	1	7.55	15	0	31	34	39	18
Sparks, Eric	0	2	9.00	4	0	4	6	4	3
Stuart, Jared	0	0	2.70	3	0	3	3	3	2
Van Gorder, Joe	6	7	5.37	20	0	105	113	62	63
Winkelsas, Joe	0	1	14.73	3	1	3	8	1	3
Zallie, Chris	4	8	5.57	23	0	95	130	39	69

NEW HAVEN

BATTING	AVG	AB	R	H	2B	3B	HR	RBI	SB
Brooks, Jeff, 3b	.339	109	15	37	7	2	5	27	2
2-team (4 Bangor)	.315	124	16	39	7	2	5	29	2
Ciraco, Darren, of	.333	99	16	33	4	0	7	19	2

BATTING	AVG	AB	R	H	2B	3B	HR	RBI	SB
Dominguez, Carlos, 2b	.235	17	4	4	0	0	0	1	1
Fera, Aaron, of	.215	181	16	39	11	1	3	23	0
2-team (37 Brockton)	.234	316	32	74	14	1	5	37	0
Fingleson, Gavin, 2b	.299	147	17	44	4	0	0	10	1
Forbes, Kevin, of	.255	306	36	78	15	3	6	30	5
Hiter, Nick, c	.236	106	9	25	6	0	1	9	0
Hurst, Jimmy, dh	.314	239	42	75	14	1	16	47	2
Johnston, P.J., 2b-of	.237	291	34	69	11	3	1	22	16
Kane, Ryan, 3b	.218	225	26	49	12	0	4	19	0
Lebron, Hector, 1b	.319	342	43	109	18	1	4	44	2
Mateo, Jose, ss	.214	295	35	63	5	0	3	23	12
Pendergrass, Tyrone, of	.193	140	14	27	2	1	1	9	7
Rich, Billy, of	.264	280	30	74	12	1	3	29	8
Santiago, Luis, 2b	.140	43	8	6	0	0	0	1	0
Shorsher, Adam, c	.301	269	40	81	18	0	7	31	2

PITCHING	W	L	ERA	G	SV	IP	H	BB	SO
Alexander, Jordy	5	3	2.78	9	0	55	50	5	53
Bengel, Buddy	0	1	5.17	8	0	15	19	7	12
Bonecio, Ryan	5	7	4.93	19	0	111	127	45	46
Brack, A.J.	2	1	3.74	20	0	33	31	15	34
Encarnacion, Orlando	3	4	5.85	15	0	60	80	29	33
2-team (3 Brockton)	3	4	5.78	18	0	67	90	34	33
Harden, Tony	4	6	4.64	19	0	110	131	39	104
Keelin, Chris	1	1	3.75	18	1	24	16	27	31
Keinath, Tim	5	7	3.56	29	0	78	76	22	56
Lambo, Luke	1	1	4.18	17	0	32	33	9	28
2-team (12 Aces)	1	4	4.50	29	0	52	56	22	42
Lee, Henry	0	0	5.40	4	0	5	9	2	2
McCarthy, Greg	1	4	2.96	21	2	27	23	15	29
McKeller, Laine	0	1	6.05	12	0	19	24	12	18
2-team (17 Bangor)	3	2	5.73	29	0	55	66	26	46
Meyer, Scott	2	0	1.17	4	0	7	10	7	3
Mindingall, Wes	3	8	4.29	23	0	86	88	38	49
Waroff, Shane	2	2	2.02	32	13	35	38	7	29
Wiley, Skip	5	8	3.97	17	0	93	99	14	53

NEW JERSEY

BATTING	AVG	AB	R	H	2B	3B	HR	RBI	SB
Almonte, Wady, of	.327	321	49	105	29	2	9	64	5
Anderson, John, of	.276	330	68	91	16	1	3	32	9
Ballon, John, 1b	.190	21	2	4	0	0	0	1	0
2-team (27 Quebec)	.289	121	21	35	10	0	6	21	0
Bassett, Mike, of	.091	33	4	3	0	0	0	0	1
Boyd, Jared, 3b	.294	17	1	5	0	0	0	1	0
Checksfield, Steven, 3b	.188	16	5	3	1	0	0	0	2
Ciraco, Darren, of	.333	33	8	11	2	1	3	11	1
2-team (28 New Haven)	.333	132	24	44	6	1	10	30	3
Conway, Craig, 2b	.285	267	40	76	12	0	2	27	5
Elder, Rick, 1b	.197	61	6	12	4	0	3	8	0
Goodman, Scott, dh-of	.279	283	38	79	21	1	7	43	3
Grijak, Kevin, 1b-of	.295	332	55	98	21	2	13	77	1
Infante, Juan, 2b-ss	.267	165	38	44	12	4	4	26	4
LaFlair, Jay, c	.244	176	29	43	8	0	6	22	2
Pagan, Carlos, c	.146	48	4	7	2	0	0	3	0
Rowan, Chris, ss	.268	287	45	77	12	3	23	63	3
*Smithlin, Zach, of	.300	273	52	82	9	1	0	16	14
Vasquez, Alberto, c	.215	130	14	28	2	5	0	10	0
Veras, Wilton, 3b	.369	320	46	118	29	1	5	59	1

PITCHING	W	L	ERA	G	SV	IP	H	BB	SO
Benitez, Fabricio	3	3	2.78	31	15	35	33	10	33
Bennett, Joel	6	4	3.72	12	0	72	69	38	80
Breslow, Craig	3	1	4.10	19	1	26	19	13	37
Crowther, Jackson	7	9	4.83	19	0	117	128	34	85
Darcy, Ryan	0	0	7.20	3	0	5	7	4	4
Figueroa, Carlos	4	3	4.73	18	0	26	24	15	23
Gomez, Carlos	0	0	6.75	11	0	13	8	14	10
Grezlovski, Ben	1	0	1.35	9	4	13	11	2	16
Guzman, Juan	0	2	15.00	2	0	6	14	4	3
Marcotte, Trevor	0	1	11.57	3	0	9	16	8	7
Miller, Josh	8	3	3.76	21	0	110	119	28	76
Myers, Aaron	7	5	3.64	20	0	116	109	26	113
Neiser, Evan	5	1	2.75	36	1	59	48	22	53
Odom, Lance	0	0	18.00	2	0	2	4	4	0
2-team (4 Bangor)	0	0	7.20	6	0	5	10	7	3
Perkins, Mike	4	2	4.91	13	1	40	53	18	33
Therneau, Dave	0	0	6.00	2	0	6	8	4	7
Whitworth, Brad	6	5	3.77	19	0	98	115	29	59
Wieben, Lou	0	0	5.66	13	0	20	24	17	21

NORTH SHORE

BATTING	AVG	AB	R	H	2B	3B	HR	RBI	SB
Agramonte, Marcos, 2b	.281	231	32	65	14	6	3	21	16

BATTING	AVG	AB	R	H	2B	3B	HR	RBI	SB
Charles, Frank, c	.276	250	27	69	12	2	3	45	1
Davilla, Vic, 1b	.330	351	67	116	14	0	14	56	0
Fischer, Rob, of	.328	244	48	80	16	2	9	38	7
Granger, Mike, 2b-3b	.231	186	27	43	11	2	1	20	0
Hastings, Joseph, of	.295	329	59	97	23	2	11	66	1
Macchi, Brian, of	.296	304	47	90	21	0	7	45	1
Mejias, Erick, 2b	.556	9	3	5	0	0	0	2	0
Mercado, Onix, c	.309	139	17	43	9	1	3	16	0
Oglesby, Travis, dh-1b	.275	273	45	75	6	0	18	64	0
Pitts, Kevin, of	.286	7	2	2	0	0	0	0	1
Sanchez, Yuri, ss	.261	295	43	77	12	10	3	45	7
Taylor, Lucas, of	.337	98	27	33	4	2	1	11	17
Teilon, Nilson, 3b-of	.305	364	68	111	20	1	11	55	4
Wootan, Tanner, 2b	.320	50	11	16	4	0	0	7	0

PITCHING	W	L	ERA	G	SV	IP	H	BB	SO
Bell, Gary	3	3	5.32	25	1	66	74	27	54
Beucler, Nate	0	0	0.00	1	0	2	3	1	1
Bicondoa, Ryan	1	5	4.54	40	21	39	47	8	41
Calvert, Klae	3	2	3.81	7	1	28	25	5	23
Dean, Aaron	6	4	6.07	17	1	86	89	35	59
Del Prete, Anthony	0	0	9.00	4	0	4	8	1	1
Dixon, Jeffrey	1	0	8.53	5	0	12	21	5	13
Gonzalez, Mario	0	0	3.86	3	0	4	4	5	3
Gordon, Adrian	2	2	3.68	9	0	36	35	17	34
Hart, Tim	4	2	4.19	26	1	66	78	27	49
Jones, Fontella	1	1	9.00	6	0	11	17	4	12
*Kelly, John	8	3	2.60	13	0	83	72	30	110
Knapp, Ben	5	3	3.21	11	0	70	68	23	45
Marichal, Miguel	1	2	7.16	15	0	27	29	17	22
Morse, Bryan	10	4	2.50	18	0	137	132	27	84
Reynoso, Edison	1	2	7.48	6	1	21	22	12	26
*Sugarman, Jeremy	10	0	2.88	11	0	75	77	17	44
Vandegriff, Nick	1	2	4.91	5	1	14	17	1	7

QUEBEC

BATTING	AVG	AB	R	H	2B	3B	HR	RBI	SB
Ballon, John, 1b	.310	100	19	31	10	0	6	20	0
Booker, Steve, of	.290	145	28	42	13	2	3	15	6
Boston, Tyson, of	.229	35	2	8	0	0	0	3	1
Bozanich, Sam, 2b	.218	197	33	43	9	1	1	13	4
Delfino, Lee, ss	.236	305	49	72	12	2	7	40	6
Emond, Benoit, of	.327	342	65	112	22	1	2	39	12
Hargrove, Taylor, dh	.000	5	0	0	0	0	0	0	1
Hopper, Shane, 3b-1b	.287	352	57	101	12	1	15	75	25
Lantigua, Eddie, 3b-1b	.290	338	52	98	19	0	18	74	8
Lepine, Olivier, c	.274	303	34	83	26	0	7	49	0
McNabb, Buck, of	.302	331	49	100	19	0	2	38	9
Melo, Juan, 2b	.309	152	29	47	8	0	7	30	6
Mercier, Andrew, c	.125	16	2	2	1	0	0	1	0
Morton, Rickie, dh-1b	.311	151	29	47	11	0	10	32	1
Quigg, Wally, dh-2b	.207	92	13	19	4	0	1	8	2
Tomlinson, Goef, of	.351	171	37	60	11	0	3	19	8
Wendt, Justin, dh	.176	34	3	6	2	0	0	2	1

PITCHING	W	L	ERA	G	SV	IP	H	BB	SO
*Abraham, Paul	0	1	0.00	7	3	6	4	3	5
*Crumpton, Lawson	3	0	0.90	3	0	20	17	0	12
Dunn, Keith	10	2	3.06	18	0	120	130	26	88
Franks, Lance	1	7	5.40	20	0	113	135	38	79
Freedman, Coogie	2	1	7.46	25	1	25	30	17	15
Fuller, Brendan	0	1	10.38	5	0	4	7	8	5
*Grezlovski, Ben	6	1	1.61	19	2	22	19	8	28
2-team (9 New Jersey)	7	1	1.51	28	6	35	30	10	44
Gutierrez, Jon	2	3	5.97	10	0	31	43	20	16
*Harris, Jeff	0	0	0.75	2	0	12	9	4	12
Hernandez, Alberto	1	0	5.14	2	0	7	6	3	7
Hoyt, Michael	6	5	4.35	34	0	41	37	23	37
*Jacinto, Paul	7	0	0.90	8	0	60	43	8	37
Johnson, Seth	1	0	0.78	12	0	23	9	6	20
Joyce, Michael	0	0	22.09	3	0	3	6	4	5
Keelin, Chris	0	0	0.00	2	0	3	2	1	2
3-team (18 New Haven, 1 Brockton)	1	1	4.50	21	1	30	20	35	36
Lawson, Brett	0	1	6.00	4	1	6	7	1	3
Major, Marc	0	0	7.71	2	0	2	3	1	4
Prata, Danny	10	3	3.99	18	0	108	107	46	60
Rodriguez, Raul	0	0	5.68	1	0	6	9	0	5
Runser, Greg	1	3	8.31	12	2	13	20	13	8
*Santos, Alex	2	1	1.06	31	22	34	19	5	49
Spigner, Chris	0	1	4.26	3	0	6	8	5	7
Turner, Jess	5	4	4.50	20	0	108	128	30	78
Waroff, Shane	1	0	0.96	7	2	9	6	6	12
2-team (32 New Haven)	3	2	1.80	39	15	45	44	13	41

FOREIGN
LEAGUES

Campeche gives Mexico a new look

BY J.J. COOPER

The last time Campeche won a Mexican League championship, Francisco "Paquin" Estrada was at the helm, a 35-year-old player/manager who still had 11 seasons left in a long playing career.

Estrada's a little older now, and he hasn't picked up a bat in a while, but after the 2004 season, he's even more of a legend in Campeche.

MEXICO

In his second stint as the Campeche manager, Estrada led the Pirates to their first title in 21 years, breaking the stranglehold that the Mexico City Red Devils and Angelopolis (formerly Mexico City) Tigers had held on the title over the past five seasons. The Red Devils and Tigers met in the finals the last five years, with the Red Devils winning three times.

It was Estrada's third title as a manager, and he became the first manager to win Mexican League titles in three different decades. He also won a championship as a player/manager with Leon in 1990.

Campeche rolled over Saltillo in the championship series, winning the best-of-seven series in five games. Danny Magee, a former Braves farmhand as a shortstop, allowed only six hits and three runs in eight innings to pick up the win in Campeche's 4-3 victory in the deciding Game 5. Jayson Bass homered three times during the series to pace the offense.

Magee was a revelation during the playoffs. After going 8-6, 3.24 during the regular season, Magee was 7-0 during the playoffs. He also picked up the victory in Game Two of the championship series, as he pitched 10 innings of the Pirates' 11-inning, 3-2 victory.

Magee emerged as a complement to Francisco Campos to give the Pirates an unstoppable pair of aces. Neither suffered a loss during the four rounds of the Mexican League playoffs.

MEL BAILEY

Francisco Campos

Magee may have been the pitching star in the championship series, but Campos was Campeche's star all season. He was named the league MVP and pitcher of the year after he strung together one of the best seasons in league history.

Campos had quietly been one of the best pitchers in the Mexican League for more than a decade. He had reached double digits in wins four different times, led the league in strikeouts in 2002, and in 10 seasons with Campeche he had never had an ERA better than 3.71. But that didn't exactly foreshadow his 2004 season.

Campos became the first pitcher in 48 years and only the fifth pitcher ever to win the Mexican League pitching Triple Crown, as he went 12-2, 1.47 with 99 strikeouts, leading the league in wins, ERA and strikeouts.

While Campos became part of Mexican League history with an outstanding single season, a pair of veteran pitchers broke career records.

Angel Moreno became the winningest lefthander in league history. Moreno went 8-6, 3.56 for Veracruz, giving him 257 wins for his career, topping Alfredo Ortiz' 255. Moreno is now the second-winningest pitcher in league history, trailing only Ramon Arano's 334 wins.

Earlier in the season, Tabasco righthander Jesus "Chito" Rios set the Mexican League record for career strikeouts, as he topped Arano's record of 2,380 strikeouts in mid-March. Rios finished the season with 2,424 strikeouts. He set the mark despite playing 11 less seasons than Arano did. Rios is also in the top five for career wins with 233.

The strikeout record was part of a solid 5-3, 3.13 season for Rios, as he bounced back from a 0-7, 4.96 season to be named the league's comeback player of the year.

One other pitching mark fell during the 2004 season. On his way to leading the league with 26 saves, Santos Hernandez set a record with 16 consecutive saves, topping Miguel Alicea's record of 15 straight, set in 1994.

STANDINGS

FIRST HALF

NORTH	W	L	GB	
Puebla Parrots	33	16	.673	—
Saltillo Sarape Makers	30	19	.612	3
Monterrey Sultans	27	22	.551	6
Tijuana Bulls	25	24	.510	8
Monclova Steelers	23	28	.451	11
Laguna Cowboys	22	28	.440	11½
Aguascalientes Rieleros	21	30	.412	13
San Luis Potosi Tuneros	18	32	.360	15½

SOUTH	W	L	PCT	GB
Mexico City Red Devils	31	20	.608	—
Angelopolis Tigers	30	21	.588	1
Tabasco Cattlemen	27	21	.563	2½
Campeche Pirates	25	25	.500	5½
Oaxaca Warriors	25	26	.490	6
Veracruz Reds	23	28	.451	8
Yucatan Lions	20	29	.408	10
Cancun Lobstermen	20	31	.392	11

SECOND HALF

NORTH	W	L	GB	
Saltillo Sarape Makers	33	15	.688	—
Puebla Parrots	30	18	.625	3
Monterrey Sultans	29	19	.604	4
Tijuana Bulls	24	24	.500	9
Aguascalientes Rieleros	24	25	.490	9½
Laguna Cowboys	23	26	.469	10½
Monclova Steelers	16	32	.333	17
San Luis Potosi Tuneros	14	34	.292	19

SOUTH	W	L	PCT	GB
Campeche Pirates	30	17	.638	—
Mexico City Red Devils	29	20	.592	2
Oaxaca Warriors	25	22	.532	5
Angelopolis Tigers	24	24	.500	6½
Yucatan Lions	23	26	.469	8
Tabasco Cattlemen	21	27	.438	9½
Veracruz Reds	21	28	.429	10
Cancun Lobstermen	20	29	.408	11

PLAYOFFS—First Round: Puebla defeated Aguascalientes 4-0; Campeche defeated Tabasco 4-1; Monterrey defeated Tijuana 4-3; Mexico City defeated Yucatan 4-1; Angelopolis defeated Oaxaca 4-1 in best-of-7 series. **Second Round:** Puebla defeated Tijuana 4-1; Campeche defeated Angelopolis 4-1; Saltillo defeated Monterrey 4-2; Mexico City defeated Oaxaca 4-0. **Semifinals:** Campeche defeated Mexico City 4-3; Saltillo defeated Puebla 4-2 in best-of-7 series. **Final:** Campeche defeated Saltillo 4-1 in best-of-7 series.

FOREIGN LEAGUES

ATTENDANCE—Tijuana 548,863; Saltillo 545,597; Monterrey 400,278; Yucatan 236,844; Laguna 195,538; Monclova 172,805; Tabasco 171,328; Puebla 138,147; Mexico City 135,471; Aguascalientes 134,635; Angelopolis 132,191; Oaxaca 102,679; Veracruz 90,816; Campeche 74,484; Cancun 72,580; San Luis Potosi 70,336.

MANAGERS: Angelopolis—Mario Mendoza/Andres Mora. **Aguascalientes**—Juan Jose Pacho. **Campeche**—Francisco Estrada. **Cancun**—Alejandro Taveras. **Laguna**—Gerardo Sanchez. **Mexico City**—Bernie Tatis/Roberto Kelly. **Monclova**—Fernando Elizondo. **Monterrey**—Dan Firova. **Oaxaca**—Houston Jimenez. **Puebla**—Enrique Reyes. **Saltillo**—Derek Bryant. **San Luis Potosi**—Juan Rodriguez. **Tabasco**—Juan Navarrette. **Tijuana**—Carlos Hernandez/Alex Ortiz/Tomas Herrera. **Veracruz**—Noe Mundro/Marco Vazquez/Rolando Camarero. **Yucatan**—Mike Easler/Eddie Diaz.

CLUB BATTING

	AVG	G	AB	R	H	2B	3B	HR	BB	SO	SB
Puebla	.318	97	3191	570	1015	182	21	74	370	497	58
Saltillo	.316	97	3146	614	995	157	10	106	458	493	37
Monterrey	.315	97	3154	550	994	159	15	93	421	402	80
Angelopolis	.304	99	3292	570	1002	152	27	138	318	450	53
Oaxaca	.304	98	3165	499	961	193	17	54	361	389	39
Mexico City	.303	100	3237	572	981	180	22	94	362	397	85
Aguascalientes	.298	100	3192	525	951	173	21	76	370	492	93
Laguna	.298	99	3166	528	942	153	10	94	360	444	28
Tijuana	.293	97	3133	535	918	172	11	86	429	406	86
Monclova	.284	99	3106	415	882	131	13	53	357	500	61
Yucatan	.282	98	3099	439	873	152	11	60	324	377	67
San Luis Potosi	.279	98	3200	428	894	160	14	83	323	519	60
Campeche	.278	97	3087	444	857	168	10	65	351	433	32
Tabasco	.274	96	2964	412	811	132	18	41	357	466	94
Veracruz	.273	100	3119	409	852	147	12	45	330	418	65
Cancun	.259	100	3062	361	793	139	13	55	282	445	23

CLUB PITCHING

	ERA	G	CG	SV	IP	H	HR	R	ER	BB	SO
Tabasco	3.58	96	6	17	776	856	47	376	309	261	365
Campeche	3.98	97	13	24	810	759	80	405	358	363	464
Monterrey	4.27	97	2	24	799	860	52	426	379	347	475
Cancun	4.35	100	7	23	811	857	65	461	392	395	360
Oaxaca	4.50	98	5	25	808	897	68	489	404	361	425
Puebla	4.54	97	2	27	796	920	91	444	402	343	406
Saltillo	4.59	97	1	31	796	872	62	462	406	372	523
Yucatan	4.59	98	4	21	808	884	76	465	412	340	460
Veracruz	4.98	100	5	30	810	981	74	507	448	268	409
Angelopolis	4.98	99	5	30	818	909	73	514	453	401	455
Mexico City	5.00	100	8	26	824	996	68	493	458	299	446
Tijuana	5.21	97	0	18	806	908	96	517	466	426	566
Aguascalientes	5.74	100	6	26	816	973	96	568	521	378	426
Monclova	5.82	99	3	20	799	1040	67	562	517	426	418
Laguna	5.97	99	3	19	795	971	108	584	528	414	453
San Luis Potosi	6.04	98	4	18	799	1041	93	598	536	376	483

INDIVIDUAL BATTING LEADERS

(Minimum 270 Plate Appearances)

	AVG	AB	R	H	2B	3B	HR	RBI	SB
Smith, Demond, Monterrey	**.405**	294	81	119	19	5	15	52	30
Munoz, Noe, Saltillo	.391	279	56	109	18	0	6	57	0
Robles, Oscar, Mexico	.381	339	72	**129**	24	5	8	64	8
Bass, Jayson, Saltillo	.373	308	93	115	19	3	16	62	13
Flores, Miguel, Monterrey	.368	326	71	120	18	2	6	46	20
Espinosa, Ramon, Laguna	.365	260	50	95	20	1	8	47	3
Burkhart, Morgan, Saltillo	.365	310	**100**	113	19	0	24	91	1
White, Derrick, Tijuana	.361	288	65	104	20	0	15	76	9
Martinez, Luis, Puebla	.361	269	43	97	17	0	4	31	1
Martinez, Greg, Oaxaca	.355	318	57	113	15	5	0	28	8
Bullett, Scott, Monterrey	.354	319	58	113	14	4	10	69	10
Martinez, Manny, Tigres	.351	345	66	121	24	3	12	47	13
Johnson, Rontrez, Aguas.	.346	373	96	**129**	29	6	14	52	**54**
Sherman, Darrell, Puebla	.345	307	74	106	9	6	2	41	7
Meyers, Chad, Mexico	.339	363	92	123	21	**10**	8	61	32
Lara, Idelfonso, Aguas.	.339	251	40	85	16	0	12	53	1
Contreras, Jose, Puebla	.337	252	50	85	16	8	4	45	19
Villalobos, Carlos, Puebla	.337	365	82	123	21	1	17	82	5
McDonald, Donzell, Tabasco	.336	238	50	80	14	4	5	24	29
Vazquez, Jorge, Tigres	.334	293	43	98	9	2	21	64	0
Rodriguez, Fernando, Laguna	.331	287	41	95	11	0	7	55	0
Robles, Javier, Tigres	.328	323	71	106	20	6	15	68	6
Castellano, Pedro, Mexico	.328	314	48	103	21	0	9	49	5
Martinez, Abel, Laguna	.328	247	47	81	10	1	9	45	4
Valencia, Carlos, Tijuana	.327	394	73	**129**	24	4	13	53	7
Smith, Bubba, Monterrey	.327	336	59	110	25	0	17	77	1
Rodriguez, Boi, Camp./Laguna	.327	306	61	100	22	2	17	62	6
Orantes, Ramon, Monterrey	.325	252	38	82	10	0	4	40	3
Romero, Wilfredo, Monclova	.325	326	53	106	21	1	6	39	21
Jimenez, Eduardo, Saltillo	.325	268	64	87	13	0	23	95	0
Hernandez, Julio, Tijuana	.323	337	79	109	25	1	6	34	4
Lucca, Lou, Cancun	.323	285	42	92	16	1	10	40	2
Connell, Lino, Veracruz	.323	372	53	120	28	2	4	48	17
Cervantes, Ivan, Oaxaca	.322	363	45	117	22	2	2	51	0
Pemberton, Rudy, Monclova	.322	298	42	96	12	1	12	53	8
Presichi, Cristian, Saltillo	.320	250	41	80	11	2	12	49	3
Brinkley, Darryl, Tij./SL Potosi	.320	266	43	85	8	0	8	42	23
Velazquez, Guillermo, Puebla	.319	301	48	96	24	0	11	59	3
Mere, Pedro, Aguascalientes	.319	320	60	102	22	2	7	68	5
Lopez, Raul, Monclova	.318	305	38	97	13	2	5	36	2
Ramirez, Omar, Veracruz	.316	351	62	111	21	1	4	31	10
Alcantara, Izzy, Laguna	.316	326	65	103	21	0	**27**	81	3
Rivera, Ruben, Campeche	.313	319	68	100	21	4	10	60	10
Quintero, Christian, Oaxaca	.313	342	56	107	28	2	9	66	10
Evans, Tom, Tabasco	.312	276	70	86	22	4	10	47	4
Iturbe, Pedro, Puebla	.311	296	51	92	20	2	10	53	2
Landaeta, Luis, Tij./Yucatan	.311	357	64	111	24	2	15	64	19
Santana, Pedro, Oaxaca	.309	392	78	121	**29**	6	10	54	12
O`Sullivan, Patrick, SL Potosi	.308	334	55	103	27	0	23	62	6
Melo, Juan, Veracruz	.307	323	56	99	21	2	14	64	10
Arredondo, Luis, Yucatan	.305	354	56	108	13	2	3	30	29
Guizar, Hector, Aguascalientes	.305	341	36	104	16	3	1	37	4
Buelna, Lorenzo, Puebla	.303	304	52	92	16	0	5	37	13
Saucedo, Roberto, Mexico	.303	357	69	108	22	0	20	**97**	7
Diaz, Remigio, SL Potosi	.302	252	31	76	10	0	3	23	9
Bojorquez, Victor, Mexico	.302	315	55	95	22	3	8	39	9
Garcia, Guillermo, Tigres	.301	282	55	85	12	0	26	68	0
Carrillo, Matias, Tigres	.300	303	49	91	13	0	13	52	4
Espino, Daniel, Cancun	.300	317	44	95	14	1	5	35	5
Gomez, Heber, Monterrey	.299	224	34	67	8	1	2	29	4
Soto, Saul, Mexico	.299	271	31	81	14	0	10	46	4
Rojas, Homar, Oaxaca	.297	273	28	81	17	0	3	51	0
Valencia, Abraham, Tijuana	.296	314	46	93	15	0	8	61	7
Morejon, Oswaldo, Yucatan	.295	359	61	106	18	3	7	48	4
Arredondo, Hernando, Tabasco	.294	265	21	78	13	1	3	33	7
Palafox, Sergio, Monclova	.293	249	41	73	12	0	7	38	4
Soriano, Ricardo, Aguas.	.292	257	48	75	12	2	4	28	3
Gastelum, Carlos A, Tigres	.289	395	55	114	6	7	3	27	15
Borges, Luis, Yucatan	.287	268	32	77	11	1	1	29	1
Rios, Eduardo, Aguas.	.285	365	51	104	17	1	18	88	3
Diaz, Edwin, Veracruz	.285	316	40	90	14	1	3	40	5
Garcia, Nick, Saltillo	.285	267	33	76	14	0	2	36	1
Sievers, Carlos, Tabasco	.281	295	48	83	20	1	7	48	8
Castro, Domingo, Monclova	.281	320	40	90	7	3	4	37	5
Fornes, Daniel, Monterrey	.281	278	44	78	15	0	9	46	2
Sanchez, Raul, Cancun	.280	322	45	90	15	7	8	49	3
Yan, Julian, Tabasco	.278	327	38	91	11	0	11	69	1
Valdez, Ramon, Campeche	.277	303	46	84	10	0	0	14	7
Ramirez, Oscar, Campeche	.276	312	44	86	19	1	7	42	4
Martinez, Ray, Mexico	.274	288	43	79	11	2	9	53	0
Mendoza, Omar, SL Potosi	.274	270	44	74	15	1	7	32	3
Arano, Eloy, Veracruz	.273	300	43	82	9	1	0	24	10
Munoz, Jose, Monclova	.272	239	42	65	9	1	3	30	5
Fernandez, Daniel, Mexico	.269	283	53	76	7	0	1	18	11
Martinez, Grimaldo, Laguna	.268	250	36	67	8	0	2	19	1
Vazquez, Gregorio, Tabasco	.265	279	31	74	8	0	2	30	5
Meza, Gonzalo, Laguna	.263	255	41	67	5	3	2	22	2
Guerrero, Sergio, Campeche	.262	317	38	83	18	2	3	30	1
Vizcarra, Roberto, Campeche	.259	259	30	67	12	0	3	35	2
Fentanes, Oscar, Veracruz	.257	257	23	66	3	0	2	27	2
Brena, Jaime, Oaxaca	.257	230	25	59	8	1	0	20	3
Garcia, Luis, Tigres	.256	301	56	77	10	2	6	45	8
Arredondo, Eduardo, Tabasco	.248	238	39	59	6	6	0	27	13
Castro, Arnoldo, Cancun	.242	260	26	63	17	0	2	16	2
Valle, Jorge, Cancun	.240	288	27	69	7	0	6	44	0
Sandoval, Jose, Mexico	.238	323	43	77	20	0	9	49	1
Salas, Heriberto, Laguna	.234	282	42	66	10	2	3	35	2
Rivera, Francisco, Veracruz	.229	253	24	58	12	0	4	33	2
Arauz, Leobardo, Yucatan	.224	254	38	57	14	1	7	28	4
Meza, Alfredo, Monterrey	.189	249	23	47	7	0	2	27	0

Other Select Players

	AVG	AB	R	H	2B	3B	HR	RBI	SB
Otanez, Willis, Campeche	.387	137	24	53	12	0	8	27	1
Rios, Armando, Tijuana	.352	105	25	37	9	1	4	26	7
Toca, Jorge, Cancun	.339	56	10	19	3	1	0	5	0
Garcia, Cornelio, Laguna	.336	146	25	49	4	1	1	17	1
Brown, Emil, Campeche	.333	105	24	35	8	0	9	26	0
Leach, Jalal, Yucatan	.320	103	10	33	3	0	2	16	2
Mejia, Roberto, Campeche	.319	144	26	46	15	0	4	21	2
Magallanes, Ever, Oaxaca	.317	218	34	69	11	0	3	26	0
Inglin, Jeff, Yucatan	.313	80	12	25	4	2	2	13	0
Miller, Orlando, Aguas./Cancun	.310	126	21	39	10	0	3	17	3

Player	AVG	AB	R	H	2B	3B	HR	RBI	SB
Bartee, Kimera, Saltillo	.308	104	23	32	8	0	1	8	5
Grijak, Kevin, Laguna	.308	143	15	42	5	0	3	22	3
Adriana, Sharnol, Yuc./Monc.	.297	148	28	44	6	0	7	22	4
Thomas, Juan, Yucatan	.292	130	20	38	12	0	5	23	0
Gil, Benji, Tijuana	.286	126	26	36	9	0	2	21	10
Flores, Kevin, Puebla	.272	114	17	31	4	1	0	7	2
Amezcua, Adan, SL Potosi	.267	221	32	59	16	1	4	29	5
Rose, Pete, Aguascalientes	.266	177	16	47	8	0	2	23	0
Encarnacion, Mario, Cancun	.256	117	16	30	7	0	3	14	0
Langaigne, Selwyn, Tijuana	.256	43	6	11	3	1	0	5	3
LeBron, Juan, Cancun	.245	151	18	37	7	0	3	21	0
Rodriguez, Carlos, SL Potosi	.244	193	22	47	11	3	3	20	0
Mosquera, Julio, Campeche	.239	176	19	42	3	0	5	30	0
Marrero, Oreste, Oaxaca	.233	73	9	17	4	0	3	16	0
Leach, Jalal, Monclova	.224	58	9	13	2	0	0	6	1
Marrero, Oreste, Veracruz	.224	67	8	15	1	1	4	13	0
Herrera, Jose, Yucatan	.222	90	3	20	5	0	0	10	2
Andrews, Shane, SL Potosi	.216	125	12	27	4	0	3	15	1
Cookson, Brent, Oaxaca	.207	29	0	6	0	0	0	5	0
Tellez, Alonso, Aguascalientes	.206	63	4	13	3	0	0	4	0
Hurst, Jimmy, Monclova	.204	54	4	11	1	0	0	6	2
Freire, Alejandro, Veracruz	.200	80	12	16	1	0	1	11	2
Jensen, Marcus, Cancun	.191	47	3	9	0	0	0	3	0
Martinez, Gabby, Cancun	.189	53	5	10	0	0	0	4	1
Jose, Felix, Mexico	.143	14	0	2	2	0	0	0	0

INDIVIDUAL PITCHING LEADERS
(Minimum 80 Innings)

	W	L	ERA	G	SV	IP	H	BB	SO
Campos, Francisco, Campeche	12	2	1.47	16	0	123	87	26	99
Fernandez, Osvaldo, Tabasco	8	6	2.69	18	0	124	117	34	68
Loya, Rigoberto, Monterrey	9	3	2.80	16	0	100	86	37	37
Ward, Bryan, Monclova	7	7	2.83	18	0	108	118	34	68
Vega, Obed, Cancun	2	5	2.93	16	0	86	88	34	37
Perez, Edgar, Cancun	3	7	3.08	19	0	91	97	29	43
Rios, Jesus, Tabasco	5	5	3.13	15	0	83	67	34	45
Ortega, Pablo, Puebla	9	5	3.17	17	0	119	132	32	57
Magee, Danny, Campeche	8	6	3.24	16	0	114	95	61	79
Valdez, Armando, Puebla	12	4	3.29	18	0	107	110	40	74
Vargas, Joel, Tabasco	4	8	3.32	19	3	84	90	26	53
Ochoa, Pablo, Monterrey	6	2	3.36	18	0	110	114	47	71
Mora, Eleazar, Oaxaca	7	4	3.46	18	0	88	104	16	35
Moreno, Angel, Veracruz	8	6	3.56	18	0	99	102	23	42
Elvira, Narciso, Campeche	7	3	3.63	16	0	89	76	40	59
Alvarez, Azael, Puebla	7	2	3.65	16	0	89	91	59	59
Rivera, Francisco, Aguas.	10	2	3.75	21	0	115	120	37	56
Alvarez, Octavio, Tabasco	7	6	3.81	17	0	99	127	17	37
Roque, Rafael, Tigres	7	4	4.02	16	0	81	70	55	74
Ramirez, Roberto, Mexico	10	5	4.07	19	0	113	127	28	44
Mairena, Ozwaldo, Mexico	7	5	4.12	14	0	83	93	28	51
Palafox, Juan, Yucatan	7	5	4.32	15	0	85	95	25	29
Elizalde, Carlos, Oaxaca	10	3	4.35	17	0	91	105	38	48
Moreno, Claudio, Mexico	9	7	4.40	22	0	117	138	41	51
Salgado, Eddie, Cancun	6	10	4.40	22	0	92	105	28	32
DeHart, Richey, Monterrey	8	5	4.42	18	0	90	105	34	60
Picota, Lenin, SLP/Yucatan	3	7	4.54	17	0	102	118	28	70
Navarro, Hector, Veracruz	5	8	4.71	18	0	94	100	38	54
Guzman, Jesus, Tigres	6	7	4.72	19	0	88	105	32	40
Navarro, Joel, Oaxaca	8	7	4.76	19	0	108	127	32	66
Gonzalez, Leonardo, Tijuana	4	6	4.80	18	0	94	107	58	80
Kelley, Rich, Vera./Puebla	7	6	4.82	19	0	98	120	40	69
Silva, Jose, Mexico	12	3	4.87	20	0	102	138	27	61
Lopez, Emigdio, Veracruz	7	5	5.05	18	0	98	139	26	50
Chavarria, Hector, Laguna	4	8	5.09	19	0	81	98	39	34
Acosta, Jasiel, Monclova	4	6	5.12	19	0	104	110	54	66
Navarro, Jose, Puebla	7	4	5.34	17	1	84	101	24	28
Campillo, Jorge, Tigres	5	5	5.38	17	0	99	120	28	66
Alvarez, Antonio, Aguas.	4	6	5.40	19	0	107	130	34	39
Gomez, Martin, Laguna	7	4	5.44	19	0	94	119	42	41
Elvira, Abraham, Aguas.	4	10	6.26	17	0	82	93	56	46
Simon, Ben, Aguas.	5	6	6.67	14	0	86	107	29	52
Madero, Francisco, Laguna	8	7	7.55	19	0	85	122	38	39

Other Select Players

	W	L	ERA	G	SV	IP	H	BB	SO
Munoz, Adan, Tigres	0	0	0.00	1	0	0	0	0	0
Henriquez, Oscar, Campeche	2	0	1.59	8	0	11	7	9	3
Webster, Daniel, Campeche	1	0	1.80	1	0	5	4	1	1
Picardo, Hipolito, Saltillo	6	0	1.91	36	20	42	40	14	32
Reyes, Carlos, Yucatan	0	0	2.57	2	0	7	10	1	5
Sinohui, David, Oaxaca	3	0	2.66	20	10	20	15	11	13
Meyer, Jake, Tijuana	2	1	2.93	6	0	31	25	18	29
McGlinchy, Kevin, Monterrey	6	2	2.99	26	1	75	78	25	40
Palacios, Vicente, Tijuana	3	0	3.12	24	0	43	47	16	22
Neri, Braulio, Tijuana	0	3	3.14	11	0	14	19	4	3
Hurtado, Edwin, Yucatan	1	3	3.24	21	8	42	40	26	27
Rivera, Oscar, Yucatan	6	5	3.30	17	0	79	71	18	50
Bourgeois, Steve, Saltillo	3	1	3.52	5	0	23	23	9	16
Hansell, Greg, Mexico	1	2	3.63	34	19	35	33	11	23
Jimenez, Jose, Oaxaca	4	4	3.65	29	1	62	56	31	35
Pina, Rafael, Tijuana	3	3	3.68	13	0	29	31	13	28
Alexander, Jordy, Cancun	1	2	3.98	6	0	32	34	5	24
Patrick, Bronswell, Mexico	1	0	4.41	3	0	16	13	6	9
Coco, Pascual, Saltillo	3	1	4.42	10	0	59	68	34	64
Aybar, Manny, Puebla	2	2	4.64	18	7	21	25	5	21
Strong, Joe, Monc./Yucatan	4	6	5.08	29	5	39	40	23	35
Cortes, David, Tijuana	0	1	5.17	14	3	16	16	6	18
Giron, Isabel, Yuc./Laguna	7	7	5.28	20	0	104	120	44	79
Rekar, Bryan, Tigres	1	1	5.40	3	0	12	14	6	5
Manning, David, Mexico	1	0	5.40	6	0	5	8	8	7
Dorame, Randey, Camp./Monc.	3	5	5.64	18	0	59	69	32	23
Serrano, Wascar, Oaxaca	2	3	5.70	8	0	36	43	19	22
Beltran, Alonso, Tijuana	4	7	5.74	15	0	69	75	37	51
Garibaldi, Cecilio, Tigres	6	1	5.75	21	0	61	80	43	31
Kelly, John, Yucatan	1	2	5.82	5	0	22	30	10	16
Harris, Jeff, Aguascalientes	0	0	6.23	5	2	4	3	6	2
Rivera, Ben, Laguna/Mexico	1	2	6.30	20	10	20	22	6	13
Woodman, Hank, Mex./Yucatan	2	3	6.23	15	4	30	35	19	20
Torres, Melqui, Mexico/Tigres	0	0	6.43	7	0	7	10	3	9
Murray, Dan, Aguascalientes	1	3	7.38	8	0	39	40	36	24
Looney, Brian, San Luis Potosi	1	10	7.80	15	0	68	94	23	38
Pacheco, Delvis, Tijuana	0	1	13.50	1	0	2	4	1	1
Bullinger, Jim, Tijuana	0	2	14.29	3	0	6	12	6	6
Deago, Roger, Tijuana	0	4	14.49	6	0	14	31	13	11
Rivera, Luis, Tigres	0	1	15.43	3	0	5	6	7	2
Pinales, Aquiles, Tabasco	0	3	31.50	4	0	2	7	5	0

Cuban season comes up golden

BY MILTON JAMAIL AND KEVIN BAXTER

Cuba reestablished its international dominance in 2004 by winning the gold medal at the Olympic Games in Athens, but the island nation also continued to lose some of its top young talent through defections.

It lost one of its best players in June when first baseman Kendry Morales and 16 others fled Cuba by boat and landed in Key West, Fla. Morales then went to the Dominican Republic to establish residency, thus making him a free agent in the eyes of Major League Baseball and free to negotiate a contract with any of 30 major league teams. He still had not signed by Oct. 30.

Despite Morales' defection, Cuba reclaimed the gold medal at the Olympics by beating Australia 6-2 in the final game. The victory avenged Cuba's only setback in Olympic competition after it was beaten by the United States in 2000 in Sydney and had to settle for silver. It previously won gold in 1992 and 1996.

The Cubans prevailed in Athens despite overhauling its national team roster since that 2000 loss. The top pitchers from team team—Jose Contreras, Jose Ibar and Maels Rodriguez—had either defected or been barred from the team. But new stars such as lefthander Adiel Palma, who was 3-0 in Athens, outfielder Frederich Cepeda and second baseman Youlieski Gourriel combined with holdovers such as shortstop Eduardo Paret, who had a crucial two-run single in the gold-medal game, catcher Ariel Pestano and pitchers Norge Vera and Pedro Luis Lazo to lead Cuba back to the top of the international baseball world.

Morales was noticeably absent from the roster. A

switch-hitter with power, the 21-year-old Morales was Cuba's top rookie in 2002. But a blossoming career unraveled when he was suspended from international competition in December 2003 because the Cuban government feared that he was planning to defect. He did so six months later.

Morales was not the only quality player to leave Cuba. In October 2003, six young Cuban players, including righthander Yamel Guevara, 21, who went 10-0 with Industriales during the 2002-2003 Serie Nacional, arrived in Florida after defecting from Cuba.

Righthander Alay Soler, 24, defected in late 2003, established residency in the Dominican Republic and became a free agent. He signed a three-year, $3 million contract with the New York Mets in July.

The hard-throwing Rodriguez, 24, also left Cuba in late 2003 but was still unsigned almost a year later. Rodriguez, who frequently touched 100 mph while playing for Cuba's national team, struggled to reach the high 80s during tryouts with major league clubs. Yobal Dueñas, 31, a veteran of the Cuban national team, signed with the New York Yankees and received a $60,000 bonus.

In Cuban domestic competition, Havana's Industriales won their second consecutive Cuban league title and their 10th overall in 2004 but they needed a two-run rally in the final inning of the final game of the playoffs to finish off their four-game sweep of Villa Clara.

Trailing Villa Clara and stellar reliever Eliecer Montes de Oca, 3-2, entering the bottom of the ninth, the Industriales started their winning rally with a double by Rudy Reyes. Pinch-hitter Yasser Ottamendi tried to bunt Reyes to third, where he could tie the game on a sacrifice fly, but beat the bunt out instead.

Shortstop Enrique Diaz then followed with a double to left-center that cleared the bases to give Havana the win in the XLIII Serie Nacional before more than 55,000 fans at Havana's Estadio Latinoamericano. The Industriales beat Sancti Spiritus and Pinar del Rio to reach the Cuban championship series while Villa Clara dominated Santiago and Granma.

The Industriales didn't even win their own division during the regular season, finishing 52-38, 2½ games back of Sancti Spiritu. But they advanced to the postseason as the Western Zone's wild-card team. Villa Clara, at 57-33, had the best record going into the playoffs.

Villa Clara's Luis Borroto went 12-3 with league bests for ERA (1.56) and strikeouts (135) in 127 innings.

On offense, Cuban Olympic star Osmani Urrutia of Las Tunas dominated the batting race, hitting .469—70 points ahead of this closest competitor. He also led with 67 RBIs, while his 16 home runs were one shy of the lead shared by Cienfurqos' Pedro Rodriguez and Sancti Spiritus' Reinier Yero.

STANDINGS

WEST

GROUP A	W	L	PCT	GB
Pinar del Rio	57	33	.633	—
Isla de la Juventud	46	43	.517	10½
Metropolitans	43	47	.478	14
Matanzas	27	63	.300	30
GROUP B	**W**	**L**	**PCT**	**GB**
Sancti Spiritus	54	35	.607	—
Industriales	52	38	.578	2½
Havana	38	51	.422	16
Cienfuegos	27	62	.303	27

EAST

GROUP C	W	L	PCT	GB
Villa Clara	57	33	.633	—
Ciego de Avila	55	34	.611	1½
Las Tunas	44	46	.489	13
Camaguey	38	52	.422	19
GROUP D	**W**	**L**	**PCT**	**GB**
Santiago de Cuba	53	37	.589	—
Granma	49	41	.544	4
Holguin	43	48	.467	11
Guantanamo	35	54	.393	17½

Playoffs—Quarterfinals: Santiago defeated Ciego de Avila 3-0; Villa Clara defeated Granma 3-0; Industriales defeated Sancti Spiritus 3-2; and Pinar del Rio defeated Isla de la Juventud 3-0 in best-of-5 series. **Semifinals:** Villa Clara defeated Santiago 4-3; and Industriales defeated Pinar del Rio 4-2 in best-of-7 series. **Finals:** Industriales defeated Villa Clara 4-0 in best-of-7 series.

INDIVIDUAL BATTING LEADERS
(Minimum 243 Plate Appearances)

	AVG	AB	R	H	2B	3B	HR	RBI
Urrutia, Osmani, Las Tunas	.469	258	51	121	23	2	16	67
Urgelles, Yoandri, Metropolitans	.399	278	47	111	29	4	5	37
Enriquez, Michel, IJ	.385	226	48	87	18	0	7	43
Machado, Roger, Ciego de Avila	.366	279	42	102	24	2	6	61
Martinez, Alexander, Cienfuegos	.360	236	22	85	10	0	0	19
Gorruiel, Yuliesky, Sancti Spiritus	.358	215	49	77	14	7	9	42
Miranda, Danny, Ciego de Avilas	.358	307	67	110	14	7	11	44
Garlobo, Yoandi, Matanzas	.355	282	41	100	14	3	12	48
Charles, Yorelvis, Ciego de Avila	.355	217	33	77	9	0	9	37
Scull, Yordanis, Las Tuna	.352	372	74	131	18	7	8	44
Borrero, Ariel, Villa Clara	.348	336	62	117	25	2	7	63
Gonzalez, Luis, Havana	.347	343	60	119	12	4	7	44
Gil, Joquel, Metropolitans	.346	266	46	92	17	0	11	32
Pedroso, Joan, Las Tunas	.345	255	59	88	16	2	15	56
Suarez, Amaury, Las Tunas	.342	348	69	119	12	3	14	59
Concepcion, Norlis, Las Tunas	.340	241	31	82	12	2	5	41
Anderson, Leslie, Camaguey	.337	332	55	112	16	3	9	50

INDIVIDUAL PITCHING LEADERS
(Minimum 90 Innings)

	W	L	ERA	G	IP	BB	SO
Borroto, Luis, Villa Clara	12	3	1.56	21	127	38	135
Betancourt, Danny, Santiago	12	4	2.03	19	129	47	101
Bueno, Francisley, Industriales	9	3	2.12	16	98	35	93
Suarez, Deinys, Industriales	10	4	2.13	15	106	35	93
Coss, Ifredi, Sancti Spiritus	10	2	2.34	17	108	28	101
Cervantes, Osmar, Ciego de Avila	9	6	2.64	21	99	42	59
Licea, Ciro, Granma	12	7	2.65	20	146	27	114
Palma, Adiel, Cienfuegos	4	7	2.66	15	95	35	96
Banos, Vladimir, Pinar del Rio	9	3	2.77	18	110	35	73
Enriquez, Roidel, Villa Clara	11	4	2.87	21	113	23	77
Lazo, Pedro, Pinar del Rio	8	5	2.93	17	101	11	75
Rodriguez, Delvis, Villa Clara	5	4	3.11	22	104	30	78
Hernandez, Noelvis, Sancti Spiritus	9	3	3.12	30	104	27	69

Seibu wins title on second chance

BY WAYNE GRACZYK

The Seibu Lions took advantage of the Pacific League's new playoff format in 2004 to parlay a second-place finish into a pennant, then went on to defeat the Central League's Chunichi Dragons in seven games to win their first Japan Series title in 12 years. It capped a season of turmoil and uncertainty about the future of Japanese baseball.

JAPAN

Seibu finished the regular season 4½ games behind first place and defending champion Fukuoka Daiei Hawks but advanced to the Japan Series by beating the third place Hokkaido Nippon Ham Fighters in a best-of-three First Stage of the P.L. playoffs, then knocking off the Hawks in the best-of-five Second Stage.

Chunichi opened up a four-game lead in the C.L. standings in late June and coasted to their first pennant since 1999, winning by a comfortable 7½ game margin over the second place Yakult Swallows. The C.L. had no playoffs.

The Lions were led by a trio of righthanded hitters: Dominican third baseman Jose Fernandez, who hit .285-33-94; Venezuelan first baseman Alex Cabrera (.280-25-62), who played in only 64 games beginning in June after he recuperated from a broken forearm suffered in spring training; and left fielder Kazuhiro Wada (.320-30-89), who also missed nearly a month of the season while playing with Japan's national team at the Athens Olympics.

Jose Fernandez

Seibu's righty fireballer Daisuke Matsuzaka, also an Olympian, led Pacific League pitchers with a 2.90 ERA while posting a 10-6 record.

For the pitching-rich Dragons, righthander Kenshin Kawakami led hurlers in both leagues in wins. He went 17-6, 3.32 and was named the Central League's MVP.

Alex Cabrera

Leading Dragons hitters were third baseman Kazuyoshi Tatsunami (.308-5-70), former major league center fielder Alex Ochoa (.294-21-89) and right fielder Kosuke Fukudome (.277-23-81), who missed the last two months of the season and the Japan Series because of his Olympic appearance and a broken hand he suffered just after his return from Athens.

Though the Hawks did not win in the playoffs, Daiei first baseman Nobuhiko Matsunaka won the Pacific League triple crown with a .358-44-120 season, also earning him league MVP honors. Nippon Ham's Panamanian slugger Fernando Seguignol tied Matsunaga with 44 homers.

A total of 65 foreigners played in Japan in 2004, and two of the Pacific League teams were guided by foreign managers. Trey Hillman's Nippon Ham Fighters finished third and made the playoffs, beating out Bobby Valentine's Chiba Lotte Marines by a half game.

Japanese baseball went into crisis mode June 13 with the announcement that two Pacific League teams, the Osaka Kintetsu Buffaloes and Orix BlueWave of Kobe, had agreed to merge. That led to a three-month tug-of-war between owners and the Japan Pro Baseball Players Union, led by Yakult Swallows catcher Atsuya Furuta.

The owners wanted to combine the Central and Pacific circuits into a single 10-team league and sought to merge two more P.L. clubs, but players and fans protested vehemently, insisting the two-league system with 12 clubs should be maintained.

Eventually, the players staged a two-day strike Sept. 18-19. That led to a compromise agreement to allow the Kintetsu-Orix merger to go through but keep the two leagues and 12 teams for the 2005 season by awarding an expansion franchise to play in Sendai, a city two hours by bullet train north of Tokyo in the Tohoku district, to replace the team lost in the Kintetsu-Orix merger.

Interleague play will also be introduced in 2005, with each team playing a home-and-away three-game series against each club in the opposite league. Central League teams will play a 146-game regular season, while the Pacific League schedule will consist of 136 regular season games plus playoffs.

CENTRAL LEAGUE

STANDINGS

	W	L	T	PCT	GB
Chunichi Dragons	79	56	3	.585	—
Yakult Swallows	72	64	2	.529	7½
Yomiuri Giants	71	64	3	.526	8
Hanshin Tigers	66	70	2	.485	13½
Hiroshima Carp	60	77	1	.438	20
Yokohama BayStars	59	76	3	.437	20

INDIVIDUAL BATTING LEADERS
(Minimum 427 Plate Appearances)

	AVG	AB	R	H	2B	3B	HR	RBI	SB
Shima, Shigenobu, Carp	.337	561	94	189	23	3	32	84	6
LaRocca, Greg, Carp	.328	436	89	143	28	2	40	101	11
Saeki, Takahiro, BayStars	.322	463	63	149	16	2	19	57	2
Takahashi, Yoshinobu, Giants	.317	426	83	135	20	1	30	79	1
Kanemoto, Tomoaki, Tigers	.317	521	92	165	32	4	34	113	5
Kokubo, Hiroki, Giants	.314	462	85	145	24	2	41	96	0
Maeda, Tomonori, Carp	.312	407	45	127	28	1	21	70	2
Shimizu, Takayuki, Giants	.308	578	86	178	39	0	16	60	4
Tatsunami, Kazuyoshi, Dragons	.308	523	68	161	25	0	5	70	5
Furuta, Atsuya, Swallows	.306	483	72	148	23	0	24	79	1
Imaoka, Makoto, Tigers	.306	572	87	175	29	0	28	83	0
Hiyama, Shinjiro, Tigers	.306	468	59	143	26	1	18	84	4
Tamura, Hitoshi, BayStars	.305	449	80	137	19	2	40	100	10
Ramirez, Alex, Swallows	.305	525	79	160	30	2	31	110	2
Ibata, Hirokazu, Dragons	.302	562	81	170	30	2	6	57	21
Kinjo, Tatsuhiko, BayStars	.302	486	53	147	15	2	13	52	0
Abe, Shinnosuke, Giants	.301	379	61	114	22	1	33	78	0
Miyamoto, Shinya, Swallows	.301	346	52	104	12	1	11	26	6
Iwamura, Akinori, Swallows	.300	533	99	160	19	0	44	103	8
Akahoshi, Norihiro, Tigers	.300	570	96	171	20	6	0	30	64
Taneda, Hitoshi, BayStars	.300	410	52	123	27	3	8	52	2
Woods, Tyrone, BayStars	.298	476	84	142	15	0	45	103	2

	AVG	AB	R	H	2B	3B	HR	RBI	SB
Ishii, Takuro, BayStars	.295	535	80	158	26	6	10	43	11
Ochoa, Alex, Dragons	.294	520	63	153	24	2	21	89	3
Araki, Masahiro, Dragons	.292	602	93	176	23	1	3	44	39
Ogata, Koichi, Carp	.292	456	91	133	20	2	26	64	4
Petagine, Roberto, Giants	.290	383	70	111	17	0	29	84	2
Nishi, Toshihisa, Giants	.289	608	106	176	27	1	28	60	3
Suzuki, Ken, Swallows	.289	470	41	136	21	0	15	65	1
Ishihara, Yoshiyuki, Carp	.288	396	32	114	22	0	6	35	0
Rhodes, Tuffy, Giants	.287	523	95	150	17	0	45	99	3
Yano, Akihiro, Tigers	.285	502	38	143	23	3	11	66	1
Sheets, Andy, Carp	.284	542	91	154	31	1	23	85	2
Fukudome, Kosuke, Dragons	.277	350	61	97	19	7	23	81	8
Arias, George, Tigers	.272	412	54	112	26	1	25	84	3
Inaba, Atsunori, Swallows	.265	437	61	116	20	3	18	45	6

Remaining U.S. and Latin Players

	AVG	AB	R	H	2B	3B	HR	RBI	SB
Matsumoto, Daniel, Swallows	.393	28	1	11	1	0	0	5	0
Linares, Omar, Dragons	.283	159	19	45	7	0	4	28	0
Martin, Billy Joe, Swallows	.241	162	18	39	10	9	6	18	0
Kinkade, Mike, Tigers	.233	86	13	20	1	1	3	7	1

INDIVIDUAL PITCHING LEADERS
(Minimum 138 Innings)

	W	L	ERA	G	SV	IP	H	BB	SO
Uehara, Koji, Giants	13	5	2.60	22	0	163	135	23	153
Yamamoto, Masahiro, Dragons	13	6	3.15	27	0	157	153	43	120
Kawashima, Ryo, Swallows	10	4	3.17	23	0	139	115	39	128
Kawakami, Kenshin, Dragons	17	7	3.32	27	0	192	173	38	176
Igawa, Kei, Tigers	14	11	3.73	29	0	200	190	54	228
Guzman, Domingo, Dragons	10	5	3.76	23	0	146	138	41	128
Fukuhara, Shinobu, Tigers	10	15	3.87	29	0	181	190	58	148
Bale, John, Carp	11	10	4.21	25	0	160	165	62	173
Miura, Daisuke, BayStars	6	8	4.25	22	0	144	158	33	135
Ishikawa, Masanori, Swallows	11	11	4.35	27	0	163	200	22	72
Kuroda, Hiroki, Carp	7	9	4.65	21	0	147	187	29	138
Kudo, Kimiyasu, Giants	10	7	4.67	23	0	139	160	33	128
Mullen, Scott, BayStars	7	10	4.71	28	0	151	182	39	87
Kisanuki, Hiroshi, Giants	7	8	5.03	31	5	140	168	50	154

Remaining U.S. and Latin Players

	W	L	ERA	G	SV	IP	H	BB	SO
Sikorski, Brian, Giants	5	3	2.67	62	5	78	76	22	83
Riggan, Jerrod, Tigers	1	1	2.84	23	4	25	23	5	14
Gonzalez, Dicky, Swallows	4	2	3.09	15	0	47	43	6	35
Williams, Jeff, Tigers	2	4	3.28	51	14	47	40	19	56
Valdes, Marc, Dragons	1	1	3.51	30	1	26	28	8	17
Bowers, Cedrick, BayStars	7	4	3.54	20	0	104	102	39	90
Morel, Ramon, Tigers	0	1	3.67	21	1	27	35	9	20
Watson, Mark, Carp	0	2	3.74	19	0	22	18	8	20
Vargas, Martin, Dragons	2	3	4.06	6	0	31	29	10	28
Myers, Rodney, Tigers	1	2	4.07	20	0	24	28	8	8
Beverlin, Jason, Swallows	9	11	4.42	22	0	136	141	65	81
Hodges, Trey, Tigers	2	3	5.31	8	0	41	40	16	29
Randel, Matt, Giants	3	2	5.45	24	1	40	39	18	42
Corey, Bryan, Giants	1	1	5.48	21	0	23	30	10	17
Mounce, Tony, Swallows	3	6	6.05	12	0	55	73	30	41
Davey, Tom, Carp	3	4	6.18	9	0	51	65	23	37
Walker, Pete, BayStars	2	4	6.80	10	0	46	63	19	23
Gaillard, Eddie, BayStars	2	2	8.31	13	0	13	15	5	5
Feliciano, Juan, Carp	0	1	15.88	3	0	11	14	10	10

PACIFIC LEAGUE

STANDINGS

	W	L	T	PCT	GB
Fukuoka Daiei Hawks	77	52	4	.597	—
Seibu Lions	74	58	1	.561	4½
Hokkaido Nippon Ham Fighters	66	65	2	.504	12
Chiba Lotte Marines	65	65	3	.500	12½
Osaka Kintetsu Buffaloes	61	70	2	.466	17
Orix BlueWave	49	82	2	.374	29

PLAYOFFS—Seibu defeated Hokkaido 2-1 in best-of-3 series; Seibu defeated Fukuoka 3-2 in best-of-5 series for league championship.

INDIVIDUAL BATTING LEADERS
(Minimum 412 Plate Appearances)

	AVG	AB	R	H	2B	3B	HR	RBI	SB
Matsunaka, Nobuhiko, Hawks	.358	478	118	171	37	1	44	120	2
Ogasawara, Michihiro, Fighters	.345	377	78	130	19	2	18	70	3
Jojima, Kenji, Hawks	.338	426	91	144	25	1	36	91	6
Iguchi, Tadahiro, Hawks	.333	510	96	170	34	2	24	89	18
Muramatsu, Akihito, BlueWave	.320	459	70	147	29	1	6	51	11
Wada, Kazuhiro, Lions	.320	394	79	126	21	1	30	89	6
Tani, Yoshitomo, BlueWave	.317	378	58	120	27	1	15	63	10
Agbayani, Benny, Marines	.315	457	89	144	31	1	35	100	8
Fukuura, Kazuya, Marines	.314	506	67	159	42	1	11	73	2
Isobe, Koichi, Buffaloes	.309	457	82	141	22	1	26	75	7
Kaizuka, Masahide, Lions	.307	384	53	118	27	2	14	75	8
Seguignol, Fernando, Fighters	.305	443	86	135	24	0	44	108	0
Omura, Naoyuki, Buffaloes	.303	498	74	151	25	2	2	34	22
Kawasaki, Munenori, Hawks	.303	564	87	171	19	8	4	45	42
Kitagawa, Hirotoshi, Buffaloes	.303	508	75	154	27	0	20	88	7
Shinjo, Tsuyoshi, Fighters	.298	504	88	150	28	3	24	79	1
Mizuguchi, Eiji, Buffaloes	.293	389	55	114	20	0	6	40	0
Ortiz, Jose, BlueWave	.289	477	70	138	28	0	24	71	4
Nakajima, Hiroyuki, Lions	.287	502	70	144	22	3	27	90	18
Kimoto, Kuniyuki, Fighters	.285	505	67	144	24	1	9	62	4
Takahashi, Shinji, Fighters	.285	404	66	115	19	2	26	84	2
Fernandez, Jose, Lions	.285	513	87	146	23	1	33	94	5
Zuleta, Julio, Hawks	.284	455	60	129	18	0	37	100	1
Valdes, Pedro, Hawks	.279	419	68	117	20	0	18	74	1
Hirano, Keiichi, BlueWave	.279	377	50	105	18	7	6	39	10
Franco, Matt, Marines	.278	439	70	122	35	2	16	65	1
Nakamura, Norihiro, Buffaloes	.274	387	59	106	16	1	19	66	0
Hori, Koichi, Marines	.261	445	70	116	23	2	14	51	5
Akada, Shogo, Lions	.259	374	68	97	18	2	9	41	16
Kaneko, Makoto, Fighters	.256	332	42	85	15	1	3	39	5
Abe, Masahiro, Buffaloes	.247	380	47	94	21	2	7	50	3

Remaining U.S. and Latin Players

	AVG	AB	R	H	2B	3B	HR	RBI	SB
Obando, Sherman, Fighters	.338	130	23	44	7	0	8	25	0
Cabrera, Alex, Lions	.280	250	47	70	14	1	25	62	0
Brown, Roosevelt, BlueWave	.269	335	45	90	23	0	15	70	2
Echevarria, Angel, Fighters	.258	306	44	79	16	0	16	54	1
Barnes, Larry, Buffaloes	.252	107	18	27	3	1	4	19	1
Valdez, Mario, Buffaloes	.213	127	21	27	9	0	9	29	0
McClain, Scott, Lions	.184	76	10	14	1	0	4	10	0

INDIVIDUAL PITCHING LEADERS
(Minimum 133 Innings)

	W	L	ERA	G	SV	IP	H	BB	SO
Matsuzaka, Daisuke, Lions	10	6	2.90	23	0	146	127	42	127
Iwakuma, Hisashi, Buffaloes	15	2	3.01	21	0	159	149	30	123
Arakaki, Nagisa, Hawks	11	8	3.28	25	0	192	173	73	177
Shimizu, Naoyuki, Marines	10	11	3.40	23	0	169	160	42	126
Watanabe, Shunsuke, Marines	12	6	3.59	23	0	150	145	42	101
Chang, Chi-Chie, Lions	9	8	3.70	22	0	146	137	57	119
Beirne, Kevin, Buffaloes	6	8	3.89	27	0	174	190	48	154
Powell, Jeremy, Buffaloes	8	8	3.90	24	0	171	173	55	112
Kanemura, Satoru, Fighters	13	8	3.93	25	0	167	157	71	114
Kawagoe, Hidetaka, BlueWave	7	9	4.17	22	0	145	161	30	91
Kobayashi, Hiroyuki, Marines	9	7	4.26	24	0	154	162	57	137
Wada, Tsuyoshi, Hawks	6	4	4.35	19	0	128	110	38	115
Mirabal, Carlos, Fighters	11	9	4.82	29	0	161	183	48	89
Motoyanagi, Kazuya, BlueWave	6	11	5.61	29	0	135	170	32	86
Saito, Kazumi, Hawks	10	7	6.26	22	0	138	139	59	120

Remaining U.S. and Latin Players

	W	L	ERA	G	SV	IP	H	BB	SO
Serafini, Dan, Marines	5	4	4.13	31	0	81	80	35	66
Gulin, Lindsay, Hawks	8	3	4.24	17	0	100	126	35	69
Carrasco, Hector, Buffaloes	8	8	5.57	53	5	76	74	37	70
Minchey, Nate, Marines	4	3	5.70	12	0	73	77	26	37
Moore, Trey, BlueWave	6	6	6.24	16	0	84	105	57	63
Rupe, Ryan, Fighters	1	4	6.67	6	0	30	41	9	20
Phillips, Jason, BlueWave	2	7	7.78	14	0	59	79	31	36
Knight, Brandon, Hawks	0	0	12.00	6	0	6	11	6	5
Voyles, Brad, Hawks	0	3	24.30	3	0	3	12	7	2
Mercado, Hector, Hawks	0	0	inf	1	0	0	1	1	0

Controversy hits Korean season

BY THOMAS ST. JOHN

The 2004 Korean Series turned into a farce as the league neglected to change the rules as they apply to tie games in the postseason. The series had three ties, which meant the best-of-seven series ended up going nine games before the defending champion Hyundai Unicorns won four games to two over Samsung. The Unicorns won their fourth title in nine years.

KOREA

The fiasco was not without its bright spots as Samsung starter Bae Yong-soo was brilliant in pitching a 10-inning no-hitter, only to end up with a no-decision when the game was called with a 0-0 score after 12 innings. According to Korean rules, a tie is declared if two teams are deadlocked after 12.

The 2004 Korean season will also be remembered as much for controversy.

Just after the all-star break, two Korean sports tabloids broke a story that some players had paid a broker to teach them how to doctor their military physicals so they would be exempt from service and could continue playing baseball. The brokers paid a fee ranging from $25,000

Cliff Brumbaugh

to $35,000 to teach players how to manipulate their urine tests to make it appear as if there was a serious kidney problem—a surefire way to avoid military service.

In Korea, all males must serve in the military for 26 months. An exemption is possible if it can be proven that there is a legitimate medical condition, but exemptions are rare.

More than 50 players, ranging from minor leaguers to star players, were implicated with about half being arrested. The investigation was still ongoing as the season ended and it was possible that up to 100 players would be evaluated. If any player was determined to be free of any kidney ailments, they would be forced to serve their time in the military.

Interestingly, the Korea Baseball Organization commissioner was not in the country for the first 10 days after the scandal broke, due to more pressing matters abroad. The players and the Korea Pro Baseball Players Association issued numerous formal apologies and statements before the KBO itself made even one public comment.

Generally, import players had stellar seasons in Korea. Two foreigners shared the league lead in wins and one narrowly missed a triple crown.

Kia's Daniel Rios and Doosan's Gary Rath both posted 17-8 records. Rios was the workhorse of the league with 223 innings, while Rath had a slightly better ERA, 2.60 against Rios' 2.87.

Righthander Mike Fyhrie (16-6, 3.32), who won nine straight games at one point in the second half, picked up his 16th win in the last game of the regular season, ensuring the first-place Unicorns would make another direct trip to the Korean Series. The team that finishes first in the regular season receives a bye to the final.

At the plate, Hyundai's Cliff Brumbaugh just missed the triple crown. He hit .343-33-105 and led the league in batting, on-base percentage and slugging percentage. He was second in home runs and hits, and third in RBIs.

The 2004 season was more than likely the last in Korea for Unicorns' slugger Shim Chong-soo, who became a free agent and was expected to test the waters in the U.S. major leagues. Shim attracted more attention than former Lions first baseman Lee Seung-yeop, who spent the 2004 season playing in Japan.

STANDINGS

	W	L	T	PCT	GB
Hyundai Unicorns	75	53	5	.586	—
Samsung Lions	73	52	8	.584	1½
Doosan Bears	70	62	1	.530	7
Kia Tigers	67	61	5	.523	8
SK Wyverns	61	64	8	.488	12½
LG Twins	59	70	4	.457	16½
Hanwha Eagles	53	74	6	.417	21½
Lotte Giants	50	72	11	.410	22

PLAYOFFS: First Round—Doosan defeated Kia 2-0 in best-of-3 series. **Second Round**—Samsung defeated Doosan 3-1 in best-of-5 series. **Finals**—Hyundai defeated Samsung 4-2-3 in best-of-7 series.

INDIVIDUAL BATTING LEADERS

	AVG	AB	R	H	HR	RBI
Cliff Brumbaugh, Hyundai	.343	475	92	163	33	105
Lee Jin-Young, SK	.342	404	74	138	15	63
Hong Song-Heun, Doosan	.329	501	62	165	14	86
Kim Tae-Kyoon, Hanwha	.323	473	76	153	23	106
Lee Byung-Kyu, LG	.323	496	95	160	14	64
Kim Ki-Tae, SK	.320	403	60	129	10	67
Lee young-Woo, Hanwha	.319	483	94	154	13	60
Yang Joon-Hyuk, Samsung	.315	497	95	151	28	103
Robert Perez, Lotte	.314	532	60	154	18	86
Park Han-Lee, Samsung	.310	503	81	156	16	63

Other North American Players

	AVG	AB	R	H	HR	RBI
Robert Perez, Lotte	.314	490	60	154	18	86
Ryan Jackson, Lotte	.300	450	53	109	7	42
Al Martin, LG	.291	358	45	104	9	52
Jay Davis, Hanwha	.291	440	70	128	19	77
Angel Pena, Hanwha	.275	131	21	36	9	27
Troy O'Leary, Samsung	.265	211	30	56	10	28
Tilson Brito, SK	.261	368	41	96	13	50
Izzy Alcantara, Doosan	.231	125	19	30	6	25
Eddy Diaz, Hanwha	.209	187	25	39	7	26
Mandy Lopez, Smsung	.162	68	6	11	3	8
Mario Encarnacion, Lotte	.083	12	1	1	0	1

INDIVIDUAL PITCHING LEADERS

	W	L	ERA	SV	IP	H	BB	SO
Park Myung-Hwan, Doosan	12	3	2.50	0	159	130	59	162
Gary Rath, Doosan	17	8	2.60	0	201	189	72	116
Bae Yong-Soo, Samsung	17	2	2.61	0	190	163	85	144
Daniel Rios, Kia	17	8	2.87	0	223	209	95	145
Kwon Oh-Joon, Samsung	11	5	3.23	2	153	128	47	142
Mike Fyhrie, Hyundai	16	6	3.32	0	182	166	70	130
Song Jin-Woo, Hanwha	11	8	3.61	1	172	162	51	100
Park Ji-Chul, Lotte	9	7	3.87	0	140	131	66	94
Oh Jae-Yong, Hyundai	10	9	3.99	0	149	135	58	113
Lee Seung-Ho, SK	15	9	3.99	0	169	160	100	145

Other North American Players

	W	L	ERA	SV	IP	H	BB	SO
Julio Manon, Kia	8	9	4.17	0	155	156	72	83
Kevin Hodges, Samsung	9	10	4.24	0	163	158	102	123
Jose Cabrera, SK	4	4	4.65	12	103	99	61	85
Mark Kiefer, Doosan	7	9	4.69	0	104	115	45	50
Brian Cooper, LG	4	4	4.75	0	61	66	29	31
Edwin Hurtado, LG	0	4	5.79	0	28	36	23	13

FOREIGN LEAGUES

Records mark exciting CPBL year

BY PAUL HUANG

With the merger of the Tawain Major League and the Chinese Professional Baseball League now a part of history, the CPBL celebrated in 2004 with what was arguably the most exciting season in the league's 15-year history.

The President Lions earned their way into the Taiwan Series by winning the first half by

TAIWAN

3½ games, while the Sinon Bulls' bumpy ride into the championship series was not determined until the last out of their regular season finale when they beat the Cobras 9-8 to narrowly edge out the Brother Elephants, the defending champs, by three percentage points.

The mid-season signings of pitcher Wu Si-yo and power hitter Lin Chih-sheng, both rookies, were the main reason the Bears were able to double their win total from 2003. Lin had 56 RBIs in 57 games while Wu went 4-0 mark in September.

But the pair of rookies were only a part of a season that was filled with exceptional performances.

Brother Elephants' cleanup hitter Peng Cheng-ming topped the 66-game league record, set by Sinon's Jay Kirkpatrick in 1998, for most games into the season with an average above .400. He extended the mark to 70, before cooling off in the final third of the season to finish at .376, which was still good enough for his second consecutive batting title.

By hitting 21 homers, Sinon slugger Chang Tai-shan became the first player to hit 20 homers in back-to-back

seasons. Chang set a single-season record of 28 for a local player in 2003.

Macoto Cobras lefthander Lin Ying-jeh broke the single-season strikeout record of 200, held by American lefty Will Flynt of the 1994 Jung-guo Bears, by three when he punched out Sinon catcher Yeh Jung-chang on three straight strikes in a rare relief appearance in his final outing.

INDIVIDUAL BATTING LEADERS

	AVG	AB	H	2B	3B	HR	RBI	SB
Peng Cheng-ming , Elephants	.376	338	127	14	3	18	66	26
Chang Tai-shan, Bulls	.337	377	127	21	0	21	94	14
Huang Chung-yi, Bulls	.312	356	111	16	1	11	57	4
Chen Rei-cheng, Elephants	.304	319	97	13	0	2	44	7
Yang Seng, Lions	.293	396	116	18	3	4	47	19
Chen Chih-yuan, Elephants	.288	393	113	18	7	12	54	20
Shih Chih-wei, Bears	.286	409	117	22	3	1	45	13
Hsieh Jia-shien, Cobras	.285	362	103	24	5	17	67	13
Cheng Jau-hang, Bulls	.279	384	107	22	3	7	54	31
Chi Jung-lin, Whales	.277	372	103	6	3	2	18	30

Other North American Hitters

	AVG	AB	H	2B	3B	HR	RBI	SB
Eduardo Rios, Bears	.271	107	29	3	0	6	19	3

INDIVIDUAL PITCHING LEADERS

	W	L	ERA	G	SV	IP	H	BB	SO
Lin Ying-jeh, Cobras	14	10	1.73	34	3	187	124	61	203
Yang Jien-fu, Bulls	15	6	1.77	27	1	173	118	77	163
Lee Ming-jing, Cobras	6	3	1.87	57	4	125	106	23	79
Pan Wei-luen, Lions	12	8	2.14	29	0	176	145	31	122
Kleber Ojima, Cobras	7	6	2.19	24	0	148	124	43	121
Wang Guo-jing, Whales	6	6	2.66	53	4	129	107	36	125
Jonathan Hurst, Elephants	17	9	2.71	32	3	176	166	45	148
Nakagomi Sin, Elephants	14	6	2.77	26	0	175	169	46	108
Kao Jien-san, Whales	10	11	2.91	32	0	167	161	62	118
Cory Bailey, Bears	11	14	2.95	33	0	211	185	103	127

Other North American Pitchers

	W	L	ERA	G	SV	IP	H	BB	SO
Michael Garcia, Lions	7	1	0.71	53	26	89	51	15	140
Dario Veras, Whales	7	1	0.81	42	20	67	38	16	83
Mel Rojas, Bulls	0	0	1.20	11	3	15	12	5	14
Ben Rivera, Cobras	2	1	1.54	16	4	23	15	8	26
Michael Lyons, Cobras	1	4	2.13	7	0	42	38	16	28
Chris Wright, Bears	6	4	2.27	16	2	99	68	39	88
Jeff Andra, Bulls	6	3	2.43	21	2	85	74	24	68
Isabel Giron, Whales	3	2	2.53	8	0	43	37	16	33
Jonathan Hurst, Elephants	17	9	2.71	32	3	176	166	45	148
Emiliano Giron, Whales	4	2	2.72	18	1	53	41	16	64
Jose Alberro, Lions	8	11	3.05	29	0	157	131	63	111
Osvaldo Martinez, Bulls	12	5	3.40	41	12	156	137	47	162
Donald Lemon, Lions	4	5	3.76	12	0	62	62	22	47

STANDINGS

FIRST HALF

	W	L	T	PCT	GB
President Lions	28	18	4	.609	—
Sinon Bulls	25	22	3	.532	3½
Brother Elephants	26	23	1	.531	3½
Macoto Cobras	26	24	0	.520	4
China Trust Whales	21	27	2	.438	8
La New Bears	18	30	2	.375	11

SECOND HALF

	W	L	T	PCT	GB
Sinon Bulls	27	21	4	.563	—
Brother Elephants	28	22	3	.560	—
President Lions	26	22	1	.542	1
China Trust Whales	24	23	0	.511	2½
La New Bears	22	26	2	.458	5
Macoto Cobras	17	30	2	.362	9½

Sun powers Beijing to another title

The defending champion Beijing Tigers rallied to win three straight games to edge Tainjin 3-2 in the best-of-five 2004 China Baseball League championship series. Led by

CHINA

center fielder Sun Ling-feng, the Tigers managed to survive three must-win games, capping the title with a 4-2 win in Game 5.

Sun had a hand in all four runs, as he scored two runs and drove in another two in Game Five. It was a fitting end for one of the league's top stars, as Sun led the league in hits (55), batting average (.382), runs (39) and stolen bases (31) during the regular season and was named the league's MVP. It was speculated that Sun might possibly get some interest from Japanese teams in the future.

Tianjin and Beijing had tied for the league's best regular season record in the four-team league, which is looked at largely as a way to help develop China's national team, which is gearing up to host the 2008 Olympics.

STANDINGS

	W	L	PCT	GB
Tianjin Lions	21	15	.583	—
Beijing Tigers	21	15	.583	—
Guandong Leopards	20	16	.556	1
Shanghai Golden Eagles	10	26	.278	11

PLAYOFFS: Beijing defeated Tianjin 3-2 in best-of-5 series.

Pitchers lead Grosseto to Italy title

Grosseto dominated professional baseball in Italy in 2004, going 47-7 to win the Serie A/1 pennant and defeating Bologna 4-2 in the best-of-seven Italy Series. It was the Tuscany club's third national championship and first since 1989.

Former big league righthander Jaime Navarro, who **_ITALY_** was the league's regular season leader in wins and tied for first with 150 strikeouts, went the distance in Games One and Four of the Italy Series. He won both contests while allowing just one run in 18 innings and was voted the series MVP.

Navarro, Oklahoma State alumnus David Rollandini and Riccardo De Santis went a combined 41-4, 1.67 for Grosseto, which had a league best 2.01 ERA. Rollandini and Navarro were Serie A/1 debutantes in 2004, but they weren't the only prominent newcomers on the Grosseto squad.

Roberto De Franceschi (.263-3-28) joined the club after spending his entire career with Nettuno. The 39-year old right fielder made his debut in 1984 and the 2004 Italy Series title was his sixth.

Grosseto led the league with a .318 average and Gabriele Ermini won the batting crown in his first season as the club's regular left fielder. Ermini, 28, had spent most of the previous nine seasons at third base. He vacated the hot corner in favor of import Johnny Carvajal.

Parma earned a playoff berth after an uncharacteristic three-year absence from the post-season. But the club batted .172 and was swept in their best-of-seven semifinal against Bologna. Former Rockies farmhand Jesus Matos pitched 16 shutout innings in the series for Bologna and won Games One and Four.

—HARVEY SAHKER

STANDINGS

	W	L	PCT	GB
Grosseto	47	7	.870	—
Bologna	43	11	.796	4
Parma	32	22	.593	15
Nettuno	30	24	.556	17
Rimini	29	25	.537	18
Paterno	24	30	.444	23
San Marino	23	31	.426	24
Modena	23	31	.426	24
Anzio	13	41	.241	34
Rho	6	48	.111	41

PLAYOFFS—Semifinals: Grosseto defeated Nettuno 4-1 and Bologna defeated Parma 4-0 in best-of-7 series. **Final:** Grosseto defeated Bologna 4-2 in best-of-7 series.

INDIVIDUAL BATTING LEADERS

	AVG	AB	R	H	2B	3B	HR	RBI	SB
Ermini, Gabriele, Grosseto	.401	177	30	71	9	2	0	34	3
Ozuna, Rafael, Grosseto	.391	179	45	70	14	6	4	50	7
Solano, Fausto, Bologna	.387	191	38	74	18	2	1	56	13
Ramos, Gizzi, Grosseto	.364	206	46	75	18	2	3	39	7
Francia, David, Grosseto	.345	171	43	59	12	4	1	20	15
Bruzon, Juan Carlos, Paterno	.338	210	39	71	4	4	2	32	8
Tamburro Robert, Modena	.337	184	28	62	13	2	0	27	9
Di Mare, Boris, Paterno	.337	190	25	64	2	0	0	16	2
Buccheri, James, Rimini	.336	152	24	51	6	1	5	29	7
Dallospedale, Davide, Bologna	.333	168	43	56	10	3	0	29	23

INDIVIDUAL PITCHING LEADERS

	W	L	ERA	G	SV	IP	H	BB	SO
Rollandini, David, Grosseto	14	1	1.16	15	0	93	55	32	82
Matos, Jesus, Bologna	14	2	1.20	17	0	127	88	24	150
Navarro, Jaime, Grosseto	15	2	1.76	18	0	133	106	27	150
De Santis, Riccardo, Grosseto	12	1	1.99	18	0	113	78	36	95
Cabalisti, Roberto, Rimini	4	3	2.04	31	4	84	57	27	65
Marchesano, Michael, Rimini	10	5	2.21	18	0	114	87	37	120
Newman, Daniel, Parma	6	2	2.28	23	2	67	48	19	60
Horn, William, San Marino	5	5	2.41	14	1	67	59	16	54
Ventura, Cipriano, Modena	8	7	2.51	18	0	150	130	26	123
Richetti, Carlo, Anzio	3	4	2.63	24	8	68	50	28	68

Record six straight for Neptunus

Neptunus defeated HCAW 3-1 in the 2004 Holland Series to win an unprecedented sixth straight Dutch national championship. It also marked a record fourth consecutive year that the two clubs went head-to-head for the Dutch Major League crown.

Righthander Rob Cordemans started Games One and **_HOLLAND_** Four for Neptunus and allowed only one earned run over 14 innings. He won both games and was voted the Holland Series MVP.

Neptunus also won the 2004 European Cup, which was held in San Marino, Italy. The Rotterdam-based club has now won five straight continental club championships. Australian Tom Becker earned the victory in Neptunus's 8-1 win in the final against Bologna (Italy). Becker has now been the winning pitcher in each of the last three European Cup finals.

HCAW's Sidney de Jong won the batting title at .361, denying Kinheim first baseman and Mariners prospect Greg Halman the Triple Crown. Halman finished at .358-4-41.

Former Orioles and Phillies hurler Calvin Maduro joined HCAW and formed a rare Dutch ex-big league duo with infielder Ralph Milliard. Both played for the Netherlands in the Athens Olympics.

Hague Tornado's southpaw Manny Olivera (9-8, 1.52) was the league's dominant pitcher. The 26-year old Barcelona native and independent league alumnus boasted the best ERA in the DML and also led the league with 142 strikeouts and 12 complete games.

—HARVEY SAHKER

STANDINGS

	W	L	T	PCT	GB
HCAW	34	6	0	.850	—
Neptunus	32	7	1	.813	1½
Hoofddorp Pioniers	27	12	1	.688	6½
Kinheim	24	15	1	.613	9½
Amsterdam Pirates	17	23	0	.425	17
Hague Tornado's	16	24	0	.400	20
Almere	12	26	2	.325	21
Sparta/Feyenoord	9	30	1	.238	24½
Oosterhout Twins	6	34	0	.150	28

PLAYOFFS—Semifinals: Neptunus defeated Hoofddorp Pioniers 3-1 and HCAW defeated Kinheim 3-0 in best-of-5 series. **Final:** Neptunus defeated HCAW 3-1 in best-of-5 series.

WINTER
LEAGUES

Dominicans win again, continue domination of Caribbean Series

BY ERIC EDWARDS

When it comes to the Caribbean Series, the Dominican Republic has established a level of dominance that even the New York Yankees would envy.

For the 10th time in 17 years, the Dominicans claimed the Caribbean Series title in 2003-04, rolling to a 5-1 record in the four-country, double round-robin tournament. The event was played in Santo Domingo, home of the Licey Tigers, the Dominican representative.

"I don't have the words to describe how overwhelmed I am by this," Dominican manager Manny Acta said. "This is the biggest thing that has happened to me in my career."

DAVID STONER

Miguel Tejada

While the Dominican Republic has dominated the Caribbean Series recently, its performance in the 2004 series was far from awe-inspiring—even with a loaded lineup. Twice the Dominicans needed extra innings to pull out victories, and on two other occasions they prevailed by just one run. But the bottom line was good enough for the frenzied, flag-waving throng that filled Santo Domingo's Quisqueya Stadium.

Only two of the 12 games were decided by more than two runs. Eight were decided by one run, and four went into extra innings.

"To be here, to win here and to celebrate here is something you can't put a price on. I would pay to live this again," said Dominican shortstop Miguel Tejada (Orioles), whose team hadn't won the series at home since 1988. "I'm grateful to the Orioles for understanding how important this was to me and letting me play."

With all the big names in the Dominican Republic's lineup, it was the No. 9 hitter in the order, a career minor leaguer imported from the United States, who made himself at home in the clutch in the final game of the series.

After the two hitters ahead of him had failed to convert on a first-and-third, no-out rally in the sixth inning, catcher Brandon Marsters delivered. Marsters (Twins)

singled through the box to score Jose Offerman (Twins) with the winning run, as the Dominicans finished off their sixth series title in the past eight years with a 4-3 victory over Puerto Rico.

Puerto Rico failed to win a game, finishing 0-6. Mexico (4-2) beat Venezuela (3-3) on the final day of the tournament to finish second. The Mexican team would have played the Dominican Republic in a tiebreaker game if the Dominicans had lost to Puerto Rico.

Unlikely Heroes

Marsters and Offerman, who reached base in four of five trips to the plate and scored three of the four Dominican runs, made sure the series didn't go to overtime.

Offerman led off the decisive sixth inning by drawing a walk and taking third on a hit-and-run single by Izzy Alcantara. Puerto Rico's starting pitcher Omar Olivares nearly escaped, striking out Mendy Lopez (Royals) and getting Abraham

2004 CARIBBEAN SERIES

Santo Domingo, Dominican Republic
Feb. 3-8, 2004

ROUND-ROBIN STANDINGS

	W	L	PCT	GB
Dominican Republic (Licey)	5	1	.833	—
Mexico (Culiacan)	4	2	.667	1
Venezuela (Aragua)	3	3	.500	2
Puerto Rico (Ponce)	0	6	.000	5

INDIVIDUAL BATTING LEADERS
(Minimum 17 Plate Appearances)

	AVG	AB	R	H	2B	3B	HR	RBI	SB
Rivera, Carlos, PR	.364	22	3	8	1	0	1	1	1
Buck, John, Dom. Rep.	.353	17	0	6	1	0	0	2	1
Alcantara, Israel, Dom. Rep.	.348	23	4	8	0	0	1	4	0
Gil, Benji, Mexico	.346	26	4	9	3	0	1	2	0
Cabrera, Miguel, Venez.	.333	24	3	8	3	1	0	2	0
Rios, Eduardo, Venez.	.333	24	5	8	1	1	2	3	0
Ordonez, Magglio, Venez.	.318	22	3	7	0	0	1	3	1
Ortiz, David, Dom. Rep.	.300	20	2	6	2	0	0	3	0
Lopez, Luis, PR	.296	27	4	8	3	0	2	5	0
Amezcua, Adan, Mexico	.292	24	1	7	1	0	0	4	0
Macias, Jose, Mexico	.286	28	4	8	2	1	1	3	1
Nieves, Melvin, Mexico	.286	14	4	4	1	0	1	4	0
Furcal, Rafael, Dom. Rep.	.263	19	3	5	0	1	0	1	0
Offerman, Jose, Dom. Rep.	.263	19	3	5	2	0	0	5	1
Pascucci, Val, PR	.263	19	4	5	1	0	1	2	0

INDIVIDUAL PITCHING LEADERS
(Minimum 5 Innings)

	W	L	ERA	G	SV	IP	H	BB	SO
Campos, Francisco, Mexico	0	0	0.00	1	0	6	3	4	5
Jimenez, Jose, Dom. Rep.	1	0	0.00	1	0	6	3	2	6
Ayala, Luis, Mexico	1	0	0.00	4	2	6	2	4	6
Hernandez, Jose, Venez.	0	0	0.00	2	0	6	4	1	4
Dessens, Elmer, Mexico	1	0	1.29	1	0	7	6	0	4
Serrano, Elio, Venez.	0	0	1.42	4	0	6	4	1	3
Burgos, Jose, PR	0	0	1.80	2	0	5	4	1	7
Roque, Rafael, Dom. Rep.	0	0	1.80	1	0	5	2	4	6
Soriano, Rafael, Dom. Rep.	1	0	2.92	2	0	12	7	1	9
Lopez, Rodrigo, Mexico	1	0	3.00	1	0	6	5	2	4

2003-04 WINTER LEAGUE ALL-STARS

Selected by Baseball America

Pos.	Player, Team (League)	Organization	AVG	AB	H	HR	RBI	SB
C	Guillermo Quiroz, Aguilas (Venez.)	Blue Jays	.299	144	43	11	24	0
1B	Juan Diaz, Caguas (P.R.)	Twins	.277	224	62	20	54	2
2B	D'Angelo Jimenez, Licey (D.R.)	Reds	.336	217	73	3	32	6
3B	Luis D. Figueroa, Carolina (P.R.)	Mariners	.422	128	54	2	24	2
SS	Omar Infante, Oriente (Venez.)	Tigers	.345	229	79	7	34	13
OF	Jason Dubois, Mesa (AFL)	Cubs	.358	120	43	9	29	2
OF	Ross Gload, Hermosillo (Mexico)	White Sox	.328	232	76	12	51	3
OF	Alexis Rios, Caguas (P.R.)	Blue Jays	.332	229	76	16	51	2
DH	Robert Perez, Lara (Venez.)	None	.295	353	104	23	66	12

			W-L	ERA	IP	H	BB	SO
SP	Francisco Campos, Mazatlan (Mex.)	White Sox	11-2	1.78	127	106	38	100
SP	Dicky Gonzalez, Carolina (P.R.)	Devil Rays	3-1	1.68	70	57	10	78
SP	Edwin Hurtado, Lara (Venez.)	Padres	9-4	2.16	121	97	25	102
SP	Rafael Soriano, Escogido (D.R.)	Mariners	2-1	0.82	55	26	19	34
RP	Francisco Rodriguez, La Guaira (Venez.)	Angels	14 SV	2.60	45	33	14	79

Big season prepares Rios for Toronto

Plenty of Latin American players grow up wanting to play in the Caribbean Series more than they'd like to reach a World Series because the former means they get to represent their home country on an international stage.

PLAYER *of the* **YEAR**

Alexis Rios, however, turned down an opportunity to play in the 2004 Caribbean Series. It wasn't because he didn't want to play for his native Puerto Rico; he just needed some rest. It was quite a year for the Blue Jays outfield prospect, who played a combined 199 games between the Double-A Eastern League regular season and playoffs, the 2003 Olympic Games qualifying tournament and the Puerto Rican League season and playoffs.

Rios said he was too exhausted to join Ponce in the Caribbean Series after it eliminated his team, Caguas, in the Puerto Rican playoffs. But he never showed evidence of that during the sea-

son. He led the Puerto Rican League with 37 RBIs, ranked second in batting at .348 and tied for second with 12 homers to earn MVP honors. He stayed hot through the playoffs, hitting .297-4-14 in 74 at-bats. That performance earned Rios, 23, Baseball America's 2003-04 Winter Player of the Year Award.

"He has power to all fields, with big, long arms, but his swing is not real long," said an NL scout who watched Rios in Puerto Rico. "He has a quick bat, and he can hit the fastball . . . and hit the good fastball."

Rios parlayed his strong winter into a big league job in 2004, making the jump from Triple-A Syracuse to Toronto in late May. He hit .286-1-28 for the Blue Jays in 428 at-bats.

Alexis Rios

PREVIOUS WINNERS

1985-1986—Wally Joyner, 1b, Mayaguez (Puerto Rico)
1986-1987—Vicente Palacios, rhp, Mexicali (Mexican Pacific)
1987-1988—Jose Nunez, rhp, Escogido (Dominican Republic)
1988-1989—Phil Stephenson, 1b, Zulia (Venezuela)
1989-1990—Edgar Martinez, 3b, San Juan (Puerto Rico)
1990-1991—Henry Rodriguez, of, Licey (Dominican Republic)
1991-1992—Wilson Alvarez, lhp, Zulia (Venezuela)
1992-1993—Matias Carrillo, of, Mexicali (Mexican Pacific)
1993-1994—John Hudek, rhp, Magallanes (Venezuela)
1994-1995—Carlos Delgado, c, San Juan (Puerto Rico)
1995-1996—Darryl Brinkley, of, Mexicali (Mexican Pacific)
1996-1997—Bartolo Colon, rhp, Aguilas (Dominican Republic)
1997-1998—Jose Hernandez, ss, Mayaguez (Puerto Rico)
1998-1999—Bob Abreu, of, Caracas (Venezuela)
1999-2000—Morgan Burkhart, 1b, Navojoa (Mexican Pacific)
2000-2001—Courtney Duncan, rhp, Caguas (Puerto Rico)
2001-2002—Ramon Hernandez, c, Pastora (Veneuzuela)
2003-2004—Arnie Munoz, lhp, Aguilas (Dominican Republic)

Nunez (Marlins) to pop out to shallow center field before Marsters poked a first-pitch sinker back up the middle to plate the game-winner.

Relievers Guillermo Mota (Dodgers) and Francis Beltran (Cubs) came on to protect the lead for Dominican starter Rafael Soriano (Mariners), who was touched for two early home runs, but stymied Puerto Rico over his final three innings of work.

Puerto Rico put runners on first and second with one out against Beltran in the ninth, but the hard-throwing righthander struck out Raul Gonzalez (Mets) and Val Pascucci (Expos) to end the game and start the Dominican Republic celebration.

Winless Puerto Rico lost four times by one run but put up a game fight against its arch-rivals in the final game.

As they did in each of their one-run losses, the Puerto Ricans took the lead early but faltered behind doses of shoddy defense and unproductive at-bats in the clutch.

Puerto Rico scored in the first inning when Carlos Baerga (Indians) tripled and scored on an error by Tejada. Puerto Rico added a solo home run by Pascucci in the second and another by Luis Lopez (Expos) in the fourth to jump out to a 3-1 lead.

By then the Dominicans were starting to figure Olivares out. Having already walked and scored on a single by Lopez to get the Dominican Republic on the board in the third inning, Offerman doubled and scored on a hit by Alcantara in the fourth to close the gap to 3-2.

Marsters began the fifth with the first of three straight singles against Olivares and scored on an errant throw to third base by Puerto Rico right fielder Juan LeBron to tie

Jose Offerman

the game.

Soriano allowed three runs over seven innings for the win. Olivares gave up 10 hits and four runs over six innings to take the loss.

Mexico Takes Second Place

In a country where Santeria, or black magic, is such a part of the culture, the rock-hard and pock-marked field at Quisqueya Stadium was never that generous in Mexico's two one-run losses to the Dominicans.

Playing for the right to sweat out the result of the Dominican Republic-Puerto Rico matchup and a possible tie-breaking game, Mexico got another outstanding effort from its bullpen, plus its first fortunate bounce of the tournament.

Mexico ended up edging Venezuela 6-5 when a perfect one-hop throw from right fielder Miguel Cabrera (Marlins) skipped off the leg of Mexican catcher Miguel Ojeda (Padres) as he slid into third base, bounding far enough away for Ojeda to scurry across the plate with the winning run.

It also benefited from the absence of Venezuela's best player; outfielder Magglio Ordonez (White Sox) flew to Miami just before the game for a prior engagement.

Mexico reliever Marc Kroon (Rockies) retired all eight batters he faced in relief of starter Rigo Beltran (Expos), and Luis Ayala (Expos) picked up his second save in as many days. Ayala was effective despite working 2⅔ innings in Mexico's 6-5 victory over Puerto Rico the night before.

"The only two games we lost were to the Dominicans, and look at the way we lost them," Mexico manager Paquin Estrada said. "We have nothing to be ashamed of."

Venezuela, which missed the 2003 series because of a nationwide strike, was again a hard-luck loser. All three of its losses in the tournament were by one run.

"A hit here or a pitch there and we could have won

this thing," Venezuela manager Welby Bailey said.

After instability in Venezuela marred the 2002-2003 winter baseball season, the 2003-2004 winter season was relatively stable. Venezuela returned to action, which enabled the Caribbean Series to return to its traditional format of taking the league champions from the four Caribbean Leagues. A year earlier, general strikes forced the early shutdown of the Venezuelan League, which forced host Puerto Rico to field two teams in the Caribbean Series.

DOMINICAN LEAGUE

In 2002-03, Licey didn't even make the Dominican League's four-team playoffs. But in 2003-04, the Tigers were the class of not only the league but the entire Caribbean.

Licey swept to the Dominican regular-season title and both sets of playoffs, before capturing its record 11th Caribbean Series title.

The Tigers had also won the most titles in Dominican League history, so 2002-03's subpar performance was a sign of the need to improve. They did that by fashioning a lineup filled from nearly top to bottom with major leaguers and former major leaguers. It paid off, as the team went 49-26 and cruised to a 3-1 victory in the best-of-5 championship series against Gigantes.

D'Angelo Jimenez

Licey shortstop D'Angelo Jimenez (Reds) led the league in hitting during the regular season, but former big leaguer Henry Rodriguez was Licey's big bat during the playoffs, as he smacked two home runs and drove in eight while hitting .625 in the championship series. But he got plenty of help from batting champion Jimenez, outfielder Eric Byrnes and outfielder Izzy Alcantara.

Licey's dominance in the championship series helped avert a potential problem. A national strike would have interfered with the final series if it had gone another game. As it was, the series was reduced to a best-of-five affair.

STANDINGS

REGULAR SEASON	W	L	PCT	GB
Licey	30	20	.600	—
Aguilas	28	22	.577	2
Azucareros	26	24	.520	4
Gigantes	26	24	.520	4
Estrellas	25	25	.500	5
Escogido	15	35	.294	15

PLAYOFFS	W	L	PCT	GB
Licey	11	4	.733	—
Gigantes	9	6	.600	2
Aguilas	9	6	.600	2
Azucareros	1	14	.083	10

Championship Series: Licey defeated Gigantes 3-1 in best-of-5 series.

TOP 10 PROSPECTS: 1. Andy Marte, 3b, Escogido (Braves). **2.** Adriano Rosario, rhp, Gigantes (Diamondbacks). **3.** Denny Bautista, rhp, Licey (Orioles). **4.** Victor Diaz, 2b, Aguilas (Mets). **5.** Felix Pie, of, Licey (Cubs). **6.** Ramon Nivar, of, Escogido (Rangers). **7.** Chad Tracy, 3b/of, Azucareros (Diamondbacks). **8.** Jose Capellan, rhp, Escogido (Braves). **9.** Jose Bautista, 3b/of, Licey (Orioles). **10.** Orlando Rodriguez, lhp, Aguilas (Dodgers).

INDIVIDUAL BATTING LEADERS
(Minimum 75 At-Bats)

	AVG	AB	R	H	2B	3B	HR	RBI	SB
Jimenez, D'Angelo, Licey	.360	136	27	49	9	2	2	20	2
Feliz, Pedro, Gigantes	.342	161	26	55	8	1	7	23	3
Gomez, Richard, Gigantes	.331	151	23	50	11	0	2	17	7
Polonia, Luis, Aguilas	.326	175	31	57	11	1	2	16	11
Diaz, Victor, Aguilas	.320	128	17	41	11	1	3	17	6
Fernandez, Alex, Aguilas	.320	125	15	40	5	0	2	20	4
Perez, Neifi, Escogido	.315	108	13	34	6	0	2	14	0
Alcantara, Izzy, Licey	.313	115	14	36	9	0	3	19	0
Olivares, Teuris, Gigantes	.312	109	17	34	7	0	3	13	1
Patterson, Jarrod, Azu.	.312	77	9	24	3	0	1	10	0
Sosa, Juan, Gigantes	.301	103	14	31	7	0	2	10	1
McKay, Cody, Licey	.300	100	6	30	4	1	2	12	0
Ramirez, Julio, Gigantes	.299	177	33	53	3	5	10	29	19
Guerrero, Wilton, Estrellas	.299	144	20	43	10	2	0	10	8
Cesar, Dionys, Aguilas	.298	94	11	28	5	1	3	16	3
Valdez, Wilson, Gigantes	.298	94	14	28	2	2	0	9	2
Febles, Carlos, Azucareros	.296	152	25	45	9	2	2	17	9
Tracy, Andy, Gigantes	.294	119	24	35	8	1	6	21	2
Nivar, Ramon, Escogido	.293	82	10	24	4	1	0	9	4
Nunez, Abraham, Estrellas	.292	178	36	52	12	0	12	35	7
Pena, Carlos, Licey	.291	134	20	39	8	2	6	28	1
Berroa, Angel, Azucareros	.289	97	11	28	5	1	1	10	6
Pena, Angel, Gigantes	.284	148	30	42	4	1	11	32	0
Ozuna, Pablo, Estrellas	.282	156	24	44	10	1	3	20	8
Offerman, Jose, Licey	.276	105	17	29	2	2	2	16	0
Burke, Jamie, Escogido	.275	91	6	25	2	0	1	10	0
Calzado, Napoleon, Estrellas	.275	91	14	25	5	0	0	8	0
Morales, Francisco, Estrellas	.272	103	14	28	5	0	6	14	0
Gomez, Alexis, Aguilas	.268	164	27	44	5	0	3	15	9
Jose, Felix, Estrellas	.266	143	19	38	6	1	4	22	2
Bautista, Jose, Licey	.265	113	26	30	4	2	2	9	3
Rogers, Ed, Estrellas	.259	112	13	29	3	1	0	11	2
Tracy, Chad, Azucareros	.258	93	11	24	2	1	5	11	1
Peralta, Jhonny, Aguilas	.257	140	21	36	6	1	4	17	3
Martinez, Felix, Aguilas	.256	125	10	32	6	0	1	11	7
German, Esteban, Azu.	.253	182	24	46	4	0	3	17	12
Belliard, Ron, Licey	.253	99	16	25	8	0	0	8	0
Almonte, Wady, Escogido	.250	88	8	22	2	0	0	6	2

INDIVIDUAL PITCHING LEADERS
(Minimum 25 Innings)

	W	L	ERA	G	SV	IP	H	BB	SO
Soriano, Rafael, Escogido	1	1	0.21	8	0	42	19	18	25
Munro, Pete, Azucareros	2	1	1.43	7	0	38	28	9	26
Linton, Doug, Aguilas	3	1	1.48	8	0	49	38	5	34
Perez, Beltran, Gigantes	3	1	1.86	9	0	39	27	13	30
De la Rosa, Maximo, Azu.	1	2	2.05	16	0	31	19	14	28
Yan, Esteban, Estrellas	5	0	2.22	11	0	65	55	9	35
#Vargas, Jose, Aguilas	0	2	2.38	20	13	23	21	7	21
Pena, Juan, Aguilas	3	1	2.48	7	0	40	35	8	25
Saipe, Mike, Azucareros	2	3	2.60	10	0	52	45	14	32
Valdez, Efrain, Estrellas	2	1	2.76	12	0	49	36	19	23
Torres, Salomon, Licey	3	1	2.76	6	0	33	31	10	27
Mateo, Julio, Escogido	2	2	2.79	9	0	42	31	9	24
Lopez, Aquilino, Gigantes	0	2	2.83	20	3	29	27	3	15
Rosario, Adriano, Gigantes	4	4	2.93	9	0	40	32	7	23
Chavez, Wilton, Licey	2	3	3.38	15	0	35	37	9	23
Ellis, Robert, Aguilas	5	2	3.48	9	0	52	59	6	33
Diaz, Felix, Licey	1	0	3.48	7	0	31	27	6	18
Manon, Julio, Licey	2	2	3.54	24	13	28	16	7	26
Roque, Rafael, Licey	0	1	3.58	11	0	38	36	12	40
Valdez, Raul, Gigantes	3	5	3.91	12	0	51	56	15	46
De Paula, Jorge, Escogido	3	2	3.98	7	0	32	36	12	27
Almanzar, Carlos, Azucareros	2	2	4.18	9	0	32	35	9	24
Santos, Victor, Escogido	1	3	4.18	7	0	32	34	12	28
Tejeda, Robinson, Aguilas	1	0	4.20	13	0	30	30	11	26
Cabrera, Jose, Aguilas	3	2	4.32	11	0	33	35	4	20
Yoshii, Masato, Estrellas	0	2	4.34	7	0	29	33	6	19
Nunez, Vladimir, Licey	1	2	4.82	8	0	28	29	5	18
Bautista, Denny, Estrellas	0	4	4.93	10	0	35	25	31	40
Coco, Pascual, Escogido	0	2	5.10	11	0	30	37	12	24
Walk, Mitch, Aguilas	1	2	5.40	12	0	38	45	13	26
Aybar, Manny, Licey	2	2	5.52	12	0	31	35	9	28

MEXICAN PACIFIC LEAGUE

According to the old mantra, good pitching beats good hitting. In the 2003-04 Mexican Pacific League playoffs, great pitching beat good pitching.

Culiacan, which did not win either half of the league's split-season schedule, won the league title over Obregon despite hitting .227 during the five-game championship series, thanks to strong pitching.

The tone of the series was set in Game One, as

Rodrigo Lopez (Orioles), Jose Silva (Cubs) and Luis Ayala (Expos) combined to limit Obregon to four hits and one run in a 2-1 win. Silva pitched 2⅓ scoreless innings of relief for the win and Ayala pitched a perfect ninth for the save.

After Obregon evened the series at 1-1, Oliver Perez (Pirates) allowed only one run in six innings of a 4-1 win, while the combo of Silva and Ayala once again pitched in with three scoreless innings of work.

Jorge Campillo continued Culiacan's pitching domination in Game Four, holding Obregon to one run in six innings in an 8-1 win that put Culiacan up 3-1 in the best-of-seven series. Lopez, Silva and Ayala closed the series out the next night in a 6-4 win, as Silva worked 2⅔ more scoreless innings for the win, while Ayala pitched a perfect ninth for his third save of the series. For the series, Culiacan had a 2.25 ERA. Ayala allowed only one hit in three innings and Silva pitched seven scoreless innings.

That strong pitching carried over into the Caribbean Series, where Mexico finished a surprisingly strong second.

STANDINGS

FIRST HALF	W	L	PCT	GB
Mazatlan	25	10	.714	—
Obregon	20	15	.571	5
Culiacan	19	16	.543	6
Hermosillo	16	18	.471	8½
Guasave	16	18	.471	8½
Los Mochis	16	19	.457	9
Navojoa	15	20	.429	10
Mexicali	12	23	.343	13

SECOND HALF	W	L	PCT	GB
Hermosillo	20	12	.625	—
Obregon	19	14	.576	1½
Culiacan	19	14	.576	1½
Guasave	17	15	.531	3
Navojoa	17	16	.515	3½
Mazatlan	15	18	.455	5½
Mexicali	13	20	.394	7½
Los Mochis	11	22	.333	9½

PLAYOFFS—Quarterfinals: Culiacan defeated Guasave 4-2, Hermosillo defeated Mazatlan 4-3 and Obregon defeated Navojoa 4-1in best-of-7 series. **Semifinals:** Culiacan defeated Hermosillo 4-2 and Obregon defeated Mazatlan 4-2 in best-of-7 series. **Finals:** Culiacan defeated Obregon 4-1 in best-of-7 series.

TOP 10 PROSPECTS: 1. Edgar Huerta, lhp, Culiacan (Padres). **.2.** Edgar Gonzalez, rhp, Obregon (Diamondbacks). **3.** Ross Gload, 1b/of, Hermosillo (White Sox). **4.** Luis C. Garcia, of, Hermosillo (Diamondbacks). **5.** Kevin Youkilis, 3b, Navojoa (Red Sox). **6.** John Gall, 1b, Mazatlan (Cardinals). **7.** Alfredo Amezaga, ss/2b, Obregon (Angels). **8.** Steve Watkins, rhp, Guasave (Padres). **9.** Jason Grabowski, of, Obregon (Rangers). **10.** Sergio Lizarraga, rhp, Culiacan (Diamondbacks).

INDIVIDUAL BATTING LEADERS
(Minimum 105 At-Bats)

	AVG	AB	R	H	2B	3B	HR	RBI	SB
Brown, Emil, Hermosillo	.388	129	27	50	12	0	7	25	6
Pemberton, Rudy, Navojoa	**.346**	191	26	66	12	0	5	27	5
Gload, Ross, Hermosillo	.328	232	36	**76**	10	1	12	**51**	3
Arredondo, Luis, Obregon	.321	196	27	63	7	2	4	22	4
Canizalez, Juan, Hermosillo	.300	223	23	67	14	2	2	24	1
Flores, Miguel, Hermosillo	.297	138	21	41	7	0	3	10	5
Franco, Matt, Hermosillo	.297	128	18	38	6	1	2	8	1
Clapinski, Chris, Mazatlan	.293	123	19	36	5	2	3	21	2
Doster, Dave, Hermosillo	.289	194	30	56	8	1	7	34	2
Pickering, Calvin, Los Mochis	.289	159	28	46	4	0	13	36	0
Gomez, Heber, Mazatlan	.288	208	31	60	13	1	5	17	4
Macias, Jose, Culiacan	.286	245	29	70	12	1	3	25	12
Smith, Demond, Guasave	.285	221	41	63	7	**3**	4	17	19
Clark, Doug, Navojoa	.284	218	26	62	4	2	4	20	14
Vazquez, Jorge, Culiacan	.284	116	14	33	7	0	3	16	0
Carrillo, Matias, Los Mochis	.282	234	34	66	8	0	10	36	3
Robles, Javier, Obregon	.280	214	26	60	12	0	6	29	0
Sherman, Darrell, Culiacan	.280	261	36	73	7	1	1	18	**23**
Verdugo, Vincente, Mazatlan	.280	161	18	45	5	0	0	13	0
Nunnally, Jon, Mazatlan	.279	208	34	58	4	0	12	37	7
Amezaga, Alfredo, Obregon	.279	226	35	63	10	1	1	13	12
White, Derrick, Obregon	.277	224	42	62	10	1	9	38	1
Gil, Geronimo, Obregon	.277	177	24	49	8	0	4	29	0
Saenz, Ricardo, Mexicali	.276	203	31	56	13	0	13	27	0
Amezcua, Adan, Culiacan	.276	185	25	51	7	0	7	18	0
Pellow, Kit, Culiacan	.275	258	42	71	9	0	14	38	2
Robles, Oscar, Navojoa	.275	204	37	56	11	0	7	22	5
Sutton, Larry, Mazatlan	.274	197	33	54	**18**	1	5	31	1
Maxwell, Jason, Obregon	.273	176	27	48	5	0	7	28	1
Mendez, Roberto, Guasave	.273	161	23	44	8	0	6	26	0
Seabol, Scott, Mazatlan	.271	133	25	36	4	0	8	30	0
Garcia, Luis, Obregon	.268	239	32	64	11	0	10	45	4
Saucedo, Robert, Mazatlan	.267	150	12	40	6	0	7	27	1
Brinkley, Darryl, Mexicali	.266	218	31	58	9	0	5	22	13
Garcia, Luis, Hermosillo	.265	166	27	44	9	0	9	34	2
Sandoval, Jose, Hermosillo	.264	220	26	58	6	0	5	32	1
Gall, John, Mazatlan	.264	121	12	32	5	0	3	14	1
Gil, Benji, Culiacan	.262	225	31	59	13	0	8	38	15
Villalobos, Carlos, Guasave	.262	187	16	49	10	0	3	19	0
Santana, Pedro, Guasave	.262	271	27	71	8	2	4	31	11
Fornes, Daniel, Mazatlan	.262	191	31	50	5	0	7	30	2
Santana, Mario, Navojoa	.262	141	15	37	6	0	1	11	3
Smith, Bubba, Mexicali	.260	242	34	63	10	0	11	35	1
Coste, Chris, Obregon	.260	200	19	52	10	1	5	26	1
Youkilis, Kevin, Navojoa	.259	112	12	29	2	0	1	13	2
Orantes, Ramon, Los Mochis	.254	244	28	62	7	0	9	28	1
Quintero, Edgar, Los Mochis	.254	114	14	29	2	2	2	16	5
Mejia, Roberto, Navojoa	.253	241	34	61	14	0	7	34	11
Burkhart, Morgan, Navojoa	.251	231	39	58	8	0	**16**	48	4
Gastelum, Sergio, Mexicali	.251	235	28	59	6	0	3	19	4
Arauz, Leobardo, Guasave	.251	167	16	42	10	3	6	30	2
Diaz, Remigio, Navojoa	.250	192	17	48	6	0	0	16	6
Brena, Jaime, Navojoa	.250	116	12	29	4	0	0	7	2
#Grabowski, Jason, Obregon	.245	229	**43**	56	8	0	9	27	14

INDIVIDUAL PITCHING LEADERS
(Minimum 35 Innings)

	W	L	ERA	G	SV	IP	H	BB	SO
Mullen, Scott, Culiacan	4	1	1.83	8	0	44	37	15	25
Garibay, Salvador, Herm.	3	0	1.83	32	1	39	28	13	16
Elizalde, Carlos, Obregon	5	1	1.91	18	0	57	47	15	48
Campos, Francisco, Mazatlan	**10**	2	**2.19**	14	0	90	79	29	**68**
Cortes, David, Hermosillo	3	2	2.29	28	9	35	26	11	35
Cannon, Jon, Hermosillo	3	1	2.39	9	0	49	26	24	43
Ortega, Pablo, Mazatlan	9	1	2.40	13	0	86	76	26	52
Delgadillo, Juan, Culiacan	4	1	2.40	23	0	41	30	22	31
Moreno, Angel, Hermosillo	4	2	2.43	13	0	56	45	31	23
Montano, Ignacio, Guasave	1	1	2.48	26	0	36	38	22	32
Diaz, Ralph, Los Mochis	1	3	2.50	22	6	40	33	15	34
Corey, Bryan, Mazatlan	0	2	2.58	37	**21**	38	32	17	33
Dingman, Craig, Obregon	3	2	2.61	33	19	38	29	10	49
Guzman, Jesus, Culiacan	8	1	2.62	22	1	69	55	25	37
Gomez, Martin, Los Mochis	3	1	2.65	30	0	54	51	19	18
Beltran, Rigo, Culiacan	5	1	2.86	11	0	63	46	27	54
Alvarez, Octavio, Navojoa	6	3	2.90	12	0	78	74	24	35
Flores, Ignacio, Gsv-Nav.	2	2	2.91	38	1	41	25	22	29
Lizarraga, Sergio, Culiacan	0	2	2.95	15	0	37	36	13	29
Campillo, Jorge, Culiacan	5	2	2.98	12	0	63	60	18	53
Elvira, Narciso, Hermosillo	3	5	3.07	14	0	76	58	28	47
Prieto, Ariel, Obregon	4	3	3.15	12	0	71	63	22	44
Mendoza, Mario, Navojoa	3	4	3.16	20	0	63	60	28	30
Chavez, Carlos, Los Mochis	3	5	3.18	36	6	40	38	17	30
Izquierdo, Hansel, Guasave	4	6	3.28	15	0	85	79	37	56
Patrick, Bronswell, Los Mochis	6	4	3.36	13	0	83	86	24	42
Watkins, Steve, Guasave	6	3	3.53	12	0	71	68	25	63
Reyes, Nate, Mexicali	2	5	3.57	18	0	58	63	21	27
Beltran, Alonso, Obregon	3	3	3.65	14	0	74	60	37	45
Moreno, Claudio, Mexicali	6	5	3.67	14	0	83	75	29	56
Palafox, Juan, Obr.-Mex.	5	5	3.90	13	0	67	68	16	35
Tequida, Mauricio, Navojoa	2	0	3.98	15	0	41	40	18	19

PUERTO RICAN LEAGUE

As he started his climb through the minors, Puerto Rican fans rarely got a chance to watch hometown hero Alexis Rios in person.

The Blue Jays prospect was the team's top draft pick in 1999, but he missed the 2001 and 2002 winter ball seasons with hand and arm injuries. But in 2003, Rios gave his home fans a taste of what U.S. minor league fans had

already seen. Rios finished second in the league in batting and home runs while leading the league in RBIs, paving the way for his eventual promotion to Toronto early in the 2004 season.

"I've missed out on this opportunity the past two winters," Rios said during the winter league season. "Every step along the way is a learning experience. My goal is within sight and I want to keep improving so I can make an impact when I do get called up."

The biggest question about Rios entering the winter season was whether he would keep up his power production. He answered some of those questions by leading the league in totals bases (106) and slugging percentage (.648). Overall, he hit .348-12-37 in 39 games.

"The kid has a world of talent; you could see that from the start," Caguas manager Mako Oliveras said. "The biggest difference is his maturity. Both physically and mentally, he has made great strides. He thrives on being the guy at the plate in clutch situations, and the ball is really flying off his bat."

Led by Rios and veteran righthander Omar Olivares, Caguas finished the regular season with the best record in the league, then cruised through the semifinals, going 9-3 in the four-team round-robin format. But in the championship series, Ponce, which had nipped at Caguas' heels during the regular season and the semifinals, outlasted Caguas for the title.

STANDINGS

REGULAR SEASON	W	L	PCT	GB
Caguas	28	20	.583	—
Ponce	28	21	.571	½
Santurce	27	23	.540	2
San Juan	27	23	.540	2
Carolina	24	25	.490	4½
Mayaguez	14	36	.280	15
PLAYOFFS	W	L	PCT	GB
Caguas	9	3	.750	—
Ponce	8	4	.667	1
Santurce	6	6	.500	3
San Juan	1	11	.083	8

CHAMPIONSHIP SERIES: Ponce defeated Caguas 5-2 in best-of-9 series.

TOP 10 PROSPECTS: 1. Alexis Rios, of, Caguas (Blue Jays). **2.** Bobby Jenks,rhp, San Juan (Angels). **3.** Adam LaRoche, 1b, Mayaguez (Braves). **4.** Michael Restovich, of, Carolina (Twins). **5.** Termel Sledge, of, Ponce (Expos). **6.** Justin Lehr, rhp, Ponce (Athletics). **7.** Justin Morneau, 1b, Carolina (Twins). **8.** Raymar Diaz, rhp, Santurce (Astros). **9.** Yadier Molina, c, Carolina (Cardinals). **10.** Simon Pond, 1b, Santurce (Blue Jays).

INDIVIDUAL BATTING LEADERS
(Minimum 75 At-Bats)

	AVG	AB	R	H	2B	3B	HR	RBI	SB
Figueroa, Luis Daniel, Carolina	**.422**	128	23	54	13	0	2	24	2
Lucca, Lou, San Juan	.368	106	26	39	5	0	11	27	1
Cancel, Robinson, Ponce	.363	80	14	29	4	0	3	11	2
Rios, Alexis, Caguas	.348	155	36	54	8	4	12	**37**	2
Bocachica, Hiram, Ponce	.339	109	21	37	8	0	6	16	7
LaRoche, Adam, Mayaguez	.333	96	18	32	6	0	7	20	1
Rodriguez, John, Santurce	.327	110	22	36	6	1	8	25	3
Sledge, Termel, Ponce	.326	95	18	31	8	0	3	12	1
McDonald, Donzell, San Juan	.325	160	38	52	8	5	6	21	**13**
Saenz, Olmedo, Carolina	.324	170	31	**55**	**17**	0	4	32	1
Garcia, Omar, San Juan	.323	133	26	43	8	0	10	28	0
Lopez, Luis, Ponce	.323	158	22	51	14	1	7	25	0
Clemente, Edgar, Carolina	.320	103	25	33	7	2	6	29	8
Pachot, John, Caguas	.319	116	12	37	9	0	4	28	0
Molina, Yadier, Carolina	.317	126	12	40	9	0	2	18	0
Ortiz, Hector, Caguas	.315	89	7	28	4	1	0	8	0
Candelaria, Ben, Santurce	.314	86	22	27	5	0	11	31	1
Nieves, Wilbert, Mayaguez	.311	103	14	32	3	0	1	17	2
Wathan, Derek, Mayaguez	.309	94	13	29	4	2	2	11	3

	AVG		R	H	2B	3B	HR	RBI	SB
Negron, Miguel, Caguas	.307	127	17	39	3	1	2	13	8
Diaz, Juan, Caguas	.307	150	29	46	10	1	12	35	2
Pagan, Angel, Ponce	.302	126	22	38	2	3	2	12	6
Rodriguez, Boi, Mayaguez	.300	120	12	36	8	1	3	18	7
Guzman, Edwards, Santurce	.299	174	27	52	9	0	7	24	3
Figueroa, Luis, Mayaguez	.298	141	20	42	6	1	3	14	4
Restovich, Michael, Carolina	.298	84	16	25	8	2	3	16	0
Munoz, Jose, Caguas	.294	153	26	45	11	0	3	14	8
Rodriguez, Victor, Carolina	.294	143	20	42	7	1	3	21	5
Martinez, Gabby, Ponce	.293	92	9	27	7	1	1	11	6
Bloomquist, Willie,. Mayaguez	.289	83	14	24	4	2	1	8	6
Valentin, John, Caguas	.289	97	18	28	8	0	8	16	0
Flores, Jose, Santurce	.287	129	21	37	9	0	0	11	10
Nieves, Raul, Ponce	.286	77	17	22	4	1	1	7	0
Marrero, Oreste, San Juan	.285	130	26	37	3	0	**14**	33	0
Espada, Josue, Carolina	.284	116	27	33	4	2	2	14	7
Gotay, Ruben, Carolina	.284	109	19	31	9	2	2	12	6
Matos, Julius, Mayaguez	.283	159	15	45	8	1	3	21	2
Velazquez, Juan, Mayaguez	.280	125	15	35	8	2	1	10	0
Sanchez, Agustin, San Juan	.277	101	16	28	4	0	1	10	0
Benitez, Yamil, San Juan	.276	123	16	34	11	0	7	19	0
Feliciano, Jesus, Santurce	.273	74	11	21	3	3	0	8	1
Diaz, Alex, Mayaguez	.270	152	19	41	3	0	8	19	2
Ortiz, Nick, Santurce	.269	93	14	25	8	1	1	8	4
Castro, Ramon, Santurce	.267	90	13	24	2	0	8	25	0
Pond, Simon, Santurce	.266	143	26	38	7	1	10	29	3
Cruz, Enrique, Ponce	.265	102	17	27	5	0	2	11	2
Curry, Mike, Mayaguez	.265	83	11	22	6	1	0	3	8
Diaz, Edwin, Santurce	.262	168	**40**	44	9	0	9	34	3
Padilla, Jorge, Caguas	.257	109	17	28	4	0	0	9	7
Cardona, Javier, Sant.-SJ	.256	90	8	23	4	0	3	10	0
Molina, Felix, Caguas	.256	90	9	23	5	1	2	10	3
Gonzalez, Raul, San Juan	.255	153	23	39	4	1	12	32	4

INDIVIDUAL PITCHING LEADERS
(Minimum 25 Innings)

	W	L	ERA	G	SV	IP	H	BB	SO
#Lehr, Justin, Ponce	1	1	1.11	19	**8**	32	17	7	17
Gonzalez, Dicky, Carolina	3	0	**1.33**	10	0	61	47	6	**64**
Small, Aaron, Santurce	4	0	2.09	8	0	47	37	11	27
Jacome, Jason, San Juan	3	3	2.56	10	0	56	40	17	40
Jenks, Bobby, San Juan	**5**	1	3.14	11	1	52	33	33	47
Cameron, Ryan, Caguas	0	1	3.18	10	0	34	24	17	16
Padilla, Juan, Caguas	0	2	3.38	23	2	29	27	10	20
Martinez, Miguel, Santurce	3	1	3.52	15	0	31	25	10	27
Vazquez, William, Santurce	1	3	3.53	10	0	36	33	14	17
#Feliciano, Pedro, Ponce	**5**	2	3.76	20	1	26	28	7	25
Alvarado, Giancarlo, Ponce	2	3	3.76	8	0	41	33	20	20
Smith, Chuck, Santurce	0	1	3.82	8	0	33	38	14	27
Rodriguez, Frank, Mayaguez	2	4	3.83	10	0	52	61	19	27
Gissell, Chris, San Juan	4	3	3.86	10	0	54	61	8	44
Nieves, Roberto, Ponce	1	2	3.86	9	0	28	18	16	17
Santiago, Jose, Carolina	4	2	3.89	21	5	37	39	21	29
Mercado, Hector, Ponce	2	2	3.91	8	0	46	44	18	30
Olivares, Omar, Caguas	**5**	2	3.91	8	0	46	39	7	34
Simon, Ben, Carolina	1	1	3.97	10	0	34	43	9	21
Flores, Randy, San Juan	0	1	4.15	10	0	30	37	13	19
Miranda, Angel, Caguas	1	1	4.15	11	0	35	40	9	24
Albaladejo, Jonathan, Maya.	3	3	4.54	8	0	40	47	10	31
Arroyo, Luis, San Juan	2	3	4.58	10	1	37	47	10	25
Collazo, William, Carolina	3	4	4.65	13	1	50	57	12	37
Osborne, Donovan, Caguas	0	1	4.71	7	0	29	25	11	18
Looney, Brian, Santurce	2	2	4.81	9	0	43	55	13	29
Enochs, Chris, Ponce	1	2	4.83	9	0	41	49	19	29
Rojas, Chris, Mayaguez	1	4	4.86	9	0	33	48	17	13
Villegas, Felix, Santurce	1	3	5.10	18	1	30	26	12	22
Navarro, Jaime, Caguas-SJ	2	6	5.23	11	0	53	58	15	41
Burgos, John, Ponce	3	0	5.28	7	0	31	40	10	19
Santiago, Tomas, Mayaguez	0	5	5.28	17	1	29	33	16	22

VENEZUELAN LEAGUE

Miguel Cabrera's year to remember didn't end in Game Six of the 2003 World Series.

The toast of Miami was also the toast of Aragua, thanks in part to his two-homer performance in the deciding game of the Venezuelan League playoffs as he drove in all four runs in Aragua's 4-1 win over Oriente in Game Six of the Venezuelan League finals.

Cabrera's two home runs provided more than enough runs for Andrew Lorraine, who allowed only one hit and one run in 5⅓ innings of work for the win, surviving a 40-

WINTER LEAGUES

minute delay when the lights went out. Francisco Butto, a Phillies prospect who emerged during the Venezuelan season, closed out the game with a scoreless ninth.

It was a happy ending to a Venezuelan season that helped start to erase the troubles of 2002-03. A year earlier, a general strike forced the league to shut down roughly two-thirds of the way through the season, canceling the playoffs and keeping the league from sending a representative to the Caribbean Series.

Cabrera didn't begin playing in Venezuela until late in the season, as he took some time to wind down after helping lead the Marlins to the World Series title. But once he arrived, he lived up to the expectations of his countrymen. In 15 regular-season games, he hit .327-4-11. He was even better once the playoffs began. He hit .288-7-15 in 20 playoff games and scored the only run in a 1-0 win in Game Five before his Game Six heroics.

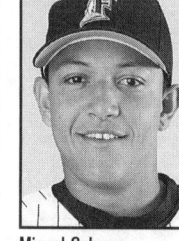

Miguel Cabrera

While Cabrera lived up to expectations, Butto was a revelation. He went 6-1, 0.96 with eight saves, striking out 36 while walking only five in 37 innings in the regular season, and batters hit only .168 off of the 21-year-old righthander. Despite working as a reliever, he finished third in the league in wins, while also ranking third in saves. In the playoffs, he saved six more games.

Another former World Series hero, Francisco Rodriguez (Angels), also left his mark, as Rodriguez was named the league's Rookie of the Year. He went 2-1, 2.62 with eight saves and 59 strikeouts in 34 innings for La Guaria. Rodriguez edged Alberto Callaspo (Angels), who hit .333-0-16 for Oriente.

STANDINGS

DIVISION OCCIDENTE	W	L	PCT	GB
Occidente Pastora	35	27	.565	—
Aragua Tigres	34	28	.548	1
Lara Cardenales	30	32	.484	5
Zulia Aguilas	22	40	.355	13
DIVISION ORIENTAL	**W**	**L**	**PCT**	**GB**
Oriente Caribes	33	29	.532	—
Caracas Leones	33	29	.532	—
La Guaira Tiburones	33	29	.532	—
Magallanes Navigators	28	34	.452	5
PLAYOFFS	**W**	**L**	**PCT**	**GB**
Aragua Tigres	10	6	.625	—
Oriente Caribes	10	6	.625	—
La Guaira Tiburones	8	8	.500	2
Caracas Leones	6	10	.375	4
Occidente Pastora	6	10	.375	4

Championship Series: Aragua defeated Oriente 4-2 in best-of-7 series.

TOP 10 PROSPECTS: 1. Felix Hernandez, rhp, Lara (Mariners). **2.** Franklin Gutierrez, of, Caracas (Dodgers). **3.** Alberto Callaspo, 2b, Oriente (Angels). **4.** Guillermo Quiroz, c, Zulia (Blue Jays). **5.** Fernando Nieve, rhp, Oriente (Astros). **6.** Hector Gimenez, c, Magallanes (Astros). **7.** Jose Lopez, ss, Magallanes (Mariners). **8.** Alex Romero, of, Aragua (Twins). **9.** Francisco Butto, rhp, Aragua (Phillies). **10.** Jose Castillo, 2b/ss, Caracas (Pirates).

INDIVIDUAL BATTING LEADERS
(Minimum 93 At-Bats)

	AVG	AB	R	H	2B	3B	HR	RBI	SB
Scutaro, Marcos, Caracas	**.359**	181	35	65	**17**	2	2	25	10
Rivera, Juan, Aragua	.351	114	22	40	10	0	5	17	0
Landaeta, Luis, Occidente	.346	231	38	**80**	14	2	14	45	5
Infante, Omar, Oriente	.343	233	**53**	**80**	13	2	7	34	13
Callaspo, Alberto, Oriente	.343	140	25	48	9	1	0	18	1
Salazar, Ruben, Aragua	.337	202	32	68	10	0	6	22	0
Chavez, Endy, Magallanes	.331	124	18	41	3	2	0	6	7
Rodriguez, Liu, La Guaira	.330	188	25	62	13	1	0	29	3
Leach, Jalal, Lara	.330	200	27	66	13	2	5	32	1
Sojo, Luis, Lara	.326	175	19	57	10	0	1	24	3
Valderrama, Carlos, Occ.	.325	126	26	41	12	0	5	14	4
Gonzalez, Luis, Oriente	.321	193	34	62	12	3	8	51	0
Maldoando, Carlos, Zulia	.321	134	19	43	4	1	6	21	0
Olmedo, Rainer, La Guaira	.318	107	17	34	4	3	0	14	0
Ugueto, Luis, Lara	.318	157	21	50	8	3	0	16	6
Redman, Tike, Zulia	.313	195	35	61	12	3	2	15	4
Freire, Alejandro, Zulia	.310	213	29	66	10	3	9	38	4
Alvarez, Nick, La Guaira	.309	178	32	55	9	0	5	23	3
Mendez, Carlos, Caracas	.309	136	17	42	6	1	3	19	0
Prieto, Alex, Caracas	.308	143	24	44	5	1	2	11	2
Langaigne, Selwyn, Lara	.308	211	31	65	11	3	5	27	3
Garcia, Douglas, Zulia	.308	117	17	36	8	2	2	15	1
Gibson, Derrick, Occidente	.307	150	21	46	5	0	10	26	0
Perez, Robert, Lara	.307	251	42	77	14	2	**15**	42	10
Perez, Tomas, Caracas	.306	206	38	63	9	2	6	36	1
Wilson, Travis, La Guaira	.303	175	29	53	10	1	9	36	1
Hernandez, Carlos, Mag.	.299	201	25	60	9	1	2	24	7
Quiroz, Guillermo, Zulia	.297	145	24	43	5	1	11	24	0
Reyes, Rene, Caracas	.297	229	42	68	13	**6**	9	37	3
Torrealba, Steve, Lara	.295	95	15	28	9	0	0	15	0
Radmanovich, Ryan, La G.	.294	109	19	32	8	1	6	17	0
Salazar, Oscar, Occidente	.292	195	38	57	11	3	8	27	1
Colon, Cris, La Guaira	.290	93	9	27	7	0	2	14	0
Swann, Pedro, Caracas	.289	218	25	63	8	0	5	26	1
Alfonzo, Eliezer, Oriente	.287	223	31	64	11	0	12	**53**	1
Romero, Alex, Aragua	.286	147	17	42	9	2	0	10	3
Bolivar, Papo, Aragua	.284	155	24	44	5	0	5	21	3
Raven, Luis, La Guaira	.281	210	26	59	7	0	9	30	1
Gimenez, Hector, Magallanes	.280	150	19	42	7	2	4	22	1
Blanco, Henry, Caracas	.276	203	36	56	**17**	2	11	51	0
Acuna, Ron, Magallanes	.276	196	26	54	9	4	4	24	3
Nieves, Jose, Occidente	.275	138	13	38	5	2	2	15	1
Colina, Javier, Occidente	.274	215	26	59	15	3	5	28	1
Paz, Richard, Magallanes	.273	121	19	33	7	1	1	11	4
Evans, Tom, Lara	.271	133	28	36	5	1	10	27	0
Raines, Tim, Aragua	.270	115	20	31	6	2	2	11	8
Castro, Ramon, Aragua	.265	170	33	45	9	2	2	13	5
#Snead, Esix, Oriente	.260	169	34	44	9	3	2	15	**15**

INDIVIDUAL PITCHING LEADERS
(Minimum 31 Innings)

	W	L	ERA	G	SV	IP	H	BB	SO
Butto, Francisco, Aragua	6	1	0.96	28	8	37	21	5	36
Nieve, Fernando, Oriente	4	1	1.88	7	0	38	24	8	46
Hurtado, Edwin, Lara	**8**	3	**2.08**	14	0	99	72	20	**86**
Serrano, Elio, Oriente	2	2	2.45	28	**14**	40	33	11	37
Murray, Dan, Aragua	3	1	2.48	14	0	58	50	19	40
Rodriguez, Francisco, La Guaira	2	1	2.62	24	8	34	26	10	59
Moreno, Victor, Aragua	1	1	2.65	26	0	34	31	13	34
Urdaneta, Lino, Caracas	0	1	2.70	30	6	33	28	12	18
Yofu, Tetsu, Oriente	0	2	2.83	8	0	35	29	21	31
Ovalles, Juan, Caracas	3	1	2.97	30	1	39	36	15	42
Pulido, Juan, Aragua	6	3	3.01	14	0	81	65	16	71
Garcia, Rosman, Aragua	4	4	3.08	10	0	50	49	13	28
Cummings, Jeremy, Zulia	3	4	3.25	11	0	53	54	9	33
Palma, Rick, Occidente	5	2	3.25	15	0	80	80	25	64
Pulsipher, Bill, La Guaira	4	1	3.40	13	0	53	66	18	34
Estrada, Horacio, Aragua	3	3	3.47	13	0	60	60	12	48
Quevedo, Ruben, Magallanes	2	3	3.50	9	0	44	37	15	33
Torrealba, Yoann, Occidente	0	3	3.55	29	7	33	34	10	20
Mata, Gustavo, La Guaira	4	1	3.66	15	0	52	52	12	35
Bouknight, Kip, Occidente	2	2	3.67	9	0	49	46	16	39
Winchester, Scott, Oriente	4	1	3.70	10	0	58	61	13	38
Duarte, Renny, Oriente	1	2	3.74	20	0	34	32	10	17
Wright, Chris, Occidente	6	2	3.81	14	0	76	70	35	51
Johnson, Mark, Caracas	2	6	3.86	14	0	70	66	21	55
Ahearne, Pat, Caracas	4	2	3.86	10	0	49	52	13	38
Powell, Brian, Magallanes	2	6	3.94	12	0	48	54	9	24
Rayborn, Kenny, Caracas	5	3	3.99	13	0	68	74	20	40
Romero, Josmir, Aragua	4	3	4.02	13	0	47	53	7	36
Lira, Felipe, La Guaira	4	6	4.20	13	0	79	90	16	51
Hernandez, Carlos, Magallanes	3	1	4.21	8	0	36	29	13	39
Pacheco, Delvis, La Guaira	3	1	4.23	25	2	45	50	19	33
Chacin, Gustavo, Lara	3	5	4.36	12	0	64	82	10	64

Statistics in **boldface** indicate league leader
#League leader but non-qualifier

COLLEGE
BASEBALL

Remember the Titans
Cal State Fullerton began the season 15-16 but finished on a 32-6 run to win the fourth national title in school history

Fullerton caps Titanic turnaround with College World Series victory

BY WILL KIMMEY

Cal State Fullerton faced a brutal early season slate that produced a 15-16 record and some scheduling second-guessing from coach George Horton.

Horton's first instinct proved right as Fullerton regrouped once conference play began, going 19-2 in the Big West and winning 32 of its final 38 games thanks to Titanic contributions from catcher Kurt Suzuki and the one-two pitching punch of Jason Windsor and Ricky Romero. The final two victories came against favored Texas in the College World Series.

Fittingly, Romero (14-4, 3.37) won the first game of the championship series before Fullerton finished the sweep with Windsor (13-4, 1.72) throwing his second complete game of the CWS and Suzuki (.413-16-87) driving in the decisive run in a 3-2 title-clinching win.

"Not to take anything away from the other Titans battling in our dugout, but what a fitting conclusion to have Jason Windsor on the mound to win it and Kurt Suzuki getting the winning hit," Fullerton coach George Horton said. "That's the way to win it."

Suzuki, a first-team All-American, was mired in a 2-for-22 CWS slump before living up to his Kurt Klutch nickname. He shot a single to left field to drive home the deciding run.

"There's no mystery that I had nothing to show for the series before that," Suzuki said. "I knew I just wanted to hit the ball somewhere. I had frustrations, but I couldn't

let that bother me. I had 24 other teammates that I was trying to win a national championship for. This is why I came to Cal State Fullerton, to be in this type of game and this type of situation."

It marked the first national title as a head coach for Horton, who served as an assistant on the 1995 Titans championship team coached by Augie Garrido, who has since moved on to Texas. Fullerton became the sixth school to win at least four titles, joining Southern California (12), Arizona State (five), Louisiana State (five), Texas (five) and Miami (four).

Windsor dominated the CWS and earned Most Outstanding Player honors, allowing just two runs in 21 innings while notching two wins and a three-inning save. He racked up 29 strikeouts against six walks while throwing 322 pitches in a nine-day span.

"I look at it on paper and I don't believe it's me," said Windsor, who won his final 12 starts of the season, a string that coincided with Fullerton's rebound from the 15-16 start. "It just feels great."

Romero experienced similar success, winning both of his starts while allowing six runs in 16 innings.

Jason Windsor

Out Of Their Depth

Texas entered the best-of-three championship series with a decided pitching edge. The Longhorns staff was the nation's deepest, and Texas had played one less game to reach the finals than the Titans.

"Pitching-wise they go eight or nine deep," Horton

JOE MIXAN

Mastering his mentor
Augie Garrido (left) congratulates George Horton

said, "but I told our guys not to worry because you only have to face one of them at a time."

Texas' greatest advantage over Fullerton looked to be in the bullpen. Because of Huston Street, Brent Cox and Buck Cody, the Longhorns entered the CWS having won 41 of 42 games in which they held a lead after five innings. But both of the Titans' victories in the championship series against Texas featured such comebacks.

Fullerton's bullpen hadn't won a game since April 18 and had recorded just five saves entering the Texas series. The question mark turned into an exclamation point during the series—Titans relievers pitched eight shutout innings at Rosenblatt Stadium.

The Titans also received an unexpected pitching boost from junior lefthander Scott Sarver. Making his second appearance since May 11, Sarver held South Carolina without a run for six-plus innings of a 4-0 win that sent the Fullerton into the championship series. Windsor worked the final three innings to finish the second Titans shutout of the Gamecocks, who hadn't been held scoreless on the year before Omaha.

Sarver's outing was nearly as unexpected as Fullerton's title run given the team's slow start after a preseason No. 4 ranking.

"This is so unbelievable, especially with what the team has been through, so much adversity," DH Felipe Garcia said. "Deep down every guy on the club knew this was possible, and it's paid off."

Pupil Bests Teacher

The title brought out mixed emotions for Horton, who instead of joining the dogpile with his players sought out the crestfallen Garrido in the Texas dugout.

"I tip-toed over there and said thanks for the opportunity," Horton said. "Who knows where I'd be without him."

Horton joined Garrido's staff at Fullerton in 1991, and they shared much during their six years together, when Garrido was Fullerton's head coach and Horton his associate head coach.

Horton had made four trips to Omaha since replacing Garrido, who left for Texas prior to the 1997 season. But he had never reached the title game before 2004. And Garrido owned four national championships, including one for the Longhorns in 2002.

Winning his first championship against the former benchmark of success at Fullerton should have been the best validation Horton could find. But it was bittersweet.

"On one hand this is equally special to accomplish this

COLLEGE WORLD SERIES

Rosenblatt Stadium, Omaha
June 18-27, 2004

STANDINGS

BRACKET ONE	W	L	RF	RA
Texas	3	0	29	11
Georgia	2	2	20	24
Arizona	1	2	15	13
Arkansas	0	2	4	20

Bracket One Final: Texas 7, Georgia 6

BRACKET TWO	W	L	RF	RA
Cal State Fullerton	3	1	15	8
South Carolina	3	2	35	24
Miami	1	2	23	26
Louisiana State	0	2	9	24

Bracket Two Finals: South Carolina 5, Cal State Fullerton 3; Cal State Fullerton 4, South Carolina 0

CHAMPIONSHIP SERIES
(Best of 3)
Saturday, June 26: Cal State Fullerton 6, Texas 4
Sunday, June 27: Cal State Fullerton 3, Texas 2

INDIVIDUAL BATTING LEADERS
(Minimum 10 Plate Appearances)

	AVG	AB	R	H	2B	3B	HR	RBI	BB
Steve Pearce, S. Carolina	.571	21	5	12	1	0	1	5	3
Dooley Prince, Texas	.529	17	4	9	2	1	0	5	1
Curtis Thigpen, Texas	.500	18	6	9	2	1	0	3	2
Trevor Crowe, Arizona	.500	14	1	7	3	0	0	0	0
J.C. Holt, Louisiana State	.500	6	1	3	1	0	0	1	2
Brian Barton, Miami	.462	13	2	6	2	0	0	1	0
Felipe Garcia, CS Fullerton	.458	24	2	11	2	0	0	7	0
Roger Tomas, Miami	.455	11	4	5	1	0	0	2	0
Jon Jay, Miami	.429	14	3	6	0	1	1	7	1
Richard Mercado, Arizona	.417	12	2	5	1	0	0	0	2

INDIVIDUAL PITCHING LEADERS
(Minimum 5 Innings)

	W	L	ERA	G	SV	IP	H	BB	SO
Scott Sarver, CS Fullerton	1	0	0.00	1	0	6	5	2	7
Chad Blackwell, S. Carolina	0	0	0.00	2	1	5	5	1	6
J.P. Howell, Texas	1	0	0.77	2	0	12	8	8	13
Jason Windsor, CS Fullerton	2	0	0.86	3	1	21	11	6	29
Will Startup, Georgia	0	0	1.12	3	1	8	6	2	9
Michael Hyle, Georgia	1	0	1.50	1	0	6	6	2	5
Sam LeCure, Texas	0	0	1.74	2	0	10	8	2	5
Cesar Carrillo, Miami	1	0	2.25	1	0	8	7	4	6
Huston Street, Texas	1	0	2.35	4	0	8	7	1	11
John Meloan, Arizona	1	0	2.84	1	0	6	5	6	5

ALL-TOURNAMENT TEAM
C—Landon Powell, South Carolina. **1B**—Steve Pearce, South Carolina. **2B**—Seth Johnston, Texas. **3B**—Bryan Triplett, South Carolina. **SS**—Roger Tomas, Miami. **OF**—Brian Barton, Miami; Trevor Crowe, Arizona; Jon Jay, Miami. **DH**—Felipe Garcia, Cal State Fullerton. **P**—Ricky Romero, Cal State Fullerton; Jason Windsor, Cal State Fullerton.

Most Outstanding Player—Jason Windsor, Cal State Fullerton.

COLLEGE BASEBALL

against your mentor that taught you so much, that built Fullerton into a great program," he said, "but my heart goes out to them because they are 180 degrees from what we are feeling right now. I think about Augie and hopefully his heart mends quickly."

Garrido and his team were so disheartened by the loss they neglected to accept their second place trophy at the post-game ceremony despite a request from NCAA tournament officials. He was curt at the following press conference, and no players were available in the locker room after that.

The Longhorns' conduct became fodder for sports talk shows around the nation, receiving almost as much attention as the entire College World Series had.

"This has received way too much attention in this neighborhood, meaning Texas," Garrido said. "So much attention has been focused on this negative stuff, instead of on the heroes on Cal State Fullerton's team. We waited

in the dugout, and frankly I didn't know there was a ceremony for the second-place trophy. I have not even picked up a first-place trophy; I've always let my players do that. There was no direction put to me in the dugout.

"I walked across the field to congratulate (Titans coach) George (Horton) and all those guys—they all played for me. I'm thrilled for them winning the championship, but we were dealing with our own emotions and our relationships at that time."

Horton said neither he nor his team were offended. "From our standpoint, nothing coach Garrido and the Texas team did detracted from our ability to enjoy our successful tournament," he said.

SEC Makes Presence Felt

It didn't always look as if the West Coast would dominate the College World Series. The Southeastern Conference proved to be college baseball's best during the regular season, and it set or tied records by getting nine tournament bids, six No. 1 seeds, five regional host sites and four CWS entries.

Every team in the eight-team SEC tournament field made regionals, with tourney winner South Carolina grabbing a No. 2 national seed. Mississippi State, the ninth team to get in, made it without participating in the SEC tournament, a precedent set by Florida in 2003. MSU had a Ratings Percentage Index among the nation's top 30, even though it was 13-17 in league play.

No other team in the 64-team tournament was four games under .500 in conference play. Four other teams—UC Irvine, Missouri, North Carolina State and Tennessee—made the field despite losing conference records.

COLLEGE WORLD SERIES CHAMPIONS: 1947-2004

Year	Champion	Coach	Record	Runner-Up	MVP
1947	California*	Clint Evans	31-10	Yale	None selected
1948	Southern California	Sam Barry	40-12	Yale	None selected
1949	Texas*	Bibb Falk	23-7	Wake Forest	Charles Teague, 2b, Wake Forest
1950	Texas	Bibb Falk	27-6	Washington State	Ray VanCleef, of, Rutgers
1951	Oklahoma*	Jack Baer	19-9	Tennessee	Sid Hatfield, 1b-p, Tennessee
1952	Holy Cross	Jack Berry	21-3	Missouri	Jim O'Neill, p, Holy Cross
1953	Michigan	Ray Fisher	21-9	Texas	J.L. Smith, p, Texas
1954	Missouri	Hi Simmons	22-4	Rollins	Tom Yewcic, c, Michigan State
1955	Wake Forest	Taylor Sanford	29-7	Western Michigan	Tom Borland, p, Oklahoma State
1956	Minnesota	Dick Siebert	33-9	Arizona	Jerry Thomas, p, Minnesota
1957	California*	George Wolfman	35-10	Penn State	Cal Emery, 1b-p, Penn State
1958	Southern California	Rod Dedeaux	35-7	Missouri	Bill Thom, p, Southern California
1959	Oklahoma State	Toby Greene	27-5	Arizona	Jim Dobson, 3b, Oklahoma State
1960	Minnesota	Dick Siebert	34-7	Southern California	John Erickson, 2b, Minnesota
1961	Southern California*	Rod Dedeaux	43-9	Oklahoma State	Littleton Fowler, p, Oklahoma State
1962	Michigan	Don Lund	31-13	Santa Clara	Bob Garibaldi, p, Santa Clara
1963	Southern California	Rod Dedeaux	37-16	Arizona	Bud Hollowell, c, Southern California
1964	Minnesota	Dick Siebert	31-12	Missouri	Joe Ferris, p, Maine
1965	Arizona State	Bobby Winkles	54-8	Ohio State	Sal Bando, 3b, Arizona State
1966	Ohio State	Marty Karow	27-6	Oklahoma State	Steve Arlin, p, Ohio State
1967	Arizona State	Bobby Winkles	53-12	Houston	Ron Davini, c, Arizona State
1968	Southern California*	Rod Dedeaux	45-14	Southern Illinois	Bill Seinsoth, 1b, Southern California
1969	Arizona State	Bobby Winkles	56-11	Tulsa	John Dolinsek, of, Arizona State
1970	Southern California	Rod Dedeaux	51-13	Florida State	Gene Ammann, p, Florida State
1971	Southern California	Rod Dedeaux	53-13	Southern Illinois	Jerry Tabb, 1b, Tulsa
1972	Southern California	Rod Dedeaux	50-13	Arizona State	Russ McQueen, p, Southern California
1973	Southern California*	Rod Dedeaux	51-11	Arizona State	Dave Winfield, of-p, Minnesota
1974	Southern California	Rod Dedeaux	50-20	Miami (Fla.)	George Milke, p, Southern California
1975	Texas	Cliff Gustafson	56-6	South Carolina	Mickey Reichenbach, 1b, Texas
1976	Arizona	Jerry Kindall	56-17	Eastern Michigan	Steve Powers, dh-p, Arizona
1977	Arizona State	Jim Brock	57-12	South Carolina	Bob Horner, 3b, Arizona State
1978	Southern California*	Rod Dedeaux	54-9	Arizona State	Rod Boxberger, p, Southern California
1979	Cal State Fullerton	Augie Garrido	60-14	Arkansas	Tony Hudson, p, Cal State Fullerton
1980	Arizona	Jerry Kindall	45-21	Hawaii	Terry Francona, of, Arizona
1981	Arizona State	Jim Brock	55-13	Oklahoma State	Stan Holmes, of, Arizona State
1982	Miami (Fla.)*	Ron Fraser	57-18	Wichita State	Dan Smith, p, Miami (Fla.)
1983	Texas*	Cliff Gustafson	66-14	Alabama	Calvin Schiraldi, p, Texas
1984	Cal State Fullerton	Augie Garrido	66-20	Texas	John Fishel, of, Cal State Fullerton
1985	Miami (Fla.)*	Ron Fraser	64-16	Texas	Greg Ellena, dh, Miami (Fla.)
1986	Arizona	Jerry Kindall	49-19	Florida State	Mike Senne, of, Arizona
1987	Stanford	Mark Marquess	53-17	Oklahoma State	Paul Carey, of, Stanford
1988	Stanford	Mark Marquess	46-23	Arizona State	Lee Plemel, p, Stanford
1989	Wichita State	Gene Stephenson	68-16	Texas	Greg Brummett, p, Wichita State
1990	Georgia	Steve Webber	52-19	Oklahoma State	Mike Rebhan, p, Georgia
1991	Louisiana State*	Skip Bertman	55-18	Wichita State	Gary Hymel, c, Louisiana State
1992	Pepperdine*	Andy Lopez	48-11	Cal State Fullerton	Phil Nevin, 3b, Cal State Fullerton
1993	Louisiana State	Skip Bertman	53-17	Wichita State	Todd Walker, 2b, Louisiana State
1994	Oklahoma*	Larry Cochell	50-17	Georgia Tech	Chip Glass, of, Oklahoma
1995	Cal State Fullerton*	Augie Garrido	57-9	Southern California	Mark Kotsay, of-p, Cal State Fullerton
1996	Louisiana State*	Skip Bertman	52-15	Miami (Fla.)	Pat Burrell, 3b, Miami
1997	Louisiana State*	Skip Bertman	57-13	Alabama	Brandon Larson, ss, Louisiana State
1998	Southern California	Mike Gillespie	49-17	Arizona State	Wes Rachels, 2b, Southern California
1999	Miami*	Jim Morris	50-13	Florida State	Marshall McDougall, 2b, Florida State
2000	Louisiana State*	Skip Bertman	52-17	Stanford	Trey Hodges, rhp, Louisiana State
2001	Miami*	Jim Morris	53-12	Stanford	Charlton Jimerson, of, Miami
2002	Texas*	Augie Garrido	57-15	South Carolina	Huston Street, rhp, Texas
2003	Rice	Wayne Graham	58-12	Stanford	John Hudgins, rhp, Stanford
2004	Cal State Fullerton	George Horton	47-22	Texas	Jason Windsor, rhp, Cal State Fullerton

*Undefeated

"Mississippi State was a good team playing in a great conference with a very good schedule," NCAA selection committe chairman Charlie Carr said. "They won enough games to get in the tournament. I'm sure coach (Ron) Polk would have liked to have won more games, but he did enough to get in."

The SEC surpassed the eight bids it received in 2001 and '03. Three other conferences tied their previous records for bids. The Atlantic Coast received six (as in 1998), as did the Big 12 ('99). The Pacific-10 earned five, which it did in a 48-team field in '97.

Major Upset

Rice was the only team from the Western Athletic Conference to make the 2004 NCAA tournament, but the Owls' postseason results were even more stunning than the combined success of the SEC. Rice looked like a solid bet to challenge for the 2004 CWS title by returning righthanders Philip Humber, Jeff Niemann and Wade Townsend, who led the Owls to the 2003 title and were all selected in the first eight picks of the 2004 draft.

The Owls opened the tournament at home against Texas Southern, a local school that earned an automatic bid by winning the Southwestern Athletic Conference tournament despite an 18-31 record. The Tigers stunned Rice 4-3 after Humber surrendered a three-run, eighth-inning home run for one of the biggest upsets in college baseball history.

Rice battled back through the loser's bracket, and beat Texas A&M once to force a deciding regional game, but couldn't complete the task.

Times Are Changing?

When Cal State Fullerton wrapped up the national championship with a sweep of Texas, it ended the College World Series one day early. Still, the June 27 date

SPORTS ON FILM

Title defense stopped by Tiger bite
Texas Southern upended Philip Humber and Rice

of the game was the latest a college baseball season had ended since the first CWS in 1947.

The 10-member NCAA Division I baseball issues committee unanimously approved four key changes to the college calendar in July, and the championships/competition cabinet approved the measures during a September meeting.

The formation of a uniform start date of March 1 headed the list of changes, which will take effect for the 2006-07 school year. The plan is flexible in that the season can begin on a February Friday if March 1 falls on a Saturday, Sunday, Monday or Tuesday.

The College World Series would be moved back one week, with corresponding regionals and super-regionals moved back as well. Feb. 1 will be the first day teams can begin spring practices.

Fall practice dates will have a major change as well, with a 45-day window installed from September though November for teams to use. Practice days would only be counted when a team actually takes the field and participates; previously practice days were counted consecutively from the first day until the final one, including dates when players did not actually practice because of poor weather or holidays.

Growing The Game

There's no better illustration of the game's growing popularity than the College World Series. The 2004 event set seven session attendance records, including the four largest crowds ever. A record 28,216 fans packed into Rosenblatt Stadium for a CWS session pitting Texas against Georgia and South Carolina against Cal State Fullerton. It was the third-largest college baseball crowd of the year—and all-time.

"I'm kind of a middle-of-the-road guy, thinking at some point this (attendance) is going to kind of level out," said Dennis Poppe, NCAA director of baseball administration. "I've been doing this for 17 years, and when we had 28,000 at a session this year, I was very

RPI RANKINGS

The Ratings Percentage Index (RPI) is a primary tool used by the NCAA in selecting at-large teams for the 64-team Division I regional field. The accompanying chart is the final, official 2004 RPI rankings, with records against Division I opponents. Ties are not included. Asterisks denote teams that did not get a regional bid; the team's final rank in Baseball America's Top 25 is noted in parentheses. College World Series teams are in boldface.

Team	Record	Team	Record
1. **Miami** (4)	50-13	26. Tennessee	38-23
2. **Texas** (2)	58-15	27. Southern Mississippi	45-19
3. **South Carolina** (3)	53-17	28. Central Florida	47-18
4. **Louisiana State** (7)	46-19	29. Oklahoma (25)	38-24
5. Arizona State (22)	41-18	30. Oral Roberts (18)	47-11
6. **Georgia** (6)	45-23	31. UC Irvine	34-23
7. Florida (16)	43-22	32. *Nebraska	36-23
8. **Cal State Fullerton** (1)	47-22	33. Mississippi State	35-24
9. **Arkansas** (5)	45-24	34. Texas Tech	37-21
10. Florida State (14)	45-23	35. North Carolina	43-21
11. Vanderbilt (17)	45-19	36. Wichita State	48-16
12. Stanford (9)	46-14	37. *Auburn	32-24
13. Georgia Tech (10)	44-21	38. Oklahoma State	38-24
14. Clemson	39-26	39. UNC Wilmington	40-23
15. Mississippi (23)	39-21	40. Coastal Carolina	40-23
16. East Carolina (8)	51-13	41. Birmingham-Southern	45-18
17. Texas A&M (20)	42-22	42. Lamar	41-16
18. Rice (11)	46-14	43. Texas Christian	39-26
19. Virginia (24)	44-15	44. Tulane (19)	41-21
20. Long Beach State (13)	40-21	45. College of Charleston	47-16
21. Notre Dame (15)	48-12	46. *Baylor	29-31
22. Washington (21)	38-20	47. *Southern California	24-32
23. Arizona (12)	36-27	48. *Houston	30-29
24. North Carolina State	36-24	49. George Mason	39-19
25. Florida Atlantic	47-17	50. Missouri	38-23

SUPER-REGIONALS

June 11-13, 16 teams, eight best-of-3 series (Winners advance to College World Series).

REGIONALS

June 4-6, 64 teams, 16 double-elimination tournaments (Winners advance to super-regionals).
* Automatic qualifier

ARIZONA

■ **Super-Regional Site:** Long Beach, Calif. (Long Beach State).
Participants: Arizona (33-24) at Long Beach State (39-19).
(Arizona wins 2-1, advances to College World Series).

☐ **Regional Site:** South Bend, Ind. (Notre Dame).
Participants: *No. 1 Notre Dame (49-10), No. 2 UC Irvine (34-21-1), No. 3 Arizona (30-24-1), *No. 4 Kent State (35-25).
Champion: Arizona (3-0). **Runner-Up:** Notre Dame (2-2).
Outstanding Player: Koley Kolberg, rhp, Arizona.

☐ **Regional Site:** Palo Alto, Calif. (Stanford).
Participants: *No. 1 Stanford (44-12), No. 2 Long Beach State (36-19), No. 3 St. John's (36-21), *No. 4 Nevada-Las Vegas (37-22).
Champion: Long Beach State (3-0). **Runner-Up:** Stanford (2-2).
Outstanding Player: Troy Tulowitzki, ss, Long Beach State.
(Long Beach State advances to meet Arizona in super-regional).

ARKANSAS

■ **Super-Regional Site:** Fayetteville, Ark. (Arkansas).
Participants: Florida State (45-21) at Arkansas (43-22).
(Arkansas wins 2-0, advances to College World Series).

☐ **Regional Site:** Fayetteville, Ark. (Arkansas).
Participants: No. 1 Arkansas (39-21), *No. 2 Wichita State (47-14), No. 3 Missouri (37-21-1), *No. 4 Le Moyne (36-19).
Champion: Arkansas (4-1). **Runner-Up:** Wichita State (2-2).
Outstanding Player: Charley Boyce, rhp, Arkansas.

☐ **Regional Site:** Tallahassee, Fla. (Florida State).
Participants: *No. 1 Florida State (42-20), *No. 2 Oklahoma State (37-22), No. 3 Central Florida (44-16), *No. 4 Bethune-Cookman (27-26).
Champion: Florida State (3-1). **Runner-Up:** Central Florida (3-2).
Outstanding Player: Bryan Zech, 2b, Florida State; Stephen Drew, ss, Florida State.
(Florida State advances to meet Arkansas in super-regional).

CAL STATE FULLERTON

■ **Super-Regional Site:** Fullerton, Calif. (Cal State Fullerton).
Participants: Tulane (41-19) at Cal State Fullerton (40-21).
(Cal State Fullerton wins 2-0, advances to College World Series).

☐ **Regional Site:** Fullerton, Calif. (Cal State Fullerton).
Participants: No. 1 Arizona State (40-16), *No. 2 Cal State Fullerton (38-20), *No. 3 Minnesota (38-21), *No. 4 Pepperdine (28-30).
Champion: Cal State Fullerton (3-1). **Runner-Up:** Pepperdine (3-2).
Outstanding Player: Jason Windsor, rhp, Cal State Fullerton.

☐ **Regional Site:** Oxford, Miss. (Mississippi).
Participants: No. 1 Mississippi (39-19), No. 2 Washington (37-18-1), No. 3 Tulane (38-19), *No. 4 Western Kentucky (34-26).
Champion: Tulane (3-0). **Runner-Up:** Washington (2-2).
Outstanding Player: Brian Bogusevic, of/lhp, Tulane.
(Tulane advances to meet Cal State Fullerton in super-regional).

GEORGIA

■ **Super-Regional Site:** Atlanta (Georgia Tech).
Participants: Georgia (41-21) at Georgia Tech (44-19).
(Georgia wins 2-0, advances to College World Series).

☐ **Regional Site:** Athens, Ga. (Georgia).
Participants: No. 1 Georgia (38-20), No. 2 Clemson (36-24), No. 3 Birmingham-Southern (46-16), No. 4 Middle Tennessee State (40-20).
Champion: Georgia (3-1). **Runner-Up:** Clemson (3-2).
Outstanding Player: Will Startup, lhp, Georgia.

☐ **Regional Site:** Atlanta (Georgia Tech).

Participants: No. 1 Georgia Tech (41-19), No. 2 Texas Tech (38-19), No. 3 Mississippi State (34-22), *No. 4 Jacksonville State (31-22).
Champion: Georgia Tech (3-0). **Runner-Up:** Texas Tech (2-2).
Outstanding Player: Eric Patterson, 2b, Georgia Tech.
(Georgia Tech advances to meet Georgia in super-regional).

LOUISIANA STATE

■ **Super-Regional Site:** Baton Rouge, La. (Louisiana State).
Participants: Texas A&M (42-20) at Louisiana State (44-17).
(Louisiana State wins 2-0, advances to College World Series).

☐ **Regional Site:** Baton Rouge, La. (Louisiana State).
Participants: No. 1 Louisiana State (41-17), No. 2 Southern Mississippi (44-17), No. 3 College of Charleston (45-14), *No. 4 Army (37-13).
Champion: Louisiana State (3-0). **Runner-Up:** College of Charleston (2-2).
Outstanding Player: Blake Gill, ss, Louisiana State.

☐ **Regional Site:** Houston (Rice).
Participants: No. 1 Rice (43-12), No. 2 Texas A&M (39-19), *No. 3 Lamar (41-14), *No. 4 Texas Southern (18-33).
Champion: Texas A&M (3-1). **Runner-Up:** Rice (3-2).
Outstanding Player: Cliff Pennington, ss, Texas A&M.
(Texas A&M advances to meet Louisiana State in super-regional).

MIAMI

■ **Super-Regional Site:** Coral Gables, Fla. (Miami).
Participants: Florida (43-20) at Miami (47-11).
(Miami wins 2-0, advances to College World Series).

☐ **Regional Site:** Coral Gables, Fla. (Miami).
Participants: No. 1 Miami (44-11), No. 2 North Carolina State (35-22), *No. 3 Florida Atlantic (45-15), *No. 4 St. Bonaventure (29-20).
Champion: Miami (3-0). **Runner-Up:** Florida Atlantic (2-2).
Outstanding Player: Jim Burt, 1b, Miami.

☐ **Regional Site:** Oklahoma City, Okla. (Oklahoma)
Participants: No. 1 Florida (40-20), No. 2 Oklahoma (37-22), No. 3 UCLA (33-27), *No. 4 Central Connecticut State (41-15-1).
Champion: Florida (3-0). **Runner-Up:** UCLA (2-2).
Outstanding Player: Ben Harrison, of, Florida.
(Florida advances to meet Miami in super-regional).

SOUTH CAROLINA

■ **Super-Regional Site:** Columbia, S.C. (South Carolina).
Participants: East Carolina (51-11) at South Carolina (48-15).
(South Carolina wins 2-0, advances to College World Series).

☐ **Regional Site:** Columbia, S.C. (South Carolina).
Participants: *No. 1 South Carolina (45-15), No. 2 North Carolina (41-19), *No. 3 Coastal Carolina (40-21), *No. 4 The Citadel (38-26).
Champion: South Carolina (3-0). **Runner-Up:** North Carolina (2-2).
Outstanding Player: Steve Pearce, 1b, South Carolina.

☐ **Regional Site:** Kinston, N.C. (East Carolina).
Participants: No. 1 East Carolina (48-11), No. 2 Tennessee (37-22), *No. 3 UNC Wilmington (38-21), *No. 4 Stony Brook (29-25).
Champion: East Carolina (3-0). **Runner-Up:** UNC Wilmington (2-2).
Outstanding Player: Greg Bunn, rhp, East Carolina.
(East Carolina advances to meet South Carolina in super-regional).

TEXAS

■ **Super-Regional Site:** Austin, Texas (Texas).
Participants: Vanderbilt (45-17) at Texas (53-13).
(Texas wins 2-0, advances to College World Series).

☐ **Regional Site:** Austin, Texas. (Texas).
Participants: No. 1 Texas (50-13), *No. 2 Oral Roberts (48-9), *No. 3 Texas Christian (38-24), *No. 4 Youngstown State (22-30).
Champion: Texas (3-0). **Runner-Up:** Oral Roberts (2-2).
Outstanding Player: Taylor Teagarden, c, Texas.

☐ **Regional Site:** Charlottesville, Va. (Virginia).
Participants: No. 1 Virginia (42-13), No. 2 Vanderbilt (42-17), No. 3 George Mason (39-17), *No. 4 Princeton (27-18).
Champion: Vanderbilt (3-0). **Runner-Up:** Virginia (2-2).
Outstanding Player: Cesar Nicolas, 1b, Vanderbilt.
(Vanderbilt advances to meet Texas in super-regional).

surprised. It just keeps growing."

The average of 23,339 fans a session also set a new record, but the 256,730 total fans fell just shy of 2003's mark of 260,091, which was accomplished with one more game.

The fan frenzy carried over to television, as ESPN's coverage of the CWS championship series drew an average of 1.32 million viewers, which represented a 7.4 percent increase from 2003's championship series. Games one and two drew the third- and fourth-best ratings of any cable sports telecasts that week.

Individual college programs also set at least 20 game and 15 season attendance records. A March game between San Diego State and Houston set the NCAA single-game attendance record as 40,106 fans packed into the first game at Petco Park, the Padres' new downtown ballpark. That event also featured local icon Tony Gwynn in the dugout for the Aztecs, as the Padres organization honored their former star before the game by naming a street after him.

The Spring Baseball Classic at Atlanta's Turner Field in May pitted Georgia against Georgia Tech and drew 28,836 fans, the second-largest crowd to ever watch a college baseball game.

"Obviously college baseball is enjoying great popularity, and one of the things I think that helps it is there's still a bit of innocence to it. The players aren't professionals yet and many won't ever be," Poppe said. "The College World Series has generated a lot of attention from that."

Comings And Goings

Detroit Mercy became the 45th Division I athletic program to drop baseball, but the move was offset by Stephen F. Austin's decision to revive its program for the 2006 season.

D-I had 285 full-time members in 2004, with 287 schools counting in the NCAA's Ratings Percentage Index, including newcomers Dallas Baptist and Northern Colorado. Utah Valley State will count in the RPI in 2005.

The end of the season also offered two dozen coaching changes. Gary Adams retired after 30 seasons, 984 wins, 11 NCAA tournament appearances and two College World Series trips at UCLA. UC Irvine coach John Savage, a former assistant at Southern California, replaced

Gary Adams

Adams. He was hired at Irvine by current UCLA athletic director Dan Guerrero, and built the Irvine program from scratch (it was resuscitated in 2002 after a decade-long hiatus) to a 2004 NCAA regional team in that short time.

COACHING CARUOSEL

Division I coaching changes since the end of the 2004 season:		
School	**Out (reason)**	**In (old job)**
Appalachian State	Troy Heustess (resigned)	Chris Pollard (Pfeiffer, N.C.)
Auburn	Steve Renfroe (fired)	Tom Slater (Florida assistant)
Canisius	Mark Notaro (resigned)	Mike McRae (Niagara)
UC Irvine	John Savage (to UCLA)	Dave Serrano (Cal State Fullerton assistant)
UCLA	Gary Adams (retired)	John Savage (UC Irvine)
George Washington	Tom Walter (to New Orleans)	Steve Mrowka (Georgia College & State)
Kent State	Rick Rembielak (to Wake Forest)	Scott Stricklin (Georgia Tech assistant)
Memphis	Dave Anderson (resigned)	Daron Schoenrock (Mississippi State assistant)
New Orleans	Randy Bush (resigned)	Tom Walter (George Washington)
Niagara	Mike McRae (to Canisius)	Chris Chernisky (Appalachian State assistant)
UNC Asheville	Matt Myers (to Auburn as assistant)	Willie Stewart (UNC Asheville assistant)
Old Dominion	Tony Guzzo (not renewed)	Jerry Meyers (South Carolina assistant)
Penn State	Joe Hindelang (retired)	Robbie Wine (Oklahoma State assistant)
Rider	Sonny Pittaro (retired)	Barry Davis (Georgia Southwestern State)
St. Joseph's	Jim Ertel (fired)	Shawn Pender (Orioles national crosschecker)
St. Peter's	Jimmy Walsh (resigned)	Derek England (high school coach)
Samford	Tim Parenton (to Florida as assistant)	Casey Dunn (Auburn assistant)
Southern Utah	Kurt Palmer (resigned)	David Eldredge (Brigham Young assistant)
Utah	Tim Esmay (Arizona State as assistant)	Bill Kinneberg (White Sox pitching instructor)
Wake Forest	George Greer (retired)	Rick Rembielak (Kent State)
Washington State	Tim Mooney (resigned)	Don Marbut (Washington State assistant)
Wright State	Ron Nischwitz (retired)	Rob Cooper (Oral Roberts assistant)
Western Michigan	Fred Decker (retired)	Randy Ford (Penn State assistant)
Xavier	John Morrey (resigned)	Dan Simonds (Miami Ohio assistant)

The Anteaters went 88-84 in his tenure.

Savage's departure opened the door at Irvine for Cal State Fullerton assistant Dave Serrano.

Two other big-name programs made changes as Auburn hired Tom Slater, the former Virginia Military coach who had spent two years as an assistant at Florida, and Wake Forest hired Rich Rembielak from Kent State. Slater replaced Steve Renfroe, who was fired after the Tigers missed the Southeastern Conference tournament with a 32-24, 12-18 record. Rembielak replaced George Greer, who retired after 17 years as Wake's coach.

Rembielak also helped shake up Georgia Tech's staff by hiring Tech assistant John Palmeiri to work for the Demon Deacons while Scott Stricklin, another Tech assistant, replaced Rembielak at Kent State.

Two other long-time coaches joined Greer in leaving the dugout on their own terms as UC Riverside's Jack Smitheran (31 years) and Rider's Sonny Pittaro (34) also retired.

Statistically Significant

■ South Carolina set six school records in a 38-0 win against Charleston Southern: runs, margin of victory (tied for the fourth-largest in NCAA history), doubles (11, tied for seventh in NCAA history), RBIs (37, tied for second), hits (35, tied for seventh) and total bases (71).

■ Twin brothers Brian and Jeff Baisley each hit home runs for South Florida in a 5-4 win against Jacksonville. Darryl and Trevor Lawhorn equaled that feat for East Carolina, but maybe that was to be expected given that Trevor rocketed 21 homers on the year, including a streak of six consecutive games with a long ball. Incidentally, Lawhorn's streak ended in the first game of a double-header against the Baisleys and South Florida, but he smacked his 15th home run of the year in the second game, and ended up with a string of 10 homers in 11 games.

■ Nebraska pitchers posted a Big 12 Conference record 43⅓ consecutive scoreless innings over five games, including four consecutive shutouts, topping the previous record of 41 (Texas, 2002). Cornhuskers senior lefthander Justin Pekarek set a school record by working 33⅓ consecutive scoreless innings of his own.

COLLEGE BASEBALL

Selected by Baseball America

| Stephen Head | Jed Lowrie | Dustin Pedroia | Danny Putnam | Kurt Suzuki |

COLLEGE BASEBALL

FIRST TEAM

Pos	Player, School	YR	Hometown	AVG	AB	R	H	2B	3B	HR	RBI	SB	Last Drafted
C	Kurt Suzuki, Cal State Fullerton	Jr.	Wailuku, Hawaii	.413	252	77	104	17	4	16	87	9	Athletics '04 (2)
1B	Mike Ferris, Miami (Ohio)	Jr.	Cincinnati	.361	208	61	75	15	2	21	62	3	Cardinals '04 (2)
2B	Jed Lowrie, Stanford	So.	Salem, Ore.	.399	233	72	93	19	4	17	68	6	Never drafted
3B	Alex Gordon, Nebraska	So.	Omaha	.365	211	64	77	18	5	18	75	12	Never drafted
SS	Dustin Pedroia, Arizona State	Jr.	Woodland, Calif.	.395	233	76	92	24	1	9	48	8	Red Sox '04 (2)
OF	Brad Corley, Mississippi State	So.	Louisville	.395	266	62	105	21	6	12	83	21	Rockies '02 (16)
OF	Eddy Martinez-Esteve, Florida State	So.	Miami	.385	270	57	104	24	3	19	81	8	Giants '04 (2)
OF	Danny Putnam, Stanford	Jr.	Escondido, Calif.	.378	249	61	94	10	4	16	62	6	Athletics '02 (1)
DH	Warner Jones, Vanderbilt	So.	Nashville	.414	268	55	111	27	3	11	74	12	Never drafted
UT	Stephen Head, Mississippi	So.	Raymond, Miss.	.357	213	39	76	13	1	11	49	0	Never drafted

Pos	Player, School	YR	Hometown	W	L	ERA	CG	SV	IP	H	BB	SO	Last Drafted
SP	Matt Fox, Central Florida	Jr.	Parkland, Fla.	14	2	1.85	6	0	112	78	32	125	Twins '04 (1)
SP	J.P. Howell, Texas	Jr.	Sacramento	15	2	2.13	4	1	135	90	53	166	Royals '04 (1)
SP	Wade Townsend, Rice	Jr.	Dripping Springs, Texas	12	0	1.80	2	2	120	74	45	148	Orioles '04 (1)
SP	Jered Weaver, Long Beach State	Jr.	Simi Valley, Calif.	15	1	1.62	3	0	144	81	21	213	Angels '04 (1)
RP	Nate Moore, Troy State	Jr.	Kinston, Ala.	9	4	1.25	0	8	65	42	16	84	Royals '04 (4)
UT	Stephen Head, Mississippi	So.	Raymond, Miss.	6	3	2.82	3	5	70	68	19	56	

SECOND TEAM

Pos	Player, School	YR	Hometown	AVG	AB	R	H	2B	3B	HR	RBI	SB	Last Drafted
C	Landon Powell, South Carolina	Sr.	New Hill, N.C.	.330	270	66	89	17	1	19	66	2	Athletics '04 (1)
1B	Josh Brady, Texas Tech	Jr.	Lubbock, Texas	.362	260	63	94	19	3	20	90	30	Brewers '04 (19)
2B	Jarrett Hoffpauir, Southern Miss.	Jr.	Vidalia, La.	.405	269	62	109	27	2	11	92	2	Cardinals '04 (6)
3B	Matt Macri, Notre Dame	Jr.	Clive, Iowa	.367	237	76	87	15	7	14	56	12	Rockies '04 (5)
SS	Stephen Drew, Florida State	Jr.	Hahira, Ga.	.344	227	68	78	14	7	17	56	12	D'backs '04 (1)
OF	Jeff Frazier, Rutgers	Jr.	Toms River, N.J.	.382	207	59	79	16	1	13	59	6	Tigers '04 (3)
OF	Chris Rahl, William & Mary	So.	Chesapeake, Va.	.389	229	73	89	10	8	20	70	42	Never drafted
OF	Richie Robnett, Fresno State	Jr.	Mojave, Ariz.	.384	229	54	88	27	3	13	51	21	Athletics '04 (1)
DH	Ryan Jones, East Carolina	Sr.	Gibsonia, Pa.	.400	215	66	86	26	4	19	69	9	Athletics '04 (22)
UT	Brian Bogusevic, Tulane	So.	Oak Lawn, Ill.	.343	230	49	79	14	4	10	68	9	Never drafted

Pos	Player, School	YR	Hometown	W	L	ERA	G	SV	IP	H	BB	SO	Last Drafted
SP	Justin Hoyman, rhp, Florida	Jr.	Melbourne, Fla.	11	2	2.71	19	0	140	116	38	89	Indians '04 (2)
SP	Philip Humber, rhp, Rice	Jr.	Carthage, Texas	13	4	2.27	20	1	115	87	37	154	Mets '04 (1)
SP	Mike Pelfrey, Wichita State	So.	Wichita	10	2	2.36	15	0	107	82	21	111	Devil Rays '02 (15)
SP	Jason Windsor, Cal State Fullerton	Sr.	Lake Forest, Calif.	13	4	1.72	22	1	163	100	24	148	Athletics '04 (3)
RP	Huston Street, Texas	Jr.	Austin, Texas	6	1	1.58	31	12	57	36	13	59	Athletics '04 (1)
UT	Brian Bogusevic, Tulane	So.	Oak Lawn, Ill.	9	5	3.70	16	0	107	114	23	82	

THIRD TEAM

Pos	Player, School	YR	Hometown	AVG	AB	R	H	2B	3B	HR	RBI	SB	Last Drafted
C	Chris Iannetta, North Carolina	Jr.	Providence, R.I.	.336	244	61	82	19	0	15	71	6	Rockies '04 (4)
1B	Jim Burt, Miami (Fla.)	Sr.	Saddle River, N.J.	.371	245	70	91	27	3	14	73	7	Mets '04 (19)
2B	Eric Patterson, Georgia Tech	Jr.	Kennesaw, Ga.	.326	264	76	86	11	5	9	49	48	Cubs '04 (8)
3B	Brad McCann, Clemson	Jr.	Duluth, Ga.	.378	249	63	94	20	0	16	65	5	Marlins '04 (5)
SS	Brian Bixler, Eastern Michigan	Jr.	Sandusky, Ohio	.453	243	74	110	18	3	8	47	31	Pirates '04 (2)
OF	J.C. Holt, Louisiana State	Jr.	Seiper, La.	.390	264	70	103	18	3	6	51	20	Braves '04 (3)
OF	Marshall Hubbard, North Carolina	Jr.	Ashland, Va.	.352	250	55	88	21	3	17	83	4	Mariners '04 (8)
OF	Eric Nielsen, UNLV	Jr.	Henderson, Nev.	.405	247	84	100	23	2	16	86	7	Blue Jays '04 (12)
DH	Jeff Fiorentino, Florida Atlantic	Jr.	Plantation, Fla.	.348	221	84	77	18	1	17	67	13	Orioles '04 (3)
UT	Joe Koshansky, Virginia	Sr.	Fairfax, Va.	.302	222	50	67	17	1	16	67	8	Rockies '04 (6)

Pos	Player, School	YR	Hometown	W	L	ERA	G	SV	IP	H	BB	SO	Last Drafted
SP	Matt Campbell, South Carolina	Jr.	Gray Court, S.C.	10	6	3.05	22	0	124	99	38	145	Royals '04 (1)
SP	Cesar Carrillo, Miami (Fla.)	So.	Hammond, Ind.	12	0	2.69	19	2	114	93	43	91	Never drafted
SP	Wade LeBlanc, Alabama	Fr.	Lake Charles, La.	8	4	2.08	16	0	113	87	26	98	Devil Rays '03 (36)
SP	Glen Perkins, Minnesota	So.	Stillwater, Minn.	9	3	2.83	16	0	111	89	21	113	Twins '04 (1)
RP	Chad Blackwell, South Carolina	Jr.	Clewiston, Fla.	4	3	2.57	37	20	63	52	14	80	Royals '04 (6)
UT	Joe Koshansky, Virginia	Sr.	Fairfax, Va.	8	3	2.98	15	0	103	83	29	80	

Weaver wins Player of Year accolade

Despite all he accomplished, Jered Weaver likely will remember the 2004 season as a disappointment.

How could he? After all he blossomed from Jeff Weaver's little brother to the best pitcher in college baseball. He enjoyed a junior season at Long Beach State that statistically rivaled Mark Prior's 2001 campaign at Southern California. Weaver set school records for strikeouts in a game (17), season (213) and career (431). He also notched first place in career wins and innings pitched.

PLAYER *of the* **YEAR**

"I don't care about any of it," Weaver said. "I care about pitching. I'm not a stat guy. I can't tell you what my ERA is. I just go out there and do what I do."

Other people cared—and the honors rolled in.

Weaver was named Baseball America's College Player of the Year.

The Angels selected him in the first round of the draft, putting him closer to fulfilling his dream of becoming a major leaguer.

Heck, he even helped topple a nemesis in Stanford, ending its streak of consecutive College World Series appearances at five. The Cardinal had bounced the Dirtbags from the tournament the last four years, and knocked brother Jeff's Fresno State team out of the postseason five years earlier.

Yet in Weaver's mind, he fell short.

"I'm here for one reason," he said midway through the season, "just to get to Omaha. It's been my dream to get drafted and be a big leaguer. But first I want to get to Omaha."

Weaver did his part to reach that goal. He was as good in his final start as he was all year in compiling a 15-1, 1.62 record. The 6-foot-7 righthander struck out 12 batters and allowed two runs—one earned—on five hits in 7⅔ innings in the super-regional opener against Arizona. But the feisty Wildcats scored four ninth-inning runs that night, then won an 11-inning 4-3 battle in the final game of the series to end Long Beach State's season one game shy of the CWS.

Weaver's unwavering desire to get to Omaha underlined his team-first attitude. He settled on Long Beach State as his college choice because he loved the program's scrappy, hard-working mindset that begat the Dirtbags nickname. He viewed his success simply as a means for his team to succeed, not a vehicle for personal stardom, though he gained that along the way.

"He doesn't want special treatment," Long Beach State coach Mike Weathers said. "The guy is a good teammate. In our program no one player is bigger than anyone else, and he fits that. They don't call him big leaguer or prima donna or whatever."

When he was not pitching, Weaver was often the first guy out of the dugout to congratulate teammates. He spent his time between starts sticking close by Weathers side, discussing in-game

Statistically dominant
Jered Weaver's season rivaled Mark Prior's 2001 efforts

strategy with the coach. "He's real interested, involved," Weathers said.

Sometimes, he got too involved. One Tuesday in late April, Weaver asked Weathers to put him on the mound during a taut, 2-1 win at UCLA. He had thrown 122 pitches and registered 14 strikeouts in seven innings the previous Friday, but told the coach he felt fine.

"He was dead serious," Weathers recalled, "so I told him, 'We don't do that.'"

Weaver might have been thinking the same thing as the final Arizona game headed to extra innings.

"He hates to lose almost more than he enjoys winning," pitching coach Troy Buckley said. "Winning is fleeting because you have to start preparing for the next time. Losing can linger because of the feeling of failure. It's pain. It leads to more concentration and discipline."

Missing out on the CWS might always haunt Weaver, no matter what success he goes on to achieve. Still, at some point in time, he'll be able to look back and remember authoring one of the greatest seasons ever by a college pitcher.

—WILL KIMMEY

PREVIOUS **WINNERS**
1981—Mike Sodders, 3b, Arizona State
1982—Jeff Ledbetter, of-lhp, Florida State
1983—Dave Magadan, 1b, Alabama
1984—Oddibe McDowell, of, Arizona State
1985—Pete Incaviglia, of, Oklahoma State
1986—Casey Close, of, Michigan
1987—Robin Ventura, 3b, Oklahoma State
1988—John Olerud, 1b-lhp, Washington State
1989—Ben McDonald, rhp, Louisiana State
1990—Mike Kelly, of, Arizona State
1991—David McCarty, 1b, Stanford
1992—Phil Nevin, 3b, Cal State Fullerton
1993—Brooks Kieschnick, dh-rhp, Texas
1994—Jason Varitek, c, Georgia Tech
1995—Todd Helton, 1b-lhp, Tennessee
1996—Kris Benson, rhp, Clemson
1997—J.D. Drew, of, Florida State
1998—Jeff Austin, rhp, Stanford
1999—Jason Jennings, rhp, Baylor
2000—Mark Teixeira, 3b, Georgia Tech
2001—Mark Prior, rhp, Southern California
2002—Khalil Greene, ss, Clemson
2003—Rickie Weeks, 2b, Southern

ROBERT OLIVER

COLLEGE BASEBALL

Fiery Perno leads Georgia to Omaha

With his season slipping away and his Georgia Bulldogs down to three outs, David Perno did the only thing he could think of: He got ejected.

Perno was tossed for arguing balls and strikes in the bottom of the eighth inning of a regional final, with Georgia trailing Clemson 6-4. But the 36-year-old Georgia alum didn't stop there. He grabbed a bucket of balls and tossed them onto the field, causing quite a ruckus. "At that point, I didn't care," Perno said after the game. "I just had to do something to fire us up."

COACH
of the **YEAR**

It worked. Georgia hit back-to-back home runs in the top of the ninth and won the game on another home run in the 10th.

Perno's knack for pushing just the right buttons proved effective all season as he guided the Bulldogs, picked by league coaches to finish 10th in the Southeastern Conference, to an SEC Eastern Divison championship and a berth in the 2004 College World Series.

Georgia won two games in Omaha and finished 45-23, the third-highest victory total in school history. Perno, who began the season on shaky ground, earned a contract extension and Baseball America's Coach of the Year award.

A trip to Omaha was the last

Pushed the right buttons
Georgia's David Perno

thing on his mind in February or April. Then the goal was Birmingham and the eight-team SEC tournament. Georgia missed out on the event a year earlier.

A return to the conference gathering was what Perno had in mind in the preseason. Forget Omaha.

The third-year head coach felt the need to remind his team in April. Georgia stumbled to a 5-7 start in the league, so Perno had the bus stop in Birmingham on a road trip to Louisiana State. Just a friendly reminder of the goal.

Georgia lost the first two games to the Tigers. But on April 18, after a pick-me-up speech by Perno, Georgia topped LSU, 12-4.

And the Bulldogs didn't stop. Georgia reeled off 11 consecutive victories after the LSU win and

closed the season 16-3. After a disappointing 1-2 in the SEC tournament, Georgia appeared on the verge of blowing the regional. Needing just one victory on the final day, the Bulldogs were three outs away from falling short.

Enter Perno in all his ball-throwing glory. "I did what I had to do to get something going," he said. "I didn't like the situation. I felt like something had to be done. I wasn't going to sit there and watch us go down like that."

Georgia carried the momentum to a sweep at rival Georgia Tech in the super-regional and into the College World Series.

In the CWS, Perno showed himself to be more than just a master motivator. In the opener, the Bulldogs bunted at Arizona's replacement third baseman. Against Texas, they stole five bases to garner an offensive advantage. And in their last game, the Bulldogs nearly rallied past Texas All-America closer Huston Street by relying on Perno's scouting report.

The entirety of Perno's work—he serves as Georgia's primary recruiter—has earned him enormous respect from his players and peers.

"You can't have any more credit given to a coach. He coached amazingly this year," reliever Will Startup said. "We pulled together as a team, and he was able to lead that ship."

—BRIAN MURPHY

Fullerton's Serrano earns top assistant honor

Dave Serrano had quite a year.

He participated in a College World Series title as Cal State Fullerton's pitching coach, and UC Irvine named him its head coach less than a month later. For his efforts, he earned the American Baseball Coach-es Association/Baseball America Assistant Coach of the Year Award.

Fullerton allowed 11 earned runs in six CWS games, and head coach George Horton credited Serrano for the pitching effort.

Dave Serrano

Serrano joined Horton at Fullerton in 1997. At Cerritos (Calif.) Junior College, Serrano played for Horton (1984-85) and served as his pitching coach (1988-90). Serrano stayed at Cerritos after Horton left for Fullerton in 1991 and then served as pitching coach at Tennessee in 1995 and 1996.

Tide's LeBlanc rolls past SEC foes to earn honors

Wade LeBlanc generated quite a bit of interest among college coaches after his junior year of high school. Well, at least those at McNeese State in his hometown of Lake Charles, La.

His velocity was down, he couldn't throw an offspeed pitch, and he couldn't command anything. He wasn't on professional scouts' radars, and outside of Lake Charles, college coaches didn't even know

FRESHMAN *of the YEAR*

who LeBlanc was—including Alabama's Jim Wells.

That was before the lanky left-hander went 16-1, 0.45 his senior year at Barbe High. "It all came together for me my senior year," LeBlanc said. "I couldn't tell you how if my life depended on it."

LeBlanc signed a letter of intent with the Cowboys, but when coach Todd Butler left before LeBlanc's freshman year to become an assistant at Alabama, new McNeese coach Chad Clement let LeBlanc out of his commitment. LeBlanc ended up following Butler to Alabama and setting school freshman records for innings (113), strikeouts (98) and complete games (eight). He also tied the record for wins (eight). He started on Friday nights in the Southeastern Conference, and still he posted a 2.08 ERA and tossed three shutouts on his way to earning Baseball America Freshman of the Year honors.

"When we did our first bullpen session with him, he certainly was as good a freshman as I've seen and probably better than I've seen, but

Freshman Friday starter Alabama's Wade LeBlanc

you never know how that's going to translate to the SEC," Wells said. "I never imagined something like this, but I knew he was going to be pretty good."

That was the book on LeBlanc after he wrapped up his stellar senior season at Barbe: He could be pretty good. He was a BA high school All-American for 2003, and the Devil Rays drafted him in the 36th round (he slipped because of signability concerns). But LeBlanc is not an overpowering pitcher, and even after he got out of his commitment to McNeese he garnered only mild interest from top Division I programs.

Now everyone is paying attention to LeBlanc. One area scout with an American League club started keeping tabs on LeBlanc though he was still two years away from draft eligibility. LeBlanc impresses with his ability to locate his pitches, mixing his high-80s fastball with an average curveball, slider and a changeup.

"He's an interesting kid," the scout said. "Not very mature physically, but he can pitch. He's an interesting prospect for us because he's still got some upside physically, so he may get better."

LeBlanc should be able to eat more innings once he fills out his 6-foot-3, 180-pound frame. He certainly has the workhorse mentality.

"I want to finish it," he said. "If I go that far, I want to be on the mound at the end of the game. I'm not scared of anybody."

—AARON FITT

FRESHMAN ALL-AMERICA TEAM

FIRST TEAM

Pos	Player, School	AVG	AB	R	H	2B	3B	HR	RBI	SB
C	Jordan Abruzzo, San Diego	.375	208	50	78	14	0	9	49	3
1B	Josh Morris, Georgia	.319	226	46	72	16	1	16	68	4
2B	Jim Negrych, Pittsburgh	.378	201	44	76	20	1	7	45	12
3B	Shelby Ford, Texas Christian	.301	249	66	75	13	3	16	56	6
SS	Chris Valaika, UC Santa Barbara	.347	222	46	77	15	3	7	38	7
OF	Chad Huffman, Texas Christian	.383	253	68	97	20	1	9	44	3
OF	Jon Jay, Miami	.368	234	51	86	14	1	6	56	19
OF	Drew Stubbs, Texas	.301	266	51	80	16	3	8	47	28
DH	Matt LaPorta, Florida	.285	130	31	37	5	0	14	37	1
UT	Anthony Smith, George Washington	.369	187	43	69	17	0	15	69	6

Pos	Player, School	W	L	ERA	G	SV	IP	H	BB	SO
SP	Ian Kennedy, Southern California	7	2	2.91	16	1	93	86	31	120
SP	Wade LeBlanc, Alabama	8	4	2.08	16	0	113	87	26	98
SP	Tim Lincecum, Washington	10	3	3.53	20	0	112	83	82	161
SP	Jason Meyer, Texas A&M	8	2	2.89	24	3	106	88	41	111
RP	Danny Gil, Miami	8	0	3.03	27	5	39	23	27	49
UT	Anthony Smith, George Washington	6	3	5.29	15	0	82	86	42	67

SECOND TEAM

C—Nick Salotti, UC Riverside (.346-10-51). **1B**—Ryne Malone, Florida State (.330-12-54). **2B**—Chris Campbell, Charleston (.332-5-63). **3B**—Austin Boggs, Texas A&M (.331-5-52). **SS**—Jason Donald, Arizona (.321-8-43). **OF**—Jake Dugger, Arkansas (.293-8-44); Clark Hardman, Cal State Fullerton (.341-0-31); Alex Presley, Mississippi (.311-6-32). **DH**—Brock Ungricht, San Diego State (.373-3-48). **UT**—Zech Zinicola, Arizona State (.280-3-26; 4-2, 3.36).

SP—Daniel Bard, North Carolina (8-4, 3.88); Clay Dirks, Louisiana State (8-2, 3.43); Andrew Miller, North Carolina (6-3, 2.93); Ryan Zink, Illinois-Chicago (9-3, 2.07). **RP**—Blair Erickson, UC Irvine (1-3, 4.10, 17 SV, 37 IP/51 SO).

COLLEGE BASEBALL

TEAM BATTING

BATTING AVERAGE	G	AVG
Eastern Kentucky	51	.375
Charleston	63	.341
Prairie View	56	.334
Nevada-Las Vegas	61	.334
Louisiana State	65	.333
Miami	63	.330
San Diego	56	.328
Southern	40	.327
Cal State Fullerton	69	.326
William & Mary	57	.326

RUNS SCORED	G	R
Nevada-Las Vegas	61	603
Georgia Tech	65	571
Texas Tech	61	554
Miami	63	542
Charleston	63	535
Florida State	68	530
New Mexico State	59	523
Wichita State	65	523
Cal State Fullerton	69	518
Louisiana State	65	515

DOUBLES	G	2B
Nevada-Las Vegas	61	159
Tennessee	62	154
Kent State	63	153
East Carolina	64	153
Utah	58	152
Cal State Fullerton	69	152

TRIPLES	G	3B
William & Mary	57	37
Arizona	64	33
McNeese State	53	31
Jackson State	49	27
New Mexico	56	26
Vanderbilt	64	26

HOME RUNS	G	HR
New Mexico State	59	115
South Carolina	70	106
East Carolina	64	100
Stanford	60	96
Southern Mississippi	64	90
Washington	60	87
Texas Tech	61	85
George Mason	58	83
Miami	63	81
Florida State	68	81

STOLEN BASES	G	SB	ATT
Jackson State	49	200	243
Pittsburgh	56	149	175
Eastern Michigan	59	147	192
Texas Tech	61	143	169
Miami	63	134	180
Northwestern State	56	131	164
Wichita State	65	130	165
Charleston Southern	58	121	165
Florida International	62	119	157
Oral Roberts	61	115	135

TEAM PITCHING

WINNING PERCENTAGE	W	L	PCT
Oral Roberts	50	11	.820
Notre Dame	51	12	.810
East Carolina	51	13	.797
Texas	58	15	.795
Miami	50	13	.794
Stanford	46	14	.767
Rice	46	14	.767
South Carolina	53	17	.757
Wichita State	49	16	.754
Virginia	44	15	.746
Charleston	47	16	.746

EARNED RUN AVERAGE	G	ERA
Rice	60	2.64
Texas	73	2.66

	G	
Oral Roberts	61	3.00
Long Beach State	61	3.11
Wichita State	65	3.13
Lamar	57	3.15
Vanderbilt	64	3.34
Alabama	55	3.34
Notre Dame	63	3.36
South Carolina	70	3.40

TEAM FIELDING

	G	AVG
Creighton	59	.982
Vanderbilt	64	.978
Rice	60	.977
North Carolina State	60	.976
East Carolina	64	.975
Long Beach State	61	.975
Nebraska	59	.975
Oral Roberts	61	.974
Stanford	60	.974
Texas	73	.974

INDIVIDUAL BATTING

BATTING AVERAGE
(Minimum 150 At-Bats)

	Yr.	AVG	G	AB	R	H	2B	3B	HR	RBI	BB	SO	SB
*Patrick Perry, Northern Colorado	Jr.	.478	50	186	53	89	27	1	13	74	26	16	2
Caleb Moore, East Tenn. State	Jr.	.455	52	202	59	92	31	1	9	45	17	18	1
Brian Bixler, Eastern Michigan	Jr.	.453	59	243	74	110	18	3	8	47	35	43	31
Stephen Carter, Eastern Ky.	Sr.	.448	46	183	50	82	14	0	1	41	21	26	21
Bryan Lange, Jackson State	Jr.	.439	49	164	50	72	17	2	3	55	20	14	29
Jim Geldhof, Central Michigan	Jr.	.427	56	227	74	97	17	4	9	68	25	27	29
Bryant Jones, Tennessee-Martin	Sr.	.425	54	226	55	96	13	3	6	33	15	25	18
Kiel Thibault, Gonzaga	So.	.424	51	205	44	87	11	3	3	35	25	17	8
Corey Wimberley, Alcorn State	Fr.	.420	42	150	51	63	8	3	0	24	20	13	40
Jonathan Woodard, Eastern Ky.	Sr.	.418	51	184	56	77	17	3	5	48	37	27	4
Nate Stone, Army	Jr.	.414	49	181	47	75	18	0	6	53	14	24	11
Warner Jones, Vanderbilt	So.	.414	64	268	55	111	27	3	11	74	11	25	12
Tim Burgess, Georgia State	Sr.	.413	49	167	33	69	19	1	7	31	32	26	4
Kurt Suzuki, CS Fullerton	Jr.	.413	69	252	78	104	17	4	16	87	50	25	9
Byron Barber, Charleston	Jr.	.410	63	261	63	107	11	3	0	58	11	12	25
Brandon Godzik, Dayton	Jr.	.407	51	162	32	66	13	0	9	53	14	23	2
Keith Stegbauer, Central Conn.	Sr.	.407	59	246	80	100	15	0	4	25	17	26	7
Dan Batz, Rhode Island	Sr.	.406	56	187	58	76	24	1	12	59	29	14	10
Jarrett Hoffpauir, Southern Miss	Jr.	.405	64	269	62	109	27	2	11	92	20	8	2
Ed Lucas, Dartmouth	Sr.	.405	42	173	47	70	17	1	4	36	15	23	3
Nolan Reimold, Bowling Green	So.	.404	47	171	42	69	14	3	13	57	25	24	4
Jeff Justice, LeMoyne	Sr.	.403	57	216	58	87	22	2	12	49	23	23	15
Eric Nielsen, Nevada-Las Vegas	Jr.	.402	61	251	84	101	23	2	16	87	30	33	7
Jeff Palumbo, George Mason	Sr.	.402	58	239	81	96	14	3	3	34	32	29	15
Ryan Jones, East Carolina	Sr.	.400	59	215	66	86	26	4	19	69	43	36	9
Tim Mascia, Florida Atlantic	So.	.400	64	225	48	90	18	0	5	59	38	21	5
Jed Lowrie, Stanford	So.	.399	60	233	72	93	19	4	17	68	50	40	6
Jeremiah Boles, Liberty	Sr.	.398	54	226	61	90	16	2	7	32	16	36	31
Jason Ruiz, Southern Utah	Jr.	.398	49	191	51	76	14	1	1	25	19	23	12
Brett Gardner, Charleston	Jr.	.397	60	237	57	94	12	9	4	51	30	30	22
Josh Mader, New Mexico	Jr.	.395	54	233	47	92	10	4	10	56	13	26	12
Hunter Pence, UT Arlington	Jr.	.395	47	190	47	75	8	5	8	35	15	23	10
Blake Adkison, Centenary	Sr.	.395	54	185	49	73	17	1	16	58	29	25	2
Brandon Green, Wichita State	Sr.	.395	65	256	38	101	27	1	2	57	28	36	7
Sean Dobson, Toledo	Sr.	.394	54	231	55	91	23	4	10	63	22	17	18
Dustin Pedroia, Arizona State	Jr.	.393	59	244	78	96	24	1	9	49	48	15	9
Thomas Myette, Dartmouth	So.	.393	40	150	39	59	16	1	2	34	14	14	4
James Cooper, Grambling	Sr.	.393	44	163	34	64	16	9	4	39	21	17	11
J.C. Holt, Louisiana State	Jr.	.393	65	270	71	106	19	3	6	52	33	40	21
Adam Lind, South Alabama	So.	.392	58	232	57	91	22	2	12	60	26	21	8
Steve Caravati, Ohio State	Jr.	.391	61	235	45	92	17	1	9	52	24	26	8
Kurt Zimniewicz, Albany	Sr.	.391	43	151	44	59	9	0	10	42	15	24	9
Chris Rahl, William & Mary	So.	.389	54	229	73	89	10	8	20	70	24	54	42
Byron Carter, Prairie View	Sr.	.389	53	175	41	68	22	0	5	52	19	22	6
Will Rhymes, William & Mary	Jr.	.388	49	188	52	73	13	4	8	35	15	12	7
Seth Bynum, Indiana	Sr.	.387	55	204	54	79	15	4	10	65	21	28	19
Brett Bolger, Eastern Kentucky	So.	.387	46	168	36	65	12	4	1	45	13	10	13
Matt Miller, Texas State	Jr.	.387	58	238	49	92	18	2	8	52	19	20	5
Brad Hayes, Arkansas State	Sr.	.386	46	171	33	66	18	0	10	45	13	25	4
Matt Adkins, Samford	So.	.386	57	223	43	86	13	7	3	48	33	37	6
Al Roach, Temple	Sr.	.385	49	179	47	69	16	0	7	41	36	25	9
Chris Westervelt, Stetson	Sr.	.385	59	205	55	79	18	0	11	56	35	33	1
Eddy Martinez-Esteve, Florida State	So.	.385	67	270	57	104	24	3	19	81	32	41	8
Brian Colopy, Ohio	Jr.	.385	52	195	41	75	17	4	2	42	26	27	9
Richie Robnett, Fresno State	So.	.384	58	229	54	88	27	3	13	50	36	41	21
Jon Zeringue, Louisiana State	Jr.	.384	65	255	56	98	19	2	12	58	26	37	3
Adam Godwin, Troy State	Jr.	.384	54	177	38	68	5	0	1	20	12	21	28
Juan Figueroa, Bethune-Cookman	Sr.	.383	55	193	48	74	15	3	8	58	33	24	5
Chad Huffman, Texas Christian	Fr.	.383	64	253	68	97	20	1	9	44	23	28	3
Matt Vanderbosch, Oral Roberts	Sr.	.383	61	240	75	92	13	7	3	52	53	40	44
Sam Herbert, Cal Poly	Sr.	.383	62	248	45	95	16	4	4	45	29	26	14
Brandon Long, Georgia Southern	Sr.	.383	56	230	58	88	12	1	8	43	25	32	9
Mark Ori, Northwestern	So.	.382	54	191	30	73	14	2	0	23	23	36	2
Jeff Frazier, Rutgers	Jr.	.382	53	207	59	79	16	1	13	59	28	27	6
Ryan Norwood, East Carolina	Jr.	.382	64	249	62	95	34	1	14	63	19	36	7

* Played for NCAA Division I provisional team

RUNS SCORED	Yr.	G	R
Eric Nielsen, Nevada-Las Vegas	Jr.	61	84
Jeff Fiorentino, Florida Atlantic	Jr.	64	84
Jeff Palumbo, George Mason	Sr.	58	81
Keith Stegbauer, Cent. Conn.	Sr.	59	80
Nick Blasi, Wichita State	Sr.	65	79
Dustin Pedroia, Arizona State	Jr.	59	78
Kurt Suzuki, CS Fullerton	Jr.	62	78
Matt Macri, Notre Dame	Jr.	61	76
Eric Patterson, Ga. Tech	Jr.	65	76
Matt Vanderbosch, Oral Roberts	.. Sr.	61	75
Phillip Coker, Charleston	So.	63	75

HITS	Yr.	G	H
Warner Jones, Vanderbilt	So.	64	111
Brian Bixler, Eastern Michigan	Jr.	59	110
Jarrett Hoffpauir, Southern Miss	Jr.	64	109
Byron Barber, Charleston	Jr.	63	107
J.C. Holt, Louisiana State	Jr.	65	106
Curtis Thigpen, Texas	Jr.	72	105
Kurt Suzuki, CS Fullerton	Jr.	69	104
Eddy Martinez-Esteve, Fla. State	.. So.	67	104
Matt Shepherd, Southern Miss	Jr.	64	104
Eric Nielsen, Nevada-Las Vegas	Jr.	61	101
Chip Grawey, UNC Wilmington	..Sr.	62	101
Brandon Green, Wichita State	Sr.	65	101
Keith Stegbauer, Central Conn.	Jr.	59	100
Ryan Patterson, Louisiana State	Jr.	65	100

SLUGGING PERCENTAGE	Yr.	G	PCT
(Minimum 150 At-Bats)			
*Patrick Perry, Northern Colorado	Jr.	50	.844
Ryan Jones, East Carolina	Sr.	59	.823
Mike Butia, James Madison	Jr.	52	.782
Chris Rahl, William & Mary	So.	54	.764
P.J. Hiser, Pittsburgh	Sr.	53	.758
Blake Adkison, Centenary	Sr.	54	.757
Mike Ferris, Miami (Ohio)	Sr.	57	.755
Alex Gordon, Nebraska	So.	59	.754
Caleb Moore, East Tenn. State	Jr.	52	.752
Nolan Reimold, Bowling Green	So.	47	.749

ON-BASE PERCENTAGE	Yr.	G	PCT
(Minimum 150 At-Bats)			
*Patrick Perry, No. Colorado	Jr.	50	.550
Stephen Carter, Eastern Kentucky	Sr.	46	.535
Brian Bixler, Eastern Michigan	Jr.	59	.519
Jonathan Woodard, Eastern Ky.	Sr.	51	.515
Chip Cannon, The Citadel	Sr.	67	.514
Mike Ferris, Miami (Ohio)	Sr.	57	.513
Kurt Suzuki, CS Fullerton	Jr.	69	.512
Ryan Jones, East Carolina	Sr.	59	.511
Tim Burgess, Georgia State	Jr.	49	.510
Caleb Moore, Eastern Kentucky	Jr.	52	.509
Eric Nielsen, Nevada-Las Vegas	Jr.	61	.508

TOTAL BASES	Yr.	G	TB
Eddy Martinez-Esteve, Fla. State	.. So.	67	191
Josh Brady, Texas Tech	Jr.	61	179
Ryan Jones, East Carolina	Sr.	59	177
Warner Jones, Vanderbilt	So.	64	177
Kurt Suzuki, CS Fullerton	Jr.	69	177
Eric Nielsen, Nevada-Las Vegas	Jr.	61	176
Chris Rahl, William & Mary	So.	54	175
Billy Becher, New Mexico State	Sr.	59	173
Ryan Norwood, East Carolina	Jr.	64	173
Jarrett Hoffpauir, Southern Miss	.. Jr.	64	173
Steve Pearce, South Carolina	Jr.	70	173
Mike Costanzo, Coastal Carolina	.. So.	62	171
Jed Lowrie, Stanford	Sr.	60	171
Ryan Patterson, Louisiana State	.. Jr.	65	169
Mike Gunning, Western Kentucky	Sr.	63	167
Brad Corley, Mississippi State	So.	59	166
Jim Burt, Miami	Sr.	63	166
Ryan Frith, Southern Mississippi...	Sr.	64	166
Marshall Hubbard, North Carolina	Jr.	64	166
Mark Jurich, Louisville	Sr.	56	165
Landon Powell, South Carolina	Sr.	70	165

DOUBLES	Yr.	G	2B
Ryan Norwood, East Carolina	Jr.	64	34
Caleb Moore, East Tenn. State	Jr.	52	31
Matt Ciaramella, Utah	Jr.	58	28
Curtis Thigpen, Texas	Jr.	72	28
Richie Robnett, Fresno State	So.	58	27
Jim Burt, Miami	Sr.	63	27
Jarrett Hoffpauir, Southern Miss.	.. Jr.	64	27
Warner Jones, Vanderbilt	So.	64	27

Jarrett Hoffpauir: 92 RBIs

	Yr.	G	3B
Matt Shepherd, Southern Miss.	.... Jr.	64	27
Brandon Green, Wichita State	...... Sr.	65	27
Ryan Jones, East Carolina	Sr.	59	26
Reed Eastley, Niagara	Jr.	54	25

TRIPLES	Yr.	G	3B
Matt Young, New Mexico	Jr.	56	12
*Ryan Olivo, Dallas Baptist	Jr.	60	10
James Cooper, Grambling	Sr.	44	9
Darryl Chever, Norfolk State	Sr.	45	9
Trevor Crowe, Arizona	So.	58	9
Brett Gardner, Charleston	Jr.	60	9
Josh LeBlanc, Southern	Jr.	36	8
B.J. Szymanski, Princeton	Jr.	45	8
Robert Benak, Md.-Eastern Shore	.. Jr.	48	8
Chris Rahl, William & Mary	So.	54	8
Mike Hughes, Illinois-Chicago	Sr.	56	8
Michael Cline, Birm.-Southern	Sr.	61	8
Ryan Klosterman, Vanderbilt	Jr.	63	8

HOME RUNS	Yr.	G	HR
Drew Moffitt, Wichita State	Sr.	62	26
Billy Becher, New Mexico State	Sr.	59	25
Ryan Frith, Southern Mississippi...	Sr.	64	22
P.J. Hiser, Pittsburgh	Sr.	53	21
Mike Ferris, Miami (Ohio)	Sr.	57	21
Jared Greenwood, West. Carolina	Jr.	59	21
Mike Costanzo, Coastal Carolina	.. So.	62	21
Trevor Lawhorn, East Carolina	Jr.	62	21
Connor Robertson, Birm.-So.	Sr.	65	21
Steve Pearce, South Carolina	Jr.	70	21
Chris Rahl, William & Mary	So.	54	20
Josh Brady, Texas Tech	Jr.	61	20
Mark Jurich, Louisville	Sr.	56	19
Brad Corley, Mississippi State	So.	59	19
Ryan Jones, East Carolina	Sr.	59	19
Eddy Martinez-Esteve, Fla. State	.. So.	67	19
Landon Powell, South Carolina	Sr.	70	19
Brendan Winn, South Carolina	Sr.	70	19
Mike Butia, James Madison	Jr.	52	18
Ty Herriott, Oakland	Sr.	54	18
Jim Fasano, Richmond	Jr.	57	18
Adrian Ballesteros, New Mx State	.. Sr.	59	18
Alex Gordon, Nebraska	So.	59	18
Cody Ehlers, Missouri	Sr.	61	18
Travis Metcalf, Kansas	Jr.	63	18
Lou Santangelo, Clemson	Jr.	64	18

RUNS BATTED IN	Yr.	G	RBI
Jarrett Hoffpauir, Southern Miss	.. Jr.	64	92
Billy Becher, New Mexico State	.... Sr.	59	90
Josh Brady, Texas Tech	Jr.	61	90
Eric Nielsen, Nevada-Las Vegas	Jr.	61	87
Kurt Suzuki, CS Fullerton	Jr.	69	87
Marshall Hubbard, North Carolina	Jr.	64	83
Cameron Blair, Texas Tech	Jr.	58	81
Chris Looze, George Mason	Jr.	58	81
Eddy Martinez-Esteve, Fla. State	.. So.	67	81
Alex Gordon, Nebraska	So.	59	75
*Patrick Perry, Northern Colorado	Jr.	50	74
Mike Costanzo, Coastal Carolina...	So.	62	74
Warner Jones, Vanderbilt	So.	64	74
Adam Innerst, George Mason	Jr.	58	73
Jim Burt, Miami	Sr.	63	73

	Yr.	G	
Mike Gunning, Western Kentucky	Sr.	63	73
Logan Sorensen, Wichita State	.... Sr.	64	73
Brent Johnson, Nevada-Las Vegas	Sr.	54	72
Drew Moffitt, Wichita State	Sr.	62	72
Derrick Peterson, Eastern Mich.	.... Sr.	59	71
Scott Simon, Northern Illinois	So.	59	71
Cody Ehlers, Missouri	Sr.	61	71
Josh Morris, Georgia	Fr.	68	71
Chris Rahl, William & Mary	So.	54	70
Kurtis Wells, Central Michigan	Jr.	57	70
Michael Mask, Texas Tech	Jr.	59	70
Ben Harrison, Florida	Sr.	63	70
Cesar Nicolas, Vanderbilt	Sr.	64	70

WALKS	Yr.	G	BB
Chip Cannon, The Citadel	Sr.	67	71
Tim Grogan, Western Kentucky	So.	63	61
Mike Ferris, Miami (Ohio)	Sr.	57	60
Drew Moffitt, Wichita State	Sr.	62	60
Tom Caple, San Diego	Sr.	56	55

STRIKEOUTS	Yr.	G	SO
Brendan Winn, South Carolina	Jr.	70	85
Drew Stubbs, Texas	Fr.	71	75
Richard Bishop, Samford	Jr.	55	74
Ryan Frith, Southern Miss	Sr.	64	73
Jeremy Pickrel, Illinois State	Jr.	47	73
Dana Tonosi, New Orleans	Sr.	53	72

TOUGHEST TO STRIKE OUT	Yr.	AB	SO	Ratio
(Minimum 125 At-Bats)				
Jarrett Hoffpauir, S. Miss	Jr.	269	8	33.6
Sam Deluca, Manhattan	Fr.	206	7	29.4
DeCarlos Hughley, Ala. State	Fr.	161	6	26.8
Matt Johnston, Western Ky.	.. Sr.	228	10	22.8
Anthony Buffone, Maryland	.. Sr.	244	11	22.2

STOLEN BASES	Yr.	G	SB	ATT
Dennis Diaz, Florida Int.	Jr.	62	50	54
Carl Lipsey, Jackson State	Jr.	47	49	57
Eric Patterson, Ga. Tech	Jr.	65	48	55
Anthony Granato, VCU	Sr.	57	44	49
Matt Vanderbosch, O. Roberts	.. Sr.	61	44	48
Clay Timpner, Central Florida	.. Jr.	65	43	49
Chris Rahl, William & Mary	.. So.	54	42	46
Kyle Brown, LeMoyne	Sr.	57	42	49
Garrett Weir, Delaware State	.. Sr.	48	42	47
Corey Wimberley, Alcorn St.	.. Fr.	42	40	46
Chris Monaco, Marshall	Jr.	51	40	52
Larry Best-Berfet, Jax	Sr.	56	40	46
Chip Grawey, UNC-W	So.	62	39	48
Ben Copeland, Pittsburgh	So.	54	37	40
Sebastien Boucher, B-Cook.	.. Jr.	55	35	44
Jermel Lomack, Pr. View	Sr.	55	35	39
Rey Rojas, High Point	Sr.	55	35	41
Chris Stanton, Va. Tech	Jr.	56	34	37
Josh Brady, Texas Tech	Jr.	61	34	38
Antoan Richardson, Vandy	.. Jr.	64	32	38

HIT BY PITCH	Yr.	G	HBP
Eric Nielsen, Nevada-Las Vegas	.... Jr.	61	27
Brad Frick, Bethune-Cookman	...... Sr.	49	26
Chris Gimenez, Nevada	Jr.	59	26
Zach Clem, Washington	So.	58	24
Byron Barber, Charleston	Jr.	63	24

Eddy Martinez-Esteve: 191 total bases

EARNED RUN AVERAGE
(Minimum 60 Innings)

	Yr.	W	L	ERA	G	GS	CG	SV	IP	H	R	ER	BB	SO
Nate Moore, Troy State	Jr.	9	4	1.25	32	0	0	8	65	42	15	9	16	84
Boyd Goodner, Arkansas	Sr.	3	3	1.50	32	0	0	0	60	55	14	10	16	46
Jered Weaver, Long Beach State	Jr.	15	1	1.63	19	19	3	0	144	81	31	26	21	213
Jason Windsor, CS Fullerton	Sr.	13	4	1.71	22	18	11	1	163	100	37	31	24	148
Wade Townsend, Rice	Jr.	12	0	1.72	18	15	2	2	120	74	29	23	45	148
Matt Fox, Central Florida	Jr.	14	2	1.85	17	17	6	0	112	78	33	23	32	125
Jon Wilson, Winthrop	Jr.	11	0	1.88	34	0	0	6	67	47	18	14	17	79
Derrick Gordon, Lamar	Fr.	7	3	1.92	18	11	2	0	66	44	18	14	35	54
Kyle Bono, Central Florida	So.	8	2	1.94	18	15	6	2	97	70	34	21	29	107
Taylor Tankersley, Alabama	Jr.	2	5	1.99	20	7	0	4	68	50	17	15	26	70
William Delage, Lamar	So.	6	0	2.00	14	12	1	0	72	53	24	16	31	68
Derek Tharpe, Tennessee	Sr.	6	1	2.01	13	13	2	0	81	66	22	18	19	84
Kris Johnson, Wichita State	Fr.	7	0	2.01	13	11	1	0	72	54	22	16	28	66
Shawn Phillips, Delaware State	Sr.	10	2	2.02	17	15	7	2	116	94	40	26	11	111
Ryan Zink, Illinois-Chicago	Fr.	9	3	2.07	19	11	6	3	96	76	31	22	15	92
Wade LeBlanc, Alabama	Fr.	8	4	2.08	16	15	8	0	113	87	37	26	26	98
J. Brent Cox, Texas	So.	6	2	2.12	37	0	0	5	64	47	16	15	19	63
Jordan Thomson, Northeastern	Sr.	8	4	2.13	14	13	6	0	85	67	29	20	12	82
J.P. Howell, Texas	Jr.	15	2	2.13	24	20	4	1	135	90	45	32	53	166
Adam Lesko, Oral Roberts	Sr.	7	1	2.15	22	8	1	0	84	70	31	20	21	49
Jonathan Ellis, The Citadel	Jr.	12	3	2.18	18	18	9	0	136	112	42	33	39	131
Matt Scherer, LeMoyne	Jr.	10	3	2.18	14	14	3	0	103	79	29	25	14	88
Mike Pelfrey, Wichita State	So.	11	2	2.19	16	16	5	0	115	86	35	28	24	125
Vern Sterry, North Carolina State	Sr.	9	2	2.20	18	16	2	0	114	92	38	28	23	106
Will Startup, Georgia	So.	7	2	2.22	33	0	0	12	81	55	28	20	23	70
Tommy Hottovy, Wichita State	Sr.	9	3	2.25	23	3	1	2	76	64	26	19	10	92
Philip Humber, Rice	Jr.	13	4	2.27	20	15	2	1	115	87	34	29	37	154
Cesar Ramos, Long Beach State	So.	12	4	2.29	19	19	1	0	134	108	41	34	35	97
Donnie Smith, Old Dominion	Jr.	6	2	2.29	20	9	2	6	86	65	26	22	25	99
Patrick Stanley, Pace	Jr.	8	4	2.30	12	12	5	0	74	56	29	19	31	69
Nolan Moser, Cal Poly	Sr.	2	1	2.31	27	1	1	9	62	46	19	16	22	52
Sam LeCure, Texas	So.	9	3	2.34	24	23	1	0	123	97	45	32	34	113
Thomas Diamond, New Orleans	Jr.	6	4	2.37	17	17	2	0	114	87	43	30	45	138
Justin Orenduff, VCU	Jr.	5	5	2.43	15	15	3	0	100	84	33	27	34	129
Jason Chavez, Southern Illinois	Jr.	5	4	2.44	16	9	2	0	74	74	32	20	34	36
Michael Gardner, UT Arlington	So.	11	3	2.49	16	15	1	0	105	84	37	29	33	77
Sean Sorrow, Oral Roberts	Sr.	9	1	2.49	19	11	2	1	87	78	30	24	20	59
Kyle Stutes, Lamar	Sr.	10	2	2.49	24	11	3	3	90	76	30	25	21	84
Andy Sonnanstine, Kent State	So.	11	4	2.52	18	18	2	0	125	122	52	35	21	117
Pat Egan, Quinnipiac	So.	7	2	2.54	11	9	6	0	60	49	21	17	13	39
Casey Lambert, Virginia	Fr.	4	1	2.54	29	1	0	8	60	51	18	17	21	40
Brett Smith, UC Irvine	Jr.	8	5	2.54	16	16	2	0	113	102	43	32	29	113
Cla Meredith, Va. Commonwealth	Jr.	7	3	2.55	26	2	0	7	67	49	27	19	12	84
Joe Piekarz, Northern Illinois	Sr.	9	5	2.55	17	16	6	0	116	112	51	33	41	96
Taylor Meier, Central Florida	Fr.	6	3	2.55	13	12	1	0	74	59	29	21	30	56

WINS

	Yr.	W	L
Jered Weaver, Long Beach State	....	Jr.	15	1
J.P. Howell, Texas	Jr.	15	2
Matt Fox, Central Florida	Jr.	14	2
Ricky Romero, CS Fullerton	So.	14	4
Dennis Bigley, Oral Roberts	Jr.	13	1
Philip Humber, Rice	Jr.	13	4
Aaron Rawl, South Carolina	Jr.	13	4
Dennis Robinson, Jacksonville	Jr.	13	4
Jason Windsor, CS Fullerton	Sr.	13	4
Cesar Carrillo, Miami	So.	12	0
Ryan Johnson, Charleston	Jr.	12	0
Wade Townsend, Rice	Jr.	12	0
Steven Carter, Coastal Carolina	Jr.	12	3
Jonathan Ellis, The Citadel	Jr.	12	3
Spencer Grogan, Oklahoma State	Jr.	12	3
Rowdy Hardy, Austin Peay	So.	12	3
Wes Letson, Birm.-Southern	Jr.	12	3
Jason Urquidez, Arizona State	Jr.	12	3
Steve Grasley, Creighton	Sr.	12	4
Ronald Hill, UNC Wilmington	Jr.	12	4
Cesar Ramos, Long Beach State	So.	12	4

LOSSES

	Yr.	W	L
Ben Rulon, Georgia State	Jr.	2	12
Bill Konecny, Xavier	So.	5	12
Doug Grant, St. Peter's	Sr.	1	11
Paul Vignola, Air Force	So.	1	11

APPEARANCES

	Yr.	G
Buck Cody, Texas	Jr.	40
J. Brent Cox, Texas	So.	37
Chad Blackwell, South Carolina	Jr.	37
Eric Roberts, Alabama-Birmingham	Jr.	37
Mike Snapp, Texas-Arlington	Sr.	36
Brandon Roznovsky, Houston	Sr.	36

Chad Blackwell: 20 saves

SAVES

	Yr.	G	SV
Chad Blackwell, South Carolina	...... Jr.	37	20
Blair Erickson, UC Irvine	Fr.	30	17
Shawn Ryan, Albany	Jr.	27	14
Ryan Schroyer, San Diego State	Sr.	28	13
Justin Ramsey, Oral Roberts	Sr.	30	13
Anthony Rea, Santa Clara	Jr.	30	13
Brett Harker, Charleston	So.	33	13
Darek Stanfield, Akron	Jr.	29	12
Ryan Doherty, Notre Dame	So.	29	12
Neil Jamison, Long Beach State	Jr.	30	12
Derrik Lutz, George Washington	Fr.	30	12
Huston Street, Texas	Jr.	31	12
Blake Cross, UNC Wilmington	Sr.	32	12
Will Startup, Georgia	So.	33	12
Michael Snapp, Texas-Arlington	Sr.	36	12

INNINGS PITCHED

	Yr.	G	IP
Jason Windsor, CS Fullerton	Sr.	22	163
Ricky Romero, CS Fullerton	So.	22	155
Koley Kolberg, Arizona	Jr.	25	149
Jered Weaver, Long Beach State	Jr.	19	144
Justin Hoyman, Florida	Jr.	19	140
Jonathan Ellis, The Citadel	Jr.	18	136

WALKS

	Yr.	IP	BB
Tim Lincecum, Washington	Fr.	112	82
Bill Konecny, Xavier	So.	79	72
Dan Graham, Xavier	So.	69	71
Grady Hinchman, Western Ky.	Jr.	105	71
Joe Reid, St. John's	Sr.	78	63

STRIKEOUTS

	Yr.	IP	SO
Jered Weaver, Long Beach State	Jr.	144	213
J.P. Howell, Texas	Jr.	135	166
Tim Lincecum, Washington	Fr.	112	161
Philip Humber, Rice	Jr.	115	154
Justin Verlander, Old Dominion	.... Jr.	106	151
Wade Townsend, Rice	Jr.	120	148
Jason Windsor, CS Fullerton	Sr.	163	148
Matt Campbell, South Carolina	...... Jr.	124	145
Thomas Diamond, New Orleans	Jr.	114	138
Mark Roberts, Oklahoma	Sr.	121	134
Jonathan Ellis, The Citadel	Jr.	136	131
David Purcey, Oklahoma	Jr.	119	130
Justin Orenduff, VCU	Jr.	100	129
R.J. Swindle, Char. Southern	Jr.	114	127
Zach Jackson, Texas A&M	Jr.	121	127
Ricky Romero, CS Fullerton	So.	155	126

STRIKEOUTS/9 INNINGS
(Minimum 50 Innings)

	Yr.	IP	SO	AVG
Jered Weaver, L.B. State	Jr.	144	213	13.3
Tim Lincecum, Washington	.. Fr.	112	161	12.9
Justin Verlander, ODU	Jr.	106	151	12.9
Bill Bray, William & Mary	Jr.	59	84	12.8
Chris Blazek, Vermont	.... So.	68	92	12.2
Josh Schmidt, Pacific	Jr.	54	73	12.2
Philip Humber, Rice	Jr.	115	154	12.1
Zach Ward, Gardner-Webb	.. So.	80	106	12.0
Zach Zuercher, Rh. Island	.. So.	93	123	11.9
Nate Moore, Troy State	Jr.	65	84	11.7
Ian Kennedy, So. California	.. Fr.	93	120	11.7
Justin Orenduff, VCU	Jr.	100	129	11.6
Mike Parisi, Manhattan	Jr.	81	104	11.6
Ryan Hamilton, Ark. State	.... Sr.	69	88	11.5
Chris Mobley, Middle Tenn.	.. Jr.	96	122	11.5

J.P. Howell: 15 wins

COMPLETE GAMES

	Yr.	GS	CG
Jason Windsor, CS Fullerton	.... Sr.	18	11
Zac Cline, West Virginia	.... Jr.	12	10
Eric Chown, Massachusetts	.... Sr.	12	9
Zach Zuercher, Rhode Island	.... So.	12	9
Jonathan Ellis, The Citadel	.... Jr.	18	9
Nick Hill, Army	Fr.	13	8
Wade LeBlanc, Alabama	.... Fr.	15	8
Adrian Duran, Morehead State	...... Jr.	15	8
Brian Jones, Mercer	.... Sr.	18	8

COLLEGE
TOP 25

BATTERS: 10 or more at-bats. **PITCHERS:** 5 or more innings.

Boldface indicates selected in 2004 draft.

1. CAL STATE FULLERTON

Coach: George Horton   **Record:** 47-22

BATTING	YR	AVG	AB	R	H	2B	3B	HR	RBI	SB
Suzuki, Kurt, c-1b	Jr.	.413	252	77	104	17	4	16	87	9
Garcia, Felipe, dh	Jr.	.353	252	39	89	18	1	6	50	0
Pilittere, P.J., 1b-c	Sr.	.351	268	54	94	18	1	4	49	2
Hardman, Clark, of-rhp	Fr.	.341	214	44	73	6	1	0	31	5
Pedroza, Sergio, of	So.	.333	195	40	65	20	1	7	39	0
Andrews, Bobby, of	Jr.	.325	83	21	27	3	0	1	15	4
Prettyman, Ronnie, 3b	Jr.	.324	262	53	85	16	5	3	38	14
Dorn, Danny, of	So.	.318	242	50	77	17	2	4	59	8
Pill, Brett, 1b	Fr.	.313	80	16	25	7	3	2	17	0
Turner, Justin, 2b	So.	.304	253	45	77	16	0	0	34	7
Davis, Blake, ss	Fr.	.295	112	24	33	6	1	2	21	6
Carroll, Mark, 2b	Jr.	.250	24	6	6	1	0	1	3	1
Walton, Neil, ss	Fr.	.237	131	19	31	4	1	0	15	4
Turgeon, Joe, of	Jr.	.231	13	10	3	0	0	0	1	1
Curtis, John, c-1b	Jr.	.208	24	4	5	1	0	0	7	0
Scobee, Shawn, of	So.	.182	22	2	4	0	0	1	4	1
Tripp, Brandon, of	Fr.	.158	19	13	3	1	0	0	0	2
Mendrin, Jake, 1b	So.	.091	11	1	1	0	0	0	0	0

PITCHING	YR	W	L	ERA	G	SV	IP	H	BB	SO
Windsor, Jason, rhp	Sr.	13	4	1.72	22	1	163	100	24	148
Sarver, Scott, lhp	Jr.	3	2	2.65	19	0	37	34	13	30
Romero, Ricky, lhp	So.	14	4	3.37	22	0	155	146	42	126
Martinez, Mike, rhp	Sr.	8	3	4.24	28	2	91	115	24	59
Gagnier, Lauren, rhp	Fr.	2	2	4.50	11	0	26	25	13	11
Pestano, Vinnie, rhp	Fr.	3	3	4.69	30	1	48	53	4	37
Schreppel, Ryan, lhp	So.	3	3	6.03	23	2	66	67	38	49
Bruyninckx, Nolan, rhp	Fr.	1	1	7.71	18	0	23	29	7	16
Hardman, Clark, rhp	Fr.	0	0	10.80	5	0	5	9	1	5

2. TEXAS

Coach: Augie Garrido   **Record:** 58-15

BATTING	YR	AVG	AB	R	H	2B	3B	HR	RBI	SB
Thigpen, Curtis, 1b-c	Jr.	.378	278	57	105	28	2	7	51	10
Kainer, Carson, of	Fr.	.335	167	31	56	9	0	3	24	3
Russ, Ryan, of	Sr.	.302	129	29	39	7	4	2	25	6
Stubbs, Drew, of	Fr.	.301	266	51	80	16	3	8	47	28
Johnston, Seth, ss	Jr.	.296	247	48	79	16	3	7	51	15
Prince, Dooley, of-dh	Jr.	.296	142	35	42	7	3	0	19	12
Hudson, Robby, ss	Jr.	.287	164	27	47	4	1	3	24	4
Reininger, J.D., 3b-dh	Jr.	.275	160	28	44	8	2	4	33	11
Teagarden, Taylor, c-1b	So.	.273	260	50	71	17	1	10	51	1
Harris, Hunter, of	Jr.	.271	133	16	36	6	3	0	21	3
Crouch, Will, dh	Jr.	.258	31	8	8	2	0	0	3	2
Warrick, Nathan, of	Fr.	.256	39	7	10	1	0	0	6	7
Dodge, Scott, of	Jr.	.250	12	2	3	0	0	0	0	0
Wheeless, Chance, 1b	Fr.	.226	62	9	14	4	0	0	10	2
Hollimon, Michael, ss	Jr.	.225	173	35	39	6	2	5	28	8
Maroul, David, 3b	Jr.	.224	116	21	26	8	0	5	16	1
Spencer, Matt, dh	Jr.	.176	17	1	3	0	0	0	1	0
Peoples, Nick, of	Fr.	.125	24	3	3	0	0	0	2	1

PITCHING	YR	W	L	ERA	G	SV	IP	H	BB	SO
Street, Huston, rhp	Jr.	6	1	1.58	31	12	57	36	13	59
Cody, Buck, lhp	Jr.	1	2	1.81	40	2	45	31	17	47
Cox, J. Brent, rhp	So.	6	2	2.12	37	5	64	47	19	63
Howell, J.P., lhp	Jr.	15	2	2.13	24	1	135	90	53	166
LeCure, Sam, rhp	So.	9	3	2.34	24	0	123	97	34	113
Yates, Kyle, rhp	Jr.	1	1	3.05	28	0	41	40	21	45
McCulloch, Kyle, rhp	Fr.	7	0	3.25	25	1	53	48	18	34
Boone, Randy, rhp	Fr.	3	1	3.27	18	0	44	46	14	30
Simmons, Justin, lhp	Sr.	10	3	4.18	18	0	90	87	33	43

3. SOUTH CAROLINA

Coach: Ray Tanner   **Record:** 53-17

BATTING	YR	AVG	AB	R	H	2B	3B	HR	RBI	SB
Pearce, Steve, 1b-3b	Jr.	.346	266	60	92	18	0	21	70	4
Powell, Landon, c	Sr.	.330	270	66	89	17	1	19	66	2
Gregg, Davy, of	Jr.	.325	228	33	74	11	1	0	26	14

	YR	AVG	AB	R	H	2B	3B	HR	RBI	SB
Tolleson, Steven, ss	So.	.316	196	40	62	14	1	4	25	7
Campell, Michael, of	So.	.312	269	45	84	14	2	14	52	7
Winn, Brendan, of	Jr.	.305	259	60	79	18	3	19	69	5
Melillo, Kevin, 2b	Jr.	.300	180	45	54	7	1	9	36	4
Triplett, Bryan, 3b-ss	Sr.	.279	.283	59	79	22	0	8	39	7
Mahoney, Ryan, c-dh	Fr.	.257	105	16	27	7	0	2	14	0
Gardiner, Nick, dh	Jr.	.244	45	6	11	2	0	0	9	0
Tommy King, 2b	Fr.	.235	98	13	23	5	0	2	8	1
Parks, Hank, dh-1b	Sr.	.225	111	13	25	2	0	6	22	1
Cash, David, if	Jr.	.217	46	7	10	1	0	0	5	1
Stanley, Mark, of	So.	.217	23	11	5	1	0	1	6	0
McDaniel, Trey, 1b	So.	.200	20	4	4	3	1	0	3	0
Reinhold, Steven, dh	Jr.	.190	21	10	4	1	0	1	3	5

PITCHING	YR	W	L	ERA	G	SV	IP	H	BB	SO
Blackwell, Chad, rhp	Jr.	4	3	2.57	37	20	63	52	14	80
Campbell, Matt, lhp	Jr.	10	6	3.05	22	0	124	99	38	145
McCamie, Zac, rhp	Jr.	7	0	3.10	21	0	58	48	10	49
Hempy, Arik, lhp	Fr.	3	1	3.27	25	1	52	38	14	49
Donald, Cliff, rhp	Jr.	2	0	3.32	22	1	41	48	8	37
Buckner, Billy, rhp	Jr.	7	2	3.32	15	0	84	77	23	105
Fletcher, Jason, rhp	Jr.	6	1	3.40	18	1	56	50	13	59
Honeycutt, Harris, rhp	Fr.	1	0	4.15	10	1	17	13	9	24
Rawl, Aaron, lhp	Jr.	13	4	4.28	20	0	122	135	17	98

4. MIAMI

Coach: Jim Morris   **Record:** 50-13

BATTING	YR	AVG	AB	R	H	2B	3B	HR	RBI	SB
Figueroa, Paco, of	Jr.	.373	102	35	38	5	2	3	19	18
Burt, Jim, 1b	Sr.	.371	245	70	91	27	3	14	73	7
Barton, Brian, of	Jr.	.371	202	55	75	10	4	6	46	17
Jay, Jon, of	Fr.	.368	234	51	86	14	1	6	56	19
Tomas, Sergio, ss	Fr.	.339	124	31	42	10	1	0	16	4
Braun, Ryan, ss-dh	Jr.	.335	155	42	52	10	1	10	45	21
Ricks, Adam, 2b	Sr.	.329	234	58	77	14	1	11	50	6
San Pedro, Erick, c	Jr.	.320	194	50	62	15	2	12	52	1
Sanchez, Gaby, 3b	Jr.	.316	231	46	73	16	0	7	47	7
Katin, Brendan, of-dh	Jr.	.283	99	26	28	6	1	6	24	5
Hooft, Joey, of	Jr.	.274	157	36	43	2	2	1	21	18
Giannotti, Richard, of	Jr.	.260	146	35	38	5	3	5	35	9
Rodriguez, Eddy, c	Fr.	.241	29	6	7	2	0	0	6	0

PITCHING	YR	W	L	ERA	G	SV	IP	H	BB	SO
Albir, Marcelo, rhp	So.	0	0	2.25	9	0	12	14	5	13
Carrillo, Cesar, rhp	So.	12	0	2.69	19	2	114	93	43	91
Lane, Andrew, lhp	So.	0	0	2.84	12	0	6	10	4	11
Chirino, Chiqui, lhp	So.	0	0	3.00	20	0	15	11	14	16
Gil, Danny, rhp	Fr.	8	0	3.03	27	5	39	23	27	49
Cockroft, J.D., lhp	Sr.	9	5	3.55	20	0	104	106	36	63
Blanco, Alex, rhp	Jr.	1	1	4.13	29	1	28	24	17	36
Camardese, Brandon, lhp	Jr.	6	3	4.20	17	0	90	78	42	63
Touchet, Dan, rhp	Sr.	5	1	4.81	14	0	49	47	17	29
Bongiovanni, Vince, rhp	Jr.	3	2	5.40	13	0	38	38	27	36
Orta, Ricky, rhp	Fr.	2	0	6.14	14	2	15	20	7	16
Perez, Chris, rhp	Fr.	0	0	7.71	11	1	19	17	18	30

5. GEORGIA

Coach: David Perno   **Record:** 45-23

BATTING	YR	AVG	AB	R	H	2B	3B	HR	RBI	SB
Holmes, Justin, ss	Sr.	.332	247	59	82	14	3	8	56	18
Wyatt, Jonathan, of	So.	.323	93	25	30	8	0	1	8	6
Morris, Josh, 1b	Fr.	.319	238	47	76	16	1	16	71	5
Smith, Josh, 3b	Jr.	.314	261	62	82	16	2	3	40	4
Szabo, Marshall, 2b	Jr.	.307	267	45	82	17	3	6	41	5
Felmy, Bobby, of	So.	.300	257	43	77	16	1	9	47	11
McDaniel, Adam, ss	Jr.	.297	37	8	11	1	0	0	4	1
Keen, Kyle, of	Fr.	.293	191	41	56	7	1	4	30	15
Side, Joey, of	Fr.	.288	243	46	70	9	1	5	35	8
Jacobs, Jason, if	Jr.	.286	133	34	38	5	1	5	28	7
Robbins, Matt, dh	Jr.	.283	46	10	13	5	0	1	9	0
Sammons, Clint, c	Jr.	.278	234	36	65	11	1	4	41	1
Thornhill, Chad, 1b	So.	.278	18	5	5	1	0	0	4	0
Smith, Derek, c	Jr.	.262	61	11	16	7	1	2	17	0

COLLEGE BASEBALL

	YR	AVG	AB	R	H	2B	3B	HR	RBI	SB
Pittman, Ryan, dh	So.	.154	26	6	4	1	0	0	5	0

PITCHING		W	L	ERA	G	SV	IP	H	BB	SO
Startup, Will, lhp	So.	7	2	2.22	33	12	81	55	23	70
Hyle, Michael, rhp	So.	8	2	2.99	16	0	87	87	32	55
Lanier, Bo, rhp	So.	4	1	3.13	24	2	46	44	19	42
Ruthven, Sean, rhp	Jr.	7	2	3.41	20	0	90	70	35	91
Dobbs, Johnny, rhp	Jr.	6	2	3.75	19	0	48	39	13	44
Lubrano, Paul, lhp	Sr.	5	4	4.64	18	0	95	100	34	63
Boggs, Mitchell, rhp	So.	2	4	4.65	19	1	31	36	16	30
Warren, Rip, lhp	Fr.	1	1	4.95	14	0	20	23	5	19
McLaughlin, Josh, rhp	Jr.	1	1	6.38	20	1	24	25	14	37
Timm, David, lhp	Jr.	1	1	7.11	6	0	19	29	9	19
Woods, Matt, rhp	Sr.	2	3	7.23	19	0	37	54	13	28
Webb, Chris, rhp	So.	0	0	9.00	5	0	6	6	3	5
Brown, Brooks, rhp	Fr.	0	0	10.22	12	1	12	17	11	19
Carroll, Joey, rhp	Fr.	1	0	12.46	5	0	9	12	6	4

6. ARKANSAS

Coach: Dave Van Horn   **Record:** 45-24

BATTING	YR	AVG	AB	R	H	2B	3B	HR	RBI	SB
Hagedorn, Brett, of-ss	Sr.	.342	73	18	25	6	0	1	21	2
Goodwin, Clay, 3b	Jr.	.319	226	49	72	13	0	4	32	4
Pratt, Haas, 1b	Sr.	.310	258	38	80	13	0	8	52	1
Hamblin, Danny, dh	Jr.	.304	253	53	77	19	1	8	42	10
Parker, Blake, c-of	Fr.	.303	165	23	50	7	0	0	21	4
Dugger, Jake, of	Fr.	.293	249	48	73	9	3	8	44	12
Hode, Scott, ss	Jr.	.293	232	30	68	14	3	7	53	5
Rowlett, Casey, of	Jr.	.292	253	47	74	10	1	3	22	22
Toops, Brady, c	Jr.	.284	215	36	61	15	0	5	30	6
Day, Devin, 2b	Jr.	.275	171	30	47	9	1	2	23	11
Merrill, Bubbs, ss	Sr.	.273	44	5	12	2	0	1	9	1
Bridges, Scott, 3b-2b	Jr.	.254	134	35	34	8	2	3	22	24
Robison, Stephen, of	Jr.	.245	53	13	13	1	0	2	7	7
Watts, Kern, of	Fr.	.149	47	12	7	0	0	0	4	2

PITCHING		W	L	ERA	G	SV	IP	H	BB	SO
Goodner, Boyd, rhp	Sr.	3	3	1.50	32	0	60	55	16	46
Boyce, Charley, rhp	So.	10	3	3.20	22	1	115	119	22	81
Sawatski, Jay, lhp	Sr.	10	3	3.38	31	7	93	104	24	86
Brannon, Clint, rhp	Jr.	4	4	3.76	20	0	105	112	30	73
Holloway, Trey, lhp	Jr.	2	2	3.77	23	1	45	52	6	16
Hall, Caton, rhp	Sr.	5	2	4.58	22	4	35	44	14	29
Maday, Daryl, rhp	Fr.	4	0	4.75	18	0	47	52	26	31
McLelland, Brian, rhp	Fr.	1	0	4.97	9	0	13	15	9	12
Stallings, Matt, rhp	So.	2	1	5.31	13	0	20	24	6	22
White, Justin, rhp	Fr.	2	3	6.08	14	0	37	50	13	15
Lennerton, Ryan, lhp	So.	0	2	6.35	11	0	23	26	7	18
Butler, Zach, rhp	So.	1	1	6.39	9	3	13	17	7	9
Gilbert, James, lhp	Fr.	0	0	9.00	5	0	6	9	4	5

7. LOUISIANA STATE

Coach: Smoke Laval   **Record:** 46-19

BATTING	YR	AVG	AB	R	H	2B	3B	HR	RBI	SB
Holt, J.C., of	Jr.	.393	270	71	106	19	3	6	52	21
Zeringue, Jon, of	Jr.	.384	255	56	98	19	2	12	57	3
Weaver, Dustin, c	Jr.	.360	50	8	18	3	0	1	12	0
Gill, Blake, 2b-ss	Jr.	.343	236	42	81	11	4	5	42	3
Patterson, Ryan, of	So.	.341	293	70	100	23	2	14	67	6
DiLiberto, Bobby, 3b	Jr.	.333	18	4	6	1	0	3	8	0
Harris, Will, 1b	So.	.329	173	38	57	9	0	7	39	0
Liuzza, Matt, c	So.	.328	229	37	75	14	0	9	45	0
Stavinoha, Nick, dh	Jr.	.323	232	46	75	17	1	8	42	3
Harris, Clay, 3b-1b	Jr.	.297	249	51	74	13	3	7	51	2
Naccarata, Ivan, 3b-2b	So.	.281	203	46	57	6	0	5	35	5
Hebert, Derek, ss	Jr.	.278	90	22	25	5	0	1	6	1
Horwath, Matt, ss	So.	.246	57	11	14	4	0	1	9	0

PITCHING		W	L	ERA	G	SV	IP	H	BB	SO
Smith, Greg, lhp	So.	2	0	2.35	22	1	31	26	13	35
Faircloth, Jordan, rhp	Jr.	3	3	2.79	26	4	58	54	13	41
Dirks, Clay, lhp	Fr.	8	2	3.43	17	1	81	83	17	66
Mestepey, Lane, lhp	Jr.	7	4	3.51	20	0	100	117	28	42
Meier, Justin, rhp	So.	6	2	3.84	18	0	101	120	28	75
Bumstead, Nate, rhp	So.	10	3	4.00	16	0	92	109	21	54
Determann, Jason, lhp	So.	6	5	4.14	20	1	76	72	16	50
Bonura, Michael, rhp	Fr.	4	0	4.46	14	0	34	33	22	31
Smith, Collin, rhp	Jr.	0	0	9.00	4	0	5	6	4	5

8. EAST CAROLINA

Coach: Randy Mazey   **Record:** 51-13

BATTING	YR	AVG	AB	R	H	2B	3B	HR	RBI	SB
Jones, Ryan, of-dh	Sr.	.400	215	66	86	26	4	19	69	9
Norwood, Ryan, 1b	Jr.	.382	249	62	95	34	1	14	63	7
Paige, Jamie, of	Jr.	.363	267	67	97	16	1	1	42	20

	YR	AVG	AB	R	H	2B	3B	HR	RBI	SB
Minicozzi, Mark, 3b	So.	.342	231	62	79	18	0	10	50	3
Costanzo, Drew, of-dh	Jr.	.320	175	37	56	11	1	5	38	4
Lawhorn, Trevor, 2b	So.	.301	256	50	77	16	0	21	66	12
Lawhorn, Darryl, of	Jr.	.298	198	40	59	11	1	10	45	8
Smith, Jake, c	So.	.293	92	10	27	3	0	2	13	0
Poppert, John, c	Sr.	.286	168	40	48	8	0	6	19	5
Lindgren, Brett, ss	Jr.	.286	42	8	12	0	0	0	3	1
Grace, Mike, of	Fr.	.281	89	14	25	4	1	5	27	1
Richardson, Billy, ss	Jr.	.234	209	35	49	5	1	2	27	15
Cavanaugh, Brian, of	Jr.	.200	25	11	5	1	1	1	5	0
Witter, Adam, c	So.	.184	38	6	7	0	0	4	10	0
Harrington, Mike, 1b-3b	Sr.	.130	23	5	3	0	0	0	4	0

PITCHING	YR	W	L	ERA	G	SV	IP	H	BB	SO
Powell, Phillip, rhp	Fr.	0	0	2.08	8	1	9	6	3	6
Bunn, Greg, rhp	Jr.	10	1	2.70	17	0	107	72	30	117
Rhodes, Kevin, rhp	So.	5	1	2.87	18	2	38	34	9	28
Andrews, Scott, lhp	So.	3	0	2.95	12	0	21	20	5	5
Harrell, Carter, rhp	So.	5	2	3.00	16	1	48	50	14	40
Bishop, Matt, rhp	Jr.	4	1	3.00	17	3	30	29	3	36
Mathews, Shane, rhp	Fr.	7	1	3.72	18	0	77	76	19	54
Flye, Mike, rhp	Fr.	2	3	3.82	19	5	33	24	11	36
Sasser, Dustin, lhp	Fr.	2	0	4.29	20	3	42	42	15	35
Connelly, P.J., rhp	Jr.	3	0	4.50	12	0	28	23	20	18
Taylor, Brody, lhp	Jr.	8	0	4.64	15	0	85	97	16	63
Brooks, Ricky, rhp	Fr.	2	3	6.32	15	0	37	44	18	30

9. STANFORD

Coach: Mark Marquess   **Record:** 46-14

BATTING	YR	AVG	AB	R	H	2B	3B	HR	RBI	SB
Lowrie, Jed, 2b-ss	So.	.399	233	72	93	19	4	17	68	6
Putnam, Danny, of	Jr.	.378	249	61	94	10	4	16	62	6
Ash, Jonny, 3b	Sr.	.372	183	55	68	6	3	5	35	2
Hall, Brian, of	Jr.	.356	236	51	84	13	4	9	52	15
Mayberry, John, 1b	So.	.333	216	53	72	11	2	16	62	9
Seawell, Ryan, dh	Fr.	.333	36	5	12	2	0	0	7	1
Lucy, Donny, c	Jr.	.313	208	53	65	10	0	12	47	5
Carter, Chris, dh	So.	.289	149	23	43	6	1	9	39	1
Fuld, Sam, of	Sr.	.273	249	62	68	5	1	4	30	9
Minaker, Chris, ss	So.	.270	174	28	47	6	0	4	33	3
Hester, John, c	So.	.265	34	2	9	3	0	0	7	2
Rapoport, Jim, of	Fr.	.250	60	10	15	0	1	0	9	1
Lewis, Chris, 2b	Jr.	.233	43	12	10	2	0	4	7	0
Sorgi, Adam, ss	Fr.	.214	70	8	15	1	0	0	5	0
Summerhays, Ben, 1b	So.	.167	12	1	2	0	0	1	0	0

PITCHING	YR	W	L	ERA	G	SV	IP	H	BB	SO
O'Hagan, David, rhp	Sr.	6	2	2.97	22	6	58	39	22	58
Ehrlich, Drew, rhp	Sr.	1	0	3.14	9	0	14	15	9	13
Quick, Kodiak, rhp	So.	1	0	3.62	16	1	27	22	13	20
Manship, Matt, rhp	So.	0	0	4.19	21	3	34	31	13	23
Leva, Matt, rhp	Fr.	6	2	4.29	14	0	36	35	11	19
Romanczuk, Mark, lhp	So.	11	3	4.31	17	0	109	112	39	94
Holler, Blake, lhp	Fr.	4	2	4.34	22	2	58	62	23	49
Gilmore, Jeff, rhp	So.	10	2	4.43	19	1	108	106	24	77
Stimpson, Jeff, rhp	Fr.	1	2	4.68	20	1	33	33	11	23
Dyer, Jonny, rhp	Jr.	1	0	4.82	7	1	9	11	1	6
Reynolds, Greg, rhp	Fr.	4	1	6.00	11	0	27	30	12	15
Jecmen, Mark, rhp	Jr.	1	0	6.64	16	0	20	21	15	24
Duda, Pete, rhp	So.	0	0	8.44	4	0	5	5	1	2

10. GEORGIA TECH

Coach: Danny Hall   **Record:** 44-21

BATTING	YR	AVG	AB	R	H	2B	3B	HR	RBI	SB
Trapani, Mike, 3b	So.	.418	79	22	33	5	0	4	17	2
Blackwood, Steven, of	So.	.359	256	71	92	22	0	4	66	7
Remole, Clifton, of-1b	Jr.	.344	259	47	89	15	2	4	56	5
Hall, Jake, of	Jr.	.333	33	8	11	4	0	0	5	0
Hawranick, Andy, c	Jr.	.330	103	24	34	7	1	2	18	1
Patterson, Eric, 2b	Jr.	.326	264	76	86	11	5	9	49	48
Boggs, Brandon, of	Jr.	.322	255	68	82	14	1	9	58	11
Owings, Micah, rhp-dh	So.	.318	255	65	81	14	0	15	64	2
Robbins, Whit, 1b	So.	.313	144	34	45	10	1	2	39	4
Hodges, Wes, 3b	Fr.	.304	184	41	56	11	4	1	31	7
Slayden, Jeremy, of	Jr.	.286	35	7	10	1	0	1	8	0
Nickeas, Mike, c	Jr.	.279	226	42	63	11	1	8	33	1
Greene, Tyler, ss	So.	.273	256	55	70	18	1	7	52	16
Lane, Cameron, if-c	Jr.	.250	28	3	7	1	0	0	5	2

PITCHING	YR	W	L	ERA	G	SV	IP	H	BB	SO
Crews, Jordan, rhp	Jr.	2	0	1.48	19	0	24	23	6	17
Wagner, Nick, rhp	Jr.	1	1	2.22	19	3	28	29	10	14
Self, Ryan, lhp	So.	0	1	3.24	26	2	17	11	5	14
Kown, Andrew, rhp	Jr.	10	1	3.46	18	0	112	109	36	96
Hyatt, Jared, rhp	Fr.	1	0	3.71	16	0	17	17	3	22

Owings, Micah, rhp	So.	9	3	3.89	18	0	113	93	43	112
Perry, Philip, rhp	Sr.	1	0	3.95	10	0	14	14	12	15
Burks, Brian, rhp	Sr.	8	6	4.67	19	0	94	105	23	76
Hyde, Lee, lhp	Fr.	5	2	5.73	16	0	49	53	20	47
Gustafson, Tim, rhp	Fr.	0	0	6.23	14	0	22	30	7	15
Goodman, John, rhp	Fr.	4	1	6.43	18	3	21	25	5	25
Walker, Aaron, lhp	Sr.	1	1	6.75	20	0	19	25	6	12
Wood, Blake, rhp	Fr.	1	2	7.84	15	0	31	40	14	23
Turner, Ryan, lhp	Fr.	1	2	7.94	15	0	23	29	12	22
Neighborgall, Jason, rhp	So.	0	1	27.00	9	1	7	6	24	11

11. RICE

Coach: Wayne Graham   **Record:** 46-14

BATTING	YR	AVG	AB	R	H	2B	3B	HR	RBI	SB
Kolkhorst, Chris, of	Sr.	.371	221	59	82	11	5	0	27	5
Townsend, Wade, rhp-dh	Jr.	.346	26	6	9	3	0	0	1	0
Janish, Paul, ss	Jr.	.345	235	52	81	16	2	9	60	5
Rodgers, Adam, c-1b	Jr.	.343	216	40	74	21	2	7	60	1
Duplessis, Lyndon, c	So.	.333	12	1	4	0	0	1	4	0
Pendleton, Lance, of	So.	.326	184	41	60	16	0	11	38	1
Rodriguez, Josh, 2b	Fr.	.306	186	36	57	9	4	2	33	6
Reagan, Travis, of	Fr.	.299	97	14	29	6	1	1	14	0
Ueckert, Matt, 1b-lhp	So.	.293	150	25	44	7	0	2	28	0
Davis, Austin, of	Sr.	.288	205	39	59	13	1	7	34	5
Morris, Adam, 3b-dh	So.	.276	174	36	48	11	1	5	28	3
Reichenbach, Clay, 3b	Jr.	.266	109	20	29	4	0	2	17	1
Moake, Matt, 2b	So.	.266	79	17	21	2	1	1	15	2
Hale, Adam, dh-rhp	Fr.	.262	141	21	37	8	2	5	25	1
Gunderson, Kyle, of	Fr.	.261	23	7	6	1	0	0	2	0
Cavanaugh, Matt, of	So.	.200	15	4	3	0	0	0	1	1

PITCHING	YR	W	L	ERA	G	SV	IP	H	BB	SO
Townsend, Wade, rhp	Jr.	12	0	1.80	18	2	120	74	45	148
Humber, Philip, rhp	Jr.	13	4	2.27	20	1	115	87	37	154
Degerman, Eddie, rhp	So.	1	1	2.70	15	2	27	21	16	39
Baker, Josh, rhp	Jr.	9	2	2.79	24	4	100	96	36	94
Niemann, Jeff, rhp	Jr.	6	3	3.02	17	3	80	59	30	94
Ueckert, Matt, lhp	So.	3	0	3.06	11	0	35	24	10	33
Pennington, Garrett, rhp	Jr.	0	0	3.38	11	1	16	15	6	15
Forester, Josh, lhp	Fr.	0	1	4.35	9	0	10	5	13	12
Hale, Adam, rhp	Fr.	1	3	4.61	11	1	14	11	6	13
Matheny, Colin, lhp	So.	0	0	5.56	10	2	11	14	3	6

12. ARIZONA

Coach: Andy Lopez   **Record:** 36-27

BATTING	YR	AVG	AB	R	H	2B	3B	HR	RBI	SB
Crowe, Trevor, of	So.	.350	203	53	71	13	9	5	33	26
Mercado, Richard, c-dh	Jr.	.342	190	30	65	7	2	4	30	0
Rhinehart, Bill, dh	Jr.	.324	142	29	46	10	1	7	26	0
Donald, Jason, ss	Fr.	.322	261	58	84	11	1	9	45	6
Van Houten, Jeff, of	Jr.	.319	216	49	69	10	6	3	40	6
Duran, Moises, 3b	Sr.	.310	213	38	66	12	3	7	49	12
Hardy, John, 2b	Jr.	.308	208	37	64	7	3	5	32	9
Brown, Jordan, 1b	So.	.306	219	37	67	11	2	13	57	1
Hundley, Nick, c	So.	.299	147	28	44	13	2	4	27	2
Reilly, Pat, 1b-dh	Jr.	.277	83	19	23	4	1	3	13	6
Boyer, Brad, of-3b	Sr.	.259	139	27	36	8	0	1	23	10
Lewis, D.J., dh	Fr.	.257	35	7	9	3	0	1	6	0
Decater, Derek, of	So.	.243	140	21	34	5	3	1	20	2
Bies, Zach, 1b	So.	.143	14	1	2	1	0	0	2	1
Taylor, Terrence, of	Sr.	.067	15	9	1	0	0	0	0	4

PITCHING	YR	W	L	ERA	G	SV	IP	H	BB	SO
Lawler, Pat, rhp	So.	0	0	4.20	8	0	15	15	5	14
Melancon, Mark, rhp	Fr.	6	4	4.33	29	3	62	57	19	46
Meloan, John, rhp	So.	10	0	4.66	18	0	93	97	45	77
Mills, Brad, lhp	Fr.	0	1	4.66	15	0	10	10	13	7
Kolberg, Koley, rhp	So.	9	7	4.70	25	2	149	183	70	123
Rodriguez, Derek, rhp	Jr.	1	3	4.74	23	7	25	26	18	12
Burns, Scott, rhp	Sr.	1	1	4.75	22	3	30	28	13	26
Jarrett, Sean, rhp	So.	0	0	4.91	8	0	15	17	5	9
Cortez, Luis, rhp	So.	3	3	6.35	11	0	45	46	26	28
Guyette, Kevin, rhp	So.	6	8	6.45	22	0	119	149	55	83

13. LONG BEACH STATE

Coach: Mike Weathers   **Record:** 40-21

BATTING	YR	AVG	AB	R	H	2B	3B	HR	RBI	SB
Vargas, Jason, dh-lhp	Jr.	.354	209	56	74	14	4	5	33	3
Boatright, Sean, of	So.	.330	100	10	33	5	0	3	23	0
Davis, Brad, c	Jr.	.329	225	39	74	9	0	4	38	4
Bowker, John, of	So.	.320	225	31	72	15	3	7	41	2
Mocny, Danny, 3b	Jr.	.318	154	24	49	6	4	4	26	4
Tulowitzki, Troy, ss	So.	.317	230	40	73	15	2	7	44	5
Buhagiar, Josh, of	Sr.	.312	173	28	54	8	1	0	13	4

Bradley, Scott, 1b	So.	.308	13	1	4	1	0	0	2	1
Hofius, Mike, 1b	Sr.	.291	213	37	62	13	2	4	48	3
Cruz, Tito, c-3b	So.	.271	48	6	13	3	0	0	2	0
Udvarhelyi, Travis, of	Sr.	.260	96	15	25	4	1	1	13	4
Sindlinger, Chuck, 2b	So.	.257	113	12	29	2	2	1	7	1
Velazco, Steve, of	Jr.	.238	105	19	25	6	0	0	17	3
Gardiner, John, of	Fr.	.192	26	5	5	0	0	0	1	2
Bruce, T.J., 3b-2b	Sr.	.186	97	11	18	4	0	0	11	3
Wolf, Tom, of	Jr.	.182	11	0	2	0	0	0	0	0
Jacobsen, Cole, 2b	Jr.	.167	24	1	4	1	0	0	0	0
Pearce, Bobby, of	Sr.	.125	16	1	2	0	0	0	1	0

PITCHING	YR	W	L	ERA	G	SV	IP	H	BB	SO
Bowdish, Andrew, rhp	Jr.	0	0	0.00	3	0	5	3	4	4
Weaver, Jered, rhp	Jr.	15	1	1.62	19	0	144	81	21	213
Ramos, Cesar, lhp	So.	12	4	2.29	19	0	134	108	35	97
Anderson, Brian, rhp	Jr.	0	2	2.98	28	2	42	39	8	39
Stout, Ross, rhp	So.	0	0	3.86	9	0	7	9	1	3
Vargas, Jason, lhp	Jr.	7	6	4.14	18	0	111	98	31	90
Jamison, Neil, rhp	Jr.	3	5	4.35	30	12	31	31	12	31
Andrade, Brett, rhp	So.	1	0	4.95	17	0	20	20	1	19
Villalobos, Brandon, lhp	Fr.	1	2	5.70	10	0	24	26	8	14
Juneau, Scott, rhp	So.	1	1	6.00	8	0	12	12	2	7
Maiques, Kenny, rhp	Fr.	0	0	8.18	12	0	11	15	5	14

14. FLORIDA STATE

Coach: Mike Martin   **Record:** 45-23

BATTING	YR	AVG	AB	R	H	2B	3B	HR	RBI	SB
Martinez-Esteve, Eddy, of-dh	So.	.385	270	57	104	24	3	19	81	8
Cheesman, Aaron, c	Jr.	.347	239	50	83	18	3	3	42	4
Drew, Stephen, ss	Jr.	.344	227	68	78	14	7	17	56	12
Zech, Bryan, 2b	Sr.	.342	260	68	89	13	0	8	46	9
Malone, Ryne, 1b-3b	Fr.	.330	203	50	67	15	3	12	54	9
Chapman, Gibbs, 3b-of	Jr.	.307	199	38	61	14	3	3	41	8
Peacher, Brant, of-dh	Fr.	.306	72	12	22	1	0	3	13	1
Robinson, Shane, of	Fr.	.280	275	52	77	18	2	1	36	9
Sauls, Matt, of	So.	.274	219	48	60	8	1	1	33	15
Diaz, Danny, c	Fr.	.250	24	4	6	1	0	0	4	0
Anderson, Dennis, 3b	Fr.	.225	138	19	31	2	0	3	19	2
Smith, Derrick, of-dh	So.	.220	109	19	24	7	1	6	25	0
Wardell, Daniel, 1b	Jr.	.211	109	28	23	9	1	4	18	0
Rojas, Louis, 1b	Fr.	.200	10	5	2	0	0	0	1	0
Manasa, Brandon, ss	So.	.130	23	10	3	0	0	0	1	2

PITCHING	YR	W	L	ERA	G	SV	IP	H	BB	SO
Lynch, Kevin, rhp	Jr.	4	4	2.43	30	5	37	38	10	34
James, Rhett, rhp	Sr.	10	3	3.36	29	3	110	100	32	93
DiBlasi, Matt, lhp	So.	0	1	3.58	24	2	28	28	11	24
Cannon, Eddie, rhp	Sr.	9	7	3.87	20	1	112	108	18	96
Chambliss, Tyler, rhp	Fr.	4	1	3.89	27	1	39	32	19	41
Schultz, Brian, lhp	Fr.	7	1	4.07	30	1	60	53	27	58
Jones, Hunter, lhp	So.	3	2	4.10	15	0	64	67	16	55
Radziwon, Frank, lhp	Jr.	1	0	5.00	11	0	9	9	6	10
Sauls, Mark, rhp	So.	6	4	5.22	20	0	91	110	40	52
Chambers, Brian, rhp	Fr.	1	0	6.45	12	0	22	32	9	17
Davis, Hunter, rhp	Jr.	0	0	7.71	21	0	19	24	15	11
Thompson, DiCarlo, rhp	Fr.	0	0	8.78	10	0	13	14	14	10

15. NOTRE DAME

Coach: Paul Mainieri   **Record:** 47-16

BATTING	YR	AVG	AB	R	H	2B	3B	HR	RBI	SB
Murray, Tim, 3b	Sr.	.538	13	0	7	0	0	0	3	0
Macri, Matt, 3b	Jr.	.367	237	76	87	15	7	14	56	12
Cooper, Craig, of	So.	.360	175	42	63	13	1	10	48	12
Lopez, Greg, ss	So.	.332	199	39	66	14	0	2	34	4
Andres, Steve, of-c	So.	.320	169	38	54	13	4	8	39	4
Gaston, Sean, c	Fr.	.316	57	11	18	3	0	0	11	4
Sollmann, Steve, 2b	Sr.	.311	151	39	47	5	1	2	23	17
Edwards, Matt, 1b	Jr.	.310	216	48	67	13	1	12	54	5
Bransfield, Matt, dh-of	So.	.306	206	44	63	12	3	12	58	0
Sisko, Zach, 2b	So.	.296	71	13	21	1	0	1	10	0
Grogan, Brennan, of	So.	.290	31	5	9	1	1	1	7	1
Sanchez, Javi, c	Sr.	.278	216	43	60	14	0	2	41	2
Dressman, Danny, of	Sr.	.264	121	25	32	7	0	0	18	2
Rizzo, Cody, of	So.	.263	175	39	46	5	1	4	29	5
Dury, Mike, 1b-lhp	Fr.	.250	16	4	4	0	0	1	3	0
Nettey, Alex, of	Fr.	.194	36	9	7	3	0	0	5	1
Fournier, Chris, 2b-of	Fr.	.190	42	9	8	1	0	0	4	0

PITCHING	YR	W	L	ERA	G	SV	IP	H	BB	SO
Whittington, Matt, lhp	Fr.	0		00.00	3	0	5	6	3	2
Johnson, Grant, rhp	Jr.	6		01.87	14	0	58	39	26	51
Bertucci, Rico, rhp	Fr.	1		01.88	12	0	14	11	0	11
Dury, Mike, lhp	Fr.	2		01.88	11	0	14	14	4	10
Doherty, Ryan, rhp	So.	5		12.38	30	12	34	19	11	46

Kapala, Dan, rhp	Fr.	2	1	2.70	28	1	40	37	16	40
Samardzija, Jeff, rhp	Fr.	5	3	2.95	20	1	64	50	17	42
Thaman, Joe, lhp	Sr.	4	1	3.35	29	1	48	37	20	34
Stewart, Jess, rhp	Fr.	7	1	3.38	12	0	40	41	8	20
Olvey, Derik, rhp	Fr.	1	0	3.52	4	0	15	14	3	7
Niesel, Chris, rhp	Jr.	8	3	3.62	18	0	102	123	20	84
Thornton, Tom, lhp	So.	9	2	3.88	16	0	100	95	24	77
Vasami, Chris, rhp	Fr.	1	0	4.63	5	0	12	13	1	7
Jones, Tyler, rhp	Jr.	0	0	21.94	9	0	5	17	4	3

16. FLORIDA

Coach: Pat McMahon **Record:** 43-22

BATTING	YR	AVG	AB	R	H	2B	3B	HR	RBI	SB
Harrison, Ben, of	Sr.	.353	238	67	84	14	0	17	71	7
Smith, C.J., 1b-of	Jr.	.341	255	63	87	16	3	14	64	7
Brooks, Daniel, of	So.	.333	12	1	4	0	0	0	2	0
Corsaletti, Jeff, of	Jr.	.323	251	47	81	12	2	5	43	11
Davis, Adam, 2b-3b	Fr.	.320	253	68	81	11	3	6	24	22
Jeroloman, Brian, c	Fr.	.318	151	22	48	4	0	1	27	1
Leclerc, Brian, of	Fr.	.312	173	28	54	13	2	6	37	0
Tordi, Justin, ss	So.	.302	235	36	71	14	0	4	41	5
LaPorta, Matt, c-dh	Fr.	.285	130	31	37	5	0	14	37	1
Tucker, Jonathan, 3b	So.	.284	268	37	76	12	4	0	28	10
Dickey, Gavin, of	Fr.	.273	22	12	6	1	0	1	4	1
Kennedy, Ryan, 2b	Fr.	.256	43	5	11	3	0	0	8	0
Barton, Stephen, dh	So.	.248	113	27	28	4	1	1	22	5
Skorupski, Jon, dh	Jr.	.231	39	11	9	3	0	1	6	0
Maley, Matt, 1b	Sr.	.185	27	4	5	2	0	0	5	1
Easley, Austin, 1b	Jr.	.175	57	10	10	5	0	0	5	0

PITCHING		W	L	ERA	G	SV	IP	H	BB	SO
O'Day, Darren, rhp	So.	8	1	2.56	26	5	60	64	10	39
Hoyman, Justin, rhp	Jr.	11	2	2.71	19	0	140	116	38	89
Falkenbach, Connor, rhp	Fr.	10	7	3.34	35	3	127	130	12	81
Boss, Tommy, rhp	Jr.	4	5	4.24	17	0	76	88	6	34
Sanabria, Adam, lhp	Jr.	1	1	4.50	11	0	20	30	3	10
Roberson, Lee, lhp	Sr.	2	1	4.84	15	2	22	26	12	17
Ball, Bryan, rhp	So.	5	1	5.04	17	1	70	84	27	27
Porter, Steven, lhp	Fr.	1	3	5.13	14	0	33	32	13	21
Pete, Mike, lhp	Jr.	1	0	6.23	12	0	17	29	5	12
Fuchs, Matt, rhp	Fr.	0	1	8.04	9	0	16	26	9	12

17. VANDERBILT

Coach: Tim Corbin **Record:** 45-19

BATTING	YR	AVG	AB	R	H	2B	3B	HR	RBI	SB
Jones, Warner, 2b	So.	.414	268	55	111	27	3	11	74	12
Klosterman, Ryan, ss	Jr.	.346	263	72	91	15	8	7	33	16
Nicolas, Cesar, 1b-dh	Sr.	.336	235	44	79	18	1	15	70	0
Baxter, Mike, 1b-dh	So.	.322	258	34	83	8	3	2	38	13
Garza, Aaron, of	Fr.	.295	166	27	49	7	3	2	31	4
Mansolino, Tony, 3b	Jr.	.274	252	31	69	9	1	5	31	7
McGraner, Matt, c	So.	.267	45	11	12	3	0	0	2	2
Richardson, Antoan, of	Jr.	.266	207	51	55	9	4	3	30	32
Douillard, Jonathan, c	Sr.	.265	189	23	50	10	1	2	14	1
Zeller, Matt, of	So.	.254	59	9	15	1	0	1	5	0
Scott, Worth, of	Sr.	.242	190	27	46	8	1	4	27	5
Shao, Stephen, of-lhp	Fr.	.211	38	4	8	3	0	0	2	0
Kleinschrodt, Bill, of	Fr.	.190	42	6	8	0	1	1	3	1
Taylor, Rucker, 2b-ss	So.	.182	11	1	2	0	0	0	1	0
Simpson, Zach, 2b	Jr.	.154	13	2	2	1	0	0	2	0

PITCHING		W	L	ERA	G	SV	IP	H	BB	SO
Moviel, Greg, lhp	Fr.	0	0	1.74	8	0	10	3	14	9
Mullins, Ryan, lhp	So.	9	3	2.58	17	0	112	104	20	98
Buschmann, Matt, rhp	So.	8	1	2.84	27	2	82	80	29	61
Sowers, Jeremy, lhp	Jr.	10	6	3.08	19	0	123	105	26	119
Rhoden, Tyler, rhp	Fr.	2	0	3.41	17	0	32	33	7	19
Shao, Stephen, lhp	Fr.	4	0	3.45	18	1	31	24	8	32
Lewis, Jensen, rhp	So.	6	4	3.49	23	2	80	77	28	69
Sues, Jeff, rhp	So.	4	1	4.57	20	1	45	45	26	45
Wagner, Michael, rhp	Fr.	1	0	4.71	13	0	21	22	19	19
Rote, Ryan, rhp	Jr.	1	4	4.94	29	11	31	32	14	39
Owen, Blake, rhp	So.	0	0	9.00	5	0	6	7	4	6

18. ORAL ROBERTS

Coach: Rob Walton **Record:** 50-11

BATTING	YR	AVG	AB	R	H	2B	3B	HR	RBI	SB
VanDerBosch, Matt, of	Sr.	.383	240	75	92	13	7	3	52	44
Hanson, Brian, 2b	Jr.	.355	231	52	82	18	1	4	53	7
Welborn, Ryan, of	Jr.	.354	175	66	62	16	1	0	21	31
Plumley, Grant, ss	Sr.	.331	251	43	83	22	1	5	64	12
Lex, Josh, 1b-c	Sr.	.330	227	51	75	14	0	11	67	7
Rivera, Ricky, of	Jr.	.320	178	37	57	12	3	8	45	3
Bigley, Dennis, 1b-rhp	Jr.	.301	146	30	44	10	1	7	29	2
Modeste, Scott, dh	Sr.	.297	74	15	22	10	0	1	23	1
Lamb, Kevin, of	Jr.	.291	86	22	25	4	1	3	13	6
Tackett, Jon, 3b	Jr.	.286	119	16	34	8	1	0	11	1
Griffin, Nate, c-3b	Sr.	.277	166	30	46	7	0	1	22	1
Tuttle, Jeff, of	Sr.	.258	62	12	16	6	0	3	13	0
Welles, Boomer, 3b	Jr.	.257	101	20	26	6	0	1	19	0

PITCHING		W	L	ERA	G	SV	IP	H	BB	SO
Towery, Dane, rhp	Jr.	1	0	2.00	19	1	27	25	15	25
Lesko, Adam, rhp	Sr.	7	1	2.15	22	0	84	70	21	49
Sorrow, Sean, rhp	Sr.	9	1	2.49	19	1	87	78	20	59
McIntyre, Taylor, lhp	So.	6	1	2.61	11	0	62	38	38	62
Bigley, Dennis, rhp	Jr.	13	1	2.91	16	0	118	95	25	100
Ramsey, Justin, rhp	Sr.	7	0	2.91	30	13	59	60	14	37
Robertson, Tim, rhp	Jr.	4	3	4.34	19	1	46	50	18	40
Recio, Rene, rhp	Jr.	1	2	5.25	5	0	12	13	5	11
Tinkler, Conner, rhp	Jr.	1	2	5.40	11	0	17	22	8	11
Hancock, Matt, lhp	Jr.	1	0	6.23	10	0	17	17	16	11

19. TULANE

Coach: Rick Jones **Record:** 41-21

BATTING	YR	AVG	AB	R	H	2B	3B	HR	RBI	SB
Barket, Matt, of	Jr.	.370	238	52	88	17	1	8	52	13
Swackhamer, Wes, of-1b	Jr.	.355	220	47	78	16	0	8	33	6
Dini, Greg, c-1b	Jr.	.354	226	37	80	17	0	11	51	1
Bogusevic, Brian, of-lhp	So.	.339	236	51	80	14	4	10	68	9
Madden, Scott, dh	Jr.	.326	46	10	15	1	0	5	16	0
Holland, Joe, 2b	Jr.	.318	245	65	78	19	1	8	32	2
Manzella, Tommy, ss	Jr.	.311	235	49	73	14	0	5	36	11
Southard, Nathan, of	So.	.297	202	36	60	12	0	6	37	5
Bormaster, Brian, 3b-c	Sr.	.291	223	48	65	9	0	6	36	2
Guidry, Tim, 3b	So.	.242	66	13	16	0	0	1	10	0
Hamilton, Mark, of	Fr.	.227	119	22	27	7	0	3	28	2
Pyle, Jason, dh	So.	.190	21	1	4	0	0	0	2	0
Mann, Matt, c	Sr.	.167	12	1	2	1	0	0	1	0
Stringer, Philip, 2b	Fr.	.136	59	9	8	1	0	1	2	4

PITCHING		W	L	ERA	G	SV	IP	H	BB	SO
Crowel, J.R., lhp	So.	8	3	3.39	17	0	104	108	30	76
Mohl, Billy, rhp	So.	6	4	3.70	15	0	80	102	16	55
Bogusevic, Brian, lhp	So.	9	6	4.19	17	0	112	128	25	84
Hahn, Cory, rhp	Sr.	9	2	4.26	15	0	89	105	15	69
Charron, Joey, lhp	Sr.	2	0	4.28	28	5	34	33	23	34
Latham, Daniel, rhp	Fr.	4	2	4.88	27	6	66	68	15	53
Goebel, Matt, rhp	So.	3	2	5.35	17	1	37	42	22	28
Kimmons, Tyler, rhp	So.	0	2	6.14	11	0	15	23	6	12

20. TEXAS A&M

Coach: Mark Johnson **Record:** 42-22

BATTING	YR	AVG	AB	R	H	2B	3B	HR	RBI	SB
Pennington, Cliff, ss	So.	.339	257	60	87	7	4	5	35	12
Boggs, Austin, 3b	Fr.	.331	260	42	86	11	3	5	52	5
Bowe, Brian, dh	Sr.	.327	49	9	16	2	1	0	4	0
Patton, Cory, of	Sr.	.326	230	49	75	18	3	11	67	3
Mavroulis, Coby, 1b	So.	.321	234	51	75	15	1	3	47	5
Schindewolf, Erik, 2b	Sr.	.311	209	69	65	12	1	4	30	5
Stinson, Craig, c	So.	.287	195	29	56	10	3	3	37	0
Bartek, Travis, of	Jr.	.287	115	26	33	6	1	1	18	4
Baldwin, Andrew, of	Jr.	.281	135	22	38	6	0	2	19	2
Infante, John, of	So.	.275	204	39	56	10	3	3	32	11
Ruggiano, Justin, dh-of	Sr.	.275	149	26	41	11	0	3	35	7
Whelan, Kevin, c-rhp	So.	.233	43	9	10	1	0	1	4	0
Scheidt, Eric, 1b	Sr.	.229	48	9	11	3	0	0	9	0
Alexander, Matt, 2b	Sr.	.184	49	6	9	3	0	1	6	0
Stroud, Todd, of-dh	Jr.	.125	24	4	3	1	1	0	4	1

PITCHING	YR	W	L	ERA	G	SV	IP	H	BB	SO
Rampy, Blake, rhp	Fr.	2	2	1.55	20	4	29	17	12	24
Cline, Jon Michael, lhp	Jr.	2	0	2.70	3	0	7	3	3	2
Meyer, Jason, lhp	Fr.	8	2	2.89	24	3	106	88	41	111
Jackson, Zach, lhp	Jr.	10	7	3.58	18	0	121	113	28	127
Creps, Austin, rhp	Fr.	2	0	4.00	13	1	27	27	8	23
Whelan, Kevin, rhp	So.	0	2	4.15	10	0	9	7	4	11
Frame, Doug, lhp	Fr.	2	1	4.21	18	0	26	30	16	35
Moore, Justin, rhp	Sr.	5	3	4.47	12	0	50	58	14	21
Donaldson, Dan, lhp	So.	1	1	4.76	15	1	34	30	23	22
Nicholson, Kyle, rhp	Fr.	3	0	5.11	21	0	37	40	18	19
Ray, Robert, rhp	So.	2	2	5.24	15	1	45	61	15	54
Marlatt, Kyle, rhp	Jr.	5	1	5.77	17	0	53	52	17	35
Soeder, Tyler, lhp	Fr.	0	0	12.00	4	0	6	8	4	4

21. WASHINGTON

Coach: Ken Knutson **Record:** 39-20

BATTING	YR	AVG	AB	R	H	2B	3B	HR	RBI	SB
Larsen, Kyle, 1b	Jr.	.344	227	44	78	16	1	11	55	1

BATTING	YR	AVG	AB	R	H	2B	3B	HR	RBI	SB
Clem, Zach, of-dh	So.	.336	214	60	72	13	0	13	47	3
Lillibridge, Brent, of-ss	So.	.317	249	65	79	16	1	11	36	18
Hathaway, Aaron, c-of	Jr.	.317	218	41	69	7	5	9	42	5
Isaacson, Greg, 2b	Sr.	.304	227	54	69	12	0	6	44	23
Batkoski, Nick, ss	Jr.	.303	165	25	50	11	2	2	33	2
Lane, Matt, c-dh	Fr.	.301	133	26	40	10	0	6	26	1
Otness, John, 3b	Sr.	.289	228	38	66	10	0	9	48	1
Johnson, Taylor, of	Jr.	.257	148	28	38	9	1	5	27	10
Mach, Tyler, dh	Fr.	.245	102	12	25	1	0	4	15	1
Burnham, Nick, of	So.	.238	21	5	5	0	0	0	1	1
Johnson, Ben, of-c	Sr.	.215	144	27	31	6	0	7	29	4
Tucker, Matt, dh	Fr.	.212	66	11	14	3	0	2	9	1
Bauer, Brian, if	So.	.200	10	3	2	0	0	0	1	0

PITCHING		W	L	ERA	G	SV	IP	H	BB	SO
Lincecum, Tim, rhp	Fr.	10	3	3.53	20	0	112	83	82	161
Parker, Kyle, rhp	Fr.	4	3	3.84	18	0	75	59	55	58
Dowling, David, lhp	Jr.	0	1	4.09	10	1	22	19	16	11
Baysinger, Trent, lhp	Sr.	3	4	4.12	29	1	74	83	19	55
Fenton, Will, rhp	Jr.	6	3	4.31	27	10	31	27	24	39
Ponzoha, Jordan, rhp	Fr.	1	0	5.32	10	0	24	27	10	24
Everitt, Keaton, rhp	So.	5	3	5.66	11	0	48	47	31	22
Kasser, Matt, rhp	So.	4	0	5.98	17	1	65	72	38	42
Villalobos, Joel, lhp	Jr.	1	0	6.35	4	0	6	4	3	6
Conover, Josh, rhp	Jr.	1	0	6.53	8	1	21	21	7	16
Lentz, Richie, rhp	Fr.	3	3	6.70	20	1	50	54	41	52
Hawkins, Jamie, lhp	Jr.	1	0	7.71	14	0	14	22	4	12

22. ARIZONA STATE
Coach: Pat Murphy   Record: 41-18

BATTING	YR	AVG	AB	R	H	2B	3B	HR	RBI	SB
Pedroia, Dustin, ss	Jr.	.393	244	78	96	24	1	9	49	9
Buck, Travis, of	So.	.373	225	64	84	16	1	9	58	13
Asanovich, Josh, 2b	Jr.	.367	150	39	55	9	2	5	41	4
Gosewisch, Tuffy, c	Jr.	.342	199	36	68	14	1	2	49	0
Walsh, Nick, 2b-of	Sr.	.329	149	31	49	7	0	0	23	6
McKenna, Ryan, of	Jr.	.326	43	9	14	2	1	1	9	1
Persichina, Joe, 1b-3b	Fr.	.320	150	27	48	7	1	1	24	3
Cook, Chris, 1b	Jr.	.309	94	21	29	7	0	5	21	1
Larish, Jeff, 1b	Jr.	.308	237	46	73	17	0	7	49	3
Curtis, Colin, of	Fr.	.300	190	37	57	11	0	5	36	12
Bocchi, Joel, c-dh	Jr.	.281	64	10	18	3	0	0	13	0
Zinicola, Zechry, rhp-dh	Jr.	.280	100	20	28	8	0	3	26	0
Cadena, Nick, of-dh	So.	.260	77	14	20	4	0	3	12	1
Dhaenens, Seth, 3b	Fr.	.250	96	27	24	3	0	0	8	3

PITCHING	YR	W	L	ERA	G	SV	IP	H	BB	SO
Zinicola, Zechry, rhp	Fr.	4	2	3.36	25	8	56	52	20	57
Urquidez, Jason, rhp	Jr.	12	3	3.41	19	0	98	90	47	94
Mousser, Jeff, rhp	Sr.	6	4	3.94	17	0	89	82	42	42
Andes, Quentin, rhp	Fr.	5	1	4.55	21	2	32	32	18	27
Bresnehan, Pat, rhp	Fr.	3	2	4.79	23	5	41	41	27	45
Averill, Erik, lhp	So.	4	4	5.19	26	2	76	83	23	56
Cassa, Pat, lhp	Fr.	3	1	5.48	21	1	48	53	25	38
Webb, Travis, lhp	Fr.	0	0	5.68	9	0	6	10	10	7
Marotz, Ty, rhp	Jr.	0	0	6.14	17	0	22	24	15	25
Blake, Josh, lhp	Fr.	1	0	6.95	14	1	22	27	16	17
Bordes, Brett, lhp	So.	3	1	8.55	13	1	34	39	31	38

23. MISSISSIPPI
Coach: Mike Bianco   Record: 39-21

BATTING	YR	AVG	AB	R	H	2B	3B	HR	RBI	SB
Head, Stephen, 1b-lhp	So.	.346	228	41	79	13	1	13	53	0
Gunther, Barry, c	Jr.	.323	164	26	53	11	1	2	28	2
Presley, Alex, of	Fr.	.311	196	34	61	11	6	6	32	9
Pettway, Brian, 3b-1b	So.	.305	203	41	62	11	0	6	31	0
Coghlan, Chris, 3b	Jr.	.302	199	40	60	11	2	2	24	3
Osteen, Cooper, 2b	Jr.	.293	239	47	70	10	1	2	27	11
Wright, Mark, of-dh	Fr.	.292	48	9	14	4	1	1	10	1
Tolbert, Matt, ss	Jr.	.290	231	32	67	11	0	2	35	11
Smith, Seth, of	Jr.	.284	225	39	64	8	1	7	40	6
Babineaux, Charlie, of	Sr.	.282	202	35	57	18	0	13	46	1
Franklin, Miles, of	Jr.	.275	51	13	14	2	1	0	8	4
Barksdale, Xan, c	Sr.	.227	22	2	5	1	0	1	4	0
Porter, Ryne, if	Fr.	.182	11	1	2	1	0	0	1	0
Donovan, Justin, if	Jr.	.083	12	1	1	0	0	0	0	0
Brashear, Justin, c	Fr.	.074	27	1	2	0	0	0	0	0

PITCHING		W	L	ERA	G	SV	IP	H	BB	SO
Fowler, Taylor, lhp	So.	1	0	0.75	7	0	12	9	7	11
Wright, Brae, lhp	So.	6	2	2.81	10	0	67	71	13	49
Head, Stephen, lhp	So.	6	3	2.82	17	5	70	68	19	56
Pettway, Brian, rhp	So.	2	3	2.93	18	2	28	29	4	29
Holliman, Mark, rhp	So.	9	3	3.05	16	0	106	101	35	101
Cupps, Anthony, rhp	So.	3	4	3.41	20	1	66	67	25	49
Thompson, Chris, rhp	Sr.	3	0	3.77	14	2	31	25	12	25
Hollomon, Chris, lhp	Jr.	1	1	4.22	3	0	11	12	4	7
Maloney, Matt, lhp	So.	1	3	4.66	11	0	48	62	6	42
Fowler, Eric, lhp	So.	3	1	5.80	15	0	59	62	20	57
Zick, Jeremy, rhp	Sr.	4	1	5.93	17	1	27	24	9	35

24. VIRGINIA
Coach: Brian O'Connor   Record: 44-15

BATTING	YR	AVG	AB	R	H	2B	3B	HR	RBI	SB
Zimmerman, Ryan, 3b	So.	.361	249	49	90	16	2	1	45	13
Koshansky, Joe, lhp-1b	Sr.	.302	222	50	67	17	1	16	67	8
Gillispie, Paul, dh-of	Sr.	.302	96	17	29	4	0	0	16	4
Dunn, Matt, of-3b	So.	.301	219	50	66	4	4	1	34	8
Mitchell, Mike, of	Fr.	.300	50	8	15	1	0	0	5	8
Ghrist, Jordan, 1b	Jr.	.300	10	2	3	1	0	0	1	0
Street, Matt, of	Jr.	.283	212	49	60	10	3	1	37	19
Darby, Josh, 1b	Fr.	.282	78	18	22	5	0	0	7	1
Hagan, Tom, of	So.	.281	114	21	32	2	2	1	22	5
Reynolds, Mark, ss	Jr.	.274	234	60	64	11	5	11	48	18
Werman, Kyle, 2b-c	Jr.	.271	192	28	52	2	0	0	28	3
Headd, Scott, c	Jr.	.260	173	33	45	16	0	1	31	2
Henry, Tim, of	Fr.	.256	172	24	44	4	3	0	20	8

PITCHING		W	L	ERA	G	SV	IP	H	BB	SO
Starr, Shooter, rhp	Sr.	3	0	1.29	11	0	14	5	13	12
Lambert, Casey, lhp	Fr.	4	1	2.54	29	8	60	51	21	40
Koshansky, Joe, lhp	Sr.	8	3	2.98	15	0	103	83	29	80
Myers, Josh, rhp	Jr.	1	0	3.12	7	0	17	18	3	12
Avery, Matt, rhp	So.	7	2	3.22	16	0	87	86	30	51
Dobies, Andrew, lhp	Jr.	6	3	3.41	16	0	108	102	30	109
Morgenthaler, Scott, lhp	Jr.	1	1	3.47	14	0	23	25	8	9
Laird, Adam, rhp	Jr.	0	0	3.77	10	0	14	19	4	10
Hickman, Canon, rhp	Sr.	8	3	4.94	19	1	24	27	8	19
Gale, Chris, rhp	Jr.	4	2	5.14	14	0	42	55	13	26
Smith, Alex, lhp	Fr.	1	0	7.13	11	0	24	32	15	14
Zimmerer, Alan, lhp	Sr.	1	0	7.71	10	0	14	29	1	9

25. OKLAHOMA
Coach: Larry Cochell   Record: 38-24

BATTING	YR	AVG	AB	R	H	2B	3B	HR	RBI	SB
Sheldon, Ole, 1b	Jr.	.367	256	48	94	19	3	4	54	3
Thornton, Eric, dh	Jr.	.337	190	31	64	13	2	8	39	0
Raley, Russell, 2b	So.	.328	241	51	79	14	2	1	24	5
Bose, Matt, 3b	Jr.	.307	199	36	61	7	1	2	32	6
Rooker, Scott, of	So.	.297	64	12	19	4	1	1	7	5
McGuire, Andrew, of	Sr.	.291	213	48	62	8	1	8	29	15
Rohlinger, Ryan, ss	Jr.	.282	177	37	50	11	0	6	32	9
Hayes, LaFringe, of	So.	.279	43	6	12	3	2	0	5	1
Scuderi, Jeff, of	Jr.	.257	206	37	53	10	2	2	30	14
Mottern, Ryan, of-rhp	Fr.	.256	39	6	10	1	1	0	7	1
Stinson, Josh, c	Fr.	.248	129	18	32	6	1	3	17	0
Herrera, Brenan, of	Jr.	.242	132	23	32	7	2	1	19	4
Lembeck, Chad, 1b	So.	.207	29	2	6	0	0	1	4	0
Hurlbutt, Blake, of	Fr.	.200	40	8	8	0	0	1	6	2
Ivey, Aaron, of	Fr.	.190	58	11	11	2	0	0	6	8
Lance, Brandon, c	So.	.157	70	6	11	2	0	0	13	0
Bradbury, Kyle, ss	Jr.	.133	30	5	4	0	0	2	3	0
Shackelford, Jon, of	Jr.	.091	11	2	1	0	0	1	2	0

PITCHING		W	L	ERA	G	SV	IP	H	BB	SO
Gooch, Tyler, rhp	Jr.	1	0	2.25	6	0	12	9	3	11
Purcey, David, lhp	Jr.	9	5	3.11	18	0	119	89	54	130
Roberts, Mark, rhp	Sr.	9	5	3.41	17	0	121	106	24	134
McCutchen, Daniel, rhp	Jr.	4	3	3.47	35	5	57	51	22	60
McAuliff, Jarod, rhp	Jr.	3	6	3.86	37	6	77	84	27	71
Brown, Casey, rhp	Sr.	5	4	4.80	21	0	54	60	23	36
Mottern, Ryan, rhp	Fr.	0	0	5.83	19	0	29	34	20	19
House, Charlie, rhp	Sr.	1	0	6.23	15	0	22	30	7	13
Swindell, Mike, rhp	Sr.	4	2	6.80	20	1	46	55	28	49
Benoit, Charles, lhp	Fr.	0	2	8.18	16	0	22	25	18	9

COLLEGE BASEBALL

2004 CONFERENCE
STANDINGS & LEADERS

*Won conference tournament
Boldface: NCAA regional participant/conference department leader

#Conference department leader who is a non-qualifier

AMERICA EAST CONFERENCE

	Conference W	L	Overall W	L
Northeastern	14	6	28	20
Maine	14	7	34	21
Albany	14	7	37	14
*Stony Brook	11	10	29	27
Vermont	10	11	18	26
Binghamton	9	11	22	21
Maryland-Baltimore County	6	15	14	38
Hartford	5	16	11	33

ALL-CONFERENCE TEAM: C—Aaron Izaryk, Jr., Maine. **1B**—Dan Schoonmaker, Sr. Albany. **2B**—Kirt Zemniewicz, Sr., Albany. **3B**—Jay Balback, Sr., Binghamton. **SS**—Joe Lamb, Jr., Albany. **OF**—Brendan Chivaro, Sr., Albany; Jeff Heriot, Jr., Northeastern; Joe Hough, So., Maine. **DH**—Derek DeGrazio, Jr., Albany. **P**—Steve Emmerthal, Sr., Albany; Jordan Thomson, Sr., Northeastern.

Player of the Year: Dan Schoonmaker, Albany. **Pitcher of the Year:** Jordan Thomson, Northeastern. **Rookie of the Year:** Miguel Magrass, Vermont. **Coach of the Year:** Jon Mueller, Albany.

INDIVIDUAL BATTING LEADERS
(Minimum 125 At-Bats)

	AVG	AB	R	H	2B	3B	HR	RBI	SB
Zimniewicz, Kirt, Albany	.391	151	44	59	9	0	10	42	9
Devins, Matt, Stony Brook	.376	157	37	59	14	2	3	29	8
DeGrazio, Derek, Albany	.369	168	32	62	12	1	6	45	1
Creek, Greg, Maine	.365	219	48	**80**	**19**	0	6	45	1
Acabbo, Ron, Hartford	.360	161	32	58	12	0	12	38	4
Barrett, Joel, Maine	.359	156	25	56	8	1	1	35	0
Heriot, Jeff, Northeastern	.355	166	41	59	9	**5**	12	39	13
Schoonmaker, Dan, Albany	.353	207	45	73	13	**5**	10	51	7
Balback, Jay, Binghamton	.348	155	40	54	15	1	**14**	45	3
Hough, Joe, Maine	.348	198	42	69	16	**5**	7	42	12
McGraw, Matt, Vermont	.344	154	23	53	9	1	2	17	0
Magrass, Miguel, Vermont	.343	169	37	58	18	2	7	**52**	1
Paquette, Miguel, Northeastern	.326	132	30	43	11	2	9	27	0
Ekelund, Leif, Vermont	.323	127	17	41	6	0	2	25	2
Lamb, Joe, Albany	.321	209	**48**	67	14	0	1	29	22
Kowalchuck, T.J., Binghamton	.320	172	39	55	10	0	8	35	2
Costello, Joe, Binghamton	.317	161	40	51	11	0	8	30	2
Clark, Zach, UMBC	.316	190	34	60	10	0	3	37	2
Brault, Kyle, Vermont	.314	140	32	44	7	2	13	42	1
Larsen, Andrew, Stony Brook	.312	202	45	63	15	1	10	37	14
Wildasin, Kyle, UMBC	.311	180	26	56	14	0	8	35	2
Geoffrey, Dean, Vermont	.305	141	28	43	9	0	1	12	5
Hitchcock, Brendon, Bing.	.305	154	30	47	10	0	4	30	2
Fortuna, Isidro, Stony Brook	.304	184	39	56	14	4	8	39	2
Eck, Brian, Hartford	.301	136	17	41	7	1	7	22	0
#Williams, Simon, Maine	.281	199	41	56	12	1	1	29	**26**

INDIVIDUAL PITCHING LEADERS
(Minimum 50 Innings)

	W	L	ERA	G	SV	IP	H	BB	SO
Thomson, Jordan, Northeastern	**8**	4	**2.13**	14	1	85	67	12	82
Lewis, Jon, Stony Brook	7	7	3.06	16	0	**100**	105	23	**93**
Vaiana, Ethan, Albany	6	1	3.08	11	1	50	43	29	36
Richard, Steve, Maine	4	2	3.09	15	0	70	58	38	63
MacDonald, Mike, Maine	6	3	3.11	15	1	93	86	27	91
Fitzgerald, Kevin, Stony Brook	7	3	3.11	17	0	90	100	16	85
Martin, Troy, Maine	5	2	3.13	15	1	75	57	30	53
Roy, Scott, Hartford	2	6	3.17	12	1	82	76	18	77
Ottavino, Adam, Northeastern	1	4	3.25	17	2	64	48	38	64
Hedrick, Justin, Northeastern	5	4	3.42	12	0	79	73	36	83
#Ryan, Shawn, Albany	0	1	3.60	**27**	**14**	25	18	18	28
Blazek, Chris, Vermont	4	3	3.86	13	0	68	49	50	92
Kroft, Adam, Albany	**8**	3	4.08	13	0	86	85	30	82
Emmerthal, Steve, Albany	**8**	3	4.48	13	0	70	85	19	72
Thomas, Kyle, Albany	4	2	4.50	14	1	56	58	22	44
Monds, Devin, Northeastern	5	4	4.66	13	0	68	61	42	44
Murphy, Nick, Albany	5	3	4.66	10	0	56	72	16	46
Stawarz, Jarrett, Hartford	4	6	4.68	12	0	65	78	16	58
Restivo, Matt, Stony Brook	2	2	4.75	20	2	53	47	31	52
Weglinski, Mike, Binghamton	3	2	4.89	13	0	50	63	22	35
Norton, Greg, Maine	4	6	4.98	17	1	69	82	24	46

ATLANTIC COAST CONFERENCE

	Conference W	L	Overall W	L
Georgia Tech	18	5	44	21
Virginia	18	6	44	15
*Florida State	16	8	45	23
North Carolina	14	10	43	21
Clemson	14	10	39	26
North Carolina State	11	12	36	24
Duke	8	16	25	31
Wake Forest	4	20	17	33
Maryland	4	20	22	34

ALL-CONFERENCE TEAM: C—Chris Iannetta, Jr., North Carolina. **1B**—Kevin Hart, Jr., Maryland. **2B**—Eric Patterson, Jr., Georgia Tech. **3B**—Ryan Zimmerman, So., Virginia. **SS**—Stephen Drew, Jr., Florida State. **OF**—Brandon Boggs, Jr., Georgia Tech; Marshall Hubbard, Jr., North Carolina; Eddy Martinez-Esteve, So., Florida State. **SP**—Daniel Bard, Fr., North Carolina; Michael Rogers, So., North Carolina State; Vern Sterry, Sr., North Carolina State. **RP**—Joey Devine, So., North Carolina State.

Player of the Year: Joe Koshansky, Virginia. **Freshman of the Year:** Daniel Bard, North Carolina. **Coach of the Year:** Brian O'Connor, Virginia.

INDIVIDUAL BATTING LEADERS
(Minimum 125 At-Bats)

	AVG	AB	R	H	2B	3B	HR	RBI	SB
Martinez-Esteve, Eddy, FSU	.385	270	57	**104**	24	3	**19**	81	8
McCann, Brad, Clemson	.379	253	64	96	20	0	16	65	6
Socorro, Javier, Duke	.369	214	41	79	14	3	1	26	6
Hart, Kevin, Maryland	.369	179	32	66	11	2	8	33	1
Zimmerman, Ryan, Virginia	.361	249	49	90	16	2	1	45	13
Ingold, Ben, Wake Forest	.361	216	48	78	14	2	3	43	12
Frazier, Will, Maryland	.360	203	45	73	17	0	10	37	2
Blackwood, Steven, Ga. Tech	.359	256	71	92	22	0	4	66	7
Maropis, Matt, Maryland	.353	201	38	71	12	4	3	31	13
Hubbard, Marshall, No. Car.	.352	250	55	88	21	3	17	**83**	4
Cheesman, Aaron, Fla. State	.347	239	50	83	18	3	3	42	4
Buffone, Anthony, Maryland	.344	244	45	84	18	0	2	34	5
Remole, Clifton, Ga. Tech	.344	259	47	89	15	2	4	56	5
Drew, Stephen, Fla. State	.344	227	68	78	14	**7**	17	56	12
Zech, Bryan, Fla. State	.342	260	68	89	13	0	8	46	9
Iannetta, Chris, No. Carolina	.336	244	61	82	19	0	15	71	6
Harvey, Kris, Clemson	.335	209	38	70	16	0	8	41	4
D'Alessio, Andy, Clemson	.333	180	29	60	10	0	4	22	2
Camp, Matt, N.C. State	.332	241	56	80	11	3	1	31	10
Malone, Ryne, Fla. State	.330	203	50	67	15	3	12	54	9
Cox, Jay, No. Carolina	.329	167	44	55	11	1	3	24	6
Hicks, David, N.C. State	.329	237	38	78	17	0	8	46	0
Mezistrano, Lee, N.C. State	.326	178	31	58	13	1	1	30	4
Patterson, Eric, Ga. Tech	.326	264	**76**	86	11	5	9	49	**48**
Boggs, Brandon, Ga. Tech	.322	255	68	82	14	1	9	58	11
Daniel, Mike, No. Carolina	.320	147	27	47	16	2	2	20	3
Owings, Micah, Ga. Tech	.318	255	61	81	14	0	15	64	2
Storrer, Travis, Clemson	.315	216	49	68	13	2	7	33	5
Robbins, Whit, Ga. Tech	.313	144	34	45	10	1	2	39	4
Scioletti, Brad, Wake Forest	.309	217	35	67	8	2	5	45	0
Mangum, Greg, No. Carolina	.308	260	57	80	10	1	2	24	16
Evans, Garrick, Clemson	.308	130	29	40	13	0	2	17	5
Chapman, Gibbs, Fla. State	.307	199	38	61	14	3	3	41	8
Layden, Tim, Duke	.307	199	39	61	13	1	6	46	7
Ellington, Matt, No. Carolina	.306	147	20	45	8	1	2	27	0
Antonelli, Matt, Wake Forest	.305	203	51	62	7	0	2	37	18
Blue, Nick, Wake Forest	.305	190	47	58	9	0	1	24	23
Hodges, Wes, Ga. Tech	.304	184	41	56	16	1	4	31	7
Triplett, Russell, Clemson	.304	240	33	73	17	0	4	41	9
Koshansky, Joe, Virginia	.302	222	50	67	17	1	16	67	8
Dunn, Matt, Virginia	.301	219	50	66	4	4	1	34	8
Santangelo, Lou, Clemson	.300	253	50	76	15	2	18	62	7
Miello, Mike, Duke	.297	145	22	43	9	2	0	21	1
LeFaivre, Steve, Wake Forest	.296	186	38	55	4	2	13	47	0
St. Julien, Jason, N.C. State	.289	211	40	61	13	1	4	33	3
Colvin, Tyler, Clemson	.289	128	21	37	10	0	2	19	4
Street, Matt, Virginia	.283	212	49	60	10	3	1	37	19
Smith, Bryan, Duke	.282	216	30	61	17	1	2	36	6
Hernandez, Brian, Duke	.282	209	28	59	7	0	1	33	0

COLLEGE BASEBALL

INDIVIDUAL PITCHING LEADERS
(Minimum 50 Innings)

	W	L	ERA	G	SV	IP	H	BB	SO
Sterry, Vern, N.C. State	9	2	**2.20**	18	0	114	92	23	106
Gross, Michael, No. Carolina	4	4	2.24	**32**	8	52	44	12	59
Lambert, Casey, Virginia	4	1	2.54	29	8	60	51	21	40
Benson, Whitley, No. Carolina	5	1	2.61	30	1	59	48	16	47
Miller, Andrew, No. Carolina	6	3	2.93	18	0	89	64	48	88
Koshansky, Joe, Virginia	8	3	2.98	15	0	103	83	29	80
Rogers, Michael, N.C. State	9	4	3.08	18	0	**117**	89	21	110
Avery, Matt, Virginia	7	2	3.22	16	0	87	86	30	51
James, Rhett, Fla. State	**10**	3	3.36	29	3	110	100	32	93
Dobies, Andrew, Virginia	6	3	3.41	16	0	108	102	30	109
Kown, Andrew, Ga. Tech	**10**	1	3.46	18	0	112	109	36	96
Woodard, Robert, No. Carolina	8	2	3.49	25	1	57	45	15	46
Cribb, Josh, Clemson	5	1	3.71	20	2	61	49	15	58
Cannon, Eddie, Fla. State	9	7	3.87	20	1	112	108	18	96
Bard, Daniel, No. Carolina	8	4	3.88	16	0	95	94	31	68
Owings, Micah, Ga. Tech	9	3	3.89	18	0	113	93	43	**112**
Bakker, Garry, No. Carolina	5	5	3.90	16	0	90	93	36	65
Pfinsgraff, Ben, Maryland	4	5	3.95	16	0	73	69	24	69
Lumsden, Tyler, Clemson	5	4	3.98	15	0	81	80	37	88
Rohrbaugh, Robert, Clemson	4	5	3.99	20	0	77	77	21	44
Schultz, Brian, Fla. State	7	1	4.07	30	1	60	53	27	58
Jones, Hunter, Fla. State	3	2	4.10	15	0	64	67	16	55
#Hogan, Patrick, Clemson	3	4	4.23	24	**10**	45	42	19	60
Otero, Danny, Duke	2	4	4.38	21	4	62	80	8	46
Kane, Sean, Maryland	1	8	4.58	13	0	75	89	29	47
Schreiber, Zach, Duke	5	5	4.60	17	0	92	100	35	79
Burks, Brian, Ga. Tech	8	6	4.67	19	0	94	105	23	76
Burke, Greg, Duke	5	7	4.73	20	2	84	96	22	71
Hart, Kevin, Maryland	3	8	5.16	14	0	68	74	24	75
Sauls, Mark, Fla. State	6	4	5.22	20	0	91	110	40	52
#Devine, Joey, N.C. State	0	4	5.25	23	**10**	36	31	18	56
Harvey, Kris, Clemson	6	0	5.40	14	0	62	73	32	52
Clem, Chris, Maryland	2	7	5.76	15	1	89	115	22	77
Keadle, Justin, Wake Forest	2	5	6.22	13	0	88	108	29	66
Layden, Tim, Duke	6	5	6.27	16	0	75	84	37	83

ATLANTIC SUN CONFERENCE

	Conference		Overall	
	W	L	W	L
Central Florida	24	6	47	18
Stetson	20	10	36	23
*Florida Atlantic	20	10	47	17
Gardner-Webb	19	11	33	25
Troy State	15	15	36	22
Campbell	14	16	23	34
Belmont	13	17	31	23
Jacksonville	12	18	25	31
Georgia State	11	19	18	36
Lipscomb	9	21	15	39
Mercer	8	22	20	35

ALL-CONFERENCE TEAM: C—Chris Westervelt, Sr., Stetson. **1B**—Jeff Fiorentino, Jr., Florida Atlantic. **2B**—Derek Hutton, Jr., Florida Atlantic. **3B**—Orlando Diaz, Sr., Jacksonville. **SS**—Alex Fonseca, So., Florida Atlantic. **OF**—Dee Brown, Jr., Central Florida; Rob Horst, Sr., Florida Atlantic; Clay Timpner, Jr., Central Florida. **DH**—Donald Brickle, So., Jacksonville. **P**—Kyle Bono, So., Central Florida; Matt Fox, Jr., Central Florida; Dennis Robinson, Jr., Jacksonville. **RP**—Nate Moore, Jr., Troy State.
Player of the Year: Chris Westervelt, Stetson. **Pitcher of the Year:** Matt Fox, Central Florida. **Freshman of the Year:** Braedyn Pruitt, Stetson. **Coach of the Year:** Jay Bergman, Central Florida.

INDIVIDUAL BATTING LEADERS
(Minimum 125 At-Bats)

	AVG	AB	R	H	2B	3B	HR	RBI	SB
Burgess, Tim, Georgia State	**.413**	167	33	69	19	1	7	31	4
Mascia, Tim, Fla. Atlantic	.400	225	48	90	18	0	5	60	5
Westervelt, Chris, Stetson	.385	205	55	79	18	0	11	56	1
Godwin, Adam, Troy State	.384	177	38	68	5	0	1	20	28
Warpool, Jason, Belmont	.375	192	43	72	18	1	11	38	8
Brown, Dee, Central Florida	.373	228	51	85	11	3	5	**68**	8
Timpner, Clay, Central Florida	.371	259	69	**96**	**20**	**6**	6	34	**43**
McBryde, Mike, Fla. Atlantic	.370	135	29	50	1	1	0	11	11
Quirello, Ryan, Gard.-Webb	.369	203	36	75	16	3	8	34	1
Zenchyk, Bryan, Stetson	.368	209	43	77	16	0	7	47	0
Maier, Lenny, Troy State	.359	145	32	52	7	1	4	38	1
Anthonsen, Joe, Campbell	.356	202	43	72	6	1	1	25	3
Hutton, Derek, Fla. Atlantic	.354	257	72	91	12	5	6	50	19
Fiorentino, Jeff, Fla. Atlantic	.348	221	**84**	77	18	1	**17**	67	13
Soukup, Dan, Belmont	.348	187	39	65	13	0	7	25	9
Clifford, Pete Jacksonville	.346	188	39	65	12	1	3	26	5
Destafano, Jon, Stetson	.346	162	40	56	7	3	3	38	4
Brown, Rusty, Florida Atlantic	.344	160	21	55	14	0	7	41	0
Still, Jon, Stetson	.343	204	43	70	16	0	2	47	1
Fonseca, Alex, Florida Atlantic	.338	195	36	66	14	3	3	43	3
O'Quinn, Casey, Troy State	.338	204	42	69	10	1	6	40	1
Pruitt, Braedyn, Stetson	.337	208	41	70	4	4	4	41	1
Newman, Justin, Georgia State	.333	177	32	59	13	1	3	18	7
McCarson, Billy, Gard.-Webb	.328	128	21	42	9	0	10	32	0
Brummett, Josh, Belmont	.325	160	33	52	10	1	6	25	7
Gomez, Dennis, Belmont	.323	155	31	50	14	1	7	29	4
Hurst, Daniel, Mercer	.322	180	33	58	14	1	5	31	3
Robinson, Clint, Troy State	.322	143	22	46	9	1	3	22	1
Bennett, Brian, Troy State	.320	128	20	41	6	0	4	16	0
Bono, Ryan, Central Florida	.316	215	33	68	16	1	2	43	0
Ray, Matt, Central Florida	.316	174	45	55	4	2	0	26	21
Randol, Jeff, Campbell	.311	190	24	59	8	5	1	33	9
Sterling, Ryan, Georgia State	.309	188	43	58	9	3	4	36	0
Rose, Chandler, Central Fla.	.308	201	30	62	16	1	1	35	3
Jordan, Shane, Stetson	.308	227	44	70	6	0	0	27	22
Hastings, Brent, Lipscomb	.308	169	34	52	10	3	4	22	11
Logan, Nate, Campbell	.306	134	17	41	6	3	1	15	0
Dobner, Brad, Belmont	.305	190	38	58	11	**6**	6	26	16
Diaz, Orlando, Jacksonville	.304	181	36	55	10	0	9	43	11
Sheffield, Brad, Troy State	.303	175	27	53	6	0	1	20	8
Priest, Mike, Campbell	.302	199	32	60	11	2	9	39	7
Alvarez, Roger, Mercer	.302	162	27	49	6	2	0	24	5
Hart, Clint, Lipscomb	.302	159	33	48	10	2	5	33	10
Lalli, Blake, Gardner-Webb	.299	201	60	14	1	8	37	3	
Blick, Jeff, Campbell	.299	194	32	58	9	0	1	18	20
Bernhard, Marshall, Cent. Fla.	.299	164	32	49	8	3	0	30	6
Brannon, Evan, Fla. Atlantic	.299	154	32	46	9	1	1	25	3

INDIVIDUAL PITCHING LEADERS
(Minimum 50 Innings)

	W	L	ERA	G	SV	IP	H	BB	SO
Moore, Nate, Troy State	9	4	1.25	**32**	8	65	42	16	84
Fox, Matt, Central Florida	**14**	2	1.85	17	0	112	78	32	**125**
Bono, Kyle, Central Florida	8	2	1.94	18	2	97	69	29	107
Meier, Taylor, Central Florida	6	3	2.53	13	0	74	59	30	56
Heacox, Ryan, Stetson	10	2	2.57	25	2	84	65	19	40
Robinson, Dennis, Jacksonville	13	4	2.85	18	0	120	121	34	76
Blackard, Cody, Belmont	5	4	2.99	13	0	72	87	8	32
Newlin, Darren, Central Florida	5	0	3.13	17	2	60	61	33	42
O'Brien, Matt, Florida Atlantic	11	3	3.14	17	0	97	100	26	72
Ward, Zach, Gardner-Webb	5	4	3.16	19	1	80	76	32	106
Saxton, Chris, Florida Atlantic	4	1	3.31	24	7	65	63	26	36
Siak, Joey, Garder-Webb	7	3	3.40	13	0	87	86	16	40
Jones, Brian, Mercer	9	6	3.46	21	1	120	117	37	87
Long, Jeff, Gardner-Webb	7	5	3.49	14	0	88	87	32	81
Jordan, Justin, Belmont	8	5	3.59	14	0	100	104	13	54
Kuwik, Seth, Lipscomb	4	8	3.54	19	2	81	84	22	48
Ingoglia, Chris, Stetson	7	3	3.62	21	0	86	83	33	50
Brickle, Donald, Jacksonville	4	4	3.63	14	0	74	91	17	31
Beam, Randy, Florida Atlantic	10	9	3.66	19	0	**123**	129	30	78
Gonzalez, Abe, Gard.-Webb	6	4	3.88	16	0	72	69	24	70
Feliciano, Milton, Georgia State	4	3	3.90	17	0	55	71	23	31
Winters, Mal, Troy State	6	3	4.04	24	1	69	83	18	65
Babyak, Joey, Campbell	4	1	4.50	21	1	58	67	28	35
Blades, Josh, Campbell	7	9	4.74	16	0	104	116	46	54
DeVries, Kyle, Jacksonville	8	4	4.80	16	0	60	84	20	49
Wikstrom, Eric, Troy State	8	4	4.82	19	0	99	128	18	66
Dixon, Ryan, Stetson	4	4	4.84	23	3	80	79	35	62
Topal, Jordan, Campbell	3	6	4.93	20	2	84	92	20	53
Terrill, Matt, Campbell	4	5	5.08	16	0	73	102	9	34

ATLANTIC-10 CONFERENCE

	Conference		Overall	
	W	L	W	L
EAST				
Rhode Island	20	4	35	20
*St. Bonaventure	14	7	29	22
Fordham	13	11	25	27
Massachusetts	10	14	19	26
Temple	10	14	23	26
St. Joseph's	4	20	10	44
WEST				
George Washington	19	5	41	18
Richmond	17	7	33	24
Duquesne	11	10	21	28
Dayton	11	13	25	28
Xavier	7	17	16	38
La Salle	5	19	20	28

ALL-CONFERENCE TEAM: C—Jeremy Bourgeois, Jr., Fordham. **1B**—Dan Batz, Sr., Rhode Island. **2B**—Tom Shanley, So., George Washington.

COLLEGE BASEBALL

	W	L	ERA	G	SV	IP	H	BB	SO
Martin, Thomas, Richmond	7	2	3.18	12	0	71	59	23	69
Holmes, Stephen, Rhode Island	5	1	3.46	14	0	75	63	30	85
Berzinskas, Rob, Richmond	6	3	3.47	17	0	73	71	24	66
Lutz, Derrik, George Wash.	3	5	3.55	30	12	51	59	21	40
McLoughlin, Matt, Richmond	3	2	3.57	20	1	58	56	25	55
Frederick, Dan, Rhode Island	7	3	3.73	15	0	82	72	32	79
Blevins, Jerry, Dayton	7	3	3.79	14	0	74	76	38	70
Sullivan, Dan, George Wash.	10	4	3.82	15	0	92	100	26	87
Trubee, Luke, Dayton	8	3	4.09	19	0	77	91	18	40
Petrutz, Adriano, St. Joseph's	2	5	4.10	12	0	53	51	39	38
Stammen, Craig, Dayton	1	6	4.26	22	9	68	82	21	61
Bolinski, Jason, Richmond	3	4	4.28	16	0	82	85	22	77
Landahl, Matt, St. Bonaventure	2	4	4.35	11	0	52	57	20	38
Haun, Adam, Duquesne	3	6	4.52	13	0	76	77	36	64
Rodriguez, David, Fordham	5	5	4.56	17	0	81	71	32	75
Reifschneider, Bob, Duquesne	4	7	4.82	13	0	80	89	28	52
Torra, Matt, Massachusetts	5	5	4.90	12	0	64	83	26	69
Hoagey, Ryan, St. Joseph's	2	8	5.00	18	0	85	102	39	57

ANDREW WOOLLEY

Notre Dame's Matt Macri

3B—Brandon Godzik, Jr., Dayton. SS—Eric Wilson, Sr., St. Bonaventure. OF—Jay Johnson, Sr., Xavier; Anthony Raglani, Jr., George Washington; Al Roach, Sr., Temple. DH—Anthony Smith, Fr., George Washington. P—Dan Sullivan, Jr., George Washington; Zach Zuercher, So., Rhode Island. RP—Derrik Lutz, Fr., George Washington.

Player of the Year: Dan Batz, Rhode Island. **Pitcher of the Year:** Zach Zuercher, Rhode Island. **Rookie of the Year:** Anthony Smith, George Washington. **Coach of the Year:** Frank Leoni, Rhode Island.

INDIVIDUAL BATTING LEADERS
(Minimum 125 At-Bats)

	AVG	AB	R	H	2B	3B	HR	RBI	SB
Godzik, Brandon, Dayton	.407	162	32	66	13	0	9	53	2
Batz, Dan, Rhode Island	.406	187	58	76	24	1	12	59	10
Nestor, Josh, Rhode Island	.395	129	27	51	7	1	4	30	3
Roach, Al, Temple	.385	179	47	69	16	0	7	41	9
Curreri, Frank, Massachusetts	.380	158	36	60	16	0	7	54	6
Flynn, Patrick, Dayton	.374	190	44	71	15	2	5	44	4
Smith, Anthony, George Wash.	.369	187	43	69	17	0	15	69	6
Wilson, Eric, St. Bonaventure	.366	186	47	68	17	1	7	40	9
Prall, Rich, La Salle	.365	170	29	62	12	0	6	29	0
Bourgeois, Jeremy, Fordham	.355	166	38	59	15	1	8	39	6
Bohnenstiehl, Nick, Dayton	.353	207	39	73	11	4	2	31	8
Tarewicz, Jason, St. Joseph's	.337	178	41	60	17	2	1	28	20
Gentile, Mike, St. Joseph's	.336	146	25	49	6	0	2	27	8
Milsom, Geoff, George Wash.	.335	164	35	55	10	0	3	34	6
Board, A.J., Richmond	.335	194	40	65	13	2	7	49	6
Maiolo, Steve, Duquesne	.333	168	34	56	9	0	3	38	8
Shanley, Tom, George Wash.	.332	211	45	70	15	0	5	36	5
Smith, Greg, Fordham	.332	199	50	66	13	2	6	33	6
Schwartzbauer, Dan, Duq.	.331	172	43	57	11	2	3	28	25
Sullivan, Matt, Rhode Island	.330	188	24	62	12	0	6	34	9
Russo, Wayne, Rhode Island	.329	149	33	49	4	1	1	20	7
Brush, Kevin, Fordham	.327	159	39	52	11	4	2	28	8
Johnson, Jay, Xavier	.326	190	32	62	11	0	6	23	13
Roberson, Ryan, Geo. Wash.	.326	233	58	76	14	1	14	61	11
Connor, Jason, Temple	.323	195	43	63	11	2	8	54	10
Thomas, Kurt, Fordham	.322	180	41	58	9	5	3	37	10
Raglani, Anthony, Geo. Wash.	.322	208	63	67	14	1	12	50	13
Parfit, Ryan, La Salle	.319	166	38	53	13	3	6	27	8
Landahl, Matt, St. Bona.	.318	195	35	62	10	1	2	32	9
Pellegrini, Brian, St. Bona.	.316	193	34	61	12	3	7	33	11
Fasano, Jim, Richmond	.316	206	43	65	15	1	18	62	2
LeNoir, Bobby, Richmond	.315	200	47	63	12	1	2	25	23
Savard, Dave, Rhode Island	.313	128	33	40	3	1	0	10	10
Quigley, John, Temple	.312	173	42	54	12	0	4	43	9
Rosenblat, Brad, Geo. Wash.	.311	183	49	57	13	1	10	43	4
Zeskind, Ben, Richmond	.311	212	50	66	23	3	1	35	14
Adler, Drew, Fordham	.310	126	29	39	6	0	0	20	7
#Short, Tim, Fordam	.257	202	38	52	9	5	2	22	9

INDIVIDUAL PITCHING LEADERS
(Minimum 50 Innings)

	W	L	ERA	G	SV	IP	H	BB	SO
#Creevy, Mike, Xavier	2	1	2.37	31	8	49	42	26	46
Wilkie, Josh, George Wash.	6	2	2.77	15	0	84	79	21	54
Zuercher, Zach, Rhode Island	8	3	2.82	17	1	93	56	44	123
Chown, Eric, Massachusetts	7	4	3.03	12	0	77	75	15	55
Cameron, Nate, St. Bonaventure	4	1	3.08	17	0	64	68	20	37

BIG EAST CONFERENCE

	Conference		Overall	
	W	L	W	L
*Notre Dame	20	6	51	12
St. John's	17	9	37	23
Pittsburgh	17	9	38	18
Boston College	15	9	32	27
Rutgers	13	11	30	23
Villanova	11	14	31	20
Virginia Tech	11	15	29	27
West Virginia	10	16	23	29
Connecticut	9	17	26	29
Seton Hall	9	17	17	33
Georgetown	8	17	25	30

ALL-CONFERENCE TEAM: C—Michael Lombardi, Sr., Georgetown. **1B**—Sean O'Brien, Fr., Virginia Tech. **2B**—Steve Sollmann, Sr., Notre Dame. **3B**—Matt Macri, Jr., Notre Dame. **SS**—Bryan Spamer, Sr., Pittsburgh. **OF**—Jason Delaney, Jr., Boston College; Jeff Frazier, Jr., Rutgers; Lee Fritz, Jr., West Virginia. **DH**—P.J. Hiser, Sr., Pittsburgh. **P**—Zac Cline, Jr., West Virginia; Nick Evangelista, Sr., Pittsburgh; Grant Johnson, Jr., Notre Dame; Chris Lambert, Jr., Boston College.

Player of the Year: P.J. Hiser, Pittsburgh. **Pitchers of the Year:** Nick Evangelista, Pittsburgh; Chris Lambert, Boston College. **Rookie of the Year:** Jim Negrych, Pittsburgh. **Coach of the Year:** Joe Jordano, Pittsburgh.

INDIVIDUAL BATTING LEADERS
(Minimum 125 At-Bats)

	AVG	AB	R	H	2B	3B	HR	RBI	SB
Frazier, Jeff, Rutgers	.382	207	59	79	16	1	13	59	6
Negrych, Jim, Pittsburgh	.378	201	44	76	20	1	7	45	12
O'Brien, Sean, Virginia Tech	.372	172	38	64	9	1	6	45	4
Peluso, Marc, Connecticut	.368	209	41	77	13	2	3	47	11
Delaney, Jason, Boston College	.368	209	46	77	14	1	9	50	4
Macri, Matt, Notre Dame	.367	237	76	87	15	7	14	56	12
Badger, Graig, Rutgers	.364	198	56	72	11	2	3	31	26
Fritz, Lee, West Virginia	.364	176	37	64	15	1	3	28	6
Cooper, Craig, Notre Dame	.360	175	42	63	13	1	10	48	12
Canuso, Rich, Rutgers	.354	195	38	69	13	0	9	47	3
Hiser, P.J., Pittsburgh	.354	198	57	70	11	3	21	67	19
Martin, Jim, St. John's	.351	225	45	79	12	0	0	26	4
Cerulo, Nick, Rutgers	.350	137	30	48	7	5	5	29	12
Lombardi, Michael, Georgetown	.348	201	27	70	15	0	4	37	1
Psomas, Grant, West Virginia	.343	198	42	68	13	1	9	45	9
Pahuta, Tim, Seton Hall	.342	193	35	66	14	3	6	37	4
Quinn, Billy, Georgetown	.341	129	17	44	11	1	5	31	2
Burke, Joe, St. John's	.340	194	28	66	11	0	1	28	8
Cline, David, Pittsburgh	.338	145	32	49	6	0	1	14	24
Leonard, Mike, Connecticut	.336	146	34	49	11	0	3	31	1
Grose, Jeff, Rutgers	.333	186	36	62	9	1	2	30	7
Scott, Joey, Seton Hall	.333	195	41	65	16	1	4	31	12
Lopez, Greg, Notre Dame	.332	199	39	66	14	0	2	34	4
Copeland, Ben, Pittsburgh	.332	217	63	72	15	7	3	37	37
Schau, Adrian, Villanova	.330	176	38	58	13	0	6	30	4
Fulda, Chris, Seton Hall	.326	181	20	59	8	2	3	33	1
Gaynor, Colin, Rutgers	.325	163	29	53	11	1	3	36	2
Cohen, Brandon, Seton Hall	.325	151	32	49	8	0	1	17	9
Petracca, Angelo, Villanova	.323	189	41	61	10	1	1	28	11
Antoniato, P.J., St. John's	.322	236	47	76	13	2	6	39	13
Posluszny, Stan, West Virginia	.322	177	29	57	13	1	6	33	6
Andres, Steve, Notre Dame	.320	169	38	54	13	4	8	39	4
Newbold, Brian, Villanova	.320	194	32	62	12	2	5	37	8
Hourigan, Jeff, Connecticut	.320	175	33	56	8	0	8	38	1
Cano, Ron, Georgetown	.320	181	30	58	12	2	1	21	8

Player	AVG	AB	R	H	2B	3B	HR	RBI	SB
Rozema, Mike, St. John's	.319	226	42	72	7	0	2	24	22
Leahy, Ryan, Boston College	.319	238	39	76	9	0	2	34	5
Seratelli, Anthony, Seton Hall	.319	166	35	53	13	2	2	27	15
Cashman, Tom, Pittsburgh	.317	183	42	58	11	2	13	45	1
Matuszek, Kyle, West Virginia	.317	139	18	44	6	0	5	26	8
Brooks, Parker, Georgetown	.316	215	36	68	14	0	1	17	12
Hershelman, Blake, St. John's	.315	213	45	67	16	0	10	48	2
Clinton, Kurtis, West Virginia	.312	173	21	54	9	1	5	39	2
Sollmann, Steve, Notre Dame	.311	151	39	47	5	1	2	23	17
Edwards, Matt, Notre Dame	.310	216	48	67	13	1	12	54	5
#Locke, Drew, Boston College	.279	233	44	65	21	1	4	41	13

INDIVIDUAL PITCHING LEADERS
(Minimum 50 Innings)

Player	W	L	ERA	G	SV	IP	H	BB	SO
Johnson, Grant, Notre Dame	6	0	1.87	14	0	58	39	26	51
#Doherty, Ryan, Notre Dame	5	1	2.38	30	12	34	19	11	46
Cline, Zac, West Virginia	8	3	2.65	12	0	78	60	22	44
Scott, Joey, Seton Hall	4	2	2.68	8	0	50	32	18	51
Delaney, Robert, St. John's	3	1	2.90	17	1	50	56	22	41
#Hansen, Craig, St. John's	2	2	2.90	31	10	40	33	16	59
Tosoni, Matt, St. John's	5	2	2.91	15	0	59	52	20	28
Samardzija, Jeff, Notre Dame	5	3	2.95	20	1	64	50	17	42
Lambert, Chris, Boston College	6	4	3.02	15	0	92	65	51	107
Evangelista, Nick, Pittsburgh	8	3	3.50	15	0	82	85	27	70
Kalb, Aaron, Rutgers	5	3	3.57	12	0	53	56	22	36
Biber, Josh, Virginia Tech	5	1	3.57	13	0	81	85	22	55
Niesel, Chris, Notre Dame	8	3	3.62	18	0	102	123	20	84
Varvaro, Anthony, St. John's	8	3	3.63	17	0	89	76	54	78
Shepard, Kevin, Boston College	8	4	3.63	14	0	92	88	41	52
Jansen, Jim, Rutgers	5	1	3.67	12	0	54	61	22	30
Wladyka, Jim, St. John's	3	3	3.81	14	1	50	52	21	33
Thornton, Tom, Notre Dame	9	2	3.88	16	0	100	95	24	77
Wells, Andrew, Virginia Tech	4	6	3.91	11	0	51	60	12	28
O'Donnel, Matt, Boston College	4	5	3.95	14	0	84	97	26	65
Gauthier, Mike, Boston College	5	3	4.03	28	5	51	51	29	36
McGinn, Brendan, Connecticut	3	5	4.08	15	0	68	89	17	47
Kuss, Andrew, Pittsburgh	4	5	4.20	15	0	75	77	33	64
Landing, Jeff, Virginia Tech	4	5	4.31	14	0	77	88	27	58
Hiser, P.J., Pittsburgh	5	1	4.40	15	1	61	70	23	49
Egbert, Jack, Rutgers	7	4	4.41	14	1	88	89	24	65
Sabo, Tim, Seton Hall	1	6	4.43	16	1	61	77	22	58
Kennedy, Ryan, Virginia Tech	5	7	4.46	15	0	85	90	33	61
Allen, Nick, Villanova	3	5	4.55	16	0	85	106	22	40
Noonan, Chris, Seton Hall	4	6	4.60	22	1	76	87	26	55
Nardozzi, Paul, Pittsburgh	6	3	4.61	15	0	55	47	30	42

Player	AVG	AB	R	H	2B	3B	HR	RBI	SB
Woods, Brad, Charleston So.	.336	217	44	73	10	1	10	36	22
Mizerany, Pat, Birm.-Southern	.336	125	18	42	3	1	0	20	0
Bogue, Matt, Birm.-Southern	.335	209	48	70	9	2	2	25	25
Repec, Matt, Winthrop	.331	236	40	78	12	0	7	48	4
Grandstrand, Brett, Co. Car.	.330	233	52	77	20	0	9	52	11
Just, Michael, Liberty	.330	197	36	65	13	0	3	26	4
Ashworth, Alan, Radford	.328	204	34	67	9	2	1	32	19
Smith, Matt, VMI	.328	201	45	66	15	5	0	27	10
Wydner, Michael, Birm.-So.	.326	193	36	63	15	0	2	36	6
Dempsey, Jacob, Winthrop	.326	227	49	74	22	4	7	47	4
Lentz, Tommy, Winthrop	.325	191	45	62	12	0	4	39	6
Fleisher, Mark, Radford	.321	184	38	59	18	0	16	52	0
Carrara, Chris, Winthrop	.321	184	47	59	11	0	2	28	13
Renta, Seby, High Point	.315	162	23	51	12	0	4	23	0
Barber, Matt, Birm.-Southern	.314	210	40	66	15	0	0	27	2
DeJesus, Michael, Co. Carolina	.313	160	37	50	8	1	3	19	3
Garcia, Carlos, Liberty	.312	199	37	62	13	2	10	47	1
Raber, Chris, Co. Carolina	.308	185	42	57	10	1	3	31	15
Ritchie, Stuart, Radford	.308	221	46	68	9	7	5	36	8
Sole, Brian, Charleston So.	.308	185	42	57	7	4	12	45	14
Ross, Jesse, Radford	.304	184	38	56	9	6	1	22	6
Dalton, Billy, Charleston So.	.304	184	31	56	8	0	2	17	14
Brown, Jeffrey, Liberty	.302	202	30	61	19	0	1	50	1
Oxendine, Chad, Co. Carolina	.302	189	27	57	12	0	2	35	2
#Cline, Michael, Birm.-So.	.298	245	57	73	14	8	4	52	28
#Rojas, Rey, High Point	.297	229	45	68	15	1	9	31	35
#Robertson, Connor, Birm.-So.	.282	262	61	74	10	2	21	69	8

INDIVIDUAL PITCHING LEADERS
(Minimum 50 Innings)

Player	W	L	ERA	G	SV	IP	H	BB	SO
Wilson, Jon, Winthrop	11	0	1.88	34	6	67	47	17	79
#Robertson, Connor, Birm.-So.	5	2	2.37	22	9	30	21	12	47
Williams, David A., UNC-A	8	3	2.84	22	2	86	74	38	71
Godwin, Mac, Birm.-Southern	6	2	3.03	17	0	71	73	31	52
Slowey, Kevin, Winthrop	9	4	3.23	17	0	120	120	10	104
Swindle, R.J., Charleston So.	8	4	3.24	18	1	114	117	30	127
Horne, David, Birm.-Southern	8	3	3.36	19	0	102	100	29	64
Mynick, Brandon, Birm.-So.	3	0	3.61	21	2	57	49	20	50
Hurry, Jake, Co. Carolina	9	3	3.72	22	0	116	104	47	93
DeLaGarza, Andy, Co. Car.	3	2	3.91	16	0	53	58	35	38
Cook, Steven, UNC-A	8	7	4.06	19	0	126	145	38	93
Graham, Tom, Radford	2	3	4.08	12	0	71	65	21	25
Carter, Steven, Co. Carolina	12	3	4.11	22	2	123	135	32	116
Rembert, Aaron UNC-A	8	7	4.20	25	3	99	122	19	72
Britnell, Josh, Birm.-Southern	4	4	4.35	17	0	81	101	30	66
Honce, Mike, Winthrop	6	5	4.41	13	0	65	70	25	53
Binda, Byron, Co. Carolina	3	5	4.45	34	9	63	54	25	72
Letson, Wes, Birm.-Southern	12	3	4.58	19	0	110	115	39	88
Zuvich, Chris, Liberty	4	3	4.69	17	0	71	76	47	75
Bissell, Brad, Charleston So.	4	10	4.76	20	0	102	113	35	79
Terry, Jason, Winthrop	2	1	4.94	16	0	55	56	15	33
Hollenbeck, J.J., VMI	4	5	4.96	18	0	85	95	27	59
Jones, Jason, Liberty	4	7	4.96	15	1	74	84	18	60
Fleisher, Mark, Radford	4	2	5.13	10	0	53	65	17	49
Fasulo, Nino, Charleston So.	5	3	5.32	24	1	64	71	21	52
Morgan, Justin, Radford	5	2	5.48	12	0	64	79	18	35

BIG SOUTH CONFERENCE

	Conference		Overall	
	W	L	W	L
Birmingham-Southern	21	3	47	18
*Coastal Carolina	16	8	40	23
Winthrop	16	8	37	23
Radford	14	10	23	30
UNC Asheville	13	11	26	31
Charleston Southern	11	13	24	34
Liberty	9	15	25	30
Virginia Military Institute	4	20	23	32
High Point	4	20	11	44

ALL-CONFERENCE TEAM: C—Ryan Griffith, Sr., Birmingham-Southern. **1B**—Mark Fleisher, Jr., Radford. **2B**—David R. Williams, So., UNC Asheville. **3B**—David Scoggin, Sr., Winthrop. **SS**—Matt Repec, So., Winthrop. **OF**—Jeremiah Boles, Sr., Liberty; Daniel Carte, So., Winthrop; Jared Walker, Sr., Birmingham-Southern. **DH**—Mike Costanzo, So., Coastal Carolina. **P**—Steven Carter, Sr., Coastal Carolina; Wes Letson, Jr., Birmingham-Southern; R.J. Swindle, Jr., Charleston Southern.

Most Valuable Player: Mike Costanzo, Coastal Carolina. **Freshman of the Year:** David A. Williams, UNC Asheville. **Coach of the Year:** Brian Shoop, Birmingham-Southern.

INDIVIDUAL BATTING LEADERS
(Minimum 125 At-Bats)

Player	AVG	AB	R	H	2B	3B	HR	RBI	SB
Boles, Jeremiah, Liberty	.398	226	61	90	16	2	7	32	31
Laurent, Phillip, Liberty	.369	203	50	75	18	3	6	62	6
Sweppenhiser, Kelly, VMI	.367	158	33	58	10	1	9	42	2
Walker, Jared, Birm.-Southern	.362	243	36	88	22	1	3	59	2
Sherman, Steve, UNC-A	.360	200	43	72	10	0	16	53	21
Costanzo, Mike, Co. Carolina	.359	231	66	83	21	2	21	74	3
Griffith, Ryan, Birm.-Southern	.349	241	44	84	12	0	10	39	6
Williams, David R., UNC-A	.345	223	37	77	13	1	4	29	16
Wohlford, Kellen, Radford	.340	209	41	71	19	4	2	30	27
Carte, Daniel, Winthrop	.339	230	54	78	14	2	10	54	16
Scoggin, David, Winthrop	.339	242	47	82	17	0	11	46	2

BIG TEN CONFERENCE

	Conference		Overall	
	W	L	W	L
*Minnesota	21	10	38	23
Ohio State	19	12	36	25
Michigan	19	13	34	26
Michigan State	19	13	33	26
Purdue	17	14	29	28
Penn State	17	15	28	29
Northwestern	14	18	26	28
Iowa	12	20	20	35
Illinois	11	21	22	33
Indiana	9	22	25	30

ALL-CONFERENCE TEAM: C—Chris Robinson, So., Illinois. **1B**—Andy Hunter, So., Minnesota. **2B**—Chris Getz, So., Michigan. **3B**—James Moreno, Sr., Michigan State. **SS**—Seth Bynum, Sr., Indiana. **OF**—Steve Caravati, Jr., Ohio State; Travis Gulick, Jr., Michigan State; Sam Steidl, Sr., Minnesota. **DH**—Brandon Roberts, Sr., Michigan. **P**—Jim Brauer, Jr., Michigan; J.A. Happ, Jr., Northwestern; Nathan Johnson, Sr., Iowa; Josh Newman, Sr., Ohio State; Glen Perkins, So., Minnesota. **RP**—Adam White, Sr., Michigan State.

Player of the Year: Steve Caravati, Ohio State. **Pitcher of the Year:** Glen Perkins, Minnesota. **Freshman of the Year:** Jacob Howell, Ohio State. **Coach of the Year:** John Anderson, Minnesota.

INDIVIDUAL BATTING LEADERS
(Minimum 125 At-Bats)

	AVG	AB	R	H	2B	3B	HR	RBI	SB
Caravati, Steve, Ohio State	.391	235	46	92	17	1	9	52	8
Bynum, Seth, Indiana	.387	204	54	79	15	4	10	65	19
Ori, Mark, Northwestern	.382	191	30	73	14	2	0	23	2
Steidl, Sam, Minnesota	.372	234	62	87	22	1	2	30	20
Roberts, Brandon, Michigan	.368	190	33	70	15	1	4	33	1
Hunter, Andy, Minnesota	.366	216	46	79	20	1	10	66	2
Getz, Chris, Michigan	.364	239	52	87	17	3	2	44	15
Robinson, Chris, Illinois	.359	181	31	65	6	0	9	38	1
Mahar, Kevin, Indiana	.359	184	40	66	10	1	14	52	8
Fornasiere, Matt, Minnesota	.353	218	46	77	14	1	6	45	14
Bohm, Kyle, Michigan	.352	216	47	76	17	1	6	52	1
Koerber, Scott, Michigan State	.352	125	27	44	11	0	7	30	1
Pohlman, Dan, Northwestern	.350	197	37	69	13	1	8	42	4
Frk, Chad, Illinois	.344	163	31	56	10	0	1	24	5
MacLean, Luke, Minnesota	.341	205	49	70	5	2	1	32	13
Howell, Jacob, Ohio State	.336	241	41	81	8	4	2	27	11
Moreno, James, Michigan State	.333	201	45	67	11	1	12	48	9
Bourquin, Ronnie, Ohio State	.333	129	25	43	8	0	5	20	0
Hilligoss, Mitch, Purdue	.327	150	23	49	5	1	2	20	6
Anderson, Drew, Ohio State	.324	253	51	82	18	5	4	30	20
Huisinga, Trevor, Illinois	.322	180	27	58	12	1	0	13	6
Morris, Erik, Michigan State	.321	221	50	71	9	1	10	44	9
Mee, Mike, Minnesota	.319	232	44	74	16	2	6	53	3
Rose, Eric, Michigan	.317	167	37	53	6	3	1	16	14
Kemp, Joe, Indiana	.317	205	43	65	16	4	7	35	3
Elder, Jake, Minnesota	.317	189	32	60	6	0	7	32	3
Mikrut, Jon, Northwestern	.316	212	30	67	10	2	7	43	0
Hastings, Ryan, Illinois	.315	168	25	53	7	1	1	20	6
Yoho, Nate, Iowa	.312	202	33	63	15	0	4	48	13
Gulick, Travis, Michigan State	.310	210	50	65	18	5	11	52	10
Heckman, Corby, Indiana	.310	184	42	57	8	3	5	33	1
Cattrysse, Alan, Michigan State	.309	204	38	63	8	2	6	31	7
Butler, Matt, Michigan	.309	217	41	67	13	0	3	44	16
Milliron, Mike, Penn State	.307	205	44	63	10	1	2	20	6
Watson, Reggie, Indiana	.307	205	41	63	12	3	3	21	25
Coles, Mike, Purdue	.307	212	40	65	17	2	4	23	13
Kunkel, Jeff, Michigan	.306	173	22	53	13	0	3	34	1
Wycklendt, Anthony, N'western	.306	183	27	56	11	4	6	34	5
Wolcott, Oliver, Michigan State	.306	216	40	66	8	4	6	31	14
Lytle, Andy, Iowa	.305	151	22	46	4	1	0	16	4
Osborn, Eric, Purdue	.304	191	26	58	10	5	3	34	6
Scheidt, A.J., Michigan	.304	230	34	70	11	1	5	42	7
Koester, Mitch, Purdue	.304	168	36	51	12	0	7	36	3
Donley, Ryan, Indiana	.303	178	33	54	6	0	6	32	6
Stephen, Jedidiah, Ohio State	.301	153	28	46	8	2	7	29	1
Wolfe, Eric, Purdue	.300	200	28	60	7	0	0	10	3

INDIVIDUAL PITCHING LEADERS
(Minimum 50 Innings)

	W	L	ERA	G	SV	IP	H	BB	SO
Happ, J.A., Northwestern	6	3	2.68	14	0	94	80	33	106
Perkins, Glen, Minnesota	9	3	2.83	16	0	111	89	21	113
Brauer, Dan, Northwestern	6	5	3.02	14	0	89	80	26	96
Gale, Bryan, Michigan State	4	5	3.12	13	0	92	87	21	93
Carroll, Jeffrey, Ohio State	5	2	3.16	18	0	51	48	17	26
Johnson, Nathan, Iowa	4	3	3.36	14	0	96	112	16	73
#Fausnaugh, Trey, Ohio State	2	1	3.50	32	9	46	51	12	26
Feldkamp, Derek, Michigan	6	5	3.59	19	4	73	69	26	51
Molldrem, Craig, Minnesota	6	3	3.62	15	1	72	67	19	41
Conroy, Jim, Illinois	6	4	3.63	12	0	57	65	10	49
Byrnes, Scott, Purdue	4	5	3.74	14	0	84	97	20	85
Hammond, Paul, Michigan	5	1	3.82	17	0	66	57	41	40
Stidfole, Sean, Penn State	6	4	3.89	16	1	76	76	23	87
Gorski, Tim, Illinois	5	2	3.95	13	0	66	73	17	42
Sattler, Dan, Purdue	4	4	3.98	12	0	54	52	24	35
Gagner, Jay, Minnesota	5	1	4.00	13	0	54	52	27	38
Newman, Josh, Ohio State	8	6	4.01	15	0	103	96	32	100
Luyster, Trent, Ohio State	4	5	4.08	20	4	82	94	25	68
Karpel, Brian, Purdue	5	5	4.12	12	0	68	63	19	36
Tressler, Aaron, Penn State	4	4	4.19	14	1	69	66	21	58
Brauer, Jim, Michigan	7	3	4.27	15	0	86	100	28	69
Pegg, Adam, Indiana	3	4	4.37	20	3	60	67	13	39
Krogman, Josh, Minnesota	4	1	4.39	14	0	53	65	37	13
Penn, Michael, Minnesota	7	6	4.46	17	0	81	84	20	44
Madsen, Mike, Ohio State	9	4	4.83	16	0	88	98	37	59
Vitielliss, Nick, Indiana	3	4	4.99	15	0	79	99	15	42
Tognetti, Phil, Michigan	4	2	5.03	27	4	54	58	20	33
Hanson, Andrew, Iowa	2	5	5.18	12	0	57	73	21	33
Lewis, Josh, Indiana	4	3	5.18	14	0	66	66	32	42
Seward, Austin, Iowa	1	5	5.21	13	0	67	86	32	39
Lortz, Brian, Indiana	3	3	5.26	16	1	51	61	15	29
Rowe, Ted, Illinois	3	8	5.32	12	0	71	83	21	43
Farrell, Jim, Penn State	3	10	5.33	15	0	78	96	31	57

BIG 12 CONFERENCE

	Conference		Overall	
	W	L	W	L
Texas	19	7	58	15
Oklahoma	19	8	38	24
Texas Tech	17	9	40	21
*Oklahoma State	15	11	38	24
Texas A&M	14	12	42	22
Baylor	13	12	29	31
Missouri	12	14	38	23
Nebraska	11	16	36	23
Kansas	7	19	31	31
Kansas State	4	23	26	30

ALL-CONFERENCE TEAM: C—Jason Jaramillo, Jr., Oklahoma State. **1B**—Josh Brady, Jr., Texas Tech. **2B**—Russell Raley, So., Oklahoma. **3B**—Alex Gordon, So., Nebraska. **SS**—Cameron Blair, Jr., Texas Tech. **OF**—Matt Baty, So., Kansas; Carson Kainer, Fr., Texas; Michael Mask, Jr., Texas Tech; Cory Patton, Sr., Texas A&M; Drew Stubbs, Fr., Texas. **DH**—Lee Laskowski, Sr., Missouri. **UT**—Curtis Thigpen, Jr., Texas. **P**—Garrett Broshuis, Jr., Missouri; J.P. Howell, Jr., Texas; Zach Jackson, Jr., Texas A&M; Jason Meyer, Fr., Texas A&M. **RP**—J. Brent Cox, So., Texas; Jarod McAuliff, Jr., Oklahoma; Huston Street, Jr., Texas

Player of the Year: Alex Gordon, Nebraska. **Pitcher of the Year:** J.P. Howell, Texas. **Newcomer of the Year:** Ole Sheldon, Oklahoma. **Freshman Player of the Year:** Drew Stubbs, Texas. **Freshman Pitcher of the Year:** Jason Meyer, Texas A&M. **Coach of the Year:** Augie Garrido, Texas.

INDIVIDUAL BATTING LEADERS
(Minimum 125 At-Bats)

	AVG	AB	R	H	2B	3B	HR	RBI	SB
Thigpen, Curtis, Texas	.378	278	57	105	28	2	7	51	10
Blair, Cameron, Texas Tech	.371	256	65	95	23	0	14	81	19
Sheldon, Ole, Oklahoma	.367	256	48	94	19	3	4	54	3
Gordon, Alex, Nebraska	.365	211	64	77	18	5	18	75	12
Ehlers, Cody, Missouri	.364	231	55	84	20	1	18	71	2
Fields, Josh, Okla. State	.362	243	54	88	21	1	10	47	2
Brady, Josh, Texas Tech	.362	260	63	94	19	3	20	90	34
Laskowski, Lee, Missouri	.355	228	42	81	13	3	8	48	3
Jaramillo, Jason, Okla. State	.350	240	48	84	12	0	8	57	0
Brees, Reid, Baylor	.355	169	33	60	17	3	3	28	0
Baty, Ryan, Kansas	.355	265	53	94	24	0	11	52	3
Haney, Josh, Texas Tech	.348	244	65	85	23	5	11	57	8
Baty, Matt, Kansas	.344	241	62	83	16	3	2	30	26
Price, Ritchie, Kansas	.339	248	50	84	4	4	1	47	7
Pennington, Cliff, Texas A&M	.339	257	60	87	7	4	5	35	12
Murphy, Steve, Kansas State	.338	198	43	67	14	1	3	40	9
Thornton, Eric, Oklahoma	.337	190	31	64	13	2	8	39	0
Mask, Michael, Texas Tech	.335	227	60	76	14	3	16	70	8
Kainer, Carson, Texas	.335	167	31	56	9	0	3	24	3
Richardson, Sean, Kansas	.332	220	47	73	15	0	12	69	8
Boone, James, Missouri	.332	205	44	68	11	4	4	37	4
Boggs, Austin, Texas A&M	.331	260	42	86	11	3	5	52	5
Raley, Russell, Oklahoma	.328	241	51	79	14	2	1	24	5
Witt, Paul, Baylor	.327	168	30	55	11	0	1	28	12
Wright, Ty, Okla. State	.327	254	57	83	16	1	5	42	9
Patton, Cory, Texas A&M	.326	230	49	75	18	3	11	67	3
Reynolds, Kyle, Baylor	.323	201	29	65	4	3	4	39	4
Mavroulis, Coby, Texas A&M	.321	234	51	75	15	1	3	47	5
Kirby, Scott, Okla. State	.316	244	46	77	19	5	6	50	3
Ryal, Rusty, Okla. State	.315	241	44	76	18	1	0	28	1
Mullinax, Jake, Nebraska	.313	217	46	68	13	2	8	34	2
Schindewolf, Erik, Texas A&M	.311	209	69	65	12	1	4	30	5
Pankratz, Mike, Baylor	.311	196	35	61	13	4	6	33	2
Tribble, Matt, Kansas	.311	228	38	71	16	3	4	46	9
Ford, Josh, Baylor	.310	216	40	67	10	3	14	43	1
Bose, Matt, Oklahoma	.307	199	36	61	7	1	2	32	6
Edwards, Madison, Texas Tech	.306	183	54	56	6	4	7	36	12
Schweitzer, Jared, Kansas	.305	164	39	50	10	0	5	15	0
Blunt, Terry, Kansas State	.305	220	54	67	12	1	4	26	15
Sutton, Drew, Baylor	.304	227	41	69	10	3	8	40	2
Delgado, Jose, Texas Tech	.303	231	62	70	10	5	4	39	24
Russ, Ryan, Texas	.302	129	29	39	7	4	2	25	6
Fuller, Cody, Texas	.302	179	50	54	11	1	2	44	27
Boyer, Jesse, Nebraska	.302	172	40	52	5	3	0	24	14
Stubbs, Drew, Texas	.301	266	51	80	16	3	8	47	28
Scholl, Andy, Kansas	.301	209	35	63	15	1	7	46	4
Simon, Keanon, Okla. State	.298	198	34	59	14	2	3	34	9
Ledbetter, Curtis, Nebraska	.297	222	31	66	16	0	8	56	2
Johnston, Seth, Texas	.296	267	48	79	16	3	7	51	15
Prince, Dooley, Texas	.296	142	35	42	7	3	0	19	12
Shockey, Colin, Nebraska	.294	197	39	58	14	0	0	27	9
McGuire, Andrew, Oklahoma	.291	213	48	62	8	1	8	29	15
Griffin, Michael, Baylor	.291	254	46	74	17	0	10	40	17

INDIVIDUAL PITCHING LEADERS
(Minimum 50 Innings)

	W	L	ERA	G	SV	IP	H	BB	SO
Street, Huston, Texas	6	1	1.58	31	12	57	36	13	59
#Cody, Buck, Texas	1	2	1.81	40	2	45	31	17	47
Cox, J. Brent, Texas	6	2	2.12	37	5	64	47	19	63
Howell, J.P., Texas	15	2	2.13	24	1	135	90	53	166
Alexander, Mark, Missouri	4	0	2.14	35	10	55	50	18	59
LeCure, Sam, Texas	9	3	2.34	24	0	123	97	34	113
Broshuis, Garrett, Missouri	11	0	2.61	17	0	114	97	24	91
Gerstner, Corey, Texas Tech	8	1	2.64	23	3	58	57	8	40
Meyer, Jason, Texas A&M	8	2	2.89	24	3	106	88	41	111
Grogan, Spencer, Okla. State	12	3	2.95	17	0	131	155	15	75
Kroenke, Zach, Nebraska	7	5	3.03	15	0	104	91	32	73
Shirek, Phil, Nebraska	5	1	3.07	15	0	70	70	34	43
Purcey, David, Oklahoma	9	5	3.11	18	0	119	89	54	130
Pekarek, Justin, Nebraska	8	1	3.16	18	0	74	66	17	75
Taylor, Trey, Baylor	6	3	3.16	16	0	91	88	26	62
McCulloch, Kyle, Texas	7	0	3.25	25	1	53	48	18	34
Roberts, Mark, Oklahoma	9	5	3.41	17	0	121	106	24	134
McCutchen, Daniel, Oklahoma	4	3	3.47	35	5	57	51	22	60
Pape, Andy, Baylor	3	2	3.48	22	0	54	49	26	36
Jackson, Zach, Texas A&M	10	7	3.58	18	0	121	113	28	127
Dessau, Erik, Missouri	6	4	3.76	14	0	69	77	20	35
McAuliff, Jarod, Oklahoma	6	2	3.86	37	6	77	84	27	71
LaMotta, Ryan, Baylor	2	5	3.88	29	3	63	57	22	55
Torres, Carlos, Kansas State	6	7	4.12	16	0	114	116	39	76
Rew, Daniel, Okla. State	5	7	4.13	20	3	85	101	26	49
Simmons, Justin, Texas	10	3	4.18	18	0	90	87	33	43
Walker, Sean, Baylor	4	6	4.24	15	0	85	93	31	42
Hill, Danny, Missouri	5	5	4.39	19	0	107	106	34	94
Culp, Nathan, Missouri	4	3	4.44	20	0	75	77	22	57
Moore, Justin, Texas A&M	5	3	4.47	12	0	50	58	14	21
Braden, Dallas, Texas Tech	6	4	4.56	17	0	99	109	21	93
Robertson, Quinton, Nebraska	4	4	4.61	16	0	57	79	15	33
Richmond, Scott, Okla. State	3	3	4.66	19	1	66	71	25	58
Cowley, Thomas, Okla. State	8	3	4.74	20	0	93	84	31	79
McGowan, Michael, Texas Tech	2	2	4.78	14	0	58	57	35	37
Brown, Casey, Oklahoma	5	4	4.80	21	0	54	60	23	36

BIG WEST CONFERENCE

	Conference		Overall	
	W	L	W	L
Cal State Fullerton	19	2	47	22
Long Beach State	14	7	40	21
UC Riverside	11	10	33	24
UC Irvine	10	11	34	23
Cal Poly	10	11	38	23
UC Santa Barbara	10	11	33	21
Pacific	5	16	20	34
Cal State Northridge	5	16	19	38

ALL-CONFERENCE TEAM: C—Kurt Suzuki, Jr., Cal State Fullerton. **1B**—Michael Paulk, So., Cal State Northridge. **2B**—Chris Malec, Jr., UC Santa Barbara. **3B**—Tony Festa, Sr., UC Riverside. **SS**—Troy Tulowitzki, So., Long Beach State. **OF**—John Bowker, So, Long Beach State; Clark Hardman, Fr., Cal State Fullerton; Sam Herbert, Sr., Cal Poly. **DH**—Brandon Roberts, So, Cal Poly. **UT**—Jason Vargas, Jr., Long Beach State. **SP**—Brett Smith, UC Irvine; Jered Weaver, Jr., Long Beach State; Jason Windsor, Sr., Cal State Fullerton. **RP**—Blair Erickson, Fr., UC Irvine.

Player of the Year: Kurt Suzuki, Cal State Fullerton. **Co-Pitchers of the Year:** Jered Weaver, Long Beach State; Jason Windsor, Cal State Fullerton. **Freshman Player of the Year:** Chris Valaika, UC Santa Barbara. **Freshman Pitcher of the Year:** Blair Erickson, UC Irvine. **Coach of the Year:** George Horton, Cal State Fullerton.

INDIVIDUAL BATTING LEADERS
(Minimum 125 At-Bats)

	AVG	AB	R	H	2B	3B	HR	RBI	SB
Suzuki, Kurt, CS Fullerton	.413	252	77	104	17	4	16	87	9
Herbert, Sam, Cal Poly	.383	248	66	95	16	4	4	45	14
Roberts, Brandon, Cal Poly	.379	232	46	88	13	3	3	44	30
Tietje, Chalon, Cal Poly	.369	236	44	87	23	0	6	58	3
Festa, Tony, UC Riverside	.367	229	45	84	11	0	8	51	5
Voita, John, CS Northridge	.358	201	46	72	10	0	10	54	1
Szabo, Jordan, UC Irvine	.357	224	39	80	10	2	5	26	4
Coit, Johnny, CS Northridge	.356	149	31	53	3	3	3	23	9
Paulk, Michael, CS Northridge	.356	225	43	80	18	1	17	59	3
Vargas, Jason, Long Beach St.	.354	209	56	74	14	4	5	33	3
Garcia, Felipe, CS Fullerton	.353	252	39	89	18	1	6	50	0
Pilittere, P.J., CS Fullerton	.351	268	54	94	18	1	4	49	2
Powers, Greg, UCSB	.349	169	41	59	10	1	3	41	6
Valaika, Chris, UCSB	.347	222	46	77	15	3	7	38	7
Salotti, Nick, UC Riverside	.346	214	32	74	17	3	10	51	0
Hardman, Clark, CS Fullerton	.341	214	44	73	6	1	0	31	5
Anderson, Matt, UC Irvine	.336	223	36	75	16	0	6	42	0
Mayo, Josh, Cal Poly	.335	212	44	71	22	1	1	36	2
Pedroza, Sergio, CS Fullerton	.333	195	40	65	20	1	7	39	0
Davis, Brad, Long Beach St.	.329	225	39	74	9	0	4	38	4
Quintana, Alberto, CS North.	.325	206	37	67	10	1	5	31	2
Prettyman, Ronnie, CS Full.	.324	262	53	85	16	5	3	38	14
Ravago, Raymond, CS North.	.323	155	32	50	10	2	5	25	4
Bigler, Brett, UC Riverside	.322	202	51	65	13	0	0	15	17
Vogt, Taylor, UCSB	.320	178	39	57	11	1	9	45	0
Bowker, John, Long Beach St.	.320	225	31	72	15	3	7	41	2
Rowe, Bill, UC Santa Barbara	.319	188	29	60	10	1	4	39	1
Dorn, Danny, CS Fullerton	.318	242	50	77	17	2	4	59	8
Mocny, Danny, Long Beach St.	.318	154	24	49	6	4	4	26	4
Taillon, Cory, Cal Poly	.317	208	26	66	8	3	0	25	4
Tulowitzki, Troy, Long Beach St.	.317	230	40	73	15	2	7	44	5
Steinmeyer, Brian, UC Riverside	.317	208	37	66	14	0	6	41	2
Buhagiar, Josh, Long Beach St.	.312	173	28	54	8	1	0	13	4
Berglund, Bret, Cal Poly	.310	184	34	57	14	0	9	43	4
Bishop, Evan, Pacific	.308	195	33	60	8	1	1	23	4
Emerick, Matt, UCSB	.308	130	23	40	5	3	0	25	4
Cunningham, Matt, UC Riverside	.306	222	47	68	15	1	4	37	12
Malec, Chris, UCSB	.306	222	49	68	11	0	4	54	4
Turner, Justin, CS Fullerton	.304	253	45	77	16	0	0	34	7
Blumenthal, Kyle, Cal Poly	.303	201	45	61	9	1	5	42	6
Harper, Aaron, Pacific	.302	222	41	61	15	3	9	37	6

INDIVIDUAL PITCHING LEADERS
(Minimum 50 Innings)

	W	L	ERA	G	SV	IP	H	BB	SO
Weaver, Jered, Long Beach St.	15	1	1.62	19	0	144	81	21	213
Windsor, Jason, CS Fullerton	13	4	1.72	22	1	163	100	24	148
Fraser, Loren, UCSB	6	1	1.94	21	2	51	51	9	36
#Schroer, Steve, UC Irvine	4	2	2.14	33	1	46	49	12	47
Ramos, Cesar, Long Beach St.	12	4	2.29	19	0	134	108	35	97
Moser, Nolan, Cal Poly	2	1	2.37	9		62	46	22	52
Smith, Brett, UC Irvine	8	5	2.54	16	0	113	102	29	113
Graham, Alex, Pacific	4	1	2.66	11	1	61	58	8	50
Romero, Ricky, CS Fullerton	14	4	3.37	22	0	155	146	42	126
Fleming, Jonathan, Cal Poly	4	1	3.48	13	0	54	41	18	44
Nicoll, Chris, UC Irvine	7	5	3.49	24	1	80	82	24	71
Shappi, A.J., UC Riverside	8	2	3.54	14	0	89	99	20	62
Schmidt, Josh, Pacific	5	3	3.67	33	7	54	54	21	73
Martinez, John, UC Riverside	9	2	3.69	17	1	112	117	18	64
Cassel, Justin, UC Irvine	4	3	3.93	19	0	66	70	22	56
#Erickson, Blair, UC Irvine	1	3	4.10	30	17	37	33	21	51
Vargas, Jason, Long Beach St.	7	6	4.14	18	0	111	98	31	90
Shull, Jimmy, Cal Poly	9	5	4.15	18	0	100	103	26	102
Martinez, Mike, CS Fullerton	8	3	4.24	28	2	91	115	24	59
LeDuc, Dennis, Cal Poly	4	4	4.85	25	3	59	73	9	36
Hochgesang, Nathan, CS North.	2	6	4.97	24	0	80	100	39	53
Morlock, Steve, UCSB	7	5	5.02	16	0	90	100	41	49
Graham, Andy, UCSB	4	4	5.08	16	0	73	88	22	34
Martin, Michael, UCSB	4	4	5.15	16	0	87	107	33	41
Swanson, Glenn, UC Irvine	6	4	5.51	17	0	83	90	32	79
Olson, Garrett, Cal Poly	7	5	5.57	18	0	84	88	38	92
Camacho, Eddy, CS Northridge	2	4	5.66	22	0	70	94	39	58
Winter, Haley, UC Riverside	3	5	5.66	19	0	62	87	21	48

COLONIAL ATHLETIC ASSOCIATION

	Conference		Overall	
	W	L	W	L
George Mason	20	4	39	19
*UNC Wilmington	17	6	40	23
William & Mary	14	10	37	20
Virginia Commonwealth	14	10	34	24
Old Dominion	13	11	26	28
Delaware	12	11	33	24
James Madison	8	16	28	26
Towson	6	18	17	35
Hofstra	3	21	14	36

ALL-CONFERENCE TEAM: C—Brian Valichka, So., Delaware. **1B**—Chris Looze, Jr., George Mason. **2B**—Will Rhymes, Jr., William & Mary. **3B**—Anthony Granato, Sr., Virginia Commonwealth. **SS**—Jeff Palumbo, Sr., George Mason. **OF**—Mike Butia, Jr., James Madison; Chip Grawey, Sr., UNC Wilmington; Chris Rahl, So., William & Mary. **DH**—Casper Wells, So., Towson. **UT**—Mike Walsh, So., Hofstra. **SP**—Stacen Gant, Jr., George Mason; Justin Verlander, Jr., Old Dominion. **RP**—Blake Cross, Sr., UNC Wilmington.

Player of the Year: Chris Rahl, William & Mary. **Defensive Player of the Year:** Jeff Palumbo, George Mason. **Rookie of the Year:** Harold Mozingo, Virginia Commonwealth. **Coach of the Year:** Bill Brown, George Mason.

INDIVIDUAL BATTING LEADERS
(Minimum 125 At-Bats)

	AVG	AB	R	H	2B	3B	HR	RBI	SB
Palumbo, Jeff, George Mason	.402	239	81	96	14	3	3	34	15
Rahl, Chris, William & Mary	.389	229	73	89	10	8	20	70	42
Rhymes, Will, William & Mary	.388	188	52	73	13	4	8	35	7
Butia, Mike, James Madison	.373	193	51	72	17	4	18	60	8
Grawey, Chip, UNC-W	.373	271	53	101	14	7	2	30	39
Valichka, Brian, Delaware	.362	188	42	68	17	3	7	27	8
Caputo, Ricky, Hofstra	.361	202	37	73	11	3	8	41	10
Heffron, Adam, Towson	.359	184	54	66	17	3	6	37	4
Granato, Anthony, VCU	.357	213	50	76	15	6	5	44	44
Sexton, Greg, William & Mary	.356	225	47	80	24	2	4	53	2
Harris, Steven, Old Dominion	.352	216	34	76	8	0	5	38	9
Schill, Nate, James Madison	.351	188	38	66	11	2	6	49	2
Cowgill, Michael, Jas. Madison	.347	213	58	74	15	1	4	30	13
Rhymes, John, William & Mary	.344	253	52	87	10	2	0	24	10
Buber, Kelly, Delaware	.343	201	38	69	11	1	9	51	2
Looze, Chris, George Mason	.340	235	58	80	23	1	17	81	2
Wells, Casper, Towson	.337	193	41	65	17	7	8	38	2
Smith, Aaron, UNC-W	.335	221	46	74	16	0	10	50	6
Van Note, Steve, Delaware	.333	243	57	81	18	3	12	58	19
Sizemore, Scott, VCU	.332	202	42	67	12	2	1	26	8
Baldwin, Bruce, George Mason	.331	242	53	80	14	2	4	47	9
Stewart, Josh, Hofstra	.330	200	46	66	16	3	7	37	16
Shimer, Nick, George Mason	.330	209	65	69	22	0	17	53	3
Walsh, Michael, Hofstra	.330	176	25	58	12	3	4	33	2
Batts, Jonathan, UNC-W	.330	176	36	58	15	0	5	33	1
Innerst, Adam, George Mason	.328	241	48	79	17	3	15	73	3
Sutton, Matt, UNC-W	.328	241	45	79	9	3	5	36	4
DeCarlo, Mike, William & Mary	.323	195	52	63	18	0	11	46	1
Meader, Joe, VCU	.321	224	50	72	14	7	4	32	16
Preston, Tim, UNC-W	.320	169	39	54	10	3	6	27	11
Moses, Mitchell, James Madison	.313	134	15	42	14	0	2	29	0
Hahn, Keith, Old Dominion	.312	141	27	44	7	0	0	14	8
Harden, Dave, Delaware	.311	225	55	70	13	3	14	56	16
Donovan, Brock, Delaware	.310	200	34	62	8	1	4	31	4
Carter, Brandon, Old Dominion	.309	194	37	60	10	1	0	24	13

INDIVIDUAL PITCHING LEADERS
(Minimum 50 Innings)

	W	L	ERA	G	SV	IP	H	BB	SO
Smith, Donnie, Old Dominion	6	2	2.29	20	6	86	65	25	99
Orenduff, Justin, VCU	5	5	2.43	15	0	100	84	34	129
Bray, Bill, William & Mary	4	4	2.44	29	8	59	46	15	84
Meredith, Cla, VCU	7	3	2.55	26	7	67	49	12	84
Gant, Stacen, George Mason	10	1	2.72	16	0	119	95	32	87
Cross, Blake, UNC-W	3	4	2.78	32	12	58	42	30	68
Beaupre, Jarame, Delaware	7	2	3.07	16	0	88	74	31	73
Kimball, Zach, UNC-W	8	5	3.26	19	0	108	100	34	74
Prendergast, Matt, VCU	8	4	3.38	16	0	99	101	27	63
Hitz, Brent, George Mason	6	0	3.45	16	0	73	68	13	42
Verlander, Justin, Old Dominion	7	6	3.49	16	0	106	90	43	151
Morrison, Josh, George Mason	5	3	3.51	22	0	59	56	13	47
Hill, Ronald, UNC-W	12	4	3.62	19	0	104	121	22	59
Moore, Jeff, UNC-W	3	0	3.86	29	0	56	56	25	47
Dagenhart, Jeff, William & Mary	7	3	3.95	19	2	84	83	35	68
Arrowood, Dana, Old Dominion	5	4	4.17	28	2	69	69	26	57
Mihalik, Mike, Delaware	5	3	4.23	17	0	104	103	39	66
Gibbons, Eric, George Mason	6	5	4.33	15	0	106	125	23	66
Burok, James, Old Dominion	2	8	4.41	16	0	65	76	23	43
Nesbitt, Greg, James Madison	2	3	4.55	13	0	59	73	9	45
Sosonko, Sean, William & Mary	4	3	4.60	17	0	59	56	26	54
Mozingo, Harold, VCU	7	4	4.68	17	1	75	60	44	82
Link, Jon, VCU	3	2	4.81	16	1	58	65	18	38
Booker, Zach, UNC-W	2	2	4.98	20	0	60	62	21	37
Peeler, Joe, Towson	5	3	5.09	12	0	58	65	17	37

CONFERENCE USA

	Conference		Overall	
	W	L	W	L
East Carolina	25	5	51	13
Tulane	21	9	41	21
Southern Mississippi	21	9	45	19
*Texas Christian	19	11	39	26
Houston	19	11	30	29
Memphis	15	14	29	28
Alabama-Birmingham	13	16	30	29
Louisville	13	17	26	30
South Florida	12	17	31	24
Charlotte	9	21	20	32
Cincinnati	6	24	15	40
St. Louis	5	24	14	41

ALL-CONFERENCE TEAM: C—Devin Ivany, Jr., South Florida. **IF**—Jarrett Hoffpauir, Jr., Southern Mississippi; Trevor Lawhorn, So., East Carolina; Ryan Norwood, Jr., East Carolina; Matt Shepherd, Jr., Southern Mississippi. **OF**—Matt Barket, Jr., Tulane; Ryan Frith, Sr., Southern Mississippi; Mark Jurich, Sr., Louisville. **DH/UT**—Ryan Jones, Sr., East Carolina. **SP**—Greg Bunn, Jr., East Carolina; J.R. Crowel, So., Tulane; Jarrett Grube, Sr., Memphis; Casey Hudspeth, Fr., South Florida. **RP**—Austin Tubb, Sr., Southern Mississippi.
Player of the Year: Ryan Jones, Sr., East Carolina. **Pitcher of the Year:** Greg Bunn, East Carolina. **Freshman of the Year:** Chad Huffman, Texas Christian. **Coach of the Year:** Randy Mazey, East Carolina.

INDIVIDUAL BATTING LEADERS
(Minimum 125 At-Bats)

	AVG	AB	R	H	2B	3B	HR	RBI	SB
Hoffpauir, Jarrett, Southern Miss	.405	269	62	109	27	2	11	92	2
Jones, Ryan, East Carolina	.400	215	46	86	26	4	19	69	9
Huffman, Chad, Texas Christian	.383	253	68	97	20	1	9	44	3
Norwood, Ryan, East Carolina	.382	249	62	95	34	1	14	63	7
Shepherd, Matt, Southern Miss	.378	275	74	104	27	6	2	41	7
Pickerell, Steve, Cincinnati	.375	192	43	72	14	1	14	46	0
Roberts, Kevin, Houston	.374	174	35	65	10	0	6	31	6
Barket, Matt, Tulane	.370	238	52	88	17	1	8	52	13
Paige, Jamie, East Carolina	.363	267	67	97	16	1	1	42	20
Rusco, Jamie, Charlotte	.362	188	41	68	12	1	14	49	3
Leslie, Myron, South Florida	.361	205	60	74	23	0	7	46	14
Nelson, Jack, Cincinnati	.360	211	39	76	14	0	7	33	1
Ivany, Devin, South Florida	.356	219	49	78	19	1	5	57	7
Swackhamer, Wes, Tulane	.355	220	47	78	16	0	8	33	6
Dini, Greg, Tulane	.354	226	37	80	17	0	11	51	1
Jurich, Mark, Louisville	.353	235	47	83	19	3	19	60	3
Bruce, Cole, Houston	.351	194	38	68	18	2	6	30	4
Adams, Austin, Texas Christian	.344	183	32	63	12	0	7	41	1
Hill, Daniel, Ala.-Birmingham	.343	230	48	79	15	2	14	52	3
Moss, Bill, Memphis	.342	149	30	51	10	2	2	10	3
Minicozzi, Mark, East Carolina	.342	231	62	79	18	0	10	50	3
Frith, Ryan, Southern Miss	.341	249	59	85	15	0	22	63	1
Willard, Adam, Charlotte	.341	208	46	71	14	1	8	35	8
Johnson, Rob, Houston	.341	229	33	78	16	0	7	46	14
Macaluso, Mike, South Florida	.341	232	48	79	13	2	2	24	15
Haley, Nick, Louisville	.340	162	38	55	6	1	2	28	5
Bogusevic, Brian, Tulane	.339	236	51	80	14	4	10	68	9
Bowker, Thomas, Charlotte	.338	204	45	69	18	0	9	30	12
Cogbill, Bo, Texas Christian	.331	242	46	80	18	2	4	52	7
Duran, German, Texas Christian	.330	191	46	63	16	0	5	27	9
McCorkle, Nathan, Ala.-Birm.	.325	209	52	68	14	1	11	50	7
Papavasiliou, Thanos, Houston	.323	130	23	42	10	2	2	33	4
Clark, Sam, Ala.-Birmingham	.321	140	27	45	6	2	3	20	9
Costanzo, Drew, East Carolina	.320	175	37	56	11	1	5	38	4
Holland, Joe, Tulane	.318	245	65	78	19	1	8	32	2
Hierlmeier, Bryan, South Florida	.317	189	50	60	10	5	11	41	3
Maddox, Marc, Southern Miss	.317	265	63	84	11	2	16	60	1
Helms, Cole, Ala.-Birmingham	.316	212	36	67	18	1	5	45	8
House, Chad, Memphis	.315	219	45	69	4	2	4	23	17
Neuman, Chris, Texas Christian	.314	258	41	81	12	3	12	58	6
Saylor, Drew, Cincinnati	.311	212	37	66	13	0	9	39	1
Rodriguez, Eugene, Ala.-Birm.	.311	196	39	61	14	0	6	40	2
Manzella, Tommy, Tulane	.311	235	49	73	14	0	5	36	11
Moll, Aaron, Cincinnati	.311	190	32	59	12	1	10	41	1
Eder, Drew, St. Louis	.310	129	21	40	9	0	3	27	3
#Moses, Ramon, Texas Christian	.292	250	50	73	10	3	4	30	23

INDIVIDUAL PITCHING LEADERS
(Minimum 50 Innings)

	W	L	ERA	G	SV	IP	H	BB	SO
Bunn, Greg, East Carolina	10	1	2.70	17	0	107	72	30	117
Findlay, Robbie, Texas Christian	6	1	2.73	32	11	56	40	22	63
Grube, Jarrett, Memphis	9	4	2.82	16	1	102	84	28	110
Roznovsky, Brandon, Houston	2	4	3.35	36	9	51	48	17	66
Crowel, J.R., Tulane	8	3	3.39	17	0	104	108	30	76
Hudspeth, Casey, South Florida	6	4	3.45	16	0	104	119	35	74
Ezell, Patrick, Southern Miss	6	2	3.57	17	0	91	101	14	73
Mohl, Billy, Tulane	6	4	3.70	15	0	80	102	16	55
Mock, Garrett, Houston	4	5	3.71	13	0	68	68	25	42
Mathews, Shane, East Carolina	7	1	3.72	18	0	77	76	19	54
Russum, Cliff, Southern Miss	6	4	3.93	13	0	71	58	37	67
Edwards, Bill, Memphis	3	5	3.97	22	3	59	55	34	42
Varner, Matt, Houston	7	4	4.03	19	0	89	99	35	69
Schmidt, Kyle, South Florida	8	4	4.07	17	0	86	75	53	64
Jerome, Clayton, Texas Christian	9	6	4.07	18	0	111	106	40	89
Bogusevic, Brian, Tulane	9	6	4.19	17	0	112	128	25	84
Underwood, Chad, Texas Christian	7	3	4.24	25	1	70	87	14	50
Hahn, Cory, Tulane	6	4	4.26	15	0	89	105	15	69
Roberts, Kevin, Houston	5	4	4.26	19	0	57	56	26	67
Lincoln, Brad, Houston	3	2	4.29	12	0	57	60	19	35
Mills, Adam, Charlotte	4	3	4.35	27	4	52	52	16	40

	W	L	ERA	G	SV	IP	H	BB	SO
Roberts, Eric, Ala.-Birmingham	5	3	4.50	37	4	80	79	25	89
Hankins, Derek, Memphis	8	5	4.58	15	0	92	96	25	114
Espineli, Eugene, Texas Christian	9	5	4.63	20	0	107	124	27	88
Taylor, Brody, East Carolina	8	0	4.64	15	0	85	97	16	63
Legg, Jacob, Ala.-Birmingham	3	4	4.74	15	0	57	67	19	28
DeWitt, Anthony, Southern Miss	10	3	4.80	17	0	94	103	35	68
Lirette, Chase, South Florida	5	4	4.84	21	2	74	78	23	59
Bird, Ryan, St. Louis	3	6	4.86	13	0	74	82	27	51

HORIZON LEAGUE

	Conference		Overall	
	W	L	W	L
Illinois-Chicago	14	8	35	21
Butler	13	11	29	30
Cleveland State	11	12	19	33
Wright State	10	11	22	34
Wisconsin-Milwaukee	9	10	23	30
Detroit	10	12	19	38
*Youngstown State	7	10	22	32

ALL-CONFERENCE TEAM: C—Bryan Vickers, Jr., Wright State. **1B**—Tim Poley, Sr., Butler. **2B**—Bryan Russo, Jr., Illinois-Chicago. **3B/P**—Ben Stanczyk, Sr., Wisconsin-Milwaukee. **SS**—Jordan DeVoir, Sr., Illinois-Chicago. **OF**—Charlie Anderson, Sr. Detroit; Mike Hughes, Sr., Illinois-Chicago; Dale Mueller, So., Butler. **DH**—Andy Bulla, So., Butler. **UT**—Justin Johnson, Jr., Illinois-Chicago. **P**—Ryan Zink, Fr., Illinois-Chicago.

Player of the Year/Pitcher of the Year: Ben Stanczyk, Wisconsin-Milwaukee. **Newcomer of the Year:** Charlie Anderson, Detroit. **Co-Coaches of the Year:** Jay Murphy, Cleveland State; Ron Nischwitz, Wright State.

INDIVIDUAL BATTING LEADERS
(Minimum 125 At-Bats)

	AVG	AB	R	H	2B	3B	HR	RBI	SB
Alexander, Matt, Wis.-Milwaukee	.381	218	42	83	14	0	3	29	5
Stanczyk, Ben, Wis.-Milwaukee	.374	195	35	73	10	1	10	43	2
Anderson, Charlie, Detroit	.366	186	42	68	17	0	14	53	2
McKinley, Justin, Butler	.365	181	32	66	13	2	4	19	12
Hughes, Mike, Illinois-Chicago	.364	214	67	78	10	8	13	61	13
Mueller, Dale, Butler	.361	191	39	69	11	4	2	29	11
Johnson, Justin, Illinois-Chicago	.361	194	42	70	12	0	8	61	1
DeVoir, Jordan, Illinois-Chicago	.356	216	45	77	10	1	2	41	7
Bulla, Andy, Butler	.355	172	27	61	12	2	4	29	6
Rosinski, Ted, Illinois-Chicago	.347	196	39	68	11	0	4	30	4
Vickers, Bryan, Wright State	.342	190	38	65	12	3	16	43	0
Reschke, Charlie, Wis.-Mil.	.340	203	43	69	15	1	7	38	8
Gord, Nelson, Illinois-Chicago	.339	186	43	63	10	0	2	27	6
Chinn, Steve, Cleveland State	.335	179	27	60	14	2	2	27	7
Russo, Bryan, Illinois-Chicago	.330	185	47	61	11	0	5	26	10
McCoy, Ross, Wis.-Milwaukee	.324	185	37	60	11	3	6	36	7
Schlabach, Kendall, Youngstown	.313	198	41	62	11	0	1	12	9
#Chapieski, Jason, Detroit	.264	201	50	53	5	2	0	9	23

INDIVIDUAL PITCHING LEADERS
(Minimum 50 Innings)

	W	L	ERA	G	SV	IP	H	BB	SO
Zink, Ryan, Illinois-Chicago	9	3	2.07	19	3	96	76	15	92
Szalewski, Tom, Illinois-Chicago	4	2	2.76	16	0	62	52	12	41
Haehnel, David, Illinois-Chicago	6	3	3.00	21	4	90	91	24	92
Byzet, Matt, Butler	6	1	3.38	13	2	56	46	24	47
Stanczyk, Ben, Wis.-Milwaukee	7	3	3.43	18	4	94	86	20	95
Costello, Craig, Butler	4	3	3.50	15	0	82	75	33	55
Dennis, Chris, Youngstown State	1	7	3.61	11	1	62	55	44	65
Michalkiewicz, Robert, Wis.-Mil.	3	6	3.95	15	0	66	72	28	36
Libeg, Kevin, Youngstown State	5	3	4.00	16	0	63	70	18	41
Hornbach, Tony, Butler	4	3	4.07	20	1	55	71	6	20
Ball, Gary, Cleveland State	3	6	4.07	13	0	60	51	28	45
Miles, Randy, Butler	5	3	4.18	21	2	75	62	32	67
#Dolske, Jed, Wis.-Milwaukee	3	5	5.17	31	6	56	72	23	27
#Behning, Luke, Butler	1	9	6.88	22	8	54	70	26	30

IVY LEAGUE

LOU GEHRIG	Conference		Overall	
	W	L	W	L
*Princeton	12	8	28	20
Columbia	8	12	14	28
Cornell	7	13	13	29
Pennsylvania	5	15	10	27
RED ROLFE	**W**	**L**	**W**	**L**
Dartmouth	15	5	25	17
Harvard	13	7	21	18
Yale	11	9	19	20
Brown	9	11	16	26

ALL-CONFERENCE TEAM: C—Schuyler Mann, Jr., Harvard. **1B/P**—Trey Hendricks, Sr., Harvard. **2B**—Steve Young, Sr., Princeton. **3B**—Tommy Myette, So., Dartmouth. **SS**—Ed Lucas, Sr., Dartmouth. **OF**—Paul Christian, So., Brown; Nate Moffie, Jr., Pennsylvania; B.J. Szymanski, Jr., Princeton; Bobby Wiginton, Jr., Brown. **DH**—Jon Slaughter, Sr., Pennsylvania. **UT**—Zak Farkes, So., Harvard. **P**—Josh Faiola, So., Dartmouth. **RP**—Brian Kappel, Jr., Princeton.

Player of the Year: Ed Lucas, Dartmouth. **Pitcher of the Year:** Stephen Perry, Dartmouth. **Rookie of the Year:** Trey Hendricks, Harvard.

INDIVIDUAL BATTING LEADERS
(Minimum 100 At-Bats)

	AVG	AB	R	H	2B	3B	HR	RBI	SB
Hendricks, Trey, Harvard	.427	143	32	61	13	1	7	34	4
Wiginton, Bobby, Brown	.415	123	38	51	10	1	3	18	8
Lucas, Ed, Dartmouth	.405	173	47	70	17	1	4	36	3
Myette, Tommy, Dartmouth	.393	150	39	59	16	1	2	34	4
Contrino, Chris, Brown	.369	149	29	55	10	1	0	34	4
Szymanski, B.J., Princeton	.362	177	44	64	10	8	6	48	11
Moffie, Nate, Penn	.362	138	32	50	9	4	8	26	6
Sawyer, Marc, Yale	.355	138	25	49	6	0	4	25	1
Young, Steve, Princeton	.354	158	47	56	6	3	1	19	15
Christian, Paul, Brown	.349	146	47	51	11	1	11	34	5
Bailey, Josh, Dartmouth	.348	135	39	47	16	1	4	29	2
Balkan, Adam, Princeton	.345	174	37	60	15	3	2	29	1
Salini, Andrew, Princeton	.344	157	36	54	11	3	2	31	3
Farkes, Zak, Harvard	.342	152	47	52	11	0	14	46	14
Nichols, Jeff, Brown	.342	155	39	53	12	2	6	32	3
Reich, Ryan, Princeton	.339	121	24	41	8	0	6	33	1
Goldblatt, Mike, Penn	.329	143	25	47	6	1	4	22	3
Leonard, Randy, Yale	.326	135	26	44	7	2	0	14	8
Speights, Jeff, Dartmouth	.324	176	32	57	11	0	8	52	1
Rodwogin, Craig, Columbia	.324	102	15	33	9	0	0	11	1
Bashelor, Will, Dartmouth	.323	130	33	42	9	0	2	19	7
Ankney, Justin, Yale	.321	159	34	51	14	1	4	14	4
Doyle, Jake, Yale	.321	131	10	42	10	0	0	22	2
Perez, Fernando, Columbia	.317	123	22	39	6	2	1	17	18
#Shirrell, Scott, Dartmouth	.295	173	48	51	10	1	5	33	8

INDIVIDUAL PITCHING LEADERS
(Minimum 40 Innings)

	W	L	ERA	G	SV	IP	H	BB	SO
Smith, Alec, Yale	6	3	3.17	10	0	60	64	15	35
#Kappel, Brian, Princeton	3	2	3.19	24	9	37	29	6	42
Sowers, Josh, Yale	3	4	3.39	11	0	61	59	17	54
Faiola, Josh, Dartmouth	5	1	3.43	9	0	66	67	14	53
Ohlendorf, Ross, Princeton	7	3	3.46	11	0	68	60	30	79
Fabian, Gavin, Princeton	4	3	3.48	11	0	75	85	4	38
Perry, Stephen, Dartmouth	6	1	3.83	8	0	49	50	20	38
Stiller, Erik, Princeton	4	3	3.96	10	0	61	60	11	47
Hollis, Jon, Yale	4	3	3.97	14	0	45	49	15	30
Hendricks, Trey, Harvard	9	2	4.09	14	2	62	62	12	46
Jennings, Sam, Brown	2	4	4.22	9	0	43	49	13	24
Grant, Tim, Dartmouth	5	4	4.57	9	0	63	63	9	42
Altman, Roy, Columbia	2	2	4.74	19	4	44	57	16	29
Bardenwerper, Tad, Cornell	2	4	4.78	11	1	49	55	18	38
Herrmann, Frank, Harvard	4	3	5.05	9	0	41	46	20	32
Cramphin, James, Brown	2	5	5.24	10	1	57	68	22	39
Grant, Jessen, Columbia	3	5	5.33	10	0	54	69	19	31

METRO ATLANTIC CONFERENCE

	Conference		Overall	
	W	L	W	L
*Le Moyne	24	3	36	21
Niagara	16	9	27	27
Manhattan	16	9	25	27
Marist	17	10	25	30
Rider	15	12	24	27
Siena	13	12	27	26
Iona	11	14	21	31
Fairfield	11	16	16	27
St. Peter's	4	23	8	34
Canisius	4	23	4	43

ALL-CONFERENCE TEAM: C—Sean Whalen, Sr., Rider. **1B**—Keith Connors, So., Le Moyne. **2B**—Anthony Aquilino, Sr., Le Moyne. **3B**—Tony Cipolla, Sr., Siena. **SS**—Blake Hanan, Sr., Siena. **OF**—Kyle Brown, Sr., Le Moyne; Jeff Justice, Sr., Le Moyne; Scott Rich, Sr., Rider. **DH**—John Fitzpatrick, So., Manhattan. **UT**—Jimmy Board, Sr., Marist. **P**—Scott Chambers, Jr., Marist; Matt Scherer, Jr., Le Moyne.

Player of the Year: Jeff Justice, Le Moyne. **Pitcher of the Year:** Matt Scherer, Le Moyne. **Relief Pitcher of the Year:** Brian Parish, Iona. **Rookie of the Year:** Bobby Blevins, Le Moyne. **Coach of the Year:** Steve Owens, Le Moyne.

INDIVIDUAL BATTING LEADERS
(Minimum 125 At-Bats)

	AVG	AB	R	H	2B	3B	HR	RBI	SB
Justice, Jeff, Le Moyne	.403	216	58	87	22	2	12	49	15
Rich, Scott, Rider	.375	200	54	75	17	3	15	45	16
Eastley, Reed, Niagara	.368	212	45	78	25	3	8	57	12
Brachold, Keith, Marist	.360	222	51	80	24	2	7	40	14
Brown, Kyle, Le Moyne	.357	213	44	76	13	1	2	34	42
Gaskin, Chris, Manhattan	.351	151	32	53	10	2	4	34	4
Cucurullo, Matt, Manhattan	.350	177	31	62	6	1	9	52	15
Cipolla, Tony, Siena	.349	192	46	67	15	2	6	40	2
Callahan, Matt, Iona	.346	208	39	72	14	1	0	22	8
Deluca, Sam, Manhattan	.345	206	37	71	14	2	1	24	11
Whalen, Sean, Rider	.343	166	25	57	16	1	4	35	0
Fortner-Villanova, Rob, Iona	.343	204	41	70	16	1	16	49	8
Fitzgerald, Tim, Niagara	.342	193	37	66	12	2	3	37	9
Alati, Mike, Niagara	.337	187	30	63	12	4	4	34	9
Buck, Kevin, Marist	.336	149	31	50	11	0	3	31	2
Towler, Bryan, Marist	.333	198	27	66	13	2	4	41	3
Hampton, Shawn, Siena	.332	199	32	66	13	2	3	38	9
Ircandia, Vince, Niagara	.332	187	57	62	13	4	4	26	22
Affronti, Mike, Le Moyne	.330	218	44	72	18	1	6	46	5
Cappello, Frank, Manhattan	.328	201	40	66	12	1	1	16	13
Perrone, Mike, Iona	.328	195	28	64	15	0	3	30	3
Rehm, Jonathan, Rider	.324	185	36	60	11	2	3	26	10
Connors, Keith, Le Moyne	.319	207	50	66	10	1	8	35	9
Fowler, Jared, St. Peter's	.315	149	16	47	7	1	3	20	1
Lepore, Justin, Marist	.315	162	25	51	8	3	3	29	3
Hansen, Brian, Le Moyne	.313	147	25	46	6	0	3	23	2
Musolf, Travis, Marist	.311	219	51	68	7	2	2	23	17
Hanan, Blake, Siena	.309	191	33	59	8	1	2	27	21
Soucy, David, Fairfield	.309	149	15	46	6	0	0	13	0
Aquilino, Anthony, Le Moyne	.308	224	42	69	20	0	4	36	8
#Bulkley, Aaron, Le Moyne	.230	161	36	37	3	5	6	20	13

INDIVIDUAL PITCHING LEADERS
(Minimum 50 Innings)

	W	L	ERA	G	SV	IP	H	BB	SO
Scherer, Matt, Le Moyne	10	3	2.18	14	0	103	79	14	88
Blevins, Bobby, Le Moyne	6	4	2.93	14	0	89	78	24	52
Maisano, Tom, Fairfield	5	1	2.96	8	0	55	53	12	40
Drechsler, Alan, Le Moyne	10	1	3.24	14	0	72	56	23	52
Kramer, Sean, Iona	6	8	3.45	18	0	107	106	30	108
Dugan, Tim, Fairfield	3	8	3.56	12	1	73	78	18	61
Lannan, John, Siena	7	3	3.84	15	0	73	67	31	54
Avery, James, Niagara	3	1	3.86	12	1	63	65	21	43
Chambers, Scott, Marist	6	6	3.90	15	0	87	91	29	71
Bitter, Ryan, Siena	6	6	3.91	14	0	99	95	24	81
#Parish, Brian, Iona	3	3	3.98	22	9	32	25	20	32
Heath, George, Marist	7	4	4.25	15	0	103	115	28	59
Robinson, Lucas, Marist	5	3	4.28	15	0	74	77	17	45
Santerre, Josh, Manhattan	7	4	4.46	17	2	79	97	26	67
Sawatzky, Josh, Niagara	6	5	4.48	13	0	76	77	35	59
Young, Matt, Fairfield	2	4	4.55	12	0	57	59	21	43
#Kosky, James, Iona	0	1	4.63	26	0	47	62	16	24
Cody, Chris, Manhattan	5	1	4.68	13	1	58	68	21	51
Grant, Ken, Siena	3	5	4.84	13	0	58	59	16	38
Spicer, Sean, St. Peter's	4	8	4.86	13	0	74	86	29	52

MID-AMERICAN CONFERENCE

	Conference		Overall	
EAST	W	L	W	L
Miami (Ohio)	14	8	36	21
*Kent State	14	10	36	27
Ohio	12	12	25	29
Akron	11	12	26	27
Marshall	10	13	27	27
Buffalo	4	18	15	39
WEST	**W**	**L**	**W**	**L**
Central Michigan	18	6	33	24
Eastern Michigan	14	10	32	27
Northern Illinois	14	10	31	28
Ball State	14	10	28	28
Bowling Green State	13	11	28	19
Toledo	8	16	20	34
Western Michigan	7	17	21	33

ALL-CONFERENCE TEAM: C—John Slone, Jr., Miami. **1B**—Mike Ferris, Jr., Miami. **2B**—Geoff Orr, So., Miami. **3B**—Jim Geldhof, Jr., Central Michigan. **SS**—Brian Bixler, Jr., Eastern Michigan. **OF**—Sean Dobson, Sr., Toledo; Todd Kimling, Sr., Eastern Michigan; Nolan Reimold, So., Bowling Green. **DH**—Anthony Gressick, So., Ohio. **UT**—Adam Rosales, Jr., Western Michigan. **P**—Ryan Ford, Sr., Eastern Michigan; Joe Piekarz, Sr., Northern Illinois; Andy Sonnanstine, So., Kent State; Keith Weiser, Fr., Miami. **RP**—Darek Stanfield, Jr., Akron.

Player of the Year: Brian Bixler, Eastern Michigan. **Pitcher of the Year:** Ryan Ford, Eastern Michigan. **Freshman of the Year:** Keith Weiser, Miami. **Coach of the Year:** Steve Jaksa, Central Michigan.

INDIVIDUAL BATTING LEADERS
(Minimum 125 At-Bats)

	AVG	AB	R	H	2B	3B	HR	RBI	SB
Bixler, Brian, Eastern Michigan	.453	243	74	110	18	3	8	47	31
Geldhof, Jim, Central Michigan	.427	227	74	97	17	4	9	68	29
Reimold, Nolan, Bowl. Green	.404	171	42	69	14	3	13	57	4
Dobson, Sean, Toledo	.394	231	55	91	23	4	10	63	18
Colopy, Brian, Ohio	.385	195	41	75	17	4	2	42	9
Gressick, Anthony, Ohio	.377	183	48	69	10	1	16	45	4
Slone, John, Miami	.375	240	59	90	15	1	8	47	16
Simon, Scott, Northern Illinois	.374	238	41	89	24	3	5	71	3
Frederick, Adam, Marshall	.374	206	46	77	11	0	3	43	13
Lipari, Jimmy, Bowling Green St.	.373	126	26	47	9	1	0	26	5
Canada, Brian, Miami	.372	199	44	74	14	0	8	52	10
Wells, Kurtis, Central Michigan	.371	229	50	85	12	2	10	70	10
Miller, Brad, Ball State	.366	216	49	79	12	1	15	58	0
Kinyon, Chad, Kent State	.365	244	53	89	19	0	15	65	1
Lawson, Eric, Bowling Green St.	.363	160	38	58	11	1	5	29	1
Ferris, Mike, Miami	.361	208	61	75	15	2	21	63	3
Hudak, Andy, Bowling Green St.	.357	140	31	50	15	0	4	32	2
Hurst, Shawn, Toledo	.356	222	47	79	16	1	9	52	5
Warnock, Jeff, Bowling Green St.	.353	133	28	47	6	3	1	21	8
Mitzel, Bryan, Central Michigan	.351	202	38	71	12	2	14	66	3
Mihalics, Jason, Buffalo	.349	218	43	76	14	5	3	25	7
Brown, Jason, Miami	.347	242	48	77	13	3	1	30	19
Marconi, Rob, Northern Illinois	.344	227	65	78	12	4	13	53	13
Rosales, Adam, Western Mich.	.343	210	57	72	17	1	10	40	16
Orr, Geoff, Miami	.341	205	41	70	16	1	8	49	9
Peterson, Derrick, East Michigan	.336	229	53	77	17	0	16	71	7
Carter, Justin, Western Michigan	.333	216	37	72	13	1	8	49	5
Sullivan, Mike, Ball State	.332	224	54	76	13	1	0	23	12
Kingsley, James, Buffalo	.332	211	30	70	20	2	7	40	1
Russell, Rich, Marshall	.331	151	33	50	14	0	8	28	0
Davis, Andrew, Kent State	.331	263	43	87	20	1	1	43	8
Crum, Jeremy, Central Michigan	.327	168	55	55	4	1	0	9	18
Franz, Marc, Ball State	.327	223	50	73	13	0	11	64	1
Resendez, Jarrod, Toledo	.317	164	46	52	7	1	12	26	8
Kimling, Todd, Eastern Michigan	.316	228	55	72	17	1	17	58	15
#Monaco, Chris, Marshall	.259	205	39	53	5	0	0	18	40

INDIVIDUAL PITCHING LEADERS
(Minimum 50 Innings)

	W	L	ERA	G	SV	IP	H	BB	SO
Sonnanstine, Andy, Kent State	11	4	2.52	18	0	125	122	21	117
Piekarz, Joe, Northern Illinois	9	5	2.55	17	0	116	112	41	96
Ford, Ryan, Eastern Michigan	11	4	2.93	16	0	120	104	47	99
#Stanfield, Darek, Akron	2	2	3.21	29	12	34	33	11	27
Bova, Chris, Ohio	5	6	3.30	14	0	93	86	33	77
Witt, Derek, Ohio	5	4	3.35	19	2	75	74	21	41
Johnson, T.J., Central Michigan	6	5	3.53	16	0	94	89	31	94
Taylor, Graham, Miami	7	6	3.57	17	0	106	128	24	72
Minor, Zach, Northern Illinois	7	4	3.61	16	0	92	78	56	77
Mathes, J.R., Western Michigan	6	4	3.64	14	1	94	100	19	87
Ness, Joe, Ball State	7	4	3.84	17	0	89	89	24	79
Liersemann, Ross, Akron	4	6	3.89	13	0	76	86	31	55
O'Rourke, Dan, Ohio	7	5	3.98	18	2	63	69	32	55
Ziroli, Steve, Marshall	3	1	4.04	23	2	56	48	19	62
Laraway, Justin, Kent State	3	3	4.12	13	0	55	65	29	49
DeGeeter, Ryan, Ball State	4	1	4.12	18	3	63	64	16	43
Dunham, Ty, Central Michigan	6	2	4.28	13	0	80	87	28	73
Weiser, Keith, Miami	8	3	4.30	19	1	84	89	29	63
Cremeans, Ryan, Central Mich.	5	3	4.30	13	0	75	90	20	66
Chrisman, Brian, Marshall	4	3	4.30	15	0	61	52	43	69
Smith, Evan, Kent State	3	4	4.30	17	1	61	70	20	50
Reineke, Chad, Miami	4	3	4.42	31	5	53	54	32	51
Koutsavlis, Chris, Marshall	4	5	4.47	15	0	89	96	26	62
Russell, Adam, Ohio	1	3	4.50	12	0	64	79	29	61

MID-CONTINENT CONFERENCE

	Conference		Overall	
	W	L	W	L
*Oral Roberts	21	1	50	11
Western Illinois	13	11	29	36
Centenary	10	11	23	31
Southern Utah	11	13	19	30
Valparaiso	11	13	20	34
Oakland	10	13	20	34
Chicago State	5	19	8	52

ALL-CONFERENCE TEAM: C—Nate Griffin, Sr., Oral Roberts; John Sullivan, Jr., Oakland. **1B**—Blake Adkison, Sr., Centenary. **2B**—Brian Hanson, Jr., Oral Roberts. **3B**—Ryan Cougill, Sr., Western Illinois. **SS**—Jason Ruiz, Jr., Southern Utah. **OF**—Amos Burgess, Jr., Southern Utah; Matt VanDerBosch, Sr., Oral Roberts; Ryan Welborn, Sr., Oral Roberts. **DH/P**—Dennis Bigley, Jr., Oral Roberts. **UT**—Josh Lex, Sr., Oral Roberts. **SP**—Sean Sorrow, Sr., Oral Roberts; Tom Starck, Sr., Valparaiso. **RP**—Adam Lesko, Jr., Oral Roberts.

Player of the Year: Dennis Bigley, Oral Roberts. **Pitcher of the Year:** Dennis Bigley, Oral Roberts. **Newcomer of the Year:** Adam Lesko, Oral Roberts. **Coach of the Year:** Rob Walton, Oral Roberts.

INDIVIDUAL BATTING LEADERS
(Minimum 125 At-Bats)

	AVG	AB	R	H	2B	3B	HR	RBI	SB
Ruiz, Jason, Southern Utah	.398	191	51	76	14	1	1	25	12
Adkison, Blake, Centenary	.395	185	49	73	17	1	16	58	2
VanDerBosch, Matt, Oral Roberts	.383	240	75	92	13	7	3	52	44
Cardone, Tony, Centenary	.377	207	38	78	14	1	1	38	8
Burgess, Amos, Southern Utah	.372	196	45	73	14	0	11	50	15
Hanson, Brian, Oral Roberts	.355	231	52	82	18	1	4	53	7
Welborn, Ryan, Oral Roberts	.354	175	66	62	16	1	0	21	31
Sullivan, John, Oakland	.348	181	34	63	10	2	12	32	4
Schultz, Blake, Western Illinois	.347	190	35	66	9	1	6	36	6
Drew, Kory, Southern Utah	.341	179	49	61	15	1	6	26	18
Herriott, Ty, Oakland	.340	197	47	67	13	1	18	50	2
Plumley, Grant, Oral Roberts	.331	251	43	83	22	1	5	64	12
Lex, Josh, Oral Roberts	.330	227	51	75	14	0	11	67	7
Arensdorff, Michael, Valparaiso	.326	193	48	63	14	0	4	21	8
Gilliam, Bobby, Centenary	.324	219	51	71	10	1	3	26	24
Cougill, Ryan, Western Illinois	.324	238	44	77	12	0	1	28	6
Rivera, Ricky, Oral Roberts	.320	178	37	57	12	3	8	45	3

INDIVIDUAL PITCHING LEADERS
(Minimum 50 Innings)

	W	L	ERA	G	SV	IP	H	BB	SO
Lesko, Adam, Oral Roberts	7	1	2.15	22	0	84	70	21	49
Sorrow, Sean, Oral Roberts	9	1	2.49	19	1	87	78	20	59
McIntyre, Taylor, Oral Roberts	6	1	2.61	11	0	62	38	38	62
Bigley, Dennis, Oral Roberts	13	1	2.91	16	0	118	95	25	100
Ramsey, Justin, Oral Roberts	7	0	2.91	30	13	59	60	14	37
Kohorst, Patrick, Western Illinois	9	5	3.03	16	1	101	84	51	74
Starck, Tom, Valparaiso	5	8	3.48	13	0	85	68	47	100
Yergin, Harvey, Valparaiso	3	5	3.66	15	0	64	60	27	43
Zimmerman, Ryan, Southern Utah	7	4	4.52	16	1	78	90	22	74
Kniebbe, Steve, Oakland	2	6	4.54	14	0	67	73	28	60
Willborn, Kevin, Centenary	5	5	4.55	18	1	87	112	21	59
Ruffing, David, Centenary	8	5	5.13	16	0	86	103	25	55

MID-EASTERN CONFERENCE

	Conference		Overall	
	W	L	W	L
*Bethune-Cookman	14	4	27	28
Delaware State	11	5	27	23
Florida A&M	9	6	22	30
North Carolina A&T	10	8	23	28
Norfolk State	8	9	17	30
Coppin State	8	10	18	32
Maryland-Eastern Shore	0	18	3	44

ALL-CONFERENCE TEAM: C—Eddie Wilson, Sr., Coppin State. **IF**—Juan Figueroa, Sr., Bethune-Cookman; Carlos Garcia, Sr., Bethune-Cookman; Virgil Priestly, Jr., Florida A&M; Juan Serrano, Fr., Norfolk State; Bret Underwood, Sr., Delaware State. **OF**—Sebastien Boucher, Jr., Bethune-Cookman; Darryl Chever, Sr., Norfolk State; Roberto Rodriguez, Sr., Bethune-Cookman. **DH**—Kelly Williams, Sr., Delaware State. **P**—Francisco Gomez, So., Bethune-Cookman; Shawn Phillips, Jr., Delaware State. **RP**—Patrick Pinkerton, Sr., Florida A&M.

Player of the Year: Sebastien Boucher, Bethune-Cookman. **Rookie of the Year:** Juan Serrano, Norfolk State. **Coach of the Year:** Mervyl Melendez, Bethune-Cookman.

INDIVIDUAL BATTING LEADERS
(Minimum 125 At-Bats)

	AVG	AB	R	H	2B	3B	HR	RBI	SB
Figueroa, Juan, Beth.-Cookman	.383	193	48	74	15	3	8	58	5
Chever, Darryl, Norfolk State	.381	160	38	61	5	9	6	30	21
Riggs, Justin, Coppin State	.360	172	45	62	13	1	11	48	5
Love, Austin, N.C. A&T	.358	173	48	62	12	1	10	40	13
Weir, Garrett, Delaware State	.356	188	52	67	17	2	0	29	42
Boucher, Sebastien, Beth.-Cook.	.352	216	57	76	8	5	1	24	37
Williams, Kelly, Delaware State	.352	196	45	69	12	2	3	38	7
Garcia, Carlos, Beth.-Cookman	.352	182	36	64	7	3	4	44	3
Serrano, Juan, Norfolk State	.352	165	33	58	10	1	3	39	4
Gamble, Charlie, N.C. A&T	.348	178	32	62	16	1	3	34	7

Rodriguez, Roberto, Beth.-Cook.	.341	170	35	58	11	3	7	39	6
Richburg, Teon, Coppin State	.340	150	39	51	12	1	4	29	15
Underwood, Bret, Del. State	.337	193	40	65	14	0	12	49	14
Jones, Jeremy, N.C. A&T	.335	188	40	63	8	1	5	27	12
Wenger, Nick, Coppin State	.330	197	34	65	14	1	3	49	6

INDIVIDUAL PITCHING LEADERS
(Minimum 50 Innings)

	W	L	ERA	G	SV	IP	H	BB	SO
Phillips, Shawn, Delaware State	10	2	2.02	17	2	116	94	11	111
Bitter, Nick, Delaware State	5	5	2.62	23	3	58	62	8	50
Hauff, Michael, N.C. A&T	6	4	3.30	14	0	87	84	27	95
Digiorgio, Ian, N.C. A&T	5	7	3.78	15	0	81	82	31	47
Conroy, Jimmy, Delaware State	3	2	4.24	18	0	64	76	25	50
Stratchko, Tommy, Coppin State	4	5	4.28	16	0	69	72	39	36
Renshaw, Andy, Norfolk State	4	6	4.35	18	4	91	105	26	69
Penrose, Nathan, Coppin State	3	1	4.50	23	5	50	61	16	24
Bornstein, Jason, Beth.-Cook.	2	4	4.56	16	0	53	55	21	46
Middleton, Tony, N.C. A&T	2	6	4.88	15	0	68	77	29	58
Rivera, Mumba, Beth.-Cook.	7	7	4.90	17	0	79	80	54	70

MISSOURI VALLEY CONFERENCE

	Conference		Overall	
	W	L	W	L
*Wichita State	28	4	49	16
Creighton	22	9	35	24
Southwest Missouri State	19	12	31	28
Southern Illinois	15	16	27	32
Evansville	12	20	28	32
Northern Iowa	12	20	25	31
Indiana State	12	20	20	37
Bradley	11	20	29	26
Illinois State	11	21	21	34

ALL-CONFERENCE TEAM: C—Jud Kindle, Sr., Southwest Missouri State. **1B**—Logan Sorensen, Sr., Wichita State. **2B**—Tony Roth, Jr., Creighton. **3B**—Brandon Green, Sr., Wichita State. **SS**—Brooks Colvin, Sr., Southwest Missouri State. **OF**—Nick Blasi, Sr., Wichita State; Drew Moffitt, Sr., Wichita State; Cody Strait, Jr., Evansville. **DH**—Pat Tumilty, Fr., Evansville. **UT**—Nathan Emrick, So., Southern Illinois. **P**—Steve Grasley, Sr., Creighton; Mike Pelfrey, So., Wichita State; Brett Sinkbeil, Fr., Southwest Missouri State. **RP**—Tommy Hottovy, Jr., Wichita State; Andrew Weber, Jr., Southern Illinois.

Co-Players of the Year: Brandon Green, Wichita State; Logan Sorensen, Wichita State. **Pitcher of the Year:** Mike Pelfrey, Wichita State. **Newcomer of the Year:** Cody Strait, Evansville. **Freshman of the Year:** Brett Sinkbeil, Southwest Missouri State. **Coach of the Year:** Ed Servais, Creighton.

INDIVIDUAL BATTING LEADERS
(Minimum 125 At-Bats)

	AVG	AB	R	H	2B	3B	HR	RBI	SB
Smith, Jonathan, Bradley	.397	136	33	54	17	0	4	35	1
Green, Brandon, Wichita State	.395	256	38	101	27	1	2	57	7
Sorensen, Logan, Wichita State	.377	244	67	92	24	1	10	73	29
Lis, Erik, Evansville	.373	220	49	82	21	1	11	58	9
Canada, Brad, Bradley	.368	201	50	74	15	3	3	42	3
Blasi, Nick, Wichita State	.366	265	79	97	16	6	10	51	21
Roth, Tony, Creighton	.356	191	44	68	17	1	5	30	19
Emrick, Nathan, So. Illinois	.353	238	36	84	10	0	1	34	15
Strait, Cody, Evansville	.350	223	53	78	12	3	11	40	15
Lara, Armando, Northern Iowa	.344	183	36	63	9	2	3	35	23
Whitney, Nate, Illinois State	.344	218	41	75	16	2	3	37	12
Grant, Dan, Northern Iowa	.342	161	34	55	14	1	8	35	4
Johnson, Mark, Wichita State	.333	186	32	62	11	0	5	34	7
Daeges, Zach, Creighton	.333	201	46	67	16	1	9	37	4
Prickett, Josh, Indiana State	.332	220	38	73	8	4	7	45	13
Rice, Paul, Bradley	.331	178	39	59	8	3	1	28	10
Dutton, Brad, Creighton	.325	160	27	52	7	1	0	19	8
Colvin, Brooks, SW Missouri	.323	186	39	60	15	1	3	27	12
Artner, Marcus, Indiana State	.322	180	30	58	10	0	1	22	2
Tumilty, Pat, Evansville	.321	168	30	54	12	2	8	49	2
Norquist, Dan, Creighton	.320	153	24	49	15	3	3	32	3
Eigsti, Jake, Indiana State	.319	188	28	60	9	5	2	30	5
Curry, Ryan, Bradley	.318	192	30	61	8	1	1	33	6
Taylor, Chris, SW Missouri	.316	136	29	43	8	0	0	16	9
Smarsh, Shawn, Wichita State	.316	193	41	61	13	1	3	31	13
Manning, Jake, SW Missouri	.316	174	30	55	7	0	7	45	8
Moran, Pat, Northern Iowa	.315	213	27	67	13	0	1	20	9
Smith, Kyle, Evansville	.313	230	49	72	9	1	0	28	19
LaCoste, Sean, Northern Iowa	.313	211	37	66	17	2	3	24	5
Kindle, Jud, SW Missouri State	.309	207	50	64	15	0	6	43	7
Aqueron, Rene, Bradley	.307	205	43	63	12	0	10	37	14
McCoola, Nick, Wichita State	.305	203	46	62	11	0	7	34	1
#Moffitt, Drew, Wichita State	.289	211	63	61	7	1	26	72	17

COLLEGE BASEBALL

INDIVIDUAL PITCHING LEADERS
(Minimum 50 Innings)

	W	L	ERA	G	SV	IP	H	BB	SO
Johnson, Kris, Wichita State	7	0	**2.01**	13	0	72	54	28	66
Pelfrey, Mike, Wichita State	11	2	2.18	16	0	115	86	24	**125**
Hottovy, Tommy, Wichita State	9	3	2.25	23	2	76	64	10	92
Chavez, Jason, Southern Illinois	5	4	2.44	16	0	74	74	34	36
Walker, Collin, Bradley	4	4	2.88	9	0	56	62	13	35
DeJong, Eric, Northern Iowa	4	4	2.91	20	2	56	45	16	40
Grasley, Steve, Creighton	**12**	4	3.00	18	1	**117**	122	23	101
Sinkbeil, Brett, SW Missouri State	7	4	3.11	15	0	84	66	34	84
#Weber, Andrew, Southern Illinois	5	1	3.13	26	**11**	37	39	14	36
Foster, Jereme, Wichita State	6	2	3.14	18	0	63	51	23	34
Drage, Derek, SW Missouri State	3	7	3.20	15	0	112	107	29	91
Gray, Jeff, SW Missouri State	8	5	3.36	18	1	83	81	30	67
Joiner, Josh, Southern Illinois	4	2	3.51	19	0	74	75	22	51
Haberer, Eric, Southern Illinois	6	3	3.54	17	1	84	78	35	60
Reese, Scott, Creighton	1	3	3.64	30	5	59	55	14	52
Goins, Derek, Bradley	5	6	3.73	12	0	70	80	15	35
Stein, Todd, Illinois State	4	6	3.98	14	1	75	80	20	68
Christensen, Micah, No. Iowa	5	1	3.99	18	1	50	53	13	56
Smith, David, SW Missouri State	3	4	4.17	14	1	54	64	24	33
Kelchen, Kory, Northern Iowa	4	5	4.22	13	0	70	70	34	48
Stanke, Cal, Evansville	5	4	4.23	12	0	66	71	31	51
Daneff, Jeff, Creighton	5	2	4.28	15	0	76	71	38	65
Zaleski, Matt, Indiana State	5	7	4.33	17	0	98	113	19	64
Marsala, Paul, SW Missouri	5	4	4.68	12	1	58	58	19	60
Zaleski, Kyle, Illinois State	3	2	4.70	25	5	69	93	16	68
#Lindsay, Adam, Indiana State	3	6	6.62	**31**	0	52	66	24	39

MOUNTAIN WEST CONFERENCE

	Conference		Overall	
	W	L	W	L
San Diego State	19	9	35	29
New Mexico	20	10	26	29
*Nevada-Las Vegas	20	10	37	24
Brigham Young	18	12	28	30
Utah	11	19	22	36
Air Force	0	28	6	49

ALL-CONFERENCE TEAM: C—Jordan Swaydan, So., San Diego State. **1F**—Rielly Embrey, Sr., San Diego State; James Guerrero, So., San Diego State; Josh Mader, Jr., New Mexico; Jared Pena, Jr., Utah; Dan Stovall, Jr., New Mexico; Brandon Taylor, Sr., Brigham Young. **OF**—Landon Burt, Sr., San Diego State; Ryan Chambers, Jr., Brigham Young; Eric Chevalier, Sr., Utah; Matt Ciaramella, So., Utah; Brent Johnson, Sr., Nevada-Las Vegas; Jake McLintock, Jr., San Diego State; Eric Nielsen, Jr., Nevada-Las Vegas; Matt Young, Jr., New Mexico. **DH/UT**—Jay Brossman, Jr., Utah; Joe Salas, Sr., New Mexico; Brock Ungricht, Fr., San Diego State. **P**—Daryl Harang, Sr., San Diego State; Paul Jacinto, Sr., Brigham Young; Drew Jenson, Sr., San Diego State; David Seccombe, Sr., Nevada-Las Vegas; Scott Shoemaker, Sr., San Diego State; Jake Vose, Sr., Nevada-Las Vegas. **RP**—Ben Scheinbaum, Sr., Nevada-Las Vegas; Ryan Schroyer, Sr., San Diego State.
Player of the Year: Eric Nielsen, Nevada-Las Vegas. **Pitcher of the Year:** Scott Shoemaker, San Diego State. **Coach of the Year:** Tony Gwynn, San Diego State.

INDIVIDUAL BATTING LEADERS
(Minimum 125 At-Bats)

	AVG	AB	R	H	2B	3B	HR	RBI	SB
Nielsen, Eric, UNLV	**.402**	251	84	101	23	2	**16**	87	7
Mader, Josh, New Mexico	.395	233	47	92	10	4	10	56	12
Parraz, Zeke, UNLV	.385	130	33	50	10	1	3	22	1
Young, Matt, New Mexico	.381	231	60	88	10	**12**	3	50	16
Ruiz, Ryan, UNLV	.377	162	56	61	14	4	6	50	12
Ungricht, Brock, San Diego St.	.373	249	49	93	21	3	3	48	5
Brossman, Jay, Utah	.369	168	40	62	11	2	2	24	4
Ciaramella, Matt, Utah	.366	243	50	89	**28**	1	13	64	9
Johnson, Brent, UNLV	.359	245	64	88	21	3	6	72	11
Embrey, Rielly, San Diego State	.353	241	48	85	19	1	5	57	0
Bolt, Karl, Air Force	.349	172	31	60	10	1	4	32	2
Pena, Jared, Utah	.348	233	44	81	24	2	8	53	5
Stovall, Daniel, New Mexico	.347	199	41	69	14	1	12	34	2
Barba, Ryan, New Mexico	.346	191	49	66	9	0	7	37	3
White, Peter, UNLV	.345	249	71	86	14	1	9	56	7
Gill, Eddie, Nev.-Las Vegas	.345	232	43	80	19	1	7	61	1
Knell, Kory, Brigham Young	.340	159	39	54	13	1	6	39	8
Murray, Sean, New Mexico	.333	219	38	73	13	2	3	34	3
D'Angelo, Andrew, UNLV	.333	207	66	69	20	1	7	44	4
Hiestand, Jeff, Brigham Young	.333	126	38	42	12	2	8	34	5
Burt, Landon, San Diego State	.321	234	61	75	11	4	6	40	**30**
Guerrero, James, San Diego St.	.318	239	51	76	10	4	4	32	12
McLintock, Jake, San Diego St.	.315	203	32	64	15	2	4	42	1
Saylor, Ben, Brigham Young	.312	224	25	70	11	0	4	40	1

Khoury, Ryan, Utah .... .310 229 41 71 13 0 6 26 6
Hill, Josh, San Diego State .... .310 129 27 40 6 3 5 29 2

INDIVIDUAL PITCHING LEADERS
(Minimum 50 Innings)

	W	L	ERA	G	SV	IP	H	BB	SO
#Schroyer, Ryan, San Diego St.	2	3	2.85	28	**13**	41	31	9	50
Shoemaker, Scott, San Diego St.	9	6	**3.99**	19	0	**113**	116	29	**110**
Harang, Daryl, San Diego State	6	6	4.34	18	0	87	99	43	74
Billings, Bruce, San Diego State	6	1	4.68	15	0	50	56	26	48
Jenson, Drew, San Diego State	2	3	4.68	22	2	65	60	23	51
Su'a, Justin, Brigham Young	2	2	5.09	13	0	58	80	11	45
Vose, Jake, UNLV	**10**	4	5.19	19	0	109	139	36	69
Fernandez, Jason, New Mexico	7	5	5.27	16	0	94	122	16	49
Herrera, Danny Ray, New Mexico	4	7	5.33	14	0	73	93	24	51
Jacinto, Paul, Brigham Young	3	9	5.55	21	3	94	110	21	70
Westmoreland, Clay, Utah	3	5	5.55	30	9	58	67	25	65
Coon, Ben, San Diego State	4	3	5.58	25	1	61	80	20	44
Seccombe, David, UNLV	9	3	5.65	16	0	94	108	27	90
Hartshorn, Chris, San Diego State	5	4	5.67	17	0	67	75	24	41
Price, Jason, Utah	4	8	5.73	21	0	108	126	43	102
Wells, Patrick, Brigham Young	7	5	5.76	17	0	105	128	30	61
Buck, Ben, Utah	6	5	6.01	**35**	0	88	133	28	49
Luca, Matt, UNLV	7	5	5.99	18	0	86	96	42	99

NORTHEAST CONFERENCE

	Conference		Overall	
	W	L	W	L
*Central Connecticut State	20	4	41	17
Quinnipiac	16	7	23	21
Monmouth	13	10	22	29
Wagner	12	11	20	29
Fairleigh Dickinson	11	13	12	28
Mount St. Mary's	10	13	25	18
Sacred Heart	10	14	12	36
Long Island	7	16	9	29
St. Francis	6	17	12	30

ALL-CONFERENCE TEAM: C—Tim D'Aquila, Sr., Central Connecticut State. **1B**—Phil Rothkugel, Jr., Central Connecticut State. **2B**—Keith Stegbauer, Sr., Central Connecticut State. **3B**—Bryan Sabatella, So., Quinnipiac. **SS**—Anthony Giudice, Sr., St. Francis. **OF**—Rob Hosgood, Sr., Central Connecticut State; Albert Marano, Sr., Quinnipiac; Jason Weszka, Sr., Mount St. Mary's.**DH**—Brett Hardie, Jr., Monmouth. **P**—Patrick Egan, So., Quinnipiac; Dustin Pease, Fr., Mount St. Mary's.
Player of the Year: Keith Stegbauer, Central Connnecticut State. **Pitcher of the Year:** Patrick Egan, Quinnipiac. **Rookie of the Year:** Dustin Pease, Mount St. Mary's. **Coach of the Year:** Dan Gooley, Quinnipiac.

INDIVIDUAL BATTING LEADERS
(Minimum 125 At-Bats)

	AVG	AB	R	H	2B	3B	HR	RBI	SB
Stegbauer, Keith, Central Conn.	**.407**	246	**80**	**100**	15	0	4	45	7
Hosgood, Rob, Central Conn.	.376	221	64	83	10	4	**9**	49	16
Weszka, Jason, Mt. St. Mary's	.367	166	40	61	11	1	3	30	8
Giudice, Anthony, St. Francis	.362	152	29	55	7	1	0	15	18
Memoli, Matt, Central Conn.	.359	192	36	69	7	1	2	36	7
Rothkugel, Phil, Central Conn.	.357	199	49	71	16	2	4	49	2
Sabatella, Bryan, Quinnipiac	.355	169	35	60	17	1	5	31	6
Mastrianni, Matt, Wagner	.352	182	34	64	12	1	3	35	4
Marano, Albert, Quinnipiac	.348	164	32	57	8	2	8	32	6
Hardie, Brett, Monmouth	.347	147	22	51	6	0	0	19	5
Schilkowski, Jamie, Sac. Heart	.346	153	18	53	11	0	0	18	0
Stormes, Burt, Mount St. Mary's	.340	150	27	51	10	0	4	31	0
Smith, Eric, Mount St. Mary's	.338	145	33	49	6	0	3	26	4
Coppola, Ricky, Quinnipiac	.338	148	24	50	11	0	0	20	2
Muldoon, Brad, Central Conn.	.325	169	38	55	5	1	1	34	**24**
Di Girolamo, John, Mt. St. Mary's	.324	148	30	48	10	3	0	24	14
DeSiena, Joe, St. Francis	.323	127	19	41	8	0	5	30	2
D'Aquila, Tim, Central Conn.	.320	231	49	74	16	5	2	**55**	12
Kotula, Joe, Mount St. Mary's	.318	173	29	55	10	0	1	31	3
Dick, Chris, Wagner	.316	171	32	54	12	0	5	28	1
Lewsey, Curtis, Sacred Heart	.316	133	12	42	8	0	3	22	7
Papa, Nick, Wagner	.314	188	29	59	**19**	5	4	38	13
Massari, Nick, Monmouth	.313	182	33	57	10	**6**	6	27	7
Sogluizzo, Troy, Wagner	.309	165	22	51	9	0	4	19	1

INDIVIDUAL PITCHING LEADERS
(Minimum 50 Innings)

	W	L	ERA	G	SV	IP	H	BB	SO
Egan, Patrick, Quinnipiac	7	2	**2.54**	11	0	60	49	13	39
Davis, Justin, Mount St. Mary's	4	4	2.61	18	1	59	67	15	53
Vitelli, Scott, Central Conn.	**9**	4	2.70	15	0	77	72	8	45
Dooley, John, Long Island	3	4	3.00	11	0	54	59	16	37
Bailey, Andrew, Wagner	6	4	3.18	15	1	76	60	34	84

Pease, Dustin, Mount St. Mary's 8 4 3.19 22 4 **85** 80 15 **88**
Ruder, Todd, Central Conn. 6 0 3.54 17 0 53 66 11 22
Keeton, Glen, Monmouth 5 2 3.58 11 0 60 56 23 49
Ristano, Chuck, Sacred Heart 4 7 3.62 13 0 72 76 18 42
Anziano, Jesse, Fair. Dickinson 5 6 3.89 14 1 72 71 19 66
Pappariella, Lewis, Central Conn. 7 3 4.12 11 0 68 64 19 46
Wakefield, Chris, Quinnipiac 4 3 4.14 11 1 54 62 18 51
Bunyan, Brian, Fair. Dickinson 2 4 4.27 12 0 59 66 30 59
Dinihanian, Adam, Sacred Heart 5 2 4.46 19 1 69 94 11 43
Peterson, Mark, Central Conn. 6 2 4.48 **24** 8 62 65 26 53
Ekberg, Ryan, Long Island 2 6 4.53 16 0 58 61 11 49
Scribner, Evan, Central Conn. 4 3 4.72 **24** 3 61 67 16 44

OHIO VALLEY CONFERENCE

	Conference		Overall	
	W	L	W	L
Austin Peay State	20	7	35	21
Eastern Illinois	17	9	26	30
*Jacksonville State	16	11	31	29
Eastern Kentucky	15	11	34	17
Southeast Missouri State	15	11	29	28
Samford	15	12	25	33
Murray State	11	16	17	35
Tennessee Tech	10	16	15	31
Tennessee-Martin	7	20	16	38
Morehead State	7	20	14	40

ALL-CONFERENCE TEAM: C—Chris Clark, Sr., Eastern Kentucky. **1B**—Will Whisenant, Jr., Eastern Kentucky. **2B**—Bryant Jones, Sr., Tennessee-Martin. **3B**—Bobby Hicks, Sr., Jacksonville State. **SS**—Kyle Haines, Sr., Eastern Illinois. **OF**—Matt Alling, So., Samford; Stephen Carter, Sr., Eastern Kentucky; Austin Stein, Jr., Jacksonville State. **DH**—Robby Goodson, Sr., Jacksonville State. **UT**—Robert Dittrich, So., Morehead State. **SP**—Rowdy Hardy, Jr., Austin Peay; Jeff Mault, Sr., Austin Peay. **RP**—Brad Smith, Jr., Southeast Missouri.

Player of the Year: Stephen Carter, Eastern Kentucky. **Pitcher of the Year:** Jeff Mault, Austin Peay. **Rookie of the Year:** Rowdy Hardy, Austin Peay. **Coach of the Year:** Tim Parenton, Samford.

INDIVIDUAL BATTING LEADERS
(Minimum 125 At-Bats)

	AVG	AB	R	H	2B	3B	HR	RBI	SB
Carter, Stephen, Eastern Ky.	**.451**	184	50	83	14	0	1	41	**21**
Jones, Bryant, Tenn.-Martin	.425	226	55	**96**	13	3	6	33	18
Woodard, Jonathan, Eastern Ky.	.418	184	56	77	17	3	5	48	4
Clark, Chris, Eastern Kentucky	.409	149	47	61	20	0	5	35	8
Bolger, Brett, Eastern Kentucky	.387	168	36	65	12	4	1	45	13
Alling, Matt, Samford	.386	223	43	86	13	**7**	3	48	6
Whisenant, Will, Eastern Ky.	.378	148	39	56	6	1	6	40	2
Hicks, Bobby, Jacksonville St.	.378	249	**64**	94	22	3	11	46	6
Walker, Jared, Austin Peay	.375	216	50	81	**23**	1	6	51	5
Horstman, Eric, SE Missouri	.368	228	61	84	19	5	2	31	13
Dittrich, Robert, Morehead State	.368	155	36	57	9	3	2	18	7
O'Dell, Chris, Eastern Kentucky	.358	159	51	57	9	1	15	43	1
Visnic, Adam, Eastern Kentucky	.355	141	29	50	6	1	0	33	0
Bracamonte, Ernie, SE Missouri	.354	229	52	81	11	1	8	51	6
Montiel, Frankie, SE Missouri	.352	199	43	70	22	3	5	42	4
Sellers, Neil, Eastern Kentucky	.351	205	58	72	18	0	12	**63**	7
Campbell, Ryan, Eastern Illinois	.347	225	49	78	22	0	7	44	3
Selvog, Brandon, Tenn. Tech	.339	183	34	62	18	2	6	30	7
Carkeek, Kevin, Eastern Illinois	.339	186	33	63	14	0	1	31	0
Chagnon, Mark, Eastern Illinois	.338	142	35	48	5	1	0	15	5
Collins, Michael, Samford	.335	224	53	75	20	0	4	21	4
Gilbert, Gary, SE Missouri St.	.333	207	37	69	15	1	5	43	2
Griggs, Clint, Murray State	.332	190	48	63	18	1	3	27	3
Smith, Tommy, Austin Peay	.331	160	21	53	12	0	1	23	0
Rima, Travis, Morehead State	.330	212	31	70	12	3	5	38	0
#Goodson, Robby, Jacksonville St.	.305	197	47	60	11	4	**17**	50	1

INDIVIDUAL PITCHING LEADERS
(Minimum 50 Innings)

	W	L	ERA	G	SV	IP	H	BB	SO
Smith, Brad, SE Missouri St.	3	2	**2.48**	**30**	**11**	54	39	16	66
Hardy, Rowdy, Austin Peay	**12**	3	2.90	18	0	**118**	116	25	91
Wynns, Bobby, Jacksonville St.	9	7	3.41	18	0	98	104	27	83
Kelley, Shawn, Austin Peay	3	3	3.45	16	0	63	66	25	51
Edens, Joseph, Samford	8	5	3.49	21	0	95	98	24	83
Mault, Jeff, Austin Peay St.	11	4	3.69	20	3	76	86	26	59
Artz, Stephen, Samford	6	5	3.70	20	3	100	104	24	**98**
Herbig, Derek, SE Missouri St.	5	4	3.72	17	0	65	62	38	77
Palmer, C.R., Jacksonville St.	9	6	3.92	18	0	103	103	31	97
Grider, Chris, Eastern Kentucky	8	4	4.13	14	0	70	70	39	81
Peach, Bart, Murray State	0	5	4.57	14	1	61	69	24	46
Kraus, Craig, Murray State	5	6	4.79	15	0	68	85	17	44
Vaculik, Chris, Eastern Illinois	5	1	5.22	14	0	50	56	18	39

Carrico, Adam, Austin Peay St. 3 6 5.34 22 4 61 68 38 49
Campbell, Casey, Morehead St. 2 7 5.80 25 1 76 99 21 49
Bachman, Dan, Eastern Ky. 5 2 5.82 12 0 65 73 44 41
Forsyth, Ryan, SE Missouri St. 4 2 5.89 22 1 70 98 38 53
#Summer, Dustin, Tenn.-Martin 2 4 7.69 **30** 0 48 96 12 29

PACIFIC-10 CONFERENCE

	Conference		Overall	
	W	L	W	L
Stanford	16	8	46	14
Washington	15	9	39	20
UCLA	14	10	35	29
Arizona State	13	11	41	18
Arizona	12	12	36	27
Oregon State	10	14	31	22
Southern California	10	14	24	32
Washington State	9	15	29	26
California	9	15	25	31

ALL-CONFERENCE TEAM: C—Jeff Clement, So., Southern California; Donny Lucy, Jr., Stanford. **1B**—Kyle Larsen, Jr., Washington; John Mayberry, Jr., Stanford. **IF**—Jonny Ash, Sr., Stanford; Trevor Crowe, So., Arizona; Ryan McCarthy, Jr., UCLA; Dustin Pedroia, Jr., Arizona State. **OF**—Travis Buck, So., Arizona State; Zach Clem, So., Washington; Jacoby Ellsbury, So., Oregon State; Brian Hall, Sr., Staford; Brent Lillibridge, So., Washington; Aaron Mathews, Jr., Oregon State; Danny Putnam, Jr., Stanford. **SP**—Casey Janssen, Sr., UCLA; Ian Kennedy, Fr., Southern California; Jake Postlewait, Sr., Oregon State; Mark Romanczuk, So., Stanford; Jason Urquidez, Jr., Arizona State. **RP**—David O'Hagan, Sr., Stanford.

Player of the Year: Jed Lowrie, Stanford. **Pitcher of the Year/Freshman of the Year:** Tim Lincecum, Washington. **Coach of the Year:** Gary Adams, UCLA.

INDIVIDUAL BATTING LEADERS
(Minimum 125 At-Bats)

	AVG	AB	R	H	2B	3B	HR	RBI	SB
Lowrie, Jed, Stanford	.399	233	72	93	19	4	**17**	**68**	6
Pedroia, Dustin, Arizona State	.393	244	**78**	**96**	24	1	9	49	9
Putnam, Danny, Stanford	.378	249	61	94	10	4	16	62	6
Buck, Travis, Arizona State	.373	225	64	84	16	1	9	58	13
Ash, Jonny, Stanford	.372	183	55	68	6	3	5	35	2
Hart, Billy, Southern California	.367	158	26	58	9	3	2	29	3
Nicholson, David, California	.367	210	50	77	14	2	1	25	6
Asanovich, Josh, Arizona State	.367	150	39	55	9	2	5	41	4
Hall, Brian, Stanford	.356	236	51	84	13	4	9	52	15
Miller, Jay, Wash. State	.355	203	43	72	13	0	2	42	5
Ellsbury, Jacoby, Oregon State	.352	196	56	69	8	2	3	20	20
Crowe, Trevor, Arizona	.350	203	53	71	13	**9**	5	33	**26**
Lissman, Mike, Oregon State	.349	146	39	51	8	0	8	34	4
Freeman, Jason, Wash. State	.344	189	42	65	13	2	1	39	12
Larsen, Kyle, Washington	.344	227	44	78	16	1	11	55	1
Mercado, Richard, Arizona	.342	190	30	65	7	2	4	30	0
Gosewisch, Tuffy, Arizona State	.342	199	36	68	14	1	2	49	0
Rubin, Kaeo, Wash. State	.341	214	64	73	16	3	5	36	2
Weiner, David, California	.338	198	35	67	9	3	9	43	3
Clem, Zach, Washington	.336	214	60	72	13	0	13	47	3
Mayberry, John, Stanford	.333	216	53	72	11	2	16	62	9
Hankerd, Cyle, So. California	.333	141	21	47	8	0	1	29	2
Walsh, Nick, Arizona State	.329	149	31	49	7	0	0	23	6
Mathews, Aaron, Oregon State	.326	227	41	74	13	6	8	49	6
Rhinehart, Bill, Arizona	.324	142	29	46	10	1	7	26	0
Thayer, Matt, UCLA	.323	217	49	70	11	5	4	33	9
Donald, Jason, Arizona	.322	261	58	84	11	1	9	45	6
Persichina, Joe, Arizona State	.320	150	27	48	7	1	1	24	3
Van Houten, Jeff, Arizona	.319	216	49	69	10	6	3	40	6
Lillibridge, Brent, Washington	.317	249	65	79	16	1	11	36	18
Hathaway, Aaron, Washington	.317	218	41	69	7	5	9	42	5
Sharpe, Blake, So. California	.316	234	37	74	11	0	2	28	7
Griffin, Preston, UCLA	.313	195	44	61	12	0	3	27	1
Lucy, Donny, Stanford	.313	208	53	65	10	0	12	47	5
Richardson, Grant, Wash. State	.311	206	33	64	9	0	13	**68**	2
Duran, Moises, Arizona	.310	213	38	66	12	3	7	49	12
Richie, Paul, Oregon State	.309	152	26	47	5	0	3	31	4
Larish, Jeff, Arizona State	.308	237	46	73	17	0	7	49	3
Hardy, John, Arizona	.308	208	34	64	7	3	5	32	9
Grossman, Chris, California	.306	134	31	41	9	0	3	32	2
Brown, Jordan, Arizona	.306	219	37	67	11	2	13	57	1
Isaacson, Greg, Washington	.304	227	54	69	12	0	6	44	23
Frost, Baron, So. California	.303	211	39	64	20	1	4	32	3
Batkoski, Nick, Washington	.303	165	25	50	11	2	2	33	2
Lane, Matt, Washington	.301	133	26	40	10	0	6	26	1
Curtis, Colin, Arizona State	.300	190	37	57	11	0	5	36	12
Hundley, Nick, Arizona	.299	147	28	44	13	2	4	27	2

COLLEGE BASEBALL

	AVG	AB	R	H	2B	3B	HR	RBI	SB
McAngus, Zach, Wash. State	.296	179	36	53	12	1	6	32	1
McCarthy, Ryan, UCLA	.295	254	42	75	15	0	15	47	7
McFeely, Shea, Oregon State	.294	180	42	53	14	2	5	38	1
Clement, Jeff, So. California	.293	198	36	58	12	1	10	43	1
Denove, Chris, UCLA	.291	213	37	62	8	1	8	47	3
Otness, John, Washington	.289	228	38	66	10	0	9	48	1
Carter, Chris, Stanford	.289	149	23	43	6	1	9	39	1

INDIVIDUAL PITCHING LEADERS
(Minimum 50 Innings)

	W	L	ERA	G	SV	IP	H	BB	SO
Gunderson, Kevin, Oregon State	6	2	2.72	22	3	50	32	16	38
Kennedy, Ian, Southern California	7	2	2.91	16	1	93	86	31	120
O'Hagan, David, Stanford	6	2	2.97	22	6	58	39	22	58
#Swanson, Matt, California	3	2	2.97	30	1	39	39	13	24
Ingram, Jesse, California	0	3	3.02	30	10	51	58	20	49
Janssen, Casey, UCLA	10	4	3.16	17	0	117	87	30	103
Zinicola, Zechry, Arizona State	4	2	3.36	25	8	56	52	20	57
Urquidez, Jason, Arizona State	12	3	3.41	19	0	98	90	47	94
Lincecum, Tim, Washington	10	3	3.53	20	0	112	83	82	161
Postlewait, Jake, Oregon State	11	3	3.72	15	0	94	92	37	55
Parker, Kyle, Washington	4	3	3.84	18	0	75	59	55	58
Mousser, Jeff, Arizona State	6	4	3.94	17	0	89	82	42	42
Baysinger, Trent, Washington	3	4	4.12	29	1	74	83	19	55
Trolia, Aaron, Washington State	6	5	4.25	16	1	78	75	34	66
Romanczuk, Mark, Stanford	11	3	4.31	17	0	109	112	39	94
Melancon, Mark, Arizona	6	4	4.33	29	3	62	57	19	46
Holler, Blake, Stanford	4	2	4.34	22	2	58	62	23	49
Gilmore, Jeff, Stanford	10	2	4.43	19	1	108	106	24	77
Johnson, David, UCLA	4	3	4.46	21	0	69	67	30	46
Gold, Adam, California	6	7	4.47	16	0	95	110	36	89
Meloan, John, Arizona	10	0	4.66	18	0	93	97	45	77
Kolberg, Koley, Arizona	9	7	4.70	25	2	149	183	70	123
Padgett, Mike, California	5	5	4.74	16	1	76	89	25	47
Wentworth, Clayton, So. California	6	2	4.80	28	0	60	71	29	61
MacKenzie, Aaron, Wash. State	6	8	4.82	17	1	108	109	36	64
Buck, Dallas, Oregon State	3	6	5.06	21	6	69	73	30	57
Baldwin, Andy, Oregon State	5	5	5.10	16	0	65	83	27	46
Alwert, Garrett, Wash. State	4	3	5.17	20	3	77	98	14	59
Averill, Erik, Arizona State	4	4	5.19	26	2	76	83	23	56
Whisler, Wes, UCLA	3	5	5.24	16	0	93	103	35	60

PATRIOT LEAGUE

	Conference		Overall	
	W	L	W	L
*Army	17	3	37	15
Lafayette	11	9	23	26
Lehigh	9	11	25	21
Holy Cross	9	11	14	22
Bucknell	7	13	20	24
Navy	7	13	14	36

ALL-CONFERENCE TEAM: C—Schuyler Williamson, Jr., Army. 1B—Jared Munde, So., Navy. 2B—Nate Stone, Jr., Army. 3B—Jesse Novalis, Sr., Lehigh. SS—Eric Hoffman, Sr., Lehigh. OF—Jason Boyd, Sr., Lafayette; Adam Rosenberg, Sr., Lafayette; Kyle Walter, So., Bucknell. DH—Frank Cortazar, Jr., Lafayette; Pete Wolf, Sr., Bucknell. SP—Nick Hill, Fr., Army; Justin Kashner, Jr., Army. RP—Burgess Nichols, Fr., Navy.
Co-Players of the Year: Adam Rosenberg, Lafayette; Schuyler Williamson, Army. Pitcher of the Year: Nick Hill, Army. Freshman of the Year: Milan Dinga, Army. Coach of the Year: Joe Sottolano, Army.

INDIVIDUAL BATTING LEADERS
(Minimum 100 At-Bats)

	AVG	AB	R	H	2B	3B	HR	RBI	SB
Stone, Nate, Army	.414	181	47	75	18	0	6	53	11
Boyd, Jason, Lafayette	.374	187	48	70	14	7	9	41	14
Walter, Kyle, Bucknell	.372	156	31	58	12	5	7	25	2
Rosenberg, Adam, Lafayette	.368	185	43	68	12	1	9	56	11
McBride, Matt, Lehigh	.366	172	36	63	20	1	3	35	2
Williamson, Schuyler, Army	.357	199	52	71	12	4	12	48	18
Bumgardner, Wes, Army	.356	149	37	53	8	5	1	21	7
Marron, Mike, Holy Cross	.346	107	13	37	3	0	0	8	4
Mahony, Chris, Bucknell	.339	127	13	43	3	1	0	22	5
Stache, Jeremy, Army	.330	185	31	61	5	2	1	37	12
Frawley, Tucker, Holy Cross	.328	137	24	45	8	0	1	20	4
Long, Justin, Army	.326	181	27	59	13	1	3	30	6
Zaszewski, John, Lehigh	.324	173	35	56	9	2	4	28	7
Dinga, Milan, Army	.323	192	51	62	9	4	2	36	3
Stoll, Ben, Bucknell	.319	160	28	51	7	2	0	18	12
Novalis, Jesse, Lehigh	.317	161	40	51	9	2	5	30	6
Wolf, Pete, Bucknell	.315	149	23	47	7	0	0	22	2
Hirschberg, Brian, Bucknell	.305	128	19	39	9	2	4	17	0
#Candeto, Craig, Navy	.276	196	29	54	7	3	3	19	20

INDIVIDUAL PITCHING LEADERS
(Minimum 40 Innings)

	W	L	ERA	G	SV	IP	H	BB	SO
Kashner, Justin, Army	7	3	2.57	13	0	77	85	22	48
Hill, Nick, Army	10	3	2.60	13	0	87	64	24	81
Greenlee, Wade, Army	4	0	2.78	19	2	45	44	2	29
Daley, Matt, Bucknell	6	2	2.82	8	0	51	33	10	49
#Mittag, Nathan, Bucknell	1	1	2.87	16	5	38	33	12	21
Miller, Matt, Holy Cross	4	2	3.20	8	0	51	59	14	29
Bigda, Drew, Holy Cross	2	4	3.24	7	0	42	41	14	29
Revelle, Matt, Lafayette	3	4	3.30	17	0	46	56	16	27
Bumgardner, Wes, Army	2	1	3.45	10	1	47	53	20	19
Muscalus, Jack, Lehigh	7	3	3.48	15	0	78	69	25	57
Soldan, Tom, Lafayette	4	4	3.52	11	0	64	68	15	41
Nichols, Burgess, Navy	2	0	3.54	18	4	48	50	12	24
Miller, Kevin, Bucknell	2	5	3.73	9	0	60	61	23	54
Hefner, Ryan, Navy	3	6	3.90	12	0	60	73	14	31
Fischetti, Paul, Lafayette	4	5	3.93	14	0	55	55	21	49
#Koessler, Joe, Navy	2	4	6.47	27	2	32	59	9	19

SOUTHEASTERN CONFERENCE

	Conference		Overall	
EAST	W	L	W	L
Georgia	19	11	45	23
*South Carolina	17	13	53	17
Florida	17	13	43	22
Vanderbilt	16	14	45	19
Tennessee	14	16	38	24
Kentucky	7	23	24	30
WEST	W	L	W	L
Arkansas	19	11	45	24
Louisiana State	18	12	46	19
Mississippi	18	12	39	21
Mississippi State	13	17	35	24
Auburn	12	18	32	24
Alabama	10	20	29	26

ALL-CONFERENCE TEAM: C—Landon Powell, Sr., South Carolina. 1B—C.J. Smith, Jr., Florida. 2B—Warner Jones, So., Vanderbilt. 3B—Josh Smith, Jr., Georgia. SS—Ryan Klosterman, Jr., Vanderbilt. OF—Brad Corley, So., Mississippi State; J.C. Holt, Jr., Louisiana State; Jon Zeringue, Jr., Louisiana State. DH—Stephen Head, So., Mississippi. SP—Mark Holliman, So., Mississippi; Justin Hoyman, Jr., Florida. RP—Chad Blackwell, Jr., South Carolina; Will Startup, So., Georgia.
Co-Players of the Year: Stephen Head, Mississippi; Jon Zeringue, Louisiana State. Pitcher of the Year: Justin Hoyman, Florida. Freshman of the Year: Wade LeBlanc, Alabama. Coaches of the Year: David Perno, Georgia; Dave Van Horn, Arkansas.

INDIVIDUAL BATTING LEADERS
(Minimum 125 At-Bats)

	AVG	AB	R	H	2B	3B	HR	RBI	SB
Jones, Warner, Vanderbilt	.414	268	55	111	27	3	11	74	12
Holt, J.C., Louisiana State	.393	270	71	106	19	3	6	52	21
Zeringue, Jon, Louisiana State	.384	255	56	98	19	2	12	57	3
Corley, Brad, Mississippi State	.380	245	60	93	12	2	19	55	4
Harrison, Ben, Florida	.353	238	67	84	14	0	17	71	7
Head, Stephen, Mississippi	.346	228	41	79	13	1	13	53	0
Klosterman, Ryan, Vanderbilt	.346	263	72	91	15	8	7	33	16
Pearce, Steve, South Carolina	.346	266	60	92	18	0	21	70	4
Gill, Blake, Louisiana State	.343	236	42	81	11	4	5	42	3
Patterson, Ryan, Louisiana State	.341	293	70	100	23	2	14	67	6
Smith, C.J., Florida	.341	255	63	87	16	3	14	64	7
Nicolas, Cesar, Vanderbilt	.336	235	44	79	18	1	15	70	0
Rice, Allen, Alabama	.333	183	39	61	9	3	1	29	11
Holmes, Justin, Georgia	.332	247	59	82	14	3	8	56	18
Graeter, Spencer, Kentucky	.332	202	42	67	11	2	4	32	1
Grace, Billy, Kentucky	.331	136	30	45	11	1	5	34	2
Suarez, Alex, Tennessee	.330	182	33	60	15	0	3	32	4
Powell, Landon, South Carolina	.330	270	66	89	17	1	19	66	2
Harris, Will, Louisiana State	.329	173	38	57	9	0	7	39	0
Stewart, Caleb, Kentucky	.329	219	50	72	20	3	10	37	4
Thomas, Clete, Auburn	.329	216	53	71	16	6	4	45	24
Liuzza, Matt, Louisiana State	.328	229	37	75	14	0	9	45	0
Breyman, Mike, Kentucky	.326	193	42	63	16	2	9	44	1
Tatum, Craig, Mississippi State	.325	237	42	77	16	0	13	60	0
Gregg, Dave, South Carolina	.325	228	33	74	11	1	0	26	14
Bush, Evan, Alabama	.324	176	35	57	12	0	8	31	1
Rea, Jeffrey, Mississippi State	.324	244	50	79	13	3	2	32	11
Iorg, Eli, Tennessee	.324	238	47	77	10	6	4	36	26
Stavinoha, Nick, Louisiana State	.323	232	46	75	17	1	8	42	3
Gunther, Barry, Mississippi	.323	164	26	53	11	1	2	28	2
Corsaletti, Jeff, Florida	.323	251	47	81	12	2	5	43	11
Scelfo, Rocky, Alabama	.322	149	22	48	10	1	1	27	5

	AVG	AB	R	H	2B	3B	HR	RBI	SB
Baxter, Mike, Vanderbilt	.322	258	34	83	8	3	2	38	13
Davis, Adam, Florida	.320	253	68	81	11	3	6	24	22
Morris, Josh, Georgia	.319	238	47	76	16	1	16	71	5
Goodwin, Clay, Arkansas	.319	226	49	72	13	0	4	32	4
Jeroloman, Brian, Florida	.318	151	22	48	4	0	1	27	1
Tolleson, Steven, So. Carolina	.316	196	40	62	14	1	4	25	7
Smith, Josh, Georgia	.314	261	62	82	16	2	3	40	4
Norrid, Kyle, Tennessee	.313	224	36	70	20	0	2	32	1
Campbell, Michael, So. Carolina	.312	269	45	84	14	2	14	52	7
Leclerc, Brian, Florida	.312	173	28	54	13	2	6	37	0
Presley, Alex, Mississippi	.311	196	34	61	11	6	6	32	9
Hunter, Joseph, Miss. State	.311	180	29	56	8	1	3	39	1
Pratt, Haas, Arkansas	.310	258	38	80	13	0	8	52	1
Szabo, Marshall, Georgia	.307	267	45	82	17	3	6	41	5
Hulett, Tug, Auburn	.306	206	43	63	12	1	0	23	2
Pettway, Brian, Mississippi	.305	203	41	62	11	0	6	31	0
Welch, Zac, Alabama	.305	190	37	58	14	1	7	46	0
Winn, Brendan, South Carolina	.305	259	60	79	18	3	19	69	5
Hamblin, Danny, Arkansas	.304	253	53	77	19	1	8	42	10
Gendron, Steve, Miss. State	.304	263	41	80	16	1	4	36	6
Parker, Blake, Arkansas	.303	165	23	50	7	0	0	21	4
Bertram, Michael, Kentucky	.303	175	36	53	10	1	1	30	1
Tordi, Justin, Florida	.302	235	36	71	14	0	4	41	5
Coghlan, Chris, Mississippi	.302	199	40	60	11	2	2	24	3
#Richardson, Antoan, Vanderbilt	.266	207	51	55	9	4	3	30	32

INDIVIDUAL PITCHING LEADERS
(Minimum 50 Innings)

	W	L	ERA	G	SV	IP	H	BB	SO
Goodner, Boyd, Arkansas	3	3	1.50	32	0	60	55	16	46
Tankersley, Taylor, Alabama	2	5	2.00	20	4	68	50	26	70
Tharpe, Derek, Tennessee	6	1	2.01	13	0	81	66	19	84
LeBlanc, Wade, Alabama	8	4	2.08	16	0	113	87	26	98
Startup, Will, Georgia	7	2	2.22	33	12	81	55	23	70
O'Day, Darren, Florida	8	1	2.56	26	5	60	64	10	39
Blackwell, Chad, South Carolina	4	3	2.57	37	20	63	52	14	80
Mullins, Ryan, Vanderbilt	9	3	2.58	17	0	112	104	20	98
Drucker, Scot, Tennessee	8	3	2.61	32	5	59	49	19	65
Hoyman, Justin, Florida	11	2	2.71	19	0	140	116	38	89
Faircloth, Jordan, Louisiana State	3	3	2.79	26	4	58	54	13	41
Wright, Brae, Mississippi	6	2	2.81	10	0	67	71	13	49
Head, Stephen, Mississippi	6	3	2.82	17	5	70	68	19	56
Buschmann, Matt, Vanderbilt	8	1	2.84	27	2	82	80	29	61
Hochevar, Luke, Tennessee	4	2	2.86	11	0	63	52	23	60
Hyle, Michael, Georgia	8	2	2.99	16	0	87	87	32	55
Campbell, Matt, South Carolina	10	6	3.05	22	0	124	99	38	145
Holliman, Mark, Mississippi	9	3	3.05	16	0	106	101	35	101
Sowers, Jeremy, Vanderbilt	10	6	3.08	19	0	123	105	26	119
McCamie, Zac, South Carolina	7	0	3.10	21	0	58	48	10	49
Boyce, Charley, Arkansas	10	3	3.20	22	1	115	119	22	81
Hempy, Arik, South Carolina	3	1	3.27	25	1	52	38	14	49
Buckner, Billy, South Carolina	7	2	3.32	15	0	84	77	23	105
Falkenborn, Connor, Florida	10	7	3.34	35	3	127	130	12	81
Sawatski, Jay, Arkansas	10	3	3.38	31	7	93	104	24	86
Fletcher, Jason, South Carolina	6	1	3.40	18	1	56	50	13	59
Ruthven, Sean, Georgia	7	2	3.41	20	0	90	70	35	91
Dirks, Clay, Louisiana State	8	2	3.43	17	1	81	83	17	66
Cobb, Craig, Tennessee	3	5	3.45	21	1	70	64	21	40
Lewis, Jensen, Vanderbilt	6	4	3.49	23	2	80	77	28	69
Mestepey, Lane, Louisiana State	7	4	3.51	20	0	100	117	28	42
Cupps, Anthony, Mississippi	3	4	3.41	20	1	66	67	25	49
Walker, Andrew, Alabama	4	1	3.71	14	0	53	54	12	51
Brannon, Clint, Arkansas	4	4	3.76	20	0	105	112	30	73
Meier, Justin, Louisiana State	6	2	3.84	18	0	101	120	28	75
Hicklen, Patrick, Tennessee	4	3	3.90	20	1	58	54	22	52
Scott, Matt, Kentucky	5	4	3.96	32	2	61	73	20	39
Bumstead, Nate, Louisiana State	10	3	4.00	16	0	92	109	21	54
#Rawl, Aaron, South Carolina	13	4	4.28	20	0	122	135	17	98

SOUTHERN CONFERENCE

	Conference		Overall	
	W	L	W	L
College of Charleston	25	5	47	16
*The Citadel	21	9	39	28
Georgia Southern	21	9	34	25
Elon	17	13	31	28
UNC Greensboro	16	14	33	21
East Tennessee State	15	15	28	30
Davidson	13	17	20	33
Western Carolina	12	18	28	31
Furman	11	19	21	33
Wofford	8	22	17	30
Appalachian State	6	24	10	43

ALL-CONFERENCE TEAM: C—Caleb Moore, Jr., East Tennessee State. **1B**—Chip Cannon, Sr., The Citadel. **2B**—Gary Morris, Jr., Elon. **3B**—Jess Easterling, Jr., Charleston. **SS**—Andy Howdeshell, Sr., East Tennessee State. **OF**—Byron Barber, Jr., Charleston; Brett Gardner, Jr., Charleston; Brandon Long, Sr., Georgia Southern. **DH**—Grant Burruss, Sr., Georgia Southern. **SP**—Jonathan Ellis, Jr., The Citadel; Ryan Johnson, Sr., Charleston. **RP**—Brett Harker, So., Charleston.

Player of the Year: Caleb Moore, East Tennessee State. **Pitcher of the Year:** Ryan Johnson, Charleston. **Freshman of the Year:** Chris Campbell, Charleston. **Coach of the Year:** John Pawlowski, Charleston.

INDIVIDUAL BATTING LEADERS
(Minimum 125 At-Bats)

	AVG	AB	R	H	2B	3B	HR	RBI	SB
Moore, Caleb, E. Tenn. State	.455	202	59	92	31	1	9	45	1
Barber, Byron, Charleston	.410	261	63	107	11	3	0	58	25
Gardner, Brett, Charleston	.397	237	57	94	12	9	4	51	22
Long, Brandon, Ga. Southern	.383	230	58	88	12	1	8	43	9
Cassedy, Case, Furman	.381	147	32	56	12	1	6	32	5
Morris, Gary, Elon	.379	232	64	88	17	1	7	36	21
Coker, Phillip, Charleston	.377	252	75	95	21	1	2	37	15
Gordon, Ryan, UNC Greensboro	.374	182	37	68	12	6	6	34	11
Dowling, Greg, Ga. Southern	.370	243	51	90	17	1	9	66	6
McGowan, Mike, West. Carolina	.362	130	21	47	14	0	3	31	1
Cannon, Chip, Citadel	.358	232	69	83	20	2	17	66	3
Howdeshell, Andy, E. Tenn. St.	.355	217	57	77	18	0	11	48	18
Hurst, Jason, Ga. Southern	.354	127	32	45	11	1	5	30	4
Church, Blake, E. Tenn. St.	.353	207	40	73	15	0	8	53	0
Easterling, Jess, Charleston	.353	207	58	73	15	1	5	53	7
Davis, Drew, Elon	.351	231	48	81	16	3	6	51	14
Payne, James, Ga. Southern	.344	253	65	87	11	1	0	18	21
Hastings, Brian, Charleston	.343	137	28	47	6	0	0	17	5
Rembert, Grant, Elon	.340	250	47	85	24	2	7	60	5
Greenwood, Jared, W. Carolina	.338	219	58	74	21	1	21	63	2
Valencia, Danny, UNC G'boro	.338	222	39	75	16	1	8	36	1
Campbell, Chris, Charleston	.332	217	42	72	22	3	5	63	5
Byrne, Shane, E. Tenn. St.	.330	230	51	76	13	5	6	39	13
Betsill, Matthew, Furman	.330	191	41	63	13	2	6	34	7
Anderson, Brett, Charleston	.328	201	66	66	12	1	16	61	6
Entrekin, Alex, Davidson	.328	198	24	65	8	0	2	32	2
Aughey, Jon, Citadel	.324	253	62	82	15	2	9	43	23
Davidiuk, A.J., Furman	.324	207	35	67	12	2	5	22	5
Economos, Mike, Ga. Southern	.323	161	28	52	7	1	3	25	6
McLain, Sam, Furman	.323	127	20	41	9	1	5	28	2
Sigmon, Brian, West. Carolina	.321	218	36	70	18	1	6	41	4
Burruss, Grant, Ga. Southern	.320	228	49	73	11	0	13	61	12
Lee, Justin, Appalachian State	.319	188	37	60	16	0	6	30	2
Stevens, Tyler, Elon	.317	224	37	71	10	0	5	47	7
Norton, Joe, Appalachian State	.314	185	32	58	9	3	5	25	8
Davis, Chris, Western Carolina	.312	240	43	75	18	1	8	36	6
Shore, Ronnie, Davidson	.312	186	28	58	9	1	0	20	8
Benefield, Eli, Davidson	.308	211	30	65	12	1	3	25	3
Erickson, Evan, Elon	.303	201	41	61	17	2	5	36	4
Ard, Chris, Citadel	.302	268	51	81	11	1	0	43	16
Roper, Todd, Western Caro.	.301	249	60	75	13	3	2	30	6
Mason, Chris, UNC Greensboro	.301	136	16	41	8	2	3	25	4
Covington, Matt, Citadel	.300	203	41	61	11	3	1	31	4
Tartaglia, Evan, Elon	.300	210	49	63	9	7	0	22	23

INDIVIDUAL PITCHING LEADERS
(Minimum 50 Innings)

	W	L	ERA	G	SV	IP	H	BB	SO
Ellis, Jonathan, Citadel	12	3	2.18	18	0	136	112	39	131
Mason, Chris, UNC Greensboro	4	1	2.36	13	0	53	45	20	46
Lairsey, Josh, Georgia Southern	4	1	3.09	14	0	64	57	20	48
Price, Reid, Charleston	7	4	3.20	16	0	101	92	39	84
Akin, Brian, Davidson	8	3	3.30	14	0	101	87	30	95
Johnson, Ryan, Charleston	12	0	3.40	14	0	87	101	20	58
Falcon, Ryan, UNC Greensboro	2	6	3.52	21	1	87	82	17	86
Chigges, Nick, Charleston	5	1	3.56	30	3	61	60	31	53
Edell, Ryan, Charleston	8	2	3.67	19	1	88	88	36	87
Carroll, John, Georgia Southern	7	4	3.79	16	1	112	122	12	90
Michael, Scooter, UNC Greensboro	9	1	3.90	14	0	81	84	19	69
Harker, Brett, Charleston	5	3	3.91	33	13	51	51	23	59
Santos, Jarrett, UNC Greensboro	9	3	3.92	34	5	87	91	22	61
Harrison, Brian, Ga. Southern	7	6	4.01	29	9	85	93	22	77
Teaford, Everett, Ga. Southern	7	6	4.07	20	1	108	123	44	113
McConnell, Caleb, West. Carolina	2	2	4.39	16	0	82	84	17	63
Garner, Matt, Elon	6	6	4.29	16	1	80	78	33	78
Beckham, Griff, Citadel	3	5	4.37	24	0	68	80	19	49
Piccola, Zach, Charleston	4	4	4.37	16	0	56	51	37	43
Cole, Lance, Elon	6	2	4.43	16	0	85	91	27	46
Egleton, Ken, Citadel	4	3	4.50	17	0	100	103	39	96
McSwain, Matt, Elon	4	4	4.57	17	0	65	66	39	72
Cannon, Chip, Citadel	5	4	4.59	17	0	98	126	24	69
Josey, Brad, Western Carolina	5	5	4.63	17	0	101	128	17	66

SOUTHLAND CONFERENCE

	Conference		Overall	
	W	L	W	L
*Lamar	18	8	41	16
Northwestern State	16	9	33	23
Texas State	16	10	32	26
Texas-Arlington	14	13	32	26
Louisiana-Monroe	12	14	30	28
Texas-San Antonio	12	14	27	31
Sam Houston State	11	14	19	30
McNeese State	11	16	24	29
Southeastern Louisiana	11	16	17	39
Nicholls State	9	16	20	29

ALL-CONFERENCE TEAM: C—Andrew Kasparek, Sr., Sam Houston State. **1B**—Ben Jones, Jr., Louisiana-Monroe. **2B**—Brandon Morgan, So., Northwestern State. **3B**—Tigger Lyles, Sr. Northwestern State. **SS**—Ryan Crew, So., Texas-San Antonio. **OF**—Josh Boop, Sr., Northwestern State; Hunter Pence, Jr., Texas-Arlington; Evan Tierce, Sr., Texas State. **DH**—Darrell Preston, Sr., Texas-Arlington. **P**—Michael Gardner, So., Texas-Arlington; Kyle Stutes, Sr., Lamar; Clayton Turner, Jr., Northwestern State.
Player of the Year/Hitter of the Year: Hunter Pence, Texas-Arlington. **Pitcher of the Year:** Kyle Stutes, Lamar. **Newcomer of the Year:** Matt Miller, Texas State. **Freshman of the Year:** Derrick Gordon, Lamar. **Coach of the Year:** Jim Gilligan, Lamar.

INDIVIDUAL BATTING LEADERS
(Minimum 125 At-Bats)

	AVG	AB	R	H	2B	3B	HR	RBI	SB
Pence, Hunter, Texas-Arlington ..	.395	190	47	75	8	5	8	35	10
Miller, Matt, Texas State	.387	238	49	92	18	2	8	52	5
Morgan, Brandon, NW State	.381	197	48	75	18	2	2	41	21
Hatch, Anthony, Nicholls State ..	.379	195	47	74	14	1	8	33	12
Kasparek, Andrew, Sam Houston	.365	156	26	57	10	0	4	28	0
Foster, Jordan, Lamar	.363	215	51	78	13	0	9	44	11
Preston, Darrell, Texas-Arlington	.362	185	27	67	16	0	3	31	5
Baker, Kasey, Texas-Arlington	.351	242	52	85	21	4	5	26	6
Craigen, Rocky, Lamar	.351	154	32	54	11	1	3	19	3
LaBorde, Justin, La.-Monroe	.350	183	34	64	16	1	6	52	2
Todesco, Lee, Texas-SA	.348	132	25	46	16	1	5	20	0
Tierce, Evan, Texas State	.343	251	54	86	17	4	5	39	20
Jones, Ben, Louisiana-Monroe ..	.338	216	48	73	17	0	14	58	2
Cooper, Mark, Texas State	.336	229	40	77	16	1	9	53	0
Lyles, Tigger, NW State	.330	194	44	64	12	2	6	34	27
Bell, Bubba, Nicholls State	.330	194	31	64	12	1	3	35	10
Boop, Josh, NW State	.329	219	54	72	10	1	3	42	29
Kingrey, Charlie, McNeese St. ..	.328	186	35	61	14	3	6	34	1
Stone, Jonathan, Sam Houston ..	.324	145	28	47	11	0	9	50	0
Tano, David, Nicholls State	.322	180	33	58	12	3	4	30	9
Jackson, Glenn, La.-Monroe	.325	206	57	67	8	4	3	19	23
Fontenot, Chris, McNeese St. ...	.319	163	30	52	10	6	3	29	8
Bruder, Paul, Texas-Arlington ...	.318	217	37	69	11	2	5	40	2
Roth, Randy, SE Louisiana	.317	189	27	60	14	0	2	22	3
Jones, Aaron, Texas State	.317	139	25	44	7	0	3	27	8
Rollinson, Ty, Louisiana-Monroe .	.315	165	29	52	5	1	4	15	7
Crew, Ryan, Texas-San Antonio ..	.310	245	41	76	14	2	9	37	7
Aulds, Jay, Louisiana-Monroe	.310	174	34	54	14	2	1	23	2
Fontenot, Josh, McNeese St.	.308	156	20	48	9	2	1	20	1
Ritchie, Jake, Nicholls State	.306	160	30	49	8	1	9	30	4
Allen, John, Lamar	.303	201	28	61	20	1	6	38	2
Nelson, Ryan, Texas-Arlington	.302	202	34	61	12	0	8	38	3
LaBorde, Lane, La.-Monroe	.301	166	29	50	5	3	4	23	2
Thoms, Hunter, NW State	.300	213	34	64	15	0	1	54	6
#Lewis, Chris, Texas-SA	.279	204	45	57	10	0	16	44	5

INDIVIDUAL PITCHING LEADERS
(Minimum 50 Innings)

	W	L	ERA	G	SV	IP	H	BB	SO
Snapp, Mike, Texas-Arlington	5	4	1.42	36	12	51	37	10	40
Gordon, Derrick, Lamar	7	3	1.92	18	0	66	44	35	54
Delage, William, Lamar	6	0	2.00	14	0	72	53	31	68
Gardner, Michael, Texas-Arlington	11	3	2.49	16	0	105	84	33	77
Stutes, Kyle, Lamar	10	2	2.49	24	3	90	76	21	84
Harris, Josh, Lamar	3	1	3.04	19	2	53	44	22	48
Colgan, Patrick, Texas State	2	2	3.17	16	1	54	58	21	46
Gultz, Michael, Texas State	5	0	3.29	28	0	55	48	19	31
Robbins, Tom, Texas State	8	6	3.34	18	0	113	105	40	81
Dorton, Russell, NW State	5	3	3.41	17	0	61	62	21	44
Turner, Clayton, NW State	10	3	3.50	16	0	100	87	42	103
Lonsbery, Daniel, NW State	5	7	3.69	16	0	95	92	34	83
Lowe, Mark, Texas-Arlington	1	4	3.74	22	3	53	54	19	48
Pierson, Blake, Texas-Arlington ...	3	1	3.99	25	0	50	50	16	22
Story, Rodney, SE Louisiana	3	6	4.14	17	1	78	83	31	50
St. Germain, Risley, SE Louisiana ...	3	4	4.17	23	5	54	55	32	53

Vander Weg, Scott, Lamar	5	4	4.19	23	1	58	58	27	58
Hebert, Robbie, Nicholls State	3	5	4.20	15	0	84	89	37	67
Craig, Dustin, Sam Houston St.	4	4	4.25	29	3	66	74	33	64
Denton, Chris, McNeese State	5	5	4.32	20	1	94	105	16	84
Stewart, Lucas, Texas-San Antonio .	4	3	4.36	17	3	54	57	19	19
Pendarvis, Chad, SE Louisiana	5	7	4.43	21	1	65	62	30	39
Begnaud, Rusty, McNeese State	6	5	4.44	17	0	93	102	25	75

SOUTHWESTERN ATHLETIC CONFERENCE

EAST	Conference		Overall	
	W	L	W	L
Mississippi Valley State	23	9	35	23
Jackson State	19	9	29	20
Alcorn State	13	17	20	22
Alabama State	11	19	18	33
Alabama A&M	8	20	13	32
WEST	W	L	W	L
Southern	19	7	26	14
*Texas Southern	15	13	19	35
Prairie View A&M	17	15	30	26
Arkansas-Pine Bluff	15	15	18	29
Grambling State	6	22	11	35

ALL-CONFERENCE TEAM: C—Ralph Johnson, Sr., Jackson State. **1B**—Nathan Purvis, Sr., Mississippi Valley State. **2B**—Corey Wimberley, Fr., Alcorn State. **3B**—Andrew Toussaint, Sr., Southern. **SS**—Mark Lewis, Jr., Arkansas-Pine Bluff. **OF**—James Cooper, Sr., Grambling State; B.J. Lange, Jr., Jackson State; Marcus Townsend, Sr., Southern. **DH**—Ricky Thomas, Fr., Prairie View A&M. **P**—Steve Acuna, Jr., Mississippi Valley State; Jose Pena, Jr., Southern.
Player of the Year/Outstanding Hitter: B.J. Lange, Jackson State. **Outstanding Pitcher:** Jose Pena, Southern. **Newcomer of the Year:** Corey Wimberley, Alcorn State.

INDIVIDUAL BATTING LEADERS
(Minimum 100 At-Bats)

	AVG	AB	R	H	2B	3B	HR	RBI	SB
Lange, B.J., Jackson State	.439	164	50	72	17	2	3	55	29
Wimberley, Corey, Alcorn St.	.420	150	52	63	8	3	0	24	40
Cooper, James, Grambling St.	.393	163	34	64	16	9	4	39	13
Nichols, Brian, Alabama State	.392	143	33	56	16	0	7	45	1
Carter, Byron, Prairie View	.389	175	41	68	22	0	5	52	6
Toussaint, Andrew, Southern	.384	146	53	56	8	4	14	54	7
Browne, Thomas, Jackson St.	.380	100	23	38	9	4	0	26	15
Purvis, Nathan, Miss. Valley St. ..	.378	127	33	48	14	0	4	30	3
LeBlanc, Joshua, Southern	.376	117	47	44	11	8	7	31	6
Miller, Gerald, Prairie View	.369	149	38	55	10	2	5	34	13
Lipsey, Carl, Jackson State	.364	151	62	55	11	1	1	27	49
Washington, Stephen, Pr. View	.356	180	53	64	14	2	9	54	17
Johnson, Ralph, Jackson State	.356	149	34	53	14	3	5	40	16
Thomas, Rickey, Prairie View	.351	171	45	60	13	1	9	53	4
Lomack, Jermel, Prairie View	.332	199	56	66	13	1	0	25	35
Wright, Aaron, Ark.-Pine Bluff	.331	118	20	39	11	1	3	25	6
Deleon, Mario, Texas Southern	.328	189	40	62	12	6	5	39	9
Penprase, Zach, Miss. Valley St. ..	.327	156	30	51	13	4	1	19	3
Nelson, Kevin, Southern	.326	141	34	46	4	2	5	45	7
Vaughn, Joseph, Prairie View	.324	185	58	60	20	2	7	37	7
Childress, Tyron, Alabama A&M	.322	121	14	39	8	0	0	27	2
Allen, Ashley, Alabama State	.322	171	45	55	9	0	1	21	11
Hall, Alvin, Alabama A&M	.322	121	25	39	8	6	2	23	5
Shinhoster, Anton, Jackson St.	.321	156	40	50	8	3	2	35	16
Ellison, Damian, Alabama A&M	.319	135	27	43	10	2	4	22	5
White, Earl, Ark.-Pine Bluff	.318	154	30	49	5	7	3	24	7
Hughley, DeCarlos, Alabama St. ...	.317	161	31	51	6	0	2	27	4
Clarke, Jermaine, Alcorn State	.316	117	25	37	6	1	3	33	7

INDIVIDUAL PITCHING LEADERS
(Minimum 40 Innings)

	W	L	ERA	G	SV	IP	H	BB	SO
Pena, Jose, Southern	8	0	2.64	11	0	48	35	9	28
Shack, Jermaine, Miss. Valley St. ..	10	4	3.10	14	0	87	73	23	77
#Cunha, Andrew, Miss. Valley St. ...	1	2	3.49	18	6	28	22	9	35
Vaughn, Jarred, Jackson State	6	4	3.56	13	0	68	65	33	49
#Quarles, Jason, Southern	1	1	3.60	21	2	20	19	14	33
Sam, Charles, Alcorn State	4	1	4.15	11	0	48	62	14	19
Daniels, Issac, Texas Southern	6	4	4.17	19	0	71	63	37	70
Acuna, Steve, Miss. Valley St.	6	2	4.43	17	0	61	62	18	43
Williams, Chad, Miss. Valley St.	5	5	4.50	14	1	58	52	17	58
Chatwin, Matt, Alcorn State	1	2	4.72	21	5	40	45	14	26
Clarke, Jermaine, Alcorn State	4	4	4.78	8	0	49	56	28	25
Poret, Corey, Southern	4	4	5.32	10	0	44	44	21	42
Law, Darrell, Grambling State	2	5	5.32	13	1	44	43	20	48
Stokely, Omar, Jackson State	2	4	5.53	15	1	54	54	40	34
Stricklen, Brandon, Tx. Southern	2	4	5.56	13	1	58	66	32	49

Coleman, Samuel, Alabama A&M 0 5 5.63 10 0 40 55 19 20
Stovall, Jonathan, Miss. Valley St. ... 5 2 5.82 15 0 51 72 10 33

SUN BELT CONFERENCE

	Conference		Overall	
	W	**L**	**W**	**L**
Middle Tennessee State	16	8	40	22
South Alabama	16	8	30	28
New Orleans	13	10	27	28
Louisiana-Lafayette	11	11	34	23
New Mexico State	12	12	33	25
*Western Kentucky	12	12	35	27
Florida International	12	12	29	33
Arkansas State	8	15	29	28
Arkansas-Little Rock	6	18	16	32

ALL-CONFERENCE TEAM: C—Kody Valverde, So., New Orleans. **1B**—Billy Becher, Sr., New Mexico State. **2B**—Eric McNamee, Jr., Middle Tennessee State. **3B**—Tim Grogan, So., Western Kentucky. **SS**—Jeff Beachum, So., Middle Tennessee State. **OF**—Matt Gunning, Sr., Western Kentucky; Adam Lind, So., South Alabama; Yahmed Yema, So., Florida International. **DH**—Justin Bourque, Sr., Louisiana-Lafayette. **UT**—Derek Phillips, Sr., Middle Tennessee State. **SP**—Thomas Diamond, Jr., New Orleans; Chris Mobley, Jr., Middle Tennessee State. **RP**—Travis Trammell, Sr., Arkansas-Little Rock.
Player of the Year: Matt Gunning, Western Kentucky. **Pitcher of the Year:** Thomas Diamond, New Orleans. **Newcomer of the Year:** Xardiel Cotto, New Mexico State. **Freshman of the Year:** P.J. Walters, South Alabama. **Coach of the Year:** Steve Peterson, Middle Tennessee State.

INDIVIDUAL BATTING LEADERS
(Minimum 125 At-Bats)

	AVG	AB	R	H	2B	3B	HR	RBI	SB
Lind, Adam, South Alabama	.392	232	57	91	22	2	12	60	8
Hayes, Brad, Arkansas State	.386	171	33	66	18	0	10	47	5
Phillips, Derek, Middle Tenn. St.	.380	187	28	71	14	1	9	41	2
Cotto, Xardiel, New Mexico St.	.379	224	72	85	12	4	11	57	8
Gunning, Matt, Western Ky.	.375	264	55	99	23	0	15	73	3
Morris, Dallas, La.-Lafayette	.373	150	41	56	9	5	12	51	8
Rio, Dominic, Western Kentucky	.372	172	29	64	8	0	3	26	2
McNamee, Eric, Middle Tenn. St.	.364	236	71	86	11	2	3	24	7
Merendino, Justin, La.-Lafayette	.348	210	56	73	21	2	7	35	13
Aranda, Mark, New Mexico St.	.346	188	51	65	14	2	16	57	0
Yema, Yahmed, Fla. International	.343	169	45	58	13	1	9	30	9
Pietro, Joe, New Orleans	.342	158	29	54	6	2	2	9	15
Skellenger, Jeff, Fla. International	.342	158	24	54	5	0	9	30	3
Burkhead, Brad, Arkansas State	.337	178	44	60	10	3	12	35	3
Aragon, Brian, Fla. International	.336	152	23	51	8	0	8	32	4
Bourque, Justin, La.-Lafayette	.333	135	25	45	12	1	6	24	6
Grogan, Tim, Western Kentucky	.332	229	56	76	15	1	13	63	1
Rayborn, Jansen, South Alabama	.332	208	39	69	19	1	7	43	5
Preau, Kevin, La.-Lafayette	.331	130	19	43	9	2	5	21	3
Rich, Chris, Arkansas State	.330	212	39	70	20	1	9	53	0
Landry, Josh, La.-Lafayette	.330	221	46	73	12	4	3	31	8
Becher, Billy, New Mexico St.	.329	234	63	77	19	1	25	90	1
Hawke, Phillip, La.-Lafayette	.329	146	33	48	9	0	10	42	2
Beachum, Jeff, Middle Tenn. St.	.326	236	41	77	10	0	4	31	14
Sirianni, Mike, Arkansas State	.326	224	58	73	17	2	2	34	2
Hawarah, Justin, South Alabama	.326	187	28	61	15	0	1	31	0
Newton, Jordan, Western Ky.	.325	197	59	64	13	4	4	32	6
Secchiari, Clark, South Alabama	.324	176	38	57	7	1	1	12	5
Ballesteros, Adrian, New Mex. St.	.320	228	50	73	15	0	18	56	0
Haefele, Aaron, Ark.-Little Rock	.315	146	27	46	7	1	0	20	3
Becker, Chris, Ark.-Little Rock	.315	197	32	62	13	0	8	46	4
Runyan, Andy, Arkansas State	.310	155	16	48	9	2	1	16	3
Lehmann, P.J., Fla. International	.308	224	41	69	7	0	3	32	13
Lopez, Michael, Fla. International	.307	189	38	58	14	0	8	42	10
#Diaz, Dennis, Fla. International	.266	241	54	64	11	3	8	33	50

INDIVIDUAL PITCHING LEADERS
(Minimum 50 Innings)

	W	L	ERA	G	SV	IP	H	BB	SO
Green, Patrick, La.-Lafayette	6	2	2.12	15	1	51	35	10	55
Diamond, Thomas, New Orleans	6	4	2.38	17	0	114	87	45	138
Fry, Cody, Ark.-Little Rock	7	4	2.54	18	0	50	38	21	24
Hernandez, Danny, Fla. Int.	7	1	2.80	27	7	55	49	17	55
Hinchman, Grady, Western Ky.	7	5	3.00	20	0	105	78	71	114
Williams, John, Middle Tenn. St.	8	4	3.06	14	0	100	88	29	109
Ardoin, Kevin, La.-Lafayette	6	2	3.30	17	0	106	105	22	95
"Trammell, Travis, Ark.-L.R.	1	2	3.45	23	7	31	22	9	35
Tharp, Stephen, Arkansas State	4	2	3.71	29	2	77	89	15	63
Church, B.J., Middle Tenn. St.	5	1	3.81	10	0	52	45	14	58
Sanders, Brandt, La.-Lafayette	2	4	3.90	26	1	60	62	20	63
Mobley, Chris, Middle Tenn. St.	7	5	3.95	16	0	96	85	42	122

Walters, P.J., South Alabama | **10** | 1 | 4.23 | 21 | 2 | **117** | 124 | 38 | 119
Worrell, Mark, Fla. International | 2 | 9 | 4.25 | 19 | 0 | 85 | 86 | 43 | 107
Kline, Steve, Middle Tenn. St. | 2 | 2 | 4.29 | 20 | 5 | 57 | 64 | 17 | 57
Birely, Grant, New Orleans | 6 | 7 | 4.42 | **35** | 6 | 55 | 61 | 20 | 62
Asher, David, Fla. International | 3 | 5 | 4.43 | 15 | 0 | 81 | 94 | 26 | 67
Edwards, Andrew, Fla. Int. | 6 | 2 | 4.58 | 15 | 0 | 77 | 77 | 25 | 66
Pecoraro, Ian, La.-Lafayette | 4 | 2 | 4.67 | 12 | 0 | 54 | 49 | 36 | 47
Simmons, Jeramy, South Alabama | 9 | 4 | 4.76 | 17 | 0 | 98 | 103 | 40 | 106
Schambough, Kraig, La.-Lafayette | 6 | 4 | 5.23 | 23 | 3 | 72 | 86 | 18 | 57
Doan, Joey, South Alabama | 4 | 8 | 5.36 | 16 | 0 | 97 | 130 | 27 | 50
Faulkner, Daniel, Western Ky. | 8 | 6 | 5.37 | 18 | 2 | 112 | 124 | 41 | 78
Hamilton, Ryan, Arkansas State | 8 | 7 | 5.37 | 26 | 5 | 68 | 76 | 24 | 88
Cherry, Brad, Ark.-Little Rock | 2 | 7 | 5.43 | 15 | 0 | 68 | 80 | 37 | 57
Martinez, J.P., New Orleans | 7 | 3 | 5.47 | 19 | 1 | 100 | 104 | 45 | 110

WEST COAST CONFERENCE

COAST	Conference		Overall	
	W	**L**	**W**	**L**
Loyola Marymount	20	7	32	22
San Diego	19	11	35	21
Gonzaga	16	11	24	27
St. Mary's	7	23	14	41
WEST	**W**	**L**	**W**	**L**
*Pepperdine	19	11	30	32
Santa Clara	16	14	27	29
San Francisco	14	16	27	32
Portland	6	24	12	44

ALL-CONFERENCE TEAM: C—Kiel Thibault, So., Gonzaga. **1B**—Brent Lewis, Sr., Pepperdine. **2B**—David Uribes, So., Pepperdine. **3B**—Bobby Carlson, Jr., Gonzaga. **SS**—Jose Ortega, Sr., San Diego. **OF**—Tom Caple, Sr., San Diego; Ryan Chiarelli, Jr., Santa Clara; Joey Prast, Sr., San Diego. **DH**—Marshall Bratton, Sr., Gonzaga. **UT**—Steve Kleen, Jr., Pepperdine. **P**—Jacob Barrack, Sr., Pepperdine; Kyle Collins, Sr., San Diego; Stephen Kahn, So., Loyola Marymount.
Player of the Year: Kiel Thibault, Gonzaga. **Pitcher of the Year:** Stephen Kahn, Loyola Marymount. **Freshman of the Year:** Jordan Abruzzo, San Diego. **Coach of the Year:** Frank Cruz, Loyola Marymount.

INDIVIDUAL BATTING LEADERS
(Minimum 125 At-Bats)

	AVG	AB	R	H	2B	3B	HR	RBI	SB
Thibault, Kiel, Gonzaga	.424	205	44	87	11	3	3	35	8
Abruzzo, Jordan, San Diego	.375	208	50	78	14	0	9	49	3
Kleen, Steve, Pepperdine	.373	225	58	84	20	1	7	56	1
Higashi, Jon, Loyola Mary.	.371	205	39	76	13	0	4	48	4
Hansen, Josh, San Diego	.369	214	44	79	8	0	6	44	5
Ortega, Jose, San Diego	.364	187	36	68	10	0	0	31	6
Carlson, Bobby, Gonzaga	.362	127	21	46	15	0	8	44	0
Chiarelli, Ryan, Santa Clara	.361	133	31	48	7	0	1	15	4
Genung, Chris, San Francisco	.361	241	40	87	22	0	6	52	1
Vetters, Travis, Portland	.353	221	36	78	10	4	3	34	7
Gaerlan, Armand, San Francisco	.351	242	44	85	14	1	3	41	3
Caple, Tom, San Diego	.345	206	54	71	16	3	3	36	4
Ruth, Keoni, San Diego	.342	225	47	77	7	2	5	40	14
Crosta, Nic, Santa Clara	.341	205	39	70	9	2	11	46	5
Jacobitz, Joe, San Francisco	.341	211	29	72	11	1	3	35	4
Salas, Luke, Pepperdine	.340	191	42	65	10	1	3	30	3
Lewis, Brent, Pepperdine	.336	223	35	75	18	1	8	52	2
Curtis, Randy, San Diego	.330	200	37	66	14	2	4	43	4
Gallagher, Delaney, St. Mary's	.330	206	38	68	16	2	2	29	3
Culpepper, Jeff, Gonzaga	.327	199	46	65	14	0	2	39	16
McGill, Clint, Loyola Marymount	.324	204	39	66	16	1	5	28	12
Sandoval, Freddy, San Diego	.323	226	45	73	16	1	9	**59**	4
Thompson, Michael, Santa Clara	.321	184	39	59	16	0	3	33	0
Uribes, David, Pepperdine	.321	262	**74**	84	15	4	7	33	**18**
Johnson, David, Gonzaga	.320	181	33	58	11	2	7	53	3
Thompson, Will, Santa Clara	.320	222	45	71	19	1	11	45	4
Tracy, Chad, Pepperdine	.320	241	34	77	15	1	**12**	47	3
Donald, Cy, San Francisco	.319	138	28	44	8	1	0	15	1
Mura, Kyle, Loyola Marymount	.317	139	27	44	8	0	6	33	2
Lockin, Billy, Loyola Marymount	.316	228	57	72	16	2	0	30	16

INDIVIDUAL PITCHING LEADERS
(Minimum 50 Innings)

	W	L	ERA	G	SV	IP	H	BB	SO
Rea, Anthony, Santa Clara	5	1	1.68	30	13	54	36	10	53
Boman, Nate, San Diego	3	1	2.26	22	6	52	44	34	69
McGuigan, Patrick, San Francisco	3	3	2.61	31	6	52	49	11	38
Kahn, Stephen, Loyola Marymount	7	3	3.61	16	1	87	89	42	80
Collins, Kyle, San Diego	7	1	3.69	18	0	93	100	31	51
Stevens, Jeff, Loyola Marymount	6	0	3.73	21	4	94	96	46	71
Tate, Derek, San Francisco	6	7	3.77	17	0	117	122	20	79
Quaglieri, Will, Loyola Marymount	5	6	3.84	16	0	94	104	29	79

	W	L	ERA	G	SV	IP	H	BB	SO
#Van Buskirk, Thomas, SC	4	2	3.89	32	0	39	36	19	31
Barrack, Jacob, Pepperdine	8	5	3.91	18	0	115	118	39	107
Oland, Bryan, St. Mary's	3	3	3.94	9	0	62	50	23	33
Wilson, Aaron, San Diego	11	3	4.02	18	0	116	118	30	71
Kometani, Kea, Pepperdine	8	6	4.05	18	0	120	145	40	85
#Kleen, Steve, Pepperdine	4	3	4.07	32	8	42	54	13	37
Peters, Matthew, Portland	3	10	4.80	15	0	90	96	25	51
Dworkis, Eric, Gonzaga	8	4	4.86	14	0	104	127	14	72
Muller, Ryan, San Francisco	4	3	4.98	19	0	60	75	18	37
Blaine, Justin, San Diego	4	3	5.10	20	2	78	98	37	58
Simo, Jordan, St. Mary's	5	9	5.20	17	0	114	138	23	48
Johnson, James, Pepperdine	1	2	5.67	24	1	54	70	18	35
Clelland, Ed, Gonzaga	5	6	5.71	14	0	88	124	24	69
McConnell, Kellan, Santa Clara	5	7	5.75	21	3	92	102	55	83
Cabral, Corey, San Jose State	6	8	5.47	16	0	97	128	29	74
#Fisherbaugh, Darrell, Hawaii	0	4	5.54	19	6	37	38	19	47
Lacy, Matt, Louisiana Tech	3	9	5.56	20	3	78	96	24	44
Cooper, Michael, Fresno State	3	8	5.58	22	2	90	110	31	57
Dewing, Brandon, San Jose State	1	9	5.66	14	0	68	74	31	42
Miller, Brandon, Fresno State	5	3	5.91	18	0	78	115	32	44
Herron, Chris, Louisiana Tech	3	3	5.96	23	0	51	68	23	32
Meyer, Clayton, Louisiana Tech	5	7	6.01	17	0	106	150	28	87
Rodriguez, Ryan, Nevada	5	7	6.09	16	0	89	119	30	71

WESTERN ATHLETIC CONFERENCE

	Conference		Overall	
	W	L	W	L
Rice	24	6	46	14
Fresno State	17	12	29	29
Nevada	14	16	30	29
Hawaii	13	16	31	24
San Jose State	11	19	23	31
Louisiana Tech	10	20	20	38

ALL-CONFERENCE TEAM: C—Brett Hayes, So., Nevada. **1B**—Kyle Spangler, Jr., Louisiana Tech. **2B**—Ryan Haag, Sr., Fresno State. **3B**—Christian Vitters, Fr., Fresno State. **SS**—Paul Janish, Jr., Rice. **OF**—Jacob Butler, Jr., Nevada; Greg Kish, Jr., Hawaii; Chris Kolkhorst, Sr., Rice; Richie Robnett, So., Fresno State. **UT**—Kevin Frandsen, Sr., San Jose State. **SP**—Ricky Bauer, Jr., Hawaii; Philip Humber, Jr., Rice; Wade Townsend, Jr., Rice. **RP**—Brad Kilby, Jr., San Jose State. **Player of the Year:** Richie Robnett, Fresno State. **Pitcher of the Year:** Wade Townsend, Rice. **Freshman of the Year:** Josh Rodriguez, Rice. **Coach of the Year:** Mike Trapasso, Hawaii.

INDIVIDUAL BATTING LEADERS
(Minimum 125 At-Bats)

	AVG	AB	R	H	2B	3B	HR	RBI	SB
Robnett, Richie, Fresno State	.384	229	54	88	27	3	13	51	21
Kolkhorst, Chris, Rice	.371	221	59	82	11	5	0	27	5
Mummy, Ben, Nevada	.367	139	37	51	9	2	8	41	2
Marcelli, Brandon, Fresno State	.358	187	33	67	12	4	7	37	5
Kish, Greg, Hawaii	.358	148	38	53	10	0	2	24	6
Butler, Jacob, Nevada	.354	229	58	81	15	0	16	58	4
Haag, Ryan, Fresno State	.352	256	58	90	18	2	4	36	20
Spangler, Kyle, Louisiana Tech	.350	203	24	71	15	0	8	41	2
Janish, Paul, Rice	.345	235	52	81	16	2	9	60	5
Gomez, David, Fresno State	.344	131	12	45	11	1	2	22	0
Rodgers, Adam, Rice	.343	216	40	74	21	2	7	60	1
Walker, Jeff, Louisiana Tech	.342	193	35	66	15	0	5	37	6
Patrick, Chris, Fresno State	.341	217	31	74	16	2	4	42	2
Finegan, Brian, Hawaii	.339	221	47	75	13	2	2	23	13
Hayes, Brett, Nevada	.337	252	53	85	10	1	8	48	8
Pendleton, Lance, Rice	.326	184	41	60	16	0	11	38	1
Inouye, Matthew, Hawaii	.326	184	33	60	20	1	5	48	13
Frandsen, Kevin, San Jose State	.321	196	34	63	14	2	2	19	4
Vitters, Christian, Fresno State	.318	217	41	69	11	2	9	42	4
Laird, Gil, Louisiana Tech	.315	165	17	52	14	1	5	25	3
Gimenez, Chris, Nevada	.314	207	57	65	11	2	14	49	6
Mercer, Joe, Nevada	.313	150	41	47	12	1	7	43	0
Omura, Isaac, Hawaii	.313	134	18	42	7	0	4	24	1
Moresi, Nick, Fresno State	.311	183	32	57	9	2	7	31	8
Sansaver, Andrew, Hawaii	.311	196	37	61	10	0	4	35	1
Lansford, Josh, San Jose State	.311	177	27	55	13	0	3	31	4
#Haygood, Brandon, La. Tech	.279	233	49	65	10	1	5	25	21
#Becktel, Travis, San Jose State	.264	178	26	47	6	5	4	27	9

INDIVIDUAL PITCHING LEADERS
(Minimum 50 Innings)

	W	L	ERA	G	SV	IP	H	BB	SO
Kilby, Brad, San Jose State	4	1	1.71	25	6	58	42	29	46
Townsend, Wade, Rice	12	0	1.80	18	2	120	74	45	148
Humber, Philip, Rice	13	4	2.27	20	1	115	87	37	154
Baker, Josh, Rice	9	2	2.79	24	4	100	96	36	94
Niemann, Jeff, Rice	6	3	3.02	17	3	80	59	30	94
McDowell, Guy, Hawaii	4	1	3.29	22	3	52	39	21	31
Bryant, Stephen, Hawaii	8	4	3.52	17	0	87	82	37	70
Bauer, Ricky, Hawaii	8	4	3.60	20	1	115	122	12	72
Durkin, Matt, San Jose State	8	5	4.49	16	0	110	101	49	103
Garza, Matt, Fresno State	6	3	4.90	27	5	90	103	34	77
Carlsen, Clary, Hawaii	6	8	5.03	16	0	93	113	24	45
Griffin, David, Fresno State	5	3	5.03	24	0	79	102	24	59
Amaya, Jose, San Jose State	1	6	5.20	21	0	62	71	34	55
Sutton, Travis, Nevada	8	5	5.43	17	0	106	126	30	62

INDEPENDENTS

	Overall	
	W	L
Miami	50	13
#Dallas Baptist	44	16
#Northern Colorado	29	23
Savannah State	24	22
Cal State Sacramento	29	32
Texas A&M-Corpus Christi	23	28
Texas-Pan American	22	31
Indiana-Purdue-Fort Wayne	20	31
New York Tech	20	32
Pace	19	31
Hawaii-Hilo	9	43

Reclassifying to Division I

INDIVIDUAL BATTING LEADERS
(Minimum 125 At-Bats)

	AVG	AB	R	H	2B	3B	HR	RBI	SB
Perry, Patrick, Nor. Colorado	.478	186	53	89	27	1	13	74	2
Allen, Trevor, Nor. Colorado	.379	198	63	75	15	3	11	52	1
Zobrist, Ben, Dallas Baptist	.378	222	57	84	15	4	8	66	22
Burt, Jim, Miami	.371	245	70	91	27	3	14	73	7
Barton, Brian, Miami	.371	202	55	75	10	4	6	46	17
Jay, Jon, Miami	.368	234	51	86	14	1	6	56	19
Smith, Tim, New York Tech	.362	188	32	68	15	0	6	34	3
Steinbach, Ryan, IP Ft. Wayne	.359	167	26	60	6	0	1	28	10
Garza, Marco, Texas-Pan Am	.356	194	44	69	10	2	1	28	11
Fremion, Dustin, IP Ft. Wayne	.356	146	30	52	6	1	0	10	17
Baker, Brad, Northern Colorado	.353	201	33	71	12	1	1	36	0
Noss, Drew, Dallas Baptist	.350	214	47	75	11	1	2	23	22
Montgomery, Cody, Dallas Baptist	.347	225	59	78	12	5	7	40	21
Holder, Drew, Dallas Baptist	.346	214	46	74	21	2	8	53	16
Olivo, Ryan, Dallas Baptist	.345	226	52	78	10	10	8	56	18
Landin, Jaime, Texas A&M CC	.338	195	47	66	14	3	2	23	5
Johnson, Craig, CS Sacramento	.337	205	54	69	13	3	4	42	18
Oligo, Kaliko, Hawaii-Hilo	.335	158	23	53	10	4	0	18	15
Braun, Ryan, Miami	.335	155	42	52	10	1	10	45	21
Tamura, Sean, Hawaii-Hilo	.333	177	24	59	12	0	0	14	11
Troxell, Craig, Nor. Colorado	.333	168	43	56	11	2	2	27	0
Binick, Kraig, New York Tech	.332	193	40	64	7	1	2	33	26
Ricks, Adam, Miami	.329	234	58	77	14	1	11	50	6
Mincey, Barry, Savannah St.	.328	137	30	45	7	1	4	31	10
Arroyo, Jack, CS Sacramento	.327	248	56	81	6	1	8	32	20
Rodriguez, Jose, Texas A&M CC	.325	191	37	62	20	0	5	44	2
Pope, Brandon, Savannah St.	.325	166	46	54	7	1	4	27	24
Smith, Caleb, IP Ft. Wayne	.325	126	9	41	6	0	0	18	5
Alamia, Louie, Texas-Pan Am	.324	182	39	59	6	5	4	28	14
San Pedro, Erick, Miami	.320	194	50	62	15	2	12	52	1
Carter, Charles, Texas A&M CC	.320	150	25	48	8	1	4	35	5

INDIVIDUAL PITCHING LEADERS
(Minimum 50 Innings)

	W	L	ERA	G	SV	IP	H	BB	SO
Stanley, Patrick, Pace	8	4	2.30	12	0	74	56	31	69
Carrillo, Cesar, Miami	12	0	2.69	19	2	114	93	43	91
Broadway, Lance, Dallas Baptist	10	2	2.82	17	0	109	108	33	102
Gilmore, Jeff, Dallas Baptist	11	3	2.85	21	0	107	100	33	59
Taylor, Randall, Dallas Baptist	9	2	2.93	16	0	68	77	11	34
Klusman, Aaron, Dallas Baptist	6	3	2.98	26	4	54	48	15	43
Cockroft, J.D., Miami	9	5	3.55	20	0	104	106	36	63
Bogy, Justin, Texas-Pan American	3	4	3.78	12	0	50	63	14	19
Rohan, Casey, IP Ft. Wayne	5	6	3.83	16	0	87	108	23	35
Katz, Ethan, CS Sacramento	9	5	4.01	16	0	110	117	52	90
Saenz, Juan, Texas-Pan American	6	3	4.02	15	0	62	48	42	63
Horvath, Jason, IP Ft. Wayne	4	9	4.09	16	0	95	110	36	71
Camardese, Brandon, Miami	6	3	4.20	17	0	90	78	42	63
Sorden, Tommy, Texas-Pan Am	2	5	4.22	15	0	70	77	44	39
Esposito, Joe, New York Tech	4	5	4.98	14	0	78	74	39	52
Garcia, Mike, Texas A&M CC	6	5	5.01	16	0	93	112	19	85
Kanellis, Justin, Pace	2	3	5.01	10	0	54	52	22	26
Reilly, Matt, Pace	1	5	5.04	15	2	61	61	30	49
O'Neil, Pat, Northern Colorado	7	3	5.08	13	0	62	65	56	50
Zachary, David, IP Ft. Wayne	5	3	5.10	13	0	55	64	25	36

Delta State wins Division II title

Delta State won its first Division II baseball championship the hard way. The Mississippi State school played

NCAA
DIVISION II

three games against defending national champion Central Missouri State, winning two of them, before outslugging Grand Valley State (Mich.) 12-8 in the 2004 D-II World Series title game in Montgomery, Ala.

The Statesmen scored in each of the first six innings against the Lakers, who had allowed just seven runs in their first three tournament games. First baseman Bert Pickard, the tournament's most outstanding player, led the Delta State onslaught with a home run, a double and four RBIs. Brett Donahoo and Eric Patten also homered for the Statesmen.

Delta State had reached the championship game twice before, in 1968 and 1978.

Central Missouri coach Darin Hendrickson guided his team to a third-place finish in his first season at the helm. Hendrickson replaced Brad Hill, who left for the head coaching position at Kansas State following the Mules' national title in 2003.

■ St. Anselm (N.H.) junior lefthander Parrish Castor struck out a school-record 20 American International (Mass.) batters in a 6-2 win. He became the sixth player in Division II history to record 20 or more strikeouts in a game.

First time's the charm in NCAA Division III Series
Oregon's George Fox won title by knocking off Eastern Connecticut State

FINAL **POLL**	
NCAA Division II	
1. Delta State (Miss.)	54-11
2. Grand Valley State (Mich.)	46-16
3. Central Missouri State	57-9
4. Rollins (Fla.)	48-12
5. Columbus State (Ga.)	40-21
6. Bryant (R.I.)	40-17
7. North Florida	41-18
8. Chico State (Calif.)	42-21
9. Kutztown (Pa.)	37-16
10. Southern Arkansas	45-15

George Fox Wins First Crown

Oregon's George Fox capped its first trip to the Division III World Series with a 6-3 win over four-time champion Eastern Connecticut State in the 2004 series, played in Grand Chute, Wis.

NCAA
DIVISION III

Tournament most outstanding player Scott Hyde allowed five hits and struck out 13 in a complete-game effort to pick up his 14th win of the season for the Bruins. Hyde went 3-0 with 30 strikeouts in 20 tournament innings.

Eastern Connecticut State (43-11) handed George Fox (40-10) its first loss of the double-elimination tournament in the first game on the final day. But in the second game, Warriors All-American lefthander Ryan DiPietro couldn't extend his season streak of 11 straight winning decisions. Right fielder Derrick Jones led George Fox offensively with

four hits, three runs and a home run. The Bruins capitalized on two Warrior errors, scoring three unearned runs.

Earlier in the day, the Bruins jumped out to a 6-0 lead but Leon Galemba doubled twice in the Warriors' seven-run fourth inning, erasing the deficit. The Warriors went on to a 12-7 win.

The two teams also met in the third round. Jones hit an RBI single in the eighth inning to propel George Fox to a 9-8 victory as Hyde pitched the final two innings, yielding no runs and striking out four to earn the win.

Hyde won 14 games on the season, while striking out 191—the second largest total in Division III history. His career strikeout total of 395 was the third best ever.

FINAL **POLL**	
NCAA Division III	
1. George Fox (Ore.)	40-10
2. Eastern Connecticut State	43-11
3. Wisconsin-Whitewater	39-9
4. Aurora (Ill.)	28-19
5. Rowan (N.J.)	41-8
6. Brockport State (N.Y.)	34-15
7. Johns Hopkins (Md.)	40-4
8. Salisbury (Md.)	37-13
9. Emory (Ga.)	42-6
10. Manchester (Ind.)	35-12

Cumberland Topples Stars

Cumberland (Tenn.) kept on hitting and No. 1-ranked Oklahoma City continued its championship game futility at the 2004 NAIA World Series, played in Lewiston, Idaho.

NAIA

Eddie Ortega (13-3) went the distance for Cumberland, throwing 149 pitches and striking out nine as the Bulldogs beat Oklahoma City 10-3 in the deciding game. It was the first national championship in any sport for the Bulldogs, who had finished second once and third twice.

Tournament MVP Donnie Burkhalter went just 1-for-4 without an RBI in the deciding game after driving in eight runs in his previous four games. But Victor Alvarez

and Craig Moreland picked up the slack with three RBIs apiece for Cumberland (59-21).

Cumberland, seeded fifth, scored at least nine runs in all five tournament game to go undefeated. The top-seeded Stars (73-7) were runners-up for a record third consecutive year.

Host Lewis-Clark State, which foiled Oklahoma City in the championship round in each of the past two years, was eliminated in the fourth round. Lewis-Clark State has won 13 national titles, including four of the previous five.

Dallas Baptist Wins Again

Sophomore righthander Stuart Sutherland, making his first start of the season, threw a perfect game as Dallas Baptist won its second consecutive National Christian

NCCAA College Athletic Association World Series title, beating Palm Beach Atlantic (Fla.) 2-0. The tournament was played in Celina, Ohio.

Dallas Baptist was a transitional Division I team in 2004, ineligible to participate in NCAA tournament play. But the Patriots went 44-16 on the season and posted eight wins against NCAA tournament teams, including Oklahoma, Oklahoma State, Texas Christian and Texas Tech.

Whistlin' Dixie: Rebels win

For the second straight year, San Jacinto (Texas) advanced to the Junior College World Series championship game with a 9-1 victory, and for the second

JUNIOR COLLEGE straight year the Gators failed to win the title. Dixie State (Utah) jumped out to a 3-0 lead after two innings and James Platt pitched six innings of one-run relief to preserve the Rebels' 4-3 win.

Dixie State became the third consecutive team from the Western district to win the title, following Southern Nevada in 2003 and Central Arizona in 2002.

Tournament MVP Matt Spring and first baseman Chad Barben each had two hits to lead Dixie State to its first championship. Spring, a fourth-round draft pick of the Devil Rays, went 12-for-25 (.480) with two homers and 10 RBIs in the tournament. Outfielder Shawn Ferguson went 13-for-28 (.464) with five homers and 15 RBIs for runner-up San Jacinto.

■ Grand Rapids (Mich.) won its second straight NJCAA

PLAYERS OF THE YEAR

Scott Hyde   A.J. Johnson

Small College: Scott Hyde, rhp, George Fox (Ore.)
Hyde almost singlehandedly led Oregon's George Fox College to the NCAA Division III World Series title, posting a 14-1, 1.99 record with 191 strikeouts in 122 innings. His strikeout total was the second highest in D-III history. Hyde, who was drafted in the seventh round by the Mets, won three games while striking out 30 in 20 innings at the World Series and was named the event's MVP.

Junior College: A.J. Johnson, of, Tallahassee (Fla.) JC
Tallahassee (Fla.) Community College outfielder A.J. Johnson was named the official state and national juco player-of-the-year, and added Baseball America national player-of-the-year honors as well. A sixth-round pick of the Pirates in the 2004 draft, Johnson .372 on the season and led the nation with 18 homers while finishing second with 88 RBIs.

Division II title, beating Lurleen B. Wallace (Ala.) 5-3 in the final. Righthander Travis Doyle spun a complete game, striking out 10. Tournament MVP Ryan Kane scored the tie-breaking run in the fourth and hit a two-run double in the fifth for Grand Rapids.

■ Richland (Texas) won its third straight NJCAA Division III championship, beating Montgomery-Germantown (Md.) 11-1 in the final. Tournament MVP Chris Palmer went 5-for-5 with two doubles and four RBIs in the victory.

■ Saddleback won its first California junior college title, beating Cypress 10-4 in the championship game. Righthander P.J. Sandoval was named the tournament MVP after pitching Saddleback to a complete-game win over host Fresno in the semi-finals.

SMALL COLLEGE ALL-AMERICA TEAM 2004

Selected by Baseball America

Pos.	Player, School	Affiliation	YR	AVG	AB	R	H	2B	3B	HR	RBI	BB	SO	SB	Drafted
C	Eric Cavers, Franklin Pierce (N.H.)	Division II	Jr.	.394	203	59	80	16	5	10	44	31	29	22	Astros (10)
1B	Tom Everidge, Sonoma State (Calif.)	Division II	Jr.	.357	230	71	82	14	3	19	69	42	38	4	Athletics (10)
2B	Kevin Sewell, Quincy (Ill.)	Division II	Sr.	.415	212	52	88	23	1	16	85	32	18	5	*Marlins
3B	Joe Dirnberger, Mesa State (Colo.)	Division II	Sr.	.461	256	100	118	31	6	15	80	14	29	14	Phillies (25)
SS	Denver Kitch, Oklahoma City	NAIA	Sr.	.401	262	98	105	14	4	18	64	17	37	36	Orioles (13)
OF	Ted Ledbetter, Oklahoma City	NAIA	Sr.	.504	232	84	117	26	0	20	90	39	20	7	Marlins (24)
OF	Jud Thigpen, Delta State (Miss.)	Division II	Sr.	.429	261	75	112	24	2	14	80	29	33	20	Not drafted
OF	Tony Wittmus, Colorado State-Pueblo	Division II	Sr.	.504	224	83	113	27	8	13	73	15	12	47	Not drafted
DH	Brandon Burgess, Sonoma State	Division II	Jr.	.357	241	71	86	14	2	20	64	23	45	14	D'backs (6)
UT	Brady Endl, Wisconsin-Whitewater	Division III	Sr.	.411	168	58	69	13	1	18	63	34	22	3	Braves (10)

Pos.	Player, School	Affiliation	YR	W	L	ERA	G	GS	CG	SV	IP	H	BB	SO	Drafted
P	Ryan DiPietro, Eastern Connecticut	Division III	So.	11	1	1.04	17	15	6	0	112	67	29	162	Not eligible
P	Mike Ekstrom, Point Loma Nazarene	NAIA	Jr.	12	5	1.96	21	21	3	0	133	99	30	128	Padres (12)
P	Evan Englebrook, Shippensburg (Pa.)	Division II	Sr.	11	1	1.78	13	13	6	0	86	58	36	113	Astros (8)
P	Scott Hyde, George Fox (Ore.)	Division III	Jr.	14	1	1.99	19	17	7	0	122	75	36	191	Mets (7)
P	Garrett Murdy, Texas A&M-Kingsville	Division II	Jr.	14	1	1.88	19	15	9	1	115	96	37	158	Astros (16)
UT	Brady Endl, Wisconsin-Whitewater	Division III	Sr.	10	2	2.34	13	13	1	0	85	74	29	103	Braves (10)

*Signed prior to draft as fifth-year senior

NCAA DIVISION II

Site: Montgomery, Ala.

Participants: Bryant, R.I. (39-15); Central Missouri State (54-6); Chico State, Calif. (42-19); Columbus State, Ga. (39-19); Delta State, Miss. (50-10); Grand Valley State, Mich. (43-15); Kutztown, Pa. (37-14); Rollins, Fla. (46-10).

Champion: Delta State (4-1).

Runner-Up: Grand Valley State (3-1).

Outstanding Player: Bert Pickard, 1b, Delta State.

DIVISION II ALL-AMERICA TEAM

Pos.	Player, School	Yr.	AVG	HR	RBI
C	Eric Cavers, Franklin Pierce (N.H.)	Jr.	.394	10	44
1B	Tim Richt, Wayne State (Neb.)	Sr.	.411	17	65
2B	Kevin Sewell, Quincy (Ill.)	Sr.	.415	16	85
3B	Matt Levering, Regis (Colo.)	Sr.	.507	15	87
SS	Robert Morgan, Valdosta State (Ga.)	Jr.	.436	9	53
UT	Joe Dirnberger, Mesa State (Colo.)	Sr.	.461	15	80
OF	Francisco Leandro, Central Missouri	Sr.	.357	16	74
	Larry Pittman, Sr., Columbus State (Ga.)	Sr.	.392	21	75
	Jud Thigpen, Delta State (Miss.)	Sr.	.429	14	80
	Tony Wittmus, Colorado State-Pueblo	Sr.	.504	13	73
DH	Chris Reed, Delta State (Miss.)	Sr.	.414	4	57

		Yr.	W	L	ERA
SP	Evan Englebrook, Shippensburg (Pa.)	Sr.	11	1	1.78
	Garrett Murdy, Texas A&M-Kingsville	Jr.	14	1	1.88
	Steve Sharpe, Central Missouri	Jr.	13	0	2.89
	Steve Sloan, Bryant (R.I.)	Jr.	10	1	1.05
RP	Brian Baker, Columbus State (Ga.)	Jr.	8	2	2.39

Player of the Year: Jud Thigpen, Delta State. **Pitcher of the Year**: Garrett Murdy, Texas A&M-Kingsville.

NATIONAL LEADERS

BATTING AVERAGE
(Minimum 100 At-Bats)

Player, School	Yr.	AB	H	AVG
Brian Medley, Longwood (Va.)	Sr.	165	85	.515
Matt Levering, Regis (Colo.)	Sr.	211	107	.507
Tony Wittmus, Colorado State-Pueblo	Sr.	224	113	.504
Brian Fryer, New Mexico Highlands	Sr.	209	103	.493
Starling Odoms, Paine (Ga.)	Jr.	171	83	.485
Justin Rozich, West Va. Wesleyan	So.	133	64	.481
Deacon Burns, Northern State (S.D.)	So.	145	69	.476
Andrew Newton, Regis (Colo.)	Sr.	198	94	.475
Troy Nunnally, Tuskegee (Ala.)	Fr.	100	47	.470
Todd Morben, Regis (Colo.)	Sr.	195	91	.467
Mike Massaro, Colorado State-Pueblo	So.	215	100	.465
Joe Dirnberger, Mesa State (Colo.)	Sr.	256	118	.461
Jason Crawford, Mesa State (Colo.)	Sr.	172	79	.459
Greg Garrison, Metro State (Colo.)	Jr.	149	67	.450

Department Leaders: Batting

Dept.	Player, School	Yr.	G	Total
R	Eric Errante, Central Missouri State	Sr.	65	103
H	Joe Dirnberger, Mesa State (Colo.)	Sr.	63	118
TB	Joe Dirnberger, Mesa State (Colo.)	Sr.	63	206
2B	Robert Morgan, Valdosta State (Ga.)	Jr.	59	32
3B	Will Bradley, Central Missouri State	Jr.	59	13
HR	Jeff Robbins, Pfeiffer (N.C.)	Sr.	55	27
RBI	Matt Levering, Regis (Colo.)	Sr.	50	87
SB	Antoine Tucker, Elizabeth City (N.C.) State	Sr.	34	59
BB	Brent Foster, Southern Arkansas	Sr.	53	51

EARNED RUN AVERAGE
(Minimum 50 Innings)

Pitcher, School	Yr.	IP	ER	ERA
Jeff Brennan, West Chester (Pa.)	Jr.	73	8	0.99
Kyle Frees, West Chester (Pa.)	Jr.	64	9	1.26
Steve Sloan, Bryant (R.I.)	Jr.	96	15	1.40
Matt Haverly, Kutztown (Pa.)	Sr.	65	11	1.53
Randy Dicken, Shippensburg (Pa.)	Jr.	74	13	1.59
Nathan Miller, Wayne State (Neb.)	Sr.	88	17	1.74
Derrick Moeves, Northern Kentucky	So.	83	16	1.74
Evan Englebrook, Shippensburg (Pa.)	Sr.	86	17	1.78
Jack Baird, Bentley (Mass.)	Sr.	84	17	1.83
Eduardo Chile, Rollins (Fla.)	So.	83	17	1.84

Department Leaders: Batting

Dept.	Player, School	Yr.	G	Total
W	Garrett Murdy, Texas A&M-Kingsville	Jr.	19	14
SV	Justin Boza, Tampa	Jr.	31	18
SO	Garrett Murdy, Texas A&M-Kingsville	Jr.	19	158

NCAA DIVISION III

Site: Grand Chute, Wis.

Participants: Aurora, Ill. (26-17); Eastern Connecticut State (39-9); George Fox, Ore. (35-9); Manchester, Ind. (35-10); Rowan, N.J. (40-6); Salisbury, Md. (37-11); SUNY-Brockport (33-13); Wisconsin-Whitewater (37-7).

Champion: George Fox (5-1).

Runner-Up: Eastern Connecticut State (4-2).

Outstanding Player: Scott Hyde, rhp, George Fox.

DIVISION III ALL-AMERICA TEAM

Pos.	Player, Team	YR	AVG	HR	RBI
C	Aaron Giza, Benedictine (Ill.)	Sr.	.479	13	61
1B	Rob Daggett, Elmhurst (Ill.)	Jr.	.422	14	60
2B	Jeremy Jirschele, Wisconsin-Oshkosh	Jr.	.431	6	59
3B	Andrew Pinckney, Emory (Ga.)	Jr.	.415	7	60
SS	David Peterson, George Fox (Ore.)	Jr.	.436	3	51
OF	Nigel Archibald, Centenary (N.J.)	Jr.	.526	12	63
	J.R. Estes, Bridgewater (Va.)	Jr.	.426	16	55
	Dwight Wildman, Eastern Connecticut	Sr.	.419	20	79
UT	Brady Endl, Wisconsin-Whitewater	Sr.	.404	18	63
	Drew Shamrock, Denison (Ohio)	Jr.	.441	9	63

		YR	W	L	ERA
P	Ryan DiPietro, Eastern Connecticut State	So.	11	1	1.04
	Brady Endl, Wisconsin-Whitewater	Sr.	10	2	2.34
	Scott Hyde, George Fox (Ore.)	Jr.	11	1	1.76
	Josh Schwartz, Rowan (N.J.)	Jr.	13	0	1.50

Player of the Year: Brady Endl, Wisconsin-Whitewater.

NATIONAL LEADERS

BATTING AVERAGE
(Minimum 100 At-Bats)

Player, School	Yr.	AB	H	AVG
Nigel Archibald, Centenary (N.J.)	Jr.	137	72	.526
Eric Cirella, Salve Regina (R.I.)	Sr.	138	71	.514
Jeff Natale, Trinity (Conn.)	Jr.	128	62	.484
Brad Groth, Elmhurst (Ill.)	Jr.	166	80	.482
Aaron Giza, Benedictine (Ill.)	Sr.	144	69	.479
Rob Morrison, Johns Hopkins (Md.)	Jr.	132	63	.477
Andy Campbell, St. John Fisher (N.Y.)	So.	148	70	.473
Matt Peetz, Wisconsin-Stevens Point	Sr.	142	66	.465
Josh Wettlaufer, St. Scholastica (Minn.)	Sr.	175	81	.463
Adam Mandel, Denison (Ohio)	Sr.	143	66	.462
Matt Miller, Wooster (Ohio)	Sr.	176	81	.460
Jason Armstrong, Trinity (Texas)	Jr.	197	90	.457
Josh Replogle, Nebraska Wesleyan	So.	103	47	.456
Richard leganiere, Utica/Rome	Jr.	108	49	.454
Tom Calistri, FDU-Florham	Jr.	139	63	.453

Department Leaders: Batting

Dept.	Player, School	Yr.	G	Total
R	Josh Wettlaufer, St. Scholastica (Minn.)	Sr.	48	77
H	Jason Armstrong, Trinity (Texas)	Sr.	47	90
TB	Dwight Wildman, Eastern Conn. State	Sr.	54	174
2B	Joe Hernandez, Wm. Paterson (N.J.)	Jr.	36	24
3B	Pat Ryan, Westfield State (Mass.)	Sr.	38	10
HR	Dwight Wildman, Eastern Conn. State	Sr.	54	20
RBI	Dwight Wildman, Eastern Conn. State	Sr.	54	79
SB	Brandon Schmitt, Piedmont (Ga.)	So.	43	50
BB	Eric Cirella, Salve Regina R.I.)	Sr.	42	42

EARNED RUN AVERAGE
(Minimum 50 Innings)

Pitcher, School	Yr.	IP	ER	ERA
Ryan DiPietro, Eastern Conn. State	So.	112	13	1.04
Dave Henninger, Messiah (Pa.)	Jr.	67	9	1.20
Tal Hendrix, Millsaps (Miss.)	So.	52	7	1.20
Jeff Wilson, Brockport State	Sr.	76	11	1.30
Luke Adkins, John Carroll (Ohio)	Sr.	65	10	1.39
Tip Fairchild, Southern Maine	So.	70	11	1.41
Joey Serfass, Eastern Conn. State	Sr.	95	15	1.42
Sam Mann, Wash. & Jefferson (Pa.)	Fr.	56	9	1.45
Josh Schwartz, Rowan (N.J.)	Jr.	108	18	1.50
Dan Howard, Johnson & Wales (Colo.)	Jr.	65	11	1.52

Department Leaders: Batting

Dept.	Player, School	Yr.	G	Total
W	Scott Hyde, George Fox (Ore.)	Jr.	19	14
SV	Aaron Roetcisoender, Pac. Luth. (Wash.)	Jr.	19	11
	Dereck Tillman, Mississippi College	Sr.	23	11
SO	Scott Hyde, George Fox (Ore.)	Jr.	19	191

NAIA

WORLD SERIES

Site: Lewiston, Idaho.
Participants: Bellevue, Neb. (54-18); Concordia, Ore. (36-20); Cumberland, Tenn. (54-21); Embry-Riddle, Fla. (51-8); Jamestown, N.D. (46-8); Lewis-Clark State, Idaho (51-8); Mount Vernon Nazarene, Ohio (39-17); Oklahoma City (70-5); Point Loma Nazarene, Calif. (44-14); William Penn, Iowa (47-13).
Champion: Cumberland (5-0).
Runner-Up: Oklahoma City (3-2).
Outstanding Player: Donnie Burkhalter, 1b, Cumberland.

NAIA ALL-AMERICA TEAM

Pos.	Player, School	YR	AVG	HR	RBI
C	Derek Brant, Grand View (Iowa)	Sr.	.426	13	67
	Justin Clarey, Mt. Vernon Nazarene (Ohio)	Sr.	.410	8	51
1B	Marcel Guevara, Bethel (Ind.)	Sr.	.464	20	65
2B	Al Estrada, Avila (Mo.)	Sr.	.477	5	37
3B	Tom Gifford, Bethel (Ind.)	Sr.	.420	14	61
SS	Denver Kitch, Oklahoma City	Sr.	.401	18	64
UT	Brian Dinkelman, McKendree (Ill.)	Sr.	.442	13	48
OF	Ted Ledbetter, Oklahoma City	Sr.	.504	20	90
	Charlie MacFarlane, Cumberland (Tenn.)	Jr.	.408	22	72
	Russell Reyes, Spalding (Ky.)	Sr.	.415	21	78
	Jose Rivas, Lyon (Ark.)	Jr.	.409	17	77
DH	Tyler Ryan, Indiana Tech	Sr.	.416	25	83

		YR	W	L	ERA
SP	Ismael Casillas, Benedictine (Kan.)	Jr.	13	2	1.79
	Mike Ekstrom, Point Loma Nazarene (Calif.)	Jr.	12	5	1.96
	E.J. Shanks, Oklahoma City	Sr.	16	1	2.89
	Rick Weber, Olivet Nazarene (Ill.)	Jr.	12	0	1.65
RP	Patrick Ryan, Embry-Riddle (Fla.)	Jr.	8	2	3.18

Player of the Year: Ted Ledbetter, Oklahoma City.

NATIONAL LEADERS

BATTING AVERAGE
(Minimum 100 At-Bats)

Player, School	Yr.	AB	H	AVG
Ted Ledbetter, Oklahoma City	Sr.	232	117	.504
Al Estrada, Avila (Mo.)	Sr.	151	72	.477
Braden Conner, Tennessee Wesleyan	Sr.	227	106	.467
Marcel Guevara, Bethel (Ind.)	Sr.	183	85	.464
R.J. Nab, Park (Mo.)	Sr.	168	76	.452
Ben Martin, St. Ambrose (Iowa)	So.	169	76	.450
Carl Galloway, Biola (Calif.)	Jr.	162	72	.444
Brian Dinkelman, McKendree (Ill.)	So.	233	103	.442
Kyle Moore, Ohio Dominican	Fr.	168	74	.440
Jon Crow, Geneva (Pa.)	Sr.	151	66	.437
Ryan Howell, St. Xavier (Ill.)	Jr.	253	110	.435
Stephen Vogt, Azusa Pacific (Calif.)	Fr.	160	69	.431
Calen Laos, Wayland Baptist (Texas)	Sr.	203	87	.429

Department Leaders: Batting

Dept.	Player, School	Yr.	G	Total
R	Scott Balster, Oklahoma City	Sr.	78	105
H	Ted Ledbetter, Oklahoma City	Sr.	72	117
	Charlie MacFarlane, Cumberland (Tenn.)	Jr.	76	117
2B	Derek Blant, Grand View (Iowa)	Sr.	59	31
3B	Several tied at			7
HR	Tyler Ryan, Indiana Tech	Sr.	59	25
RBI	Ted Ledbetter, Oklahoma City	Sr.	72	90
SB	Chris Lebeda, Bethany (Kan.)	Jr.	54	58

EARNED RUN AVERAGE
(Minimum 50 Innings)

Pitcher, School	Yr.	IP	ER	ERA
Jeremy Helms, Bethany (Kan.)	Sr.	67	8	1.09
Joe Williams, St. Xavier (Ill.)	Sr.	88	13	1.33
Tyler Piatz, William Penn (Iowa)	Jr.	115	20	1.56
Jon Kars, Missouri Baptist	Sr.	86	15	1.58
Rick Weber, Olivet Nazarene (Ill.)	Jr.	93	17	1.65
Ismael Casillas, Benedictine (Kan.)	Jr.	106	21	1.80
Pete Bynum, Indiana Tech	Sr.	83	17	1.84
B.J. Jenkins, Trevecca Nazarene (Tenn.)	Sr.	82	17	1.87
Dean Mitchell, Trevecca Nazarene (Tenn.)	Sr.	92	20	1.96
Chris Ofat, Ohio Dominican	Sr.	92	23	2.25
Edgar Galindo, William Penn (Iowa)	Jr.	96	24	2.25
Jason Halstead, Brewton Parker (Ga.)	Sr.	55	14	2.29
Eric Hedstrom, Northwestern (Minn.)	Sr.	59	15	2.29

Department Leaders: Pitching

Dept.	Player, School	Yr.	G	Total
W	E.J. Shanks, Oklahoma City	Sr.	19	16
SO	Jesse Hoover, Indiana Tech	Sr.	14	137

JUNIOR COLLEGE

DIVISION I WORLD SERIES

Site: Grand Junction, Colo.
Participants: Dixie State, Utah (46-13); Grayson County, Texas (44-16); Indian Hills, Iowa (30-34); Meridian, Miss. (46-10); Middle Georgia (44-17); Pensacola, Fla. (34-18); Potomac State, W.Va. (31-20); San Jacinto, Texas (36-20); Seminole State, Okla. (33-25); Seward County, Kan. (45-14).
Champion: Dixie State (5-1).
Runner-Up: San Jacinto (5-2).
Outstanding Player: Matt Spring, c, Dixie State.

ALL-AMERICA TEAM

C—Jesse Shriner, Lamar (Colo.). **INF**—Scott Campbell, Lamar (Colo.); Isa Garcia, Blinn (Texas); Jonathan Malo, Northeastern Oklahoma A&M; Van Pope, Meridien (Miss.). **OF**—James Bennett, Dodge City (Kan.); A.J. Johnson, Tallahassee (Fla.); Matt Richardson, John A. Logan (Ill.). **DH**—Roberto Martinez, Howard (Texas). **P**—Jesse Litsch, South Florida; Johnny Lujan, New Mexico; Josh Wahpepah, Cowley County (Kan.).

Player of the Year: A.J. Johnson, Tallahassee (Fla.).

NATIONAL LEADERS

BATTING AVERAGE
(Minimum 125 At-Bats)

Player, School	AB	H	AVG
Jonathan Malo, NE Oklahoma A&M	143	70	.490
Yosvany Almario, Miami-Dade	160	77	.481
Josh Payne, Clarendon (Texas)	148	71	.480
Bobby Getty, Olney Central (Ill.)	174	81	.466
Brandon Buckman, Garden City (Kan.)	202	93	.460
Matt Goyea, Jefferson (Mo.)	168	77	.458
Isa Garcia, Blinn (Texas)	176	79	.449
Roberto Martinez, Howard (Texas)	194	87	.448
Brandon Jones, Tallahassee (Fla.)	235	105	.447
Scott Mitchell, Howard (Texas)	180	80	.444

Department Leaders: Batting

Dept.	Player, School	G	Total
HR	A.J. Johnson, Tallahassee (Fla.)	57	18
	Matt Richardson, John A. Logan (Ill.)	49	18
RBI	Phil Britton, Olney Central (Ill.)	58	89
SB	Vince Rodden, Johnson County (Kan.)	55	64

EARNED RUN AVERAGE
(Minimum 50 Innings)

Player, School	IP	ER	ERA
Doug Mathis, Central Arizona	83	6	0.65
Luis Cota, South Mountain (Ariz.)	93	9	0.87
Nick Montgomery, Young Harris (Ga.)	74	8	0.96
Gilbert DeLaVara, Pima (Ariz.)	93	11	1.07

Department Leaders: Pitching

Dept.	Player, School	G	Total
W	Adam Howard, Walters State (Tenn.)	15	14
SV	Drew Buford, Southwest Tennessee	34	14
SO	Brandon Jones, Olive-Harley (Ill.)	17	146

DIVISION II WORLD SERIES

Site: Millington, Tenn.
Participants: Connecticut-Avery Point (39-5); Elgin, Ill. (40-26); Grand Rapids, Mich. (39-15); Iowa Central (49-12); Lenoir, N.C. (33-15); Louisiana State-Eunice (46-10); Lurleen B. Wallace, Ala. (41-16); Mesa, Ariz. (42-19).
Champion: Grand Rapids (4-0).
Runner-Up: Lurleen B. Wallace (3-2).
Outstanding Player: Ryan Kane, of, Grand Rapids.

DIVISION III WORLD SERIES

Site: Batavia, NY.
Participants: Gloucester County, N.J. (42-11); Jamestown, N.Y. (21-6); Joliet, Ill. (34-28); Massasoit, Mass. (31-12-1); Minnesota State (27-15); Montgomery, Md. (33-18); Richland, Texas (45-16); Ulster County, N.Y. (29-13);
Champion: Richland (4-0).
Runner-Up: Montgomery (3-2).
Outstanding Player: Chris Palmer, dh, Richland.

CALIFORNIA CC STATE CHAMPIONSHIP

Site: Fresno, Calif.
Participants: Cypress (26-13); Fresno City (33-7); Ohlone (23-17); Saddleback (28-12).
Champion: Saddleback (3-0).
Runner-Up: Cypress (2-2).

HIGH SCHOOL
BASEBALL

Chatsworth runs table, repeats as nation's No. 1 high school club

BY ALAN MATTHEWS

Chatsworth High became the first California school in 2003 to finish atop Baseball America's high school poll in the 11-year history of the rankings. The Chancellors liked the view from the top so much that they ran the table in 2004, compiling a perfect 35-0 record and repeating as the No. 1 team in the BA/National High School Baseball Coaches Association Top 50.

"Losing to us is unacceptable and no one takes it very well," senior right-hander/outfielder Jason Dominguez said. "But no one said at the beginning of the season we were going to go undefeated. It goes without saying, because we expect to go out and win every game."

Dominguez and his teammates met those lofty expectations. The Chancellors set a California record

Atop the heap
Chatsworth celebrates its second straight city section championship at Dodger Stadium

with 50 consecutive victories dating back to a 3-0 loss to Tucson's Sabino High in April, 2003. They won their final 15 games that year and never let off the accelerator as they motored through their 2004 schedule.

The season concluded with a 7-1 win over San Pedro High (31-4) at Dodger Stadium in the California Interscholastic Federation division IV city section title game. It was the second straight sectional title for Chatsworth (California does not have a state championship) and its fourth in the past six years. Chatsworth has also earned a top-20 ranking in six of the past seven seasons.

Model Of Consistency

Similar to 2003, Chatsworth's climb to the top spot was gradual and steady. The Chancellors lost 10 seniors off their previous year's club, including three Division I signees, the most notable of which was righthander Justin Cassel, the team's ace. While Cassel was putting together a strong freshman campaign at UC Irvine, Dominguez and his younger brother Matt were leading the Chancellors' charge up the rankings.

Despite the defections, the public school with an enrolment of 3,300 was ranked No. 24 in BA's preseason poll. With six seniors, a junior and—a rarity in any major prep program—two freshmen headlining the roster, Chatsworth cracked the top 10 on May 1. The following two weeks saw five of the nation's top six teams stumble and when Tomball High was ousted from the Texas Class 5-A playoffs May 22, Chatsworth's rise to the top spot was complete.

Dominguez, who signed with Pepperdine and went

undrafted because of signability concerns, relished his role as the staff's top arm and offensive stalwart. He hit .490-6-35 and was perfect atop the mound, going 13-0, 1.38.

He got the nod in the sectional final against San Pedro and was dominant in front of an estimated crowd of 3,500, tossing a complete game, allowing five hits and a run with seven strikeouts.

"I've been waiting four years for that," Dominguez said. "I knew this was the last game of my career. There's only one way to go out and that's winning."

Cruise Control

The one-sided affair was something Chatsworth was accustomed to. The Chancellors cruised to run-rule wins in 17 of their 35 games, outscoring their opposition 372-67. They batted .418 as a team and set a school record with 49 home runs.

It all began with senior second baseman Willie Cabrera, who held down the leadoff spot a year after a knee injury ended his junior season early. Cabrera led the team in average (.545) and runs (60) but more significantly provided the pivotal play Chatsworth needed to complete the season undefeated.

The Chancellors trailed Kennedy High of Granada Hills 7-1 in the semifinals of the sectional playoffs before Cabrera hit a solo homer to lead off the fourth inning. The home run sparked a rally, with Chatsworth scoring five times in the inning and plating four more in the fifth on its way to a 10-7 victory.

"It was one of the biggest hits of the season, if not the

Baseball America's final Top 50 national high school poll is selected in conjunction with the National High School Baseball Coaches Association.

Team	Record	Accomplishment	Top Player
1. Chatsworth (Calif.) HS	35-0	CIF sectional champion	Jason Dominguez, rhp/of
2. Moody HS, Corpus Christi, Texas	42-1	State 5-A champion	*Luis Flores, c/rhp
3. Farragut HS, Knoxville, Tenn.	46-2	State 3-A champion	Kyle Waldrop, rhp/1b
4. Riverside HS, Greer, S.C.	30-2	State 3-A champion	Brad Chalk, of/lhp
5. Columbus (Ga.) HS	35-2	State 4-A champion	*Iain Sebastian, rhp/3b
6. La Cueva HS, Albuquerque	28-0	State 5-A champion	James Parr, rhp/ss
7. Owasso (Okla.) HS	34-3	State 6-A champion	Dallas Trahern, rhp/ss
8. Nova HS, Fort Lauderdale	29-3	State 5-A champion	Anthony Swarzak, rhp
9. Monsignor Pace HS, Opa Locka, Fla.	24-2		Gio Gonzalez, lhp
10. Tomball (Texas) HS	32-3		Troy Patton, lhp
11. Villa Park (Calif.) HS	26-3		Mark Trumbo, rhp/ss
12. Chaparral HS, Scottsdale, Ariz.	31-2	State 4-A champion	*Ike Davis, 1b/lhp
13. Destrehan (La.) HS	33-2		*Beau Jones, lhp
14. La Quinta HS, Westminster, Calif.	28-2		*Brandon Laird, 3b
15. Cypress Bay HS, Weston, Fla.	30-2	State 6-A champion	Eric English, rhp
16. Germantown Academy, Fort Washington, Pa.	32-2	State independent champ	Sean Grieve, of
17. St. Francis HS, Mountain View, Calif.	29-3		*Jared Lansford, 3b/rhp
18. Gulliver Prep, Miami	27-6	State 3-A champion	Christian Garcia, rhp
19. Moeller HS, Cincinnati	28-3	State Group I champion	Andrew Brackman, rhp
20. Reno (Nev.) HS	36-5	State 4-A champion	Jeff Schoenbachler, lhp
21. Wilcox HS, Santa Clara, Calif.	30-4	CIF sectional champion	Donald Brandt, lhp
22. Flower Mound (Texas) HS	37-8	Texas 5-A runner-up	*Paul Kelley, ss
23. James Monroe HS, Bronx, N.Y.	43-2	City public school champ	#Danny Almonte, lhp
24. Westminster Academy, Fort Lauderdale	27-3		Brian Van Kirk, c
25. Jenison (Mich.) HS	34-2	State Division I runner-up	Anthony Clausen, of
26. Fallbrook (Calif.) HS	30-5	CIF sectional runner-up	Brock Bardeen, of
27. Wolfson HS, Jacksonville	27-5	State 5-A runner-up	Eric Hurley, rhp
28. Edwardsville (Ill.) HS	35-4		Shawn Seibert, rhp
29. The Woodlands (Texas) HS	32-6		Jordan Dodson, rhp
30. Goddard (Kan.) HS	23-2	State 6-A champion	Travis Banwart, rhp
31. Tampa Jesuit HS	28-3		Michael Branham, rhp
32. Rose HS, Greenville, N.C.	27-5	State 4-A champion	Kevin Hodges, rhp/of
33. Crespi HS, Encino, Calif.	27-5	CIF sectional runner-up	Trevor Plouffe, ss/rhp
34. Auburn (Wash.) HS	21-1		K.C. Herren, of
35. Santaluces HS, Lake Worth, Fla.	25-3		Chris Eberhart, rhp
36. Mission Bay HS, San Diego	27-7	CIF sectional champion	Matt Bush, ss/rhp
37. Lowell HS, San Francisco	29-4	TransBay champion	*Charlie Cutler, c
38. Rockhurst HS, Kansas City, Mo.	26-3	State 4-A runner-up	Ryan Bennett, ss
39. La Grange (Texas) HS	33-1	Texas 3-A champion	Homer Bailey, rhp
40. T.C. Roberson HS, Arden, N.C.	25-1		*Cameron Maybin, of
41. Deering HS, Portland, Maine.	24-0	State A champion	*Ryan Flaherty, ss
42. Milton HS, Alpharetta, Ga.	29-7	State 5-A champion	Dexter Fowler, of
43. Lamar HS, Houston	29-3		Joe Savery, lhp/of
44. Foothill HS, Santa Ana, Calif.	23-5		Phil Hughes, rhp
45. Bryant (Ark.) HS	31-3	State 5-A runner-up	*Travis Wood, lhp
46. Petal (Miss.) HS	33-5	District VII champion	Kyle Edwards, lhp/1b
47. St. Mark's HS, Wilmington, Del.	23-1	State champion	*John Dischert, lhp
48. Spring (Texas) HS	36-9		Sam Demel, rhp
49. Sikeston (Mo.) HS	27-2		Blake DeWitt, ss
50. Bishop Eustace Prep, Pennsauken, N.J.	28-3	State Parochial B champion	#Bill Rowell, ss

* Junior # Sophomore

biggest," coach Tom Meusborn said. "Here was a guy chasing a record. We're trailing in that game and seven was the most we had given up all year. When Willie hit that home run, you just got the feeling, 'OK, here we go.' "

Cabrera's home run fueled Chatsworth's comeback and also broke the California record for hits in a season, topping current Rangers catcher Gerald Laird's mark of 68, set with La Quinta High in 1998. Cabrera finished the season with 72 hits.

Dominguez batted behind Cabrera and was followed in Chatsworth's order by his little brother Matt, a 5-foot-10, 175-pound freshman. The younger Dominguez set a state freshman record with 65 RBIs to go along with a .461

average and eight homers, and was named the state's top freshman.

The 14-year-old third baseman figures to extend the school's long tradition of winning for three more years, a tradition Chatsworth's critics claim is built on a foundation of inferior competition.

Many coaches in Southern California complain that Chatsworth piles up victories and gaudy stats against weaker city section teams that don't have the high-round draft picks that some of the suburban Orange County schools produce year-in and year-out.

Meusborn, however, feels his schedule is legitimate, and contends his team deserves its lofty status.

HIGH SCHOOL BASEBALL

"We've played our schedule every year for the last 15 years and I think it speaks for itself," said Meusborn, who is 373-80 in that time as head coach. "We're playing in the San Fernando Valley and we went to Las Vegas and played five games in three days and won all five.

"We've heard that . . . we don't play a tough tourney schedule, but we feel like we did play a good schedule. We just go out and try and win, whomever we're playing."

The Chancellors will have to listen to their critics throughout another offseason. But once again, they'll own the preeminent of bragging rights: Baseball America's No. 1 team.

Ranks Of The Undefeated

In addition to Chatsworth High, two other teams ranked in BA's top 50 ran the table in 2004.

■ La Cueva High of Albuquerque wrapped up another undefeated season with three consecutive shutouts in the New Mexico Class 5-A playoffs. La Cueva (28-0) won its second successive state title, extending its winning streak to 58 games—10 short of the record set by New York's Archbishop Molloy High from 1963-66.

Senior infielder/righthander Jordan Pacheco threw a three-hitter in the championship game, tossing 61 pitches over six innings in an 11-0 win over Clovis High.

Senior shortstop/righthander James Parr struck out eight and allowed six hits in a complete-game, 5-0 victory over Las Cruces High in the semifinals. Parr, who was drafted by the Braves in the fourth round, touched 95 mph in the outing.

■ No better example of baseball's increased popularity at the grassroots level could be found than in Maine, hardly regarded as a baseball hotbed.

But when undefeated Deering High met Mt. Ararat High in the state Class A baseball championship in mid-June, the game had to be moved to Hadlock Field, home of the Double-A Eastern League's Portland Sea Dogs, and 6,770 fans showed up to watch.

Deering (24-0) won the game, 6-1, and the state title, handing righthander Mark Rogers his only loss of the season. Rogers had been the first high school pitcher selected in the draft—and the first-ever prep first-rounder from Maine—several days earlier.

Lone Star state standout
Luis Flores carried Moody High

On Pace To Be No. 1

Less than a week before the Florida state playoffs began, Miami's Monsignor Pace, then the nation's No. 1 high school team, got rid of its best player. Then it went and lost in the first round, ending its season.

Gio Gonzalez, the ace lefthander for Pace, was dismissed from the team along with his brother Max. Their dismissals came after a public argument between their mother Yolanda and Pace coach Tom Duffin that witnesses say stemmed from Max' lack of playing time.

After transferring from Hialeah High before the season, Gio Gonzalez quickly became Pace's ace. Max, a junior catcher and outfielder, struggled to get playing time on the talented team, BA's preseason No. 2 squad.

The situation had been discussed before but apparently reached a breaking point after Pace's regular season finale April 29, an 8-0 win over Florida Christian. Max did not play, and a witness said Mrs. Gonzalez and Duffin got into an argument that spread to the dugout, involving both Gio and Max.

"I did everything in my power to try and live with the situation, and it got to the point where it was a distraction and we had to move on," Duffin said. "There was team policy rule that was broken, and the integrity of the baseball program is not going to be threatened and there's not one man that is bigger than the program."

Yolanda Gonzalez declined comment. Gonzalez' father, Max Sr., said: "We don't know what happened. The coach hasn't told us anything. The coach never talked to my wife."

Gonzalez, who signed with the White Sox for $850,000 as a supplemental first-round pick, was disappointed that he didn't get another opportunity to pitch before the draft, but he might not have anyway because the Spartans were ousted in the first round of the playoffs.

State Champs, Alas

Moody High of Corpus Christi claimed its first-ever Texas 5-A title with a 6-1 win over Flower Mound High, and ended the season No. 2 behind Chatsworth. The Trojans (42-1) inched up the rankings from No. 28 in the preseason with a hard-nosed team comprised of a young nucleus of players and a righthander/catcher that dealt his way into prospect status.

Junior Luis Flores, a second-team All-American, did not allow an earned run in 91 innings, going 14-0 with 160 strikeouts and eight walks, while batting .405-5-40.

Moody received remarkable production throughout its lineup. Senior center fielder/catcher Jeremy Sauceda, the team's leadoff batter, hit .453, scored 56 runs and was 31 for 34 in stolen base attempts. Alfredo Joseph was a 15th-round draft pick of the Devil Rays.

Approximately 6,000 fans packed Round Rock's Dell Diamond for the title game, many of whom made the 4½ hour trip from Corpus Christi. The Trojans were making their seventh trip to the semifinal round of the state playoffs but had never won the title.

■ Knoxville's Farragut High ranked in the top three for the second year in a row—second in 2003 after going 48-1 and third in 2004 after going 46-2.

The Admirals cruised through the postseason with a bevy of double-digit wins behind a potent one-two pitching punch of sophomore lefthander Rob Catapano and senior righthander Kyle Waldrop.

At 5-foot-11, Catapano's size and approach presented a stark contrast to the hard-throwing 6-foot-5 Waldrop.

"One reason why we are both successful is because we would play each district team twice and each pitched against them once," Waldrop said. "It was just two totally opposite looks, and it's hard to make that adjustment."

Catapano was 12-0, 1.05 with 103 strikeouts and 14 walks, allowing just 34 hits on the season. He tossed a four-hitter, surrendering one run in Farragut's state semi-

ANDREW WOOLLEY

Bailey brands name as nation's best

BY ALAN MATTHEWS

Prior to the 2004 Texas Class 3-A title game, Homer Bailey felt the need to make one phone call. Rockwall High catcher Preston Clark and Bailey played together in the inaugural AFLAC All-America Classic the previous August and Bailey wanted Clark's advice as his LaGrange team met Forney High, a team Clark faced earlier in the year.

PLAYER *of the* **YEAR**

"He basically said 'Go after 'em,'" Bailey said.

Bailey could have saved the airtime.

The hard-throwing, easygoing righthander went right after 'em every time out, including in the title game, which he won with a complete-game outing to cap his senior season with a perfect record, the school's third state championship and Baseball America's High School Player of the Year honor.

Bailey entered the 2004 season as an intriguing prospect, but had not separated himself from the promising crop of high school pitchers in the draft class. By the time the draft rolled around he was widely considered the No. 1 high school pitcher.

His mid-90s fastball, power downer curveball and smooth, simple mechanics made him one of the most sought-after players in the draft and persuaded the Reds to pop him with the seventh-overall pick.

"He was the top high school pitcher on our board," Reds scouting director Terry Reynolds said.

ANDREW WOOLLEY

Homer Bailey

Bailey went 15-0 with two saves and an 0.68 ERA. In 20 appearances spanning 93 innings, he struck out 201, walked 19 and posted a .117 opponent average. He did not allow an earned run until his eighth outing and never seemed fazed, regardless of whom he faced or how many scouts lined the bleachers.

He was the winning pitcher when La Grange beat Forney for the Class 3-A Texas tile in 2001 as a freshman and again in 2004, making for a pair of extraordinary bookends to his high school career.

"It really didn't hit me until I got home," Bailey said. "My parents said look back at what you did. I reflected on it and dwelled on it, and it was almost too good to be true. Two state titles, a first-round pick . . . I've accomplished almost everything a high school player can accomplish."

In his final game, Bailey struck out 14, recording strikeouts on 10 of the game's final 12 outs with his last pitch registering 96 mph for a swinging strike-three. He also went 2-for-3 at the plate, including a first-inning, two-run double to lead La Grange to the 10-4 win.

His composure and maturity were two factors that impressed scouts most. For the Reds, it was his consistency and knack for showing up with clutch performances on the biggest stages that sold them.

"I think he's one of those kids that, because he won a state championship as a freshman, he's had to the wear that bull's-eye on his back for years," Reynolds said. "He has to be at his best because every time he goes out there, they're going to try and beat him. We thought he held up to that situation every time.

"No matter what the situation was—whether it was a high school game, a summer league game or whatever—he brought his 'A' game and nothing ruffled him. He just went out there and did it."

PREVIOUS **WINNERS**

1992—Preston Wilson, of-rhp, Bamberg-Ehrhardt (S.C.) HS
1993—Trot Nixon, of-lhp, New Hanover HS, Wilmington, N.C.
1994—Doug Million, lhp, Sarasota (Fla.) HS
1995—Ben Davis, c, Malvern (Pa.) Prep
1996—Matt White, rhp, Waynesboro Area (Pa.) HS
1997—Darnell McDonald, of, Cherry Creek HS, Englewood, Colo.
1998—Drew Henson, 3b-rhp, Brighton (Mich.) HS
1999—Josh Hamilton, of-lhp, Athens Drive HS, Raleigh, N.C.
2000—Matt Harrington, rhp, Palmdale (Calif.) HS
2001—Joe Mauer, c, Cretin-Derham Hall, St. Paul, Minn.
2002—Scott Kazmir, lhp, Cypress Falls HS, Houston
2003—Jeff Allison, rhp, Veterans Memorial HS, Peabody, Mass.

final victory over Munford High.

Waldrop handled the rest, holding Halls High—a school that lost twice to the Admirals in the regular season—to an unearned run off three hits to cap a perfect 14-0 campaign. Working on two days' rest, Waldrop threw 97 pitches—69 for strikes—in the 3-1 win.

"The overall pressure of being the big favorite of the tournament and it being the last high school game of my career, there were definitely some nerves," said Waldrop, who spurned a scholarship to Vanderbilt to sign a $1 million bonus contract with the Twins as a first-round pick.

"Going 94-3 over two seasons is kind of unheard of," he said. "When I look back over my career I will be amazed at the number of games we played and the number of wins we put together."

Prepster Sets Record With 40 K's

Major milestones are usually accompanied by lavish celebrations. But when Illinois high school pitcher Joe Labek set a national record for strikeouts in a game with

40, there was no tickertape. He didn't dance off the mound. His team didn't even win.

Ridgewood High fell to Evergreen Park High 2-1 in a 24-inning game played over two days, a week apart in suburban Chicago. Labek gave a yeoman's effort, pitching the final 21 innings of the game for Ridgewood and striking out 40, but he gave up a run in the top of the 24th to take the loss.

"I felt bad for Joe," Ridgewood coach Paul Frerking said. "He pitches great and loses that game. Nobody was interested (in the strikeouts). You lose that game and it just took the wind out a little."

Labek said he was unaware of his strikeout total though he thought it was "somewhere in the 30s" when he came off the mound and saw all the "K" signs fans had posted along a fence. He learned it was an Illinois record when he read a story about the performance in the Chicago Tribune, but didn't realize it was a national record until told by a Baseball America reporter.

Labek came on in relief in the fourth inning of a

HIGH SCHOOL BASEBALL

2004 HIGH SCHOOL ALL-AMERICA TEAM

Philip Hughes	Mark Rogers	Chris Nelson	Trevor Plouffe

Selected by Baseball America

*Junior

FIRST TEAM

Pos.	Player	School, Hometown	AVG	AB	R	H	2B	3B	HR	RBI	SB	Drafted
C	Neil Walker	Pine Richland HS, Gibsonia, Pa.	.657	67	41	44	9	1	13	42	9	Pirates (1)
IF	Matt Bush	Mission Bay HS, San Diego	.447	123	46	55	11	1	11	33	12	Padres (1)
IF	Blake DeWitt	Sikeston (Mo.) HS	.558	86	49	48	11	1	14	48	11	Dodgers (1)
IF	Chris Nelson	Redan HS, Decatur, Ga.	.552	87	54	48	11	2	8	44	29	Rockies (1)
IF	*Justin Upton	Great Bridge HS, Chesapeake, Va.	.569	58	35	33	9	0	8	30	30	Not eligible
OF	Dexter Fowler	Milton HS, Alpharetta, Ga.	.457	105	38	48	14	2	14	37	23	Rockies (14)
OF	Greg Golson	John Connally HS, Austin, Texas	.487	78	32	38	9	3	4	26	20	Phillies (1)
OF	Warren McFadden	Nova HS, Davie, Fla.	.555	90	48	50	16	1	11	50	28	Not drafted
UT	Trevor Plouffe	Crespi HS, Encino, Calif.	.481	81	30	39	8	2	6	29	12	Twins (1)
UT	Kyle Waldrop	Farragut HS, Knoxville	.493	148	70	73	26	5	16	67	3	Twins (1)

Pos.	Player	School, Hometown	W	L	ERA	G	SV	IP	H	BB	SO	Drafted
P	Homer Bailey	La Grange (Texas) HS	15	0	0.68	20	2	93	36	19	201	Reds (1)
P	Phil Hughes	Foothill HS, Santa Ana, Calif.	9	1	0.69	10	0	61	40	3	83	Yankees (1)
P	Eric Hurley	Wolfson HS, Jacksonville	15	1	0.73	17	1	105	45	13	154	Rangers (1)
P	Troy Patton	Tomball (Texas) HS	12	0	0.91	14	1	77	24	24	142	Astros (9)
P	Mark Rogers	Mt. Ararat HS, Topsham, Me.	9	1	0.52	11	1	67	14	14	166	Brewers (1)
UT	Trevor Plouffe	Crespi HS, Encino, Calif.	12	2	0.78	15	1	89	60	23	111	
UT	Kyle Waldrop	Farragut HS, Knoxville	14	0	0.15	16	0	91	39	7	118	

SECOND TEAM

Pos.	Player	School, Hometown	AVG	AB	R	H	2B	3B	HR	RBI	SB	Drafted
C	Ed Easley	Olive Branch (Miss.) HS	.490	98	42	48	11	0	12	50	0	Not drafted
IF	Reid Brignac	St. Amant (La.) HS	.417	127	41	53	19	2	11	58	7	Devil Rays (2)
IF	Eric Campbell	Gibson Southern HS, Fort Branch, Ind.	.506	79	43	40	15	0	12	33	7	Braves (2)
IF	Cale Iorg	Karns HS, Knoxville	.505	99	49	50	9	5	13	52	29	Devil Rays (16)
IF	Eddie Prasch	Milton HS, Alpharetta, Ga.	.463	123	55	57	15	1	13	54	20	Pirates (3)
OF	K.C. Herren	Auburn (Wash.) HS	.556	50	27	29	5	1	7	28	20	Rangers (2)
OF	*Sean O'Sullivan	Valhalla HS, El Cajon, Calif.	.617	99	50	61	16	1	16	50	15	Not eligible
OF	Patrick White	Daphne (Ala.) HS	.487	117	51	57	13	4	12	48	28	Angels (4)
UT	Dallas Trahern	Owasso (Okla.) HS	.450	111	42	50	16	0	13	54	8	Tigers (34)
UT	Mark Trumbo	Villa Park (Calif.) HS	.421	88	30	37	7	0	9	36	2	Angles (18)

Pos.	Player	School, Hometown	W	L	ERA	G	SV	IP	H	BB	SO	Drafted
P	Michael Branham	Jesuit HS, Tampa	11	2	0.88	14	1	80	39	21	160	Dodgers (39)
P	*Luis Flores	Moody HS, Corpus Christi, Texas	14	0	0.00	14	0	91	28	8	160	Not eligible
P	Scott Elbert	Seneca (Mo.) HS	6	2	0.52	8	0	54	13	14	114	Dodgers (1)
P	Jay Rainville	Bishop Hendricken HS, Warwick, R.I.	9	0	0.12	11	1	59	26	5	92	Twins (1-S)
P	Anthony Swarzak	Nova HS, Davie, Fla.	12	2	0.33	15	1	87	40	19	140	Twins (2)
UT	Dallas Trahern	Owasso (Okla.) HS	11	0	1.37	11	0	67	46	20	79	
UT	Mark Trumbo	Villa Park (Calif.) HS	10	2	2.20	16	1	73	52	34	89	

scoreless game against Evergreen Park May 17. He tossed nine shutout innings with 18 strikeouts, three hits and a walk, but Ridgewood also couldn't score. The game was suspended after 12 innings due to darkness, and Labek and his teammates figured the game wouldn't be completed because of heavy rain in the area and the approaching end of the regular season.

When Ridgewood went on to sweep a doubleheader against Riverside Brookfield High three days later, with Labek tossing a shutout in the second game, striking out 12, Ridgewood was left tied with Riverside Brookfield in their conference standings. So the Ridgewood-Evergreen Park game had to be finished.

Frerking sent Labek back out for Ridgewood, figuring it would take an inning or two to snap the tie. Labek

struck out the first nine batters he faced before getting a groundout, followed by four more strikeouts to run his total to 31.

Finally in the 19th inning, Evergreen snapped the scoreless tie when Labek issued one of his three walks, a single, a sacrifice and a wild pitch. But Ridgewood answered in the bottom of the inning, scoring on a two-out balk to tie it at 1-1.

The game remained deadlocked through the 23rd, when Labek tied the all-time national mark, notching his 37th strikeout of the game to work out of a jam. The previous record for strikeouts in an extra-inning game was 37, set by Billy Brimm of Asher (Okla.) High in 1971 in a 17-inning game.

Labek gave up a leadoff double in the 24th and

walked the next batter intentionally. He broke the record against the next hitter before a bloop single brought home the go-ahead run. He struck out the next two hitters to reach 40, but Ridgewood couldn't score in the bottom half, making for a sour ending to an epic outing.

The game was also the longest in Illinois high school history.

West Doubles Up East In AFLAC

In a tightly-contested second annual AFLAC All-American High School Classic, played at Cal Ripken Stadium in Aberdeen, Md., the West beat the East 4-2 in front of 4,006 fans and a throng of scouts and college recruiters.

The two teams, made up of 40 of the nation's top ris-

ing high school seniors, combined for 28 strikeouts, the final two coming with the bases loaded in the ninth inning by righthander Ryan DeLaughter from Denton Ryan High in Denton, Texas.

DeLaughter loaded the bases and allowed the game-tying run to reach scoring position with three walks and a single before buckling down with two strikeouts to seal the victory.

Ike Davis, a modest, sure-handed first baseman from Chaparral High in Scottsdale, Ariz., curled a high fly ball inside the right-field foul pole for a solo home run in the bottom of the second to give the West a 2-1 lead it would not relinquish. Davis, who also struck out twice in three at-bats, was named the game's most valuable player.

STATE HIGH SCHOOL CHAMPIONS, 2004

ALABAMA. 6-A: Pelham HS (31-10). **5-A:** Charles Henderson HS, Troy (33-11). **4-A:** #Hokes Bluff HS, Gadsden (31-10). **3-A:** Florence Central HS (31-8). **2-A:** Sumiton Christian HS. **1-A:** American Christian HS.

ALASKA. Kodiak HS (17-0).

ARIZONA. 5-A: #Hamilton HS, Chandler (30-8). **4-A:** *#Chaparral HS, Scottsdale (31-2). **3-A:** Fountain Hills HS (28-4). **2-A:** Scottsdale Christian Academy (24-3). **1-A:** Duncan HS (18-3).

ARKANSAS. 5-A: North Little Rock HS (22-11). **4-A:** Batesville HS (31-5). **3-A:** Central Arkansas Christian HS, North Little Rock (33-5). **2-A:** Junction City HS (28-9). **1-A:** Taylor HS (23-7).

CALIFORNIA. No state championship

COLORADO. 5-A: Thunder Ridge HS, Highlands Ranch (18-8). **4-A:** Niwot HS, Longmont (25-1). **3-A:** #Eaton HS (22-3). **2-A:** Academy of Charter, Pueblo (25-0).

CONNECTICUT. LL: Danbury HS (24-2). **L:** RHAM HS, Hebron (21-3). **M:** Sheehan-Wallingford (15-10). **S:** #Immaculate HS, Danbury (15-8).

DELAWARE. #St. Mark's HS, Wilmington (22-1).

FLORIDA. 6-A: *Cypress Bay HS, Weston (30-2). **5-A:** *Nova HS, Fort Lauderdale (29-3). **4-A:** Rockledge HS (18-13). **3-A:** *Gulliver Prep, Miami (26-6). **2-A:** Florida Christian HS, Miami (21-10). **1-A:** Summit Christian HS, West Palm Beach (20-9).

GEORGIA. 5-A: *Milton HS, Alpharetta (29-7). **4-A:** *Columbus HS (35-2). **3-A:** Northgate HS, Newnan (31-5). **2-A:** Bacon County HS, Alma. **1-A:** Lakeview Academy, Gainesville (31-9).

HAWAII. Punahou HS, Honolulu (20-6).

IDAHO. 5-A: Timberline HS, Boise (25-5). **4-A:** Hillcrest HS, Idaho Falls. **3-A:** South Fremont HS, Saint Anthony. **2-A:** Kamiah HS.

ILLINOIS. 2-A: Notre Dame HS, Niles (34-9). **A:** Harrisburg HS (35-5). **Summer:** Lyons Township HS, La Grange (22-12).

INDIANA. 4-A: Lawrence Central HS, Indianapolis (27-7). **3-A:** New Palestine HS (30-4). **2-A:** Hammond Noll (21-11). **1-A:** Central Catholic HS, Lafayette (27-8).

IOWA (summer schedule). **4-A:** #West Des Moines Valley HS (36-10). **3-A:** Assumption HS, Davenport (34-7). **2-A:** Mid-Prairie Community HS, Wellman (31-10). **1-A:** Martensdale-St. Mary HS, Martensdale (35-3).

KANSAS. 6-A: Goddard HS (23-2). **5-A:** Seaman HS, Topeka (32-2). **4-A:** #Bishop

Ward HS, Kansas City (20-8). **3-A:** Lyons HS (15-9). **2-A/1-A:** St. Mary's Colgan HS, Pittsburg (24-2).

KENTUCKY. Christian County HS, Hopkinsville (25-11).

LOUISIANA. 5-A: St. Amant HS (31-9). **4-A:** Dutchtown HS, Geismar. **3-A:** Parkview Baptist HS, Baton Rouge (23-14). **2-A:** Episcopal HS.

MAINE. A: #*Deering HS, Portland (24-0). **B:** Cape Elizabeth HS (16-4). **C:** George Stevens Academy, Blue Hill (17-3).

MARYLAND. 4-A: Bowie HS (25-1). **3-A:** Centennial HS, Ellicott City (21-4). **2-A:** Liberty HS, Sykesville (20-3). **1-A:** Cambridge-South Dorchester HS, Cambridge. **A:** Mt. St. Joseph HS, Baltimore (28-6). **B:** St. Mary's HS, Annapolis (19-10).

MASSACHUSETTS. I: Xaverian HS, Westwood. **II.** Hopkinton HS (23-2). **III:** Bishop Fenwick HS, Peabody.

MICHIGAN. I. Pioneer, Ann Arbor (37-4). **II:** Divine Child HS, Dearborn (37-7). **III:** Homer HS (38-0).

MINNESOTA. 3-A: Eden Prairie HS (24-6). **2-A:** Jackson County Central HS (24-5). **1-A:** St. Mary's HS, Sleepy Eye (24-4).

MISSISSIPPI. 5-A: #Oak Grove HS, Hattiesburg (30-7). **4-A:** Brookhaven HS (30-8). **3-A:** Purvis HS (32-6). **2-A:** Enterprise-Clarke HS (27-8). **1-A:** Cathedral HS, Natchez (29-4). **Private:** Jackson Prep (27-8).

MISSOURI. 4-A: Vianney HS, St. Louis (22-7). **3-A:** Ozark HS (29-4). **2-A:**Hallsville HS (23-2). **1-A:** Archie HS (18-4).

NEBRASKA. Creighton Prep, Omaha (26-9).

NEVADA. 4-A: Reno HS (36-5). **3-A:** #Bishop Manogue HS, Reno. **2-A:** #Faith Lutheran HS, Las Vegas.

NEW HAMPSHIRE. L: Londonderry HS. **M:** Farmington HS (19-1). **S:** Lisbon Regional HS.

NEW JERSEY. IV: Morristown HS (23-7). **III:** Wall HS, Belmar (28-7). **II:** Rutherford HS (22-6). **I:** New Milford HS (25-3). **Parochial A:** St. Joseph HS, Hammonton (28-5). **Parochial B:** Bishop Eustace Prep, Pennsauken (28-5).

NEW MEXICO. 5-A: #*La Cueva HS, Albuquerque (28-0). **4-A:** Deming HS (23-5). **3-A:** St. Michael's HS, Santa Fe. **2-A/1-A:** Loving HS (22-1).

NEW YORK. A: Columbia HS, East Greenbush. **B:** Windsor Central HS. **C:** Friends Academy, Locust Valley. **D:** Northstar Christian Academy, Rochester.

NORTH CAROLINA. 4-A: #*J.H. Rose HS, Greenville (28-5). **3-A:** West Brunswick HS,

Shallotte (22-9). **2-A:** #East Rutherford HS, Forest City (32-3). **1-A:** #South Stokes HS, Walnut Cove (30-3).

NORTH DAKOTA. A: Dickinson HS (30-5). **B:** Cavalier HS (23-9).

OHIO. I: Moeller HS, Cincinnati (28-3). **II:** Walsh Jesuit HS, Stow (29-5). **III:** New Albany (18-12). **IV:** #Newark Catholic HS, Newark (29-5).

OKLAHOMA. 6-A: #*Owasso HS (34-3). **5-A:** Bishop Kelley HS, Tulsa (34-8). **4-A:** Skiatook HS (23-13). **3-A:** Sulphur HS (34-5). **2-A:** #Latta HS, Ada (31-7).

OREGON. 4-A: Lake Oswego HS (25-4). **3-A:** Henry HS, Keizer (27-3). **2-A/1-A:** Santiam Christian HS, Adair Village (26-4).

PENNSYLVANIA. 3-A: Chambersburg Area HS (25-4). **2-A:** Northeastern HS, Manchester (24-4). **1-A:** Neshannock HS, New Castle (24-1).

RHODE ISLAND. A: #*Bishop Hendricken HS, Warwick (28-4). **B:** Smithfield HS.

SOUTH CAROLINA. 4-A: Mauldin HS (28-5). **3-A:** #*Riverside HS, Greer (30-2). **2-A:** Cheraw HS. **1-A:** Johnsonville HS.

TENNESSEE. 3-A: #*Farragut HS, Knoxville (46-2). **2-A:** Milan HS (41-3). **1-A:** Goodpasture Christian HS, Madison (40-5).

TEXAS. 5-A: Moody HS, Corpus Christi (42-1). **4-A:** Boerne HS (32-5). **3-A:** La Grange HS (33-1). **2-A:** Central Heights HS, Nacogdoches (37-2). **1-A:** Shiner HS (23-9).

UTAH. 5-A: Alta HS, Sandy (22-3). **4-A:** Timpanogos HS, Orem (24-3). **3-A:** Bear River HS, Garland (26-3). **2-A:** #Juan Diego HS, Draper (19-6).

VERMONT. I: Brattleboro Union HS (14-6). **II:** Oxbow HS, Bradford (15-5). **III:** Bellows Free Academy, Fairfax (19-1). **IV:** Rochester (13-7).

VIRGINIA. 3-A: Western Branch HS, Chesapeake (20-8). **2-A:** Tunstall HS, Dry Fork (16-7). **1-A:** Mathews HS (23-3).

WASHINGTON. 4-A: South Ridge HS, Kennewick (19-9). **3-A:** Issaquah HS (22-4). **2-A:** Port Townsend HS. **1-A:** Archbishop Murphy HS, Everett. **B:** #DeSales Catholic HS, Walla Walla.

WASHINGTON, D.C. #Woodrow Wilson HS (19-7).

WEST VIRGINIA. 3-A: Ripley HS (27-7). **2-A:** Weir HS, Weirton (25-7). **1-A:** Pendleton County HS, Franklin (32-5).

WISCONSIN. I: Appleton West HS (19-7). **II:** Edgewood HS, Madison (17-9). **III:** Catholic Central HS, Burlington (18-8). **Summer:** Oak Creek HS (20-14).

* Ranked in Baseball America/National High School Baseball Coaches Association poll   # Repeat champion

AMATEUR
BASEBALL

New-look Cuba wins Olympic gold; defending champ U.S. on sidelines

BY JOHN MANUEL

With a nearly new cast of players and a familiar formula, Cuba claimed Olympic gold in baseball in 2004 for the third time in four Olympiads.

A four-run sixth inning lifted Cuba to a 6-2 victory over the surprise team of the tournament, Australia, in the gold-medal game.

Cuba previously earned gold medals in the 1992 and 1996 Olympics, but had to settle for silver in 2000 in Sydney, Australia. That's when a team of future big leaguers, led by current Brewers righthander Ben Sheets, led the United States to the gold medal.

The Cubans prevailed in Athens, Greece, despite having turned over its national team to a younger group of position players since that 2000 loss.

Cuba celebrates its latest gold-medal triumph
Beats surprising Australia in final game of Athens Olympics

The top pitchers from its 2000 silver-medal team—Jose Contreras, Jose Ibar and Maels Rodriguez—had either defected or been barred from the team. Nevertheless, new stars such as veteran lefthander Adiel Palma (who was 3-0 in Athens), outfielder Frederich Cepeda and second baseman Youlieski Gourriel combined with holdovers such as shortstop Eduardo Paret (who had a crucial two-run single in the gold-medal game), catcher Ariel Pestano and pitchers Norge Vera and Pedro Luis Lazo to lead Cuba back to the top of the international baseball world.

"It's very important for us not just to come to the Olympics, but to win a gold medal," Cepeda said. "Baseball is our national sport, and it's very important for us to win. We wanted to win for Cuba and our families back home."

A New Reign

Cuba lost once in Athens, with a 6-3 defeat to Japan in the round-robin. Japan sent a team of top players from its major leagues to Athens, but settled for the bronze medal because of two losses to Australia, one in the round-robin and one in the semifinals.

Righthander Chris Oxspring (Padres) and lefthander Jeff Williams, who pitches professionally in Japan, combined for a 1-0 shutout for the Aussies in the semis, dashing Japan's hopes for gold. Australia took home the silver medal, its first medal in Olympic baseball competition.

The Aussies weren't overwhelmed in the gold-medal game, but Cuba's international experience proved too much for Australia starter John Stephens (Red Sox). Holding a 2-1 lead in the top of the sixth on the strength of a two-run homer by Cepeda, Cuba scored four times to put the game out of reach. Osmani Urrutia, Cepeda

Chris Oxspring

and Pestano—who led the tournament with a .514 average and 14 RBIs—opened the frame with singles to load the bases. Eriel Sanchez and Paret then drove in two runs apiece with a single and a double for a five-run cushion.

Australia rallied to score one in the eighth, and chased Palma in the ninth with consecutive singles by Gavin Fingleson (New Haven, independent) and Brett Roneberg (Red Sox). Reliever Danny Betancourt came on to face Dave Nilsson, and the best Australian player in major league history just missed a three-run homer on the second pitch. Center fielder Carlos Tabares made the catch on the edge of the warning track, though, and Betancourt retired Williams and indy leaguer Brendan Kingman to end the game.

Right before the top of the fifth inning, Australia manager Jon Deeble was ejected from the game after protesting a call made in the fourth inning. With two outs and two runners on base, Thomas Brice (White Sox) hit a deep fly ball to center field, and umpires ruled that Tabares made the catch, while Australia protested that the ball hit the wall before Tabares caught it.

"There were a number of missed calls that hurt our team," Deeble said. "For example, six umpires couldn't tell if the ball hit the center-field wall or not."

However, Australia was, in Deeble's words, satisfied with a medal, particularly after its dismal 2-5 showing as the host nation in Sydney in 2000. This time, Australia lost its first two games of the tournament, but won five of its next six games before losing in the gold-medal game. Their satisfaction came at the expense of Japan, which took the bronze by beating Canada 11-2.

Tide Turned

Early in the competition, it appeared that Japan and Canada might battle for gold. But Japan couldn't beat the Australians, losing 9-4 in the round-robin for its only loss, then dropping a 1-0 decision in the semifinals. Oxspring, who pitched at Triple-A Portland during the 2004 regular season, kept the Japanese off the board for

AMATEUR BASEBALL

6⅔ innings. Williams, who pitched in Japan for the Hanshin Tigers, came on to get the last seven outs and notch the save.

"It's by far the greatest victory in my career," said Oxspring, who won both his starts in Athens and didn't give up a run in 14⅔ innings. "I actually don't know if I can pitch any better."

Japan came back from the upset to win the bronze, an accomplishment the team tried to be proud of, even though it had entered the games with loftier aspirations.

"We were here to get the gold medal," said manager Kiyoshi Nakahata, who replaced Shigeo Nagahima after a stroke sidelined Nagahima prior to the Games. "We could not meet those expectations. However, we played very well. There is nothing shameful about how this team played, and the Olympics play an important role in spreading . . . baseball to the world."

The Canadian team couldn't overcome the loss of two top players prior to the Games, lefthander Jeff Francis and first baseman Justin Morneau. Morneau was called up by the Minnesota Twins in July and was already in double digits in home runs as the Olympics ended. Francis, the Minor League Player of the Year, was denied access to Canada's Olympic team by the Colorado Rockies and made his big league debut as the Olympics ended.

Even without Francis and Morneau, Canada was six outs away from playing for gold. It led Cuba 3-2 in the semifinal before Cuba rallied for six runs in the eighth inning off relievers Chris Begg (Giants), who took the loss, and ex-big leaguer Chris Mears (Tigers). Canada rallied for two runs in the ninth to close to within 8-5 and had the tying run at the plate in ex-big leaguer Kevin Nicholson (Pirates), but his fly ball to left field was caught on the warning track by Cepeda.

Japanese lefty Tsuyoshi Wada then held Canada in check in the bronze-medal game while Japan pounded righthander Mike Johnson, another former big leaguer, for seven runs in the first four innings.

The Olympic baseball tournament went off smoothly, with games played at two sites in Athens and in front of sizable and enthusiastic, though inexperienced, crowds. The host Greeks, fielding a team of Greek-Americans ranging from big league veterans like Clay Bellinger (Orioles) to stockbroker Laurence Heisler, played in front of capacity crowds every game but finished just 1-6 in a disappointing showing.

If they paid any attention, they picked up on one other fact. In international baseball, Cuba remains king.

Format Changes

The United States was conspicuous in the baseball tournament only in its absence. Team USA failed to qualify and sat out the games—all because of an upset 2-1 loss to Mexico in the quarterfinals of the November 2003 America's qualifying tournament.

But USA Baseball, the American baseball governing body, got a victory after the Olympics when the International Baseball Federation adjusted how teams qualify for the 2008 Olympic baseball tournament, giving teams that fail to earn spots in their continental qualifiers another chance and eliminating the one-and-done medal-round format.

Qualification will be broken into two phases. Two teams from the Americas, one from Asia and one from Europe will qualify through continental tournaments, which must be completed by Oct. 30, 2007. The other

Athens, Greece
Aug. 15-25, 2004

ROUND-ROBIN STANDINGS

	W	L	RF	RA		W	L	RF	RA
Japan	6	1	49	20	Taiwan	3	4	24	28
Cuba	6	1	41	17	Netherlands	2	5	29	55
Canada	5	2	39	17	Greece	1	6	24	49
Australia	4	3	49	30	Italy	1	6	19	58

SEMIFINALS: Australia 1, Japan 0; Cuba 8, Canada 5.
GOLD MEDAL: Cuba 6, Australia 2. **BRONZE MEDAL:** Japan 11, Canada 2.

INDIVIDUAL BATTING LEADERS
(Minimum 25 At-Bats)

	AVG	AB	R	H	2B	3B	HR	RBI	SB
Ariel Pestano, Cuba	.514	35	7	18	5	0	1	14	0
Shinya Miyamoto, Japan	.500	36	9	18	1	0	0	3	1
Frederich Cepeda, Cuba	.455	33	10	15	3	0	1	5	0
Chin-Feng Chen, Taiwan	.407	27	2	11	3	0	1	8	2
Kenji Jojima, Japan	.378	37	8	14	5	0	2	7	0
Brett Roneberg, Australia	.361	36	5	13	1	0	3	7	1
Eriel Sanchez, Cuba	.360	25	5	9	1	0	1	9	0
Peter Orr, Canada	.353	34	8	12	1	1	1	8	2
Gavin Fingleson, Australia	.351	37	6	13	0	0	2	9	1
Nick Markakis, Greece	.346	26	3	9	1	1	1	6	0
Eugene Kingsale, Neth.	.346	26	3	9	3	1	1	5	1
Yulieski Gourriel, Cuba	.343	35	8	12	1	0	0	4	1
Kazuhiro Wada, Japan	.333	33	5	11	4	0	2	6	0
Osmani Urrutia, Cuba	.333	33	6	11	0	0	1	5	0
Kosuke Fukudome, Japan	.316	38	11	12	2	0	3	10	0
Pete LaForest, Canada	.308	26	3	8	1	0	2	8	0
Glenn Williams, Australia	.297	37	6	11	2	0	1	3	0
David Nilsson, Australia	.296	27	6	8	1	0	1	3	0
Eduardo Paret, Cuba	.294	34	6	10	1	1	0	5	0
Yosh. Takahashi, Japan	.289	38	9	11	1	0	3	8	0
Atsushi Fujimoto, Japan	.276	29	7	8	2	0	1	4	1
Jim Buccheri, Italy	.269	26	2	7	4	0	1	4	0
Michel Enriquez, Cuba	.263	38	6	10	0	0	2	6	0

INDIVIDUAL PITCHING LEADERS
(Minimum 10 Innings)

	W	L	ERA	G	SV	IP	H	BB	SO
Chris Oxspring, Australia	2	0	0.00	2	2	15	6	1	10
Norge Vera, Cuba	1	0	0.69	3	0	13	7	6	11
Norberto Gonzalez, Cuba	1	0	0.75	3	1	12	9	0	8
Wei-Lun Pan, Taiwan	2	0	0.75	2	0	12	2	4	6
Adiel Palma, Cuba	3	0	1.40	4	0	19	12	10	16
Tsuyoshi Wada, Japan	2	0	1.50	2	0	12	7	5	13
Shawn Hill, Canada	1	0	1.64	2	0	11	7	4	6
Daisuke Matsuzaka, Japan	1	1	1.69	2	0	16	12	4	20
Chien-Ming Wang, Taiwan	1	0	1.98	2	0	14	11	2	3
Koji Uehara, Japan	1	0	2.08	2	0	13	12	3	10
Michael Marchesano, Italy	0	2	2.84	2	0	13	14	4	4
Mel Melehes, Greece	0	2	3.00	2	0	12	10	3	4
Chih-Chia Chang, Taiwan	0	1	3.00	2	0	12	7	6	18
Danny Betancourt, Cuba	1	0	3.46	5	2	13	5	4	12
Naoyuki Shimizu, Japan	1	0	3.73	2	0	10	9	3	14
Jason Dickson, Canada	1	1	4.09	2	0	11	11	2	3

three spots in the eight-team Olympic tournament (other than host China, which gets an automatic berth) will come from the top three finishers in an eight-team qualifying tournament held early in 2008. The tournament will include the third- and fourth-place teams from the America's qualifier, the second- and third-place teams from Asia, the second- and third-place teams from Europe and the top teams from Africa and Oceania.

In addition, qualification will be based on a round-robin format, with single-elimination games removed altogether.

"This new format almost certainly insures the top seven baseball countries in the world plus the host nation will qualify," USA Baseball executive director/CEO Paul Seiler said. "We believe it is more in keeping with the traditional baseball competition, where advancement in a tournament is built upon the overall strength of your team, not just the ability to win or lose a single game."

TEAM USA AMATEUR

BY WILL KIMMEY AND ALAN MATTHEWS

All's well that ends well might be the most succinct way to sum up the summer of 2004 for USA Baseball's college national team.

Team USA swept through the second World University Championship in Taiwan with an 8-0 record thanks to three come-from-behind victories. Two such wins came in the final and semifinal as Team USA fell behind 2-0 in each game. DH Jeff Clement (Southern California) hit an eighth-inning grand slam to erase a 2-1 deficit against Taiwan to send the team into the gold medal game, where center fielder Drew Stubbs (Texas) capped a string of four unanswered runs with a two-run single to beat Japan 4-2.

The pitching staff allowed just nine earned runs in the championships and went 31⅓ consecutive innings without allowing a run at one point during the round-robin portion of the competition, finishing with a 1.19 ERA and .155 opponent average. The bullpen never allowed a run thanks to a pair of righthanders. Closer J. Brent Cox (Texas) had four saves in the tournament, often following excellent set-up work from Joey Devine (North Carolina State).

"Our pitching staff really carried us. All of our guys were unbelievable," outfielder Travis Buck (Arizona State) said. "We just had to get a couple of runs and then give it to Cox and Devine."

Yet had things played out according to that simple formula all summer, the events in Taiwan might not have been as memorable. The Americans arrived at the tournament with a 10-7 record, which included a 2-7

USA Baseball's most successful team in 2004
College national team wins gold at World University Games

mark against their top competition as they were swept in five games in Japan and went 2-2 against Taiwan in Durham, N.C. Coach Frank Cruz (Loyola Marymount) chided his players about a lack of energy as they put forth inconsistent, lackadaisical efforts riddled with errors in the field and poor offensive execution.

The coaching staff and players said facing that adversity ended up turning into a positive.

"I think it definitely helped us," Buck said. "It made us become more serious to gel as one unit. It took us a while to do that."

A key moment came in the Durham Bulls Athletic Park locker room following the final game against Taiwan, a 4-1 loss that included three Team USA errors.

"Coach told us we were the most talented team and that there was no reason we should be losing," Cox said. "When he finished his speech, he asked if anyone had anything to say. I was so frustrated at the time I stood up and said we can't go back home in the fall and have people talking about us, saying we're the worst USA team ever. We were tired of getting our butts kicked."

Other players also spoke up before Stanford's John Mayberry Jr., normally a reserved type, said his piece and then had the team end the discussion by putting their hands in a circle and breaking with a "USA!"

"That was good for some of the guys to get involved and not have it all coming from the coaches," Cruz said. "They made the adjustments. There was no coaching genius on our part."

Everyone involved with the team could sense a change in Taiwan. First, the party arrived there and had a few days to adjust to the time change and

TEAM USA: COLLEGE NATIONAL TEAM

Season Statistics (18-7)

HEAD COACH: Frank Cruz (Loyola Marymount)

BATTING	Avg.	AB	R	H	2B	3B	HR	RBI	SB	College	Class
Ryan Zimmerman, 3b	.468	77	25	36	12	1	4	27	3	Virginia	So.
Travis Buck, of	.412	68	17	28	2	1	2	14	5	Arizona State	So.
Alex Gordon, 1b-3b	.388	67	18	26	5	0	4	12	2	Nebraska	So.
Drew Stubbs, of	.319	69	14	22	6	1	0	9	5	Texas	Fr.
Brett Hayes, of-c	.315	54	5	17	2	0	0	6	1	Nevada	So.
Taylor Teagarden, c	.309	55	10	17	6	0	1	7	0	Texas	So.
Troy Tulowitzki, ss	.299	77	17	23	3	1	4	18	0	Long Beach State	So.
Trevor Crowe, of	.295	78	11	23	8	3	0	11	5	Arizona	So.
Jeff Clement, c	.275	69	11	19	2	0	3	15	2	Southern California	So.
John Mayberry, 1b-of	.254	59	16	15	1	0	2	9	3	Stanford	So.
Chris Valaika, 2b-ss	.239	46	2	11	1	2	1	10	1	UC Santa Barbara	Fr.
Jed Lowrie, 2b	.230	61	12	14	6	1	1	13	5	Stanford	So.

PITCHING	W	L	ERA	G	SV	IP	H	BB	SO	College	Class
Joey Devine	1	0	0.55	10	0	16	9	8	26	North Carolina State	So.
Ricky Romero	3	1	1.57	5	0	29	13	9	30	Cal State Fullerton	So.
J. Brent Cox	2	1	2.08	12	4	17	8	7	25	Texas	So.
Luke Hochevar	1	0	2.73	1	0	33	29	11	38	Tennessee	So.
Mark Romanczuk	3	1	2.95	8	0	18	12	6	21	Stanford	So.
Mike Pelfrey	1	1	3.24	6	0	17	23	5	20	Wichita State	So.
Cesar Ramos	3	2	3.33	7	0	27	25	3	21	Long Beach State	So.
Ian Kennedy	3	1	3.81	6	0	26	21	10	40	Southern California	Fr.
Stephan Kahn	0	0	4.72	8	1	13	12	8	15	Loyola Marymount	So.
Daniel Bard	0	0	6.55	8	0	11	11	7	8	North Carolina	Fr.

environment, a luxury it hadn't previously been afforded between a trip to Japan, back to the U.S. and then over to the Far East again. Then, the extra rest combined with a sense of urgency helped the players get up for the games.

"Everybody was up in the dugout cheering in Taiwan," Cox said. "Before everybody was kind of relaxing like it was summer ball. I would say it wasn't so much people just playing for themselves as it was a summer ball (mentality). I played in Liberal, Kansas, last summer and we'd hang out and go shoot rabbits and then play some baseball.

"Team USA isn't the same thing. You're playing for your country. There's more on the line. After (we got to Taiwan), everybody was playing for the right reasons."

That was apparent in the team's first game. Team USA took the field against the host nation as more than 5,000 of its fans looked on. First baseman Alex Gordon (Nebraska) drove in both U.S. runs with a 2-for-3 effort in that game, which served as the beginning of an impressive hot streak that netted him offensive MVP honors for the tournament. He hit .524 with two home runs, eight runs scored and five RBIs.

Third baseman Ryan Zimmerman (Virginia) continued his hot hitting in Taiwan, finishing the summer as the team's leader in batting, doubles, RBIs, runs, slugging percentage and on-base percentage. His .468 average was the best in Team USA history, breaking Dave McCarty's record set in 1990.

"It's definitely a great feeling to have this kind of success on this team," Zimmerman said. "I didn't come here thinking I'd be the leading hitter or home run guy."

Zimmerman tied with Gordon and shortstop Troy Tulowitzki (Long Beach State) for the lead in home runs. Buck hit .400 in Taiwan to join Zimmerman as the members of the summer .400 club.

Stubbs hit .407 in Taiwan and delivered the game-winning RBIs in the gold-medal game after hitting .262 earlier in the summer. While Stubbs' hit was key, no player delivered a more timely at-bat than Clement in the semifinal win against Taiwan. His slump came in Taiwan, where he was just 5-for-24. Team USA was six outs from having to scrap for a bronze medal when Clement launched a monstrous home run.

"When he hit that grand slam, we knew it was our tournament and that we were going to win," Buck said. Cox began celebrating in the bullpen before entering the game to record the save, as he did in Team USA's final three games.

It was only fitting that Team USA won the gold medal by first beating Taiwan, which entered with a better team than the one it sent to Durham earlier in the summer, and then Japan.

"I think the losing, looking back, I'm glad that's the way it happened," Cox said. "I like winning, and maybe we didn't have to lose all five in Japan, but it definitely helped."

TEAM USA: JUNIOR NATIONAL TEAM

World Junior Championship, Taipei City, Taiwan (4–2, Fourth Place)
Head Coach: Marc Johnson (Cherry Creek HS, Englewood, Colo.)

BATTING	AVG	AB	R	H	2B	3B	HR	RBI	SB	High School, Hometown
Brandon Snyder, 3b-c	.421	19	3	8	2	0	0	6	0	Westfield HS, Centreville, Va.
Justin Upton, ss	.417	24	8	10	0	4	1	5	2	Great Bridge HS, Chesapeake, Va.
Kyle Russell, of	.368	19	5	7	3	1	1	8	0	Tomball (Texas) HS
Ike Davis, 1b-lhp	.316	19	3	6	2	0	0	6	1	Chaparral HS, Scottsdale, Ariz.
David Cooper, of	.316	19	6	6	1	0	0	2	0	Tokay HS, Lodi, Calif.
Randy Molina, of-1b	.286	14	2	4	2	0	0	3	0	South Gate (Calif.) HS
Robert Lara, c	.250	8	2	2	0	0	0	0	0	Nova HS, Davie, Fla.
Brandon Laird, 2b	.208	24	2	5	1	0	0	2	0	La Quinta HS, Westminster, Calif.
Buster Posey, rhp-3b	.200	5	1	1	0	0	0	1	0	Lee County HS, Leesburg, Ga.
Andrew McCutchen, of	.133	15	6	2	0	0	0	1	0	Fort Meade (Fla.) HS
Landon Hernandez, c	.111	9	1	1	0	0	0	0	0	Desert Christian HS, Indio, Calif.
Austin Yount, rhp	.000	6	0	0	0	0	0	0	0	Chaparral HS, Scottsdale, Ariz.
Sean O'Sullivan, 3b-rhp	.000	5	0	0	0	0	0	0	0	Valhalla HS, El Cajon, Calif.

PITCHING	W	L	ERA	G	SV	IP	H	BB	SO	High School, Hometown
Ike Davis	1	0	0.00	2	0	6	3	0	10	Chaparral HS, Scottsdale, Ariz.
Joseph Parigi	0	0	0.00	2	0	4	1	4	6	Monterey (Calif.) HS
Buster Posey	0	1	1.23	2	0	7	6	7	7	Lee County HS, Leesburg, Ga.
Austin Yount	1	0	1.42	2	0	6	4	2	7	Chaparral HS, Scottsdale, Ariz.
Sean O'Sullivan	0	1	2.57	2	0	7	8	1	10	Valhalla HS, El Cajon, Calif.
Eric Massingham	1	0	3.00	1	0	6	6	2	4	De La Salle HS, Concord, Calif.
Jonathan Niese	0	0	4.50	1	0	2	3	2	2	Defiance (Ohio) HS
Tyson Ross	1	0	4.50	2	0	2	2	1	4	Bishop O'Dowd HS, Oakland
Erik Davis	0	0	6.75	2	0	7	6	4	5	Mountain View (Calif.) HS
Brandon Laird	0	0	15.43	2	0	2	3	2	1	La Quinta HS, Westminster, Calif.

TEAM USA: YOUTH NATIONAL TEAM

Pan-Am Championship Qualifier, Lagos De Moreno, Mexico (7–2, Silver Medal)
Head Coach: Tom Succow (Brophy Prep, Phoenix)

BATTING	AVG	AB	R	H	2B	3B	HR	RBI	SB	High School, Hometown
Colton Willems, rhp	1.000	2	1	2	1	0	0	2	0	John Carroll HS, Fort Pierce, Fla.
Robert Stock, rhp	1.000	1	1	1	0	0	1	3	0	Agoura (Calif.) HS
Chris Huseby, rhp	.750	4	2	3	0	0	1	4	0	Martin County HS, Stuart, Fla.
Blake Dean, lhp	.600	5	2	3	1	0	0	1	0	Crestview (Fla.) HS
Matt Newman, of	.424	33	15	14	3	0	1	4	2	Brophy Prep, Glendale, Ariz.
Chris Marrero, ss-3b	.417	36	15	15	0	0	5	16	1	Monsignor Pace HS, Opa Locka, Fla.
Greg Peavey, rhp-of-3b	.400	25	12	10	1	1	0	6	3	Hudson's Bay HS, Vancouver, Wash.
Ryan Aguayo, 2b-ss	.345	29	13	10	3	0	1	11	1	Servite HS, Anaheim
Hank Conger, c-3b	.333	36	6	12	2	0	1	11	0	Huntington Beach (Calif.) HS
Max Sapp, c	.333	27	5	9	3	0	3	11	0	Bishop Moore HS, Windermere, Fla.
Joey Wong, 2b	.333	9	3	3	0	0	0	3	0	Sprague HS, Salem, Ore.
Brett Anderson, lhp	.286	7	1	2	1	0	0	1	0	Stillwater (Okla.) HS
Iden Nazario, 1b	.280	25	13	7	4	0	2	6	0	Southridge HS, Miami
Ryan Knox, of	.278	18	4	5	1	0	0	6	1	King HS, Riverside, Calif.
Steven Figueroa, rhp-of	.250	4	2	1	0	0	0	1	0	Haines City (Fla.) HS
Michael Main, of-rhp	.200	35	8	7	1	1	1	9	3	De Land HS, Deltona, Fla.
John Tolisano, 2b	.200	10	4	2	1	0	0	3	0	Estero HS, Sanibel, Fla.
Shawn Tolleson, rhp	.200	5	2	1	0	0	0	0	0	Allen (Texas) HS

PITCHING	W	L	ERA	G	SV	IP	H	BB	SO	High School, Hometown
Colton Willems	0	0	0.00	2	1	5	7	2	5	John Carroll HS, Fort Pierce, Fla.
Robert Stock	0	0	0.00	3	0	4	1	4	3	Agoura (Calif.) HS
Blake Dean	2	0	0.82	2	0	11	8	8	16	Crestview (Fla.) HS
Chris Huseby	2	0	1.35	2	0	7	8	5	10	Martin County HS, Stuart, Fla.
Greg Peavey	0	1	1.88	2	0	14	11	8	15	Hudson's Bay HS, Vancouver, Wash.
Michael Main	0	1	2.25	2	0	4	7	3	6	De Land HS, Deltona, Fla.
Shawn Tolleson	1	0	3.24	2	0	8	5	4	12	Allen (Texas) HS
Brett Anderson	2	0	3.65	2	0	12	11	5	24	Stillwater (Okla.) HS
Steven Figueroa	0	0	9.00	1	0	3	2	4	4	Haines City (Fla.) HS

WORLD UNIVERSITY GAMES
Tainan, Taiwan
July 24-Aug. 1, 2004

ROUND-ROBIN STANDINGS

	W	L	RF	RA
United States	6	0	43	8
Japan	5	1	32	11
Korea	4	2	45	10
Taiwan	3	3	34	10
Czech Republic	2	4	12	44
Canada	1	5	10	62
Mexico	0	6	15	46

SEMI-FINALS: United States 5, Taiwan 2; Japan 5, Korea 0. **GOLD-MEDAL GAME:** United States 4, Japan 2. **BRONZE-MEDAL GAME:** Korea 3, Taiwan 1.

INDIVIDUAL LEADERS: AVG: Ryan Zimmerman, United States .643. **HR:** Carlos Sosa, Mexico 3. **RBI:** Keun-woo Jeong, Korea 12. **ERA:** Sung-wei Tseng, Taiwan 0.00.

MVP: Ryan Zimmerman, 3b, United States.

TEAM USA
Tournament Statistics

BATTING	AVG	AB	R	H	2B	3B	HR	RBI	SB
Alex Gordon, 1b	.524	21	8	11	1	0	2	5	0
Drew Stubbs, of	.407	27	6	11	3	1	0	5	0
Travis Buck, of	.400	25	5	10	0	1	0	1	1
Ryan Zimmerman, 3b	.375	24	9	9	4	0	1	2	1
Taylor Teagarden, c	.360	25	4	9	3	0	0	3	0
Troy Tulowitzki, ss	.286	28	6	8	0	1	2	10	0
Brett Hayes, of-dh	.286	21	2	6	1	0	0	4	0
Jeff Clement, dh-c	.208	24	3	5	0	0	1	8	0
Chris Valaika, 2b	.200	15	1	3	0	0	0	2	0
Trevor Crowe, of	.182	22	2	4	2	1	0	2	1
Jed Lowrie, 2b	.143	14	2	2	1	1	0	3	0
John Mayberry Jr., 1b	.000	8	4	0	0	0	0	2	0

PITCHING	W	L	ERA	G	SV	IP	H	BB	SO
Mark Romanczuk	1	0	0.00	2	0	9	3	2	11
Joey Devine	1	0	0.00	3	0	5	3	1	7
J. Brent Cox	1	0	0.00	5	4	5	0	4	9
Cesar Ramos	1	0	0.00	2	0	5	1	1	4
Mike Pelfrey	0	0	0.00	1	0	3	3	0	4
Stephen Kahn	0	0	0.00	2	0	2	1	2	1
Daniel Bard	0	0	0.00	2	0	2	0	0	1
Ricky Romero	1	0	1.42	2	0	13	6	5	14
Ian Kennedy	2	0	1.59	2	0	11	8	2	17
Luke Hochevar	1	0	3.46	2	0	13	12	3	14

WORLD JUNIOR CHAMPIONSHIP
Taipei City, Taiwan
Sept. 3-12, 2004

ROUND-ROBIN STANDINGS

POOL A	W	L	RF	RA
Japan	4	0	28	9
United States	3	1	23	14
Taiwan	2	2	27	9
The Netherlands	1	3	11	23
Germany	0	4	9	43

POOL B	W	L	RF	RA
Cuba	5	0	41	7

Korea	4	1	34	7
Italy	2	3	16	24
Panama	2	3	25	30
Australia	2	3	24	26
South Africa	0	5	2	48

SEMI-FINALS: Cancelled.
GOLD-MEDAL GAME: Cuba 4, Japan 0. **BRONZE-MEDAL GAME:** Korea 10, United States 5.
ALL-TOURNAMENT TEAM: C—Kai Gronauer, Germany. **1B**—Syunji Sato, Japan. **2B**—Yoilan Cerse, Cuba. **3B**—Adalberto Ibarra, Cuba. **SS**—Ji-Soo Kim, Korea. **OF**—Yuan-Chin Chu, Taiwan; Ryan McMillan, Australia; Andrea Santolupo, Italy. **P**—Yadier Pedroso, Cuba; Alain Sanchez, Cuba.

PAN AMERICAN YOUTH CHAMPIONSHIP
Qualifier/2005 World Youth Tournament
Lagos De Moreno, Mexico
Sept. 3-12, 2004

ROUND-ROBIN STANDINGS

	W	L	RF	RA
United States	7	1	109	28
Cuba	7	1	88	25
Mexico	6	2	70	47
Brazil	6	3	74	48
Venezuela	6	3	85	63
Colombia	3	5	35	66
Aruba	2	6	39	78
Argentina	1	7	30	70
Guatemala	0	8	14	105

GOLD-MEDAL GAME: Cuba 3, United States 0. **BRONZE-MEDAL GAME:** None (Mexico awarded third place).

INDIVIDUAL BATTING LEADERS
(Minimum 20 Plate Appearances)

BATTING	AVG	AB	R	H	2B	3B	HR	RBI	SB
Jesus Gomez, Venez.	.500	24	6	12	4	0	1	11	0
Wellinson Viana, Brazil	.500	30	12	15	4	1	1	12	0
Adrian Ruiz, Mexico	.474	19	6	9	0	0	0	3	1
Yogey Perez, Cuba	.448	29	10	13	1	0	0	9	0
Ryan Aguayo, U.S.	.444	27	13	12	3	0	1	11	1
Yasmany Viera, Cuba	.429	28	9	12	2	0	0	4	0
Juan Serrano, Cuba	.423	26	5	11	1	0	1	8	0
Rene Chavez, Mexico	.423	26	10	11	2	1	0	8	3
Carlos Mesa, Cuba	.419	31	10	13	1	3	1	11	2
Matt Newman, U.S.	.414	29	15	12	3	0	1	3	2
Chris Marrero, U.S.	.412	34	15	14	0	0	5	17	1
Alvaro Gutierrez, Venez.	.409	22	9	9	3	0	1	6	1
Juan Aponte, Venez.	.400	25	10	10	6	0	1	6	1

INDIVIDUAL PITCHING LEADERS
(Minimum 10 Innings)

PITCHING	W	L	ERA	G	SV	IP	H	BB	SO
Humberto Gutierrez, Mex.	2	0	0.59	2	0	15	7	2	13
Blake Dean, United States	2	0	0.82	2	0	11	8	8	16
Juan Serrano, Cuba	2	0	0.86	3	0	21	13	4	28
Yasmany Leon, Cuba	2	0	1.50	2	0	12	7	6	14
Felipe Natel, Brazil	3	0	1.93	3	0	14	13	8	9
Meldrick Solognier, Aruba	1	1	2.70	3	0	10	16	3	8
Ezequiel Lopez, Argentina	1	1	3.45	2	0	16	16	5	20
Eric Arias, Argentina	0	0	4.09	3	0	11	11	1	8
Andres Rosales, Colombia	2	1	4.16	3	0	17	16	18	18
Christian Diaz, Aruba	0	1	4.61	4	0	14	20	13	6

In other words, all's well that ends well.

Juniors' Streak Halted

While the eastern United States suffered through the worst hurricane season in decades in 2004, USA Baseball's junior national team suffered a setback—in part because of torrential rains in September, also—across the globe in Taiwan.

Saturated fields and heavy rainfall led to an abbreviated tournament format at the 11-nation World Junior Championship in Taipei City, ultimately costing Team USA a chance to play for a gold medal. The Americans finished fourth.

Cuba (7-0) successfully defended its 2002 world title by blanking Japan (5-1) 4-0 to win gold at the biennial event comprised of players 18-and-under.

Team USA (4-2) was slated to meet Cuba in the semifinals but both semifinal-round games were cancelled. Cuba and Japan advanced to the gold-medal game based on pool-play records. International Baseball Federation officials ruled Team USA and Korea (5-1) would play for bronze because they were the next highest seeds.

The juniors lost 10-5, stranding 13 runners in the bronze-medal game, which lasted three hours and 42

minutes and was played in a steady rain. The loss ended USA Baseball's 20-year streak of having earned a medal at the World Championship.

"It was a long day but we have no excuses," Team USA coach Marc Johnson said. "We came out and were simply outplayed by Korea. I wish we would have played better, but the fact of the matter is that Korea simply beat us at our game."

Catcher Brandon Snyder, a senior at Westfield High in Centreville, Va., led Team USA with a .421 average and hit safely in all six games. Shortstop Justin Upton (Great Bridge High, Chesapeake, Va.) led the squad in runs (eight), hits (10), triples (four), total bases (21) and slugging percentage (.875).

The event marked the first time in international competition at the 18-and-under level professional players were allowed to compete. Australia and Panama each recruited minor league players from their nations to participate, a practice that is allowed by International Baseball Federation rules and regulations but has never been exercised.

Cuba also won the nine-nation Pan American Youth Championship in Encarnacion de Diaz, Mexico. USA Baseball's youth national team, comprised of players 16-and-under, earned a silver medal, thus qualifying for the 2005 World Youth Championship slated for Aug. 19-30 in Monterrey, Mexico, along with Cuba and Mexico.

Cuban pitcher Raidel Borges tossed seven shutout innings, allowing four hits and six walks, in Cuba's 3-0 gold-medal game victory. Cuban second baseman Pavel Quesada went 2-for-3 with two RBIs and a run.

The United States averaged 15.3 runs and 14.7 hits in its seven round-robin victories. Both Team USA losses came to Cuba.

Juniors Chris Marrero (Monsignor Pace High, Opa Locka, Fla.) and Matt Newman (Brophy Prep, Glendale, Ariz.) paced the youth offense. Marrero led the tournament in home runs with five and RBIs with 16 while Newman posted a .424 average with eight walks and two stolen bases in nine games.

The youth squad sent righthander Greg Peavey to the mound in both battles against Cuba, including the gold-medal game. The junior righthander from Hudson's Bay High in Vancouver, Wash., pitched admirably, despite

Weaver wins Amateur award

Righthander Jered Weaver swept every major individual honor in college baseball in 2004, capping the hardware run by earning the Golden Spikes Award.

GOLDEN SPIKES

Weaver became the first Long Beach State player to win the Golden Spikes, given annually to the nation's top amateur baseball player by USA Baseball and sponsored by the Major League Baseball Players Association.

He also won Baseball America's College Player of the Year honor and the first Roger Clemens Award for college baseball's best Division I pitcher.

"I never expected any of these awards to come, so to even be among the top five amateur players in the country, that's a very big honor," Weaver said.

"This past season, I just tried to keep my team in ballgames, and I was able to do that."

Weaver beat Stephen Head (Mississippi), Dustin Pedroia (Arizona State), Huston Street (Texas) and Wade Townsend (Rice) for the award. He went 15-1, 1.62 with 213 strikeouts, the sixth-best single-season mark in NCAA history, as a junior.

Weaver, the 12th-overall pick in the June draft by the Angels, ranks as Long Beach State's all-time leader in wins (37), strikeouts (431) and innings (370) and also holds school records for strikeouts in a game (17) and season.

He set a Team USA record with an 0.38 ERA in the summer of 2003, working 45⅔ consecutive scoreless innings before allowing two runs to Cuba in the gold-medal game at the Pan American Games.

"Jered's magnificent collegiate career in which he dominated the headlines and posted incredible numbers, certainly proves he was the most outstanding amateur player this year," said Paul Seiler, USA Baseball executive director and CEO. "We're also excited that Jered played such an instrumental role in helping Team USA capture a silver medal at the 2003 Pan Am Games, and we're very happy for the LBSU baseball program and their head coach, Mike Weathers."

Jered Weaver
RICH ABEL

PREVIOUS WINNERS

1978	Bob Horner, 3b, Arizona State
1979	Tim Wallach, 1b, Cal State Fullerton
1980	Terry Francona, of, Arizona
1981	Mike Fuentes, of, Florida State
1982	Augie Schmidt, ss, New Orleans
1983	Dave Magadan, 1b, Alabama
1984	Oddibe McDowell, of, Arizona State
1985	Will Clark, 1b, Mississippi State
1986	Mike Loynd, rhp, Florida State
1987	Jim Abbott, lhp, Michigan
1988	Robin Ventura, 3b, Oklahoma State
1989	Ben McDonald, rhp, Louisiana State
1990	Alex Fernandez, rhp, Miami-Dade CC
1991	Mike Kelly, of, Arizona State
1992	Phil Nevin, 3b, Cal State Fullerton
1993	Darren Dreifort, rhp-dh, Wichita State
1994	Jason Varitek, c, Georgia Tech
1995	Mark Kotsay, of-lhp, Cal State Fullerton
1996	Travis Lee, 1b, San Diego State
1997	J.D. Drew, of, Florida State
1998	Pat Burrell, 3b, Miami
1999	Jason Jennings, rhp-dh, Baylor
2000	Kip Bouknight, rhp, South Carolina
2001	Mark Prior, rhp, Southern California
2002	Khalil Greene, ss, Clemson
2003	Rickie Weeks, 2b, Southern

coming away without a win. He tossed 14 innings, allowing 11 hits, while striking out 15.

Cuban righthander Juan Serrano struck out 15 over 11 innings in Cuba's 3-2, extra-inning win over the youth national team during round-robin play in the event's most entertaining affair.

Lefthander Brett Anderson, a junior at Stillwater (Okla.) High and the son of Oklahoma State baseball coach Frank Anderson, was Team USA's most successful pitcher. He went 2-0, 3.65 with 24 strikeouts and five walks.

The event's format was changed when Venezuela failed to show for the tournament. Cuba and Team USA, the top two seeds from pool play, still met for the championship but the third and fourth seeds were slated to play for the final of three World Youth Championship qualifying spots from the Americas. However, the third-place game was not played, and Mexico, the team with the third-best record (based on tiebreakers) automatically received the final bid.

AMATEUR BASEBALL

Carte wins summer league honor

BY WILL KIMMEY

Daniel Carte didn't go to high school in Florida, Texas or California. He doesn't play in a major Division I conference.

PLAYER
of the **YEAR**

Still, scouts weren't oblivious to his talents. Yes, the talent chasers had labeled Carte an "interesting guy" even before his impressive performance in the Cape Cod League in 2004.

Yet it's a wonder what becoming the sixth Cape player ever to reach double-figures in home runs and stolen bases can do for a 6-foot, 190-pound outfielder from Winthrop.

Long-term, it may have moved Carte into the top two or three rounds of the June 2005 draft. In the short term, it earned the Hurricane (W.Va.) High product Baseball America's Summer Player of the Year award.

"He already had an interesting resume, but this summer kind of put an exclamation point on it," Falmouth coach Jeff Trundy said.

Carte paced the Cape Cod League in home runs (11), RBIs (38) and slugging percentage (.560) while adding those 13 steals and batting .308 to earn league MVP honors. He also helped lead Falmouth to the league's championship series, where it eventually lost the title to Yarmouth-Dennis in an 11-inning clincher.

"Going out facing the best competition everyday, you really can't expect to do as well as I did," Carte said.

Carte's efforts over a lengthy summer slate helped him edge out Virginia third baseman Ryan Zimmerman, who led Team USA in average, homers and RBIs, for the award.

Even without the same familiar roots as many Cape participants, Carte didn't feel the need to prove he belonged among them. After all, he had served as Winthrop's top hitter during his first two years there, netting first-team Freshman All-America honors in 2003. He hit .339/.436/.548 for Winthrop as a sophomore.

"He's a very tough kid mentally," Winthrop coach Joe Hudak said. "He's a good hitter, but (mental toughness) is his greatest strength."

Carte put that trait on display after starting the season 0-for-19.

"A lot of kids that would have come here and gone 0-for-19 might have lost their confidence and had a bad summer," Trundy said. "Even at 0-for-19, I felt he was having great at-bats, that he was almost there but not quite.

"Maybe he was trying to do a little too much the first few weeks of the season."

Carte's first hit was a game-winning home run, and his next two hits also left the park. That was really the last time any pitcher had an advantage against Carte.

"Once I started hitting, it felt great," Carte said.

He liked the feeling enough that he didn't bother to stop hitting the rest of the summer.

Daniel Carte

2004 SUMMER LEAGUE ALL-AMERICA TEAM

Selected by Baseball America

FIRST TEAM

Pos.	Player	Team (League)	College	AVG	AB	R	H	HR	RBI
C	Nick Hundley	Alexandria (Northwoods)	Arizona	.293	150	27	44	4	27
1B	Eric Lis	Colleyville (Texas)	Evansville	.418	177	30	74	6	35
2B	Cameron Blair	Fairbanks (Alaska)	Texas Tech	.333	117	40	39	11	27
3B	Ryan Zimmerman	Team USA	Virginia	.468	77	25	36	4	27
SS	Cliff Pennington	Falmouth (Cape Cod)	Texas A&M	.277	148	26	41	3	20
OF	Travis Buck	Team USA	Arizona State	.412	68	17	28	2	14
	Daniel Carte	Falmouth (Cape Cod)	Winthrop	.308	159	30	49	11	38
	Matt Spencer	Colleyville (Texas)	Texas	.367	166	29	61	12	41
DH	Alex Gordon	Team USA	Nebraska	.388	67	18	26	4	12
UT	Zack Kalter	Berkshire (NECBL)	So. California	.353	119	26	42	5	21

Pos.	Pitcher	Team (League)	College	W	L	ERA	IP	H	BB	SO
SP	Dallas Buck	Falmouth (Cape Cod)	Oregon State	4	1	0.77	58	26	20	65
	Matt Goyen	Brewster (Cape Cod)	Ga. College	5	2	1.25	58	42	14	80
	Ryan Mullins	Chatham (Cape Cod)	Vanderbilt	5	1	1.82	54	37	7	64
	Garrett Olson	Anch. Bucs (Alaska)	Cal Poly	9	0	0.67	67	43	10	69
RP	Craig Hansen	Harwich (Cape Cod)	St. John's	1	1	0.00	22	9	2	41
UT	Zack Kalter	Berkshire (N. England)	So. California	1	1	1.47	43	35	12	34

SECOND TEAM

C—Jeff Clement, Team USA (Southern California). **1B**—Scott Simon, Mat-Su/Alaska (Northern Illinois). **2B**—Jim Negrych, Keene/New England (Pittsburgh). **3B**—Jeremy Terni, Winchester/Valley (Southern Connecticut State). **SS**—Tyler Greene, Orleans/Cape Cod (Georgia Tech). **OF**—Jon Love, Front Royal/Valley (Kennesaw State, Ga.); Ryan Patterson, Brewster/Cape Cod (Louisiana State); A.J. Van Slyke, Bluff City/Central Illinois (Kansas). **DH**—Jordan Brown, Orleans/Cape Cod (Arizona). **UT**—Mike Costanzo, Hyannis/Cape Cod (Coastal Carolina).

SP—Lance Broadway, Wisconsin/Northwoods (Dallas Baptist); Kyle Parker, Aloha/Pacific International (Washington); Ricky Romero, Team USA (Cal State Fullerton); Mike Wagner, Winchester/Valley (Vanderbilt). **RP**—Kevin Whelan, Wareham/Cape Cod (Texas A&M).

BY WILL KIMMEY AND ALLAN SIMPSON

Yarmouth-Dennis and Falmouth posted the two best records during the 2004 Cape Cod League regular season, with Y-D finishing one game better. In the playoffs, the Red Sox again narrowly edged the Commodores, needing 11 innings to pull out an 8-4 win to win the best-of-3 championship series in two straight games.

Y-D scored twice in the top of the ninth to force extra innings before scoring four times in the 11th on a wild pitch, a squeeze play and a two-run home run by Nick Moresi (Fresno State). Red Sox shortstop Ryan Rohlinger (Oklahoma) and righthander Josh Faiola (Dartmouth) shared playoff MVP honors.

Timely hitting was a summer-long trend for Y-D. In a league always dominated by pitching, the Red Sox had a team ERA (2.93) that ranked next to last. But they led the Cape League with 197 runs, and catcher Frank Curreri (Massachusetts) led the league with a .432 on-base per-

Dallas Buck

centage and Matt LaPorta's (Florida) nine home runs ranked second.

Falmouth may have had the Cape Cod League's best individual talent, however. Led by manager of the year Jeff Trundy, the Commodores had seven of the league's 20 best prospects. They boasted the league's MVP in outfielder Daniel Carte (Winthrop), who led the league in home runs (11), RBIs (38) and slugging per-

centage (.560) while becoming the sixth player to reach double figures in homers and steals (13). Falmouth righthander Dallas Buck (Oregon State) led the league with an 0.77 ERA.

While Yarmouth-Dennis and Falmouth often did it with their bats, pitching still ruled the rest of the Cape. Chatham offered the league's best one-two punch in lefthanders Andrew Miller (North Carolina) and Ryan Mullins (Vanderbilt). Mullins produced better numbers (5-1, 1.82) with his pinpoint control, while Miller (2-0, 2.03) showed the better stuff and had two of his best outings in games that didn't count. He struck out the side four times in four innings against Falmouth before the game was cancelled because of fog, then punched out all three batters he faced in the all-star game.

Perfect Knights Take NBC Title

The Aloha (Ore.) Knights are owned by Penny Knight, wife of Nike founder and CEO Phil Knight. In true Nike tradition, the Knights went from rags to riches in winning the 70th annual National Baseball Congress World Series in Wichita, Kan.

The Knights entered the 44-team, double-elimination tournament with just a 27-26 record but relied on solid pitching and defense to reel off seven straight wins, becoming the first team since the Jayhawk League's El Dorado (Kan.) Broncos in 1998 to go undefeated.

Righthander Kyle Parker, a rising sophomore at Washington, stopped the Mat-Su (Alaska) Miners, the tournament's best hitting team, on five hits in the decid-

ing game, winning 7-0.

It was Parker's second impressive outing of the tournament, but because the all-tournament team and MVP trophy were awarded the night before the finale, Parker wasn't recognized for his complete-game effort. Instead, he took great pleasure in striking out Mat-Su first baseman Scott Simon (Northern Illinois) four times. Simon, who was 19-for-33 (.576) in eight previous games, had been named the tournament MVP.

"Kyle took it as a challenge facing that kid," Knights manager Geoff Loomis said.

Pitching and defense led the Knights to the title in only their second appearance in the NBC tournament. They allowed 12 runs in seven games while committing just two errors.

"We were kind of the underdog team going in—one game over .500—and a lot of people

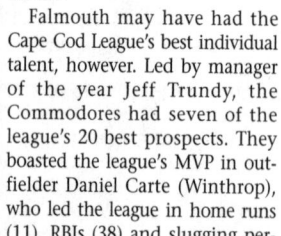

Kyle Parker

doubted us," Parker said. "We wanted to show people we belonged and we deserve this."

Parker and Nate Fogle, a rising junior at Oregon State, started four games for the Knights and went 3-0, 0.58 between them, while striking out 32 in 31 innings. Fogle, who threw a shutout in the tournament opener, was named to the all-tournament team.

Pitching Shines In Other Summer Leagues

■ The Alaska League was a pitcher's league in 2004, with the league's best pitching prospects leading the Anchorage Bucs and Mat-Su Miners to the league's two berths in the annual National Baseball Congress World Series. Mat-Su, which won the Alaska League pennant by a game over the Bucs and Peninsula Oilers, eliminated the Bucs in a loser's bracket game at the NBC tournament. Bucs lefthander Garrett Olson, who led the Alaska League with a 0.88 ERA and was named the league's top prospect, spun 16 scoreless innings at the NBC World Series, earning all-tournament honors.

■ Madison, which posted the Northwoods League's best record at 42-21 to net manager of the year honors for Darrell Handelsman, won its first NWL title. It swept the best-of-3 series with an 11-inning win in game two against Duluth, which was making its first playoff appearance in its second year of existence. Still the story of the year was Wisconsin righthander Lance Broadway. He tossed a 15-strikeout no-hitter against Alexandria en route to leading the league with a 1.80 ERA and 95 strikeouts in 65 innings. He transferred from Dallas Baptist to Texas Christian for his junior year.

■ A new summer league sprung up in 2004, with the initial Texas Collegiate League title going to Coppell, which beat Graham two games to one. All three games were one-run affairs. Coppell second baseman Matt Young (New Mexico) earned series MVP honors with a pair of home runs in the second game. Graham reached the finals behind righthander Alex Rollin (California), who went 6-0, 0.00 with three saves and 39 strikeouts in 37 innings. He was named pitcher of the year.

NCAA-CERTIFIED

CAPE COD LEAGUE

EAST	W	L	T	PCT	Pts
Yarmouth-Dennis Red Sox	26	17	1	.602	53
Brewster Whitecaps	23	21	0	.523	46
Orleans Cardinals	22	21	1	.511	45
Chatham Athletics	21	23	0	.477	42
Harwich Mariners	20	24	1	.455	40

WEST	W	L	T	PCT	Pts
Falmouth Commodores	25	18	1	.580	51
Hyannis Mets	21	22	1	.489	43
Cotuit Kettleers	20	23	1	.466	41
Wareham Gatemen	20	24	0	.455	40
Bourne Braves	19	24	1	.443	39

PLAYOFFS—Semifinals: Yarmouth-Dennis defeated Brewster 2-0 and Falmouth defeated Hyannis 2-1 in best-of-3 series. **Final:** Yarmouth-Dennis defeated Falmouth 2-0 in best-of-3 series.

ALL-STAR TEAM: C—Frank Curreri, Yarmouth-Dennis (Massachusetts); Chris Robinson, Hyannis (Illinois). **1B**—Mike Costanzo, Hyannis (Coastal Carolina). **2B**—Warner Jones, Wareham (Vanderbilt). **3B**—Matt Antonelli, Falmouth (Wake Forest). **SS**—Tyler Greene, Orleans (Georgia Tech). **IF**—Cliff Pennington, Falmouth (Texas A&M); Will Rhymes, Brewster (William & Mary). **OF**—Daniel Carte, Falmouth (Winthrop); Ben Copeland, Harwich (Pittsburgh); Ryan Patterson, Brewster (Louisiana State); Danny Perales, Falmouth (Southern California). **DH**—Jordan Brown, Orleans (Arizona); Pat Reilly, Hyannis (Arizona). **SP**—Dan Brauer, Harwich (Northwestern); Dallas Buck, Falmouth (Oregon State); Matt Goyen, Brewster (Georgia College); Mike Madsen, Bourne (Ohio State); Ryan Mullins, Chatham (Vanderbilt). **RP**—Craig Hansen, Harwich (St. John's); Kevin Whelan, Wareham (Texas A&M).

Most Valuable Player: Daniel Carte, of, Falmouth. **Outstanding Pitcher:** Matt Goyen, lhp, Brewster. **Manager of the Year:** Jeff Trundy, Falmouth.

TOP 20 PROSPECTS: 1. Andrew Miller, lhp, Chatham (North Carolina). **2.** Tyler Greene, ss, Orleans (Georgia Tech). **3.** Craig Hansen, rhp, Harwich (St. John's). **4.** Dallas Buck, rhp, Falmouth (Oregon State). **5.** Stephen Head, 1b/lhp, Chatham (Mississippi). **6.** Mark McCormick, rhp, Wareham (Baylor). **7.** Daniel Carte, of, Falmouth (Winthrop). **8.** Ryan Mullins, lhp, Chatham (Vanderbilt). **9.** Cliff Pennington, ss, Falmouth (Texas A&M). **10.** Kevin Whelan, rhp, Wareham (Texas A&M). **11.** Robert Ray, rhp, Wareham (Texas A&M). **12.** Chris Leroux, rhp, Falmouth (Winthrop). **13.** Zach Ward, rhp, Harwich (Gardner-Webb). **14.** Mark Hamilton, 1b, Falmouth (Tulane). **15.** Micah Owings, of/rhp, Bourne (Georgia Tech). **16.** Justin Maxwell, of, Cotuit (Maryland). **17.** Jacoby Ellsbury, of, Falmouth (Oregon State). **18.** Matt Antonelli, 3b, Falmouth (Wake Forest). **19.** Mike Costanzo, 1b/rhp, Hyannis (Coastal Carolina). **20.** Clete Thomas, of, Harwich (Auburn).

INDIVIDUAL BATTING LEADERS
(Minimum 118 Plate Appearances)

	AVG	AB	R	H	2B	3B	HR	RBI	SB
Patterson, Ryan, Brewster	.327	110	19	36	6	0	5	25	5
Reilly, Pat, Hyannis	.327	101	14	33	2	1	2	12	10
Brown, Jordan, Orleans	.318	132	21	42	8	0	5	28	2
Rhymes, Will, Brewster	.308	159	21	49	5	0	1	5	9
Harris, Bryan, Cotuit	.308	156	17	48	9	1	3	21	3
Carte, Daniel, Falmouth	.308	159	30	49	5	1	11	38	13
Jones, Warner, Wareham	.303	188	19	57	16	1	0	21	3
Perales, Danny, Falmouth	.296	142	19	42	10	1	3	16	3
Greene, Tyler, Orleans	.296	125	23	37	7	3	1	13	13
Curreri, Frank, Yar.-Dennis	.293	133	23	39	3	0	2	15	3

INDIVIDUAL PITCHING LEADERS
(Minimum 35 Innings)

	W	L	ERA	G	SV	IP	H	BB	SO
Buck, Dallas, Falmouth	4	1	0.77	10	0	58	26	20	65
McCormick, Mark, Wareham	2	1	0.93	6	0	39	20	17	47
Ward, Zach, Harwich	2	3	1.05	9	0	43	27	22	57
Huff, David, Chatham	3	3	1.09	12	0	49	37	9	48
Goyen, Matt, Brewster	5	2	1.25	9	0	58	42	14	80
Madsen, Mike, Bourne	5	1	1.31	7	0	48	24	16	32
Self, Ryan, Orleans	0	3	1.43	16	5	38	18	17	28
LaMotta, Ryan, Harwich	3	0	1.47	14	0	37	31	9	30
McCutchen, Daniel, Y-D	5	1	1.58	8	0	46	32	12	43
Averill, Erik, Orleans	5	3	1.70	10	1	64	50	15	62

Cape Cod League's No.1 prospect Chatham lefthander Andrew Miller

CARL KLINE

BOURNE

BATTING	AVG	AB	R	H	2B	3B	HR	RBI	SB
Boesch, Brennan, of	.138	109	8	15	2	0	0	8	0
Caravati, Steve, of	.235	17	3	4	1	0	0	1	0
Creek, Greg, 1b	.242	161	11	39	9	0	0	15	2
Day, Larry, c	.071	14	1	1	0	0	0	0	0
Easley, Austin, of	.173	104	7	18	2	0	1	5	5
Figueroa, Paco, of-ss	.220	50	6	11	2	0	0	4	2
Hawranick, Andy, c	.100	100	5	10	0	1	0	6	1
Hunter, Joseph, of	.179	56	8	10	2	0	0	4	1
Ivany, Devin, c	.190	21	2	4	1	0	0	3	0
Larsen, Andrew, of	.180	50	6	9	1	0	0	2	0
Mangum, Greg, 2b	.176	136	13	24	4	0	0	7	10
Mascia, Tim, of	.238	147	16	35	5	1	0	4	2
Owings, Micah, p-dh	.345	58	4	20	2	0	2	10	0
Padgett, Kyle, 3b	.239	138	11	33	9	0	1	8	3
Simokaitis, Joe, ss	.169	124	5	21	2	0	0	10	3
Sorgi, Adam, 3b-ss	.162	37	2	6	2	0	1	1	0
Stinson, Craig, c	.177	62	2	11	3	0	1	5	1
Valiente, Rob, of	.000	3	0	0	0	0	0	0	0

PITCHING	W	L	ERA	G	SV	IP	H	BB	SO
Bloss, Tom	0	2	3.86	9	0	19	19	5	15
Bongiovanni, Vince	0	1	0.48	4	1	19	11	4	15
Davidson, Daniel	0	0	1.80	3	0	5	3	2	4
Donaldson, Dan	1	0	1.96	12	2	23	22	8	14
Goodman, John	2	0	1.32	10	2	27	12	3	17
Lewis, John	3	3	1.81	8	0	50	38	10	38
Madsen, Mike	5	1	1.31	7	0	48	24	16	32
Mittag, Nathan	0	1	2.25	4	0	12	10	5	5
Neighborgall, Jason	0	2	11.25	4	0	8	8	13	10
Norton, Greg	0	1	5.32	10	1	22	19	11	14
Owings, Micah	1	1	0.69	4	1	13	10	3	19
Reynolds, Greg	4	3	2.27	9	0	40	26	16	31
Schimdt, Kyle	2	6	4.30	10	0	46	48	28	41
Slorp, Andrew	0	1	3.90	11	2	28	27	12	19
Smith, Greg	1	2	2.16	6	0	33	28	16	32

BREWSTER

BATTING	AVG	AB	R	H	2B	3B	HR	RBI	SB
Albano, Marco, ss	.077	39	3	3	0	0	0	1	1
Boone, James, of	.224	134	18	30	4	0	1	13	6
Braun, Ryan, ss	.180	50	9	9	1	0	1	2	4
Campbell, Michael, of	.277	83	6	23	3	0	1	10	2
Cooper, Craig, of	.217	129	11	28	6	0	3	17	4
Hunter, Andy, 1b	.277	119	12	33	7	0	0	7	0

	AVG	AB	R	H	2B	3B	HR	RBI	SB
Jarosinski, Brian, of	.250	28	1	7	1	1	0	2	1
Patterson, Ryan, of	.327	110	19	36	6	0	5	25	5
Rasmussen, Eric, c	.000	2	0	0	0	0	0	0	0
Rhymes, Will, 2b	.308	159	21	49	5	0	1	5	9
Roberson, Ryan, 1b-3b	.272	125	13	34	5	1	5	23	0
Sanchez, Gaby, 3b	.235	132	11	31	8	1	2	11	0
Tolleson, Steven, ss	.280	100	12	28	3	0	1	5	6
Tucker, J.B., c	.177	79	4	14	5	0	2	9	0
Twomley, Jason, of	.211	19	2	4	0	1	0	0	0
Wagner, Mark, c	.173	98	7	17	6	0	0	4	0
Zeskind, Ben, dh	.200	35	5	7	1	0	1	3	0

PITCHING	W	L	ERA	G	SV	IP	H	BB	SO
Avery, Matt	4	1	1.99	6	0	32	31	10	22
Carrillo, Cesar	1	0	1.50	2	0	6	7	1	8
Cleveland, Brett	0	1	0.87	6	0	10	11	0	11
Crews, Jordan	1	0	2.25	17	3	24	26	2	13
Cribb, Josh	3	3	4.00	8	0	45	42	21	43
Cronin, John	0	1	4.15	8	2	9	11	4	6
Davidson, Phillip	2	3	3.23	14	0	47	41	18	35
Determann, Jason	1	2	2.20	14	3	33	24	4	38
Erickson, Blair	0	0	2.25	4	2	4	0	4	4
Falcon, Ryan	3	3	2.27	13	1	40	34	14	57
Gold, Adam	2	3	3.73	9	0	51	40	15	39
Goyen, Matt	5	2	1.25	9	0	58	42	14	80
Lonergan, Scott	1	2	3.75	12	0	24	26	8	29
Matheny, Colin	0	0	18.00	2	0	2	4	3	2
Powers, Trevor	0	0	0.00	1	0	1	0	0	1

CHATHAM

BATTING	AVG	AB	R	H	2B	3B	HR	RBI	SB
Bono, Ryan, 1b-c	.215	163	9	35	4	0	1	14	1
Camp, Matt, ss	.224	156	19	35	4	0	1	8	6
Defendis, Johnny, of	.197	132	9	26	6	0	0	12	0
Demmink, Herm, 3b-2b	.143	28	1	4	0	0	0	0	0
Derba, Nick, 3b	.143	42	2	6	0	0	0	0	0
Dillon, Zack, c	.179	95	4	17	3	0	0	7	0
Getz, Chris, 2b-ss	.293	116	24	34	3	0	0	3	1
Grose, Jeff, of	.216	102	9	22	1	0	0	4	2
Head, Steven, 1b	.271	118	11	32	5	1	3	15	3
Jacobsen, Rob, of	.137	102	9	14	0	0	1	2	3
Mura, Kyle, 3b	.091	11	1	1	0	0	0	0	0
Muyco, Jake, c	.102	49	4	5	1	0	0	3	0
Shanley, Tom, 3b-2b	.183	126	10	23	4	0	0	6	5
Storrer, Travis, of-2b	.238	151	13	36	7	0	0	18	3

PITCHING	W	L	ERA	G	SV	IP	H	BB	SO
Adamski, Brian	0	0	0.00	1	0	0	0	1	0
Avery, James	3	1	5.04	9	0	30	34	17	31
Billek, Mike	0	3	5.52	8	0	15	16	3	19
Bono, Kyle	1	0	0.00	12	7	16	5	5	22
Cassel, Justin	0	4	3.16	7	0	37	33	16	37
Cody, Chris	0	2	2.92	5	0	12	11	6	16
Fabian, Gavin	0	1	8.31	1	0	4	7	3	1
Fenton, Will	1	1	1.59	5	0	6	3	2	11
Huff, David	3	3	1.09	12	0	49	37	9	48
Miller, Andrew	2	0	2.03	7	0	40	19	26	48
Mullins, Ryan	5	1	1.82	7	0	54	37	7	64
Parnell, Robert	0	0	2.00	14	2	18	19	5	13
Paschal, Bobby	0	4	5.55	6	0	24	28	13	12
Sittig, Billy	1	0	0.00	7	0	13	9	4	9
Swanson, Glen	4	3	2.81	8	0	51	36	6	50
Walz, Erik	0	0	0.00	1	0	3	3	1	1
Woodard, Robert	2	2	1.56	8	1	17	12	6	16

COTUIT

BATTING	AVG	AB	R	H	2B	3B	HR	RBI	SB
Ames, Rodney, 1b	1.000	2	0	2	0	0	0	0	0
Beamon, Calvin, of	.056	18	1	1	0	0	0	1	0
Boyer, Brad, of-2b	.282	110	21	31	3	3	6	17	7
Crabtree, Ben, c	.200	10	0	2	0	0	0	1	0
DeCarlo, Mike, c	.109	46	3	5	0	0	2	4	1
Diaz, Dennis, of	.239	142	11	34	2	0	0	12	14
Donald, Jason, ss	.206	102	10	21	4	0	2	6	1
Egelton, Ken, 2b-of	.125	24	2	3	1	0	1	3	0
Emrick, Nathan, c-1b	.198	106	3	21	1	1	0	5	2
Felmy, Bobby, of	.230	87	13	20	4	0	0	2	9
Harris, Bryan, 1b-3b	.308	156	17	48	9	1	3	21	3
Hayes, Brett, c-2b	.000	9	0	0	0	0	0	0	0
Headley, Chase, 3b	.242	124	11	30	3	0	3	17	7
Ingold, Ben, ss	.167	66	3	11	1	0	1	7	1
Maxwell, Justin, of	.263	57	10	15	4	0	1	3	9
Pearce, Steve, c-1b-ss	.277	83	15	23	4	0	1	7	3
Sipp, Tony, of-p	.258	31	4	8	0	0	0	2	5
Southard, Nathan, of	.180	122	14	22	7	0	3	10	6
Strickland, Geoff, 2b	.225	138	16	31	7	3	0	6	7

PITCHERS	W	L	ERA	G	SV	IP	H	BB	SO
Balkan, Adam	0	0	20.25	1	0	1	2	2	0
Cahalan, Ryan	6	1	2.74	29	3	49	50	20	31
Daniels, Adam	0	1	6.27	7	0	19	14	10	20
Egelton, Ken	1	1	5.71	10	1	17	17	10	15
Evans, Cody	1	2	3.51	9	0	51	43	16	41
Faircloth, Jordan	3	4	2.59	22	2	42	43	9	29
Harris, Bryan	0	0	9.00	3	0	2	2	2	3
Hudspeth, Casey	2	3	2.59	10	2	49	39	14	32
Koehler, Michael	0	1	4.85	10	0	13	17	6	7
Luca, Matthew	1	2	2.59	9	0	42	42	21	24
Marlatt, Kyle	2	3	4.81	9	0	43	53	11	25
Miller, Shawn	1	0	0.00	1	0	6	3	0	5
Ramsey, Saunders	3	5	2.38	21	4	42	43	11	38
Sipp, Tony	0	0	1.00	5	2	18	13	6	21
Strickland, Geoff	0	0	10.13	1	0	3	0	3	1

FALMOUTH

BATTING	AVG	AB	R	H	2B	3B	HR	RBI	SB
Antonelli, Matt, 3b	.280	150	26	42	3	0	2	13	9
Bogusevic, Brian, of-p	.183	71	9	13	2	0	0	5	7
Carte, Daniel, of	.308	159	30	49	5	1	11	38	13
Christian, Paul, dh-of	.204	93	7	19	3	0	2	12	0
Delaney, Jason, 3b-1b	.206	68	6	14	2	0	0	4	0
Ellsbury, Jacoby, of	.245	110	20	27	2	3	1	7	12
Gunther, Barry, c	.200	55	4	11	2	0	0	3	1
Hale, Adam, of	.160	25	2	4	1	0	0	1	0
Hamilton, Mark, 1b	.254	130	14	33	5	0	7	29	1
Harvey, Kris, of-p	.294	17	3	5	1	0	1	3	0
Hernandez, Chris	.000	11	0	0	0	0	0	0	0
Leroux, Chris, 1b-c	.167	6	0	1	0	0	0	1	0
Lewis, Chris, 2b	.193	145	13	28	1	1	2	11	6
Looze, Chris, 1b	.233	30	3	7	3	0	1	1	0
Pennington, Cliff, ss	.277	148	26	41	8	1	3	20	21
Perales, Danny, of	.296	142	19	42	10	1	3	16	3
Ray, John, c	.182	55	8	10	2	0	2	6	0
Roberts, Kevin, 2b-p	.150	20	3	3	1	0	0	0	0
Smith, Anthony, p-dh	.000	1	0	0	0	0	0	0	0

PITCHING	W	L	ERA	G	SV	IP	H	BB	SO
Bartleski, Phil	5	3	1.96	8	0	46	35	8	32
Bogusevic, Brian	0	0	0.00	5	0	6	3	1	7
Buck, Dallas	4	1	0.77	10	0	58	26	20	65
Connelly, P.J.	2	3	1.72	6	0	31	19	16	22
Hale, Adam	0	0	9.00	7	0	10	12	6	14
Harvey, Kris	0	0	0.00	1	0	2	1	1	1
Leroux, Chris	2	1	2.08	19	2	26	13	9	38
Lewis, Jensen	4	0	1.73	8	0	52	36	15	53
Phelps, Mike	2	2	5.04	14	1	25	24	12	28
Rice, Tim	0	0	0.00	1	0	2	3	2	2
Roberts, Kevin	0	1	1.64	10	2	11	7	8	16
Ruhlman, Jayson	3	2	2.77	9	0	49	40	24	55
Smith, Anthony	0	1	0.00	5	1	3	1	4	6
Sullivan, Dan	0	0	11.57	2	0	5	8	4	2
Webber, Nick	3	1	3.91	20	1	23	21	20	29
Young, Kyle	0	3	3.92	9	0	44	41	14	33

HARWICH

BATTING	AVG	AB	R	H	2B	3B	HR	RBI	SB
Aughey, Jon, 2b	.267	105	18	28	8	0	3	10	3
Becker, Dave, c	.208	24	3	5	0	0	0	0	0
Bell, Josh, c	.161	56	5	9	1	0	1	4	0
Copeland, Ben, of	.271	140	21	38	1	0	3	11	12
Davidson, Drew, of	.206	126	14	26	5	0	1	13	5
Eymann, Eric, ss	.161	124	10	20	3	0	0	3	0
Grogan, Tim, 3b	.175	143	7	25	4	0	1	16	2
Heriot, Jeff, c	.000	4	0	0	0	0	0	0	0
Holder, James, 1b	.179	134	7	24	4	0	3	9	0
Lillibridge, Brent, of-ss	.208	144	13	30	5	1	4	10	16
Lyons, Charles, c-1b	.158	19	3	3	2	0	0	2	0
Magrass, Miguel, 3b	.133	15	0	2	0	0	0	1	1
Mavroulis, Coby, 1b	.159	63	4	10	2	0	0	3	0
Pankratz, Mike, of	.195	41	7	8	2	0	1	3	0
Slone, Chris, c	.244	131	13	32	3	0	0	12	8
Stadanlick, Ryan, of	.100	20	1	2	0	0	0	0	0
Thomas, Clete, of	.241	116	17	28	5	3	3	15	8

PITCHING	W	L	ERA	G	SV	IP	H	BB	SO
Brauer, Dan	6	2	1.90	8	0	47	31	20	65
Hansen, Craig	1	1	0.00	20	10	22	9	2	41
Kroenke, Zach	1	4	4.93	10	0	35	28	19	28
LaMotta, Ryan	3	0	1.47	14	0	37	31	9	30
Lynch, Kevin	3	1	2.74	12	0	23	20	7	25
Monds, Sonny	0	0	1.19	11	1	23	12	13	19
Mulvey, Kevin	1	3	2.75	8	0	39	25	20	31
Rice, Tim	0	0	8.10	2	0	3	6	3	6

	W	L	ERA	G	SV	IP	H	BB	SO
Sabo, Tim	0	5	4.14	9	0	50	47	22	53
Stadalick, Ryan	0	0	5.91	10	0	11	6	12	9
Varvaro, Anthony	3	5	3.50	9	0	54	40	31	50
Ward, Zach	2	3	1.05	9	0	43	27	22	57

HYANNIS

BATTING	AVG	AB	R	H	2B	3B	HR	RBI	SB
Baxter, Mike, 3b	.267	165	18	44	1	1	1	16	6
Costantino, Mike, ss	.222	99	16	22	5	0	0	8	1
Costanzo, Mike, 1b-p	.234	167	25	39	8	1	6	30	1
Holland, Joe, 2b	.266	154	17	41	8	0	0	24	1
Inouye, Matt, of	.137	102	12	14	1	0	0	4	8
Keen, Kyle, of	.268	123	13	33	3	1	0	9	5
Locke, Drew, of	.167	24	2	4	0	0	0	1	1
Miller, Jay, of	.256	133	20	34	5	0	0	9	3
Ponder, Brandon, 2b	.333	9	1	3	1	0	0	1	0
Reilly, Pat, dh-1b	.327	101	14	33	2	1	2	12	10
Robinson, Chris, c	.292	106	12	31	8	1	1	13	0
Robinson, Shane, of	.252	107	10	27	5	1	1	11	7
Rose, Chandler, ss	.071	14	0	1	0	0	0	0	0
Stinson, Josh, c	.250	80	7	20	1	1	0	6	0
Tordi, Justin, ss	.160	75	5	12	2	0	1	8	0

PITCHING	W	L	ERA	G	SV	IP	H	BB	SO
Adamski, Bryan	0	0	9.00	1	0	2	4	1	0
Boone, Randy	1	0	1.08	10	0	17	13	4	16
Buschmann, Matt	4	3	3.29	9	0	55	62	10	39
Costanzo, Mike	1	1	0.00	13	4	16	7	9	24
Fiorenza, Drew	1	3	2.45	11	0	15	12	19	12
Horne, David	0	3	4.38	7	0	12	11	5	10
Kennedy, Ryan	2	2	2.36	9	0	53	42	20	41
Lanier, Bo	1	1	0.64	12	5	14	8	9	16
Lara, Luis	0	0	1.29	2	1	7	3	1	2
Martinez, Joe	2	5	2.84	9	0	57	41	15	56
McCulloch, Kyle	1	1	4.79	7	0	21	27	9	28
Olisky, Ken	1	0	12.00	3	0	3	5	2	0
Sauls, Mark	3	1	1.90	9	0	52	39	15	38
Taylor, Justin	1	2	3.80	10	1	24	32	9	30
Wlodarczyk, Mike	4	0	2.08	8	0	43	44	12	33

ORLEANS

BATTING	AVG	AB	R	H	2B	3B	HR	RBI	SB
Anderson, Matt, 3b	.102	49	4	5	0	0	0	4	0
Barton, Brian, of	.250	104	8	26	2	1	3	13	4
Blackwood, Steven, of	.274	164	18	45	3	0	0	15	3
Brown, Jordan, 1b	.318	132	21	42	8	0	5	28	2
Butera, Drew, c-3b	.182	137	7	25	4	0	0	10	0
Cooksey, Matt, of	.124	121	20	15	1	1	1	5	7
Curtis, Colin, of	.223	157	16	35	7	0	3	20	9
Dhaenens, Seth, 3b	.207	58	5	12	0	0	0	5	1
Greene, Tyler, ss	.296	125	23	37	7	3	1	13	13
Gronkowski, Gordie, 1b	.125	24	2	3	1	0	0	0	0
Payne, James, of	.167	18	2	3	0	0	0	1	1
Richardson, Antoan, of	.107	28	1	3	0	0	0	2	3
Richardson, Sean, c	.153	98	8	15	2	1	2	9	4
Rivera, Alex, 2b-ss	.212	132	13	28	3	0	0	4	10
Sharpe, Blake, 2b	.138	80	7	11	0	0	0	3	2
Uribes, David, 2b	.222	9	0	2	0	0	0	1	0

PITCHING	W	L	ERA	G	SV	IP	H	BB	SO
Albritton, Daniel	0	0	2.08	5	2	9	6	2	6
Averill, Erik	5	3	1.70	10	1	64	50	15	62
Benoit, Charles	3	1	2.45	12	1	37	34	16	30
Carroll, John	1	2	6.07	5	0	13	16	3	13
Hakey, Patrick	0	0	0.00	1	0	3	1	0	2
Hicks, Romas	1	0	1.71	15	3	26	21	8	29
Nicoll, Chris	4	1	1.70	9	0	53	36	15	42
Robinson, Dennis	1	3	2.31	8	0	47	41	9	32
Rohrbaugh, Robert	1	4	2.25	7	0	40	28	10	35
Seibly, Evan	1	1	5.40	4	0	7	9	2	6
Self, Ryan	0	3	1.43	16	5	38	18	17	28
Torra, Matt	3	1	4.26	11	0	32	30	8	33
Touchet, Dan	2	2	2.82	9	2	22	18	5	18
Woody, Abe	0	0	4.50	2	0	2	3	1	3

WAREHAM

BATTING	AVG	AB	R	H	2B	3B	HR	RBI	SB
Adams, Austin, of	.093	54	5	5	3	0	0	4	2
Alling, Matt, of	.167	18	1	3	1	0	0	1	0
Bell, Mike, 3b	.357	42	9	15	2	0	2	5	3
Brashear, Justin, c-1b	.189	95	9	18	4	0	2	10	0
Bullock, Tyler, c	.150	100	11	15	3	0	1	6	0
Farkes, Zak, 3b-1b	.188	144	15	27	6	2	1	14	7
Gutierrez, Chris, ss	.267	176	16	47	6	0	3	13	7
Hernandez, Mike, of	.290	107	13	31	7	0	0	7	4
Jones, Warner, 2b	.303	188	19	57	16	1	0	21	3

	AVG	AB	R	H	2B	3B	HR	RBI	SB
Kainer, Carson, of	.181	94	9	17	4	1	1	10	4
Reynolds, Kyle, 3b	.233	60	6	14	1	1	0	1	1
Robbins, Whit, 1b	.270	74	4	20	4	0	0	4	0
Rodgers, Adam, 1b-c	.143	70	6	10	4	0	2	5	1
Salsgiver, Lance, of-p	.286	105	13	30	5	1	1	11	4
Tully, Travis, of	.225	129	14	29	4	0	0	10	7
Whelan, Kevin, c	.071	14	2	1	1	0	0	2	1

PITCHING	W	L	ERA	G	SV	IP	H	BB	SO
Bullock, Tyler	0	0	3.18	5	0	6	5	1	4
Cupps, Anthony	1	1	3.48	10	2	41	37	12	25
Forester, Josh	0	0	12.60	8	0	5	6	12	7
Furnish, Brad	1	1	2.00	4	0	27	18	6	31
Gant, Jamie	3	4	4.86	13	2	17	21	7	15
Horne, Alan	3	3	3.71	8	0	34	34	16	45
McCormick, Mark	2	1	0.93	6	0	39	20	17	47
Ray, Robert	2	1	1.93	15	0	33	21	18	57
Salsgiver, Lance	0	1	15.43	7	0	2	6	1	0
Sowers, Josh	0	2	2.17	14	0	29	21	8	31
Taylor, Trey	1	2	3.20	8	0	39	45	18	27
Thornton, Tom	3	5	3.81	9	0	52	56	14	35
Trent, Adam	2	2	3.06	7	0	32	34	15	33
Whelan, Kevin	2	2	0.42	18	11	22	9	6	31
Wiggins, Peter	1	0	1.04	4	0	9	8	4	8

YARMOUTH-DENNIS

BATTING	AVG	AB	R	H	2B	3B	HR	RBI	SB
Anthonsen, Joe, 2b	.229	140	34	32	4	0	0	18	14
Butler, Jacob, of-p	.087	23	3	2	1	0	0	3	1
Byrne, Bryan, 3b-1b	.269	26	4	7	2	0	1	6	1
Crabtree, Ben, c	.238	84	5	20	1	0	2	11	0
Curreri, Frank, c-of	.293	133	23	39	3	0	2	15	3
Davis, Adam, of-ss	.268	149	17	40	4	1	3	13	14
Finigan, P.J., ss-p	.000	3	0	0	0	0	0	0	0
Gerdes, Chase, of	.182	11	3	2	0	0	0	1	2
Glasgow, Ramon, of	.200	5	2	1	0	0	0	1	0
Harris, William, 1b	.256	86	8	22	6	0	3	13	0
Hodges, Wes, 3b-of	.159	88	8	14	2	0	2	11	2
Kleen, Steven, 1b	.118	17	1	2	1	0	0	2	0
LaPorta, Matt, dh-of	.234	145	20	34	3	0	9	20	3
Mahoney, Larry, 1b-3b	.000	2	0	0	0	0	0	0	0
Moresi, Nick, of	.265	113	18	30	5	1	6	17	5
Rapoport, Jim, of	.217	152	18	33	6	3	1	14	12
Ray, Matt, of-2b	.179	28	4	5	1	0	1	2	3
Rohlinger, Ryan, ss-3b	.258	151	16	39	6	1	0	15	7
Vitters, Christian, 1b-3b	.186	59	12	11	1	1	0	2	0

PITCHING	W	L	ERA	G	SV	IP	H	BB	SO
Blaine, Justin	4	2	2.53	12	0	46	33	15	56
Butler, Jacob	1	0	6.35	1	0	6	6	3	8
Butler, Joshua	2	2	2.81	11	2	32	29	7	28
Faiola, Joshua	3	2	1.14	18	9	24	16	4	40
Finigan, P.J.	0	0	2.08	4	0	9	6	5	11
Harker, Brett	1	1	3.25	20	1	28	24	15	22
Holler, Blake	1	1	3.79	15	1	19	14	13	16
Hyde, Lee	3	2	3.02	8	0	48	40	15	50
Keadle, Justin	5	1	3.44	9	0	50	45	13	49
Kleen, Steven	0	0	0.00	4	0	5	3	0	5
Majors, Tommie	0	0	40.50	1	0	1	2	2	2
McCutchen, Daniel	5	1	1.58	8	0	46	32	12	43
Meier, Justin	0	2	5.79	11	2	14	10	9	16
Morrow, Brandon	1	4	3.82	8	0	33	29	13	40
Van Allen, Cory	0	0	2.43	11	1	30	22	12	24

OTHER NCAA-CERTIFIED LEAGUES

ATLANTIC COLLEGIATE LEAGUE

WOLFF	W	L	PCT	GB
Quakertown Blazers	26	14	.650	—
Jersey Pilots	26	14	.650	—
Lehigh Valley Catz	22	18	.550	4
New Jersey Colts	13	27	.325	13

KAISER	W	L	PCT	GB
Stamford Robins	20	20	.500	—
Metro New York Cadets	20	20	.500	—
New York Generals	19	21	.475	1
Long Island Collegians	14	26	.350	6

PLAYOFFS: Quarterfinals—Stamford defeated New York and Quakertown defeated Lehigh Valley in one-game qualifiers. **Semifinals**—Stamford defeated Metro New York 2-0 and Jersey defeated Quakertown 2-1 in best-of-3 series. **Final**—Jersey defeated Stamford in one-game championship.

AMATEUR BASEBALL

Most Valuable Player: Barrett Ward, Lehigh Valley Catz (Central Arkansas). **Outstanding Pitcher:** Brian Honeyman, rhp, Metro New York Cadets (St. Francis).

TOP 10 PROSPECTS: 1. Jeff Sues, rhp, New Jersey (Vanderbilt). **2.** Steve McFarland, rhp, Stamford (Pace). **3.** Todd Martin, of, New Jersey (Tennessee). **4.** Kyle Collins, rhp, Quakertown (Lehigh). **5.** Aaron Kalb, rhp, Jersey (Rutgers). **6.** Ross Boudreaux, c, Lehigh Valley (Southern Arkansas). **7.** David Welch, lhp, Lehigh Valley (Texarkana, Texas, JC). **8.** Milton Feliciano, rhp, Metro New York (Georgia State). **9.** Mike LeFort, rhp, Stamford (Rhode Island). **10.** Doug Anderson, ss, Jersey (Fairfield).

INDIVIDUAL BATTING LEADERS
(Minimum 100 Plate Appearances)

	AVG	AB	R	H	2B	3B	HR	RBI	SB
Sabatella, Bryan, Long Island	.351	134	16	47	10	2	3	27	2
Kuklick, Clay, Quakertown	.350	103	22	36	10	0	1	18	1
Ward, Barrett, Lehigh Valley	.336	137	21	46	5	1	1	20	25
Iacono, Sal, Metro New York	.333	120	17	40	8	0	3	24	3
Hook, Steve, Jersey	.330	115	24	38	6	2	6	25	8
Deluca, Sam, New York	.317	126	17	40	11	0	1	15	3
Garcia, Daniel, Metro New York	.314	118	12	37	8	0	2	14	1
Smith, Curtis, Lehigh Valley	.313	115	19	36	4	1	1	7	23
Holden, Joe, Long Island	.313	147	26	46	8	3	3	21	7
Parfitt, Ryan, Quakertown	.313	147	22	46	6	5	1	18	8
Haney, Joe, Stamford	.312	109	24	34	5	1	0	7	20
Lert, Jordan, New York	.304	92	16	28	2	1	2	18	3
Jones, Kyle, Quakertown	.303	122	18	37	10	0	4	30	0
Donovan, Dennis, Stamford	.301	133	23	40	3	0	0	14	3
Devanney, Ken, Long Island	.299	127	16	38	11	0	1	17	2

INDIVIDUAL PITCHING LEADERS
(Minimum 30 Innings)

	W	L	ERA	G	SV	IP	H	BB	SO
Honeyman, Brian, Metro New York	4	1	0.39	10	1	46	29	10	35
Sues, Jeff, New Jersey	4	1	1.12	7	0	40	20	15	44
Battista, Mike, Jersey	6	0	1.25	9	1	50	48	9	31
Kalb, Aaron, Jersey	3	2	1.60	9	0	51	36	19	53
Bergstrom, Mike, Quakertown	4	3	1.83	8	0	39	37	7	26
Collina, Kyle, Quakertown	4	1	1.85	10	1	44	39	14	49
Zollweg, Mike, New Jersey	1	4	1.86	11	0	48	43	11	25
Feliciano, Milton, Metro New York	4	0	2.01	6	0	40	39	11	26
Bunyan, Brian, New York	6	1	2.10	12	0	64	42	23	63
Welch, David, Lehigh Valley	3	1	2.30	8	0	47	39	10	47

CENTRAL ILLINOIS COLLEGIATE LEAGUE

	W	L	PCT	GB
Twin City Stars	28	15	.651	—
Bluff City Bombers	25	18	.581	3
Danville Dans	23	21	.523	5 ½
Quincy Gems	22	21	.512	6
Galesburg Pioneers	17	26	.395	11
Springfield Rifles	15	29	.341	13 ½

PLAYOFFS: Semifinals—Twin City defeated Quincy 2-0 and Bluff City defeated Danville 2-1 in best-of-3 series. **Final**—Bluff City defeated Twin City 2-0 in best-of-3 series.

Most Valuable Player Year: A.J. Van Slyke, of, Bluff City (Kansas). **Pitchers of the Year:** Nathan Culp, lhp, Bluff City (Missouri); Josh Johnson, rhp, Danville (Mississippi State); Ned Schauff, lhp, Twin City (Illinois State); Eric Theisen, rhp, Twin City (Illinois State).

TOP 10 PROSPECTS: 1. Josh Johnson, rhp, Danville (Mississippi State). **2.** P.J. Finegan, ss/rhp, Springfield (Southern Illinois). **3.** A.J. Van Slyke, of, Bluff City (Kansas). **4.** Nate Culp, lhp, Bluff City (Missouri). **5.** Ty Davis, rhp, Danville (Vanderbilt). **6.** Eric Dessau, rhp, Bluff City (Missouri). **7.** Paul Coleman, lhp, Danville (Pepperdine). **8.** Chris Coghlan, 3b, Danville (Mississippi). **9.** Jeff Rea, 2b, Danville (Mississippi State). **10.** Eric Theisen, rhp, Twin City (Illinois State).

INDIVIDUAL BATTING LEADERS
(Minimum 100 Plate Appearances)

	AVG	AB	R	H	2B	3B	HR	RBI	SB
Van Slyke, A.J., Bluff City	.402	174	51	70	15	2	9	40	19
Reynolds, Kevin, Quincy	.358	106	21	38	10	1	0	12	10
Peden, Scott, Bluff City	.347	150	23	52	17	0	2	43	3
Dinkelman, Brian, Twin City	.335	176	25	59	12	3	0	25	14
Rice, Paul, Galesburg	.331	148	24	49	7	3	0	12	8
Nelson, Jack, Twin City	.329	155	22	51	11	1	4	32	1
Jackson, Carlos, Bluff City	.319	160	45	51	5	3	2	16	26
Jones, J.T., Twin City	.316	158	22	50	6	1	0	16	0
Coghlan, Chris, Danville	.313	160	22	47	10	1	1	30	13
Rea, Jeffrey, Danville	.302	169	30	51	8	2	3	28	5
Busch, Jeremy, Twin City	.299	167	29	50	14	2	0	18	13
Desmond, Geoff, Danville	.295	149	16	44	6	0	3	22	2
Tumilty, Pat, Quincy	.292	161	24	47	9	2	5	30	6

Votaw, Matt, Danville	.291	148	22	43	8	3	1	15	4
Scherer, Scott, Springfield	.290	145	19	42	7	1	1	19	10
Moake, Matt, Bluff City	.290	93	18	27	2	1	0	9	7
Gerst, Matt, Bluff City	.287	150	20	43	12	0	3	29	4
Kyes, J.R., Springfield	.286	133	23	38	9	2	2	15	1

INDIVIDUAL PITCHING LEADERS
(Minimum 30 Innings)

	W	L	ERA	G	SV	IP	H	BB	SO
Davis, Ty, Danville	3	1	1.31	16	3	34	24	14	40
Himes, Drew, Twin City	4	1	1.38	12	0	46	37	14	30
Jones, Kyle, Bluff City	4	2	1.79	16	0	45	29	24	42
Theisen, Eric, Twin City	6	1	1.99	11	0	63	53	20	43
Dessau, Erik, Bluff City	5	2	2.05	10	0	66	55	10	47
Johnson, Josh, Danville	5	1	2.17	10	0	54	38	17	61
Tyler, Adam, Bluff City	1	3	2.20	11	0	33	27	19	10
Schauff, Ned, Twin City	5	0	2.25	9	0	60	46	14	50
Stone, Brad, Quincy	2	3	2.48	10	0	65	53	25	55
Hammond, Steve, Danville	3	2	2.66	8	0	44	46	16	45
Culp, Nathan, Bluff City	7	0	2.79	12	0	61	50	16	48
Harvot, Tony, Twin City	6	2	2.81	15	3	42	43	17	43

COASTAL PLAIN LEAGUE

NORTH	W	L	PCT	GB
+*Edenton Steamers	32	11	.739	—
Peninsula Pilots	29	18	.617	5
Outer Banks Daredevils	23	22	.511	10
Petersburg Generals	15	30	.333	18

SOUTH	W	L	PCT	GB
+*Wilson Tobs	28	22	.560	—
Florence RedWolves	23	24	.489	3 ½
Wilmington Sharks	24	27	.471	4 ½
Fayetteville SwampDogs	21	27	.438	6

WEST	W	L	PCT	GB
*Thomasville Hi-Toms	26	24	.520	—
Asheboro Copperheads	23	24	.489	1 ½
+Gastonia Grizzlies	24	27	.471	2 ½
Spartanburg Stingers	17	29	.370	7

+First-half champion. *Second-half champion
PETTIT CUP TOURNAMENT: Edenton (4-0) defeated Outer Banks (3-2) in championship game of eight-team tournament.

Player of the Year: Tommy Lentz, of, Spartanburg (Winthrop). **Pitcher of the Year:** Jeff DeMara, rhp, Peninsula (Virginia Military Institute).

TOP 10 PROSPECTS: 1. Chris Rahl, of, Peninsula (William & Mary). **2.** Jason Neighborgall, rhp, Fayetteville (Georgia Tech). **3.** Steve Singleton, ss, Thomasville (San Diego). **4.** Keith Beauregard, of, Outer Banks (St. Anselm). **5.** Edgar Ramirez, rhp, Edenton (Florida International). **6.** Danny Powers, rhp, Edenton (Central Missouri State). **7.** Blake Maxwell, rhp, Fayetteville (Methodist, N.C.). **8.** Brian York, 3b/of, Asheboro (Pfeiffer, N.C.). **9.** Chris Cahill, rhp, Edenton (Florida Gulf Coast). **10.** Dusty Bensko, 1b/rhp, Wilmington (Illinois).

INDIVIDUAL BATTING LEADERS
(Minimum 100 Plate Appearances)

	AVG	AB	R	H	2B	3B	HR	RBI	SB
York, Brian, Asheboro	.360	164	35	59	12	2	2	26	16
Dempsey, Jacob, Outer Banks	.345	168	31	58	14	0	7	36	1
Lentz, Tommy, Spartanburg	.335	158	53	16	0	9	33	6	
Henry, Justin, Thomasville	.335	185	39	62	12	2	2	22	13
Singleton, Steve, Thomasville	.327	150	30	49	13	0	7	27	4
Goree, Trent, Thomasville	.324	148	18	48	11	0	1	16	8
Williamson, Schuyler, Pen.	.318	151	28	48	8	0	4	17	13
Sweppenhiser, Kelly, Pen.	.316	152	30	48	9	2	4	28	1
Grace, Mike, Outer Banks	.311	90	20	28	11	0	6	23	1
Godwin, Adam, Gastonia	.309	149	33	46	3	2	0	11	29
Khoury, Ryan, Edenton	.308	143	30	44	11	0	3	19	12
Forbes, David, Fayetteville	.307	127	14	39	7	0	1	12	1
Beauregard, Keith, OB	.306	180	39	55	15	1	3	25	10
Landin, Jaime, Edenton	.305	131	25	40	12	1	1	12	5
Rahl, Chris, Peninsula	.304	184	26	56	4	1	0	28	27
Barber, Byron, Florence	.304	158	29	48	7	0	1	25	13
Davin, Quentin, Gastonia	.303	178	31	54	8	1	1	18	28
Cox, Jay, Fayetteville	.301	146	16	44	10	1	2	32	2
Ard, Chris, Florence	.300	160	23	48	3	0	0	20	14
Gibson, Ian, Gastonia	.298	181	16	54	9	0	2	26	1
Edmondson, Jerod, OB	.298	168	29	50	15	0	3	29	5
Stewart, Josh, Asheboro	.298	124	30	37	5	1	0	10	20

INDIVIDUAL PITCHING LEADERS
(Minimum 30 Innings)

	W	L	ERA	G	SV	IP	H	BB	SO
Jones, Blake, Fayetteville	2	2	0.81	11	0	44	28	13	47

Gemma, Daniel, Edenton	3	0	1.05	11	0	52	35	18	40
Powers, Danny, Edenton	5	2	1.29	7	0	42	33	3	51
Barnes, Brian, Peninsula	5	0	1.29	19	1	35	30	10	34
Walker, Erik, Wilson	3	2	1.31	19	9	41	30	11	50
Rollins, Heath, Florence	4	0	1.39	7	0	45	25	14	50
Cantrell, Jonathan, Fayetteville	5	3	1.46	11	0	56	37	14	56
Eubanks, Aaron, Wilson	4	2	1.65	12	2	55	45	18	42
Henyan, Pete, Edenton	6	1	1.66	10	0	49	35	23	39
Koliscak, Cory, Asheboro	1	2	1.71	22	8	32	23	13	35
Sutton, Josh, Florence	2	2	2.03	15	1	40	32	16	29
Nasiatka, Ryan, Gastonia	1	2	2.16	9	0	33	25	15	22
Tilley, Chad, Gastonia	4	1	2.21	15	2	37	32	10	34
Brown, Eric, Fayetteville	3	3	2.25	13	0	56	48	24	52
Wood, Rick, Thomasville	2	1	2.25	7	0	44	35	9	36
Bronder, Steve, Outer Banks	3	3	2.25	18	2	32	27	12	41

GREAT LAKES LEAGUE

	W	L	PCT	Pts
Lima Locos	26	14	.650	52
Delaware Cows	24	13	.649	48
Columbus All-Americans	23	13	.639	46
Stark County Terriers	24	18	.571	48
Grand Lake Mariners	21	16	.568	42
Indianapolis One Crown	18	25	.419	36
Pittsburgh Pandas	16	22	.421	32
Southern Ohio Copperheads	16	23	.410	32
Youngstown Express	6	32	.158	12

PLAYOFFS: Lima (4-1) defeated Delaware (2-2) in championship game of six-team, double elimination tournament.

ALL-STAR TEAM: C—Andy Busch, Columbus (Ohio Wesleyan); Steve Hill, Indianapolis (San Jacinto, Texas, CC). **1B**—Aaron Hauser, Delaware (John Logan, Ill., CC); Brad Miller, Stark County (Ball State). **2B**—Jason Bucholtz, Columbus (Ball State). **3B**—Jake Frank, Columbus (Wooster, Ohio). **SS**—Ryan Steinbach, Lima (Indiana-Purdue-Fort Wayne). **UT**—Joe Mihalics, Southern Ohio (New York-Buffalo). **OF**—Aaron Bulkley, Grand Lake (Le Moyne); Alan Cattrysse, Lima (Michigan State); Bobby Getty, Delaware (Olney Central, Ill., CC); Billy Grace, Grand Lake (Kentucky). **DH**—Kurt Eichorn, Delaware (Kent State). **P**—Chris Cummings, Lima (Marshall); Ross Liersemann, Grand Lake (Akron); Joe Ness, Columbus (Ball State); Drew Shamrock, Lima (Denison); David Zachary, Grand Lake (Indiana-Purdue-Fort Wayne). **RP**—Rony Mercado, Lima (Suffolk, Mass.).

Player of the Year: Brad Miller, 1b, Stark County. **Pitcher of the Year**: Joe Ness, rhp, Columbus.

TOP 10 PROSPECTS: **1.** Joe Ness, rhp Columbus (Ball State). **2.** Aaron Bulkley, of, Grand Lake (Le Moyne). **3.** Chris Cummings, rhp, Lima (Marshall). **4.** Andy Busch, c, Columbus (Ohio Wesleyan). **5.** Ben Snyder, lhp, Columbus (Ball State). **6.** Brad Miller, 1b, Stark County (Ball State). **7.** Aaron Tennyson, lhp, Grand Lake (Kentucky). **8.** Chad Wagler, rhp, Stark County (Kent State). **9.** Justin Thomas, lhp, Columbus (Youngstown State). **10.** Ross Liersemann, rhp, Grand Lake (Akron).

INDIVIDUAL BATTING LEADERS
(Minimum 100 Plate Appearances)

	AVG	AB	R	H	2B	3B	HR	RBI	SB
Getty, Bobby, Delaware	.409	93	26	38	9	1	2	20	5
Hauser, Aaron, Delaware	.379	132	27	50	5	2	6	32	5
Miller, Brad, Stark County	.374	139	28	52	10	0	4	35	2
Busch, Andy, Columbus	.356	104	13	37	11	1	7	26	0
Onderlinde, Chris, Indianapolis	.345	110	14	38	3	0	1	12	1
Frank, Jake, Columbus	.345	119	31	41	10	1	1	17	3
Eichorn, Kurt, Delaware	.343	108	21	37	9	0	2	20	3
Bucholtz, Jason, Columbus	.337	101	18	34	6	0	1	12	9
Cattrysse, Alan, Lima	.333	132	22	44	8	0	2	11	14
Ayers, Allen, Columbus	.333	111	20	37	5	1	1	22	14
Binick, Kraig, Lima	.330	100	19	33	3	0	1	11	13
Godzik, Brandon, Delaware	.328	116	15	38	9	2	1	26	5
Dygert, Kyle, Southern Ohio	.314	102	17	32	9	3	1	23	1
Steinbach, Ryan, Lima	.313	99	23	31	3	0	0	13	13
Alvarez, Victor, Southern Ohio	.312	128	30	40	6	1	1	12	14

INDIVIDUAL PITCHING LEADERS
(Minimum 30 innings)

	W	L	ERA	G	SV	IP	H	BB	SO
DeMark, Mike, Pittsburgh	3	4	1.52	9	2	47	37	17	39
Biddle, George, Delaware	5	1	1.54	9	0	41	38	10	24
Shamrock, Drew, Lima	5	2	1.62	7	0	39	30	8	37
Cummings, Chris, Lima	4	1	1.89	6	0	38	26	19	51
Ness, Joe, Columbus	5	1	1.93	7	0	51	31	14	50
Lepore, Paul, Stark County	3	1	1.95	8	0	37	28	17	30
Stammen, Craig, Lima	5	1	2.81	8	1	42	42	13	39
Wagler, Chad, Stark County	4	2	2.81	7	0	42	40	7	36
Thomas, Justin, Columbus	3	2	2.95	9	1	43	40	12	36
Hunton, Brock, Delaware	2	1	2.97	7	1	36	40	11	33

NEW ENGLAND COLLEGIATE LEAGUE

NORTH	W	L	PCT	GB
Keene Swamp Bats	26	16	.619	—
North Adams SteepleCats	24	18	.571	2
Sanford Mainers	23	19	.548	3
Vermont Mountaineers	21	21	.500	5
Concord Quarry Dogs	20	22	.476	6
Mill City All Americans	19	23	.452	7

SOUTH	W	L	PCT	GB
Newport Gulls	26	15	.634	—
Manchester Silkworms	24	17	.585	2
Riverpoint Royals	20	20	.500	5½
Torrington Twisters	19	23	.452	7½
Holyoke Giants	17	25	.405	9½
Berkshire Dukes	16	26	.381	10½
Danbury Westerners	15	25	.375	10½

PLAYOFFS: Quarterfinals—Keene defeated Vermont 2-0, Sanford defeated North Adams 2-1, Newport defeated Torrington 2-1 and Riverpoint defeated Manchester 2-1 in best-of-3 series. **Semifinals**—Sanford defeated Keene 2-1 and Newport defeated Riverpoint 2-1 in best-of-3 series. **Final**—Sanford defeated Newport 2-1 in best-of-3 series.

ALL-STAR TEAM: C—Jordan Newton, Danbury (Western Kentucky). **1B**—Chris Colabello, Mill City (Assumption, Mass.). **2B**—Jim Negrych, Keene (Pittsburgh). **3B**—Chris Stanton, Newport (Virginia Tech). **SS**—P.J. Antoniato, Manchester (St. John's). **OF**—Ryan Chambers, Newport (Brigham Young); John McDonald, North Adams (Valdosta State, Ga.); Zack Kalter, Berkshire (Pasadena, Calif., CC). **DH**—Brian Vickers, North Adams (Wright State). **P**—Scott Chambers, North Adams (Marist); Zack Kalter, Berkshire (Pasadena, Calif., CC); Kevin Slowery, Sanford (Winthrop).

Co-Most Valuable Players: Jim Negrych, Keene; Chris Stanton, Newport. **Most Outstanding Pitcher:** Kevin Slowery, Sanford.

TOP 10 PROSPECTS: **1.** Richie Lentz, rhp, Newport (Washington). **2.** Zack Kalter, of/rhp, Berkshire (Pasadena, Calif., CC). **3.** Ryan Crew, ss/rhp, Sanford (Texas-San Antonio). **4.** Brooks Brown, rhp, Keene (Georgia). **5.** Jim Negrych, 2b, Keene (Pittsburgh). **6.** Jordan Newton, c, Danbury (Western Kentucky). **7.** Andrew Bailey, rhp, Mill City (Wagner). **8.** Ryan Turner, lhp, Keene (Georgia Tech). **9.** Chris Stanton, 3b/of, Newport (Virginia Tech). **10.** P.J. Antoniato, ss, Manchester (St. John's).

INDIVIDUAL BATTING LEADERS
(Minimum 100 Plate Appearances)

	AVG	AB	R	H	2B	3B	HR	RBI	SB
Stanton, Chris, Newport	.405	148	40	60	10	3	1	20	21
McDonald, John, North Adams	.367	150	28	55	11	2	3	22	8
Eastley, Reed, Danbury	.362	141	35	51	14	1	4	24	9
Negrych, Jim, Keene	.354	144	36	51	12	0	9	39	14
Kalter, Zack, Berkshire	.353	119	26	42	8	3	5	21	15
Locke, Drew, Newport	.349	106	18	37	11	0	3	28	6
Crew, Ryan, Sanford	.346	156	24	54	12	3	6	30	11
Colabello, Chris, Mill City	.345	148	25	51	7	2	8	33	2
Olson, Garrett, Keene	.333	138	23	46	4	0	1	20	4
Grimes, Scott, North Adams	.328	131	28	43	7	1	6	24	6
Tewksbary, Bobby, Concord	.320	147	27	47	13	2	2	16	3
Rath, Brian, Riverpoint	.316	133	21	42	7	0	0	19	2
Thomas, Devin, Concord	.316	114	17	36	6	0	3	14	2
Taylor, Brandon, Mill City	.314	156	20	49	14	3	1	17	18
Binkoski, Tim, Manchester	.311	132	16	41	3	3	2	20	3
Kozusko, Matt, Berkshire	.309	149	18	46	4	3	4	26	0
Carey, Jason, Vermont	.308	143	25	44	9	1	2	16	18
Antoniato, P.J., Manchester	.306	170	22	52	7	2	0	13	7
Chamber, Ryan, Newport	.306	147	31	45	9	0	7	25	13
Iorg, Eli, Torrington	.304	148	25	45	8	5	3	15	11

INDIVIDUAL PITCHING LEADERS
(Minimum 35 innings)

	W	L	ERA	G	SV	IP	H	BB	SO
Turner, Ryan, Keene	5	0	1.24	9	1	44	27	11	40
Slowery, Kevin, Sanford	4	1	1.44	8	0	50	36	4	59
Kalter, Zack, Berkshire	1	1	1.47	8	0	43	35	12	34
Cobb, Craig, Sanford	4	3	1.78	8	0	51	40	9	24
Chambers, Scott, North Adams	5	1	1.83	8	0	59	31	34	69
Hourigan, Jeff, Torrington	5	2	1.83	8	0	54	32	17	55
Dunn, Brooks, Newport	4	0	1.84	10	2	49	48	12	38
Harrison, Brian, Keene	3	2	2.09	7	1	39	31	2	38
Hammond, Paul, Torrington	1	3	2.11	8	0	47	34	16	52
Heckert, Mitch, Manchester	3	1	2.15	18	4	38	33	4	47
Mooney, Mike, Manchester	5	1	2.20	16	2	41	31	15	31
Franco, T.J., Torrington	3	3	2.24	8	0	56	49	10	63
DiPietro, Ryan, Manchester	4	2	2.28	8	0	55	35	31	57
Honce, Mike, Sanford	2	2	2.36	8	0	42	35	17	23
Herrmann, Frank, Berkshire	3	1	2.49	8	1	47	40	11	36

NEW YORK COLLEGIATE LEAGUE

EAST	W	L	PCT	GB
Glens Falls Golden Eagles	31	10	.756	—
Amsterdam Mohawks	23	18	.561	8
Saratoga Phillies	20	20	.500	10½
Watertown Wizards	20	22	.476	11½
Plattsburgh Thunder	18	23	.439	13
Mohawk Valley Cobras	10	26	.277	18½

WEST	W	L	PCT	GB
Hornell Dodgers	31	11	.738	—
Allegany County Nitros	30	12	.714	1
Alfred A's	24	16	.600	6
Geneva Red Wings	17	25	.415	14
Genesee Valley Riverbats	14	28	.333	17
Wayne Valley Raptors	10	32	.238	21

PLAYOFFS: Semifinals—Amsterdam defeated Glens Falls 2-0 and Hornell defeated Allegany County 2-0 in best-of-3 series. **Final**—Amsterdam defeated Hornell 2-0 in best-of-3 series.

ALL-STAR TEAM: C—Caleb Mangum, Saratoga (North Carolina State). **1B**—Chris Carlson, Glens Falls (Kansas State). **IF**—Jeremy Goldschmeding, Glen Falls (Michigan); Dietrich Jache, Alfred (Northwestern); Kevin McCarroll, Alfred (Oxnard, Calif., JC). **OF**—James Barksdale, Allegany County (North Alabama); Joe Glevenyak, Plattsburgh (Marshall); David Williams, Glens Falls (Rutgers). **DH**—John Allman, Amsterdam (Kansas). **UT**—Bryan Minkel, Alfred (Pepperdine). **SP**—Dan Griffin, Saratoga (Niagara); Chris Ryan, Allegany County (Midland, Texas, JC); Gian Testa, Amsterdam (Cleveland State); Brett Zamzow, Glens Falls (Navarro JC). **RP**—Shawn Ryan, Glens Falls (Albany).

Most Valuable Player: Terry Blunt, of, Glens Falls (Kansas State). **Pitcher of the Year:** Derrick Gordon, Amsterdam (Lamar).

NORTHWOODS LEAGUE

NORTH	W	L	PCT	GB
*St. Cloud River Bats	33	31	.516	—
Thunder Bay Border Cats	32	32	.500	1
+Duluth Huskies	31	32	.492	1½
Alexandria Beetles	25	39	.391	8
Mankato MoonDogs	21	43	.328	12

SOUTH	W	L	PCT	GB
+Madison Mallards	42	22	.656	—
Rochester Honkers	36	26	.581	5
*La Crosse Loggers	34	30	.531	8
Wisconsin Woodchucks	32	31	.508	9½
Waterloo Bucks	32	32	.500	10

* First-half champion.+ Second-half champion.

PLAYOFFS—Semifinals: Madison defeated La Crosse 2-0 and Duluth defeated St. Cloud 2-1 in best-of-3 series. **Final:** Madison defeated Duluth 2-0 in best-of-3 series.

ALL-STAR TEAM: C—Brandon Ketron, St. Cloud (Union, Tenn.); Joe Muich, Rochester (Wichita State). **1B**—Phillip Hawke, Waterloo (Louisiana-Lafayette). **2B**—Jon Schemmel, St. Cloud (Concordia-St. Paul). **3B**—Matt Einspahr, La Crosse (California). **SS**—John Shelby, Waterloo (Kentucky). **IF**—Chad Frk, Madison (Illinois). **OF**—Zach Daeges, Thunder Bay (Creighton); Aaron Grant, Mankato (UC Riverside); Jay Johnson, Madison (Xavier); Ryan Rogowski, Madison (Illinois); Andy Scholl, Duluth (Kansas). **DH**—Kody Valverde, Duluth (New Orleans). **P**—Ricky Bauer, Madison (Hawaii); Lance Broadway, Wisconsin (Dallas Baptist); Rick Cavaiani, Wisconsin (Wisconsin-Milwaukee); Don Czyz, Rochester (Kansas); Chad Epperson, Waterloo (Iowa Western CC); Nick Hall, Alexandria (Northern Illinois); Ben Huffman, Wisconsin (Wisconsin-Oshkosh); Jason Mills, St. Cloud (George Mason); Steve Plucinski, Duluth (Lakeland, Ohio, CC); Andy Sigerich, Madison (Illinois); Ben Stanczyk, La Crosse (Wisconsin-Milwaukee); Ryan Zink, Madison (Illinois-Chicago).

Most Valuable Player: Phillip Hawke, Waterloo.

TOP 10 PROSPECTS: 1. Lance Broadway, rhp, Wisconsin (Dallas Baptist). **2.** Max Scherzer, rhp, La Crosse (Missouri). **3.** Ryan Zink, rhp, Madison (Illinois-Chicago). **4.** Nick Hundley, c/of, Alexandria (Arizona). **5.** John Shelby, ss, Waterloo (Kentucky). **6.** Phillip Hawke, 1b, Waterloo (Louisiana-Lafayette). **7.** John Gaub, lhp, St. Cloud (Minnesota). **8.** Jay Johnson, of, Madison (Xavier). **9.** Ben Stanczyk, rhp, La Crosse (Wisconsin-Milwaukee). **10.** Mark Melancon, rhp, Duluth (Arizona).

INDIVIDUAL BATTING LEADERS
(Minimum 150 Plate Appearances)

	AVG	AB	R	H	2B	3B	HR	RBI	SB
Stewart, Tim, Alexandria	.346	159	25	55	15	0	3	24	4
Johnson, Jay, Madison	.325	209	38	68	6	2	3	28	19
Muich, Joe, Rochester	.322	180	20	58	12	0	3	28	2
Grant, Aaron, Mankato	.321	168	33	54	9	2	1	23	11
Schemmel, Jon, St. Cloud	.318	201	39	64	5	0	0	12	5
Ketron, Brandon, St. Cloud	.317	205	24	65	11	0	5	33	2
Valverde, Kody, Duluth	.307	192	33	59	11	1	5	25	2
Hawke, Phillip, Waterloo	.301	206	34	62	10	0	11	41	3
Frk, Chad, Madison	.299	194	22	58	7	1	1	19	4
Mueller, Dale, La Crosse	.296	223	31	66	9	0	2	18	20
Scholl, Andy, Duluth	.294	221	33	65	21	0	2	33	3
Einspahr, Matt, La Crosse	.293	229	25	67	12	1	2	22	5
Jirschele, Jeremy, Wisconsin	.293	225	39	66	19	0	2	27	12
Hundley, Nick, Alexandria	.293	150	27	44	12	1	4	27	5
Corsaletti, Jeff, Rochester	.293	140	28	41	4	1	3	21	6

INDIVIDUAL PITCHING LEADERS
(Minimum 50 Innings)

	W	L	ERA	G	SV	IP	H	BB	SO
Broadway, Lance, Wisconsin	5	1	1.80	9	0	65	40	17	95
Plucinski, Steve, Duluth	4	1	1.92	17	6	52	38	19	64
Stanczyk, Ben, La Crosse	5	4	2.03	10	0	71	62	15	86
Zink, Ryan, Madison	4	6	2.10	12	0	81	53	15	81
Hall, Nick, Alexandria	3	1	2.17	11	0	58	46	34	42
Phillips, Billy, Madison	6	2	2.38	11	0	68	54	16	60
Huffman, Ben, Wisconsin	7	3	2.47	12	0	87	62	23	88
Eiler, Jake, Madison	6	2	2.51	11	0	65	64	20	51
Bauer, Ricky, Madison	7	2	2.60	10	0	66	45	12	46
Kohrs, Josh, St. Cloud	5	2	2.62	10	0	58	42	28	49
Brettl, Jimmy, Thunder Bay	4	3	2.70	21	1	67	55	19	57

VALLEY LEAGUE

NORTH	W	L	PCT	GB
Winchester Royals	29	15	.659	—
Luray Wranglers	23	21	.523	6
New Market Rebels	23	21	.523	6
Front Royal Cardinals	21	23	.477	8
Loudoun Rangers	15	28	.357	13½

SOUTH	W	L	PCT	GB
Harrisonburg Turks	30	14	.682	—
Staunton Braves	25	19	.568	5
Woodstock River Bandits	20	24	.455	10
Covington Lumberjacks	18	26	.409	12
Waynesboro Generals	15	28	.349	14½

PLAYOFFS: Semifinals—Winchester defeated Harrisonburg 3-0 and New Market defeated Staunton 3-1 in best-of-5 series. **Final**—Winchester defeated Staunton 2-0 in best-of-3 series.

ALL-STAR TEAM: C—Matt Weglarz, Harrisonburg (Southwest Missouri State). **1B**—Joe Kemp, Harrisonburg (Indiana). **2B**—Jeff Beachum, Staunton (Middle Tennessee State). **3B**—Jeremy Terni, Winchester (Southern Connecticut State). **SS**—Gered Mochizuki, Harrisonburg (Yavapai, Ariz., JC). **OF**—Jon Love, Front Royal (Kennesaw State, Ga.); Bruce Sprowl, Winchester (Louisiana State); Reggie Watson, Harrisonburg (Indiana). **DH**—Marion Knowles, New Market (North Florida). **UT**—Jon Hancock, Luray (Mississippi). **SP**—Hunter Abercrombie, Staunton (Tallahassee, Fla., CC); Tim Gudex, Harrisonburg (Iowa); Mike Wagner, Winchester (Vanderbilt). **RP**—Chris Dennis, Winchester (Auburn); Derek Lutz, Front Royal (George Washington).

Co-Most Valuable Players: Jon Love, Front Royal; Jeremy Terni, Winchester.

TOP 10 PROSPECTS: 1. Chris Dennis, rhp, Winchester (Auburn). **2.** Mike Wagner, rhp, Winchester (Vanderbilt). **3.** Jon Jay, of, Staunton (Miami). **4.** Brendan Katin, of, Covington (Miami). **5.** Omar Aguilar, rhp, Covington (Merced, Calif., CC). **6.** Joe Kemp, 1b, Harrisonburg (Indiana). **7.** Jon Love, of, Front Royal (Kennesaw State, Ga.). **8.** Chris Perez, rhp, Staunton (Miami). **9.** Kyle Dubois, rhp, Woodstock (Manatee, Fla., JC). **10.** Chase Tucker, lhp, Staunton (Panola, Texas, JC).

INDIVIDUAL BATTING LEADERS
(Minimum 100 Plate Appearances)

	AVG	AB	R	H	2B	3B	HR	RBI	SB
Kemp, Joe, Harrisonburg	.396	149	34	59	8	3	4	38	5
Love, Jon, Front Royal	.374	171	46	64	13	0	16	48	2
Terni, Jeremy, Winchester	.364	162	28	59	8	1	12	54	5
Mochizuki, Gered, Harrisonburg	.343	143	26	49	6	1	2	27	9
Sprowl, Bruce, Winchester	.340	200	46	68	13	0	6	26	21
Beachum, Jeff, Staunton	.337	172	20	58	9	1	0	22	6
Sain, Derek, Winchester	.337	104	19	35	5	0	1	11	7
Koski, Kevin, Harrisonburg	.331	145	37	48	5	0	0	14	9
Skorupski, Jon, Front Royal	.331	139	20	46	15	0	9	28	1
Watson, Reggie, Harrisonburg	.323	155	37	50	5	0	0	20	26
Murphy, Daniel, Luray	.317	142	24	45	6	0	2	17	14
Weglarz, Matt, Harrisonburg	.313	150	14	47	9	0	1	34	3

Hierlmeier, Bryan, Woodstock	.310	168	37	52	10	3	4	18	12
Walter, Kyle, Winchester	.308	156	30	48	9	2	5	22	9
Selvog, Brandon, Waynesboro	.306	160	28	49	8	0	4	13	9
Knowles, Marion, New Market	.306	134	32	41	5	0	5	21	11

INDIVIDUAL PITCHING LEADERS
(Minimum 40 Innings)

	W	L	ERA	G	SV	IP	H	BB	SO
Hernandez, Danny, Luray	6	2	1.35	20	3	47	24	19	59
Wagner, Mike, Winchester	6	0	1.79	10	1	55	45	7	75
Abercrombie, Hunter, Staunton	4	1	1.91	10	0	57	43	9	44
Stidfole, Sean, Winchester	4	2	2.01	11	0	58	44	25	76
Schwartz, Josh, Waynesboro	3	4	2.10	8	0	60	41	23	73
Gudex, Tim, Harrisonburg	4	1	2.25	14	2	68	59	18	89
Faris, Stephen, New Market	5	2	2.26	9	0	64	56	10	55
Glafenhein, Caleb, Staunton	2	4	2.47	23	2	40	37	15	40
Frontz, Neal, Loudoun	2	5	2.64	9	0	61	45	19	62
Gonzalez, Alexander, Woodstock	4	3	2.66	10	0	68	48	24	73

NON-AFFILIATED LEAGUES

ALASKA LEAGUE

	W	L	PCT	GB	OVERALL W	OVERALL L
*Mat-Su Miners	22	13	.629	—	27	15
*Anchorage Bucs	21	14	.600	1	32	15
Kenai Peninsula Oilers	21	14	.600	1	26	18
Alaska Goldpanners	20	15	.571	2	29	16
Anchorage Glacier Pilots	14	21	.400	8	21	24
Athletes In Action	7	28	.200	15	9	32

*Qualified for National Baseball Congress World Series

ALL-STAR TEAM: C—Brian Jeroloman, Goldpanners (Florida). **1B**—Nick Kliebert, Kenai (Pepperdine). **2B**—Cameron Blair, Goldpanners (Texas Tech). **3B**—Isaac Omura, Bucs (Hawaii). **SS**—Matt Barber, Athletes In Action (Birmingham Southern). **OF**—Travis Becktel, Bucs (San Jose State); Brandon Roberts, Bucs (Cal Poly); Israel Victor, Athletes In Action (Dallas Baptist). **DH**—Paul Keck, Goldpanners (Chabot, Calif., JC). **UT**—Matt Baty, Glacier Pilots (Kansas). **P**—Eric Butkiewicz, Kenai (Maryland-Baltimore County); Chris Malone, Mat-Su (San Joaquin Delta, Calif., JC); Chris Mason, Mat-Su (UNC Greensboro); Garrett Olson, Bucs (Cal Poly); Sean Timmons, Goldpanners. **RP**—Tim Robertson, Kenai (Oral Roberts).

Player of the Year: Cameron Blair, 2b, Goldpanners.

TOP 10 PROSPECTS: 1. Garrett Olson, lhp, Bucs (Cal Poly). **2.** Jeff Gilmore, rhp, Mat-Su (Stanford). **3.** Chris Malone, rhp, Mat-Su (San Joaquin Delta, Calif., JC). **4.** Cameron Blair, 2b, Goldpanners (Texas Tech). **5.** John Hester, c, Mat-Su (Stanford). **6.** Travis Becktel, of, Bucs (San Jose State). **7.** Steve Morlock, rhp, Kenai (UC Santa Barbara). **8.** Kenny Maiques, rhp, Goldpanners (Long Beach State). **9.** Matt Manship, rhp, Mat-Su (Stanford). **10.** Brandon Roberts, of, Bucs (Cal Poly).

INDIVIDUAL BATTING LEADERS
(Minimum 110 Plate Appearances)

	AVG	AB	R	H	2B	3B	HR	RBI	SB
Roberts, Brandon, Bucs	.369	149	35	55	6	2	1	19	12
Omura, Isaac, Bucs	.345	174	29	60	15	3	2	29	5
Kliebert, Nick, Kenai	.331	166	32	55	16	0	1	28	5
Simon, Scott, Mat-Su	.323	164	18	53	6	3	2	29	3
Balmer, Allen, Goldpanners	.314	137	20	43	10	0	1	15	1
Jeroloman, Brian, Goldpanners	.314	102	18	32	6	0	2	15	1
Minaker, Chris, Kenai	.311	135	24	42	7	0	3	23	4
Barber, Matt, AIA	.311	119	15	37	4	1	0	10	5
Satin, Josh, Mat-Su	.309	149	33	46	12	2	4	31	5
Becktel, Travis, Bucs	.308	159	31	49	8	6	3	34	6
Baty, Matt, Glacier Pilots	.306	160	25	49	8	2	0	10	17
Dahl, Andy, Kenai	.305	167	29	51	6	1	1	20	18
Keck, Paul, Goldpanners	.305	128	22	39	7	1	4	25	1
Victor, Israel, AIA	.304	112	22	34	8	1	2	12	3
Blair, Cameron, Goldpanners	.298	121	33	36	4	1	11	27	12
Hester, John, Mat-Su	.293	140	24	41	12	1	1	20	3
Faulkner, Nathan, Kenai	.290	131	23	38	4	0	4	26	10
Paulk, Michael, Glacier Pilots	.288	153	25	44	7	2	2	17	4
Mortensen, Trevor, G'panners	.285	158	25	45	6	1	0	14	14
Mehl, Truan, Bucs	.284	176	25	50	7	3	0	15	12

INDIVIDUAL PITCHING LEADERS
(Minimum 35 innings)

	W	L	ERA	G	SV	IP	H	BB	SO
Olson, Garrett, Bucs	7	0	0.88	7	0	51	34	8	53
Malone, Chris, Mat-Su	6	1	1.99	9	0	54	33	13	56
Butkiewicz, Eric, Kenai	2	1	2.06	23	1	44	31	19	29
Mason, Chris, Mat-Su	7	1	2.09	9	0	65	59	22	56
Wood, Blake, Bucs	3	3	2.34	7	0	42	32	9	39

Tomasiewicz, Kevin, Mat-Su	4	4	2.63	8	0	51	45	18	33
Stimpson, Jeff, Goldpanners	2	3	2.66	9	0	47	47	24	43
Pape, Andy, Bucs	4	2	2.66	15	0	44	35	14	26
Wordekemper, Eric, Glacier Pilots	1	2	2.85	9	0	60	49	19	48
Fisher, Carlos, Goldpanners	3	2	3.23	7	0	39	39	19	35
Morlock, Steve, Kenai	6	2	3.36	9	0	56	46	15	61
Hamblet, Reid, Goldpanners	3	3	3.55	8	0	46	47	11	55
Timmons, Sean, Goldpanners	5	1	3.59	8	0	53	60	10	28
Bordes, Brett, Bucs	2	2	3.63	7	0	40	41	25	32
Serrato, Oscar, Kenai	4	2	3.73	12	1	51	47	24	36

CLARK GRIFFITH LEAGUE

	W	L	PCT	GB
Bethesda Big Train	29	13	.690	—
Herndon Braves	28	14	.667	1
Silver Spring-Takoma Thunderbolts	26	15	.634	2 ½
Vienna Senators	23	19	.547	6
Fauquier Gators	19	22	.463	9 ½
Baltimore Pride	15	27	.357	14
Reston Hawks	6	36	.143	23

Co-Most Valuable Players: Michael McKenry, c, Bethesda (Middle Tennessee State); Joey Testa, of, Fauquier (Gardner-Webb).

TOP 10 PROSPECTS: 1. Adam Mills, rhp, Silver Spring (UNC Charlotte). **2.** Brad LaNinfa, 1b, Bethesda (Mississippi State). **3.** J.J. Hollenback, rhp, Herndon (Virginia Military). **4.** Michael McKenry, c, Bethesda (Middle Tennessee State). **5.** Jon Link, rhp, Herndon (Virginia Commonwealth). **6.** Brandon Bowser, of, Herndon (James Madison). **7.** Daniel Burton, of/1b, Vienna (Louisville). **8.** Manny Burriss, ss/2b, Vienna (Kent State). **9.** Chris Rhoades, rhp, Bethesda (Towson). **10.** Keith Moreland, rhp, Bethesda (UNC Charlotte).

INDIVIDUAL BATTING LEADERS
(Minimum 100 Plate Appearances)

	AVG	AB	R	H	2B	3B	HR	RBI	SB
Bowser, Brandon, Herndon	.361	169	34	61	13	2	4	31	11
Testa, Joey, Fauquier	.356	132	16	47	6	0	0	7	7
LaNinfa, Brian, Bethesda	.333	123	23	41	10	1	3	27	2
McKenry, Michael, Bethesda	.321	106	15	34	5	0	7	17	0
Towler, Bryan, Fauqier	.319	138	16	44	9	1	1	17	5
Good, Braxton, Herndon	.318	110	24	35	3	0	4	9	7
Teller, Rhett, Herndon	.315	143	26	45	12	0	7	25	0
Burton, Daniel, Vienna	.305	154	29	47	12	5	4	34	14
Greene, Andrew, SS-Takoma	.301	143	30	43	5	2	0	8	18
Jones, Michael, Baltimore	.300	130	11	39	8	1	3	24	0
Capece, Matt, SS-Takoma	.298	161	27	48	3	2	0	21	9
Yarbrough, Charlie, Reston	.298	141	11	42	7	1	7	28	1
Prosise, Nick, Vienna	.292	130	19	38	8	2	1	23	3
Scott, Steven, Reston	.291	141	9	41	6	1	2	13	2
Cuevas, Trey, Bethesda	.287	101	14	29	11	0	1	17	2

INDIVIDUAL PITCHING LEADERS
(Minimum 35 innings)

	W	L	ERA	G	SV	IP	H	BB	SO
Mills, Adam, SS-Takoma	6	0	1.04	15	5	69	41	15	56
Moreland, Keith, Bethesda	6	1	1.16	10	1	47	24	15	41
Redd, Adam, Bethesda	3	1	1.19	6	0	38	26	12	32
Belanger, Ryan, Vienna	4	2	1.25	11	1	58	28	14	45
Stone, Philip, Herndon	4	0	1.25	9	0	43	26	15	49
Rhoades, Chris, Bethesda	4	2	1.51	9	0	60	41	19	60
Link, Jon, Herndon	7	1	1.88	12	0	72	49	19	64
Hollenbeck, J.J., Herndon	3	5	1.91	12	0	66	57	11	87
Mills, Randy, Vienna	3	1	1.93	16	3	47	26	21	49
Baron, Casey, Bethesda	5	2	1.93	9	0	51	44	12	43

JAYHAWK LEAGUE

	W	L	PCT	GB
*El Dorado Broncos	21	12	.636	—
*Hays Larks	14	10	.583	2 ½
Liberal BeeJays	14	17	.452	6
Nevada Griffons	12	16	.429	6 ½
Elkhart Dusters	12	18	.400	7 ½

*Qualified for National Baseball Congress World Series

TOP 10 PROSPECTS: 1. Matt Green, rhp, El Dorado (Louisiana-Monroe). **2.** Mike McCallister, of, Liberal (Alabama). **3.** Kevin Russo, ss, Hays (San Jacinto, Texas, JC). **4.** Stephen Marek, rhp, San Jacinto, Texas, JC). **5.** Anthony Hatch, 1b/3b, El Dorado (Nicholls State). **6.** Nolan Reimold, of, Hays (Bowling Green State). **7.** Gilbert Delavera, lhp, Elkhart (Pima, Ariz., CC). **8.** Bob Reifschneider, rhp, Hays (Duquesne). **9.** Matt Rainey, rhp, Hays (Odessa, Texas, JC). **10.** Trent Lare, lhp, Nevada (Coffeyville, Kan., CC).

INDIVIDUAL BATTING LEADERS
(Minimum 75 Plate Appearances)

	AVG	AB	R	H	2B	3B	HR	RBI	SB
Hatch, Anthony, El Dorado	.425	106	24	45	12	0	4	32	8
Russo, Kevin, Hays	.374	107	19	40	9	0	6	24	4
Fortenberry, Seth, Hays	.358	81	17	29	8	1	3	21	9
Batlle, Aaron, Hays	.356	104	23	37	7	0	5	25	0
Dimercurio, J.R., El Dorado	.333	108	17	36	2	0	5	26	1
Reimold, Nolan, Hays	.327	113	29	37	7	2	6	28	6
Zimmerman, Cory, Liberal	.326	89	15	29	5	1	2	19	1
Van Hook, Clay, Liberal	.326	89	23	29	1	0	0	9	2
Nichol, Mickey, Nevada	.320	97	10	31	5	0	1	9	5
Leal, Andrew, Elkhart	.306	72	11	22	6	0	5	16	0
Stevens, Justin, Liberal	.294	109	21	32	10	0	5	24	0
Ryal, Rusty, El Dorado	.293	92	15	27	5	1	2	16	4
White, Dwayne, El Dorado	.293	92	16	27	3	1	1	10	10
Myers, Jared, El Dorado	.292	65	22	19	6	1	1	8	11
Bell, Bubba, El Dorado	.288	73	13	21	3	0	2	11	2

INDIVIDUAL PITCHING LEADERS
(Minimum 20 Innings)

	W	L	ERA	G	SV	IP	H	BB	SO
Trevino, Toro, El Dorado	3	0	0.90	4	1	20	14	6	18
Jones, Rusty, El Dorado	4	0	0.96	6	0	38	30	8	34
Costi, Justin, El Dorado	3	1	2.48	5	0	29	17	7	33
Green, Matt, El Dorado	4	1	2.57	8	1	42	28	18	51
Reischnei, Bob, Hays	4	2	3.00	7	0	48	46	10	47
Deseg, Gomez, Liberal	2	3	3.04	7	0	24	30	12	31
Delavara, Gilbert, Elkhart	2	1	3.30	8	1	30	19	4	31
Ofat, Chris, Hays	2	2	3.34	5	0	32	31	4	24
Edens, Joe, Hays	2	1	3.41	6	0	32	33	7	24
Cohn, Kevin, Elkhart	3	2	3.44	8	1	30	16	20

PACIFIC INTERNATIONAL LEAGUE

INTERNATIONAL	W	L	PCT	GB	OVERALL W	L
Wenatchee AppleSox	24	12	.667	—	36	16
Kelowna Falcons	22	14	.611	2	34	21
Bellingham Bells	21	15	.583	3	26	18
Langley Blaze	17	19	.472	7	17	20
Spokane RiverHawks	6	30	.167	18	10	31

NATIONAL	W	L	PCT	GB	W	L
Bend Elks	24	12	.667	—	42	21
*Seattle Studs	24	12	.667	—	31	19
*Aloha Knights	17	19	.472	7	34	26
Kirkland Kodiaks	17	19	.472	7	23	24
Portland Kings	14	22	.389	10	23	23
Everett Merchants	12	24	.333	12	16	31

PLAYOFFS: Semifinals—Kelowna defeated Wenatchee 2-0 and Bend defeated Kirkland 2-0 in best-of-3 series. **Final**—Bend defeated Kelowna 2-0 in best-of-3 series.

*Qualified for National Baseball Congress World Series

ALL-STAR TEAM: C—Jason Anderson, Wenatchee (Howard, Texas, JC). **1B**—Cole Gillespie, Wenatchee (Oregon State). **2B**—Louie Hernandez, Bellingham (UC Riverside). **3B**—Mike Rundle, Bend (Gonzaga). **SS**—Nick Batkoski, Seattle (Washington). **OF**—Aaron Coiteux, Aloha (Concordia, Ore.); Jake Dickinson, Kelowna (Arkansas Tech); Kaeo Rubin, Aloha (Washington State). **DH**—Dave Bingham, Kirkland. **UT**—Seth McCauley, Kirkland (Lewis-Clark State). **P**—Nate Fogle, Aloha (Mt. Hood, Ore., CC); Justin Goodrich, Kelowna (Harding, Ark.); Nate Kuhns, Seattle (Lewis-Clark State); Kyle Parker, Aloha (Washington); Dane Renkert, Bellingham (Washington State); Ben Rowe, Bend (Oregon State); Kyle Wright, Wenatchee (Columbia Basin, Wash., CC).

Most Valuable Player: Aaron Coiteux, of, Aloha.

TOP 10 PROSPECTS: 1. Tim Lincecum, rhp, Seattle (Washington). **2.** Kyle Parker, rhp, Aloha (Washington). **3.** Cole Gillespie, 1b, Wenatchee (Oregon State). **4.** Zach Clem, 3b/of, Bellingham (Washington). **5.** Andrew Lefave, of, Everett (Edmonds, Wash., CC). **6.** Josh McLaughlin, rhp, Kelowna (Georgia). **7.** Nate Fogle, rhp, Aloha (Mt. Hood, Ore., CC). **8.** Taylor Johnson, rhp, Seattle (Washington). **9.** Chad Decker, lhp, Aloha (UC Riverside). **10.** Nick Batkoski, ss, Seattle (Washington).

INDIVIDUAL BATTING LEADERS
(Minimum 75 Plate Appearances)

	AVG	AB	R	H	2B	3B	HR	RBI	SB
Coiteux, Aaron, Aloha	.417	120	31	50	12	2	1	19	13
Gillespie, Cole, Wenatchee	.402	122	36	49	9	1	5	27	5
Dickinson, Jake, Kelowna	.394	104	28	41	8	0	4	22	4
Morrison, Josh, Kelowna	.390	82	13	32	8	0	0	13	0
Anderson, Jason, Wenatchee	.385	156	25	60	13	1	2	20	0
Rubin, Kaeo, Aloha	.381	97	23	37	8	0	3	15	0
Lindsey, Shawn, Seattle	.379	132	31	50	9	2	3	31	7

McCauley, Seth, Kirkland	.377	106	18	40	7	1	4	29	1
Dias, Chad, Seattle	.376	141	33	53	10	0	8	39	1
Stevenson, Ryan, Spokane	.373	110	20	41	8	8	1	18	11

INDIVIDUAL PITCHING LEADERS
(Minimum 20 Innings)

	W	L	ERA	G	SV	IP	H	BB	SO
Fogle, Nate, Aloha	4	1	1.64	6	1	44	29	15	46
Renkert, Dane, Bellingham	6	0	1.83	11	2	34	21	10	34
Kasser, Matt, Aloha	1	3	1.87	5	0	34	28	15	24
Harmon, Brandon, Wenatchee	4	2	2.25	8	0	36	31	11	30
Cebula, Nick, Seattle	3	1	2.35	11	3	23	10	11	21
Hill, Josh, Wenatchee	0	0	2.38	12	5	23	20	8	22
Rowe, Ben, Bend	3	3	2.49	11	3	47	40	17	33
Merritt, Cory, Bend	3	0	2.57	10	1	21	19	9	18
Cannell, Alan, Spokane	0	3	2.61	4	0	21	29	3	12
Jensen, Jeff, Bend	2	1	2.64	7	0	31	29	6	11
Parker, Kyle, Aloha	4	1	2.66	6	0	44	30	14	47

TEXAS COLLEGIATE LEAGUE

ROGERS HORNSBY	W	L	PCT	GB
Graham Roungnecks	31	21	.596	—
Weatherford Wranglers	29	22	.569	1½
Mineral Wells Steam	22	30	.423	9
Granbury Generals	17	35	.327	14

TRIS SPEAKER	W	L	PCT	GB
McKinney Marshals	33	17	.660	—
Coppell Copperheads	30	21	.588	3½
Colleyville-Grapevine LoneStars	25	27	.481	9
Highland Park Blue Sox	19	33	.365	15

PLAYOFFS: Semifinals—Coppell defeated McKinney 2-0 and Graham defeated Weatherford 2-1 in best-of-3 series. **Final**—Coppell defeated Graham 2-1 in best-of-3 series.

ALL-STAR TEAM: C—Blake Parker, Coppell (Arkansas). **1B**—Erik Lis, Colleyville-Grapevine (Evansville). **2B**—Gibbs Chapman, Highland Park (Florida State). **3B**—Ryan Hill, Highland Park (Texas A&M). **SS**—Michael Hollimon, Colleyville-Grapevine (Texas). **OF**—J.J. Estrada, Granbury (Texas Christian); Trey Rachal, McKinney (Oklahoma State); Matt Spencer, Colleyville-Grapevine (Texas). **DH**—Robbie Winn, Weatherford (Weatherford, Texas, CC). **P**—Drew Johnson, Coppell (Texas); Matt Ueckert, Coppell (Rice). **RP**—Cameron Johnson, Weatherford (California); Alex Rollin, Graham (California).

Player of the Year: Erik Lis, 1b, Colleyville-Grapevine. **Pitcher of the Year:** Alex Rollin, rhp, Graham.

TOP 10 PROSPECTS: 1. Drew Johnson, rhp, Coppell (Texas). **2.** Bryce Cox, rhp, McKinney (Paris, Texas, JC). **3.** Eric Lis, 1b, Colleyville-Grapevine (Evansville). **4.** German Duran, ss, Coppell (Texas Christian). **5.** Matt Spencer, of, Colleyville-Grapevine (Texas). **6.** Braedyn Pruitt, 3b, Weatherford (Stetson). **7.** Adam Morris, 3b, McKinney (Rice). **8.** Travis Reagan, c, Weatherford (Rice). **9.** Pete Duda, rhp, Weatherford (Stanford). **10.** Ryan Tacker, rhp, Coppell (Navarro, Texas, JC).

INDIVIDUAL BATTING LEADERS
(Minimum 75 Plate Appearances)

	AVG	AB	R	H	2B	3B	HR	RBI	SB
Lis, Erik, Colleyville-Grapevine	.418	177	30	74	11	2	6	35	7
Spencer, Matt, Colley.-Grape.	.367	166	29	61	10	0	12	41	8
Rachal, Trey, McKinney	.359	167	28	60	8	0	4	23	8
Winn, Robbie, Weatherford	.351	151	17	53	14	0	4	25	1
Pill, Brett, Coppell	.346	104	21	36	9	1	4	28	5
Chapman, Gibbs, High. Park	.327	147	34	48	8	1	9	24	10
Hollimon, Michael, C-G	.323	124	28	40	9	1	7	21	9
Kimbrough, Brandon, MW	.320	97	12	31	1	0	3	14	4
Hill, Ryan, Highland Park	.318	192	29	61	11	0	5	29	4
Alamia, Louis, McKinney	.317	161	38	51	12	0	1	14	10
Morris, Adam, McKinney	.312	141	26	44	9	0	6	23	3
Estrada, J.J., Granbury	.312	186	30	58	16	1	6	36	17
Burton, Blake, Highland Park	.310	145	20	45	13	0	2	22	1
Shaffer, Stephen, Weatherford	.308	65	15	20	3	0	0	6	3

INDIVIDUAL PITCHING LEADERS
(Minimum 20 Innings)

	W	L	ERA	G	SV	IP	H	BB	SO
Rollin, Alex, Graham	6	0	0.00	12	3	37	25	15	39
Melek, Nate, Highland Park	3	0	0.69	4	0	26	11	11	28
Stallings, Matt, Coppell	4	1	0.94	13	2	29	22	9	26
Johnson, Cameron, Weatherford	7	1	1.60	18	3	39	34	14	40
Creps, Austin, McKinney	3	0	1.69	12	1	21	20	5	24
Ueckert, Matt, Coppell	4	2	1.81	11	0	55	31	14	63
Parker, Taylor, Coppell	1	0	1.82	8	0	35	23	12	23
Johnson, Drew, Coppell	4	3	1.82	12	2	59	54	18	72
Hering, Hart, Weatherford	1	1	1.91	17	6	28	21	8	33
Herrera, Bryan, Coppell	1	2	2.05	14	4	22	14	15	21

YOUTH BASEBALL

BY ALLAN SIMPSON

After losing the international final to Japan in each of the previous three years, Curacao finally broke through in 2004 to win its first Little League World Series (11-12) and the first ever by a team from the Caribbean.

Curacao (6-0) beat Mexico, 4-0, to win the international final and then defeated Thousand Oaks, Calif., the United States champion, 5-2 in the final. The 16-team tournament was played in Williamsport, Pa., with the final game attracting a throng of 35,000 fans.

A two-run homer by Jurickson Profar staked Curacao to a 3-0 first-inning lead against Thousand Oaks, which was 22-0 in district, state, regional and World Series play entering the final. Five-foot-11, 168-pound righthander Carlos Pineda (2-0) made the lead stand up as he blanked the Americans through five innings, while striking out 11. Thousand Oaks scored both its runs off Pineda in the sixth and final inning, before Jonathan Schoop, Curacao's No. 2 pitcher, came on to get the final two outs.

In the tournament's third-place game, Richmond, Texas, defeated Mexico 5-0 as righthander Randal Grichuk struck out 11 and tied a tournament record with his 12th hit. Grichuk, who also appeared in the 2003 World Series, led the tournament with four home runs.

Taiwan, which won the last of 17 Little League World Series titles in 1996, returned to the series for the first time after voluntarily withdrawing in 1998 amid charges it recruited players from outside the strict geographical boundaries mandated by Little League. Taiwan failed to advance to the international division final, after losing to Panama and Curacao.

■ Tampa's Palma Ceia/Bayshore Little League arrived at the Junior League World Series (13-14) two days late because of the effects of Hurricane Charley, which ravaged Florida's Gulf Coast, but strung together six straight wins to win the 2004 title, beating Venezuela 5-2 in the final. The tournament was played in Taylor, Mich.

Peto Kirkwood hit two homers in the deciding game, giving him five for the tournament, tying a record, while teammate Mike Lashbrook went 4-for-4 to give him a tournament record-tying 15 hits overall.

■ Host South Carolina captured the Big League World Series (17-18) for the second year in a row, beating Pennsylvania 9-1 in the 2004 final. The tournament was

Maybin building own legacy

BY BILL BALLEW

Cameron Maybin, 17, has first-hand experience regarding the impact of legacies on the game. In fact, the the 6-foot-3, 195-pound outfielder seems to make history virtually every time he steps on the field, which led to yet another honor as Baseball America's 2004 Youth Player of the Year.

PLAYER *of the* **YEAR**

"Playing baseball is all I've ever wanted to do," said Maybin, a senior at T.C. Roberson High in Arden, N.C. "When I was in first grade, I wrote a picture book about how I wanted to play for the Asheville Tourists when I grew up. My dad and I laugh about that now, but that's how long I've wanted to play the game."

Maybin has worked out with the Tourists during pregame drills and was hitting home runs during batting practice at age 14. He also served two years as a Tourists bat-boy, which carries a legacy unlike any other in the minor leagues. Among those that previously manned the position include author Thomas Wolfe, Tourists general manager Ron McKee,

**Connie Mack World Series star
North Carolina's Cameron Maybin**

University of North Carolina head basketball coach Roy Williams, future Hall of Famer Cal Ripken Jr., and Atlanta Braves rookie Charles Thomas.

"Hanging around the club-house and taking BP with the Tourists, that was so big for me," Maybin said. "By watching and talking with the players, it taught me how important it is to take care of the little stuff. I think it gave me a more professional approach to the game."

Maybin went on to meet every challenge in 2004, beginning with leading Roberson to 25 straight

wins. On the season, he hit .536-8-41.

Maybin joined Cincinnati's Midland Redskins for the second summer and led the team to the Connie Mack World Series title with a record-breaking performance. Maybin won the batting title and was tabbed the tournament MVP while hitting five home runs. Overall, he hit .464-11-61 for the Redskins.

Joe Hayden, who founded the Midland program more than 40 years ago, has managed his share of standouts while winning nine Connie Mack titles since 1984. According to Hayden, the comparisons between Maybin and Ken Griffey Jr., a former Midland player, are not unfair.

"There's a lot of resemblance between the two," Hayden said. "They've both got all five tools and they have the same instincts in the outfield and at the plate. Kenny matured quicker at 16, while Cameron matured at 17. But otherwise, they're very similar."

PREVIOUS **WINNERS**

2002—Delmon Young, of, Camarillo, Calif.
2003—Nick Adenhart, rhp, Williamsport, Md.

played in Easley, S.C.

The South Carolina team was comprised of players from area schools, including a nucleus of seven from Riverside High in nearby Greer. Riverside (29-1 in 2003, 30-2 in 2004) repeated as state 3-A champions and finished fourth in the Baseball America/National High School Baseball Coaches Association final top 50 poll for the second straight year.

"These guys know how to win," South Carolina coach Gregg Powell said. "They play well together."

Lefthander Marc Young, who went undefeated as a junior and senior at Riverside High, won the final two games of the tournament for South Carolina. He worked the final two innings in relief in the semifinals and threw a complete game against Pennsylvania in the final. Young was a 29th-round pick of the Orioles in the 2004 draft.

Maybin Powers Midland

Led by outfielder Cameron Maybin's record-breaking performance, Cincinnati's Midland Redskins returned to the winner's circle at the 2004 Connie Mack World Series, played in Farmington, N.M.

Maybin, a rising senior at T.C. Roberson High in Arden, N.C., and a projected first-round pick in the 2005 draft, hit five home runs as Midland overcame a first-round loss to win five straight games and the title. The Redskins beat previously-unbeaten Phoenix Subia 8-6 and 10-6 on the final night of the eight-team, double elimination tournament.

The win was the first for Midland since 1998, but the ninth since 1984. The team ended the 2004 season with a 58-7 record.

Maybin won the batting title and was named the tournament's most valuable player. In a semifinal game against the Florida Bombers, he went 4-for-4 and set a tournament record with three home runs.

The Bombers earned a trip to the tournament by defeating the East Cobb (Ga.) Yankees, winners of three of the five previous Connie Mack World Series, in regional play.

Maine School Wins Legion Title

Portland, Maine, proved its baseball talent matches any high school-aged group in the country as it went undefeated in winning the 2004 American Legion World Series, played in Corvallis, Ore.

Portland's Deering High went 24-0 during the spring and was one of only three undefeated teams in the BA/NHSBCA Top 50. It beat Mt. Ararat High righthander Mark Rogers, the first high school pitcher drafted in June, for the Maine state Class A title before nearly 7,000 at Portland's Hadlock Park. And yet Deering was ranked only 41st in the BA/NHSBCA final poll. California's Chatsworth High, one of the undefeated team, was crowned the national champion for the second year in row. New Mexico's La Cueva High, the other, ranked sixth.

With a team that was kept intact for Legion play, Deering (37-4) went 10-1 in regional and national play and beat Kennewick, Wash. (58-9), 2-0, in the championship game. It was the first Legion title for a Maine team and the first for a team from New England in 67 years.

Righthander Mike Powers blanked Kennewick on one hit through eight innings in the championship game, getting last inning relief help from outfielder/closer Ryan Reid. Reid, the team's best player and a James Madison recruit, led Portland with a 5-0, 1.27 record and won the Bob Feller Award for most strikeouts (29 in 21 innings) in regional and national play.

Mexico Captures Ripken Crown

Mexico won the Cal Ripken World Series (11-12) for the second year in a row, scoring twice in the last inning to beat West Raleigh, N.C., 4-3. The 15-team tournament was played in Aberdeen, Md.

Mexico allowed one run in its previous five games entering the final, getting two outstanding pitching performances from righthander Michael Alvarez. He no-hit Korea, winning 7-0, with 11 strikeouts in the semi-finals and one-hit the Dominican Republic, winning 8-0, while striking out 16—one short of the single-game record. He didn't walk a batter in either game.

■ San Gabriel Valley, Calif., won a record eighth Babe Ruth League 16-18 World Series title, beating Worcester, Mass., 8-2 in the championship game, played in Newark, Ohio. Tournament MVP Bill Spottiswood, a sophomore at Glendale (Calif.) Junior College, had a single, home run and three RBIs in the deciding game after pitching a complete game, eight-hitter in a 10-3 win over Mineral Area, Mo., in the semifinals.

East Cobb Triumphs Again

The East Cobb Astros continued their amazing run in AAU's 16-year-old Junior Olympics competition by winning the baseball championship for the eighth time in nine years. The event was held in Des Moines, Iowa.

The Astros won nine straight games, including six by shutout, and beat the San Jose Vipers in the final, 8-2. Lefthander Josh Smoker, from Calhoun High in Sugar Valley, Ga., was the winning pitcher in the final game. He also pitched a perfect game earlier in the tournament.

East Cobb, 80-7 on the year, also won the Continental Amateur Baseball Association 16-year-old for the third year in a row.

■ East Cobb's 14-year-old team breezed through the 2004 PONY League World Series, played in Washington, Pa., winning four straight games, including a 3-1 win over Mililani, Hawaii, in the final. East Cobb last won the PONY League title in 1985.

Righthander Jake Davies was the big star for East Cobb, winning two games and hitting three homers. In addition to pitching a one-hitter against Mililani, he doubled in his team's first run, homered in his second at-bat and hit a single that scored his team's third run. Davies is the younger brother of Atlanta Braves pitching prospect Kyle Davies, one of the most celebrated players in the history of the highly successful East Cobb program.

■ The Maryland Orioles won the All-American Amateur Baseball Association (20-and-under) title for the second straight year and 22nd time by a team from Baltimore, beating 12-time champion New Orleans 2-1 in the championship game of the 60th annual tournament, played in Johnstown, Pa.

Lefthander Joe Krebs (Navarro, Texas, JC) struck out 12, walked none and allowed four hits in going the distance against New Orleans after working the final three innings of an 8-4, 12-inning marathon that the Orioles (50-8) had won earlier in the day against host Johnstown to advance to the final. Krebs was named the tournament's MVP.

BASEBALL FOR **THE AGES**

BY ALLAN SIMPSON

Baseball America's annual Baseball For the Ages selection brings together players from every age, every level and every region. But they share one thing in common: They're the best baseball players in the country—if not the world—at their ages.

The universal youth baseball cutoff date of Aug. 1 is used to establish a player's age.

12 **CODY POLK, lhp-1b, North Richland Hills, Texas**
The 5-foot-8, 150-pound Polk was the ace pitcher for the Texas Rattlers, the nation's No. 1-ranked team in his age group in 2002 and 2003. At one point, the Rattlers strung together 57 straight wins. At 18-0, he went unbeaten in 2004 for the second season in a row as the Rattlers went 68-6. While Polk didn't lead his team to a national title as he did in 2003, when he was the MVP of the United States Specialty Sports Association (USSSA) Majors World Series, he pitched all of his team's big games—and beat all the nation's top-ranked teams. He was invited to join the Texas Steel at one of

Cody Polk

Cooperstown Dreamspark's weekly 80-team tournaments, and excelled as the Steel won the title. He hit .778-9-21 in 12 games and went 2-for-4 with three RBIs as the Steel beat the No. 1 seed Miami Mudcats 10-3 in the championship game.

13 **ZAK SINCLAIR, rhp-ss, McDonald, Pa.**
The 6-foot-4, 175-pound Sinclair did it all in 2004 for Pennsylvania's Beaver Valley Red, the nation's top-ranked

Zak Sinclair

13-year-old team. He pitched, he played shortstop, he hit cleanup and he was his team's fastest runner. At the premier event for 13-year-olds, the USSSA Elite World Series, he earned MVP honors as the Red went unbeaten. Sinclair showcased an 86 mph fastball and 72-74 mph slider, and worked only his team's most important games as the Red amassed a 61-3 record. He went 13-0 with a sub-1.00 ERA and also had four saves while striking out 178 in 82 innings. He threw

five no-hitters. Sinclair also played a big role with the bat, hitting .608 with 28 home runs.

14 **ROBERT STOCK, rhp, Westlake Village, Calif.**
Stock has been one of the top players in his age group for three years running. He earned runner-up honors as a 12-year-old before earning his due in 2003 at 13, when his fastball was clocked at 89 mph. He dialed the pitch up to 91 in the spring as a freshman closer at Agoura High, to 92 at an Area Code Games tryout in Sacramento in July and to 93 at the Team USA youth team trials in August. Stock was the youngest player ever selected to USA Baseball's national youth team, which qualified for the 2005 World Youth Championship by finishing second at a qualifying tournament in Mexico in September. Used as a closer, he threw four scoreless innings and also hit a

walk-off home run in his only at-bat.

15 **MICHAEL MAIN, rhp-of, Deltona, Fla.**
Main was the runner-up at 14, and his skills continue to be extremely advanced for his age. He has already been rated the No. 1 high school player in the Draft Class of 2007. Though only 6-foot-1 and 165 pounds, Main is extremely athletic and has excellent arm strength. His fastball was clocked at 94 mph in September, when he helped lead Team USA's national youth squad to a second-place finish in an America's qualifying tournament for the 2005 World Youth championship. Main's skills aren't limited to the mound, how-

Michael Main

ever. He's been timed in the 60-yard dash in 6.6 seconds and is a superior defender, capable of playing almost any position. As a freshman at DeLand High, he led his team in hitting with a .407 average.

16 **JUSTIN UPTON, ss, Chesapeake, Va.**
Upton was the nation's best 14-year-old in 2002 and best 15-year-old in 2003, and completed a rare hat trick by being named the best 16-year-old. He's followed almost the same career path as his older brother B.J., the 19-year-old honoree. He earned first-team All-America honors as a junior at Great Bridge High in Chesapeake, while hitting .565-8-23 with 30 stolen bases. He was named the inaugural winner of the Jackie Robinson award as AFLAC's national player of the year. Upton starred for Team USA at the World Junior Championship, where he hit .417-1-5 and led Team USA with eight runs and four triples.

17 **CAMERON MAYBIN, of, T.C. Roberson HS, Arden, N.C.**
Justin Upton is the top prospect for the 2005 draft, but Maybin went a long way toward closing the gap on the Virginia high school shortstop in 2004. He hit .536-8-41 for T.C. Roberson High, which lost its only game in the North Carolina 3-A playoffs. He starred for Cincinnati's Midland Redskins, who went 57-7 and went on to win their ninth Connie Mack World Series in 21 years. Maybin was named the series MVP after winning the batting title (.571), tying a Series record with five home runs and setting a single-game mark with three. He hit .464-11-61 overall for the Redskins.

18 **DELMON YOUNG, of, Devil Rays**
Young was the first player selected in the 2003 draft. After sitting out the remainder of that season while negotiating a $5.8 million major league deal, he broke into pro ball in 2004 with an outstanding season at low Class A Charleston, S.C. He led the South Atlantic League in RBIs with 116 while hitting .322 with 25 homers, and was selected as the league's top major league prospect.

19 **B.J. UPTON, ss, Devil Rays**
Upton became the first teenager to homer in a big league game since the Pirates' Aramis Ramirez in 1998, when he went deep Aug. 17, 2004, against the Angels. He hit .258-4-12 in 158 at-bats in his first exposure to big league pitching. Prior to his promotion to Tampa Bay, Upton sizzled in both the Triple-A International League, hitting .311-12-36 in 264 at-bats for Durham, and Double-A Southern League, where he hit .327-2-25 for Montgomery.

WINNERS AGES 20-25

20. Zack Greinke, rhp, Royals
21. Miguel Cabrera, of, Marlins
22. Carl Crawford, of, Devil Rays
23. Jake Peavy, rhp, Padres
24. Albert Pujols, rhp, Cardinals
25. Adrian Beltre, 3b, Dodgers

AMATEUR BASEBALL

TEAM USA
HEADQUARTERS: Durham, N.C.

COLLEGE TEAM

Event	Site	Champion	Runner-up
World University Games	Tainan City, Taiwan	United States	Japan

JUNIOR TEAM (18-and-Under)

World Championship	Taipei, Taiwan	Cuba	Japan

YOUTH TEAM (16-and-Under)

COPABE Pan Am Championship	Aguascalientes, Mexico	Cuba	United States
USA Junior Olympics—East	Jupiter, Fla.	Southeast Texas Sun Devils	Miami Tigers
USA Junior Olympics—West	Peoria/Sunrise, Ariz.	Chino (Calif.) Tigers	Placentia (Calif.) Mustangs Elite

ALL-AMERICAN AMATEUR BASEBALL ASSOCIATION (AAABA)
HEADQUARTERS: Zanesville, Ohio

World Series (21-and-Under)	Johnstown, Pa.	Maryland Orioles	New Orleans

AMATEUR ATHLETIC UNION (AAU)
HEADQUARTERS: Lake Buena Vista, Fla.

8-and-Under	Concord, N.C.	West Palm (Fla.) Diamond Dawgs	Carolina Mustangs
9-and-Under	Orlando	Hawaii Warriors	Florida Xtreme
10-and-Under (60-foot)	Des Moines	West Des Moines Diamondbacks	Eden Prairie (Minn.) Black
10-and-Under (65-foot)	Charlotte	Central Florida Express	Carolina Lightning
11-and-Under (60-foot)	Des Moines	South Des Moines Hitmen	Fort Dodge (Kan.) White Sox
11-and-Under (70-foot)	Orlando	Tampa Ball Players	California Park Bums
12-and-Under	Burnsville, Minn.	Greenville (S.C.) Gators	Virginia Performance Baseball
13-and-Under (80-foot)	Knoxville	East Cobb (Ga.) Astros	Knoxville Yard Dogs
13-and-Under (90-foot)	Myrtle Beach, S.C.	Massachusetts Lightning Baseball	St. Petersburg Stingers
14-and-Under (90-foot)	Sarasota, Fla.	California Starmaker Sharks	Tampa Gators
15-and-Under	Virginia Beach, Va.	Tri-State Arsenal-Navy	South Charlotte Panthers
Junior Olympics/16 & U	Des Moines	East Cobb (Ga.) Astros	San Jose Vipers
17-and-Under	Kingsport, Tenn.	Myrtle Beach (S.C.) Jr. Pelicans	Texas Braves
18-and-Under	Orlando	Savannah (Ga.) Chain	Baton Rouge White Sox

AMERICAN AMATEUR BASEBALL CONGRESS (AABC)
HEADQUARTERS: Marshall, Mich.

Roberto Clemente (8 & U)	McDonough, Ga.	Knoxville Stars	Puerto Rico
Willie Mays (9 & U)	Tulsa	Sykesville (Md.) Cyclones	Midwest City (Okla.) Warriors
Willie Mays (10 & U)	Catano, P.R.	Puerto Rico	Knoxville Stars
Pee Wee Reese (11 & U)	Brooklyn, N.Y.	Weston (Fla.) Rattlers	Baltimore Buzz
Pee Wee Reese (12 & U)	Toa Baja, P.R.	Los Potros, P.R.	Toa Baja, P.R.
Sandy Koufax (13 & U)	Battle Creek, Mich.	Miami	Calvary, Pa.
Sandy Koufax (14 & U)	Rockford, Ill.	Dallas Giants	Riverdale, Ga.
Mickey Mantle (16 & U)	McKinney, Texas	Long Island (N.Y.) Titans	Dallas D-Bats 15
Connie Mack (18 & U)	Farmington, N.M.	Midland (Ohio) Redskins	Phoenix Subia
Stan Musial (open)	Battle Creek, Mich.	Atlanta	Battle Creek, Mich.

AMERICAN LEGION BASEBALL
HEADQUARTERS: Indianapolis

World Series (19 & U)	Corvallis, Ore.	Portland, Maine	Kennewick, Wash.

BABE RUTH BASEBALL
HEADQUARTERS: Trenton, N.J.

Cal Ripken (10 & U)	Vincennes, Ind.	Fort Carolina, Fla.	South Lexington, Ky.
Cal Ripken (11-12)	Aberdeen, Md.	Mexico	West Raleigh, N.C.
13-year-old	Van Buren, Ark.	Tri Valley, Calif.	Beaverton, Ore.
14-year-old	Wilson, N.C.	Honolulu	Harris Township, Ind.
13-15-year-olds	Longview, Wash.	Jefferson Parish, La.	El Segundo, Calif.
16-year-old	Leesburg, Va.	Syracuse, N.Y.	Loudoun County, Va.
16-18-year-old	Newark, Ohio	San Gabriel, Calif.	Worcester, Mass.

CONTINENTAL AMATEUR BASEBALL ASSOCIATION (CABA)
HEADQUARTERS: Westerville, Ohio

9-and-Under	Charles City, Iowa	Omaha Pacesetters	Arcadia, Calif.
10-and-Under	Marietta, Ga.	Columbus (Ohio) Sharks	East Cobb (Ga.) Cubs
11-and-Under	Marion, Ohio	Cincinnati Lakota Braves	San Juan, P.R.
12-and-Under	Cincinnati	East Cobb (Ga.) Astros	Dublin (Ohio) Green Sox
13-and-Under	Broken Arrow, Okla.	Brooklyn Bergen Beach	Tulsa Aces
14-and-Under (54-foot)	Dublin, Ohio	Washington Cannons	Seattle Stars
14-and-Under (60-foot)	Monterey Park, Calif.	Snohomish County (Wash.) Express	Maywood (Calif.) Giants
15-and-Under	Crystal Lake, Ill.	Seattle Stars	Japan
16-and-Under	Marietta, Ga.	East Cobb (Ga.) Astros	Columbus (Ohio) Jaguars
High school age	Euclid, Ohio	Brooklyn Bergen Beach	Ann Arbor, Mich.
18-and-Under	Homestead, Fla.	South Florida Spartans	Maryland Monarchs
18-and-Under (wood)	Charleston, S.C.	South Carolina Diamond Devils	East Cobb (Ga.) A's
College	Aurora, Ill.	Northern Kentucky Bandits	Wheaton (Ill.) White Sox

COOPERSTOWN DREAMSPARK
HEADQUARTERS: Salisbury, N.C.

Tournament of Champions (12)	Cooperstown, N.Y.	Huntington Beach (Calif.) Vikings	California OC Juice

DIXIE BASEBALL
HEADQUARTERS: Montgomery, Ala.

Dixie Youth (9-10)	Muscle Shoals, Ala.	Montgomery (Ala.) AUM Gold	Bossier City, La.
Dixie Youth (12 & U)	Muscle Shoals, Ala.	Goodlettsville, Tenn.	Bartow, Fla.
Junior Dixie Boys 13	Aiken, S.C.	Troy, Ala.	Decatur, Ala.
Dixie Boys (13-14)	La Grange, Ga.	Hartsville, S.C.	Columbus County, N.C.
Dixie Pre-Majors (15-16)	Guntersville, Ala.	Shelby-Tipton, Tenn.	West Monroe, La.
Dixie Majors (15-18)	Monroe, La.	Polk County, Fla.	Monroe, La.

DIZZY DEAN BASEBALL
HEADQUARTERS: Hernando, Miss.

8-and-Under	Southaven, Miss.	Hobgood (Ga.) Heat	Gardendale, Ala.

9-and-Under	Southaven, Miss.	Gardendale, Ala.	Northport (Ala.) Blue
10-and-Under	Moody, Ala.	Huffman, Ala.	Tallahassee, Fla.
11-and-Under	Jasper, Tenn.	Tallahassee (Fla.) Myers Park	Pensacola (Fla.) Brent
12-and-Under	Moody, Ala.	Tallahassee, Fla.	Kenner, La.
13-and-Under	Southaven, Miss.	Cantonment, Fla.	Hamilton, Miss.
14-and-Under	Southaven, Miss.	St. Petersburg Fossil Park	Northport (Ala.) Red
Junior (15-16)	Southaven, Miss.	Frederick, Md.	Lufkin, Texas
Senior (17-19)	Southaven, Miss.	Boynton, Ga.	Tri-Cities, Tenn.
High school	Starkville, Miss.	Lufkin, Texas	Tupelo, Miss.

HAP DUMONT BASEBALL/National Baseball Congress — HEADQUARTERS: Wichita

8-and-Under	Midwest City, Okla.	Oklahoma City Sooners	Lawrence (Kan.) Detonators
9-and-Under	Bartlett, Tenn.	Wichita Sluggers	Topeka (Kan.) Cathawks
10-and-Under	Harrison, Ark.	Memphis Tigers	Wichita Young Guns
11-and-Under	Oklahoma City	Brockfield (Ill.) Scorpions	Wichita Cardinals
12-and-Under	Greenfield, Ind.	Sioux City (Iowa) Stars	Indianapolis Prospects
13-and-Under	Tunica, Miss.	Houston Mudbugs	Columbus (Miss.) Dirty Dozen
14-and-Under	Casper, Wyo.	Oklahoma City 89ers	Pittsburg, Kan.
15-and-Under	Kearny, Mo.	Tulsa Redhawks	West Chester, Ohio
16-and-Under	Horn Lake, Miss.	Mississippi Tigers	Louisiana Wildcats
18-and-Under	Wichita	Springfield (Mo.) Rebels	Texas Blackhawks 18

LITTLE LEAGUE BASEBALL — HEADQUARTERS: Williamsport, Pa.

Little League (11-12)	Williamsport, Pa.	Willemstad, Curacao	Thousand Oaks, Calif.
Junior League (13-14)	Taylor, Mich.	Tampa	Punto Fijo, Venez.
Senior League (15-16)	Bangor, Me.	Freehold Township, N.J.	Oxnard, Calif.
Big League (17-18)	Easley, S.C.	South Carolina	Pennsylvania

NATIONAL AMATEUR BASEBALL FEDERATION (NABF) — HEADQUARTERS: Bowie, Md.

Freshman (12 & U)	Hopkinsville, Ky.	Maryland Orioles	Johnny Appleseed (Ohio)
Sophomore (14 & U)	Joplin, Mo.	Nashville Donelson Knights	Maryland Orioles
Junior (16 & U)	Northville, Mich.	Bayside (N.Y.) Yankees	Indiana Bulls
High School (17 & U)	Millington, Tenn.	Mississippi Stars	Team Ontario
Senior (18 & U)	Jackson, Miss.	Pennsylvania Diamond Dogs	Indiana Bulls
College (22 & U)	Toledo	Twin City (Ill.) Scrappers	Michigan Bulls
Major (open)	Louisville	Brunswick (Md.) Orioles	Fort Wayne, Ind.

PERFECT GAME/WORLD WOOD BAT ASSOCIATION SUMMER CHAMPIONSHIPS — HEADQUARTER: Cedar Rapids, Iowa

15-and-Under	Marietta, Ga.	NorCal	Atlanta Blue Jays
16-and-Under	Chicago	Florida Red Wings	Upper Deck-Chicago
17-and-Under	Marietta, Ga.	Houston Kyle Chapman	South Texas Sliders-Navy
18-and-Under	Marietta, Ga.	South Carolina Diamond Devils	East Cobb (Ga.) Braves

PONY BASEBALL — HEADQUARTERS: Washington, Pa.

Mustang (9-10)	Irving, Texas	Miami Tamiami	Levittown, Pa.
Bronco (11-12)	Monterey, Calif.	Tampa Wellswood	Caguas, P.R.
Pony (13)	Chino Hills, Calif.	Chino Hills, Calif.	Anaheim
Pony (13-14)	Washington, Pa.	East Cobb (Ga.) Astros	Mililani, Hawaii
Colt (15-16)	Lafayette, Ind.	North Tampa	Canovanas, P.R.
Palomino (17-18)	Santa Clara, Calif.	Santa Clara (Calif.) Red Sox	Orange County (Calif.) Renegades

REVIVING BASEBALL IN INNER CITIES (RBI) — HEADQUARTERS: New York

Junior (13-15)	Detroit	Puerto Rico	Miami
Senior (16-18)	Detroit	Miami	Philadelphia

U.S. AMATEUR BASEBALL ASSOCIATION (USABA) — HEADQUARTERS: Edmonds, Wash.

13-and-Under	Hoquiam, Wash.	Hoquiam, Wash.	Shelton, Wash.
14-and-Under	Pasco, Wash.	San Leandro, Calif.	Kennewick, Wash.
15-and-Under	Mianer, Nev.	Sonora, Calif.	Las Vegas, Nev.
16-and-Under	Pasco, Wash.	Yakima, Wash.	Kennewick, Wash.

U.S. AMATEUR BASEBALL FEDERATION (USABF) — HEADQUARTERS: Coronado, Calif.

11-and-Under	San Diego	Encinitas (Calif.) Red	Seattle Stars
12-and-Under	San Diego	Tucson Show	Tucson Bandits
13-and-Under	San Diego	Seattle Stars	Washington Cannons
14-and-Under	San Diego	San Diego Dugout	Team Mexico
15-and-Under	San Diego	San Diego Bulldogs	San Diego Sun Devils
16-and-Under	San Diego	Encinitas (Calif.) Reds	San Diego Crew
18-and-Under (wood)	San Diego	California Night Hawks	Riverside (Calif.) ABD

U.S. SPECIALTY SPORTS ASSOCIATION (USSSA) — HEADQUARTERS: Petersburg, Va.

9-and-Under/Majors	St. Louis	Houston Banditos-Black	Louisiana Baseball Academy
10-and-Under/Majors	Henderson, Nev.	Houston Banditos-Black	California Yankees
11-and-Under/Majors	Nevada, Mo.	Rocky Mountain (Colo.) Steel	Omaha Tigers
11-and-Under/Majors Elite	Orlando	San Diego Stars	Broward (Fla.) Bulldogs
12-and-Under/Majors	Kansas City, Mo.	Mac & Seitz (Kan.) Indians	Iowa Predators
12-and-Under/Majors Elite	Orlando	Texas Express	California HB Vikings
13-and-Under/Majors	Kansas City, Mo.	Mac & Seitz (Mo.) Indians	St. Louis Gateway Grizzlies
13-and-Under/Majors Elite	Orlando	Beaver Valley (Pa.) Red	Knoxville Yard Dogs
14-and-Under/Majors Elite	Orlando	Scottsdale (Ariz.) Storm	Richmond (Va.) Braves National
15-and-Under/Majors	Orlando	Atlanta Blue Jays	Weston (Fla.) Lightning
16-and-Under/Majors	Orlando	Georgia Stars	Palm Beach County, Fla.
17-and-Under/Majors	Lexington, Ky.	Kansas City (Kan.) White Sox	Kentucky Players Edge Elite
18-and-Under/Majors	Nashville	Midwest (Mo.) Prospects	Indiana Mustangs

AMATEUR BASEBALL

DRAFT

Padres settle on local product Bush, but feel-good angle quickly sours

BY JIM CALLIS

A month before the 2004 draft, the Padres narrowed their candidates for the No. 1 overall pick to three collegians: shortstop Stephen Drew (Florida State) and righthanders Jeff Niemann (Rice) and Jered Weaver (Long Beach State). With six days to go, San Diego general manager Kevin Towers said his club was leaning heavily toward Drew.

The teams picking immediately behind the Padres began to plan accordingly. As late as June 4, three days before the draft, Drew still appeared to be San Diego's choice.

Then several clubs' draft boards were thrown into chaos after owner John Moore and Towers met and decided that the cost of signing Drew exceeded their impression of his worth. Local Mission Bay High shortstop Matt Bush was at home watching the Padres play the Brewers on television that evening when he decided to take matters into his own hands. He placed a call to area scout Tim McWilliam.

Rosy picture in San Diego
Matt Bush is flanked by Padres GM Kevin Towers, left, and scouting director Bill Gayton

"I knew the Padres had never made a final decision," Bush said. "They were looking at Stephen Drew at the time, but I was still in the mix. I've always been a Padres fan, and I really wanted to be a Padre. I called Tim and told him I wanted to be a Padre."

McWilliam called Gayton but couldn't reach him in San Diego's draft war room. McWilliam eventually got through to West Coast crosschecker Chris Gwynn, who relayed Bush's interest to Gayton. Suddenly, the feeling was mutual.

"I've been in the business for a long time, and this is the first time this has happened in the first round," Gayton said. "It's unique, but this is what you hope for. You want players who want to be a part of your organization."

The next day, a large Padres contingent took a break from draft planning and ventured to San Diego State to watch Bush play in the California Interscholastic Federation Division III championship game against crosstown rival St. Augustine High. Bush went 4-for-5, setting a state record with 214 career hits, and threw a complete-game four-hitter in a 13-4 victory.

"Probably Saturday we knew this was going to go down," Gayton said. "We had been in the draft room for over a week when we went out to SDSU to see that game. We had been trying to fly under the radar, and I guess we did a pretty good job until

that day. I know that night was the first night in a while that I slept well."

On June 6, the day before the draft, the Padres and Bush's advisers, Greg Genske and Kenny Felder (a former Brewers first-round pick) of Moorad Sports Management, hammered out the parameters of a $3.15 million bonus agreement. The deal, which was officially announced June 9, represents the lowest for a No. 1 overall pick since 2000, when San Diego area high schooler Adrian Gonzalez signed for $3 million with the Marlins.

The Padres insisted that their choice was not based primarily on finances. They didn't deny that money always enters into decisions at the top of the draft, but they said they viewed Bush as the best high school prospect in the draft. The bottom line was that they thought he was a better value at $3.15 million then any of their other targets would be wherever their final price tags ended up.

Had San Diego not chosen Bush, he likely would have gone to either the Indians or the Reds as the sixth or seventh pick. A pure shortstop, he had the best defensive skills and the most arm strength (he has been clocked up to 96 mph on the mound) of any position player available. Though at 5-foot-10 and 170 pounds he's the smallest No. 1 pick ever, he's athletic and the Padres liked his offensive potential.

Legal Troubles, Offensive Woes

Bush became the first No. 1 overall choice selected by his hometown team since the Twins tabbed St. Paul catcher Joe Mauer in 2001. But the feel-good,

FIRST-ROUND **BONUSES**		
1989-2004		
Year	Average	Change
1989	$176,000	—
1990	246,000	+39.7%
1991	355,000	+44.3%
1992	482,000	+35.8%
1993	611,000	+26.8%
1994	790,000	+29.3%
1995	913,000	+15.6%
1996*	924,000	+1.2%
1997	1,326,000	+43.5%
1998	1,638,000	+23.5%
1999	1,810,000	+10.5%
2000	1,873,000	+3.5%
2001	2,154,000	+15.0%
2002	2,107,000	-2.2%
2003	1,766,000	-16.2%
2004#	1,645,000	-6.9%

*1996 average doesn't include four loophole free agents who didn't sign with the teams that picked them.
#2004 average doesn't include five first-rounders still in negotiations with clubs.
Figures rounded to nearest thousand dollars.

local-kid-makes-good angle quickly turned sour.

On June 20, two days before he was to make his pro debut in the Rookie-level Arizona League, Bush was arrested at 1 a.m. in Peoria, Ariz.

A Peoria police department spokesman said Bush, 18, and his older brother Jeremy, 23, tried to enter a bar named McDuffy's across the street from the Padres' minor league and spring-training complex. Bush was denied access because he was underage, and the brothers then tried to force their way in and scuffled with bouncers. Bush was charged one felony (aggravated assault, which was later dismissed) and three misdemeanors (disorderly conduct, trespassing, underage consumption of alcohol).

San Diego suspended Bush for a month and threatened to void his bonus agreement. The Padres reportedly wanted to rewrite the deal to include conduct clauses, though neither side would comment on the specifics.

"I believe in the theory of redemption," Moores said. "Everybody gets a second chance. I've had multiple second chances, and I think we ought to give this kid at least one, too. But we expect him to toe the line and be the best baseball player he can be."

After he got back on the diamond, Bush struggled. In 28 games between the AZL and the short-season Northwest League, he batted .192 with 26 strikeouts and 17 errors. Though Baseball America ranked Bush as the fifth-best prospect in the AZL, managers were generally underwhelmed.

"He didn't impress me that much, but he'll be OK," Athletics Ruben manager Escalera said, "His bat has a way to go. He swings too hard and he tries to lift the ball too much."

MLB Closes Window On Townsend

At the end of the 2004 regular season, an unprecedented six first-rounders had yet to agree to terms. Right-hander Justin Verlander, picked second overall by the Tigers, signed Oct. 22 and four of the five remaining selections were expected to eventually sign, though perhaps not until early in 2005. The sixth was Rice righthander Wade Townsend, the eighth overall choice by the Orioles.

Baltimore scouting director Tony DeMacio was prepared to select Redan High (Stone Mountain, Ga.) shortstop Chris Nelson on draft day. But right before the pick came up, Orioles owner Peter Angelos insisted his club

Three of a kind
Rice pitchers Jeff Niemann, Philip Humber and Wade Townsend were all first-rounders

take a college pitcher who would sign at or below Major League Baseball's recommended bonus for the No. 8 slot, approximately $2.2 million.

The Orioles offered Townsend $1.85 million, the same below-market bonus they signed seventh overall pick Nick Markakis for in 2003. Not only did Townsend decline, but he also reportedly blew up at Orioles executive vice president Jim Beattie later in the summer when the offer hadn't changed.

Both sides still hoped they could come to terms. But Townsend decided not to sit around doing nothing, so he returned to Rice once classes began on Aug. 23 so he could finish the final semester he needed to complete his degree in history. In addition to earning first-team All-America honors on the field, Townsend also was named the academic all-American of the year for NCAA Division I baseball.

MLB draft rule 4-H states: "A player who is selected at the Summer Meeting and returns to school in the fall without signing a contract shall be subject to selection at the next Summer Meeting at which the player is eligible." But Townsend and his agent, Casey Close, sought to find a loophole by sending a letter to MLB that formalized their relationship and effectively terminated Townsend's college eligibility.

Close cited a section of MLB's draft rules interpretation handbook that reads: "A college player is a student who is eligible to play baseball on an intercollegiate baseball team fielded by the student's four-year college/university and sanctioned by a national collegiate governing body." Thus, Close reasoned, Townsend couldn't be considered a college player because he no longer was eligible to play baseball.

"If the buzzword is eligible, that only means you have to be eligible," Close said. "There's no question here. Wade formalized his representation and is no longer eligible to play college baseball."

MLB, however, didn't agree with Close's interpretation, and ruled on Sept. 15 that the negotiating window closed when Townsend set foot in class. The commissioner's office wanted to avoid a situation where the NCAA could reinstate Townsend's eligibility while he was still discussing a contract with the Orioles.

FIRST-ROUND TRENDS

Year	College	High School	Hitters	Pitchers	Average Bonus	Change
1999	15	15	10	*20	$1,810,000	+10.5%
2000	12	18	13	17	1,873,000	+3.5%
2001	18	12	10	*20	*2,154,000	+15.0%
2002	14	16	14	16	2,107,000	-2.2%
2003	18	12	*20	10	1,766,000	-16.2%
2004	17	13	11	19	#1,704,000	-3.5%

*Draft record.
#2004 average doesn't include four first-rounders still in negotiations with clubs.
NOTE: College includes junior college selections. Average bonuses rounded to nearest thousand.

BILL BAPTIST

DRAFT

In early October, Close acknowledged hearing from MLB but said there would be other efforts made to re-open negotiations, possibly through legal action. "While we're not surprised with Major League Baseball's initial reaction," Close said, "it's not the end of the road." If Townsend has to re-enter the 2005 draft, Close said he would complete his degree in December, begin working out at IMG's Florida complex in January and possibly pitch for an independent league club to showcase his stuff.

Meanwhile, Nelson went immediately after Townsend at No. 9 to the Rockies. He quickly signed for $2.15 million and had a banner pro debut, batting .347 and earning acclaim as the No. 1 prospect in the Rookie-level Pioneer League. The Orioles informed DeMacio, who wasn't allowed to take the player he wanted, that his contract wouldn't be renewed when it expired at the end of October.

Top Prospects Drop To 12th, 15th Picks

Verlander's signing with Detroit came just eight days after the Tigers declared they were no longer interested in the Old Dominion righthander. He was signed to a contract that provided a $3.12 million bonus with a guarantee of $4.5 million and a maximum value of $5.6 million.

Verlander's father Richard, a former union representative with the Communication Workers of America who participated in numerous negotiations, played a key role in getting the contract negotiated. After the Tigers had broken off negotiations, he called scouting director Greg Smith.

"There comes a time when the parties need to reach out personally," Richard Verlander said.

Smith said the Tigers had "turned the page" on the Verlander negotiations and had no interest in signing him. The team notified agent Mike Milchin of SFX that it was withdrawing its offer. But the family subsequently contacted the Tigers directly to move the deal forward.

"It was a very difficult decision to make at the time we made it," Smith said. "What happened when Mr. Verlander called is a dialogue was established that hadn't been there before and we were able to get this done."

The other four unsigned first-rounders fell into two groups. The pair of righthanders who went right behind Verlander—Rice's Philip Humber (No. 3, Mets) and

MAJOR LEAGUE CONTRACTS

Though only one player had signed a major league contract in 2004 prior to Nov. 1, it was expected that most of the four remaining first-round picks that remained unsigned would ink big league deals. Through Nov. 1, the number of major league contracts signed since Bo Jackson agreed to a major league deal with the Royals in 1986 as a condition of his being pried away from a promising NFL career, is 24. Here's the full list, including the bonus the player received as well as the amount guaranteed in major league salaries and roster bonuses.

Year	Club (Round)	Player, Pos.	Bonus	Guar. Amount
1986	Royals (4)	Bo Jackson, of	$100,000	$1,066,000
1989	Orioles (1)	Ben McDonald, rhp	350,000	824,000
	Blue Jays (3)	John Olerud, 1b	575,000	800,000
1990	Athletics (1)	*Todd Van Poppel, rhp	500,000	1,200,000
1992	Angels (1)	Pete Janicki, rhp	90,000	215,000
1993	Mariners (1)	*Alex Rodriguez, ss	1,000,000	1,300,000
1998	Phillies (1)	Pat Burrell, 1b-of	3,150,000	8,000,000
	Cardinals (1)	J.D. Drew, of	3,000,000	7,000,000
	Cardinals (2)	Chad Hutchinson, rhp	2,300,000	3,400,000
1999	Marlins (1)	*Josh Beckett, rhp	3,625,000	7,000,000
	Tigers (1)	Eric Munson, c	3,500,000	6,750,000
2000	Reds (1)	*David Espinosa, ss	None	2,950,000
	Reds (2)	Dane Sardinha, c	None	1,950,000
	Padres (2)	Xavier Nady, 3b	1,100,000	2,850,000
	Devil Rays (5)	Jace Brewer, ss	450,000	1,200,000
2001	Cubs (1)	Mark Prior, rhp	4,000,000	10,500,000
	Devil Rays (1)	Dewon Brazelton, rhp	4,200,000	4,800,000
	Rangers (1)	Mark Teixeira, 3b	4,500,000	9,500,000
2002	+Orioles (1)	Adam Loewen, lhp	3,200,000	4,020,000
	Indians (1)	Jeremy Guthrie, rhp	3,000,000	4,000,000
	Rockies (4)	Jeff Baker, 3b	200,000	2,000,000
2003	Devil Rays (1)	*Delmon Young, of	3,700,000	5,800,000
	Brewers (1)	Rickie Weeks, 2b	3,600,000	4,790,000
2004	Tigers (1)	Justin Verlander, rhp	3,120,000	4,500,000

* High school signee
\# Secondary phase + Draft-and-follow, signed the following year

Niemann (No. 4, Devil Rays)—seemed to be waiting for the others to sign first. And the two consensus top prospects in the draft, Weaver (No. 12, Angels) and Drew (No. 15, Diamondbacks), seemed destined to be get the biggest deals and be the last to reach an agreement.

As the draft began, there was no clear destination for Weaver or Drew, Baseball America's top-rated pitcher and hitter in the 2004 crop. Weaver reportedly wanted an eight-figure deal similar to the record $10.5 million guarantee Mark Prior got from the Cubs as the No. 2 choice in 2001, and Drew was believed to be seeking a package close to the

Jered Weaver

$9.5 million Mark Teixeira got from the Rangers as the No. 5 pick in the same draft. Both Weaver and Drew are advised by Scott Boras, who's anathema to several clubs.

"When you're dealing with Boras, if his player is head and shoulders above everyone else, you have no problem dealing with him," a National League scouting director said. "But Jered Weaver is not Mark Prior. He's a good competitor and he has great command, but he's not a No. 1 starter in the big leagues right now. You'd rather spend that money elsewhere."

The Angels decided to spend their money on Weaver. New owner Arte Moreno wasn't shy about shelling out $145.75 million to sign free agents such as Vladimir Guerrero and Bartolo Colon during the previous offseason, but Anaheim had focused solely on high school players in the days leading up to the draft.

New Angels scouting director Eddie Bane said he didn't

HISTORICAL SIGNIFICANCE

First-round bonuses took a pronounced drop in 2003 and 2004—subject to the eventual signing of five unsigned first-rounders in 2004—and predictably no significant bonus records were set. Below are the 10 largest bonuses for players who signed with the teams that drafted them (for those players who signed major league contracts, only the cash bonus is noted):

Player, Pos.	Club, Year (Round)	Bonus
1. Joe Borchard, of	White Sox '00 (1)	$5,300,000
2. Joe Mauer, c	Twins '01 (1)	5,150,000
3. B.J. Upton, ss	Devil Rays '02 (1)	4,600,000
4. *Mark Teixeira, 3b	Rangers '01 (1)	4,500,000
5. *Dewon Brazelton, rhp	Devil Rays '01 (1)	4,200,000
	Gavin Floyd, rhp	Phillies '01 (1)	4,200,000
7. *Mark Prior, rhp	Cubs '01 (1)	4,000,000
	Bryan Bullington, rhp	Pirates '02 (1)	4,000,000
9. Josh Hamilton, of	Devil Rays '99 (1)	3,960,000
10. Corey Patterson, of	Cubs '98 (1)	3,700,000
	*Delmon Young, of	Devil Rays '03 (1)	3,700,000

*Signed major league contract

DRAFT '04 TOP 100 PICKS

Signing bonuses do not include scholarships, incentive bonus plans or salaries from a major league contract.
*Highest level of professional baseball attained   +College Senior

Rank, Team, Player, Pos.	Hometown	School	Bonus	Birthdate	B-T	Ht.	Wt.	AVG	AB	R	H	2B	3B	HR	RBI	SB	*'04 Assignment
1. Padres, Matt Bush, ss	Mission Bay HS	El Cajon, Calif.	$3,150,000	2-8-86	R-R	5-10	170	.447	123	46	55	11	1	11	33	12	Eugene (A)
9. Rockies, Chris Nelson, ss	Redan HS	Decatur, Ga.	2,150,000	9-3-85	R-R	6-0	176	.552	87	54	48	11	2	8	44	29	Casper (R)
11. Pirates, Neil Walker, c	Pine Richland HS	Gibsonsia, Pa.	1,950,000	9-10-85	B-R	6-3	205	.656	64	39	42	9	1	12	41	9	Williamsport (A)
14. Royals, Billy Butler, 3b	Wolfson HS	Jacksonville	1,400,000	4-18-86	R-R	6-1	225	.426	68	33	29	4	1	4	13	11	Idaho Falls (R)
15. D'backs, Stephen Drew, ss	Florida State U.	Hahira, Ga.	DNS	3-16-83	L-R	6-0	185	.344	227	68	78	14	7	17	56	12	Did not sign
18. White Sox, Josh Fields, 3b	Oklahoma State U.	Stillwater, Okla.	1,550,000	12-14-82	R-R	6-2	210	.362	243	54	88	21	1	10	47	2	Winston-Salem (R)
20. Twins, Trevor Plouffe, ss	Crespi HS	Encino, Calif.	1,500,000	6-15-86	R-R	6-1	175	.481	81	30	39	8	2	6	29	12	Elizabethton (R)
21. Phillies, Greg Golson, of	John Connally HS	Austin, Texas	1,475,000	9-17-85	R-R	6-0	190	.487	78	32	38	9	3	4	26	20	GCL Phillies (R)
+Athletics, Landon Powell, c	U. of South Carolina	Apex, N.C.	1,000,000	3-19-82	B-R	6-3	235	.328	268	66	88	17	1	19	66	2	Vancouver (A)
26. Athletics, Richie Robnett, of	Fresno State U.	Visalia, Calif.	1,325,000	9-17-83	L-L	5-10	195	.384	229	54	88	27	3	13	51	21	Vancouver (A)
28. Dodgers, Blake DeWitt, ss	Sikeston HS	Sikeston, Mo.	1,200,000	8-20-85	L-R	5-11	175	.558	86	49	48	11	1	14	48	11	Ogden (R)
Athletics, Danny Putnam, of	Stanford U.	Escondido, Calif.	950,000	9-17-82	L-L	5-10	200	.378	249	61	94	10	4	16	62	6	Kane County (A)
37. Yankees, Jon Poterson, c	Chandler HS	Chandler, Ariz.	925,000	2-10-86	B-R	6-1	215	.424	85	36	36	6	1	13	35	7	GCL Yankees (R)
45. Devil Rays, Reid Brignac, ss	St. Amant HS	St. Amant, La.	795,000	1-16-86	L-R	6-3	170	.417	127	41	53	19	2	11	58	7	Charleston (A)
48. Reds, B.J. Szymanski, of	Princeton U.	Wichita Falls, Texas	725,000	10-1-82	B-R	6-5	210	.362	177	44	64	10	8	6	40	11	Billings (R)
50. Rockies, Seth Smith, of	U. of Mississippi	Jackson, Miss.	690,000	9-30-82	L-L	6-3	215	.284	225	39	64	8	1	7	40	6	Tri-City (A)
51. Rangers, K.C. Herren, of	Auburn HS	Auburn, Wash.	675,000	8-21-85	R-R	6-0	210	.580	50	27	29	5	1	7	28	20	AZL Rangers (R)
52. Pirates, Brian Bixler, ss	Eastern Michigan U.	Sandusky, Ohio	670,000	10-22-82	R-R	6-1	188	.453	243	74	110	18	3	8	47	31	Williamsport (A)
54. Expos, Erick San Pedro, c	U. of Miami	Hialeah, Fla.	650,000	10-5-83	R-R	6-0	205	.320	194	50	62	15	2	12	52	1	Savannah (A)
56. D'backs, Jon Zeringue, of	Louisiana State U.	Thibodeaux, La.	630,000	3-29-83	R-R	6-2	215	.384	255	56	98	19	2	12	57	3	Lancaster (A)
57. Blue Jays, Curtis Thigpen, c	U. of Texas	Forney, Texas	625,000	4-19-83	R-R	6-0	188	.378	278	57	105	28	2	7	51	10	Auburn (A)
59. White Sox, Donny Lucy, c	Stanford U.	Fallbrook, Calif.	525,000	8-8-82	R-R	6-3	210	.313	208	53	65	10	0	12	47	5	Great Falls (R)
60. Cardinals, Mike Ferris, 1b	Miami (Ohio) U.	Cincinnati	600,000	12-31-82	L-L	6-1	220	.361	208	61	75	15	2	21	62	3	New Jersey (A)
62. Phillies, Jason Jaramillo, c	Oklahoma State U.	Franksville, Wis.	585,000	10-9-82	B-R	6-0	200	.350	240	48	84	12	0	8	57	0	Batavia (A)
64. Astros, Hunter Pence, of	U. of Texas-Arlington	Arlington, Texas	575,000	4-13-83	R-R	6-4	210	.395	190	47	75	8	5	9	35	10	Tri-City (A)
65. Red Sox, Dustin Pedroia, ss	Arizona State U.	Woodland, Calif.	575,000	8-17-83	R-R	5-9	180	.393	244	78	96	24	1	9	49	9	Sarasota (A)
67. Athletics, Kurt Suzuki, c	Cal State Fullerton	Wailuku, Hawaii	550,000	10-4-83	R-R	5-11	200	.413	252	77	104	17	4	16	87	9	Vancouver (A)
70. Giants, Eddy Martinez-Esteve, of	Florida State U.	Miami	537,500	7-14-83	R-R	6-2	215	.385	270	57	104	24	3	19	81	8	San Jose (A)
71. Braves, Eric Campbell, 3b	Gibson Southern HS	Owensville, Ind.	500,000	8-6-85	R-R	6-0	195	.506	79	43	40	15	0	12	33	7	Rome (A)
72. Padres, Billy Killian, c	Chippewa Hills HS	Stanwood, Mich.	450,000	6-12-86	R-R	6-1	190	.632	68	34	43	9	7	5	22	4	Portland (AAA)
73. Tigers, Jeff Frazier, of	Rutgers U.	Toms River, N.J.	500,000	8-10-82	R-R	6-3	195	.382	207	59	79	16	1	13	59	6	Oneonta (A)
78. Reds, Craig Tatum, c	Mississippi State U.	Hattiesburg, Miss.	450,000	3-18-83	R-R	6-1	215	.325	237	42	77	16	0	13	60	0	Billings (R)
79. Orioles, Jeff Fiorentino, of	Florida Atlantic U.	Plantation, Fla.	450,000	4-14-83	L-R	6-1	190	.348	221	84	77	18	1	17	67	13	Delmarva (A)
82. Pirates, Eddie Prasch, 3b	Milton HS	Alpharetta, Ga.	500,000	1-25-86	L-L	6-1	180	.463	123	55	57	15	1	5	54	20	GCL Pirates (R)
83. Blue Jays, Adam Lind, 1b	U. of South Alabama	Anderson, Ind.	445,000	7-17-83	L-L	6-2	195	.392	232	57	91	22	2	12	60	8	Auburn (A)
84. Expos, Ian Desmond, ss	Sarasota HS	Sarasota, Fla.	430,000	9-20-85	R-R	6-2	185	.410	78	37	32	8	3	4	21	8	Vermont (A)
85. Royals, Josh Johnson, ss	Middleton HS	Tampa	410,000	1-11-86	R-R	5-11	170	.509	57	27	29	8	0	4	9	28	Burlington (A)
88. Dodgers, Cory Dunlap, 1b	Contra Costa (Calif.) CC	Alameda, Calif.	430,000	4-13-84	L-L	6-0	205	.500	120	30	60	20	0	4	35	2	Ogden (R)
93. Mariners, Matt Tuiasosopo, ss	Woodinville HS	Woodinville, Wash.	2,290,000	5-10-86	R-R	6-2	220	.366	61	20	22	5	0	1	14	13	Everett (A)
94. Astros, Jordan Parraz, of	CC of Southern Nevada	Las Vegas, Nev.	400,000	10-8-84	R-R	6-3	220	.359	131	28	47	10	0	2	29	13	Greeneville (R)
96. Cubs, Mark Reed, c	Bonita HS	La Verne, Calif.	650,000	4-13-86	L-R	5-11	175	.525	59	29	31	15	2	3	25	14	AZL Cubs (R)
98. Marlins, Greg Burns, of	Walnut HS	Pomona, Calif.	395,000	11-7-86	L-L	6-2	185	.462	91	24	42	9	2	4	23	15	GCL Marlins (R)
100. Giants, John Bowker, of	Long Beach State U.	Sacramento	405,000	7-8-83	L-L	6-2	190	.320	225	31	72	15	3	7	41	2	Salem-Keizer (A)

Rank, Team, Player, Pos.	Hometown	School	Bonus	Birthdate	B-T	Ht.	Wt.	W-L	ERA	G	SV	IP	H	BB	SO	*'04 Assignment
2. Tigers, Justin Verlander, rhp	Old Dominion U.	Goochland, Va.	$3,150,000	2-20-83	R-R	6-5	200	7-6	3.49	16	0	106	90	43	151	DNP—Signed late
3. Mets, Philip Humber, rhp	Rice U.	Carthage, Texas	DNS	12-21-82	R-R	6-4	220	13-4	2.27	20	1	115	87	37	154	Did not sign
4. Devil Rays, Jeff Niemann, rhp	Rice U.	Houston	DNS	2-28-83	R-R	6-9	205	6-3	3.02	17	3	80	59	30	94	Did not sign
5. Brewers, Mark Rogers, rhp	Mt. Ararat HS	Orr's Island, Maine	2,200,000	1-30-86	R-R	6-2	205	9-0	0.11	10	1	63	10	11	158	AZL Brewers (R)
6. Indians, Jeremy Sowers, lhp	Vanderbilt U.	Louisville, Ky.	2,475,000	5-17-83	L-L	6-1	165	10-6	3.08	19	0	123	105	26	119	DNP—Signed late
7. Reds, Homer Bailey, rhp	La Grange HS	La Grange, Texas	2,300,000	5-3-86	R-R	6-4	185	12-0	0.29	16	2	73	23	10	169	GCL Reds (R)

DRAFT

Signing bonuses do not include scholarships, incentive bonus plans or salaries from a major league contract.
*Highest level of professional baseball attained

Rank	Team, Player, Pos.	School	Hometown	Bonus	Birthdate	B-T	Ht.	Wt.	W-L	ERA	G	SV	IP	H	BB	SO	*
8	Orioles. Wade Townsend, rhp	Rice U.	Dripping Springs, Texas	DNS	2-22-83	R-R	6-4	225	12-0	1.80	18	0	120	74	45	148	Did not sign
10	Rangers. Thomas Diamond, rhp	U. of New Orleans	Metairie, La.	2,025,000	4-6-83	R-R	6-3	230	6-4	2.38	17	0	114	87	45	138	Clinton (A)
12	Angels. Jered Weaver, rhp	Long Beach State U.	Simi Valley, Calif.	DNS	10-4-82	R-R	6-7	205	15-1	1.62	19	0	144	81	21	213	Did not sign
13	Expos. Bill Bray, lhp	Coll. of William & Mary	Virginia Beach	1,750,000	6-5-83	L-L	6-3	215	4-4	2.96	24	6	49	40	12	69	Brevard County (A)
16	Blue Jays. David Purcey, lhp	U. of Oklahoma	Dallas	1,600,000	4-22-82	L-L	6-5	240	9-5	3.11	18	0	119	89	54	130	Auburn (A)
17	Dodgers. Scott Elbert, lhp	Seneca HS	Seneca, Mo.	1,575,000	5-13-85	L-L	6-2	190	6-2	0.52	8	0	54	13	14	114	Ogden (R)
19	Cardinals. Chris Lambert, rhp	Boston College	Manchester, N.H.	1,525,000	3-8-83	R-R	6-1	205	6-4	3.02	15	0	92	65	51	107	Peoria (A)
22	Yankees. Glen Perkins, lhp	U. of Minnesota	Stillwater, Minn.	1,425,000	3-2-83	L-L	6-0	200	9-3	2.83	16	0	111	89	21	113	Quad Cities (A)
23	Yankees. Philip Hughes, rhp	Foothill HS	Santa Ana, Calif.	1,400,000	6-24-86	R-R	6-4	190	9-1	0.69	10	0	61	40	3	83	GCL Yankees (R)
25	Twins. Kyle Waldrop, rhp	Farragut HS	Knoxville, Tenn.	1,000,000	10-27-85	R-R	6-4	190	14-0	0.15	16	0	91	39	7	118	Elizabethton (R)
27	Marlins. Taylor Tankersley, lhp	U. of Alabama	Vicksburg, Miss.	1,300,000	3-7-83	L-L	6-1	220	2-5	2.00	20	4	68	50	26	70	Jamestown (A)
29	Royals. Matt Campbell, lhp	U. of South Carolina	Simpsonville, S.C.	1,100,000	12-27-82	L-L	6-2	170	10-5	2.90	21	0	118	92	36	138	Idaho Falls (R)
30	Rangers. Eric Hurley, rhp	Wolfson HS	Jacksonville	1,050,000	9-17-85	R-R	6-4	195	15-1	0.73	17	1	105	45	13	154	Spokane (A)
31	Royals. J.P. Howell, lhp	U. of Texas	Sacramento	1,000,000	4-25-83	L-L	6-0	180	15-2	2.13	24	1	135	90	53	166	Idaho Falls (R)
32	Blue Jays. Zach Jackson, lhp	Texas A&M U.	Cranberry Township, Pa.	1,017,500	5-13-83	L-L	6-5	220	10-7	3.58	18	0	121	113	28	127	Auburn (A)
33	Dodgers. Justin Orenduff, rhp	Virginia Commonwealth U.	Chesapeake, Va.	1,000,000	5-27-83	R-R	6-4	205	5-5	2.43	15	0	100	84	34	129	Ogden (R)
34	White Sox. Tyler Lumsden, lhp	Clemson U.	Roanoke, Va.	975,000	5-9-83	L-L	6-3	200	5-4	3.98	15	0	81	80	37	88	Winston-Salem (A)
35	Twins. Matt Fox, rhp	U. of Central Florida	Coral Springs, Fla.	950,000	12-4-82	R-R	6-3	192	14-2	1.85	17	0	112	78	32	125	Elizabethton (R)
38	White Sox. Gio Gonzalez, lhp	Monsignor Pace HS	Miami	850,000	9-19-85	R-L	5-11	180	6-0	1.37	8	0	41	18	17	87	Kannapolis (A)
39	Twins. Jay Rainville, rhp	Bishop Hendricken HS	Pawtucket, R.I.	875,000	10-16-85	R-R	6-3	230	9-0	0.12	11	0	59	26	5	92	GCL Twins (R)
40	Athletics. Huston Street, rhp	U. of Texas	Round Rock, Texas	800,000	8-2-83	R-R	6-0	190	6-1	1.58	31	12	57	36	13	59	Sacramento (AAA)
41	Yankees. Jeff Marquez, rhp	Sacramento CC	Vacaville, Calif.	790,000	8-10-84	R-R	6-2	175	8-2	1.98	18	2	60	45	16	64	Staten Island (A)
42	Yankees. Brett Smith, rhp	UC Irvine	La Habra, Calif.	800,000	8-12-83	R-R	6-5	190	8-5	2.54	16	0	113	94	22	113	DNP—Signed late
43	Tigers. Eric Beattie, rhp	U. of Tampa	Valrico, Fla.	800,000	4-2-83	R-R	6-3	190	10-5	3.38	16	0	104	101	27	127	DNP—Signed late
44	Mets. Matt Durkin, rhp	San Jose State U.	San Jose, Calif.	800,000	2-22-83	R-R	6-4	220	8-5	4.49	16	0	61	34	49	103	DNP—Signed late
46	Brewers. Yovani Gallardo, rhp	Trimble Tech	Fort Worth, Texas	725,000	2-27-86	R-R	6-2	195	5-4	1.38	11	0	60	30	10	143	Beloit (A)
47	Indians. Josh Hoyman, rhp	U. of Florida	Cocoa, Fla.	725,000	4-17-82	L-R	6-3	195	11-2	2.71	19	0	140	116	38	89	Mahoning Valley (A)
49	Athletics. Michael Rogers, rhp	North Carolina State U.	Hamilton, N.J.	700,000	10-24-82	R-R	6-1	195	9-4	3.08	18	0	117	89	21	110	Vancouver (A)
53	White Sox. Wes Whisler, lhp	UCLA	Noblesville, Ind.	660,000	4-7-83	L-L	6-5	235	3-5	5.24	16	0	93	103	35	60	Winston-Salem (A)
55	Royals. Billy Buckner, rhp	U. of South Carolina	Convers, Ga.	635,000	8-27-83	R-R	6-2	215	7-2	3.32	15	0	84	77	23	105	Idaho Falls (R)
58	Dodgers. Blake Johnson, rhp	Parkview Baptist HS	Baton Rouge, La.	600,000	6-14-85	R-R	6-3	185	8-3	1.31	12	0	64	39	15	116	Ogden (R)
61	Twins. Anthony Swarzak, rhp	Nova HS	Fort Lauderdale, Fla.	575,000	9-10-85	R-R	6-4	195	12-2	0.33	15	1	87	40	19	140	GCL Twins (R)
63	Royals. Erik Cordier, rhp	Southern Door HS	Sturgeon Bay, Wis.	575,000	2-25-86	R-R	6-3	195	5-1	0.97	8	0	29	6	15	61	AZL Royals (R)
66	Cubs. Grant Johnson, rhp	U. of Notre Dame	Burr Ridge, Ill.	1,260,000	5-26-83	R-R	6-6	220	6-0	1.87	14	0	58	39	26	51	DNP—Signed late
68	Marlins. Jason Vargas, lhp	Long Beach State U.	Apple Valley, Calif.	525,000	2-2-83	L-L	6-0	215	7-6	4.14	18	0	111	98	31	90	Greensboro (A)
74	Devil Rays. Wade Davis, rhp	Lake Wales HS	Lake Wales, Fla.	480,000	9-7-85	R-R	6-5	220	8-4	2.40	13	0	94	76	26	117	Princeton (R)
75	Brewers. Josh Wahpepah, rhp	Gulf Coast (Fla.) CC	Kenner, La.	475,000	4-3-83	L-L	6-3	220	4-3	2.24	12	0	86	71	32	72	Helena (R)
77	Indians. Scott Lewis, lhp	Ohio State U.	Wash. Ct. House, Ohio	460,000	9-26-83	L-L	6-1	170	11-1	1.24	17	0	85	47	14	114	Mahoning Valley (A)
81	Rockies. Steven Register, rhp	Auburn U.	Columbus, Ga.	450,000	5-16-83	R-R	6-1	185	1-0	3.48	22	8	21	20	6	23	Tri-City (A)
81	Rangers. Michael Schlact, rhp	Wheeler HS	Marietta, Ga.	455,000	12-9-85	R-R	6-7	205	7-0	4.02	13	0	56	55	16	52	AZL Rangers (R)
86	D'backs. Garrett Mock, rhp	U. of Houston	Grand Prairie, Texas	440,000	4-25-83	R-R	6-4	215	6-6	1.14	13	1	68	68	25	42	South Bend (A)
87	+Blue Jays. Danny Hill, rhp	U. of Missouri	Weimar, Texas	275,000	11-5-81	R-R	6-0	200	4-5	3.71	19	0	107	106	34	94	Auburn (A)
89	White Sox. Grant Hansen, rhp	Oklahoma City U.	Edmond, Okla.	430,000	2-25-83	R-R	6-6	225	13-0	2.42	16	0	89	78	35	60	Great Falls (R)
90	Cardinals. Eric Haberer, lhp	Southern Illinois U.	Bloomington, Ill.	422,500	9-14-82	L-L	6-2	205	7-3	3.54	17	1	84	78	35	60	New Jersey (A)
91	Twins. Eduardo Morlan, rhp	Coral Park HS	Miami	420,000	3-1-86	R-R	6-2	210	7-3	2.41	12	0	61	43	22	92	GCL Twins (R)
92	Phillies. J.A. Happ, lhp	Northwestern U.	Peru, Ill.	420,000	10-19-82	L-L	6-5	205	6-3	2.68	14	0	94	80	33	106	Batavia (A)
95	Red Sox. Andrew Dobies, lhp	U. of Virginia	Wexford, Pa.	400,000	4-20-83	L-L	6-1	180	6-3	3.41	16	0	108	102	30	109	Lowell (A)
97	+Athletics. Jason Windsor, rhp	Cal State Fullerton	Lake Forest, Calif.	270,000	7-16-82	R-R	6-2	220	13-4	1.72	22	1	163	100	24	148	Kane County (A)
99	Yankees. Christian Garcia, rhp	Gulliver Prep	Miami	390,000	8-24-85	R-R	6-4	175	7-1	1.09	11	2	45	24	16	55	GCL Yankees (R)

know until two minutes before the draft that he'd definitely get the opportunity to choose Weaver.

"We did our homework," Bane said. "We started when Jered first got to Long Beach. I watched him in intrasquad games back in January. All our guys had seen him. We didn't back off because of reports in the paper. We do our stuff privately. We were prepared if he was there at 12 to take him."

The Diamondbacks had zeroed in on college lefthanders before Drew fell to them. He ranked second on their draft board, trailing only Weaver, and scouting director Mike Rizzo said Arizona couldn't pass him up.

Stephen Drew

"We understand why Stephen Drew was there at the 15th pick in the country, but I wasn't afraid of it," Rizzo said. "This guy doesn't come around every year. I don't think there's a guy with Stephen Drew ability in every draft."

While the Angels hadn't moved beyond the preliminary stages with Weaver as of late October, negotiations between the Diamondbacks and Drew briefly heated up in late August.

Drew registered for his senior year at Florida State and was set to attend his first class on Aug. 31 before changing his mind and withdrawing. Arizona offered him a four-year big league contract including a bonus of more than $3 million (a team record) and the potential to make more than $7 million.

The Drew camp claims the Diamondbacks agreed at the time of the draft that Drew was worth $8 million to $10 million. The team denies making any such assurances. Further complicating matters was Arizona's front-office shakeup, with former agent Jeff Moorad replacing Jerry Colangelo as CEO.

Baseball sources said the Diamondbacks had become wary of exceeding the commissioner's office's recommendation for Drew's bonus because they feared drawing the wrath of other owners, who must approve Moorad's role. That approval already was less than certain because owners may be wary of an ex-agent taking over a club, especially one who has angered some teams and had conflicts with agents—including a bitter rivalry with Boras. Diamondbacks general partner Ken Kendrick denied a link between Moorad's pending confirmation and the Drew negotiations.

First-Round Bonuses Stay Down

MLB efforts to keep signings bonuses down worked better than it ever could have dreamed in 2003, as first-rounders averaged just $1.766 million, the lowest figure since 1998 and down a record 16.2 percent from the previous year. MLB roughly maintained the status quo in 2004.

The first 25 first-rounders to sign received an average of

NO. 1 PICKS, 1965–2004

Year Club, Player, Pos.	School	Hometown	Highest Level (G#)	2004 Team	Bonus
1965 A's. Rick Monday, of	Arizona State U.	Santa Monica, Calif.	Majors (1,996)	Out of Baseball	$104,000
1966 Mets. Steve Chilcott, c	Antelope Valley HS	Lancaster, Calif.	Triple-A (2)	Out of Baseball	75,000
1967 Yankees. Ron Blomberg, 1b	Druid Hills HS	Atlanta	Majors (461)	Out of Baseball	75,000
1968 Mets. Tim Foli, ss	Notre Dame HS	Sherman Oaks, Calif.	Majors (1,696)	Out of Baseball	75,000
1969 Senators. Jeff Burroughs, of	Wilson HS	Long Beach, Calif.	Majors (1,689)	Out of Baseball	88,000
1970 Padres. Mike Ivie, c	Walker HS	Decatur, Ga.	Majors (857)	Out of Baseball	80,000
1971 White Sox. Danny Goodwin, c	Central HS	Peoria, Ill.	Majors (252)	Out of Baseball	DNS
1972 Padres. Dave Roberts, 3b	U. of Oregon	Corvallis, Ore.	Majors (709)	Out of Baseball	60,000
1973 Rangers. David Clyde, lhp	Westchester, HS	Houston	Majors (84)	Out of Baseball	125,000
1974 Padres. Bill Almon, ss	Brown U.	Warwick, R.I.	Majors (1,236)	Out of Baseball	90,000
1975 Angels. Danny Goodwin, c	Southern U.	Peoria, Ill.	Majors (252)	Out of Baseball	125,000
1976 Astros. Floyd Bannister, lhp	Arizona State U.	Seattle	Majors (431)	Out of Baseball	100,000
1977 White Sox. Harold Baines, of	St. Michaels HS	St. Michaels, Md.	Majors (2,830)	Out of Baseball	40,000
1978 Braves. Bob Horner, 3b	Arizona State U.	Glendale, Ariz.	Majors (1,020)	Out of Baseball	175,000
1979 Mariners. Al Chambers, of	Harris HS	Harrisburg, Pa.	Majors (57)	Out of Baseball	60,000
1980 Mets. Darryl Strawberry, of	Crenshaw HS	Los Angeles	Majors (1,583)	Out of Baseball	152,500
1981 Mariners. Mike Moore, rhp	Oral Roberts U.	Eakly, Okla.	Majors (450)	Out of Baseball	100,000
1982 Cubs. Shawon Dunston, ss	Jefferson HS	New York	Majors (1,750)	Out of Baseball	100,000
1983 Twins. Tim Belcher, rhp	Mt. Vernon Naz. Coll.	Sparta, Ohio	Majors (362)	Out of Baseball	DNS
1984 Mets. Shawn Abner, of	Mechanicsburg HS	Mechanicsburg, Pa.	Majors (392)	Out of Baseball	150,000
1985 Brewers. B.J. Surhoff, c	U. of North Carolina	Rye, N.Y.	Majors (2,222)	Orioles	150,000
1986 Pirates. Jeff King, 3b	U. of Arkansas	Colorado Springs	Majors (1,201)	Out of Baseball	160,000
1987 Mariners. Ken Griffey Jr., of	Moeller HS	Cincinnati	Majors (2,007)	Reds	169,000
1988 Padres. Andy Benes, rhp	U. of Evansville	Evansville, Ind.	Majors (403)	Out of Baseball	235,000
1989 Orioles. Ben McDonald, rhp	Louisiana State U.	Denham Springs, La.	Majors (211)	Out of Baseball	*350,000
1990 Braves. Chipper Jones, ss	The Bolles School	Jacksonville	Majors (1,542)	Braves	275,000
1991 Yankees. Brien Taylor, lhp	East Carteret HS	Beaufort, N.C.	Double-A (27)	Out of Baseball	1,550,000
1992 Astros. Phil Nevin, 3b	Cal State Fullerton	Placentia, Calif.	Majors (985)	Padres	700,000
1993 Mariners. Alex Rodriguez, ss	West. Christian HS	Miami	Majors (1,430)	Yankees	*1,000,000
1994 Mets. Paul Wilson, rhp	Florida State U.	Orlando, Fla.	Majors (161)	Reds	1,550,000
1995 Angels. Darin Erstad, of	U. of Nebraska	Jamestown, N.D.	Majors (1,127)	Angels	1,575,000
1996 Pirates. Kris Benson, rhp	Clemson U.	Kennesaw, Ga.	Majors (137)	Pirates	2,000,000
1997 Tigers. Matt Anderson, rhp	Rice U.	Louisville, Ky.	Majors (245)	Tigers (AAA)	2,505,000
1998 Phillies. Pat Burrell, 3b	U. of Miami	Boulder Creek, Calif.	Majors (696)	Phillies	*3,150,000
1999 Devil Rays. Josh Hamilton, of	Athens Drive HS	Raleigh, N.C.	Double-A (23)	Did not play	3,960,000
2000 Marlins. Adrian Gonzalez, 1b	Eastside HS	Chula Vista, Calif.	Majors (16)	Rangers	3,000,000
2001 Twins. Joe Mauer, c	Cretin-Derham Hall	St. Paul, Minn.	Majors (35)	Twins	5,150,000
2002 Pirates. Bryan Bullington, rhp	Ball State U.	Fishers, Ind.	Class AA (26)	Pirates (AA)	4,000,000
2003 Devil Rays. Delmon Young, of	Camarillo HS	Camarillo, Calif.	Class A (131)	Devil Rays (A)	*3,700,000
2004 Padres. Matt Bush, ss	Mission Bay HS	El Cajon, Calif.	Class A (8)	Padres (A)	3,150,000

*Received major league contract with guaranteed incentives #No. of games at that level DNS—Did not sign

$1.704 million in bonus money. That represented just a 3.8 percent increase over the average $1.641 million bonus for those same slots in 2003.

The four first-round picks still negotiating with clubs may receive the five highest bonuses in the 2004 draft, so the overall average will rise. Even so, that figure is unlikely to exceed the $2 million threshold that was crossed in both 2001 and 2002.

Bush's $3.15 million bonus paled in comparison to recent No. 1 picks. Delmon Young got a $3.7 million bonus as part of a $5.8 million big league contract from the Devil Rays as the top choice in 2003. Bryan Bullington signed with the Pirates for $4 million in 2002, while Joe Mauer received $5.15 million from the Twins in 2001.

Though bonus money has decreased significantly from the beginning of the decade, teams had little trouble signing players. Only 19 of the 311 players selected in the first 10 rounds in 2004 hadn't come to terms by late October, the second-lowest total in draft history. The record (not including draft-and-follows) for the first 10 rounds is 15 unsigned players, established in 2003.

Every high school player selected in the first three rounds signed, an unprecedented feat in draft annals. The 2003 draft was the first in which every prep player taken in the first two rounds agreed to terms.

Big Money Lower In Draft

While first-round money stayed flat, several bonus records were shattered in lower rounds in 2004.

The Mariners, who gave up their first two picks as free-agent compensation, chose Woodinville (Wash.) High shortstop Matt Tuiasosopo with their top choice and signed him for $2.29 million. Tuiasosopo surpassed the third-round mark of $2 million set by Drew Henson (Yankees, 1998) and fellow Washington high school product Grady Sizemore (Expos, 2000).

Like Henson and Sizemore, Tuiasosopo's price tag was bolstered by his ability as a quarterback. He was a top recruit of the University of Washington, where he might have pushed for playing time as a true freshman. His

DOUBLE THEIR **PLEASURE**

Vanderbilt lefthander Jeremy Sowers became the 12th player in draft history to be selected in the first round of two different June drafts. (That includes only the regular phase, from the June 1965-86 drafts. The 20th overall pick out of high school in 2001 by the Reds, who made little effort to sign him, Sowers received a $2.475 million bonus from the Indians as the No. 6 pick in 2004.

Player, Pos., School	First Time	College	Second Time
Randy Scarbery, rhp, HS—Fresno	Astros, 1970 (7th)	Southern California	Athletics, 1973 (23rd)
Mike Miley, ss, HS—New Orleans	Reds, 1971 (24th)	Louisiana State	Angels, 1974 (10th)
Danny Goodwin, c, HS—Peoria, Ill.	White Sox, 1971 (1st)	Southern	Angels, 1975 (1st)
Mike Sullivan, lhp, HS—Woodbridge, Va.	Athletics, 1976 (24th)	Clemson	Reds, 1979 (22nd)
Brad DuVall, rhp, Virginia Tech	Orioles, 1987 (15th)	Virginia Tech	Cardinals, 1988 (23rd)
Alex Fernandez, rhp, HS—Miami	Brewers, 1988 (24th)	Miami-Dade CC South	White Sox, 1990 (4th)
Calvin Murray, of, HS—Dallas	Indians, 1989 (11th)	Texas	Giants, 1992 (7th)
Charles Johnson, c, HS—Fort Pierce, Fla.	Expos, 1989 (10th)	Miami	Marlins, 1992 (28th)
John Burke, rhp, Florida	Astros, 1991 (6th)	Florida	Rockies, 1992 (27th)
Jason Varitek, c, Georgia Tech	Twins, 1993 (21st)	Georgia Tech	Mariners, 1994 (14th)
J.D. Drew, of, Florida State	Phillies, 1997 (2nd)	Florida State	Cardinals, 1998 (5th)
Jeremy Sowers, lhp, HS—Louisville	Reds, 2001 (20th)	Vanderbilt	Indians, 2004 (6th)

BONUS RECORDS BY ROUND

Round	Player, Pos, Team	Year	Bonus
1st	Joe Borchard, of, White Sox	2000	$5,300,000
S-1st	Michael Garciaparra, ss, Mariners	2001	$2,000,000
2nd	Jason Young, rhp, Rockies	2000	$2,750,000
3rd	Matt Tuiasosopo, ss, Mariners	2004	$2,290,000
4th	Zach Miner, rhp, Braves	2000	$1,250,000
5th	Matt McClendon, rhp, Braves	1999	$900,000
6th	Quan Cosby, of, Angels	2001	$825,000
7th	Tyler Adamczyk, rhp, Cardinals	2001	$1,000,000
8th	Kyle Boone, rhp, Red Sox	2004	$432,000
9th	Jason Middlebrook, rhp, Padres	1996	$750,000
10th	Luis Cota, rhp, Royals*	2003	$1,050,000
11th	Kiki Bengoechea, rhp, Rangers	2002	$550,000
12th	Mike Rozier, lhp, Red Sox	2004	$1,575,000
Post-12th	Sean Henn, lhp, Yankees*	2000	$1,701,000

*Signed next year as draft-and-follow.

father Manu (with the NFL's Seahawks) and older brothers Marques and Zach (with the Huskies) all played football in Seattle, but Matt chose a different path.

"As the process went on, I finally realized that this is what I want to do," Tuiasosopo said. "It wasn't too hard to let go of football. Every morning when I woke up, this was what I thought about doing. I'm glad I made this choice. Playing baseball every day is the best job a kid could ask for."

His performance is the best the Mariners could have asked for. Tuiasosopo hit .412 and earned No. 1 prospect honors in the Arizona League, then held his own in the Northwest League as an 18-year-old against much older players. He showed five-tool potential at both spots, and the only question he raised was whether he'll grow too big for a shortstop.

Twice in 10 days, clubs shattered baseball's bonus record for non-draft-and-follows after the 10th round. On Aug. 14, the Angels gave 18th-rounder Mark Trumbo $1.425 million. The Red Sox trumped that on Aug. 24 when they signed 12th-rounder Mike Rozier for $1.575 million.

The old standard was the $1 million that 39th-round infielder Andy LaRoche got from the Dodgers in 2003. The draft-and-follow mark is the $1.701 million the Yankees gave lefthander Sean Henn in 2001 after taking him in the 26th round a year earlier.

For the third time in four years, the Red Sox forfeited their first-round pick to sign a free agent. They believe they compensated with Rozier, a lefthander from Henry County High in Stockbridge, Ga. Rozier has a consistent 88-92 mph fastball that touches 94 and a curveball that shows flashes of becoming a well above-average pitch.

"We're excited about this," Boston scouting director David Chadd said. "We didn't have a first-round pick, but we value this guy as a first-round arm."

It was widely known that Trumbo wanted a seven-figure bonus to give up a baseball scholarship from the University of Southern California. And it's no secret that Moreno has deep pockets and is willing to dig into them in order to improve the Angels.

So Trumbo's deal wasn't a surprise. But this was: Anaheim is making him a full-time third baseman.

Baseball America ranked the Villa Park (Calif.) High product as the No. 31 prospect for the 2004 draft—as a righthanded pitcher. But the more the Angels scouted him during the summer, the more excited they got about tapping into his powerful bat on a full-time basis.

"We didn't do a great job doing our homework on his

Record bonus for 18th-rounder
Angels sign third baseman Mark Trumbo for $1.425 million

LARRY GOREN

bat before the draft," Bane said. "But we did a great job during the summer. Every time our scouts would go to see the guy, balls were jumping all over the place."

Two 14th-round picks got unprecedented bonuses for their round. Williamsport (Md.) High righthander Nick Adenhart opened 2004 as the nation's top high school prospect but injured his elbow in May and required Tommy John surgery. Nevertheless, the Angels invested a low-round pick and a $710,000 bonus in hopes he'll regain his low-90s fastball and devastating curveball.

Milton High (Alpharetta, Ga.) outfielder Dexter Fowler was one of the top athletes in the draft and had the five-tool ability to go in the first round. But his commitment to the University of Miami clouded his signability, and he lasted until the Rockies took him in the 14th round, three picks ahead of Adenhart.

Colorado still didn't figure to sign Fowler until it saved $9.25 million on Larry Walker's contact by trading him to the Cardinals on Aug. 6. The Rockies began putting that saving to use 11 days later by signing Fowler for $925,000.

Rice, Drew Family Have Historic Trios

■ When Rice's Humber, Niemann and Townsend went in the first eight picks, they became the highest drafted trio of teammates ever. Michigan (Rick Leach, Steve Howe and Steve Perry in 1979) and Fresno State (Steve Hosey, Eddie Zosky and Tom Goodwin in 1989) are the only other colleges to produce three first-rounders in one draft.

■ Drew made his family the first to produce three first-round selections. Brothers J.D. (Phillies, 1997; Cardinals, 1998) and Tim (Indians, 1997) spent 2004 in the Braves organization, J.D. in the majors and Tim mostly in Triple-A. Incidentally, J.D., who also is represented by Boras, was the last college first-round pick before Townsend to go unsigned.

Eric Hurley

■ Wolfson High (Jacksonville, Fla.) third baseman Billy Butler (No. 14, Royals) and righthander Eric Hurley (No. 30, Rangers) became the fifth pair of high school teammates to go in the first round of the same draft. Cordova High's (Rancho Cordova, Calif.) Mike Ondina and Jerry Manuel were the first to do so in 1972.

Next came Michael Cuddyer and John Curtice from Great Bridge High (Chesapeake, Va.) in 1997, followed by Matt Wheatland and Scott Heard from Rancho Bernardo High (San Diego) in 2000 and Clint Everts and Scott Kazmir from Cypress Falls High (Houston) in 2002.

■ As usual, the draft was a family affair. Besides Drew, three other draftees had ties to former first-round picks. Weaver's brother Jeff was a Tigers first-rounder in 1998. White Sox 12th-rounder Daron Roberts' father Dave was the No. 1 overall pick by the Padres in 1972, and Rangers 30th-rounder Wally Backman Jr.'s dad was a Mets first-rounder in 1977. Three former Cy Young Award winners had their sons drafted: Frank Viola Jr. (White Sox, 29th round), Drew Saberhagen (Athletics, 38th; son of Bret) and Peter Vuckovich Jr. (White Sox, 48th round). The White Sox also drafted Ken Williams Jr., the son of their general manager, in the 36th round. The Red Sox picked Nick Francona, whose father Terry is their big league manager, in the 40th.

DRAFT 2004

CLUB-BY-CLUB SELECTIONS

Order of selection in parentheses • **Boldface** indicates player signed • *Player still eligible to sign

ANAHEIM ANGELS (12)

1. *Jered Weaver, rhp, Long Beach State U.
2. (Choice to White Sox as compensation for Type A free agent Bartolo Colon).
3. (Choice to Blue Jays as compensation for Type A free agent Kelvim Escobar).
4. Patrick White, of, Daphne (Ala.) HS
5. **Luis Rivera, of, Ramon Vila Mayo HS, Rio Piedras, P.R.**
6. **Josh LeBlanc, 2b, Southern U.**
7. **Bill Layman, rhp, U. of North Florida**
8. **Freddy Sandoval, 3b, U. of San Diego**
9. **Hainley Statia, ss, Trinity Christian Academy, Boynton Beach, Fla.**
10. **Doug Reinhardt, 3b, Santa Margarita Catholic HS, Laguna Beach, Calif.**
11. **Clifton Remole, 1b, Georgia Tech**
12. **Tyler Johnson, of, Haskell (Okla.) HS**
13. **Andrew Toussaint, 3b, Southern U.**
14. **Nick Adenhart, rhp, Williamsport (Md.) HS**
15. Adam Crabtree, rhp, Phillips Academy, Andover, Mass.
16. **Chris Waters, rhp, U. of North Florida**
17. **Ryan Aldridge, rhp, Middle Georgia JC**
18. **Mark Trumbo, rhp, Villa Park HS, Orange, Calif.**
19. **David Hernandez, rhp, Miami-Dade CC South**
20. **D.T. McDowell, of, Tucker HS, Atlanta**
21. Stan Posluszny, of, West Virginia U.
22. Matt Moore, 3b, Newhall, Calif.
23. **Ben Johnson, c, U. of Washington**
24. **Nate Sutton, 2b, UC Santa Barbara**
25. **Casey Mutter, rhp, Cal State San Bernardino**
26. **Jaime Douglas, lhp, U. of Central Florida**
27. **Martin Maldonado, c, Dr. Juan J. Maunez Pimentel HS, Naguabo, P.R.**
28. Cristen Tapia, 1b, Tucson (Ariz.) Magnet HS
29. **Billy Edwards, rhp, U. of Memphis**
30. Alan Horne, rhp, Chipola (Fla.) JC
31. Ricky Bambino, c, Sierra (Calif.) JC
32. **Brooks Shankle, 3b, U. of Texas-San Antonio**
33. **Frederic Carney, rhp, Regis (Colo.) U.**
34. **Bobby Cassevah, rhp, Pace (Fla.) HS**
35. **Nick Green, rhp, Darton (Ga.) JC**
36. John Mariotti, rhp, Gulf Coast (Fla.) JC
37. Clayton Trenary, of, Central Florida CC
38. **Rich Giannotti, rhp, U. of Miami**
39. **Mike Sweeney, lhp, St. Petersburg (Fla.) CC**
40. Stephen Marek, rhp, San Jacinto (Texas) JC
41. William Cooper, rhp, Shelton State (Ala.) JC
42. Patrick Warfle, of, Daytona Beach (Fla.) CC
43. Chris Lombardo, rhp, Etiwanda (Calif.) HS
44. Grant Harper, of, San Pedro (Calif.) HS
45. Andrew Colon, rhp, Choctawhatchee HS, Fort Walton Beach, Fla.
46. Marquez Smith, 3b, Daytona Beach (Fla.) JC
47. Erik Davis, rhp, Mountain View (Calif.) HS
48. Julian Laurean, 2b, Chandler-Gilbert (Ariz.) CC
49. Nick Dashnaw, rhp, Santa Clarita (Calif.) Christian HS
50. Abel Nieves, 2b, Middle Georgia JC

ARIZONA DIAMONDBACKS (15)

1. *Stephen Drew, ss, Florida State U.
2. **Jon Zeringue, of, Louisiana State U.**
3. **Garrett Mock, rhp, U. of Houston**
4. **Ross Ohlendorf, rhp, Princeton U.**
5. *Cesar Nicolas, 1b, Vanderbilt U.
6. **Brandon Burgess, of, Sonoma State (Calif.) U.**
7. **Koley Kolberg, rhp, U. of Arizona**
8. Jimmy Shull, rhp, Cal Poly U.
9. **A.J. Shappi, rhp, UC Riverside**
10. **Steven Jackson, rhp, Clemson U.**
11. *Darryl Lawhorn, of, East Carolina U.
12. **Richard Mercado, c, U. of Arizona**
13. Antoan Richardson, of, Vanderbilt U.
14. **Lester Contreras, ss, St. Petersburg (Fla.) JC**
15. **Dan Pohlman, c, Northwestern U.**
16. **Mark Reynolds, ss, U. of Virginia**
17. **Chris Carter, 1b, Stanford U.**

18. **Vince Davis, lhp, Southern U.**
19. **Derek Bruce, ss, Lewis-Clark State (Idaho) College**
20. **Edwin Roman, of, Princeton (Ind.) Community HS**
21. **Chris Thompson, rhp, U. of Mississippi**
22. **Luis Lajara, of, Santo Domingo, D.R.**
23. **Travis Gulick, of, Michigan State U.**
24. **Trey Hendricks, 1b, Harvard U.**
25. **Todd Stein, lhp, Illinois State U.**
26. **Eric Schindewolf, 2b, Texas A&M U.**
27. **Garrett Bauer, lhp, Missouri Baptist College**
28. **Ramon Downing, 2b, Wabash Valley (Ill.) CC**
29. Chris Bowen, lhp, U. of Maryland
30. **Kevin Williams, of, U. of South Alabama**
31. **Marcus Townsend, of, Southern U.**
32. **Josh Buhagier, of, Long Beach State U.**
33. Joseph Campbell, 3b, Fremd HS, Palatine, Ill.
34. David Hernandez, rhp, Cosumnes River (Calif.) JC
35. Jo Jo Batten, 2b, Middle Georgia JC
36. Craig Heyer, rhp, Coronado HS, Scottsdale, Ariz.
37. **Billy Lockin, ss, Loyola Marymount U.**
38. Lorenzo Church, rhp, Misison Bay HS, San Diego, Calif.
39. Michael Jarman, lhp, Edmond North HS, Edmond, Okla.
40. Ulrich Snijders, c, Trinity Christian Academy, West Palm Beach, Fla.
41. **Frank Curreri, c, U. of Massachusetts**
42. Brandon Pullen, lhp, Idaho Falls (Idaho) HS
43. Brandon White, 3b, Surry (N.C.) CC
44. **Adam Howard, rhp, Walters State (Tenn.) CC**
45. Ryan McKibben, rhp, Aliso Niguel HS, Aliso Viejo, Calif.
46. Ryan Castellanos, 3b, CC of Southern Nevada
47. Eduardo Baeza, rhp, Mission (Calif.) JC
48. Ryan Mooradian, lhp, Essex (Md.) CC
49. Carlos Soto, of, Wabash Valley (Ill.) CC
50. Kyler Newby, rhp, Mesa (Ariz.) CC

ATLANTA BRAVES (30)

1. (Choice to Rangers as compensation for Type B free agent John Thomson).
2. **Eric Campbell, 3b, Gibson Southern HS, Owensville, Ind.**
3. **J.C. Holt, 2b, Louisiana State U.**
4. **James Parr, rhp, La Cueva HS, Albuquerque**
5. **Van Pope, 3b, Meridian (Miss.) JC**
6. **Clint Sammons, c, U. of Georgia**
7. **Trae Wiggins, lhp, Brewton Parker (Ga.) College**
8. **Derrick Arnold, ss, Tallahassee (Fla.) CC**
9. **Jeff Katz, rhp, Cheshire (Conn.) HS**
10. **Brady Endl, lhp, U. of Wisconsin-Whitewater**
11. **Wes Letson, lhp, Birmingham-Southern College**
12. **Jeff Long, rhp, Gardner-Webb U.**
13. **Todd Blackford, rhp, Triton HS, Bourbon, Ind.**
14. **Mike Rozema, ss, St. John's U.**
15. **Jason Paul, rhp, Southern New Hampshire U.**
16. **Zach Schreiber, rhp, Duke U.**
17. **Jon Mark Owings, of, Gainesville (Ga.) HS**
18. Brad Emaus, ss, East Coweta HS, Sharpsburg, Ga.
19. **Scott Brazeale, ss, Berkeley HS, Moncks Corner, S.C.**
20. Christian Marrero, of, Monsignor Pace HS, Miami
21. **Tyler Wilson, lhp, Andalusia (Ala.) HS**
22. **Troy Harp, c, Middle Tennessee State U.**
23. Austin Hyatt, rhp, Marietta (Ga.) HS
24. Josh Flores, of, Lincoln-Way Central HS, New Lenox, Ill.
25. Judson Norton, rhp, Manatee (Fla.) CC
26. **Adam Parliament, of, El Paso (Texas) CC**
27. Tyler Flowers, c/1b, Blessed Trinity HS, Marietta, Ga.
28. Joey Lieberman, 1b, Meridian (Miss.) CC
29. Trevion Griffin, of, Lurleen B. Wallace (Ala.) JC
30. Kurt Houck, rhp, Boyertown (Pa.) HS
31. Jamie Richmond, rhp, Cawthraw SS, Mississauga, Ont.
32. Clay Caulfield, rhp, Lawrence Park Collegiate HS, Toronto
33. Brian Murphy, rhp, Torrey Pines HS, San Diego
34. Luis Sanchez, ss, Puerto Rico Baseball Academy, Caguas, P.R.
35. Shawn Lee, c, Gosnell (Ark.) HS
36. Phillip Britton, c, Olney Central (Ill.) JC
37. Joshua Ward, rhp, Seminole HS, Donalsonville, Ga.
38. Ryan Horton, lhp, Bishop Moore HS, Orlando
39. Sean Doolittle, lhp, Shawnee HS, Medford, N.J.

40. Jared Shaffer, ss, Kiski Area HS, Vandergrift, Pa.
41. Steven Creswell, lhp, Rim of the World HS, Crestline, Calif.
42. Eric Farris, ss, Hamilton HS, Chandler, Ariz.
43. Adam Myers, rhp, Herbert Hoover HS, Clendenin, W.Va.
44. Daniel Rios, 1b, JC of the Sequoias (Calif.)
45. Jesse Warren, lhp, Western Alamance HS, Elon College, N.C.
46. Marcus Covington, rhp, Louisburg (N.C.) JC
47. Kevin Camacho, rhp, Santa Fe Springs (Calif.) HS
48. Eric Evans, lhp, UMS Wright HS, Mobile, Ala.
49. William Tanner, rhp, White Knoll HS, Lexington, S.C.
50. Eric Gonzalez, rhp, Cochise County (Ariz.) CC

BALTIMORE ORIOLES (8)

1. Wade Townsend, rhp, Rice U.
2. (Choice to Athletics as compensation for Type A free agent Miguel Tejada).
3. **Jeff Fiorentino, c/1b, Florida Atlantic U.**
4. **Brad Bergesen, rhp, Foothill HS, Pleasanton, Calif.**
5. **C.J. Smith, of, U. of Florida**
6. **Bryce Chamberlin, rhp, Washington State U.**
7. Seth Johnston, 2b, U. of Texas
8. **David Haehnel, lhp, U. of Illinois-Chicago**
9. **Joey Howell, of, Santaluces HS, West Palm Beach, Fla.**
10. **Drew Moffitt, of, Wichita State U.**
11. **Kevin Hart, rhp/1b, U. of Maryland**
12. **Dan Puente, c, Bradley U.**
13. **Denver Kitch, ss, Oklahoma City U.**
14. **Kyle Schmidt, rhp, U. of South Florida**
15. Will Venable, of, Princeton U.
16. **Andy Schindling, rhp, St. John's Collegiate HS, Bowie, Md.**
17. **Kyle Boehm, rhp, Oakland U.**
18. **Trent Baysinger, lhp, U. of Washington**
19. Matt McGuirk, of, Arlington Heights HS, Fort Worth
20. **Jonathan Tucker, 2b, U. of Florida**
21. **Ryan Finan, 1b, Lamar U.**
22. **Rob Marconi, 3b, Northern Illinois U.**
23. **Ryan Schwabe, lhp, U. of Louisiana-Monroe**
24. Dale Mollenhauer, ss, Pine Richland HS, Gibsonia, Pa.
25. **Zach Minor, lhp, Northern Illinois U.**
26. **Kevin Kotch, c, Cecil (Md.) CC**
27. **Cody Wargo, c, Indiana U.**
28. Alex Graham, rhp, U. of the Pacific
29. Marc Young, lhp, Riverside HS, Greer, S.C.
30. Jaime Garcia, lhp, Sharyland (Texas) HS
31. Matthew Garnett, lhp, Bakersfield (Calif.) JC
32. Jeff Jeffords, rhp, Spartanburg Methodist (S.C.) JC
33. Jared Elmore, rhp, Raymond (Miss.) HS
34. Nick Burns, c, Palomar (Calif.) CC
35. Drew Crisp, ss, Riverside HS, Greer, S.C.
36. Derik Drewett, rhp, U. of Arkansas-Fort Smith JC
37. Ian Harrington, lhp, Bellevue (Wash.) CC
38. Adam Crisp, of, Riverside HS, Greer, S.C.
39. Larry Hill, lhp, Smithson Valley HS, Spring Branch, Texas
40. Jason Roach, lhp, Sacramento CC
41. Demetrios Marinos, c, Steinert HS, Hamilton, N.J.
42. Brian Blackburn, c, Kellogg (Mich.) CC
43. Bryan Casey, c, Kofa HS, Yuma, Ariz.
44. Leonardo Calderon, lhp, Puerto Rico Baseball Academy, Loiza, P.R.
45. **Samuel Basta, lhp, Marquette University HS, Milwaukee**
46. Casey Larson, of, Paso Robles (Calif.) HS
47. Bailey Daniels, rhp, Manteo (N.C.) HS
48. Matt Lane, rhp, Iowa Western CC
49. **Clifton Turner, of, CC of Baltimore-Catonsville**
50. Michael Banks, rhp, Lake Michigan JC

BOSTON RED SOX (24)

1. (Choice to Athletics as compensation for Type A free agent Keith Foulke).
2. **Dustin Pedroia, ss, Arizona State U.**
3. **Andrew Dobies, lhp, U. of Virginia**
4. **Tommy Hottovy, lhp, Wichita State U.**
5. **Ryan Schroyer, rhp, San Diego State U.**
6. **Cla Meredith, rhp, Virginia Commonwealth U.**
7. **Pat Perry, c, U. of Northern Colorado**
8. **Kyle Bono, rhp, U. of Central Florida**
9. **Matt Vanderbosch, of, Oral Roberts U.**
10. Steve Pearce, 1b, U. of South Carolina
11. **Ryan Phillips, lhp, Barton County (Kan.) CC**
12. **Mike Rozier, lhp, Henry County HS, Stockbridge, Ga.**
13. **Matt Ciaramella, of, U. of Utah**
14. **R.J. Swindle, rhp, Charleston Southern U.**
15. **Dustin Kelly, ss, Cuesta (Calif.) JC**
16. Matt Clarkson, c, U. of Arkansas-Fort Smith JC
17. Jeremy Haynes, of, Madison County HS, Madison, Fla.

18. Randy Beam, lhp, Florida Atlantic U.
19. **Logan Sorensen, 1b, Wichita State U.**
20. Brian Van Kirk, c, Westminster Academy, Fort Lauderdale, Fla.
21. **Chuck Jeroloman, ss, Auburn U.**
22. **John Burgess, 1b, Georgia State U.**
23. **Matt Goodson, rhp, U. of Texas**
24. Matt Spencer, 1b, Morristown West HS, Morristown, Tenn.
25. Michael Jones, of, Arizona Western JC
26. Jake Renshaw, rhp, Ventura (Calif.) JC
27. Justin Phillabaum, rhp, Royal Palm Beach HS, West Palm Beach, Fla.
28. **Michael James, rhp, U. of Connecticut**
29. **David Seccombe, rhp, U. of Nevada-Las Vegas** (voided)
30. **Drew Ehrlich, rhp, Stanford U.**
31. Brendan Winn, of, U. of South Carolina
32. Brad Hertzler, lhp, East Providence (R.I.) HS
33. **John Wells, lhp, Timber Creek HS, Orlando**
34. **Andrew Pinckney, 3b, Emory U.**
35. Bo Lanier, rhp, U. of Georgia
36. **Cooper Eddy, rhp, U. of New Mexico**
37. Glenn Swanson, lhp, UC Irvine
38. Colby Summer, rhp, U. of Hawaii
39. Zak Farkes, ss, Harvard U.
40. Nick Francona, lhp, Lawrenceville HS, Yardley, Pa.
41. Steven Edlefsen, ss, Barton County (Kan.) CC
42. Kyle Peter, of, Archbishop O'Hara HS, Kansas City, Mo.
43. Tyler Latham, rhp, Hewitt-Trussville HS, Trussville, Ala.
44. Beau Mills, 3b, Golden West HS, Visalia, Calif.
45. Adam Campbell, 3b, U. of British Columbia
46. **Tom Caple, of, U. of San Diego**
47. **Austin Easley, 1b, U. of Florida**
48. Felipe Garcia, c/1b, Cal State Fullerton
49. Blake Tillett, lhp, Brandon (Fla.) HS
50. Raudel Alfonso, rhp, Hialeah (Fla.) HS

CHICAGO CUBS (25)

1. (Choice to Twins as compensation for Type A free agent LaTroy Hawkins)
2. **Grant Johnson, rhp, Notre Dame U.**
3. **Mark Reed, c, Bonita HS, La Verne, Calif.**
4. **Chris Shaver, lhp, College of William & Mary**
5. Adrian Ortiz, of, Puerto Rico Baseball Academy, Caguas, P.R.
6. **Tim Layden, lhp, Duke U.**
7. **Mitch Atkins, rhp, Northeast Guilford HS, Browns Summit, N.C.**
8. **Eric Patterson, 2b, Georgia Tech**
9. **Ryan Norwood, 1b, East Carolina U.**
10. **Sam Fuld, of, Stanford U.**
11. **Jonathan Hunton, rhp, Lamar U.**
12. **Sean Gallagher, rhp, St. Thomas Aquinas HS, Fort Lauderdale, Fla.**
13. Ryan Moorer, rhp, Veterans Memorial HS, Peabody, Mass.
14. Eli Iorg, of, U. of Tennessee
15. **Alfred Joseph, of, Moody HS, Corpus Christi, Texas**
16. **J.R. Mathes, lhp, Western Michigan U.**
17. **Jeremy Blevins, lhp, U. of Dayton**
18. **Jake Marsello, rhp, Boston College**
19. Micah Owings, rhp, Georgia Tech
20. Trey Taylor, lhp, Baylor U.
21. **Will Fenton, rhp, U. of Washington**
22. Walter Diaz, ss, Braddock HS, Miami
23. **Chris Gaskin, 1b, Manhattan College**
24. Jeff Culpepper, of, Gonzaga U.
25. Casey Erickson, rhp, Glenwood HS, Chatham, Ill.
26. Paul Cinder, rhp, Lake Mary HS, Longwood Fla.
27. **Jason Kosow, rhp, Babson (N.H.) College**
28. **Jon Douillard, c, Vanderbilt U.**
29. **Mike Svetlic, 2b, UCLA**
30. **Russ Canzler, 3b, Hazleton Area HS, Conyngham, Pa.**
31. **Jesse Estrada, rhp, Grayson County (Texas) JC**
32. Cody Gilbert, 3b, Lincoln HS, Vincennes, Ind.
33. Randy Brown, of, Jonesboro (Ga.) HS
34. Dustin Bamberg, c, Winter Haven (Fla.) HS
35. Drew O'Connell, rhp, Barrington HS, South Barrington, Ill.
36. Colby Wark, rhp, Redmond HS, Terrebonne, Ore.
37. Michael Hyle, rhp, U. of Georgia
38. Kurt Eichorn, of, Kent State U.
39. Trent Luyster, lhp, Ohio State U.
40. Marcus Crockett, of, St. Bernard HS, Inglewood, Calif.
41. Kenn Kasparek, rhp, Weimar (Texas) HS
42. **Ryan Morgan, 3b, Boston College**
43. Adam Daniels, lhp, Eastern Oklahoma State JC
44. **Zane Green, of, Clemson U.**
45. Christopher Dunkin, c, La Porte (Texas) HS
46. Greg Fudacz, lhp, Cle Elum-Roslyn HS, Cle Elum, Wash.
47. Andrew Liebel, rhp, Damien HS, Pomona, Calif.
48. **Olin Wick, c, U. of Puget Sound**

49. Brandon Harmon, rhp, Columbia Basin (Wash.) JC
50. **Gerald Miller, of, Prarie View A&M U.**

CHICAGO WHITE SOX (18)

1. **Josh Fields, 3b, Oklahoma State U.**
1. **Tyler Lumsden, lhp, Clemson U.** (Supplemental choice—34th—for loss of Type A free agent Bartolo Colon)
1. **Gio Gonzalez, lhp, Monsignor Pace HS, Miami** (Supplemental choice—38th—for loss of Type A free agent Tom Gordon)
2. **Wes Whisler, lhp, UCLA** (Choice from Angels as compensation for Colon)
2. **Donny Lucy, c, Stanford U.**
2. **Ray Liotta, lhp, Gulf Coast (Fla.) CC** (Choice from Yankees as compensation for Gordon)
3. **Grant Hansen, rhp, Oklahoma City U.**
4. **Lucas Harrell, rhp, Ozark (Mo.) HS**
5. **Brandon Allen, of, Montgomery (Texas) HS**
6. **Adam Russell, rhp, Ohio U.**
7. **Tim Murphey, lhp, Glacock County HS, Gibson, Ga.**
8. **Nick Lemon, rhp, Brigham Young U.**
9. **Ryan McCarthy, 3b, UCLA**
10. **Adam Ricks, 2b, U. of Miami**
11. **Garry Bakker, rhp, U. of North Carolina**
12. **Daron Roberts, of, Cal State San Bernardino**
13. **John Egbert, rhp, Rutgers U.**
14. **Michael Swain, 3b, Wabash Valley (Ill.) JC**
15. **Carlos Torres, rhp, Kansas State U.**
16. **Fernando Alvarez, of, Florida International U.**
17. Jacob Wild, rhp, Bakersfield (Calif.) JC
18. Brett Scarpetta, rhp, Hononegah HS, Rockton, Ill.
19. **Caleb Cooper, 3b, Cal State Hayward**
20. Michael Dubee, rhp, Riverview HS, Sarasota, Fla.
21. Brian Flores, lhp, Carlsbad (N.M.) HS
22. Matt Mansilla, ss, American Heritage HS, Pembroke, Fla.
23. **Derek McNeil, ss, St. Leo (Fla.) College**
24. **Josh Hansen, c, U. of San Diego**
25. Justin Sincock, rhp, Millikan HS, Long Beach, Calif.
26. Danny Jordan, 3b, Gulliver Prep, Miami
27. Logan Williamson, lhp, Pensacola (Fla.) JC
28. Greg Young, of, Delaware Tech JC
29. **Frank Viola, rhp, Florida CC**
30. **Matt Zaleski, rhp, Indiana State U.**
31. Nichols Walters, lhp, Mountain Ridge HS, Glendale, Ariz.
32. Eric Sheridan, rhp, Saddleback (Calif.) JC
33. Brandon Cooney, rhp, Broward (Fla.) CC
34. **Mario Suarez, 3b, Florida International U.**
35. **Evan Tartaglia, of, Elon U.**
36. Ken Williams, of, Plainfield (Ill.) HS
37. Robert Grinestaff, c, Okaloosa-Walton (Fla.) CC
38. Shaun Spearman, ss, St. Pius X HS, Atlanta
39. James Leigh, lhp, Bryant (Ark.) HS
40. **Justin Roelle, lhp, Iowa Western CC**
41. Matthew Rozier, rhp, Meridian (Miss.) CC
42. Michael Schower, lhp, Riverview HS, Sarasota, Fla.
43. Ian Murray, rhp, Jefferson (Mo.) JC
44. Steven Muck, rhp, Covington Catholic HS, Park Hills, Ky.
45. Jason Sullivan, rhp, Crowder (Mo.) JC
46. Jason Rodriquez, ss, Alta Loma HS, Rancho Cucamonga, Calif.
47. Richard O'Brien, c, Little Rock, Ark.
48. **Peter Vuckovich, c, Clarion (Pa.) U.**
49. **Dennis Guest, 2b, St. Joseph's (Ind.) College**
50. Bryan Wagner, rhp, Thunderbird HS, Phoenix

CINCINNATI REDS (7)

1. **Homer Bailey, rhp, La Grange (Texas) HS**
2. **B.J. Szymanski, of, Princeton U.**
3. **Craig Tatum, c, Mississippi State U.**
4. **Rafael Gonzalez, rhp, George Washington HS, Bronx, N.Y.**
5. **Paul Janish, ss, Rice U.**
6. **Lonny Roa, c, Puerto Rico Baseball Academy, San Juan**
7. **Philippe Valiquette, lhp, Edouard Montpetit HS, St. Laurent, Quebec**
8. **Greg Goetz, lhp, Bellevue (Wash.) CC**
9. **Trevor Lawhorn, 2b, East Carolina U.**
10. **Terrell Young, rhp, Grenada (Miss.) HS**
11. Jason Urquidez, rhp, Arizona State U.
12. **Cody Strait, of, U. of Evansville**
13. **Drew Anderson, 2b, Ohio State U.**
14. **Jared Sanders, rhp, Oregon State U.**
15. **J.D. Reininger, 3b, U. of Texas**
16. **Travis Kaats, rhp, of Grand Canyon U.**
17. Milton Loo, ss, Molokai HS, Hoolehua, Hawaii
18. **Charles O'Neal, lhp, Chipola (Fla.) JC**

19. **Drew Jenson, lhp, San Diego State U.**
20. **Robert Coello, c, Okaloosa-Walton (Fla.) CC**
21. **Blake Honey, ss, Lafayette County HS, Lewisville, Ark.**
22. **Matt Levering, 3b, Regis (Colo.) U.**
23. **Pedro Hawkins, of, Green River (Wash.) CC**
24. **Adam Gillihan, rhp, Crowder (Mo.) JC**
25. Robbie Nickols, lhp, Sabino HS, Tucson
26. **Johnny Dillard, rhp, Southwestern Oklahoma State U.**
27. **James Langham, of, Georgia College & State U.**
28. Donnie Ecker, of, Los Altos (Calif.) HS
29. **Terrance Sparks, lhp, Prairie View A&M U.**
30. **David Griffin, lhp, Fresno State U.**
31. Jacob Arrieta, rhp, Plano East HS, Plano, Texas
32. **Robbie Wachman, rhp, Valdosta State (Ga.) U.**
33. Dylan Moseley, rhp, Arkansas HS, Texarkana, Ark.
34. **Drew Phillips, ss, Northwestern Oklahoma State U.**
35. Robert Palencia, rhp, Monsignor Pace HS, Opa Locka, Fla.
36. **T.J. Johnson, lhp, Central Michigan U.**
37. Andrew Wells, of, Union HS, Tulsa, Okla.
38. Robert Orton, c, Florida Atlantic U.
39. Mario Colletto, 1b, Simi Valley (Calif.) HS
40. **Brad Morenko, rhp, Oakland U.**
41. Scott Mueller, rhp, Greenway HS, Phoenix
42. Ben Price, ss, Terra Linda HS, San Rafael, Calif.
43. **Ben Parker, rhp, Huston-Tillotson (Texas) College**
44. Jacob Long, c, Johansen HS, Modesto, Calif.
45. **Brandon Roberts, of, U. of Michigan**
46. Justin Glover, 1b, Westside HS, Houston
47. Bradley Jarrell, 1b, Denham Springs (La.) HS
48. **Brad Key, 3b, U. of South Carolina-Aiken**
49. Tyler Cales, rhp, James Madison HS, San Antonio
50. Juan Buck, of, East HS, Anchorage, Alaska

CLEVELAND INDIANS (6)

1. **Jeremy Sowers, lhp, Vanderbilt U.**
2. **Justin Hoyman, rhp, U. of Florida**
3. **Scott Lewis, lhp, Ohio State U.**
4. **Chuck Lofgren, lhp-of, Serra HS, Burlingame, Calif.**
5. **Mike Butia, of, James Madison U.**
6. **Cody Bunkelman, rhp, Itasca (Minn.) CC**
7. **Mark Jecmen, rhp, Stanford U.**
8. **Justin Pekarek, lhp, U. of Nebraska**
9. **Chris Niesel, rhp, Notre Dame U.**
10. Reinaldo Alicano, of, Josefina Barcelo HS, Guaynabo, P.R.
11. Brian Logan, lhp, Varina HS, Richmond, Va.
12. Jordan Chambless, rhp, Calallen HS, Corpus Christi, Texas
13. **Jason Denham, of, Deer Valley HS, Antioch, Calif.**
14. Jeff Sues, rhp, Vanderbilt U.
15. **Brian Finegan, ss, U. of Hawaii**
16. Josh Williamson, rhp, Columbia Basin (Wash.) CC
17. **Marshall Szabo, 2b, U. of Georgia**
18. Danny Calvert, rhp, Hutchinson (Kan.) CC
19. **Chris Gimenez, of, U. of Nevada**
20. **Derrick Peterson, 3b, Eastern Michigan U.**
21. Carlton Smith, rhp, Piscataway (N.J.) HS
22. Jeff Corsaletti, of, U. of Florida
23. **Michael Storey, lhp, Bellevue West HS, Bellevue, Neb.**
24. **Wyatt Toregas, c, Virginia Tech**
25. David Newman, lhp, San Jacinto (Texas) JC
26. **Justin Holmes, ss, U. of Georgia**
27. **Adrian Schau, rhp, Villanova U.**
28. Doodle Hicks, lhp, Virginia HS, Bristol, Va.
29. **P.J. Hiser, of, U. of Pittsburgh**
30. **Alfred Ard, of, Southern U.**
31. Doug Pickens, c, Brother Rice HS, West Bloomfield, Mich.
32. **Kyle Collins, rhp, U. of San Diego**
33. **Paul Lubrano, lhp, U. of Georgia**
34. Ashton Shewey, lhp, Payson (Ariz.) HS
35. **Ryan Knippschild, lhp, U. of Kansas**
36. Jeff Kamrath, rhp, U. of Virginia
37. Blake Gill, 2b, Louisiana State U.
38. **Jose Amaya, rhp, San Jose State U.**
39. Preston Clark, c, Rockwall (Texas) HS
40. **Dustin Roddy, rhp, Nicholls State U.**
41. David Coulon, lhp, Hanford (Calif.) HS
42. **Josh Harris, rhp, Lamar U.**
43. Trevor Mortensen, of, Santa Ana (Calif.) JC
44. Phil Shirek, rhp, U. of Nebraska
45. **Tony Sipp, lhp, Clemson U.**
46. Chris Sosa, of, West Hills (Calif.) JC
47. Tyler Beranek, 1b, Waukesha (Wis.) South HS
48. Brian Winings, rhp, U. of Pennsylvania
49. Jose Chavez, ss, Santa Ana (Calif.) JC
50. Tim Battaglia, rhp, U. of Minnesota-Duluth

COLORADO ROCKIES (9)

1. Chris Nelson, ss, Redan HS, Decatur, Ga.
2. Seth Smith, of, U. of Mississippi
3. Steven Register, rhp, Auburn U.
4. Chris Iannetta, c, U. of North Carolina
5. Matt Macri, 3b, Notre Dame U.
6. Joe Koshansky, 1b, U. of Virginia
7. Jake Postlewait, lhp, Oregon State U.
8. Jim Miller, rhp, U. of Louisiana-Monroe
9. Dustin Hahn, 3b, Sacramento CC
10. Jarrett Grube, rhp, U. of Memphis
11. Chris Buechner, rhp, Lamar U.
12. David Patton, rhp, Green River (Wash.) CC
13. Matt Miller, of, Texas State U.
14. Dexter Fowler, of, Milton HS, Alpharetta, Ga.
15. Justin Nelson, of, U. of California
16. Patrick Stanley, rhp, Pace U.
17. Dominick Foster, rhp, Buchanan HS, Clovis, Calif.
18. Jeff Dragicevich, ss, U. of California
19. Josh Newman, lhp, Ohio State U.
20. Rene Garcia, rhp, Sunnyside HS, Tuscon, Ariz.
21. Matt Prendergast, rhp, Virginia Commonwealth U.
22. Stephen Edsall, rhp, Rollins (Fla.) College
23. Jason Metzger, lhp, UNC Greensboro
24. Rob Hosgood, of, Central Connecticut State U.
25. Aaron Lovett, rhp, Brownstown (Ill.) HS
26. Kyle Wilson, c, Fresno State U.
27. Andrew Koubek, lhp, Eau Gallie HS, Melbourne, Fla.
28. Steven Thomas, rhp, Texas Tech
29. Kyle Foster, lhp, Castle Rock (Wash.) HS
30. Michael Criswell, lhp, Lincoln HS, Tallahassee, Fla.
31. Xavier Cedeno, lhp, Asuncioan Rodriguez HS, Desal, P.R.
32. Jackie Davidson, rhp, Richland (Texas) CC
33. Justin Jameson, of, Southern Union (Ala.) JC
34. Richard Crowell, of, East Los Angeles JC
35. Josiah Cowden, rhp, Cypress Community Christian HS, Kingwood, Texas
36. Jeremey White, lhp, Caly Poly Ponoma
37. Todd Frazier, of, Toms River (N.J.) South HS
38. Reidier Gonzalez, rhp, St. Petersburg (Fla.) JC
39. Jonathan Santos, ss, Puerto Rico Baseball Academy, Caguas, P.R.
40. Gary McKissick, lhp, Itawamba (Miss.) JC
41. Chris Henry, lhp, San Joaquin Delta (Calif.) JC
42. Colt Sedbrook, 2b, Broomfield (Colo.) HS
43. Tony Snow, rhp, Edmonds (Wash.) CC
44. Justin Keadle, rhp, Wake Forest U.
45. Colby Lehman, lhp, Bishop (Calif.) HS
46. Kody Keroher, rhp, Solano (Calif.) JC
47. Josh Banda, of, Cypress (Calif.) JC
48. J.T. LaFountain, c, U. of Louisville
49. Brian Brohm, of, Trinity HS, Louisville
50. Andy Goff, 2b, Mt. Lebanon HS, Pittsburgh

Rockies first-rounder
Georgia high school shortstop Chris Nelson

30. Josh Lee, 1b, McMurray (Texas) U.
31. Leonardo Grullon, of, U. of South Florida
32. Nate Bumstead, rhp, Louisiana State U.
33. Kevin Brower, rhp, U. of North Carolina
34. Dallas Trahern, rhp, Owasso (Okla.) HS
35. Clay Britton, of, Weatherford (Texas) JC
36. Travis DeBondt, of, Bakersfield (Calif.) CC
37. Ramon Navarro, ss, Triton (Ill.) JC
38. Jamaal Peoples, of, Philadelphia (Miss.) HS
39. Adrian Bowens, ss, Lumberton (Miss.) HS
40. Kevin McAtee, 1b, Regis Jesuit HS, Littleton, Colo.
41. Bryan Sheffield, of, Williston (Fla.) HS
42. Trenton Lare, lhp, Coffeville (Kan.) CC
43. Chris Schwinden, rhp, Golden West HS, Visalia, Calif.
44. Tyler Fockler, rhp, Scotts Valley (Calif.) HS
45. Lionel Roberts, 1b, John McDonogh HS, New Orleans
46. Alec Sheppard, rhp, Colorado Springs (Colo.) Christian School
47. Rene Recio, rhp, Oral Roberts U.
48. Bernard Williams, of, East Marion HS, Columbia, Miss.
49. Dominic De la Osa, ss, Archbishop Carroll HS, Coral Gables, Fla.
50. Maxwell Leon, 2b, South Mountain (Ariz.) JC

DETROIT TIGERS (2)

1. Justin Verlander, rhp, Old Dominion U.
2. Eric Beattie, rhp, U. of Tampa
3. Jeff Frazier, of, Rutgers U.
4. Collin Mahoney, rhp, Clemson U.
5. Andrew Kown, rhp, Georgia Tech
6. Brent Dlugach, ss, U. of Memphis
7. Chris Carpenter, rhp, Bryan (Ohio) HS
8. Luke French, lhp, Heritage HS, Littleton, Colo.
9. Brandon Timm, of, Broken Arrow (Okla.) HS
10. Cory Middleton, ss, Escambia HS, Pensacola, Fla.
11. Josh Kauten, rhp, Illinois State U.
12. Cole Miller, c, JC of the Siskiyous (Calif.)
13. Brooks Colvin, ss, Southwest Missouri State U.
14. James Skelton, c, West Covina (Calif.) HS
15. Matt O'Brien, rhp, Florida Atlantic U.
16. Steve Young, 2b, Princeton U.
17. Dan Konecny, rhp, Northwestern U.
18. Chris Martin, rhp, Arlington (Texas) HS
19. Tyler Jacobson, rhp, Central Arizona JC
20. Ed Clelland, lhp, Gonzaga U.
21. Matthew Righter, rhp, Johns Hopkins U.
22. Thomas Royals, rhp, Pearl River (Miss.) CC
23. Vince Berry, of, Triton (Ill) JC
24. Jordan Foster, of, Lamar U.
25. Robbie Tulk, rhp, UC Davis
26. Thad McBurrows, lhp, Lake Wales (Fla.) HS
27. Dominic Carmosino, lhp, Oakland U.
28. Brian Hensen, lhp, Elon U.
29. Octavio Amezquita, ss, U. of the Pacific

FLORIDA MARLINS (27)

1. Taylor Tankersley, lhp, U. of Alabama
2. Jason Vargas, lhp, Long Beach State U.
3. Greg Burns, of, Walnut HS, West Covina, Calif.
4. Jamar Walton, of, Greensville County HS, Emporia, Va.
5. Brad Davis, c, Long Beach State U.
6. Brad McCann, 3b, Clemson U.
7. Jared Gaston, of, Walters State (Tenn.) JC
8. Craig Molldrem, rhp, U. of Minnesota
9. Joe Pietro, of, U. of New Orleans
10. Brett Carroll, 3b, Middle Tennessee State U.
11. Daniel Barone, rhp, Sonoma State (Calif.) U.
12. Jeff Gogal, lhp, Montclair State (N.J.) U.
13. Steve Gendron, ss/3b, Mississippi State U.
14. Patrick Hogan, rhp, Clemson U.
15. Brandon Verley, of, Columbia HS, White Salmon, Wash.
16. Brian Cleveland, ss, U. of Tennessee
17. Barry Gunther, c, U. of Mississippi
18. Nathan Messner, 3b, Muncy (Pa.) HS
19. John Parker Wilson, c, Hoover (Ala.) HS
20. Rhett James, rhp, Florida State U.
21. Marcus Davis, of, East Central (Miss.) JC
22. Chris Mobley, rhp, Middle Tennessee State U.
23. Ted Ledbetter, of, Oklahoma City U.
24. Jeff Lacher, rhp, Mississippi State U.
25. Agustin Montanez, ss, Ramon Vila Mayo HS, Rio Piedras, P.R.
26. Kevin Turmail, rhp, St. Louis CC-Forest Park
27. Brian Hoff, rhp, UC Riverside
28. Charles Blackmon, lhp, North Gwinnett HS, Suwanee, Ga.

29. **Aaron Easton, rhp, U. of Massachusetts-Lowell**
30. Josepth Munn, lhp, Foothill HS, Pleasanton, Calif.
31. **Parrish Castor, lhp, St. Anselm (N.H.) College**
32. Jared Petrovich, lhp, Shamokin Area HS, Coal Township. Pa.
33. **Clay Westmoreland, rhp, U. of Utah**
34. **Jarrett Santos, rhp, UNC Greensboro**
35. Drew Shetrone, rhp, Seminole (Fla.) CC
36. Sebastien Vendette, rhp, Ahuntsic College HS, Laval, Quebec
37. **Juan Figueroa, 1b, Bethune-Cookman College**
38. Zach Barrett, of, Reitz Memorial HS, Evansville, Ind.
39. **Beau McMillan, 2b, Lynn (Fla.) U.**
40. Gerald Watson, 2b, Central Catholic HS, Morgan City, La.
41. Jake Taylor, 3b, Canyon Springs HS, Moreno Valley, Calif.
42. Steve Santos, rhp, Diablo Valley (Calif.) CC
43. Reyes Dorado, rhp, A.B. Miller HS, Fontana, Calif.
44. Charles Jestice, rhp, Memorial HS, Tulsa, Okla.
45. Matt Bates, rhp, Illinois Valley CC
46. Jared Johnson, rhp, Central Arizona JC
47. Michael Mulholland, lhp, Lincoln Trail (Ill.) JC
48. Brady Decker, rhp, Red Hill HS, Bridgeport, Ill.
49. Chris Kirkland, c, South Doyle HS, Knoxville, Tenn.
50. Saunders Ramsey, rhp, Mississippi State U.

HOUSTON ASTROS (23)

1. (Choice to Astros as compensation for Type A free agent Andy Pettitte)
2. **Hunter Pence, of, U. of Texas-Arlington**
3. **Jordan Parraz, of, CC of Southern Nevada**
4. **Lou Santangelo, c, Clemson U.**
5. **Mitch Einertson, 2b, Rancho Buena Vista HS, Oceanside, Calif.**
6. **Ben Zobrist, ss, Dallas Baptist U.**
7. **Andy Alvarado, rhp, Chabot (Calif.) JC**
8. **Evan Englebrook, rhp, Shippensburg (Pa.) U.**
9. **Troy Patton, lhp, Tomball HS, Magnolia, Texas**
10. **Eric Cavers, c, Franklin Pierce (N.H.) College**
11. **Jonny Ash, 2b, Stanford U.**
12. **Bryan Triplett, ss, U. of South Carolina**
13. **Chad Reineke, rhp, Miami (Ohio) U.**
14. **Ole Sheldon, 1b, U. of Oklahoma**
15. **Drew Sutton, ss, Baylor U.**
16. **Garrett Murdy, rhp, Texas A&M U.-Kingsville**
17. **Beau Torbert, of, Faulkner (Ala.) U.**
18. **Chris Clark, c, Eastern Kentucky U.**
19. Jared Clark, rhp, Valencia (Calif.) HS
20. **J.R. Towles, c, North Central Texas JC**
21. **Ryan Reed, of, Louisiana State U.-Eunice JC**
22. **Matt Brown, rhp, U. of California**
23. **Jeff Wigdahl, lhp, St. Mary's (Texas) U.**
24. **Brandon Averill, 3b, UCLA**
25. Andrew Darnell, of, Castro Valley (Calif.) HS
26. **Jared Brite, rhp, Kansas State U.**
27. **Casey Brown, rhp, U. of Oklahoma**
28. **Chris Sotro, rhp, Cal Poly Poloma**
29. **Brad James, rhp, North Central Texas JC**
30. **Luke Barganier, of, Temple (Texas) JC**
31. **Chris Uhle, ss, Eastern Illinois U.**
32. **Neil Sellers, 3b, Eastern Kentucky U.**
33. **James Cooper, of, Grambling State U.**
34. Nick Cobler, lhp, Strake Jesuit College Prep, Houston
35. Kyle Woodruff, rhp, Leland HS, San Jose, Calif.
36. **Anthony DeWitt, rhp, U. of Southern Mississippi**
37. **Brad Chedister, rhp, Louisiana Tech**
38. Brandon Todd, rhp, Central Florida CC
39. Zachary Williams, rhp, Lindsay (Okla.) HS
40. Dane Ponciano, c, Mount Miguel HS, Grossmont, Calif.
41. Casey McCleskey, of, Burkburnett (Texas) HS
42. Josh Smith, rhp, Riverside (Calif.) CC
43. Tom Rafferty, of, Temple (Texas) JC
44. Vladimir Frias, ss, Chipola (Fla.) JC
45. Chris Siewert, ss, CC of Southern Nevada
46. **Anthony Adler, rhp, U. of Texas-Dallas**
47. Corey Bass, rhp, Pearl River (Miss.) CC
48. Eric Epperson, of, Arlington Heights HS, Fort Worth, Texas
49. Matthew Gardner, c, Andrews (Texas) HS
50. Victor Ferrante, rhp, Solano (Calif.) JC

KANSAS CITY ROYALS (14)

1. **Billy Butler, 1b/3b, Wolfson HS, Jacksonville**
1. **Matt Campbell, lhp, U. of South Carolina** (Choice from Giants as compensation for Type B free agent Michael Tucker)
1. **J.P. Howell, lhp, U. of Texas** (Supplemental choice—31st—for loss of Type A free agent Raul Ibanez)
2. **Billy Buckner, rhp, U. of South Carolina**
2. **Erik Cordier, rhp, Southern Door HS, Sturgeon Bay, Wis.** (Choice from Mariners as compensation for Ibanez)

3. Josh Johnson, ss, Middleton HS, Tampa
4. Nate Moore, rhp, Troy State U.
5. **Henry Barrera, rhp, Rosemead (Calif.) HS**
6. **Chad Blackwell, rhp, U. of South Carolina**
7. **Patrick Green, rhp, U. Louisiana-Lafayette**
8. **Ed Lucas, ss, Dartmouth U.**
9. **Chris McConnell, ss, Delsea HS, Franklinville, N.J.**
10. **Bobby Beeson, lhp, Southern Arkansas U.**
11. **Josh Haney, 2b, Texas Tech**
12. **Brad Hayes, 3b, Arkansas State U.**
13. **Travis Trammell, rhp, U. of Arkansas-Little Rock**
14. Kyle Howe, rhp, North Kitsap HS, Poulsbo, Wash.
15. Gilbert De La Vara, lhp, Pima (Ariz.) CC
16. **Patrick Hicklen, rhp, U. of Tennessee**
17. Adam Trent, rhp, Ooltewah, Tenn.
18. **Andrew Coffey, lhp, Mingus Union HS, Cottonwood, Ariz.**
19. Kade Keowen, 1b, Central HS, Baton Rouge, La.
20. **Adam Rowe, lhp, Mt. Vernon Nazarene (Ohio) College**
21. Andrew Underwood, rhp, Fresno CC
22. **Ethien Santana, of, Laredo (Texas) CC**
23. O.D. Gonzalez, of, Broward (Fla.) CC
24. Myles Ioane, lhp, Waiakea HS, Hilo, Hawaii
25. Garrick Evans, of, Clemson U.
26. **Nick Cerulo, c, Rutgers U.**
27. **Zane Carlson, rhp, Baylor U.**
28. Marty Beno, rhp, Horn Lake HS, Lake Cormorant, Miss.
29. Riley Hollingsworth, rhp, Minden (La.) HS
30. Kris Krise, rhp, JC of the Canyons (Calif.)
31. Kevin Clark, of, Armwood HS, Seffner, Fla.
32. Tyler Hogan, of, Servite HS, Anaheim
33. Jimmy Wallace, rhp, Pratt (Kan.) CC
34. **Kyle Crist, rhp, U. of California**
35. Vincent Biancamano, ss, Cactus HS, Glendale Ariz.
36. Eric Krebs, rhp, Alvin (Texas) CC
37. Kyle Hartz, of, De Anza (Calif.) JC
38. Kenneth Herndon, rhp, Mosley HS, Lynn Haven, Fla.
39. Will Jostock, rhp, Lapeer West HS, Lapeer, Mich.
40. Johnnie Santangelo, rhp, Bossier Parish (La.) CC
41. Kendall Thurman, rhp, Angelina (Texas) JC
42. Anthony Marbry, rhp, Jackson State (Tenn.) CC
43. Tyler Brown, rhp, Lane (Ore.) CC
44. Ty Sarchet, rhp, Kalani HS, Honolulu
45. Jacob Myking, c, Kalaheo HS, Kailua, Hawaii
46. Randy Rundgren, ss, Mid-Pacific Institute, Honolulu
47. Mark Serrano, rhp, Downey (Calif.) HS
48. Ernie Medina, rhp, San Jacinto (Calif.) HS
49. Tyler Jennings, of, Daphne (Ala.) HS
50. **Jefferson Infante, c, Ramapo (N.J.) College**

LOS ANGELES DODGERS (17)

1. **Scott Elbert, lhp, Seneca (Mo.) HS**
1. **Blake DeWitt, ss, Sikeston (Mo.) HS** (Choice from Yankees as compensation for Type A free agent Paul Quantrill)
1. **Justin Orenduff, rhp, Virginia Commonwealth U.** (Supplemental choice—33rd—for loss of Quantrill)
2. **Blake Johnson, rhp, Parkview Baptist HS, Baton Rouge**
3. **Cory Dunlap, 1b, Contra Costa (Calif) JC**
4. **Javy Guerra, rhp, Denton Ryan HS, Denton, Texas**
5. **Anthony Raglani, of, George Washington U.**
6. **Daniel Batz, 1b, U. of Rhode Island**
7. **Barry Richmond, of, Spartanburg Methodist (S.C.) JC**
8. **Brandon Medero-Stullz, c, Barbara Goleman HS, Hialeah, Fla.**
9. **David Nicholson, 3b, U. of California**
10. **Cory Wade, rhp, Kentucky Wesleyan College**
11. **Chris Westervelt, c, Stetson U.**
12. **Sam Steidl, of, U. of Minnesota**
13. Jeff Larish, of, Arizona State U.
14. **Brian Akin, rhp, Davidson College**
15. Joe Savery, lhp, Lamar HS, Bellaire, Texas
16. Chase Dardar, rhp, Delgado (La.) CC
17. Danny Forrer, lhp, Chipola (Fla.) JC
18. **Matt Paul, 2b, Southern U.**
19. David Price, lhp, Blackman HS, Murfreesboro, Tenn.
20. **Mark Alexander, rhp, U. of Missouri**
21. **Justin Simmons, lhp, U. of Texas**
22. **Kyle Wilson, rhp, UCLA**
23. **Kenny Plaisance, rhp, Louisiana State U.-Eunice JC**
24. Kody Kaiser, ss, Santa Fe HS, Edmond, Okla.
25. **Justin Ruggiano, of, Texas A&M U.**
26. Ben Petralli, c, Weatherford (Texas) HS
27. Levander Graves, c, Dillon (S.C.) HS
28. Brett Lawler, 1b, San Jacinto (Texas) JC
29. Ryan Strieby, 1b, Edmonds (Wash.) CC
30. Paul Gran, ss, Bothell (Wash.) HS

31. Ryan Koch, rhp, Osceola HS, Pinellas Park, Fla.
32. Mike Stutes, rhp, Lake Oswego (Ore.) HS
33. James Gilbert, rhp, Chabot (Calif.) JC
34. Chris LeMay, lhp, Kwantlen (B.C.) College
35. Lynn Henry, of, Buras (La.) HS
36. Mike Burgher, of, Shorecrest HS, Seattle
37. Jeremy Brown, of, Pratt (Kan.) CC
38. Justin Crist, 2b, Chandler-Gilbert (Ariz.) CC
39. Michael Branham, rhp, Jesuit HS, Tampa
40. Brandon Carter, ss, Old Dominion U.
41. Troy Grundy, rhp, Carbon HS, North Price, Utah
42. Chris Johnson, rhp, Cabell-Midland HS, Huntington, W.Va.
43. Davis Bilardello, lhp, Vero Beach (Fla.) HS
44. Kyle Rapp, lhp, Wabash Valley (Ill.) CC
45. Michael Hernandez, of, Connors State (Okla.) CC
46. Andrew Brewer, rhp, Metro Christian Academy, Tulsa, Okla.
47. Bobby Bratton, ss, Columbia (Tenn.) Central HS
48. Giuseppe Norrito, rhp, Nova Southeastern U.
49. Scott Bates, c, Salado HS, Belton, Texas
50. Ross Hoffman, 1b, Bakersfield (Calif.) CC

MILWAUKEE BREWERS (5)

1. **Mark Rogers, rhp, Mt. Ararat HS, Orr's Island, Maine**
2. **Yovani Gallardo, rhp, Trimble Tech, Fort Worth**
3. **Josh Wahpepah, rhp, Cowley County (Kan.) CC**
4. **Josh Baker, rhp, Rice U.**
5. **Angel Salome, c, George Washington HS, Bronx, N.Y.**
6. **Stephen Chapman, of, Marianna (Fla.) HS**
7. **Craig Langille, rhp, Charles Allen HS, Bedford, Nova Scotia**
8. **Brandon Parillo, lhp, Marina HS, Huntington Beach, Calif.**
9. **Derek DeCarlo, rhp, Florida International U.**
10. **Steve Sollmann, 2b, Notre Dame U.**
11. **Lenny Leclercq, ss, West Vigo HS, Terre Haute, Ind.**
12. Andrew Albers, lhp, John Paul II HS, North Battleford, Sask.
13. **Angel Ayala, 1b, Lino Padron Rivera HS, Vega Baja, P.R.**
14. **Grant Richardson, 1b, Washington State U.**
15. **David Johnson, rhp, UCLA**
16. **Alexandre Periard, rhp, Poly Deux-Montagnes HS, St. Eustache, Quebec**
17. Lorenzo Cain, of, Madison County HS, Madison, Fla.
18. Darren Ford, of, Vineland (N.J.) HS
19. **Josh Brady, of, Texas Tech**
20. Jose Garcia, rhp, Indians Hills (Iowa) CC
21. Drew Bowman, lhp, Dakota Ridge HS, Morrison, Colo.
22. Matt Kretzschmar, rhp, San Pedro (Calif.) HS
23. Tony Festa, 3b, UC Riverside
24. Jose Delgado, rhp, Puerto Rico Baseball Academy, Caguas, P.R.
25. Sean Morgan, rhp, Clements HS, Sugar Land, Texas
26. Dustin Timm, rhp, U. of Nebraska
27. Ty Pryor, rhp, Olympia HS, Orlando
28. Ronnie Prettyman, 3b, Cal State Fullerton
29. Ryan Paterson, rhp, Lake Cowichan HS, Duncan, B.C.
30. Brian Johnson, rhp, East Islip (N.Y.) HS
31. Kanekoa Texeira, rhp, Kamehameha HS, Kula, Hawaii
32. Joel Needham, rhp, UC Davis
33. Luis Bernal, rhp, Pima (Ariz.) CC
34. Kris Dabrowiecki, rhp, Ursula Franklin Academy, Toronto
35. Chris Copot, c, John Diefenbaker HS, Prince Albert, Sask.
36. Stephen Barnes, rhp, First Coast HS, Jacksonville
37. Sean McCraw, c, Alvin (Texas) HS
38. Donald Jordat, rhp, Summit Christian HS, Lake Worth, Fla.
39. Jeremy Bloor, lhp, Grand Rapids (Mich.) CC
40. Chris Rickey, lhp, Reno (Nev.) HS
41. James Coker, lhp, Spartanburg Methodist (S.C.) JC
42. Josh Louis, rhp, Temple (Texas) JC
43. Brandon Jasper, 1b, Newport Harbor HS, Cerritos, Calif.
44. Jon Mungle, of, Mississippi State U.
45. Deik Scram, of, Cowley County (Kan.) CC
46. Louis Metzner, rhp, Langley, B.C.
47. Derek Miller, lhp, U. of Vermont
48. Brandon Glover, of, McKinney (Texas) HS
49. Shane Buriff, lhp, Sickles HS, Tampa
50. Chad Miller, 1b, Chandler-Gilbert (Ariz.) CC

MINNESOTA TWINS (20)

1. **Trevor Plouffe, ss, Crespi HS, Northridge, Calif.**
1. **Glen Perkins, lhp, U. of Minnesota** (Choice from Mariners as compensation for Type A free agent Eddie Guardado)
1. **Kyle Waldrop, rhp, Farragut HS, Knoxville** (Choice from Cubs as compensation for Type A free agent LaTroy Hawkins).
1. **Matt Fox, rhp, U. of Central Florida** (Supplemental choice—35th—for loss of Guardado)
1. **Jay Rainville, rhp, Bishop Hendricken HS, Pawtucket, R.I.** (Supplemental choice—39th—for loss of Hawkins)

2. **Anthony Swarzak, rhp, Nova HS, Fort Lauderdale**
3. **Eduardo Morlan, rhp, Coral Park HS, Miami**
4. **Mark Robinson, of, Mountain View HS, El Monte, Calif**
5. **Jeff Schoenbachler, lhp, Reno (Nev.) HS**
6. **Patrick Bryant, rhp, Pensacola Catholic HS, Gulf Breeze, Fla.**
7. **John Williams, lhp, Middle Tennessee State U.**
8. **Jay Sawatski, lhp, U. of Arkansas**
9. **J.P. Martinez, rhp, U. of New Orleans**
10. **Jeremy Pickrel, of, Illinois State U.**
11. **Kyle Aselton, lhp, Oregon State U.**
12. Shane Boyd, rhp, U. of Kentucky
13. Walter Patton, rhp, Lincoln Land (Ill.) CC
14. **Javi Sanchez, c, U. of Notre Dame**
15. **Juan Portes, ss, Malden, Mass.**
16. **Matt Tolbert, ss, U. of Mississippi**
17. Eammon Portice, rhp, Fort Lauderdale HS, Oakland Park, Fla.
18. Josh Rose, rhp, Mariner HS, Cape Coral, Fla.
19. Tate Casey, rhp, Longview (Texas) HS
20. Tim Lahey, c, Princeton U.
21. Joseph Abellera, 3b, Hopkins HS, Minnetonka, Minn.
22. Vincent Scarduzio, lhp, Jupiter Community HS, Jupiter, Fla.
23. Tim Arnold, lhp, Fallbrook (Calif.) HS
24. Garrett White, lhp, San Jacinto (Texas) JC
25. Joe Welsh, lhp, Grand Rapids (Mich.) CC
26. Deacon Burns, of, Northern State (S.D.) U.
27. Landon Burt, of, San Diego State U.
28. Aaron Craig, rhp, Century HS, Rochester, Minn.
29. Ricky Prady, rhp, Sebastian River HS, Sebastian, Fla.
30. Daniel Berg, 3b, Texarkana (Texas) JC
31. Jason Laird, rhp, Henry County HS, Hampton, Ga.
32. Nolan Mulligan, rhp, Broward (Fla.) CC
33. Sean Kalmen, rhp, Katella HS, Anaheim
34. Rene Tosoni, of, Terry Fox SS, Port Coquitlam, B.C.
35. Jeff Mousser, rhp, Arizona State U.
36. John Thies, lhp, Meramec (Mo.) CC
37. Gregory D'Oleo, c, Ramon Vila Mayo HS, Toa Baja, P.R.
38. Josh Land, of, Okaloosa-Walton (Fla.) CC
39. Danny Santiesteban, of, Palm Beach (Fla.) CC
40. Justin Otto, rhp, Chandler (Okla.) HS
41. Eric Sweeney, rhp, Mt. Carmel HS, San Diego
42. Greg Schilling, lhp, Broward (Fla.) CC
43. Robbie Hebert, rhp, Nicholls State U.
44. Tony Joiner, of, Haines City (Fla.) HS
45. Lance Lofton, 3b, Connally HS, Waco, Texas
46. Matt Rizzotti, 1b, Archbishop Molloy HS, Jamaica, N.Y.
47. Chris Petrie, of, Lake City (Fla.) CC
48. Ryne Nelson, rhp, Dickinson (Texas) HS
49. Nicholas Bleau, lhp, Gulf Coast (Fla.) CC
50. Taylor Cameron, rhp, Cypress (Calif.) JC

MONTREAL EXPOS (13)

1. **Bill Bray, lhp, College of William & Mary**
2. **Erick San Pedro, c, U. of Miami**
3. **Ian Desmond, ss, Sarasota (Fla.) HS**
4. **Collin Balester, rhp, Huntington Beach (Calif.) HS**
5. **Greg Bunn, rhp, East Carolina U.**
6. **Devin Ivany, c, U. of South Florida**
7. **Marvin Lowrance, of, Golden West (Calif.) JC**
8. **Leonard Davis, 3b, Fresno (Calif.) CC**
9. **Brandon Conway, ss, Frederick (Md.) CC**
10. **Duron Legrande, of, North Carolina A&T U.**
11. **David Trahan, rhp, Alvin (Texas) JC**
12. Robert Mosebach, of, Hillsborough (Fla.) CC
13. **David Travis, 2b, Southern Wesleyan (S.C.) U.**
14. **Lyndsey Simmons, c, New York Tech**
15. Michael Wlodarczyk, lhp, Boston College
16. **Thomas Wilson, lhp, Catawba (N.C.) College**
17. **John Poppert, c, East Carolina U.**
18. **Matt Perks, rhp, Mercer County (N.J.) CC**
19. **Ben Cox, rhp, Lamar U.**
20. **Wendell Yost, lhp, Averett (Va.) U.**
21. Ibrahim Lopez, of, Puerto Rico Baseball Academy, Carolina, P.R.
22. Aaron Jackson, rhp, St. Augustine (Fla.) HS
23. Ryan Harrison, rhp, South Carroll HS, Woodbine, Md.
24. Steven Hornostaj, ss, St. David Catholic HS, Waterloo, Ont.
25. Steven Cook, rhp, UNC Asheville
26. Gabe Suarez, ss, South Mountain (Ariz.) CC
27. Ladd Hall, rhp, Arizona State U.
28. Chris Lugo, rhp, Hudson Catholic HS, Hoboken, N.J.
29. Steven Hirschfeld, rhp, Grand County HS, Moab, Utah
30. Brendan Murphy, 1b, Garden City (Kan.) CC
31. P.J. Treadaway, rhp, Archbishop Hannan HS, Carrier, Miss.
32. Matt Averitt, rhp, New Mexico JC
33. Chris Whisenhunt, lhp, Fort Worth Christian HS, North Richland Hills,

Tex
34. Brett Campbell, rhp, Kennesaw State (Ga.) U.
35. Rudy Garza, rhp, Hill (Texas) JC
36. Todd Nicholas, lhp, Troy State U.
37. Jamie Gant, rhp, Mississippi State U.
38. Daniel Cooper, rhp, Costa Mesa (Calif.) HS
39. Brian Peacock, c, Manatee (Fla.) JC
40. **Melvin Perez, 3b, George Washington HS, Bronx, N.Y.**
41. Joseph Dunigan, of, St. Ignatius Prep, Chicago
42. Brent Gaphardt, lhp, Dundalk (Md.) CC
43. Andy Gale, rhp, Philips Exeter Academy, Durham, N.H.
44. Phillip Vale, ss, Bellevue Christian HS, Clyde Hill, Wash.
45. Austin Reilly, ss, Fort Worth (Texas) Country Day HS
46. Robert Molinaro, ss, American Heritage HS, Boca Raton, Fla.
47. Jonathan Del Franco, rhp, Bridgewater-Raritan HS, Bridgewater, N.J.
48. Carlos Ceron, rhp, Miami-Dade CC North
49. Patrick Kanakevich, rhp, Georgetown Prep, Rockville, Md.
50. Joel Collins, c, Cardinal Carter SS, Richmond Hill, Ont.

1. *Philip Humber, rhp, Rice U.
2. **Matt Durkin, rhp, San Jose State U.**
3. **Gaby Hernandez, rhp, Belen Jesuit HS, Miami**
4. **Aaron Hathaway, c, U. of Washington**
5. **Nick Evans, 3b, St. Mary's HS, Phoenix**
6. **Ryan Coultas, ss, UC Davis**
7. **Scott Hyde, rhp, George Fox (Ore.) College**
8. Neil Jamison, rhp, Long Beach State U.
9. **Mike Carp, 1b, Lakewood (Calif.) HS**
10. **Brahiam Maldonado, of, St. Francis HS, Loiza, P.R.**
11. **Josh Wyrick, of, Porterville (Calif.) CC**
12. **Jeff Landing, rhp, Virginia Tech**
13. Martinez Allen, of, Dunnellon (Fla.) HS
14. Brad Meyers, rhp, Servite HS, Yorba Linda, Calif.
15. **Grant Psomas, ss, West Virginia U.**
16. **Parris Austin, of, Douglas County HS, Douglasville, Ga.**
17. **Joe Williams, lhp, St. Xavier (Ill.) U.**
18. **Kyle Brown, of, LeMoyne College**
19. **Jim Burt, 1b, U. of Miami**
20. **Sean Henry, ss, Diablo Valley (Calif.) JC**
21. Tim Smith, of, Birchmount Park HS, Scarborough, Ont.
22. **Caleb Stewart, of, U. of Kentucky**
23. **Michael Devaney, rhp, Concordia (Ore.) U.**
24. **Bryan Zech, 2b, Florida State U.**
25. **Jonathan Castillo, rhp, Miami-Dade CC South**
26. **Rafael Arroyo, c, Cal State Los Angeles**
27. **Bryant Suggs, of, Hillsborough (Fla.) CC**
28. **Armand Gaerlan, ss, U. of San Francisco**
29. **Mike Swindell, rhp, U. of Oklahoma**
30. **Blake Eager, rhp, Metropolitan State (Colo.) U.**
31. Erin Jones, rhp, Francis Marion (S.C.) U.
32. Jason James, of, Kishwaukee (Ill.) JC
33. **Matt Fisher, 2b, UC Irvine**
34. Jeremiah Lokken, of, Eagle View Academy, Jacksonville, Fla.
35. Garret Halleran, rhp, Central Arizona JC
36. Jake Harrington, rhp, Northeastern (Colo.) JC
37. Bradley Burns, rhp, Lookeba Sickles HS, Gracemont, Okla.
38. Zack Sterner, rhp, Franklin (Pa.) Regional HS
39. Bryan Lee, rhp, Cuesta (Calif.) JC
40. Julio Rodriguez, of, Manuel Mendez Liceaga HS, San Sebastian, P.R.
41. Jacob Ruckle, rhp, Mohave HS, Bullhead City, Ariz.
42. Jim Brauer, rhp, U. of Michigan
43. Ian Thurman-Kelly, lhp, Eastern New Mexico U.
44. Lance Scoggins, lhp, Okaloosa-Walton (Fla.) CC
45. Daniel McDonald, rhp, Morris Hills HS, Rockaway, N.J.
46. Jeremy Hefner, rhp, Perkins (Okla.) Tryon HS
47. Ryan Paul, lhp, Los Angeles Pierce JC
48. Morgan Carlile, lhp, Three Oaks HS, Summerside, Prince Edward Island
49. Daniel Buller, lhp, Fresno CC
50. Sean Cunningham, lhp, Bullard HS, Fresno

1. **Philip Hughes, rhp, Foothill HS, Santa Ana, Calif.** (Choice from Astros as compensation for Type A free agent Andy Pettitte)
1. (Choice to Dodgers as compensation for loss of Type A free agent Paul Quantrill)
1. **Jon Poterson, c, Chandler (Ariz.) HS** (Supplemental choice—37th—for loss of Pettitte)
1. **Jeff Marquez, rhp, Sacramento CC** (Supplemental choice—41st—for loss of Type A free agent David Wells)
2. **Brett Smith, rhp, UC Irvine** (Choice from Padres as compensation for Wells)
2. (Choice to White Sox as compensation for Type A free agent Tom

Gordon)
3. **Christian Garcia, rhp, Gulliver Prep, Miami**
4. **Jason Jones, rhp, Liberty U.**
5. **Jesse Hoover, rhp, Indiana Tech**
6. **Nate Phillips, ss, Grace Prep Academy, Roanoke, Texas**
7. Alex Garabedian, c, Columbus HS, Miami
8. **Mike Martinez, rhp, Cal State Fullerton**
9. **Grant Plumley, ss, Oral Roberts U.**
10. **Ben Scheinbaum, lhp, U. of Nevada-Las Vegas**
11. **Cody Ehlers, 1b, U. of Missouri**
12. **Rod Allen, of, Oklahoma State U.**
13. **P.J. Pilittere, c, Cal State Fullerton**
14. **Ben Jones, 1b, U. of Louisiana-Monroe**
15. **Robert Villanova, of, Iona College**
16. **Ryan Haag, 2b, Fresno State U.**
17. **Evan Tierce, of, Texas State U.**
18. **Yosvany Almario-Cabrera, 3b, Miami-Dade CC South**
19. **Jordan DeVoir, ss, U. of Illinois-Chicago**
20. **Jose Tadeo, rhp, Culver-Stockton (Mo.) College**
21. **Scott Rich, of, Rider U.**
22. Patrick Caldwell, lhp, Yavapai (Ariz.) JC
23. Jamarkus James, of, Grand Prairie (Texas) HS
24. Ryan Tabor, lhp, CC of Southern Nevada
25. Garrison Campfield, rhp, Navarro (Texas) JC
26. **Sean Kramer, lhp, Iona College**
27. Jeremiah Shepherd, rhp, Texarkana (Texas) JC
28. Jacob McCarter, rhp, Navarro (Texas) JC
29. Kyle Ginley, rhp, Dunnellon (Fla.) HS
30. Jonathan Lindenberger, rhp, San Jacinto (Texas) JC
31. Grant Duff, rhp, JC of the Sequoias (Calif.)
32. Clint Preisendorfer, lhp, La Jolla (Calif.) Country Day HS
33. Michael Dunn, 1b, CC of Southern Nevada
34. Jonathan Bertschinger, of, Navarro (Texas) JC
35. Michael Hale, lhp, Ball State U.
36. Matt Harrington, rhp, Fort Worth Cats (Central League)
37. Ryan Rote, rhp, Vanderbilt U.
38. Joseph Krebs, lhp, Navarro (Texas) JC
39. Tim LeMaster, of, Perry Meridian HS, Indianapolis
40. **Nathan Griffin, c, Oral Roberts U.**
41. Mike Lomba, lhp, Sacramento CC
42. Ronald Ball, rhp, Cypress (Calif.) JC
43. Keaton Hougen, rhp, Wylie (Texas) HS
44. Harrison Ashmore, rhp, Mansfield (Texas) HS
45. Drew Fiorenza, rhp, Middle Georgia JC
46. Juan Velazquez, rhp, Grossmont (Calif.) CC
47. Justin O'Bannon, rhp, San Jacinto (Texas) JC
48. Erik Morrison, ss, Arroyo Grande (Calif.) HS
49. Andrew Spaulding, of, Purcell Marian HS, Cincinnati
50. Chris Davis, 3b, Longview (Texas) HS

1. **Landon Powell, c, U. of South Carolina** (Choice from Red Sox as compensation for Type A free agent Keith Foulke)
1. **Richie Robnett, of, Fresno State U.**
1. **Danny Putnam, of, Stanford U.** (Supplemental choice—36th—for loss of Foulke)
1. **Huston Street, rhp, U. of Texas** (Supplemental choice—40th—for loss of Type A free agent Miguel Tejada)
2. **Michael Rogers, rhp, North Carolina State U.** (Choice from Orioles as compensation for Tejada)
2. **Kurt Suzuki, c, Cal State Fullerton**
3. **Jason Windsor, rhp, Cal State Fullerton**
4. **Ryan Webb, rhp, Clearwater Central Catholic HS, Palm Harbor, Fla.**
5. **Kevin Melillo, 2b, U. of South Carolina**
6. **Derek Tharpe, lhp, U. of Tennessee**
7. **Jarod McAuliff, rhp, U. of Oklahoma**
8. **Myron Leslie, 3b, U. of South Florida**
9. **Chad Boyd, of, El Camino Real HS, West Hills, Calif.**
10. **Tom Everidge, 1b, Sonoma State (Calif.) U.**
11. **Steve Sharpe, rhp, Central Missouri State U.**
12. **Nick Blasi, of, Wichita State U.**
13. **Scott Drucker, rhp, U. of Tennessee**
14. Jorge Charry, rhp, Puerto Rico Baseball Academy, Fajardo, P.R.
15. **Ryan Ford, lhp, Eastern Michigan U.**
16. **Tyler Best, c, Lewis-Clark State (Idaho) College**
17. **Clay Tichota, rhp, Regis (Colo.) U.**
18. Jeremy Slayden, of, Georgia Tech
19. **Ryan Ruiz, 2b, U. of Nevada-Las Vegas**
20. **Robert Semerano, rhp, Fordham U.**
21. **Chalon Tietje, of, Cal Poly U.**
22. **Ryan Jones, of, East Carolina U.** (voided)
23. **Shawn Martinez, rhp, Colorado State U.-Pueblo**
24. **Dallas Braden, lhp, Texas Tech**
25. Jim Conroy, rhp, U. of Illinois

26. Steven Carter, rhp, Coastal Carolina U.
27. Clayton Turner, rhp, Northwestern State U.
28. Andre Piper-Jordan, of, Everett (Wash.) CC
29. Wesley Long, ss, U. of Alabama-Huntsville
30. Haas Pratt, 1b, U. of Arkansas
31. Connor Robertson, rhp, Birmingham-Southern College
32. Jeff Gray, rhp, Southwest Missouri State U.
33. Scott Fairbanks, rhp, Lewis-Clark State (Idaho) College
34. Yusuf Carter, of, El Paso (Texas) CC
35. Broc Coffman, lhp, Lower Columbia (Wash.) JC
36. Matt Cassel, rhp, U. of Southern California
37. Beau Seabury, c, Skajit Valley (Wash.) CC
38. Drew Saberhagen, 1b/lhp, Calabasas (Calif.) HS
39. Joseph Florio, 2b, Blair Academy, Blairstown, N.J.
40. Danny Figueroa, of, U. of Miami

PHILADELPHIA PHILLIES (21)

1. Greg Golson, of, John Connally HS, Austin
2. Jason Jaramillo, c, Oklahoma State U.
3. J.A. Happ, lhp, Northwestern U.
4. Louis Marson, c, Coronado HS, Scottsdale, Ariz.
5. Andy Baldwin, rhp, Oregon State U.
6. Sean Gamble, of, Auburn U.
7. John Hardy, 2b, U. of Arizona
8. Sam Orr, ss, Biola (Calif.) U.
9. Andy Macfarlane, of, Treasure Valley (Ore.) CC
10. Charles Cresswell, c, Perryton (Texas) HS
11. Carl Galloway, 1b, Biola (Calif.) U.
12. Joe Bisenius, rhp, Oklahoma City U.
13. James Adkins, lhp, Wilson Central HS, Mt. Juliet, Tenn.
14. Jason Martinez, lhp, Mesa State (Colo.) College
15. Zac Cline, lhp, West Virginia U.
16. Kyle Allen, lhp, Lewis-Clark State (Idaho) College
17. Ryan Frith, of, U. of Southern Mississippi
18. Greg Isaacson, 2b, U. of Washington
19. Jacob Barrack, rhp, Pepperdine U.
20. Nathan Johnson, rhp, U. of Iowa
21. Buck Shaw, 1b, Connors State (Okla.) JC
22. Anthony Buffone, 3b, U. of Maryland
23. Kevin Rose, rhp, U. of San Francisco
24. Aaron Wilson, rhp, U. of San Diego
25. Joe Dirnberger, 3b, Mesa State (Colo.) College
26. Nick Evangelista, rhp, U. of Pittsburgh
27. Jason Appel, of, John F. Kennedy HS, Plainview, N.Y.
28. Chris Raulinaitis, rhp, Sacramento CC
29. Josh Mader, ss, U. of New Mexico
30. Kevin Shepard, lhp, Boston College
31. Jesse Kovacs, ss, U. of the Pacific
32. Nick Shimer, 3b, George Mason U.
33. Clary Carlsen, rhp, U. of Hawaii
34. Alex McEnaney, rhp, Royal Palm Beach HS, West Palm Beach, Fla
35. Derek Brant, c, Grand View (Iowa) College
36. Andrew Romine, ss, Trabuco Hills HS, Mission Viejo, Calif.
37. Steve Marquardt, 3b, Kennewick (Wash.) HS
38. James Brown, rhp, Brunswick (Ga.) HS
39. Dusty Brabender, rhp, Oregon (Wis.) HS
40. Michael Mihalik, rhp, U. of Delaware
41. Bryce Massanari, c, Centennial HS, Las Vegas, Nev.
42. Curt Miaso, of, Chaparral HS, Scottsdale, Ariz.
43. Jerome Wooley, of, Columbia HS, Decatur, Ga.
44. Erik Morris, c, Michigan State U.
45. Lucas Miranda, 3b, Ferndale (Calif.) HS
46. Aaron Brown, rhp, Clear Creek HS, League City, Texas
47. Brendan Lafferty, lhp, Poly HS, Riverside, Calif.
48. Steven Lopez, c, Yavapai (Ariz.) JC
49. Willie Mays, of, Bryan Station HS, Lexington, Ky.
50. Matt Johnson, 1b, Bryan HS, Omaha

PITTSBURGH PIRATES (11)

1. Neil Walker, c, Pine Richland HS, Gibsonia, Pa.
2. Brian Bixler, ss, Eastern Michigan U.
3. Eddie Prasch, 3b, Milton HS, Alpharetta, Ga.
4. Joe Bauserman, rhp, Lincoln HS, Tallahassee, Fla.
5. Kyle Bloom, lhp, Illinois State U.
6. A.J. Johnson, of, Tallahassee (Fla.) CC
7. Jason Quarles, rhp, Southern U.
8. Eric Ridener, rhp, Taravella HS, Coral Springs, Fla.
9. Christopher Covington, of, Brookwood HS, Snellville, Ga.
10. Derek Hankins, rhp, U. of Memphis
11. Matt Guillory, rhp, U. of Louisiana-Monroe
12. J.P. Padron, 3b, Clear Creek HS, League City, Texas
13. Brett Grandstrand, 2b, Coastal Carolina U.
14. Jermel Lomack, 2b, Prairie View A&M U.
15. John Slone, c, Miami (Ohio) U.

16. Ryan Herbort, rhp, Northwest Whitfield HS, Dalton, Ga.
17. Matt Bishop, rhp, East Carolina U.
18. Cory Luebke, lhp, Marion HS, Maria Stein, Ohio
19. Brad Clapp, rhp, Juanita HS, Kirkland, Wash.
20. Brandon Reddinger, c, Washington State U.
21. Derek Drage, rhp, Southwest Missouri State U.
22. Mike Hofius, 1b, Long Beach State U.
23. Dustin Craig, rhp, Sam Houston State U.
24. Joe Salas, lhp, U. of New Mexico
25. Kevin Miller, rhp, Bucknell U.
26. Jason Tweedy, ss, Newark (Calif.) Memorial HS
27. Scott Loeffler, c, Lake City (Fla.) CC
28. Pat McAnaney, lhp, Westhill HS, Syracuse, N.Y.
29. Christian Romple, c, Big Bend (Wash.) CC
30. Issael Gonzalez, 2b, Edouard Montpetit HS, Quebec
31. Oliver Marmol, ss, Dr. Phillips HS, Orlando
32. Chris Palma, rhp, JC of the Canyons (Calif.)
33. Justin Byler, c, Warren G. Harding HS, Warren, Ohio
34. Nick Beghtol, c, Mountainview HS, Fort Collins, Colo.
35. Jeff Robinson, rhp, Roswell (Ga.) HS
36. Jose Nunez, ss, Puerto Rico Baseball Academy, Caguas, P.R.
37. Tim Rice, lhp, U. of Richmond
38. Keith Pedersen, lhp, Glide (Ore.) HS
39. Todd Redmond, rhp, St. Petersburg (Fla.) CC
40. Jeremy Horst, lhp, Iowa Western CC
41. Daniel Schwartzbauer, ss, Duquesne U.
42. Mikel McIntyre, of, Diablo Valley (Calif.) JC
43. Stephen Ashcraft, of, Brentwood (Tenn.) HS
44. Sean Setzer, 1b, Woodrow Wilson HS, Portland, Ore.
45. Corey Kemp, c, Centennial HS, Franklin, Tenn.
46. Josh Scofield, lhp, Newport HS, Bellevue, Wash.
47. Zach Phillips, rhp, Lee County HS, Sanford, N.C.
48. Ricardo Rivas, rhp, El Paso (Texas) CC
49. Patrick Wandtke, lhp, West Orange HS, Winter Garden, Fla.
50. Brock Lindeke, c, Soquel (Calif.) HS

ST. LOUIS CARDINALS (19)

1. Chris Lambert, rhp, Boston College
2. Mike Ferris, 1b, Miami (Ohio) U.
3. Eric Haberer, lhp, Southern Illinois U.
4. Donnie Smith, rhp, Old Dominion U.
5. Wes Swackhamer, of, Tulane U.
6. Jarrett Hoffpauir, 2b, U. of Southern Mississippi
7. Buck Cody, lhp, U. of Texas
8. Matt Shepherd, ss, U. of Southern Mississippi
9. Mike Parisi, rhp, Manhattan College
10. Brady Toops, c, U. of Arkansas
11. Simon Williams, of, U. of Maine
12. Mark Worrell, rhp, Florida International U.
13. Daniel Nelson, ss, Los Angeles Pierce JC
14. Jake Mullinax, 2b, U. of Nebraska
15. Jeremy Zick, rhp, U. of Mississippi
16. Matt Scherer, lhp, LeMoyne College
17. Chris Noonan, lhp, Seton Hall U.
18. Cameron Blair, ss, Texas Tech
19. Das Jesson, 3b, Cal State Los Angeles
20. Chad Gabriel, of, Santa Ana (Calif.) JC
21. Mike Sillman, rhp, U. of Nebraska
22. Billy Becker, 1b, New Mexico State U.
23. Phillip Andersen, rhp, Chandler-Gilbert (Ariz.) CC
24. Jose Delgado, 2b, Texas Tech
25. Mike Miller, of, Cal State Los Angeles
26. Steven Sherman, of, UNC Asheville
27. Christian Reyes, c, Jose M. Pestrana HS, Aguas Buenas, P.R.
28. Chris Della Rocco, rhp, Monmouth U.
29. Cory Taillon, c, Cal Poly U.
30. Brandon Marcelli, c, Fresno State U.
31. Daniel Baysinger, rhp, Cornell U.
32. Austin Tubb, rhp, U. of Southern Mississippi
33. Michael Gross, rhp, U. of North Carolina
34. Brett Cooley, 1b, U. of Houston
35. Brian Parish, rhp, Iona College
36. Chris Bova, rhp, Ohio U.
37. Chris Patrick, ss, Fresno State U.
38. Adam Burton, c, U. of Arkansas-Monticello
39. Sam Herbert, of, Cal Poly U.
40. Sean Dobson, of, U. of Toledo
41. Mark Broome, 3b, Delta State (Miss.) U.
42. Joe Rigoli, 1b, Parsippany (N.J.) HS
43. Jessen Grant, rhp, Columbia U.
44. Quinton Robertson, rhp, U. of Nebraska
45. Gregg Pleeter, rhp, Fairleigh Dickinson U.
46. Matt Johnson, rhp, Eupora (Miss.) HS
47. Nicholas Dinapoli, of, Buena HS, Ventura, Calif.

SAN DIEGO PADRES (1)

1. Matt Bush, ss, Mission Bay HS, San Diego
2. (Choice to Yankees as compensation for Type A free agent David Wells)
3. Billy Killian, c, Chippewa Hills HS, Stanwood, Mich
4. Daryl Jones, 1b, Westchester HS, Gardena, Calif.
5. Sean Kazmar, ss, CC of Southern Nevada
6. Jonathon Ellis, rhp, The Citadel
7. Ricky Steik, rhp, Golden West (Calif.) JC
8. Vern Sterry, rhp, North Carolina State U.
9. David O'Hagan, rhp, Stanford U.
10. Chris Kolkhorst, of, Rice U.
11. Matt Varner, rhp, U. of Houston
12. Mike Ekstrom, rhp, Pt. Loma Nazarene (Calif.) U.
13. Jake Vose, rhp, U. of Nevada-Las Vegas
14. Matt Montgomery, rhp, Okaloosa-Walton (Fla.) JC
15. Brandon Thomson, lhp, Gilbert (Ariz.) HS
16. Ben Krosschell, rhp, Highlands Ranch (Colo.) HS
17. Clayton Hamilton, rhp, Penn State U.
18. Michael Moon, 3b, U. of Southern California
19. Craig Johnson, of, Sacramento State U.
20. Brian Fryer, of, New Mexico Highlands U.
21. Gary Gallegos, lhp, Biola (Calif.) U.
22. Kyle Stutes, lhp, Lamar U.
23. Rielly Embrey, 1b, San Diego State U.
24. Jodam Rivera, ss, Puerto Rico Baseball Academy, Hatillo, P.R.
25. Brian Burks, rhp, Georgia Tech
26. Kelvin Vazquez, ss, Indians Hills (Iowa) CC
27. Orlando Diaz, 3b, Jacksonville U.
28. B.J. Jenkins, rhp, Trevecca Nazarene (Tenn.) U.
29. E.J. Shanks, rhp, Oklahoma City U.
30. Adam Kroft, rhp, U. of Albany
31. Matt Thayer, of, UCLA
32. Toddric Johnson, of, Meridian (Miss.) JC
33. Adam Miller, rhp, Indian Hills (Iowa) CC
34. Gary Moran, rhp, Fresno CC
35. Josh Bartusick, 1b, Golden West (Calif.) JC
36. Chorye Spoone, rhp, CC of Baltimore-Catonsville
37. Erik Lovett, of, Louisburg (N.C.) JC
38. Michael Lorentson, lhp, Malvern Prep, Springfield, Pa.
39. Robert Spain, 3b, Norman (Okla.) HS
40. Brandon Kintzler, rhp, Dixie State (Utah) JC
41. Taylor Bennett, rhp, Okaloosa-Walton (Fla.) CC
42. Kyle Blanks, 1b, Moriarty HS, Edgewood, N.M.
43. Zach Shadle, rhp, Tacoma (Wash.) JC
44. Omar Kadir, rhp, Lethbridge (Alberta) CC
45. Cameron Nickell, of, Columbia State (Tenn.) CC
46. Aaron Breit, rhp, Thomas More Prep HS, Hays, Kan.
47. Sean Cunningham, 3b, Sinclair SS, Whitby, Ont.
48. David Minor, of, South Hagerstown (Md.) HS
49. Brandon Tuten, rhp, Mt. Pleasant (Tenn.) HS
50. Brian Joynt, 1b, Indian Hills (Iowa) CC

SAN FRANCISCO GIANTS (29)

1. (Choice to Royals as compensation for Type A free agent Michael Tucker)
2. Eddy Martinez-Esteve, of, Florida State U.
3. John Bowker, of, Long Beach State U.
4. Clay Timpner, of, U. of Central Florida
5. Garrett Broshuis, rhp, U. of Missouri
6. Justin Hedrick, rhp, Northeastern U.
7. Will Thompson, 1b, Santa Clara U.
8. Omar Aguilar, rhp, Merced (Calif.) JC
9. Jamie Arnesen, lhp, Liberty HS, Bakersfield, Calif.
10. Spencer Grogan, lhp, Oklahoma State U.
11. Darrin Sack, rhp, Sonoma State (Calif.) U.
12. Kevin Frandsen, 2b, San Jose State U.
13. Thomas Martin, lhp, U. of Richmond
14. Eugene Espinelli, lhp, Texas Christian U.
15. Jeff Palumbo, ss, George Mason U.
16. Emmanuel Cividanes, of, Broward (Fla.) CC
17. Jordan Thomson, rhp, Northeastern U.
18. Jeremiah Luster, ss, Oceanside (Calif.) HS
19. Nathan Pendley, lhp, Oregon State U.
20. Rickey Putman, rhp, U. of Houston
21. Simon Klink, 3b, Purdue U.
22. Doug MacKay, rhp, U. of Utah
23. Brad Groth, ss, Elmhurst (Ill.) College
24. Matt Raguse, rhp, Miami (Ohio) U.
25. John Acha, 3b, Sacramento State U.
26. Trevor Wohlgemuth, rhp, Northern Illinois U.
27. Jonathan Sanchez, lhp, Ohio Dominican College
28. Charlie Babineaux, of, U. of Mississippi

---

29. Ryan Shaver, rhp, Lower Columbia (Wash.) JC
30. Kevin Jenson, rhp, Loyola Marymount U.
31. Kyle Haines, ss, Eastern Illinois U.
32. Morgan Brinson, rhp, Walnut Grove SS, Langley, B.C.
33. Judson Richards, 1b, Point Loma Nazarene (Calif.) U.
34. Jacob Coash, lhp, JC of the Canyons (Calif.)
35. Tim Grant, rhp, Dartmouth College
36. Buster Lussier, rhp, Diman Vocational HS, Fall River, Mass.
37. Erik Meyer, rhp, Eastern Washington U.
38. Tyson Brummett, rhp, Central Arizona JC
39. Brad Schwarzenbach, rhp, St. John Bosco HS, Bellflower, Calif.
40. Mac Nelson, c, Timpanogas HS, Cedar Hills, Utah
41. Chase Smith, rhp, U. of Central Oklahoma
42. Ryan Addition, rhp, Western HS, Davie, Fla.
43. Jack Spradlin, lhp, Southwestern (Calif.) JC
44. T.J. Gornati, rhp, U. of Pittsburgh
45. Kris Gibson, 1b, San Francisco State U.
46. David Quinowski, lhp, Redlands (Calif.) HS
47. Matt Minor, rhp, U. of Nevada-Las Vegas
48. Benny Cepeda, rhp, Ohio Dominican College
49. Michael Santoro, of, Northern Illinois U.
50. Garrett Lingle, 2b, Mission Bay HS, San Diego

SEATTLE MARINERS (22)

1. (Choice to Twins as compensation for Type A free agent Eddie Guardado)
2. (Choice to Royals as compensation for Type A free agent Raul Ibanez)
3. Matt Tuiasosopo, ss, Woodinville (Wash.) HS
4. Rob Johnson, c, U. of Houston
5. Mark Lowe, rhp, U. of Texas-Arlington
6. Jermaine Brock, of, Ottawa Hills HS, Grand Rapids, Mich.
7. Sebastien Boucher, of, Bethune-Cookman College
8. Marshall Hubbard, of, U. of North Carolina
9. Jeff Dominguez, ss, Puerto Rico Baseball Academy, Carolina, P.R.
10. Eric Carter, rhp, Delaware State U.
11. Michael Saunders, 3b, Lambrick Park SS, Victoria, B.C.
12. Steve Uhlmansiek, lhp, Wichita State U.
13. Kris Kasarjian, of, Los Angeles Pierce JC
14. Brent Johnson, of, U. of Nevada-Las Vegas
15. Brent Thomas, of, Bellevue (Wash.) CC
16. Chad Fillinger, rhp, Santa Clara U.
17. J.P. Arencibia, c, Westminster Christian HS, Miami
18. Jack Arroyo, 2b, Sacramento State U.
19. Brandon Green, ss, Wichita State U.
20. Brian Chavez, ss, Quartz Hill HS, Palmdale, Calif.
21. Mumba Rivera, rhp, Bethune-Cookman College
22. David Hall, of, San Diego State U.
23. Ben Summerhays, 1b, Stanford U.
24. Greg Slee, c, Huntington (Ind.) College
25. Joe Jacobitz, c, U. of San Francisco
26. Zach Ashwood, lhp, The Colony (Texas) HS
27. Aaron Trolia, rhp, Washington State U.
28. Adam Brandt, lhp, Otterbrien (Ohio) College
29. Mike Ciccotelli, lhp, Villanova U.
30. Rollie Gibson, lhp, Fresno CC
31. Chad Rothford, 1b, Fresno CC
32. Don Clement, rhp, Colorado State U.-Pueblo
33. Marquise Liverpool, of, Don Bosco Prep, Ramsey, N.J.
34. Duke Welker, rhp, Woodinville (Wash.) HS
35. Brandon Javis, ss, Cross Creek HS, Augusta, Ga.
36. Nick Hagadone, lhp, Sumner (Wash.) HS
37. James Russell, lhp, Heritage HS, Colleyville, Texas
38. Harold Williams, lhp, Mt. San Jacinto (Calif.) JC
39. Jacob Opitz, ss, Heritage HS, Littleton, Colo.
40. Michael Schilling, rhp, Fresno CC
41. Garrett Parcell, rhp, Norco (Calif.) HS
42. Erwin Jacobo, 3b, Braddock HS, Miami
43. Luis Coste, of, Puerto Rico Baseball Academy, San Juan, P.R.
44. Felix Martinez, of, Broward (Fla.) CC
45. Dwayne Lynah, of, Spartanburg Methodist (S.C.) JC
46. Daniel Martin, of, Indian River (Fla.) CC
47. Andrew McDonald, c, Sahuaro HS, Tucson, Ariz.
48. Zachary Walden, c, Stockbridge HS, McDonough, Ga.
49. Andrew Reichard, rhp, Seminole (Fla.) JC
50. Leighton Autrey, of, Navarro (Texas) JC

TAMPA BAY DEVIL RAYS (4)

1. *Jeff Niemann, rhp, Rice U.
2. Reid Brignac, ss, St. Amant (La.) HS
3. Wade Davis, rhp, Lake Wales (Fla.) HS
4. Matt Spring, c, Dixie State (Utah) JC
5. Jacob McGee, lhp, Edward Reed HS, Sparks, Nev.
6. Ryan Royster, of, Churchill HS, Eugene, Ore.
7. Fernando Perez, of, Columbia U.

8. Rhyne Hughes, 1b, Pearl River (Miss.) CC
9. Joseph Muro, rhp, Mt. San Antonio (Calif.) JC
10. Matt Walker, rhp, Central HS, Baton Rouge, La.
11. Josh Asanovich, 2b, Arizona State U.
12. Chris Cunningham, of, South Suburban (Ill.) JC
13. Andy Sonnanstine, rhp, Kent State U.
14. Woods Fines, rhp, Northwood HS, Pittsboro, N.C.
15. Ken Brock, lhp, Lane (Ore.) CC
16. Cale Iorg, ss, Karns HS, Knoxville, Tenn.
17. Marcus Barriger, rhp, Armstrong Atlantic State (Ga.) U.
18. James Scholzen, ss, Hurricane (Utah) HS
19. Chris Nowak, 3b, U. of South Carolina-Spartanburg
20. Matt Duryea, lhp, Marshfield HS, North Bend, Ore.
21. Pat Breen, of, U. of Houston
22. Ryan Bitter, rhp, Siena College
23. Logan Wiens, 1b, Merced (Calif.) HS
24. Francisco Leandro, of, Central Missouri State U.
25. Deunte Heath, rhp, Lake City (Fla.) CC
26. Alex Crooks, 1b, East Los Angeles CC
27. Matt Goyen, lhp, Georgia College & State U.
28. Nick Wagner, rhp, Georgia Tech
29. Daniel McCutchen, rhp, U. of Oklahoma
30. Aaron Walker, lhp, Georgia Tech
31. John Rodriguez, lhp, Pearl River (Miss.) CC
32. Matt Rainey, rhp, Odessa (Texas) JC
33. Patrick Cottrell, ss, U. of West Florida
34. Grant Theophilus, rhp, Cypress (Calif.) JC
35. Billy Evers, rhp, Eckerd (Fla.) College
36. Ryan Davis, 3b, Chaparral HS, Scottsdale, Ariz.
37. Brian McCormick, c, Arundel HS, Gambrills, Md.
38. Ryan Conan, ss, Archbishop Mitty HS, San Jose, Calif.
39. Drew Bigda, lhp, College of the Holy Cross
40. Jason Dean, of, Sacramento CC
41. J.T. Hall, of, Southwest Mississippi JC
42. Matt Ware, lhp, Quartz Hill HS, Lancaster, Calif.
43. John Price, lhp, U. of Mobile
44. Matt Fields, 1b, Rainier Beach HS, Seattle
45. Robbie Bouman, ss, Tusculum (Tenn.) College
46. Chris Kelly, rhp, Jacksonville U.
47. Ben Lanier, ss, Kinston (N.C.) HS
48. Andrew Gray, 1b, Holy Spirit HS, Tuscaloosa, Ala.
49. Patrick Mahoney, c, Lincoln HS, Des Moines, Iowa
50. Jerrylee Scott, ss, Livonia (La.) HS

TEXAS RANGERS (10)

1. Thomas Diamond, rhp, U. of New Orleans
1. Eric Hurley, rhp, Wolfson HS, Jacksonville (Choice from Braves as compensation for Type B free agent John Thomson)
2. K.C. Herren, of, Auburn (Wash.) HS
3. Micheal Schlact, rhp, Wheeler HS, Marietta, Ga.
4. Brandon Boggs, of, Georgia Tech
5. Mike Nickeas, c, Georgia Tech
6. Bill Susdorf, of, UCLA
7. Ben Harrison, of, U. of Florida
8. Mark Roberts, rhp, U. of Oklahoma
9. Jim Fasano, 1b, U. of Richmond
10. Justin Maxwell, of, U. of Maryland
11. Travis Metcalf, 3b, U. of Kansas
12. Kevin Ardoin, rhp, U. of Louisiana-Lafayette
13. Kyle Rogers, rhp, Ball HS, Galveston, Texas
14. Tug Hulett, 2b, Auburn U.
15. John Lujan, rhp, New Mexico JC
16. Jarrad Burcie, rhp, Tarleton State (Texas) U.
17. Nic Crosta, of, Santa Clara U.
18. Freddy Thon, 1b, Brevard (Fla.) CC
19. Marc Cornell, rhp, Ohio U.
20. Shawn Phillips, rhp, Delaware State U.
21. Bobby Lenoir, ss, U. of Richmond
22. Ryan Griffith, c, Birmingham-Southern College
23. Zachary Phillips, lhp, Galt Union HS, Galt, Calif.
24. Charles Isbell, rhp, Temescal Canyon HS, Lake Elsinore, Calif.
25. Ben Foster, lhp, Tennessee Temple U.
26. J.D. Cockroft, lhp, U. of Miami
27. Marlon Melendez, rhp, Chemeketa (Ore.) CC
28. Brett Zamzow, rhp, Navarro (Texas) JC
29. Justin Klipp, rhp, Cuesta (Calif.) JC
30. Wally Backman, ss, Crook County HS, Prineville, Ore.

31. Nicholas Casanova, rhp, Canyon HS, Corona, Calif.
32. Michael Mask, of, Texas Tech
33. Luis Rodriguez, ss, New Mexico JC
34. Clint Brannon, lhp, U. of Arkansas
35. Sam Demel, rhp, Spring (Texas) HS
36. Jesse Ingram, rhp, U. of California
37. Justin Lensch, lhp, U. of Louisiana-Monroe
38. Craig Hurba, c, Mt. Olive (N.C.) College
39. Jose Torres, of, East Los Angeles JC
40. Tony Irvin, rhp, Hillsborough (Fla.) JC
41. Clayton Jerome, rhp, Texas Christian U.
42. Joe Kemp, of, Indiana U.
43. Austin Faught, lhp, U. of Louisiana-Lafayette
44. Joe Franklin, 3b, Dawson (Mont.) CC
45. Jeffrey Hoffner, rhp, Yavapai (Ariz.) JC
46. Arthur Hill, rhp, Mt. San Jacinto (Calif.) JC
47. Kellan McConnell, rhp, Santa Clara U.
48. Brian Capon, c, Saddleback (Calif.) JC
49. Adam Resendez, of, Boswell HS, Fort Worth
50. Ivan Ramirez, lhp, UC Santa Barbara

TORONTO BLUE JAYS (16)

1. David Purcey, lhp, U. of Oklahoma
1. Zach Jackson, lhp, Texas A&M U. (Supplemental choice—32nd—for loss of Type A free agent Kelvim Escobar)
2. Curtis Thigpen, c, U. of Texas
3. Adam Lind, 1b, U. of South Alabama (Choice from Angels as compensation for Escobar)
3. Danny Hill, rhp, U. of Missouri
4. Casey Janssen, rhp, UCLA
5. Ryan Klosterman, ss, Vanderbilt U.
6. Cory Patton, of, Texas A&M U.
7. Randy Dicken, rhp, Shippensburg (Pa.) U.
8. Chip Cannon, 1b, The Citadel
9. Joey Metropoulos, 1b, U. of Southern California
10. Brian Hall, 2b, Stanford U.
11. Kristian Bell, rhp, Blinn (Texas) CC
12. Eric Nielsen, of, U. of Nevada-Las Vegas
13. Kyle Yates, rhp, U. of Texas
14. Jordan Timm, lhp, U. of Wisconsin-Oshkosh
15. Mike MacDonald, rhp, U. of Maine
16. Jose Castro, ss, Puerto Rico Baseball Academy, Caguas, P.R.
17. Michael Cooper, rhp, Santa Ana (Calif.) JC
18. Joey McLaughlin, rhp, Oklahoma City U.
19. Aaron Mathews, of, Oregon State U.
20. Bobby Scott, rhp, Stelly's SS, Saanich, B.C.
21. Scott Roy, rhp, U. of Hartford
22. Joe Wice, lhp, Dixie State (Utah) CC
23. Daryl Harang, lhp, San Diego State U.
24. Jesse Litsch, rhp, South Florida CC
25. Jason Armstrong, ss, Trinity (Texas) U.
26. Brian Bormaster, c, Tulane U.
27. Casey McKenzie, rhp, U. of Tampa
28. Josh Lex, c, Oral Roberts U.
29. Michael Macaluso, ss, U. of South Florida
30. Cory Hahn, rhp, Tulane U.
31. Paul Franko, 3b, Scottsdale (Ariz.) CC
32. Aaron Tressler, rhp, Penn State U.
33. Greg Powers, 3b, UC Santa Barbara
34. Derek Tate, lhp, U. of San Francisco
35. Charles Anderson, of, U. of Detroit
36. David Hicks, 1b, North Carolina State U.
37. Anthony Garibaldi, 3b, Southeastern Louisiana U.
38. Ben Humphrey, 1b, Olney (Ill.) Central JC
39. Matthew Trink, rhp, Yavapai (Ariz.) JC
40. Jacob Vasquez, 1b, Santa Ana (Calif.) JC
41. Derek Feldkamp, rhp, U. of Michigan
42. Jon Hesketh, lhp, Brookswood SS, Langley, B.C.
43. Chad Beck, rhp, Panola (Texas) JC
44. Eddie Cannon, rhp, Florida State U.
45. Rodrick Ratliff, rhp, Labette (Kan.) CC
46. Brok Butcher, rhp, Santa Barbara (Calif.) CC
47. Colin Quarles, rhp, Melbourne (Fla.) HS
48. Ryan Harris, ss, San Bernardino (Calif.) Valley CC
49. Brad Miller, 1b, Ball State U.
50. Jordan Lennerton, 1b, Brookswood SS, Langley, B.C.

APPENDIX

Pete Ambrosina, a second/third baseman who played for two years in the Cardinals organization, died as the result of a car accident May 27, in Knoxville, Tenn. He was 34. Ambrosina was drafted by the Cardinals in the 14th round of the 1994 draft. He spent two seasons in the Cardinals system.

George Bamberger, former manager of the Brewers and Mets, died April 4, in Redington Beach, Fla. He was 80. Bamberger managed the Brewers from 1978-1980, the Mets from 1982-1983 and then the Brewers again from 1985-1986. He finished with a 458-478 career record in six seasons as a manager. He also appeared in 10 games with the Giants and Orioles as a righthander in the early 1950s, going 0-0, 9.42.

Earl Battey, one of the best catchers of the 1960s, died Nov. 15, 2003, in Gainesville, Fla. He was 68. Battey broke into the majors with the White Sox in 1955. He spent five seasons as a backup, but once he joined the Washington Senators in 1960, Battey blossomed. He hit .270-15-60 in 1960 and earned his first of three consecutive Gold Gloves. Battey was a four-time all-star (for the Senators and, after they moved, Minnesota Twins), hitting .302-17-55 in 1961 and .297-6-60 in 1965.

John Blatnik, an outfielder who hit .260-6-45 for the Phillies in 1948, died Jan. 21 in Lansing, Ohio. He was 82. Blatnik's 1948 season was his only full season in the majors. He had 18 more at-bats with the Phillies and Cardinals over the next two seasons.

Ray Boone, an infielder who spent 13 years in major leagues, died Oct. 17 in San Diego. He was 81. Boone's career began in 1942 but was put on hold from 1943-45 due to military service. He returned in 1946 and played in the minors until 1948, when the Indians called him up. He played with the Indians until 1953, when he was traded to the Tigers, where he had his best years. He hit .296-26-114 in 1953, .295-20-85 in '54, .284-20-116 in '55 and .308-25-81 in '56. He also played for the White Sox, Kansas City Athletics, Milwaukee Braves and Red Sox. He became a long-time scout for the Red Sox after his playing career ended, signing Curt Schilling among others, and was the original member of the first family to have three generations in the major leagues. He was followed by his son Bob and two grandsons, Bret and Aaron, who are still active in the major leagues.

Hank Borowy, a righthander who helped the Yankees and Cubs make it to the World Series in the 1940's, died Aug. 23 in Brick, N.J. He was 88. Borowy was one of the last remaining members of the Cubs' 1945 World Series' team. He reached the majors in 1942 and helped the Yankees to the World Series in 1943. He had another strong season with that club in 1944, going 17-12, 2.63, before joining the Cubs, where he played for three more seasons before joining the Phillies in 1949, where he went 12-12, 4.20.

Lee Bowen, the Florida State Seminoles radio announcer, died July 16 in Tallahassee, Fla. He was 47. Bowen worked as the radio voice of the Seminoles baseball team for 15 years.

Charlie Bowles, a righthander who spent parts of two seasons with the Philadelphia Athletics, died Dec. 23 in Hickory, N.C. He was 86. While Bowles made the majors, his legacy might be more notable because of his baseball travels. Over an 18-year pro career, he made 31 different stops, playing for 26 different teams. He broke into pro ball with Daytona Beach (Florida State) in 1936 and had a cup of coffee with the A's in 1943, going 1-1, 3.00 in 18 innings. He missed the 1944 season while in military service, but returned to go 0-3, 5.18 for the A's in 1945.

Bob Boyd, a first baseman you spent parts of eight seasons in the majors, died Sept. 7 in Wichita, Kan. He was 78. Boyd had a distinguished minor league career, but it took him seven seasons to make it to the majors. He reached the majors in 1953 with the White Sox, hitting .297 in 165 at-bats, and returned to the majors in 1956 with the Orioles. He stayed in the big leagues through the 1961 season, hitting .293-19-75 for his career.

Harry Breechen, a lefthander who spent 12 seasons with the St. Louis Cardinals and Browns, died Jan. 17 in Ada, Okla. He was 89. Breechen twice led the National League in ERA, including a 20-7, 2.24 season in 1948 when he also led in strikeouts (149). He made two all-star appearances (in 1947 and '48) and finished fifth in MVP balloting in 1948. Breechen had a stretch of five straight seasons with 15 or more wins.

Ken Brett, the youngest player to pitch in the World Series, died Nov. 18 in Spokane, Wash., of a brain tumor. He was 55. Brett pitched for the Red Sox against the Cardinals in the 1967 World Series, when he was just 19 years and one month old. The brother of Royals third baseman George Brett, Brett went 83-85, 3.93 in a 14-year major league career. He was also known as one of the best-hitting pitchers of all time. Brett set a record for pitchers when he homered in

Ken Brett

four consecutive games in 1973. He finished his career hitting .262-10-44 in 347 at-bats.

Jack Brewer, a righthander who spent parts of three seasons with the New York Giants, died Nov. 30 in Sun City, Calif. He was 84. Brewer broke into the majors in 1944, going 1-4, 5.56 for the Giants. He rebounded in 1945 to go 8-6, 3.83 for the Giants.

Ernest Burke, a Negro Leagues pitcher who also spent time in the minors as a third baseman, died Jan. 31 in Baltimore. He was 79. After serving in the Marines during World War II, Burke broke into the Negro Leagues as a righthander in 1947. He went 4-1 for Baltimore the next season, then entered Organized Baseball as part of the first wave of players who helped to integrate the game.

Ed Burtschy, a righthander who pitched five seasons in the majors, died May 2, in Delhi Township, Ohio.

He was 82. Burtschy broke into the majors in 1950 with the Athletics. His debut was actually a mistake—manager Connie Mack summoned Burtschy thinking that a righthander was coming to the plate, but by the time he realized a lefty was batting, Burtschy was already in the game. Burtschy's best major league season was 1954, when he went 5-4, 3.79 for the A's.

Ivan Calderon, a 10-year major leaguer who was an all-star in 1990, died Dec. 27 in Loiza, P.R. He was 41. Signed by the Mariners in 1979, Calderon broke into the majors with the Mariners in 1984, but he's best remembered with the White Sox. He hit .293-28-83 in 1987 and hit 14 home runs in each of the next three seasons before putting together his all-star season in 1990, when he hit .300-19-75.

Ken Caminiti, a three-time all-star third baseman, died Oct. 10 in New York. He was 41. Caminiti, an Astros third-round pick in 1984, is probably best known for his stint with the Padres, where he played from 1994-1998. He had his best year in 1996 when he hit .326-40-130 and won the National League MVP award. He made his only appearance in the World Series in 1998 with the Padres. Caminiti broke into the majors with the Astros in 1987 and spent six seasons as the team's everyday third baseman before he was part of an 11-player swap between the Padres and Astros. After his stint with the Padres, Caminiti returned to Houston for the 1999 and 2000 seasons and split 2001, his final season, between the Rangers and Braves. Caminiti retired after that season. He was arrested for drug use shortly after his career was over and also admitted to using steroids during his career. He finished his career with a .272 average, 239 home runs and 983 RBIs.

Ken Caminiti

John Cerutti, a TV broadcaster and lefthander who pitched seven seasons in the majors, died Oct. 3 in Toronto. He was 44. Cerutti reached the majors with the Blue Jays in 1985 and had two of his best years with Toronto in 1987 (11-4, 4.40) and 1989 (11-11, 3.07). He stayed with the Blue Jays through the 1990 season and spent 1991 with the Tigers before retiring. Cerutti began broadcasting Blue Jays games in 1997 and spent the last three years as lead analyst for Rogers Sportsnet.

Gary Coleman, a lefthander who played five seasons in the major leagues, died May 14 in Wolfeboro, N.H. He was 72. Coleman was 7-25, 4.58 for his career, making stops with the Yankees, Athletics and Orioles.

Al Corwin, a righthander who spent parts of five seasons with the New York Giants, died Oct. 23 in Geneva, Ill. He was 76. Corwin was 18-10, 3.98 in his major league career.

Bob Cremins, a lefthander who made four appearances with the 1927 Red Sox, died March 27 in Pelham, N.Y. Cremins was 0-0, 5.06 in five innings.

Alfred Cuccinello, a second baseman who played briefly for the New York Giants, died March 29 in New York City. He was 89. In 1936, Cuccinello hit .248-4-20 in his only year in the major leagues.

Rob Derksen, a Baltimore Orioles scout and the manager of the Greek Olympic baseball team, died June 16 in New York City. He was 44. Derksen was a 16th-round draft pick of the Brewers in 1982. After a brief minor league career, he spent the next 20 years as a coach and scout, making a name for himself as a proponent of international baseball.

Jim Devlin, a catcher who had one at-bat with the Indians in 1944, died Jan. 15 in Danville, Pa. He was 81.

Taylor Duncan, a first-round pick of the Braves in 1971, died Jan. 3 in Asheville, N.C. He was 50. A third baseman for most of his career, Duncan was dealt with catcher Earl Williams to the Orioles in a trade that brought Davey Johnson to the Braves. Duncan made the majors with the Cardinals in 1977, hitting .333-1-2 in 12 at-bats. He spent the next season with the Athletics, hitting .257-2-37 in his only significant time in the majors.

Sammy Dunn, a two-time national high school coach of the year, died Oct. 3, in Vestavia Hills, Ala. He was 52. Dunn was Alabama's most decorated high school baseball coach, leading Vestavia Hills High to the No. 1 ranking in the Baseball America/National High School Baseball Coaches Association final poll in 1998.

Hal Epps, an outfielder who spent parts of four seasons in the majors, died on Aug. 26 in Houston. He was 90. Epps hit .253-1-23 with the Cardinals, Browns and Athletics.

Joe Falls, a longtime sportswriter for the Detroit News and a member of the Baseball Hall of Fame, died Aug. 11 in Detroit. He was 76. Falls covered 50 World Series during a long and varied 58-year sportswriting career. He broke into journalism as a copy boy with the Associated Press in 1945, but he came to fame in Detroit, where he moved in 1953 and wrote for the next 50 years. He worked as a Tigers beat writer, columnist and sports editor during stints at the Detroit Times, Detroit News and Detroit Free-Press.

Charlie Fox, a major league manager for seven years, died Feb. 16 in Stanford, Calif. He was 82. Fox made it to the majors in his first pro season, jumping to the New York Giants for three games (and hitting .429) in his only major league stint. He became a coach for the Giants in 1965 and took over managing the team about a third of the way through the 1970 season, leading it to a 67-51 record. The next season, he led the Giants to the playoffs, where they were knocked out in the National League Championship Series by the Pirates. Fox managed another 2½ seasons with the Giants before being fired. He later served as interim manager with the Expos (1976) and Cubs (1983).

Hershell Freeman, a righthander who played for the Red Sox and Reds in the 1950's, died Jan. 17 in Orlando, Fla. He was 75. Freeman blossomed into one of the better relievers in the game in 1955, going 7-4, 2.16 with 11 saves for the Reds. He followed it up with a 14-5, 3.40 season with 18 saves in 1956. He made another 52 appearances out of the pen in 1957, but a shoulder injury cut his career short in 1958.

Floyd Giebell, a righthander who spent parts of three seasons in the majors, died April 28, in Wilkesboro,

N.C. He was 94. Giebell made his major league debut with the Tigers in 1939, going 1-1, 3.00.

Tony Giuliani, a catcher who spent parts of six seasons in the majors and several years as a scout, died Oct. 8 in Minneapolis, Minn. He was 91. Giuliani played for the Browns, Senators and Dodgers in a major league career that stretched from 1937-1941 and 1943. Giuliani became a scout with the Senators after his career ended and followed the team when it moved to Minnesota in 1961. He stayed with the organization until he retired in 1987.

Tom Glaviano, a third baseman who spent five seasons in the majors, died Jan. 19 in Sacramento. He was 80. Glaviano hit .257-24-108 with the Cardinals and Phillies in a career that stretched from 1949-1953.

Mike Goliat, a second baseman who spent parts of four seasons in the majors, died Jan. 13 in Seven Hills, Ohio. He was 78. Goliat hit .225-20-99 in four seasons with the Phillies and Browns.

Ruben Gomez, a righthander who played for five major league teams in a 10-year career, died July 26 in Carolina, P.R. He was 77. Gomez was one of the first prominent Puerto Rican major leaguers, going 76-86, 4.09 from 1953-67.

George Hausmann, a second baseman who spent three seasons with the Giants, died June 16 in Boerne, Texas. He was 88. Hausmann spent six seasons in the minors before getting the call to the big leagues. He hit .268-3-78 in three seasons with the Giants (1944-1945, 1949), but was best known for being one of the players suspended for talking to the Mexican League, which was trying to develop into a major league.

Thomas Hesketh, a righthander who spent four seasons in the minors, died May 18, in Cincinnati. He was 75. Hesketh began his career in 1948 with McAlester (Sooner State) and went 11-9, 3.79.

Avitus "Vedie" Himsl, a longtime major league coach who also had a six-year playing career, died March 15 in Chicago. He was 86. Once his playing career was over, Himsl stayed in the game as a coach and manager. He coached in the big leagues with the Cubs from 1960-1964 and had a long-time minor league coaching career.

Paul Hopkins, believed to be the oldest living major leaguer at the time of his death, died Jan. 2 in Deep River, Conn. He was 99. Hopkins starred at Colgate from 1924-26 before making his pro debut for New Haven (Eastern) in 1927. After going 3-7, 3.62 for New Haven, he joined the Washington Senators at the end of the 1927 season and earned a spot in the record books. On Sept. 29, 1927, the righthander gave up Babe Ruth's record-tying 59th home run of the season.

Cowan Hyde, a Negro Leaguer who was one of the fastest players in baseball in the 1940s, died Nov. 20 in St. Louis. He was 95. Hyde tried out for the Memphis Red Sox as a 14-year-old, but he didn't break into baseball until five years later when he hit .190 for the Sox. He spent most of the next two decades with Memphis as a speedy outfielder. He made all-star teams in 1943 and '46.

Curtis Johnson, a pitcher for the Negro Leagues' Kansas City Monarchs, died Jan. 27 in St. Louis. His age at death was not known. Johnson played briefly with the Monarchs in 1950, when the team was struggling to survive the defection of players to Organized Baseball.

Darrell Johnson, former manager of the Boston Red Sox died May 3, in Fairfield, Calif. He was 75. After taking over the Red Sox in 1974, Johnson led the Red Sox to the legendary 1975 World Series, where the Red Sox extended the Reds to seven games before losing. He didn't get a chance to lead the team back to the World Series the next season as he was fired 86 games into the season. As a player, Johnson made it to the majors for six years as a catcher. Johnson also managed the expansion Seattle Mariners, beginning in 1977.

Mack Jones, an outfielder who spent 10 years in the major leagues, died June 8, in Atlanta. He was 65. Jones spent the majority of his major league career with the Braves and hit .252-133-415 over 10 seasons.

John "Spider" Jorgensen, a third baseman who spent five seasons with the Brooklyn Dodgers and New York Giants, died Nov. 6, 2003, in Rancho Cucamonga, Calif. He was 84. A teammate of Jackie Robinson with the Montreal Royals in 1946, Jorgensen and Robinson made their major league debuts on the same day in 1947. Jorgensen hit .274-5-67 as the Dodgers' everyday third baseman, his only season with a full-time major league job. He never had more than 134 at-bats in four more major league seasons.

Joe Just, a catcher who spent parts of two seasons with the Reds, died Nov. 22, 2004, in Franklin, Va. He was 87.

Hub Kittle, a longtime pitcher, manager, general manager and coach, died Feb. 10. He was 86. Kittle broke into baseball with the Los Angeles Angels in 1936 and had a lengthy career as a minor league pitcher and manager. He was named The Sporting News minor league executive of the year in 1960. He later served as a major league pitching coach for the Astros (1971-75) and Cardinals (1981-83), winning a World Series ring with the Cardinals in 1982. At the time of his death, Kittle was working as a special assignment instructor for the Mariners.

Irvin Lacrouts, a first baseman who played three seasons in the minor leagues, died May 12, in Kenner, La. He was 81. His best season was his last, as he hit .257-5-48 for Houma (Evangeline) in 1948.

Joe Lafata, a first baseman/outfielder who played three seasons in the majors, died May 6, in Roseville, Mich. He was 82. Lafata hit .225-5-34 in three major league stints from 1947-1949.

Tony Lupien, a first baseman who spent six seasons in the major leagues in the 1940s, died July 9 in Norwich, Vt. He was 87. Lupien hit .268-18-230 with the Red Sox, Phillies and White Sox.

Carmen Mauro, an outfielder who played parts of four seasons in the major leagues, died Dec. 19, 2003, in Carmichael, Calif. He was 77. Mauro made it to the majors with Cubs for a three-game stint in 1948, hitting an inside-the-park home run for his first major league hit. He also played for the Dodgers, Senators and Athletics. He later became the baseball coach at Cuesta (Calif.) Junior College.

Tug McGraw, a reliever who recorded the final out of

APPENDIX

the Phillies' only World Series title, died Jan. 5 in Nashville. He was 59. McGraw was a member of the

Tug McGraw

1969 Amazin' Mets, going 9-3, 2.25 with 12 saves. He also helped the 1973 Mets to the World Series by going 5-6, 3.86 with 25 saves, but he is probably best remembered for his 1980 season, when he went 5-4, 1.47 with 20 saves for the Phillies and struck out Willie Wilson to finish the World Series. Overall, McGraw went 96-92, 3.14 with 180 saves.

Wayne McLeland, a righthander who briefly pitched for the Tigers, died May 8, in Houston. He was 79. McLeland went 0-1, 8.18 for Detroit in 11 innings in 1951, and 0-0, 9.00 in a four-inning stint in 1952.

Ray Medeiros, a middle infielder who played one game in the major leagues, died June 6, 2003 in San Mateo, Calif. He was 77. Medeiros made his pro debut in 1945 when he entered a game as a pinch runner for the Reds. He didn't get a chance to hit before being sent to Trenton (Inter-State) and he never returned to the majors.

Lloyd Merriman, an outfielder who spent five seasons in the majors, died Jan. 20 in Fresno. He was 79. Merriman hit .242-12-117 with the Reds and Cubs.

Bob Murphy, voice of the Mets for virtually the team's entire history, died Aug. 3 in Palm Beach, Fla. He was 80. Murphy began broadcasting major league games in 1954, working for the Red Sox through 1959. He called Orioles games in 1960 and '61 before taking over as the first voice of the Mets on April 11, 1962 and he called more than 6,000 games over the next 42 years. He stepped down after broadcasting on Bob Murphy Night on Sept. 25, 2003. "For me, Bob Murphy and the Mets were one," Mets pitcher Al Leiter said. "I can't tell you how many games I listened to in my car and in my room growing up."

Samuel Nahem, a righthander who spent parts of four seasons in the majors, died April 19, in Berkeley, Calif. He was 88. Nahem went 10-8, 4.69 in 224 innings with the Dodgers, Cardinals and Phillies.

Leslie Narum, a righthander who split 12 seasons between the majors and minors, died May 17 in Clearwater, Fla. He was 63. Narum broke into the majors with the Orioles in 1963, going 0-0, 3.00. Over the next four seasons, he went 14-27, 4.48 in 388 innings with the Senators.

Paul Owens, a player, manager and general manager who was instrumental in putting together the Phillies' only World Series champion in 1980, died Dec. 26 in Woodbury, N.J. Owens had a 48-year career in the Phillies organization. He started as a player/manager in 1955, and worked as a scout and farm director before becoming GM in 1972. He helped build the Phillies into Eastern Division winners in 1976, '77 and '78 and World Series champs in 1980. He also served as interim manager on the Phillies' 1983 pennant winners.

Doug Pappas, a writer who specialized in covering the business of baseball, died in Texas on May 22. He

was 42. Pappas was the chairman of the Society for America Baseball Research's Business of Baseball committee.

Norman Paulson, a baseball photographer for more than 50 years and a business manager for several minor league teams, died Jan. 10 in New Port Richey, Fla. He was 87. Paulson served as business manager of teams in the Three-I, Evangeline and Central Leagues. He stepped down as a business manager in 1949, but he spent much of the next 50 years photographing major and minor leaguers for various newspapers, including The Sporting News.

Clark Powell, an intern for the Portland Beavers, died June 10, near Salem, Ore. He was 23. Powell was involved in a one-car accident on Interstate 5 near his hometown of Salem, Ore. He was interning with the Beavers and the Portland Timbers soccer team at the time of his death.

Ewald Pyle, a lefthander who spent parts of five seasons in the majors, died Jan. 10 in DuQuoin, Ill. He was 93. Pyle went 11-21, 5.03 over a five-year major league career. He broke into the majors with the Browns in 1939 and also spent time with the Senators, Giants and Braves.

Hal Reniff, a righthander who played seven seasons in the major leagues, died Sept. 7 in Ontario, Calif. He was 66. Reniff carved out a solid career as a reliever for the Yankees from 1961-1967, going 21-23, 3.27 with 45 saves.

Lawrence Ritter, author of several notable baseball books, died Feb. 15 in New York City. He was 81. Ritter's "The Glory of Our Times" is considered one of the best baseball histories ever written. He recorded oral histories from great players of the early 1900s, turning them into a book that helped spark interest in baseball and the way it was played during the dead ball era.

Jim Russo, a scout for the Orioles for 33 years, died Feb. 8 in Wildwood, Mo. He was 81. Russo spent 33 years as a scout for the Orioles, signing Jim Palmer, Dave McNally, Eddie Watt, Boog Powell and Davey Johnson. In 2003, the Orioles named an award for the club's top scout in Russo's honor.

Andy Seminick, a member of the Philadelphia "Whiz Kids," died Feb. 22 in Melbourne, Fla. He was 83. Seminick broke into the majors with the Phillies in 1943 and became the team's starting catcher in 1946. He earned an All-Star Game appearance in 1949 and was a key part of the Phillies pennant winners the next season. Over a 15-year career, he hit .243-164-556.

Sonny Senerchia, who made it to the big leagues as a third baseman but also spent four minor league seasons primarily as a pitcher, died Nov. 1 in Freehold, N.J. He was 72. Senerchia had 100 at-bats with the Pirates in 1951. He hit .220-3-11 and was back in the minors in 1953. He moved to the mound in 1955, spending four seasons as a pitcher in the minors before retiring.

Marge Schott, the outspoken former owner of the Cincinnati Reds, died March 2, 2004 in Cincinnati. She was 75. While Schott's tenure as Reds owner is remembered more for its lowlights than highlights, the team did win the 1990 World Series under her

ownership, and the team was usually competitive. Schott built her fortune after taking over her late husband's business empire upon his death in 1968. She purchased the Reds in 1984. During the final years of her ownership Schott became known more for her politically incorrect comments than for the success of her franchise. Schott stepped down as president and CEO in 1996 while facing a possible suspension amid increasing pressure from other team owners. In 1999 she sold all but one of her shares in the team and her limited partners soon voted her out as controlling partner.

Marge Schott

Jim Sheehan, a catcher who played one game in the majors, died Dec. 2, in New Haven. He was 88. Sheehan's only taste of the big leagues came before he played an inning in the minors. A Fordham star when Vince Lombardi was on the school's football team, Sheehan went straight to the majors in 1936, going 0-for-4 for the Giants.

Warren Spahn, the winningest lefthander in major league history and a 14-time all-star, died Nov. 24 in Broken Arrow, Okla. He was 82. Spahn won 363 games, even though he didn't make the majors for good until he was 25. He spent four games with the Braves in 1942, but was demoted by manager Casey Stengel after he refused to throw at a batter. Spahn then went into the Army, earning a Purple Heart for his service as an infantryman in the Battle of the Bulge. After returning from the war, Spahn got his first full season in the majors in 1946, going 8-5, 2.93. It was the only time he didn't reach double figures in wins over the next 17 seasons. He posted a winning record in his first 18 years and topped 20 wins 13 times, leading the National League in wins eight times. Spahn also led the league in ERA in 1947 (2.33), '53 (2.10) and '61 (3.01). He had his first losing record as a 43-year-old in 1964 and stuck

Warren Spahn

around for one more season, struggling with the Mets and Giants. He then played in the Mexican League in 1966. He had a couple of stints on the mound while managing Tulsa (Pacific Coast) in 1967, delaying his induction into the Hall of Fame until 1973.

John Stoneman, an outfielder who had a 10-game stint with the White Sox, died Jan. 1 in Owasso, Okla. He was 85. Stoneman hit .120-1-3 in 25 at-bats with the White Sox in 1933.

Johnny Sturm, a first baseman who played one season in the major leagues, died Oct. 8 in St. Louis. He was 88. Sturm got his only chance with the Yankees in 1941 and hit .239-3-36.

Gus Suhr, a fixture at first base for the Pirates in the 1930s, died Jan. 15 in Scottsdale, Ariz. He was 98. Suhr had an exceptional minor league career that included

a .381-51-177 season for San Francisco in 1929, which earned him a spot with the Pirates. He hit .286-17-107 as a National League rookie in 1930. As Pittsburgh's everyday first baseman, he led the league in games played three times. Suhr reached double digits in triples in eight different seasons and made an All-Star Game appearance in 1936 with a .312-11-118 season.

John Tankersly, a longtime coach for Prairie View A&M, died Oct. 27. He was 80. A member of the Texas Black Sports Hall of Fame, Tankersley was 370-723 in a three-decade career as the Prairie View coach.

Ted Tappe, an outfielder who spent parts of three seasons in the majors, died Feb. 13 in Wenatchee, Wash. He was 73. Tappe homered in his first major and minor league at-bats. He had a meteoric rise, jumping to the Reds as a 19-year-old. In 1955, Tappe got his only extended major league action with the Cubs, hitting .260-4-10 in 23 games.

Bernard Uhalt, an outfielder who played one season in the major leagues, died Sept. 3 in Walnut Creek, Calif. He was 93. Uhalt hit .242-0-16 for the White Sox in 1934.

Randy Waddill, a scout with the Giants, Phillies and Braves, died July 30 in Tampa. He was 58. Waddill made a brief appearance in the minors as a player, but made a more lasting impact as a scout and coach for 37 years. He had worked as a scout for the Giants since 1993.

Leon "Daddy Wags" Wagner, one of the first stars of the Los Angeles Angels, died Jan. 3 in Los Angeles. He was 69. Wagner broke into the majors with the Giants in 1958, but it was with the expansion Angels that Wagner established himself as one of the American League's better power hitters. He made two All-Star Game appearances, topped 20 homers three times with the Indians and finished fourth in American League MVP voting in 1964.

Ron Walker, an infielder who spent five years in the minors, died April 16 in a single-car accident in Medford Township, N.J. He was 28. Walker was an eighth-round pick of the Cubs in 1997 out of Old Dominion.

Max West, an outfielder/first baseman who spent six seasons with the Boston Braves, died Dec. 31, 2003, in Sierra Madre, Calif. He was 87. An all-star in 1940, West broke into the majors with the Boston Braves in 1938. He reached double figures in home runs in five of the next six seasons, and finished fifth in the National League in home runs in 1942, when he hit .254-16-56. His best season was in 1939, when he hit .285-19-82.

Don Wheeler, a catcher who spent one season with the White Sox, died Dec. 10, 2003, in Bloomington, Minn. He was 81. Wheeler hit .240-1-22 in 67 games.

John Henry Williams, son of Ted Williams and a former minor and independent league first baseman, died March 6 in Los Angeles of leukemia. He was 35. Williams is best known publicly for his fight with his half-sister over whether their father's body should be frozen at a cryonics lab in Arizona. His baseball career began at the age of 33, when the Red Sox signed him to a minor league contract as a favor to his father. He did not register a hit in six at-bats for the Gulf Coast League Red Sox in 2002 before being released in the offseason.

INDEX
MAJOR AND MINOR LEAGUE CLUBS

APPENDIX

ALL THROUGH 2005

Subscribing is easy and you'll save more than 30% off the cover price!

We know the Almanac has a valuable place on your bookshelf as the essential reference for baseball happenings in 2004.

But what about all the exciting action on and off the field that takes place in the new year? From spring training to winter leagues—including the most complete draft coverage anywhere, a front-row seat at the College World Series and statistics for every minor league team—Baseball America magazine is the best source for baseball information. Since 1981, BA has been finding the prospects and tracking them from the bushes to the big leagues. That means you get comprehensive reporting and commentary every step of the way.

When you subscribe to Baseball America, you also gain access to BaseballAmerica.com premium content.

So join the team now to receive Baseball America every other week, and be the first to know about today's rising stars.

It's baseball news you can't get anywhere else.

magazine • books • website

BaseballAmerica.com